The Norton Anthology of World Masterpieces

FOURTH EDITION

VOLUME 2

VOLUME 1

MASTERPIECES OF THE ANCIENT WORLD • Knox

MASTERPIECES OF THE MIDDLE AGES • McGalliard

MASTERPIECES OF THE RENAISSANCE • Pasinetti

VOLUME 2

MASTERPIECES OF NEOCLASSICISM • Hugo

MASTERPIECES OF ROMANTICISM • Hugo

MASTERPIECES OF REALISM AND NATURALISM • Wellek

MASTERPIECES OF THE MODERN WORLD • Douglas / Lawall

A COMPANION VOLUME

MASTERPIECES OF THE ORIENT
Edited by G. L. Anderson
Available in Enlarged and Shorter Editions

The Norton Anthology of World Masterpieces

FOURTH EDITION

Maynard Mack, *General Editor*
Yale University

Bernard M. W. Knox
Center for Hellenic Studies

John C. McGalliard
The University of Iowa

P. M. Pasinetti
University of California, Los Angeles

Howard E. Hugo
Late of the University of California, Berkeley

René Wellek
Yale University

Kenneth Douglas
Late of Yale University

Sarah Lawall
University of Massachusetts, Amherst

VOLUME 2
Literature of Western Culture since the Renaissance

W·W· NORTON & COMPANY· *NEW YORK* · *LONDON*

W. W. Norton & Company, Inc. 500 Fifth Avenue, New York, N.Y. 10110

BOOK DESIGN BY JOHN WOODLOCK

Library of Congress Cataloging in Publication Data
Main entry under title:
The Norton anthology of world masterpieces.
Fourth ed. edited by M. Mack published in 1973 under
title: World masterpieces.
Includes indexes.
CONTENTS: v. 1. Literature of Western culture through the Renaissance.—v. 2. Literature of Western culture since the Renaissance.
1. Literature—Collections. I. Mack, Maynard,
1909– II. Mack, Maynard, 1909– ed.
World masterpieces.
PN6014.M1382 1979 808.8 78–26744

6 7 8 9 0

ISBN 0-393-95040-9 CLOTH
ISBN 0-393-95050-6 PBK.

Anna Akhamatova: "Requiem," translated by Robin Kemball, copyright 1976 by Ardis, in Anna Akhamatova, *Selected Poems*, ed. Walter Arndt, Ann Arbor: Ardis, 1976.
Charles Baudelaire: "Spleen", "Correspondances", "Les Fenêtres" by Charles Baudelaire excerpted from *French Poetry* From Baudelaire to the Present with English prose Translation. Translated by Elaine Marks. Copyright © 1962 by Dell Publishing Co., Inc. Reprinted by permission of Dell Publishing Co., Inc.
William Blake: Text from *The Poetry and Prose of William Blake*, edited by David V. Erdmann and Harold Bloom, published by Doubleday & Company, Inc.
Jorge Luis Borges: "The Lottery in Babylon," translated by John M. Fein, from Jorge Luis Borges, *Labyrinths*. Copyright © 1962 by New Directions Publishing Corporation. Reprinted by permission of New Directions Publishing Corporation and Penguin Books Ltd.
Bertold Brecht: "Mother Courage and Her Childien" from *Collected Plays of Bertolt Brecht*, Volume 5, edited and translated by Ralph Manheim and John Willet. Copyright © 1972 by Stefan S. Brecht. Reprinted by permission of Random House, Inc. and Eyre Methuen, Ltd.
Albert Camus: "The Renegade" from *Exile and the Kingdom*, by Albert Camus, translated by Justin O'Brien. Copyright © 1957, 1958 by Alfred A. Knopf, Inc. Reprinted by permission of Alfred A. Knopf, Inc. and Hamish Hamilton Ltd.
François René de Chateaubriand: "René" from *Atala and René*, translated by Irving Putter (University of California, 1957). Reprinted with the permission of the publishers.
Anton Chekhov: "The Cherry Orchard" from *The Portable Chekhov*, translated by Avrahm Yarmolinsky. Copyright 1947, © 1975 by the Viking Press, Inc. Reprinted by permission of Viking Penguin Inc.
Emily Dickinson: Reprinted by permission of the publishers and the Trustees Amherst College from *The Poems of Emily Dickinson*, edited by Thomas H. Johnson, (Cambridge, Mass.: The Belknap Press of Harvard University Press, copyright © 1951, 1955 by the President and Fellows of Harvard College. Poems #341 and #657, copyright 1929 by Martha Dickinson Bianchi. Copyright © 1957 by Mary L. Hampson. From *The Complete Poems of Emily Dickinson* edited by Thomas H. Johnson, by permission of Little, Brown and Company.
Fyodor Dostoevsky: "Notes From Underground" from *White Nights and Other Stories* by Fyodor Dostoevsky translated by Constance Garnett. Reprinted by permission of William Heinemann, Ltd.
T. S. Eliot: Selections from *Collected Poems 1909–1962* by T. S. Eliot. Copyright 1963 by Harcourt Brace Jovanovich, Inc.; copyright © 1963, 1964 by T. S. Eliot. Reprinted by permission of Harcourt Brace Jovanovich, Inc. and Faber and Faber, Ltd.
William Faulkner: "Old Man" from *The Wild Palms* by William Faulkner. Copyright 1939 and renewed 1967 by Mrs. William Faulkner and Mrs. Paul D. Summers. Reprinted by permission of Random House, Inc., the Author's Literary Estate, and Chatto and Windus Ltd.
Gustave Flaubert: *Madame Bovary* translated by Paul De Man. Copyright © 1965 by W. W. Norton & Company, Inc. Reprinted by permission of the publisher.
André Gide: "The Return of the Prodigal Son" reprinted from *French Stories* edited and translated by Wallace Fowlie. Copyright © 1960 by Bantam Books, Inc. All rights reserved. Original story copyright © 1949 by Editions Gallimard. Reprinted with permission of the publishers.
Johann Wolfgang Von Goethe: From Goethe's *Faust*, translated by Louis MacNeice. Copyright 1951 by Louis MacNeice. Reprinted by permission of Oxford University Press, Inc. and Faber and Faber Ltd.
Henrik Ibsen: "Hedda Gabler" from *Hedda Gabler and Three Other Plays* translated by Michael Meyer. Copyright © 1961 by Michael Meyer. Used by permission of Doubleday & Company, Inc.
James Joyce: From *A Portrait of the Artist as a Young Man* by James Joyce. Copyright 1916 by B. W. Huebsch, 1944 by Nora Joyce. Copyright © 1964 by the Estate of James Joyce. All rights reserved. Reprinted by permission of Viking Penguin Inc.
Franz Kafka: "The Metamorphosis." Reprinted by permission of Schocken Books, Inc. and Martin Secker & Warburg Limited, from *The Penal Colony* by Franz Kafka. Copyright © 1948 by Schocken Books, Inc.; copyright renewed © 1975 by Schocken Books, Inc.
Jean de la Fontaine: "The Fox and the Crow" from *The Fables of La Fontaine*, translated by Marianne Moore. Copyright 1952 by Marianne Moore. "The Grasshopper and the Ant", "The Frog Who Would Be an Ox", "The Town Rat and the Country Rat", "The Wolf and the Lamb", "The Oak and the Reed" from *The Fables of La Fontaine* translated by Marianne Moore. Copyright 1954 by Marianne Moore. Reprinted by permission of Viking Penguin Inc. "The Dairymaid and Her Milk-Pot" from *The Fables of La Fontaine*, translated by Marianne Moore. Copyright 1954 by Marianne Moore. Reprinted by permission of Viking Penguin Inc. and Clive Driver, Literary Executor of the Estate of Marianne C. Moore.
D. H. Lawrence: "The Odour of Chrysanthemums" from *The Complete Short Stories of D. H. Lawrence*, vol. II. All rights reserved. Reprinted by permission of Viking Penguin Inc., William Heinemann Ltd., Laurence Pollinger Ltd., and the Estate of the late Mrs. Frieda Lawrence Ravagli.
Stéphane Mallarmé: "Sainte" from *The Poems of Mallarmé* translated by Roger Fry. Copyright 1951 by New Directions Publishing Corporation. Reprinted by permission of New Directions and Mrs. Pamela Diamand.
Thomas Mann: "Tonio Kröger" copyright 1936 and renewed 1964 by Alfred A. Knopf, Inc. Reprinted from *Stories of Three Decades*, by Thomas Mann, translated by H. T. Lowe-Porter, by permission of Alfred A. Knopf, Inc. and Martin Secker & Warburg Limited.
Herman Melville: "Billy Budd" reprinted in its entirety by permission of the publishers from *Melville's Billy Budd* edited by Frederick Barron Freeman and corrected by Elizabeth Treeman (Cambridge, Mass.; Harvard University Press, 1948). Copyright 1948, © 1956 by The President and Fellows of Harvard College.

Contents

Masterpieces of Romanticism

Masterpieces of Nineteenth-Century Realism and Naturalism

Masterpieces of the Modern World

Preface to the Fourth Edition

This fourth edition is, we think, the best to date. Notable additions to the selections from the ancient world, the middle ages, the romantic poets, and the moderns combine with the introduction of important new authors and several brilliant new translations to make the volumes now before you an immensely flexible, practical, and attractive instrument for teaching the literature of the western world. (For those who wish to extend their courses to include Eastern literatures, we recommend a companion anthology, *Masterpieces of the Orient*, edited by G. L. Anderson, available from the publisher in 397- and 846-page versions.)

Our representation of the twentieth century has been particularly enriched. In this edition there appear for the first time no fewer than eight major modern writers: Wallace Stevens (eleven poems); Virginia Woolf (a short story); Anna Akhmatova (a lyric sequence); Katherine Anne Porter (a short novel); Bertolt Brecht (a full-length play); Jorge Luis Borges and Vladimir Nabokov (a short story by each); and Richard Wright (the chilling first story from *Uncle Tom's Children*, "Big Boy Leaves Home"). And though the canon of authentic masters is better established for earlier periods, and our additions to these periods have therefore mostly been enlargements of existing selections rather than additions of previously unrepresented writers, there have also been a few of the latter: the anonymous authors of the Anglo-Saxon *Dream of the Rood* and the Middle English *Sir Gawain and the Green Knight*, the latter in the incomparable translation by Marie Borroff, and Emily Dickinson (fifteen poems).

We have also made a handful of substitutions. The replacement of Euripides' *The Trojan Women* by his *Hippolytus* permits interesting crossweavings when Racine's *Phaedra* is reached. Ibsen's *Hedda Gabler*, replacing his *The Wild Duck*, invites some fascinating comparisons not only with Euripides' and Racine's Phaedra but (for those with an eye to representative cultural symbols) with

Emma Bovary, Mother Courage, and the heroine of Katherine Anne Porter's *Pale Horse, Pale Rider*. The long opening chapter of Proust's *Remembrance of Things Past*, which we have substituted for his account of the soirée at the Marquise de Saint-Euverte's, affords a more concise entry into the author's themes and methods while supplying at the same time a psychological wellhead in the evolution of the modern American novel, to be placed beside its other sources in the self-enclosed linguistic game-worlds of Borges and the often almost unmediated transcriptions of raw experience in Wright. The two other substitutions have a similar intent. Mann's *Tonio Kröger* replaces his *Felix Krull* because it comments so poignantly on the deep cleavage between life and art, action and contemplation, which characterizes modern culture generally; and Faulkner's *Old Man* replaces his "Delta Autumn" because it is painted on so much broader a canvas of American life and experience. For the teacher who thrives on experiment and exploration, as most of us do, these exchanges are transparent gains.

To the selections from authors already represented, we have been able to add in this edition substantial new portions of the *Odyssey* and the *Aeneid*, two complete books of Wordsworth's *The Prelude* in the preferred 1805 text, further poems by Shelley (all the Shelley poems in *World Masterpieces* are now given in the definitive text lately edited from the manuscripts by Donald Reiman), Keats, Tennyson (not only additional poems but a selection from *In Memoriam* preserving the shape and progression of the whole), and Whitman.

To make this expansion possible we have been obliged to forgo a scattering of works for which our teacher-users assure us they lack time and inclination. Partly in the same interest, we have returned to first principles, and have excluded from this edition most lyric poetry in translation. We have always held (see the Note on Translation which concludes this volume) that lyric poetry loses too much in translation to warrant extensive treatment in either a survey anthology or a survey course; and the reports from our experiment with a large infusion of such poetry in the third edition confirm us in our original conviction. (By way of compensation, we have increased the quantity and variety of lyric poetry in English.)

Finally, our translations. We have always been vigilant about these, as our long-time users know, and have tried with each successive edition to make improvements. We believe we have succeeded in doing so again. A long consideration of the two great modern verse translations of the *Iliad* has persuaded us to give our vote in this edition to Robert Fitzgerald, whose unmatched *Odyssey* we have already used for several years. With less reluctance but some regret, we have also let go Dryden's elegant rendering of

Lucretius in favor of Rolfe Humphries' version, unquestionably more comfortable for a twentieth-century eye and ear. Allen Mandelbaum's fine *Aeneid,* winner of the National Book Award, has replaced C. Day Lewis's on somewhat similar grounds, and Joseph Sheed's *Confessions* of St. Augustine brings a vernacular lucidity where Elizabethan syntax reigned before. To all our translators new and old, not forgetting Rex Warner for our new *Hippolytus,* Robin Kemball for our version of Akhmatova's *Requiem,* and Ralph Manheim for our *Mother Courage and Her Children,* we offer hearty thanks, and to their publishers as well.

In conclusion, we welcome a new colleague, Professor Sarah Lawall of the Comparative Literature department of the University of Massachusetts, Amherst, to our collegium of editors. The revisions in the current Introduction to the Modern World, and the texts, notes, introductions, and bibliographies for the authors and works newly added are all hers, and we look forward to her further collaboration in editions yet to come. We must, unhappily, at this same time record the grievous losses of Kenneth Douglas by accidental death, and Howard E. Hugo, taken from us prematurely by illness. Kenneth and Howard were among the original seven editors of this anthology, and by their judicious choices they probably brought more recalcitrant students to an appreciation of neoclassic, romantic, and modern world writing than any other anthologists in history. We applaud their work and honor their memory. *Si monumentum requiris, circumspice.*

The Editors

Preface

World Masterpieces is an anthology of Western literature, based on principles which we believe to be sound, but which have not always been sufficiently observed, we feel, in the existing anthologies in this field.

We have sought to make the range of readings in this collection unusually wide and varied. Its contents reach in time from Genesis and the *Iliad* to Nabokov and Camus, and the literatures represented include English, Irish, American, Russian, German, Scandinavian, French, Italian, Spanish, Argentine, Latin, Hebrew, and Greek. The literatures of the Far East have been omitted, on the ground that the principal aim of a course in world literature is to bring American students into living contact with their own Western tradition, and that this aim cannot be adequately realized in a single course if they must also be introduced to a very different tradition, one requiring extended treatment to be correctly understood. (We refer those who wish to incorporate Eastern literatures into their courses to a companion anthology, *Masterpieces of the Orient*, edited by G. L. Anderson.) Twentieth-century literature has been represented with particular fullness, because we feel that it is important for students to grasp the continuity of literature.

World Masterpieces is predominantly an anthology of imaginative literature. We have not tried to cover the entire history of the West in print, and have avoided filling our pages with philosophy, political theory, theology, historiography, and the like. This principle was adopted not because we disapprove of coming at the history of an epoch by way of literature, but because imaginative literature, in our view, itself best defines the character of its epoch: great monuments of art, we would be inclined to say, furnish the *best* documents for history. They lead us deeper into the meaning of a past age than other modes of writing do, because they convey its unformulated aspirations and intuitions as well as its conscious theorems and ideals; and yet, being timeless, they have also an unmatched appeal to our own age. For this reason, we have admitted into *World Masterpieces* only works which have something important to say to modern readers, and we have made it a point to interpret them with reference not only to their time but to ours. Teacher and student will find here a number of selections which they have not encountered before in a text of this kind.

We are convinced that effective understanding of any author depends upon studying an autonomous and substantial piece of his work: a whole drama, a whole story, at least a whole canto or book of a long poem. Our anthology therefore contains no snippets. Where it has been necessary to represent a long work by extracts, they are large extracts, forming a coherent whole. These considerations have also affected our treatment of lyric poems. Experience leads us to the conclusion that lyric poetry cannot be taught with full success in translation, and that very short poems, in whatever language, are nearly useless in a survey of these dimensions. We have accordingly excluded almost all *short* lyrics, and, with rare exceptions, all lyric poetry in foreign languages. We have preferred to represent the romantic movement, in which the lyric becomes a dominant form, with selections in English from the major English and American poets. This is not a flawless solution to the problem, but it seems to us better than printing many pages of inferior translations.

Since nothing has so deterred students from enjoying the great masterpieces of the classical and modern foreign languages as translations in an English idiom that is no longer alive, we have done our best to use translations which show a feeling for the English language as it is written and spoken today. Thus we offer here, with some pride, Robert Fitzgerald's *Iliad* and *Odyssey*; Louis MacNeice's *Agamemnon* and his *Faust*; Rex Warner's *Medea* and *Hippolytus*; Allen Mandelbaum's *Aeneid*; Mark Musa's *Inferno* (with selections from *Purgatorio* and *Paradiso* in Lawrence Binyon's translation); Samuel Putnam's *Don Quixote*; and many other renderings of equal quality.

Our introductions—in consonance with the scheme of the book —emphasize criticism rather than history. While providing all that seems to us necessary in the way of historical background (and supplying biographical summaries in the appendix following each introduction), we aim to give the student primarily a critical and analytical discussion of the works themselves. We try to suggest what these works have to say to us today, and why they should be valued now. In every instance, we seek to go beneath the usual generalizations about periods and philosophies, and to focus on men and books.

Our annotations of the texts are, we believe, exceptionally full and helpful. In a number of cases, these texts are annotated in this anthology for the first time. In one instance, we have been able to supply for a work the best-known notes on it in English, those of C. H. Grandgent to the *Divine Comedy*. Every care has been taken to furnish accurate and generous bibliographies as a guide to further reading.

In sum, we have sought to compile a new anthology, a text new in every sense—new in its emphasis on imaginative literature, on major authors, on wholes and large excerpts, on modern translations, on critical rather than historical treatment of texts, and, pervasively, on the tastes and values of our own time.

The Editors

The Norton Anthology of World Masterpieces

FOURTH EDITION

VOLUME 2

Masterpieces of Neoclassicism

EDITED BY
HOWARD E. HUGO
Late of the University of California, Berkeley

FROM MOLIÈRE TO DIDEROT

Words such as "Reformation" and "Renaissance" are rich in connotations of drastic alteration, rebirth, and revolt—the new arising from the old and the old interpreted with sudden vigor and apparent heterodoxy. Not so are the names given at the time or by posterity to the last half of the seventeenth century and the first half of the eighteenth: the "neoclassical" period, the "Age of Reason," the "Enlightenment," the "Century of Light." Here are terms indicative of relative quiescence, the triumph of consolidation and harmony over innovation and disorder. There is some truth in these phrases, but not the whole truth.

While men have never ceased to invigorate their thought by returning to the masterpieces of Greece and Rome, the special task of the Renaissance—to bring back to life a world bypassed or partly forgotten—seemed finished by the end of the seventeenth century. The "Quarrel of the Ancients and the Moderns" (to be referred to again later on) was fought with an acerbity that happily cost nobody's blood. Was modern man inferior, equal, or possibly superior to his glorious classical ancestors? Whatever their answer, the participants in the "Quarrel" recognized continuity with the great minds of classical antiquity. Similarly the religious strife occasioned by Protestant attacks on the institution of the Roman Catholic Church lost its acrimony. Conflicts henceforward were likely to be between nations, not sects, and to concern politics and the balance of power instead of the individual's private relation to God. True, Louis XIV's revocation of the Edict of Nantes in 1685 upsets any easy picture of the gradual emergence of religious toleration, for the "Sun King" thereby denied to Protestants the right to practice their own variety of Christianity. Yet the French Regency repented that monarch's action some thirty years later, and in 1689 the English Toleration Acts set a broad pattern slowly emulated by most European commonwealths.

Political and economic wars, on the other hand, abounded: struggles about Spanish, Austrian, Polish, and Bavarian successions; various Silesian engagements; the war between Peter the Great and Charles XII of Sweden; ancillary combats in the New World and in the recently colonized East. Nationalistic marches and countermarches fill the years we now consider. The punctilio and formal splendor portrayed in Chapter 3 of Voltaire's *Candide* (in this volume) is that author's ironical commentary on his own best of all possible worlds from the point of view of man's organized inhumanity to man. Certainly it cannot be said that peace elected the Enlightenment as the moment to proclaim "olives of endless age." Yet fortunately the horrible slaughter of the Thirty Years' War (1618-1648) was not soon repeated. Europe had almost two hundred years from the start of that catastrophe before undergoing devastation on a similar scale. Then the battles of Napoleon's *Grande Armée* and his opponents involved hundreds, not merely tens, of thousands.

Classical Greece viewed its gods as residing serenely on Mount Olympus. Neoclassicism produced a pantheon of monarchs who enacted comparable roles within a more human, but also more elegant, environment. The modern state had arisen from its feudal antecedents; and kings, both absolute and enlightened, tended more and more to symbolize the aspirations of the countries they headed. At first glance the age seems to be dominated by the lengthening shadows of its rulers. What other epoch, for instance, could boast three political personalities of the order of Peter and Catherine of Russia, and Frederick II of Prussia—all called "the Great"? Add to them Maria Theresa of Austria and the Holy Roman Empire, with her forty-year reign; the radiant figure of Louis XIV; and the less spectacular but equally important English monarchs—Anne and her Hanoverian descendants, the first three Georges.

Nevertheless, the growth of certain theories about kingship made the condition of royalty less secure. Simpler medieval and Renaissance assumptions had invested earthly rulers with divine rights (even if the problem of Church and State, pope and emperor, persisted). When for example the English under Cromwell executed Charles I—to the horror of many contemporary Europeans—John Milton, in his *Tenure of Kings and Magistrates* (1649), attempted to justify the regicide by invoking precedents, history, common sense, and Holy Scripture. A true king, said Milton, enjoys his office by "the eminence of his wisdom and integrity." A tyrant, in contradistinction, "reigns only for himself and his faction." But his arguments for and against monarchy were slowly superseded by the notion that men live together by virtue of a social contract—the theme of such disparate thinkers as Hobbes, Locke, Rousseau, and many of the French *philosophes*. At the start of the eighteenth century a monarch, acting *in loco parentis*, was still generally considered necessary for the state, particularly if the royal prerogatives were circumscribed by custom or constitution. The age of neoclassicism and the Enlightenment accepted its rulers, but in good rationalist fashion attempted to define their station and duties within an orderly civil society. Future generations were to find more radical and violent solutions. Chapter 26 of *Candide* is strangely prophetic of the shape of things to come. Here the six indigent and dispossessed kings convening at the Carnival of Venice are portrayed as ultimately inferior to the commoner, Candide, who joins them: "Who is this fellow who is able to give a hundred times as much as any of us, and who gives it?"

These are broad cultural and political characteristics of the age. When we turn from them to the contributions of the philosophers of the period, generalization becomes more difficult: Descartes, Spinoza, Locke, Leibnitz, Berkeley, Hume, La Mettrie, D'Alembert, Holbach—what common denominator will reconcile such differing minds? Yet most thinkers manifested two tendencies. First, they challenged traditional Christianity and classical philosophy by posing questions of a complex and problematic nature and thus helped to bring about what Paul Hazard has called a crisis in European thought. And second, they stressed that man's mind alone is the sole judge of the readings we make of the universe, of God, and of man; they assumed, as almost no earlier philosophers had done, that the cosmos conforms to what human experience and our judgments and abstractions seem to prove. They were, in short, *rationalists*, although many of them would be surprised at being so labeled.

In England, Sir Francis Bacon had earlier laid down a program for new scientific studies, although for him these were but dimly ascertained. Induction was to be the tool whereby we would derive "axioms from the senses and particulars, rising by a gradual and unbroken ascent, so that it [i.e., the inductive method] arrives at the most general axioms last of all. This is the true way, but as yet untried." (*Novum organum*, 1620). His comment may seem relevant chiefly to the growth of the physical sciences, as indeed it was. Nevertheless, it also helped to determine the cast of thought in the subsequent century.

Descartes' *Discourse of Method (Discours de la méthode*, 1637) indicated that he was no Baconian worshiper of induction; yet he insisted on starting from one certain "truth" of observation—"I think, therefore I am"—in building up a philosophical system. Perhaps most important,

Descartes sharpened the distinction between mind and matter, spirit and body. After him philosophers tended to fall into one camp or the other: either asserting, as "idealists" (like Berkeley), that all reality is ultimately mind and spirit; or, as materialists (like Hobbes and many of the more extreme French *philosophes*), that reality is finally reduced to the world of matter. But whatever their beliefs, they all held one belief in common. To these thinkers the universe made *rational* sense; it possessed a discernible pattern; it moved according to fixed scientific and mathematical laws. And here the early scientists came to the aid of their more abstract-minded colleagues, with Newton making the greatest contribution; for it was he who synthesized the scientific work done from Copernicus to his own day, to produce a plausible and orderly picture of the material universe, the "Newtonian world-machine." At least two writers included in this portion of the anthology—Pope and Voltaire—wrote with full conviction of its existence.

TYPES OF NEOCLASSICISM—MOLIÈRE AND RACINE

Seventeenth-century religious conflicts created a strongly centralized Catholic France, particularly after the revocation of the Edict of Nantes in 1685, which effectively ended French Protestantism. The emergence of a strongly centralized Catholic France may be viewed in one aspect as a triumph of the Counter Reformation—the various efforts taken by the Roman Catholic Church, in the face of the Protestant Reformation, to strengthen doctrine and dogma. Yet this monolithic new commonwealth had secular antecedents. Under Louis XIV Versailles and Paris were soon felt to be what Rome had been under Augustus Caesar, and the line from Greece and Rome to France was asserted to be direct and unbroken. Racine and Molière wrote in a milieu that united Renaissance and Counter Reformation. Whatever the precise ingredients may have been, seventeenth-century French neoclassicism emerges as a combination of these cultural forces, one religious and the other secular. Stated in other terms, two conceptions of the human condition were in opposition—man in a state of grace and man in a state of nature.

Even the famous "Quarrel of the Ancients and the Moderns," mentioned earlier, was symptomatic of the tension between these antithetical outlooks. The Renaissance had extolled classical, pagan antiquity and made it the model for human conduct and aspiration. But now the possibility gained credence that modern man might *excel* the Greeks and Romans and not merely emulate them in an effort to regain a lost golden age. Hence the birth of the idea of progress in history—a concept relatively new to mankind, and one hard to reconcile with the Christian notion of man's fall from his pristine felicity. The "Moderns" were those who insisted that modern culture could equal or surpass that of the classical period; the "Ancients," those who joined literary modesty to something very like a Christian sense of imperfection. Yet while one side felt itself to be an inglorious heir and the other a superior son, *all* were convinced that they were neoclassic, a happy synthesis of the ancient and modern.

MOLIÈRE

Within this cultural environment of neoclassicism, France's two greatest dramatists, one in the comic and one in the tragic vein, wrote their plays. Molière, the comic dramatist, leaned heavily toward the pole of the natural, rational, and humanistic. His concern is not with metaphysics or with an eventual state of eternal salvation. He portrays man as a product of the social order. As Sainte-Beuve long ago pointed out, Molière's characters are untouched by any thought of Christian grace. Only one of his plays, the famous *Tartuffe* (1664), is concerned with a near-religious theme, and even this work is preoccupied more with an analysis of mundane hypocrisy than with the assessment of true belief. Each of Molière's plays is actually an *exemplum* and a critical study of the failure to conform to an ideal of urbanity, solid pragmatism, worldly common sense, good taste, and moderation—all the secular virtues of antiquity and Louis XIV's new state. Both Tartuffe and Orgon are ludicrous, for each fails to meet these criteria of behavior. Tartuffe is a rogue and a scoundrel, a hypocrite whose apparent religiosity and asceticism are eventually unmasked. Orgon is a dupe, in whom Molière satirizes the solid, middle-class citizen. Orgon's false values impel him to give his daughter a "good" marriage against her wishes, disinherit his son, sign over his property to Tartuffe, and himself be tricked by a fashionable rascal who uses pretended piety as an excuse for financial gain and amatory satisfaction.

Voltaire's description of true comedy as "the speaking picture of the follies and foibles of a nation" can readily be applied to Molière's plays. Actually Voltaire had the Greek comic playwright Aristophanes in mind; to compare Molière with Aristophanes is to see once more how close was the bond between neoclassicism and classical antiquity. Aristophanes' panorama of Athenian citizens displays the same infinite variety as Molière's collection taken from the Parisian scene. Stock characters were easily drawn from two societies where social stratification was menaced by a rising commercialism, and the resulting *parvenu* became material for the satirist's pen. Finally the problems of the day—political, religious, educational, ethical—served as subject matter for both Aristophanes and Molière. From the Greek playwright through the Latin authors Plautus and Terence and later the creators of the Italian Renaissance *commedia dell' arte*, the tradition of classical comedy moves to Molière. The topical issues may no longer interest us—arranged marriages, the excessive refinement of precious fops, and so on—but the classical vision of man in society rather than man the individual, the ideals of universality and rationality, these transcend the local and the temporary.

RACINE

When we move from the racy, realistic style of comedy to Racine's lofty language of tragedy, more comprehension of the age and its conventions is required. It has always been difficult for the English reader, accustomed to the apparent looseness and gusto of Shakespearean drama, to savor the French playwright's decorous elegance. We are puzzled by the careful control and compression insisted on through adherence to the unities of time, place, and action; by the intrusion of long, distracted monologues, the alternating debatelike interchange between characters, and the operalike duets, and by the circumlocution of the vocabulary.

Racine's model for *Phaedra* (*Phèdre*, 1677) was the *Hippolytus* of Euripides. Racine assures us in his preface that he has retained all that is suitable from the Greek tragedy—and added to it ingredients which make it more pertinent to the audience of his own time. In Euripides' drama the protagonist is not Phaedra but Hippolytus, depicted as a follower of Artemis (Diana) and thus bound by vows of rigid chastity. This condition leads him into *hubris* (overweening human pride) toward Aphrodite (Venus) and thus brings Nemesis (judgment) upon him —all according to the conventional Greek view of life. Phaedra appears in only two scenes, never face to face with Hippolytus; and her death occurs halfway through the play. No doubt the more thoughtful, discerning members of Euripides' audience caught a note of his own skepticism about the dubious ethics of the gods; but the action of the drama is satisfying on a human level alone, since the cause of Hippolytus' downfall is the pride implicit in his excessive, vehement denial of Phaedra. For the story of Theseus, Racine was indebted also to Plutarch's life of Theseus; and possibly, although he denied it, to the *Phaedra* (alternatively entitled *Hippolytus*) of the Roman Stoic Seneca. In Seneca's play Hippolytus is portrayed as a Stoic philosopher; Phaedra, not Hippolytus, suffers the wrath of Venus; and while he remains technically the protagonist, Phaedra is the focal figure, with her shameless love mixed with guilt. No divinities enter Seneca's declamatory, rhetorical drama, and Venus is the mere personification of passion.

Like his Greek predecessor and like Milton in *Samson Agonistes*, Racine deals with one terrible day—the culmination of previous events and states of feeling—and his technique is in keeping also with the tenets of French classical drama. He concentrates not on the pale Hippolytus, who even in Euripides' drama seems more a passive instrument of two rival goddesses than an active protagonist, but rather on the tormented, passion-racked Phaedra. She becomes a Greek woman with a Christian conscience, for the peculiar remorse Racine has his heroine exhibit when once she is aware of her illicit love is an emotion that was unknown to the ancient world.[1] Within her soul the fundamental conflict is between one overwhelming passion and the restraining power of reason. Her tragic flaw, to use the Aristotelian phrase, is her abnegation of rational responsibility for her moral conduct. The entire play is a slow unfolding, rather than a record of the development, of this fatal weakness. Only the most insensitive reader could be unaffected by Racine's skillfully conveyed, intricate psychological analysis—the cognizance of forces deep within the well of the unconscious that imperil the tenuously held supremacy of the intellect—and by the tone of majestic, dignified sadness.

TYPES OF NEOCLASSICISM—LA ROCHEFOUCAULD, LA FONTAINE

The word *moraliste* which describes these two authors is difficult to translate into English. Naturally "moralist" is the cognate, but for us the word has overtones of someone preaching a definite moral code and employing didactic persuasion. This description does not quite fit the *moraliste*. From Montaigne and Pascal to Gide, Camus, and Sartre, French literature has abounded with writers employing all the traditional literary forms—as well as diaries, notebooks, fables, essays, and aphorisms—to present a total "morality" and outlook on life, a commentary based on observations about the given elements, the *données*, of human nature. Generally the *moraliste* says, "This is the way human nature is"—not, "This is the way human nature should be." Satire is occasionally the mode of expression, but seldom evoked with any burning desire to correct man's vices and foibles. The animal universe of La Fontaine is emblematic of our own, where silly geese, clever foxes, pretentious frogs, and lazy grasshoppers sketch the rich varieties of human foolishness. But even here the human comedy seems more to be observed and savored than censured. To exercise the intellect in an acute dissection of motives and conduct is an end in itself.

LA ROCHEFOUCAULD

La Rochefoucauld's *Maxims* (from which we have excerpted nearly sixty from more than three hundred) shocked his contemporaries when first they appeared in 1665. The modern reader, insulated against shock by his post-Freudian worldliness, may do well to ponder *Maxim* 384: "We ought never to be

1. So intense is her self-recrimination that some critics have attributed it to Racine's Jansenist background. The Jansenist order was a group within the Catholic Church concerned chiefly with the Augustinian concept of predestination and Divine Election. This preoccupation, as well as their general austerity and asceticism, links the Jansenists to Calvinism and the Puritan movement in England. The order was bitterly opposed by the Jesuits, and the Jansenist center at Port-Royal was destroyed in 1709-1710. Like the heroine of Euripides' tragedy, Racine's Phaedra implies that the gods have brought about her destruction. It is also possible to interpret her assertion in Jansenist-Christian terms as referring to a fall from grace.

surprised, save that we can still be surprised." The social milieu and the course of La Rochefoucauld's career offer some explanation for the mood of acerbity and bitter reflectiveness, even downright cynicism, in these pithy statements. When he was a young man, La Rochefoucauld's family and the class to which he belonged still enjoyed real power and prestige. But the age of Richelieu and later the reign of Louis XIV witnessed a steady decline of both these factors. What privileges the nobility entertained were increasingly the gift of monarchs and ministers whose concern was the consolidation of royal prerogatives. Moreover, failure and defeat marked La Rochefoucauld's active life, both politically and militarily. His castle was burned in the wars of the *Fronde*, a natural son was killed in battle, near-blindness for himself came as the result of a wound. Poverty and the infidelity of several mistresses scarcely contributed to produce in him a vision of life as bliss, and in his *Memoirs* (1662) can be traced a pattern of deepening disillusionment. Yet such data only partially explain the cast of La Rochefoucauld's mind, which had a genius like Newton's for reducing complex phenomena to a single simple (and also over-simple) principle.

La Rochefoucauld, indeed, accomplished for the domain of human nature what Machiavelli had achieved for statecraft some centuries earlier, and accomplished it with such apparent stark simplicity of phrasing that we are often dazzled. *Maxim* 218 is a good example. "Hypocrisy is the tribute that vice pays to virtue" ("L'hypocrisie est un hommage que le vice rend à la vertu"). Here four abstractions, carefully balanced in pairs, occur within barely twice as many words. Vice and virtue we are accustomed to consider in opposition, but hypocrisy coupled with homage or tribute startles the mind, so that the relation between vice and virtue takes on new dimensions.

One other characteristic of La Rochefoucauld's commentaries is the generality of his expression. A major tenet of neoclassical criticism, Continental and English, was the asserted superiority of the universal statement over the particular, the generic class over the individual. Hence the *Maxims*, delivered in a tone of assurance that twentieth-century man with his dubieties might well covet, deliberately aim at the typical rather than at the unique. Sainte-Beuve aptly described La Rochefoucauld as "the polished misanthrope, insinuating and smiling," and while the tender-minded may be appalled at the aphorist's ruthless dissection of love, honor, friendship, and the like, they will be hard pressed to phrase a rebuttal with such precision combined with such grandeur of generality.

LA FONTAINE

La Fontaine's *Fables* describe a more genial world than that of his cynical contemporary. They too, especially in the abstract statements that conclude most of the little tales in verse, have all of mankind as their concern, and their association with children's literature is more apparent than real. Though La Fontaine shrewdly dedicated the first six books of *Fables* to France's most important child, the six-year-old son of Louis XIV, obviously his talking animals are far removed from the inanities of Donald Duck and his friends, and from those conversing beasts in today's comic strips ostensibly created to delight the juvenile reader. His pungent tags—e.g., "Every flatterer lives at the expense of the person who listens to him" ("Chaque flatteur vit au dépens de celui qui l'écoute") —are not the sort of observations that bring chortles to the nursery. The timeless appeal of his tales, full of anecdotal skill and psychological subtlety, is better summed up in Alexander Pope's neoclassical dictum: "True wit is Nature to advantage dressed,/ What oft was thought, but ne'er so well expressed:/ Something whose truth convinced at sight we find. . . ." La Fontaine's borrowings from Aesop, Phaedrus, and other minor Greek and Latin fabulists may also be thus explained. They are in keeping with the aesthetics of an age that felt its chief artistic merit to lie in perpetuating and renewing the classical tradition. Perhaps the highest compliment paid to these *Fables* is the remark of the critic who submitted that if the world were suddenly shattered, the next day (if man were permitted to reconstruct its animalian content) the birds and beasts would behave precisely as they are made to do by La Fontaine.

As modern readers and hence heirs willy-nilly to romanticism and the cultural tradition of the last one hundred and fifty years, we may feel that these two seventeenth-century writers are excessively objective and impersonal. We are accustomed to veiled autobiography in literature, where the "I" of the artist is never far from his creation. Romantic affinities for the peculiarities of each individual have blunted our appreciation of the grandeur of generality, where human nature is viewed as a totality, permanent and unchanging, and the task of the man of letters is to treat mankind in its public rather than its private context. La Rochefoucauld's and La Fontaine's minds, critical and decorous, chary of enthusiasm and aristocratically scornful of democratic friendliness (today's "togetherness"), may strike us as chilly. They speak with a *courage de tête* (literally, "courage of the head") and a surety we often attribute to intellectual arrogance. Finally, they lack the solemnity that our own Age of Anxiety too often confuses with profundity. They are witty and seemingly casual. Their grace, ease, and apparent simplicity deceive us. It is good to remember Horace Walpole's remark, "The world is a comedy to those that think, a tragedy to those who feel." With them, as with Voltaire, the rapid play of mind over human experience should not obscure an underlying seriousness of intention.

TOWARD THE ENLIGHTENMENT—POPE

In our day, or within the last twenty-five years, we have become accustomed to seeing our own cultural milieu, and that of our immediate predecessors, defined only in terms which are deprecatory, negative, or cynical—for example, "the Jazz Age," "the Lost Generation," "the Age of Anxiety," or "the Age of Longing." Hence, we are not well equipped to appreciate the eighteenth century, when for the first time in history men announced to each other and to posterity that theirs was an Age of Reason, an *Enlightenment*. Voltaire, in his *Last Remarks on the "Pensées of M. Pascal*, exclaimed with joy, "What a light has burst over Europe within the last few years! It first illuminated all the princes of the North; it has even come into the universities. It is the light of common sense!" Crane Brinton epitomizes the movement in *Ideas and Men* (1950) when he speaks of "the belief that all human beings can attain here on this earth a state of perfection hitherto in the West thought to be possible only for Christians in a state of grace, and for them only after death."

Traditional Christianity had been securely moored by a pair of anchors: *faith* ("the substance of things hoped for, and the evidence of things not seen") and *reason*. The two elements were always linked in an unstable combination. To watch the progress of thought in the seventeenth century is to see the latter gradually usurp the position of the former. Biblical exegesis had succeeded in weakening the concept of the biblical God of miracles. Of what practical use were the records of an obscure Hebrew tribe for the "modern" man who trusted in his subjective rational capabilities, and for whom the wonders of the orderly universe were disclosed daily by contemporary scientists and philosophers? Reason, rapidly assuming a state of near-deification, could show men how to control themselves and their environment. Furthermore this same environment—nature—began to seem increasingly benign as man explored its previously concealed workings.

Deism became the most satisfying metaphysical position for most intellectuals. Taking their departure from the traditional arguments of "first cause" and "design" which were used to demonstrate the existence of God, they could conceive of a Supreme Being—*Monsieur l'Être*, a French wit said—who was an impersonal cosmic clockmaker, the prime mover of Newton's vast mechanical machine, remote and abstract. In short, one now invented a God to whom one could not pray and from whom one could not expect forgiveness. (Voltaire once wrote an article describing the fallacy of prayer, finding the act impious, superfluous, and ineffective.) The doctrinal handbook of the Middle Ages had been the *Summa theologica* of St. Thomas Aquinas; the Century of Light was to produce its *Encyclopedia* (*Encyclopédie*), a joint effort published from 1751 to 1776 by the leading French *philosophes*, edited by Diderot, and designed to popularize and disseminate the new doctrines.

Deism attempted to reconcile Christianity with "modern" rationalism. In one sense this was nothing new. We must remember that from the very start, Christian thinkers—St. Paul and the early Church fathers—faced the task of amalgamating Hebraic ideas about a revealed Messiah, the Son of God, with Greek rationalist philosophy. Many centuries later it was inevitable that for intellectuals imbued with scientific attitudes, the revelatory aspects of Christianity—invoking that same God who spoke to Pascal—would retreat before more analytical approaches. The period when modern philosophy was formed can be placed between Galileo (1564–1642) and Leibnitz (1646–1716). While differences between interim thinkers such as Hobbes, Spinoza, and Descartes may seem to be more paramount than similarities, these men were unanimous in their rejection of medieval logic and in their insistence that the axioms of the new mathematical physics were consonant with the authentic workings of the universe. The omniscience and activity of God has to conform with the same laws He had established, and there could be no room for divine caprice and arbitrary conduct. The critical climate of the age is succinctly revealed in Alexander Pope's epitaph intended for Sir Isaac Newton's tomb in Westminster Abbey. "Nature and Nature's Laws lay hid in Night:/ God said, *Let Newton be!* and all was Light."

Hence Deistic thinkers constructed or adumbrated complicated philosophic abstractions such as the Great Chain of Being, plenitude, and the principle of sufficient reason. Gottfried Wilhelm Leibnitz, himself a respectable figure in the history of philosophy, was responsible for much of the dissemination of the new doctrine, mostly through the writings of his more superficial disciples. Leibnitz's hypothesis of "many possible worlds"—which in less capable hands became a theory of "the best of all possible worlds"—ran somewhat as follows. God considered an infinite number of possible worlds before the Creation; but His final decision was to make a world where good predominates over evil. A cosmos *without* evil would actually not have been as "good" as one where evil is a minor ingredient, since many "goods" are related to certain evils. (For example, by definition the existence of free will implies the possibility of sin, for there must be an alternative upon which to exercise the power of free choice. God therefore invented the forbidden apple, and Adam's fall ensued.) According to this view, the world contains a preponderance of good over evil in the long run, and the evil it does possess is no argument against God's benevolence. Reduced to finite, human terms, this philosophical outlook became known as *Optimism*. The student must be careful not to confuse it with our everyday use of the word.

Pope's *Essay on Man* (1733-1734)—the first epistle of which appears in the present volume—

has often been interpreted as a poetic expression of the Deistic outlook we have just sketched, and even some present-day critics fall into this easy error. Pope was unusually aware of the intellectual currents of his age, and many of his turns of phrase do reflect the philosophical terminology we associate with the extreme exponents of the Enlightenment. Generally speaking, however, the *Essay* offers us arguments that stretch from Plato and the Stoics through the leading apologists for both Catholic and Protestant Christianity. Milton and Racine, each in his own way, synthesized a pagan, classical humanism with Christian ideology. Pope joins their company and speaks for his age by adding his voice to a chorus of his predecessors. His aim in the *Essay* is to bring home traditional wisdom by stating it superbly and to place Augustan man in a universal picture of mankind. He is concerned with a vision of common humanity transcending the idiosyncracies of place and personality.

The point of departure of the poem, as in *Paradise Lost*, is individual man confronted by the problem of evil. The analogy with *Paradise Lost* is strengthened by the image of the garden—now extended to include the whole world in which man dwells. (We shall see Voltaire return to the same compelling metaphor at the conclusion of *Candide.*) The four epistles treat man in his relations to the universe, to himself as a sentient being, to society and finally to happiness and eventual salvation. The first epistle is our concern.

A logical progression in ideas marks the ten parts of this epistle. At the start it is rebellious man who questions the ways of God. Man the microcosm sets out to assert himself against the macrocosm of the universe, and immediately confronts his finitude: "Can a part contain the whole?" We are but a portion of a universe, he has to learn—the mid-point in a Great Chain of Being, stretching from the smallest particle of inanimate matter to God Himself, and by definition we cannot envisage the grand scheme that the cosmic order embraces. Man's knowledge is "measured to his state and place"; to seek more is to exhibit classical *hubris,* Christian pride; not until Goethe's *Faust* will the problem be stated with added complications. The fallacy in our critique of the structure of the world at large, says Pope, is a too-rapid identification of the over-all pattern of divine providence with personal desire.

Pope then proceeds to examine the three causes of evil. First there are the catastrophes brought about by natural causes—the earthquakes and tempests that seem to defy human explanation, but are phenomena generated "not by partial, but by gen'ral laws." Next there are the limitations inherent in being "Man," a specific link of the Chain of Being: "The bliss of Man . . . / Is not to act or think beyond mankind." Finally, there is moral evil, man's misuse of the capabilities given him, capabilities which are summed up in the gift of reason bestowed upon man alone, while the lower orders—all equipped with their proper capabilities—do not share this ultimate, crowning dispensation. The triumphant final line of this epistle, "One truth is clear, WHATEVER IS, IS RIGHT," is an assertion about the rationale of the universe, and *not* a statement—though it has been often so misconstrued—that individual life is essentially rosy, blissful, or untroubled. Like his contemporary Swift, Pope was all too aware that man is merely *rationis capax*—a creature *capable* of reason, the attribute necessary if the individual is to harmonize his will with the cosmic framework.

But the modesty exhibited by Pope did not carry over to all his contemporaries and successors in the Enlightenment. As Pope saw it, the problem of evil was finally insoluble and humanity finally an enigma: "The glory, jest, and riddle of the world." Although outright revelation was minimized, faith and mystery were still present in Pope's vision. But when treated by lesser minds and lesser poets, the concepts he expounded became ridiculous. Moreover, complicated philosophical abstractions, such as the Great Chain of Being, plenitude, and the principle of sufficient reason, always tend to absurdity when oversimplified. The popularizers of the theories of the Enlightenment usually forgot, with rationalist zeal, that the identity of God's will with man's was an issue over which the best minds had *tentatively* speculated.

The selections from Swift and Voltaire that follow *An Essay on Man* in this volume treat with equal seriousness the state of man in the universe; even if satire is the vehicle of expression—grim with Swift, often extravagantly comic with Voltaire. Pope's *The Rape of the Lock*, "an heroi-comical poem," as he called it, illustrates another important aspect of the eighteenth century: the sheer delight in absurdity, wit, good humor, and human frivolity. The poem is not, however, without its serious moments ("The hungry judges soon the sentence sign,/ And wretches hang that jurymen may dine"); and while the dominant tone is bantering and gay, the poem is really about a serious subject, the destruction of society by its disarray of values. The objects on the heroine's dressing table reflect the jumble ("Here files of pins extend their shining rows,/ Puffs, powders, patches, Bibles, billet-doux") as does Ariel's speech warning of impending disaster:

> Whether the nymph shall
> break Diana's law,
> Or some frail china jar receive
> a flaw,
> Or stain her honor or her new
> brocade,
> Forget her prayers, or miss a
> masquerade,
> Or lose her heart, or necklace,
> at a ball;
> Or whether Heaven has
> doomed that Shock must
> fall.

The gaity and wit is engendered chiefly by the application of epic devices to a ridiculous situation and Pope's educated readers must have revelled in his parodic use of materials and devices from Homer, Virgil, and Milton. *The Rape of the Lock* is unequaled as an exposé of upper-class Augustan society, with its lapdogs, card games, and fashionable wigs, elegant dress, cosmetics, jewelry, and so forth. It is a society where no one seems to work and where social graces and distinctions are all important. From this poem the line goes directly to the plays of Oscar Wilde in the late nineteenth century and to the writings of Noel Coward and Evelyn Waugh in our own time. After finishing *The Rape of the Lock*, we return with increased concern to the empty antics, not only of our own time, with its jet-set and Hollywood, but to those of all men everywhere whose sense of values has been tragically confused.

SWIFT

Despite the fact that Swift's *Gulliver's Travels* antedates Pope's *Essay on Man* by some seven years, the texts are presented here in reverse chronological order. It has previously been stated that Pope's philosophical position is not to be confused with popular ideas of Optimism, and that for him man's existence ultimately remains an enigma. Nevertheless, there is a tone in the *Essay* of qualified ebullience, effected by those hearty heroic couplets which march down the page with the assurance of a regiment of guards. While a central concern for both authors is man's pride, in this poem Pope deals with moral dereliction in a series of measured abstract statements. Swift's corrosive satire shows us in a more concrete form—as does Voltaire's *Candide* which follows the *Travels* in this volume—what shapes folly and vice take. Pope told Swift in a letter (1730), "I am just now planning, or rather writing, a book [*The Essay on Man*] to make mankind look upon this life with comfort and pleasure, and put morality in a good humour." Against this genial statement, we have Swift saying to Pope (1725), "I have employed my time . . . in finishing, correcting, and transcribing my Travels . . . the chief end I propose to myself in all my labours is to *vex* [our italics] the world rather than divert it." Voltaire might have said the same about *Candide*.

The first three parts of *Gulliver* present no great difficulties in their interpretation. The diminutive Lilliputians reveal in their physical stature their spiritual and moral pettiness. The inhabitants of Brobdingnag again enable Swift to show "real" mankind's vanity from yet another perspective, when the ruler of that land of giants punctures Gulliver's portrayal of the "glories" of European civilization, reducing him to sullen silence. In an arresting anticipation of our own century's anxieties about technology, the excursion to Laputa displays the follies of an intellectualism divorced from feeling.

In the fourth and last voyage (which we present here) Swift splits man into two parts, symbolized by the horselike Houyhnhnms "wholly governed by reason," and the bestial Yahoos without "the least tincture of reason"—a species that Gulliver slowly comes to believe is really the human race, whereas he himself is merely a Yahoo possessing clothes. This is the portion of the *Travels* that early earned for Swift the reputation of being a bitter misanthrope. In 1851, Thackeray lectured to Victorian ladies and cautioned them not to read Part IV. "As for the moral, I think it horrible, shameful, unmanly, blasphemous . . . [Swift is] a monster gibbering shrieks, and gnashing imprecations against mankind." More recently the late Aldous Huxley (whose novel *Brave New World* owes much to Swiftian techniques) commented, "Swift never could forgive man for being a vertebrate animal as well as an immortal soul."

Though modern critical commentary about Part Four has been widely divergent, on one point there has been a fair degree of unanimity: Gulliver, when last we see him, back in England, writing his adventures is not to be identified with Swift. He has been driven to near-madness when he realizes that he can never attain the rationality of his Houyhnhnm masters, from whom he has taken a tearful farewell; and he even prefers the company of his horses and groom (who at least *smells* like a horse) to that of his family. That Swift intended Gulliver's attitude to be ludicrous seems attested by the author's use of verses written by Pope, to preface the second edition of *Gulliver*. One poem is a comic-plaintive appeal by Gulliver's wife, that he return to his neglected marital responsibilities. "Why then that dirty Stable-boy thy Care?/ What mean those Visits to the Sorrel Mare?" More important is the letter to Pope in 1725, already mentioned, which would seem to show—as does Swift's whole career—that he never subscribed to his antihero's glacial contempt for humanity. "I have ever hated all nations, professions, and communities, and my love is towards individuals . . . principally I hate and detest that animal called man, although I heartily love John, Peter, Thomas, and so forth. . . . I have got materials towards a treatise proving the falsity of that definition *animal rationale* [rational animal]; and to show it should be only *rationis capax* [capable of reason]."

R. S. Crane has shown that, in Latin textbooks on logic, familiar to Swift's educated readers, *homo est animal rationale* ("Man is a rational animal") has as its frequent antithesis, *equus est animal hinnibile* ("A horse is a whinnying animal"). This raises a second critical problem. If the Yahoos indubitably possess all of mankind's worst qualities, what of the gentle Houyhnhnms, exalted by Gulliver as ideal? True, being "wholly governed by reason" they seem devoid of all the emotions that motivate human depravity; and they, no doubt, emblemize the general Augustan disapproval of undisciplined passions, as impediments in the search for "truth." Yet the Houyhnhnm's simplistic and functional vocabulary (a lie is "the thing that is not") and their stoic attitude toward love, child-raising, and death suggest a life barren and lacking in vitality. Gulliver discovers that their name means "the perfection of nature"; and the complacency in which this view of themselves eventuates makes them lack the desirable "human" trait of curiosity, all their opinions being extremely limited and positive. That Gulliver admires their ability to thread needles and to carry trays is as much a comment on him as on them.

What is the final result of their teaching and example upon Gulliver? He sees the kindly Portuguese captain who rescues him as another Yahoo, albeit a good Yahoo. He writes his four voyages after his return to England to demonstrate that all human vices and frailties are attributable to pride; yet his own smug sense of alienation makes him guilty of that same sin. Both he and the Houyhnhnms lack love, the highest of the Christian virtues ("Faith, Hope, and Charity [*caritas*], and the greatest of these is Charity"). Though Swift's more than thirty years as dean of Dublin's St. Patrick's Cathedral has sometimes been seen as simply another example of the Erastianism of the English church, it seems finally more convincing to regard him as a compassionate Christian thinker for whom *caritas*—or its lack—was central to the human condition.

VOLTAIRE AND THE ENLIGHTENMENT

The younger Voltaire began as an Optimist and embraced these ideas in his early *Discourse in Verse on Mankind* (*Discours en vers sur l'homme*, 1738). For a time it may have appeared to him, particularly since he participated in the writing of the *Encyclopédie*, that he and his fellow philosophers were leading the rest of humanity toward a revival of the golden age on earth by dint of unaided "reason." But the course of Voltaire's own life and the pattern of his intellectual development brought about inevitable disillusion.

Tragedy has been described as a pattern in which theory is destroyed by a fact. For Voltaire and many of his contemporaries, the stubborn fact that threatened to destroy the theories of the Century of Light was the Lisbon earthquake of November 1, 1755, when an estimated thirty to fifty thousand persons perished—ironically on All Saints' Day, when the churches were crowded. It was the greatest natural catastrophe in Western Europe since Pompeii disappeared under Vesuvius' lava. In 1756 Voltaire wrote his first bitter rebuttal of the Optimists, the *Poem on the Disaster of Lisbon* (*Poème sur le désastre de Lisbonne*). He revaluated the self-satisfied cosmic acceptance of these philosophers as complacent, negative fatalism. For him it was "an insult to the sadness of our existence"—we who are "Tormented atoms on this pile of mud/ Swallowed up by death, the mere playthings of Fate." Voltaire's concluding line in the poem expresses his *respect* for God and his *love* for humanity.

The major work that grew out of Voltaire's disgust with Optimistic metaphysics was *Candide.* Written with incredible speed in 1758 (he claimed in three days) and out of white-hot indignation, it was published in 1759 and ran to some forty editions within twenty years. Like Dante, Voltaire immortalized his enemies. Pangloss, Candide's mentor, is a caricature of the Optimistic philosophers Christian Wolf(f) and Leibnitz. Jean-Jacques Rousseau, Voltaire's intellectual enemy (he once remarked, "If Rousseau is dead, it's one scoundrel the less"), flattered himself into believing that the portrait was of him. But Voltaire's satiric concern with individual thinkers was peripheral, and the truth is that his main target was a system, a way of looking at the world. Here he joins the company of great French *moralistes* we have earlier discussed. The framework for *Candide* is one that was popular with seventeenth- and eighteenth-century writers—the exotic romance, the travel story. The romancer could use such a story to satisfy the age's desire for vicarious voyaging and knowledge of distant, strange lands. The satirist could use it to indulge in contemporary and often dangerous criticism without fear of persecution. The philosopher could use it to reinforce the rationalists' conviction that all men are basically alike—children of "reason."

But we must not ignore the subtle ingredient added by Voltaire, the element that gives the book its distinctive flavor. This is Voltaire's *parody* of his literary models. The tale is a satire, almost a burlesque, of the romance, the adventure story, and the pedagogical novel. Did a novel ever contain more ridiculous improbabilities? Within a rigid formal structure (ten chapters in the Old World, ten in the New World, and the last ten back in Europe and Asia Minor) we are presented with dozens of recognition scenes, most of them accompanied by appropriate flashbacks as the once-lost character tells his tale to the wondering Candide. "I am consoled by one thing," says the ingenuous young man. "We see that we often meet people we thought we should never meet again." The recognition device is an excellent way to impose a design upon what otherwise would be a series of loosely linked adventures. It is also Voltaire's ironical commentary on storybook life in comparison with our own sorry existence, where the lost stay lost and the dead remain dead. Several of the major "deaths" in the story fortunately turn out to be not permanent; but half of Lisbon, two entire armies, the inhabitants of one ship and two castles, and miscellaneous llamas, monkeys, and sheep are summarily dispatched. A dim view of this best of all possible worlds!

In a later tale, *The Simple Fellow* (*L'Ingénu*, 1767), Voltaire has a priest tell the wandering Huron hero that God must have great designs for him, since He moves the young man about so freely. To this the Indian retorts that more likely the devil plans his itinerary. Candide never descends to such pessimism, even when at last he recovers his beloved Cunégonde, now a haggard washerwoman on the shores of the Bosphorus. Perhaps it is the vision of Eldorado that saves

Candide (and Voltaire) from complete despair. For a brief time the hero is allowed to dwell in a never-never land, a composite of all the utopian dreams of the Enlightenment.

The nineteenth-century writer Flaubert said that *Candide* was a book that made you want to gnash your teeth. Flaubert also commented that the conclusion of *Candide*, with its admonition to work, may be "serene and stupid, like life itself." Yet the garden must be cultivated. In a letter written in 1759, Voltaire remarked, "I have read a great deal; I have found nothing but uncertainties, lies, fanaticisms, and I am just about in the same certainty concerning our existence as I was when I was a suckling babe; I much prefer to plant, to sow, to build, and above all to be free." Voltaire seems to say that the answer is neither a complacent acceptance of existence —Optimism—nor an equally fatuous condemnation—pessimism —but rather an intermediate path which may be called *meliorism*.

LIVES, WRITINGS, AND CRITICISM

Biographical and critical works are listed only if they are available in English.

JEAN-BAPTISTE POQUELIN MOLIÈRE

LIFE. Born in Paris in 1622 as Jean-Baptiste Poquelin. His father was upholsterer to the king. Molière attended the Jesuit school at Clermont and later studied under the famous "libertine" and Epicurean philosopher Gassendi. At about the age of twenty-five he joined the Illustrious Theater (*Illustre Théâtre*), a company of traveling players formed by the Béjart family. From 1646 to 1658 Molière and his troupe toured the provinces, playing mostly short pieces after the fashion of the Italian *commedia dell' arte*. In 1658 the players were ordered to perform before Louis XIV in Paris, and soon after their initial success they became the Troupe de Monsieur, enjoying royal patronage. Despite the intrigues of rival companies, particularly that of the Hôtel de Bourgogne, Molière's prestige increased; and when his theater of the Petit Bourbon was demolished, the king gave him the Palais-Royal theater in 1661. Molière married Armande Béjart in 1662—an unfortunate match, since his enemies spread the scandal that she was his daughter by a former mistress, Madeleine Béjart, although in reality the women were sisters. *Tartuffe,* a study in religious hypocrisy, first produced in 1664, embroiled the playwright with certain groups in the Church. The king was forced to ban it, but Molière succeeded in having the play published and reperformed by 1669. In 1673, although ailing, the author-actor insisted on playing the lead role in his *Imaginary Invalid*, and he died a few hours after a performance on February 17, 1673. The Church refused him burial; but Louis XIV interceded at the pleas of his widow, and a compromise was effected.

CHIEF WRITINGS. Molière's first great success was *The High-Brow Ladies* (*Les Précieuses ridicules*, 1659), a satire on the intellectual pretensions of Parisian fashionable society. Approximately two dozen comedies can be definitely identified as his own. Among these are *The School for Husbands* (*L'École des maris*, 1661); *Don Juan* (1665)—a treatment of the legendary hero; *The Misanthrope* (*Le Misanthrope*, 1666); *Tartuffe*(1664-1669); *The Miser* (*L'Avare*, 1668); *The Bourgeois Gentleman* (*Le Bourgeois Gentilhomme*, 1670); *The Wise Ladies* (*Les Femmes savantes*, 1672); and his last play, *The Imaginary Invalid* (*Le Malade imaginaire*, 1673). *The Bourgeois Gentleman* was first performed at Chambord on November 14, 1670, and in Paris on November 29. Molière played the part of M. Jourdain. It is actually entitled a "comedy-ballet"; the court composer Lully (Lulli) wrote the incidental music for the play and sang the role of the Mufti. The part of Lucile was taken by Molière's wife.

BIOGRAPHY AND CRITICISM. Karl Mantzius, *Molière* (1908), is a good factual account of the author's life. C. H. C. Wright, *French Classicism* (1920), offers a brief survey of the period; Martin Turnell, *The Classical Moment* (1947), includes studies of Molière, Racine, and Corneille; W. G. Moore, *Molière: A New Criticism* (1950), is a recent study in English, as are J. D. Hubert, *Molière and the Comedy of Intellect* (1962) and D. B. Wyndham Lewis, *Molière: The Comic Mask* (1959).

Recommended also are the chapter on Molière in E. Auerbach, *Mimesis* (1953); L. Grossman, *Men and Masks: A Study of Molière* (1963); and R. McBride, *The Sceptical Vision of Molière* (1977).

JEAN RACINE

LIFE. Born in 1639 in the Valois district, eighty miles from Paris. His father was a government official. Racine attended the College de Beauvais, and from 1655 to 1659 studied at the Jansenist center of Port-Royal, when that institution was at its peak. (Pascal wrote his *Provincial Letters*, the *Provinciales*, dealing with Port-Royal, in 1656 and 1657.) Racine came to Paris in 1660, encouraged by a friend, the poet La Fontaine. His early plays were failures, and he went into seclusion at Uzès, in Provence—for an interval of retirement similar to Milton's Horton period. He returned to Paris early in 1663, received the patronage of the court and the nobility, and soon came to be one of the leading playwrights, along with Molière and Corneille. He left Paris in 1677, officially to write history; married Catherine de Romanet (after earlier liaisons with two of his actresses); and returned to Port-Royal—a move indicative of his increasing piety and interest in religious speculation. (Most of his seven children became nuns or priests.) He led the life of the affluent country gentleman, interrupted by occasional trips to Paris and by missions as historiographer on Louis XIV's campaigns during the period from 1678 to 1693. Racine died in 1699 and was buried at Port-Royal. His body was exhumed when the place was destroyed in 1711, and he was placed next to Pascal at the church of St. Étienne-du-Mont in Paris.

CHIEF WRITINGS. Racine's plays, twelve in all, consist of an early comedy, *The Suitors* (*Les Plaideurs*, 1668), based on Aristophanes; two tragedies, *The Thebaid (La Thébaïde*, 1664), and *Alexander the Great (Alexander le Grand*, 1665), both imitative of Corneille; seven "profane" or secular tragedies; and two biblical dramas. His first major writing was *Andromache* (*Andromaque*, 1667), and this play enjoyed a success almost as great as that of the famous *Cid* of Corneille. *Britannicus* followed in 1669, *Bérénice* in 1670, *Mithridates* (*Mithridate*) in 1673—three tragedies whose sources were classical historians: Tacitus, Suetonius, and Plutarch. *Bajazet* (1672), marked an excursion into oriental *decor;* it is perhaps the most contemporary of Racine's plays, since despite the exotic locale, the plot—according to Racine—came from an adventure that had taken place only thirty years before. Both *Iphegenia* (*Iphigénie*, 1674), and *Phaedra* (*Phèdre*, 1677), were modeled on plays by Euripides. The latter was performed at the Hôtel de Bourgogne, the theater used by Molière's rivals; and it was after the play's success that Racine went into semiretirement. Twelve years later, at the request of Mme. de Maintenon, Racine wrote his first biblical drama, *Esther* (1689); this, like *Athalia* (*Athalie*, 1691), dealt with Old Testament material, and both plays were designed for performance at Mme. de Maintenon's school for girls at Saint-Cyr.

BIOGRAPHY AND CRITICISM. An excellent biography of the playwright, A. F. B. Clark, *Racine* (1939), may be supplemented by M. Duclaux, *The Life of Racine* (1925); K. Vossler, *Racine* (1926). C. H. C. Wright, *French Classicism* (1920), and Martin Turnell, *The Classical Moment* (1947), are recommended for background material. A recent and interesting study of Racine's plays is V. Orgel, *A New View of the Plays of Racine* (1948); a valuable edition of *Phèdre* has been prepared by R. C. Knight (1943); and translations by Lacy Lockert of several of Racine's plays—including *Phèdre*—in rhymed alexandrine couplets were published in 1936. E. Auerbach's chapter on Racine in *Mimesis* (1953) is excellent; and there is also G. Brereton, *Jean Racine: A Critical Biography* (1951); K. Wheatley, *Racine and English Classicism* (1956); M. Bowra, *The Simplicity of Racine* (1956); and the chapters on Racine in W. Sypher, *Four Stages of Renaissance Style* (1955) and in F. Fergusson, *The Idea of a Theater* (1949). More recently, there is B. Weinberg, *The Art of Jean Racine* (1963); P. France, *Racine's Rhetoric* (1965); O. de Mourgues, *Racine: Or, The Triumph of Relevance* (1967); a series of essays about Racine edited by R. C. Knight (1969); P. H. Nurse, *Classical Voices* (1971), with a chapter on Racine; M. Turnell, *Jean Racine: Dramatist* (1972); and G. Pocock, *Corneille and Racine* (1973).

FRANÇOIS, DUC DE LA ROCHEFOUCAULD

LIFE. Born on September 15, 1613, in Paris as Prince de Marcillac, La Rochefoucauld later received the title of Duke. He had an early army career. At 16 (in 1629), the year he married, he came to court. Through Mme. de Chevreuse he became attached to Anne of Austria, Louis XIII's wife, whose escape to Brussels he once tried to effect. He spent eight days in the Bastille, and was then exiled to his family estates after eight years of intriguing at Court. When Anne became regent, La Rochefoucauld opposed her advisor, Mazarin. La Rochefoucauld fought on the side of the Prince de Condé in the two outbreaks during Louis XIV's minority: the *Fronde of the Parlement* (1648–1649), and the *Fronde of the Princes* (1650–1653), and was wounded in 1652. He spent the remainder of his life as close friend to Mme. de Sablé, Mme. de La Fayette, and Mme. de Sevigné, whose salons were intellectual centers in Paris. He died March 17, 1680—legend has it in the arms of the theologian Bossuet.

CHIEF WRITINGS. His *Maxims* were first published anonymously in 1665; the last augmented edition appeared in 1678. La Rochefoucauld's *Memoirs* (1662) are chiefly concerned with his experiences as a *Frondeur*.

BIOGRAPHY AND CRITICISM: E. Gosse, *Three French Moralists* (1918); H. A. Grubbs, *The Originality of La Rochefoucauld's Maxims* (1929); M. Bishop, *The Life and Adventures of La Rochefoucauld* (1951); Sister M. F. Zeller, *New Aspects of La Rochefoucauld's Style* (1954); and W. G. Moore, *La Rochefoucauld* (1969).

JEAN DE LA FONTAINE

LIFE. Born July 8, 1621, at Château-Thierry in Compiègne, where his father was chief huntsman and forester on the royal preserves. At one time La Fontaine briefly considered entering holy orders; he studied law, was admitted to the bar, but never practised. He married Marie Héricart when he was 26 (in 1647); they were separated in 1649. An indolent life in the provinces was succeeded after 1656 by an equally pleasant existence in Paris, where he was the favorite of various elegant ladies: the dowager Duchesse d'Orléans, Mme. de la Sablière (at whose residence he lived for many years), Mme. d'Hervart. Nicolas Fouquet, Superintendent of Finance (1653-1661) under Louis XIV, became his patron. When Fouquet fell, denounced by Colbert and others for his dubious financial operations, La Fontaine readily found other benefactors to guarantee him a life devoid of monetary worries. Molière, Racine, and Boileau were his close friends. He became a member of the French Academy in 1684; La Fontaine was on the side of the "Ancients" in the famous literary quarrel between the Ancients and the Moderns. Epicurean and skeptic, by temperament inclined toward neither philosophy nor religion, he increased his Christian devotions after a serious illness in 1692. He died April 13, 1695.

CHIEF WRITINGS. The *Fables*, published in twelve books (1668, 1678–1679, 1694) were his masterpiece. Other works included *Stories and Tales in Verse* (1664), mainly imitations from Ariosto and Boccaccio.

BIOGRAPHY AND CRITICISM. F. Hamel, *La Fontaine* (1912); P. A. Wadsworth, *Young La Fontaine* (1952); M. Sutherland, *La Fontaine* (1953); M. Guiton, *La Fontaine: Poet and Counterpoet* (1961).

ALEXANDER POPE

LIFE. Born in May 21, 1688, in London, Pope was the son of a retired linen merchant. Because of his Roman Catholic parentage, Pope was excluded from an academic or political career; indeed, in 1700 the family was forced to move to Binfield in Windsor Forest to comply with the law forbidding Roman Catholics to live within ten miles of London. In the closing years of Queen Anne's reign he was closely associated with Whig journalists and pamphleteers, including Addison; later he joined literary forces with those Tories (Swift, Gay, Arbuthnot, and others) who styled themselves the Scriblerus Club. He was the first English poet to achieve financial independence through his writings, and in 1718 he bought a small estate at Twickenham, on the Thames outside of London. There he spent the rest of his life writing, entertaining his friends, and amusing himself with landscape gardening. He was never in good health—tiny in size, he later became afflicted with tubercular curvature of the spine—and he once referred to "this long disease, my life." He died of dropsy on May 30, 1744.

CHIEF WRITINGS. Pope devoted his youth to the study of Latin verse and of the technique of his predecessor John Dryden. His *Pastorals* were published when he was twenty-one, although he insisted that he had written them when he was sixteen. His translations of Homer's *Iliad* (1715-1720) and *Odyssey* (1725-1726), brought him fame and financial success: for the former he received over five thousand pounds, equal today to well above a hundred thousand dollars. The *Essay on Criticism* (1711), states the essential literary canons of the day, even as the *Essay on Man* (1733-1734) is the repository for much of the philosophic doctrine of Deism. The bulk of Pope's poetry, apart from the translations, is satiric; works of this type include *The Rape of the Lock* (1711-1714), the four *Moral Essays* (1731-1733), the *Epistle to Dr. Arbuthnot* (1735), and *The Dunciad* (1729-1743).

BIOGRAPHY AND CRITICISM. Biographies include the life by W. J. Courthope, in *The Works of Alexander Pope*, edited by W. Elwin and W. J. Courthope, Vol. V (1889); E. Sitwell, *Alexander Pope* (1930); G. Sherburn, *The Early Career of Alexander Pope* (1934); B. Dobrée, *Alexander Pope* (1951). For the background, A. O. Lovejoy, *The Great Chain of Being* (1933); J. Sutherland, *A Preface to Eighteenth Century Poetry* (1948); and B. Willey, *The Eighteenth Century Background* (1940), are recommended Valuable general studies on Pope's poetry are F. R. Leavis, *Revaluations* (1936); G. Tillotson, *The Poetry of Pope* (1933); R. A. Brower, *Alexander Pope: The Poetry of Allusion* (1959); and T. R. Edwards, *This Dark Estate: A Reading of Pope* (1963). For *An Essay on Man*, consult the introduction to the poem in the Twickenham edition, edited by M. Mack (1950), and Ernest Tuveson, "An Essay on Man and 'The Way of Ideas'", *Journal of English Literary History*, XXVI (September, 1959). There is also the *Correspondence*, edited by G. Sherburne (1957). More recent studies are *Essential Articles for the Study of Alexander Pope*, edited by M. Mack (1964); M. Nicolson and G. Rousseau, *This Long Disease: Alexander Pope and the Sciences* (1968); J. A. Jones, *Pope's Couplet Art* (1969); M. Mack, *The Garden and the City* (1969); H. D. Weinbrot, *The Formal Strain* (1969); D. H. White, *Pope and the Context of Controversy: The Manipulation of Ideas in* An Essay on Man (1970); and J. Reeves, *The Reputation and Writing of Alexander Pope* (1976); H. Erskine-Hill, *The Social Milieu of Pope* (1975).

JONATHAN SWIFT

LIFE. Born on November 30, 1667, in Dublin, of English parents. Educated at Kilkenny Grammar School and Trinity College, Dublin. In 1688 or early 1689, the political troubles occasioned by James II's abdication and his invasion of Ireland drove Swift and other Anglo-Irish to England. Between 1689 and 1699 he resided intermittently in the household of his kinsman, Sir William Temple, at Moor Park. There he met Esther Johnson, the daughter of Sir William's steward. She was the object of Swift's strong affection until her death in 1728, and she inspired the famous *Journal to Stella*, Stella being the name he gave her. (These were journal-letters written between 1710 and 1713, when he was in England and she in Ireland and first published in 1766. By 1716 rumors spread that they were secretly married, but this has never been verified.) In 1692 he received the M.A. degree from Oxford, and in 1695 he was ordained a priest in the Anglican Church. He was installed as dean of St. Patrick's Cathedral in Dublin in 1713. Swift wrote his first political tract in 1701 in defense of impeached Whig statesmen; but in 1710 he left that party to become an ardent Tory, feeling that the Whigs insufficiently supported the Anglican Church in Ireland. As spokesman for the Tories, he became the most effective political journalist of the time. His friends numbered many of the leading writers and intellectuals of the day: Addison, Steele, Gay, Prior, Congreve, Oxford, Bolingbroke, and Pope; indeed, he stayed with Pope at Twickenham in the summer of 1726, a year before his last visit to England. In 1742 he was judged to be "of unsound mind and memory," and guardians were appointed to handle his affairs. He died on October 19, 1745, leaving the bulk of his estate to found a hospital for the insane.

CHIEF WRITINGS. *A Tale of a Tub* and *The Battle of the Books* (1704) first displayed Swift's satiric genius. These were followed by *The Bickerstaff Papers* (1709) and *An Argument against Abolishing Christianity* (1711). The *Journal to Stella* has already been mentioned. Under the pseudonym of "M. B. Drapier," Swift published a series of public letters in 1724 attacking English policies in Ireland. Although most of Dublin knew him to be the author, no one came forward to accept the three-hundred-pound reward offered by the British to reveal information about Drapier. These letters established Swift as an Irish national hero, which he still is today. *Gulliver's Travels* was published in London in 1726, and *A Modest Proposal* in 1729.

BIOGRAPHY AND CRITICISM. H. Craik, *The Life of Jonathan Swift* (1882); L. Stephen, *Swift* (1882, in *English Men of Letters*); C. Van Doren, *Swift* (1930); R. Quintana, *The Mind and Art of Jonathan Swift* (1936); A. E. Case, *Four Essays on Gulliver's Travels* (1945); B. Ackworth, *Swift* (1948); W. B. Ewald, *Swift* (1954); I. Ehrenpreis, *The Personality of Jonathan Swift* (1958); K. Williams, *Jonathan Swift and the Age of Compromise* (1959); I. Ehrenpreis, *Swift: The Man, His Works and the Age*, vol. I, *Mr. Swift and His Contemporaries* (1962), vol. II, *Dr. Swift* (1967); E. W. Rosenheim, *Swift and the Satirist's Art* (1963); H. Davis, *Jonathan Swift: Essays on His Satire and Other Studies* (1964); books containing substantial sections on Swift include M. Price, *To the Palace of Wisdom* (1964), and R. Paulson, *The Fictions of Satire* (1967); W. B. Carnochan, *Lemuel Gulliver's Mirror for Man* (1969); D. Donoghue, *Swift* (1969). See also *Swift*, a collection of critical essays, edited by E. Tuveson (1964); *Gulliver's Travels*, an annotated text with critical essays, edited by R. A. Greenberg (1970); D. Ward, *Jonathan Swift* (1973); and A. L. Rowse, *Jonathan Swift, Major Prophet* (1976).

FRANCOIS-MARIE AROUET DE VOLTAIRE

LIFE. Born on November 21, 1694, in Paris, as François-Marie Arouet. His father was a minor treasury official, originally from Poitou. Voltaire attended a Jesuit school and later undertook and abandoned the study of law. He spent eleven months in the Bastille (1717–1718), imprisoned by *lettre de cachet*, for writing satiric verses about the aristocracy. By 1718 he was using the name Voltaire. Literary and social success soon followed; speculations in the Compagnie des Indes made him wealthy by 1726. That same year the Chevalier de Rohan had him beaten and again sent to the Bastille, and 1726–1729 saw him in exile, mostly in England. From 1734 to 1749 he pursued philosophical, historical, and scientific studies, and became the companion of Mme. du Châtelet on her estate at Cirey. His election to the French Academy took place in 1746. From 1750 to 1753 he stayed with Frederick the Great of Prussia, at Potsdam, after Louis XV had failed to give him sufficient patronage. That unstable alliance broke in 1753. Soon after, Voltaire bought adjacent property in France and Switzerland, and settled first at his château, Les Délices, just outside Geneva, and then at nearby Ferney, on French soil. It was from there that he, as the foremost representative of the Enlightenment, directed his campaigns against intolerance and injustice. He made a triumphant return to Paris in 1778, and died there on May 30.

CHIEF WRITINGS. Voltaire's first serious work was a tragedy on Greek lines, *Oedipus* (*Oedipe,* 1715). His epic, *The Henriad* (*La Henriade*)—in praise of the tolerance of Henry IV—was published in 1728. His stay in England produced the *Letters on the English* (*Lettres sur les Anglais,* 1733); but before that, in 1731, appeared the *History of Charles XII* (*Histoire de Charles XII*) of Sweden—perhaps the first "modern" history. *Zadig* (1748), was his first famous philosophical tale, and *Candide* (1759), marked the summit of his achievement in this genre. Another major historical enterprise was *The Century of Louis XIV* (*Le Siècle de Louis XIV,* 1751). His *Philosophical Dictionary* (*Dictionnaire philosophique,* 1764) may be considered most typical both of Voltaire and of the Encyclopedists. In quantity, Voltaire's correspondence is almost unequaled, since he wrote to virtually every important intellectual, social, and political figure of his age.

BIOGRAPHY AND CRITICISM. Good biographies and studies of Voltaire are H. N. Brailsford, *Voltaire* (1935); R. Aldington, *Voltaire* (1934); G. Brandes, *The Life of Voltaire* (undated); and N. Torrey, *The Spirit of Voltaire* (1938). The best edition of *Candide*—to which this editor is greatly indebted—is by A. Morize, 1913. Also recommended are more recent studies: I. O. Wade, *Voltaire and "Candide"* (1959); P. Gay, *Voltaire's Politics: The Poet as Realist* (1961); two articles by W. Bottiglia in *Publications of the Modern Language Association,* "Candide's Garden," LXVI (September, 1951); N. Mitford, *Voltaire in Love* (1957); "The Eldorado Episode in *Candide,*" LXXIII (September, 1958); T. Besterman, *Voltaire* (1969); and J. Hearsey, *Voltaire* (1976).

JEAN-BAPTISTE POQUELIN MOLIÈRE (1622–1673)

Tartuffe or The Imposter (Le Tartuffe ou L'Imposteur) *

Preface

Here is a comedy that has excited a good deal of discussion and that has been under attack for a long time; and the persons who are mocked by it have made it plain that they are more powerful in France than all whom my plays have satirized up to this time. Noblemen, ladies of fashion, cuckolds, and doctors all kindly consented to their presentation,[1] which they themselves seemed to enjoy along with everyone else; but hypocrites do not understand banter: they became angry at once, and found it strange that I was bold enough to represent their actions and to care to describe a profession shared by so many good men. This is a crime for which they cannot forgive me, and they have taken up arms against my comedy in a terrible rage. They were careful not to attack it at the point that had wounded them: they are too crafty for that and too clever to reveal their true character. In keeping with their lofty custom, they have used the cause of God to mask their private interests; and *Tartuffe*, they say, is a play that offends piety: it is filled with abominations from beginning to end, and nowhere is there a line that does not deserve to be burned. Every syllable is wicked, the very gestures are criminal, and the slightest glance, turn of the head, or step from right to left conceals mysteries that they are able to explain to my disadvantage. In vain did I submit the play to the criticism of my friends and the scrutiny of the public: all the corrections I could make, the judgment of the king and queen who saw the play,[2] the approval of great princes and ministers of state who honored it with their presence. the opinion of good men who found it worthwhile, all this did not help. They will not let go of their prey, and every day of the week they have pious zealots abusing me in public and damning me out of charity.

I would care very little about all they might say except that their devices make enemies of men whom I respect and gain the support of genuinely good men, whose faith they know and who, because of

* Molière's *Tartuffe* translated by Richard Wilbur.

The first version of *Tartuffe* was performed in 1664 and the second in 1667. The third and final version was published in March, 1669, accompanied by this preface. When a second edition of the third version was printed in June, 1669, Molière added his three petitions to Louis XIV; they follow the preface.

1. a reference to some of Molière's earlier plays, such as *Les Précieuses ridicules* and *L'École des femmes*.

2. Louis XIV was married to Marie Thérèse of Austria.

the warmth of their piety, readily accept the impressions that others present to them. And it is this which forces me to defend myself. Especially to the truly devout do I wish to vindicate my play, and I beg of them with all my heart not to condemn it before seeing it, to rid themselves of preconceptions, and not aid the cause of men dishonored by their actions.

If one takes the trouble to examine my comedy in good faith, he will surely see that my intentions are innocent throughout, and tend in no way to make fun of what men revere; that I have presented the subject with all the precautions that its delicacy imposes; and that I have used all the art and skill that I could to distinguish clearly the character of the hypocrite from that of the truly devout man. For that purpose I used two whole acts to prepare the appearance of my scoundrel. Never is there a moment's doubt about his character; he is known at once from the qualities I have given him; and from one end of the play to the other, he does not say a word, he does not perform an action which does not depict to the audience the character of a wicked man, and which does not bring out in sharp relief the character of the truly good man which I oppose to it.

I know full well that by way of reply, these gentlemen try to insinuate that it is not the role of the theater to speak of these matters; but with their permission, I ask them on what do they base this fine doctrine. It is a proposition they advance as no more than a supposition, for which they offer not a shred of proof; and surely it would not be difficult to show them that comedy, for the ancients, had its origin in religion and constituted a part of its ceremonies; that our neighbors, the Spaniards, have hardly a single holiday celebration in which a comedy is not a part; and that even here in France, it owes its birth to the efforts of a religious brotherhood who still own the Hôtel de Bourgogne, where the most important mystery plays of our faith were presented[3]; that you can still find comedies printed in gothic letters under the name of a learned doctor of the Sorbonne[4]; and without going so far, in our own day the religious dramas of Pierre Corneille[5] have been performed to the admiration of all France.

If the function of comedy is to correct men's vices, I do not see why any should be exempt. Such a condition in our society would be much more dangerous than the thing itself; and we have seen that the theater is admirably suited to provide correction. The most forceful lines of a serious moral statement are usually less powerful than

3. a reference to the *Confrérie de la Passion et Résurrection de Notre-Seigneur* (the Fraternity of the Passion and Resurrection of Our Saviour), founded in 1402. The Hôtel de Bourgogne was a rival theater of Molière.

4. probably Maitre Jehan Michel, a medical doctor who wrote mystery plays.

5. Pierre Corneille (1606–1684) and Racine were France's two greatest writers of classic tragedy. The two dramas Molière doubtlessly had in mind were *Polyeucte* (1643) and *Théodore, vierge et martyre* (1645).

those of satire; and nothing will reform most men better than the depiction of their faults. It is a vigorous blow to vices to expose them to public laughter. Criticism is taken lightly, but men will not tolerate satire. They are quite willing to be mean, but they never like to be ridiculed.

I have been attacked for having placed words of piety in the mouth of my impostor. Could I avoid doing so in order to represent properly the character of a hypocrite? It seemed to me sufficient to reveal the criminal motives which make him speak as he does, and I have eliminated all ceremonial phrases, which nonetheless he would not have been found using incorrectly. Yet some say that in the fourth act he sets forth a vicious morality; but is not this a morality which everyone has heard again and again? Does my comedy say anything new here? And is there any fear that ideas so thoroughly detested by everyone can make an impression on men's minds; that I make them dangerous by presenting them in the theater; that they acquire authority from the lips of a scoundrel? There is not the slightest suggestion of any of this; and one must either approve the comedy of *Tartuffe* or condemn all comedies in general.

This has indeed been done in a furious way for some time now, and never was the theater so much abused.[6] I cannot deny that there were Church Fathers who condemned comedy; but neither will it be denied me that there were some who looked on it somewhat more favorably. Thus authority, on which censure is supposed to depend, is destroyed by this disagreement; and the only conclusion that can be drawn from this difference of opinion among men enlightened by the same wisdom is that they viewed comedy in different ways, and that some considered it in its purity, while others regarded it in its corruption and confused it with all those wretched performances which have been rightly called performances of filth.

And in fact, since we should talk about things rather than words, and since most misunderstanding comes from including contrary notions in the same word, we need only to remove the veil of ambiguity and look at comedy in itself to see if it warrants condemnation. It will surely be recognized that as it is nothing more than a clever poem which corrects men's faults by means of agreeable lessons, it cannot be condemned without injustice. And if we listened to the voice of ancient times on this matter, it would tell us that its most famous philosophers have praised comedy—they who professed so austere a wisdom and who ceaselessly denounced the vices of their times. It would tell us that Aristotle spent his evenings at the theater[7] and took the trouble to reduce the art of making comedies to

6. Molière had in mind Nicole's two attacks on the theater: *Visionnaires* (1666) and *Traité de Comédie,* the Prince de Conti's *Traité de Comédie* (1666).

7. a reference to Aristotle's *Poetics* (composed between 335 and 322 B.C., the year of his death).

rules. It would tell us that some of its greatest and most honored men took pride in writing comedies themselves[8]; and that others did not disdain to recite them in public; that Greece expressed its admiration for this art by means of handsome prizes and magnificent theaters to honor it; and finally, that in Rome this same art also received extraordinary honors; I do not speak of Rome run riot under the license of the emperors, but of disciplined Rome, governed by the wisdom of the consuls, and in the age of the full vigor of Roman dignity.

I admit that there have been times when comedy became corrupt. And what do men not corrupt every day? There is nothing so innocent that men cannot turn it to crime; nothing so beneficial that its values cannot be reversed; nothing so good in itself that it cannot be put to bad uses. Medical knowledge benefits mankind and is revered as one of our most wonderful possessions; and yet there was a time when it fell into discredit, and was often used to poison men. Philosophy is a gift of Heaven; it has been given to us to bring us to the knowledge of a God by contemplating the wonders of nature; and yet we know that often it has been turned away from its function and has been used openly in support of impiety. Even the holiest of things are not immune from human corruption, and every day we see scoundrels who use and abuse piety, and wickedly make it serve the greatest of crimes. But this does not prevent one from making the necessary distinctions. We do not confuse in the same false inference the goodness of things that are corrupted with the wickedness of the corrupt. The function of an art is always distinguished from its misuse; and as medicine is not forbidden because it was banned in Rome,[9] nor philosophy because it was publicly condemned in Athens,[10] we should not suppress comedy simply because it has been condemned at certain times. This censure was justified then for reasons which no longer apply today; it was limited to what was then seen; and we should not seize on these limits, apply them more rigidly than is necessary, and include in our condemnation the innocent along with the guilty. The comedy that this censure attacked is in no way the comedy that we want to defend. We must be careful not to confuse the one with the other. There may be two persons whose morals may be completely different. They may have no resemblance to one another except in their names, and it would be a terrible injustice to want to condemn Olympia, who is a good woman, because there is also an Olympia who is lewd. Such procedures would make for great confusion everywhere. Everything under the sun

8. The Roman consul and general responsible for the final destruction of Carthage in 146 B.C., Scipio Africanus Minor (*ca.* 185-129 B.C.), collaborated with the writer of comedies, Terence (Publius Terentius Afer, *ca.* 195 or 185-*ca.* 159 B.C.).

9. Pliny the Elder says that the Romans expelled their doctors at the same time that the Greeks did theirs.

10. an allusion to Socrates' condemnation to death.

would be condemned; now since this rigor is not applied to the countless instances of abuse we see every day, the same should hold for comedy, and those plays should be approved in which instruction and virtue reign supreme.

I know there are some so delicate that they cannot tolerate a comedy, who say that the most decent are the most dangerous, that the passions they present are all the more moving because they are virtuous, and that men's feelings are stirred by these presentations. I do not see what great crime it is to be affected by the sight of a generous passion; and this utter insensitivity to which they would lead us is indeed a high degree of virtue! I wonder if so great a perfection resides within the strength of human nature, and I wonder if it is not better to try to correct and moderate men's passions than to try to suppress them altogether. I grant that there are places better to visit than the theater; and if we want to condemn every single thing that does not bear directly on God and our salvation, it is right that comedy be included, and I should willingly grant that it be condemned along with everything else. But if we admit, as is in fact true, that the exercise of piety will permit interruptions, and that men need amusement, I maintain that there is none more innocent than comedy. I have dwelled too long on this matter. Let me finish with the words of a great prince on the comedy, *Tartuffe*.[11]

Eight days after it had been banned, a play called *Scaramouche the Hermit*[12] was performed before the court; and the king, on his way out, said to this great prince: "I should really like to know why the persons who make so much noise about Molière's comedy do not say a word about *Scaramouche*." To which the prince replied, "It is because the comedy of *Scaramouche* makes fun of Heaven and religion, which these gentlemen do not care about at all, but that of Molière makes fun of *them*, and that is what they cannot bear."

THE AUTHOR

First Petition[13]

(presented to the King on the comedy of Tartuffe)

Sire,

As the duty of comedy is to correct men by amusing them, I be-

11. One of Molière's benefactors who liked the play was the Prince de Condé; de Condé had *Tartuffe* read to him and also privately performed for him.

12. A troupe of Italian comedians had just performed the licentious farce, where a hermit dressed as a monk makes love to a married woman, announcing that *questo e per mortificar la carne* ("this is to mortify the flesh").

13. The first of the three *petitions* or *placets* to Louis XIV concerning the play. On May 12, 1664, *Tartuffe*—or at least the first three acts roughly as they now stand—was performed at Versailles. A cabal unfavorable to Molière, including the Archbishop of Paris, Hardouin de Péréfixe, Queen-Mother Anne of Austria, certain influential courtiers, and the Brotherhood or Company of the Holy Sacrament (formed in 1627 to enforce morality), arranged that the play be banned and Molière censured.

lieved that in my occupation I could do nothing better than attack the vices of my age by making them ridiculous; and as hypocrisy is undoubtedly one of the most common, most improper, and most dangerous, I thought, Sire, that I would perform a service for all good men of your kingdom if I wrote a comedy which denounced hypocrites and placed in proper view all of the contrived poses of these incredibly virtuous men, all of the concealed villainies of these counterfeit believers who would trap others with a fraudulent piety and a pretended virtue.

I have written this comedy, Sire, with all the care and caution that the delicacy of the subject demands; and so as to maintain all the more properly the admiration and respect due to truly devout men, I have delineated my character as sharply as I could; I have left no room for doubt; I have removed all that might confuse good with evil, and have used for this painting only the specific colors and essential lines that make one instantly recognize a true and brazen hypocrite.

Nevertheless, all my precautions have been to no avail. Others have taken advantage of the delicacy of your feelings on religious matters, and they have been able to deceive you on the only side of your character which lies open to deception: your respect for holy things. By underhanded means, the Tartuffes have skillfully gained Your Majesty's favor, and the models have succeeded in eliminating the copy, no matter how innocent it may have been and no matter what resemblance was found between them.

Although the suppression of this work was a serious blow for me, my misfortune was nonetheless softened by the way in which Your Majesty explained his attitude on the matter; and I believed, Sire, that Your Majesty removed any cause I had for complaint, as you were kind enough to declare that you found nothing in this comedy that you would forbid me to present in public.

Yet, despite this glorious declaration of the greatest and most enlightened king in the world, despite the approval of the Papal Legate[14] and of most of our churchmen, all of whom, at private readings of my work, agreed with the views of Your Majesty, despite all this, a book has appeared by a certain priest[15] which boldly contradicts all of these noble judgments. Your Majesty expressed himself in vain, and the Papal Legate and churchmen gave their opinion to no avail: sight unseen, my comedy is diabolical, and so is my brain; I am a devil garbed in flesh and disguised as a man,[16] a libertine, a disbeliever who deserves a punishment that will set an example. It is not

14. Cardinal Legate Chigi, nephew to Pope Alexander VII, heard a reading of *Tartuffe* at Fontainebleau on August 4, 1664.

15. Pierre Roullé, the curate of St. Barthélémy, who wrote a scathing attack on the play and sent his book to the king.

16. Molière took some of these phrases from Roullé.

enough that fire expiate my crime in public, for that would be letting me off too easily: the generous piety of this good man will not stop there; he will not allow me to find any mercy in the sight of God; he demands that I be damned, and that will settle the matter.

This book, Sire, was presented to Your Majesty; and I am sure that you see for yourself how unpleasant it is for me to be exposed daily to the insults of these gentlemen, what harm these abuses will do my reputation if they must be tolerated, and finally, how important it is for me to clear myself of these false charges and let the public know that my comedy is nothing more than what they want it to be. I will not ask, Sire, for what I need for the sake of my reputation and the innocence of my work: enlightened kings such as you do not need to be told what is wished of them; like God, they see what we need and know better than we what they should give us. It is enough for me to place my interests in Your Majesty's hands, and I respectfully await whatever you may care to command.

(August, 1664)

Second Petition[17]

(presented to the King in his camp before the city of Lille, in Flanders)

Sire,

It is bold indeed for me to ask a favor of a great monarch in the midst of his glorious victories; but in my present situation, Sire, where will I find protection anywhere but where I seek it, and to whom can I appeal against the authority of the power that crushes me,[18] if not to the source of power and authority, the just dispenser of absolute law, the sovereign judge and master of all?

My comedy, Sire, has not enjoyed the kindnesses of Your Majesty. All to no avail, I produced it under the title of *The Hypocrite* and disguised the principal character as a man of the world; in vain I gave him a little hat, long hair, a wide collar, a sword, and lace clothing,[19] softened the action and carefully eliminated all that I thought might provide even the shadow of grounds for discontent on the part of the famous models of the portrait I wished to present; nothing did any good. The conspiracy of opposition revived even at mere conjecture of what the play would be like. They found a way

17. On August 5, 1667, *Tartuffe* was performed at the Palais-Royal. The opposition—headed by the First President of Parliament—brought in the police, and the play was stopped. Since Louis was campaigning in Flanders, friends of Molière brought the second *placet* to Lille. Louis had always been favorable toward the playwright; in August, 1665, Molière's company, the *Troupe de Monsieur* (nominally sponsored by Louis's brother Philippe, Duc d'Orléans) had become the *Troupe du Roi*.

18. President de Lanvignon, in charge of the Paris police.

19. There is evidence that in 1664 Tartuffe played his role dressed in a cassock, thus allying him more directly to the clergy.

of persuading those who in all other matters plainly insist that they are not to be deceived. No sooner did my comedy appear than it was struck down by the very power which should impose respect; and all that I could do to save myself from the fury of this tempest was to say that Your Majesty had given me permission to present the play and I did not think it was necessary to ask this permission of others, since only Your Majesty could have refused it.

I have no doubt, Sire, that the men whom I depict in my comedy will employ every means possible to influence Your Majesty, and will use, as they have used already, those truly good men who are all the more easily deceived because they judge of others by themselves.[20] They know how to display all of their aims in the most favorable light; yet, no matter how pious they may seem, it is surely not the interests of God which stir them; they have proven this often enough in the comedies they have allowed to be performed hundreds of times without making the least objection. Those plays attacked only piety and religion, for which they care very little; but this play attacks and makes fun of them, and that is what they cannot bear. They will never forgive me for unmasking their hypocrisy in the eyes of everyone. And I am sure that they will not neglect to tell Your Majesty that people are shocked by my comedy. But the simple truth, Sire, is that all Paris is shocked only by its ban, that the most scrupulous persons have found its presentation worthwhile, and men are astounded that individuals of such known integrity should show so great a deference to people whom everyone should abominate and who are so clearly opposed to the true piety which they profess.

I respectfully await the judgment that Your Majesty will deign to pronounce; but it is certain, Sire, that I need not think of writing comedies if the Tartuffes are triumphant, if they thereby seize the right to persecute me more than ever, and find fault with even the most innocent lines that flow from my pen.

Let your goodness, Sire, give me protection against their envenomed rage, and allow me, at your return from so glorious a campaign, to relieve Your Majesty from the fatigue of his conquests, give him innocent pleasures after such noble accomplishments, and make the monarch laugh who makes all Europe tremble!

(*August, 1667*)

20. Molière apparently did not know that de Lanvignon had been affiliated with the Company of the Holy Sacrament for the previous ten years.

Third Petition

(*presented to the King*)

Sire,

A very honest doctor[21] whose patient I have the honor to be, promises and will legally contract to make me live another thirty years if I can obtain a favor for him from Your Majesty. I told him of his promise that I do not deserve so much, and that I should be glad to help him if he will merely agree not to kill me. This favor, Sire, is a post of canon at your royal chapel of Vincennes, made vacant by death.

May I dare to ask for this favor from Your Majesty on the very day of the glorious resurrection of *Tartuffe*, brought back to life by your goodness? By this first favor I have been reconciled with the devout, and the second will reconcile me with the doctors.[22] Undoubtedly this would be too much grace for me at one time, but perhaps it would not be too much for Your Majesty, and I await your answer to my petition with respectful hope.

(*February*, 1669)

21. a physician friend, M. de Mauvillain, who helped Molière with some of the medical details of *Le Malade imaginaire*.

22. Doctors are ridiculed to varying degrees in earlier plays of Molière: *Dom Juan*, *L'Amour médecin*, and *Le Médecin malgré lui*.

Characters†

MME PERNELLE, *Orgon's mother*
ORGON, *Elmire's husband*
ELMIRE, *Orgon's wife*
DAMIS, *Orgon's son, Elmire's stepson*
MARIANE, *Orgon's daughter, Elmire's stepdaughter, in love with Valère*
VALERE, *in love with Mariane*
CLEANTE, *Orgon's brother-in-law*

† The name Tartuffe has been traced back to an older word associated with liar or charlatan: *truffer*, "to deceive" or "to cheat". Then there was also the Italian actor, Tartufo, physically deformed and truffle-shaped. Most of the other names are typical of this genre of court-comedy and possess rather elegant connotations of pastoral and *bergerie*. Dorine would be a *demoiselle de compagne* and not a mere maid; that is, a female companion to Mariane of roughly the same social status. This in part accounts for the liberties she takes in conversation with Orgon, Madame Pernelle, and others. Her name is short for Théodorine.

TARTUFFE, *a hypocrite*
DORINE, *Mariane's lady's-maid*
M. LOYAL, *a bailiff*
A POLICE OFFICER
FLIPOTE, *Mme Pernelle's maid*

The SCENE *throughout: Orgon's house in Paris*

Act I

SCENE 1. *Madame Pernelle and Flipote, her maid, Elmire, Mariane, Dorine, Damis, Cleante*

MADAME PERNELLE. Come, come, Flipote; it's time I left this place.
ELMIRE. I can't keep up, you walk at such a pace.
MADAME PERNELLE. Don't trouble, child; no need to show me out.
It's not your manners I'm concerned about.
ELMIRE. We merely pay you the respect we owe. 5
But, Mother, why this hurry? Must you go?
MADAME PERNELLE. I must. This house appals me. No one in it
Will pay attention for a single minute.
I offer good advice, but you won't hear it.
Children, I take my leave much vexed in spirit. 10
You all break in and chatter on and on.
It's like a madhouse with the keeper gone.
DORINE. If . . .
MADAME PERNELLE. Girl, you talk too much, and I'm afraid
You're far too saucy for a lady's-maid.
You push in everywhere and have your say. 15
DAMIS. But . . .
MADAME PERNELLE. You, boy, grow more foolish every day.
To think my grandson should be such a dunce!
I've said a hundred times, if I've said it once,
That if you keep the course on which you've started,
You'll leave your worthy father broken-hearted. 20
MARIANE. I think . . .
MADAME PERNELLE. And you, his sister, seem so pure,
So shy, so innocent, and so demure.
But you know what they say about still waters.
I pity parents with secretive daughters.
ELMIRE. Now, Mother . . .

12. *Madhouse:* in the original, *la cour du roi Pétaud,* the Court of King Pétaud where all are masters; a house of misrule.

MADAME PERNELLE. And as for you, child, let me add
That your behavior is extremely bad, 25
And a poor example for these children, too.
Their dear, dead mother did far better than you.
You're much too free with money, and I'm distressed
To see you so elaborately dressed. 30
When it's one's husband that one aims to please,
One has no need of costly fripperies.

CLEANTE. Oh, Madam, really . . .

MADAME PERNELLE. You are her Brother, Sir,
And I respect and love you; yet if I were
My son, this lady's good and pious spouse, 35
I wouldn't make you welcome in my house.
You're full of worldly counsels which, I fear,
Aren't suitable for decent folk to hear.
I've spoken bluntly, Sir; but it behooves us
Not to mince words when righteous fervor moves us. 40

DAMIS. Your man Tartuffe is full of holy speeches . . .

MADAME PERNELLE. And practises precisely what he preaches.
He's a fine man, and should be listened to.
I will not hear him mocked by fools like you.

DAMIS. Good God! Do you expect me to submit 45
To the tyranny of that carping hypocrite?
Must we forgo all joys and satisfactions
Because that bigot censures all our actions?

DORINE. To hear him talk—and he talks all the time—
There's nothing one can do that's not a crime. 50
He rails at everything, your dear Tartuffe.

MADAME PERNELLE. Whatever he reproves deserves reproof.
He's out to save your souls, and all of you
Must love him, as my son would have you do.

DAMIS. Ah no, Grandmother, I could never take 55
To such a rascal, even for my father's sake.
That's how I feel, and I shall not dissemble.
His every action makes me seethe and tremble,
With helpless anger, and I have no doubt
That he and I will shortly have it out. 60

DORINE. Surely it is a shame and a disgrace
To see this man usurp the master's place—
To see this beggar who, when first he came,
Had not a shoe or shoestring to his name
So far forget himself that he behaves 65
As if the house were his, and we his slaves.

MADAME PERNELLE. Well, mark my words, your souls would fare far better

If you obeyed his precepts to the letter.

DORINE. You see him as a saint. I'm far less awed;
In fact, I see right through him. He's a fraud. 70

MADAME PERNELLE. Nonsense!

DORINE. His man Laurent's the same, or worse;
I'd not trust either with a penny purse.

MADAME PERNELLE. I can't say what his servant's morals may be;
His own great goodness I can guarantee.
You all regard him with distaste and fear 75
Because he tells you what you're loath to hear,
Condemns your sins, points out your moral flaws,
And humbly strives to further Heaven's cause.

DORINE. If sin is all that bothers him, why is it
He's so upset when folk drop in to visit? 80
Is Heaven so outraged by a social call
That he must prophesy against us all?
I'll tell you what I think: if you ask me,
He's jealous of my mistress' company.

MADAME PERNELLE. Rubbish! [*To* ELMIRE] He's not alone, child, in complaining 85
Of all of your promiscuous entertaining.
Why, the whole neighborhood's upset, I know,
By all these carriages that come and go,
With crowds of guests parading in and out
And noisy servants loitering about. 90
In all of this, I'm sure there's nothing vicious;
But why give people cause to be suspicious?

CLEANTE. They need no cause; they'll talk in any case.
Madam, this world would be a joyless place
If, fearing what malicious tongues might say, 95
We locked our doors and turned our friends away.
And even if one did so dreary a thing,
D' you think those tongues would cease their chattering?
One can't fight slander; it's a losing battle;
Let us instead ignore their tittle-tattle. 100
Let's strive to live by conscience' clear decrees,
And let the gossips gossip as they please.

DORINE. If there is talk against us, I know the source:
It's Daphne and her little husband, of course.
Those who have greatest cause for guilt and shame 105
Are quickest to besmirch a neighbor's name.
When there's a chance for libel, they never miss it;
When something can be made to seem illicit
They're off at once to spread the joyous news,

Adding to fact what fantasies they choose. 110
By talking up their neighbor's indiscretions
They seek to camouflage their own transgressions,
Hoping that others' innocent affairs
Will lend a hue of innocence to theirs,
Or that their own black guilt will come to seem 115
Part of a general shady color-scheme.

MADAME PERNELLE. All that is quite irrelevant. I doubt
That anyone's more virtuous and devout
Than dear Orante; and I'm informed that she
Condemns your mode of life most vehemently. 120

DORINE. Oh, yes, she's strict, devout, and has no taint
Of worldliness; in short, she seems a saint.
But it was time which taught her that disguise;
She's thus because she can't be otherwise.
So long as her attractions could enthrall, 125
She flounced and flirted and enjoyed it all,
But now that they're no longer what they were
She quits a world which fast is quitting her,
And wears a veil of virtue to conceal
Her bankrupt beauty and her lost appeal. 130
That's what becomes of old coquettes today:
Distressed when all their lovers fall away,
They see no recourse but to play the prude,
And so confer a style on solitude.
Thereafter, they're severe with everyone, 135
Condemning all our actions, pardoning none,
And claiming to be pure, austere, and zealous
When, if the truth were known, they're merely jealous,
And cannot bear to see another know
The pleasures time has forced them to forgo. 140

MADAME PERNELLE. [*Initially to* ELMIRE] That sort of talk is what you like to hear;
Therefore you'd have us all keep still, my dear,
While Madam rattles on the livelong day.
Nevertheless, I mean to have my say.
I tell you that you're blest to have Tartuffe 145
Dwelling, as my son's guest, beneath this roof;
That Heaven has sent him to forestall its wrath
By leading you, once more, to the true path;
That all he reprehends is reprehensible,
And that you'd better heed him, and be sensible. 150
These visits, balls, and parties in which you revel

141. *That sort of talk:* in the original, a reference to a collection of novels about chivalry found in *La Bibliothèque bleue* (*The Blue Library*), written for children.

Are nothing but inventions of the Devil.
One never hears a word that's edifying:
Nothing but chaff and foolishness and lying,
As well as vicious gossip in which one's neighbor 155
Is cut to bits with épée, foil, and saber.
People of sense are driven half-insane
At such affairs, where noise and folly reign
And reputations perish thick and fast.
As a wise preacher said on Sunday last, 160
Parties are Towers of Babylon, because
The guests all babble on with never a pause;
And then he told a story which, I think . . .
[*To* CLEANTE] I heard that laugh, Sir, and I saw that wink!
Go find your silly friends and laugh some more! 165
Enough; I'm going; don't show me to the door.
I leave this household much dismayed and vexed;
I cannot say when I shall see you next.
[*Slapping* FLIPOTE] Wake up, don't stand there gaping into space!
I'll slap some sense into that stupid face. 170
Move, move, you slut.

SCENE 2. *Cléante, Dorine*

CLEANTE. I think I'll stay behind;
I want no further pieces of her mind.
How that old lady . . .
DORINE. Oh, what wouldn't she say
If she could hear you speak of her that way!
She'd thank you for the *lady*, but I'm sure 5
She'd find the *old* a little premature.
CLEANTE. My, what a scene she made, and what a din!
And how this man Tartuffe has taken her in!
DORINE. Yes, but her son is even worse deceived;
His folly must be seen to be believed. 10
In the late troubles, he played an able part
And served his king with wise and loyal heart,
But he's quite lost his senses since he fell
Beneath Tartuffe's infatuating spell.
He calls him brother, and loves him as his life, 15
Preferring him to mother, child, or wife.
In him and him alone will he confide;
He's made him his confessor and his guide;

161. *Towers of Babylon:* i.e. Tower of Babel. Mme. Pernelle's malapropism is the cause of Cléante's laughter.

11. *the late troubles:* a series of political disturbances during the minority of Louis XIV. Specifically these consisted of the *Fronde* ("opposition") of the Parlement (1648-1649) and the *Fronde* of the Princes (1650-1653). Orgon is depicted as supporting Louis XIV in these outbreaks and their resolution.

He pets and pampers him with love more tender
Than any pretty maiden could engender, 20
Gives him the place of honor when they dine,
Delights to see him gorging like a swine,
Stuffs him with dainties till his guts distend,
And when he belches, cries "God bless you, friend!"
In short, he's mad; he worships him; he dotes; 25
His deeds he marvels at, his words, he quotes,
Thinking each act a miracle, each word
Oracular as those that Moses heard.
Tartuffe, much pleased to find so easy a victim,
Has in a hundred ways beguiled and tricked him, 30
Milked him of money, and with his permission
Established here a sort of Inquisition.
Even Laurent, his lackey, dares to give
Us arrogant advice on how to live;
He sermonizes us in thundering tones 35
And confiscates our ribbons and colognes.
Last week he tore a kerchief into pieces
Because he found it pressed in a *Life of Jesus:*
He said it was a sin to juxtapose
Unholy vanities and holy prose. 40

SCENE 3. *Elmire, Mariane, Damis, Cléante, Dorine*

ELMIRE. [*To* CLEANTE] You did well not to follow; she stood in the door
And said *verbatim* all she'd said before.
I saw my husband coming. I think I'd best
Go upstairs now, and take a little rest.
CLEANTE. I'll wait and greet him here; then I must go. 5
I've really only time to say hello.
DAMIS. Sound him about my sister's wedding, please.
I think Tartuffe's against it, and that he's
Been urging Father to withdraw his blessing.
As you well know, I'd find that most distressing. 10
Unless my sister and Valère can marry,
My hopes to wed *his* sister will miscarry.
And I'm determined . . .
DORINE. He's coming.

SCENE 4. *Orgon, Cléante, Dorine*

ORGON. Ah, Brother, good-day.
CLEANTE. Well, welcome back. I'm sorry I can't stay.

37. Laurent's act is more salacious than the translation might suggest.

How was the country? Blooming, I trust, and green?
ORGON. Excuse me, Brother; just one moment.
[*To* DORINE] Dorine . . .
[*To* CLEANTE] To put my mind at rest, I always learn 5
The household news the moment I return.
[*To* DORINE] Has all been well, these two days I've been gone?
How are the family? What's been going on?
DORINE. Your wife, two days ago, had a bad fever,
And a fierce headache which refused to leave her. 10
ORGON. Ah. And Tartuffe?
DORINE. Tartuffe? Why, he's round and red,
Bursting with health, and excellently fed.
ORGON. Poor fellow!
DORINE. That night, the mistress was unable
To take a single bite at the dinner-table.
Her headache-pains, she said, were simply hellish. 15
ORGON. Ah. And Tartuffe?
DORINE. He ate his meal with relish,
And zealously devoured in her presence
A leg of mutton and a brace of pheasants.
ORGON. Poor fellow!
DORINE. Well, the pains continued strong,
And so she tossed and tossed the whole night long, 20
Now icy-cold, now burning like a flame.
We sat beside her bed till morning came.
ORGON. Ah. And Tartuffe?
DORINE. Why, having eaten, he rose
And sought his room, already in a doze,
Got into his warm bed, and snored away 25
In perfect peace until the break of day.
ORGON. Poor fellow!
DORINE. After much ado, we talked her
Into dispatching someone for the doctor.
He bled her, and the fever quickly fell.
ORGON. Ah. And Tartuffe?
DORINE. He bore it very well. 30
To keep his cheerfulness at any cost,
And make up for the blood *Madame* had lost,
He drank, at lunch, four beakers full of port.
ORGON. Poor fellow!
DORINE. Both are doing well, in short.
I'll go and tell *Madame* that you've expressed 35
Keen sympathy and anxious interest.

SCENE 5. *Orgon, Cléante*

CLEANTE. That girl was laughing in your face, and though
I've no wish to offend you, even so

I'm bound to say that she had some excuse.
How can you possibly be such a goose?
Are you so dazed by this man's hocus-pocus 5
That all the world, save him, is out of focus?
You've given him clothing, shelter, food, and care;
Why must you also . . .

ORGON. Brother, stop right there.
You do not know the man of whom you speak.

CLEANTE. I grant you that. But my judgment's not so weak 10
That I can't tell, by his effect on others . . .

ORGON. Ah, when you meet him, you two will be like brothers!
There's been no loftier soul since time began.
He is a man who . . . a man who . . . an excellent man.
To keep his precepts is to be reborn, 15
And view this dunghill of a world with scorn.
Yes, thanks to him I'm a changed man indeed.
Under his tutelage my soul's been freed
From earthly loves, and every human tie:
My mother, children, brother, and wife could die, 20
And I'd not feel a single moment's pain.

CLEANTE. That's a fine sentiment, Brother; most humane.

ORGON. Oh, had you seen Tartuffe as I first knew him,
Your heart, like mine, would have surrendered to him.
He used to come into our church each day 25
And humbly kneel nearby, and start to pray.
He'd draw the eyes of everybody there
By the deep fervor of his heartfelt prayer;
He'd sigh and weep, and sometimes with a sound
Of rapture he would bend and kiss the ground; 30
And when I rose to go, he'd run before
To offer me holy-water at the door.
His serving-man, no less devout than he,
Informed me of his master's poverty;
I gave him gifts, but in his humbleness 35
He'd beg me every time to give him less.
"Oh, that's too much," he'd cry, "too much by twice!
I don't deserve it. The half, Sir, would suffice."
And when I wouldn't take it back, he'd share
Half of it with the poor, right then and there. 40
At length, Heaven prompted me to take him in
To dwell with us, and free our souls from sin.
He guides our lives, and to protect my honor
Stays by my wife, and keeps an eye upon her;
He tells me whom she sees, and all she does, 41
And seems more jealous than I ever was!
And how austere he is! Why, he can detect
A moral sin where you would least suspect;

In smallest trifles, he's extremely strict.
Last week, his conscience was severely pricked 50
Because, while praying, he had caught a flea
And killed it, so he felt, too wrathfully.

CLEANTE. Good God, man! Have you lost your common sense—
Or is this all some joke at my expense?
How can you stand there and in all sobriety . . . 55

ORGON. Brother, your language savors of impiety.
Too much free-thinking's made your faith unsteady,
And as I've warned you many times already,
'Twill get you into trouble before you're through.

CLEANTE. So I've been told before by dupes like you: 60
Being blind, you'd have all others blind as well;
The clear-eyed man you call an infidel,
And he who sees through humbug and pretense
Is charged, by you, with want of reverence.
Spare me your warnings, Brother; I have no fear 65
Of speaking out, for you and Heaven to hear,
Against affected zeal and pious knavery.
There's true and false in piety, as in bravery,
And just as those whose courage shines the most
In battle, are the least inclined to boast, 70
So those whose hearts are truly pure and lowly
Don't make a flashy show of being holy.
There's a vast difference, so it seems to me,
Between true piety and hypocrisy:
How do you fail to see it, may I ask? 75
Is not a face quite different from a mask?
Cannot sincerity and cunning art,
Realty and semblance, be told apart?
Are scarecrows just like men, and do you hold
That a false coin is just as good as gold? 80
Ah, Brother, man's a strangely fashioned creature
Who seldom is content to follow Nature,
But recklessly pursues his inclination
Beyond the narrow bounds of moderation,
And often, by transgressing Reason's laws, 85
Perverts, a lofty aim or noble cause.
A passing observation, but it applies.

ORGON. I see, dear Brother, that you're profoundly wise;
You harbor all the insight of the age.
You are our one clear mind, our only sage, 90

50-52. *Last week . . . wrathfully:* In the *Golden Legend* (*Legenda santorum*), a popular collection of the lives of the saints written in the thirteenth century, it is said of St. Marcarius the Elder (d. 390) that he dwelt naked in the desert for six months, a penance he felt appropriate for having killed a flea.

The era's oracle, its Cato too,
And all mankind are fools compared to you.

CLEANTE. Brother, I don't pretend to be a sage,
Nor have I all the wisdom of the age.
There's just one insight I would dare to claim: 95
I know that true and false are not the same;
And just as there is nothing I more revere
Than a soul whose faith is steadfast and sincere,
Nothing that I more cherish and admire
Than honest zeal and true religious fire, 100
So there is nothing that I find more base
Than specious piety's dishonest face—
Than these bold mountebanks, these histrios
Whose impious mummeries and hollow shows
Exploit our love of Heaven, and make a jest 105
Of all that men think holiest and best;
These calculating souls who offer prayers
Not to their Maker, but as public wares,
And seek to buy respect and reputation
With lifted eyes and sighs of exaltation; 110
These charlatans, I say, whose pilgrim souls
Proceed, by way of Heaven, toward earthly goals,
Who weep and pray and swindle and extort,
Who preach the monkish life, but haunt the court,
Who make their zeal the partner of their vice— 115
Such men are vengeful, sly, and cold as ice,
And when there is an enemy to defame
They cloak their spite in fair religion's name,
Their private spleen and malice being made
To seem a high and virtuous crusade, 120
Until, to mankind's reverent applause,
They crucify their foe in Heaven's cause.
Such knaves are all too common; yet, for the wise,
True piety isn't hard to recognize,
And, happily, these present times provide us 125
With bright examples to instruct and guide us.
Consider Ariston and Périandre;
Look at Oronte, Alcidamas, Clitandre;
Their virtue is acknowledged; who could doubt it?
But you won't hear them beat the drum about it. 130
They're never ostentatious, never vain,
And their religion's moderate and humane;
It's not their way to criticize and chide:

127-128. ***Ariston . . . Clitandre:*** vaguely Greek and Roman names derived from the elegant literature of the day; not names of actual persons.

They think censoriousness a mark of pride,
And therefore, letting others preach and rave, 135
They show, by deeds, how Christians should behave.
They think no evil of their fellow man,
But judge of him as kindly as they can.
They don't intrigue and wangle and conspire;
To lead a good life is their one desire; 140
The sinner wakes no rancorous hate in them;
It is the sin alone which they condemn;
Nor do they try to show a fiercer zeal
For Heaven's cause than Heaven itself could feel.
These men I honor, these men I advocate 145
As models for us all to emulate.
Your man is not their sort at all, I fear:
And, while your praise of him is quite sincere,
I think that you've been dreadfully deluded.

ORGON. Now then, dear Brother, is your speech concluded? 150
CLEANTE. Why, yes.
ORGON. Your servant, Sir. [*He turns to go.*]
CLEANTE. No, Brother; wait.
There's one more matter. You agreed of late
That young Valère might have your daughter's hand.
ORGON. I did.
CLEANTE. And set the date, I understand.
ORGON. Quite so.
CLEANTE. You've now postponed it; is that true? 155
ORGON. No doubt.
CLEANTE. The match no longer pleases you?
ORGON. Who knows?
CLEANTE. D'you mean to go back on your word?
ORGON. I won't say that.
CLEANTE. Has anything occurred
Which might entitle you to break your pledge?
ORGON. Perhaps.
CLEANTE. Why must you hem, and haw, and hedge?
The boy asked me to sound you in this affair . . . 160
ORGON. It's been a pleasure.
CLEANTE. But what shall I tell Valère?
ORGON. Whatever you like.
CLEANTE. But what have you decided?
What are your plans?
ORGON. I plan, Sir, to be guided
By Heaven's will.
CLEANTE. Come, Brother, don't talk rot. 165
You've given Valère your word; will you keep it, or not?

ORGON. Good day.

CLEANTE. This looks like poor Valère's undoing;
I'll go and warn him that there's trouble brewing.

Act II

SCENE 1. *Orgon, Mariane*

ORGON. Mariane.

MARIANE. Yes, Father?

ORGON. A word with you; come here.

MARIANE. What are you looking for?

ORGON. [*Peering into a small closet*] Eavesdroppers, dear.
I'm making sure we shan't be overheard.
Someone in there could catch our every word.
Ah, good, we're safe. Now, Mariane, my child, 5
You're a sweet girl who's tractable and mild,
Whom I hold dear, and think most highly of.

MARIANE. I'm deeply grateful, Father, for your love.

ORGON. That's well said, Daughter; and you can repay me
If, in all things, you'll cheerfully obey me. 10

MARIANE. To please you, Sir, is what delights me best.

ORGON. Good, good. Now, what d'you think of Tartuffe, our guest?

MARIANE. I, Sir?

ORGON. Yes. Weigh your answer; think it through.

MARIANE. Oh, dear. I'll say whatever you wish me to.

ORGON. That's wisely said, my Daughter. Say of him, then, 15
That he's the very worthiest of men,
And that you're fond of him, and would rejoice
In being his wife, if that should be my choice.
Well?

MARIANE. What

ORGON. What's that?

MARIANE. I . . .

ORGON. Well?

MARIANE. Forgive me, pray.

ORGON. Did you not hear me?

MARIANE. Of *whom*, Sir, must I say 20
That I am fond of him, and would rejoice
In being his wife, if that should be your choice?

ORGON. Why, of Tartuffe.

MARIANE. But, Father, that's false, you know.
Why would you have me say what isn't so?

ORGON. Because I am resolved it shall be true. 25
That it's my wish should be enough for you.

MARIANE. You can't mean, Father . . .

ORGON. Yes, Tartuffe shall be
Allied by marriage to this family,
And he's to be your husband, is that clear?
It's a father's privilege . . .

SCENE 2. *Dorine, Orgon, Mariane*

ORGON. [*To* DORINE] What are you doing in here?
Is curiosity so fierce a passion
With you, that you must eavesdrop in this fashion?
DORINE. There's lately been a rumor going about—
Based on some hunch or chance remark, no doubt— 5
That you mean Mariane to wed Tartuffe.
I've laughed it off, of course, as just a spoof.
ORGON. You find it so incredible?
DORINE. Yes, I do.
I won't accept that story, even from you.
ORGON. Well, you'll believe it when the thing is done. 10
DORINE. Yes, yes, of course. Go on and have your fun.
ORGON. I've never been more serious in my life.
DORINE. Ha!
ORGON. Daughter, I mean it; you're to be his wife.
DORINE. No, don't believe your father; it's all a hoax.
ORGON. See here, young woman . . .
DORINE. Come, Sir, no more jokes;
You can't fool us. 15
ORGON. How dare you talk that way?
DORINE. All right, then: we believe you, sad to say.
But how a man like you, who looks so wise
And wears a moustache of such splendid size,
Can be so foolish as to . . .
ORGON. Silence, please! 20
My girl, you take too many liberties.
I'm master here, as you must not forget.
DORINE. Do let's discuss this calmly; don't be upset.
You can't be serious, Sir, about this plan.
What should that bigot want with Mariane? 25
Praying and fasting ought to keep him busy.
And then, in terms of wealth and rank, what is he?
Why should a man of property like you
Pick out a beggar son-in-law?
ORGON. That will do.
Speak of his poverty with reverence. 30

29. *Allied by marriage:* This assertion is important and more than a mere device in the plot of the play. The second *placet* or petition insists that Tartuffe be costumed as a layman, and Orgon's plan for him to marry again asserts Tartuffe's position in the laity. In the 1664 version of the play Tartuffe had been dressed in a cassock suggestive of the priesthood, and Molière was now anxious to avoid any suggestion of this kind.

His is a pure and saintly indigence
Which far transcends all worldly pride and pelf.
He lost his fortune, as he says himself,
Because he cared for Heaven alone, and so
Was careless of his interests here below. 35
I mean to get him out of his present straits
And help him to recover his estates—
Which, in his part of the world, have no small fame.
Poor though he is, he's a gentleman just the same.

DORINE. Yes, so he tells us; and, Sir, it seems to me 40
Such pride goes very ill with piety.
A man whose spirit spurns this dungy earth
Ought not to brag of lands and noble birth;
Such worldly arrogance will hardly square
With meek devotion and the life of prayer. 45
. . . But this approach, I see, has drawn a blank;
Let's speak, then, of his person, not his rank.
Doesn't it seem to you a trifle grim
To give a girl like her to a man like him?
When two are so ill-suited, can't you see 50
What the sad consequence is bound to be?
A young girl's virtue is imperilled, Sir,
When such a marriage is imposed on her;
For if one's bridegroom isn't to one's taste,
It's hardly an inducement to be chaste, 55
And many a man with horns upon his brow
Has made his wife the thing that she is now.
It's hard to be a faithful wife, in short,
To certain husbands of a certain sort,
And he who gives his daughter to a man she hates 60
Must answer for her sins at Heaven's gates.
Think, Sir, before you play so risky a role.

ORGON. This servant-girl presumes to save my soul!

DORINE. You would do well to ponder what I've said.

ORGON. Daughter, we'll disregard this dunderhead. 65
Just trust your father's judgment. Oh, I'm aware
That I once promised you to young Valère;
But now I hear he gambles, which greatly shocks me;
What's more, I've doubts about his orthodoxy.
His visits to church, I note, are very few. 70

DORINE. Would you have him go at the same hours as you,
And kneel nearby, to be sure of being seen?

ORGON. I can dispense with such remarks, Dorine.
[*To* MARIANE] Tartuffe, however, is sure of Heaven's blessing.
And that's the only treasure worth possessing. 75
This match will bring you joys beyond all measure;
Your cup will overflow with every pleasure;

You two will interchange your faithful loves
Like two sweet cherubs, or two turtle-doves.
No harsh word shall be heard, no frown be seen, 80
And he shall make you happy as a queen.

DORINE. And she'll make him a cuckold, just wait and see.

ORGON. What language!

DORINE. Oh, he's a man of destiny;
He's *made* for horns, and what the stars demand
Your daughter's virtue surely can't withstand. 85

ORGON. Don't interrupt me further. Why can't you learn
That certain things are none of your concern?

DORINE. It's for your own sake that I interfere.

[*She repeatedly interrupts* ORGON *just as he is turning to speak to his daughter.*]

ORGON. Most kind of you. Now, hold your tongue, d'you hear?

DORINE. If I didn't love you . . .

ORGON. Spare me your affection. 90

DORINE. I'll love you, Sir, in spite of your objection.

ORGON. Blast!

DORINE. I can't bear, Sir, for your honor's sake,
To let you make this ludicrous mistake.

ORGON. You mean to go on talking?

DORINE. If I didn't protest
This sinful marriage, my conscience couldn't rest. 95

ORGON. If you don't hold your tongue, you little shrew . . .

DORINE. What, lost your temper? A pious man like you?

ORGON. Yes! Yes! You talk and talk. I'm maddened by it.
Once and for all, I tell you to be quiet.

DORINE. Well, I'll be quiet. But I'll be thinking hard. 100

ORGON. Think all you like, but you had better guard
That saucy tongue of yours, or I'll . . .
[*Turning back to* MARIANE] Now, child,
I've weighed this matter fully.

DORINE. [*Aside*] It drives me wild
That I can't speak.

[ORGON *turns his head, and she is silent.*]

ORGON. Tartuffe is no young dandy,
But, still, his person . . .

DORINE. [*Aside*] Is as sweet as candy. 105

ORGON. Is such that, even if you shouldn't care
For his other merits . . .

[*He turns and stands facing* DORINE, *arms crossed.*]

DORINE. [*Aside*] They'll make a lovely pair.
If I were she, no man would marry me
Against my inclination, and go scot-free.

He'd learn, before the wedding-day was over, 110
How readily a wife can find a lover.

ORGON. [*To* DORINE] It seems you treat my orders as a joke.

DORINE. Why, what's the matter? 'Twas not to you I spoke.

ORGON. What *were* you doing?

DORINE. Talking to myself, that's all.

ORGON. Ah! [*Aside*] One more bit of impudence and gall, 115
And I shall give her a good slap in the face.

[*He puts himself in position to slap her;* DORINE, *whenever he glances at her, stands immobile and silent.*]

Daughter, you shall accept, and with good grace,
The husband I've selected . . . Your wedding-day . . .
[*To* DORINE] Why don't you talk to yourself?

DORINE. I've nothing to say.

ORGON. Come, just one word.

DORINE. No thank you, Sir. I pass. 120

ORGON. Come, speak; I'm waiting.

DORINE. I'd not be such an ass.

ORGON. [*Turning to* MARIANE] In short, dear Daughter, I mean to be obeyed,
And you must bow to the sound choice I've made.

DORINE. [*Moving away*] I'd not wed such a monster, even in jest.

[ORGON *attempts to slap her, but misses.*]

ORGON. Daughter, that maid of yours is a thorough pest; 125
She makes me sinfully annoyed and nettled.
I can't speak further; my nerves are too unsettled.
She's so upset me by her insolent talk,
I'll calm myself by going for a walk.

SCENE 3. *Dorine, Mariane*

DORINE. [*Returning*] Well, have you lost your tongue, girl? Must I play
Your part, and say the lines you ought to say?
Faced with a fate so hideous and absurd,
Can you not utter one dissenting word?

MARIANE. What good would it do? A father's power is great. 5

DORINE. Resist him now, or it will be too late.

MARIANE. But . . .

DORINE. Tell him one cannot love at a father's whim;
That you shall marry for yourself, not him;
That since it's you who are to be the bride,
It's you, not he, who must be satisfied; 10
And that if his Tartuffe is so sublime,
He's free to marry him at any time.

MARIANE. I've bowed so long to Father's strict control,

I couldn't oppose him now, to save my soul. 14
DORINE. Come, come, Mariane. Do listen to reason, won't you?
Valère has asked your hand. Do you love him, or don't you?
MARIANE. Oh, how unjust of you! What can you mean
By asking such a question, dear Dorine?
You know the depth of my affection for him;
I've told you a hundred times how I adore him. 20
DORINE. I don't believe in everything I hear;
Who knows if your professions were sincere?
MARIANE. They were, Dorine, and you do me wrong to doubt it;
Heaven knows that I've been all too frank about it.
DORINE. You love him, then?
MARIANE. Oh, more than I can express. 25
DORINE. And he, I take it, cares for you no less?
MARIANE. I think so.
DORINE. And you both, with equal fire,
Burn to be married?
MARIANE. That is our one desire.
DORINE. What of Tartuffe, then? What of your father's plan?
MARIANE. I'll kill myself, if I'm forced to wed that man. 30
DORINE. I hadn't thought of that recourse. How splendid!
Just die, and all your troubles will be ended!
A fine solution. Oh, it maddens me
To hear you talk in that self-pitying key.
MARIANE. Dorine, how harsh you are! It's most unfair. 35
You have no sympathy for my despair.
DORINE. I've none at all for people who talk drivel
And, faced with difficulties, whine and snivel.
MARIANE. No doubt I'm timid, but it would be wrong . . .
DORINE. True love requires a heart that's firm and strong. 40
MARIANE. I'm strong in my affection for Valère,
But coping with my father is his affair.
DORINE. But if your father's brain has grown so cracked
Over his dear Tartuffe that he can retract
His blessing, though your wedding-day was named, 45
It's surely not Valère who's to be blamed.
MARIANE. If I defied my father, as you suggest,
Would it not seem unmaidenly, at best?
Shall I defend my love at the expense
Of brazenness and disobedience? 50
Shall I parade my heart's desires, and flaunt . . .
DORINE. No, I ask nothing of you. Clearly you want
To be Madame Tartuffe, and I feel bound
Not to oppose a wish so very sound.
What right have I to criticize the match? 55

Indeed, my dear, the man's a brilliant catch.
Monsieur Tartuffe! Now, there's a man of weight!
Yes, yes, Monsieur Tartuffe, I'm bound to state,
Is quite a person; that's not to be denied;
'Twill be no little thing to be his bride. 60
The world already rings with his renown;
He's a great noble—in his native town;
His ears are red, he has a pink complexion,
And all in all, he'll suit you to perfection.

MARIANE. Dear God!

DORINE. Oh, how triumphant you will feel 65
At having caught a husband so ideal!

MARIANE. Oh, do stop teasing, and use your cleverness
To get me out of this appalling mess.
Advise me, and I'll do whatever you say.

DORINE. Ah, no, a dutiful daughter must obey 70
Her father, even if he weds her to an ape.
You've a bright future; why struggle to escape?
Tartuffe will take you back where his family lives,
To a small town aswarm with relatives—
Uncles and cousins whom you'll be charmed to meet. 75
You'll be received at once by the elite,
Calling upon the bailiff's wife, no less—
Even, perhaps, upon the mayoress,
Who'll sit you down in the *best* kitchen chair.
Then, once a year, you'll dance at the village fair 80
To the drone of bagpipes—two of them, in fact—
And see a puppet-show, or an animal act.
Your husband . . .

MARIANE. Oh, you turn my blood to ice!
Stop torturing me, and give me your advice.

DORINE. [*Threatening to go*] Your servant, Madam.

MARIANE. Dorine, I
beg of you . . . 85

DORINE. No, you deserve it; this marriage must go through.

MARIANE. Dorine!

DORINE. No.

MARIANE. Not Tartuffe! You know I think him . . .

77. *bailiff:* a high-ranking official in the judiciary, not simply a sheriff's deputy as today.

78. *mayoress:* the wife of a tax collector (*élu*), an important official controlling imports, elected by the Estates General.

79. *the best chair:* In elegant society of Molière's day, there was a hierarchy of seats and the use of each was determined by rank. The seats descended from *fauteuils, chaises, perroquets, tabourets,* to *pliants.* Thus Mariane would get the lowest seat in the room.

82. *puppet-show . . . act:* in the original, *fagotin,* literally a monkey dressed up in a man's clothing.

DORINE. Tartuffe's your cup of tea, and you shall drink him.
MARIANE. I've always told you everything, and relied . . .
DORINE. No. You deserve to be tartuffified. 90
MARIANE. Well, since you mock me and refuse to care,
I'll henceforth seek my solace in despair:
Despair shall be my counsellor and friend,
And help me bring my sorrows to an end. [*She starts to leave.*]
DORINE. There now, come back; my anger has subsided. 95
You do deserve some pity, I've decided.
MARIANE. Dorine, if Father makes me undergo
This dreadful martyrdom, I'll die, I know.
DORINE. Don't fret; it won't be difficult to discover
Some plan of action . . . But here's Valère, your lover. 100

SCENE 4. *Valère, Mariane, Dorine*

VALERE. Madam, I've just received some wondrous news
Regarding which I'd like to hear your views.
MARIANE. What news?
VALERE. You're marrying Tartuffe.
MARIANE. I find
That Father does have such a match in mind.
VALERE. Your father, Madam . . .
MARIANE. . . . has just this minute said
That it's Tartuffe he wishes me to wed. 5
VALERE. Can he be serious?
MARIANE. Oh, indeed he can;
He's clearly set his heart upon the plan.
VALERE. And what position do you propose to take,
Madam?
MARIANE. Why—I don't know.
VALERE. For heaven's sake— 10
You don't know?
MARIANE. No.
VALERE. Well, well!
MARIANE. Advise me, do.
VALERE. Marry the man. That's my advice to you.
MARIANE. That's your advice?
VALERE. Yes.
MARIANE. Truly?
VALERE. Oh, absolutely.
You couldn't choose more wisely, more astutely.
MARIANE. Thanks for this counsel; I'll follow it, of course. 15
VALERE. Do, do; I'm sure 'twill cost you no remorse.
MARIANE. To give it didn't cause your heart to break.
VALERE. I gave it, Madam, only for your sake.
MARIANE. And it's for your sake that I take it, Sir.

DORINE. [*Withdrawing to the rear of the stage*]
Let's see which fool will prove the stubborner. 20
VALERE. So! I am nothing to you, and it was flat
Deception when you . . .
MARIANE. Please, enough of that.
You've told me plainly that I should agree
To wed the man my father's chosen for me,
And since you've deigned to counsel me so wisely, 25
I promise, Sir, to do as you advise me.
VALERE. Ah, no, 'twas not by me that you were swayed.
No, your decision was already made;
Though now, to save appearances, you protest
That you're betraying me at my behest. 30
MARIANE. Just as you say.
VALERE. Quite so. And I now see
That you were never truly in love with me.
MARIANE. Alas, you're free to think so if you choose.
VALERE. I choose to think so, and here's a bit of news:
You've spurned my hand, but I know where to turn 35
For kinder treatment, as you shall quickly learn.
MARIANE. I'm sure you do. Your noble qualities
Inspire affection . . .
VALERE. Forget my qualities, please.
They don't inspire you overmuch, I find.
But there's another lady I have in mind 40
Whose sweet and generous nature will not scorn
To compensate me for the loss I've borne.
MARIANE. I'm no great loss, and I'm sure that you'll transfer
Your heart quite painlessly from me to her.
VALERE. I'll do my best to take it in my stride. 45
The pain I feel at being cast aside
Time and forgetfulness may put an end to.
Or if I can't forget, I shall pretend to.
No self-respecting person is expected
To go on loving once he's been rejected. 50
MARIANE. Now, that's a fine, high-minded sentiment.
VALERE. One to which any sane man would assent.
Would you prefer it if I pined away
In hopeless passion till my dying day?
Am I to yield you to a rival's arms 55
And not console myself with other charms?
MARIANE. Go then; console yourself; don't hesitate.
I wish you to; indeed, I cannot wait.
VALERE. You wish me to?
MARIANE. Yes.
VALERE. That's the final straw.

Madam, farewell. Your wish shall be my law. 60

[*He starts to leave, and then returns: this repeatedly.*]

MARIANE. Splendid.

VALERE. [*Coming back again*]

This breach, remember, is of your making; It's you who've driven me to the step I'm taking.

MARIANE. Of course.

VALERE. [*Coming back again*] Remember, too, that I am merely Following your example.

MARIANE. I see that clearly.

VALERE. Enough. I'll go and do your bidding, then. 65

MARIANE. Good.

VALERE. [*Coming back again*] You shall never see my face again.

MARIANE. Excellent.

VALERE. [*Walking to the door, then turning about*]

Yes?

MARIANE. What?

VALERE. What's that? What did you say?

MARIANE. Nothing. You're dreaming.

VALERE. Ah. Well, I'm on my way.

Farewell, *Madame*. [*He moves slowly away.*]

MARIANE. Farewell.

DORINE. [*To* MARIANE] If you ask me,

Both of you are as mad as mad can be. 70

Do stop this nonsense, now. I've only let you

Squabble so long to see where it would get you.

Whoa there, Monsieur Valère!

[*She goes and seizes* VALERE *by the arm; he makes a great show of resistance.*]

VALERE. What's this, Dorine?

DORINE. Come here.

VALERE. No, no, my heart's too full of spleen.

Don't hold me back; her wish must be obeyed. 75

DORINE. Stop!

VALERE. It's too late now; my decision's made.

DORINE. Oh, pooh!

MARIANE. [*Aside*] He hates the sight of me, that's plain.

I'll go, and so deliver him from pain.

DORINE. [*Leaving* VALERE, *running after* MARIANE]

And now *you* run away! Come back.

MARIANE. No, no.

Nothing you say will keep me here. Let go! 80

VALERE. [*Aside*] She cannot bear my presence, I perceive.

To spare her further torment, I shall leave.

DORINE. [*Leaving* MARIANE, *running after* VALERE]
Again! You'll not escape, Sir; don't you try it.
Come here, you two. Stop fussing and be quiet.
[*She takes* VALERE *by the hand, then* MARIANE, *and draws them together.*]
VALERE. [*To* DORINE] What do you want of me? 85
MARIANE. [*To* DORINE] What is the point of this?
DORINE. We're going to have a little armistice.
[*To* VALERE] Now, weren't you silly to get so overheated?
VALERE. Didn't you see how badly I was treated?
DORINE. [*To* MARIANE] Aren't you a simpleton, to have lost your head?
MARIANE. Didn't you hear the hateful things he said? 90
DORINE. [*To* VALERE] You're both great fools. Her sole desire, Valère,
Is to be yours in marriage. To that I'll swear.
[*To* MARIANE] He loves you only, and he wants no wife
But you, Mariane. On that I'll stake my life. 95
MARIANE. [*To* VALERE] Then why you advised me so, I cannot see.
VALERE. [*To* MARIANE] On such a question, why ask advice of *me?*
DORINE. Oh, you're impossible. Give me your hands, you two.
[*To* VALERE] Yours first.
VALERE. [*Giving* DORINE *his hand*] But why?
DORINE. [*To* MARIANE] And now a hand from you.
MARIANE. [*Also giving* DORINE *her hand*]
What are you doing?
DORINE. There: a perfect fit. 100
You suit each other better than you'll admit.
[VALERE *and* MARIANE *hold hands for some time without looking at each other.*]
VALERE. [*Turning toward* MARIANE]
Ah, come, don't be so haughty. Give a man
A look of kindness, won't you, Mariane?
[MARIANE *turns toward* VALERE *and smiles.*]
DORINE. I tell you, lovers are completely mad!
VALERE. [*To* MARIANE] Now come, confess that you were very bad
To hurt my feelings as you did just now. 105
I have a just complaint, you must allow.
MARIANE. *You* must allow that you were most unpleasant . . .
DORINE. Let's table that discussion for the present;
Your father has a plan which must be stopped. 110
MARIANE. Advise us, then; what means must we adopt?
DORINE. We'll use all manner of means, and all at once.
[*To* MARIANE] Your father's addled; he's acting like a dunce.
Therefore you'd better humor the old fossil.
Pretend to yield to him, be sweet and docile, 115
And then postpone, as often as necessary,

The day on which you have agreed to marry.
You'll thus gain time, and time will turn the trick.
Sometimes, for instance, you'll be taken sick,
And that will seem good reason for delay; 120
Or some bad omen will make you change the day—
You'll dream of muddy water, or you'll pass
A dead man's hearse, or break a looking-glass.
If all else fails, no man can marry you
Unless you take his ring and say "I do." 125
But now, let's separate. If they should find
Us talking here, our plot might be divined.
[*To* VALERE]Go to your friends, and tell them what's occurred,
And have them urge her father to keep his word.
Meanwhile, we'll stir her brother into action, 130
And get Elmire, as well, to join our faction.
Good-bye.

VALERE. [*To* MARIANE] Though each of us will do his best,
It's your true heart on which my hopes shall rest.

MARIANE. [*To* VALERE] Regardless of what Father may decide,
None but Valère shall claim me as his bride. 135

VALERE. Oh, how those words content me! Come what will . . .

DORINE. Oh, lovers, lovers! Their tongues are never still.
Be off, now.

VALERE. [*Turning to go, then turning back.*]
One last word . . .

DORINE. No time to chat:
You leave by this door; and *you* leave by that.
[DORINE *pushes them, by the shoulders, toward opposing doors.*]

Act III

SCENE 1. *Damis, Dorine*

DAMIS. May lightning strike me even as I speak,
May all men call me cowardly and weak,
If any fear or scruple holds me back
From settling things, at once, with that great quack!

DORINE. Now, don't give way to violent emotion. 5
Your father's merely talked about this notion,
And words and deeds are far from being one.
Much that is talked about is never done.

DAMIS. No, I must stop that scoundrel's machinations;
I'll go and tell him off; I'm out of patience. 10

130. *Elmire:* Orgon's second wife.

DORINE. Do calm down and be practical. I had rather
My mistress dealt with him—and with your father.
She has some influence with Tartuffe, I've noted.
He hangs upon her words, seems most devoted,
And may, indeed, be smitten by her charm. 15
Pray Heaven it's true! 'Twould do our cause no harm.
She sent for him, just now, to sound him out
On this affair you're so incensed about;
She'll find out where he stands, and tell him, too,
What dreadful strife and trouble will ensue 20
If he lends countenance to your father's plan.
I couldn't get in to see him, but his man
Says that he's almost finished with his prayers.
Go, now. I'll catch him when he comes downstairs.
DAMIS. I want to hear this conference, and I will. 25
DORINE. No, they must be alone.
DAMIS. Oh, I'll keep still.
DORINE. Not you. I know your temper. You'd start a brawl,
And shout and stamp your foot and spoil it all.
Go on.
DAMIS. I won't; I have a perfect right . . . 30
DORINE. Lord, you're a nuisance! He's coming; get out of sight.
[DAMIS *conceals himself in a closet at the rear of the stage.*]

SCENE 2. *Tartuffe, Dorine*

TARTUFFE. [*Observing* DORINE, *and calling to his manservant offstage*] Hang up my hair-shirt, put my scourge in place,
And pray, Laurent, for Heaven's perpetual grace.
I'm going to the prison now, to share
My last few coins with the poor wretches there.
DORINE. [*Aside*] Dear God, what affectation! What a fake! 5
TARTUFFE. You wished to see me?
DORINE. Yes . . .
TARTUFFE. [*Taking a handkerchief from his pocket*]
For mercy's sake,
Please take this handkerchief, before you speak.
DORINE. What?
TARTUFFE. Cover that bosom, girl. The flesh is weak,
And unclean thoughts are difficult to control.
Such sights as that can undermine the soul. 10
DORINE. Your soul, it seems, has very poor defenses,

8. *Cover that bosom:* The Brotherhood of the Holy Sacrament (*cf.* note 13, p. 27) practiced almsgiving to prisoners and kept a careful, censorious check on female wearing apparel if they deemed it lascivious. Thus, Molière's audience would have identified Tartuffe as sympathetic—hypocritically—to the aims of the organization.

And flesh makes quite an impact on your senses.
It's strange that you're so easily excited;
My own desires are not so soon ignited,
And if I saw you naked as a beast, 15
Not all your hide would tempt me in the least.

TARTUFFE. Girl, speak more modestly; unless you do,
I shall be forced to take my leave of you.

DORINE. Oh, no, it's I who must be on my way;
I've just one little message to convey. 20
Madame is coming down, and begs you, Sir,
To wait and have a word or two with her.

TARTUFFE. Gladly.

DORINE. [*Aside*] *That* had a softening effect!
I think my guess about him was correct.

TARTUFFE. Will she be long?

DORINE. No: that's her step I hear. 25
Ah, here she is, and I shall disappear.

SCENE 3. *Elmire, Tartuffe*

TARTUFFE. May Heaven, whose infinite goodness we adore,
Preserve your body and soul forevermore,
And bless your days, and answer thus the plea
Of one who is its humblest votary.

ELMIRE. I thank you for that pious wish. But please, 5
Do take a chair and let's be more at ease.
[*They sit down.*]

TARTUFFE. I trust that you are once more well and strong?

ELMIRE. Oh, yes: the fever didn't last for long.

TARTUFFE. My prayers are too unworthy, I am sure,
To have gained from Heaven this most gracious cure; 10
But lately, Madam, my every supplication
Has had for object your recuperation.

ELMIRE. You shouldn't have troubled so. I don't deserve it.

TARTUFFE. Your health is priceless, Madam, and to preserve it
I'd gladly give my own, in all sincerity. 15

ELMIRE. Sir, you outdo us all in Christian charity.
You've been most kind. I count myself your debtor.

TARTUFFE. 'Twas nothing, Madam. I long to serve you better.

ELMIRE. There's a private matter I'm anxious to discuss.
I'm glad there's no one here to hinder us. 20

TARTUFFE. I too am glad; it floods my heart with bliss
To find myself alone with you like this.
For just this chance I've prayed with all my power—
But prayed in vain, until this happy hour.

ELMIRE. This won't take long, Sir, and I hope you'll be 25

Entirely frank and unconstrained with me.
TARTUFFE. Indeed, there's nothing I had rather do
Than bare my inmost heart and soul to you.
First, let me say that what remarks I've made
About the constant visits you are paid 30
Were prompted not by any mean emotion,
But rather by a pure and deep devotion,
A fervent zeal . . .
ELMIRE. No need for explanation.
Your sole concern, I'm sure, was my salvation.
TARTUFFE. [*Taking* ELMIRE'*s hand and pressing her fingertips*]
Quite so; and such great fervor do I feel . . . 35
ELMIRE. Ooh! Please! You're pinching!
TARTUFFE. 'Twas from excess of zeal.
I never meant to cause you pain, I swear.
I'd rather . . . [*He places his hand on* ELMIRE'*s knee.*]
ELMIRE. What can your hand be doing there?
TARTUFFE. Feeling your gown: what soft, fine-woven stuff!
ELMIRE. Please, I'm extremely ticklish. That's enough. 40
[*She draws her chair away;* TARTUFFE *pulls his after her.*]
TARTUFFE. [*Fondling the lace collar of her gown*]
My, my, what lovely lacework on your dress!
The workmanship's miraculous, no less.
I've not seen anything to equal it.
ELMIRE. Yes, quite. But let's talk business for a bit.
They say my husband means to break his word 45
And give his daughter to you, Sir. Had you heard?
TARTUFFE. He did once mention it. But I confess
I dream of quite a different happiness.
It's elsewhere, Madam, that my eyes discern
The promise of that bliss for which I yearn. 50
ELMIRE. I see: you care for nothing here below.
TARTUFFE. Ah, well—my heart's not made of stone, you know.
ELMIRE. All your desires mount heavenward, I'm sure,
In scorn of all that's earthly and impure.
TARTUFFE. A love of heavenly beauty does not preclude 55
A proper love for earthly pulchritude;
Our senses are quite rightly captivated
By perfect works our Maker has created.
Some glory clings to all that Heaven has made;
In you, all Heaven's marvels are displayed. 60
On that fair face, such beauties have been lavished,
The eyes are dazzled and the heart is ravished;
How could I look on you, O flawless creature,
And not adore the Author of all Nature,

Feeling a love both passionate and pure 65
For you, his triumph of self-portraiture?
At first, I trembled lest that love should be
A subtle snare that Hell had laid for me;
I vowed to flee the sight of you, eschewing
A rapture that might prove my soul's undoing; 70
But soon, fair being, I became aware
That my deep passion could be made to square
With rectitude, and with my bounden duty,
I thereupon surrendered to your beauty.
It is, I know, presumptuous on my part 75
To bring you this poor offering of my heart,
And it is not my merit, Heaven knows,
But your compassion on which my hopes repose.
You are my peace, my solace, my salvation;
On you depends my bliss—or desolation; 80
I bide your judgment and, as you think best,
I shall be either miserable or blest.

ELMIRE. Your declaration is most gallant, Sir,
But don't you think it's out of character?
You'd have done better to restrain your passion 85
And think before you spoke in such a fashion.
It ill becomes a pious man like you . . .

TARTUFFE. I may be pious, but I'm human too:
With your celestial charms before his eyes,
A man has not the power to be wise. 90
I know such words sound strangely, coming from me,
But I'm no angel, nor was meant to be,
And if you blame my passion, you must needs
Reproach as well the charms on which it feeds.
Your loveliness I had no sooner seen 95
Than you became my soul's unrivalled queen;
Before your seraph glance, divinely sweet,
My heart's defenses crumbled in defeat,
And nothing fasting, prayer, or tears might do
Could stay my spirit from adoring you. 100
My eyes, my sighs have told you in the past
What now my lips make bold to say at last,
And if, in your great goodness, you will deign
To look upon your slave, and ease his pain,—
If, in compassion for my soul's distress, 105
You'll stoop to comfort my unworthiness,
I'll raise to you, in thanks for that sweet manna,
An endless hymn, an infinite hosanna.
With me, of course, there need be no anxiety,

No fear of scandal or of notoriety. 110
These young court gallants, whom all the ladies fancy,
Are vain in speech, in action rash and chancy;
When they succeed in love, the world soon knows it;
No favor's granted them but they disclose it
And by the looseness of their tongues profane 115
The very altar where their hearts have lain.
Men of my sort, however, love discreetly,
And one may trust our reticence completely.
My keen concern for my good name insures
The absolute security of yours; 120
In short, I offer you, my dear Elmire,
Love without scandal, pleasure without fear.

ELMIRE. I've heard your well-turned speeches to the end,
And what you urge I clearly apprehend.
Aren't you afraid that I may take a notion 125
To tell my husband of your warm devotion,
And that, supposing he were duly told,
His feelings toward you might grow rather cold?

TARTUFFE. I know, dear lady, that your exceeding charity
Will lead your heart to pardon my temerity; 130
That you'll excuse my violent affection
As human weakness, human imperfection;
And that—O fairest!—you will bear in mind
That I'm but flesh and blood, and am not blind.

ELMIRE. Some women might do otherwise, perhaps, 135
But I shall be discreet about your lapse;
I'll tell my husband nothing of what's occurred
If, in return, you'll give your solemn word
To advocate as forcefully as you can
The marriage of Valère and Mariane, 140
Renouncing all desire to dispossess
Another of his rightful happiness,
And . . .

SCENE 4. *Damis, Elmire, Tartuffe*

DAMIS. [*Emerging from the closet where he has been hiding*]
No! We'll not hush up this vile affair;
I heard it all inside that closet there,
Where Heaven, in order to confound the pride
Of this great rascal, prompted me to hide.
Ah, now I have my long-awaited chance 5
To punish his deceit and arrogance,
And give my father clear and shocking proof
Of the black character of his dear Tartuffe.

ELMIRE. Ah no, Damis; I'll be content if he
Will study to deserve my leniency. 10
I've promised silence—don't make me break my word;
To make a scandal would be too absurd.
Good wives laugh off such trifles, and forget them;
Why should they tell their husbands, and upset them?
DAMIS. You have your reasons for taking such a course, 15
And I have reasons, too, of equal force.
To spare him now would be insanely wrong.
I've swallowed my just wrath for far too long
And watched this insolent bigot bringing strife
And bitterness into our family life. 20
Too long he's meddled in my father's affairs,
Thwarting my marriage-hopes, and poor Valère's.
It's high time that my father was undeceived,
And now I've proof that can't be disbelieved—
Proof that was furnished me by Heaven above. 25
It's too good not to take advantage of.
This is my chance, and I deserve to lose it
If, for one moment, I hesitate to use it.
ELMIRE. Damis . . .
DAMIS. No, I must do what I think right.
Madam, my heart is bursting with delight, 30
And, say whatever you will, I'll not consent
To lose the sweet revenge on which I'm bent.
I'll settle matters without more ado;
And here, most opportunely, is my cue.

SCENE 5. *Orgon, Damis, Tartuffe, Elmire*

DAMIS. Father, I'm glad you've joined us. Let us advise you
Of some fresh news which doubtless will surprise you.
You've just now been repaid with interest
For all your loving-kindness to our guest.
He's proved his warm and grateful feelings toward you; 5
It's with a pair of horns he would reward you.
Yes, I surprised him with your wife, and heard
His whole adulterous offer, every word.
She, with her all too gentle disposition,
Would not have told you of his proposition; 10
But I shall not make terms with brazen lechery,
And feel that not to tell you would be treachery.

34. *My cue:* In the original stage directions, Tartuffe now reads silently from his breviary—in the Roman Catholic Church, the book containing the Divine Office for each day, which those in holy orders are required to recite.

ELMIRE. And I hold that one's husband's peace of mind
Should not be spoilt by tattle of this kind.
One's honor doesn't require it: to be proficient 15
In keeping men at bay is quite sufficient.
These are my sentiments, and I wish, Damis,
That you had heeded me and held your peace.

SCENE 6. *Orgon, Damis, Tartuffe*

ORGON. Can it be true, this dreadful thing I hear?
TARTUFFE. Yes, Brother, I'm a wicked man, I fear:
A wretched sinner, all depraved and twisted,
The greatest villain that has ever existed.
My life's one heap of crimes, which grows each minute; 5
There's naught but foulness and corruption in it;
And I perceive that Heaven, outraged by me,
Has chosen this occasion to mortify me.
Charge me with any deed you wish to name;
I'll not defend myself, but take the blame. 10
Believe what you are told, and drive Tartuffe
Like some base criminal from beneath your roof;
Yes, drive me hence, and with a parting curse:
I shan't protest, for I deserve far worse.
ORGON. [*To* DAMIS] Ah, you deceitful boy, how dare you try 15
To stain his purity with so foul a lie?
DAMIS. What! Are you taken in by such a bluff?
Did you not hear . . . ?
ORGON. Enough, you rogue, enough!
TARTUFFE. Ah, Brother, let him speak: you're being unjust.
Believe his story; the boy deserves your trust. 20
Why, after all, should you have faith in me?
How can you know what I might do, or be?
Is it on my good actions that you base
Your favor? Do you trust my pious face?
Ah, no, don't be deceived by hollow shows; 25
I'm far, alas, from being what men suppose;
Though the world takes me for a man of worth,
I'm truly the most worthless man on earth.
[*To* DAMIS]
Yes, my dear son, speak out now: call me the chief
Of sinners, a wretch, a murderer, a thief; 30
Load me with all the names men most abhor;
I'll not complain; I've earned them all, and more;
I'll kneel here while you pour them on my head
As a just punishment for the life I've led.

ORGON. [*To* TARTUFFE] This is too much, dear Brother.
[*To* DAMIS] Have you no heart?
DAMIS. Are you so hoodwinked by this rascal's art . . . ? 35
ORGON. Be still, you monster.
[*To* TARTUFFE] Brother, I pray you, rise.
[*To* DAMIS] Villain!
DAMIS. But . . .
ORGON. Silence!
DAMIS. Can't you realize . . . ?
ORGON. Just one word more, and I'll tear you limb from limb.
TARTUFFE. In God's name, Brother, don't be harsh with him. 40
I'd rather far be tortured at the stake
Than see him bear one scratch for my poor sake.
ORGON. [*To* DAMIS] Ingrate!
TARTUFFE If I must beg you, on bended knee,
To pardon him . . .
ORGON. [*Falling to his knees, addressing Tartuffe*]
Such goodness cannot be!
[*To* DAMIS] *Now, there's* true charity!
DAMIS. What, you . . . ?
ORGON. Villain, be still! 45
I know your motives; I know you wish him ill:
Yes, all of you—wife, children, servants, all—
Conspire against him and desire his fall,
Employing every shameful trick you can
To alienate me from this saintly man. 50
Ah, but the more you seek to drive him away,
The more I'll do to keep him. Without delay,
I'll spite this household and confound its pride
By giving him my daughter as his bride.
DAMIS. You're going to force her to accept his hand? 55
ORGON. Yes, and this very night, d'you understand?
I shall defy you all, and make it clear
That I'm the one who gives the orders here.
Come, wretch, kneel down and clasp his blessed feet,
And ask his pardon for your black deceit. 60
DAMIS. I ask that swindler's pardon? Why, I'd rather . . .
ORGON. So! You insult him, and defy your father!
A stick! A stick! [*To* TARTUFFE] No, no—release me, do.
[*To* DAMIS.] Out of my house this minute! Be off with you,
And never dare set foot in it again. 65
DAMIS. Well, I shall go, but . . .
ORGON. Well, go quickly, then.
I disinherit you; an empty purse
Is all you'll get from me—except my curse!

SCENE 7. *Orgon, Tartuffe*

ORGON. How he blasphemed your goodness! What a son!
TARTUFFE. Forgive him, Lord, as I've already done.
[*To* ORGON] You can't know how it hurts when someone tries
To blacken me in my dear Brother's eyes.
ORGON. Ahh!
TARTUFFE. The mere thought of such ingratitude 5
Plunges my soul into so dark a mood . . .
Such horror grips my heart . . . I gasp for breath,
And cannot speak, and feel myself near death.
ORGON. [*He runs, in tears, to the door through which he has just driven his son.*]
You blackguard! Why did I spare you? Why did I not
Break you in little pieces on the spot? 10
Compose yourself, and don't be hurt, dear friend.
TARTUFFE. These scenes, these dreadful quarrels, have got to end.
I've much upset your household, and I perceive
That the best thing will be for me to leave.
ORGON. What are you saying!
TARTUFFE. They're all against me here;
They'd have you think me false and insincere. 15
ORGON. Ah, what of that? Have I ceased believing in you?
TARTUFFE. Their adverse talk will certainly continue,
And charges which you now repudiate
You may find credible at a later date. 20
ORGON. No, Brother, never.
TARTUFFE. Brother, a wife can sway
Her husband's mind in many a subtle way.
ORGON. No, no.
TARTUFFE. To leave at once is the solution;
Thus only can I end their persecution.
ORGON. No, no, I'll not allow it; you shall remain. 25
TARTUFFE. Ah, well; 'twill mean much martyrdom and pain,
But if you wish it . . .
ORGON. Ah!
TARTUFFE. Enough; so be it.
But one thing must be settled, as I see it.
For your dear honor, and for our friendship's sake,
There's one precaution I feel bound to take. 30
I shall avoid your wife, and keep away . . .
ORGON. No, you shall not, whatever they may say.
It pleases me to vex them, and for spite
I'd have them see you with her day and night.
What's more, I'm going to drive them to despair 35

By making you my only son and heir;
This very day, I'll give to you alone
Clear deed and title to everything I own.
A dear, good friend and son-in-law-to-be
Is more than wife, or child, or kin to me. 40
Will you accept my offer, dearest son?

TARTUFFE. In all things, let the will of Heaven be done.

ORGON. Poor fellow! Come, we'll go draw up the deed.
Then let them burst with disappointed greed!

Act IV

SCENE 1. *Cleante, Tartuffe*

CLEANTE. Yes, all the town's discussing it, and truly,
Their comments do not flatter you unduly.
I'm glad we've met, Sir, and I'll give my view
Of this sad matter in a word or two.
As for who's guilty, that I shan't discuss; 5
Let's say it was Damis who caused the fuss;
Assuming, then, that you have been ill-used
By young Damis, and groundlessly accused,
Ought not a Christian to forgive, and ought
He not to stifle every vengeful thought? 10
Should you stand by and watch a father make
His only son an exile for your sake?
Again I tell you frankly, be advised:
The whole town, high and low, is scandalized;
This quarrel must be mended, and my advice is 15
Not to push matters to a further crisis.
No, sacrifice your wrath to God above,
And help Damis regain his father's love.

TARTUFFE. Alas, for my part I should take great joy
In doing so. I've nothing against the boy. 20
I pardon all, I harbor no resentment;
To serve him would afford me much contentment.
But Heaven's interest will not have it so:
If he comes back, then I shall have to go.
After his conduct—so extreme, so vicious— 25
Our further intercourse would look suspicious.
God knows what people would think! Why, they'd describe
My goodness to him as a sort of bribe;
They'd say that out of guilt I made pretense
Of loving-kindness and benevolence— 30
That, fearing my accuser's tongue, I strove

To buy his silence with a show of love.
CLEANTE. Your reasoning is badly warped and stretched,
And these excuses, Sir, are most far-fetched.
Why put yourself in charge of Heaven's cause? 35
Does Heaven need our help to enforce its laws?
Leave vengeance to the Lord Sir; while we live,
Our duty's not to punish, but forgive;
And what the Lord commands, we should obey
Without regard to what the world may say. 40
What! Shall the fear of being misunderstood
Prevent our doing what is right and good?
No, no: let's simply do what Heaven ordains,
And let no other thoughts perplex our brains.
TARTUFFE. Again, Sir, let me say that I've forgiven 45
Damis, and thus obeyed the laws of Heaven;
But I am not commanded by the Bible
To live with one who smears my name with libel.
CLEANTE. Were you commanded, Sir, to indulge the whim
Of poor Orgon, and to encourage him 50
In suddenly transferring to your name
A large estate to which you have no claim?
TARTUFFE. 'Twould never occur to those who know me best
To think I acted from self-interest.
The treasures of this world I quite despise; 55
Their specious glitter does not charm my eyes;
And if I have resigned myself to taking
The gift which my dear Brother insists on making,
I do so only, as he well understands,
Lest so much wealth fall into wicked hands, 60
Lest those to whom it might descend in time
Turn it to purposes of sin and crime,
And not, as I shall do, make use of it
For Heaven's glory and mankind's benefit.
CLEANTE. Forget these trumped-up fears. Your argument 65
Is one the rightful heir might well resent;
It *is* a moral burden to inherit
Such wealth, but give Damis a chance to bear it.
And would it not be worse to be accused
Of swindling, than to see that wealth misused? 70
I'm shocked that you allowed Orgon to broach
This matter, and that you feel no self-reproach;
Does true religion teach that lawful heirs
May freely be deprived of what is theirs?
And if the Lord has told you in your heart 75
That you and young Damis must dwell apart,

Would it not be the decent thing to beat
A generous and honorable retreat,
Rather than let the son of the house be sent,
For your convenience, into banishment? 80
Sir, if you wish to prove the honesty
Of your intentions . . .

TARTUFFE. Sir, it is a half past three.
I've certain pious duties to attend to,
And hope my prompt departure won't offend you.

CLEANTE. [*Alone*] Damn.

SCENE 2. *Elmire, Mariane, Cleante, Dorine*

DORINE. Stay, Sir, and help Mariane, for Heaven's sake!
She's suffering so, I fear her heart will break.
Her father's plan to marry her off tonight
Has put the poor child in a desperate plight.
I hear him coming. Let's stand together, now, 5
And see if we can't change his mind, somehow,
About this match we all deplore and fear.

SCENE 3. *Orgon, Elmire, Mariane, Cleante, Dorine*

ORGON. Hah! Glad to find you all assembled here.
[*To* MARIANE] This contract, child, contains your happiness,
And what it says I think your heart can guess.

MARIANE. [*Falling to her knees*]
Sir, by that Heaven which sees me here distressed,
And by whatever else can move your breast, 5
Do not employ a father's power, I pray you,
To crush my heart and force it to obey you,
Nor by your harsh commands oppress me so
That I'll begrudge the duty which I owe—
And do not so embitter and enslave me 10
That I shall hate the very life you gave me.
If my sweet hopes must perish, if you refuse
To give me to the one I've dared to choose,
Spare me at least—I beg you, I implore—
The pain of wedding one whom I abhor; 15
And do not, by a heartless use of force,
Drive me to contemplate some desperate course.

ORGON. [*Feeling himself touched by her*]
Be firm, my soul. No human weakness, now.

MARIANE. I don't resent your love for him. Allow
Your heart free rein, Sir; give him your property, 20
And if that's not enough, take mine from me;
He's welcome to my money; take it, do,

But don't, I pray, include my person too.
Spare me, I beg you; and let me end the tale
Of my sad days behind a convent veil. 25

ORGON. A convent! Hah! When crossed in their amours,
All lovesick girls have the same thought as yours.
Get up! The more you loathe the man, and dread him,
The more ennobling it will be to wed him.
Marry Tartuffe, and mortify your flesh! 30
Enough; don't start that whimpering afresh.

DORINE. But why . . . ?

ORGON. Be still, there. Speak when you're spoken to.
Not one more bit of impudence out of you.

CLEANTE. If I may offer a word of counsel here . . .

ORGON. Brother, in counselling you have no peer; 35
All your advice is forceful, sound, and clever;
I don't propose to follow it, however.

ELMIRE. [*To* ORGON] I am amazed, and don't know what to say;
Your blindness simply takes my breath away.
You are indeed bewitched, to take no warning 40
From our account of what occurred this morning.

ORGON. Madam, I know a few plain facts, and one
Is that you're partial to my rascal son;
Hence, when he sought to make Tartuffe the victim
Of a base lie, you dared not contradict him. 45
Ah, but you underplayed your part, my pet;
You should have looked more angry, more upset.

ELMIRE. When men make overtures, must we reply
With righteous anger and a battle-cry?
Must we turn back their amorous advances 50
With sharp reproaches and with fiery glances?
Myself, I find such offers merely amusing,
And make no scenes and fusses in refusing;
My taste is for good-natured rectitude,
And I dislike the savage sort of prude 55
Who guards her virtue with her teeth and claws,
And tears men's eyes out for the slightest cause:
The Lord preserve me from such honor as that,
Which bites and scratches like an alley-cat!
I've found that a polite and cool rebuff 60
Discourages a lover quite enough.

ORGON. I know the facts, and I shall not be shaken.

ELMIRE. I marvel at your power to be mistaken.
Would it, I wonder, carry weight with you
If I could *show* you that our tale was true? 65

ORGON. Show me?

ELMIRE. Yes.
ORGON. Rot.
ELMIRE. Come, what if I found a way
To make you see the facts as plain as day?
ORGON. Nonsense.
ELMIRE. Do answer me; don't be absurd.
I'm not now asking you to trust our word.
Suppose that from some hiding-place in here 70
You learned the whole sad truth by eye and ear—
What would you say of your good friend, after that?
ORGON. Why, I'd say . . . nothing, by Jehoshaphat!
It can't be true.
ELMIRE. You've been too long deceived,
And I'm quite tired of being disbelieved. 75
Come now: let's put my statements to the test,
And you shall see the truth made manifest.
ORGON. I'll take that challenge. Now do your uttermost.
We'll see how you make good your empty boast.
ELMIRE. [*To* DORINE] Send him to me.
DORINE. He's crafty; it may be hard
To catch the cunning scoundrel off his guard. 80
ELMIRE. No, amorous men are gullible. Their conceit
So blinds them that they're never hard to cheat.
Have him come down. [*To* CLEANTE *&* MARIANE] Please leave us, for a bit.

SCENE 4. *Elmire, Orgon*

ELMIRE. Pull up this table, and get under it.
ORGON. What?
ELMIRE. It's essential that you be well-hidden.
ORGON. Why there?
ELMIRE. Oh, Heavens! Just do as you are bidden.
I have my plans; we'll soon see how they fare.
Under the table, now; and once you're there, 5
Take care that you are neither seen nor heard.
ORGON. Well, I'll indulge you, since I gave my word
To see you through this infantile charade.
ELMIRE. Once it is over, you'll be glad we played.
[*To her husband, who is now under the table*]
I'm going to act quite strangely, now, and you 10
Must not be shocked at anything I do.
Whatever I may say, you must excuse
As part of that deceit I'm forced to use.
I shall employ sweet speeches in the task
Of making that impostor drop his mask; 15

I'll give encouragement to his bold desires,
And furnish fuel to his amorous fires.
Since it's for your sake, and for his destruction,
That I shall seem to yield to his seduction,
I'll gladly stop whenever you decide 20
That all your doubts are fully satisfied.
I'll count on you, as soon as you have seen
What sort of man he is, to intervene,
And not expose me to his odious lust
One moment longer than you feel you must. 25
Remember: you're to save me from my plight
Whenever . . . He's coming! Hush! Keep out of sight!

SCENE 5. *Tartuffe, Elmire, Orgon*

TARTUFFE. You wish to have a word with me, I'm told.
ELMIRE. Yes, I've a little secret to unfold.
Before I speak, however, it would be wise
To close that door, and look about for spies.
[TARTUFFE *goes to the door, closes it, and returns.*]
The very last thing that must happen now 5
Is a repetition of this morning's row.
I've never been so badly caught off guard.
Oh, how I feared for you! You saw how hard
I tried to make that troublesome Damis
Control his dreadful temper, and hold his peace. 10
In my confusion, I didn't have the sense
Simply to contradict his evidence;
But as it happened, that was for the best,
And all has worked out in our interest.
This storm has only bettered your position; 15
My husband doesn't have the least suspicion,
And now, in mockery of those who do,
He bids me be continually with you.
And that is why, quite fearless of reproof,
I now can be alone with my Tartuffe, 20
And why my heart—perhaps too quick to yield—
Feels free to let its passion be revealed.
TARTUFFE. Madam, your words confuse me. Not long ago,
You spoke in quite a different style, you know.
ELMIRE. Ah, Sir, if that refusal made you smart, 25
It's little that you know of woman's heart,
Or what that heart is trying to convey
When it resists in such a feeble way!
Always, at first, our modesty prevents
The frank avowal of tender sentiments: 30

However high the passion which inflames us,
Still, to confess its power somehow shames us.
Thus we reluct, at first, yet in a tone
Which tells you that our heart is overthrown,
That what our lips deny, our pulse confesses, 35
And that, in time, all noes will turn to yesses.
I fear my words are all too frank and free,
And a poor proof of woman's modesty;
But since I'm started, tell me, if you will—
Would I have tried to make Damis be still, 40
Would I have listened, calm and unoffended,
Until your lengthy offer of love was ended,
And been so very mild in my reaction,
Had your sweet words not given me satisfaction?
And when I tried to force you to undo 45
The marriage-plans my husband has in view,
What did my urgent pleading signify
If not that I admired you, and that I
Deplored the thought that someone else might own
Part of a heart I wished for mine alone? 50

TARTUFFE. Madam, no happiness is so complete
As when, from lips we love, come words so sweet;
Their nectar floods my every sense, and drains
In honeyed rivulets through all my veins.
To please you is my joy, my only goal; 55
Your love is the restorer of my soul;
And yet I must beg leave, now, to confess
Some lingering doubts as to my happiness.
Might this not be a trick? Might not the catch
Be that you wish me to break off the match 60
With Mariane, and so have feigned to love me?
I shan't quite trust your fond opinion of me
Until the feelings you've expressed so sweetly
Are demonstrated somewhat more concretely,
And you have shown, by certain kind concessions, 65
That I may put my faith in your professions.

ELMIRE. [*She coughs, to warn her husband.*] Why be in such a hurry? Must my heart
Exhaust its bounty at the very start?
To make that sweet admission cost me dear,
But you'll not be content, it would appear, 70
Unless my store of favors is disbursed
To the last farthing, and at the very first.

TARTUFFE. The less we merit, the less we dare to hope,
And with our doubts, mere words can never cope.

We trust no promised bliss till we receive it; 75
Not till a joy is ours can we believe it.
I, who so little merit your esteem,
Can't credit this fulfillment of my dream,
And shan't believe it, Madam, until I savor
Some palpable assurance of your favor. 80

ELMIRE. My, how tyrannical your love can be,
And how it flusters and perplexes me!
How furiously you take one's heart in hand,
And make your every wish a fierce command!
Come, must you hound and harry me to death? 85
Will you not give me time to catch my breath?
Can it be right to press me with such force,
Give me no quarter, show me no remorse,
And take advantage, by your stern insistence,
Of the fond feelings which weaken my resistance? 90

TARTUFFE. Well, if you look with favor upon my love,
Why, then, begrudge me some clear proof thereof?

ELMIRE. But how can I consent without offense
To Heaven, toward which you feel such reverence?

TARTUFFE. If Heaven is all that holds you back, don't worry. 95
I can remove that hindrance in a hurry.
Nothing of that sort need obstruct our path.

ELMIRE. Must one not be afraid of Heaven's wrath?

TARTUFFE. Madam, forget such fears, and be my pupil,
And I shall teach you how to conquer scruple. 100
Some joys, it's true, are wrong in Heaven's eyes;
Yet Heaven is not averse to compromise;
There is a science, lately formulated,
Whereby one's conscience may be liberated,
And any wrongful act you care to mention 105
May be redeemed by purity of intention.
I'll teach you, Madam, the secrets of that science;
Meanwhile, just place on me your full reliance.
Assuage my keen desires, and feel no dread:
The sin, if any, shall be on my head. 110
[ELMIRE *coughs, this time more loudly.*]
You've a bad cough.

ELMIRE. Yes, yes. It's bad indeed.

TARTUFFE. [*Producing a little paper bag*]
A bit of licorice may be what you need.

ELMIRE. No, I've a stubborn cold, it seems. I'm sure it
Will take much more than licorice to cure it.

104. ***Whereby . . . liberated:*** Molière appended his own footnote to this line: "It is a scoundrel who speaks."

TARTUFFE. How aggravating.
ELMIRE. Oh, more than I can say. 115
TARTUFFE. If you're still troubled, think of things this way:
No one shall know our joys, save us alone,
And there's no evil till the act is known;
It's scandal, Madam, which makes it an offense,
And it's no sin to sin in confidence. 120
ELMIRE. [*Having coughed once more*]
Well, clearly I must do as you require,
And yield to your importunate desire.
It is apparent, now, that nothing less
Will satisfy you, and so I acquiesce.
To go so far is much against my will; 125
I'm vexed that it should come to this; but still,
Since you are so determined on it, since you
Will not allow mere language to convince you,
And since you ask for concrete evidence, I
See nothing for it, now, but to comply. 130
If this is sinful, if I'm wrong to do it,
So much the worse for him who drove me to it.
The fault can surely not be charged to me.
TARTUFFE. Madam, the fault is mine, if fault there be,
And . . .
ELMIRE. Open the door a little, and peek out; 135
I wouldn't want my husband poking about.
TARTUFFE. Why worry about the man? Each day he grows
More gullible; one can lead him by the nose.
To find us here would fill him with delight,
And if he saw the worst, he'd doubt his sight. 140
ELMIRE. Nevertheless, do step out for a minute
Into the hall, and see that no one's in it.

SCENE 6. *Orgon, Elmire*

ORGON. [*Coming out from under the table*]
That man's a perfect monster, I must admit!
I'm simply stunned. I can't get over it.
ELMIRE. What, coming out so soon? How premature!
Get back in hiding, and wait until you're sure.
Stay till the end, and be convinced completely; 5
We mustn't stop till things are proved concretely.
ORGON. Hell never harbored anything so vicious!
ELMIRE. Tut, don't be hasty. Try to be judicious.
Wait, and be certain that there's no mistake.
No jumping to conclusions, for Heaven's sake! 10
[*She places* ORGON *behind her, as* TARTUFFE *re-enters.*]

SCENE 7. *Tartuffe, Elmire, Orgon*

TARTUFFE. [*Not seeing* ORGON]
Madam, all things have worked out to perfection;
I've given the neighboring rooms a full inspection;
No one's about; and now I may at last . . .
ORGON. [*Intercepting him*] Hold on, my passionate fellow, not so fast!
I should advise a little more restraint. 5
Well, so you thought you'd fool me, my dear saint!
How soon you wearied of the saintly life—
Wedding my daughter, and coveting my wife!
I've long suspected you, and had a feeling
That soon I'd catch you at your double-dealing. 10
Just now, you've given me evidence galore;
It's quite enough; I have no wish for more.
ELMIRE. [*To* TARTUFFE] I'm sorry to have treated you so slyly,
But circumstances forced me to be wily.
TARTUFFE. Brother, you can't think . . .
ORGON. No more talk from you;
Just leave this household, without more ado. 15
TARTUFFE. What I intended . . .
ORGON. That seems fairly clear.
Spare me your falsehoods and get out of here.
TARTUFFE. No, I'm the master, and you're the one to go!
This house belongs to me, I'll have you know, 20
And I shall show you that you can't hurt *me*
By this contemptible conspiracy,
That those who cross me know not what they do,
And that I've means to expose and punish you,
Avenge offended Heaven, and make you grieve 25
That ever you dared order me to leave.

SCENE 8. *Elmire, Orgon*

ELMIRE. What was the point of all that angry chatter?
ORGON. Dear God, I'm worried. This is no laughing matter.
ELMIRE. How so?
ORGON. I fear I understood his drift.
I'm much disturbed about that deed of gift.
ELMIRE. You gave him . . . ?
ORGON. Yes, it's all been drawn and signed.
But one thing more is weighing on my mind. 5
ELMIRE. What's that?
ORGON. I'll tell you; but first let's see if there's
A certain strong-box in his room upstairs.

Act V

SCENE 1. *Orgon, Cleante*

CLEANTE. Where are you going so fast?
ORGON. God knows!
CLEANTE. Then wait;
Let's have a conference, and deliberate
On how this situation's to be met.
ORGON. That strong-box has me utterly upset;
This is the worst of many, many shocks. 5
CLEANTE. Is there some fearful mystery in that box?
ORGON. My poor friend Argas brought that box to me
With his own hands, in utmost secrecy;
'Twas on the very morning of his flight.
It's full of papers which, if they came to light, 10
Would ruin him—or such is my impression.
CLEANTE. Then why did you let it out of your possession?
ORGON. Those papers vexed my conscience, and it seemed best
To ask the counsel of my pious guest.
The cunning scoundrel got me to agree 15
To leave the strong-box in his custody,
So that, in case of an investigation,
I could employ a slight equivocation
And swear I didn't have it, and thereby,
At no expense to conscience, tell a lie. 20
CLEANTE. It looks to me as if you're out on a limb.
Trusting him with that box, and offering him
That deed of gift, were actions of a kind
Which scarcely indicate a prudent mind.
With two such weapons, he has the upper hand, 25
And since you're vulnerable, as matters stand,
You erred once more in bringing him to bay.
You should have acted in some subtler way.
ORGON. Just think of it: behind that fervent face,
A heart so wicked, and a soul so base! 30
I took him in, a hungry beggar, and then . . .
Enough, by God! I'm through with pious men:
Henceforth I'll hate the whole false brotherhood,
And persecute them worse than Satan could.
CLEANTE. Ah, there you go—extravagant as ever! 35
Why can you not be rational? You never
Manage to take the middle course, it seems,
But jump, instead, between absurd extremes.
You've recognized your recent grave mistake

In falling victim to a pious fake; 40
Now, to correct that error, must you embrace
An even greater error in its place,
And judge our worthy neighbors as a whole
By what you've learned of one corrupted soul?
Come, just because one rascal made you swallow 45
A show of zeal which turned out to be hollow,
Shall you conclude that all men are deceivers,
And that, today, there are no true believers?
Let atheists make that foolish inference;
Learn to distinguish virtue from pretense, 50
Be cautious in bestowing admiration,
And cultivate a sober moderation.
Don't humor fraud, but also don't asperse
True piety; the latter fault is worse,
And it is best to err, if err one must, 55
As you have done, upon the side of trust.

SCENE 2. *Damis, Orgon, Cléante*

DAMIS. Father, I hear that scoundrel's uttered threats
Against you; that he pridefully forgets
How, in his need, he was befriended by you,
And means to use your gifts to crucify you.
ORGON. It's true, my boy. I'm too distressed for tears. 5
DAMIS. Leave it to me, Sir; let me trim his ears.
Faced with such insolence, we must not waver.
I shall rejoice in doing you the favor
Of cutting short his life, and your distress.
CLEANTE. What a display of young hotheadedness! 10
Do learn to moderate your fits of rage.
In this just kingdom, this enlightened age,
One does not settle things by violence.

SCENE 3. *Madame Pernelle, Mariane, Elmire, Dorine, Damis, Orgon, Cléante*

MADAME PERNELLE. I hear strange tales of very strange events.
ORGON. Yes, strange events which these two eyes beheld.
The man's ingratitude is unparalleled.
I save a wretched pauper from starvation,
House him, and treat him like a blood relation, 5
Shower him every day with my largesse,
Give him my daughter, and all that I possess;
And meanwhile the unconscionable knave
Tries to induce my wife to misbehave;
And not content with such extreme rascality, 10

Now threatens me with my own liberality,
And aims, by taking base advantage of
The gifts I gave him out of Christian love,
To drive me from my house, a ruined man,
And make me end a pauper, as he began. 15

DORINE. Poor fellow!

MADAME PERNELLE. No, my son, I'll never bring
Myself to think him guilty of such a thing.

ORGON. How's that?

MADAME PERNELLE. The righteous always were maligned.

ORGON. Speak clearly, Mother. Say what's on your mind.

MADAME PERNELLE. I mean that I can smell a rat, my dear.
You know how everybody hates him, here. 20

ORGON. That has no bearing on the case at all.

MADAME PERNELLE. I told you a hundred times, when you were small,
That virtue in this world is hated ever;
Malicious men may die, but malice never. 25

ORGON. No doubt that's true, but how does it apply?

MADAME PERNELLE. They've turned you against him by a clever lie.

ORGON. I've told you, I was there and saw it done.

MADAME PERNELLE. Ah, slanderers will stop at nothing, Son.

ORGON. Mother, I'll lose my temper . . . For the last time, 30
I tell you I was witness to the crime.

MADAME PERNELLE. The tongues of spite are busy night and noon,
And to their venom no man is immune.

ORGON. You're talking nonsense. Can't you realize
I saw it; saw it; saw it with my eyes? 35
Saw, do you understand me? Must I shout it
Into your ears before you'll cease to doubt it?

MADAME PERNELLE. Appearances can deceive, my son. Dear me,
We cannot always judge by what we see.

ORGON. Drat! Drat!

MADAME PERNELLE. One often interprets things awry; 40
Good can seem evil to a suspicious eye.

ORGON. Was I to see his pawing at Elmire
As an act of charity?

MADAME PERNELLE. Till his guilt is clear,
A man deserves the benefit of the doubt.
You should have waited, to see how things turned out. 45

ORGON. Great God in Heaven, what more proof did I need?
Was I to sit there, watching, until he'd . . .
You drive me to the brink of impropriety.

MADAME PERNELLE. No, no, a man of such surpassing piety

Could not do such a thing. You cannot shake me. 50
I don't believe it, and you shall not make me.
ORGON. You vex me so that, if you weren't my mother,
I'd say to you . . . some dreadful thing or other.
DORINE. It's your turn now, Sir, not to be listened to;
You'd not trust us, and now she won't trust you. 55
CLEANTE. My friends, we're wasting time which should be spent
In facing up to our predicament.
I fear that scoundrel's threats weren't made in sport.
DAMIS. Do you think he'd have the nerve to go to court?
ELMIRE. I'm sure he won't: they'd find it all too crude 60
A case of swindling and ingratitude.
CLEANTE. Don't be too sure. He won't be at a loss
To give his claims a high and righteous gloss;
And clever rogues with far less valid cause
Have trapped their victims in a web of laws. 65
I say again that to antagonize
A man so strongly armed was most unwise.
ORGON. I know it; but the man's appalling cheek
Outraged me so, I couldn't control my pique.
CLEANTE. I wish to Heaven that we could devise 70
Some truce between you, or some compromise.
ELMIRE. If I had known what cards he held, I'd not
Have roused his anger by my little plot.
ORGON. [*To* DORINE, *as* M. LOYAL *enters*] What is that fellow looking for? Who is he?
Go talk to him—and tell him that I'm busy. 75

SCENE 4. *Monsieur Loyal, Madame Pernelle, Orgon, Damis, Mariane, Dorine, Elmire, Cléante*

MONSIEUR LOYAL. Good day, dear sister. Kindly let me see
Your master.
DORINE. He's involved with company,
And cannot be disturbed just now, I fear.
MONSIEUR LOYAL. I hate to intrude; but what has brought me here
Will not disturb your master, in any event. 5
Indeed, my news will make him most content.
DORINE. Your name?
MONSIEUR LOYAL. Just say that I bring greetings from
Monsieur Tartuffe, on whose behalf I've come.
DORINE. [*To* ORGON] Sir, he's a very gracious man, and bears
A message from Tartuffe, which, he declares, 10
Will make you most content.

CLEANTE. Upon my word,
I think this man had best be seen, and heard.
ORGON. Perhaps he has some settlement to suggest.
How shall I treat him? What manner would be best?
CLEANTE. Control your anger, and if he should mention 15
Some fair adjustment, give him your full attention.
MONSIEUR LOYAL. Good health to you, good Sir. May Heaven confound
Your enemies, and may your joys abound.
ORGON. [*Aside, to* CLEANTE] A gentle salutation: it confirms
My guess that he is here to offer terms. 20
MONSIEUR LOYAL. I've always held your family most dear;
I served your father, Sir, for many a year.
ORGON. Sir, I must ask your pardon; to my shame,
I cannot now recall your face or name.
MONSIEUR LOYAL. Loyal's my name; I come from Normandy, 25
And I'm a bailiff, in all modesty.
For forty years, praise God, it's been my boast
To serve with honor in that vital post,
And I am here, Sir, if you will permit
The liberty, to serve you with this writ . . . 30
ORGON. To—*what?*
MONSIEUR LOYAL. Now, please, Sir, let us have no friction:
It's nothing but an order of eviction.
You are to move your goods and family out
And make way for new occupants, without
Deferment or delay, and give the keys . . . 35
ORGON. I? Leave this house?
MONSIEUR LOYAL. Why yes, Sir, if you please.
This house, Sir, from the cellar to the roof,
Belongs now to the good Monsieur Tartuffe,
And he is lord and master of your estate
By virtue of a deed of present date, 40
Drawn in due form, with clearest legal phrasing . . .
DAMIS. Your insolence is utterly amazing!
MONSIEUR LOYAL. Young man, my business here is not with you
But with your wise and temperate father, who,
Like every worthy citizen, stands in awe 45
Of justice, and would never obstruct the law.
ORGON. But . . .
MONSIEUR LOYAL. Not for a million, Sir, would you rebel
Against authority; I know that well.
You'll not make trouble, Sir, or interfere
With the execution of my duties here. 50
DAMIS. Someone may execute a smart tattoo

On that black jacket of yours, before you're through.

MONSIEUR LOYAL. Sir, bid your son be silent. I'd much regret
Having to mention such a nasty threat
Of violence, in writing my report. 55

DORINE. [*Aside*] This man Loyal's a most disloyal sort!

MONSIEUR LOYAL. I love all men of upright character,
And when I agreed to serve these papers, Sir,
It was your feelings that I had in mind.
I couldn't bear to see the case assigned 60
To someone else, who might esteem you less
And so subject you to unpleasantness.

ORGON. What's more unpleasant than telling a man to leave
His house and home?

MONSIEUR LOYAL. You'd like a short reprieve?
If you desire it, Sir, I shall not press you, 65
But wait until tomorrow to dispossess you.
Splendid. I'll come and spend the night here, then,
Most quietly, with half a score of men.
For form's sake, you might bring me, just before
You go to bed, the keys to the front door. 70
My men, I promise, will be on their best
Behavior, and will not disturb your rest.
But bright and early, Sir, you must be quick
And move out all your furniture, every stick:
The men I've chosen are both young and strong, 75
And with their help it shouldn't take you long.
In short, I'll make things pleasant and convenient,
And since I'm being so extremely lenient,
Please show me, Sir, a like consideration,
And give me your entire cooperation. 80

ORGON. [*Aside*] I may be all but bankrupt, but I vow
I'd give a hundred louis, here and now,
Just for the pleasure of landing one good clout
Right on the end of that complacent snout.

CLEANTE. Careful; don't make things worse.

DAMIS. My bootsole itches
To give that beggar a good kick in the breeches. 85

DORINE. Monsieur Loyal, I'd love to hear the whack
Of a stout stick across your fine broad back.

MONSIEUR LOYAL. Take care: a woman too may go to jail if
She uses threatening language to a bailiff. 90

CLEANTE. Enough, enough, Sir. This must not go on.
Give me that paper, please, and then begone.

52. *black jacket:* in the original, *just-aucorps à longues basques,* a close-fitting, long black coat with skirts, the customary dress of a bailiff.

MONSIEUR LOYAL. Well, *au revoir*. God give you all good cheer!
ORGON. May God confound you, and him who sent you here!

SCENE 5. *Orgon, Cleante, Mariane, Elmire, Madame Pernelle, Dorine, Damis*

ORGON. Now, Mother, was I right or not? This writ
Should change your notion of Tartuffe a bit.
Do you perceive his villainy at last?
MADAME PERNELLE. I'm thunderstruck. I'm utterly aghast.
DORINE. Oh, come, be fair. You mustn't take offense 5
At this new proof of his benevolence.
He's acting out of selfless love, I know.
Material things enslave the soul, and so
He kindly has arranged your liberation
From all that might endanger your salvation. 10
ORGON. Will you not ever hold your tongue, you dunce?
CLEANTE. Come, you must take some action, and at once.
ELMIRE. Go tell the world of the low trick he's tried.
The deed of gift is surely nullified
By such behavior, and public rage will not 15
Permit the wretch to carry out his plot.

SCENE 6. *Valère, Orgon, Cléante, Elmire, Mariane, Madame Pernelle, Damis, Dorine*

VALERE. Sir, though I hate to bring you more bad news,
Such is the danger that I cannot choose.
A friend who is extremely close to me
And knows my interest in your family
Has, for my sake, presumed to violate 5
The secrecy that's due to things of state,
And sends me word that you are in a plight
From which your one salvation lies in flight.
That scoundrel who's imposed upon you so
Denounced you to the King an hour ago 10
And, as supporting evidence, displayed
The strong-box of a certain renegade
Whose secret papers, so he testified,
You had disloyally agreed to hide.
I don't know just what charges may be pressed, 15
But there's a warrant out for your arrest;
Tartuffe has been instructed, furthermore,
To guide the arresting officer to your door.
CLEANTE. He's clearly done this to facilitate
His seizure of your house and your estate. 20

ORGON. That man, I must say, is a vicious beast!
VALERE. You can't afford to delay, Sir, in the least.
My carriage is outside, to take you hence;
This thousand louis should cover all expense.
Let's lose no time, or you shall be undone; 25
The sole defense, in this case, is to run.
I shall go with you all the way, and place you
In a safe refuge to which they'll never trace you.
ORGON. Alas, dear boy, I wish that I could show you
My gratitude for everything I owe you. 30
But now is not the time; I pray the Lord
That I may live to give you your reward.
Farewell, my dears; be careful . . .
CLEANTE. Brother, hurry.
We shall take care of things; you needn't worry.

SCENE 7. *The Officer, Tartuffe, Valère, Orgon, Elmire, Mariane, Madame Pernelle, Dorine, Cléante, Damis*

TARTUFFE. Gently, Sir, Gently; stay right where you are.
No need for haste; your lodging isn't far.
You're off to prison, by order of the Prince.
ORGON. This is the crowning blow, you wretch; and since
It means my total ruin and defeat, 5
Your villainy is now at last complete.
TARTUFFE. You needn't try to provoke me; it's no use.
Those who serve Heaven must expect abuse.
CLEANTE. You are indeed most patient, sweet, and blameless.
DORINE. How he exploits the name of Heaven! It's shameless. 10
TARTUFFE. Your taunts and mockeries are all for naught;
To do my duty is my only thought.
MARIANE. Your love of duty is most meritorious,
And what you've done is little short of glorious.
TARTUFFE. All deeds are glorious, Madam, which obey 15
The sovereign prince who sent me here today.
ORGON. I rescued you when you were destitute;
Have you forgotten that, you thankless brute?
TARTUFFE. No, no, I well remember everything;
But my first duty is to serve my King. 20
That obligation is so paramount
That other claims, beside it, do not count;
And for it I would sacrifice my wife,
My family, my friend, or my own life.
ELMIRE. Hypocrite!
DORINE. All that we most revere, he uses 25
To cloak his plots and camouflage his ruses.

CLEANTE. If it is true that you are animated
By pure and loyal zeal, as you have stated,
Why was this zeal not roused until you'd sought
To make Orgon a cuckold, and been caught? 30
Why weren't you moved to give your evidence
Until your outraged host had driven you hence?
I shan't say that the gift of all his treasure
Ought to have damped your zeal in any measure;
But if he is a traitor, as you declare, 35
How could you condescend to be his heir?

TARTUFFE. [*To the* OFFICER] Sir, spare me all this clamor; it's growing shrill.
Please carry out your orders, if you will.

OFFICER. Yes, I've delayed too long, Sir. Thank you kindly.
You're just the proper person to remind me. 40
Come, you are off to join the other boarders
In the King's prison, according to his orders.

TARTUFFE. Who? I, Sir?

OFFICER. Yes.

TARTUFFE. To prison? This can't be true!

OFFICER. I owe an explanation, but not to you.
[*To* ORGON] Sir, all is well; rest easy, and be grateful. 45
We serve a Prince to whom all sham is hateful,
A Prince who sees into our inmost hearts,
And can't be fooled by any trickster's arts.
His royal soul, though generous and human,
Views all things with discernment and acumen; 50
His sovereign reason is not lightly swayed,
And all his judgments are discreetly weighed.
He honors righteous men of every kind,
And yet his zeal for virtue is not blind,
Nor does his love of piety numb his wits 55
And make him tolerant of hypocrites.
'Twas hardly likely that this man could cozen
A King who's foiled such liars by the dozen.
With one keen glance, the King perceived the whole
Perverseness and corruption of his soul, 60
And thus high Heaven's justice was displayed:
Betraying you, the rogue stood self-betrayed.
The King soon recognized Tartuffe as one
Notorious by another name, who'd done
So many vicious crimes that one could fill 65

39. *police officer:* in the original, *un exempt*. He would actually have been a gentleman from the king's personal bodyguard with the rank of lieutenant-colonel or "master of the camp."

Ten volumes with them, and be writing still.
But to be brief: our sovereign was appalled
By this man's treachery toward you, which he called
The last, worst villainy of a vile career,
And bade me follow the impostor here 70
To see how gross his impudence could be,
And force him to restore your property.
Your private papers, by the King's command,
I hereby seize and give into your hand.
The King, by royal order, invalidates 75
The deed which gave this rascal your estates,
And pardons, furthermore, your grave offense
In harboring an exile's documents.
By these decrees, our Prince rewards you for
Your loyal deeds in the late civil war, 80
And shows how heartfelt is his satisfaction
In recompensing any worthy action,
How much he prizes merit, and how he makes
More of men's virtues than of their mistakes.

DORINE. Heaven be praised!

MADAME PERNELLE. I breathe again, at last. 85

ELMIRE. We're safe.

MARIANE. I can't believe the danger's past.

ORGON. [*To* TARTUFFE]. Well, traitor, now you see . . .

CLEANTE. Ah, brother, please,
Let's not descend to such indignities.
Leave the poor wretch to his unhappy fate,
And don't say anything to aggravate 90
His present woes; but rather hope that he
Will soon embrace an honest piety,
And mend his ways, and by a true repentance
Move our just King to moderate his sentence.
Meanwhile, go kneel before your sovereign's throne 95
And thank him for the mercies he has shown.

ORGON. Well said: let's go at once and, gladly kneeling,
Express the gratitude which all are feeling.
Then, when that first great duty has been done,
We'll turn with pleasure to a second one, 100
And give Valère, whose love has proven so true,
The wedded happiness which is his due.

80. ***late civil war:*** a reference to Orgon's role in supporting the king during the Fronde (see note 11, p. 36).

JEAN RACINE
(1639–1699)
Phaedra (Phèdre) *
Preface †

Behold another tragedy whose theme is borrowed from Euripides! Although I have followed a rather different path than did this author for the course of the action, I have not failed to embellish my play with everything that seemed to me to be striking in his. While I took from him only the simple idea of the character of Phaedra, I might say that I owe to him perhaps the most logical elements of his stagecraft. I am not at all surprised that this character has had such a happy success since the days of Euripides, and that moreover it has been so successful in our own century, since the character has all the qualities required by Aristotle for the tragic hero that are proper for the raising of pity and terror. In all truth, Phaedra is neither completely guilty nor completely innocent. She is plunged by her fate, and by the anger of the gods, into an illegitimate passion for which she feels horror from the very start. She makes every attempt to surmount it. . . .

I have even taken care to make her a little less repellent than she is in classical tragedy, where she herself resolves to accuse Hippolytus. I believed that calumny was too low and too black to put in the mouth of a princess who otherwise showed such noble and virtuous feelings. This baseness seemed to me more fitting for a nurse, who could possess more servile inclinations, and who nevertheless only delivered this false accusation to save the life and honor of her mistress. . . .

Hippolytus, in Euripides and in Seneca, is accused of having in effect seduced his stepmother. . . . But here he is merely accused of planning to do it. I wished to spare Theseus a confusion in his character which might have made him less appealing to the audience.

Concerning the character of Hippolytus, I have noticed that among the Ancients Euripides was blamed for representing him as a philosopher free from any imperfection. The result was that the death of the young prince caused more indignation than pity. I

* Translated by Robert Lowell. The original play was written in rhymed hexameter (or Alexandrine) couplets; Lowell's version is in pentameter (or Heroic) couplets, the verse form of Pope's "The Rape of the Lock" and "An Essay on Man," but Lowell observes that his couplet is "run on, avoids inversion and alliteration, and loosens its rhythm with shifted accents and occasional extra syllables. . . ."

† From the Preface published with the first edition in March, 1677. Translated by Howard E. Hugo.

thought I should give him some weakness which would make him slightly culpable in his relations with his father, without however, robbing him of the magnanimity with which he spares Phaedra's honor, and let himself be charged without implicating her. I term "weakness" that passion that he bears for Aricia, in spite of himself: she who is the daughter and the sister of his father's mortal enemies. . . .

To conclude, I do not yet dare state that this play is my best tragedy. . . . What I can affirm is that I have never written one where virtue is brought more to light than in this. The slightest errors are severely punished here. The mere idea of crime is regarded with as much horror as the crime itself. . . . Passions are only revealed to the eyes to show all the disorder that they cause; and vice here is painted in colors so that one may recognize it and hate its hideousness. . . . This is what the first tragic poets always maintained. Their theater was a school where virtue was no less well taught than in the schools of philosophy. . . .

Characters

THESEUS (THÉSÉE), *son of Ægeus and king of Athens*
PHAEDRA (PHÈDRE), *wife of Theseus and daughter of Minos and Pasiphaë*
HIPPOLYTUS (HIPPOLYTE), *son of Theseus and Antiope, queen of the Amazons*
THERAMENES (THÉRAMÈNE), *tutor of Theseus*
ARICIA (ARICIE), *princess of the blood royal of Athens*
OENONE, *Phaedra's nurse and confidante*
ISMENE (ISMENE), *Aricia's confidante*
PANOPE, *Phaedra's lady in waiting*
GUARDS

The SCENE *is laid at Troezen, a town in the Peloponnesus, on the south shore of the Saronic Gulf, opposite Athens.*

Act 1

SCENE I. *Hippolytus, Theramenes*

HIPPOLYTUS. No, no, my friend, we're off! Six months have passed
since Father heard the ocean howl and cast
his galley on the Aegean's skull-white froth.
Listen! The blank sea calls us—off, off, off!
I'll follow Father to the fountainhead 5
and marsh of hell. We're off. Alive or dead,
I'll find him.

THERAMENES. Where, my lord? I've sent a host of veteran seamen up and down the coast;

each village, creek and cove from here to Crete
has been ransacked and questioned by my fleet; 10
my flagship skirted Hades' rapids, furled
sail there a day, and scoured the underworld.
Have you fresh news? New hopes? One even doubts
if noble Theseus wants his whereabouts
discovered. Does he need helpers to share 15
the plunder of his latest love affair;
a shipload of spectators and his son
to watch him ruin his last Amazon—
some creature, taller than a man, whose tanned
and single bosom slithers from his hand, 20
when he leaps to crush her like a waterfall
of honeysuckle?

HIPPOLYTUS. You are cynical,
my friend. Your insinuations wrong a king,
sick as myself of his philandering.
His heart is Phaedra's and no rivals dare 25
to challenge Phaedra's sole possession there.
I sail to find my father. The command
of duty calls me from this stifling land.

THERAMENES. This stifling land? Is that how you deride
this gentle province where you used to ride 30
the bridle-paths, pursuing happiness?
You cured your orphaned childhood's loneliness
and found a peace here you preferred to all
the blaze of Athens' brawling protocol.
A rage for exploits blinds you. Your disease is boredom. 35

HIPPOLYTUS. Friend, this kingdom lost its peace,
when Father left my mother for defiled
bull-serviced Pasiphaë's child. The child
of homicidal Minos is our queen!

THERAMENES. Yes, Phaedra reigns and rules here. I have seen 40
you crouch before her outbursts like a cur.
When she first met you, she refused to stir
until your father drove you out of court.
The news is better now; our friends report
the queen is dying. Will you cross the seas, 45
desert your party and abandon Greece?

11. *Hades' rapids:* The river Acheron in Epirus was thought to flow into the Underworld.

18. *Amazon:* that tribe of Greek women who spent their time in warfare and hunting.

20. *single bosom:* a reference to the legend that the Amazons cut off the right breast in order to draw their bows further.

45. *queen:* i.e., Phaedra, daughter of Minos of Crete and of Pasiphaë, sister to Circe. Enamored of a white bull sent by Poseidon, Pasiphaë consequently gave birth to the Minotaur, the Cretan monster later slain by Theseus. Thus Phaedra was half-sister to the Minotaur.

Why flee from Phaedra? Phaedra fears the night
less than she fears the day that strives to light
the universal ennui of her eye—
this dying woman, who desires to die! 50

HIPPOLYTUS. No, I despise her Cretan vanity,
hysteria and idle cruelty.
I fear Aricia; she alone survives
the blood-feud that destroyed her brothers' lives.

THERAMENES. Prince, Prince, forgive my laughter. Must you fly 55
beyond the limits of the world and die,
floating in flotsam, friendless, far from help,
and clubbed to death by Tartars in the kelp?
Why arm the shrinking violet with a knife?
Do you hate Aricia, and fear for your life, 60
Prince?

HIPPOLYTUS. If I hated her, I'd trust myself and stay.

THERAMENES. Shall I explain you to yourself?
Prince, you have ceased to be that hard-mouthed, proud
and pure Hippolytus, who scorned the crowd
of common lovers once and rose above 65
your wayward father by despising love.
Now you justify your father, and you feel
love's poison running through you, now you kneel
and breathe the heavy incense, and a god
possesses you and revels in your blood! 70
Are you in love?

HIPPOLYTUS. Theramenes, when I call
and cry for help, you push me to the wall.
Why do you plague me, and try to make me fear
the qualities you taught me to revere?
I sucked in prudence with my mother's milk. 75
Antiope, no harlot draped in silk,
first hardened me. I was my mother's son
and not my father's. When the Amazon,
my mother, was dethroned, my mind approved
her lessons more than ever. I still loved 80
her bristling chastity. Later, you told
stories about my father's deeds that made me hold

53-54. *survives . . . lives:* According to one legend, Aegeus, father of Theseus, was the adopted son of Pandion. Pallas, Pandion's second son, had in turn fifty sons. These were the Pallantids and all brothers to Aricia; Theseus killed them because they threatened his own kingship of Athens.

76. *Antiope:* an Amazon, and sister to Hippolyta, the queen of the Amazons. Antiope was beloved by Theseus, who carried her off to Athens. The Amazons then invaded Attica (Athens) in an effort to recover Antiope, but they were defeated in battle and Hippolyta lost her life. Antiope's son by Theseus was Hippolytus.

81. *chastity:* The Amazons were traditionally scornful of love.

back judgment—how he stood for Hercules,
a second Hercules who cleared the Cretan seas
of pirates, throttled Scirron, Cercyon, 85
Procrustes, Sinnis, and the giant man
of Epidaurus writhing in his gore.
He pierced the maze and killed the Minotaur.
Other things turned my stomach: that long list
of women, all refusing to resist. 90
Helen, caught up with all her honeyed flesh
from Sparta; Periboea, young and fresh,
already tired of Salinis. A hundred more,
their names forgotten by my father—whore
and virgin, child and mother, all deceived, 95
if their protestations can be believed!
Ariadne declaiming to the rocks,
her sister, Phaedra, kidnapped. Phaedra locks
the gate at last! You know how often I
would weary, fall to nodding and deny 100
the possiblity of hearing the whole
ignoble, dull, insipid boast unroll.
And now I too must fall. The gods have made me creep.
How can I be in love? I have no specious heap
of honors, friend. No mastered monsters drape 105
my shoulders—Theseus' excuse to rape
at will. Suppose I chose a woman. Why
choose an orphan? Aricia is eternally
cut off from marriage, lest she breed
successors to her fierce brothers, and seed 110
the land with treason. Father only grants
her life on one condition. This—he wants
no bridal torch to burn for her. Unwooed
and childless, she must answer for the blood
her brothers shed. How can I marry her, 115
gaily subvert our kingdom's character,
and sail on the high seas of love?

THERAMENES. You'll prove
nothing by reason, for you are in love.
Theseus' injustice to Aricia throws
her in the light; your eyes he wished to close 120

91. *Helen:* famed as the most beautiful of women, daughter of Zeus and Leda, sister of Castor and Pollux, later the wife of Menelaus of Sparta. When still a young girl, she was abducted by Theseus and Pirithoüs (king of the Lapiths in Thessaly). Her brothers rescued her and brought her back home to Leda and Leda's husband, Tyndareus.

92. *Periboea:* mother of Ajax.

93. *Salinis:* Salamis, island in the Gulf of Aegina on the eastern shore of Greece, off which the Greeks later defeated the Persians in a naval battle, 480 B.C.

97. *Ariadne:* Phaedra's sister, deserted by Theseus after she rescued him from the Minotaur.

are open. She dazzles you. Her pitiful
seclusion makes her doubly terrible.
Does this innocent passion freeze your blood?
There's sweetness in it. Is your only good
the dismal famine of your chastity? 125
You shun your father's path? Where would you be,
Prince, if Antiope had never burned
chastely for Theseus? Love, my lord, has turned
the head of Hercules, and thousands—fired
the forge of Vulcan! All your uninspired, 130
cold moralizing is nothing, Prince. You have changed!
Now no one sees you riding, half-deranged
along the sand-bars, where you drove your horse
and foaming chariot with all your force,
tilting and staggering upright through the surf— 135
far from their usual course across the turf.
The woods are quiet . . . How your eyes hang down!
You often murmur and forget to frown.
All's out, Prince. You're in love; you burn. Flames, flames,
Prince! A dissimulated sickness maims 140
The youthful quickness of your daring. Does
lovely Aricia haunt you?

HIPPOLYTUS. Friend, spare us.
I sail to find my father.

THERAMENES. Will you see
Phaedra before you go?

HIPPOLYTUS. I mean to be
here when she comes. Go, tell her. I will do 145
my duty. Wait, I see her nurse. What new
troubles torment her?

SCENE II. *Hippolytus, Theramenes, Oenone*

OENONE. Who has griefs like mine,
my lord? I cannot help the queen in her decline.
Although I sit beside her day and night,
she shuts her eyes and withers in my sight. 150
An eternal tumult roisters through her head,
panics her sleep, and drags her from her bed.
Just now she fled me at the prime
of day to see the sun for the last time.
She's coming.

HIPPOLYTUS. So! I'll steal away. My flight 155
removes a hateful object from her sight.

127. *Antiope:* Hippolytus' mother.

SCENE III. *Phaedra, Oenone*

PHAEDRA. Dearest, we'll go no further. I must rest.
I'll sit here. My emotions shake my breast,
the sunlight throws black bars across my eyes.
My knees give. If I fall, why should I rise, 160
Nurse?

OENONE. Heaven help us! Let me comfort you.

PHAEDRA. Tear off these gross, official rings, undo
these royal veils. They drag me to the ground.
Why have you frilled me, laced me, crowned me, and wound
my hair in turrets? All your skill torments 165
and chokes me. I am crushed by ornaments.
Everything hurts me, and drags me to my knees!

OENONE. Now this, now that, Madam. You never cease
commanding us, then cancelling your commands.
You feel your strength return, summon all hands 170
to dress you like a bride, then say you choke!
We open all the windows, fetch a cloak,
rush you outdoors. It's no use, you decide
that sunlight kills you, and only want to hide.

PHAEDRA. I feel the heavens' royal radiance cool 175
and fail, as if it feared my terrible
shame has destroyed its right to shine on men.
I'll never look upon the sun again.

OENONE. Renunciation or renunciation!
Now you slander the source of your creation. 180
Why do you run to death and tear your hair?

PHAEDRA. Oh God, take me to some sunless forest lair . . .
There hoof-beats raise a dust-cloud, and my eye
follows a horseman outlined on the sky!

OENONE. What's this, my lady?

PHAEDRA. I have lost my mind. 185
Where am I? Oh forget my words! I find
I've lost the habit now of talking sense.
My face is red and guilty—evidence
of treason! I've betrayed my darkest fears,
Nurse, and my eyes, despite me, fill with tears. 190

OENONE. Lady, if you must weep, weep for your silence
that filled your days and mine with violence.
Ah deaf to argument and numb to care,
you have no mercy. Spare me, spare
yourself. Your blood is like polluted water, 195

178. *sun:* i.e., Helios, the sun-god, father of Pasiphaë, Phaedra's mother.

184. *horseman:* Phaedra is thinking of Hippolytus.

fouling a mind desiring its own slaughter.
The sun has died and shadows filled the skies
thrice now, since you have closed your eyes;
the day has broken through the night's content
thrice now, since you have tasted nourishment. 200
Is your salvation from your terrified
conscience this passive, servile suicide?
Lady, your madness harms the gods who gave
you life, betrays your husband. Who will save
your children? Your downfall will orphan them, 205
deprive them of their kingdom, and condemn
their lives and future to the discipline
of one who abhors you and all your kin,
a tyrant suckled by an amazon,
Hippolytus . . .

PHAEDRA. Oh God!

OENONE. You still hate someone; 210
thank heaven for that, Madam!

PHAEDRA. You spoke his name!

OENONE. Hippolytus, Hippolytus! There's hope
in hatred, Lady. Give your anger rope.
I love your anger. If the winds of love
and fury stir you, you will live. Above 215
your children towers this foreigner, this child
of Scythian cannibals, now wild
to ruin the kingdom, master Greece, and choke
the children of the gods beneath his yoke.
Why dawdle? Why deliberate at length? 220
Oh, gather up your dissipated strength.

PHAEDRA. I've lived too long.

OENONE. Always, always agonized!
Is your conscience still stunned and paralyzed?
Do you think you have washed your hands in blood?

PHAEDRA. Thank God, my hands are clean still. Would to God 225
my heart were innocent!

OENONE. Your heart, your heart!
What have you done that tears your soul apart?

PHAEDRA. I've said too much. Oenone, let me die;
by dying I shall escape blasphemy.

OENONE. Search for another hand to close your eyes. 230
Oh cruel Queen, I see that you despise
my sorrow and devotion. I'll die first,

205. *children:* Phaedra's sons, Acamas and Demophöon.

217. *Scythian cannibals:* Scythia, the home of the Amazons, was for the ancient Greeks associated with barbarians.

and end the anguish of this service cursed
by your perversity. A thousand roads
always lie open to the killing gods. 235
I'll choose the nearest. Lady, tell me how
Oenone's love has failed you. Will you allow
your nurse to die, your nurse, who gave up all—
nation, parents, children, to serve in thrall.
I saved you from your mother, King Minos' wife! 240
Will your death pay me for giving up my life?

PHAEDRA. What I could tell you, I have told you. Nurse,
only my silence saves me from the curse
of heaven.

OENONE. How could you tell me anything
worse than watching you dying?

PHAEDRA. I would bring 245
my life and rank dishonor. What can I say
to save myself, or put off death a day.

OENONE. Ah Lady, I implore you by my tears
and by your suffering body. Heaven hears,
and knows the truth already. Let me see. 250

PHAEDRA. Stand up.

OENONE. Your hesitation's killing me!

PHAEDRA. What can I tell you? How the gods reprove me!

OENONE. Speak!

PHAEDRA. On Venus, murdering Venus! love
gored Pasiphaë with the bull.

OENONE. Forget
your mother! When she died, she paid her debt. 255

PHAEDRA. Oh Ariadne, oh my Sister, lost
for love of Theseus on that rocky coast.

OENONE. Lady, what nervous languor makes you rave
against your family; they are in the grave.

PHAEDRA. Remorseless Aphrodite drives me. I, 260
my race's last and worst love-victim, die.

OENONE. Are you in love?

PHAEDRA. I am insane with love!

OENONE. Who is he?

PHAEDRA. I'll tell you. Nothing love can do could
equal . . . Nurse, I am in love. The shame
kills me. I love the . . . Do not ask his name. 265

OENONE. Who?

PHAEDRA. Nurse, you know my old loathing for the son
of Theseus and the barbarous amazon?

257. ***rocky coast:*** **Theseus abandoned Ariadne on the island of Naxos, off the southern coast of Greece in the Aegean Sea.**

OENONE. Hippolytus! My God, oh my God!
PHAEDRA. You,
not I, have named him.
OENONE. What can you do,
but die? Your words have turned my blood to ice. 270
Oh righteous heavens, must the blasphemies
of Pasiphaë fall upon her daughter?
Her Furies strike us down across the water.
Why did we come here?
PHAEDRA. My evil comes from farther off. In May, 275
in brilliant Athens, on my marriage day,
I turned aside for shelter from the smile
of Theseus. Death was frowning in an aisle—
Hippolytus! I saw his face, turned white!
My lost and dazzled eyes saw only night, 280
capricious burnings flickered through my bleak
abandoned flesh. I could not breathe or speak
I faced my flaming executioner,
Aphrodite, my mother's murderer!
I tried to calm her wrath by flowers and praise, 285
I built her a temple, fretted months and days
on decoration. I even hoped to find
symbols and stays for my distracted mind,
searching the guts of sacrificial steers.
Yet when my erring passions, mutineers 290
to virtue, offered incense at the shrine
of love, I failed to silence the malign
Goddess, Alas, my hungry open mouth,
thirsting with adoration, tasted drouth—
Venus resigned her altar to my new lord— 295
and even while I was praying, I adored
Hippolytus above the sacred flame,
now offered to his name I could not name.
I fled him, yet he stormed me in disguise,
and seemed to watch me from his father's eyes. 300
I even turned against myself, screwed up
my slack courage to fury, and would not stop
shrieking and raging, till half-dead with love
and the hatred of a stepmother, I drove
Hippolytus in exile from the rest 305
and strenuous wardship of his father's breast.
Then I could breathe, Oenone; he was gone;
my lazy, nerveless days meandered on
through dreams and daydreams, like a stately carriage
touring the level landscape of my marriage. 310

Yet nothing worked. My husband sent me here
to Troezen, far from Athens; once again the dear
face shattered me; I saw Hippolytus
each day, and felt my ancient, venomous
passion tear my body limb from limb; 315
naked Venus was clawing down her victim.
What could I do? Each moment, terrified
by loose diseased emotions, now I cried
for death to save my glory and expel
my gloomy frenzy from this world, my hell. 320
And yet your tears and words bewildered me,
and so endangered my tranquillity,
at last I spoke. Nurse, I shall not repent,
if you will leave me the passive content
of dry silence and solitude. 325

SCENE IV. *Phaedra, Oenone, Panope*

PANOPE. My heart breaks. Would to God, I could refuse
to tell your majesty my evil news.
The King is dead! Listen, the heavens ring
with shouts and lamentations for the King.

PHAEDRA. The King is dead? What's this?

PANOPE. In vain 330
you beg the gods to send him back again.
Hippolytus has heard the true report,
he is already heading for the port.

PHAEDRA. Oh God!

PANOPE. They've heard in Athens. Everyone
is joining factions—some salute your son, 335
others are calling for Hippolytus;
they want him to reform and harden us—
even Aricia claims the loyalty
of a fanatical minority.
The Prince's captains have recalled their men. 340
His flag is up and now he sails again
for Athens. Queen, if he appear there now,
he'll drag the people with him!

OENONE. Stop, allow
the Queen a little respite for her grief.
She hears you, and will act for our relief. 345

SCENE V. *Phaedra, Oenone*

OENONE. I'd given up persuading you to live;
death was your refuge, only death could give

you peace and save your troubled glory. I
myself desired to follow you, and die.
But this catastrophe prescribes new laws: 350
the king is dead, and for the king who was.
fate offers you his kingdom. You have a son;
he should be king! If you abandon
him, he'll be a slave. The gods, his ancestors,
will curse and drive you on your fatal course. 355
Live! Who'll condemn you if you love and woo
the Prince? Your stepson is no kin to you,
now that your royal husband's death has cut
and freed you from the throttling marriage-knot.
Do not torment the Prince with persecution, 360
and give a leader to the revolution;
no, win his friendship, bind him to your side.
Give him this city and its countryside.
He will renounce the walls of Athens, piled
stone on stone by Minerva for your child. 365
Stand with Hippolytus, annihilate
Aricia's faction, and possess the state!

PHAEDRA. So be it! Your superior force has won.
I will live if compassion for my son,
devotion to the Prince, and love of power 370
can give me courage in this fearful hour.

Act 2

SCENE I. *Aricia, Ismene*

ARICIA. What's this? The Prince has sent a messenger?
The Prince begs me to wait and meet him here?
The Prince begs! Goose, you've lost your feeble wits!

ISMENE. Lady, be calm. These are the benefits
of Theseus' death: first Prince Hippolytus 5
comes courting favors; soon the populous
cities of Greece will follow—they will eat
out of your hand, Princess, and kiss your feet.

ARICIA. This felon's hand, this slave's! My dear, your news
is only frivolous gossip, I refuse 10
to hope.

ISMENE. Ah Princess, the just powers of hell
have struck. Theseus has joined your brothers!

ARICIA. Tell
me how he died.

365. *Minerva:* the Greek Goddess Athene, patroness of Athens.

ISMENE. Princess, fearful tales
are circulating. Sailors saw his sails,
his infamous black sails, spin round and round 15
in Charybdis' whirlpool; all hands were drowned.
Yet others say on better evidence
that Theseus and Pirithoüs passed the dense
darkness of hell to rape Persephone.
Pirithoüs was murdered by the hound; 20
Theseus, still living, was buried in the ground.
ARICIA. This is an old wives' tale. Only the dead
enter the underworld, and see the bed
of Queen Persephone. What brought him there?
ISMENE. Princess, the King is dead—dead! Everywhere 25
men know and mourn. Already our worshipping
townsmen acclaim Hippolytus for their king;
in her great palace, Phaedra, the self-styled
regent, rages and trembles for her child.
ARICIA. What makes you think the puritanical 30
son of Theseus is human. Will he recall
my sentence and relent?
ISMENE. I know he will.
ARICIA. You know nothing about him. He would kill
a woman, rather than be kind to one.
That wolf-cub of a fighting amazon 35
hates me above all women. He would walk
from here to hell, rather than hear me talk.
ISMENE. Do you know Hippolytus? Listen to me.
His famous, blasphemous frigidity,
what is it, when you've seen him close at hand? 40
I've watched him like a hawk, and seen him stand
shaking beside you—all his reputation
for hating womenkind bears no relation
to what I saw. He couldn't take his eyes
off you! His eyes speak what his tongue denies. 45
ARICIA. I can't believe you. Your story's absurd!
How greedily I listen to each word!
Ismene, you know me, you know how my heart
was reared on death, and always set apart
from what it cherished—can this plaything of 50
the gods and furies feel the peace of love?

16. *Charybdis:* in mythology, the destroying daughter of Poseidon and Gaea who lived beneath a large rock bearing her name, on the Sicilian side of the narrows between Sicily and Italy, and opposite Scylla—the cave at these same straits where the goddess-monster Scylla lived.

18-19. *Pirithoüs . . . Persephone:* Theseus went with Pirithoüs, king of the Lapiths, to Hades to help him steal Persephone. Hercules freed Theseus, whom Pluto had imprisoned, but could not free Pirithoüs, who was later killed.

What sights I've seen, Ismene! "Heads will roll,"
my brothers told me, "we will rule." I, the sole
survivor of those fabulous kings, who tilled
the soil of Greece, have seen my brothers killed, 55
six brothers murdered! In a single hour,
the tyrant, Theseus, lopped them in their flower.
The monster spared my life, and yet decreed
the torments of this childless life I lead
in exile, where no Greek can look on me; 60
my forced, perpetual virginity
preserves his crown; no son shall bear my name
or blow my brothers' ashes into flame.
Ismene, you know how well his tyranny
favors my temperament and strengthens me 65
to guard the honor of my reputation;
his rigor fortified my inclination.
How could I test his son's civilities?
I'd never even seen him with my eyes!
I'd never seen him. I'd restrained my eye, 70
that giddy nerve, from dwelling thoughtlessly
upon his outward grace and beauty—on mere
embellishments of nature, a veneer
the Prince himself despises and ignores.
My heart loves nobler virtues, and adores 75
in him his father's hard intelligence.
He has his father's daring and a sense
of honor his father lacks. Let me confess,
I love him for his lofty haughtiness
never submitted to a woman's yoke. 80
How could Phaedra's splendid marriage provoke
my jealousy? Have I so little pride,
I'd snatch at a rake's heart, a heart denied
to none—all riddled, opened up to let
thousands pass in like water through a net? 85
To carry sorrows to a heart, alone
untouched by passion, inflexible as stone,
to fasten my dominion on a force
as nervous as a never-harnessed horse—
this stirs me, this enflames me. Devilish Zeus 90
is easier mastered than Hippolytus;
heaven's love-infatuated emperor
confers less glory on his conqueror!
Ismene, I'm afraid. Why should I boast?
His very virtues I admire most 95
threaten to rise and throw me from the brink

of hope. What girlish folly made me think
Hippolytus could love Aricia?

ISMENE. Here
he is. He loves you, Princess. Have no fear.

SCENE II. *Aricia, Ismene, Hippolytus*

HIPPOLYTUS. Princess, before 100
I leave here, I must tell you what's in store
for you in Greece. Alas, my father's dead.
The fierce forebodings that disquieted
my peace are true. Death, only death, could hide
his valor from this world he pacified. 105
The homicidal Fates will not release
the comrade, friend and peer of Hercules.
Princess, I trust your hate will not resent
honors whose justice is self-evident.
A single hope alleviates my grief, 110
Princess, I hope to offer you relief.
I now revoke a law whose cruelty
has pained my conscience. Princess, you are free
to marry. Oh enjoy this province, whose
honest, unhesitating subjects choose 115
Hippolytus for king. Live free as air,
here, free as I am, much more free!

ARICIA. I dare
not hope. You are too gracious. Can you free
Aricia from your father's stern decree?

HIPPOLYTUS. Princess, the Athenian people, torn in two 120
between myself and Phaedra's son, want you.

ARICIA. Want me, my Lord!

HIPPOLYTUS. I've no illusions. Lame
Athenian precedents condemn my claim,
because my mother was a foreigner.
But what is that? If my only rival were 125
my younger brother, his minority
would clear my legal disability.
However, a better claim than his or mine
now favors you, ennobled by the line
of great Erectheus. Your direct descent 130
sets you before my father; he was only lent

124. *foreigner:* In Euripides' time, Athenian law made the son of an Athenian and a non-Greek woman illegitimate. Hippolytus' mother was Antiope the Amazon. Yet in Racine, and in Euripides, it is not made clear why Phaedra's childen do not suffer from the same liability.

130. *Erectheus:* son of Hephaestus and Gaea, brought up secretly by Athene in her temple. He subsequently became king of Athens, where he introduced her cult.

this kingdom by adoption. Once the common
Athenian, dazed by Theseus' superhuman
energies, had no longing to exhume
the rights that rushed your brothers to their doom. 135
Now Athens calls you home; the ancient feud
too long has stained the sacred olive wood;
blood festers in the furrows of our soil
to blight its fruits and scorch the farmer's toil.
This province suits me; let the vines of Crete 140
offer my brother a secure retreat.
The rest is yours. All Attica is yours;
I go to win you what your right assures.

ARICIA. Am I awake, my lord? Your sayings seem
like weird phantasmagoria in a dream. 145
How can your sparkling promises be true?
Some god, my lord, some god, has entered you!
How justly you are worshiped in this town;
oh how the truth surpasses your renown!
You wish to endow me with your heritage! 150
I only hoped you would not hate me. This rage
your father felt, how can you put it by
and treat me kindly?

HIPPOLYTUS. Princess, is my eye
blind to beauty? Am I a bear, a bull, a boar,
some abortion fathered by the Minotaur? 155
Some one-eyed Cyclops, able to resist
Aricia's loveliness and still exist?
How can a man stand up against your grace?

ARICIA. My lord, my lord!

HIPPOLYTUS. I cannot hide my face,
Princess! I'm driven. Why does my violence 160
so silence reason and intelligence?
Must I be still, and let my adoration
simmer away in silent resignation?
Princess, I've lost all power to restrain
myself. You see a madman, whose insane 165
pride hated love, and hoped to sit ashore,
watching the galleys founder in the war;
I was Diana's liegeman, dressed in steel.
I hoped to trample love beneath my heel—

156. *Cyclops:* one-eyed giants possessing vast strength, generally thought by the Greeks to dwell in Sicily, where they lived in a lawless and cannibalistic fashion.

168-170. ***Diana's liegeman . . . flaming Venus:*** In the original play by Euripides, even more is made of Hippolytus worshipping Artemis (Diana), to the exclusion of Aphrodite (Venus), and the latter goddess' jealousy brings about his destruction.

alas, the flaming Venus burns me down, 170
I am the last dependent on her crown.
What left me charred and writhing in her clutch?
A single moment and a single touch.
Six months now, bounding like a wounded stag,
I've tried to shake this poisoned dart, and drag 175
myself to safety from your eyes that blind
when present, and when absent leave behind
volleys of burning arrows in my mind.
Ah Princess, shall I dive into the sea,
or steal the wings of Icarus to flee 180
love's Midas' touch that turns my world to gold?
Your image drives me stumbling through the cold,
floods my deserted forest caves with light,
darkens the day and dazzles through my night.
I'm grafted to your side by all I see; 185
all things unite us and imprison me.
I have no courage for the Spartan exercise
that trained my hand and steeled my energies.
Where are my horses? I forget their names.
My triumphs with my chariot at the games 190
no longer give me strength to mount a horse.
The ocean drives me shuddering from its shores.
Does such a savage conquest make you blush?
My boorish gestures, headlong cries that rush
at you like formless monsters from the sea? 195
Ah, Princess, hear me! Your serenity
must pardon the distortions of a weak
and new-born lover, forced by you to speak
love's foreign language, words that snarl and yelp . . .
I never could have spoken without your help. 200

SCENE III. *Aricia, Ismene, Hippolytus, Theramenes*

THERAMENES. I announce the Queen. She comes hurriedly,
looking for you.

HIPPOLYTUS. For me!

THERAMENES. Don't ask me why;
she insisted. I promised I'd prevail
on you to speak with her before you sail. 205

HIPPOLYTUS. What can she want to hear? What can I say?

180. *Icarus:* son of Daedalus. With his father he escaped from Minos of Crete by means of wings made from feathers and wax. Despite Daedalus' warnings, Icarus flew too high; the sun melted the wax, and he fell into the sea.

181. *Midas:* King of Phrygia, to whom the god Dionysus granted the wish that all he touched might be changed to gold.

ARICIA. Wait for her, here! You cannot turn away.
Forget her malice. Hating her will serve
no purpose. Wait for her! Her tears deserve
your pity.

HIPPOLYTUS. You're going, Princess? And I must go 210
to Athens, far from you. How shall I know
if you accept my love.

ARICIA. My lord, pursue
your gracious promise. Do what you must do,
make Athens tributary to my rule.
Nothing you offer is unacceptable; 215
yet this empire, so great, so glorious,
is the least precious of your gifts to us.

SCENE IV. *Hippolytus, Theramenes*

HIPPOLYTUS. We're ready. Wait, the Queen's here. I need you.
You must interrupt this tedious interview.
Hurry down to the ship, then rush back, pale 220
And breathless. Say the wind's up and we must sail.

SCENE V. *Hippolytus, Oenone, Phaedra*

PHAEDRA. He's here! Why does he scowl and look away
from me? What shall I do? What shall I say?

OENONE. Speak for your son, he has no other patron.

PHAEDRA. Why are you so impatient to be gone 225
from us, my lord? Stay! we will weep together.
Pity my son; he too has lost his father.
My own death's near. Rebellion, sick with wrongs,
now like a sea-beast, lifts its slimey prongs,
its muck, its jelly. You alone now stand 230
to save the state. Who else can understand
a mother? I forget. You will not hear
me! An enemy deserves no pity. I fear
your anger. Must my son, your brother, Prince,
be punished for his cruel mother's sins? 235

HIPPOLYTUS. I've no such thoughts.

PHAEDRA. I persecuted you
blindly, and now you have good reason to
return my impudence. How could you find
the motivation of this heart and mind
that scourged and tortured you, till you began 240
to lose the calm composure of a man,
and dwindle to a harsh and sullen boy,
a thing of ice, unable to enjoy
the charms of any civilized resource

except the heavy friendship of your horse, 245
that whirled you far from women, court and throne,
to course the savage woods for wolves alone?
You have good reason, yet if pain's a measure,
no one has less deserved your stern displeasure.
My lord, no one has more deserved compassion. 250

HIPPOLYTUS. Lady, I understand a mother's passion,
a mother jealous for her children's rights.
How can she spare a first wife's son? Long nights
of plotting, devious ways of quarrelling—
a madhouse! What else can remarriage bring? 255
Another would have shown equal hostility,
pushed her advantage more outrageously.

PHAEDRA. My lord, if you had known how far my love
and yearning have exalted me above
this usual weakness . . . Our afflicting kinship 260
is ending . . .

HIPPOLYTUS. Madame, the precious minutes slip
by, I fatigue you. Fight against your fears.
Perhaps Poseidon has listened to our tears,
perhaps your husband's still alive. He hears
us, he is surging home—only a short 265
day's cruise conceals him, as he scuds for port.

PHAEDRA. That's folly, my lord. Who has twice visited
black Hades and the river of the dead
and returned? No, the poisonous Acheron
never lets go. Theseus drifts on and on, 270
a gutted galley on that clotted waste—
he woos, he wins Persephone, the chaste . . .
What am I saying? Theseus is not dead.
He lives in you. He speaks, he's taller by a head,
I see him, touch him, and my heart—a reef . . . 275
Ah Prince, I wander. Love betrays my grief . . .

HIPPOLYTUS. No, no, my father lives. Lady, the blind
furies release him; in your loyal mind,
love's fullness holds him, and he cannot die.

PHAEDRA. I hunger for Theseus. Always in my eye 280
he wanders, not as he appeared in hell,
lascivious eulogist of any belle
he found there, from the lowest to the Queen;
no, faithful, airy, just a little mean
through virtue, charming all, yet young and new, 285
as we would paint a god—as I now see you!
Your valiant shyness would have graced his speech,

263. *Poseidon:* Neptune, god of the sea, son of Cronus and Rhea.

he would have had your stature, eyes, and reach,
Prince, when he flashed across our Cretan waters,
the loved enslaver of King Minos' daughters. 200
Where were you? How could he conscript the flower
of Athens' youth against my father's power,
and ignore you? You were too young, they say;
you should have voyaged as a stowaway.
No dawdling bypath would have saved our bull, 295
when your just vengeance thundered through its skull.
There, light of foot, and certain of your goal,
you would have struck my brother's monstrous soul,
and pierced our maze's slow meanders, led
by Ariadne and her subtle thread. 300
By Ariadne? Prince *I* would have fought
for precedence; my every flaming thought,
love-quickened, would have shot you through the dark,
straight as an arrow to your quaking mark.
Could I have waited, panting, perishing, 305
entrusting your survival to a string,
like Ariadne, when she skulked behind,
there at the portal, to bemuse her mind
among the solemn cloisters of the porch?
No, Phaedra would have snatched your burning torch, 310
and lunged before you, reeling like a priest
of Dionysus to distract the beast.
I would have reached the final corridor
a lap before you, and killed the Minotaur!
Lost in the labyrinth, and at your side, 315
would it have mattered, if I lived or died?

HIPPOLYTUS. What are you saying, Madam? You forget
my father is your husband!

PHAEDRA. I have let
you see my grief for Theseus! How could I
forget my honor and my majesty,
Prince?

HIPPOLYTUS. Madame, forgive me! My foolish youth 320
conjectured hideous untruths from your truth.
I cannot face my insolence. Farewell . . .

PHAEDRA. You monster! You understood me too well!
Why do you hang there, speechless, petrified,
polite! My mind whirls. What have I to hide? 325
Phaedra in all her madness stands before you.
I love you! Fool, I love you, I adore you!
Do not imagine that my mind approved
my first defection, Prince, or that I loved

your youth light-heartedly, and fed my treason 330
with cowardly compliance, till I lost my reason.
I wished to hate you, but the gods corrupt
us; though I never suffered their abrupt
seductions, shattering advances, I
too bear their sensual lightnings in my thigh. 335
I too am dying. I have felt the heat
that drove my mother through the fields of Crete,
the bride of Minos, dying for the full
magnetic April thunders of the bull.
I struggled with my sickness, but I found 340
no grace or magic to preserve my sound
intelligence and honor from this lust,
plowing my body with its horny thrust.
At first I fled you, and when this fell short
of safety, Prince, I exiled you from court. 345
Alas, my violence to resist you made
my face inhuman, hateful. I was afraid
to kiss my husband lest I love his son.
I made you fear me (this was easily done);
you loathed me more, I ached for you no less. 350
Misfortune magnified your loveliness.
I grew so wrung and wasted, men mistook
me for the Sibyl. If you could bear to look
your eyes would tell you. Do you believe my passion
is voluntary? That my obscene confession 355
is some dark trick, some oily artifice?
I came to beg you not to sacrifice
my son, already uncerain of his life.
Ridiculous, mad embassy, for a wife
who loves her stepson! Prince, I only spoke 360
about myself! Avenge yourself, invoke
your father; a worse monster threatens you
than any Theseus ever fought and slew.
The wife of Theseus loves Hippolytus!
See, Prince! Look, this monster, ravenous 365
for her execution, will not flinch.
I want your sword's spasmodic final inch.

OENONE. Madam, put down this weapon. Your distress
attracts the people. Fly these witnesses.
Hurry! Stop kneeling! What a time to pray! 370

353. *Sibyl*: originally the daughter of Dardanus and Neso, who had prophetic powers. Later the name was used about many old women who could foretell the future. Apollo granted the Cumaean Sibyl a lifetime of a thousand years, but not lasting youth.

SCENE VI. *Theramenes, Hippolytus*

THERAMENES. Is this Phaedra, fleeing, or rather dragged away
sobbing? Where is your sword? Who tore
this empty scabbard from your belt?

HIPPOLYTUS. No more!
Oh let me get away! I face disaster.
Horrors unnerve me. Help! I cannot master 375
my terror. Phaedra . . . No, I won't expose
her. No! Something I do not dare disclose . . .

THERAMENES. Our ship is ready, but before you leave,
listen! Prince, what we never would believe
has happened: Athens has voted for your brother. 380
The citizens have made him king. His mother
is regent.

HIPPOLYTUS. Phaedra is in power!

THERAMENES. An envoy sent from Athens came this hour
to place the scepter in her hands. Her son
is king.

HIPPOLYTUS. Almighty gods, you know this woman! 385
Is it her spotless virtue you reward?

THERAMENES. I've heard a rumor. Someone swam aboard
a ship off Epirus. He claims the King
is still alive. I've searched. I know the thing
is nonsense.

HIPPOLYTUS. Search! Nothing must be neglected. 390
If the king's dead, I'll rouse the disaffected
people, crown Aricia, and place our lands,
our people, and our lives in worthy hands.

Act 3

SCENE I. *Phaedra, Oenone*

PHAEDRA. Why do my people rush to crown me queen?
Who can even want to see me? They have seen
my downfall. Will their praise deliver me?
Oh bury me at the bottom of the sea!
Nurse, I have said too much! Led on by you, 5
I've said what no one should have listened to.
He listened. How could he pretend my drift
was hidden? Something held him, and made him shift
his ground . . . He only wanted to depart
and hide, while I was pouring out my heart. 10
Oh how his blushing multiplied my shame!
Why did you hold me back! You are to blame,

Oenone. But for you, I would have killed
myself. Would he have stood there, iron-willed
and merciless, while I fell upon his sword? 15
He would have snatched it, held me, and restored
my life. No! No!

OENONE. Control yourself! No peace
comes from surrendering to your disease,
Madam. Oh daughter of the kings of Crete,
why are you weeping and fawning at the feet 20
of this barbarian, less afraid of fate
than of a woman? You must rule the state.

PHAEDRA. Can I, who have no courage to restrain
the insurrection of my passions, reign?
Will the Athenians trust their sovereignty 25
to me? Love's despotism is crushing me,
I am ruined.

OENONE. Fly!

PHAEDRA. How can I leave him?

OENONE. Lady, you have already banished him.
Can't you take flight?

PHAEDRA. The time for flight has passed.
He knows me now. I rushed beyond the last 30
limits of modesty, when I confessed.
Hope was no longer blasting through my breast;
I was resigned to hopelessness and death,
and gasping out my last innocent breath,
Oenone, when you forced me back to life. 35
You thought I was no longer Theseus' wife,
and let me feel that I was free to love.

OENONE. I would have done anything to remove
your danger. Whether I'm guilty or innocent
is all the same to me. Your punishment 40
should fall on one who tried to kill you, not
on poor Oenone. Lady, you must plot
and sacrifice this monster, whose unjust
abhorence left you dying in the dust.
Oh humble him, undo him, oh despise 45
him! Lady, you must see him with my eyes.

PHAEDRA. Oenone, he was nourished in the woods;
he is all shyness and ungracious moods
because the forests left him half-inhuman.
He's never heard love spoken by a woman! 50
We've gone too far. Oenone, we're unwise;
perhaps the young man's silence was surprise.

OENONE. His mother, the amazon, was never moved
by men.

PHAEDRA. The boy exists. She must have loved!
OENONE. He has a sullen hatred for our sex. 55
PHAEDRA. Oh, all the better; rivals will not vex
my chances. Your advice is out of season;
now you must serve my frenzy, not my reason!
You tell me love has never touched his heart;
we'll look, we'll find an undefended part. 60
He's turned his bronze prows seaward; look, the wind
already blows like a trumpeter behind
his bulging canvas! The Acropolis
of Athens and its empire shall be his!
Hurry, Oenone, hunt the young man down, 65
blind him with dazzling visions of the crown.
Go tell him I relinquish my command,
I only want the guidance of his hand.
Let him assume these powers that weary me,
he will instruct my son in sovereignty. 70
Perhaps he will adopt my son, and be
the son and mother's one divinity!
Oenone, rush to him, use every means
to bend and win him; if he fears the Queen's
too proud, he'll listen to her slave. Plead, groan, 75
insist, say I am giving him my throne . . .
No, say I'm dying!

SCENE II. *Phaedra*

PHAEDRA. Implacable Aphrodite, now you see
the depths to which your tireless cruelty
has driven Phaedra—here is my bosom;
every thrust and arrow has struck home! 80
Oh Goddess, if you hunger for renown,
rise now, and shoot a worthier victim down!
Conquer the barbarous Hippolytus,
who mocks the graces and the power of Venus,
and gazes on your godhead with disgust. 85
Avenge me, Venus! See, my cause is just,
my cause is yours. Oh bend him to my will! . . .
You're back, Oenone? Does he hate me still?

SCENE III. *Phaedra, Oenone*

OENONE. Your love is folly, dash it from your soul,
gather your scattered pride and self-control, 90
Madam! I've seen the royal ship arrive.
Theseus is back, Theseus is still alive!
Thousands of voices thunder from the docks.
People are waving flags and climbing rocks.

While I was looking for Hippolytus . . . 95

PHAEDRA. My husband's living! Must you trouble us
by talking? What am I living for?
He lives, Oenone, let me hear no more
about it.

OENONE. Why?

PHAEDRA. I told you, but my fears
were stilled, alas, and smothered by your tears. 100
Had I died this morning, I might have faced
the gods. I heeded you and die disgraced!

OENONE. You are disgraced!

PHAEDRA. Oh Gods of wrath,
how far I've travelled on my dangerous path!
I go to meet my husband; at his side 105
will stand Hippolytus. How shall I hide
my thick adulterous passion for this youth,
who has rejected me, and knows the truth?
Will the stern Prince stand smiling and approve
the labored histrionics of my love 110
for Theseus, see my lips, still languishing
for his, betray his father and his King?
Will he not draw his sword and strike me dead?
Suppose he spares me? What if nothing's said?
Am I a gorgon, or Circe, or the infidel 115
Medea, stifled by the flames of hell,
yet rising like Aphrodite from the sea,
refreshed and radiant with indecency?
Can I kiss Theseus with dissembled poise?
I think each stone and pillar has a voice. 120
The very dust rises to disabuse
my husband—to defame me and accuse!
Oenone, I want to die. Death will give
me freedom; oh it's nothing not to live;
death to the unhappy's no catastrophe! 125
I fear the name that must live after me,
and crush my son until the end of time.
Is his inheritance his mother's crime,
his right to curse me, when my pollution stains

115-116. *gorgon . . . Medea:* The Gorgons were three sisters, the most famed being Medusa; they were frightful in appearance, with snakes in their hair, large mouths and irregular teeth, and flaming eyes; they were winged, and had claws. Circe, Pasiphaë's sister, was a magician who lived on the island of Aeaea. Her chief feat was changing Odysseus' men into swine. Medea, at one time beloved by Jason when he was questing for the Golden Fleece, had a notably bloodthirsty career: she strewed her brother's limbs on the sea, killed Jason's uncle by persuading his daughters to cut him up in small pieces and boil them in a cauldron, killed Jason's second wife with a poisoned bridal robe, and murdered the two children she had had by Jason.

the blood of heaven bubbling in his veins? 130
The day will come, alas, the day will come,
when nothing will be left to save him from
the voices of despair. If he should live
he'll flee his subjects like a fugitive.

OENONE. He has my pity. Who has ever built 135
firmer foundations to expose her guilt?
But why expose your son? Is your contribution
for his defense to serve the prosecution?
Suppose you kill yourself? The world will say
you fled your outraged husband in dismay. 140
Could there be stronger evidence and proof
than Phaedra crushed beneath the horse's hoof
of blasphemous self-destruction to convince
the crowds who'll dance attendance on the Prince?
The crowds will mob your children when they hear 145
their defamation by a foreigner!
Wouldn't you rather see earth bury us?
Tell me, do you still love Hippolytus?

PHAEDRA. I see him as a beast, who'd murder us.

OENONE. Madam, let the positions be reversed! 150
You fear the Prince; you must accuse him first.
Who'll dare assert your story is untrue,
if all the evidence shall speak for you:
your present grief, your past despair of mind,
the Prince's sword so luckily left behind? 155
Do you think Theseus will oppose his son's
second exile? He has consented once!

PHAEDRA. How dare I take this murderous, plunging course?

OENONE. I tremble, Lady, I too feel remorse.
If death could rescue you from infamy, 160
Madam, I too would follow you and die.
Help me by being silent. I will speak
in such a way the King will only seek
a bloodless exile to assert his rights.
A father is still a father when he smites, 165
You shudder at this evil sacrifice,
but nothing's evil or too high a price
to save your menaced honor from defeat.
Ah Minos, Minos, you defended Crete
by killing young men? Help us! If the cost 170
for saving Phaedra is a holocaust
of virtue, Minos, you must sanctify
our undertaking, or watch your daughter die.
I see the King.

PHAEDRA. I see Hippolytus!

SCENE IV. *Phaedra, Theseus, Hippolytus, Oenone*

THESEUS. Fate's heard me, Phaedra, and removed the bar 175
that kept me from your arms.
PHAEDRA. Theseus, stop where you are!
Your raptures and endearments are profane.
Your arm must never comfort me again.
You have been wronged, the gods who spared your life 180
have used your absence to disgrace your wife,
unworthy now to please you or come near.
My only refuge is to disappear.

SCENE V. *Theseus, Hippolytus*

THESEUS. What a strange welcome! This bewilders me.
My son, what's happened?
HIPPOLYTUS. Phaedra holds the key. 185
Ask Phaedra. If you love me, let me leave
this kingdom. I'm determined to achieve
some action that will show my strength. I fear
Phaedra. I am afraid of living here,
THESEUS. My son, you want to leave me?
HIPPOLYTUS. I never sought 190
her grace or favor. Your decision brought
her here from Athens. Your desires prevailed
against my judgment, Father, when you sailed
leaving Phaedra and Aricia in my care.
I've done my duty, now I must prepare 195
for sterner actions, I must test my skill
on monsters far more dangerous to kill
than any wolf or eagle in this wood.
Release me, I too must prove my manhood.
Oh Father, you were hardly half my age, 200
when herds of giants writhed before your rage—
you were already famous as the scourge
of insolence. Our people saw you purge
the pirates from the shores of Greece and Thrace,
the harmless merchantman was free to race 205
the winds, and weary Hercules could pause
from slaughter, knowing you upheld his cause.
The world revered you. I am still unknown;
even my mother's deeds surpass my own.
Some tyrants have escaped you; let me meet 210
with them and throw their bodies at your feet.

I'll drag them from their wolf-holes; if I die,
my death will show I struggled worthily.
Oh, Father, raise me from oblivion;
my deeds shall tell the universe I am your son. 215

THESEUS. What do I see? Oh gods, what horror drives
my queen and children fleeing for their lives
before me? If so little warmth remains,
oh why did you release me from my chains?
Why am I hated, and so little loved? 220
I had a friend, just one. His folly moved
me till I aided his conspiracy
to ravish Queen Persephone.
The gods, tormented by our blasphemous
designs, befogged our minds and blinded us— 225
we invaded Epirus instead of hell.
There a diseased and subtle tyrant fell
upon us as we slept, and while I stood
by, helpless, monsters crazed for human blood
consumed Pirithoüs. I myself was chained 230
fast in a death-deep dungeon. I remained
six months there, then the gods had pity,
and put me in possession of the city.
I killed the tyrant; now his body feasts
the famished, pampered bellies of his beasts. 235
At last, I voyaged home, cast anchor, furled
my sails. When I was rushing to my world—
what am I saying? When my heart and soul
were mine again, unable to control
themselves for longing—who receives me? All run 240
and shun me, as if I were a skelcton.
Now I myself begin to feel the fear
I inspire. I wish I were a prisoner
again or dead. Speak! Phaedra says my home
was outraged. Who betrayed me? Someone come 245
and tell me. I have fought for Greece. Will Greece,
sustained by Theseus, give my enemies
asylum in my household? Tell me why
I've no avenger? Is my son a spy?
You will not answer. I must know my fate. 250
Suspicion chokes me, while I hesitate
and stand here pleading. Wait, let no one stir.
Phaedra shall tell me what has troubled her.

221. *a friend:* Pirithoüs.
226. *Epirus:* a district in western Greece, on the Ionian Sea.

SCENE VI. *Hippolytus*

HIPPOLYTUS. What now? His anger turns my blood to ice.
Will Phaedra, always uncertain, sacrifice 255
herself? What will she tell the King? How hot
the air's becoming here! I feel the rot
of love seeping like poison through this house.
I feel the pollution. I cannot rouse
my former loyalties. When I try to gather 260
the necessary strength to face my father,
my mind spins with some dark presentiment . . .
How can such terror touch the innocent?
I LOVE ARICIA! Father, I confess
my treason to you is my happiness! 265
I LOVE ARICIA! Will this bring you joy,
our love you have no power to destroy?

Act 4

SCENE I. *Theseus, Oenone*

THESEUS. What's this, you tell me he dishonors me,
and has assaulted Phaedra's chastity?
Oh heavy fortune, I no longer know
who loves me, who I am, or where I go.
Who has ever seen such disloyalty 5
after such love? Such sly audacity!
His youth made no impression on her soul,
so he fell back on force to reach his goal!
I recognize this perjured sword; I gave
him this myself to teach him to be brave! 10
Oh Zeus, are blood-ties no impediment?
Phaedra tried to save him from punishment!
Why did her silence spare this parricide?
OENONE. She hoped to spare a trusting father's pride.
She felt so sickened by your son's attempt, 15
his hot eyes leering at her with contempt,
she had no wish to live. She read out her will
to me, then lifted up her arm to kill
herself. I struck the sword out of her hand.
Fainting, she babbled the secret she had planned 20
to bury with her in the grave. My ears
unwillingly interpreted her tears.
THESEUS. Oh traitor! I know why he seemed to blanch
and toss with terror like an aspen branch
when Phaedra saw him. Now I know why he stood 25
back, then embraced me so coldly he froze my blood.

Was Athens the first stage for his obscene
attentions? Did he dare attack the Queen
before our marriage?

OENONE. Remember her disgust
and hate then? She already feared his lust. 30

THESEUS. And when I sailed, this started up again?

OENONE. I've hidden nothing. Do you want your pain
redoubled? Phaedra calls me. Let me go,
and save her. I have told you what I know.

SCENE II. *Theseus, Hippolytus*

THESEUS. My son returns! Oh God, reserved and cool, 35
dressed in a casual freedom that could fool
the sharpest. Is it right his brows should blaze
and dazzle me with virtue's sacred rays?
Are there not signs? Should not ADULTERER
in looping scarlet script be branded there? 40

HIPPOLYTUS. What cares becloud your kingly countenance,
Father! What is this irritated glance?
Tell me! Are you afraid to trust your son?

THESEUS. How dare you stand here? May the great Zeus stone
me, if I let my fondness and your birth 45
protect you! Is my strength which rid the earth
of brigands paralysed? Am I so sick
and senile, any coward with a stick
can strike me? Am I a schoolboy's target? Oh God,
am I food for vultures? Some carrion you must prod 50
and poke to see if it's alive or dead?
Your hands are moist and itching for my bed,
Coward! Wasn't begetting you enough
dishonor to destroy me? Must I snuff
your perjured life, my own son's life, and stain 55
a thousand glories? Let the gods restrain
my fury! Fly! live hated and alone—
there are places where my name may be unknown.
Go, find them, follow your disastrous star
through filth; if I discover where you are, 60
I'll add another body to the hill
of vermin I've extinguished by my skill.
Fly from me, let the grieving storm-winds bear
your contagion from me. You corrupt the air.
I call upon Poseidon. Help me, Lord 65
of Ocean, help your servant! Once my sword
heaped crucified assassins on your shore
and let them burn like beacons. God, you swore

my first request would be fulfilled. My first!
I never made it. Even through the worst 70
torments of Epirus I held my peace;
no threat or torture brought me to my knees
beseeching favors; even then I knew
some greater project was reserved for you!
Poseidon, now I kneel. Avenge me, dash 75
my incestuous son against your rocks, and wash
his dishonor from my household; wave on wave
of roaring nothingness shall be his grave.

HIPPOLYTUS. Phaedra accuses me of lawless love!
Phaedra! My heart stops, I can hardly move 80
my lips and answer. I have no defense,
if you condemn me without evidence.

THESEUS. Oh coward, you were counting on the Queen
to hide your brutal insolence and screen
your outrage with her weakness! You forgot 85
something. You dropped your sword and spoiled your plot.
You should have kept it. Surely you had time
to kill the only witness to your crime!

HIPPOLYTUS. Why do I stand this, and forbear to clear
away these lies, and let the truth appear? 90
I could so easily. Where would you be,
if I spoke out? Respect my loyalty,
Father, respect your own intelligence.
Examine me. What am I? My defense
is my whole life. When have I wavered, when 95
have I pursued the vices of young men?
Father, you have no scaffolding to rig
your charges on. Small crimes precede the big.
Phaedra accused me of attempting rape!
Am I some Proteus, who can change his shape? 100
Nature despises such disparities.
Vice, like virtue, advances by degrees.
Bred by Antiope to manly arms,
I hate the fever of this lust that warms
the loins and rots the spirit. I was taught 105
uprightness by Theramenes. I fought
with wolves, tamed horses, gave my soul to sport,
and shunned the joys of women and the court.
I dislike praise, but those who know me best
grant me one virtue—it's that I detest 110
the very crimes of which I am accused.

100 *Proteus:* an old man of the ocean, keeper of Poseidon's seals, capable of assuming any form he wished.

How often you yourself have been amused
and puzzled by my love of purity,
pushed to the point of crudeness. By the sea
and in the forest, I have filled my heart 115
with freedom, far from women.

THESEUS. When this part
was dropped, could only Phaedra violate
the cold abyss of your immaculate
reptilian soul. How could this funeral urn
contain a heart, a living heart, or burn 120
for any woman but my wife?

HIPPOLYTUS. Ah no!
Father, I too have seen my passions blow
into a tempest. Why should I conceal
my true offense? I feel, Father, I feel
what other young men feel. I love, I love 125
Aricia. Father, I love the sister of
your worst enemies. I worship her!
I only feel and breathe and live for her!

THESEUS. You love Aricia? God! No, this is meant
to blind my eyes and throw me off the scent. 130

HIPPOLYTUS. Father, for six months I have done my worst
to kill this passion. You shall be the first
to know . . . You frown still. Nothing can remove
your dark obsession. Father, what will prove
my innocence? I swear by earth and sky, 135
and nature's solemn, shining majesty . . .

THESEUS. Oaths and religion are the common cant
of all betrayers. If you wish to taunt
me, find a better prop than blasphemy.

HIPPOLYTUS. All's blasphemy to eyes that cannot see. 140
Could even Phaedra bear me such ill will?

THESEUS. Phaedra, Phaedra! Name her again, I'll kill
you! My hand's already on my sword.

HIPPOLYTUS. Explain
my terms of exile. What do you ordain?

THESEUS. Sail out across the ocean. Everywhere 145
on earth and under heaven is too near.

HIPPOLYTUS. Who'll take me in? Oh who will pity me,
and give me bread, if you abandon me?

THESEUS. You'll find fitting companions. Look for friends
who honor everything that most offends. 150
Pimps and jackals who praise adultery

116. *women:* In Euripides' play, much is made of Hippolytus' allegiance to Artemis (Diana), the "queen and huntress, chaste and fair."

and incest will protect your purity!
HIPPOLYTUS. Adultery! Is it your privilege
to fling this word in my teeth? I've reached the edge
of madness . . . No, I'll say no more. Compare 155
my breeding with Phaedra's. Think and beware . . .
She had a mother . . . No, I must not speak.
THESEUS. You devil, you'll attack the queen still weak
from your assault. How can you stand and face
your father? Must I drive you from this place 160
with my own hand. Run off, or I will flog
you with the flat of my sword like a dog!

SCENE III. *Theseus*

THESEUS. You go to your inevitable fate,
Child—by the river immortals venerate.
Poseidon gave his word. You cannot fly: 165
death and the gods march on invisibly.
I loved you once; despite your perfidy,
my bowels writhe inside me. Must you die?
Yes; I am in too deep now to draw back.
What son has placed his father on such a rack? 170
What father groans for such a monstrous birth?
Oh gods, your thunder throws me to the earth.

SCENE IV. *Theseus, Phaedra*

PHAEDRA. Theseus, I heard the deluge of your voice,
and stand here trembling. If there's time for choice,
hold back your hand, still bloodless; spare your race! 175
I supplicate you, I kneel here for grace.
Oh, Theseus, Theseus, will you drench the earth
with your own blood? His virtue, youth and birth
cry out for him. Is he already slain
by you for me—spare me this incestuous pain! 180
THESEUS. Phaedra, my son's blood has not touched my hand;
and yet I'll be avenged. On sea and land,
spirits, the swift of foot, shall track him down
Poseidon owes me this. Why do you frown?
PHAEDRA. Poseidon owes you this? What have you done 185
in anger?
THESEUS. What! You wish to help my son?
No, stir my anger, back me to the hilt,
call for blacker colors to paint his guilt.
Lash, strike and drive me on! You cannot guess

164. *river:* the Styx, the chief river in Hades and sacred to the gods themselves, so that their most binding oath was by the Styx. If such an oath were broken, the god would lie as one dead for a year.

the nerve and fury of his wickedness. 190
Phaedra, he slandered your sincerity,
he told me your accusation was a lie.
He swore he loved Aricia, he wants to wed
Aricia. . . .

PHAEDRA. What, my lord!

THESEUS. That's what he said.
Of course, I scorn his shallow artifice. 195
Help me, Poseidon, hear me, sacrifice
my son. I seek the altar. Come! Let us both
kneel down and beg the gods to keep their oath.

SCENE V. *Phaedra*

PHAEDRA. My husband's gone, still rumbling his own name
and fame. He has no inkling of the flame 200
his words have started. If he hadn't spoken,
I might have . . . I was on my feet, I'd broken
loose from Oenone, and had just begun
to say I know not what to save his son.
Who knows how far I would have gone? Remorse, 205
longing and anguish shook me with such force,
I might have told the truth and suffered death,
before this revelation stopped my breath:
Hippolytus is not insensible,
only insensible to me! His dull 210
heart chases shadows. He is glad to rest
upon Aricia's adolescent breast!
Oh thin abstraction! When I saw his firm
repugnance spurn my passion like a worm,
I thought he had some magic to withstand 215
the lure of any woman in the land,
and now I see a schoolgirl leads the boy,
as simply as her puppy or a toy.
Was I about to perish for this sham,
this panting hypocrite? Perhaps I am 220
the only woman that he could refuse!

SCENE VI. *Phaedra, Oenone*

PHAEDRA. Oenone, dearest, have you heard the news?

OENONE. No, I know nothing, but I am afraid.
How can I follow you? You have betrayed
your life and children. What have you revealed, 225
Madam?

PHAEDRA. I have a rival in the field,
Oenone.

OENONE. What?

PHAEDRA. Oenone, he's in love—
this howling monster, able to disprove
my beauty, mock my passion, scorn each prayer,
and face me like a tiger in its lair— 230
he's tamed, the beast is harnessed to a cart;
Aricia's found an entrance to his heart.

OENONE. Aricia?

PHAEDRA. Nurse, my last calamity
has come. This is the bottom of the sea,
All that preceded this had little force— 235
the flames of lust, the horrors of remorse,
the prim refusal by my grim young master,
were only feeble hints of this disaster.
They love each other! Passion blinded me.
I let them blind me, let them meet and see 240
each other freely! Was such bounty wrong?
Oenone, you have known this all along,
you must have seen their meetings, watched them sneak
off to their forest, playing hide-and-seek!
Alas, such rendezvous are no offence: 245
innocent nature smiles of innocence,
for them each natural impulse was allowed,
each day was summer and without a cloud.
Oenone, nature hated me. I fled
its light, as if a price were on my head. 250
I shut my eyes and hungered for my end.
Death was the only God my vows could bend.
And even while my desolation served
me gall and tears, I knew I was observed;
I never had security or leisure 255
for honest weeping, but must steal this pleasure.
Oh hideous pomp; a monarch only wears
the robes of majesty to hide her tears!

OENONE. How can their folly help them? They will never
enjoy its fruit. 260

PHAEDRA. Ugh, they will love forever—
even while I am talking, they embrace,
they scorn me, they are laughing in my face!
In the teeth of exile, I hear them swear
they will be true forever, everywhere.
Oenone, have pity on my jealous rage; 265
I'll kill this happiness that jeers at age.
I'll summon Theseus; hate shall answer hate!
I'll drive my husband to annihilate
Aricia—let no trivial punishment,

her instant death, or bloodless banishment . . . 270
What am I saying? Have I lost my mind?
I am jealous, and call my husband! Bind
me, gag me; I am frothing with desire.
My husband is alive, and I'm on fire!
For whom? Hippolytus. When I have said 275
his name, blood fills my eyes, my heart stops dead.
Imposture, incest, murder! I have passed
the limits of damnation; now at last,
my lover's lifeblood is my single good.
Nothing else cools my murderous thirst for blood. 280
Yet I live on! I live, looked down upon
by my progenitor, the sacred sun,
by Zeus, by Europa, by the universe
of gods and stars, my ancestors. They curse
their daughter. Let me die. In the great night 285
of Hades, I'll find shelter from their sight.
What am I saying? I've no place to turn:
Minos, my father, holds the judge's urn.
The gods have placed damnation in his hands,
the shades in Hades follow his commands. 290
Will he not shake and curse his fatal star
that brings his daughter trembling to his bar?
His child by Pasiphaë forced to tell
a thousand sins unclassified in hell?
Father, when you interpret what I speak, 295
I fear your fortitude will be too weak
to hold the urn. I see you fumbling for
new punishments for crimes unknown before.
You'll be your own child's executioner!
You cannot kill me; look, my murderer 300
is Venus, who destroyed our family;
Father, she has already murdered me.
I killed myself—and what is worse I wasted
my life for pleasures I have never tasted.
My lover flees me still, and my last gasp 305
is for the fleeting flesh I failed to clasp.

OENONE. Madam, Madam, cast off this groundless terror!
Is love now an unprecedented error?
You love! What then! You love! Accept your fate.
You're not the first to sail into this strait. 310

283. *Europa:* Carried off by Zeus in the form of a bull, Europa conceived three children by him, of whom one was Minos, Phaedra's father.

288. *judge's urn:* After his death, Minos of Crete became, along with his brother Rhadamanthus, one of the judges of souls in the Underworld. The urn held the lots which determined to what abode in the Underworld the souls of the dead were to be sent.

Will chaos overturn the earth and Jove,
because a mortal woman is in love?
Such accidents are easy, all too common.
A woman must submit to being woman.
You curse a failure in the source of things. 315
Venus has feasted on the hearts of kings;
even the gods, man's judges, feel desire,
Zeus learned to live with his adulterous fire.

PHAEDRA. Must I still listen and drink your poisoned breath?
My death's redoubled on the edge of death. 320
I'd fled Hippolytus and I was free
till your entreaties stabbed and blinded me,
and dragged me howling to the pit of lust.
Oenone, I was learning to be just.
You fed my malice. Attacking the young Prince 325
was not enough; you clothed him with my sins.
You wished to kill him; he is dying now,
because of you, and Theseus' brutal vow.
You watch my torture; I'm the last ungorged
scrap rooting in this trap your plots have forged. 330
What binds you to me? Leave me, go, and die,
may your punishment be to terrify
all those who ruin princes by their lies,
hints, acquiescence, filth, and blasphemies—
panders who grease the grooves of inclination, 335
and lure our willing bodies from salvation.
Go die, go frighten false flatterers, the worst
friends the gods can give to kings they've cursed!

OENONE. I have given all and left all for her service,
almighty gods! I have been paid my price! 340

Act 5

SCENE I. *Hippolytus, Aricia*

ARICIA. Take a stand, speak the truth, if you respect
your father's glory and your life. Protect
yourself! I'm nothing to you. You consent
without a struggle to your banishment.
If you are weary of Aricia, go; 5
at least do something to prevent the blow
that dooms your honor and existence—both
at a stroke! Your father must recall his oath;
there is time still, but if the truth's concealed,
you offer your accuser a free field. 10
Speak to your father!

HIPPOLYTUS. I've already said

what's lawful. Shall I point to his soiled bed,
tell Athens how his marriage was foresworn,
make Theseus curse the day that he was born?
My aching heart recoils. I only want 15
God and Aricia for my confidants.
See how I love you; love makes me confide
in you this horror I have tried to hide
from my own heart. My faith must not be broken;
forget, if possible, what I have spoken. 20
Ah Princess, if even a whisper slips
past you, it will perjure your pure lips
God's justice is committed to the cause
of those who love him, and uphold his laws;
sooner or later, heaven itself will rise 25
in wrath and punish Phaedra's blasphemies.
I must not. If I rip away her mask,
I'll kill my father. Give me what I ask.
Do this! Then throw away your chains; it's right
for you to follow me, and share my flight. 30
Fly from this prison; here the vices seethe
and simmer, virtue has no air to breathe.
In the confusion of my exile, none
will even notice that Aricia's gone.
Banished and broken, Princess, I am still 35
a force in Greece. Your guards obey my will,
powerful intercessors wish us well:
our neighbors, Argos' citadel
is armed, and in Mycenae our allies
will shelter us, if lying Phaedra tries 40
to hurry us from our paternal throne,
and steal our sacred titles for her son.
The gods are ours, they urge us to attack.
Why do you tremble, falter and hold back?
Your interests drive me to this sacrifice. 45
While I'm on fire, your blood has changed to ice.
Princess, is exile more than you can face?

ARICIA. Exile with you, my lord? What sweeter place
is under heaven? Standing at your side,
I'd let the universe and heaven slide. 50
You're my one love, my king, but can I hope
for peace and honor, Prince, if I elope
unmarried? This . . . I wasn't questioning
the decency of flying from the King.
Is he my father? Only an abject 55

38. *Argos:* chief city in Argolis, in the northeastern Peloponnesus.
39. *Mycenae:* also in Argolis, and center of the Mycenaean civilization, with close Cretan connections.

spirit honors tyrants with respect.
You say you love me. Prince, I am afraid.

HIPPOLYTUS. Aricia, you shall never be betrayed;
accept me! Let our love be sanctified,
then flee from your oppressor as my bride. 60
Bear witness, oh you gods, our love released
by danger, needs no temple or a priest.
It's faith, not ceremonial, that saves.
Here at the city gates, among these graves
the resting places of my ancient line, 65
there stands a sacred temple and a shrine.
Here, where no mortal ever swore in vain,
here in these shadows, where eternal pain
is ready to engulf the perjurer;
here heaven's scepter quivers to confer 70
its final sanction; here, my Love, we'll kneel,
and pray the gods to consecrate and seal
our love. Zeus, the father of the world will stand
here as your father and bestow your hand.
Only the pure shall be our witnesses: 75
Hera, the guarantor of marriages,
Demeter and the virgin Artemis.

ARICIA. The King is coming. Fly. I'll stay and meet
his anger here and cover your retreat.
Hurry. Be off, send me some friend to guide 80
my timid footsteps, husband, to your side.

SCENE II. *Theseus, Ismene, Aricia*

THESEUS. Oh God, illuminate my troubled mind.
Show me the answer I have failed to find.

ARICIA. Go, Ismene, be ready to escape.

SCENE III. *Theseus, Aricia*

THESEUS. Princess, you are disturbed. You twist your cape 85
and blush. The Prince was talking to you. Why
is he running?

ARICIA. We've said our last goodbye,
my lord.

THESEUS. I see the beauty of your eyes
moves even my son, and you have gained a prize
no woman hoped for.

ARICIA. He hasn't taken on 90
your hatred for me, though he is your son.

76. *Hera . . . Demeter:* Hera was Zeus's wife, hence queen of the gods. She was closelv associated with marriage. Demeter, the daughter of Cronus and Rhea, mother of Persephone, was also associated with marriage and fertility.

THESEUS. I follow. I can hear the oaths he swore.
He knelt, he wept. He has done this before
and worse. You are deceived.

ARICIA. Deceived, my lord?

THESEUS. Princess, are you so rich? Can you afford 95
to hunger for this lover that my queen
rejected? Your betrayer loves my wife.

ARICIA. How can you bear to blacken his pure life?
Is kingship only for the blind and strong,
unable to distinguish right from wrong? 100
What insolent prerogative obscures
a light that shines in every eye but yours?
You have betrayed him to his enemies.
What more, my lord? Repent your blasphemies.
Are you not fearful lest the gods so loathe 105
and hate you they will gratify your oath?
Fear God, my lord, fear God. How many times
he grants men's wishes to expose their crimes.

THESEUS. Love blinds you, Princess, and beclouds your reason.
Your outburst cannot cover up his treason. 110
My trust's in witnesses that cannot lie.
I have seen Phaedra's tears. She tried to die.

ARICIA. Take care, your Highness. When your killing hand
drove all the thieves and reptiles from the land,
you missed one monster, one was left alive, 115
one.... No, I must not name her, Sire, or strive
to save your helpless son; he wants to spare
your reputation. Let me go. I dare
not stay here. If I stayed I'd be too weak
to keep my promise. I'd be forced to speak. 120

SCENE V. *Theseus*

THESEUS. What was she saying? I must try to reach
the meaning of her interrupted speech.
Is it a pitfall? A conspiracy?
Are they plotting together to torture me?
Why did I let the rash, wild girl depart? 125
What is this whisper crying in my heart?
A secret pity fills my soul with pain.
I must question Oenone once again.
My guards summon Oenone to the throne.
Quick, bring her. I must talk with her alone. 130

SCENE V. *Theseus, Panope*

PANOPE. The Queen's deranged, your Highness. Some accursed
madness is driving her; some fury stalks

behind her back, possesses her, and talks
its evil through her, and blasphemes the world.
She cursed Oenone. Now Oenone's hurled 135
herself into the ocean Sire, and drowned.
Why did she do it? No reason can be found.

THESEUS. Oenone's drowned?

PANOPE. Her death has brought no peace.
The cries of Phaedra's troubled soul increase.
Now driven by some sinister unrest, 140
she snatches up her children to her breast,
pets them and weeps, till something makes her scoff
at her affection and she drives them off.
Her glance is drunken and irregular,
she looks through us and wonders who we are; 145
thrice she has started letters to you, Sire,
thrice tossed the shredded fragments in the fire.
Oh call her to you. Help her!

THESEUS. The nurse is drowned? Phaedra wishes to die?
Oh gods! Summon my son. Let him defend 150
himself, tell him I'm ready to attend.
I want him!

[*Exit* PANOPE.]

Neptune, hear me, spare my son!
My vengeance was too hastily begun.
Oh why was I so eager to believe
Oenone's accusation? The gods deceive 155
the victims they are ready to destroy!

SCENE VI. *Theseus, Theramenes*

THESEUS. Here is Theramenes. Where is my boy,
my first-born? He was yours to guard and keep.
Where is he? Answer me. What's this? You weep?

THERAMENES. Oh, tardy, futile grief, his blood is shed. 160
My lord, your son, Hippolytus, is dead.

THESEUS. Oh gods, have mercy!

THERAMENES. I saw him die. The most
lovely and innocent of men is lost.

THESEUS. He's dead? The gods have hurried him away
and killed him? . . . just as I began to pray . . . 165
What sudden thunderbolt has struck him down?

THERAMENES. We'd started out, and hardly left the town.
He held the reins; a few feet to his rear,
a single, silent guard held up a spear.
He followed the Mycenae highroad, deep 170
in thought, reins dangling, as if half asleep;
his famous horses, only he could hold,

trudged on with lowered heads, and sometimes rolled
their dull eyes slowly—they seemed to have caught
their master's melancholy, and aped his thought. 175
Then all at once winds struck us like a fist,
we heard a sudden roaring through the mist;
from underground a voice in agony
answered the prolonged groaning of the sea.
We shook, the horses' manes rose on their heads, 180
and now against a sky of blacks and reds,
we saw the flat waves hump into a mountain
of green-white water rising like a fountain,
as it reached land and crashed with a last roar
to shatter like a galley on the shore. 185
Out of its fragments rose a monster, half
dragon, half bull; a mouth that seemed to laugh
drooled venom on its dirty yellow scales
and python belly forking to three tails.
The shore was shaken like a tuning fork, 190
ships bounced on the stung sea like bits of cork,
the earth moved, and the sun spun round and round,
a sulphur-colored venom swept the ground.
We fled; each felt his useless courage falter,
and sought asylum at a nearby altar. 195
Only the Prince remained; he wheeled about,
and hurled a javelin through the monster's snout.
Each kept advancing. Flung from the Prince's arm,
dart after dart struck where the blood was warm.
The monster in its death-throes felt defeat, 200
and bounded howling to the horses' feet.
There its stretched gullet and its armor broke,
and drenched the chariot with blood and smoke,
and then the horses, terror-struck, stampeded.
Their master's whip and shouting went unheeded, 205
they dragged his breathless body to the spray.
Their red mouths bit the bloody surf, men say
Poseidon stood beside them, that the god
was stabbing at their bellies with a goad.
Their terror drove them crashing on a cliff, 210
the chariot crashed in two, they ran as if
the Furies screamed and crackled in their manes,
their fallen hero tangled in the reins,
jounced on the rocks behind them. The sweet light
of heaven never will expunge this sight: 215
the horses that Hippolytus had tamed,

212. ***Furies:*** **Roman name *(Furiae)* for the Greek Erinyes—the three winged goddesses of vengeance, with snakes for hair, named Alecto, Tisiphone, and Megaera.**

now dragged him headlong, and their mad hooves maimed
his face past recognition. When he tried
to call them, calling only terrified;
faster and ever faster moved their feet, 220
his body was a piece of bloody meat.
The cliffs and ocean trembled to our shout,
at last their panic failed, they turned about,
and stopped not far from where those hallowed graves,
the Prince's fathers, overlook the waves. 225
I ran on breathless, guards were at my back,
my master's blood had left a generous track.
The stones were red, each thistle in the mud
was stuck with bits of hair and skin and blood.
I came upon him, called; he stretched his right 230
hand to me, blinked his eyes, then closed them tight.
"I die," he whispered, "it's the gods' desire.
Friend, stand between Aricia and my sire—
some day enlightened, softened, disabused,
he will lament his son, falsely accused; 235
then when at last he wishes to appease
my soul, he'll treat my lover well, release
and honor Aricia. . . ." On this word, he died.
Only a broken body testified
he'd lived and loved once. On the sand now lies 240
something his father will not recognize.

THESEUS. My son, my son! Alas, I stand alone
before the gods. I never can atone.

THERAMENES. Meanwhile, Aricia, rushing down the path,
approached us. She was fleeing from your wrath, 245
my lord, and wished to make Hippolytus
her husband in God's eyes. Then nearing us,
she saw the signs of struggle in the waste,
she saw (oh what a sight) her love defaced,
her young love lying lifeless on the sand. 250
At first she hardly seemed to understand;
while staring at the body in the grass,
she kept on asking where her lover was.
At last the black and fearful truth broke through
her desolation! She seemed to curse the blue 255
and murdering ocean as she caught his head
up in her lap; then fainting lay half dead,
until Ismene somehow summoned back her breath,
restored the child to life—or rather death.
I come, great King, to urge my final task, 260
your dying son's last outcry was to ask
mercy for poor Aricia, for his bride.
Now Phaedra comes. She killed him. She has lied.

SCENE VII. *Theseus, Phaedra, Panope*

THESEUS. Ah Phaedra, you have won. He's dead. A man
was killed. Were you watching? His horses ran 265
him down, and tore his body limb from limb.
Poseidon struck him, Theseus murdered him.
I served you! Tell me why Oenone died?
Was it to save you? Is her suicide
A proof of your truth? No, since he's dead, I must 270
accept your evidence, just or unjust.
I must believe my faith has been abused;
you have accused him; he shall stand accused.
He's friendless even in the world below.
There the shades fear him! Am I forced to know 275
the truth? Truth cannot bring my son to life.
If fathers murder, shall I kill my wife
too? Leave me, Phaedra. Far from you, exiled
from Greece, I will lament my murdered child.
I am a murdered gladiator, whirled 280
in black circles. I want to leave the world;
my whole life rises to increase my guilt—
all those dazzled, dazzling eyes, my glory built
on killing killers. Less known, less magnified,
I might escape, and find a place to hide. 285
Stand back, Poseidon. I know the gods are hard
to please. I pleased you. This is my reward:
I killed my son. I killed him! Only a god
spares enemies, and wants his servants' blood!

PHAEDRA. No, Theseus, I must disobey your prayer. 290
Listen to me. I'm dying. I declare
Hippolytus was innocent.

THESEUS. Ah Phaedra, on your evidence, I sent
him to his death. Do you ask me to forgive
my son's assassin? Can I let you live? 295

PHAEDRA. My time's too short, your highness. It was I,
who lusted for your son with my hot eye.
The flames of Aphrodite maddened me;
I loathed myself, and yearned outrageously
like a starved wolf to fall upon the sheep. 300
I wished to hold him to me in my sleep
and dreamt I had him. Then Oenone's tears,
troubled my mind; she played upon my fears,
until her pleading forced me to declare
I loved your son. He scorned me. In despair, 305
I plotted with my nurse, and our conspiracy
made you believe your son assaulted me.
Oenone's punished; fleeing from my wrath,
she drowned herself, and found a too easy path

to death and hell. Perhaps you wonder why 310
I still survive her, and refuse to die?
Theseus, I stand before you to absolve
your noble son. Sire, only this resolve
upheld me, and made me throw down my knife.
I've chosen a slower way to end my life— 315
Medea's poison; chills already dart
along my boiling veins and squeeze my heart.
A cold composure I have never known
gives me a moment's poise. I stand alone
and seem to see my outraged husband fade 320
and waver into death's dissolving shade.
My eyes at last give up their light, and see
the day they've soiled resume its purity.

PANOPE. She's dead, my lord.

THESEUS. Would God, all memory
of her and me had died with her! Now I 325
must live. This knowledge that has come too late
must give me strength and help me expiate
my sacrilegious vow. Let's go, I'll pay
my son the honors he has earned today.
His father's tears shall mingle with his blood. 330
My love that did my son so little good
asks mercy from his spirit. I declare
Aricia is my daughter and my heir.

324-325. ***Would . . . her:*** The performances of the *Comédie Française* traditionally end with this line, the remainder being regarded as anticlimactic.

FRANÇOIS, DUC DE LA ROCHEFOUCAULD
(1613–1680)
Maxims*

5. The continuance of our passions no more depends on us than does the continuance of our lives.

6. Passion often makes a fool out of the ablest of men, and renders ability to the silliest.

9. The passions show an unfair and personal bias, which makes them dangerous to follow; and one should beware of them, even when they seem the most reasonable.

* First published 1665; last augmented edition 1678. Translated by Howard E. Hugo. La Rochefoucauld published five editions during his lifetime (1665, 1666, 1671, 1675, 1678), in the process of which he added new maxims and rewrote some of the earlier ones.

14. Men are apt not only to forget kindness and injuries; they even hate those who have benefited them, and cease to hate those who have wronged them. Diligence in rewarding good and punishing evil seems to them a bondage to which they will scarcely submit.

17. The modesty of happy persons comes from the peace of mind which good fortune lends to their spirits.

19. We all have strength enough to bear the misfortunes of others.

22. Philosophy easily triumphs over past and future evils; but present evils triumph over philosophy.

25. It requires greater virtue to bear good fortune than bad.

26. Neither the sun nor death can be looked at steadily.

38. We make our promises according to our hopes, and keep them according to our fears.

43. Man often believes he leads, when indeed he is being led; and while his mind directs him toward one goal, his heart drags him unconsciously toward another.

49. We are never as happy or as unhappy as we imagine ourselves to be.

64. Truth does not accomplish as much good in the world, as its counterfeits work evil.

72. If you judge love by most of its results, it seems more akin to hate than to friendship.

76. With true loves as with ghosts: everyone speaks of them, but few have seen them.

78. For most of mankind, love of justice is nothing more than the fear of suffering injustice.

93. The old love to give good advice, to console themselves for no longer being in a condition to give bad examples.

98. Each speaks well of his heart, and no one dares speak so well about his mind.

102. The head is forever fooled by the heart.

119. We are so accustomed to disguising ourselves from others, that we end by disguising ourselves from ourselves.

123. We would scarcely ever enjoy ourselves, if we never flattered ourselves.

132. It is easier to be wise for others than to be wise about oneself.

136. There are those who would never have been in love, had they never heard about love.

149. To refuse praise means that you want to be praised twice.

155. Some disgusting persons possess virtue, and others also exist who are pleasing with all their blemishes.

169. Although sloth and timidity impel us toward our duty, often our virtue gets all the credit.

174. We would do better to employ our intelligence in coping with present misfortunes, than in foreseeing those which might happen to us.

185. Evil, like good, has its own heroes.

190. Only great men can possess great faults.

195. What often prohibits us from abandonment to a single vice is that we own many more.

210. As we grow old, we become sillier and wiser.

218. Hypocrisy is a tribute that vice pays to virtue.

235. We easily console ourselves when our friends suffer disgrace, if the occasion serves to bring out our affection for them.

259. The pleasure of love is in loving; and we are happier in our own passion than in the passion we inspire.

298. For most of mankind, gratitude is no more than a secret wish to receive even greater benefits.

303. No matter how many nice things they say about us, we never learn anything new.

304. We often pardon those who bore us; we can never forgive those whom we bore.

308. Moderation has been made a virtue in order to curb the ambition of the great, and also to console those who are mediocre in either fortune or merit.

310. Sometimes occasions occur in life from whence you have to be slightly mad in order to extricate yourself.

326. Ridicule hurts our honor more than does dishonor itself.

327. We admit our small failings only in order to persuade others that we have no greater ones.

354. Certain defects, when placed in a good setting, shine more brilliantly than virtue itself.

384. We ought never to be surprised, save that we can still be surprised.

391. Fate never seems so blind as she does to those she has not favored.

392. One should cope with luck as one does with health: enjoy it when things go well, be patient when things go badly, and never take recourse to extreme remedies except in the last resort.

409. We would often be ashamed of our finest acts, if the world were aware of the motives behind them.

417. In love, first cured is best cured.

422. All the passions cause us to make mistakes, but love causes us to make the most ridiculous ones.

428. We easily forgive our friends those faults that personally do not touch us.

429. Women in love forgive major indiscretions more easily than they do small infidelities.

439. We would scarcely wish zealously for things, if we really understood the things we wanted.

442. We try to ennoble those faults which we do not wish to correct.

445. Weakness, rather than virtue, is vice's adversary.

453. In major affairs, we should strive less to create situations than to profit from those already present.

458. Our enemies come closer in their judgments about us than we ever do about ourselves.

464. There exist extremes of well-being and misery that go beyond our sensibility and imagination.

496. Quarrels would not last long, if the wrong were only on one side.

499. Ordinarily one pays no attention to a woman's first love-affair until she has had a second.

15. In the misfortunes of our best friends, we always find something not displeasing.[1]

1. *In . . . displeasing:* from Barbin's *Supplementary Maxims* (1693).

JEAN DE LA FONTAINE
(1621–1695)
Fables*

The Grasshopper and the Ant[a]

Until fall, a grasshopper
Chose to chirr;
With starvation as foe
When northeasters would blow,
And not even a gnat's residue 5
Or caterpillar's to chew,
She chirred a recurrent chant
Of want beside an ant,
Begging it to rescue her
With some seeds it could spare 10
Till the following year's fell.
"By August you shall have them all,
Interest and principal."
Share one's seeds? Now what is worse
For any ant to do? 15
Ours asked, "When fair, what brought you through?"
—"I sang for those who might pass by chance—
Night and day, an't you please."
—"Sang, you say? You have put me at ease.
A singer! Excellent. Now dance." 20

The Fox and the Crow[b]

On his airy perch among the branches
Master Crow was holding cheese in his beak.
Master Fox, whose pose suggested fragrances,
Said in language which of course I cannot speak,
"Aha, superb Sir Ebony, well met. 5
How black! who else boasts your metallic jet!
If your warbling were unique,
Rest assured, as you are sleek,

* The original title: *Aesop's Fables Rendered into Verse by M. de La Fontaine.* Aesop, a slave of Samos, reputedly lived in the sixth century B.C., although his actual existence is doutbful. But fables were early collected under his name. The English translation is by Marianne Moore.

a. Book I, No. 1; Aesop No. 134. (Aesop, a slave of Samos, reputedly lived in the 6th century B.C., although his actual existence is doubtful. But fables were early collected under his name.)

b. Book I, No. 2; Aesop, No. 204. Cf. also Phaedrus (Latin fabulist, first century A.D.), I, 13.

One would say that our wood had hatched nightingales."
All aglow, Master Crow tried to run a few scales, 10
Risking trills and intervals,
Dropping the prize as his huge beak sang false.
The fox pounced on the cheese and remarked, "My dear sir,
Learn that every flatterer
Lives at the flattered listener's cost: 15
A lesson worth more than the cheese that you lost."
The tardy learner, smarting under ridicule,
Swore he'd learned his last lesson as somebody's fool.

The Frog Who Would Be an Ox[c]

That great ox, built just right!
Eying the beast, although at best
A mere egg's height or less, the frog mustered might
And spread out and swelled and expanded his chest
To approximate the ox, his despair; 5
Then said to another frog, "Compare:
I'm his size. See, now I need not defer."
"Still small."—"Now?"—"By no means."—"Now I am not outclassed."
"Not nearly large enough." The poor envier
Burst; overtested at last. 10
Our world is full of mentalities quite as crude:
The man of trade must house himself so kings would stare;
Each small prince's deputies are everywhere.
Each marquis has pages—a multitude.

The Town Rat and the Country Rat[d]

In this ancient parable,
Town rat proffered country rat
A fashionable meal
As a change from this and that,

Where on a rug from Turkey, 5
A feast for two was ready.
Fond fancy alone could see
The pair's joint ecstasy.

c. Book I, No. 3; Aesop No. 420; Phaedrus, I, 24.

d. Book I, No. 9; Aesop, No. 301; Horace, *Satires*, II, 6.

Fine food made each's plate replete—
More dainties there than greed could paint, 10
But as they were about to eat,
Noises were heard; the pair felt faint.

At the door, sniff and smell.
What was scratching steadily?
Both frightened ill, half fell, 15
Then fled confusedly.

When they had dared to reappear,
In seclusion with relief,
The city rat resumed, "My dear,
Come now, divide the beef." 20

—"I have dined," the field rat said;
"Be my guest, pray, a day hence,
Though you'll not find, I am afraid,
Similar magnificence.

Yet I'm never in danger: I've supped, 25
Carefree from year to year;
And so farewell. What is good cheer
Which death threats can disrupt?"

The Wolf and the Lamb[e]

Force has the best of any argument:
Soon proved by the story which I present.

A thirsty lamb was drinking where
A brook ran crystal clear.
Up came a wolf who had been lured there 5
By hunger, since it was a spot where prey might be.
"Soiling it, intrepid transgressor?" the wolf growled,
"Leaving me to drink what you fouled?
Such impropriety involves a penalty."
—"Bear with me," the lamb said, "your Majesty. 10
I've not trespassed anywhere.
I'm twenty feet from where you were;
Am here, where what you can't drink went
In its descent;
And to be mathematical, 15

e. Book I, No. 10; Phaedrus. I, 1.

How have I possibly by what I have done
Polluted water of your own?"
—"You stirred the mud." Bloodthirsty minds are small.
"And the past year as well, I know you slandered me."
—"How?" the lamb asked. "I, unweaned, born recently— 20
This very year? I still require home care."
—"Your brother then, you've one somewhere."
—"But I have none."—"It was some relative then;
All of you sheep are unfair;
You, your shepherds, and the dogs they train. 25
I have a debt to myself to discharge."
Dragged down a wooded gully,
The small was eaten by the large
Unconditionally.

The Oak and the Reed[f]

The oak said to the reed, "You grow
Too unprotectedly. Nature has been unfair;
A tiny wren alights, and you are bending low;
If a fitful breath of air
Should freshen till ripples show, 5
You heed her and lower your head;
Whereas my parasol makes welcome shade each day
And like the Caucasus need never sway,
However it is buffeted.
Your so-called hurricanes are too faint to fear. 10
Would that you'd been born beneath this towering tent I've made,
Which could afford you ample shade;
Your hazards would not be severe:
I'd shield you when the lightning played;
But grow you will, time and again, 15
On the misty fringe of the wind's domain.
I perceive that you are grievously oppressed."
The rush said, "Bless you for fearing that I might be distressed;
It is you alone whom the winds should alarm.
I bend and do not break. You've seemed consistently 20
Impervious to harm—
Erect when blasts rushed to and fro;
As for the end, who can foresee how things will go?"
Relentless wind was on them instantly—
A fury of destruction 25
Which the North had nursed in some haunt known to none.
The bulrush bent, but not the tree.

f. Book I, No. 22; Aesop, Nos. 143 and 180.

Confusion rose to a roar,
Until the hurricane threw prone
That thing of kingly height whose head had all but touched
God's throne— 30
Who had shot his root to the threshold of Death's door.

The Dairymaid and Her Milk-Pot[g]

Perrette's milk-pot fitted her head-mat just right—
Neatly quilted to grip the pot tight.
Then she set off to market and surely walked well,
In her short muslin dress that encouraged long strides,
Since to make better time she wore shoes with low heel 5
And had tucked up her skirt at the sides.
Like summer attire her head had grown light,
Thinking of what she'd have bought by night.
In exchange for the milk, since supposing it gone,
She'd buy ten times ten eggs and three hens could be set. 10
Taking care all hatched out, she'd not lose more than one
And said, "Then there'll be pullets to sell.
I'll raise them at home; it is quite within reason,
Since shrewd Master Fox will be doing well
If I can't shortly buy a young pig and grow bacon. 15
The one I had bought would be almost half grown;
He'd need next to no feed—almost nothing at all;
When he's sold I'll have funds—good hard cash to count on.
Then with room at the barn for some stock in the stall,
I could buy cow and calf if the pig had sold high; 20
If I'd not had a loss, I'd add sheep by and by."
Perrette skipped for joy as she dreamt of what she'd bought.
The crock crashed. Farewell, cow, calf, fat pig, eggs not
hatched out.
The mistress of wealth grieved to forfeit forever
The profits that were mounting. 25
How ask her husband to forgive her
Lest he beat her as was fitting?
And thus ended the farce we have watched:
Don't count your chickens before they are hatched.

Whom does a daydream not entrance?
Have castles in air no romance? 30
Picrochole, Pyrrhus, Perrette—a fool's or wisdom's mirth—
Every hearth can give them birth.

g. Book VII, No. 10. Source is Bonaventure des Périers, *Novella* 14.

32. *Picrochole . . . Perrette:* names that belong to the seventeenth-century tradition of the pastoral (*bergerie*), where elegant aristocrats played at being shepherds and shepherdesses.

Each of us loves a daydream—the fondest think on earth,
Illusion has a charm to which our minds succumb; 35
Since it captures whatever has worth.
All hearts are ours, we pluck each plum.
When alone, I tower so tall that the bravest shiver.
I crush and see Persian emperors suffer.
I am a king, an idol. 40
My head is diademed with gems that rain:
Then the king's deep problems by some unjust reversal,
Are Jean de La Fontaine's again.

ALEXANDER POPE
(1688–1744)

The Rape of the Lock* †

AN HEROI-COMICAL POEM

Nolueram, Belinda, tuos violare capillos;
sed juvat hoc precibus me tribuisse tuis.
—MARTIAL

TO MRS. ARABELLA FERMOR

MADAM,

It will be in vain to deny that I have some regard for this piece, since I dedicate it to you. Yet you may bear me witness, it was intended only to divert a few young ladies, who have good sense and

* Text and notes by Samuel Holt Monk.

† *The Rape of the Lock* is based upon an actual episode that provoked a quarrel between two prominent Catholic families. Pope's friend John Caryll, to whom the poem is addressed (l. 3), suggested that Pope write it, in the hope that a little laughter might serve to soothe ruffled tempers. Lord Petre had cut off a lock of hair from the head of the lovely Arabella Fermor (often spelled "Farmer" and doubtless so pronounced), much to the indignation of the lady and her relatives. In its original version of two cantos and 334 lines, published in 1712, *The Rape of the Lock* was a great success. In 1713 a new version was undertaken against the advice of Addison, who considered the poem perfect as it was first written. Pope greatly expanded the earlier version, adding the delightful "machinery" (i.e., the supernatural agents in epic action) of the Sylphs, Belinda's toilet, the card game, and the visit to the Cave of Spleen in Canto IV. In 1717, with the addition of Clarissa's speech on good humor, the poem assumed its final form.

With supreme tact, delicate fancy, playful wit, and the gentlest satire, Pope elaborated the trivial episode which occasioned the poem into the semblance of an epic in miniature, the most nearly perfect "heroi-comical poem" in English. The poem abounds in parodies and echoes of the *Iliad,* the *Aeneid,* and *Paradise Lost,* thus constantly forcing the reader to compare small things with great. The familiar devices of epic are observed, but the incidents or characters are beautifully proportioned to the scale of mock epic. The *Rape* tells of war, but it is the drawing-room war between the sexes; it has its heroes and heroines, but they are beaux and belles; it has its supernatural characters ("machinery") but they are Sylphs (borrowed, as Pope tells us in his engaging dedicatory letter, from Rosicrucian lore)—creatures of the air, the souls of dead coquettes, with tasks apgood humor enough to laugh not only at their sex's little unguarded follies, but at their own. But it was communicated with the air of a secret, it soon found its way into the world. An imperfect copy having been offered to a bookseller, you had the good nature for my sake to consent to the publication of one more correct; this I was forced to, before I had executed half my design, for the machinery was entirely wanting to complete it.

The machinery, Madam, is a term invented by the critics, to signify that part which the deities, angels, or demons are made to act in a poem; for the ancient poets are in one respect like many modern ladies: let an action be never so trivial in itself, they always make it appear of the utmost importance. These machines I determined to raise on a very new and odd foundation, the Rosicrucian [1] doctrine of spirits.

I know how disagreeable it is to make use of hard words before a lady; but 'tis so much the concern of a poet to have his works understood, and particularly by your sex, that you must give me leave to explain two or three difficult terms.

The Rosicrucians are a people I must bring you acquainted with. The best account I know of them is in a French book called *Le Comte de Gabalis*,[2] which both in its title and size is so like a novel, that many of the fair sex have read it for one by mistake. According to these gentlemen, the four elements are inhabited by spirits, which they call Sylphs, Gnomes, Nymphs, and Salamanders. The Gnomes or Demons of earth delight in mischief; but the Sylphs, whose habitation is in the air, are the best-conditioned creatures imaginable. For they say, any mortals may enjoy the most intimate familiarities with these gentle spirits, upon a condition very easy to all true adepts, an inviolate preservation of chastity.

As to the following cantos, all the passages of them are as fabulous as the vision at the beginning, or the transformation at the end; (except the loss of your hair, which I always mention

---

propriate to their nature—or the Gnome Umbriel, once a prude on earth; it has its epic game, played on the "velvet plain" of the card table, its feasting heroes, who sip coffee and gossip, its battle, fought with the clichés of compliment and conceits, with frowns and angry glances, with snuff and a bodkin; it has the traditional epic journey to the underworld—here the Cave of Spleen, emblematic of the peevish ill nature of spoiled and hypochondriacal women. And Pope creates a world in which these actions take place, a world that is dense with beautiful objects: brocades, ivory and tortoise shell, cosmetics and diamonds, lacquered furniture, silver teapot, delicate chinaware. It is a world that is constantly in motion and that sparkles and glitters with light, whether the light of the sun, or of Belinda's eyes, or that light into which the "fluid" bodies of the Sylphs seem to dissolve as they flutter in the shrouds and around the mast of Belinda's ship. Though Pope laughs at this world and its creatures—and remembers that a grimmer, darker world surrounds it (III.19–24 and V. 145–148)—he makes us very much aware of its beauty and its charm.

The epigraph may be translated, "I was unwilling, Belinda, to ravish your locks; but I rejoice to have conceded this to your prayers" (Martial, *Epigrams* XII.lxxxiv.1–2). Pope substituted his heroine for Martial's Polytimus. The epigraph is intended to suggest that the poem was published at Miss Fermor's request.

1. a system of arcane philosophy introduced into England from Germany in the seventeenth century.

2. by the Abbé de Montfaucon de Villars, published in 1670.

with reverence). The human persons are as fictitious as the airy ones; and the character of Belinda, as it is now managed, resembles you in nothing but in beauty.

If this poem had as many graces as there are in your person, or in your mind, yet I could never hope it should pass through the world half so uncensured as you have done. But let its fortune be what it will, mine is happy enough, to have given me this occasion of assuring you that I am, with the truest esteem,

MADAM,

Your most obedient, humble servant,

A. POPE

Canto I

What dire offense from amorous causes springs,
What mighty contests rise from trivial things,
I sing—This verse to Caryll, Muse! is due:
This, even Belinda may vouchsafe to view:
Slight is the subject, but not so the praise, 5
If she inspire, and he approve my lays.
Say what strange motive, Goddess! could compel
A well-bred lord to assault a gentle belle?
Oh, say what stranger cause, yet unexplored,
Could make a gentle belle reject a lord? 10
In tasks so bold can little men engage,
And in soft bosoms dwells such mighty rage?
Sol through white curtains shot a timorous ray,
And oped those eyes that must eclipse the day.
Now lapdogs give themselves the rousing shake, 15
And sleepless lovers just at twelve awake:
Thrice rung the bell, the slipper knocked the ground,
And the pressed watch returned a silver sound.
Belinda still her downy pillow pressed,
Her guardian Sylph prolonged the balmy rest: 20
'Twas he had summoned to her silent bed
The morning dream that hovered o'er her head.
A youth more glittering than a birthnight beau
(That even in slumber caused her cheek to glow)
Seemed to her ear his winning lips to lay, 25
And thus in whispers said, or seemed to say:
"Fairest of mortals, thou distinguished care
Of thousand bright inhabitants of air!
If e'er one vision touched thy infant thought,
Of all the nurse and all the priest have taught, 30
Of airy elves by moonlight shadows seen,
The silver token, and the circled green,

17. Belinda thus summons her maid. A *pressed watch* chimes the hour and the quarter-hour when the stem is pressed down.
23. Courtiers wore especially fine clothes on the sovereign's birthday.
32. *silver token:* According to popular belief, fairies skim off the cream from jugs of milk left standing overnight and leave a coin in payment. *the circled green:* Rings of bright green grass, which are common in England even in winter, were held to be due to the round dances of fairies.

Or virgins visited by angel powers,
With golden crowns and wreaths of heavenly flowers,
Hear and believe! thy own importance know, 35
Nor bound thy narrow views to things below.
Some secret truths, from learned pride concealed,
To maids alone and children are revealed:
What though no credit doubting wits may give?
The fair and innocent shall still believe. 40
Know, then, unnumbered spirits round thee fly,
The light militia of the lower sky:
These, though unseen, are ever on the wing,
Hang o'er the box, and hover round the Ring.
Think what an equipage thou hast in air, 45
And view with scorn two pages and a chair.
As now your own, our beings were of old,
And once enclosed in woman's beauteous mold;
Thence, by a soft transition, we repair
From earthly vehicles to these of air. 50
Think not, when woman's transient breath is fled,
That all her vanities at once are dead:
Succeeding vanities she still regards,
And though she plays no more, o'erlooks the cards.
Her joy in gilded chariots, when alive, 55
And love of ombre, after death survive.
For when the Fair in all their pride expire,
To their first elements their souls retire:
The sprites of fiery termagants in flame
Mount up, and take a Salamander's name. 60
Soft yielding minds to water glide away,
And sip, with Nymphs, their elemental tea.
The graver prude sinks downward to a Gnome,
In search of mischief still on earth to roam.
The light coquettes in Sylphs aloft repair, 65
And sport and flutter in the fields of air.
"Know further yet; whoever fair and chaste
Rejects mankind, is by some Sylph embraced:
For spirits, freed from mortal laws, with ease
Assume what sexes and what shapes they please. 70
What guards the purity of melting maids,
In courtly balls, and midnight masquerades,
Safe from the treacherous friend, the daring spark,
The glance by day, the whisper in the dark,
When kind occasion prompts their warm desires, 75

44. *box* in the theater and the fashionable circular drive (*Ring*) in Hyde Park.

46. *chair:* Sedan chair.

56. *ombre:* The popular card game. See III.27 ff. and note.

58. *element:* The four elements out of which all things were believed to have been made were fire, water, earth, and air. One or another of these elements was supposed to be predominant in both the physical and psychological make-up of each human being. In this context they are spoken of as "humors."

60 ff. Pope borrowed his supernatural beings from Rosicrucian mythology. Each element was inhabited by a spirit, as the following lines explain. The salamander is a lizardlike animal, in antiquity believed to live in fire.

62. *tea:* Pronounce *tay*.

When music softens, and when dancing fires?
'Tis but their Sylph, the wise Celestials know,
Though Honor is the word with men below.
"Some nymphs there are, too conscious of their face,
For life predestined to the Gnomes' embrace. 80
These swell their prospects and exalt their pride,
When offers are disdained, and love denied:
Then gay ideas crowd the vacant brain,
While peers, and dukes, and all their sweeping train,
And garters, stars, and coronets appear, 85
And in soft sounds, 'your Grace' salutes their ear.
'Tis these that early taint the female soul,
Instruct the eyes of young coquettes to roll,
Teach infant cheeks a bidden blush to know,
And little hearts to flutter at a beau. 90
"Oft, when the world imagine women stray,
The Sylphs through mystic mazes guide their way,
Through all the giddy circle they pursue,
And old impertinence expel by new.
What tender maid but must a victim fall 95
To one man's treat, but for another's ball?
When Florio speaks what virgin could withstand,
If gentle Damon did not squeeze her hand?
With varying vanities, from every part,
They shift the moving toyshop of their heart; 100
Where wigs with wigs, with sword-knots sword-knots strive,
Beaux banish beaux, and coaches coaches drive.
This erring mortals levity may call;
Oh, blind to truth! the Sylphs contrive it all.
"Of these am I, who thy protection claim, 105
A watchful sprite, and Ariel is my name.
Late, as I ranged the crystal wilds of air,
In the clear mirror of thy ruling star
I saw, alas! some dread event impend,
Ere to the main this morning sun descend, 110
But Heaven reveals not what, or how, or where:
Warned by the Sylph, O pious maid, beware!
This to disclose is all thy guardian can:
Beware of all, but most beware of Man!"
He said; when Shock, who thought she slept too long, 115
Leaped up, and waked his mistress with his tongue.
'Twas then, Belinda, if report say true,
Thy eyes first opened on a billet-doux;
Wounds, charms, and ardors were no sooner read,
But all the vision vanished from thy head. 120
And now, unveiled, the toilet stands displayed,
Each silver vase in mystic order laid.
First, robed in white, the nymph intent adores,
With head uncovered, the cosmetic powers.

83. *gay ideas:* images.
100. *toyshop:* a shop stocked with baubles and trifles.
115. *Shock:* Belinda's lapdog.

A heavenly image in the glass appears; 125
To that she bends, to that her eyes she rears.
The inferior priestess, at her altar's side,
Trembling begins the sacred rites of Pride.
Unnumbered treasures ope at once, and here
The various offerings of the world appear; 130
From each she nicely culls with curious toil,
And decks the goddess with the glittering spoil.
This casket India's glowing gems unlocks,
And all Arabia breathes from yonder box.
The tortoise here and elephant unite, 135
Transformed to combs, the speckled and the white.
Here files of pins extend their shining rows,
Puffs, powders, patches, Bibles, billet-doux.
Now awful Beauty puts on all its arms;
The fair each moment rises in her charms, 140
Repairs her smiles, awakens every grace,
And calls forth all the wonders of her face;
Sees by degrees a purer blush arise,
And keener lightnings quicken in her eyes.
The busy Sylphs surround their darling care, 145
These set the head, and those divide the hair,
Some fold the sleeve, whilst others plait the gown;
And Betty's praised for labors not her own.

Canto II

Not with more glories, in the ethereal plain,
The sun first rises o'er the purpled main,
Than, issuing forth, the rival of his beams
Launched on the bosom of the silver Thames.
Fair nymphs and well-dressed youths around her shone, 5
But every eye was fixed on her alone.
On her white breast a sparkling cross she wore,
Which Jews might kiss, and infidels adore.
Her lively looks a sprightly mind disclose,
Quick as her eyes, and as unfixed as those: 10
Favors to none, to all she smiles extends;
Oft she rejects, but never once offends.
Bright as the sun, her eyes the gazers strike,
And, like the sun, they shine on all alike.
Yet graceful ease, and sweetness void of pride, 15
Might hide her faults, if belles had faults to hide:
If to her share some female errors fall,
Look on her face, and you'll forget 'em all.
This nymph, to the destruction of mankind,
Nourished two locks which graceful hung behind 20
In equal curls, and well conspired to deck
With shining ringlets the smooth ivory neck.
Love in these labyrinths his slaves detains,
And mighty hearts are held in slender chains.

148. *Betty's:* Belinda's maid, the "inferior priestess" mentioned in line 127.

With hairy springes we the birds betray, 25
Slight lines of hair surprise the finny prey,
Fair tresses man's imperial race ensnare,
And beauty draws us with a single hair.
The adventurous Baron the bright locks admired,
He saw, he wished, and to the prize aspired. 30
Resolved to win, he meditates the way,
By force to ravish, or by fraud betray;
For when success a lover's toil attends,
Few ask if fraud or force attained his ends.
For this, ere Phoebus rose, he had implored 35
Propitious Heaven, and every power adored,
But chiefly Love—to Love an altar built,
Of twelve vast French romances, neatly gilt.
There lay three garters, half a pair of gloves,
And all the trophies of his former loves. 40
With tender billet-doux he lights the pyre,
And breathes three amorous sighs to raise the fire.
Then prostrate falls, and begs with ardent eyes
Soon to obtain, and long possess the prize:
The powers gave ear, and granted half his prayer, 45
The rest the winds dispersed in empty air.
But now secure the painted vessel glides,
The sunbeams trembling on the floating tides,
While melting music steals upon the sky,
And softened sounds along the waters die. 50
Smooth flow the waves, the zephyrs gently play,
Belinda smiled, and all the world was gay.
All but the Sylph—with careful thoughts oppressed,
The impending woe sat heavy on his breast.
He summons straight his denizens of air; 55
The lucid squadrons round the sails repair:
Soft o'er the shrouds aërial whispers breathe
That seemed but zephyrs to the train beneath.
Some to the sun their insect-wings unfold,
Waft on the breeze, or sink in clouds of gold. 60
Transparent forms too fine for mortal sight,
Their fluid bodies half dissolved in light,
Loose to the wind their airy garments flew,
Thin glittering textures of the filmy dew,
Dipped in the richest tincture of the skies, 65
Where light disports in ever-mingling dyes,
While every beam new transient colors flings,
Colors that change whene'er they wave their wings.
Amid the circle, on the gilded mast,
Superior by the head was Ariel placed; 70
His purple pinions opening to the sun,

25. ***springes:*** snares; pronounced *sprinjez.*
71. ***purple:*** In eighteenth-century poetic diction, the word might mean "blood-red," "purple," or simply (as is likely here) "brightly colored." The word derives from Virgil, *Eclogue* IX. 40, ***purpureous.*** An example of the Latinate nature of some poetic diction of the period.

He raised his azure wand, and thus begun:
"Ye Sylphs and Sylphids, to your chief give ear!
Fays, Fairies, Genii, Elves, and Daemons, hear!
Ye know the spheres and various tasks assigned
By laws eternal to the aërial kind. 75
Some in the fields of purest ether play,
And bask and whiten in the blaze of day.
Some guide the course of wandering orbs on high,
Or roll the planets through the boundless sky. 80
Some less refined, beneath the moon's pale light
Pursue the stars that shoot athwart the night,
Or suck the mists in grosser air below,
Or dip their pinions in the painted bow,
Or brew fierce tempests on the wintry main, 85
Or o'er the glebe distill the kindly rain.
Others on earth o'er human race preside,
Watch all their ways, and all their actions guide:
Of these the chief the care of nations own,
And guard with arms divine the British Throne. 90
"Our humbler province is to tend the Fair,
Not a less pleasing, though less glorious care:
To save the powder from too rude a gale,
Nor let the imprisoned essences exhale;
To draw fresh colors from the vernal flowers; 95
To steal from rainbows e'er they drop in showers
A brighter wash; to curl their waving hairs,
Assist their blushes, and inspire their airs;
Nay oft, in dreams invention we bestow,
To change a flounce, or add a furbelow. 100
"This day black omens threat the brightest fair,
That e'er deserved a watchful spirit's care;
Some dire disaster, or by force or slight,
But what, or where, the Fates have wrapped in night:
Whether the nymph shall break Diana's law, 105
Or some frail china jar receive a flaw,
Or stain her honor or her new brocade,
Forget her prayers, or miss a masquerade,
Or lose her heart, or necklace, at a ball;
Or whether Heaven has doomed that Shock must fall. 110
Haste, then, ye spirits! to your charge repair:
The fluttering fan be Zephyretta's care;
The drops to thee, Brillante, we consign;
And, Momentilla, let the watch be thine;
Do thou, Crispissa, tend her favorite Lock; 115
Ariel himself shall be the guard of Shock.
"To fifty chosen Sylphs, of special note,
We trust the important charge, the petticoat;

86. *glebe:* cultivated field.
97. *wash:* cosmetic lotion.
105. *Diana:* was the goddess of chastity.
113. *drops:* diamond earrings. Observe the appropriateness of the names of the Sylphs to their assigned functions.
115. *Crispissa:* From Latin *crispere,* to curl.

Oft have we known that sevenfold fence to fail,
Though stiff with hoops, and armed with ribs of whale. 120
Form a strong line about the silver bound,
And guard the wide circumference around.
"Whatever spirit, careless of his charge,
His post neglects, or leaves the fair at large,
Shall feel sharp vengeance soon o'ertake his sins, 125
Be stopped in vials, or transfixed with pins,
Or plunged in lakes of bitter washes lie,
Or wedged whole ages in a bodkin's eye;
Gums and pomatums shall his flight restrain,
While clogged he beats his silken wings in vain, 130
Or alum styptics with contracting power
Shrink his thin essence like a riveled flower:
Or, as Ixion fixed, the wretch shall feel
The giddy motion of the whirling mill,
In fumes of burning chocolate shall glow, 135
And tremble at the sea that froths below!"
He spoke; the spirits from the sails descend;
Some, orb in orb, around the nymph extend;
Some thread the mazy ringlets of her hair;
Some hang upon the pendants of her ear: 140
With beating hearts the dire event they wait,
Anxious, and trembling for the birth of Fate.

Canto III

Close by those meads, forever crowned with flowers,
Where Thames with pride surveys his rising towers,
There stands a structure of majestic frame,
Which from the neighboring Hampton takes its name.
Here Britain's statesmen oft the fall foredoom 5
Of foreign tyrants and of nymphs at home;
Here thou, great Anna! whom three realms obey,
Dost sometimes counsel take—and sometimes tea.
Hither the heroes and the nymphs resort,
To taste awhile the pleasures of a court; 10
In various talk the instructive hours they passed,
Who gave the ball, or paid the visit last;
One speaks the glory of the British Queen,
And one describes a charming Indian screen;
A third interprets motions, looks, and eyes; 15
At every word a reputation dies.
Snuff, or the fan, supply each pause of chat,
With singing, laughing, ogling, and all that.
Meanwhile, declining from the noon of day,
The sun obliquely shoots his burning ray; 20

128. ***bodkin's eye:*** a blunt needle with a large eye, used for drawing ribbon through eyelets in the edging of women's garments.

132. ***riveled:*** To "rivel" is to "contract into wrinkles and corrugations" (Johnson's *Dictionary*).

133. ***Ixion:*** In the Greek myth Ixion was punished in the underworld by being bound on an ever-turning wheel.

4. Hampton Court, the royal palace, about fifteen miles up the Thames from London.

The hungry judges soon the sentence sign,
And wretches hang that jurymen may dine;
The merchant from the Exchange returns in peace,
And the long labors of the toilet cease.
Belinda now, whom thirst of fame invites, 25
Burns to encounter two adventurous knights,
At ombre singly to decide their doom,
And swells her breast with conquests yet to come.
Straight the three bands prepare in arms to join,
Each band the number of the sacred nine. 30
Soon as she spreads her hand, the aërial guard
Descend, and sit on each important card:
First Ariel perched upon a Matadore,
Then each according to the rank they bore;
For Sylphs, yet mindful of their ancient race, 35
Are, as when women, wondrous fond of place.
Behold, four Kings in majesty revered,
With hoary whiskers and a forky beard;
And four fair Queens whose hands sustain a flower,
The expressive emblem of their softer power; 40
Four Knaves in garbs succinct, a trusty band,
Caps on their heads, and halberts in their hand;
And parti-colored troops, a shining train,
Draw forth to combat on the velvet plain.
The skillful nymph reviews her force with care; 45
"Let Spades be trumps!" she said, and trumps they were.
Now move to war her sable Matadores,
In show like leaders of the swarthy Moors.
Spadillio first, unconquerable lord!
Led off two captive trumps, and swept the board. 50
As many more Manillio forced to yield,
And marched a victor from the verdant field.
Him Basto followed, but his fate more hard
Gained but one trump and one plebeian card.
With his broad saber next, a chief in years, 55
The hoary Majesty of Spades appears,
Puts forth one manly leg, to sight revealed,
The rest his many-colored robe concealed.
The rebel Knave, who dares his prince engage,
Proves the just victim of his royal rage. 60
Even mighty Pam, that kings and queens o'erthrew
And mowed down armies in the fights of loo,

27. *ombre:* the game which Belinda plays against the Baron and another young man which is too complicated for complete explication here. Pope has carefully arranged the cards so that Belinda wins. The Baron's hand is strong enough to be a threat, but the third player's is of little account. The hand is played exactly according to the rules of ombre, and Pope's description of the cards is equally accurate. Each player holds nine cards (l. 30). The "Matadores" (l. 33), when spades are trumps, are "Spadillio" (l. 49), the ace of spades; "Manillio" (l. 51), the two of spades; "Basto" (l. 53), the ace of clubs; Belinda holds all three of these. (For a more complete description of ombre, see Appendix C, *The Rape of the Lock and Other Poems,* ed. Geoffrey Tillotson in the Twickenham Edition of Pope's poems, vol. 2.)

41. *garbs succinct:* girded up.

61. *Pam:* the knave of clubs, the highest trump in the game of loo.

Sad chance of war! now destitute of aid,
Falls undistinguished by the victor Spade.
 Thus far both armies to Belinda yield; 65
Now to the Baron fate inclines the field.
His warlike amazon her host invades,
The imperial consort of the crown of Spades.
The Club's black tyrant first her victim died,
Spite of his haughty mien and barbarous pride. 70
What boots the regal circle on his head,
His giant limbs, in state unwieldy spread?
That long behind he trails his pompous robe,
And of all monarchs only grasps the globe?
 The Baron now his Diamonds pours apace; 75
The embroidered King who shows but half his face,
And his refulgent Queen, with powers combined
Of broken troops an easy conquest find.
Clubs, Diamonds, Hearts, in wild disorder seen,
With throngs promiscuous strew the level green. 80
Thus when dispersed a routed army runs,
Of Asia's troops, and Afric's sable sons,
With like confusion different nations fly,
Of various habit, and of various dye,
The pierced battalions disunited fall 85
In heaps on heaps; one fate o'erwhelms them all.
 The Knave of Diamonds tries his wily arts,
And wins (oh, shameful chance!) the Queen of Hearts.
At this, the blood the virgin's cheek forsook,
A livid paleness spreads o'er all her look; 90
She sees, and trembles at the approaching ill,
Just in the jaws of ruin, and Codille,
And now (as oft in some distempered state)
On one nice trick depends the general fate.
An Ace of Hearts steps forth: the King unseen 95
Lurked in her hand, and mourned his captive Queen.
He springs to vengeance with an eager pace,
And falls like thunder on the prostrate Ace.
The nymph exulting fills with shouts the sky,
The walls, the woods, and long canals reply. 100
 O thoughtless mortals! ever blind to fate,
Too soon dejected, and too soon elate:
Sudden these honors shall be snatched away,
And cursed forever this victorious day.
 For lo! the board with cups and spoons is crowned, 105
The berries crackle, and the mill turns round;
On shining altars of Japan they raise
The silver lamp; the fiery spirits blaze:
From silver spouts the grateful liquors glide,
While China's earth receives the smoking tide. 110
At once they gratify their scent and taste,

92. *Codille:* the term applied to losing a hand at cards.

106. *the mill turns round:* i.e., coffee is roasted and ground.

107. *shining altars of Japan:* i.e., small, lacquered tables. The word "altars" suggests the ritualistic character of coffee-drinking in Belinda's world.

And frequent cups prolong the rich repast.
Straight hover round the fair her airy band;
Some, as she sipped, the fuming liquor fanned,
Some o'er her lap their careful plumes displayed, 115
Trembling, and conscious of the rich brocade.
Coffee (which makes the politician wise,
And see through all things with his half-shut eyes)
Sent up in vapors to the Baron's brain
New stratagems, the radiant Lock to gain. 120
Ah, cease, rash youth! desist ere 'tis too late,
Fear the just Gods, and think of Scylla's fate!
Changed to a bird, and sent to flit in air,
She dearly pays for Nisus' injured hair!
But when to mischief mortals bend their will, 125
How soon they find fit instruments of ill!
Just then, Clarissa drew with tempting grace
A two-edged weapon from her shining case:
So ladies in romance assist their knight,
Present the spear, and arm him for the fight. 130
He takes the gift with reverence, and extends
The little engine on his fingers' ends;
This just behind Belinda's neck he spread,
As o'er the fragrant steams she bends her head.
Swift to the Lock a thousand sprites repair, 135
A thousand wings, by turns, blow back the hair,
And thrice they twitched the diamond in her ear,
Thrice she looked back, and thrice the foe drew near.
Just in that instant, anxious Ariel sought
The close recesses of the virgin's thought; 140
As on the nosegay in her breast reclined,
He watched the ideas rising in her mind,
Sudden he viewed, in spite of all her art,
An earthly lover lurking at her heart.
Amazed, confused, he found his power expired, 145
Resigned to fate, and with a sigh retired.
The Peer now spreads the glittering forfex wide,
To enclose the Lock; now joins it, to divide.
Even then, before the fatal engine closed,
A wretched Sylph too fondly interposed; 150
Fate urged the shears, and cut the Sylph in twain
(But airy substance soon unites again):
The meeting points the sacred hair dissever
From the fair head, forever, and forever!
Then flashed the living lightning from her eyes, 155
And screams of horror rend the affrighted skies.
Not louder shrieks to pitying heaven are cast,
When husbands, or when lapdogs breathe their last;

122. *Scylla's fate:* Scylla, daughter of Nisus, was turned into a sea bird because, for the sake of her love for Minos of Crete, who was besieging her father's city of Megara, she cut from her father's head the purple lock on which his safety depended. She is not the Scylla of "Scylla and Charybdis."

147. *forfex:* scissors.

Or when rich china vessels fallen from high,
In glittering dust and painted fragments lie! 160
"Let wreaths of triumph now my temples twine,"
The victor cried, "the glorious prize is mine!
While fish in streams, or birds delight in air,
Or in a coach and six the British Fair,
As long as *Atalantis* shall be read, 165
Or the small pillow grace a lady's bed,
While visits shall be paid on solemn days,
When numerous wax-lights in bright order blaze,
While nymphs take treats, or assignations give,
So long my honor, name, and praise shall live! 170
What Time would spare, from Steel receives its date,
And monuments, like men, submit to fate!
Steel could the labor of the Gods destroy,
And strike to dust the imperial towers of Troy;
Steel could the works of mortal pride confound, 175
And hew triumphal arches to the ground.
What wonder then, fair nymph! thy hairs should feel,
The conquering force of unresisted Steel?"

Canto IV

But anxious cares the pensive nymph oppressed,
And secret passions labored in her breast.
Not youthful kings in battle seized alive,
Not scornful virgins who their charms survive,
Not ardent lovers robbed of all their bliss, 5
Not ancient ladies when refused a kiss,
Not tyrants fierce that unrepenting die,
Not Cynthia when her manteau's pinned awry,
E'er felt such rage, resentment, and despair,
As thou, sad virgin! for thy ravished hair. 10
For, that sad moment, when the Sylphs withdrew
And Ariel weeping from Belinda flew,
Umbriel, a dusky, melancholy sprite
As ever sullied the fair face of light,
Down to the central earth, his proper scene, 15
Repaired to search the gloomy Cave of Spleen.
Swift on his sooty pinions flits the Gnome,
And in a vapor reached the dismal dome.
No cheerful breeze this sullen region knows,
The dreaded east is all the wind that blows. 20
Here in a grotto, sheltered close from air,
And screened in shades from day's detested glare,
She sighs forever on her pensive bed,
Pain at her side, and Megrim at her head.

165. *Atalantis:* Mrs. Manley's *New Atalantis* (1709) was notorious for its thinly concealed allusions to contemporary scandals.
8. *manteau's:* negligee or loose robe.
13. *Umbriel:* the name suggests shade and darkness.
16. *Cave of Spleen:* ill humor.
24. *Megrim:* headache.

Two handmaids wait the throne: alike in place, 25
But differing far in figure and in face.
Here stood Ill-Nature like an ancient maid,
Her wrinkled form in black and white arrayed;
With store of prayers for mornings, nights, and noons,
Her hand is filled; her bosom with lampoons. 30
There Affectation, with a sickly mien,
Shows in her cheek the roses of eighteen,
Practiced to lisp, and hang the head aside,
Faints into airs, and languishes with pride,
On the rich quilt sinks with becoming woe, 35
Wrapped in a gown, for sickness and for show.
The fair ones feel such maladies as these,
When each new nightdress gives a new disease.
A constant vapor o'er the palace flies,
Strange phantoms rising as the mists arise; 40
Dreadful as hermit's dreams in haunted shades,
Or bright as visions of expiring maids.
Now glaring fiends, and snakes on rolling spires,
Pale specters, gaping tombs, and purple fires;
Now lakes of liquid gold, Elysian scenes, 45
And crystal domes, and angels in machines.
Unnumbered throngs on every side are seen
Of bodies changed to various forms by Spleen.
Here living teapots stand, one arm held out,
One bent; the handle this, and that the spout: 50
A pipkin there, like Homer's tripod, walks;
Here sighs a jar, and there a goose pie talks;
Men prove with child, as powerful fancy works,
And maids, turned bottles, call aloud for corks.
Safe passed the Gnome through this fantastic band, 55
A branch of healing spleenwort in his hand.
Then thus addressed the Power: "Hail, wayward Queen!
Who rule the sex to fifty from fifteen:
Parent of vapors and of female wit,
Who give the hysteric or poetic fit, 60
On various tempers act by various ways,
Make some take physic, others scribble plays;
Who cause the proud their visits to delay,
And send the godly in a pet to pray.
A nymph there is that all your power disdains, 65
And thousands more in equal mirth maintains.
But oh! if e'er thy Gnome could spoil a grace,

39. *vapor:* emblematic of "the vapors," i.e., hypochondria, melancholy, peevishness, often affected by fashionable women.

43. *rolling spires:* coils.

46. *angels in machines:* mechanical devices used in the theaters for spectacular effects. The fantasies of neurotic women here merge with the sensational stage effects popular with contemporary audiences.

51. *pipkin:* an earthen pot. In *Iliad* XVIII.373–377, Vulcan furnishes the gods with self-propelling "tripods" (three-legged stools).

56. *spleenwort:* an herb, efficacious against the spleen. Pope alludes to the golden bough that Aeneas and the Cumaean sybil carry with them for protection into the underworld in *Aeneid* VI.

Or raise a pimple on a beauteous face,
Like citron-waters matrons' cheeks inflame,
Or change complexions at a losing game; 70
If e'er with airy horns I planted heads,
Or rumpled petticoats, or tumbled beds,
Or caused suspicion when no soul was rude,
Or discomposed the headdress of a prude,
Or e'er to costive lapdog gave disease, 75
Which not the tears of brightest eyes could ease,
Hear me, and touch Belinda with chagrin:
That single act gives half the world the spleen."
  The Goddess with a discontented air
Seems to reject him though she grants his prayer. 80
A wondrous bag with both her hands she binds,
Like that where once Ulysses held the winds;
There she collects the force of female lungs,
Sighs, sobs, and passions, and the war of tongues.
A vial next she fills with fainting fears, 85
Soft sorrows, melting griefs, and flowing tears.
The Gnome rejoicing bears her gifts away,
Spreads his black wings, and slowly mounts to day.
  Sunk in Thalestris' arms the nymph he found,
Her eyes dejected and her hair unbound. 90
Full o'er their heads the swelling bag he rent,
And all the Furies issued at the vent.
Belinda burns with more than mortal ire,
And fierce Thalestris fans the rising fire.
"O wretched maid!" she spread her hands, and cried 95
(While Hampton's echoes, "Wretched maid!" replied),
"Was it for this you took such constant care
The bodkin, comb, and essence to prepare?
For this your locks in paper durance bound,
For this with torturing irons wreathed around? 100
For this with fillets strained your tender head,
And bravely bore the double loads of lead?
Gods! shall the ravisher display your hair,
While the fops envy, and the ladies stare!
Honor forbid! at whose unrivaled shrine 105
Ease, pleasure, virtue, all, our sex resign.
Methinks already I your tears survey,

69. *citron-waters:* brandy flavored with orange or lemon peel.

71. *horns:* the symbol of the cuckold, the man whose wife has been unfaithful to him; here "airy," because they exist only in the jealous suspicions of the husband, the victim of the mischievous Umbriel.

77. *chagrin:* ill humor.

82. *Winds: Aeolus* (later conceived of as god of the winds) gave Ulysses a bag containing all the winds adverse to his voyage home. When his ship was in sight of Ithaca, his companions opened the bag and the storms that ensued drove Ulysses far away (*Odyssey* X.19 ff.).

89. *Thalestris':* The name is borrowed from a queen of the Amazons, hence a fierce and warlike woman. Thalestris, according to legend, traveled 30 days in order to have a child by Alexander the Great. Plutarch denies the story.

102. *double loads of lead:* the frame on which the elaborate coiffures of the day were arranged.

Already hear the horrid things they say,
Already see you a degraded toast,
And all your honor in a whisper lost! 110
How shall I, then, your helpless fame defend?
'Twill then be infamy to seem your friend!
And shall this prize, the inestimable prize,
Exposed through crystal to the gazing eyes,
And heightened by the diamond's circling rays, 115
On that rapacious hand forever blaze?
Sooner shall grass in Hyde Park Circus grow,
And wits take lodgings in the sound of Bow;
Sooner let earth, air, sea, to chaos fall,
Men, monkeys, lapdogs, parrots, perish all!" 120
She said; then raging to Sir Plume repairs,
And bids her beau demand the precious hairs
(Sir Plume of amber snuffbox justly vain,
And the nice conduct of a clouded cane).
With earnest eyes, and round unthinking face, 125
He first the snuffbox opened, then the case,
And thus broke out—"My Lord, why, what the devil!
Z——ds! damn the lock! 'fore Gad, you must be civil!
Plague on't! 'tis past a jest—nay prithee, pox!
Give her the hair"—he spoke, and rapped his box. 130
"It grieves me much," replied the Peer again,
"Who speaks so well should ever speak in vain.
But by this Lock, this sacred Lock I swear
(Which never more shall join its parted hair;
Which never more its honors shall renew, 135
Clipped from the lovely head where late it grew),
That while my nostrils draw the vital air,
This hand, which won it, shall forever wear."
He spoke, and speaking, in proud triumph spread
The long-contended honors of her head. 140
But Umbriel, hateful Gnome, forbears not so;
He breaks the vial whence the sorrows flow.
Then see! the nymph in beauteous grief appears,
Her eyes half languishing, half drowned in tears;
On her heaved bosom hung her drooping head, 145
Which with a sigh she raised, and thus she said:
"Forever cursed be this detested day,
Which snatched my best, my favorite curl away!
Happy! ah, ten times happy had I been,
If Hampton Court these eyes had never seen! 150
Yet am not I the first mistaken maid,
By love of courts to numerous ills betrayed.
Oh, had I rather unadmired remained
In some lone isle, or distant northern land;
Where the gilt chariot never marks the way, 155
Where none learn ombre, none e'er taste bohea!

118. A person born within sound of the bells of St. Mary-le-Bow in Cheapside is said to be a cockney. No fashionable wit would have so vulgar an address.

140. *honors:* ornaments, hence locks; a Latinism.

156. *bohea:* a costly sort of tea.

There kept my charms concealed from mortal eye,
Like roses that in deserts bloom and die.
What moved my mind with youthful lords to roam?
Oh, had I stayed, and said my prayers at home! 160
'Twas this the morning omens seemed to tell,
Thrice from my trembling hand the patch box fell;
The tottering china shook without a wind,
Nay, Poll sat mute, and Shock was most unkind!
A Sylph too warned me of the threats of fate, 165
In mystic visions, now believed too late!
See the poor remnants of these slighted hairs!
My hands shall rend what e'en thy rapine spares.
These in two sable ringlets taught to break,
Once gave new beauties to the snowy neck; 170
The sister lock now sits uncouth, alone,
And in its fellow's fate foresees its own;
Uncurled it hangs, the fatal shears demands,
And tempts once more thy sacrilegious hands.
Oh, hadst thou, cruel! been content to seize 175
Hairs less in sight, or any hairs but these!"

Canto V

She said: the pitying audience melt in tears.
But Fate and Jove had stopped the Baron's ears.
In vain Thalestris with reproach assails,
For who can move when fair Belinda fails?
Not half so fixed the Trojan could remain, 5
While Anna begged and Dido raged in vain.
Then grave Clarissa graceful waved her fan;
Silence ensued, and thus the nymph began:
"Say why are beauties praised and honored most,
The wise man's passion, and the vain man's toast? 10
Why decked with all that land and sea afford,
Why angels called, and angel-like adored?
Why round our coaches crowd the white-gloved beaux,
Why bows the side box from its inmost rows?
How vain are all these glories, all our pains, 15
Unless good sense preserve what beauty gains;
That men may say when we the front box grace,
'Behold the first in virtue as in face!'
Oh! if to dance all night, and dress all day,
Charmed the smallpox, or chased old age away, 20
Who would not scorn what housewife's cares produce,
Or who would learn one earthly thing of use?
To patch, nay ogle, might become a saint,
Nor could it sure be such a sin to paint.

162. *patch box:* a box to hold the ornamental patches of court plaster worn on the face by both sexes. Cf. *Spectator* 81.
5. *the Trojan:* Aeneas, who forsook Dido at the bidding of the gods, despite her reproaches and the supplications of her sister Anna. Virgil compares him to a steadfast oak that withstands a storm (*Aeneid* IV.437–443).
9–34. The speech is a close parody of Pope's own translation of the speech of Sarpedon to Glaucus, first published in 1709 and slightly revised in his version of the *Iliad* (XII.371–396).

But since, alas! frail beauty must decay, 25
Curled or uncurled, since locks will turn to gray;
Since painted, or not painted, all shall fade,
And she who scorns a man must die a maid;
What then remains but well our power to use,
And keep good humor still whate'er we lose? 30
And trust me, dear, good humor can prevail
When airs, and flights, and screams, and scolding fail.
Beauties in vain their pretty eyes may roll;
Charms strike the sight, but merit wins the soul."

So spoke the dame, but no applause ensued; 35
Belinda frowned, Thalestris called her prude.
"To arms, to arms!" the fierce virago cries,
And swift as lightning to the combat flies.
All side in parties, and begin the attack;
Fans clap, silks rustle, and tough whalebones crack; 40
Heroes' and heroines' shouts confusedly rise,
And bass and treble voices strike the skies.
No common weapons in their hands are found,
Like Gods they fight, nor dread a mortal wound.

So when bold Homer makes the Gods engage, 45
And heavenly breasts with human passions rage;
'Gainst Pallas, Mars; Latona, Hermes arms;
And all Olympus rings with loud alarms:
Jove's thunder roars, heaven trembles all around,
Blue Neptune storms, the bellowing deeps resound: 50
Earth shakes her nodding towers, the ground gives way,
And the pale ghosts start at the flash of day!

Triumphant Umbriel on a sconce's height
Clapped his glad wings, and sat to view the fight:
Propped on the bodkin spears, the sprites survey 55
The growing combat, or assist the fray.

While through the press enraged Thalestris flies,
And scatters death around from both her eyes,
A beau and witling perished in the throng,
One died in metaphor, and one in song. 60
"O cruel nymph! a living death I bear,"
Cried Dapperwit, and sunk beside his chair.
A mournful glance Sir Fopling upwards cast,
"Those eyes are made so killing"—was his last.
Thus on Maeander's flowery margin lies 65
The expiring swan, and as he sings he dies.

When bold Sir Plume had drawn Clarissa down,
Chloe stepped in, and killed him with a frown;
She smiled to see the doughty hero slain,
But, at her smile, the beau revived again. 70

Now Jove suspends his golden scales in air,
Weighs the men's wits against the lady's hair;
The doubtful beam long nods from side to side;
At length the wits mount up, the hairs subside.

See, fierce Belinda on the Baron flies, 75

With more than usual lightning in her eyes;
Nor feared the chief the unequal fight to try,
Who sought no more than on his foe to die.
  But this bold lord with manly strength endued,
She with one finger and a thumb subdued: 80
Just where the breath of life his nostrils drew,
A charge of snuff the wily virgin threw;
The Gnomes direct, to every atom just,
The pungent grains of titillating dust.
Sudden, with starting tears each eye o'erflows, 85
And the high dome re-echoes to his nose.
  "Now meet thy fate," incensed Belinda cried,
And drew a deadly bodkin from her side.
(The same, his ancient personage to deck,
Her great-great-grandsire wore about his neck, 90
In three seal rings; which after, melted down,
Formed a vast buckle for his widow's gown:
Her infant grandame's whistle next it grew,
The bells she jingled, and the whistle blew;
Then in a bodkin graced her mother's hairs, 95
Which long she wore, and now Belinda wears.)
  "Boast not my fall," he cried, "insulting foe!
Thou by some other shalt be laid as low.
Nor think to die dejects my lofty mind:
All that I dread is leaving you behind! 100
Rather than so, ah, let me still survive,
And burn in Cupid's flames—but burn alive."
  "Restore the Lock!" she cries; and all around
"Restore the Lock!" the vaulted roofs rebound.
Not fierce Othello in so loud a strain 105
Roared for the handkerchief that caused his pain.
But see how oft ambitious aims are crossed,
And chiefs contend till all the prize is lost!
The lock, obtained with guilt, and kept with pain,
In every place is sought, but sought in vain: 110
With such a prize no mortal must be blessed,
So Heaven decrees! with Heaven who can contest?
  Some thought it mounted to the lunar sphere,
Since all things lost on earth are treasured there.
There heroes' wits are kept in ponderous vases, 115
And beaux' in snuffboxes and tweezer cases.
There broken vows and deathbed alms are found,
And lovers' hearts with ends of riband bound,
The courtier's promises, and sick man's prayers,
The smiles of harlots, and the tears of heirs, 120
Cages for gnats, and chains to yoke a flea,
Dried butterflies, and tomes of casuistry.
  But trust the Muse—she saw it upward rise,

88. ***deadly bodkin:*** an ornamental pin shaped like a dagger, to be worn in the hair.

105–106. *Othello* III.iv.

Though marked by none but quick, poetic eyes
(So Rome's great founder to the heavens withdrew, 125
To Proculus alone confessed in view);
A sudden star, it shot through liquid air,
And drew behind a radiant trail of hair.
Not Berenice's locks first rose so bright,
The heavens bespangling with disheveled light. 130
The Sylphs behold it kindling as it flies,
And pleased pursue its progress through the skies.
This the beau monde shall from the Mall survey,
And hail with music its propitious ray.
This the blest lover shall for Venus take, 135
And send up vows from Rosamonda's Lake.
This Partridge soon shall view in cloudless skys,
When next he looks through Galileo's eyes;
And hence the egregious wizard shall foredoom
The fate of Louis, and the fall of Rome. 140
Then cease, bright nymph! to mourn thy ravished hair,
Which adds new glory to the shining sphere!
Not all the tresses that fair head can boast,
Shall draw such envy as the Lock you lost.
For, after all the murders of your eye, 145
When, after millions slain, yourself shall die:
When those fair suns shall set, as set they must,
And all those tresses shall be laid in dust,
This Lock the Muse shall consecrate to fame,
And 'midst the stars inscribe Belinda's name. 150

1712 1714

125. Romulus, the "founder" and first king of Rome, was snatched to heaven in a storm cloud while reviewing his army in the Campus Martius (Livy I. xvi).
129. Berenice, the wife of Ptolemy III, dedicated a lock of her hair to the gods to ensure her husband's safe return from war. It was turned into a constellation.
133. *the Mall:* a walk laid out by Charles II in St. Jame's Park, a resort for strollers of all sorts.
136. *Rosamonda's Lake:* in St. James's Park; associated with unhappy lovers.
137. John Partridge, the astrologer whose annually published predictions had been amusingly satirized by Swift and other wits in 1708.
138. *Galileo's eyes:* i.e., a telescope.

An Essay on Man*

TO HENRY ST. JOHN, LORD BOLINGBROKE

Epistle I

ARGUMENT OF THE NATURE AND STATE OF MAN, WITH RESPECT TO THE UNIVERSE. Of man in the abstract—I. That we can judge only with regard to our own system, being ignorant of the relations

* The four parts of the *Essay* were published separately and anonymously between February, 1733, and January, 1734. Pope probably started the poem in 1729 and finished it before 1732.

of systems and things, ver. 17, &c.—II. That man is not to be deemed imperfect, but a being suited to his place and rank in the creation, agreeable to the general order of things, and conformable to ends and relations to him unknown, ver. 35, &c.—III. That it is partly upon his ignorance of future events, and partly upon the hope of a future state, that all his happiness in the present depends, ver. 77, &c.—IV. The pride of aiming at more knowledge, and pretending to more perfection, the cause of man's error and misery. The impiety of putting himself in the place of God, and judging of the fitness or unfitness, perfection or imperfection, justice or injustice of his dispensations, ver. 113, &c.—V. The absurdity of conceiting himself the final cause of the creation, or expecting that perfection in the moral world which is not in the natural, ver. 131, &c.—VI. The unreasonableness of his complaints against Providence, while on the one hand he demands the perfections of the angels, and on the other the bodily qualifications of the brutes; though, to possess any of the sensitive faculties in a higher degree, would render him miserable, ver. 173, &c.—VII. That throughout the whole visible world, an universal order and gradation in the sensual and mental faculties is observed, which causes a subordination of creature to creature, and of all creatures to man. The gradations of sense, instinct, thought, reflection, reason: that reason alone countervails all the other faculties, ver. 207.—VIII. How much further this order and subordination of living creatures may extend, above and below us; were any part of which broken, not that part only, but the whole connected creation must be destroyed, ver. 233—IX. The extravagance, madness, and pride of such a desire, ver. 259.—X. The consequence of all, the absolute submission due to Providence, both as to our present and future state, ver. 281, &c., to the end.

Awake, my St. John! leave all meaner things
To low ambition, and the pride of Kings.
Let us (since Life can little more supply
Than just to look about us and to die)
Expatiate free o'er all this scene of Man; 5
A mighty maze! but not without a plan;
A Wild, where weeds and flow'rs promiscuous shoot;
Or Garden, tempting with forbidden fruit.
Together let us beat this ample field,
Try what the open, what the covert yield; 10
The latent tracts, the giddy heights, explore
Of all who blindly creep, or sightless soar;

1. *St. John:* Pope's friend, who had thus far neglected to keep his part of their friendly bargain: Pope was to write his philosophical speculations in verse, Bolingbroke was to write his in prose.

Eye Nature's walks, shoot Folly as it flies,
And catch the Manners living as they rise;
Laugh where we must, be candid where we can; 15
But vindicate the ways of God to man.
I. Say first, of God above, or Man below,
What can we reason, but from what we know?
Of Man, what see we but his station here,
From which to reason, or to which refer? 20
Through worlds unnumbered though the God be known,
'Tis ours to trace him only in our own.
He, who through vast immensity can pierce,
See worlds on worlds compose one universe,
Observe how system into system runs, 25
What other planets circle other suns,
What varied Being peoples ev'ry star,
May tell why Heav'n has made us as we are.
But of this frame the bearings, and the ties,
The strong connections, nice dependencies, 30
Gradations just, has thy pervading soul
Looked through? or can a part contain the whole?
Is the great chain, that draws all to agree,
And drawn supports, upheld by God, or thee?
II. Presumptuous Man! the reason wouldst thou find, 35
Why formed so weak, so little, and so blind?
First, if thou canst, the harder reason guess,
Why formed no weaker, blinder, and no less?
Ask of thy mother earth, why oaks are made
Taller or stronger than the weeds they shade? 40
Or ask of yonder argent fields above,
Why Jove's satellites are less than JOVE?
Of Systems possible, if 'tis confest.
That Wisdom infinite must form the best,
Where all must full or not coherent be, 45
And all that rises, rise in due degree;
Then, in the scale of reas'ning life, 'tis plain,
There must be, somewhere, such a rank as Man:
And all the question (wrangle e'er so long)
Is only this, if God has placed him wrong? 50
Respecting Man, whatever wrong we call,

16. *vindicate . . . man:* compare Milton's *Paradise Lost*, Book I, l. 26. Pope's theme is essentially the same as Milton's, and even the opening image of the garden reminds us of the earlier poet's "Paradise."

33. *the great chain:* the popular eighteenth-century notion of the Great Chain of Being, in which elements of the universe took their places in a hierarchy ranging from the lowest matter to God.

45. *full:* According to the principle of plenitude, there can be no gaps in the Chain.

May, must be right, as relative to all.
In human works, though laboured on with pain,
A thousand movements scarce one purpose gain;
In God's, one single can its end produce; 55
Yet serves to second too some other use.
So Man, who here seems principal alone,
Perhaps acts second to some sphere unknown,
Touches some wheel, or verges to some goal;
'Tis but a part we see, and not a whole. 60
  When the proud steed shall know why Man restrains
His fiery course, or drives him o'er the plains;
When the dull Ox, why now he breaks the clod,
Is now a victim, and now Egypt's God:
Then shall Man's pride and dullness comprehend 65
His actions', passions', being's use and end;
Why doing, suff'ring, checked, impelled; and why
This hour a slave, the next a deity.
  Then say not Man's imperfect, Heav'n in fault;
Say rather, Man's as perfect as he ought: 70
His knowledge measured to his state and place;
His time a moment, and a point his space.
If to be perfect in a certain sphere,
What matter, soon or late, or here or there?
The blest to-day is as completely so, 75
As who began a thousand years ago.
  III. Heav'n from all creatures hides the book of Fate,
All but the page prescribed, their present state:
From brutes what men, from men what spirits know:
Or who could suffer Being here below? 80
The lamb thy riot dooms to bleed to-day,
Had he thy Reason, would he skip and play?
Pleased to the last, he crops the flow'ry food,
And licks the hand just raised to shed his blood.
Oh blindness to the future! kindly giv'n, 85
That each may fill the circle marked by Heav'n:
Who sees with equal eye, as God of all,
A hero perish, or a sparrow fall,
Atoms or systems into ruin hurled,
And now a bubble burst, and now a world. 90
  Hope humbly then; with trembling pinions soar;
Wait the great teacher Death; and God adore.
What future bliss, he gives not thee to know,
But gives that Hope to be thy blessing now.
Hope springs eternal in the human breast: 95
Man never Is, but always To be blest:

The soul, uneasy and confined from home,
Rests and expatiates in a life to come.
   Lo, the poor Indian! whose untutored mind
Sees God in clouds, or hears him in the wind; 100
His soul, proud Science never taught to stray
Far as the solar walk, or milky way;
Yet simple Nature to his hope has giv'n,
Behind the cloud-topt hill, an humbler heav'n;
Some safer world in depth of woods embraced, 105
Some happier island in the wat'ry waste,
Where slaves once more their native land behold,
No fiends torment, no Christians thirst for gold.
To Be, contents his natural desire,
He asks no Angel's wing, no Seraph's fire; 110
But thinks, admitted to that equal sky,
His faithful dog shall bear him company.
   IV. Go, wiser thou! and, in thy scale of sense,
Weigh thy Opinion against Providence;
Call imperfection what thou fanciest such, 115
Say, here he gives too little, there too much:
Destroy all Creatures for thy sport or gust,
Yet cry, If Man's unhappy, God's unjust;
If Man alone engross not Heav'n's high care,
Alone made perfect here, immortal there: 120
Snatch from his hand the balance and the rod,
Re-judge his justice, be the GOD of GOD.
In Pride, in reas'ning Pride, our error lies;
All quit their sphere, and rush into the skies.
Pride still is aiming at the blest abodes, 125
Men would be Angels, Angels would be Gods.
Aspiring to be Gods, if Angels fell,
Aspiring to be Angels, Men rebel:
And who but wishes to invert the laws
Of ORDER, sins against th' Eternal Cause. 130
   V. Ask for what end the heav'nly bodies shine,
Earth for whose use? Pride answers, "'Tis for mine:
For me kind Nature wakes her genial Pow'r,
Suckles each herb, and spreads out ev'ry flow'r;
Annual for me, the grape, the rose, renew, 135
The juice nectareous, and the balmy dew;
For me, the mine a thousand treasures brings;
For me, health gushes from a thousand springs;
Seas roll to waft me, suns to light me rise;
My footstool earth, my canopy the skies." 140
   But errs not Nature from this gracious end,

From burning suns when livid deaths descend,
When earthquakes swallow, or when tempests sweep
Towns to one grave, whole nations to the deep?
"No," 'tis replied, "the first Almighty Cause 145
Acts not by partial, but by gen'ral laws;
Th' exceptions few; some change since all began:
And what created perfect?"—Why then Man?
If the great end be human happiness,
Then Nature deviates; and can man do less? 150
As much that end a constant course requires
Of show'rs and sunshine, as of man's desires;
As much eternal springs and cloudless skies,
As Men forever temp'rate, calm, and wise.
If plagues or earthquakes break not Heav'n's design, 155
Why then a Borgia, or a Catiline?
Who knows but He whose hand the lightning forms,
Who heaves old Ocean, and who wings the storms;
Pours fierce Ambition in a Cæsar's mind,
Or turns young Ammon loose to scourge mankind? 160
From pride, from pride, our very reas'ning springs;
Account for moral, as for nat'ral things:
Why charge we Heav'n in those, in these acquit?
In both, to reason right is to submit.
  Better for Us, perhaps, it might appear, 165
Were there all harmony, all virtue here;
That never air or ocean felt the wind;
That never passion discomposed the mind.
But ALL subsists by elemental strife;
And Passions are the elements of Life. 170
The gen'ral ORDER, since the whole began,
Is kept in Nature, and is kept in Man.
  VI. What would this Man? Now upward will he soar,
And little less than Angel, would be more;
Now looking downwards, just as grieved appears 175
To want the strength of bulls, the fur of bears.
Made for his use all creatures if he call,
Say what their use, had he the pow'rs of all?
Nature to these, without profusion, kind,
The proper organs, proper pow'rs assigned; 180
Each seeming want compensated of course,
Here with degrees of swiftness, there of force;
All in exact proportion to the state;

156. *Borgia:* Cesare Borgia (1476–1507), Italian prince notorious for his crimes. *Catiline:* Roman who conspired against the state in 63 B.C.

160. *Ammon:* Alexander the Great, who when he visited the oracle of Zeus Ammon in Egypt was hailed by the priest there as son of the god.

Nothing to add, and nothing to abate.
Each beast, each insect, happy in its own: 185
Is Heav'n unkind to Man, and Man alone?
Shall he alone, whom rational we call,
Be pleased with nothing, if not blessed with all?
  The bliss of Man (could Pride that blessing find)
Is not to act or think beyond mankind; 190
No pow'rs of body or of soul to share,
But what his nature and his state can bear.
Why has not Man a microscopic eye?
For this plain reason, Man is not a Fly.
Say what the use, were finer optics giv'n, 195
T' inspect a mite, not comprehend the heav'n?
Or touch, if tremblingly alive all o'er,
To smart and agonize at ev'ry pore?
Or quick effluvia darting through the brain,
Die of a rose in aromatic pain? 200
If nature thundered in his op'ning ears,
And stunned him with the music of the spheres,
How would he wish that Heav'n had left him still
The whisp'ring Zephyr, and the purling rill?
Who finds not Providence all good and wise, 205
Alike in what it gives, and what denies?
  VII. Far as Creation's ample range extends,
The scale of sensual, mental pow'rs ascends:
Mark how it mounts, to Man's imperial race,
From the green myriads in the peopled grass: 210
What modes of sight betwixt each wide extreme,
The mole's dim curtain, and the lynx's beam:
Of smell, the headlong lioness between,
And hound sagacious on the tainted green:
Of hearing, from the life that fills the Flood, 215
To that which warbles through the vernal wood:
The spider's touch, how exquisitely fine!
Feels at each thread, and lives along the line:
In the nice bee, what sense so subtly true
From pois'nous herbs extracts the healing dew? 220
How Instinct varies in the grov'lling swine,
Compared, half-reas'ning elephant, with thine!
'Twixt that, and Reason, what a nice barrier,
For ever sep'rate, yet for ever near!
Remembrance and Reflection how allied; 225

195. *optics:* eyes.
199. *effluvia:* stream of minute particles.
202. *music . . . spheres:* the old notion that the movement of the planets created a "higher" music.
212. *dim curtain:* the mole's poor vision. *lynx's beam:* Legend made this animal one of the keenest-sighted.
214. *sagacious:* here meaning "exceptionally quick of scent."

What thin partitions Sense from Thought divide:
And Middle natures, how they long to join,
Yet never pass th' insuperable line!
Without this just gradation, could they be
Subjected, these to those, or all to thee? 230
The pow'rs of all subdued by thee alone,
Is not thy Reason all these pow'rs in one?
VIII. See, through this air, this ocean, and this earth,
All matter quick, and bursting into birth.
Above, how high, progressive life may go! 235
Around, how wide! how deep extend below!
Vast chain of Being! which from God began,
Natures ethereal, human, angel, man,
Beast, bird, fish, insect, what no eye can see,
No glass can reach; from Infinite to thee, 240
From thee to Nothing.—On superior pow'rs
Were we to press, inferior might on ours:
Or in the full creation leave a void,
Where, one step broken, the great scale's destroyed:
From Nature's chain whatever link you strike, 245
Tenth or ten thousandth, breaks the chain alike.
And, if each system in gradation roll
Alike essential to th' amazing Whole,
The least confusion but in one, not all
That system only, but the Whole must fall. 250
Let Earth unbalanced from her orbit fly,
Planets and Suns run lawless through the sky;
Let ruling angels from their spheres be hurled,
Being on Being wrecked, and world on world;
Heav'n's whole foundations to their center nod, 255
And Nature trembles to the throne of God.
All this dread Order break—for whom? for thee?
Vile worm!—oh Madness! Pride! Impiety!
IX. What if the foot, ordained the dust to tread,
Or hand, to toil, aspired to be the head? 260
What if the head, the eye, or ear repined
To serve mere engines to the ruling Mind?
Just as absurd for any part to claim
To be another, in this gen'ral frame:
Just as absurd, to mourn the tasks or pains, 265
The great directing Mind of All ordains.
All are but parts of one stupendous whole,
Whose body Nature is, and God the soul;
That, changed through all, and yet in all the same;

227. *Middle natures:* animals that seem to share the characteristics of several different classes; for example, the duck-billed platypus.

Great in the earth, as in th' ethereal frame; 270
Warms in the sun, refreshes in the breeze,
Glows in the stars, and blossoms in the trees,
Lives through all life, extends through all extent,
Spreads undivided, operates unspent;
Breathes in our soul, informs our mortal part, 275
As full, as perfect, in a hair as heart;
As full, as perfect, in vile Man that mourns,
As the rapt Seraph that adores and burns:
To him no high, no low, no great, no small;
He fills, he bounds, connects, and equals all. 280

X. Cease then, nor ORDER imperfection name:
Our proper bliss depends on what we blame.
Know thy own point: this kind, this due degree
Of blindness, weakness, Heav'n bestows on thee.
Submit.—In this, or any other sphere, 285
Secure to be as blest as thou canst bear:
Safe in the hand of one disposing Pow'r,
Or in the natal, or the mortal hour.
All Nature is but Art, unknown to thee;
All Chance, Direction, which thou canst not see; 290
All Discord, Harmony not understood;
All partial Evil, universal Good:
And, spite of Pride, in erring Reason's spite,
One truth is clear, WHATEVER IS, IS RIGHT.

294. Epistle II deals with "the Nature and State of Man with respect to himself, as an Individual"; Epistle III examines "the Nature and State of Man with respect to Society"; and the last Epistle concerns "the Nature and State of Man with respect to Happiness.")

JONATHAN SWIFT
(1667–1745)

Gulliver's Travels*

A Letter from Captain Gulliver to His Cousin Sympson[1]

I hope you will be ready to own publicly, whenever you shall be called to it, that by your great and frequent urgency you prevailed on me to publish a very loose and uncorrect account of my travels; with direction to hire some young gentlemen of either University to put them in order, and correct the style, as my Cousin Dampier[2] did by my advice, in his book called *A Voyage round the World*. But I do not remember I gave you power to consent that anything should be omitted, and much less that anything should be inserted: therefore, as to the latter, I do here renounce everything of that kind; particularly a paragraph about her Majesty the late Queen Anne, of most pious and glorious memory; although I did reverence and esteem her more than any of human species. But you, or your interpolator, ought to have considered that as it was not my inclination, so was it not decent to praise any animal of our composition before my master Houyhnhnm; and besides, the fact was altogether false; for to my knowledge, being in England during some part of her Majesty's reign, she did govern by a chief Minister; nay, even by two successively; the first whereof was the Lord of Godolphin, and the second the Lord of Oxford; so that you have made me *say*

* Abridged. Swift's full title for this work was *Travels into Several Remote Nations of the World. In Four Parts. By Lemuel Gulliver, First a Surgeon, and then a Captain of several Ships*. Originally published in London in 1726. The text is based on the Dublin edition of Swift's works (1735).

Lemuel Gulliver, the narrator, makes four voyages to "several remote nations of the world," and this volume contains the last. He is a ship's surgeon; Swift takes great care to portray him as the average man—in short, all of us, or how we see ourselves. In Voyage I he is shipwrecked in the empire of Lilliput, amid a race of tiny people not quite six inches tall. His early pleasure at being a giant among pygmies turns to disillusionment when they are revealed in all their ambition, pettiness, malice, and cruelty. Part I turns out to be a bitter commentary on contemporary British politics, with clearly identifiable persons and parties.

In the second voyage, Gulliver is abandoned by his crew in Brobdingnag, where the inhabitants are ten times his size. In contradistinction to the nasty Lilliputians, the Brobdingnagians emerge as a kindly race, governed by a wise and benevolent prince who is shocked by Gulliver's naïve conception of the excellences of British and European institutions which the prince shows to be sham glories.

Laputa (voyage three) is peopled mainly by philosophers and scientists, some recognizable as members of the British Royal Academy; Swift attacks what for him were the absurdities of theoretical and abstract reasoning in economics, science, and politics.

1. In this letter, first published in 1735, Swift complains, among other matters, of the alterations in his original text made by the publisher, Benjamin Motte, in the interest of what he considered political discretion.

2. William Dampier (1652–1715), the explorer, whose account of his circumnavigation of the globe Swift had read.

the thing that was not. Likewise, in the account of the Academy of Projectors, and several passages of my discourse to my master Houyhnhnm, you have either omitted some material circumstances, or minced or changed them in such a manner, that I do hardly know mine own work. When I formerly hinted to you something of this in a letter, you were pleased to answer that you were afraid of giving offense; that people in power were very watchful over the press; and apt not only to interpret, but to punish everything which looked like an *inuendo* (as I think you called it). But pray, how could that which I spoke so many years ago, and at above five thousand leagues distance, in another reign, be applied to any of the Yahoos, who now are said to govern the herd; especially, at a time when I little thought on or feared the unhappiness of living under them. Have not I the most reason to complain, when I see these very Yahoos carried by Houyhnhnms in a vehicle, as if these were brutes, and those the rational creatures? And, indeed, to avoid so monstrous and detestable a sight was one principal motive of my retirement hither.[3]

Thus much I thought proper to tell you in relation to yourself, and to the trust I reposed in you.

I do in the next place complain of my own great want of judgment, in being prevailed upon by the intreaties and false reasonings of you and some others, very much against mine own opinion, to suffer my travels to be published. Pray bring to your mind how often I desired you to consider, when you insisted on the motive of public good, that the Yahoos were a species of animals utterly incapable of amendment by precepts or examples; and so it hath proved; for instead of seeing a full stop put to all abuses and corruptions, at least in this little island, as I had reason to expect, behold, after above six months warning. I cannot learn that my book hath produced one single effect according to mine intentions; I desired you would let me know by a letter, when party and faction were extinguished; judges learned and upright; pleaders honest and modest, with some tincture of common sense; and Smithfield[4] blazing with pyramids of law books; the young nobility's education entirely changed; the physicians banished; the female Yahoos abounding in virtue, honor, truth, and good sense; courts and levees of great ministers thoroughly weeded and swept; wit, merit, and learning rewarded; all disgracers of the press in prose and verse, condemned to eat nothing but their own cotton, and quench their thirst with their own ink. These, and a thousand other reformations, I firmly counted upon by your encouragement; as indeed they were plainly deducible from the precepts delivered in my book. And, it must be owned that seven months were a sufficient time to correct every vice and folly to which Yahoos are subject; if their natures had

3. To Nottinghamshire.

4. A part of London containing many bookshops.

been capable of the least disposition to virtue or wisdom; yet so far have you been from answering mine expectation in any of your letters, that on the contrary, you are loading our carrier every week with libels, and keys, and reflections, and memoirs, and second parts; wherein I see myself accused of reflecting upon great statesfolk; of degrading human nature (for so they have still the confidence to style it) and of abusing the female sex. I find likewise, that the writers of those bundles are not agreed among themselves; for some of them will not allow me to be author of mine own travels; and others make me author of books to which I am wholly a stranger.

I find likewise that your printer hath been so careless as to confound the times, and mistake the dates of my several voyages and returns; neither assigning the true year, or the true month, or day of the month; and I hear the original manuscript is all destroyed, since the publication of my book. Neither have I any copy left; however, I have sent you some corrections, which you may insert, if ever there should be a second edition; and yet I cannot stand to them, but shall leave that matter to my judicious and candid readers, to adjust it as they please.

I hear some of our sea Yahoos find fault with my sea language, as not proper in many parts, nor now in use. I cannot help it. In my first voyages, while I was young, I was instructed by the oldest mariners, and learned to speak as they did. But I have since found that the sea Yahoos are apt, like the land ones, to become new fangled in their words; which the latter change every year; insomuch, as I remember upon each return to mine own country, their old dialect was so altered, that I could hardly understand the new. And I observe, when any Yahoo comes from London out of curiosity to visit me at mine own house, we neither of us are able to deliver our conceptions in a manner intelligible to the other.

If the censure of Yahoos could any way affect me, I should have great reason to complain that some of them are so bold as to think my book of travels a mere fiction out of mine own brain; and have gone so far as to drop hints that the Houyhnhnms, and Yahoos have no more existence than the inhabitants of Utopia.

Indeed I must confess that as to the people of Lilliput, Brobdingrag (for so the word should have been spelled, and not erroneously Brobdingnag) and Laputa, I have never yet heard of any Yahoo so presumptuous as to dispute their being, or the facts I have related concerning them; because the truth immediately strikes every reader with conviction. And, is there less probability in my account of the Houyhnhnms or Yahoos, when it is manifest as to the latter, there are so many thousands even in this city, who only differ from their brother brutes in Houyhnhnmland, because they use a sort of a jabber, and do not go naked. I wrote for their amendment, and not their approbation. The united praise of the whole race would be of less consequence to me, than the neighing of those two degenerate Houyhnhnms I keep in my stable; because, from these, degenerate as they are, I still improve in some virtues, without any mixture of vice.

Do these miserable animals presume to think that I am so far degenerated as to defend my veracity; Yahoo as I am, it is well known through all Houyhnhnmland, that by the instructions and example of my illustrious master, I was able in the compass of two years (although I confess with the utmost difficulty) to remove that infernal habit of lying, shuffling, deceiving, and equivocating, so deeply rooted in the very souls of all my species; especially the Europeans.

I have other complaints to make upon this vexatious occasion; but I forbear troubling myself or you any further. I must freely confess that since my last return, some corruptions of my Yahoo nature have revived in me by conversing with a few of your species, and particularly those of mine own family, by an unavoidable necessity; else I should never have attempted so absurd a project as that of reforming the Yahoo race in this kingdom; but I have now done with all such visionary schemes for ever.

1727? 1735

The Publisher to the Reader

The author of these travels, Mr. Lemuel Gulliver, is my ancient and intimate friend; there is likewise some relation between us by the mother's side. About three years ago Mr. Gulliver, growing weary of the concourse of curious people coming to him at his house in Redriff,[5] made a small purchase of land, with a convenient house, near Newark, in Nottinghamshire, his native country; where he now lives retired, yet in good esteem among his neighbors.

Although Mr. Gulliver were born in Nottinghamshire, where his father dwelt, yet I have heard him say his family came from Oxfordshire; to confirm which, I have observed in the churchyard at Banbury, in that county, several tombs and monuments of the Gullivers.

Before he quitted Redriff, he left the custody of the following papers in my hands, with the liberty to dispose of them as I should think fit. I have carefully perused them three times; the style is very plain and simple; and the only fault I find is that the author, after the manner of travelers, is a little too circumstantial. There is an air of truth apparent through the whole; and indeed the author was so distinguished for his veracity, that it became a sort of proverb among his neighbors at Redriff, when anyone affirmed a thing, to say, it was as true as if Mr. Gulliver had spoke it.

5. **Rotherhithe, a district in southern London then frequented by sailors.**

By the advice of several worthy persons, to whom, with the author's permission, I communicated these papers, I now venture to send them into the world; hoping they may be, at least for some time, a better entertainment to our young noblemen, than the common scribbles of politics and party.

This volume would have been at least twice as large, if I had not made bold to strike out innumerable passages relating to the winds and tides, as well as to the variations and bearings in the several voyages; together with the minute descriptions of the management of the ship in storms, in the style of sailors; likewise the account of the longitudes and latitudes, wherein I have reason to apprehend that Mr. Gulliver may be a little dissatisfied; but I was resolved to fit the work as much as possible to the general capacity of readers. However, if my own ignorance in sea affairs shall have led me to commit some mistakes, I alone am answerable for them; and if any traveler hath a curiosity to see the whole work at large, as it came from the hand of the author, I will be ready to gratify him.

As for any further particulars relating to the author, the reader will receive satisfaction from the first pages of the book.

RICHARD SYMPSON

Part IV. A Voyage to the Country of the Houyhnhnms [6]

CHAPTER I. *The Author sets out as Captain of a ship. His men conspire against him, confine him a long time to his cabin, set him on shore in an unknown land. He travels up into the country. The Yahoos, a strange sort of animal, described. The Author meets two Houyhnhnms.*

I continued at home with my wife and children about five months in a very happy condition, if I could have learned the lesson of knowing when I was well. I left my poor wife big with child, and accepted an advantageous offer made me to be Captain of the *Adventure*, a stout merchantman of 350 tons; for I understood navigation well, and being grown weary of a surgeon's employment at sea, which however I could exercise upon occasion, I took a skillful young man of that calling, one Robert Purefoy, into my ship. We set sail from Portsmouth upon the 7th day of September, 1710; on the 14th we met with Captain Pocock of Bristol, at Tenariff,[7] who was going to the Bay of Campeachy [8] to cut logwood. On the 16th he was parted from us by a storm; I heard since my return that his ship foundered and none escaped, but one cabin boy. He was an honest man and a good sailor, but a little too positive in his own opinions, which was the cause of his destruction,

6. Pronounced Hwin-ims, the word suggests a horse neighing.
7. Largest of the Canary Islands, off northwest Africa in the Atlantic.
8. Probably Campeche, in southeast Mexico, on the western side of the Yucatan peninsula.

as it hath been of several others. For if he had followed my advice, he might at this time have been safe at home with his family as well as myself.

I had several men died in my ship of calentures,[9] so that I was forced to get recruits out of Barbadoes and the Leeward Islands,[10] where I touched by the direction of the merchants who employed me; which I had soon too much cause to repent, for I found afterwards that most of them had been buccaneers. I had fifty hands on board; and my orders were that I should trade with the Indians in the South Sea, and make what discoveries I could. These rogues whom I had picked up debauched my other men, and they all formed a conspiracy to seize the ship and secure me; which they did one morning, rushing into my cabin, and binding me hand and foot, threatening to throw me overboard, if I offered to stir. I told them I was their prisoner, and would submit. This they made me swear to do, and then unbound me, only fastening one of my legs with a chain near my bed, and placed a sentry at my door with his piece charged, who was commanded to shoot me dead if I attempted my liberty. They sent me down victuals and drink, and took the government of the ship to themselves. Their design was to turn pirates and plunder the Spaniards, which they could not do, till they got more men. But first they resolved to sell the goods in the ship, and then go to Madagascar for recruits, several among them having died since my confinement. They sailed many weeks, and traded with the Indians; but I knew not what course they took, being kept close prisoner in my cabin, and expecting nothing less than to be murdered, as they often threatened me.

Upon the 9th day of May, 1711, one James Welch came down to my cabin; and said he had orders from the Captain to set me ashore. I expostulated with him, but in vain; neither would he so much as tell me who their new Captain was. They forced me into the longboat, letting me put on my best suit of clothes, which were as good as new, and a small bundle of linen, but no arms except my hanger;[11] and they were so civil as not to search my pockets, into which I conveyed what money I had, with some other little necessaries. They rowed about a league, and then set me down on a strand. I desired them to tell me what country it was; they all swore, they knew no more than myself, but said that the Captain (as they called him) was resolved, after they had sold the lading, to get rid of me in the first place where they discovered land. They pushed off immediately, advising me to make haste, for fear of being overtaken by the tide, and bade me farewell.

In this desolate condition I advanced forward, and soon got upon firm ground, where I sat down on a bank to rest myself, and con-

9. Tropical fever.

10. Barbados is an island in the British West Indies. The Leeward Islands are the northern group of the Lesser Antilles in the West Indies, extending southeast from Puerto Rico to the Windward Isles.

11. A hanger was a small sword.

sider what I had best to do. When I was a little refreshed, I went up into the country, resolving to deliver myself to the first savages I should meet, and purchase my life from them by some bracelets, glass rings, and other toys, which sailors usually provide themselves with in those voyages, and whereof I had some about me. The land was divided by long rows of trees, not regularly planted, but naturally growing; there was great plenty of grass, and several fields of oats. I walked very circumspectly for fear of being surprised, or suddenly shot with an arrow from behind, or on either side. I fell into a beaten road, where I saw many tracks of human feet, and some of cows, but most of horses. At last I beheld several animals in a field, and one or two of the same kind sitting in trees. Their shape was very singular, and deformed, which a little discomposed me, so that I lay down behind a thicket to observe them better. Some of them coming forward near the place where I lay, gave me an opportunity of distinctly marking their form. Their heads and breasts were covered with a thick hair, some frizzled and others lank; they had beards like goats, and a long ridge of hair down their backs, and the fore parts of their legs and feet; but the rest of their bodies were bare, so that I might see their skins, which were of a brown buff color. They had no tails, nor any hair at all on their buttocks, except about the anus; which, I presume Nature had placed there to defend them as they sat on the ground; for this posture they used, as well as lying down, and often stood on their hind feet. They climbed high trees, as nimbly as a squirrel, for they had strong extended claws before and behind, terminating in sharp points, and hooked. They would often spring, and bound, and leap with prodigious agility. The females were not so large as the males; they had long lank hair on their heads, and only a sort of down on the rest of their bodies, except about the anus, and pudenda.[12] Their dugs hung between their forefeet, and often reached almost to the ground as they walked. The hair of both sexes was of several colors, brown, red, black, and yellow. Upon the whole, I never beheld in all my travels so disagreeable an animal, or one against which I naturally conceived so strong an antipathy. So that thinking I had seen enough, full of contempt and aversion, I got up and pursued the beaten road, hoping it might direct me to the cabin of some Indian: I had not gone far when I met one of these creatures full in my way, and coming up directly to me. The ugly monster, when he saw me, distorted several ways every feature of his visage, and stared as at an object he had never seen before; then approaching nearer, lifted up his forepaw, whether out of curiosity or mischief, I could not tell; but I drew my hanger, and gave him a good blow with the flat side of it; for I durst not strike him with the edge, fearing the inhabitants might be provoked against me, if they should come to know that I had killed or maimed any of their cattle. When the beast felt the smart, he drew back, and roared so loud, that a herd of

12. The genital area.

at least forty came flocking about me from the next field, howling and making odious faces; but I ran to the body of a tree, and leaning my back against it, kept them off, by waving my hanger. Several of this cursed brood getting hold of the branches behind, leaped up into the tree, from whence they began to discharge their excrements on my head; however, I escaped pretty well, by sticking close to the stem of the tree, but was almost stifled with the filth, which fell about me on every side.

In the midst of this distress, I observed them all to run away on a sudden as fast as they could; at which I ventured to leave the tree, and pursue the road, wondering what it was that could put them into this fright. But looking on my left hand, I saw a horse walking softly in the field; which my persecutors having sooner discovered, was the cause of their flight. The horse started a little when he came near me, but soon recovering himself, looked full in my face with manifest tokens of wonder; he viewed my hands and feet, walking round me several times. I would have pursued my journey, but he placed himself directly in the way, yet looking with a very mild aspect, never offering the least violence. We stood gazing at each other for some time; at last I took the boldness, to reach my hand towards his neck, with a design to stroke it; using the common style and whistle of jockies when they are going to handle a strange horse. But, this animal seeming to receive my civilities with disdain, shook his head, and bent his brows, softly raising up his left forefoot to remove my hand. Then he neighed three or four times, but in so different a cadence, that I almost began to think he was speaking to himself in some language of his own.

While he and I were thus employed, another horse came up; who applying himself to the first in a very formal manner, they gently struck each others right hoof before, neighing several times by turns, and varying the sound, which seemed to be almost articulate. They went some paces off, as if it were to confer together, walking side by side, backward and forward, like persons deliberating upon some affair of weight; but often turning their eyes towards me, as it were to watch that I might not escape. I was amazed to see such actions and behavior in brute beasts; and concluded with myself that if the inhabitants of this country were endued with a proportionable degree of reason, they must needs be the wisest people upon earth. This thought gave me so much comfort, that I resolved to go forward until I could discover some house or village, or meet with any of the natives, leaving the two horses to discourse together as they pleased. But the first, who was a dapple grey, observing me to steal off, neighed after me in so expressive a tone that I fancied myself to understand what he meant; whereupon I turned back, and came near him, to expect his farther commands; but concealing my fear as much as I could; for I began to be in some pain, how this adventure might terminate; and the reader will easily believe I did not much like my present situation.

The two horses came up close to me, looking with great earnestness upon my face and hands. The grey steed rubbed my hat all round with his right fore hoof, and discomposed it so much that I was forced to adjust it better, by taking it off, and settling it again; whereat both he and his companion (who was a brown bay) appeared to be much surprised; the latter felt the lappet of my coat, and finding it to hang loose about me, they both looked with new signs of wonder. He stroked my right hand, seeming to admire the softness, and color; but he squeezed it so hard between his hoof and his pastern,[13] that I was forced to roar; after which they both touched me with all possible tenderness. They were under great perplexity about my shoes and stockings, which they felt very often, neighing to each other, and using various gestures, not unlike those of a philosopher, when he would attempt to solve some new and difficult phenomenon.

Upon the whole, the behavior of these animals was so orderly and rational, so acute and judicious, that I at last concluded, they must needs be magicians, who had thus metamorphosed themselves upon some design; and seeing a stranger in the way, were resolved to divert themselves with him; or perhaps were really amazed at the sight of a man so very different in habit, feature, and complexion from those who might probably live in so remote a climate. Upon the strength of this reasoning, I ventured to address them in the following manner: "Gentlemen, if you be conjurers, as I have good cause to believe, you can understand any language; therefore I make bold to let your worships know that I am a poor distressed Englishman, driven by his misfortunes upon your coast; and I entreat one of you, to let me ride upon his back, as if he were a real horse, to some house or village, where I can be relieved. In return of which favor, I will make you a present of this knife and bracelet" (taking them out of my pocket). The two creatures stood silent while I spoke, seeming to listen with great attention; and when I had ended, they neighed frequently towards each other, as if they were engaged in serious conversation. I plainly observed, that their language expressed the passions very well, and the words might with little pains be resolved into an alphabet more easily than the Chinese.

I could frequently distinguish the word *Yahoo*, which was repeated by each of them several times; and although it were impossible for me to conjecture what it meant, yet while the two horses were busy in conversation, I endeavored to practice this word upon my tongue; and as soon as they were silent, I boldly pronounced "Yahoo" in a loud voice, imitating, at the same time, as near as I could, the neighing of a horse; at which they were both visibly sur-

13. "The pastern of a horse . . . is the distance between the joint next the foot, and the coronet of the hoof." The definition is taken from the first edition of the *Encyclopaedia Britannica* (1768–1771), a work we shall subsequently refer to as *E.B.*

prised, and the grey repeated the same word twice, as if he meant to teach me the right accent, wherein I spoke after him as well as I could, and found myself perceivably to improve every time, although very far from any degree of perfection. Then the bay tried me with a second word, much harder to be pronounced; but reducing it to the English orthography, may be spelt thus, *Houyhnhnm.* I did not succeed in this so well as the former, but after two or three farther trials, I had better fortune; and they both appeared amazed at my capacity.

After some farther discourse, which I then conjectured might relate to me, the two friends took their leaves, with the same compliment of striking each other's hoof; and the grey made me signs that I should walk before him; wherein I thought it prudent to comply, till I could find a better director. When I offered to slacken my pace, he would cry, "Hhuun, Hhuun"; I guessed his meaning, and gave him to understand, as well as I could that I was weary, and not able to walk faster; upon which, he would stand a while to let me rest.

Chapter II. *The Author conducted by a Houyhnhnm to his house. The house described. The Author's reception. The food of the Houyhnhnms. The Author in distress for want of meat is at last relieved. His manner of feeding in that country.*

Having traveled about three miles, we came to a long kind of building, made of timber, stuck in the ground, and wattled across; the roof was low, and covered with straw. I now began to be a little comforted, and took out some toys, which travelers usually carry for presents to the savage Indians of America and other parts, in hopes the people of the house would be thereby encouraged to receive me kindly. The horse made me a sign to go in first; it was a large room with a smooth clay floor, and a rack and manger extending the whole length on one side. There were three nags, and two mares, not eating, but some of them sitting down upon their hams, which I very much wondered at; but wondered more to see the rest employed in domestic business; the last seemed but ordinary cattle; however this confirmed my first opinion, that a people who could so far civilize brute animals must needs excel in wisdom all the nations of the world. The grey came in just after, and thereby prevented any ill treatment, which the others might have given me. He neighed to them several times in a style of authority, and received answers.

Beyond this room there were three others, reaching the length of the house, to which you passed through three doors, opposite to each other, in the manner of a vista; we went through the second room towards the third; here the grey walked in first, beckoning me to attend; I waited in the second room, and got ready my presents, for the master and mistress of the house; they were two knives, three bracelets of false pearl, a small looking glass and a bead necklace. The horse neighed three or four times, and I waited to hear some answers in a human voice, but I heard no other returns than in the same dialect, only one or two a little shriller than his. I began to think that this house must belong to some person of great note among them, because there appeared so much ceremony before I could gain admittance. But, that a man of quality should be served all by horses, was beyond my comprehension. I feared my brain was disturbed by my sufferings and misfortunes; I roused myself, and looked about me in the room where I was left alone; this was furnished as the first, only after a more elegant manner. I rubbed my eyes often, but the same objects still occurred. I pinched my arms and sides, to awake myself, hoping I might be in a dream. I then absolutely concluded that all these appearances could be nothing else but necromancy and magic. But I had no time to pursue these reflections; for the grey horse came to the door, and made me a sign to follow him into the third room; where I saw a very comely mare, together with a colt and foal, sitting on their haunches, upon mats of straw, not unartfully made, and perfectly neat and clean.

The mare soon after my entrance, rose from her mat, and coming up close, after having nicely observed my hands and face, gave me a most contemptuous look; then turning to the horse, I heard the word Yahoo often repeated betwixt them; the meaning of which word I could not then comprehend, although it were the first I had learned to pronounce; but I was soon better informed, to my everlasting mortification: for the horse beckoning to me with his head, and repeating the word, "Hhuun, Hhuun," as he did upon the road, which I understood was to attend him, led me out into a kind of court, where was another building at some distance from the house. Here we entered, and I saw three of those detestable creatures, which I first met after my landing, feeding upon roots, and the flesh of some animals, which I afterwards found to be that of asses and dogs, and now and then a cow dead by accident or disease. They were all tied by the neck with strong withes,[14] fastened to a beam; they held their food between the claws of their forefeet, and tore it with their teeth.

The master horse ordered a sorrel nag, one of his servants, to untie the largest of these animals, and take him into a yard. The beast and I were brought close together; and our countenances diligently compared, both by master and servant, who thereupon repeated several times the word "Yahoo." My horror and astonishment are not to be described, when I observed, in this abominable animal, a perfect human figure; the face of it indeed was flat and broad, the nose depressed, the lips large, and the mouth wide; but these differences are common to all savage nations, where the lineaments of the countenance are distorted by the natives suffering their infants

14. Fibers braided into rope.

to lie groveling on the earth, or by carrying them on their backs, nuzzling with their face against the mother's shoulders. The fore-feet of the Yahoo differed from my hands in nothing else but the length of the nails, the coarseness and brownness of the palms, and the hairiness on the backs. There was the same resemblance between our feet, with the same differences, which I knew very well, although the horses did not, because of my shoes and stockings; the same in every part of our bodies, except as to hairiness and color, which I have already described.

The great difficulty that seemed to stick with the two horses was to see the rest of my body so very different from that of a Yahoo, for which I was obliged to my clothes, whereof they had no conception; the sorrel nag offered me a root, which he held (after their manner, as we shall describe in its proper place) between his hoof and pastern; I took it in my hand, and having smelled it, returned it to him again as civilly as I could. He brought out of the Yahoo's kennel a piece of ass's flesh, but it smelled so offensively that I turned from it with loathing; he then threw it to the Yahoo, by whom it was greedily devoured. He afterwards showed me a wisp of hay, and a fetlock[15] full of oats; but I shook my head, to signify that neither of these were food for me. And indeed, I now apprehended that I must absolutely starve, if I did not get to some of my own species; for as to those filthy Yahoos, although there were few greater lovers of mankind, at that time, than myself, yet I confess I never saw any sensitive being so detestable on all accounts; and the more I came near them, the more hateful they grew, while I stayed in that country. This the master horse observed by my behavior, and therefore sent the Yahoo back to his kennel. He then put his forehoof to his mouth, at which I was much surprised, although he did it with ease, and with a motion that appeared perfectly natural; and made other signs to know what I would eat; but I could not return him such an answer as he was able to apprehend; and if he had understood me, I did not see how it was possible to contrive any way for finding myself nourishment. While we were thus engaged, I observed a cow passing by; whereupon I pointed to her, and expressed a desire to let me go and milk her. This had its effect; for he led me back into the house, and ordered a mare-servant to open a room, where a good store of milk lay in earthen and wooden vessels, after a very orderly and cleanly manner. She gave me a large bowl full, of which I drank very heartily, and found myself well refreshed.

About noon I saw coming towards the house a kind of vehicle, drawn like a sledge by four Yahoos. There was in it an old steed, who seemed to be of quality; he alighted with his hind feet forward, having by accident got a hurt in his left forefoot. He came to dine with our horse, who received him with great civility. They dined in the best room, and had oats boiled in milk for the second

15. "A tuft of hair growing behind the pastern joint of many horses; for those of a low size have scarce any such tuft." *E.B.*

course, which the old horse eat warm, but the rest cold. Their mangers were placed circular in the middle of the room, and divided into several partitions, round which they sat on their haunches upon bosses of straw. In the middle was a large rack with angles answering to every partition of the manger. So that each horse and mare eat their own hay, and their own mash of oats and milk, with much decency and regularity. The behavior of the young colt and foal appeared very modest; and that of the master and mistress extremely cheerful and complaisant to their guest. The grey ordered me to stand by him; and much discourse passed between him and his friend concerning me, as I found by the stranger's often looking on me, and the frequent repetition of the word Yahoo.

I happened to wear my gloves; which the master grey observing, seemed perplexed; discovering signs of wonder what I had done to my forefeet; he put his hoof three or four times to them, as if he would signify, that I should reduce them to their former shape, which I presently did, pulling off both my gloves, and putting them into my pocket. This occasioned farther talk, and I saw the company was pleased with my behavior, whereof I soon found the good effects. I was ordered to speak the few words I understood; and while they were at dinner, the master taught me the names for oats, milk, fire, water, and some others which I could readily pronounce after him, having from my youth a great facility in learning languages.

When dinner was done, the master horse took me aside, and by signs and words made me understand the concern he was in that I had nothing to eat. Oats in their tongue are called *hlunnh.* This word I pronounced two or three times; for although I had refused them at first, yet upon second thoughts, I considered that I could contrive to make a kind of bread, which might be sufficient with milk to keep me alive, till I could make my escape to some other country, and to creatures of my own species. The horse immediately ordered a white mare-servant of his family to bring me a good quantity of oats in a sort of wooden tray. These I heated before the fire as well as I could, and rubbed them till the husks came off, which I made a shift to winnow from the grain; I ground and beat them between two stones, then took water, and made them into a paste or cake, which I toasted at the fire, and eat warm with milk. It was at first a very insipid diet, although common enough in many parts of Europe, but grew tolerable by time; and having been often reduced to hard fare in my life, this was not the first experiment I had made how easily nature is satisfied. And I cannot but observe that I never had one hour's sickness, while I staid in this island. It is true, I sometimes made a shift to catch a rabbit, or bird, by springes[16] made of Yahoos' hairs; and I often gathered wholesome herbs, which I boiled, or eat as salads with my bread; and now and then, for a rarity, I made a little butter, and drank the whey. I was

16. Traps.

at first at a great loss for salt; but custom soon reconciled the want of it; and I am confident that the frequent use of salt among us is an effect of luxury, and was first introduced only as a provocative to drink; except where it is necessary for preserving of flesh in long voyages, or in places remote from great markets. For we observe no animal to be fond of it but man;[17] and as to myself, when I left this country, it was a great while before I could endure the taste of it in anything that I eat.

This is enough to say upon the subject of my diet, wherewith other travelers fill their books, as if the readers were personally concerned whether we fare well or ill. However, it was necessary to mention this matter, lest the world should think it impossible that I could find sustenance for three years in such a country, and among such inhabitants.

When it grew towards evening, the master horse ordered a place for me to lodge in; it was but six yards from the house, and separated from the stable of the Yahoos. Here I got some straw, and covering myself with my own clothes, slept very sound. But I was in a short time better accommodated, as the reader shall know hereafter, when I come to treat more particularly about my way of living.

CHAPTER III. *The Author studious to learn the language, the Houyhnhnm his master assists in teaching him. The language described. Several Houyhnhnms of quality come out of curiosity to see the Author. He gives his master a short account of his voyage.*

My principal endeavor was to learn the language, which my master (for so I shall henceforth call him) and his children, and every servant of his house were desirous to teach me. For they looked upon it as a prodigy, that a brute animal should discover such marks of a rational creature. I pointed to everything, and enquired the name of it, which I wrote down in my journal book when I was alone, and corrected my bad accent, by desiring those of the family to pronounce it often. In this employment, a sorrel nag, one of the under servants, was very ready to assist me.

In speaking, they pronounce through the nose and throat, and their language approaches nearest to the High Dutch or German, of any I know in Europe; but is much more graceful and significant. The Emperor Charles V made almost the same observation, when he said, that if he were to speak to his horse, it should be in High Dutch.[18]

The curiosity and impatience of my master were so great, that he spent many hours of his leisure to instruct me. He was convinced (as he afterwards told me) that I must be a Yahoo, but my

17. Gulliver's error: many animals are very fond of salt.

18. Charles was reputed to have said he would address his God in Spanish, his mistress in Italian, and his horse in German.

teachableness, civility, and cleanliness astonished him; which were qualities altogether so opposite to those animals. He was most perplexed about my clothes, reasoning sometimes with himself whether they were a part of my body; for I never pulled them off till the family were asleep, and got them on before they waked in the morning. My master was eager to learn from whence I came; how I acquired those appearances of reason, which I discovered in all my actions; and to know my story from my own mouth, which he hoped he should soon do by the great proficiency I made in learning and pronouncing their words and sentences. To help my memory, I formed all I learned into the English alphabet, and writ the words down with the translations. This last, after some time, I ventured to do in my master's presence. It cost me much trouble to explain to him what I was doing; for the inhabitants have not the least idea of books or literature.

In about ten weeks time I was able to understand most of his questions; and in three months could give him some tolerable answers. He was extremely curious to know from what part of the country I came, and how I was taught to imitate a rational creature; because the Yahoos (whom he saw I exactly resembled in my head, hands, and face, that were only visible) with some appearance of cunning, and the strongest disposition to mischief, were observed to be the most unteachable of all brutes. I answered that I came over the sea, from a far place, with many others of my own kind, in a great hollow vessel made of the bodies of trees; that my companions forced me to land on this coast, and then left me to shift for myself. It was with some difficulty, and by the help of many signs, that I brought him to understand me. He replied that I must needs be mistaken, or that I *said the thing which was not*. (For they have no word in their language to express lying or falsehood.) He knew it was impossible that there could be a country beyond the sea, or that a parcel of brutes could move a wooden vessel whither they pleased upon water. He was sure no Houyhnhnm alive could make such a vessel, or would trust Yahoos to manage it.

The word Houyhnhnm, in their tongue, signifies a Horse; and in its etymology, the Perfection of Nature. I told my master that I was at a loss for expression, but would improve as fast as I could; and hoped in a short time I should be able to tell him wonders; he was pleased to direct his own mare, his colt, and foal, and the servants of the family to take all opportunities of instructing me; and every day for two or three hours, he was at the same pains himself; several horses and mares of quality in the neighborhood came often to our house, upon the report spread of a wonderful Yahoo, that could speak like a Houyhnhnm, and seemed in his words and actions to discover some glimmerings of reason. These delighted to converse with me; they put many questions, and received such answers as I was able to return. By all which advantages,

I made so great a progress, that in five months from my arrival, I understood whatever was spoke, and could express myself tolerably well.

The Houyhnhnms who came to visit my master, out of a design of seeing and talking with me, could hardly believe me to be a right Yahoo, because my body had a different covering from others of my kind. They were astonished to observe me without the usual hair or skin, except on my head, face, and hands; but I discovered that secret to my master, upon an accident, which happened about a fortnight[19] before.

I have already told the reader, that every night when the family were gone to bed, it was my custom to strip and cover myself with my clothes; it happened one morning early, that my master sent for me, by the sorrel nag, who was his valet; when he came, I was fast asleep, my clothes fallen off on one side, and my shirt above my waist. I awaked at the noise he made, and observed him to deliver his message in some disorder; after which he went to my master, and in a great fright gave him a very confused account of what he had seen; this I presently discovered; for going as soon as I was dressed, to pay my attendance upon his honor, he asked me the meaning of what his servant had reported; that I was not the same thing when I slept as I appeared to be at other times; that his valet assured him, some part of me was white, some yellow, at least not so white, and some brown.

I had hitherto concealed the secret of my dress, in order to distinguish myself as much as possible, from that cursed race of Yahoos; but now I found it in vain to do so any longer. Besides, I considered that my clothes and shoes would soon wear out, which already were in a declining condition, and must be supplied by some contrivance from the hides of Yahoos, or other brutes; whereby the whole secret would be known. I therefore told my master, that in the country from whence I came, those of my kind always covered their bodies with the hairs of certain animals prepared by art, as well for decency, as to avoid inclemencies of air both hot and cold; of which, as to my own person I would give him immediate conviction, if he pleased to command me; only desiring his excuse, if I did not expose those parts that nature taught us to conceal. He said, my discourse was all very strange, but especially the last part; for he could not understand why Nature should teach us to conceal what Nature had given. That neither himself nor family were ashamed of any parts of their bodies; but however I might do as I pleased. Whereupon, I first unbuttoned my coat, and pulled it off. I did the same with my waistcoat; I drew off my shoes, stockings, and breeches. I let my shirt down to my waist, and drew up the bottom, fastening it like a girdle about my middle to hide my nakedness.

19. Two weeks.

My master observed the whole performance with great signs of curiosity and admiration. He took up all my clothes in his pastern, one piece after another, and examined them diligently; he then stroked my body very gently, and looked round me several times; after which he said, it was plain I must be a perfect Yahoo; but that I differed very much from the rest of my species, in the whiteness and smoothness of my skin, my want of hair in several parts of my body, the shape and shortness of my claws behind and before, and my affectation of walking continually on my two hinder feet. He desired to see no more; and gave me leave to put on my clothes again, for I was shuddering with cold.

I expressed my uneasiness at his giving me so often the appellation of Yahoo, an odious animal, for which I had so utter an hatred and contempt. I begged he would forbear applying that word to me, and take the same order in his family, and among his friends whom he suffered to see me. I requested likewise, that the secret of my having a false covering to my body might be known to none but himself, at least as long as my present clothing should last; for as to what the sorrel nag his valet had observed, his honor might command him to conceal it.

All this my master very graciously consented to; and thus the secret was kept till my clothes began to wear out, which I was forced to supply by several contrivances, that shall hereafter be mentioned. In the meantime, he desired I would go on with my utmost diligence to learn their language, because he was more astonished at my capacity for speech and reason, than at the figure of my body, whether it were covered or no; adding that he waited with some impatience to hear the wonders which I promised to tell him.

From thenceforward he doubled the pains he had been at to instruct me; he brought me into all company, and made them treat me with civility, because, as he told them privately, this would put me into good humor, and make me more diverting.

Every day when I waited on him, beside the trouble he was at in teaching, he would ask me several questions concerning myself, which I answered as well as I could; and by those means he had already received some general ideas, although very imperfect. It would be tedious to relate the several steps, by which I advanced to a more regular conversation, but the first account I gave of myself in any order and length was to this purpose:

That, I came from a very far country, as I already had attempted to tell him, with about fifty more of my own species; that we traveled upon the seas, in a great hollow vessel made of wood, and larger than his honor's house. I described the ship to him in the best terms I could; and explained by the help of my handkerchief displayed, how it was driven forward by the wind. That, upon a quarrel among us, I was set on shore on this coast, where I walked forward without knowing whither, till he delivered me from the persecution of those execrable Yahoos. He asked me who made the ship, and how it was possible that the Houyhnhnms of my country would leave it to the management of brutes? My answer was that I durst proceed no farther in my relation, unless he would give me his word and honor that he would not be offended; and then I would tell him the wonders I had so often promised. He agreed; and I went on by assuring him, that the ship was made by creatures like myself, who in all the countries I had traveled, as well as in my own, were the only governing, rational animals; and that upon my arrival hither, I was as much astonished to see the Houyhnhnms act like rational beings, as he or his friends could be in finding some marks of reason in a creature he was pleased to call a Yahoo; to which I owned my resemblance in every part, but could not account for their degenerate and brutal nature. I said farther, that if good fortune ever restored me to my native country, to relate my travels hither, as I resolved to do; everybody would believe that I *said the thing which was not*; that I invented the story out of my own head; and with all possible respect to himself, his family, and friends, and under his promise of not being offended, our countrymen would hardly think it probable, that a Houyhnhnm should be the presiding creature of a nation, and a Yahoo the brute.

CHAPTER IV. *The Houyhnhnms' notion of truth and falsehood. The author's discourse disapproved by his master. The author gives a more particular account of himself, and the accidents of his voyage.*

My master heard me with great appearances of uneasiness in his countenance; because *doubting* or *not believing* are so little known in this country, that the inhabitants cannot tell how to behave themselves under such circumstances. And I remember in frequent discourses with my master concerning the nature of manhood, in other parts of the world, having occasion to talk of *lying* and *false representation,* it was with much difficulty that he comprehended what I meant; although he had otherwise a most acute judgment. For he argued thus: that the use of speech was to make us understand one another, and to receive information of facts; now if anyone *said the thing which was not,* these ends were defeated; because I cannot properly be said to understand him; and I am so far from receiving information, that he leaves me worse than in ignorance; for I am led to believe a thing *black* when it is *white,* and *short* when it is *long.* And these were all the notions he had concerning that faculty of *lying,* so perfectly well understood, and so universally practiced among human creatures.

To return from this digression; when I asserted that the Yahoos were the only governing animals in my country, which my master said was altogether past his conception, he desired to know, whether we had Houyhnhnms among us, and what was their employment; I told him we had great numbers; that in summer they grazed in the fields, and in winter were kept in houses, with hay and oats, where Yahoo servants were employed to rub their skins smooth, comb their manes, pick their feet, serve them with food, and make their beds. "I understand you well," said my master; "it is now very plain from all you have spoken, that whatever share of reason the Yahoos pretend to, the Houyhnhnms are your masters; I heartily wish our Yahoos would be so tractable." I begged his honor would please to excuse me from proceeding any farther, because I was very certain that the account he expected from me would be highly displeasing. But he insisted in commanding me to let him know the best and the worst; I told him he should be obeyed. I owned that the Houyhnhnms among us, whom we called Horses, were the most generous[20] and comely animal we had; that they excelled in strength and swiftness; and when they belonged to persons of quality, employed in traveling, racing, and drawing chariots, they were treated with much kindness and care, till they fell into diseases, or became foundered in the feet; but then they were sold, and used to all kind of drudgery till they died; after which their skins were stripped and sold for what they were worth, and their bodies left to be devoured by dogs and birds of prey. But the common race of horses had not so good fortune, being kept by farmers and carriers, and other mean people, who put them to greater labor, and feed them worse. I described as well as I could, our way of riding; the shape and use of a bridle, a saddle, a spur, and a whip; of harness and wheels. I added, that we fastened plates of a certain hard substance called iron at the bottom of their feet, to preserve their hoofs from being broken by the stony ways on which we often traveled.

My master, after some expressions of great indignation, wondered how we dared to venture upon a Houyhnhnm's back; for he was sure, that the weakest servant in his house would be able to shake off the strongest Yahoo; or by lying down, and rolling upon his back, squeeze the brute to death. I answered that our horses were trained up from three or four years old to the several uses we intended them for; that if any of them proved intolerably vicious, they were employed for carriages; that they were severely beaten while they were young for any mischievous tricks; that the males, designed for the common use of riding or draught, were generally castrated about two years after their birth, to take down their spirits, and make them more tame and gentle; that they were indeed sensible of rewards and punishments; but his honor would please to consider that they had not the least tincture of reason any more than the Yahoos in this country.

It put me to the pains of many circumlocutions to give my master a right idea of what I spoke; for their language doth not abound in variety of words, because their wants and passions are fewer than

20. Noble.

among us. But it is impossible to express his noble resentment at our savage treatment of the Houyhnhnm race; particularly after I had explained the manner and use of castrating horses among us, to hinder them from propagating their kind, and to render them more servile. He said, if it were possible there could be any country where Yahoos alone were endued with reason, they certainly must be the governing animal, because reason will in time always prevail against brutal strength. But, considering the frame of our bodies, and especially of mine, he thought no creature of equal bulk was so ill-contrived for employing that reason in the common offices of life; whereupon he desired to know whether those among whom I lived resembled me or the Yahoos of his country. I assured him that I was as well shaped as most of my age; but the younger and the females were much more soft and tender, and the skins of the latter generally as white as milk. He said I differed indeed from other Yahoos, being much more cleanly, and not altogether so deformed; but in point of real advantage, he thought I differed for the worse. That my nails were of no use either to my fore or hinder feet; as to my forefeet, he could not properly call them by that name, for he never observed me to walk upon them; that they were too soft to bear the ground; that I generally went with them uncovered, neither was the covering I sometimes wore on them of the same shape, or so strong as that on my feet behind. That I could not walk with any security; for if either of my hinder feet slipped, I must inevitably fall. He then began to find fault with other parts of my body; the flatness of my face, the prominence of my nose, my eyes placed directly in front, so that I could not look on either side without turning my head; that I was not able to feed myself without lifting one of my forefeet to my mouth; and therefore nature had placed those joints to answer that necessity. He knew not what could be the use of those several clefts and divisions in my feet behind; that these were too soft to bear the hardness and sharpness of stones without a covering made from the skin of some other brute; that my whole body wanted a fence against heat and cold, which I was forced to put on and off every day with tediousness and trouble. And lastly, that he observed every animal in his country naturally to abhor the Yahoos, whom the weaker avoided, and the stronger drove from them. So that supposing us to have the gift of reason, he could not see how it were possible to cure that natural antipathy which every creature discovered against us; nor consequently, how we could tame and render them serviceable. However, he would (as he said) debate the matter no farther, because he was more desirous to know my own story, the country where I was born, and the several actions and events of my life before I came hither.

I assured him how extremely desirous I was that he should be satisfied in every point; but I doubted much whether it would be possible for me to explain myself on several subjects whereof his honor could have no conception, because I saw nothing in his country to which I could resemble them. That however, I would do my best, and strive to express myself by similitudes, humbly desiring his assistance when I wanted proper words; which he was pleased to promise me.

I said, my birth was of honest parents, in an island called England, which was remote from this country, as many days journey as the strongest of his honor's servants could travel in the annual course of the sun. That I was bred a surgeon, whose trade it is to cure wounds and hurts in the body, got by accident or violence. That my country was governed by a female man, whom we called a queen.[21] That I left it to get riches, whereby I might maintain myself and family when I should return. That in my last voyage, I was Commander of the ship and had about fifty Yahoos under me, many of which died at sea, and I was forced to supply them by others picked out from several nations. That our ship was twice in danger of being sunk; the first time by a great storm, and the second, by striking against a rock. Here my master interposed, by asking me, how I could persuade strangers out of different countries to venture with me, after the losses I had sustained, and the hazards I had run. I said, they were fellows of desperate fortunes, forced to fly from the places of their birth, on account of their poverty or their crimes. Some were undone by lawsuits; others spent all they had in drinking, whoring, and gaming; others fled for treason; many for murder, theft, poisoning, robbery, perjury, forgery, coining false money; for committing rapes or sodomy; for flying from their colors, or deserting to the enemy; and most of them had broken prison. None of these durst return to their native countries for fear of being hanged, or of starving in a jail; and therefore were under a necessity of seeking a livelihood in other places.

During this discourse, my master was pleased often to interrupt me. I had made use of many circumlocutions in describing to him the nature of the several crimes, for which most of our crew had been forced to fly their country. This labor took up several days conversation before he was able to comprehend me. He was wholly at a loss to know what could be the use or necessity of practicing those vices. To clear up which I endeavored to give him some ideas of the desire of power and riches; of the terrible effects of lust, intemperance, malice, and envy. All this I was forced to define and describe by putting of cases, and making suppositions. After which, like one whose imagination was struck with something never seen or heard of before, he would lift up his eyes with amazement and indignation. Power, government, war, law, punishment, and a thousand other things had no terms, wherein that language could express them; which made the difficulty almost insuperable to give my master any conception of what I meant; but being of an excellent understanding, much improved by con-

21. Queen Anne (1665–1714), last Stuart ruler.

templation and converse, he at last arrived at a competent knowledge of what human nature in our parts of the world is capable to perform; and desired I would give him some particular account of that land, which we call Europe, especially, of my own country.

CHAPTER V. *The Author, at his master's commands, informs him of the state of England. The causes of war among the princes of Europe. The Author begins to explain the English Constitution.*

The reader may please to observe that the following extract of many conversations I had with my master contains a summary of the most material points, which were discoursed at several times for above two years; his honor often desiring fuller satisfaction as I farther improved in the Houyhnhnm tongue. I laid before him, as well as I could, the whole state of Europe; I discoursed of trade and manufactures, of arts and sciences; and the answers I gave to all the questions he made, as they arose upon several subjects, were a fund of conversation not to be exhausted. But I shall here only set down the substance of what passed between us concerning my own country, reducing it into order as well as I can, without any regard to time or other circumstances, while I strictly adhere to truth. My only concern is that I shall hardly be able to do justice to my master's arguments and expressions; which must needs suffer by my want of capacity, as well as by a translation into our barbarous English.

In obedience therefore to his honor's commands, I related to him the Revolution under the Prince of Orange; the long war with France entered into by the said Prince, and renewed by his successor the present queen; wherein the greatest powers of Christendom were engaged, and which still continued. I computed at his request, that about a million of Yahoos might have been killed in the whole progress of it; and perhaps a hundred or more cities taken, and five times as many ships burned or sunk.[22]

He asked me what were the usual causes or motives that made one country to go to war with another. I answered, they were innumerable; but I should only mention a few of the chief. Sometimes the ambition of princes, who never think they have land or people enough to govern; sometimes the corruption of ministers, who engage their master in a war in order to stifle or divert the clamor of the subjects against their evil administration. Difference in opinions hath cost many millions of lives; for instance, whether flesh be bread, or bread be flesh; whether the juice of a certain berry be blood or wine; whether whistling be a vice or a virtue; whether it be better to kiss a post, or throw it into the fire; what is the best color for a coat, whether black, white, red, or grey; and

22. Gulliver relates recent English history: the Glorious Revolution of 1688 and the War of Spanish Succession (1703–1713). He greatly exaggerates the casualties in the war.

whether it should be long or short, narrow or wide, dirty or clean;[23] with many more. Neither are any wars so furious and bloody, or of so long continuance, as those occasioned by difference in opinion, especially if it be in things indifferent.

Sometimes the quarrel between two princes is to decide which of them shall dispossess a third of his dominions, where neither of them pretend to any right. Sometimes one prince quarreleth with another, for fear the other should quarrel with him. Sometimes a war is entered upon, because the enemy is too strong, and sometimes because he is too weak. Sometimes our neighbors want the things which we have, or have the things which we want; and we both fight, till they take ours or give us theirs. It is a very justifiable cause of war to invade a country after the people have been wasted by famine, destroyed by pestilence, or embroiled by factions amongst themselves. It is justifiable to enter into a war against our nearest ally, when one of his towns lies convenient for us, or a territory of land, that would render our dominions round and compact. If a prince send forces into a nation, where the people are poor and ignorant, he may lawfully put half of them to death, and make slaves of the rest, in order to civilize and reduce them from their barbarous way of living. It is a very kingly, honorable, and frequent practice, when one prince desires the assistance of another to secure him against an invasion, that the assistant, when he hath driven out the invader, should seize on the dominions himself, and kill, imprison, or banish the prince he came to relieve. Alliance by blood or marriage is a sufficient cause of war between princes; and the nearer the kindred is, the greater is their disposition to quarrel; poor nations are hungry, and rich nations are proud; and pride and hunger will ever be at variance. For these reasons, the trade of a soldier is held the most honorable of all others: because a soldier is a Yahoo hired to kill in cold blood as many of his own species, who have never offended him, as possibly he can.

There is likewise a kind of beggarly princes in Europe, not able to make war by themselves, who hire out their troops to richer nations for so much a day to each man; of which they keep three fourths to themselves, and it is the best part of their maintenance; such are those in many northern parts of Europe.

"What you have told me," said my master, "upon the subject of war, doth indeed discover most admirably the effects of that reason you pretend to; however, it is happy that the shame is greater than the danger; and that Nature hath left you utterly uncapable of doing much mischief; for your mouths lying flat with your faces, you can hardly bite each other to any purpose, unless by

23. Gulliver refers to the religious controversies of the Reformation and Counter Reformation: the doctrine of transubstantiation, the use of music in church services, the veneration of the crucifix, and the wearing of priestly vestments.

consent. Then, as to the claws upon your feet before and behind, they are so short and tender, that one of our Yahoos would drive a dozen of yours before him. And therefore in recounting the numbers of those who have been killed in battle, I cannot but think that you have *said the thing which is not*."

I could not forbear shaking my head and smiling a little at his ignorance. And, being no stranger to the art of war, I gave him a description of cannons, culverins, muskets, carabines, pistols, bullets, powder, swords, bayonets, battles, sieges, retreats, attacks, undermines, countermines, bombardments, sea fights; ships sunk with a thousand men; twenty thousand killed on each side; dying groans, limbs flying in the air; smoke, noise, confusion, trampling to death under horses' feet; flight, pursuit, victory; fields strewed with carcasses left for food to dogs, and wolves, and birds of prey; plundering, stripping, ravishing, burning, and destroying. And, to set forth the valor of my own dear countrymen, I assured him that I had seen them blow up a hundred enemies at once in a siege, and as many in a ship; and beheld the dead bodies drop down in pieces from the clouds, to the great diversion of all the spectators.

I was going on to more particulars, when my master commanded me silence. He said, whoever understood the nature of Yahoos might easily believe it possible for so vile an animal, to be capable of every action I had named, if their strength and cunning equaled their malice. But, as my discourse had increased his abhorrence of the whole species, so he found it gave him a disturbance in his mind, to which he was wholly a stranger before. He thought his ears being used to such abominable words, might by degrees admit them with less detestation. That, although he hated the Yahoos of this country, yet he no more blamed them for their odious qualities, than he did a *gnnayh* (a bird of prey) for its cruelty, or a sharp stone for cutting his hoof. But, when a creature pretending to reason could be capable of such enormities, he dreaded lest the corruption of that faculty might be worse than brutality itself. He seemed therefore confident, that instead of reason, we were only possessed of some quality fitted to increase our natural vices; as the reflection from a troubled stream returns the image of an ill-shapen body, not only larger, but more distorted.

He added that he had heard too much upon the subject of war, both in this and some former discourses. There was another point which a little perplexed him at present. I had said that some of our crew left their country on account of being ruined by law: that I had already explained the meaning of the word; but he was at a loss how it should come to pass, that the law which was intended for every man's preservation, should be any man's ruin. Therefore he desired to be farther satisfied what I meant by law, and the dispensers thereof, according to the present practice in my own country; because he thought nature and reason were sufficient guides for a reasonable animal, as we pretended to be, in showing us what we ought to do, and what to avoid.

I assured his honor that law was a science wherein I had not much conversed, further than by employing advocates, in vain, upon some injustices that had been done me. However, I would give him all the satisfaction I was able.

I said there was a society of men among us, bred up from their youth in the art of proving by words multiplied for the purpose, that white is black, and black is white, according as they are paid. To this society all the rest of the people are slaves.

"For example. If my neighbor hath a mind to my cow, he hires a lawyer to prove that he ought to have my cow from me. I must then hire another to defend my right; it being against all rules of law that any man should be allowed to speak for himself. Now in this case, I who am the true owner lie under two great disadvantages. First, my lawyer being practiced almost from his cradle in defending falsehood is quite out of his element when he would be an advocate for justice, which as an office unnatural, he always attempts with great awkwardness, if not with ill-will. The second disadvantage is that my lawyer must proceed with great caution, or else he will be reprimanded by the judges, and abhorred by his brethren, as one who would lessen the practice of the law. And therefore I have but two methods to preserve my cow. The first is to gain over my adversary's lawyer with a double fee; who will then betray his client, by insinuating that he hath justice on his side. The second way is for my lawyer to make my cause appear as unjust as he can; by allowing the cow to belong to my adversary; and this if it be skillfully done, will certainly bespeak the favor of the bench.

"Now, your honor is to know that these judges are persons appointed to decide all controversies of property, as well as for the trial of criminals; and picked out from the most dextrous lawyers who are grown old or lazy; and having been biased all their lives against truth and equity, lie under such a fatal necessity of favoring fraud, perjury, and oppression, that I have known some of them to have refused a large bribe from the side where justice lay, rather than injure the faculty,[24] by doing anything unbecoming their nature or their office.

"It is a maxim among these lawyers, that whatever hath been done before may legally be done again; and therefore they take special care to record all the decisions formerly made against common justice and the general reason of mankind. These, under the name of *precedents*, they produce as authorities to justify the most iniquitous opinions; and the judges never fail of directing accordingly.

24. Profession.

"In pleading, they studiously avoid entering into the merits of the cause; but are loud, violent, and tedious in dwelling upon all circumstances which are not to the purpose. For instance, in the case already mentioned, they never desire to know what claim or title my adversary hath to my cow; but whether the said cow were red or black; her horns long or short; whether the field I graze her in be round or square; whether she were milked at home or abroad; what diseases she is subject to, and the like. After which they consult precedents, adjourn the cause, from time to time, and in ten, twenty, or thirty years come to an issue.

"It is likewise to be observed, that this society hath a peculiar cant and jargon of their own, that no other mortal can understand, and wherein all their laws are written, which they take special care to multiply; whereby they have wholly confounded the very essence of truth and falsehood, of right and wrong; so that it will take thirty years to decide whether the field, left me by my ancestors for six generations, belong to me, or to a stranger three hundred miles off.

"In the trial of persons accused for crimes against the state, the method is much more short and commendable: the judge first sends to sound the disposition of those in power; after which he can easily hang or save the criminal, strictly preserving all the forms of law."

Here my master interposing said it was a pity that creatures endowed with such prodigious abilities of mind as these lawyers, by the description I gave of them must certainly be, were not rather encouraged to be instructors of others in wisdom and knowledge. In answer to which, I assured his honor that in all points out of their own trade, they were usually the most ignorant and stupid generation among us, the most despicable in common conversation, avowed enemies to all knowledge and learning; and equally disposed to pervert the general reason of mankind, in every other subject of discourse as in that of their own profession.

Chapter VI. *A continuation of the state of England, under Queen Anne. The character of a first minister in the courts of Europe.*

My master was yet wholly at a loss to understand what motives could incite this race of lawyers to perplex, disquiet, and weary themselves by engaging in a confederacy of injustice, merely for the sake of injuring their fellow animals; neither could he comprehend what I meant in saying they did it for hire. Whereupon I was at much pains to describe to him the use of money, the materials it was made of, and the value of the metals; that when a Yahoo had got a great store of his precious substance, he was able to purchase whatever he had a mind to; the finest clothing, the noblest houses, great tracts of land, the most costly meats and drinks; and have his choice of the most beautiful females. Therefore since money alone was able to perform all these feats, our Yahoos thought they could never have enough of it to spend or to save, as they found themselves inclined from their natural bent either to profusion or avarice. That the rich man enjoyed the fruit of the poor man's labor, and the latter were a thousand to one in proportion to the former. That the bulk of our people was forced to live miserably, by laboring every day for small wages to make a few live plentifully. I enlarged myself much on these and many other particulars to the same purpose, but his honor was still to seek,[7] for he went upon a supposition that all animals had a title to their share in the productions of the earth; and especially those who presided over the rest. Therefore he desired I would let him know what these costly meats were, and how any of us happened to want[25] them. Whereupon I enumerated as many sorts as came into my head, with the various methods of dressing them, which could not be done without sending vessels by sea to every part of the world, as well for liquors to drink, as for sauces, and innumerable other conveniencies. I assured him, that this whole globe of earth must be at least three times gone round, before one of our better female Yahoos could get her breakfast, or a cup to put it in. He said, "That must needs be a miserable country which cannot furnish food for its own inhabitants." But what he chiefly wondered at, was how such vast tracts of ground as I described, should be wholly without fresh water, and the people put to the necessity of sending over the sea for drink. I replied that England (the dear place of my nativity) was computed to produce three times the quantity of food, more than its inhabitants are able to consume, as well as liquors extracted from grain, or pressed out of the fruit of certain trees, which made excellent drink; and the same proportion in every other convenience of life. But, in order to feed the luxury and intemperance of the males, and the vanity of the females, we sent away the greatest part of our necessary things to other countries, from whence in return we brought the materials of diseases, folly, and vice, to spend among ourselves. Hence it follows of necessity, that vast numbers of our people are compelled to seek their livelihood by begging, robbing, stealing, cheating, pimping, forswearing, flattering, suborning,[26] forging, gaming, lying, fawning, hectoring, voting, scribbling, star gazing, poisoning, whoring, canting, libeling, freethinking, and the like occupations; every one of which terms, I was at much pains to make him understand.

That, wine was not imported among us from foreign countries, to supply the want of water or other drinks, but because it was a sort of liquid which made us merry, by putting us out of our senses; diverted all melancholy thoughts, begat wild extravagant imaginations in the brain, raised our hopes, and banished our

25. Lack.

26. "Subornation of perjury consists in tampering with persons who are to swear in judgment, by directing them how they are to dispose; and it is punished with the pains of perjury." *E.B.*

fears; suspended every office of reason for a time, and deprived us of the use of our limbs, until we fell into a profound sleep; although it must be confessed, that we always awaked sick and dispirited; and that the use of this liquor filled us with diseases, which made our lives uncomfortable and short.

But beside all this, the bulk of our people supported themselves by furnishing the necessities or conveniencies of life to the rich, and to each other. For instance, when I am at home and dressed as I ought to be, I carry on my body the workmanship of an hundred tradesmen; the building and furniture of my house employ as many more; and five times the number to adorn my wife.

I was going on to tell him of another sort of people, who get their livelihood by attending the sick; having upon some occasions informed his honor that many of my crew had died of diseases. But here it was with the utmost difficulty that I brought him to apprehend what I meant. He could easily conceive that a Houyhnhnm grew weak and heavy a few days before his death; or by some accident might hurt a limb. But that nature, who worketh all things to perfection, should suffer any pains to breed in our bodies, he thought impossible; and desired to know the reason of so unaccountable an evil. I told him, we fed on a thousand things which operated contrary to each other; that we eat when we were not hungry, and drank without the provocation of thirst; that we sat whole nights drinking strong liquors without eating a bit, which disposed us to sloth, inflamed our bodies, and precipitated or prevented digestion. That, prostitute female Yahoos acquired a certain malady, which bred rottenness in the bones of those who fell into their embraces; that this and many other diseases were propagated from father to son; so that great numbers come into the world with complicated maladies upon them; that it would be endless to give him a catalogue of all diseases incident to human bodies; for they could not be fewer than five or six hundred, spread over every limb, and joint; in short, every part, external and intestine, having diseases appropriated to each. To remedy which, there was a sort of people bred up among us, in the profession or pretense of curing the sick. And because I had some skill in the faculty, I would in gratitude to his honor let him know the whole mystery and method by which they proceed.

Their fundamental is that all diseases arise from repletion; from whence they conclude, that a great evacuation of the body is necessary, either through the natural passage, or upwards at the mouth. Their next business is, from herbs, minerals, gums, oils, shells, salts, juices, seaweed, excrements, barks of trees, serpents, toads, frogs, spiders, dead men's flesh and bones, birds, beasts and fishes, to form a composition for smell and taste the most abominable, nauseous, and detestable, that they can possibly contrive, which the stomach immediately rejects with loathing, and this they call a vomit. Or else from the same storehouse, with some other poisonous additions, they command us to take in at the orifice above or below (just as the physician then happens to be disposed) a medicine equally annoying and disgustful to the bowels; which relaxing the belly, drives down all before it; and this they call a purge, or a clyster. For nature (as the physicians allege) having intended the superior anterior orifice only for the intromission of solids and liquids, and the inferior posterior for ejection, these artists ingeniously considering that in all diseases nature is forced out of her seat; therefore to replace her in it, the body must be treated in a manner directly contrary, but interchanging the use of each orifice; forcing solids and liquids in at the anus, and making evacuations at the mouth.

But, besides real diseases, we are subject to many that are only imaginary, for which the physicians have invented imaginary cures; these have their several names, and so have the drugs that are proper for them; and with these our female Yahoos are always infested.

One great excellency in this tribe is their skill at prognostics, wherein they seldom fail; their predictions in real diseases, when they rise to any degree of malignity, generally portending death, which is always in their power, when recovery is not, and therefore, upon any unexpected signs of amendment, after they have pronounced their sentence rather than be accused as false prophets, they know how to approve[27] their sagacity to the world by a seasonable dose.

They are likewise of special use to husbands and wives, who are grown weary of their mates; to eldest sons, to great ministers of state, and often to princes.

I had formerly upon occasion discoursed with my master upon the nature of government in general, and particularly of our own excellent constitution, deservedly the wonder and envy of the whole world. But having here accidently mentioned a minister of state, he commanded me some time after to inform him what species of Yahoo I particularly meant by that appellation.

I told him that a first or chief minister of state, whom I intended to describe, was a creature wholly exempt from joy and grief, love and hatred, pity and anger; at least makes use of no other passions but a violent desire of wealth, power, and titles; that he applies his words to all uses, except to the indication of his mind; that he never tells a truth, but with an intent that you should take it for a lie; nor a lie, but with a design that you should take it for a truth; that those he speaks worst of behind their backs are in the surest way to preferment; and whenever he begins to praise you to others or to yourself, you are from that day forlorn. The worst mark you can receive is a promise, especially when it is confirmed

27. Prove.

with an oath; after which every wise man retires, and gives over all hopes.

There are three methods by which a man may rise to be chief minister: the first is by knowing how with prudence to dispose of a wife, a daughter, or a sister; the second, by betraying or undermining his predecessor; and the third is by a furious zeal in public assemblies against the corruptions of the court. But a wise prince would rather choose to employ those who practice the last of these methods; because such zealots prove always the most obsequious and subservient to the will and passions of their master. That, these ministers having all employments at their disposal, preserve themselves in power by bribing the majority of a senate or great council; and at last by an expedient called an Act of Indemnity (whereof I described the nature to him) they secure themselves from after reckonings, and retire from the public, laden with the spoils of the nation.

The palace of a chief minister is a seminary to breed up others in his own trade; the pages, lackies, and porter, by imitating their master, become ministers of state in their several districts, and learn to excel in the three principal ingredients, of insolence, lying, and bribery. Accordingly, they have a subaltern court paid to them by persons of the best rank; and sometimes by the force of dexterity and impudence, arrive through several gradations to be successors to their lord.

He is usually governed by a decayed wench, or favorite footman, who are the tunnels through which all graces are conveyed, and may properly be called, in the last resort, the governors of the kingdom.

One day, my master, having heard me mention the nobility of my country, was pleased to make me a compliment which I could not pretend to deserve: that, he was sure, I must have been born of some noble family, because I far exceeded in shape, color, and cleanliness, all the Yahoos of his nation, although I seemed to fail in strength, and agility, which must be imputed to my different way of living from those other brutes; and besides, I was not only endowed with the faculty of speech, but likewise with some rudiments of reason, to a degree, that with all his acquaintance I passed for a prodigy.

He made me observe, that among the Houyhnhnms, the white, the sorrel, and the iron grey were not so exactly shaped as the bay, the dapple grey, and the black; nor born with equal talents of mind, or a capacity to improve them; and therefore continued always in the condition of servants, without ever aspiring to match out of their own race, which in that country would be reckoned monstrous and unnatural.

I made his honor my most humble acknowledgments for the

good opinion he was pleased to conceive of me; but assured him at the same time, that my birth was of the lower sort, having been born of plain, honest parents, who were just able to give me a tolerable education; that, nobility among us was altogether a different thing from the idea he had of it; that, our young noblemen are bred from their childhood in idleness and luxury; that, as soon as years will permit, they consume their vigor, and contract odious diseases among lewd females; and when their fortunes are almost ruined, they marry some woman of mean birth, disagreeable person, and unsound constitution, merely for the sake of money, whom they hate and despise. That, the productions of such marriages are generally scrofulous, rickety or deformed children; by which means the family seldom continues above three generations, unless the wife take care to provide a healthy father among her neighbors, or domestics, in order to improve and continue the breed. That a weak diseased body, a meager countenance, and sallow complexion are the true marks of noble blood; and a healthy robust appearance is so disgraceful in a man of quality, that the world concludes his real father to have been a groom or a coachman. The imperfections of his mind run parallel with those of his body; being a composition of spleen, dullness, ignorance, caprice, sensuality, and pride.

Without the consent of this illustrious body, no law can be enacted, repealed, or altered, and these nobles have likewise the decision of all our possessions without appeal.

Chapter VII. *The Author's great love of his native country. His master's observations upon the constitution and administration of England, as described by the Author, with parallel cases and comparisons. His master's observations upon human nature.*

The reader may be disposed to wonder how I could prevail on myself to give so free a representation of my own species, among a race of mortals who were already too apt to conceive the vilest opinion of humankind, from that entire congruity betwixt me and their Yahoos. But I must freely confess that the many virtues of those excellent quadrupeds placed in opposite view to human corruptions had so far opened my eyes, and enlarged my understanding, that I began to view the actions and passions of man in a very different light; and to think the honor of my own kind not worth managing; which, besides, it was impossible for me to do before a person of so acute a judgment as my master, who daily convinced me of a thousand faults in myself, whereof I had not the least perception before, and which with us would never be numbered even among human infirmities. I had likewise learned from his example an utter detestation of all falsehood or disguise; and truth appeared so amiable to me, that I determined upon sacrificing everything to it.

Let me deal so candidly with the reader as to confess that there was yet a much stronger motive for the freedom I took in my representation of things. I had not been a year in this country, before I contracted such a love and veneration for the inhabitants, that I entered on a firm resolution never to return to humankind, but to pass the rest of my life among these admirable Houyhnhnms in the contemplation and practice of every virtue; where I could have no example or incitement to vice. But it was decreed by fortune, my perpetual enemy, that so great a felicity should not fall to my share. However, it is now some comfort to reflect that in what I said of my countrymen, I extenuated their faults as much as I durst before so strict an examiner; and upon every article, gave as favorable a turn as the matter would bear. For, indeed, who is there alive that will not be swayed by his bias and partiality to the place of his birth?

I have related the substance of several conversations I had with my master, during the greatest part of the time I had the honor to be in his service; but have indeed for brevity sake omitted much more than is here set down.

When I had answered all his questions, and his curiosity seemed to be fully satisfied; he sent for me one morning early, and commanding me to sit down at some distance (an honor which he had never before conferred upon me), he said he had been very seriously considering my whole story, as far as it related both to myself and my country; that, he looked upon us as a sort of animals to whose share, by what accident he could not conjecture, some small pittance of reason had fallen, whereof we made no other use than by its assistance to aggravate our natural corruptions, and to acquire new ones which nature had not given us. That we disarmed ourselves of the few abilities she had bestowed; had been very successful in multiplying our original wants, and seemed to spend our whole lives in vain endeavors to supply them by our own inventions. That, as to myself, it was manifest I had neither the strength or agility of a common Yahoo; that I walked infirmly on my hinder feet; had found out a contrivance to make my claws of no use or defense, and to remove the hair from my chin, which was intended as a shelter from the sun and the weather. Lastly, that I could neither run with speed, nor climb trees like my brethren (as he called them) the Yahoos in this country.

That our institutions of government and law were plainly owing to our gross defects in reason, and by consequence, in virtue; because reason alone is sufficient to govern a rational creature; which was therefore a character we had no pretense to challenge, even from the account I had given of my own people; although he manifestly perceived, that in order to favor them, I had concealed many particulars, and often *said the thing which was not.*

He was the more confirmed in this opinion, because he observed that I agreed in every feature of my body with other Yahoos, except where it was to my real disadvantage in point of strength, speed, and activity, the shortness of my claws, and some other particulars where nature had no part; so, from the representation I had given him of our lives, our manners, and our actions, he found as near a resemblance in the disposition of our minds. He said the Yahoos were known to hate one another more than they did any different species of animals; and the reason usually assigned was the odiousness of their own shapes, which all could see in the rest, but not in themselves. He had therefore begun to think it not unwise in us to cover our bodies, and by that invention, conceal many of our deformities from each other, which would else be hardly supportable. But he now found he had been mistaken; and that the dissentions of those brutes in his country were owing to the same cause with ours, as I had described them. For, if (said he) you throw among five Yahoos as much food as would be sufficient for fifty, they will, instead of eating peaceably, fall together by the ears, each single one impatient to have all to itself; and therefore a servant was usually employed to stand by while they were feeding abroad, and those kept at home were tied at a distance from each other. That, if a cow died of age or accident, before a Houyhnhnm could secure it for his own Yahoos, those in the neighborhood would come in herds to seize it, and then would ensue such a battle as I had described, with terrible wounds made by their claws on both sides, although they seldom were able to kill one another, for want of such convenient instruments of death as we had invented. At other times the like battles have been fought between the Yahoos of several neighborhoods without any visible cause; those of one district watching all opportunities to surprise the next before they are prepared. But if they find their project hath miscarried, they return home, and for want of enemies, engage in what I call a civil war among themselves.

That, in some fields of his country, there are certain shining stones of several colors, whereof the Yahoos are violently fond; and when part of these stones are fixed in the earth, as it sometimes happeneth, they will dig with their claws for whole days to get them out, and carry them away, and hide them by heaps in their kennels; but still looking round with great caution, for fear their comrades should find out their treasure. My master said he could never discover the reason of this unnatural appetite, or how these stones could be of any use to a Yahoo; but now he believed it might proceed from the same principle of avarice, which I had ascribed to mankind. That he had once, by way of experiment, privately removed a heap of these stones from the place where one of his Yahoos had buried it, whereupon, the sordid animal missing his treasure, by his loud lamenting brought the whole herd to the place, there miserably howled, then fell to biting and tearing the rest; began to pine away, would neither eat nor sleep, nor work, till he ordered a servant privately to convey the stones into the same hole, and hide them as before; which when his Yahoo had found, he presently recovered his spirits and good humor; but took care to remove them to a better hiding place; and hath ever since been a very serviceable brute.

My master farther assured me, which I also observed myself; that in the fields where these shining stones abound, the fiercest and most frequent battles are fought, occasioned by perpetual inroads of the neighboring Yahoos.

He said it was common when two Yahoos discovered such a stone in a field, and were contending which of them should be the proprietor, a third would take the advantage, and carry it away from them both; which my master would needs contend to have some resemblance with our suits at law; wherein I thought it for our credit not to undeceive him; since the decision he mentioned was much more equitable than many decrees among us; because the plaintiff and defendant there lost nothing beside the stone they contended for; whereas our courts of equity would never have dismissed the cause while either of them had anything left.

My master continuing his discourse said there was nothing that rendered the Yahoos more odious, than their undistinguished appetite to devour everything that came in their way, whether herbs, roots, berries, corrupted flesh of animals, or all mingled together; and it was peculiar in their temper, that they were fonder of what they could get by rapine or stealth at a greater distance, than much better food provided for them at home. If their prey held out, they would eat till they were ready to burst, after which nature had pointed out to them a certain root that gave them a general evacuation.

There was also another kind of root very juicy, but something rare and difficult to be found, which the Yahoos fought for with much eagerness, and would suck it with great delight; it produced the same effects that wine hath upon us. It would make them sometimes hug, and sometimes tear one another; they would howl and grin, and chatter, and reel, and tumble, and then fall asleep in the mud.

I did indeed observe that the Yahoos were the only animals in this country subject to any diseases; which however, were much fewer than horses have among us, and contracted not by any ill treatment they meet with, but by the nastiness and greediness of that sordid brute. Neither has their language any more than a general appellation for those maladies; which is borrowed from the name of the beast, and called *Hnea Yahoo*, or the Yahoo's Evil; and the cure prescribed is a mixture of their own dung and urine, forcibly put down the Yahoo's throat. This I have since often known to have been taken with success, and do here freely recommend it to my countrymen, for the public good, as an admirable specific against all diseases produced by repletion.

As to learning, government, arts, manufactures, and the like, my master confessed he could find little or no resemblance between the Yahoos of that country and those in ours. For he only meant to observe what parity there was in our natures. He had heard indeed some curious Houyhnhnms observe that in most herds there was a sort of ruling Yahoo (as among us there is generally some leading or principal stag in a park) who was always more deformed in body, and mischievous in disposition, than any of the rest. That this leader had usually a favorite as like himself as he could get, whose employment was to lick his master's feet and posteriors, and drive the female Yahoos to his kennel; for which he was now and then rewarded with a piece of ass's flesh. This favorite is hated by the whole herd; and therefore to protect himself, keeps always near the person of his leader. He usually continues in office till a worse can be found; but the very moment he is discarded, his successor, at the head of all the Yahoos in that district, young and old, male and female, come in a body, and discharge their excrements upon him from head to foot. But how far this might be applicable to our courts and favorites, and ministers of state, my master said I could best determine.

I durst make no return to this malicious insinuation, which debased human understanding below the sagacity of a common hound, who hath judgment enough to distinguish and follow the cry of the ablest dog in the pack, without being ever mistaken.

My master told me there were some qualities remarkable in the Yahoos, which he had not observed me to mention, or at least very slightly, in the accounts I had given him of humankind. He said, those animals, like other brutes, had their females in common; but in this they differed, that the she-Yahoo would admit the male while she was pregnant; and that the hes would quarrel and fight with the females as fiercely as with each other. Both which practices were such degrees of infamous brutality, that no other sensitive creature ever arrived at.

Another thing he wondered at in the Yahoos was their strange disposition to nastiness and dirt; whereas there appears to be a natural love of cleanliness in all other animals. As to the two former accusations, I was glad to let them pass without any reply, because I had not a word to offer upon them in defense of my species, which otherwise I certainly had done from my own inclinations. But I could have easily vindicated humankind from the imputation of singularity upon the last article, if there had been any swine in that country (as unluckily for me there were not) which although it may be a sweeter quadruped than a Yahoo, cannot I humbly conceive in justice pretend to more cleanliness; and so his honor himself must have owned, if he had seen their filthy way of feeding, and their custom of wallowing and sleeping in the mud.

My master likewise mentioned another quality, which his servants had discovered in several Yahoos, and to him was wholly unaccountable. He said, a fancy would sometimes take a Yahoo, to retire into a corner, to lie down and howl, and groan, and spurn away all that came near him, although he were young and fat, and wanted neither food nor water; nor did the servants imagine what could possibly ail him. And the only remedy they found was to set him to hard work, after which he would infallibly come to himself. To this I was silent out of partiality to my own kind; yet here I could plainly discover the true seeds of spleen,[28] which only seizeth on the lazy, the luxurious, and the rich; who, if they were forced to undergo the same regimen, I would undertake for the cure.

His Honor had farther observed, that a female Yahoo would often stand behind a bank or a bush, to gaze on the young males passing by, and then appear, and hide, using many antic gestures and grimaces; at which time it was observed, that she had a most offensive smell; and when any of the males advanced, would slowly retire, looking back, and with a counterfeit show of fear, run off into some convenient place where she knew the male would follow her.

At other times, if a female stranger came among them, three or four of her own sex would get about her, and stare and chatter, and grin, and smell her all over; and then turn off with gestures that seemed to express contempt and disdain.

Perhaps my master might refine a little in these speculations, which he had drawn from what he observed himself, or had been told by others; however, I could not reflect without some amazement, and much sorrow, that the rudiments of lewdness, coquetry, censure, and scandal, should have place by instinct in womankind.

I expected every moment that my master would accuse the Yahoos of those unnatural appetites in both sexes, so common among us. But nature it seems hath not been so expert a schoolmistress; and these politer pleasures are entirely the productions of art and reason, on our side of the globe.

CHAPTER VIII. *The Author relateth several particulars of the Yahoos. The great virtues of the Houyhnhnms. The education and exercises of their youth. Their general assembly.*

As I ought to have understood human nature much better than I supposed it possible for my master to do, so it was easy to apply

28. Hypochondria.

the character he gave of the Yahoos to myself and my countrymen; and I believed I could yet make farther discoveries from my own observation. I therefore often begged his honor to let me go among the herds of Yahoos in the neighborhood; to which he always very graciously consented, being perfectly convinced that the hatred I bore those brutes would never suffer me to be corrupted by them; and his honor ordered one of his servants, a strong sorrel nag, very honest and good-natured, to be my guard; without whose protection I durst not undertake such adventures. For I have already told the reader how much I was pestered by those odious animals upon my first arrival. I afterwards failed very narrowly three or four times of falling into their clutches, when I happened to stray at any distance without my hanger. And I have reason to believe, they had some imagination that I was of their own species, which I often assisted myself, by stripping up my sleeves, and shewing my naked arms and breast in their sight, when my protector was with me; at which times they would approach as near as they durst, and imitate my actions after the manner of monkeys, but ever with great signs of hatred; as a tame jackdaw with cap and stockings is always persecuted by the wild ones, when he happens to be got among them.

They are prodigiously nimble from their infancy; however, I once caught a young male of three years old, and endeavored by all marks of tenderness to make it quiet; but the little imp fell a squalling, scratching, and biting with such violence, that I was forced to let it go; and it was high time, for a whole troop of old ones came about us at the noise; but finding the cub was safe (for away it ran) and my sorrel nag being by, they durst not venture near us. I observed the young animal's flesh to smell very rank, and the stink was somewhat between a weasel and a fox, but much more disagreeable. I forgot another circumstance (and perhaps I might have the reader's pardon, if it were wholly omitted) that while I held the odious vermin in my hands, it voided its filthy excrements of a yellow liquid substance, all over my clothes; but by good fortune there was a small brook hard by, where I washed myself as clean as I could; although I durst not come into my master's presence until I were sufficiently aired.

By what I could discover, the Yahoos appear to be the most unteachable of all animals, their capacities never reaching higher than to draw or carry burdens. Yet I am of opinion, this defect ariseth chiefly from a perverse, restive disposition. For they are cunning, malicious, treacherous and revengeful. They are strong and hardy, but of a cowardly spirit, and by consequence insolent, abject, and cruel. It is observed that the red-haired of both sexes are more libidinous and mischievous than the rest, whom yet they much exceed in strength and activity.

The Houyhnhnms keep the Yahoos for present use in huts not far from the house; but the rest are sent abroad to certain fields, where they dig up roots, eat several kinds of herbs, and search about for carrion, or sometimes catch weasels and *luhimuhs* (a sort of wild rat) which they greedily devour. Nature hath taught them to dig deep holes with their nails on the side of a rising ground, wherein they lie by themselves; only the kennels of the females are larger, sufficient to hold two or three cubs.

They swim from their infancy like frogs, and are able to continue long under water, where they often take fish, which the females carry home to their young. And upon this occasion, I hope the reader will pardon my relating an odd adventure.

Being one day abroad with my protector the sorrel nag, and the weather exceeding hot, I entreated him to let me bathe in a river that was near. He consented, and I immediately stripped myself stark naked, and went down softly into the stream. It happened that a young female Yahoo standing behind a bank, saw the whole proceeding; and inflamed by desire, as the nag and I conjectured, came running with all speed, and leaped into the water within five yards of the place where I bathed. I was never in my life so terribly frighted; the nag was grazing at some distance, not suspecting any harm; she embraced me after a most fulsome manner; I roared as loud as I could, and the nag came galloping towards me, whereupon she quitted her grasp, with the utmost reluctancy, and leaped upon the opposite bank, where she stood gazing and howling all the time I was putting on my clothes.

This was matter of diversion to my master and his family, as well as of mortification to myself. For now I could no longer deny that I was a real Yahoo, in every limb and feature, since the females had a natural propensity to me as one of their own species; neither was the hair of this brute of a red color (which might have been some excuse for an appetite a little irregular) but black as a sloe, and her countenance did not make an appearance altogether so hideous as the rest of the kind; for I think, she could not be above eleven years old.

Having already lived three years in this country, the reader I suppose will expect that I should, like other travelers, give him some account of the manners and customs of its inhabitants, which it was indeed my principal study to learn.

As these noble Houyhnhnms are endowed by Nature with a general disposition to all virtues, and have no conceptions or ideas of what is evil in a rational creature; so their grand maxim is to cultivate reason, and to be wholly governed by it. Neither is reason among them a point problematical as with us, where men can argue with plausibility on both sides of a question; but strikes you with immediate conviction; as it must needs do where it is not mingled, obscured, or discolored by passion and interest. I remember it was with extreme difficulty that I could bring my master to understand the meaning of the word "opinion," or how a point could be disputable; because reason taught us to affirm or deny only where we are certain; and beyond our knowledge we cannot do either. So that controversies, wranglings, disputes, and positiveness in false or dubious propositions are evils unknown among the Houyhnhnms. In the like manner when I used to explain to him our several systems of natural philosophy, he would laugh that a creature pretending to reason should value itself upon the knowledge of other people's conjectures, and in things, where that knowledge, if it were certain, could be of no use. Wherein he agreed entirely with the sentiments of Socrates, as Plato delivers them, which I mention as the highest honor I can do that prince of philosophers. I have often since reflected what destruction such a doctrine would make in the libraries of Europe; and how many paths to fame would be then shut up in the learned world.

Friendship and benevolence are the two principal virtues among the Houyhnhnms; and these not confined to particular objects, but universal to the whole race. For a stranger from the remotest part is equally treated with the nearest neighbor, and wherever he goes, looks upon himself as at home. They preserve decency and civility in the highest degrees, but are altogether ignorant of ceremony. They have no fondness[29] for their colts or foals; but the care they take in educating them proceedeth entirely from the dictates of reason. And I observed my master to show the same affection to his neighbor's issue that he had for his own. They will have it that nature teaches them to love the whole species, and it is reason only that maketh a distinction of persons, where there is a superior degree of virtue.

When the matron Houyhnhnms have produced one of each sex, they no longer accompany with their consorts, except they lose one of their issue by some casualty, which very seldom happens; but in such a case they meet again; or when the like accident befalls a person whose wife is past bearing, some other couple bestows on him one of their own colts, and then go together a second time, until the mother be pregnant. This caution is necessary to prevent the country from being overburdened with numbers. But the race of inferior Houyhnhnms bred up to be servants is not so strictly limited upon this article; these are allowed to produce three of each sex, to be domestics in the noble families.

In their marriages they are exactly careful to choose such colors as will not make any disagreeable mixture in the breed. Strength is chiefly valued in the male, and comeliness in the female; not upon the account of love, but to preserve the race from degenerating; for, where a female happens to excel in strength, a consort is

29. Excessive doting.

chosen with regard to comeliness. Courtship, love, presents, jointures, settlements, have no place in their thoughts, or terms whereby to express them in their language. The young couple meet and are joined, merely because it is the determination of their parents and friends; it is what they see done every day; and they look upon it as one of the necessary actions in a reasonable being. But the violation of marriage, or any other unchastity, was never heard of; and the married pair pass their lives with the same friendship and mutual benevolence that they bear to all others of the same species who come in their way, without jealousy, fondness, quarreling, or discontent.

In educating the youth of both sexes, their method is admirable, and highly deserveth our imitation. These are not suffered to taste a grain of oats, except upon certain days, till eighteen years old; nor milk, but very rarely; and in summer they graze two hours in the morning, and as many in the evening, which their parents likewise observe; but the servants are not allowed above half that time; and a great part of the grass is brought home, which they eat at the most convenient hours, when they can be best spared from work.

Temperance, industry, exercise, and cleanliness are the lessons equally enjoined to the young ones of both sexes; and my master thought it monstrous in us to give the females a different kind of education from the males, except in some articles of domestic management; whereby, as he truly observed, one half of our natives were good for nothing but bringing children into the world; and to trust the care of their children to such useless animals, he said was yet a greater instance of brutality.

But the Houyhnhnms train up their youth to strength, speed, and hardiness, by exercising them in running races up and down steep hills, or over hard stony grounds; and when they are all in a sweat, they are ordered to leap over head and ears into a pond or a river. Four times a year the youth of certain districts meet to show their proficiency in running, and leaping, and other feats of strength or agility; where the victor is rewarded with a song made in his or her praise. On this festival the servants drive a herd of Yahoos into the field, laden with hay, and oats, and milk for a repast to the Houyhnhnms; after which these brutes are immediately driven back again, for fear of being noisome to the assembly.

Every fourth year, at the vernal equinox,[30] there is a representative council of the whole nation, which meets in a plain about twenty miles from our house, and continueth about five or six days. Here they inquire into the state and condition of the several districts; whether they abound or be deficient in hay or oats, or cows or Yahoos? And wherever there is any want (which is but seldom) it is immediately supplied by unanimous consent and contribution.

30. About March 21, when the sun's center crosses the celestial equator southward, and night and day are of equal length over the entire earth.

Here likewise the regulation of children is settled: as for instance, if a Houyhnhnm hath two males, he changeth one of them with another who hath two females, and when a child hath been lost by any casualty, where the mother is past breeding, it is determined what family in the district shall breed another to supply the loss.

CHAPTER IX. *A grand debate at the general assembly of the Houyhnhnms, and how it was determined. The learning of the Houyhnhnms. Their buildings. Their manner of burials. The defectiveness of their language.*

One of these grand assemblies was held in my time, about three months before my departure, whither my master went as the representative of our district. In this council was resumed their old debate, and indeed, the only debate that ever happened in their country; whereof my master after his return gave me a very particular account.

The question to be debated was whether the Yahoos should be exterminated from the face of the earth. One of the members for the affirmative offered several arguments of great strength and weight, alleging that, as the Yahoos were the most filthy, noisome, and deformed animal which nature ever produced, so they were the most restive and indocible, mischievous, and malicious; they would privately suck the teats of the Houyhnhnms' cows; kill and devour their cats, trample down their oats and grass, if they were not continually watched; and commit a thousand other extravagancies. He took notice of a general tradition, that Yahoos had not been always in their country, but that many ages ago, two of these brutes appeared together upon a mountain; whether produced by the heat of the sun upon corrupted mud and slime, or from the ooze and froth of the sea, was never known. That these Yahoos engendered, and their brood in a short time grew so numerous as to overrun and infest the whole nation. That the Houyhnhnms to get rid of this evil, made a general hunting, and at last enclosed the whole herd; and destroying the older, every Houyhnhnm kept two young ones in a kennel, and brought them to such a degree of tameness as an animal so savage by nature can be capable of acquiring, using them for draft and carriage. That there seemed to be much truth in this tradition, and that those creatures could not be *ylnhniamshy* (or aborigines of the land) because of the violent hatred the Houyhnhnms as well as all other animals bore them; which although their evil disposition sufficiently deserved, could never have arrived at so high a degree, if they had been aborigines, or else they would have long since been rooted out. That the inhabitants taking a fancy to use the service of the Yahoos, had very imprudently neglected to cultivate the breed of asses, which were a comely animal, easily kept, more tame and orderly, without any offensive smell, strong enough for labor, although they yield to the other in agility of body; and if their braying be no agreeable sound, it is far preferable to the horrible howlings of the Yahoos.

Several others declared their sentiments to the same purpose, when my master proposed an expedient to the assembly, whereof he had indeed borrowed the hint from me. He approved of the tradition, mentioned by the honorable member, who spoke before; and affirmed, that the two Yahoos said to be first seen among them, had been driven thither over the sea; that coming to land, and being forsaken by their companions, they retired to the mountains, and degenerating by degrees, became in process of time much more savage than those of their own species in the country from whence these two originals came. The reason of his assertion was that he had now in his possession a certain wonderful Yahoo (meaning myself) which most of them had heard of, and many of them had seen. He then related to them how he first found me; that my body was all covered with an artificial composure of the skins and hairs of other animals; that I spoke in a language of my own, and had thoroughly learned theirs; that I had related to him the accidents which brought me thither; that when he saw me without my covering, I was an exact Yahoo in every part, only of a whiter color, less hairy and with shorter claws. He added how I had endeavored to persuade him that in my own and other countries the Yahoos acted as the governing, rational animal, and held the Houyhnhnms in servitude; that he observed in me all the qualities of a Yahoo, only a little more civilized by some tincture of reason, which however was in a degree as far inferior to the Houyhnhnm race as the Yahoos of their country were to me; that among other things, I mentioned a custom we had of castrating Houyhnhnms when they were young, in order to render them tame; that the operation was easy and safe; that it was no shame to learn wisdom from brutes, as industry is taught by the ant, and building by the swallow (for so I translate the world *lyhannh*, although it be a much larger fowl). That this invention might be practiced upon the younger Yahoos here, which, besides rendering them tractable and fitter for use, would in an age put an end to the whole species without destroying life. That in the meantime the Houyhnhnms should be exhorted to cultivate the breed of asses, which, as they are in all respects more valuable brutes, so they have this advantage, to be fit for service at five years old, which the others are not till twelve.

This was all my master thought fit to tell me at that time, of what passed in the grand council. But he was pleased to conceal one particular, which related personally to myself, whereof I soon felt the unhappy effect, as the reader will know in its proper place, and from whence I date all the succeeding misfortunes of my life.

The Houyhnhnms have no letters, and consequently, their knowledge is all traditional. But there happening few events of any moment among a people so well united, naturally disposed to every virtue, wholly governed by reason, and cut off from all commerce with other nations, the historical part is easily preserved without burdening their memories. I have already observed that they are subject to no diseases, and therefore can have no need of physicians. However, they have excellent medicines composed of herbs, to cure accidental bruises and cuts in the pastern or frog of the foot by sharp stones, as well as other maims and hurts in the several parts of the body.

They calculate the year by the revolution of the sun and the moon, but use no subdivisions into weeks. They are well enough acquainted with the motions of those two luminaries, and understand the nature of eclipses; and this is the utmost progress of their astronomy.

In poetry they must be allowed to excell all other mortals; wherein the justness of their similes, and the minuteness, as well as exactness of their descriptions, are indeed inimitable. Their verses abound very much in both of these, and usually contain either some exalted notions of friendship and benevolence, or the praises of those who were victors in races and other bodily exercises. Their buildings, although very rude and simple, are not inconvenient, but well contrived to defend them from all injuries of cold and heat. They have a kind of tree, which at forty years old loosens in the root, and falls with the first storm; it grows very straight, and being pointed like stakes with a sharp stone (for the Houyhnhnms know not the use of iron), they stick them erect in the ground about ten inches asunder, and then weave in oat straw, or sometimes wattles, betwixt them. The roof is made after the same manner, and so are the doors.

The Houyhnhnms use the hollow part between the pastern and the hoof of their forefeet as we do our hands, and this with greater dexterity than I could at first imagine. I have seen a white mare of our family thread a needle (which I lent her on purpose) with that joint. They milk their cows, reap their oats, and do all the work which requires hands in the same manner. They have a kind of hard flints, which by grinding against other stones they form into instruments that serve instead of wedges, axes, and hammers. With tools made of these flints, they likewise cut their hay, and reap their oats, which there groweth naturally in several fields; the Yahoos draw home the sheaves in carriages, and the servants tread them in certain covered huts, to get out the grain, which is kept in stores. They make a rude kind of earthen and wooden vessels, and bake the former in the sun.

If they can avoid casualties, they die only of old age, and are buried in the obscurest places that can be found, their friends and relations expressing neither joy nor grief at their departure; nor does the dying person discover the least regret that he is leaving the world, any more than if he were upon returning home from a visit to one of his neighbors; I remember my master having once made an appointment with a friend and his family to come to his house upon some affair of importance; on the day fixed, the mistress and her two children came very late; she made two excuses, first for her husband, who, as she said, happened that very morning to *lhnuwnh*. The word is strongly expressive in their language, but not easily rendered into English; it signifies, *to retire to his first Mother*. Her excuse for not coming sooner was that her husband dying late in the morning, she was a good while consulting her servants about a convenient place where his body should be laid; and I observed she behaved herself at our house, as cheerfully as the rest; she died about three months after.

They live generally to seventy or seventy-five years, very seldom to fourscore; some weeks before their death they feel a gradual decay, but without pain. During this time they are much visited by their friends, because they cannot go abroad with their usual ease and satisfaction. However, about ten days before their death, which they seldom fail in computing, they return the visits that have been made by those who are nearest in the neighborhood, being carried in a convenient sledge drawn by Yahoos; which vehicle they use, not only upon this occasion, but when they grow old, upon long journeys, or when they are lamed by any accident. And therefore when the dying Houyhnhnms return those visits, they take a solemn leave of their friends, as if they were going to some remote part of the country, where they designed to pass the rest of their lives.

I know not whether it may be worth observing, that the Houyhnhnms have no word in their language to express anything that is evil, except what they borrow from the deformities or ill qualities of the Yahoos. Thus they denote the folly of a servant, an omission of a child, a stone that cuts their feet, a continuance of foul or unseasonable weather, and the like, by adding to each the epithet of Yahoo. For instance, *hhnm Yahoo, whnaholm Yahoo, ynlhmndwihlma Yahoo*, and an ill-contrived house, *ynholmhnmrohlnw Yahoo*.

I could with great pleasure enlarge farther upon the manners and virtues of this excellent people; but intending in a short time to publish a volume by itself expressly upon that subject, I refer the reader thither. And in the meantime, proceed to relate my own sad catastrophe.

CHAPTER X. *The Author's economy, and happy life among the Houyhnhnms. His great improvement in virtue, by conversing with them. Their conversations. The Author hath notice given him by his master that he must depart from the country. He falls into a swoon for grief, but submits. He contrives and finishes a canoe, by the help of a fellow servant, and puts to sea at a venture.*

I had settled my little economy to my own heart's content. My master had ordered a room to be made for me after their manner, about six yards from the house; the sides and floors of which I plastered with clay, and covered with rush mats of my own contriving; I had beaten hemp, which there grows wild, and made of it a sort of ticking; this I filled with the feathers of several birds I had taken with springes made of Yahoos' hairs, and were excellent food. I had worked two chairs with my knife, the sorrel nag helping me in the grosser and more laborious part. When my clothes were worn to rags, I made myself others with the skins of rabbits, and of a certain beautiful animal about the same size, called *nnuhnoh*, the skin of which is covered with a fine down. Of these I likewise made very tolerable stockings. I soled my shoes with wood which I cut from a tree, and fitted to the upper leather, and when this was worn out, I supplied it with the skins of Yahoos, dried in the sun. I often got honey out of hollow trees, which I mingled with water, or eat it with my bread. No man could more verify the truth of these two maxims, that *Nature is very easily satisfied*; and, that *Necessity is the mother of invention*. I enjoyed perfect health of body, and tranquility of mind; I did not feel the treachery or inconstancy of a friend, nor the inquiries of a secret or open enemy. I had no occasion of bribing, flattering, or pimping to procure the favor of any great man, or of his minion. I wanted no fence against fraud or oppression; here was neither physician to destroy my body, nor lawyer to ruin my fortune; no informer to watch my words and actions, or forge accusations against me for hire; here were no gibers, censurers, backbiters, pickpockets, highwaymen, housebreakers, attorneys, bawds, buffoons, gamesters, politicians, wits, splenetics, tedious talkers, controvertists, ravishers, murderers, robbers, virtuosos; no leaders or followers of party and faction; no encouragers to vice, by seducement or examples; no dungeons, axes, gibbets, whipping posts, or pillories; no cheating shopkeepers or mechanics; no pride, vanity or affectation; no fops, bullies, drunkards, strolling whores, or poxes; no ranting, lewd, expensive wives; no stupid, proud pedants; no importunate, overbearing, quarrelsome, noisy, roaring, empty, conceited, swearing companions; no scoundrels raised from the dust upon the merit of their vices; or nobility thrown into it on account of their virtues; no lords, fiddlers, judges, or dancing masters.

I had the favor of being admitted to several Houyhnhnms, who came to visit or dine with my master; where his honor graciously suffered me to wait in the room, and listen to their discourse. Both he and his company would often descend to ask me questions, and receive my answers. I had also sometimes the honor of attending my master in his visits to others. I never presumed to speak, except in answer to a question; and then I did it with inward regret, because it was a loss of so much time for improving myself; but I was infinitely delighted with the station of an humble auditor in such conversations, where nothing passed but what was useful, expressed in the fewest and most significant words; where (as I have already said) the greatest decency was observed, without the least degree of ceremony; where no person spoke without being pleased himself, and pleasing his companions; where there was no interruption, tediousness, heat, or difference of sentiments. They have a notion, that when people are met together, a short silence doth much improve conversation; this I found to be true; for during those little intermissions of talk, new ideas would arise in their minds, which very much enlivened the discourse. Their subjects are generally on friendship and benevolence; on order and economy; sometimes upon the visible operations of nature, or ancient traditions; upon the bounds and limits of virtue; upon the unerring rules of reason; or upon some determinations, to be taken at the next great assembly; and often upon the various excellencies of poetry. I may add, without vanity, that my presence often gave them sufficient matter for discourse, because it afforded my master an occasion of letting his friends into the history of me and my country, upon which they were all pleased to discant in a manner not very advantageous to human kind; and for that reason I shall not repeat what they said; only I may be allowed to observe that his honor, to my great admiration, appeared to understand the nature of Yahoos much better than myself. He went through all our vices and follies, and discovered many which I had never mentioned to him; by only supposing what qualities a Yahoo of their country, with a small proportion of reason, might be capable of exerting; and concluded, with too much probability, how vile as well as miserable such a creature must be.

I freely confess, that all the little knowledge I have of any value was acquired by the lectures I received from my master, and from hearing the discourses of him and his friends; to which I should be prouder to listen, than to dictate to the greatest and wisest assembly in Europe. I admired the strength, comeliness, and speed of the inhabitants; and such a constellation of virtues in such amiable persons produced in me the highest veneration. At first, indeed, I did not feel that natural awe which the Yahoos and all other animals bear towards them; but it grew upon me by degrees, much sooner than I imagined, and was mingled with a respectful love and gratitude, that they would condescend to distinguish me from the rest of my species.

When I thought of my family, my friends, my countrymen, or human race in general, I considered them as they really were, Yahoos in shape and disposition, perhaps a little more civilized, and qualified with the gift of speech; but making no other use of reason than to improve and multiply those vices, whereof their brethren in this country had only the share that nature allotted them. When I happened to behold the reflection of my own form in a lake or fountain, I turned away my face in horror and detestation of myself, and could better endure the sight of a common Yahoo than of my own person. By conversing with the Houyhnhnms, and looking upon them with delight, I fell to imitate their gait and gesture, which is now grown into a habit; and my friends often tell me in a blunt way, that I trot like a horse; which, however, I take for a great compliment; neither shall I disown, that in speaking I am apt to fall into the voice and manner of the Houyhnhnms, and hear myself ridiculed on that account without the least mortification.

In the midst of this happiness, when I looked upon myself to be fully settled for life, my master sent for me one morning a little earlier than his usual hour. I observed by his countenance that he was in some perplexity, and at a loss how to begin what he had to speak. After a short silence, he told me, he did not know how I would take what he was going to say; that, in the last general assembly, when the affair of the Yahoos was entered upon, the representatives had taken offense at his keeping a Yahoo (meaning myself) in his family more like a Houyhnhnm than a brute animal. That he was known frequently to converse with me, as if he could receive some advantage of pleasure in my company; that such a practice was not agreeable to reason or nature, or a thing ever heard of before among them. The assembly did therefore exhort him, either to employ me like the rest of my species, or command me to swim back to the place from whence I came. That the first of these expedients was utterly rejected by all the Houyhnhnms who had ever seen me at his house or their own; for, they alleged, that because I had some rudiments of reason, added to the natural pravity of those animals, it was to be feared, I might be able to seduce them into the woody and mountainous parts of the country, and bring them in troops by night to destroy the Houyhnhnms' cattle, as being naturally of the ravenous kind, and averse from labor.

My master added that he was daily pressed by the Houyhnhnms of the neighborhood to have the assembly's exhortation executed, which he could not put off much longer. He doubted it would be impossible for me to swim to another country; and therefore wished I would contrive some sort of vehicle resembling those I had described to him, that might carry me on the sea; in which work I should have the assistance of his own servants, as well as those of his neighbors. He concluded that for his own part he could have been content to keep me in his service as long as I lived; because he found I had cured myself of some bad habits and dispositions, by endeavoring, as far as my inferior nature was capable, to imitate the Houyhnhnms.

I should here observe to the reader, that a decree of the general assembly in this country is expressed by the word *hnhloayn*, which signifies an exhortation, as near as I can render it; for they have no conception how a rational creature can be compelled, but only advised, or exhorted; because no person can disobey reason without giving up his claim to be a rational creature.

I was struck with the utmost grief and despair at my master's discourse; and being unable to support the agonies I was under, I fell into a swoon at his feet; when I came to myself, he told me that he concluded I had been dead (for these people are subject to no such imbecilities of nature). I answered, in a faint voice, that death would have been too great an happiness; that although I could not blame the assembly's exhortation, or the urgency of his friends; yet in my weak and corrupt judgment, I thought it might consist with reason to have been less rigorous. That I could not swim a league, and probably the nearest land to theirs might be distant above an hundred; that many materials, necessary for making a small vessel to carry me off, were wholly wanting in this country, which, however, I would attempt in obedience and gratitude to his honor, although I concluded the thing to be impossible, and therefore looked on myself as already devoted[31] to destruction. That the certain prospect of an unnatural death was the least of my evils; for, supposing I should escape with life by some strange adventure, how could I think with temper[32] of passing my days among Yahoos, and relapsing into my old corruptions, for want of examples to lead and keep me within the paths of virtue. That I knew too well upon what solid reasons all the determinations of the wise Houyhnhnms were founded, not to be shaken by arguments of mine, a miserable Yahoo; and therefore after presenting him with my humble thanks for the offer of his servants' assistance in making a vessel, and desiring a reasonable time for so difficult a work, I told him I would endeavor to preserve a wretched being; and, if ever I returned to England, was not without hopes of being useful to my own species by celebrating the praises of the renowned Houyhnhnms, and proposing their virtues to the imitation of mankind.

My master in a few words made me a very gracious reply, allowed me the space of two months to finish my boat, and ordered the sorrel nag, my fellow servant (for so at this distance I may presume to call him), to follow my instructions, because I told my master that his help would be sufficient, and I knew he had a tenderness for me.

In his company my first business was to go to that part of the coast where my rebellious crew had ordered me to be set on shore. I got upon a height, and looking on every side into the sea, fancied I saw a small island towards the northeast; I took out my pocket glass, and could then clearly distinguish it about five leagues off, as I computed; but it appeared to the sorrel nag to be only a blue cloud; for, as he had no conception of any country besides his own, so he

31. Doomed.

32. Equanimity.

could not be as expert in distinguishing remote objects at sea, as we who so much converse in that element.

After I had discovered this island, I considered no farther; but resolved, it should, if possible, be the first place of my banishment, leaving the consequence to fortune.

I returned home, and consulting with the sorrel nag, we went into a copse at some distance, where I with my knife, and he with a sharp flint fastened very artificially,[33] after their manner, to a wooden handle, cut down several oak wattles about the thickness of a walking staff, and some larger pieces. But I shall not trouble the reader with a particular description of my own mechanics; let it suffice to say, that in six weeks time, with the help of the sorrel nag, who performed the parts that required most labor, I finished a sort of Indian canoe; but much larger, covering it with the skins of Yahoos, well stitched together, with hempen threads of my own making. My sail was likewise composed of the skins of the same animal; but I made use of the youngest I could get, the older being too tough and thick; and I likewise provided myself with four paddles. I laid in a stock of boiled flesh, of rabbits and fowls; and took with me two vessels, one filled with milk, and the other with water.

I tried my canoe in a large pond near my master's house, and then corrected in it what was amiss, stopping all the chinks with Yahoo's tallow, till I found it staunch, and able to bear me and my freight. And when it was as complete as I could possibly make it, I had it drawn on a carriage very gently by Yahoos, to the seaside, under the conduct of the sorrel nag and another servant.

When all was ready, and the day came for my departure, I took leave of my master and lady, and the whole family, my eyes flowing with tears and my heart quite sunk with grief. But his honor, out of curiosity, and perhaps (if I may speak it without vanity) partly out of kindness, was determined to see me in my canoe; and got several of his neighboring friends to accompany him. I was forced to wait above an hour for the tide, and then observing the wind very fortunately bearing towards the island to which I intended to steer my course, I took a second leave of my master; but as I was going to prostrate myself to kiss his hoof, he did me the honor to raise it gently to my mouth. I am not ignorant how much I have been censured for mentioning this last particular. Detractors are pleased to think it improbable that so illustrious a person should descend to give so great a mark of distinction to a creature so inferior as I. Neither have I forgot how apt some travelers are to boast of extraordinary favors they have received. But, if these censurers were better acquainted with the noble and courteous disposition of the Houyhnhnms, they would soon change their opinion. I paid my respects to the rest of the Houyhnhnms in his honor's company; then getting into my canoe, I pushed off from shore.

33. Adroitly.

CHAPTER XI. *The Author's dangerous voyage. He arrives at New Holland, hoping to settle there. Is wounded with an arrow by one of the natives. Is seized and carried by force into a Portuguese ship. The great civilities of the Captain. The Author arrives at England.*

I began this desperate voyage on February 15, 1714/5,[34] at 9 o'clock in the morning. The wind was very favorable; however, I made use at first only of my paddles; but considering I should soon be weary, and that the wind might probably chop about, I ventured to set up my little sail; and thus, with the help of the tide, I went at the rate of a league and a half an hour, as near as I could guess. My master and his friends continued on the shore, till I was almost out of sight; and I often heard the sorrel nag (who always loved me) crying out, "*Hnuy illa nyha maiah Yahoo,*" ("Take care of thyself, gentle Yahoo").

My design was, if possible, to discover some small island uninhabited, yet sufficient by my labor to furnish me with necessaries of life, which I would have thought a greater happiness than to be first minister in the politest court of Europe, so horrible was the idea I conceived of returning to live in the society and under the government of Yahoos. For in such a solitude as I desired, I could at least enjoy my own thoughts, and reflect with delight on the virtues of those inimitable Houyhnhnms, without any opportunity of degenerating into the vices and corruptions of my own species.

The reader may remember what I related when my crew conspired against me, and confined me to my cabin, how I continued there several weeks, without knowing what course we took; and when I was put ashore in the longboat, how the sailors told me with oaths, whether true or false, that they knew not in what part of the world we were. However, I did then believe us to be about 10 degrees southward of the Cape of Good Hope, or about 45 degrees southern latitude, as I gathered from some general words I overheard among them, being I supposed to the southeast in their intended voyage to Madagascar. And although this were but little better than conjecture, yet I resolved to steer my course eastward, hoping to reach the southwest coast of New Holland, and perhaps some such island as I desired, lying westward of it. The wind was full west, and by six in the evening I computed I had gone eastward at least eighteen leagues; when I spied a very small island about half a league off, which I soon reached. It was nothing but a rock with one creek,[35] naturally arched by the force of tempests. Here I put in my canoe, and climbing a part of the rock, I could plainly discover land to the east, extending from south to north. I lay all night in my canoe; and repeating my voyage early in the morning, I arrived in seven hours to the southeast point of New Holland.[36] This confirmed me in the opinion I have long entertained, that the maps and

34. I.e., 1714. The year began on March 25th.

35. A bay.

36. Present-day Union of South Africa.

charts place this country at least three degrees more to the east than it really is; which thought I communicated many years ago to my worthy friend Mr. Herman Moll,[37] and gave him my reasons for it, although he hath rather chosen to follow other authors.

I saw no inhabitants in the place where I landed; and being unarmed, I was afraid of venturing far into the country. I found some shellfish on the shore, and eat them raw, not daring to kindle a fire, for fear of being discovered by the natives. I continued three days feeding on oysters and limpets, to save my own provisions; and I fortunately found a brook of excellent water, which gave me great relief.

On the fourth day, venturing out early a little too far, I saw twenty or thirty natives upon a height, not above five hundred yards from me. They were stark naked, men, women, and children round a fire, as I could discover by the smoke. One of them spied me, and gave notice to the rest; five of them advanced towards me, leaving the women and children at the fire. I made what haste I could to the shore, and getting into my canoe, shoved off; the savages observing me retreat, ran after me; and before I could get far enough into the sea, discharged an arrow, which wounded me deeply on the inside of my left knee. (I shall carry the mark to my grave.) I apprehended the arrow might be poisoned; and paddling out of the reach of their darts (being a calm day) I made a shift to suck the wound, and dress it as well as I could.

I was at a loss what to do, for I durst not return to the same landing place, but stood to the north, and was forced to paddle; for the wind, although very gentle, was against me, blowing northwest. As I was looking about for a secure landing place, I saw a sail to the north northeast, which appearing every minute more visible, I was in some doubt whether I should wait for them or no; but at last my detestation of the Yahoo race prevailed; and turning my canoe, I sailed and paddled together to the south, and got into the same creek from whence I set out in the morning, choosing rather to trust myself among these barbarians than live with European Yahoos. I drew up my canoe as close as I could to the shore, and hid myself behind a stone by the little brook, which, as I have already said, was excellent water.

The ship came within half a league of this creek, and sent out her longboat with vessels to take in fresh water (for the place it seems was very well known), but I did not observe it until the boat was almost on shore; and it was too late to seek another hiding place. The seamen at their landing observed my canoe, and rummaging it all over, easily conjectured that the owner could not be far off. Four of them well armed searched every cranny and lurking hole, till at last they found me flat on my face behind the stone. They gazed a while in admiration at my strange uncouth dress;

37. A famous contemporary map maker.

my coat made of skins, my wooden-soled shoes, and my furred stockings; from whence, however, they concluded I was not a native of the place, who all go naked. One of the seamen in Portuguese bid me rise, and asked who I was. I understood that language very well, and getting upon my feet, said I was a poor Yahoo, banished from the Houyhnhnms, and desired they would please to let me depart. They admired to hear me answer them in their own tongue, and saw by my complexion I must be an European; but were at a loss to know what I meant by Yahoos and Houyhnhnms, and at the same time fell a laughing at my strange tone in speaking, which resembled the neighing of a horse. I trembled all the while betwixt fear and hatred; I again desired leave to depart, and was gently moving to my canoe; but they laid hold on me, desiring to know what country I was of? whence I came? with many other questions. I told them I was born in England, from whence I came about five years ago, and then their country and ours was at peace. I therefore hoped they would not treat me as an enemy, since I meant them no harm, but was a poor Yahoo, seeking some desolate place where to pass the remainder of his unfortunate life.

When they began to talk, I thought I never heard or saw any thing so unnatural; for it appeared to me as monstrous as if a dog or a cow should speak in England, or a Yahoo in Houyhnhnmland. The honest Portuguese were equally amazed at my strange dress, and the odd manner of delivering my words, which however they understood very well. They spoke to me with great humanity, and said they were sure their Captain would carry me *gratis* to Lisbon, from whence I might return to my own country; that two of the seamen would go back to the ship, to inform the Captain of what they had seen, and receive his orders; in the meantime, unless I would give my solemn oath not to fly, they would secure me by force. I thought it best to comply with their proposal. They were very curious to know my story, but I gave them very little satisfaction; and they all conjectured, that my misfortunes had impaired my reason. In two hours the boat, which went laden with vessels of water, returned with the Captain's commands to fetch me on board. I fell on my knees to preserve my liberty; but all was in vain, and the men having tied me with cords, heaved me into the boat, from whence I was taken into the ship, and from thence into the Captain's cabin.

His name was Pedro de Mendez; he was a very courteous and generous person; he entreated me to give some account of myself, and desired to know what I would eat or drink; said I should be used as well as himself, and spoke so many obliging things, that I wondered to find such civilities from a Yahoo. However, I remained silent and sullen; I was ready to faint at the very smell of him and his men. At last I desired something to eat out of my own canoe; but he ordered me a chicken and some excellent wine, and then directed that I should be put to bed in a very clean cabin. I would not undress myself, but lay on the bedclothes; and in half an hour stole out, when I thought the crew was at dinner; and getting to the side of the ship, was going to leap into the sea, and swim for my life, rather than continue among Yahoos. But one of the seamen prevented me, and having informed the Captain, I was chained to my cabin.

After dinner Don Pedro came to me, and desired to know my reason for so desperate an attempt; assured me he only meant to do me all the service he was able; and spoke so very movingly, that at last I descended to treat him like an animal which had some little portion of reason. I gave him a very short relation of my voyage; of the conspiracy against me by my own men; of the country where they set me on shore, and of my five years residence there. All which he looked upon as if it were a dream or a vision; whereat I took great offense; for I had quite forgot the faculty of lying, so peculiar to Yahoos in all countries where they preside, and consequently the disposition of suspecting truth in others of their own species. I asked him whether it were the custom of his country to *say the thing that was not?* I assured him I had almost forgot what he meant by falsehood; and if I had lived a thousand years in Houyhnhnmland, I should never have heard a lie from the meanest servant. That I was altogether indifferent whether he believed me or no; but however, in return for his favors, I would give so much allowance to the corruption of his nature, as to answer any objection he would please to make; and he might easily discover the truth.

The Captain, a wise man, after many endeavors to catch me tripping in some part of my story, at last began to have a better opinion of my veracity. But he added that since I professed so inviolable an attachment to truth, I must give him my word of honor to bear him company in this voyage without attempting anything against my life; or else he would continue me a prisoner till we arrived at Lisbon. I gave him the promise he required; but at the same time protested that I would suffer the greatest hardships rather than return to live among Yahoos.

Our voyage passed without any considerable accident. In gratitude to the Captain I sometimes sat with him at his earnest request, and strove to conceal my antipathy against humankind, although it often broke out; which he suffered to pass without observation. But the greatest part of the day, I confined myself to my cabin, to avoid seeing any of the crew. The Captain had often entreated me to strip myself of my savage dress, and offered to lend me the best suit of clothes he had. This I would not be prevailed on to accept, abhorring to cover myself with anything that had been on the back of a Yahoo. I only desired he would lend me two clean shirts, which having been washed since he wore them, I believed would not so much defile me. These I changed every second day, and washed them myself.

We arrived at Lisbon, Nov. 5, 1715. At our landing, the Captain forced me to cover myself with his cloak, to prevent the rabble from crowding about me. I was conveyed to his own house; and at my earnest request, he led me up to the highest room backwards.[38] I conjured him to conceal from all persons what I had told him of the Houyhnhnms; because the least hint of such a story would not only draw numbers of people to see me, but probably put me in danger of being imprisoned, or burned by the Inquisition. The Captain persuaded me to accept a suit of clothes newly made; but I would not suffer the tailor to take my measure; however, Don Pedro being almost of my size, they fitted me well enough. He accoutred me with other necessaries, all new, which I aired for twenty-four hours before I would use them.

The Captain had no wife, nor above three servants, none of which were suffered to attend at meals; and his whole deportment was so obliging, added to very good human understanding, that I really began to tolerate his company. He gained so far upon me, that I ventured to look out of the back window. By degrees I was brought into another room, from whence I peeped into the street, but drew my head back in a fright. In a week's time he seduced me down to the door. I found my terror gradually lessened, but my hatred and contempt seemed to increase. I was at last bold enough to walk the street in his company, but kept my nose well stopped with rue, or sometimes with tobacco.

In ten days, Don Pedro, to whom I had given some account of my domestic affairs, put it upon me as a point of honor and conscience that I ought to return to my native country, and live at home with my wife and children. He told me there was an English ship in the port just ready to sail, and he would furnish me with all things necessary. It would be tedious to repeat his arguments, and my contradictions. He said it was altogether impossible to find such a solitary island as I had desired to live in; but I might command in my own house, and pass my time in a manner as recluse as I pleased.

I complied at last, finding I could not do better. I left Lisbon the 24th day of November, in an English merchantman, but who was the Master I never inquired. Don Pedro accompanied me to the ship, and lent me twenty pounds. He took kind leave of me, and embraced me at parting; which I bore as well as I could. During this last voyage I had no commerce with the Master, or any of his men; but pretending I was sick kept close in my cabin. On the fifth of December, 1715, we cast anchor in the Downs about nine in the morning, and at three in the afternoon I got safe to my house at Redriff.

My wife and family received me with great surprise and joy, because they concluded me certainly dead; but I must freely confess, the sight of them filled me only with hatred, disgust, and con-

38. At the rear.

tempt; and the more, by reflecting on the near alliance I had to them. For, although since my unfortunate exile from the Houyhnhnm country, I had compelled myself to tolerate the sight of Yahoos, and to converse with Don Pedro de Mendez; yet my memory and imaginations were perpetually filled with the virtues and ideas of those exalted Houyhnhnms. And when I began to consider that by copulating with one of the Yahoo species, I had become a parent of more, it struck me with the utmost shame, confusion, and horror.

As soon as I entered the house, my wife took me in her arms, and kissed me; at which, having not been used to the touch of that odious animal for so many years, I fell in a swoon for almost an hour. At the time I am writing, it is five years since my last return to England; during the first year I could not endure my wife or children in my presence, the very smell of them was intolerable; much less could I suffer them to eat in the same room. To this hour they dare not presume to touch my bread, or drink out of the same cup; neither was I ever able to let one of them take me by the hand. The first money I laid out was to buy two young stone-horses,[39] which I keep in a good stable, and next to them the groom is my greatest favorite; for I feel my spirits revived by the smell he contracts in the stable. My horses understand me tolerably well; I converse with them at least four hours every day. They are strangers to bridle or saddle; they live in great amity with me, and friendship to each other.

CHAPTER XII. *The Author's veracity. His design in publishing this work. His censure of those travelers who swerve from the truth. The Author clears himself from any sinister ends in writing. An objection answered. The method of planting colonies. His native country commended. The right of the crown to those countries described by the Author is justified. The difficulty of conquering them. The Author takes his last leave of the reader; proposeth his manner of living for the future; gives good advice, and concludeth.*

Thus, gentle reader, I have given thee a faithful history of my travels for sixteen years, and above seven months; wherein I have not been so studious of ornament as of truth. I could perhaps like others have astonished thee with strange improbable tales; but I rather chose to relate plain matter of fact in the simplest manner and style; because my principal design was to inform, and not to amuse thee.

It is easy for us who travel into remote countries, which are seldom visited by Englishmen or other Europeans, to form descriptions of wonderful animals both at sea and land. Whereas a traveler's chief aim should be to make men wiser and better, and to improve their minds by the bad as well as good example of

39. Stallions.

what they deliver concerning foreign places.

I could heartily wish a law were enacted, that every traveler, before he were permitted to publish his voyages, should be obliged to make oath before the Lord High Chancellor that all he intended to print was absolutely true to the best of his knowledge; for then the world would no longer be deceived as it usually is, while some writers, to make their works pass the better upon the public, impose the grossest falsities on the unwary reader. I have perused several books of travels with great delight in my younger days; but, having since gone over most parts of the globe, and been able to contradict many fabulous accounts from my own observation, it hath given me a great disgust against this part of reading, and some indignation to see the credulity of mankind so impudently abused. Therefore, since my acquaintance were pleased to think my poor endeavors might not be unacceptable to my country; I imposed on myself as a maxim, never to be swerved from, that I would *strictly adhere to truth*; neither indeed can I be ever under the least temptation to vary from it, while I retain in my mind the lectures and example of my noble master, and the other illustrious Houyhnhnms, of whom I had so long the honor to be an humble hearer.

> *——Nec si miserum Fortuna Sinonem*
> *Finxit, vanum etiam, mendacemque improba finget.*[40]

I know very well how little reputation is to be got by writings which require neither genius nor learning, nor indeed any other talent, except a good memory, or an exact *Journal.* I know likewise, that writers of travels, like dictionary-makers, are sunk into oblivion by the weight and bulk of those who come last, and therefore lie uppermost. And it is highly probable that such travelers who shall hereafter visit the countries described in this work of mine, may be detecting my errors (if there be any) and adding many new discoveries of their own, jostle me out of vogue, and stand in my place, making the world forget that ever I was an author. This indeed would be too great a mortification if I wrote for fame; but, as my sole intention was the PUBLIC GOOD, I cannot be altogether disappointed. For, who can read the virtues I have mentioned in the glorious Houyhnhnms, without being ashamed of his own vices, when he considers himself as the reasoning, governing animal of his country? I shall say nothing of those remote nations where Yahoos preside; amongst which the least corrupted are the Brobdingnagians, whose wise maxims in morality and government it would be our happiness to observe. But I forbear descanting further, and rather leave the judicious reader to his own remarks and applications.

40. Virgil, *Aeneid* II. 79–80. "* * * nor if Fortune had moulded Simon for misery, will she also in spite mould him as false and lying."

I am not a little pleased that this work of mine can possibly meet with no censurers; for what objections can be made against a writer who relates only plain facts that happened in such distant countries, where we have not the least interest with respect either to trade or negotiations? I have carefully avoided every fault with which common writers of travels are often too justly charged. Besides, I meddle not the least with any party, but write without passion, prejudice, or ill-will against any man or number of men whatsoever. I write for the noblest end, to inform and instruct mankind, over whom I may, without breach of modesty, pretend to some superiority, from the advantages I received by conversing so long among the most accomplished Houyhnhnms. I write without any view towards profit or praise. I never suffer a word to pass that may look like reflection, or possibly give the least offense even to those who are most ready to take it. So that, I hope, I may with justice pronounce myself an Author perfectly blameless; against whom the tribes of answerers, considerers, observers, reflectors, detecters, remarkers will never be able to find matter for exercising their talents.

I confess it was whispered to me that I was bound in duty as a subject of England, to have given in a memorial to a secretary of state, at my first coming over; because, whatever lands are discovered by a subject, belong to the Crown. But I doubt whether our conquests in the countries I treat of would be as easy as those of Ferdinando Cortez over the naked Americans.[41] The Lilliputians, I think, are hardly worth the charge of a fleet and army to reduce them; and I question whether it might be prudent or safe to attempt the Brobdingnagians; or, whether an English army would be much at their ease with the Flying Island over their heads. The Houyhnhnms, indeed, appear not to be so well prepared for war, a science to which they are perfect strangers, and especially against missive weapons. However, supposing myself to be a minister of state, I could never give my advice for invading them. Their prudence, unanimity, unacquaintedness with fear, and their love of their country would amply supply all defects in the military art. Imagine twenty thousand of them breaking into the midst of an European army, confounding the ranks, overturning the carriages, battering the warriors' faces into mummy,[42] by terrible yerks[43] from their hinder hoofs: for they would well deserve the character given to Augustus, *Recalcitrat undique tutus*.[44] But instead of proposals for conquering that magnanimous nation, I rather wish they were in a capacity or disposition to send a sufficient number of their inhabitants for civilizing Europe; by teaching us the first principles of Honor, Justice, Truth, Temperance,

41. Swift is referring to Hernando Cortez (1485–1547), who destroyed the Aztec Empire.

42. Pulp.

43. Kicks.

44. Horace, *Satires* II.i.20. "* * * he kicks backward, at every point on his guard."

public Spirit, Fortitude, Chastity, Friendship, Benevolence, and Fidelity. The names of all which Virtues are still retained among us in most languages, and are to be met with in modern as well as ancient authors, which I am able to assert from my own small reading.

But I had another reason which made me less forward to enlarge his majesty's dominions by my discoveries: to say the truth, I had conceived a few scruples with relation to the distributive justice of princes upon those occasions. For instance, a crew of pirates are driven by a storm they know not whither; at length a boy discovers land from the topmast; they go on shore to rob and plunder; they see an harmless people, are entertained with kindness, they give the country a new name, they take formal possession of it for the king, they set up a rotton plank or a stone for a memorial, they murder two or three dozen of the natives, bring away a couple more by force for a sample, return home, and get their pardon. Here commences a new dominion acquired with a title by Divine Right. Ships are sent with the first opportunity; the natives driven out or destroyed, their princes tortured to discover their gold; a free license given to all acts of inhumanity and lust; the earth reeking with the blood of its inhabitants: and this execrable crew of butchers employed in so pious an expedition is a *modern colony* sent to convert and civilize an idolatrous and barbarous people.

But this description, I confess, doth by no means affect the British nation, who may be an example to the whole world for their wisdom, care, and justice in planting colonies; their liberal endowments for the advancement of religion and learning; their choice of devout and able pastors to propagate Christianity; their caution in stocking their provinces with people of sober lives and conversations from this the Mother Kingdom; their strict regard to the distribution of justice, in supplying the civil administration through all their colonies with officers of the greatest abilities, utter strangers to corruption: and to crown all, by sending the most vigilant and virtuous governors, who have no other views than the happiness of the people over whom they preside, and the honor of the king their master.

But, as those countries which I have described do not appear to have any desire of being conquered, and enslaved, murdered, or driven out by colonies, nor abound either in gold, silver, sugar, or tobacco, I did humbly conceive they were by no means proper objects of our zeal, our valor, or our interest. However, if those whom it may concern, think fit to be of another opinion, I am ready to depose, when I shall be lawfully called, that no European did ever visit these countries before me. I mean, if the inhabitants ought to be believed.

But, as to the formality of taking possession in my sovereign's name, it never came once into my thoughts; and if it had, yet as my affairs then stood, I should perhaps in point of prudence and self-preservation have put it off to a better opportunity.

Having thus answered the only objection that can be raised against me as a traveler, I here take a final leave of my courteous readers, and return to enjoy my own speculations in my little garden at Redriff; to apply those excellent lessons of virtue which I learned among the Houyhnhnms; to instruct the Yahoos of my own family as far as I shall find them docible animals; to behold my figure often in a glass, and thus if possible habituate myself by time to tolerate the sight of a human creature; to lament the brutality of Houyhnhnms in my own country, but always treat their persons with respect, for the sake of my noble master, his family, his friends, and the whole Houyhnhnm race, whom these of ours have the honor to resemble in all their lineaments, however their intellectuals came to degenerate.

I began last week to permit my wife to sit at dinner with me, at the farthest end of a long table; and to answer (but with the utmost brevity) the few questions I ask her. Yet the smell of a Yahoo continuing very offensive, I always keep my nose well stopped with rue, lavender, or tobacco leaves. And although it be hard for a man late in life to remove old habits, I am not altogether out of hopes in some time to suffer a neighbor Yahoo in my company, without the apprehensions I am yet under of his teeth or his claws.

My reconcilement to the Yahoo kind in general might not be so difficult, if they would be content with those vices and follies only which nature hath entitled them to. I am not in the least provoked at the sight of a lawyer, a pickpocket, a colonel, a fool, a lord, a gamester, a politician, a whoremonger, a physician, an evidence, a suborner, an attorney, a traitor, or the like: this is all according to the due course of things. But when I behold a lump of deformity, and diseases both in body and mind, smitten with pride, it immediately breaks all the measures of my patience; neither shall I be ever able to comprehend how such an animal and such a vice could tally together. The wise and virtuous Houyhnhnms, who abound in all excellencies that can adorn a rational creature, have no name for this vice in their language, which hath no terms to express anything that is evil, except those whereby they describe the detestable qualities of their Yahoos, among which they were not able to distinguish this of pride, for want of thoroughly understanding human nature, as it showeth itself in other countries, where that animal presides. But I, who had more experience, could plainly observe some rudiments of it among the wild Yahoos.

But the Houyhnhnms, who live under the government of reason, are no more proud of the good qualities they possess, than I should be for not wanting a leg or an arm, which no man in his wits would boast of, although he must be miserable without them. I dwell the longer upon this subject from the desire I have to make the society of an English Yahoo by any means not insupportable; and therefore I here entreat those who have any tincture of this absurd vice, that they will not presume to appear in my sight.

1726, 1735

FRANÇOIS-MARIE AROUET DE VOLTAIRE
(1694–1778)
Candide, or Optimism*

translated from the German of Doctor Ralph with the additions which were found in the Doctor's pocket when he died at Minden in the Year of Our Lord 1759

CHAPTER 1
How Candide Was Brought up in a Fine Castle and How He Was Driven Therefrom

There lived in Westphalia,[1] in the castle of the Baron of Thunder-Ten-Tronckh, a young man on whom nature had bestowed the perfection of gentle manners. His features admirably expressed his soul, he combined an honest mind with great simplicity of heart; and I think it was for this reason that they called him Candide. The old servants of the house suspected that he was the son of the Baron's sister by a respectable, honest gentleman of the neighborhood, whom she had refused to marry because he could prove only seventy-one quarterings,[2] the rest of his family tree having been lost in the passage of time.

The Baron was one of the most mighty lords of Westphalia, for his castle had a door and windows. His great hall was even hung with a tapestry. The dogs of his courtyard made up a hunting pack on occasion, with the stableboys as huntsmen; the village priest was his grand almoner. They all called him "My Lord," and laughed at his stories.

The Baroness, who weighed in the neighborhood of three hundred and fifty pounds, was greatly respected for that reason, and did the honors of the house with a dignity which rendered her even more imposing. Her daughter Cunégonde,[3] aged seventeen, was a ruddy-cheeked girl, fresh, plump, and desirable. The Baron's son seemed in every way worthy of his father. The tutor Pangloss was the oracle of the household, and little Candide listened to his lectures with all the good faith of his age and character.

Pangloss gave instruction in metaphysico-theologico-cosmoloonigology.[4] He proved admirably that there cannot possibly be an effect

* Translated with notes by Robert M. Adams.

1. Westphalia is a province of western Germany, near Holland and the lower Rhineland. Flat, boggy, and drab, it is noted chiefly for its excellent ham. In a letter to his niece, written during his German expedition of 1750, Voltaire described the "vast, sad, sterile, detestable countryside of Westphalia."

2. Quarterings are genealogical divisions of one's family tree. Seventy-one of them is a grotesque number to have, representing something over 2,000 years of uninterrupted nobility.

3. Cunégonde gets her odd name from Kunigunda, wife to Emperor Henry II, who walked barefoot and blindfolded on red-hot irons to prove her chastity; Pangloss gets his name from Greek words meaning all-tongue.

4. The "looney" I have buried in this burlesque word corresponds to a buried *nigaud*—"booby" in the French. Christian Wolff, disciple of Leibniz, invented and popularized the word "cosmology."

without a cause and that in this best of all possible worlds[5] the Baron's castle was the best of all castles and his wife the best of all possible Baronesses.

—It is clear, said he, that things cannot be otherwise than they are, for since everything is made to serve an end, everything necessarily serves the best end. Observe: noses were made to support spectacles, hence we have spectacles. Legs, as anyone can plainly see, were made to be breeched, and so we have breeches. Stones were made to be shaped and to build castles with; thus My Lord has a fine castle, for the greatest Baron in the province should have the finest house; and since pigs were made to be eaten, we eat pork all year round.[6] Consequently, those who say everything is well are uttering mere stupidities; they should say everything is for the best.

Candide listened attentively and believed implicitly; for he found Miss Cunégonde exceedingly pretty, though he never had the courage to tell her so. He decided that after the happiness of being born Baron of Thunder-Ten-Tronckh, the second order of happiness was to be Miss Cunégonde; the third was seeing her every day, and the fourth was listening to Master Pangloss, the greatest philosopher in the province and consequently in the entire world.

One day, while Cunégonde was walking near the castle in the little woods that they called a park, she saw Dr. Pangloss in the underbrush; he was giving a lesson in experimental physics to her mother's maid, a very attractive and obedient brunette. As Miss Cunégonde had a natural bent for the sciences, she watched breathlessly the repeated experiments which were going on; she saw clearly the doctor's sufficient reason, observed both cause and effect, and returned to the house in a distracted and pensive frame of mind, yearning for knowledge and dreaming that she might be the sufficient reason of young Candide—who might also be hers.

As she was returning to the castle, she met Candide, and blushed; Candide blushed too. She greeted him in a faltering tone of voice; and Candide talked to her without knowing what he was saying. Next day, as everyone was rising from the dinner table, Cunégonde and Candide found themselves behind a screen; Cunégonde dropped her handkerchief, Candide picked it up; she held his hand quite innocently, he kissed her hand quite innocently

5. These catch phrases, echoed by popularizers of Leibniz, make reference to the determinism of his system, its linking of cause with effect, and its optimism. As his correspondence indicates, Voltaire habitually thought of Leibniz's philosophy (which, having been published in definitive form as early as 1710, had been in the air for a long time) in terms of these catch phrases.

6. The argument from design supposes that everything in this world exists for a specific reason; Voltaire objects not to the argument as a whole, but to the abuse of it. He grants, for example, that noses were made to smell and stomachs to digest but denies that feet were made to put shoes on or stones to be cut up into building blocks. His full view finds expression in the article on "causes finales" in the *Philosophical Dictionary*.

with remarkable vivacity and emotion; their lips met, their eyes lit up, their knees trembled, their hands wandered. The Baron of Thunder-Ten-Tronckh passed by the screen and, taking note of this cause and this effect, drove Candide out of the castle by kicking him vigorously on the backside. Cunégonde fainted; as soon as she recovered, the Baroness slapped her face; and everything was confusion in the most beautiful and agreeable of all possible castles.

CHAPTER 2
What Happened to Candide Among the Bulgars[7]

Candide, ejected from the earthly paradise, wandered for a long time without knowing where he was going, weeping, raising his eyes to heaven, and gazing back frequently on the most beautiful of castles which contained the most beautiful of Baron's daughters. He slept without eating, in a furrow of a plowed field, while the snow drifted over him; next morning, numb with cold, he dragged himself into the neighboring village, which was called Waldberghoff-trarbk-dikdorff; he was penniless, famished, and exhausted. At the door of a tavern he paused forlornly. Two men dressed in blue[8] took note of him:

—Look, chum, said one of them, there's a likely young fellow of just about the right size.

They approached Candide and invited him very politely to dine with them.

—Gentlemen, Candide replied with charming modesty, I'm honored by your invitation, but I really don't have enough money to pay my share.

—My dear sir, said one of the blues, people of your appearance and your merit don't have to pay; aren't you five feet five inches tall?

—Yes, gentlemen, that is indeed my stature, said he, making a bow.

—Then, sir, you must be seated at once; not only will we pay your bill this time, we will never allow a man like you to be short of money; for men were made only to render one another mutual aid.

—You are quite right, said Candide; it is just as Dr. Pangloss always told me, and I see clearly that everything is for the best.

They beg him to accept a couple of crowns, he takes them, and offers an I.O.U.; they won't hear of it, and all sit down at table

7. Voltaire chose this name to represent the Prussian troops of Frederick the Great because he wanted to make an insinuation of pederasty against both the soldiers and their master. *Cf.* French *bougre,* English "bugger."

8. The recruiting officers of Frederick the Great, much feared in eighteenth-century Europe, wore blue uniforms. Frederick had a passion for sorting out his soldiers by size; several of his regiments would accept only six-footers.

together.

—Don't you love dearly . . . ?

—I do indeed, says he, I dearly love Miss Cunégonde.

—No, no, says one of the gentlemen, we are asking if you don't love dearly the King of the Bulgars.

—Not in the least, says he, I never laid eyes on him.

—What's that you say? He's the most charming of kings, and we must drink his health.

—Oh, gladly, gentlemen; and he drinks.

—That will do, they tell him; you are now the bulwark, the support, the defender, the hero of the Bulgars; your fortune is made and your future assured.

Promptly they slip irons on his legs and lead him to the regiment. There they cause him to right face, left face, present arms, order arms, aim, fire, doubletime, and they give him thirty strokes of the rod. Next day he does the drill a little less awkwardly and gets only twenty strokes; the third day, they give him only ten, and he is regarded by his comrades as a prodigy.

Candide, quite thunderstruck, did not yet understand very clearly how he was a hero. One fine spring morning he took it into his head to go for a walk, stepping straight out as if it were a privilege of the human race, as of animals in general, to use his legs as he chose.[9] He had scarcely covered two leagues when four other heroes, each six feet tall, overtook him, bound him, and threw him into a dungeon. At the court-martial they asked which he preferred, to be flogged thirty-six times by the entire regiment or to receive summarily a dozen bullets in the brain. In vain did he argue that the human will is free and insist that he preferred neither alternative; he had to choose; by virtue of the divine gift called "liberty" he decided to run the gauntlet thirty-six times, and actually endured two floggings. The regiment was composed of two thousand men. That made four thousand strokes, which laid open every muscle and nerve from his nape to his butt. As they were preparing for the third beating, Candide, who could endure no more, begged as a special favor that they would have the goodness to smash his head. His plea was granted; they bandaged his eyes and made him kneel down. The King of the Bulgars, passing by at this moment, was told of the culprit's crime; and as this king had a rare genius, he understood, from everything they told him of Candide, that this was a

9. This episode was suggested by the experience of a Frenchman named Courtilz, who had deserted from the Prussian army and been bastionadoed for it. Voltaire intervened with Frederick to gain his release. But it also reflects the story that Wolff, Leibniz's disciple, got into trouble with Frederick's father when someone reported that his doctrine denying free will had encouraged several soldiers to desert. "The argument of the grenadier," who was said to have pleaded pre-established harmony to justify his desertion, so infuriated the king that he had Wolff expelled from the country.

young metaphysician, extremely ignorant of the ways of the world, so he granted his royal pardon, with a generosity which will be praised in every newspaper in every age. A worthy surgeon cured Candide in three weeks with the ointments described by Dioscorides.[1] He already had a bit of skin back and was able to walk when the King of the Bulgars went to war with the King of the Abares.[2]

CHAPTER 3
How Candide Escaped from the Bulgars, and What Became of Him

Nothing could have been so fine, so brisk, so brilliant, so well-drilled as the two armies. The trumpets, the fifes, the oboes, the drums, and the cannon produced such a harmony as was never heard in hell. First the cannons battered down about six thousand men on each side; then volleys of musket fire removed from the best of worlds about nine or ten thousand rascals who were cluttering up its surface. The bayonet was a sufficient reason for the demise of several thousand others. Total casualties might well amount to thirty thousand men or so. Candide, who was trembling like a philosopher, hid himself as best he could while this heroic butchery was going on.

Finally, while the two kings in their respective camps celebrated the victory by having *Te Deums* sung, Candide undertook to do his reasoning of cause and effect somewhere else. Passing by mounds of the dead and dying, he came to a nearby village which had been burnt to the ground. It was an Abare village, which the Bulgars had burned, in strict accordance with the laws of war. Here old men, stunned from beatings, watched the last agonies of their butchered wives, who still clutched their infants to their bleeding breasts; there, disemboweled girls, who had first satisfied the natural needs of various heroes, breathed their last; others, half-scorched in the flames, begged for their death stroke. Scattered brains and severed limbs littered the ground.

Candide fled as fast as he could to another village; this one belonged to the Bulgars, and the heroes of the Abare cause had given it the same treatment. Climbing over ruins and stumbling over corpses, Candide finally made his way out of the war area, carrying

1. Dioscorides' treatise on *materia medica,* dating from the first century A.D., was not the most up to date.
2. The name "Abares" actually designates a tribe of semicivilized Scythians, who might be supposed at war with the Bulgars; allegorically, the Abares are the French, who opposed the Prussians in the conflict known to hindsight history as the Seven Years' War (1756–1763). For Voltaire, at the moment of writing *Candide,* it was simply the current war. One notes that according to the title page of 1761, "Doctor Ralph," the dummy author of *Candide,* himself perished at the battle of Minden (Westphalia) in 1759.

a little food in his knapsack and never ceasing to dream of Miss Cunégonde. His supplies gave out when he reached Holland; but having heard that everyone in that country was rich and a Christian, he felt confident of being treated as well as he had been in the castle of the Baron before he was kicked out for the love of Miss Cunégonde.

He asked alms of several grave personages, who all told him that if he continued to beg, he would be shut up in a house of correction and set to hard labor.

Finally he approached a man who had just been talking to a large crowd for an hour on end; the topic was charity. Looking doubtfully at him, the orator demanded:

—What are you doing here? Are you here to serve the good cause?

—There is no effect without a cause, said Candide modestly; all events are linked by the chain of necessity and arranged for the best. I had to be driven away from Miss Cunégonde, I had to run the gauntlet, I have to beg my bread until I can earn it; none of this could have happened otherwise.

—Look here, friend, said the orator, do you think the Pope is Antichrist?[3]

—I haven't considered the matter, said Candide; but whether he is or not, I'm in need of bread.

—You don't deserve any, said the other; away with you, you rascal, you rogue, never come near me as long as you live.

Meanwhile, the orator's wife had put her head out of the window, and, seeing a man who was not sure the Pope was Antichrist, emptied over his head a pot full of —— Scandalous! The excesses into which women are led by religious zeal!

A man who had never been baptized, a good Anabaptist[4] named Jacques, saw this cruel and heartless treatment being inflicted on one of his fellow creatures, a featherless biped possessing a soul[5]; he took Candide home with him, washed him off, gave him bread and beer, presented him with two florins, and even undertook to give him a job in his Persian-rug factory—for these items are widely manufactured in Holland. Candide, in an ecstasy of gratitude, cried out:

—Master Pangloss was right indeed when he told me everything

3. Voltaire is satirizing extreme Protestant sects that have sometimes seemed to make hatred of Rome the sum and substance of their creed.
4. Holland, as the home of religious liberty, had offered asylum to the Anabaptists, whose radical views on property and religious discipline had made them unpopular during the sixteenth century. Granted tolerance, they settled down into respectable burghers. Since this behavior confirmed some of Voltaire's major theses, he had a high opinion of contemporary Anabaptists.
5. Plato's famous minimal definition of a man, which he corrected by the addition of a soul to distinguish man from a plucked chicken. The point is that the Anabaptist sympathizes with men simply because they are human.

is for the best in this world; for I am touched by your kindness far more than by the harshness of that black-coated gentleman and his wife.

Next day, while taking a stroll about town, he met a beggar who was covered with pustules, his eyes were sunken, the end of his nose rotted off, his mouth twisted, his teeth black, he had a croaking voice and a hacking cough, and spat a tooth every time he tried to speak.

CHAPTER 4
How Candide Met His Old Philosophy Tutor, Doctor Pangloss, and What Came of It

Candide, more touched by compassion even than by horror, gave this ghastly beggar the two florins that he himself had received from his honest Anabaptist friend Jacques. The phantom stared at him, burst into tears, and fell on his neck. Candide drew back in terror.

—Alas, said one wretch to the other, don't you recognize your dear Pangloss any more?

—What are you saying? You, my dear master! you, in this horrible condition? What misfortune has befallen you? Why are you no longer in the most beautiful of castles? What has happened to Miss Cunégonde, that pearl among young ladies, that masterpiece of Nature?

—I am perishing, said Pangloss.

—Candide promptly led him into the Anabaptist's stable, where he gave him a crust of bread, and when he had recovered: —Well, said he, Cunégonde?

—Dead, said the other.

Candide fainted. His friend brought him around with a bit of sour vinegar which happened to be in the stable. Candide opened his eyes.

—Cunégonde, dead! Ah, best of worlds, what's become of you now? But how did she die? It wasn't of grief at seeing me kicked out of her noble father's elegant castle?

—Not at all, said Pangloss; she was disemboweled by the Bulgar soldiers, after having been raped to the absolute limit of human endurance; they smashed the Baron's head when he tried to defend her, cut the Baroness to bits, and treated my poor pupil exactly like his sister.[6] As for the castle, not one stone was left on another, not a shed, not a sheep, not a duck, not a tree; but we had the satisfaction of revenge, for the Abares did exactly the same thing to a

6. The theme of homosexuality which attaches to Cunégonde's brother seems to have no general satiric point, but its presence is unmistakable. See Chapters 14, 15, and 28.

nearby barony belonging to a Bulgar nobleman.

At this tale Candide fainted again; but having returned to his senses and said everything appropriate to the occasion, he asked about the cause and effect, the sufficient reason, which had reduced Pangloss to his present pitiful state.

—Alas, said he, it was love; love, the consolation of the human race, the preservative of the universe, the soul of all sensitive beings, love, gentle love.

—Unhappy man, said Candide, I too have had some experience of this love, the sovereign of hearts, the soul of our souls; and it never got me anything but a single kiss and twenty kicks in the rear. How could this lovely cause produce in you such a disgusting effect?

Pangloss replied as follows: —My dear Candide! you knew Paquette, that pretty maidservant to our august Baroness. In her arms I tasted the delights of paradise, which directly caused these torments of hell, from which I am now suffering. She was infected with the disease, and has perhaps died of it. Paquette received this present from an erudite Franciscan, who took the pains to trace it back to its source; for he had it from an elderly countess, who picked it up from a captain of cavalry, who acquired it from a marquise, who caught it from a page, who had received it from a Jesuit, who during his novitiate got it directly from one of the companions of Christopher Columbus.[7] As for me, I shall not give it to anyone, for I am a dying man.

—Oh, Pangloss, cried Candide, that's a very strange genealogy. Isn't the devil at the root of the whole thing?

—Not at all, replied that great man; it's an indispensable part of the best of worlds, a necessary ingredient; if Columbus had not caught, on an American island, this sickness which attacks the source of generation and sometimes prevents generation entirely—which thus strikes at and defeats the greatest end of Nature herself—we should have neither chocolate nor cochineal. It must also be noted that until the present time this malady, like religious controversy, has been wholly confined to the continent of Europe. Turks, Indians, Persians, Chinese, Siamese, and Japanese know nothing of it as yet; but there is a sufficient reason for which they in turn will make its acquaintance in a couple of centuries. Meanwhile, it has made splendid progress among us, especially among those big armies of honest, well-trained mercenaries who decide the destinies of nations. You can be sure that when thirty thousand men fight a pitched battle against the same number of the enemy, there will be about twenty thousand with the pox on either side.

7. Syphilis was the first contribution of the New World to the happiness of the Old. Voltaire's information comes from Astruc, *Traité des maladies vénériennes* (1734).

—Remarkable indeed, said Candide, but we must see about curing you.

—And how can I do that, said Pangloss, seeing I don't have a cent to my name? There's not a doctor in the whole world who will let your blood or give you an enema without demanding a fee. If you can't pay yourself, you must find someone to pay for you.

These last words decided Candide; he hastened to implore the help of his charitable Anabaptist, Jacques, and painted such a moving picture of his friend's wretched state that the good man did not hesitate to take in Pangloss and have him cured at his own expense. In the course of the cure, Pangloss lost only an eye and an ear. Since he wrote a fine hand and knew arithmetic, the Anabaptist made him his bookkeeper. At the end of two months, being obliged to go to Lisbon on business, he took his two philosophers on the boat with him. Pangloss still maintained that everything was for the best, but Jacques didn't agree with him.

—It must be, said he, that men have corrupted Nature, for they are not born wolves, yet that is what they become. God gave them neither twenty-four-pound cannon nor bayonets, yet they have manufactured both in order to destroy themselves. Bankruptcies have the same effect, and so does the justice which seizes the goods of bankrupts in order to prevent the creditors from getting them.[8]

—It was all indispensable, replied the one-eyed doctor, since private misfortunes make for public welfare, and therefore the more private misfortunes there are, the better everything is.

While he was reasoning, the air grew dark, the winds blew from all directions, and the vessel was attacked by a horrible tempest within sight of Lisbon harbor.

CHAPTER 5
Tempest, Shipwreck, Earthquake, and What Happened to Doctor Pangloss, Candide, and the Anabaptist, Jacques

Half of the passengers, weakened by the frightful anguish of seasickness and the distress of tossing about on stormy waters, were incapable of noticing their danger. The other half shrieked aloud and fell to their prayers, the sails were ripped to shreds, the masts snapped, the vessel opened at the seams. Everyone worked who could stir, nobody listened for orders or issued them. The Anabaptist was lending a hand in the after part of the ship when a frantic sailor struck him and knocked him to the deck; but just at that moment, the sailor lurched so violently that he fell head first over the side, where he hung, clutching a fragment of the broken mast.

8. Voltaire had suffered losses from various bankruptcy proceedings, which lend a personal edge to his satire here, besides diverting its point a bit.

The good Jacques ran to his aid, and helped him to climb back on board, but in the process was himself thrown into the sea under the very eyes of the sailor, who allowed him to drown without even glancing at him. Candide rushed to the rail, and saw his benefactor rise for a moment to the surface, then sink forever. He wanted to dive to his rescue; but the philosopher Pangloss prevented him by proving that the bay of Lisbon had been formed expressly for this Anabaptist to drown in. While he was proving the point *a priori*, the vessel opened up and everyone perished except for Pangloss, Candide, and the brutal sailor who had caused the virtuous Anabaptist to drown; this rascal swam easily to shore, while Pangloss and Candide drifted there on a plank.

When they had recovered a bit of energy, they set out for Lisbon; they still had a little money with which they hoped to stave off hunger after escaping the storm.

Scarcely had they set foot in the town, still bewailing the loss of their benefactor, when they felt the earth quake underfoot; the sea was lashed to a froth, burst into the port, and smashed all the vessels lying at anchor there. Whirlwinds of fire and ash swirled through the streets and public squares; houses crumbled, roofs came crashing down on foundations, foundations split; thirty thousand inhabitants of every age and either sex were crushed in the ruins.[9] The sailor whistled through his teeth, and said with an oath: —There'll be something to pick up here.

—What can be the sufficient reason of this phenomenon? asked Pangloss.

—The Last Judgment is here, cried Candide.

But the sailor ran directly into the middle of the ruins, heedless of danger in his eagerness for gain; he found some money, laid violent hands on it, got drunk, and, having slept off his wine, bought the favors of the first streetwalker he could find amid the ruins of smashed houses, amid corpses and suffering victims on every hand. Pangloss however tugged at his sleeve.

—My friend, said he, this is not good form at all; your behavior falls short of that required by the universal reason; it's untimely, to say the least.

—Bloody hell, said the other, I'm a sailor, born in Batavia; I've been four times to Japan and stamped four times on the crucifix[1]; get out of here with your universal reason.

9. The great Lisbon earthquake and fire occurred on November 1, 1755; between thirty and forty thousand deaths resulted.

1. The Japanese, originally receptive to foreign visitors, grew fearful that priests and proselytizers were merely advance agents of empire, and expelled both the Portuguese and Spanish early in the seventeenth century. Only the Dutch were allowed to retain a small foothold, under humiliating conditions, of which the notion of stamping on the crucifix is symbolic. It was never what Voltaire suggests here, an actual requirement for entering the country.

Some falling stonework had struck Candide; he lay prostrate in the street, covered with rubble, and calling to Pangloss: —For pity's sake bring me a little wine and oil; I'm dying.

—This earthquake is nothing novel, Pangloss replied; the city of Lima, in South America, underwent much the same sort of tremor, last year; same causes, same effects; there is surely a vein of sulphur under the earth's surface reaching from Lima to Lisbon.

—Nothing is more probable, said Candide; but, for God's sake, a little oil and wine.

—What do you mean, probable? replied the philosopher; I regard the case as proved.

Candide fainted and Pangloss brought him some water from a nearby fountain.

Next day, as they wandered amid the ruins, they found a little food which restored some of their strength. Then they fell to work like the others, bringing relief to those of the inhabitants who had escaped death. Some of the citizens whom they rescued gave them a dinner as good as was possible under the circumstances; it is true that the meal was a melancholy one, and the guests watered their bread with tears; but Pangloss consoled them by proving that things could not possibly be otherwise.

—For, said he, all this is for the best, since if there is a volcano at Lisbon, it cannot be somewhere else, since it is unthinkable that things should not be where they are, since everything is well.

A little man in black, an officer of the Inquisition,[2] who was sitting beside him, politely took up the question, and said: —It would seem that the gentleman does not believe in original sin, since if everything is for the best, man has not fallen and is not liable to eternal punishment.

—I most humbly beg pardon of your excellency, Pangloss answered, even more politely, but the fall of man and the curse of original sin entered necessarily into the best of all possible worlds.

—Then you do not believe in free will? said the officer.

—Your excellency must excuse me, said Pangloss; free will agrees very well with absolute necessity, for it was necessary that we should be free, since a will which is determined . . .

Pangloss was in the middle of his sentence, when the officer nodded significantly to the attendant who was pouring him a glass of port, or Oporto, wine.

2. Specifically, a *familier* or *poursuivant*, an undercover agent with powers of arrest.

CHAPTER 6
How They Made a Fine Auto-da-Fé to Prevent Earthquakes, and How Candide Was Whipped

After the earthquake had wiped out three quarters of Lisbon, the learned men of the land could find no more effective way of averting total destruction than to give the people a fine auto-da-fé[3]; the University of Coimbra had established that the spectacle of several persons being roasted over a slow fire with full ceremonial rites is an infallible specific against earthquakes.

In consequence, the authorities had rounded up a Biscayan convicted of marrying a woman who had stood godmother to his child, and two Portuguese who while eating a chicken had set aside a bit of bacon used for seasoning.[4] After dinner, men came with ropes to tie up Doctor Pangloss and his disciple Candide, one for talking and the other for listening with an air of approval; both were taken separately to a set of remarkably cool apartments, where the glare of the sun is never bothersome; eight days later they were both dressed in *san-benitos* and crowned with paper mitres[5]; Candide's mitre and *san-benito* were decorated with inverted flames and with devils who had neither tails nor claws; but Pangloss's devils had both tails and claws, and his flames stood upright. Wearing these costumes, they marched in a procession, and listened to a very touching sermon, followed by a beautiful concert of plainsong. Candide was flogged in cadence to the music; the Biscayan and the two men who had avoided bacon were burned, and Pangloss was hanged, though hanging is not customary. On the same day there was another earthquake, causing frightful damage.[6]

Candide, stunned, stupefied, despairing, bleeding, trembling, said to himself: —If this is the best of all possible worlds, what are the others like? The flogging is not so bad, I was flogged by the Bulgars. But oh my dear Pangloss, greatest of philosophers, was it necessary for me to watch you being hanged, for no reason that I can see? Oh my dear Anabaptist, best of men, was it necessary that you should be drowned in the port? Oh Miss Cunégonde, pearl of young ladies, was it necessary that you should have your belly slit open?

He was being led away, barely able to stand, lectured, lashed, ab-

3. Literally, "act of faith," a public ceremony of repentance and humiliation. Such an auto-da-fé was actually held in Lisbon, June 20, 1756.
4. The Biscayan's fault lay in marrying someone within the forbidden bounds of relationship, an act of spiritual incest. The men who declined pork or bacon were understood to be crypto-Jews.
5. The cone-shaped paper cap (intended to resemble a bishop's mitre) and flowing yellow cape were customary garb for those pleading before the Inquisition.
6. In fact, the second quake occurred December 21, 1755.

solved, and blessed, when an old woman approached and said, —My son, be of good cheer and follow me.

CHAPTER 7
How an Old Woman Took Care of Candide, and How He Regained What He Loved

Candide was of very bad cheer, but he followed the old woman to a shanty; she gave him a jar of ointment to rub himself, left him food and drink; she showed him a tidy little bed; next to it was a suit of clothing.

—Eat, drink, sleep, she said; and may Our Lady of Atocha, Our Lord St. Anthony of Padua, and Our Lord St. James of Compostela watch over you. I will be back tomorrow.

Candide, still completely astonished by everything he had seen and suffered, and even more by the old woman's kindness, offered to kiss her hand.

—It's not *my* hand you should be kissing, said she. I'll be back tomorrow; rub yourself with the ointment, eat and sleep.

In spite of his many sufferings, Candide ate and slept. Next day the old woman returned bringing breakfast; she looked at his back and rubbed it herself with another ointment; she came back with lunch; and then she returned in the evening, bringing supper. Next day she repeated the same routine.

—Who are you? Candide asked continually. Who told you to be so kind to me? How can I ever repay you?

The good woman answered not a word; she returned in the evening, and without food.

—Come with me, says she, and don't speak a word.

Taking him by the hand, she walks out into the countryside with him for about a quarter of a mile; they reach an isolated house, quite surrounded by gardens and ditches. The old woman knocks at a little gate, it opens. She takes Candide up a secret stairway to a gilded room furnished with a fine brocaded sofa; there she leaves him, closes the door, disappears. Candide stood as if entranced; his life, which had seemed like a nightmare so far, was now starting to look like a delightful dream.

Soon the old woman returned; on her feeble shoulder leaned a trembling woman, of a splendid figure, glittering in diamonds, and veiled.

—Remove the veil, said the old woman to Candide.

The young man stepped timidly forward, and lifted the veil. What an event! What a surprise! Could it be Miss Cunégonde? Yes, it really was! She herself! His knees give way, speech fails him, he falls at her feet, Cunégonde collapses on the sofa. The old woman plies them with brandy, they return to their senses, they exchange words. At first they could utter only broken phrases, questions and answers at cross purposes, sighs, tears, exclamations. The old woman warned them not to make too much noise, and left them alone.

—Then it's really you, said Candide, you're alive, I've found you again in Portugal. Then you never were raped? You never had your belly ripped open, as the philosopher Pangloss assured me?

—Oh yes, said the lovely Cunégonde, but one doesn't always die of these two accidents.

—But your father and mother were murdered then?

—All too true, said Cunégonde, in tears.

—And your brother?

—Killed too.

—And why are you in Portugal? and how did you know I was here? and by what device did you have me brought to this house?

—I shall tell you everything, the lady replied; but first you must tell me what has happened to you since that first innocent kiss we exchanged and the kicking you got because of it.

Candide obeyed her with profound respect; and though he was overcome, though his voice was weak and hesitant, though he still had twinges of pain from his beating, he described as simply as possible everything that had happened to him since the time of their separation. Cunégonde lifted her eyes to heaven; she wept at the death of the good Anabaptist and at that of Pangloss; after which she told the following story to Candide, who listened to every word while he gazed on her with hungry eyes.

CHAPTER 8
Cunégonde's Story

—I was in my bed and fast asleep when heaven chose to send the Bulgars into our castle of Thunder-Ten-Tronckh. They butchered my father and brother, and hacked my mother to bits. An enormous Bulgar, six feet tall, seeing that I had swooned from horror at the scene, set about raping me; at that I recovered my senses, I screamed and scratched, bit and fought, I tried to tear the eyes out of that big Bulgar—not realizing that everything which had happened in my father's castle was a mere matter of routine. The brute then stabbed me with a knife on my left thigh, where I still bear the scar.

—What a pity! I should very much like to see it, said the simple Candide.

—You shall, said Cunégonde; but shall I go on?

—Please do, said Candide.

So she took up the thread of her tale: —A Bulgar captain appeared, he saw me covered with blood and the soldier too intent to get up. Shocked by the monster's failure to come to attention, the captain killed him on my body. He then had my wound dressed, and took me off to his quarters, as a prisoner of war. I laundered his few shirts and did his cooking; he found me attractive, I confess it, and I won't deny that he was a handsome fellow, with a smooth, white skin; apart from that, however, little wit, little philosophical training; it was evident that he had not been brought up by Doctor Pangloss. After three months, he had lost all his money and grown sick of me; so he sold me to a jew named Don Issachar, who traded in Holland and Portugal, and who was mad after women. This jew developed a mighty passion for my person, but he got nowhere with it; I held him off better than I had done with the Bulgar soldier; for though a person of honor may be raped once, her virtue is only strengthened by the experience. In order to keep me hidden, the jew brought me to his country house, which you see here. Till then I had thought there was nothing on earth so beautiful as the castle of Thunder-Ten-Tronckh; I was now undeceived.

—One day the Grand Inquisitor took notice of me at mass; he ogled me a good deal, and made known that he must talk to me on a matter of secret business. I was taken to his palace; I told him of my rank; he pointed out that it was beneath my dignity to belong to an Israelite. A suggestion was then conveyed to Don Issachar that he should turn me over to My Lord the Inquisitor. Don Issachar, who is court banker and a man of standing, refused out of hand. The inquisitor threatened him with an auto-da-fé. Finally my jew, fearing for his life, struck a bargain by which the house and I would belong to both of them as joint tenants; the jew would get Mondays, Wednesdays, and the Sabbath, the inquisitor would get the other days of the week. That has been the arrangement for six months now. There have been quarrels; sometimes it has not been clear whether the night from Saturday to Sunday belonged to the old or the new dispensation. For my part, I have so far been able to hold both of them off; and that, I think, is why they are both still in love with me.

—Finally, in order to avert further divine punishment by earthquake, and to terrify Don Issachar, My Lord the Inquisitor chose to celebrate an auto-da-fé. He did me the honor of inviting me to attend. I had an excellent seat; the ladies were served with refreshments between the mass and the execution. To tell you the truth, I was horrified to see them burn alive those two jews and that decent Biscayan who had married his child's godmother; but what was my surprise, my terror, my grief, when I saw, huddled in a *san-benito* and wearing a mitre, someone who looked like Pangloss! I rubbed my eyes, I watched his every move, I saw him hanged; and I fell back in a swoon. Scarcely had I come to my senses again, when I saw you stripped for the lash; that was the peak of my horror, consternation, grief, and despair. I may tell you, by the way, that your skin is even whiter and more delicate than that of my Bulgar captain. Seeing you, then, redoubled the torments which were already overwhelming me. I shrieked aloud, I wanted to call out, 'Let him go, you brutes!' but my voice died within me, and my cries would have been useless. When you had been thoroughly thrashed: 'How can it be,' I asked myself, 'that agreeable Candide and wise Pangloss have come to Lisbon, one to receive a hundred whiplashes, the other to be hanged by order of My Lord the Inquisitor, whose mistress I am? Pangloss must have deceived me cruelly when he told me that all is for the best in this world.'

—Frantic, exhausted, half out of my senses, and ready to die of weakness, I felt as if my mind were choked with the massacre of my father, my mother, my brother, with the arrogance of that ugly Bulgar soldier, with the knife slash he inflicted on me, my slavery, my cookery, my Bulgar captain, my nasty Don Issachar, my abominable inquisitor, with the hanging of Doctor Pangloss, with that great plainsong *miserere* which they sang while they flogged you—and above all, my mind was full of the kiss which I gave you behind the screen, on the day I saw you for the last time. I praised God, who had brought you back to me after so many trials. I asked my old woman to look out for you, and to bring you here as soon as she could. She did just as I asked; I have had the indescribable joy of seeing you again, hearing you and talking with you once more. But you must be frightfully hungry; I am, myself; let us begin with a dinner.

So then and there they sat down to table; and after dinner, they adjourned to that fine brocaded sofa, which has already been mentioned; and there they were when the eminent Don Issachar, one of the masters of the house, appeared. It was the day of the Sabbath; he was arriving to assert his rights and express his tender passion.

CHAPTER 9
What Happened to Cunégonde, Candide, the Grand Inquisitor, and a Jew

This Issachar was the most choleric Hebrew seen in Israel since the Babylonian captivity.

—What's this, says he, you bitch of a Christian, you're not satisfied with the Grand Inquisitor? Do I have to share you with this rascal, too?

So saying, he drew a long dagger, with which he always went

armed, and, supposing his opponent defenceless, flung himself on Candide. But our good Westphalian had received from the old woman, along with his suit of clothes, a fine sword. Out it came, and though his manners were of the gentlest, in short order he laid the Israelite stiff and cold on the floor, at the feet of the lovely Cunégonde.

—Holy Virgin! she cried. What will become of me now? A man killed in my house! If the police find out, we're done for.

—If Pangloss had not been hanged, said Candide, he would give us good advice in this hour of need, for he was a great philosopher. Lacking him, let's ask the old woman.

She was a sensible body, and was just starting to give her opinion of the situation, when another little door opened. It was just one o'clock in the morning, Sunday morning. This day belonged to the inquisitor. In he came, and found the whipped Candide with a sword in his hand, a corpse at his feet, Cunégonde in terror, and an old woman giving them both good advice.

Here now is what passed through Candide's mind in this instant of time; this is how he reasoned: —If this holy man calls for help, he will certainly have me burned, and perhaps Cunégonde as well; he has already had me whipped without mercy; he is my rival; I have already killed once; why hesitate?

It was a quick, clear chain of reasoning; without giving the inquisitor time to recover from his surprise, he ran him through, and laid him beside the jew.

—Here you've done it again, said Cunégonde; there's no hope for us now. We'll be excommunicated, our last hour has come. How is it that you, who were born so gentle, could kill in two minutes a jew and a prelate?

—My dear girl, replied Candide, when a man is in love, jealous, and just whipped by the Inquisition, he is no longer himself.

The old woman now spoke up and said:—There are three Andalusian steeds in the stable, with their saddles and bridles; our brave Candide must get them ready: my lady has some gold coin and diamonds; let's take to horse at once, though I can only ride on one buttock; we will go to Cadiz. The weather is as fine as can be, and it is pleasant to travel in the cool of the evening.

Promptly, Candide saddled the three horses. Cunégonde, the old woman, and he covered thirty miles without a stop. While they were fleeing, the Holy Brotherhood[7] came to investigate the house; they buried the inquisitor in a fine church, and threw Issachar on the dunghill.

Candide, Cunégonde, and the old woman were already in the lit-

7. A semireligious order with police powers, very active in eighteenth-century Spain.

tle town of Avacena, in the middle of the Sierra Morena; and there, as they sat in a country inn, they had this conversation.

CHAPTER 10
In Deep Distress, Candide, Cunégonde, and the Old Woman Reach Cadiz; They Put to Sea

—Who then could have robbed me of my gold and diamonds? said Cunégonde, in tears. How shall we live? what shall we do? where shall I find other inquisitors and jews to give me some more?

—Ah, said the old woman, I strongly suspect that reverend Franciscan friar who shared the inn with us yesterday at Badajoz. God save me from judging him unfairly! But he came into our room twice, and he left long before us.

—Alas, said Candide, the good Pangloss often proved to me that the fruits of the earth are a common heritage of all, to which each man has equal right. On these principles, the Franciscan should at least have left us enough to finish our journey. You have nothing at all, my dear Cunégonde?

—Not a maravedi, said she.

—What to do? said Candide.

—We'll sell one of the horses, said the old woman; I'll ride on the croup behind my mistress, though only on one buttock, and so we will get to Cadiz.

There was in the same inn a Benedictine prior; he bought the horse cheap. Candide, Cunégonde, and the old woman passed through Lucena, Chillas, and Lebrixa, and finally reached Cadiz. There a fleet was being fitted out and an army assembled, to reason with the Jesuit fathers in Paraguay, who were accused of fomenting among their flock a revolt against the kings of Spain and Portugal near the town of St. Sacrement.[8] Candide, having served in the Bulgar army, performed the Bulgar manual of arms before the general of the little army with such grace, swiftness, dexterity, fire, and agility, that they gave him a company of infantry to command. So here he is, a captain; and off he sails with Miss Cunégonde, the old woman, two valets, and the two Andalusian steeds which had belonged to My Lord the Grand Inquisitor of Portugal.

Throughout the crossing, they spent a great deal of time reasoning about the philosophy of poor Pangloss.

—We are destined, in the end, for another universe, said Candide; no doubt that is the one where everything is well. For in

8. Actually, Colonia del Sacramento. Voltaire took great interest in the Jesuit role in Paraguay, which he has much oversimplified and largely misrepresented here in the interests of his satire. In 1750 they did, however, offer armed resistance to an agreement made between Spain and Portugal. They were subdued and expelled in 1769.

this one, it must be admitted, there is some reason to grieve over our physical and moral state.

—I love you with all my heart, said Cunégonde; but my soul is still harrowed by thoughts of what I have seen and suffered.

—All will be well, replied Candide; the sea of this new world is already better than those of Europe, calmer and with steadier winds. Surely it is the New World which is the best of all possible worlds.

—God grant it, said Cunégonde; but I have been so horribly unhappy in the world so far, that my heart is almost dead to hope.

—You pity yourselves, the old woman told them; but you have had no such misfortunes as mine.

Cunégonde nearly broke out laughing; she found the old woman comic in pretending to be more unhappy than she.

—Ah, you poor old thing, said she, unless you've been raped by two Bulgars, been stabbed twice in the belly, seen two of your castles destroyed, witnessed the murder of two of your mothers and two of your fathers, and watched two of your lovers being whipped in an auto-da-fé, I do not see how you can have had it worse than me. Besides, I was born a baroness, with seventy-two quarterings, and I have worked in a scullery.

—My lady, replied the old woman, you do not know my birth and rank; and if I showed you my rear end, you would not talk as you do, you might even speak with less assurance.

These words inspired great curiosity in Candide and Cunégonde, which the old woman satisfied with this story.

CHAPTER 11
The Old Woman's Story

—My eyes were not always bloodshot and red-rimmed, my nose did not always touch my chin, and I was not born a servant. I am in fact the daughter of Pope Urban the Tenth and the Princess of Palestrina.[9] Till the age of fourteen, I lived in a palace so splendid that all the castles of all your German barons would not have served it as a stable; a single one of my dresses was worth more than all the assembled magnificence of Westphalia. I grew in beauty, in charm, in talent, surrounded by pleasures, dignities, and glowing visions of the future. Already I was inspiring the young men to love; my breast was formed—and what a breast! white, firm, with the shape of the Venus de Medici; and what eyes! what lashes, what black brows! What fire flashed from my glances and outshone the glitter

9. Voltaire left behind a comment on this passage, a note first published in 1829: "Note the extreme discretion of the author; hitherto there has never been a pope named Urban X; he avoided attributing a bastard to a known pope. What circumspection! what an exquisite conscience!"

of the stars, as the local poets used to tell me! The women who helped me dress and undress fell into ecstasies, whether they looked at me from in front or behind; and all the men wanted to be in their place.

—I was engaged to the ruling prince of Massa-Carrara; and what a prince he was! as handsome as I, softness and charm compounded, brilliantly witty, and madly in love with me. I loved him in return as one loves for the first time, with a devotion approaching idolatry. The wedding preparations had been made, with a splendor and magnificence never heard of before; nothing but celebrations, masks, and comic operas, uninterruptedly; and all Italy composed in my honor sonnets of which not one was even passable. I had almost attained the very peak of bliss, when an old marquise who had been the mistress of my prince invited him to her house for a cup of chocolate. He died in less than two hours, amid horrifying convulsions. But that was only a trifle. My mother, in complete despair (though less afflicted than I), wished to escape for a while the oppressive atmosphere of grief. She owned a handsome property near Gaeta.[1] We embarked on a papal galley gilded like the altar of St. Peter's in Rome. Suddenly a pirate ship from Salé swept down and boarded us. Our soldiers defended themselves as papal troops usually do; falling on their knees and throwing down their arms, they begged of the corsair absolution *in articulo mortis*.[2]

—They were promptly stripped as naked as monkeys, and so was my mother, and so were our maids of honor, and so was I too. It's a very remarkable thing, the energy these gentlemen put into stripping people. But what surprised me even more was that they stuck their fingers in a place where we women usually admit only a syringe. This ceremony seemed a bit odd to me, as foreign usages always do when one hasn't traveled. They only wanted to see if we didn't have some diamonds hidden there; and I soon learned that it's a custom of long standing among the genteel folk who swarm the seas. I learned that my lords the very religious knights of Malta never overlook this ceremony when they capture Turks, whether male or female; it's one of those international laws which have never been questioned.

—I won't try to explain how painful it is for a young princess to be carried off into slavery in Morocco with her mother. You can imagine everything we had to suffer on the pirate ship. My mother was still very beautiful; our maids of honor, our mere chambermaids, were more charming than anything one could find in all Africa. As for myself, I was ravishing, I was loveliness and grace su-

1. About halfway between Rome and Naples.
2. Literally, when at the point of death. Absolution from a corsair in the act of murdering one is of very dubious validity.

preme, and I was a virgin. I did not remain so for long; the flower which had been kept for the handsome prince of Massa-Carrara was plucked by the corsair captain; he was an abominable negro, who thought he was doing me a great favor. My Lady the Princess of Palestrina and I must have been strong indeed to bear what we did during our journey to Morocco. But on with my story; these are such common matters that they are not worth describing.

—Morocco was knee deep in blood when we arrived. Of the fifty sons of the emperor Muley-Ismael,[3] each had his faction, which produced in effect fifty civil wars, of blacks against blacks, of blacks against browns, halfbreeds against halfbreeds; throughout the length and breadth of the empire, nothing but one continual carnage.

—Scarcely had we stepped ashore, when some negroes of a faction hostile to my captor arrived to take charge of his plunder. After the diamonds and gold, we women were the most prized possessions. I was now witness of a struggle such as you never see in the temperate climate of Europe. Northern people don't have hot blood; they don't feel the absolute fury for women which is common in Africa. Europeans seem to have milk in their veins; it is vitriol or liquid fire which pulses through these people around Mount Atlas. The fight for possession of us raged with the fury of the lions, tigers, and poisonous vipers of that land. A Moor snatched my mother by the right arm, the first mate held her by the left; a Moorish soldier grabbed one leg, one of our pirates the other. In a moment's time almost all our girls were being dragged four different ways. My captain held me behind him while with his scimitar he killed everyone who braved his fury. At last I saw all our Italian women, including my mother, torn to pieces, cut to bits, murdered by the monsters who were fighting over them. My captive companions, their captors, soldiers, sailors, blacks, browns, whites, mulattoes, and at last my captain, all were killed, and I remained half dead on a mountain of corpses. Similar scenes were occurring, as is well known, for more than three hundred leagues around, without anyone skimping on the five prayers a day decreed by Mohammed.

—With great pain, I untangled myself from this vast heap of bleeding bodies, and dragged myself under a great orange tree by a neighboring brook, where I collapsed, from terror, exhaustion, horror, despair, and hunger. Shortly, my weary mind surrendered to a sleep which was more of a swoon than a rest. I was in this state of weakness and languor, between life and death, when I felt myself

3. Having reigned for more than fifty years, a potent and ruthless sultan of Morocco, he died in 1727 and left his kingdom in much the condition described.

touched by something which moved over my body. Opening my eyes, I saw a white man, rather attractive, who was groaning and saying under his breath: '*O che sciagura d'essere senza coglioni!*'[4]

CHAPTER 12
The Old Woman's Story Continued

—Amazed and delighted to hear my native tongue, and no less surprised by what this man was saying, I told him that there were worse evils than those he was complaining of. In a few words, I described to him the horrors I had undergone, and then fainted again. He carried me to a nearby house, put me to bed, gave me something to eat, served me, flattered me, comforted me, told me he had never seen anyone so lovely, and added that he had never before regretted so much the loss of what nobody could give him back.

'I was born at Naples, he told me, where they caponize two or three thousand children every year; some die of it, others acquire a voice more beautiful than any woman's, still others go on to become governors of kingdoms.[5] The operation was a great success with me, and I became court musician to the Princess of Palestrina . . .'

'Of my mother,' I exclaimed.

'Of your mother,' cried he, bursting into tears; 'then you must be the princess whom I raised till she was six, and who already gave promise of becoming as beautiful as you are now!'

'I am that very princess; my mother lies dead, not a hundred yards from here, buried under a pile of corpses.'

—I told him my adventures, he told me his: that he had been sent by a Christian power to the King of Morocco, to conclude a treaty granting him gunpowder, cannon, and ships with which to liquidate the traders of the other Christian powers.

'My mission is concluded,' said this honest eunuch; 'I shall take ship at Ceuta and bring you back to Italy. *Ma che sciagura d'essere senza coglioni!*'

—I thanked him with tears of gratitude, and instead of returning me to Italy, he took me to Algiers and sold me to the dey of that country. Hardly had the sale taken place, when that plague which has made the rounds of Africa, Asia, and Europe broke out in full fury at Algiers. You have seen earthquakes; but tell me, young lady, have you ever had the plague?

—Never, replied the baroness.

—If you had had it, said the old woman, you would agree that it is far worse than an earthquake. It is very frequent in Africa, and I

4. "Oh what a misfortune to have no testicles!"
5. The castrato Farinelli (1705–1782), originally a singer, came to exercise considerable political influence on the Kings of Spain, Philip V and Ferdinand VI.

had it. Imagine, if you will, the situation of a pope's daughter, fifteen years old, who in three months' time had experienced poverty, slavery, had been raped almost every day, had seen her mother quartered, had suffered from famine and war, and who now was dying of pestilence in Algiers. As a matter of fact, I did not die; but the eunuch and the dey and nearly the entire seraglio of Algiers perished.

—When the first horrors of this ghastly plague had passed, the slaves of the dey were sold. A merchant bought me and took me to Tunis; there he sold me to another merchant, who resold me at Tripoli; from Tripoli I was sold to Alexandria, from Alexandria resold to Smyrna, from Smyrna to Constantinople. I ended by belonging to an aga of janizaries, who was shortly ordered to defend Azov against the besieging Russians.[6]

—The aga, who was a gallant soldier, took his whole seraglio with him, and established us in a little fort amid the Maeotian marshes,[7] guarded by two black eunuchs and twenty soldiers. Our side killed a prodigious number of Russians, but they paid us back nicely. Azov was put to fire and sword without respect for age or sex; only our little fort continued to resist, and the enemy determined to starve us out. The twenty janizaries had sworn never to surrender. Reduced to the last extremities of hunger, they were forced to eat our two eunuchs, lest they violate their oaths. After several more days, they decided to eat the women too.

—We had an imam,[8] very pious and sympathetic, who delivered an excellent sermon, persuading them not to kill us altogether.

'Just cut off a single rumpsteak from each of these ladies,' he said, 'and you'll have a fine meal. Then if you should need another, you can come back in a few days and have as much again; heaven will bless your charitable action, and you will be saved.'

—His eloquence was splendid, and he persuaded them. We underwent this horrible operation. The imam treated us all with the ointment that they use on newly circumcised children. We were at the point of death.

—Scarcely had the janizaries finished the meal for which we furnished the materials, when the Russians appeared in flat-bottomed boats; not a janizary escaped. The Russians paid no attention to the state we were in; but there are French physicians everywhere, and one of them, who knew his trade, took care of us. He cured us, and I shall remember all my life that when my wounds were healed, he made me a proposition. For the rest, he counselled us simply to

6. Azov, near the mouth of the Don, was besieged by the Russians under Peter the Great in 1695–1696. The janizaries were an élite corps of the Ottoman armies.

7. The Roman name of the so-called Sea of Azov, a shallow swampy lake near the town.

8. In effect, a chaplain.

have patience, assuring us that the same thing had happened in several other sieges, and that it was according to the laws of war.

—As soon as my companions could walk, we were herded off to Moscow. In the division of booty, I fell to a boyar who made me work in his garden, and gave me twenty whiplashes a day; but when he was broken on the wheel after about two years, with thirty other boyars, over some little court intrigue,[9] I seized the occasion; I ran away; I crossed all Russia; I was for a long time a chambermaid in Riga, then at Rostock, Vismara, Leipzig, Cassel, Utrecht, Leyden, The Hague, Rotterdam; I grew old in misery and shame, having only half a backside and remembering always that I was the daughter of a Pope; a hundred times I wanted to kill myself, but always I loved life more. This ridiculous weakness is perhaps one of our worst instincts; is anything more stupid than choosing to carry a burden that really one wants to cast on the ground? to hold existence in horror, and yet to cling to it? to fondle the serpent which devours us till it has eaten out our heart?

—In the countries through which I have been forced to wander, in the taverns where I have had to work, I have seen a vast number of people who hated their existence; but I never saw more than a dozen who deliberately put an end to their own misery: three negroes, four Englishmen, four Genevans, and a German professor named Robeck.[1] My last post was as servant to the jew Don Issachar; he attached me to your service, my lovely one; and I attached myself to your destiny, till I have become more concerned with your fate than with my own. I would not even have mentioned my own misfortunes, if you had not irked me a bit, and if it weren't the custom, on shipboard, to pass the time with stories. In a word, my lady, I have had some experience of the world, I know it; why not try this diversion? Ask every passenger on this ship to tell you his story, and if you find a single one who has not often cursed the day of his birth, who has not often told himself that he is the most miserable of men, then you may throw me overboard head first.

9. Voltaire had in mind an ineffectual conspiracy against Peter the Great known as the "revolt of the strelitz" or musketeers, which took place in 1698. Though easily put down, it provoked from the emperor a massive and atrocious program of reprisals.

1. Johann Robeck (1672–1739) published a treatise advocating suicide and showed his conviction by drowning himself. But he waited till he was 67 before putting his theory to the test. For a larger view of the issue, see L. G. Crocker, "The Discussion of Suicide in the 18th Century," *Journal of the History of Ideas,* XIII, 47–72 (1952).

CHAPTER 13
How Candide Was Forced to Leave the Lovely Cunégonde and the Old Woman

Having heard out the old woman's story, the lovely Cunégonde paid her the respects which were appropriate to a person of her rank and merit. She took up the wager as well, and got all the passengers, one after another, to tell her their adventures. She and Candide had to agree that the old woman had been right.

—It's certainly too bad, said Candide, that the wise Pangloss was hanged, contrary to the custom of autos-da-fé; he would have admirable things to say of the physical evil and moral evil which cover land and sea, and I might feel within me the impulse to dare to raise several polite objections.

As the passengers recited their stories, the boat made steady progress, and presently landed at Buenos Aires. Cunégonde, Captain Candide, and the old woman went to call on the governor, Don Fernando d'Ibaraa y Figueroa y Mascarenes y Lampourdos y Souza. This nobleman had the pride appropriate to a man with so many names. He addressed everyone with the most aristocratic disdain, pointing his nose so loftily, raising his voice so mercilessly, lording it so splendidly, and assuming so arrogant a pose, that everyone who met him wanted to kick him. He loved women to the point of fury; and Cunégonde seemed to him the most beautiful creature he had ever seen. The first thing he did was to ask directly if she were the captain's wife. His manner of asking this question disturbed Candide; he did not dare say she was his wife, because in fact she was not; he did not dare say she was his sister, because she wasn't that either; and though this polite lie was once common enough among the ancients,[2] and sometimes serves moderns very well, he was too pure of heart to tell a lie.

—Miss Cunégonde, said he, is betrothed to me, and we humbly beg your excellency to perform the ceremony for us.

Don Fernando d'Ibaraa y Figueroa y Mascarenes y Lampourdos y Souza twirled his moustache, smiled sardonically, and ordered Captain Candide to go drill his company. Candide obeyed. Left alone with My Lady Cunégonde, the governor declared his passion, and protested that he would marry her tomorrow, in church or in any other manner, as it pleased her charming self. Cunégonde asked for a quarter-hour to collect herself, consult the old woman, and make up her mind.

The old woman said to Cunégonde: —My lady, you have

2. Voltaire has in mind Abraham's adventures with Sarah (Genesis xii) and Isaac's with Rebecca (Genesis xxvi).

seventy-two quarterings and not one penny; if you wish, you may be the wife of the greatest lord in South America, who has a really handsome moustache; are you going to insist on your absolute fidelity? You have already been raped by the Bulgars; a jew and an inquisitor have enjoyed your favors; miseries entitle one to privileges. I assure you that in your position I would make no scruple of marrying My Lord the Governor, and making the fortune of Captain Candide.

While the old woman was talking with all the prudence of age and experience, there came into the harbor a small ship bearing an alcalde and some alguazils.[3] This is what had happened.

As the old woman had very shrewdly guessed, it was a long-sleeved Franciscan who stole Cunégonde's gold and jewels in the town of Badajoz, when she and Candide were in flight. The monk tried to sell some of the gems to a jeweler, who recognized them as belonging to the Grand Inquisitor. Before he was hanged, the Franciscan confessed that he had stolen them, indicating who his victims were and where they were going. The flight of Cunégonde and Candide was already known. They were traced to Cadiz, and a vessel was hastily dispatched in pursuit of them. This vessel was now in the port of Buenos Aires. The rumor spread that an alcalde was aboard, in pursuit of the murderers of My Lord the Grand Inquisitor. The shrewd old woman saw at once what was to be done.

—You cannot escape, she told Cunégonde, and you have nothing to fear. You are not the one who killed my lord, and, besides, the governor, who is in love with you, won't let you be mistreated. Sit tight.

And then she ran straight to Candide: —Get out of town, she said, or you'll be burned within the hour.

There was not a moment to lose; but how to leave Cunégonde, and where to go?

CHAPTER 14

How Candide and Cacambo Were Received by the Jesuits of Paraguay

Candide had brought from Cadiz a valet of the type one often finds in the provinces of Spain and in the colonies. He was one quarter Spanish, son of a halfbreed in the Tucuman[4]; he had been choirboy, sacristan, sailor, monk, merchant, soldier, and lackey. His name was Cacambo, and he was very fond of his master because his

3. Police officers.

4. A city and province of Argentina, to the northwest of Buenos Aires, just at the juncture of the Andes and the Grand Chaco.

master was a very good man. In hot haste he saddled the two Andalusian steeds.

—Hurry, master, do as the old woman says; let's get going and leave this town without a backward look.

Candide wept: —O my beloved Cunégonde! must I leave you now, just when the governor is about to marry us! Cunégonde, brought from so far, what will ever become of you?

—She'll become what she can, said Cacambo; women can always find something to do with themselves; God sees to it; let's get going.

—Where are you taking me? where are we going? what will we do without Cunégonde? said Candide.

—By Saint James of Compostela, said Cacambo, you were going to make war against the Jesuits, now we'll go make war for them. I know the roads pretty well, I'll bring you to their country, they will be delighted to have a captain who knows the Bulgar drill; you'll make a prodigious fortune. If you don't get your rights in one world, you will find them in another. And isn't it pleasant to see new things and do new things?

—Then you've already been in Paraguay? said Candide.

—Indeed I have, replied Cacambo; I was cook in the College of the Assumption, and I know the government of Los Padres[5] as I know the streets of Cadiz. It's an admirable thing, this government. The kingdom is more than three hundred leagues across; it is divided into thirty provinces. Los Padres own everything in it, and the people nothing; it's a masterpiece of reason and justice. I myself know nothing so wonderful as Los Padres, who in this hemisphere make war on the kings of Spain and Portugal, but in Europe hear their confessions; who kill Spaniards here, and in Madrid send them to heaven; that really tickles me; let's get moving, you're going to be the happiest of men. Won't Los Padres be delighted when they learn they have a captain who knows the Bulgar drill!

As soon as they reached the first barricade, Cacambo told the frontier guard that a captain wished to speak with My Lord the Commander. A Paraguayan officer ran to inform headquarters by laying the news at the feet of the commander. Candide and Cacambo were first disarmed and deprived of their Andalusian horses. They were then placed between two files of soldiers; the commander was at the end, his three-cornered hat on his head, his cassock drawn up, a sword at his side, and a pike in his hand. He nods, and twenty-four soldiers surround the newcomers. A sergeant then informs them that they must wait, that the commander cannot talk to them, since the reverend father provincial has forbidden all

5. The Jesuit fathers. R. B. Cunningham-Grahame has written an account of the Jesuits in Paraguay 1607–1767, under the title *A Vanished Arcadia*.

Spaniards from speaking, except in his presence, and from remaining more than three hours in the country.[6]

—And where is the reverend father provincial? says Cacambo.

—He is reviewing his troops after having said mass, the sergeant replies, and you'll only be able to kiss his spurs in three hours.

—But, says Cacambo, my master the captain, who, like me, is dying from hunger, is not Spanish at all, he is German; can't we have some breakfast while waiting for his reverence?

The sergeant promptly went off to report this speech to the commander.

—God be praised, said this worthy; since he is German, I can talk to him; bring him into my bower.

Candide was immediately led into a leafy nook surrounded by a handsome colonnade of green and gold marble and trellises amid which sported parrots, birds of paradise,[7] humming birds, guinea fowl, and all the rarest species of birds. An excellent breakfast was prepared in golden vessels; and while the Paraguayans ate corn out of wooden bowls in the open fields under the glare of the sun, the reverend father commander entered into his bower.

He was a very handsome young man, with an open face, rather blonde in coloring, with ruddy complexion, arched eyebrows, liquid eyes, pink ears, bright red lips, and an air of pride, but a pride somehow different from that of a Spaniard or a Jesuit. Their confiscated weapons were restored to Candide and Cacambo, as well as their Andalusian horses; Cacambo fed them oats alongside the bower, always keeping an eye on them for fear of an ambush.

First Candide kissed the hem of the commander's cassock, then they sat down at the table.

—So you are German? said the Jesuit, speaking in that language.

—Yes, your reverence, said Candide.

As they spoke these words, both men looked at one another with great surprise, and another emotion which they could not control.

—From what part of Germany do you come? said the Jesuit.

—From the nasty province of Westphalia, said Candide; I was born in the castle of Thunder-Ten-Tronckh.

—Merciful heavens! cries the commander. Is it possible?

—What a miracle! exclaims Candide.

6. In fact, the Jesuits, who had organized their Indian parishes into villages under a system of tribal communism, did their best to discourage contact with the outside world.

7. In this passage and several later ones, Voltaire uses in conjunction two words, both of which mean humming bird. The French system of classifying humming birds, based on the work of the celebrated Buffon, distinguishes *oiseaux-mouches* with straight bills from *colibris* with curved bills. This distinction is wholly fallacious. Humming birds have all manner of shaped bills, and the division of species must be made on other grounds entirely. At the expense of ornithological accuracy, I have therefore introduced birds of paradise to get the requisite sense of glitter and sheen.

—Can it be you? asks the commander.

—It's impossible, says Candide.

They both fall back in their chairs, they embrace they shed streams of tears.

—What, can it be you, reverend father! you, the brother of the lovely Cunégonde! you, who were killed by the Bulgars! you, the son of My Lord the Baron! you, a Jesuit in Paraguay! It's a mad world, indeed it is. Oh, Pangloss! Pangloss! how happy you would be, if you hadn't been hanged.

The commander dismissed his negro slaves and the Paraguayans who served his drink in crystal goblets. He thanked God and Saint Ignatius a thousand times, he clasped Candide in his arms, their faces were bathed in tears.

—You would be even more astonished, even more delighted, even more beside yourself, said Candide, if I told you that My Lady Cunégonde, your sister, who you thought was disemboweled, is enjoying good health.

—Where?

—Not far from here, in the house of the governor of Buenos Aires; and to think that I came to make war on you!

Each word they spoke in this long conversation added another miracle. Their souls danced on their tongues, hung eagerly at their ears, glittered in their eyes. As they were Germans, they sat a long time at table, waiting for the reverend father provincial; and the commander spoke in these terms to his dear Candide.

CHAPTER 15
How Candide Killed the Brother of His Dear Cunégonde

—All my life long I shall remember the horrible day when I saw my father and mother murdered and my sister raped. When the Bulgars left, that adorable sister of mine was nowhere to be found; so they loaded a cart with my mother, my father, myself, two serving girls, and three little murdered boys, to carry us all off for burial in a Jesuit chapel some two leagues from our ancestral castle. A Jesuit sprinkled us with holy water; it was horribly salty, and a few drops got into my eyes; the father noticed that my lid made a little tremor; putting his hand on my heart, he felt it beat; I was rescued, and at the end of three weeks was as good as new. You know, my dear Candide, that I was a very pretty boy; I became even more so; the reverend father Croust,[8] superior of the abbey, conceived a most tender friendship for me; he accepted me as a novice, and shortly after, I was sent to Rome. The Father General had need of

8. It is the name of a Jesuit rector at Colmar with whom Voltaire had quarreled in 1754.

a resupply of young German Jesuits. The rulers of Paraguay accept as few Spanish Jesuits as they can; they prefer foreigners, whom they think they can control better. I was judged fit, by the Father General, to labor in this vineyard. So we set off, a Pole, a Tyrolean, and myself. Upon our arrival, I was honored with the posts of sub-deacon and lieutenant; today I am a colonel and a priest. We are giving a vigorous reception to the King of Spain's men; I assure you they will be excommunicated as well as trounced on the battlefield. Providence has sent you to help us. But is it really true that my dear sister, Cunégonde, is in the neighborhood, with the governor of Buenos Aires?

Candide reassured him with a solemn oath that nothing could be more true. Their tears began to flow again.

The baron could not weary of embracing Candide; he called him his brother, his savior.

—Ah, my dear Candide, said he, maybe together we will be able to enter the town as conquerors, and be united with my sister Cunégonde.

—That is all I desire, said Candide; I was expecting to marry her, and I still hope to.

—You insolent dog, replied the baron, you would have the effrontery to marry my sister, who has seventy-two quarterings! It's a piece of presumption for you even to mention such a crazy project in my presence.

Candide, terrified by this speech, answered: —Most reverend father, all the quarterings in the world don't affect this case; I have rescued your sister out of the arms of a jew and an inquisitor; she has many obligations to me, she wants to marry me. Master Pangloss always taught me that men are equal; and I shall certainly marry her.

—We'll see about that, you scoundrel, said the Jesuit baron of Thunder-Ten-Tronckh; and so saying, he gave him a blow across the face with the flat of his sword. Candide immediately drew his own sword and thrust it up to the hilt in the baron's belly; but as he drew it forth all dripping, he began to weep.

—Alas, dear God! said he, I have killed my old master, my friend, my brother-in-law; I am the best man in the world, and here are three men I've killed already, and two of the three were priests.

Cacambo, who was standing guard at the entry of the bower, came running.

—We can do nothing but sell our lives dearly, said his master; someone will certainly come; we must die fighting.

Cacambo, who had been in similar scrapes before, did not lose his head; he took the Jesuit's cassock, which the commander had been wearing, and put it on Candide; he stuck the dead man's square hat on Candide's head, and forced him onto horseback. Everything was done in the wink of an eye.

—Let's ride, master; everyone will take you for a Jesuit on his way to deliver orders; and we will have passed the frontier before anyone can come after us.

Even as he was pronouncing these words, he charged off, crying in Spanish: —Way, make way for the reverend father colonel!

CHAPTER 16

What Happened to the Two Travelers with Two Girls, Two Monkeys, and the Savages Named Biglugs

Candide and his valet were over the frontier before anyone in the camp knew of the death of the German Jesuit. Foresighted Cacambo had taken care to fill his satchel with bread, chocolate, ham, fruit, and several bottles of wine. They pushed their Andalusian horses forward into unknown country, where there were no roads. Finally a broad prairie divided by several streams opened before them. Our two travelers turned their horses loose to graze; Cacambo suggested that they eat too, and promptly set the example. But Candide said: —How can you expect me to eat ham when I have killed the son of My Lord the Baron, and am now condemned never to see the lovely Cunégonde for the rest of my life? Why should I drag out my miserable days, since I must exist far from her in in the depths of despair and remorse? And what will the *Journal de Trévoux* say of all this?[9]

Though he talked this way, he did not neglect the food. Night fell. The two wanderers heard a few weak cries which seemed to be voiced by women. They could not tell whether the cries expressed grief or joy; but they leaped at once to their feet, with that uneasy suspicion which one always feels in an unknown country. The outcry arose from two girls, completely naked, who were running swiftly along the edge of the meadow, pursued by two monkeys who snapped at their buttocks. Candide was moved to pity; he had learned marksmanship with the Bulgars, and could have knocked a nut off a bush without touching the leaves. He raised his Spanish rifle, fired twice, and killed the two monkeys.

—God be praised, my dear Cacambo! I've saved these two poor creatures from great danger. Though I committed a sin in killing an inquisitor and a Jesuit, I've redeemed myself by saving the lives of two girls. Perhaps they are two ladies of rank, and this good deed may gain us special advantages in the country.

He had more to say, but his mouth shut suddenly when he

9. A journal published by the Jesuit order, founded in 1701 and consistently hostile to Voltaire.

saw the girls embracing the monkeys tenderly, weeping over their bodies, and filling the air with lamentations.

—I wasn't looking for quite so much generosity of spirit, said he to Cacambo; the latter replied: —You've really fixed things this time, master; you've killed the two lovers of these young ladies.

—Their lovers! Impossible! You must be joking, Cacambo; how can I believe you?

—My dear master, Cacambo replied, you're always astonished by everything. Why do you think it so strange that in some countries monkeys succeed in obtaining the good graces of women? They are one quarter human, just as I am one quarter Spanish.

—Alas, Candide replied, I do remember now hearing Master Pangloss say that such things used to happen, and that from these mixtures there arose pans, fauns, and satyrs, and that these creatures had appeared to various grand figures of antiquity; but I took all that for fables.

—You should be convinced now, said Cacambo; it's true, and you see how people make mistakes who haven't received a measure of education. But what I fear is that these girls may get us into real trouble.

These sensible reflections led Candide to leave the field and to hide in a wood. There he dined with Cacambo; and there both of them, having duly cursed the inquisitor of Portugal, the governor of Buenos Aires, and the baron, went to sleep on a bed of moss. When they woke up, they found themselves unable to move; the reason was that during the night the Biglugs,[1] natives of the country, to whom the girls had complained of them, had tied them down with cords of bark. They were surrounded by fifty naked Biglugs, armed with arrows, clubs, and stone axes. Some were boiling a caldron of water, others were preparing spits, and all cried out: —It's a Jesuit, a Jesuit! We'll be revenged and have a good meal; let's eat some Jesuit, eat some Jesuit!

—I told you, my dear master, said Cacambo sadly, I said those two girls would play us a dirty trick.

Candide, noting the caldron and spits, cried out: —We are surely going to be roasted or boiled. Ah, what would Master Pangloss say if he could see these men in a state of nature? All is for the best, I agree; but I must say it seems hard to have lost Miss Cunégonde and to be stuck on a spit by the Biglugs.

Cacambo did not lose his head.

—Don't give up hope, said he to the disconsolate Candide; I

1. Voltaire's name is "Oreillons" from Spanish "Orejones," a name mentioned in Garcilaso de Vega's *Historia General del Perú* (1609), on which Voltaire drew for many of the details in his picture of South America. See Richard A. Brooks, "Voltaire and Garcilaso de Vega" in *Studies in Voltaire and the 18th Century,* XXX, 189-204.

understand a little of the jargon these people speak, and I'm going to talk to them.

—Don't forget to remind them, said Candide, of the frightful inhumanity of eating their fellow men, and that Christian ethics forbid it.

—Gentlemen, said Cacambo, you have a mind to eat a Jesuit today? An excellent idea; nothing is more proper than to treat one's enemies so. Indeed, the law of nature teaches us to kill our neighbor, and that's how men behave the whole world over. Though we Europeans don't exercise our right to eat our neighbors, the reason is simply that we find it easy to get a good meal elsewhere; but you don't have our resources, and we certainly agree that it's better to eat your enemies than to let the crows and vultures have the fruit of your victory. But, gentlemen, you wouldn't want to eat your friends. You think you will be spitting a Jesuit, and it's your defender, the enemy of your enemies, whom you will be roasting. For my part, I was born in your country; the gentleman whom you see is my master, and far from being a Jesuit, he has just killed a Jesuit, the robe he is wearing was stripped from him; that's why you have taken a dislike to him. To prove that I am telling the truth, take his robe and bring it to the nearest frontier of the kingdom of Los Padres; find out for yourselves if my master didn't kill a Jesuit officer. It won't take long; if you find that I have lied, you can still eat us. But if I've told the truth, you know too well the principles of public justice, customs, and laws, not to spare our lives.

The Biglugs found this discourse perfectly reasonable; they appointed chiefs to go posthaste and find out the truth; the two messengers performed their task like men of sense, and quickly returned bringing good news. The Biglugs untied their two prisoners, treated them with great politeness, offered them girls, gave them refreshments, and led them back to the border of their state, crying joyously: —He isn't a Jesuit, he isn't a Jesuit!

Candide could not weary of exclaiming over his preservation.

—What a people! he said. What men! what customs! If I had not had the good luck to run a sword through the body of Miss Cunégonde's brother, I would have been eaten on the spot! But, after all, it seems that uncorrupted nature is good, since these folk, instead of eating me, showed me a thousand kindnesses as soon as they knew I was not a Jesuit.

CHAPTER 17

Arrival of Candide and His Servant at the Country of Eldorado,[2] and What They Saw There

When they were out of the land of the Biglugs, Cacambo said to Candide: —You see that this hemisphere is no better than the other; take my advice, and let's get back to Europe as soon as possible.

—How to get back, asked Candide, and where to go? If I go to my own land, the Bulgars and Abares are murdering everyone in sight; if I go to Portugal, they'll burn me alive; if we stay here, we risk being skewered any day. But how can I ever leave that part of the world where Miss Cunégonde lives?

—Let's go toward Cayenne, said Cacambo, we shall find some Frenchmen there, for they go all over the world; they can help us; perhaps God will take pity on us.

To get to Cayenne was not easy; they knew more or less which way to go, but mountains, rivers, cliffs, robbers, and savages obstructed the way everywhere. Their horses died of weariness; their food was eaten; they subsisted for one whole month on wild fruits, and at last they found themselves by a little river fringed with coconut trees, which gave them both life and hope.

Cacambo, who was as full of good advice as the old woman, said to Candide: —We can go no further, we've walked ourselves out; I see an abandoned canoe on the bank, let's fill it with coconuts, get into the boat, and float with the current; a river always leads to some inhabited spot or other. If we don't find anything pleasant, at least we may find something new.

—Let's go, said Candide, and let Providence be our guide.

They floated some leagues between banks sometimes flowery, sometimes sandy, now steep, now level. The river widened steadily; finally it disappeared into a chasm of frightful rocks that rose high into the heavens.[3] The two travelers had the audacity to float with the current into this chasm. The river, narrowly confined, drove them onward with horrible speed and a fearful roar. After twenty-four hours, they saw daylight once more; but their canoe was smashed on the snags. They had to drag themselves from rock to rock for an entire league; at last they emerged to an immense horizon, ringed with remote mountains. The countryside was tended for pleasure as well as profit; everywhere the useful was joined to the agreeable. The roads were covered, or rather decorated, with ele-

2. The myth of this land of gold somewhere in Central or South America had been widespread since the sixteenth century.

3. This journey down an underground river is probably adapted from a similar episode in the story of Sinbad the Sailor.

gantly shaped carriages made of a glittering material, carrying men and women of singular beauty, and drawn by great red sheep which were faster than the finest horses of Andalusia, Tetuan, and Mequinez.

—Here now, said Candide, is a country that's better than Westphalia.

Along with Cacambo, he climbed out of the river at the first village he could see. Some children of the town, dressed in rags of gold brocade, were playing quoits at the village gate; our two men from the other world paused to watch them; their quoits were rather large, yellow, red, and green, and they glittered with a singular luster. On a whim, the travelers picked up several; they were of gold, emeralds, and rubies, and the least of them would have been the greatest ornament of the Great Mogul's throne.

—Surely, said Cacambo, these quoit players are the children of the king of the country.

The village schoolmaster appeared at that moment, to call them back to school.

—And there, said Candide, is the tutor of the royal household.

The little rascals quickly gave up their game, leaving on the ground their quoits and playthings. Candide picked them up, ran to the schoolmaster, and presented them to him humbly, giving him to understand by sign language that their royal highnesses had forgotten their gold and jewels. With a smile, the schoolmaster tossed them to the ground, glanced quickly but with great surprise at Candide's face, and went his way.

The travelers did not fail to pick up the gold, rubies, and emeralds.

—Where in the world are we? cried Candide. The children of this land must be well trained, since they are taught contempt for gold and jewels.

Cacambo was as much surprised as Candide. At last they came to the finest house of the village; it was built like a European palace. A crowd of people surrounded the door, and even more were in the entry; delightful music was heard, and a delicious aroma of cooking filled the air. Cacambo went up to the door, listened, and reported that they were talking Peruvian; that was his native language, for every reader must know that Cacambo was born in Tucuman, in a village where they talk that language exclusively.

—I'll act as interpreter, he told Candide; it's an hotel, let's go in.

Promptly two boys and two girls of the staff, dressed in cloth of gold, and wearing ribbons in their hair, invited them to sit at the host's table. The meal consisted of four soups, each one garnished with a brace of parakeets, a boiled condor which weighed two hundred pounds, two roast monkeys of an excellent flavor, three hundred birds of paradise in one dish and six hundred humming birds in another, exquisite stews, delicious pastries, the whole thing served up in plates of what looked like rock crystal. The boys and girls of the staff poured them various beverages made from sugar cane.

The diners were for the most part merchants and travelers, all extremely polite, who questioned Cacambo with the most discreet circumspection, and answered his questions very directly.

When the meal was over, Cacambo as well as Candide supposed he could settle his bill handsomely by tossing onto the table two of those big pieces of gold which they had picked up; but the host and hostess burst out laughing, and for a long time nearly split their sides. Finally they subsided.

—Gentlemen, said the host, we see clearly that you're foreigners; we don't meet many of you here. Please excuse our laughing when you offered us in payment a couple of pebbles from the roadside. No doubt you don't have any of our local currency, but you don't need it to eat here. All the hotels established for the promotion of commerce are maintained by the state. You have had meager entertainment here, for we are only a poor town; but everywhere else you will be given the sort of welcome you deserve.

Cacambo translated for Candide all the host's explanations, and Candide listened to them with the same admiration and astonishment that his friend Cacambo showed in reporting them.

—What is this country, then, said they to one another, unknown to the rest of the world, and where nature itself is so different from our own? This probably is the country where everything is for the best; for it's absolutely necessary that such a country should exist somewhere. And whatever Master Pangloss said of the matter, I have often had occasion to notice that things went badly in Westphalia.

CHAPTER 18
What They Saw in the Land of Eldorado

Cacambo revealed his curiosity to the host, and the host told him: —I am an ignorant man and content to remain so; but we have here an old man, retired from the court, who is the most knowing person in the kingdom, and the most talkative.

Thereupon he brought Cacambo to the old man's house. Candide now played second fiddle, and acted as servant to his own valet. They entered an austere little house, for the door was merely of silver and the paneling of the rooms was only gold, though so tastefully wrought that the finest paneling would not surpass it. If the truth must be told, the lobby was only decorated with rubies and emeralds; but the patterns in which they were arranged atoned for the extreme simplicity.

The old man received the two strangers on a sofa stuffed with bird-of-paradise feathers, and offered them several drinks in diamond carafes; then he satisfied their curiosity in these terms.

—I am a hundred and seventy-two years old, and I heard from my late father, who was liveryman to the king, about the astonishing revolutions in Peru which he had seen. Our land here was formerly part of the kingdom of the Incas, who rashly left it in order to conquer another part of the world, and who were ultimately destroyed by the Spaniards. The wisest princes of their house were those who had never left their native valley; they decreed, with the consent of the nation, that henceforth no inhabitant of our little kingdom should ever leave it; and this rule is what has preserved our innocence and our happiness. The Spaniards heard vague rumors about this land, they called it El Dorado; and an English knight named Raleigh[4] even came somewhere close to it about a hundred years ago; but as we are surrounded by unscalable mountains and precipices, we have managed so far to remain hidden from the rapacity of the European nations, who have an inconceivable rage for the pebbles and mud of our land, and who, in order to get some, would butcher us all to the last man.

The conversation was a long one; it turned on the form of the government, the national customs, on women, public shows, the arts. At last Candide, whose taste always ran to metaphysics, told Cacambo to ask if the country had any religion.

The old man grew a bit red.

—How's that? he said. Can you have any doubt of it? Do you suppose we are altogether thankless scoundrels?

Cacambo asked meekly what was the religion of Eldorado. The old man flushed again.

—Can there be two religions? he asked. I suppose our religion is the same as everyone's, we worship God from morning to evening.

—Then you worship a single deity? said Cacambo, who acted throughout as interpreter of the questions of Candide.

—It's obvious, said the old man, that there aren't two or three or four of them. I must say the people of your world ask very remarkable questions.

Candide could not weary of putting questions to this good old man; he wanted to know how the people of Eldorado prayed to God.

—We don't pray to him at all, said the good and respectable

4. *The Discovery of Guiana*, published in 1595, described Sir Walter Raleigh's infatuation with the myth of Eldorado and served to spread the story still further.

sage; we have nothing to ask him for, since everything we need has already been granted; we thank God continually.

Candide was interested in seeing the priests; he had Cacambo ask where they were. The old gentleman smiled.

—My friends, said he, we are all priests; the king and all the heads of household sing formal psalms of thanksgiving every morning, and five or six thousand voices accompany them.

—What! you have no monks to teach, argue, govern, intrigue, and burn at the stake everyone who disagrees with them?

—We should have to be mad, said the old man; here we are all of the same mind, and we don't understand what you're up to with your monks.

Candide was overjoyed at all these speeches, and said to himself: —This is very different from Westphalia and the castle of My Lord the Baron; if our friend Pangloss had seen Eldorado, he wouldn't have called the castle of Thunder-Ten-Tronckh the finest thing on earth; to know the world one must travel.

After this long conversation, the old gentleman ordered a carriage with six sheep made ready, and gave the two travelers twelve of his servants for their journey to the court.

—Excuse me, said he, if old age deprives me of the honor of accompanying you. The king will receive you after a style which will not altogether displease you, and you will doubtless make allowance for the customs of the country if there are any you do not like.

Candide and Cacambo climbed into the coach; the six sheep flew like the wind, and in less than four hours they reached the king's palace at the edge of the capital. The entryway was two hundred and twenty feet high and a hundred wide; it is impossible to describe all the materials of which it was made. But you can imagine how much finer it was than those pebbles and sand which we call gold and jewels.

Twenty beautiful girls of the guard detail welcomed Candide and Cacambo as they stepped from the carriage, took them to the baths, and dressed them in robes woven of humming-bird feathers; then the high officials of the crown, both male and female, led them to the royal chamber between two long lines, each of a thousand musicians, as is customary. As they approached the throne room, Cacambo asked an officer what was the proper method of greeting his majesty: if one fell to one's knees or on one's belly; if one put one's hands on one's head or on one's rear; if one licked up the dust of the earth—in a word, what was the proper form?[5]

—The ceremony, said the officer, is to embrace the king and kiss him on both cheeks.

5. Candide's questions are probably derived from those of Gulliver on a similar occasion; see *Gulliver's Travels*, Book IV.

Candide and Cacambo fell on the neck of his majesty, who received them with all the dignity imaginable, and asked them politely to dine.

In the interim, they were taken about to see the city, the public buildings rising to the clouds, the public markets and arcades, the fountains of pure water and of rose water, those of sugar cane liquors which flowed perpetually in the great plazas paved with a sort of stone which gave off odors of gillyflower and rose petals. Candide asked to see the supreme court and the hall of parliament; they told him there was no such thing, that lawsuits were unknown. He asked if there were prisons, and was told there were not. What surprised him more, and gave him most pleasure, was the palace of sciences, in which he saw a gallery two thousand paces long, entirely filled with mathematical and physical instruments.

Having passed the whole afternoon seeing only a thousandth part of the city, they returned to the king's palace. Candide sat down to dinner with his majesty, his own valet Cacambo, and several ladies. Never was better food served, and never did a host preside more jovially than his majesty. Cacambo explained the king's witty sayings to Candide, and even when translated they still seemed witty. Of all the things which astonished Candide, this was not, in his eyes, the least astonishing.

They passed a month in this refuge. Candide never tired of saying to Cacambo: —It's true, my friend, I'll say it again, the castle where I was born does not compare with the land where we now are; but Miss Cunégonde is not here, and you doubtless have a mistress somewhere in Europe. If we stay here, we shall be just like everybody else, whereas if we go back to our own world, taking with us just a dozen sheep loaded with Eldorado pebbles, we shall be richer than all the kings put together, we shall have no more inquisitors to fear, and we shall easily be able to retake Miss Cunégonde.

This harangue pleased Cacambo; wandering is such pleasure, it gives a man such prestige at home to be able to talk of what he has seen abroad, that the two happy men resolved to be so no longer, but to take their leave of his majesty.

—You are making a foolish mistake, the king told them; I know very well that my kingdom is nothing much; but when you are pretty comfortable somewhere, you had better stay there. Of course I have no right to keep strangers against their will, that sort of tyranny is not in keeping with our laws or our customs; all men are free; depart when you will, but the way out is very difficult. You cannot possibly go up the river by which you miraculously came; it runs too swiftly through its underground caves. The mountains which surround my land are ten thousand feet high, and steep as walls; each one is more than ten leagues across; the only way down is over precipices. But since you really must go, I shall order my engineers to make a machine which can carry you conveniently. When we take you over the mountains, nobody will be able to go with you, for my subjects have sworn never to leave their refuge, and they are too sensible to break their vows. Other than that, ask of me what you please.

—We only request of your majesty, Cacambo said, a few sheep loaded with provisions, some pebbles, and some of the mud of your country.

The king laughed.

—I simply can't understand, said he, the passion you Europeans have for our yellow mud; but take all you want, and much good may it do you.

He promptly gave orders to his technicians to make a machine for lifting these two extraordinary men out of his kingdom. Three thousand good physicists worked at the problem; the machine was ready in two weeks' time, and cost no more than twenty million pounds sterling, in the money of the country. Cacambo and Candide were placed in the machine; there were two great sheep, saddled and bridled to serve them as steeds when they had cleared the mountains, twenty pack sheep with provisions, thirty which carried presents consisting of the rarities of the country, and fifty loaded with gold, jewels, and diamonds. The king bade tender farewell to the two vagabonds.

It made a fine spectacle, their departure, and the ingenious way in which they were hoisted with their sheep up to the top of the mountains. The technicians bade them good-bye after bringing them to safety, and Candide had now no other desire and no other object than to go and present his sheep to Miss Cunégonde.

—We have, said he, enough to pay off the governor of Buenos Aires—if, indeed, a price can be placed on Miss Cunégonde. Let us go to Cayenne, take ship there, and then see what kingdom we can find to buy up.

CHAPTER 19

What Happened to Them at Surinam, and How Candide Got to Know Martin

The first day was pleasant enough for our travelers. They were encouraged by the idea of possessing more treasures than Asia, Europe, and Africa could bring together. Candide, in transports, carved the name of Cunégonde on the trees. On the second day two of their sheep bogged down in a swamp and were lost with their loads; two other sheep died of fatigue a few days later; seven or eight others starved to death in a desert; still others fell, a little after, from precipices. Finally, after a hundred days' march, they had only two sheep left. Candide told Cacambo: —My friend, you see how the riches of this world are fleeting; the only solid things are virtue and the joy of seeing Miss Cunégonde again.

—I agree, said Cacambo, but we still have two sheep, laden with more treasure than the king of Spain will ever have; and I see in the distance a town which I suspect is Surinam; it belongs to the Dutch. We are at the end of our trials and on the threshold of our happiness.

As they drew near the town, they discovered a negro stretched on the ground with only half his clothes left, that is, a pair of blue drawers; the poor fellow was also missing his left leg and his right hand.

—Good Lord, said Candide in Dutch, what are you doing in that horrible condition, my friend?

—I am waiting for my master, Mr. Vanderdendur,[6] the famous merchant, answered the negro.

—Is Mr. Vanderdendur, Candide asked, the man who treated you this way?

—Yes, sir, said the negro, that's how things are around here. Twice a year we get a pair of linen drawers to wear. If we catch a finger in the sugar mill where we work, they cut off our hand; if we try to run away, they cut off our leg: I have undergone both these experiences. This is the price of the sugar you eat in Europe. And yet, when my mother sold me for ten Patagonian crowns on the coast of Guinea, she said to me: 'My dear child, bless our witch doctors, reverence them always, they will make your life happy; you have the honor of being a slave to our white masters, and in this way you are making the fortune of your father and mother.' Alas! I don't know if I made their fortunes, but they certainly did not make mine. The dogs, monkeys, and parrots are a thousand times less unhappy than we are. The Dutch witch doctors who converted me tell me every Sunday that we are all sons of Adam, black and white alike. I am no genealogist; but if these preachers are right, we must all be remote cousins; and you must admit no one could treat his own flesh and blood in a more horrible fashion.

—Oh Pangloss! cried Candide, you had no notion of these abominations! I'm through, I must give up your optimism after all.

—What's optimism? said Cacambo.

—Alas, said Candide, it is a mania for saying things are well

6. A name perhaps intended to suggest VanDuren, a Dutch bookseller with whom Voltaire had quarreled. In particular, the incident of gradually raising one's price recalls VanDuren, to whom Voltaire had successively offered 1,000, 1,500, 2,000, and 3,000 florins for the return of the manuscript of Frederick the Great's *Anti-Machiavel.*

when one is in hell.

And he shed bitter tears as he looked at his negro, and he was still weeping as he entered Surinam.

The first thing they asked was if there was not some vessel in port which could be sent to Buenos Aires. The man they asked was a Spanish merchant who undertook to make an honest bargain with them. They arranged to meet in a cafe; Candide and the faithful Cacambo, with their two sheep, went there to meet with him.

Candide, who always said exactly what was in his heart, told the Spaniard of his adventures, and confessed that he wanted to recapture Miss Cunégonde.

—I shall take good care *not* to send you to Buenos Aires, said the merchant; I should be hanged, and so would you. The lovely Cunégonde is his lordship's favorite mistress.

This was a thunderstroke for Candide; he wept for a long time; finally he drew Cacambo aside.

—Here, my friend, said he, is what you must do. Each one of us has in his pockets five or six millions' worth of diamonds; you are cleverer than I; go get Miss Cunégonde in Buenos Aires. If the governor makes a fuss, give him a million; if that doesn't convince him, give him two millions; you never killed an inquisitor, nobody will suspect you. I'll fit out another boat and go wait for you in Venice. That is a free country, where one need have no fear either of Bulgars or Abares or jews or inquisitors.

Cacambo approved of this wise decision. He was in despair at leaving a good master who had become a bosom friend; but the pleasure of serving him overcame the grief of leaving him. They embraced, and shed a few tears; Candide urged him not to forget the good old woman. Cacambo departed that very same day; he was a very good fellow, that Cacambo.

Candide remained for some time in Surinam, waiting for another merchant to take him to Italy, along with the two sheep which were left him. He hired servants and bought everything necessary for the long voyage; finally Mr. Vanderdendur, master of a big ship, came calling.

—How much will you charge, Candide asked this man, to take me to Venice—myself, my servants, my luggage, and those two sheep over there?

The merchant set a price of ten thousand piastres; Candide did not blink an eye.

—Oh ho, said the prudent Vanderdendur to himself, this stranger pays out ten thousand piastres at once, he must be pretty well fixed.

Then, returning a moment later, he made known that he could not set sail under twenty thousand.

—All right, you shall have them, said Candide.

—Whew, said the merchant softly to himself, this man gives twenty thousand piastres as easily as ten.

He came back again to say he could not go to Venice for less than thirty thousand piastres.

—All right, thirty then, said Candide.

—Ah ha, said the Dutch merchant, again speaking to himself; so thirty thousand piastres mean nothing to this man; no doubt the two sheep are loaded with immense treasures; let's say no more; we'll pick up the thirty thousand piastres first, and then we'll see.

Candide sold two little diamonds, the least of which was worth more than all the money demanded by the merchant. He paid him in advance. The two sheep were taken aboard. Candide followed in a little boat, to board the vessel at its anchorage. The merchant bides his time, sets sail, and makes his escape with a favoring wind. Candide, aghast and stupified, soon loses him from view.

—Alas, he cries, now there is a trick worthy of the old world!

He returns to shore sunk in misery; for he had lost riches enough to make the fortunes of twenty monarchs.

Now he rushes to the house of the Dutch magistrate, and, being a bit disturbed, he knocks loudly at the door; goes in, tells the story of what happened, and shouts a bit louder than is customary. The judge begins by fining him ten thousand piastres for making such a racket; then he listens patiently to the story, promises to look into the matter as soon as the merchant comes back, and charges another ten thousand piastres as the costs of the hearing.

This legal proceeding completed the despair of Candide. In fact he had experienced miseries a thousand times more painful, but the coldness of the judge, and that of the merchant who had robbed him, roused his bile and plunged him into a black melancholy. The malice of men rose up before his spirit in all its ugliness, and his mind dwelt only on gloomy thoughts. Finally, when a French vessel was ready to leave for Bordeaux, since he had no more diamond-laden sheep to transport, he took a cabin at a fair price, and made it known in the town that he would pay passage and keep, plus two thousand piastres, to any honest man who wanted to make the journey with him, on condition that this man must be the most disgusted with his own condition and the most unhappy man in the province.

This drew such a crowd of applicants as a fleet could not have held. Candide wanted to choose among the leading candidates, so he picked out about twenty who seemed companionable enough, and of whom each pretended to be more miserable than all the others. He brought them together at his inn and gave them a dinner, on condition that each would swear to tell truthfully his entire history. He would select as his companion the most truly miserable and rightly discontented man, and among the others he would distribute various gifts.

The meeting lasted till four in the morning. Candide, as he listened to all the stories, remembered what the old woman had told him on the trip to Buenos Aires, and of the wager she had made, that there was nobody on the boat who had not undergone great misfortunes. At every story that was told him, he thought of Pangloss.

—That Pangloss, he said, would be hard put to prove his system. I wish he was here. Certainly if everything goes well, it is in Eldorado and not in the rest of the world.

At last he decided in favor of a poor scholar who had worked ten years for the booksellers of Amsterdam. He decided that there was no trade in the world with which one should be more disgusted.

This scholar, who was in fact a good man, had been robbed by his wife, beaten by his son, and deserted by his daughter, who had got herself abducted by a Portuguese. He had just been fired from the little job on which he existed; and the preachers of Surinam were persecuting him because they took him for a Socinian.[7] The others, it is true, were at least as unhappy as he, but Candide hoped the scholar would prove more amusing on the voyage. All his rivals declared that Candide was doing them a great injustice, but he pacified them with a hundred piastres apiece.

CHAPTER 20
What Happened to Candide and Martin at Sea

The old scholar, whose name was Martin, now set sail with Candide for Bordeaux. Both men had seen and suffered much; and even if the vessel had been sailing from Surinam to Japan via the Cape of Good Hope, they would have been able to keep themselves amused with instances of moral evil and physical evil during the entire trip.

However, Candide had one great advantage over Martin, that he still hoped to see Miss Cunégonde again, and Martin had nothing to hope for; besides, he had gold and diamonds, and though he had lost a hundred big red sheep loaded with the greatest treasures of the earth, though he had always at his heart a memory of the Dutch merchant's villainy, yet, when he thought of the wealth that remained in his hands, and when he talked of Cunégonde, especially just after a good dinner, he still inclined to the system of Pangloss.

7. A follower of Faustus and Laelius Socinus, sixteenth-century Polish theologians, who proposed a form of "rational" Christianity which exalted the rational conscience and minimized such mysteries as the trinity. The Socinians, by a special irony, were vigorous optimists.

—But what about you, Monsieur Martin, he asked the scholar, what do you think of all that? What is your idea of moral evil and physical evil?

—Sir, answered Martin, those priests accused me of being a Socinian, but the truth is that I am a Manichee.[8]

—You're joking, said Candide; there aren't any more Manichees in the world.

—There's me, said Martin; I don't know what to do about it, but I can't think otherwise.

—You must be possessed of the devil, said Candide.

—He's mixed up with so many things of this world, said Martin, that he may be in me as well as elsewhere; but I assure you, as I survey this globe, or globule, I think that God has abandoned it to some evil spirit—all of it except Eldorado. I have scarcely seen one town which did not wish to destroy its neighboring town, no family which did not wish to exterminate some other family. Everywhere the weak loathe the powerful, before whom they cringe, and the powerful treat them like brute cattle, to be sold for their meat and fleece. A million regimented assassins roam Europe from one end to the other, plying the trades of murder and robbery in an organized way for a living, because there is no more honest form of work for them; and in the cities which seem to enjoy peace and where the arts are flourishing, men are devoured by more envy, cares, and anxieties than a whole town experiences when it's under siege. Private griefs are worse even than public trials. In a word, I have seen so much and suffered so much, that I am a Manichee.

—Still there is some good, said Candide.

—That may be, said Martin, but I don't know it.

In the middle of this discussion, the rumble of cannon was heard. From minute to minute the noise grew louder. Everyone reached for his spyglass. At a distance of some three miles they saw two vessels fighting; the wind brought both of them so close to the French vessel that they had a pleasantly comfortable seat to watch the fight. Presently one of the vessels caught the other with a broadside so low and so square as to send it to the bottom. Candide and Martin saw clearly a hundred men on the deck of the sinking ship; they all raised their hands to heaven, uttering fearful shrieks; and in a moment everything was swallowed up.

—Well, said Martin, that is how men treat one another.

8. Mani, a Persian mage and philosopher of the third century A.D., taught (probably under the influence of traditions stemming from Zoroaster and the worshippers of the sun god Mithra) that the earth is a field of dispute between two almost equal powers, one of light and one of darkness, both of which must be propitiated. Saint Augustine was much exercised by the heresy, to which he was at one time himself addicted, and Voltaire came to some knowledge of it through the encyclopedic learning of the seventeenth century scholar Pierre Bayle.

—It is true, said Candide, there's something devilish in this business.

As they chatted, he noticed something of a striking red color floating near the sunken vessel. They sent out a boat to investigate; it was one of his sheep. Candide was more joyful to recover this one sheep than he had been afflicted to lose a hundred of them, all loaded with big Eldorado diamonds.

The French captain soon learned that the captain of the victorious vessel was Spanish and that of the sunken vessel was a Dutch pirate. It was the same man who had robbed Candide. The enormous riches which this rascal had stolen were sunk beside him in the sea, and nothing was saved but a single sheep.

—You see, said Candide to Martin, crime is punished sometimes; this scoundrel of a Dutch merchant has met the fate he deserved.

—Yes, said Martin; but did the passengers aboard his ship have to perish too? God punished the scoundrel, and the devil drowned the others.

Meanwhile the French and Spanish vessels continued on their journey, and Candide continued his talks with Martin. They disputed for fifteen days in a row, and at the end of that time were just as much in agreement as at the beginning. But at least they were talking, they exchanged their ideas, they consoled one another. Candide caressed his sheep.

—Since I have found you again, said he, I may well rediscover Miss Cunégonde.

CHAPTER 21
Candide and Martin Approach the Coast of France: They Reason Together

At last the coast of France came in view.

—Have you ever been in France, Monsieur Martin? asked Candide.

—Yes, said Martin, I have visited several provinces. There are some where half the inhabitants are crazy, others where they are too sly, still others where they are quite gentle and stupid, some where they venture on wit; in all of them the principal occupation is lovemaking, the second is slander, and the third stupid talk.

—But, Monsieur Martin, were you ever in Paris?

—Yes, I've been in Paris; it contains specimens of all these types; it is a chaos, a mob, in which everyone is seeking pleasure and where hardly anyone finds it, at least from what I have seen. I did not live there for long; as I arrived, I was robbed of everything I possessed by thieves at the fair of St. Germain; I myself was taken for a thief, and spent eight days in jail, after which I took a proofreader's job to earn enough money to return on foot to Holland. I knew the writing gang, the intriguing gang, the gang with fits and convulsions.[9] They say there are some very civilized people in that town; I'd like to think so.

—I myself have no desire to visit France, said Candide; you no doubt realize that when one has spent a month in Eldorado, there is nothing else on earth one wants to see, except Miss Cunégonde. I am going to wait for her at Venice; we will cross France simply to get to Italy; wouldn't you like to come with me?

—Gladly, said Martin; they say Venice is good only for the Venetian nobles, but that on the other hand they treat foreigners very well when they have plenty of money. I don't have any; you do, so I'll follow you anywhere.

—By the way, said Candide, do you believe the earth was originally all ocean, as they assure us in that big book belonging to the ship's captain?[1]

—I don't believe that stuff, said Martin, nor any of the dreams which people have been peddling for some time now.

—But why, then, was this world formed at all? asked Candide.

—To drive us mad, answered Martin.

—Aren't you astonished, Candide went on, at the love which those two girls showed for the monkeys in the land of the Biglugs that I told you about?

—Not at all, said Martin, I see nothing strange in these sentiments; I have seen so many extraordinary things that nothing seems extraordinary any more.

—Do you believe, asked Candide, that men have always massacred one another as they do today? That they have always been liars, traitors, ingrates, thieves, weaklings, sneaks, cowards, backbiters, gluttons, drunkards, misers, climbers, killers, calumniators, sensualists, fanatics, hypocrites, and fools?

—Do you believe, said Martin, that hawks have always eaten pigeons when they could get them?

—Of course, said Candide.

—Well, said Martin, if hawks have always had the same character, why do you suppose that men have changed?

—Oh, said Candide, there's a great deal of difference, because freedom of the will . . .

As they were disputing in this manner, they reached Bordeaux.

9. The Jansenists, a sect of strict Catholics, became notorious for spiritual ecstasies. Their public displays reached a height during the 1720's, and Voltaire described them in *Le Siècle de Louis XIV* (chap. 37), as well as in the article on "Convulsions" in the *Philosophical Dictionary*.

1. The Bible. Voltaire is straining at a dark passage in Genesis 1.

CHAPTER 22

What Happened in France to Candide and Martin

Candide paused in Bordeaux only long enough to sell a couple of Dorado pebbles and to fit himself out with a fine two-seater carriage, for he could no longer do without his philosopher Martin; only he was very unhappy to part with his sheep, which he left to the academy of science in Bordeaux. They proposed, as the theme of that year's prize contest, the discovery of why the wool of the sheep was red; and the prize was awarded to a northern scholar who demonstrated[2] by A plus B minus C divided by Z that the sheep ought to be red and die of sheep rot.

But all the travelers with whom Candide talked in the roadside inns told him: —We are going to Paris.

This general consensus finally inspired in him too a desire to see the capital; it was not much out of his road to Venice.

He entered through the Faubourg Saint-Marceau,[3] and thought he was in the meanest village of Westphalia.

Scarcely was Candide in his hotel, when he came down with a mild illness caused by exhaustion. As he was wearing an enormous diamond ring, and people had noticed among his luggage a tremendously heavy safe, he soon found at his bedside two doctors whom he had not called, several intimate friends who never left him alone, and two pious ladies who helped to warm his broth. Martin said: —I remember that I too was ill on my first trip to Paris; I was very poor; and as I had neither friends, pious ladies, nor doctors, I got well.

However, as a result of medicines and bleedings, Candide's illness became serious. A resident of the neighborhood came to ask him politely to fill out a ticket, to be delivered to the porter of the other world.[4] Candide wanted nothing to do with it. The pious ladies assured him it was a new fashion; Candide replied that he wasn't a man of fashion. Martin wanted to throw the resident out the window. The cleric swore that without the ticket they wouldn't bury Candide. Martin swore that he would bury the cleric if he continued to be a nuisance. The quarrel grew heated; Martin took him by the shoulders and threw him bodily out the door; all of which caused a great scandal, from which developed a legal case.

2. The satire is pointed at Maupertuis Le Lapon, philosopher and mathematician, whom Voltaire had accused of trying to adduce mathematical proofs of the existence of God and whose algebraic formulae were easily ridiculed.

3. A district on the left bank, notably grubby in the eighteenth century. " 'As I entered [Paris] through the Faubourg Saint-Marceau, I saw nothing but dirty stinking little streets, ugly black houses, a general air of squalor and poverty, beggars, carters, menders of clothes, sellers of herb-drinks and old hats,' J.-J. Rousseau, *Confessions*, Book IV."

4. In the middle of the eighteenth century, it became customary to require persons who were grievously ill to sign *billets de confession*, without which they could not be given absolution, admitted to the last sacraments, or buried in consecrated ground.

Candide got better; and during his convalescence he had very good company in to dine. They played cards for money; and Candide was quite surprised that none of the aces were ever dealt to him, and Martin was not surprised at all.

Among those who did the honors of the town for Candide there was a little abbé from Perigord, one of those busy fellows, always bright, always useful, assured, obsequious, and obliging, who waylay passing strangers, tell them the scandal of the town, and offer them pleasures at any price they want to pay. This fellow first took Candide and Martin to the theatre. A new tragedy was being played. Candide found himself seated next to a group of wits. That did not keep him from shedding a few tears in the course of some perfectly played scenes. One of the commentators beside him remarked during the intermission: —You are quite mistaken to weep, this actress is very bad indeed; the actor who plays with her is even worse; and the play is even worse than the actors in it. The author knows not a word of Arabic, though the action takes place in Arabia; and besides, he is a man who doesn't believe in innate ideas.[5] Tomorrow I will show you twenty pamphlets written against him.[6]

—Tell me, sir, said Candide to the abbé, how many plays are there for performance in France?

—Five or six thousand, replied the other.

—That's a lot, said Candide; how many of them are any good?

—Fifteen or sixteen, was the answer.

—That's a lot, said Martin.

Candide was very pleased with an actress who took the part of Queen Elizabeth in a rather dull tragedy[7] that still gets played from time to time.

—I like this actress very much, he said to Martin, she bears a slight resemblance to Miss Cunégonde; I should like to meet her.

The abbé from Perigord offered to introduce him. Candide, raised in Germany, asked what was the protocol, how one behaved in France with queens of England.

—You must distinguish, said the abbé; in the provinces, you take them to an inn; at Paris they are respected while still attractive, and thrown on the dunghill when they are dead.[8]

—Queens on the dunghill! said Candide.

—Yes indeed, said Martin, the abbé is right; I was in Paris when

5. Descartes proposed certain ideas as innate, Voltaire followed Locke in categorically denying innate ideas. The point is simply that in faction fights all the issues get muddled together.

6. Here begins a long passage interpolated by Voltaire in 1761; it ends on p. 280.

7. *Le Comte d'Essex* by Thomas Corneille.

8. Voltaire engaged in a long and vigorous campaign against the rule that actors and actresses could not be buried in consecrated ground. The superstition probably arose from a feeling that by assuming false identities they denied their own souls.

Miss Monime herself[9] passed, as they say, from this life to the other; she was refused what these folk call 'the honors of burial,' that is, the right to rot with all the beggars of the district in a dirty cemetery; she was buried all alone by her troupe at the corner of the Rue de Bourgogne; this must have been very disagreeable to her, for she had a noble character.

—That was extremely rude, said Candide.

—What do you expect? said Martin; that is how these folk are. Imagine all the contradictions, all the incompatibilities you can, and you will see them in the government, the courts, the churches, and the plays of this crazy nation.

—Is it true that they are always laughing in Paris? asked Candide.

—Yes, said the abbé, but with a kind of rage too; when people complain of things, they do so amid explosions of laughter; they even laugh as they perform the most detestable actions.

—Who was that fat swine, said Candide, who spoke so nastily about the play over which I was weeping, and the actors who gave me so much pleasure?

—He is a living illness, answered the abbé, who makes a business of slandering all the plays and books; he hates the successful ones, as eunuchs hate successful lovers; he's one of those literary snakes who live on filth and venom; he's a folliculator . . .

—What's this word *folliculator*? asked Candide.

—It's a folio filler, said the abbé, a Fréron.[1]

It was after this fashion that Candide, Martin, and the abbé from Perigord chatted on the stairway as they watched the crowd leaving the theatre.

—Although I'm in a great hurry to see Miss Cunégonde again, said Candide, I would very much like to dine with Miss Clairon,[2] for she seemed to me admirable.

The abbé was not the man to approach Miss Clairon, who saw only good company.

—She has an engagement tonight, he said; but I shall have the honor of introducing you to a lady of quality, and there you will get to know Paris as if you had lived here four years.

Candide, who was curious by nature, allowed himself to be brought to the lady's house, in the depths of the Faubourg St.-

9. Adrienne Lecouvreur (1690–1730), so called because she made her debut as Monime in Racine's *Mithridate*. Voltaire had assisted at her secret midnight funeral and wrote an indignant poem about it.

1. A successful and popular journalist, who had attacked several of Voltaire's plays, including *Tancrède*. Voltaire had a fine story that the devil attended the first night of *Tancrède* disguised as Fréron: when a lady in the balcony wept at the play's pathos, her tear dropped on the devil's nose; he thought it was holy water and shook it off—psha! psha! G. Desnoiresterres, *Voltaire et Jean-Jacques Rousseau*, pp. 3–4.

2. Actually Claire Leris (1723–1803). She had played the lead role in *Tancrède* and was for many years a leading figure on the Paris stage.

Honoré; they were playing faro[3]; twelve melancholy punters held in their hands a little sheaf of cards, blank summaries of their bad luck. Silence reigned supreme, the punters were pallid, the banker uneasy; and the lady of the house, seated beside the pitiless banker, watched with the eyes of a lynx for the various illegal redoublings and bets at long odds which the players tried to signal by folding the corners of their cards; she had them unfolded with a determination which was severe but polite, and concealed her anger lest she lose her customers. The lady caused herself to be known as the Marquise of Parolignac.[4] Her daughter, fifteen years old, sat among the punters and tipped off her mother with a wink to the sharp practices of these unhappy players when they tried to recoup their losses. The abbé from Perigord, Candide, and Martin came in; nobody arose or greeted them or looked at them; all were lost in the study of their cards.

—My Lady the Baroness of Thunder-Ten-Tronckh was more civil, thought Candide.

However, the abbé whispered in the ear of the marquise, who, half rising, honored Candide with a gracious smile and Martin with a truly noble nod; she gave a seat and dealt a hand of cards to Candide, who lost fifty thousand francs in two turns; after which they had a very merry supper. Everyone was amazed that Candide was not upset over his losses; the lackeys, talking together in their usual lackey language, said: —He must be some English milord.

The supper was like most Parisian suppers: first silence, then an indistinguishable rush of words; then jokes, mostly insipid, false news, bad logic, a little politics, a great deal of malice. They even talked of new books.

—Have you seen the new novel by Dr. Gauchat, the theologian?[5] asked the abbé from Perigord.

—Oh yes, answered one of the guests; but I couldn't finish it. We have a horde of impudent scribblers nowadays, but all of them put together don't match the impudence of this Gauchat, this doctor of theology. I have been so struck by the enormous number of detestable books which are swamping us that I have taken up punting at faro.

—And the *Collected Essays* of Archdeacon T——[6] asked the abbé, what do you think of them?

3. A game of cards, about which it is necessary to know only that a number of punters play against a banker or dealer. The pack is dealt out two cards at a time, and each player may bet on any card as much as he pleases. The sharp practices of the punters consist essentially of tricks for increasing their winnings without corresponding risks.

4. A *paroli* is an illegal redoubling of one's bet; her name therefore implies a title grounded in cardsharping.

5. He had written against Voltaire, and Voltaire suspected him (wrongly) of having committed a novel, *L'Oracle des nouveaux philosophes*.

6. His name was Trublet, and he had said, among other disagreeable things, that Voltaire's epic poem, the *Henriade*, made him yawn and that Voltaire's genius was "the perfection of mediocrity."

—Ah, said Madame de Parolignac, what a frightful bore he is! He takes such pains to tell you what everyone knows; he discourses so learnedly on matters which aren't worth a casual remark! He plunders, and not even wittily, the wit of other people! He spoils what he plunders, he's disgusting! But he'll never disgust me again; a couple of pages of the archdeacon have been enough for me.

There was at table a man of learning and taste, who supported the marquise on this point. They talked next of tragedies; the lady asked why there were tragedies which played well enough but which were wholly unreadable. The man of taste explained very clearly how a play could have a certain interest and yet little merit otherwise; he showed succinctly that it was not enough to conduct a couple of intrigues, such as one can find in any novel, and which never fail to excite the spectator's interest; but that one must be new without being grotesque, frequently touch the sublime but never depart from the natural; that one must know the human heart and give it words; that one must be a great poet without allowing any character in the play to sound like a poet; and that one must know the language perfectly, speak it purely, and maintain a continual harmony without ever sacrificing sense to mere sound.

—Whoever, he added, does not observe all these rules may write one or two tragedies which succeed in the theatre, but he will never be ranked among the good writers; there are very few good tragedies; some are idylls in well-written, well-rhymed dialogue, others are political arguments which put the audience to sleep, or revolting pomposities; still others are the fantasies of enthusiasts, barbarous in style, incoherent in logic, full of long speeches to the gods because the author does not know how to address men, full of false maxims and emphatic commonplaces.

Candide listened attentively to this speech and conceived a high opinion of the speaker; and as the marquise had placed him by her side, he turned to ask her who was this man who spoke so well.

—He is a scholar, said the lady, who never plays cards and whom the abbé sometimes brings to my house for supper; he knows all about tragedies and books, and has himself written a tragedy that was hissed from the stage and a book, the only copy of which ever seen outside his publisher's office was dedicated to me.

—What a great man, said Candide, he's Pangloss all over.

Then, turning to him, he said: —Sir, you doubtless think everything is for the best in the physical as well as the moral universe, and that nothing could be otherwise than as it is?

—Not at all, sir, replied the scholar, I believe nothing of the sort. I find that everything goes wrong in our world; that nobody knows his place in society or his duty, what he's doing or what he ought to be doing, and that outside of mealtimes, which are cheerful and congenial enough, all the rest of the day is spent in useless quarrels, as of Jansenists against Molinists,[7] parliament-men against churchmen, literary men against literary men, courtiers against courtiers, financiers against the plebs, wives against husbands, relatives against relatives—it's one unending warfare.

Candide answered: —I have seen worse; but a wise man, who has since had the misfortune to be hanged, taught me that everything was marvelously well arranged. Troubles are just the shadows in a beautiful picture.

—Your hanged philosopher was joking, said Martin; the shadows are horrible ugly blots.

—It is human beings who make the blots, said Candide, and they can't do otherwise.

—Then it isn't their fault, said Martin.

Most of the faro players, who understood this sort of talk not at all, kept on drinking; Martin disputed with the scholar, and Candide told part of his story to the lady of the house.

After supper, the marquise brought Candide into her room and sat him down on a divan.

—Well, she said to him, are you still madly in love with Miss Cunégonde of Thunder-Ten-Tronckh?

—Yes, ma'am, replied Candide. The marquise turned upon him a tender smile.

—You answer like a young man of Westphalia, said she; a Frenchman would have told me: 'It is true that I have been in love with Miss Cunégonde; but since seeing you, madame, I fear that I love her no longer.'

—Alas, ma'am, said Candide, I will answer any way you want.

—Your passion for her, said the marquise, began when you picked up her handkerchief; I prefer that you should pick up my garter.

—Gladly, said Candide, and picked it up.

—But I also want you to put it back on, said the lady; and Candide put it on again.

—Look you now, said the lady, you are a foreigner; my Paris lovers I sometimes cause to languish for two weeks or so, but to you I surrender the very first night, because we must render the honors of the country to a young man from Westphalia.

The beauty, who had seen two enormous diamonds on the two hands of her young friend, praised them so sincerely that from the fingers of Candide they passed over to the fingers of the marquise.

As he returned home with his Perigord abbé, Candide felt

7. The Jansenists (from Corneille Jansen, 1585–1638) were a relatively strict party of religious reform; the Molinists (from Luis Molina) were the party of the Jesuits. Their central issue of controversy was the relative importance of divine grace and human will to the salvation of man.

some remorse at having been unfaithful to Miss Cunégonde; the abbé sympathized with his grief; he had only a small share in the fifty thousand francs which Candide lost at cards, and in the proceeds of the two diamonds which had been half-given, half-extorted. His scheme was to profit, as much as he could, from the advantage of knowing Candide. He spoke at length of Cunégonde, and Candide told him that he would beg forgiveness for his beloved for his infidelity when he met her at Venice.

The Perigordian overflowed with politeness and unction, taking a tender interest in everything Candide said, everything he did, and everything he wanted to do.[8]

—Well, sir, said he, so you have an assignation at Venice?

—Yes indeed, sir, I do, said Candide; it is absolutely imperative that I go there to find Miss Cunégonde.

And then, carried away by the pleasure of talking about his love, he recounted, as he often did, a part of his adventures with that illustrious lady of Westphalia.

—I suppose, said the abbé, that Miss Cunégonde has a fine wit and writes charming letters.

—I never received a single letter from her, said Candide; for, as you can imagine, after being driven out of the castle for love of her, I couldn't write; shortly I learned that she was dead; then I rediscovered her; then I lost her again, and I have now sent, to a place more than twentyfive hundred leagues from here, a special agent whose return I am expecting.

The abbé listened carefully, and looked a bit dreamy. He soon took his leave of the two strangers, after embracing them tenderly. Next day Candide, when he woke up, received a letter, to the following effect:

—Dear sir, my very dear lover, I have been lying sick in this town for a week, I have just learned that you are here. I would fly to your arms if I could move. I heard that you had passed through Bordeaux; that was where I left the faithful Cacambo and the old woman, who are soon to follow me here. The governor of Buenos Aires took everything, but left me your heart. Come; your presence will either return me to life or cause me to die of joy.

8. Here ends the long passage interpolated by Voltaire in 1761, which began on p. 273. In the original version the transition was managed as follows. After the "commentator's" speech, ending: —Tomorrow I will show you twenty pamphlets written against him.

—Sir, said the abbé from Perigord, do you notice that young person over there with the attractive face and the delicate figure? She would only cost you ten thousand francs a month, and for fifty thousand crowns of diamonds . . .

—I could spare her only a day or or two, replied Candide, because I have an urgent appointment at Venice.

Next night after supper, the sly Perigordian overflowed with politeness and assiduity.

—Well, sir, said he, so you have an assignation at Venice?

This charming letter, coming so unexpectedly, filled Candide with inexpressible delight, while the illness of his dear Cunégonde covered him with grief. Torn between these two feelings, he took gold and diamonds, and had himself brought, with Martin, to the hotel where Miss Cunégonde was lodging. Trembling with emotion, he enters the room; his heart thumps, his voice breaks. He tries to open the curtains of the bed, he asks to have some lights.

—Absolutely forbidden, says the serving girl; light will be the death of her.

And abruptly she pulls shut the curtain.

—My dear Cunégonde, says Candide in tears, how are you feeling? If you can't see me, won't you at least speak to me?

—She can't talk, says the servant.

But then she draws forth from the bed a plump hand, over which Candide weeps a long time, and which he fills with diamonds, meanwhile leaving a bag of gold on the chair.

Amid his transports, there arrives a bailiff followed by the abbé from Perigord and a strong-arm squad.

—These here are the suspicious foreigners? says the officer; and he has them seized and orders his bullies to drag them off to jail.

—They don't treat visitors like this in Eldorado, says Candide.

—I am more a Manichee than ever, says Martin.

—But, please sir, where are you taking us? says Candide.

—To the lowest hole in the dungeons, says the bailiff.

Martin, having regained his self-possession, decided that the lady who pretended to be Cunégonde was a cheat, the abbé from Perigord was another cheat who had imposed on Candide's innocence, and the bailiff still another cheat, of whom it would be easy to get rid.

Rather than submit to the forms of justice, Candide, enlightened by Martin's advice and eager for his own part to see the real Cunégonde again, offered the bailiff three little diamonds worth about three thousand pistoles apiece.

—Ah, my dear sir! cried the man with the ivory staff, even if you have committed every crime imaginable, you are the most honest man in the world. Three diamonds! each one worth three thousand pistoles! My dear sir! I would gladly die for you, rather than take you to jail. All foreigners get arrested here; but let me manage it; I have a brother at Dieppe in Normandy; I'll take you to him; and if you have a bit of a diamond to give him, he'll take care of you, just like me.

—And why do they arrest all foreigners? asked Candide.

The abbé from Perigord spoke up and said: —It's because a beggar from Atrebatum[9] listened to some stupidities; that made him commit a parricide, not like the one of May, 1610, but like the one of December, 1594, much on the order of several other crimes committed in other years and other months by other beggars who had listened to stupidities.

The bailiff then explained what it was all about.[1]

—Foh! what beasts! cried Candide. What! monstrous behavior of this sort from a people who sing and dance? As soon as I can, let me get out of this country, where the monkeys provoke the tigers. In my own country I've lived with bears; only in Eldorado are there proper men. In the name of God, sir bailiff, get me to Venice where I can wait for Miss Cunégonde.

—I can only get you to Lower Normandy, said the guardsman. He had the irons removed at once, said there had been a mistake, dismissed his gang, and took Candide and Martin to Dieppe, where he left them with his brother. There was a little Dutch ship at anchor. The Norman, changed by three more diamonds into the most helpful of men, put Candide and his people aboard the vessel, which was bound for Portsmouth in England. It wasn't on the way to Venice, but Candide felt like a man just let out of hell; and he hoped to get back on the road to Venice at the first possible occasion.

CHAPTER 23

Candide and Martin Pass the Shores of England; What They See There

—Ah, Pangloss! Pangloss! Ah, Martin! Martin! Ah, my darling Cunégonde! What is this world of ours? sighed Candide on the Dutch vessel.

—Something crazy, something abominable, Martin replied.

—You have been in England; are people as crazy there as in France?

—It's a different sort of crazy, said Martin. You know that these two nations have been at war over a few acres of snow near Canada, and that they are spending on this fine struggle more than Canada itself is worth.[2] As for telling you if there are more people

9. The Latin name for the district of Artois, from which came Robert-François Damiens, who tried to stab Louis XV in 1757. The assassination failed, like that of Châtel, who tried to kill Henri Quatre in 1594, but unlike that of Ravaillac, who succeeded in killing him in 1610.

1. The point, in fact, is not too clear since arresting foreigners is an indirect way at best to guard against home-grown fanatics, and the position of the abbé from Perigord in the whole transaction remains confused. Has he called in the officer just to get rid of Candide? If so, why is he sardonic about the very suspicions he is trying to foster? Candide's reaction is to the notion that Frenchmen should be capable of political assassination at all; it seems excessive.

2. The wars of the French and English over Canada dragged intermittently through the eighteenth century till the

in one country or the other who need a strait jacket, that is a judgment too fine for my understanding; I know only that the people we are going to visit are eaten up with melancholy.

As they chatted thus, the vessel touched at Portsmouth. A multitude of people covered the shore, watching closely a rather bulky man who was kneeling, his eyes blindfolded, on the deck of a man-of-war. Four soldiers, stationed directly in front of this man, fired three bullets apiece into his brain, as peaceably as you would want; and the whole assemblage went home, in great satisfaction.[3]

—What's all this about? asked Candide. What devil is everywhere at work?

He asked who was that big man who had just been killed with so much ceremony.

—It was an admiral, they told him.

—And why kill this admiral?

—The reason, they told him, is that he didn't kill enough people; he gave battle to a French admiral, and it was found that he didn't get close enough to him.

—But, said Candide, the French admiral was just as far from the English admiral as the English admiral was from the French admiral.

—That's perfectly true, came the answer; but in this country it is useful from time to time to kill one admiral in order to encourage the others.

Candide was so stunned and shocked at what he saw and heard, that he would not even set foot ashore; he arranged with the Dutch merchant (without even caring if he was robbed, as at Surinam) to be taken forthwith to Venice.

The merchant was ready in two days; they coasted along France, they passed within sight of Lisbon, and Candide quivered. They entered the straits, crossed the Mediterranean, and finally landed at Venice.

—God be praised, said Candide, embracing Martin; here I shall recover the lovely Cunégonde. I trust Cacambo as I would myself. All is well, all goes well, all goes as well as possible.

CHAPTER 24
About Paquette and Brother Giroflée

As soon as he was in Venice, he had a search made for Cacambo in all the inns, all the cafés, all the stews—and found no trace of

peace of Paris sealed England's conquest (1763). Voltaire thought the French should concentrate on developing Louisiana where the Jesuit influence was less marked.

3. Candide has witnessed the execution of Admiral John Byng, defeated off Minorca by the French fleet under Galisonnière and executed by firing squad on March 14, 1757. Voltaire had intervened to avert the execution.

him. Every day he sent to investigate the vessels and coastal traders; no news of Cacambo.

—How's this? said he to Martin. I have had time to go from Surinam to Bordeaux, from Bordeaux to Paris, from Paris to Dieppe, from Dieppe to Portsmouth, to skirt Portugal and Spain, cross the Mediterranean, and spend several months at Venice—and the lovely Cunégonde has not come yet! In her place, I have met only that impersonator and that abbé from Perigord. Cunégonde is dead, without a doubt; and nothing remains for me too but death. Oh, it would have been better to stay in the earthly paradise of Eldorado than to return to this accursed Europe. How right you are, my dear Martin; all is but illusion and disaster.

He fell into a black melancholy, and refused to attend the fashionable operas or take part in the other diversions of the carnival season; not a single lady tempted him in the slightest. Martin told him: —You're a real simpleton if you think a half-breed valet with five or six millions in his pockets will go to the end of the world to get your mistress and bring her to Venice for you. If he finds her, he'll take her for himself; if he doesn't, he'll take another. I advise you to forget about your servant Cacambo and your mistress Cunégonde.

Martin was not very comforting. Candide's melancholy increased, and Martin never wearied of showing him that there is little virtue and little happiness on this earth, except perhaps in Eldorado, where nobody can go.

While they were discussing this important matter and still waiting for Cunégonde, Candide noticed in St. Mark's Square a young Theatine[4] monk who had given his arm to a girl. The Theatine seemed fresh, plump, and flourishing; his eyes were bright, his manner cocky, his glance brilliant, his step proud. The girl was very pretty, and singing aloud; she glanced lovingly at her Theatine, and from time to time pinched his plump cheeks.

—At least you must admit, said Candide to Martin, that these people are happy. Until now I have not found in the whole inhabited earth, except Eldorado, anything but miserable people. But this girl and this monk, I'd be willing to bet, are very happy creatures.

—I'll bet they aren't, said Martin.

—We have only to ask them to dinner, said Candide, and we'll find out if I'm wrong.

Promptly he approached them, made his compliments, and invited them to his inn for a meal of macaroni, Lombardy partridges, and caviar, washed down with wine from Montepulciano, Cyprus,

4. A Catholic order founded in 1524 by Cardinal Cajetan and G. P. Caraffa, later Pope Paul IV.

and Samos, and some Lacrima Christi. The girl blushed but the Theatine accepted gladly, and the girl followed him, watching Candide with an expression of surprise and confusion, darkened by several tears. Scarcely had she entered the room when she said to Candide: —What, can it be that Master Candide no longer knows Paquette?

At these words Candide, who had not yet looked carefully at her because he was preoccupied with Cunégonde, said to her: —Ah, my poor child! so you are the one who put Doctor Pangloss in the fine fix where I last saw him.

—Alas, sir, I was the one, said Paquette; I see you know all about it. I heard of the horrible misfortunes which befell the whole household of My Lady the Baroness and the lovely Cunégonde. I swear to you that my own fate has been just as unhappy. I was perfectly innocent when you knew me. A Franciscan, who was my confessor, easily seduced me. The consequences were frightful; shortly after My Lord the Baron had driven you out with great kicks on the backside, I too was forced to leave the castle. If a famous doctor had not taken pity on me, I would have died. Out of gratitude, I became for some time the mistress of this doctor. His wife, who was jealous to the point of frenzy, beat me mercilessly every day; she was a gorgon. The doctor was the ugliest of men, and I the most miserable creature on earth, being continually beaten for a man I did not love. You will understand, sir, how dangerous it is for a nagging woman to be married to a doctor. This man, enraged by his wife's ways, one day gave her as a cold cure a medicine so potent that in two hours' time she died amid horrible convulsions. Her relatives brought suit against the bereaved husband; he fled the country, and I was put in prison. My innocence would never have saved me if I had not been rather pretty. The judge set me free on condition that he should become the doctor's successor. I was shortly replaced in this post by another girl, dismissed without any payment, and obliged to continue this abominable trade which you men find so pleasant and which for us is nothing but a bottomless pit of misery. I went to ply the trade in Venice. Ah, my dear sir, if you could imagine what it is like to have to caress indiscriminately an old merchant, a lawyer, a monk, a gondolier, an abbé; to be subjected to every sort of insult and outrage; to be reduced, time and again, to borrowing a skirt in order to go have it lifted by some disgusting man; to be robbed by this fellow of what one has gained from that; to be shaken down by the police, and to have before one only the prospect of a hideous old age, a hospital, and a dunghill, you will conclude that I am one of the most miserable creatures in the world.

Thus Paquette poured forth her heart to the good Candide in a hotel room, while Martin sat listening nearby. At last he said to Candide: —You see, I've already won half my bet.

Brother Giroflée[5] had remained in the dining room, and was having a drink before dinner.

—But how's this? said Candide to Paquette. You looked so happy, so joyous, when I met you; you were singing, you caressed the Theatine with such a natural air of delight; you seemed to me just as happy as you now say you are miserable.

—Ah, sir, replied Paquette, that's another one of the miseries of this business; yesterday I was robbed and beaten by an officer, and today I have to seem in good humor in order to please a monk.

Candide wanted no more; he conceded that Martin was right. They sat down to table with Paquette and the Theatine; the meal was amusing enough, and when it was over, the company spoke out among themselves with some frankness.

—Father, said Candide to the monk, you seem to me a man whom all the world might envy; the flower of health glows in your cheek, your features radiate pleasure; you have a pretty girl for your diversion, and you seem very happy with your life as a Theatine.

—Upon my word, sir, said Brother Giroflée, I wish that all the Theatines were at the bottom of the sea. A hundred times I have been tempted to set fire to my convent, and go turn Turk. My parents forced me, when I was fifteen years old, to put on this detestable robe, so they could leave more money to a cursed older brother of mine, may God confound him! Jealousy, faction, and fury spring up, by natural law, within the walls of convents. It is true, I have preached a few bad sermons which earned me a little money, half of which the prior stole from me; the remainder serves to keep me in girls. But when I have to go back to the monastery at night, I'm ready to smash my head against the walls of my cell; and all my fellow monks are in the same fix.

Martin turned to Candide and said with his customary coolness: —Well, haven't I won the whole bet?

Candide gave two thousand piastres to Paquette and a thousand to Brother Giroflée.

—I assure you, said he, that with that they will be happy.

—I don't believe so, said Martin; your piastres may make them even more unhappy than they were before.

—That may be, said Candide; but one thing comforts me, I note that people often turn up whom one never expected to see again; it may well be that, having rediscovered my red sheep and Paquette, I will also rediscover Cunégonde.

5. His name means "gillyflower," and Paquette means "daisy." They are lilies of the field who spin not, neither do they reap.

—I hope, said Martin, that she will some day make you happy; but I very much doubt it.

—You're a hard man, said Candide.

—I've lived, said Martin.

—But look at these gondoliers, said Candide; aren't they always singing?

—You don't see them at home, said Martin, with their wives and squalling children. The doge has his troubles, the gondoliers theirs. It's true that on the whole one is better off as a gondolier than as a doge; but the difference is so slight, I don't suppose it's worth the trouble of discussing.

—There's a lot of talk here, said Candide, of this Senator Pococurante,[6] who has a fine palace on the Brenta and is hospitable to foreigners. They say he is a man who has never known a moment's grief.

—I'd like to see such a rare specimen, said Martin.

Candide promptly sent to Lord Pococurante, asking permission to call on him tomorrow.

CHAPTER 25
Visit to Lord Pococurante, Venetian Nobleman

Candide and Martin took a gondola on the Brenta, and soon reached the palace of the noble Pococurante. The gardens were large and filled with beautiful marble statues; the palace was handsomely designed. The master of the house, sixty years old and very rich, received his two inquisitive visitors perfectly politely, but with very little warmth; Candide was disconcerted and Martin not at all displeased.

First two pretty and neatly dressed girls served chocolate, which they whipped to a froth. Candide could not forbear praising their beauty, their grace, their skill.

—They are pretty good creatures, said Pococurante; I sometimes have them into my bed, for I'm tired of the ladies of the town, with their stupid tricks, quarrels, jealousies, fits of ill humor and petty pride, and all the sonnets one has to make or order for them; but, after all, these two girls are starting to bore me too.

After lunch, Candide strolled through a long gallery, and was amazed at the beauty of the pictures. He asked who was the painter of the two finest.

—They are by Raphael, said the senator; I bought them for a lot of money, out of vanity, some years ago; people say they're the finest in Italy, but they don't please me at all; the colors have all turned brown, the figures aren't well modeled and don't stand out

6. His name means "small care."

enough, the draperies bear no resemblance to real cloth. In a word, whatever people may say, I don't find in them a real imitation of nature. I like a picture only when I can see in it a touch of nature itself, and there are none of this sort. I have many paintings, but I no longer look at them.

As they waited for dinner, Pococurante ordered a concerto performed. Candide found the music delightful.

—That noise? said Pococurante. It may amuse you for half an hour, but if it goes on any longer, it tires everybody though no one dares to admit it. Music today is only the art of performing difficult pieces, and what is merely difficult cannot please for long. Perhaps I should prefer the opera, if they had not found ways to make it revolting and monstrous. Anyone who likes bad tragedies set to music is welcome to them; in these performances the scenes serve only to introduce, inappropriately, two or three ridiculous songs designed to show off the actress's sound box. Anyone who wants to, or who can, is welcome to swoon with pleasure at the sight of a castrate wriggling through the role of Caesar or Cato, and strutting awkwardly about the stage. For my part, I have long since given up these paltry trifles which are called the glory of modern Italy, and for which monarchs pay such ruinous prices.

Candide argued a bit, but timidly; Martin was entirely of a mind with the senator.

They sat down to dinner, and after an excellent meal adjourned to the library. Candide, seeing a copy of Homer[7] in a splendid binding, complimented the noble lord on his good taste.

—That is an author, said he, who was the special delight of great Pangloss, the best philosopher in all Germany.

—He's no special delight of mine, said Pococurante coldly. I was once made to believe that I took pleasure in reading him; but that constant recital of fights which are all alike, those gods who are always interfering but never decisively, that Helen who is the cause of the war and then scarcely takes any part in the story, that Troy which is always under siege and never taken—all that bores me to tears. I have sometimes asked scholars if reading it bored them as much as it bores me; everyone who answered frankly told me the book dropped from his hands like lead, but that they had to have it in their libraries as a monument of antiquity, like those old rusty coins which can't be used in real trade.

—Your Excellence doesn't hold the same opinion of Virgil? said Candide.

7. Since the mid-sixteenth century, when Julius Caesar Scaliger established the dogma, it had been customary to prefer Virgil to Homer. Voltaire's youthful judgments, as delivered in the *Essai sur la poésie épique* (1728), are here summarized with minor revisions—upward for Ariosto, downward for Milton.

—I concede, said Pococurante, that the second, fourth, and sixth books of his *Aeneid* are fine; but as for his pious Aeneas, and strong Cloanthes, and faithful Achates, and little Ascanius, and that imbecile King Latinus, and middle-class Amata, and insipid Lavinia, I don't suppose there was ever anything so cold and unpleasant. I prefer Tasso and those sleepwalkers' stories of Ariosto.

—Dare I ask, sir, said Candide, if you don't get great enjoyment from reading Horace?

—There are some maxims there, said Pococurante, from which a man of the world can profit, and which, because they are formed into vigorous couplets, are more easily remembered; but I care very little for his trip to Brindisi, his description of a bad dinner, or his account of a quibblers' squabble between some fellow Pupilus, whose words he says *were full of pus,* and another whose words *were full of vinegar.*[8] I feel nothing but extreme disgust at his verses against old women and witches; and I can't see what's so great in his telling his friend Maecenas that if he is raised by him to the ranks of lyric poets, he will strike the stars with his lofty forehead. Fools admire everything in a well-known author. I read only for my own pleasure; I like only what is in my style.

Candide, who had been trained never to judge for himself, was much astonished by what he heard; and Martin found Pococurante's way of thinking quite rational.

—Oh, here is a copy of Cicero, said Candide. Now this great man I suppose you're never tired of reading.

—I never read him at all, replied the Venetian. What do I care whether he pleaded for Rabirius or Cluentius? As a judge, I have my hands full of lawsuits. I might like his philosophical works better, but when I saw that he had doubts about everything, I concluded that I knew as much as he did, and that I needed no help to be ignorant.

—Ah, here are eighty volumes of collected papers from a scientific academy, cried Martin; maybe there is something good in them.

—There would be indeed, said Pococurante, if one of these silly authors had merely discovered a new way of making pins; but in all those volumes there is nothing but empty systems, not a single useful discovery.

—What a lot of stage plays I see over there, said Candide, some in Italian, some in Spanish and French.

—Yes, said the senator, three thousand of them, and not three dozen good ones. As for those collections of sermons, which all to-

8. The reference is to Horace, *Satires* I. vii; Pococurante, with gentlemanly negligence, has corrupted Rupilius to Pupilus. Horace's poems against witches are *Epodes* V, VIII, XII; the one about striking the stars with his lofty forehead is *Odes* I.i.

gether are not worth a page of Seneca, and all these heavy volumes of theology, you may be sure I never open them, nor does anybody else.

Martin noticed some shelves full of English books.

—I suppose, said he, that a republican must delight in most of these books written in the land of liberty.

—Yes, replied Pococurante, it's a fine thing to write as you think; it is mankind's privilege. In all our Italy, people write only what they do not think; men who inhabit the land of the Caesars and Antonines dare not have an idea without the permission of a Dominican. I would rejoice in the freedom that breathes through English genius, if partisan passions did not corrupt all that is good in that precious freedom.

Candide, noting a Milton, asked if he did not consider this author a great man.

—Who? said Pococurante. That barbarian who made a long commentary on the first chapter of Genesis in ten books of crabbed verse? That clumsy imitator of the Greeks, who disfigures creation itself, and while Moses represents the eternal being as creating the world with a word, has the messiah take a big compass out of a heavenly cupboard in order to design his work? You expect me to admire the man who spoiled Tasso's hell and devil? who disguises Lucifer now as a toad, now as a pigmy? who makes him rehash the same arguments a hundred times over? who makes him argue theology? and who, taking seriously Ariosto's comic story of the invention of firearms, has the devils shooting off cannon in heaven? Neither I nor anyone else in Italy has been able to enjoy these gloomy extravagances. The marriage of Sin and Death, and the monster that Sin gives birth to, will nauseate any man whose taste is at all refined; and his long description of a hospital is good only for a gravedigger. This obscure, extravagant, and disgusting poem was despised at its birth; I treat it today as it was treated in its own country by its contemporaries. Anyhow, I say what I think, and care very little whether other people agree with me.

Candide was a little cast down by this speech; he respected Homer, and had a little affection for Milton.

—Alas, he said under his breath to Martin, I'm afraid this man will have a supreme contempt for our German poets.

—No harm in that, said Martin.

—Oh what a superior man, said Candide, still speaking softly, what a great genius this Pococurante must be! Nothing can please him.

Having thus looked over all the books, they went down into the garden. Candide praised its many beauties.

—I know nothing in such bad taste, said the master of the house;

we have nothing but trifles here; tomorrow I am going to have one set out on a nobler design.

When the two visitors had taken leave of his excellency: —Well now, said Candide to Martin, you must agree that this was the happiest of all men, for he is superior to everything he possesses.

—Don't you see, said Martin, that he is disgusted with everything he possesses? Plato said, a long time ago, that the best stomachs are not those which refuse all food.

—But, said Candide, isn't there pleasure in criticizing everything, in seeing faults where other people think they see beauties?

—That is to say, Martin replied, that there's pleasure in having no pleasure?

—Oh well, said Candide, then I am the only happy man . . . or will be, when I see Miss Cunégonde again.

—It's always a good thing to have hope, said Martin.

But the days and the weeks slipped past; Cacambo did not come back, and Candide was so buried in his grief, that he did not even notice that Paquette and Brother Giroflée had neglected to come and thank him.

CHAPTER 26
About a Supper that Candide and Martin Had with Six Strangers, and Who They Were

One evening when Candide, accompanied by Martin, was about to sit down for dinner with the strangers staying in his hotel, a man with a soot-colored face came up behind him, took him by the arm, and said: —Be ready to leave with us, don't miss out.

He turned and saw Cacambo. Only the sight of Cunégonde could have astonished and pleased him more. He nearly went mad with joy. He embraced his dear friend.

—Cunégonde is here, no doubt? Where is she? Bring me to her, let me die of joy in her presence.

—Cunégonde is not here at all, said Cacambo, she is at Constantinople.

—Good Heavens, at Constantinople! but if she were in China, I must fly there, let's go.

—We will leave after supper, said Cacambo; I can tell you no more; I am a slave, my owner is looking for me, I must go wait on him at table; mum's the word; eat your supper and be prepared.

Candide, torn between joy and grief, delighted to have seen his faithful agent again, astonished to find him a slave, full of the idea of recovering his mistress, his heart in a turmoil, his mind in a whirl, sat down to eat with Martin, who was watching all these events coolly, and with six strangers who had come to pass the carnival season at Venice.

Cacambo, who was pouring wine for one of the strangers, leaned respectfully over his master at the end of the meal, and said to him: —Sire, Your Majesty may leave when he pleases, the vessel is ready.

Having said these words, he exited. The diners looked at one another in silent amazement, when another servant, approaching his master, said to him: —Sire, Your Majesty's litter is at Padua, and the bark awaits you.

The master nodded, and the servant vanished. All the diners looked at one another again, and the general amazement redoubled. A third servant, approaching a third stranger, said to him: —Sire, take my word for it, Your Majesty must stay here no longer; I shall get everything ready.

Then he too disappeared.

Candide and Martin had no doubt, now, that it was a carnival masquerade. A fourth servant spoke to a fourth master: —Your majesty will leave when he pleases—and went out like the others. A fifth followed suit. But the sixth servant spoke differently to the sixth stranger, who sat next to Candide. He said: —My word, sire, they'll give no more credit to Your Majesty, nor to me either; we could very well spend the night in the lockup, you and I. I've got to look out for myself, so good-bye to you.

When all the servants had left, the six strangers, Candide, and Martin remained under a pall of silence. Finally Candide broke it.

—Gentlemen, said he, here's a funny kind of joke. Why are you all royalty? I assure you that Martin and I aren't.

Cacambo's master spoke up gravely then, and said in Italian: —This is no joke, my name is Achmet the Third.[9] I was grand sultan for several years; then, as I had dethroned my brother, my nephew dethroned me. My viziers had their throats cut; I was allowed to end my days in the old seraglio. My nephew, the Grand Sultan Mahmoud, sometimes lets me travel for my health; and I have come to spend the carnival season at Venice.

A young man who sat next to Achmet spoke after him, and said: —My name is Ivan; I was once emperor of all the Russias.[1] I was dethroned while still in my cradle; my father and mother were locked up, and I was raised in prison; I sometimes have permission to travel, though always under guard, and I have come to spend the carnival season at Venice.

The third said: —I am Charles Edward, king of England[2]; my

9. His dates are 1673–1736; he was deposed in 1730.

1. Ivan VI reigned from his birth in 1740 till 1756, then was confined in the Schlusselberg, and executed in 1764.

2. This is the Young Pretender (1720–1788), known to his supporters as Bonnie Prince Charlie. The defeat so theatrically described took place at Culloden, April 16, 1746.

father yielded me his rights to the kingdom, and I fought to uphold them; but they tore out the hearts of eight hundred of my partisans, and flung them in their faces. I have been in prison; now I am going to Rome, to visit the king, my father, dethroned like me and my grandfather; and I have come to pass the carnival season at Venice.

The fourth king then spoke up, and said: —I am a king of the Poles[3]; the luck of war has deprived me of my hereditary estates; my father suffered the same losses; I submit to Providence like Sultan Achmet, Emperor Ivan, and King Charles Edward, to whom I hope heaven grants long lives; and I have come to pass the carnival season at Venice.

The fifth said: —I too am a king of the Poles[4]; I lost my kingdom twice, but Providence gave me another state, in which I have been able to do more good than all the Sarmatian kings ever managed to do on the banks of the Vistula. I too have submitted to Providence, and I have come to pass the carnival season at Venice.

It remained for the sixth monarch to speak.

—Gentlemen, said he, I am no such great lord as you, but I have in fact been a king like any other. I am Theodore; I was elected king of Corsica.[5] People used to call me *Your Majesty*, and now they barely call me *Sir;* I used to coin currency, and now I don't have a cent; I used to have two secretaries of state, and now I scarcely have a valet; I have sat on a throne, and for a long time in London I was in jail, on the straw; and I may well be treated the same way here, though I have come, like your majesties, to pass the carnival season at Venice.

The five other kings listened to his story with noble compassion. Each one of them gave twenty sequins to King Theodore, so that he might buy a suit and some shirts; Candide gave him a diamond worth two thousand sequins.

—Who in the world, said the five kings, is this private citizen who is in a position to give a hundred times as much as any of us, and who actually gives it?[6]

3. Augustus III (1696–1763), Elector of Saxony and King of Poland, dethroned by Frederick the Great in 1756.

4. Stanislas Leczinski (1677–1766), father-in-law of Louis XV, who abdicated the throne of Poland in 1736, was made Duke of Lorraine and in that capacity befriended Voltaire.

5. Theodore von Neuhof (1690–1756), an authentic Westphalian, an adventurer and a soldier of fortune, who in 1736 was (for about eight months) the elected king of Corsica. He spent time in an Amsterdam as well as a London debtor's prison.

6. A late correction of Voltaire's makes this passage read: —Who is this man who is in a position to give a hundred times as much as any of us, and who actually gives it? Are you a king too, sir?

—No, gentlemen, and I have no desire to be.

But this reading, though Voltaire's on good authority, produces a conflict with Candide's previous remark: —Why are you all royalty? I assure you that Martin and I aren't.

Thus, it has seemed better for literary reasons to follow an earlier reading. Voltaire was very conscious of his situation as a man richer than many princes; in 1758 he had money

Just as they were rising from dinner, there arrived at the same establishment four most serene highnesses, who had also lost their kingdoms through the luck of war, and who came to spend the rest of the carnival season at Venice. But Candide never bothered even to look at these newcomers because he was only concerned to go find his dear Cunégonde at Constantinople.

CHAPTER 27
Candide's Trip to Constantinople

Faithful Cacambo had already arranged with the Turkish captain who was returning Sultan Achmet to Constantinople to make room for Candide and Martin on board. Both men boarded ship after prostrating themselves before his miserable highness. On the way, Candide said to Martin: —Six dethroned kings that we had dinner with! and yet among those six there was one on whom I had to bestow charity! Perhaps there are other princes even more unfortunate. I myself have only lost a hundred sheep, and now I am flying to the arms of Cunégonde. My dear Martin, once again Pangloss is proved right, all is for the best.

—I hope so, said Martin.

—But, said Candide, that was a most unlikely experience we had at Venice. Nobody ever saw, or heard tell of, six dethroned kings eating together at an inn.

—It is no more extraordinary, said Martin, than most of the things that have happened to us. Kings are frequently dethroned; and as for the honor we had from dining with them, that's a trifle which doesn't deserve our notice.[7]

Scarcely was Candide on board than he fell on the neck of his former servant, his friend Cacambo.

—Well! said he, what is Cunégonde doing? Is she still a marvel of beauty? Does she still love me? How is her health? No doubt you have bought her a palace at Constantinople.

—My dear master, answered Cacambo, Cunégonde is washing dishes on the shores of the Propontis, in the house of a prince who has very few dishes to wash; she is a slave in the house of a onetime king named Ragotski,[8] to whom the Great Turk allows three crowns a day in his exile; but, what is worse than all this, she has lost all her beauty and become horribly ugly.

on loan to no fewer than three highnesses, Charles Eugene, Duke of Wurtemburg; Charles Theodore, Elector Palatine; and the Duke of Saxe-Gotha.

7. Another late change adds the following question: —What does it matter whom you dine with as long as you fare well at table?

I have omitted it, again on literary grounds (the observation is too heavy and commonplace), despite its superior claim to a position in the text.

8. Francis Leopold Rakoczy (1676–1735) who was briefly king of Transylvania in the early eighteenth century. After 1720 he was interned in Turkey.

—Ah, beautiful or ugly, said Candide, I am an honest man, and my duty is to love her forever. But how can she be reduced to this wretched state with the five or six millions that you had?

—All right, said Cacambo, didn't I have to give two millions to Señor don Fernando d'Ibaraa y Figueroa y Mascarenes y Lampourdos y Souza, governor of Buenos Aires, for his permission to carry off Miss Cunégonde? And didn't a pirate cleverly strip us of the rest? And didn't this pirate carry us off to Cape Matapan, to Melos, Nicaria, Samos, Petra, to the Dardanelles, Marmora, Scutari? Cunégonde and the old woman are working for the prince I told you about, and I am the slave of the dethroned sultan.

—What a lot of fearful calamities linked one to the other, said Candide. But after all, I still have a few diamonds, I shall easily deliver Cunégonde. What a pity that she's become so ugly!

Then, turning toward Martin, he asked: —Who in your opinion is more to be pitied, the Emperor Achmet, the Emperor Ivan, King Charles Edward, or myself?

—I have no idea, said Martin; I would have to enter your hearts in order to tell.

—Ah, said Candide, if Pangloss were here, he would know and he would tell us.

—I can't imagine, said Martin, what scales your Pangloss would use to weigh out the miseries of men and value their griefs. All I will venture is that the earth holds millions of men who deserve our pity a hundred times more than King Charles Edward, Emperor Ivan, or Sultan Achmet.

—You may well be right, said Candide.

In a few days they arrived at the Black Sea canal. Candide began by repurchasing Cacambo at an exorbitant price; then, without losing an instant, he flung himself and his companions into a galley to go search out Cunégonde on the shores of Propontis, however ugly she might be.

There were in the chain gang two convicts who bent clumsily to the oar, and on whose bare shoulders the Levantine[9] captain delivered from time to time a few lashes with a bullwhip. Candide naturally noticed them more than the other galley slaves, and out of pity came closer to them. Certain features of their disfigured faces seemed to him to bear a slight resemblance to Pangloss and to that wretched Jesuit, that baron, that brother of Miss Cunégonde. The notion stirred and saddened him. He looked at them more closely.

—To tell you the truth, he said to Cacambo, if I hadn't seen Master Pangloss hanged, and if I hadn't been so miserable as to murder the baron, I should think they were rowing in this very galley.

9. From the eastern Mediterranean.

At the names of 'baron' and 'Pangloss' the two convicts gave a great cry, sat still on their bench, and dropped their oars. The Levantine captain came running, and the bullwhip lashes redoubled.

—Stop, stop, captain, cried Candide. I'll give you as much money as you want.

—What, can it be Candide? cried one of the convicts.

—What, can it be Candide? cried the other.

—Is this a dream? said Candide. Am I awake or asleep? Am I in this galley? Is that My Lord the Baron, whom I killed? Is that Master Pangloss, whom I saw hanged?

—It is indeed, they replied.

—What, is that the great philosopher? said Martin.

—Now, sir, Mr. Levantine Captain, said Candide, how much money do you want for the ransom of My Lord Thunder-Ten-Tronckh, one of the first barons of the empire, and Master Pangloss, the deepest metaphysician in all Germany?

—Dog of a Christian, replied the Levantine captain, since these two dogs of Christian convicts are barons and metaphysicians, which is no doubt a great honor in their country, you will give me fifty thousand sequins for them.

—You shall have them, sir, take me back to Constantinople and you shall be paid on the spot. Or no, take me to Miss Cunégonde.

The Levantine captain, at Candide's first word, had turned his bow toward the town, and he had them rowed there as swiftly as a bird cleaves the air.

A hundred times Candide embraced the baron and Pangloss.

—And how does it happen I didn't kill you, my dear baron? and my dear Pangloss, how can you be alive after being hanged? and why are you both rowing in the galleys of Turkey?

—Is it really true that my dear sister is in this country? asked the baron.

—Yes, answered Cacambo.

—And do I really see again my dear Candide? cried Pangloss.

Candide introduced Martin and Cacambo. They all embraced; they all talked at once. The galley flew, already they were back in port. A jew was called, and Candide sold him for fifty thousand sequins a diamond worth a hundred thousand, while he protested by Abraham that he could not possibly give more for it. Candide immediately ransomed the baron and Pangloss. The latter threw himself at the feet of his liberator, and bathed them with tears; the former thanked him with a nod, and promised to repay this bit of money at the first opportunity.

—But is it really possible that my sister is in Turkey? said he.

—Nothing is more possible, replied Cacambo, since she is a dishwasher in the house of a prince of Transylvania.

At once two more jews were called; Candide sold some more diamonds; and they all departed in another galley to the rescue of Cunégonde.

CHAPTER 28
What Happened to Candide, Cunégonde, Pangloss, Martin, &c.

—Let me beg your pardon once more, said Candide to the baron, pardon me, reverend father, for having run you through the body with my sword.

—Don't mention it, replied the baron. I was a little too hasty myself, I confess it; but since you want to know the misfortune which brought me to the galleys, I'll tell you. After being cured of my wound by the brother who was apothecary to the college, I was attacked and abducted by a Spanish raiding party; they jailed me in Buenos Aires at the time when my sister had just left. I asked to be sent to Rome, to the father general. Instead, I was named to serve as almoner in Constantinople, under the French ambassador. I had not been a week on this job when I chanced one evening on a very handsome young ichoglan.[1] The evening was hot; the young man wanted to take a swim; I seized the occasion, and went with him. I did not know that it is a capital offense for a Christian to be found naked with a young Moslem. A cadi sentenced me to receive a hundred blows with a cane on the soles of my feet, and then to be sent to the galleys. I don't suppose there was ever such a horrible miscarriage of justice. But I would like to know why my sister is in the kitchen of a Transylvanian king exiled among Turks.

—But how about you, my dear Pangloss, said Candide; how is it possible that we have met again?

—It is true, said Pangloss, that you saw me hanged; in the normal course of things, I should have been burned, but you recall that a cloudburst occurred just as they were about to roast me. So much rain fell that they despaired of lighting the fire; thus I was hanged, for lack of anything better to do with me. A surgeon bought my body, carried me off to his house, and dissected me. First he made a cross-shaped incision in me, from the navel to the clavicle. No one could have been worse hanged than I was. In fact, the executioner of the high ceremonials of the Holy Inquisition, who was a subdeacon, burned people marvelously well, but he was not in the way of hanging them. The rope was wet, and tightened badly; it caught on a knot; in short, I was still breathing. The cross-

1. A page to the sultan.

shaped incision made me scream so loudly that the surgeon fell over backwards; he thought he was dissecting the devil, fled in an agony of fear, and fell downstairs in his flight. His wife ran in, at the noise, from a nearby room; she found me stretched out on the table with my cross-shaped incision, was even more frightened than her husband, fled, and fell over him. When they had recovered a little, I heard her say to him: 'My dear, what were you thinking of, trying to dissect a heretic? Don't you know those people are always possessed of the devil? I'm going to get the priest and have him exorcised.' At these words, I shuddered, and collected my last remaining energies to cry: 'Have mercy on me!' At last the Portuguese barber[2] took courage; he sewed me up again; his wife even nursed me; in two weeks I was up and about. The barber found me a job and made me lackey to a Knight of Malta who was going to Venice; and when this master could no longer pay me, I took service under a Venetian merchant, whom I followed to Constantinople.

—One day it occurred to me to enter a mosque; no one was there but an old imam and a very attractive young worshipper who was saying her prayers. Her bosom was completely bare; and between her two breasts she had a lovely bouquet of tulips, roses, anemones, buttercups, hyacinths, and primroses. She dropped her bouquet, I picked it up, and returned it to her with the most respectful attentions. I was so long getting it back in place that the imam grew angry, and, seeing that I was a Christian, he called the guard. They took me before the cadi, who sentenced me to receive a hundred blows with a cane on the soles of my feet, and then to be sent to the galleys. I was chained to the same galley and precisely the same bench as My Lord the Baron. There were in this galley four young fellows from Marseilles, five Neapolitan priests, and two Corfu monks, who assured us that these things happen every day. My Lord the Baron asserted that he had suffered a greater injustice than I; I, on the other hand, proposed that it was much more permissible to replace a bouquet in a bosom than to be found naked with an ichoglan. We were arguing the point continually, and getting twenty lashes a day with the bullwhip, when the chain of events within this universe brought you to our galley, and you ransomed us.

—Well, my dear Pangloss, Candide said to him, now that you have been hanged, dissected, beaten to a pulp, and sentenced to the galleys, do you still think everything is for the best in this world?

—I am still of my first opinion, replied Pangloss; for after all I am a philosopher, and it would not be right for me to recant since Leibniz could not possibly be wrong, and besides pre-established harmony is the finest notion in the world, like the plenum and subtle matter.[3]

2. The two callings of barber and surgeon, since they both involved sharp instruments, were interchangeable in the early days of medicine.

CHAPTER 29
How Candide Found Cunégonde and the Old Woman Again

While Candide, the baron, Pangloss, Martin, and Cacambo were telling one another their stories, while they were disputing over the contingent or non-contingent events of this universe, while they were arguing over effects and causes, over moral evil and physical evil, over liberty and necessity, and over the consolations available to one in a Turkish galley, they arrived at the shores of Propontis and the house of the prince of Transylvania. The first sight to meet their eyes was Cunégonde and the old woman, who were hanging out towels on lines to dry.

The baron paled at what he saw. The tender lover Candide, seeing his lovely Cunégonde with her skin weathered, her eyes bloodshot, her breasts fallen, her cheeks seamed, her arms red and scaly, recoiled three steps in horror, and then advanced only out of politeness. She embraced Candide and her brother; everyone embraced the old woman; Candide ransomed them both.

There was a little farm in the neighborhood; the old woman suggested that Candide occupy it until some better fate should befall the group. Cunégonde did not know she was ugly, no one had told her; she reminded Candide of his promises in so firm a tone that the good Candide did not dare to refuse her. So he went to tell the baron that he was going to marry his sister.

—Never will I endure, said the baron, such baseness on her part, such insolence on yours; this shame at least I will not put up with; why, my sister's children would not be able to enter the Chapters in Germany.[4] No, my sister will never marry anyone but a baron of the empire.

Cunégonde threw herself at his feet, and bathed them with her tears; he was inflexible.

—You absolute idiot, Candide told him, I rescued you from the galleys, I paid your ransom, I paid your sister's; she was washing dishes, she is ugly, I am good enough to make her my wife, and you still presume to oppose it! If I followed my impulses, I would kill you all over again.

—You may kill me again, said the baron, but you will not marry my sister while I am alive.

3. Rigorous determinism requires that there be no empty spaces in the universe, so wherever it seems empty, one posits the existence of the "plenum." "Subtle matter" describes the soul, the mind, and all spiritual agencies—which can, therefore, be supposed subject to the influence and control of the great world machine, which is, of course, visibly material. Both are concepts needed to round out the system of optimistic determinism.

4. Knightly assemblies.

CHAPTER 30
Conclusion

At heart, Candide had no real wish to marry Cunégonde; but the baron's extreme impertinence decided him in favor of the marriage, and Cunégonde was so eager for it that he could not back out. He consulted Pangloss, Martin, and the faithful Cacambo. Pangloss drew up a fine treatise, in which he proved that the baron had no right over his sister and that she could, according to all the laws of the empire, marry Candide morganatically.[5] Martin said they should throw the baron into the sea. Cacambo thought they should send him back to the Levantine captain to finish his time in the galleys, and then send him to the father general in Rome by the first vessel. This seemed the best idea; the old woman approved, and nothing was said to his sister; the plan was executed, at modest expense, and they had the double pleasure of snaring a Jesuit and punishing the pride of a German baron.

It is quite natural to suppose that after so many misfortunes, Candide, married to his mistress, and living with the philosopher Pangloss, the philosopher Martin, the prudent Cacambo, and the old woman—having, besides, brought back so many diamonds from the land of the ancient Incas—must have led the most agreeable life in the world. But he was so cheated by the jews[6] that nothing was left but his little farm; his wife, growing every day more ugly, became sour-tempered and insupportable; the old woman was ailing and even more ill-humored than Cunégonde. Cacambo, who worked in the garden and went into Constantinople to sell vegetables, was worn out with toil, and cursed his fate. Pangloss was in despair at being unable to shine in some German university. As for Martin, he was firmly persuaded that things are just as bad wherever you are; he endured in patience. Candide, Martin, and Pangloss sometimes argued over metaphysics and morals. Before the windows of the farmhouse they often watched the passage of boats bearing effendis, pashas, and cadis into exile on Lemnos, Mytilene, and Erzeroum; they saw other cadis, other pashas, other effendis coming, to take the place of the exiles and to be exiled in their turn. They saw various heads, neatly impaled, to be set up at the Sublime Porte.[7] These sights gave fresh impetus to their discussions; and

5. A morganatic marriage confers no rights on the partner of lower rank or on the offspring. Pangloss always uses more language than anyone else to achieve fewer results.

6. Voltaire's anti-Semitism, derived from various unhappy experiences with Jewish financiers, is not the most attractive aspect of his personality.

7. The gate of the sultan's palace is often used by extension to describe his government as a whole. But it was in fact a real gate where the heads of traitors and public enemies were gruesomely exposed.

when they were not arguing, the boredom was so fierce that one day the old woman ventured to say: —I should like to know which is worse, being raped a hundred times by negro pirates, having a buttock cut off, running the gauntlet in the Bulgar army, being flogged and hanged in an auto-da-fé, being dissected and rowing in the galleys—experiencing, in a word, all the miseries through which we have passed—or else just sitting here and doing nothing?

—It's a hard question, said Candide.

These words gave rise to new reflections, and Martin in particular concluded that man was bound to live either in convulsions of misery or in the lethargy of boredom. Candide did not agree, but expressed no positive opinion. Pangloss asserted that he had always suffered horribly; but having once declared that everything was marvelously well, he continued to repeat the opinion and didn't believe a word of it.

One thing served to confirm Martin in his detestable opinions, to make Candide hesitate more than ever, and to embarrass Pangloss. It was the arrival one day at their farm of Paquette and Brother Giroflée, who were in the last stages of misery. They had quickly run through their three thousand piastres, had split up, made up, quarreled, been jailed, escaped, and finally Brother Giroflée had turned Turk. Paquette continued to ply her trade everywhere, and no longer made any money at it.

—I told you, said Martin to Candide, that your gifts would soon be squandered and would only render them more unhappy. You have spent millions of piastres, you and Cacambo, and you are no more happy than Brother Giroflée and Paquette.

—Ah ha, said Pangloss to Paquette, so destiny has brought you back in our midst, my poor girl! Do you realize you cost me the end of my nose, one eye, and an ear? And look at you now! eh! what a world it is, after all!

This new adventure caused them to philosophize more than ever. There was in the neighborhood a very famous dervish, who was said to be the best philosopher in Turkey; they went to ask his advice. Pangloss was spokesman, and he said: —Master, we have come to ask you to tell us why such a strange animal as man was created.

—What are you getting into? answered the dervish. Is it any of your business?

—But, reverend father, said Candide, there's a horrible lot of evil on the face of the earth.

—What does it matter, said the dervish, whether there's good or evil? When his highness sends a ship to Egypt, does he worry whether the mice on board are comfortable or not?

—What shall we do then? asked Pangloss.

—Hold your tongue, said the dervish.

—I had hoped, said Pangloss, to reason a while with you concerning effects and causes, the best of possible worlds, the origin of evil, the nature of the soul, and pre-established harmony.

At these words, the dervish slammed the door in their faces.

During this interview, word was spreading that at Constantinople they had just strangled two viziers of the divan,[8] as well as the mufti, and impaled several of their friends. This catastrophe made a great and general sensation for several hours. Pangloss, Candide, and Martin, as they returned to their little farm, passed a good old man who was enjoying the cool of the day at his doorstep under a grove of orange trees. Pangloss, who was as inquisitive as he was explanatory, asked the name of the mufti who had been strangled.

—I know nothing of it, said the good man, and I have never cared to know the name of a single mufti or vizier. I am completely ignorant of the episode you are discussing. I presume that in general those who meddle in public business sometimes perish miserably, and that they deserve their fate; but I never listen to the news from Constantinople; I am satisfied with sending the fruits of my garden to be sold there.

Having spoken these words, he asked the strangers into his house; his two daughters and two sons offered them various sherbets which they had made themselves, Turkish cream flavored with candied citron, orange, lemon, lime, pineapple, pistachio, and mocha coffee uncontaminated by the inferior coffee of Batavia and the East Indies. After which the two daughters of this good Moslem perfumed the beards of Candide, Pangloss, and Martin.

—You must possess, Candide said to the Turk, an enormous and splendid property?

I have only twenty acres, replied the Turk; I cultivate them with my children, and the work keeps us from three great evils, boredom, vice, and poverty.

Candide, as he walked back to his farm, meditated deeply over the words of the Turk. He said to Pangloss and Martin: —This good old man seems to have found himself a fate preferable to that of the six kings with whom we had the honor of dining.

—Great place, said Pangloss, is very perilous in the judgment of all the philosophers; for, after all, Eglon, king of the Moabites, was murdered by Ehud; Absalom was hung up by the hair and pierced with three darts; King Nadab, son of Jeroboam, was killed by Baasha; King Elah by Zimri; Ahaziah by Jehu; Athaliah by Jehoiada; and Kings Jehoiakim, Jeconiah, and Zedekiah were enslaved. You know how death came to Croesus, Astyages, Darius, Dionysius of Syracuse, Pyrrhus, Perseus, Hannibal, Jugurtha, Ariovistus, Caesar, Pompey, Nero, Otho, Vitellius, Domitian, Rich-

8. Intimate advisers of the sultan.

ard II of England, Edward II, Henry VI, Richard III, Mary Stuart, Charles I, the three Henrys of France, and the Emperor Henry IV? You know . . .

—I know also, said Candide, that we must cultivate our garden.

—You are perfectly right, said Pangloss; for when man was put into the garden of Eden, he was put there *ut operaretur eum,* so that he should work it; this proves that man was not born to take his ease.

—Let's work without speculating, said Martin; it's the only way of rendering life bearable.

The whole little group entered into this laudable scheme; each one began to exercise his talents. The little plot yielded fine crops. Cunégonde was, to tell the truth, remarkably ugly; but she became an excellent pastry cook. Paquette took up embroidery; the old woman did the laundry. Everyone, down even to Brother Giroflée, did something useful; he became a very adequate carpenter, and even an honest man; and Pangloss sometimes used to say to Candide: —All events are linked together in the best of possible worlds; for, after all, if you had not been driven from a fine castle by being kicked in the backside for love of Miss Cunégonde, if you hadn't been sent before the Inquisition, if you hadn't traveled across America on foot, if you hadn't given a good sword thrust to the baron, if you hadn't lost all your sheep from the good land of Eldorado, you wouldn't be sitting here eating candied citron and pistachios.

—That is very well put, said Candide, but we must cultivate our garden.

Masterpieces of Romanticism

EDITED BY
HOWARD E. HUGO
Late of the University of California, Berkeley

FROM ROUSSEAU TO MELVILLE

Only a little over a hundred years separate Rousseau's completion of his *Confessions* (1770) from Melville's *Billy Budd* (1891). Though there are broader chronological stretches in other sections of this anthology, one may venture to say that few periods offer more radical shifts in man's entire outlook than do these years. In fact one measure of the works we have selected is the awareness their authors show (often more implicit than explicit) of such mutations.

"Everything goes to the people and deserts the kings, even literary themes, which descend from royal misfortunes to private misfortunes, from Priam to Birotteau"—so lamented the Goncourt brothers in 1866. From Homer's great monarch of Troy to Balzac's perfume manufacturer in Paris in the 1830's there is a vast movement, not only in time but also in the human spirit—a movement from the heroic hero that still interested Shakespeare and Racine to the unheroic hero of the nineteenth-century bourgeoisie. The dates 1775, 1789, 1830, and 1848 (all falling within the confines of this portion of the anthology) mark years of revolution when middle-class protests against the *status quo* emerged with various degrees of violence. Only one major monarch—Charles I of England—was deposed in the seventeenth century. By contrast, the reader will recall having met six kings in Chapter 26 of *Candide,* all impoverished and in exile. The nineteenth century was to see political alterations unanticipated by political theorists, as "the divinity [that] doth hedge a king" was examined with rational suspicion, and monarchical and aristocratic powers were curtailed or abolished. The firing of "the shot heard round the world" at Concord (1775) and the fall of the Bastille (1789) mark dramatic moments which made actual the abstract political thought of eighteenth-century philosophers (with their paper constitutions, social contracts, declarations of the rights of man, and plans for perpetual peace). By 1850, it seemed to many political liberals that the bourgeoisie was politically and socially canonized. Continental revolutions in 1830 and 1848 and legislative reforms in England (chiefly in 1832) may have disappointed a few radicals by their compromises; but on the whole, the ascendancy of the middle class was guaranteed.

The change just outlined was "horizontal," cutting across national boundaries. The Enlightenment had set the goal, for the rational man, of being a "citizen of the world"; later eighteenth-century thought and nineteenth-century romanticism moved from such universality toward the phenomenon known as nationalism. Rousseau's claim for personal uniqueness was expanded to apply to the individuality of the *Volk*, the nation, or the race. Nationalism was curiously intertwined with political liberalism from the French Revolution on. At times "vertical" national interests even superseded more generous ideas of man's brotherhood and the abolition of world-wide tyranny. The Year One, announced in Paris in September, 1792, was intended to inaugurate a new egalitarian millennium for the *entire* human race; yet twelve years later Napoleon was crowned Emperor of the French.

Whitman could combine both attitudes, the mystique of racial uniqueness and the ideal of an all-inclusive political democracy.

> Come, I will make the continent indissoluble,
> I will make the most splendid race the sun ever shone upon.
> What we believe in waits latent forever through all the continents,
> Invites no one, promises nothing, sits in calmness and light, is positive and composed, knows no discouragement,
> Waiting patiently, waiting its time.

The amalgam of political liberalism and nationalism was not rare: many thinkers, the Italian liberal Mazzini, for example, regarded nationalism as a necessary stage before man reached true awareness of humanity as a whole. From 1815 to 1853 the comparative absence of all warfare save colonial engagements seemed to display the relative harmlessness of nationalism. We have had the dubious advantage of another hundred years of history, to watch nationalism flourishing in its full horror.

Political upheavals in this period had their counterpart in the Industrial Revolution, which indeed accentuated notions of "class" and "nation" and began the transformation of most of Western Europe from an agrarian to a primarily industrial culture. The Reformation had earlier underscored the dignity and necessity of individual labor, and had indicated a connection between spiritual and material prudence and enterprise. With the growth of wealth, industry, manufacturing, and colonies came a need for more comprehensive theories. Adam Smith's *Wealth of Nations* (1776) set the pattern for subsequent economic speculation and practice: the laissez-faire state, permitting free trade, free markets, and free competition, in keeping with what Smith termed the "obvious and simple system of natural liberty." The advocacy of economic liberalism places Smith and his followers squarely within the tradition of middle-class liberalism, broadly defined. The modern reader should note Smith's assumption that economic individualism, without any form of government regulation, will result in public benefit and ultimate harmony. This difference in viewpoint distinguishes the early liberal from his spiritual descendants, who enlarged, rather than circumscribed, the scope of governmental function.

The Industrial Revolution was made possible by the technological innovations of applied science. One thinks of the steam engine perfected by James Watt toward the end of the eighteenth century; George Stephenson's locomotive, built in 1814; the telegraph, in 1844, and so on. What theology had been to the Middle Ages, science was to become to the nineteenth century. While Milton could write *Paradise Lost* (1667) relatively untroubled by scientific investigations (and only twenty years before Newton's *Principia*), Pope, in his *Essay on Man* (1733-1734), rejoiced in the wonders of the physical universe which scientists seemed daily to reveal, and writers after Pope found themselves situated in a world where science was increasingly important. To the already established abstract field of mathematics were slowly added the more empirical studies of astronomy, physics, geology, and chemistry. Shortly after 1800, biology became a recognized area of study, as scientists dealt more and more systematically with the organic as well as the inorganic. When Auguste Comte expounded his "Positive philosophy" in the 1820's, and spoke of the need of an additional "life science" (sociology), the definition of the scientific disciplines seemed complete. Comte divided human history into "religious-superstitious," "philosophical," and "scientific-positivistic" periods, and announced that the world was now enjoying the last of the three.

The trends we have just discussed inevitably gave rise to countertrends. The rise of the bourgeoisie and of democratic egalitarianism had opponents—not only defenders of privilege, and those who could say with Talleyrand, "No man not alive before 1789 knows the sweetness of life," but also those who anticipated the horrible potentialities implicit in "the revolt of the masses," later described by Ortega y Gasset. The "liberating" impulses of early nineteenth-century nationalism too frequently evolved into aggressive national pride or, worse, into rampant racism. The exponents of a free mercantile economy, assuming without justification that man's individual actions will naturally produce economic harmony, inspired economists like Karl Marx to correct the balance by elaborating theories according to which the independent capitalist would disappear altogether in the inexorable class struggle that (in Marx's view) he was helping to create. Finally, the faith in progress and the future which science apparently underwrote—the belief that man was destined to be biologically, materially, and morally better—was from its inception queried by those who feared the sin of pride, whether defined in Christian or in classical terms, and by those who resented the displacement of absolute truth by the relative, pragmatic truths which science asserted.

If some common direction is sought beneath these manifold tendencies, it may be found in the rise of secularity and in what the historian Lecky called "a declining sense of the miraculous." Medieval man knew that he lived in God's world, and Christianity had permeated every aspect of daily living. Whether the Reformation came as a symptom or a cause of weakened faith, the existence in the West of several hundred churches in 1700, in comparison with one Church in 1300, indicated doubts and questionings where once had been absolute doctrinal certainty. Politics and economics were increasingly shorn of theocratic presuppositions; and by the time of the Age of Reason, religious truth itself had to pass the tests of empirical and rational inquiry. Naturally there were individual thinkers, and even mass movements, who protested the departure from Christian orthodoxy; but, in general, during the first half of the nineteenth century, Christianity for the intellectual was absorbed into what Comte called vaguely "a religion of humanity." (Christianity for the average man often was summed up in a remark attributed to Lord Melbourne: "No man has more respect for the Christian religion than I have, but really, when it comes to intruding it into private life. . . .")

In 1859, Darwin published his *Origin of Species*. At first hailed with delight by many critics—for did not evolution make progress as *real* as the law of gravitation, and even coincide with ideas of Christian teleology?—Darwin's book was soon attacked by churchmen for destroying certain fundamentalist theses, and the fight between religion and science began in earnest. More important, as the century moved on, certain deeper minds were disturbed by the new conceptions of a universe from which mind and spirit seemed excluded, where chance determined change, where "survival of the fittest" and "natural selection" suggested that might and force won over right, and where moral laws were illusory fictions. Herbert Spencer's remark—"Nature's discipline is a little cruel that it may be very kind"—was then regarded either as small comfort or as downright erroneous. Many perplexed souls would have found Melville's lines in *Clarel* (1876) an expression of their own dubieties.

> Yea, ape and angel, strife and old debate—
> The harps of heaven and the dreary gongs of hell;
> Science the feud can only aggravate—
> No umpire she betwixt the chimes and knell:
> The running battle of the star and clod
> Shall run for ever—if there be no God.

It is within this climate of opinion that romanticism ends and realism begins.

ROMANTICISM—SENTIMENT AND NATURE

The preceding remarks range far ahead of the first works in this section. Let us return briefly to the mid-eighteenth century, when, in the period of transition from the Enlightenment to romanticism, certain philosophical, political, and cultural presuppositions at one time thought to be eternally true were discussed, then criticized, then finally abandoned. Once again we are faced with the fact that men very radically change their opinions within a relatively short span of history. Out of the mass of attitudes and ideas, we abstract two which seem particularly significant: the change in the concept of nature and the growing importance attributed to the sentiments, feelings, emotions, passions.

Frederick the Great, onetime patron of Voltaire, described *Candide* as "Job in modern dress," and it is good to remember that the Book of Job ends in mystery. In *Candide* the same mystery is posed en route, although the work itself ends with acceptance. Why does evil exist in the universe? Why does the good man suffer? What is the relation of God to mankind? Does the cosmos run according to some rational scheme comprehensible to the human mind? Eighteenth-century science and mathematics had seemed to confirm the mechanistic view that all parts of nature were intelligible. Yet an increasing number of dark spots on the once illuminated intellectual horizon puzzled and confused later thinkers. Nature was to remain the comforting talisman for romanticism that it had been for the Age of Reason, but we shall see that "nature" came to be redefined. The romantics were as anxious as their classical and neoclassical forbears to fathom the riddle of man in his world, but henceforth it was felt that perhaps the heart—the emotions—and not the head held the key to ultimate comprehension of the universe. To understand this change, we must examine the growing cult of sentiment in the eighteenth century.

It would be foolish to imagine that at a certain moment people stopped thinking and began feeling. The Enlightenment had made much of the "moral sense," and the early decades of the eighteenth century had enjoyed an honest tear with innumerable sentimental novels and plays. But on the whole the deliberate exploitation of the emotions had been held suspect; and if ultimate values—laws about the cosmos, the arts, society, and so on—were at stake, those areas of the psyche which related to the feelings were conceived to be irrelevant. Spinoza, in *Of Human Bondage, or The Power of the Affections* (1667) said, "In so far as men are subject to passions, they cannot be said to agree in nature." The idiosyncrasy resulting from adherence to personal emotion rather than to the generally accepted principles of reason was not considered ideal material for literature in a period unusually dedicated to ideas of universality, social man, communication between minds, and conformity to classical norms. Then, for reasons that are still not clear, philosophical introspection, reverie, the melancholy heart became fashionable. The brooding, solitary daydreamer came into his own, with varieties of "spleen," "the blue devils," *Weltschmerz* ("world sorrow"), *le mal du siècle* ("the sickness of the century"). Rousseau's *Confessions* (1781-1788), filled with this kind of passionate unrest, were hailed by a reading public already assured of the primacy of the emotions.

I am commencing [said Rousseau] an undertaking, hitherto without precedent, and which will never find an imitator. I desire to set before my fellow-men the likeness of a man in all the truth of nature, and that man is myself. Myself alone! I know the feelings of my heart, and I know men. I am not made like any of those I have seen; I venture to believe that I am not made like any of those who are in existence.

From the objective norms that were the delight of the Age of Reason, we turn to the subjective, innate, indefinable, and *unique* core of each individual. The "man of feeling" (the phrase forms the title of a popular novel by the Scottish writer, Henry MacKenzie, published in 1771) replaced the elegant conversationalist of the salon, coffee house, and boudoir. And his feelings were mostly mournful. Earlier eighteenth-century sentimental literature had displayed *both* pleasurable and painful experiences, enriched by laughter and tears. The romantics endeavored to show that sensibility was not equated with happiness, and romantic literature in general is rarely comical or amusing. Pushkin does occasionally smile wryly, but after the manner of Byron, whom he so admired: "And if I laugh at any mortal thing, 'Tis that I may not weep." In Rousseau's novel, *Julie ou La Nouvelle Héloïse* (*Julia, or The New Héloïse,* 1761), the young hero Saint-Preux exclaims poignantly, "For me there is only a single way to be happy, but there are millions of ways to be miserable."

For the romantics, the so-called "tender passion"—love—gained pre-eminence among all the feelings. The modern colloquial usage of "romantic" with connotations of moon-June-spoon is in part a legacy from that period. With the exception of Racine's *Phèdre,* the preceding section of this anthology contains, significantly, no literature dealing with love. Candide voyages from continent to continent to find his elusive Cunégonde, but her chief virtue—physical indestructibility—scarcely qualifies her for the role of a *romantic* heroine. The eighteenth century—despite its finesse, social decorum, and elegance—abounds with works displaying the relations between the sexes as surprisingly lusty and earthy, or as a kind of psychological game with possession the assumed goal of the male partner. Against such amorous franchise the romantics rebelled. We shall watch Faust and Margaret, among other heroes and heroines, asserting that love is a genuine spiritual entity and a condition eagerly to be coveted—not for purposes of physical satisfaction but because unhappy as the condition may be, life is meaningless unless we exist in that state of morose delight.

Even as the age brought a revaluation of the less ratiocinative, more intuitive processes of the psyche, it also brought new colorings to the concept of nature. From classical antiquity through most of the eighteenth century, the word *nature* had meant the totality of existence, the entire cosmos—animate and inanimate—with its laws and activity, and when it meant anything less than this, it had usually meant the whole nature of man—common human nature. But in the cult of nature inspired by the romantic movement, the term came to mean something much more limited: the physical world apart from man's achievements—that is, the landscape and countryside, the sea and mountains. In a sense this idealization of nature was no innovation. The Hebraic-Christian tradition had begun with a garden. Pagan antiquity in Greece and Rome had produced pastorals and bucolics, in which the vision of the simple life in close proximity to animals and the land was portrayed. But the cleavage that Rousseau and his heirs now felt to exist between the individual and his environment led to a redefinition of "nature." Neoclassical society, polished and polite, had been essentially urban, although the philosopher-gentleman could enjoy the country as a respite from strenuous city life with its Court and Parliament, salons and coffee houses, wit and conversation. The formal garden—like Voltaire's at Ferney, with two head gardeners and twenty laborers—may be taken as a symbol of what was held to be a happy compromise between the country's annoying miscellaneousness and civilized mankind's love of order. As Dr. Johnson, Voltaire's contemporary, put it: "Sir, they who are content to live in the country are fit for it."

In the passage above from Rousseau, he stated that he is psychologically unique and like no other man past or present. From this sense of acute individuality, it is only a short step to a feeling of being alien and misunderstood. If our insensitive contemporaries reject us, we can always find comfort in the great sympathetic soul of nature—nature who "never did betray/The heart that loved her."

The heroes of later eighteenth-century literature move out from the confines of city and drawing room to the seas and forests. By the early nineteenth century the new hero has become stereotyped and hostility to organized society a cliché. If any member of society gained the romantic's approbation, it was generally the simple rustic who—like the innocent child—was close to nature and therefore morally purer than his sophisticated fellows. Primitivism long had interested the rationalist thinkers, and the untutored mind afforded the *philosophes* fascinating material for their studies of general mankind, although for this purpose distant, exotic savages (Voltaire's *Oreillons*, for instance) were more pleasing and more conveniently remote than the local peasantry. Later eighteenth-century expansions of this concept marked a shift from mere interest in the Noble Savage to positive approval. Serious doubts were raised as to the validity of urbanity and cultivation and about the notion of progress itself. Perhaps the unspoiled savage partook of a Golden Age where hearts rather than purses were gold, where there was no *mine* or *thine*, no artificial legislation, no social hierarchy. Though Rousseau's "natural man" drew a shout of derision from Voltaire, who saw men once more getting down on all fours in abdication of their rational-human capabilities, Voltaire was fighting a rearguard action, and the success of a work he ridiculed proved it. Few literary productions have attained the popularity of the Ossian poems (1760-1763), ostensibly translated by James Macpherson. *Fingal* and *Temora*, two "epics" in the group, depicted early Scottish-Celtic-"Erse" days in an elegiac, melancholy tone. What critics seemed most to admire was the *goodness* of all the characters. The poems of Ossian, for example, were among the favorite reading of a most unprimitive figure—Napoleon. That Macpherson's work was later proved a forgery in no way diminished his incredible influence. Twenty-five years afterward, Bernardin de Saint-Pierre published *Paul and Virginia* (*Paul et Virginie*, 1788), in which the life of decadent Europe was contrasted unfavorably with life on an unspoiled, Eden-like island. "Here there is merely wooden furniture, but there you find serene faces and hearts of gold."

France had been the Continental fortress of the Age of Reason, as our selection of readings in the preceding section of the anthology indicates. The headquarters of the new ideology moved to the "misty" north and Germany. That country demonstrated conscious romantic symptoms during the 1770's with its "Storm and Stress" (*Sturm und Drang*) movement in literature—led by a coterie of young writers fired by naturalistic, anti-French, anticlassical feeling. In their twenties, they were impregnated with notions about "genius" that should transcend any fettering rules and standards, convinced of the primacy of the passions over the meddling intellect, desirous of writing simple folk poetry stemming directly from the heart of the race, anxious to identify the spirit of man with the spirit of the new "nature," and, finally, eager to use literature as a vehicle in the search for philosophic truth—the pursuit of the Absolute, the underlying reality of existence. This was one of the first *avant-garde* groups. Among those who contributed to the "Storm and Stress" movement was Johann Wolfgang von Goethe. His *Faust*, Part I, begun during these years, is an illustration of the fully developed romantic mood.

ROMANTICISM AND THE METAPHYSICAL QUEST—GOETHE'S *FAUST*

Goethe, speaking of *Faust* to his friend and amanuensis Eckermann, once commented, "I think that I have given them a bone to pick." Seldom in Western literature has a work been so provocative to its audience; yet many a critic has sunk deep in the morass of intellectualism when attempting to explicate the play. The average reader will find *Faust* difficult going. He will be aware that there is more to it than meets the eye, although perhaps his feeling of disquietude will overbalance any pleasure the reading has afforded. If he is honest with himself, however, he will be forced to one conclusion upon completing *Faust:* he has been in the presence of one of the greatest of the world's masterpieces. Such an experience *should* lead to healthy confusion, since the reader—with the artist—has just taken a plunge into the unknown.

The first part of *Faust* was published by Goethe in 1808. Many years had gone into its creation. His so-called *Ur-Faust* ("early" or "primitive" *Faust*) was written between 1770 and 1775, and *Faust, a Fragment*, appeared in 1790. Behind Goethe's extensive labors lay the whole legend of the Renaissance scholar, Dr. Faustus, who quested after universal knowledge by means of white magic—that is, orthodox science—and the more terrible instrument of black magic. A real Johannes Faustus lived from 1480 to 1540. His adventures, much embroidered, were related by Johannes Spies twenty-seven years later, and these became the subject for innumerable puppet shows and popular folk-dramas throughout the seventeenth and eighteenth centuries in Germany. Hence from childhood on, the Faust myth was familiar to Goethe; and from the time he was twenty until he died at eighty-two, the theme never left his imagination. To trace the slow genesis of *Faust*, Part I, and later *Faust*, Part II (the sequel published posthumously in 1833), is fascinating to the scholar, but dull for the student. The important fact to be grasped is simple. Once again, as in Greek tragedy and Racine's

Phèdre, we have the playwright using traditional, legendary, even mythical material.

The "Prologue in Heaven" Benedetto Croce has called "the jest of a great artist . . . deliberately archaic, and slightly in the style of Voltaire." We should not be misled by its cosmic humor and high irony. It must be read with care, for the key to subsequent events is found in the dialogue between God and Mephistopheles. The paean of the Archangels in praise of the wonderful universe is succeeded by the nay-sayer's insouciant remarks. Like Satan in the Book of Job (the opening scene is obviously modeled on Job 1:6-12 and 2:1-6) Goethe's devil has just returned "from going to and fro in the earth, and from walking up and down on it." What he has seen has only increased his contempt for that silly grasshopper, man. The angels may place man a little lower than themselves. Mephistopheles finds restless mankind scarcely an improvement over primordial chaos. Already we note that Mephistopheles' quarrel is not with man or with Faust; his challenge is leveled at God and His fitness as a creator!

Then follows the *first* wager, which is between God and a fallen divinity. Faust is discontented, says Mephistopheles. That beautiful gift of reason has induced nothing but fatal curiosity. His bewilderment, answers God, is temporary; and He turns Faust over to this most cynical of devils for the rest of his life. No holds are barred for Mephistopheles. He is given *carte blanche* to lure Faust in any fashion. The cryptic language may obscure the real issue for the reader. Here is no simple temptation to be naughty. Mephistopheles' aim is to undermine Faust's whole *moral* sense, the awareness that values of good and evil do exist despite man's difficulties in defining them. A being of searchings and questionings, living a life of constant aspiration toward goals but dimly seen—this, as described by God, is the being He has created in His own image. We shall see shortly how the terms of the *second* pact between man and devil are an attempt on Mephistopheles' part to stop this vital activity, thus implicitly defeating God's description of life as an eternal Becoming.

Such a vitalistic and dynamic interpretation of the human condition is the essence of romantic philosophy. Christianity had posited a state of grace, and Christian thought is the history of attempts to determine how erring man might finally enjoy eternal bliss. The Enlightenment, ignoring the mystery of faith implicit in Christian doctrine, had expanded the element of reason to be an end in itself. Romanticism, suddenly aware of dynamic (even irrational) principles underlying both man and nature, took striving—tentative progression and development, and pure endeavor—and made it the defining quality of mankind. In the second part of *Faust* (about which we shall speak briefly later on), Goethe has a chorus of angels proclaim, "Should a man strive with all his heart/ Heaven can foil the devil." The paradox of *Faust* is that of a man finally redeemed by a God whose reality Faust doubts. Goethe has written a modern *Divine Comedy* paralleling Dante's, but it is "divine comedy" of the profoundest irony.

Following the prologue we move from heaven to earth—a shift in background reminiscent of the epic. The setting of the opening of the play is traditional: "a high-vaulted narrow *Gothic* room." It reminds us of Goethe's role in the "Storm and Stress" group, the young writers of Germany who were anxious to rescue the native scene, and also the Middle Ages, and also Shakespeare (their idol), from the undervaluations of the Enlightenment—by which they meant France and French neoclassicism. The late C. S. Lewis, in *The Screwtape Letters* (1942), pointed out how "the long, dull, monstrous years of middle-aged prosperity or middle-aged adversity are excellent campaigning weapons" for the devil, and Goethe's Heinrich Faust is in the full maturity of worldly success. He owns everything—and nothing. He as polymath has investigated the entire field of human knowledge to find a chaos of relativism. A simple three-meal-a-day life is impossible for him. He cherishes a passion for the Absolute which his pedantic assistant Wagner cannot comprehend. Black magic yields little save despair. Death is one road to possession of final truth, but a childhood memory of naïve faith averts suicide. At this critical stage Mephistopheles enters (first in the guise of a poodle, and we remember that the Greek root of the word *cynic* means "dog"). The real action of the play begins.

The Prince of Darkness is a gentleman, and the devil soon abandons his earlier disguises for the elegant costume of the polished gallant and wit. He had minced no words when he said previously, "I am the Spirit which always denies" (*"Ich bin der Geist der stets verneint"*). Now he offers *his* wager to Faust. Their pact is a corollary of the one we witnessed in Heaven. An interesting point, however, is that Faust frames the terms. We have already indicated that God's picture of Mephistopheles does not coincide with the devil's view of himself. The relation of the tempter to Faust presents us with an additional facet to his character, for Mephistopheles never really understands the nature of his companion's problem. *If* Mephistopheles can destroy Faust's sense of aspiration, *if* Faust can say of any single moment in time that *this* is complete fulfillment of desire—then the devil wins, and God and man are defeated. Such repose and satiety would represent an end to striving. It would also—and here is the subtle touch—mean a cessation of Faust's moral awareness. By the achievement of a final "good" on earth, the whole conception of good and evil as being in a state of development would be denied. Faust examines existence in terms of a question that only modern man could conceive;

certainly it was unknown to the Greeks with their feeling for limitation. Is a life of tireless movement toward an undefined goal worth living? And the devil (orthodox conservative and traditionalist that he is) can hardly be expected to grasp such a radical query.

The varieties of pleasure that the devil parades before the hero are proffered in an effort to supply *the* moment of complete satisfaction, and thus obfuscate Faust's values. Mephistopheles almost wins with Margaret (Gretchen). But love is more complicated than mere sex, and Faust's love comes to mean the acme of human aspiration. From love he learns to break through the bonds of his individual ego and to see his state in humanity. Margaret's tragedy enhances rather than diminishes Faust's moral sensibility, and Mephistopheles is a puzzled, disappointed sensualist when he takes Faust back to Gretchen's dungeon for the last poignant scene in the play. It is essential that the reader comprehend how much the author stresses the nature of Faust's affection, how love is raised to the level of a high philosophical concept. Stendhal showed only his lack of perception when he remarked: "Goethe gives Faust the Devil for a friend; and with this powerful ally, Faust does what we have all done at the age of twenty—he seduces a seamstress."

Even before the first part of *Faust* was published, Goethe thought of writing a second drama where the hero would turn from individual to social concerns. From approximately 1800 to 1831 Goethe worked on *Faust*, Part II, a play designed principally to be read. To read it is, in the words of one critic, "a pilgrimage from which few have returned safe and sound." Few works in modern times present us with such a conglomeration of shifting symbols, and we move from mystery to mystery, carried forward by Goethe's incomparable verse and brilliant ideas. A "Classical Walpurgis Night" synthesizes ancient Greece and the Gothic north. Goethe returns to the older Faust legend to have his aging protagonist marry Helen of Troy, now a widow after the death of Menelaus. Their union begets Euphorion (the spirit of new humanity; it is said that Goethe had Byron in mind as his model). Faust also undertakes a military career to save a shaky kingdom from falling. The ultimate activity pursued by Faust consists in reclaiming land from the sea, and he sees the vision of a new, happy community composed of industrious mankind. *This* is at last the consummate moment for him, and Mephistopheles—a nearly exhausted tempter—wins the wager in a dubious victory. But Faust's satisfaction is potential rather than actual: the vision lies in the indeterminate future for which he strives. The angels rescue Faust's soul from the forces of evil and bear him in triumph to heaven. Goethe's God seems to say that Faust's errors are necessary imperfections of man's growth. Imperfections in time are perfections in eternity. Faust's has been a "good" life. The final lines of the great drama, declaimed by the *Chorus Mysticus* in heaven, sum up the author's profound affirmation of existence.

> All that is past of us
> Was but reflected;
> All that was lost in us
> Here is corrected;
> All indescribables
> Here we descry;
> Eternal Womanhead
> Leads us on high.
> [*Das Ewig-Weibliche / Zieht uns hinan*]

BLAKE

Virtually unknown as a poet in his own lifetime, Blake was considered at the best eccentric, at the worst insane, by most of the few late nineteenth-century critics who read him at all. As recently as 1933, A. E. Housman (in the *Name and Nature of Poetry*) made that same psychic disability a virtue that gives us "poetry neat, or adulterated with so little meaning that nothing except poetic emotion is perceived and matters." Only within the last several generations has Blake's "madness" come to be viewed as obscurity, stemming from his attempt to synthesize experience into a unified whole. He once wrote: "I must create a system or be enslav'd by another man's." Such servitude would scarcely have been congenial to the artist who described himself as "I, William Blake, a Mental Prince." As for obscurity, here is Blake again: "You say that I want somebody to Elucidate my Ideas. But you ought to know that What is Grand is necessarily obscure to Weak men. That which can be made Explicit to the Idiot is not worth my care."

This remark effectively seems to gainsay any effort to subject Blake's work to critical scrutiny. An additional problem is that he was a self-proclaimed mystic, a category of person that ordinary minds find puzzling. At the age of four he claimed he saw God looking at him through the window. When he was somewhat older, he beheld a tree filled with angels, "their bright wings bespangling the boughs like stars." (There is evidence that for reporting this vision, his father gave him a sound beating). Of one of his poems, he commented: "I dare not pretend to be anything other than the Secretary; the Authors are in Eternity." In the same vein, his wife told a friend that she saw relatively little of her husband, since he was "always in Paradise." Later, we have the account of a witness that, shortly before Blake died, "his eyes brightened and he burst out singing of the things he saw in Heaven."

How then can we grapple with a mind in one sense so resolutely defiant of interpretation, and in another sense so unearthly? Our best approach, I think, is to examine first the things he disliked.

The outbreak of the French Revolution in 1789 meant for Blake the advent of the millenium—an attitude he shared with Wordsworth, Southey, Coleridge, and Hazlitt, all younger contemporaries. Unlike them, however, he never completely abandoned his high hopes. Longer poems such as *America, The Visions of the Daughters of Albion,* and *The French Revolution* chronicle his political radicalism, as do many of the lyrics in *The Songs of Experience.* Among his friends were William Godwin, whose *Political Justice* (1793) preached a kind of benevolent anarchism; Dr. Price, whose famous sermon in 1789 provoked Edmund Burke to answer it with his conservative *Reflections on the Revolution in France* (1790); and Tom Paine, who had to flee from England to escape prosecution for his *Rights of Man.* Kings, tyrannical laws, social and economic inequality, war: these were for Blake just a few of the examples in mankind's history of cruelty and misery to be put against the virtues of "Mercy, Pity, Peace and Love"—as set forth in his poem, "The Divine Image," in *Songs of Innocence.*

For Blake, political oppression was merely one aspect of modern man's depravity. Individual morality also reflected humanity's fall from primal innocence. The "Proverbs of Hell" in *The Marriage of Heaven and Hell* can be read as his attack on an ethic composed principally of cant and hypocrisy. In the field of sexual morality, for instance, he was most daring and advanced by the standards of his day. W. H. Auden remarks that "The whole of Freud's teaching may be found in *The Marriage.*" This is hyperbolic. Nevertheless, Blake looked forward with uncanny prescience to many twentieth-century theories about sexual repression and its often damaging consequences. He seemed to have felt that man, partly through an inordinate intellectualism that inhibited the emotions (Freud's Ego and Id), had lost his capacity for genuine love.

"Intellectualism" was another object of Blake's animosity: the entire body of eighteenth-century philosophy as he construed it was rationalist, analytic, mechanistic, essentially inhumane, cold, and dead. One need only contrast Pope's couplet, "Nature and Nature's Laws lay hid in Night,/ God said, 'Let Newton be!' and all was Light," with Blake's rejoinder, "May God us keep/ From Single vision & Newton's sleep!" "Single vision" meant scientific and abstract reasoning, where the imagination—for Blake the highest of human faculties—was rigorously excluded. Thus he lumped together disparate thinkers like Bacon, Newton, Voltaire, Locke, Hume, Gibbon, Rousseau, and the Deists as the opposition. They comprise an odd company when, for example, we recall the intellectual hostility between Rousseau and Voltaire. But for Blake they all shared in a lowest common denominator, their skepticism about revealed religion. *There Is No Natural Religion* is the title of one of his tracts. In another (*To the Deists*) he thunders, "You, Deists, profess yourselves the Enemies of Christianity, and you are so; you are also the Enemies of the Human Race & of Universal Nature."

It follows as a corollary that

Blake would strike down all of classical literature, revered by the Augustans as well as by his own educated contemporaries. This can be partly explained by his total lack of formal schooling, except for drawing instruction, not to mention his resentment against the upper classes. But it is also true that his deep religiosity and extreme Protestantism, with the Bible as the sole avatar of wisdom and ultimate truth, compelled him to castigate the pagan authors. (After all, did not Milton, writing in his old age, have Christ reject the classics in favor of the Old Testament, in Book IV of *Paradise Regained?*) Blake's Preface to *Milton,* opens with an assault upon the classics: "The Stolen and Perverted Writings of Homer & Ovid, of Plato & Cicero, which all Men ought to condemn, are set up by artifice against the Sublime of the Bible." In painting, Blake's other medium of artistic expression, his special target was Sir Joshua Reynolds, first president of the Royal Academy, whose fashionable portraits seemed to him examples of a sterile classicism. He dismissed Reynolds tersely: "This man was hired to depress art."

In the same manner he condemned eighteenth-century neoclassic poetry, as, in their diverse ways, Wordsworth and Keats were later to do. "The languid strings do scarcely move! The sound is forc'd, the notes are few." ("*To the Muses*"). In contrast, his own short lyrics drew on folk poetry—if in that category we include hymns, street ballads, metrical versions of the psalms, and popular poems like Isaac Watt's *Divine and Moral Songs.* In the later and longer "prophetic" poems he also departed from the traditional rhymed couplet, to an unrhymed, loose, accentual verse having from four to eight stresses to a line. In the Preface to *Jerusalem,* he tells how he first considered using blank verse, only to discard it: "I therefore have produced a variety in every line, both of cadences & number of syllables. Every word and every letter is studied and put into its fit place; the terrific numbers are reserved for the terrific parts, the mild & gentle for the mild & gentle parts, and the prosaic for inferior parts; all are necessary to each other."

So much for Blake's polemics in matters political, cultural, and esthetic. His abhorrence of institutionalized religion likewise is evident in the poems. His break from Swedenborg, described in *The Marriage of Heaven and Hell,* stemmed partly from his conviction that his former mentor was merely setting up another Church—a proof for him that once more men were superimposing dogma and "man-forg'd manacles" on the original teachings of Jesus, thereby ironically restoring the very "Law" that Christ had transcended. Some of his ideas strike modern minds as at the very least absurd. He was convinced, for instance, that Christ once came to England; that the British were really one of the Lost Tribes of Israel (a belief still held by the group known as "British Israelites"); and that Noah, Shem, Abraham, and other figures in the Old Testament were Druids. "All things Begin & End in Albion's [i.e., England's] Ancient Druid Rocky Shore." As for his own role: "My Work . . . is an Endeavour to Restore what the Ancients call'd the Golden Age."

Yet basically his theology—he would have resented this abstract word applied to himself—is a set of variations, original and complex, on traditional Christian ideas about man's Fall and hopeful redemption. *The Songs of Innocence* delineate the life of happy, idyllic childhood: presexual and with images drawn chiefly from the countryside. The animals are wild but benign; the poems speak of birds, springtime, dawn, and dewy fields. This for Blake was also the Garden of Adam and Eve, before they committed disobedience against God by eating the apple from the Tree of Knowledge. The pristine condition of our first parents was repeated throughout history, and indeed Blake saw this role reenacted in each individual life.

The Songs of Experience take us to a somber world: one that is sick and diseased by lust and greed, adult-controlled and urban, with nature replaced by churches, factories, and alehouses; the once happy child now subjected to parental, religious, and political tyranny, often pathetically lost and wandering in a universe that rejects him. Abstract reasoning has supplanted the feelings. The imagery sometimes is taken from dream or nightmare. The pastoral and daylight decor of *The Songs of Innocence* ominously shifts to night, frost, thunder, winter, seas, and dark forests.

Yet for Blake this is a stage that must be traversed and accepted, since Good and Evil coexist. The self now realizes that it is fallen from innocence, but it also comes to know through "experience" that it has the capacity for the awareness of a higher reality. "Everything will appear, as it is, Infinite." The simple Piper we meet in the Introduction to *The Songs of Innocence* gives way in *Experience* to the Bard, a prophet and seer. And that Bard is Blake himself. Only now is the attainment of the third realm possible. Blake called it "Beulah," a word from the Old Testament meaning "marriage." Thus each individual goes from happy childhood through the harsh despotism of the human and divine parent (the latter is "Old Nobodaddy," Blake's conception of the angry God of the Old Testament), at last recognizing Christ and the "human form divine."

Blake's later prophetic books are not represented here, but a short summary of the mythological creatures he conceived for them may illuminate the works we have selected. The Four Zoas (from "beast" in Greek)—Luvah, Urizen, Tharmas, and Urthona—represent man's bodily components (loins, head, heart, and legs) as well as his qualities (love–emotion, wisdom–reason, power–the senses, and imagination–spirit). Critics have worked out these categories to reveal a fairly consistent system, in which they relate to the four elements of fire, air, earth, and water; the times of the day, the four seasons, the four Gospels, the sense organs (nose, eye, tongue, and ear); the professions (weaver, ploughman, shepherd, and blacksmith). The Fall for Blake meant that this fourfold unity was destroyed. Cultural history he saw as now the triumph of one Zoa, now another, but always at the expense of the rest—to negate the last and affirmative line in *The Marriage of Heaven and Hell*, "For every thing that lives is Holy."

Blake held that imagination was the sole route by which a world that the intellectualism of eighteenth-century philosophy had left mechanical and lifeless, could be revivified. "I know of no other Christianity and of no other Gospel than of the liberty both of the body & mind to exercise the Divine Arts of Imagination, Imagination, the real & eternal world of which this Vegetable Universe is but a faint shadow, & in which we shall live in our Eternal or Imaginative Bodies when these Vegetable Mortal Bodies are no more." One last quotation demonstrates Blake's creed that true art and religion are conjoined: "A poet, a painter, a musician, an architect: the man or woman who is not one of these is not a Christian. . . . Jesus & His apostles were all artists. . . . The whole business of man is the arts."

ENGLISH ROMANTIC VERSE

WORDSWORTH

In 1800 Wordsworth's Preface to the *Lyrical Ballads* appeared—the first English romantic manifesto in the arts, in which the author was primarily concerned with a new poetics for a new era. The *Lyrical Ballads*, the work of both William Wordsworth and Samuel Taylor Coleridge, had originally been published in 1798. The Preface written by Wordsworth in 1800 for the second edition of the poems, stands as an apology for the techniques of both poets, although Wordsworth was chiefly interested in defending himself.

Included in the 1800 volume was "Tintern Abbey" ("Lines Composed a Few Miles above Tintern Abbey . . ."). This poem is a meditation in three parts: the description of the scene, the account of the poet's gradually maturing conception of nature and his relation to it, and finally the apostrophe to his sister Dorothy. To the modern reader the work seems innocent enough and scarcely revolutionary in thought or technique. Properly to estimate the poem's literary worth, we must remember the poetic tradition against which Wordsworth was rebelling and some of the doctrine presented in the Preface of 1800.

Wordsworth's aim (already outlined in the Advertisement to the 1798 *Lyrical Ballads*) was to write in "the language of conversation in the middle and lower classes of society," not in what seemed to him the flowery poetic diction which the Age of Reason ordinarily employed in pastoral and descriptive poetry. That he regarded "Tintern Abbey" as a departure from conventional forms is best illustrated by his own tentative feelings concerning its classification. "I have not ventured to call this Poem an Ode; but it was written with the hope that in the transitions and the impassioned music of the versification, would be found the principal requisites, of this species of composition." The composition of the work, blending present sensations with past memories ("Five years have past"), exemplifies Wordsworth's definition of poetry as "emotion recollected in tranquility." Despite the simple vocabulary and the obvious effort to write in a blank-verse medium close to prose, critics have questioned how far the style of "Tintern Abbey" actually resembles the language of conversation in the middle and lower classes.

Perhaps most important in the poem is the pervading pantheistic sentiment, the notion of the world soul immanent in every part of nature. "Tintern Abbey" displays in miniature what Wordsworth's long poem, *The Prelude* (1798-1805), was to show on a grander scale. It traces the growth of the poet's mind from a naïve childhood association with nature based on mere physical sensations to a final vision where the individual soul and "the still, sad music of humanity" are made one with the outer world of external shapes and forms. For Wordsworth the "sense sublime / Of something far more deeply interfused" is not merely the occasion conducive to the poetic experience. It is also the credo of pantheism.

The "Ode on Intimations of Immortality" (1807) recapitulates much of Wordsworth's attitude in "Tintern Abbey"; yet the pattern of spiritual and artistic crisis, followed by explanation and finally consolation, gives the "Ode" an intensity modern readers may find lacking in the earlier poem. From the Platonic notion of an existence before birth, Wordsworth moves to the babe and to the child—each much closer than the adult (and the poet) to the pristine, visionary state where the soul was one with pure Being and God. The frequent use of images referring to light is significant. What he poignantly states is the problem of sustaining "the visionary gleam . . . the glory and the dream." For its loss, to Wordsworth and to many romantic poets, meant not merely a dearth of poetry but a loss of contact with the underlying spirit of the universe. By relating poetry to metaphysics—and exalting it to a quasi-religious, quasi-mystical level—the romantics were giving even the lyric new necessity and new dignity; but they also demonstrated how difficult it was to capture and to retain the moment of poetic inspiration.

COLERIDGE

The same belief in the high intent and lofty office of the poet was shared by Coleridge, but he approached his craft with a style and technique different, and in some ways diametrically opposed, to those of Wordsworth. Like Wordsworth he revolted against the artifice of eighteenth-century verse, but Coleridge was interested less in recreating the "real language of men" than in returning to the older poetry of humble people —the ballad and the folk song, Furthermore, he felt that the new poetry had to revive the ancient sense of awe and wonder that primitive men displayed toward the universe. While employing the strange and the supernatural, he attempted to forge a set of poetic symbols that might make poetry not mere entertainment but an instrument of metaphysical knowledge. Later studies in German Idealistic philosophers (Kant, Schelling, Fichte) were to intensify his temperamental bent toward intellectual speculation, Coleridge's belief in the power of the imagination to peer into the workings of the cosmos augmented his conviction that poetry was a form of truth, and that art was to mediate between man and nature. As it had been for his predecessor William Blake, the poetic symbol was for Coleridge a hieroglyphic of reality; and *Kubla Khan* (ca. 1800) displayed in practice what he later expanded into theory. Unlike Wordsworth, who could never squarely face the problem of rhyme and meter—are they part of the "real language of men?"—Coleridge found these aspects of verse necessary to raise language to its highest capacity, where poetry acts as verbal incantation—a conception anticipating the idea of "evocative magic" later introduced by the symbolist poet Baudelaire.

BYRON AND THE ROMANTIC HERO

No single figure served better to answer the demand for a romantic hero than did Byron. In 1812, as he said, he awoke to find himself famous when the public welcomed the first two cantos of *Childe Harold's Pilgrimage*. For the modern reader, one problem is to disentangle his life, his works, and the myth that arose about them both. Handsome, debonair, elegant—the English aristocrat rejected by the society he treated with contempt—he swaggered through his thirty-six years with the brilliance of a consummate actor. When he spoke of his poetry as the pageant of his bleeding heart, he satisfied the age's taste for the literary confession. The role he played as the satanic dandy, the fallen angel, extended his influence outside England to the Continent, where a young generation—already filled with sentiments of *taedium vitae*, melancholia, *accidia*, "spleen," *Weltschmerz*, and *mal du siècle*—saw in him and in his writings the incarnation of their own feelings.

To understand *Don Juan* (1819-1824), it is necessary first to consider certain aspects of eighteenth-century poetry. The Augustan age had been concerned with social man, the general species rather than the peculiarities of the individual; Hence satire, as we have previously seen, was a favorite form, for it could serve to correct deviations from norms of attitude and behavior. By the same token, lyric poetry—typically intimate, personal, and written not to project some universal truth but rather to evoke a private, unique feeling—was generally considered least important in the hierarchy of poetic genres. But romanticism, stressing the imagination, the emotions, and the private instead of the public phase of life, naturally turned to lyric poetry for its medium.

Don Juan represents a peculiar amalgam of both attitudes. On the one hand, the haunting poignancy of the Juan-Haidée episode is an echo of Byron's own love affairs, the poetic statement of the man who could write the following lines to the Countess Guiccioli: "You, who are my only and my last love, who are my only joy, the delight of my life—you who are my only hope—you who were—at least for a moment—all mine—you have gone away—and I remain here alone and desolate." The love of Juan and Haidée, placed in the exotic setting so dear to the romantics eager to escape from the mediocrity of a hum drum existence, is transmitted to the reader in poetry expressive of excited passion in accordance with Byron's own definition of his art. The lovers personify the protest of innocent, natural goodness against the claims of a cynical, worldly, materialistic society; they fulfill the romantic dream of primitive man happy in a state of nature:

> They were alone, but not alone as they
> Who shut in chambers think it loneliness;
> The silent ocean, and the starlight bay,
> The twilight glow, which momently grew less,
> The voiceless sands, and dropping caves, that lay
> Around them, made them to each other press . . .

On the other hand, we are faced with Byron's affection for eighteenth-century verse and the affinities between him and the Augustan poets, especially Pope. Despite his debt to other English romantic writers, he tended to be critical of them: he deplored the vulgarity of the so-called "cockney" style of Keats, the sentimental and formless effusions of Southey and Wordsworth, the metaphysical vagaries of Coleridge, the confused symbolism of Shelley. The earlier masters of the terse, sharp, concise heroic couplet were his ideal. Although he referred to Pope as "that bitter Queen Anne's man," it was from Pope that he learned the power of devices such as antithesis and deliberate anticlimax, calculated bathos produced by the "art of sinking," and the sudden intrusion of the critical intellect after a rhapsodic outpouring of the feelings. Other resemblances to the literature of the preceding century are easy to discern. Fielding had called his novel *Joseph Andrews* (1742) "a comic epic poem in prose." Byron too returns to the epic form: the heroic becomes mock-heroic, the epic machinery is burlesqued and parodied ("Hail, Muse! *et caetera*"), the once doughty deeds turn into a series of boudoir escapades and picaresque rogueries, and this satiric grand tour opens in the mood of French bedroom farce or Restoration comedy.

Yet it is impossible to define Byron's special complexity solely in terms of a synthesis of neoclassicism with romanticism. The explanation lies within his own personality, and to some extent within romanticism itself. The mixture of ardor and cynicism apparent in Canto II of *Don Juan*—the counterpoint of sympathy against cool detachment—is only one facet of the tensions within the poet: he is the impertinent skeptic and fre-thinker never able to suppress memories of a rigid Presbyterian childhood; the great lover of the autobiographical portrait and the real man eternally seeking fulfill-ment in love and too quick to discover boredom and satiety; the weary champion of liberty and egalitarianism dying at Mis-solonghi, and the aristocrat con-scious of his station and title. Typical of the man who was ever posturing but always frank with himself is Byron's state-ment concerning *Don Juan:* "It . . . is meant to be a little quietly facetious about everything." But we remember the lines within the poem that perhaps reveal more of the author than his explicit assertion would allow. "And if I laugh at any mortal thing,/ 'Tis that I may not weep." In short, Byron exhibits one facet of what we now call *romantic irony*. In verbal irony, a statement means some-thing different from what it seems to say. But romantic irony results from the individual's compartmentalizing his person-ality, so that the "thinking ego" watches the "feeling ego" with objectivity and the human be-ing, split between factor and spectator, experiences a desire to plunge into life and an equally strong urge to stand apart from it. An earlier writer, Horace Wal-pole, had said, "The world is a comedy to those that think, a tragedy to those that feel." It is almost as if certain romantics had discovered that the same person could do both and would consequently be doomed to re-main in a state of unstable equilibrium.

SHELLEY

Wordsworth and Coleridge proclaimed the new movement in the *Lyrical Ballads* of 1798-1800; Shelley and Keats estab-lished romantic verse as *the* po-etic tradition of the period. In the poems by them offered here, we see the fulfillment of certain qualities associated with roman-tic poetry: the attempted musi-calization of verse, with the em-phasis on sound rather than on sense; a skillful metrical tech-nique; a keen eye for the particu-larities of nature, and the em-ployment of existing verse forms (combined with experimenta-tion) to achieve special effects. In the "Ode to the West Wind" (1820), it may be said that Shel-ley takes his point of departure from Wordsworth. There is the same evocation of nature (al-though a wilder, more spectacu-lar landscape than ever Words-worth described); there is even a similar regret for powers pos-sessed by the child and lost in maturity:

> If . . .
> I were as in my boyhood, and could be
> The comrade of thy wanderings over heaven.

On the other hand, we see that already in Shelley a poetic dic-tion has been developed—per-haps not that of the eighteenth century, but an equally stylized use of language. The imagery, the choice of words, the alterna-tion of moods of fierce passion and abject despair are a far cry from Wordsworth's attempt to write in the speech of common men. Indeed, Shelley criticized his predecessor for "failing to distinguish between simplicity of intellect and silly foolishness," and he feared that an unexalted poetry approaching too close to prose would be no poetry at all.

Outweighing these differences is the fact that the attitude expressed in the "Ode to the West Wind" represents an intensification of Wordsworth's ideas. One feels that the wind, for example, is more than a convenient aspect of nature in which the author wishes to lose his identity. It becomes a symbol for the intuited perception Shelley believed the poet to possess—a power at once preserving and destroying, serene and terrible, joyful and sad. Hence the final section is the key both to Shelley's own reforming zeal and to the growing conviction on the part of romantic poets that they—to use his phrase—were the "unacknowledged legislators of the world." The thoughts that will be driven "over the universe/Like withered leaves to quicken a new birth!" will bring about "Spring"—the utopian dream of free, happy humanity. Whether Shelley was writing pamphlets to the Irish people pleading for moral reform as the necessary precondition for political and social change (addresses he then scattered by balloons and glass bottles!) or creating visions—by means of a complex of allegories and symbols—of the perfect future world in *Prometheus Unbound* (1820), this missionary zeal never left him.

KEATS

In the case of Keats and the "Ode to a Nightingale" (1820), again a brief reconsideration of the purpose of the earlier *Lyrical Ballads* is pertinent. While the aim of Wordsworth was primarily to recreate the "real language of men" (most of the Preface deals with *Wordsworth's* part in the program), Coleridge's poetic contributions and his later theorizing indicate that *his* intentions differed from those of his colleague. Coleridge was convinced that the new poetry had to revive the ancient sense of awe and wonder that primitive man displayed toward the universe. By employing the strange, the wonderful, and the supernatural he attempted to fashion a set of poetic symbols—"hieroglyphics of reality"—that might make poetry an instrument of metaphysical knowledge rather than mere entertainment.

This is the aspect of romantic tradition to which the "Ode to a Nightingale" belongs. The opening tone of despair and the desire to flee may seem simply to place the poem in the category of romantic escapist literature. But the curious spell, almost an enchantment, occasioned by the bird's song brings about an infinitely more complicated progression of ideas and emotions than any mere evasion-wish could prompt. The mutability of life, the sadness of an existence "where men sit and hear each other groan," the transiency of love, beauty, and the present, are contrasted with the eternal truth of myth and history—"The voice I hear this passing night was heard / In ancient days by emperor and clown"—and with the permanence of death itself. When the nightingale departs with the thrice-reiterated (and perhaps onomatopoetic) "Adieu!" we are left with a question. Which is the reality: the vision, the dream, or the "real" life to which the poet returns when the imaginative act is over? "Fled is that music:—do I wake or sleep?"

In short, the "Ode to a Nightingale" serves to embody two concepts essential for an understanding of Keats's verse and important for an adequate comprehension of what many romantic poets were trying to accomplish. Keats spoke of what he called "negative capability," describing it as the moment of artistic inspiration when the poet achieved a kind of self-annihilation—complete absorption in the object contemplated—and arrived "at that trembling, delicate, snail-horn perception of Beauty." Moreover, this instant was not only the occasion for poetic creation: for Keats it was then that the barrier between the individual ego and the world beyond this world dropped, and he partook of "fellowship with essence." Once more we are presented with the example of a romantic attempting to employ poetry—even the short lyric—as a means of exploring reality. If we perhaps cannot share the romantics' ultimate faith and grasp their curious convictions, at least we may sympathize with the boldness of their quest.

CHATEAUBRIAND AND THE ROMANTIC HERO

While a royalist exile in England, Chateaubriand conceived of a plan to write an apology for Christianity, wherein certain fictional tales would serve as *exempla* to illustrate the efficacy of true belief. He had flirted with philosophical skepticism in his youth. The statement he made about his conversion is interesting: "My conviction came from the heart; I wept and I believed." Anxious to return to France, he was unsure about the reception such an ambitious work, *The Genius of Christianity* (*Le Génie du Christianisme*), would obtain. He produced *Atala* (1801) as a trial balloon, and the results were highly gratifying. A rapid sequence of events in 1802 displays the changing temper of the times. On April 8 Napoleon signed a Concordat with the pope, restoring the Church to France after ten years of enforced secularism. On April 14 *The Genius of Christianity* was published, including both *Atala* and *René*. On April 18 a *Te Deum* was sung in Notre Dame Cathedral in Paris, with all the ancient splendor of the *ancien régime*, to celebrate peace between Church and State. That fantastic creation of the Revolution, the Goddess of Reason, was dethroned; and the Madonna returned to supplant her. Thus a changing religious mood contributed to ensure the triumph of Chateaubriand's book. His decision in 1805 to reprint *Atala* and *René* apart from the larger work shows that his impressive arguments in the *Genius* had been brushed aside by the common reader who preferred imaginative enjoyment to moral edification. This is the impression one receives from three contemporaries. "I read *René*, and I shuddered," said Sainte-Beuve. George Sand, leading female novelist who preferred a male *nom de plume,* behaved true-to-form when she commented, "It seemed that René was myself." Maurice de Guérin confided to his *Journal,* "This reading [of *René*] soaked my soul like rain from a storm." *René* came to be for the youth of France in the 1810's and 1820's what Goethe's *Werther* (1774) had been for readers across the Rhine a generation earlier. In each case social and philosophical dislocations had produced a state of mind such that a single book articulated sentiments dimly felt. With *René* the eternal theme of moral man in immoral society received a new local habitation and a name.

Behind the creation of this *novella* lay Chateaubriand's grander plan, and *René* is best comprehended if the author's ideas—sometimes barely implicit in the story—are sketched. *The Genius of Christianity* starts with an attack on the *Encyclopédie*—"that tower of Babel of science and reason." Chateaubriand then takes recourse to history. Christianity is *better* because it represents an emotional increase over all prior faiths, and even Adam's fall was caused by his sterile intellectualism before he succumbed to the temptation. Chateaubriand's digressions deal less with the intelligent design of the circumambient universe often celebrated by the Deists than with its aesthetic charms and beauty. "The Christian God is poetically superior to ancient Jupiter," he declares—a declaration that must have been surprising to theologians in Rome, Geneva, and Canterbury; and also both Testaments are more moving *qua* literature than the classics of Greece and Rome. Theologians had always emphasized that man's sojourn on earth was but a temporary phase. Chateaubriand reverts to their idea and reaffirms the role of the Christian pilgrim-voyager, faced with salvation or damnation, whose emotional intensity is an improvement on pagan intellect. Gothic architecture, ecclesiastical ruins and tombs, remind the Christian of his dim mortality; the aspiration of the church spire pointing toward heaven displays a yearning for divinity that the more "horizontal" dimensions of Greek temples can never possess. Finally, in a chapter entitled *About the Vagueness of the Passions* ("Du Vague des Passions"), he cites the contribution that Christianity has made in canonizing the emotion of love, and lists famous lovers, all postdating the birth of Christ. For him progress meant not mere intellectual aggrandizement, the progress of the *philosophes.* "The more that people advance in civilization, the more increases this condition of the *vagueness* of the passions." Christian love, an aspect of such "vagueness," meant a salutary synthesis of *eros* and *agape,* profane and sacred love, in Chateaubriand's mind. Thus *René* is in part an *exemplum,* in which the incestuous feelings of brother and sister clash with Amelia's Christian decision to enter a convent, and René is made to feel the full horror of his illicit passion. Yet the resulting unalleviated melancholy exalts him as a hero of sensibility above crasser fellow men. Here lay René's appeal to the readers who discovered in him a paradigm for their own conditions.

Romantic themes abound in the novel: the hero's childhood is unhappy in that he is misunderstood by others; nature responds like a violin to his fluctuating moods; incestuous love tragically distinguishes him from his happier but duller contemporaries. Most romantic of all, perhaps, are his voyages. Candide, that epitome of the rationalist in search of a better world, travels extensively, and the eighteenth century fairly swarms with accounts of young men who take the Grand Tour to fill out their education and acquaint themselves with the ways of polite society. But the romantic voyage which frames René's lugubrious narrative adds a new element. Here the hero moves from civilization and the company of insensitive fellow beings toward an unknown, exotic, mysterious terrain, where there is always the promise—though rarely the fulfillment—that the jaded soul will discover peace. Thus we gradually arrive at those curious romantic voyages of the imagination, quests we normally associate with the world of dreams: Hoffmann's *Tales,* Coleridge's *Ancient Mariner,* Melville's *Moby Dick*—works that look ahead to Rimbaud's *Drunken Ship* (*Bateau ivre*) and the bizarre universe of Franz Kafka with that castle forever out of reach. "Anywhere out of this world," cried Baudelaire in a dialogue he undertook with his soul (from *The Spleen of Paris,* 1869). "Life is a hospital where every invalid wants to exchange his bed for someone else's."

LATER ROMANTICISM AND THE VICTORIAN PERIOD

The earlier romantics had been conscious of living in an epoch of radical mutations and innovations in every sphere of activity. Dark voyages into the unknown such as the Ancient Mariner's were prerequisite for utopian visions such as Faust's at the end of the second part of Goethe's play. The poets felt with an intensity unequaled since the Renaissance that they were spearheading civilization. Hence Shelley could write in all conviction, "Poets are the unacknowledged legislators of the world." Perhaps the world had been callous to the exalted utterances of its prophets. A *new* society, a *new* golden age was about to be born, and there the artist-seer would come into his own. Earlier, William Blake could command his contemporaries to listen to the poet ("Hear the voice of the Bard! / Who Present, Past, & Future, sees").

Alas, the *new* society voted in its own legislation, without Shelley's aid, and it ignored a simple visionary like Blake. The marriage between life and art that in the romantic era had seemed eternal now dissolved; and the Victorian poets either tried unsuccessfully to effect a reunion or sang a sad elegiac strain. The future utopia that had gleamed so beautifully turned out to have smoke pouring from its ugly chimneys, and it was populated not by a pure, happy humanity but rather by a humanity mass-produced. The Industrial Revolution had slowly transformed England from an agrarian to a mechanized, urban nation. Romantic metaphysics gave way to scientific social theories; and Coleridge's high-flown speculations about life were matched by the cooler, more practical hypotheses of Jeremy Bentham and John Stuart Mill, for whom the glow of reason shone brighter than it ever did in the Enlightenment. When the French thinker Auguste Comte described man's history in terms of religious-superstitious, philosophical, and scientific-positivistic periods, and announced that the world was now enjoying the emancipated last of these three epochs, he spoke for most of the intellectuals of his age. In such an era, the fruit of mechanical, scientific, materialistic progress, what was the role of the poet? Indeed, what was the place of poetry? If, as the critic Thomas Love Peacock said, perhaps ironically, "poetry was the mental rattle that awakened the attention of intellect in the infancy of civil society," then there could be little need for the ministrations of poetry in humanity's *adult* condition.

Victorian writers had several alternatives, and most of the authors vacillated among them. They could come to grips with the new "utilitarian" environment and extol its dubious virtues. A century before, Young had written, "Is 'Merchant' an inglorious name? / No! Fit for Pindar such a theme." Actually, the novel—the unique art form produced by middle-class, urban, liberal society—was better suited than the lyric for praising the entrepreneur, but scientific progress had its own poetic apologists. Tennyson himself, in his more optimistic moments, could speak of "the ringing grooves of change" (after a too-hasty glimpse of a railroad track), or write such twaddle as this:

Dash back that ocean with a pier,
Strew yonder mountain flat;
A railway there, a tunnel here—
Mix me this zone with that.

The modern gadgets had their fascination for the poet, ever anxious to extend the subject matter of his craft, and there was always the possibility that the new Iron Monster might be tamed.

Or the poets could return again to the dim, happy, idyllic past. Earlier romanticism had developed an awareness of distant periods and places which until then had been misunderstood or only vaguely comprehended: the medieval era, Greece, the East, primitive cultures. Victorian literature intensified interest in some of these. The cult of the Middle Ages, for example, was strengthened when in the 1830's and the 1840's aesthetic escapism was augmented by the religious hunger for dogma in the Oxford Movement and by the aristocratic, semifeudal conservatism of the Young England group. Or one could seek the solace of nature as an answer to trapped individualism. But Darwinian theory showed a nature "red in tooth and claw," and even beatific nature loses its powers of assuaging the hurt soul when one is forced to flee to it. To quote the modern poet Peter Viereck, there was soot on the ivory tower. The Victorian poets were uncomfortable, confused, baffled by necessary compromises, unsure of their function or of the world in which they lived.

TENNYSON

Tennyson has been hailed as the spokesman for Victorian England. It would be safer to call him the spokesman for Victorian poets. A contemporary said that Tennyson "looked as if he might have written the *Iliad.*" But the leonine, bearded face, the apparent gruff masculinity, the proto-Kiplingese heartiness found in "The Charge of the Light Brigade" (1854), were coupled with acute sensitivity, melancholia, and a capacity for pathos that had to answer as a capacity for passion. Such poems as "Locksley Hall" (1842) and "Ulysses" (1842), with their notes of courage, uplift, and praise of the active life, are counterbalanced—indeed outweighed—by the pessimistic tranquility of "The Passing of Arthur" (1842, 1869) and the quiet, sad contemplativeness of many of his short lyrics. Tennyson's material success (he became, to use the phrase of his friend Dickens, a "household word") in no way diminished his disquietude. He saw all too clearly the process he describes in the opening of "Tithonus" (1860):

The woods decay, the woods decay
 and fall,
The vapours weep their burthen to
 the ground,
Man comes and tills the field and
 lies beneath,
And after many a summer dies the
 swan.

This message was not likely to influence a generation interested in "muscular, jocular Christianity," the expansion of the Empire, investments at six per cent, and improved steam engines.

BROWNING

Browning is an example of a more vigorous Victorian writer, and one is tempted to speculate about how much his years in Italy contributed to his lustier, more robust outlook and expression. In any case he fulfilled the romantic myth of the Anglo-Saxon blossoming in the climate of the warm south. His early poems, from *Pauline* (1833) to *Sordello* (1840), exemplify a conception of poetry which had been intensified by the romantic movement—the view of poetry as the confessional, the place where the poet pours out his own intimate spiritual doubts, perhaps using the thin disguise of imaginary characters. Browning's inability to attain the slightest popular favor in this genre led him to try the drama. For almost ten years he devoted himself exclusively to the composition of a series of equally unsuccessful plays, in which he attempted to join Shakespearean effects with Bulwer-Lyttonian melodrama. The greatness of his later poems came from the union of what he had learned from these two failures, in the triumphant synthesis of the dramatic monologue. Here sensitive psychological analysis was conceived within the framework of the dramatic situation. Even Browning's shorter lyrics often share this quality, when the lyric catches the moment of sudden insight, but we are also keenly aware of narrative, atmosphere, and situation. "The Bishop Orders His Tomb" (1845) unites the private intensity of lyric self-expression with the objectivity of the dramatic form, and it may be regarded as one of Browning's most impressive dramatic monologues.

Carlyle's contrast of Tennyson and Browning is the revealing comment of a keen contemporary: "Alfred knows how to jingle; Browning does not." Browning's ebullience is a cheerful contrast to Tennyson's tenderness. The Victorian writer, as we have suggested, could either grapple with the new ideas of his times or retreat; Browning certainly chose the first alternative. His philosophical point of view was a blend of conventional Christianity and Neoplatonism with the new scientific concepts of emergent, creative evolution. Yet Browning's roots were in the Italian Renaissance and the Elizabethan age. Consequently his love poetry, which came close to violating the Great Taboo of Grundyism, appeared daring and unconventional when held up against the "lollypoppism" (Carlyle's word) of Tennyson and Tennyson's imitators. Not since John Donne had love been anatomized with such incisions.

AMERICAN ROMANTICISM

The history of American literature is the story of the slow emergence of native elements and the gradual assimilation of foreign schools. It was simpler to throw off a political yoke in 1776 than it was to abandon a servile aping of English culture. Yet by the mid-nineteenth century, certain writers had demonstrated to all that the New World was no longer rude and unlettered. Cooper, Hawthorne, and Melville, in the novel, Emerson in philosophy, and Poe and Whitman were caught up in the general ambience of romanticism. To the movement, however, they added certain temperamental and national qualities—contributions which make American romanticism worthy of special attention.

WHITMAN

Whitman stands for all the romantic aspirations toward brotherhood, humanity, freedom, and liberty. Once more we return to the notion of the bard-seer who would speak for the nation. "I will not descend among professors," cried the latter-day prophet who physically so resembled his Old Testament forebears; and his remark makes our comments seem presumptuous. The apparent artlessness of Whitman's prolix verse is apt to obscure its sources in the Bible, Shakespeare, "Ossian," nineteenth-century bombastic political oratory, Italian opera, and the traditional American love of unfettered liberty and hatred of restraint. In one sense, Whitman's free verse fulfills the romantic dream of a prose that would be poetry, and William James described *Leaves of Grass* as "thousands of images of patient, homely, American life." Like Wordsworth's milder departure from previous poetic diction, Whitman's rejection of the "genteel tradition" resulted from a determination to express the sentiments of the common, ordinary man—"and all the men that were born are also my brothers." Emerson had transplanted German idealism to domestic soil, where it became the major element in American transcendentalism. Whitman's ideas were often close to those of his philosopher-contemporary, and his "noiseless patient spider" might serve as an image for the Emersonian life process —spirit working through the natural phenomena of the universe. The grandeur and dignity of Whitman's writing is coupled with pagan sensuality, a lusty, hearty gusto for existence, and a constant contact with the earth. When he said, "Arnold gives me the feeling that he hates to touch the dirt," Whitman not only rendered a critique of his Victorian colleague but also revealed his own position. The entire—and in our time somewhat faded—hopes of a young agrarian country emerge from his lines. With Whitman we are always outside on the open road or amid the loving comradeship of the crowded city —never confined or disheartened, since implicit in the voice of the people is the romantic faith in an ideal community.

DICKINSON

The world of Emily Dickinson's poetry is something like the world in which she chose to live. During her mature years she seldom left her father's house and grounds, and her poems also work within stringent limits. They are short—the longest is but fifty lines. They exclude most of what we take to be the real world, for she is not much interested in the great issues and events of her time, or of earlier times either; her allusions are not to myth or history or literature but to the Bible, which serves her for all three. There are few people in her poems, and she is sour about most of them ("She dealt her pretty words like Blades," "He preached upon 'Breadth' till it argued him narrow"). Like the Soul in one of her poems (303), she took what little she wanted from human society, and resolutely shut out the rest.

The society of nature is another matter, for Dickinson wrote much about the creatures and phenomena she so intently observed. " 'Nature' is what we see," she begins a poem, but goes on to claim more: "Nay —Nature is Heaven." "A Bird came down the Walk" (328) begins as the report of a seeing eye, offered without moralizing: "He bit an Angleworm in halves / And ate the fellow, raw." But the poem, like the bird, takes flight in the last six lines, the dry, half-scientific account giving way to a visionary image as the air becomes palpable, silvery and buoyant. When natural forces take on body, the body is often that of an animal; lightning becomes an "electric Moccasin," striking as swiftly and dangerously as a poisonous snake. Even a steam locomotive—several tons of cast-iron machine hurtling purposefully along steel rails— cavorts through the landscape like a colt. "Possibility" is imagined in terms of sky and trees. When she describes as her occupation "The spreading wide my narrow Hands / To gather Paradise" (657), it is not a heavenly but an earthly paradise that she means.

Indeed, Dickinson was profoundly skeptical about God's heaven, and mistrustful of its divine architect. As an adolescent she was sent to a seminary, and saw most of her relatives swept up in the religious revivals of the 1850's; later in life she continued to attend church (the forms of her poems owe much to the rhythms and rhyme schemes of the Protestant hymnal, as well as to the English ballad stanza), and had close friends among the clergy; but conventional religion never "took." She believes—"I know that He exists"—but protests against a faceless God that remains silent in the all too visible face of human misery, who often mistreats and toys with His most devoted servants. Christ she admires for human qualities, especially humility and sacrifice, but does not accept him as fulfilling a divine purpose. Her many Biblical quotations and allusions, then, express not devoutness but a more complex mixture of wishfulness and New England hardheadedness, of playfulness and resentment. When the locomotive "neigh[s] like Boanerges" (*Sons of thunder*, Christ's name for two disciples), we catch her satiric amusement at priestly blowhards thundering from the pulpit. But Dickinson also begins a poem, "Of course—I prayed— / And did God care?," comparing God's silence to the sound of a bird stamping its foot in air. Heaven, she concluded in a poem (1551) written four years before her death, is a will o' the wisp, its promises seductive but illusory. "Who has not found the Heaven—below—Will fail of it above."

Dickinson's religious unorthodoxy is one of many reasons that have been advanced to explain why all but a handful of her 1775 surviving poems remained unpublished until years after her death. This fact, like much else about her life, can probably never be fully explained. Its effect, however, if not its cause, was that she could confide her poems to paper as if to a diary or journal, and therefore express and explore feelings too appalling to make public. For there are hundreds of Dickinson poems obsessed with mental anguish, feelings of loss, and death. "There's a certain slant of light" (258) anticipates many more clinical but hardly more convincing descriptions of depression, of despair triggered by the most irrelevant stimuli; "After great pain, a formal feeling comes" (341) renders no less accurately the way the body (or the mind) defends itself against too painful a wound by going into shock. "I like a look of agony," she says, amazingly, "Because I know it's true." If God remains silent, useless to one in such misery, relief can still be found—in death. Even in her twenties she was writing poems that claim the "privilege" of death, and from 1861 onward she meditates ceaselessly on death; more, she acts it out again and again, sometimes with eerie detachment ("I heard a Fly buzz—when I died," 465), sometimes with mounting excitement ("Because I could not stop for Death," 712).

Unlike her suicidal American descendants of the 1960's, such as Sylvia Plath, Emily Dickinson was content to wait until death came for her. Fame came more slowly, and because her editors of the 1890's kept back many of the darker, more complex, and unchurchly poems which now seem so characteristic of her, a just assessment was even slower in coming. (Some of her poems appeared first as late as 1945, and a collected, scholarly edition of all her work was not available until 1955.) Now, however, we can see through the apparent fragility and quaintness of her work to find the individuality and strength it so evidently has, and see her effort to find and create a heaven on earth as the hard-won affirmation of one who also knew its hell.

MELVILLE

Moby-Dick (1851) is the summit of Melville's achievement. For forty more years he continued—to quote his own line—"to wrestle with the angel—Art," but he poignantly said in the early 1860's, "The work I was born to do is done." The modern reader of *Pierre* (1852), *The Confidence-Man* (1857), and *Billy Budd* (finished shortly before his death in 1891) may disagree with Melville's modesty. In *Moby-Dick* almost all the romantic themes are brought together and re-examined, often to their peril and ultimate rejection. The easy, happy pantheism of Wordsworth and Emerson and the cult of nature of Rousseau, Melville supplants with an insight more ambiguous, even terrible, where the inscrutable God revealed is the God of Blake's Tiger. The romantic utopian dream of an egalitarian democracy is brought up against the equally compelling notion of the role of the great man, the leader, in history. The romantic interpretation of science as the handmaid of human progress, the instrument by which man may discover final truths, is found suspect. The romantic vindication of Christianity in the face of what was construed to be eighteenth-century mechanism is likewise held inadequate.

Melville completed *Billy Budd* forty years after the publication of his monumental, but ill-received, *Moby-Dick*. He probably began the tale in 1886. By 1888 the story as we read it had taken shape within his mind, but he kept revising it until the year he died. Mrs. Melville regarded the work as unfinished and made her own emendations. It was not published until 1924.

Billy Budd is set in the years immediately after the French Revolution, when romantic hopes for the beginning of a great new age ran highest. The special phenomenon of naval mutiny seems to have obsessed Melville. He had participated in a mutiny aboard the whaler *Lucy Ann* when he was a seaman not much older than his hero. In his writings he frequently alluded to the mutiny aboard the U.S. brig *Somers* in 1842, when his cousin Guert Gansevoort helped to condemn a rebellious midshipman to death by hanging. He also wrote about fictional mutinies in *Benito Cereno* and in the interpolated narrative about the *Town-Ho* in *Moby-Dick*. In all these instances, Melville's sympathy for this form of protest against constituted authority takes on certain romantic configurations, if we identify the romantic movement politically with the age of revolution.

The innocence of the passive protagonist, who goes down before the demands of social and perhaps cosmic justice, places Billy Budd among those milder romantic heroes who share the traits of the unspoiled, unsophisticated primitive and the blameless child trailing his Wordsworthian clouds of glory, still untouched by the corruption of adulthood and what Shelley called "the world's slow stain." Billy is also isolated, set apart from his fellows by his physical beauty—an outward sign of inner harmonies—and his speech impediment. Here he becomes a paler manifestation of Rousseau's claim for extreme individualism: "I venture to believe that I am not made like any of those [men] who are in existence."

As for the story, we know from Melville's sketches that Claggart was slowly developed as the antagonist, with overtones of some of Shakespeare's villains and of Milton's Satan. Similarly, Captain Vere finally emerged as a kind of father-image, a perplexing figure of the older man torn between his respect for law and his humane and decent impulses. As in *Moby Dick*, Melville came back to the theme of good and evil that always occupied his mind.

As with his great novel, critical interpretations of *Billy Budd* have varied widely. Some critics, like the late John Middleton Murry, have seen it as Melville's "last will and spiritual testament," and the author's final acceptance of the universe. ("God bless Captain Vere," sings out Bill, at the very moment of his execution). But others have viewed *Billy Budd* as the last expression of Melville's protest against the order of existence. Billy's sacrificial death has been construed to make him a Christ-figure; and it is at least true that the story, like many of Melville's is rich in Christian symbols and images . But Melville's lifelong ambivalence toward traditional Christianity makes this thesis problematical, although provocative. In any case, Billy's death is occasioned at least in part by the inexorable demands of society, that key concept of the nineteenth century.

LIVES, WRITINGS, AND CRITICISM

Biographical and critical works are listed only if they are available in English.

JEAN-JACQUES ROUSSEAU

LIFE. Born on June 28, 1712, in Geneva, son of a watchmaker. Unhappy as an engraver's apprentice, he left home while still in his teens, and for a time lived with Mme. de Warens—the first of many female protectors. He led a peripatetic existence and held many positions: as music teacher, secretary, footman, government official under the king of Sardinia, clerk in the Bureau of Taxes in Paris (where he settled in 1745). There he lived with Thérèse le Vasseur, with whom he had five children (all deposited at an orphanage). In 1756 Mme. d'Épinay invited him to live on her estate at Montmorency. Official criticism of his books several times forced Rousseau, like Voltaire, to leave France for Switzerland; in 1766 he traveled to England as guest of the philosopher David Hume. He was permitted to return to Paris in 1770 on condition that he write nothing against government or religion. Rousseau died on July 3, 1778, at Ermenonville. His body was brought to the Pantheon in Paris in 1794, during the Revolution.

CHIEF WRITINGS. His writings fall into four categories: Works involving music: *On Modern Music* (*Dissertation sur la musique moderne,* 1743); *Letter on French Music* (*Lettre sur la musique française,* 1752); *Musical Dictionary* (*Dictionnaire de musique,* 1767); and an opera, *The Village Soothsayer* (*Le Devin du village,* 1752). Political writings: *Concerning the Origin of Inequality among Men* (*Discours sur l'origine et les fondements de l'inégalité parmi les hommes,* 1754) and *The Social Contract* (*Le Contrat social,* 1762). A book, nominally a novel, on education: *Emile* (1762). Autobiographical productions: a novel, *Julie, or the New Heloise* (*Julie, ou La Nouvelle Héloïse,* 1761); the *Confessions,* composed between 1765 and 1770, published in 1781–1788; and *Musings of a Solitary Stroller (Les Rêveries du promeneur solitaire),* composed between 1776 and 1778, published in 1782.

BIOGRAPHY AND CRITICISM. J. Morley, *Rousseau* (1873, revised 1886); F. Macdonald, *Rousseau* (1906); I. Babbitt, *Rousseau and Romanticism* (1919); M. B. Ellis, *Julie: A Synthesis of Rousseau's Thought* (1949); E. Cassirer, "Rousseau," in *Rousseau, Kant, Goethe* (1945): H. Höffding, *Rousseau and His Philosophy* (1930); Frances Winwar, *Jean-Jacques Rousseau: Conscience of a Era* (1961); F. C. Green, *Jean-Jacques Rousseau: A Critical Study of His Life and Writings* (1955). Excellent is the series of essays about the author in *Yale French Studies,* No. 28 (1962). There are also J. Guéhenno, *Jean-Jacques Rousseau* (1966); W. and A. Durant, *Rousseau and Revolution* (1968); J. McManners, *The Social Contract and Rousseau's Revolt against Society* (1968); W. Blanchard, *Rousseau and the Spirit of Revolt* (1968); M. Einaudi, *The Early Rousseau* (1968); Sir G. de Beer, *Jean-Jacques Rousseau and his World* (1972); R. Grimsley, *The Philosophy of Rousseau*; and L. G. Crocker, *Jean-Jacques Rousseau: A New Interpretative Analysis of his Works* (1973).

JOHANN WOLFGANG VON GOETHE

LIFE. Born on August 28, 1749, in Frankfurt-am-Main, Germany. From 1765 to 1768 Goethe attended Leipzig University, then the center of French culture in Germany. It was at the end of that time that he met Suzanna von Klettenberg, eminent Pietist and mystic, who interested him in the theosophy of the period. At the University of Strassburg, in 1770–1771, he made the acquaintance of Gottfried Herder, leader of the new German literary movement later called the "Storm and Stress" (*Sturm und Drang*) movement. Herder showed the young writer the importance of Shakespeare (as opposed to the French neoclassic authors) and interested him in folk songs and in the need for an indigenous German literature. On a series of trips to Switzerland he began his scientific and philosophical studies. In 1775 Goethe moved to Weimar, and there his long friendship with the reigning duke, Karl August, began. He also received the first of several government appointments which guaranteed him financial independence. From 1786 to 1788 he took his famous Italian trip. He met the author Schiller in 1794, and their fruitful relationship was terminated only by the latter's death in 1805. Goethe married Christiane Vulpius in 1806 and subsequently legitimitized the son they had had some twelve years earlier. In 1808 occurred his meeting with Napoleon, an encounter mutually impressive; and four years later he met Beethoven. From 1823 to 1832 he was in the daily company of Johann Peter Eckermann, who was thus able to record, in his *Conversations with Goethe (Gespräche mit Goethe,* 1836–1848), all the commentary and criticism that Goethe's long life had accumulated. Goethe's presence made Weimar a cultural mecca for twenty years, and during that period there was scarcely a prominent European intellectual who did not come there to pay his respects. He died on March 22, 1832.

CHIEF WRITINGS. Goethe's earliest verse is in the rococo tradition of French and German eighteenth-century poetry. It was not until he was influenced by Herder—and until his many love affairs took on a more serious cast—that he achieved writing of high stature. His first great play, *Götz von Berlichingen,*1773), was a product of his Shakespeare studies and his enthusiasm for the preromantic "Storm and Stress" movement. About the same time, he started the first of many sketches for *Faust,* Part I. *The Sorrows of Young Werther* (*Die Leiden des jungen Werthers*), the short novel that inflamed the youth of Europe as did no other book before or after, was published in 1774. Goethe's increasing interest in classical literature led to the creation of such plays as *Iphigenia* (*Iphigenie auf Tauris,* 1787), and *Torquato Tasso* (1790) and the epic-idyll *Hermann and Dorothea* (*Hermann und Dorothea,* 1798). His two largest novels were *Wilhelm Meister's Apprenticeship* (*Wilhelm Meisters Lehrjahre,* 1795–1796), and *Wilhelm Meister's Travels* (*Wilhelm Meisters Wanderjahre,* 1821). *Faust,* Part I, appeared in 1808; *Faust,* Part II, completed in 1831, was published in 1833. Goethe's fame as a lyric poet rests on the many volumes of verse he wrote, from his first *Poems* (*Gedichte,* 1771) through the *Roman Elegies* (*Romische Elegien,* 1795); *Ballads* (*Balladen,* 1798); the enigmatic *West-East Divan* (*Westöstlicher Diwan,* 1819); and the last great *Marienbad Elegies* (*Marienbad Elegien,* 1823). His scientific writings fill several volumes. Most of Goethe's critical commentary is found in the penetrating *Truth and Poetry* (*Dichtung und Wahrheit,* 1811–1833).

BIOGRAPHY AND CRITICISM. Biographies and general studies of Goethe include A. Bielschowsky, *Life of Goethe* (1905–1908); K. Viëtor, *Goethe the Poet*(1949); E. Ludwig, *Goethe*(1928); B. Fairley, *A Study of Goethe* (1948); T. Mann, *Essays of Three Decades*

(1947), and introduction to *The Permanent Goethe* (1948); A. Schweitzer, Goethe (1949); E. M. Wilkinson and L. A. Willoughby, *Goethe, Poet and Thinker* (1962); H. Hatfield, *Goethe* (1963); B. Croce, *Goethe* (1923); W. H. Bruford, *Culture and Society in Classical Weimar* (1962). For *Faust,* consult D. J. Enright, *Commentary on Goethe's Faust* (1949); F. M. Stawell and G. L. Dickinson, *Goethe and Faust* (1928); E. M. Butler, *The Myth of the Magus* (1948) and *The Fortunes of Faust* (1952); S. Atkins, *Goethe's Faust: A Literary Analysis* (1958); P. M. Palmer and R. P. More, *Sources of the Faust Tradition* (1910); G. Santayana, "Goethe," in *Three Philosophical Poets* (1910); A. Gillies, *Goethe's Faust: An Interpretation* (1957); R. Peacock, *Goethe's Major Plays* (1959); E. Mason, *Goethe's Faust* (1967); G. Lukacs, *Goethe and His Age* (1969); L. Dieckmann, *Goethe's Faust* (1972); and the essays and commentary in W. Arndt and C. Hamlin, *Faust* (a Norton Critical Edition, 1976).

WILLIAM BLAKE

LIFE. Born on November 28, 1757. His father was a London hosier. At fourteen he was apprenticed to James Basire, engraver to the London Society of Antiquaries and the new Royal Academy. He married Catherine Boucher in 1782; the marriage was childless. His friendship with the painter Fuseli and the sculptor Flaxman influenced his own painting style, and in 1788 he began to develop his engraving process. In the same year, he became interested in the Swedenborgian movement. In 1800 he moved to Felpham at the invitation of his patron William Hayley. In August, 1803, his bodily eviction of John Scholfield, a private in the Royal Dragoons, from his garden led to an indictment for assault and sedition—the latter a hanging offense, since England and France were at war. He was acquitted in 1804. He had returned to London in 1803, where he remained the rest of his life. In 1818 he met John Linnell, who—with a small group of young painters—became one of Blake's few devoted admirers. He died on August 12, 1827.

CHIEF WRITINGS AND ENGRAVINGS. His first and only conventionally published book of poems was *Poetical Sketches* (1783). His first engraved works were *There Is No Natural Religion* and *All Religions Are One* (1788), followed by *The Songs of Innocence* and *The Book of Thel* (1789). *The Songs of Innocence* was the first example of Blake's illuminated printing, where poems and illustrations were engraved on copper plates, printed, and then painted by hand. Then followed *America* and *Visions of the Daughters of Albion, The Marriage of Heaven and Hell* (1793); *Songs of Innocence and of Experience, Europe, The First Book of Urizen* (1794); *The Book of Ahania, The Book of Los,* and *The Songs of Los* (1795). He probably began *Vala,* his first poem of epic length, in 1797. This was later to become *The Four Zoas,* on which he worked until 1806; but it was never engraved or put in final form. *Milton* and *Jerusalem,* each with fifty and a hundred plates, are dated 1804. Other etchings were illustrations for Young's *Night Thoughts* (1785–1797), Chaucer's *Canterbury Tales,* Spenser's *Fairie Queene,* Milton's *Paradise Lost* (1805–1808); *The Book of Job* (1823–1825), Bunyan's *Pilgrim's Progress* (1824), and Dante's *Divine Comedy* (1825–1826). Blake's laborious method of pictorial composition combined with poetry meant that he struck off few copies of his original work: twenty-seven copies of *Songs of Innocence and Experience* (complete and incomplete), nine of *The Marriage of Heaven and Hell,* and even fewer of *Milton* and *Jerusalem.* The definitive edition of Blake's works is *The Poetry and Prose of William Blake,* edited by D. V. Erdman and H. Bloom (1965).

BIOGRAPHY AND CRITICISM. Alexander Gilchrist, *Life of William Blake* (1863), completed by Anne Gilchrist and the Rossetti brothers after Gilchrist's death in 1861, first called attention to Blake. W. B. Yeats, and E. J. Ellis (1893) brought out a three-volume edition, including a biography, of what was then known of his works. S. F. Damon, in *William Blake: His Philosophy and Symbols* (1924), began modern Blake studies; and later published also *The Blake Dictionary: The Ideas and Symbols of William Blake* (1965). Other valuable studies include M. Schorer, *William Blake: The Politics of Vision* (1946); N. Frye, *Fearful Symmetry* (1947); J. Bronowski, *A Man without a Mask* (1943); D. Erdman, *Blake: Prophet against Empire* (1954); P. Fisher, *The Valley of Vision* (1961); H. M. Margoliouth, *William Blake* (1951); H. Adams, *William Blake: A Reading of the Shorter Poems* (1963); B. Blackstone, *English Blake* (1949); H. Bloom, *Blake's Apocalypse* (1964); R. Gleckner, *The Piper and the Bard* (1959); E. D. Hirsch, *Innocence and Experience: An Introduction to William Blake* (1964); K. Raine, *Blake and Tradition* (1968); J. Hagstrum, *William Blake Poet and Painter* (1964); **Blake, a collection of critical essays edited by N. Frye (1966); K. Raine, *Blake and Tradition* (1968); E. D. Hirsch. *Innocence and Experience* (1969); J. Beer, *Blake's Humanism* (1968); R. Lister, *Blake* (1968); M. Paley, *Energy and*** *the Imagination* (1971); J. Bronowski, *William Blake and the Age of Revolution* (1972); D. G. Gillham, *William Blake* (1973); and M. Klonsky, *William Blake* (1977).

WILLIAM WORDSWORTH

LIFE. Born on April 7, 1770, at Cockermouth, Cumberland. His father was an attorney. Wordsworth had three brothers and a sister, Dorothy; she later played a large part in his intellectual development. He attended St. John's College, Cambridge, from 1787 to 1791, and spent the following year in France. There he met Annette Vallon, by whom he had a daughter. Like Coleridge, whom he met in 1795, he soon lost sympathy with the cause of the French Revolution, and like Coleridge, he was strongly influenced by the philosophical and social theories of William Godwin. In 1797 Wordsworth and Dorothy moved to Alfoxeden, close to Nether Stowey, where Coleridge lived. There he and Coleridge conceived the idea for collaborating on the *Lyrical Ballads;* these important poems appeared anonymously in 1798, commissioned by the publisher Cottle. In 1799 Wordsworth and his sister settled in the Lake District of northwest England. In 1802 he inherited his father's estate, and in the same year married Mary Hutchinson, who eventually bore him five children. In 1813 he was appointed to the office of stamp distributor, a comfortable sinecure. As he grew older, his earliest radicalism—both political and aesthetic—grew dimmer; it is significant that he opposed the Catholic Emancipation Bill, the Reform Bill of 1832, and the successive extensions of the ballot. In 1843 he succeeded Southey as poet laureate. He died on April 23, 1850.

CHIEF WRITINGS. Wordsworth's early work (verse composed up to 1791) reflects the dominant poetic taste of the late eighteenth century: it consists largely of conventional sonnets, Spenserian stanzas, "Gothic" verse, and folksong imitations. His acquaintance with Godwin seemed to deepen Wordsworth's seriousness and sensibilities, and this was evident in his new humanitarianism, his attitude toward nature, and his interest in psychology. As with Coleridge, the years of Wordsworth's greatest and richest productivity were from 1797 to 1807, the period not only of the *Lyrical Ballads* but also of *The Prelude,* composed between 1798 and 1805, and the "Ode on Intimations of Immortality," composed between 1802 and 1806. Except for the famous Preface to the *Lyrical Ballads,* Wordsworth—unlike Coleridge—wrote little prose. Much of his later verse (from 1807 until 1850) is occasional poetry.

BIOGRAPHY AND CRITICISM. For the author's life, see G. M. Harper, *Wordsworth* (1916-1929); *Letters of William and Dorothy Wordsworth,* edited by E. de Selincourt (1941); and M. Elwin, *The First Romantics* (1948). The following general studies of Wordsworth as a poet are recommended: J. W. Beach, *The Concept of Nature in Nineteenth Century English Poetry* (1936); C. M. Bowra, "Wordsworth," in *The Romantic Imagination* (1949); G. W. Knight, *The Starlit Dome* (1941); *Wordsworth and Coleridge Studies,* edited by E. L. Griggs (1939); S. Banerjee, *Critical Theories and Poetic Practice in the Lyrical Ballads* (1931); N. P. Stallknecht, *Strange Seas of Thought*(1945); R. D. Havens, *The Mind of a Poet* (1950); Helen Darbishire, *The Poet Wordsworth* (1950); *Centenary Studies,* edited by G. T. Dunklin (1951); M. H. Abrams, *The Mirror and the Lamp* (1953); F. Danby, *The Simple Wordsworth* (1960); D. Ferry, *The Limits of Mortality: An Essay on Wordsworth's Major Poems* (1960); J. C. Smith, *A Study of Wordsworth* (1961); C. Clarke, *Romantic Paradox* (1962); G. Hartman, *Wordsworth's Poetry* (1964); D. Perkins, *Wordsworth and the Poetry of Sincerity* (1964); C. Salvesen, *The Landscape of Memory* (1965); J. Scoggins, *Imagination and Fancy* (1965); A. King, *Wordsworth and the Artist's Vision* (1966); B. Groom, *The Unity of Wordsworth's Poetry* (1967); M. Rader, *Wordsworth: A Philosophical Approach* (1967); G. Durrant, *William Wordsworth* (1969); M. H. Abrams, *Natural Supernaturalism: Tradition and Revolution in Romantic Literature* (1971); J. Onorato, *The Character of the Poet: Wordsworth in "The Prelude"* (1972); A. O. Wlecke, *Wordsworth and the Sublime* (1973); P. D. Sheats, *The Making of Wordsworth's Poetry* (1973); A. Grob, *The Philosophic Mind* (1974); F. D. McConnell, *The Confessional Imagination* (1975); M. Jacobus, *Tradition and Experiment in Wordsworth's Lyrical Ballads* (1976); and S. Parrish, *The Prelude 1798–1799* (1977).

SAMUEL TAYLOR COLERIDGE

LIFE. Born on October 21, 1772, at Ottery St. Mary. His father was a clergyman. Coleridge attended Jesus College, Cambridge, from 1791 to 1793. In 1795 he married Sara Fricker, who bore him three children. Like Wordsworth and Southey, he did not long retain his initial enthusiasm for the French Revolution, and he also soon abandoned his plans, made with Southey, for founding a perfect society, or "pantisocracy," on the banks of the Susquehanna River, in America. He met Wordsworth in 1795, and they developed their idea for poetic collaboration in the *Lyrical Ballads,* published in 1798 Difficulties with his wife led to eventual separation, in 1810, and Coleridge became increasingly addicted to opium. He spent his last twenty years in lecturing, writing, and brilliant talk. He died on July 25, 1834.

CHIEF WRITINGS. Almost all of Coleridge's poetry dates from the period between 1797 and 1807, when he worked with Wordsworth, and it is a curious coincidence that both poets felt a distinct loss in poetic power after the latter year. His early philosophical studies had been among the works of the British empiricists thinkers, but a trip to Germany introduced Coleridge to the writings of Kant, Schelling, and Fichte. His own prose—including the *Biographia Literaria* (1817) and the posthumous *Table Talk and Anima Poetae*—reflects the outlook of German Idealism. The depth of his critical insights and his awareness of Continental ideas make Coleridge the leading theoretician for English romanticism, despite the cloudiness of his thinking and the opacity of his literary style.

BIOGRAPHY AND CRITICISM. Good biographies are E. K. Chambers, *Samuel Taylor Coleridge* (1938) and H. I. 'A. Fausset, *Samuel Taylor Coleridge* (1926). General studies of the poet's thought are found in C. M. Bowra, "Coleridge," in *The Romantic Imagination* (1949), and B. Willey, *Nineteenth Century Studies* (1950); M. Schulz, *The Poetic Voices of Coleridge* (1963); J. H. Muirhead, *Coleridge as Philosopher* (1930); M. H. Abrams, *The Mirror and the Lamp* (1953); I. A. Richards, *Coleridge on Imagination* (1934); M. Suther, *The Dark Night of Samuel Taylor Coleridge* (1960); J. Appleyard, *Coleridge's Philosophy of Literature* (1965); M. Suther, *Visions of Xanadu* (1965); G. Watson, *Coleridge the Poet* (1966); G. Yarlott, *Coleridge and the Abyssinian Maid* (1967); P. Adair, *The Waking Dream* (1968); W. Bate, *Coleridge* (1968); T. McFarland, *Coleridge and the Pantheist Tradition* (1969); B. Willey, *Coleridge* (1971). For special studies of *Kubla Khan*, see J. L. Lowes, *The Road to Xanadu* (1927); J. Charpentier, *Coleridge the Sublime Somnambulist* (1929); G. W. Knight, *The Starlit Dome* (1941); R. C. Bald, "Coleridge," in *Nineteenth Century Studies*, edited by H. Davis (1940); J. V. Baker, *The Sacred River* (1957); E. L. Griggs, "Coleridge and Opium," *Huntington Library Quarterly*, XVII (1965); D. F. Mercer, "The Symbolism of *Kubla Khan*," *Journal of Aesthetics*, XII (1953); E. Schneider, *Coleridge, Opium, and Kubla Khan* (1953); N. Fruman, *Coleridge, the Damaged Archangel* (1972); J. Cornwell, *Coleridge* (1973); and J. Beer, *Coleridge's Poetic Intelligence* (1975).

GEORGE GORDON, LORD BYRON

LIFE. Born on January 22, 1788, to Captain "Mad Jack" and Catherine Gordon Byron. He succeeded his great-uncle to the title and estate (Newstead Abbey) in 1798. He was educated at Harrow from 1801 to 1805 and at Trinity College, Cambridge, from 1805 to 1808. In 1809–1811 he traveled in Portugal, Spain, Albania, and the Near East. His life was marked by a series of love affairs: with Mary Chaworth, in 1803; with Lady Caroline Lamb, in 1812–1813; allegedly with his half sister Augusta; and later with Teresa, Countess Guiccioli. He married Anne Isabelle Milbanke, and they separated after the birth of their child late in 1815. His daughter Allegra was born of a liaison with Claire Clairmont. Byron left England permanently in 1816 to live in Italy. In 1823 he went to Greece to aid the fight against the Turks; he died of a fever at Missolonghi on April 19, 1824.

CHIEF WRITINGS. His first poems appeared in 1807; *Childe Harold's Pilgrimage* (1812–1818), an autobiographical travel poem, won him fame, which was further guaranteed by a series of verse dramas appearing between 1813 and 1821: *The Giaour, The Corsair, Lara, Manfred, Cain, Sardanapalus. English Bards and Scotch Reviewers* (1809); *A Vision of Judgment* (1822); and *Don Juan* (1819–1824) are the satires for which he is best known today.

BIOGRAPHY AND CRITICISM. E. C. Mayne, *Byron* (1912, revised 1924); P. Quennell, *Byron* (1934); W. J. Calvert, *Byron, Romantic Paradox* (1935). For criticism see C. M. Fuess, *Lord Byron as a Satirist in Verse* (1912); T. S. Eliot, "Byron," in *From Anne to Victoria*, edited by B. Dobree (1937), and Matthew Arnold, "Byron," in *Essays in Criticism, Second Series* (1888). Helpful studies of *Don Juan* are P. G. Trueblood, *The Flowering of Byron's Genius* (1945); J. Austen, *The Story of Don Juan* (1939), and L. Kronenberger, introduction to the Modern Library edition of *Don Juan* (1951). Other studies of Byron include W. H. Marshall, *The Structure of Byron's Major Poems* (1963); P. Thorslev, *The Byronic Hero* (1962); A. Rutherford, *Byron: A Critical Study* (1961); P. West, *Byron and the Spoiler's Art* (1960); L. Marchand, *Byron* (1957); D. L. Moore, *The Late Lord Byron* (1961), a study of his posthumous fame and notoriety; E. J. Lovell, Jr., *Byron: The Record of a Quest* (1950); G. M. Ridenour, *The Style of "Don Juan"* (1960). A variorum edition of *Don Juan*, edited by T. E. Steffan and W. W. Pratt, appeared in four volumes in 1957. More recent studies are L. Marchand, *Byron's Poetry* (1966); R. Gleckner, *Byron and the Ruins of Para-*

dise (1967); M. Cooke, *The Blind Man Traces the Circle* (1969); J. McGann, *Fiery Dust: Byron's Poetic Development* (1969).

PERCY BYSSHE SHELLEY

LIFE. Born on August 4. 1792, in Sussex, to Timothy and Elizabeth Shelley; his father was a country squire, and his grandfather was Sir Bysshe Shelley. He attended Eton from 1804 to 1810 and Oxford in 1810-1811, until he was sent down for writing *The Necessity of Atheism.* In 1811 he married Harriet Westbrook; they had two children. During these early years he was interested in Irish emancipation and land reclamation. He ran away with Mary Wollstonecraft Godwin in 1814. Shortly after Harriet's suicide they married and had several children. He met Byron in 1816; Keats, Hunt, and Hazlitt in 1817. In 1816 he visited Switzerland, and in 1818 left England for Italy, where he saw much of Byron. He was drowned on July 8, 1822, while sailing from Livorno to Lerici.

CHIEF WRITINGS. Shelley's poems, which range from short personal lyrics to long philosophical, allegorical works, include the utopian *Queen Mab* (1813); the portrait of the poet-youth in *Alastor* (1816); the satiric *Witch of Atlas* (1820); the visionary-philosophical *Prometheus Unbound* (1820); the defense of free love. *Epipsychidion* (1821); the elegy *Adonais* (1821), written in memory of Keats; and lyrics such as "Lines Written among the Euganean Hills" (1818); the "Ode to the West Wind" (1820); "The Cloud" (1820); "To a Skylark" (1820). He also wrote a verse play, *The Cenci* (1819) and the essay "A Defence of Poetry" (first published in 1840).

BIOGRAPHY AND CRITICISM. N. I. White, *Shelley* (1940); K. N. Cameron, *The Young Shelley* (1950); F. E. Lea, *Shelley and the Romantic Revolution* (1945); J. W. Beach, "Shelley," in *The Concept of Nature in Nineteenth Century English Poetry* (1936); J. Barrell, *Shelley and the Thought of His Time* (1947); T. S. Eliot, "Shelley and Keats," in *The Use of Poetry and the Use of Criticism* (1933); Carlos Baker, *Shelley's Major Poetry: The Fabric of a Vision* (1948); C. S. Lewis, *Rehabilitations* (1939); C. M. Bowra, "Shelley," in *The Romantic Imagination* (1949); A. M. D. Hughes, *The Nascent Mind of Shelley* (1947); E. Blunden, *Shelley: A Life Story* (1946); R. Fogle, *The Imagery of Keats and Shelley* (1949); P. Butler, *Shelley's Idols of the Cave* (1954); H. Bloom, *Shelley's Mythmaking* (1959); E. Wasserman, *The Subtler Language* (1959); Sylvia Norman, *Flight of the Skylark: The Development of Shelley's Reputation* (1955); M. Wilson, *Shelley's Later Poetry* (1959); D. G. King-Hele, *Shelley: His Thought and Work* (1960); R. Woodman, *The Apocalyptic Vision in the Poetry of Shelley* (1964); J. Fuller, *Shelley* (1968); S. Reiter, *A Study of Shelley's Poetry* (1968); E. Wasserman, *Shelley* (1971); K. N. Cameron, *Shelley, the Golden Years* (1974); and R. L. Holmes, *Shelley: the Pursuit* (1974).

JOHN KEATS

LIFE. Born on October 31, 1795. His father, Thomas Keats, was an hostler at the Swan and Hoop Inn in London. He attended school at Enfield, where his friend Charles Cowden Clarke, the headmaster's son, encouraged his literary inclinations. He was apprenticed to a druggist and surgeon from 1811 to 1814, and was licensed as an apothecary in 1816. His friends Haydon and Severn encouraged Keats' interest in the fine arts. He joined Leigh Hunt's literary circle in 1816, and there came to know Shelley, Hazlitt, and Lamb. Study, writing, several walking tours, and a love affair with Fanny Brawne (to whom he was engaged in 1819) made up his brief life. In 1820 he went to Italy, hoping to cure his tuberculosis, but he died in Rome on February 23, 1821.

CHIEF WRITINGS. His *Poems* (1817) evoked favorable comment and enjoyed a small sale. The long mythological poem *Endymion* (1818) was attacked by Tory reviews (*Blackwood's and the Quarterly*) for its "uncouth language" typical of the "Cockney School," with which Keats was associated because of his friendship with the liberal Leigh Hunt and his circle. *Lamia, Isabella, The Eve of St. Agnes and Other Poems,* the volume which included the great odes, was published in 1820, and met with better success from the critics. The unfinished *Fall of Hyperion,* a Miltonic poem in blank verse, appeared posthumously, in 1856-1857.

BIOGRAPHY AND CRITICISM. S. Colvin, *John Keats: His Life and Poetry* (1917); Amy Lowell, *John Keats* (1925); D. Hewlett, *A Life of John Keats* (1938); *Letters of John Keats,* edited by M. B. Forman (1935); *The Keats Circle: Letters and Papers,* edited by H. E. Rollins (1948). M. R. Ridley, *Keats's Craftsmanship* (1934); C. M. Bowra, "Keats," in *The Romantic Imagination* (1949); T. S. Eliot, "Shelley and Keats," in *The Use of Poetry and the Use of Criticism* (1933); W. J. Bate, *The Stylistic Development of Keats* (1945); G. W. Knight, *The Starlit Dome* (1941); B. I. Evans, *Keats* (1934); C. D. Thorpe, *The Mind of Keats* (1926); R. H. Fogle, *The Imagery of Keats and Shelley* (1949); E. Wasserman, *The Finer Tone* (1953);

Aileen Ward, *John Keats: The Making of a Poet* (1963); H. T. Lyon, *Keats's Well-Read Urn* (1958), a collection of comments about the "Ode on a Grecian Urn"; R. Gittings, *The Mask of Keats* (1956); E. C. Pettet, *On the Poetry of Keats* (1957); W. J. Bate, *John Keats* (1963); B. Blackstone, *The Consecrated Urn* (1959); W. Evert, *Aesthetic and Myth in the Poetry of Keats* (1965); D. Bush, *John Keats* (1967); I. Jack, *Keats and the Mirror of Art* (1967); R. Gittings, *John Keats: The Living Year* (1954), and *John Keats* (1968); M. Goldberg, *The Poetics of Romanticism: Toward a Reading of John Keats* (1969); M. Dickstein, *Keats and His Poetry* (1971); C. Ricks, *Keats and Embarrassment* (1974); S. M. Sperry, *Keats the Poet* (1973); and R. M. Ryan, Keats: *The Religious Sense* (1976).

FRANÇOIS RENÉ DE CHATEAUBRIAND

LIFE. Born September 4, 1768, at Combourg, St. Malo, Brittany, to a noble family allied to both the Spanish and English ruling houses. Chateaubriand obtained a lieutenant's commission in the army, just before the Revolution in 1789. In 1791 he spent five months in North America, returning in January, 1792. He married Céleste Buisson de la Vigne. He joined the royalist, counter-Revolutionary forces, and was wounded at the battle of Valmy (1792). Chateaubriand left (May, 1793) for exile in England, where he lived as a teacher and translator. His mother died in 1798; Chateaubriand, hitherto mildly skeptical, became an ardent Catholic ("I wept and I believed"). He returned to France in 1800. The success of *The Genius of Christianity* (1802) was in part responsible for Napoleon's appointing him to two diplomatic posts, one to the Vatican. He resigned after the execution of the Duc D'Enghien, traveled extensively in Italy, Greece, and the Holy Land (1806–1807), then retired to his country estate at Aulnay. He was appointed by Louis XVIII as Minister of the Interior (1815). In 1818 he became the lover of Mme. de Recamier, who was but one of his many mistresses. He was appointed ambassador to Berlin in 1821, to London in 1822 and Foreign Minister in 1823; Charles X made him ambassador to Rome in 1828. He retired from politics when the Bourbons fell in 1830. His last years were spent writing and traveling. Chateaubriand died July 4, 1848.

CHIEF WRITINGS. *The Essay on Revolutions* was his first work: it was politically ambiguous, and at times anticlerical. *Atala* (1801) was a pilot study intended to test the future reception of *The Genius of Christianity* (1802), into which it was incorporated—the book that included *René* and *The Martyrs*. (The latter was an epic treating the early persecution of the Christians under Domitian). *An Itinerary from Paris to Jerusalem* (1811) described his travels; *Memoirs from Beyond the Grave* (published 1849–1850) was his autobiography.

BIOGRAPHY AND CRITICISM. A. Maurois, *Chateaubriand* (1938); J. Evans, *Chateaubriand* (1939); T. C. Walker, *Chateaubriand's Nature Scenery* (1946).

ALFRED, LORD TENNYSON

LIFE. Born on August 6, 1809, in Somersby, into the family of an Anglican clergyman. An unhappy four years at school were succeeded by tutoring at home and finally by Trinity College, Cambridge, at nineteen. There he founded a literary society, The Apostles, with his friend Arthur Hallam, who died at sea in 1833. The poet became engaged to Emily Sellwood in 1836, but did not marry her till 1850. A pension, granted in 1845 and his appointment as poet laureate, in 1850 eased his financial difficulties. After 1850 he lived quietly at Twickenham (where Pope had once made his home), on the Isle of Wight, and at Aldworth. In 1884 Gladstone created him the first Baron Tennyson. He died on October 6, 1892.

CHIEF WRITINGS. In 1827, with his brother Charles, Tennyson published *Poems by Two Brothers*. The savage critical attack made on *Poems, Chiefly Lyrical* (1830) and *Poems* (1832) led to a nine-year silence. Hallam's death, the eventual subject of *In Memoriam* (1849), was also a great blow. The 1842 collection of *Poems* met with success, and from that date Tennyson became increasingly the poetic spokesman for Victorian England. *The Princess* (1847, revised 1855), *Maud* (1855), and *The Idylls of the King* (first published 1859, final version 1885) were among his most popular works.

BIOGRAPHY AND CRITICISM. The interesting biographies by Hallam Tennyson (1898) and Charles Tennyson (1949) reflect the point of view of the son and grandson respectively. Other biographical works are H. G. Nicholson, *Tennyson* (1923, 1925); and T. R. Lounsbury, *Life and Times of Tennyson* (1915). A standard critical study is W. J. Rolfe, *Poetic and Dramatic Works of Tennyson* (1898). Other commentary is available in F. L. Lucas, *Ten Victorian Poets* (1940); W. H. Auden, *Introduction to Selected Poems* (1944); P. Baum, *Tennyson Sixty Years After* (1948); and T. S. Eliot, "Tennyson," in *Essays Ancient and Modern* (1936). There is also J. Buckley, *Tennyson: The Growth of a Poet* (1961); *Critical Essays on the Poetry of Tennyson,* edited by J. Kilham (1960); Valerie Pitt, *Tennyson Laureate* (1962); Joanna Richardson, *The Pre-Eminent Victorian* (1962); and C. Ricks, *Tennyson* (1972).

ROBERT BROWNING

LIFE. Born on May 7, 1812, in Camberwell, son of a clerk in the Bank of England who later became an affluent banker. He attended the University of London and traveled extensively on the Continent, visiting Italy for the first time in 1834. During the thirties and forties Browning moved in the literary circles of Wordsworth, Dickens, Carlyle, and Leigh Hunt. His marriage to Elizabeth

Barrett in 1846 was one of the great "romantic" alliances of the century. For fifteen years they lived chiefly in Italy. After her death in 1861 Browning returned to London. He went back to the Continent frequently and died at his son's home in Venice on December 12, 1889.

Chief Writings. Browning's early poems *Pauline* (1833), *Paracelsus,* (1835), and *Sordello* (1840), reflect a strong Shelleyan influence. Between 1841 and 1846 appeared a series of lyrics, dramatic monologues (the genre he made famous), and closet dramas which won him literary and popular acclaim. The poems in *Bells and Pomegranates* (1841-1846), *Men and Women* (1855), and *Dramatis Personae* (1864) all exemplify the dramatic cast he gave to lyric verse. Browning's largest, perhaps greatest work is *The Ring and the Book* (1868-1869), a series of monologues in blank verse based on a Renaissance murder trial.

Biography and Criticism. There are biographies of value by A. Symons (1886, revised 1906); E. Dowden (1904); W. H. Griffin and H. C. Minchin (1910); F. M. Sim (1923), and O. Burdett (1933). F. Winwar, *The Immortal Lovers* (1950), is a fictionalized account of Browning's life with his poetess-wife. W. C. De Vane, *A Browning Handbook* (1935), is the single most important work for the student. A. A. Brockington, *Browning and the Twentieth Century* (1932); C. N. Wenger, *The Aesthetics of Browning* (1924); and F. L. Lucas, *Ten Victorian Poets* (1940), are provocative. To these might be added P. Honon, *Browning's Characters* (1962); R. A. King, Jr., *The Bow and the Lyre: The Art of Robert Browning* (1957); Betty Miller, *Robert Browning: A Portrait* (1952); W. O. Raymond, *The Infinite Moment* (1950); J. Williams, *Robert Browning* (1967); T. Blackburn, *Robert Browning: A Study of His Poetry* (1967); W. Shaw, *The Dialectical Temper: The Rhetorical Art of Robert Browning* (1967); N. Crowell, *The Convex Glass* (1968); B. Melchiori, *Browning's Poetry of Reticence* (1968); and I. Jack, *Browning's Major Poetry* (1973).

WALT WHITMAN

Life. Born Walter Whitman (he shortened his name to distinguish it from his father's) on May 31, 1819, in Long Island. While he was still a child, his family moved to Brooklyn, New York. As a young man, Whitman was a schoolteacher and occasional author. In 1841 he became a journalist in New York City. After a varied life as a builder, bookstore proprietor, journalist, and poet, he went to Washington to work as a government clerk. There, as a volunteer nurse, he had firsthand experience with the Civil War wounded. Whitman settled in Camden, New Jersey, in 1873—the year he suffered his inital attack of paralysis—and died there on March 26, 1892.

Chief Writings. Whitman's earliest writings include much bad verse and one novel, a temperance tract. His journalistic efforts led to extensive reading, and by the 1840's he was an ardent admirer of Emerson and the New England Transcendentalist school, and a Jeffersonian Democrat. *Leaves of Grass* was first published in 1855, and Whitman continued to supplement and revise this important book of verse throughout his lifetime. *Drum Taps*—the result of his observations during the Civil War—appeared in 1865. *Democratic Vistas* (1871), a volume of essays, embodied his political and philosophical ideas about the future of America.

Biography and Criticism. Whitman's *Complete Writings* were issued in 1902. Biographies include those by Whitman's friend John Burroughs, (1895); B. Perry (1906); J. Bailey (1926); and E. Holloway (1926). For critical interpretations see G. Santayana, "The Poetry of Barbarism," in *Interpretations of Poetry and Religion* (1900); N. Foerster, *American Criticism* (1928); V. L. Parrington, "The Culture of the Seventies," in *Main Currents of American Thought* (1927-1930); and F. O. Matthiessen, *American Renaissance* (1941). L. Untermeyer, *Poetry and Prose of Walt Whitman* (1948), contains a critical essay and bibliography. Other studies include R. Asselineau, *The Evolution of Walt Whitman* (1960); R. Chase, *Walt Whitman Reconsidered* (1955); R. H. Pearce, *The Continuity of American Poetry* (1961); J. E. Miller, Jr., *A Critical Guide to Leaves of Grass* (1957); G. W. Allen, *The Solitary Singer: A Critical Biography of Walt Whitman* (1959) and *Walt Whitman as Man, Poet, and Legend* (1962), a collection of essays; H. Waskow, *Whitman: Explorations in Form* (1966); *Walt Whitman: The Critical Heritage*, edited by M. Hindus (1971); and J. J. Rubin, *The Historic Whitman* (1974).

EMILY DICKINSON

Life. Emily Dickinson was born December 19, 1830, in Amherst, Massachusetts. Her father, Edward Dickinson, was to become a leading citizen of the town, a prominent lawyer, the treasurer of Amherst College, and for one term a Representative in Congress; her mother, Emily Norcross Dickinson, was supportive, and self-effacing as befitted a New England society wife, but evidently little more. At home and at the Amherst Academy, Emily Dickinson had unusual opportunities for intellectual growth, and rapidly developed a strong and unconforming personality. Sent away to the Mount Holyoke Female Seminary in the Autumn of 1847, perhaps to encourage in her a more conventionally womanly attitude, she was back in Amherst for good by the next summer.

The last 38 years of Emily Dickinson's life are almost bare of incident, at least the kind of incident that makes biographies. Until her death she lived in her father's house; she never married; she seldom traveled, and in 1869 could tell a correspondent, "I do not cross my Father's ground to any House or Town." Despite these self-appointed boundaries, however, her letters show her emotional life to have been anything but impoverished. She was an affectionate daughter and sister, and she kept up a continual correspondence with a circle of friends, among them Charles Wadsworth, a Philadelphia preacher who from 1855 until his death in 1882 was her "closest earthly friend" (though they seldom met), and Samuel Bowles, editor of the Springfield *Republican*, a married man with whom she may have been in love.

Her most important correspondence was with the Boston writer and critic Thomas Wentworth Higginson, for it was by his agency that her poetry was ultimately to be published. In the late 1850s she had begun writing poems, and by 1862 she had compiled about 300 of them, copied out on sheets of paper folded and stitched together as if in imitation of the gatherings of a book. When Higginson's "Letter to a Young Contributor" appeared in the *Atlantic Monthly* in April 1862, Dickinson immediately responded by asking his evaluation of her poems, and though slow to appreciate her originality and power, he began a correspondence with her that lasted off and on until her death. He also came to visit her in Amherst—this was in 1870, when she had become a recluse—commenting afterwards, "I never was with any one who drained my nerve power so much." She had done most of the talking, and her mercurial intelligence had set a pace he could not possibly match.

When Emily Dickinson died on May 15, 1886, after a two-year illness, only seven of her poems had appeared, and those anonymously. She had nonetheless continued to write almost to the end, and left behind her 1775 poems. Higginson and another friend, Mabel Todd Loomis, selected those they liked best for a volume (published in 1890) that was enormously popular and was soon followed by two more; other volumes continued to appear until 1945. In 1955, the complete poems were published for the first time in an edition discarding the previous editions' thematic arrangement, titles, and normalized texts in favor of a chronological ordering of the poems as Emily Dickinson actually left them.

Biography and Criticism. *The Poems of Emily Dickinson*, (3 vols., 1955), edited by Thomas H. Johnson, is the standard edition of her work; a reader's edition is *The Complete Poems* (1960) and a selection is published as *Final Harvest* (1961), both also edited by Johnson. Dickinson's *Letters* (3 vols., 1958) are a valuable supplement. The standard biography is R. B. Sewall, *The Life of Emily Dickinson* (1976), and the most current bibliography is *Emily Dickinson, an Annotated Bibliography* (1970) edited by W. J. Buckingham. Recommended are H. W. Wells, *Introduction to Emily Dickinson* (1946); T. H. Johnson, *Emily Dickinson: An Interpretive Biography* (1955); C. R. Anderson, *Emily Dickinson's Poetry* (1960); J. Leyda, *The Years and Hours of Emily Dickinson* (1960); A. J. Gelpi, *Emily Dickinson: The Mind of the Poet* (1965); and R. Weisbuch, *Emily Dickinson's Poetry.*

HERMAN MELVILLE

Life. Born on August 1, 1819, in New York City, of New England and Hudson River Dutch stock. His father's death in 1832 left the family in reduced financial condition (a state from which Melville never escaped until his wife received an inheritance in 1878); and after teaching school, storekeeping, and clerking in a bank, he shipped aboard the Liverpool packet *St. Lawrence* in 1839-1840. He again taught school briefly upon his return, made a trip to the Midwest in 1840, and in January, 1841, sailed aboard the whaler *Acushnet* from New Bedford, bound for the South Seas. He jumped ship in the Marquesas in 1842, lived for a month among the Taipis (Typess), joined the Australian whaler *Lucy Ann*, where he participated in a mutiny, became a harpooner aboard the Nantucket whaler *Charles & Henry*, and after fourteen weeks in Hawaii enlisted as an ordinary seaman aboard the frigate *United States*, where he served from August, 1843, to October, 1844. Melville married Elizabeth Shaw, daughter of the Massachusetts chief justice, in 1847. By 1850 they had settled in Pittsfield, Massachusetts, where Melville concentrated on a career in letters. He made a brief trip to England in 1849. His attempts to obtain a foreign consulate failed, and his lecture tours were equally unsuccessful. He visited Hawthorne in England in 1856; toured Italy, Greece, the Near East, and the Holy Land in 1857; and in 1860 sailed for San Francisco aboard a clipper commanded by his brother Thomas. The Melville family, which included four children, moved to New York City in 1864, and in 1867 he took a position at the Custom House, which he held until 1885. Melville's last years were passed in relative obscurity. He died on September 28, 1891.

Chief Writings. Melville's early novels, based on his seafaring experiences, achieved popularity; these are *Typee* (1846), *Omoo* (1847), *Redburn* (1849), and *White-Jacket* (1850). He moved toward allegory with *Mardi* (1849); and the mild reception the publice gave *Moby-Dick* (1851) indicated increasing puzzlement at his writing. In his remaining forty years he wrote novels, short stories, and poetry which met with small favor. The prose includes *Pierre* (1852); *Israel Potter* (1855); *The Piazza Tales* (1856), containing "Bartleby the Scrivener," "Benito Cereno," and other stories; *The Confidence Man* (1857); and *Billy Budd* (written 1888-1891, first published in 1924). *Battle-Pieces* (1866) is a volume of poems about the Civil War. The rest of Melville's verse consists of *Clarel,* (1876), a long narrative poem; *John Marr and Other Sailors* (1888); and *Timoleon* (1891). The last two were privately printed in editions of twenty-five copies.

Biography and Criticism. Full-length studies of Melville begin with R. Weaver (1921); followed by J. Freeman (1926); L. Mumford (1929); W. E. Sedgwick (1944); C. Olson, *Call Me Ishmael* (1947); R. Chase (1949); G. Stone (1949); N. Arvin (1950); and L. Howard (1951). The interested reader should also consult F. O. Matthiessen, *American Renaissance* (1941); J. Leyda, *The Melville Log* (1951); L. Thompson, *Melville's Quarrel with God* (1952); D. H. Lawrence, *Studies in Classic American Literature* (1923); C. Feidelson, *Symbolism and American Literature* (1953); R. W. B. Lewis, *The American Adam* (1955); E. Rosenberry, *Melville and the Comic Spirit* (1955); P. Miller, *The Raven and the Whale* (1956); W. Berthoff, *The Example of Melville* (1962); M. Bowen, *The Long Encounter* (1961); J. Miller, Jr., *A Reader's Guide to Herman Melville* (1962); H. Franklin, *The Wake of the Gods: Melville's Mythology* (1963); G. Allen, *Herman Melville and His World* (1971); A. Lebowitz, *Progress into Science: A Study of Melville's Heroes* (1971); M. Pops, *The Melville Archetype* (1971); J. Seelye, *Melville: The Ironic Diagram* (1971).

JEAN-JACQUES ROUSSEAU

(1712–1778)

Confessions*

Part I

BOOK I

[The Years 1712–1719.] I am commencing an undertaking, hitherto without precedent, and which will never find an imitator. I desire to set before my fellows the likeness of a man in all the truth of nature, and that man myself.

Myself alone! I know the feelings of my heart, and I know men. I am not made like any of those I have seen; I venture to believe that I am not made like any of those who are in existence. If I am not better, at least I am different. Whether Nature has acted rightly or wrongly in destroying the mould in which she cast me, can only be decided after I have been read.

Let the trumpet of the Day of Judgment sound when it will, I will present myself before the Sovereign Judge with this book in my hand. I will say boldly: "This is what I have done, what I have thought, what I was. I have told the good and the bad with equal frankness. I have neither omitted anything bad, nor interpolated anything good. If I have occasionally made use of some immaterial embellishments, this has only been in order to fill a gap caused by lack of memory. I may have assumed the truth of that which I knew might have been true, never of that which I knew to be false. I have shown myself as I was: mean and contemptible, good,

* Completed in 1770; published in 1781–1788. The selections reprinted here are from *The Confessions of Jean-Jacques Rousseau,* Everyman's Library, E. P. Dutton and Co., Inc., New York.

high-minded and sublime, according as I was one or the other. I have unveiled my inmost self even as Thou hast seen it, O Eternal Being. Gather round me the countless host of my fellow-men; let them hear my confessions, lament for my unworthiness, and blush for my imperfections. Then let each of them in turn reveal, with the same frankness, the secrets of his heart at the foot of the Throne, and say, if he dare, '*I was better than that man!*' " . . .

I felt before I thought: this is the common lot of humanity. I experienced it more than others. I do not know what I did until I was five or six years old. I do not know how I learned to read; I only remember my earliest reading, and the effect it had upon me; from that time I date my uninterrupted self-consciousness. My mother had left some romances behind her, which my father and I began to read after supper. At first it was only a question of practising me in reading by the aid of amusing books; but soon the interest became so lively, that we used to read in turns without stopping, and spent whole nights in this occupation. We were unable to leave off until the volume was finished. Sometimes, my father, hearing the swallows begin to twitter in the early morning, would say, quite ashamed, "Let us go to bed; I am more of a child than yourself."

In a short time I acquired, by this dangerous method, not only extreme facility in reading and understanding what I read, but a knowledge of the passions that was unique in a child of my age. I had no idea of things in themselves, although all the feelings of actual life were already known to me. I had conceived nothing, but felt everything. These confused emotions which I felt one after the other, certainly did not warp the reasoning powers which I did not as yet possess; but they shaped them in me of a peculiar stamp, and gave me odd and romantic notions of human life, of which experience and reflection have never been able wholly to cure me. . . .

How could I become wicked, when I had nothing but examples of gentleness before my eyes, and none around me but the best people in the world? My father, my aunt, my nurse, my relations, our friends, our neighbours, all who surrounded me, did not, it is true, obey me, but they loved me; and I loved them in return. My wishes were so little excited and so little opposed, that it did not occur to me to have any. I can swear that, until I served under a master, I never knew what a fancy was. Except during the time I spent in reading or writing in my father's company, or when my nurse took me for a walk, I was always with my aunt, sitting or standing by her side, watching her at her embroidery or listening to her singing; and I was content. Her cheerfulness, her gentleness and her pleasant face have stamped so deep and lively an impression on my mind that I can still see her manner, look, and attitude; I remember her affectionate language: I could describe what clothes she wore and how her head was dressed, not forgetting the two little curls of black hair on her temples, which she wore in accordance with the fashion of the time.

I am convinced that it is to her I owe the taste, or rather passion, for music, which only became fully developed in me a long time afterwards. She knew a prodigious number of tunes and songs which she used to sing in a very thin, gentle voice. This excellent woman's cheerfulness of soul banished dreaminess and melancholy from herself and all around her. The attraction which her singing possessed for me was so great, that not only have several of her songs always remained in my memory, but even now, when I have lost her, and as I grew older, many of them, totally forgotten since the days of my childhood, return to my mind with inexpressible charm. Would anyone believe that I, an old dotard, eaten up by cares and troubles, sometime find myself weeping like a child, when I mumble one of those little airs in a voice already broken and trembling?

. . . I have spent my life in idle longing, without saying a word, in the presence of those whom I loved most. Too bashful to declare my taste, I at least satisfied it in situations which had reference to it and kept up the idea of it. To lie at the feet of an imperious mistress, to obey her commands, to ask her forgiveness—this was for me a sweet enjoyment; and, the more my lively imagination heated my blood, the more I presented the appearance of a bashful lover. It may be easily imagined that this manner of making love does not lead to very speedy results, and is not very dangerous to the virtue of those who are its object. For this reason I have rarely possessed, but have none the less enjoyed myself in my own way —that is to say, in imagination. Thus it has happened that my senses, in harmony with my timid disposition and my romantic spirit, have kept my sentiments pure and my morals blameless, owing to the very tastes which, combined with a little more impudence, might have plunged me into the most brutal sensuality. . . .

I am a man of very strong passions, and, while I am stirred by them, nothing can equal my impetuosity; I forget all discretion, all feelings of respect, fear and decency; I am cynical, impudent, violent and fearless; no feeling of shame keeps me back, no danger frightens me; with the exception of the single object which occupies my thoughts, the universe is nothing to me. But all this lasts only for a moment, and the following moment plunges me into complete annihilation. In my calmer moments I am indolence and timidity itself; everything frightens and discourages me; a fly, buzzing past, alarms me; a word which I have to say, a gesture which I have to make, terrifies my idleness; fear and shame overpower me to such an extent that I would gladly hide myself from the sight of my fellow-creatures. If I have to act, I do not know what to do; if I have to speak, I do not know what to say; if anyone looks at me, I am put out of countenance. When I am strongly moved I sometimes know how to find the right words, but in ordinary conversation I can find absolutely nothing, and my condition is unbearable for the simple reason that I am obliged to speak. . . .

Add to this, that none of my prevailing tastes centre in things that can be bought. I want nothing but unadulterated pleasures, and money poisons all. For instance, I am fond of the pleasures of the table; but, as I cannot endure either the constraint of good society or the drunkenness of the tavern, I can only enjoy them with a friend; alone, I cannot do so, for my imagination then occupies itself with other things, and eating affords me no pleasure. If my heated blood longs for women, my excited heart longs still more for affection. Women who could be bought for money would lose for me all their charms; I even doubt whether it would be in me to make use of them. I find it the same with all pleasures within my reach; unless they cost me nothing, I find them insipid. I only love those enjoyments which belong to no one but the first man who knows how to enjoy them.

. . . I worship freedom; I abhor restraint, trouble, dependence. As long as the money in my purse lasts, it assures my independence; it relieves me of the trouble of finding expedients to replenish it, a necessity which always inspired me with dread; but the fear of seeing it exhausted makes me hoard it carefully. The money which a man possesses is the instrument of freedom; that which we eagerly pursue is the instrument of slavery. Therefore I hold fast to that which I have, and desire nothing.

My disinterestedness is, therefore, nothing but idleness; the pleasure of possession is not worth the trouble of acquisition. In like manner, my extravagance is nothing but idleness; when the opportunity of spending agreeably presents itself, it cannot be too profitably employed. Money tempts me less than things, because between money and the possession of the desired object there is always an intermediary, whereas between the thing itself and the enjoyment of it there is none. If I see the thing, it tempts me; if I only see the means of gaining possession of it, it does not. For this reason I have committed thefts, and even now I sometimes pilfer trifles which tempt me, and which I prefer to take rather than to ask for; but neither when a child nor a grown-up man do I ever remember to have robbed anyone of a farthing, except on one occasion, fifteen years ago, when I stole seven *livres* ten *sous*. . . .

BOOK II

[The Years 1728–1731.] . . . I have drawn the great moral lesson, perhaps the only one of any practical value, to avoid those situations of life which bring our duties into conflict with our interests, and which show us our own advantage in the misfortunes of others; for it is certain that, in such situations, however sincere our love of virtue, we must, sooner or later, inevitably grow weak without perceiving it, and become unjust and wicked in act, without having ceased to be just and good in our hearts.

This principle, deeply imprinted on the bottom of my heart, which, although somewhat late, in practice guided my whole conduct, is one of those which have caused me to appear a very strange and foolish creature in the eyes of the world, and, above all, amongst my acquaintances. I have been reproached with wanting to pose as an original, and different from others. In reality, I have never troubled about acting like other people or differently from them. I sincerely desired to do what was right. I withdrew, as far as it lay in my power, from situations which opposed my interests to those of others, and might, consequently, inspire me with a secret, though involuntary, desire of injuring them.

. . . I loved too sincerely, too completely, I venture to say, to be able to be happy easily. Never have passions been at once more lively and purer than mine; never has love been tenderer, truer, more disinterested. I would have sacrificed my happiness a thousand times for that of the person whom I loved; her reputation was dearer to me than my life, and I would never have wished to endanger her repose for a single moment for all the pleasures of enjoyment. This feeling has made me employ such carefulness, such secrecy, and such precaution in my undertakings, that none of them have ever been successful. My want of success with women has always been caused by my excessive love for them. . . .

BOOK III

[The Years 1731–1732.] . . . I only felt the full strength of my attachment when I no longer saw her.[1] When I saw her, I was only content; but, during her absence, my restlessness became painful. The need of living with her caused me outbreaks of tenderness which often ended in tears. I shall never forget how, on the day of a great festival, while she was at vespers, I went for a walk outside the town, my heart full of her image and a burning desire to spend my life with her. I had sense enough to see that at present this was impossible, and that the happiness which I enjoyed so deeply could only be short. This gave to my reflections a tinge of melancholy, about which, however, there was nothing gloomy, and which was tempered by flattering hopes. The sound of the bells, which always singularly affects me, the song of the birds, the beauty of the daylight, the enchanting landscape, the scattered country dwellings in which my fancy placed our common home—all these produced upon me an impression so vivid, tender, melancholy and touching, that I saw myself transported, as it were, in ecstasy, into that happy time and place, wherein my heart, possessing all the happiness it could desire, tasted it with inexpressible rapture, without even a thought of sensual pleasure. I never remember to have plunged into the future

1. Rousseau refers here to Mme. de Warens, whom he also calls "mamma."

with greater force and illusion than on that occasion; and what has struck me most in the recollection of this dream after it had been realised, is that I have found things again exactly as I had imagined them. If ever the dream of a man awake resembled a prophetic vision, it was assuredly that dream of mine. I was only deceived in the imaginary duration; for the days, the years, and our whole life were spent in serene and undisturbed tranquillity, whereas in reality it lasted only for a moment. Alas! my most lasting happiness belongs to a dream, the fulfilment of which was almost immediately followed by the awakening. . . .

Two things, almost incompatible, are united in me in a manner which I am unable to understand: a very ardent temperament, lively and tumultuous passions, and, at the same time, slowly developed and confused ideas, which never present themselves until it is too late. One might say that my heart and my mind do not belong to the same person. Feeling takes possession of my soul more rapidly than a flash of lightning; but, instead of illuminating, inflames and dazzles me. I feel everything and see nothing. I am carried away by my passions, but stupid; in order to think, I must be cool. The astonishing thing is that, notwithstanding, I exhibit tolerably sound judgment, penetration, even finesse, if I am not hurried; with sufficient leisure I can compose excellent impromptus; but I have never said or done anything worthy of notice on the spur of the moment. I could carry on a very clever conversation through the post, as the Spaniards are said to carry on a game of chess. When I read of that Duke of Savoy, who turned round on his journey, in order to cry, "At your throat, Parisian huckster," I said, "There you have myself!"

This sluggishness of thought, combined with such liveliness of feeling, not only enters into my conversation, but I feel it even when alone and at work. My ideas arrange themselves in my head with almost incredible difficulty; they circulate in it with uncertain sound, and ferment till they excite and heat me, and make my heart beat fast; and, in the midst of this excitement, I see nothing clearly and am unable to write a single word—I am obliged to wait. Imperceptibly this great agitation subsides, the confusion clears up, everything takes its proper place, but slowly, and only after a period of long and confused agitation. . . .

BOOK IV

[The Years 1731–1732.] . . . I returned, not to Nyon, but to Lausanne. I wanted to sate myself with the sight of this beautiful lake, which is there seen in its greatest extent. Few of the secret motives which have determined me to act have been more rational. Things seen at a distance are rarely powerful enough to make me act. The uncertainty of the future has always made me look upon plans, which need considerable time to carry them out, as decoys for fools. I indulge in hopes like others, provided it costs me nothing to support them; but if they require continued attention, I have done with it. The least trifling pleasure which is within my reach tempts me more than the joys of Paradise. However, I make an exception of the pleasure which is followed by pain; this has no temptation for me, because I love only pure enjoyments, and these a man never has when he knows that he is preparing for himself repentance and regret. . . .

Why is it that, having found so many good people in my youth, I find so few in my later years? Is their race extinct? No; but the class in which I am obliged to look for them now, is no longer the same as that in which I found them. Among the people, where great passions only speak at intervals, the sentiments of nature make themselves more frequently heard; in the higher ranks they are absolutely stifled, and, under the mask of sentiment, it is only interest or vanity that speaks.

. . . Whenever I approach the Canton of Vaud, I am conscious of an impression in which the remembrance of Madame de Warens, who was born there, of my father who lived there, of Mademoiselle de Vulson who enjoyed the first fruits of my youthful love, of several pleasure trips which I made there when a child and, I believe, some other exciting cause, more mysterious and more powerful than all this, is combined. When the burning desire of this happy and peaceful life, which flees from me and for which I was born, inflames my imagination, it is always the Canton of Vaud, near the lake, in the midst of enchanting scenery, to which it draws me. I feel that I must have an orchard on the shore of this lake and no other, that I must have a loyal friend, a loving wife, a cow, and a little boat. I shall never enjoy perfect happiness on earth until I have all that. I laugh at the simplicity with which I have several times visited this country merely in search of this imaginary happiness. I was always surprised to find its inhabitants, especially the women, of quite a different character from that which I expected. How contradictory it appeared to me! The country and its inhabitants have never seemed to me made for each other.

During this journey to Vévay, walking along the beautiful shore, I abandoned myself to the sweetest melancholy. My heart eagerly flung itself into a thousand innocent raptures; I was filled with emotion, I sighed and wept like a child. How often have I stopped to weep to my heart's content, and, sitting on a large stone, amused myself with looking at my tears falling into the water! . . .

How greatly did the entrance into Paris belie the idea I had formed of it! The external decorations of Turin, the beauty of its streets, the symmetry and regularity of the houses, had made me look for something quite different in Paris. I had imagined to myself a city of most imposing aspect, as beautiful as it was large, where nothing was to be seen but splendid streets and palaces of gold and marble. Entering by the suburb of St. Marceau, I saw nothing but dirty and stinking little streets, ugly black houses, a general air of slovenliness and poverty, beggars, carters, menders of old clothes, criers of decoctions and old hats. All this, from the outset, struck me so forcibly, that all the real magnificence I have since seen in Paris has been unable to destroy this first impression, and I have always retained a secret dislike against residence in this capital. I may say that the whole time, during which I afterwards lived there, was employed solely in trying to find means to enable me to live away from it.

Such is the fruit of a too lively imagination, which exaggerates beyond human exaggeration, and is always ready to see more than it has been told to expect. I had heard Paris so much praised, that I had represented it to myself as the ancient Babylon, where, if I had ever visited it, I should, perhaps, have found as much to take off from the picture which I had drawn of it. The same thing happened to me at the Opera, whither I hastened to go the day after my arrival. The same thing happened to me later at Versailles; and again, when I saw the sea for the first time; and the same thing will always happen to me, when I see anything which has been too loudly announced; for it is impossible for men, and difficult for Nature herself, to surpass the exuberance of my imagination.

. . . The sight of the country, a succession of pleasant views, the open air, a good appetite, the sound health which walking gives me, the free life of the inns, the absence of all that makes me conscious of my dependent position, of all that reminds me of my condition—all this sets my soul free, gives me greater boldness of thought, throws me, so to speak, into the immensity of things, so that I can combine, select, and appropriate them at pleasure, without fear or restraint. I dispose of Nature in its entirety as its lord and master; my heart, roaming from object to object, mingles and identifies itself with those which soothe it, wraps itself up in charming fancies, and is intoxicated with delicious sensations. If, in order to render them permanent, I amuse myself by describing them by myself, what vigorous outlines, what fresh colouring, what power of expression I give them!

. . . At night I lay in the open air, and, stretched on the ground or on a bench, slept as calmly as upon a bed of roses. I remember, especially, that I spent a delightful night outside the city, on a road which ran by the side of the Rhône or Saône, I do not remember which. Raised gardens, with terraces, bordered the other side of the road. It had been very hot during the day; the evening was delightful; the dew moistened the parched grass; the night was calm, without a breath of wind; the air was fresh, without being cold; the sun, having gone down, had left in the sky red vapours, the reflection of which cast a rose-red tint upon the water; the trees on the terraces were full of nightingales answering one another. I walked on in a kind of ecstasy, abandoning my heart and senses to the enjoyment of all, only regretting, with a sigh, that I was obliged to enjoy it alone. Absorbed in my delightful reverie, I continued my walk late into the night, without noticing that I was tired. At last, I noticed it. I threw myself with a feeling of delight upon the shelf of a sort of niche or false door let into a terrace wall; the canopy of my bed was formed by the tops of trees; a nightingale was perched just over my head, and lulled me to sleep with his song; my slumbers were sweet, my awaking was still sweeter. . . .

In relating my journeys, as in making them, I do not know how to stop. My heart beat with joy when I drew near to my dear mamma, but I walked no faster. I like to walk at my ease, and to stop when I like. A wandering life is what I want. To walk through a beautiful country in fine weather, without being obliged to hurry, and with a pleasant prospect at the end, is of all kinds of life the one most suited to my taste. My idea of a beautiful country is already known. No flat country, however beautiful, has ever seemed so to my eyes. I must have mountain torrents, rocks, firs, dark forests, mountains, steep roads to climb or descend, precipices at my side to frighten me. . . .

BOOK V

[The Years 1732–1736.] . . . It is sometimes said that the sword wears out the scabbard. That is my history. My passions have made me live, and my passions have killed me. What passions? will be asked. Trifles, the most childish things in the world, which, however, excited me as much as if the possession of Helen or the throne of the universe had been at stake. In the first place—women. When I possessed one, my senses were calm; my heart, never. The needs of love devoured me in the midst of enjoyment; I had a tender mother, a dear friend; but I needed a mistress. I imagined one in her place; I represented her to myself in a thousand forms, in order to deceive myself. If I had thought that I held mamma in my arms when I embraced her, these embraces would have been no less lively, but all my desires would have been extinguished; I should have sobbed from affection, but I should never have felt any enjoyment. Enjoyment! Does this ever fall to the lot of man? If I had ever, a single time in my life, tasted all the delights of love in their fulness, I do not believe that my frail existence could have endured it; I should have died on the spot.

Thus I was burning with love, without an object; and it is this state, perhaps, that is most exhausting. I was restless, tormented by the hopeless condition of poor mamma's affairs, and her imprudent conduct, which were bound to ruin her completely at no distant date. My cruel imagination, which always anticipates misfortunes, exhibited this particular one to me continually, in all its extent and in all its results. I already saw myself compelled by want to separate from her to whom I had devoted my life, and without whom I could not enjoy it. Thus my soul was ever in a state of agitation; I was devoured alternately by desires and fears. . . .

BOOK VI

[The Year 1736.] . . . At this period commences the brief happiness of my life; here approach the peaceful, but rapid moments which have given me the right to say, *I have lived.* Precious and regretted moments! begin again for me your delightful course; and, if it be possible, pass more slowly in succession through my memory, than you did in your fugitive reality. What can I do, to prolong, as I should like, this touching and simple narrative, to repeat the same things over and over again, without wearying my readers by such repetition, any more than I was wearied of them myself, when I recommenced the life again and again? If all this consisted of facts, actions, and words, I could describe, and in a manner, give an idea of them; but how is it possible to describe what was neither said nor done, nor even thought, but enjoyed and felt, without being able to assign any other reason for my happiness than this simple feeling? I got up at sunrise, and was happy; I walked, and was happy; I saw mamma, and was happy; I left her, and was happy; I roamed the forests and hills, I wandered in the valleys, I read, I did nothing, I worked in the garden, I picked the fruit, I helped in the work of the house, and happiness followed me everywhere—happiness, which could not be referred to any definite object, but dwelt entirely within myself, and which never left me for a single instant. . . .

I should much like to know, whether the same childish ideas ever enter the hearts of other men as sometimes enter mine. In the midst of my studies, in the course of a life as blameless as a man could have led, the fear of hell still frequently troubled me. I asked myself: "In what state am I? If I were to die this moment, should I be damned?" According to my Jansenists, there was no doubt about the matter; but, according to my conscience, I thought differently. Always fearful, and a prey to cruel uncertainty, I had recourse to the most laughable expedients to escape from it, for which I would unhesitatingly have anyone locked up as a madman if I saw him doing as I did. One day, while musing upon this melancholy subject, I mechanically amused myself by throwing stones against the trunks of trees with my usual good aim, that is to say, without hardly hitting one. While engaged in this useful exercise, it occurred to me to draw a prognostic from it to calm my anxiety. I said to myself: "I will throw this stone at the tree opposite; if I hit it, I am saved; if I miss it, I am damned." While speaking, I threw my stone with a trembling hand and a terrible palpitation of the heart, but with so successful an aim that it hit the tree right in the middle, which, to tell the truth, was no very difficult feat, for I had been careful to choose a tree with a thick trunk close at hand. From that time I have never had any doubt about my salvation! When I recall this characteristic incident, I do not know whether to laugh or cry at myself. You great men, who are most certainly laughing, may congratulate yourselves; but do not mock my wretchedness, for I swear to you that I feel it deeply. . . .

JOHANN WOLFGANG VON GOETHE

(1749–1832)

Faust*

Prologue in Heaven[a]

The LORD. *The* HEAVENLY HOSTS. MEPHISTOPHELES[b] *following.*

[*The* THREE ARCHANGELS *step forward.*]

RAPHAEL. The chanting sun, as ever, rivals
The chanting of his brother spheres
And marches round his destined circuit—
A march that thunders in our ears.
His aspect cheers the Hosts of Heaven 5
Though what his essence none can say;
These inconceivable creations
Keep the high state of their first day.

GABRIEL. And swift, with inconceivable swiftness,
The earth's full splendour rolls around, 10
Celestial radiance alternating
With a dread night too deep to sound;
The sea against the rocks' deep bases
Comes foaming up in far-flung force,
And rock and sea go whirling onward 15
In the swift spheres' eternal course.

MICHAEL. And storms in rivalry are raging
From sea to land, from land to sea,
In frenzy forge the world a girdle
From which no inmost part is free. 20
The blight of lightning flaming yonder
Marks where the thunder-bolt will play;
And yet Thine envoys, Lord, revere

* From *Goethe's Faust*, translated by Louis MacNeice. Copyright 1951 by Louis MacNeice. Reprinted by permission of Oxford University Press, Inc. Part I was first published in 1808. Goethe's Dedication and the Prologue at the Theater have not been included, since neither is part of the play itself. All of Part I, except for a few minor omissions made by the translator (indicated in the footnotes), is reprinted here.

a. probably written in 1798. The scene is patterned on Job 1:6–12 and 2:1–6.

b. The origin of the name is still debatable. It may come from Hebrew, Persian, or Greek, with such meanings as "destroyer-liar," "no friend of Faust," "no friend of light."

The gentle movement of Thy day.
CHOIR OF ANGELS. Thine aspect cheers the Hosts of Heaven 25
Though what Thine essence none can say,
And all Thy loftiest creations
Keep the high state of their first day.
[*Enter* MEPHISTOPHELES.]
MEPHISTOPHELES. Since you, O Lord, once more approach and ask
If business down with us be light or heavy— 30
And in the past you've usually welcomed me—
That's why you see me also at your levee.
Excuse me, I can't manage lofty words—
Not though your whole court jeer and find me low;
My pathos certainly would make you laugh 35
Had you not left off laughing long ago.
Your suns and worlds mean nothing much to me;
How men torment themselves, that's all I see.
The little god of the world, one can't reshape, reshade him;
He is as strange to-day as that first day you made him. 40
His life would be not so bad, not quite,
Had you not granted him a gleam of Heaven's light;
He calls it Reason, uses it not the least
Except to be more beastly than any beast.
He seems to me—if your Honour does not mind— 45
Like a grasshopper—the long-legged kind—
That's always in flight and leaps as it flies along
And then in the grass strikes up its same old song.
I could only wish he confined himself to the grass!
He thrusts his nose into every filth, alas. 50
LORD. Mephistopheles, have you no other news?
Do you always come here to accuse?
Is nothing ever right in your eyes on earth?
MEPHISTOPHELES. No, Lord! I find things there as downright bad as ever.
I am sorry for men's days of dread and dearth; 55
Poor things, *my* wish to plague 'em isn't fervent.
LORD. Do you know Faust?
MEPHISTOPHELES. The Doctor?
LORD. Aye, my servant.
MEPHISTOPHELES. Indeed! He serves you oddly enough, I think. 60
The fool has no earthly habits in meat and drink.
The ferment in him drives him wide and far,
That he is mad he too has almost guessed;
He demands of heaven each fairest star

58. *Doctor:* i.e., doctor of philosophy.
60. *you:* In the German text, Mephistopheles shifts from *du* to *ihr*, indicating his lack of respect for God.

And of earth each highest joy and best, 65
And all that is new and all that is far
Can bring no calm to the deep-sea swell of his breast.

LORD. Now he may serve me only gropingly,
Soon I shall lead him into the light.
The gardener knows when the sapling first turns green 70
That flowers and fruit will make the future bright.

MEPHISTOPHELES. What do you wager? You will lose him yet,
Provided *you* give *me* permission
To steer him gently the course I set.

LORD. So long as he walks the earth alive, 75
So long you may try what enters your head;
Men make mistakes as long as they strive.

MEPHISTOPHELES. I thank you for that; as regards the dead,
The dead have never taken my fancy.
I favour cheeks that are full and rosy-red; 80
No corpse is welcome to my house;
I work as the cat does with the mouse.

LORD. Very well; you have my permission.
Divert this soul from its primal source
And carry it, if you can seize it, 85
Down with you upon your course—
And stand ashamed when you must needs admit:
A good man with his groping intuitions
Still knows the path that is true and fit.

MEPHISTOPHELES. All right—but it won't last for long. 90
I'm not afraid my bet will turn out wrong.
And, if my aim prove true and strong,
Allow me to triumph wholeheartedly.
Dust shall he eat—and greedily—
Like my cousin the Snake renowned in tale and song. 95

LORD. That too you are free to give a trial;
I have never hated the likes of you.
Of all the spirits of denial
The joker is the last that I eschew.
Man finds relaxation too attractive— 100
Too fond too soon of unconditional rest;
Which is why I am pleased to give him a companion
Who lures and thrusts and must, as devil, be active.
But ye, true sons of Heaven, it is your duty
To take your joy in the living wealth of beauty. 105
The changing Essence which ever works and lives
Wall you around with love, serene, secure!
And that which floats in flickering appearance

95. ***Snake:*** **the serpent in Genesis, who tempted Adam and Eve.**

Fix ye it firm in thoughts that must endure.
CHOIR OF ANGELS. Thine aspect cheers the Hosts of Heaven 110
Though what Thine essence none can say,
And all Thy loftiest creations
Keep the high state of their first day.
[*Heaven closes.*]
MEPHISTOPHELES. [*Alone*] I like to see the Old One now and then
And try to keep relations on the level. 115
It's really decent of so great a person
To talk so humanely even to the Devil.

The First Part of the Tragedy

NIGHT

In a high-vaulted narrow Gothic room FAUST, *restless, in a chair at his desk.*

FAUST. Here stand I, ach, Philosophy
Behind me and Law and Medicine too
And, to my cost, Theology—
All these I have sweated through and through
And now you see me a poor fool 5
As wise as when I entered school!
They call me Master, they call me Doctor,
Ten years now I have dragged my college
Along by the nose through zig and zag
Through up and down and round and round 10
And this is all that I have found—
The impossibility of knowledge!
It is this that burns away my heart;
Of course I am cleverer than the quacks,
Than master and doctor, than clerk and priest, 15
I suffer no scruple or doubt in the least,
I have no qualms about devil or burning,
Which is just why all joy is torn from me,
I cannot presume to make use of my learning,
I cannot presume I could open my mind 20
To proselytize and improve mankind.

Besides, I have neither goods nor gold,
Neither reputation nor rank in the world;
No dog would choose to continue so!
Which is why I have given myself to Magic 25
To see if the Spirit may grant me to know
Through its force and its voice full many a secret,

May spare the sour sweat that I used to pour out
In talking of what I know nothing about,
May grant me to learn what it is that girds 30
The world together in its inmost being,
That the seeing its whole germination, the seeing
Its workings, may end my traffic in words.

O couldst thou, light of the full moon,
Look now thy last upon my pain, 35
Thou for whom I have sat belated
So many midnights here and waited
Till, over books and papers, thou
Didst shine, sad friend, upon my brow!
O could I but walk to and fro 40
On mountain heights in thy dear glow
Or float with spirits round mountain eyries
Or weave through fields thy glances glean
And freed from all miasmal theories
Bathe in thy dew and wash me clean! 45

Oh! Am I still stuck in this jail?
This God-damned dreary hole in the wall
Where even the lovely light of heaven
Breaks wanly through the painted panes!
Cooped up among these heaps of books 50
Gnawed by worms, coated with dust,
Round which to the top of the Gothic vault
A smoke-stained paper forms a crust.
Retorts and canisters lie pell-mell
And pyramids of instruments, 55
The junk of centuries, dense and mat—
Your world, man! World? They call it that!

And yet you ask why your poor heart
Cramped in your breast should feel such fear,
Why an unspecified misery 60
Should throw your life so out of gear?
Instead of the living natural world
For which God made all men his sons
You hold a reeking mouldering court
Among assorted skeletons. 65

Away! There is a world outside!
And this one book of mystic art
Which Nostradamus wrote himself,

68. ***Nostradamus:*** Latin name of the French astrologer and physician Michel de Notredame, born in 1503. His collection of rhymed prophecies, ***The Centuries***, appeared in 1555.

Is this not adequate guard and guide?
By this you can tell the course of the stars, 70
By this, once Nature gives the word,
The soul begins to stir and dawn,
A spirit by a spirit heard.
In vain your barren studies here
Construe the signs of sanctity. 75
You Spirits, you are hovering near;
If you can hear me, answer me!

[*He opens the book and perceives the sign of the Macrocosm.*[a]]

Ha! What a river of wonder at this vision
Bursts upon all my senses in one flood!
And I feel young, the holy joy of life 80
Glows new, flows fresh, through nerve and blood!
Was it a god designed this hieroglyph to calm
The storm which but now raged inside me,
To pour upon my heart such balm,
And by some secret urge to guide me 85
Where all the powers of Nature stand unveiled around me?
Am I a God? It grows so light!
And through the clear-cut symbol on this page
My soul comes face to face with all creating Nature.
At last I understand the dictum of the sage: 90
'The spiritual world is always open,
Your mind is closed, your heart is dead;
Rise, young man, and plunge undaunted
Your earthly breast in the morning red.'

[*He contemplates the sign.*]

Into one Whole how all things blend, 95
Function and live within each other!
Passing gold buckets to each other
How heavenly powers ascend, descend!
The odour of grace upon their wings,
They thrust from heaven through earthly things 100
And as all sing so *the* All sings!

What a fine show! Aye, but only a show!
Infinite Nature, where can I tap thy veins?
Where are thy breasts, those well-springs of all life
On which hang heaven and earth, 105
Towards which my dry breast strains?
They well up, they give drink, but I feel drought and dearth.

a. literally, "the great world"; the universe as a whole.

[*He turns the pages and perceives the sign of the* EARTH SPIRIT.]

How differently this new sign works upon me!
Thy sign, thou Spirit of the Earth, 'tis thine
And thou art nearer to me. 110
At once I feel my powers unfurled,
At once I glow as from new wine
And feel inspired to venture into the world,
To cope with the fortunes of earth benign or malign,
To enter the ring with the storm, to grapple and clinch, 115
To enter the jaws of the shipwreck and never flinch.
Over me comes a mist,
The moon muffles her light,
The lamp goes dark.
The air goes damp. Red beams flash 120
Around my head. There blows
A kind of a shudder down from the vault
And seizes on me.
It is thou must be hovering round me, come at my prayers!
Spirit, unveil thyself! 125
My heart, oh my heart, how it tears!
And how each and all of my senses
Seem burrowing upwards towards new light, new breath!
I feel my heart has surrendered, I have no more defences.
Come then! Come! Even if it prove my death! 130

[*He seizes the book and solemnly pronounces the sign of the* EARTH SPIRIT. *There is a flash of red flame and the* SPIRIT *appears in it.*]

SPIRIT. Who calls upon me?
FAUST. Appalling vision!
SPIRIT. You have long been sucking at my sphere,
Now by main force you have drawn me here
And now— 135
FAUST. No! Not to be endured!
SPIRIT. With prayers and with pantings you have procured
The sight of my face and the sound of my voice—
Now I am here. What a pitiable shivering
Seizes the Superman. Where is the call of your soul? 140
Where the breast which created a world in itself
And carried and fostered it, swelling up, joyfully quivering,
Raising itself to a level with Us, the Spirits?
Where are you, Faust, whose voice rang out to me,

109. *Spirit of the Earth:* The Macrocosm represented the ordered, harmonious universe in its totality; this figure seems to be a symbol for the energy of terrestrial nature—neither good nor bad, merely powerful.

Who with every nerve so thrust yourself upon me? 145
Are you the thing that at a whiff of my breath
Trembles throughout its living frame,
A poor worm crawling off, askance, askew?

FAUST. Shall I yield to Thee, Thou shape of flame?
I am Faust, I can hold my own with Thee. 150

SPIRIT. In the floods of life, in the storm of work,
In ebb and flow,
In warp and weft,
Cradle and grave,
An eternal sea, 155
A changing patchwork,
A glowing life,
At the whirring loom of Time I weave
The living clothes of the Deity.

FAUST. Thou who dost rove the wide world round, 160
Busy Spirit, how near I feel to Thee!

SPIRIT. You are like that Spirit which you can grasp,
Not me!

[*The* SPIRIT *vanishes.*]

FAUST. Not Thee!
Whom then? 165
I who am Godhead's image,
Am I not even like Thee!

[*A knocking on the door.*]

Death! I know who that is. My assistant!
So ends my happiest, fairest hour.
The crawling pedant must interrupt 170
My visions at their fullest flower!

[WAGNER *enters in dressing-gown and nightcap, a lamp in his hand.*]

WAGNER. Excuse me but I heard your voice declaiming—
A passage doubtless from those old Greek plays.
That is an art from which I would gladly profit,
It has its advantages nowadays. 175
And I've often heard folks say it's true
A preacher can learn something from an actor.

FAUST. Yes, when the preacher is an actor too;
Which is a not uncommon factor.

WAGNER. Ah, when your study binds up your whole existence 180
And you scarcely can see the world on a holiday
Or through a spyglass—and always from a distance—
How can your rhetoric make it walk your way?

FAUST. Unless you feel it, you cannot gallop it down,
Unless it thrust up from your soul 185

Forcing the hearts of all your audience
With a primal joy beyond control.
Sit there for ever with scissors and paste!
Gather men's leavings for a rehash
And blow up a little paltry flicker 190
Out of your own little heap of ash!
It will win you claps from apes and toddlers—
Supposing your palate welcome such—
But heart can never awaken a spark in heart
Unless your own heart keep in touch. 195

WAGNER. However, it is the delivery wins all ears
And I know that I am still far, too far, in arrears.

FAUST. Win your effects by honest means,
Eschew the cap and bells of the fool!
True insight and true sense will make 200
Their point without the rhetoric school
And, given a thought that must be heard,
Is there such need to chase a word?
Yes, your so glittering purple patches
In which you make cat's cradles of humanity 205
Are like the foggy wind which whispers in the autumn
Through barren leaves—a fruitless vanity.

WAGNER. Ah God, we know that art
Is long and short our life!
Often enough my analytical labours 210
Pester both brain and heart.
How hard it is to attain the means
By which one climbs to the fountain head;
Before a poor devil can reach the halfway house,
Like as not he is dead. 215

FAUST. Your manuscript, is that your holy well
A draught of which for ever quenches thirst?
You have achieved no true refreshment
Unless you can tap your own soul first.

WAGNER. Excuse me—it is considerable gratification 220
To transport oneself into the spirit of times past,
To observe what a wise man thought before our days
And how we now have brought his ideas to consummation.

FAUST. Oh yes, consummated in heaven!
There is a book, my friend, and its seals are seven— 225
The times that have been put on the shelf.
Your so-called spirit of such times
Is at bottom merely the spirit of the gentry
In whom each time reflects itself,

225. *its seals are seven:* See Revelation 5:1.

And at that it often makes one weep 230
And at the first glance run away,
A lumber-room and a rubbish heap,
At best an heroic puppet play
With excellent pragmatical Buts and Yets
Such as are suitable to marionettes. 235

WAGNER. And yet the world! The heart and spirit of men!
We all would wish to understand the same.

FAUST. Yes, what is known as understanding—
But who dare call the child by his real name?
The few who have known anything about it, 240
Whose hearts unwisely overbrimmed and spake,
Who showed the mob their feelings and their visions,
Have ended on the cross or at the stake.
My friend, I beg you, the night is now far gone;
We must break off for this occasion. 245

WAGNER. I'd have been happy sitting on and on
To continue such a learned conversation.
To-morrow however, as it is Easter Day,
I shall put you some further questions if I may.
Having given myself to knowledge heart and soul 250
I have a good share of it, now I would like the whole.

[*Exit* WAGNER.]

FAUST. [*Alone*] To think this head should still bring hope to birth
Sticking like glue to hackneyed rags and tags,
Delving with greedy hand for treasure
And glad when it finds an earthworm in the earth! 255

That such a human voice should here intrude
Where spiritual fulness only now enclosed me!
And yet, my God, you poorest of all the sons
Of earth, this time you have earned my gratitude.
For you have snatched me away from that despair 260
Which was ripe and ready to destroy my mind;
Beside that gigantic vision I could not find
My normal self; only a dwarf was there.

I, image of the Godhead, who deemed myself but now
On the brink of the mirror of eternal truth and seeing 265
My rapturous fill of the blaze of clearest Heaven,
Having stripped off my earthly being;
I, more than an angel, I whose boundless urge
To flow through Nature's veins and in the act of creation
To revel it like the gods—what a divination, 270

What an act of daring—and what an expiation!
One thundering word has swept me over the verge.

To boast myself thine equal I do not dare.
Granted I owned the power to draw thee down,
I lacked the power to hold thee there. 275
In that blest moment I felt myself,
Felt myself so small, so great;
Cruelly thou didst thrust me back
Into man's uncertain fate.
Who will teach me? What must I shun? 280
Or must I go where that impulse drives?
Alas, our very actions like our sufferings
Put a brake upon our lives.
Upon the highest concepts of the mind
There grows an alien and more alien mould; 285
When we have reached what in this world is good
That which is better is labelled a fraud, a blind.
What gave us life, feelings of highest worth,
Go dead amidst the madding crowds of earth.

Where once Imagination on daring wing 290
Reached out to the Eternal, full of hope,
Now, that the eddies of time have shipwrecked chance on chance,
She is contented with a narrow scope.
Care makes her nest forthwith in the heart's deep places,
And there contrives her secret sorrows, 295
Rocks herself restlessly, destroying rest and joy;
And always she is putting on new faces,
Will appear as your home, as those that you love within it,
As fire or water, poison or steel;
You tremble at every blow that you do not feel 300
And what you never lose you must weep for every minute.

I am not like the gods—that I too deeply feel—
No, I am like the worm that burrows through the dust
Which, as it keeps itself alive in the dust,
Is annulled and buried by some casual heel. 305

Is it not dust that on a thousand shelves
Narrows this high wall round me so?
The junk that with its thousandfold tawdriness
In this moth world keeps me so low?
Shall I find here what I require? 310
Read maybe in a thousand books how men
Have in the general run tortured themselves,

With but a lucky one now and then?
Why do you grin at me, you hollow skull?
To point out that your brain was once, like mine, confused 315
And looked for the easy day but in the difficult dusk,
Lusting for truth was led astray and abused?
You instruments, I know you are mocking me
With cog and crank and cylinder.
I stood at the door, you were to be the key; 320
A key with intricate wards—but the bolt declines to stir.
Mysterious in the light of day
Nature lets none unveil her; if she refuse
To make some revelation to your spirit
You cannot force her with levers and with screws. 325
You ancient gear I have never used, it is only
Because my father used you that I retain you.
You ancient scroll, you have been turning black
Since first the dim lamp smoked upon this desk to stain you.
Far better to have squandered the little I have 330
Than loaded with that little to stay sweating here.
Whatever legacy your fathers left you,
To own it you must earn it dear.
The thing that you fail to use is a load of lead;
The moment can only use what the moment itself has bred. 335

But why do my eyes fasten upon that spot?
Is that little bottle a magnet to my sight?
Why do I feel of a sudden this lovely illumination
As when the moon flows round us in a dark wood at night?

Bottle, unique little bottle, I salute you 340
As now I devoutly lift you down. In you
I honour human invention and human skill.
You, the quintessence of all sweet narcotics,
The extract of all rare and deadly powers,
I am your master—show me your good will! 345
I look on you, my sorrow is mitigated,
I hold you and my struggles are abated,
The flood-tide of my spirit ebbs away, away.
The mirroring waters glitter at my feet,
I am escorted forth on the high seas, 350
Allured towards new shores by a new day.
A fiery chariot floats on nimble wings
Down to me and I feel myself upbuoyed
To blaze a new trail through the upper air

326–327. *gear . . . father:* Later we find that Faust's father was a doctor of medicine.

Into new spheres of energy unalloyed. 355
Oh this high life, this heavenly rapture! Do *you*
Merit this, you, a moment ago a worm?
Merit it? Aye—only turn your back on the sun
Which enchants the earth, turn your back and be firm!
And brace yourself to tear asunder the gates 360
Which everyone longs to shuffle past if he can;
Now is the time to act and acting prove
That God's height need not lower the merit of Man;
Nor tremble at that dark pit in which our fancy
Condemns itself to torments of its own framing, 365
But struggle on and upwards to that passage
At the narrow mouth of which all hell is flaming.
Be calm and take this step, though you should fall
Beyond it into nothing—nothing at all.

And you, you loving-cup of shining crystal— 370
I have not given a thought to you for years—
Down you come now out of your ancient chest!
You glittered at my ancestors' junketings
Enlivening the serious guest
When with you in his hand he proceeded to toast his neighbour— 375
But to-day no neighbour will take you from my hand.
Here is a juice that makes one drunk in a wink;
It fills you full, you cup, with its brown flood.
It was I who made this, I who had it drawn;
So let my whole soul now make my last drink 380
A high and gala greeting, a toast to the dawn!

[*He raises the cup to his mouth. There is an outburst of bells and choirs.*]

CHORUS OF ANGELS. Christ is arisen!
Joy to mortality
Whom its own fatally
Earth-bound mortality 385
Bound in a prison.

FAUST. What a deep booming, what a ringing tone
Pulls back the cup from my lips—and with such power!
So soon are you announcing, you deep bells,
Easter Day's first festive hour? 390
You choirs, do you raise so soon the solacing hymn
That once round the night of the grave rang out from the seraphim

381. *dawn:* See l. 248.
382. *Christ is arisen!:* first line of an old medieval Easter hymn, freely adapted by Goethe.

As man's new covenant and dower?

CHORUS OF WOMEN. With balm and with spices
'Twas we laid him out, 395
We who tended him,
Faithful, devout;
We wound him in linen,
Made all clean where he lay,
Alas—to discover 400
Christ gone away.

CHORUS OF ANGELS. Christ is arisen!
The loving one! Blest
After enduring the
Grievous, the curing, the 405
Chastening test.

FAUST. You heavenly music, strong as you are kind,
Why do you search me out in the dust?
Better ring forth where men have open hearts!
I hear your message, my faith it is that lags behind; 410
And miracle is the favourite child of faith.
Those spheres whence peals the gospel of forgiving,
Those are beyond what I can dare,
And yet, so used am I from childhood to this sound,
It even now summons me back to living. 415
Once I could feel the kiss of heavenly love
Rain down through the calm and solemn Sabbath air,
Could find a prophecy in the full-toned bell,
A spasm of happiness in a prayer.
An ineffably sweet longing bound me 420
To quest at random through field and wood
Where among countless burning tears
I felt a world rise up around me.
This hymn announced the lively games of youth, the lovely
Freedom of Spring's own festival; 425
Now with its childlike feelings memory holds me back
From the last and gravest step of all.
But you, sweet songs of heaven, keep sounding forth!
My tears well up, I belong once more to earth.

CHORUS OF DISCIPLES. Now has the Buried One, 430
Lowliness ended,
Living in lordliness,
Lordly ascended;
He in the zest of birth

394–401. *With balm . . . away:* Goethe makes free use of the New Testament here. None of the Evangelists says that Christ was laid in the tomb by women. According to Mark and Luke, they came on the third day *intending* to anoint the body, but He was gone from the tomb.

Near to creating light; 435
We on the breast of earth
Still in frustrating night!
He left us, his own ones,
Pining upon this spot,
Ah, and lamenting, 440
Master, thy lot.

CHORUS OF ANGELS. Christ is arisen
From the womb of decay!
Burst from your prison,
Rejoice in the day! 445
Praising him actively,
Practising charity,
Giving alms brotherly,
Preaching him wanderingly,
Promising sanctity, 450
You have your Master near,
You have him here!

EASTER HOLIDAY

Holidaymakers of all kinds come out through the city gate.[a]

FIRST STUDENT. Lord, these strapping wenches they go a lick!
Hurry up, brother, we must give 'em an escort.
My programme for to-day is a strong ale,
A pipe of shag and a girl who's got up chic.

FIRST GIRL. Look! Will you look at the handsome boys! 5
Really and truly its degrading;
They could walk out with the best of us
And they have to run round scullery-maiding!

SECOND STUDENT. Hold on, hold on! There are two coming up behind
With a very pretty taste in dress; 10
One of those girls is a neighbour of mine,
She appeals to me, I must confess.
You see how quietly they go
And yet in the end they'll be taking *us* in tow.

BEGGAR. [*Singing*] Good gentlemen and lovely ladies, 15
Rosy of cheek and neat of dress,
Be kind enough to look upon me
And see and comfort my distress.
Leave me not here a hopeless busker!

a. It has been shown that Goethe had Frankfurt-am-Main in mind for this scene, and the "gate" referred to is the Sachsenhausen Tor, or Affenthor. The translator omits a few lines here which include other local references—to a hunting lodge, or *Forsthaus*, two miles southwest of the gate; to an inn called the Gerbermühle on the Main River; and to a village, probably Oberrad.

Only the giver can be gay. 20
A day when all the town rejoices,
Make it for me a harvest day.

FIRST BURGHER. I know nothing better on Sundays or on holidays
Than to have a chat about war and warlike pother
When far away, in Turkey say, 25
The peoples are socking one another.
One stands at the window, drinks one's half of mild,
And sees the painted ships glide down the waterways;
Then in the evening one goes happily home
And blesses peace and peaceful days. 30

SECOND BURGHER. Yes indeed, neighbour! That is all right with me.
They can break heads if they like it so
And churn up everything topsyturvy.
But at home let us keep the status quo.

OLD WOMAN. Eh, but how smart they look! Pretty young things! 35
Whoever saw you should adore you!
But not so haughty! It's all right—
Tell me your wish and I can get it for you.

FIRST GIRL. Come, Agatha! Such witches I avoid
In public places—it's much wiser really; 40
It's true, she helped me on St. Andrew's night
To see my future sweetheart clearly.

SECOND GIRL. Yes, mine she showed me in a crystal,
A soldier type with dashing chaps behind him;
I look around, I seek him everywhere 45
And yet—and yet I never find him.

SOLDIERS. [*Singing*] Castles with towering
Walls to maintain them,
Girls who have suitors
But to disdain them, 50
Would I could gain them!
Bold is the venture,
Lordly the pay.

Hark to the trumpets!
They may be crying 55
Summons to gladness,
Summons to dying.
Life is a storming!
Life is a splendour!
Maidens and castles 60
Have to surrender.

41. ***St. Andrew's night:*** **Actually, St. Andrew's eve, November 29. This was the traditional time for young girls to consult fortunetellers about their future lovers or husbands.**

Bold is the venture,
Lordly the pay;
Later the soldiers
Go marching away. 65

[FAUST *and* WAGNER *are now walking off on the road to the village.*]

FAUST. River and brook are freed from ice
By the lovely enlivening glance of spring
And hope grows green throughout the dale;
Ancient winter, weakening,
Has fallen back on the rugged mountains 70
And launches thence his Parthian shafts
Which are merely impotent showers of hail
Streaking over the greening mead;
But the sun who tolerates nothing white
Amidst all this shaping and stirring of seed, 75
Wants to enliven the world with colour
And, flowers being lacking, in their lieu
Takes colourful crowds to mend the view.
Turn round and look back from this rise
Towards the town. From the gloomy gate 80
Look, can you see them surging forth—
A harlequin-coloured crowd in fête!
Sunning themselves with one accord
In homage to the risen Lord
For they themselves to-day have risen: 85
Out of the dismal room in the slum,
Out of each shop and factory prison,
Out of the stuffiness of the garret,
Out of the squash of the narrow streets,
Out of the churches' reverend night— 90
One and all have been raised to light.
Look, only look, how quickly the gardens
And fields are sprinkled with the throng,
How the river all its length and breadth
Bears so many pleasure-boats along, 95
And almost sinking from its load
How this last dinghy moves away.
Even on the furthest mountain tracks
Gay rags continue to look gay.
Already I hear the hum of the village, 100
Here is the plain man's real heaven—
Great and small in a riot of fun;
Here I'm a man—and dare be one.

WAGNER. Doctor, to take a walk with you

Is a profit and a privilege for me 105
But I wouldn't lose my way alone round here,
Sworn foe that I am of all vulgarity.
This fiddling, screaming, skittle-playing,
Are sounds I loathe beyond all measure;
They run amuck as if the devil were in them 110
And call it music, call it pleasure.

[*They have now reached the village.*]

OLD PEASANT. Doctor, it is most good of you
Not to look down on us to-day
And, pillar of learning that you are,
To mill around with folk at play. 115
So take this most particular jug
Which we have filled for you at the tap,
This is a pledge and I pray aloud
That it quench your thirst and more mayhap:
As many drops as this can give, 120
So many days extra may you live.

FAUST. Thank you for such a reviving beer
And now—good health to all men here.

[*The people collect round him.*]

OLD PEASANT. Of a truth, Doctor, you have done rightly
To appear on this day when all are glad, 125
Seeing how in times past you proved
Our own good friend when days were bad.
Many a man stands here alive
Whom your father found in the grip
Of a raging fever and tore him thence 130
When he put paid to the pestilence.
You too—you were a youngster then—
Where any was ill you went your round,
Right many a corpse left home feet first
But you came out of it safe and sound, 135
From many a gruelling trial—Aye,
The helper got help from the Helper on high.

CROWD. Health to the trusty man. We pray
He may live to help us many a day.

FAUST. Kneel to the One on high, our friend 140
Who teaches us helpers, who help can send.

[FAUST *and* WAGNER *leave the* CROWD *and move on.*]

WAGNER. You great man, how your heart must leap
To be so honoured by the masses!
How happy is he who has such talents

129. *your father:* See l. 327 in the preceding scene. The old German Faust legend made Faust's father a peasant; but Nostradamus (see note to l. 68 in the preceding scene) and Paracelsus (1493–1541), two physician-astrologers closely linked to the Faust myth, were famous for their plague-curing remedies.

And from them such a crop can reap! 145
The father points you out to his boy,
They all ask questions, run and jostle,
The fiddles and the dancers pause
And, as you pass, they stand in rows
And caps go hurtling in the sky; 150
They almost kneel to you as though
The eucharist were passing by.

FAUST. Only a few steps more up to that stone!
Here, after our walk, we will take a rest.
Here I have often sat, thoughtful, alone, 155
Torturing myself with prayer and fast.
Rich in hope and firm in faith,
With tears and sighs to seven times seven
I thought I could end that epidemic
And force the hand of the Lord of Heaven. 160
But now the crowd's applause sounds to me like derision.
O could you only read in my inmost heart
How little father and son
Merited their great reputation!
My father was a worthy man who worked in the dark, 165
Who in good faith but on his own wise
Brooded on Nature and her holy circles
With laborious whimsicalities;
Who used to collect the connoisseurs
Into the kitchen and locked inside 170
Its black walls pour together divers
Ingredients of countless recipes;
Such was our medicine, the patients died
And no one counted the survivors.
And thus we with our hellish powders 175
Raged more perniciously than the plague
Throughout this district—valley and town.
Myself I have given the poison to thousands;
They drooped away, *I* must live on to sample
The brazen murderers' renown. 180

WAGNER. How can you let that weigh so heavily?
Does not a good man do enough
If he works at the art that he has received
Conscientiously and scrupulously?
As a young man you honour your father, 185
What he can teach, you take with a will;
As a man you widen the range of knowledge
And your son's range may be wider still.

FAUST. Happy the man who swamped in this sea of Error
Still hopes to struggle up through the watery wall; 190
What we don't know is exactly what we need

And what we know fulfils no need at all.
But let us not with such sad thoughts
Make this good hour an hour undone!
Look how the cottages on the green 195
Shine in the glow of the evening sun!
He backs away, gives way, the day is overspent,
He hurries off to foster life elsewhere.
Would I could press on his trail, on his trail for ever—
Alas that I have no wings to raise me into the air! 200
Then I should see in an everlasting sunset
The quiet world before my feet unfold,
All of its peaks on fire, all of its vales becalmed,
And the silver brook dispersed in streams of gold.
Not the wild peaks with all their chasms 205
Could interrupt my godlike flight;
Already the bays of the sea that the sun has warmed
Unfurl upon my marvelling sight.
But in the end the sungod seems to sink away,
Yet the new impulse sets me again in motion, 210
I hasten on to drink his eternal light,
With night behind me and before me day,
Above me heaven and below me ocean.
A beautiful dream—yet the sun leaves me behind.
Alas, it is not so easy for earthly wing 215
To fly on level terms with the wings of the mind.
Yet born with each of us is the instinct
That struggles upwards and away
When over our heads, lost in the blue,
The lark pours out her vibrant lay; 220
When over rugged pine-clad ranges
The eagle hangs on outspread wings
And over lake and over plain
We see the homeward-struggling crane.

WAGNER. I myself have often had moments of fancifulness 225
But I never experienced yet an urge like this.
Woods and fields need only a quick look
And I shall never envy the bird its pinions.
How differently the joys of the mind's dominions
Draw us from page to page, from book to book. 230
That's what makes winter nights lovely and snug—
The blissful life that warms you through your body—
And, ah, should you unroll a worthwhile manuscript,
You bring all heaven down into your study.

FAUST. You are only conscious of one impulse. Never 235
Seek an acquaintance with the other.
Two souls, alas, cohabit in my breast,
A contract one of them desires to sever.

The one like a rough lover clings
To the world with the tentacles of its senses; 240
The other lifts itself to Elysian Fields
Out of the mist on powerful wings.
Oh, if there be spirits in the air,
Princes that weave their way between heaven and earth,
Come down to me from the golden atmosphere 245
And carry me off to a new and colourful life.
Aye, if I only had a magic mantle
On which I could fly abroad, a-voyaging,
I would not barter it for the costliest raiment,
Not even for the mantle of a king. 250

WAGNER. Do not invoke the notorious host
Deployed in streams upon the wind,
Preparing danger in a thousand forms
From every quarter for mankind.
Thrusting upon you from the North 255
Come fanged spirits with arrow tongues;
From the lands of morning they come parching
To feed themselves upon your lungs;
The South despatches from the desert
Incendiary hordes against your brain 260
And the West a swarm which first refreshes,
Then drowns both you and field and plain.
They are glad to listen, adepts at doing harm,
Glad to obey and so throw dust in our eyes;
They make believe that they are sent from heaven 265
And lisp like angels, telling lies.
But let us move! The world has already gone grey,
The air is beginning to cool and the mist to fall.
It's in the evening one really values home—
But why do you look so astonished, standing there, staring that way? 270
What's there to see in the dusk that's worth the trouble?

FAUST. The black dog, do you mark him ranging through corn and stubble?

WAGNER. I noticed him long ago; he struck me as nothing much.

FAUST. Have a good look at the brute. What do you take him for?

WAGNER. For a poodle who, as is the way of such, 275
Is trailing his master, worrying out the scent.

FAUST. But don't you perceive how in wide spirals around us
He is getting nearer and nearer of set intent?
And, unless I'm wrong, a running fire
Eddies behind him in his wake. 280

WAGNER. I can see nothing but a black poodle;
It must be your eyes have caused this mistake.

FAUST. He is casting, it seems to me, fine nooses of magic

About our feet as a snare.
WAGNER. *I* see him leaping round us uncertainly, timidly, 285
Finding instead of his master two strangers there.
FAUST. The circle narrows; now he is near.
WAGNER. Just a dog, you see; no phantoms here.
He growls and hesitates, grovels on the green
And wags his tail. Pure dog routine. 290
FAUST. Heel, sir, heel! Come, fellow, come!
WAGNER. He is a real poodle noodle.
Stand still and he'll sit up and beg;
Speak to him and he's all over you;
Lose something and he'll fetch it quick, 295
He'll jump in the water after your stick.
FAUST. I think you're right, I cannot find a trace
Of a spirit here; it is all a matter of training.
WAGNER. If a dog is well brought up, a wise man even
Can come to be fond of him in such a case. 300
Yes, he fully deserves your name upon his collar,
He whom the students have found so apt a scholar.

FAUST'S STUDY

He enters with the poodle.

FAUST. I have forsaken field and meadow
Which night has laid in a deep bed,
Night that wakes our better soul
With a holy and foreboding dread.
Now wild desires are wrapped in sleep 5
And all the deeds that burn and break,
The love of Man is waking now,
The love of God begins to wake.

Poodle! Quiet! Don't run hither and thither!
Leave my threshold! Why are you snuffling there? 10
Lie down behind the stove and rest.
Here's a cushion; it's my best.
Out of doors on the mountain paths
You kept us amused by running riot;
But as my protégé at home 15
You'll only be welcome if you're quiet.

Ah, when in our narrow cell
The lamp once more imparts good cheer,
Then in our bosom—in the heart
That knows itself—then things grow clear. 20
Reason once more begins to speak
And the blooms of hope once more to spread;
One hankers for the brooks of life,
Ah, and for life's fountain head.

Don't growl, you poodle! That animal sound 25
Is not in tune with the holy music
By which my soul is girdled round.
We are used to human beings who jeer
At what they do not understand,
Who grouse at the good and the beautiful 30
Which often causes them much ado;
But must a dog snarl at it too?

But, ah, already, for all my good intentions
I feel contentment ebbing away in my breast.
Why must the stream so soon run dry 35
And we be left once more athirst?
I have experienced this so often;
Yet this defect has its compensation,
We learn to prize the supernatural
And hanker after revelation, 40
Which burns most bright and wins assent
Most in the New Testament.
I feel impelled to open the master text
And this once, with true dedication,
Take the sacred original 45
And make in my mother tongue my own translation.
[*He opens a Bible.*]
It is written: In the beginning was the Word.
Here I am stuck at once. Who will help me on?
I am unable to grant the Word such merit,
I must translate it differently 50
If I am truly illumined by the spirit.
It is written: In the beginning was the Mind.
But why should my pen scour
So quickly ahead? Consider that first line well.
Is it the Mind that effects and creates all things? 55
It *should* read: In the beginning was the Power.
Yet, even as I am changing what I have writ,
Something warns me not to abide by it.
The spirit prompts me, I see in a flash what I need,
And write: In the beginning was the Deed! 60

Dog! If we two are to share this room,
Leave off your baying,
Leave off your barking!
I can't have such a fellow staying
Around me causing all this bother. 65
One of us or the other

43. *master text:* i.e., the Greek.

47. *In the beginning . . . Word:* John 1:1.

Will have to leave the cell.
Well?
I don't really like to eject you so
But the door is open, you may go. 70

But what? What do I see?
Can this really happen naturally?
Is it a fact or is it a fraud?
My dog is growing so long and broad!
He raises himself mightily, 75
That is not a dog's anatomy!
What a phantom have I brought to my house!
He already looks like a river horse
With fiery eyes and frightful jaws—
Aha! But I can give you pause! 80
For such a hybrid out of hell
Solomon's Key is a good spell.

[SPIRITS *are heard in the passage.*]

SPIRITS. Captured within there is one of us!
Wait without, follow him none of us!
Like a fox in a snare 85
An old hell-cat's trembling there.
But on the alert!
Fly against and athwart,
To starboard and port,
And he's out with a spurt! 90
If help you can take him,
Do not forsake him!
For often, to earn it, he
Helped our fraternity.

FAUST. First, to confront the beast, 95
Be the Spell of the Four released:
Salamander shall glow,
Undine shall coil,
Sylph shall vanish
And gnome shall toil. 100
One without sense
Of the elements,
Of their force
And proper course,
The spirits would never 105
Own him for master.
Vanish in flames,
Salamander!

82. *Solomon's Key:* the *Clavicula Salomonis*, a standard work used by magicians for conjuring; in many medieval legends, Solomon was noted as a great magician.

96. *Spell of the Four:* Salamanders were spirits of fire; undines, of water; sylphs, of air; and gnomes, of earth.

Commingle in babble of streams,
Undine! 110
Shine meteor-like and majestic,
Sylph!
Bring help domestic,
Lubber-fiend! Lubber-fiend!
Step out of him and make an end! 115
None of the Four
Is the creature's core.
He lies quite quiet and grins at me,
I have not yet worked him injury.
To exercise you 120
I'll have to chastise you.
Are you, rapscallion,
A displaced devil?
This sign can level
Each dark battalion; 125
Look at this sign!
He swells up already with bristling spine.
You outcast! Heed it—
This name! Can you read it?
The unbegotten one, 130
Unpronounceable,
Poured throughout Paradise,
Heinously wounded one?
Behind the stove, bound by my spells,
Look, like an elephant it swells, 135
Filling up all the space and more,
It threatens to melt away in mist.
Down from the ceiling! Down before—!
Down at your master's feet! Desist!
You see, I have not proved a liar; 140
I can burn you up with holy fire!
Do not await
The triply glowing light!
Do not await
My strongest brand of necromancy! 145

[*The mist subsides and* MEPHISTOPHELES *comes forward from behind the stove, dressed like a travelling scholar.*]

MEPHISTOPHELES. What is the noise about? What might the gentleman fancy?

FAUST. So that is what the poodle had inside him!
A travelling scholar? That casus makes me laugh.

MEPHISTOPHELES. My compliments to the learned gentleman.
You have put me a sweat—not half! 150

143. *triply glowing light:* perhaps the Trinity, or a triangle with divergent rays.

FAUST. What is your name?
MEPHISTOPHELES. The question strikes me as petty
For one who holds the Word in such low repute,
Who, far withdrawn from all mere surface,
Aims only at the Essential Root. 155
FAUST. With you, you gentry, what is essential
The name more often than not supplies,
As is indeed only too patent
When they call you Fly-God, Corrupter, Father of Lies.
All right, who are you then? 160
MEPHISTOPHELES. A part of that Power
Which always wills evil, always procures good.
FAUST. What do you mean by this conundrum?
MEPHISTOPHELES. I am the Spirit which always denies.
And quite rightly; whatever has a beginning 165
Deserves to have an undoing;
It would be better if nothing began at all.
Thus everything that you call
Sin, destruction, Evil in short,
Is my own element, my resort. 170
FAUST. You call yourself a part, yet you stand before me whole?
MEPHISTOPHELES. This is the unassuming truth.
Whereas mankind, that little world of fools,
Commonly takes itself for a whole—
I am a part of the Part which in the beginning was all, 175
A part of the darkness which gave birth to light,
To that haughty light which is struggling now to usurp
The ancient rank and realm of its mother Night,
And yet has no success, try as it will,
Being bound and clamped by bodies still. 180
It streams from bodies, bodies it beautifies,
A body clogs it when it would run,
And so, I hope, it won't be long
Till, bodies and all, it is undone.
FAUST. Ah, now I know your honourable profession! 185
You cannot destroy on a large scale,
So you are trying it on a small.
MEPHISTOPHELES. And, candidly, not getting far at all.
That which stands over against the Nothing,
The Something, I mean this awkward world, 190
For all my endeavours up to date
I have failed to get it under foot
With waves, with storms, with earthquakes, fire—

153. *Word:* See l. 47 in this scene.
159. *Fly-God:* an almost literal translation of the name of the Philistine deity Beelzebub.
176. *darkness:* Mephistopheles here speaks as the Prince of Darkness, the rôle in Christianity acquired by the devil from the Persian Manichaean deity Ahriman.

Sea and land after all stay put.
And this damned stuff, the brood of beasts and men, 195
There is no coming to grips with them;
I've already buried heaps of them!
And always new blood, fresh blood, circulates again.
So it goes on, it's enough to drive one crazy.
A thousand embryos extricate themselves 200
From air, from water and from earth
In wet and dry and hot and cold.
Had I not made a corner in fire
I should find myself without a berth.

FAUST. So you when faced with the ever stirring, 205
The creative force, the beneficent,
Counter with your cold devil's fist
Spitefully clenched but impotent.
You curious son of Chaos, why
Not turn your hand to something else? 210

MEPHISTOPHELES. We will give it our serious attention—
But more on that subject by and by.
Might I for this time take my leave?

FAUST. Why you ask I cannot see.
I have already made your acquaintance; 215
When you feel like it, call on me.
Here is the window, here is the door—
And a chimney too—if it comes to that.

MEPHISTOPHELES. I must confess; there's a slight impediment
That stops me making my exit pat, 220
The pentagram upon your threshold—

FAUST. So the witch's foot is giving you trouble?
Then tell me, since you're worried by that spell,
How did you ever enter, child of Hell?
How was a spirit like you betrayed? 225

MEPHISTOPHELES. You study that sign! It's not well made;
One of its corners, do you see,
The outside one's not quite intact.

FAUST. A happy accident in fact!
Which means you're in my custody? 230
I did not intend to set a gin.

MEPHISTOPHELES. The dog—he noticed nothing, jumping in;
The case has now turned round about
And I, the devil, can't get out.

FAUST. Then why not leave there by the window? 235

MEPHISTOPHELES. It is a law for devils and phantoms all:
By the way that we slip in by the same we must take our
leave.

221. *pentagram:* a magic five-pointed star designed to keep away evil spirits, principally the female incubus or witch.
222. *witch's foot:* the pentagram.

One's free in the first, in the second one's a thrall.

FAUST. So Hell itself has its regulations?
That's excellent; a contract in that case 240
Could be made with you, you gentry—and definite?

MEPHISTOPHELES. What we promise, you will enjoy with no reservations,
Nothing will be nipped off from it.
But all this needs a little explaining
And will keep till our next heart-to-heart; 245
But now I beg and doubly beg you:
Let me, just for now, depart.

FAUST. But wait yet a minute and consent
To tell me first some news of moment.

MEPHISTOPHELES. Let me go now! I'll soon be back 250
To be questioned to your heart's content.

FAUST. It was not I laid a trap for you,
You thrust your own head in the noose.
A devil in the hand's worth two in hell!
The second time he'll be longer loose. 255

MEPHISTOPHELES. If you so wish it, I'm prepared
To keep you company and stay;
Provided that by my arts the time
Be to your betterment whiled away.

FAUST. I am in favour, carry on— 260
But let your art be a pleasing one.

MEPHISTOPHELES. My friend, your senses will have more
Gratification in this hour
Than in a year's monotony.
What the delicate spirits sing to you 265
And the beauties that they bring to you
Are no empty, idle wizardry.
You'll have your sense of smell delighted,
Your palate in due course excited,
Your feelings rapt enchantingly. 270
Preparation? There's no need,
We are all here. Strike up! Proceed!

[*The* SPIRITS *sing.*]

SPIRITS. Vanish, you darkling
Arches above him,
That a more witching 275
Blue and enriching
Sky may look in!
If only the darkling
Clouds were unravelled!
Small stars are sparkling, 280
Suns are more gently
Shining within!

Spiritual beauty
Of the children of Heaven
Swaying and bowing 285
Floats in the air,
Leanings and longings
Follow them there;
And ribbons of raiment
The breezes have caught 290
Cover the country,
Cover the arbour
Where, drowning in thought,
Lovers exchange their
Pledges for life. 295
Arbour on arbour!
Creepers run rife!
Grapes in great wreathing
Clusters are poured into
Vats that are seething, 300
Wines that are foaming
Pour out in rivulets
Rippling and roaming
Through crystalline stones,
Leaving the sight of 305
The highlands behind them,
Widening to lakes
Amid the delight of
Green-growing foothills.
And the winged creatures 310
Sipping their ecstasy,
Sunwards they fly,
Fly to discover
The glittering islands
Which bob on the wave-tops 315
Deceiving the eye.
There we can hear
Huzzaing in chorus,
A landscape of dancers
Extending before us, 320
All in the open,
Free as the air.
Some of them climbing
Over the peaks,
Some of them swimming 325
Over the lakes,
Or floating in space—
All towards existence,
All towards the distance

Of stars that will love them, 330
The blessing of grace.

MEPHISTOPHELES. He is asleep. That's fine, you airy, dainty youngsters
You have sung him a real cradle song.
For this performance I am in your debt.
You are not yet the man to hold the devil for long. 335
Play round him with your sweet dream trickeries
And sink him in a sea of untruth!
But to break the spell upon this threshold
What I need now is a rat's tooth.
And I needn't bother to wave a wand, 340
I can hear one rustling already, he'll soon respond.
The lord of rats, the lord of mice,
Of flies, frogs, bugs and lice,
Commands you to come out of that
And gnaw away this threshold, rat, 345
While he takes oil and gives it a few—
So there you come hopping? Quick on your cue!
Now get on the job! The obstructing point
Is on the edge and right in front.
One bite more and the work's done. 350
Now, Faust, till we meet again, dream on!

FAUST. [*Waking*] Am I defrauded then once more?
Does the throng of spirits vanish away like fog
To prove that the devil appeared to me in a dream
But what escaped was only a dog? 355

FAUST'S STUDY

The same room. Later.

FAUST. Who's knocking? Come in! *Now* who wants to annoy me?
MEPHISTOPHELES. [*Outside door*] It's I.
FAUST. Come in!
MEPHISTOPHELES. [*Outside door*]
You must say 'Come in' three times.
FAUST. Come in then! 5
MEPHISTOPHELES. [*Entering*] Thank you; you overjoy me.
We two, I hope, we shall be good friends;
To chase those megrims of yours away
I am here like a fine young squire to-day,
In a suit of scarlet trimmed with gold 10
And a little cape of stiff brocade,
With a cock's feather in my hat
And at my side a long sharp blade,

9. *a fine young squire:* In the popular plays based on the Faust legend, the devil often appeared as a monk when the play catered to a Protestant audience, and as a cavalier when the audience was predominantly Catholic.

And the most succinct advice I can give
Is that you dress up just like me, 15
So that uninhibited and free
You may find out what it means to live.

FAUST. The pain of earth's constricted life, I fancy,
Will pierce me still, whatever my attire;
I am too old for mere amusement, 20
Too young to be without desire.
How can the world dispel my doubt?
You must do without, you must do without!
That is the everlasting song
Which rings in every ear, which rings, 25
And which to us our whole life long
Every hour hoarsely sings.
I wake in the morning only to feel appalled,
My eyes with bitter tears could run
To see the day which in its course 30
Will not fulfil a wish for me, not one;
The day which whittles away with obstinate carping
All pleasures—even those of anticipation,
Which makes a thousand grimaces to obstruct
My heart when it is stirring in creation. 35
And again, when night comes down, in anguish
I must stretch out upon my bed
And again no rest is granted me,
For wild dreams fill my mind with dread.
The God who dwells within my bosom 40
Can make my inmost soul react;
The God who sways my every power
Is powerless with external fact.
And so existence weighs upon my breast
And I long for death and life—life I detest. 45

MEPHISTOPHELES. Yet death is never a wholly welcome guest.

FAUST. O happy is he whom death in the dazzle of victory
Crowns with the bloody laurel in the battling swirl!
Or he whom after the mad and breakneck dance
He comes upon in the arms of a girl! 50
O to have sunk away, delighted, deleted,
Before the Spirit of the Earth, before his might!

MEPHISTOPHELES. Yet I know someone who failed to drink
A brown juice on a certain night.

FAUST. Your hobby is espionage—is it not? 55

MEPHISTOPHELES. Oh I'm not omniscient—but I know a lot.

FAUST. Whereas that tumult in my soul
Was stilled by sweet familiar chimes
Which cozened the child that yet was in me
With echoes of more happy times, 60

I now curse all things that encompass
The soul with lures and jugglery
And bind it in this dungeon of grief
With trickery and flattery.
Cursed in advance be the high opinion 65
That serves our spirit for a cloak!
Cursed be the dazzle of appearance
Which bows our senses to its yoke!
Cursed be the lying dreams of glory,
The illusion that our name survives! 70
Cursed be the flattering things we own,
Servants and ploughs, children and wives!
Cursed be Mammon when with his treasures
He makes us play the adventurous man
Or when for our luxurious pleasures 75
He duly spreads the soft divan!
A curse on the balsam of the grape!
A curse on the love that rides for a fall!
A curse on hope! A curse on faith!
And a curse on patience most of all! 80

[*The invisible* SPIRITS *sing again.*]

SPIRITS. Woe! Woe!
You have destroyed it,
The beautiful world;
By your violent hand
'Tis downward hurled! 85
A half-god has dashed it asunder!
From under
We bear off the rubble to nowhere
And ponder
Sadly the beauty departed. 90
Magnipotent
One among men,
Magnificent
Build it again,
Build it again in your breast! 95
Let a new course of life
Begin
With vision abounding
And new songs resounding
To welcome it in! 100

MEPHISTOPHELES. These are the juniors
Of my faction.
Hear how precociously they counsel

73. *Mammon:* the Aramaic word for "riches," used in the New Testament; medieval writers interpreted the word as a proper noun, the name of the devil, as representing covetousness or avarice.

Pleasure and action.
Out and away 105
From your lonely day
Which dries your senses and your juices
Their melody seduces.

Stop playing with your grief which battens
Like a vulture on your life, your mind! 110
The worst of company would make you feel
That you are a man among mankind.
Not that it's really my proposition
To shove you among the common men:
Though I'm not one of the Upper Ten, 115
If you would like a coalition
With me for your career through life,
I am quite ready to fit in,
I'm yours before you can say knife.
I am your comrade; 120
If you so crave,
I am your servant, I am your slave.

FAUST. And what have I to undertake in return?

MEPHISTOPHELES. Oh it's early days to discuss what that is.

FAUST. No, no, the devil is an egoist 125
And ready to do nothing gratis
Which is to benefit a stranger.
Tell me your terms and don't prevaricate!
A servant like you in the house is a danger.

MEPHISTOPHELES. I will bind myself to your service in this world,
To be at your beck and never rest nor slack;
When we meet again on the other side,
In the same coin you shall pay me back.

FAUST. The other side gives me little trouble;
First batter this present world to rubble, 135
Then the other may rise—if that's the plan.
This earth is where my springs of joy have started,
And this sun shines on me when broken-hearted;
If I can first from them be parted,
Then let happen what will and can! 140
I wish to hear no more about it—
Whether there too men hate and love
Or whether in those spheres too, in the future,
There is a Below or an Above.

MEPHISTOPHELES. With such an outlook you can risk it. 145
Sign on the line! In these next days you will get
Ravishing samples of my arts;
I am giving you what never man saw yet.

FAUST. Poor devil, can *you* give anything ever?
Was a human spirit in its high endeavour 150
Even once understood by one of your breed?
Have you got food which fails to feed?
Or red gold which, never at rest,
Like mercury runs away through the hand?
A game at which one never wins? 155
A girl who, even when on my breast,
Pledges herself to my neighbour with her eyes?
The divine and lovely delight of honour
Which falls like a falling star and dies?
Show me the fruits which, before they are plucked, decay 160
And the trees which day after day renew their green!

MEPHISTOPHELES. Such a commission doesn't alarm me,
I have such treasures to purvey.
But, my good friend, the time draws on when we
Should be glad to feast at our ease on something good. 165

FAUST. If ever I stretch myself on a bed of ease,
Then I am finished! Is that understood?
If ever your flatteries can coax me
To be pleased with myself, if ever you cast
A spell of pleasure that can hoax me— 170
Then let *that* day be my last!
That's my wager!

MEPHISTOPHELES. Done!

FAUST. Let's shake!
If ever I say to the passing moment 175
'Linger a while! Thou art so fair!'
Then you may cast me into fetters,
I will gladly perish then and there!
Then you may set the death-bell tolling,
Then from my service you are free, 180
The clock may stop, its hand may fall,
And that be the end of time for me!

MEPHISTOPHELES. Think what you're saying, we shall not forget it.

FAUST. And you are fully within your rights;
I have made no mad or outrageous claim. 185
If I stay as I am, I am a slave—
Whether yours or another's, it's all the same.

MEPHISTOPHELES. I shall this very day at the College Banquet
Enter your service with no more ado,
But just one point—As a life-and-death insurance 190
I must trouble you for a line or two.

FAUST. So you, you pedant, you too like things in writing?
Have you never known a man? Or a man's word? Never?

188. *College Banquet:* actually the *Doctorschmaus,* or dinner given by a successful candidate for a Ph.D. degree.

Is it not enough that my word of mouth
Puts all my days in bond for ever? 195
Does not the world rage on in all its streams
And shall a promise hamper *me?*
Yet this illusion reigns within our hearts
And from it who would be gladly free?
Happy the man who can inwardly keep his word; 200
Whatever the cost, he will not be loath to pay!
But a parchment, duly inscribed and sealed,
Is a bogey from which all wince away.
The word dies on the tip of the pen
And wax and leather lord it then. 205
What do you, evil spirit, require?
Bronze, marble, parchment, paper?
Quill or chisel or pencil of slate?
You may choose whichever you desire.

MEPHISTOPHELES. How can you so exaggerate 210
With such a hectic rhetoric?
Any little snippet is quite good—
And you sign it with one little drop of blood.

FAUST. If that is enough and is some use,
One may as well pander to your fad. 215

MEPHISTOPHELES. Blood is a very special juice.

FAUST. Only do not fear that I shall break this contract.
What I promise is nothing more
Than what all my powers are striving for.
I have puffed myself up too much, it is only 220
Your sort that really fits my case.
The great Earth Spirit has despised me
And Nature shuts the door in my face.
The thread of thoughts is snapped asunder,
I have long loathed knowledge in all its fashions. 225
In the depths of sensuality
Let us now quench our glowing passions!
And at once make ready every wonder
Of unpenetrated sorcery!
Let us cast ourselves into the torrent of time, 230
Into the whirl of eventfulness,
Where disappointment and success,
Pleasure and pain may chop and change
As chop and change they will and can;
It is restless action makes the man. 235

MEPHISTOPHELES. No limit is fixed for you, no bound;
If you'd like to nibble at everything

213. *blood:* This method of confirming an agreement with the devil is older than the Faust legend—in which it always appears—and is partly a parody of the rôle of blood in the Christian Sacrament.

Or to seize upon something flying round—
Well, may you have a run for your money!
But seize your chance and don't be funny! 240

FAUST. I've told you, it is no question of happiness.
The most painful joy, enamoured hate, enlivening
Disgust—I devote myself to all excess.
My breast, now cured of its appetite for knowledge,
From now is open to all and every smart, 245
And what is allotted to the whole of mankind
That will I sample in my inmost heart,
Grasping the highest and lowest with my spirit,
Piling men's weal and woe upon my neck,
To extend myself to embrace all human selves 250
And to founder in the end, like them, a wreck.

MEPHISTOPHELES. O believe *me*, who have been chewing
These iron rations many a thousand year,
No human being can digest
This stuff, from the cradle to the bier. 255
This universe—believe a devil—
Was made for no one but a god!
He exists in eternal light
But *us* he has brought into the darkness
While *your* sole portion is day and night. 260

FAUST. I will all the same!

MEPHISTOPHELES. That's very nice.
There's only one thing I find wrong;
Time is short, art is long.
You could do with a little artistic advice. 265
Confederate with one of the poets
And let him flog his imagination
To heap all virtues on your head,
A head with such a reputation:
Lion's bravery, 270
Stag's velocity,
Fire of Italy,
Northern tenacity.
Let *him* find out the secret art
Of combining craft with a noble heart 275
And of being in love like a young man,
Hotly, but working to a plan.
Such a person—*I'd* like to meet him;
'Mr. Microcosm' is how I'd greet him.

FAUST. What am I then if fate must bar 280
My efforts to reach that crown of humanity
After which all my senses strive?

279. ***Mr. Microcosm:*** **i.e., man viewed as the epitome of the universe.**

MEPHISTOPHELES. You are in the end . . . what you are.
You can put on full-bottomed wigs with a million locks,
You can put on stilts instead of your socks, 285
You remain for ever what you are.

FAUST. I feel my endeavours have not been worth a pin
When I raked together the treasures of the human mind,
If at the end I but sit down to find
No new force welling up within. 290
I have not a hair's breadth more of height,
I am no nearer the Infinite.

MEPHISTOPHELES. My very good sir, you look at things
Just in the way that people do;
We must be cleverer than that 295
Or the joys of life will escape from you.
Hell! You have surely hands and feet,
Also a head and you-know-what;
The pleasures I gather on the wing,
Are they less mine? Of course they're not! 300
Suppose I can afford six stallions,
I can add that horse-power to my score
And dash along and be a proper man
As if my legs were twenty-four.
So good-bye to thinking! On your toes! 305
The world's before us. Quick! Here goes!
I tell you, a chap who's intellectual
Is like a beast on a blasted heath
Driven in circles by a demon
While a fine green meadow lies round beneath. 310

FAUST. How do we start?

MEPHISTOPHELES. We just say go—and skip.
But please get ready for this pleasure trip.
[*Exit* FAUST.]
Only look down on knowledge and reason,
The highest gifts that men can prize, 315
Only allow the spirit of lies
To confirm you in magic and illusion,
And then I have you body and soul.
Fate has given this man a spirit
Which is always pressing onwards, beyond control, 320
And whose mad striving overleaps
All joys of the earth between pole and pole.
Him shall I drag through the wilds of life
And through the flats of meaninglessness,
I shall make him flounder and gape and stick 325
And to tease his insatiableness
Hang meat and drink in the air before his watering lips;
In vain he will pray to slake his inner thirst,

And even had he not sold himself to the devil
He would be equally accursed.[a] 330
[*Re-enter* FAUST.]
FAUST. And now, where are we going?
MEPHISTOPHELES. Wherever you please.
The small world, then the great for us.
With what pleasure and what profit
You will roister through the syllabus! 335
FAUST. But I, with this long beard of mine,
I lack the easy social touch,
I know the experiment is doomed;
Out in the world I never could fit in much.
I feel so small in company 340
I'll be embarrassed constantly.
MEPHISTOPHELES. My friend, it will solve itself, any such mis giving;
Just trust yourself and you'll learn the art of living.
FAUST. Well, then, how do we leave home?
Where are your grooms? Your coach and horses? 345
MEPHISTOPHELES. We merely spread this mantle wide,
It will bear us off on airy courses.
But do not on this noble voyage
Cumber yourself with heavy baggage.
A little inflammable gas which I'll prepare 350
Will lift us quickly into the air.
If we travel light we shall cleave the sky like a knife.
Congratulations on your new course of life![b]

THE WITCH'S KITCHEN[c]

Every sort of witch prop. A large cauldron hangs over the fire. MONKEYS *sit around it, seen through the fumes.*

MEPHISTOPHELES. Look, what a pretty species of monkey!
She is the kitchen-maid, he is the flunkey.
It seems your mistress isn't at home?
MONKEYS. Out at a rout!
Out and about! 5
By the chimney spout!
MEPHISTOPHELES. How long does she keep it up at night?
MONKEYS. As long as we warm our paws at this fire.

a. Between Faust's exit and entrance, the translator omits a scene in which Mephistopheles cynically interviews one of Faust's students.

350. *gas:* indicative of Goethe's scientific interests. The first hydrogen balloon was sent aloft in Paris in 1783, and several letters by Goethe refer to this new experiment.

b. The translator omits the next scene, in Auerbach's Cellar, where Faust and Mephistopheles join a group of genial drinking companions and Mephistopheles performs the trick—traditional in early Faust stories—of making wine flow from the table.

c. Certain transpositions have been made in this scene. [Translator's note.]

MEPHISTOPHELES. How do you like these delicate animals?
FAUST. I never saw such an outré sight. 10
I find it nauseating, this crazy witchcraft!
Do you promise me that I shall improve
In this cesspit of insanity?
Do I need advice from an old hag?
And can this filthy brew remove 15
Thirty years from my age? O vanity,
If you know nothing better than this!
My hope has already vanished away.
Surely Nature, surely a noble spirit
Has brought some better balm to the light of day? 20
MEPHISTOPHELES. My friend, you once more talk to the point.
There is also a natural means of rejuvenation;
But that is written in another book
And is a chapter that needs some explanation.
FAUST. I want to know it. 25
MEPHISTOPHELES. Right. There is a means requires
No money, no physician, and no witch:
Away with you this moment back to the land,
And there begin to dig and ditch,
Confine yourself, confine your mind, 30
In a narrow round, ever repeating,
Let your diet be of the simplest kind,
Live with the beasts like a beast and do not think it cheating
To use your own manure to insure your crops are weighty!
Believe me, that is the best means 35
To keep you young till you are eighty.
FAUST. I am not used to it, I cannot change
My nature and take the spade in hand.
The narrow life is not my style at all.
MEPHISTOPHELES. Then it's a job for the witch to arrange. 40
FAUST. The hag—but why do we need just her?
Can you yourself not brew the drink?
MEPHISTOPHELES. A pretty pastime! I'd prefer
To build a thousand bridges in that time.
It is not only art and science 45
That this work needs but patience too.
A quiet spirit is busy at it for years
And time but fortifies the subtle brew.
And the most wonderful ingredients
Go into it—you couldn't fake it! 50

11. *crazy witchcraft:* In composing this scene, Goethe may have had in mind certain paintings by the Flemish artists David Teniers the Younger (1610–1690) and Pieter Breughel the Younger (1564?–1638).

44. *bridges:* The folk legend existed that the devil built bridges at the request of men. As a reward, he caught either the first or the thirteenth soul to cross each new bridge.

The devil taught it her, I admit;
The devil, however, cannot make it.
Tell me, you monkeys, you damned puppets,
What are you doing with that great globe?

HE-MONKEY. This is the world: 55
It rises and falls
And rolls every minute;
It rings like glass—
But how soon it breaks!
And there's nothing in it. 60
It glitters here
And here still more:
I am alive!
O my son, my dear,
Keep away, keep away! 65
You are bound to die!
The shards are sharp,
It was made of clay.

[FAUST *has meanwhile been gazing in a mirror.*]

FAUST. What do I see in this magic mirror?
What a heavenly image to appear! 70
O Love, lend me the swiftest of your wings
And waft me away into her sphere!
But, alas, when I do not keep this distance,
If to go nearer I but dare
I can see her only as if there were mist in the air— 75
The fairest image of a woman!
But can Woman be so fair?
In that shape in the mirror must I see the quintessence
Of all the heavens—reclining there?
Can such a thing be found on earth? 80

MEPHISTOPHELES. Naturally, when a God works six days like a black
And at the end of it slaps himself on the back,
Something should come of it of some worth.
For this occasion look your fill.
I can smell you out a sweetheart as good as this, 85
And happy the man who has the luck
To bear her home to wedded bliss.

[*The* WITCH *enters down the chimney—violently.*]

WITCH. What goes on here?
Who are you two?
What d'you want here? 90
Who has sneaked through?
May the fever of fire
Harrow your marrow!

MEPHISTOPHELES. Don't you know me, you bag of bones? You monster, you!

Don't you know your lord and master? 95
What prevents me striking you
And your monkey spirits, smashing you up like plaster?
Has my red doublet no more claim to fame?
Can you not recognize the cock's feather?
Have I concealed my countenance? 100
Must I myself announce my name?

WITCH. My lord, excuse this rude reception.
It is only I miss your cloven foot.
And where is your usual brace of ravens?

MEPHISTOPHELES. I'll forgive you this once, as an exception; 105
Admittedly some time has pass't
Since we two saw each other last.
Culture too, which is licking the whole world level,
Has latterly even reached the devil.
The Nordic spook no longer commands a sale; 110
Where can you see horns, claws or tail?
And as regards the foot, which is my *sine qua non*,
It would prejudice me in the social sphere;
Accordingly, as many young men have done,
I have worn false calves this many a year. 115

WITCH. Really and truly I'm knocked flat
To see Lord Satan here again!

MEPHISTOPHELES. Woman, you must not call me that!

WITCH. Why! What harm is there in the name?

MEPHISTOPHELES. Satan has long been a myth without sense or
sinew; 120
Not that it helps humanity all the same,
They are quit of the Evil One but the evil ones continue.
You may call me the Noble Baron, that should do;
I am a cavalier among other cavaliers,
You needn't doubt my blood is blue— 125
[*He makes an indecent gesture.*]

WITCH. Ha! Ha! Always true to type!
You still have the humour of a guttersnipe!

MEPHISTOPHELES. Observe my technique, my friend—not a single
hitch;
This is the way to get round a witch.

WITCH. Now tell me, gentlemen, what do you want? 130

MEPHISTOPHELES. A good glass of your well-known juice.
And please let us have your oldest vintage;
When it's been kept it's twice the use.

WITCH. Delighted! Why, there's some here on the shelf—
I now and then take a nip myself— 135
And, besides, this bottle no longer stinks;

104. *brace of ravens:* Perhaps Goethe was thinking of the Norse god Odin, who owned two such birds: Hugin (Thought) and Munin (Memory).

You're welcome while I've a drop to give.
[*Aside*] But, if this man is unprepared when he drinks,
You very well know he has not an hour to live.

MEPHISTOPHELES. He's a good friend and it should set him up; 140
I'd gladly grant him the best of your kitchen,
So draw your circle and do your witching
And give the man a decent cup.

[*The* WITCH *begins her conjuration.*]

FAUST. But, tell me, how will this mend my status?
These lunatic gestures, this absurd apparatus, 145
This most distasteful conjuring trick—
I've known it all, it makes me sick.

MEPHISTOPHELES. Pooh, that's just fooling, get it in focus,
And don't be such a prig for goodness' sake!
As a doctor she must do her hocus-pocus 150
So that when you have drunk your medicine it will take.

WITCH. The lofty power
That is wisdom's dower,
Concealed from great and clever,
Don't use your brain 155
And that's your gain—
No trouble whatsoever.

FAUST. What nonsense is she saying to us?
My head is splitting; I've the sensation
Of listening to a hundred thousand 160
Idiots giving a mass recitation.

MEPHISTOPHELES. Enough, enough, you excellent Sibyl!
Give us your drink and fill the cup
Full to the brim and don't delay!
This draught will do my friend no injury; 165
He is a man of more than one degree
And has drunk plenty in his day.

[*The* WITCH *gives* FAUST *the cup.*]

Now lower it quickly. Bottoms up!
And your heart will begin to glow and perk.
Now out of the circle! You mustn't rest. 170

WITCH. I hope the little drink will work.

MEPHISTOPHELES. [*To* WITCH] And you, if there's anything you want, all right;
Just mention it to me on Walpurgis Night.
[*To* FAUST] Come now, follow me instantly!
You've got to perspire, it's necessary, 175
That the drug may pervade you inside and out.

173. ***Walpurgis Night:*** the eve of May Day (May 1), when witches are supposed to assemble on the Brocken, a peak in the Harz Mountains.

I can teach you later to value lordly leisure
And you soon will learn with intensest pleasure
How Cupid stirs within and bounds about.

FAUST. Just one more look, one quick look, in the mirror! 180
That woman was too fair to be true.

MEPHISTOPHELES. No, no! The paragon of womanhood
Will soon be revealed in the flesh to you.
[*Aside*] With a drink like this in you, take care—
You'll soon see Helens everywhere. 185

IN THE STREET

FAUST *accosts* GRETCHEN *as she passes.*

FAUST. My pretty young lady, might I venture
To offer you my arm and my escort too?

GRETCHEN. I'm not a young lady nor am I pretty
And I can get home without help from you.
[*She releases herself and goes off.*]

FAUST. By Heaven, she's beautiful, this child! 5
I have never seen her parallel.
So decorous, so virtuous,
And just a little pert as well.
The light of her cheek, her lip so red,
I shall remember till I'm dead! 10
The way that she cast down her eye
Is stamped on my heart as with a die;
And the way that she got rid of me
Was a most ravishing thing to see!
[*Enter* MEPHISTOPHELES.]
Listen to me! Get me that girl! 15

MEPHISTOPHELES. Which one?

FAUST. The one that just went past.

MEPHISTOPHELES. She? She was coming from her priest,
Absolved from her sins one and all;
I'd crept up near the confessional. 20
An innocent thing. Innocent? Yes!
At church with nothing to confess!
Over that girl I have no power.

FAUST. Yet she's fourteen if she's an hour.

MEPHISTOPHELES. Why, you're talking like Randy Dick 25
Who covets every lovely flower
And all the favours, all the laurels,
He fancies are for him to pick;

185. *Helens:* Faust marries Helen of Troy in the second part of *Faust*.
25. *Randy Dick:* in the original German, "Hans Liederlich"—i.e., a profligate, since *liederlich* means "careless" or "dissolute."

But it doesn't always work out like that.
FAUST. My dear Professor of Ancient Morals, 30
Spare me your trite morality!
I tell you straight—and hear me right—
Unless this object of delight
Lies in my arms this very night,
At midnight we part company. 35
MEPHISTOPHELES. Haven't you heard: more haste less speed?
A fortnight is the least I need
Even to work up an occasion.
FAUST. If I had only seven hours clear,
I should not need the devil here 40
To bring *this* quest to consummation.
MEPHISTOPHELES. It's almost French, your line of talk;
I only ask you not to worry.
Why make your conquest in a hurry?
The pleasure is less by a long chalk 45
Than when you first by hook and by crook
Have squeezed your doll and moulded her,
Using all manner of poppycock
That foreign novels keep in stock.
FAUST. I am keen enough without all that. 50
MEPHISTOPHELES. Now, joking apart and without aspersion,
You cannot expect, I tell you flat,
This beautiful child in quick reversion.
Immune to all direct attack—
We must lay our plots behind her back. 55
FAUST. Get me something of my angel's!
Carry me to her place of rest!
Get me a garter of my love's!
Get me a kerchief from her breast!
MEPHISTOPHELES. That you may see the diligent fashion 60
In which I shall abet your passion,
We won't let a moment waste away,
I will take you to her room to-day.
FAUST. And shall I see her? Have her?
MEPHISTOPHELES. No! 65
She will be visiting a neighbour.
But you in the meanwhile, quite alone,
Can stay in her aura in her room
And feast your fill on joys to come.
FAUST. Can we go now? 70
MEPHISTOPHELES. It is still too soon.

30. *Professor:* in the original German, Herr Magister Lobesan ("Master Worshipful")—stuffed shirt, or academic prig.

FAUST Then a present for her! Get me one!
[*Exit* FAUST.]
MEPHISTOPHELES. Presents already? Fine. A certain hit!
I know plenty of pretty places
And of long-buried jewel-cases; 75
I must take stock of them a bit.

GRETCHEN'S ROOM

GRETCHEN. [*Alone, doing her hair*] I'd give a lot to be able to say
Who the gentleman was to-day.
He cut a fine figure certainly
And is sprung from nobility;
His face showed that—Besides, you see, 5
He'd otherwise not have behaved so forwardly.
[*She goes out; then* MEPHISTOPHELES *and* FAUST *enter.*]
MEPHISTOPHELES. Come in—very quietly—Only come in!
FAUST. [*After a silence*] I ask you: please leave me alone!
MEPHISTOPHELES. Not all girls keep their room so clean.
FAUST. [*Looking around*] Welcome, sweet gleaming of the gloaming 10
That through this sanctuary falls aslope!
Seize on my heart, sweet fever of love
That lives and languishes on the dews of hope!
What a feeling of quiet breathes around me,
Of order, of contentedness! 15
What fulness in this poverty,
And in this cell what blessedness!

Here I could while away hour after hour.
It was here, O Nature, that your fleeting dreams
Brought this born angel to full flower. 20
Here lay the child and the warm life
Filled and grew in her gentle breast,
And here the pure and holy threads
Wove a shape of the heavenliest.

And you! What brought you here to-day? 25
Why do I feel this deep dismay?
What do you want here? Why is your heart so sore?
Unhappy Faust! You are Faust no more.

Is this an enchanted atmosphere?
To have her at once was all my aim, 30
Yet I feel my will dissolve in a lovesick dream.
Are we the sport of every current of air?

And were she this moment to walk in,
You would pay for this outrage, how you would pay!
The big man, now, alas, so small, 35
Would lie at her feet melted away.

MEPHISTOPHELES. Quick! I can see her coming below.

FAUST. Out, yes out! I'll never come back!

MEPHISTOPHELES. Here is a casket, it's middling heavy,
I picked it up in a place I know. 40
Only put it at once here in the cupboard,
I swear she won't believe her eyes;
I put some nice little trinkets in it
In order to win a different prize.
Still child is child and a game's a game. 45

FAUST. I don't know; shall I?

MEPHISTOPHELES. You ask? For shame!
Do you perhaps intend to keep the spoil?
Then I advise Your Lustfulness
To save these hours that are so precious 50
And save me any further toil.
I hope you aren't avaricious.
After scratching my head so much and twisting my hands—
[*He puts the casket in the cupboard.*]
Now quick! We depart!
In order to sway the dear young thing 55
To meet the dearest wish of your heart;
And *you* assume
A look that belongs to the lecture room,
As if Physics and Metaphysics too
Stood grey as life in front of you! 60
Come on!
[*They go out; then* GRETCHEN *reappears.*]

GRETCHEN. It is so sultry, so fusty here,
And it's not even so warm outside.
I feel as if I don't know what—
I wish my mother would appear. 65
I'm trembling all over from top to toe—
I'm a silly girl to get frightened so.
[*She sings as she undresses.*]
There was a king in Thule
Was faithful to the grave,

68. *Thule:* the fabled *ultima Thule* of Latin literature—those distant lands just beyond the reach of every explorer. In Roman times, the phrase probably denoted the Shetland Islands. Goethe wrote this ballad in 1774; it was published and set to music in 1782. The poem also served as the inspiration for the slow movement of Mendelssohn's *Italian Symphony*.

To whom his dying lady 70
A golden winecup gave.

He drained it at every banquet—
A treasure none could buy;
Whenever he filled and drank it
The tears o'erflowed his eye. 75

And when his days were numbered
He numbered land and pelf;
He left his heir his kingdom,
The cup he kept himself.

He sat at the royal table 80
With his knights of high degree
In the lofty hall of his fathers
In the castle on the sea.

There stood the old man drinking
The last of the living glow, 85
Then threw the sacred winecup
Into the waves below.

He saw it fall and falter
And founder in the main;
His eyelids fell, thereafter 90
He never drank again.

[*She opens the cupboard to put away her clothes and sees the casket.*]

How did this lovely casket get in here?
I locked the cupboard, I'm quite sure.
But what can be in it? It's very queer.
Perhaps someone left it here in pawn 95
And my mother gave him a loan on it.
Here's a little key tied on with tape—
I've a good mind to open it.
What is all this? My God! But see!
I have never come across such things. 100
Jewels—that would suit a countess
At a really grand festivity.
To whom can these splendid things belong?

[*She tries on the jewels and looks in the looking-glass.*]

If only the ear-rings belonged to me!
They make one look quite differently. 105
What is the use of looks and youth?
That's all very well and fine in truth

But people leave it all alone,
They praise you and pity you in one;
Gold is their sole 110
Concern and goal.
Alas for us who have none!

A WALK

Elsewhere and later. MEPHISTOPHELES *joins* FAUST.

MEPHISTOPHELES. By every despised love! By the elements of hell!
I wish I knew something worse to provide a curse as well!
FAUST. What's the trouble? What's biting you?
I never saw such a face in my life.
MEPHISTOPHELES. I would sell myself to the devil this minute 5
If only I weren't a devil too.
FAUST. What is it? Are you mad? Or sick?
It suits you to rage like a lunatic!
MEPHISTOPHELES. Imagine! The jewels that Gretchen got,
A priest has gone and scooped the lot! 10
Her mother got wind of it and she
At once had the horrors secretly.
That woman has a nose beyond compare,
She's always snuffling in the Book of Prayer,
And can tell by how each object smells 15
If it is sacred or something else;
So the scent of the jewels tells her clear
There's nothing very blessed here.
'My child,' she cries, 'unrighteous wealth
Invests the soul, infects the health. 20
We'll dedicate it to the Virgin
And *she'll* make heavenly manna burgeon!'
Gretchen's face, you could see it fall;
She thought: 'It's a gift-horse after all,
And he *can't* be lacking in sanctity 25
Who brought it here so handsomely!'
The mother had a priest along
And had hardly started up her song
Before he thought things looked all right
And said: 'Very proper and above board! 30
Self-control is its own reward.
The Church has an excellent appetite,
She has swallowed whole countries and the question
Has never arisen of indigestion.
Only the Church, my dears, can take 35
Ill-gotten goods without stomach-ache!'

FAUST. That is a custom the world through,
A Jew and a king observe it too.
MEPHISTOPHELES. So brooch, ring, chain he swipes at speed
As if they were merely chicken-feed, 40
Thanks them no more and no less for the casket
Than for a pound of nuts in a basket,
Promises Heaven will provide
And leaves them extremely edified.
FAUST. And Gretchen? 45
MEPHISTOPHELES. Sits and worries there,
Doesn't know what to do and doesn't care,
Thinks day and night on gold and gem,
Still more on the man who presented them.
FAUST. My sweetheart's grief distresses me. 50
Get her more jewels instantly!
The first lot barely deserved the name.
MEPHISTOPHELES. So the gentleman thinks it all a nursery game!
FAUST. Do what I tell you and get it right;
Don't let her neighbour out of your sight. 55
And don't be a sloppy devil; contrive
A new set of jewels. Look alive!
[*Exit* FAUST.]
MEPHISTOPHELES. Yes, my dear sir, with all my heart.
This is the way that a fool in love
Puffs away to amuse his lady 60
Sun and moon and the stars above.

MARTHA'S HOUSE

MARTHA. [*Alone*] My dear husband, God forgive him,
His behaviour has *not* been without a flaw!
Careers away out into the world
And leaves me alone to sleep on straw.
And yet I never trod on his toes, 5
I loved him with all my heart, God knows. [*Sobs.*]
Perhaps he is even dead—O fate!
If I'd only a death certificate!
[GRETCHEN *enters.*]
GRETCHEN. Frau Martha!
MARTHA. Gretelchen! What's up? 10
GRETCHEN. My legs are sinking under me,
I've just discovered in my cupboard
Another casket—of ebony,
And things inside it, such a store,
Far richer than the lot before. 15
MARTHA. You mustn't mention it to your mother;

She'd take it straight to the priest—like the other.
GRETCHEN. But only look! Just look at this!
MARTHA. O you lucky little Miss!
GRETCHEN. I daren't appear in the street, I'm afraid, 20
Or in church either, thus arrayed.
MARTHA. Just you visit me often here
And put on the jewels secretly!
Walk up and down for an hour in front of my glass
And that will be fun for you and me; 25
And then an occasion may offer, a holiday,
Where one can let them be seen in a gradual way;
A necklace to start with, then a pearl ear-ring; your mother
Most likely won't see; if she does one can think up something or other.
GRETCHEN. But who brought these two cases, who could it be? 30
It doesn't seem quite right to me.
[*Knocking.*]
My God! My mother? Is that her?
MARTHA. It is a stranger. Come in, sir!
[*Enter* MEPHISTOPHELES.]
MEPHISTOPHELES. I have made so free as to walk straight in;
The ladies will pardon me? May I begin 35
By inquiring for a Frau Martha Schwerdtlein?
MARTHA. That's me. What might the gentleman want?
MEPHISTOPHELES. [*Aside to* MARTHA] Now I know who you are, that's enough for me;
You have very distinguished company.
Forgive my bursting in so soon; 40
I will call again in the afternoon.
MARTHA. Imagine, child, in the name of Piety!
The gentleman takes you for society.
GRETCHEN. I'm a poor young thing, not at all refined;
My God, the gentleman is too kind. 45
These jewels and ornaments aren't my own.
MEPHISTOPHELES. Oh, it's not the jewellery alone;
She has a presence, a look so keen—
How delighted I am that I may remain.
MARTHA. What is your news? I cannot wait— 50
MEPHISTOPHELES. I wish I'd a better tale to relate.
I trust this will not earn me a beating:
Your husband is dead and sends his greeting.
MARTHA. Dead? The good soul? Oh why! Oh why!
My husband is dead! Oh I shall die! 55
GRETCHEN. Oh don't, dear woman, despair so.

36. *Schwerdtlein:* literally. "little sword." Her husband is a soldier.

MEPHISTOPHELES. Listen to my tale of woe!
GRETCHEN. Now, while I live, may I never love;
  Such a loss would bring me to my grave.
MEPHISTOPHELES. Joy must have grief, grief must have joy. 60
MARTHA. How was his end? Oh tell it me.
MEPHISTOPHELES. He lies buried in Padua
  At the church of Holy Anthony,
  In properly consecrated ground
  Where he sleeps for ever cool and sound. 65
MARTHA. Have you nothing else for me? Is that all?
MEPHISTOPHELES. Yes, a request; it's heavy and fat.
  You must have three hundred masses said for his soul.
  My pockets are empty apart from that.
MARTHA. What! Not a trinket? Not a token? 70
  What every prentice keeps at the bottom of his bag
  And saves it up as a souvenir
  And would sooner starve and sooner beg—
MEPHISTOPHELES. Madam, you make me quite heart-broken.
  But, really and truly, he didn't squander his money. 75
  And, besides, he repented his mistakes,
  Yes, and lamented still more his unlucky breaks.
GRETCHEN. Alas that men should be so unlucky!
  Be assured I shall often pray that he may find rest above.
MEPHISTOPHELES. *You* deserve to be taken straight to the altar; 80
  You are a child a man could love.
GRETCHEN. No, no, it's not yet time for that.
MEPHISTOPHELES. Then, if not a husband, a lover will do.
  It's one of the greatest gifts of Heaven
  To hold in one's arms a thing like you. 85
GRETCHEN. That is not the custom of our race.
MEPHISTOPHELES. Custom or not, it's what takes place.
MARTHA. But tell me!
MEPHISTOPHELES. His deathbed, where I stood,
  Was something better than a dungheap— 90
  Half-rotten straw; however, he died like a Christian
  And found he had still a great many debts to make good.
  How thoroughly, he cried, I must hate myself
  To leave my job and my wife like that on the shelf!
  When I remember it, I die! 95
  If only she would forgive me here below!
MARTHA. Good man! I have forgiven him long ago.
MEPHISTOPHELES. All the same, God knows, she was more at fault
    than I.

63. *Anthony:* Mephistopheles' lie acquires added irony from the fact that this is one of Padua's most famous churches, its basilica holding the bones of St. Anthony.

MARTHA. That's a lie! To think he lied at the point of death!
MEPHISTOPHELES. He certainly fibbed a bit with his last breath, 100
If I'm half a judge of the situation.
I had no need, said he, to gape for recreation;
First getting children, then getting bread to feed 'em—
And bread in the widest sense, you know—
And I couldn't even eat my share in peace. 105
MARTHA. So all my love, my loyalty, went for naught,
My toiling and moiling without cease!
MEPHISTOPHELES. Not at all; he gave it profoundest thought.
When I left Malta—that was how he began—
I prayed for my wife and children like one demented 110
And Heaven heard me and consented
To let us capture a Turkish merchantman,
With a treasure for the Sultan himself on board.
Well, bravery got its due reward
And I myself, as was only fit, 115
I got a decent cut of it.
MARTHA. Eh! Eh! How? Where? Has he perhaps buried it?
MEPHISTOPHELES. Who knows where the four winds now have carried it?
As he lounged round Naples, quite unknown,
A pretty lady made him her friend, 120
She was so fond of him, so devoted,
He wore her colours at his blessed end.
MARTHA. The crook! The robber of his children!
Could no misery, no poverty,
Check the scandalous life he led! 125
MEPHISTOPHELES. You see! That is just why he's dead.
However, if I were placed like you,
I would mourn him modestly for a year
While looking round for someone new.
MARTHA. Ah God! My first one was so dear, 130
His like in this world will be hard to discover.
There could hardly be a more sweet little fool than mine.
It was only he was too fond of playing the rover,
And of foreign women and foreign wine,
And of the God-damned gaming-table. 135
MEPHISTOPHELES. Now, now, he might have still got by
If he on his part had been able
To follow your suit and wink an eye.
With that proviso, I swear, I too
Would give an engagement ring to you. 140
MARTHA. The gentleman is pleased to be witty.
MEPHISTOPHELES. [*Aside*] I had better go while the going's good;

She'd hold the devil to his word, she would!
And how is it with *your* heart, my pretty?
GRETCHEN. What does the gentleman mean? 145
MEPHISTOPHELES. [*Aside*] Good, innocent child!
Farewell, ladies!
GRETCHEN. Farewell!
MARTHA. O quickly! Tell me;
I'd like to have the evidence filed 150
Where, how and when my treasure died and was buried.
I have always liked things orderly and decent
And to read of his death in the weeklies would be pleasant.
MEPHISTOPHELES. Yes, Madam, when two witnesses are agreed,
The truth, as we all know, is guaranteed; 155
And I have a friend, an excellent sort,
I'll get him to swear you this in court.
I'll bring him here.
MARTHA. O yes! Please do!
MEPHISTOPHELES. And the young lady will be here too? 160
He's an honest lad. He's been around,
His politeness to ladies is profound.
GRETCHEN. I'll be all blushes in his presence.
MEPHISTOPHELES. No king on earth should so affect you.
MARTHA. Behind the house there—in my garden— 165
This evening—both of you—we'll expect you.

IN THE STREET

FAUST. How is it? Going ahead? Will it soon come right?
MEPHISTOPHELES. Excellent! Do I find you all on fire?
Gretchen is yours before many days expire.
You will see her at Martha's, her neighbour's house to-night
And that's a woman with a special vocation, 5
As it were, for the bawd-cum-gipsy occupation.
FAUST. Good!
MEPHISTOPHELES. But there is something *we* must do.
FAUST. One good turn deserves another. True.
MEPHISTOPHELES. It only means the legal attesting 10
That her husband's played-out limbs are resting
At Padua in consecrated ground.
FAUST. Very smart! I suppose we begin by going to Padua!
MEPHISTOPHELES. There's no need for that. What a simple lad you are!
Only bear witness and don't ask questions. 15
FAUST. The scheme's at an end if you have no better suggestions.
MEPHISTOPHELES. Oh there you go! What sanctity!
Is this the first time in your life

You have committed perjury?
God and the world and all that moves therein, 20
Man and the way his emotions and thoughts take place,
Have you not given downright definitions
Of these with an iron breast and a brazen face?
And if you will only look below the surface,
You must confess you knew as much of these 25
As you know to-day of Herr Schwerdtlein's late decease.

FAUST. You are and remain a sophist and a liar.

MEPHISTOPHELES. Quite so—if that is as deep as you'll inquire.
Won't you to-morrow on your honour
Befool poor Gretchen and swear before her 30
That all your soul is set upon her?

FAUST. And from my heart.

MEPHISTOPHELES. That's nice of you!
And your talk of eternal faith and love,
Of one single passion enthroned above 35
All others—will that be heartfelt too?

FAUST. Stop! It will! If I have feeling, if I
Feel this emotion, this commotion,
And can find no name to call it by;
If then I sweep the world with all my senses casting 40
Around for words and all the highest titles
And call this flame which burns my vitals
Endless, everlasting, everlasting,
Is that a devilish game of lies?

MEPHISTOPHELES. I'm right all the same. 45

FAUST. Listen! Mark this well,
I beg you, and spare me talking till I'm hoarse:
The man who *will* be right, provided he has a tongue,
Why, he'll be right of course.
But come, I'm tired of listening to your voice; 50
You're right, the more so since I have no choice.

MARTHA'S GARDEN

They are walking in pairs: MARTHA *with* MEPHISTOPHELES, GRETCHEN *on* FAUST'S *arm.*

GRETCHEN. The gentleman's only indulging me, I feel,
And condescending, to put me to shame.
You travellers are all the same,
You put up with things out of sheer good will.
I know too well that my poor conversation 5
Can't entertain a person of your station.

FAUST. One glance from you, one word, entertains me more

Than all this world's wisdom and lore.
[*He kisses her hand.*]
GRETCHEN. Don't go to such inconvenience! How could you kiss my hand?
It is so ugly, it is so rough. 10
I have had to work at Heaven knows what!
My mother's exacting, true enough.
[*They pass on.*]
MARTHA. And you, sir, do you always move round like this?
MEPHISTOPHELES. Oh, business and duty keep us up to the minute!
With what regret one often leaves a place 15
And yet one cannot ever linger in it.
MARTHA. That may go in one's salad days—
To rush all over the world at random;
But the evil time comes on apace
And to drag oneself to the grave a lonely bachelor 20
Is never much good in any case.
MEPHISTOPHELES. The prospect alarms me at a distant glance.
MARTHA. Then, worthy sir, be wise while you have the chance.
[*They pass on.*]
GRETCHEN. Yes, out of sight, out of mind!
You are polite to your finger-ends 25
But you have lots of clever friends
Who must leave *me* so far behind.
FAUST. Believe me, dearest, what the world calls clever
More often is vanity and narrowness.
GRETCHEN. What? 30
FAUST. Alas that simplicity, that innocence,
Cannot assess itself and its sacred value ever!
That humility, lowliness, the highest gifts
That living Nature has shared out to men—
GRETCHEN. Only think of *me* one little minute, 35
I shall have time enough to think of you again.
FAUST. You are much alone, I suppose?
GRETCHEN. Yes, our household's only small
But it needs running after all.
We have no maid; I must cook and sweep and knit 40
And sew and be always on the run,
And my mother looks into every detail—
Each single one.
Not that she has such need to keep expenses down;
We could spread ourselves more than some others do; 45
My father left us a decent property,

14. ***business:*** **Mephistopheles speaks as a traveling salesman.**

A little house with a garden outside town.
However, my days at the present are pretty quiet;
My brother's in the army,
My little sister is dead. 50
The child indeed had worn me to a thread;
Still, all that trouble, I'd have it again, I'd try it,
I loved her so.

FAUST. An angel, if she was like you!

GRETCHEN. I brought her up, she was very fond of me. 55
She was born after my father died,
We gave my mother up for lost,
Her life was at such a low, low tide,
And she only got better slowly, bit by bit;
The poor little creature, she could not even 60
Think for a minute of suckling it;
And so I brought her up quite alone
On milk and water; so she became my own.
On my own arm, on my own knee,
She smiled and kicked, grew fair to see. 65

FAUST. You felt, I am sure, the purest happiness.

GRETCHEN. Yes; and—be sure—many an hour of distress.
The little one's cradle stood at night
Beside my bed; she could hardly stir
But I was awake, 70
Now having to give her milk, now into my bed with her,
Now, if she went on crying, try to stop her
By getting up and dandling her up and down the room,
And then first thing in the morning stand at the copper;
Then off to the market and attend to the range, 75
And so on day after day, never a change.
Living like that, one can't always feel one's best;
But food tastes better for it, so does rest.
[*They pass on.*]

MARTHA. No, the poor women don't come out of it well,
A *vieux garçon* is a hard nut to crack. 80

MEPHISTOPHELES. It only rests with you and your like
To put me on a better tack.

MARTHA. Tell me, sir: have you never met someone you fancy?
Has your heart been nowhere involved among the girls?

MEPHISTOPHELES. The proverb says: A man's own fireside 85
And a good wife are gold and pearls.

MARTHA. I mean, have you never felt any inclination?

MEPHISTOPHELES. I've generally been received with all consideration.

MARTHA. What I wanted to say: has your heart never been serious?

MEPHISTOPHELES. To make a joke to a woman is always precarious.

MARTHA. Oh you don't understand me!

MEPHISTOPHELES. Now *that* I really mind!

But I do understand—that you are very kind.

[*They pass on.*]

FAUST. You knew me again, you little angel,

As soon as you saw me enter the garden? 95

GRETCHEN. Didn't you see me cast down my eyes?

FAUST. And the liberty that I took you pardon?

The impudence that reared its head

When you lately left the cathedral door.

GRETCHEN. I was upset; it had never happened before; 100

No one could ever say anything bad of me—

Oh can he, I thought, have seen in my behaviour

Any cheekiness, any impropriety?

The idea, it seemed, had come to you pat:

'I can treat this woman just like that'. 105

I must admit I did not know what it was

In my heart that began to make me change my view,

But indeed I was angry with myself because

I could not be angrier with you.

FAUST. Sweet love! 110

GRETCHEN. Wait a moment!

[*She plucks a flower and starts picking off the petals.*]

FAUST. What is that? A bouquet?

GRETCHEN. No, only a game.

FAUST. A what?

GRETCHEN. You will laugh at me. Go away! 115

[GRETCHEN *murmurs.*]

FAUST. What are you murmuring?

GRETCHEN. Loves me—Loves me not—

FAUST. You flower from Heaven's garden plot!

GRETCHEN. Loves me—Not—Loves me—Not—

Loves me! 120

FAUST. Yes, child. What this flower has told you

Regard it as God's oracle. He loves you!

Do you know the meaning of that? He loves you!

[*He takes her hands.*]

GRETCHEN. Oh I feel so strange.

FAUST. Don't shudder. Let this look, 125

Let this clasp of the hand tell you

What mouth can never express:

To give oneself up utterly and feel

A rapture which must be everlasting.

Everlasting! Its end would be despair. 130
No; no end! No end!
[*She breaks away from him and runs off. After a moment's thought he follows her.*]
MARTHA. [*Approaching*] The night's coming on.
MEPHISTOPHELES. Yes—and we must go.
MARTHA. I would ask you to remain here longer
But this is a terrible place, you know. 135
It's as if no one were able to shape at
Any vocation or recreation
But must have his neighbour's comings and goings to gape at
And, whatever one does, the talk is unleashed, unfurled.
And our little couple? 140
MEPHISTOPHELES. Carefree birds of summer!
Flown to the summerhouse.
MARTHA. He seems to like her.
MEPHISTOPHELES. And vice versa. That is the way of the world.

A SUMMERHOUSE

GRETCHEN *runs in and hides behind the door.*

GRETCHEN. He comes!
FAUST. [*Entering*] You rogue! Teasing me so!
I've caught you!
[*He kisses her.*]
GRETCHEN. Dearest! I love you so!
[MEPHISTOPHELES *knocks.*]
FAUST. Who's there? 5
MEPHISTOPHELES. A friend.
FAUST. A brute!
MEPHISTOPHELES. It is time to part, you know.
MARTHA. [*Joining them*] Yes, it is late, sir.
FAUST. May I not see you home? 10
GRETCHEN. My mother would—Farewell!
FAUST. I must go then?
Farewell!
MARTHA. Adieu!
GRETCHEN. Let us soon meet again! 15
[FAUST *and* MEPHISTOPHELES *leave.*]
Dear God! A man of such a kind,
What things must go on in his mind!
I can only blush when he talks to me;
Whatever he says, I must agree.
Poor silly child, I cannot see 20
What it is he finds in me.

FOREST AND CAVERN

FAUST. [*Alone*] Exalted Spirit, you gave me, gave me all
I prayed for. Aye, and it is not in vain
That you have turned your face in fire upon me.
You gave me glorious Nature for my kingdom
With power to feel her and enjoy her. Nor 5
Is it a mere cold wondering glance you grant me
But you allow me to gaze into her depths
Even as into the bosom of a friend.
Aye, you parade the ranks of living things
Before me and you teach me to know my brothers 10
In the quiet copse, in the water, in the air.
And when the storm growls and snarls in the forest
And the giant pine falls headlong, bearing away
And crushing its neighbours, bough and bole and all,
With whose dull fall the hollow hill resounds, 15
Then do you carry me off to a sheltered cave
And show me myself, and wonders of my own breast
Unveil themselves in their deep mystery.
And now that the clear moon rises on my eyes
To soften things, now floating up before me 20
From walls of rocks and from the dripping covert
Come silver forms of the past which soothe and temper
The dour delight I find in contemplation.

That nothing perfect falls to men, oh now
I feel that true. In addition to the rapture 25
Which brings me near and nearer to the gods
You gave me that companion whom already
I cannot do without, though cold and brazen
He lowers me in my own eyes and with
One whispered word can turn your gifts to nothing. 30
He is always busily fanning in my breast
A fire of longing for that lovely image.
So do I stagger from desire to enjoyment
And in enjoyment languish for desire.

[MEPHISTOPHELES *enters*.]

MEPHISTOPHELES. Haven't you yet had enough of this kind of life? 35
How can it still appeal to you?
It is all very well to try it once,
Then one should switch to something new.

FAUST. I wish you had something else to do
On my better days than come plaguing me. 40

MEPHISTOPHELES. Now, now! I'd gladly leave you alone;

You needn't suggest it seriously.
So rude and farouche and mad a friend
Would certainly be little loss.
One has one's hands full without end! 45
One can never read in the gentleman's face
What he likes or what should be left alone.

FAUST. That is exactly the right tone!
He must be thanked for causing me ennui.

MEPHISTOPHELES. Poor son of earth, what sort of life 50
Would you have led were it not for me?
The flim-flams of imagination,
I have cured you of those for many a day.
But for me, this terrestrial ball
Would already have seen you flounce away. 55
Why behave as an owl behaves
Moping in rocky clefts and caves?
Why do you nourish yourself like a toad that sips
From moss that oozes, stone that drips?
A pretty pastime to contrive! 60
The doctor in you is still alive.

FAUST. Do you comprehend what a new and vital power
This wandering in the wilderness has given me?
Aye, with even an inkling of such joy,
You would be devil enough to grudge it me. 65

MEPHISTOPHELES. A supernatural gratification!
To lie on the mountain tops in the dark and dew
Rapturously embracing earth and heaven,
Swelling yourself to a godhead, ferreting through
The marrow of the earth with divination, 70
To feel in your breast the whole six days of creation,
To enjoy I know not what in arrogant might
And then, with the Old Adam discarded quite,
To overflow into all things in ecstasy;
After all which your lofty intuition 75
[*He makes a gesture.*]
Will end—hm—unmentionably.

FAUST. Shame on you!

MEPHISTOPHELES. Am I to blame?
You have the right to be moral and cry shame!
One must not mention to the modest ear 80
What the modest heart is ever agog to hear.
And, in a word, you are welcome to the pleasure
Of lying to yourself in measure;
But this deception will not last.

61. ***doctor:*** **i.e., the doctor of philosophy.**

Already overdriven again, 85
If this goes on you must collapse,
Mad or tormented or aghast.
Enough of this! Back there your love is sitting
And all her world seems sad and small;
You are never absent from her mind, 90
Her love for you is more than all.
At first your passion came overflowing
Like a brook that the melted snows have bolstered high;
You have poured your passion into her heart
And now your brook once more is dry. 95
I think, instead of lording it here above
In the woods, the great man might think fit
In view of that poor ninny's love
To make her some return for it.
She finds the time wretchedly long; 100
She stands at the window, watches the clouds
As over the old town walls they roll away.
'If I had the wings of a dove'—so runs her song
Half the night and all the day.
Now she is cheerful, mostly low, 105
Now has spent all her tears,
Now calm again, it appears,
But always loves you so.

FAUST. You snake! You snake!

MEPHISTOPHELES. [*Aside*] Ha! It begins to take! 110

FAUST. You outcast! Take yourself away
And do not name that lovely woman.
Do not bring back the desire for her sweet body
Upon my senses that are half astray.

MEPHISTOPHELES. Where's this to end? She thinks you have run
off, 115
And so you have—about half and half.

FAUST. I am still near her, though far removed,
Her image must be always in my head;
I already envy the body of the Lord
When her lips rest upon the holy bread. 120

MEPHISTOPHELES. Very well, my friend. I have often envied you
Those two young roes that are twins, I mean her two—

FAUST. Pimp! Get away!

MEPHISTOPHELES. Fine! So you scold? I must laugh.
The God who created girl and boy 125
Knew very well the high vocation
Which facilitates their joy.
But come, this is a fine excuse for gloom!

You should take the road to your sweetheart's room,
Rather than that to death, you know. 130

FAUST. What is the joy of heaven in her arms?
Even when I catch fire upon her breast
Do I not always sense her woe?
Am I not the runaway? The man without a home?
The monster restless and purposeless 135
Who roared like a waterfall from rock to rock in foam
Greedily raging towards the precipice?
And she on the bank in childlike innocence
In a little hut on the little alpine plot
And all her little household world 140
Concentrated in that spot.
And I, the loathed of God,
I was not satisfied
To seize and crush to powder
The rocks on the river side! 145
Her too, her peace, I must undermine as well!
This was the sacrifice I owed to Hell!
Help, Devil, to shorten my time of torment!
What must be, must be; hasten it!
Let her fate hurtle down with mine, 150
Let us go together to the pit!

MEPHISTOPHELES. How it glows again, how it boils again!
Go in and comfort her, my foolish friend!
When such a blockhead sees no outlet
He thinks at once it is the end. 155
Long live the man who does not flinch!
But you've a devil in you, somewhere there.
I know of nothing on earth more unattractive
Than your devil who feels despair.

GRETCHEN'S ROOM

GRETCHEN *is alone, singing at the spinning-wheel.*

GRETCHEN. My peace is gone,
My heart is sore,
I shall find it never
And never more.

He has left my room 5
An empty tomb,
He has gone and all
My world is gall.

My poor head

Is all astray,
My poor mind
Fallen away. 10

My peace is gone,
My heart is sore,
I shall find it never 15
And never more.

'Tis he that I look through
The window to see,
He that I open
The door for—he! 20

His gait, his figure,
So grand, so high!
The smile of his mouth,
The power of his eye,

And the magic stream 25
Of his words—what bliss!
The clasp of his hand
And, ah, his kiss!

My peace is gone,
My heart is sore, 30
I shall find it never
And never more.

My heart's desire
Is so strong, so vast;
Ah, could I seize him 35
And hold him fast

And kiss him for ever
Night and day—
And on his kisses
Pass away! 40

MARTHA'S GARDEN

GRETCHEN. Promise me, Heinrich!
FAUST. If I can!
GRETCHEN. Tell me: how do you stand in regard to religion?
You are indeed a good, good man
But I think you give it scant attention. 5
FAUST. Leave that, my child! You feel what I feel for you;

1. *Heinrich:* i.e., Faust. In the legend, Faust's first name was generally Johann (John). Goethe changed it to Heinrich (Henry).

For those I love I would give my life and none
Will I deprive of his sentiments and his church.
GRETCHEN. That is not right; one must believe thereon.
FAUST. Must one? 10
GRETCHEN. If only I had some influence!
Nor do you honour the holy sacraments.
FAUST. I honour them.
GRETCHEN. Yes, but not with any zest.
When were you last at mass, when were you last confessed? 15
Do you believe in God?
FAUST. My darling, who dare say:
I believe in God?
Ask professor or priest,
Their answers will make an odd 20
Mockery of you.
GRETCHEN. You don't believe, you mean?
FAUST. Do not misunderstand me, my love, my queen!
Who can name him?
Admit on the spot: 25
I believe in him?
And who can dare
To perceive and declare:
I believe in him not?
The All-Embracing One, 30
All-Upholding One,
Does he not embrace, uphold,
You, me, Himself?
Does not the Heaven vault itself above us?
Is not the earth established fast below? 35
And with their friendly glances do not
Eternal stars rise over us?
Do not my eyes look into yours,
And all things thrust
Into your head, into your heart, 40
And weave in everlasting mystery
Invisibly, visibly, around you?
Fill your heart with *this*, great as it is,
And when this feeling grants you perfect bliss,
Then call it what you will— 45
Happiness! Heart! Love! God!
I have no name for it!
Feeling is all;
Name is mere sound and reek
Clouding Heaven's light. 50
GRETCHEN. That sounds quite good and right;

And much as the priest might speak,
Only not word for word.

FAUST. It is what all hearts have heard
In all the places heavenly day can reach, 55
Each in his own speech;
Why not I in mine?

GRETCHEN. I could almost accept it, you make it sound so fine,
Still there is something in it that shouldn't be;
For you have no Christianity. 60

FAUST. Dear child!

GRETCHEN. It has long been a grief to me
To see you in such company.

FAUST. You mean?

GRETCHEN. The man who goes about with you, 65
I hate him in my soul, right through and through.
And nothing has given my heart
In my whole life so keen a smart
As that man's face, so dire, so grim.

FAUST. Dear poppet, don't be afraid of him! 70

GRETCHEN. My blood is troubled by his presence.
All other people, I wish them well;
But much as I may long to see you,
He gives me a horror I cannot tell,
And I think he's a man too none can trust. 75
God forgive me if I'm unjust.

FAUST. Such queer fish too must have room to swim.

GRETCHEN. I wouldn't live with the like of him!
Whenever that man comes to the door,
He looks in so sarcastically, 80
Half angrily,
One can see he feels no sympathy;
It is written on his face so clear
There is not a soul he can hold dear.
I feel so cosy in your arms, 85
So warm and free from all restraint,
And his presence ties me up inside.

FAUST. You angel, with your wild alarms!

GRETCHEN. It makes me feel so ill, so faint,
That, if he merely happens to join us, 90
I even think I have no more love for you.
Besides, when he's there, I could never pray,
And that is eating my heart away;
You, Heinrich, you must feel it too.

FAUST. You suffer from an antipathy. 95

GRETCHEN. Now I must go.

FAUST. Oh, can I never rest
One little hour hanging upon your breast,
Pressing both breast on breast and soul on soul?
GRETCHEN. Ah, if I only slept alone! 100
I'd gladly leave the door unlatched for you to-night;
My mother, however, sleeps so light
And if she found us there, I own
I should fall dead upon the spot.
FAUST. You angel, there is no fear of that. 105
Here's a little flask. Three drops are all
It needs—in her drink—to cover nature
In a deep sleep, a gentle pall.
GRETCHEN. What would I not do for your sake!
I hope it will do her no injury. 110
FAUST. My love, do you think that of me?
GRETCHEN. Dearest, I've only to look at you
And I do not know what drives me to meet your will
I have already done so much for you
That little more is left me to fulfil. 115
[*She goes out—and* MEPHISTOPHELES *enters.*]
MEPHISTOPHELES. The monkey! Is she gone?
FAUST. Have you been spying again?
MEPHISTOPHELES. I have taken pretty good note of it,
The doctor has been catechised—
And much, I hope, to his benefit; 120
The girls are really keen to be advised
If a man belongs to the old simple-and-pious school.
'If he stand that', they think, 'he'll stand *our* rule.'
FAUST. You, you monster, cannot see
How this true and loving soul 125
For whom faith is her whole
Being and the only road
To beatitude, must feel a holy horror
Having to count her beloved lost for good.
MEPHISTOPHELES. You supersensual, sensual buck, 130
Led by the nose by the girl you court!
FAUST. O you abortion of fire and muck!
MEPHISTOPHELES. And she also has skill in physiognomy;
In my presence she feels she doesn't know what,
She reads some hidden sense behind my little mask, 135
She feels that I am assuredly a genius—
Maybe the devil if she dared to ask.
Now: to-night—
FAUST. What is to-night to you?
MEPHISTOPHELES. I have my pleasure in it too. 140

AT THE WELL

GRETCHEN *and* LIESCHEN *with pitchers.*

LIESCHEN. Haven't you heard about Barbara? Not what's passed?
GRETCHEN. Not a word. I go out very little.
LIESCHEN. It's true, Sibylla told me to-day:
She has made a fool of herself at last.
So much for her fine airs! 5
GRETCHEN. Why?
LIESCHEN. It stinks!
Now she feeds two when she eats and drinks.
GRETCHEN. Ah!
LIESCHEN. Yes; she has got her deserts in the end. 10
What a time she's been hanging on her friend!
Going the rounds
To the dances and the amusement grounds,
She had to be always the first in the line,
He was always standing her cakes and wine; 15
She thought her looks so mighty fine,
She was so brazen she didn't waver
To take the presents that he gave her.
Such cuddlings and such carryings on—
But now the pretty flower is gone. 20
GRETCHEN. Poor thing!
LIESCHEN. Is that the way you feel?
When we were at the spinning-wheel
And mother kept us upstairs at night,
She was below with her heart's delight; 25
On the bench or in the shady alley
They never had long enough to dally.
But now she must grovel in the dirt,
Do penance in church in a hair shirt.
GRETCHEN. But surely he will marry her. 30
LIESCHEN. He'd be a fool! A smart young chap
Has plenty of other casks to tap.
Besides he's gone.
GRETCHEN. That's not right.
LIESCHEN. If she hooks him she won't get off light! 35
The boys will tear her wreath in half
And we shall strew her door with chaff.
[LIESCHEN *goes off.*]

3. *Sibylla:* a friend of Gretchen's; not to be confused with the "Sibyl" named in l. 162 of the scene in the witch's kitchen.

37. *chaff:* in contrast to the bridal bouquet. In Germany this treatment was reserved for girls who had "fallen."

GRETCHEN. [*Going home*] What scorn I used to pour upon her
When a poor maiden lost her honour!
My tongue could never find a name 40
Bad enough for another's shame!
I thought it black and I blackened it,
It was never black enough to fit,
And I blessed myself and acted proud—
And now I too am under a cloud. 45
Yet, God! What drove me to this pass,
It was all so good, so dear, alas!

RAMPARTS

In a niche in the wall is an image of the Mater Dolorosa.[a] *In front of it* GRETCHEN *is putting fresh flowers in the pots.*

GRETCHEN. Mary, bow down,
Beneath thy woeful crown,
Thy gracious face on me undone!

The sword in thy heart,
Smart upon smart, 5
Thou lookest up to thy dear son;

Sending up sighs
To the Father which rise
For his grief and for thine own.

Who can gauge 10
What torments rage
Through the whole of me and how—
How my poor heart is troubled in me,
How fears and longings undermine me?
Only thou knowest, only thou! 15

Wherever I may go,
What woe, what woe, what woe
Is growing beneath my heart!
Alas, I am hardly alone,
I moan, I moan, I moan 20
And my heart falls apart.

The flower-pots in my window
I watered with tears, ah me,
When in the early morning
I picked these flowers for thee. 25

a. literally, "sorrowful mother"; i.e., the Virgin Mary.

Not sooner in my bedroom
The sun's first rays were shed
Than I in deepest sorrow
Sat waking on my bed.

Save me from shame and death in one! 30
Ah, bow down
Thou of the woeful crown,
Thy gracious face on me undone.

NIGHT SCENE AT GRETCHEN'S DOOR

VALENTINE. When I was at some drinking bout
Where big talk tends to blossom out,
And my companions raised their voice
To praise the maidens of their choice
And drowned their praises in their drink, 5
Then I would sit and never blink,
Propped on my elbow listening
To all their brags and blustering.
Then smiling I would stroke my beard
And raise the bumper in my hand 10
And say: 'Each fellow to his taste!
But is there one in all the land
To hold a candle to my own
Dear sister, Gretchen? No, there's none!'
Hear! Hear! Kling! Kling! It went around; 15
Some cried: 'His judgment is quite sound,
She is the pearl of womanhood!'
That shut those boasters up for good.
And now! It would make one tear one's hair
And run up walls in one's despair! 20
Each filthy fellow in the place
Can sneer and jeer at my disgrace!
And I, like a man who's deep in debt,
Every chance word must make me sweat.
I could smash their heads for them if I tried— 25
I could not tell them that they lied.

[FAUST *and* MEPHISTOPHELES *enter.*]

VALENTINE. Who comes there, slinking? Who comes there?
If I mistake not, they're a pair.
If it's he, I'll scrag him on the spot;
He'll be dead before he knows what's what! 30
FAUST. How from the window of the sacristy there
The undying lamp sends up its little flicker

Which glimmers sideways weak and weaker
And round it presses the dark air.
My heart too feels its night, its noose. 35

MEPHISTOPHELES. And I feel like a tom-cat on the loose,
Brushing along the fire escape
And round the walls, a stealthy shape;
Moreover I feel quite virtuous,
Just a bit burglarious, a bit lecherous. 40
You see, I'm already haunted to the marrow
By the glorious Walpurgis Night.
It returns to us the day after to-morrow,
Then one knows why one's awake all right.

FAUST. I'd like some ornament, some ring, 45
For my dear mistress. I feel sad
To visit her without anything.

MEPHISTOPHELES. It's really nothing to regret—
That you needn't pay for what you get.
Now that the stars are gems on heaven's brocade, 50
You shall hear a real masterpiece.
I will sing her a moral serenade
That her folly may increase.

[*He sings to the guitar.*]

MEPHISTOPHELES. Catherine, my dear,
What? Waiting here 55
At your lover's door
When the stars of the night are fading?
Oh don't begin!
When he lifts the pin,
A maid goes in— 60
But she won't come out a maiden.

So think aright!
Grant him delight
And it's good night,
You poor, poor things—Don't linger! 65
A girl who's wise
Will hide her prize
From robber's eyes—
Unless she's a ring on her finger.

[VALENTINE *comes forward.*]

VALENTINE. Damn you! Who're you seducing here? 70
You damned pied piper! You magician!
First to the devil with your guitar!

54–69. *Catherine . . . finger:* adapted by Goethe from Shakespeare's *Hamlet*, Act IV, Scene 5.

Then to the devil with the musician!
MEPHISTOPHELES. The guitar is finished. Look, it's broken in two.
VALENTINE. Now then, to break your heads for you! 75
MEPHISTOPHELES. Doctor! Courage! All you can muster!
Stick by me and do as I say!
Quick now, draw your feather duster!
I'll parry his blows, so thrust away!
VALENTINE. Then parry that! 80
MEPHISTOPHELES. Why not, why not?
VALENTINE. And that!
MEPHISTOPHELES. Of course.
VALENTINE. Is he the devil or what?
What's this? My hand's already lamed. 85
MEPHISTOPHELES. Strike, you!
VALENTINE. Oh!
[VALENTINE *falls.*]
MEPHISTOPHELES. Now the lout is tamed!
But we must go! Vanish in the wink of an eye!
They're already raising a murderous hue and cry. 90
MARTHA. [*At the window*] Come out! Come out!
GRETCHEN. [*At the window*] Bring a light!
MARTHA. [*As before*] There's a row and a scuffle, they're having a fight.
MAN. Here's one on the ground; he's dead.
MARTHA. [*Coming out*] The murderers, have they gone? 95
GRETCHEN. [*Coming out*] Who's here?
MAN. Your mother's son.
GRETCHEN. O God! What pain! O God!
VALENTINE. I am dying—that's soon said
And sooner done, no doubt.
Why do you women stand howling and wailing? 100
Come round and hear me out.
[*They all gather round him.*]
Look, my Gretchen, you're young still,
You have not yet sufficient skill,
You bungle things a bit.
Here is a tip—you need no more— 105
Since you are once for all a whore,
Then make a job of it!
GRETCHEN. My brother? O God! Is it I you blame!
VALENTINE. Leave our Lord God out of the game!
What is done I'm afraid is done, 110
As one starts one must carry on.
You began with one man on the sly,

There will be more of them by and by,
And when a dozen have done with you
The whole town will have you too. 115

When Shame is born, she first appears
In this world in secrecy,
And the veil of night is drawn so tight
Over her head and ears;
Yes, people would kill her and forget her. 120
But she grows still more and more
And brazenly roams from door to door
And yet her appearance grows no better.
The more her face creates dismay,
The more she seeks the light of day. 125

Indeed I see the time draw on
When all good people in this town
Will turn aside from you, you tart,
As from a corpse in the plague cart.
Then your heart will sink within you, 130
When they look you in the eye!
It's good-bye to your golden chains!
And church-going and mass—good-bye!
No nice lace collars any more
To make you proud on the dancing floor! 135
No, in some dark and filthy nook
You'll hide with beggars and crippled folk
And, if God pardon you, he may;
You are cursed on earth till your dying day.

MARTHA. Commend your soul to the mercy of God! 140
Will you add slander to your load?

VALENTINE. If I could get at your withered body,
You bawd, you sinner born and hardened!
Then I should hope that all my sins
And in full measure might be pardoned. 145

GRETCHEN. My brother! O hell's misery!

VALENTINE. I tell you: let your weeping be.
When you and your honour came to part,
It was you that stabbed me to the heart.
I go to God through the sleep of death, 150
A soldier—brave to his last breath.
[*He dies.*]

CATHEDRAL

Organ and anthem. GRETCHEN *in the congregation. An* EVIL SPIRIT *whispers to her over her shoulder.*

EVIL SPIRIT. How different it all was
Gretchen, when you came here
All innocent to the altar,
Out of the worn-out little book
Lisping your prayers, 5
Half a child's game,
Half God in the heart!
Gretchen!
How is your head?
And your heart— 10
What are its crimes?
Do you pray for your mother's soul, who thanks to you
And your sleeping draught overslept into a long, long
pain?
And whose blood stains your threshold?
Yes, and already under your heart 15
Does it not grow and quicken
And torture itself and you
With its foreboding presence?

GRETCHEN. Alas! Alas!
If I could get rid of the thoughts 20
Which course through my head hither and thither
Despite me!

CHOIR. Dies irae, dies illa
Solvet saeclum in favilla.

[*The organ plays.*] 25

EVIL SPIRIT. Agony seizes you!
The trumpet sounds!
The graves tremble
And your heart
From its ashen rest
To fiery torment 30
Comes up recreated
Trembling too!

GRETCHEN. Oh to escape from here!
I feel as if the organ
Were stifling me, 35
And the music dissolving
My heart in its depths.

CHOIR. Judex ergo cum sedebit,
Quidquid latet adparebit,

23–24. *Dies . . . favilla:* Day of wrath, that day that dissolves the world into ashes. (The choir is singing the famous thirteenth-century hymn by Thomas Celano.)

38–40. *Judex . . . remanebit:* When the judge shall be seated, what is hidden shall appear, nothing shall remain unavenged.

Nil inultum remanebit. 40

GRETCHEN. I cannot breathe!
The pillars of the walls
Are round my throat!
The vaulted roof
Chokes me!—Air! 45

EVIL SPIRIT. Hide yourself! Nor sin nor shame
Remains hidden.
Air? Light?
Woe to you!

CHOIR. Quid sum miser tunc dicturus? 50
Quem patronum rogaturus?
Cum vix justus sit securus.

EVIL SPIRIT. The blessed turn
Their faces from you.
The pure shudder 55
To reach out their hands to you.
Woe!

CHOIR. Quid sum miser tunc dicturus?

GRETCHEN. Neighbour! Help! Your smelling bottle!
[*She faints.*]

WALPURGIS NIGHT

FAUST *and* MEPHISTOPHELES *making their way through the Hartz Mountains.*

MEPHISTOPHELES. A broomstick—don't you long for such a conveyance?
I'd find the coarsest he-goat some assistance.
Taking this road, our goal is still in the distance.

FAUST. No, so long as my legs are not in abeyance,
I can make do with this knotted stick. 5
What is the use of going too quick?
To creep along each labyrinthine valley,
Then climb this scarp, downwards from which
The bubbling spring makes its eternal sally,
This is the spice that makes such journeys rich. 10
Already the spring is weaving through the birches,
Even the pine already feels the spring;
Should not our bodies too give it some purchase?

MEPHISTOPHELES. Candidly—*I* don't feel a thing.
In my body all is winter, 15
I would prefer a route through frost and snow.
How sadly the imperfect disc

50–52. *Quid . . . securus:* What shall I say in my wretchedness? To whom shall I appeal when scarcely the righteous man is safe?

Of the red moon rises with belated glow
And the light it gives is bad, at every step
One runs into some rock or tree! 20
Permit me to ask a will o' the wisp.
I see one there, he's burning heartily.
Ahoy, my friend! Might I call on you to help us?
Why do you blaze away there to no purpose?
Be so good as to light us along our road. 25

WILL O' THE WISP. I only hope my sense of your mightiness
Will control my natural flightiness;
A zigzag course is our accustomed mode.

MEPHISTOPHELES. Ha! Ha! So it's men you want to imitate.
In the name of the Devil you go straight 30
Or I'll blow out your flickering, dickering light!

WILL O' THE WISP. You're the head of the house, I can see that all right,
You are welcome to use me at your convenience.
But remember, the mountain is magic-mad to-day
And, if a will o' the wisp is to show you the way, 35
You too must show a little lenience.

FAUST, MEPHISTOPHELES, WILL O' THE WISP. [*Singing successively*]

Into realms of dreams and witchcraft
We, it seems, have found an ingress.
Lead us well and show your woodcraft,
That we may make rapid progress 40
Through these wide and desert spaces.

Trees on trees—how each one races,
Pushing past—how each one hastens!
And the crags that make obeisance!
And the rocks with long-nosed faces— 45
Hear them snorting, hear them blowing!

Through the stones and lawns are flowing
Brook and brooklet, downward hustling.
Is that song—or is it rustling?
Sweet, sad notes of love—a relic— 50
Voices from those days angelic?
Thus we hope, we love—how vainly!
Echo like an ancient rumour
Calls again, yes, calls back plainly.

Now—Tu-whit!—we near the purlieu 55
Of—Tu-whoo!—owl, jay and curlew;
Are they all in waking humour?

21. *will o' the wisp:* the Jack o' lantern, or ignis fatuus. In German folklore, this was thought of as leading travelers to their destruction.

In the bushes are those lizards—
Straggling legs and bloated gizzards?
And the roots like snakes around us 60
Coil from crag and sandy cranny,
Stretch their mad and strange antennae
Grasping at us to confound us;
Stretch from gnarled and living timber
Towards the passer-by their limber 65
Polyp-suckers!
And in legions
Through these mossy, heathy regions
Mice, all colours, come cavorting!
And above, a serried cohort, 70
Fly the glow-worms as our escort—
More confusing than escorting.

Tell me what our real case is!
Are we stuck or are we going?
Rocks and trees, they all seem flying 75
Round and round and making faces,
And the will o' the wisps are blowing
Up so big and multiplying.

MEPHISTOPHELES. Hold my coat-tails, hold on tight!
Standing on this central height 80
Marvelling see how far and wide
Mammon lights the peaks inside.

FAUST. How strangely through the mountain hollows
A sad light gleams as of morning-red
And like a hound upon the scent 85
Probes the gorges' deepest bed!
Here fumes arise, there vapours float,
Here veils of mist catch sudden fire
Which creeps along, a flimsy thread,
Then fountains up, a towering spire. 90
Here a whole stretch it winds its way
With a hundred veins throughout the glen,
And here in the narrow neck of the pass
Is suddenly one strand again.
There, near by, are dancing sparks 95
Sprinkled around like golden sand.
But look! The conflagration climbs
The crags' full height, hand over hand.

MEPHISTOPHELES. Does not Sir Mammon light his palace

82. *Mammon:* See the note to l. 73, p. 427. Mammon is portrayed as leading a group of fallen angels in digging out gold and gems from the ground of Hell, presumably for Satan's palace in Milton's *Paradise Lost,* Book I, ll.. 678 ff.

In splendid style for this occasion? 100
You are lucky to have seen it;
Already I sense the noisy guests' invasion.

FAUST. How the Wind Hag rages through the air!
What blows she rains upon the nape of my neck!

MEPHISTOPHELES. You must clamp yourself to the ancient ribs of the rock 105
Or she'll hurl you into this gorge, to find your grave down there.
A mist is thickening the night.
Hark to the crashing of the trees!
The owls are flying off in fright.
And the ever-green palaces— 110
Hark to their pillars sundering!
Branches moaning and breaking!
Tree-trunks mightily thundering!
Roots creaking and yawning!
Tree upon tree in appalling 115
Confusion crashing and falling,
And through the wreckage on the scarps
The winds are hissing and howling.
Do you hear those voices in the air?
Far-off voices? Voices near? 120
Aye, the whole length of the mountain side
The witch-song streams in a crazy tide.

WITCHES. [*In chorus*]. The witches enter the Brocken scene,
The stubble is yellow, the corn is green.
There assembles the mighty horde, 125
Urian sits aloft as lord.
So we go—over stock and stone—
Farting witch on stinking goat.

A VOICE. But ancient Baubo comes alone,
She rides on a mother sow—take note. 130

CHORUS. So honour to whom honour is due!
Let Mother Baubo head the queue!
A strapping sow and Mother on top
And we'll come after, neck and crop.

The way is broad, the way is long, 135
How is this for a crazy throng?
The pitchfork pricks, the broomstick pokes,
The mother bursts and the child chokes.

VOICE FROM ABOVE. Come along, come along, from Felsensee!

VOICES FROM BELOW. We'd like to mount with you straight away.
We wash ourselves clean behind and before 141

126. *Urian:* a name for the devil.
129. *Baubo:* In Greek mythology, the nurse of Demeter, noted for her obscenity and bestiality.

But we are barren for evermore.

CHORUS. The wind is silent, the star's in flight,
The sad moon hides herself from sight.
The soughing of the magic choir 145
Scatters a thousand sparks of fire.

VOICE FROM BELOW. Wait! Wait!

VOICE FROM ABOVE. Who calls there from the cleft in the rock?

VOICE FROM BELOW. Don't leave me behind! Don't leave me behind!
Three hundred years I've been struggling up 150
And I can never reach the top;
I want to be with my own kind.

CHORUS. Ride on a broom or ride on a stick,
Ride on a fork or a goat—but quick!
Who cannot to-night achieve the climb 155
Is lost and damned till the end of time.

HALF-WITCH. So long, so long, I've been on the trot;
How far ahead the rest have got!
At home I have neither peace nor cheer
And yet I do not find it here. 160

CHORUS. Their ointment makes the witches hale,
A rag will make a decent sail
And any trough a ship for flight;
You'll never fly, if not to-night.
Once at the peak, you circle round 165
And then you sweep along the ground
And cover the heath far and wide—
Witchhood in swarms on every side.
[*The* WITCHES *land.*]

MEPHISTOPHELES. What a push and a crush and a rush and a clatter!
How they sizzle and whisk, how they babble and batter! 170
Kindle and sparkle and blaze and stink!
A true witch-element, I think.
Only stick to me or we shall be swept apart!
Where are you?

FAUST. Here! 175

MEPHISTOPHELES. What! Carried so far already!
I must show myself the master on this ground.
Room! Here comes Voland! Room, sweet rabble! Steady!
Here, Doctor, catch hold of me. Let's make one bound
Out of this milling crowd and so get clear. 180
Even for the likes of me it's *too* mad here.

178. *Voland:* one of Mephistopheles' names for himself. *Voland,* or *Valand,* is an old German word for "evil fiend."

There's something yonder casting a peculiar glare,
Something attracts me towards those bushes.
Come with me! We will slip in there.

FAUST. You spirit of contradiction! Go on though! I'll follow. 185
You have shown yourself a clever fellow. Quite!
We visit the Brocken on Walpurgis Night
To shut ourselves away in this lonely hollow!

MEPHISTOPHELES. Only look—what motley flames!
It's a little club for fun and games 190
One's not alone with a few, you know.

FAUST. I'd rather be above there though.
Already there's fire and whorls of smoke.
The Prince of Evil is drawing the folk;
Many a riddle must there be solved. 195

MEPHISTOPHELES. And many a new one too evolved.
Let the great world, if it likes, run riot;
We will set up here in quiet.
It is a custom of old date
To make one's own small worlds within the great. 200
I see young witches here, bare to the buff,
And old ones dressed—wisely enough.
If only for my sake, do come on;
It's little trouble and great fun.
I hear some music being let loose too. 205
What a damned clack! It's what one must get used to.
Come along! Come along! You have no choice.
I'll lead the way and sponsor you
And you'll be obliged to me anew.
What do you say? This milieu isn't small. 210
Just look! You can see no end to it at all.
A hundred fires are blazing in a row;
They dance and gossip and cook and drink and court—
Tell me where there is better sport!

FAUST. Do you intend, to introduce us here, 215
To play the devil or the sorcerer?

MEPHISTOPHELES. I am quite accustomed to go incognito
But one wears one's orders on gala days, you know.
I have no garter for identification
But my cloven foot has here some reputation. 220
See that snail? Creeping up slow and steady?
Her sensitive feelers have already
Sensed out something odd in me.
Here I could *not* hide my identity.

187. *Walpurgis Night:* the eve of May Day (May 1).

219. *garter:* i.e., he has no decoration of nobility, such as the Order of the Garter.

But come! Let us go the round of the fires 225
And I'll play go-between to your desires.

COSTER-WITCH. Gentlemen, don't pass me by!
Don't miss your opportunity!
Inspect my wares with careful eye;
I have a great variety. 230
And yet there is nothing on my stall
Whose like on earth you could not find,
That in its time has done no small
Harm to the world and to mankind.
No dagger which has not drunk of blood, 235
No goblet which has not poured its hot and searing
Poison into some healthy frame,
No gewgaw which has not ruined some endearing
Woman, no sword which has not been used to hack
A bond in two and stab a partner in the back. 240

MEPHISTOPHELES. Auntie! You are behind the times.
Past and done with! Past and done!
You must go in for novelties!
You'll lose our custom if you've none.

FAUST. I mustn't go crazy unawares! 245
This is a fair to end all fairs.

MEPHISTOPHELES. The whole crowd's forcing its way above;
You find you're shoved though you may think you shove.

FAUST. Who then is that?

MEPHISTOPHELES. Look well at Madam; 250
That's Lilith.

FAUST. Who?

MEPHISTOPHELES. First wife of Adam.
Be on your guard against her lovely hair,
That shining ornament which has no match; 255
Any young man whom those fair toils can catch,
She will not quickly loose him from her snare.

FAUST. Look, an old and a young one, there they sit.
They have already frisked a bit.

MEPHISTOPHELES. No rest to-night for 'em, not a chance. 260
They're starting again. Come on! Let's join the dance.

[FAUST *dances with a* YOUNG WITCH.]

FAUST. A lovely dream once came to me
In which I saw an apple tree,

227. *Coster-Witch:* The original, *Trödelhexe,* literally means "a witch (dealing in) old rags and clothes."

251. *Lilith:* According to an old rabbinical legend, Adam's first wife (the "female" mentioned in Genesis 1:27) was Lilith. After Eve was created, Lilith became a ghost who seduced men and inflicted evil upon children.

On which two lovely apples shine,
They beckon me, I start to climb. 265

YOUNG WITCH. Those little fruit you long for so
Just as in Eden long ago.
Joy runs through me, through and through;
My garden bears its apples too.

[FAUST *breaks away from the dance.*]

MEPHISTOPHELES. Why did you let that lovely maiden go 270
Who danced with you and so sweetly sang?

FAUST. Ugh, in the middle of it there sprang
Out of her mouth a little red mouse.

MEPHISTOPHELES. Why complain? That's nothing out of the way;
You should be thankful it wasn't grey. 275
In an hour of love! What a senseless grouse!

FAUST. And then I saw—

MEPHISTOPHELES. What?

FAUST. Mephisto, look over there!
Do you see a girl in the distance, pale and fair? 280
Who drags herself, only slowly, from the place?
And seems to walk with fetters on her feet?
I must tell you that I think I see
Something of dear Gretchen in her face.

MEPHISTOPHELES. That can do no good! Let it alone! Beware! 285
It is a lifeless phantom, an image of air.
It is a bad thing to behold;
Its cold look makes the blood of man run cold,
One turns to stone almost upon the spot;
You have heard of Medusa, have you not? 290

FAUST. Indeed, they are the eyes of one who is dead,
Unclosed by loving hands, left open, void.
That is the breast which Gretchen offered me,
And that is the sweet body I enjoyed.

MEPHISTOPHELES. That is mere magic, you gullible fool! She
can 295
Appear in the shape of his love to every man.

FAUST. What ravishment! What pain! Oh stay!
That look! I cannot turn away!
How strange that that adorable neck
In one red thread should be arrayed 300
As thin as the back of a knife-blade.

MEPHISTOPHELES. You are quite correct! I see it too.
She can also carry her head under her arm,

290. *Medusa:* the Gorgon, with hair made of serpents, whose glance turned men to stone. She was finally killed by Perseus, and her head was given to Athene.

Perseus has cut it off for her.
Always this love of things untrue![a] 305
[A CHOIR *is heard, pianissimo.*]
CHOIR. Drifting cloud and gauzy mist
Brighten and dissever.
Breeze on the leaf and wind in the reeds
And all is gone for ever.

DREARY DAY—OPEN COUNTRY

FAUST. In misery! In despair! Long on the earth a wretched wanderer, now a prisoner! A criminal cooped in a dungeon for horrible torments, that dear and luckless creature! To end so! So! Perfidious, worthless spirit—and this you have kept from me! Stand, Just stand there! Roll your devilish eyes spitefully round in your head! Stand and brave me with your unbearable presence! A prisoner! In irremediable misery! Abandoned to evil spirits, to judging, unfeeling man! And I in the meantime—you lull me with stale diversions, you hide her worsening plight from me, you abandon her to perdition!

MEPHISTOPHELES. She is not the first.

FAUST. Dog! Loathsome monster! Change him, Thou eternal Spirit! Change this serpent back to his shape of a dog, in which he often delighted to trot before me at night—to roll about at the feet of the harmless wanderer and, as he tripped, to sink his teeth in his shoulders. Change him back to his fancy-shape that he may crouch in the sand on his belly before me, that I may trample over his vileness!

Not the first, you say! O the pity of it! What human soul can grasp that more than one creature has sunk to the depth of this misery, that the first did not pay off the guilt of all the rest, writhing and racked in death before the eyes of the Ever-Pardoning! It pierces me to my marrow and core, the torment of this one girl—and you grin calmly at the fate of thousands!

MEPHISTOPHELES. Now we're already back at our wits' end—the point where your human intelligence snaps. Why do you enter our company, if you can't carry it through? So you want to fly—and have no head for heights? Did we force ourselves on you—or you on us?

FAUST. Do not bare at me so those greedy fangs of yours! You sicken me! O great and glorious Spirit, Thou who didst deign to appear to me, Thou who knowest my heart and my soul, why fetter me to this odious partner who grazes on mischief and laps up destruction?

a. The Walpurgis Night's Dream, which is always cut from performances of *Faust,* is omitted. It occurs between l. 305 and l. 306 of our text.

MEPHISTOPHELES. Have you finished?

FAUST. Save her! Or woe to you! The most withering curse upon you for thousands of years!

MEPHISTOPHELES. I cannot undo the avenger's bonds, his bolts I cannot open. Save her! Who was it plunged her into ruin? I or you?

[FAUST *looks wildly around.*]

MEPHISTOPHELES. Are you snatching at the thunder? Luckily, that is forbidden you wretched mortals. To smash to pieces his innocent critic, that is the way the tyrant relieves himself when in difficulties.

FAUST. Bring me to her! She shall be free!

MEPHISTOPHELES. And what of the risk you will run? Let me tell you; the town is still tainted with blood-guilt from your hand. Over the site of the murder there float avenging spirits who await the returning murderer.

FAUST. That too from *you?* Murder and death of a world on your monstrous head! Take me to her, I tell you; set her free!

MEPHISTOPHELES. I will take you, and what I *can* do—listen! Am I omnipotent in heaven and earth? I will cast a cloud on the gaoler's senses; do you get hold of the keys and carry her out with your own human hands. I meanwhile wait, my magic horses are ready, I carry you off. That much I can manage.

FAUST. Away! Away!

NIGHT

FAUST *and* MEPHISTOPHELES *fly past on black horses.*

FAUST. What do they weave round the Gallows Rock?
MEPHISTOPHELES. Can't tell what they're cooking and hatching.
FAUST. Floating up, floating down, bending, descending.
MEPHISTOPHELES. A witch corporation.
FAUST. Black mass, black water. 5
MEPHISTOPHELES. Come on! Come on!

DUNGEON

FAUST *with a bunch of keys and a lamp, in front of an iron door.*

FAUST. A long unwonted trembling seizes me,
The woe of all mankind seizes me fast.
It is here she lives, behind these dripping walls,
Her crime was but a dream too good to last!
And *you*, Faust, waver at the door? 5
You fear to see your love once more?
Go in at once—or her hope of life is past.

1. *Gallows Rock:* the masonry supporting a gallows.

[*He tries the key.* GRETCHEN *starts singing inside.*]

GRETCHEN. My mother, the whore,
Who took my life!
My father, the rogue, 10
Who ate my flesh!
My little sister
My bones did lay
In a cool, cool glen;
And there I turned to a pretty little wren; 15
Fly away! Fly away!

[FAUST *opens the lock.*]

FAUST. She does not suspect that her lover is listening—
To the chains clanking, the straw rustling.

[*He enters.*]

GRETCHEN. Oh! They come! O death! It's hard! Hard!

FAUST. Quiet! I come to set you free. 20

[*She throws herself at his feet.*]

GRETCHEN. If you are human, feel my misery.

FAUST. Do not cry out—you will wake the guard.

[*He takes hold of the chains to unlock them.*]

GRETCHEN. [*On her knees*] Who has given you this power,
Hangman, so to grieve me?
To fetch me at this midnight hour! 25
Have pity! O reprieve me!
Will to-morrow not serve when the bells are rung?

[*She gets up.*]

I am still so young, I am still so young!
Is my death so near?
I was pretty too, that was what brought me here. 30
My lover was by, he's far to-day;
My wreath lies torn, my flowers have been thrown away.
Don't seize on me so violently!
What have I done to you? Let me be!
Let me not vainly beg and implore; 35
You know I have never seen you before.

FAUST. Can I survive this misery?

GRETCHEN. I am now completely in your power.
Only let me first suckle my child.
This night I cherished it, hour by hour; 40
To torture me they took it away
And now I murdered it, so they say.
And I shall never be happy again.
People make ballads about me—the heartless crew!
An old story ends like this— 45
Must mine too?

[FAUST *throws himself on the ground.*]

FAUST. Look! At your feet a lover lies
To loose you from your miseries.

[GRETCHEN *throws herself beside him.*]

GRETCHEN. O, let us call on the saints on bended knee!
Beneath these steps—but see— 50
Beneath this sill
The cauldron of Hell!
And within,
The Evil One in his fury
Raising a din! 55

FAUST. Gretchen! Gretchen!

GRETCHEN. That was my lover's voice!

[*She springs up: the chains fall off.*]

I heard him calling. Where can he be?
No one shall stop me. I am free!
Quick! My arms round his neck! 60
And lie upon his bosom! Quick!
He called 'Gretchen!' He stood at the door.
Through the whole of Hell's racket and roar,
Through the threats and jeers and from far beyond
I heard that voice so sweet, so fond. 65

FAUST. It is I!

GRETCHEN. It's you? Oh say so once again!

[*She clasps him.*]

It is! It is! Where now is all my pain?
And where the anguish of my captivity?
It's you; you have come to rescue me! 70
I am saved!
The street is back with me straight away
Where I saw you that first day,
And the happy garden too
Where Martha and I awaited you. 75

FAUST. Come! Come!

GRETCHEN. Oh stay with me, oh do!
Where *you* stay, I would like to, too.

FAUST. Hurry!
If you don't, 80
The penalty will be sore.

GRETCHEN. What! Can you kiss no more?
So short an absence, dear, as this
And you've forgotten how to kiss!
Why do I feel so afraid, clasping your neck? 85
In the old days your words, your looks,
Were a heavenly flood I could not check

And you kissed me as if you would smother me—
Kiss me now!
Or I'll kiss you! 90
[*She kisses him.*]
Oh your lips are cold as stone!
And dumb!
What has become
Of your love?
Who has robbed me of my own? 95
[*She turns away from him.*]

FAUST. Come! Follow me, my love! Be bold!
I will cherish you after a thousandfold.
Only follow me now! That is all I ask of you.

GRETCHEN. And is it you then? Really? Is it true?

FAUST. It is! But come! 100

GRETCHEN. You are undoing each chain,
You take me to your arms again.
How comes it you are not afraid of me?
Do you know, my love, *whom* you are setting free?

FAUST. Come! The deep night is passing by and beyond. 105

GRETCHEN. My mother, I have murdered her;
I drowned my child in the pond.
Was it not a gift to you and me?
To you too—You! Are you what you seem?
Give me your hand! It is not a dream! 110
Your dear hand—but, oh, it's wet!
Wipe it off! I think
There is blood on it.
Oh God! What have you done?
Put up your sword, 115
I beg you to.

FAUST. Let what is gone be gone!
You are killing me.

GRETCHEN. No! *You* must live on!
I will tell you about the graves— 120
You must get them put right
At morning light;
Give the best place to my mother,
The one next door to my brother,
Me a shade to the side— 125
A gap, but not too wide.
And the little one on my right breast.
No one else shall share my rest.
When it was you, when I could clasp you,
That was a sweet, a lovely day! 130

But I no longer can attain it,
I feel I must use force to grasp you,
As if you were thrusting me away.
And yet it's you and you look so kind, so just.
FAUST. If you feel it's I, then come with me! You must! 135
GRETCHEN. Outside there?
FAUST. Into the air!
GRETCHEN. If the grave is there
And death on the watch, then come!
Hence to the final rest of the tomb 140
And not a step beyond—
You are going now? O Heinrich, if *I* could too!
FAUST. You can! The door is open. Only respond!
GRETCHEN. I dare not go out; for me there is no more hope.
They are lying in wait for me; what use is flight? 145
To have to beg, it is so pitiable
And that with a conscience black as night!
So pitiable to tramp through foreign lands—
And in the end I must fall into their hands!
FAUST. I shall stay by you. 150
GRETCHEN. Be quick! Be quick!
Save your poor child!
Go! Straight up the path—
Along by the brook—
Over the bridge— 155
Into the wood—
Left where the plank is—
In the pond!
Catch hold of it quickly!
It's trying to rise, 160
It's kicking still!
Save it! Save it!
FAUST. Collect yourself!
One step—just one—and you are free.
GRETCHEN. If only we were past the hill! 165
There sits my mother on a stone—
My brain goes cold and dead—
There sits my mother on a stone—
And wags and wags her head.
No sign, no nod, her head is such a weight 170
She'll wake no more, she slept so late.
She slept that we might sport and play.
What a time that was of holiday!
FAUST. If prayer and argument are no resource,
I will risk saving you by force. 175

GRETCHEN. No! I will have no violence! Let me go!
Don't seize me in that murderous grip!
I have done everything else for you, you know.

FAUST. My love! My love! The day is dawning!

GRETCHEN. Day! Yes, it's growing day! The last day breaks on me! 180
My wedding day it was to be!
Tell no one you had been before with Gretchen.
Alas for my garland!
There's no more chance!
We shall meet again— 185
But not at the dance.
The people are thronging—but silently;
Street and square
Cannot hold them there.
The bell tolls—it tolls for *me*. 190
How they seize me, bind me, like a slave!
Already I'm swept away to the block.
Already there jabs at every neck,
The sharp blade which jabs at mine.
The world lies mute as the grave. 195

FAUST. I wish I had never been born!

[MEPHISTOPHELES *appears outside.*]

MEPHISTOPHELES. Away! Or you are lost.
Futile wavering! Waiting and prating!
My horses are shivering,
The dawn's at the door. 200

GRETCHEN. What rises up from the floor?
It's he! Send him away! It's he!
What does he want in the holy place?
It is I he wants!

FAUST. You shall live! 205

GRETCHEN. Judgment of God! I have given myself to Thee!

MEPHISTOPHELES. [*To* FAUST] Come! Or I'll leave you both in the lurch.

GRETCHEN. O Father, save me! I am Thine!
You angels! Hosts of the Heavenly Church,
Guard me, stand round in serried line! 210
Heinrich! I shudder to look at you.

MEPHISTOPHELES. She is condemned!

VOICE FROM ABOVE. Redeemed!

MEPHISTOPHELES. Follow me!

[*He vanishes with* FAUST.]

VOICE [*From within, dying away*] Heinrich! Heinrich! 215

WILLIAM BLAKE*

(1757–1827)

From SONGS OF INNOCENCE AND OF EXPERIENCE

SHEWING THE TWO CONTRARY STATES OF THE HUMAN SOUL

From Songs of Innocence†

1789

The Author & Printer W Blake

Introduction

Piping down the valleys wild
Piping songs of pleasant glee
On a cloud I saw a child,
And he laughing said to me,

"Pipe a song about a Lamb"; 5
So I piped with merry chear;
"Piper pipe that song again"—
So I piped, he wept to hear.

"Drop thy pipe thy happy pipe
Sing thy songs of happy chear"; 10
So I sung the same again
While he wept with joy to hear.

"Piper sit thee down and write
In a book that all may read"—
So he vanish'd from my sight. 15
And I pluck'd a hollow reed,

And I made a rural pen,
And I stain'd the water clear,
And I wrote my happy songs
Every child may joy to hear. 20

1789

* The text for all of Blake's works is that of *The Poetry and Prose of William Blake*, edited by David V. Erdman and Harold Bloom (New York: Doubleday and Company. Inc., 1965).

† *Songs of Innocence* (1789) was later combined with *Songs of Experience* (1794); and the poems were etched and accompanied by Blake's illustrations, the process accomplished by copper engravings stamped on paper, then colored by hand. (Blake had to cut a mirror image for the text of each poem, a laborious process). In later copies, Blake was not always consistent about the order of the poems, and sometimes poems from *Songs of Innocence* were transferred to *Songs of Experience*. The order we have used follows Blake's own original instructions, written in a memorandum. "Innocence" as a word appears frequently in eighteenth-century discussions of pastoral poetry, associated with "simplicity."

18. *stain'd:* perhaps an allusion to Blake preparing watercolors to tint the engravings.

The Lamb

Little Lamb, who made thee?
Dost thou know who made thee?
Gave thee life & bid thee feed,
By the stream & o'er the mead;
Gave thee clothing of delight, 5
Softest clothing wooly bright;
Gave thee such a tender voice,
Making all the vales rejoice!
Little Lamb who made thee?
Dost thou know who made thee? 10

Little Lamb I'll tell thee,
Little Lamb I'll tell thee!
He is callèd by thy name,
For he calls himself a Lamb:
He is meek & he is mild, 15
He became a little child:
I a child & thou a lamb,
We are callèd by his name.
Little Lamb God bless thee.
Little Lamb God bless thee. 20

1789

18. ***his name:*** **a Christian child is called by the name of Christ.**

The Little Black Boy*

My mother bore me in the southern wild,
And I am black, but O! my soul is white;
White as an angel is the English child:
But I am black as if bereav'd of light.

My mother taught me underneath a tree, 5
And sitting down before the heat of day,
She took me on her lap and kissèd me,
And pointing to the east, began to say:

"Look on the rising sun: there God does live,
And gives his light, and gives his heat away; 10
And flowers and trees and beasts and men receive
Comfort in morning, joy in the noon day.

"And we are put on earth a little space,
That we may learn to bear the beams of love,
And these black bodies and this sun-burnt face 15
Is but a cloud, and like a shady grove.

***** ***The Little Black Boy:*** **F. W. Bateson mentions that Blake's father was said to have been a Moravian, a small Protestant sect in England engaged in missionary activity.**

"For when our souls have learn'd the heat to bear,
The cloud will vanish; we shall hear his voice,
Saying: 'Come out from the grove, my love & care,
And round my golden tent like lambs rejoice.' " 20

Thus did my mother say, and kissèd me;
And thus I say to little English boy:
When I from black and he from white cloud free,
And round the tent of God like lambs we joy,

I'll shade him from the heat till he can bear 25
To lean in joy upon our father's knee;
And then I'll stand and stroke his silver hair,
And be like him, and he will then love me.

1789

Holy Thursday

'Twas on a Holy Thursday, their innocent faces clean,
The children walking two & two, in red & blue & green,
Grey headed beadles walk'd before with wands as white as snow,
Till into the high dome of Paul's they like Thames' waters flow.

O what a multitude they seemd, these flowers of London town! 5
Seated in companies they sit with radiance all their own.
The hum of multitudes was there, but multitudes of lambs,
Thousands of little boys & girls raising their innocent hands.

Now like a mighty wind they raise to heaven the voice of song,
Or like harmonious thunderings the seats of heaven among. 10
Beneath them sit the aged men, wise guardians of the poor;
Then cherish pity, lest you drive an angel from your door.

ca. 1784 1789

1. *Thursday:* Ascension Day, forty days after Easter, when children from charity schools were marched to St. Paul's Cathedral.

2. *red & blue & green:* each school had its own distinctive uniform.

3. *beadles:* ushers and minor functionaries, whose job was to maintain order.

11. *wise guardians:* the governors of the Charity Schools, not the Poor Law Guardians.

12. *Hebrews 13:* "Be not forgetful to entertain strangers; for thereby some have entertained angels unawares."

The Chimney Sweeper

When my mother died I was very young,
And my father sold me while yet my tongue
Could scarcely cry " 'weep! 'weep! 'weep! 'weep!"
So your chimneys I sweep & in soot I sleep.

2. *sold me:* It was common practice in Blake's day for fathers to sell, or indenture, their children for this task. The average age of the child has been estimated at six and seven; they were generally employed for seven years, until they were too large for the task of ascending the chimneys.

3. *weep:* the child's lisping effort to say "sweep," as he walks the streets looking for work.

There's little Tom Dacre, who cried when his head 5
That curl'd like a lambs back, was shav'd, so I said,
"Hush, Tom! never mind it, for when your head's bare,
You know that the soot cannot spoil your white hair."

And so he was quiet, & that very night,
As Tom was a-sleeping he had such a sight! 10
That thousands of sweepers, Dick, Joe, Ned, & Jack,
Were all of them lock'd up in coffins of black;

And by came an Angel who had a bright key,
And he open'd the coffins & set them all free;
Then down a green plain, leaping, laughing they run, 15
And wash in a river and shine in the Sun;

Then naked & white, all their bags left behind,
They rise upon clouds, and sport in the wind.
And the Angel told Tom, if he'd be a good boy,
He'd have God for his father & never want joy. 20

And so Tom awoke; and we rose in the dark
And got with our bags & our brushes to work.
Tho' the morning was cold, Tom was happy & warm;
So if all do their duty, they need not fear harm.

1789

17. ***naked:*** **They climbed up the chimneys naked.**

From Songs of Experience

1794

The Author & Printer W Blake

Introduction

Hear the voice of the Bard!
Who Present, Past, & Future sees;
Whose ears have heard
The Holy Word
That walk'd among the ancient trees; 5

Calling the lapséd Soul
And weeping in the evening dew;
That might controll
The starry pole,
And fallen, fallen light renew! 10

5. *trees:* Genesis 3:8: "And [Adam and Eve] heard the voice of the Lord God walking in the garden in the cool of the day." Blake's ambiguous use of pronouns makes for interpretative difficulties. It would seem that "The Holy Word" (Jehovah, the Old Testament deity) calls "the lapsed soul," and weeps—not the Bard.

"O Earth, O Earth, return!
Arise from out the dewy grass;
Night is worn,
And the morn
Rises from the slumberous mass. 15

"Turn away no more;
Why wilt thou turn away?
The starry floor
The watry shore
Is giv'n thee till the break of day." 20

1794

20. *till:* only until.

Earth's Answer

Earth rais'd up her head,
From the darkness dread & drear.
Her light fled:
Stony dread!
And her locks cover'd with grey despair. 5

"Prison'd on watry shore
Starry Jealousy does keep my den,
Cold and hoar
Weeping o'er
I hear the Father of the ancient men. 10

"Selfish father of men,
Cruel, jealous, selfish fear!
Can delight
Chain'd in night
The virgins of youth and morning bear? 15

"Does spring hide its joy
When buds and blossoms grow?
Does the sower
Sow by night,
Or the plowman in darkness plow? 20

"Break this heavy chain
That does freeze my bones around;
Selfish! vain!
Eternal bane!
That free Love with bondage bound." 25

1790–1792 1794

10. *father:* In Blake's later prophetic works one of the four Zoas, representing the four chief faculties of man, is Urizen. In general he stood for the orthodox conception of the Divine Creator, sometimes Jehovah in the Old Testament, often the God conceived by Newton and Locke; in all instances a tyrant associated with excessive rationalism, sexual repression, the opponent of the imagination and creativity. This may be "the Holy Word" in "Introduction."

The Tyger

Tyger! Tyger! burning bright
In the forests of the night,
What immortal hand or eye
Could frame thy fearful symmetry?

In what distant deeps or skies 5
Burnt the fire of thine eyes?
On what wings dare he aspire?
What the hand, dare seize the fire?

And what shoulder, & what art,
Could twist the sinews of thy heart? 10
And when thy heart began to beat,
What dread hand? & what dread feet?

What the hammer? what the chain?
In what furnace was thy brain?
What the anvil? what dread grasp 15
Dare its deadly terrors clasp?

When the stars threw down their spears,
And water'd heaven with their tears,
Did he smile his work to see?
Did he who made the Lamb make thee? 20

Tyger! Tyger! burning bright
In the forests of the night,
What immortal hand or eye
Dare frame thy fearful symmetry?

1790–1792 1794

5. *deeps:* oceans, or possibly volcanoes.

12. *feet:* A first draft of this poem, found in the Rossetti manuscript, had this line followed by "Could fetch it from the furnace deep"—deleted in the final version. This accounts for a certain grammatical ambiguity at the end of the third stanza.

15. *anvil:* In Blake's mythology, Los—the spirit of prophecy—was also a divine blacksmith.

19. *smile:* possibly a reference to Genesis where, after each day's creation, the phrase "and God saw that it was good" is repeated.

The Sick Rose

O Rose, thou art sick.
The invisible worm
That flies in the night
In the howling storm

Has found out thy bed 5
Of crimson joy,
And his dark secret love
Does thy life destroy.

1790–1792 1794

London

I wander thro' each charter'd street,
Near where the charter'd Thames does flow,
And mark in every face I meet
Marks of weakness, marks of woe.

In every cry of every Man, 5
In every Infant's cry of fear,
In every voice, in every ban,
The mind-forg'd manacles I hear.

How the Chimney-sweeper's cry
Every blackning Church appalls; 10
And the hapless Soldier's sigh
Runs in blood down Palace walls.

But most thro' midnight streets I hear
How the youthful Harlot's curse
Blasts the new-born Infant's tear, 15
And blights with plagues the Marriage hearse.

1790–1792 1794

1. *charter'd:* given liberty or freedom, but also taken over as private property.
7. *ban:* a prohibition, also possibly a marriage ban—notice of intended matrimony.
15. *tear:* The harlot infects the parents with venereal disease, and thus the infant is inflicted with prenatal blindness.
16. *hearse:* The marriage coach becomes a funeral hearse.

The Chimney Sweeper

A little black thing among the snow
Crying "'weep, 'weep," in notes of woe!
"Where are thy father & mother? say?"
"They are both gone up to the church to pray.

"Because I was happy upon the heath, 5
And smil'd among the winter's snow;
They clothéd me in the clothes of death,
And taught me to sing the notes of woe.

"And because I am happy, & dance & sing,
They think they have done me no injury, 10
And are gone to praise God & his Priest & King,
Who make up a heaven of our misery."

1790–1792 1794

9. *sing:* it has been suggested that this may allude to an annual dance of London sweeps and milkmaids on May Day.

The Marriage of Heaven and Hell*

PLATE 2

The Argument

Rintrah [1] roars & shakes his fires in the burdend air;
Hungry clouds swag on the deep.

Once meek, and in a perilous path,
The just man kept his course along
The vale of death. 5

Roses are planted where thorns grow,
And on the barren heath
Sing the honey bees.

Then the perilous path was planted,
And a river, and a spring, 10
On every cliff and tomb;
And on the bleached bones
Red clay [2] brought forth;

Till the villain left the paths of ease,
To walk in perilous paths, and drive 15
The just man into barren climes.

Now the sneaking serpent walks
In mild humility,
And the just man rages in the wilds
Where lions roam. 20

Rintrah roars & shakes his fires in the burdend air;
Hungry clouds swag [3] on the deep.

PLATE 3

As a new heaven is begun and it is now thirty-three years[4] since its advent, the Eternal Hell[5] revives. And lo! Swendenborg is the Angel sitting at the tomb; his writings are the linen clothes[6] folded

* Engraved, probably in 1792, with twenty-five plates. Blake wrote this satire—if the work can be classified within any one genre—partly to ridicule Emanuel Swedenborg (1688–1772), the visionary Swedish theologian, whose writings Blake had earlier admired. But the attack is far broader, directed against conventional and orthodox Christian morality and theology; which to Blake meant man's self-subjugation to restraints and prohibitions against values he deemed positive: energy, action, freedom, passion, genius, abundance.

1. In Blake's prophetic works a wrathful prophet, who resembles Elijah in the Old Testament as well as St. John the Baptist in the New.

2. the meaning of "Adam" in Hebrew.

3. sway, lower, sag, sink down.

4. Blake probably began writing the *Marriage* in 1790, thirty-three years after Swedenborg had predicted that the Last Judgment and the coming of the Kingdom of Heaven would begin in 1757—also the year of Blake's birth. Blake's own age in 1790 is that of Christ's at the time of the Resurrection from the tomb. He must also have been attracted by the Trinitarian aspects of the number thirty-three.

5. This is the contrary state ironically brought into being by Swedenborg's false New Heaven.

6. the garments wrapped around the dead body of Jesus.

up. Now is the dominion of Edom, & the return of Adam into Paradise; see Isaiah xxxiv & XXXV Chap.[7]

Without Contraries is no progression. Attraction and Repulsion, Reason and Energy, Love and Hate, are necessary to Human existence.

From these contraries spring what the religious call Good & Evil. Good is the passive that obeys Reason. Evil is the active springing from Energy.

Good is Heaven. Evil is Hell.

PLATE 4

The voice of the Devil

All Bibles or sacred codes have been the causes of the following Errors:

1. That Man has two real existing principles; Viz: a Body & a Soul.

2. That Energy, calld Evil, is alone from the Body, & that Reason, calld Good, is alone from the Soul.[8]

3. That God will torment Man in Eternity for following his Energies. But the following Contraries to these are True:

1. Man has no Body distinct from his Soul; for that calld Body is a portion of Soul discernd by the five Senses, the chief inlets of Soul in this age.

2. Energy is the only life, and is from the Body; and Reason is the bound or outward circumference of Energy.

3. Energy is Eternal Delight

PLATE 5

Those who restrain desire, do so because theirs is weak enough to be restrained; and the restrainer or reason usurps its place & governs the unwilling.

And being restraind, it by degrees becomes passive, till it is only the shadow of desire.

The history of this is written in *Paradise Lost*,[9] & the Governor or Reason is call'd Messiah.

And the original Archangel, or possessor of the command of the

7. Edom is the kingdom of Esau, brother of Jacob, who stole from Esau the blessing of their dying father, Isaac (Genesis 28:40). In Isaiah 63, Edom is also a place from whence comes a man whose clothes are stained with the blood of his victim: "the day of vengeance is in mine heart, and the year of my redeemed is come"—a period Blake interprets as the time when Adam would regain his lost Paradise. Isaiah 34 prophesies the destruction of the wicked; Isaiah 35 foretells the redemption to follow. It has been suggested—since many of Blake's writings contain covert references to the current political situation—that Edom may be France in 1790. In that case, the man coming from Edom represents the spirit of the French revolution being for Blake a sign of the immanent redemption of mankind.

8. Blake denied the separateness of the soul and the body.

9. This section contains Blake's "diabolical" reading of Milton's poem.

heavenly host, is calld the Devil or Satan, and his children are call'd Sin & Death.[10]

But in the Book of Job, Milton's Messiah is call'd Satan.

For this history has been adopted by both parties.

It indeed appear'd to Reason as if Desire was cast out; but the Devil's account is, that the Messi[PL 6]ah fell, & formed a heaven of what he stole from the Abyss.

This is shewn in the Gospel, where he prays to the Father to send the comforter or Desire that Reason may have Ideas to build on; the Jehovah of the Bible being no other than he who dwells in flaming fire. Know that after Christ's death, he became Jehovah.

But in Milton, the Father is Destiny, the Son, a Ratio[11] of the five senses, & the Holy-ghost, Vacuum!

Note. The reason Milton wrote in fetters when he wrote of Angels & God, and at liberty when of Devils & Hell, is because he was a true Poet and of the Devil's party without knowing it.

A Memorable Fancy[12]

As I was walking among the fires of hell, delighted with the enjoyments of Genius, which to Angels look like torment and insanity, I collected some of their Proverbs; thinking that as the sayings used in a nation mark its character, so the Proverbs of Hell shew the nature of Infernal wisdom better than any description of buildings or garments.

When I came home, on the abyss of the five senses, where a flat sided steep frowns over the present world, I saw a mighty Devil[13] folded in black clouds, hovering on the sides of the rock; with cor-[PL 7]roding fires he wrote the following sentence now perceived by the minds of men, & read by them on earth:

> How do you know but ev'ry Bird that cuts the airy way,
> Is an immense world of delight, clos'd by your senses five?

Proverbs of Hell[14]

In seed time learn, in harvest teach, in winter enjoy.
Drive your cart and your plow over the bones of the dead.
The road of excess leads to the palace of wisdom.
Prudence is a rich ugly old maid courted by Incapacity.

10. In Book II, lines 745 ff., of *Paradise Lost*, Satan gives birth to Sin, then incestuously conceives Death with her.

11. Latin for both "sum" and "reason." Blake refers to Locke and his empirical philosophy, where the mind's cognitions are limited to what the five senses apprehend.

12. A parody of what Swedenborg called his "Memorable Relations"—his visions, where he often described "buildings" and "garments."

13. this may be Blake, and the "corroding fires" the acid with which he etched his plates.

14. Blake's parody of the Book of Proverbs in the Old Testament.

He who desires but acts not, breeds pestilence.
The cut worm forgives the plow.
Dip him in the river who loves water.
A fool sees not the same tree that a wise man sees.
He whose face gives no light, shall never become a star.
Eternity is in love with the productions of time.
The busy bee has no time for sorrow.
The hours of folly are measur'd by the clock; but of wisdom, no clock can measure.
All wholsom food is caught without a net or a trap.
Bring out number, weight, & measure in a year of dearth.
No bird soars too high, if he soars with his own wings.
A dead body revenges not injuries.
The most sublime act is to set another before you.
If the fool would persist in his folly he would become wise.
Folly is the cloke of knavery.
Shame is Pride's cloke.

PLATE 8

Prisons are built with stones of Law, Brothels with bricks of Religion.
The pride of the peacock is the glory of God.
The lust of the goat is the bounty of God.
The wrath of the lion is the wisdom of God.
The nakedness of woman is the work of God.
Excess of sorrow laughs. Excess of joy weeps.
The roaring of lions, the howling of wolves, the raging of the stormy sea, and the destructive sword, are portions of eternity too great for the eye of man.
The fox condemns the trap, not himself.
Joys impregnate. Sorrows bring forth.
Let man wear the fell of the lion, woman the fleece of the sheep.
The bird a nest, the spider a web, man friendship.
The selfish, smiling fool & the sullen, frowning fool shall be both thought wise, that they may be a rod.
What is now proved was once only imagin'd.
The rat, the mouse, the fox, the rabbit watch the roots; the lion, the tyger, the horse, the elephant, watch the fruits.
The cistern contains: the fountain overflows.
One thought fills immensity.
Always be ready to speak your mind, and a base man will avoid you.
Every thing possible to be believ'd is an image of truth.
The eagle never lost so much time as when he submitted to learn of the crow.

PLATE 9

The fox provides for himself, but God provides for the lion.
Think in the morning, Act in the noon, Eat in the evening, Sleep in the night.
He who has sufferd you to impose on him knows you.
As the plow follows words, so God rewards prayers.
The tygers of wrath are wiser than the horses of instruction.

Expect poison from the standing water.
You never know what is enough unless you know what is more than enough.
Listen to the fools reproach! it is a kingly title!
The eyes of fire, the nostrils of air, the mouth of water, the beard of earth.
The weak in courage is strong in cunning.
The apple tree never asks the beech how he shall grow, nor the lion the horse, how he shall take his prey.
The thankful reciever bears a plentiful harvest.
If others had not been foolish, we should be so.
The soul of sweet delight can never be defil'd.
When thou seest an Eagle, thou seest a portion of Genius; lift up thy head!
As the catterpiller chooses the fairest leaves to lay her eggs on, so the priest lays his curse on the fairest joys.
To create a little flower is the labour of ages.
Damn braces: Bless relaxes.
The best wine is the oldest, the best water the newest.
Prayers plow not! Praises reap not!
Joys laugh not! Sorrows weep not!

PLATE 10

The head Sublime, the heart Pathos, the genitals Beauty, the hands & feet Proportion.
As the air to a bird or the sea to a fish, so is contempt to the contemptible.
The crow wish'd every thing was black, the owl that every thing was white.
Exuberance is Beauty.
If the lion was advised by the fox, he would be cunning.
Improvement makes strait roads, but the crooked roads without Improvement are roads of Genius.
Sooner murder an infant in its cradle than nurse unacted desires.
Where man is not, nature is barren.
Truth can never be told so as to be understood, and not be believ'd.
Enough! or Too much.

PLATE 11

The ancient Poets animated all sensible objects with Gods or Geniuses, calling them by the names and adorning them with the properties of woods, rivers, mountains, lakes, cities, nations, and whatever their enlarged & numerous senses could percieve.

And particularly they studied the genius of each city & country, placing it under its mental deity.

Till a system was formed, which some took advantage of & enslav'd the vulgar by attempting to realize or abstract the mental deities from their objects; thus began Priesthood,

Choosing forms of worship from poetic tales.
And at length they pronounced that the Gods had ordered such things.
Thus men forgot that All deities reside in the human breast.

PLATE 12

A Memorable Fancy

The Prophets Isaiah and Ezekiel dined with me, and I asked them how they dared so roundly to assert that God spake to them; and whether they did not think at the time that they would be misunderstood, & so be the cause of imposition.

Isaiah answer'd: "I saw no God, nor heard any, in a finite organical perception; but my senses discover'd the infinite in every thing, and as I was then perswaded, & remain confirm'd, that the voice of honest indignation is the voice of God, I cared not for consequences, but wrote."

Then I asked: "Does a firm perswasion that a thing is so, make it so?"

He replied: "All poets believe that it does, & in ages of imagination this firm perswasion removed mountains; but many are not capable of a firm perswasion of any thing."

Then Ezekiel said: "The philosophy of the East taught the first principles of human perception. Some nations held one principle for the origin & some another; we of Israel taught that the Poetic Genius (as you now call it) was the first principle and all the others merely derivative, which was the cause of our despising the Priests & Philosophers of other countries, and prophecying that all Gods [PL 13] would at last be proved to originate in ours & to be the tributaries of the Poetic Genius; it was this that our great poet, King David, desired so fervently & invokes so patheticly, saying by this he conquers enemies & governs kingdoms; and we so loved our God, that we cursed in his name all the deities of surrounding nations, and asserted that they had rebelled; from these opinions the vulgar came to think that all nations would at last be subject to the Jews."

"This," said he, "like all firm perswasions, is come to pass, for all nations believe the Jews' code and worship the Jews' god, and what greater subjection can be?"

I heard this with some wonder, & must confess my own conviction. After dinner I ask'd Isaiah to favour the world with his lost works; he said none of equal value was lost. Ezekiel said the same of his.

I also asked Isaiah what made him go naked and barefoot[15] three

15. See Isaiah 20:2–3, where the Lord told Isaiah to go "naked and barefoot" for three years. Diogenes (412?–323 B.C.) was the Greek cynic philosopher, whose renunciation of conventional behavior created the legend that he also renounced clothes.

years? He answerd, "the same that made our friend Diogenes, the Grecian."

I then asked Ezekiel why he eat dung, & lay so long on his right & left side?[16] He answered, "the desire of raising other men into a perception of the infinite; this the North American tribes practise, & is he honest who resists his genius or conscience only for the sake of present ease or gratification?"

PLATE 14

The ancient tradition that the world will be consumed in fire at the end of six thousand years is true, as I have heard from Hell.

For the cherub with his flaming sword is hereby commanded to leave his guard at tree of life;[17] and when he does, the whole creation will be consumed, and appear infinite and holy, whereas it now appears finite & corrupt.

This will come to pass by an improvement of sensual enjoyment.

But first the notion that man has a body distinct from his soul is to be expunged; this I shall do, by printing in the infernal method, by corrosives, which in Hell are salutary and medicinal, melting apparent surfaces away, and displaying the infinite which was hid.

If the doors of perception were cleansed every thing would appear to man as it is, infinite.

For man has closed himself up, till he sees all things thro' narrow chinks of his cavern.

PLATE 15

A Memorable Fancy

I was in a Printing house in Hell & saw the method in which knowledge is transmitted from generation to generation.[18]

In the first chamber was a Dragon-Man, clearing away the rubbish from a cave's mouth; within, a number of Dragons were hollowing the cave.

In the second chamber was a Viper folding round the rock & the cave, and others adorning it with gold, silver, and precious stones.

In the third chamber was an Eagle with wings and feathers of air; he caused the inside of the cave to be infinite; around were numbers of Eagle-like men, who built palaces in the immense cliffs.

In the fourth chamber were Lions of flaming fire, raging around & melting the metals into living fluids.

16. See Ezekiel 4:4–6, where the Lord commanded the prophet to obey these instructions.

17. See Genesis 3:24. After the Lord drove Adam and Eve from the Garden of Eden, he stationed Cherubims and a flaming sword "to keep the way of the tree of life."

18. See earlier notes about Blake's own methods of engraving and printing. (p. 441, n.†; p. 450, n.13).

In the fifth chamber were Unnam'd forms, which cast the metals into the expanse.

There they were receiv'd by Men who occupied the sixth chamber, and took the forms of books & were arranged in libraries.

PLATE 16

The Giants[19] who formed this world into its sensual existence, and now seem to live in it in chains, are in truth the causes of its life & the sources of all activity; but the chains are the cunning of weak and tame minds which have power to resist energy; according to the proverb, the weak in courage is strong in cunning.

Thus one portion of being is the Prolific, the other, the Devouring: to the Devourer it seems as if the producer was in his chains; but it is not so, he only takes portions of existence and fancies that the whole.

But the Prolific would cease to be Prolific unless the Devourer as a sea received the excess of his delights.

Some will say, "Is not God alone the Prolific?" I answer, "God only Acts & Is, in existing beings or Men."

These two classes of men are always upon earth, & they should be enemies; whoever tries [PL 17] to reconcile them seeks to destroy existence.

Religion is an endeavour to reconcile the two.

Note. Jesus Christ did not wish to unite but to separate them, as in the Parable of sheep and goats! & he says, "I came not to send Peace but a Sword."[20]

Messiah or Satan or Tempter was formerly thought to be one of the Antediluvians[21] who are our Energies.

A Memorable Fancy

An Angel came to me and said: "O pitiable foolish young man! O horrible! O dreadful state! consider the hot burning dungeon thou art preparing for thyself to all eternity, to which thou art going in such career."

I said: "Perhaps you will be willing to shew me my eternal lot, & we will contemplate together upon it and see whether your lot or mine is most desirable."

So he took me thro' a stable[22] thro' a church & down into the

19. These are man's creative energies, called by Blake "the Prolific." Their necessary contrary is "the Devourer."

20. See Matthew 25: 32–33 for the parable of the sheep and the goats; Christ's statement is in Matthew 10:34.

21. Those who lived before the Flood.

22. Perhaps a reference to Jesus's birthplace, followed by the church founded in His name, and the vault that Blake sees to be the "burial" of that same institution in his own day.

church vault at the end of which was a mill;[23] thro' the mill we went, and came to a cave; down the winding cavern we groped our tedious way till a void boundless as a nether sky appeard beneath us, & we held by the roots of trees and hung over this immensity, but I said: "If you please, we will commit ourselves to this void, and see whether Providence is here also, if you will not I will." But he answerd: "Do not presume, O young man, but as we here remain, behold thy lot which will soon appear when the darkness passes away."

So I remaind with him sitting in the twisted [PL 18] root of an oak; he was suspended in a fungus which hung with the head downward into the deep.

By degrees we beheld the infinite Abyss, fiery as the smoke of a burning city; beneath us at an immense distance was the sun, black but shining; round it were fiery tracks on which revolv'd vast spiders, crawling after their prey, which flew, or rather swum in the infinite deep, in the most terrific shapes of animals sprung from corruption; & the air was full of them, & seemd composed of them; these are Devils, and are called Powers of the air. I now asked my companion which was my eternal lot? he said, "Between the black & white spiders."

But now, from between the black & white spiders a cloud and fire burst and rolled thro the deep, blackning all beneath, so that the nether deep grew black as a sea & rolled with a terrible noise; beneath us was nothing now to be seen but a black tempest, till looking east between the clouds & the waves, we saw a cataract of blood mixed with fire, and not many stones throw from us appeard and sunk again the scaly fold of a monstrous serpent. At last to the east, distant about three degrees, appeard a fiery crest above the waves. Slowly it reared like a ridge of golden rocks till we discovered two globes of crimson fire, from which the sea fled away in clouds of smoke; and now we saw it was the head of Leviathan; his forehead was divided into streaks of green & purple like those on a tyger's forehead: soon we saw his mouth & red gills hang just above the raging foam, tinging the black deep with beams of blood, advancing toward [PL 19] us with all the fury of a spiritual existence.

My friend the Angel climb'd up from his station into the mill; I remain'd alone, & then this appearance was no more, but I found myself sitting on a pleasant bank beside a river by moon light, hearing a harper who sung to the harp, & his theme was: "The man who never alters his opinion is like standing water, & breeds reptiles of the mind."

But I arose, and sought for the mill, & there I found my Angel, who surprised asked me how I escaped?

23. Always a symbol for Blake of modern industrialism and also analytic philosophy, "grinding" out barren intellectual speculations.

I answerd: "All that we saw was owing to your metaphysics: for when you ran away, I found myself on a bank by moonlight hearing a harper. But now we have seen my eternal lot, shall I shew you yours? He laughd at my proposal; but I by force suddenly caught him in my arms, & flew westerly thro' the night, till we were elevated above the earth's shadow; then I flung myself with him directly into the body of the sun; here I clothed myself in white, & taking in my hand Swedenborg's volumes, sunk from the glorious clime, and passed all the planets till we came to Saturn; here I staid to rest & then leap'd into the void between Saturn & the fixed stars.

"Here," said I, "is your lot, in this space, if space it may be calld." Soon we saw the stable and the church, & I took him to the altar and open'd the Bible, and lo! it was a deep pit, into which I descended, driving the Angel before me; soon we saw seven houses[24] of brick; one we enterd; in it were a [PL 20] number of monkeys, baboons, & all of that species, chaind by the middle, grinning and snatching at one another, but withheld by the shortness of their chains: however, I saw that they sometimes grew numerous, and then the weak were caught by the strong, and with a grinning aspect, first coupled with & then devourd, by plucking off first one limb and then another till the body was left a helpless trunk. This, after grinning & kissing it with seeming fondness, they devourd too; and here & there I saw one savourily picking the flesh off of his own tail; as the stench terribly annoyd us both, we went into the mill, & I in my hand brought the skeleton of a body, which in the mill was Aristotle's Analytics.[25]

So the Angel said: "Thy phantasy has imposed upon me, & thou oughtest to be ashamed."

I answerd: "We impose on one another, & it is but lost time to converse with you whose works are only Analytics."

Opposition is true Friendship.

PLATE 21

I have always found that Angels have the vanity to speak of themselves as the only wise; this they do with a confident insolence sprouting from systematic reasoning.

Thus Swedenborg boasts that what he writes is new; tho' it is only the Contents or Index of already publish'd books.

A man carried a monkey about for a shew, & because he was a little wiser than the monkey, grew vain, and conciev'd himself as much wiser than seven men. It is so with Swedenborg; he shews the folly of churches & exposes hypocrites, till he imagines that all are religious, & himself the single [PL 22] one on earth that ever broke

24. See Revelations 1:4; the "seven churches which are in Asia" to which St. John the Divine addresses his book.

25. Aristotle's treatises on logic.

a net.

Now hear a plain fact: Swedenborg has not written one new truth. Now hear another: he has written all the old falshoods.

And now hear the reason: He conversed with Angels who are all religious, & conversed not with Devils, who all hate religion, for he was incapable thro' his conceited notions.

Thus Swedenborg's writings are a recapitulation of all superficial opinions, and an analysis of the more sublime, but no further.

Have now another plain fact: Any man of mechanical talents may from the writings of Paracelsus or Jacob Behmen[26] produce ten thousand volumes of equal value with Swedenborg's, and from those of Dante or Shakespear, an infinite number.

But when he has done this, let him not say that he knows better than his master, for he only holds a candle in sunshine.

A Memorable Fancy

Once I saw a Devil in a flame of fire, who arose before an Angel that sat on a cloud, and the Devil utterd these words:

"The worship of God is, Honouring his gifts in other men, each according to his genius, and loving the [PL 23] greatest men best; those who envy or calumniate great men hate God, for there is no other God."

The Angel hearing this became almost blue; but mastering himself, he grew yellow, & at last white, pink, & smiling, and then replied:

"Thou Idolater, is not God One? & is not he visible in Jesus Christ? and has not Jesus Christ given his sanction to the law of ten commandments, and are not all other men fools, sinners, & nothings?"

The Devil answer'd; "Bray[27] a fool in a mortar with wheat, yet shall not his folly be beaten out of him; if Jesus Christ is the greatest man, you ought to love him in the greatest degree; now hear how he has given his sanction to the law of ten commandments: did he not mock at the sabbath, and so mock the sabbath's God? murder those who were murderd because of him? turn away the law from the woman taken in adultery? steal the labor of others to support him? bear false witness when he omitted making a defence before Pilate? covet when he pray'd for his disciples, and when he bid them shake off the dust of their feet against such as refused to lodge them? I tell you, no virtue can exist without breaking these ten commandments. Jesus was all virtue, and acted from im[PL

26. Paracelsus (ca. 1490–1541), Swiss physician, alchemist, Neoplatonist; Jakob Böhme (1575–1624), a German shoemaker, mystic, and theologian.

27. crush, pulverize, break into small pieces.

24]pulse, not from rules."

When he had so spoken, I beheld the Angel, who stretched out his arms, embracing the flame of fire, & he was consumed and arose as Elijah.[28]

Note. This Angel, who is now become a Devil, is my particular friend; we often read the Bible together in its infernal or diabolical sense, which the world shall have if they behave well.

I have also The Bible of Hell, which the world shall have whether they will or no.

One Law for the Lion & Ox is Oppression.

1790–1793 1790–1793

PLATE 25

A Song of Liberty[29]

1. The Eternal Female groand! it was heard over all the Earth.
2. Albion's[30] coast is sick, silent; the American meadows faint!
3. Shadows of Prophecy shiver along by the lakes and the rivers and mutter across the ocean: France, rend down thy dungeon![31]
4. Golden Spain, burst the barriers of old Rome!
5. Cast thy keys, O Rome, into the deep down falling, even to eternity down falling,
6. And weep.
7. In her trembling hands she took the new born terror, howling.
8. On those infinite mountains of light now barr'd out by the Atlantic sea,[32] the new born fire stood before the starry king!
9. Flag'd with grey brow'd snows and thunderous visages, the jealous wings wav'd over the deep.
10. The speary hand burned aloft, unbuckled was the shield, forth went the hand of jealousy among the flaming hair, and [PL 26] hurl'd the new born wonder thro' the starry night.
11. The fire, the fire, is falling!
12. Look up! look up! O citizen of London, enlarge thy countenance! O Jew, leave counting gold! return to thy oil and wine. O African! black African! (Go, wingéd thought, widen his forehead.)

28. See "Argument," note 1.

29. Blake etched this poem in 1792, and usually bound it with the *Marriage* as an appendix or coda. It tells of contemporary events in France, and the birth of the spirit of Revolution (whom he later called Orc, the temporal name for the Zoa, Luvah), who fights with Urizen (see "Earth's answer," note on line 10).

30. Albion is England.

31. The Bastille fell on July 14, 1789.

32. the legendary continent of Atlantis, frequently used by Blake to symbolize man's condition before the Fall, or the realm of the imagination now covered by the waters of modern mechanistic thinking.

13. The fiery limbs, the flaming hair, shot like the sinking sun into the western sea.
14. Wak'd from his eternal sleep, the hoary element roaring fled away:
15. Down rushd, beating his wings in vain, the jealous king; his grey brow'd councellors, thunderous warriors, curl'd veterans, among helms, and shields, and chariots, horses, elephants; banners, castles, slings and rocks,
16. Falling, rushing, ruining! buried in the ruins, on Urthona's dens;[33]
17. All night beneath the ruins; then, their sullen flames, faded, emerge round the gloomy king,
18. With thunder and fire, leading his starry hosts thro' the waste wilderness [PL 27] he promulgates his ten commands, glancing his beamy eyelids over the deep in dark dismay,
19. Where the son of fire in his eastern cloud, while the morning plumes her golden breast,
20. Spurning the clouds written with curses, stamps the stony law to dust, loosing the eternal horses from the dens of night, crying:

Empire is no more! and now the lion & wolf shall cease.[34]

CHORUS

Let the Priests of the Raven of dawn, no longer in deadly black, with hoarse note curse the sons of joy. Nor his accepted brethren, whom, tyrant, he calls free, lay the bound or build the roof. Nor pale religious letchery call that virginity, that wishes but acts not!

For every thing that lives is Holy.

1792 1792

33. probably from "earth-owner." In the later Prophetic Books, Urthona becomes an emblem for creative and imaginative power.

34. See Isaiah 65:17–25, and his prophecy of "new heavens and a new earth," when "the wolf and the lamb shall feed together, and the lion shall eat straw like the bullock."

Mock on, Mock on, Voltaire, Rousseau

Mock on, Mock on, Voltaire, Rousseau;
Mock on, Mock on, 'tis all in vain.
You throw the sand against the wind,
And the wind blows it back again.

And every sand becomes a Gem 5
Reflected in the beams divine;
Blown back, they blind the mocking Eye,
But still in Israel's paths they shine.

The Atoms of Democritus
And Newton's Particles of light 10
Are sands upon the Red sea shore,
Where Israel's tents do shine so bright.

1800–1803

9. *Democritus:* Greek philosopher (460?–362? B.C.) who advanced a theory that all things are merely patterns of atoms.

10. *Particles:* Newton's corpuscular theory of light. For Blake, both men were condemned as materialists.

And Did Those Feet*

And did those feet in ancient time
Walk upon England's mountains green?
And was the holy Lamb of God
On England's pleasant pastures seen?

And did the Countenance Divine 5
Shine forth upon our clouded hills?
And was Jerusalem builded here,
Among these dark Satanic Mills? [2]

Bring me my Bow of burning gold:
Bring me my Arrows of desire: 10
Bring me my Spear: O clouds unfold!
Bring me my Chariot of fire!

I will not cease from Mental Fight,
Nor shall my Sword sleep in my hand,
Till we have built Jerusalem 15
In England's green & pleasant Land.

ca. 1804–1810

* These stanzas appear in the *Preface to Milton*, shortest of Blake's major prophetic books.

1. *feet:* a reference to an ancient legend that Jesus came to England with Joseph of Arimathea.

8. *mills:* possibly industrial England, but "mills" also meant for Blake eighteenth-century arid, mechanistic philosophy.

WILLIAM WORDSWORTH

(1770–1850)

Lines

COMPOSED A FEW MILES ABOVE TINTERN ABBEY, ON REVISITING THE BANKS OF THE WYE DURING A TOUR. JULY 13, 1798.*

Five years have past; five summers, with the length
Of five long winters! and again I hear
These waters, rolling from their mountain-springs

* First published in 1798 in *Lyrical Ballads.*

With a soft inland murmur.—Once again
Do I behold these steep and lofty cliffs, 5
That on a wild secluded scene impress
Thoughts of more deep seclusion; and connect
The landscape with the quiet of the sky.
The day is come when I again repose
Here, under this dark sycamore, and view 10
These plots of cottage-ground, these orchard-tufts,
Which at this season, with their unripe fruits,
Are clad in one green hue, and lose themselves
'Mid groves and copses. Once again I see
These hedge-rows, hardly hedge-rows, little lines 15
Of sportive wood run wild: these pastoral farms,
Green to the very door; and wreaths of smoke
Sent up, in silence, from among the trees!
With some uncertain notice, as might seem
Of vagrant dwellers in the houseless woods, 20
Or of some Hermit's cave, where by his fire
The Hermit sits alone.

These beauteous forms,
Through a long absence, have not been to me
As is a landscape to a blind man's eye:
But oft, in lonely rooms, and 'mid the din 25
Of towns and cities, I have owed to them,
In hours of weariness, sensations sweet,
Felt in the blood, and felt along the heart;
And passing even into my purer mind,
With tranquil restoration:—feelings too 30
Of unremembered pleasure: such, perhaps,
As have no slight or trivial influence
On that best portion of a good man's life,
His little, nameless, unremembered, acts
Of kindness and of love. Nor less, I trust, 35
To them I may have owed another gift,
Of aspect more sublime; that blessed mood,
In which the burthen of the mystery,
In which the heavy and the weary weight
Of all this unintelligible world, 40
Is lightened:—that serene and blessed mood,
In which the affections gently lead us on,—
Until, the breath of this corporeal frame
And even the motion of our human blood
Almost suspended, we are laid asleep 45
In body, and become a living soul:

While with an eye made quiet by the power
Of harmony, and the deep power of joy,
We see into the life of things.

If this
Be but a vain belief, yet, oh! how oft— 50
In darkness and amid the many shapes
Of joyless daylight; when the fretful stir
Unprofitable, and the fever of the world,
Have hung upon the beatings of my heart—
How oft, in spirit, have I turned to thee, 55
O sylvan Wye! thou wanderer thro' the woods,
How often has my spirit turned to thee!

And now, with gleams of half-extinguished thought
With many recognitions dim and faint,
And somewhat of a sad perplexity, 60
The picture of the mind revives again:
While here I stand, not only with the sense
Of present pleasure, but with pleasing thoughts
That in this moment there is life and food
For future years. And so I dare to hope, 65
Though changed, no doubt, from what I was when first
I came among these hills; when like a roe
I bounded o'er the mountains, by the sides
Of the deep rivers, and the lonely streams,
Wherever nature led: more like a man 70
Flying from something that he dreads than one
Who sought the thing he loved. For nature then
(The coarser pleasures of my boyish days,
And their glad animal movements all gone by)
To me was all in all.—I cannot paint 75
What then I was. The sounding cataract
Haunted me like a passion: the tall rock,
The mountain, and the deep and gloomy wood,
Their colours and their forms, were then to me
An appetite; a feeling and a love, 80
That had no need for a remoter charm,
By thought supplied, nor any interest
Unborrowed from the eye.—That time is past,
And all its aching joys are now no more,
And all its dizzy raptures. Not for this 85
Faint I, nor mourn nor murmur; other gifts
Have followed; for such loss, I would believe,
Abundant recompense. For I have learned

To look on nature, not as in the hour
Of thoughtless youth; but hearing oftentimes 90
The still, sad music of humanity,
Nor harsh nor grating, though of ample power
To chasten and subdue. And I have felt
A presence that disturbs me with the joy
Of elevated thoughts; a sense sublime 95
Of something far more deeply interfused,
Whose dwelling is the light of setting suns,
And the round ocean and the living air,
And the blue sky, and in the mind of man:
A motion and a spirit, that impels 100
All thinking things, all objects of all thought,
And rolls through all things. Therefore am I still
A lover of the meadows and the woods,
And mountains; and of all that we behold
From this green earth; of all the mighty world 105
Of eye, and ear,—both what they half create,
And what perceive; well pleased to recognise
In nature and the language of the sense
The anchor of my purest thoughts, the nurse,
The guide, the guardian of my heart, and soul 110
Of all my moral being.

Nor perchance,
If I were not thus taught, should I the more
Suffer my genial spirits to decay:
For thou art with me here upon the banks
Of this fair river; thou my dearest Friend, 115
My dear, dear Friend; and in thy voice I catch
The language of my former heart, and read
My former pleasures in the shooting lights
Of thy wild eyes. Oh! yet a little while
May I behold in thee what I was once, 120
My dear, dear Sister! and this prayer I make,
Knowing that Nature never did betray
The heart that loved her; 'tis her privilege,
Through all the years of this our life, to lead
From joy to joy: for she can so inform 125
The mind that is within us, so impress
With quietness and beauty, and so feed
With lofty thoughts, that neither evil tongues,
Rash judgments, nor the sneers of selfish men,
Nor greetings where no kindness is, nor all 130
The dreary intercourse of daily life,

Shall e'er prevail against us, or disturb
Our cheerful faith, that all which we behold
Is full of blessings. Therefore let the moon
Shine on thee in thy solitary walk; 135
And let the misty mountain-winds be free
To blow against thee: and, in after years,
When these wild ecstasies shall be matured
Into a sober pleasure; when thy mind
Shall be a mansion for all lovely forms, 140
Thy memory be as a dwelling-place
For all sweet sounds and harmonies; oh! then,
If solitude, or fear, or pain, or grief
Should be thy portion, with what healing thoughts
Of tender joy wilt thou remember me, 145
And these my exhortations! Nor, perchance—
If I should be where I no more can hear
Thy voice, nor catch from thy wild eyes these gleams
Of past existence—wilt thou then forget
That on the banks of this delightful stream 150
We stood together; and that I, so long
A worshipper of Nature, hither came
Unwearied in that service: rather say
With warmer love—oh! with far deeper zeal
Of holier love. Nor wilt thou then forget 155
That after many wanderings, many years
Of absence, these steep woods and lofty cliffs,
And this green pastoral landscape, were to me
More dear, both for themselves and for thy sake!

Ode*

INTIMATIONS OF IMMORTALITY FROM RECOLLECTIONS OF EARLY CHILDHOOD

The Child is father of the Man;
And I could wish my days to be
Bound each to each by natural piety.

I

There was a time when meadow, grove, and stream,
The earth, and every common sight,
To me did seem
Apparelled in celestial light,
The glory and the freshness of a dream. 5
It is not now as it hath been of yore;—
Turn wheresoe'er I may,

*** Written between 1802 and 1806; published in 1807.**

By night or day,
The things which I have seen I now can see no more.

II

The Rainbow comes and goes 10
And lovely is the Rose;
The Moon doth with delight
Look round her when the heavens are bare,
Waters on a starry night
Are beautiful and fair; 15
The sunshine is a glorious birth;
But yet I know, where'er I go,
That there hath past away a glory from the earth.

III

Now, while the birds thus sing a joyous song,
And while the young lambs bound 20
As to the tabor's sound,
To me alone there came a thought of grief:
A timely utterance gave that thought relief,
And I again am strong:
The cataracts blow their trumpets from the steep; 25
No more shall grief of mine the season wrong;
I hear the Echoes through the mountains throng,
The Winds come to me from the fields of sleep,
And all the earth is gay;
Land and sea 30
Give themselves up to jollity,
And with the heart of May
Doth every Beast keep holiday;—
Thou Child of Joy,
Shout round me, let me hear thy shouts, thou happy 35
Shepherd-boy!

IV

Ye blessèd Creatures, I have heard the call
Ye to each other make; I see
The heavens laugh with you in your jubilee;
My heart is at your festival, 40
My head hath its coronal,
The fulness of your bliss, I feel—I feel it all.
Oh evil day! if I were sullen
While Earth herself is adorning,
This sweet May-morning, 45
And the Children are culling
On every side,
In a thousand valleys far and wide,
Fresh flowers; while the sun shines warm,
And the Babe leaps upon his Mother's arm:— 50

I hear, I hear, with joy I hear!
—But there's a Tree, of many, one,
A single Field which I have looked upon,
Both of them speak of something that is gone:
The Pansy at my feet 55
Doth the same tale repeat:
Whither is fled the visionary gleam?
Where is it now, the glory and the dream?

V

Our birth is but a sleep and a forgetting:
The Soul that rises with us, our life's Star, 60
Hath had elsewhere its setting,
And cometh from afar:
Not in entire forgetfulness,
And not in utter nakedness,
But trailing clouds of glory do we come 65
From God, who is our home:
Heaven lies about us in our infancy!
Shades of the prison-house begin to close
Upon the growing Boy,
But He beholds the light, and whence it flows, 70
He sees it in his joy;
The Youth, who daily farther from the east
Must travel, still is Nature's Priest,
And by the vision splendid
Is on his way attended; 75
At length the Man perceives it die away,
And fade into the light of common day.

VI

Earth fills her lap with pleasures of her own;
Yearnings she hath in her own natural kind,
And, even with something of a Mother's mind, 80
And no unworthy aim,
The homely Nurse doth all she can
To make her Foster-child, her Inmate, Man,
Forget the glories he hath known,
And that imperial palace whence he came. 85

VII

Behold the Child among his new-born blisses,
A six years' Darling of a pigmy size!
See, where 'mid work of his own hand he lies,
Fretted by sallies of his mother's kisses,
With light upon him from his father's eyes! 90
See, at his feet, some little plan or chart,
Some fragment from his dream of human life,

Shaped by himself with newly-learned art;
  A wedding or a festival,
  A mourning or a funeral; 95
    And this hath now his heart,
  And unto this he frames his song
    Then will he fit his tongue
To dialogues of business, love, or strife;
    But it will not be long 100
    Ere this will be thrown aside,
    And with new joy and pride
The little Actor cons another part;
Filling from time to time his 'humorous stage'
With all the Persons, down to palsied Age, 105
That Life brings with her in her equipage;
    As if his whole vocation
    Were endless imitation.

VIII

Thou, whose exterior semblance doth belie
    Thy Soul's immensity; 110
Thou best Philosopher, who yet dost keep
Thy heritage, thou Eye among the blind,
That, deaf and silent, read'st the eternal deep,
Haunted for ever by the eternal mind,—
    Mighty Prophet! Seer blest! 115
    On whom those truths do rest,
Which we are toiling all our lives to find,
In darkness lost, the darkness of the grave;
Thou, over whom thy Immortality
Broods like the Day, a Master o'er a Slave, 120
A presence which is not to be put by;
      [To whom the grave
Is but a lonely bed without the sense or sight
    Of day or the warm light
A place of thought where we in waiting lie;] 125
Thou little Child, yet glorious in the might
Of heaven-born freedom on thy being's height,
Why with such earnest pains dost thou provoke
The years to bring the inevitable yoke,
Thus blindly with thy blessedness at strife? 130
Full soon thy Soul shall have her earthly freight,
And custom lie upon thee with a weight,
Heavy as frost, and deep almost as life!

122–125. *To whom . . . lie:* These lines were included in the "Ode" in the 1807 and 1815 editions of Wordsworth's poems but were omitted in the 1820 and subsequent editions, as a result of Coleridge's severe censure of them.

IX

O joy! that in our embers
Is something that doth live, 135
That nature yet remembers
What was so fugitive!
The thought of our past years in me doth breed
Perpetual benediction: not indeed
For that which is most worthy to be blest; 140
Delight and liberty, the simple creed
Of Childhood, whether busy or at rest,
With new-fledged hope still fluttering in his breast—
Not for these I raise
The song of thanks and praise; 145
But for those obstinate questionings
Of sense and outward things,
Fallings from us, vanishings;
Blank misgivings of a Creature
Moving about in worlds not realized, 150
High instincts before which our mortal Nature
Did tremble like a guilty Thing surprised:
But for those first affections,
Those shadowy recollections,
Which, be they what they may, 155
Are yet the fountain-light of all our day,
Are yet a master-light of all our seeing;
Uphold us, cherish, and have power to make
Our noisy years seem moments in the being
Of the eternal Silence: truths that wake, 160
To perish never:
Which neither listlessness, nor mad endeavour,
Nor Man nor Boy,
Nor all that is at enmity with joy,
Can utterly abolish or destroy! 165
Hence in a season of calm weather
Though inland far we be,
Our Souls have sight of that immortal sea
Which brought us hither,
Can in a moment travel thither, 170
And see the Children sport upon the shore,
And hear the mighty waters rolling evermore.

X

Then sing, ye Birds, sing, sing a joyous song!
And let the young Lambs bound
As to the tabor's sound! 175
We in thought will join your throng,
Ye that pipe and ye that play,
Ye that through your hearts to-day

Feel the gladness of the May!
What though the radiance which was once so bright 180
Be now for ever taken from my sight,
Though nothing can bring back the hour
Of splendour in the grass, of glory in the flower;
We will grieve not, rather find
Strength in what remains behind; 185
In the primal sympathy
Which having been must ever be;
In the soothing thoughts that spring
Out of human suffering;
In the faith that looks through death, 190
In years that bring the philosophic mind.

XI

And O, ye Fountains, Meadows, Hills, and Groves,
Forebode not any severing of our loves!
Yet in my heart of hearts I feel your might;
I only have relinquished one delight 195
To live beneath your more habitual sway.
I love the Brooks which down their channels fret,
Even more than when I tripped lightly as they;
The innocent brightness of a new-born Day
Is lovely yet; 200
The Clouds that gather round the setting sun
Do take a sober colouring from an eye
That hath kept watch o'er man's mortality;
Another race hath been, and other palms are won.
Thanks to the human heart by which we live, 205
Thanks to its tenderness, its joys, and fears,
To me the meanest flower that blows can give
Thoughts that do often lie too deep for tears.

Composed upon Westminster Bridge, September 3, 1802*

Earth has not anything to show more fair:
Dull would he be of soul who could pass by
A sight so touching in its majesty;
This City now doth, like a garment, wear
The beauty of the morning; silent, bare, 5
Ships, towers, domes, theatres, and temples lie
Open unto the fields, and to the sky;
All bright and glittering in the smokeless air.

* Published in 1807. "Composed on the roof of a coach on my way to France" (Wordsworth), on July 31, not September 3. The conflict of feelings attending Wordsworth's brief return to France, where he had first gone in 1791-1792 sympathetic to the revolution and had been the lover of Annette Vallon and the father of her child, evoked a number of personal and political sonnets.

Never did sun more beautifully steep
In his first splendour, valley, rock, or hill; 10
Ne'er saw I, never felt, a calm so deep!
The river glideth at his own sweet will:
Dear God! the very houses seem asleep;
And all that mighty heart is lying still!

The World Is Too Much with Us †

The world is too much with us; late and soon,
Getting and spending, we lay waste our powers
Little we see in Nature that is ours;
We have given our hearts away, a sordid boon!
This Sea that bares her bosom to the moon, 5
The winds that will be howling at all hours,
And are up-gathered now like sleeping flowers,
For this, for everything, we are out of tune;
It moves us not.—Great God! I'd rather be
A Pagan suckled in a creed outworn; 10
So might I, standing on this pleasant lea,
Have glimpses that would make me less forlorn;
Have sight of Proteus rising from the sea;
Or hear old Triton blow his wreathèd horn.

The Prelude*

Book I

INTRODUCTION—CHILDHOOD AND SCHOOL-TIME

Oh there is blessing in this gentle breeze
That blows from the green fields and from the clouds
And from the sky: it beats against my cheek,

† Written in 1806; published in 1807.
4. *boon:* gift; *sordid* refers to the act of giving the heart away.
14. *Proteus:* an old man of the sea who, in the *Odyssey,* can assume a variety of shapes. *Triton:* a sea deity, usually represented as blowing on a conch shell.

*Early in 1798, Wordsworth conceived the idea of writing a poem about the growth of his own mind and his development as a poet. Originally, this was intended to make part of a longer philosophical poem, *The Recluse, or Views on Man, Nature, and Society;* but in 1799 he had decided to make the spiritual autobiography an independent work, prefatory to the grander project, and had completed a first version of the first two books. By May 1805 he had finished a first version of the poem in thirteen books, dedicated to his friend Coleridge and called simply "Poem, Title not yet fixed upon." For the rest of his long life Wordsworth continued to revise and expand the poem, and at his death in 1850 it remained known only to members of the Wordsworth circle. It was however published three months later by Mrs. Wordsworth, who gave it its present title. The 1805 version remained unpublished until 1926, and the two-part version until 1974. Doubtless other phases of the poem's evolution will be reconstructed from the copious manuscripts, demonstrating further the growth of the poet's mind.

We offer here the opening and conclusion of the poem in the 1805 text, Books I and XIII. (The 1850 text has fourteen books because Wordsworth divided Book X of the 1805 text, "Residence in France," into two parts.) Though the 1805 text is less polished than that of 1850, it registers a hospitality to experience of every sort and a glowing exuberance of outlook that make it in most respects a more telling record of the growth of a poet's mind than the sedater poem published in 1850.

And seems half-conscious of the joy it gives.
O welcome Messenger! O welcome Friend! 5
A captive greets thee, coming from a house
Of bondage, from yon City's walls set free,
A prison where he hath been long immured.
Now I am free, enfranchised and at large.
May fix my habitation where I will. 10
What dwelling shall receive me? In what Vale
Shall be my harbor? Underneath what grove
Shall I take up my home, and what sweet stream
Shall with its murmur lull me to my rest?
The earth is all before me: with a heart 15
Joyous, nor scared at its own liberty,
I look about, and should the guide I choose
Be nothing better than a wandering cloud,
I cannot miss my way. I breathe again;
Trances of thought and mountings of the mind 20
Come fast upon me: it is shaken off,
As by miraculous gift 'tis shaken off,
That burthen of my own unnatural self,
The heavy weight of many a weary day
Not mine, and such as were not made for me. 25
Long months of peace (if such bold word accord
With any promises of human life),
Long months of ease and undisturbed delight
Are mine in prospect; whither shall I turn
By road or pathway or through open field, 30
Or shall a twig or any floating thing
Upon the river, point me out my course?

Enough that I am free; for months to come
May dedicate myself to chosen tasks;
May quit the tiresome sea and dwell on shore, 35
If not a Settler on the soil, at least
To drink wild water, and to pluck green herbs,
And gather fruits fresh from their native bough.
Nay more, if I may trust myself, this hour
Hath brought a gift that consecrates my joy; 40
For I, methought, while the sweet breath of Heaven
Was blowing on my body, felt within
A corresponding mild creative breeze,
A vital breeze which traveled gently on
O'er things which it had made, and is become 45
A tempest; a redundant energy
Vexing its own creation. 'Tis a power
That does not come unrecognized, a storm,
Which, breaking up a long-continued frost

7. *yon City*: London, where Wordsworth had been living from February, 1793, to September, 1795.

Brings with it vernal promises, the hope 50
Of active days, of dignity and thought,
Of prowess in an honorable field,
Pure passions, virtue, knowledge, and delight,
The holy life of music and of verse.

Thus far, O Friend! did I, not used to make 55
A present joy the matter of my Song,
Pour out, that day, my soul in measured strains
Even in the very words which I have here
Recorded: to the open fields I told
A prophecy: poetic numbers came 60
Spontaneously, and clothed in priestly robe
My spirit, thus singled out, as it might seem,
For holy services: great hopes were mine;
My own voice cheered me, and, far more, the mind's
Internal echo of the imperfect sound; 65
To both I listened, drawing from them both
A cheerful confidence in things to come.

Whereat, being not unwilling now to give
A respite to this passion, I paced on
Gently, with careless steps; and came, erelong, 70
To a green shady place where down I sate
Beneath a tree, slackening my thoughts by choice,
And settling into gentler happiness.
'Twas Autumn, and a calm and placid day,
With warmth as much as needed from a sun 75
Two hours declin'd towards the west, a day
With silver clouds, and sunshine on the grass,
And, in the sheltered grove where I was couched
A perfect stillness. On the ground I lay
Passing through many thoughts, yet mainly such 80
As to myself pertained. I made a choice
Of one sweet Vale whither my steps should turn
And saw, methought, the very house and fields
Present before my eyes: nor did I fail
To add, meanwhile, assurance of some work 85
Of glory, there forthwith to be begun,
Perhaps, too, there performed. Thus long I lay
Cheered by the genial pillow of the earth
Beneath my head, soothed by a sense of touch
From the warm ground, that balanced me, else lost 90
Entirely, seeing nought, nought hearing, save
When here and there, about the grove of Oaks
Where was my bed, an acorn from the trees
Fell audibly, and with a startling sound.

55. *Friend*: Samuel Taylor Coleridge, frequently mentioned in the poem, and the only person outside the Wordsworth family to have read it during the poet's lifetime. Cf. XIII: 269 and 372.

86. *forthwith*: Immediately.

Thus occupied in mind, I lingered here 95
Contented, nor rose up until the sun
Had almost touched the horizon, bidding then
A farewell to the City left behind,
Even with the chance equipment of that hour
I journeyed towards the Vale that I had chosen. 100
It was a splendid evening; and my soul
Did once again make trial of the strength
Restored to her afresh; nor did she want
Eolian visitations; but the harp
Was soon defrauded, and the banded host 105
Of harmony dispersed in straggling sounds
And, lastly, utter silence. "Be it so,
It is an injury," said I, "to this day
To think of any thing but present joy."
So like a Peasant I pursued my road 110
Beneath the evening sun, nor had one wish
Again to bend the sabbath of that time
To a servile yoke. What need of many words?
A pleasant loitering journey, through two days
Continued, brought me to my hermitage. 115

I spare to speak, my Friend, of what ensued,
The admiration and the love, the life
In common things; the endless store of things
Rare, or at least so seeming, every day
Found all about me in one neighborhood, 120
The self-congratulation, the complete
Composure, and the happiness entire.
But speedily a longing in me rose
To brace myself to some determined aim,
Reading or thinking, either to lay up 125
New stores, or rescue from decay the old
By timely interference, I had hopes
Still higher, that with a frame of outward life,
I might endue, might fix in a visible home
Some portion of those phantoms of conceit 130
That had been floating loose about so long,
And to such Beings temperately deal forth
The many feelings that oppressed my heart.
But I have been discouraged; gleams of light
Flash often from the East, then disappear 135
And mock me with a sky that ripens not
Into a steady morning: if my mind,
Remembering the sweet promise of the past,
Would gladly grapple with some noble theme,

104. *Eolian visitations*: I.e., stirrings of inspiration; the image is of the Aeolian harp, an instrument played by the wind passing through its strings.

114. *journey*: About fifty miles.

129. *endue*: Supply.

130. *conceit*: Thought, imagination.

Vain is her wish; where'er she turns she finds 140
Impediments from day to day renewed.

And now it would content me to yield up
Those lofty hopes awhile for present gifts
Of humbler industry. But, O dear Friend!
The Poet, gentle creature as he is, 145
Hath, like the Lover, his unruly times;
His fits when he is neither sick nor well,
Though no distress be near him but his own
Unmanageable thoughts. The mind itself
The meditative mind, best pleased, perhaps, 150
While she, as duteous as the Mother Dove,
Sits brooding, lives not always to that end,
But hath less quiet instincts, goadings on
That drive her as in trouble through the groves.
With me is now such passion, which I blame 155
No otherwise than as it lasts too long.

When, as becomes a man who would prepare
For such a glorious work, I through myself
Make rigorous inquisition, the report
Is often cheering; for I neither seem 160
To lack, that first great gift! the vital soul,
Nor general truths which are themselves a sort
Of Elements and Agents, Under-Powers,
Subordinate helpers of the living mind.
Nor am I naked in external things, 165
Forms, images; nor numerous other aids
Of less regard, though won perhaps with toil,
And needful to build up a Poet's praise.
Time, place, and manners, these I seek, and these
I find in plenteous store; but nowhere such 170
As may be singled out with steady choice;
No little Band of yet remembered names
Whom I, in perfect confidence, might hope
To summon back from lonesome banishment
And make them inmates in the hearts of men 175
Now living, or to live in times to come.
Sometimes, mistaking vainly, as I fear,
Proud spring-tide swellings for a regular sea,
I settle on some British theme, some old
Romantic tale, by Milton left unsung; 180
More often resting at some gentle place
Within the groves of Chivalry, I pipe
Among the Shepherds, with reposing Knights
Sit by a Fountain-side, and hear their tales.

180. *Milton*: Wordsworth's first ambition is to emulate Milton, England's last epic poet, and the opening of Book I is rich with epic and Miltonic allusions.

183–184. *Chivalry . . . shepherds*: Refers to the chivalric romances and pastoral poetry of an earlier time, and perhaps specifically to Edmund Spenser's Arthurian "epic," *The Faerie Queene*.

Sometimes, more sternly moved, I would relate 185
How vanquished Mithridates northward passed,
And, hidden in the cloud of years, became
That Odin, Father of a Race, by whom
Perish'd the Roman Empire: how the Friends
And Followers of Sertorius, out of Spain 190
Flying, found shelter in the Fortunate Isles;
And left their usages, their arts, and laws,
To disappear by a slow gradual death;
To dwindle and to perish one by one
Starved in those narrow bounds: but not the Soul 195
Of Liberty, which fifteen hundred years
Survived, and, when the European came
With skill and power that could not be withstood,
Did, like a pestilence, maintain its hold,
And wasted down by glorious death that Race 200
Of natural Heroes; or I would record
How in tyrannic times some unknown man,
Unheard of in the Chronicles of Kings,
Suffered in silence for the love of truth;
How that one Frenchman, through continued force 205
Of meditation on the inhuman deeds
Of the first Conquerors of the Indian Isles,
Went single in his ministry across
The Ocean, not to comfort the Oppressed,
But, like a thirsty wind, to roam about, 210
Withering the Oppressor: how Gustavus found
Help at his need in Dalecarlia's Mines:
How Wallace fought for Scotland, left the name
Of Wallace to be found like a wild flower,
All over his dear Country, left the deeds 215
Of Wallace, like a family of Ghosts,
To people the steep rocks and river banks,
Her natural sanctuaries, with a local soul
Of independence and stern liberty.
Sometimes it suits me better to shape out 220
Some Tale from my own heart, more near akin
To my own passions and habitual thoughts,
Some variegated story, in the main
Lofty, with interchange of gentler things.
But deadening admonitions will succeed 225

186–191. *Mithridates . . . Fortunate Isles*: The connections made between the Asian king Mithridates II and the Norse god Odin, and between the Roman general Quintus Sertorius and the Fortunate Isles (the Canaries), come from Wordsworth's reading in Plutarch's *Lives* and Gibbon's *Decline and Fall of the Roman Empire*.

205. *Frenchman*: Dominique de Georges, who in 1568 went to Florida to avenge the massacre of a French colony there by the Spaniards.

211. *Gustavus*: Gustav Vasa, later Gustavus I (1496–1560), who led a revolt that freed Sweden from Denmark.

212. *Dalecarlia's Mines*: Gustavus, captured by the Danes, escaped to Dalecarlia, a region of southern Sweden, where he disguised himself as a miner to prevent capture.

214. *Wallace*: Patriot hero of Scotland (1272–1305), who fought against Edward I of England.

And the whole beauteous Fabric seems to lack
Foundation, and, withal, appears throughout
Shadowy and unsubstantial. Then, last wish,
My last and favorite aspiration! then
I yearn towards some philosophic Song 230
Of Truth that cherishes our daily life;
With meditations passionate from deep
Recesses in man's heart, immortal verse
Thoughtfully fitted to the Orphean lyre;
But from this awful burthen I full soon 235
Take refuge, and beguile myself with trust
That mellower years will bring a riper mind
And clearer insight. Thus from day to day
I live, a mockery of the brotherhood
Of vice and virtue, with no skill to part 240
Vague longing that is bred by want of power
From paramount impulse not to be withstood,
A timorous capacity from prudence;
From circumspection, infinite delay.
Humility and modest awe themselves 245
Betray me, serving ofen for a cloak
To a more subtle selfishness, that now
Doth lock my functions up in blank reserve;
Now dupes me by an over-anxious eye
That with a false activity beats off 250
Simplicity and self-presented truth.
—Ah! better far than this, to stray about
Voluptuously through fields and rural walks,
And ask no record of the hours, given up
To vacant musing, unreproved neglect 255
Of all things, and deliberate holiday;
Far better never to have heard the name
Of zeal and just ambition, than to live
Thus baffled by a mind that every hour
Turns recreant to her task, takes heart again, 260
Then feels immediately some hollow thought
Hang like an interdict upon her hopes.
This is my lot; for either still I find
Some imperfection in the chosen theme,
Or see of absolute accomplishment 265
Much wanting, so much wanting, in myself,
That I recoil and droop, and seek repose
In listlessness from vain perplexity,
Unprofitably traveling towards the grave,
Like a false steward who hath much received 270
And renders nothing back.—Was it for this
That one, the fairest of all Rivers, loved

227. *withal*: In addition.
234. *the Orphean lyre*: The harp of Orpheus, legendary musician whose playing could tame animals as well as charm humans and gods.
260. *recreant*: Unfaithful.

To blend his murmurs with my Nurse's song,
And from his alder shades and rocky falls,
And from his fords and shallows, sent a voice 275
That flowed along my dreams? For this, didst Thou,
O Derwent! traveling over the green Plains
Near my "sweet Birthplace," didst thou, beauteous Stream,
Make ceaseless music through the night and day
Which with its steady cadence, tempering 280
Our human waywardness, composed my thoughts
To more than infant softness, giving me,
Among the fretful dwellings of mankind,
A foretaste, a dim earnest, of the calm
That Nature breathes among the hills and groves. 285
When, having left his Mountains, to the Towers
Of Cockermouth that beauteous River came,
Behind my Father's House he passed, close by,
Along the margin of our Terrace Walk.
He was a Playmate whom we dearly loved. 290
Oh! many a time have I, a five years' Child,
A naked Boy, in one delightful Rill,
A little Mill-race severed from his stream,
Made one long bathing of a summer's day,
Basked in the sun, and plunged, and basked again 295
Alternate all a summer's day, or coursed
Over the sandy fields, leaping through groves
Of yellow grunsel, or when crag and hill,
The woods, and distant Skiddaw's lofty height,
Were bronzed with a deep radiance, stood alone 300
Beneath the sky, as if I had been born
On Indian Plains, and from my Mother's hut
Had run abroad in wantonness, to sport,
A naked Savage, in the thunder shower.

Fair seed-time had my soul, and I grew up 305
Fostered alike by beauty and by fear;
Much favor'd in my birthplace, and no less
In that beloved Vale to which, erelong,
I was transplanted. Well I call to mind
('Twas at an early age, ere I had seen 310
Nine summers) when upon the mountain slope
The frost and breath of frosty wind had snapped
The last autumnal crocus, 'twas my joy
To wander half the night among the Cliffs
And the smooth Hollows, where the woodcocks ran 315
Along the open turf. In thought and wish
That time, my shoulder all with springes hung,

277. *Derwent*: The river that flows through Cockermouth, close to the house where Wordsworth was born.

299. *Skiddaw*: One of the highest peaks in the Lake District, near Cockermouth.

308. *Vale*: Esthwaite, where the poet attended school at Hawkshead.

317. *springes*: Snares for birds.

I was a fell destroyer. On the heights
Scudding away from snare to snare, I plied
My anxious visitation, hurrying on, 320
Still hurrying, hurrying onward; moon and stars
Were shining o'er my head; I was alone,
And seemed to be a trouble to the peace
That was among them. Sometimes it befell
In these night-wanderings, that a strong desire 325
O'erpowered my better reason, and the bird
Which was the captive of another's toils
Became my prey; and, when the deed was done
I heard among the solitary hills
Low breathings coming after me, and sounds 330
Of undistinguishable motion, steps
Almost as silent as the turf they trod.
Nor less in springtime when on southern banks
The shining sun had from his knot of leaves
Decoyed the primrose flower, and when the Vales 335
And woods were warm, was I a plunderer then
In the high places, on the lonesome peaks
Where'er, among the mountains and the winds,
The Mother Bird had built her lodge. Though mean
My object, and inglorious, yet the end 340
Was not ignoble. Oh! when I have hung
Above the raven's nest, by knots of grass
And half-inch fissures in the slippery rock
But ill sustained, and almost, as it seemed,
Suspended by the blast which blew amain, 345
Shouldering the naked crag; Oh! at that time,
While on the perilous ridge I hung alone,
With what strange utterance did the loud dry wind
Blow through my ears! the sky seemed not a sky
Of earth, and with what motion mov'd the clouds! 350

The mind of Man is framed even like the breath
And harmony of music. There is a dark
Invisible workmanship that reconciles
Discordant elements, and makes them move
In one society. Ah me! that all 355
The terrors, all the early miseries
Regrets, vexations, lassitudes, that all
The thoughts and feelings which have been infused
Into my mind, should ever have made up
The calm existence that is mine when I 360
Am worthy of myself! Praise to the end!
Thanks likewise for the means! But I believe
That Nature, oftentimes, when she would frame
A favored Being, from his earliest dawn

318. *fell*: Fierce.

345. *amain*: With full force.

Of infancy doth open up the clouds, 365
As at the touch of lightning, seeking him
With gentlest visitation; not the less,
Though haply aiming at the self-same end,
Does it delight her sometimes to employ
Severer interventions, ministry 370
More palpable, and so she dealt with me.

One evening (surely I was led by her)
I went alone into a Shepherd's Boat,
A Skiff that to a Willow tree was tied
Within a rocky Cave, its usual home. 375
'Twas by the shores of Patterdale, a Vale
Wherein I was a Stranger, thither come
A School-boy Traveler, at the Holidays.
Forth rambled from the Village Inn alone
No sooner had I sight of this small Skiff, 380
Discovered thus by unexpected chance,
Than I unloosed her tether and embarked.
The moon was up, the Lake was shining clear
Among the hoary mountains; from the Shore
I pushed, and struck the oars and struck again 385
In cadence, and my little Boat moved on
Even like a Man who walks with stately step
Though bent on speed. It was an act of stealth
And troubled pleasure; not without the voice
Of mountain-echoes did my Boat move on, 390
Leaving behind her still on either side
Small circles glittering idly in the moon,
Until they melted all into one track
Of sparkling light. A rocky Steep uprose
Above the Cavern of the Willow tree 395
And now, as suited one who proudly rowed
With his best skill, I fixed a steady view
Upon the top of that same craggy ridge,
The bound of the horizon, for behind
Was nothing but the stars and the grey sky. 400
She was an elfin Pinnace; lustily
I dipped my oars into the silent Lake,
And, as I rose upon the stroke, my Boat
Went heaving through the water, like a Swan;
When from behind that craggy Steep, till then 405
The bound of the horizon, a huge Cliff,
As if with voluntary power instinct,
Upreared its head. I struck, and struck again,
And, growing still in stature, the huge Cliff

376. *Patterdale*: A town near Ullswater, one of the Lakes.
363. *frame*: Shape.
368. *haply*: Perhaps.
384. *hoary*: Ancient; also white-topped, as if with age.
401. *Pinnace*: Small boat that can be sailed or rowed.

Rose up between me and the stars, and still, 410
With measured motion, like a living thing,
Strode after me. With trembling hands I turned,
And through the silent water stole my way
Back to the Cavern of the Willow tree.
There, in her mooring-place, I left my Bark, 415
And, through the meadows homeward went, with grave
And serious thoughts; and after I had seen
That spectacle, for many days, my brain
Worked with a dim and undetermined sense
Of unknown modes of being; in my thoughts 420
There was a darkness, call it solitude,
Or blank desertion, no familiar shapes
Of hourly objects, images of trees,
Of sea or sky, no colors of green fields;
But huge and mighty Forms that do not live 425
Like living men moved slowly through the mind
By day and were the trouble of my dreams.

Wisdom and Spirit of the universe!
Thou Soul that art the eternity of thought!
That giv'st to forms and images a breath 430
And everlasting motion! not in vain,
By day or star-light thus from my first dawn
Of Childhood didst Thou intertwine for me
The passions that build up our human Soul,
Not with the mean and vulgar works of Man, 435
But with high objects, with enduring things,
With life and nature, purifying thus
The elements of feeling and of thought,
And sanctifying, by such discipline,
Both pain and fear, until we recognize 440
A grandeur in the beatings of the heart.

Nor was this fellowship vouchsafed to me
With stinted kindness. In November days,
When vapors, rolling down the valleys, made
A lonely scene more lonesome; among woods 445
At noon, and 'mid the calm of summer nights,
When, by the margin of the trembling Lake,
Beneath the gloomy hills I homeward went
In solitude, such intercourse was mine;
And by the waters all the summer long.
'Twas mine among the fields both day and night, 450

And in the frosty season, when the sun
Was set, and visible for many a mile
The cottage windows through the twilight blazed,

442. ***vouchsafed***: Given.

I heeded not the summons:—happy time 455
It was, indeed, for all of us; to me
It was a time of rapture: clear and loud
The village clock tolled six; I wheeled about,
Proud and exulting, like an untired horse,
That cares not for his home.—All shod with steel, 460
We hissed along the polished ice, in games
Confederate, imitative of the chase
And woodland pleasures, the resounding horn,
The Pack loud bellowing, and the hunted hare.
So through the darkness and the cold we flew, 465
And not a voice was idle; with the din,
Meanwhile, the precipices rang aloud,
The leafless trees, and every icy crag
Tinkled like iron, while the distant hills
Into the tumult sent an alien sound 470
Of melancholy, not unnoticed, while the stars,
Eastward, were sparkling clear, and in the west
The orange sky of evening died away.

Not seldom from the uproar I retired
Into a silent bay, or sportively 475
Glanced sideway, leaving the tumultuous throng,
To cut across the image of a star
That gleamed upon the ice: and oftentimes
When we had given our bodies to the wind,
And all the shadowy banks, on either side, 480
Came sweeping through the darkness, spinning still
The rapid line of motion; then at once
Have I, reclining back upon my heels,
Stopped short, yet still the solitary Cliffs
Wheeled by me, even as if the earth had rolled 485
With visible motion her diurnal round;
Behind me did they stretch in solemn train
Feebler and feebler, and I stood and watched
Till all was tranquil as a dreamless sleep.

Ye Presences of Nature, in the sky 490
And on the earth! Ye Visions of the hills!
And Souls of lonely places! can I think
A vulgar hope was yours when Ye employed
Such ministry, when Ye through many a year
Haunting me thus among my boyish sports, 495
On caves and trees, upon the woods and hills,
Impressed upon all forms the characters
Of danger or desire, and thus did make
The surface of the universal earth

476. *glanced*: Moved swiftly.

With triumph, and delight, and hope, and fear, 500
Work like a sea?
Not uselessly employed,
I might pursue this theme through every change
Of exercise and play, to which the year
Did summon us in its delightful round.

We were a noisy crew, the sun in heaven 505
Beheld not vales more beautiful than ours,
Nor saw a race in happiness and joy
More worthy of the ground where they were sown.
I would record with no reluctant voice
The woods of autumn and their hazel bowers 510
With milk-white clusters hung; the rod and line,
True symbol of the foolishness of hope,
Which with its strong enchantment led us on
By rocks and pools, shut out from every star
All the green summer, to forlorn cascades 515
Among the windings of the mountain brooks.
—Unfading recollections! at this hour
The heart is almost mine with which I felt
From some hill-top, on sunny afternoons
The Kite high up among the fleecy clouds 520
Pull at its rein, like an impatient Courser,
Or, from the meadows sent on gusty days,
Beheld her breast the wind, then suddenly
Dashed headlong; and rejected by the storm.

Ye lowly Cottages in which we dwelt, 525
A ministration of your own was yours,
A sanctity, a safeguard, and a love!
Can I forget you, being as you were
So beautiful among the pleasant fields
In which ye stood? Or can I here forget 530
The plain and seemly countenance with which
Ye dealt out your plain comforts? Yet had ye
Delights and exultations of your own.
Eager and never weary we pursued
Our home amusements by the warm peat-fire 535
At evening; when with pencil and with slate,
In square divisions parcelled out, and all
With crosses and with cyphers scribbled o'er,
We schemed and puzzled, head opposed to head
In strife too humble to be named in Verse. 540
Or round the naked table, snow-white deal,
Cherry or maple, sate in close array,

525. *Cottages*: Students at Hawkshead boarded in the village; and for nine years Wordsworth lived in Anne Tyson's cottage.

538. *cyphers*: Zeroes.

541. *deal*: Planks of fir or pine.

And to the combat, Loo or Whist, led on
A thick-ribbed Army; not as in the world
Neglected and ungratefully thrown by 545
Even for the very service they had wrought,
But husbanded through many a long campaign.
Uncouth assemblage was it, where no few
Had changed their functions, some, plebeian cards,
Which Fate beyond the promise of their birth 550
Had glorified, and called to represent
The persons of departed Potentates.
Oh! with what echoes on the Board they fell!
Ironic Diamonds, Clubs, Hearts, Diamonds, Spades,
A congregation piteously akin. 555
Cheap matter did they give to boyish wit,
Those sooty knaves, precipitated down
With scoffs and taunts, like Vulcan out of Heaven,
The paramount Ace, a moon in her eclipse,
Queens, gleaming through their splendor's last decay, 560
And Monarchs, surly at the wrongs sustained
By royal visages. Meanwhile, abroad
The heavy rain was falling, or the frost
Raged bitterly, with keen and silent tooth,
And, interrupting oft the impassioned game, 565
From Esthwaite's neighboring Lake the splitting ice,
While it sank down towards the water, sent,
Among the meadows and the hills, its long
And dismal yellings, like the noise of wolves
When they are howling round the Bothnic Main. 570

Nor, sedulous as I have been to trace
How Nature by extrinsic passion first
Peopled my mind with beauteous forms or grand,
And made me love them, may I here forget
How other pleasures have been mine, and joys 575
Of subtler origin; how I have felt,
Not seldom, even in that tempestuous time,
Those hallowed and pure motions of the sense
Which seem, in their simplicity, to own
An intellectual charm, that calm delight 580
Which, if I err not, surely must belong
To those first-born affinities that fit
Our new existence to existing things,
And, in our dawn of being, constitute
The bond of union betwixt life and joy. 585

543. *Loo or Whist*: Card games.
544. *Army*: The game is an imitation of Pope's *Rape of the Lock*, III, ll. 25–98.
557. *knaves*: I.e., Jacks.
558. *Vulcan*: Also known as Hephaestus, blacksmith and god of fire, crippled when his father Zeus threw him out of Heaven. Cf. Milton, *Paradise Lost*, I, 738–46.
570. *Bothnic Main*: The Gulf of Bothnia, between Sweden and Finland.
572. *extrinsic passion*: Feelings for the superficial pleasures of nature.

Yes, I remember, when the changeful earth,
And twice five seasons on my mind had stamped
The faces of the moving year, even then,
A Child, I held unconscious intercourse
With the eternal Beauty, drinking in 590
A pure organic pleasure from the lines
Of curling mist, or from the level plain
Of waters color'd by the steady clouds.

The Sands of Westmoreland, the Creeks and Bays
Of Cumbria's rocky limits, they can tell 595
How when the Sea threw off his evening shade
And to the Shepherd's huts beneath the crags
Did send sweet notice of the rising moon,
How I have stood, to fancies such as these,
Engrafted in the tenderness of thought, 600
A stranger, linking with the spectacle
No conscious memory of a kindred sight,
And bringing with me no peculiar sense
Of quietness or peace, yet I have stood,
Even while mine eye has moved o'er three long leagues 605
Of shining water, gathering, as it seemed,
Through every hair-breadth of that field of light,
New pleasure, like a bee among the flowers.

Thus, often in those fits of vulgar joy
Which, through all seasons, on a child's pursuits 610
Are prompt attendants, 'mid that giddy bliss
Which, like a tempest, works along the blood
And is forgotten; even then I felt
Gleams like the flashing of a shield; the earth
And common face of Nature spake to me 615
Rememberable things; sometimes, 'tis true,
By chance collisions and quaint accidents
Like those ill-sorted unions, work supposed
Of evil-minded fairies, yet not vain
Nor profitless, if haply they impress'd 620
Collateral objects and appearances,
Albeit lifeless then, and doomed to sleep
Until maturer seasons called them forth
To impregnate and to elevate the mind.
—And if the vulgar joy by its own weight 625
Wearied itself out of the memory,
The scenes which were a witness of that joy
Remained, in their substantial lineaments
Depicted on the brain, and to the eye

594–595. *Westmoreland . . . Cumbria*: Counties on England's west coast near the Scottish border. (*Cumbria*: Cumberland.)

600. *Engrafted*: I.e., grafted.

605. *three . . . leagues*: Nine miles.

609. *vulgar*: Common, ordinary.

Were visible, a daily sight; and thus 630
By the impressive discipline of fear,
By pleasure and repeated happiness,
So frequently repeated, and by force
Of obscure feelings representative
Of joys that were forgotten, these same scenes, 635
So beauteous and majestic in themselves,
Though yet the day was distant, did at length
Become habitually dear, and all
Their hues and forms were by invisible links
Allied to the affections. I began 640
My story early, feeling as I fear,
The weakness of a human love, for days
Disowned by memory, ere the birth of spring
Planting my snowdrops among winter snows.
Nor will it seem to thee, my Friend! so prompt 645
In sympathy, that I have lengthened out,
With fond and feeble tongue, a tedious tale.
Meanwhile, my hope has been that I might fetch
Invigorating thoughts from former years,
Might fix the wavering balance of my mind, 650
And haply meet reproaches, too, whose power
May spur me on, in manhood now mature,
To honorable toil. Yet should these hopes
Be vain, and thus should neither I be taught
To understand myself, nor thou to know 655
With better knowledge how the heart was framed
Of him thou lovest, need I dread from thee
Harsh judgments, if I am so loth to quit
Those recollected hours that have the charm
Of visionary things, and lovely forms 660
And sweet sensations that throw back our life
And almost make our Infancy itself
A visible scene, on which the sun is shining?

One end hereby at least hath been attained,
My mind hath been revived, and if this mood 665
Desert me not, I will forthwith bring down,
Through later years, the story of my life.
The road lies plain before me; 'tis a theme
Single and of determined bounds; and hence
I choose it rather at this time, than work 670
Of ampler or more varied argument.

[The course of *The Prelude* may be gathered from the titles of the eleven intervening books: II. School-Time (continued); III. Residence at Cambridge; IV. Summer Vacation; V. Books; VI. Cambridge and the Alps; VII. Residence in London; VIII. Retrospect

640. *affections*: Mild emotions. 658. *loth*: Reluctant.

—Love of Nature Leading to Love of Mankind; IX. Residence in France; X. Residence in France and French Revolution; XI. Imagination, how Impaired and Restored; XII. Same Subject (continued)]

Book XIII

CONCLUSION

In one of these excursions, traveling then
Through Wales on foot, and with a youthful Friend,
I left Bethhelert's huts at couching-time,
And westward took my way to see the sun
Rise from the top of Snowdon. Having reached 5
The Cottage at the Mountain's foot, we there
Roused up the Shepherd, who by ancient right
Of office is the Stranger's usual guide;
And after short refreshment sallied forth.

It was a Summer's night, a close warm night, 10
Wan, dull and glaring, with a dripping mist
Low-hung and thick that covered all the sky,
Half threatening storm and rain; but on we went
Unchecked, being full of heart and having faith
In our tried Pilot. Little could we see 15
Hemmed round on every side with fog and damp,
And, after ordinary travelers' chat
With our Conductor, silently we sank
Each into commerce with his private thoughts:
Thus did we breast the ascent, and by myself 20
Was nothing either seen or heard the while
Which took me from my musings, save that once
The Shepherd's Cur did to his own great joy
Unearth a hedgehog in the mountain crags
Round which he made a barking turbulent. 25
This small adventure, for even such it seemed
In that wild place and at the dead of night,
Being over and forgotten, on we wound
In silence as before. With forehead bent
Earthward, as if in opposition set 30
Against an enemy, I panted up
With eager pace, and no less eager thoughts.
Thus might we wear perhaps an hour away,
Ascending at loose distance each from each,
And I, as chanced, the foremost of the Band; 35
When at my feet the ground appeared to brighten,

1–5. In either 1791 or 1793, Wordsworth and Robert Coles (a companion with whom he also toured the Alps, cf. Bk. VI) climbed Mt. Snowdon, Wales's highest mountain (3560 ft.). They left at evening ("couching-time") from the village of Bethgelert (or Bethhelert).

And with a step or two seemed brighter still;
Nor had I time to ask the cause of this,
For instantly a Light upon the turf
Fell like a flash; I looked about, and lo! 40
The Moon stood naked in the Heavens, at height
Immense above my head, and on the shore
I found myself of a huge sea of mist,
Which, meek and silent, rested at my feet:
A hundred hills their dusky backs upheaved 45
All over this still Ocean, and beyond,
Far, far beyond, the vapors shot themselves,
In headlands, tongues, and promontory shapes,
Into the Sea, the real Sea, that seemed
To dwindle, and give up its majesty, 50
Usurped upon as far as sight could reach.
Meanwhile, the Moon looked down upon this show
In single glory, and we stood, the mist
Touching our very feet; and from the shore
At distance not the third part of a mile 55
Was a blue chasm; a fracture in the vapor,
A deep and gloomy breathing-place through which
Mounted the roar of waters, torrents, streams
Innumerable, roaring with one voice.
The universal spectacle throughout 60
Was shaped for admiration and delight,
Grand in itself alone, but in that breach
Through which the homeless voice of waters rose,
That dark deep thoroughfare had Nature lodged
The Soul, the Imagination of the whole. 65

A meditation rose in me that night
Upon the lonely Mountain when the scene
Had passed away, and it appeared to me
The perfect image of a mighty Mind,
Of one that feeds upon infinity, 70
That is exalted by an underpresence,
The sense of God, or whatsoe'er is dim
Or vast in its own being, above all
One function of such mind had Nature there
Exhibited by putting forth, and that 75
With circumstance most awful and sublime,
That domination which she oftentimes
Exerts upon the outward face of things,
So moulds them, and endues, abstracts, combines,
Or by abrupt and unhabitual influence 80
Doth make one object so impress itself
Upon all others, and pervade them so
That even the grossest minds must see and hear
And cannot choose but feel. The Power which these
Acknowledge when thus moved, which Nature thus 85

Thrusts forth upon the senses, is the express
Resemblance, in the fullness of its strength
Made visible, a genuine Counterpart
And Brother of the glorious faculty
Which higher minds bear with them as their own. 90
That is the very spirit in which they deal
With all the objects of the universe;
They from their native selves can send abroad
Like transformations, for themselves create
A like existence, and, whene'er it is 95
Created for them, catch it by an instinct;
Them the enduring and the transient both
Serve to exalt; they build up greatest things
From least suggestions, ever on the watch,
Willing to work and to be wrought upon, 100
They need not extraordinary calls
To rouse them, in a world of life they live,
By sensible impressions not enthralled,
But quickened, roused, and made thereby more apt
To hold communion with the invisible world. 105
Such minds are truly from the Deity,
For they are Powers; and hence the highest bliss
That can be known is theirs, the consciousness
Of whom they are habitually infused
Through every image, and through every thought, 110
And all impressions; hence religion, faith,
And endless occupation for the soul
Whether discursive or intuitive;
Hence sovereignty within and peace at will
Emotion which best foresight need not fear 115
Most worthy then of trust when most intense.
Hence cheerfulness in every act of life
Hence truth in moral judgments and delight
That fails not in the external universe.

Oh! who is he that hath his whole life long 120
Preserved, enlarged, this freedom in himself?
For this alone is genuine Liberty:
Witness, ye Solitudes! where I received
My earliest visitations, careless then
Of what was given me, and where now I roam, 125
A meditative, oft a suffering Man,
And yet, I trust, with undiminished powers,
Witness, whatever falls my better mind,
Revolving with the accidents of life,

89. *glorious faculty*: The imagination.
100. *wrought*: I.e., worked.
103. *sensible*: Of the senses.
113. *discursive or intuitive*: The former faculty is rational and scientific; the latter is immediate and depends more on the emotions and the imagination. While here both modes seem balanced, throughout the *Prelude* and his other writings Wordsworth—like most Romantics—regards the "intuitive" as superior.

May have sustained, that, howsoe'er misled, 130
I never, in the quest of right and wrong,
Did tamper with myself from private aims;
Nor was in any of my hopes the dupe
Of selfish passions; nor did wilfully
Yield ever to mean cares and low pursuits; 135
But rather did with jealousy shrink back
From every combination that might aid
The tendency, too potent in itself,
Of habit to enslave the mind, I mean
Oppress it by the laws of vulgar sense, 140
And substitute a universe of death,
The falsest of all worlds, in place of that
Which is divine and true. To fear and love,
To love as first and chief, for there fear ends,
Be this ascribed; to early intercourse, 145
In presence of sublime and lovely forms,
With the adverse principles of pain and joy,
Evil as one is rashly named by those
Who know not what they say. By love, for here
Do we begin and end, all grandeur comes, 150
All truth and beauty, from pervading love,
That gone, we are as dust, Behold the fields
In balmy spring-time, full of rising flowers
And happy creatures; see that Pair, the Lamb
And the Lamb's Mother, and their tender ways 155
Shall touch thee to the heart; in some green bower
Rest, and be not alone, but have thou there
The One who is thy choice of all the world,
There linger, lulled and lost, and rapt away,
Be happy to thy fill; thou call'st this love 160
And so it is, but there is higher love
Than this, a love that comes into the heart
With awe and a diffusive sentiment;
Thy love is human merely; this proceeds
More from the brooding Soul, and is divine. 165

This love more intellectual cannot be
Without Imagination, which, in truth,
Is but another name for absolute strength
And clearest insight, amplitude of mind,

140. *vulgar*: Ordinary.

156–165. Here, and elsewhere in the Conclusion, Wordsworth changed or inserted passages after completing the 1805 version that make the moment of revelation accord with orthodox Christian belief. Here is the 1850 version: ". . . thou callest this love, / And not inaptly so, for love it is, / Far as it carries thee. In some green bower / Rest, and be not alone, but have thou there / The One who is thy choice of all the world: / There linger, listening, gazing, with delight / Impassioned, but delight how pitiable! / Unless this love by a still higher love / Be hallowed, love that breathes not without awe; / Love that adores, but on the knees of prayer, / By heaven inspired; that frees from chains the soul, / Bearing, in union with the purest, best, / Of earth-born passions, on the wings of praise / A mutual tribute to the Almighty's Throne."

And reason in her most exalted mood. 170
This faculty hath been the moving soul
Of our long labor: we have traced the stream
From darkness, and the very place of birth
In its blind cavern, whence is faintly heard
The sound of waters; followed it to light 175
And open day, accompanied its course
Among the ways of Nature, afterwards
Lost sight of it bewildered and engulfed,
Then given it greeting, as it rose once more
With strength, reflecting in its solemn breast 180
The works of man and face of human life,
And lastly, from its progress have we drawn
The feeling of life endless, the great thought
By which we live, Infinity and God.
Imagination having been our theme, 185
So also hath that intellectual love,
For they are each in each, and cannot stand
Dividually.—Here must thou be, O Man!
Strength to thyself; no Helper hast thou here;
Here keepest thou thy individual state: 190
No other can divide with thee this work,
No secondary hand can intervene
To fashion this ability; 'tis thine,
The prime and vital principle is thine
In the recesses of thy nature, far 195
From any reach of outward fellowship,
Else is not thine at all. But joy to him,
Oh, joy to him who here hath sown, hath laid
Here the foundations of his future years!
For all that friendship, all that love can do, 200
All that a darling countenance can look
Or dear voice utter to complete the man,
Perfect him, made imperfect in himself,
All shall be his: and he whose soul hath risen
Up to the height of feeling intellect 205
Shall want no humbler tenderness, his heart
Be tender as a nursing Mother's heart;
Of female softness shall his life be full,
Of little loves and delicate desires,
Mild interests and gentlest sympathies. 210

Child of my Parents! Sister of my Soul!
Elsewhere have streams of gratitude been breathed
To thee for all the early tenderness
Which I from thee imbibed. And true it is
That later seasons owed to thee no less; 215

188. *Dividually*: Apart from each other.

211. *Child of my Parents!*: His sister Dorothy.

For, spite of thy sweet influence and the touch
Of other kindred hands that opened out
The springs of tender thought in infancy,
And spite of all which singly I had watched
Of elegance, and each minuter charm 220
In nature and in life, still to the last
Even to the very going out of youth,
The period which our Story now hath reached,
I too exclusively esteemed that love,
And sought that beauty, which, as Milton sings, 225
Hath terror in it. Thou didst soften down
This over-sternness; but for thee, sweet Friend,
My soul, too reckless of mild grace, had been
Far longer what by Nature it was framed,
Longer retained its countenance severe, 230
A rock with torrents roaring, with the clouds
Familiar, and a favorite of the Stars:
But thou didst plant its crevices with flowers,
Hang it with shrubs that twinkle in the breeze,
And teach the little birds to build their nests 235
And warble in its chambers. At a time
When Nature, destined to remain so long
Foremost in my affections, had fallen back
Into a second place, well pleased to be
A handmaid to a nobler than herself, 240
When every day brought with it some new sense
Of exquisite regard for common things,
And all the earth was budding with these gifts
Of more refined humanity, thy breath,
Dear Sister, was a kind of gentler spring 245
That went before my steps.
With such a theme,
Coleridge! with this my argument, of thee
Shall I be silent? O most loving Soul!
Placed on this earth to love and understand,
And from thy presence shed the light of love, 250
Shall I be mute ere thou be spoken of?
Thy gentle Spirit to my heart of hearts
Did also find its way; and thus the life
Of all things and the mighty unity
In all which we behold, and feel, and are, 255
Admitted more habitually a mild
Interposition, and closelier gathering thoughts
Of man and his concerns, such as become
A human Creature, be he who he may!
Poet, or destined for a humbler name; 260
And so the deep enthusiastic joy,

225. *Milton*: In *Paradise Lost*, IX, 489–91.

240. *handmaid*: Servant.

The rapture of the Hallelujah sent
From all that breathes and is, was chastened, stemmed
And balanced by a Reason which indeed
Is reason; duty and pathetic truth; 265
And God and Man divided, as they ought,
Between them the great system of the world
Where Man is sphered, and which God animates.

And now, O Friend! this history is brought
To its appointed close: the discipline 270
And consummation of the Poet's mind,
In everything that stood most prominent,
Have faithfully been pictured; we have reached
The time (which was our object from the first)
When we may, not presumptuously, I hope, 275
Suppose my powers so far confirmed, and such
My knowledge, as to make me capable
Of building up a work that should endure.
Yet much hath been omitted, as need was;
Of Books how much! and even of the other wealth 280
That is collected among woods and fields,
Far more: for Nature's secondary grace,
That outward illustration which is hers,
Hath hitherto been barely touched upon,
The charm more superficial, and yet sweet 285
Which from her works finds way, contemplated
As they hold forth a genuine counterpart
And softening mirror of the moral world.

Yes, having tracked the main essential Power,
Imagination, up her way sublime, 290
In turn might Fancy also be pursued
Through all her transmigrations, till she too
Was purified, had learned to ply her craft
By judgment steadied. Then might we return
And in the Rivers and the Groves behold 295
Another face, might hear them from all sides
Calling upon the more instructed mind
To link their images with subtle skill
Sometimes, and by elaborate research
With forms and definite appearances 300
Of human life, presenting them sometimes
To the involuntary sympathy
Of our internal being, satisfied
And soothed with a conception of delight
Where meditation cannot come, which thought 305
Could never heighten. Above all how much

265. *pathetic*: Emotional.
291. *Fancy*: Or fantasy, the power of uncontrolled imagination.

Still nearer to ourselves we overlook
In human nature and that marvelous world
As studied first in my own heart, and then
In life among the passions of mankind 310
And qualities commixed and modified
By the infinite varieties and shades
Of individual character. Therein
It was for me (this justice bids me say)
No useless preparation to have been 315
The pupil of a public School, and forced
In hardy independence, to stand up
Amid conflicting passions, and the shock
Of various tempers, to endure and note
What was not understood though known to be; 320
Among the mysteries of love and hate,
Honor and shame, looking to right and left,
Unchecked by innocence too delicate
And moral notions too intolerant,
Sympathies too contracted. Hence, when called 325
To take a station among Men, the step
Was easier, the transition more secure,
More profitable also; for the mind
Learns from such timely exercise to keep
In wholesome separation the two natures, 330
The one that feels, the other that observes.

Yet one word more of personal circumstance,
Not needless, as it seems, be added here.
Since I withdrew unwillingly from France,
The Story hath demanded less regard 335
To time and place; and where I lived, and how
Hath been no longer scrupulously marked.
Three years, until a permanent abode
Received me with that Sister of my heart
Who ought by rights the dearest to have been 340
Conspicuous through this biographic Verse,
Star seldom utterly concealed from view,
I led an undomestic Wanderer's life,
In London chiefly was my home, and thence
Excursively, as personal friendships, chance 345
Or inclination led, or slender means

311. *commixed*: Mixed together.

316. *public School*: Not in the American sense; in Britain, "public" schools are what we would call "private." The implied alternative here is to have been educated at home (or to have educated oneself).

334. Wordsworth had gone to France in 1791, an enthusiast of the Revolution. When he left in 1792 that enthusiasm had not yet given way to disillusion at the excesses committed in the Revolution's name. Doubtless some of his unwillingness stemmed from his affair with Annette Vallon, with whom he had an illegitimate daughter.

338. *permanent abode*: The house he shared with his sister Dorothy at Racedown, in Dorset, or the house at Grasmere in the Lake Country where he lived with his wife; Wordsworth's meaning is not clear.

Gave leave, I roamed about from place to place
Tarrying in pleasant nooks, wherever found
Through England or through Wales. A Youth (he bore
The name of Calvert; it shall live, if words 350
Of mine can give it life), without respect
To prejudice or custom, having hope
That I had some endowments by which good
Might be promoted, in his last decay
From his own Family withdrawing part 355
Of no redundant Patrimony, did
By a Bequest sufficient for my needs
Enable me to pause for choice, and walk
At large and unrestrained, nor damped too soon
By mortal cares. Himself no Poet, yet 360
Far less a common Spirit of the world,
He deemed that my pursuits and labors lay
Apart from all that leads to wealth, or even
Perhaps to necessary maintenance,
Without some hazard to the finer sense; 365
He cleared a passage for me, and the stream
Flowed in the bent of Nature.

Having now
Told what best merits mention, further pains
Our present purpose seems not to require,
And I have other tasks. Call back to mind 370
The mood in which this Poem was begun,
O Friend! the termination of my course
Is nearer now, much nearer; yet even then
In that distraction and intense desire
I said unto the life which I had lived, 375
Where art thou? Hear I not a voice from thee
Which 'tis reproach to hear? Anon I rose
As if on wings, and saw beneath me stretched
Vast prospect of the world which I had been
And was; and hence this Song, which like a lark 380
I have protracted, in the unwearied Heavens
Singing, and often with more plaintive voice
Attempered to the sorrows of the earth;
Yet cent'ring all in love, and in the end
All gratulant if rightly understood. 385

Whether to me shall be allotted life,
And with life power to accomplish aught of worth
Sufficient to excuse me in men's sight
For having given this Record of myself,
Is all uncertain: but, beloved Friend, 390

350. *Calvert*: Raisley Calvert, a consumptive whom Wordsworth attended through his last illness, and who left the poet a legacy of £900 which freed him from financial need, and thus enabled him to write.

377. *Anon*: Immediately.

385. *gratulant*: Grateful.

When, looking back thou seest in clearer view
Than any sweetest sight of yesterday
That summer when on Quantock's grassy Hills
Far ranging, and among her sylvan Combs,
Thou in delicious words, with happy heart, 395
Didst speak the Vision of that Ancient Man,
The bright-eyed Mariner, and rueful woes
Didst utter of the Lady Christabel;
And I, associate with such labor, walked
Murmuring of him who, joyous hap! was found, 400
After the perils of his moonlight ride
Near the loud Waterfall; or her who sate
In misery near the miserable Thorn;
When thou dost to that summer turn thy thoughts,
And hast before thee all which then we were, 405
To thee, in memory of that happiness
It will be known, by thee at least, my Friend,
Felt, that the history of a Poet's mind
Is labor not unworthy of regard:
To thee the work shall justify itself. 410

The last and later portions of this Gift
Which I for Thee design, have been prepared
In times which have from those wherein we first
Together wantoned in wild Poesy,
Differed thus far, that they have been, my Friend, 415
Times of much sorrow, of a private grief
Keen and enduring, which the frame of mind
That in this mediative History
Hath been described, more deeply makes me feel;
Yet likewise hath enabled me to bear 420
More firmly; and a comfort now, a hope,
One of the dearest which this life can give,
Is mine; that Thou art near, and wilt be soon
Restored to us in renovated health;
When, after the first mingling of our tears, 425
'Mong other consolations we may find
Some pleasure from this Offering of my love.

Oh! yet a few short years of useful life,
And all will be complete, thy race be run,
Thy monument of glory will be raised. 430

394. *Combs*: Narrow valleys.
394–403. *Quantock . . . Thorn*: Wordsworth lived at Alfoxden from July, 1797, until September, 1798, and Coleridge at nearby Nether Stowey. The Quantock Hills are also nearby. Coleridge wrote both *The Ancient Mariner* and *Christabel* there in late autumn, 1797. "Him" (l. 400) is a reference to Wordsworth's *Idiot Boy*, which he composed along with *The Thorn* (l. 403) in 1798.
414. *wantoned*: Luxuriated.
416. *private grief*: The death of Wordsworth's brother John in February 1805.

Then, though, too weak to tread the ways of truth,
This Age fall back to old idolatry,
Though men return to servitude as fast
As the tide ebbs, to ignominy and shame
By Nations sink together, we shall still 435
Find solace in the knowledge which we have,
Blessed with true happiness if we may be
United helpers forward of a day
Of firmer trust, joint-laborers in a work
(Should Providence such grace to us vouchsafe) 440
Of their redemption, surely yet to come.
Prophets of Nature, we to them will speak
A lasting inspiration, sanctified
By reason and by truth; what we have loved,
Others will love; and we may teach them how; 445
Instruct them how the mind of man becomes
A thousand times more beautiful than the earth
On which he dwells, above this Frame of things
(Which, 'mid all revolution in the hopes
And fears of men, doth still remain unchanged) 450
In beauty exalted, as it is itself
Of substance and of fabric more divine.

439. *joint-laborers*: A reference to *The Lyrical Ballads* (1798).

SAMUEL TAYLOR COLERIDGE (1772–1834)

Kubla Khan*

OR, A VISION IN A DREAM, A FRAGMENT

The following fragment is here published at the request of a poet of great and deserved celebrity [Lord Byron], and, as far as the Author's own opinions are concerned, rather as a psychological curiosity, than on the ground of any supposed poetic merits.

In the summer of the year 1797, the Author, then in ill health, had retired to a lonely farm-house between Porlock and Linton, on the Exmoore confines of Somerset and Devonshire.[1] In consequence of a slight indisposition, an anodyne had been prescribed, from the effects of which he fell asleep in his chair at the moment that he

* The poem was first published together with *Christabel* and *The Pains of Sleep* in 1816. E. H. Coleridge dates the poem 1798; it may actually have been written in 1799 or as late as 1800.

1. A high moorland shared by the two southwestern counties in England of Devonshire and Somerset.

was reading the following sentence, or words of the same substance, in "Purchas's Pilgrimage"[2]: "Here the Khan Kubla commanded a palace to be built, and a stately garden thereunto. And thus ten miles of fertile ground were inclosed with a wall." The Author continued for about three hours in a profound sleep, at least of the external senses, during which time he has the most vivid confidence, that he could not have composed less than from two to three hundred lines; if that indeed can be called composition in which all the images rose up before him as things, with a parallel production of the correspondent expressions, without any sensation or consciousness of effort.[3] On awaking he appeared to himself to have a distinct recollection of the whole, and taking his pen, ink, and paper, instantly and eagerly wrote down the lines that are here preserved. At this moment he was unfortunately called out by a person on business from Porlock, and detained by him above an hour, and on his return to his room, found, to his no small surprise and mortification, that though he still retained some vague and dim recollection of the general purport of the vision yet, with the exception of some eight or ten scattered lines and images, all the rest had passed away like the images on the surface of a stream into which a stone has been cast, but, alas! without the after restoration of the latter!

> Then all the charm
> Is broken—all that phantom-world so fair
> Vanishes, and a thousand circlets spread,
> And each mis-shape['s] the other. Stay awhile,
> Poor youth! who scarcely dar'st lift up thine eyes—
> The stream will soon renew its smoothness, soon
> The visions will return! And lo, he stays,
> And soon the fragments dim of lovely forms
> Come trembling back, unite, and now once more
> The pool becomes a mirror.[4]

Yet from the still surviving recollections in his mind, the Author has frequently purposed to finish for himself what had been originally, as it were, given to him.

Σαμερον αδιον ασω:[5] but the to-morrow is yet to come.

2. Samuel Purchas (1575?–1626) published *Purchas his Pilgrimage, or Relations of the World and the Religions observed in all Ages* in 1613. The passage in Purchas is slightly different: "In Xamdu did Cublai Can build a stately Palace, encompassing sixteene miles of plaine ground with a wall, wherein are fertile meddowes, pleasant Springs, delightfull Streames, and all sorts of beasts of chase and game, and in the middest thereof a sumptuous house of pleasure, which may be removed from place to place" (Book IV, Chap. 13).

3. Coleridge's statement that he dreamed the poem and wrote down what he could later remember *verbatim* has been queried, most recently by medical opinion. The belief that opium produces special dreams, or even any dreams at all, seems to lack confirmation.

4. From Coleridge's poem *The Picture; or, the Lover's Resolution*, lines 91–100.

5. From Theocritus, *Idylls*, I, 132: "to sing a sweeter song tomorrow."

In Xanadu did Kubla Khan
A stately pleasure-dome decree:
Where Alph, the sacred river, ran
Through caverns measureless to man
   Down to a sunless sea. 5
So twice five miles of fertile ground
With walls and towers were girdled round:
And there were gardens bright with sinuous rills,
Where blossomed many an incense-bearing tree;
And here were forests ancient as the hills, 10
Enfolding sunny spots of greenery.

But oh! that deep romantic chasm which slanted
Down the green hill athwart a cedarn cover!
A savage place! as holy and enchanted
As e'er beneath a waning moon was haunted 15
By woman wailing for her demon-lover!
And from this chasm, with ceaseless turmoil seething,
As if this earth in fast thick pants were breathing,
A mighty fountain momently was forced:
Amid whose swift half-intermitted burst 20
Huge fragments vaulted like rebounding hail,
Or chaffy grain beneath the thresher's flail:
And 'mid these dancing rocks at once and ever
It flung up momently the sacred river.
Five miles meandering with a mazy motion 25
Through wood and dale the sacred river ran,
Then reached the caverns measureless to man,
And sank in tumult to a lifeless ocean:
And 'mid this tumult Kubla heard from far
Ancestral voices prophesying war! 30
   The shadow of the dome of pleasure
   Floated midway on the waves;
   Where was heard the mingled measure
   From the fountain and the caves.
It was a miracle of rare device, 35
A sunny pleasure-dome with caves of ice!

   A damsel with a dulcimer
   In a vision once I saw:
   It was an Abyssinian maid,
   And on her dulcimer she played, 40

1. *Kubla Khan:* Mongol emperor (1215?–1294), visited by Marco Polo.
3. *Alph:* J. L. Lowes, in *The Road to Xanadu* (1927), thinks that Coleridge may have had in mind the river Alpheus —linked with the Nile—mentioned by Virgil.

Singing of Mount Abora.
Could I revive within me
Her symphony and song,
To such a deep delight 'twould win me,
That with music loud and long, 45
I would build that dome in air,
That sunny dome! those caves of ice!
And all who heard should see them there,
And all should cry, Beware! Beware!
His flashing eyes, his floating hair! 50
Weave a circle round him thrice,
And close your eyes with holy dread,
For he on honey-dew hath fed,
And drunk the milk of Paradise.

41. *Mount Abora:* Lowes argues that this may have been "Mt. Amara," mentioned by Milton in *Paradise Lost* (IV, 28), or Amhara in Samuel Johnson's *Rasselas*.

Dejection: An Ode*

Late, late yestreen I saw the new Moon,
With the old Moon in her arms;
And I fear, I fear, my Master dear!
We shall have a deadly storm.
Ballad of Sir Patrick Spence 5

I

Well! If the Bard was weather-wise, who made
The grand old ballad of Sir Patrick Spence,
This night, so tranquil now, will not go hence
Unroused by winds, that ply a busier trade
Than those which mould yon cloud in lazy flakes, 10
Or the dull sobbing draft, that moans and rakes
Upon the strings of this Aeolian lute,
Which better far were mute.
For lo! the New-moon winter-bright!
And overspread with phantom light, 15
(With swimming phantom light o'erspread
But rimmed and circled by a silver thread)
I see the old Moon in her lap, foretelling
The coming-on of rain and squally blast.

* Written April 4, 1802. First published in the *Morning Post,* October 4, 1802. The first version was addressed to Sara Hutchinson, a close friend, and it is she who was originally meant in the opening of lines 30, 52, and 143. In later versions Colerdge changed the references to "William," "Edmund," and finally "Lady."

12. *Aeolian lute:* a frame fitted with strings or wires which produce musical tones when the wind hits them. Named after Aeolus, god of the winds.

And oh! that even now the gust were swelling, 20
  And the slant night-shower driving loud and fast!
Those sounds which oft have raised me, whilst they awed,
    And sent my soul abroad,
Might now perhaps their wonted impulse give,
Might startle this dull pain, and make it move and live! 25

II

A grief without a pang, void, dark, and drear,
  A stifled, drowsy, unimpassioned grief,
  Which finds no natural outlet, no relief,
    In word, or sigh, or tear—
O Lady! in this wan and heartless mood, 30
To other thoughts by yonder throstle woo'd,
  All this long eve, so balmy and serene,
Have I been gazing on the western sky,
  And its peculiar tint of yellow green:
And still I gaze—and with how blank an eye! 35
And those thin clouds above, in flakes and bars,
That give away their motion to the stars;
Those stars, that glide behind them or between,
Now sparkling, now bedimmed, but always seen:
Yon crescent Moon, as fixed as if it grew 40
In its own cloudless, starless lake of blue;
I see them all so excellently fair,
I see, not feel, how beautiful they are!

III

    My genial spirits fail;
    And what can these avail 45
  To lift the smothering weight from off my breast?
    It were a vain endeavour,
    Though I should gaze for ever
  On that green light that lingers in the west:
  I may not hope from outward forms to win 50
  The passion and the life, whose fountains are within.

IV

  O Lady! we receive but what we give,
  And in our life alone does Nature live:
  Ours is her wedding garment, ours her shroud!
    And would we aught behold, of higher worth, 55
  Than that inanimate cold world allowed

24. *wonted:* accustomed.
31. *throstle:* the song-thrush.
44. *genial spirits:* Coleridge's generative spirits; in short, his creativity. The first version was written soon after Wordsworth had composed the first four stanzas of the *Ode on Intimations of Immortality,* and the themes are similar.

To the poor loveless ever-anxious crowd,
  Ah! from the soul itself must issue forth
A light, a glory, a fair luminous cloud
    Enveloping the Earth— 60
And from the soul itself must there be sent
  A sweet and potent voice, of its own birth,
Of all sweet sounds the life and element!

V

O pure of heart! thou need'st not ask of me
What this strong music in the soul may be! 65
What, and wherein doth exist,
This light, this glory, this fair luminous mist,
This beautiful and beauty-making power.
  Joy, virtuous Lady! Joy that ne'er was given,
Save to the pure, and in their purest hour, 70
Life, and Life's effluence, cloud at once and shower,
Joy, Lady! is the spirit and the power,
Which wedding Nature to us gives in dower
  A new Earth and new Heaven,
Undreamt of by the sensual and the proud— 75
Joy is the sweet voice, Joy the luminous cloud—
    We in ourselves rejoice!
And thence flows all that charms or ear or sight,
  All melodies the echoes of that voice,
All colours a suffusion from that light. 80

VI

There was a time when, though my path was rough,
  This joy within me dallied with distress,
And all misfortunes were but as the stuff
  Whence Fancy made me dreams of happiness:
For hope grew round me, like the twining vine, 85
And fruits, and foliage, not my own, seemed mine.
But now afflictions bow me down to earth:
Nor care I that they rob me of my mirth;
    But oh! each visitation
Suspends what nature gave me at my birth, 90
  My shaping spirit of Imagination.
For not to think of what I needs must feel,
  But to be still and patient, all I can;
And haply by abstruse research to steal
  From my own nature all the natural man— 95
  This was my sole resource, my only plan:

84. *Fancy:* Coleridge made much of the distinction between "fancy" and the "imagination" (line 86). Fancy makes pleasant combinations of images (*cf.* lines 78–79); the Imagination is a higher faculty of the mind that combines images in such a way that they create a higher reality, a poetic "truth" more valid than that which is perceived by the ordinary senses.

89. *visitation:* of the misfortunes and afflictions in line 82.

Till that which suits a part infects the whole,
And now is almost grown the habit of my soul.

VII

Hence, viper thoughts, that coil around my mind,
Reality's dark dream! 100
I turn from you, and listen to the wind,
Which long has raved unnoticed. What a scream
Of agony by torture lengthened out
That lute sent forth! Thou Wind that rav'st without,
Bare crag, or mountain-tairn, or blasted tree, 105
Or pine-grove whither woodman never clomb,
Or lonely house, long held the witches' home,
Methinks were fitter instruments for thee,
Mad Lutanist! who in this month of showers,
Of dark-brown gardens, and of peeping flowers, 110
Mak'st Devils' yule with worse than wintry song,
The blossoms, buds, and timorous leaves among.
Thou Actor, perfect in all tragic sounds!
Thou mighty Poet, e'en to frenzy bold!
What tell'st thou now about? 115
'Tis of the rushing of an host in rout,
With groans, of trampled men, with smarting wounds—
At once they groan with pain, and shudder with the cold!
But hush! there is a pause of deepest silence!
And all that noise, as of a rushing crowd, 120
With groans, and tremulous shudderings—all is over—
It tells another tale, with sounds less deep and loud!
A tale of less affright,
And tempered with delight,
As Otway's self had framed the tender lay,— 125
'Tis of a little child
Upon a lonesome wild,
Not far from home, but she hath lost her way:
And now moans low in bitter grief and fear,
And now screams loud, and hopes to make her mother hear. 130

VIII

'Tis midnight, but small thoughts have I of sleep.
Full seldom may my friend such vigils keep!
Visit her, gentle Sleep! with wings of healing,
And may this storm be but a mountain-birth,
May all the stars hang bright above her dwelling, 135
Silent as though they watched the sleeping Earth!
With light heart may she rise,
Gay fancy, cheerful eyes,

105. ***mountain-tairn:*** tarn or small mountain lake.
109. ***Mad Lutanist:*** the storm wind in line 99.
111. ***Devil's yule:*** Originally, yule was a heathen feast.
116. ***host:*** an army.
122. ***another tale:*** the story of Wordsworth's *Lucy Gray*.
125. ***Otway's self:*** originally "William" (Wordsworth). Thomas Otway (1652-1685) was a tragic dramatist.

Joy lift her spirit, joy attune her voice;
To her may all things live, from pole to pole, 140
Their life the eddying of her living soul!
O simple spirit, guided from above,
Dear Lady! friend devoutest of my choice,
Thus mayest thou ever, evermore rejoice.

GEORGE GORDON, LORD BYRON
(1788–1824)

Don Juan

*Canto II**

I

Oh ye! who teach the ingenuous youth of nations,
Holland, France, England, Germany, or Spain,
I pray ye flog them upon all occasions,
It mends their morals, never mind the pain:
The best of mothers and of educations 5
In Juan's case were but employed in vain,
Since, in a way that's rather of the oddest, he
Became divested of his native modesty.

II

Had he but been placed at a public school,
In the third form, or even in the fourth, 10
His daily task had kept his fancy cool,
At least, had he been nurtured in the north—
Spain may prove an exception to the rule,
But then exceptions always prove its worth—
A lad of sixteen causing a divorce 15
Puzzled his tutors very much, of course.

III

I can't say that it puzzles me at all,
If all things be considered; first, there was
His lady-mother, mathematical,
A——never mind;—his tutor, an old ass; 20
A pretty woman—(that's quite natural,
Or else the thing had hardly come to pass)
A husband rather old, not much in unity
With his young wife—a time, and opportunity.

* Written between December 13, 1818 and January 20, 1819; published on July 15, 1819.

6. *vain:* In Canto I Byron describes his hero Juan, born in Seville to a pedantic mother and an unfaithful father. Juan's mother, Donna Inez, is soon widowed; and despite Juan's careful education, he succumbs to the charms of the young Julia, married to a much older husband. A bedroom farce ensues, with Juan hiding under Julia's bedclothes. Juan escapes, but the scandal breaks. Don Alfonso, Julia's husband, sues for divorce, and Donna Inez orders her son to leave Spain by way of Cadiz.

IV

Well—well; the world must turn upon its axis,
And all mankind turn with it, heads or tails,
And live and die, make love and pay our taxes,
And as the veering wind shifts, shift our sails;
The king commands us, and the doctor quacks us,
The priest instructs, and so our life exhales,
A little breath, love, wine, ambition, fame,
Fighting, devotion, dust,—perhaps a name.

V

I said, that Juan had been sent to Cadiz—
A pretty town, I recollect it well—
'Tis where the mart of colonial trade is,
(Or was, before Peru learned to rebel,)
And such sweet girls—I mean, such graceful ladies,
Their very walk would make your bosom swell;
I can't describe it, though so much it strike,
Nor liken it—I never saw the like:

VI

An Arab horse, a stately stag, a barb
New broke, a cameleopard, a gazelle,
No—none of these will do;—and then their garb,
Their veil and petticoat—Alas! to dwell
Upon such things would very near absorb
A canto—then their feet and ankles,—well,
Thank Heaven I've got no metaphor quite ready,
(And so, my sober Muse—come, let's be steady—

VII

Chaste Muse!—well, if you must, you must)—the veil
Thrown back a moment with the glancing hand,
While the o'erpowering eye, that turns you pale,
Flashes into the heart:—All sunny land
Of love! when I forget you, may I fail
To——say my prayers—but never was there plann'd
A dress through which the eyes give such a volley,
Excepting the Venetian Fazzioli.

VIII

But to our tale: the Donna Inez sent
Her son to Cadiz only to embark;

36. *Peru:* Between 1810 and 1825 the Spanish and Portuguese colonies in South America were in a state of rebellion. Peru became an independent nation in 1821, two years after this canto was written.

41. *barb:* breed of horse imported from Barbary, in North Africa.

42. *cameleopard:* giraffe.

56. *Fazzioli:* "literally, the little handkerchiefs—the veils most availing of St. Mark." [Byron's note.]

To stay there had not answered her intent,
  But why?—we leave the reader in the dark— 60
'Twas for a voyage the young man was meant,
  As if a Spanish ship were Noah's ark,
To wean him from the wickedness of earth,
And send him like a dove of promise forth.

IX

Don Juan bade his valet pack his things 65
  According to direction, then received
A lecture and some money: for four springs
  He was to travel; and though Inez grieved
(As every kind of parting has its stings),
  She hoped he would improve—perhaps believed: 70
A letter, too, she gave (he never read it)
Of good advice—and two or three of credit.

X

In the mean time, to pass her hours away,
  Brave Inez now set up a Sunday school
For naughty children, who would rather play 75
  (Like truant rogues) the devil, or the fool;
Infants of three years old were taught that day,
  Dunces were whipt, or set upon a stool:
The great success of Juan's education
Spurred her to teach another generation. 80

XI

Juan embarked—the ship got under way,
  The wind was fair, the water passing rough;
A devil of a sea rolls in that bay,
  As I, who've crossed it oft, know well enough;
And, standing upon deck, the dashing spray 85
  Flies in one's face, and makes it weather-tough:
And there he stood to take, and take again,
His first—perhaps his last—farewell of Spain.

XII

I can't but say it is an awkward sight
  To see one's native land receding through 90
The growing waters; it unmans one quite,
  Especially when life is rather new:
I recollect Great Britain's coast looks white,
  But almost every other country's blue,
When gazing on them, mystified by distance, 95
We enter on our nautical existence.

XIII

So Juan stood, bewildered on the deck:
  The wind sung, cordage strained, and sailors swore,
And the ship creaked, the town became a speck,
  From which away so fair and fast they bore. 100
The best of remedies is a beef-steak
  Against sea-sickness: try it, sir, before
You sneer, and I assure you this is true,
For I have found it answer—so may you.

XIV

Don Juan stood, and, gazing from the stern, 105
  Beheld his native Spain receding far:
First partings form a lesson hard to learn,
  Even nations feel this when they go to war;
There is a sort of unexprest concern,
  A kind of shock that sets one's heart ajar: 110
At leaving even the most unpleasant people
And places, one keeps looking at the steeple.

XV

But Juan had got many things to leave,
  His mother, and a mistress, and no wife,
So that he had much better cause to grieve 115
  Than many persons more advanced in life;
And if we now and then a sigh must heave
  At quitting even those we quit in strife,
No doubt we weep for those the heart endears—
That is, till deeper griefs congeal our tears. 120

XVI

So Juan wept, as wept the captive Jews
  By Babel's waters, still remembering Sion:
I'd weep,—but mine is not a weeping Muse,
  And such light griefs are not a thing to die on;
Young men should travel, if but to amuse 125
  Themselves; and the next time their servants tie on
Behind their carriages their new portmanteau,
Perhaps it may be lined with this my canto.

XVII

And Juan wept, and much he sighed and thought,
  While his salt tears dropped into the salt sea, 130

121. *Jews:* a reference to the Babylonian captivity (586–538 B.C.), which began when Nebuchadnezzar captured and destroyed Jerusalem, and the Jews were carried off in bondage. See Psalm 137.

"Sweets to the sweet;" (I like so much to quote;
You must excuse this extract—'tis where she,
The Queen of Denmark, for Ophelia brought
Flowers to the grave;) and, sobbing often, he
Reflected on his present situation, 135
And seriously resolved on reformation.

XVIII

"Farewell, my Spain! a long farewell!" he cried,
"Perhaps I may revisit thee no more,
But die, as many an exiled heart hath died,
Of its own thirst to see again thy shore: 140
Farewell, where Guadalquivir's waters glide!
Farewell, my mother! and, since all is o'er,
Farewell, too, dearest Julia—(here he drew
Her letter out again, and read it through.)

XIX

"And oh! if e'er I should forget, I swear— 145
But that's impossible, and cannot be—
Sooner shall this blue ocean melt to air,
Sooner shall earth resolve itself to sea,
Than I resign thine image, oh, my fair!
Or think of anything, excepting thee; 150
A mind diseased no remedy can physic—
(Here the ship gave a lurch, and he grew sea-sick.)

XX

"Sooner shall heaven kiss earth—(here he fell sicker)
Oh, Julia, what is every other woe?—
(For God's sake let me have a glass of liquor; 155
Pedro, Battista, help me down below.)
Julia, my love—(you rascal, Pedro, quicker)—
Oh, Julia!—(this curst vessel pitches so)—
Beloved Julia, hear me still beseeching!"
(Here he grew inarticulate with retching.) 160

XXI

He felt that chilling heaviness of heart,
Or rather stomach, which, alas! attends,
Beyond the best apothecary's art,
The loss of love, the treachery of friends,
Or death of those we dote on, when a part 165

131. *"Sweets to the sweet": Hamlet*, Act V, Scene 1, l. 266 (l. 31 in our text).

141. *Guadalquivir:* the river by which Cadiz is situated.

Of us dies with them as each fond hope ends:
No doubt he would have been much more pathetic,
But the sea acted as a strong emetic.

XXII

Love's capricious power: I've known it hold
Out through a fever caused by its own heat, 170
But be much puzzled by a cough and cold,
And find a quinsy very hard to treat;
Against all noble maladies he's bold,
But vulgar illnesses don't like to meet,
Nor that a sneeze should interrupt his sigh, 175
Nor inflammations redden his blind eye.

XXIII

But worse of all is nausea, or a pain
About the lower region of the bowels;
Love, who heroically breathes a vein,
Shrinks from the application of hot towels, 180
And purgatives are dangerous to his reign,
Sea-sickness death: his love was perfect, how else
Could Juan's passion, while the billows roar,
Resist his stomach, ne'er at sea before?

XXIV

The ship, called the most holy *Trinidada*, 185
Was steering duly for the port Leghorn;
For there the Spanish family Moncada
Were settled long ere Juan's sire was born:
They were relations, and for them he had a
Letter of introduction, which the morn 190
Of his departure had been sent him by
His Spanish friends for those in Italy.

XXV

His suite consisted of three servants and
A tutor, the licentiate Pedrillo,
Who several languages did understand, 195
But now lay sick and speechless on his pillow,
And, rocking in his hammock, longed for land,
His headache being increased by every billow;

172. *quinsy:* inflammation of the throat.
179. *breathes:* lances.
185. *Trinidada:* Trinity.
186. *Leghorn:* Livorno, a port on the western coast of Italy, north of Rome.
194. *licentiate:* person holding a university degree, adjudged competent to teach.

And the waves oozing through the port-hole made
His berth a little damp, and him afraid. 200

XXVI

'Twas not without some reason, for the wind
Increased at night, until it blew a gale;
And though 'twas not much to a naval mind,
Some landsmen would have looked a little pale,
For sailors are, in fact, a different kind: 205
At sunset they began to take in sail,
For the sky showed it would come on to blow,
And carry away, perhaps, a mast or so.

XXVII

At one o'clock the wind with sudden shift
Threw the ship right into the trough of the sea, 210
Which struck her aft, and made an awkward rift,
Started the stern-post, also shattered the
Whole of her stern-frame, and, ere she could lift
Herself from out her present jeopardy,
The rudder tore away: 'twas time to sound 215
The pumps, and there were four feet water found.

XXVIII

One gang of people instantly was put
Upon the pumps, and the remainder set
To get up part of the cargo, and what not;
But they could not come at the leak as yet; 220
At last they did get at it really, but
Still their salvation was an even bet:
The water rushed through in a way quite puzzling,
While they thrust sheets, shirts, jackets, bales of muslin,

XXIX

Into the opening; but all such ingredients 225
Would have been in vain, and they must have gone down,
Despite of all their efforts and expedients,
But for the pumps: I'm glad to make them known
To all the brother tars who may have need hence,
For fifty tons of water were upthrown 230
By them per hour, and they all had been undone,
But for the maker, Mr. Mann, of London.

201. *wind:* Although Bryon maintained that all his sea descriptions came from personal experience, it is now known that he borrowed much from Sir G. Dalzell's *Shipwrecks and Disasters at Sea* (1812).

XXX

As day advanced the weather seemed to abate,
  And then the leak they reckoned to reduce,
And keep the ship afloat, though three feet yet 235
  Kept two hand and one chain-pump still in use.
The wind blew fresh again: as it grew late
  A squall came on, and while some guns broke loose,
A gust—which all descriptive power transcends—
Laid with one blast the ship on her beam ends. 240

XXXI

There she lay, motionless, and seemed upset;
  The water left the hold, and washed the decks,
And made a scene men do not soon forget;
  For they remember battles, fires, and wrecks,
Or any other thing that brings regret, 245
  Or breaks their hopes, or hearts, or heads, or necks;
Thus drownings are much talked of by the divers,
And swimmers, who may chance to be survivors.

XXXII

Immediately the masts were cut away,
  Both main and mizen: first the mizen went, 250
The main-mast followed; but the ship still lay
  Like a mere log, and baffled our intent.
Foremast and bowsprit were cut down, and they
  Eased her at last (although we never meant
To part with all till every hope was blighted), 255
And then with violence the old ship righted.

XXXIII

It may be easily supposed, while this
  Was going on, some people were unquiet,
That passengers would find it much amiss
  To lose their lives, as well as spoil their diet; 260
That even the able seaman, deeming his
  Days nearly o'er, might be disposed to riot,
As upon such occasions tars will ask
For grog, and sometimes drink rum from the cask.

XXXIV

There's nought, no doubt, so much the spirit calms 265
  As rum and true religion: thus it was,
Some plundered, some drank spirits, some sung psalms,
  The high wind made the treble, and as bass

The hoarse harsh waves kept time; fright cured the qualms
  Of all the luckless landsmen's sea-sick maws: 270
Strange sounds of wailing, blasphemy, devotion,
Clamoured in chorus to the roaring ocean.

XXXV

Perhaps more mischief had been done, but for
  Our Juan, who, with sense beyond his years,
Got to the spirit-room, and stood before 275
  It with a pair of pistols; and their fears,
As if Death were more dreadful by his door
  Of fire than water, spite of oaths and tears,
Kept still aloof the crew, who, ere they sunk,
Thought it would be becoming to die drunk. 280

XXXVI

"Give us more grog," they cried, "for it will be
  All one an hour hence." Juan answered, "No!
'Tis true that death awaits both you and me,
  But let us die like men, not sink below
Like brutes:"—and thus his dangerous post kept he, 285
  And none liked to anticipate the blow;
And even Pedrillo, his most reverend tutor,
Was for some rum a disappointed suitor.

XXXVII

The good old gentleman was quite aghast,
  And made a loud and pious lamentation; 290
Repented all his sins, and made a last
  Irrevocable vow of reformation;
Nothing should tempt him more (this peril past)
  To quit his academic occupation,
In cloisters of the classic Salamanca, 295
To follow Juan's wake, like Sancho Panca.

XXXVIII

But now there came a flash of hope once more;
  Day broke, and the wind lulled: the masts were gone;
The leak increased; shoals round her, but no shore,
  The vessel swam, yet still she held her own. 300
They tried the pumps again, and though before
  Their desperate efforts seemed all useless grown,

295. *Salamanca:* city in eastern Spain, possessing the oldest university (founded 1230) on the Iberian peninsula.

296. *Sancho Panca:* Sancho Panza, the knight's servant in Cervantes' *Don Quixote.*

A glimpse of sunshine set some hands to bale—
The stronger pumped, the weaker thrummed a sail.

XXXIX

Under the vessel's keel the sail was passed, 305
And for the moment it had some effect;
But with a leak, and not a stick of mast,
Nor rag of canvas, what could they expect?
But still 'tis best to struggle to the last,
'Tis never too late to be wholly wrecked: 310
And though 'tis true that man can only die once,
'Tis not so pleasant in the Gulf of Lyons.

XL

There winds and waves had hurled them, and from thence,
Without their will, they carried them away;
For they were forced with steering to dispense, 315
And never had as yet a quiet day
On which they might repose, or even commence
A jurymast or rudder, or could say
The ship would swim an hour, which, by good luck,
Still swam—though not exactly like a duck. 320

XLI

The wind, in fact, perhaps, was rather less,
But the ship laboured so, they scarce could hope
To weather out much longer; the distress
Was also great with which they had to cope
For want of water, and their solid mess 325
Was scant enough: in vain the telescope
Was used—nor sail nor shore appeared in sight,
Nought but the heavy sea, and coming night.

XLII

Again the weather threatened,—again blew
A gale, and in the fore and after hold 330
Water appeared; yet, though the people knew
All this, the most were patient, and some bold,
Until the chains and leathers were worn through
Of all our pumps:—a wreck complete she rolled,

304. *thrummed:* To thrum a sail is to roughen its surface by sewing pieces of rope yarn to it. Such a sail, greased and tarred, would be passed under the hull of a leaking ship and heaved tight in an effort to stanch the leak.

312. *Gulf of Lyons:* off the southern coast of France, between Marseilles and the Spanish border.

318. *jurymast:* temporary mast in place of one broken or lost.

At mercy of the waves, whose mercies are 335
Like human beings during civil war.

XLIII

Then came the carpenter, at last, with tears
  In his rough eyes, and told the captain, he
Could do no more: he was a man in years,
  And long had voyaged through many a stormy sea, 340
And if he wept at length, they were not fears
  That made his eyelids as a woman's be,
But he, poor fellow, had a wife and children,
Two things for dying people quite bewildering.

XLIV

The ship was evidently settling now 345
  Fast by the head; and, all distinction gone,
Some went to prayers again, and made a vow
  Of candles to their saints—but there were none
To pay them with; and some looked o'er the bow;
  Some hoisted out the boats; and there was one 350
That begged Pedrillo for an absolution,
Who told him to be damned—in his confusion.

XLV

Some lashed them in their hammocks; some put on
  Their best clothes, as if going to a fair;
Some cursed the day on which they saw the sun, 355
  And gnashed their teeth, and howling, tore their hair;
And others went on as they had begun,
  Getting the boats out, being well aware
That a tight boat will live in a rough sea,
Unless with breakers close beneath her lee. 360

XLVI

The worst of all was, that in their condition,
  Having been several days in great distress,
'Twas difficult to get out such provision
  As now might render their long suffering less:
Men, even when dying, dislike inanition; 365
  Their stock was damaged by the weather's stress:
Two casks of biscuit, and a keg of butter,
Were all that could be thrown into the cutter.

XLVII

But in the long-boat they contrived to stow
  Some pounds of bread, though injured by the wet: 370

Water, a twenty-gallon cask or so;
  Six flasks of wine: and they contrived to get
A portion of their beef up from below,
  And with a piece of pork, moreover, met,
But scarce enough to serve them for a luncheon— 375
Then there was rum, eight gallons in a puncheon.

XLVIII

The other boats, the yawl and pinnace, had
  Been stove in the beginning of the gale;
And the long-boat's condition was but bad,
  As there were but two blankets for a sail, 380
And one for a mast, which a young lad
  Threw in by good luck over the ship's rail;
And two boats could not hold, far less be stored,
To save one half the people then on board.

XLIX

'Twas twilight, and the sunless day went down 385
  Over the waste of waters; like a veil,
Which, if withdrawn, would but disclose the frown
  Of one whose hate is masked but to assail.
Thus to their hopeless eyes the night was shown,
  And grimly darkled o'er the faces pale, 390
And the dim desolate deep: twelve days had Fear
Been their familiar, and now Death was here.

L

Some trial had been making at a raft,
  With little hope in such a rolling sea,
A sort of thing at which one would have laughed, 395
  If any laughter at such times could be,
Unless with people who too much have quaffed,
  And have a kind of wild and horrid glee,
Half epileptical, and half hysterical:—
Their preservation would have been a miracle. 400

LI

At half-past eight o'clock, booms, hencoops, spars,
  And all things, for a chance, had been cast loose
That still could keep afloat the struggling tars,
  For yet they strove, although of no great use:
There was no light in heaven but a few stars, 405
  The boats put off o'ercrowded with their crews;

376. ***puncheon:*** large cask, holding from 72 to 120 gallons.

She gave a heel, and then a lurch to port,
And, going down head foremost—sunk, in short.

LII

Then rose from sea to sky the wild farewell—
Then shrieked the timid, and stood still the brave— 410
Then some leaped overboard with dreadful yell,
As eager to anticipate their grave;
And the sea yawned around her like a hell,
And down she sucked with her the whirling wave,
Like one who grapples with his enemy, 415
And strives to strangle him before he die.

LIII

And first one universal shriek there rushed,
Louder than the loud ocean, like a crash
Of echoing thunder; and then all was hushed,
Save the wild wind and the remorseless dash 420
Of billows; but at intervals there gushed,
Accompanied with a convulsive splash,
A solitary shriek, the bubbling cry
Of some strong swimmer in his agony.

LIV

The boats, as stated, had got off before, 425
And in them crowded several of the crew;
And yet their present hope was hardly more
Than what it had been, for so strong it blew
There was slight chance of reaching any shore;
And then they were too many, though so few— 430
Nine in the cutter, thirty in the boat,
Were counted in them when they got afloat.

LV

All the rest perished; near two hundred souls
Had left their bodies; and what's worse, alas!
When over Catholics the ocean rolls, 435
They must wait several weeks before a mass
Takes off one peck of purgatorial coals,
Because, till people know what's come to pass,
They won't lay out their money on the dead—
It costs three francs for every mass that's said. 440

LVI

Juan got into the long-boat, and there
Contrived to help Pedrillo to a place;

It seemed as if they had exchanged their care,
For Juan wore the magisterial face
Which courage gives, while poor Pedrillo's pair 445
Of eyes were crying for their owner's case:
Battista, though (a name called shortly Tita),
Was lost by getting at some aqua-vita.

LVII

Pedro, his valet, too, he tried to save,
But the same cause, conducive to his loss, 450
Left him so drunk, he jumped into the wave,
As o'er the cutter's edge he tried to cross,
And so he found a wine-and-watery grave;
They could not rescue him although so close,
Because the sea ran higher every minute, 455
And for the boat—the crew kept crowding in it.

LVIII

A small old spaniel—which had been Don Jóse's,
His father's, whom he loved, as ye may think,
For on such things the memory reposes
With tenderness—stood howling on the brink, 460
Knowing, (dogs have such intellectual noses!)
No doubt, the vessel was about to sink;
And Juan caught him up, and ere he stepped
Off threw him in, then after him he leaped.

LIX

He also stuffed his money where he could 465
About his person, and Pedrillo's too,
Who let him do, in fact, whate'er he would,
Not knowing what himself to say, or do,
As every rising wave his dread renewed;
But Juan, trusting they might still get through, 470
And deeming there were remedies for any ill,
Thus re-embarked his tutor and his spaniel.

LX

'Twas a rough night, and blew so stiffly yet,
That the sail was becalmed between the seas,
Though on the wave's high top too much to set, 475
They dared not take it in for all the breeze:
Each sea curled o'er the stern, and kept them wet,
And made them bale without a moment's ease,

448. *aqua-vita:* brandy.

So that themselves as well as hopes were damped,
And the poor little cutter quickly swamped. 480

LXI

Nine souls more went in her: the long-boat still
Kept above water, with an oar for mast,
Two blankets stitched together, answering ill
Instead of sail, were to the oar made fast:
Though every wave rolled menacing to fill, 485
And present peril all before surpassed,
They grieved for those who perished with the cutter,
And also for the biscuit-casks and butter.

LXII

The sun rose red and fiery, a sure sign
Of the continuance of the gale: to run 490
Before the sea until it should grow fine,
Was all that for the present could be done:
A few tea-spoonfuls of their rum and wine
Were served out to the people, who begun
To faint, and damaged bread wet through the bags, 495
And most of them had little clothes but rags.

LXIII

They counted thirty, crowded in a space
Which left scarce room for motion or exertion;
They did their best to modify their case,
One half sate up, though numbed with the immersion, 500
While t'other half were laid down in their place,
At watch and watch; thus, shivering like the tertian
Ague in its cold fit, they filled their boat,
With nothing but the sky for a great coat.

LXIV

'Tis very certain the desire of life 505
Prolongs it: this is obvious to physicians,
When patients, neither plagued with friends nor wife,
Survive through very desperate conditions,
Because they still can hope, nor shines the knife
Nor shears of Atropos before their visions: 510
Despair of all recovery spoils longevity,
And makes men's miseries of alarming brevity.

489. *fiery:* Compare the sailors' adage: "Red sky at night, sailors' delight; / Red sky at morning, sailors take warning."
502–503. *tertian ague:* a fever whose symptoms recur every third day, as in certain types of malaria.
510. *Atropos:* in Greek mythology the third of the three Fates, the one who cuts the thread of life.

LXV

'Tis said that persons living on annuities
  Are longer lived than others,—God knows why,
Unless to plague the grantors,—yet so true it is, 515
  That some, I really think, *do* never die;
Of any creditors the worst a Jew it is,
  And *that's* their mode of furnishing supply:
In my young days they lent me cash that way,
Which I found very troublesome to pay. 520

LXVI

'Tis thus with people in an open boat,
  They live upon the love of life, and bear
More than can be believed, or even thought,
  And stand like rocks the tempest's wear and tear;
And hardship still has been the sailor's lot, 525
  Since Noah's ark went cruising here and there;
She had a curious crew as well as cargo,
Like the first old Greek privateer, the Argo.

LXVII

But man is a carnivorous production,
  And must have meals, at least one meal a day; 530
He cannot live, like woodcocks, upon suction,
  But, like the shark and tiger, must have prey;
Although his anatomical construction
  Bears vegetables, in a grumbling way,
Your labouring people think beyond all question 535
Beef, veal, and mutton, better for digestion.

LXVIII

And thus it was with this our hapless crew;
  For on the third day there came on a calm,
And though at first their strength it might renew,
  And lying on their weariness like balm, 540
Lulled them like turtles sleeping on the blue
  Of ocean, when they woke they felt a qualm,
And fell all ravenously on their provision,
Instead of hoarding it with due precision.

LXIX

The consequence was easily foreseen— 545
  They ate up all they had, and drank their wine,

528. *Argo:* the ship—named after its builder, Argus—in which Jason and his followers sailed to find the Golden Fleece.

In spite of all remonstrances, and then
On what, in fact, next day were they to dine?
They hoped the wind would rise, these foolish men!
And carry them to shore; these hopes were fine, 550
But as they had but one oar, and that brittle,
It would have been more wise to save their victual.

LXX

The fourth day came, but not a breath of air,
And Ocean slumbered like an unweaned child;
The fifth day, and their boat lay floating there, 555
The sea and sky were blue, and clear, and mild—
With their one oar (I wish they had had a pair)
What could they do? and hunger's rage grew wild:
So Juan's spaniel, spite of his entreating,
Was killed, and portioned out for present eating. 560

LXXI

On the sixth day they fed upon his hide,
And Juan, who had still refused, because
The creature was his father's dog that died,
Now feeling all the vulture in his jaws,
With some remorse received (though first denied) 565
As a great favour one of the fore-paws,
Which he divided with Pedrillo, who
Devoured it, longing for the other too.

LXXII

The seventh day, and no wind—the burning sun
Blistered and scorched, and, stagnant on the sea, 570
They lay like carcasses; and hope was none,
Save in the breeze that came not: savagely
They glared upon each other—all was done,
Water, and wine, and food,—and you might see
The longings of the cannibal arise 575
(Although they spoke not) in their wolfish eyes.

LXXIII

At length one whispered to his companion, who
Whispered another, and thus it went round,
And then into a hoarser murmur grew,
An ominous, and wild, and desperate sound; 580
And when his comrade's thought each sufferer knew,
'Twas but his own, suppressed till now, he found:
And out they spoke of lots for flesh and blood,
And who should die to be his fellow's food.

LXXIV

But ere they came to this, they that day shared 585
Some leathern caps, and what remained of shoes;
And then they looked around them, and despaired,
And none to be the sacrifice would choose;
At length the lots were torn up, and prepared,
But of materials that must shock the Muse— 590
Having no paper, for the want of better,
They took by force from Juan Julia's letter.

LXXV

Then lots were made, and marked, and mixed, and handed
In silent horror, and their distribution
Lulled even the savage hunger which demanded, 595
Like the Promethean vulture, this pollution;
None in particular had sought or planned it,
'Twas nature gnawed them to this resolution,
By which none were permitted to be neuter—
And the lot fell on Juan's luckless tutor. 600

LXXVI

He but requested to be bled to death:
The surgeon had his instruments, and bled
Pedrillo, and so gently ebbed his breath,
You hardly could perceive when he was dead.
He died as born, a Catholic in faith, 605
Like most in the belief in which they're bred,
And first a little crucifix he kissed,
And then held out his jugular and wrist.

LXXVII

The surgeon, as there was no other fee,
Had his first choice of morsels for his pains; 610
But being thirstiest at the moment, he
Preferred a draught from the fast-flowing veins:
Part was divided, part thrown in the sea,
And such things as the entrails and the brains
Regaled two sharks, who followed o'er the billow— 615
The sailors ate the rest of poor Pedrillo.

LXXVIII

The sailors ate him, all save three or four,
Who were not quite so fond of animal food;

596. *Promethean vulture:* According to Greek mythology (see Aeschylus, *Prometheus Bound*), Prometheus was chained to a rock on Mount Caucasus where vultures and eagles tore at him.

To these was added Juan, who, before
  Refusing his own spaniel, hardly could 620
Feel now his appetite increased much more;
  'Twas not to be expected that he should,
Even in extremity of their disaster,
Dine with them on his pastor and his master.

LXXIX

'Twas better that he did not; for, in fact, 625
  The consequence was awful in the extreme;
For they, who were most ravenous in the act,
  Went raging mad—Lord! how they did blaspheme!
And foam, and roll, with strange convulsions racked,
  Drinking salt-water like a mountain-stream; 630
Tearing, and grinning, howling, screeching, swearing,
And, with hyæna-laughter, died despairing.

LXXX

Their numbers were much thinned by this infliction
  And all the rest were thin enough, Heaven knows;
And some of them had lost their recollection, 635
  Happier than they who still perceived their woes;
But others pondered on a new dissection,
  As if not warned sufficiently by those
Who had already perished, suffering madly,
For having used their appetites so sadly. 640

LXXXI

And next they thought upon the master's mate,
  As fattest; but he saved himself, because,
Besides being much averse from such a fate,
  There were some other reasons: the first was,
He had been rather indisposed of late; 645
  And that which chiefly proved his saving clause,
Was a small present made to him at Cadiz,
By general subscription of the ladies.

LXXXII

Of poor Pedrillo something still remained,
  But was used sparingly,—some were afraid, 650
And others still their appetites constrained,
  Or but at times a little supper made;
All except Juan, who throughout abstained,

647. *present:* i.e., he had contracted a venereal disease.

Chewing a piece of bamboo, and some lead:
At length they caught two boobies, and a noddy, 655
And then they left off eating the dead body.

LXXXIII

And if Pedrillo's fate should shocking be,
Remember Ugolino condescends
To eat the head of his arch-enemy
The moment after he politely ends 660
His tale: if foes be food in hell, at sea
'Tis surely fair to dine upon our friends,
When shipwreck's short allowance grows too scanty,
Without being much more horrible than Dante.

LXXXIV

And the same night there fell a shower of rain, 665
For which their mouths gaped, like the cracks of earth
When dried to summer dust; till taught by pain,
Men really know not what good water's worth;
If you had been in Turkey or in Spain,
Or with a famished boat's-crew had your berth, 670
Or in the desert heard the camel's bell,
You'd wish yourself where Truth is—in a well.

LXXXV

It poured down torrents, but they were no richer,
Until they found a ragged piece of sheet,
Which served them as a sort of spongy pitcher, 675
And when they deemed its moisture was complete,
They wrung it out, and though a thirsty ditcher
Might not have thought the scanty draught so sweet
As a full pot of porter, to their thinking
They ne'er till now had known the joys of drinking. 680

LXXXVI

And their baked lips, with many a bloody crack,
Sucked in the moisture, which like nectar streamed;
Their throats were ovens, their swoln tongues were black
As the rich man's in hell, who vainly screamed
To beg the beggar, who could not rain back 685
A drop of dew, when every drop had seemed
To taste of heaven—If this be true, indeed,
Some Christians have a comfortable creed.

658. *Ugolino:* See Dante's *Inferno*, Canto XXXIII. Ugolino, placed in the circle of traitors, tells his story to Dante and then returns to gnaw on the skull of his enemy.

683–686. *tongues . . . dew:* See the episode of the rich man and Lazarus in Luke 16:19–24.

LXXXVII

There were two fathers in this ghastly crew,
And with them their two sons, of whom the one 690
Was more robust and hardy to the view,
But he died early; and when he was gone,
His nearest messmate told his sire, who threw
One glance at him, and said, "Heaven's will be done!
I can do nothing," and he saw him thrown 695
Into the deep without a tear or groan.

LXXXVIII

The other father had a weaklier child,
Of a soft cheek, and aspect delicate;
But the boy bore up long, and with a mild
And patient spirit held aloof his fate; 700
Little he said, and now and then he smiled,
As if to win a part from off the weight
He saw increasing on his father's heart,
With the deep deadly thought, that they must part.

LXXXIX

And o'er him bent his sire, and never raised 705
His eyes from off his face, but wiped the foam
From his pale lips, and ever on him gazed,
And when the wished-for shower at length was come,
And the boy's eyes, which the dull film half glazed,
Brightened, and for a moment seemed to roam, 710
He squeezed from out a rag some drops of rain
Into his dying child's mouth—but in vain.

XC

The boy expired—the father held the clay,
And looked upon it long; and when at last
Death left no doubt, and the dead burthen lay 715
Stiff on his heart, and pulse and hope were past,
He watched it wistfully, until away
'Twas borne by the rude wave wherein 'twas cast;
Then he himself sunk down all dumb and shivering,
And gave no signs of life, save his limbs quivering. 720

XCI

Now overheard a rainbow, bursting through
The scattering clouds, shone, spanning the dark sea,
Resting its bright base on the quivering blue;
And all within its arch appeared to be

Clearer than that without, and its wide hue 725
 Waxed broad and waving, like a banner free,
Then changed like to a bow that's bent, and then
Forsook the dim eyes of these shipwrecked men.

XCII

It changed, of course; a heavenly chameleon,
 The airy child of vapour and the sun, 730
Brought forth in purple, cradled in vermilion,
 Baptized in molten gold, and swathed in dun,
Glittering like crescents o'er a Turk's pavilion,
 And blending every colour into one,
Just like a black eye in a recent scuffle 735
(For sometimes we must box without the muffle).

XCIII

Our shipwrecked seamen thought it a good omen—
 It is as well to think so, now and then;
'Twas an old custom of the Greek and Roman,
 And may become of great advantage when 740
Folks are discouraged; and most surely no men
 Had greater need to nerve themselves again
Than these, and so this rainbow looked like hope—
Quite a celestial kaleidoscope.

XCIV

About this time a beautiful white bird, 745
 Web-footed, not unlike a dove in size
And plumage (probably it might have erred
 Upon its course), passed oft before their eyes,
And tried to perch, although it saw and heard
 The men within the boat, and in this guise 750
It came and went, and fluttered round them till
Night fell:—this seemed a better omen still.

XCV

But in this case I also must remark,
 'Twas well this bird of promise did not perch,
Because the tackle of our shattered bark 755
 Was not so safe for roosting as a church;
And had it been the dove from Noah's ark,
 Returning there from her successful search,
Which in their way that moment chanced to fall,
They would have eat her, olive-branch and all. 760

736. *muffle:* a boxing glove (originally, a leather restraining glove for lunatics).

XCVI

With twilight it again came on to blow,
  But not with violence; the stars shone out,
The boat made way; yet now they were so low,
  They knew not where nor what they were about;
Some fancied they saw land, and some said "No!" 765
  The frequent fog-banks gave them cause to doubt—
Some swore that they heard breakers, others guns,
And all mistook about the latter once.

XCVII

As morning broke, the light wind died away,
  When he who had the watch sung out and swore, 770
If 'twas not land that rose with the sun's ray,
  He wished that land he never might see more:
And the rest rubbed their eyes, and saw a bay,
  Or thought they saw, and shaped their course for shore;
For shore it was, and gradually grew 775
Distinct, and high, and palpable to view.

XCVIII

And then of these some part burst into tears,
  And others, looking with a stupid stare,
Could not yet separate their hopes from fears,
  And seemed as if they had no further care; 780
While a few prayed—(the first time for some years)—
  And at the bottom of the boat three were
Asleep: they shook them by the hand and head,
And tried to awaken them, but found them dead.

XCIX

The day before, fast sleeping on the water, 785
  They found a turtle of the hawk's-bill kind,
And by good fortune, gliding softly, caught her,
  Which yielded a day's life, and to their mind
Proved even still a more nutritious matter,
  Because it left encouragement behind: 790
They thought that in such perils, more than chance
Had sent them this for their deliverance.

C

The land appeared a high and rocky coast,
  And higher grew the mountains as they drew,
Set by a current, toward it: they were lost 795
  In various conjectures, for none knew

CIX

With slow and staggering effort he arose, 865
But sunk again upon his bleeding knee
And quivering hand; and then he looked for those
Who long had been his mates upon the sea;
But none of them appeared to share his woes,
Save one, a corpse, from out the famished three, 870
Who died two days before, and now had found
An unknown barren beach for burial-ground.

CX

And as he gazed, his dizzy brain spun fast,
And down he sunk; and as he sunk, the sand
Swam round and round, and all his senses passed: 875
He fell upon his side, and his stretched hand
Drooped dripping on the oar (their jury-mast),
And, like a withered lily, on the land
His slender frame and pallid aspect lay,
As fair a thing as e'er was formed of clay. 880

CXI

How long in his damp trance young Juan lay
He knew not, for the earth was gone for him,
And time had nothing more of night nor day
For his congealing blood, and senses dim;
And how this heavy faintness passed away 885
He knew not, till each painful pulse and limb,
And tingling vein, seemed throbbing back to life,
For Death, though vanquished, still retired with strife.

CXII

His eyes he opened, shut, again unclosed,
For all was doubt and dizziness; he thought 890
He still was in the boat, and had but dozed,
And felt again with his despair o'erwrought,
And wished it death in which he had reposed,
And then once more his feelings back were brought,
And slowly by his swimming eyes was seen 895
A lovely female face of seventeen.

CXIII

'Twas bending close o'er his, and the small mouth
Seemed almost prying into his for breath;

896 ff. *female face . . .* : In keeping with the mock-epic tone of the poem, Byron obviously borrows this scene from Homer's *Odyssey* (Book VI), where Odysseus is treated in similar fashion by Nausicaä—daughter of King Alcinous—in the land of the Phaeacians.

And chafing him, the soft warm hand of youth
  Recalled his answering spirits back from death; 900
And, bathing his chill temples, tried to soothe
  Each pulse to animation, till beneath
Its gentle touch and trembling care, a sigh
To these kind efforts made a low reply.

CXIV

Then was the cordial poured, and mantle flung 905
  Around his scarce-clad limbs; and the fair arm
Raised higher the faint head which o'er it hung;
  And her transparent cheek, all pure and warm,
Pillowed his death-like forehead; then she wrung
  His dewy curls, long drenched by every storm; 910
And watched with eagerness each throb that drew
A sigh from his heaved bosom—and hers, too.

CXV

And lifting him with care into the cave,
  The gentle girl, and her attendant,—one
Young, yet her elder, and of brow less grave, 915
  And more robust of figure—then begun
To kindle fire, and as the new flames gave
  Light to the rocks that roofed them, which the sun
Had never seen, the maid, or whatsoe'er
She was, appeared distinct, and tall, and fair. 920

CXVI

Her brow was overhung with coins of gold,
  That sparkled o'er the auburn of her hair,
Her clustering hair, whose longer locks were rolled
  In braids behind; and though her stature were
Even of the highest for a female mould, 925
  They nearly reached her heel; and in her air
There was a something which bespoke command,
As one who was a lady in the land.

CXVII

Her hair, I said, was auburn; but her eyes
  Were black as death, their lashes the same hue, 930
Of downcast length, in whose silk shadow lies
  Deepest attraction; for when to the view
Forth from its raven fringe the full glance flies,
  Ne'er with such force the swiftest arrow flew;
'Tis as the snake late coiled, who pours his length, 935
And hurls at once his venom and his strength.

CXVIII

Her brow was white and low, her cheek's pure dye
  Like twilight rosy still with the set sun;
Short upper lip—sweet lips! that make us sigh
  Ever to have seen such; for she was one 940
Fit for the model of a statuary
  (A race of mere impostors, when all's done—
I've seen much finer women, ripe and real,
Than all the nonsense of their stone ideal).

CXIX

I'll tell you why I say so, for 'tis just 945
  One should not rail without a decent cause:
There was an Irish lady, to whose bust
  I ne'er saw justice done, and yet she was
A frequent model; and if e'er she must
  Yield to stern Time and Nature's wrinkling laws, 950
They will destroy a face which mortal thought
Ne'er compassed, nor less mortal chisel wrought.

CXX

And such was she, the lady of the cave:
  Her dress was very different from the Spanish,
Simpler, and yet of colours not so grave; 955
  For, as you know, the Spanish women banish
Bright hues when out of doors, and yet, while wave
  Around them (what I hope will never vanish)
The basquina and the mantilla, they
Seem at the same time mystical and gay. 960

CXXI

But with our damsel this was not the case:
  Her dress was many-coloured, finely spun;
Her locks curled negligently round her face,
  But through them gold and gems profusely shone:
Her girdle sparkled, and the richest lace 965
  Flowed in her veil, and many a precious stone
Flashed on her little hand; but, what was shocking,
Her small snow feet had slippers, but no stocking.

CXXII

The other female's dress was not unlike,
  But of inferior materials: she 970

959. ***basquina:*** Spanish ornamented petticoat. ***mantilla:*** lace veil covering the head and shoulders.

Had not so many ornaments to strike
  Her hair had silver only, bound to be
Her dowry; and her veil, in form alike,
  Was coarser; and her air, though firm, less free;
Her hair was thicker, but less long; her eyes 975
As black, but quicker, and of smaller size.

CXXIII

And these two tended him, and cheered him both
  With food and raiment, and those soft attentions,
Which are—(as I must own)—of female growth,
  And have ten thousand delicate inventions: 980
They made a most superior mess of broth,
  A thing which poesy but seldom mentions,
But the best dish that e'er was cooked since Homer's
Achilles ordered dinner for new comers.

CXXIV

I'll tell you who they were, this female pair, 985
  Lest they should seem princesses in disguise;
Besides, I hate all mystery, and that air
  Of clap-trap, which your recent poets prize;
And so, in short, the girls they really were
  They shall appear before your curious eyes, 990
Mistress and maid; the first was only daughter
Of an old man, who lived upon the water.

CXXV

A fisherman he had been in his youth,
  And still a sort of fisherman was he;
But other speculations were, in sooth, 995
  Added to his connexion with the sea,
Perhaps not so respectable, in truth:
  A little smuggling, and some piracy,
Left him, at last, the sole of many masters
Of an ill-gotten million of piastres. 1000

CXXVI

A fisher, therefore, was he,—though of men,
  Like Peter the Apostle,—and he fished
For wandering merchant vessels, now and then,

984. *dinner:* a reference to the feast given by Achilles for Ajax, Odysseus, and Phoenix in Homer's *Iliad,* Book IX.

1000. *piastres:* Both a Spanish silver coin and a small Turkish coin were so called.

1001–1002. *of men . . . Peter the Apostle:* See Matthew 4:19 and Mark 1:17.

And sometimes caught as many as he wished;
The cargoes he confiscated, and gain 1005
He sought in the slave-market, too, and dished
Full many a morsel for that Turkish trade,
By which, no doubt, a good deal may be made.

CXXVII

He was a Greek, and on his isle had built
(One of the wild and smaller Cyclades) 1010
A very handsome house from out his guilt,
And there he lived exceedingly at ease;
Heaven knows what cash he got, or blood he spilt,
A sad old fellow was he, if you please;
But this I know, it was a spacious building, 1015
Full of barbaric carving, paint, and gilding.

CXXVIII

He had an only daughter, called Haidée,
The greatest heiress of the Eastern Isles;
Besides, so very beautiful was she,
Her dowry was as nothing to her smiles: 1020
Still in her teens, and like a lovely tree
She grew to womanhood, and between whiles
Rejected several suitors, just to learn
How to accept a better in his turn.

CXXIX

And walking out upon the beach, below 1025
The cliff,—towards sunset, on that day she found,
Insensible,—not dead, but nearly so,—
Don Juan, almost famished, and half drowned;
But being naked, she was shocked, you know,
Yet deemed herself in common pity bound, 1030
As far as in her lay, "to take him in,
A stranger" dying, with so white a skin.

CXXX

But taking him into her father's house
Was not exactly the best way to save,
But like conveying to the cat the mouse, 1035
Or people in a trance into their grave;
Because the good old man had so much "*νους*,"
Unlike the honest Arab thieves so brave,
He would have hospitably cured the stranger
And sold him instantly when out of danger. 1040

1037. *νους*: "mind" or "spirit" (Greek); pronounced "nowse."

CXXXI

And therefore, with her maid, she thought it best
 (A virgin always on her maid relies)
To place him in the cave for present rest:
 And when, at last, he opened his black eyes,
Their charity increased about their guest; 1045
 And their compassion grew to such a size,
It opened half the turnpike gates to heaven—
(St. Paul says, 'tis the toll which must be given).

CXXXII

They made a fire,—but such a fire as they
 Upon the moment could contrive with such 1050
Materials as were cast up round the bay,—
 Some broken planks, and oars, that to the touch
Were nearly tinder, since so long they lay
 A mast was almost crumbled to a crutch;
But, by God's grace, here wrecks were in such plenty, 1055
That there was fuel to have furnished twenty.

CXXXIII

He had a bed of furs, and a pelisse,
 For Haidée stripped her sables off to make
His couch; and, that he might be more at ease,
 And warm, in case by chance he should awake, 1060
They also gave a petticoat apiece,
 She and her maid,—and promised by daybreak
To pay him a fresh visit, with a dish
For breakfast, of eggs, coffee, bread, and fish.

CXXXIV

And thus they left him to his lone repose: 1065
 Juan slept like a top, or like the dead,
Who sleep at last, perhaps (God only knows),
 Just for the present; and in his lulled head
Not even a vision of his former woes
 Throbbed in accursèd dreams, which sometimes spread 1070
Unwelcome visions of our former years,
Till the eye, cheated, opens thick with tears.

CXXXV

Young Juan slept all dreamless:—but the maid,
 Who smoothed his pillow, as she left the den
Looked back upon him, and a moment staid, 1075

1048. *St. Paul:* See I Corinthians 13:1–13.

And turned, believing that he called again.
He slumbered; yet she thought, at least she said
(The heart will slip, even as the tongue and pen),
He had pronounced her name—but she forgot
That at this moment Juan knew it not. 1080

CXXXVI

And pensive to her father's house she went,
Enjoining silence strict to Zoe, who
Better than her knew what, in fact, she meant,
She being wiser by a year or two:
A year or two's an age when rightly spent, 1085
And Zoe spent hers, as most women do,
In gaining all that useful sort of knowledge
Which is acquired in Nature's good old college.

CXXXVII

The morn broke, and found Juan slumbering still
Fast in his cave, and nothing clashed upon 1090
His rest: the rushing of the neighbouring rill,
And the young beams of the excluded sun,
Troubled him not, and he might sleep his fill;
And need he had of slumber yet, for none
Had suffered more—his hardships were comparative 1095
To those related in my grand-dad's "Narrative."

CXXXVIII

Not so Haidée: she sadly tossed and tumbled,
And started from her sleep, and turning o'er,
Dreamed of a thousand wrecks, o'er which she stumbled,
And handsome corpses strewed upon the shore; 1100
And woke her maid so early that she grumbled,
And called her father's old slaves up, who swore
In several oaths—Armenian, Turk, and Greek—
They knew not what to think of such a freak.

CXXXIX

But up she got, and up she made them get, 1105
With some pretence about the sun, that makes
Sweet skies just when he rises, or is set;
And 'tis, no doubt, a sight to see when breaks
Bright Phœbus, while the mountains still are wet

1096. *"Narrative"*: The poet drew upon his grandfather's *Narrative* . . . (1768), the tale of a shipwreck off the coast of Chile in 1741. John Byron (1723–1786) sailed as a midshipman aboard the *Wager*, one of Lord Anson's squadron in his famous voyage around the world.

With mist, and every bird with him awakes, 1110
And night is flung off like a mourning suit
Worn for a husband,—or some other brute.

CXL

I say, the sun is a most glorious sight:
I've seen him rise full oft, indeed of late
I have sat up on purpose all the night, 1115
Which hastens, as physicians say, one's fate;
And so all ye, who would be in the right
In health and purse, begin your day to date
From daybreak, and when coffined at four-score
Engrave upon the plate, you rose at four. 1120

CXLI

And Haidée met the morning face to face;
Her own was freshest, though a feverish flush
Had dyed it with the headlong blood, whose race
From heart to cheek is curbed into a blush,
Like to a torrent which a mountain's base, 1125
That overpowers some Alpine river's rush,
Checks to a lake, whose waves in circles spread;
Or the Red Sea—but the sea is not red.

CXLII

And down the cliff the island virgin came,
And near the cave her quick light footsteps drew, 1130
While the sun smiled on her with his first flame,
And young Aurora kissed her lips with dew,
Taking her for a sister; just the same
Mistake you would have made on seeing the two,
Although the mortal, quite as fresh and fair, 1135
Had all the advantage, too, of not being air.

CXLIII

And when into the cavern Haidée stepped
All timidly, yet rapidly, she saw
That like an infant Juan sweetly slept;
And then she stopped, and stood as if in awe 1140
(For sleep is awful), and on tiptoe crept
And wrapt him closer, lest the air, too raw,
Should reach his blood, then o'er him still as death
Bent, with hushed lips, that drank his scarce-drawn breath.

1132. *Aurora:* Roman name for Eos, goddess of the dawn.

CXLIV

And thus like to an angel o'er the dying 1145
  Who die in righteousness, she leaned; and there
All tranquilly the shipwrecked boy was lying,
  As o'er him lay the calm and stirless air:
But Zoe the meantime some eggs was frying,
  Since, after all, no doubt the youthful pair 1150
Must breakfast, and betimes—lest they should ask it,
She drew out her provision from the basket.

CXLV

She knew that the best feelings must have victual,
  And that a shipwrecked youth would hungry be;
Besides, being less in love, she yawned a little, 1155
  And felt her veins chilled by the neighbouring sea;
And so, she cooked their breakfast to a tittle;
  I can't say that she gave them any tea,
But there were eggs, fruit, coffee, bread, fish, honey,
With Scio wine,—and all for love, not money. 1160

CXLVI

And Zoe, when the eggs were ready, and
  The coffee made, would fain have wakened Juan;
But Haidée stopped her with her quick small hand,
  And without a word, a sign her finger drew on
Her lip, which Zoe needs must understand; 1165
  And, the first breakfast spoilt, prepared a new one,
Because her mistress would not let her break
That sleep which seemed as it would ne'er awake.

CXLVII

For still he lay, and on his thin worn cheek
  A purple hectic played like dying day 1170
On the snow-tops of distant hills; the streak
  Of sufferance yet upon his forehead lay,
Where the blue veins looked shadowy, shrunk, and weak;
  And his black curls were dewy with the spray,
Which weighed upon them yet, all damp and salt, 1175
Mixed with the stony vapours of the vault.

CXLVIII

And she bent o'er him, and he lay beneath,
  Hushed as the babe upon its mother's breast,
Drooped as the willow when no winds can breathe,
  Lulled like the depth of ocean when at rest, 1180

Fair as the crowning rose of the whole wreath,
  Soft as the callow cygnet in its nest;
In short, he was a very pretty fellow,
Although his woes had turned him rather yellow.

CXLIX

He woke and gazed, and would have slept again, 1185
  But the fair face which met his eyes forbade
Those eyes to close, though weariness and pain
  Had further sleep a further pleasure made;
For woman's face was never formed in vain
  For Juan, so that even when he prayed 1190
He turned from grisly saints, and martyrs hairy,
To the sweet portraits of the Virgin Mary.

CL

And thus upon his elbow he arose,
  And looked upon the lady, in whose cheek
The pale contended with the purple rose, 1195
  As with an effort she began to speak;
Her eyes were eloquent, her words would pose,
  Although she told him, in good modern Greek,
With an Ionian accent, low and sweet,
That he was faint, and must not talk, but eat. 1200

CLI

Now Juan could not understand a word,
  Being no Grecian; but he had an ear,
And her voice was the warble of a bird,
  So soft, so sweet, so delicately clear,
That finer, simpler, music ne'er was heard; 1205
  The sort of sound we echo with a tear,
Without knowing why—an overpowering tone,
Whence melody descends as from a throne.

CLII

And Juan gazed as one who is awoke
  By a distant organ, doubting if he be 1210
Not yet a dreamer, till the spell is broke
  By the watchman, or some such reality,
Or by one's early valet's cursèd knock;
  At least it is a heavy sound to me,
Who like a morning slumber—for the night 1215
Shows stars and women in a better light.

CLIII

And Juan, too, was helped out from his dream,
  Or sleep, or whatsoe'er it was, by feeling
A most prodigious appetite; the steam
  Of Zoe's cookery no doubt was stealing 1220
Upon his senses, and the kindling beam
  Of the new fire, which Zoe kept up, kneeling,
To stir her viands, made him quite awake
And long for food, but chiefly a beef-steak.

CLIV

But beef is rare within these oxless isles; 1225
  Goat's flesh there is, no doubt, and kid, and mutton,
And, when a holiday upon them smiles,
  A joint upon their barbarous spits they put on:
But this occurs but seldom, between whiles,
  For some of these are rocks with scarce a hut on; 1230
Others are fair and fertile, among which
This, though not large, was one of the most rich.

CLV

I say that beef is rare, and can't help thinking
  That the old fable of the Minotaur—
From which our modern rivals, rightly shrinking, 1235
  Condemn the royal lady's taste who wore
A cow's shape for a mask—was only (sinking
  The allegory) a mere type, no more,
That Pasiphae promoted breeding cattle,
To make the Cretans bloodier in battle. 1240

CLVI

For we all know that English people are
  Fed upon beef—I won't say much of beer,
Because 'tis liquor only, and being far
  From this my subject, has no business here;
We know, too, they are very fond of war, 1245
  A pleasure—like all pleasures—rather dear;
So were the Cretans—from which I infer
That beef and battles both were owing to her.

CLVII

But to resume. The languid Juan raised
  His head upon his elbow, and he saw 1250
A sight on which he had not lately gazed,

1234–1239. *Minotaur . . . Pasiphae:* The Minotaur was the offspring of Pasiphae and the bull sent to Minos, king of Crete. The beast was eventually slain by Theseus.

As all his latter meals had been quite raw,
Three or four things, for which the Lord be praised,
And, feeling still the famished vulture gnaw,
He fell upon whate'er was offered, like 1255
A priest, a shark, an alderman, or pike.

CLVIII

He ate, and he was well supplied; and she
Who watched him like a mother, would have fed
Him past all bounds, because she smiled to see
Such appetite in one she had deemed dead: 1260
But Zoe, being older than Haidée,
Knew (by tradition, for she ne'er had read)
That famished people must be slowly nurst,
And fed by spoonfuls, else they always burst.

CLIX

And so she took the liberty to state, 1265
Rather by deeds than words, because the case
Was urgent, that the gentleman, whose fate
Had made her mistress quit her bed to trace
The sea-shore at this hour, must leave his plate,
Unless he wished to die upon the place— 1270
She snatched it, and refused another morsel,
Saying, he had gorged enough to make a horse ill.

CLX

Next they—he being naked, save a tattered
Pair of scarce decent trowsers—went to work,
And in the fire his recent rags they scattered, 1275
And dressed him, for the present, like a Turk,
Or Greek—that is, although it not much mattered,
Omitting turban, slippers, pistols, dirk,—
They furnished him, entire, except some stitches,
With a clean shirt, and very spacious britches. 1280

CLXI

And then fair Haidée tried her tongue at speaking,
But not a word could Juan comprehend,
Although he listened so that the young Greek in
Her earnestness would ne'er have made an end;
And, as he interrupted not, went eking 1285
Her speech out to her protégé and friend,
Till pausing at the last her breath to take,
She saw he did not understand Romaic.

1288. *Romaic:* the vernacular language of modern Greece.

CLXII

And then she had recourse to nods, and signs,
  And smiles, and sparkles of the speaking eye, 1290
And read (the only book she could) the lines
  Of his fair face, and found, by sympathy,
The answer eloquent, where the soul shines
  And darts in one quick glance a long reply;
And thus in every look she saw exprest 1295
A world of words, and things at which she guessed.

CLXIII

And now, by dint of fingers and of eyes,
  And words repeated after her, he took
A lesson in her tongue; but by surmise,
  No doubt, less of her language than her look: 1300
As he who studies fervently the skies
  Turns oftener to the stars than to his book,
Thus Juan learned his alpha beta better
From Haidée's glance than any graven letter.

CLXIV

'Tis pleasing to be schooled in a strange tongue 1305
  By female lips and eyes—that is, I mean,
When both the teacher and the taught are young,
  As was the case, at least, where I have been;
They smile so when one's right, and when one's wrong
  They smile still more and then there intervene 1310
Pressure of hands, perhaps even a chaste kiss;—
I learned the little that I know by this:

CLXV

That is, some words of Spanish, Turk, and Greek,
  Italian not at all, having no teachers;
Much English I cannot pretend to speak, 1315
  Learning that language chiefly from its preachers,
Barrow, South, Tillotson, whom every week
  I study, also Blair, the highest reachers
Of eloquence in piety and prose—
I hate your poets, so read none of those. 1320

CLXVI

As for the ladies, I have nought to say,
  A wanderer from the British world of fashion,

1317–1318. *Barrow . . . Blair:* Isaac Barrow (1630–1677), preacher and professor of Greek at Cambridge; Robert South (1634–1716), court preacher to Charles II; John Tillotson (1630–1694), archbishop of Canterbury; Hugh Blair (1699–1746), Scottish preacher and professor of rhetoric.

Where I, like other "dogs, have had my day,"
  Like other men, too, may have had my passion—
But that, like other things, has passed away, 1325
  And all her fools whom I *could* lay the lash on:
Foes, friends, men, women, now are nought to me
But dreams of what has been, no more to be.

CLXVII

Return we to Don Juan. He begun
  To hear new words, and to repeat them; but 1330
Some feelings, universal as the sun,
  Were such as could not in his breast be shut
More than within the bosom of a nun:
  He was in love,—as you would be, no doubt,
With a young benefactress,—so was she, 1335
Just in the way we very often see.

CLXVIII

And every day by daybreak—rather early
  For Juan, who was somewhat fond of rest,—
She came into the cave, but it was merely
  To see her bird reposing in his nest; 1340
And she would softly stir his locks so curly,
  Without disturbing her yet slumbering guest,
Breathing all gently o'er his cheek and mouth,
As o'er a bed of roses the sweet south.

CLXIX

And every morn his colour freshlier came, 1345
  And every day helped on his convalescence;
'Twas well, because health in the human frame
  Is pleasant, besides being true love's essence,
For health and idleness to passion's flame
  Are oil and gunpowder; and some good lessons 1350
Are also learnt from Ceres and from Bacchus,
Without whom Venus will not long attack us.

CLXX

While Venus fills the heart (without heart really
  Love, though good always, is not quite so good),
Ceres presents a plate of vermicelli,— 1355
  For love must be sustained like flesh and blood,
While Bacchus pours out wine, or hands a jelly:

1351. *Ceres:* the Roman goddess of agriculture—here equivalent to foods made of grain.

Eggs, oysters, too, are amatory food;
But who is their purveyor from above
Heaven knows—it may be Neptune, Pan, or Jove. 1360

CLXXI

When Juan woke he found some good things ready,
A bath, a breakfast, and the finest eyes
That ever made a youthful heart less steady,
Besides her maid's, as pretty for their size;
But I have spoken of all this already— 1365
And repetition's tiresome and unwise,—
Well—Juan, after bathing in the sea,
Came always back to coffee and Haidée.

CLXXII

Both were so young, and one so innocent,
That bathing passed for nothing; Juan seemed 1370
To her, as 'twere, the kind of being sent,
Of whom these two years she had nightly dreamed,
A something to be loved, a creature meant
To be her happiness, and whom she deemed
To render happy: all who joy would win 1375
Must share it,—Happiness was born a twin.

CLXXIII

It was such a pleasure to behold him, such
Enlargement of existence to partake
Nature with him, to thrill beneath his touch,
To watch him slumbering, and to see him wake; 1380
To live with him for ever were too much;
But then the thought of parting made her quake:
He was her own, her ocean-treasure, cast
Like a rich wreck—her first love, and her last.

CLXXIV

And thus a moon rolled on, and fair Haidée 1385
Paid daily visits to her boy, and took
Such plentiful precautions, that still he
Remained unknown within his craggy nook;
At last her father's prows put out to sea,
For certain merchantmen upon the look, 1390
Not as of yore to carry off an Io,
But three Ragusan vessels bound for Scio.

1391. *Io:* beloved by Zeus, and changed by him into a heifer to protect her from his wife, Hera. See Aeschylus, *Prometheus Bound.*

1392. *Ragusan:* from Ragusa, a port in modern Yugoslavia, on the Adriatic. *Scio:* an island in the Aegean, northeast of Athens.

CLXXV

Then came her freedom, for she had no mother,
  So that, her father being at sea, she was
Free as a married woman, or such other 1395
  Female, as where she likes she may freely pass,
Without even the encumbrance of a brother,
  The freest she that ever gazed on glass:
I speak of Christian lands in this comparison,
Where wives, at least, are seldom kept in garrison. 1400

CLXXVI

Now she prolonged her visits and her talk
  (For they must talk), and he had learnt to say
So much as to propose to take a walk,—
  For little had he wandered since the day
On which, like a young flower snapped from the stalk, 1405
  Drooping and dewy on the beach he lay,—
And thus they walked out in the afternoon,
And saw the sun set opposite the moon.

CLXXVII

It was a wild and breaker-beaten coast,
  With cliffs above, and a broad sandy shore, 1410
Guarded by shoals and rocks as by an host,
  With here and there a creek, whose aspect wore
A better welcome to the tempest-tost;
  And rarely ceased the haughty billow's roar,
Save on the dead long summer days, which make 1415
The outstretched ocean glitter like a lake.

CLXXVIII

And the small ripple spilt upon the beach
  Scarcely o'erpassed the cream of your champagne,
When o'er the brim the sparkling bumpers reach,
  That spring-dew of the spirit! the heart's rain! 1420
Few things surpass old wine; and they may preach
  Who please,—the more because they preach in vain,—
Let us have wine and women, mirth and laughter,
Sermons and soda-water the day after.

CLXXIX

Man, being reasonable, must get drunk; 1425
  The best of life is but intoxication:
Glory, the grape, love, gold, in these are sunk
  The hopes of all men, and of every nation;

Without their sap, how branchless were the trunk
  Of life's strange tree, so fruitful on occasion! 1430
But to return,—Get very drunk; and when
  You wake with headache, you shall see what then.

CLXXX

Ring for your valet—bid him quickly bring
  Some hock and soda-water, then you'll know
A pleasure worthy Xerxes the great king; 1435
  For not the blest sherbet, sublimed with snow,
Nor the first sparkle of the desert spring,
  Nor Burgundy in all its sunset glow,
After long travel, ennui, love, or slaughter,
Vie with that draught of hock and soda-water. 1440

CLXXXI

The coast—I think it was the coast that I
  Was just describing—Yes, it *was* the coast—
Lay at this period quiet as the sky,
  The sands untumbled, the blue waves untost,
And all was stillness, save the sea-birds' cry, 1445
  And dolphin's leap, and little billow crost
By some low rock or shelve, that made it fret
Against the boundary it scarcely wet.

CLXXXII

And forth they wandered, her sire being gone,
  As I have said, upon an expedition; 1450
And mother, brother, guardian, she had none,
  Save Zoe, who, although with due precision
She waited on her lady with the sun,
  Thought daily service was her only mission,
Bringing warm water, wreathing her long tresses, 1455
And asking now and then for cast-off dresses.

CLXXXIII

It was the cooling hour, just when the rounded
  Red sun sinks down behind the azure hill,
Which then seems as if the whole earth is bounded,
  Circling all nature, hushed, and dim, and still, 1460
With the far mountain-crescent half surrounded
  On one side, and the deep sea calm and chill,
Upon the other, and the rosy sky,
With one star sparkling through it like an eye.

1435. *Xerxes:* king of Persia and son of Darius. Xerxes (519–465 B.C.) bridged the Hellespont, invaded Greece, defeated the Spartans at Thermopylae, and was finally beaten by the Greeks at Salamis in 480 B.C.

CLXXXIV

And thus they wandered forth, hand in hand, 1465
Over the shining pebbles and the shells,
Glided along the smooth and hardened sand,
And in the worn and wild receptacles
Worked by the storms, yet worked as it were planned,
In hollow halls, with sparry roofs and cells, 1470
They turned to rest; and, each clasped by an arm,
Yielded to the deep twilight's purple charm.

CLXXXV

They looked up to the sky, whose floating glow
Spread like a rosy ocean, vast and bright;
They gazed upon the glittering sea below, 1475
Whence the broad moon rose circling into sight;
They heard the waves splash, and the wind so low,
And saw each other's dark eyes darting light
Into each other—and, beholding this,
Their lips drew near, and clung into a kiss; 1480

CLXXXVI

A long, long kiss, a kiss of youth, and love,
And beauty, all concentrating like rays
Into one focus, kindled from above;
Such kisses as belong to early days,
Where heart, and soul, and sense, in concert move, 1485
And the blood's lava, and the pulse a blaze,
Each kiss a heart-quake,—for a kiss's strength,
I think it must be reckoned by its length.

CLXXXVII

By length I mean duration; theirs endured
Heaven knows how long—no doubt they never reckoned; 1490
And if they had, they could not have secured
The sum of their sensations to a second:
They had not spoken; but they felt allured,
As if their souls and lips each other beckoned,
Which, being joined, like swarming bees they clung— 1495
Their hearts the flowers from whence the honey sprung.

CLXXXVIII

They were alone, but not alone as they
Who shut in chambers think it loneliness;
The silent ocean, and the starlight bay,
The twilight glow, which momently grew less, 1500

The voiceless sands, and dropping caves, that lay
  Around them, made them to each other press,
As if there were no life beneath the sky
  Save theirs, and that their life could never die.

CLXXXIX

They feared no eyes nor ears on that lone beach, 1505
  They felt no terrors from the night; they were
All in all to each other; though their speech
  Was broken words, they *thought* a language there,—
And all the burning tongues the passions teach
  Found in one sigh the best interpreter 1510
Of nature's oracle—first love,—that all
Which Eve has left her daughters since her fall.

CXC

Haidée spoke not of scruples, asked no vows,
  Nor offered any; she had never heard
Of plight and promises to be a spouse, 1515
  Or perils by a loving maid incurred;
She was all which pure ignorance allows,
  And flew to her young mate like a young bird,
And never having dreamt of falsehood, she
Had not one word to say of constancy. 1520

CXCI

She loved, and was beloved—she adored,
  And she was worshipped; after nature's fashion,
Their intense souls, into each other poured,
  If souls could die, had perished in that passion,—
But by degrees their senses were restored, 1525
  Again to be o'ercome, again to dash on;
And, beating 'gainst *his* bosom, Haidée's heart
Felt as if never more to beat apart.

CXCII

Alas! they were so young, so beautiful,
  So lonely, loving, helpless, and the hour 1530
Was that in which the heart is always full,
  And, having o'er itself no further power,
Prompts deeds eternity cannot annul,
  But pays off moments in an endless shower
Of hell-fire—all prepared for people giving 1535
Pleasure or pain to one another living.

CXCIII

Alas; for Juan and Haidée! they were
  So loving and so lovely—till then never,
Excepting our first parents, such a pair
  Had run the risk of being damned for ever; 1540
And Haidée, being devout as well as fair,
  Had, doubtless, heard about the Stygian river,
And hell and purgatory—but forgot
Just in the very crisis she should not.

CXCIV

They look upon each other, and their eyes 1545
  Gleam in the moonlight; and her white arm clasps
Round Juan's head, and his around her lies
  Half buried in the tresses which it grasps;
She sits upon his knee, and drinks his sighs,
  He hers, until they end in broken gasps; 1550
And thus they form a group that's quite antique,
Half naked, loving, natural, and Greek.

CXCV

And when those deep and burning moments passed,
  And Juan sunk to sleep within her arms,
She slept not, but all tenderly, though fast, 1555
  Sustained his head upon her bosom's charms;
And now and then her eye to heaven is cast,
  And then on the pale cheek her breast now warms,
Pillowed on her o'erflowing heart, which pants
With all it granted, and with all it grants. 1560

CXCVI

An infant when it gazes on a light,
  A child the moment when it drains the breast,
A devotee when soars the Host in sight,
  An Arab with a stranger for a guest,
A sailor when the prize has struck in fight, 1565
  A miser filling his most hoarded chest,
Feel rapture; but not such true joy are reaping
As they who watch o'er what they love while sleeping.

CXCVII

For there it lies so tranquil, so beloved,
  All that it hath of life with us is living; 1570
So gentle, stirless, helpless, and unmoved,

And all unconscious of the joy 'tis giving;
All it hath felt, inflicted, passed, and proved,
Hushed into depths beyond the watcher's diving;
There lies the thing we love with all its errors 1575
And all its charms, like death without its terrors.

CXCVIII

The lady watched her lover—and that hour
Of Love's, and Night's, and Ocean's solitude,
O'erflowed her soul with their united power;
Amidst the barren sand and rocks so rude 1580
She and her wave-born love had made their bower,
Where nought upon their passion could intrude,
And all the stars that crowded the blue space
Saw nothing happier than her glowing face.

CXCIX

Alas! the love of women! it is known 1585
To be a lovely and a fearful thing;
For all of theirs upon that die is thrown,
And if 'tis lost, life hath no more to bring
To them but mockeries of the past alone,
And their revenge is as the tiger's spring, 1590
Deadly, and quick, and crushing; yet, as real
Torture is theirs, what they inflict they feel.

CC

They are right; for man to man so oft unjust,
Is always so to women; one sole bond
Awaits them, treachery is all their trust; 1595
Taught to conceal, their bursting hearts despond
Over their idol, till some wealthier lust
Buys them in marriage—and what rests beyond?
A thankless husband, next a faithless lover,
Then dressing, nursing, praying, and all's over. 1600

CCI

Some take a lover, some take drams or prayers,
Some mind their household, others dissipation,
Some run away, and but exchange their cares,
Losing the advantage of a virtuous station;
Few changes e'er can better their affairs, 1605
Theirs being an unnatural situation,
From the dull palace to the dirty hovel:
Some play the devil, and then write a novel.

1608. *novel:* Lady Caroline Lamb (1785–1828), infatuated with Byron, wrote a thinly veiled autobiographical novel about their affair after her

CCII

Haidée was Nature's bride, and knew not this:
  Haidée was Passion's child, born where the sun 1610
Showers triple light, and scorches even the kiss
  Of his gazelle-eyed daughters; she was one
Made to love, to feel that she was his
  Who was her chosen: what was said or done
Elsewhere was nothing. She had nought to fear, 1615
Hope, care, nor love beyond,—her heart beat *here*.

CCIII

And oh! that quickening of the heart, that beat!
  How much it costs us! yet each rising throb
Is in its cause as its effect so sweet,
  That Wisdom, ever on the watch to rob 1620
Joy of its alchemy, and to repeat
  Fine truths; even Conscience, too, has a tough job
To make us understand each good old maxim,
So good—I wonder Castlereagh don't tax 'em.

CCIV

And now 'twas done—on the lone shore were plighted 1625
  Their hearts; the stars, their nuptial torches, shed
Beauty upon the beautiful they lighted:
  Ocean their witness, and the cave their bed.
By their own feelings hallowed and united,
  Their priest was Solitude, and they were wed: 1630
And they were happy, for to their young eyes
Each was an angel, and earth paradise.

CCV

Oh, Love! of whom great Cæsar was the suitor,
  Titus the master, Anthony the slave,
Horace, Catullus, scholars, Ovid tutor, 1635
  Sappho the sage blue-stocking, in whose grave
All those may leap who rather would be neuter—
  (Leucadia's rock still overlooks the wave)—
Oh, Love! thou art the very god of evil,
For, after all, we cannot call thee devil. 1640

rupture with him. The book, *Glenarvon* (1816), was later republished as *The Fatal Passion* (1865). It was Lady Caroline who said of Byron that he was "mad, bad, and dangerous to know." The sight of his funeral in 1824 permanently deranged her mind.

1624. *Castlereagh:* Viscount Castlereagh (1769–1822), British foreign secretary between 1812 and 1822.

1634. *Titus:* Titus Flavius Vespasianus, Roman emperor from 79 to 81 A.D., called "the love and delight of the human race" for his virtues.

1638. *Leucadia's rock:* a promontory on the island of Leucadia, or Leucas, from which unhappy lovers—notably the poetess Sappho—were said to have leaped into the sea.

CCVI

Thou makest the chaste connubial state precarious,
  And jestest with the brows of mightiest men:
Cæsar and Pompey, Mahomet, Belisarius,
  Have much employed the muse of history's pen:
Their lives and fortunes were extremely various, 1645
  Such worthies Time will never see again;
Yet to these four in three things the same luck holds,
They all were heroes, conquerors, and cuckolds.

CCVII

Thou makest philosophers; there's Epicurus
  And Aristippus, a material crew! 1650
Who to immoral courses would allure us
  By theories quite practicable too;
If only from the devil they would insure us,
  How pleasant were the maxim (not quite new),
"Eat, drink, and love; what can the rest avail us?" 1655
So said the royal sage Sardanapalus.

CCVIII

But Juan! had he quite forgotten Julia?
  And should he have forgotten her so soon?
I can't but say it seems to me most truly a
  Perplexing question; but, no doubt, the moon 1660
Does these things for us, and whenever newly a
  Strong palpitation rises, 'tis her boon,
Else how the devil is it that fresh features
Have such a charm for us poor human creatures?

CCIX

I hate inconstancy—I loathe, detest, 1665
  Abhor, condemn, abjure the mortal made
Of such quicksilver clay that in his breast
  No permanent foundation can be laid;
Love, constant love, has been my constant guest,
  And yet last night, being at a masquerade, 1670
I saw the prettiest creature, fresh from Milan,
Which gave me some sensations like a villain.

1642. *brows:* alluding to the horns reputed to appear on the foreheads of cuckolds.
1643. *Belisarius:* military commander during the reign (527–565 A.D.) of the Roman emperor Justinian.
1650. *Aristippus:* born about 428 B.C., founder of the Cyrenaic (hedonistic) school of philosophy.
1656. *Sardanapalus:* last king of Assyria, according to legend notorious for effeminacy and love of luxury. He was the central character of Byron's play *Sardanapalus* (1821).

CCX

But soon Philosophy came to my aid,
  And whispered, "Think of every sacred tie!"
"I will, my dear Philosophy!" I said, 1675
  "But then her teeth, and then, oh, Heaven! her eye!
I'll just inquire if she be wife or maid,
  Or neither—out of curiosity."
"Stop!" cried Philosophy, with air so Grecian
(Though she was masqued then as a fair Venetian); 1680

CCXI

"Stop!" so I stopped.—But to return: that which
  Men call inconstancy is nothing more
Than admiration due where nature's rich
  Profusion with young beauty cover o'er
Some favoured object; and as in the niche 1685
  A lovely statue we almost adore,
This sort of adoration of the real
Is but a heightening of the "beau ideal."

CCXII

'Tis the perception of the beautiful,
  A fine extension of the faculties, 1690
Platonic, universal, wonderful,
  Drawn from the stars, and filtered through the skies,
Without which life would be extremely dull;
  In short, it is the use of our own eyes,
With one or two small senses added, just 1695
To hint that flesh is formed of fiery dust.

CCXIII

Yet 'tis a painful feeling, and unwilling,
  For surely if we always could perceive
In the same object graces quite as killing
  As when she rose upon us like an Eve, 1700
'Twould save us many a heart-ache, many a shilling
  (For we must get them any how, or grieve),
Whereas, if one sole lady pleased for ever,
How pleasant for the heart, as well as liver!

CCXIV

The heart is like the sky, a part of heaven, 1705
  But changes night and day, too, like the sky;
Now o'er it clouds and thunder must be driven,
  And darkness and destruction as on high:
But when it hath been scorched, and pierced, and riven,
  Its storms expire in water-drops; the eye 1710

Pours forth at last the heart's blood turned to tears,
Which makes the English climate of our years.

CCXV

The liver is the lazaret of bile,
  But very rarely executes its function,
For the first passion stays there such a while, 1715
  That all the rest creep in and form a junction,
Like knots of vipers on a dunghill's soil,
  Rage, fear, hate, jealousy, revenge, compunction,
So that all mischiefs spring up from this entrail,
Like earthquakes from the hidden fire called "central." 1720

CCXVI

In the mean time, without proceeding more
  In this anatomy, I've finished now
Two hundred and odd stanzas as before,
  That being about the number I'll allow
Each canto of the twelve, or twenty-four; 1725
  And, laying down my pen, I make my bow,
Leaving Don Juan and Haidée to plead
For them and theirs with all who deign to read.

1726. *pen:* Cantos III through XVI were published between August, 1821, and March, 1824, and the fragmentary Canto XVII first appeared in 1903. The love affair is interrupted by the entrance of Haidée's father, Lambro; and Juan is sold as a slave, while Haidée dies of a broken heart. After a sojourn at the Sultan's court at Constantinople, where he becomes the lover of the Sultana Gulbeyaz and the concubine Dudú, Juan joins the Russian army besieging the Turks in Ismail. He later is the recipient of the affections of Catherine the Great, and eventually goes to England. Here he enters the elegant society of the day, and the poem breaks off with Juan's affair with the Duchess of Fitz-Fulke.

PERCY BYSSHE SHELLEY

(1792–1822)

Stanzas written in Dejection—December 1818, Near Naples*

The Sun is warm, the sky is clear,
The waves are dancing fast and bright,
Blue isles and snowy mountains wear
The purple noon's transparent might,
The breath of the moist earth is light 5
Around its unexpanded buds;
Like many a voice of one delight
The winds, the birds, the Ocean-floods;
The City's voice itself is soft, like Solitude's.

* Written in 1816; published in 1817. Shelley's dejection arose from the suicide of his first wife, the recent death of his baby daughter, and his own ill health and other worries.

I see the Deep's untrampled floor 10
With green and purple seaweeds strown;
I see the waves upon the shore
Like light dissolved in star-showers, thrown;
I sit upon the sands alone;
The lightning of the noontide Ocean 15
Is flashing round me, and a tone
Arises from its measured motion,
How sweet! did any heart now share in my emotion.

Alas, I have nor hope nor health
Nor peace within nor clam around, 20
Nor that content surpassing wealth
The sage in meditation found,
And walked with inward glory crowned;
Nor fame nor power nor love nor leisure—
Others I see whom these surround, 25
Smiling they live and call life pleasure:
To me that cup has been dealt in another measure.

Yet now despair itself is mild,
Even as the winds and waters are;
I could lie down like a tired child 30
And weep away the life of care
Which I have borne and yet must bear
Till Death like Sleep might steal on me,
And I might feel in the warm air
My cheek grow cold, and hear the Sea 35
Breathe o'er my dying brain its last monotony.

Some might lament that I were cold,
As I, when this sweet day is gone,
Which my lost heart, too soon grown old,
Insults with this untimely moan— 40
They might lament,—for I am one
Whom men love not, and yet regret;
Unlike this day, which, when the Sun
Shall on its stainless glory set,
Will linger though enjoyed, like joy in Memory yet. 45

England in 1819*

An old, mad, blind, despised, and dying King;
Princes, the dregs of their dull race, who flow
Through public scorn,—mud from a muddy spring;
Rulers who neither see nor feel nor know,

* Written in that year, but published in 1839.
1. *King*: George III (1738–1820).
2. *Princes*: His sons, including the Prince-Regent, whose dissolute behavior gave rise to public scandals.

But leechlike to their fainting country cling 5
Till they drop, blind in blood, without a blow.
A people starved and stabbed in th'untilled field;
An army, whom liberticide and prey
Makes as a two-edged sword to all who wield;
Golden and sanguine laws which tempt and slay; 10
Religion Christless, Godless—a book sealed;
A senate, Time's worst statute, unrepealed—
Are graves from which a glorious Phantom may
Burst, to illumine our tempestuous day.

10. *golden*: I.e., bought; the laws favor the rich and powerful. *sanguine*: Bloody, causing bloodshed.
12. *Time's worst statute*: The law by which Roman Catholics and dissenters from the state religion (Anglicanism) were curtailed in their civil liberties.

Ode to the West Wind*

I

O wild West Wind, thou breath of Autumn's being,
Thou, from whose unseen presence the leaves dead
Are driven, like ghosts from an enchanter fleeing,

Yellow, and black, and pale, and hectic red,
Pestilence-stricken multitudes: O Thou, 5
Who chariotest to their dark wintry bed

The winged seeds, where they lie cold and low,
Each like a corpse within its grave, until
Thine azure sister of the Spring shall blow

Her clarion o'er the dreaming earth, and fill 10
(Driving sweet buds like flocks to feed in air)
With living hues and odors plain and hill:

Wild Spirit, which are moving everywhere;
Destroyer and Preserver; hear, O hear!

II

Thou on whose stream, 'mid the steep sky's commotion, 15
Loose clouds like Earth's decaying leaves are shed,
Shook from the tangled boughs of Heaven and Ocean,

Angels of rain and lightning; there are spread
On the blue surface of thine aery surge,
Like the bright hair uplifted from the head 20

Of some fierce Mænad, even from the dim verge
Of the horizon to the zenith's height,
The locks of the approaching storm. Thou Dirge

* Written in 1819; published in 1820.
10. *clarion*: Trumpet.
21. *Mænad*: Or bacchante, ecstatic female worshiper of Bacchus, god of wine.

Of the dying year, to which this closing night
Will be the dome of a vast sepulchre, 25
Vaulted with all thy congregated might

Of vapors, from whose solid atmosphere
Black rain and fire and hail will burst: O hear!

III

Thou who didst waken from his summer dreams
The blue Mediterranean, where he lay, 30
Lulled by the coil of his crystalline streams,

Beside a pumice isle in Baiæ's bay,
And saw in sleep old palaces and towers
Quivering within the wave's intenser day,

All overgrown with azure moss and flowers 35
So sweet, the sense faints picturing them! Thou
For whose path the Atlantic's level powers

Cleave themselves into chasms, while far below
The sea-blooms and the oozy woods which wear
The sapless foliage of the ocean, know 40

Thy voice, and suddenly grow grey with fear,
And tremble and despoil themselves: O hear!

IV

If I were a dead leaf thou mightest bear;
If I were a swift cloud to fly with thee;
A wave to pant beneath thy power, and share 45

The impulse of thy strength, only less free
Than thou, O Uncontrollable! If even
I were as in my boyhood, and could be

The comrade of thy wanderings over Heaven,
As then, when to outstrip thy skiey speed 50
Scarce seemed a vision; I would ne'er have striven

As thus with thee in prayer in my sore need.
Oh! lift me as a wave, a leaf, a cloud!
I fall upon the thorns of life! I bleed!

A heavy weight of hours has chained and bowed 55
One too like thee: tameless, and swift, and proud.

32. *Baiæ's bay*: West of Naples; the Roman emperors built villas there. *pumice*: A volcanic rock.
42. *despoil*: Plunder.

V

Make my thy lyre, even as the forest is:
What if my leaves are falling like its own!
The tumult of thy mighty harmonies

Will take from both a deep, autumnal tone, 60
Sweet though in sadness. Be thou, Spirit fierce,
My spirit! Be thou me, impetuous one!

Drive my dead thoughts over the universe
Like withered leaves to quicken a new birth!
And, by the incantation of this verse, 65

Scatter, as from an unextinguished hearth
Ashes and sparks, my words among mankind!
Be through my lips to unawakened Earth

The trumpet of a prophecy! O Wind,
If Winter comes, can Spring be far behind? 70

A Defence of Poetry*

. . . Poetry is the record of the best and happiest moments of the happiest and best minds. We are aware of evanescent visitations of thought and feeling sometimes associated with place or person, sometimes regarding our own mind alone, and always arising unforeseen and departing unbidden, but elevating and delightful beyond all expression: so that even in the desire and the regret they leave, there cannot but be pleasure, participating as it does in the nature of its object. It is as it were the interpentration of a diviner nature through our own; but its footsteps are like those of a wind over a sea, which the coming calm erases, and whose traces remain only as on the wrinkled sand which paves it. These and corresponding conditions of being are experienced principally by those of the most delicate sensibility and the most enlarged imagination; and the state of mind produced by them is at war with every base desire. The enthusiasm of virtue, love, patriotism, and friendship is essentially linked with these emotions, and whilst they last, self appears as what it is, an atom to a Universe. Poets are not only subject to these experiences as spirits of the most refined organization, but they can color all that they combine with the evanescent hues of this ethereal

57. *lyre*: Ancient harp. The allusion is also to the aeolian harp, an instrument played upon by the wind, and a frequent image for the poet played upon by inspiration.

*** Written in 1821; first published in 1840. Our selection is the conclusion of the essay.**

world; a word, a trait in the representation of a scene or a passion, will touch the enchanted chord, and reanimate, in those who have ever experienced these emotions, the sleeping, the cold, the buried image of the past. Poetry thus makes immortal all that is best and most beautiful in the world; it arrests the vanishing apparitions which haunt the interlunations[1] of life, and veiling them or[2] in language or in form sends them forth among mankind, bearing sweet news of kindred joy to those with whom their sisters abide—abide, because there is no portal of expression from the caverns of the spirit which they inhabit into the universe of things. Poetry redeems from decay the visitations of the divinity in man. * * *

The first part of these remarks has related to Poetry in its elements and principles; and it has been shown, as well as the narrow limits assigned them would permit, that what is called poetry, in a restricted sense, has a common source with all other forms of order and of beauty according to which the materials of human life are susceptible of being arranged, and which is poetry in an universal sense.

The second part[3] will have for its object an application of these principles to the present state of the cultivation of Poetry, and a defence of the attempt to idealize the modern forms of manners and opinion, and compel them into a subordination to the imaginative and creative faculty. For the literature of England, an energetic development of which has ever preceded or accompanied a great and free development of the national will, has arisen as it were from a new birth. In spite of the low-thoughted envy which would undervalue contemporary merit, our own will be a memorable age in intellectual achievements, and we live among such philosophers and poets as surpass beyond comparison any who have appeared since the last national struggle for civil and religious liberty.[4] The most unfailing herald, companion, and follower the awakening of a great people to work a beneficial change in opinion or institution, is Poetry. At such periods there is an accumulation of the power of communicating and receiving intense and impassioned conceptions respecting man and nature. The persons in whom this power resides, may often, as far as regards many portions of their nature, have little apparent correspondence with that spirit of good of which they are the ministers. But even whilst they deny and abjure, they are yet compelled to serve, the Power which is seated upon the throne of their own soul. It is impossible to read the compositions of the most celebrated writers of the present day without being startled with the electric life which burns within their words. They measure the circumference and sound the depths of human nature with a comprehensive and all-penetrating spirit, and they are them-

1. Dark periods between the old and new moon.
2. Either.
3. The second part was never written.
4. The English Civil War; the great poet of that age was Milton.

selves perhaps the most sincerely astonished at its manifestations, for it is less their spirit than the spirit of the age. Poets are the hierophants[5] of an unapprehended inspiration, the mirrors of the gigantic shadows which futurity casts upon the present, the words which express what they understand not; the trumpets which sing to battle, and feel not what they inspire: the influence which is moved not, but moves. Poets are the unacknowledged legislators of the World.

JOHN KEATS
(1795–1821)

On First Looking into Chapman's Homer*

Much have I traveled in the realms of gold,
  And many goodly states and kingdoms seen;
  Round many western islands have I been
Which bards in fealty to Apollo hold.
Oft of one wide expanse had I been told 5
  That deep-browed Homer ruled as his demesne;
  Yet did I never breathe its pure serene
Till I heard Chapman speak out loud and bold:
Then felt I like some watcher of the skies
  When a new planet swims into his ken; 10
Or like stout Cortez when with eagle eyes
  He stared at the Pacific—and all his men
Looked at each other with a wild surmise—
  Silent, upon a peak in Darien.

Bright Star*

Bright star, would I were steadfast as thou art—
  Not in lone splendor hung aloft the night
And watching, with eternal lids apart,
  Like nature's patient, sleepless Eremite,
The moving waters at their priestlike task 5
  Of pure ablution round earth's human shores,

5. Interpreters, as priests who interpret sacred mysteries.

* Written and published in 1816. Keats's friend and former teacher Charles Cowden Clarke had introduced Keats to George Chapman's translations of the *Iliad* (1611) and the *Odyssey* (1616) the night before this poem was written.

4. *Apollo*: God of poetic inspiration.

6. *demesne*: Realm, kingdom.

7. *serene*: Calm atmosphere.

11. *Cortez*: In fact, Balboa, not Cortez, was the European explorer who first saw the Pacific from Darien, Panama.

* Written in 1819; published in 1838. Formerly thought to be Keats's last sonnet, written on his voyage to Italy in September, 1820; but a manuscript proves it to have been composed a year earlier.

4. *Eremite*: Hermit.

6. *ablution*: Ritual cleansing.

Or gazing on the new soft fallen mask
 Of snow upon the mountains and the moors—
No—yet still steadfast, still unchangeable,
 Pillowed upon my fair love's ripening breast, 10
To feel forever its soft fall and swell,
 Awake forever in a sweet unrest,
Still, still to hear her tender-taken breath,
And so live ever—or else swoon to death.

La Belle Dame Sans Merci*

O what can ail thee, knight at arms,
 Alone and palely loitering?
The sedge has withered from the lake
 And no birds sing!

O what can ail thee, knight at arms, 5
 So haggard, and so woebegone?
The squirrel's granary is full
 And the harvest's done.

I see a lily on thy brow
 With anguish moist and fever dew, 10
And on thy cheeks a fading rose
 Fast withereth too.

I met a lady in the meads,
 Full beautiful, a faery's child,
Her hair was long, her foot was light 15
 And her eyes were wild.

I made a garland for her head,
 And bracelets too, and fragrant zone;
She looked at me as she did love
 And made sweet moan. 20

I set her on my pacing steed
 And nothing else saw all day long,
For sidelong would she bend and sing
 A faery's song.

She found me roots of relish sweet, 25
 And honey wild, and manna dew,
And sure in language strange she said
 "I love thee true."

* Written 1819; published 1820. First version. The title is from a medieval poem by Alain Chartier: "The Beautiful Lady without Pity."

13. *meads*: Meadows.

18. *zone*: Girdle.

26. *manna*: The supernatural substance with which God fed the Hebrews in the Wilderness. Cf. *Exodus* 16, *Numbers* 11:7–8, and Joshua 5:12.

She took me to her elfin grot
And there she wept and sighed full sore, 30
And there I shut her wild wild eyes
With kisses four.

And there she lulléd me asleep,
And there I dreamed, ah woe betide!
The latest dream I ever dreamt 35
On the cold hill side.

I saw pale kings, and princes too,
Pale warriors, death-pale were they all;
They cried, "La belle dame sans merci
Thee hath in thrall!" 40

I saw their starved lips in the gloam
With horrid warning gapéd wide,
And I awoke, and found me here
On the cold hill's side.

And this is why I sojourn here, 45
Alone and palely loitering;
Though the sedge withered from the lake
And no birds sing.

Ode on a Grecian Urn*

I

Thou still unravished bride of quietness,
Thou foster-child of silence and slow time,
Sylvan historian, who canst thus express
A flowery tale more sweetly than our rhyme:
What leaf-fringed legend haunts about thy shape 5
Of deities or of mortals, or of both,
In Tempe or the dales of Arcady?
What men or gods are these? What maidens loth?
What mad pursuit? What struggle to escape?
What pipes and timbrels? What wild ecstasy? 10

29. *grot*: Cavern.
30. *full sore*: With great grief.
35. *latest*: Last.
40. *thrall*: Bondage.
41. *gloam*: Twilight.
* Written in 1819; published in 1820. Keats's Hellenism is nowhere more apparent than in this ode, which may have been inspired by his reading in Lemprière's *Classical Dictionary*, and by his acquaintance with various classical antiquities on exhibit in London.
7. *Tempe . . . Arcady:* Tempe is a valley in Thessaly between Mount Olympus and Mount Ossa; Arcady is a mountainous region in the Peloponnese, traditionally regarded as the place of ideal rustic, bucolic contentment.

II

Heard melodies are sweet, but those unheard
  Are sweeter; therefore, ye soft pipes, play on;
Not to the sensual ear, but, more endeared,
  Pipe to the spirit ditties of no tone:
Fair youth, beneath the trees, thou canst not leave 15
  Thy song, nor ever can those trees be bare;
    Bold lover, never, never canst thou kiss,
Though winning near the goal—yet, do not grieve;
    She cannot fade, though thou hast not thy bliss,
  For ever wilt thou love, and she be fair! 20

III

Ah, happy, happy boughs! that cannot shed
  Your leaves, nor ever bid the Spring adieu;
And, happy melodist, unwearièd,
  For ever piping songs for ever new;
More happy love! more happy, happy love! 25
  For ever warm and still to be enjoyed,
    For ever panting, and for ever young;
All breathing human passion far above,
  That leaves a heart high-sorrowful and cloyed,
    A burning forehead, and a parching tongue. 30

IV

Who are these coming to the sacrifice?
  To what green altar, O mysterious priest,
Lead'st thou that heifer lowing at the skies,
  And all her silken flanks with garlands drest?
What little town by river or sea shore, 35
  Or mountain-built with peaceful citadel,
    Is emptied of this folk, this pious morn?
And, little town, thy streets for evermore
  Will silent be; and not a soul to tell
    Why thou art desolate, can e'er return. 40

V

O Attic shape! Fair attitude! with brede
  Of marble men and maidens overwrought,
With forest branches and the trodden weed;
  Thou, silent form, dost tease us out of thought
As doth eternity: Cold Pastoral! 45
  When old age shall this generation waste,
    Thou shalt remain, in midst of other woe
Than ours, a friend to man, to whom thou say'st,
  "Beauty is truth, truth beauty,"—that is all
    Ye know on earth, and all ye need to know. 50

41. *brede:* pattern.

Ode to a Nightingale*

I

My heart aches, and a drowsy numbness pains
My sense, as though of hemlock I had drunk,
Or emptied some dull opiate to the drains
One minute past, and Lethe-wards had sunk:
'Tis not through envy of thy happy lot, 5
But being too happy in thy happiness,
That thou, light-winged Dryad of the trees,
In some melodious plot
Of beechen green, and shadows numberless,
Singest of summer in full-throated ease. 10

II

O for a draught of vintage! that hath been
Cooled a long age in the deep-delved earth,
Tasting of Flora and the country green,
Dance, and Provençal song, and sunburnt mirth!
O for a beaker full of the warm South! 15
Full of the true, the blushful Hippocrene,
With beaded bubbles winking at the brim,
And purple-stained mouth;
That I might drink, and leave the world unseen,
And with thee fade away into the forest dim: 20

III

Fade far away, dissolve, and quite forget
What thou among the leaves hast never known,
The weariness, the fever, and the fret
Here, where men sit and hear each other groan;
Where palsy shakes a few, sad, last grey hairs, 25
Where youth grows pale, and spectre-thin, and dies;
Where but to think is to be full of sorrow
And leaden-eyed despairs;
Where beauty cannot keep her lustrous eyes,
Or new love pine at them beyond tomorrow. 30

IV

Away! away! for I will fly to thee,
Not charioted by Bacchus and his pards,

* Written in 1819; published in 1820.

4. *Lethe-wards:* i.e., toward Lethe, the river of forgetfulness in Greek mythology.

7. *Dryad:* wood nymph.

14. *Provençal:* Provence was the district in France associated with the troubadours.

16. *Hippocrene:* the fountain on Mount Helicon, in Boeotia (a part of Greece), sacred to the Muse of poetry.

32. *pards:* leopards. Bacchus (Dionysus) was traditionally supposed to be accompanied by leopards, lions, goats, and so on.

But on the viewless wings of Poesy,
Though the dull brain perplexes and retards:
Already with thee! tender is the night, 35
And haply the Queen-Moon is on her throne,
Clustered around by all her starry Fays;
But here there is no light,
Save what from heaven is with the breezes blown
Through verdurous glooms and winding mossy ways. 40

V

I cannot see what flowers are at my feet,
Nor what soft incense hangs upon the boughs,
But, in embalmèd darkness, guess each sweet
Wherewith the seasonable month endows
The grass, the thicket, and the fruit-tree wild; 45
White hawthorn, and the pastoral eglantine;
Fast-fading violets covered up in leaves;
And mid-May's eldest child,
The coming musk-rose, full of dewy wine,
The murmurous haunt of flies on summer eves. 50

VI

Darkling I listen; and for many a time
I have been half in love with easeful Death,
Called him soft names in many a mused rhyme,
To take into the air my quiet breath;
Now more than ever seems it rich to die, 55
To cease upon the midnight with no pain,
While thou art pouring forth thy soul abroad
In such an ecstasy!
Still wouldst thou sing, and I have ears in vain—
To thy high requiem become a sod. 60

VII

Thou wast not born for death, immortal Bird!
No hungry generations tread thee down;
The voice I hear this passing night was heard
In ancient days by emperor and clown:
Perhaps the self-same song that found a path 65
Through the sad heart of Ruth, when, sick for home,
She stood in tears amid the alien corn;
The same that ofttimes hath
Charmed magic casements, opening on the foam
Of perilous seas, in faery lands forlorn. 70

66. ***Ruth:*** See Ruth 1:16. After her Israelite husband died, she returned to his native land with her mother-in-law.

VIII

Forlorn! the very word is like a bell
  To toll me back from thee to my sole self!
Adieu! the fancy cannot cheat so well
  As she is famed to do, deceiving elf.
Adieu! adieu! thy plaintive anthem fades 75
  Past the near meadows, over the still stream,
    Up the hill-side; and now 'tis buried deep
      In the next valley-glades:
  Was it a vision, or a waking dream?
    Fled is that music:—do I wake or sleep? 80

Ode on Melancholy*

1

No, no, go not to Lethe, neither twist
  Wolfsbane, tight-rooted, for its poisonous wine;
Nor suffer thy pale forehead to be kissed
  By nightshade, ruby grape of Proserpine;
Make not your rosary of yew-berries, 5
  Nor let the beetle, nor the death-moth be
    Your mournful Psyche, nor the downy owl
A partner in your sorrow's mysteries;
  For shade to shade will come too drowsily,
    And drown the wakeful anguish of the soul. 10

2

But when the melancholy fit shall fall
  Sudden from heaven like a weeping cloud,
That fosters the droop-headed flowers all,
  And hides the green hill in an April shroud;
Then glut thy sorrow on a morning rose, 15
  Or on the rainbow of the salt sand-wave,
    Or on the wealth of globèd peonies;
Or if thy mistress some rich anger shows,
  Imprison her soft hand, and let her rave,
    And feed deep, deep upon her peerless eyes. . 20

3

She dwells with Beauty—Beauty that must die;
  And Joy, whose hand is ever at his lips
Bidding adieu; and aching Pleasure nigh,
  Turning to Poison while the bee-mouth sips:

* Written 1819; published 1820.

1. *Lethe*: The river of forgetfulness in Hades.

2–4. *Wolfsbane . . . nightshade*: Plants from which poisons are derived.

4. *Proserpine*: Wife of Pluto, queen of the Underworld.

5. *yew-berries*: Emblematic of death.

6. *beetle . . . death-moth*: Creatures associated (like the other elements in this stanza) with melancholy, twilight, oblivion, death. The death's head moth has markings that resemble a skull; the beetle, from whose shape comes the scarab found in Egyptian tombs, was an emblem of death.

7. *Psyche*: The soul, portrayed by the Greeks as a butterfly.

21. *She*: Melancholy.

Aye, in the very temple of Delight 25
Veiled Melancholy has her sov'reign shrine,
Though seen of none save him whose strenuous tongue
Can burst Joy's grape against his palate fine;
His soul shall taste the sadness of her might,
And be among her cloudy trophies hung. 30

Ode: To Autumn*

I

Season of mists and mellow fruitfulness,
Close bosom-friend of the maturing sun;
Conspiring with him how to load and bless
With fruit the vines that round the thatch-eves run;
To bend with apples the mossed cottage-trees, 5
And fill all fruit with ripeness to the core;
To swell the gourd, and plump the hazel shells
With a sweet kernel; to set budding more,
And still more, later flowers for the bees,
Until they think warm days will never cease, 10
For Summer has o'er-brimmed their clammy cells.

II

Who hath not seen thee oft amid thy store?
Sometimes whoever seeks abroad may find
Thee sitting careless on a granary floor,
Thy hair soft-lifted by the winnowing wind; 15
Or on a half-reaped furrow sound asleep,
Drowsed with the fume of poppies, while thy hook
Spares the next swath and all its twinèd flowers:
And sometimes like a gleaner thou dost keep
Steady thy laden head across a brook; 20
Or by a cyder-press, with patient look,
Thou watchest the last oozings hours by hours.

III

Where are the songs of Spring? Ay, where are they?
Think not of them, thou hast thy music too,—
While barrèd clouds bloom the soft-dying day, 25
And touch the stubble-plains with rosy hue;
Then in a wailful choir the small gnats mourn
Among the river sallows, borne aloft
Or sinking as the light wind lives or dies;
And full-grown lambs loud bleat from hilly bourn; 30
Hedge-crickets sing; and now with treble soft
The red-breast whistles from a garden-croft;
And gathering swallows twitter in the skies.

30. *trophies*: The Greeks placed war trophies in their temples to commemorate victories.

* **Written in 1819; published in 1820.**

FRANÇOIS RENÉ DE CHATEAUBRIAND
(1768–1848)

René*

On arriving among the Natchez René[1] was obliged to take a wife in order to conform to the Indian customs; but he did not live with her. His melancholy nature drew him constantly away into the depths of the woods. There he would spend entire days in solitude, a savage among the savages. Aside from Chactas, his foster father, and Father Souël, a missionary at Fort Rosalie, he had given up all fellowship with men. These two elders had acquired a powerful influence over his heart, Chactas, through his kindly indulgence, and Father Souël, on the contrary, through his extreme severity. Since the beaver hunt, when the blind sachem[2] had told his adventures to René, the young man had consistently refused to talk about his own. And yet both Chactas and the missionary keenly desired to know what sorrow had driven this well-born European to the strange decision of retiring into the wildernesses of Louisiana. René had always claimed that he would not tell his story because it was too insignificant, limited as it was to his thoughts and feelings. "As for the circumstance which induced me to leave for America," he added, "that must forever be buried in oblivion."

Thus several years[3] went by, and the two elders were unable to draw his secret from him. One day, however, he received a letter from Europe, through the Office of Foreign Missions, which so increased his sadness that he felt he had to flee even from his old friends. Now more than ever they exhorted him to open his heart to them. And so great was their tact, so gentle their manner, and so deep the respect they commanded, that he finally felt obliged to yield. He therefore set a day to tell them, not the adventures of his life, for he had never had any, but the innermost feelings of his soul.

On the twenty-first day of the month the Indians call the "moon of flowers," René went to the cabin of Chactas. Giving his arm to the sachem, he led him to a spot under a sassafras tree on the bank of the Meschacebe.[4] Soon afterwards Father Souël arrived at the meeting place. Day was breaking. Off on the plain, some distance

* Translated by Irving Putter (University of California Press, 1957) and reprinted with the permission of the publishers. *René* was included in Chateaubriand's *Genius of Christianity* (1802), a long work designed to illustrate its subtitle: *The Poetic and Moral Beauties of Christianity*. Atala, also in the volume, had appeared a year earlier, partly to test the public's reception.

1. *René:* He appears in *Atala* as the melancholy youth who has fled Europe for Louisiana in 1725, and to whom the Indian sage tells the sad tale of his love for Atala.

2. *sachem:* chief.

3. *several years:* René, killed in 1730, tells his story sometime between 1728 and 1730.

4. *Meschacebe:* Mississippi.

away, the Natchez village could be seen with its grove of mulberry trees and its cabins which looked like beehives. The French colony and Fort Rosalie were visible on the river bank at the right. Tents, half-built houses, fortresses just begun, hosts of negroes clearing tracts of land, groups of white men and Indians, all offered a striking contrast of social and primitive ways in this limited space. Towards the east, in the background of this setting, the sun was just beginning to show behind the jagged peaks of the Appalachians, which stood forth like azure symbols against the golden reaches of the sky. In the west, the Meschacebe rolled its waves in majestic stillness, forming for the picture a border of indescribable grandeur.

For some time the young man and the missionary stood marveling at this splendid scene and pitying the sachem who could no longer enjoy it. Then Father Souël and Chactas sat down on the grass at the foot of the tree. René took his place between them, hesitated a moment, and then began speaking in the following manner.

As I open my story, I cannot stifle a feeling of shame. The peace in your hearts, respected elders, and the calm of nature all about me make me blush for the disorder and turmoil of my soul.

How you will pity me! How wretched my perpetual anxieties will seem to you! You who have passed through all the hardships of life, what will you think of a young man with neither strength nor moral courage, who finds the source of his torments within himself, and can hardly lament any misfortunes save those he has brought on himself? Alas! Do not condemn him too severely; he has already been harshly punished!

I cost my mother[5] her life as I came into this world and had to be drawn from her womb with an instrument. My father gave his blessing to my brother because he saw in him his elder son; as for me, I was soon abandoned to strange hands and brought up far from my father's roof.

I was spirited in temper and erratic by nature. As I alternated turbulence and joy with silence and sadness, I would gather my young friends around me, then leave them suddenly and go off to sit by myself watching the swift clouds or listening to the rain falling among the leaves.

Each autumn I would return to the family château,[6] off in the midst of the forests, near a lake in a remote province.

I was timid and inhibited in my father's presence, and found freedom and contentment only with my sister Amelia.[7] We were

5. *mother:* Actually Chateaubriand's mother died in 1798, when he was thirty.

6. *château:* The author's home was a castle at Combourg, on the sea near St. Malo in Brittany.

7. *Amelia:* closely modeled on Chateaubriand's sister Lucile, born in 1764.

closely bound together by our tender affinities in mood and taste; my sister was only slightly older than I. We loved to climb the hillside together or go sailing on the lake or wander through the woods under the falling leaves, and even now memories of those rambles fill my soul with delight. O illusions of childhood and homeland, can your sweetness ever fade away?

Sometimes we strolled in silence hearkening to the muffled rumbling of the autumn or the crackling of the dry leaves trailing sadly under our feet. In our innocent games we ran after the swallow in the meadows or the rainbow on the storm-swept hills. At other times we would whisper poetry inspired in us by the spectacle of nature. In my youth I courted the Muses. Nothing is more poetic than a heart of sixteen in all the pristine freshness of its passions. The morning of life is like the morning of the day, pure, picturesque, and harmonious.

On Sundays and holidays I often stood in the deep woods as the sound of the distant bell drifted through the trees, calling from the temple to the man of the fields. Leaning against the trunk of an elm, I would listen in rapt silence to the devout tolling. Each tremor of the resounding bronze would waft into my guileless soul the innocence of country ways, the calm of solitude, the beauty of religion, and the cherished melancholy of memories out of my early childhood! Oh! What churlish heart has never started at the sound of the bells in his birthplace, those bells which trembled with joy over his cradle, which rang out the dawn of his life, which signaled his first heartbeat, announcing to all surrounding places the reverent gladness of his father, the ineffable anguish and supreme joy of his mother! All is embraced in that magical revery which engulfs us at the sound of our native bell—faith, family, homeland, the cradle and the grave, the past and the future.

True enough, Amelia and I enjoyed these solemn, tender thoughts far more than did others, for in the depths of our heart we both had a strain of sadness, given us by God or our mother.

Meanwhile my father was attacked by a disease which brought him to his grave in a short time. He passed away in my arms, and I learned to know death from the lips of the very person who had given me life. The impression was profound; it is vivid still. It was the first time that the immortality of the soul was clearly present before my eyes. I could not believe that this lifeless body was the creator of my thought; I felt it had to come from some other source, and, in my religious sorrow, close akin to joy, I hoped one day to join the spirit of my father.

Another circumstance fixed this lofty idea even more firmly in my mind. My father's features had taken on a sublime quality in his coffin. Why should this astonishing mystery not be an indication of our immortality? Could not all-knowing death have stamped the secrets of another universe on the brow of its victim? And why could the tomb not have some great vision of eternity?

Overcome with grief Amelia had withdrawn to the seclusion of a tower from which she could hear the chanting of the priests in the funeral procession and the death knell reverberating under the vaults of the Gothic château.

I accompanied my father to his last abode, and the earth closed over his remains. Eternity and oblivion pressed down on him with all their weight, and that very evening the indifferent passer-by trod over his grave. Aside from his daughter and son, it was already as though he had never existed.

Then I had to leave the family shelter, which my brother had inherited. Amelia and I went to live with some aged relatives.

Pausing before the deceptive paths of life, I considered them one by one, but dared not set out along any of them. Amelia would frequently speak of the joy of the religious life, adding that I was the only bond still holding her to the outside world; and her eyes would fix themselves upon me sadly.

With my heart stirred by these devout talks, I would often make by way toward a monastery close by my new dwelling. Once I was even tempted to retire within its walls forever. Happy are they who reach the end of their travels without ever leaving the harbor and have never, as have I, dragged their barren days out over the face of the earth!

In our endless agitation we Europeans are obliged to erect lonely retreats for ourselves. The greater the turmoil and din in our hearts, the more we are drawn to calmness and silence. These shelters in my country are always open to the sad and weak. Often they are hidden in little valleys, which seem to harbor in their bosom a vague feeling of sorrow and a hope for a future refuge. Sometimes, too, they are found in high places where the religious soul, like some mountain plant, seems to rise toward heaven, offering up its perfumes.

I can still see the majestic mingling of waters and forests around that ancient abbey, where I hoped to shelter my life from the whims of fate; I still wander at eventide in those reverberating, solitary cloisters. When the moon cast its wan light on the pillars of the arcades and outlined their shadow on the opposite wall, I would stop to contemplate the cross marking the burial ground and the tall grass growing among the tombstones. O men who once lived far removed from the world and have passed from the silence of life to the silence of death, how your tombs filled my soul with disgust for this earth!

Whether it was my natural instability or a dislike of the monastic life, I do not know, but I changed my plans and decided to go abroad. As I bade my sister farewell, she clasped me in her arms in an almost joyful gesture, as though she were happy to see me leave, and I could not repress a bitter thought about the inconstancy of human affections.

Nevertheless, I set forth all alone and full of spirit on the stormy ocean of the world, though I knew neither its safe ports nor its perilous reefs. First I visited peoples[8] who exist no more. I went and sat among the ruins of Rome and Greece, those countries of virile and brilliant memory, where palaces are buried in the dust and royal mausoleums hidden beneath the brambles. O power of nature and weakness of man! A blade of grass will pierce through the hardest marble of these tombs, while their weight can never be lifted by all these mighty dead!

Sometimes a tall column rose up solitary in a waste land, as a great thought may spring from a soul ravaged by time and sorrow.

I meditated on these monuments at every hour and through all the incidents of the day. Sometimes, I watched the same sun which had shone down on the foundation of these cities now setting majestically over their ruins; soon afterwards, the moon rose between crumbling funeral urns into a cloudless sky, bathing the tombs in pallid light. Often in the faint, dream-wafting rays of that planet, I thought I saw the Spirit of Memory sitting pensive by my side.

But I grew weary of searching through graveyards, where too often I stirred up only the dust of a crime-ridden past.

I was anxious to see if living races had more virtue and less suffering to offer than those which had vanished. One day, as I was walking in a large city, I passed through a secluded and deserted courtyard behind a palace. There I noticed a statue pointing to a spot made famous by a certain sacrifice. I was struck by the stillness of the surroundings; only the wind moaned weakly around the tragic marble. Workmen were lying about indifferently at the foot of the statue or whistled as they hewed out stones. I asked them what the monument meant; some knew little indeed, while the others were totally oblivious of the catastrophe it commemorated. Nothing could indicate so vividly the true import of human events and the vanity of our existence. What has become of those figures whose fame was so widespread? Time has taken a step and the face of the earth has been made over.

In my travels I especially sought out artists and those inspired poets whose lyres glorify the gods and the joy of peoples who honor their laws, their religion, and their dead. These singers come of a

8. *I visited peoples:* Chateaubriand's own romantic voyaging came after the publication of *René*.

divine race and possess the only sure power which heaven has granted earth. Their life is at once innocent and sublime. They speak like immortals or little children. They explain the laws of the universe and cannot themselves understand the most elementary concerns of life. They have marvelous intuitions of death and die with no consciousness of it, like new-born infants.

On the mountain peaks of Caledonia, the last bard[9] ever heard in those wildernesses sang me poems which had once consoled a hero in his old age. We were sitting on four stones overgrown with moss; at our feet ran a brook, and in the distance the roebuck strayed among the ruins of a tower, while from the seas the wind whistled in over the waste land of Cona. The Christian faith, itself a daughter of the lofty mountains, has now placed crosses over the monuments of Morven heroes and plucked the harp of David on the banks of the very stream where once the harp of Ossian sighed. Loving peace even as the divinities of Selma loved war, it now shepherds flocks where Fingal once joined battle and has strewn angels of peace amongst clouds once occupied by murderous phantoms.

Ancient, lovely Italy offered me its host of masterworks. With what reverent and poetic awe I wandered through those vast edifices consecrated to religion by the arts! What a labyrinth of columns! What a sequence of arches and vaults! How beautiful are the echoes circling round those domes like the rolling of waves in the ocean, like the murmur of winds in the forest or the voice of God in his temple! The architect seems to build the poet's thoughts and make them accessible to the senses.

And yet with all my effort what had I learned until then? I had discovered nothing stable among the ancients and nothing beautiful among the moderns. The past and present are imperfect statues —one, quite disfigured, drawn from the ruins of the ages, and the other still devoid of its future perfection.

But, my old friends, you who have lived so long in the wilderness, you especially will be surprised that I have not once spoken of the glories of nature in this story of my travels.

One day I climbed to the summit of Etna, that great volcano burning in the middle of an island. Above me, I saw the sun rising in the vast reaches of the horizon, while at my feet Sicily shrank to a point and the sea retreated into the distant spaces. In this vertical view of the picture the rivers seemed little more than lines traced on a map. But while on one side I observed this sight, on the

9. *last bard:* All references in this paragraph are to MacPherson's *Poems of Ossian* (1760–1763), which Chateaubriand knew in the Letourneur translation. MacPherson claimed to have discovered Gaelic (Erse) poems, including an epic *Fingal*, by a third-century blind bard Ossian, which MacPherson published in English translation. Though spurious, their popularity was immense throughout Europe. Caledonia here is Scotland; Cona and Morven are in that country; Selma is northern Ireland (near modern Belfast), where the fighting in *Fingal* takes place.

other my eye plunged into the depths of Etna's crater, whose bowels I saw blazing between billows of black smoke.

A young man full of passion, sitting at the mouth of a volcano and weeping over mortal men whose dwellings he could barely distinguish far off below him—O revered elders! Such a creature is doubtless worthy only of your pity! But think what you may, such a picture reveals my character and my whole being. Just so, throughout my life, I have had before my eyes an immense creation which I could barely discern, while a chasm yawned at my side.

As he uttered these last words René grew silent and soon sank into revery. Father Souël looked at him in surprise, while the blind and aged sachem, not hearing the young man's voice any more, did not know what to make of this silence.

René had fixed his eyes on a group of Indians gaily passing through the plain. Suddenly his countenance softened, and tears fell from his eyes.

"Happy Indians," he exclaimed, "oh, why can I not enjoy the peace which always goes with you! While my fruitless wanderings led me through so many lands, you, sitting quietly under your oaks, let the days slip by without counting them. Your needs were your only guide, and, far better than I, you have reached wisdom's goal through your play and your sleep—like children. Your soul may sometimes have been touched by the melancholy of extreme happiness, but you emerged soon enough from this fleeting sadness, and your eyes rose toward heaven, tenderly seeking the mysterious presence which takes pity on the poor Indian."

Here René's voice broke again, and the young man bowed his head. Chactas held his hands out in the shadows, and, touching his son's arm, he exclaimed, deeply moved, "My son! My dear son!" The ring of his voice drew René from his revery, and, blushing at his weakness, he begged his father to forgive him.

Then the aged Indian spoke thus: "My young friend, a heart such as yours cannot be placid; but you must try to temper your character, which has already brought you so much grief. Do not be surprised that you suffer more than others from the experiences of life; a great soul necessarily holds more sorrow than a little one. Go on with your story. You have taken us through part of Europe; now tell us about your own country. As you know, I have seen France and am deeply attached to it. I would like to hear of the great chief who has now passed on, and whose magnificent cabin[10] I once visited. My child, I live only for the past. An old man with his memories is like a decrepit oak in our woods; no longer able to

10. ***great chief . . . cabin:*** **Louis XIV and Versailles.**

adorn itself with its own foliage, it is obliged to cover its nakedness with foreign plants which have taken root on its ancient boughs."

Calmed by these words, René once more took up the story of his heart.

Alas, father, I cannot tell you about that great century, for I saw only the end of it as a child; it had already drawn to a close when I returned to my land. Never has a more astonishing, nor a more sudden change taken place in a people. From the loftiness of genius, from respect for religion and dignity in manners everything suddenly degenerated to cleverness and godlessness and corruption.

So it had been useless indeed to try to find something in my own country to calm this anxiety, this burning desire which pursues me everywhere. Studying the world had taught me nothing, and yet I had lost the freshness of innocence.

By her strange behavior, my sister seemed bent on increasing my gloom. She had left Paris a few days before my arrival, and when I wrote that I expected to join her, she hastened to dissuade me, claiming she did not know where her business might take her. How sadly I reflected on human affection. It cools in our presence and vanishes in our absence; in adversity it grows weak and in good fortune weaker still.

Soon I found myself lonelier in my native land than I had been on foreign soil. I was tempted to plunge for a time into a totally new environment which I could not understand and which did not understand me. My heart was not yet wasted by any kind of passion, and I sought to find someone to whom I could become attached. But I soon discovered that I was giving more of myself than I was receiving of others. It was neither lofty language nor deep feeling which the world asked of me. I was simply reducing my being to the level of society. Everywhere I was taken for an impractical dreamer. Ashamed of the role I was playing and increasingly repulsed by men and things, I finally decided to retire to some smaller community where I could live completely by myself.

At first I was happy enough in this secluded, independent life. Unknown by everyone, I could mingle with the crowd—that vast desert of men! Often I would sit in some lonely church, where I could spend hour after hour in meditation. I saw poor women prostrating themselves before the Almighty or sinners kneeling at the seat of penitence. None emerged from this retreat without a more serene expression, and the muffled noises drifting in from outside seemed like waves of passion or storms of the world subsiding at the foot of the Lord's temple. Mighty God, who from Thy solitude couldst see my tears falling in that holy shelter, Thou knowest how many times I threw myself at Thy feet, imploring Thee to relieve me of the weight of my existence or make over the old man within me! Ah, who has never felt a need of regeneration, of growing young in the waters of the spring and refreshing his soul in the fountain of life? Who does not sometimes feel himself crushed by the burden of his own corruption and incapable of anything great or noble or just!

When night had closed in I would start back to my retreat, pausing on the bridges to watch the sunset. As the great star kindled the mists of the city, it seemed to swing slowly in a golden fluid like the pendulum of some clock of the ages. Then I retired with the night through a labyrinth of solitary streets. As I passed lights shining in the dwellings of men, I imagined myself among the scenes of sorrow and joy which they revealed, and I reflected that under all those roofs sheltering so many people, I had not a single friend. In the midst of these thoughts, the hour began tolling in measured cadence from the tower of the Gothic cathedral, and its message was taken up from church to church in a wide range of tones and distances. Alas!! Every hour in society lays open a grave and draws fresh tears.

But this life, which at first was so delightful, soon became intolerable. I grew weary of constantly repeating the same scenes and the same thoughts, and I began to search my soul to discover what I really sought. I did not know; but suddenly it occurred to me that I might be happy in the woods. Immediately I resolved to adopt a country exile where I could spend the rest of my days, for, though scarcely begun, my life had already consumed centuries.

I adopted this plan with the ardor typical of all my projects and left at once to retire into seclusion in some rustic cabin, just as previously I had left to travel around the world.

People accuse me of being unpredictable in my tastes, of being unable for long to cherish any single illusion. They consider me the victim of an imagination which plunges toward the end of all pleasures as though it suffered from their duration. They accuse me of forever overreaching the goal I can achieve. Alas! I am only in search of some unknown good, whose intuition pursues me relentlessly. Am I to blame if everywhere I find limitations, if all that is finite I consider worthless? And yet, I feel that I love the monotony in the feelings of life, and, if I were still foolish enough to believe in happiness, I would seek it in an orderly existence.

Total solitude and the spectacle of nature soon brought me to a state almost impossiblé to describe. Practically bereft of relatives and friends on earth, and never having been in love, I was furiously driven by an excess of life. Sometimes I blushed suddenly and felt torrents of burning lava surging through my heart. Sometimes I would cry out involuntarily, and the night was disturbed both by my dreams and by sleepless cares. I felt I needed something to fill the vast emptiness of my existence. I went down into the valley and up on the mountain, calling, with all the strength of my desire, for the ideal creature of some future passion. I embraced her in the winds and thought I heard her in the river's moaning. Everything became this vision of my imagination—the stars in the skies and the very principle of life in the universe.

Nevertheless, this state of calm and anxiety, of poverty and wealth was not wholly without charm. One day I amused myself by stripping the leaves from a willow branch, one by one, and throwing them into the stream, attaching a thought to each leaf as the current carried it off. A king in fear of losing his crown in a sudden revolution does not feel sharper pangs of anguish than did I, as I watched each peril threatening the remains of my bough. O frailty of mortal man! O childishness of the human heart, which never grows old! How infantile our haughty reason can become! And yet how many men attach their existence to such petty things as my willow leaves!

How can I describe the host of fleeting sensations I felt in my rambles? The echoes of passion in the emptiness of a lonely heart are like the murmurings of wind and water in the silence of the wilderness—they offer their joy, but cannot be portrayed.

Autumn came upon me in the midst of this uncertainty, and I welcomed the stormy months with exhilaration. Sometimes I wished I were one of those warriors who wander amongst winds, clouds, and phantoms, while at other times I was envious even of the shepherd's lot, as I watched him warming his hands by the humble brushwood fire he had built in a corner of the woods. I listened to his melancholy airs and remembered that in every land the natural song of man is sad, even when it renders happiness. Our heart is a defective instrument, a lyre with several chords missing, which forces us to express our joyful moods in notes meant for lamentation.

During the day I roamed the great heath with its forests in the distance. How little I needed to wander off in revery—a dry leaf blown before me by the wind, a cabin with smoke drifting up through the bare tree tops, the moss trembling in the north wind on the trunk of an oak, an isolated rock, or a lonely pond where the withered reed whispered . . . The solitary steeple far off in the valley often drew my attention. Many times, too, my eyes followed birds of passage as they flew overhead. I imagined the unknown shores and distant climes for which they were bound—and how I would have loved to be on their wings! A deep intuition tormented me; I felt that I was no more than a traveler myself, but a voice from heaven seemed to be telling me, "Man, the season for thy migration is not yet come; wait for the wind of death to spring up, then wilt thou spread thy wings and fly toward those unexplored realms for which thy heart longs."

Rise swiftly, coveted storms, coming to bear me off to the spaces of another life! This was my plea, as I plunged ahead with great strides, my face all aflame and the wind whistling through my hair, feeling neither rain nor frost, bewitched, tormented, and virtually possessed by the demon of my heart.

At night, when the fierce wind shook my hut and the rain fell in torrents on my roof, as I looked out through my window and saw the moon furrowing the thick clouds like a pallid vessel ploughing through the waves, it seemed to me that life grew so strong in the depths of my heart that I had the power to create worlds. Ah, if only I could have shared with someone else the delight I felt! O Lord, if only Thou hadst given me a woman after my heart's desire, if Thou hadst drawn from my side an Eve, as Thou didst once for our first father, and brought her to me by the hand . . . Heavenly beauty! I would have knelt down before you, and then, clasping you in my arms, I would have begged the Eternal Being to grant you the rest of my life!

Alas! I was alone, alone in the world! A mysterious apathy gradually took hold of my body. My aversion for life, which I had felt as a child, was returning with renewed intensity. Soon my heart supplied no more nourishment for my thought, and I was aware of my existence only in a deep sense of weariness.

For some time I struggled against my malady, but only half-heartedly, with no firm will to conquer it. Finally, unable to find any cure for this strange wound of my heart, which was nowhere and everywhere, I resolved to give up my life.[11]

Priest of the Almighty, now listening to my story, forgive this poor creature whom Heaven had almost stripped of his reason. I was imbued with faith, and I reasoned like a sinner; my heart loved God, and my mind knew Him not. My actions, my words, my feelings, my thoughts were nothing but contradictions, enigmas, and lies. But does man always know what he wishes, and is he always sure of what he thinks?

Affection, society, and seclusion, everything was slipping away from me at once. I had tried everything, and everything had proved disastrous. Rejected by the world and abandoned by Amelia, what had I left now that solitude had failed me? It was the last support which I had hoped could save me, and now I felt it too giving way and dropping into the abyss!

Having decided to rid myself of life's burden, I now resolved to use the full consciousness of my mind in committing this desperate

11. *resolved . . . life:* In his *Memories from Beyond the Grave,* Chateaubriand mentions he once tried suicide as a youth, but the gun failed to fire.

act. Nothing made it necessary to take action quickly. I did not set a definite time for my death, so that I might savor the final moments of my existence in long, full draughts and gather all my strength, like the men of antiquity, to feel my soul escaping.

I felt obliged, however, to make arrangements about my worldly goods and had to write to Amelia. A few complaints escaped me concerning her neglect, and doubtless I let her sense the tenderness which overcome my heart as I wrote. Nevertheless, I thought I had succeeded in concealing my secret; but my sister was accustomed to reading into the recesses of my heart, and she guessed it at once. She was alarmed at the restrained tone of my letter and at my questions about business matters, which had never before concerned me. Instead of answering she came to see me at once with no advance warning.

To realize how bitter my sorrow was later to be and how delighted I was now to see Amelia again, you must understand that she was the only person in the world I had ever loved, and all my feelings converged in her with the sweetness of my childhood memories. And so I welcomed Amelia with a kind of ecstasy in my heart. It had been so long since I had found someone who could understand me and to whom I could reveal my soul!

Throwing herself in my arms, Amelia said to me: "How ungrateful! You want to die and your sister is still alive! You doubt her heart! Don't explain and don't apologize, I know everything; I guessed your intention as though I had been with you. Do you suppose I can be misled, I who watched the first stirrings of your heart? So this is your unhappy character, your dislikes and injustices! Swear to me, while I press you to my heart, swear that this is the last time you will give in to your foolishness; make an oath never to try to take your life again."

As she uttered these words, Amelia looked at me compassionately, tenderly, covering my brow with kisses; she was almost a mother, she was something more tender. Alas! Once again my heart opened out to life's every joy. Like a child, I had only to be consoled, and I quickly surrendered to Amelia's influence. She insisted on a solemn oath, and I readily swore it, not suspecting that I could ever again be unhappy.

Thus we spent more than a month getting used to the delight of being together again. When, instead of finding myself alone in the morning, I heard my sister's voice, I felt a thrill of joy and contentment. Amelia had received some divine attribute from nature. Her soul had the same innocent grace as her body; her feelings were surpassingly gentle, and in her manner there was nothing but softness and a certain dreamy quality. It seemed as though her heart, her thought, and her voice were all sighing in harmony. From her womanly side came her shyness and love, while her purity and melody were angelic.

But the time had come when I was to atone for all my erratic ways. In my madness I had gone so far as to hope some calamity would strike me, so that I might at least have some real reason for suffering—it was a terrible wish, which God in His anger has granted all too well!

O my friends, what am I about to reveal to you! See how these tears flow from my eyes. Can I even . . . Only a few days ago nothing could have torn this secret from me . . . But now, it is all over!

Still, O revered elders, let this story be buried in silence forever; remember that it was meant to be told only under this tree in the wilderness.

Winter was drawing to a close, when I became aware that Amelia was losing her health and repose, even as she was beginning to restore them to me. She was growing thin, her eyes became hollow, her manner listless, and her voice unsteady. People or solitude, my absence or presence, night or day—everything frightened her. Involuntary sighs would die on her lips. Sometimes long distances would not tire her out, and at other times she could barely move about. She would take up her work and set it down, open a book and find it impossible to read, begin a sentence and not finish it, and then she would suddenly burst into tears and go off to pray.

I tried vainly to discover her secret. When I pressed her in my arms and questioned her, she smilingly answered that she was like myself—she did not know what was wrong with her.

Thus three months went by, and each day her state grew worse. The source of her tears seemed to be a mysterious correspondence she was having, for she appeared calmer or more disturbed according to the letters she received. Finally one morning as the time for breakfast had passed, I went up to her rooms. I knocked, but received no answer. I pushed the door ajar; no one was in the room. On the mantel there was an envelope addressed to me. Snatching it up with trembling fingers, I tore it open and read this letter, which will remain with me forever to discourage any possible feeling of joy.

To René:

"My brother, Heaven bears me witness that I would give up my life a thousand times to spare you one moment's grief. But miserable as I am, I can do nothing to make you happy. Forgive me, then, for stealing away from you as though I were guilty. I could never have resisted your pleas, and yet I had to leave. . . . Lord, have pity on me!

"You know, René, that the religious life has always attracted me. Now the time has come to heed Heaven's call. Only why have I waited so long? God is punishing me for it. It was for you alone that I remained in the world . . . But forgive me; I am upset by the sadness of having to leave you.

"Dear brother, it is only now that I feel the full need of those retreats which I have heard you condemn so often. There are certain sorrows which separate us from men forever; were it not for such shelters, what would become of some unfortunate women! . . . I am convinced that you, too, would find rest in these religious havens, for the world has nothing to offer which is worthy of you.

"I shall not remind you of your oath; I know how reliable your word is. You have sworn it, and you will go on living for my sake. Is there anything more pitiful than thinking constantly of suicide? For a man of your character it is easy to die. Believe me, it is far more difficult to live.

"But, my brother, you must give up this solitude at once; it is not good for you. Try to find some kind of occupation. I realize that you bitterly despise the usual necessity of 'becoming established' in France. But you must not scorn all the experience and wisdom of our fathers. Dear René, it is better to resemble ordinary men a little more and be a little less miserable.

"Perhaps you will find relief from your cares in marriage. A wife and children would take up your days. And what woman would not try to make you happy! The ardor of your soul, the beauty of your thought, your noble, passionate air, that proud and tender expression in your eyes, everything would assure you of her love and loyalty. Ah, how joyfully she would clasp you in her arms and press you to her heart! How her eyes and her thoughts would always be fixed on you to shield you from the slightest pain! In your presence she would become all love and innocence; you would feel that you had found a sister again.

"I am leaving for the convent of B——. It is a cloister built by the edge of the sea and wholly suited to the state of my soul. At night, from within my cell, I shall hear the murmur of the waves as they lap against the convent walls. I shall dream of those walks we once took through the woods, when we fancied we heard the sound of the sea in the tops of the waving pines. Beloved childhood friend, will I ever see you again? Though hardly older than you, I once rocked you in your cradle. Many times we used to sleep together. Ah, if we might one day be together again in the same tomb! But no, I must sleep alone beneath the icy marble of that sanctuary where girls who have never known love rest in eternal peace.

"I do not know whether you will succeed in reading these lines, blurred as they are by my tears. After all, sweet friend, a little sooner or a little later, would we not have had to part? Need I speak of

the uncertainty and emptiness of life? You remember young M——
whose ship was lost off the island of Mauritius.[12] When you received his last letter a few months after his death, his earthly remains did not even exist any more, and just when you began to mourn for him in Europe, others in the Indies were ending their mourning. What can man be, then, when his memory perishes so quickly! When some of his friends learn of his death, others are already consoled! Tell me, dear, beloved René, will my memory, too, vanish so quickly from your heart? O my brother, I tear myself away from you in earthly time only that we may not be parted in eternity.

AMELIA

"P.S. I am enclosing the deed of my worldly goods. I hope you will not reject this token of my affection."

Had lightning struck at my feet I could not have been seized by greater panic. What secret was Amelia hiding from me? Who was forcing her into the religious life so suddenly? And had she reconciled me to life through her tender affection only to abandon me now so abruptly? Oh, why had she come back to turn me aside from my plan? A feeling of pity had brought her back to me, but now, tired of her disagreeable duty, she was impatiently leaving me to my misery, though I had no one but her in all the world. People imagine they have done something wonderful when they have kept a man from death! Such were my sad reflections. Then, examining my own feelings, I said, "Ungrateful Amelia, if you were in my place, if, like myself, you were lost in the void of your existence, ah, you would not be forsaken by your bother!"

And yet, as I reread the letter, I felt in its tone something so sad, so tender, that my heart melted completely. Suddenly I had a thought which gave me hope. It occurred to me that Amelia might have fallen in love with a man, and dared not admit it. This suspicion seemed to explain her melancholy, her mysterious correspondence, and the passionate tone pervading her letter. I wrote to her at once, begging her to open her heart to me. Her answer was not long in coming, but revealed nothing about her secret. She wrote only that she had obtained dispensation from the novitiate and was about to pronounce her vows.

I was exasperated by Amelia's stubbornness, by the enigma of her words, and her lack of confidence in my affection. After hesitating a little about what I would do next, I decided to go to B—— to attempt one last effort to win back my sister. On my way I had to pass through the region where I was brought up. When I caught sight of the woods where I had spent the only happy moments of

12. *Mauritius:* in the Indian Ocean.

my life I could not hold back my tears, and I found it impossible to resist the temptation of bidding them a last farewell.[13]

My elder brother had sold the family heritage, and the new owner did not live on the estate. I went up to the château through a long lane of pines. Walking across the deserted courtyard I stopped to gaze at the closed or partly broken windows, the thistle growing at the foot of the walls, the leaves strewn over the threshold of the doors, and that lonely stone stairway where so often I had seen my father and his faithful servants. The steps were already covered with moss, and yellow stock grew between the loose, shaky stones. A new caretaker brusquely opened the doors for me. When I hesitated in crossing the threshold, the fellow exclaimed: "Well, are you going to do what that strange woman did who was here a few days ago? She fainted as she was about to come in, and I had to carry her back to her carriage." It was easy enough for me to recognize the "strange woman" who, like myself, had come back to this spot to find memories and tears!

Drying my eyes with a handkerchief I entered the dwelling of my ancestors. I paced through the resounding halls where nothing could be heard but the beat of my foosteps. The chambers were barely lit by a faint glimmer filtering in through the closed shutters. First I went to see the room where my mother had given her life to bring me into the world, then the room to which my father used to retire, after that the one where I had slept in my cradle, and finally the one where my sister had received my first confessions into the bosom of her love. Everywhere the rooms were neglected, and spiders spun their webs in the abandoned beds. I left the château abruptly and strode quickly away, never daring to turn my head. How sweet, but how fleeting, are those moments spent together by brothers and sisters in their younger years under the wing of their aged parents! The family of man endures but a day, and then God's breath scatters it away like smoke. The son barely knows the father or the father the son, the brother the sister or the sister the brother! The oak sees its acorns take root all around it; it is not so with the children of men!

Arriving at B—— I was taken to the convent, where I asked for an opportunity to speak with my sister. I was told she could not see anybody. I wrote to her, and she replied that, as she was about to be consecrated to God,[14] she was not permitted to turn her thought to the world, and if I loved her, I would avoid burdening her with my sorrow. To this she added: "However, if you plan to appear at

13. *farewell:* Chateaubriand saw the old château at Combourg in 1791, just before he left for America, and revisited it once more in 1801.

14. *consecrated to God:* Chateaubriand's sister Lucile never entered a convent, but was briefly married when she was 32 to a man over twice her age. She died at the age of 40.

the altar on the day of my profession, be pleased to serve as my father. It is the only role worthy of your courage, and the only fitting one for our affection and my peace of mind."

This cold determination resisting my burning affection threw me into a violent rage. There were times when I was about to return where I had come from; then, again, I wanted to stay for the sole purpose of disturbing the sacrifice. Hell even goaded me on with the thought of stabbing myself in the church and mingling my last sighs with the vows tearing my sister away from me. The mother superior of the convent sent word that a bench had been prepared for me in the sanctuary and invited me to attend the ceremony, which was to take place the very next day.

At daybreak I heard the first sound of the bells . . . About ten o'clock I dragged myself to the convent in a deathlike stupor. Nothing can ever again be tragic to a man who has witnessed such a spectacle, nor can anything ever again be painful for one who has lived through it. The church was filled with a huge throng. I was led to the bench in the sanctuary, and immediately I fell on my knees, practically unconscious of where I was or what I intended to do. The priest was already at the altar. Suddenly the mysterious grille swung open and Amelia came forward resplendent in all the finery of the world. So beautiful was she, so divinely radiant her countenance, that she brought a gasp of surprise and admiration from the onlookers. Overcome by the glorious sorrow of her saintly figure and crushed by the grandeur of religion, I saw all my plans of violence crumbling. My strength left me. I felt myself bound by an all-powerful hand, and, instead of blasphemy and threats, I could find in my heart only profound adoration and sighs of humility.

Amelia took her place beneath a canopy, and the sacrifice began by the light of torches amid flowers and aromas which lent their charm to this great renunciation. At the offertory the priest put off all his ornaments, keeping only a linen tunic; then, mounting the pulpit, he described in a simple, moving discourse the joy of the virgin who is consecrated to the Lord. As he pronounced the words, "She appeared like the incense consumed in the fire," deep calm and heavenly fragrances seemed to spread through the audience. It was as if the mystic dove had spread its wings to offer its shelter, while angels seemed to hover over the altar and fly back toward heaven with crowns and perfumes.

Ending his discourse, the priest donned his vestments once more and went on with the sacrifice. Sustained by two young sisters, Amelia knelt down on the bottom step of the altar. Then someone came to get me in order that I might fulfill my role as a father. At the sound of my faltering steps in the sanctuary Amelia was about to collapse. I was placed beside the priest for I was to offer him the scissors. At that moment once again I suddenly felt my passion flame up within me. I was about to burst out in fury, when Amelia recovered her courage and darted such a sad and reproachful glance at me that I was transfixed. Religion was triumphant. Taking advantage of my confusion, Amelia boldly brought her head forward; under the holy blades her magnificent tresses fell in every direction. Her worldly ornaments were replaced by a long muslin robe, which sacrificed none of her appeal. The cares of her brow vanished under a linen headband, and the mysterious veil, that two-fold symbol of virginity and religion, was placed on her shorn head. Never had she appeared so beautiful. The penitent's eye was fixed on the dust of the world, while her soul was already in heaven.

However, Amelia had not yet pronounced her vows, and in order to die for the world she had to pass through the tomb. She therefore lay down on the marble slab, and over her was spread a pall, while a torch burned at each of the four corners. With his stole round his neck and his book in his hand, the priest began the service for the dead. The young virgins took it up. O joys of religion, you are powerful indeed, but oh, how terrible! I was obliged to kneel beside this mournful sight. Suddenly a confused murmur emerged from under the shroud, and as I leaned over, my ears were struck by these dreadful words, audible only to myself: "Merciful God, let me never again rise from this deathbed, and may Thy blessings be lavished on my brother, who has never shared my forbidden passion!"[15]

With these words escaping from the bier the horrible truth suddenly grew clear, and I lost control of my senses. Falling across the death sheet I pressed my sister in my arms and cried out: "Chaste spouse of Christ, receive this last embrace through the chill of death and the depths of eternity which already have parted you from your brother!"

This impulse, this cry, and these tears disturbed the ceremony. The priest interrupted himself, the sisters shut the grille, the crowd pushed forward toward the altar, and I was carried away unconscious. Surely I was not grateful to those who revived me! Opening my eyes, I learned that the sacrifice had been consummated, and my sister had been taken with a violent fever. She sent word begging me not to try to see her again. O misery of my life—a sister fearing to talk to her brother, and a brother afraid of having his sister hear his voice! I left the convent as though it were the place of atonement which prepares us in flames for the blessed life, and where all has been lost, as it is in hell—save hope.

15. *forbidden passion:* Some scholars have tried to demonstrate that Amelia's incestuous love had a basis in Chateaubriand's reciprocated affection for his sister Lucile. It is perhaps safest to recall that incest became a popular romantic theme: in Gothic novels, Goethe's *Wilhelm Meister,* Shelley's *Cenci,* Byron's *Manfred,* etc.

There is strength in our soul to sustain us in our own misfortunes, but to become the involuntary cause of someone else's misfortune is completely unbearable. Now that I understood my sister's grief, I imagined how she must have suffered. Several things which I had been unable to understand now became clear—the joy tinged with sadness which my sister had felt when I was leaving on my travels, the efforts she made to avoid me when I had returned, and at the same time, the weakness which kept her from entering a convent for so long. In her sorrow she must have tried to convince herself that she could yet be cured! As for the secret correspondence which had so deceived me—that was apparently made up of her plans to retire from the world and her arrangements for dispensation from the novitiate, as well as the transfer of her property to me.

O my friends, now I knew what it meant to shed tears for grief which was far from imaginary! My emotions, which had been vague for so long, now seized avidly upon this, its first prey. I even felt a kind of unexpected satisfaction in the fullness of my anguish, and I became aware, with a sense of hidden joy, that sorrow is not a feeling which consumes itself like pleasure.

I had wanted to withdraw from the world before receiving the Almighty's command—that was a great crime. God had sent me Amelia both to save and to punish me. Thus does every guilty thought and forbidden act bring on disorder and sorrow. Amelia had begged me to continue living, and I owed it to her not to aggravate her woes. Besides—how strange it seems!—now that my sorrows were real, I no longer wished to die. My grief had become an immediate concern occupying my every moment, so thoroughly is my heart molded of weariness and misery!

And so I suddenly settled on another plan of action; I determined to leave Europe and go to America.[16] At that very time, in the port of B——, they were fitting out a fleet of ships bound for Louisiana. I made arrangements with one of the captains, wrote to Amelia about my plan, and prepared to leave.

My sister had been at the gates of death, but God had reserved for her the supreme crown of virgins and chose not to call her to Him so soon. Her trials on earth were prolonged. Coming down once again into life's painful path she went courageously forward as a heroine in the face of affliction; bent under the cross she saw in her struggles the certainty of triumph and overwhelming glory in her overwhelming woe.

The sale to my brother of what little property I still had, the long preparations of the convoy, and unfavorable winds, all held me in

16. *America:* Chateaubriand spent some five months in America (1791–1792), though it is doubtful whether he saw the "Meschacebe."

port a long time. Each morning I would go for news of Amelia, and always I returned with new reasons for weeping and admiring.

I wandered endlessly about the convent at the edge of the sea. Often I would notice, in a little grilled window overlooking the deserted beach, a nun sitting in a pensive attitude. She was meditating as she gazed out over the broad ocean, where some vessel could be seen sailing toward the ends of the earth. Several times, in the moonlight, I again saw the nun at the bars of the same window. With the star of night shining down upon her, she was contemplating the sea, listening, it seemed, to the sound of the waves breaking sadly on the lonely shores.

I can still hear the bell in the silence of the night calling the sisters to vigils and prayer. As it tolled in slow rhythm and the virgins moved silently toward the altar of the Almighty, I hastened to the convent. There, alone at the foot of the walls, I would listen in reverent rapture to the last strains of the hymns, as they blended beneath the temple vaults with the gentle murmur of the waves.

I do not know why all these things, which should have intensified my anguish, served instead to soften its sting. My tears were less bitter when I shed them out there on those rocks in the wind. My very grief, which was so rare, bore within itself some remedy; for there is joy in the uncommon, even if it is an uncommon calamity. This almost gave me hope that my sister too might become less miserable.

A letter I received from her before my departure seemed to confirm this feeling. Amelia pitied me tenderly for my sorrow, and assured me that time was healing her wound. "I have not given up hoping for happiness," she wrote. "The very immensity of my sacrifice calms me somewhat, now that it is all over. The simplicity of my companions, the purity of their vows, the regularity of their life, everything spreads its healing balm over my days. When I hear the storms raging and the sea bird beating its wings at my window, I, poor dove of heaven, reflect on my joy in finding a shelter from the tempest. Here is the holy mountain, the lofty summit where we hear the last faint murmurs of the earth and the opening harmonies of heaven. It is here that religion gently beguiles a tender soul. For the most violent passion it substitutes a kind of burning chastity in which lover and virgin are at one. It purifies every sigh, it makes the ephemeral flame inviolate, and it blends its divine calm and innocence with the remains of confusion and worldly joy in a heart seeking rest and a life seeking solitude."

I do not know what heaven still holds in store for me, or whether it meant to warn me that everywhere my steps would be harried by storms. The order was given for our fleet to set sail; as the sun began sinking, several vessels had already weighed anchor. I made arrangements to spend the last night on shore writing my farewell letter to Amelia. Around midnight, as my attention was absorbed in my thoughts and tears moistened my paper, my ear was suddenly drawn to the wailing of the winds. As I listened, cannon shots of alarm could be heard through the storm, together with the knell tolling in the convent. I plunged out to the shore where all was deserted and nothing could be heard but the roar of the surf. I sat down on a rock. On one side I could see the vast expanse of shimmering waves, and on the other the somber walls of the convent vaguely reaching up and fading away in the skies. A dim light shone out from the grilled window. O my Amelia! Was it you, on your knees at the foot of the cross, praying to the God of Tempests to spare your unhappy brother? Storm on the waves, and calm in your retreat; men shattered on the reefs before an unshakeable haven; infinity on the other side of a cell wall; the tossing lights of ships, and the motionless beacon of the convent; the uncertain lot of the seaman, and the vestal's vision in a single day of all the days of her life; and yet, O Amelia, a soul such as yours, stormy as the ocean; a catastrophe more dreadful than the mariner's—this whole picture is still deeply engraved in my memory.

Sun of this new sky, now witness to my tears, echoes of American shores repeating these accents, it was on the morrow of that terrible night that I leaned over the ship's stern and watched my native land disappearing forever! Long I stood there and gazed for the last time at the trees of my country swaying on the shore and the height of the convent sinking over the horizon.

As René came to the end of his story he drew a sheet of paper from his breast and gave it to Father Souël; then, throwing himself into the arms of Chactas and stifling his sobs, he waited as the missionary read through the letter.

It came from the mother superior of B——, and described the last hours in the life of Sister Amelia of Mercy, who had died a victim of her zeal and charity, while caring for companions stricken by a contagious disease. The entire community was inconsolable, and Amelia was regarded as a saint. The mother superior added that in her thirty years as head of the house she had never seen a sister so gentle and calm in disposition and none so happy to be relieved of the world's tribulations.

Chactas clasped René in his arms; the old man was weeping. "My child," he said to his son, "how I wish Father Aubry[17] were here. He could draw from the depths of his heart a strange calm which could pacify storms and yet seemed akin to them. He was

17. *Father Aubry:* the missionary in *Atala,* who shelters the two Indian lovers. It is Aubry who with Chactas buries Atala, after she commits suicide.

the moon on a stormy night. The moving clouds are powerless to carry it along in their flight; pure and unperturbed, it advances serenely above them. Alas, as for me, everything disturbs me and carries me away!"

Until now Father Souël had listened to René's story with a severe countenance and without uttering a word. Although inwardly warm-hearted, he presented to the world an inflexible character. It was the sachem's tenderness which made him break his silence.

"Nothing," he began, "nothing in your story deserves the pity you are now being shown. I see a young man infatuated with illusions, satisfied with nothing, withdrawn from the burdens of society, and wrapped up in idle dreams. A man is not superior, sir, because he sees the world in a dismal light. Only those of limited vision can hate men and life. Look a little farther and you will soon be convinced that all those griefs about which you complain are absolutely nothing. Why, what a shame not to be able to think of the only real misfortune in your life without having to blush! All the purity, all the virtue and faith, and all the crowns of a saint can scarcely make the very idea of your troubles tolerable. Your sister has atoned for her sin, but if I must speak frankly, I fear that through some terrible justice, that confession, emerging from the depths of the tomb, has in turn stirred up your own soul. What do you do all alone in the woods using up your days and neglecting all your duties? You will tell me that saints have retired to the wilderness. Yes, but they were there weeping and subduing their passions, while you seem to be wasting your time inflaming your own. Presumptuous youth, you thought man sufficient unto himself. Know now that solitude is bad for the man who does not live with God. It increases the soul's power while robbing it at the same time of every opportunity to find expression. Whoever has been endowed with talent must devote it to serving his fellow men, for if he does not make use of it, he is first punished by an inner misery, and sooner or later Heaven visits on him a fearful retribution."

Disturbed and humiliated by these words, René raised his head from the bosom of Chactas. The blind sachem began to smile, and this smile of the lips, unrelated as it was to the expression in his eyes, seemed to possess some mysterious, heavenly quality. "My son," said the old man who had once loved Atala, "he speaks severely to both of us; he is reprimanding the old man and the young, and he is right. Yes, you must give up this strange life, which holds nothing but care. Happiness can be found only in the common paths.

"One day the Meschacebe, while yet rather close to its source, grew weary of being only a limpid stream. It called for snows from the mountains, waters from the rivers, and rains from the tempests, and it overran its banks and laid waste its lovely forests. At first the haughty stream applauded its own power. But soon, seeing how everything grew barren along its path and how it now flowed abandoned in its solitude with its waters always troubled, it longed once again for the humble bed which nature had prepared for it, and it pined for the birds and the flowers, the trees and the streams which were once its modest companions along its peaceful course."

Chactas grew silent, and off in the reeds of the Meschacebe the flamingo's call could be heard announcing a storm for the middle of the day. The three friends started back toward their cabins. René walked silently between the missionary, who was praying, and the blind sachem, who kept feeling his way. It is said that, encouraged by the two elders, René returned to his wife, but still found no happiness. Soon afterwards, along with Chactas and Father Souël, he perished in the massacres of the French and Natchez in Louisiana. They still point out a rock where he would go off and sit in the setting sun.

ALFRED, LORD TENNYSON

(1809–1892)

Ulysses*

It little profits that an idle king,
By this still hearth, among these barren crags,
Matched with an agèd wife, I mete and dole
Unequal laws unto a savage race,
That hoard, and sleep, and feed, and know not me. 5
I cannot rest from travel. I will drink
Life to the lees. All time I have enjoyed
Greatly, have suffered greatly, both with those
That loved me, and alone; on shore, and when
Through scudding drifts the rainy Hyades 10
Vext the dim sea. I am become a name;
For always roaming with a hungry heart
Much have I seen and known,—cities of men
And manners, climates, councils, governments,
Myself not least, but honored of them all,— 15
And drunk delight of battle with my peers,
Far on the ringing plains of windy Troy.
I am a part of all that I have met;
Yet all experience is an arch where-through
Gleams that untravelled world whose margin fades 20

* 1842.

3. *wife:* Penelope. Ulysses is pictured here long after his travels back from Troy.

10. *Hyades:* A cluster of seven stars in the constellation of Taurus. The ancients supposed that when they rose with the sun, rainy weather would follow.

Forever and forever when I move.
How dull it is to pause, to make an end,
To rust unburnished, not to shine in use!
As though to breathe were life! Life piled on life
Were all too little, and of one to me 25
Little remains; but every hour is saved
From that eternal silence, something more,
A bringer of new things; and vile it were
For some three suns to store and hoard myself,
And this gray spirit yearning in desire 30
To follow knowledge like a sinking star,
Beyond the utmost bound of human thought.
This is my son, mine own Telemachus,
To whom I leave the scepter and the isle—
Well-loved of me, discerning to fulfill 35
This labor, by slow prudence to make mild
A rugged people, and through soft degrees
Subdue them to the useful and the good.
Most blameless is he, centered in the sphere
Of common duties, decent not to fail 40
In offices of tenderness, and pay
Meet adoration to my household gods,
When I am gone. He works his work, I mine.
There lies the port; the vessel puffs her sail;
There gloom the dark broad seas. My mariners, 45
Souls that have toiled, and wrought, and thought with me—
That ever with a frolic welcome took
The thunder and the sunshine, and opposed
Free hearts, free foreheads—you and I are old;
Old age hath yet his honor and his toil; 50
Death closes all. But something ere the end,
Some work of noble note, may yet be done,
Not unbecoming men that strove with gods.
The lights begin to twinkle from the rocks;
The long day wanes; the slow moon climbs; the deep 55
Moans round with many voices. Come, my friends,
'Tis not too late to seek a newer world.
Push off, and sitting well in order smite
The sounding furrows; for my purpose holds
To sail beyond the sunset, and the baths 60
Of all the western stars, until I die.
It may be that the gulfs will wash us down;

34. *isle:* Ithaca.
63. *Happy Isles:* in Greek myth, the abode of the warriors after death.
64. *Achilles:* comrade-in-arms of Ulysses at Troy.

It may be we shall touch the Happy Isles,
And see the great Achilles, whom we knew.
Though much is taken, much abides; and though 65
We are not now that strength which in old days
Moved earth and heaven, that which we are, we are;
One equal temper of heroic hearts,
Made weak by time and fate, but strong in will
To strive, to seek, to find, and not to yield. 70

Tithonus*

The woods decay, the woods decay and fall,
The vapors weep their burthen to the ground,
Man comes and tills the field and lies beneath,
And after many a summer dies the swan.
Me only cruel immortality 5
Consumes; I wither slowly in thine arms,
Here at the quiet limit of the world,
A white-haired shadow roaming like a dream
The ever-silent spaces of the East,
Far-folded mists, and gleaming halls of morn. 10
Alas! for this gray shadow, once a man—
So glorious in his beauty and thy choice,
Who madest him thy chosen, that he seemed
To his great heart none other than a God!
I asked thee, "Give me immortality." 15
Then didst thou grant mine asking with a smile,
Like wealthy men who care not how they give.
But thy strong Hours indignant worked their wills,
And beat me down and marred and wasted me,
And thou, they could not end me, left me maimed 20
To dwell in presence of immortal youth,
Immortal age beside immortal youth,
And all I was in ashes. Can thy love,
Thy beauty, make amends, though even now,
Close over us, the silver star, thy guide, 25
Shines in those tremulous eyes that fill with tears
To hear me? Let me go; take back thy gift.
Why should a man desire in any way
To vary from the kindly race of men,
Or pass beyond the goal of ordinance 30
Where all should pause, as is most meet for all?

* Written in 1833, revised in 1859 for publication in 1860. Tithonus was a prince of Troy loved by Aurora, goddess of dawn, in whose palace he is depicted as living. She obtained for him from Zeus the gift of immortality, but not of eternal youth.

18. *Hours*: Or *Horae*, goddesses of the seasons and of growth and decay.

25. *Silver star*: The morning star that precedes the dawn.

31. *meet*: Suitable.

A soft air fans the cloud apart; there comes
A glimpse of that dark world where I was born.
Once more the old mysterious glimmer steals
From thy pure brows, and from thy shoulders pure, 35
And bosom beating with a heart renewed.
Thy cheek begins to redden through the gloom,
Thy sweet eyes brighten slowly close to mine,
Ere yet they blind the stars, and the wild team
Which love thee, yearning for thy yoke, arise, 40
And shake the darkness from their loosened manes,
And beat the twilight into flakes of fire.
Lo! ever thus thou growest beautiful
In silence, then before thine answer given
Departest, and thy tears are on my cheek. 45
Why wilt thou ever scare me with thy tears,
And make me tremble lest a saying learnt,
In days far-off, on that dark earth, be true?
"The Gods themselves cannot recall their gifts."
Ay me! ay me! with what another heart 50
In days far-off, and with what other eyes
I used to watch—if I be he that watched—
The lucid outline forming round thee; saw
The dim curls kindle into sunny rings;
Changed with thy mystic change, and felt my blood 55
Glow with the glow that slowly crimsoned all
Thy presence and thy portals, while I lay,
Mouth, forehead, eyelids, growing dewy-warm
With kisses balmier than half-opening buds
Of April, and could hear the lips that kissed 60
Whispering I knew not what of wild and sweet,
Like that strange song I heard Apollo sing,
While Ilion like a mist rose into towers.
Yet hold me not forever in thine East;
How can my nature longer mix with thine? 65
Coldly thy rosy shadows bathe me, cold
Are all thy lights, and cold my wrinkled feet
Upon thy glimmering thresholds, when the steam
Floats up from those dim fields about the homes
Of happy men that have the power to die, 70
And grassy barrows of the happier dead.
Release me, and restore me to the ground.
Thou seest all things, thou wilt see my grave;
Thou wilt renew thy beauty morn by morn,
I earth in earth forget these empty courts, 75
And thee returning on thy silver wheels.

39. *wild team*: Of supernatural horses; they draw Aurora's chariot into the sky at dawn.

62. *Apollo*: God of music and patron of Troy. According to legend, the walls of Troy (Ilion) were raised by the sound of his song.

71. *barrows*: Burial mounds.

From *The Princess**

The Splendor Falls on Castle Walls

The splendor falls on castle walls
  And snowy summits old in story;
The long light shakes across the lakes,
  And the wild cataract leaps in glory.
Blow, bugle, blow, set the wild echoes flying, 5
Blow, bugle; answer, echoes, dying, dying, dying.

O, hark, O, hear! how thin and clear,
  And thinner, clearer, farther going!
O, sweet and far from cliff and scar
  The horns of Elfland faintly blowing! 10
Blow, let us hear the purple glens replying,
Blow, bugle; answer, echoes, dying, dying, dying.

O love, they die in yon rich sky,
  They faint on hill or field or river;
Our echoes roll from soul to soul, 15
  And grow forever and forever.
Blow, bugle, blow, set the wild echoes flying,
And answer, echoes, answer, dying, dying, dying.

Tears, Idle Tears

Tears, idle tears, I know not what they mean,
Tears from the depth of some divine despair
Rise in the heart, and gather to the eyes,
In looking on the happy autumn-fields,
And thinking of the days that are no more. 5

Fresh as the first beam glittering on a sail,
That brings our friends up from the underworld,
Sad as the last which reddens over one
That sinks with all we love below the verge;
So sad, so fresh, the days that are no more. 10

Ah, sad and strange as in dark summer dawns
The earliest pipe of half-awakened birds
To dying ears, when unto dying eyes
The casement slowly grows a glimmering square;
So sad, so strange, the days that are no more. 15

* Long narrative poem on the wooing by Prince Hilarion of Princess Ida, founder of a women's college and leader of its feminist faculty and students. The four songs printed here, interludes that reflect and obliquely comment on the situation, were published variously in 1847 and 1850.

9. *scar*: Another name for a rocky cliff.

Dear as remembered kisses after death,
And sweet as those by hopeless fancy feigned
On lips that are for others; deep as love,
Deep as first love, and wild with all regret;
O Death in Life, the days that are no more! 20

Now Sleeps the Crimson Petal

Now sleeps the crimson petal, now the white;
Nor waves the cypress in the palace walk;
Nor winks the gold fin in the porphyry font.
The firefly wakens; waken thou with me.

Now droops the milk-white peacock like a ghost, 5
And like a ghost she glimmers on to me.

Now lies the Earth all Danaë to the stars,
And all thy heart lies open unto me.

Now slides the silent meteor on, and leaves
A shining furrow, as thy thoughts in me. 10

Now folds the lily all her sweetness up,
And slips into the bosom of the lake.
So fold thyself, my dearest, thou, and slip
Into my bosom and be lost in me.

Come Down, O Maid

Come down, O maid, from yonder mountain height.
What pleasure lives in height (the shepherd sang),
In height and cold, the splendor of the hills?
But cease to move so near the heavens, and cease
To glide a sunbeam by the blasted pine, 5
To sit a star upon the sparkling spire;
And come, for Love is of the valley, come,
For Love is of the valley, come thou down
And find him; by the happy threshold, he,
Or hand in hand with Plenty in the maize, 10
Or red with spurted purple of the vats,
Or foxlike in the vine; nor cares to walk
With Death and Morning on the Silver Horns,
Nor wilt thou snare him in the white ravine,
Nor find him dropped upon the firths of ice, 15
That huddling slant in furrow-cloven falls
To roll the torrent out of dusky doors.

3. *porphyry*: A hard, dark red rock.
7. *Danaë*: Princess of ancient Greece; shut away by her father in a tower open only to the sky, she was visited by Zeus, ruler of the gods, who assumed the form of a golden shower.
10. *maize*: Corn.
12. *foxlike in the vine*: Refers to "the little foxes that spoil the vineyard." [*Song of Solomon* 2:15.]
13. *Horns*: Mountaintops (as in Matterhorn).
15. *firths of ice*: Glaciers.

But follow; let the torrent dance thee down
To find him in the valley; let the wild
Lean-headed eagles yelp alone, and leave 20
The monstrous ledges there to slope, and spill
Their thousand wreaths of dangling water-smoke,
That like a broken purpose waste in air.
So waste not thou, but come; for all the vales
Await thee; azure pillars of the hearth 25
Arise to thee; the children call, and I
Thy shepherd pipe, and sweet is every sound,
Sweeter thy voice, but every sound is sweet;
Myriads of rivulets hurrying through the lawn,
The moan of doves in immemorial elms, 30
And murmuring of innumerable bees.

In Memoriam A. H. H.*

Obit. MDCCCXXXIII

[*Prologue*]

Strong Son of God, immortal Love,
  Whom we, that have not seen thy face,
  By faith, and faith alone, embrace,
Believing where we cannot prove;

Thine are these orbs of light and shade; 5
  Thou madest Life in man and brute;
  Thou madest Death; and lo, thy foot
Is on the skull which thou hast made.

25. *pillars*: Of smoke.

* In his second year at Trinity College, Cambridge (1828), Tennyson met Arthur Hallam. Hallam, a vivid and magnetic young man who was expected by his elders and his contemporaries to become one of England's outstanding future leaders, befriended Tennyson, encouraged him to write, and introduced him into an eminent undergraduate society called the "Apostles," whose members concerned themselves with the social, religious, scientific, and literary issues of the day. In 1830, Hallam having by now become engaged to Tennyson's sister, the two young men went together to Spain to deliver money to the Spanish revolutionaries, and two years later toured the Rhineland. Then, suddenly, Hallam died in Vienna at the age of twenty-two. The 133 lyrics that make up *In Memoriam* were intermittently composed over the next seventeen years and first published in 1850. The poem brought Tennyson immediate fame, such that he was appointed to succeed Wordsworth as Poet Laureate of England and was able to support himself by his writings.

The cycle of poems is unified by a striking stanza form which, though it had been used as early as the Sixteenth Century, is now identified with *In Memoriam,* and by the recurring celebrations of Christmas (stanzas 28, 78, and 104–6) which, as A. C. Bradley has suggested, mark the stages of a progression from personal grief for Hallam to thoughts of the problem of survival after death, to the affirmation of faith and hope, and to a final vision of Hallam as the forerunner of a new human race that would transcend its present condition. This abridgment of *In Memoriam* is designed to preserve this shape without omitting any of the most memorable lyrics.

1. Cf 1 John 4:8, 15. "He that loveth not knoweth not God; for God is love." "Whosoever shall confess that Jesus is the Son of God, God dwelleth in him, and he in God."

5. *orbs . . . shade*: I.e., the earth and the planets, part of each of which is sunlit, the rest in shadow.

7–8. I.e., Christ crushes Death underfoot, a common motif in painting and sculpture.

Thou wilt not leave us in the dust:
  Thou madest man, he knows not why, 10
  He thinks he was not made to die;
And thou hast made him: thou art just.

Thou seemest human and divine,
  The highest, holiest manhood, thou.
  Our wills are ours, we know not how; 15
Our wills are ours, to make them thine.

Our little systems have their day;
  They have their day and cease to be;
  They are but broken lights of thee,
And thou, O Lord, art more than they. 20

We have but faith: we cannot know,
  For knowledge is of things we see;
  And yet we trust it comes from thee,
A beam in darkness: let it grow.

Let knowledge grow from more to more, 25
  But more of reverence in us dwell;
  That mind and soul, according well,
May make one music as before,

But vaster. We are fools and slight;
  We mock thee when we do not fear: 30
  But help thy foolish ones to bear;
Help thy vain worlds to bear thy light.

Forgive what seemed my sin in me,
  What seemed my worth since I began;
  For merit lives from man to man, 35
And not from man, O Lord, to thee.

Forgive my grief for one removed,
  Thy creature, whom I found so fair.
  I trust he lives in thee, and there
I find him worthier to be loved. 40

Forgive these wild and wandering cries,
  Confusions of a wasted youth;
  Forgive them where they fail in truth,
And in thy wisdom make me wise.

17. *systems*: Transient theological and philosophical systems, contrasted with the enduring systems of the stars.
19. *broken*: Refracted, as by a prism.
28. *before*: I.e., in times when faith and knowledge were still harmonious.
32. *bear thy light*: I.e., both survive the radiance and convey it.
42. *wasted*: Laid waste (by Hallam's loss).

1

I held it truth, with him who sings
  To one clear harp in divers tones,
  That men may rise on stepping-stones
Of their dead selves to higher things.

But who shall so forecast the years (5)
  And find in loss a gain to match?
  Or reach a hand through time to catch
The far-off interest of tears?

Let Love clasp Grief lest both be drowned,
  Let darkness keep her raven gloss. (10)
  Ah, sweeter to be drunk with loss,
To dance with Death, to beat the ground,

Than that the victor Hours should scorn
  The long result of love, and boast,
  "Behold the man that loved and lost, (15)
But all he was is overworn."

2

Old yew, which graspest at the stones
  That name the underlying dead,
  Thy fibers net the dreamless head,
Thy roots are wrapt about the bones.

The seasons bring the flower again, (5)
  And bring the firstling to the flock;
  And in the dusk of thee the clock
Beats out the little lives of men.

O, not for thee the glow, the bloom,
  Who changest not in any gale, (10)
  Nor branding summer suns avail
To touch thy thousand years of gloom;

And gazing on thee, sullen tree,
  Sick for thy stubborn hardihood,
  I seem to fail from out my blood (15)
And grow incorporate into thee.

1. *him*: Goethe, who in the second part of *Faust* and elsewhere voices his conception of spiritual progress through the outgrowing of one's former selves.
2. *divers*: Various.
5–8. But who, in the grip of an immediate loss, can look ahead to some future compensating gain? or grasp whatever future reward ("interest") that present loss may someday bring?
13. *Hours*: Or Horae, goddesses of growth and decay.
16. *overworn*: Worn out, exhausted.
1. *yew*: Evergreen capable of attaining to great age; hence often planted in graveyards as symbol of immortality.
14. *for*: With longing for. *constant*: The yew does not change with the seasons.

3

O Sorrow, cruel fellowship,
O Priestess in the vaults of Death,
O sweet and bitter in a breath,
What whispers from thy lying lip?

"The stars," she whispers, "blindly run; 5
A web is woven across the sky;
From out waste places comes a cry,
And murmurs from the dying sun;

"And all the phantom, Nature, stands—
With all the music in her tone, 10
A hollow echo of my own,—
A hollow form with empty hands."

And shall I take a thing so blind,
Embrace her as my natural good;
Or crush her, like a vice of blood, 15
Upon the threshold of the mind?

* * *

5

I sometimes hold it half a sin
To put in words the grief I feel;
For words, like Nature, half reveal
And half conceal the Soul within.

But, for the unquiet heart and brain, 5
A use in measured language lies;
The sad mechanic exercise,
Like dull narcotics, numbing pain.

In words, like weeds, I'll wrap me o'er,
Like coarsest clothes against the cold; 10
But that large grief which these enfold
Is given in outline and no more.

* * *

7

Dark house, by which once more I stand
Here in the long unlovely street,
Doors, where my heart was used to beat
So quickly, waiting for a hand,

4. *lying*: I.e., because grief for a dead loved one may inspire the conviction that the universe is simply a machine running down, wholly indifferent to human lives and values (as in 5–12).

5. *she*: Sorrow.

9. *weeds*: Garments (with allusion to mourning garments).

1. *house*: The Hallam family residence.

A hand that can be clasped no more— 5
  Behold me, for I cannot sleep,
  And like a guilty thing I creep
At earliest morning to the door.

He is not here; but far away
  The noise of life begins again, 10
  And ghastly through the drizzling rain
On the bald street breaks the blank day.

* * *

10

I hear the noise about thy keel;
  I hear the bell struck in the night;
  I see the cabin-window bright;
I see the sailor at the wheel.

Thou bring'st the sailor to his wife, 5
  And traveled men from foreign lands;
  And letters unto trembling hands;
And, thy dark freight, a vanished life.

So bring him; we have idle dreams;
  This look of quiet flatters thus 10
  Our home-bred fancies. O, to us,
The fools of habit, sweeter seems

To rest beneath the clover sod,
  That takes the sunshine and the rains,
  Or where the kneeling hamlet drains 15
The chalice of the grapes of God;

Than if with thee the roaring wells
  Should gulf him fathom-deep in brine,
  And hands so often clasped in mine,
Should toss with tangle and with shells. 20

11

Calm is the morn without a sound,
  Calm as to suit a calmer grief,
  And only through the faded leaf
The chestnut pattering to the ground;

1. *keel*: Of the ship bringing Hallam's body back from Vienna, where he had died on 15 September 1833, aged 22.

13–16. Alternate modes of burial: in the churchyard or under the chancel where worshippers kneel for the Sacrament.

20. *tangle*: Seaweed.

1–5. The time is September, when Hallam's body is still en route; the poet is at his home in Somersby among the high wolds (open uplands) of Lincolnshire.

Calm and deep peace on this high wold, 5
And on these dews that drench the furze,
And all the silvery gossamers
That twinkle into green and gold;

Calm and still light on yon great plain
That sweeps with all its autumn bowers, 10
And crowded farms and lessening towers,
To mingle with the bounding main;

Calm and deep peace in this wide air,
These leaves that redden to the fall,
And in my heart, if calm at all, 15
If any calm, a calm despair;

Calm on the seas, and silver sleep,
And waves that sway themselves in rest,
And dead calm in that noble breast
Which heaves but with the heaving deep. 20

* * *

15

Tonight the winds begin to rise
And roar from yonder dropping day;
The last red leaf is whirled away,
The rooks are blown about the skies;

The forest cracked, the waters curled, 5
The cattle huddled on the lea;
And wildly dashed on tower and tree
The sunbeam strikes along the world:

And but for fancies, which aver
That all thy motions gently pass 10
Athwart a plane of molten glass,
I scarce could brook the strain and stir

That makes the barren branches loud;
And but for fear it is not so,
The wild unrest that lives in woe 15
Would dote and pore on yonder cloud

4. *rooks*: European crow-like birds.
6. *lea*: Pasture.
9–16. In the midst of a gathering storm, the poet's imagination soothes him with the fancy that Hallam's ship moves gently toward England on a glass-calm sea. Only a fear that this fancy may delude him (and Hallam's crossing be really in danger) prevents the stormy unrest within him from romantically luxuriating in the stormy sunset all around him.
12. *brook*: Endure.

That rises upward always higher,
  And onward drags a laboring breast,
  And topples round the dreary west,
A looming bastion fringed with fire. 20

16

What words are these have fall'n from me?
  Can calm despair and wild unrest
  Be tenants of a single breast,
Or Sorrow such a changeling be?

Or doth she only seem to take 5
  The touch of change in calm or storm,
  But knows no more of transient form
In her deep self, than some dead lake

That holds the shadow of a lark
  Hung in the shadow of a heaven? 10
  Or has the shock, so harshly given,
Confused me like the unhappy bark

That strikes by night a craggy shelf,
  And staggers blindly ere she sink?
  And stunned me from my power to think 15
And all my knowledge of myself;

And made me that delirious man
  Whose fancy fuses old and new,
  And flashes into false and true,
And mingles all without a plan? 20

* * *

19

The Danube to the Severn gave
  The darkened heart that beat no more;
  They laid him by the pleasant shore,
And in the hearing of the wave.

There twice a day the Severn fills; 5
  The salt sea-water passes by,
  And hushes half the babbling Wye,
And makes a silence in the hills.

2. *despair and wild unrest*: The moods of the preceding sections: 11 and 15.

12. *bark*: Ship.

1. Vienna, where Hallam died, is on the Danube; the church at Clevedon, Somersetshire, where he was buried, is on the Severn.

3–4. Tennyson was not present at the funeral and did not learn till years later that Hallam had been buried in the church, not in the graveyard by the river.

5–8. The tides reach far up the Bristol channel into the Severn and the Wye, its tributary.

The Wye is hushed nor moved along,
And hushed my deepest grief of all, 10
When filled with tears that cannot fall,
I brim with sorrow drowning song.

The tide flows down, the wave again
Is vocal in its wooded walls;
My deeper anguish also falls, 15
And I can speak a little then.

* * *

21

I sing to him that rests below,
And, since the grasses round me wave,
I take the grasses of the grave,
And make them pipes whereon to blow.

The traveler hears me now and then, 5
And sometimes harshly will he speak:
"This fellow would make weakness weak,
And melt the waxen hearts of men."

Another answers: "Let him be,
He loves to make parade of pain, 10
That with his piping he may gain
The praise that comes to constancy."

A third is wroth: "Is this an hour
For private sorrow's barren song,
When more and more the people throng 15
The chairs and thrones of civil power?

"A time to sicken and to swoon,
When Science reaches forth her arms
To feel from world to world, and charms
Her secret from the latest moon?" 20

Behold, ye speak an idle thing;
Ye never knew the sacred dust.
I do but sing because I must,
And pipe but as the linnets sing;

4. ***pipes***: Alluding to the pipes of mourning shepherds in pastoral elegy, the genre to which *In Memoriam* in part belongs.

5–20. The poet foresees the criticisms that will be leveled at such a poem as *In Memoriam*.

13. *wroth*: Very angry.

15–16 Alluding to the revolutionary movements of the age in England and France.

18–20. From 1846 to 1848, astronomers discovered the planet Neptune, the moon of Neptune, the satellites of Uranus, and the eighth moon of Saturn.

And one is glad; her note is gay, 25
  For now her little ones have ranged;
  And one is sad; her note is changed,
Because her brood is stolen away.

22

The path by which we twain did go,
  Which led by tracts that pleased us well,
  Through four sweet years arose and fell,
From flower to flower, from snow to snow;

And we with singing cheered the way, 5
  And, crowned with all the season lent,
  From April on to April went,
And glad at heart from May to May.

But where the path we walked began
  To slant the fifth autumnal slope, 10
  As we descended following Hope,
There sat the Shadow feared of man;

Who broke our fair companionship,
  And spread his mantle dark and cold,
  And wrapt thee formless in the fold, 15
And dulled the murmur on thy lip,

And bore thee where I could not see
  Nor follow, tho' I walk in haste,
  And think that somewhere in the waste
The Shadow sits and waits for me. 20

23

Now, sometimes in my sorrow shut,
  Or breaking into song by fits,
  Alone, alone, to where he sits,
The Shadow cloaked from head to foot,

Who keeps the keys of all the creeds, 5
  I wander, often falling lame,
  And looking back to whence I came,
Or on to where the pathway leads;

And crying, How changed from where it ran
  Through lands where not a leaf was dumb, 10
  But all the lavish hills would hum
The murmur of a happy Pan;

19. *waste*: Wasteland.

9–24. The poet recalls the happiness of life's "pathway" when he and Hallam traveled it together in their Cambridge studies.

12. *Pan*: God of flocks and shepherds, and hence of pastoral poetry like these verses.

When each by turns was guide to each,
And Fancy light from Fancy caught,
And Thought leapt out to wed with Thought 15
Ere Thought could wed itself with Speech;

And all we met was fair and good,
And all was good that Time could bring,
And all the secret of the Spring
Moved in the chambers of the blood; 20

And many an old philosophy
On Argive heights divinely sang,
And round us all the thicket rang
To many a flute of Arcady.

* * *

27

I envy not in any moods
The captive void of noble rage,
The linnet born within the cage,
That never knew the summer woods;

I envy not the beast that takes 5
His license in the field of time,
Unfettered by the sense of crime,
To whom a conscience never wakes;

Nor, what may count itself as blest,
The heart that never plighted troth 10
But stagnates in the weeds of sloth;
Nor any want-begotten rest.

I hold it true, whate'er befall;
I feel it, when I sorrow most;
'Tis better to have loved and lost 15
Than never to have loved at all.

28

The time draws near the birth of Christ.
The moon is hid, the night is still;
The Christmas bells from hill to hill
Answer each other in the mist.

21–24. I.e., they were like shepherds on the hills of Greece when what is now "old philosophy" was brand new; or on the plains of Arcady (home of pastoral poetry) when pastoral poetry was young.

5–6. *takes . . . time*: Does whatever his appetites direct, conscious of nothing but the temporal world.

10. *plighted troth*: Became engaged to be married.

12. *want-begotten rest*: I.e., any rest that comes from a lack or deficiency—specifically, from a failure to be fully human and therefore vulnerable.

1–4. It is the first Christmas after Hallam's death, and bellringers are ringing changes on the bells of four neighboring village churches.

Four voices of four hamlets round, 5
  From far and near, on mead and moor,
  Swell out and fail, as if a door
Were shut between me and the sound;

Each voice four changes on the wind,
  That now dilate, and now decrease, 10
  Peace and goodwill, goodwill and peace,
Peace and goodwill, to all mankind.

This year I slept and woke with pain,
  I almost wished no more to wake,
  And that my hold on life would break 15
Before I heard those bells again;

But they my troubled spirit rule,
  For they controlled me when a boy;
  They bring me sorrow touched with joy,
The merry, merry bells of Yule. 20

* * *

50

Be near me when my light is low,
  When the blood creeps, and the nerves prick
  And tingle; and the heart is sick,
And all the wheels of being slow.

Be near me when the sensuous frame 5
  Is racked with pangs that conquer trust;
  And Time, a maniac scattering dust,
And Life, a Fury slinging flame.

Be near me when my faith is dry,
  And men the flies of latter spring, 10
  That lay their eggs, and sting and sting
And weave their petty cells and die.

Be near me when I fade away,
  To point the term of human strife,
  And on the low dark verge of life 15
The twilight of eternal day.

* * *

54

O, yet we trust that somehow good
  Will be the final goal of ill,
  To pangs of nature, sins of will,
Defects of doubt, and taints of blood;

6. *mead and moor*: Meadow and wasteland.
7. *dust*: The dust from which life comes and to which it returns.
8. *flame*: The Furies of Greek myth carry torches.

That nothing walks with aimless feet; 5
That not one life shall be destroyed,
Or cast as rubbish to the void,
When God hath made the pile complete;

That not a worm is cloven in vain;
That not a moth with vain desire 10
Is shriveled in a fruitless fire,
Or but subserves another's gain.

Behold, we know not anything;
I can but trust that good shall fall
At last—far off—at last, to all, 15
And every winter change to spring.

So runs my dream; but what am I?
An infant crying in the night;
An infant crying for the light,
And with no language but a cry. 20

55

The wish, that of the living whole
No life may fail beyond the grave,
Derives it not from what we have
The likest God within the soul?

Are God and Nature then at strife, 5
That Nature lends such evil dreams?
So careful of the type she seems,
So careless of the single life,

That I, considering everywhere
Her secret meaning in her deeds, 10
And finding that of fifty seeds
She often brings but one to bear,

I falter where I firmly trod,
And falling with my weight of cares
Upon the great world's altar-stairs 15
That slope through darkness up to God,

I stretch lame hands of faith, and grope,
And gather dust and chaff, and call
To what I feel is Lord of all,
And faintly trust the larger hope. 20

7–8. *careful . . . careless*: The significance of Nature's prodigality and destructiveness was widely debated during Tennyson's lifetime. *type*: Species.

19. *Lord of all*: Cf. Prologue, line 1n.
20. *the larger hope*: That there is some form of immortality for individuals.

56

"So careful of the type?" but no.
From scarpèd cliff and quarried stone
She cries, "A thousand types are gone;
I care for nothing, all shall go.

"Thou makest thine appeal to me: 5
I bring to life, I bring to death;
The spirit does but mean the breath:
I know no more." And he, shall he,

Man, her last work, who seemed so fair,
Such splendid purpose in his eyes, 10
Who rolled the psalm to wintry skies,
Who built him fanes of fruitless prayer,

Who trusted God was love indeed
And love Creation's final law—
Though Nature, red in tooth and claw 15
With ravin, shrieked against his creed—

Who loved, who suffered countless ills,
Who battled for the True, the Just,
Be blown about the desert dust,
Or sealed within the iron hills? 20

No more? A monster then, a dream,
A discord. Dragons of the prime,
That tare each other in their slime,
Were mellow music matched with him.

O life as futile, then, as frail! 25
O for thy voice to soothe and bless!
What hope of answer, or redress?
Behind the veile, behind the veil.

* * *

78

Again at Christmas did we weave
The holly round the Christmas hearth;
The silent snow possessed the earth,
And calmly fell our Christmas-eve:

2. *scarpèd*: Shorn away vertically to expose the rock strata of different ages.
3. That whole species had disappeared, not merely individuals, had become evident from Charles Lyell's researches, published in his *Principles of Geology* (3 vols., 1830–33) and *Elements of Geology* (1838).
12. *fanes*: Temples.
13. *God was love*: As claimed for example in 1 John 4:8.
17. *ravin*: Prey.
20. I.e., like other fossils.
22. *Dragons . . . prime*: Prehistoric creatures.
26. *thy voice*: Hallam's.
27. *veil*: Death.
1. *Christmas*: In 1834.

The yule-clog sparkled keen with frost, 5
No wing of wind the region swept,
But over all things brooding slept
The quiet sense of something lost.

As in the winters left behind,
Again our ancient games had place, 10
The mimic picture's breathing grace,
And dance and song and hoodman-blind.

Who showed a token of distress?
No single tear, no mark of pain:
O sorrow, then can sorrow wane? 15
O grief, can grief be changed to less?

O last regret, regret can die!
No—mixt with all this mystic frame,
Her deep relations are the same,
But with long use her tears are dry. 20

* * *

95

By night we lingered on the lawn,
For underfoot the herb was dry;
And genial warmth; and o'er the sky
The silvery haze of summer drawn;

And calm that let the tapers burn 5
Unwavering; not a cricket chirred;
The brook alone far-off was heard,
And on the board the fluttering urn.

And bats went round in fragrant skies,
And wheeled or lit the filmy shapes 10
That haunt the dusk, with ermine capes
And woolly breasts and beaded eyes;

While now we sang old songs that pealed
From knoll to knoll, where, couched at ease,
The white kine glimmered, and the trees 15
Laid their dark arms about the field.

But when those others, one by one,
Withdrew themselves from me and night,
And in the house light after light
Went out, and I was all alone, 20

5. *yule-clog*: Yule log.
11. *mimic picture*: The game may be charades.
12. *hoodman-blind*: Blind man's bluff.
1. *lawn*: At Somersby (above, Section 11, lines 1–5 and note).
8. *board*: Table. *fluttering urn*: Boiling tea-urn.
10–11. *filmy shapes . . . ermine capes*: Night moths, especially the ermine moth.
15. *kine*: Cattle.

A hunger seized my heart; I read
  Of that glad year which once had been,
  In those fall'n leaves which kept their green,
The noble letters of the dead.

And strangely on the silence broke 25
  The silent-speaking words, and strange
  Was love's dumb cry defying change
To test his worth; and strangely spoke

The faith, the vigor, bold to dwell
  On doubts that drive the coward back, 30
  And keen thro' wordy snares to track
Suggestion to her inmost cell.

So word by word, and line by line,
  The dead man touched me from the past,
  And all at once it seemed at last 35
The living soul was flashed on mine,

And mine in this was wound, and whirled
  About empyreal heights of thought,
  And came on that which is, and caught
The deep pulsations of the world, 40

Æonian music measuring out
  The steps of Time—the shocks of Chance—
  The blows of Death. At length my trance
Was canceled, stricken through with doubt.

Vague words! but ah, how hard to frame 45
  In matter-molded forms of speech,
  Or even for intellect to reach
Through memory that which I became;

Till now the doubtful dusk revealed
  The knolls once more where, couched at ease, 50
  The white kine glimmered, and the trees
Laid their dark arms about the field;

And sucked from out the distant gloom
  A breeze began to tremble o'er
  The large leaves of the sycamore, 55
And fluctuate all the still perfume,

22. *glad year*: The entire period of Tennyson's and Hallam's friendship.

35–44. In a visionary moment, the poet believes he has made contact with ultimate reality; that reality proves to be the process of eternal change as sensed in "The deep pulsations of the world" and in the "music" of Time's passing aeons.

38. *empyreal*: Sublime.

41. *Aeonian*: Age-old.

45–46. I.e., it is impossible to express in words a mystical experience.

And gathering freshlier overhead
  Rock'd the full-foliaged elms, and swung
  The heavy-folded rose, and flung
The lilies to and fro, and said, 60

"The dawn, the dawn," and died away;
  And East and West, without a breath,
  Mixt their dim lights, like life and death,
To broaden into boundless day.

* * *

106

Ring out, wild bells, to the wild sky,
  The flying cloud, the frosty light:
  The year is dying in the night;
Ring out, wild bells, and let him die.

Ring out the old, ring in the new, 5
  Ring, happy bells, across the snow:
  The year is going, let him go;
Ring out the false, ring in the true.

Ring out the grief that saps the mind,
  For those that here we see no more; 10
  Ring out the feud of rich and poor,
Ring in redress to all mankind.

Ring out a slowly dying cause,
  And ancient forms of party strife;
  Ring in the nobler modes of life, 15
With sweeter manners, purer laws.

Ring out the want, the care, the sin,
  The faithless coldness of the times;
  Ring out, ring out my mournful rhymes,
But ring the fuller minstrel in. 20

Ring out false pride in place and blood,
  The civic slander and the spite;
  Ring in the love of truth and right,
Ring in the common love of good.

Ring out old shapes of foul disease; 25
  Ring out the narrowing lust of gold;
  Ring out the thousand wars of old,
Ring in the thousand years of peace.

3. It is New Year's eve, the third since Hallam's death.

28–29. The poet has in mind Revelation 20, where it is said that Satan will be bound in chains for a thousand years, during which time the martyrs will be "priests of God and of Christ, and shall reign with him."

Ring in the valiant man and free,
  The larger heart, the kindlier hand; 30
  Ring out the darkness of the land,
Ring in the Christ that is to be.

* * *

118

Contemplate all this work of Time,
  The giant laboring in his youth;
  Nor dream of human love and truth,
As dying Nature's earth and lime;

But trust that those we call the dead 5
  Are breathers of an ampler day
  For ever nobler ends. They say,
The solid earth whereon we tread

In tracts of fluent heat began,
  And grew to seeming-random forms, 10
  The seeming prey of cyclic storms,
Till at the last arose the man;

Who throve and branched from clime to clime,
  The herald of a higher race,
  And of himself in higher place, 15
If so he type this work of time

Within himself, from more to more;
  Or, crown'd with attributes of woe
  Like glories, move his course, and show
That life is not as idle ore, 20

But iron dug from central gloom,
  And heated hot with burning fears,
  And dipt in baths of hissing tears,
And battered with the shocks of doom

To shape and use. Arise and fly 25
  The reeling Faun, the sensual feast;
  Move upward, working out the beast,
And let the ape and tiger die.

* * *

32. Tennyson believed a time would come when disputes over creeds would cease and the spirit of Christ would triumph.

1–28. The poet takes here a more inclusive view of Evolution than that which troubled him in sections 54–56. He is able to believe now that those who die evolve to higher states of being (3–8); and while he is willing to entertain the nebular theory of the origin of things as a theory (7–12), he also insists that man has an evolutionary destiny of his own, if he will but "Move upward, working out the beast" (13–28).

4. *earth and lime*: The products of the decay of flesh and bone.

14–19. I.e., it may be that man is not Evolution's final product but merely a harbinger of a greater race to come; or it may be that man can fit himself to become that higher race by moral effort, and suffering.

16. *type*: Copy, emulate.

124

That which we dare invoke to bless;
Our dearest faith; our ghastliest doubt;
He, They, One, All; within, without;
The Power in darkness whom we guess,—

I found Him not in world or sun, 5
Or eagle's wing, or insect's eye,
Nor through the questions men may try,
The petty cobwebs we have spun.

If e'er when faith had fallen asleep,
I heard a voice, "believe no more," 10
And heard an ever-breaking shore
That tumbled in the Godless deep,

A warmth within the beast would melt
The freezing reason's colder part,
And like a man in wrath the heart 15
Stood up and answered, "I have felt."

No, like a child in doubt and fear:
But that blind clamor made me wise;
Then was I as a child that cries,
But, crying, knows his father near; 20

And what I am beheld again
What is, and no man understands;
And out of darkness came the hands
That reach through nature, molding men.

[*Epilogue*]

Today the grave is bright for me,
For them the light of life increased,
Who stay to share the morning feast, 75
Who rest tonight beside the sea.

3. *He, They, One, All*: Christ, as part of the Trinity, seen as three elements and as indivisible.

5–16. The poet has found God neither through the inductive arguments from design (e.g., the aptness of an eagle's wing or an insect's eye for its function suggests a Designer) nor through the questions of inductive logic, but from his own suffering experience.

13–16. Tennyson evidently has in mind Pascal's statement that the heart has reasons that the mind knows not of.

17–24. The poet now recurs to but sees beyond the situation in which he found himself in Section 54.

22. *and*: I.e., and what.

73–144. The Epilogue to *In Memoriam* celebrates the wedding of the poet's sister Cecilia to his friend Edmund Lushington (10 October 1842) and brings the poem of mourning full circle to its conclusion in a marriage and in the prospect of a new birth.

74. *them*: The new husband and wife.

Let all my genial spirits advance
  To meet and greet a whiter sun;
  My drooping memory will not shun
The foaming grape of eastern France. 80

It circles round, and fancy plays,
  And hearts are warmed and faces bloom,
  As drinking health to bride and groom
We wish them store of happy days.

Nor count me all to blame if I 85
  Conjecture of a stiller guest,
  Perchance, perchance, among the rest,
And, though in silence, wishing joy.

But they must go, the time draws on,
  And those white-favored horses wait; 90
  They rise, but linger; it is late;
Farewell, we kiss, and they are gone.

A shade falls on us like the dark
  From little cloudlets on the grass,
  But sweeps away as out we pass 95
To range the woods, to roam the park,

Discussing how their courtship grew,
  And talk of others that are wed,
  And how she looked, and what he said,,
And back we come at fall of dew. 100

Again the feast, the speech, the glee,
  The shade of passing thought, the wealth
  Of words and wit, the double health,
The crowning cup, the three-times-three,

And last the dance;—till I retire. 105
  Dumb is that tower which spake so loud,
  And high in heaven the streaming cloud,
And on the downs a rising fire:

And rise, O moon, from younder down,
  Till over down and over dale 110
  All night the shining vapor sail
And pass the silent-lighted town,

78. *whiter*: More joyous and hopeful because of the marriage.
80. *foaming grape*: Champagne.
86. *guest*: Hallam.
90. *white-favored*: Caparisoned for the wedding.
104. *three-times-three*: Rousing cheers.
106. *tower*: Church tower where wedding bells recently rang.

The white-faced halls, the glancing rills,
  And catch at every mountain head,
  And o'er the friths that branch and spread 115
Their sleeping silver through the hills;

And touch with shade the bridal doors,
  With tender gloom the roof, the wall;
  And breaking let the splendor fall
To spangle all the happy shores 120

By which they rest, and ocean sounds,
  And, star and system rolling past,
  A soul shall draw from out the vast
And strike his being into bounds,

And, moved through life of lower phase, 125
  Result in man, be born and think,
  And act and love, a closer link
Betwixt us and the crowning race

Of those that, eye to eye, shall look
  On knowledge; under whose command 130
  Is Earth and Earth's, and in their hand
Is Nature like an open book;

No longer half-akin to brute,
  For all we thought and loved and did,
  And hoped, and suffer'd, is but seed 135
Of what in them is flower and fruit;

Whereof the man that with me trod
  This planet was a noble type
  Appearing ere the times were ripe,
That friend of mine who lives in God, 140

That God, which ever lives and loves,
  One God, one law, one element,
  And one far-off divine event,
To which the whole creation moves.

115. *friths*: Arms of the sea.

123–30. I.e., a child will be born of this union, will recapitulate as an embryo in the womb the successive stages of human evolution, will subsequently by thought, act, and love evolve a moral being, and so in the end will bring the human species closer to those higher lives that Hallam's life heralded. In this way, a triple series of evolutions—physical before birth, moral during life, spiritual after death—draws mankind and the whole creation to a planned destiny.

129. *eye to eye*: Tennyson seems to have in mind throughout this stanza 1 Corinthians 13:9–12, where it is said that we see *now* as through a glass darkly, but *then* face to face.

ROBERT BROWNING

(1812–1889)

The Bishop Orders His Tomb at Saint Praxed's Church†

ROME, 15—

Vanity, saith the preacher, vanity!
Draw round my bed: is Anselm keeping back?
Nephews—sons mine . . . ah God, I know not! Well—
She, men would have to be your mother once,
Old Gandolf envied me, so fair she was! 5
What's done is done, and she is dead beside,
Dead long ago, and I am Bishop since,
And as she died so must we die ourselves,
And thence ye may perceive the world's a dream.
Life, how and what is it? As here I lie 10
In this state-chamber, dying by degrees,
Hours and long hours in the dead night, I ask
'Do I live, am I dead?' Peace, peace seems all.
Saint Praxed's ever was the church for peace;
And so, about this tomb of mine. I fought 15
With tooth and nail to save my niche, ye know:
—Old Gandolf cozened me, despite my care;
Shrewd was that snatch from out the corner South
He graced his carrion with, God curse the same!
Yet still my niche is not so cramped but thence 20
One sees the pulpit o' the epistle-side,
And somewhat of the choir, those silent seats,
And up into the aery dome where live
The angels, and a sunbeam's sure to lurk:
And I shall fill my slab of basalt there, 25
And 'neath my tabernacle take my rest,
With those nine columns round me, two and two,
The odd one at my feet where Anselm stands:
Peach-blossom marble all, the rare, the ripe
As fresh-poured red wine of a mighty pulse. 30
—Old Gandolf with his paltry onion-stone,

† Published in 1845. The Bishop, his tomb, and the character Gandolf are all fictional. Saint Praxed's church, seen by Browning in 1844, is named after a second-century Roman virgin.

1. *Vanity:* See Ecclesiastes 1:2. *preacher:* the author of Ecclesiastes.

5. *Gandolf:* the Bishop's predecessor.

21. *epistle-side:* i.e., the right side as the congregation faces the altar.

26. *tabernacle:* here, the canopy over his tomb.

31. *onion-stone:* a lesser grade of green marble.

Put me where I may look at him! True peach,
Rosy and flawless: how I earned the prize!
Draw close: that conflagration of my church
—What then? So much was saved if aught were missed! 35
My sons, ye would not be my death? Go dig
The white-grape vineyard where the oil-press stood,
Drop water gently till the surface sink,
And if ye find . . . Ah God, I know not, I! . . .
Bedded in store of rotten fig-leaves soft, 40
And corded up in a tight olive-frail,
Some lump, ah God, of lapis lazuli,
Big as a Jew's head cut off at the nape,
Blue as a vein o'er the Madonna's breast . . .
Sons, all have I bequeathed you, villas, all, 45
That brave Frascati villa with its bath,
So, let the blue lump poise between my knees,
Like God the Father's globe on both his hands
Ye worship in the Jesu Church so gay,
For Gandolf shall not choose but see and burst! 50
Swift as a weaver's shuttle fleet our years:
Man goeth to the grave, and where is he?
Did I say basalt for my slab, sons? Black—
'Twas ever antique-black I meant! How else
Shall ye contrast my frieze to come beneath? 55
The bas-relief in bronze ye promised me,
Those Pans and Nymphs ye wot of, and perchance
Some tripod, thyrsus, with a vase or so,
The Saviour at his sermon on the mount,
Saint Praxed in a glory, and one Pan 60
Ready to twitch the Nymph's last garment off,
And Moses with the tables . . . but I know
Ye mark me not! What do they whisper thee,
Child of my bowels, Anselm? Ah, ye hope
To revel down my villas while I gasp 65
Bricked o'er with beggar's mouldy travertine
Which Gandolf from his tomb-top chuckles at!
Nay, boys, ye love me—all of jasper, then!

41. *olive-frail:* basket made of rushes, for figs, raisins, olives, and so on.
42. *lapis lazuli:* a bright-blue semi-precious stone.
46. *Frascati:* a wealthy Roman suburb.
49. *Jesu Church:* the principal Jesuit church in Rome, off what came to be called the Corso Vittorio Emanuela.
51. *shuttle:* See Job 7:6.
54. *antique-black:* a grade of good marble.
56. *bas-relief:* a shallow carving or sculpture.
57. *Pans:* images of Greek nature deities.
58. *thyrsus:* a staff tipped with a pine cone, associated with the Greek god Bacchus.
62. *tables:* the stone tablets on which the Decalogue was inscribed.
66. *travertine:* a cheap, flaky Italian building stone.
68. *jasper:* reddish quartz.

'Tis jasper ye stand pledged to, lest I grieve.
My bath must needs be left behind, alas! 70
One block, pure green as a pistachio-nut,
There's plenty jasper somewhere in the world—
And have I not Saint Praxed's ear to pray
Horses for ye, and brown Greek manuscripts,
And mistresses with great smooth marbly limbs? 75
—That's if ye carve my epitaph aright,
Choice Latin, picked phrase, Tully's every word,
No gaudy ware like Gandolf's second line—
Tully, my masters? Ulpian serves his need!
And then how I shall lie through centuries, 80
And hear the blessed mutter of the mass,
And see God made and eaten all day long,
And feel the steady candle-flame, and taste
Good strong thick stupefying incense-smoke!
For as I lie here, hours of the dead night, 85
Dying in state and by such slow degrees,
I fold my arms as if they clasped a crook,
And stretch my feet forth straight as stone can point,
And let the bedclothes, for a mortcloth, drop
Into great laps and folds of sculptor's-work: 90
And as yon tapers dwindle, and strange thoughts
Grow, with a certain humming in my ears,
About the life before I lived this life.
And this life too, popes, cardinals and priests,
Saint Praxed at his sermon on the mount, 95
Your tall pale mother with her talking eyes,
And new-found agate urns as fresh as day,
And marble's language, Latin pure, discreet,
—Aha, *Elucescebat* quoth our friend?
No Tully, said I, Ulpian at the best! 100
Evil and brief hath been my pilgrimage.
All lapis, all, sons! Else I give the Pope
My villas! Will ye ever eat my heart?
Ever your eyes were as a lizard's quick,
They glitter like your mother's for my soul, 105
Or ye would heighten my impoverished frieze,
Piece out its starved design, and fill my vase

77. *Tully:* Cicero.
79. *Ulpian:* Ulpianus Domitius (170–228 A.D.), lawyer, secretary to Emperor Alexander Severus, writer of nonclassical Latin.
82. *eaten:* a reference to the sacrament of Communion.
87. *crook:* the bishop's crosier.
89. *mortcloth:* funeral pall or winding sheet.
95. *his sermon:* Browning's implication is evidently that the Bishop is unaware that St. Prassede was a woman.
99. *Elucescebat:* "He was illustrious," or "famous"; in classical Latin the word would be *elucebat. Elucescebat* is an example of the less elegant Latin associated with Ulpian's era.

With grapes, and add a vizor and a Term,
And to the tripod ye would tie a lynx
That in his struggle throws the thyrsus down, 110
To comfort me on my entablature
Whereon I am to lie till I must ask
'Do I live, am I dead?' There, leave me, there!
For ye have stabbed me with ingratitude
To death—ye wish it—God, ye wish it! Stone— 115
Gritstone, a-crumble! Clammy squares which sweat
As if the corpse they keep were oozing through—
And no more lapis to delight the world!
Well go! I bless ye. Fewer tapers there,
But in a row: and, going, turn your backs 120
—Ay, like departing altar-ministrants,
And leave me in my church, the church for peace,
That I may watch at leisure if he leers—
Old Gandolf, at me, from his onion-stone,
As still he envied me, so fair she was! 125

WALT WHITMAN
(1819–1892)
Song of Myself*

1

I celebrate myself, and sing myself,
And what I assume you shall assume,
For every atom belonging to me as good belongs to you.

I loafe and invite my soul,
I lean and loafe at my ease observing a spear of summer grass. 5

My tongue, every atom of my blood, form'd from this soil, this air,
Born here of parents born here from parents the same, and their
parents the same,
I, now thirty-seven years old in perfect health begin,
Hoping to cease not till death.

Creeds and schools in abeyance, 10
Retiring back a while sufficed at what they are, but never forgotten,

108. *vizor:* mask. *Term:* a carved head atop a square pedestal.
111. *entablature:* in classical architecture, the wall resting upon the columns, consisting of the architrave, frieze, and cornice.
116. *Gritstone:* a coarse, poor-grade sandstone.
* Selected sections. First published in 1855. Our text is from the 1891–1892 edition of *Leaves of Grass,* the so-called Deathbed Edition.

I harbor for good or bad, I permit to speak at every hazard,
Nature without check with original energy.

4

Trippers and askers surround me,
People I meet, the effect upon me of my early life or the ward and
city I live in, or the nation,
The latest dates, discoveries, inventions, societies, authors old and 15
new,
My dinner, dress, associates, looks, compliments, dues,
The real or fancied indifference of some man or woman I love,
The sickness of one of my folks or of myself, or ill-doing or loss or
lack of money, or depressions or exaltations,
Battles, the horrors of fratricidal war, the fever of doubtful news,
the fitful events; 20
These come to me days and nights and go from me again,
But they are not the Me myself.

Apart from the pulling and hauling stands what I am,
Stands amused, complacent, compassionating, idle, unitary,
Looks down, is erect, or bends an arm on an impalpable certain rest,
Looking with side-curved head curious what will come next, 26
Both in and out of the game and watching and wondering at it.

Backward I see in my own days where I sweated through fog with
linguists and contenders,
I have no mockings or arguments, I witness and wait.

7

Has any one supposed it lucky to be born? 30
I hasten to inform him or her it is just as lucky to die, and I know it.

I pass death with the dying and birth with the new-wash'd babe,
and am not contain'd between my hat and boots,
And peruse manifold objects, no two alike and every one good,
The earth good and the stars good, and their adjuncts all good.

I am not an earth nor an adjunct of an earth, 35
I am the mate and companion of people, all just as immortal and
fathomless as myself,
(They do not know how immortal, but I know.)

Every kind for itself and its own, for me mine male and female,
For me those that have been boys and that love women,
For me the man that is proud and feels how it stings to be slighted,
For me the sweet-heart and the old maid, for me mothers and the
mothers of mothers, 41
For me lips that have smiled, eyes that have shed tears,
For me children and the begetters of children.

Undrape! you are not guilty to me, nor stale nor discarded,
I see through the broadcloth and gingham whether or no, 45
And am around, tenacious, acquisitive, tireless, and cannot be shaken away.

16

I am of old and young, of the foolish as much as the wise,
Regardless of others, ever regardful of others,
Maternal as well as paternal, a child as well as a man,
Stuff'd with the stuff that is coarse and stuff'd with the stuff that is fine, 50
One of the Nation of many nations, the smallest the same and the largest the same,
A Southerner soon as a Northerner, a planter nonchalant and hospitable down by the Oconee I live,
A Yankee bound my own way ready for trade, my joints the limberest joints on earth and the sternest joints on earth,
A Kentuckian walking the vale of the Elkhorn in my deer-skin leggings, a Louisianian or Georgian,
A boatman over lakes or bays or along coasts, a Hoosier, Badger, Buckeye; 55
At home on Kanadian snow-shoes or up in the bush, or with fishermen off Newfoundland,
At home in the fleet of ice-boats, sailing with the rest and tacking,
At home on the hills of Vermont or in the woods of Maine, or the Texan ranch,
Comrade of Californians, comrade of free North-Westerners, (loving their big proportions,)
Comrade of raftsmen and coalmen, comrade of all who shake hands and welcome to drink and meat, 60
A learner with the simplest, a teacher of the thoughtfullest,
A novice beginning yet experient of myriads of seasons,
Of every hue and caste am I, of every rank and religion,
A farmer, mechanic, artist, gentleman, sailor, quaker,
Prisoner, fancy-man, rowdy, lawyer, physician, priest. 65

I resist any thing better than my own diversity,
Breathe the air but leave plenty after me,
And am not stuck up, and am in my place.

(The moth and the fish-eggs are in their place,
The bright suns I see and the dark suns I cannot see are in their place, 70
The palpable is in its place and the impalpable is in its place.)

21

I am the poet of the Body and I am the poet of the Soul,
The pleasures of heaven are with me and the pains of hell are with me,
The first I graft and increase upon myself, the latter I translate into a new tongue.

I am the poet of the woman the same as the man,
And I say it is as great to be a woman as to be a man,
And I say there is nothing greater than the mother of men.

I chant the chant of dilation or pride,
We have had ducking and deprecating about enough,
I show that size is only development. 80

Have you outstript the rest? are you the President?
It is a trifle, they will more than arrive there every one, and still pass on.

I am he that walks with the tender and growing night,
I call to the earth and sea half-held by the night.

Press close bare-bosom'd night—press close magnetic nourishing night! 85
Night of south winds—night of the large few stars!
Still nodding night—mad naked summer night.

Smile O voluptuous cool-breath'd earth!
Earth of the slumbering and liquid trees!
Earth of departed sunset—earth of the mountains misty-topt! 90
Earth of the vitreous pour of the full moon just tinged with blue!
Earth of shine and dark mottling the tide of the river!
Earth of the limpid gray of clouds brighter and clearer for my sake!
Far-swooping elbow'd earth—rich apple-blossom'd earth!
Smile, for your lover comes. 95

Prodigal, you have given me love—therefore I to you give love!
O unspeakable passionate love.

24

Walt Whitman, a kosmos, of Manhattan the son,
Turbulent, fleshy, sensual, eating, drinking and breeding,
No sentimentalist, no stander above men and women or apart from them, 100
No more modest than immodest.

Unscrew the locks from the doors!
Unscrew the doors themselves from their jambs!

Whoever degrades another degrades me,
And whatever is done or said returns at last to me. 105

Through me the afflatus surging and surging, through me the current and index.

I speak the pass-word primeval, I give the sign of democracy,
By God! I will accept nothing which all cannot have their counterpart of on the same terms.

. . .

32

I think I could turn and live with animals, they are so placid and self-contain'd,
I stand and look at them long and long. 110

They do not sweat and whine about their condition,
They do not lie awake in the dark and weep for their sins,
They do not make me sick discussing their duty to God,
Not one is dissatisfied, not one is demented with the mania of owning things,
Not one kneels to another, nor to his kind that lived thousands of years ago, 115
Not one is respectable or unhappy over the whole earth.
So they show their relations to me and I accept them,
They bring me tokens of myself, they evince them plainly in their possession.

I wonder where they get those tokens,
Did I pass that way huge times ago and negligently drop them? 120

Myself moving forward then and now and forever,
Gathering and showing more always and with velocity,
Infinite and omnigenous, and the like of these among them,
Not too exclusive toward the reachers of my remembrancers,
Picking out here one that I love, and now go with him on brotherly terms. 125

A gigantic beauty of a stallion, fresh and responsive to my caresses,
Head high in the forehead, wide between the ears,
Limbs glossy and supple, tail dusting the ground,
Eyes full of sparkling wickedness, ears finely cut, flexibly moving.

His nostrils dilate as my heels embrace him, 130
His well-built limbs tremble with pleasure as we race around and return.
I but use you a minute, then I resign you, stallion,
Why do I need your paces when I myself out-gallop them?
Even as I stand or sit passing faster than you.

46

I know I have the best of time and space, and was never measured and never will be measured. 135

I tramp a perpetual journey, (come listen all!)
My signs are a rain-proof coat, good shoes, and a staff cut from the woods,
No friend of mine takes his ease in my chair,
I have no chair, no church, no philosophy,
I lead no man to a dinner-table, library, exchange, 140
But each man and each woman of you I lead upon a knoll,
My left hand hooking you round the waist,
My right hand pointing to landscapes of continents and the public road.

Not I, not any one else can travel that road for you,
You must travel it for yourself. 145

It is not far, it is within reach,
Perhaps you have been on it since you were born and did not know,
Perhaps it is everywhere on water and on land.

Shoulder your duds dear son, and I will mine, and let us hasten forth,
Wonderful cities and free nations we shall fetch as we go. 150

. . .

51

The past and present wilt—I have fill'd them, emptied them,
And proceed to fill my next fold of the future.

Listener up there! what have you to confide to me?
Look in my face while I snuff the sidle of evening,
(Talk honestly, no one else hears you, and I stay only a minute longer.) 155

Do I contradict myself?
Very well then I contradict myself,
(I am large, I contain multitudes.)

I concentrate toward them that are nigh, I wait on the door-slab.

Who has done his day's work? who will soonest be through with
his supper? 160
Who wishes to walk with me?

Will you speak before I am gone? will you prove already too late?

52

The spotted hawk swoops by and accuses me, he complains of my
gab and my loitering.

I too am not a bit tamed, I too am untranslatable,
I sound my barbaric yawp over the roofs of the world. 165

The last scud of day holds back for me,
It flings my likeness after the rest and true as any on the shadow'd
wilds,
It coaxes me to the vapor and the dusk.

I depart as air, I shake my white locks at the runaway sun,
I effuse my flesh in eddies, and drift it in lacy jags. 170

I bequeath myself to the dirt to grow from the grass I love,
If you want me again look for me under your boot-soles.

You will hardly know who I am or what I mean,
But I shall be good health to you nevertheless,
And filter and fibre your blood. 175

Failing to fetch me at first keep encouraged,
Missing me one place search another,
I stop somewhere waiting for you.

Out of the Cradle Endlessly Rocking*

Out of the cradle endlessly rocking,
Out of the mocking-bird's throat, the musical shuttle,
Out of the Ninth-month midnight,
Over the sterile sands and the fields beyond, where the child leaving
his bed wander'd alone, bareheaded, barefoot,
Down from the shower'd halo, 5
Up from the mystic play of shadows twining and twisting as if they
were alive,
Out from the patches of briers and blackberries,

* First published in 1859 as "A Child's Reminiscence"; incorporated with the present title into the third edition of *Leaves of Grass* (1860).

3. *Ninth-month*: September, in Quaker usage.

From the memories of the bird that chanted to me,
From your memories sad brother, from the fitful risings and fallings
I heard,
From under that yellow half-moon late-risen and swollen as if with
tears, 10
From those beginning notes of yearning and love there in the mist,
From the thousand responses of my heart never to cease,
From the myriad thence-arous'd words,
From the word stronger and more delicious than any,
From such as now they start the scene revisiting, 15
As a flock, twittering, rising, or overhead passing,
Borne hither, ere all eludes me, hurriedly,
A man, yet by these tears a little boy again,
Throwing myself on the sand, confronting the waves,
I, chanter of pains and joys, uniter of here and hereafter, 20
Taking all hints to use them, but swiftly leaping beyond them,
A reminiscence sing.

Once Paumanok,
When the lilac-scent was in the air and Fifth-month grass was
growing,
Up this seashore in some briers, 25
Two feather'd guests from Alabama, two together,
And their nest, and four light-green eggs spotted with brown,
And every day the he-bird to and fro near at hand,
And every day the she-bird crouch'd on her nest, silent, with bright
eyes,
And every day I, a curious boy, never too close, never disturibing
them, 30
Cautiously peering, absorbing, translating.

Shine! shine! shine!
Pour down your warmth, great sun!
While we bask, we two together.

Two together! 35
Winds blow south, or winds blow north,
Day come white, or night come black,
Home, or rivers and mountains from home,
Singing all time, minding no time,
While we two keep together. 40

Till of a sudden,
Maybe kill'd, unknown to her mate,
One forenoon the she-bird crouch'd not on the nest,
Nor return'd that afternoon, nor the next,
Nor ever appear'd again. 45

23. *Paumanok*: The Indian name for Long Island, where Whitman grew up.

24. *Fifth-month*: May.

And thenceforward all summer in the sound of the sea,
And at night under the full of the moon in calmer weather,
Over the hoarse surging of the sea,
Or flitting from brier to brier by day,
I saw, I heard at intervals the remaining one, the he-bird, 50
The solitary guest from Alabama.

Blow! blow! blow!
Blow up sea-winds along Paumanok's shore;
I wait and I wait till you blow my mate to me.

Yes, when the stars glisten'd, 55
All night long on the prong of a moss-scallop'd stake,
Down almost amid the slapping waves,
Sat the lone singer wonderful causing tears.

He call'd on his mate,
He pour'd forth the meanings which I of all men know. 60

Yes my brother I know,
The rest might not, but I have treasur'd every note,
For more than once dimly down to the beach gliding,
Silent, avoiding the moonbeams, blending myself with the shadows,
Recalling now the obscure shapes, the echoes, the sounds and sights
after their sorts, 65
The white arms out in the breakers tirelessly tossing,
I, with bare feet, a child, the wind wafting my hair,
Listen'd long and long.

Listen'd to keep, to sing, now translating the notes,
Following you my brother. 70

Soothe! soothe! soothe!
Close on its wave soothes the wave behind,
And again another behind embracing and lapping, every one close,
But my love soothes not me, not me.

Low hangs the moon, it rose late, 75
It is lagging—O I think it is heavy with love, with love.

O madly the sea pushes upon the land,
With love, with love.

O night! do I not see my love fluttering out among the breakers?
What is that little black thing I see there in the white? 80

Loud! loud! loud!
Loud I call to you, my love!
High and clear I shoot my voice over the waves,
Surely you must know who is here, is here,
You must know who I am, my love. 85

Low-hanging moon!
What is that dusky spot in your brown yellow?
O it is the shape, the shape of my mate!
O moon do not keep her from me any longer.

Land! land! O land! 90
Whichever way I turn, O I think you could give me my mate back again if you only would,
For I am almost sure I see her dimly whichever way I look.

O rising stars!
Perhaps the one I want so much will rise, will rise with some of you.

O throat! O trembling throat! 95
Sound clearer through the atmosphere!
Pierce the woods, the earth,
Somewhere listening to catch you must be the one I want.

Shake out carols!
Solitary here, the night's carols! 100
Carols of lonesome love! death's carols!
Carols under that lagging, yellow, waning moon!
O under that moon where she droops almost down into the sea!
O reckless despairing carols.

But soft! sink low! 105
Soft! let me just murmur,
And do you wait a moment you husky-nois'd sea,
For somewhere I believe I heard my mate responding to me,
So faint, I must be still, be still to listen,
But not altogether still, for then she might not come immediately to me. 110

Hither my love!
Here I am! here!
With this just-sustain'd note I announce myself to you,
This gentle call is for you my love, for you.

Do not be decoy'd elsewhere, 115
That is the whistle of the wind, it is not my voice,
That is the fluttering, the fluttering of the spray,
Those are the shadows of leaves.

O darkness! O in vain!
O I am very sick and sorrowful. 120

O brown halo in the sky near the moon, drooping upon the sea!
O troubled reflection in the sea!
O throat! O throbbing heart!
And I singing uselessly, uselessly all the night.

O past! O happy life! O songs of joy! 125
In the air, in the woods, over fields,
Loved! loved! loved! loved! loved!
But my mate no more, no more with me!
We two together no more.

The aria sinking, 130
All else continuing, the stars shining,
The winds blowing, the notes of the bird continuous echoing,
With angry moans the fierce old mother incessantly moaning,
On the sands of Paumanok's shore gray and rustling,
The yellow half-moon enlarged, sagging down, drooping, the face of the sea almost touching, 135
The boy ecstatic, with his bare feet the waves, with his hair the atmosphere dallying,
The love in the heart long pent, now loose, now at last tumultously bursting,
The aria's meaning, the ears, the soul, swiftly depositing,
The strange tears down the cheeks coursing,
The colloquy there, the trio, each uttering, 140
The undertone, the savage old mother incessantly crying,
To the boy's soul's questions sullenly timing, some drown'd secret hissing,
To the outsetting bard.

Demon or bird! (said the boy's soul,)
Is it indeed toward your mate you sing? or is it really to me? 145
For I, that was a child, my tongue's use sleeping, now I have heard you,

Now in a moment I know what I am for, I awake,
And already a thousand singers, a thousand songs, clearer, louder and more sorrowful than yours,
A thousand warbling echoes have started to life within me, never to die.

O you singer solitary, singing by yourself, projecting me, 150
O solitary me listening, never more shall I cease perpetuating you,
Never more shall I escape, never more the reverberations,
Never more the cries of unsatisfied love be absent from me,
Never again leave me to be the peaceful child I was before what there in the night,
By the sea under the yellow and sagging moon, 155
The messenger there arous'd, the fire, the sweet hell within,
The unknown want, the destiny of me.

O give me the clue! (it lurks in the night here somewhere,)
O if I am to have so much, let me have more!

130. *aria*: A solo song, in opera.
137. *pent*: Shut in.
140. *trio*: Operatic ensemble of three singers.

A word then, (for I will conquer it,) 160
The word final, superior to all,
Subtle, sent up—what is it?—I listen;
Are you whispering it, and have been all the time, you sea-waves?
Is that it from your liquid rims and wet sands?

Whereto answering, the sea, 165
Delaying not, hurrying not,
Whisper'd me through the night, and very plainly before daybreak,
Lisp'd to me the low and delicious word death,
And again death, death, death, death,
Hissing melodious, neither like the bird nor like my arous'd child's
heart, 170
But edging near as privately for me rustling at my feet,
Creeping thence steadily up to my ears and laving me softly all
over,
Death, death, death, death, death.

Which I do not forget,
But fuse the song of my dusky demon and brother, 175
That he sang to me in the moonlight on Paumanok's gray beach,
With the thousand responsive songs at random,
My own songs awaked from that hour,
And with them the key, the word up from the waves,
The word of the sweetest song and all songs, 180
That strong and delicious word which, creeping to my feet,
(Or like some old crone rocking the cradle, swathed in sweet gar-
ments, bending aside,)
The sea whisper'd me.

A Noiseless Patient Spider*

A noiseless patient spider,
I mark'd where on a little promontory it stood isolated,
Mark'd how to explore the vacant vast surrounding,
It launch'd forth filament, filament, filament, out of itself,
Ever unreeling them, ever tirelessly speeding them. 5

And you O my soul where you stand,
Surrounded, detached, in measureless oceans of space,
Ceaselessly musing, venturing, throwing, seeking the spheres to
connect them,
Till the bridge you will need be form'd, till the ductile anchor hold,
Till the gossamer thread you fling catch somewhere, O my soul. 10

* First published 1862–1863; revised 1881.

EMILY DICKINSON

(1830–1886)

165[a]

A *Wounded* Deer—leaps highest—
I've heard the Hunter tell—
'Tis but the Ecstasy of *death*—
And then the Brake is still!

The *Smitten* Rock that gushes! 5
The *trampled* Steel that springs!
A Cheek is always redder
Just where the Hectic stings!

Mirth is the Mail of Anguish—
In which it Cautious Arm, 10
Lest anybody spy the blood
And "you're hurt" exclaim!

258[b]

There's a certain Slant of light,
Winter Afternoons—
That oppresses, like the Heft
Of Cathedral Tunes—

Heavenly Hurt, it gives us— 5
We can find no scar,
But internal difference,
Where the Meanings, are—

None may teach it—Any—
'Tis the Seal Despair— 10
An imperial affliction
Sent us of the Air—

When it comes, the Landscape listens—
Shadows—hold their breath—
When it goes, 'tis like the Distance 15
On the look of Death—

303[c]

The Soul selects her own Society—
Then—shuts the Door—
To her divine Majority—
Present no more—

a. Written *c.* 1860; published in 1890.
4. *Brake*: Thicket.
5. *Smitten Rock . . . gushes*: As when Moses struck a rock with his rod and it gave forth water for the Israelites to drink. [*Exodus* 17:6.]
8. *Hectic*: Fever, especially tuberculosis.
9. *Mail*: Armor.
b. Written *c.* 1861; published in 1890.
c. Written *c.* 1862; published in 1890.

Unmoved—she notes the Chariots—pausing 5
At her low Gate—
Unmoved—an Emperor be kneeling
Upon her Mat—

I've known her—from an ample nation—
Choose One— 10
Then—close the Valves of her attention—
Like Stone—

328[d]

A Bird came down the Walk—
He did not know I saw—
He bit an Angleworm in halves
And ate the fellow, raw,

And then he drank a Dew 5
From a convenient Grass—
And then hopped sidewise to the Wall
To let a Beetle pass—

He glanced with rapid eyes
That hurried all around— 10
They looked like frightened Beads, I thought—
He stirred his Velvet Head

Like one in danger, Cautious,
I offered him a Crumb
And he unrolled his feathers 15
And rowed him softer home—

Than Oars divide the Ocean,
Too silver for a seam—
Or Butterflies, off Banks of Noon
Leap, plashless as they swim. 20

341[e]

After great pain, a formal feeling comes—
The Nerves sit ceremonious, like Tombs—
The stiff Heart questions was it He, that bore,
And Yesterday, or Centuries before?

The Feet, merchanical, go round— 5
Of Ground, or Air, or Ought—
A Wooden way
Regardless grown,
A Quartz contentment, like a stone—

d. Written *c.* 1862; published in 1891.
e. Written *c.* 1862; published in 1929.

6. *Ought*: Zero.

This is the Hour of Lead— 10
Remembered, if outlived,
As Freezing persons, recollect the Snow—
First—Chill—then Stupor—then the letting go—

435[f]

Much Madness is divinest Sense—
To a discerning Eye—
Much Sense—the starkest Madness—
'Tis the Majority
In this, as All, prevail— 5
Assent—and you are sane—
Demur—you're straightway dangerous—
And handled with a Chain—

465[g]

I heard a Fly buzz—when I died—
The Stillness in the Room
Was like the Stillness in the Air—
Between the Heaves of Storm—

The Eyes around—had wrung them dry— 5
And Breaths were gathering firm
For that last Onset—when the King
Be witnessed—in the Room—

I willed my Keepsakes—Signed away
What portion of me be 10
Assignable—and then it was
There interposed a Fly—

With Blue—uncertain stumbling Buzz—
Between the light—and me—
And then the Windows failed—and then 15
I could not see to see—

585[h]

I like to see it lap the Miles—
And lick the Valleys up—
And stop to feed itself at Tanks—
And then—prodigious step

Around a Pile of Mountains— 5
And supercilious peer
In Shanties—by the sides of Roads—
And then a Quarry pare

To fit its Ribs
And crawl between 10

f. Written *c.* 1862; published in 1890.
g. Written *c.* 1862; published in 1896.
h. Written *c.* 1862; published in 1891.

Complaining all the while
In horrid—hooting stanza—
Then chase itself down Hill—

And neigh like Boanerges—
Then—punctual as a Star 15
Stop—docile and omnipotent
At its own stable door—

612[i]

It would have starved a Gnat—
To live so small as I—
And yet I was a living Child—
With Food's necessity

Upon me—like a Claw— 5
I could no more remove
Than I could coax a Leech away—
Or make a Dragon—move—

Nor like the Gnat—had I—
The privilege to fly 10
And seek a Dinner for myself—
How mightier He—than I—

Nor like Himself—the Art
Upon the Window Pane
To gad my little Being out— 15
And not begin—again—

632[j]

The Brain—is wider than the Sky—
For—put them side by side—
The one the other will contain
With ease—and You—beside—

The Brain is deeper than the sea— 5
For—hold them—Blue to Blue—
The one the other will absorb—
As Sponges—Buckets—do—

The Brain is just the weight of God—
For—Heft them—Pound for Pound— 10
And they will differ—if they do—
As Syllable from Sound—

657[k]

I dwell in Possibility—
A fairer House than Prose—

14. *Boanerges*: "Sons of thunder," name given by Jesus to the brothers and disciples James and John, presumably because they were thunderous preachers.

i. Written *c.* 1862; published in 1945.
j. Written *c.* 1862; published in 1896.
k. Written *c.* 1862; published in 1929.

More numberous of Windows—
Superior—for Doors—

Of Chambers as the Cedars— 5
Impregnable of Eye—
And for an Everlasting Roof
The Gambrels of the Sky—

Of Visitors—the fairest—
For Occupation—This— 10
The spreading wide my narrow Hands
To gather Paradise—

712[l]

Because I could not stop for Death—
He kindly stopped for me—
The Carriage held but just Ourselves—
And Immortality.

We slowly drove—He knew no haste 5
And I had put away
My labor and my leisure too,
For His Civility—

We passed the School, where Children strove
At Recess—in the Ring— 10
We passed the Fields of Gazing Grain—
We passed the Setting Sun—

Or rather—He passed Us—
The Dews drew quivering and chill—
For only Gossamer, my Gown— 15
My Tippet—only Tulle—

We paused before a House that seemed
A Swelling of the Ground—
The Roof was scarcely visible—
The Cornice—in the Ground— 20

Since then—'tis Centuries—and yet
Feels shorter than the Day
I first surmised the Horses' Heads
Were toward Eternity—

1129[m]

Tell all the Truth but tell it slant—
Success in Circuit lies
Too bright for our infirm Delight
The Truth's superb surprise
As Lightning to the Children eased 5

8. *Gambrels*: Slopes, as in the large, arched roofs often seen on barns.
l. Written *c.* 1863; published in 1890.

16. *Tippet*: A scarf, usually of heavy material. *Tulle*: Fine silken netting.
m. Written *c.* 1868; published in 1945.

With explanation kind
The Truth must dazzle gradually
Or every man be blind—

1207[n]

He preached upon "Breadth" till it argued him narrow—
The Broad are too broad to define
And of "Truth" until it proclaimed him a Liar—
The Truth never flaunted a Sign—

Simplicity fled from his counterfeit presence 5
As Gold the Pyrites would shun—
What confusion would cover the innocent Jesus
To meet so enabled a Man!

1551[o]

Those—dying then,
Knew where they went—
They went to God's Right Hand—
That Hand is amputated now
And God cannot be found— 5

The abdication of Belief
Makes the Behavior small—
Better an ignis fatuus
Than no illume at all—

1593[p]

There came a Wind like a Bugle—
It quivered through the Grass
And a Green Chill upon the Heat
So ominous did pass
We barred the Windows and the Doors 5
As from an Emerald Ghost—
The Doom's electric Moccasin
That very instant passed—
On a strange Mob of panting Trees
And Fences fled away 10
And Rivers where the Houses ran
Those looked that lived—that Day—
The Bell within the steeple wild
The flying tidings told—
How much can come 15
And much can go,
And yet abide the World!

n. Written *c.* 1872; published in 1891.
6. *Pyrites*: Iron bisulphide, sometimes called "fool's gold."
8. *enabled*: Competent.
o. Written *c.* 1882; published in 1945.
3. *God's Right Hand*: Reference is to the *Apostles' Creed*: "[Jesus Christ] sitteth on the right hand of God. . . ."
8. *ignis fatuus*: Will o' the wisp; a pale, flickering light sometimes seen over marshland at night and mistaken by travelers for a sign of human habitation, thus luring them on into the swamp.
p. Written *c.* 1883; published in 1891.
7. *Moccasin*: Or water moccasin, a poisonous snake.

HERMAN MELVILLE
(1819–1891)
Billy Budd*

Preface[1]

The year 1797, the year of this narrative, belongs to a period which as every thinker now feels, involved a crisis for Christendom not exceeded in its undetermined momentousness at the time by any other era whereof there is record. The opening proposition made by the Spirit of that Age involved rectification of the Old World's hereditary wrongs. In France, to some extent, this was bloodily effected. But what then? Straightway the Revolution itself become a wrong-doer, one more oppressive than the kings. Under Napoleon it enthroned upstart kings, and initiated that prolonged agony of continual war whose final throe was Waterloo. During those years not the wisest could have foreseen that the outcome of all would be what to some thinkers apparently it has since turned out to be—a political advance along nearly the whole line for Europeans.

Now, as elsewhere hinted, it was something caught from the Revolutionary Spirit that at Spithead emboldened the man-of-war's men to rise against real abuses, long-standing ones, and afterwards at the Nore to make inordinate and aggressive demands[2]—successful resistance to which was confirmed only when the ringleaders were

* Reprinted in its entirety by permission of the publishers from *Melville's Billy Budd*, edited by Frederick Barron Freeman and corrected by Elizabeth Treeman (Cambridge, Mass.: Harvard University Press). Copyright 1948, © 1956 by The President and Fellows of Harvard College.

The story was left as a semifinal draft by Melville at his death. It was posthumously published as *Billy Budd, Foretopman* in 1924, as a supplement to *The Works* * (1922-1924). This was not strictly edited, but subsequent editions have been based on it. The text below represents a collation with the original manuscript in the Houghton Library of Harvard University by Miss Treeman, an assistant editor of Harvard University Press. Where additional punctuation is absolutely necessary for clarity, it has been inserted in square brackets. A few interpolated words and all words not entirely clear in the manuscript have also been placed in square brackets. A few important variant readings left standing in the manuscript are shown in footnotes. Melville's chapter divisions are different from those in the 1924 edition, and we have followed his manuscript in this matter also. Spelling is corrected.**

In 1962 Harrison Hayford and Merton M. Sealts, Jr., published an edition that differs from the one printed here in several particulars of varying importance (they suggest, for example, that Melville's intended title was *Billy Budd / Sailor / An Inside Narrative*). As Lawrence Thompson has pointed out in *American Literature* (March, 1964), it will never be possible to determine Melville's precise intention in all its details. Consequently, major differences are mentioned in the footnotes, but no attempt has been made to record all minor disputed readings.

1. This preface appeared in the first publication of this work in 1924. Hayford and Sealts reject the preface.

2. There were a series of mutinies in the British fleet during the Napoleonic wars. The first, on April 15, 1797, was at the Spithead, the roadstead between Portsmouth and the Isle of Wight, and another was at a sandbank in the Thames estuary. The mutineers were all hanged.

hung for an admonitory spectacle to the anchored fleet. Yet in a way analogous to the operation of the Revolution at large—the Great Mutiny, though by Englishmen naturally deemed monstrous at the time, doubtless gave the first latent prompting to most important reforms in the British navy.

I

In the time before steamships, or then more frequently than now, a stroller along the docks of any considerable sea-port would occasionally have his attention arrested by a group of bronzed mariners, man-of-war's men or merchant-sailors in holiday attire ashore on liberty. In certain instances they would flank, or, like a body-guard quite surround some superior figure of their own class, moving along with them like Aldebaran among the lesser lights of his constellation.[3] That signal object was the "Handsome Sailor" of the less prosaic time alike of the military and merchant navies. With no perceptible trace of the vainglorious about him, rather with the off-hand unaffectedness of natural regality, he seemed to accept the spontaneous homage of his shipmates. A somewhat remarkable instance recurs to me. In Liverpool,[4] now half a century ago I saw under the shadow of the great dingy street-wall of Prince's Dock (an obstruction long since removed) a common sailor, so intensely black that he must needs have been a native African of the unadulterate blood of Ham.[5] A symmetric figure much above the average height. The two ends of a gay silk handkerchief thrown loose about the neck danced upon the displayed ebony of his chest; in his ears were big hoops of gold, and a Scotch Highland bonnet with a tartan band set off his shapely head.

It was a hot noon in July; and his face, lustrous with persipiration, beamed with barbaric good humor. In jovial sallies right and left[,] his white teeth flashing into view, he rollicked along, the centre of a company of his shipmates. These were made up of such an assortment of tribes and complexions as would have well fitted them to be marched up by Anacharsis Cloots before the bar of the first French Assembly as Representatives of the Human Race.[6] At each spon-

3. a star of the first magnitude in the constellation of Taurus (the "Bull"), frequently used in navigation.

4. Melville served abroad the Liverpool packet *St. Lawrence* on his first sea voyage; his novel *Redburn* (1849) documents some of his experiences in Liverpool.

5. The word *Ham* derives from the Hebrew for "swarthy". Ham, the second son of Noah, was cursed by his father for mocking him. Later, it was thought that a black skin was the result of the curse. "Hamitic" languages include Somali, Berber, Tuareg, and Galla.

6. Jean Baptiste du Val-de-Grâce, Baron de Cloots (1755-1794) is mentioned in Carlyle's *French Revolution.* Cloots, or Clootz, assembled a crowd of assorted nationalities and introduced them at the French National Assembly during the Revolution. Cloots' zany idealism appealed to Melville, and he described the crew of the *Pequod* in *Moby Dick* as "an Anarcharsis Clootz deputation from all the isles of the sea."

taneous tribute rendered by the wayfarers to this black pagod[7] of a fellow—the tribute of a pause and stare, and less frequent an exclamation,—the motley retinue showed that they took that sort of pride in the evoker of it which the Assyrian priests doubtless showed for their grand sculptured Bull when the faithful prostrated themselves.[8]

To return.

If in some cases a bit of a nautical Murat[9] in setting forth his person ashore, the handsome sailor of the period in question evinced nothing of the dandified Billy-be-Damn, an amusing character all but extinct now, but occasionally to be encountered, and in a form yet more amusing than the original, at the tiller of the boats on the tempestuous Erie Canal or, more likely, vaporing in the groggeries along the tow-path. Invariably a proficient in his perilous calling, he was also more or less of a mighty boxer or wrestler. It was strength and beauty. Tales of his prowess were recited. Ashore he was the champion; afloat the spokesman; on every suitable occasion always foremost. Close-reefing topsails in a gale, there he was, astride the weather yard-arm-end foot in the Flemish horse as "stirrup," both hands tugging at the "earring" as at a bridle, in very much the attitude of young Alexander curbing the fiery Bucephalus.[10] A superb figure, tossed up as by the horns of Taurus[11] against the thunderous sky, cheerily hallooing to the strenuous file along the spar.

The moral nature was seldom out of keeping with the physical make. Indeed, except as toned by the former, the comeliness and power, always attractive in masculine conjunction, hardly could have drawn the sort of honest homage the Handsome Sailor in some examples received from his less gifted associates.

Such a cynosure, at least in aspect, and something such too in nature, though with important variations made apparent as the story proceeds, was welkin-eyed[12] Billy Budd, or Baby Budd as more familiarly under circumstances hereafter to be given he at last came to be called[,] aged twenty-one, a foretopman[13] of the British fleet toward the close of the last decade of the eighteenth century. It was not very long prior to the time of the narration that follows that he had entered the King's Service, having been impressed on the Narrow Seas from a homeward-bound English merchantman into a seventy-four

7. pagoda.

8. In Assyrian bas-reliefs, the bull is prominent as a figure of worship.

9. Joachim Murat (1767-1815), Marshal of France and king of Naples, was Napoleon's brother-in-law and famous chiefly as a playboy and dandy.

10. Melville is alluding to one of the most hazardous activities engaged in by a sailor on a square-rigged ship. The "Flemish horse" was the footrope beneath the yard whose sail he was furling. Bucephalus (Greek: "ox-headed") was Alexander the Great's horse.

11. *Cf.* note 3.

12. eyes accustomed to looking at the vaulted heavens above.

13. junior to a maintopman like Jack Chase.

outward-bound, H.M.S. *Indomitable*[14]; which ship, as was not unusual in those hurried days having been obliged to put to sea short of her proper complement of men. Plump upon Billy at first sight in the gangway the boarding officer Lieutenant Ratcliffe pounced, even before the merchantman's crew was formally mustered on the quarter-deck[15] for his deliberate inspection. And him only he elected. For whether it was because the other men when ranged before him showed to ill advantage after Billy, or whether he had some scruples in view of the merchantman being rather short-handed, however it might be, the officer contented himself with his first spontaneous choice. To the surprise of the ship's company, though much to the Lieutenant's satisfaction Billy made no demur. But, indeed, any demur would have been as idle as the protest of a goldfinch popped into a cage.

Noting this uncomplaining acquiescence, all but cheerful one might say, the shipmates turned a surprised glance of silent reproach at the sailor. The shipmaster was one of those worthy mortals found in every vocation even the humbler ones—the sort of person whom everybody agrees in calling "a respectable man." And—nor so strange to report as it may appear to be—though a ploughman of the troubled waters, life-long contending with the intractable elements, there was nothing this honest soul at heart loved better than simple peace and quiet. For the rest, he was fifty or thereabouts, a little inclined to corpulence, a prepossessing face unwhiskered, and of an agreeable color—a rather full face, humanely intelligent in expression. On a fair day with a fair wind and all going well, a certain musical chime in his voice seemed to be the veritable unobstructed outcome of the innermost man. He had much prudence, much conscientiousness, and there were occasions when these virtues were the cause of overmuch disquietude in him. On a passage, so long as his craft was in any proximity to land, no sleep for Captain Graveling. He took to heart those serious responsibilities not so heavily borne by some shipmasters.

Now while Billy Budd was down in the forecastle getting his kit together, the *Indomitable*'s lieutenant, burly and bluff, nowise disconcerted by Captain Graveling's omitting to proffer the customary hospitalities on an occassion so unwelcome to him, an omission simply caused by preoccupation of thought, unceremoniously invited

14. British naval commanders were then permitted by law to complete the complement of their crews by "impressing" (forcing into service aboard their own ships) foreign seamen. The Narrow Seas: the English Channel and the waters between England and Ireland. A *seventy-four* ship: a third-rate ship of the line, equivalent to a light cruiser today; the rating referred only to the number of guns.

15. the ceremonial part of the ship, near the stern.

himself into the cabin, and also to a flask from the spirit-locker, a receptacle which his experienced eye instantly discovered. In fact he was one of those sea-dogs in whom all the hardship and peril of naval life in the great prolonged wars of his time never impaired the natural instinct for sensuous enjoyment. His duty he always faithfully did; but duty is sometimes a dry obligation, and he was for irrigating its aridity, whensoever possible, with a fertilizing decoction of strong waters. For the cabin's proprietor there was nothing left but to play the part of the enforced host with whatever grace and alacrity were practicable. As necessary adjuncts to the flask, he silently placed tumbler and water-jug before the irrepressible guest. But excusing himself from partaking just then, [he] dismally watched the unembarrassed office deliberately diluting his grog a little, then tossing it off in three swallows, pushing the empty tumbler away, yet not so far as to be beyond easy reach, at the same [time] settling himself in his seat and smacking his lips with high satisfaction, looking straight at the host.

These proceedings over, the Master broke the silence; and there lurked a rueful reproach in the tone of his voice; "Lieutenant, you are going to take my best man from me, the jewel of 'em."

"Yes, I know" rejoined the other, immediately drawing back the tumbler preliminary to a replenishing; "Yes, I know. Sorry."

"Beg pardon, but you don't understand, Lieutenant. See here now. Before I shipped that young fellow, my forecastle[16] was a rat-pit of quarrels. It was black times, I tell you, aboard the '*Rights*' here.[17] I was worried to that degree my pipe had no comfort for me. But Billy came; and it was like a Catholic priest striking peace in an Irish shindy.[18] Not that he preached to them or said or did anything in particular; but a virtue went out of him, sugaring the sour ones. They took to him like hornets to treacle; all but the buffer of the gang, the big shaggy chap with the fire-red whiskers. He indeed out of envy, perhaps, of the newcomer, and thinking such a 'sweet and pleasant fellow,' as he mockingly designated him to the others, could hardly have the spirit of a game-cock, must needs bestir himself in trying to get up an ugly row with him. Billy forebore with him and reasoned with him in a pleasant way—he is something like myself, lieutenant, to whom aught like a quarrel is hateful—but nothing served. So, in the second dog-watch[19] one day the Red Whiskers

16. the forepart, or foc'sle, of a ship, where ordinary seamen lived.

17. Named for Thomas Paine's *The Rights of Man* (1791), a defense of the French Revolution. Melville may have chosen the name to underscore the political theme of the tale.

18. originally a spree, here associated with a row or a fight.

19. At sea the day is divided into six four-hour watches. The 4 to 8 p.m. watch is further divided into two short or "dogged" watches of two hours each in order to rotate the time of day that any given crew member stands watch.

in presence of the others, under pretence of showing Billy just whence a sirloin steak was cut—for the fellow had once been a butcher—insultingly gave him a dig under the ribs. Quick as lightning Billy let fly his arm. I dare say he never meant to do quite as much as he did, but anyhow he gave the burly fool a terrible drubbing. It took about half a minute, I should think. And, lord bless you, the lubber was astonished at the celerity. And will you believe it, Lieutenant, the Red Whiskers now really loves Billy—loves him, or is the biggest hypocrite that ever I heard of. But they all love him. Some of 'em do his washing, darn his old trousers for him; the carpenter is at odd times making a pretty little chest of drawers for him. Anybody will do anything for Billy Budd; and it's the happy family here. But now, Lieutenant, if that young fellow goes—I know how it will be aboard the '*Rights*.' Not again very soon shall I, coming up from dinner, lean over the capstan smoking a quiet pipe—no, not very soon again, I think. Ay, Lieutenant, you are going to take away the jewel of 'em; you are going to take away my peacemaker!" And with that the good soul had really some ado in checking a rising sob.

"Well," said the officer who had listened with amused interest to all this, and now waxing merry with his tipple; "Well, blessed are the peacemakers especially the fighting peacemakers! And such are the seventy-four beauties some of which you see poking their noses out of the port-holes of yonder war-ship lying-to for me" pointing thro' the cabin window at the *Indomitable*. "But courage! don't look so downhearted, man. Why, I pledge you in advance the royal approbation. Rest assured that His Majesty will be delighted to know that in a time when his hard tack[20] is not sought for by sailors with such avidity as should be; a time also when some shipmasters privily resent the borrowing from them a tar or two for the service; His Majesty, I say, will be delighted to learn that *one* shipmaster at least cheerfully surrenders to the King, the flower of his flock, a sailor who with equal loyalty makes no dissent.—But where's my beauty? Ah," looking through the cabin's open door "Here he comes; and by Jove—lugging along his chest—Apollo with his portmanteau!—My man," stepping out to him, "you can't take that big box aboard a warship. The boxes there are mostly shot-boxes. Put your duds in a bag, lad. Boot and saddle for the cavalryman, bag and hammock for the man-of-war's man."

The transfer from chest to bag was made. And, after seeing his man into the cutter and then following him down, the lieutenant pushed off from the *Rights-of-Man*. That was the merchant-ship's

20. literally, a biscuit; often, all shipboard fare.

name; tho' by her master and crew abbreviated in sailor fashion into the *Rights.* The hard-headed Dundee[21] owner was a staunch admirer of Thomas Paine whose book in rejoinder to Burke's arraignment of the French Revolution had then been published for some time and had gone everywhere. In christening his vessel after the title of Paine's volume the man of Dundee was something like his contemporary shipowner, Stephen Girard[22] of Philadelphia, whose sympathies, alike with his native land and its liberal philosophers, he evinced by naming his ships after Voltaire, Diderot, and so forth.

But now, when the boat swept under the merchant-man's stern, and officer and oarsmen were noting—some bitterly and others with a grin,—the name emblazoned there; just then it was that the new recruit jumped up from the bow where the coxswain[23] had directed him to sit, and waving [his] hat to his silent shipmates sorrowfully looking over at him from the taffrail,[24] bade the lads a genial good-bye. Then, making a salutation as to the ship herself, "And good-bye to you too, old *Rights of Man.*"

"Down, Sir!" roared the lieutenant, instantly assuming all the rigor of his rank, though with difficulty repressing a smile.

To be sure, Billy's action was a terrible breach of naval decorum. But in that decorum he had never been instructed; in consideration of which the lieutenant would hardly have been so energetic in reproof but for the concluding farewell to the ship. This he rather took as meant to convey a covert sally on the new recruit's part, a sly slur at impressment in general, and that of himself in especial. And yet, more likely, if satire it was in effect, it was hardly so by intention, for Billy tho' happily endowed with the gayety of high health, youth, and a free heart, was yet by no means of a satirical turn. The will to it and the sinister dexterity were alike wanting. To deal in double meanings and insinuations of any sort was quite foreign to his nature.

As to his enforced enlistment, that he seemed to take pretty much as he was wont to take any vicissitude of weather. Like the animals, though no philosopher, he was, without knowing it, practically a fatalist. And, it may be, that he rather liked his adventurous turn in his affairs, which promised an opening into novel scenes and martial excitements.

Aboard the *Indomitable* our merchant-sailor was forthwith rated as an able-seaman and assigned to the starboard watch of the foretop.[25] He was soon at home in the service, not at all disliked for

21. a port on the Firth of Tay in Scotland.

22. Girard (1750-1831), who emigrated from France when he was twenty-seven, became a wealthy banker and shipowner.

23. a petty-officer, the helmsman of a small boat.

24. at the stern of a ship.

25. The three ascending grades are ordinary, able, and leading seamen. Another grouping is: boys, able-bodied seamen, and ordinary seamen. A ship's crew is divided into port and starboard watches. The foretop watch assigned to Billy suggests his excellence as a seaman; according to Melville, this station was superior to a watch at the waist ot

his unpretentious good looks and a sort of genial happy-go-lucky air. No merrier man in his mess; in marked contrast to certain other individuals included like himself among the impressed portion of the ship's company; for these when not actively employed were sometimes, and more particularly in the last dog-watch when the drawing near of twilight induced revery, apt to fall into a saddish mood which in some partook of sullenness. But they were not so young as our foretopman, and no few of them must have known a hearth of some sort, others may have had wives and children left, too probably, in uncertain circumstances, and hardly any but must have had acknowledged kith and kin, while for Billy, as will shortly be seen, his entire family was practically invested in himself.

2

Though our new-made foretopman was well received in the top and on the gun-decks, hardly here was he that cynosure he had previously been among those minor ship's companies of the merchant marine, with which companies only had he hitherto consorted.

He was young; and despite his all but fully developed frame in aspect looked even younger than he really was, owing to a lingering adolescent expression in the as yet smooth face all but feminine in purity of natural complexion but where, thanks to his seagoing, the lily was quite suppressed and the rose had some ado visibly to flush through the tan.

To one essentially such a novice in the complexities of factitious life, the abrupt transition from his former and simpler sphere to the ampler and more knowing world of a great warship; this might well have abashed him had there been any conceit or vanity in his composition. Among her miscellaneous multitude, the *Indomitable* mustered several individuals who however inferior in grade were of no common natural stamp, sailors more signally susceptive of that air which continuous martial discipline and repeated presence in battle can in some degree impart even to the average man. As the *handsome sailor* Billy Budd's position aboard the seventy-four was something analogous to that of a rustic beauty transplanted from the provinces and brought into competition with the highborn dames of the court. But this change of circumstances he scarce noted. As little did he observe that something about him provoked an ambiguous smile in one or two harder faces among the blue-jackets. Nor less unaware was he of the peculiar favorable effect his person and demeanor had upon the more intelligent gentlemen of the quarter-deck.[26] Nor could this well have been otherwise. Cast in a mould peculiar to the finest physical examples of those Englishmen in whom the Saxon strain would seem not at all to partake of any Norman or other admixture, he showed in face that humane look

a ship or the afterguard, both of which entailed deck duties.

26. the officers.

of reposeful good nature which the Greek sculptor in some instances gave to his heroic strong man, Hercules. But this again was subtly modified by another and pervasive quality. The ear, small and shapely, the arch of the foot, the curve in mouth and nostril, even the indurated hand dyed to the orange-tawny of the toucan's bill,[27] a hand telling alike of the halyards[28] and tar-bucket; but, above all, something in the mobile expression, and every chance attitude and movement, something suggestive of a mother eminently favored by Love and the Graces; all this strangely indicated a lineage in direct contradiction to his lot. The mysteriousness here, became less mysterious through a matter-of-fact elicited when Billy at the capstan was being formally mustered into the service. Asked by the officer, a small brisk little gentleman as it chanced among other questions, his place of birth, he replied, "Please, Sir, I don't know."

"Don't know where you were born?—Who was your father?"

"God knows, Sir."

Struck by the straightforward simplicity of these replies, the officer next asked "Do you know anything about your beginning?"

"No, Sir. But I have heard that I was found in a pretty silk-lined basket hanging one morning from the knocker of a good man's door in Bristol[.]"[29]

"*Found* say you? Well," throwing back his head and looking up and down the new recruit; "Well[,] it turns out to have been a pretty good find. Hope they'll find some more like you, my man; the fleet sadly needs them."

Yes, Billy Budd was a foundling, a presumable bye-blow,[30] and, evidently, no ignoble one. Noble descent was as evident in him as in a blood horse.

For the rest, with little or no sharpness of faculty or any trace of the wisdom of the serpent, nor yet quite a dove,[31] he possessed that kind and degree of intelligence going along with the unconventional rectitude of a sound human creature, one to whom not yet has been proffered the questionable apple of knowledge. He was illiterate; he could not read, but he could sing, and like the illiterate nightingale was sometimes the composer of his own song.

Of self-consciousness he seemed to have little or none, or about as much as we may reasonably impute to a dog of Saint Bernard's breed.

Habitually living with the elements and knowing little more of the land than as a beach, or, rather, that portion of the terraqueous globe

27. *toucans:* birds, noted for their large bill and striking coloration, inhabiting the tropical regions of South and Central America.

28. ropes used to raise and lower or to "haul the yards," the spars from which the square sails are suspended.

29. a major English seaport.

30. Usually "by-blow," an illegitimate child.

31. *Cf.* Matthew 10:16: "Behold, I send you forth as sheep in the midst of wolves: be ye therefore as wise as serpents, and harmless as doves."

providentially set apart for dance-houses doxies and tapsters, in short what sailors call a "fiddlers' green,"[32] his simple nature remained unsophisticated by those moral obliquities which are not in every case incompatible with that manufacturable thing known as respectability. But are sailors, frequenters of "fiddlers'-greens," without vices? No; but less often than with landsmen do their vices, so called, partake of crookedness of heart, seeming less to proceed from viciousness than exuberance of vitality after long constraint; frank manifestations in accordance with natural law. By his original constitution aided by the cooperating influences of his lot, Billy in many respects was little more than a sort of upright barbarian, much such perhaps as Adam presumably might have been ere the urbane Serpent wriggled himself into his company.

And here be it submitted that apparently going to corroborate the doctrine of man's fall, a doctrine now popularly ignored, it is observable that where certain virtues pristine and unadulterate peculiarly characterize anybody in the external uniform of civilization, they will upon scrutiny seem not to be derived from custom or convention, but rather to be out of keeping with these, as if indeed exceptionally transmitted from a period prior to Cain's city[33] and citified man. The character marked by such qualities has to an unvitiated taste an untampered-with flavor like that of berries, while the man thoroughly civilized even in a fair specimen of the breed has to the same moral palate a questionable smack as of a compounded wine. To any stray inheritor of these primitive qualities found, like Caspar Hauser,[34] wandering dazed in any Christian capital of our time the good-natured poet's famous invocation, near two thousand years ago, of the good rustic out of his latitude in the Rome of the Cesars, still appropriately holds:—

> "Honest and poor, faithful in word and thought
> What has thee, Fabian, to the city brought."[35]

Though our Handsome Sailor had as much of masculine beauty as one can expect anywhere to see; nevertheless, like the beautiful woman in one of Hawthorne's minor tales,[36] there was just one thing amiss in him. No visible blemish indeed, as with the lady; no, but an occasional liability to a vocal defect. Though in the hour of elemental uproar or peril, he was everything that a sailor should be, yet under sudden provocation of strong heart-feeling his voice otherwise singularly musical, as if expressive of the harmony within, was apt to

32. *doxies:* prostitutes. *fiddler's green:* a sailor's utopia.

33. *i.e.,* in the time of the Garden of Eden. Cain "builded a city" in *Genesis* 4:16-17.

34. a German foundling (1817-1833) who claimed to have been brought up in a primitive wildness. In his autobiography (1828), he described his childhood as a prisoner.

35. Martial, *Epigrams,* I. iv. 1-2; Cowley's translation in the Bohn edition.

36. *The Birthmark.*

develop an organic hesitancy, in fact more or less of a stutter or even worse. In this particular Billy was a striking instance that the arch interferer, the envious marplot of Eden[37] still has more or less to do with every human consignment to this planet of earth. In every case, one way or another he is sure to slip in his little card, as much as to remind us—I too have a hand here.

The avowal of such an imperfection in the Handsome Sailor should be evidence not alone that he is not presented as a conventional hero, but also that the story in which he is the main figure is no romance.

3

At the time of Billy Budd's arbitrary enlistment into the *Indomitable* that ship was on her way to join the Mediterranean fleet. No long time elasped before the junction was effected. As one of that fleet the seventy-four participated in its movements, tho' at times on account of her superior sailing qualities, in the absence of frigates,[38] despatched on separate duty as a scout and at times on less temporary service. But with all this the story has little concernment, restricted as it is to the inner life of one particular ship and the career of an individual sailor.

It was the summer of 1797. In the April of that year had occurred the commotion at Spithead followed in May by a second and yet more serious outbreak in the fleet at the Nore. The latter is known, and without exaggeration in the epithet, as the Great Mutiny. It was indeed a demonstration more menacing to England than the contemporary manifestoes and conquering and proselyting armies of the French Directory.[39]

To the British Empire the Nore Mutiny was what a strike in the fire-brigade would be to London threatened by general arson. In a crisis when the kingdom might well have anticipated the famous signal that some years later published along the naval line of battle what it was that upon occasion England expected of Englishmen,[40] *that* was the time when at the mast-heads of the three-deckers and seventy-fours moored in her own roadstead—a fleet, the right arm of a Power then all but the sole free conservative one of the Old World, the blue-jackets, to be numbered by thousands[,] ran up with huzzas the British colors with the union and cross wiped out;[41] by that cancellation transmuting the flag of founded law and freedom defined, into the enemy's red meteor of unbridled and unbounded

37. *marplot:* one who destroys or defeats a plot or design; here, Satan.
38. ships mounting from 28 to 60 guns chiefly on the main deck, too small for line of battle.
39. the five directors who governed France from 1795 to 1799.
40. A reference to Lord Nelson's signal before the battle at Trafalgar (October 21, 1805): "England expects every man to do his duty!"
41. the British Union Jack, with the crosses of St. Andrew, St. George, and St. Patrick (the patron saints of Scotland, England, and Ireland).

revolt. Reasonable discontent growing out of practical grievances in the fleet had been ignited into irrational combustion as by live cinders blown across the Channel from France in flames.

The event converted into irony for a time those spirited strains of Dibdin[42]—as a song-writer no mean auxiliary to the English Government at the European conjuncture—strains celebrating, among other things, the patriotic devotion of the British tar:

"And as for my life, 'tis the Kings!"

Such an episode in the Island's grand naval story her naval historians naturally abridge; one of them (G.P.R. James) candidly acknowledging that fain would he pass it over did not "impartiality forbid fastidiousness." And yet his mention is less a narration than a reference, having to do hardly at all with details. Nor are these readily to be found in the libraries. Like some other events in every age befalling states everywhere including America the Great Mutiny was of such character that national pride along with views of policy would fain shade it off into the historical background. Such events can not be ignored, but there is a considerate way of historically treating them. If a well-constituted individual refrains from blazoning aught amiss or calamitous in his family; a nation in the like circumstance may without reproach be equally discreet.

Though after parleyings between Government and the ringleaders, and concessions by the former as to some glaring abuses, the first uprising—that at Spithead—with difficulty was put down, or matters for the time pacified; yet at the Nore the unforeseen renewal of insurrection on a yet larger scale, and emphasized in the conferences that ensued by demands deemed by the authorities not only inadmissible but aggressively insolent, indicated—if the Red Flag did not sufficiently do so[—]what was the spirit animating the men. Final suppression, however, there was; but only made possible perhaps by the unswerving loyalty of the marine corps a[nd] voluntary resumption of loyalty among influential sections of the crews.

To some extent the Nore Mutiny may be regarded as analogous to the distempering irruption of contagious fever in a frame constitutionally sound, and which anon throws it off.

At all events, of these thousands of mutineers were some of the tars who not so very long afterwards—whether wholly prompted thereto by patriotism, or pugnacious instinct, or by both,—helped to win a coronet for Nelson at the Nile, and the naval crown of crowns for him at Trafalgar.[43] To the mutineers those battles and especially

42. Charles Dibdin (1745-1814), English dramatist, chiefly remembered for his sea chanteys.

43. A reference to Nelson's victory over the French (at Aboukir) in 1798, for which he was made a baronet; his victory at Trafalgar (1805) is considered one of the greatest in naval history.

Trafalgar were a plenary absolution and a grand one: For all that goes to make up scenic naval display, heroic magnificence in arms, those battles especially Trafalgar stand unmatched in human annals.

4

Concerning "The greatest sailor since the world began."

Tennyson?[44]

In this matter of writing, resolve as one may to keep to the main road, some by-paths have an enticement not readily to be withstood. I am going to err into such a by-path. If the reader will keep me company I shall be glad. At the least we can promise ourselves that pleasure which is wickedly said to be in sinning, for a literary sin the divergence will be.

Very likely it is no new remark that the inventions of our time have at last brought about a change in sea-warfare in degree corresponding to the revolution in all warfare effected by the original introduction from China into Europe of gunpowder. The first European fire-arm, a clumsy contrivance, was, as is well known, scouted by no few of the knights as a base implement, good enough peradventure for weavers too craven to stand up crossing steel with steel in frank fight. But as ashore knightly valor tho' shorn of its blazonry did not cease with the knights, neither on the seas though nowadays in encounters there a certain kind of displayed gallantry be fallen out of date as hardly applicable under changed circumstances, did the nobler qualities of such naval magnates as Don John of Austria, Doria, Van Tromp, Jean Bart, the long line of British Admirals and the American Decaturs of 1812 become obsolete with their wooden walls.[45]

Nevertheless, to anybody who can hold the Present at its worth without being inappreciative of the Past, it may be forgiven, if to such an one the solitary old hulk at Portsmouth, Nelson's *Victory*,[46] seems to float there, not alone as the decaying monument of a fame incorruptible, but also as a poetic reproach, softened by its picturesqueness, to the *Monitors*[47] and yet mightier hulls of the Euro-

44. The question mark inserted by Melville suggests that he intended to check it before publication. The quotation is line 7 in Tennyson's "Ode on the Death of the Duke of Wellington" (1852); it should read, "The greatest sailor since our world began."

45. Don Juan of Austria (1547-1578) commanded the fleet of the Holy League against the Turks at Lepanto in 1571, the last major sea battle where oaredships predominated; Andrea Doria (1468-1560) liberated Genoa from the Turks; Maarten Van Tromp (1596-1653) was a Dutch admiral who fought successfully against the English under Charles II; Jean Bart (1651?-1702) was a French captain who battled the Dutch; Stephen Decatur (1779-1820) is best remembered for his victories over the Barbary Coast pirates at Tripoli and his over the British in the War of 1812. *wooden walls:* Iron-clad ships (see note 47) made all wooden ships obsolete.

46. Nelson's flagship at Trafalgar, still moored at Portsmouth.

47. John Ericsson's ironclad, launched in 1862 to fight the Confederate *Merrimac;* that battle effectively ended the era of wooden and sail-propelled battleships.

pean iron-clads. And this not altogether because such craft are unsightly, unavoidably lacking the symmetry and grand lines of the old battle-ships, but equally for other reasons.

There are some, perhaps, who while not altogether inaccessible to that poetic reproach just alluded to, may yet on behalf of the new order, be disposed to parry it; and this to the extent of iconoclasm, if need be. For example, prompted by the sight of the star inserted in the *Victory's* quarter-deck designating the spot where the Great Sailor fell, these martial utilitarians may suggest considerations implying that Nelson's ornate publication of his person in battle was not only unnecessary, but not military, nay, savored of foolhardiness and vanity. They may add, too, that at Trafalgar it was in effect nothing less than a challenge to death; and death came; and that but for his bravado the victorious Admiral might possibly have survived the battle, and so, instead of having his sagacious dying injunctions overruled by his immediate successor in command he himself when the contest was decided might have brought his shattered fleet to anchor, a proceeding which might have averted the deplorable loss of life by shipwreck in the elemental tempest that followed the martial one.

Well, should we set aside the more disputable point whether for various reasons it was possible to anchor the fleet, then plausibly enough the Benthamites[48] of war may urge the above.

But the *might-have-been* is but boggy ground to build on. And, certainly, in foresight as to the larger issue of an encounter, and anxious preparations for it—buoying the deadly way and mapping it out, as at Copenhagen[49]—few commanders have been so painstakingly circumspect as this same reckless declarer of his person in fight.

Personal prudence even when dictated by quite other than selfish considerations surely is no special virtue in a military man; while an excessive love of glory, impassioning a less burning impulse, the honest sense of duty, is the first. If the name *Wellington* is not so much of a trumpet to the blood as the simpler name *Nelson*, the reason for this may perhaps be inferred from the above. Alfred[50] in his funeral ode on the victor of Waterloo ventures not to call him the greatest soldier of all time, tho' in the same ode he invokes Nelson as "the greatest sailor since the world began."

At Trafalgar Nelson on the brink of opening the fight sat down and wrote his last brief will and testament. If under the presentiment of the most magnificent of all victories to be crowned by his

48. Utilitarian thinkers and followers of Jeremy Bentham (1748-1832), famous for his theory that "the greatest happiness of the greatest number is the foundation of morals and legislation." Melville uses the word derogatively.

49. another of Nelson's victories, in 1801.

50. Tennyson; *cf.* note 44.

own glorious death, a sort of priestly motive led him to dress his person in the jewelled vouchers of his own shining deeds; if thus to have adorned himself for the altar and the sacrifice were indeed vainglory, then affection and fustian is each more heroic line in the great epics and dramas, since in such lines the poet but embodies in verse those exaltations of sentiment that a nature like Nelson, the opportunity being given, vitalizes into acts.

5

Yes, the outbreak at the Nore was put down. But not every grievance was redressed. If the contractors, for example, were no longer permitted to ply some practices peculiar to their tribe everywhere, such as providing shoddy cloth, rations not sound, or false in the measure, not the less impressment, for one thing, went on. By custom sanctioned for centuries, and judicially maintained by a Lord Chancellor as late as Mansfield,[51] that mode of manning the fleet, a mode now fallen into a sort of abeyance but never formally renounced, it was not practicable to give up in those years. Its abrogation would have crippled the indispensable fleet, one wholly under canvas, no steam-power, its innumerable sails and thousands of cannon, everything in short, worked by muscle alone; a fleet the more insatiate in demand for men, because then multiplying its ship[s] of all grades against contingencies present and to come of the convulsed Continent.

Discontent foreran the Two Mutinies, and more or less it lurkingly survived them. Hence it was not unreasonable to apprehend some return of trouble sporadic or general. One instance of such apprehensions: In the same year with this story, Nelson, then Vice Admiral Sir Horatio, being with the fleet off the Spanish coast, was directed by the Admiral in command to shift his pennant from the *Captain* to the *Theseus;* and for this reason: that the latter ship having newly arrived on the station from home where it had taken part in the Great Mutiny, danger was apprehended from the temper of the men; and it was thought that an officer like Nelson was the one, not indeed to terrorize the crew into base subjection, but to win them, by force of his mere presence back to an allegiance if not as enthusiatic as his own, yet as true. So it was that for a time on more than one quarter-deck anxiety did exist. At sea precautionary vigilance was strained against relapse. At short notice an engagement might come on. When it did, the lieutenants assigned to batteries felt it incumbent on them, in some instances, to stand with drawn swords behind the men working the guns.

51. William Murray, Baron Mansfield (1705-1793), Lord Chief Justice of Great Britain from 1756 and later a cabinet minister (1773-1788).

6

But on board the seventy-four in which Billy now swung his hammock, very little in the manner of the men and nothing obvious in the demeanor of the officers would have suggested to an ordinary observer that the Great Mutiny was a recent event. In their general bearing and conduct the commissioned officers of a war-ship naturally take their tone from the commander, that is if he have that ascendancy of character that ought to be his.

Captain the Honorable Edward Fairfax Vere, to give his full title, was a bachelor of forty or thereabouts, a sailor of distinction even in a time prolific of renowned seamen. Though allied to the higher nobility his advancement had not been altogether owing to influences connected with that circumstance. He had seen much service, been in various engagements, always acquitting himself as an officer mindful of the welfare of his men, but never tolerating an infraction of discipline; thoroughly versed in the science of his profession, and intrepid to the verge of temerity, though never injudiciously so. For his gallantry in the West Indian waters as flag-lieutenant under Rodney in that Admiral's crowning victory over De Grasse,[52] he was made a post-captain.

Ashore in the garb of a civilian scarce anyone would have taken him for a sailor, more especially that he never garnished unprofessional talk with nautical terms, and grave in his bearing, evinced little appreciation of mere humor. It was not out of keeping with these traits that on a passage when nothing demanded his paramount action, he was the most undemonstrative of men. Any landsmen observing this gentleman not conspicuous by his stature and wearing no pronounced insignia, emerging from his cabin to the open deck, and noting the silent deference of the officers retiring to leeward,[53] might have taken him for the King's guest, a civilian aboard the King's-ship[,] some highly honorable discreet envoy on his way to an important post. But in fact this unobtrusiveness of demeanor may have proceeded from a certain unaffected modesty of manhood sometimes accompanying a resolute nature, a modesty evinced at all times not calling for pronounced action, and which shown in any rank of life suggests a virtue aristocratic in kind.

As with some others engaged in various departments of the world's more heroic activities, Captain Vere though practical enough upon occasion would at times betray a certain dreaminess of mood. Standing alone on the weather-side of the quarter deck, one hand holding by the rigging he would absently gaze off at the blank sea. At the

52. The British admiral George Brydges, Baron Rodney (1719-1792) defeated the French Admiral De Grasse off Dominica, in the Leeward Islands, in 1782.

53. the side of the ship away from the direction of the wind, as opposed to "windward."

presentation to him then of some minor matter interrupting the current of his thoughts he would show more or less irascibility; but instantly he would control it.

In the navy he was popularly known by the appellation—Starry Vere. How such a designation happened to fall upon one who whatever his sturdy qualities was without any brilliant ones was in this wise: A favorite kinsman, Lord Denton, a free-hearted fellow, had been the first to meet and congratulate him upon his return to England from his West Indian cruise; and but the day previous turning over a copy of Andrew Marvell's[54] poems had lighted, not for the first time however, upon the lines entitled *Appleton House,* the name of one of the seats of their common ancestor, a hero in the German wars of the seventeenth century, in which poem occur the lines,

> "This 'tis to have been from the first
> In a domestic heaven nursed,
> Under the discipline severe
> Of Fairfax and the starry Vere[.]"

And so, upon embracing his cousin fresh from Rodney's great victory wherein he had played so gallant a part, brimming over with just family pride in the sailor of their house, he exuberantly exclaimed, "Give ye joy, Ed; give ye joy, my starry Vere!" This got currency, and the novel prefix serving in familiar parlance readily to distinguish the *Indomitable*'s Captain from another Vere his senior, a distant relative an officer of like rank in the navy, it remained permanently attached to the surname.

7

In view of the part that the commander of the *Indomitable* plays in scenes shortly to follow, it may be well to fill out that sketch of him outlined in the previous chapter.

Aside from his qualities as a sea-officer Captain Vere was an exceptional character. Unlike no few of England's renowned sailors, long and arduous service with signal devotion to it, had not resulted in absorbing and *salting* the entire man. He had a marked leaning toward everything intellectual. He loved books, never going to sea without a newly replenished library, compact but of the best. The isolated leisure, in some cases so wearisome, falling at intervals to commanders even during a war-cruise, never was tedious to Captain Vere. With nothing of that literary taste which less heeds the thing conveyed than the vehicle, his bias was towards those books to which every serious mind of superior order occupying any active post of authority in the world, naturally inclines: books treating of actual

54. English lyric poet (1621-1678).

men and events no matter of what era—history, biography and unconventional writers, who, free from cant and convention, like Montaigne, honestly and in the spirit of common sense philosophize upon realities.

In this line of reading he found confirmation of his own more reasoned thoughts—confirmation which he had vainly sought in social converse, so that as touching most fundamental topics, there had got to be established in him some positive convictions, which he forefelt would abide in him essentially unmodified so long as his intelligent part remained unimpaired. In view of the troubled period in which his lot was cast this was well for him. His settled convictions were as a dyke against those invading waters of novel opinion social political and otherwise, which carried away as in a torrent no few minds in those days, minds by nature not inferior to his own. While other members of that aristocracy to which by birth he belonged were incensed at the innovators mainly because their theories were inimical to the privileged classes, not alone Captain Vere disinterestedly opposed them because they seemed to him incapable of embodiment in lasting institutions, but at war with the peace of the world and the true welfare of mankind.

With minds less stored than his and less earnest, some officers of his rank, with whom at times he would necessarily consort, found him lacking in the companionable quality, a dry and bookish gentleman as they deemed. Upon any chance withdrawal from their company one would be apt to say to another, something like this: "Vere is a noble fellow, Starry Vere. Spite the gazettes,[55] Sir Horatio["] meaning him with the Lord title[56] ["]is at bottom scarce a better seaman or fighter. But between you and me now don't you think there is a queer streak of the pedantic running thro' him? Yes, like the King's yarn in a coil of navy-rope?["][57]

Some apparent ground there was for this sort of confidential criticism; since not only did the Captain's discourse never fall into the jocosely familiar, but in illustrating of any point touching the stirring personages and events of the time he would be as apt to cite some historic character or incident of antiquity as that he would cite from the moderns. He seemed unmindful of the circumstance that to his bluff company such remote allusions however pertinent they might really be were altogether alien to men whose reading was mainly confined to the journals. But considerateness in such matters is not easy to natures constituted like Captain Vere's. Their honesty prescribes to them directness, sometimes far-reaching like that of a migratory fowl that in its flight never heeds when it crosses a frontier.

55. the official gazettes that printed accounts of naval careers and honors.
56. Lord Nelson.
57. This may be a reference to the thread worked into hempen cable to mark it as belonging to the Royal Navy.

8

The lieutenants and other commissioned gentlemen forming Captain Vere's staff it is not necessary here to particularize, nor needs it to make any mention of any of the warrant-officers.[58] But among the petty-officers was one who having much to do with the story, may as well be forthwith introduced. His portrait I essay, but shall never hit it. This was John Claggart, the Master-at-arms.[59] But that sea-title may to landsmen seem somewhat equivocal. Originally doubtless that petty-officer's function was the instruction of the men in the use of arms, sword or cutlas. But very long ago, owing to the advance in gunnery making hand-to-hand encounters less frequent and giving to nitre and sulphur the preeminence over steel, that function ceased; the master-at-arms of a great war-ship becoming a sort of Chief of Police charged among other matters with the duty of preserving order on the populous lower gun-decks.

Claggart was a man about five and thirty, somewhat spare and tall, yet of no ill figure upon the whole. His hand was too small and shapely to have been accustomed to hard toil. The face was a notable one; the features all except the chin cleanly cut as those on a Greek medallion; yet the chin, beardless as Tecumseh's,[60] had something of strange protuberant heaviness in its make that recalled the prints of the Rev. Dr. Titus Oates, the historic deponent with the clerical drawl in the time of Charles II and the fraud of the alleged Popish Plot.[61] It served Claggart in his office that his eye could cast a tutoring glance. His brow was of the sort phrenologically[62] associated with more than average intellect; silken jet curls partly clustering over it, making a foil to the pallor below, a pallor tinged with a faint shade of amber akin to the hue of time-tinted marbles of old. This complexion, singularly contrasting with the red or deeply bronzed visages of the sailors, and in part the result of his official seclusion from the sunlight, tho it was not exactly displeasing, nevertheless seemed to hint of something defective or abnormal in the constitution and blood. But his general aspect and manner were so suggestive of an education and career incongruous with his naval function that when not actively engaged in it he looked like a man of high quality, social and moral, who for reasons of his own was keeping incog.[63] Nothing was known of his former life. It might be that he was an

58. officers midway in rank between commissioned and noncommissioned officers. Originally they held their rank by a warrant as distinct from a commission.

59. the principal police officer and small-arms instructor.

60. the Shawnee chief (1768?-1813) who attempted to unite the Indian tribes against the United States.

61. In 1678 Oates (1649-1705) invented a plot which accused Jesuits of planning to assassinate Charles II, burn London, and slaughter English Protestants. As a result many English Roman Catholics were persecuted and killed.

62. Phrenology is the study of the shape of the skull as indicative of mental faculties.

63. *incognito:* unrecognized.

Englishman; and yet there lurked a bit of accent in his speech suggesting that possibly he was not such by birth, but through naturalization in early childhood. Among certain grizzled sea-gossips of the gun-decks and forecastle went a rumor perdue that the master-at-arms was a *chevalier* who had volunteered into the King's navy by way of compounding for some mysterious swindle whereof he had been arraigned at the King's Bench.[64] The fact that nobody could substantiate this report was, of course, nothing against its secret currency. Such a rumor once started on the gun-decks in reference to almost anyone below the rank of a commissioned officer would, during the period assigned to this narrative, have seemed not altogether wanting in credibility to the tarry old wiseacres of a man-of-war crew. And indeed a man of Claggart's accomplishments, without prior nautical experience entering the navy at mature life, as he did, and necessarily allotted at the start to the lowest grade in it; a man too who never made allusion to his previous life ashore; these were circumstances which in the dearth of exact knowlege as to his true antecedents opened to the invidious a vague field for unfavorable surmise.

But the sailors' dog-watch gossip concerning him derived a vague plausibility from the fact that now for some period the British Navy could so little afford to be squeamish in the matter of keeping up the muster-rolls, that not only were press-gangs notoriously abroad both afloat and ashore, but there was little or no secret about another matter, namely that the London police were at liberty to capture any able-bodied suspect, any questionable fellow at large and summarily ship him to the dockyard or fleet. Furthermore, even among voluntary enlistments there were instances where the motive thereto partook neither of patriotic impulse nor yet of a random desire to experience a bit of sea-life and martial adventure. Insolvent debtors of minor grade, together with the promiscuous lame ducks of morality found in the Navy a convenient and secure refuge. Secure, because once enlisted aboard a King's-Ship, they were as much in sanctuary, as the transgressor of the Middle Ages harboring himself under the shadow of the altar. Such sanctioned irregularities, which for obvious reasons the Government would hardly think to parade at the time and which consequently, and as affecting the least influential class of mankind, have all but dropped into oblivion, lend color to something for the truth whereof I do not vouch, and hence have some scruple in stating; something I remember having seen in print though the book I can not recall; but the same thing was personally communicated to me now more than forty years ago by an old pensioner in a cocked hat with whom I had a most interesting talk on the terrace at Greenwich, a Baltimore negro, a Trafalgar

64. formerly the supreme court of common law in Great Britain.

man.[65] It was to this effect: In the case of a warship short of hands whose speedy sailing was imperative, the deficient quota in lack of any other way of making it good, would be eked out by draughts culled direct from the jails. For reasons previously suggested it would not perhaps be easy at the present day directly to prove or disprove the allegation. But allowed as a verity, how significant would it be of England's straits at the time confronted by those wars which like a flight of harpies rose shrieking from the din and dust of the fallen Bastille.[66] That era appears measurably clear to us who look back at it, and but read of it. But to the grandfathers of us graybeards, the more thoughtful of them, the genius of it presented an aspect like that of Camoen's Spirit of the Cape,[67] an eclipsing menace mysterious and prodigious. Not America was exempt from apprehension. At the height of Napoleon's unexampled conquests, there were Americans who had fought at Bunker Hill who looked forward to the possibility that the Atlantic might prove no barrier against the ultimate schemes of this French upstart from the revolutionary chaos who seemed in act of fulfilling judgment prefigured in the Apocalypse.

But the less credence was to be given to the gun-deck talk touching Claggart, seeing that no man holding his office in a man-of-war can ever hope to be popular with the crew. Besides, in derogatory comments upon anyone against whom they have a grudge, or for any reason or no reason mislike, sailors are much like landsmen, they are apt to exaggerate or romance it.

About as much was really known to the *Indomitable's* tars of the master-at-arms' career before entering the service as an astronomer knows about a comet's travels prior to its first observable appearance in the sky. The verdict of the sea quidnuncs[68] has been cited only by way of showing what sort of moral impression the man made upon rude uncultivated natures whose conceptions of human wickedness were necessarily of the narrowest, limited to ideas of vulgar rascality, —a thief among the swinging hammocks during a night-watch, or the man-brokers and land-sharks of the sea-ports.

It was no gossip, however, but fact, that though, as before hinted, Claggart upon his entrance into the navy was, as a novice, assigned to the least honorable section of a man-of-war's crew,[69] embracing the drudgery, he did not long remain there.

The superior capacity he immediately evinced, his constitutional

65. a Trafalgar veteran at Greenwich Hospital near London, a home for retired personnel.

66. figuratively the fall of the Bastille (July 14, 1789) signaling the beginning of the Napoleonic wars.

67. The Portuguese poet Luiz Vaz de Camoëns (Camões, 1524-1580), in his epic poem the *Lusiads,* has a monster named Adamastor who attempts to destroy Vasco de Gama and his crew.

68. Latin, "what now"; an inquisitive person, a gossip, a busybody.

69. the waist of the ship on the gun deck, where the duties included attending to the sewage and drainage.

sobriety, ingratiating deference to superiors, together with a peculiar ferreting genius manifested on a singular occasion, all this capped by a certain austere patriotism abruptly advanced him to the position of master-at-arms.

Of this maritime Chief of Police the ship's-corporals, so called, were the immediate subordinates, and compliant ones; and this, as is to be noted in some business departments ashore, almost to a degree inconsistent with entire moral volition. His place put various converging wires of underground influence under the Chief's control, capable when astutely worked thro his understrappers of operating to the mysterious discomfort[,] if nothing worse, of any of the sea-commonalty.

9

Life in the fore-top well agreed with Billy Budd. There, when not actually engaged on the yards yet higher aloft, the topmen, who as such had been picked out for youth and activity, constituted an aerial club lounging at ease against the smaller stun'sails rolled up into cushions, spinning yarns like the lazy gods, and frequently amused with what was going on in the busy world of the decks below. No wonder then that a young fellow of Billy's disposition was well content in such society. Giving no cause of offence to anybody, he was always alert at a call. So in the merchant service it had been with him. But now such a punctiliousness in duty was shown that his topmates would sometimes good-naturedly laugh at him for it. This heightened alacrity had its cause, namely, the impression made upon him by the first formal gangway-punishment he had ever witnessed, which befell the day following his impressment. It had been incurred by a little fellow, young, a novice[,]an after-guardsman absent from his assigned post when the ship was being put about[70] a dereliction resulting in a rather serious hitch to that manœuvre, one demanding instantaneous promptitude in letting go and making fast. When Billy saw the culprit's naked back under the scourge gridironed with red welts, and worse; when he marked the dire expression on the liberated man's face as with his woolen shirt flung over him by the executioner he rushed forward from the spot to bury himself in the crowd, Billy was horrified. He resolved that never through remissness would he make himself liable to such a visitation or do or omit aught that might merit even verbal reproof. What then was his surprise and concern when ultimately he found himself getting into petty trouble occasionally about such matters as the stowage of his bag or something amiss in his hammock, matters under the police oversight of the ship's-corporals of the lower decks, and which brought down on

70. The afterguard was responsible for handling the braces and sheets of the main and mizzen sails when the ship was "put about" or headed up into the wind making a 90-degree turn.

him a vague threat from one of them.

So heedful in all things as he was, how could this be? He could not understand it, and it more than vexed him. When he spoke to his young topmates about it they were either lightly incredulous or found something comical in his unconcealed anxiety. "Is it your bag, Billy?" said one "well, sew yourself up in it, bully boy, and then you'll be sure to know if anybody meddles with it."

Now there was a veteran aboard who because his years began to disqualify him for more active work had been recently assigned duty as main-mast-man in his watch, looking to the gear belayed at the rail roundabout that great spar near the deck. At off-times the foretopman had picked up some acquaintance with him, and now in his trouble it occurred to him that he might be the sort of person to go to for wise counsel. He was an old Dansker[71] long anglicized in the service, of few words, many wrinkles and some honorable scars. His wizened face, time-tinted and weather-stained to the complexion of an antique parchment, was here and there peppered blue by the chance explosion of a gun-cartridge in action. He was an *Agamemnon*-man; some two years prior to the time of this story having served under Nelson when but Sir Horatio in that ship immortal in naval memory, and which[,] dismantled and in part broken up to her bare ribs[,] is seen a grand skeleton in Haydon's etching.[72] As one of a boarding-party from the *Agamemnon* he had received a cut slantwise along one temple and cheek leaving a long pale scar like a streak of dawn's light falling athwart the dark visage. It was on account of that scar and the affair in which it was known that he had received it, as well as from his blue-peppered complexion that the Dansker went among the *Indomitable*'s crew by the name of "Board-her-in-the smoke."

Now the first time that his small weazel-eyes happened to light on Billy Budd, a certain grim internal merriment set all his ancient wrinkles into antic play. Was it that his eccentric unsentimental old sapience primitive in its kind saw or thought it saw something which in contrast with the war-ship's environment looked oddly incongruous in the handsome sailor? But after slyly studying him at intervals, the old Merlin's[73] equivocal merriment was modified; for now when the twain would meet, it would start in his face a quizzing sort of look, but it would be but momentary and sometimes replaced by an expression of speculative query as to what might eventually befall a nature like that, dropped into a world not without some mantraps and against whose subtleties simple courage lacking experience

71. Dane.

72. probably Sir Francis Seymour Haden (1818-1910), whose etching of the breaking-up of the *Agamemnon*, one of Lord Nelson's commands, was published in 1870. Benjamin Robert Haydon (1786-1846), a friend of Keats, was a popular historical painter.

73. King Arthur's court magician.

and address and without any touch of defensive ugliness, is of little avail; and where such innocence as man is capable of does yet in a moral emergency not always sharpen the faculties or enlighten the will.

However it was the Dansker in his ascetic way rather took to Billy. Nor was this only because of a certain philosophic interest in such a character. There was another cause. While the old man's eccentricities, sometimes bordering on the ursine,[74] repelled the juniors, Billy, undeterred thereby, revering him as a salt hero would make advances, never passing the old Agamemnon-man without a salutation marked by that respect which is seldom lost on the aged however crabbed at times or whatever their station in life.

There was a vein of dry humor, or what not, in the mast-man; and whether in freak of patriarchal irony touching Billy's youth and athletic frame, or for some other and more recondite reason, from the first in addressing him he always substituted Baby for Billy. The Dansker in fact being the originator of the name by which the foretopman eventually became known aboard ship.

Well then, in his mysterious little difficulty going in quest of the wrinkled one, Billy found him off duty in a dog-watch ruminating by himself seated on a shot-box of the upper gun-deck now and then surveying with a somewhat cynical regard certain of the more swaggering promenaders there. Billy recounted his trouble, again wondering how it all happened. The salt seer attentively listened, accompanying the foretopman's recital with queer twitchings of his wrinkles and problematical little sparkles of his small ferret eyes. Making an end of his story, the foretopman asked, "And now, Dansker, do tell me what you think of it."

The old man, shoving up the front of his tarpaulin and deliberately rubbing the long slant scar at the point where it entered the thin hair, laconically said, "Baby Budd, *Jemmy Legs*"[75] (meaning the master-at-arms) "is down on you[.]"

"*Jemmy Legs!*" ejaculated Billy his welkin eyes expanding, "what for? Why he calls me *the sweet and pleasant young fellow*, they tell me."

"Does he so?" grinned the grizzled one; then said "Ay[,] Baby Lad[,] a sweet voice has *Jemmy Legs*."

"No, not always. But to me he has. I seldom pass him but there comes a pleasant word."

"And that's because he's down upon you, Baby Budd."

Such reiteration along with the manner of it, incomprehensible to a novice, disturbed Billy almost as much as the mystery for which he had sought explanation. Something less unpleasingly oracular he

74. bearlike.
75. "Jimmy Legs," a disparaging nickname for the master-at-arms, still used in the American navy.

tried to extract; but the old sea-Chiron[76] thinking perhaps that for the nonce he had sufficiently instructed his young Achilles, pursed his lips, gathered all his wrinkles together and would commit himself to nothing further.

Years, and those experiences which befall certain shrewder men subordinated life-long to the will of superiors, all this had developed in the Dansker the pithy guarded cynicism that was his leading characteristic.

10

The next day an incident served to confirm Billy Budd in his incredulity as to the Dansker's strange summing up of the case submitted. The ship at noon going large before the wind was rolling on her course, and he below at dinner and engaged in some sportful talk with the members of his mess, chanced in a sudden lurch to spill the entire contents of his soup-pan upon the new scrubbed deck. Claggart, the Master-at-arms, official rattan[77] in hand, happened to be passing along the battery in a bay of which the mess was lodged, and the greasy liquid streamed just across his path. Stepping over it, he was proceeding on his way without comment, since the matter was nothing to take notice of under the circumstances, when he happened to observe who it was that had done the spilling. His countenance changed. Pausing, he was about to ejaculate something hasty at the sailor, but checked himself, and pointing down to the streaming soup, playfull tapped him from behind with his rattan, saying in a low musical voice peculiar to him at times "Handsomely done, my lad! And handsome is as handsome did it too!" And with that passed on. Not noted by Bill as not coming within his view was the involuntary smile, or rather grimace, that accompanied Claggart's equivocal words. Aridly it drew down the thin corner of his shapely mouth. But everybody taking his remark as meant for humorous, and at which therefore as coming from a superior they were bound to laugh, "with counterfeited glee"[78] acted accordingly; and Billy tickled, it may be, by the allusion to his being the handsome sailor, merrily joined in; then addressing his messmates exclaimed "There now, who says that Jemmy Legs is down on me!" "And who said he was, Beauty?" demanded one Donald with some surprise. Whereat the foretopman looked a little foolish recalling that it was only one person. Board-her-in-the-smoke who had suggested what to him was the smoky idea that this master-at-arms was in any peculiar way hostile to him. Meantime that functionary resuming his path must have momentarily worn some expression less guarded than that of the bitter

76. Chiron the Centaur (half man and half horse), skilled in healing and the wisest of his species; the teacher of Achilles, Hercules, and Aesculapius.

77. swagger stick, light whip.

78. *Cf.* Oliver Goldsmith, "The Deserted Village," line 201. The reference is to the severe schoolmaster in the poem.

smile, and usurping the face from the heart, some distorting expression perhaps, for a drummer-boy heedlessly frolicking along from the opposite direction and chancing to come into light collision with his person was strangely disconcerted by his aspect. Nor was the impression lessened when the official impulsively giving him a sharp cut with the rattan, vehemently exclaimed "Look where you go!"

11

What was the matter with the master-at-arms? And, be the matter what it might, how could it have direct relation to Billy Budd with whom prior to the affair of the spilled soup he had never come into any special contact official or otherwise? What indeed could the trouble have to do with one so little inclined to give offence as the merchant-ship's *peacemaker*, even him who in Claggart's own phrase was "the sweet and pleasant young fellow?["] Yes, why should *Jemmy Legs*, to borrow the Dansker's expression, be *down* on the Handsome Sailor? But, at heart and not for nothing, as the late chance encounter may indicate to the discerning, down on him, secretly down on him, he assuredly was.

Now to invent something touching the more private career of Claggart, something involving Billy Budd, of which something the latter should be wholly ignorant, some romantic incident implying that Claggart's knowledge of the young blue-jacket began at some period anterior to catching sight of him on board the seventy-four—all this, not so difficult to do, might avail in a way more or less interesting to account for whatever of enigma may appear to lurk in the case. But in fact there was nothing of the sort. And yet the cause, necessarily to be assumed as the sole one assignable, is in its very realism as much charged with that prime element of Radcliffian romance, *the mysterious*, as any that the ingenuity of the author of the *Mysteries of Udolpho* could devise.[79] For what can more partake of the mysterious than an antipathy spontaneous and profound such as is evoked in certain exceptional mortals by the mere aspect of some other mortal, however harmless he may be? if not called forth by this very harmlessness itself.

Now there can exist no irritating juxtaposition of dissimilar personalities comparable to that which is possible aboard a great war-ship fully manned and at sea. There, every day among all ranks almost every man comes into more or less of contact with almost every other man. Wholly there to avoid even the sight of an aggravating object one must needs give it Jonah's toss[80] or jump overboard himself. Imagine how all this might eventually operate on some peculiar

79. Mrs. Ann Radcliffe (1764-1823) was the author of this immensely popular Gothic novel.

80. Jonah 1:15: "So they took up Jonah, and cast him forth into the sea." A nautical expression, when an unlucky object or person is put overboard.

human creature the direct reverse of a saint?

But for the adequate comprehending of Claggart by a normal nature these hints are insufficient. To pass from a normal nature to him one must cross "the deadly space between." And this is best done by indirection.

Long ago an honest scholar my senior, said to me in reference to one who like himself is now no more, a man so unimpeachably respectable that against him nothing was ever openly said tho' among the few something was whispered, "Yes, X—— is a nut not to be cracked by the tap of a lady's fan. You are aware that I am the adherent of no organized religion much less of any philosophy built into a system. Well, for all that, I think that to try and get into X——, enter his labyrinth and get out again, without a clue derived from some source other than what is known as *knowledge of the world*—that were hardly possible, at least for me."

"Why" said I, "X——however singular a study to some, is yet human, and knowledge of the world assuredly implies the knowledge of human nature, and in most of its varieties."

"Yes, but a superficial knowledge of it, serving ordinary purposes. But for anything deeper, I am not certain whether to know the world and to know human nature be not two distinct branches of knowledge, which while they may coexist in the same heart, yet either may exist with little or nothing of the other. Nay, in an average man of the world, his constant rubbing with it blunts that fine spiritual insight indispensable to the understanding of the essential in certain exceptional characters, whether evil ones or good. In a matter of some importance I have seen a girl wind an old lawyer about her little finger. Nor was it the dotage of senile love. Nothing of the sort. But he knew law better than he knew the girl's heart. Coke and Blackstone[81] hardly shed so much light into obscure spiritual places as the Hebrew prophets. And who were they? Mostly recluses."

At the time my inexperience was such that I did not quite see the drift of all this. It may be that I see it now. And, indeed, if that lexicon which is based on Holy Writ were any longer popular, one might with less difficulty define and denominate certain phenomenal men. As it is, one must turn to some authority not liable to the charge of being tinctured with the Biblical element.

In a list of definitions included in the authentic translation of Plato, a list attributed to him, occurs this: "Natural Depravity: a depravity according to nature." A definition which tho' savoring of Calvinism, by no means involves Calvin's dogmas as to total mankind. Evidently its intent makes it applicable but to individuals.

81. Sir Edward Coke (1552-1634) and Sir William Blackstone (1723-1780), famous British jurists and writers on the law.

Not many are the examples of this depravity which the gallows and jail supply. At any rate for notable instances, since these have no vulgar alloy of the brute in them, but invariably are dominated by intellectuality, one must go elsewhere. Civilization, especially if of the austerer sort, is auspicious to it. It folds itself in the mantle of respectability. It has its certain negative virtues serving as silent auxiliaries. It never allows wine to get within its guard. It it not going too far to say that it is without vices or small sins. There is a phenomenal pride in it that excludes them from anything mercenary or avaricious. In short the depravity here meant partakes nothing of the sordid or sensual. It is serious, but free from acerbity. Though no flatterer of mankind it never speaks ill of it.

But the thing which in eminent instances signalizes so exceptional a nature is this: though the man's even temper and discreet bearing would seem to intimate a mind peculiarly subject to the law of reason, not the less in his heart he would seem to riot in complete exemption from that law[,] having apparently little to do with reason further than to employ it as an ambidexter implement for effecting the irrational. That is to say: Toward the accomplishment of an aim which in wantonness of malignity would seem to partake of the insane, he will direct a cool judgement sagacious and sound.

These men are true madmen, and of the most dangerous sort, for their lunacy is not continuous but occasional[,] evoked by some special object; it is probably secretive, which is as much to say it is self-contained, so that when moreover, most active[,] it is to the average mind not distinguishable from sanity, and for the reason above suggested that whatever its aims may be, and the aim is never declared—the method and the outward proceeding are always perfectly rational.

Now something such an one was Claggart, in whom was the mania of an evil nature, not engendered by vicious training or corrupting books or licentious living, but born with him and innate, in short "a depravity according to nature."

12

Lawyers, Experts, Clergy: An Episode[82]

By the way, can it be the phenomenon, disowned or at least concealed, that in some criminal cases puzzles the courts? For this cause have our juries at times not only to endure the prolonged contentions of lawyers with their fees, but also the yet more perplexing strife of the medical experts with theirs?—But why leave it to them? why not subpoena as well the clerical proficients? Their vocation bringing them into peculiar contact with so many human beings, and sometimes in their least guarded hour, in interviews very much more confidential than those of physician and patient; this would

82. In their edition Hayford and Sealts reject this episode.

seem to qualify them to know something about those intricacies involved in the question of moral responsibility; whether in a given case, say, the crime proceeded from mania in the brain or rabies of the heart. As to any differences among themselves these clerical proficients might develop on the stand, these could hardly be greater than the direct contradictions exchanged between the remunerated medical experts.

Dark sayings are these, some will say. But why? Is it because they somewhat savor of Holy Writ in its phrase "mysteries of iniquity"?[83] If they do, such savor was far from being intended for little will it commend these pages to many a reader of to-day.

The point of the present story turning on the hidden nature of the master-at-arms has necessitated this chapter. With an added hint or two in connection with the incident at the mess, the resumed narrative must be left to vindicate, as it may, its own credibility.

13

Pale ire, envy and despair[84]

That Claggart's figure was not amiss, and his face, save the chin, well moulded, has already been said. Of these favorable points he seemed not insensible, for he was not only neat but careful in his dress. But the form of Billy Budd was heroic; and if his face was without the intellectual look of the pallid Claggart's, not the less was it lit, like his, from within, though from a different source. The bonfire in his heart made luminous the rose-tan in his cheek.

In view of the marked contrast between the persons of the twain, it is more than probable that when the master-at-arms in the scene last given applied to the sailor the proverb *Handsome is as handsome does;* he there let escape an ironic inkling, not caught by the young sailors who heard it, as to what it was that had first moved him against Billy, namely, his significant personal beauty.

Now envy and antipathy passions irreconcilable in reason, nevertheless in fact may spring conjoined like Chang and Eng[85] in one birth. Is Envy then such a monster? Well, though many an arraigned mortal has in hopes of mitigated penalty pleaded guilty to horrible actions, did ever anybody seriously confess to envy? Something there is in it universally felt to be more shameful than even felonious crime. And not only does everybody disown it but the better sort are inclined to incredulity when it is in earnest imputed to an intelligent man. But since its lodgement is in the heart not the brain, no degree of intellect supplies a guarantee against it. But Claggart's

83. II *Thessalonians,* ii:7: "For the mystery of iniquity doth already work * * *." The text is concerned with the principle of evil in nature.

84. In Milton's *Paradise Lost,* Book IV, 1. 115. As he approaches the Garden of Eden, Satan's face "thrice changed" with these emotions.

85. famous Siamese twins (1811-1874), who toured the United States.

was no vulgar form of the passion. Nor, as directed toward Billy Budd did it partake of that streak of apprehensive jealousy that marred Saul's visage perturbedly brooding on the comely young David.[86] Claggart's envy struck deeper. If askance he eyed the good looks, cheery health and frank enjoyment of young life in Billy Budd, it was because these [went] along with a nature that as Claggart magnetically felt, had in its simplicity never willed malice or experienced the reactionary bite of that serpent. To him, the spirit lodged within Billy, and looking out from his welkin eyes as from windows, that ineffability it was which made the dimple in his dyed cheek, suppled his joints, and dancing in his yellow curls made him preeminently the Handsome Sailor. One person excepted the master-at-arms was perhaps the only man in the ship intellectually capable of adequately appreciating the moral phenomenon presented in Billy Budd. And the insight but intensified his passion, which assuming various secret forms within him, at times assumed that of cynic disdain—disdain of innocence—To be nothing more than innocent! Yet in an aesthetic way he saw the charm of it, the courageous free-and-easy temper of it, and fain would have shared it, but he despaired of it.

With no power to annul the elemental evil in him, tho readily enough he could hide it; apprehending the good, but powerless to be it; a nature like Claggart's surcharged with energy as such natures almost invariably are, what recourse is left to it but to recoil upon itself and like the scorpion for which the Creator alone is responsible, act out to the end of the part allotted it.

14

Passion, and passion in its profoundest, is not a thing demanding a palatial stage whereon to play its part. Down among the groundlings,[87] among the beggars and rakers of the garbage, profound passion is enacted. And the circumstances that provoke it, however trivial or mean, are no measure of its power. In the present instance the stage is a scrubbed gun-deck, and one of the external provocations a man-of-war's-man's spilled soup.

Now when the Master-at-arms noticed whence came that greasy fluid streaming before his feet, he must have taken it—to some extent wilfully, perhaps—not for the mere accident it assuredly was, but for the sly escape of a spontaneous feeling on Billy's part more or less answering to the antipathy on his own. In effect a foolish demonstration he must have thought, and very harmless, like the futile kick of a heifer, which yet were the heifer a shod stallion, would not be so harmless. Even so was it that into the gall of

86. In I Samuel 16:18, 18:8*ff.*, it is suggested that David's military successes, as well as his personal popularity with the Jews, brought about Saul's envy and dislike.

87. the part of the audience which stood on the ground in an Elizabethan theater; the poorest spectators.

Claggart's envy he infused the vitriol of his contempt. But the incident confirmed to him certain tell-tale reports purveyed to his ear by *Squeak*, one of his more cunning Corporals, a grizzled little man, so nicknamed by the sailors on account of his squeaky voice, and sharp visage ferreting about the dark corners of the lower decks after interlopers, satirically suggesting to them the idea of a rat in a cellar.

From his Chief's employing him as an implicit tool in laying little traps for the worriment of the Foretopman—for it was from the Master-at-arms that the petty persecutions heretofore adverted to had proceeded—the corporal having naturally enough concluded that his master could have no love for the sailor, made it his business, faithful understrapper that he was, to foment the ill blood by perverting to his Chief certain innocent frolics of the good natured Foretopman, besides inventing for his mouth sundry contumelious epithets he claimed to have overheard him let fall. The Master-at-arms never suspected the veracity of these reports, more especially as to the epithets, for he well knew how secretly unpopular may become a master-at-arms[,] at least a master-at-arms of those days zealous in his function, and how the blue-jackets shoot at him in private their raillery and wit; the nickname by which he goes among them (*Jemmy Legs*) implying under the form of merriment their cherished disrespect and dislike.

But in view of the greediness of hate for patrolmen it hardly needed a purveyor to feed Claggart's passion. An uncommon prudence is habitual with the subtler depravity, for it has everything to hide. And in case of an injury but suspected, its secretiveness voluntarily cuts if off from enlightenment or disillusion; and, not unreluctantly, action is taken upon surmise as upon certainty. And the retaliation is apt to be in monstrous disproportion to the supposed offence; for when in anybody was revenge in its exactions aught else but an inordinate usurer. But how with Claggart's conscience? For though consciences are unlike as foreheads, every intelligence, not excluding the Scriptural devils who "believe and tremble," has one. But Claggart's conscience being but the lawyer to his will, made ogres of trifles, probably arguing that the motive imputed to Billy in spilling the soup just when he did, together with the epithets alleged, these, if nothing more, made a strong case against him; nay, justified animosity into a sort of retributive righteousness. The Pharisee is the Guy Fawkes[88] prowling in the hid chambers underlying the Claggarts. And they can really form no conception of an unreciprocated malice. Probably, the master-at-arms' clandestine persecution of Billy was started to try the temper of the man; but it

88. *Pharisee*: a follower of a Jewish sect (*c.* 135 B.C.-A.D. 135) known for its strict observance of the Torah. The term has come to mean anyone of extremely rigid and dogmatic persuasion. *Guy Fawkes*: one of the instigators of the Gunpowder Plot, the plan to blow up the Houses of Parliament and King James I on November 5, 1605.

had **not** developed any quality in him that enmity could make official use of or even pervert into plausible self-justification; so that the occurrence at the mess, petty if it were, was a welcome one to that peculiar conscience assigned to be the private mentor of Claggart; And for the rest, not improbably it put him upon new experiments.

15

Not many days after the last incident narrated something befell Billy Budd that more gravelled him than aught that had previously occurred.

It was a warm night for the latitude; and the Foretopman, whose watch at the time was properly below, was dozing on the uppermost deck whither he had ascended from his hot hammock one of hundreds suspended so closely wedged together over a lower gun-deck that there was little or no swing to them. He lay as in the shadow of a hill-side, stretched under the lee of the booms, a piled ridge of spare spars amidships between foremast and mainmast and among which the ship's largest boat, the launch, was stowed. Alongside of three other slumberers from below, he lay near that end of the booms which approaches the foremast; his station aloft on duty as a foretopman being just over the deck-station of the forecastlemen, entitling him according to usage to make himself more or less at home in that neighborhood.

Presently he was stirred into semi-consciousness by somebody, who must have previously sounded the sleep of the others, touching his shoulder, and then as the Foretopman raised his head, breathing into his ear in a quick whisper, "Slip into the lee forechains,[89] Billy; there is something in the wind. Don't speak. Quick, I will meet you there;" and disappeared.

Now Billy like sundry other essentially good-natured ones had some of the weaknesses inseparable from essential good nature; and among these was a reluctance, almost an incapacity of plumply saying *no* to an abrupt proposition not obviously absurd, on the face of it, nor obviously unfriendly, nor iniquitous. And being of warm blood he had not the phlegm tacitly to negative any proposition by unresponsive inaction. Like his sense of fear, his apprehension as to aught outside of the honest and natural was seldom very quick. Besides, upon the present occasion, the drowse from his sleep still hung upon him.

However it was, he mechanically rose, and sleepily wondering what could be in the wind, betook himself to the designated place, a narrow platform, one of six, outside of the high bulwarks and screened by the great dead-eyes[90] and multiple columned lanyards of the shrouds and back-stays; and, in a great war-ship of that time, of

89. platforms near the bow, designed to carry the lower shrouds of the foremast out from the side of the ship.

90. wooden blocks through which lanyards (short lengths of line) are threaded.

dimensions commensurate [with the] hull's magnitude; a tarry balcony in short overhanging the sea, and so secluded that one mariner of the *Indomitable*, a non-conformist[91] old tar of a serious turn, made it even in daytime his private oratory.

In this retired nook the stranger soon joined Billy Budd. There was no moon as yet; a haze obscured the star-light. He could not distinctly see the stranger's face. Yet from something in the outline and carriage, Billy took him to be, and correctly, for one of the afterguard.[92]

"Hist! Billy," said the man in the same quick cautionary whisper as before; "You were impressed, weren't you? Well, so was I"; and he paused, as to mark the effect. But Billy not knowing exactly what to make of this said nothing. Then the other: "We are not the only impressed ones, Billy. There's a gang of us.—Couldn't you—help—at a pinch?["]

"What do you mean?["] demanded Billy here thoroughly shaking off his drowse.

"Hist, hist!["] the hurried whisper now growing husky, ["] see here"; and the man held up two small objects faintly twinkling in the nightlight; "see, they are yours, Billy, if you'll only—"

But Billy broke in, and in his resentful eagerness to deliver himself his vocal infirmity somewhat intruded: "D-D-Damme, I don't know what you are d-d-driving at, or what you mean, but you had better g-g-go where you belong!" For the moment the fellow, as confounded, did not stir; and Billy springing to his feet, said "If you d-don't start I'll t-t-toss you back over the r-rail!" There was no mistaking this and the mysterious emissary decamped disappearing in the direction of the mainmast in the shadow of the booms.

"Hallo, what's the matter?" here came growling from a forecastleman awakened from his deck-doze by Billy's raised voice. And as the foretopman reappeared and was recognized by him; "Ah, *Beauty*, is it you? Well, something must have been the matter for you st-st-stuttered."

"O," rejoined Billy, now mastering the impediment; "I found an afterguardsman in our part of the ship here and I bid him be off where he belongs."

"And is that all you did about it, foretopman?" gruffly demanded another, an irascible old fellow of brick-colored visage and hair, and who was known to his associate forecastlemen as *Red Pepper*; "Such sneaks I should like to marry to the gunner's daughter!" by that expression meaning that he would like to subject them to disciplinary castigation over a gun.

However, Billy's rendering of the matter satisfactorily accounted

91. a Protestant dissenter from the Church of England.
92. *cf.* note 70.

to these inquirers for the brief commotion, since of all the sections of a ship's company the forecastlemen, veterans for the most part and bigoted in their sea-prejudices, are the most jealous in resenting territorial encroachments, especially on the part of any of the afterguard, of whom they have but a sorry opinion, chiefly landsmen, never going aloft except to reef or furl the mainsail, and in no wise competent to handle a marlinspike[93] or turn in a *dead-eye*, say.

16

This incident sorely puzzled Billy Budd. It was an entirely new experience; the first time in his life that he had ever been personally approached in underhand intriguing fashion. Prior to this encounter he had known nothing of the afterguardsman, the two men being stationed wide apart, one forward and aloft during his watch, the other on deck and aft.

What could it mean? And could they reallly be guineas,[94] those two glittering objects the interloper had held up to his (Billy's)[95] eyes? Where could the fellow get guineas? Why even buttons spare buttons[96] are not so plentiful at sea. The more he turned the matter over, the more he was non-plussed, and made uneasy and discomforted. In his disgustful recoil from an overture which tho' he but ill comprehended he instinctively knew must involve evil of some sort, Billy Budd was like a young horse fresh from the pasture suddenly inhaling a vile whiff from some chemical factory and by repeated snortings tries to get it out of his nostrils and lungs. This frame of mind barred all desire of holding further parley with the fellow, even were it but for the purpose of gaining some enlightenment as to his design in approaching him. And yet he was not without natural curiosity to see how such a visitor in the dark would look in broad day.

He espied him the following afternoon in his first dog-watch below[,]one of the smokers on that forward part of the upper gun deck allotted to the pipe.[97] He recognized him by his general cut and build, more than by his round freckled face and glassy eyes of pale blue, veiled with lashes all but white. And yet Billy was a bit uncertain whether indeed it were he—yonder chap about his own age chatting and laughing in free-hearted way, leaning against a gun; a genial young fellow enough to look at, and something of a rattle-

93. an iron tool tapering to a point, used to separate the strands in a length of rope.

94. *guinea*: an English gold coin, not minted after 1813, worth about 21 shillings.

95. The parentheses around "Billy's" suggests that Melville may have intended to delete it.

96. *even buttons spare buttons:* Melville may have intended to delete the first "buttons."

97. Enlisted men were allowed to smoke on the galley on the forward upper gun deck. This ship had three decks in this order: lower gun deck, upper gun deck, and spar deck.

brain, to all appearance. Rather chubby too for a sailor even an afterguardsman. In short the last man in the world, one would think, to be overburthened with thoughts, especially those perilous thoughts that must needs belong to a conspirator in any serious project, or even to the underling of such a conspirator.

Altho' Billy was not aware of it, the fellow, with a side-long watchful glance had perceived Billy first, and then noting that Billy was looking at him, thereupon nodded a familiar sort of friendly recognition as to an old acquaintance, without interrupting the talk he was engaged in with the group of smokers. A day or two afterwards chancing in the evening promenade on a gun deck, to pass Billy, he offered a flying word of good-fellowship as it were, which by its unexpectedness, and equivocalness under the circumstances so embarrassed Billy that he knew not how to respond to it, and let it go unnoticed.

Billy was now left more at a loss than before. The ineffectual speculation into which he was led was so disturbingly alien to him that he did his best to smother [it]. It never entered his mind that here was a matter which from its extreme questionableness, it was his duty as a loyal blue-jacket to report in the proper quarter. And, probably, had such a step been suggested to him, he would have been deterred from taking it by the thought, one of novice-magnanimity, that it would savor overmuch of the dirty work of a telltale. He kept the thing to himself. Yet upon one occasion, he could not forbear a little disburthening himself to the old Dansker, tempted thereto perhaps by the infiluence of a balmy night when the ship lay becalmed; the twain, silent for the most part, sitting together on deck, their heads propped against the bulwarks. But it was only a partial and anonymous account that Billy gave, the unfounded scruples above referred to preventing full disclosure to anybody. Upon hearing Billy's version, the sage Dansker seemed to divine more than he was told; and after a little meditation during which his wrinkles were pursed as into a point, quite effacing for the time that quizzing expression his face sometimes wore,—"Didn't I say so, Baby Budd?"

"Say what?" demanded Billy.

"Why, *Jemmy Legs* is *down* on you."

"And what" rejoined Billy in amazement, "has *Jemmy Legs* to do with that cracked afterguardsman?"

"Ho, it was an afterguardsman then. A cat's-paw, a cat's-paw!" And with that exclamation, which, whether it had reference to a light puff of air just then coming over the calm sea, or subtler relation to the afterguardsman, there is no telling, the old Merlin gave a twisting wrench with his black teeth at his plug of tobacco, vouchsafing no reply to Billy's impetuous question, tho' now repeated, for it was his wont to relapse into grim silence when interrogated in skeptical sort as to any of his sententious oracles, not always very clear ones, rather partaking of that obscurity which invests most Delphic deliverances[98] from any quarter.

Long experience had very likely brought this old man to that bitter prudence which never interferes in aught and never gives advice.

17

Yes, despite the Dansker's pithy insistence as to the Master-at-arms being at the bottom of these strange experiences of Billy on board the *Indomitable,* the young sailor was ready to ascribe them to almost anybody but the man who, to use Billy's own expression, "always had a pleasant word for him." This is to be wondered at. Yet not so much to be wondered at. In certain matters, some sailors even in mature life remain unsophisticated enough. But a young seafarer of the disposition of our athletic Foretopman, is much of a child-man. And yet a child's utter innocence is but its blank ignorance, and the innocence more or less wanes as intelligence waxes. But in Billy Budd intelligence, such as it was, had advanced, while yet his simple mindedness remained for the most part unaffected. Experience is a teacher indeed; yet did Billy's years make his experience small. Besides, he had none of that intuitive knowledge of the bad which in natures not good or incompletely so foreruns experience, and therefore may pertain, as in some instances it too clearly does pertain, even to youth.

And what could Billy know of man except of man as a mere sailor? And the old-fashioned sailor, the veritable man-before-the-mast, the sailor from boyhood up, he, tho' indeed of the same species as a landsman is in some respects singularly distinct from him. The sailor is frankness, the landsman is finesse. Life is not a game with the sailor, demanding the long head; no intricate game of chess where few moves are made in straightforwardness, and ends are attained by indirection; an oblique, tedious, barren game hardly worth that poor candle burnt out in playing it.[99]

Yes, as a class, sailors are in character a juvenile race. Even their deviations are marked by juvenility. And this more especially holding true with the sailors of Billy's time. Then, too, certain things which apply to all sailors, do more pointedly operate here and there, upon the junior one. Every sailor, too is accustomed to obey orders without debating them; his life afloat is externally ruled for him; he is not brought into that promiscuous commerce with mankind where unobstructed free agency on equal terms—equal superficially, at least—

98. a reference to the Pythian priestess, whose pronouncements in verse had to be interpreted by a priest. Her shrine was at Delphi.

99. *Cf.* Shakespeare, *Macbeth,* Act V, Scene 5, 11. 23–26: "* * * Out, out, brief candle! / Life's but a walking shadow, a poor player, / That struts and frets his hour upon the stage / And then is heard no more. * * *"

soon teaches one that unless upon occasion he exercise a distrust keen in proportion to the fairness of the appearance, some foul turn may be served him. A ruled undemonstrative distrustfulness is so habitual, not with business-men so much, as with men who know their kind in less shallow relations than business, namely, certain men-of-the-world, that they come at last to employ it all but unconsciously; and some of them would very likely feel real surprise at being charged with it as one of their general characteristics.

18

But after the little matter at the mess Billy Budd no more found himself in strange trouble at times about his hammock or his clothes-bag or what not. While, as to that smile that occasionally sunned him, and the pleasant passing word, these were if not more frequent, yet if anything more pronounced that before.

But for all that, there were certain other demonstrations now. When Claggart's unobserved glance happened to light on belted Billy rolling along the upper gun-deck in the leisure of the second dog-watch exchanging passing broadsides of fun with other young promenaders in the crowd; that glance would follow the cheerful sea-Hyperion[100] with a settled meditative and melancholy expression, his eyes strangely suffused with incipient feverish tears. Then would Claggart look like the man of sorrows.[101] Yes, and sometimes the melancholy expression would have in it a touch of soft yearning, as if Claggart could even have loved Billy but for fate and ban. But this was an evanescence, and quickly repented of, as it were, by an immitigable look, pinching and shrivelling the visage into the momentary semblance of a wrinkled walnut. But sometimes catching sight in advance of the foretopman coming in his direction, he would, upon their nearing, step aside a little to let him pass, dwelling upon Billy for the moment with the glittering dental satire of a Guise.[102] But upon any abrupt unforeseen encounter a red light would[flash] forth from his eye like a spark from an anvil in a dusk smithy. That quick fierce light was a strange one, darted from orbs which in repose were of a color nearest approaching a deeper violet, the softest of shades.

Tho' some of these caprices of the pit could not but be observed by their object, yet were they beyond the construing of such a nature. And the *thews* of Billy were hardly compatible with that sort of sensitive spiritual organisation which in some cases instinctively conveys to ignorant innocence an admonition of the proximity of the malign. He thought the Master-at-arms acted in a manner rather queer at

100. in Greek mythology, the Titan god who came to be identified with Apollo, the god of youth and beauty.

101. In *Isaiah* 53:3, the Lord's servant is described as "despised and rejected of men; a man of sorrows, and acquainted with grief."

102. Henri de Guise (1550-1588), remembered chiefly for his conspiratorial activities and his ability, like Claudius in *Hamlet*, to "smile, and smile, and be a villain."

times. That was all. But the occasional frank air and pleasant word went for what they purported to be, the young sailor never having heard as yet of the "too fair-spoken man."

Had the foretopman been conscious of having done or said anything to provoke the ill will of the official, it would have been different with him, and his sight might have been purged if not sharpened. As it was[,] innocence was his blinder.

So was it with him in yet another matter. Two minor officers—the Armorer and Captain of the Hold,[103] with whom he had never exchanged a word, his position in the ship not bringing him into contact with them; these men now for the first began to cast upon Billy when they chanced to encounter him, that peculiar glance which evidences that the man from whom it comes has been some way tampered with and to the prejudice of him upon whom the glance lights. Never did it occur to Billy as a thing to be noted or a thing suspicious, tho' he well knew the fact, that the Armorer and Captain of the Hold, with the ship's-yeoman,[104] apothecary, and others of that grade, were by naval usage, mess-mates of the master-at-arms, men with ears convenient to his confidential tongue.

But the general popularity that our *Handsome Sailor's* manly forwardness upon occasion, and[his] irresistible good nature[,] indicating no mental superiority tending to excite an invidious feeling; this good will on the part of most of his shipmates made him the less to concern himself about such mute aspects toward him as those whereto allusion has just been made.

As to the afterguardsman, tho' Billy for reasons already given necessarily saw little of him, yet when the two did happen to meet, invariably came the fellow's off-hand cheerful recognition, sometimes accompanied by a passing pleasant word or two. Whatever that equivocal young person's original design may really have been, or the design of which he might have been the deputy, certain it was from his manner upon these occasions, that he had wholly dropped it.

It was as if his precocity of crookedness (and every vulgar villain is precocious) had for once deceived him, and the man he had sought to entrap as a simpleton had, through his very simplicity ignorantly baffled him.

But shrewd ones may opine that it was hardly possible for Billy to refrain from going up to the afterguardsman and bluntly demanding to know his purpose in the initial interview, so abruptly closed in the fore-chains. Shrewd ones may also think it but natural in Billy to set about sounding some of the other impressed men of the ship in order to discover what basis, if any, there was for the emissary's obscure suggestions as to plotting disaffection aboard. Yes, [the]

103. *Armorer:* the petty-officer in charge of the ship's arms; *Captain of the Hold:* the petty-officer in charge of stowing the hold.

104. the petty-officer in charge of stores.

shrewd may so think. But something more, or rather, something else than mere shrewdness is perhaps needful for the due understanding of such a character as Billy Budd's.

As to Claggart, the monomania in the man—if that indeed it were—as involuntarily disclosed by starts in the manifestations detailed, yet in general covered over by his self-contained and rational demeanor; this, like a subterranean fire was eating its way deeper and deeper in him. Something decisive must come of it.

19

After the mysterious interview in the fore-chains, the one so abruptly ended there by Billy, nothing especially German[105] to the story occurred until the events now about to be narrated.

Elsewhere it has been said that in the lack of frigates (of course better sailers than line-of-battle ships) in the English squadron up the Straits[106] at that period, the *Indomitable* was occasionally employed not only as an available substitute for a scout, but at times on detached service of more important kind. This was not alone because of her sailing qualities, not common in a ship of her rate, but quite as much, probably, that the character of her commander, it was thought, specially adapted him for any duty where under unforeseen difficulties a prompt initiative might have to be taken in some matter demanding knowledge and ability in addition to those qualities implied in good seamanship. It was on an expedition of the latter sort, a somewhat distant one, and when the *Indomitable* was almost at her furthest remove from the fleet that in the latter part of an afternoon-watch she unexpectedly came in sight of a ship of the enemy. It proved to be a frigate. The latter perceiving thro' the glass that the weight of men and metal would be heavily against her, invoking her light heels crowded sail to get away. After a chase urged almost against hope and lasting until about the middle of the first dog-watch, she signally succeeded in effecting her escape.

Not long after the pursuit had been given up, and ere the excitement incident thereto had altogether waned away, the Master-at-Arms ascending from his cavernous sphere made his appearance cap in hand by the mainmast respectfully waiting the notice of Captain Vere then solitary walking the weather-side of the quarter-deck, doubtless somewhat chafed at the failure of the pursuit. The spot where Claggart stood was the place allotted to men of lesser grades seeking some more particular interview either with the officer-of-the-deck or the Captain himself. But from the latter it was not often that a sailor or petty-officer of those days would seek a hearing; only some exceptional cause, would, according to established custom, have warranted that.

Presently, just as the Commander absorbed in his reflections was

105. *i.e.*, "germane" or "akin."
106. the British Mediterranean Fleet, sailing from the Straits of Gibraltar.

on the point of turning aft in his promenade, he became sensible of Claggart's presence, and saw the doffed cap held in deferential expectancy. Here be it said that Captain Vere's personal knowledge of this petty-officer had only begun at the time of the ship's last sailing from home, Claggart then for the first, in transfer from a ship detained for repairs, supplying on board the *Indomitable* the place of a previous master-at-arms disabled and ashore.

No sooner did the Commander observe who it was that now deferentially stood awaiting his notice, than a peculiar expression came over him. It was not unlike that which uncontrollably will flit across the countenance of one at unawares encountering a person who though known to him indeed has hardly been long enough known for thorough knowledge, but something in whose aspect nevertheless now for the first provokes a vaguely repellent distaste. But coming to a stand, and resuming much of his wonted official manner, save that a sort of impatience lurked in the intonation of the opening word, he said "Well? what is it, Master-at-Arms?"

With the air of a subordinate grieved at the necessity of being a messenger of ill tidings, and while conscientiously determined to be frank, yet equally resolved upon shunning overstatement, Claggart at this invitation or rather summons to disburthen, spoke up. What he said, conveyed in the language of no uneducated man, was to the effect following if not altogether in these words, namely, that during the chase and preparations for the possible encounter he had seen enough to convince him that at least one sailor aboard was a dangerous character in a ship mustering some who not only had taken a guilty part in the late serious troubles, but others also who, like the man in question, had entered His Majesty's service under another form than enlistment.

At this point Captain Vere with some impatience, interrupted him: "Be direct, man; say impressed men."

Claggart made a gesture of subservience, and proceeded.

Quite lately he (Claggart) had begun to suspect that on the gundecks some sort of movement prompted by the sailor in question was covertly going on, but he had not thought himself warranted in reporting the suspicion so long as it remained indistinct. But from what he had that afternoon observed in the man referred to the suspicion of something clandestine going on had advanced to a point less removed from certainty. He deeply felt, he added, the serious responsibility assumed in making a report involving such possible consequences to the individual mainly concerned, besides tending to augment those natural anxieties which every naval commander must feel in view of extraordinary outbreaks so recent as those which, he sorrowfully said it, it needed not to name.

Now at the first broaching of the matter Captain Vere taken by surprise could not wholly dissemble his disquietude. But as Claggart went on, the former's aspect changed into restiveness under something in the witness' manner in giving his testimony. However, he refrained from interrupting him. And Claggart, continuing, concluded with this:

"God forbid, your honor, that the *Indomitable*'s should be the experience of the—"

"Never mind that!" here peremptorily broke in the superior, his face altering with anger, instinctively divining the ship that the other was about to name, one in which the Nore Mutiny had assumed a singularly tragical character that for a time jeopardized the life of its commander. Under the circumstances he was indignant at the purposed allusion. When the commissioned officers themselves were on all occasions very heedful how they referred to the recent events, for a petty-officer unnecessarily to allude to them in the presence of his Captain, this struck him as a most immodest presumption. Besides, to his quick sense of self-respect, it even looked under the circumstances something like an attempt to alarm him. Nor at first was he without some surprise that one who so far as he had hitherto come under his notice had shown considerable tact in his function should in this particular evince such lack of it.

But these thoughts and kindred dubious ones flitting across his mind were suddenly replaced by an intuitional surmise which though as yet obscure in form served practically to affect his reception of the ill tidings. Certain it is, that long versed in everything pertaining to the complicated gun-deck life, which like every other form of life, has its secret mines and dubious side, the side popularly disclaimed, Captain Vere did not permit himself to be unduly disturbed by the general tenor of his subordinate's report. Furthermore, if in view of recent events prompt action should be taken at the first palpable sign of recurring insubordination, for all that, not judicious would it be, he thought, to keep the idea of lingering disaffection alive by undue forwardness in crediting an informer even if his own subordinate and charged among other things with police surveillance of the crew. This feeling would not perhaps have so prevailed with him were it not that upon a prior occasion the patriotic zeal officially evinced by Claggart had somewhat irritated him as appearing rather supersensible and strained. Furthermore, something even in the official's self-possessed and somewhat ostentatious manner in making his specifications strangely reminded him of a bandsman, a perjurous witness in a capital case before a court-martial ashore of which when a lieutenant he Captain Vere had been a member.

Now the peremptory check given to Claggart in the matter of the arrested allusion was quickly followed up by this: "You say that there is at least one dangerous man aboard. Name him."

"William Budd. A foretopman, your honor—"

"William Budd" repeated Captain Vere with unfeigned astonishment; "and mean you the man that Lieutenant Ratcliffe took from the merchantman not very long ago— the young fellow who seems to be so popular with the men—Billy, the Handsome Sailor, as they call him?["]

"The same, your honor; but for all his youth and good looks, a deep one. Not for nothing does he insinuate himself into the good will of his shipmates, since at the least all hands will at a pinch say a good word for him at all hazards. Did Lieutenant Ratcliffe happen to tell your honor of that adroit fling of Budd's, jumping up in the cutter's bow under the merchantman's stern when he was being taken off? It is even masqued by that sort of good humored air that at heart he resents his impressment. You have but noted his fair cheek. A man-trap may be under his ruddy-tipped daisies."

Now the *Handsome Sailor* as a signal figure among the crew had naturally enough attracted the Captain's attention from the first. Tho' in general not very demonstrative to his officers, he had congratulated Lieutenant Ratcliffe upon his good fortune in lighting on such a fine specimen of the genus homo, who in the nude might have posed for a statue of young Adam before the Fall.

As to Billy's adieu to the ship *Rights-of-Man,* which the boarding lieutenant had indeed reported to him but in a deferential way more as a good story than aught else, Captain Vere[,] tho mistakenly understanding it as a satiric sally, had but thought so much the better of the impressed man for it; as a military sailor, admiring the spirit that could take an arbitrary enlistment so merrily and sensibly. The foretopman's conduct, too, so far as it had fallen under the Captain's notice had confirmed the first happy augury, while the new recruit's qualities as a *sailor-man* seemed to be such that he had thought of recommending him to the executive officer for promotion to a place that would more frequently bring him under his own observation, namely, the captaincy of the mizzen-top, replacing there in the starboard watch a man not so young whom partly for that reason he deemed less fitted for the post. Be it parenthesized here that since the mizzen-top-men having not to handle such breadths of heavy canvas as the lower sails on the main-mast and fore-mast, a young man if of the right stuff not only seems best adapted to duty there, but in fact is generally selected for the captaincy of that top, and the company under him are light hands and often but striplings. In sum, Captain Vere had from the beginning deemed Billy Budd to be what in the naval parlance of the time was called a "King's *bargain*[,]" that is to say, for His Britannic Majesty's navy a capital investment at small outlay or none at all.

After a brief pause during which the reminiscences above mentioned passed vividly through his mind and he weighed the import of Claggart's last suggestion conveyed in the phrase "pitfall under the clover,"[107] and the more he weighed it the less reliance he felt in the informer's good faith. Suddenly[108] he turned upon him and in a low voice: "Do you come to me, master-at-arms[,] with so foggy a tale? As to Budd, cite me an act or spoken word of his confirmatory of what you in general charge against him. Stay," drawing nearer to him "heed what you speak. Just now, and in a case like this, there is a yard-arm-end for the false-witness."

"Ah, your honor!" sighed Claggart mildly shaking his shapely head as in sad deprecation of such unmerited severity of tone. Then, bridling—erecting himself as in virtuous self-assertion, he circumstantially alleged certain words and acts, which collectively, if credited, led to presumptions mortally inculpating Budd. And for some of these averments, he added, substantiating proof was not far.

With gray eyes impatient and distrustful essaying to fathom to the bottom Claggart's calm violet ones, Captain Vere again heard him out; then for the moment stood ruminating. The mood he evinced, Claggart—himself for the time liberated from the other's scrutiny—steadily regarded with a look difficult to render,—a look curious of the operation of his tactics, a look such as might have been that of the spokesman of the envious children of Jacob deceptively imposing upon the troubled patriarch the blood-dyed coat of young Joseph.[109]

Though something exceptional in the moral quality of Captain Vere made him, in earnest encounter with a fellow-man, a veritable touch-stone of that man's essential nature, yet now as to Claggart and what was really going on in him his feeling partook less of intuitional conviction than of strong suspicion clogged by strange dubieties. The perplexity he evinced proceeded less from aught touching the man informed against—as Claggart doubtless opined—than from considerations how best to act in regard to the informer. At first indeed he was naturally for summoning that substantiation of his allegations which Claggart said was at hand. But such a proceeding would result in the matter at once getting abroad, which in the present stage of it, he thought, might undesirably affect the ship's company. If Claggart was a false witness,—that closed the

107. *Cf.* "A man-trap * * * under his * * * daisies," ending the third paragraph above. There Melville had first written, then crossed out, "a pitfall under his ruddy clover," the words that Captain Vere remembers here. The discrepancy might have been corrected had Melville seen the manuscript through press.

108. The manuscript reads, "good faith, suddenly * * *," an obvious comma splice between two sentences. It was the first edition.

109. Genesis 37:31–32: "And they took Joseph's coat, and killed a kid of the goats, and dipped the coat in the blood; and they sent the coat of many colours, and they brought it to their father; and said, This have we found: know now whether it be thy son's coat or no."

affair. And therefore before trying the accusation, he would first practically test the accuser; and he thought this could be done in a quiet undemonstrative way.

The measure he determined upon involved a shifting of the scene, a transfer to a place less exposed to observation than the broad quarter-deck. For although the few gun-room officers there at the time had, in due observance of naval etiquette, withdrawn to leeward the moment Captain Vere had begun his promenade on the deck's weather-side; and tho' during the colloquy with Claggart they of course ventured not to diminish the distance; and though throughout the interview Captain Vere's voice was far from high, and Claggart's silvery and low; and the wind in the cordage and the wash of the sea helped the more to put them beyond ear-shot; nevertheless, the interview's continuance already had attracted observation from some topmen aloft and other sailors in the waist or further forward.

Having determined upon his measures, Captain Vere forthwith took action. Abruptly turning to Claggart he asked "Master-at-arms, is it now Budd's watch aloft?"

"No, your honor." Whereupon, "Mr. Wilkes!" summoning the nearest midshipman, "tell Albert to come to me." Albert was the Captain's hammock-boy, a sort of sea-valet in whose discretion and fidelity his master had much confidence. The lad appeared. "You know Budd the foretopman?"

"I do, Sir."

"Go find him. It is his watch off. Manage to tell him out of ear-shot that he is wanted aft. Contrive it that he speaks to nobody. Keep him in talk yourself. And not till you get well aft here, not till then let him know that the place where he is wanted is my cabin. You understand. Go.—Master-at-Arms, show yourself on the decks below, and when you think it time for Albert to be coming with his man, stand by quietly to follow the sailor in."

20

Now when the foretopman found himself closeted there, as it were, in the cabin with the Captain and Claggart, he was surprised enough. But it was a surprise unaccompanied by apprehension or distrust. To an immature nature essentially honest and humane, forewarning intimations of subtler danger from one's kind come tardily if at all. The only thing that took shape in the young sailor's mind was this: Yes, the Captain, I have always thought, looks kindly upon me. Wonder if he's going to make me his coxswain. I should like that. And maybe now he is going to ask the master-at-arms about me.

"Shut the door there, sentry," said the commander; "stand without, and let nobody come in.—Now, master-at-arms, tell this man to his face what you told of him to me;" and stood prepared to scrutinize the mutually confronting visages.

With the measured step and calm collected air of an asylum-physician approaching in the public hall some patient beginning to show indications of a coming paroxysm, Claggart deliberately advanced within short range of Billy, and mesmerically looking him in the eye, briefly recapitulated the accusation.

Not at first did Billy take it in. When he did, the rose-tan of his cheek looked struck as by white leprosy. He stood like one impaled and gagged. Meanwhile the accuser's eyes removing not as yet from the blue dilated ones, underwent a phenomenal change, their wonted rich violet color blurring into a muddy purple. Those lights of human intelligence losing human expression, gelidly protruding like the alien eyes of certain uncatalogued creatures of the deep. The first mesmeric glance was one of serpent fascination; the last was as the hungry lurch of the torpedo-fish.

"Speak, man!" said Captain Vere to the transfixed one struck by his aspect even more than by Claggart's, "Speak! defend yourself." Which appeal caused but a strange dumb gesturing and gurgling in Billy; amazement at such an accusation to suddenly sprung on inexperienced nonage; this, and, it may be horror of the accuser, serving to bring out his lurking defect and in this instance for the time intensifying it into a convulsed tongue-tie; while the intent head and entire form straining forward in an agony of ineffectual eagerness to obey the injunction to speak and defend himself, gave an expression to the face like that of a condemned Vestal priestess in the moment of being buried alive, and in the first struggle against suffocation.[110]

Though at the time Captain Vere was quite ignorant of Billy's liability to vocal impediment, he now immediately divined it, since vividly Billy's aspect recalled to him that of a bright young schoolmate of his whom he had once seen struck by much the same startling impotence in the act of eagerly rising in the class to be foremost in response to a testing question put to it by the master. Going close up to the young sailor, and laying a soothing hand on his shoulder, he said[:] "There is no hurry, my boy. Take your time, take your time." Contrary to the effect intended, these words so fatherly in tone, doubtless touching Billy's heart to the quick, prompted yet more violent efforts at utterance—efforts soon ending for the time in confirming the paralysis, and bringing to his face an expression which was as a crucifixion to behold. The next instant, quick as the flame from a discharged cannon at night, his right arm shot out, and Claggart dropped to the deck. Whether intentionally or but owing to the young athlete's superior height, the blow had taken effect full upon the forehead, so shapely and intellectual-look-

110. the punishment given to Vestal Virgins in Rome if they violated their vows.

ing a feature in the master-at-arms; so that the body fell over lengthwise, like a heavy plank tilted from erectness. A gasp or two, and he lay motionless.

"Fated boy," breathed Captain Vere in tone so low as to be almost a whisper, "what have you done! But here, help me."

The twain raised the felled one from the loins up into a sitting position. The spare form flexibly acquiesced, but inertly. It was like handling a dead snake. They lowered it back. Regaining erectness Captain Vere with one hand covering his face stood to all appearance as impassive as the object at his feet. Was he absorbed in taking in all the bearings of the event and what was best not only now at once to be done, but also in the sequel? Slowly he uncovered his face; and the effect was as if the moon emerging from eclipse should reappear with quite another aspect than that which had gone into hiding. The father in him, manifested towards Billy thus far in the scene, was replaced by the military disciplinarian. In his official tone he bade the foretopman retire to a state-room aft, (pointing it out) and there remain till thence summoned. This order Billy in silence mechanically obeyed. Then going to the cabin-door where it opened on the quarter-deck, Captain Vere said to the sentry without, "Tell somebody to send Albert here." When the lad appeared his master so contrived it that he should not catch sight of the prone one. "Albert," he said to him, "tell the Surgeon I wish to see him. You need not come back till called." When the Surgeon entered—a self-poised character of that grave sense and experience that hardly anything could take him aback,—Captain Vere advanced to meet him, thus unconsciously intercepting his view of Claggart and interrupting the other's wonted ceremonious salutation, said, "Nay, tell me how it is with yonder man," directing his attention to the prostrate one.

The Surgeon looked, and for all his self-command, somewhat started at the abrupt revelation. On Claggart's always pallid complexion, thick black blood was now oozing from nostril and ear. To the gazer's professional eye it was unmistakably no living man that he saw.

"Is it so then?["] said Captain Vere intently watching him. "I thought it. But verify it." Whereupon the customary tests confirmed the Surgeon's first glance, who now looking up in unfeigned concern, cast a look of intense inquisitiveness upon his superior. But Captain Vere, with one hand to his brow, was standing motionless. Suddenly, catching the Surgeon's arm convulsively, he exclaimed, pointing down to the body—"It is the divine judgment on Ananias![111] Look!"

Disturbed by the excited manner he had never before observed in

111. Acts 5: 3-5: "Peter said, Ananias * * * thou hast not lied unto men, but unto God. And Ananias hearing these words fell down, and gave up the ghost."

the *Indomitable*'s Captain, and as yet wholly ignorant of the affair, the prudent Surgeon nevertheless held his peace, only again looking an earnest interrogation as to what it was that had resulted in such a tragedy.

But Captain Vere was now again motionless standing absorbed in thought. But again starting, he vehemently exclaimed—"Struck dead by an angel of God! Yet the angel must hang![")]

At these passionate interjections, mere incoherences to the listener as yet unapprised of the antecedents, the Surgeon was profoundly discomposed. But now as recollecting himself, Captain Vere in less harsh tone briefly related the circumstances leading up to the event.

["]But come; we must despatch" he added. ["]Help me to remove him (meaning the body) to yonder compartment,["] designating one opposite that where the foretopman remained immured. Anew disturbed by a request that as implying a desire for secrecy, seemed unaccountably strange to him, there was nothing for the subordinate to do but comply.

"Go now" said Captain Vere with something of his wonted manner—["]Go now, I shall presently call a drum-head court.[112] Tell the lieutenants what has happened, and tell Mr. Mordant," meaning the captain of marines, "and charge them to keep the matter to themselves."

21

Full of disquietude and misgiving the Surgeon left the cabin. Was Captain Vere suddenly affected in his mind, or was it but a transient excitement, brought about by so strange and extraordinary a happening? As to the drum-head court, it struck the Surgeon as impolitic, if nothing more. The thing to do, he thought, was to place Billy Budd in confinement and in a way dictated by usage, and postpone further action in so extraordinary a case, to such time as they should rejoin the squadron, and then refer it to the Admiral. He recalled the unwonted agitation of Captain Vere and his excited exclamations so at variance with his normal manner. Was he unhinged? But assuming that he is, it is not so susceptible of proof. What then can he do? No more trying situation is conceivable than that of an officer subordinate under a Captain whom he suspects to be, not mad indeed, but yet not quite unaffected in his intellect. To argue his order to him would be insolence. To resist him would be mutiny.

In obedience to Captain Vere he communicated what had happened to the lieutenants & captain of marines; saying nothing as to the Captain's state. They fully shared his own surprise and concern.

112. a court-martial, originally held around an upturned drum, to try offenses committed during military operations.

Like him too they seemed to think that such a matter should be preferred to the Admiral.

22

Who in the rainbow can draw the line where the violet tint ends and the orange tint begins? Distinctly we see the difference of the colors, but where exactly does the one first blendingly enter into the other? So with sanity and insanity. In pronounced cases there is no question about them. But in some supposed cases, in various degrees supposedly less pronounced, to draw the exact line of demarkation few will undertake tho for a fee some professional experts will. There is nothing namable but that some men will undertake to do it for pay.

Whether Captain Vere, as the Surgeon professionally and privately surmised, was really the sudden victim of any degree of aberration, one must determine for himself by such light as this narrative may afford.

[That] the unhappy event which has been narrated could not have happened at a worse juncture was but too true. For it was close on the heel of the suppressed insurrections, an aftertime very critical to naval authority, demanding from every English sea-commander two qualities not readily interfusable—prudence and rigor. Moreover there was something crucial in the case.

In the jugglery of circumstances preceding and attending the event on board the *Indomitable* and in the light of that martial code whereby it was formally to be judged, innocence and guilt personified in Claggart and Budd in effect changed places. In a legal view the apparent victim of the tragedy was he who had sought to victimize a man blameless; and the indisputable deed of the latter, navally regarded, constituted the most heinous of military crimes. Yet more. The essential right and wrong involved in the matter, the clearer that might be, so much the worse for the responsibility of a loyal sea-commander inasmuch as he was not authorized to determine the matter on that primitive basis.

Small wonder then that the *Indomitable*'s Captain though in general a man of rapid decision, felt that circumspectness not less than promptitude was necessary. Until he could decide upon his course, and in each detail; and not only so, but until the concluding measure was upon the point of being enacted, he deemed it advisable, in view of all the circumstances to guard as much as possible against publicity. Here he may or may not have erred. Certain it is however that subsequently in the confidential talk of more than one or two gun-rooms and cabins he was not a little criticized by some officers, a fact imputed by his friends and vehemently by his cousin Jack Denton to professional jealousy of *Starry Vere*. Some imaginative ground for invidious comment there was. The maintenance of secrecy in the matter, the confining all knowledge of it for a time to the place where the homicide occurred, the quarter-deck cabin; in these particulars lurked some resemblance to the policy adopted in those tragedies of the palace which have occurred more than once in the capital founded by Peter the Barbarian.[113]

The case indeed was such that fain would the *Indomitable*'s captain have deferred taking any action whatever respecting it further than to keep the foretopman a close prisoner till the ship rejoined the squadron and then submitting the matter to the judgement of his Admiral.

But a true military officer is in one particular like a true monk. Not with more of self-abnegation will the latter keep his vows of monastic obedience than the former his vows of allegiance to martial duty.

Feeling that unless quick action was taken on it, the deed of the foretopman, so soon as it should be known on the gun-decks would tend to awaken any slumbering embers of the Nore among the crew, a sense of the urgency of the case overruled in Captain Vere every other consideration. But tho' a conscientious disciplinarian he was no lover of authority for mere authority's sake. Very far was he from embracing opportunities for monopolizing to himself the perils of moral responsibility[,] none at least that could properly be referred to an official superior or shared with him by his official equals or even subordinates. So thinking[,] he was glad it would not be at variance with usage to turn the matter over to a summary court of his own officers, reserving to himself as the one on whom the ultimate accountability would rest, the right of maintaining a supervision of it, or formally or informally interposing at need. Accordingly a drum-head court was summarily convened, he electing the individuals composing it, the First Lieutenant, the Captain of marines, and the Sailing Master.

In associating an officer of marines with the sea-lieutenants in a case having to do with a sailor the Commander perhaps deviated from general custom. He was prompted thereto by the circumstance that he took that soldier to be a judicious person, thoughtful, and not altogether incapable of grappling with a difficult case unprecedented in his prior experience. Yet even as to him he was not without some latent misgiving, for withal he was an extremely good-natured man, an enjoyer of his dinner, a sound sleeper, and inclined to obesity. [A] man who tho' he would always maintain his manhood in battle might not prove altogether reliable in a moral dilemma involving aught of the tragic. As to the First Lieutenant and the Sailing Master Captain Vere could not but be aware that though honest natures, of approved gallantry upon occasion[,] their intelligence was mostly confined to the matter of active seamanship and

113. St. Petersburg, founded by Peter the Great in 1703.

the fighting demands of their profession. The court was held in the same cabin where the unfortunate affair had taken place. This cabin, the Commander's, embraced the entire area under the poop-deck. Aft, and on either side[,] was a small state-room[;] the one room temporarily a jail & the other a dead-house[,] and a yet smaller compartment leaving a space between, expanding forward into a goodly oblong of length coinciding with the ship's beam. A skylight of moderate dimension was overhead and at each end of the oblong space were two sashed port-hole windows easily convertible back into embrasures for short carronades.

All being quickly in readiness, Billy Budd was arraigned, Captain Vere necessarily appearing as the sole witness in the case, and as such temporarily sinking his rank, though singularly maintaining it in a matter apparently trivial, namely, that he testified from the ship's weather-side[,] with that object having caused the court to sit on the lee-side. Concisely he narrated all that had led up to the catastrophe, omitting nothing in Claggart's accusation and deposing as to the manner in which the prisoner had received it. At his testimony the three officers glanced with no little surprise at Billy Budd, the last man they would have suspected either of the mutinous design alleged by Claggart or the undeniable deed he himself had done.

The First Lieutenant[,] taking judicial primacy and turning toward the prisoner, said, "Captain Vere has spoken. Is it or is it not as Captain Vere says?" In response came syllables not so much impeded in the utterance as might have been anticipated. They were these: "Captain Vere tells the truth. It is just as Captain Vere says, but it is not as the Master-at-Arms said. I have eaten the King's bread and I am true to the King."

"I believe you, my man" said the witness[,] his voice indicating a suppressed emotion not otherwise betrayed.

"God will bless you for that, Your Honor!" not without stammering said Billy, and all but broke down. But immediately was recalled to self-control by another question, to which with the same emotional difficulty of utterance he said "No, there was no malice between us. I never bore malice against the Master-at-arms. I am sorry that he is dead. I did not mean to kill him. Could I have used my tongue I would not have struck him. But he foully lied to my face and in presence of my Captain, and I had to say something, and I could only say it with a blow, God help me!"

In the impulsive above-board manner of the frank one[,] the court saw confirmed all that was implied in words that just previously had perplexed them[,] coming as they did from the testifier to the tragedy and promptly following Billy's impassioned disclaimer of mutinous intent—Captain Vere's words, "I believe you, my man."

Next it was asked of him whether he knew of or suspected aught savoring of incipient trouble (meaning mutiny, tho' the explicit term was avoided) going on in any section of the ship's company.

The reply lingered. This was naturally imputed by the court to the same vocal embarrassment which had retarded or obstructed previous answers. But in main it was otherwise here; the question immediately recalling to Billy's mind the interview with the afterguardsman in the fore-chains. But an innate repugnance to playing a part at all approaching that of an informer against one's own shipmates—the same erring sense of uninstructed honor which had stood in the way of his reporting the matter at the time though as a loyal man-of-war-man it was incumbent on him[,] and failure so to do if charged against him and proven, would have subjected him to the heaviest of penalties; this, with the blind feeling now his, that nothing really was being hatched, prevailed with him. When the answer came it was a negative.

"One question more," said the officer of marines now first speaking and with a troubled earnestness, "You tell us that what the Master-at-arms said against you was a lie. Now why should he have so lied, so maliciously lied, since you declare there was no malice between you?"

At that question unintentionally touching on a spiritual sphere wholly obscure to Billy's thoughts, he was nonplussed, evincing a confusion indeed that some observers, such as can readily be imagined, would have construed into involuntary evidence of hidden guilt. Nevertheless he strove some way to answer, but all at once relinquished the vain endeavor, at the same time turning an appealing glance towards Captain Vere as deeming him his best helper and friend. Captain Vere who had been seated for a time rose to his feet, addressing the interrogator. "The question you put to him comes naturally enough. But how can he rightly answer it? or anybody else? unless indeed it be he who lies within there" designating the compartment where lay the corpse. "But the prone one there will not rise to our summons. In effect, tho', as it seems to me, the point you make is hardly material. Quite aside from any conceivable motive actuating the Master-at-arms, and irrespective of the provocation to the blow, a martial court must needs in the present case confine its attention to the blow's consequence, which consequence justly is to be deemed not otherwise than as the striker's deed."

This utterance the full significance of which it was not at all likely that Billy took in, nevertheless caused him to turn a wistful interrogative look toward the speaker, a look in its dumb expressiveness not unlike that which a dog of generous breed might turn upon his master seeking in his face some elucidation of a previous gesture ambiguous to the canine intelligence. Nor was the same utterance without marked effect upon the three officers, more especially the soldier. Couched in it seemed to them a meaning unanticipated, involving a prejudgement on the speaker's part. It served to augment a mentsl disturbance previously evident enough.

The soldier once more spoke; in a tone of suggestive dubiety addressing at once his associates and Captain Vere: "Nobody is present—none of the ship's company, I mean, who might shed lateral light, if any is to be had, upon what remains mysterious in this matter."

"That is thoughtfully put" said Captain Vere; "I see your drift. Ay, there is a mystery; but, to use a Scriptural phrase, it is 'a mystery of iniquity,' a matter for psychologic theologians to discuss. But what has a military court to do with it? Not to add that for us any possible investigation of it is cut off by the lasting tongue-tie of—him—in yonder," again designating the mortuary state-room ["]The prisoner's deed,—with that alone we have to do."

To this, and particularly the closing reiteration, the marine soldier knowing not how aptly to reply, sadly abstained from saying aught. The First Lieutenant who at the outset had not unnaturally assumed primacy in the court, now overrulingly instructed by a glance from Captain Vere, a glance more effective than words, resumed that primacy. Turning to the prisoner, "Budd," he said, and scarce in equable tones, "Budd, if you have aught further to say for yourself, say it now."

Upon this the young sailor turned another quick glance toward Captain Vere; then, as taking a hint from that aspect, a hint confirming his own instinct that silence was now best, replied to the Lieutenant "I have said all, Sir."

The marine—the same who had been the sentinel without the cabin-door at the time that the foretopman followed by the master-at-arms, entered it—he, standing by the sailor throughout these judicial proceedings, was now directed to take him back to the after compartment originally assigned to the prisoner and his custodian. As the twain disappeared from view, the three officers as partially liberated from some inward constraint associated with Billy's mere presence, simultaneously stirred in their seats. They exchanged looks of troubled indecision, yet feeling that decide they must and without long delay. As for Captain Vere, he for the time stood unconsciously with his back toward them, apparently in one of his absent fits, gazing out from a sashed port-hole to windward upon the monotonous blank of the twilight sea. But the court's silence continuing, broken only at moments by brief consultations in low earnest tones, this seemed to arm him and energize him. Turning, he to-and-fro paced the cabin athwart; in the returning ascent to windward, climbing the slant deck in the ship's lee roll; without knowing it symbolizing thus in his action a mind resolute to surmount difficulties even if against primitive instincts strong as the wind and the sea. Presently he came to a stand before the three. After scanning their faces he stood less as mustering his thoughts for expression, than as one only deliberating how best to put them to well-meaning men not intellectually mature, men with whom it was necessary to demonstrate certain principles that were axioms to himself. Similar impatience as to talking is perhaps one reason that deters some minds from addressing any popular assemblies.

When speak he did, something both in the substance of what he said and his manner of saying it, showed the influence of unshared studies modifying and tempering the practical training of an active career. This, along with his phraseology now and then was suggestive of the grounds whereon rested that imputation of a certain pedantry socially alleged against him by certain naval men of wholly practical cast, captains who nevertheless would frankly concede that His Majesty's navy mustered no more efficient officer of their grade than *Starry Vere*.

What he said was to this effect: "Hitherto I have been but the witness, little more; and I should hardly think now to take another tone, that of your coadjutor, for the time, did I not perceive in you,—at the crisis too—a troubled hesitancy, proceeding, I doubt not from the clash of military duty with moral scruple—scruple vitalized by compassion. For the compassion how can I otherwise than share it. But, mindful of paramount obligations I strive against scruples that may tend to enervate decision. Not, gentlemen, that I hide from myself that the case is an exceptional one. Speculatively regarded, it well might be referred to a jury of casuists. But for us here acting not as casuists or moralists, it is a case practical, and under martial law practically to be dealt with.

"But your scruples: do they move as in a dusk? Challenge them. Make them advance and declare themselves. Come now: do they import something like this: If, mindless of palliating circumstances, we are bound to regard the death of the Master-at-arms as the prisoner's deed, then does that deed constitute a capital crime whereof the penalty is a mortal one. But in natural justice is nothing but the prisoner's overt act to be considered? How can we adjudge to summary and shameful death a fellow-creature innocent before God, and whom we feel to be so?—Does that state it aright? You sign sad assent. Well, I too feel that, the full force of that. It is Nature. But do these buttons that we wear attest that our allegiance is to Nature? No, to the King. Though the ocean, which is inviolate Nature primeval, tho' this be the element where we move and have our being as sailors, yet as the King's officers lies our duty in a sphere correspondingly natural? So little is that true, that in receiving our commissions we in the most important regards ceased to be natural free-agents. When war is declared are we the commissioned fighters previously consulted? We fight at command. If our judgements approve the war, that is but coincidence. So in other particulars. So now. For suppose condemnation to follow these present proceedings. Would it be so much we ourselves that would condemn as it would be martial law operating through us? For that law and the rigour of it, we are not responsible. Our vowed responsibility is in this: That however pitilessly that law may operate, we nevertheless adhere to it and administer it.

["] But the exceptional in the matter moves the hearts within you. Even so too is mine moved. But let not warm hearts betray heads that should be cool. Ashore in a criminal case will an upright judge allow himself off the bench to be waylaid by some tender kinswoman of the accused seeking to touch him with her tearful plea? Well the heart here denotes the feminine in man[114] is as that piteous woman, and hard tho' it be[,] she must here be ruled out."

He paused, earnestly studying them for a moment; then resumed.

"But something in your aspect seems to urge that it is not solely the heart that moves in you, but also the conscience, the private conscience. But tell me whether or not, occupying the position we do, private conscience should not yield to that imperial one formulated in the code under which alone we officially proceed?"

Here the three men moved in their seats, less convinced than agitated by the course of an argument troubling but the more the spontaneous conflict within.

Perceiving which, the speaker paused for a moment; then abruptly changing his tone, went on.

"To steady us a bit, let us recur to the facts.—In war-time at sea a man-of-war's-man strikes his superior in grade, and the blow kills. Apart from its effect the blow itself is, according to the Articles of War,[115] a capital crime. Furthermore—"

"Ay, Sir," emotionally broke in the officer of marines, "in one sense it was. But surely Budd purposed neither mutiny nor homicide."

"Surely not. my good man. And before a court less arbitrary and more merciful than a martial one, that plea would largely extenuate. At the Last Assizes[116] it shall acquit. But how here? We proceed under the law of the Mutiny Act.[117] In feature no child can resemble his father more than that Act resembles in spirit the thing from which it derives—War. In His Majesty['s] service—in this ship indeed—there are Englishmen forced to fight for the King against their will. Against their conscience, for aught we know. Tho' as their fellow-creatures some of us may appreciate their position, yet as navy officers, what reck we of it? Still less recks the enemy. Our impressed men he would fain cut down in the same swath with our volunteers. As regards the enemy's naval conscripts, some of whom may even share our own abhorrence of the regicidal French Directory,[118] it is the same on our side. War looks but to the frontage,

114. the comma in the manuscript is deleted here.

115. regulations governing the behavior of military and naval forces.

116. Assizes are the highest courts of appeal in Great Britain. Here Melville means the Last Judgment.

117. The original Mutiny Act (1689) and successive acts passed by the British Parliaments applied only to the army; the navy followed the King's Regulations and Admiralty Instructions of 1772.

118. The governing body of France at the time of this story.

the appearance. And the Mutiny Act, War's child, takes after the father. Budd's intent or non-intent is nothing to the purpose.

["]But while, put to it by those anxieties in you which I can not but respect, I only repeat myself—while thus strangely we prolong proceedings that should be summary—the enemy may be sighted and an engagement result. We must do; and one of two things must we do—condemn or let go."

"Can we not convict and yet mitigate the penalty?" asked the junior Lieutenant here speaking, and falteringly, for the first.

"Lieutenant, were that clearly lawful for us under the circumstances consider the consequences of such clemency. The people" (meaning the ship's company) "have native-sense; most of them are familiar with our naval usage and tradition; and how would they take it? Even could you explain to them—which our official position forbids—they, long moulded by arbitrary discipline have not that kind of intelligent responsiveness that might qualify them to comprehend and discriminate. No, to the people the foretopman's deed however it be worded in the announcement will be plain homicide committed in a flagrant act of mutiny. What penalty for that should follow, they know. But it does not follow. *Why?* they will ruminate. You know what sailors are. Will they not revert to the recent outbreak at the Nore? Ay. They know the well-founded alarm—the panic it struck throughout England. Your clement sentence they would account pusillanimous. They would think that we flinch, that we are afraid of them—afraid of practising a lawful rigor singularly demanded at this juncture lest it should provoke new troubles. What shame to us such a conjecture on their part, and how deadly to discipline. You see then, whither prompted by duty and the law I steadfastly drive. But I beseech you, my friends, do not take me amiss. I feel as you do for this unfortunate boy. But did he know our hearts, I take him to be of that generous nature that he would feel even for us on whom in this military necessity so heavy a compulsion is laid."

With that, crossing the deck he resumed his place by the sashed port-hole tacitly leaving the three to come to a decision. On the cabin's opposite side the troubled court sat silent. Loyal lieges, plain and practical, though at bottom they dissented from some points Captain Vere had put to them, they were without the faculty, hardly had the inclination to gainsay one whom they felt to be an earnest man, one too not less their superior in mind than in naval rank. But it is not improbable that even such of his words as were not without influence over them, less came home to them than his closing appeal to their instinct as sea-officers in the forethought he threw out as to the practical consequences to discipline, considering the unconfirmed tone of the fleet at the time, should a man-of-war's-man['s] violent killing at sea of a superior in grade be allowed to pass for aught else than a capital crime demanding prompt infliction of the penalty.

Not unlikely they were brought to something more or less akin to that harassed frame of mind which in the year 1842 actuated the commander of the U.S. brig-of-war *Somers*[119] to resolve, under the so-called Articles of War, Articles modelled upon the English Mutiny Act, to resolve upon the execution at sea of a midshipman and two petty-officers as mutineers designing the seizure of the brig. Which resolution was carried out though in a time of peace and within not many days sail of home. An act vindicated by a naval court of inquiry subsequently convened ashore. History, and here cited without comment. True, the circumstances on board the *Somers* were different from those on board the *Indomitable*. But the urgency felt, well-warranted or otherwise, was much the same.

Says a writer whom few know, "Forty years after a battle it is easy for a non-combatant to reason about how it ought to have been fought. It is another thing personally and under fire to direct the fighting while involved in the obscuring smoke of it. Much so with respect to other emergencies involving considerations both practical and moral, and when it is imperative promptly to act. The greater the fog the more it imperils the steamer, and speed is put on tho' at the hazard of running somebody down. Little ween the snug card-players in the cabin of the responsibilities of the sleepless man on the bridge."

In brief, Billy Budd was formally convicted and sentenced to be hung at the yard-arm in the early morning-watch, it being now night. Otherwise, as is customary in such cases, the sentence would forthwith have been carried out. In war-time on the field or in the fleet, a mortal punishment decreed by a drum-head court—on the field sometimes decreed by but a nod from the General—follows without delay on the heel of conviction without appeal.

23

It was Captain Vere himself who of his own motion communicated the finding of the court to the prisoner; for that purpose going to the compartment where he was in custody and bidding the marine there to withdraw for the time.

Beyond the communication of the sentence what took place at this interview was never known. But in view of the character of the twain briefly closeted in that state-room, each radically sharing in the rarer qualities of our nature—so rare indeed as to be all but incredible to average minds however much cultivated—some conjectures may be ventured.

119. Melville's cousin, Guert Gansevoort, was first lieutenant of the *Somers* at the time of a mutiny. The incident seems to have impressed Melville, and perhaps it was in the back of his mind when he wrote *Billy Budd*.

It would have been in consonance with the spirit of Captain Vere should he on this occasion have concealed nothing from the condemned one—should he indeed have frankly disclosed to him the part he himself had played in bringing about the decision, at the same time revealing his actuating motives. On Billy's side it is not improbable that such a confession would have been received in much the same spirit that prompted it. Not without a sort of joy indeed he might have appreciated the brave opinion of him implied in his Captain making such a confidant of him. Nor, as to the sentence itself could he have been insensible that it was imparted to him as to one not afraid to die. Even more may have been. Captain Vere in [the] end may have developed the passion sometimes latent under a[n] exterior stoical or indifferent. He was old enough to have been Billy's father. The austere devotee of military duty letting himself melt back into what remains primeval in our formalized humanity may in [the] end have caught Billy to his heart even as Abraham may have caught young Isaac on the brink of resolutely offering him up in obedience to the exacting behest.[120] But there is no telling the sacrament, seldom if in any case revealed to the gadding world wherever under circumstances at all akin to those here attempted to be set forth two of great Nature's nobler order embrace. There is privacy at the time, inviolable to the survivor, and holy oblivion the sequel to each diviner magnanimity, providentially covers all at last.

The first to encounter Captain Vere in act of leaving the compartment was the senior Lieutenant. The face he beheld, for the moment one expressive of the agony of the strong, was to that officer, tho' a man of fifty, a startling revelation. That the condemned one suffered less than he who mainly had effected the condemnation was apparently indicated by the former's exclamation in the scene soon perforce to be touched upon.

24

Of a series of incidents within a brief term rapidly following each other, the adequate narration may take up a term less brief, especially if explanation or comment here and there seem requisite to the better understanding of such incidents. Between the entrance into the cabin of him who never left it alive, and him who when he did leave it left it as one condemned to die; between this and the closeted interview just given less than an hour and a half had elapsed. It was an interval long enough however to awaken speculations among no few of the ship's company as to what it was that could be detaining

120. Genesis 22: 1-18: "God did tempt Abraham, and said * * * Take now thy son, thine only son Isaac, whom thou lovest * * * and offer him * * * for a burnt offering * * * And Abraham bound Isaac his son, and laid him on the altar upon the wood. And Abraham stretched forth his hand, and took the knife to slay his son. And the angel of the Lord said, Lay not thine hand upon the lad, neither do thou anything unto him: for now I know that thou fearest God. And, saith the Lord, I will bless thee * * * because thou hast obeyed my voice."

in the cabin the master-at-arms and the sailor; for a rumor that both of them had been seen to enter it and neither of them had been seen to emerge, this rumor had got abroad upon the gun-decks and in the tops; the people of a great warship being in one respect like villagers taking microscopic note of every outward movement or non-movement going on. When therefore in weather not at all tempestuous all hands were called in the second dog-watch, a summons under such circumstances not usual in those hours, the crew were not wholly unprepared for some announcement extraordinary, one having connection too with the continued absence of the two men from their wonted haunts.

There was a moderate sea at the time; and the moon, newly risen and near to being at its full, silvered the white spar-deck wherever not blotted by the clear-cut shadows horizontally thrown of fixtures and moving men. On either side the quarter-deck the marine guard under arms was drawn up; and Captain Vere standing in his place surrounded by all the ward-room officers, addressed his men. In so doing his manner showed neither more nor less than that property pertaining to his supreme position aboard his own ship. In clear terms and concise he told them what had taken place in the cabin; that the master-at-arms was dead; that he who had killed him had been already tried by a summary court and condemned to death; and that the execution would take place in the early morning watch. The word *mutiny* was not named in what he said. He refrained too from making the occasion an opportunity for any preachment as to the maintenance of discipline, thinking perhaps that under existing circumstances in the navy the consequence of violating discipline should be made to speak for itself.

Their captain's announcement was listened to by the throng of standing sailors in a dumbness like that of a seated congregation of believers in hell listening to the clergyman's announcement of his Calvinistic text.

At the close, however, a confused murmur went up. It began to wax. All but instantly, then, at a sign, it was pierced and suppressed by shrill whistles of the Boatswain and his Mates piping down one watch.

To be prepared for burial Claggart's body was delivered to certain petty-officers of his mess. And here, not to clog the sequel with lateral matters, it may be added that at a suitable hour, the Master-at-arms was committed to the sea with every funeral honor properly belonging to his naval grade.

In this proceeding as in every public one growing out of the tragedy strict adherence to usage was observed. Nor in any point could it have been at all deviated from, either with respect to Claggart or Billy Budd[,] without begetting undesirable speculations in the ship's company, sailors, and more particularly men-of-war's men, being of all men the greatest sticklers for usage.

For similar cause, all communication between Captain Vere and the condemned one ended with the closeted interview already given, the latter being now surrendered to the ordinary routine preliminary to the end. This transfer under guard from the Captain's quarters was effected without unusual precautions—at least no visible ones.

If possible not to let the men so much as surmise that their officers anticipate aught amiss from them is the tacit rule in a military ship. And the more that some sort of trouble should really be apprehended the more do the officers keep that apprehension to themselves; tho' not the less unostentatious vigilance may be augmented.

In the present instance the sentry placed over the prisoner had strict orders to let no one have communication with him but the Chaplain. And certain unobtrusive measures were taken absolutely to insure this point.

25

In a seventy-four of the old order the deck known as the upper gun-deck was the one covered over by the spar-deck which last though not without its armament was for the most part exposed to the weather. In general it was at all hours free from hammocks; those of the crew swinging on the lower gun-deck, and berth-deck, the latter being not only a dormitory but also the place for the stowing of the sailors' bags, and on both sides lined with the large chests or movable pantries of the many messes of the men.

On the starboard side of the *Indomitable*'s upper gun-deck, behold Billy Budd under sentry lying prone in irons in one of the bays formed by the regular spacing of the guns comprising the batteries on either side. All these pieces were of the heavier calibre of that period. Mounted on lumbering wooden carriages they were hampered with cumbersome harness of breeching and strong side-tackles for running them out. Guns and carriages, together with the long rammers and shorter lintstocks lodged in loops overhead—all these, as customary, were painted black; and the heavy hempen breechings tarred to the same tint, wore the like livery of the undertakers. In contrast with the funereal hue of these surroundings the prone sailor's exterior apparel, white *jumper* and white duck trousers, each more or less soiled, dimly glimmered in the obscure light of the bay like a patch of discolored snow in early April lingering at some upland cave's black mouth. In effect he is already in his shroud or the garments that shall serve him in lieu of one. Over him but scarce illuminating him, two battle-lanterns swing from two massive beams of the deck above. Fed with the oil supplied by the war-contractors (whose gains, honest or otherwise, are in every land an anticipated portion of the harvest of death) with flickering splashes of dirty yellow light they pollute the pale moonshine[,] all but ineffectually struggling in obstructed flecks thro the open ports from which the tompioned[121] cannon protrude. Other lanterns at intervals serve but to bring out somewhat the obscurer bays which like small confessionals or side-chapels in a cathedral branch from the long dim-vistaed broad aisle between the two batteries of that covered tier.

Such was the deck where now lay the Handsome Sailor. Through the rose-tan of his complexion, no pallor could have shown. It would have taken days of sequestration from the winds and the sun to have brought about the effacement of that. But the skeleton in the cheekbone at the point of its angle was just beginning delicately to be defined under the warm-tinted skin. In fervid hearts self-contained some brief experiences devour our human tissue as secret fire in a ship's hold consumes cotton in the bale.

But now lying between the two guns, as nipped in the vice of fate, Billy's agony, mainly proceeding from a generous young heart's virgin experience of the diabolical incarnate and effective in some men—the tension of that agony was over now. It survived not the something healing in the closeted interview with Captain Vere. Without movement, he lay as in a trance. That adolescent expression previously noted as his, taking on something akin to the look of a slumbering child in the cradle when the warm hearth-glow of the still chamber at night plays on the dimples that at whiles mysteriously form in the cheek, silently coming and going there. For now and then in the gyved one's trance a serene happy light born of some wandering reminiscence or dream would diffuse itself over his face, and then wane away only anew to return.

The Chaplain coming to see him and finding him thus, and perceiving no sign that he was conscious of his presence, attentively regarded him for a space, then slipping aside, withdrew for the time, peradventure feeling that even he the minister of Christ tho' receiving his stipend from Mars had no consolation to proffer which could result in a peace transcending that which he beheld. But in the small hours he came again. And the prisoner now awake to his surroundings noticed his approach and civilly, all but cheerfully, welcomed him. But it was to little purpose that in the interview following the good man sought to bring Billy Budd to some godly understanding that he must die, and at dawn. True, Billy himself freely referred to his death as a thing close at hand; but it was something in the way that children will refer to death in general, who yet among their other sports will play a funeral with hearse and mourners.

Not that like children Billy was incapable of conceiving what death really is. No, but he was wholly without irrational fear of it, a fear more prevalent in highly civilized communities than those

121. usually "tampioned": plugged with a tampion, which fits into the muzzle of a gun not in use.

so-called barbarous ones which in all respects stand nearer to unadulterate Nature. And, as elsewhere said, a barbarian Billy radically was; as much so, for all the costume, as his countrymen the British captives, living trophies, made to march in the Roman triumph of Germanicus.[122] Quite as much so as those later barbarians, young men probably, and picked specimens among the earlier British converts to Christianity, at least nominally such and taken to Rome (as today converts from lesser isles of the sea may be taken to London) of whom the Pope of that time, admiring the strangeness of their personal beauty so unlike the Italian stamp, their clear ruddy complexion and curled flaxen locks, exclaimed, "Angles" (meaning *English* the modern derivative) "Angles do you call them? And is it because they look so like angels?"[123] Had it been later in time one would think that the Pope had in mind Fra Angelico's seraphs some of whom, plucking apples in gardens of the Hesperides[124] have the faint rose-bud complexion of the more beautiful English girls.

If in vain the good Chaplain sought to impress the young barbarian with ideas of death akin to those conveyed in the skull, dial, and crossbones on old tombstones; equally futile to all appearance were his efforts to bring home the thought of salvation and a Saviour. Billy listened, but less out of awe or reverence perhaps than from a certain natural politeness; doubtless at bottom regarding all that in much the same way that most mariners of his class take any discourse abstract or out of the common one of the work-a-day world. And this sailor-way of taking clerical discourse is not wholly unlike the way in which the pioneer of Christianity full of transcendent miracles was received long ago on tropic isles by any superior *savage* so called—a Tahitian say of Captain Cook's time or shortly after that time.[125] Out of natural courtesy he received, but did not appropriate. It was like a gift placed in the palm of an outreached hand upon which the fingers do not close.

But the *Indomitable*'s Chaplain was a discreet man possessing the good sense of a good heart. So he insisted not in his vocation here. At the instance of Captain Vere, a lieutenant had apprised him of pretty much everything as to Billy; and since he felt that innocence was even a better thing than religion wherewith to go to Judgement, he reluctantly withdrew; but in his emotion not without first performing an act strange enough in an Englishman, and under the circumstances yet more so in any regular priest. Stooping over, he kissed on the fair cheek his fellow-man, a felon in martial law, one who though on the confines of death he felt he could never convert

122. Germanicus Caesar (15 B.C.–A.D. 19) was granted a triumph in Rome in A.D. 17.

123. The anecdote, told in Bede's *Ecclesiastical History of the English People,* is about Pope Gregory the Great (540?–604).

124. Fra Angelico, the Florentine-painter Giovanni da Fiesole (1387–1455). Originally the Hesperides were nymphs, daughters of Atlas. They dwelled on an enchanted island in the western sea, guarding a tree bearing golden apples.

125. James Cook (1728–1779) was in Tahiti in 1769 and in 1772–1775.

to a dogma; nor for all that did he fear for his future.

Marvel not that having been made acquainted with the young sailor's essential innocence (an irruption of heretic thought hard to suppress) the worthy man lifted not a finger to avert the doom of such a martyr to martial discipline. So to do would not only have been as idle as invoking the desert, but would also have been an audacious transgression of the bounds of his function, one as exactly prescribed to him by military law as that of the boatswain or any other naval officer. Bluntly put, a chaplain is the minister of the Prince of Peace serving in the host of the God of War—Mars. As such, he is as incongruous as that musket of Blücher etc.[126] at Christmas. Why then is he there? Because he indirectly subserves the purpose attested by the cannon; because too he lends the sanction of the religion of the meek to that which practically is the abrogation of everything but brute Force.

26

The night so luminous on the spar-deck but otherwise on the cavernous ones below, levels so like the tiered galleries in a coal-mine—the luminous night passed away. But, like the prophet in the chariot disappearing in heaven and dropping his mantle to Elisha,[127] the withdrawing night transferred its pale robe to the breaking day. A meek shy light appeared in the East, where stretched a diaphanous fleece of white furrowed vapor. That light slowly waxed. Suddenly *eight bells*[128] was struck aft, responded to by one louder metallic stroke from forward. It was four o'clock in the morning. Instantly the silver whistles were heard summoning all hands to witness punishment. Up through the great hatchways rimmed with racks of heavy shot, the watch below came pouring overspreading with the watch already on deck the space between the mainmast and foremast including that occupied by the capacious *launch* and the black booms tiered on either side of it, boat and booms making a summit of observation for the powder-boys and younger tars. A different group comprising one watch of topmen leaned over the rail of that sea-balcony, no small one in a seventy-four, looking down on the crowd below. Man or boy none spake but in whisper, and few spake at all. Captain Vere—as before, the central figure among the assembled commissioned officers—stood nigh the break of the poop-deck facing forward. Just below him on the quarter-deck the marines in full equipment were drawn up much as at the scene of the promulgated sentence.

126. The manuscript is illegible, and "Blücher etc." is a conjectural reading. If the word is "Blücher," Melville was referring to the Prussian Field Marshal Blücher (1742-1819) who, with Wellington, defeated Napoleon at Waterloo.

127. *Cf.* II, *Kings* 2:11–13: "There appeared a chariot of fire, and horses of fire, and parted them both asunder; and Elijah went up by a whirlwind into heaven. And Elisha * * * took up * * * the mantle of Elijah that fell from him."

128. Aboard ship a bell is struck every half hour; thus eight bells are struck at the end of a four-hour watch. Here it is 4 A.M.

At sea in the old time, the execution by halter of a military sailor was generally from the fore-yard. In the present instance, for special reasons the main-yard was assigned. Under an arm of that lee yard[129] the prisoner was presently brought up, the Chaplain attending him. It was noted at the time and remarked upon afterwards, that in this final scene the good man evinced little or nothing of the perfunctory. Brief speech indeed he had with the condemned one, but the genuine Gospel was less on his tongue than in his aspect and manner towards him. The final preparations personal to the latter being speedily brought to an end by two boatswain's-mates, the consummation impended. Billy stood facing aft. At the penultimate moment, his words, his only ones, words wholly unobstructed in the utterance were these—"God bless Captain Vere!" Syllables so unanticipated coming from one with the ignominious hemp about his neck—a conventional felon's benediction directed aft towards the quarters of honor; syllables too delivered in the clear melody of a singing-bird on the point of launching from the twig, had a phenomenal effect, not unenhanced by the rare personal beauty of the young sailor spiritualized now thro' late experiences so poignantly profound.

Without volition as it were, as if indeed the ship's populace were but the vehicles of some vocal current electric, with one voice from alow and aloft came a resonant sympathetic echo—"God bless Captain Vere!" And yet at that instant Billy alone must have been in their hearts, even as he was in their eyes.

At the pronounced words and the spontaneous echo that voluminously rebounded them, Captain Vere, either thro stoic self-control or a sort of momentary paralysis induced by emotional shock, stood erectly rigid as a musket in the ship-armorer's rack.

The hull deliberately recovering from the periodic roll to leeward was just regaining an even keel, when the last signal[,] a preconcerted dumb one[,] was given. At the same moment it chanced that the vapory fleece hanging low in the East, was shot thro with a soft glory as of the fleece of the Lamb of God seen in mystical vision[,] and simultaneously therewith, watched by the wedged mass of upturned faces, Billy ascended; and, ascending, took the full rose of the dawn.

In the pinioned figure, arrived at the yard-end, to the wonder of all no motion was apparent[,] none save that created by the ship's motion, in moderate weather so majestic in a great ship ponderously cannoned.

End of Chapter

129. In the manuscript, Melville wrote both "weather" and "lee" above the word "yard." It is not clear why Captain Vere chooses the mainyard over the foreyard. The yards are the horizontal spars from which the square sails are suspended. Certain critics, who make Billy a Christ-figure, have suggested that the choice was dictated by the three masts, so that Billy would be raised to the central "cross," reminiscent of the Crucifixion.

27
A digression

When some days afterward in reference to the singularity just mentioned, the Purser a rather ruddy rotund person more accurate as an accountant than profound as a philosopher, said at mess to the Surgeon, "What testimony to the force lodged in will-power" the latter—saturnine spare and tall, one in whom a discreet causticity went along with a manner less genial than polite, replied, "Your pardon, Mr. Purser. In a hanging scientifically conducted—and under special orders I myself directed how Budd's was to be effected—any movement following the completed suspension and originating in the body suspended, such movement indicates mechanical spasm in the muscular system. Hence the absence of that is no more attributable to will-power as you call it than to horse-power—begging your pardon."

"But this muscular spasm you speak of, is not that in a degree more or less invariable in these cases?[")]

"Assuredly so, Mr. Purser."

"How then, my good sir, do you account for its absence in this instance?"

"Mr. Purser, it is clear that your sense of the singularity in this matter equals not mine. You account for it by what you call will-power a term not yet included in the lexicon of science. For me I do not, with my present knowledge pretend to account for it at all. Even should we assume the hypothesis that at the first touch of the halyards the action of Budd's heart, intensified by extraordinary emotion at its climax, abruptly stopt—much like a watch when in carelessly winding it up you strain at the finish, thus snapping the chain—even under that hypothesis how account for the phenomenon that followed."

"You admit then that the absence of spasmodic movement was phenomenal."

["]It was phenomenal, Mr. Purser, in the sense that it was an appearance the cause of which is not immediately to be assigned."

["]But tell me, my dear Sir,["] pertinaciously continued the other, "was the man's death effected by the halter, or was it a species of euthanasia?["][130]

"*Euthanasia,* Mr. Purser, is something like your *will-power*: I doubt its authenticity as a scientific term—begging your pardon again. It is at once imaginative and metaphysical,—in short, Greek. But" abruptly changing his tone "there is a case in the sick-bay that I do not care to leave to my assistants. Beg your pardon, but excuse me." And rising from the mess he formally withdrew.

28

The silence at the moment of execution and for a moment or two

130. from the Greek, a quiet and easy death.

continuing thereafter, a silence but emphasized by the regular wash of the sea against the hull or the flutter of a sail caused by the helmsman's eyes being tempted astray, this emphasized silence was gradually disturbed by a sound not easily to be verbally rendered. Whoever has heard the freshet-wave of a torrent suddenly swelled by pouring showers in tropical mountains, showers not shared by the plain; whoever has heard the first muffled murmur of its sloping advance through precipitous woods, may form some conception of the sound now heard. The seeming remoteness of its source was because of its murmurous indistinctness since it came from close-by, even from the men massed on the ship's open deck. Being inarticulate, it was dubious in significance further than it seemed to indicate some capricious revulsion of thought or feeling such as mobs ashore are liable to, in the present instance possibly implying a sullen revocation on the men's part of their involuntary echoing of Billy's benediction. But ere the murmur had time to wax into clamor it was met by a strategic command, the more telling that it came with abrupt unexpectedness.

"Pipe down the starboard watch Boatswain, and see that they go."

Shrill as the shriek of the sea-hawk the whistles of the Boatswain and his Mates pierced that ominous low sound, dissipating it; and yielding to the mechanism of discipline the throng was thinned by one half. For the remainder most of them were set to temporary employments connected with trimming the yards and so forth, business readily to be got up to serve occasion by any officer-of-the-deck.

Now each proceeding that follows a mortal sentence pronounced at sea by a drum-head court is characterised by promptitude not perceptibly merging into hurry, tho bordering that. The hammock, the one which had been Billy's bed when alive, having already been ballasted with shot and otherwise prepared to serve for his canvas coffin, the last offices of the sea-undertakers, the Sail-Maker's Mates, were now speedily completed. When everything was in readiness a second call for all hands made necessary by the strategic movement before mentioned was sounded and now to witness burial.

The details of his closing formality it needs not to give. But when the tilted plank let slide its freight into the sea, a second strange human murmur was heard, blended now with another inarticulate sound proceeding from certain larger sea-fowl whose attention having been attracted by the peculiar commotion in the water resulting from the heavy sloped dive of the shotted hammock into the sea, flew screaming to the spot. So near the hull did they come, that the stridor[131] or bony creak of their gaunt double-jointed pinions was audible. As the ship under light airs passed on, leaving the burial-spot astern, they still kept circling it low down with the moving shadow of their outstretched wings and the croaked requiem of their cries.

131. a grating, harsh, high-pitched sound.

Upon sailors as superstitious as those of the age preceding ours, men-of-war's men too who had just beheld the prodigy of repose in the form suspended in air and now foundering in the deeps; to such mariners the action of the sea-fowl tho' dictated by mere animal greed for prey, was big with no prosaic significance. An uncertain movement began among them, in which some encroachment was made. It was tolerated but for a moment. For suddenly the drum beat to quarters, which familiar sound happening at least twice every day, had upon the present occasion a signal peremptoriness in it. True martial discipline long continued superinduces in average man a sort of impulse [of] docility whose operation at the official sound of command much resembles in its promptitude the effect of an instinct.

The drum-beat dissolved the multitude, distributing most of them along the batteries of the two covered gun-decks. There, as wont, the guns' crews stood by their respective cannon erect and silent. In due course the First Officer, sword under arm and standing in his place on the quarter-deck[,] formally received the successive reports of the sworded Lieutenants commanding the sections of batteries below; the last of which reports being made[,] the summed report he delivered with the customary salute to the Commander. All this occupied time, which in the present case, was the object of beating to quarters at an hour prior to the customary one. That such variance from usage was authorized by an officer like Captain Vere, a martinet as some deemed him, was evidence of the necessity for unusual action implied in what he deemed to be temporarily the mood of his men. "With mankind" he would say "forms, measured forms are everything; and that is the import couched in the story of Orpheus[132] with his lyre spell-binding the wild denizens of the wood." And this he once applied to the disruption of forms going on across the Channel and the consequences thereof.

At this unwonted muster at quarters, all proceeded as at the regular hour. The band on the quarter-deck played a sacred air. After which the Chaplain went thro' the customary morning service. That done, the drum beat the retreat, and toned by music and religious rites subserving the discipline & purpose of war, the men in their wonted orderly manner, dispersed to the places allotted them when not at the guns.

And now it was full day. The fleece of low-hanging vapor had vanished, licked up by the sun that late had so glorified it. And the circumambient air in the clearness of its serenity was like smooth white marble in the polished block not yet removed from the marbledealer's yard.

132. In Greek mythology, Orpheus was the son of Oeagrus and the Muse Calliope. When he played his lyre and sang, wild animals were charmed, trees and stones followed him, fish left the water in which they swam, and birds flew about his head.

29

The symmetry of form attainable in pure fiction can not so readily be achieved in a narration essentially having less to do with fable than with fact. Truth uncompromisingly told will always have its ragged edges; hence the conclusion of such a narration is apt to be less finished than an architectural finial.

How it fared with the Handsome Sailor during the year of the Great Mutiny has been faithfully given. But tho' properly the story ends with his life, something in way of sequel will not be amiss. Three brief chapters will suffice.

In the general re-christening under the Directory of the craft originally forming the navy of the French monarchy, the *St. Louis* line-of-battle ship was named the *Athéiste.* Such a name, like some other substituted ones in the Revolutionary fleet while proclaiming the infidel audacity of the ruling power was yet, tho' not so intended to be, the aptest name, if one consider it, ever given to a war-ship; far more so indeed than the *Devastation,* the *Erebus* (the *Hell*) and similar names bestowed upon fighting-ships.

On the return-passage to the English fleet from the detached cruise during which occurred the events already recorded, the *Indomitable* fell in with the *Athéiste.* An engagement ensued; during which Captain Vere in the act of putting his ship alongside the enemy with a view of throwing his boarders across her bulwarks, was hit by a musket-ball from a port-hole of the enemy's main cabin. More than disabled he dropped to the deck and was carried below to the same cock-pit[133] where some of his men already lay. The senior Lieutenant took command. Under him the enemy was finally captured and though much crippled was by rare good fortune successfully taken into Gibraltar, an English port not very distant from the scene of the fight. There, Captain Vere with the rest of the wounded was put ashore. He lingered for some days, but the end came. Unhappily he was cut off too early for the Nile and Trafalgar.[134] The spirit that spite its philosophic austerity may yet have indulged in the most secret of all passions, ambition, never attained to the fulness of fame.

Not long before death while lying under the influence of that magical drug which soothing the physical frame mysteriously operates on the subtler element in man, he was heard to murmur words inexplicable to his attendant—"Billy Budd, Billy Budd." That these were not the accents of remorse, would seem clear from what the attendant said to the *Indomitable*'s senior officer of marines who[,] as the most reluctant to condemn of the members of the drum-head court, too well knew[,] tho' here he kept the knowledge to himself, who Billy Budd was.

133. in the after-part of the deck below the lower gun deck; during battle it was converted into a sick bay.

134. Nelson's great victories over the French in 1798 and 1805.

30

Some few weeks after the execution, among other matters under the head of *News from the Mediterranean,* there appeared in a naval chronicle of the time, an authorized weekly publication, an account of the affair. It was doubtless for the most part written in good faith, tho' the medium, partly rumor, through which the facts must have reached the writer, served to deflect and in part falsify them. The account was as follows:—

"On the tenth of the last month a deplorable occurrence took place on board H.M.S. *Indomitable*. John Claggart, the ship's master-at-arms, discovering that some sort of plot was incipient among an inferior section of the ship's company, and that the ring-leader was one William Budd; he, Claggart in the act of arraigning the man before the Captain was vindictively stabbed to the heart by the suddenly drawn sheath-knife of Budd.

["]The deed and the implement employed, sufficiently suggest that tho' mustered into the service under an English name the assassin was no Englishman, but one of those aliens adopting English cognomens whom the present extraordinary necessities of the Service have caused to be admitted into it in considerable numbers.

["]The enormity of the crime and the extreme depravity of the criminal, appear the greater in view of the character of the victim, a middle-aged man respectable and discreet, belonging to that minor official grade, the petty-officers, upon whom, as none know better than the commissioned gentlemen, the efficiency of His Majesty's navy so largely depends. His function was a responsible one; at once onerous & thankless and his fidelity in it the greater because of his strong patriotic impulse. In this instance as in so many other instances in these days, the character of this unfortunate man signally refutes, if refutation were needed, that peevish saying attributed to the late Dr. Johnson, that patriotism is the last refuge of a scoundrel.[135]

["]The criminal paid the penalty of his crime. The promptitude of the punishment has proved salutary. Nothing amiss is now apprehended aboard H.M.S. *Indomitable*."

The above, appearing in a publication now long ago superannuated and forgotten[,] is all that hitherto has stood in human record to attest what manner of men respectively were John Claggart and Billy Budd[.]

31

Everything is for a term remarkable in navies. Any tangible object associated with some striking incident of the service is converted

135. Dr. Samuel Johnson (1709–1784), a noted English critic, man of letters, and lexicographer. The quotation about patriotism is in James Boswell's *Life of Johnson* (1791).

into a monument. The spar from which the Foretopman was suspended, was for some few years kept trace of by the bluejackets. Their knowledge followed it from ship to dock-yard and again from dock-yard to ship, still pursuing it even when at last reduced to a mere dock-yard boom. To them a chip of it was as a piece of the Cross. Ignorant tho' they were of the secret facts of the tragedy, and not thinking but that the penalty was somehow unavoidably inflicted from the naval point of view, for all that they instinctively felt that Billy was a sort of man as incapable of mutiny as of wilful murder. They recalled the fresh young image of the Handsome Sailor, that face never deformed by a sneer or subtler vile freak of the heart within. Their impression of him was doubtless deepened by the fact that he was gone, and in a measure mysteriously gone. At the time on the gun decks of the *Indomitable* the general estimate of his nature and its unconscious simplicity eventually found rude utterance from another foretopman[,] one of his own watch[,] gifted, as some sailors are, with an artless poetic temperament; the tarry hands made some lines which after circulating among the shipboard crew for a while, finally got rudely printed at Portsmouth as a ballad. The title given to it was the sailor's.

Billy in the Darbies[136]

Good of the Chaplain to enter Lone Bay
And down on his marrow-bones here and pray
For the likes just o' me, Billy Budd.—But look:
Through the port comes the moon-shine astray!
It tips the guard's cutlas and silvers this nook;
But 'twill die in the dawning of Billy's last day.
A jewel-block they'll make of me tomorrow,
Pendant pearl from the yard-arm-end
Like the ear-drop I gave to Bristol Molly—
O, 'tis me, not the sentence they'll suspend.
Ay, Ay, all is up; and I must up too
Early in the morning, aloft from alow.
On an empty stomach, now, never it would do.
They'll give me a nibble—bit o' biscuit ere I go.
Sure, a messmate will reach me the last parting cup;
But, turning heads away from the hoist and the belay,
Heaven knows who will have the running of me up!
No pipe to those halyards.—But aren't it all sham?
A blur's in my eyes; it is dreaming that I am.
A hatchet to my hawser? all adrift to go?
The drum roll to grog,[137] and Billy never know?

136. *darbies:* slang for handcuffs, irons, or fetters.
137. a mixture of rum diluted with water.

But Donald he has promised to stand by the plank;
So I'll shake a friendly hand ere I sink.
But—no! It is dead then I'll be, come to think.—
I remember Taff the Welshman when he sank.
And his cheek it was like the budding pink[.]
But me they'll lash me in hammock, drop me deep.
Fathoms down, fathoms down, how I'll dream fast asleep.
I feel it stealing now. Sentry, are you there?
Just ease this darbies at the wrist, and roll me over fair,
I am sleepy, and the oozy weeds about me twist.

END OF BOOK April 19th 1891

Masterpieces of Nineteenth-Century Realism and Naturalism

EDITED BY
RENÉ WELLEK
Sterling Professor of Comparative Literature, Yale University

As was indicated in the preceding introduction, the nineteenth century is the century of greatest change in the history of Western civilization. The upheavals following the French Revolution broke up the old order of Europe. The Holy Roman Empire and the Papal States were dissolved. Nationalism, nourished by the political and social aspirations of the middle classes, grew by leaps and bounds. "Liberty" became the main political slogan of the century. In different countries and different decades it meant different things: here liberation from the rule of the foreigner, there the emancipation of the serf; here the removal of economic restrictions on trade and manufacturing, there the introduction of a constitution, free speech, parliamentary institutions. Almost all over Europe, the middle classes established their effective rule, though monarchs often remained in more or less nominal power. Two large European countries, Germany and Italy, achieved their centuries-old dreams of political unification. The predominance of France, still marked at the beginning of the century, was broken, and England—or rather Great Britain—ruled the sea throughout the century. The smaller European nations, especially in the Balkans, began to emancipate themselves from foreign rule.

These major political changes were caused by, and in their turn caused, great social and economic changes. The Industrial Revolution which had begun in England in the eighteenth century spread over the Continent and transformed living conditions radically. The enormous increase in the speed and availability of transportation due to the development of railroads and steamships, the greatly increased urbanization following from the establishment of industries, changed the whole pattern of human life in most countries, and made possible, within a century, an unprecedented increase in the population (as much as threefold in most European countries), which was also fostered by the advances of medicine and hygiene. The increase of widespread wealth and prosperity is, in spite of the wretched living conditions and other hardships of the early factory workers, an undeniable fact. The barriers between the social classes diminished appreciably almost everywhere: both the social and the political power of the aristocracy declined. The industrial laborer began to be felt as a political force.

These social and economic changes were closely bound up with shifts in the prevailing outlooks and philosophies. Technological innovation is impossible without the discoveries of science. The scientific outlook, hitherto dominant only in a comparatively limited area, spread widely and permeated almost all fields of human thought and endeavor. It raised enormous hopes for the future betterment of man's condition on earth, especially when Darwin's evolutionary theories fortified the earlier, vaguer faith in unlimited progress. "Liberty," "science," "progress," "evolution" are the concepts which define the mental atmosphere of the nineteenth century.

But tendencies hostile to these were by no means absent. Feudal or Catholic conservatism succeeded, especially in Austria-Hungary, in Russia, and in much of the south of Europe, in preserving old regimes, and the philosophies of a conservative and religious society were reformulated in modern terms. At the same time, in England the very assumptions of the new industrial middle-class society were powerfully attacked by writers such as Carlyle and Ruskin who recommended a return to medieval forms of social co-operation and handicraft. The industrial civilization of the nineteenth century was also opposed by the fierce individualism of many artists and thinkers who were unhappy in the ugly commercial "Philistine" society of the age. The writings of Nietzsche, toward the end of the century, and the whole movement of "art for art's sake," which asserted the independence of the artist from society, are the most obvious symptoms of this revolt. The free-enterprise system and the liberalism of the ruling middle classes also early clashed with the rising proletariat, which was won over to diverse forms of socialism, preaching a new collectivism with the stress on equality. Socialism could have Christian or romantic motivations, or it could become "scientific" and revolutionary, as Marx's brand of socialism (a certain stage of which he called "communism") claimed to be.

While up through the eighteenth century religion was, at least in name, a major force in European civilization, in the nineteenth century there was a marked decrease in its influence on both the intellectual leaders and the masses. Local intense revivals of religious consciousness, such as the Oxford Movement in England, did occur, and the traditional religious institutions were preserved everywhere, but the impact of science on religion was such that many tenets of the old faiths crumbled. The discoveries of astronomy, geology, evolutionary biology, archaeology, and biblical criticism forced, almost everywhere, a restatement of the old creeds. Religion, especially in the Protestant countries, was frequently confined to an inner feeling of religiosity or to a system of morality which preserved the ancient Christian virtues. During the early nineteenth century, in Germany, Hegel and his predecessors and followers tried to interpret the world in spiritual terms outside the bounds of traditional religion. There were many attempts even late in the century to restate this view, but the methods and discoveries of science seemed to invalidate it, and various formulas which took science as their base in building new lay religions of hope in humanity gained popularity. French Positivism, English utilitarianism, the evolutionism of Herbert Spencer, are some of the best-known examples. Meanwhile, for the first time in history, at least in Europe, profoundly pessimistic and atheistic philosophies arose, of which Schopenhauer's was the most subtle, while a purely physical materialism was the most widespread. Thus the whole gamut of views of the universe was represented during the century in new and impressive formulations.

The plastic arts did not show a similar vitality. For a long time, in most countries, painting and architecture floundered in a sterile eclecticism, in a bewildering variety of historical masquerades in which the neo-Gothic style was replaced by the neo-Renaissance and that by the neo-Baroque and other decorative revivals of past forms. Only in France, painting, with the impressionists, found a new style which was genuinely original. In music the highly romantic art of Richard Wagner attracted most attention, but the individual national schools either continued in their tradition, like Italian opera (Verdi) or founded an idiom of their own, often based on a revival of folklore, as in Russia (Tchaikovsky), Poland (Chopin), Bohemia (Dvořák), and Norway (Grieg).

But literature was the most representative and the most widely influential art of the nineteenth century. It found new forms and methods and expressed the social and intellectual situation of the time most fully and memorably.

After the great wave of the international romantic movement had spent its force in the fourth decade of the nineteenth century, European literature moved in the direction of what is usually called *realism*. Realism was not a coherent general movement which established itself unchallenged for a long period of time, as classicism had succeeded in doing during the eighteenth century. There were many authors in the nineteenth century who continued to practice a substantially romantic art (Tennyson and Hugo, for example); there were even movements which upheld a definitely romantic "escapist," antirealist program, such as that of the Pre-Raphaelites in England or the Parnassians in France. But, with whatever exceptions and reservations, in retrospect the nineteenth century appears as the period of the great realistic writers: Flaubert in France, Dostoevsky and Tolstoy in Russia, Dickens in England, James in America, Ibsen in Norway.

What is meant by realism? The term, in literary use (there is a much older philosophical use), apparently dates back to the Germans at the turn of the century—to Schiller and the Schlegels. It cropped up in France as early as 1826 but became a commonly accepted literary and artistic slogan only in the 1850's. (A review called *Réalisme* began publication in 1856, and a critic, Champfleury, published a volume of critical articles with the title *Le Réalisme* in the following year.) Since then the word has been bandied about, discussed, analyzed, and abused as all slogans are. It is frequently confused with naturalism, an ancient philosophical term for materialism, epicureanism, or any secularism. As a specifically literary term, it crystallized only in France. In French, as in English, naturalist means, of course, simply student of nature, and the analogy between the writer and the naturalist, specifically the botanist and zoologist, was ready at hand. Emile Zola, in the Preface to a new edition of his early novel, *Thérèse Raquin* (1866), proclaimed the naturalist creed most boldly. His book, he claims, is "an analytical labor on two living bodies like that of a surgeon on corpses." He proudly counts himself among the group of "naturalist writers."

The program of the groups of writers and critics who used these terms can be easily summarized. The realists wanted a truthful representation in literature of reality—that is, of contemporary life and manners. They thought of their method as inductive, observational, and hence "objective." The personality of the author was to be suppressed, or was at least to recede into the background, since reality was to be seen "as it is." The naturalistic program, as formulated by Zola, was substantially the same except that Zola put greater stress on the analogies to science, considering the procedure of the novelist as identical with that of the experimenting scientist. He also more definitely and exclusively embraced the philosophy of scientific materialism, with its deterministic implications, its stress on heredity and environment, while the older realists were not always so clear in drawing the philosophical consequences. These French theories were anticipated, paralleled, or imitated all over the world of Western literature. In Germany, the movement called Young Germany, with which Heine was associated, had propounded a substantially antiromantic realistic program as early as the thirties, but versions of the French theories definitely triumphed there only in the 1880's. In Russia, as early as the forties, the most prominent critic of the time, Vissarion Belinsky, praised the "natural" school of Russian fiction, which described contemporary Russia with fidelity. Italy also, from the late seventies on, produced an analogous movement, which called itself *verismo*. The English-speaking countries were the last to adopt the critical programs and slogans of the Continent: George Moore and George Gissing brought the French theories to England in the late eighties, and in the United States William Dean Howells began his campaign for realism in 1886, when he became editor of *Harper's Magazine*. Realistic and naturalistic theories of literature have since been widely accepted in spite of many twentieth-century criticisms and the whole general trend of twentieth-century literature. Especially in the United States, the contemporary novel is usually considered naturalistic and judged by standards of nature and truth. The officially promoted doctrine in Russia is called "socialist Realism."

The slogans "realism" and "naturalism" were thus new in the nineteenth century. They served as effective formulas directed against the romantic creed. Truth, contemporaneity, and objectivity were the obvious counterparts of romantic imagination, of romantic historicism and its glorification of the past, and of romantic subjectivity, the exaltation of the ego and the individual. But, of course, the emphasis on truth and objectivity was not really new: these qualities had been demanded by many older, classical theories of imitation, and in the eighteenth century there were great writers such as Diderot who wanted a literal "imitation of life" even on the stage.

The practice of realism, it could be argued, is very old indeed. There are realistic scenes in the *Odyssey*, and there is plenty of realism in ancient comedy and satire, in medieval stories (fabliaux) like some of Chaucer's and Boccaccio's, in many Elizabethan plays, in the Spanish rogue novels, in the English eighteenth-century novel beginning with Defoe, and so on almost ad infinitum. But while it would be easy to find in early literature anticipations of almost every single element of modern realism, still the systematic description of contemporary society, with a serious purpose, often even with a tragic tone as well, and with sympathy for heroes drawn from the middle and lower classes, was a real innovation of the nineteenth century.

It is usually rash to explain a literary movement in social and political terms. But the new realistic art surely has something to do with the triumph of the middle classes in France after the July revolution in 1830, and in England after the passage of the Reform Bill in 1832, and with the increasing influence of the middle classes in almost every country. Russia is somewhat of an exception as no large middle class could develop there during the nineteenth century. An absolute feudal regime continued in power and the special character of most of Russian literature must be due to this distinction, but even in Russia there emerged an "intelligentsia" (the term comes from Russia) which was open to Western ideas and was highly critical of the czarist regime and its official "ideology." But while much nineteenth-century literature reflects the triumph of the middle classes, it would be an error to think of the great realistic writers as spokesmen or mouthpieces of the society they described. Balzac was politically a Catholic monarchist who applauded the Bourbon restoration after the fall of Napoleon, but he had an extraordinary imaginative insight into the processes leading to the victory of the middle classes. Flaubert despised the middle-class society of the Third Empire with an intense hatred and the pride of a self-conscious artist. Dickens became increasingly critical of the middle classes and the assumptions of industrial civilization. Dostoevsky, though he took part in a conspiracy against the Russian government early in his life and spent ten years in exile in Siberia, became the propounder of an extremely conservative nationalistic and religious creed which was definitely directed against the revolutionary forces in Russia. Tolstoy, himself a count and a landowner, was violent in his criticism of the czarist regime, especially later in his life, but he cannot be described as friendly to the middle classes, to the aims of the democratic movements in Western Europe, or to the science of the time. Ibsen's political attitude is that of a proud individualist who condemns the "compact majority" and its tyranny. Possibly all art is critical of its society, but in the nineteenth century this criticism became much more explicit, as social and political issues became much more urgent or, at least, were regarded as more urgent by the writing groups. To a far greater degree than in earlier centuries, writers felt their isolation from society, viewed the structure and problems of the prevailing order as debatable and reformable, and in spite of all demands for objectivity became, in many cases, social propagandists and reformers in their own right.

The program of realism, while defensible enough as a reaction against romanticism, raises critical questions which were not answered theoretically by its defenders. What is meant by "truth" of representation? Photographic copying? This seems the implication of many famous pronouncements. "A novel is a mirror walking along the road," said Stendhal as early as 1830. But such statements can hardly be taken literally. All art must select and represent; it cannot be and has never been a simple transcript of reality. What such analogies are intended to convey is rather a claim for an all-inclusiveness of subject matter, a protest against the exclusion of themes which before were considered "low," "sordid," or "trivial" (like the puddles along the road the mirror walks). Chekhov formulated this protest with the usual parallel between the scientist and the writer: "To a chemist nothing on earth is unclean. A writer must be as objective as a chemist; he must abandon the subjective line: he must know that dungheaps play a very respectable part in a landscape, and that evil passions are as inherent in life as good ones." Thus the "truth" of realistic art includes the sordid, the low, the disgusting, and the evil; and, the implication is, the subject is treated objectively, without interference and falsification by the artist's personality and his own desires. But in practice, while the realistic artist succeeded in expanding the themes of art, he could not fulfill the demand for total objectivity. Works of art are written by human beings and inevitably express their personalities and their points of view. As Conrad admitted, "even the most artful of writers will give himself (and his morality) away in about every third sentence." Objectivity, in the sense which Zola had in mind when he proposed a scientific method in the writing of novels and conceived of the novelist as a sociologist collecting human documents, is impossible in practice. When it has been attempted, it has led only to bad art, to dullness and the display of inert materials, to the confusion between the art of the novel and reporting, "documentation." The demand for "objectivity" can be understood only as a demand for a specific method of narration, in which the author does not interfere explicitly, in his own name, and as a rejection of personal themes of introspection and reverie.

The realistic program, while it has made innumerable new subjects available to art, also implies a narrowing of its themes and methods—a condemnation of the fantastic, the historical, the remote, the idealized, the "unsullied," the idyllic. Realism professes to present us with a "slice of life." But one should recognize that it is an artistic method and convention like any other. Romantic art could, without offending its readers, use coincidences, improbabilities, and even impossibilities, which were not, theoretically at least, tolerated in realistic art. Ibsen, for instance, avoided many older conventions of the stage: asides, soliloquies, eavesdropping, sudden unmotivated appearances of new characters, and so on; but his dramas have their own marked conventions, which seem today almost as "unnatural" as those of the romantics. Realistic theories of literature cannot be upheld in their literal sense; objective and impersonal truth is unobtainable, at least in art, since all art is a "making," a creating of a world of symbols which differs radically from the world which we call reality. The value of realism lies in its negation of the conventions of romanticism, its expansion of the themes of art, and its new demonstration (never forgotten by artists) that literature has to deal also with its time and society and has, at its best, an insight into reality (not only social reality) which is not necessarily identical with that of science. Many of the great writers make us "realize" the world of their time, evoke an imaginative picture of it which seems truer and will last longer than that of historians and sociologists. But this achievement is due to their imagination and their art, or craft, two requisites which realistic theory tended to forget or minimize.

When we observe the actual practice of the great realistic

writers of the nineteenth century, we notice a sharp contradiction between theory and practice, and an independent evolution of the art of the novel which is obscured for us if we pay too much attention to the theories and slogans of the time, even those that the authors themselves propounded. Flaubert, the high priest of a cult of "art for art's sake," the most consistent advocate of absolute objectivity, was actually, at least in a good half of his work, a writer of romantic fantasies of blood and gold, flesh and jewels. There is some truth in his saying that Madame Bovary is himself, for in the drab story of a provincial adulteress he castigated his own romanticism and romantic dreams.

So too with Dostoevsky. Although some of his settings resemble those of the "grime novel," he is actually a writer of high tragedy, of a drama of ideas in which ordinary reality is transformed into a symbol of the spiritual world. His technique is closely associated with Balzac's (it is significant that his first publication was a translation of Balzac's *Eugénie Grandet*) and thus with many devices of the sensational melodramatic novel of French romanticism. Tolstoy's art is more concretely real than that of any of the other great masters mentioned, yet he is, at the same time, the most personal and even literally autobiographical author in the history of the novel—a writer, besides, who knows nothing of detachment toward social and religious problems, but frankly preaches his own very peculiar religion. And if we turn to Ibsen, we find essentially the same situation. Ibsen began as a writer of historical and fantastic dramas and slowly returned to a style which is fundamentally symbolist. All his later plays are organized by symbols, from the duck of *The Wild Duck* (1884) to the white horses in *Rosmersholm* (1886) and the tower in *The Master Builder* (1892). Even Zola, the propounder of the most scientific theory, was in practice a novelist who used the most extreme devices of melodrama and symbolism. In *Germinal* (1885), his novel of mining, the mine is the central symbol, alive as an animal, heaving, breathing. It would be an odd reader who could find literal truth in the final catastrophe of the cave-in or even in such "naturalistic" scenes as a dance where the beer oozes from the nostrils of the drinkers.

One could assert, in short, that all the great realists were at bottom romanticists, but it is probably wiser to conclude that they were simply artists who created worlds of imagination and knew (at least instinctively) that in art one can say something about reality only through symbols. The attempts at documentary art, at mere reporting and transcribing, are today forgotten.

FLAUBERT, *MADAME BOVARY*

Flaubert's novel, *Madame Bovary* (1856), is deservedly considered the showpiece of French realism. It would be impossible to find a novel, certainly before Flaubert, in which humble persons in a humble setting are treated with such seriousness, restraint, verisimilitude, and imaginative clarity. At first sight, *Madame Bovary* is a solidly documented and clearly visualized account of life in a village of the French province of Normandy sometime in the forties of the last century. We meet a whole spectrum of social types found in such a time and place: the doctor (actually a "health officer" with a lower degree), a pharmacist, a storekeeper, a notary and his clerk, a tax collector, a woman innkeeper and her stableboy, the priest and his sacristan, a neighboring landowner, and a farmer. We are told the story of a young peasant woman brought up in a convent, who marries a dull man and commits adultery first with a ruthless philanderer and then with a spineless younger man. Overwhelmed by debts concealed from her unsuspecting husband, faced by sudden demands for repayment, disillusioned in love, rebuffed by everybody who might help her, she commits suicide by poisoning herself with arsenic. Nothing seems simpler and more ordinary, and the manner of telling seems completely objective, detached, impersonal. A case is presented which is observed with almost scientific curiosity. The descriptions are obviously accurate, sometimes based on expert knowledge; the clubfoot operation and the effects of arsenic poisoning agree with medical evidence. The setting—the topography of the two villages, the interior of the houses, the inn, the pharmacy, the city of Rouen, the cathedral there, the river landscape, and the particular things and sounds—imprints itself vividly on our memory. Every detail serves its purpose of characterization—from the absurd cap of the schoolboy Charles to the mirror and the crucifix in the deathbed scene; from the sound of Binet's lathe turning out napkin rings to the tap of the stableboy's wooden leg. "The technique of *Madame Bovary* has become the model of all novels" (Albert Thibaudet).

But surely the book could not have kept its grip on modern readers if it were only a superbly accurate description of provincial life in France (as the added subtitle, *Mœurs de province,* suggests). The book transcends its time and place if one thinks of Emma Bovary as the type of the unfulfilled dreamer, as the failed and foiled romanticist, as a female Don Quixote, corrupted by sentimental reading, caught in a trap of circumstance, pitiful and to be pitied in her horrible self-inflicted death.

This central theme has, however, remained ambiguous. What attracted and shocked readers was the uncertainty about the author's attitude toward Emma, particularly at the time of publication when readers were accustomed to being told clearly by addresses and comments what they were to think of the actions and morals of the characters of a novel. *Madame Bovary,* at publication, caused a scandal. The review (*Revue de Paris*) in which it was published serially and the author were hauled into court for immorality and blasphemy and the prosecutor described the book as an incitement to adultery and atheism. In his rebuttal, the defense counsel argued that the novel is rather a highly moral work in which adultery is punished even excessively. Flaubert was acquitted but neither the prosecutor nor the defending attorney interpreted the book correctly. It is neither a salacious novel nor a didactic tract. Some parts of the book are frankly satirical (and thus far from purely objective): The gross village priest who cannot even understand the distress of Emma is flanked by the fussy, shallow, pseudoscientific, enlightened, "progressive" pharmacist Homais. Though they argue and quarrel they are finally reduced to a common level when they eat and snore at the wake next to Emma's corpse. The rightly famous scene of the country fair satirizes and parodies the pompous rhetoric of the officials extolling the glories of agriculture, counterpointing it to the equally platitudinous love talk of Rodolphe and the lowing of the cattle in an amalgam which reduces men and women to a common level of animality. Even Emma is not spared: Her sentimental religiosity, her taste for luxury, her financial improvidence are diagnosed as disguised eroticism. She would not have minded if Rodolphe had drawn a pistol against her husband. In her desperate search for escape she asks Léon to steal for her. In the last attempt to get money she is ready to sell herself. She is indifferent to her child, deceitful even in small matters. Her longing for sensual satisfaction becomes, in the scenes with Léon in the hotel at Rouen, frantic and corrupt. The author weighed the scales against her: She married an excessively stupid and insensitive man; she met two callous lovers; she is tricked by a merciless usurer; she is utterly alone at last. When Charles meeting Rodolphe after her death and after he had discovered her infidelities tells him, ineptly, awkwardly: "It was the fault of destiny," the author expressly approves of this saying. The novel conveys a sense of inexorable determinism, of the vanity of dreaming, of the impossibility of escape from one's nature and station. It conveys a sense of despair, of man's and woman's alienation in an incomprehensible universe but also a hatred for all the stupidity, mediocrity and baseness of people there and everywhere. (Flaubert called them "bourgeois," but included the proletarian masses in his contempt). Emma is pitied because she has, at least, a spark of discontent, the yearning to escape the cage of her existence. But baseness triumphs and the book ends with a sudden change to the present tense: "Homais has just received the cross of the Legion of Honor."

This sense of the inexorable, the fatal, the inescapable is secured also by the precision and firmness of Flaubert's style and the carefully planned architectonics of his composition. If we mean by style the systematic exploitation of the syntactical and lexical possibilities of a language we must class Flaubert with the great stylists: the exact descriptive epithet, the one right word (*le mot juste*) even when he uses the most trivial cliché or the most recondite scientific term coheres with the skillful modulations and rhythms of the sentences, the organization of the paragraphs and the divisions of the sections which are grouped around a series of pictorial scenes: the schoolroom, the rustic wedding, the ball, the visit to the priest, the country fair, the ride in the woods, the clubfoot operation, the opera, the cathedral, the cab ride, the deathbed, to mention only the most memorable.

Madame Bovary is constantly cited as an example for the handling of narrative perspective. The story begins in the schoolroom ostensibly told by a schoolfellow (the word "we" is used in the first pages); it shifts then to the narration of an omniscient author and, off and on, narrows to the point of view of Emma. Much is seen only through her eyes, but one cannot say that the author identifies with her or enters her mind sympathetically. He keeps his distance and on occasion conveys his own opinion. He is not averse even to moral judgments: He speaks of Emma's hardhearted and tightfisted peasant nature (p. 797), he refers to her corruption (p. 890), and Rodolphe is several times condemned for his brutality and cynicism (pp. 843, 888, 976). In the description of extreme unction (p. 987) the author pronounces solemnly his forgiveness (which he suggests would be also God's) for her coveting all worldly goods, her greediness "for the warm breeze and scents of love," and even her sensuality and lust. But mostly Flaubert depicts the scenes by simple description or reproduction of speech or imagined silent reflections. Things and people become at times symbolic even in an obtrusive way: the wedding bouquet, the plate of boiled beef, and the apparition of the blind beggar who turns up conveniently at the hour of Emma's death. Much is said about her which she could not have observed herself. The famous saying "Madame Bovary c'est moi" cannot be traced back to an earlier date than 1909 when it is reported on distant hearsay in René Descharmes, *Flaubert avant 1857* (p. 103). There are dozens of passages in the letters during the composition of *Madame Bovary* which express Flaubert's distaste for the "vulgarity of his subject," "the fetid smell of the milieu," and his opinion of Emma Bovary as "a woman of false poetry and false sentiments." Usually he defends his choice of theme as a "prodigious *tour de force*," as "an act of crude will power," as "a deliberate made-up thing" though we suspect him sometimes of exaggerating his efforts in order to impress his correspondent in Paris, a facile and prolific novelist and poetess, Louise Colet.

Still, the saying "Madame Bovary c'est moi" has been widely quoted and accepted because it contains a kernel of truth. In Emma, Flaubert combats his own vices of daydreaming, romanticism, exoticism, of which he thought he could cure himself by writing this antiromantic book. But the identification with Emma distracts us from noticing Flaubert's deepseated sympathies with the slowwitted, abused, but honest and loving Charles who rightly opens and closes the book and for the other good people: Emma's father, the farmer Rouault, kind and distressed by all he could not foresee; Justin, the pharmacist's apprentice adoring Emma from afar, praying on her grave; the clubfoot stableboy tortured and exploited for a dream of medical reputation; poor neglected Berthe sent to the cotton mill; the old peasant woman at the fair who for fifty-four years of service got a medal worth twenty-five francs; and even the blind beggar with his horrible skin disease. Moreover, there is the admirable Dr. Larivière who appears fleetingly like an apparition from a saner, loftier world of good sense and professional devotion. Thus it seems unjust of Martin Turnell to say that the novel is "an onslaught on the whole basis of human feeling and on all spiritual and moral values."

In Flaubert's mind, the novel was also an assertion of the redeeming power of art. His long struggle with its composition, which took him more than five years of grinding drudgery: five days in which he had written a single page, five or six pages in a week, twenty-five pages in six weeks, thirteen pages in seven weeks, a whole night spent in hunting for the right adjective; the ruthless pruning to which he subjected his enormous manuscript, eliminating many fine touches, similes, metaphors, and descriptions of elusive mental states (as a study of the manuscripts has shown) were to him a victory of art over reality, a passionate search for Beauty, which he knew to be an illusion. But one wonders whether the conflict of Flaubert's scientific detachment and cruel observation with the intense adoration of beauty, the thirst for calculated purity and structure, for "style" as perfection, can be resolved. He tried to achieve this synthesis in *Madame Bovary*. Watching this struggle between heterogeneous elements, and even opposites, should explain some of the fascination of the book.

DOSTOEVSKY, *NOTES FROM UNDERGROUND*

Dostoevsky, like every great writer, can be approached in different ways and read on different levels. We can try to understand him as a religious philosopher, a political commentator, a psychologist, and a novelist, and if we know much about his fascinating and varied life, we can interpret his works as biographical.

The biographical interpretation is the one that has been pushed furthest. The lurid crimes of Dostoevsky's characters (such as the rape of a young girl) have been ascribed to him, and all his novels have been studied as if they constituted a great personal confession. Dostoevsky certainly did use many of his experiences in his books (as every writer does): he several times described the feelings of a man facing a firing squad as he himself faced it on December 22, 1849, only to be reprieved at the last moment. His writings also reflect his years in Siberia: four years working in a loghouse, in chains, as he describes it in an oddly impersonal book, *Memoirs from the House of the Dead* (1862), and six more years as a common soldier on the borders of Mongolia, in a small, remote provincial town. Similarly, he used the experience of his disease (epilepsy), ascribing great spiritual significance to the ecstatic rapture preceding the actual seizure. He assigned his disease to both his most angelic "good" man, the "Idiot," Prince Myshkin, and his most diabolical, inhuman figure, the cold-blooded unsexed murderer of the old Karamazov, the flunky Smerdyakov. Dostoevsky also used something of his experiences in Germany, where in the 1860's he succumbed to a passion for gambling which he overcame only much later, during his second marriage. The short novel *The Gambler* (1866) gives an especially vivid account of this life and its moods.

There are other autobiographical elements in Dostoevsky's works, but it seems a gross misunderstanding of his methods and the procedures of art in general to conclude from his writings (as Thomas Mann has done) that he was a "saint and criminal" in one. Dostoevsky, after all, was an extremely hard worker who wrote and rewrote some twenty volumes. He was a novelist who employed the methods of the French sensational novel; he was constantly on the lookout for the most striking occurrences —the most shocking crimes and the most horrible disasters and scandals—because only in such fictional situations could he exalt his characters to their highest pitch, bringing out the clash of ideas and temperaments, revealing the deepest layers of their souls. But these fictions cannot be taken as literal transcripts of reality and actual experience.

Whole books have been written to explain Dostoevsky's religious philosophy and conception of man. The Russian philosopher Berdayev concludes his excellent study by saying, "So great is the value of Dostoevsky that to have produced him is by itself sufficient justification for the existence of the Russian people in the world." But there is no need for such extravagance. Dostoevsky's philosophy of religion is rather a personal version of extreme mystical Christianity, and assumes flesh and blood only in the context of the novels. Reduced to the bare bones of abstract propositions, it amounts to saying that man is fallen but is free to choose between evil and Christ. And choosing Christ means taking upon oneself the burden of humanity in love and pity, since "everybody is guilty for all and before all." Hence in Dostoevsky there is tremendous stress on personal freedom of choice, and his affirmation of the worth of every individual is combined, paradoxically, with an equal insistence on the substantial identity of all men, their equality before God, the bond of love which unites them.

Dostoevsky also develops a philosophy of history, with practical political implications, based upon this point of view. According to him, the West is in complete decay; only Russia has preserved Christianity in its original form. The West is either Catholic—and Catholicism is condemned by Dostoevsky as an attempt to force salvation by magic and authority—or bourgeois, and hence materialistic and fallen away from Christ; or socialist, and socialism is to Dostoevsky identical with atheism, as it dreams of a utopia in which man would not be free to choose even at the expense of suffering. Dostoevsky—who himself had belonged to a revolutionary group and come into contact with Russian revolutionaries abroad—had an extraordinary insight into the mentality of the Russian underground. In *The Possessed* (1871-1872) he gave a lurid satiric picture of these would-be saviors of Russia and mankind. But while he was afraid of the revolution, Dostoevsky himself hoped and prophesied that Russia would save Europe from the dangers of communism, as Russia alone was the uncorrupted Christian land. Put in terms of political propositions (as Dostoevsky himself preached them in his journal, *The Diary of a Writer*, 1876-1881), what he propounds is a conservative Russian nationalism with messianic hopes for Russian Christianity. It is hard to imagine a political creed more remote from present-day realities.

When translated into abstractions, Dostoevsky's psychology is as unimpressive as his political theory. It is merely a derivative of theories propounded by German writers about the unconscious, the role of dreams, the ambivalence of human feelings. What makes it electric in the novels is his ability to dramatize it in scenes of sudden revulsions, in characters who in today's terminology would be called split personalities, in people twisted by isolation, lust, humiliation, and resentment. The dreams of Raskolnikov may be interpreted according to Freudian psychology, but to the reader without any knowledge of science they are comprehensible in their place in the novel and function as warnings and anticipations.

Dostoevsky is first of all an artist—a novelist who succeeded in using his ideas (many old and venerable, many new and fantastic) and psychological insights for the writing of stories of absorbing interest. As an artist, Dostoevsky treated the novel like a drama, constructing it in large, vivid scenes which end with a scandal or a crime or some act of violence, filling it with unforgettable "stagelike" figures torn by great passions and swayed by great ideas. Then he set this world in an environment of St. Petersburg slums, or of towns, monasteries, and country houses, all so vividly realized that we forget how the setting, the figures, and the ideas melt together into one cosmos of the imagination only remotely and obliquely related to any reality of nineteenth-century Russia. We take part in a great drama of pride and humility, good and evil, in a huge allegory of man's search for God and himself. We understand and share in this world because it is not merely Russia in the nineteenth century, where people could hardly have talked and behaved as Dostoevsky's people do, but a myth of humanity, universalized as all art is.

Notes from Underground (1864) precedes the four great novels, *Crime and Punishment* (1866), *The Idiot* (1868), *The Possessed*, and *The Brothers Karamazov* (1880). The *Notes* can be viewed as a prologue, an introduction to the cycle of the four great novels, an anticipation of the mature Dostoevsky's method and thought. Though it cannot compare in dramatic power and scope with these, the story has its own peculiar and original artistry. It is made up of two parts, at first glance seemingly independent: the monologue of the Underground man and the confession which he makes about himself, called "À Propos of the Wet Snow." The monologue, though it includes no action, is dramatic—a long address to an imaginary hostile reader, whom the Underground man ridicules, defies, jeers at, but also flatters. The confession is an autobiographical reminiscence of the Underground man. It describes events which occurred long before the delivery of the monologue, but it functions as a confirmation in concrete terms of the self-portrait drawn in the monologue and as an explanation of the isolation of the hero.

The narrative of the confession is a comic variation on the old theme of the rescue of a fallen woman from vice, a seesaw series of humiliations permitting Dostoevsky to display all the cruelty of his probing psychology. The hero, out of spite and craving for human company, forces himself into the company of former schoolfellows and is shamefully humiliated by them. He reasserts his ego (as he cannot revenge himself on them) in the company of a humble prostitute by impressing her with florid and moving speeches, which he knows to be insincere, about her horrible future. Ironically, he converts her, but when she comes to him and surprises him in a degrading scene with his servant, he humiliates her again. When, even then, she understands and forgives and thus shows her moral superiority, he crowns his spite by deliberately misunderstanding her and forcing money on her. She is the moral victor and the Underground man returns to his hideout to jeer at humanity. It is hard not to feel that we are shown a tortured and twisted soul almost too despicable to elicit our compassion.

Still it would be a complete misunderstanding of Dostoevsky's story to take the philosophy expounded jeeringly in the long monologue of the first part merely as the irrational railings of a sick soul. The Underground man, though abject and spiteful, represents not only a specific Russian type of the time—the intellectual divorced from the soil and his nation—but also modern humanity, even Everyman, and, strangely enough, even the author, who through the mouth of this despicable character, as through a mask, expresses his boldest and most intimate convictions. In spite of all the exaggerated pathos, wild paradox, and jeering irony used by the speaker, his self-criticism and his criticism of society and history must be taken seriously and interpreted patiently if we are to extract the meaning accepted by Dostoevsky.

The Underground man is the hyperconscious man who examines himself as if in a mirror, and sees himself with pitiless candor. His very self-consciousness cripples his will and poisons his feelings. He cannot escape from his ego; he knows that he has acted badly toward the girl but at the same time he cannot help acting as he does. He knows that he is alone, that there is no bridge from him to humanity, that the world is hostile to him, and that he is being humiliated by everybody he meets. But though he resents the humiliation, he cannot help courting it, provoking it, and liking it in his perverse manner. He understands (and knows from his own experience) that man is not good but enjoys evil and destruction.

His self-criticism widens, then, into a criticism of the assumptions of modern civilization, of nineteenth-century optimism about human nature and progress, of utilitarianism, and of all kinds of utopias. It is possible to identify definite allusions to a contemporary novel by a radical socialist and revolutionary, Chernyshevsky, entitled *What Shall We Do?* (1863), but we do not need to know the exact target of Dostoevsky's satire to recognize what he attacks: the view that man is good, that he always seeks his enlightened self-interest, that science propounds immutable truths, and that a paradise on earth will be just around the corner once society is reformed along scientific lines. In a series of vivid symbols these assumptions are represented, parodied, exposed. Science says that "twice two makes four" but the Underground man laughs that "twice two makes five is sometimes a very charming thing too." Science means to him (and to Dostoevsky) the victory of the doctrine of fatality, of iron necessity, of determinism, and thus finally of death. Man would become an "organ-stop," a "piano-key," if deterministic science were valid.

Equally disastrous are the implications of the social philosophy of liberalism and of socialism (which Dostoevsky considers its necessary consequence). Man, in this view, need only follow his enlightened self-interest, need only be rational, and he will become noble and good and the earth will be a place of prosperity and peace. But the Underground man knows that this conception of man is entirely false. What if mankind does not follow, and never will follow, its own enlightened self-interest, is consciously and purposely irrational, even bloodthirsty and evil? History seems to the Underground man to speak a clear language: ". . . civilization has made mankind if not more bloodthirsty, at least more vilely, more loathsomely bloodthirsty." Man wills the irrational and evil because he does not want to become an organ-stop, a piano key, because he wants to be left with the freedom to choose between good and evil. This freedom of choice, even at the expense of chaos and destruction, is what makes him man.

Actually, man loves something other than his well-being and happiness, loves even suffering and pain, because he is a man and not an animal inhabiting some great organized rational "ant-heap." The ant-heap, the hen house, the block of tenements, and finally the Crystal Palace (then the newest wonder of architecture, a great hall of iron and glass erected for the Universal Exhibition in London) are the images used by the Underground man to represent his hated utopia. The heroine of *What Shall We Do?* had dreamed of a building, made of cast iron and glass and placed in the middle of a beautiful garden where there would be eternal spring and summer, eternal joy. Dostoevsky had recognized there the utopian dream of Fourier, the French socialist whom he had admired in his youth and whose ideals he had come to hate with a fierce revulsion. But we must realize that the Underground man, and Dostoevsky, despises this "ant heap," this perfectly organized society of robots, in the name of something higher, in the name of freedom. Dostoevsky does not believe that man can achieve freedom and happiness at the same time; he thinks that man can buy happiness only at the expense of freedom, and all utopian schemes seem to him devices to lure man into the yoke of slavery. This freedom is, of course, not political freedom but freedom of choice, indeterminism, even caprice and willfulness, in the paradoxical formulation of the Underground man.

There are hints at a positive solution only in the one section (Section X), which was mutilated by the censor. A letter by Dostoevsky to his brother about the "swine of a censor who let through the passages where I jeered at everything and blasphemed ostensibly" refers to the fact that he "suppressed everything where I drew the conclusion that faith in Christ is needed." In Section XI of the present text (and Dostoevsky never restored the suppressed passages) the Underground man says merely, "I am lying because I know myself that it is not underground that is better, but something different, quite different, for which I am thirsting, but which I cannot find!" This "something . . . quite different" all the other writings of Dostoevsky show to be the voluntary following of Christ even at the expense of suffering and pain.

In a paradoxical form, through the mouth of one of his vilest characters, Dostoevsky reveals in the story his view of man and history—of the evil in man's nature and of the blood and tragedy in history—and his criticism of the optimistic, utilitarian, utopian, progressive view of man which was spreading to Russia from the West during the nineteenth century and which found its most devoted adherents in the Russian revolutionaries. Preoccupied with criticism, Dostoevsky does not here suggest any positive remedy. But if we understand the *Notes* we can understand how Raskolnikov, the murderer out of intellect in *Crime and Punishment*, can find salvation at last, and how Dmitri, the guilty-guiltless parricide of *The Brothers Karamazov*, can sing his hymn to joy in the Siberian mines. We can even understand the legend of the Great Inquisitor told by Ivan Karamazov, in which we meet the same criticism of a utopia (this time that of Catholicism) and the same exaltation of human freedom even at the price of suffering.

TOLSTOY, *THE DEATH OF IVÁN ILYICH*

Tolstoy excited the interest of the West mainly as a public figure: a count owning large estates who decided to give up his wealth and live like a simple

Russian peasant—to dress in a blouse, to eat peasant food, and even to plow the fields and make shoes with his own hands. Tragically, this renunciation involved him in a conflict with his wife and family; at the age of eighty-two he left his home and died in a stationmaster's house (at Astápovo, in 1910). By then he had become the leader of a religious cult, the propounder of a new religion. It was, in substance, a highly simplified primitive Christianity which he put into a few moral commands (such as, "Do not resist evil") and from which he drew, with radical consistency, a complete condemnation of modern civilization: the state, courts and law, war, patriotism, marriage, modern art and literature, science and medicine. In debating this Christian anarchism people have tended to forget that Tolstoy established his command of the public ear as a novelist, or they have exaggerated the contrast between the early worldly novelist and the later prophet.

In his youth, Tolstoy served as a Russian artillery officer in the little wars against the mountain tribes of the Caucasus and in the Crimean War against the English and French. His reputation in Russia was at first based on his war stories. In 1862 he married and settled down on his estate, Yásnaya Polyána, where he wrote his enormous novel *War and Peace* (1865-1869). The book made him famous in Russia but was not translated into English until long afterward. Superficially, *War and Peace* is a historical novel about the Napoleonic invasion of Russia in 1812, a huge swarming epic of a nation's resistance to the foreigner. Tolstoy himself interprets history in general as a struggle of anonymous collective forces which are moved by unknown irrational impulses, waves of communal feeling. Heroes, great men, are actually not heroes but merely insignificant puppets; the best general is the one who does nothing to prevent the unknown course of Providence. But *War and Peace* is not only an impressive and vivid panorama of historical events but also the profound story—centered in two main characters, Pierre Bezúkhov and Prince Andrey Bolkónsky—of a search for the meaning of life. Andrey finds the meaning of life in love and forgiveness of his enemies. Pierre, at the end of a long groping struggle, an education by suffering, finds it in an acceptance of ordinary existence, its duties and pleasures, the family, the continuity of the race.

Tolstoy's next long novel, *Anna Karénina* (1875-1877), resumes this second thread of *War and Peace*. It is a novel of contemporary manners, a narrative of adultery and suicide. But this vivid story, told with incomparable concrete imagination, is counterpointed and framed by a second story, that of Levin, another seeker after the meaning of life, a figure who represents the author as Pierre did in the earlier book; the work ends with a promise of solution, with the ideal of a life in which we should "remember God." Thus *Anna Karénina* also anticipates the approaching crisis in Tolstoy's life. When it came, with the sudden revulsion he describes in *A Con-*

fession (1879), he condemned his earlier books and spent the next years in writing pamphlets and tracts expounding his religion. Later, he returned to the writing of fiction, now regarded entirely as a means of presenting his creed. The earlier novels seemed to him unclear in their message, overdetailed in their method. Hence Tolstoy tried to simplify his art; he wrote plays with a thesis, stories which are like fables or parables, and one long, rather inferior novel, *The Resurrection* (1899), his most savage satire on Russian and modern institutions.

But surely if we look back on all of Tolstoy's work, we must recognize its complete continuity. From the very beginning Tolstoy was a Rousseauist. As early as 1851, when he was in the Caucasus, his diary announced his intention of founding a new, simplified religion. Even as a young man on his estate he had lived quite simply, like a peasant, except for occasional sprees and debauches. He had been horrified by war from the very beginning, though he admired the heroism of the individual soldier and had remnants of patriotic feeling. All his books concern the same theme, the good life, and they all say that the good life lies outside of civilization, near to the soil, in simplicity and humility, in love of one's neighbor. Power, the lust for power, luxury, are always evil.

As a novelist Tolstoy is rooted in the tradition of the older realism. He read and knew the English writers of the eighteenth century, and also Thackeray and Trollope. He did not care for the recent French writers (he was strong in his disapproval of Flaubert) except for Maupassant, who struck him as truthful and useful in his struggle against hypocrisy. Tolstoy's long novels are loosely plotted, though they have large over-all designs. They work by little scenes vividly visualized, by an accumulation of exact detail. Each character is drawn by means of repeated emphasis on certain physical traits, like Pierre's shortsightedness and his hairy, clumsy hands, or Princess Marya's luminous eyes, the red patches on her face, and her shuffling gait. This concretely realized surface, however, everywhere recedes into depths: to the depiction of disease, delirium, and death and to glimpses into eternity. In *War and Peace* the blue sky is the recurrent symbol for the metaphysical relationships of man. Tolstoy is so robust, has his feet so firmly on the ground, presents what he sees with such clarity and objectivity, that one can be easily deluded into considering his dominating quality to be physical, sensual, antithetical to Dostoevsky's spirituality. The contrasts between the two greatest Russian novelists are indeed obvious. While Tolstoy's method can be called epic, Dostoevsky's is dramatic; while Tolstoy's view of man is Rousseauistic, Dostoevsky stresses the fall of man; while Tolstoy rejects history and status, Dostoevsky appeals to the past and wants a hierarchical society, and so on. But these profound differences should not obscure one basic similarity: the deep spirituality of both, their rejection of the basic materialism and the conception of truth propounded by modern science and theorists of realism.

The Death of Iván Ilyich (1886) belongs to the period after Tolstoy's religious conversion when he slowly returned to fiction writing. It represents a happy medium between the early and late manner of Tolstoy. Its story and moral are simple and obvious, as always with Tolstoy (in contrast to Dostoevsky). And it says what almost all of his works are intended to convey—that man is leading the wrong kind of life, that he should return to essentials, to "nature." In *The Death of Iván Ilyich* Tolstoy combines a savage satire on the futility and hypocrisy of conventional life with a powerful symbolic presentation of man's isolation in the struggle with death and of man's hope for a final resurrection. Iván Ilyich is a Russian judge, an official, but he is also the average man of the prosperous middle classes of his time and ours, and he is also Everyman confronted with disease and dying and death. He is an ordinary person, neither virtuous nor particularly vicious, a "go-getter" in his profession, a "family man," as marriages go, who has children but has drifted apart from his wife. Through his disease, which comes about by a trivial accident in the trivial business of fixing a curtain, Iván Ilyich is slowly awakened to self-consciousness and a realization of the falsity of his life and ambitions. The isolation which disease imposes upon him, the wall of hypocrisy erected around him by his family and his doctors, his suffering and pain, drive him slowly to the recognition of *It*, to a knowledge, not merely theoretical but proved on his pulses, of his own mortality. At first he would like simply to return to his former pleasant and normal life—even in the last days of his illness, knowing he must die, he screams in his agony, "I won't!"—but at the end, struggling in the black sack into which he is being pushed, he sees the light at the bottom. " 'Death is finished,' he said to himself. 'It is no more!' "

All the people around him are egotists and hypocrites: his wife, who can remember only how she suffered during his agony; his daughter, who thinks only of the delay in her marriage; his colleagues, who speculate only about the room his death will make for promotions in the court; the doctors, who think only of the name of the disease and not of the patient; all except his shy and frightened son, Vásya, and the servant Gerásim. Gerásim is a healthy peasant lad, assistant to the butler, but because he is near to nature, he is free from hypocrisy, helps his master to be comfortable, and even mentions death, while all the others conceal the truth from him. The doctors, especially, are shown as mere specialists, inhuman and selfish. The first doctor is like a judge, like Iván himself when he sat in court, summing up and cutting off further questions of the patient (or is it the prisoner?). The satire at points appears ineffectively harsh in its violence, but it will not seem exceptional to those who know the older Tolstoy's general attitude toward courts, medicine, marriage, and even modern literature. The cult of art is jeered at, in small touches, only incidentally; it belongs, according to Tolstoy, to the falsities of modern civilization, alongside marriage (which merely hides bestial sensuality), and science (which merely hides rapacity and ignorance).

The story is deliberately deprived of any element of suspense, not only by the announcement contained in the title but by the technique of the cutback. We first hear of Iván Ilyich's death and see the reaction of the widow and friends, and only then listen to the story of his life. The detail, as always in Tolstoy, is superbly concrete and realistic: he does not shy away from the smell of disease, the physical necessity of using a commode, or the sound of screaming. He can employ the creaking of a hassock as a recurrent motif to point up the comedy of hypocrisy played by the widow and her visitor. He can seriously and tragically use the humble image of a black sack or the illusion of the movement of a train.

But all this naturalistic detail serves the one purpose of making us realize, as Iván Ilyich realizes, that not only Caius is mortal but you and I also, and that the life of most of us civilized people is a great lie because it disguises and ignores its dark background, the metaphysical abyss, the reality of Death. While the presentation of *The Death of Iván Ilyich* approaches, at moments, the tone of a legend or fable ("Iván Ilyich's life had been most simple and most ordinary and therefore most terrible"), Tolstoy in this story manages to stay within the concrete situation of our society and to combine the aesthetic method of realism with the universalizing power of symbolic art.

IBSEN, *HEDDA GABLER*

Ibsen's plays can be viewed as the culmination point of the *bourgeois* drama which has flourished fitfully, in France and Germany particularly, since the eighteenth century, when Diderot advocated and wrote plays about the middle classes, their "conditions" and problems. But his works can also be seen as the fountainhead of much modern drama—of the plays of Shaw and Galsworthy, who discuss social problems, and of Maeterlinck and Chekhov, who have learned from the later "symbolist" Ibsen. After a long period of incubation and experimentation with romantic and historical themes, Ibsen wrote a series of "problem" plays, beginning with *The Pillars of Society* (1877), which in their time created a furor by their fearless criticism of the nineteenth-century social scene: the subjection of women, hypocrisy, hereditary disease, seamy politics, and corrupt journalism. He wrote these plays using naturalistic modes of presentation: ordinary colloquial speech, a simple setting in a drawing room or study, a natural way of introducing or dismissing characters. Ibsen had learned from the "well-made" Parisian play (typified by those of Scribe) how to confine his action to one climactic situation and how gradually to uncover the past by retrogressive exposition. But he went far beyond it in technical skill and intellectual honesty.

The success of Ibsen's problem plays was international. But we must not forget that he was a Norwegian, the first writer of his small nation (its population at that time was less than two million) to win a reputation outside of Norway. Ibsen more than anyone else widened the scope of world literature beyond the confines of the great modern nations, which had entered its community roughly in this order: Italy, Spain, France, England, Germany, Russia. Since the time of Ibsen, the other small nations have begun to play their part in the concert of European literature. Paradoxically, however, Ibsen rejected his own land. He had dreamed of becoming a great national poet, but in 1864 he left his country for voluntary exile in Italy, Germany, and Austria. In exile, he wrote the plays depicting Norwegian society—a stuffy, provincial middle class, redeemed, in Ibsen's eyes, by single upright, even fiery, individuals of initiative and courage.

Ibsen could hardly have survived his time if he had been merely a painter of society, a dialectician of social issues, and a magnificent technician of the theater. Many of his discussions are now dated. We smile at some of the doings in *A Doll's House* (1879) and *Ghosts* (1881). His stagecraft is not unusual, even on Broadway. But Ibsen stays with us because he has more to offer—because he was an artist who managed to create, at his best, works of poetry which, under their mask of sardonic humor, express his dream of humanity reborn by intelligence and self-sacrifice.

Hedda Gabler (1890) surprised and puzzled the large audience all over Europe that Ibsen had won in the 1880's. The play shows nothing of Ibsen's reforming zeal: no general theme emerges which could be used in spreading progressive ideas such as the emancipation of women dramatized in *A Doll's House* (1879), nor is the play an example of Ibsen's peculiar technique of retrospective revelation exhibited in *Rosmersholm* (1886). At first glance it seems mainly a study of a complex, exceptional, and even unique woman. Henry James, reviewing the first English performance, saw it as the picture of "a state of nerves as well as of soul, a state of temper, of health, of chagrin, of despair." Undoubtedly, Hedda is the central figure of the play, but she is no conventional heroine. She behaves atrociously to everyone with whom she comes in contact, and her moral sense is thoroughly defective: she is perverse, egotistical, sadistic, callous, even evil and demonic, truly a *femme fatale*. Still, this impression, while not mistaken, ignores another side of her personality and her situation. The play is, after all, a tragedy (though there are comic touches) and we are to feel pity and terror. Hedda is not simply evil and perverse. We must imagine her as distinguished, well-bred, proud, beautiful, and even grand in her defiance of her surroundings and in the final gesture of her suicide. Not for nothing have great actresses excelled in this role. We must pity her as a tortured, tormented creature caught in a web of circumstance, as a victim, in spite of her lashings-out to dominate and control the fate of those around her.

We are carefully prepared to understand her heritage. She is General Gabler's daughter. Ibsen tells us himself (in a letter to Count Moritz Prozor, 4 December 1890) that "I intended to indicate thereby that as a personality she is to be regarded rather as her father's daughter than as her husband's wife." She has inherited an aristocratic view of life. Her father's portrait hangs in her apartment. His pistols tell of the code of honor and the ready escape they offer in a self-inflicted death. Hedda lives in Norway, in the nineteenth century, in a stuffy, provincial, middle-class society, and is acutely, even morbidly afraid of scandal. She has, to her own regret, rejected the advances of Eilert, theatrically threatening him with her father's pistol. She envies Thea for the boldness with which she deserted her husband to follow Eilert. She admires Eilert for his escapades, which she romanticizes with the recurrent metaphor of his returning with "vine-leaves in his hair." But she cannot break out of the narrow confines of her society. She is not an emancipated woman.

When she is almost thirty, in reduced circumstances, she accepts a suitable husband, Jörgen Tesman. The marriage of convenience turns out to be a ghastly error for which she cannot forgive herself: Tesman is an amiable bore absorbed in his research into the "Domestic Industries of Brabant during the Middle Ages." His expectations of a professorship in his home town turn out to be uncertain. He has gone into debt, even to his guileless old aunt, in renting an expensive house and, supreme humiliation for her, Hedda is with child by him. The dream of luxury, of becoming a hostess, of keeping thoroughbred horses, is shattered the very first day after their return from the prolonged honeymoon which for Tesman was also a trip to rummage around in archives. Hedda is deeply stirred by the return of Eilert, her first suitor. She seems vaguely to think of a new relationship, at least, by spoiling his friendship with Thea. She plays with the attentions of Judge Brack. But everything quickly comes to nought: she is trapped in her marriage, unable and unwilling to become unfaithful to her husband; she is deeply disappointed by Eilert's ugly death, saying, "Everything I touch seems destined to turn into something mean and farcical." She fears the scandal which will follow when her role in Eilert's suicide is discovered and she is called before the police; she can avoid it only by coming under the power of Judge Brack, who is prepared to blackmail her with his knowledge of the circumstances. Her plot to destroy Thea and Eilert's brainchild is frustrated by Thea's having preserved notes and drafts which Thea eagerly starts to reconstruct with the help of Tesman. Still, while Hedda is in a terrible *impasse*, her suicide remains a shock, an abrupt, even absurd deed, eliciting the final line from the commonsensical Judge Brack: "Good God—people don't do things like that!" But we must assume that Hedda had pondered suicide long before: the pistol she gave to Eilert implies an unspoken suicide pact. He bungled it; she does it the right way, dying in beauty, shot in the temple and not in the abdomen.

The play is not, however, simply a character study, though Hedda is an extraordinarily complex, contradictory, subtle woman whose portrait, at least on the stage, could not be easily paralleled before Ibsen. It is also an extremely effective, swiftly moving play of action, deftly plotted in its clashes and climaxes. At the end of Act I Hedda seems to have won. The Tesmans, husband and aunt, are put in their place. Thea is lured into making confidences. The scene in Act II in which Hedda appeals to Eilert's pride in his independence and induces him to join in Judge Brack's party is a superb display of Hedda's power and skill. Act II ends with Eilert going off and the two women left alone in their tense though suppressed antagonism. Act III ends with Hedda alone, burning the precious manuscript about the "forces that will shape our civilization and the direction in which that civilization may develop," an obvious contrast to Tesman's research into an irrelevant past. (Ibsen himself always believed in progress, in a utopia he called "the Third Empire.")

The action is compressed into about thirty-six hours and located in a house where only the moving of furniture (the piano into the back room) or the change of light or costumes indicates the passing of time. Tesman is something of a fool. He is totally unaware of Hedda's inner turmoil, he obtusely misunderstands allusions to her pregnancy, he comically encourages the advances of Judge Brack, he complacently settles down to the task of assembling the fragments of Eilert's manuscript, recognizing that "putting other people's papers into order is rather my specialty." Though he seems amiably domestic in his love for his aunts, proud of having won Hedda, ambitious to provide an elegant home for her, his behavior is by no means above reproach. He envies and fears Eilert, gloats over his bad reputation, surreptitiously brings home the lost manuscript, conceals its recovery from Thea; when Hedda tells of its being burned, he is at first shocked, reacting comically with the legal phrase about "appropriating lost property," but is then easily persuaded to accept it when Hedda tells him that she did it for his sake and completely won over when she reveals her pregnancy. After Eilert's death he feels, however, some guilt and tries to make up by helping in the reconstruction of the manuscript, now that his rival no longer threatens his career. Tesman is given strong speech mannerisms: the frequent use of "what?" which Hedda, commenting at the end on the progress of the work on the manuscript, imitates sarcastically, and the use of "fancy that." His last inappropriate words, "She's shot herself! Shot herself in the head! Fancy that!", lend a grotesque touch to the tragic end. Aunt Juliana belongs with him: she is a fussy, kindly person, proud of her nephew, awed by his new wife, eager to help with the expected baby, but also easily consoled after the death of her sister: "There's always some poor invalid who needs care and attention."

Judge Brack is a "man of the world," a sensualist who hardly conceals his desire to make Hedda his mistress, by blackmail if necessary, and is dismayed when she escapes his clutches: in his easy-going philosophy "people usually learn to accept the inevitable."

The other pair, Eilert Loevborg and Thea Elvsted, are sharply contrasted. Thea had the courage to leave her husband; she is devoted to Eilert and seems to have cured him of his addiction to drink but fears that he cannot resist a new temptation. Eilert tells Hedda unkindly that Thea is "stupid," and there is some truth to that, inasmuch as she is so easily taken in by Hedda. Her quick settling down to work on the manuscript after Eilert's death suggests some obtuseness, though we must, presumably, excuse it as a theatrical foreshortening.

Eilert, we must assume, is some kind of genius. His book, we have to take on trust, is an important work. We are told that he had squandered an inheritance, had engaged in orgies, and had regaled Hedda with tales of his exploits before she chased him with her pistol. When he comes back to town, ostensibly reformed, dressed conventionally, he immediately starts courting Hedda again. Stung by her contempt for his abstinence, he rushes off to Brack's party, which degenerates into a disgraceful brawl in a house of ill fame. His relapse and the loss of the manuscript destroy his self-esteem and hope for any future. He accepts Hedda's pistol but dies an ignominious, ugly death. We see Eilert mainly reflected in Hedda's imagination as a figure of pagan freedom who, she thinks, has done something noble, beautiful, and courageous in "rising from the feast of life so early." She dies in beauty as she wanted Eilert to die.

This aesthetic suicide must seem to us a supremely futile gesture of revolt. Ibsen always admired the great rebels, the fighters for freedom, but *Hedda Gabler* will appear almost a parodic version of his persistent theme: the individual against society, defying it and escaping it in death.

CHEKHOV, *THE CHERRY ORCHARD*

Chekhov differs sharply from the two giants of Russian literature. His work is of smaller scope. With the exception of an immature, forgotten novel and a travel book, he never wrote anything but short stories and plays. He belongs, furthermore, to a very different moral and spiritual atmosphere. Chekhov had studied medicine, and practiced it for a time. He shared the scientific outlook of his age and had too skeptical a mind to believe in Christianity or in any metaphysical system. He confessed that an intelligent believer was a puzzle to him. His attitude toward his materials and characters is detached, "objective." He is thus much more in the stream of Western realism than either Tolstoy or Dostoevsky, and his affinities with Maupassant (to whom he is related also in technical matters) are obvious. But extended reading of Chekhov does convey an impression of his view of life. There is implied in his stories a philosophy of kindness and humanity, a sense of the unexplainable mystery of life, a sense, especially, of man's utter loneliness in this universe and among his fellow men. Chekhov's pessimism has nothing of the defiance of the universe or the horror at it which we meet in other writers with similar attitudes; it is somehow merely sad, pathetic, and yet also comforting and comfortable.

The Russia depicted in Chekhov's stories and plays is of a later period than that presented by Tolstoy and Dostoevsky. It seems to be nearing its end; there is a sense of decadence and frustration which heralds the approach of the catastrophe. The aristocracy still keeps up a beautiful front, but is losing its fight without much resistance, resignedly. Officialdom is stupid and venal. The Church is backward and narrow-minded. The intelligentsia are hopelessly ineffectual, futile, lost in the provinces or absorbed in their egos. The peasants live subject to the lowest degradations of poverty and drink, apparently rather aggravated than improved since the much-heralded emancipation of the serfs in 1861. There seems no hope for society except in a gradual spread of enlightenment, good sense, and hygiene, for Chekhov is skeptical of the revolution and revolutionaries as well as of Tolstoy's followers.

The plays of Chekhov seem to go furthest in the direction of naturalism, the depiction of a "slice of life" on stage. Compared to Ibsen's plays they seem plotless; they could be described as a succession of little scenes, composed like a mosaic or like the dots on an impressionist painting. The characters often do not engage in the usual dialogue; they speak often in little soliloquies, hardly justified by the situation and they often do not listen to the words of their ostensible partners. They seem alone even in a crowd. Human communication seems difficult and even impossible. There is no clear message, no zeal for social reform; life seems to flow quietly, even sluggishly, until interrupted by some desperate outbreak or even a pistol shot.

Chekhov's last play, *The Cherry Orchard* (composed in 1903, first performed at the Moscow Art Theatre on January 17, 1904) differs, however, from this pattern in several respects. It has a strongly articulated central theme: the loss of the orchard, and it has a composition which roughly follows the traditional scheme of a well-made play. Arrival and departure from the very same room, the nursery, frame the two other acts: the outdoor idyll of Act II and the dance in Act III. Act III is the turning point of the action: Lopahin appears and announces, somewhat shamefacedly, that he has bought the estate. The orchard was lost from the very beginning—there is no real struggle to prevent its sale—but still the news of Lopahin's purchase is a surprise as he had no intention of buying it but did so only when during the auction sale a rival seemed to have a chance of acquiring it. A leading action runs its course, and one may even argue, many—too many—subplots crisscross each other: the shy and awkward love affair of the student Trofimov and the gay daughter Anya; the love triangle among the three dependents, Yepihodov, the unlucky clerk, Dunyasha, the silly chambermaid, and Yasha, the conceited and insolent footman. Varya, the practical, spinsterish stepdaughter, has her troubles with Lopahin, and Simeonov-Pishchik is beset by the same financial problems as the owners of the orchard and is rescued by the discovery of some white clay on his estate. The German governess Charlotta drifts around alluding to her obscure origins and past. There are undeveloped references to events preceding the action on stage: the lover in Paris, the drowned boy Grisha, but there is no revelation of the past as in Ibsen, no mystery, no intrigue.

While the events on the stage follow each other naturally, though hardly always in a logical, causal order, a symbolic device is used conspicuously: In Act II after a pause, "suddenly a distant sound is heard, coming from the sky as it were, the sound of a snapping string, mournfully dying away." It occurs again at the very end of the play followed by "the stroke of an ax felling a tree far away in the orchard." An attempt is made to explain this sound at its first occurrence as a bucket's fall in a far away pit, or as the cries of a heron or an owl, but the effect is weird and even supernatural; it establishes an ominous mood. Even the orchard carries more than its obvious meaning: It is white, drowned in blossoms when the party arrives in the spring; it is bare and desolate in the autumn when the axes are heard cutting it down. "The old bark on the trees gleams faintly, and the cherry trees seem to be dreaming of things that happened a hundred, two hundred years ago and to be tormented by painful visions," declaims Trofimov, defining his feeling for the orchard as a symbol of repression and serfdom. For Lubov Ranevskaya it is an image of her lost innocence and of the happier past, while Lopahin sees it only as an investment. It seems to draw together the meaning of the play.

But what is this meaning? Can we even decide whether it is a tragedy or a comedy? It has been commonly seen as the tragedy of the downfall of the Russian aristocracy (or more correctly, the landed gentry) victimized by the newly rich, upstart peasantry. One could see the play as depicting the defeat of a group of feckless people at the hand of a ruthless "developer" who destroys nature and natural beauty for profit. Or one can see it as prophesying, through the mouth of the student Trofimov, the approaching end of feudal Russia and the coming happier future. Soviet interpretations and performances lean that way.

Surely none of these interpretations can withstand inspection of the actual text of the play. They all run counter to Chekhov's professed intentions. He called the play a comedy. In a letter of September 15, 1903, he declared expressly that the play "has not turned out as drama but as comedy, in places even a farce" and a few days later (September 21, 1903) he wrote that "the whole play is gay and frivolous." Chekhov did not like the staging of the play at the Moscow Art Theatre and complained of its tearful tone and its slow pace. He objected that "they obstinately call my play a drama in playbill and newspaper advertisements" while he had called it a comedy (April 10, 1904).

No doubt, there are many comical and even farcical characters and scenes in the play. Charlotta with her dog eating nuts, her card tricks, her ventriloquism, her disappearing acts, is a clownish figure. Gayev, the landowner, though "suave and elegant," is a windbag obsessed by his passion for billiards, constantly popping candy into his mouth, telling the waiters in a restaurant about the "decadents" in Paris. Yepihodov, the clerk, carries a revolver and, threatening suicide, asks foolishly whether you have read Buckle (the English historian) and complains of his ill-luck: a spider on his chest, a cockroach in his drink. Simeonov-Pishchik empties a whole bottle of pills, eats a gallon and a half of cucumbers, quotes Nietzsche supposedly recommending the forging of banknotes and, fat as he is, puffs and prances at the dance ordering the "cavaliers aux genoux." Even the serious characters are put into ludicrous predicaments: Trofimov falls down the stairs; Lopahin, coming to announce the purchase of the estate, is almost hit with a stick by Varya (and was hit in the original version). Lopahin, teasing his intended Varya, "moos like a cow." The ball with the Jewish orchestra, the hunting for the galoshes, and the champagne drinking by Yasha in the last act have all a touch of absurdity. The grand speeches, Gayev's addresses to the bookcase and to nature or Trofimov's about "mankind going forward" and "All Russia is our orchard," are undercut by the contrast between the sentiment and the character: Gayev is callous and shallow, the "eternal student" Trofimov never did a stitch of work. He is properly ridiculed and insulted by Lubov for his scant beard and his silly professions of being "above love." One can sympathize with Chekhov's irritation at the pervading gloom imposed by the Moscow production.

Still, I believe, we cannot, in spite of the author, completely dismiss the genuine pathos of the central situation and of the central figure, Lubov Ranevskaya. Whatever one may say about her recklessness in financial matters and her guilt in relation to her lover in France, we must feel her deep attachment to the house and the orchard, to the past and her lost innocence, clearly and unhumorously expressed in the first act on her arrival, again and again at the impending sale of the estate, and finally at the parting from her house: "Oh, my orchard—my dear, sweet, beautiful orchard! . . . My life, my youth, my happiness—Goodbye!" That Gayev, before the final parting, seems to have overcome the sense of loss and even looks forward to his job in the bank and that Lubov acknowledges that her "nerves are better" and that "she sleeps well" testifies to the indestructible spirit of brother and sister, but cannot minimize the sense of loss, the pathos of parting, the nostalgia for happier times. Nor is the conception of Lopahin simple. Chekhov emphasized, in a letter to Konstantin Stanislavsky who was to play the part, that "Lopahin is a decent person in the full sense of the word, and his bearing must be that of a completely dignified and intelligent man." He is not, he says, a profiteering peasant (*kulachok*, October 30, 1903). He admires Lubov and thinks of her with gratitude. He senses the beauty of the poppies in his fields. Even the scene of the abortive encounter with Varya at the end has its quiet pathos in spite of all its awkwardness and the comic touches such as the reference to the broken thermometer. Firs, the old valet, aged eighty-six, may be grotesque in his deafness and his nostalgia for the good old days of serfdom, but the very last scene when we see him abandoned in the locked-up house surely concludes the play on a note of desolation and even despair.

Chekhov, we must conclude, achieved a highly original and even paradoxical blend of comedy and tragedy or rather of farce and pathos. The play gives a social picture firmly set in a specific historical time: the dissolution of the landed gentry, the rise of the peasant, the encroachment of the city; but it does not propound an obvious social thesis. Chekhov, in his tolerance and tenderness, in his distrust of ideologies and heroics, extends his sympathy to all his characters (with the exception of the crudely ambitious valet Yasha). The glow of his humanity, untrammeled by time and place, keeps *The Cherry Orchard* alive in quite different social and political conditions, as it has the universalizing power of great art.

LIVES, WRITINGS, AND CRITICISM

Biographical and critical works are listed only if they are available in English.

GUSTAVE FLAUBERT

LIFE. Born at Rouen, Normandy, on December 12, 1821, to the chief surgeon of the Hôtel Dieu. Flaubert was extremely precocious: by the age of sixteen he was writing stories in the romantic taste, which were published only after his death. In 1840 he went to Paris to study law (he had received his baccalaureate from the local *lycée*), but he failed in his examinations, and in 1843 suffered a sudden nervous breakdown which kept him at home. In 1846 he moved to Croisset, just outside of Rouen on the Seine, where he made his home for the rest of his life, devoting himself to writing. The same year, in Paris, Flaubert met Louise Colet, a minor poetess and lady about town, who became his mistress. In 1849-1851 he visited the Levant, traveling extensively in Greece, Syria, and Egypt. After his return he settled down to the writing of *Madame Bovary,* which took him five full years. *Madame Bovary* was a great popular success. An attempt was made to suppress it, however, and a lawsuit ensued, charging Flaubert with immorality. In 1857 he was acquitted of this charge. The remainder of his life was uneventful. He made occasional trips to Paris, and one trip, in 1860, to

Tunisia to see the ruins of Carthage in preparation for the writing of his novel *Salammbô*. Flaubert died at Croisset on May 8, 1880.

CHIEF WRITINGS. *Madame Bovary* (1856); *Salammbô* (1862); *The Sentimental Education* (*L'Éducation sentimentale*, 1869); *The Temptation of St. Anthony* (*La Tentation de Saint Antoine*, 1874); *Three Tales* (*Trois Contes*, 1877), including "A Simple Heart" ("Un Coeur simple"); *Bouvard and Pécuchet* (*Bouvard et Pécuchet*, a posthumous novel, unfinished, 1881).

BIOGRAPHY AND CRITICISM. Erich Auerbach, "In the Hôtel de la Mole," in *Mimesis: The Representation of Reality in Western Literature*, translated by Willard Trask (1953); Benjamin F. Bart, *Flaubert* (1967); *Madame Bovary and the Critics*, edited by Benjamin F. Bart (1966); Victor Brombert, *The Novels of Flaubert* (1966); *Gustave Flaubert: Madame Bovary. Backgrounds and Sources: Essays in Criticism*, edited by Paul de Man (1965); Raymond D. Giraud, *The Unheroic Hero in the Novels of Stendhal, Balzac, and Flaubert* (1957); *Flaubert: A Collection of Critical Essays*, edited by Raymond D. Giraud (1964); Alison Fairlie, *Flaubert: Madam Bovary* (1962); Henry James, "Gustave Flaubert," in *Notes on Novelists* (1914); Harry Levin, "Flaubert," in *The Gates of Horn: A Study of Five French Realists* (1963); Percy Lubbock, chapters 5 and 6 in *The Craft of Fiction* (1921); Maurice Nadau, *The Greatness of Flaubert*, translated by Barbara Bray (1972); Georges Poulet, "Flaubert," in *The Metamorphoses of the Circle*, translated by Carley Dawson and Eliott Coleman (1967); Philip Spencer, *Flaubert: A Biography* (1952); Enid Starkie, *Flaubert: The Making of the Master* (1967); Francis Steegmuller, *Flaubert and Madame Bovary* (1939, new ed. 1950); Margaret G. Tillett, *On Reading Flaubert* (1961); Anthony Thorlby, *Gustave Flaubert and the Art of Realism* (1957); Martin Turnell, "Flaubert," in *The Novel in France* (1951).

FYODOR DOSTOEVSKY

LIFE. Fyodor Mikhailovich Dostoevsky, born in Moscow on October 30, 1821. His father was a staff doctor at the Hospital for the Poor. Later he acquired an estate and serfs. In 1839 he was killed by one of his peasants in a quarrel. Dostoevsky was sent to the Military Engineering Academy in St. Petersburg, from which he graduated in 1843. He became a civil servant, a draftsman in the St. Petersburg Engineering Corps, but resigned soon because he feared that he would be transferred to the provinces when his writing was discovered. His first novel, *Poor People* (1846), proved a great success with the critics; his second, *The Double* (1846), which followed immediately, was a failure.

Subsequently, Dostoevsky became involved in the Petrashevsky circle, a secret society of antigovernment and socialist tendencies. He was arrested on April 23, 1849, and condemned to be shot. On December 22 he was led to public execution, but he was reprieved at the last moment and sent to penal servitude in Siberia (near Omsk), where he worked for four years in a stockade, wearing fetters, completely cut off from communications with Russia. On his release in February, 1854, he was assigned as a common soldier to Semipalatinsk, a small town near the Mongolian frontier. There he received several promotions (eventually becoming an ensign); his rank of nobility, forfeited by his sentence, was restored; and he married the widow of a customs official. In July, 1859, Dostoevsky was permitted to return to Russia, and finally, in December, 1859, to St. Petersburg—after ten years of his life had been spent in Siberia.

In the last year of his exile, Dostoevsky had resumed writing, and in 1861, shortly after his return, he founded a review, *Time (Vremya)*. This was suppressed in 1863, though Dostoevsky had changed his political opinions and was now strongly nationalistic and conservative in outlook. He made his first trip to France and England in 1862, and traveled in Europe again in 1863 and 1865, in order to follow a young woman friend, Apollinaria Suslova, and to indulge in gambling. After his wife's death in 1864, and another unsuccessful journalistic venture, *The Epoch* (*Epokha*), 1864-1865, Dostoevsky was for a time almost crushed by gambling debts, emotional entanglements, and frequent epileptic seizures. He barely managed to return from Germany in 1865. In the winter of 1866 he wrote *Crime and Punishment*, and before he had finished it, dictated a shorter novel, *The Gambler*, to meet a deadline. He married his secretary, Anna Grigoryevna Snitkina, early in 1867 and left Russia with her to avoid his creditors. For years they wandered over Germany, Italy, and Switzerland, frequently in abject poverty. Their first child died. In 1871, when the initial chapters of *The Possessed* proved a popular success, Dostoevsky returned to St. Petersburg. He became the editor of a weekly, *The Citizen* (*Grazhdanin*), for a short time and then published a periodical written by himself, *The Diary of a Writer* (1876-1881), which won great acclaim. Honors and some prosperity came to him. At a Pushkin anniversary celebrated in Moscow in 1880 he gave the main speech. But soon after his return to St. Petersburg he died, on January 28, 1881, not yet sixty years old.

CHIEF WRITINGS. *Memoirs from the*

House of the Dead (1862); *Notes from Underground* (1864); *Crime and Punishment* (1866); *The Idiot* (1869); *The Possessed* (1871-1872); *The Raw Youth* (1875); *The Brothers Karamazov* (1880).

BIOGRAPHY AND CRITICISM. Monroe C. Beardsley, "Dostoyevsky's Metaphor of the 'Underground,'" *Journal of the History of Ideas*, III (June, 1942), 265-290; Maurice Beebe and Christopher Newton, "Dostoevsky in English: A Checklist of Criticism and Translations" in *Modern Fiction Studies* IV (1958); Nikolay N. Berdayev, *Dostoievsky: An Interpretation* (1934, new ed. 1957); R. P. Blackmur, "Studies in Dostoevsky," in *Eleven Essays in the European Novel* (1964); E. H. Carr, *Dostoevsky, 1821–1881: A New Biography* (1931); Richard Curle, *Characters of Dostoevsky: Studies from Four Novels* (1950); *Fyodor Dostoevsky: Notes from Underground*, edited by Robert G. Durgy, translated by Serge Shishkoff, criticism and analysis (1969); Donald Fanger, *Dostoevsky and Romantic Realism* (1965); Joseph Frank, "Nihilism and *Notes from Underground*," in *Sewanee Review* LXIX (1961); Sigmund Freud, "Dostoievski and Parricide," in *Partisan Review* XIV (1945), 530–44; Vyacheslav Ivanov, *Freedom and the Tragic Life: A Study in Dostoevsky* (1952); Robert L. Jackson, *The Underground Man in Russian Literature* (1958), and *Dostoevsky's Quest for Form* (1966); Janko Lavrin, *Dostoevski: A Study* (1947); David Magarshack, *Dostoevsky* (1962); Konstantin Mochulsky, *Dostoevsky: Life and Work*, translated by Michael Minihan (1967); Middleton Murry, *Fyodor Dostoevsky: A Critical Study* (1916); Richard Peace, *Dostoevsky: An Examination of the Major Novels* (1971); Ernest J. Simmons, *Dostoevski, The Making of a Novelist* (1940); George Steiner, *Tolstoy or Dostoevsky* (1959); Victor Terras, *The Young Dostoevsky, 1846–1849* (1969); Edward Wasiolek, *Dostoevsky: The Major Fiction* (1964); *Dostoevsky: A Collection of Critical Essays*, edited by René Wellek (1962); Avrahm Yarmolinsky, *Dostoevsky: A Study in His Ideology* (1921), and *Dostoevsky: A Life* (1934); L. A. Zander, *Dostoevsky*, translated by Natalie Duddington (1948); Stefan Zweig, *Three Masters: Balzac, Dickens, Dostoevsky* (1930). See also M. M. Bakhtin, *Problems of Dostoevsky's Poetics*, translated by R. W. Rostel (1973); Joseph Frank, *Dostoevsky: The Seeds of Revolt, 1821–1849* (1976); Leonid Grossman, *Dostoevsky*, translated by Mary Mackler (1974); Michael Holquist, *Dostoevsky and the Novel* (1977); Malcolm V. Jones, *Dostoevsky: The Novel of Discord* (1976); Alex de Jonge, *Dostoevsky and the Age of Intensity* (1975); and Robert Lord *Dostoevsky: Essays and Perspectives* (1970).

LEO TOLSTOY

LIFE. Born at Yásnaya Polyána, his mother's estate near Tula (about 130 miles south of Moscow), on August 28, 1828. His father was a retired lieutenant colonel; one of his ancestors, the first count, had served Peter the Great as an ambassador. His mother's father was a Russian general in chief. Tolstoy lost both parents early in his life and was brought up by aunts. He went to the University of Kazan between 1844 and 1847, drifted along aimlessly for a few years more, and in 1851 became a cadet in the Caucasus. As an artillery officer he saw action in the wars with the mountain tribes and again, in 1854-1855, during the Crimean War against the French and English. Tolstoy had written fictional reminiscences of his childhood while he was in the Caucasus, and during the Crimean War he wrote war stories which established his literary reputation. For some years he lived on his estate, where he founded and himself taught an extremely "progressive" school for peasant children. He made two trips to western Europe, in 1857 and in 1860-1861. In 1862 he married the daughter of a physician, Sonya Bers, who bore him thirteen children. In the first years of his married life, between 1863 and 1869, he wrote *War and Peace*, and between 1873 and 1877 composed *Anna Karénina*. After this, a religious crisis came over him, which he described in 1879 in *A Confession*. The next years were devoted to the writing of tracts—attacks on orthodoxy, the government, and the cult of art, and elaborations of his own religious creed. Only slowly did Tolstoy return to the writing of fiction. His longest later book was *The Resurrection*. In 1901 Tolstoy was excommunicated. A disagreement with his wife about the nature of the good life and about financial matters sharpened into a conflict over his last will, which finally led to a complete break: he left home in the company of a doctor friend. He caught cold on the train journey south and died in the house of the stationmaster of Astápovo, on November 20, 1910.

CHIEF WRITINGS. *The Cossacks* (1863); *War and Peace* (1865-1869); *Anna Karénina* (1875-1877); *A Confession* (1879); *The Death of Iván Ilyich* (1886); *The Power of Darkness* (1886); *The Kreutzer Sonata* (1889); *Master and Man* (1895); *What Is Art?* (1897); *The Resurrection* (1899); *Hadji Murad* (1896-1904).

BIOGRAPHY AND CRITICISM. John Bayley, *Tolstoy and the Novel* (1962); Isaiah Berlin, *The Hedgehog and the Fox: An Essay on Tolstoy's View of History* (1953); R. F. Christian, *Tolstoy's "War and Peace": A Study* (1962), and *Tolstoy: A Critical Introduction* (1969); Maxim Gorky, *Rem-*

iniscences of Tolstoy (1921); Janko Lavrin, *Tolstoy* (1946); Derrick Leon, *Tolstoy: His Life and Work* (1944); Georg Lukács, "Tolstoy," in *Studies in European Realism,* translated by E. Bone (1950); Thomas Mann, "Goethe and Tolstoy," in *Essays of Three Decades,* translated by H. T. Lowe-Porter (1947); *Tolstoy: A Collection of Critical Essays,* edited by Ralph E. Matlaw (1967); Aylmer Maude, *The Life of Tolstoy* (2 vols, 1908–1910); D. S. Merezhkovsky, *Tolstoy as Man and Artist* (1902); Renato Poggioli, "A Portrait of Tolstoy as Alceste," in *The Phoenix and the Spider* (1957); Philip Rahv, "The Death of Ivan Ilyich and Joseph K." and "Tolstoy: The Green Twig and the Black Trunk," in *Image and Idea* (1949); Theodore Redpath, *Tolstoy* (1960); Ernest J. Simmons, *Leo Tolstoy* (1946), and *An Introduction to Tolstoy's Writings* (1968); Logan Speirs, *Tolstoy and Chekhov* (1971); George Steiner, *Tolstoy or Dostoevsky* (1959); Stefan Zweig, *Adepts in Self-Portraiture* (*Casanova, Stendhal, Tolstoy*), translated by E. and C. Paul (1952). See also E. G. Greenwood, *Tolstoy: The Comprehensive Vision* (1975), and Logan Speirs, *Tolstoy and Chekhov,* (1971).

HENRIK IBSEN

LIFE. Born at Skien, in Norway, on March 20, 1828. His family had sunk into poverty and finally complete bankruptcy. In 1844, at the age of sixteen, Ibsen was sent to Grimstad, another small coastal town, as an apothecary's apprentice. There he lived in almost complete isolation and cut himself off from his family, except for his sister Hedvig. In 1850 he managed to get to Oslo (then Christiana) and to enroll at the university. But he never passed his examinations and in the following year left for Bergen, where he had acquired the position of playwright and assistant stage manager at the newly founded Norwegian Theater. Ibsen supplied the small theater with several historical and romantic plays. In 1857 he was appointed artistic director at the Møllergate Theater in Christiana, and a year later he married Susannah Thoresen. *Love's Comedy* (1862) was his first major success on the stage. Ibsen was then deeply affected by Scandinavianism, the movement for the solidarity of the Northern nations, and when in 1864 Norway refused to do anything to support Denmark in her war with Prussia and Austria over Schleswig-Holstein, he was so disgusted with his country that he left it for what he thought would be permanent exile. After that, Ibsen led a life of wandering. He lived in Rome, in Dresden, in Munich, and in smaller summer resorts, and during this time wrote all his later plays. *The Wild Duck* was written in Gossensass, in the Austrian Alps, in 1884. He paid a visit to Norway in 1885, but returned again to Germany. Only in 1891, when he was sixty-three, did Ibsen return to Christiana for good. He was then famous and widely honored, but lived a very retired life. In 1900 he suffered a stroke which made him a complete invalid for the last years of his life. He died on May 23, 1906, at Christiana.

CHIEF WRITINGS. (All of the works listed are plays.) *A Doll's House* (1879); *Ghosts* (1881); *An Enemy of the People* (1882); *The Wild Duck* (1884); *Rosmersholm* (1886); *The Lady from the Sea* (1888); *Hedda Gabler* (1890); *The Master Builder* (1892).

BIOGRAPHY AND CRITICISM. Eric Bentley, "Wagner and Ibsen: A Contrast," in *The Playwright as Thinker* (1946), and "Ibsen, Pro and Con," in *In Search of Theater* (1959); *Contemporary Approaches to Ibsen,* edited by Alex Bolckmans (1966); Muriel C. Bradbrook, *Ibsen: The Norwegian* (1948); Robert Brustein, "Henrik Ibsen," in *The Theater of Revolt* (1964); Brian W. Downs, *Ibsen: The Intellectual Background* (1946), and *A Study of Six Plays by Ibsen* (1950); *Ibsen: A Collection of Critical Essays,* edited by Rolf Fjelds (1965); Hans Heiberg, *Ibsen: A Portrait of the Artist,* translated by Joan Tate (1969); Orley I. Holtan, *Mythic Patterns in Ibsen's Last Plays* (1970); Theodore Jorgensen, *Henrik Ibsen: A Study in Art and Personality* (1945); G. Wilson Knight, *Ibsen* (1962); Halvdan Koht, *Life of Ibsen,* translated by E. Haugen and N. E. Santiello (2 vols., 1971); Janko Lavrin, *Ibsen: An Approach* (1950); F. L. Lucas, *The Drama of Ibsen and Strindberg* (1962); James W. McFarlane, *Ibsen and the Temper of Norwegian Literature* (1960), and *Discussions of Henrik Ibsen* (1962), and *Henrik Ibsen: A Critical Anthology* (1970); Michael Meyer, *Ibsen: A Biography* (1971); Kenneth Muir, *Last Periods of Shakespeare, Racine, Ibsen* (1961); John Northam, *Ibsen's Dramatic Method: A Study of the Prose Dramas* (1953); George Bernard Shaw, *The Quintessence of Ibsenism* (1891, 3rd enl. ed., 1913); Peter F. D. Tennant, *Ibsen's Dramatic Technique* (1948); Maurice J. Valency, *The Flower and the Castle: An Introduction to Modern Drama* (1963); Hermann J. Weigand, *The Modern Ibsen* (1925); Raymond Williams, *Modern Tragedy* (1966); A. E. Zucker, *Henrik Ibsen: The Master Builder* (1927). See also Jens Arup, "On 'Hedda Gabler' " in *Orbis Litterarum* XII (1957); Eva Le Gallienne, *Preface to Ibsen's 'Hedda Gabler',* (1953); and Henry James, "On the Occasion of 'Hedda Gabler'," in *Essays in London and Elsewhere* (1893) and in *The Scenic Art,* edited by Allan Wade (1948).

ANTON CHEKHOV

LIFE. Anton Pavlovich Chekhov, born on January 17, 1860, at Taganrog, a small town on the Sea of Azov. His father was a grocer and haberdasher; his grandfather, a serf who had bought

his freedom. Chekhov's father went bankrupt in 1876, and the family moved to Moscow, leaving Anton to finish school in his home town. After his graduation in 1879, he followed his family to Moscow, where he studied medicine. In order to earn additional money for his family and himself, he started to write humorous sketches and stories for magazines. In 1884 he became a doctor and published his first collection of stories, *Tales of Melpomene*. In the same year he had his first hemorrhage. All the rest of his life he struggled against tuberculosis. His first play, *Ivanov*, was performed in 1887. Three years later, he undertook an arduous journey through Siberia to the island of Sakhalin (north of Japan) and back by boat through the Suez Canal. He saw there the Russian penal settlements and wrote a moving account of his trip in *Sakhalin Island* (1892). In 1898 his play *The Sea Gull* was a great success at the Moscow Art Theater. The next year he moved to Yalta, in the Crimea, and in 1901 married the actress Olga Knipper. He died on July 2, 1904, at Badenweiler in the Black Forest.

CHIEF WRITINGS. Chekhov's stories, which first appeared in scattered magazines, have been collected in many variously titled volumes. The plays were performed in this order: *Ivanov* (1887); *The Sea Gull* (1896); *Uncle Vanya* (1899); *The Three Sisters* (1901); *The Cherry Orchard* (1904); they have been translated by Constance Garnett, 2 vols., 1924.

BIOGRAPHY AND CRITICISM. W. H. Bruford, *Chekhov and His Russia* (1948) and *Anton Chekhov* (1957); Korney Chukovsky, *Chekhov the Man*, trans. by Pauline Rose (1945); Thomas Adam Eekman, *A. Čechov, 1860-1960. Some Essays* (1960); Oliver Elton, "Chekhov" in *Essays and Addresses* (1939); Francis Fergusson, "*Ghosts* and *The Cherry Orchard*," in *The Idea of a Theater* (1949); Anna Heifetz (Sherman), *Chekhov in English: A List of Works by and about Him*, ed. by A. Yarmolinsky (1949); Ronald Hingley, *Chekhov, A Biographical and Critical Study* (1950); *Chekhov: A Collection of Critical Essays*, edited by Robert L. Jackson (1967); David Magarshack, *Chekhov the Dramatist* (1952), and *Chekhov: A Life* (1952); Leon Shestov, *Chekhov and Other Essays*, edited by Sidney Monas (1966); Ernest J. Simmons, *Chekhov: A Biography* (1962); Logan Speirs, *Tolstoy and Chekhov* (1971); L. J. Styan, *Chekhov in Performance: A Commentary on the Major Plays* (1971); Maurice Valency, *The Breaking Spring: The Plays of Anton Chekhov* (1966).

GUSTAVE FLAUBERT

(1821–1880)

Madame Bovary*

[*Editor's Note.* An explanation of the plot and the stage business is needed to understand properly the performance in *Madame Bovary* of the opera *Lucia di Lammermoor*, which occurs on pages 910-16 of this text. The French libretto by Alp. Royer and Gust. Vaez[1] (published in Brussels in 1839) must be consulted, as it differs greatly from the original Italian libretto by Salvatore Cammarano and resembles only distantly the novel by Walter Scott. The story is one of family hatred: Edgar, the owner of the castle of Ravenswood in the Scottish Highlands, has been expelled by Lord Henry Ashton who had killed his father. He is in hiding as an outlaw. He loves and is loved clandestinely by Lucy, Lord Henry's sister. The opera opens with a hunting scene on the grounds of Ravenswood castle where Henry, his forester called Gilbert (Normanno in the Italian), and other followers comb the grounds for traces of a mysterious stranger whom they suspect to be the outcast Edgar. They are joined by Lord Arthur who is a suitor for Lucy's hand and is favored by her brother as he can save him from financial ruin. Arthur declares his love for Lucy (no such scene is in the Italian). Lucy in the next scene prepares to meet Edgar in a secluded spot; she gives a purse to Gilbert whom she believes to be her friend though Gilbert is actually scheming with Lord Henry against her. (The scene is not in the Italian original.) Then Lucy is left alone and sings a cavatina beginning: "Que n'avons-nous des ailes." Edgar appears then, played by Lagardy, a fictional tenor. He tells of his hatred for Lucy's brother because of the death of his father. He had sworn vengeance but is ready to forget it in his love for her. Edgar has to leave on a mission to France but in parting the lovers pledge their troth and exchange rings. The stretto contains the words, "Une fleur pour ma tombe," "donne une larme à l'exilé," phrases alluded to in Flaubert's account.

Charles is so obtuse that he thinks that Edgar is torturing Lucy, and Emma has to tell him that he is her lover. Charles protests that he heard him vowing vengeance on her family. He had heard him saying: "J'ai juré vengeance et guerre." Charles has also heard Lord Arthur say, "J'aime Lucie et m'en crois aimé," and has seen Lord Arthur going off with her father arm in arm. But Charles obviously takes her brother Henry for her father.

The second act begins with Gilbert telling his master Henry that he slipped Lucy's ring from the sleeping Edgar, had made a

*A substantially new translation by Paul De Man.

1. A pseudonym of J. N. G. Van Niewenhuysen.

copy and will produce it in order to convince Lucy of Edgar's faithlessness. Charles mistakes the false ring which is shown Lucy for a love gift sent by Edgar. The business with the rings replaced an analogous deception with forged letters in the Italian libretto. Lucy appears dressed for the wedding with Lord Arthur, unhappily resisting and imploring, reminding Emma of her own wedding day and the contrast with her false joy soon turned to bitterness. Brandishing a sword Edgar suddenly returns voicing his indignation. There follows a sextet (Lucy, Henry, Edgar, Raimondo the minister, Arthur, Gilbert) which suggests to Emma her desire to flee and to be carried off as Edgar wants to carry off Lucy. But the marriage contract has been signed and Edgar curses her. The third act does not interest Emma any more as Léon has appeared in the interval. She does not care for the scene between Lord Henry and his retainer (called here "servant") Gilbert who introduces a disguised stranger, Edgar of course. The duet between Henry Lord Ashton and Edgar reaffirms their mutual hatred. The mad scene follows. Lucy flees the marriage chamber; she has stabbed her husband and gone mad. She dreams of Edgar and dies. The great aria which was considered the climax of coloratura singing was lost on Emma absorbed in Léon.

One must asume that Flaubert had the French libretto in front of him or remembered its wordings and stage business accurately.[2] A modern reader who knows the Italian libretto from recordings may be puzzled by the discrepancies, and ascribe to Flaubert's imagination or confused memory what is actually an accurate description of the French version.—R.W.]

Part One

I

We were in class when the headmaster came in, followed by a new boy, not wearing the school uniform, and a school servant carrying a large desk. Those who had been asleep woke up, and every one rose as if just surprised at his work.

The headmaster made a sign to us to sit down. Then, turning to the teacher, he said to him in a low voice:

"Monsieur Roger, here is a pupil whom I recommend to your care; he'll be in the second. If his work and conduct are satisfactory, he will go into one of the upper classes, as becomes his age."

The new boy, standing in the corner behind the door so that he could hardly be seen, was a country lad of about fifteen, and taller than any of us. His hair was cut square on his forehead like a village choir boy; he looked reliable, but very ill at ease. Although he was

2. Flaubert had seen the opera first in Rouen in 1840 and again in Constantinople in November 1850.

not broad-shouldered, his short jacket of green cloth with black buttons must have been tight about the armholes, and showed at the opening of the cuffs red wrists accustomed to being bare. His legs, in blue stockings, looked out from beneath yellowish trousers, drawn tight by suspenders. He wore stout, ill-cleaned, hob-nailed boots.

We began reciting the lesson. He listened with all his ears, as attentive as if at a sermon, not daring even to cross his legs or lean on his elbow; and when at two o'clock the bell rang, the master was obliged to tell him to fall into line with the rest of us.

When we came back to work, we were in the habit of throwing our caps on the ground so as to have our hands more free; we used from the door to toss them under the desk, so that they hit against the wall and made a lot of dust: it was the fad of the moment.

But, whether he had not noticed the trick, or did not dare to attempt it, the new boy was still holding his cap on his knees even after prayers were over. It was one of those head-gears of composite order, in which we can find traces of the bear- and the coonskin, the shako, the bowler, and the cotton nightcap; one of those poor things, in fine, whose dumb ugliness has depths of expression, like an imbecile's face. Ovoid and stiffened with whalebone, it began with three circular strips; then came in succession lozenges of velvet and rabbit fur separated by a red band; after that a sort of bag that ended in a cardboard polygon covered with complicated braiding, from which hung, at the end of a long thin cord, small twisted gold threads in the manner of a tassel. The cap was new; its peak shone.

"Rise," said the master.

He stood up; his cap fell. The whole class began to laugh. He stooped to pick it up. A neighbour knocked it down again with his elbow; he picked it up once more.

"Get rid of your helmet," said the master, who liked to joke.

There was a burst of laughter from the boys, which so thoroughly put the poor lad out of countenance that he did not know whether to keep his cap in his hand, leave it on the ground, or put it on his head. He sat down again and placed it on his knee.

"Rise," repeated the master, "and tell me your name."

The new boy articulated in a stammering voice an unintelligible name.

"Again!"

The same sputtering of syllables was heard, drowned by the tittering of the class.

"Louder!" cried the master; "louder!"

The new boy then took a supreme resolution, opened an inordinately large mouth, and shouted at the top of his voice as if calling some one, the word "Charbovari."

A hubbub broke out, rose in *crescendo* with bursts of shrill voices (they yelled, barked, stamped, repeated "Charbovari! Charbovari!"), then died away into single notes, growing quieter only with great difficulty, and now and again suddenly recommencing along the line of a seat from where rose here and there, like a damp cracker going off, a stifled laugh.

However, amid a rain of penalties, order was gradually re-established in the class; and the master having succeeded in catching the name of "Charles Bovary," having had it dictated to him, spelt out, and re-read, at once ordered the poor devil to go and sit down on the punishment form at the foot of the master's desk. He got up, but before going hesitated.

"What are you looking for?" asked the master.

"My c-c-c-cap," said the new boy shyly, casting troubled looks round him.

"Five hundred verses for all the class!" shouted in a furious voice, stopped, like the *Quos ego*,[1] a fresh outburst. "Silence!" continued the master indignantly, wiping his brow with his handkerchief, which he had just taken from his cap. As to you, Bovary, you will conjugate '*ridiculus sum*' twenty times." Then, in a gentler tone, "Come, you'll find your cap again; it hasn't been stolen."

Quiet was restored. Heads bent over desks, and the new boy remained for two hours in an exemplary attitude, although from time to time some paper pellet flipped from the tip of a pen came bang in his face. But he wiped his face with one hand and continued motionless, his eyes lowered.

In the evening, at study hall, he pulled out his sleeveguards from his desk, arranged his small belongings, and carefully ruled his paper. We saw him working conscientiously, looking up every word in the dictionary, and taking the greatest pains. Thanks, no doubt, to the willingness he showed, he had not to go down to the class below. But though he knew his rules passably, he lacked all elegance in composition. It was the curé of his village who had taught him his first Latin; his parents, from motives of economy, having sent him to school as late as possible.

His father, Monsieur Charles Denis Bartolomé Bovary, retired assistant-surgeon-major, compromised about 1812 in certain conscription scandals, and forced at this time to leave the service, had taken advantage of his fine figure to get hold of a dowry of sixty thousand francs in the person of a hosier's daughter who had fallen in love with his good looks. He was a fine man, a great talker,

1. Neptune becalming the winds in the *Aeneid* (I.135)

making his spurs ring as he walked, wearing whiskers that ran into his moustache, his fingers always garnished with rings; he dressed in loud colours, had the dash of a military man with the easy go of a commercial traveller. Once married, he lived for three or four years on his wife's fortune, dining well, rising late, smoking long porcelain pipes, not coming in at night till after the theatre, and haunting cafés. The father-in-law died, leaving little; he was indignant at this, tried his hand at the textile business, lost some money in it, then retired to the country, where he thought he would make the land pay off. But, as he knew no more about farming than calico, as he rode his horses instead of sending them to plough, drank his cider in bottle instead of selling it in cask, ate the finest poultry in his farmyard, and greased his hunting-boots with the fat of his pigs, he was not long in finding out that he would do better to give up all speculation.

For two hundred francs[2] a year he managed to rent on the border of the provinces of Caux and Picardy, a kind of place half farm, half private house; and here, soured, eaten up with regrets, cursing his luck, jealous of every one, he shut himself up at the age of forty-five, sick of men, he said, and determined to live in peace.

His wife had adored him once on a time; she had loved him with a thousand servilities that had only estranged him the more. Lively once, expansive and affectionate, in growing older she had become (after the fashion of wine that, exposed to air, turns to vinegar) ill-tempered, grumbling, irritable. She had suffered so much without complaint at first, when she had seen him going after all the village harlots, and when a score of bad houses sent him back to her at night, weary, stinking drunk. Then her pride revolted. After that she was silent, burying her anger in a dumb stoicism that she maintained till her death. She was constantly going about looking after business matters. She called on the lawyers, the judges, remembered when notes fell due, got them renewed, and at home ironed, sewed, washed, looked after the workmen, paid the accounts, while he, troubling himself about nothing, eternally besotted in a sleepy sulkiness from which he only roused himself to say nasty things to her, sat smoking by the fire and spitting into the cinders.

When she had a child, it had to be sent out to nurse. When he came home, the lad was spoilt as if he were a prince. His mother stuffed him with jam; his father let him run about barefoot, and, playing the philosopher, even said he might as well go about quite

2. It is very difficult to transpose monetary values from 1840 into present-day figures, since relationships between the actual value of the franc, the cost of living, and the relative cost of specific items (such as rent, real estate, etc.) have undergone fundamental changes. One would not be too far off the mark by reading present-day dollars for Flaubert's francs; that would show Madame Bovary destroyed, at the end of the book, by an 8,000-dollar debt.

naked like the young of animals. As opposed to the maternal ideas, he had a certain virile idea of childhood on which he sought to mould his son, wishing him to be brought up hardily, like a Spartan, to give him a strong constitution. He sent him to bed without any fire, taught him to drink off large draughts of rum and to jeer at religious processions. But, peaceable by nature, the boy responded poorly to his attempts. His mother always kept him near her; she cut out cardboard pictures for him, told him tales, entertained him with monologues full of melancholy gaiety, chatting and fondling in endless baby-talk. In her life's isolation she transferred on the child's head all her scattered, broken little vanities. She dreamed of high station; she already saw him, tall, handsome, clever, settled as an engineer or in the law. She taught him to read, and even on an old piano she had taught him two or three sentimental ballads. But to all this Monsieur Bovary, caring little for arts and letters, said "It was not worth while. Would they ever have the means to send him to a public school, to buy him a practice, or start him in business? Besides, with brashness a man can always make his way in the world." Madame Bovary bit her lips, and the child knocked about the village.

He followed the farm laborers, drove away with clods of earth the ravens that were flying about. He ate blackberries along the hedges, minded the geese with a long switch, went hay-making during harvest, ran about in the woods, played hopscotch under the church porch on rainy days, and at great fêtes begged the beadle to let him toll the bells, that he might hang all his weight on the long rope and feel himself borne upward by it in its swing.

So he grew like an oak; he was strong of hand, ruddy of complexion.

When he was twelve years old his mother had her own way; he began his lessons. The curé took him in hand; but the lessons were so short and irregular that they could not be of much use. They were given at spare moments in the sacristy, standing up, hurriedly, between a baptism and a burial; or else the curé, if he had not to go out, sent for his pupil after the *Angelus*. They went up to his room and settled down; the flies and moths fluttered round the candle. It was close, the child fell asleep, and the good man, beginning to doze with his hands on his stomach, was soon snoring with his mouth wide open. On other occasions, when Monsieur le Curé, on his way back after administering the holy oil to some sick person in the neighborhood, caught sight of Charles playing about the fields, he called him, lectured him for a quarter of an hour, and took advantage of the occasion to make him conjugate his verb at the foot of a tree. The rain interrupted them or an acquaintance passed. All the same he was always pleased with him, and even said the "young man" had a very good memory.

Charles could not go on like this. Madame Bovary took strong steps. Ashamed, or rather tired out, Monsieur Bovary gave in without a struggle, and they waited one year longer, so that the child could take his first communion.

Six months more passed, and the year after Charles was finally sent to school at Rouen. His father took him there towards the end of October, at the time of the St. Romain fair.

It would now be impossible for any of us to remember any thing about him. He was a youth of even temperament, who played in playtime, worked in school-hours, was attentive in class, slept well in the dormitory, and ate well in the refectory. He had for guardian a hardware merchant in the Rue Ganterie, who took him out once a month on Sundays after his shop was shut, sent him for a walk on the quay to look at the boats, and then brought him back to college at seven o'clock before supper. Every Thursday evening he wrote a long letter to his mother with red ink and three wax seals; then he went over his history note-books, or read an old volume of "Anarchasis"[3] that was lying about the study. When he went for walks he talked to the servant, who, like himself, came from the country.

By dint of hard work he kept always about the middle of the class; once even he got an honor mark in natural history. But at the end of his third year his parents withdrew him from the school to make him study medicine, convinced that he could make it to the bachelor's degree by himself.

His mother chose a room for him on the fourth floor of a dyer's she knew, overlooking the Eau-de-Robec.[4] She made arrangements for his board, got him furniture, table and two chairs, sent home for an old cherry-tree bedstead, and bought besides a small cast-iron stove with the supply of wood that was to warm her poor child. Then at the end of a week she departed, after a thousand injunctions to be good now that he was going to be left to himself.

The course list that he read on the notice-board stunned him: lectures on anatomy, lectures on pathology, lectures on physiology, lectures on pharmacy, lectures on botany and clinical medicine, and therapeutics, without counting hygiene and materia medica—all names of whose etymologies he was ignorant, and that were to him as so many doors to sanctuaries filled with magnificent darkness.

He understood nothing of it all; it was all very well to listen—he did not follow. Still he worked; he had bound note-books, he attended all the courses, never missed a single lecture. He did his little

3. *Voyage du jeune Anarchasis en Grèce* (1788) was a popular account of ancient Greece, by Jean-Jacques Barthélemy (1716–1795).

4. Small river, now covered up, that flows through the poorest neighborhood of Rouen, used as a sewer by the factories that border it, thus suggesting Flaubert's description as "*une ignoble petite Venise.*"

daily task like a mill-horse, who goes round and round with his eyes bandaged, not knowing what work it is grinding out.

To spare him expense his mother sent him every week by the carrier a piece of veal baked in the oven, with which he lunched when he came back from the hospital, while he sat kicking his feet against the wall. After this he had to run off to lectures, to the operation-room, to the hospital, and return to his home at the other end of the town. In the evening, after the poor dinner of his landlord, he went back to his room and set to work again in his wet clothes, that smoked as he sat in front of the hot stove.

On the fine summer evenings, at the time when the close streets are empty, when the servants are playing shuttle-cock at the doors, he opened his window and leaned out. The river, that makes of this quarter of Rouen a wretched little Venice, flowed beneath him, between the bridges and the railings, yellow, violet, or blue. Working men, kneeling on the banks, washed their bare arms in the water. On poles projecting from the attics, skeins of cotton were drying in the air. Opposite, beyond the roofs, spread the pure sky with the red sun setting. How pleasant it must be at home! How fresh under the beech-tree! And he expanded his nostrils to breathe in the sweet odours of the country which did not reach him.

He grew thin, his figure became taller, his face took a saddened look that made it almost interesting.

Passively, through indifference, he abandoned all the resolutions he had made. Once he missed a lecture; the next day all the lectures; and, enjoying his idleness, little by little he gave up work altogether.

He got into the habit of going to the cafés, and had a passion for dominoes. To shut himself up every evening in the dirty public room, to push about on marble tables the small sheep-bones with black dots, seemed to him a fine proof of his freedom, which raised him in his own esteem. It was beginning to see life, the sweetness of stolen pleasures; and when he entered, he put his hand on the door-handle with a joy almost sensual. Then many things compressed within him expanded; he learned by heart student songs and sang them at gatherings, became enthusiastic about Béranger,[5] learnt how to make punch, and, finally how to make love.

Thanks to these preparatory labors, he failed completely in his examination for his degree of *officier de santé*.[6] He was expected

5. Pierre-Jean de Béranger (1780–1857) was an extremely popular writer of songs often exalting the glories of the empire of Napoleon I.

6. The degree of Officier de Santé, instituted during the Revolution, was a kind of second-class medical degree, well below the doctorate. The student was allowed to attend a medical school without having passed the equivalence of the *baccalauréat*. He could only practice in

home the same night to celebrate his success.

He started on foot, stopped at the beginning of the village, sent for his mother, and told her all. She excused him, threw the blame of his failure on the injustice of the examiners, encouraged him a little, and took upon herself to set matters straight. It was only five years later that Monsieur Bovary knew the truth; it was old then, and he accepted it. Moreover, he could not believe that a man born of him could be a fool.

So Charles set to work again and crammed for his examination, ceaselessly learning all the old questions by heart. He passed pretty well. What a happy day for his mother! They gave a grand dinner.

Where should he go to practise? To Tostes, where there was only one old doctor. For a long time Madame Bovary had been on the look-out for his death, and the old fellow had barely been packed off when Charles was installed, opposite his place, as his successor.

But it was not everything to have brought up a son, to have had him taught medicine, and discovered Tostes, where he could practise it; he must have a wife. She found him one—the widow of a bailiff at Dieppe, who was forty-five and had an income of twelve hundred francs.

Though she was ugly, as dry as a bone, her face with as many pimples as the spring has buds, Madame Dubuc had no lack of suitors. To attain her ends Madame Bovary had to oust them all, and she even succeeded in very cleverly baffling the intrigues of a pork-butcher backed up by the priests.

Charles had seen in marriage the advent of an easier life, thinking he would be more free to do as he liked with himself and his money. But his wife was master; he had to say this and not say that in company, to fast every Friday, dress as she liked, harass at her bidding those patients who did not pay. She opened his letters, watched his comings and goings, and listened at the partition-wall when women came to consult him in his surgery.

She had to have her chocolate every morning, attentions without end. She constantly complained of her nerves, her chest, her liver. The noise of footsteps made her ill; when people went away, solitude became odious to her; if they came back, it was doubtless to see her die. When Charles returned in the evening, she stretched forth two long thin arms from beneath the sheets, put them round his neck, and having made him sit down on the edge of the bed, began to talk to him of her troubles: he was neglecting her, he loved another. She had been warned she would be unhappy; and she ended by asking him for a dose of medicine and a little more love.

---

the department in which the diploma had been conferred (Bovary is thus tied down to the vicinity of Rouen) and was not allowed to perform major operations except in the presence of a full-fledged doctor. The diploma was suppressed in 1892.

II

One night towards eleven o'clock they were awakened by the noise of a horse pulling up outside their door. The maid opened the garret-window and parleyed for some time with a man in the street below. He came for the doctor, had a letter for him. Nastasie came downstairs shivering and undid the locks and bolts one after the other. The man left his horse, and, following the servant, suddenly came in behind her. He pulled out from his wool cap with grey top-knots a letter wrapped up in a rag and presented it gingerly to Charles, who rested on his elbow on the pillow to read it. Nastasie, standing near the bed, held the light. Madame in modesty had turned to the wall and showed only her back.

This letter, sealed with a small seal in blue wax, begged Monsieur Bovary to come immediately to the farm of the Bertaux to set a broken leg. Now from Tostes to the Bertaux was a good fifteen miles across country by way of Longueville and Saint-Victor. It was a dark night; Madame Bovary junior was afraid of accidents for her husband. So it was decided the stable-boy should go on first; Charles would start three hours later when the moon rose. A boy was to be sent to meet him, in order to show him the way to the farm and open the gates for him.

Towards four o'clock in the morning, Charles, well wrapped up in his cloak, set out for the Bertaux. Still sleepy from the warmth of his bed, he let himself be lulled by the quiet trot of his horse. When it stopped of its own accord in front of those holes surrounded with thorns that are dug on the margin of furrows, Charles awoke with a start, suddenly remembered the broken leg, and tried to call to mind all the fractures he knew. The rain had stopped, day was breaking, and on the branches of the leafless trees birds roosted motionless, their little feathers bristling in the cold morning wind. The flat country stretched as far as eye could see, and the tufts of trees around the farms seemed, at long intervals, like dark violet stains on the vast grey surface, fading on the horizon into the gloom of the sky. Charles from time to time opened his eyes but his mind grew weary, and sleep coming upon him, he soon fell into a doze wherein his recent sensations blending with memories, he became conscious of a double self, at once student and married man, lying in his bed as but now, and crossing the operation theatre as of old. The warm smell of poultices mingled in his brain with the fresh odour of dew; he heard the iron rings rattling along the curtain-rods of the bed and saw his wife sleeping . . . As he passed Vassonville he came upon a boy sitting on the grass at the edge of a ditch.

"Are you the doctor?" asked the child.

And on Charles's answer he took his wooden shoes in his hands and ran on in front of him.

The *officier de santé,* riding along, gathered from his guide's talk that Monsieur Rouault must be one of the well-to-do farmers. He had broken his leg the evening before on his way home from a Twelfth-night feast at a neighbor's. His wife had been dead for two years. There was only his daughter, who helped him to keep house, with him.

The ruts were becoming deeper; they were approaching the Bertaux. The little farmboy, slipping through a hole in the hedge, disappeared; then he came back to the end of a courtyard to open the gate. The horse slipped on the wet grass; Charles had to stoop to pass under the branches. The watchdogs in their kennels barked, dragging at their chains. As he entered the Bertaux the horse took fright and stumbled.

It was a substantial-looking farm. In the stables, over the top of the open doors, one could see great cart-horses quietly feeding from new racks. Right along the outbuildings extended a large dunghill, smoking at the top, while amidst fowls and turkeys five or six peacocks, the luxury of Cauchois farmyards, were foraging around. The sheepfold was long, the barn high, with walls smooth as a hand. Under the cart-shed were two large carts and four ploughs, with their whips, shafts and harnesses complete, whose fleeces of blue wool were getting soiled by the fine dust that fell from the graneries. The courtyard sloped upwards, planted with trees set out symmetrically, and the chattering noise of a flock of geese was heard near the pond.

A young woman in a blue merino dress with three flounces came to the threshold of the door to receive Monsieur Bovary; she led him to the kitchen, where a large fire was blazing. The servants' breakfast was boiling beside it in small pots of all sizes. Some damp clothes were drying inside the chimney-corner. The shovel, tongs, and the nozzle of the bellows, all of colossal size, shone like polished steel, while along the walls hung many pots and pans in which the clear flame of the hearth, mingling with the first rays of the sun coming in through the window, was mirrored fitfully.

Charles went up to the first floor to see the patient. He found him in his bed, sweating under his bed-clothes, having thrown his cotton nightcap right away from him. He was a fat little man of fifty, with white skin and blue eyes, the fore part of his head bald, and he wore ear-rings. By his side on a chair stood a large decanter of brandy, from which he poured himself out a little from time to time to keep up his spirits; but as soon as he caught sight of the doctor his elation subsided, and instead of swearing, as he had been doing for the last twelve hours, he began to groan feebly.

The fracture was a simple one, without any kind of complication. Charles could not have hoped for an easier case. Then calling to mind the devices of his masters at the bedside of patients, he comforted the sufferer with all sorts of kindly remarks, those caresses of the surgeon that are like the oil they put on scalpels. In order to make some splints a bundle of laths was brought up from the carthouse. Charles selected one, cut it into two pieces and planed it with a fragment of windowpane, while the servant tore up sheets to make bandages, and Mademoiselle Emma tried to sew some pads. As she was a long time before she found her workcase, her father grew impatient; she did not answer, but as she sewed she pricked her fingers, which she then put to her mouth to suck them.

Charles was surprised at the whiteness of her nails. They were shiny, delicate at the tips, more polished than the ivory of Dieppe, and almond-shaped. Yet her hand was not beautiful, perhaps not white enough, and a little hard at the knuckles; besides, it was too long, with no soft inflections in the outlines. Her real beauty was in her eyes. Although brown, they seemed black because of the lashes, and her look came at you frankly, with a candid boldness.

The bandaging over, the doctor was invited by Monsieur Rouault himself to have a bite before he left.

Charles went down into the room on the ground-floor. Knives and forks and silver goblets were laid for two on a little table at the foot of a huge bed that had a canopy of printed cotton with figures representing Turks. There was an odor of iris-root and damp sheets that escaped from a large oak chest opposite the window. On the floor in corners were sacks of flour stuck upright in rows. These were the overflow from the neighboring granary, to which three stone steps led. By way of decoration for the apartment, hanging to a nail in the middle of the wall, whose green paint scaled off from the effects of the saltpeter, was a crayon head of Minerva in a gold frame, underneath which was written in Gothic letters "To my dear Papa."

First they spoke of the patient, then of the weather, of the great cold, of the wolves that infested the fields at night. Mademoiselle Rouault did not at all like the country, especially now that she had to look after the farm almost alone. As the room was chilly, she shivered as she ate. This showed something of her full lips, that she had a habit of biting when silent.

Her neck stood out from a white turned-down collar. Her hair, whose two black folds seemed each of a single piece, so smooth were they, was parted in the middle by a delicate line that curved slightly with the curve of the head; and, just showing the tip of the ear, it was joined behind in a thick chignon, with a wavy movement at the temples that the country doctor saw now for the first time in his life. The upper part of her cheek was rose-coloured. Like a man, she wore a tortoise-shell eyeglass thrust between two buttons of her blouse.

When Charles, after bidding farewell to old Rouault, returned to the room before leaving, he found her standing, her forehead against the window, looking into the garden, where the beanpoles had been knocked down by the wind. She turned around. "Are you looking for something?" she asked.

"My riding crop, if you please," he answered.

He began rummaging on the bed, behind the doors, under the chairs. It had fallen to the ground, between the sacks and the wall. Mademoiselle Emma saw it, and bent over the flour sacks. Charles out of politeness made a dash also, and as he stretched out his arm, at the same moment felt his breast brush against the back of the young girl bending beneath him. She drew herself up, scarlet, and looked at him over her shoulder as she handed him his riding crop.

Instead of returning to the Bertaux in three days as he had promised, he went back the very next day, then regularly twice a week, without counting the visits he paid now and then as if by accident.

Everything, moreover, went well; the patient progressed favorably; and when, at the end of forty-six days, old Rouault was seen trying to walk alone in his "den," Monsieur Bovary began to be looked upon as a man of great capacity. Old Rouault said that he could not have been cured better by the first doctor of Yvetot, or even of Rouen.

As to Charles, he did not stay to ask himself why it was a pleasure to him to go to the Bertaux. Had he done so, he would, no doubt have attributed his zeal to the importance of the case, or perhaps to the money he hoped to make by it. Was it for this, however, that his visits to the farm formed a delightful exception to the barren occupations of his life? On these days he rose early, set off at a gallop, urging on his horse, then got down to wipe his boots in the grass and put on black gloves before entering. He liked seeing himself enter the courtyard, and noticing the gate turn against his shoulder, the cock crow on the wall, the farmboys run to meet him. He liked the granary and the stables; he liked old Rouault, who pressed his hand and called him his saviour; he liked the small wooden shoes of Mademoiselle Emma on the scoured flags of the kitchen—her high heels made her a little taller; and when she walked in front of him, the wooden soles springing up quickly struck with a sharp sound against the leather of her boots.

She always reconducted him to the first step of the porch. When his horse had not yet been brought round she stayed there. They had said "Good-bye"; there was no more talking. The open air wrapped her round, playing with the soft down on the back of her neck, or blew to and fro on her hips her apron-strings, that fluttered like streamers. Once, during a thaw, the bark of the trees in the yard was oozing, the snow melted on the roofs of the buildings; she stood on the threshold, went to fetch her sunshade and opened it. The parasol, made of an iridescent silk that let the sunlight sift through, colored the white skin of her face with shifting reflections. Beneath it, she smiled at the gentle warmth; drops of water fell one by one on the taut silk.

During the first period of Charles's visits to the Bertaux, the younger Madame Bovary never failed to inquire after the invalid, and she had even chosen in the book that she kept on a system of double entry a clean blank page for Monsieur Rouault. But when she heard he had a daughter, she began to make inquiries, and she learnt that Mademoiselle Rouault, brought up at the Ursuline Convent, had received what is called "a good education"; and so knew dancing, geography, drawing, how to embroider and play the piano. That was the last straw.

"So that's why he looks so beaming when he goes to see her," she thought. "That's why he puts on his new waistcoat regardless of the rain. Ah! that woman! that woman!"

And she detested her instinctively. At first she solaced herself by allusions that Charles did not understand, then by casual observations that he let pass for fear of a storm, finally by open apostrophes to which he knew no reply.—Why did he go back to the Bertaux now that Monsieur Rouault was cured and that the bill was still unpaid? Ah! it was because a certain person was there, some one who knew how to talk, to embroider, to be witty. So that was what he liked; he wanted city girls! And she went on:

"Imagine old Rouault's daughter being taken for a city girl! The grandfather was a shepherd and a cousin of theirs barely escaped being sentenced for nearly killing someone in a brawl. Hardly a reason to put on airs, or showing herself in church dressed in silk, like a countess. If it hadn't been for the colza crop last year, the old fellow would have been hard put paying his arrears."

For very weariness Charles left off going to the Bertaux. Héloïse made him swear, his hand on the prayer-book, that he would go there no more, after much sobbing and many kisses, in a great outburst of love. He obeyed then, but the strength of his desire protested against the servility of his conduct; and he thought, with a kind of naïve hypocrisy, that this interdict to see her gave him a sort of right to love her. And then the widow was thin; she had long teeth; wore in all weathers a little black shawl, the edge of which hung down between her shoulder-blades; her bony figure was sheathed in her clothes as if they were a scabbard; they were too short, and displayed her ankles with the laces of her large boots crossed over grey stockings.

Charles's mother came to see them from time to time, but after a few days the daughter-in-law seemed to put her own edge on her, and then, like two knives, they scarified him with their reflections and observations. It was wrong of him to eat so much. Why did he always offer a free drink to everyone who came along? How stubborn of him not to put on flannel underwear!

In the spring it came about that a notary at Ingouville, who managed the widow Dubuc's property, one fine day vanished, taking with him all the money in his office. Héloïse, it is true, still owned, besides a share in a boat valued at six thousand francs, her house in the Rue St. François; and yet, with all this fortune that had been so trumpeted abroad, nothing, excepting perhaps a little furniture and a few clothes, had appeared in the household. The matter had to be gone into. The house at Dieppe was found to be eaten up with mortgages to its foundations; what she had placed with the notary God only knew, and her share in the boat did not exceed three thousand francs. She had lied, the good lady! In his exasperation, Monsieur Bovary the elder, smashing a chair on the stone floor, accused his wife of having caused the misfortune of their son by harnessing him to such a harridan, whose harness wasn't worth her hide. They came to Tostes. Explanations followed. There were scenes. Héloïse in tears, throwing her arms about her husband, conjured him to defend her from his parents. Charles tried to speak up for her. They grew angry and left the house.

But "the blow had struck home." A week after, as she was hanging up some washing in her yard, she was seized with a spitting of blood, and the next day, while Charles had his back turned and was closing the window curtains, she said, "O God!" gave a sigh and fainted. She was dead! What a surprise!

When all was over at the cemetery Charles went home. He found no one downstairs; he went up to the first floor to their room, saw her dress still hanging at the foot of the alcove; then leaning against the writing-table, he stayed until the evening, buried in a sorrowful reverie. She had loved him after all!

III

One morning old Rouault brought Charles the money for setting his leg—seventy-five francs in forty-sou pieces, and a turkey. He had heard of his loss, and consoled him as well as he could.

"I know what it is," said he, clapping him on the shoulder; "I've been through it. When I lost my poor wife, I went into the field to be alone. I fell at the foot of a tree; I cried; I called on God; I talked nonsense to Him. I wanted to be like the moles that I saw on the branches, their insides swarming with maggots, in short, dead, and an end of it. And when I thought that there were others at that very moment, with their wives in their arms, I struck great blows on the earth with my stick. I almost went out of my mind, to the point of not eating; the very idea of going to a café disgusted me—you wouldn't believe it. Well, very slowly, one day following another, a spring on a winter, and an autumn after a summer, this wore away, piece by piece, crumb by crumb; it passed away, it is gone, I should say it has sunk; for something always remains inside, as we would say—a weight here, at one's heart. But since it is the lot of all of us, one must not give way altogether, and, because others have died, want to die too. You must pull yourself together, Monsieur Bovary. It will pass away. Come and see us; my daughter thinks of you time and again, you know, and she says you are forgetting her. Spring will soon be here. We'll have you shoot a rabbit in the field to help you get over your sorrows."

Charles followed his advice. He went back to the Bertaux. He found all as he had left it, that is to say, as it was five months ago. The pear trees were already in blossom, and Farmer Rouault, on his legs again, came and went, making the farm more lively.

Thinking it his duty to heap the greatest attention upon the doctor because of his sad situation, he begged him not to take his hat off, spoke to him in whispers as if he had been ill, and even pretended to be angry because nothing lighter had been prepared for him than for the others, such as a little custard or stewed pears. He told stories. Charles found himself laughing, but the remembrance of his wife suddenly coming back to him depressed him. Coffee was brought in; he thought no more about her.

He thought less of her as he grew accustomed to living alone. The new delight of independence soon made his loneliness bearable. He could now change his meal-times, go in or out without explanation, and when he was very tired stretch himself at full length on his bed. So he nursed and coddled himself and accepted the consolations that were offered him. On the other hand, the death of his wife had not served him ill in his business, since for a month people had been saying, "The poor young man! what a loss!" His name had been talked about, his practice had increased; and, moreover, he could go to the Bertaux just as he liked. He had an aimless hope, and a vague happiness; he thought himself better looking as he brushed his whiskers before the looking-glass.

One day he got there about three o'clock. Everybody was in the fields. He went into the kitchen, but did not at once catch sight of Emma; the outside shutters were closed. Through the chinks of the wood the sun sent across the flooring long fine rays that were broken at the corners of the furniture and trembled along the ceiling. Some flies on the table were crawling up the glasses that had been used, and buzzing as they drowned themselves in the dregs of the cider. The daylight that came in by the chimney made velvet of the soot at the back of the fireplace, and touched with blue the cold cinders. Between the window and the hearth Emma was sewing; she wore no scarf; he could see small drops of perspiration on her bare shoulders.

After the fashion of country folks she asked him to have something to drink. He said no; she insisted, and at last laughingly offered to have a glass of liqueur with him. So she went to fetch a bottle of curaçoa from the cupboard, reached down two small glasses, filled one to the brim, poured scarcely anything into the other, and, after having clinked glasses, carried hers to her mouth. As it was almost empty she bent back to drink, her head thrown back, her lips pouting, her neck straining. She laughed at getting none, while with the tip of her tongue passing between her small teeth she licked drop by drop the bottom of her glass.

She sat down again and took up her work, a white cotton stocking she was darning. She worked with her head bent down; she did not speak, nor did Charles. The air coming in under the door blew a little dust over the stone floor; he watched it drift along, and heard nothing but the throbbing in his head and the faint clucking of a hen that had laid an egg in the yard. Emma from time to time cooled her cheeks with the palms of her hands, and cooled these again on the knobs of the huge fire-dogs.

She complained of suffering since the beginning of the spring from giddiness; she asked if sea-baths would do her any good; she began talking of her convent, Charles of his school; words came to them. They went up into her bed-room. She showed him her old music-books, the little prizes she had won, and the oak-leaf crowns, left at the bottom of a cupboard. She spoke to him, too, of her mother, of the country, and even showed him the bed in the garden where, on the first Friday of every month, she gathered flowers to put on her mother's tomb. But their gardener understood nothing about it; servants were so careless. She would have dearly liked, if only for the winter, to live in town, although the length of the fine days made the country perhaps even more wearisome in the summer. And, according to what she was saying, her voice was clear, sharp, or, suddenly all languor, lingering out in modulations that ended almost in murmurs as she spoke to herself, now joyous, opening big naïve eyes, then with her eyelids half closed, her look full of boredom, her thoughts wandering.

Going home at night, Charles went over her words one by one, trying to recall them, to fill out their sense, that he might piece out the life she had lived before he knew her. But he never saw her in his thoughts other than he had seen her the first time, or as he had just left her. Then he asked himself what would become of her—if she would be married, and to whom? Alas! old Rouault was rich, and she!—so beautiful! But Emma's face always rose before his eyes, and a monotone, like the humming of a top, sounded in his ears, "If you should marry after all! if you should marry!" At night he could not sleep; his throat was parched; he was thirsty. He got up to drink from the water-bottle and opened the window. The night was covered with stars, a warm wind blowing in the distance; the dogs were barking. He turned his head towards the Bertaux.

Thinking that, after all, he had nothing to lose, Charles promised himself to ask her in marriage at the earliest opportunity, but each time the fear of not finding the right words sealed his lips.

Old Rouault would not have been sorry to be rid of his daughter, who was of no use to him in the house. In his heart he excused her, thinking her too clever for farming, a calling under the ban of Heaven, since one never saw a millionaire in it. Far from having made a fortune, the old man was losing every year; for if he was good at bargaining and enjoyed the dodges of the trade, he was the poorest of growers or farm managers. He did not willingly take his hands out of his pockets, and did not spare expense for his own comforts, liking to eat and to sleep well, and never to suffer from the cold. He liked old cider, underdone legs of mutton, brandied coffee well beaten up. He took his meals in the kitchen, alone, opposite the fire on a little table brought to him already laid as on the stage.

When, therefore, he perceived that Charles's cheeks grew flushed if near his daughter, which meant that he would propose one of these days, he mulled over the entire matter beforehand. He certainly thought him somewhat weak, not quite the son-in-law he would have liked, but he was said to be well-behaved, prudent with his money as well as learned, and no doubt would not make too many difficulties about the dowry. Now, as old Rouault would soon be forced to sell twenty-two acres of his land as he owed a good deal to the mason, to the harnessmaker, and as the shaft of the cider-press wanted renewing, "If he asks for her," he said to himself, "I'll give her to him."

In the early fall Charles went to spend three days at the Bertaux. The last had passed like the others in procrastinating from hour to hour. Old Rouault was seeing him off; they were walking along a dirt road full of ruts; they were about to part. This was the time. Charles gave himself as far as to the corner of the hedge, and at last, when past it . . .

"Monsieur Rouault," he murmured, "I should like to say something to you."

They stopped. Charles was silent.

"Well, tell me your story. Don't I know all about it?" said old

Rouault, laughing softly.

"Monsieur Rouault—Monsieur Rouault," stammered Charles.

"I ask nothing better," the farmer went on. "Although, no doubt, the little one agrees with me, still we must ask her opinion. So you get off—I'll go back home. If it is 'yes,' you needn't return because of all the people around, and besides it would upset her too much. But so that you may not be biting your fingernails with impatience, I'll open wide the outer shutter of the window against the wall; you can see it from the back by leaning over the hedge."

And he went off.

Charles fastened his horse to a tree; he ran into the road and waited. Half-an-hour passed, then he counted nineteen minutes by his watch. Suddenly a noise was heard against the wall; the shutter had been thrown back; the hook was still quivering.

The next day by nine o'clock he was at the farm. Emma blushed as he entered, and she gave a little forced laugh to hide her embarrassment. Old Rouault embraced his future son-in-law. The discussion of money matters was put off; moreover, there was plenty of time before them, as the marriage could not decently take place till Charles was out of mourning, that is to say, about the spring of the next year.

The winter passed waiting for this. Mademoiselle Rouault was busy with her trousseau. Part of it was ordered at Rouen, and she made herself slips and nightcaps after fashionplates that she borrowed. When Charles visited the farmer, the preparations for the wedding were talked over; they wondered in what room they should have dinner; they dreamed of the number of dishes that would be wanted, and what should be the entrées.

Emma would, on the contrary, have preferred to have a midnight wedding with torches, but old Rouault could not understand such an idea. So there was a wedding at which forty-three persons were present, at which they remained sixteen hours at table, began again the next day, and even carried a little into the following days.

IV

The guests arrived early in carriages, in one-horse chaises, two-wheeled cars, old open gigs, vans with leather curtains, and the young people from the nearer villages in carts, in which they stood up in rows, holding on to the sides so as not to fall, going at a trot and well shaken up. Some came from a distance of thirty miles, from Goderville, from Normanville, and from Cany. All the relatives of both families had been invited, old quarrels had been patched up and near-forgotten acquaintances written to for the occasion.

From time to time one heard the crack of a whip behind the hedge; then the gates opened, a chaise entered. Galloping up to the foot of the steps, it stopped short and emptied its load. They got down from all sides, rubbing knees and stretching arms. The ladies, wearing bonnets, had on dresses in the town fashion, gold watch chains, pelerines with the ends tucked into belts, or little coloured scarfs fastened down behind with a pin, and that left the back of the neck bare. The boys, dressed like their papas, seemed uncomfortable in their new clothes (many that day were wearing their first pair of boots), and by their sides, speaking never a word, wearing the white dress of their first communion lengthened for the occasion, were some big girls of fourteen or sixteen, cousins or elder sisters no doubt, scarlet, bewildered, their hair greasy with rose-pomade, and very much afraid of dirtying their gloves. As there were not enough stable-boys to unharness all the carriages, the gentlemen turned up their sleeves and set about it themselves. According to their different social positions they wore tail-coats, overcoats, shooting-jackets, cutaway-coats: fine tail-coats, redolent of family respectability, that only came out of the wardrobe on state occasions; overcoats with long tails flapping in the wind and round capes and pockets like sacks; shooting-jackets of coarse cloth, generally worn with a cap with a brass-bound peak; very short cutaway-coats with two small buttons in the back, close together like a pair of eyes, and the tails of which seemed cut out of one piece by a carpenter's hatchet. Some, too (but these, you may be sure, would sit at the bottom of the table), wore their best smocks—that is to say, with collars turned down to the shoulders, the back gathered into small plaits and the waist fastened very low down with a stitched belt.

And the shirts stood out from the chests like armour breastplates! Everyone had just had his hair cut; ears stood out from the heads; they had been close-shaven; a few, even, who had had to get up before daybreak, and not been able to see to shave, had diagonal gashes under their noses or cuts the size of a three-franc piece along the jaws, which the fresh air had enflamed during the trip, so that the great white beaming faces were mottled here and there with red spots.

The mairie was a mile and a half from the farm, and they went there on foot, returning in the same way after the ceremony in the church. The procession, first united like one long coloured scarf that undulated across the fields, along the narrow path winding amid the green wheat, soon lengthened out, and broke up into different groups that loitered to talk. The fiddler walked in front with his violin, gay with ribbons at its pegs. Then came the married pair, the relatives, the friends, all following pell-mell; the children stayed behind amusing themselves plucking the bell-flowers from oat-ears, or playing amongst themselves unseen. Emma's dress, too long, trailed a little on the ground; from time to time she stopped to pull it up, and then delicately, with her gloved hands, she picked off the coarse grass and the thistles, while Charles, empty handed, waited till she had finished. Old Rouault, with a new silk hat and the cuffs of his black coat covering his hands up to the nails, gave his arm to Madame Bovary senior. As to Monsieur Bovary senior, who, heartily despising all these people, had come simply in a frock-coat of military cut with one row of buttons—he was exchanging barroom banter with a blond young farmgirl. She bowed, blushed, and did not know what to say. The other wedding guests talked business or played tricks behind each other's backs, egging each other on in advance for the fun that was to come. Those who listened could always catch the squeaking of the fiddler, who went on playing across the fields. When he saw that the rest were far behind he stopped to take breath, slowly rosined his bow, so that the strings should squeak all the louder, then set off again, by turns lowering and raising the neck of his violin, the better to mark time for himself. The noise of the instrument drove away the little birds from afar.

The table was laid under the cart-shed. On it were four roasts of beef, six chicken fricassées, stewed veal, three legs of mutton, and in the middle a fine roast sucking-pig, flanked by four pork sausages with sorrel. At the corners were decanters of brandy. Sweet bottled-cider frothed round the corks, and all the glasses had been filled to the brim with wine beforehand. Large dishes of yellow cream, that trembled with the least shake of the table, had designed on their smooth surface the initials of the newly wedded pair in nonpareil arabesques. A confectioner of Yvetot had been entrusted with the pies and candies. As he had only just started out in the neighborhood, he had taken a lot of trouble, and at dessert he himself brought in a wedding cake that provoked loud cries of wonderment. At its base there was a square of blue cardboard, representing a temple with porticoes, colonnades, and stucco statuettes all round, and in the niches constellations of gilt paper stars; then on the second level was a dungeon of Savoy cake, surrounded by many fortifications in candied angelica, almonds, raisins, and quarters of oranges; and finally, on the upper platform a green field with rocks set in lakes of jam, nutshell boats, and a small Cupid balancing himself in a chocolate swing whose two uprights ended in real roses for balls at the top.

Until night they ate. When any of them were too tired of sitting, they went out for a stroll in the yard, or for a game of darts in the granary, and then returned to table. Some towards the end went to sleep and snored. But with the coffee every one woke up. Then they began songs, showed off tricks, raised heavy weights, competed to see who could pass his head under his arm while keeping a thumb on the table, tried lifting carts on their shoulders, made bawdy jokes, kissed the women. At night when they left, the horses, stuffed up to the nostrils with oats, could hardly be got into the shafts; they kicked, reared, the harness broke, their masters laughed or swore; and all night in the light of the moon along country roads there were runaway carts at full gallop plunging into the ditches, jumping over yard after yard of stones, clambering up the hills, with women leaning out from the tilt to catch hold of the reins.

Those who stayed at the Bertaux spent the night drinking in the kitchen. The children had fallen asleep under the seats.

The bride had begged her father to be spared the usual marriage pleasantries. However, a fishmonger, one of their cousins (who had brought a pair of soles for his wedding present), began to squirt water from his mouth through the keyhole, when old Rouault came up just in time to stop him, and explain to him that the distinguished position of his son-in-law would not allow of such liberties. The cousin was not easily convinced. In his heart he accused old Rouault of being proud, and he joined four or five other guests in a corner, who, through mere chance, had been served the poorer cuts of meat several times over and also considered themselves ill-treated. They were whispering about their host, hoping with covered hints that he would ruin himself.

Madame Bovary, senior, had not opened her mouth all day. She had been consulted neither as to the dress of her daughter-in-law nor as to the arrangement of the feast; she went to bed early. Her husband, instead of following her, sent to Saint-Victor for some cigars, and smoked till daybreak, drinking kirsch-punch, a mixture unknown to the company that added even more to the consideration in which he was held.

Charles, who was anything but quick-witted, did not shine at the wedding. He answered feebly to the puns, *doubles entendres*, compliments, and the customary pleasantries that were dutifully aimed at him as soon as the soup appeared.

The next day, on the other hand, he seemed another man. It was he who might rather have been taken for the virgin of the evening before, whilst the bride gave no sign that revealed anything. The shrewdest did not know what to make of it, and they looked at her when she passed near them with an unbounded concentration of mind. But Charles concealed nothing. He called her "my wife," addressed her by the familiar "tu," asked for her of everyone, looked for her everywhere, and often he dragged her into the yards, where he could be seen from far between the trees, putting his arm round her waist, and walking half-bending over her, ruffling the collar of her blouse with his head.

Two days after the wedding the married pair left. Charles, on account of his patients, could not be away longer. Old Rouault had them driven back in his cart, and himself accompanied them as far as Vassonville. Here he embraced his daughter for the last time, got down, and went his way. When he had gone about a hundred paces he stopped, and as he saw the cart disappearing, its wheels turning in the dust, he gave a deep sigh. Then he remembered his wedding, the old times, the first pregnancy of his wife; he, too, had been very happy the day when he had taken her from her father to his home, and had carried her off riding pillion, trotting through the snow, for it was near Christmas-time, and the country was all white. She held him by one arm, her basket hanging from the other; the wind blew the long lace of her Cauchois headdress so that it sometimes flapped across his mouth, and when he turned his head he saw near him, on his shoulder, her little rosy face, smiling silently under the gold bands of her cap. To warm her hands she put them from time to time in his breast. How long ago it all was! Their son would have been thirty by now. Then he looked back and saw nothing on the road. He felt dreary as an empty house; and tender memories mingling with sad thoughts in his brain, addled by the fumes of the feast, he felt inclined for a moment to take a turn towards the church. As he was afraid, however, that this sight would make him even sadder, he went right away home.

Monsieur and Madame Charles arrived at Tostes about six o'clock. The neighbors came to the windows to see their doctor's new wife.

The old servant presented herself, curtsied to her, apologised for not having dinner ready, and suggested that madame, in the meantime, should look over her house.

V

The brick front was just in a line with the street, or rather the road. Behind the door hung a cloak with a small collar, a bridle, and a black leather cap, and on the floor, in a corner, were a pair of leggings, still covered with dry mud. On the right was the one room that was both dining and sitting room. A canary-yellow paper, relieved at the top by a garland of pale flowers, was puckered everywhere over the badly-stretched canvas; white calico curtains with a red border hung crossways the length of the window; and on the narrow mantelpiece a clock with a head of Hippocrates shone resplendent between two plate candlesticks under oval shades. On the other side of the passage was Charles's consulting-room, a little room about six paces wide, with a table, three chairs, and an office-chair. Volumes of the "Dictionary of Medical Science," uncut, but the binding rather the worse for the successive sales through which they had gone, occupied almost alone the six shelves of a pinewood bookcase. The smell of sauces penetrated through the walls when he saw patients, just as in the kitchen one could hear the people coughing in the consulting-room and recounting their whole histories. Then, opening on the yard, where the stable was, came a large dilapidated room with a stove, now used as a wood-house, cellar, and pantry, full of old rubbish, of empty casks, discarded garden tools, and a mass of dusty things whose use it was impossible to guess.

The garden, longer than wide, ran between two mud walls covered with espaliered apricot trees, to a thorn hedge that separated it from the field. In the middle was a slate sundial on a brick pedestal; four flower-beds with eglantines surrounded symmetrically the more useful vegetable garden. Right at the bottom, under the spruce bushes, a plaster priest was reading his breviary.

Emma went upstairs. The first room was not furnished, but in the second, the conjugal bedroom, was a mahogany bedstead in an alcove with red drapery. A shell-box adorned the chest of drawers, and on the secretary near the window a bouquet of orange blossoms tied with white satin ribbons stood in a bottle. It was a bride's bouquet: the other one's. She looked at it. Charles noticed; he took the bouquet, carried it to the attic, while Emma seated in an armchair (they were putting her things down around her) thought of her bridal flowers packed up in a bandbox, and wondered, dreaming, what would be done with them if she were to die.

During the first days she kept busy thinking about changes in the house. She took the shades off the candlesticks, had new wall-paper put up, the staircase repainted, and seats made in the garden round the sundial; she even inquired how she could get a basin with a jet fountain and fishes. Finally her husband, knowing that she liked to drive out, picked up a second-hand dogcart, which, with new lamps and a splashboard in striped leather, looked almost like a tilbury.

He was happy then, and without a care in the world. A meal together, a walk in the evening on the highroad, a gesture of her hands over her hair, the sight of her straw hat hanging from the window-fastener, and many other things of which he had never suspected how pleasant they could be, now made up the endless round of his happiness. In bed, in the morning, by her side, on the pillow, he watched the sunlight sinking into the down on her fair cheek, half hidden by the ribbons of her nightcap. Seen thus closely, her eyes looked to him enlarged, especially when, on waking up, she opened and shut her eyelids rapidly many times. Black in the shade, dark blue in broad daylight, they had, as it were, depths of successive colors that, more opaque in the center, grew more transparent towards the surface of the eye. His own eyes lost themselves in these depths and he could see himself mirrored in miniature, down to his shoulders, with his scarf round his head and the top of his shirt open. He rose. She came to the window to see him off, and stayed leaning on the sill between two pots of geranium, clad in her dressing-gown hanging loosely about her. Charles, in the street, buckled his spurs, his foot on the mounting stone, while she talked to him from above, picking with her mouth some scrap of flower or leaf that she blew out at him and which, eddying, floating, described semicircles in the air like a bird, caught before it reached the ground in the ill-groomed mane of the old white mare standing motionless at the door. Charles from horseback threw her a kiss; she answered with a nod; she shut the window, and he set off. And then, along the endless dusty ribbon of the highroad, along the deep lanes that the trees bent over as in arbours, along paths where the wheat reached to the knees, with the sun on his back and the morning air in his nostrils, his heart full of the joys of the past night, his mind at rest, his flesh at ease, he went on, re-chewing his happiness, like those who after dinner taste again the truffles which they are digesting.

Until now what good had he had of his life? His time at school, when he remained shut up within the high walls, alone, in the midst of companions richer than he or cleverer at their work, who laughed at his accent, who jeered at his clothes, and whose mothers came to the school with cakes in their muffs? Later on, when he studied medicine, and never had his purse full enough to take out dancing some little work-girl who would have become his mistress? Afterwards, he had lived fourteen months with the widow, whose feet in bed were cold as icicles. But now he had for life this beautiful woman whom he adored. For him the universe did not extend beyond the silky circumference of her petticoat. He reproached himself for not loving her enough; he wanted to see her again, turned back quickly, ran up the stairs with a beating heart. Emma, in her room, was dressing; he came up on tiptoe, kissed her back; she cried out in surprise.

He could not keep from constantly touching her comb, her rings, her scarf; sometimes he gave her great sounding kisses with all his mouth on her cheeks, or else little kisses in a row all along her bare arm from the tip of her fingers up to her shoulder, and she put him away half-smiling, half-annoyed, as one does with a clinging child.

Before marriage she thought herself in love; but since the happiness that should have followed failed to come, she must, she thought, have been mistaken. And Emma tried to find out what one meant exactly in life by the words *bliss, passion, ecstasy*, that had seemed to her so beautiful in books.

VI

She had read "Paul and Virginia,"[7] and she had dreamed of the little bamboo-house, the negro Domingo, the dog Fidèle, but above all of the sweet friendship of some dear little brother, who seeks red fruit for you on trees taller than steeples, or who runs barefoot over the sand, bringing you a bird's nest.

When she was thirteen, her father himself took her to town to

7. *Paul et Virginie* (1784) is a story of the sentimental and tragic love of two young people on the tropical island of Ile de France (today, Mauritius). It was the most popular work of Bernardin de Saint-Pierre (1737–1814).

place her in the convent. They stopped at an inn in the St. Gervais quarter, where, at their supper, they used painted plates that set forth the story of Mademoiselle de la Vallière.[8] The explanatory legends, chipped here and there by the scratching of knives, all glorified religion, the tendernesses of the heart, and the pomps of court.

Far from being bored at first at the convent, she took pleasure in the society of the good sisters, who, to amuse her, took her to the chapel, which one entered from the refectory by a long corridor. She played very little during recreation hours, knew her catechism well, and it was she who always answered the Vicar's difficult questions. Living thus, without ever leaving the warm atmosphere of the class-rooms, and amid these pale-faced women wearing rosaries with brass crosses, she was softly lulled by the mystic languor exhaled in the perfumes of the altar, the freshness of the holy water, and the lights of the tapers. Instead of following mass, she looked at the pious vignettes with their azure borders in her book, and she loved the sick lamb, the sacred heart pierced with sharp arrows, or the poor Jesus sinking beneath the cross he carried. She tried, by way of mortification, to eat nothing a whole day. She puzzled her head to find some vow to fulfil.

When she went to confession, she invented little sins in order that she might stay there longer, kneeling in the shadow, her hands joined, her face against the grating beneath the whispering of the priest. The comparisons of betrothed, husband, celestial lover, and eternal marriage, that recur in sermons, stirred within her soul depths of unexpected sweetness.

In the evening, before prayers, there was some religious reading in the study. On week-nights it was some abstract of sacred history or the Lectures of the Abbé Frayssinous,[9] and on Sundays passages from the "Génie du Christianisme,"[10] as a recreation. How she listened at first to the sonorous lamentations of romantic melancholy re-echoing through the world and eternity! If her childhood had been spent in the shops of a busy city section, she might perhaps have opened her heart to those lyrical invasions of Nature, which usually come to us only through translation in books. But she knew the country too well; she knew the lowing of cattle, the milking, the ploughs. Accustomed to the quieter aspects of life, she turned instead to its tumultuous parts. She loved the sea only for the sake of its storms, and the green only when it was scattered among ruins. She had to gain some personal profit from things and she rejected as

8. One of Louis XIV's mistresses, whose mythologized character is familiar to all readers of Alexandre Dumas's *Le Vicomte de Bragelonne* (a sequel to *The Three Musketeers*).

9. Denis de Frayssinous (1765–1841) was a popular preacher who wrote a *Défense du Christianisme* (1825). Under Louis XVIII he became a bishop and minister of ecclesiastical affairs.

10. *Le Génie du Christianisme* (1802) by François-René de Chateaubriand (1768–1848) was an enormously influential book celebrating the truths and beauties of Roman Catholicism, just before Napoleon's concordat with Rome.

useless whatever did not contribute to the immediate satisfaction of her heart's desires—being of a temperament more sentimental than artistic, looking for emotions, not landscapes.

At the convent there was an old maid who came for a week each month to mend the linen. Patronised by the clergy, because she belonged to an ancient family of noblemen ruined by the Revolution, she dined in the refectory at the table of the good sisters, and after the meal chatted with them for a while before going back to her work. The girls often slipped out from the study to go and see her. She knew by heart the love-songs of the last century, and sang them in a low voice as she stitched away. She told stories, gave them news, ran their errands in the town, and on the sly lent the big girls some of the novels, that she always carried in the pockets of her apron, and of which the lady herself swallowed long chapters in the intervals of her work. They were all about love, lovers, sweethearts, persecuted ladies fainting in lonely pavilions, postilions killed at every relay, horses ridden to death on every page, sombre forests, heart-aches, vows, sobs, tears and kisses, little boatrides by moonlight, nightingales in shady groves, gentlemen brave as lions, gentle as lambs, virtuous as no one ever was, always well dressed, and weeping like fountains. For six months, then, a fifteen year old Emma dirtied her hands with the greasy dust of old lending libraries. With Walter Scott, later on, she fell in love with historical events, dreamed of guardrooms, old oak chests and minstrels. She would have liked to live in some old manor-house, like those long-waisted chatelaines who, in the shade of pointed arches, spent their days leaning on the stone, chin in hand, watching a white-plumed knight galloping on his black horse from the distant fields. At this time she had a cult for Mary Stuart and enthusiastic veneration for illustrious or unhappy women. Joan of Arc, Héloïse,[11] Agnès Sorel,[12] the beautiful Ferronière, and Clémence Isaure stood out to her like comets in the dark immensity of history, where also were seen, lost in shadow, and all unconnected, St. Louis[13] with his oak, the dying Bayard,[14] some cruelties of Louis XI,[15] a little of St. Bartholomew's,[16] the plume of the Béarnais, and always the remembrance of

11. Héloise was famous for her love affair with the philosopher Abelard (1101–1164).

12. Agnès Sorel (1422–1450) was a mistress of Charles VII, rumored to have been poisoned by the future Louis XI; "*la belle Ferronière*" (died in 1540) was one of François I's mistresses, wife of the lawyer Le Ferron who is said to have contracted syphilis for the mere satisfaction of passing it on to the king; Clémence Isaure is a half-fictional lady from Toulouse (fourteenth century), popularized in a novel by Florian as an incarnation of the mystical poetry of the troubadours.

13. St. Louis was King of France, Louis IX (1215–1270). He led the seventh and eighth crusades. He was canonized in 1297. According to tradition he dispensed justice under an oak tree at Vincennes (near Paris).

14. Bayard (Pierre du Terrail, seigneur de, 1473–1524) was one of the most famous French captains, distinguishing himself by feats of bravery during the wars of Francis I. He was killed in 1524. Dying, he chided the connétable de Bourbon for his treason in a famous speech.

15. Louis XI was born in 1421 and was king from 1461 to 1483. He ruthlessly suppressed the rebellious noblemen.

16. St. Bartholomew was the massacre of the Protestants ordered by Catherine de Medici in the night of August 23, 1572.

the painted plates glorifying Louis XIV.

In the music-class, the ballads she sang were all about little angels with golden wings, madonnas, lagunes, gondoliers; harmless-sounding compositions that, in spite of the inanity of the style and the vagueness of the melody, enabled one to catch a glimpse of the tantalizing phantasmagoria of sentimental realities. Some of her companions brought keepsakes given them as new year's gifts to the convent. These had to be hidden; it was quite an undertaking; they were read in the dormitory. Delicately handling the beautiful satin bindings, Emma looked with dazzled eyes at the names of the unknown authors, who had signed their verses for the most part as counts or viscounts.

She trembled as she blew back the thin transparent paper over the engraving and saw it folded in two and fall gently against the page. Here behind the balustrade of a balcony was a young man in a short cloak, holding in his arms a young girl in a white dress who was wearing an alms-bag at her belt; or there were nameless portraits of English ladies with fair curls, who looked at you from under their round straw hats with their large clear eyes. Some could be seen lounging in their carriages, gliding through parks, a greyhound bounding along ahead of the equipage, driven at a trot by two small postilions in white breeches. Others, dreaming on sofas with an open letter, gazed at the moon through a slightly open window half draped by a black curtain. The innocent ones, a tear on their cheeks, were kissing doves through the bars of a Gothic cage, or, smiling, their heads on one side, were plucking the leaves of a marguerite with their taper fingers, that curved at the tips like peaked shoes. And you, too, were there, Sultans with long pipes reclining beneath arbours in the arms of Bayadères; Giaours, curved swords, fezzes; and you especially, pale landscapes of dithyrambic lands, that often show us at once palm-trees and firs, tigers on the right, a lion to the left, Tartar minarets on the horizon, Roman ruins in the foreground with some kneeling camels besides; the whole framed by a very neat virgin forest, and with a great perpendicular sunbeam trembling in the water, where, sharply edged on a steel-grey background, white swans are swimming here and there.

And the shade of the oil lamp fastened to the wall above Emma's head lighted up all these pictures of the world, that passed before her one by one in the silence of the dormitory, and to the distant noise of some belated carriage still rolling down the Boulevards.

When her mother died she cried much the first few days. She had a funeral picture made with the hair of the deceased, and, in a letter sent to the Bertaux full of sad reflections on life, she asked to be buried later on in the same grave. The old man thought she must be ill, and came to see her. Emma was secretly pleased that she had reached at a first attempt the rare ideal of delicate lives, never attained by mediocre hearts. She let herself meander along with Lamartine, listened to harps on lakes, to all the songs of dying swans, to the falling of the leaves, the pure virgins ascending to heaven, and the voice of the Eternal discoursing down the valleys. She soon grew tired but wouldn't admit it, continued from habit first, then out of vanity, and at last was surprised to feel herself consoled, and with no more sadness at heart than wrinkles on her brow.

The good nuns, who had been so sure of her vocation, perceived with great astonishment that Mademoiselle Rouault seemed to be slipping from them. They had indeed been so lavish to her of prayers, retreats, novenas, and sermons, they had so often preached the respect due to saints and martyrs, and given so much good advice as to the modesty of the body and the salvation of her soul, that she did as tightly reigned horses: she pulled up short and the bit slipped from her teeth. This nature, positive in the midst of its enthusiasms, that had loved the church for the sake of the flowers, and music for the words of the songs, and literature for the passions it excites, rebelled against the mysteries of faith as it had rebelled against discipline, as something alien to her constitution. When her father took her from school, no one was sorry to see her go. The Lady Superior even thought that she had of late been less than reverent toward the community.

Emma, at home once more, first took pleasure in ruling over servants, then grew disgusted with the country and missed her convent. When Charles came to the Bertaux for the first time, she thought herself quite disillusioned, with nothing more to learn, and nothing more to feel.

But the uneasiness of her new position, or perhaps the disturbance caused by the presence of this man, had sufficed to make her believe that she at last felt that wondrous passion which, till then, like a great bird with rose-coloured wings, hung in the splendor of poetic skies;—and now she could not think that the calm in which she lived was the happiness of her dreams.

VII

She thought, sometimes, that, after all, this was the happiest time of her life: the honeymoon, as people called it. To taste the full sweetness of it, it would no doubt have been necessary to fly to those lands with sonorous names where the days after marriage are full of the most suave laziness! In post-chaises behind blue silken curtains, one rides slowly up steep roads, listening to the song of the postilion re-echoed by the mountains, along with the bells of goats and the muffled sound of a waterfall. At sunset on the shores of gulfs one breathes in the perfume of lemon-trees; then in the evening on the villa-terraces above, one looks hand in hand at the stars, making plans for the future. It seemed to her that certain places on earth must bring happiness, as a plant peculiar to the soil, and that cannot thrive elsewhere. Why could not she lean over balconies in Swiss châlets, or enshrine her melancholy in a Scotch cottage, with a husband dressed in a black velvet coat with long tails, and thin shoes, a pointed hat and frills?

Perhaps she would have liked to confide all these things to some one. But how tell an undefinable uneasiness, changing as the clouds, unstable as the winds? Words failed her and, by the same token, the opportunity, the courage.

If Charles had but wished it, if he had guessed, if his look had but once met her thought, it seemed to her that a sudden bounty would have come from her heart, as the fruit falls from a tree when shaken by a hand. But as the intimacy of their life became deeper, the greater became the gulf that kept them apart.

Charles's conversation was commonplace as a street pavement, and every one's ideas trooped through it in their everyday garb, without exciting emotion, laughter, or thought. He had never had the curiosity, he said, while he lived at Rouen, to go to the theatre to see the actors from Paris. He could neither swim, nor fence, nor shoot, and one day he could not explain some term of horsemanship to her that she had come across in a novel.

A man, on the contrary, should he not know everything, excel in manifold activities, initiate you into the energies of passion, the refinements of life, all mysteries? But this one taught nothing, knew nothing, wished nothing. He thought her happy; and she resented this easy calm, this serene heaviness, the very happiness she gave him.

Sometimes she would draw; and it was great amusement to Charles to stand there bolt upright and watch her bend over her paper, with eyes half-closed the better to see her work, or rolling, between her fingers, little bread-pellets. As to the piano, the more quickly her fingers glided over it the more he wondered. She struck the notes with aplomb, and ran from top to bottom of the keyboard without a break. Thus shaken up, the old instrument, whose strings buzzed, could be heard at the other end of the village when the window was open, and often the bailiff's clerk, passing along the highroad bareheaded and in slippers, stopped to listen, his sheet of paper in his hand.

Emma, on the other hand, knew how to look after her house. She sent the patients' accounts in well-phrased letters that had no suggestion of a bill. When they had a neighbor to dinner on Sundays, she managed to have some tasty dish, knew how to pile the plums in pyramids on vine-leaves, how to serve jam turned out on a plate, and even spoke of buying finger bowls for dessert. From all this much consideration was extended to Bovary.

Charles finished by rising in his own esteem for possessing such a wife. He showed with pride in the sitting-room two small pencil sketches by her that he had had framed in very large frames, and hung up against the wall-paper by long green cords. People returning from mass saw him standing on his doorstep, wearing beautiful carpet slippers.

He came home late—at ten o'clock, at midnight sometimes. Then he asked for something to eat, and as the servant had gone to bed, Emma waited on him. He took off his coat to dine more at his ease. He told her, one after the other, the people he had met, the villages where he had been, the prescriptions he had written, and, well pleased with himself, he finished the remainder of the boiled beef, peeled the crust of his cheese, munched an apple, finished the wine, and then went to bed, lay on his back and snored.

As he had been for a long time accustomed to wear nightcaps, his handkerchief would not keep down over his ears, so that his hair in the morning was all dishevelled and whitened with the feathers of the pillow, whose strings came untied during the night. He always wore thick boots that had two long creases over the instep running obliquely towards the ankle, while the upper part continued in a straight line as if stretched on a wooden foot. He said that this was quite good enough for someone who lived in the country.

His mother approved of his thrift, for she came to see him as before, after there had been some violent row at her place; and yet the elder Madame Bovary seemed prejudiced against her daughter-in-law. She thought she was living above her means; the wood, sugar and candles vanished as in a large establishment, and the amount of stovewood used in the kitchen would have been enough for twenty-five courses. She straightened the linen chests, and taught her to keep an eye on the butcher when he brought the meat. Emma had to accept these lessons lavished upon her, and the words "daughter" and "mother" were exchanged all day long, accompanied by little quiverings of the lips, each one uttering sweet words in a voice trembling with anger.

In Madame Dubuc's time the old woman felt that she was still the favourite; but now the love of Charles for Emma seemed to her a desertion from her tenderness, an encroachment upon what was hers, and she watched her son's happiness in sad silence, as a ruined man looks through the windows at people dining in his old house. She recalled to him as remembrances her troubles and her sacrifices, and, comparing these with Emma's casual ways, came to the conclusion that it was not reasonable to adore her so exclusively.

Charles knew not what to answer: he respected his mother, and he loved his wife infinitely; he considered the judgment of the one infallible, and yet he thought the conduct of the other irreproachable. When Madame Bovary had gone, he tried timidly and in the same terms to hazard one or two of the more anodyne observations he had heard from his mamma. Emma proved to him with a word that he was mistaken, and sent him off to his patients.

And yet, in accord with theories she believed right, she wanted to experience love with him. By moonlight in the garden she recited all the passionate rhymes she knew by heart, and, sighing, sang to him many melancholy adagios; but she found herself as calm after this as before, and Charles seemed neither more amorous, nor more moved.

When she had thus for a while struck the flint on her heart without getting a spark, incapable, moreover, of understanding what she did not experience or of believing anything that did not take on a conventional form, she persuaded herself without difficulty that Charles's passion was no longer very ardent. His outbursts became regular; he embraced her at certain fixed times. It was one habit among other habits, like a familiar dessert after the monotony of dinner.

A gamekeeper, whom the doctor had cured of a lung infection, had given madame a little Italian greyhound; she took her out walking, for she went out sometimes in order to be alone for a moment, and not to see before her eyes the eternal garden and the dusty road.

She went as far as the beeches of Banneville, near the deserted pavilion which forms an angle on the field side of the wall. Amidst the grass of the ditches grow long reeds with sharp-edged leaves that cut you.

She began by looking round her to see if nothing had changed since she had last been there. She found again in the same places the foxgloves and wallflowers, the beds of nettles growing round the big stones, and the patches of lichen along the three windows, whose shutters, always closed, were rotting away on their rusty iron bars. Her thoughts, aimless at first, wandered at random, like her greyhound, who ran round and round in the fields, yelping after the yellow butterflies, chasing the field-mice, or nibbling the poppies on the edge of a wheatfield. Then gradually her ideas took definite shape, and, sitting on the grass that she dug up with little pricks of her sunshade, Emma repeated to herself:—Why, for Heaven's sake, did I marry?

She asked herself if by some other chance combination it would not have been possible to meet another man; and she tried to imagine what would have been these unrealised events, this different life, this unknown husband. All, surely, could not be like this one. He might have been handsome, witty, distinguished, attractive, like, no doubt, the men her old companions of the convent had married. What were they doing now? In town, among the crowded streets, the buzzing theatres and the lights of the ball-room, they were living lives where the heart expands and the senses blossom out. As for her, her life was cold as a garret facing north, and ennui, the silent spider, was weaving its web in the darkness, in every corner of her heart. She recalled graduation day, when she mounted the platform to receive her little wreaths. With her hair in long plaits, in her white frock and open prunella shoes she had a pretty way, and when she went back to her seat, the gentlemen bent over to congratulate her; the courtyard was full of carriages; farewells were called to her through their windows; the music-master with his violin-case bowed in passing by. How far off all this! How far away!

She called Djali,[17] took her between her knees, and smoothed the long, delicate head, saying, "Come, kiss your mistress, you who are free of cares."

Then noting the melancholy face of the graceful animal, who yawned slowly, she softened, and comparing her to herself, spoke to her aloud as to somebody in pain whom one is consoling.

Occasionally there came gusts of wind, breezes from the sea rolling in one sweep over the whole plateau of the Caux country, which brought to these fields a salt freshness. The rushes, close to the ground, whistled; the branches of the beech trees trembled in a swift rustling, while their crowns, ceaselessly swaying, kept up a deep murmur. Emma drew her shawl round her shoulders and rose.

In the avenue a green light dimmed by the leaves lit up the short moss that crackled softly beneath her feet. The sun was setting; the sky showed red between the branches, and the trunks of the trees, uniform, and planted in a straight line, seemed a brown colonnade standing out against a background of gold. A fear took hold of her; she called Djali, and hurriedly returned to Tostes by the highroad, threw herself into an armchair, and for the rest of the evening did not speak.

But towards the end of September something extraordinary befell her: she was invited by the Marquis d'Andervilliers to Vaubyessard.

Secretary of State under the Restoration, the Marquis, anxious to re-enter political life, had long since been preparing for his candidature to the Chamber of Deputies. In the winter he distributed a great deal of firewood, and in the Conseil Général always enthusiastically demanded new roads for his arrondissement. During the height of the Summer heat he had suffered from an abcess in the mouth, which Charles had cured as if by miracle by giving a timely

17. Djali is the name of the little she-goat in Hugo's *Notre Dame de Paris.*

little touch with the lancet. The steward sent to Tostes to pay for the operation reported in the evening that he had seen some superb cherries in the doctor's little garden. Now cherry-trees did not thrive at Vaubyessard; the Marquis asked Bovary for some offshoots. He made it his business to thank him personally and, on that occasion, saw Emma. He thought she had a pretty figure, and that she did not greet him like a peasant; so that he did not think he was going beyond the bounds of condescension, nor, on the other hand, making a mistake, in inviting the young couple.

One Wednesday at three o'clock, Monsieur and Madame Bovary, seated in their dog-cart, set out for Vaubyessard, with a great trunk strapped on behind and a hat-box in front on the apron. Besides these Charles held a carton between his knees.

They arrived at nightfall, just as the lamps in the park were being lit to show the way for the carriages.

VIII

The château, a modern building in Italian style, with two projecting wings and three flights of steps, lay at the foot of an immense lawn, on which some cows were grazing among clumps of large trees set out at regular intervals, while large beds of arbutus, rhododendron, syringas and snowballs bulged out their irregular clusters of green along the curve of the gravel path. A river flowed under a bridge; through the mist one could distinguish buildings with thatched roofs scattered over the field bordered by two gently-sloping well-timbered hillocks, and in the background amid the trees rose in two parallel lines the coach-houses and stables, all that was left of the ruined old château.

Charles's dog-cart pulled up before the middle flight of steps; servants appeared; the Marquis came forward, and offering his arm to the doctor's wife, conducted her to the vestibule.

It was paved with marble slabs and seemed very lofty; the sound of footsteps and that of voices re-echoed through it as in a church. Opposite rose a straight staircase, and on the left a gallery overlooking the garden led to the billiard room, from where the click of the ivory balls could be heard immediately upon entering. As she crossed it to go to the drawing-room, Emma saw standing round the table men with grave faces, their chins resting on high cravats. They all wore orders, and smiled silently as they made their strokes. On the dark wainscoting of the walls large gold frames bore at the bottom names written in black letters. She read: "Jean-Antoine d'Andervilliers d'Yverbonville, Count de la Vaubyessard and Baron de la Fresnaye, killed at the battle of Coutras[18] on the 20th of October 1587." And on another: "Jean-Antoine-Henry-Guy d'Andervilliers de la Vaubyessard, Admiral of France and Chevalier of

18. Battle of Coutras (in the Gironde) was won by Henri de Navarre against the Duke de Joyeuse (1587).

the Order of St. Michael, wounded at the battle of the Hougue-Saint-Vaast on the 29th of May 1692; died at Vaubyessard on the 23rd of January 1693." One could hardly make out the next ones, for the light of the lamps lowered over the green cloth threw a dim shadow round the room. Burnishing the horizontal pictures, it broke up in delicate lines among the cracks in the varnish, and from all these great black squares framed in gold stood out here and there some lighter portion of the painting—a pale brow, two eyes that looked at you, wigs resting on the powdered shoulder of red coats, or the buckle of a garter above a well-rounded calf.

The Marquis opened the drawing-room door; one of the ladies (the Marquise herself) came to meet Emma. She made her sit down by her on an ottoman, and began talking to her as amicably as if she had known her a long time. She was a woman of about forty, with fine shoulders, a hook nose, a drawling voice, and on this evening she wore over her brown hair a simple guipure fichu that fell in a point at the back. A blond young woman sat by her side in a high-backed chair, and gentlemen with flowers in their button-holes were talking to ladies round the fire.

At seven dinner was served. The men, who were in the majority, sat down at the first table in the vestibule; the ladies at the second in the dining-room with the Marquis and Marquise.

Emma, on entering, felt herself wrapped round as by a warm breeze, a blending of the perfume of flowers and of the fine linen, of the fumes of the roasts and the odour of the truffles. The candles in the candelabra threw their lights on the silver dish covers; the cut crystal, covered with a fine mist of steam, reflected pale rays of light; bouquets were placed in a row the whole length of the table; and in the large-bordered plates each napkin, arranged after the fashion of a bishop's mitre, held between its two gaping folds a small oval-shaped roll. The red claws of lobsters hung over the dishes; rich fruit in woven baskets was piled up on moss; the quails were dressed in their own plumage, smoke was rising; and in silk stockings, knee-breeches, white cravat, and frilled shirt, the steward, grave as a judge, passed between the shoulders of the guests, offering ready-carved dishes and, with a flick of the spoon, landed on one's plate the piece one had chosen. On the large porcelain stove inlaid with copper baguettes the statue of a woman, draped to the chin, gazed motionless on the crowded room.

Madame Bovary noticed that many ladies had not put their gloves in their glasses.[19]

At the upper end of the table, alone amongst all these women,

19. The ladies in the provinces, unlike their Paris counterparts, did not drink wine at public dinner parties, and signified their intention by putting their gloves in their wine-glasses. The fact that they fail to do so suggests to Emma the high degree of sophistication of the company.

bent over his full plate, and his napkin tied round his neck like a child, an old man sat eating, letting drops of gravy drip from his mouth. His eyes were bloodshot, and he wore his hair in a little queue tied with a black ribbon. He was the Marquis's father-in-law, the old Duke de Laverdière, once on a time favourite of the Count d'Artois, in the days of the Marquis de Conflans' hunting-parties at le Vaudreuil, and had been, it was said, the lover of Queen Marie Antoinette, between Monsieur de Coigny and Monsieur de Lauzun. He had lived a life of loud dissipation, full of duels, bets, elopements; he had squandered his fortune and frightened all his family. A servant behind his chair shouted in his ear, in reply to his mutterings, the names of the dishes that he pointed to, and constantly Emma's eyes turned involuntarily to this old man with hanging lips, as to something extraordinary. He had lived at court and slept in the bed of queens!

Iced champagne was poured out. Emma shivered all over as she felt its cold in her mouth. She had never seen pomegranates nor tasted pineapples. Even the powdered sugar seemed to her whiter and finer than elsewhere.

The ladies afterwards retired to their rooms to prepare for the ball.

Emma made her toilette with the fastidious care of an actress on her début. She did her hair according to the directions of the hairdresser, and put on the barege dress spread out upon the bed. Charles's trousers were tight across the belly.

"My trouser-straps will be rather awkward for dancing," he said.

"Dancing?" repeated Emma.

"Yes!"

"Why, you must be mad! They would make fun of you; stay in your place, as it becomes a doctor."

Charles was silent. He walked up and down waiting for Emma to finish dressing.

He saw her from behind in the mirror between two lights. Her black eyes seemed blacker than ever. Her hair, gently undulating towards the ears, shone with a blue lustre; a rose in her chignon trembled on its mobile stalk, with artificial dewdrops on the tip of the leaves. She wore a gown of pale saffron trimmed with three bouquets of pompon roses mixed with green.

Charles came and kissed her on her shoulder.

"Don't touch me!" she cried; "I'll be all rumpled."

One could hear the flourish of the violin and the notes of a horn. She went downstairs restraining herself from running.

Dancing had begun. Guests were arriving and crowding the room. She sat down on a bench near the door.

The quadrille over, the floor was occupied by groups of talking men and by servants in livery bearing large trays. Along the line of seated women painted fans were fluttering, bouquets half-hid smiling faces, and gold-stoppered scent-bottles were turned in half-clenched hands, with white gloves outlining the nail and tightening on the flesh at the wrists. Lace trimmings, diamond brooches, medallion bracelets trembled on blouses, gleamed on breasts, clinked on bare arms. The hair, well smoothed over the temples and knotted at the nape, bore crowns, or bunches, or sprays of myosotis, jasmine, pomegranate blossoms, wheat-sprays and corn-flowers. Calmly seated in their places, mothers with forbidding countenances were wearing red turbans.

Emma's heart beat rather faster when, her partner holding her by the tips of the fingers, she took her place in a line with the dancers, and waited for the first note to start. But her emotion soon vanished, and, swaying to the rhythm of the orchestra, she glided forward with slight movements of the neck. A smile rose to her lips at certain delicate phrases of the violin, that sometimes played alone while the other instruments were silent; one could hear the clear clink of the louis d'or that were being thrown down upon the card-tables in the next room; then all struck in again, the trumpet uttered its sonorous note, feet marked time, skirts swelled and rustled, hands touched and parted; the same eyes that had been lowered returned to gaze at you again.

A few men (some fifteen or so), of twenty-five to forty, scattered here and there among the dancers or talking at the doorways, distinguished themselves from the crowd by a certain family-air, whatever their differences in age, dress, or countenance.

Their clothes, better made, seemed of finer cloth, and their hair, brought forward in curls towards the temples, glossy with more delicate pomades. They had the complexion of wealth,—that clear complexion that is heightened by the pallor of porcelain, the shimmer of satin, the veneer of old furniture, and that a well-ordered diet of exquisite food maintains at its best. Their necks moved easily in their low cravats, their long whiskers fell over their turned-down collars, they wiped their lips upon handkerchiefs with embroidered initials that gave forth a subtle perfume. Those who were beginning to grow old had an air of youth, while there was something mature in the faces of the young. Their indifferent eyes had the appeased expression of daily-satiated passions, and through all their gentleness of manner pierced that peculiar brutality that stems from a steady command over half-tame things, for the exercise of one's strength and the amusement of one's vanity—the handling of thoroughbred horses and the society of loose women.

A few steps from Emma a gentleman in a blue coat was talking of Italy with a pale young woman wearing a parure of pearls. They were praising the width of the columns of St. Peter's, Tivoli,

Vesuvius, Castellamare,[20] and the Cascine,[21] the roses of Genoa, the Coliseum by moonlight. With her other ear Emma was listening to a conversation full of words she did not understand. A circle gathered round a very young man who the week before had beaten "Miss Arabella," and "Romulus," and won two thousand louis jumping a ditch in England. One complained that his racehorses were growing fat; another of the printers' errors that had disfigured the name of his horse.

The atmosphere of the ball was heavy; the lamps were growing dim. Guests were flocking to the billiard-room. A servant got upon a chair and broke the window-panes. At the crash of the glass Madame Bovary turned her head and saw in the garden the faces of peasants pressed against the window looking in at them. Then the memory of the Bertaux came back to her. She saw the farm again, the muddy pond, her father in his apron under the apple-trees, and she saw herself again as formerly, skimming with her finger the cream off the milk-pans in the dairy. But in the splendor of the present hour her past life, so distinct until then, faded away completely, and she almost doubted having lived it. She was there; beyond the ball was only shadow overspreading all the rest. She was eating a maraschino ice that she held with her left hand in a silver-gilt cup, her eyes half-closed, and the spoon between her teeth.

A lady near her dropped her fan. A gentleman was passing.

"Would you be good enough," said the lady, "to pick up my fan that has fallen behind the sofa?"

The gentleman bowed, and as he moved to stretch out his arm, Emma saw the hand of the young woman throw something white, folded in a triangle, into his hat. The gentleman picking up the fan, respectfully offered it to the lady; she thanked him with a nod and breathed in the smell of her bouquet.

After supper, consisting of plenty of Spanish and Rhine wines, bisque and almond-cream soups, Trafalgar puddings and all sorts of cold meats with jellies that trembled in the dishes, the carriages began to leave one after the other. Raising the corners of the muslin curtain, one could see the light of their lanterns glimmering through the darkness. The seats began to empty, some card-players were still left; the musicians were cooling the tips of their fingers on their tongues. Charles was half asleep, his back propped against a door.

At three o'clock the cotillion began. Emma did not know how to waltz. Every one was waltzing, Mademoiselle d'Andervilliers herself and the Marquis; only the guests staying at the castle were still there, about a dozen persons.

One of the waltzers, however, who was addressed as Viscount, and whose low cut waistcoat seemed moulded to his chest, came a

20. Castellamare, a port south of Naples.

21. Cascine, a park near Florence.

second time to ask Madame Bovary to dance, assuring her that he would guide her, and that she would get through it very well.

They began slowly, then increased in speed. They turned; all around them was turning, the lamps, the furniture, the wainscoting, the floor, like a disc on a pivot. On passing near the doors the train of Emma's dress caught against his trousers. Their legs intertwined; he looked down at her; she raised her eyes to his. A torpor seized her and she stopped. They started again, at an even faster pace; the Viscount, sweeping her along, disappeared with her to the end of the gallery, where, panting, she almost fell, and for a moment rested her head upon his breast. And then, still turning, but more slowly, he guided her back to her seat. She leaned back against the wall and covered her eyes with her hands.

When she opened them again, in the middle of the drawing-room three waltzers were kneeling before a lady sitting on a stool. She chose the Viscount, and the violin struck up once more.

Every one looked at them. They kept passing by, she with rigid body, her chin bent down, and he always in the same pose, his figure curved, his elbow rounded, his chin thrown forward. That woman knew how to waltz! They kept it up a long time, and tired out all the others.

Then they talked a few moments longer, and after the good-nights, or rather good-mornings, the guests of the château retired to bed.

Charles dragged himself up by the banister. His knees were giving way under him. For five consecutive hours, he had stood bolt upright at the card-tables, watching them play whist, without understanding anything about it, and it was with a deep sigh of relief that he pulled off his boots.

Emma threw a shawl over her shoulders, opened the window, and leant out.

The night was dark; some drops of rain were falling. She breathed in the damp wind that refreshed her eyelids. The music of the ball was still echoing in her ears, and she tried to keep herself awake in order to prolong the illusion of this luxurious life that she would soon have to give up.

Day began to break. She looked long at the windows of the château, trying to guess which were the rooms of all those she had noticed the evening before. She would have wanted to know their lives, to penetrate into them, to blend with them.

But she was shivering with cold. She undressed, and cowered down between the sheets against Charles, who was asleep.

There were a great many people to luncheon. The meal lasted ten minutes; to the doctor's astonishment, no liqueurs were served. Next, Mademoiselle d'Andervilliers collected some rolls in a small basket to take them to the swans on the ornamental waters, and they went for a walk in the hothouses, where strange plants, bristling with hairs, rose in pyramids under hanging vases from where fell, as from overfilled nests of serpents, long green cords interlacing. The orangery, at the other end, led by a covered way to the tenant houses of the château. The Marquis, to amuse the young woman, took her to see the stables. Above the basket-shaped racks porcelain slabs bore the names of the horses in black letters. Each animal in its stall whisked its tail when any one came near and clicked his tongue. The boards of the harness-room shone like the flooring of a drawing-room. The carriage harness was piled up in the middle against two twisted columns, and the bits, the whips, the spurs, the curbs, were lined up in a row all along the wall.

Charles, meanwhile, went to ask a groom to harness his horse. The dog-cart was brought to the foot of the steps, and all the parcels being crammed in, the Bovarys paid their respects to the Marquis and the Marquise and set out again for Tostes.

Emma watched the turning wheels in silence. Charles, on the extreme edge of the seat, held the reins with his arms spread far apart, and the little horse ambled along in the shafts that were too big for him. The loose reins hanging over his crupper were wet with foam, and the box fastened behind bumped regularly against the cart.

They were on the heights of Thibourville when suddenly some horsemen with cigars between their lips passed, laughing. Emma thought she recognised the Viscount, turned back, and caught on the horizon only the movement of the heads rising or falling with the unequal cadence of the trot or gallop.

A mile farther on they had to stop to mend with some string the traces that had broken.

But Charles, giving a last look to the harness, saw something on the ground between his horse's legs, and he picked up a cigar-case with a green silk border and a crest in the centre like the door of a carriage.

"There are even two cigars in it," said he; "they'll do for this evening after dinner."

"Since when do you smoke?" she asked.

"Sometimes, when I get a chance."

He put his find in his pocket and whipped up the nag.

When they reached home the dinner was not ready. Madame lost her temper. Nastasie answered rudely.

"Leave the room!" said Emma. "You are being insolent. I'll dismiss you."

For dinner there was onion soup and a piece of veal with sorrel. Charles, seated opposite Emma, rubbed his hands gleefully.

"How good it is to be at home again!"

Nastasie could be heard crying. He was rather fond of the poor girl. She had formerly, during the wearisome time of his widowhood, kept him company many an evening. She had been his first patient, his oldest acquaintance in the place.

"Have you dismissed her for good?" he asked at last.

"Yes. Who is to prevent me?" she replied.

Then they warmed themselves in the kitchen while their room was being made ready. Charles began to smoke. He smoked with lips protruded, spitting every moment, drawing back at every puff.

"You'll make yourself ill," she said scornfully.

He put down his cigar and ran to swallow a glass of cold water at the pump. Seizing the cigar case, Emma threw it quickly to the back of the cupboard.

The next day was a long one. She walked about her little garden, up and down the same walks, stopping before the beds, before the fruit tree, before the plaster priest, looking with amazement at all these things of the past that she knew so well. How far off the ball seemed already! What was it that thus set so far asunder the morning of the day before yesterday and the evening of to-day? Her journey to Vaubyessard had made a gap in her life, like the huge crevasses that a thunderstorm will sometimes carve in the mountains, in the course of a single night. Still she was resigned. She devoutly put away in her drawers her beautiful dress, down to the satin shoes whose soles were yellowed with the slippery wax of the dancing floor. Her heart resembled them: in its contact with wealth, something had rubbed off on it that could not be removed.

The memory of this ball, then, became an occupation for Emma. Whenever Wednesday came round she said to herself as she awoke, "Ah! I was there a week—a fortnight—three weeks ago." And little by little the faces grew confused in her remembrance. She forgot the tune of the quadrilles; she no longer saw the liveries and the guest-houses so distinctly; some of the details faded but the wistful feeling remained with her.

IX

Often when Charles was out she took from the cupboard, between the folds of the linen where she had left it, the green silk cigar-case.

She looked at it, opened it, and even smelt the odour of the lining, a mixture of verbena and tobacco. Whose was it? . . . The Viscount's? Perhaps it was a present from his mistress. It had been embroidered on some rosewood frame, a pretty piece of furniture, hidden from all eyes, that had occupied many hours, and over which had fallen the soft curls of the pensive worker. A breath of love had passed over the stitches on the canvas; each prick of the needle had fixed there a hope or a memory, and all those interwoven threads of silk were but the continued extension of the same silent passion. And then one morning the Viscount had taken it away with him. Of what had they spoken when it lay upon the wide-mantelled chimneys between flower-vases and Pompadour clocks? She was at Tostes; he was at Paris now, far away! What was this Paris like? What a boundless name! She repeated it in a low voice, for the mere pleasure of it; it rang in her ears like a great cathedral bell; it shone before her eyes, even on the labels of her jars of pomade.

At night, when the carts passed under her windows, carrying fish to Paris to the tune of "la Marjolaine," she awoke, and listened to the noise of the iron-bound wheels, which, as they gained the country road, was soon deadened by the earth. "They will be there tomorrow!" she said to herself.

And she followed them in thought up and down the hills, crossing villages, gliding along the highroads by the light of the stars. At the end of some indefinite distance there was always a confused spot, into which her dream died.

She bought a plan of Paris, and with the tip of her finger on the map she walked about the capital. She went up the boulevards, stopping at every turn, between the lines of the streets, in front of the white squares that represented the houses. At last she would close the lids of her weary eyes, and see in the darkness the gas jets flaring in the wind and the steps of carriages lowered noisily in front of the theatre-entrances.

She subscribed to "La Corbeille," a ladies' magazine, and the "Sylphe des Salons." She devoured, without skipping a word, all the accounts of first nights, races, and soirées, took an interest in the début of a singer, in the opening of a new shop. She knew the latest fashions, the addresses of the best tailors, the days of the Bois and the Opera. In Eugène Sue[22] she studied descriptions of furniture; she read Balzac and George Sand,[23] seeking in them imaginary satisfaction for her own desires. She even brought her book to the table, and turned over the pages while Charles ate and talked to her. The memory of the Viscount always cropped up in everything she read. She made comparisons between him and the fictional characters in her books. But the circle of which he was the centre gradually widened round him, and the aureole that he bore, fading from his form and extending beyond his image, lit up her other dreams.

Paris, more vague than the ocean, glimmered before Emma's eyes with a silvery glow. The many lives that stirred amid this tumult

22. Eugène Sue (1804–1857) a popular novelist, extremely successful at that period, both as a writer and as a fashionable dandy.

23. George Sand (pseudonym of Aurore Dupín), prolific woman novelist (1803–1876).

were, however, divided into parts, classed as distinct pictures. Emma perceived only two or three that hid from her all the rest, and in themselves represented all humanity. The world of ambassadors moved over polished floors in drawing-rooms lined with mirrors, round oval tables covered with velvet and gold-fringed cloths. There were dresses with trains, deep mysteries, anguish hidden beneath smiles. Then came the society of the duchesses; all were pale; all got up at four o'clock; the women, poor angels, wore English point on their petticoats; and the men, their talents hidden under a frivolous appearance, rode horses to death at pleasure parties, spent the summer season at Baden, and ended up, on reaching their forties, by marrying heiresses. In the private rooms of restaurants, where one dines after midnight by the light of wax candles, the colorful crowd of writers and actresses held sway. They were prodigal as kings, full of ambitious ideals and fantastic frenzies. They lived far above all others, among the storms that rage between heaven and earth, partaking of the sublime. As for the rest of the world, it was lost, with no particular place, and as if non-existent. Anyway, the nearer things were the more her thoughts turned away from them. All her immediate surroundings, the wearisome countryside, the petty-bourgeois stupidity, the mediocrity of existence seemed to her the exception, an exception in which she had been caught by a stroke of fate, while beyond stretched as far as eye could see an immense land of joys and passions. In her wistfulness, she confused the sensuous pleasures of luxury with the delights of the heart, elegance of manners with delicacy of sentiment. Did not love, like Indian plants, need a special soil, a special temperature? Sighs by moonlight, long embraces, tears flowing over yielded hands, all the passions of the flesh and the languors of tenderness seemed to her inseparable from the balconies of great castles where life flows idly by, from boudoirs with silken curtains and thick carpets, well-filled flower-stands, a bed on a raised daïs, and from the flashing of precious stones and the golden braids of liveries.

The boy from the post-office who came to groom the mare every morning passed through the passage with his heavy wooden shoes; there were holes in his apron; his feet were bare in his slippers. And this was the groom in knee-breeches with whom she had to be content! His work done, he did not come back again all day, for Charles on his return put up his horse himself, unsaddled it and put on the halter, while the maid brought a bundle of straw and threw it as best she could into the manger.

To replace Nastasie (who finally left Tostes shedding torrents of tears) Emma hired a young girl of fourteen, an orphan with a sweet face. She forbade her wearing cotton caps, taught her to address her in the third person, to bring a glass of water on a plate, to knock before coming into a room, to iron, starch, and to dress her; she wanted to make a lady's-maid of her. The new servant obeyed without a murmur, so as not to be dismissed; and as madame usually left the key in the sideboard, Félicité every evening took a small supply of sugar that she ate alone in her bed after she had said her prayers.

Sometimes in the afternoon she went across the road to chat with the coachmen. Madame stayed upstairs.

She wore an open dressing-gown, that showed under the shawl-shaped collar a pleated blouse with three gold buttons. Her belt was a corded girdle with great tassels, and her small wine-red slippers had a large knot of ribbon that fell over her instep. She had bought herself a blotter, writing-case, pen-holder, and envelopes although she had no one to write to; she dusted her shelf, looked at herself in the mirror, picked up a book, and then, dreaming between the lines, let it drop on her knees. She longed to travel or to go back to her convent. She wanted to die, but she also wanted to live in Paris.

Charles trotted over the country-roads in snow and rain. He ate omelettes on farmhouse tables, poked his arm into damp beds, received the tepid spurt of blood-letting in his face, listened to death-rattles, examined basins, turned over a good deal of dirty linen; but every evening he found a blazing fire, his dinner ready, easy-chairs, and a well-dressed woman, charming and so freshly scented that it was impossible to say where the perfume came from; it might have been her skin that communicated its fragrance to her blouse.

She delighted him by numerous attentions; now it was some new way of arranging paper sconces for the candles, a flounce that she altered on her gown, or an extraordinary name for some very simple dish that the servant had spoilt, but that Charles swallowed with pleasure to the last mouthful. At Rouen she saw some ladies who wore a bundle of charms hanging from their watch-chains; she bought some. She wanted for her mantelpiece two large blue glass vases, and some time after an ivory nécessaire with a silver-gilt thimble. The less Charles understood these refinements the more they seduced him. They added something to the pleasure of the senses and to the comfort of his fireside. It was like a golden dust sanding all along the narrow path of his life.

He was well, looked well; his reputation was firmly established. The country-folk loved him because he was not proud. He petted the children, never went to the public-house, and, moreover, his good behavior inspired confidence. He was specially successful with heavy colds and chest ailments. Being much afraid of killing his patients, Charles, in fact, only prescribed sedatives, from time to time an emetic, a footbath, or leeches. It was not that he was afraid of surgery; he bled people copiously like horses, and for the pulling of teeth the strength of his grasp was second to no one.

Finally, to keep up with the times, he subscribed to "La Ruche Médicale," a new journal whose prospectus had been sent him. He read it a little after dinner, but in about five minutes, the warmth of the room added to the effect of his dinner sent him to sleep; and he sat there, his chin on his two hands and his hair spreading like a mane to the foot of the lamp. Emma looked at him and shrugged her shoulders. Why at least, was not her husband one of those silently determined men who work at their books all night, and at last, when at sixty the age of rhumatism was upon them, wear a string of medals on their ill-fitting black coat? She would have wished this name of Bovary, which was hers, to be illustrious, to see it displayed at the booksellers', repeated in the newspapers, known to all France. But Charles had no ambition. An Yvetot doctor whom he had lately met in consultation had somewhat humiliated him at the very bedside of the patient, before the assembled relatives. When, in the evening, Charles told this incident Emma inveighed loudly against his colleague. Charles was much touched. He kissed her forehead with a tear in his eyes. But she was angered with shame; she felt a wild desire to strike him; she went to open the window in the passage and breathed in the fresh air to calm herself.

"What a man! what a man!" she said in a low voice, biting her lips.

She was becoming more irritated with him. As he grew older his manner grew coarser; at dessert he cut the corks of the empty bottles; after eating he cleaned his teeth with his tongue; in eating his soup he made a gurgling noise with every spoonful; and, as he was getting fatter, the puffed-out cheeks seemed to push the eyes, always small, up to the temples.

Sometimes Emma tucked the red borders of his undervest into his waistcoat, rearranged his cravat, and threw away the faded gloves he was going to put on; and this was not, as he fancied, for his sake; it was for herself, by an expansion of selfishness, of nervous irritation. At other times, she told him what she had been reading, some passage in a novel, a new play, or an anecdote from high society found in a newspaper story; for, after all, Charles was someone to talk to, an ever-open ear, an ever-ready approbation. She even confided many a thing to her greyhound! She would have done so to the logs in the fireplace or to the pendulum of the clock.

All the while, however, she was waiting in her heart for something to happen. Like shipwrecked sailors, she turned despairing eyes upon the solitude of her life, seeking afar some white sail in the mists of the horizon. She did not know what this act of fortune would be, what wind would bring it, towards what shore it would drive her, if it would be a rowboat or an ocean liner with three decks, carrying anguish or laden to the gunwales with bliss. But each morning, as she awoke, she hoped it would come that day; she listened to every sound, sprang up with a start, wondered that it did not come; then at sunset, always more saddened, she longed for the next day.

Spring came round. With the first warm weather, when the pear-trees began to blossom, she had fainting-spells.

From the beginning of July she counted off on her fingers how many weeks there were to October, thinking that perhaps the Marquis d'Andervilliers would give another ball at Vaubyessard. But all September passed without letters or visits.

After the shock of this disappointment her heart once more remained empty, and then the same series of identical days recommenced.

So now they would keep following one another, always the same, immovable, and bringing nothing new. Other lives, however flat, had at least the chance of some event. One adventure sometimes brought with it infinite consequences and the scene changed. But nothing happened to her; God had willed it so! The future was a dark corridor, with its door at the end shut tight.

She gave up music. What was the good of playing? Who would hear her? Since she could never, in a velvet gown with short sleeves, striking with her light fingers the ivory keys of an Erard concert piano, feel the murmur of ecstasy envelop her like a breeze, it was not worth while boring herself with practising. Her drawing card-board and her embroidery she left in the cupboard. What was the use? What was the use? Sewing irritated her.

"I have read everything," she said to herself.

And she sat there, letting the tongs grow red-hot or looking at the rain falling.

How sad she was on Sundays when vespers sounded! She listened with dull attention to each stroke of the cracked bell. A cat slowly walking over some roof put up his back in the pale rays of the sun. The wind on the highroad blew up clouds of dust. A dog sometimes howled in the distance; and the bell, keeping time, continued at regular intervals its monotonous ringing that died away over the fields.

Then the people came out from church. The women had waxed their wooden shoes, the farmers wore new smocks, and with the little bareheaded children skipping along in front of them, all were going home. And till nightfall, five or six men, always the same, stayed playing at corks in front of the large door of the inn.

The winter was severe. Every morning, the windows were covered with rime, and the light that shone through them, dim as through ground-glass, sometimes did not change the whole day long. At four o'clock the lamp had to be lighted.

On fine days she went down into the garden. The dew had left a silver lace on the cabbages with long transparent threads spreading from one to the other. No birds were to be heard; everything seemed asleep, the fruit tree covered with straw, and the vine, like a great sick serpent under the coping of the wall, along which, on drawing near, one saw the many-footed woodlice crawling. Under the spruce by the hedgerow, the curé in the three-cornered hat reading his breviary had lost his right foot, and the very plaster, scaling off with the frost, had left white scabs on his face.

Then she went up again, shut her door, put on coals, and fainting with the heat of the hearth, felt her boredom weigh more heavily than ever. She would have liked to go down and talk to the maid, but a sense of shame restrained her.

Every day at the same time the schoolmaster in a black skull-cap opened the shutters of his house, and the village policeman, wearing his sword over his blouse, passed by. Night and morning the post-horses, three by three, crossed the street to water at the pond. From time to time the bell of a café would tinkle, and when it was windy one could hear the little brass basins that served as signs for the hairdresser's shop creaking on their two rods. The shop was decorated with an old engraving of a fashion-plate stuck against a window-pane and with the wax bust of a woman with yellow hair. He, too, the hairdresser, lamented his wasted calling, his hopeless future, and dreaming of some shop in a big town—at Rouen, for example, overlooking the harbour, near the theatre—he walked up and down all day from the mairie to the church, sombre and waiting for customers. When Madame Bovary looked up, she always saw him there, like a sentinel on duty, with his skull-cap over his ears and his woolen jacket.

Sometimes in the afternoon outside the window of her room, the head of a man appeared, a swarthy head with black whiskers, smiling slowly, with a broad, gentle smile that showed his white teeth. A waltz began, and on the barrel-organ, in a little drawing-room, dancers the size of a finger, women in pink turbans, Tyrolians in jackets, monkeys in frock-coats, gentlemen in knee breeches, turned and turned between the armchairs, the sofas and the tables, reflected in small pieces of mirror that strips of paper held together at the corners. The man turned the handle, looking to the right, to the left and up at the windows. Now and again, while he shot out a long squirt of brown saliva against the milestone, he lifted his instrument with his knee, to relieve his shoulder from the pressure of the hard straps; and now, doleful and drawling, or merry and hurried, the music issued forth from the box, droning through a curtain of pink taffeta underneath an ornate brass grill. They were airs played in other places at the theatres, sung in drawing-rooms, danced to at night under lighted lustres, echoes of the world that reached even to Emma. Endless sarabands ran through her head, and, like an Oriental dancing-girl on the flowers of a carpet, her thoughts leapt with the notes, swung from dream to dream, from sadness to sadness. When the man had caught some pennies in his cap he drew down an old cover of blue cloth, hitched his organ on to his back, and went off with a heavy tread. She watched him going.

But it was above all the meal-times that were unbearable to her, in this small room on the ground-floor, with its smoking stove, its creaking door, the walls that sweated, the damp pavement; all the bitterness of life seemed served up on her plate, and with the smoke of the boiled beef there rose from her secret soul waves of nauseous disgust. Charles was a slow eater; she played with a few nuts, or, leaning on her elbow, amused herself drawing lines along the oil-cloth table-cover with the point of her knife.

She now let everybody in her household go its own way, and the elder Madame Bovary, when she came to spend part of Lent at Tostes, was much surprised at the change. She who was formerly so careful, so dainty, now spent whole days without dressing, wore grey cotton stockings, and used tallow candles to light the house. She kept saying they must be economical since they were not rich, adding that she was very contented, very happy, that Tostes pleased her very much, and other such statements that left her mother-in-law speechless. Besides, Emma no longer seemed inclined to follow her advice; on one occasion, when Madame Bovary had thought fit to maintain that masters ought to keep an eye on the religion of their servants, she had answered with a look so angry and a smile so cold that the old lady preferred to let the matter drop.

Emma was growing difficult, capricious. She ordered dishes for herself, then she did not touch them; one day drank only pure milk, and the next cups of tea by the dozen. Often she persisted in not going out, then, stifling, threw open the windows and put on light dresses. After she had well scolded her maid she gave her presents or sent her out to see neighbors. She sometimes threw beggars all the silver in her purse, although she was by no means tender-hearted or easily accessible to the feelings of others; like most country-bred people, she always retained in her soul something of the horny hardness of the paternal hands.

Towards the end of February old Rouault, in memory of his cure, personally brought a superb turkey to his son-in-law, and stayed three days at Tostes. Charles being with his patients, Emma kept him company. He smoked in the room, spat on the andirons, talked farming, calves, cows, poultry, and municipal council, so that when he left she closed the door on him with a feeling of satisfaction that surprised even herself. Moreover she no longer concealed her contempt for anything or anybody, and at times expressed singular opinions, finding fault with whatever others approved, and approving things perverse and immoral, all of which left her husband wide-eyed.

Would this misery last for ever? Would she never escape from it? Yet she was the equal of all the women who were living happily. She had seen duchesses at Vaubyessard with clumsier waists and commoner ways, and she hated the divine injustice of God. She leant her head against the walls to weep; she longed for lives of adventure, for masked balls, for shameless pleasures that were bound, she thought, to initiate her to ecstacies she had not yet experienced.

She grew pale and suffered from palpitations of the heart. Charles prescribed valerian drops and camphor baths. Everything that was tried only seemed to irritate her the more.

On certain days she chattered with feverish profusion, and this overexcitement was suddenly followed by a state of torpor, in which she remained without speaking, without moving. What then revived her was to pour a bottle of eau-de-cologne over her arms.

As she was constantly complaining about Tostes, Charles fancied that her illness was no doubt due to some local cause, and, struck by this idea, he began to think seriously of setting up practice elsewhere.

From that moment she drank vinegar to lose weight, contracted a sharp little cough, and lost all appetite.

It cost Charles much to give up Tostes after living there four years, just when he was beginning to get somewhere. Yet if it must be! He took her to Rouen to see his old master. It was a nervous condition; she needed a change of air.

After some looking around, Charles discovered that the doctor of a considerable market-town in the arrondissement of Neufchâtel, a former Polish refugee, had vanished a week earlier. Then he wrote to the local pharmacist to ask the size of the population, the distance from the nearest doctor, how much his predecessor had earned in a year, and so forth; and the answer being satisfactory, he made up his mind to move towards the spring, if Emma's health did not improve.

One day when, in view of her departure, she was tidying a drawer, something pricked her finger. It was a wire of her wedding-bouquet. The orange blossoms were yellow with dust and the silver-bordered satin ribbons frayed at the edges. She threw it into the fire. It flared up more quickly than dry straw. Then it was like a red bush in the cinders, slowly shrinking away. She watched it burn. The little pasteboard berries burst, the wire twisted, the gold lace melted; and the shrivelled paper petals, fluttering like black butterflies at the back of the stove, at last flew up the chimney.

When they left Tostes in the month of March, Madame Bovary was pregnant.

Part Two

I

Yonville-l'Abbaye (named after an old Capuchin abbey of which not even the ruins remain), is a market-town some twenty miles from Rouen, between the Abbeville and Beauvais roads. It lies at the foot of a valley watered by the Rieule, a little river that runs into the Andelle after turning three water-mills near its mouth; it contains a few trout and, on Sundays, the village boys entertain themselves by fishing.

Leaving the main road at la Boissière, one reaches the height of les Leux from where the valley comes into view. The river that runs through it has divided the area into two very distinct regions: on the left are pastures, while the right consists of tilled land. The meadow stretches under a bulge of low hills to join at the back with the pasture land of the Bray country, while on the eastern side, the plain, gently rising, broadens out, showing as far as the eye can reach its blond wheatfields. The water, flowing through the grass, divides with a white line the color of the meadows from that of the ploughed fields, and the country is like a great unfolded mantle with a green velvet cape bordered with a fringe of silver.

On the horizon rise the oaks of the forest of Argueil, with the steeps of the Saint-Jean hills scarred from top to bottom with red irregular lines; they are rain-tracks, and these brick-tones standing out in narrow streaks against the grey colour of the mountain are due to the high iron content of the springs that flow beyond in the neighboring country.

These are the confines of Normandy, Picardy, and the Ile-de-France, a mongrel land whose language, like its landscape, is without accent or character. The worst Neufchâtel cheeses in the arrondissement are made here; and, on the other hand, farming is costly because so much manure is needed to enrich this brittle soil, full of sand and stones.

Up to 1835 no practicable road for getting to Yonville existed, but about this time a cross-road was cut, joining the Abbeville to the Amiens highway; it is occasionally used by the Rouen teamsters on their way to Flanders. Yonville-l'Abbaye has remained stationary in spite of its "new outlet." Instead of improving the soil they persist in keeping up the pasture lands, however depreciated they may be in value, and the lazy village, growing away from the plain, has naturally spread riverwards. It is seen from afar sprawling along the banks like a cowherd taking a nap by the side of the river.

At the foot of the hill beyond the bridge begins a roadway, planted with young aspens that leads in a straight line to the first houses in the place. These, fenced in by hedges, are in the middle of courtyards full of straggling buildings, wine-presses, cart-sheds, and distilleries scattered under thick trees, with ladders, poles, or scythes hooked over the branches. The thatched roofs, like fur caps drawn over eyes, reach down over about a third of the low windows, whose coarse convex glasses have bull's eyes in the middle, like the bottom of a bottle. A meagre pear-tree may be found leaning against some plaster wall crossed by black beams, and one enters the ground-floors through a door with a small swing-gate that keeps out the chicks when they pilfer, on the threshold, crumbs of bread steeped in cider. Gradually the courtyards grow narrower, the houses closer together, and the fences disappear; a bundle of ferns swings under a window from the end of a broomstick; there is a blacksmith's forge and then a wheelwright's, with two or three new carts outside that partly block the way. Then across an open space appears a white house at the end of a round lawn ornamented by a Cupid, his finger on his lips. Two cast-iron jars flank the high porch, copper signs gleam on the door. It is the notary's house, the finest in the place.

The church is on the other side of the street, twenty paces farther down, at the entrance of the square. The little graveyard that surrounds it, closed in by a breast-high wall, is so full of graves that the old stones, level with the ground, form a continuous pavement, on which the grass has, by itself, marked out regular green squares. The church was rebuilt during the last years of the reign of Charles X.[24] The wooden roof is beginning to rot from the top, and here and there black hollows appear in the blue paint. Over the door, where the organ should be, is a gallery for the men, with a spiral staircase that reverberates under the weight of their wooden shoes.

The daylight coming through the plain glass windows falls obliquely upon the pews perpendicular to the walls, here and there adorned with a straw mat inscribed, in large letters, with the name of some parishioner. Further on, where the nave grows narrow, the confessional faces a small Madonna, clothed in satin, wearing a tulle veil sprinkled with silver stars and with cheeks stained red like an idol of the Sandwich Islands;[25] finally, a painted copy entitled "The Holy Family, a gift from the Minister of the Interior," flanked

24. Charles X (1757–1836), son of Louis XV, was the last Bourbon king; he was expelled by the July Revolution (1830).

25. Sandwich Islands is the old name for Hawaii. They were named after John Montagu, fourth Earl of Sandwich (1718–1792) who served as first Lord of Admiralty when the islands were discovered.

by four candlesticks, crowns the main altar and rounds off the view. The choir stalls, of pine wood, have been left unpainted.

The market, that is to say, a tiled roof supported by some twenty posts, occupies by itself about half the public square of Yonville. The town hall, constructed "after the designs of a Paris architect," is a sort of Greek temple that forms the corner next to the pharmacy. On the ground-floor are three Ionic columns and on the first floor a gallery with arched windows, while the crowning frieze is occupied by a Gallic cock, resting one foot upon the Charter[26] and holding in the other the scales of Justice.

But what catches the eye most of all is Mr. Homais' pharmacy, right across from the Lion d'Or. In the evening especially its lamp is lit up and the red and green jars that embellish his shop-front cast their colored reflection far across the street; beyond them, as in a Bengal light, the silhouette of the pharmacist can be seen leaning over his desk. His house is plastered from top to bottom with inscriptions written in longhand, in round, in lower case: "Vichy, Seltzer and Barrège waters, depurative gum drops, Raspail patent medicine, Arabian racahout, Darcet lozenges, Regnault ointment, trusses, baths, laxative chocolate, etc." And the signboard, which stretches all the breadth of the shop, bears in gold letters "Homais, Pharmacist." Then at the back of the shop, behind the great scales fixed to the counter, the word "Laboratory" appears on a scroll above a glass door on which, about half-way up, the word Homais is once more repeated in gold letters on a black ground.

Beyond this there is nothing to see at Yonville. The street (the only one) a gunshot long and flanked by a few shops on either side stops short at the turn of the high road. Turning right and following the foot of the Saint-Jean hills one soon reaches the graveyard.

At the time of the cholera epidemic, a piece of wall was pulled down and three acres of land purchased in order to make more room, but the new area is almost deserted; the tombs, as heretofore, continue to crowd together towards the gate. The keeper, who is at once gravedigger and church sexton (thus making a double profit out of the parish corpses), has taken advantage of the unused plot of ground to plant potatoes. From year to year, however, his small field grows smaller, and when there is an epidemic, he does not know whether to rejoice at the deaths or regret the added graves.

"You feed on the dead, Lestiboudois!" the curé told him one day.

This grim remark made him reflect; it checked him for some time; but to this day he carries on the cultivation of his little tubers, and even maintains stoutly that they grow naturally.

Since the events about to be narrated, nothing in fact has changed at Yonville. The tin tricolour flag still swings at the top of

26. The *Charte constitutionelle de la France*, basis of the French constitution after the Revolution, bestowed in 1814 by Louis XVIII and revised in 1830, after the downfall of Charles X.

the church-steeple; the two streamers at the novelty store still flutter in the wind; the spongy white lumps, the pharmacist's foetuses, rot more and more in their cloudy alcohol, and above the big door of the inn the old golden lion, faded by rain, still shows passers-by its poodle mane.

On the evening when the Bovarys were to arrive at Yonville, the widow Lefrançois, the landlady of this inn, was so busy that she sweated great drops as she moved her saucepans around. To-morrow was market-day. The meat had to be cut beforehand, the chickens drawn, the soup and coffee made. Moreover, she had the boarders' meal to see to, and that of the doctor, his wife, and their maid; the billiard-room was echoing with bursts of laughter; three millers in the small parlour were calling for brandy; the wood was blazing, the charcoal crackling, and on the long kitchen-table, amid the quarters of raw mutton, rose piles of plates that rattled with the shaking of the block on which spinach was being chopped. From the poultry-yard was heard the screaming of the chickens whom the servant was chasing in order to wring their necks.

A slightly pockmarked man in green leather slippers, and wearing a velvet cap with a gold tassel, was warming his back at the chimney. His face expressed nothing but self-satisfaction, and he appeared as calmly established in life as the gold-finch suspended over his head in its wicker cage: he was the pharmacist.

"Artémise!" shouted the innkeeper, "chop some wood, fill the water bottles, bring some brandy, hurry up! If only I knew what dessert to offer the guests you are expecting! Good heavens! Those furniture-movers are beginning their racket in the billiard-room again; and their van has been left before the front door! The 'Hirondelle' might crash into it when it draws up. Call Polyte and tell him to put it away . . . Imagine, Monsieur Homais, that since morning they have had about fifteen games, and drunk eight pots of cider! . . . Why they'll tear my billiard-cloth to pieces!" she went on, looking at them from a distance, her strainer in her hand.

"That wouldn't be much of a loss," replied Monsieur Homais. "You would buy another."

"Another billiard-table!" exclaimed the widow.

"Since that one is coming to pieces, Madame Lefrançois. I tell you again you are doing yourself harm, much harm! And besides, players now want narrow pockets and heavy cues. They don't play the way they used to, everything is changed! One must keep pace with the times! Just look at Tellier!"

The hostess grew red with anger. The pharmacist added:

"You may say what you like; his table is better than yours; and if one were to think, for example, of getting up a patriotic tournament for Polish independence or for the victims of the Lyon floods . . ."[27]

"It isn't beggars like him that'll frighten us," interrupted the landlady, shrugging her fat shoulders. "Come, come, Monsieur Homais; as long as the 'Lion d'Or' exists people will come to it. We are no fly-by-nights, we have feathered our nest! While one of these days you'll find the 'Café Français' closed with a fine poster on the shutters. Change my billiard-table!" she went on, speaking to herself, "the table that comes in so handy for folding the washing, and on which, in the hunting season, I have slept six visitors! . . . But what can be keeping the slowpoke of a Hivert?"

"Are you waiting for him to serve your gentlemen's dinner?"

"Wait for him! And what about Monsieur Binet? As the clock strikes six you'll see him come in, for he hasn't his equal under the sun for punctuality. He must always have his seat in the small parlour. He'd rather die than eat anywhere else. And he is finicky! and particular about his cider! Not like monsieur Léon; he sometimes comes at seven, or even half-past, and he doesn't so much as look at what he eats. Such a nice young man! Never speaks a cross word!"

"Well, you see, there's a great difference between an educated man and a former army man who is now a tax-collector."

Six o'clock struck. Binet came in.

He was dressed in a blue frock-coat falling in a straight line round his thin body, and his leather cap, with its lappets knotted over the top of his head with string, showed under the turned-up peak a bald forehead, flattened by the constant wearing of a helmet. He wore a black cloth vest, a hair collar, grey trousers, and, all the year round, well-blacked boots, that had two parallel swellings where the big toes protruded. Not a hair stood out from the regular line of fair whiskers, which, encircling his jaws, framed like a garden border his long, wan face, with smallish eyes and a hooked nose. Clever at all games of cards, a good hunter, and writing a fine hand, he had at home a lathe, and amused himself by turning napkin-rings, with which he crammed his house, jealous as an artist and selfish as a bourgeois.

He went to the small parlour, but the three millers had to be got out first, and during the whole time necessary for resetting the table, Binet remained silent in his place near the stove. Then he shut the door and took off his cap as usual.

"Politeness will not wear out his tongue," said the pharmacist, as soon as he was alone with the hostess.

"He never talks more," she replied. "Last week I had two travel-

27. The allusion dates the action of the novel as taking place in 1840; during the winter of 1840, the Rhône overflowed with catastrophic results. At the same time, Louis Philippe was under steady attack for his failure to offer sufficient assistance to the victims of the repression that followed the insurrection of Warsaw (1831).

ling salesmen here selling cloth, really a cheerful pair, who spent the night telling jokes. They made me weep with laughter but he, he stood there mute as a fish, never opened his mouth."

"Yes," said the pharmacist, "no imagination, no wit, nothing that makes a man shine in society."

"Yet they say he is a man of means," objected the landlady.

"Of means?" replied the pharmacist. "He? In his own line, perhaps," he added in a calmer tone. And he went on:

"Now, that a businessman with numerous connections, a lawyer, a doctor, a pharmacist, should be thus absent-minded, that they should become whimsical or even peevish, I can understand; such cases are cited in history. But at least it is because they are thinking of something. How often hasn't it happened to me, for instance, to look on my desk for my pen when I had to write out a label, merely to discover, at last, that I had put it behind my ear?"

Madame Lefrançois just then went to the door to see if the "Hirondelle" was not coming. She started. A man dressed in black suddenly came into the kitchen. By the last gleam of the twilight one could see that he was red-faced and powerfully built.

"What can I do for you, Monsieur le curé?" asked the hostess, as she reached down a copper candlestick from the row of candles. "Will you have something to drink? A thimbleful of *Cassis?* A glass of wine?"

The priest declined very politely. He had come for his umbrella, that he had forgotten the other day at the Ernemont convent, and after asking Madame Lefrançois to have it sent to him at the rectory in the evening, he left for the church; the Angelus was ringing.

When the pharmacist no longer heard the noise of his boots along the square, he confessed that he had found the priest's behaviour just now very unbecoming. This refusal to take any refreshment seemed to him the most odious hypocrisy; all priests tippled on the sly, and were trying to bring back the days of the tithe.

The landlady took up the defence of her curé.

"Besides, he could double up four men like you over his knee. Last year he helped our people to bring in the hay, he carried as many as six bales at once, he is so strong."

"Bravo!" said the pharmacist. "Now just send your daughters to confess to such vigorous fellows! I, if I were the Government, I'd have the priests bled once a month. Yes, Madame Lefrançois, every month—a good phlebotomy, in the interests of the police and morals."

"Be quiet, Monsieur Homais. You are a godless man! You have no religion."

The chemist replied:

"I have a religion, my religion, and I even have more than all these others with their mummeries and their juggling. I adore God, on the contrary. I believe in the Supreme Being, in a Creator, whatever he may be. I care little who has placed us here below to fulfill our duties as citizens and parents; but I don't need to go to church to kiss silver plates, and fatten, out of my pocket, a lot of good-for-nothings who live better than we do. For one can know him as well in a wood, in a field, or even contemplating the ethereal heavens like the ancients. My God is the God of Socrates, of Franklin, of Voltaire, and of Béranger! I support the *Profession de Foi du Vicaire savoyard*[28] and the immortal principles of '89! And I can't admit of an old boy of a God who takes walks in his garden with a cane in his hand, who lodges his friends in the belly of whales, dies uttering a cry, and rises again at the end of three days; things absurd in themselves, and completely opposed, moreover, to all physical laws, which proves to us, by the way, that priests have always wallowed in squalid ignorance, and tried to drag whole nations down after them."

He stopped, looked around as if expecting to find an audience, for in his enthusiasm the pharmacist had for a moment fancied himself in the midst of the town council. But the landlady no longer heard him; she was listening to a distant rolling. One could distinguish the noise of a carriage mingled with the clattering of loose horseshoes that beat against the ground, and at last the "Hirondelle" stopped at the door.

It was a yellow box on two large wheels, that, reaching to the tilt, prevented travellers from seeing the road and dirtied their shoulders. The small panes of narrow windows rattled in their frames when the coach was closed, and retained here and there patches of mud amid the old layers of dust, that not even storms of rain had altogether washed away. It was drawn by three horses, the first a leader, and when it came down-hill its lower side jolted against the ground.

Some of the inhabitants of Yonville came out into the square; they all spoke at once, asking for news, for explanations of the delay, for their orders. Hivert did not know whom to answer first. He ran the errands in town for the entire village. He went to the shops and brought back rolls of leather for the shoemaker, old iron for the farrier, a barrel of herrings for his mistress, hats from the hat-shop and wigs from the hairdresser, and all along the road on his return journey he distributed his parcels, throwing them over fences as he stood upright on his seat and shouted at the top of his voice, while his horses went their own way.

An accident had delayed him. Madame Bovary's greyhound had escaped across the field. They had whistled for him a quarter of an

28. *Profession du Foi du Vicaire savoyard* (1762) is Rousseau's declaration of faith in God, a religion of his heart, coupled with a criticism of revealed religion. It is included in Book IV of his pedagogic treatise *Émile* but was frequently reprinted as an independent pamphlet.

hour; Hivert had even gone back a mile and a half expecting every moment to catch sight of her; but they had been forced to resume the journey. Emma had wept, grown angry; she had accused Charles of this misfortune. Monsieur Lheureux, a draper, who happened to be in the coach with her, had tried to console her by a number of examples of lost dogs recognising their masters at the end of long years. He had been told of one, he said, who had come back to Paris from Constantinople. Another had gone one hundred and fifty miles in a straight line, and swum four rivers; and his own father had owned a poodle, which, after twelve years of absence, had all of a sudden jumped on his back in the street as he was going to dine in town.

II

Emma got out first, then Félicité, Monsieur Lheureux, and a nurse, and they had to wake up Charles in his corner, where he had slept soundly since night set in.

Homais introduced himself; he offered his homages to madame and his respects to monsieur; said he was charmed to have been able to render them some slight service, and added cordially that he had taken the liberty to join them at dinner, his wife being away.

When Madame Bovary entered the kitchen she went up to the fireplace. With two fingertips she caught her dress at the knee, and having thus pulled it up to her ankle, held out her black-booted foot to the fire above the revolving leg of mutton. The flame lit up the whole of her, casting its harsh light over the pattern of her gown, the fine pores of her fair skin, and even her eyelids, when she blinked from time to time. A great red glow passed over her with the wind, blowing through the half-open door.

On the other side of the fireplace, a fair-haired young man watched her in silence.

As he was frequently bored at Yonville, where he was a clerk at Maître Guilleumin, the notary, Monsieur Léon Dupuis (the second of the *Lion d'Or*'s daily customers) often delayed his dinner-hour in the hope that some traveller might come to the inn, with whom he could chat in the evening. On the days when his work was done early, he had, for want of something else to do, to come punctually, and endure from soup to cheese a *tête-à-tête* with Binet. It was therefore with delight that he accepted the hostess's suggestion that he should dine in company with the newcomers, and they passed into the large parlour where Madame Lefrançois, hoping to make an impression, had had the table laid for four.

Homais asked to be allowed to keep on his skull-cap, for fear of catching cold; then, turning to his neighbor:

"Madame is no doubt a little fatigued; one gets so frightfully shaken up in our *Hirondelle*."

"That is true," replied Emma; "but moving about always amuses me. I like a change."

"It is so tedious," sighed the clerk, "to be always riveted to the same places."

"If you were like me," said Charles, "constantly obliged to be in the saddle" . . .

"But," Léon went on, addressing himself to Madame Bovary, "nothing, it seems to me, is more pleasant—when one can," he added.

"Moreover," said the pharmacist, "the practice of medicine is not very hard work in our part of the world, for the state of our roads allows us the use of gigs, and generally, as the farmers are well off, they pay pretty well. We have, medically speaking, besides the ordinary cases of enteritis, bronchitis, bilious affections, &c., now and then a few intermittent fevers at harvest-time; but on the whole, little of a serious nature, nothing special to note, unless it be a great deal of scrofula, due, no doubt, to the deplorable hygienic conditions of our peasant dwellings. Ah! you will find many prejudices to combat, Monsieur Bovary, much obstinacy of routine, with which all the efforts of your science will daily come into collision; for people still have recourse to novenas, to relics, to the priest, rather than come straight to the doctor or the pharmacist. The climate, however, is truly not too bad, and we even have a few nonagenarians in our parish. The thermometer (I have made some observations) falls in winter to 4 degrees, and in the hottest season rises to 25 or 30 degrees Centigrade at the outside, which gives us 24 degrees Réaumur as the maximum, or otherwise stated 54 degrees Fahrenheit (English scale), not more. And, as a matter of fact, we are sheltered from the north winds by the forest of Argueil on the one side, from the west winds by the Saint Jean hills on the other; and this heat, moreover, which, on account of the watery vapours given off by the river and the considerable number of cattle in the fields, which, as you know, exhale much ammonia, that is to say, nitrogen, hydrogen, and oxygen (no, nitrogen and hydrogen alone), and which sucking up the humus from the soil, mixing together all those different emanations, unites them into a single bundle, so to speak, and combining with the electricity diffused through the atmosphere, when there is any, might in the long-run, as in tropical countries, engender poisonous fumes,—this heat, I say, finds itself perfectly tempered on the side from where it comes, or rather from where it ought to come, that is the south side, by the south-eastern winds, which, having cooled themselves in crossing the Seine, reach us sometimes all at once like blasts from Russia!"

"Do you at least have some walks in the neighborhood?" continued Madame Bovary, speaking to the young man.

"Oh, very few," he answered. "There is a place they call La Pâture, on the top of the hill, on the edge of the forest. Sometimes, on Sundays, I go and stay there with a book, watching the sunset."

"I think there is nothing so beautiful as sunsets," she resumed; "but especially by the seashore."

"Oh, I love the sea!" said Monsieur Léon.

"And doesn't it seem to you," continued Madame Bovary, "that the mind travels more freely on this limitless expanse, of which the contemplation elevates the soul, gives ideas of the infinite, the ideal?"

"It is the same with mountainous landscapes," continued Léon. "A cousin of mine who travelled in Switzerland last year told me that one could not picture to oneself the poetry of the lakes, the charm of the waterfalls, the gigantic effect of the glaciers. One sees pines of incredible size across torrents, cottages suspended over precipices, and, a thousand feet below one, whole valleys when the clouds open. Such spectacles must stir to enthusiasm, incline to prayer, to ecstasy; and I no longer wonder why a celebrated musician, in order to stimulate his imagination, was in the habit of playing the piano before some imposing view."

"Do you play?" she asked.

"No, but I am very fond of music," he replied.

"Ah! don't you listen to him, Madame Bovary," interrupted Homais, bending over his plate. "That's sheer modesty. Why, my friend, the other day in your room you were singing 'L'Ange Gardien[29] to perfection. I heard you from the laboratory. You articulated with the skill of an actor."

Léon rented a small room at the pharmacist's, on the second floor overlooking the Square. He blushed at the compliment of his landlord, who had already turned to the doctor, and was enumerating to him, one after the other, all the principal inhabitants of Yonville. He was telling anecdotes, giving information; no one knew just how wealthy the notary was and there were, of course, the Tuvaches who put up a considerable front.

Emma continued, "And what music do you prefer?"

"Oh, German music; that which makes you dream."

"Have you been to the opera?"

"Not yet; but I shall go next year, when I'll be living in Paris to get a law degree."

"As I had the honour of putting it to your husband," said the pharmacist, "with regard to this poor Yanoda who has run away, you will find yourself, thanks to his extravagance, in the possession of one of the most comfortable houses of Yonville. Its greatest convenience for a doctor is a door giving on the Walk, where one

29. A sentimental romance written by Mme. Pauline Duchambre, author of several such songs that appeared in the keepsakes.

can go in and out unseen. Moreover, it contains everything that is useful in a household—a laundry, kitchen with pantry, sitting-room, fruit bins, etc. He was a gay dog, who didn't care what he spent. At the end of the garden, by the side of the water, he had an arbour built just for the purpose of drinking beer in summer; and if madame is fond of gardening she will be able . . . "

"My wife doesn't care to," said Charles; "although she has been advised to take exercise, she prefers always sitting in her room reading."

"Just like me," replied Léon. "And indeed, what is better than to sit by one's fireside in the evening with a book, while the wind beats against the window and the lamp is burning? . . ."

"What, indeed?" she said, fixing her large black eyes wide open upon him.

"One thinks of nothing," he continued; "the hours slip by. Without having to move, we walk through the countries of our imagination, and your thought, blending with the fiction, toys with the details, follows the outline of the adventures. It mingles with the characters, and it seems you are living their lives, that your own heart beats in their breast."

"That is true! that is true!" she said.

"Has it ever happened to you," Léon went on, "to discover some vague idea of one's own in a book, some dim image that comes back to you from afar, and as the fullest expression of your own slightest sentiment?"

"I have experienced it," she replied.

"That is why," he said, "I especially love the poets. I think verse more tender than prose, and that it makes one weep more easily."

"Still in the long-run it is tiring," continued Emma, "and now, on the contrary, I have come to love stories that rush breathlessly along, that frighten one. I detest commonplace heroes and moderate feelings, as one finds them in nature."

"You are right," observed the clerk, "since these works fail to touch the heart, they miss, it seems to me, the true end of art. It is so sweet, amid all the disenchantments of life, to be able to dwell in thought upon noble characters, pure affections, and pictures of happiness. For myself, living here far from the world, this is my one distraction. But there is so little to do in Yonville!"

"Like Tostes, no doubt," replied Emma; "and so I always subscribed to a lending library."

"If madame will do me the honor of making use of it," said the pharmacist, who had just caught the last words, "I have at her disposal a library composed of the best authors, Voltaire, Rousseau, Delille,[30] Walter Scott, the 'Echo des Feuilletons'; and in addition I

30. Jacques Delille (1738–1813) wrote idyllic descriptive poems; *Les Jardins* (1782) is best known.

receive various periodicals, among them the 'Fanal de Rouen' daily, being privileged to act as its correspondent for the districts of Buchy, Forges, Neufchâtel, Yonville, and vicinity."

They had been at the table for two hours and a half, for Artémise, the maid, listlessly dragged her slippered feet over the tile-floor, brought in the plates one by one, forgot everything, understood nothing and constantly left the door of the billiard-room half open, so that the handle kept beating against the wall with its hooks.

Unconsciously, Léon, while talking, had placed his foot on one of the bars of the chair on which Madame Bovery was sitting. She wore a small blue silk necktie, which held upright, stiff as a ruff, a pleated batiste collar, and with the movements of her head the lower part of her face gently sunk into the linen or rose from it. Thus side by side, while Charles and the pharmacist chatted, they entered into one of those vague conversations where the hazard of all that is said brings you back to the fixed centre of a common sympathy. The Paris theatres, titles of novels, new quadrilles, and the world they did not know; Tostes, where she had lived, and Yonville, where they were; they examined all, talked of everything till the end of dinner.

When coffee was served Félicité left to prepare the room in the new house, and the guests soon rose from the table. Madame Lefrançois was asleep near the cinders, while the stable-boy, lantern in hand, was waiting to show Monsieur and Madame Bovary the way home. Bits of straw stuck in his red hair, and his left leg had a limp. When he had taken in his other hand the curé's umbrella, they started.

The town was asleep; the pillars of the market threw great shadows; the earth was all grey as on a summer's night.

But as the doctor's house was only some fifty paces from the inn, they had to say good-night almost immediately, and the company dispersed.

As soon as she entered the hallway, Emma felt the cold of the plaster fall about her shoulders like damp linen. The walls were new and the wooden stairs creaked. In their bedroom, on the first floor, a whitish light passed through the curtainless windows. She could catch glimpses of tree-tops, and beyond, the fields, half-drowned in the fog that lay like smoke over the course of the river. In the middle of the room, pell-mell, were scattered drawers, bottles, curtain-rods, gilt poles, with mattresses on the chairs and basins on the floor—the two men who had brought the furniture had left everything about carelessly.

This was the fourth time that she had slept in a strange place. The first was the day she went to the convent; the second, of her arrival at Tostes; the third, at Vaubyessard; and this was the fourth; and it so happened that each one had marked in her life a new beginning. She did not believe that things could remain the same in different places, and since the portion of her life that lay behind her had been bad, no doubt that which remained to be lived would be better.

III

The next day, as she was getting up, she saw the clerk on the Place. She had on a dressing-gown. He looked up and bowed. She nodded quickly and reclosed the window.

Léon waited all day for six o'clock in the evening to come, but on going to the inn, he found only Monsieur Binet already seated at the table.

The dinner of the evening before had been a considerable event for him; he had never till then talked for two hours consecutively to a "lady." How then had he been able to express, and in such language, so many things that he could not have said so well before? He was usually shy, and maintained that reserve which partakes at once of modesty and dissimulation. At Yonville, his manners were generally admired. He listened to the opinions of the older people, and seemed to have moderate political views, a rare thing for a young man. Then he had some accomplishments; he painted in water-colours, could read music, and readily talked literature after dinner when he did not play cards. Monsieur Homais respected him for his education; Madame Homais liked him for his good-nature, for he often took the little Homais into the garden—little brats who were always dirty, very much spoilt, and somewhat slow-moving, like their mother. They were looked after by the maid and by Justin, the pharmacist's apprentice, a second cousin of Monsieur Homais, who had been taken into the house out of charity and was also being put to work as a servant.

The druggist proved the best of neighbors. He advised Madame Bovary as to the tradespeople, sent expressly for his own cider merchant, tasted the wine himself, and saw that the casks were properly placed in the cellar; he explained how to stock up cheaply on butter, and made an arrangement with Lestiboudois, the sacristan, who, besides his ecclesiastical and funereal functions, looked after the main gardens at Yonville by the hour or the year, according to the wishes of the customers.

The need of looking after others was not the only thing that urged the pharmacist to such obsequious cordiality; there was a plan underneath it all.

He had infringed the law of the 19th Ventôse, year xi., article 1,[31] which forbade all persons not having a diploma to practise medicine; so that, after certain anonymous denunciations, Homais had

31. Ventôse ("windy") was the sixth month of the calendar established by the French Republic (from February 19 to March 20). The government of the Republic made the new year begin on September 22, 1792; thus the Year xi is 1801, and the 19th Ventôse March 10.

been summoned to Rouen to see the royal prosecutor in his private office; the magistrate receiving him standing up, ermine on shoulder and cap on head. It was in the morning, before the court opened. In the corridors one heard the heavy boots of the gendarmes walking past, and like a far-off noise great locks that were shut. The druggist's ears tingled as if he were about to have a stroke; he saw the depths of dungeons, his family in tears, his shop sold, all the jars dispersed; and he was obliged to enter a café and take a glass of rum and soda water to recover his spirits.

Little by little the memory of this reprimand grew fainter, and he continued, as heretofore, to give anodyne consultations in his back-parlour. But the mayor resented it, his colleagues were jealous, he had everything and everyone to fear; gaining over Monsieur Bovary by his attentions was to earn his gratitude, and prevent his speaking out later on, should he notice anything. So every morning Homais brought him the paper, and often in the afternoon left his shop for a few moments to have a chat with the Doctor.

Charles was depressed: he had no patients. He remained seated for hours without speaking, went into his consulting-room to sleep, or watched his wife sewing. Then for diversion he tried to work as a handyman around the house; he even tried to decorate the attic with some paint that had been left behind by the painters. But money matters worried him. He had spent so much for repairs at Tostes, for madame's toilette, and for the moving, that the whole dowry, over three thousand écus, had slipped away in two years. Then how many things had been spoilt or lost during their move from Tostes to Yonville, without counting the plaster curé, who, thrown out of the carriage by a particularly severe jolt, had broken in a thousand pieces on the pavement of Quincampoix!

A more positive worry came to distract him, namely, the pregnancy of his wife. As the time of birth approached he cherished her more. It was another bond of the flesh between them, and, as it were, a continued sentiment of a more complex union. When he caught sight of her indolent walk or watched her figure filling out over her uncorseted hips, when he had the opportunity to look at her undisturbed taking tired poses in her armchair, then his happiness knew no bounds; he got up, embraced her, passed his hands over her face, called her little mamma, wanted to make her dance, and, half-laughing, half-crying, uttered all kinds of caressing pleasantries that came into his head. The idea of having begotten a child delighted him. Now he wanted nothing more. He knew all there was to know of human life and sat down to enjoy it serenely, his elbows planted on the table as for a good meal.

Emma at first felt a great astonishment; then was anxious to be delivered that she might know what it felt like to be a mother. But not being able to spend as much as she would have liked on a suspended cradle with rose silk curtains, and embroidered caps, in a fit of bitterness she gave up looking for the layette altogether and had it all made by a village seamstress, without choosing or discussing anything.

Thus she did not amuse herself with those preparations that stimulate the tenderness of mothers, and so her affection was perhaps impaired from the start.

As Charles, however, spoke of the baby at every meal, she soon began to think of him more steadily.

She hoped for a son; he would be strong and dark; she would call him George; and this idea of having a male child was like an expected revenge for all her impotence in the past. A man, at least, is free; he can explore all passions and all countries, overcome obstacles, taste of the most distant pleasures. But a woman is always hampered. Being inert as well as pliable, she has against her the weakness of the flesh and the inequity of the law. Like the veil held to her hat by a ribbon, her will flutters in every breeze; she is always drawn by some desire, restrained by some rule of conduct.

She gave birth on a Sunday at about six o'clock, as the sun was rising.

"It is a girl!" said Charles.

She turned her head away and fainted.

Madame Homais, as well as Madame Lefrançois of the Lion d'Or, almost immediately came running in to embrace her. The pharmacist, as a man of discretion, only offered a few provisional felicitations through the half-opened door. He asked to see the child, and thought it well made.

During her recovery, she spent much time seeking a name for her daughter. First she went over all names that have Italian endings, such as Clara, Louisa, Amanda, Atala; she liked Galsuinde pretty well, and Yseult or Léocadie still better. Charles wanted the child to be called after her mother; Emma opposed this. They ran over the calendar from end to end, and then consulted outsiders.

"Monsieur Léon," said the chemist, "with whom I was talking about it the other day, wonders why you do not choose Madeleine. It is very much in fashion just now."

But Monsieur Bovary's mother protested loudly against this name of a sinner. As to Monsieur Homais, he had a preference for all names that recalled some great man, an illustrious fact, or a generous idea, and it was in accordance with this system that he had baptized his four children. Thus Napoleon represented glory and Franklin liberty; Irma was perhaps a concession to romanticism, but Athalie[32] was a homage to the greatest masterpiece of the French stage. For his philosophical convictions did not interfere with his

32. *Athalie* is a tragedy by Jean Racine (1639–1699) written in 1691 for the pupils of Saint-Cyr. Racine had abandoned the regular stage after a spiritual crisis and wrote two sacred tragedies *Esther* and *Athalie* for the young girls of Saint-Cyr.

artistic tastes; in him the thinker did not stifle the man of sentiment; he could make distinctions, make allowances for imagination and fanaticism. In this tragedy, for example, he found fault with the ideas, but admired the style; he detested the conception, but applauded all the details, and loathed the characters while he grew enthusiastic over their dialogue. When he read the fine passages he was transported, but when he thought that the Catholics would use it to their advantage, he was disconsolate; and in this confusion of sentiments in which he was involved he would have liked both to crown Racine with both his hands and take him to task for a good quarter of an hour.

At last Emma remembered that at the château of Vaubyessard she had heard the Marquise call a young lady Berthe; from that moment this name was chosen; and as old Rouault could not come, Monsieur Homais was requested to be godfather. His gifts were all products from his establishment, to wit: six boxes of jujubes, a whole jar of racahout, three cakes of marsh-mallow paste, and six sticks of sugar-candy that he had come across in a cupboard. On the evening of the ceremony there was a grand dinner; the curé was present; there was much excitement. Towards liqueur time, Monsieur Homais began singing "Le Dieu des bonnes gens."[33] Monsieur Léon sang a barcarolle, and the elder Madame Bovary, who was godmother, a romance of the time of the Empire; finally, M. Bovary, senior, insisted on having the child brought down, and began baptizing it with a glass of champagne that he poured over its head. This mockery of the first of the sacraments aroused the indignation of the Abbé Bournisien; Father Bovary replied by a quotation from "La Guerre des Dieux";[34] the curé wanted to leave; the ladies implored, Homais interfered; they succeeded in making the priest sit down again, and he quietly went on with the half-finished coffee in his saucer.

Monsieur Bovary père stayed at Yonville a month, dazzling the natives by a superb soldier's cap with silver tassels that he wore in the morning when he smoked his pipe in the square. Being also in the habit of drinking a good deal of brandy, he often sent the servant to the Lion d'Or to buy him a bottle, which was put down to his son's account, and to perfume his handkerchiefs he used up his daughter-in-law's whole supply of eau-de-cologne.

The latter did not at all dislike his company. He had knocked about the world, he talked about Berlin, Vienna, and Strasbourg, of his soldier times, of his mistresses, of the brilliant dinner-parties he had attended; then he was amiable, and sometimes even, either on the stairs or in the garden, would catch her by the waist, exclaiming:

33. "Le Dieu des Bonnes Gens" is a deistic song by Béranger (see p. 757, n.5).

34. "La Guerre des Dieux" ("The War of the Gods") is a satirical poem by Evarite-Désiré Deforge (later Viscount de Parny, 1753–1814) published in 1799. It ridicules the Christian religion.

"Charles, you better watch out!"

Then the elder Madame Bovary became alarmed for her son's happiness, and fearing that her husband might in the long run have an immoral influence upon the ideas of the young woman, she speeded up their departure. Perhaps she had more serious reasons for uneasiness. Monsieur Bovary was the man to stop at nothing.

One day Emma was suddenly seized with the desire to see her little girl, who had been put to nurse with the carpenter's wife, and, without looking at the calendar to see whether the six weeks of the Virgin[35] were yet passed, she set out for the Rollets' house, situated at the extreme end of the village, between the highroad and the fields.

It was mid-day, the shutters of the houses were closed, and the slate roofs that glittered beneath the fierce light of the blue sky seemed to strike sparks from the crest of their gables. A heavy wind was blowing; Emma felt weak as she walked; the stones of the pavement hurt her; she was doubtful whether she would not go home again, or enter somewhere to rest.

At that moment Monsieur Léon came out from a neighboring door with a bundle of papers under his arm. He came to greet her, and stood in the shade in front of Lheureux's shop under the projecting grey awning.

Madame Bovary said she was going to see her baby, but that she was getting tired.

"If . . ." said Léon, not daring to go on.

"Have you any business to attend to?" she asked.

And on the clerk's negative answer, she begged him to accompany her. That same evening this was known in Yonville, and Madame Tuvache, the mayor's wife, declared in the presence of her maid that Madame Bovary was jeopardizing her good name.

To get to the nurse's it was necessary to turn to the left on leaving the street, as if heading for the cemetery, and to follow between little houses and yards a small path bordered with privet hedges. They were in bloom, and so were the speedwells, eglantines, thistles, and the sweetbriar that sprang up from the thickets. Through openings in the hedges one could see into the huts, some pig on a dung-heap, or tethered cows rubbing their horns against the trunk of trees. The two, side by side, walked slowly, she leaning upon him, and he restraining his pace, which he regulated by hers; in front of them flies were buzzing in the warm air.

They recognised the house by an old walnut-tree which shaded it. Low and covered with brown tiles, there hung outside it, beneath the attic-window, a string of onions. Faggots upright against a thorn fence surrounded a bed of lettuces, a few square feet of lavender,

35. Originally the six weeks that separate Christmas from Purification (Feb. 2nd); in those days, the normal period of confinement for a woman after childbirth.

and sweet peas strung on sticks. Dirty water was running here and there on the grass, and all round were several indefinite rags, knitted stockings, a red flannel undershirt, and a large sheet of coarse linen spread over the hedge. At the noise of the gate the wet nurse appeared with a baby she was suckling on one arm. With her other hand she was pulling along a poor puny little boy, his face covered with a scrofulous rash, the son of a Rouen hosier, whom his parents, too taken up with their business, left in the country.

"Go in," she said; "your baby is there asleep."

The room on the ground-floor, the only one in the dwelling, had at its farther end, against the wall, a large bed without curtains, while a kneading-trough took up the side by the window, one pane of which was mended with a piece of blue paper. In the corner behind the door, shining hob-nailed shoes stood in a row under the slab of the washstand, near a bottle of oil with a feather stuck in its mouth; a Mathieu Laensberg[36] lay on the dusty mantelpiece amid gunflints, candle-ends, and bits of tinder. Finally, the last extravagance in the room was a picture representing Fame blowing her trumpets, cut out, no doubt, from some perfumer's prospectus and nailed to the wall with six wooden shoe-pegs.

Emma's child was asleep in a wicker-cradle. She took it up in the wrapping that enveloped it and began singing softly as she rocked it to and fro.

Léon walked up and down the room; it seemed strange to him to see this beautiful woman in her silk dress in the midst of all this poverty. Madame Bovary blushed; he turned away, thinking perhaps there had been an impertinent look in his eyes. Then she put back the little girl, who had just thrown up over her collar. The nurse at once came to dry her, protesting that it wouldn't show.

"You should see some of the other tricks she plays on me," she said. "I always seem to be sponging her off. If you would have the goodness to order Camus, the grocer, to let me have a little soap; it would really be more convenient for you, as I needn't trouble you then."

"All right, all right!" said Emma. "Good-bye, Madame Rollet."

And she went out, wiping her shoes at the door.

The woman accompanied her to the end of the garden, complaining all the time of the trouble she had getting up nights.

"I'm so worn out sometimes that I drop asleep on my chair. You could at least give me a pound of ground coffee; that'd last me a month, and I'd take it in the morning with some milk."

After having submitted to her thanks, Madame Bovary left. She had gone a little way down the path when, at the sound of wooden shoes, she turned round. It was the nurse.

36. A farmer's almanac, begun in 1635 by Mathieu Laensberg, frequently found in farms and country houses.

"What is it?"

Then the peasant woman, taking her aside behind an elm tree, began talking to her of her husband, who with his trade and six francs a year that the captain . . .

"Hurry up with your story," said Emma.

"Well," the nurse went on, heaving sighs between each word, "I'm afraid he'll be put out seeing me have coffee alone, you know men . . ."

"But I just told you you'll get some," Emma repeated; "I will give you some. Leave me alone!"

"Oh, my dear lady! you see, his wounds give him terrible cramps in the chest. He even says that cider weakens him."

"Do make haste, Mère Rollet!"

"Well," the latter continued, making a curtsey, "if it weren't asking too much," and she curtsied once more, "if you would"—and her eyes begged—"a jar of brandy," she said at last, "and I'd rub your little one's feet with it; they're as tender as your tongue."

Once they were rid of the nurse, Emma again took Monsieur Léon's arm. She walked fast for some time, then more slowly, and looking straight in front of her, her eyes rested on the shoulder of the young man, whose frock-coat had a black-velvet collar. His brown hair fell over it, straight and carefully combed. She noticed his nails, which were longer than one wore them in Yonville. It was one of the clerk's chief concerns to trim them, and for this purpose he kept a special knife in his writing-desk.

They returned to Yonville by the water-side. In the warm season the bank, wider than at other times, showed to their foot the garden walls from where a few steps led to the river. It flowed noiselessly, swift, and cold to the eye; long, thin grasses huddled together in it as the current drove them, and spread themselves upon the limpid water like streaming hair. Sometimes at the top of the reeds or on the leaf of a water-lily an insect with fine legs crawled or rested. The sun pierced with a ray the small blue bubbles of the waves that broke successively on the bank; branchless old willows mirrored their grey barks in the water; beyond, all around, the meadows seemed empty. It was the dinner-hour at the farms, and the young woman and her companion heard nothing as they walked but the fall of their steps on the earth of the path, the words they spoke, and the sound of Emma's dress rustling round her.

The walls of the gardens, crested with pieces of broken bottle, were heated like the glass roof of a hothouse. Wallflowers had sprung up between the bricks, and with the tip of her open parasol Madame Bovary, as she passed, made some of their faded flowers crumble into yellow dust, or else a spray of overhanging honeysuckle and clematis would catch in the fringe of the parasol and scrape for a moment over the silk.

They were talking of a troupe of Spanish dancers who were expected shortly at the Rouen theatre.

"Are you going?" she asked.

"If I can," he answered.

Had they nothing else to say to one another? Yet their eyes were full of more serious speech, and while they forced themselves to find trivial phrases, they felt the same languor stealing over them both; it was like the deep, continuous murmur of the soul dominating that of their voices. Surprised with wonder at this strange sweetness, they did not think of speaking of the sensation or of seeking its cause. Future joys are like tropical shores; like a fragrant breeze, they extend their innate softness to the immense inland world of past experience, and we are lulled by this intoxication into forgetting the unseen horizons beyond.

In one place the ground had been trodden down by the cattle; they had to step on large green stones put here and there in the mud. She often stopped a moment to look where to place her foot, and tottering on the stone that shook, her arms outspread, her form bent forward with a look of indecision, she would laugh, afraid of falling into the puddles of water.

When they arrived in front of her garden, Madame Bovary opened the little gate, ran up the steps and disappeared.

Léon returned to his office. His employer was away; he just glanced at the briefs, then cut himself a pen, and finally took up his hat and went out.

He went to La Pâture at the top of the Argueil hills at the beginning of the forest; he stretched out under the pines and watched the sky through his fingers.

"How bored I am!" he said to himself, "how bored I am!"

He thought he was to be pitied for living in this village, with Homais for a friend and Monsieur Guillaumin for master. The latter, entirely absorbed by his business, wearing gold-rimmed spectacles and red whiskers over a white cravat, understood nothing of mental refinements, although he affected a stiff English manner, which in the beginning had impressed the clerk.

As for Madame Homais, she was the best wife in Normandy, gentle as a sheep, loving her children, her father, her mother, her cousins, weeping for others' woes, letting everything go in her household, and detesting corsets; but so slow of movement, such a bore to listen to, so common in appearance, and of such restricted conversation, that although she was thirty and he only twenty, although they slept in rooms next each other and he spoke to her daily, he never thought that she might be a woman to anyone, or that she possessed anything else of her sex than the gown.

And what else was there? Binet, a few shopkeepers, two or three innkeepers, the curé, and, finally, Monsieur Tuvache, the mayor, with his two sons, rich, haughty, obtuse people, who farmed their own lands and had feasts among themselves, devout Christians at that, but altogether unbearable as companions.

But from the general background of all these human faces the figure of Emma stood out isolated and yet farthest off; for between her and him he seemed to sense a vague abyss.

In the beginning he had called on her several times along with the pharmacist. Charles had not appeared particularly anxious to see him again, and Léon did not know what to do between his fear of being indiscreet and the desire for an intimacy that seemed almost impossible.

IV

When the first cold days set in Emma left her bedroom for the parlour, a long, low-ceilinged room, with on the mantelpiece a large bunch of coral spread out against the looking-glass. Seated in her armchair near the window, she could see the villagers pass along the pavement.

Twice a day Léon went from his office to the Lion d'Or. Emma could watch him coming from afar; she leant forward listening, and the young man glided past the curtain, always dressed in the same way, and without turning his head. But in the twilight, when, her chin resting on her left hand, she let her begun embroidery fall on her knees, she often shuddered at the apparition of this shadow suddenly gliding past. She would get up and order the table to be laid.

Monsieur Homais called at dinner-time. Skull-cap in hand, he came in on tiptoe, in order to disturb no one, always repeating the same phrase, "Good evening, everybody." Then, when he had taken his seat at table between them, he asked the doctor about his patients, and the latter consulted him as to the probability of their payment. Next they talked of "what was in the paper." By this hour of the day, Homais knew it almost by heart, and he repeated from beginning to end, including the comments of the journalist, all the stories of individual catastrophes that had occurred in France or abroad. But the subject becoming exhausted, he was not slow in throwing out some remarks on the dishes before him. Sometimes even, half-rising, he delicately pointed out to madame the tenderest morsel, or turning to the maid, gave her some advice on the manipulation of stews and the hygiene of seasoning. He talked aroma, osmazome, juices, and gelatine in a bewildering manner. Moreover, Homais, with his head fuller of recipes than his shop of jars, excelled in making all kinds of preserves, vinegars, and sweet liqueurs; he knew also all the latest inventions in economic stoves, together with the art of preserving cheeses and of curing sick wines.

At eight o'clock Justin came to fetch him to shut up the shop. Then Monsieur Homais gave him a sly look, especially if Félicité was there, for he had noticed that his apprentice was fond of the doctor's house.

"The young man," he said, "is beginning to have ideas, and the devil take me if I don't believe he's in love with your maid!"

But a more serious fault with which he reproached Justin was his constantly listening to conversation. On Sunday, for example, one could not get him out of the parlor, even when Madame Homais called him to fetch the children, who had fallen asleep in the armchairs, dragging down with their backs the overwide slip-covers.

Not many people came to the pharmacist's evening parties, his scandal-mongering and political opinions having successfully alienated various persons. The clerk never failed to be there. As soon as he heard the bell he ran to meet Madame Bovary, took her shawl, and put away under the shop-counter the heavy overshoes she wore when it snowed.

First they played some hands at trente-et-un; next Monsieur Homais played écarté with Emma; Léon standing behind her, gave advice. Standing up with his hands on the back of her chair, he saw the teeth of her comb that bit into her chignon. With every movement that she made to throw her cards the right side of her dress was drawn up. From her turned-up hair a dark colour fell over her back, and growing gradually paler, lost itself little by little in the shade. Her dress dropped on both sides of her chair, blowing out into many folds before it spread on the floor. When Léon occasionally felt the sole of his boot resting on it, he drew back as if he had trodden on something alive.

When the game of cards was over, the pharmacist and the Doctor played dominoes, and Emma, changing her place, leant her elbow on the table, turning over the pages of "L'Illustration." She had brought her ladies' journal with her. Léon sat down near her; they looked at the engravings together, and waited for one another at the bottom of the pages. She often begged him to read her the verses; Léon declaimed them in a languid voice, to which he carefully gave a dying fall in the love passages. But the noise of the dominoes annoyed him. Monsieur Homais was strong at the game; he could beat Charles and give him a double-six. Then the three hundred finished, they both stretched in front of the fire, and were soon asleep. The fire was dying out in the cinders; the teapot was empty, Léon was still reading. Emma listened to him, mechanically turning round the lampshade, its gauze decorated with painted clowns in carriages, and tightrope dancers with balancing-poles.

Léon stopped, pointing with a gesture to his sleeping audience; then they talked in low tones, and their conversation seemed the sweeter to them because it was unheard.

Thus a kind of bond was established between them, a constant exchange of books and of romances. Little inclined to jealousy, Monsieur Bovary thought nothing of it.

On his birthday he received a beautiful phrenological head, all marked with figures to the thorax and painted blue. This was a gift of the clerk's. He showed him many other attentions, to the point of running errands for him at Rouen: and a novel having made the mania for cactuses fashionable, Léon bought some for Madame Bovary, bringing them back on his knees in the "Hirondelle," pricking his fingers on their hard spikes.

She had a railed shelf suspended against her window to hold the pots. The clerk, too, had his small hanging garden; they saw each other tending their flowers at their windows.

One of the village windows was even more often occupied; for on Sundays from morning to night, and every morning when the weather was bright, one could see at an attic-window the profile of Monsieur Binet bending over his lathe; its monotonous humming could be heard at the Lion d'Or.

One evening on coming home Léon found in his room a rug in velvet and wool with leaves on a pale ground. He called Madame Homais, Monsieur Homais, Justin, the children, the cook; he spoke of it to his employer; every one wanted to see this rug. Why did the doctor's wife give the clerk presents? It looked odd; and they decided that he must be her lover.

He gave plenty of reason for this belief, so ceaselessly did he talk of her charms and of her wit; so much so, that Binet once roughly interrupted him:

"What do I care since I'm not one of her friends?"

He tortured himself to find out how he could make his declaration to her, and always halting between the fear of displeasing her and the shame of being such a coward, he wept with discouragement and desire. Then he took energetic resolutions, wrote letters that he tore up, put it off to times that he again deferred. Often he set out with the determination to dare all; but this resolution soon deserted him in Emma's presence; and when Charles, dropping in, invited him to jump into his carriage to go with him to see some patient in the neighborhood, he at once accepted, bowed to madame, and left. Wasn't the husband also a part of her after all?

As for Emma, she did not ask herself whether she loved him. Love, she thought, must come suddenly, with great outbursts and lightnings,—a hurricane of the skies, which sweeps down on life, upsets everything, uproots the will like a leaf and carries away the heart as in an abyss. She did not know that on the terrace of houses the rain makes lakes when the pipes are choked, and she would thus have remained safe in her ignorance when she suddenly discovered a rent in the wall.

V

It was a Sunday in February, an afternoon when the snow was falling.

Monsieur and Madame Bovary, Homais, and Monsieur Léon had all gone to see a yarn-mill that was being built in the valley a mile and a half from Yonville. The druggist had taken Napoleon and Athalie to give them some exercise, and Justin accompanied them, carrying the umbrellas over his shoulder.

Nothing, however, could be less worth seeing than this sight. A great piece of waste ground, on which, amid a mass of sand and stones, were scattered a few rusty cogwheels, surrounded by a long rectangular building pierced with numerous little windows. The building was unfinished; the sky could be seen through the beams of the roofing. Attached to the ridgepole of the gable a bunch of straw mixed with corn-ears fluttered its tricoloured ribbons in the wind.

Homais was talking. He explained to the company the future importance of this establishment, computed the strength of the floorings, the thickness of the walls, and regretted extremely not having a yard-stick such as Monsieur Binet possessed for his own special use.

Emma, who had taken his arm, bent lightly against his shoulder, and she looked at the sun's disc shining afar through the mist with pale splendour. She turned; there was Charles. His cap was drawn down over his eyebrows, and his two thick lips were trembling, which added a look of stupidity to his face; his very back, his calm back, was irritating to behold, and she saw all his platitude spelled out right there, on his very coat.

While she was considering him thus, savoring her irritation with a sort of depraved pleasure, Léon made a step forward. The cold that made him pale seemed to add a more gentle languor to his face; between his cravat and his neck the somewhat loose collar of his shirt showed the skin; some of his ear was showing beneath a lock of hair, and his large blue eyes, raised to the clouds, seemed to Emma more limpid and more beautiful than those mountain-lakes which mirror the heavens.

"Look out there!" suddenly cried the pharmacist.

And he ran to his son, who had just jumped into a pile of lime in order to whiten his boots. Overcome by his father's reproaches, Napoleon began to howl, while Justin dried his shoes with a wisp of straw. But a knife was needed; Charles offered his.

"Ah!" she said to herself, "he carries a knife in his pocket like a peasant."

It was beginning to snow and they turned back to Yonville.

In the evening Madame Bovary did not go to her neighbor's, and when Charles had left and she felt herself alone, the comparison again forced itself upon her, almost with the clarity of direct sensation, and with that lengthening of perspective which memory gives to things. Looking from her bed at the bright fire that was burning, she still saw, as she had down there, Léon standing up with one hand bending his cane, and with the other holding Athalie, who was quietly sucking a piece of ice. She thought him charming; she could not tear herself away from him; she recalled his other attitudes on other days, the words he had spoken, the sound of his voice, his whole person; and she repeated, pouting out her lips as if for a kiss:

"Yes, charming! charming! Is he not in love?" . . . she asked herself; "but with whom? . . . With me!"

All the evidence asserted itself at once; her heart leapt. The flame of the fire threw a joyous light upon the ceiling; she turned on her back, stretched out her arms.

Then began the eternal lamentation: "Oh, if Heaven had but willed it! And why not? What prevented it?"

When Charles came home at midnight, she seemed to have just awakened, and as he made a noise undressing, she complained of a headache, then asked casually what had happened that evening.

"Monsieur Léon," he said, "went to his room early."

She could not help smiling, and she fell asleep, her soul filled with a new delight.

The next day, at dusk, she received a visit from Monsieur Lheureux, the owner of the local general store.

He was a smart man, this shopkeeper.

Born in Gascony but bred a Norman, he grafted upon his southern volubility the cunning of the Cauchois. His fat, flabby, beardless face seemed dyed by a decoction of liquorice, and his white hair made even more vivid the keen brilliance of his small black eyes. No one knew what he had been formerly; some said he was a peddler, others that he was a banker at Routot. One thing was certain: he could make complex figurings in his head that would have frightened Binet himself. Polite to obsequiousness, he always held himself with his back bent in the attitude of one who bows or who invites.

After leaving at the door his black-bordered hat, he put down a green cardboard box on the table, and began by complaining to madame, with many civilities, that he should have remained till that day without the benefit of her confidence. A poor shop like his was not made to attract a lady of fashion; he stressed the words; yet she had only to command, and he would undertake to provide her with anything she might wish, whether it be lingerie or knitwear, hats or dresses, for he went to town regularly four times a month. He was connected with the best houses. His name could be mentioned at the "Trois Frères," at the "Barbe d'Or," or at the "Grand Sauvage"; all these gentlemen knew him inside out. Today, then, he had come to show madame, in passing, various articles he happened to have by an unusual stroke of luck. And he pulled out half-a-dozen embroidered collars from the box.

Madame Bovary examined them.

"I don't need anything," she said.

Then Monsieur Lheureux delicately exhibited three Algerian scarves, several packages of English needles, a pair of straw slippers, and, finally, four eggcups in cocoa-nut wood, carved in open work by convicts. Then, with both hands on the table, his neck stretched out, leaning forward with open mouth, he watched Emma's gaze wander undecided over the merchandise. From time to time, as if to remove some dust, he flicked his nail against the silk of the scarves spread out at full length, and they rustled with a little noise, making the gold spangles of the material sparkle like stars in the greenish twilight.

"How much are they?"

"A mere trifle," he replied, "a mere trifle. But there's no hurry; whenever it's convenient. We are no Jews."

She reflected for a few moments, and ended by again declining Monsieur Lheureux's offer. Showing no concern, he replied:

"Very well! Better luck next time. I have always got on with ladies . . . even if I didn't with my own!"

Emma smiled.

"I wanted to tell you," he went on good-naturedly, after his joke, "that it isn't the money I should trouble about. Why, I could give you some, if need be."

She made a gesture of surprise.

"Ah!" he said quickly and in a low voice, "I shouldn't have to go far to find you some, rely on that."

And he began asking after Père Tellier, the owner of the "Café Français," who was being treated by Monsieur Bovary at the time.

"What's the matter with Père Tellier? He makes the whole house shake with his coughing, and I'm afraid he'll soon need a pine coat rather than a flannel jacket. He certainly lived it up when he was young! These people, madame, they never know when to stop! He burned himself up with brandy. Still it's sad, all the same, to see an acquaintance go."

And while he fastened up his box he discoursed about the doctor's patients.

"It's the weather, no doubt," he said, looking frowningly at the floor, "that causes these illnesses. I myself don't feel just right. One of these days I shall even have to consult the doctor for a pain I have in my back. Well, good-bye, Madame Bovary. At your service; your very humble servant."

And he gently closed the door behind him.

Emma had her dinner served in her bedroom on a tray by the fireside; she took a long time eating; everything seemed wonderful.

"How good I was!" she said to herself, thinking of the scarves.

She heard steps on the stairs. It was Léon. She got up and took from the chest of drawers the first pile of dusters to be hemmed. When he came in she seemed very busy.

The conversation languished; Madame Bovary let it drop every few minutes, while he himself seemed quite embarrassed. Seated on a low chair near the fire, he kept turning the ivory thimble case with his fingers. She stitched on, or from time to time turned down the hem of the cloth with her nail. She did not speak; he was silent, captivated by her silence, as he would have been by her speech.

"Poor fellow!" she thought.

"How have I displeased her?" he asked himself.

At last, however, Léon said that one of these days, he had to go to Rouen on business.

"Your music subscription has expired; shall I renew it?"

"No," she replied.

"Why?"

"Because . . ."

And pursing her lips she slowly drew a long stitch of grey thread.

This work irritated Léon. It seemed to roughen the ends of her fingers. A gallant phrase came into his head, but he did not risk it.

"Then you are giving it up?" he went on.

"What?" she asked hurriedly. "Music? Ah! yes! Have I not my house to look after, my husband to attend to, a thousand things, in fact, many duties that must be considered first?"

She looked at the clock. Charles was late. Then she affected anxiety. Two or three times she even repeated, "He is so good!"

The clerk was fond of Monsieur Bovary. But this tenderness on his behalf came as an unpleasant surprise; still, he sang his praise: everyone did, he said, especially the pharmacist.

"Ah! he is a good man," continued Emma.

"Certainly," replied the clerk.

And he began talking of Madame Homais, whose very untidy appearance generally made them laugh.

"What does it matter?" interrupted Emma. "A good housewife does not trouble about her appearance."

Then she relapsed into silence.

It was the same on the following days; her talks, her manners, everything changed. She took interest in the housework, went to church regularly, and looked after her maid with more severity.

She took Berthe away from the nurse. When visitors called, Félicité brought her in, and Madame Bovary undressed her to show off her limbs. She claimed to love children; they were her consolation, her joy, her passion, and she accompanied her caresses with lyrical outbursts that would have reminded any one but the Yonvillians of Sachette[37] in "Notre Dame de Paris."[38]

When Charles came home he found his slippers put to warm near the fire. His waistcoat now never wanted lining, nor his shirt buttons, and it was quite a pleasure to see in the cupboard the nightcaps arranged in piles of the same height. She no longer grumbled as before when asked to take a walk in the garden; what he proposed was always done, although she never anticipated the wishes to which she submitted without a murmur; and when Léon saw him sit by his fireside after dinner, his two hands on his stomach, his two feet on the fender, his cheeks flushed with wine, his eyes moist with happiness, the child crawling along the carpet, and this woman with the slender waist who came behind his armchair to kiss his forehead:

"What madness!" he said to himself. "How could I ever hope to reach her?"

She seemed so virtuous and inaccessible to him that he lost all hope, even the faintest. But, by thus renouncing her, he made her ascend to extraordinary heights. She transcended, in his eyes, those sensuous attributes which were forever out of his reach; and in his heart she rose forever, soaring away from him like a winged apotheosis. It was one of those pure feelings that do not interfere with life, that are cultivated for their rarity, and whose loss would afflict more than their fulfilment rejoices.

Emma grew thinner, her cheeks paler, her face longer. With her black hair, her large eyes, her straight nose, her birdlike walk, and always silent now, did she not seem to be passing through life scarcely touching it, bearing on her brow the slight mark of a sublime destiny? She was so sad and so calm, at once so gentle and so reserved, that near her one came under the spell of an icy charm, as we shudder in churches at the perfume of the flowers mingling with the cold of the marble. Even others could not fail to be impressed. The pharmacist said:

"She is a real lady! She would not be out of place in a sous-préfecture!"

37. Sachette ("sackcloth"); Paguette la Chantefleurie is the mother of Agnes, the girl abducted by gypsies who takes the name Esmeralda. She worshipped a shoe of her stolen child.

38. *Notre Dame de Paris* (1831) is a historical novel by Victor Hugo (1802–1885).

The housewives admired her thrift, the patients her politeness, the poor her charity.

But she was eaten up with desires, with rage, with hate. The rigid folds of her dress covered a tormented heart of which her chaste lips never spoke. She was in love with Léon, and sought solitude that she might more easily delight in his image. His physical presence troubled the voluptuousness of this meditation. Emma thrilled at the sound of his step; then in his presence the emotion subsided, and afterwards there remained in her only an immense astonishment that ended in sorrow.

Léon did not know that when he left her in despair she rose after he had gone to see him in the street. She concerned herself about his comings and goings; she watched his face; she invented quite a story to find an excuse for going to his room. She envied the pharmacist's wife for sleeping under the same roof, and her thoughts constantly centered upon this house, like the Lion d'Or pigeons who alighted there to dip their pink feet and white wings in the rainpipes. But the more Emma grew conscious of her love, the more she repressed it, hoping thus to hide and to stifle her true feeling. She would have liked Léon to know, and she imagined circumstances, catastrophes that would make this possible. What restrained her was, no doubt, idleness and fear, as well as a sense of shame. She thought she had repulsed him too much, that the time was past, that all was lost. Then, pride, the joy of being able to say to herself, "I am virtuous," and to look at herself in the mirror striking resigned poses, consoled her a little for the sacrifice she thought she was making.

Then the desires of the flesh, the longing for money, and the melancholy of passion all blended into one suffering, and instead of putting it out of her mind, she made her thoughts cling to it, urging herself to pain and seeking everywhere the opportunity to revive it. A poorly served dish, a half open door would aggravate her; she bewailed the clothes she did not have, the happiness she had missed, her overexalted dreams, her too cramped home.

What exasperated her was that Charles did not seem to be aware of her torment. His conviction that he was making her happy looked to her a stupid insult, and his self-assurance on this point sheer ingratitude. For whom, then, was she being virtuous? Was it not for him, the obstacle to all happiness, the cause of all misery, and, as it were, the sharp clasp of that complex strap that buckled her in all sides?

Thus he became the butt of all the hatred resulting from her frustrations; but all efforts to conquer them augmented her suffering—for this useless humiliation still added to her despair and widened the gap between them. His very gentleness would drive her at times to rebellion. Domestic mediocrity urged her on to wild extravagance, matrimonial tenderness to adulterous desires. She would have liked

Charles to beat her, that she might have a better right to hate him, to revenge herself upon him. She was surprised sometimes at the shocking thoughts that came into her head, and she had to go on smiling, to hear repeated to her at all hours that she was happy, to pretend to be happy and let it be believed.

Yet, at moments, she loathed this hypocrisy. She was tempted to flee somewhere with Léon and try a new life; but at once a dark, shapeless chasm would open within her soul.

"Besides, he no longer loves me," she thought. "What is to become of me? What help can I hope for, what consolation, what relief?"

Such thoughts would leave her shattered, exhausted, frozen, sobbing silently, with flowing tears.

"Why don't you tell monsieur?" the maid asked her when she came in during these crises.

"It is nerves," said Emma. "Don't mention it to him, he would worry."

"Ah! yes," Félicité went on, "you are just like La Guérine, the daughter of Père Guérin, the fisherman at le Pollet,[39] that I used to know at Dieppe before I came to see you. She was so sad, so sad, that to see her standing on the threshold of her house, she looked like a winding-sheet spread out before the door. Her illness, it appears, was a kind of fog that she had in the head, and the doctors could do nothing about it, neither could the priest. When she had a bad spell, she went off by herself to the sea-shore, so that the customs officer, going his rounds, often found her flat on her face, crying on the pebbles. Then, after her marriage, it stopped, they say."

"But with me," replied Emma, "it was after marriage that it began."

VI

One evening when she was sitting by the open window, watching Lestiboudois, the sexton, trim the boxwood, she suddenly heard the Angelus ringing.

It was the beginning of April, when the primroses are in bloom, and a warm wind blows over the newly-turned flower beds, and the gardens, like women, seem to be getting ready for the summer dances. Through the bars of the arbour and away beyond, the river could be seen in the fields, meandering through the grass in sinuous curves. The evening vapors rose between the leafless poplars, touching their outlines with a violet tint, paler and more transparent than a subtle gauze caught amidst their branches. Cattle moved around in the distance; neither their steps nor their lowing could be heard; and the bell, still ringing through the air, kept up its peaceful lamentation.

39. Suburb of Dieppe, where the fishermen live.

This repeated tinkling stirred in the young woman distant memories of her youth and school-days. She remembered the great candlesticks that rose above the vases full of flowers on the altar, and the tabernacle with its small columns. She would have liked to be once more lost in the long line of white veils, marked off here and there by the stiff black hoods of the good sisters bending over their praying-chairs. At mass on Sundays, when she looked up, she saw the gentle face of the Virgin amid the blue smoke of the rising incense. The image awoke a tender emotion in her; she felt limp and helpless, like the down of a bird whirled by the tempest, and it was unconsciously that she went towards the church, ready for any kind of devotion, provided she could humble her soul and lose all sense of selfhood.

On the Square she met Lestiboudois on his way back, for, in order not to lose out on a full day's wages, he preferred to interrupt his gardening-work and go ring the Angelus when it suited him best. Besides, the earlier ringing warned the boys that catechism time had come.

Already a few who had arrived were playing marbles on the stones of the cemetery. Others, astride the wall, swung their legs, trampling with their wooden shoes the large nettles that grew between the little enclosure and the newest graves. This was the only green spot. All the rest was but stones, always covered with a fine dust, in spite of Lestiboudois' broom.

The children played around in their socks, as if they were on their own ground. The shouts of their voices could be heard through the humming of the bell. The noise subsided with the swinging of the great rope that, hanging from the top of the belfry, dragged its end on the ground. Swallows flitted to and fro uttering little cries, cutting the air with the edge of their wings, and swiftly returned to their yellow nests under the eave-tiles of the coping. At the end of the church a lamp was burning, the wick of a night-light hung up in a glass. Seen from a distance, it looked like a white stain trembling in the oil. A long ray of the sun fell across the nave and seemed to darken the lower sides and the corners.

"Where is the priest?" Madame Bovary asked one of the boys, who was entertaining himself by shaking the turnstile in its too loose socket.

"He is coming," he answered.

Indeed, the door of the rectory creaked and the Abbé Bournisien appeared; the children fled in a heap into the church.

"The little brats!" muttered the priest, "always the same!" Then, picking up a ragged catechism on which he had stepped:

"They have respect for nothing!"

But, as soon as he caught sight of Madame Bovary:

"Excuse me," he said; "I did not recognise you."

He thrust the catechism into his pocket, and stopped, balancing the heavy key of the sacristy between his two fingers.

The full light of the setting sun upon his face made the cloth of his cassock, shiny at the elbows and frayed at the hem, seem paler. Grease and tobacco stains ran along his broad chest, following the line of his buttons, growing sparser in the vicinity of his neckcloth, in which rested the massive folds of his red chin; it was dotted with yellow spots that disappeared beneath the coarse hair of his greyish beard. He had just eaten his dinner, and was breathing noisily.

"And how are you?" he added.

"Not well," replied Emma; "I am suffering."

"So do I," answered the priest. "The first heat of the year is hard to bear, isn't it? But, after all, we are born to suffer, as St. Paul says. But, what does Monsieur Bovary think of it?"

"He!" she said with a gesture of contempt.

"What!" he replied, genuinely surprised, "doesn't he prescribe something for you?"

"Ah!" said Emma, "it is no earthly remedy I need."

But the curé time and again was looking into the church, where the kneeling boys were shouldering one another, and tumbling over like packs of cards.

"I should like to know . . ." she went on.

"You look out, Riboudet," the priest cried angrily, "I'll box your ears, you scoundrel!" Then turning to Emma. "He's Boudet the carpenter's son; his parents are well off, and let him do just as he pleases. Yet he could learn quickly if he would, for he is very sharp. And so sometimes for a joke I call him *Ri*boudet (like the road one takes to go to Maromme), and I even say '*Mon* Riboudet.' Ha! ha! '*Mont* Riboudet.' The other day I repeated this little joke to the bishop, and he laughed. Can you imagine? He deigned to laugh. And how is Monsieur Bovary?"

She seemed not to hear him. And he went on . . .

"Always very busy, no doubt; for he and I are certainly the busiest people in the parish. But he is doctor of the body," he added with a thick laugh, "and I of the soul."

She fixed her pleading eyes upon the priest. "Yes," she said, "you solace all sorrows."

"Ah! don't tell me of it, Madame Bovary. This morning I had to go to Bas-Diauville for a cow was all swollen; they thought it was under a spell. All their cows, I don't know how it is . . . But pardon me! Longuemarre and Boudet! Bless me! Will you stop it?"

And he bounded into the church.

The boys were just then clustering round the large desk, climbing over the cantor's footstool, opening the missal; and others on tiptoe were just about to venture into the confessional. But the priest suddenly distributed a shower of blows among them. Seizing them by the collars of their coats, he lifted them from the ground, and deposited them on their knees on the stones of the choir, firmly, as if he meant to plant them there.

"Yes," said he, when he returned to Emma, unfolding his large cotton handkerchief, one corner of which he put between his teeth, "farmers are much to be pitied."

"Others, too," she replied.

"Certainly. Workingmen in the cities, for instance."

"I wasn't thinking of them . . ."

"Oh, but excuse me! I've known housewives there, virtuous women, I assure you, real saints, who didn't even have bread to eat."

"But those," replied Emma, and the corners of her mouth twitched as she spoke, "those, Monsieur le Curé, who have bread and have no . . ."

"Fire in the winter," said the priest.

"Oh, what does it matter?"

"What! What does it matter? It seems to me that when one has firing and food . . . for, after all . . ."

"My God! my God!" she sighed.

"Do you feel unwell?" he asked, approaching her anxiously. "It is indigestion, no doubt? You must get home, Madame Bovary; drink a little tea, that will strengthen you, or else a glass of fresh water with a little moist sugar."

"Why?"

And she looked like one awaking from a dream.

"Well, you see, you were putting your hand to your forehead. I thought you felt faint."

Then, bethinking himself: "But you were asking me something? What was it? I don't remember."

"I? Oh, nothing . . . nothing," Emma repeated.

And the glance she cast round her slowly fell upon the old man in the cassock. They looked at each other face to face without speaking.

"Well then, Madame Bovary," he said at last, "excuse me, but duty comes first as the saying goes; I must look after my brats. The first communion will soon be upon us, and I fear we shall be behind, as ever. So after Ascension Day I regularly keep them an extra hour every Wednesday. Poor children! One cannot lead them too soon into the path of the Lord . . . he himself advised us to do so, through the mouth of his Divine Son. Good health to you, madame; my respects to your husband."

And he went into the church making a genuflexion as soon as he reached the door.

Emma saw him disappear between the double row of benches, walking with heavy tread, his head a little bent over his shoulder, and with his two half-open hands stretched sidewards.

Then she turned on her heel all of one piece, like a statue on a pivot, and went homewards. But the loud voice of the priest, the clear voices of the boys still reached her ears, and pursued her:

"Are you a Christian?"

"Yes, I am a Christian."

"What is a Christian?"

"He who, being baptized . . . baptized . . . baptized . . ."

She climbed the steps of the staircase holding on to the banisters, and when she was in her room threw herself into an arm-chair.

The whitish light of the window-panes was softly wavering. The pieces of furniture seemed more frozen in their places, about to lose themselves in the shadow as in an ocean of darkness. The fire was out, the clock went on ticking, and Emma vaguely wondered at this calm of all things while within herself there was such tumult. But little Berthe was there, between the window and the work-table, tottering on her knitted shoes, and trying to reach the end of her mother's apron-strings.

"Leave me alone," Emma said, pushing her back with her hand.

The little girl soon came up closer against her knees, and leaning on them with her arms, she looked up with her large blue eyes, while a small thread of clear saliva drooled from her lips on to the silk of her apron.

"Leave me alone," repeated the young woman quite angrily.

Her expression frightened the child, who began to scream.

"Will you leave me alone?" she said, forcing her away with her elbow.

Berthe fell at the foot of the chest of drawers against the brass handle; she cut her cheek, blood appeared. Madame Bovary rushed to lift her up, broke the bell-rope, called for the maid with all her might, and she was just going to curse herself when Charles appeared. It was dinner time; he was coming home.

"Look, dear!" said Emma calmly, "the child fell down while she was playing, and she hurt herself."

Charles reassured her; it was only a slight cut, and he went for some adhesive plaster.

Madame Bovary did not go downstairs to the dining-room; she wished to remain alone to look after the child. Then watching her sleep, the little anxiety she still felt gradually wore off, and she seemed very stupid to herself, and very kind to have been so worried just now at so little. Berthe, in fact, no longer cried. Her breathing now imperceptibly raised the cotton covering. Big tears lay in the corner of the half-closed eyelids, through whose lashes one could see two pale sunken pupils; the adhesive plaster on her cheek pulled the skin aside.

"It is very strange," thought Emma, "how ugly this child is!"

When at eleven o'clock Charles came back from the pharmacist's shop, where he had gone after dinner to return the remainder of the plaster, he found his wife standing by the cradle.

"I assure you it's nothing," he said, kissing her on the forehead. "Don't worry, my poor darling; you will make yourself ill."

He had stayed a long time at the pharmacist's. Although he had not seemed much concerned, Homais, nevertheless, had exerted himself to buoy him up, to "raise his spirits." Then they had talked of the various dangers that threaten childhood, of the carelessness of servants. Madame Homais knew what he meant: she still carried on her chest the scars of a load of charcoal that a cook dropped on her when she was a child. Hence that her kind parents took all sorts of precautions. The knives were not sharpened, nor the floors waxed; there were iron gratings in front of the windows and strong bars across the fireplace. In spite of their spirit, the little Homais could not stir without some one watching them; at the slightest cold their father stuffed them with cough-syrups; and until they turned four they all were mercilessly forced to use padded headwear. This, it is true, was a fancy of Madame Homais'; her husband was secretly afflicted by it. Fearing the possible consequences of such compression to the intellectual organs, he even went so far as to say to her:

"Do you want to make them into Caribs or Botocudos?"

Charles, however, had several times tried to interrupt the conversation.

"I would like a word with you," he whispered, addressing the clerk who preceded him on the stairs.

"Can he suspect anything?" Léon asked himself. His heart beat faster, and all sorts of conjectures occured to him.

At last, Charles, having closed the door behind him, begged him to inquire at Rouen after the price of a fine daguerreotype. It was a sentimental surprise he intended for his wife, a delicate attention: his own portrait in black tail coat. But he wanted first to know how much it would cost. It wouldn't cause Monsieur Léon too much trouble to find out, since he went to town almost every week.

Why? Monsieur Homais suspected some love affair, an intrigue. But he was mistaken. Léon was carrying on no flirtations. He was sadder than ever, as Madame Lefrançois saw from the amount of food he left on his plate. To find out more about it she questioned the tax-collector. Binet answered roughly that he wasn't being paid to spy on him.

All the same, his companion's behavior seemed very strange to him, for Léon often threw himself back in his chair, and stretching out his arms, complained vaguely about life.

"It's because you have no distractions," said the collector.

"What distractions?"

"If I were you I'd have a lathe."

"But I don't know how to turn," answered the clerk.

"Ah! that's true," said the other, rubbing his chin with an air of mingled contempt and satisfaction.

Léon was weary of loving without success; moreover, he was beginning to feel that depression caused by the repetition of the same life, with no interest to inspire and no hope to sustain it. He was so bored with Yonville and the Yonvillers, that the sight of certain persons, of certain houses, irritated him beyond endurance; and the pharmacist, good companion though he was, was becoming absolutely unbearable to him. Yet the prospect of a new condition of life frightened as much as it seduced him.

This apprehension soon changed into impatience, and then Paris beckoned from afar with the music of its masked balls, the laughter of the grisettes. Since he was to go to law-school there anyway, why not set out at once? Who prevented him? And, inwardly, he began making preparations; he arranged his occupations beforehand. In his mind, he decorated an apartment. He would lead an artist's life there! He would take guitar lessons! He would have a dressing-gown, a Basque béret, blue velvet slippers! He already admired two crossed foils over his chimney-piece, with a skull on the guitar above them.

The main difficulty was to obtain his mother's consent, though nothing could seem more reasonable. Even his employer advised him to go to some other law office where he could learn more rapidly. Taking a middle course, then, Léon looked for some position as second clerk in Rouen; found none, and at last wrote his mother a long letter full of details, in which he set forth the reasons for going to live in Paris at once. She consented.

He did not hurry. Every day for a month Hivert carried boxes, valises, parcels for him from Yonville to Rouen and from Rouen to Yonville; and when Léon had rounded out his wardrobe, had his three armchairs restuffed, bought a supply of neckties, in a word, had made more preparations than for a trip round the world, he put it off from week to week, until he received a second letter from his mother urging him to leave, since he wanted to pass his examination before the vacation.

When the moment for the farewells had come, Madame Homais wept, Justin sobbed; Homais, as a strong man, concealed his emotion; he wished to carry his friend's overcoat himself as far as the gate of the notary, who was taking Léon to Rouen in his carriage. The latter had just time to bid farewell to Monsieur Bovary.

When he reached the head of the stairs he stopped, he was so out of breath. When he entered, Madame Bovary rose hurriedly.

"It is I again!" said Léon.

"I was sure of it!"

She bit her lips, and a rush of blood flowing under her skin made her red from the roots of her hair to the top of her collar. She remained standing, leaning with her shoulder against the wainscot.

"The doctor is not here?" he went on.

"He is out."

She repeated:

"He is out."

Then there was silence. They looked one at the other, and their thoughts, united in the same agony, clung together like two hearts in a passionate embrace.

"I would like to kiss little Berthe good-bye," said Léon.

Emma went down a few steps and called Félicité.

He threw one long look around him that took in the walls, the shelves, the fireplace, as if to appropriate everything, to carry it with him.

She returned, and the servant brought Berthe, who was swinging an upside down windmill at the end of a string. Léon kissed her several times on the neck.

"Good-bye poor child! good-bye, dear little one! good-bye!" And he gave her back to her mother.

"Take her away," she said.

They remained alone—Madame Bovary, her back turned, her face pressed against a window-pane; Léon held his cap in his hand, tapping it softly against his thigh.

"It is going to rain," said Emma.

"I have a coat," he answered.

"Ah!"

She turned round, her chin lowered, her forehead bent forward. The light covered it to the curve of the eyebrows, like a single piece of marble, without revealing what Emma was seeing on the horizon or what she was thinking within herself.

"Well, good-bye," he sighed.

She raised her head with a quick movement.

"Yes, good-bye . . . go!"

They faced each other; he held out his hand; she hesitated.

"In the English manner, then," she said, offering him her hand and forcing a laugh.

Léon felt it between his fingers, and the very substance of all his being seemed to pass into that moist palm.

He opened his hand; their eyes met again, and he disappeared. When he reached the market-place, he stopped and hid behind a pillar to look for the last time at this white house with the four green blinds. He thought he saw a shadow behind the window in the room; but the curtain, sliding along the rod as though no one were touching it, slowly opened its long oblique folds, that spread out all at once, and thus hung straight and motionless as a plaster wall. Léon ran away.

From afar he saw his employer's buggy in the road, and by it a man in a coarse apron holding the horse. Homais and Monsieur Guillaumin were talking. They were waiting for him.

"Embrace me," said the pharmacist with tears in his eyes. "Here is your coat, my good friend. Mind the cold; take care of yourself; don't overdo it!"

"Come, Léon, jump in," said the notary.

Homais bent over the splash-board, and in a voice broken by sobs uttered these three sad words:

"A pleasant journey!"

"Good-night," said Monsieur Guillaumin. "Go ahead!"

They departed and Homais went home.

Madame Bovary had opened her window that looked out over the garden and watched the clouds. They were gathering round the sunset in the direction of Rouen, and rolling back swiftly in black swirls, behind which the great rays of the sun looked out like the golden arrows of a suspended trophy, while the rest of the empty heavens was white as porcelain. But a gust of wind bowed the poplars, and suddenly the rain fell; it rattled against the green leaves. Then the sun reappeared, the hens clucked, sparrows shook their wings in the damp thickets, and the pools of water on the gravel as they flowed away carried off the pink flowers of an acacia.

"Ah! how far off he must be already!" she thought.

Monsieur Homais, as usual, came at half-past six during dinner.

"Well," said he, "so we've sent off our young friend!"

"So it seems," replied the doctor.

Then, turning on his chair: "Any news at home?"

"Nothing much. Only my wife was a little out of sorts this afternoon. You know women—a nothing upsets them, especially my wife. And we shouldn't object to that, since their nervous system is much more fragile than ours."

"Poor Léon!" said Charles. "How will he live at Paris? Will he get used to it?"

Madame Bovary sighed.

"Of course!" said the pharmacist, smacking his lips. "The late night suppers! the masked balls, the champagne—he won't be losing his time, I assure you."

"I don't think he'll go wrong," objected Bovary.

"Nor do I," said Monsieur Homais quickly; "although he'll have to do like the rest for fear of passing for a Jesuit. And you don't know what a life those jokers lead in the Latin quarter, actresses and the rest! Besides, students are thought a great deal of in Paris. Provided they have a few accomplishments, they are received in the best society; there are even ladies of the Faubourg Saint-Germain[40] who fall in love with them, which later gives them opportunities for making very good matches."

"But," said the doctor, "I fear for him that . . . down there . . ."

"You are right," interrupted the pharmacist, "that is the other side of the coin. And you are constantly obliged to keep your hand in your pocket there. Let us say, for instance, you are in a public garden. A fellow appears, well dressed, even wearing a decoration, and whom one would take for a diplomat. He addresses you, you chat with him; he forces himself upon you; offers you a pinch of snuff, or picks up your hat. Then you become more intimate; he takes you to a café, invites you to his countryhouse, introduces you, between two drinks, to all sorts of people; and three-fourths of the time it's only to get hold of your money or involve you in some shady deal"

"That is true," said Charles; "but I was thinking specially of illnesses—of typhoid fever, for example, that attacks students from the provinces."

Emma shuddered.

"Because of the change of diet," continued the pharmacist, "and of the resulting upset for the whole system. And then the water at Paris, don't you know! The dishes at restaurants, all the spiced food, end by heating the blood, and are not worth, whatever people may say of them, a good hearty stew. As for me, I have always preferred home cooking; it is healthier. So when I was studying pharmacy at Rouen, I boarded in a boarding-house; and dined with the professors."

And thus he went on, expounding his general opinions and his personal preferences, until Justin came to fetch him for a mulled egg for a customer.

"Not a moment's peace!" he cried; "always at it! I can't go out for a minute! Like a plough-horse, I have always to be sweating blood and water! What drudgery!" Then, when he was at the door, "By the way, do you know the news?"

"What news?"

"It is very likely," Homais went on, raising his eyebrows and assuming one of his gravest expressions, "that the agricultural fair

40. Faubourg Saint-Germain is the aristocratic quarter of Paris.

of the Seine-Inférieure will be held this year at Yonville-l'Abbaye."

The rumor, at all events, is going the round. This morning the paper alluded to it. It would be of the utmost importance for our district. But we'll talk it over later. I can see, thank you; Justin has the lantern."

VII

The next day was a dreary one for Emma. Everything seemed shrouded in an atmosphere of bleakness that hung darkly over the outward aspect of things, and sorrow blew into her soul with gentle moans, as the winter wind makes in ruined castles. Her reverie was that of things gone forever, the exhaustion that seizes you after everything is done; the pain, in short, caused by the interruption of a familiar motion, the sudden halting of a long drawn out vibration.

As on the return from Vaubyessard, when the quadrilles were running in her head, she was full of a gloomy melancholy, of a numb despair. Léon reappeared, taller, handsomer, more charming, more vague. Though separated from her, he had not left her; he was there, and the walls of the house seemed to hold his shadow. She could not detach her eyes from the carpet where he had walked, from those empty chairs where he had sat. The river still flowed on and slowly drove its ripples along the slippery banks. They had often walked there listening to the murmur of the waves over the moss-covered pebbles. How bright the sun had been! What happy afternoons they had known, alone, in the shade at the end of the garden! He read aloud, bare-headed, sitting on a footstool of dry sticks; the fresh wind of the meadow set trembling the leaves of the book and the nasturtiums of the arbour. Ah! he was gone, the only charm of her life, the only possible hope of joy. Why had she not seized this happiness when it came to her? Why did she not keep him from leaving, beg him on her knees, when he was about to flee from her? And she cursed herself for not having loved Léon. She thirsted for his lips. She wanted to run after him, to throw herself into his arms and say to him, "It is I; I am yours." But Emma recoiled beforehand at the difficulties of the enterprise, and her desires, increased by regret, became only the more acute.

Henceforth the memory of Léon was the center of her boredom; it burnt there more brightly than the fires left by travellers on the snow of a Russian steppe. She threw herself at his image, pressed herself against it; she stirred carefully the dying embers, sought all around her anything that could make it flare; and the most distant reminiscences, like the most immediate occasions, what she experienced as well as what she imagined, her wasted voluptuous desires that were unsatisfied, her projects of happiness that crackled in the wind like dead boughs, her sterile virtue, her lost hopes, the yoke of domesticity,—she gathered it all up, took everything, and made it all serve as fuel for her melancholy.

The flames, however, subsided, either because the supply had exhausted itself, or because it had been piled up too much. Love, little by little, was quelled by absence; regret stifled beneath habit; and the bright fire that had empurpled her pale sky was overspread and faded by degrees. In her slumbering conscience, she took her disgust for her husband for aspirations towards her lover, the burning of hate for the warmth of tenderness; but as the tempest still raged, and as passion burnt itself down to the very cinders, and no help came, no sun rose, there was night on all sides, and she was lost in the terrible cold that pierced her through.

Then the evil days of Tostes began again. She thought herself now far more unhappy; for she had the experience of grief, with the certainty that it would not end.

A woman who had consented to such sacrifices could well allow herself certain whims. She bought a gothic prie-Dieu, and in a month spent fourteen francs on lemons for polishing her nails; she wrote to Rouen for a blue cashmere gown; she chose one of Lheureux's finest scarves, and wore it knotted round her waist over her dressing-gown; thus dressed, she lay stretched out on the couch with closed blinds.

She often changed her hairdo; she did her hair *à la Chinoise*, in flowing curls, in plaited coils; she parted it on one side and rolled it under, like a man's.

She wanted to learn Italian; she bought dictionaries, a grammar, and a supply of white paper. She tried serious reading, history, and philosophy. Sometimes in the night Charles woke up with a start, thinking he was being called to a patient:

"I'm coming," he stammered.

It was the noise of a match Emma had struck to relight the lamp. But her reading fared like her pieces of embroidery, all of which, only just begun, filled her cupboard; she took it up, left it, passed on to other books.

She had attacks in which she could easily have been driven to commit any folly. She maintained one day, to contradict her husband, that she could drink off a large glass of brandy, and, as Charles was stupid enough to dare her to, she swallowed the brandy to the last drop.

In spite of her vaporish airs (as the housewives of Yonville called them), Emma, all the same, never seemed gay, and usually she had at the corners of her mouth that immobile contraction that puckers the faces of old maids, and those of men whose ambition has failed. She was pale all over, white as a sheet; the skin of her nose was drawn at the nostrils, her eyes had a vague look. After discovering three grey hairs on her temples, she talked much of her old age.

She often had spells. One day she even spat blood, and, as Charles fussed round her showing his anxiety . . .

"Bah!" she answered, "what does it matter?"

Charles fled to his study and wept there, both his elbows on the table, sitting in his office chair under the phrenological head.

Then he wrote to his mother to beg her to come, and they had many long consultations together on the subject of Emma.

What should they decide? What was to be done since she rejected all medical treatment?

"Do you know what your wife wants?" replied Madame Bovary senior. "She wants to be forced to occupy herself with some manual work. If she were obliged, like so many others, to earn her living, she wouldn't have these vapors, that come to her from a lot of ideas she stuffs into her head, and from the idleness in which she lives."

"Yet she is always busy," said Charles.

"Ah! always busy at what? Reading novels, bad books, works against religion, and in which they mock at priests in speeches taken from Voltaire. But all that leads you far astray, my poor child. A person who has no religion is bound to go astray."

So it was decided to keep Emma from reading novels. The enterprise did not seem easy. The old lady took it upon herself: She was, when she passed through Rouen, to go herself to the lending library and represent that Emma had discontinued her subscription. Would they not have a right to call in the police if the bookseller persisted all the same in his poisonous trade?

The farewells of mother and daughter-in-law were cold. During the three weeks that they had been together they had not exchanged half-a-dozen words except for the usual questions and greetings when they met at table and in the evening before going to bed.

Madame Bovary left on a Wednesday, the market-day at Yonville.

Since morning, the Square had been crowded by end on end of carts, which, with their shafts in the air, spread all along the line of houses from the church to the inn. On the other side there were canvas booths for the sale of cotton goods, blankets, and woolen stockings, together with harness for horses, and packages of blue ribbon, whose ends fluttered in the wind. The coarse hardware was spread out on the ground between pyramids of eggs and hampers of cheeses showing pieces of sticky straw. Near the wheat threshers clucking hens passed their necks through the bars of flat cages. The crowds piled up in one place and refused to budge; they threatened at times to smash the window of the pharmacy. On

Wednesdays his shop was never empty, and the people pushed in less to buy drugs than for consultations, so great was Homais' reputation in the neighboring villages. His unshakable assurance deeply impresssed the country people. They considered him a greater doctor than all the doctors.

Emma was standing in the open window (she often did so: in the provinces, the window takes the place of the theatre and the promenade) and she amused herself with watching the rustic crowd, when she saw a gentleman in a green velvet coat. Although he was wearing heavy boots, he had on yellow gloves; he was coming towards the doctor's house, followed by a worried looking peasant with lowered head and quite a thoughtful air.

"Can I see the doctor?" he asked Justin, who was talking on the doorsteps with Félicité.

And, mistaking him for a servant of the house, he added,

"Tell him that M. Rodolphe Boulanger *de la* Huchette is here."

It was not out of affectation that the new arrival added "*de la* Huchette" to his name, but to make himself the better known. La Huchette, in fact, was an estate near Yonville, where he had just bought the château and two farms that he cultivated himself, without, however, taking too many pains. He lived as a bachelor, and was supposed to have an income of "at least fifteen thousand francs a year."

Charles came into the room. Monsieur Boulanger introduced his man, who wanted to be bled because he felt "as if ants were crawling all over him."

"It will clear me out," was his answer to all reasonable objections.

So Bovary brought a bandage and a basin, and asked Justin to hold it. Then addressing the peasant, who was already turning pale:

"Don't be scared, my friend."

"No, no, sir," said the other; "go ahead!"

And with an air of bravado he held out his heavy arm. At the prick of the lancet the blood spurted out, splashing against the looking-glass.

"Hold the basin nearer," exclaimed Charles.

"Look!" said the peasant, "one would swear it was a little fountain flowing. How red my blood is! That's a good sign, isn't it?"

"Sometimes," answered the officier de santé, "one feels nothing at first, and them they start fainting, especially when they're strong like this one."

At these words the peasant dropped the lancet-case he was holding back of his chair. A shudder of his shoulders made the chair-back creak. His hat fell off.

"I thought as much," said Bovary, pressing his finger on the vein.

The basin was beginning to tremble in Justin's hands; his knees shook, he turned pale.

"My wife! get my wife!" called Charles.

With one bound she rushed down the staircase.

"Vinegar," he cried. "Lord, two at a time!"

And he was so upset he could hardly put on the compress.

"It is nothing," said Monsieur Boulanger quietly, taking Justin in his arms. He seated him on the table with his back resting against the wall.

Madame Bovary opened the collar of his shirt. The strings of his shirt had got into a knot, and she was for some minutes moving her light fingers about the young fellow's neck. Then she poured some vinegar on her cambric handkerchief; she moistened his temples with little dabs, and then blew delicately upon them.

The ploughman revived, but Justin remained unconscious. His eyeballs disappeared in their whites like blue flowers in milk.

"We must hide this from him," said Charles.

Madame Bovary took the basin to put it under the table. With the movement she made in bending down, her dress (it was a summer dress with four flounces, yellow, long in the waist and wide in the skirt) spread out around on the tiles; and as Emma, stooping, staggered a little in stretching out her arms, the pull of her dress made it hug more closely the line of her bosom. Then she went to fetch a bottle of water, and she was melting some pieces of sugar when the pharmacist arrived. The maid had gone for him at the height of the confusion; seeing his pupil with his eyes open he gave a sigh of relief; then going round him he looked at him from head to foot.

"You fool!" he said, "you're a real fool! A capital idiot! And all that for a little blood-letting! and coming from a fellow who isn't afraid of anything! a real squirrel, climbing to incredible heights in order to steal nuts! You can be proud of yourself! showing a fine talent for the pharmaceutical profession; for, later on, you may be called before the courts of justice in serious circumstances, to enlighten the consciences of the magistrates, and you would have to keep your head then, to reason, show yourself a man, or else pass for an imbecile."

Justin did not answer. The pharmacist went on:

"Who asked you to come? You are always pestering the doctor and madame. Anyway, on Wednesday, I need you in the shop. There are over 20 people there now waiting to be served. I left them just out of concern for you. Get going! hurry! Wait for me there and keep an eye on the jars."

When Justin, who was rearranging his clothes, had gone, they talked for a little while about fainting-fits. Madame Bovary had never fainted.

"That is most unusual for a lady," said Monsieur Boulanger; "but some people are very susceptible. Thus in a duel, I have seen a witness faint away at the mere sound of the loading of pistols."

"As for me," said the pharmacist, "the sight of other people's blood doesn't affect me in the least, but the mere thought of my own flowing would make me faint if I reflected upon it too much."

Monsieur Boulanger, however, dismissed his servant and told him to be quiet, now that his whim was satisfied.

"It gave me the opportunity of making your acquaintance," he added, and he looked at Emma as he said this.

Then he put three francs on the corner of the table, bowed casually, and went out.

He soon had crossed to the other bank of the river (this was his way back to La Huchette), and Emma saw him in the meadow, walking under the poplars, slackening his pace now and then as one who reflects.

"She is nice, very nice, that doctor's wife," he said to himself. "Fine teeth, black eyes, a dainty foot, a figure like a Parisienne's. Where the devil does she come from? Where did that boor ever pick her up?"

Monsieur Rodolphe Boulanger was thirty-four; he combined brutality of temperament with a shrewd judgment, having had much experience with women and being something of a connoisseur. This one had seemed pretty to him; so he kept dreaming about her and her husband.

"I think he is very stupid. She must be tired of him, no doubt. He has dirty nails, and hasn't shaven for three days. While he is trotting after his patients, she sits there mending socks. How bored she gets! How she'd want to be in the city and go dancing every night! Poor little woman! She is gaping after love like a carp on the kitchen table after water. Three gallant words and she'd adore me, I'm sure of it. She'd be tender, charming. Yes; but how get rid of her afterwards?"

The prospect of love's involvements brought to mind, by contrast, his present mistress. She was an actress in Rouen whom he kept, and when he had pondered over this image, even in memory he found himself satiated.

"Madame Bovary," he thought, "is much prettier, much fresher too. Virginie is decidedly beginning to grow fat. Her enthusiasms bore me to tears. And that habit of hers of eating prawns all the time . . . !"

The fields were empty; around him Rodolphe only heard the

noise of the grass as it rubbed against his boots, and the chirping of the cricket hidden away among the oats. He again saw Emma in her room, dressed as he had seen her, and he undressed her.

"Oh, I will have her," he cried, smashing, with a blow of his cane, a clod of earth before him.

At once, he began to consider the strategy. He wondered:

"Where shall we meet? And how? We shall always be having the brat on our hands, and the maid, the neighbors, the husband, all sorts of worries. Bah!" he concluded, "it would be too time-consuming!"

Then he started again:

"But she really has eyes that bore into your heart. And that pale complexion! And I, who love pale women!"

When he reached the top of the Argueil hills he had made up his mind.

"All that remains is to create the proper opportunity. Well, I will call in now and then, I'll send game and poultry; I'll have myself bled, if need be. We shall become friends; I'll invite them to my place. Of course!" he added, "the agricultural fair is coming on; she'll be there, I'll see her. We'll begin boldly, for that's the surest way."

VIII

At last it came, the much-awaited agricultural fair. Ever since the morning of the great day, the villagers, on their doorsteps, were discussing the preparations. The facade of the townhall had been hung with garlands of ivy; a tent had been erected in a meadow for the banquet; and in the middle of the Place, in front of the church, a kind of a small cannon was to announce the arrival of the prefect and the names of the fortunate farmers who had won prizes. The National Guard of Buchy (there was none at Yonville) had come to join the corps of firemen, of whom Binet was captain. On that day he wore a collar even higher than usual; and, tightly buttoned in his tunic, his figure was so stiff and motionless that all life seemed to be confined to his legs, which moved in time with the music, with a single motion. As there was some rivalry between the tax-collector and the colonel, both, to show off their talents, drilled their men separately. The red epaulettes and the black breastplates kept parading up and down, one after the other; there was no end to it, and it constantly began again. Never had there been such a display of pomp. Several citizens had washed down their houses the evening before; tricolor flags hung from half-open windows; all the cafés were full; and in the lovely weather the starched caps, the golden crosses, and the colored neckerchiefs seemed whiter than snow, shone in the sun, and relieved with their motley colors the somber monotony of the frock-coats and blue smocks. The neighboring farmers' wives, when they got off their horses, removed the long pin with which they had gathered their dresses tight around them for fear of getting them spattered; while their husbands protected their hats by covering them with handkerchiefs, of which they held one corner in their teeth.

The crowd came into the main street from both ends of the village. People poured in from the lanes, the alleys, the houses; and from time to time one heard the banging of doors closing behind ladies of the town in cotton gloves, who were going out to see the fête. Most admired of all were two long lamp-stands covered with lanterns, that flanked a platform on which the authorities were to sit. Aside from this, a kind of pole had been placed against the four columns of the townhall, each bearing a small standard of greenish cloth, embellished with inscriptions in gold letters. On one was written, "To Commerce"; on the other, "To Agriculture"; on the third, "To Industry"; and on the fourth, "To the Fine Arts".

But the jubilation that brightened all faces seemed to darken that of Madame Lefrançois, the innkeeper. Standing on her kitchen-steps she muttered to herself:

"How stupid! How stupid they are with their canvas booth! Do they think the prefect will be glad to dine down there under a tent like a gipsy? They call all this fussing for the good of the town! As if it helped the town to send to Neufchâtel for the keeper of a cookshop! And for whom? For cowheads! for tramps!"

The pharmacist passed by. He was wearing a frock-coat, nankeen trousers, beaver shoes, and, to everyone's surprise, a hat—a low crowned hat.

"Your servant," he said. "Excuse me, I am in a hurry."

And as the fat widow asked where he was going . . .

"It seems odd to you, doesn't it, I who am always more cooped up in my laboratory than the man's rat in his cheese."

"What cheese?" asked the landlady.

"Oh, nothing, never mind!" Homais continued. "I merely wished to convey to you, Madame Lefrançois, that I usually live at home like a recluse. To-day, however, considering the circumstances, it is necessary . . ."

"Oh, are you going down there?" she said contemptuously.

"Yes, I am going," replied the pharmacist, astonished. "Am I not a member of the Advisory committee?"

Mère Lefrançois looked at him for a few moments, and ended by saying with a smile:

"That's another matter! But is agriculture any of your business? Do you understand anything about it?"

"Certainly I understand it, since I am a pharmacist,—that is to say, a chemist. And the object of chemistry, Madame Lefrançois, being the knowledge of the reciprocal and molecular action of all natural bodies, it follows that agriculture is comprised within its domain. And, in fact, the composition of the manure, the fermentation of liquids, the analyses of gases, and the effects of miasmas, what, I ask you, is all this, if it isn't chemistry, pure and simple?"

The landlady did not answer. Homais went on:

"Do you think that to be an agriculturist it is necessary to have tilled the earth or fattened fowls oneself? It is much more important to know the composition of the substances in question—the geological strata, the atmospheric actions, the quality of the soil, the minerals, the waters, the density of the different bodies, their capillarity, and what not. And one must be master of all the principles of hygiene in order to direct, criticise the construction of buildings, the feeding of animals; the diet of the servants. And, moreover, Madame Lefrançois, one must know botany, be able to distinguish between plants, you understand, which are the wholesome and those that are deleterious, which are unproductive and which nutritive, if it is well to pull them up here and re-sow them there, to propagate some, destroy others; in brief, one must keep pace with science by reading publications and papers, be always on the alert to detect improvements."

The landlady never took her eyes off the "Café Français" and the pharmacist went on:

"Would to God our agriculturists were chemists, or that at least they would pay more attention to the counsels of science. Thus lately I myself wrote a substantial paper, a memoir of over seventy-two pages, entitled, 'Cider, its Manufacture and its Effects, together with some New Reflections on this Subject,' that I sent to the Agricultural Society in Rouen, and which even procured me the honor of being received among its members—Section, Agriculture; Class, Pomology. Well, if my work had been given to the public . . ."

But the pharmacist stopped, so distracted did Madame Lefrançois seem.

"Just look at them!" she said. "It's past comprehension! Such a hash-house!" And with a shrug of the shoulders that stretched out the stitches of her sweater, she pointed with both hands at the rival establishment, from where singing erupted. "Well, it won't last long," she added, "It'll be over before a week."

Homais drew back in surprise. She came down three steps and whispered in his ear:

"What! you didn't know it? They'll foreclose this week. It's Lheureux who does the selling; he killed them off with his notes."

"What a dreadful catastrophe!" exclaimed the pharmacist, who always found expressions that filled all imaginable circumstances.

Then the landlady began telling him this story, that she had heard from Theodore, Monsieur Guillaumin's servant, and although she detested Tellier, she blamed Lheureux. He was "a wheedler, a fawner."

"There!" she said. "Look at him! There he goes down the square; he is greeting Madame Bovary, who's wearing a green hat. And she is on Monsieur Boulanger's arm."

"Madame Bovary!" exclaimed Homais. "I must go at once and pay her my respects. Perhaps she'll be pleased to have a seat in the enclosure under the peristyle." And, without heeding Madame Lefrançois, who was calling him back for more gossip, the pharmacist walked off rapidly with a smile on his face and his walk jauntier than ever, bowing copiously to right and left, and taking up much room with the large tails of his frock-coat that fluttered behind him in the wind.

Rodolphe having caught sight of him from afar, quickened his pace, but Madame Bovary couldn't keep up; so he walked more slowly, and, smiling at her, said roughly:

"It's only to get away from that fat fellow, you know, the pharmacist."

She nudged him with her elbow.

"How shall I understand that?" he asked himself.

And, walking on, he looked at her out of the corner of his eyes.

Her profile was so calm that it revealed nothing.

It stood out in the light from the oval of her hat that was tied with pale ribbons like waving rushes. Her eyes with their long curved lashes looked straight before her, and though wide open, they seemed slightly slanted at the cheek-bones, because of the blood pulsing gently under the delicate skin. A rosy light shone through the partition between her nostrils. Her head was bent upon her shoulder, and the tips of her teeth shone through her lips like pearls.

"Is she making fun of me?" thought Rodolphe.

Emma's gesture, however, had only been meant for a warning; for Monsieur Lheureux was accompanying them, and spoke now and again as if to enter into the conversation.

"What a beautiful day! Everybody is outside! The wind is from the east!"

Neither Madame Bovary nor Rodolphe answered him, but their slightest movement made him draw near saying, "I beg your pardon!" and raising his hat.

When they reached the blacksmith's house, instead of following the road up to the fence, Rodolphe suddenly turned down a path, drawing Madame Bovary with him. He called out:

"Good evening, Monsieur Lheureux! We'll see you soon!"

"How you got rid of him!" she said, laughing.

"Why," he went on, "allow oneself to be intruded upon by others? And as to-day I have the happiness of being with you . . ."

Emma blushed. He did not finish his sentence. Then he talked of the fine weather and of the pleasure of walking on the grass. A few daisies had sprung up again.

"Here are some pretty Easter daisies," he said, "and enough to provide oracles for all the lovers in the vicinity."

He added,

"Shall I pick some? What do you think?"

"Are you in love?" she asked, coughing a little.

"H'm, h'm! who knows?" answered Rodolphe.

The meadow was beginning to fill up, and the housewives were hustling about with their great umbrellas, their baskets, and their babies. One often had to make way for a long file of country girls, servant-maids with blue stockings, flat shoes and silver rings, who smelt of milk when one passed close to them. They walked along holding one another by the hand, and thus they spread over the whole field from the row of open trees to the banquet tent. But this was the judging time, and the farmers one after the other entered a kind of enclosure formed by ropes supported on sticks.

The beasts were there, their noses turned toward the rope, and making a confused line with their unequal rumps. Drowsy pigs were burrowing in the earth with their snouts, calves were lowing and bleating; the cows, one leg folded under them stretched their bellies on the grass, slowly chewing their cud, and blinking their heavy eyelids at the gnats that buzzed around them. Ploughmen with bare arms were holding by the halter prancing stallions that neighed with dilated nostrils looking in the direction of the mares. These stood quietly, stretching out their heads and flowing manes, while their foals rested in their shadow, or sucked them from time to time. And above the long undulation of these crowded bodies one saw some white mane rising in the wind like a wave, or some sharp horns sticking out, and the heads of men running about. Apart, outside the enclosure, a hundred paces off, was a large black bull, muzzled, with an iron ring in its nostrils, and who moved no more than if he had been in bronze. A child in rags was holding him by a rope.

Between the two lines the committee-men were walking with heavy steps, examining each animal, then consulting one another in a low voice. One who seemed of more importance now and then took notes in a book as he walked along. This was the president of the jury, Monsieur Derozerays de la Panville. As soon as he recognised Rodolphe he came forward quickly, and smiling amiably, said:

"What! Monsieur Boulanger, you are deserting us?"

Rodolphe protested that he would come. But when the president had disappeared:

"To tell the truth," he said, "I shall not go. Your company is better than his."

And while poking fun at the show, Rodolphe, to move about more easily, showed the gendarme his blue card, and even stopped now and then in front of some fine beast, which Madame Bovary did not at all admire. He noticed this, and began jeering at the Yonville ladies and their dresses; then he apologised for his own casual attire. It had the inconsistency of things at once common-place and refined which enchants or exasperates the ordinary man because he suspects that it reveals an unconventional existence, a dubious morality, the affectations of the artist, and, above all, a certain contempt for established conventions. The wind, blowing up his batiste shirt with pleated cuffs revealed a waistcoat of grey linen, and his broad-striped trousers disclosed at the ankle nankeen boots with patent leather gaiters. These were so polished that they re-flected the grass. He trampled on horse's dung, one hand in the pocket of his jacket and his straw hat tilted on one side.

"Anyway," he added, "when one lives in the country. . . ."

"Nothing is worth while," said Emma.

"That is true," replied Rodolphe. "To think that not one of these people is capable of understanding even the cut of a coat!"

Then they talked about provincial mediocrity, of the lives it stifles, the lost illusions.

"No wonder," said Rodolphe, "that I am more and more sinking in gloom."

"You!" she said in astonishment; "I thought you very light-hearted."

"Oh, yes, it seems that way because I know how to wear a mask of mockery in society, and yet, how many a time at the sight of a cemetery by moonlight have I not asked myself whether it were not better to join those sleeping there!"

"Oh! and your friends?" she said. "How can you forget them."

"My friends! What friends? Have I any? Who cares about me?" And he followed up the last words with a kind of hissing whistle.

They were obliged to separate because of a great pile of chairs that a man was carrying behind them. He was so overladen that one could only see the tips of his wooden shoes and the ends of his two outstretched arms. It was Lestiboudois, the gravedigger, who was carrying the church chairs about amongst the people. Alive to all that concerned his interests, he had hit upon this means of turning the agricultural show to his advantage, and his idea was succeeding, for he no longer knew which way to turn. In fact, the villagers, who were tired and hot, quarrelled for these seats, whose straw smelt of incense, and they leant against the thick backs, stained with the wax of candles, with a certain veneration.

Madame Bovary again took Rodolphe's arm; he went on as if speaking to himself:

"Yes, I have missed so many things. Always alone! Ah! if I had some aim in life, if I had met some love, if I had found some one! Oh, how I would have spent all the energy of which I am capable, surmounted everything, overcome everything!"

"Yet it seems to me," said Emma, "that you are not to be pitied."

"Ah! you think so?" said Rodolphe.

"For, after all," she went on, "you are free . . ."

She hesitated,

"Rich . . ."

"Don't mock me," he replied.

And she protested that she was not mocking him, when the sound of a cannon was heard; immediately all began crowding one another towards the village.

It was a false alarm. The prefect seemed not to be coming, and the members of the jury felt much embarrassed, not knowing if they ought to begin the meeting or wait longer.

At last, at the end of the Place a large hired landau appeared, drawn by two thin horses, generously whipped by a coachman in a white hat. Binet had only just time to shout, "Present arms!" and the colonel to imitate him. There was a rush towards the guns; every one pushed forward. A few even forgot their collars.

But the prefectoral coach seemed to sense the trouble, for the two yoked nags, dawdling in their harness, came at a slow trot in front of the townhall at the very moment when the National Guard and firemen deployed, beating time with their boots.

"Present arms!" shouted Binet.

"Halt!" shouted the colonel. "By the left flank, march!"

And after presenting arms, during which the clang of the band, letting loose, rang out like a brass kettle rolling downstairs, all the guns were lowered.

Then was seen stepping down from the carriage a gentleman in a short coat with silver braiding, with bald brow, and wearing a tuft of hair at the back of his head, of a sallow complexion and the most benign of aspects. His eyes, very large and covered by heavy lids, were half-closed to look at the crowd, while at the same time he raised his sharp nose, and forced a smile upon his sunken mouth. He recognised the mayor by his scarf, and explained to him that the prefect was not able to come. He himself was a councillor at the prefecture; then he added a few apologies. Monsieur Tuvache reciprocated with polite compliments, humbly acknowledged by the other; and they remained thus, face to face, their foreheads almost touching, surrounded by members of the jury, the municipal council, the notable personages, the National Guard and the crowd. The councillor pressing his little cocked hat to his breast repeated his greetings, while Tuvache, bent like a bow, also smiled, stammered, tried to say something, protested his devotion to the monarchy and the honor that was being done to Yonville.

Hippolyte, the groom from the inn, took the head of the horses from the coachman, and, limping along with his clubfoot, led them to the door of the "Lion d'Or" where a number of peasants collected to look at the carriage. The drum beat, the howitzer thundered, and the gentlemen one by one mounted the platform, where they sat down in red utrecht velvet arm-chairs that had been lent by Madame Tuvache.

All these people looked alike. Their fair flabby faces, somewhat tanned by the sun, were the color of sweet cider, and their puffy whiskers emerged from stiff collars, kept up by white cravats with broad bows. All the waistcoats were of velvet, double-breasted; all the watches had, at the end of a long ribbon, an oval seal; all rested their two hands on their thighs, carefully stretching the stride of their trousers, whose unspunged glossy cloth shone more brilliantly than the leather of their heavy boots.

The ladies of the company stood at the back under the porch between the pillars, while the common herd was opposite, standing up or sitting on chairs. Lestiboudois had brought there all the chairs that he had moved from the field, and he even kept running back every minute to fetch others from the church. He caused such confusion with this piece of business that one had great difficulty in getting to the small steps of the platform.

"I think," said Monsieur Lheureux to the pharmacist who was heading for his seat, "that they ought to have put up two Venetian masts with something rather severe and rich for ornaments; it would have been a very pretty sight."

"Certainly," replied Homais; "but what can you expect? The mayor took everything on his own shoulders. He hasn't much taste. Poor Tuvache! he is completely devoid of what is called the genius of art."

Meanwhile, Rodolphe and Madame Bovary had ascended to the first floor of the townhall, to the "council-room," and, as it was empty, he suggested that they could enjoy the sight there more comfortably. He fetched three chairs from the round table under the bust of the monarch, and having carried them to one of the windows, they sat down together.

There was commotion on the platform, long whisperings, much parleying. At last the councillor got up. It was known by now that his name was Lieuvain, and in the crowd the name was now passing from lip to lip. After he had reshuffled a few pages, and bent over them to see better, he began:

"Gentlemen! May I be permitted first of all (before addressing you on the object of our meeting to-day, and this sentiment will, I am sure, be shared by you all), may I be permitted, I say, to pay a tribute to the higher administration, to the government, to the monarch, gentlemen, our sovereign, to that beloved king, to whom no branch of public or private prosperity is a matter of indifference, and who directs with a hand at once so firm and wise the chariot of the state amid the incessant perils of a stormy sea, knowing, moreover, how to make peace respected as well as war, industry, commerce, agriculture, and the fine arts."

"I ought," said Rodolphe, "to get back a little further."

"Why?" said Emma.

But at this moment the voice of the councillor rose to an extraordinary pitch. He declaimed—

"This is no longer the time, gentlemen, when civil discord made blood flow in our market squares, when the landowner, the businessman, the working-man himself, lying down to peaceful sleep, trembled lest he should be awakened suddenly by the noise of alarming tocsins, when the most subversive doctrines audaciously sapped foundations . . ."

"Well, some one down there might see me," Rodolphe resumed, "then I should have to invent excuses for a fortnight; and with my bad reputation . . ."

"Oh, you are slandering yourself," said Emma.

"No! It is dreadful, I assure you."

"But, gentlemen," continued the councillor, "if, banishing from my memory the remembrance of these sad pictures, I carry my eyes back to the present situation of our dear country, what do I see there? Everywhere commerce and the arts are flourishing; everywhere new means of communication, like so many new arteries in the body politic, establish within it new relations. Our great industrial centers have recovered all their activity; religion, more consolidated, smiles in all hearts; our ports are full, confidence is born again, and France breathes once more! . . . ."

"Besides," added Rodolphe, "perhaps from the world's point of view they are right."

"How so?" she asked.

"What!" said he. "Don't you know that there are souls constantly tormented? They need by turns to dream and to act, the purest passions and the most turbulent joys, and thus they fling themselves into all sorts of fantasies, of follies."

Then she looked at him as one looks at a traveler who has voyaged over strange lands, and went on:

"We have not even this distraction, we poor women!"

"A sad distraction, for happiness isn't found in it."

"But is it ever found?" she asked.

"Yes; one day it comes," he answered.

"And this is what you have understood," said the councillor. "You, farmers, agricultural laborers! you pacific pioneers of a work that belongs wholly to civilisation! you, men of progress and morality, you have understood, I say, that political storms are even more redoubtable than atmospheric disturbances!"

"A day comes," repeated Rodolphe, "one is near despair. Then the horizon expands; it is as if a voice cried, 'It is here!' You feel the need of confiding the whole of your life, of giving everything, sacrificing everything to this person. There is no need for explanations; one understands each other, having met before in dreams!" (And he looked at her.) "At last, here it is, this treasure so sought after, here before you. It glitters, it flashes; yet one still doubts, one does not believe it; one remains dazzled, as if one went out from darkness into light."

And as he ended Rodolphe suited the action to the word. He passed his hand over his face, like a man about to faint. Then he let it fall on Emma's. She drew hers back. But the councillor was still reading.

"And who would be surprised at it, gentlemen? He only who was so blind, so imprisoned (I do not fear to say it), so imprisoned by the prejudices of another age as still to misunderstand the spirit of our rural populations. Where, indeed, is more patriotism to be found than in the country, greater devotion to the public welfare, in a word, more intelligence? And, gentlemen, I do not mean that superficial intelligence, vain ornament of idle minds, but rather that profound and balanced intelligence that applies itself above all else to useful objects, thus contributing to the good of all, to the common amelioration and to the support of the state, born of respect for law and the practice of duty . . ."

"Ah! again!" said Rodolphe. "Always 'duty.' I am sick of the word. They are a lot of old jackasses in woolen vests and old bigots with foot-warmers and rosaries who constantly drone into our ears

'Duty, duty!' Ah! by Jove! as if one's real duty were not to feel what is great, cherish the beautiful, and not accept all the conventions of society with the hypocrisy it forces upon us."

"Yet . . . yet . . ." objected Madame Bovary.

"No, no! Why cry out against the passions? Are they not the one beautiful thing on earth, the source of heroism, of enthusiasm, of poetry, music, the arts, in a word, of everything?"

"But one must," said Emma, "to some extent bow to the opinion of the world and accept its morality."

"Ah, but there are two moralities," he replied, "the petty one, the morality of small men that constantly keeps changing, but yells itself hoarse; crude and loud like the crowd of imbeciles that you see down there. But the other, the eternal, that is about us and above, like the landscape that surrounds us, and the blue heavens that give us light."

Monsieur Lieuvain had just wiped his mouth with a pocket-handkerchief. He continued:

"It would be presumptuous of me, gentlemen, to point out to you the uses of agriculture. Who supplies our wants, who provides our means of subsistence, if not the farmer? It is the farmer, gentlemen, who sows with laborious hand the fertile furrows of the country, brings forth the wheat, which, being ground, is made into a powder by means of ingenious machinery, issues from there under the name of flour, and is then transported to our cities, soon delivered to the baker, who makes it into food for poor and rich alike. Again, is it not the farmer who fattens his flocks in the pastures in order to provide us with warm clothing? For how should we clothe or nourish ourselves without his labor? And, gentlemen, is it even necessary to go so far for examples? Who has not frequently reflected on all the momentous things that we get out of that modest animal, the ornament of poultry-yards, that provides us at once with a soft pillow for our bed, with succulent flesh for our tables, and eggs? But I should never end if I were to enumerate one after the other all the different products which the earth, well cultivated, like a generous mother, lavishes upon her children. Here it is the vine; elsewhere apple trees for cider; there colza; further, cheeses; and flax; gentlemen, let us not forget flax, which has made such great strides forward these last years and to which I call your special attention!"

He had no need to call it, for all the mouths of the multitude were wide open, as if to drink in his words. Tuvache by his side listened to him with staring eyes. Monsieur Derozerays from time to time softly closed his eyelids, and farther on the pharmacist, with his son Napoleon between his knees, put his hand behind his ear in order not to lose a syllable. The chins of the other members of the jury nodded slowly up and down in their waistcoats in sign of approval. The firemen at the foot of the platform rested on their bayonets; and Binet, motionless, stood with out-turned elbows, the point of his sabre in the air. Perhaps he could hear, but he certainly couldn't see a thing, for the visor of his helmet fell down on his nose. His lieutenant, the youngest son of Monsieur Tuvache, had an even bigger one; it was so large that he could hardly keep it on, in spite of the cotton scarf that peeped out from underneath. He wore a smile of childlike innocence, and his thin pale face, dripping with sweat, expressed satisfaction, some exhaustion and sleepiness.

The square was crowded up to the houses. People were leaning on their elbows at all the windows, others were standing on their doorsteps, and Justin, in front of the pharmacy, seemed fascinated by the spectacle. In spite of the silence Monsieur Lieuvain's voice was lost in the air. It reached you in fragments of phrases, interrupted here and there by the creaking of chairs in the crowd; then, the long bellowing of an ox would suddenly burst forth from behind, or else the bleating of the lambs, who answered one another from street to street. Even the cowherds and shepherds had driven their beasts this far, and one could hear their lowing from time to time, while with their tongues they tore down some scrap of foliage that hung over their muzzles.

Rodolphe had drawn nearer to Emma, and was whispering hurriedly in her ear:

"Doesn't this conspiracy of society revolt you? Is there a single sentiment it does not condemn? The noblest instincts, the purest feelings are persecuted, slandered; and if at length two poor souls do meet, all is organized in such a way as to keep them from becoming one. Yet they will try, they will call to each other. Not in vain, for sooner or later, be it in six or ten years, they will come together in love; for fate has decreed it, and they are born for each other."

His arms were folded across his knees, and thus lifting his face at her from close by, he looked fixedly at her. She noticed in his eyes small golden lines radiating from the black pupils; she even smelt the perfume of the pomade that made his hair glossy. Then something gave way in her; she recalled the Viscount who had waltzed with her at Vaubyessard, and whose beard exhaled a similar scent of vanilla and lemon, and mechanically she half-closed her eyes the better to breathe it in. But in making this movement, as she leant back in her chair, she saw in the distance, right on the line of the horizon, the old diligence the "Hirondelle," that was slowly descending the hill of Leux, dragging after it a long trail of dust. It was in this yellow carriage that Léon had so often come back to her, and by this route down there that he had gone for ever. She fancied she saw him opposite at his window; then all grew confused; clouds gathered; it seemed to her that she was again turning in the waltz under the light of the lustres on the arm of the Viscount, and that Léon was not far away, that he was coming . . . and yet all the time she was conscious of Rodolphe's head by her side. The sweetness of this sensation revived her past desires, and like grains of sand under a gust of wind, they swirled around in the subtle breath of the perfume that diffused over her soul. She breathed deeply several times to drink in the freshness of the ivy round the columns. She took off her gloves and wiped her hands; then she fanned her face with her handkerchief while she kept hearing, through the throbbing of her temples, the murmur of the crowd and the voice of the councillor intoning his phrases.

He was saying:

"Persevere! listen neither to the suggestions of routine, nor to the over-hasty councils of a rash empiricism. Apply yourselves, above all, to the amelioration of the soil, to good manures, to the development of the breeds, whether equine, bovine, ovine, or porcine. May these shows be to you pacific arenas, where the victor in leaving will hold forth a hand to the vanquished, and will fraternise with him in the hope of even greater success. And you, aged servants! humble helpers, whose hard labor no Government up to this day has taken into consideration, receive the reward of your silent virtues, and be assured that the state henceforward has its eye upon you; that it encourages you, protects you; that it will accede to your just demands, and alleviate as much as possible the heavy burden of your painful sacrifices."

Monsieur Lieuvain sat down; Monsieur Derozerays got up, beginning another speech. His was not perhaps so florid as that of the councillor, but it stood out by a more direct style, that is to say, by more specific knowledge and more elevated considerations. Thus the praise of the Government took up less space; religion and agriculture more. He showed the relation between both, and how they had always contributed to civilisation. Rodolphe was talking dreams, forebodings, magnetism with Madame Bovary. Going back to the cradle of society, the orator painted those fierce times when men lived on acorns in the heart of woods. Then they had left off the skins of beasts, had put on cloth, tilled the soil, planted the vine. Was this a good, or wasn't there more harm than good in this discovery? That was the problem to which Monsieur Derozerays addressed himself. From magnetism little by little Rodolphe had come to affinities, and while the president was citing Cincinnatus[41] and his plough, Diocletian[42] planting his cabbages, and the Emperors

41. Cincinnatus was a Roman Consul (460 B.C.), who was supposedly called to his office while found plowing.

42. Diocletian (245–313) was Roman emperor from 284 to 305. He resigned in 305 and retired to Salone, (now Split) in Dalmatia, to cultivate his garden.

of China inaugurating the year by the sowing of seed, the young man was explaining to the young woman that these irresistible attractions find their cause in some previous state of existence.

"Take us, for instance," he said, "how did we happen to meet? What chance willed it? It was because across infinite distances, like two streams uniting, our particular inclinations pushed us toward one another."

And he seized her hand; she did not withdraw it.

"First prize for general farming!" announced the president.

"—Just now, for example, when I went to your home . . . ."

"To Mr. Bizat of Quincampoix."

"—Did I know I would accompany you?"

"Seventy francs!"

"—A hundred times I tried to leave; yet I followed you and stayed . . ."

"For manures!"

"—As I would stay to-night, to-morrow, all other days, all my life!"

"To Monsieur Caron of Argueil, a gold medal!"

"—For I have never enjoyed anyone's company so much."

"To Monsieur Bain of Givry-Saint-Martin."

"—And I will never forget you."

"For a merino ram . . ."

"—Whereas you will forget me; I'll pass through your life as a mere shadow . . ."

"To Monsieur Belot of Notre-Dame."

"—But no, tell me there can be a place for me in your thoughts, in your life, can't there?"

"Hog! first prize equally divided between Messrs. Lehérissé and Cullembourg, sixty francs!"

Rodolphe was holding her hand on his; it was warm and quivering like a captive dove that wants to fly away; perhaps she was trying to take it away or perhaps she was answering his pressure, at any rate, she moved her fingers; he exclaimed

"Oh, thank you! You do not repulse me! You are kind! You understand that I am yours! Let me see you, let me look at you!"

A gust of wind that blew in at the window ruffled the cloth on the table, and in the square below all the large bonnets rose up like the fluttering wings of white butterflies.

"Use of oil-cakes!" continued the president.

He was hurrying now: "Flemish manure, flax-growing, drainage, long term leases . . . domestic service."

Rodolphe was no longer speaking. They looked at each other. As their desire increased, their dry lips trembled and languidly, effortlessly, their fingers intertwined.

"Catherine Nicaise Elizabeth Leroux, of Sassetot-la-Guerrière, for fifty-four years of service at the same farm, a silver medal—value, twenty-five francs!"

"Where is Catherine Leroux?" repeated the councillor.

She did not appear, and one could hear whispering voices:

"Go ahead!"

"No."

"To the left!"

"Don't be afraid!"

"Oh, how stupid she is!"

"Well, is she there?" cried Tuvache.

"Yes; here she is."

"Then what's she waiting for?"

There came forward on the platform a frightened-looking little old lady who seemed to shrink within her poor clothes. On her feet she wore heavy wooden shoes, and from her hips hung a large blue apron. Her pale face framed in a borderless cap was more wrinkled than a withered russet apple, and from the sleeves of her red jacket looked out two large hands with gnarled joints. The dust from the barns, washing soda and grease from the wool had so encrusted, roughened, hardened them that they seemed dirty, although they had been rinsed in clear water; and by dint of long service they remained half open, as if to bear humble witness of so much suffering endured. Something of monastic rigidity dignified her. No trace of sadness or tenderness weakened her pale face. Having lived so long among animals, she had taken on their silent and tranquil ways. It was the first time that she found herself in the midst of so large a company; and inwardly scared by the flags, the drums, the gentlemen in frock-coats, and the decorations of the councillor, she stood motionless, not knowing whether she should advance or run away, nor why the crowd was cheering and the jury smiling at her. Thus, a half century of servitude confronted these beaming bourgeois.

"Step forward, venerable Catherine Nicaise Elizabeth Leroux!" said the councillor, who had taken the list of prize-winners from the president; and, looking at the piece of paper and the old woman by turns, he repeated in a fatherly tone:

"Step forward, step forward!"

"Are you deaf?" said Tuvache, who was jumping around in his arm-chair; and he began shouting in her ear, "Fifty-four years of service. A silver medal! Twenty-five francs! For you!"

Then, when she had her medal, she looked at it, and a smile of beatitude spread over her face; and as she walked away they could hear her muttering:

"I'll give it to our curé at home, to say some masses for me!"

"What fanaticism!" exclaimed the pharmacist, leaning across to the notary.

The meeting was over, the crowd dispersed, and now that the speeches had been read, everything fell back into place again, and everything into the old grooves; the masters bullied the servants, the servants beat the animals, indolent victors returning to their stables with a green wreath between their horns.

The National Guards, however, had climbed up to the second floor of the townhall; brioches were stuck on their bayonets, and the drummer of the battalion carried a basket with bottles. Madame Bovary took Rodolphe's arm; he saw her home; they separated at her door; then he walked about alone in the meadow while waiting for the banquet to start.

The feast was long, noisy, ill served; the guests were so crowded that they could hardly move their elbows; and the narrow planks that served as benches almost broke under their weight. They ate huge amounts. Each one stuffed himself with all he could lay hands on. Sweat stood on every brow, and a whitish steam, like the vapour of a stream on an autumn morning, floated above the table between the hanging lamps. Rodolphe, leaning against the canvas of the tent, was thinking so intently of Emma that he heard nothing. Behind him on the grass the servants were piling up the dirty plates, his neighbors were talking; he did not answer them; they filled his glass, and there was silence in his thoughts in spite of the noise around him. He was dreaming of what she had said, of the line of her lips; her face, as in a magic mirror, shone on the plates of the shakos, the folds of her gown fell along the walls, and endless days of love unrolled before him in the future.

He saw her again in the evening during the fireworks, but she was with her husband, Madame Homais, and the pharmacist, who was worrying about the danger of stray rockets. Time and again he left the company to give some advice to Binet.

The fireworks sent to Monsieur Tuvache had, through an excess of caution, been locked in his cellar; so the damp powder would not light, and the main piece, that was to represent a dragon biting his tail, failed completely. From time to time, a meagre Roman-candle went off; then the gaping crowd sent up a roar that mingled with the giggling of the women who were being tickled in the darkness. Emma silently nestled against Charles's shoulder; then, raising her chin, she watched the luminous rays of the rockets against the dark sky. Rodolphe gazed at her in the light of the burning lanterns.

One by one, they went out. Stars appeared. A few drops of rain began to fall. She tied her scarf over her bare head.

At this moment the councillor's carriage came out from the inn. His coachman, who was drunk, suddenly fell asleep, and one could see the mass of his body from afar above the hood, framed by the two lanterns, swaying from right to left with the motion of the springs.

"Truly," said the pharmacist, "severe measures should be taken against drunkenness! I should like to see written up weekly at the door of the townhall on a board *ad hoc* the names of all those who during the week got intoxicated on alcohol. Besides, with regard to statistics, one would thus have, as it were, public records that one could refer to if needed . . . But excuse me!"

And he once more ran off to the captain. The latter was returning to see his lathe.

"You might do well," said Homais to him, "to send one of your men, or to go yourself . . ."

"Oh, leave me alone!" answered the tax-collector. "I'm telling you everything is taken care of."

"There is nothing for you to worry about," said the pharmacist, when he returned to his friends. "Monsieur Binet has assured me that all precautions have been taken. No sparks have fallen; the pumps are full. Let's go to bed."

"I can certainly use some sleep," said Madame Homais with a huge yawn. "But never mind; we've had a beautiful day for our fete."

Rodolphe repeated in a low voice, and with a tender look, "Oh, yes! very beautiful!"

And after a final good night, they parted ways.

Two days later, in the "Fanal de Rouen," there was a long article on the show. Homais had composed it on the spur of the moment, the very morning after the banquet.

"Why these festoons, these flowers, these garlands? Whereto was the crowd hurrying, like the waves of a furious sea under the torrents of a tropical sun pouring its heat upon our meadows?"

Then he spoke of the condition of the peasants. Certainly the Government was doing much, but not enough. "Be bold!" he told them; "a thousand reforms are needed; let us carry them out! Then, reporting on the entry of the councillor, he did not forget "the martial spirit of our militia," nor "our dazzling village maidens," nor the "bald-headed elders like patriarchs, some of whom, left over from our immortal phalanxes, still felt their hearts beat at the manly sound of the drums." He cited himself among the first of the members of the jury, and he even called attention in a note to the fact that Monsieur Homais, pharmacist, had sent a memoir on cider to the agricultural society. When he came to the distribution of the prizes, he painted the joy of the prize-winners in dithyrambic strophes. "The father embraced the son, the brother the brother, the husband his wife. More than one showed his humble medal with pride; and no doubt when he got home to his good housewife, he hung it up weeping on the modest walls of his cottage.

"About six o'clock a banquet prepared in the meadow of Monsieur Leigeard brought together the main participants in the festivities. The utmost merriment reigned throughout. Several toasts were proposed: Monsieur Lieuvain, To the king! Monsieur Tuvache, To the prefect! Monsieur Derozerays, To Agriculture! Monsieur Homais, To the twin sisters, Industry and Fine Arts! Monsieur Leplichey, To Improvements! At night some brilliant fireworks suddenly lit up the sky. It was a real kaleidoscope, an operatic scene; and for a moment our little locality might have thought itself transported into the midst of a dream from the 'Thousand and One Nights.'

"Let us state that no untoward event disturbed this family meeting."

And he added: "Only the absence of the clergy was noted. No doubt the priests do not understand progress in the same way. Just as you please, *messieurs de Loyola!*"[43]

IX

Six weeks passed. Rodolphe did not come again. At last one evening he appeared.

The day after the fair he told himself:

"Let's not go back too soon; that would be a mistake."

And at the end of a week he had gone off hunting. After the hunting he first feared that too much time had passed, and then he reasoned thus:

"If she loved me from the first day, impatience must make her love me even more. Let's persist!"

And he knew that his calculation had been right when, on entering the room, he saw Emma turn pale.

She was alone. Night was falling. The small muslin curtain along the windows deepened the twilight, and the gilding of the barometer, on which the rays of the sun fell, shone in the looking-glass between the meshes of the coral.

Rodolphe remained standing, and Emma hardly answered his first conventional phrases.

"I have been busy," he said, "I have been ill."

"Nothing serious?" she cried.

"Well," said Rodolphe, sitting down at her side on a footstool, "no . . . It was because I did not want to come back."

"Why?"

"Can't you guess?"

He looked at her again, but so hard that she lowered her head, blushing. He pursued:

"Emma . . ."

"Monsieur!" she exclaimed, drawing back a little.

"Ah! you see," he replied in a melancholy voice, "that I was right

43. Messieurs de Loyola, or Jesuits. Ignatius Loyola (1491–1556), a Spaniard, founded the Order of the Jesuits in 1534. The Jesuits were expelled from France in 1762.

not to come back; for this name, this name that fills my whole soul, and that escaped me, you forbid me its use! Madame Bovary! . . . why, the whole world calls you thus! Moreover, it is not your name; it is the name of another!"

He repeated,

"Of another!"

And he hid his face in his hands.

"Yes, I think of you constantly! . . . The thought of you drives me to despair. Ah! forgive me! . . . I'll go . . . Adieu . . . I'll go far away, so far that you will never hear of me again; yet . . . today . . . I don't know what force made me come here. For one does not struggle against Heaven; it is impossible to resist the smile of angels; one is carried away by the beautiful, the lovely, the adorable."

It was the first time that Emma had heard such words addressed to her, and her pride unfolded languidly in the warmth of this language, like someone stretching in a hot bath.

"But if I didn't come," he continued, "if I couldn't see you, at least I have gazed long on all that surrounds you. At night, every night, I arose; I came here; I watched your house, the roof glimmering in the moon, the trees in the garden swaying before your window, and the little lamp, a gleam shining through the window-panes in the darkness. Ah! you never knew that there, so near you, so far from you, was a poor wretch . . ."

She turned towards him with a sob.

"Oh, you are kind!" she said.

"No, I love you, that is all! You do not doubt that! Tell me; one word, one single word!"

And Rodolphe imperceptibly glided from the footstool to the ground; but a sound of wooden shoes was heard in the kitchen, and he noticed that the door of the room was not closed.

"You would do an act of charity," he went on, rising, "if you accepted to gratify a whim!" It was to visit her home, he wished to see it, and since Madame Bovary could see no objection to this, they both rose just when Charles came in.

"Good morning, doctor," Rodolphe said to him.

Flattered by this unexpected title, Charles launched into elaborate displays of politeness. Of this the other took advantage to pull himself together.

"Madame was speaking to me," he then said, "about her health."

Charles interrupted; she was indeed giving him thousands of worries; her palpitations were beginning again. Then Rodolphe asked if riding would not be helpful.

"Certainly! excellent, just the thing! What a good idea! You ought to try it."

And as she objected that she had no horse, Monsieur Rodolphe offered one. She refused his offer; he did not insist. Then to explain his visit he said that his ploughman, the man of the blood-letting, still suffered from dizziness.

"I'll drop by," said Bovary.

"No, no! I'll send him to you; we'll come; that will be more convenient for you."

"Ah! very good! I thank you."

And as soon as they were alone, "Why don't you accept Monsieur Boulanger's offer? It was so gracious of him."

She seemed to pout, invented a thousand excuses, and finally declared that perhaps it would look odd.

"That's the least of my worries!" said Charles, turning on his heel. "Health first! You are making a mistake."

"Could I go riding without proper clothes?"

"You must order a riding outfit," he answered.

The riding-habit decided her.

When it was ready, Charles wrote to Monsieur Boulanger that his wife was able to accept his invitation and thanked him in advance for his kindness.

The next day at noon Rodolphe appeared at Charles's door with two saddle-horses. One had pink rosettes at his ears and a deerskin side-saddle.

Rodolphe had put on high soft boots, assuming that she had never seen the likes of them. In fact, Emma was charmed with his appearance as he stood on the landing in his great velvet coat and white corduroy breeches. She was ready; she was waiting for him.

Justin escaped from the store to watch her depart, and the pharmacist himself also came out. He was giving Monsieur Boulanger some good advice.

"An accident happens so easily. Be careful! Your horses may be skittish!"

She heard a noise above her; it was Félicité drumming on the window-panes to amuse little Berthe. The child blew her a kiss; her mother answered with a wave of her whip.

"Have a pleasant ride!" cried Monsieur Homais. "Be careful! above all, be careful!"

And he flourished his newspaper as he saw them disappear.

As soon as he felt the ground, Emma's horse set off at a gallop. Rodolphe galloped by her side. Now and then they exchanged a word. With slightly bent head, her hand well up, and her right arm stretched out, she gave herself up to the cadence of the movement that rocked her in her saddle.

At the bottom of the hill Rodolphe gave his horse its head; they set off together at a bound, then at the top suddenly the horses stopped, and her large blue veil fell about her.

It was early in October. There was fog over the land. Hazy clouds hovered on the horizon between the outlines of the hills; others, rent asunder, floated up and disappeared. Sometimes through a rift in the clouds, beneath a ray of sunshine, gleamed from afar the roofs of Yonville, with the gardens at the water's edge, the yards, the walls and the church steeple. Emma half closed her eyes to pick out her house, and never had this poor village where she lived appeared so small. From the height on which they were the whole valley seemed an immense pale lake sending off its vapour into the air. Clumps of trees here and there stood out like black rocks, and the tall lines of the poplars that rose above the mist were like a beach stirred by the wind.

By the side, on the grass between the pines, a brown light shimmered in the warm atmosphere. The earth, ruddy like the powder of tobacco, deadened the noise of their steps, and as they walked, the horses kicked up fallen pine cones before them.

Rodolphe and Emma thus skirted the woods. She turned away from time to time to avoid his look, and then she saw only the line of pine trunks, whose monotonous succession made her a little giddy. The horses were panting; the leather of the saddles creaked.

Just as they were entering the forest the sun came out.

"God is with us!" said Rodolphe.

"Do you think so?" she said.

"Forward! forward!" he continued.

He clucked with his tongue. The horses set off at a trot.

Long ferns by the roadside caught in Emma's stirrup. Rodolphe leant forward and removed them as they rode along. At other times, to turn aside the branches, he passed close to her, and Emma felt his knee brushing against her leg. The sky was blue now. The leaves no longer stirred. There were spaces full of heather in flower, and patches of purple alternated with the confused tangle of the trees, grey, fawn, or golden colored, according to the nature of their leaves. Often in the thicket one could hear the fluttering of wings, or else the hoarse, soft cry of the ravens flying off amidst the oaks.

They dismounted. Rodolphe fastened up the horses. She walked on in front on the moss between the paths.

But her long dress got in her way, although she held it up by the skirt; and Rodolphe, walking behind her, saw between the black cloth and the black shoe the delicacy of her white stocking, that seemed to him as if it were a part of her nakedness.

She stopped.

"I am tired," she said.

"Come, try some more," he went on. "Courage!"

Some hundred paces further on she stopped again, and through her veil, that fell sideways from her man's hat over her hips, her face appeared in a bluish transparency as if she were floating under azure waves.

"But where are we going?"

He did not answer. She was breathing irregularly. Rodolphe looked round him biting his moustache.

They came to a larger space which had been cleared of undergrowth. They sat down on the trunk of a fallen tree, and Rodolphe began speaking to her of his love.

He did not frighten her at first with compliments. He was calm, serious, melancholy.

Emma listened to him with bowed head, and stirred the bits of wood on the ground with the tip of her foot.

But at the words, "Are not our destinies now forever united?"

"Oh, no!" she replied. "You know they aren't. It is impossible!"

She rose to go. He seized her by the wrist. She stopped. Then, having gazed at him for a few moments with an amorous and moist look, she said hurriedly:

"Well let's not speak of it again! Where are the horses? Let's go back."

He made a gesture of anger and annoyance. She repeated:

"Where are the horses? Where are the horses?"

Then smiling a strange smile, looking straight at her, his teeth set, he advanced with outstretched arms. She recoiled trembling. She stammered:

"Oh, you frighten me! You hurt me! Take me back!"

"If it must be," he went on, his face changing; and he again became respectful, caressing, timid. She gave him her arm. They went back. He said:

"What was the matter with you? Why? I do not understand. You were mistaken, no doubt. In my soul you are as a Madonna on a pedestal, in a place lofty, secure, immaculate. But I cannot live without you! I need your eyes, your voice, your thought! Be my friend, my sister, my angel!"

And he stretched out his arm and caught her by the waist. Gently she tried to disengage herself. He supported her thus as they walked along.

They heard the two horses browsing on the leaves.

"Not quite yet!" said Rodolphe. "Stay a minute longer! Please stay!"

He drew her farther on to a small pool where duckweeds made a greenness on the water. Faded waterlilies lay motionless between the reeds. At the noise of their steps in the grass, frogs jumped away to hide themselves.

"I shouldn't, I shouldn't!" she said. "I am out of my mind listening to you!"

"Why? . . . Emma! Emma!"

"Oh, Rodolphe! . . ." she said slowly and she pressed against his shoulder.

The cloth of her dress clung to the velvet of his coat. She threw back her white neck which swelled in a sigh, and, faltering, weeping, and hiding her face in her hands, with one long shudder, she abandoned herself to him.

The shades of night were falling; the horizontal sun passing between the branches dazzled the eyes. Here and there around her, in the leaves or on the ground, trembled luminous patches, as if humming-birds flying about had scattered their feathers. Silence was everywhere; something sweet seemed to come forth from the trees. She felt her heartbeat return, and the blood coursing through her flesh like a river of milk. Then far away, beyond the wood, on the other hills, she heard a vague prolonged cry, a voice which lingered, and in silence she heard it mingling like music with the last pulsations of her throbbing nerves. Rodolphe, a cigar between his lips, was mending with his penknife one of the two broken bridles.

They returned to Yonville by the same road. On the mud they saw again the traces of their horses side by side, the same thickets, the same stones in the grass; nothing around them seemed changed; and yet for her something had happened more stupendous than if the mountains had moved in their places. Rodolphe now and again bent forward and took her hand to kiss it.

She was charming on horseback—upright, with her slender waist, her knee bent on the mane of her horse, her face somewhat flushed by the fresh air in the red of the evening.

On entering Yonville she made her horse prance in the road.

People looked at her from the windows.

At dinner her husband thought she looked well, but she pretended not to hear him when he inquired about her ride, and she remained sitting there with her elbow at the side of her plate between the two lighted candles.

"Emma!" he said.

"What?"

"Well, I spent the afternoon at Monsieur Alexandre's. He has an old filly, still very fine, just a little broken in the knees, and that could be bought, I am sure, for a hundred crowns." He added, "And thinking it might please you, I have reserved her . . . I bought her . . . Have I done right? Do tell me!"

She nodded her head in assent; then a quarter of an hour later:

"Are you going out to-night?" she asked.

"Yes. Why?"

"Oh, nothing, nothing, dear!"

And as soon as she had got rid of Charles she went and shut herself up in her room.

At first she felt stunned; she saw the trees, the paths, the ditches, Rodolphe, and she again felt the pressure of his arms, while the leaves rustled and the reeds whistled.

But when she saw herself in the mirror she wondered at her face. Never had her eyes been so large, so black, nor so deep. Something subtle about her being transfigured her.

She repeated: "I have a lover! a lover!" delighting at the idea as if a second puberty had come to her. So at last she was to know those joys of love, that fever of happiness of which she had despaired! She was entering upon a marvelous world where all would be passion, ecstasy, delirium. She felt herself surrounded by an endless rapture. A blue space surrounded her and ordinary existence appeared only intermittently between these heights, dark and far away beneath her.

Then she recalled the heroines of the books that she had read, and the lyric legion of these adulterous women began to sing in her memory with the voice of sisters that charmed her. She became herself, as it were, an actual part of these lyrical imaginings; at long last, as she saw herself among those lovers she had so envied, she fulfilled the love-dream of her youth. Besides, Emma felt a satisfaction of revenge. How she had suffered! But she had won out at last, and the love so long pent up erupted in joyous outbursts. She tasted it without remorse, without anxiety, without concern.

The next day brought a new-discovered sweetness. They exchanged vows. She told him of her sorrows. Rodolphe interrupted her with kisses; and she, looking at him through half-closed eyes, asked him to call her again by her name and to say that he loved her. They were in the forest, as yesterday, this time in the hut of some *sabot* makers. The walls were of straw, and the roof so low they had to stoop. They were seated side by side on a bed of dry leaves.

From that day on they wrote to one another regularly every evening. Emma placed her letter at the end of the garden, by the river, in a crack of the wall. Rodolphe came to fetch it, and put another in its place that she always accused of being too short.

One morning, when Charles had gone out before daybreak, she felt the urge to see Rodolphe at once. She would go quickly to La Huchette, stay there an hour, and be back again at Yonville while every one was still asleep. The idea made her breathless with desire, and she soon found herself in the middle of the field, walking with rapid steps, without looking behind her.

Day was just breaking. Emma recognised her lover's house from a distance. Its two dove-tailed weathercocks stood out black against the pale dawn.

Beyond the farmyard there was a separate building that she assumed must be the château. She entered it as if the doors at her approach had opened wide of their own accord. A large straight staircase led up to the corridor. Emma raised the latch of a door, and suddenly at the end of the room she saw a man sleeping. It was Rodolphe. She uttered a cry.

"You here? You here?" he repeated. "How did you manage to come? Ah! your dress is wet."

"I love you!" she answered, winding her arm around his neck.

This first bold attempt having been successful, now every time Charles went out early Emma dressed quickly and slipped on tiptoe down the steps that led to the waterside.

But when the cow plank was taken up, she had to follow the walls alongside the river; the bank was slippery; to keep from falling, she had to catch hold of the tufts of faded wall-flowers. Then she went across ploughed fields, stumbling, her thin shoes sinking in the heavy mud. Her scarf, knotted round her head, fluttered to the wind in the meadows. She was afraid of the oxen; she began to run; she arrived out of breath, with rosy cheeks, and breathing out from her whole person a fresh perfume of sap, of verdure, of the open air. At this hour Rodolphe was still asleep. It was like a spring morning bursting into his room.

The golden curtains along the windows let a heavy, whitish light filter into the room. Emma would find her way gropingly, with blinking eyes, the drops of dew hanging from her hair, making a topaz halo around her face. Rodolphe, laughing, would draw her to him and press her to his breast.

Then she inspected the room, opened the drawers of the tables, combed her hair with his comb, and looked at herself in his shaving mirror. Often she put between her teeth the big pipe that lay on the bedtable, amongst lemons and pieces of sugar near the water bottle.

It took them a good quarter of an hour to say good-bye. Then Emma cried: she would have wished never to leave Rodolphe. Something stronger than herself drew her to him; until, one day, when she arrived unexpectedly, he frowned as one put out.

"What is wrong?" she said. "Are you ill? tell me!"

He ended up declaring earnestly that her visits were too dangerous and that she was compromising herself.

X

Gradually Rodolphe's fears took possession of her. At first, love had intoxicated her, and she had thought of nothing beyond. But now that he was indispensable to her life, she feared losing the smallest part of his love or upsetting him in the least. When she came back from his house, she looked all about her, anxiously watching every form that passed in the horizon, and every village window from which she could be seen. She listened for steps, cries, the noise of the ploughs, and she stopped short, white, and trembling more than the aspen leaves swaying overhead.

One morning as she was thus returning, she suddenly thought she saw the long barrel of a carbine that seemed to be aimed at her. It stuck out sideways from the end of a small barrel half-buried in the grass on the edge of a ditch. Emma, half-fainting with terror, nevertheless walked on, and a man stepped out of the barrel like a Jack-in-the-box jumping out of his cage. He had gaiters buckled up to the knees, his cap pulled down over his eyes; his lips shivered in the cold and his nose was red. It was Captain Binet lying in ambush for wild ducks.

"You ought to have called out long ago!" he exclaimed. "When one sees a gun, one should always give warning."

The tax-collector was thus trying to hide his own fright, for a prefectorial order prohibited duck-hunting except in boats, Monsieur Binet, despite his respect for the laws, was breaking the law and he expected to see the garde champêtre turn up any moment. But this anxiety whetted his pleasure, and, all alone in his barrel, he congratulated himself on his luck and his cleverness.

The sight of Emma seemed to relieve him of a great weight, and he at once opened the conversation.

"Pretty cold, isn't it; it's nippy!"

Emma didn't answer. He pursued:

"You're certainly off to an early start today."

"Yes," she stammered; "I am just coming from the nurse who is keeping my child."

"Ah, yes indeed, yes indeed. As for myself, I am here, just as you see me, since break of day; but the weather is so muggy, that unless one had the bird at the mouth of the gun . . ."

"Good day, Monsieur Binet," she interrupted, turning her back on him.

"Your servant, madame," he replied drily.

And he went back into his barrel.

Emma regretted having left the tax-collector so abruptly. No doubt he would jump to the worst conclusions. The story about the nurse was the weakest possible excuse, for every one at Yonville knew that the Bovary baby had been at home with her parents for a year. Besides, no one was living in this direction; this path led only to La Huchette. Binet, then, could not fail to guess where she came from, and he would not remain silent; he would talk, that was certain. She remained until evening racking her brain with every lie she could think up, but the image of that idiot with his game bag would not leave her.

Seeing her so gloomy, Charles proposed after dinner to take her to the pharmacist by way of distraction, and the first person she caught sight of in the shop was him again, the tax-collector! He was standing in front of the counter, lit up by the gleams of the red jar, saying:

"Could I have half an ounce of vitriol, please?"

"Justin," cried the pharmacist, "bring us the sulphuric acid."

Then to Emma, who was going up to Madame Homais' room, "Don't go up, it's not worth the trouble, she is just coming down. Why not warm yourself by the fire . . . Excuse me . . . Good-day, doctor" (for the pharmacist much enjoyed pronouncing the word "doctor," as if addressing another by it reflected on himself some of the grandeur of the title). "Justin, take care not to upset the mortars! You'd better fetch some chairs from the little room; you know very well that the arm-chairs are not to be taken out of the drawing-room."

And he was just about to put his arm-chair back in its place when Binet asked him for half an ounce of sugar acid.

"Sugar acid!" said the pharmacist contemptuously, "never heard of it! There is no such thing. Perhaps it is Oxalic acid you want. It is Oxalic, isn't it?"

Binet explained that he wanted a corrosive to make himself some copper-water with which to remove rust from his hunting things. Emma shuddered. The pharmacist was saying:

"Indeed, the dampness we're having is certainly not propitious."

"Nevertheless," replied the tax-collector, with a sly look, "some people seem to like it." She was stifling.

"And give me . . ."

"Will he never go?" she thought.

"Half an ounce of resin and turpentine, four ounces of beeswax, and three half ounces of animal charcoal, if you please, to clean the leather of my togs."

The druggist was beginning to cut the wax when Madame Homais appeared with Irma in her arms, Napoleon by her side, and Athalie following. She sat down on the velvet seat by the window, and the boy squatted down on a footstool, while his eldest sister hovered round the jujube box near her papa. The latter was filling funnels and corking phials, sticking on labels, making up parcels. Around him all were silent; only from time to time could one hear the weights jingling in the scales, and a few words of advice from the pharmacist to his apprentice.

"And how is your little girl?" Madame Homais asked suddenly.

"Silence!" exclaimed her husband, who was writing down some

figures on a scratch pad.

"Why didn't you bring her?" she went on in a low voice.

"Hush! hush!" said Emma, pointing a finger at the pharmacist.

But Binet, quite absorbed in checking over his bill, had probably heard nothing. At last he went out. Then Emma, relieved, uttered a deep sigh.

"How heavily you are breathing!" said Madame Homais.

"It is so hot in here," she replied.

So the next day they agreed to arrange their rendezvous. Emma wanted to bribe her servant with a present, but it would be better to find some safe house at Yonville. Rodolphe promised to look for one.

All through the winter, three or four times a week, in the dead of night he came to the garden. Emma had on purpose taken away the key of the gate, letting Charles think it was lost.

To call her, Rodolphe threw a handful of sand at the shutters. She jumped up with a start; but sometimes he had to wait, for Charles had the habit of talking endlessly by the fireside.

She was wild with impatience; if her eyes could have done it, they would have hurled him out of the window. At last she would begin to undress, then take up a book, and go on reading very quietly as if the book amused her. But Charles, who was in bed, would call her to bed.

"Come, now, Emma," he said, "it is time."

"Yes, I am coming," she answered.

Then, as the candles shone in his eyes, he turned to the wall and fell asleep. She escaped, holding her breath, smiling, half undressed.

Rodolphe had a large cloak; he wrapped it around her, and putting his arm round her waist, he drew her without a word to the end of the garden.

It was in the arbour, on the same bench of half rotten sticks where formerly Léon had stared at her so amorously on the summer evenings. She never thought of him now.

The stars shone through the leafless jasmine branches. Behind them they heard the river flowing, and now and again on the bank the rustling of the dry reeds. Masses of deeper darkness stood out here and there in the night and sometimes, shaken with one single motion, they would rise up and sway like immense black waves pressing forward to engulf them. The cold of the nights made them clasp each other more tightly; the sighs of their lips seemed to them deeper; their eyes, that they could hardly see, larger; and in the midst of the silence words softly spoken would fall on their souls with a crystalline sound, that echoed in endless reverberations.

When the night was rainy, they took refuge in the consulting-room between the cart-shed and the stable. She would light one of the kitchen candles that she had hidden behind the books. Rodolphe settled down there as if at home. The sight of the library, of the desk, of the entire room, in fine, would arouse his mirth; and he could not refrain from making jokes at Charles' expense despite Emma's embarrassment. She would have liked to see him more serious, and even on occasions more dramatic; as, for example, when she thought she heard a noise of approaching steps in the alley.

"Some one is coming!" she said.

He blew out the light.

"Have you your pistols?"

"Why?"

"Why, to defend yourself," replied Emma.

"From your husband? Oh, the poor fellow!" And Rodolphe finished his sentence with a gesture that said, "I could crush him with a flip of my finger."

She was awed at his bravery, although she felt in it a sort of indecency and a naïve coarseness that scandalised her.

Rodolphe reflected a good deal on the pistol incident. If she had spoken in earnest, he thought it most ridiculous, even odious; for he had no reason whatever to hate the good Charles, not exactly being devoured by jealousy; and in this same connection, Emma had made him a solemn promise that he did not think in the best of taste.

Besides, she was becoming dreadfully sentimental. She had insisted on exchanging miniatures; handfuls of hair had been cut off, and now she was asking for a ring—a real wedding-ring, in token of eternal union. She often spoke to him of the evening chimes, of the "voices of nature." Then she talked to him of their respective mothers. Rodolphe's had died twenty years ago. Emma none the less consoled him with conventional phrases, like those one would use with a bereaved child; sometimes she even said to him, gazing at the moon:

"I am sure that, from up there, both approve our love."

But she was so pretty! He had possessed so few women of similar ingenuousness. This love without debauchery was a new experience for him, and, drawing him out of his lazy habits, caressed at once his pride and his sensuality. Although his bourgeois common sense disapproved of it, Emma's exaltations, deep down in his heart, enchanted him, since they were directed his way. Then, sure of her love, he no longer made an effort, and insensibly his manner changed.

No longer, did he, as before, find words so tender that they made her cry, nor passionate caresses that drove her into ecstasy; their great love, in which she had lived immersed, seemed to run out beneath her, like the water of a river absorbed by its own bed; and she could see the bottom. She would not believe it; she redoubled in tenderness, and Rodolphe concealed his indifference less and less.

She did not know if she regretted having yielded to him, or whether she did not wish, on the contrary, to love him even more. The humiliation of having given in turned into resentment, tempered by their voluptuous pleasures. It was not tenderness; it was like a continual seduction. He held her fully in his power; she almost feared him.

On the surface, however, things seemed calm enough, Rodolphe having carried out his adultery just as he had wanted; and at the end of six months, when the spring-time came, they were to one another like a married couple, tranquilly keeping up a domestic flame.

It was the time of year when old Rouault sent his turkey in rememberance of the setting of his leg. The present always arrived with a letter. Emma cut the string that tied it to the basket, and read the following lines:

> My Dear Children,—I hope this will find you in good health, and that it will be as good as the others, for it seems to me a little more tender, if I may venture to say so, and heavier. But next time, for a change, I'll give you a turkeycock, unless you would prefer a capon; and send me back the hamper, if you please, with the two old ones. I have had an accident with sheds; the coverings flew off one windy night among the trees. The harvest has not been overgood either. Finally, I don't know when I shall come to see you. It is so difficult now to leave the house since I am alone, my poor Emma.

Here there was a break in the lines as if the old fellow had dropped his pen to dream a little while.

> "As for myself, I am very well, except for a cold I caught the other day at Yvetot, where I had gone to hire a shepherd, having got rid of mine because no cooking was good enough for his taste. We are to be pitied with rascals like him! Moreover, he was dishonest.
>
> I heard from a peddler who had a tooth pulled out when he passed through your part of the country this winter, that Bovary was as usual working hard. That doesn't surprise me; and he showed me his tooth; we had some coffee together. I asked him if he had seen you, and he said no, but that he had seen two horses in the stables, from which I conclude that business is looking up. So much the better, my dear children, and may God send you every imaginable happiness!
>
> It grieves me not yet to have seen my dear little grand-daughter, Berthe Bovary. I have planted an Orleans plum-tree for her in the garden under your room, and I won't have it touched until we can

make jam from it, that I will keep in the cupboard for her when she comes.

Good-bye, my dear children. I kiss you, my girl, you too, my son-in-law, and the little one on both cheeks. I am, with best compliments, your loving father.

THEODORE ROUAULT

She held the coarse paper in her fingers for some minutes. A continuous stream of spelling mistakes ran through the letter, and Emma followed the kindly thought that cackled right through it like a hen half hidden in a hedge of thorns. The writing had been dried with ashes from the hearth, for a little grey powder slipped from the letter on her dress, and she almost thought she saw her father bending over the hearth to take up the tongs. How long since she had been with him, sitting on the footstool in the chimney-corner, where she used to burn the end of a stick in the crackling flame of the sea-sedges! She remembered the summer evenings all full of sunshine. The colts whinnied when one passed by, and galloped, galloped . . . Under her window there was a beehive and at times, the bees wheeling round in the light, struck against her window like rebounding balls of gold. What happiness she had known at that time, what freedom, what hope! What a wealth of illusions! It was all gone now. She had lost them one by one, at every stage in the growth of her soul, in the succession of her conditions; maidenhood, marriage and love—shedding them along her path like a traveller who leaves something of his wealth at every inn along his road.

But who was it, then, who made her so unhappy? What extraordinary catastrophe had destroyed her life? And she raised her head, as if seeking around her for the cause of all that suffering.

An April sunray was dancing on the china in the shelves; the fire burned; beneath her slippers she felt the softness of the carpet; the day was bright, the air warm, and she heard her child shouting with laughter.

In fact, the little girl was just then rolling on the lawn in the new-mown grass. She was lying flat on her stomach at the top of a rick. The maid was holding her by her skirt. Lestiboudois was raking by her side, and every time he came near she bent forward, beating the air with both her arms.

"Bring her to me," said her mother, rushing over to kiss her. "How I love you, my poor child! How I love you!"

Then noticing that the tips of her ears were rather dirty, she rang at once for warm water, and washed her, changed her underwear, her stockings, her shoes, asked a thousand questions about her health, as if on the return from a long journey, and finally, kissing her again and crying a little, she gave her back to the maid, who was dumbfounded at this sudden outburst.

That evening Rodolphe found her more reserved than usual.

"It will blow over," he thought, "a passing whim . . ."

And he missed three successive rendezvous. When he did appear, her attitude was cold, almost contemptuous.

"Ah! you're wasting time, sweetheart!"

And he pretended not to notice her melancholy sighs, nor the handkerchief she pulled out.

Then Emma knew what it was to repent!

She even wondered why she hated Charles; wouldn't it have been better trying to love him? But he offered little hold for these reawakened sentiments, so she remained rather embarrassed with her sacrificial intentions until the pharmacist provided her with a timely opportunity.

XI

He had recently read a paper praising a new method for curing club-foot, and since he was a partisan of progress, he conceived the patriotic idea that Yonville should show its pioneering spirit by having some club-foot operations performed there.

"Look here," he told Emma, "what do we risk?" and he ticked off on his fingers the advantages of the attempt, "success practically assured, relief and better appearance for the patient, quick fame for the surgeon. Why, for example, should not your husband relieve poor Hippolyte of the 'Lion d'Or'? He is bound to tell all passing travellers about his cure, and then" (Homais lowered his voice and looked round him) "who is to prevent me from sending a short piece on the subject to the paper? And! My God! an article gets around . . . people talk about it . . . it snowballs! And who knows? who knows?"

After all, Bovary might very well succeed. Emma had no reason to suppose he lacked skill, it would be a satisfaction for her to have urged him to a step by which his reputation and fortune would be increased! She only longed to lean on something more solid than love.

Pressed by her and the pharmacist, Charles allowed himself to be persuaded. He sent to Rouen for Dr. Duval's volume, and every evening, with his head between his hands, he embarked on his reading assignment.

While he struggled with the equinus, varus and valgus—that is to say, *katastrephopody*, *endostrephopody*, and *exostrephopody*, or in other words, the various deviations of the foot, to the inside, outside, or downwards, as well as with *hypostrephopody* and *anastrephopody* or torsion below and contraction above,—Monsieur Homais was trying out all possible arguments on the stable boy in order to persuade him to submit to the operation.

"At the very most you'll feel a slight pain, a small prick, like a little blood letting, less than the extraction of certain corns."

Hippolyte thought it over, rolling his stupid eyes.

"Anyway," continued the pharmacist, "it is none of my business. I am telling you this for your own sake! out of pure humanity! I would like to see you freed from that hideous caudication as well as that swaying in your lumbar region which, whatever you say, must considerably interfere with the proper performance of your work."

Then Homais represented to him how much more dashing and nimble he would feel afterwards, and even hinted that he would be more likely to please the women; and the stable boy broke into a stupid grin. Then he attacked him through his vanity:

"Come on, act like a man! Think what would have happened if you had been called into the army, and had to fight under our national banner! . . . Ah! Hippolyte!"

And Homais left him, declaring that he could not understand such blindness, such obstinacy, in refusing the benefits of science.

The poor wretch finally gave in, for it was like a conspiracy. Binet, who never interfered with other people's business, Madame Lefrançois, Artémise, the neighbors, even the mayor, Monsieur Tuvache—every one tried to convince him by lecture and reproof; but what finally won him over was that it would cost him nothing. Bovary even undertook to provide the machine for the operation. This generosity was an idea of Emma's, and Charles consented to it, thinking in his heart of hearts that his wife was an angel.

So with the advice of the pharmacist, and after three fresh starts, he had a kind of box made by the carpenter, with the assistance of the locksmith; it weighed about eight pounds, for iron, wood, sheet-iron, leather, screws, and nuts had not been spared.

Yet, to know which of Hippolyte's tendons had to be cut, it was necessary first of all to find out what kind of club-foot he had.

His foot almost formed a straight line with the leg, which, however, did not prevent it from being turned in, so that it was an equinus combined with something of a varus, or else a slight varus with a strong tendency to equinus. But on the equine foot, wide indeed as a horse's hoof, with its horny skin, and large toes, whose black nails resembled the nails of a horse shoe, the cripple ran about like a deer from morn till night. He was constantly to be seen on the Square, jumping round the carts, thrusting his limping foot forwards. He seemed even stronger on that leg than the other. By dint of hard service it had acquired, as it were, moral qualities of patience and energy; and when he was given some heavy work to do, he would support himself on it in preference to the sound one.

Now, as it was an equinus, it was necessary to cut the Achilles tendon first; if need be, the anterior tibial muscle could be seen to afterwards to take care of the varus. For the doctor did not dare to risk both operations at once; he was already sufficiently worried for fear of injuring some important region that he did not know.

Neither Ambroise Paré, applying a ligature to an artery, for the first time since Celsus did it fifteen centuries before; nor Dupuytren, cutting open abscesses through a thick layer of brain; nor Gensoul on first removing the superior maxilla, had hearts that trembled, hands that shook, minds that strained as Monsieur Bovary's when he approached Hippolyte, his tenotomy knife between his fingers. Just as in a hospital, near by on a table lay a heap of lint, with waxed thread, many bandages—a pyramid of bandages—every bandage to be found at the pharmacy. It was Monsieur Homais who since morning had been organising all these preparations, as much to dazzle the multitude as to keep up his illusions. Charles pierced the skin; a dry crackling was heard. The tendon was cut, the operation over. Hippolyte could not believe his eyes: he bent over Bovary's hands to cover them with kisses.

"Come, be calm," said the pharmacist; "later on you will show your gratitude to your benefactor."

And he went down to report the result to five or six bystanders who were waiting in the yard, and who fancied that Hippolyte would reappear walking straight up. Then Charles, having strapped his patient into the machine, went home, where Emma was anxiously waiting for him on the doorstep. She threw herself on his neck; they sat down at the table; he ate much, and at dessert he even wanted to take a cup of coffee, a luxury he only permitted himself on Sundays when there was company.

The evening was charming, full of shared conversation and common dreams. They talked about their future success, of the improvements to be made in their house; with his rising reputation, he saw his comforts increasing, his wife always loving him; and she was happy to refresh herself with a new sentiment, healthier and purer, and to feel at last some tenderness for this poor man who adored her. The thought of Rodolphe for one moment passed through her mind, but her eyes turned again to Charles; she even noticed with surprise that he had rather handsome teeth.

They were in bed when Monsieur Homais, sidestepping the cook, suddenly entered the room, holding in his hand a newly written sheet of paper. It was the article he intended for the "Fanal de Rouen." He brought it them to read.

"You read it," said Bovary.

He read:

" 'Braving the prejudices that still spread over the face of Europe like a net, the light nevertheless begins to penetrate into our country places. Thus on Tuesday our little town of Yonville found itself the scene of a surgical operation which was at the same time an act of loftiest philanthropy. Monsieur Bovary, one of our most distinguished practitioners . . ."

"Oh, that is too much! too much!" said Charles, choking with emotion.

—"But certainly not! far from it! . . . 'operated on a club-foot.' I have not used the scientific term, because you know in newspapers . . . not everyone would understand . . . the masses, after all, must . . ."

"Certainly," said Bovary; "please go on!"

"I proceed," said the pharmacist. " 'Monsieur Bovary, one of our most distinguished practitioners, performed an operation on a club-footed man, one Hippolyte Tautain, stable-man for the last twenty-five years at the hotel of the "Lion d'Or," kept by Widow Lefrancois, at the Place d'Armes. The novelty of the experiment and the general interest in the patient had attracted such a number of people that a crowd gathered on the threshold of the establishment. The operation, moverover, was performed as if by magic, and barely a few drops of blood appeared on the skin, as though to say that the rebellious tendon had at last given way under the efforts of the medical arts. The patient, strangely enough (we affirm it *de visu*) complained of no pain. His condition up to the present time leaves nothing to be desired. Everything tends to show that his convalescence will be brief; and who knows if, at our next village festivity we shall not see our good Hippolyte appear in the midst of a bacchic dance, surrounded by a group of gay companions, and thus bear witness to all assembled, by his spirit and his capers, of his total recovery? Honor, then, to those generous men of science! Honor to those tireless spirits who consecrate their vigils to the improvement and relief of their kind! Honor to them! Hasn't the time come to cry out that the blind shall see, the deaf hear, the lame walk? What fanaticism formerly promised to a few elect, science now accomplishes for all men. We shall keep our readers informed as to the subsequent progression of this remarkable cure.' "

All this did not prevent Mère Lefrançois from coming five days later, scared out of her wits and shouting:

"Help! he is dying! I am going out of my mind!"

Charles rushed to the "Lion d'Or," and the pharmacist, who caught sight of him passing along the Square without a hat, left his shop. He arrived himself breathless, flushed, anxious, and asked from every one who was going up the stairs:

"What can be the matter with our interesting patient?"

The interesting patient was writhing, in dreadful convulsions, so violent that the contraption in which his foot was locked almost beat down the wall.

With many precautions, in order not to disturb the position of the limb, the box was removed, and an awful spectacle came into view. The outlines of the foot disappeared in such a swelling that the entire skin seemed about to burst; moreover, the leg was covered with bruises caused by the famous machine. Hippolyte had abundantly complained, but nobody had paid any attention to him; now they admitted he might have some grounds for protest and he was freed for a few hours. But hardly had the oedema somewhat gone down, that the two specialists thought fit to put back the limb in the machine, strapping it even tighter to speed up matters. At last, three days after, when Hippolyte could not stand it any longer, they once more removed the machine, and were much surprised at the result they saw. A livid tumescence spread over the entire leg, and a black liquid oozed from several blisters. Things had taken a turn for the worse. Hippolyte was getting bored, and Mère Lefrançois had him installed in the little room near the kitchen, so that he might at least have some distraction.

But the tax-collector, who dined there every day, complained bitterly of such companionship. Then Hippolyte was removed to the billiard-room.

He lay there moaning under his heavy blankets, pale and unshaven, with sunken eyes; from time to time he rubbed his sweating head over the fly-covered pillow. Madame Bovary came to see him. She brought him linen for his poultices; she comforted, and encouraged him. Besides, he did not want for company, especially on market days, when farmers around him were hitting the billiard balls around and fencing with the cues while they drank, sang and brawled.

"How are things?" they would say, clapping him on the shoulder. "Ah! not so well from what we hear. But that's your fault. You should do this! do that!"

And then they told him stories of people who had all been cured by other means. Then by way of consolation they added:

"You pamper yourself too much! You should get up; you coddle yourself like a king. Just the same, old boy, you do smell pretty awful!"

Gangrene was indeed spreading higher and higher. It made Bovary ill to think of it. He came every hour, every moment. Hippolyte looked at him with terrified eyes and sobbed:

"When will I be cured?—Oh, please save me! . . . How unhappy I am! . . . How unhappy I am!"

And the doctor left him, prescribing a strict diet.

"Don't listen to him," said Mère Lefrançois. "Haven't they tortured you enough already? You'll grow still weaker. Here! swallow this."

And she gave him some strong broth, a slice of mutton, a piece of bacon, and sometimes small glasses of brandy, that he had not the strength to put to his lips.

The abbé Bournisien, hearing that he was growing worse, asked to see him. He began by pitying his sufferings, declaring at the same time that he ought to rejoice since it was the will of the Lord, and hasten to reconcile himself with Heaven.

"For," said the ecclesiastic in a paternal tone, "you rather neglected your duties; you were rarely seen at divine worship. How many years is it since you approached the holy table? I understand that your work, that the whirl of the world may have distracted you from your salvation. But now the time has come. Yet don't despair. I have known great sinners, who, about to appear before God (you are not yet at this point I know), had implored His mercy, and who certainly died in a truly repenting frame of mind. Let us hope that, like them, you will set us a good example! Thus, as a precaution, what is to prevent you from saying morning and evening a Hail Mary and an Our Father? Yes, do that, for my sake, to oblige me. That won't cost you anything. Will you promise me?"

The poor devil promised. The curé came back day after day. He chatted with the landlady, and even told anecdotes interspersed with jokes and puns that Hippolyte did not understand. Then, as soon as he could, he would return to religious considerations, putting on an appropriate expression.

His zeal seemed to bring results, for the club-foot soon manifested a desire to go on a pilgrimage to Bon-Secours if he were cured; to which Monsieur Bournisien replied that he saw no objection; two precautions were better than one; moreover, it certainly could do no harm.

The pharmacist was incensed by what he called the priest's machinations; they were prejudicial, he said, to Hippolyte's convalescence, and he kept repeating to Madame Lefrançois, "Leave him alone! leave him alone! You're ruining his morale with your mysticism."

But the good woman would no longer listen to him; she blamed him for being the cause of it all. In sheer rebellion, she hung near the patient's bedside a well-filled basin of holy water and a sprig of boxwood.

Religion, however, seemed no more able than surgery to bring relief and the irresistible putrefaction kept spreading from the foot to the groin. It was all very well to vary the potions and change the poultices; the muscles each day rotted more and more; Charles replied by an affirmative nod of the head when Mére Lefrançois asked him if she could not, as a last resort, send for Monsieur Canivet, a famous surgeon from Neufchâtel.

Charles' fifty-year old colleague, a doctor of medicine with a well established practice and a solid self confidence, did not refrain from laughing disdainfully when he had uncovered the leg, gangrened to the knee. Then having flatly declared that it must be amputated, he went off to the pharmacist's to rail at the asses who could have reduced a poor man to such a state. Shaking Monsieur Homais by his coat-button, he shouted for everyone to hear:

"That is what you get from listening to the fads from Paris! What will they come up with next, these gentlemen from the capital! It is like strabismus, chloroform, lithotrity, monstrosities the Government ought to prohibit. But they want to be clever and cram you full of remedies without troubling about the consequences. We are not so clever out here, not we! We are no specialists, no cure-alls, no fancy talkers! We are practitioners; we cure people, and we wouldn't dream of operating on someone who is in perfect health. Straighten club-feet! As if one could straighten club-feet indeed! It is as if one wished to make a hunchback straight!"

Homais suffered as he listened to this discourse, and he concealed his discomfort beneath a courtier's smile; for he needed to humour Monsieur Canivet, whose prescriptions sometimes came as far as Yonville. So he did not take up the defence of Bovary; he did not even make a single remark, and, renouncing his principles, he sacrificed his dignity to the more serious interests of his business.

This thigh amputation by Doctor Canivet was a great event in the village. On that day all the inhabitants got up earlier, and the Grande Rue, crowded as it was, had something lugubrious about it, as though one were preparing for an execution. At the grocers they discussed Hippolyte's illness; the shops did no business, and Madame Tuvache, the mayor's wife, did not stir from her window, such was her impatience to see the surgeon arrive.

He came in his gig, which he drove himself. The springs of the right side had all given way beneath his corpulence and the carriage tilted a little as it rolled along, revealing on the cushion near him a large case covered in red sheep-leather, whose three brass clasps shone grandly.

Like a whirlwind, the doctor entered the porch of the Lion d'Or and, shouting loudly, he ordered to unharness. Then he went into the stable to see that his horse was eating his oats all right; for on arriving at a patient's he first of all looked after his mare and his gig. The habit made people say, "Ah, that Monsieur Canivet, what a character!" but he was the more esteemed for his composure. The universe as a whole might have been blown apart, and he would not have changed the least of his habits.

Homais introduced himself.

"I count on you," said the doctor. "Are you ready? Come along!"

But the pharmacist blushingly confessed that he was too sensitive to witness such an operation.

"When one is a simple spectator," he said, "the imagination, you know, is easily impressed. And then, my nerves are so . . ."

"Bah!" interrupted Canivet; "on the contrary, you seem like the apoplectic type to me. But I am not surprised, for you gentlemen pharmacists are always poking about your kitchens, which must end by spoiling your constitutions. Now just look at me. I get up every day at four o'clock; I shave with cold water (and am never cold). I don't wear flannel underwear, and I never catch cold; my carcass is good enough! I take things in my stride, philosophically, as they come my way. That is why I am not squeamish like you, and it doesn't matter to me whether I carve up a Christian or the first fowl that comes my way. Habit, you'll say . . . mere habit! . . ."

Then, without any consideration for Hippolyte, who was sweating with agony between his sheets, these gentlemen began a conversation, in which the druggist compared the coolness of a surgeon to that of a general; and this comparison was pleasing to Canivet, who held forth on the demands of his art. He looked upon it as a sacred office, although the ordinary practitioners dishonored it. At last, coming back to the patient, he examined the bandages brought by Homais, the same that had appeared for the club-foot, and asked for some one to hold the limb for him. Lestiboudois was sent for, and Monsieur Canivet having turned up his sleeves, passed into the billiard-room, while the druggist stayed with Artémise and the landlady, both whiter than their aprons, and with ears strained towards the door.

Meanwhile, Bovary didn't dare to stir from his house.

He kept downstairs in the sitting-room by the side of the fireless chimney, his chin on his breast, his hands clasped, his eyes staring. "What a misfortune," he thought, "what a disappointment!" Yet, he had taken all possible precautions. Luck must have been against him. All the same, if Hippolyte died later on, he would be considered the murderer. And how would he defend himself against the questions his patients were bound to ask him during his calls? Maybe, after all, he had made some slip. He thought and thought, but nothing came. The most famous surgeons also made mistakes. But no one would ever believe that; on the contrary, people would laugh, jeer! The news would spread as far as Neufchâtel, as Rouen, everywhere! Who could say if his colleagues would not write against him? Polemics would ensue; he would have to answer in the papers. Hippolyte might even prosecute him. He saw himself dishonored, ruined, lost; and his imagination, assailed by numberless hypotheses, tossed amongst them like an empty cask dragged out to sea and pitched about by the waves.

Emma, opposite, watched him; she did not share his humiliation; she felt another—that of having imagined that such a man could have any worth, as if twenty times already she had not sufficiently perceived his mediocrity.

Charles was pacing the room. His boots creaked on the floor.

"Sit down," she said; "you irritate me!"

He sat down again.

How was it that she—she, who was so intelligent—could have allowed herself to be deceived again? Moreover, what madness had driven her to ruin her life by continual sacrifices? She recalled all her instincts of luxury, all the privations of her soul, the sordidness of marriage, of the household, her dreams sinking into the mire like wounded swallows; all that she had longed for, all that she had denied herself, all that she might have had! And for what? for what?

In the midst of the silence that hung over the village a heart-rending cry pierced the air. Bovary turned white as a sheet. She knit her brows with a nervous gesture, then returned to her thought. And it was for him, for this creature, for this man, who understood nothing, who felt nothing! For he sat there as if nothing had happened, not even suspecting that the ridicule of his name would henceforth sully hers as well as his. She had made efforts to love him, and she had repented with tears for having yielded to another!

"But it was perhaps a valgus after all!" exclaimed Bovary suddenly, interrupting his meditations.

At the unexpected shock of this phrase falling on her thought like a leaden bullet on a silver plate, Emma shuddered and raised her head in an effort to find out what he meant to say; and they gazed at one another in silence, almost amazed to see each other, so far sundered were they by their respective states of consciousness. Charles gazed at her with the dull look of a drunken man, while he listened motionless to the last cries of the sufferer, following each other in long-drawn modulations, broken by sharp spasms like the far-off howling of some beast being slaughtered. Emma bit her wan lips, and rolling between her fingers a piece of wood she had peeled from the coral-tree, fixed on Charles the burning glance of her eyes like two arrows of fire about to dart forth. Everything in him irritated her now; his face, his dress, all the things he did not say, his whole person, in short, his existence. She repented of her past virtue as of a crime, and what still remained of it crumbled away beneath the furious blows of her pride. She revelled in all the evil ironies of triumphant adultery. The memory of her lover came back to her with irresistible, dizzying attractions; she threw her whole soul towards this image, carried by renewed passion; and Charles seemed to her as removed from her life, as eternally absent, as incongruous and annihilated, as if he were dying under her very eyes.

There was a sound of steps on the pavement. Charles looked up, and through the lowered blinds he saw Dr. Canivet standing in broad sunshine at the corner of the market, wiping his brow with his handerchief. Homais, behind him, was carrying a large red bag in his hand, and both were going towards the pharmacy.

Then with a feeling of sudden tenderness and discouragement Charles turned to his wife and said:

"Oh, kiss me, my dear!"

"Don't touch me!" she cried, flushed with anger.

"What is it? what is it?" he repeated, in utter bewilderment. "Don't be upset! calm down! You know that I love you . . . come! . . ."

"Stop it!" she cried with a terrible look.

And rushing from the room, Emma closed the door so violently that the barometer fell from the wall and smashed on the floor.

Charles sank back into his arm-chair thoroughly shaken, wondering what could have come over her, imagining it might be some nervous disease, weeping, and vaguely feeling something fatal and incomprehensible was whirling around him.

When Rodolphe came to the garden that evening, he found his mistress waiting for him at the foot of the steps on the lowest stair. They threw their arms round one another, and all their rancor melted like snow beneath the warmth of that kiss.

XII

Their love resumed its course. Often in the middle of the day, Emma would suddenly write to him, then beckon Justin through the window; he quickly untied his apron and flew to La Huchette. Rodolphe would come; she had to tell him again how bored she was, that her husband was odious, her life dreadful.

"What do you expect me to do about it?" he asked one day impatiently.

"Ah, if only you wanted . . ."

She was sitting on the floor between his knees, her hair loosened, staring in a void.

"Wanted what?" said Rodolphe.

She sighed.

"We would go and live elsewhere . . . anywhere . . ."

"Are you out of your mind!" he said laughing. "How could we?"

She mentioned it again; he pretended not to understand, and changed the subject. What he did not understand was all this worry about so simple an affair as love. But she had a motive, a reason that gave added grounds to her attachment.

Her tenderness, in fact, grew daily as her repulsion toward her husband increased. The more she yielded to the one, the more she loathed the other. Never did Charles seem so unattractive, slow-witted, clumsy and vulgar as when she met him after her rendezvous with Rodolphe. Then while playing the part of the virtuous wife, she would burn with passion at the thought of his head, the black curl falling over the sun-tanned brow; of his figure, both elegant and strong, of the man so experienced in his thought, so impetuous in his desires! It was for him that she filed her nails with a sculptor's care, that there was never enough cold-cream for her skin, nor patchouli for her handkerchiefs. She loaded herself with bracelets, rings, and necklaces. When she expected him, she filled her two large blue glass vases with roses, and prepared herself and her room like a courtesan receiving a prince. The servant was kept busy steadily laundering her linen, and all day Félicité did not stir from the kitchen, where little Justin, who often kept her company, watched her at work.

With his elbows on the long board on which she was ironing, he greedily watched all these women's garments spread out about him, the dimity petticoats, the fichus, the collars, and the drawers with running strings, wide at the hips and narrowing below.

"What is that for?" asked the young boy, passing his hand over the crinoline or the hooks and eyes.

"Why, haven't you ever seen anything?" Félicité answered laughing. "As if your mistress, Madame Homais, didn't wear the same."

"Oh, well, Madame Homais . . ."

And he added thoughtfully,

"Is she a lady like Madame?"

But Félicité grew impatient of seeing him hanging round her. She was six years older than he, and Theodore, Monsieur Guillaumin's servant, was beginning to pay court to her.

"Leave me alone," she said, moving her pot of starch. "You'd better be off and pound almonds; you are always snooping around women. Before you bother with such things, naughty boy, wait till you've got a beard to your chin."

"Oh, don't be cross! I'll go and clean her boots."

And he hurriedly took down Emma's boots from the shelf all coated with mud—the mud of the rendezvous—that crumbled into powder beneath his fingers, and that he watched as it gently rose in a ray of sunlight.

"How scared you are of spoiling them!" said the maid, who wasn't so particular when she cleaned them herself, because if the boots looked slightly worn Madame would give them to her.

Emma kept a number in her cupboard that she squandered one after the other, without Charles allowing himself the slightest observation.

He also spent three hundred francs for a wooden leg that she thought had to be given to Hippolyte. The top was covered with cork, and it had spring joints, a complicated mechanism, covered over by black trowsers ending in a patent-leather boot. But Hippolyte didn't dare use such a handsome leg every day, and he begged Madame Bovary to get him another more convenient one. The doctor, of course, had to pay for this purchase as well.

So little by little the stable-boy returned to work. One saw him running about the village as before, and when Charles heard from afar the tap of the wooden leg on the pavement, he quickly went in another direction.

It was Monsieur Lheureux, the shopkeeper, who had ordered the wooden leg. This provided him with an excuse for visiting Emma. He chatted with her about the new goods from Paris, about a thousand feminine trifles, made himself very obliging and never asked for his money. Emma yielded to this lazy mode of satisfying all her caprices. When she wanted to give Rodolphe a handsome riding-crop from an umbrella store in Rouen, Monsieur Lheureux placed it on her table the very next week.

But the next day he called on her with a bill for two hundred and seventy francs, not counting the centimes. Emma was much embarrassed; all the drawers of the writing-table were empty; they owed over a fortnight's wages to Lestiboudois, six months to the maid, and there were several other bills. Bovary was impatiently waiting to hear from Monsieur Derozeray who was in the habit of settling every year about Midsummer.

She succeeded at first in putting off Lheureux. At last he lost patience; he was being sued; he was short of capital and unless he could collect on some of his accounts, he would be forced to take back all the goods she had received.

"Oh, very well, take them!" said Emma.

"I was only joking," he replied; "the only thing I regret is the riding crop. Well, I'll have to ask Monsieur to return it to me."

"No, no!" she said.

"Ah! I've got you!" thought Lheureux.

And, certain of his discovery, he went out muttering to himself and with his usual low whistle . . .

"Good! we shall see! we shall see!"

She was wondering how to handle the situation when the maid entered and put on the mantelpiece a small roll of blue paper "with the compliments of Monsieur Derozeray." Emma grasped it, tore it open. It contained fifteen napoleons: the account paid in full. Hearing Charles on the stairs, she threw the money to the back of her drawer, and took out the key.

Three days later, Lheureux returned.

"I have a suggestion to make," he said. "If, instead of the sum, agreed on, you would take. . . ."

"Here it is," she said handing him fourteen napoleons.

The shopkeeper was taken aback. Then, to conceal his disappointment, he was profuse in apologies and offers of service, all of which Emma declined; she remained a few moments fingering in the pocket of her apron the two five-franc pieces of change he had returned to her. She told herself she would economise in order to pay back later . . . "Bah!," she thought, "he'll forget all about it."

Besides the riding-crop with its silver-gilt top, Rodolphe had received a signet with the motto *Amor nel cor,* furthermore, a scarf for a muffler, and, finally, a cigar-case exactly like the Viscount's, that Charles had formerly picked up in the road, and that Emma had kept. These presents, however, humiliated him; he refused several; she insisted, and he ended by obeying, thinking her tyrannical and over-exacting.

Then she had strange ideas.

"When midnight strikes," she said, "you must think of me."

And if he confessed that he had not thought of her, there were floods of reproaches that always ended with the eternal question:

"Do you love me?"

"Why, of course I love you," he answered.

"A great deal?"

"Certainly!"

"You haven't loved any others?"

"Did you think you'd got a virgin?" he exclaimed laughing.

Emma cried, and he tried to console her, adorning his protestations with puns.

"Oh," she went on, "I love you! I love you so that I could not live without you, do you see? There are times when I long to see you again, when I am torn by all the anger of love. I ask myself, where is he? Perhaps he is talking to other women. They smile upon him; he approaches. Oh no; no one else pleases you. There are some more beautiful, but I love you best. I know how to love best. I am your servant, your concubine! You are my king, my idol! You are good, you are beautiful, you are clever, you are strong!"

He had so often heard these things said that they did not strike him as original. Emma was like all his mistresses; and the charm of novelty, gradually falling away like a garment, laid bare the eternal monotony of passion, that has always the same shape and the same language. He was unable to see, this man so full of experience, the variety of feelings hidden within the same expressions. Since libertine or venal lips had murmured similar phrases, he only faintly believed in the candor of Emma's; he thought one should beware of exaggerated declarations which only serve to cloak a tepid love; as though the abundance of one's soul did not sometimes overflow with empty metaphors, since no one ever has been able to give the exact measure of his needs, his concepts, or his sorrows. The human tongue is like a cracked cauldron on which we beat out tunes to set a bear dancing when we would make the stars weep with our melodies.

But with the superiority of critical insight of the person who holds back his emotions in any engagement, Rodolphe perceived that there were other pleasures to be exploited in this love. He discarded all modesty as inconvenient. He treated her without consideration. And he made her into something at once malleable and corrupt. It was an idiotic sort of attachment, full of admiration on his side and voluptuousness on hers, a beatitude which left her numb; and her soul sunk deep into this intoxication and drowned in it, all shrivelled up, like the duke of Clarence[44] in his butt of malmsey.

Solely as a result of her amorous practices, Madame Bovary began to change in appearance. Her glances were bolder, her speech freer; she even went as far as to go out walking with Rodolphe, a cigarette in her mouth, "just to scandalize the town"; finally, those who had doubted doubted no longer when they saw her descend one day from the Hirondelle wearing a tight-fitting waistcoat cut like a man's. And Madame Bovary senior who, after a frightful scene with her husband, had come to seek refuge with her son, was not the least scandalized lady in town. Many other things displeased her too: first of all, Charles had not followed her advice in banning novels from the house; then, the "tone" of the house upset her; she allowed herself to make observations, and there were arguments, especially, on one occasion, concerning Felicité.

The previous evening, while crossing the corridor, Madame Bovary senior had come upon her in the company of a man of about forty wearing a brown collar, who on hearing footsteps, had quickly fled from the kitchen. Emma had burst out laughing; but the good woman was furious, declaring that anyone who took morality seriously ought to keep an eye on their servant's behavior.

"What kind of society do you come from?" asked the daughter-in-law, with so impertinent a look that Madame Bovary asked her if

44. The duke of Clarence was the younger brother of King Edward IV of England and the elder brother of Richard Duke of Gloucester. He was condemned to death for treason and, according to rumor, drowned in a butt of malmsey (a sweet aromatic wine) in February 1478. See Shakespeare, *Richard III*, Act 1, sc. 4, l. 155.

she were not perhaps defending her own case.

"Get out!" said the young woman, rising in fury.

"Emma! . . . Mother! . . ." cried Charles, trying to reconcile them.

But both had fled in their exasperation. Emma was stamping her feet as she repeated:

"Oh! what manners! What a peasant!"

He ran to his mother; she was beside herself. She stammered:

"How insolent she is! and how flighty! worse perhaps!"

And she was ready to leave at once if the other did not apologise. So Charles went back again to his wife and implored her to give way; he threw himself at her feet; finally, she said:

"Very well! I'll go to her."

And she actually held out her hand to her mother-in-law with the dignity of a marquise as she said:

"Excuse me, madame."

Then, having returned to her room, she threw herself flat on her bed and cried there like a child, her face buried in the pillow.

She and Rodolphe had agreed that in the event of anything extraordinary occurring, she should fasten a small piece of white paper to the blind, so that if by chance he happened to be in Yonville, he could hurry to the lane behind the house. Emma made the signal; she had been waiting three-quarters of an hour when she suddenly caught sight of Rodolphe at the corner of the square. She felt tempted to open the window and call him, but he had already disappeared. She fell back in despair.

Soon, however, it seemed to her that someone was walking on the pavement. It was he, no doubt. She went downstairs, crossed the yard. He was there outside. She threw herself into his arms.

"Watch out!" he said.

"Ah! if only you knew!" she replied.

And she began telling him everything, hurriedly, disjointedly, exaggerating the facts, inventing many, and with so many digressions that he understood nothing at all.

"Come now, my poor angel, be brave, console yourself, be patient!"

"But I have been patient; I have suffered for four years. A love like ours ought to show itself in the face of heaven. They torture me! I can bear it no longer! Save me!"

She clung to Rodolphe. Her eyes, full of tears, flashed like flames beneath a wave; her panting made her breast rise and fall; never had she seemed more lovely, so much so that he lost his head and said:

"What do you want me to do?"

"Take me away," she cried, "carry me off! . . . I beg you!"

She pressed her lips against his mouth, as if to capture the unhoped for consent the moment it was breathed forth in a kiss.

"But . . ." Rodolphe began.

"What?"

"Your little girl!"

She reflected a few moments, then replied:

"We'll take her with us, there is no other way!"

"What a woman!" he said to himself, watching her as she went. For she had run into the garden. Some one was calling her.

On the following days the elder Madame Bovary was much surprised at the change in her daughter-in-law. Emma, in fact, was showing herself more docile, and even carried her deference to the point of asking for a recipe for pickles.

Was it the better to deceive them both? Or did she wish by a sort of voluptuous stoicism to feel the more profoundly the bitterness of the things she was about to leave? But she paid no heed to them; on the contrary, she lived as lost in the anticipated delight of her coming happiness. It was an eternal subject for conversation with Rodolphe. She leant on his shoulder murmuring:

"Think, we will soon be in the mail-coach! Can you imagine? Is it possible? It seems to me that the moment the carriage will start, it will be as if we were rising in a balloon, as if we were setting out for the clouds. Do you know that I count the hours? . . . Don't you?"

Never had Madame Bovary been so beautiful as at this period; she had that indefinable beauty that results from joy, from enthusiasm, from success, and that expresses the harmony between temperament and circumstances. Her cravings, her sorrows, her sensuous pleasures and her ever-young illusions had slowly brought her to full maturity, and she blossomed forth in the fulness of her being, like a flower feeding on manure, on rain, wind and sunshine. Her half-closed eyelids seemed perfectly shaped for the long languid glances that escaped from them; her breathing dilated the fine nostrils and raised the fleshy corners of her mouth, shaded in the light by a slight black down. Some artist skilled in corruption seemed to have devised the shape of her hair as it fell on her neck, coiled in a heavy mass, casually reassembled after being loosened daily in adultery. Her voice now took more mellow inflections, her figure also; something subtle and penetrating escaped even from the folds of her gown and from the line of her foot. Charles thought her exquisite and altogether irresistible, as when they were first married.

When he came home in the middle of the night, he did not dare to wake her. The porcelain night-light threw a round trembling gleam upon the ceiling, and the drawn curtains of the little cot formed as it were a white hut standing out in the shade by the bedside. Charles looked at them. He seemed to hear the light breathing of his child. She would grow big now; every season would bring rapid progress. He already saw her coming from school as the day drew in, laughing, with ink-stains on her jacket, and carrying her basket on her arm. Then she would have to be sent to a boarding-school; that would cost much; how was it to be done? He kept thinking about it. He thought of renting a small farm in the neighborhood, that he would supervise every morning on his way to his patients. He would not spend what he brought in; he would put it in the savings-bank. Then he would invest in some stocks, he didn't know which; besides, his practice would increase; he counted on it, for he wanted Berthe to be well-educated, to be accomplished, to learn to play the piano. Ah! how pretty she would be later on when she was fifteen, when, resembling her mother, she would, like her, wear large straw hats in the summer-time; from a distance they would be taken for two sisters. He pictured her to himself working in the evening by their side beneath the light of the lamp; she would embroider him slippers; she would look after the house; she would fill all the home with her charm and her gaiety. At last, they would think of her marriage; they would find her some good young fellow with a steady business; he would make her happy; this would last for ever.

Emma was not asleep; she pretended to be; and while he dozed off by her side she awakened to other dreams.

To the gallop of four horses she was carried away for a week towards a new land, from where they would never return. They went on and on, their arms entwined, without speaking a word. Often from the top of a mountain there suddenly appeared some splendid city with domes, and bridges, and ships, forests of lemon trees, and cathedrals of white marble, their pointed steeples crowned with storks' nests. The horses slowed down to a walk because of the wide pavement, and on the ground there were bouquets of flowers, offered by women dressed in red. They heard the chiming of bells, the neighing of mules, together with the murmur of guitars and the noise of fountains, whose rising spray refreshed heaps of fruit arranged like a pyramid at the foot of pale statues that smiled beneath playing waters. And then, one night they came to a fishing village, where brown nets were drying in the wind along the cliffs and in front of the huts. It was there that they would stay; they would live in a low, flat-roofed house, shaded by a palm-tree, in the heart of a gulf, by the sea. They would row in gondolas, swing in hammocks, and their existence would be easy and free as their wide silk gowns, warm and star-spangled as the nights they would contemplate. However, in the immensity of this future that she conjured up, nothing specific stood out; the days, all magnificent, resembled each other like waves; and the vision swayed in the horizon, infinite, harmonised, azure, and bathed in sunshine. But the child began to cough in her cot or Bovary snored more loudly, and Emma did not fall asleep till morning, when the dawn whitened the windows, and when little Justin was already in the square taking down the shutters of the pharmacy.

She had sent for Monsieur Lheureux, and had said to him:

"I want a cloak—a large lined cloak with a deep collar."

"You are going on a journey?" he asked.

"No; but . . . never mind. I count on you to get it in a hurry."

He bowed.

"Besides, I shall want," she went on, "a trunk . . . not too heavy . . . a handy size."

"Yes, yes, I understand. About three feet by a foot and a half, as they are being made just now."

"And a travelling bag."

"No question about it," thought Lheureux, "she is up to something."

"And," said Madame Bovary, taking her watch from her belt, "take this; you can pay yourself out of it."

But the shopkeeper protested that it was not necessary; as if he didn't know and trust her. She was being childish!

She insisted, however, on his taking at least the chain, and Lheureux had already put it in his pocket and was going, when she called him back.

"You will leave everything at your place. As to the cloak"—she seemed to be reflecting—"do not bring it either; you can give me the maker's address, and tell him to have it ready for me."

It was the next month that they were to run away. She was to leave Yonville as if she was going on some business to Rouen. Rodolphe would have booked the seats, obtained the passports, and even have written to Paris in order to have the whole mail-coach reserved for them as far as Marseilles, where they would buy a carriage, and go on from there straight by the Genoa road. She would have sent her luggage to Lheureux, from where it would be taken directly to the "Hirondelle," so that no one would have any suspicion. And in all this there never was any allusion to the child. Rodolphe avoided the subject; it may be that he had forgotten about it.

He wished to have two more weeks before him to arrange some affairs; then at the end of a week he wanted two more; then he said he as ill; next he went on a journey. The month of August passed, and, after all these delays, they decided that it was to be irrevocably fixed for the 4th September—a Monday.

At last the Saturday before arrived.

Rodolphe came in the evening earlier than usual.

"Is everything ready?" she asked him.

"Yes."

Then they walked round a garden-bed, and sat down near the terrace on the kerb-stone of the wall.

"You are sad," said Emma.

"No; why?"

And yet he looked at her strangely, though with tenderness.

"Is it because you are going away?" she went on; "because you are leaving behind what is dear to you, your own life? I can understand that . . . But I have nothing in the world! You are everything I have, and I'll be everything to you. I'll be your family, your country; I'll look after you, I'll love you."

"How sweet you are!" he said, taking her in his arms.

"Am I really?" she said with a voluptuous laugh. "Do you love me? Swear it then!"

"Do I love you? Do I? But I adore you, my love!"

The moon, full and purple-colored, was rising right out of the earth at the end of the meadow. It rose quickly between the branches of the poplar trees, partly hidden as by a tattered black curtain. Then it appeared dazzling white, lighting up the empty sky; slowing down, it let fall upon the river a great stain that broke up into an infinity of stars; and the silver sheen seemed to writhe through the very depths like a headless serpent covered with luminous scales; it also resembled some monster candelabra from which sparkling diamonds fell like molten drops. The soft night was about them; masses of shadow filled the branches. Emma, her eyes half closed, breathed in with deep sighs the fresh wind that was blowing. They did not speak, caught as they were in their dream. The tenderness of the old days came back to their hearts, full and silent as the flowing river, with the soft perfume of the syringas, and threw across their memories shadows more immense and more sombre than those of the still willows that lengthened out over the grass. Often some night-animal, hedgehog or weasel, setting out on the hunt, disturbed the lovers, or sometimes they heard a ripe peach fall by itself from the tree.

"Ah! what a lovely night!" said Rodolphe.

"We shall have others," replied Emma.

Then, as if speaking to herself:

"Yes, it will be good to travel. And yet, why should my heart be so heavy? Is it dread of the unknown? The weight of old habits? . . . Or else? No, it is the excess of happiness. How weak I am! You must forgive me!"

"There is still time!" he cried. "Think! You may regret it later!"

"Never!" she cried impetuously.

And, drawing closer to him:

"What ill could come to me? There is no desert, no precipice, no ocean I would not traverse with you. The longer we live together the more it will be like an embrace, every day closer, more complete. There will be nothing to trouble us, no cares, no obstacle. We shall be alone, all to ourselves forever . . . Say something, answer me!"

At regular intervals he answered, "Yes . . . Yes . . ." She had passed her hands through his hair, and she repeated in a childlike voice through her tears:

"Rodolphe! Rodolphe! . . . Sweet little Rodolphe!"

Midnight struck.

"Midnight!" she said. "Come, it is to-morrow. One more day!"

He rose to go; and as if the movement he made had been the signal for their flight, Emma suddenly seemed gay:

"You have the passports?"

"Yes."

"You are forgetting nothing?"

"No."

"Are you sure?"

"Absolutely."

"You'll be waiting for me at the Hotel de Provence, won't you? . . . at noon?"

He nodded.

"Till to-morrow then!" said Emma in a last caress; and she watched him go.

He did not turn round. She ran after him, and, leaning over the water's edge between the bushes:

"Till to-morrow!" she cried.

He was already on the other side of the river and walking fast across the meadow.

After a few moments Rodolphe stopped; and when he saw her with her white gown gradually fade away in the shade like a ghost, his heart beat so wildly that he had to support himself against a tree.

"What a fool I am!" he said, swearing a dreadful oath. "All the same, she was the prettiest mistress ever."

And immediately Emma's beauty, with all the pleasures of their love, came back to him. For a moment he weakened, but then he rebelled against her.

"For, after all," he exclaimed, gesticulating, "I can't exile myself, and with a child on my hands to boot!"

He was saying these things to strengthen his determination.

"And besides, the worries, the cost! No, no, a thousand times no! It would have been too stupid."

XIII

No sooner was Rodolphe at home than he sat down quickly at his desk under the stag's head that hung as a trophy on the wall. But when he had the pen between his fingers, he could think of nothing, so that, resting on his elbows, he began to reflect. Emma seemed to him to have receded into a far-off past, as if the resolution he had taken had suddenly placed an immeasurable distance between them.

In order to recapture something of her presence, he fetched from the cupboard at the bedside an old Rheims cookie-box, in which he usually kept his love letters. An odour of dry dust and withered roses emanated from it. First he saw a handkerchief stained with pale drops. It was a handkerchief of hers. Once when they were walking her nose had bled; he had forgotten it. Near it, almost too large for the box, was Emma's miniature: her dress seemed pretentious to him, and her languishing look in the worst possible taste. Then, from looking at this image and recalling the memory of the original, Emma's features little by little grew confused in his remembrance, as if the living and the painted face, rubbing one against the other, had erased each other. Finally, he read some of her letters; they were full of explanations relating to their journey, short, technical, and urgent, like business notes. He wanted to see the long ones again, those of old times. In order to find them at the bottom of the box, Rodolphe disturbed all the others, and mechanically began rummaging among this mass of papers and things, finding pell-mell bouquets, garters, a black mask, pins, and hair . . . lots of hair! Some dark, some fair, some, catching in the hinges of the box, even broke when he opened it.

Following his memories, he examined the writing and the style of the letters, as varied as their spelling. They were tender or jovial, facetious, melancholy; there were some that asked for love, others that asked for money. A word recalled faces to him, certain gestures, the sound of a voice; sometimes, however, he remembered nothing at all.

All these women, crowding into his consciousness, rather shrank in size, levelled down by the uniformity of his feeling. Seizing the letters at random, he amused himself for a while by letting them cascade from his right into his left hand. At last, bored and weary, Rodolphe took back the box to the cupboard, saying to himself: "What a lot of nonsense!"

Which summed up his opinion; for pleasures, like schoolboys in a school courtyard, had so trampled upon his heart that no green thing was left; whatever entered there, more heedless than children, did not even, like them, leave a name carved upon the wall.

"Come," he said, "let's go."

He wrote:

> Courage, Emma! you must be brave! I don't want to be the one to ruin your life . . .

"After all, that's true," thought Rodolphe. "I am acting in her interest; I am honest."

> Have you carefully weighed your resolution? Do you know to what an abyss I was dragging you, poor angel? No, you don't, I assure you. You were coming confident and fearless, believing in a future happiness . . . Ah! the wretched creatures we are! We nearly lost our minds!

Rodolphe paused to think of some good excuse.

"If I told her that I lost all my money? No! Besides, that would stop nothing. It would all start again later on. As if one could make women like that listen to reason!"

He thought for a moment, then added:

> I shall not forget you, believe me; and I shall forever have a profound devotion for you; but some day, sooner or later, this ardour (such is the fate of human things) would doubtlessly have diminished. Weariness would have been unavoidable, and who knows if I would not even have had the atrocious pain of witnessing your remorse, of sharing it myself, since I would have been its cause? The mere idea of the grief that would come to you tortures me, Emma. Forget me! Why did I ever know you? Why were you so beautiful? Is it my fault? God, no! only fate is to blame!

"That's a word that always helps," he said to himself.

> Ah, if you had been one of those shallow women of which there are so many, I might, out of selfishness, have tried an experiment, in that case without danger for you. But your exquisite sensitivity, at once your charm and your torment, has prevented you from understanding, adorable woman that you are, the falseness of our future position. I myself had not fully realized this till now; I was living in the bliss of this ideal happiness as under the shade of a poisonous tree, without forseeing the consequences.

"She may suspect that it is out of stinginess that I am giving her up . . . But never mind, let's get this over with!"

> This is a cruel world, Emma. Wherever we might have gone, it would have persecuted us. You would have had to put up with indiscreet questions, calumny, contempt, insult perhaps. Imagine you being insulted! It is unbearable! . . . I who would place you on a throne! I who bear with me your memory as a talisman! For I am going to punish myself by exile for all the ill I have done you. I am going away. I don't know where, I am too close to madness to think. Farewell! Continue to be good! Remember the unfortu-

nate man who caused your undoing. Teach my name to your child; let her repeat it in her prayers.

The wicks of the candles flickered. Rodolphe got up to close the window, and when he sat down again:

"I think that covers it. Ah, let me add this for fear she might pursue me here."

I shall be far away when you read these sad lines, for I have wished to flee as quickly as possible to shun the temptation of seeing you again. No weakness! I shall return, and perhaps later on we shall be able to talk coldly of our past love. Adieu!

And there was a last "adieu" divided into two words: "A Dieu!" which he thought in very excellent taste.

"Now how am I to sign?" he asked himself. " 'Yours devotedly?' No! 'Your friend?' Yes, that's it."

YOUR FRIEND.

He re-read his letter and thought it quite good.

"Poor little woman!" he thought tenderly. "She'll think me harder than a rock. There ought to have been some tears on this; but I can't cry; it isn't my fault." Then, having emptied some water into a glass, Rodolphe dipped his finger into it, and let a big drop fall on the paper, making a pale stain on the ink. Then looking for a seal, he came upon the one "*Amor nel cor*."

"Hardly the right thing under the circumstances . . . But who cares?"

Whereupon he smoked three pipes and went to bed.

Upon arising the next morning—around two o'clock in the afternoon, for he had slept late—Rodolphe had a basket of apricots picked. He put his letter at the bottom under some vine leaves, and at once ordered Girard, his ploughman, to take it with care to Madame Bovary. They used to correspond this way before and he would send her fruit or game according to season.

"If she asks about me," he said, "tell her that I have gone on a journey. You must give the basket to her herself, into her own hands. Get going now, and be careful!"

Girard put on his new smock, knotted his handkerchief round the apricots, and, walking heavily in his hobnailed boots, quietly made his way to Yonville.

When he got to the house, Madame Bovary was arranging a bundle of linen on the kitchen-table with Félicité.

"Here," said the ploughboy, "is something for you from my master."

She was seized with apprehension, and as she sought in her pocket for some small change, she looked at the peasant with haggard eyes, while he himself stared at her with amazement, not understanding how such a small present could stir up such violent emotions. Finally he left. Félicité stayed. She could bear it no longer; she ran into the sitting room as if to take the apricots there, overturned the basket, tore away the leaves, found the letter, opened it, and, as if pursued by some fearful fire, Emma flew in terror to her room.

Charles was there; she saw him; he spoke to her; she heard nothing, and she ran quickly up the stairs, breathless, distraught, crazed, and ever holding this horrible piece of paper, that crackled between her fingers like a plate of sheet-iron. On the second floor she stopped before the closed attic-door.

Then she tried to calm herself; she recalled the letter; she must finish it but she didn't dare. Where and how was she to read it? She would be seen!

"Here," she thought, "I'll be safe here."

Emma pushed open the door and went in.

The slates projected a heavy heat that gripped her temples, stifled her; she dragged herself to the closed window, drew back the bolt, and the dazzling sunlight burst in.

Opposite, beyond the roofs, the open country stretched as far as the eye could reach. Down below, underneath her, the village square was empty; the stones of the pavement glittered, the weathercocks on the houses stood motionless. At the corner of the street, from a lower story, rose a kind of humming with strident modulations. It was Binet turning.

She leant against the window-frame, and re-read the letter with angry sneers. But the more she concentrated on it, the more confused she grew. She could see him, hear him, feel his embrace; the throbbing of her heart, beating irregularly in her breast like the blows of a battering ram, grew faster and faster. She looked about her wishing that the earth might crumble. Why not end it all? What restrained her? She was free. She advanced, looked at the paving-stones, saying to herself, "Jump! jump!"

The ray of light reflected straight from below drew the weight of her body towards the abyss. The ground of the village square seemed to tilt over and climb up the walls, the floor to pitch forward like in a tossing boat. She was right at the edge, almost hanging, surrounded by vast space. The blue of the sky invaded her, the air was whirling in her hollow head; she had but to yield, to let herself be taken; and the humming of the lathe never ceased, like an angry voice calling her.

"My wife! my wife!" cried Charles.

She stopped.

"Where have you gone? Come here!"

The thought that she had just escaped from death almost made her faint with terror. She closed her eyes; then she started at the touch of a hand on her sleeve; it was Félicité.

"Monsieur is waiting for you, madame; the soup is on the table."

And she had to go down! and sit at the table!

She tried to eat. The food choked her. Then she unfolded her napkin as if to examine the darns, and really tried to concentrate on this work, counting the stitches in the linen. Suddenly she remembered the letter. How had she lost it? Where could it be found? But she felt such weariness of spirit that she could not even invent a pretext for leaving the table. Then she became a coward; she was afraid of Charles; he knew all, that was certain! Just then, he said, in an odd tone:

"We are not likely to see Monsieur Rodolphe soon again, it seems."

"Who told you?" she said, shuddering.

"Who told me!" he replied, rather astonished at her abrupt tone. "Why, Girard, whom I met just now at the door of the Café Français. He has gone on a journey, or is about to go."

She could not suppress a sob.

"What is so surprising about that? He goes away like that from time to time for a change, and I certainly can't blame him. A bachelor, and rich as he is! And from what I hear, he isn't exactly starved for pleasures, our friend! he enjoys life. Monsieur Langlois told me . . ."

He stopped for propriety's sake because the maid had just come in.

She collected the apricots that were strewn over the sideboard and put them back in the basket. Charles, unaware that his wife had turned scarlet, had them brought to him, took one, and bit into it.

"Perfect!" he said; "have a taste!"

And he handed her the basket, which she gently put away from her.

"Smell them! Such perfume!" he insisted, moving it back and forth under her nose.

"I am choking," she exclaimed, leaping up.

By sheer willpower, she succeeded in forcing back the spasm.

"It is nothing," she said, "it is nothing! Just nerves. Sit down and eat."

For she dreaded most of all that he would question her, try to help and not leave her to herself.

Charles, to obey her, sat down again, and he spat the stones of the apricots into his hands, afterwards putting them on his plate.

Suddenly a blue tilbury passed across the square at a rapid trot. Emma uttered a cry and fell back rigid on the floor.

After many hesitations, Rodolphe had finally decided to set out for Rouen. Now, as from La Huchette to Buchy there is no other way than by Yonville, he had to go through the village, and Emma had recognised him by the rays of the lanterns, which like lightning flashed through the twilight.

The general commotion which broke out in the house brought the pharmacist over in a hurry. The table, with all the plates, had been knocked over; sauce, meat, knives, the salt, and cruet-stand were strewn over the room; Charles was calling for help; Berthe, scared, was crying; and Félicité, whose hands trembled, was unlacing her mistress, whose whole body shivered convulsively.

"I'll run to my laboratory for some aromatic vinegar," said the pharmacist.

Then as she opened her eyes on smelling the bottle:

"I thought so," he said, "this thing would resuscitate a corpse!"

"Speak to us," said Charles "try to recover! It is Charles, who loves you . . . Do you know me? Look, here is your little girl; kiss her, darling!"

The child stretched out her arms to cling to her mother's neck. But turning away her head, Emma said in a broken voice:

"No, no . . . I want no one!"

She fainted again. They carried her to her bed.

She lay there stretched at full length, her lips apart, her eyelids closed, her hands open, motionless, and white as a waxen image. Two streams of tears flowed from her eyes and fell slowly upon the pillow.

Charles stood at the back of the alcove, and the pharmacist, near him, maintained the meditative silence that is fitting on the serious occasions of life.

"Don't worry," he said, touching his elbow; "I think the paroxysm is past."

"Yes, she is resting a little now," answered Charles, watching her sleep. "Poor girl! poor girl! She has dropped off now!"

Then Homais asked how the accident had occurred. Charles answered that she had been taken ill suddenly while she was eating some apricots.

"Extraordinary!" continued the pharmacist. "It is quite possible that the apricots caused the syncope. Some natures are so sensitive to certain smells; it would even be a very fine question to study both from a pathological and physiological point of view. The priests know all about it; that's why they use aromatics in all their ceremonies. It is to stupefy the senses and to bring on ecstasies,—a thing, moreover, very easy in persons of the weaker sex, who are more sensitive than we are. Some are reported fainting at the smell of burnt horn, or fresh bread . . ."

"Be careful not to wake her!" warned Bovary.

But the pharmacist was not to be stopped. "Not only," he resumed, "are human beings subject to such anomalies, but animals also. You are of course not ignorant of the singularly aphrodisiac effect produced by the *Nepeta cataria*, vulgarly called catnip, on the feline race; and, on the other hand, to quote an example whose authenticity I can vouch for, Bridaux (one of my old schoolmates, at present established in the Rue Malpalu) owns a dog that falls into convulsions as soon as you hold out a snuff-box to him. He often performs the experiment before his friends at his summer-house in Bois-Guillaume. Could you believe that a simple sternutative could cause such damage to a quadrupedal organism? Wouldn't you agree that it is extremely curious?"

"Yes," said Charles, who was not listening.

"It just goes to show," pursued the pharmacist, smiling with benign self-satisfaction, "the numberless irregularities of the nervous system. With regard to madame, I must say that she has always seemed extremely susceptible to me. And so I should by no means recommend to you, my dear friend, any of those so-called remedies that, under the pretence of attacking the symptoms, attack the constitution. No, no gratuitous medications! Diet, that is all; sedatives, emollients, dulcifiers. And then, don't you think we ought to stimulate the imagination?"

"In what way? How?" said Bovary.

"Ah, that is the problem. 'That is the question' (he said it in English) as I lately read in a newspaper."

But Emma, awaking, cried out:

"The letter! Where is the letter?"

They thought she was delirious; and she was by midnight. Brain-fever had set in.

For forty-three days Charles did not leave her. He gave up all his patients; he no longer went to bed; he was constantly feeling her pulse, applying mustard plasters and cold-water compresses. He sent Justin as far as Neufchâtel for ice; the ice melted on the way; he sent him back again. He called Monsieur Canivet into consultation; he sent for Dr. Larivière, his old master, from Rouen; he was in despair. What alarmed him most was Emma's prostration, for she did not speak, did not listen, did not even seem to suffer—as if both her body and her soul were resting after all their tribulations.

About the middle of October she could sit up in bed supported by pillows. Charles wept when he saw her eat her first piece of bread and jam. Her strength returned; she got up for a few hours of an afternoon, and one day, when she felt better, he tried to take her, leaning on his arm, for a walk round the garden. The sand of the paths was disappearing beneath the dead leaves; she walked slowly, dragging her slippers, and leaning against Charles's shoulder. She smiled all the time.

They went thus to the end of the garden near the terrace. She drew herself up slowly, shading her eyes with her hand. She looked far off, as far as she could, but on the horizon were only great bonfires of grass smoking on the hills.

"You will tire yourself, darling!" said Bovary.

And, pushing her gently to make her enter the arbour: "Sit down on this seat; you'll be comfortable."

"Oh! no; not there!" she said in a faltering voice.

She was seized with giddiness, and that evening, she suffered a relapse, less specific in character, it is true, and with more complex symptoms. At times it was her heart that troubled her, then her head or her limbs; she had vomitings, in which Charles thought he detected the first signs of cancer.

And, on top of all this, the poor fellow had money troubles!

XIV

To begin with, he did not know how to reimburse Monsieur Homais for all the drugs he had supplied and although, as a doctor, he could have forgone paying for them, he blushed at the thought of such an obligation. Then the expenses of the household, now that the maid was in charge, became staggering. Bills flooded the house; the tradesmen grumbled; Monsieur Lheureux especially harassed him. At the height of Emma's illness, he had taken advantage of the situation to increase his bill; he hurriedly brought the cloak, the travelling-bag, two trunks instead of one, and a number of other things. Charles protested in vain; the shopkeeper rudely replied that the merchandise had been ordered and that he had no intention of taking it back. Besides, it would interfere with madame's convalescence; the doctor had better think it over; in short, he was resolved to sue him rather than give up his rights and take it off his hands. Charles subsequently ordered them sent back to the shop. Félicité forgot and, having other things on his mind, Charles thought no more about it. Monsieur Lheureux did not desist and, alternating threats with whines, he finally forced Bovary into signing him a six months' promissory note. But hardly had he signed the note than a bold idea occurred to him: he meant to borrow a thousand francs from Lheureux. So, with an embarrassed air, he asked if he could get them, adding that it would be for a year, at any interest. Lheureux ran off to his shop, brought back the money, and dictated another note, by which Bovary undertook to pay to his order on the 1st of September next the sum of one thousand and seventy francs, which, with the hundred and eighty already agreed to, made just twelve hundred and fifty. He was thus lending at six per cent in addition to one-fourth for commission; and since the merchandise brought him a good third profit at least, he stood to make one hundred and thirty francs in twelve months. He hoped that the business would not stop there; that the notes would not be paid on time and would have to be renewed, and that his puny little investment, thriving in the doctor's care like a patient in a rest home, would return to him one day considerably plumper, fat enough to burst the bag.

All of Lheureux's enterprises were thriving. He got the franchise for supplying the Neufchâtel hospital with cider; Monsieur Guillaumin promised him some shares in the turf-bogs of Gaumesnil, and he dreamt of establishing a new coach service between Argueil and Rouen, which no doubt would not be long in putting the ramshackle van of the "Lion d'Or" out of business. Travelling faster, at a cheaper rate, and carrying more luggage, it would concentrate into his hands all of Yonville's business.

Charles often wondered how he would ever be able to pay back so much money next year. He tried to think of solutions, such as applying to his father or selling something. But his father would be deaf, and he—he had nothing to sell. He foresaw such difficulties that he quickly dismissed so disagreeable a subject of meditation from his mind. He reproached himself with forgetting Emma, as if, all his thoughts belonging to this woman, it was robbing her of something not to be constantly thinking of her.

It was a severe winter. Madame Bovary's convalescence was slow. On good days they wheeled her arm-chair to the window that overlooked the square, for she now disliked the garden, and the blinds on that side were always down. She wanted her horse to be sold; what she formerly liked now displeased her. The limit of her concerns seemed to be her own health. She stayed in bed taking light meals, rang for the maid to inquire about her tea or merely to chat. The snow on the market-roof threw a white, still light into the room; then the rain began to fall; and every day Emma would wait with a kind of anxiety for the inevitable return of some trifling event that was of little or no concern to her. The most important was the arrival of the "Hirondelle" in the evening. Then the innkeeper would shout and other voices answered, while Hippolyte's lantern, as he took down the luggage from the roof, was like a star in the darkness. At noontime, Charles came home; then he left again; next she took some broth, and towards five o'clock, as night fell, the children coming back from school, dragging their wooden shoes along the pavement, beat with their rulers against the clapper of the shutters.

Around this time of day, Monsieur Bournisien came to see her. He inquired after her health, gave her news, exhorted her to religion in a playful, gossipy tone that was not without charm. The mere sight of his cassock comforted her.

Once, at the height of her illness, she thought she was about to die and asked for communion; and while they were making the preparations in her room for the sacrament, while they were clearing the night table of its medicine bottles and turning it into an altar, and while Félicité was strewing dahlia flowers on the floor, Emma felt some power passing over her that freed her from her pains, from all perception, from all feeling. Her body, relieved, no longer thought; another life was beginning; it seemed to her that her being, mounting toward God, would be annihilated in that love like a burning incense that melts into vapour. The bed-clothes were sprinkled with holy water, the priest drew the white host from the holy pyx and she fainted with celestial joy as she advanced her lips to accept the body of the Saviour presented to her. The curtains of the alcove floated gently round her like clouds, and the rays of the two tapers burning on the night table seemed to shine like dazzling halos. Then she let her head fall back, fancying she heard in space the music of seraphic harps, and perceived in an azure sky, on a golden throne in the midst of saints holding green palms, God the Father, resplendent with majesty, who ordered to earth angels with wings of fire to carry her away in their arms.

This splendid vision dwelt in her memory as the most beautiful thing that it was possible to dream, so that now she strove to recall her sensation; it was still with her, albeit in a less overpowering manner, but with the same profound sweetness. Her soul, tortured by pride, at length found rest in Christian humility, and, tasting the joy of weakness, she saw within herself the destruction of her will opening wide the gates for heavenly grace to conquer her. She realised the existence of a bliss that could replace happiness, another love beyond all loves, without pause and without end, that would grow forever! Amid the illusions of her hope, she saw a state of purity floating above the earth, mingling with heaven. She wanted to become a saint. She bought rosaries and wore holy medals; she wished to have in her room, by the side of her bed, a reliquary set in emeralds that she might kiss it every evening.

The priest was delighted with her new state of mind, although he couldn't help worrying that Emma's excessive fervor might lead to heresy, to extravagance. But not being much versed in these matters once they went beyond a certain point he wrote to Monsieur Boulard, the bishop's bookseller, to send him "something first rate for a lady with a very distinguished mind." With as much concern as if he were shipping kitchen ware to savages, the bookseller made a random package of whatever happened to be current in the religious booktrade at the time. It contained little question and answer manuals, pamphlets written in the brusque tone of Joseph de Maistre,[45] pseudo-novels in rose-coloured bindings and a sugary style, manufactured by sentimental seminarists or penitent blue-stockings.

45. Joseph de Maistre (1753–1821) was the main theorist of Catholic conservatism. His books, *Du Pape* (1819) and *Soirées de Saint-Petersbourg* (1821), defended the power of the pope and the sovereign king and argued that the reign of evil on earth has to be curbed by authority.

There were titles such as "Consider carefully: the Man of the World at the Feet of the Virgin Mary, by Monsieur de * * *, decorated with many Orders"; "The Errors of Voltaire, for the Use of the Young," &c.

Madame Bovary's mind was not yet sufficiently clear to apply herself seriously to anything; moreover, she began this reading in too great a hurry. She grew provoked at the doctrines of religion; the arrogance of the polemic writings displeased her by their ferocious attacks on people she did not know; and the secular stories, sprinkled with religious seasoning, seemed to her written in such ignorance of the world, that they rather led her away from the truths she wanted to see confirmed. Nevertheless, she persevered; and when the volume slipped from her hands, she fancied herself seized with the finest Catholic melancholy ever conceived by an ethereal soul.

As for the memory of Rodolphe, she had locked it away in the deepest recesses of her heart, and it remained there solemn and motionless as a pharaoh's mummy in a catacomb. A fragance escaped from this embalmed love, that, penetrating through everything, perfumed with tenderness the immaculate atmosphere in which she longed to live. When she knelt on her Gothic prie-Dieu, she addressed to the Lord the same suave words that she had murmured formerly to her lover in the outpourings of adultery. She was searching for faith; but no delights descended from the heavens, and she arose with aching limbs and the vague feeling that she was being cheated.

Yet she thought this search all the more admirable, and in the pride of her devoutness Emma compared herself to those grand ladies of long ago whose glory she had dreamed of over a portrait of La Vallière, and who, trailing with so much majesty the lace-trimmed trains of their long gowns, retired into solitude to shed at the feet of Christ the tears of hearts that life had wounded.

Then she indulged in excessive charity. She sewed clothes for the poor, she sent wood to women in childbirth; and on coming home one day, Charles found three tramps eating soup in the kitchen. Her little girl, whom her husband had sent back to the nurse during her illness, returned home. She wanted to teach her to read; even Berthe's crying no longer irritated her. She was resigned, universally tolerant. Her speech was full of elevated expressions. She would say:

"Is your stomach-ache any better, my angel?"

The elder Madame Bovary couldn't find fault with anything except perhaps this mania of knitting jackets for orphans instead of mending her own dishtowels; but, harassed with domestic quarrels, the good woman took pleasure in this quiet house, and she even stayed there till after Easter, to escape the sarcasms of old Bovary, who never failed to order a big pork sausage on Good Friday.

Besides the companionship of her mother-in-law, who strengthened her resolutions somewhat by the rigor of her judgment and her stern appearance, Emma almost every day had other visitors: Madame Langlois, Madame Caron, Madame Dubreuil, Madame Tuvache, and regularly from two to five o'clock the sterling Madame Homais who, for her part, had never believed any of the gossip about her neighbor. The Homais children also came to see her, accompanied by Justin. He went up with them to her bedroom, and remained standing near the door without daring to move or to utter a word. Often enough Madame Bovary, taking no heed of him, would start dressing. She began by taking out her comb and tossing her head, in a brusk gesture, and when for the first time the poor boy saw this mass of hair fall in ringlets to her knees, it was as if he entered suddenly into a new and strange world, whose splendour terrified him.

Emma probably did not notice his silent attentions or his timidity. She had no inkling that love, which presumably had left her life forever, was pulsating right there, under that coarse shirt, in that adolescent heart open to the emanations of her beauty. Besides, she now wrapped all things in the same mood of indifference, she combined gentleness of speech with such haughty looks, affected such contradictory ways, that one could no longer distinguish selfishness from charity, or corruption from virtue. One evening, for example, she first got angry with the maid, who had asked to go out, and stammered as she tried to find some pretext; then suddenly:

"So you love him, don't you?" she said.

And without waiting for an answer from Félicité, who was blushing, she added sadly:

"All right! run along, and have a good time!"

In early spring she had the garden all changed around, over Bovary's objections; yet he was pleased to see her at last express some will of her own. She did so more and more as her strength returned. First, she found occasion to expel Mère Rollet, the nurse, who during her convalescence had taken to visiting the kitchen in the company of her two nurslings and her young boarder, whose appetite surpassed that of a cannibal. She cut down on the visits of the Homais family, gradually freed herself from the other visitors, and even went to church less assiduously, to the great approval of the pharmacist, who remarked to her:

"I suspect you were beginning to fall for the priest's sales talk!"

As before, Monsieur Bournisien would drop in every day after catechism class. He preferred to take the air in the "grove," as he called the arbour. This was the time when Charles came home. They were hot; some sweet cider was brought out, and they drank together to madame's complete recovery.

Binet was often there, that is to say, a little lower down against the terrace wall, fishing for crayfish. Bovary invited him to have a drink, and he proved to be a real expert on the uncorking of the stone bottles.

Looking around with utter self-satisfaction, first at his companions, then at the furthest confines of the landscape, he would say: "You must first hold the bottle perpendicularly on the table, and after the strings are cut, press the cork upwards inch by inch, gently, very gently—the way they handle soda water in restaurants."

But during his demonstration the cider often spurted right into their faces, and the priest, laughing his thick laugh, would never fail to make his little joke:

"Its excellence certainly strikes the eye!"

He was undoubtedly a kindly fellow and one day he was not even scandalised at the pharmacist, who advised Charles to give madame some distraction by taking her to the theatre at Rouen to hear the illustrious tenor, Lagardy. Homais, surprised at this silence, wanted to know his opinion, and the priest declared that he considered music less dangerous for morals than literature.

But the pharmacist took up the defence of letters. The theatre, he contended, served to decry prejudices and, while pretending to amuse, it taught virtue.

"*Castigat ridendo mores,*[46] Monsieur Bournisien! Look at most of Voltaire's tragedies: they contain a wealth of philosophical considerations that make them into a real school of morals and diplomacy for the people."

"I," said Binet, "once saw a play called the 'Gamin de Paris,'[47] in which there is a really fine part of an old general. He settles the account of a rich young fellow who has seduced a working girl, and at the end . . ."

"Of course," pursued Homais, "there is bad literature as there is bad pharmacy, but to condemn in a lump the most important of the fine arts seems to me a stupidity, a Gothic aberration worthy of the abominable times that imprisoned Galileo."[48]

"I know very well," objected the curé, "that there are good works, good authors. Still, the very fact of crowding people of different sexes into the same room, made to look enticing by displays of worldly pomp, these pagan disguises, the makeup, the lights, the effeminate voices, all this must, in the long-run, engender

46. *Castigat ridendo mores:* "It [comedy] reproves the manners, through laughter"—a slogan for comedy invented by the poet Jean de Santeuil (1630–1697), and given to the harlequin Dominique to put it on the curtain of his theater.

47. *Gamin de Paris* is a comedy by Bayard and Vanderbusch performed in 1836 in Paris.

48. Galileo Galilei (1564–1642), the astronomer, was confined to his house in Arcetri (near Florence) after his book propounding the view that the earth circled around the sun was condemned by the Inquisition (in 1633).

a certain mental libertinage, give rise to immodest thoughts and impure temptations. Such, at any rate, is the opinion of all the church fathers. Moreover," he added, suddenly assuming a mystic tone of voice while he rolled a pinch of snuff between his fingers, "if the Church has condemned the theatre, she must be right; we must bow to her decrees."

"Why," asked the druggist, "should she excommunicate actors when formerly they used to take part openly in religious ceremonies? They would play right in the middle of the choir and perform a kind of farce called "mystery plays" that frequently offended against the laws of decency."

The curé merely groaned and the pharmacist persisted:

"It's like in the Bible; you know . . . there are things in it . . . certain details . . . I'd call them downright daring . . . bordering on obscenity!"

And as Monsieur Bournisien signaled his annoyance:

"Ah! you'll admit that it is not a book to place in the hands of a young girl, and I wouldn't at all like it if Athalie . . ."

"But it is the Protestants, and not we," protested the other impatiently, "who recommend the Bible."

"All the same," said Homais. "I am surprised that in our days, in this century of enlightenment, any one should still persist in proscribing an intellectual relaxation that is inoffensive, morally uplifting, and sometimes even good for the health—isn't that right, doctor?"

"Quite," the doctor replied in a non-committal tone, either because, sharing the same ideas, he wished to offend no one, or else because he simply had no ideas on the subject.

The conversation seemed at an end when the pharmacist thought fit to try a parting shot.

"I've known priests who put on civilian clothes to go watch burlesque shows."

"Come, come!" said the curé.

"Ah yes, I've known some!"

And, separating the words, he repeated:

"I—have—known—some!"

"Well, they did wrong," said Bournisien, prepared to listen to anything with resignation.

"And they didn't stop at that, either!" persisted the pharmacist.

"That's enough! . . ." exclaimed the priest, looking so fierce that the other thought safe to retreat.

"I only mean to say," he replied in a much less aggressive tone, "that tolerance is the surest way to draw people to religion."

"That is true! that is true!" conceded the priest, sitting down again.

But he stayed only a few minutes. Hardly had he left that Monsieur Homais said to the doctor:

"That's what I call a good fight! See how I found his weak spot? I didn't give him much of a chance . . . Now take my advice. Take madame to the theatre, if only to get for once the better of one of these rooks! If someone could keep the store in my absence, I'd go with you. But hurry! Lagardy is only going to give one performance; he's going to play in England for a tremendous fee. From what I hear, he's quite a character. He's simply loaded with money! He travels with three mistresses and a cook. All these great artists burn the candle at both ends; they need to lead a dissolute life to stir the imagination of the public. But they die at the poorhouse, because they don't have the sense to save their money when it comes in. Well, enjoy your dinner! See you to-morrow."

This theatre idea quickly grew in Bovary's mind; he at once communicated it to his wife, who at first refused, alleging the fatigue, the worry, the expense; but, for once, Charles did not give in, so sure was he that this occasion would do her good. He saw nothing to prevent it: his mother had sent three hundred francs he no longer counted on, the current bills were far from staggering and Lheureux's notes were not due for such a long time that he could dismiss them from his mind. Besides, imagining that she was refusing out of consideration for him, he insisted all the more, until she finally consented. The next day at eight o'clock they set out in the "Hirondelle."

The pharmacist, who had nothing whatever to keep him at Yonville but fancied himself to be indispensable, sighed with envy as he saw them go.

"Well, a pleasant journey!" he said to them; "happy mortals that you are!"

Then addressing himself to Emma, who was wearing a blue silk gown with four flounces:

"You are prettier than ever. You'll make quite an impression in Rouen."

The diligence stopped at the "Croix-Rouge" on the Place Beavoisine. It was a typical provincial inn, with large stables and small bedrooms and chickens in the courtyard, picking at the oats under the muddy gigs of travelling salesmen;—a fine old place, with worm-eaten balconies that creak in the wind on winter nights, always crowded, noisy and full of food, its black tables stained with coffee and brandy, the thick windows yellowed by flies, the napkins spotted with cheap red wine. Like farmboys dressed in Sunday-clothes, the place still reeks of the country; it has a café on the street and a vegetable-garden on the back. Charles at once set out on his errands. He confused stage-boxes and gallery, orchestra seats and regular boxes, asked for explanations which he did not understand, was sent from the box-office to the manager, came back to the inn, returned to the theatre and ended up by crossing the full length of the town, from theatre to outer boulevard, several times.

Madame bought herself a hat, gloves, and a bouquet. Monsieur worried greatly about missing the beginning, and, without having had time to swallow a plate of soup, they arrived at the gates of the theatre well before opening time.

XV

The crowd was lined up against the wall, evenly distributed on both sides of the entrance rails. At the corner of the neighbouring streets huge bills, printed in Gothic letters, announced "Lucie de Lammermoor-Lagardy-Opera &c."[49] The weather was fine, the people hot; sweat trickled among fancy coiffures and pocket handkerchiefs were mopping red foreheads; now and then a warm wind that blew from the river gently stirred the edges of the canvass awnings hanging from the doors of the cafés. A little lower down, however, one was refreshed by a current of icy air that smelt of tallow, leather, and oil, breathed forth from the Rue des Charrettes with its huge, dark warehouses resounding with the noise of rolling barrels.

For fear of seeming ridiculous, Emma first wanted to take a little stroll in the harbor, and Bovary carefully kept clutching the tickets in his trouser pockets, pressed against his stomach.

Her heart began to beat as soon as she reached the entrance hall. She involuntarily smiled with vanity on seeing the crowd rushing to the right by the other corridor while she went up the staircase to the reserved seats. She was as pleased as a child to push the large tapestried door open with her finger; she breathed deeply the dusty smell of the lobbies, and when she was seated in her box she drew herself up with the self-assurance of a duchess.

The theatre was beginning to fill; opera-glasses were taken from their cases, and the subscribers greeted and bowed as they spotted each other at a distance. They sought relief from the pressures of commerce in the arts, but, unable to take their minds off business matters, they still talked about cotton, spirits of wine, or indigo. The placid and meek heads of the old men, with their pale whitish hair and complexion, resembled silver medals tarnished by lead fumes. The young beaux were strutting about in the orchestra, exhibiting their pink or apple-green cravats under their gaping waistcoats; sitting above them, Madame Bovary admired how they leant the tight-drawn palm of their yellow gloves on the golden knobs of their canes.

49. *Lucia di Lammermoor* is an opera by Gaetano Donizetti (1797–1848) first performed in Naples in 1835 (in Paris in 1837). It is based on Walter Scott's novel, *The Bride of Lammermoor* (1819). **See the extended note p. 740.**

Now the lights of the orchestra were lit; the chandelier, let down from the ceiling, threw the sudden gaiety of its sparkling crystals over the theatre; then the musicians began to file in; and first there was the protracted hubbub of roaring cellos, squeaking violins, blaring trumpets and piping flutes. But three knocks were heard on the stage, a rolling of drums began, the brass instruments played some chords, and the curtain rose, discovering a country-scene.

It was the cross-roads of a wood, with a fountain on the left, shaded by an oak tree. Peasants and lords with tartans over their shoulders were singing a hunting-song in chorus; a captain suddenly appeared, who evoked the spirit of evil by lifting both his arms to heaven. Another followed; they departed, and the hunters started afresh.

She felt herself carried back to the reading of her youth, into the midst of Walter Scott. She seemed to hear through the mist the sound of the Scotch bagpipes re-echoing over the moors. Her remembrance of the novel helping her to understand the libretto, she followed the story phrase by phrase, while the burst of music dispersed the fleeting thoughts that came back to her. She gave herself up to the flow of the melodies, and felt all her being vibrate as if the violin bows were being drawn over her nerves. Her eyes could hardly take in all the costumes, the scenery, the actors, the painted trees that shook whenever someone walked, and the velvet caps, cloaks, swords—all those imaginary things that vibrated in the music as in the atmosphere of another world. But a young woman stepped forward, throwing a purse to a squire in green. She was left alone on the stage, and the flute was heard like the murmur of a fountain or the warbling of birds. Lucie bravely attacked her cavatina in G major. She begged for love, longed for wings. Emma, too, would have liked to flee away from life, locked in a passionate embrace. Suddenly Edgar Lagardy appeared.

He had that splendid pallor that gives something of the majesty of marble to the ardent races of the South. His vigourous form was tightly clad in a brown-coloured doublet; a small chiselled dagger swung against his left thigh, and he rolled languid eyes while flashing his white teeth. They said that a Polish princess having heard him sing one night on the beach at Biarritz, where he used to be a boatsman, had fallen in love with him. She had lost her entire fortune for his sake. He had deserted her for other women, and this sentimental fame did not fail to enhance his artistic reputation. A skilled ham actor, he never forgot to have a phrase on his seductiveness and his sensitive soul inserted in the accounts about him. He had a fine voice, colossal aplomb, more temperament than intelligence, more pathos than lyric feeling; all this made for an admirable charlatan type, in which there was something of the hairdresser as well as of the bullfighter.

From the first scene he brought down the house. He pressed

Lucie in his arms, he left her, he came back, he seemed desperate; he had outbursts of rage, then elegiac gurglings of infinite sweetness, and tones like sobs and kisses escaped from his bare throat. Emma bent forward to see him, scratching the velvet of the box with her nails. Her heart filled with these melodious lamentations that were accompanied by the lugubrious moanings of the double-bases, like the cries of the drowning in the tumult of a tempest. She recognised all the intoxication and the anguish that had brought her close to death. The voice of the prima donna seemed to echo her own conscience, and the whole fictional story seemed to capture something of her own life. But no one on earth had loved her with such love. He had not wept like Edgar that last moonlit night when they had said "Till tomorrow! Till tomorrow! . . ." The theatre rang with cheers; they repeated the entire stretto; the lovers spoke of the flowers on their tomb, of vows, exile, fate, hopes; and when they uttered the final farewell, Emma gave a sharp cry that mingled with the vibrations of the last chords.

"But why," asked Bovary, "is that lord torturing her like that?"

"No, no!" she answered; "he is her lover!"

"Yet he vows vengeance on her family, while the other one who came on before said, 'I love Lucie and she loves me!' Besides, he went off with her father arm in arm. For he certainly is her father, isn't he—the ugly little man with a cock's feather in his hat?"

Despite Emma's explanations, as soon as the recitative duet began in which Gilbert lays bare his abominable machinations to his master Ashton, Charles, seeing the false engagement ring that is to deceive Lucie, thought it was a love-gift sent by Edgar. He confessed, moreover, that he did not understand the story because of the music, which interfered very much with the words.

"What does it matter?" said Emma. "Do be quiet!"

"Yes, but you know," he went on, leaning against her shoulder, "I like to understand things."

"Be quiet! be quiet!" she cried impatiently.

Lucie came on, half supported by her women, a wreath of orange blossoms in her hair, and paler than the white satin of her gown. Emma dreamed of her marriage day; she saw herself at home again among the fields in the little path as they walked to the church. Why didn't she, like this woman, resist and implore? Instead, she had walked joyously and unwittingly towards the abyss . . . Ah! if in the freshness of her beauty, before the degradation of marriage and the disillusions of adultery, she could have anchored her life upon some great, strong heart! Virtue, affection, sensuous pleasure and duty would have combined to give her eternal bliss. But such happiness, she realized, was a lie, a mockery to taunt desire. She knew now how small the passions were that art magnified. So, striving for detachment, Emma resolved to see in this reproduction of her sorrows a mere formal fiction for the entertainment of the eye, and she smiled inwardly in scornful pity when from behind the velvet curtains at the back of the stage a man appeared in a black cloak.

His large Spanish hat fell at a gesture he made, and immediately the instruments and the singers began the sextet. Edgar, flashing with fury, dominated all the others with his clearer voice; Ashton hurled homicidal provocations at him in deep notes; Lucie uttered her shrill lament; Arthur sang modulated asides in a middle register and the deep basso of the minister pealed forth like an organ, while the female voices re-echoed his words in a delightful chorus. They were lined up in one single gesticulating row, breathing forth anger, vengeance, jealousy, terror, mercy and surprise all at once from their open mouths. The outraged lover brandished his naked sword; his lace ruff rose and fell jerkily with the movements of his chest, and he walked from right to left with long strides, clanking against the boards the silver-gilt spurs of his soft, flaring boots. She thought that he must have inexhaustible supplies of love in him to lavish it upon the crowd with such effusion. All her attempts at critical detachment were swept away by the poetic power of the acting, and, drawn to the man by the illusion of the part, she tried to imagine his life—extraordinary, magnificent, notorious, the life that could have been hers if fate had willed it. If only they had met! He would have loved her, they would have travelled together through all the kingdoms of Europe from capital to capital, sharing in his success and in his hardships, picking up the flowers thrown to him, mending his clothes. Every night, hidden behind the golden lattice of her box, she would have drunk in eagerly the expansions of this soul that would have sung for her alone; from the stage, even as he acted, he would have looked at her. A mad idea took possession of her: he was looking at her right now! She longed to run to his arms, to take refuge in his strength, as in the incarnation of love itself, and to say to him, to cry out, "Take me away! carry me with you! let us leave! All my passion and all my dreams are yours!"

The curtain fell.

The smell of gas mingled with the people's breath and the waving fans made the air even more suffocating. Emma wanted to go out; the crowd filled the corridors, and she fell back in her armchair with palpitations that choked her. Charles, fearing that she would faint, ran to the refreshment-room to get a glass of orgeat.

He had great difficulty in getting back to his seat, for as he was holding the glass in his hands, his elbows bumped into someone at every step; he even spilt three-fourths on the shoulders of a Rouen lady in short sleeves, who feeling the cold liquid running down her back, started to scream like a peacock, as if she were being murdered. Her mill-owner husband lashed out at his clumsiness, and while she used her handkerchief to wipe off the stains from her handsome cherry-coloured taffeta gown, he angrily muttered about indemnity, costs, reimbursement. Charles was quite out of breath when he finally reached his wife:

"I thought I'd never make it. What a crowd! . . . What a crowd!"

And he added:

"Just guess whom I met up there! Monsieur Léon!"

"Léon?"

"Himself! He's coming along to pay his respects."

And as he finished these words the ex-clerk of Yonville entered the box.

He held out his hand with the casual ease of a gentleman; and Madame Bovary extended hers, yielding no doubt to the pressure of a stronger will. She had not felt it since that spring evening when the rain fell upon the green leaves, and they had said good-bye while standing near the window. But soon recalling herself to the necessities of the situation, she managed to shake off the torpor of her memories, and began stammering a few hurried words.

"Ah! good evening . . . What, you here?"

"Silence!" cried a voice from the orchestra, for the third act was beginning.

"So you are at Rouen?"

"Yes."

"And since when?"

"Be quiet! Throw them out!"

People were looking at them; they fell silent.

But from that moment she listened no more; and the chorus of the guests, the scene between Ashton and his servant, the grand duet in D major, all became more distant, as if the instruments had grown less sonorous and the characters more remote. She remembered the card games at the pharmacist, the walk to the nurse, the poetry readings in the arbour, the tête-à-têtes by the fireside—all the sadness of their love, so calm and so protracted, so discreet, so tender, and that she had nevertheless forgotten. And why had he come back? What combination of circumstances had brought him back into her life? He was standing behind her, leaning with his shoulder against the wall of the box; now and again she felt herself shudder as she felt the warmth of his breath on her hair.

"Do you find this amusing?" he said, bending over her so closely that the end of his moustache brushed her cheek.

She replied flippantly:

"Heavens, no! not particularly."

Then he suggested that they leave the theatre and have an ice somewhere.

"Oh, not yet; let us stay," said Bovary. "Her hair's undone; this is going to be tragic."

But the madness scene did not interest Emma, and she thought the singer was overacting.

"She screams too loud," she said, turning to Charles who was listening.

"Yes . . . perhaps . . . a little," he replied, torn between his genuine enjoyment and his respect for his wife's opinion.

Then Léon sighed:

"Don't you find it hot . . ."

"Unbearably so! Yes!"

"Don't you feel well?" Bovary inquired.

"Yes, I am stifling; let's go."

Monsieur Léon draped her long lace shawl carefully about her shoulders, and the three of them left and sat down near the harbor, on the terrace of a café. First they spoke of her illness, although Emma interrupted Charles from time to time, for fear, she said, of boring Monsieur Léon; and the latter told them that he had come to spend two years in a big Rouen law firm, in order to gain some experience of how business is conducted in Normandy—so different from Paris. Then he inquired after Berthe, the Homais, Mère Lefrançois, and as they had, in the husband's presence, nothing more to say to one another, the conversation soon came to an end.

People coming out of the theatre walked along the pavement, humming or shouting at the top of their voices, "*O bel ange, ma Lucie!*" Then Léon, playing the dilettante, began to talk music. He had seen Tamburini, Rubini, Persiani, Grisi,[50] and, compared with them, Lagardy, despite his grand outbursts, was nowhere.

"Yet," interrupted Charles, who was slowly sipping his rum-sherbet, "they say that he is quite admirable in the last act. I regret leaving before the end, just when I was beginning to enjoy myself."

"Why," said the clerk, "he will soon give another performance."

But Charles replied that they had to leave the next day. "Unless," he added, turning to his wife, "you'd like to stay by yourself, my darling?"

And changing his tactics at the unexpected opportunity that presented itself to his hopes, the young man sang the praises of Lagardy in the last aria. It was really superb, sublime. Then Charles insisted:

"You'll come back on Sunday. Come, make up your mind. If you feel that this is doing you the least bit of good, you shouldn't

50. Antonio Tamburini (1800–1876), Gian-Battista Rubini (1795–1854), Fanny Facchinardi Persiani (who was the first Lucia), and Ciulia Grisi (1811–1869) were all famous Bel-Canto singers who appeared in Paris in the operas of Rossini and Donizetti.

hesitate to stay."

The adjoining tables, however, were emptying; a waiter came and stood discreetly near them. Charles, who understood, took out his purse; the clerk held back his arm, and made a point of leaving two extra pieces of silver that he made chink on the marble.

"I am really sorry," said Bovary," for all the money you are . . ."

The other silenced him with a gesture of affable disdain and, taking his hat, said:

"So, we are agreed, to-morrow at six o'clock?"

Charles explained once more that he could not absent himself longer, but that nothing prevented Emma . . .

"But," she stammered, with a strange smile, "I don't know if I ought . . ."

"Well, you must think it over. Sleep over it and we'll see in the morning."

Then, to Léon, who was walking along with them:

"Now that you are in our part of the world, I hope you'll come and have dinner with us from time to time."

The clerk declared he would not fail to do so, being obliged, moreover, to go to Yonville on some business for his office. And they parted before the passage Saint-Herbland just as the cathedral struck half-past eleven.

Part Three

I

Monsieur Léon, while studying law, had been a fairly assiduous customer at the Chaumière, a dance-hall where he was particularly successful with the grisettes who thought him distinguished looking. He was the best-mannered of the students; he wore his hair neither too long nor too short, didn't spend all his quarter's money on the first day of the month, and kept on good terms with his professors. As for excesses, he had always abstained from them, as much from cowardice as from refinement.

Often when he stayed in his room to read, or else when sitting in the evening under the linden-trees of the Luxembourg,[51] he let his law-code fall to the ground, and the memory of Emma came back to him. But gradually this feeling grew weaker, and other desires took the upperhand, although the original passion still acted through them. For Léon did not lose all hope; there was for him, as it were, a vague promise floating in the future, like a golden fruit suspended from some fantastic tree.

51. Luxembourg refers to the gardens of the Palace of Luxembourg (built between 1615 and 1620 for Marie de Medici). The gardens are open to the public and much frequented by students, as they are near the Sorbonne.

Then, seeing her again after three years of absence, his passion reawakened. He must, he thought, finally make up his mind to possess her. Moreover, his timidity had worn off in the gay company of his student days, and he returned to the provinces in utter contempt of whoever had not set foot on the asphalt of the boulevards. In the presence of a genuine Parisienne, in the house of some famous physician surrounded by honors and luxury, the poor clerk would no doubt have trembled like a child; but here, on the quais of Rouen, with the wife of a small country-doctor, he felt at his ease, sure to shine. Self-confidence depends on environment: one does not speak in the same tone in the drawing room than in the kitchen; and the wealthy woman seems to have about her, to guard her virtue, all her bank-notes, like an armour, in the lining of her corset.

On leaving the Bovarys the night before, Léon had followed them through the streets at a distance; when he saw them enter the Croix-Rouge, he returned home and spent the night planning his strategy.

So the next afternoon about five o'clock he walked into the kitchen of the inn, pale and apprehensive, driven by a coward's resolution that stops at nothing.

"Monsieur isn't in," a servant told him.

This seemed to him a good omen. He went upstairs.

She didn't seem surprised at his arrival; on the contrary, she apologized for having failed to tell him where they were staying.

"Oh, I guessed it!" said Léon.

He pretended he had found her by chance, guided by instinct. When he saw her smile, he tried to repair his blunder by telling her he had spent the morning looking for her in all the hotels in the town.

"So you have made up your mind to stay?" he added.

"Yes," she said, "and I shouldn't have. One should avoid getting used to inaccessible pleasures when one is burdened by so many responsibilities . . ."

"Oh, I can imagine . . ."

"No, you can't, you are not a woman."

But men too had their trials, and the conversation started off by some philosphical considerations. Emma expatiated on the frailty of earthly affections, and the eternal isolation that stifles the human heart.

To show off, or in a naive imitation of this melancholy which stirred his own, the young man declared that he had been dreadfully despondent. He was bored by the law, attracted by other vocations and his mother had never ceased to harrass him in all her letters. As they talked, they stated the reasons for their respective unhappiness with more precision and they felt a shared exaltation in this growing confidence. But they sometimes stopped short of revealing their thought in full, and then sought to invent a phrase that might nevertheless express it. She did not confess her passion for another; he did not say that he had forgotten her.

Perhaps he no longer remembered the suppers with girls after masked balls; and no doubt she did not recollect the rendezvous of old when she ran across the fields in the morning to her lover's house. The noises of the town hardly reached them, and the room seemed small, as if to bring them even closer together in their solitude. Emma, in a dimity dressing gown, leant her chignon against the back of the old arm-chair; the yellow wall-paper formed, as it were, a golden background behind her, and her bare head was reflected in the mirror with the white parting in the middle, the tip of her ears peeping out from the folds of her hair.

"How bad of me!" she said, "you must forgive me for boring you with my eternal complaints."

"No, never, never!"

"If only you knew," she went on, raising to the ceiling her beautiful eyes, in which a tear was trembling, "if only you knew all I dreamed!"

"So did I! Oh, I too have suffered! Often I went out; I went away. I left, dragging myself along the quays, seeking distraction amid the din of the crowd without being able to banish the heaviness that weighed upon me. In an engraver's shop on the boulevard I found an Italian print of one of the Muses. She is draped in a tunic, and she is looking at the moon, with forget-me-nots in her flowing hair. Something continually drove me there, I would stay for hour after hour."

Then, in a trembling voice:

"She looked a little like you."

Madame Bovary turned away her head that he might not see the irrepressible smile she felt rising to her lips.

"Often," he went on, "I wrote you letters that I tore up."

She did not answer. He continued;

"I sometimes fancied that some chance would bring you. I thought I recognised you at street-corners, and I ran after carriages when I saw a shawl or a veil like yours flutter in the window . . ."

She seemed resolved to let him speak without interruption. With arms crossed and her head lowered, she stared at the rosettes on her slippers, and from time to time moved her toes under the satin. At last she sighed.

"But what I find worst of all is to drag out, as I do, a useless existence. If our pains could be of use to some one, we should find consolation in the thought of the sacrifice."

He started off in praise of virtue, duty, and silent immolation, having himself an incredible longing for self-sacrifice that he could not satisfy.

"What I would like," she said "is to work in a hospital as a nursing Sister."

"Unfortunately," he replied, "no such holy vocations are open to men, and I can think of no profession . . . except perhaps a doctor's . . ."

With a slight shrug of the shoulders, Emma interrupted him to speak of her illness, which had almost killed her. How she regretted her cure! if she had died, she would not now be suffering. Léon was quick to express his own longing for "the quiet of the tomb"; one night, he had even made his will, asking to be buried in that beautiful coverlet with velvet stripes he had received from her. For this was how they would have wished to be, each setting up an ideal to which they were now trying to adapt their past life. Besides, speech is like a rolling machine that always stretches the sentiment it expresses.

But this made-up story of the coverlet made her ask:

"Why?"

"Why?" He hesitated.

"Because I loved you so!"

And congratulating himself at having surmounted the obstacle, Léon watched her face out of the corner of his eye.

It was like the sky when a gust of wind sweeps the clouds away. The mass of darkening sad thoughts lifted from her blue eyes; her whole face shone.

He waited. At last she replied:

"I always suspected it."

Then they went over all the trifling events of that far-off existence, of which the joys and sorrows had just been conjured up by that one word. He remembered the clematis arbour, the dresses she had worn, the furniture of her room, the entire house.

"And our poor cactuses, where are they?"

"The cold killed them this winter."

"How often did I think of them! I see them again as they looked when on summer mornings the sun shone on your blinds, and I saw your two bare arms among the flowers.

"Poor friend!" she said, holding out her hand.

Léon swiftly pressed his lips to it. Then, when he had taken a deep breath:

"In those days, you were like an incomprehensible power to me which held me captive. Once, for instance, I came to see you, but you probably don't remember."

"I do," she said; "go on."

"You were downstairs in the hall, ready to go out, standing on the last stair; you were wearing a hat with small blue flowers; and without being invited, in spite of myself, I went with you. But I grew more and more conscious of my folly every moment, and I kept walking by your side, not daring to follow you completely but unable to leave. When you went into a shop, I waited in the street, and I watched you through the window taking off your gloves and counting the change on the counter. Then you rang at Madame Tuvache's; you were let in, and I stood like an idiot in front of the great heavy door that had closed after you."

Madame Bovary, as she listened to him, wondered that she was so old. All these things reappearing before her seemed to expand her existence; it was like some sentimental immensity to which she returned; and from time to time she said in a low voice, her eyes half closed:

"Yes, it is true . . . it is true . . ."

They heard eight o'clock strike on the different towers that surround the Place Beauvoisine, a neighborhood of schools, churches, and large empty private dwellings. They no longer spoke, but as they looked upon each other, they felt their heads whirl, as if waves of sound had escaped from their fixed glances. They were hand in hand now, and the past, the future, reminiscences and dreams, all were confounded in the sweetness of this ecstasy. Night was darkening over the walls, leaving visible only, half hidden in the shade, the coarse colours of four bills representing scenes from *La Tour de Nesle*,[52] with Spanish and French captions underneath. Through the sash-window they could see a patch of sky between the pointed roofs.

She rose to light two wax-candles on the chest of drawers, then she sat down again.

"Well . . . ?" said Léon.

"Well . . . ?" she replied.

He was wondering how to resume the interrupted conversation, when she said to him:

"How is it that no one until now has ever expressed such sentiments to me?"

The clerk retorted that idealistic natures rarely found understanding. But he had loved her from the very first moment; the thought of their possible happiness filled him with despair. If only they had met earlier, by some stroke of chance, they would have been forever bound together.

"I have sometimes thought of it," she went on.

"What a dream!" murmured Léon.

And fingering gently the blue border of her long white belt, he

52. A melodrama by Alexandre Dumas the elder (1803–1870) and Gaillardet (1832) in which Marie de Bourgogne, famous for her crimes, is the main heroine.

added,

"Who prevents us from starting all over again?"

"No, my friend," she replied; "I am too old . . . You are too young . . . forget me! Others will love you . . . you will love them."

"Not as I love you!"

"What a child you are! Come, let us be sensible, I want it."

She told him again that their love was impossible, that they must remain, as before, like brother and sister to each other.

Was she speaking seriously? No doubt Emma did not herself know, absorbed as she was by the charm of the seduction and the necessity of defending herself; looking tenderly at the young man, she gently repulsed the timid caresses that his trembling hands attempted.

"Ah! forgive me!" he cried, drawing back.

Emma was seized with a vague fear at this shyness, more dangerous to her than the boldness of Rodolphe when he advanced to her open-armed. No man had ever seemed to her so beautiful. His demeanor suggested an exquisite candor. He lowered his long curling eyelashes. The soft skin of his cheek was flushed, she thought, with desire for her, and Emma felt an invincible longing to press her lips to it. Then, leaning towards the clock as if to see the time:

"How late it is!" she exclaimed. "How we have been chattering!"

He understood the hint and took up his hat.

"You made me forget about the opera! And poor Bovary who left me here especially for that! Monsieur Lormeaux, of the Rue Grand-Pont, was to take me and his wife."

And there would be no other opportunity, as she was to leave the next day.

"Really?" said Léon.

"Yes."

"But I must see you again," he went on. "I had something to tell you . . ."

"What?"

"Something . . . important, serious. I cannot possibly let you go like this. If only you knew . . . Listen to me . . . Haven't you understood? Can't you guess?"

"You made yourself very clear" said Emma.

"Ah! you can jest! But you shouldn't. Have mercy, and allow me to see you again . . . only once . . . one single time."

"Well . . ."

She stopped; then, as if changing her mind:

"But not here!"

"Wherever you say."

"Will you . . ."

She seemed to think; then suddenly:

"To-morrow at eleven o'clock in the cathedral."

"I shall be there," he cried, seizing her hands, which she withdrew.

And as they were both standing up, he behind and Emma with lowered head, he stooped over her and pressed long kisses on her neck.

"You are crazy, you are crazy!" she cried between bursts of laughter, as the kisses multiplied.

Then bending his head over her shoulder, he seemed to beg the consent of her eyes, but when they met his, they seemed icy and distant.

Léon took three paces backwards. He stopped on the threshold; then he whispered in a trembling voice:

"Till to-morrow."

She answered with a nod, and vanished like a bird into the next room.

In the evening Emma wrote the clerk an interminable letter, in which she cancelled the rendezvous; all was over between them; they must not, for the sake of their happiness, meet again. But when the letter was finished, as she did not know Léon's address, she was puzzled.

"I'll give it to him myself," she said; "he'll come."

The next morning, humming a tune while he stood on his balcony by the open window, Léon polished his shoes with special care. He put on white trousers, silken socks, a green coat, emptied all the scent he had into his handkerchief, then having had his hair curled, he uncurled it again, in order to give it a more natural elegance.

"It is still too early," he thought, looking at the barber's cuckoo-clock, that pointed to the hour of nine.

He read an old fashion journal, went out, smoked a cigar, walked up three streets, thought the time had come and walked slowly towards the porch of Notre Dame.

It was a beautiful summer morning. Silver sparkled in the window of the jeweler's store and the light, falling obliquely on the cathedral, threw shimmering reflections on the edges of the grey stones; a flock of birds fluttered in the grey sky round the trefoiled turrets; the square, resounding with cries, was fragrant with the flowers that bordered the pavement, roses, jasmines, carnations, narcissus, and tuberoses, unevenly spaced out between moist grasses, catnip, and chickweed for the birds; the fountains gurgled in the center, and under large umbrellas, amidst heaps of piled up mellons, bare-headed flower vendors wrapped bunches of violets in pieces of paper.

The young man took one. It was the first time that he had

bought flowers for a woman, and his breast, as he smelt them, swelled with pride, as if this homage that he meant for another had been reflected upon himself.

But he was afraid of being seen and resolutely entered the church.

The verger was just then standing on the threshold in the middle of the left doorway, under the figure of Salomé dancing, known in Rouen as the "dancing Marianne". He wore a feather cap, a rapier dangled against his leg and he looked more majestic than a cardinal, as shining as a pyx.

He came towards Léon, and, with the bland benign smile of a priest when questioning a child, asked:

"I gather that Monsieur is a visitor in this town? Would Monsieur care to be shown the church?"

"No!" said Léon.

And he first went round the lower aisles. Then he went out to look at the Place. Emma was not coming yet, so he returned as far as the choir.

The nave was reflected in the full fonts together with the base of the arches and some fragments of the stained glass windows. But the reflections of the painted glass, broken by the marble rim, were continued farther on upon the pavement, like a many-coloured carpet. The broad daylight from outside entered the church in three enormous rays through the three opened portals. From time to time a sacristan crossed the far end of the church, making the sidewise genuflection of a hurried worshipper in the direction of the altar. The crystal lustres hung motionless. In the choir a silver lamp was burning, and from the side chapels and dark places of the church sounds like sighs arose, together with the clang of a closing grating that echoed under the lofty vaults.

Léon walked solemnly alongside the walls. Life had never seemed so good to him. She would soon appear, charming and agitated, looking back to see if anyone was watching her—with her flounced dress, her gold eyeglass, her delicate shoes, with all sorts of elegant trifles that he had never been allowed to taste, and with the ineffable seduction of yielding virtue. The church was set around her like a huge boudoir; the arches bent down to shelter in their darkness the avowal of her love; the windows shone resplendent to light up her face, and the censers would burn that she might appear like an angel amid sweet-smelling clouds.

Meanwhile, she did not come. He sat down on a chair, and his eyes fell upon a blue stained window representing boatmen carrying baskets. He looked at it long, attentively, and he counted the scales of the fishes and the button-holes of the doublets, while his thoughts wandered off in search of Emma.

The verger, left to himself, resented the presence of someone who dared to admire the cathedral without his assistance. He considered this a shocking way to behave, robbing him of his due, close to committing sacrilege.

There was a rustle of silk on the pavement, the edge of a hat, a hooded cape—it was she! Léon rose and ran to meet her.

Emma was pale. She walked hurriedly.

"Read this!" she said, holding out a piece of paper to him. "Oh, no!"

And she abruptly withdrew her hand to enter the chapel of the Virgin, where, kneeling on a chair, she began to pray.

The young man was irritated by this display of piety; then he nevertheless felt a certain charm in seeing her thus lost in devotions in the middle of a rendezvous, like an Andalusian marquise; then he grew bored, for she seemed to go on for ever.

Emma prayed, or rather tried to pray, hoping that some sudden resolution might descend to her from heaven; and to draw down divine aid she filled her eyes with the splendors of the tabernacle. She breathed in the perfumes of the full-blown flowers in the large vases, and listened to the stillness of the church—a stillness that only heightened the tumult in her own heart.

She rose, and they were about to leave, when the verger quickly approached:

"Madame is perhaps a stranger here? Madame would like to visit the church?"

"Oh, no!" the clerk cried.

"Why not?" she said.

For, with her expiring virtue, she clung to the Virgin, the sculptures, the tombs—to anything.

Then, in order to do things right, the verger took them to the entrance near the square, where, pointing out with his cane a large circle of black stones, without inscription or carving:

"This," he said majestically, "is the circumference of the beautiful bell of Ambroise. It weighed forty thousand pounds. There was not its equal in all Europe. The workman who cast it died of joy . . ."

"Let's go," said Léon.

The old man started off again; then, having got back to the chapel of the Virgin, he waved his arm in a theatrical gesture of demonstration, and, prouder than a country squire showing his orchard, he announced:

"This simple stone covers Pierre de Brézé, lord of Varenne and of Brissac, grand marshal of Poitou, and governor of Normandy, who died at the battle of Montlhéry on the 16th of July, 1465."

Léon was furiously biting his lips of impatience.

"And on the right, this gentleman in full armour, on the prancing horse, is his grandson, Louis de Brézé, lord of Breval and of Montchauvet, Count de Maulevrier, Baron de Mauny, chamberlain to the king, Knight of the Order, and also governor of Normandy; he died on the 23rd of July, 1531—a Sunday, as the inscription specifies; and below, this figure, about to descend into the tomb, portrays the same person. How could one conceive of a better way to depict the void of human destiny?"

Madame Bovary lifted her eyeglass. Motionless, Léon watched her without even trying to protest, to make a gesture, so discouraged was he by this double display of idle talk and indifference.

Nothing could stop the guide:

"Near him, this kneeling woman who weeps is his spouse, Diane de Poitiers, comtesse de Brézé, duchesse de Valentinois, born in 1499, died in 1566, and to the left, the one with the child is the Holy Virgin. Now if you turn to this side, you will see the tombs of the Ambroise. They were both cardinals and archbishops of Rouen. That one was minister under Louis XII. He did a great deal for the cathedral. In his will he left thirty thousand gold crowns for the poor."

And without ceasing to talk, he pushed them into a chapel crowded with wooden railings; he pushed some aside and discovered a kind of wooden block that looked vaguely like a poorly carved statue.

"It seems hard to believe," he sighed sadly, "but this used to adorn the tomb of Richard Coeur de Lion,[53] King of England and Duke of Normandy. It was the Calvinists, Monsieur, who reduced it to this condition. They were mean enough to bury it in the earth, under the episcopal throne of Monseigneur the bishop. You can see from here the door by which Monseigneur passes to his house. Let's move on to the gargoyle windows."

But Léon hastily extracted some silver coins from his pocket and seized Emma's arm. The verger stood dumbfounded, not able to understand this untimely munificence when there were still so many things for the stranger to see. He called after him:

"Monsieur! The steeple! the steeple!"[54]

"No, thank you!" said Léon.

"You are missing the best! It is four hundred and forty feet high, nine less than the great pyramid of Egypt. It is all cast iron, it . . ."

Léon was fleeing, for it seemed to him that his love, that for nearly two hours had been frozen in the church like the stones, would now vanish like a vapor through that sort of truncated fun-

53. Richard Coeur de Lion, the Lion Hearted (born 1175), was king of England from 1189–1199. He died at the siege of the Castle of Châlus.

54. The Cathedral of Rouen built in the Gothic style in stages from the thirteenth century to the early sixteenth, got a high cast iron spire (485 feet), which is generally considered a tasteless disfigurement. Construction was begun in 1824 but not finished until 1876.

nel, rectangular cage or open chimney that rises so grotesquely from the cathedral like the extravagant brainchild of some fantastic roofer.

"But where are we going?" she said.

He pushed on without answering, and Madame Bovary was already dipping her finger in the holy water when behind them they heard a panting breath interrupted by the regular sound of a tapping cane. Léon turned around.

"Monsieur!"

"What is it?"

And he recognised the verger, holding under his arms and bracing against his stomach some twenty large volumes, all of them works on the cathedral.

"Idiot!" muttered Léon, rushing out of the church.

A boy was playing on the sidewalk:

"Go and get me a cab!"

The child bounded off like a ball by the rue des Quatre-Vents; then they were alone a few minutes, face to face, and a little embarrassed.

"Oh Léon! Truly . . . I don't know . . . if I should . . ."

She simpered. Then, in a serious tone:

"It's very improper, you know, it isn't done."

"Everybody does it in Paris!" replied the clerk.

This, like a decisive argument, entirely convinced her. She had made up her mind.

But no cab arrived. Léon shuddered at the thought that she might return into the church. At last the cab appeared.

"At least, you should go out by the northern gate," cried the verger, who was left alone on the threshold, "and look at the Ressurection, the Last Judgment, Paradise, King David, and the damned burning in the flames of Hell!"

"Where to, sir?" asked the coachman.

"Anywhere!" said Léon, pushing Emma into the cab.

And the lumbering machine set out.

It went down the Rue Grand-Pont, crossed the Place des Arts, the Quai Napoleon, the Pont Neuf, and stopped short before the statue of Pierre Corneille.

"Go on," cried a voice that came from within.

The cab went on again, and as soon as it reached the Carrefour Lafayette, set off down-hill, and entered the railroad station at a gallop.

"No, straight on!" cried the same voice.

The cab came out by the gate, and soon having reached the Mall, trotted quietly beneath the elm-trees. The coachman wiped his brow, put his leather hat between his knees, and drove his carriage beyond the side alley by the meadow to the margin of the waters.

It went along by the river, along the towing-path paved with sharp pebbles, and for a long while in the direction of Oyssel, beyond the islands.

But suddenly it turned sideways across Quatremares, Sotteville, La Grande-Chaussée, the Rue d'Elbeuf, and made its third halt in front of the Jardin des Plantes.

"Get on, will you?" cried the voice more furiously.

And at once resuming its course, it passed by Saint Sever, by the Quai des Curandiers, the Quai aux Meules, once more over the bridge, by the Place du Champ de Mars, and behind the hospital gardens, where old men in black coats were walking in the sun along the ivy-covered terraces. It went up the Boulevard Bouvreuil, along the Boulevard Cauchoise, then the whole of Mont-Riboudet to the Deville hills.

It came back; and then, without any fixed plan or direction, wandered about at random. The cab was seen at Saint-Pol, at Lescure, at Mont Gargan, at La Rougue-Marc and Place du Gaillardbois; in the Rue Maladrerie, Rue Dinanderie, before Saint-Romain, Saint-Vivien, Saint-Maclou, Saint-Nicaise—in front of the Customs, at the Basse-Vieille-Tour, the "Trois Pipes," and the Cimetière monumental. From time to time the coachman on his seat cast despairing glances at the passing cafés. He could not understand what furious locomotive urge prevented these people from ever coming to a stop. Time and again he would try, but exclamations of anger would at once burst forth behind him. Then he would whip his two sweating nags, but he no longer bothered dodging bumps in the road; the cab would hook on to things on all sides but he couldn't have cared less, demoralised as he was, almost weeping with thirst, fatigue and despair.

Near the harbor, among the trucks and the barrels, and along the street corners and the sidewalks, bourgeois stared in wonder at this thing unheard of in the provinces: a cab with all blinds drawn that reappeared incessantly, more tightly sealed than a tomb and tossed around like a ship on the waves.

One time, around noon, in the open country, just as the sun beat most fiercely against the old plated lanterns, a bare hand appeared under the yellow canvass curtain, and threw out some scraps of paper that scattered in the wind, alighting further off like white butterflies on a field of red clover all in bloom.

Then, at about six o'clock the carriage stopped in a back street of the Beauvoisine Quarter, and a woman got out, walking with her veil down and without looking back.

II

On reaching the inn, Madame Bovary was surprised not to see

the stage coach. Hivert had waited for her fifty-three minutes, but finally left without her.

Nothing forced her to go, but she had promised to return that same evening. Moreover, Charles expected her, and in her heart she felt already that cowardly docility that is for some women at once the chastisement and atonement of adultery.

She packed her bag quickly, paid her bill, took a cab in the yard, hurrying on the driver, urging him on, every moment inquiring about time and distance traversed. He succeeded in catching up with the Hirondelle as it neared the first houses of Quincampoix.

Hardly was she seated in her corner that she closed her eyes, and opened them at the foot of the hill, when from afar she recognised Félicité, who was on the look-out in front of the blacksmith's. Hivert pulled up his horses, and the maid, reaching up to the window, said in a tone of mystery:

"Madame, you must go at once to Monsieur Homais. It's for something urgent."

The village was silent as usual. At the corner of the streets little pink mounds lay smoking in the air, for this was the time for jam-making, and every one at Yonville prepared his supply on the same day. But in front of the pharmacist's shop one might admire a far larger heap; it surpassed the others with the superiority that a laboratory must have over domestic ovens, a general need over individual fancy.

She went in. The big arm chair had fallen over and even the "Fanal de Rouen" lay on the ground, outspread between two pestles. She pushed open the door of the hall, and in the middle of the kitchen, amid brown jars full of picked currants, powdered and lump sugar, scales on the table and pans on the fire, she saw assembled all the Homais, big and little, with aprons reaching to their chins, and holding forks in their hands. Justin was standing with bowed head, and the pharmacist was screaming:

"Who told you to go fetch it in the *Capharnaum?*"

"What is it? What is the matter?"

"What is it?" replied the pharmacist. "We are making jelly; it is cooking; but it threatens to boil over because there is too much juice, and I ask for another pan. Then this one here, out of laziness, goes to my laboratory, and dares to take the key to the capharnaum from the nail!"

This name had been given to a small room under the eaves, crammed with the tools and the goods of his trade. He often spent long hours there alone, labelling, decanting, and packaging. He looked upon it not as a simple store-room, but as a veritable sanctuary from where the creations of his own hands were to set forth: pills, lotions and potions that would spread far and wide his rising fame. No one in the world was allowed to set foot there, and he revered it to the point of sweeping it himself. If the pharmacy, open to all comers, was the stage where he displayed his pride, the Capharnaum was the refuge where in selfish concentration, Homais indulged in his most relished pursuits. Therefore, Justin's thoughtlessness seemed to him a monstrous piece of irreverence, and, his face redder than the currants, he continued:

"Yes, the key to the Capharnaum! The key that locks up the acids and caustic alkalis! To go and get a spare pan! a pan with a lid! and that I shall perhaps never use! Everything is of importance in the delicate operations of our art! One must maintain the proper distinctions, and not employ for nearly domestic purposes what is destined for pharmaceutical science! It is as if one were to carve a fowl with a scalpel; as if a magistrate . . ."

"Quiet down," Madame Homais was saying.

And Athalie, pulling at his coat, cried:

"Papa! papa!"

"No, leave me alone!" the pharmacist cried, "leave me alone! I tell you, I might as well be running a grocery store. Just keep at it, don't mind me and break everything to pieces! Smash the test-tubes, let the leeches loose, burn the marshmallows, put pickles in the medical jars, tear up the bandages!"

"I thought you wanted to . . ."

"In a moment . . . Do you know what risks you took? Didn't you see something in the corner, on the left, on the third shelf? Speak! Answer me! Say something!"

"I . . . don't . . . know . . ." stammered the boy.

"Ah! you don't know! Well, *I* do! You saw a bottle of blue glass sealed with yellow wax, that contains a white powder carefully marked *Dangerous!* And do you know what is in it? Arsenic! And you go and touch it! You take a pan that stands right next to it!"

"Right next to it!" cried Madame Homais, clasping her hands. "Arsenic! You might have poisoned us all."

And the children began to scream as if they already felt dreadful stomach pains.

"Or poison a patient!" continued the pharmacist. "Do you want to see me dragged into court like a common criminal? or taken to the scaffold? As if you didn't know how careful one has to be in handling chemicals, even I who spent my life doing nothing else. Often I am horrified when I think of my responsibility; the Government persecutes us, and the absurd legislation that rules us is a veritable Damocles' sword suspended over our heads."

Emma gave up trying to find out what they wanted her for, and the pharmacist continued without pausing for breath:

"That is how you thank us for the many kindnesses we have shown you! That is how you reward me for the truly paternal care that I lavish on you! Where would you be if I hadn't taken you in hand? What would you be doing? Who provides you with food, education, clothes, and all the means to rise to a respectable level in society? But if you want to get there, you'll have to learn to pull hard at the oars—get callouses on your hands, as they saying goes. *Fabricando fit faber, age quod agis.*" [55]

He was so exasperated he quoted Latin. He would have used Chinese or Greenlandic had he known them, for he was rocked by one of these crises in which the soul reveals all it contains, just as the storm lays bare the ocean from the seaweed on the shore down to the sand on its deepest bottom.

And he went on:

"I am beginning to regret that I ever took you in charge! I would have done a lot better if I'd let you wallow in poverty and filth, where you were born. The best you can hope for is to be a cowhand. You are not fit to be a scientist! You hardly know how to stick on a label! And there you are, dwelling with me snug as a parson, living in clover, taking your ease!"

Emma turned in despair to Madame Homais:

"I was told to come . . . "

"Heavens!" the lady exclaimed in a mournful tone "How am I to tell you? . . . Such a misfortune!"

She could not finish. The pharmacist was thundering:

"Empty it! Clean it! Take it back! And hurry!"

And seizing Justin by the collar of his apron, he shook him so vigorously that a book fell out of his pocket. The boy stooped, but Homais was the quicker, and, having picked up the volume, he stared at it with bulging eyes and open mouth.

"Conjugal . . . love!" he said, slowly separating the two words. "Ah! very good! very good! very pretty! And with illustrations! . . . Truly, this is too much!"

Madame Homais drew near.

"No, don't touch it!"

The children wanted to look at the pictures.

"Leave the room," he said imperiously.

They went out.

First he walked up and down, with the open book in his hand, rolling his eyes, choking, fuming, apoplectic. Then he came straight to his apprentice, and, planting himself in front of him with folded arms:

"So you are blessed with all the vices under the sun, you little wretch? Watch out! you are following a dangerous path! . . . Did

55. *Fabricando fit Faber, age quod agis* ("Do what you do"), the artisan becomes proficient through practice; practice what you are supposed to do.

it never occur to you that this infamous book might fall into the hands of my children, kindle a spark in their minds, tarnish the purity of Athalie, corrupt Napoleon! He is close to being a man. Are you quite sure, at least, that they have not read it? Can you certify to me . . ."

"But, Monsieur," said Emma, "you wished to tell me . . ."

"Oh yes, madame . . . your father-in-law is dead."

Indeed, the elder Bovary had suddenly died from a stroke the evening before, as he got up from the table; overanxious to spare Emma's sensitive nerves, Charles had asked Monsieur Homais to break the horrible news to her as carefully as possible.

Homais had meditated at length over his speech; he had rounded, polished it, given it the proper cadence; it was a masterpiece of prudence and transitions, of subtle turns and delicacy; but anger had got the better of rhetoric.

Emma, abandoning all hope to learn any further details, left the pharmacy; for Monsieur Homais had resumed his vituperations. He was growing calmer, however, and was now grumbling in a paternal tone whilst he fanned himself with his skull-cap.

"It is not that I entirely disapprove of the book. The author was a doctor! It contains scientific information that a man might well want to know; I'd go as far as saying that he ought to know. But later . . . later! You should at least wait till you are yourself full-grown, and your character formed."

When Emma knocked at the door, Charles, who was waiting for her, came forward with open arms and said in a tearful voice:

"Ah! my dear wife. . . ."

And he leant over gently to kiss her. But at the contact of his lips the memory of the other returned; she passed her hand over her face and shuddered.

Yet, she answered:

"Yes, I know . . . I know . . ."

He showed her the letter in which his mother told the event without any sentimental hypocrisy. Her only regret was that her husband had not received the consolation of religion; he had died at Doudeville, in the street, at the door of a café after a patriotic dinner with some ex-officers.

Emma gave him back the letter; then at dinner, for appearance's sake, she affected a lack of appetite. But as he urged her to try, she resolutely began eating, while Charles opposite her sat motionless and dejected.

Now and then he raised his head and gave her a long, distressed look. Once he sighed:

"I'd have liked to see him again!"

She was silent. At last, realizing that she must say something:

"How old was your father?" she asked.

"Fifty-eight."

"Ah!"

And that was all.

A quarter of an hour later, he added: "My poor mother! what will become of her now?"

She made a gesture of ignorance.

Seeing her so taciturn, Charles imagined her much affected, and forced himself to say nothing, not to reawaken this sorrow which moved him. And, shaking off his own:

"Did you enjoy yourself yesterday?" he asked.

"Yes."

When the cloth was removed, Bovary did not rise, nor did Emma; and as she looked at him, the monotony of the spectacle drove little by little all pity from her heart. He seemed to her paltry, weak, a nonentity—a sorry creature in every way. How to get rid of him? What an interminable evening! She felt a stupor invading her, as if from opium fumes.

They heard the sharp noise of a wooden leg on the boards of the entrance hall. It was Hippolyte bringing back Emma's luggage.

To put them down, he had to bring around his wooden stump painfully in a quarter circle.

"He doesn't even seem to remember" she thought, looking at the poor devil, whose coarse red hair was wet with perspiration.

Bovary was searching for a coin at the bottom of his purse; he did not seem to realize how humiliating the man's presence was for him, standing there as the living embodiment of his hopeless ineptitude.

"Oh, you have a pretty bouquet," he said, noticing Léon's violets on the mantlepiece.

"Yes," she replied indifferently; "it's a bouquet I bought just now . . . from a beggar-woman."

Charles picked up the flowers and, bathing his tear-stained eyes in their freshness, he delicately sniffed their perfume. She took them quickly from his hand and put them in a glass of water.

The next day the elder Madame Bovary arrived. She and her son spent much time weeping. Pretending to be busy in the house, Emma managed to stay by herself.

The following day, they had to discuss together the arrangements for the period of mourning. They went and sat down with their workboxes by the waterside under the arbor.

Charles was thinking of his father, and was surprised to feel so much affection for this man, whom up till now he thought he cared little about. The older Madame Bovary was thinking of her husband. The worst days of the past seemed enviable to her. All was forgotten beneath the instinctive regret of such a long habit, and from time to time, while sewing, a big tear rolled down her nose and hung suspened there a moment.

Emma was thinking that it was scarcely forty-eight hours since they had been together, far from the world, lost in ecstasy, and not having eyes enough to gaze upon each other. She tried to recall the slightest details of that past day. But the presence of her husband and mother-in-law bothered her. She would have liked to stop hearing and seeing, in order to keep intact the stillness of her love; but, try as she would, the memory would vanish under the impact of outer sensations.

She was removing the lining of a dress, and the strips were scattered around her. Mother Bovary, without looking up, kept her scissors busy, and Charles, in his felt slippers and his old brown coat that he used as a dressing gown, sat in silence with both hands in his pockets; near them Berthe, in a little white apron, was raking the sandwalks with her spade.

Suddenly they saw Monsieur Lheureux, the storekeeper, come in through the gate.

He came to offer his services "on this sad occasion." Emma replied that none were needed, but the shopkeeper wouldn't take no for an answer.

"I beg your pardon," he said, "but I should like to have a word in private."

Then, in a low voice, he added:

"It is about this little matter . . . you know . . ." Charles turned crimson.

"Oh yes . . . of course."

And, in his confusion, he turned to his wife:

"Darling, could you perhaps . . . ?"

She seemed to understand him, for she rose; and Charles said to his mother:

"Nothing important. Some household trifle, I suppose."

Fearing her reproaches, he didn't want her to know about the note.

As soon as they were alone, Monsieur Lheureux began by congratulating Emma outspokenly on the inheritance, then talked of this and that, the fruit trees, the harvest, his own health which had endless ups and downs. He had to work like a devil and, regardless of what people thought, didn't make enough to buy butter for his bread.

Emma let him talk. She had been so dreadfully bored, these last two days!

"And so you're quite well again?" he went on. "Believe me, your husband was in quite a state. He's a good fellow, though we did have a little misunderstanding."

She asked what the misunderstanding was about, for Charles had told her nothing of the dispute about the goods supplied to her.

"As if you didn't know!" exclaimed Lheureux. "It was about your little caprice . . . the trunks."

He had drawn his hat over his eyes, and, with his hands behind his back, smiling and whistling, he looked straight at her in an unbearable manner. Did he suspect anything? She was lost in all kinds of apprehensions. Finally he said:

"We made it up, and I've come to propose still another arrangement."

He offered to renew the note Bovary had signed. The doctor, of course, would do as he pleased; he was not to trouble himself, especially just now, when he would have a lot to attend to.

"It seems to me he'd do well to turn it all over to some one else,—to you for example. With a power of attorney it could be easily managed, and then the two of us could have our little business transactions together . . ."

She did not understand. He did not insist, and brought the conversation back to his trade; it was impossible that Madame didn't need anything. He would send her a black barège, twelve yards, just enough to make a dress.

"The one you've on is good enough for the house, but you want another for calls. I saw that the very moment that I came in. I've got a quick eye for these things!"

He did not send the material, he brought it. Then he came again to take her measurements; he came again on other pretexts, always trying to make himself agreeable, useful, like a vassal serving his master, as Homais might have put it, and never failing to drop a hint about the power of attorney. He never mentioned the note. She didn't think of it; although Charles doubtlessly had mentioned something at the beginning of her convalescence, so many emotions had passed through her head that she no longer remembered it. Besides, she made it a point never to bring up any money questions. Charles' mother seemed surprised at this, and attributed the change in her ways to the religious sentiments she had contracted during her illness.

But as soon as she left, Emma greatly astounded Bovary by her practical good sense. They would have to make inquiries, look into the mortgages, decide whether it would be more advantageous to sell by auction or by other means.

She quoted legal jargon at random, and grand words such as "order", "the future", "foresight". She constantly exaggerated the difficulties of settling his father's affairs; at last, one day she showed him the rough draft of a power of attorney to manage and administer his business, arrange all notes, sign and endorse all bills, pay all sums, etc. She had profited by Lheureux's lessons.

Charles naively asked her where this paper came from.

"From Master Guillaumin."

And with the utmost coolness she added:

"I don't trust him overmuch. Notaries have such a bad reputation. Perhaps we ought to consult . . . But the only person we know . . . There is no one."

"Unless perhaps Léon . . ." replied Charles, who was thinking.

But it was difficult to explain matters by letter. Then she offered to make the journey. He refused. She insisted. It was quite a contest of mutual consideration. At last she exclaimed, in a childish tone of mock-rebellion:

"No, enough, I will!"

"How good you are!" he said, kissing her on the forehead.

The next morning she set out in the "Hirondelle" for Rouen to consult Monsieur Léon, and she stayed there three days.

III

They were three full, exquisite, magnificent days—a true honeymoon. They stayed at the Hôtel-de-Boulogne, on the harbor; and they lived there behind drawn blinds and closed doors, with flowers on the floor, and iced fruit syrups that were brought them early in the morning.

Towards evening they took a covered boat and went to dine on one of the islands.

At this time of the day, one could hear the caulking irons sound against the hulls in the dockyard. Tar smoke rose up between the trees and large oily patches floated on the water, undulating unevenly in the purple sunlight like surfaces of Florentine bronze.

They drifted down among moored ships whose long slanting cables grazed lightly the top of their boat.

The sounds of the city gradually fainted in the distance, the rattling of carriages, the tumult of voices, the yelping of dogs on the decks of barges. She loosened her hat and they landed on their island.

They sat down in the low-ceilinged room of a tavern with black fishing-nets hanging across the door. They ate fried smelts, cream and cherries. They lay down upon the grass, kissed behind the poplar trees; like two Robinson Crusoes, they would gladly have lived forever in this spot; in their bliss, it seemed to them the most magnificent place on earth. It was not the first time that they had seen trees, a blue sky, meadows; or heard the water flow and the wind blow in the branches. But they had never really felt any of this; it was as if nature had not existed before, or had only begun to be beautiful since the gratification of their desires.

At nightfall they returned. The boat glided along the shores of the islands. They stayed below, hidden in darkness, without saying a word. The square-tipped oars sounded against the iron oar-locks; in the stillness, they seemed to mark time like the beat of a metronome, while the rope that trailed behind never ceased its gentle splash against the water.

One night the moon rose, and they did not fail to make fine phrases about how melancholical and poetic it appeared to them. She even began to sing:

> One night, do you remember,
> We were sailing . . .

Her thin musical voice died away over the water; Léon could hear the wind-borne trills pass by him like a fluttering of wings.

She faced him, leaning against the wall of the cabin while the moon shone through the open blinds. Her black dress, falling around her like a fan, made her seem more slender, taller. Her head was raised, her hands clapsed, her eyes turned towards heaven. At times the shadow of the willows hid her completely; then she reappeared suddenly, like a vision in the moonlight.

Léon, on the floor by her side, found under his hand a ribbon of scarlet silk.

The boatman looked at it, and said at last:

"Perhaps it belongs to the party I took out the other day. They were a jolly bunch of ladies and gentlemen, with cakes, champagne, trumpets—everything in style! There was one especially, a tall handsome man with small moustaches, who was the life of the party. They kept asking him 'Come on, Adolphe—or Dodolphe, or something like that—tell us a story . . .' "

She shuddered.

"Don't you feel well?" Léon inquired, coming closer.

"Oh, it's nothing! Just a chill from the cold night air."

"He's another one who seems to have no trouble finding women," the old sailor added softly, intending to pay Léon a compliment.

Then, spitting on his hands, he took the oars again.

Yet the time to part had come. The farewells were sad. He was to send his letters to Mère Rollet, and she gave him such precise instructions about a double envelope that he was much impressed with her shrewdness in love matters.

"So you can guarantee me that everything is in order?" she said with her last kiss.

"Yes, certainly."

"But why," he thought afterwards as he came back through the streets alone, "is she so very anxious to get this power of attorney?"

IV

Léon soon put on superior airs with his friends, avoided their company, and completely neglected his work.

He waited for her letters, read and re-read them. He wrote to her. He called her to mind with all the strength of his desires and of his memories. Instead of lessening with absence, his longing to see her kept growing to the point where, one Saturday morning he escaped from his office.

When, from the summit of the hill, he saw in the valley below the church-spire with its metal flag swinging in the wind, he felt that delight mingled with triumphant vanity and selfish benevolence that millionaires must experience when they come back to their native village.

He went prowling around round her house. A light was burning in the kitchen. He watched for her shadow behind the curtains, but nothing appeared.

Mère Lefrançois, on seeing him, uttered many exclamations. She thought he had grown taller and thinner, while Artémise, on the contrary, thought him stouter and darker.

He ate in the little dining-room, as in the past, but alone, without the tax collector; for Binet, tired of waiting for the "Hirondelle," had definitely moved his meal an hour earlier. Now he dined punctually at five, which didn't keep him from complaining that the rickety old carriage was late.

Léon finally made up his mind, and knocked at the doctor's door. Madame was in her room, and did not come down for a quarter of an hour. The doctor seemed delighted to see him, but he never left the house that evening, nor the next day.

He saw her alone in the evening, very late, behind the garden in the lane;—in the lane, as with the other one! It was a stormy night, and they talked under an umbrella by lightning flashes.

They couldn't bear the thought of parting.

"I'd rather die!" said Emma.

She seized his arm convulsively, and wept.

"Good bye! When shall I see you again?"

They came back again to embrace once more, and it was then that she promised him to find soon, no matter how, some assured way of meeting in freedom at least once a week. Emma was certain to find a way. She was generally in a hopeful frame of mind: the inheritance money was bound to come in soon.

On the strength of it she bought a pair of yellow curtains with large stripes for her room; Monsieur Lheureux had recommended them as a particularly good buy. She dreamt of getting a carpet, and Lheureux, declaring that it wasn't that much of an investment after all, politely undertook to supply her with one. She could no longer do without his services. Twenty times a day she sent for him, and he at once interrupted whatever he was doing, without a murmur. Neither could people understand why Mére Rollet ate at her house every day, and even paid her private visits.

It was about this time, in the early part of the Winter, that a sudden urge to make music seemed to come over her.

One evening when Charles was listening to her, she began the same piece four times over, each time with much vexation, while he, totally oblivious to her mistakes, exclaimed:

"Bravo! . . . Very good! . . . Don't stop. Keep going!"

"Oh, no. It's awful! My fingers are much too rusty!"

The next day he begged her to play for him again.

"Very well, if you wish."

And Charles had to confess that she had slipped a little. She played wrong notes and blundered; then, stopping short:

"Ah! it's no use. I ought to take some lessons, but . . ."

Biting her lip, she added:

"Twenty francs a lesson, that's too expensive!"

"Maybe it is . . . a little," said Charles with a stupid giggle. "But it seems to me that one might be able to do it for less; for there are artists of little reputation, who are often better than the celebrities."

"Find them!" said Emma.

The next day on coming home, he gave her a sly look, and finally could no longer repress what he had to say:

"How stubborn you can be at times! I went to Barfuchéres today. Well, Madame Liégard assured me that her three daughters, who go to school at Miséricorde, take lessons at fifty sous apiece, and that from an excellent teacher!"

She shrugged her shoulders and did not open her piano again.

But whenever she passed in front of it (provided Bovary was present), she sighed:

"Ah! my poor piano!"

And whenever someone came to call, she did not fail to inform them that she had given up music, and could not begin again now for important reasons. People would commiserate. What a pity! She had so much talent! They even spoke to Bovary about it. They put him to shame, especially the pharmacist.

"You are wrong. One should never let any natural faculties lie fallow. Besides, just think, my good friend, that by inducing madame to study, you are economising on the subsequent musical education of your child. For my own part, I think that mothers ought themselves to instruct their children. It's an idea of Rousseau's, still rather new perhaps, but bound to win out sooner or later, like vaccination and breast-feeding."

So Charles returned once more to this question of the piano. Emma replied bitterly that it would be better to sell it. Poor piano!

it had given his vanity so many satisfactions that to see it go was for Bovary, in an undefinable manner, like Emma's partial suicide.

"If you really want it . . ." he said, "a lesson from time to time wouldn't ruin us after all."

"But lessons," she replied, "are only of use if one persists."

And this is how she managed to obtain her husband's permission to go to town once a week to see her lover. At the end of a month she was even considered to have made considerable progress.

V

She went on Thursdays. She got up and dressed silently, in order not to awaken Charles, who would have reproached her for getting ready too early. Then she walked up and down, stood at the windows, and looked out over the Square. The early dawn was broadening between the pillars of the market, and the pharmacy, still boarded up, showed in the pale light of the dawn the large letters of the signboard.

When the clock pointed to a quarter past seven, she went to the "Lion d'Or," where a yawning Artémise unlocked the door for her. She would poke the fire in Madame's honor, and Emma remained alone in the kitchen. Now and again she went out. Hivert was leisurely harnessing his horses while listening to the Mère Lefrançois who, sticking her head and night cap through a window, was instructing him on his errands and giving him explanations that would have bewildered any one else. Emma tapped her boots on the cobblestones of the yard.

At last, when he had eaten his soup, put on his cloak, lighted his pipe, and grasped his whip, he calmly took his place on the seat.

The "Hirondelle" started at a slow trot, and for about a mile stopped time and again to pick up waiting passengers along the roadside, before their house-gates. Those who had booked seats the night before kept it waiting; some even were still in bed in their houses. Hivert called, shouted, swore; then he got down from his seat and knocked loudly at the doors. The wind blew through the cracked windows.

Gradually, the four benches filled up. The carriage rolled off; rows of apple-trees followed one upon another, and the road between its two long ditches, full of yellow water, rose, constantly narrowing towards the horizon.

Emma knew every inch of the road: after a certain meadow there was a sign post, then a barn or roadmender's hut. Sometimes, in hope of being surprised, she would close her eyes, but she never lost a clear sense of the distance still to be covered.

At last the brick houses began to follow one another more closely, the earth resounded beneath the wheels, the "Hirondelle" glided between the gardens, revealing through an occasional opening, statues, a summer pavillion, trimmed yew trees, a swing. Then all at once, the city came into sight.

Sloping down like an amphitheatre, and drowned in the fog, it overflowed unevenly beyond its bridges. Then the open country mounted again in a monotonous sweep until it touched in the distance the elusive line of the pale sky. Seen thus from above, the whole landscape seemed frozen, like a picture; the anchored ships were massed in one corner, the river curved round the foot of the green hills, and the oblong islands looked like giant fishes lying motionless on the water. The factory chimneys belched forth immense plumes of brown smoke, their tips carried off in the wind. One heard the rumbling of the foundries, mingled with the clear chimes of the churches, dimly outlined in the fog. The leafless trees on the boulevards seemed violet thickets in the midst of the houses, and the roofs, shining from the rain, threw back unequal reflections, according to the heights of the various districts. From time to time a gust of wind would drive the clouds towards the slopes of Saint Catherine, like aerial waves breaking silently against a cliff.

Something seemed to emanate from this mass of human lives that left her dizzy; her heart swelled as though the hundred and twenty thousand souls palpitating there had all at once wafted to her the passions with which her imagination had endowed them. Her love grew in the presence of this vastness, and filled with the tumult of the vague murmuring which rose from below. She poured it out, onto the squares, the avenues, the streets; and the old Norman city spread out before her like some incredible capital, a Babylon into which she was about to enter. She lifted the window with both hands to lean out, drinking in the breeze; the three horses galloped, the stones grated in the mud, the diligence rocked, and Hivert, from afar, hailed the carts on the road, while the well-to-do residents of Bois Guillaume sedately descended the hill to town in their little family carriages.

The coach made a stop at the city gates; Emma undid her overshoes, put on other gloves, rearranged her shawl, and some twenty paces farther she descended from the "Hirondelle."

The town was beginning to awake. Shop-boys in caps were polishing the front windows of the stores, and women, with baskets balanced on their hips, would stand on the street corners calling out from time to time some sonorous cry. She walked with downcast eyes, close to the walls, and smiling with pleasure beneath her lowered black veil.

For fear of being seen, she did not usually take the most direct road. She would plunge into dark alleys, and emerge, all in a sweat, near the little fountain at the beginning of the Rue Nationale. This was the quarter of the theaters, cabarets, and prostitutes. Often, a cart loaded with shaking scenery passed close by her. Waiters in aprons were sprinkling sand on the flagstones between green shrubs. There was a smell of absinthe, cigars and oysters.

She turned a corner; she recognised him by his curling hair that escaped from beneath his hat.

Léon kept on walking ahead of her along the sidewalk. She followed him into the hotel. He went up, opened the door, entered — What an embrace!

Then, after the kisses, the words rushed forth. They told each other the sorrows of the week, the forebodings, the anxiety for the letters; but now everything was forgotten; they gazed at each other with voluptuous laughs, and tender names.

The bed was a large one, made of mahogany and shaped like a boat. The red silk curtains which hung from the ceiling, were gathered together too low, close to the lyre-shaped headboards;—and nothing in the world was so lovely as her brown hair and white skin set off against that deep crimson color, when with a gesture of modesty, she closed her arms and hid her face in her hands.

The warm room, with its subdued carpet, its frivolous ornaments and its soft light, seemed made for the intimacies of passion. The curtain-rods, ending in arrows, the brass pegs and the great balls of the andirons would suddenly light up if a ray of sunlight entered. On the chimney, between the candelabra there were two of those pink shells in which one hears the murmur of the sea when one holds them against one's ear.

How they loved that room, so full of gaiety, despite its somewhat faded splendour! They always found the furniture arranged the same way, and sometimes hairpins, that she had forgotten the Thursday before, under the pedestal of the clock. They lunched by the fireside on a little round table, inlaid with rosewood. Emma carved, put bits on his plate while playing all sorts of coquettish tricks; she would laugh a ringing libertine laugh when the froth from the champagne overflowed the fragile glass onto the rings of her fingers. They were so completely lost in the possession of each other that they thought themselves in their own house, that they would go on living there until separated by death, like an eternally young married couple. They said "our room," "our carpet," she even said "my slippers," referring to the gift Léon had bought to satisfy a whim of hers. They were rose-colored satin, bordered with swansdown. When she sat on his lap, her leg, which was then too short, hung in the air, and the dainty shoe having no back, was held on only by the toes of her bare foot.

He savoured for the first time the inexpressible delights of feminine refinement. He had never encountered this grace of language, this direction in dress, these poses of a weary dove. He admired the exaltation of her soul and the lace on her petticoat. Besides, was she not a "woman of the world", and a married woman! in short a real mistress!

According to her changing moods, in turn meditative and gay, talkative and silent, passionate and langorous, she awakened in him a thousand desires, called up instincts or memories. She was the mistress of all the novels, the heroine of all the dramas, the vague "she" of all the volumes of verse. On her shoulders, he rediscovered the amber color of the "Odalisque au Bain";[56] her waist was long like the feudal chatelaines; she resembled Musset's "Femme Pâle de Barcelone."[57] Above all, she was his Angel.

It often seemed to him that his soul, fleeing toward her, broke like a wave against the contours of her head, and was drawn irrisistibly down into the whiteness of her breast.

He knelt on the ground before her; and resting his elbows on her lap, he would gaze at her smilingly, his face uplifted.

She bent over him, and murmured, as if choking with intoxication:

"Oh! don't move! don't speak! Look at me! There is something so tender that comes from your eyes. It does me so much good!"

She called him child.

"Do you love me, child?"

And she never heard his reply, his lips always rose so fast to find her mouth.

There was a little bronze cupid on the clock, who simpered as he held up his arms under a golden garland. They had laughed at it many a time, but when they had to part everything seemed serious.

Motionless, they looked at each other and kept repeating:

"Till Thursday! . . . Till Thursday! . . ."

Suddenly she would take his head between her hands and kiss him quickly on the forehead while crying "Adieu" and rush down the stairs.

She went next to a hairdresser in the Rue de la Comédie to have her hair arranged. Night would be falling; they lit the gas in the shop.

She heard the bell in the theatre calling the actors to the performance; and she saw white-faced men and women in faded dresses pass by on the other side of the street and enter in at the stage door.

It was hot in the little low-ceilinged room with its stove humming amidst the wigs and pommades. The smell of the tongs together with the oily hands that were manipulating her hair, would soon stupefy her and she would begin to doze a bit in her dressing gown.

56. Famous painting by Jean Auguste Dominique Ingres.

57. Alfred de Musset frequently incarnates, for Flaubert, the type of stilted romantic sentimentality he despises.

Often, as he did her hair, the man offered her tickets for a masked ball.

Then she left! She remounted the streets; reached the Croix Rouge, retrieved her overshoes which she had hidden under the bench that morning, and settled into her place among the impatient passengers. The other passengers got out at the foot of the hill in order to spare the horses. She remained alone in the carriage.

At every turn, they could see more and more of the city below, forming a luminous mist above the mass of houses. Emma knelt on the cushions, and let her eyes wander over the dazzling light. She sobbed, called to Léon, sent him tender words and kisses which were lost in the wind.

There was a wretched creature on the hillside, who would wander about with his stick right in the midst of the carriages. A mass of rags covered his shoulders, and an old staved-in beaver hat, shaped like a basin, hid his face; but when he took it off he revealed two gaping bloody orbits in the place of eyelids. The flesh hung in red strips; and from them flowed a liquid which congealed into green scales reaching down to his nose with its black nostrils, which kept sniffing convulsively. To speak to you he threw back his head with an idiotic laugh;—then his blueish eyeballs, rolling round and round, would rub against the open wound near the temples.

He sang a little song as he followed the carriages:

> Often the warmth of a summer day
> Makes a young girl dream her heart away.

And all the rest was about birds and sunshine and green leaves.

Sometimes he would appear behind Emma, his head bare. She would draw back with a cry. Hivert liked to tease him. He would advise him to get a booth at the Saint Romain fair, or else ask him, laughing, how his girl friend was.

Often the coach was already in motion when his hat would be thrust violently in at the window, while he clung with his other arm to the footboard, between the spattering of the wheels. His voice, at first weak and quavering, would grow sharp. It lingered into the night like an inarticulate lament of some vague despair; and, heard through the jingling of the horses' bells, the murmuring of the trees, and the rumble of the empty coach, it had something so distant and sad that it filled Emma with dread. It went to the very depths of her soul, like a whirlwind in an abyss, and carried her away to a boundless realm of melancholy. But Hivert, noticing a weight behind, would lash out savagely at the blind man with his whip. The thong lashed his wounds and he fell back into the mud with a shriek.

The passengers in the Hirondelle would all finally drop off to sleep, some with their mouths open, others their chins pressed against their chests, leaning on their neighbor's shoulder, or with their arm passed through the strap, all the time swaying regularly with the jolting of the carriage; and the sight of the lantern, that was swinging back and forth outside and reflecting on the rumps of the shaft horses, penetrated into the coach through the chocolate-colored curtains, throwing blood-red shadows over all those motionless beings within. Emma, drunk with grief, shivered under her coat and felt her feet grow colder and colder, with death in her soul.

Charles at home would be waiting for her; the "Hirondelle" was always late on Thursdays. Madame arrived at last! She scarcely kissed the child. The dinner was not ready, no matter! She excused the cook. The girl now seemed allowed to do just as she liked.

Often her husband, noting her pallor, asked if she were unwell.

"No," said Emma.

"But," he replied, "you seem so strange this evening."

"Oh, it's nothing! nothing!"

There were even days when she had no sooner come in than she went up to her room; and Justin, who would happen to be there, moved about noiselessly, more adroit at helping her than the best of maids. He put the matches ready, the candlestick, a book, arranged her nightgown, turned back the bedclothes.

"All right," she'd say "that's fine, get going!"

For he stood there, his hands hanging down and his eyes wide open, as if enmeshed in the innumerable threads of a sudden reverie.

The following day was frightful, and those that came after still more unbearable, because of her impatience to once again seize her happiness,—this fierce lust, enflamed by recent memories, which on the seventh day would erupt freely within Léon's embraces. His own passion was manifested by continual expressions of wonder and gratitude. Emma tasted this love discreetly, and with all her being, nourished it by every tender device she knew, and trembled a little that some day it might be lost.

She often said to him, with a sweet melancholy in her voice:

"Ah! you too, you will leave me! You will marry! You will be like all the others."

He asked:

"What others?"

"Why, like all men," she replied.

Then added, repulsing him with a languid movement:

"You are all of you wretches!"

One day, as they were talking philosophically of earthly disillusions she happened to mention (in order to provoke his jealousy, or perhaps through some irrisistible urge to confide in him) that in the past, before she knew him, she had loved someone else. "Not like you," she went on quickly, swearing on the head of her child "that nothing had happened."

The young man believed her, but none the less questioned her to find out what kind of a man *He* was.

"He was a ship's captain, my dear."

Was this not preventing any inquiry, and, at the same time, assuming a higher ground because of the aura of fascination which is supposed to surround a man who must have been of warlike nature and accustomed to receive homage?

The clerk then felt the lowliness of his position; he longed for epaulettes, crosses, titles. These things would please her; he suspected as much from her extravagant habits.

However, Emma never mentioned a number of her most extravagant ideas, such as her desire to have a blue tilbury to drive into Rouen, drawn by an English horse and driven by a groom in turned down boots. It was Justin who had inspired her with this whim, by begging her to take him into service as footman; and if the privation of it did not lessen the pleasure of her arrival at each of their weekly rendez-vous, it certainly augmented the bitterness of the return.

Often, when they were talking together of Paris, she would end by murmuring,

"Ah, how happy we could be living there."

"Are we not happy?" the young man would gently ask, passing his hands over her hair.

"Yes, that is true," she said. "I am mad: kiss me!"

To her husband she was more charming than ever. She made him pistachio-creams and played him waltzes after dinner. He thought himself the most fortunate of men, and Emma was without uneasiness, when, suddenly one evening:

"It is Mademoiselle Lempereur, isn't it, who gives you lessons?"

"Yes."

"Well, I saw her just now," Charles went on, "at Madame Liégard's. I spoke to her about you; and she doesn't know you."

This was like a thunderbolt. However, she replied quite naturally:

"She must have forgotten my name."

"But perhaps," said the doctor, "there are several Demoiselles Lempereur at Rouen who are music teachers."

"Possibly!"

Then she added quickly:

"Nevertheless, I have her receipts, here! Look."

And she went to the writing-table, ransacked all the drawers, mixed up the papers, and at last lost her head so completely that Charles earnestly begged her not to take so much trouble about those wretched receipts.

"Oh! I will find them," she said.

And, in fact, on the following Friday, as Charles was putting on one of his boots in the dark closet where his clothes were kept, he felt a piece of paper between the leather and his sock. He took it out and read:

"Received, for three months' lessons and several pieces of music, the sum of sixty-three francs.—FELICIE LEMPEREUR, professor of music."

"How the devil did it get into my boots?"

"It must," she replied, "have fallen from the old box of bills that is on the edge of the shelf."

From that moment on, her existence was one long tissue of lies, in which she wrapped her love as under a veil in order to hide it. It became a need, an obsession, a delight, to such a point that, if she claimed to have walked on the right side of the street the previous day, one could be sure she had walked on the left.

One morning, when she had gone, as usual, rather lightly clothed, it suddenly began to snow, and as Charles was watching the weather from the window, he caught sight of Monsieur Bournisien in the chaise of Monsieur Tuvache, who was driving him to Rouen. Then he went down to give the priest a thick shawl that he was to hand over to Emma as soon as he reached the Croix-Rouge. When he got to the inn, Monsieur Bournisien asked for the wife of the Yonville doctor. The landlady replied that she very rarely came to her establishment. So that evening, when he recognised Madame Bovary in the "Hirondelle," the curé told her his dilemma, without, however, appearing to attach much importance to it, for he began praising a preacher who was doing wonders at the Cathedral, and whom all the ladies were rushing to hear.

Still, even if he had not asked for any explanations, others, later on, might prove less discreet. So she thought it would be a good idea to get out of the coach at the Croix Rouge each time she came so that the good folk of her village seeing her on the stairs would not become suspicious.

One day, however, Monsieur Lheureux met her coming out of the Hôtel de Boulogne on Léon's arm; and she was frightened, thinking he would gossip. He was not such a fool.

But three days after he came to her room, shut the door, and said:

"I must have some money."

She declared she could not give him any. Lheureux began to moan, reminding her of all the favors he had done her.

In fact, of the two bills signed by Charles, Emma up to the present had paid only one. As to the second, the shopkeeper, at her request, had consented to replace it by another, which again had been renewed for a long date. Then he drew from his pocket a list of goods not paid for; to wit, the curtains, the carpet, the material for the arm-chairs, several dresses, and diverse articles of dress, totalling in all a sum of about two thousand francs.

She hung her head; he continued:

"But if you haven't any ready money, you do have some property."

And he called to her attention a miserable little shack situated at Barneville, near Aumale, that brought in almost nothing. It had formerly been part of a small farm sold by Monsieur Bovary senior; for Lheureux knew everything, even down to the number of acres and the names of the neighbors.

"If I were in your place," he said, "I'd get it off my hands, and have some money left over."

She pointed out the difficulty of finding a buyer; he said he thought he could find one; but she asked him how she should manage to sell it.

"Haven't you your power of attorney?" he replied.

The phrase came to her like a breath of fresh air. "Leave me the bill," said Emma.

"Oh, it isn't worth while," answered Lheureux.

He came back the following week boasting that after having gone to a great deal of trouble, he had finally tracked down a certain man named Langlois, who had had his eye on the property for a long time but had never mentioned a price.

"Never mind the price!" she cried.

On the contrary, he said, they must take their time and sound the fellow out. The affair was certainly worth the trouble of a trip, and, as she could not undertake it, he offered to go to the place and bargain with Langlois. On his return he announced that the purchaser proposed four thousand francs.

Emma's heart rose at this news.

"Frankly," he added, "that's a good price."

She drew half the sum at once, and when she was about to pay her account the shopkeeper said:

"It grieves me, it really does, to see you give up such a considerable sum of money as that all at once." She stared at the bank notes and began to dream of the countless rendez-vous with Léon that those two thousand francs represented.

"What! What do you mean!" she stammered.

"Oh!" he went on, laughing good-naturedly, "one puts anything one likes on receipts. Don't you think I know what household affairs are?"

And he looked at her fixedly, while in his hand he held two long papers which he kept sliding between his nails. At last, opening his billfold, he spread out on the table four bills to order, each for a thousand francs.

"Sign these," he said, "and keep it all!"

She cried out, scandalised.

"But if I give you the balance," replied Monsieur Lheureux impudently, "isn't that doing you a service?"

And taking a pen he wrote at the bottom of the account, "Received from Madame Bovary four thousand francs."

"What is there to worry about, since in six months you'll draw the arrears for your cottage, and I don't make the last bill due till after you've been paid?"

Emma was becoming somewhat confused in her calculations and her ears rang as though gold pieces were bursting out of their bags and tinkling onto the floor all around her. At last Lheureux explained that he had a very good friend named Vinçart, a banker in Rouen, who would discount these four bills. Then he himself would hand over to madame the remainder after the actual debt was paid.

But instead of two thousand francs he brought her only eighteen hundred, for his friend Vinçart (which was "only fair") had deducted two hundred francs for commission and discount.

Then he carelessly asked for a receipt.

"You understand . . . in business . . . sometimes . . . And with the date, please don't forget the date."

A whole horizon of new possibilities now opened up before Emma. She was wise enough to set aside three thousand francs, with which the first three bills were paid when they fell due; but the fourth happened to arrive at the house on a Thursday, and a stunned Charles patiently awaited his wife's return for an explanation.

If she had not told him about this note, it was only to spare him such domestic worries; she sat on his lap, caressed him, cooed at him, gave a long enumeration of all the indispensable things that had been got on credit.

"Really, you must confess, considering the number of things, it isn't too expensive."

Charles, at his wit's end, soon had recourse to the eternal Lheureux, who promised to arrange everything if Charles would sign two more notes, one of which was for seven hundred francs and would be payable in three months. To take care of this he wrote his mother a pathetic letter. Instead of sending a reply she came herself; and when Emma wanted to know whether he had got anything out of her:

"Yes," he replied; "but she wants to see the account."

The next morning at daybreak Emma ran to Lheureux to beg him to make out another account for not more than a thousand francs: for to show the one for four thousand it would be necessary to say that she had paid two-thirds, and confess, consequently, the sale of the property, for the transaction had been well handled by the shopkeeper and only came to light later on.

Despite the low price of each article, Madame Bovary senior of course thought the expenditure extravagant.

"Couldn't you do without a carpet? Why did you re-cover the arm-chairs? In my time there was a single arm-chair in a house, for elderly persons,—at any rate it was so at my mother's, who was a respectable woman, I assure you.—Everybody can't be rich! No fortune can hold out against waste! I should be ashamed to pamper myself as you do! And yet I am old. I need looking after . . . and look at this! Look at this! alterations! frills and finery! What is that! silk for lining at two francs; . . . when you get jaconet for ten sous, or even for eight which does just as well!"

Emma lying on a lounge, replied as calmly as she could "Ah! Madame, enough! enough! . . ."

The other went on lecturing her, predicting they would end in the workhouse. But it was Bovary's fault. Luckily he had promised to destroy that power of attorney.

"What?"

"Ah! he swore he would," went on the good woman.

Emma opened the window, called Charles, and the poor fellow was obliged to confess the promise torn from him by his mother.

Emma disappeared, then came back quickly, and majestically handed her a large sheet of paper.

"Thank you," said the old woman. And she threw the power of attorney into the fire.

Emma began to laugh, a strident, piercing, continuous laugh; she had an attack of hysterics.

"Oh! my God!" cried Charles. "Ah! You are in the wrong too! You come here and make scenes with her! . . ."

His mother, shrugging her shoulders, declared it was "all put on."

But Charles, rebelling for the first time, took his wife's part, so that Madame Bovary senior said she would leave. She went the very next day, and on the threshold, as he was trying to detain her, she replied:

"No, no! You love her better than me, and you are right. It is natural. Take care of yourself! . . . for I'm not likely to be back again soon to 'make scenes' as you say."

Charles nevertheless was very crestfallen before Emma, who did not hide the resentment she still felt at his want of confidence, and it needed many prayers before she would consent to another power of attorney. He even accompanied her to Monsieur Guillaumin to have a second one, just like the other, drawn up.

"I know how it is," said the notary; "a man of science can't be worried with the practical details of life."

And Charles felt relieved by this comfortable reflection, which gave his weakness the flattering appearance of higher preoccupation.

How exalted she was the following Thursday at the hotel in their room with Léon! She laughed, cried, sang, sent for sherbets, wanted to smoke cigarettes, seemed to him wild and extravagant, but adorable, superb.

He did not know what combination of forces within her was driving her to throw herself so recklessly after the pleasures of life. She became irritable, greedy, voluptuous. She walked boldly through the streets with him, her head high, unconcerned, she said, about being compromised. At times, however, Emma shuddered at the sudden thought of meeting Rodolphe, for it seemed to her that, although they were separated forever, she was not completely free from the power he held over her.

One night she did not return to Yonville at all. Charles lost his head with anxiety, and little Berthe refusing to go to bed without her mamma, sobbed as though her heart would break. Justin had gone out searching the road at random. Monsieur Homais even had left his pharmacy.

At last, at eleven o'clock, able to bear it no longer, Charles harnessed his chaise, jumped in, whipped up his horse, and reached the Croix-Rouge about two o'clock in the morning. No one there! He thought that the clerk had perhaps seen her; but where did he live? Happily, Charles remembered his employer's address, and rushed off there.

Day was breaking, and he could make out some letters over the door; he knocked. Some one, without opening the door, shouted out the required information and added a generous number of insults concerning people who disturb others in the middle of the night.

The house inhabited by the clerk had neither bell, knocker, nor porter. Charles beat on the shutters with his fists. A policeman happened to pass by; he felt nervous and left.

"What a fool I am" he said. "M. Lormeaux must have asked her to stay to dinner."

The Lormeaux no longer lived in Rouen.

"She probably stayed to look after Madame Dubreuil. Oh, but Madame Dubreuil has been dead these ten months . . . Then where can she be?"

An idea occurred to him. At a café he asked for a Directory, and hurriedly looked for the name of Mademoiselle Lempereur, who turned out to live at No. 74 Rue de la Renelle-des-Maroquiniers.

As he was turning into the street, Emma herself appeared at the other end of it; he threw himself upon her rather than embraced her, crying:

"What kept you yesterday?"

"I was not well."

"What! . . . Where! . . . How! . . ."

She passed her hand over her forehead and answered,

"At Mme. Lempereur's."

"I was sure of it! I was just on my way there."

"Oh!" said Emma. "It's not worth while now. She just stepped out a minute ago; don't get so excited. I will never feel free, you understand, if the slightest delay is going to make you lose your head like this."

This was a sort of permission that she gave herself, so as to get perfect freedom in her escapades. And she took full and free advantage of it. Whenever she was seized with the desire to see Léon, she would set out upon any pretext whatever, and if he were not expecting her that day, she would go to fetch him at his office.

It was a great delight at first, but soon he no longer concealed the truth, which was, that his master complained very much about these interruptions.

"Oh, who cares!" she said, "come along."

And he slipped out.

She wanted him to dress all in black, and grow a pointed beard, to look like the portraits of Louis XIII.[58] She asked to see his rooms and found them lacking in taste. This embarrassed him but she paid no attention; she then advised him to buy curtains like hers, and when he objected to the expense:

"Ah! ah! you hold onto your pennies!" she said laughing.

Each time Léon had to tell her everything that he had done since their last meeting. She asked him for some verses—some verses "for herself," a "love poem" in honor of her. But he never succeeded in getting a rhyme for the second verse; and at last ended by copying a sonnet from a Keepsake.

He did this less from vanity, than simply out of a desire to please her. He never questioned her ideas; he accepted all her tastes; he was becoming her mistress rather than she his. She had tender words and kisses that thrilled his soul. Where could she have learnt this corruption so deep and well masked as to be almost unseizable?

VI

On his trips to see her, Léon often dined at the pharmacist's, and he felt obliged out of politeness to invite him in turn.

"With pleasure!" Monsieur Homais had replied; "besides, I must

58. Louis XIII (born 1601, king 1610–1643) was the father of Louis XIV.

recharge my mind a bit, for I am getting rusty here. We'll go to the theatre, to the restaurant. We'll do the town."

"Oh, my dear!" tenderly murmured Madame Homais, alarmed at the vague perils he was preparing to brave.

"Well, what? Do you think I'm not sufficiently ruining my health living here amid the continual emanations of the pharmacy? But there! That's just like a woman! They are jealous of science, and then are opposed to our taking the most legitimate distractions. No matter! Count upon me. One of these days I shall turn up at Rouen, and we'll paint the town together."

The pharmacist would formerly have taken good care not to use such an expression, but he was cultivating a flippant Parisian manner which he thought very stylish; and, like his neighbor, Madame Bovary, he questioned the clerk avidly about life in the capital; he even used slang in order to impress . . . the "bourgeois", saying "flip", "cool", "sweet", "neat-o", and "I must break it up", for "I must leave."

So one Thursday Emma was surprised to meet Monsieur Homais in the kitchen of the "Lion d'Or," wearing a traveller's costume, that is to say, wrapped in an old cloak which no one knew he had, while he carried a valise in one hand and the foot-warmer of his establishment in the other. He had confided his intentions to no one, for fear of causing the public anxiety by his absence.

The prospect of seeing again the scenes of his youth no doubt excited him for he never stopped talking during the whole trip; the coach had barely stopped when he leaped out in search of Léon; and in vain the clerk struggled to free himself. M. Homais dragged him off to the flashy Cafe de la Normandie, where he entered majestically, without taking off his hat, for he thought it highly provincial to uncover in any public place.

Emma waited for Léon three quarters of an hour. At last she ran to his office, and, lost in all sorts of conjectures, accusing him of indifference, and reproaching herself for her weakness, she spent the afternoon, her face pressed against the window-panes.

At two o'clock they were still at table opposite each other. The large room was emptying; the stove-pipe, in the shape of a palm-tree, spread its gilt leaves over the white ceiling; and near them, just outside the window, in the full sun, a little fountain gurgled into a white basin, where, among the watercress and asparagus, sluggish lobsters stretched out their claws towards a heap of quail lying on their sides.

Homais relished it all. He was more intoxicated by the luxury than by the fine food and drink, but nevertheless, the Pommard wine began to go to his head, and by the time the "omelette au rhum" appeared, he began expounding scandalous theories on women. What attracted him above all else, was "chic." He adored an elegant outfit and hairdo in a well-furnished apartment, and when it came to their physical proportions, he didn't mind them on the plump side.

Léon watched the clock in despair. The pharmacist went on drinking, eating, and talking.

"You must be completely deprived here in Rouen," he said suddenly. "But then the object of your affections doesn't live far away."

And, when the other blushed:

"Come now, be frank. Can you deny that at Yonville . . ."

The young man began to stammer.

"At Madame Bovary's, can you deny that you were courting . . ."

"Whom do you mean?"

"The maid!"

He was not joking; but vanity getting the better of his judgement, Léon protested indignantly in spite of himself. Besides, he only liked dark women.

"I approve of your taste," said the pharmacist; "they have more temperament."

And whispering into his friend's ear, he pointed out the symptoms by which one could detect temperament in a woman. He even launched into an ethnographic digression: the German was romantic, the French woman licentious, the Italian passionate.

"And negresses?" asked the clerk.

"They are for artistic tastes!" said Homais. "Waiter! Two demitasses!"

"Shall we go?" asked Léon, at last reaching the end of his patience.

"Yes" said Homais in English.

But before leaving he wanted to see the proprietor of the establishment and made him a few compliments. Then the young man, to be alone, alleged he had some business engagement.

"Ah! I will escort you," said Homais.

And all the while he was walking through the streets with him he talked of his wife, his children, of their future, and of his business; told him in what a dilapidated condition he had found it, and to what a state of perfection he had now raised it.

When they arrived in front of the Hôtel de Boulogne, Léon left him abruptly, ran up the stairs, and found his mistress almost hysterical.

On hearing the name of the pharmacist, she flew into a passion. Nevertheless, he kept overwhelming her with good reasons; it wasn't his fault; didn't she know Homais? Could she believe that he would prefer his company? But she turned away; he held her back, and falling on his knees, he encircled her waist with his arm, in a pose at once langorous, passionate, and imploring.

She stood there looking at him, her large flashing eyes were serious, almost terrible. Then her tears clouded them over, her pink eyelids lowered, and she gave him her hands. Léon was just pressing them to his lips when a servant appeared to say that someone wanted to see the gentleman.

"You will come back?" she said.

"Yes."

"But when?"

"Immediately."

"It's a trick," said the pharmacist, when he saw Léon. "I wanted to interrupt this visit, that seemed to me to annoy you. Let's go and have a glass of *garus*[59] at Bridoux'."

Léon swore that he must get back to his office. Then the pharmacist began making jokes about legal papers and procedure.

"Forget about Cujas[60] and Barthole[61] a bit, what the Devil! Who's going to stop you? Be a man! Let's go to Bridoux'. You'll see his dog. It's very interesting."

And as the clerk still insisted:

"I'll go with you. I'll read a paper while I wait for you, or thumb through a code."

Léon, bewildered by Emma's anger, Monsieur Homais' chatter, and perhaps, by the heaviness of the luncheon, was undecided, and, as though he were under the spell of the pharmacist who kept repeating:

"Let's go to Bridoux'. It's just by here, in the Rue Malpalu."

Then, out of cowardice, out of stupidity, out of that undefinable necessity that leads us towards those actions we are most set against, he allowed himself to be led off to Bridoux'; they found him in his small courtyard overseeing three workmen who panted as they turned the huge wheel of a selza water machine. Homais gave them some advice; he embraced Bridoux; they drank some garus. Twenty times Léon tried to escape, but the other seized him by the arm saying:

"Wait a minute! I'm coming! We'll go to the Fanal de Rouen' to see the fellows there. I'll introduce you to Thomassin."

He finally got rid of him, however, and flew to the hotel. Emma was gone.

She had just left in exasperation. She detested him now. His failure to come as he had promised she took as an insult, and she looked for other reasons for separating from him: he was incapable

59. A liqueur named after its inventor, Garus.

60. Jacques Cugar (1522–1590) was a famous jurist who interpreted Roman Law in contemporary terms.

61. Barthole, or Bartole, was an early Italian jurist (1313–1357) in Bologna.

of heroism, weak, banal, more spiritless than a woman, avaricious, and timorous as well.

Later when she was calmer, she realized that she had doubtless been unjust to him. But the picking apart of those we love always alienates us from them. One must not touch one's idols, a little of the gilt always comes off on one's fingers.

They gradually began to talk more frequently of matters outside their love, and in the letters that Emma wrote him she spoke of flowers, poetry, the moon and the stars, naïve resources of a waning passion striving to keep itself alive by all external aids. She was constantly promising herself a profound happiness on her next trip; then she confessed to herself that she had felt nothing extraordinary. This disappointment quickly gave way to a new hope, and Emma returned to him more avid and inflamed than before. She undressed brutally, ripping off the thin laces of her corset so violently that they would whistle round her hips like a gliding snake. She went on tiptoe, barefooted, to see once more that the door was locked, then with one movement, she would let her clothes fall at once to the ground;—then, pale and serious, without a word, she would throw herself against his breast with a long shudder.

Yet there was upon that brow covered with cold drops, on those stammering lips, in those wild eyes, in the grip of those arms, something strange, vague and sinister that seemed to Léon to be subtly gliding between them to force them apart.

He did not dare to question her; but finding how experienced she was, he told himself that she must have passed through all the extremes of both pleasure and pain. What had once charmed now frightened him a little. Furthermore, he revolted against the daily increased absorption of his personality into hers. He resented her, because of this constant victory. He even strove not to love her; then, when he heard the creaking of her boots, he felt his courage desert him, like drunkards at the sight of strong liquor.

It is true, she showered him with every sort of attention, from exotic foods, to little coquettish refinements in her dress and languishing glances. She used to bring roses from Yonville hidden in her bosom which she would toss up into his face; she was worried about his health, advised him how he should behave; and in order to bind him closer to her, hoping perhaps that heaven would take her part, she hung a medal of the Virgin round his neck. She inquired like a virtuous mother about his companions. She said to him:

"Don't see them; don't go out; only think of us; love me!"

She would have liked to be able to watch over his life, and the idea occurred to her of having him followed in the streets. Near the hotel there was always a kind of vagabond who accosted travellers, and who would surely not refuse . . . But her pride revolted at this.

"Ah! So what! What does it matter if he betrays me! What do I care?"

One day, when they had parted early and she was returning alone along the boulevard, she saw the walls of her convent; she sat down on a bench in the shade of the elms. How calm her life had been in those days! How she envied her first undefinable sentiments of love which she had tried to construct from the books she read.

The first months of her marriage, her rides in the forest, the viscount who had waltzed with her, and Lagardy singing, all repassed before her eyes . . . And Léon suddenly appeared to her as far off as the others.

"I do love him!" she said to herself.

No matter! She was not happy, she never had been. Why was her life so unsatisfactory, why did everything she leaned on instantly rot and give way? . . . But suppose there existed somewhere some one strong and beautiful, a man of valor, passionate yet refined, the heart of a poet in the form of an angel, a bronze stringed lyre, playing elegaic epithalamia to the heavens, why might she not someday happen on him? What a vain thought! Besides, nothing was worth the trouble of seeking it; everything was a lie. Every smile concealed a yawn of boredom, every joy a curse, every pleasure its own disgust, and the sweetest kisses left upon your lips only the unattainable desire for a greater delight.

A coarse metallic rattle sounded around her, and the convent bell struck four. And it seemed to her that she had been sitting on that bench since the beginning of time. But an infinity of time can be compressed into a minute like a crowd of people into a small space.

Emma lived all absorbed in her passions and worried no more about money matters than an archduchess.

There came a day, however, when a seedy looking man with a red face and a bald head came to her house, saying he had been sent by Monsieur Vinçart of Rouen. He took out the pins that held together the side-pockets of his long green overcoat, stuck them into his sleeve, and politely handed her a paper.

It was a bill for seven hundred francs, signed by her, and which Lheureux, in spite of all his promises had endorsed to Vinçart.

She sent her servant for him. He could not come.

Then the stranger who had remained standing, casting around him to the right and left curious glances which were hidden behind his blond eyebrows, asked with an innocent air:

"What answer am I to take Vinçart?"

"Well!" said Emma, "tell him . . . that I haven't got it . . . I'll pay him next week . . . He must wait . . . yes, next week."

And the fellow went without another word.

But the next day at twelve o'clock she received a summons, and the sight of the stamped paper, on which appeared several times in large letters, "Maître Hereng, bailiff at Buchy," so frightened her that she rushed in all haste to Lheureux. She found him in his shop, tying up a parcel.

"At your service," he said. "What can I do for you?"

But Lheureux continued what he was doing, aided by a young girl of about thirteen, somewhat hunchbacked, who was both his clerk and his servant.

Then, his sabots clattering on the wooden planks of the shop, he mounted in front of Madame Bovary to the second floor and showed her into a narrow closet, where, in a large pine wood desk, lay some ledgers, protected by an iron bar laid horizontally across them and padlocked down. Against the wall, under some remnants of calico, one caught sight of a safe, but of such dimensions that it must contain something besides promisory notes and cash. Monsieur Lheureux, in fact, went in for pawnbroking, and it was there that he had put Madame Bovary's gold chain, together with the earrings of poor old Tellier, who had been forced, at last, to sell his café, and had bought a small grocery store in Quincampoix, where he was dying of catarrh amongst his candles, that were less yellow than his face.

Lheureux sat down in a large cane arm-chair, saying:

"What's new?"

"Look here!"

"Well, what do you want me to do about it?"

Then she lost her temper, reminding him that he had promised not to endorse her notes away. He admitted it.

"But I was pressed myself; they were holding a knife against my throat too."

"And what will happen now?" she went on.

"Oh, it's very simple; a judgment and then a seizure . . . that's about it!"

Emma kept down a desire to strike him, and asked gently if there was no way of quieting Monsieur Vinçart.

"Oh, sure! appease Vinçart, indeed! You don't know him; he's fiercer than an Arab!"

Nevertheless, Monsieur Lheureux had to help her.

"All right then, listen, it seems to me that I've been pretty good to you so far."

And opening one of his ledgers:

"Look!" he said.

Then moving his finger up the page:

"Let's see . . . let's see . . . ! August 3d, two hundred francs . . . June 17th, a hundred and fifty . . . March 23d, forty-six . . . In April . . ."

He stopped, as if afraid of making some mistake.

"I won't even mention the bills signed by Monsieur Bovary, one for seven hundred francs, and another for three hundred. As to the little payments on your account and the interest, I'd never get to the end of the list, I can't figure that high. I'll have nothing more to do with it."

She wept; she even called him "her good Monsieur Lheureux." But he always fell back upon "that rascal Vinçart." Besides, he hadn't a penny, no one was paying him these days, they were eating his coat off his back, a poor shopkeeper like himself couldn't advance money.

Emma was silent, and Monsieur Lheureux, who was biting the feathers of a quill, no doubt became uneasy at her silence, for he went on:

"Perhaps, if something were paid on this, one of these days . . . I might . . ."

"Well," she said, "as soon as the balance on the Barneville property . . ."

"What? . . ."

And on hearing that Langlois had not yet paid he seemed much surprised. Then in a honied voice:

"Then we'll agree, what do you say to . . . ?"

"Oh! Whatever you say!"

On this he closed his eyes to reflect, wrote down a few figures, and saying that this was really going to hurt him, it was a risky affair, that he was "bleeding" himself for her, he wrote out four bills for two hundred and fifty francs each, to fall due month by month.

"Provided that Vinçart will listen to me! However, it's settled. I don't back down on my word. I'm as square as a brick."

Next he carelessly showed her several new goods; not one of which, however, was in his opinion worthy of madame.

"When I think that there's a dress that costs seven cents a yard and guaranteed color-fast! And they actually swallow it all down! Of course you understand one doesn't tell them what it really is!" He hoped by this confession of chicanery towards others to convince her of his honesty with her.

Then he called her back to show her three yards of guipure that he had lately picked up "at a sale."

"Isn't it lovely?" said Lheureux. "It is very much used now for the backs of arm-chairs. It's quite the rage."

And, quicker than a juggler, he wrapped up the guipure in some blue paper and put it in Emma's hands.

"But at least let me know . . ."

"Yes, some other time," he replied, turning on his heel.

That same evening she urged Bovary to write to his mother, to ask her to send at once the whole of the balance due from the father's estate. The mother-in-law replied that she had nothing more: that the liquidation was complete, and, aside from Barneville, there remained for them an income of six hundred francs, that she would pay them punctually.

Madame Bovary then sent bills to two or three patients, and was soon making great use of this method which turned out to be very successful. She was always careful to add a postscript: "Do not mention this to my husband; you know how proud he is . . . forgive my having to . . . your humble servant. . . ." There were a few complaints; she intercepted them.

To get money she began selling her old gloves, her old hats, all sorts of old odds and ends, and she bargained rapaciously, her peasant blood standing her in good stead. Then on her trips to town she searched the second hand stores for nick-nacks which she was sure, if no one else, Monsieur Lheureux would certainly take off her hands. She bought ostrich feathers, Chinese porcelain, and trunks; she borrowed from Félicité, from Madame Lefrançois, from the landlady at the "Croix Rouge," from everybody, no matter where. With the money she at last received from Barneville she paid two bills; the other fifteen hundred francs fell due. She renewed the notes, and then renewed them again!

Sometimes, it is true, she tried to add up her accounts, but the results were always so staggering, she couldn't believe they were possible. Then she would begin over again, soon get confused, leave everything where it was and forget about it.

The house was a dreary place now! Tradesmen were seen leaving it with angry faces. Handkerchiefs hung drying on the stoves, and little Berthe, to the great scandal of Madame Homais, wore stockings with holes in them. If Charles timidly ventured a remark, she would snap back at him savagely that it certainly wasn't her fault!

What was the meaning of all these fits of temper? He explained everything by her old nervous illness, and reproaching himself with having taken her infirmities for faults, accused himself of egotism, and longed to go and take her in his arms.

"Ah, no!" he said to himself; "I would only annoy her."

And he stayed where he was.

After dinner he would walk about alone in the garden; he took little Berthe on his lap and unfolding his medical journal, tried to teach her to read. But the child, who had never had any schooling at all, would soon open wide her large eyes in bewilderment and begin to cry. Then he would comfort her; he fetched water in her watering can to make rivers on the sand path, or broke off branches from the privet hedges to plant trees in the flower beds. This did not spoil the garden much, which was now overgrown with long weeds. They owed Lestiboudois for so many day's wages. Then the child would grow cold and ask for her mother.

"Go call your nurse," said Charles. "You know, my darling, that mama does not like to be disturbed!"

Autumn was setting in, and the leaves were already falling—as they had two years ago when she was ill!—Where would it all end! . . . And he would continue to pace up and down, his hands behind his back.

Madame was in her room. No one was allowed to enter. There she stayed from morning to night, listless and hardly dressed, from time to time lighting a tablet of Turkish incense she had bought at the shop of an Algerian in Rouen. In order to get rid of this sleeping man stretched out beside her at night, she finally managed by continual badgering to relegate him to a room on the third floor; then she would read until morning, lurid novels where there would be scenes of orgies, violence and bloodshed. Often she would be seized by a sudden terror and cry out. Charles would come running.

"Oh! Leave me alone!" she would say.

Or at other times, when she was burnt more fiercely by that inner flame which her adultery kept feeding, panting and overcome with desire, she would throw open the window breathing in the chill air and letting the wind blow back her hair which hung too heavy on her neck, and, looking up at the stars, she would long for the love of a prince. She thought of him, of Léon. She would then have given anything for a single one of those meetings which would appease her.

These were her gala days. She was determined that they should be magnificent! When he could not pay all the expenses himself, she made up the deficit liberally, which happened pretty well every time. He tried to convince her that they would be just as well off somewhere else, in a more modest hotel, but she always found some objection.

One day she drew six small silver-gilt spoons from her bag (they were old Rouault's wedding present), begging him to pawn them at once for her; Léon obeyed, although the errand annoyed him. He was afraid of compromising himself.

Then, on reflection, he began to think that his mistress was beginning to behave rather strangely, and perhaps they were not wrong in wishing to separate him from her.

In fact, some one had sent his mother a long anonymous letter to warn her that he was "ruining himself with a married woman"; and immediately the good woman had visions of the eternal bug-a-boo of every family, that is to say, that vague and terrible creature, the siren, the fantastic monster which makes its home in the treacherous depths of love. She wrote to Maître Dubocage, his employer, who behaved perfectly in the affair. He kept him for three quarters of an hour trying to open his eyes, to warn him of the abyss into which he was falling. Such an intrigue would damage him later on in his career. He implored him to break with her, and, if he would not make this sacrifice in his own interest, to do it at least for his, Dubocage's sake.

Léon finally swore he would not see Emma again; and he reproached himself with not having kept his word, considering all the trouble and reproaches she was likely to bring down on him, not counting the jokes made by his fellow clerks as they sat around the stove in the morning. Besides, he was soon to be head clerk; it was time to settle down. So he gave up his flute, his exalted sentiments, his poetic imagination; for every bourgeois in the flush of his youth, were it but for a day, a moment, has believed himself capable of immense passions, of lofty enterprises. The most mediocre libertine has dreamed of sultanas; every notary bears within him the débris of a poet.

He was bored now when Emma suddenly began to sob on his breast; and his heart, like the people who can only stand a certain amount of music, became drowsy through indifference to the vibrations of a love whose subtleties he could no longer distinguish.

They knew one another too well to experience any of those sudden surprises which multiply the enjoyment of a possession a hundredfold. She was as sick of him as he was weary of her. Emma found again in adultery all the platitudes of marriage.

But how to get rid of him? Then, though she felt humiliated by the sordidity of such a happiness, she clung to it out of habit, or out of degeneration; she pursued it more desperately than ever, destroying every pleasure by always wishing for it to be too great. She blamed Léon for her disappointed hopes, as if he had betrayed her; and she even longed for some catastrophe that would bring about their separation, since she had not the courage to do it herself.

She none the less went on writing him love letters, in keeping with the notion that a woman must write to her lover.

But while writing to him, it was another man she saw, a phantom fashioned out of her most ardent memories, of her favorite books, her strongest desires, and at last he became so real, so tangible, that her heart beat wildly in awe and admiration, though unable to see him distinctly, for, like a god, he was hidden beneath the abundance of his attributes. He dwelt in that azure land where silken ladders swung from balconies in the moonlight, beneath a flower-scented breeze. She felt him near her; he was coming and would ravish her entire being in a kiss. Then she would fall back to earth again shattered; for these vague ecstasies of imaginary love, would exhaust her more than the wildest orgies.

She now felt a constant pain throughout her body. Often she even received summonses, stamped paper that she barely looked at. She would have liked not to be alive, or to be always asleep.

On the day of Mid-Lent she did not return to Yonville; that evening she went to a masked ball. She wore velvet breeches, red stockings, a peruke, and a three-cornered hat cocked over one ear. She danced all night to the wild sounds of the trombones; people gathered around her, and in the morning she found herself on the steps of the theatre together with five or six other masked dancers, dressed as stevadores or sailors, friends of Léon's who were talking about going out to find some supper.

The neighboring cafés were full. They found a dreadful looking restaurant at the harbor, where the proprietor showed them to a little room on the fifth floor.

The men were whispering in a corner, no doubt consulting about expenses. There were a clerk, two medical students, and a shop assistant: what company for her! As to the women, Emma soon perceived from the tone of their voices that most of them probably came from the lowest class. This frightened her, she drew back her chair and lowered her eyes.

The others began to eat; she ate nothing. Her head was on fire, her eyes smarted, and her skin was ice-cold. In her head she seemed to feel the floor of the ball-room rebounding again beneath the rhythmical pulsation of thousands of dancing feet. The smell of punch and cigar smoke made her dizzy. She fainted: they carried her to the window.

Day was breaking, and a large purple stain was spreading across the pale sky in the direction of the St. Catherine hills. The ashen river was shivering in the wind; there was no one on the bridges; the street lamps were going out.

She came to herself, however, and began to think of Berthe asleep at home in the maid's room. But just then a cart loaded with long strips of iron passed by, and made a deafening metallic vibration against the walls of the house.

She abruptly slipped out of the room; removed her costume; told Léon she had to return; and found herself alone at last in the Hôtel de Boulogne. Everything, herself included, was now unbearable to her. She would have liked to take wing like a bird, and fly off far away to become young again in the realms of immaculate purity.

She left the hotel, crossed the Boulevard, the Place Cauchoise, and the Faubourg, as far as an open street that overlooked the park. She walked rapidly, the fresh air calmed her; and, little by little, the faces of the crowd, the masks, the quadrilles, the lights, the supper, those women, all, disappeared like rising mists. Then, reaching the "Croix-Rouge," she threw herself on the bed in her little room on the second floor, where there were pictures of the "Tour de Nesle." At four o'clock Hivert awoke her.

When she got home, Félicité showed her a grey paper stuck behind the clock. She read:

"In virtue of the seizure in execution of a judgment."

What judgment . . . ? As a matter of fact, the evening before another paper had been brought that she had not yet seen, and she was stunned by these words:

"By power of the king, the law, and the courts, Mme. Bovary is hereby ordered . . ."

Then, skipping several lines, she read:

"Within twenty-four hours, at the latest . . ." But what? "To pay the sum of eight thousand francs." There was even written at the bottom of the page, "She will be constrained thereto by every form of law, and notably by a writ of distraint on her furniture and effects."

What should she do? . . . In twenty-four hours; tomorrow! Lheureux, she thought, probably wanted to frighten her again, for, all at once, she saw through his manoeuvres, the reason for his favors. The only thing that reassured her was the extraordinary amount of the figure.

Nevertheless, as a result of buying and not paying, of borrowing, signing notes, and renewing these notes which grew ever larger each time they fell due, she had ended by preparing a capital for Monsieur Lheureux which he was impatiently waiting to collect to use in his own financial speculations.

She went over to his place, assuming an air of indifference.

"Do you know what has happened to me? It's a joke, I'm sure!"

"No."

"What do you mean?"

He slowly turned around, and, folding his arms, said to her:

"Did you think, my dear lady, that I was going to go on to the end of time providing you with merchandise and cash, just for the love of God? I certainly have to get back what I laid out, let's be fair."

She objected to the amount of the debt.

"Ah! Too bad! The court has recognised it! There's a judgment. You've been notified. Besides, it isn't my fault. It's Vinçart's."

"But couldn't you . . . ?"

"No! Not a single thing!"

"But . . . Still . . . let's talk it over."

And she began beating about the bush; she had known nothing about it . . . it was a surprise . . .

"Whose fault is that?" said Lheureux, bowing ironically. "While I'm slaving like a nigger, you go gallivanting about."

"Ah! Don't preach to me!"

"It never does any harm," he replied.

She turned coward; she implored him; she even pressed her pretty white and slender hand against the shopkeeper's knee.

"There, that'll do! Any one'd think you wanted to seduce me!"

"You are a wretch!" she cried.

"Oh, oh! What a fuss you are making!"

"I will show you up. I'll tell my husband . . ."

"All right! I too, I'll show your husband something!"

And Lheureux drew from his strong box the receipt for eighteen hundred francs that she had given him when Vinçart had discounted the bills.

"Do you think," he added, "that he won't catch on to your little theft, the poor dear man?"

She collapsed, more overcome than if felled by the blow of a club. He was walking up and down from the window to the bureau, repeating all the while:

"I'll show him all right . . . I'll show him all right . . . " Then he approached her, and said in a soft voice:

"It's no fun, I know; but after all it hasn't killed anyone, and, since that is the only way that is left for you paying back my money . . ."

"But where am I to get any?" said Emma, wringing her hands.

"Bah! when one has friends like you!"

And he looked at her with such a knowing and terrible stare, that she shuddered to the very core of her heart.

"I promise you," she said, "I'll sign . . ."

"I've enough of your signatures!"

"I will sell something else . . ."

"Oh come!" he said, shrugging his shoulders. "You've nothing left to sell."

And he called through the peep-hole that looked down into the shop:

"Annette, don't forget the three coupons of No. 14."

The servant appeared; Emma caught the hint and asked how much money would be needed to put a stop to the proceedings.

"It is too late."

"But if I were to bring you several thousand francs, a quarter of the sum, a third, almost all?"

"No; it's no use!"

And he pushed her gently towards the staircase.

"I implore you, Monsieur Lheureux, just a few days more!"

She was sobbing.

"Ah that's good! let's have some tears!"

"You'll drive me to do something desperate!"

"Don't make me laugh!" said he, shutting the door.

VII

She was stoical the next day when Maître Hareng, the bailiff, with two assistants arrived at her house to draw up inventory for the seizure.

They began with Bovary's consulting-room, and did not write down the phrenological head, which was considered an "instrument of his profession"; but in the kitchen they counted the plates, the saucepans, the chairs, the candlesticks, and in the bedroom all the nick-nacks on the wall-shelf. They examined her dresses, the linen, the dressing-room; and her whole existence, to its most intimate details, was stretched out like a cadavre in an autopsy before the eyes of these three men.

Maître Hareng, buttoned up in his thin black coat, wearing a white choker and very tight foot-straps, repeated from time to time:

"Allow me madame? Allow me?"

Often he uttered exclamations:

"Charming! very pretty."

Then he began writing again, dipping his pen into the horn inkstand he carried in his left hand.

When they had done with the rooms they went up to the attic, She kept a desk there in which Rodolphe's letters were locked. It had to be opened.

"Ah! a correspondence!" said Maître Hareng, with a discreet smile. "But allow me! for I must make sure the box contains nothing else." And he tipped up the papers lightly, as if to let the napoleons fall out. This made her furious to see this coarse hand, with red moist fingers like slugs, touching these pages against which her heart had beaten.

They went at last! Félicité came back. Emma had sent her out to watch for Bovary in order to keep him away, and they hastily installed the man set to guard the seizure, in the attic, where he swore he would not stir.

During the evening Charles seemed to her careworn. Emma watched him with a look of anguish, fancying she saw an accusation in every line of his face. Then, when her eyes wandered over the chimney-piece ornamented with Chinese screens, over the large curtains, the arm-chairs, all those things that had softened the bitterness of her life, remorse seized her, or rather an immense regret, that, far from destroying her passion, rather irritated it. Charles placidly poked the fire, both his feet on the andirons.

Once the man, no doubt bored in his hiding-place, made a slight noise.

"Is any one walking upstairs?" said Charles.

"No," she replied; "it is a window that has been left open, and is banging in the wind."

The next day which was Sunday, she went to Rouen to call on all the brokers whose names she knew. They were either in the country, or away on a trip. She was not discouraged; and those whom she did manage to see she asked for money, insisting that she absolutely had to have it, that she would pay it back. Some laughed in her face; all refused.

At two o'clock she ran to Léon's apartment, and knocked at the door. No one answered. At length he appeared.

"What brings you here?"

"Am I disturbing you?"

"No . . . but . . ." And he admitted that his landlord didn't like his having "women" there.

"I must speak to you," she went on.

Then he took down the key, but she stopped him.

"No, no! Over there, in our home!"

And they went to their room at the Hôtel de Boulogne.

On arriving she drank off a large glass of water. She was very pale. She said to him:

"Léon, I have a favor to ask you."

And, shaking him by both hands which she held tightly in hers, she added:

"Listen, I must have eight thousand francs."

"But you are mad!"

"Not yet."

And thereupon, telling him the story of the seizure, she explained her distress to him; for Charles knew nothing of it; her mother-in-law detested her; old Rouault could do nothing; but he, Léon, he would set about finding this indispensable sum . . .

"But what do you want me . . . ?"

"What a coward you are!" she cried.

Then he said stupidly, "You're making things out to be worse than they are. Your fellow there could probably be quieted with three thousand francs."

All the more reason to try and do something; it was inconceivable that they couldn't find three thousand francs. Besides, Léon could sign the notes instead of her.

"Go! try! you must! run! . . . Oh! Try! try! I will love you so!"

He went out, and came back at the end of an hour, saying, with a solemn face:

"I have been to three people . . . with no success!"

Then they sat there facing each other on either side of the

fireplace, motionless, without speaking. Emma shrugged her shoulders as she tapped her foot impatiently. He heard her murmur:

"If I were in your place I'd certainly find some!"

"Where?"

"At your office."

And she looked at him.

A diabolical determination showed in her burning eyes which were half closed in a lascivious and encouraging manner;—so that the young man felt himself growing weak beneath the mute will of this woman who was urging him to commit a crime. Then he was afraid, and to avoid any explanation he smote his forehead crying:

"Morel is coming back tonight! He will not refuse me, I hope" (this was one of his friends, the son of a very rich merchant); "and I will bring it you to-morrow," he added.

Emma did not seem to welcome this new hope with all the joy he had expected. Did she suspect the lie? He went on, blushing:

"However, if you don't see me by three o'clock, do not wait for me, my darling. I must leave now, forgive me. Good-bye!"

He pressed her hand, but it felt quite lifeless. Emma had no strength left for any sentiment whatever.

Four o'clock struck; and she rose to return to Yonville, mechanically obeying the force of old habits.

The weather was beautiful; it was one of those March days, clear and sharp, when the sun shines in a perfectly white sky. The people of Rouen, dressed in their Sunday-clothes, seemed happy as they strolled by. She reached the Place du Parvis. People were coming out of the cathedral after vespers; the crowd flowed out through the three portals like a river through the three arches of a bridge, and in the middle, more immobile than a rock, stood the verger.

Then she remembered the day when, eager and full of hope, she had entered beneath this large nave, that had opened out before her, less profound than her love; and she walked on weeping beneath her veil, dazed, staggering, almost fainting.

"Look out!" cried a voice issuing from behind a carriage gate which was swinging open.

She stopped to let pass a black horse, prancing between the shafts of a tilbury, driven by a gentleman dressed in sables. Who was it? She knew him . . . The carriage sprang forward and disappeared.

Why, it was he, the Viscount! She turned away; the street was empty. She was so crushed, so sad, that she had to lean against a wall to keep herself from falling.

Then she thought she had been mistaken.

How could she tell? Everything, within herself and without, was abandoning her. She felt that she was lost, that she was wandering about at random within undefinable abysses, and she was almost happy, on reaching the "Croix Rouge," to see the good Homais, who was watching a large box full of pharmaceutical stores being hoisted on to the "Hirondelle"; holding in his hand a silk handkerchief containing six "cheminots" for his wife.

Madame Homais was very fond of these small, heavy rolls shaped like turbans which are eaten during Lent with salt butter: a last relic of Gothic fare, going back, perhaps, to the Crusades, and with which the hardy Normans would stuff themselves in times gone-by, thinking that they saw, illuminated in the golden light of the torches, between the tankards of Hippocras[62] and the gigantic slabs of meat, the heads of Saracens to be devoured. The druggist's wife crunched them up as they had done, heroically, in spite of her wretched teeth; so whenever Homais made a trip to town, he never failed to bring her home some which he bought at the great baker's in the Rue Massacre.

"Charmed to see you," he said, offering Emma a hand to help her into the "Hirondelle."

Then he tied his "cheminots" to the baggage net and remained with his head bare and his arms folded in an attitude pensive and Napoleonic.

But when the blind man appeared as usual at the foot of the hill he exclaimed indignantly:

"I can't understand why the authorities continue to tolerate such criminal occupations! These unfortunate people should be locked up, forced to do some work. I give you my word, Progress marches at a snail's pace! We are paddling about in a state of total barbarism!"

The blind man held out his hat which flapped about in the window as though it were a pocket in the upholstery which had come loose.

"This," said the pharmacist, "is a scrofulous disease."

And though he knew the poor devil, he pretended to see him for the first time, muttering such words as "cornea," "opaque cornea," "sclerotic," "facies," then asked him in a paternal tone:

"My friend, have you suffered long from this dreadful affliction? Instead of getting drunk in the café you would do better to follow a diet."

He advised him to drink good wine, good beer and to eat good roasts of meat. The blind man went on with his song. He actually seemed almost insane. At last Monsieur Homais opened his purse.

"Now there's a sou; give me back two liards: don't forget what I told you, you'll find it does you good."

Hivert openly cast some doubt on its efficacy. But the druggist said that he would cure the man himself with an antiphlogistic salve of his own composition, and he gave his address: "Monsieur

62. Hippocras (Hippocrates, the Greek physician) was an aromatic, highly spiced wine of medieval Europe.

Homais, near the market, everyone knows me."

"All right!" said Hivert, "in payment, you can 'put on your act' for us."

The blind man squatted down on his haunches with his head thrown back, and rolling his greenish eyes and sticking out his tongue, he rubbed his stomach with both hands while uttering a sort of low howl like a famished dog. Emma, overcome with disgust, threw him a five franc piece over her shoulder. It was all her fortune. It seemed like a grand thing to her to throw it away like this.

The coach had already started again when Monsieur Homais suddenly leaned out of the window and shouted:

"No farinacious foods or dairy products, wear woolen clothing next to the skin, and expose the diseased areas to the smoke of juniper berries."

The sight of the familiar things that passed before her eyes gradually diverted Emma from her present suffering. An intolerable fatigue overwhelmed her, and she reached home stupefied, discouraged, almost asleep.

"Let come what may!" she told herself.

Besides, anything could happen. Couldn't some extraordinary event occur at any moment? Lheureux might even die.

At nine o'clock in the morning she was awakened by the sound of voices in the square. A crowd around the market was reading a large bill fixed to one of the posts, and she saw Justin climb on a milepost and tear down the bill. The local policeman had just seized him by the collar. Monsieur Homais came out of his shop, and Mère Lefrançois, in the midst of the crowd, was talking the loudest of all.

"Madame! madame!" cried Félicité, running in, "it's an outrage!"

And the poor girl, all in tears, handed her a yellow paper that she had just torn off the door. Emma read with a glance that her furniture was for sale.

Then they looked at one another in silence. Servant and master had no secrets from each other. At last Félicité whispered:

"If I were you, madame, I'd go see Monsieur Guillaumin."

"You think so?"

The question meant:

"You who know all about the house from the butler, has the master sometimes spoken of me?"

"Yes, you'd do well to go there."

She dressed, put on her black gown, and her cape with jet beads, and that she might not be seen (there was still a crowd on the Square), she took the path by the river, outside the village.

She was out of breath when she reached the notary's gate. The sky was sombre, and a little snow was falling.

At the sound of the bell, Theodore in a red waistcoat appeared on the steps; he came to open the door with a casual air, as if she were an old acquaintance, and showed her into the dining-room.

A large porcelain stove crackled beneath a cactus that filled up the niche in the wall, and in black wood frames against the oak-stained paper hung Steuben's[63] "Esmeralda" and Schopin's "Putiphar."[64] The ready-laid table, the two silver chafing-dishes, the crystal door-knobs, the parquet and the furniture, all shone with a scrupulous, English cleanliness; the windows were ornamented at each corner with stained glass.

"Now this," thought Emma, "is the kind of dining-room I ought to have."

The notary came in. With his left hand, he pressed his palm-embroidered dressing gown against his body, while with his other hand he quickly took off and replaced his brown velvet skullcap, which he wore jauntily cocked to the right. After circling around his bald cranium, the end of three strains of blond hair stuck out from underneath the cap.

After he had offered her a seat he sat down to breakfast, apologising profusely for his rudeness.

"I have come," she said, "to beg you, sir . . ."

"What, madame? I am listening."

And she began telling him about her situation.

Monsieur Guillaumin knew all about it. He was working in secret partnership with the shopkeeper, who always provided him with the capital for the mortgage loans he was asked to arrange.

So he knew (and better than she herself) the long story of these notes, small at first, bearing the names of several endorsers, made out for long terms and constantly renewed up to the day when, gathering together all the protested notes, the shopkeeper had asked his friend Vinçart to take in his own name all the necessary legal steps to collect the money, not wishing to appear as a shark in the eyes of his fellow-citizens.

She mingled her story with recriminations against Lheureux, to which the notary from time to time gave meaningless replies. Eating his cutlet and drinking his tea, he buried his chin in his sky-blue cravat, into which were thrust two diamond pins, held together by a small gold chain; and he smiled a singular smile, in a sugary, ambiguous fashion. Noticing that her feet were damp:

"Do get closer to the stove," he said, "put your feet up against the porcelain."

She was afraid of dirtying it but the notary replied gallantly:

63. Karl Steuben (1788–1856) was a German history painter. Esmeralda is the gypsy girl in Hugo's *Notre Dame de Paris* (a picture, "Esmeralda et Quasimodo"—the Dwarf—was exhibited in 1839).

64. Schopin was (with a different spelling) the brother of the composer Chopin. Putiphar is the official of the court of Egypt who was Joseph's master—the wife of Putiphar tried to seduce him. The picture represents the seduction scene.

"Pretty things never spoil anything."

Then she tried to appeal to his better feelings and, growing moved herself, she began telling him about the tightness of her household, her worries, her wants. He could understand that—such an elegant woman!—and, without interrupting his lunch, he turned completely round towards her, so that his knee brushed against her boot; the sole was beginning to curl in the heat of the stove.

But when she asked for three thousand francs, his lips drew tight and he said how sorry he was not to have had the management of her capital before, for there were hundreds of ways very convenient, even for a lady, of turning her money to account. In the turf-pits of Gaumesnil or in Le Havre real estate, they could have ventured, with hardly any risk, on some excellent speculations; and he let her consume herself with rage at the thought of the fabulous sums that she would certainly have made.

"How was it," he went on, "that you didn't come to me?"

"I don't know," she said.

"Why not? Did I frighten you so much? It is I, on the contrary, who ought to complain. We hardly know one another; yet I am very devoted to you. You do not doubt that any longer, I hope?"

He held out his hand, took hers, kissed it greedily, then held it on his knee; and he played delicately with her fingers, while muttering thousands of compliments.

His bland voice rustled like a running brook; a light shone in his eyes through the glimmering of his spectacles, and his hand was advancing up Emma's sleeve to press her arm. She felt against her cheek his panting breath. This man was intolerable.

She sprang to her feet and told him:

"Sir, I am waiting."

"For what?" said the notary, who suddenly became very pale.

"This money."

"But . . ."

Then, yielding to an irresistible wave of desire:

"Well then, . . . yes!"

He dragged himself towards her on his knees, regardless of his dressing gown.

"I beg you, stay! I love you!"

He seized her by the waist. Madame Bovary's face flushed purple. She recoiled with a terrible look, exclaiming:

"You shamelessly take advantage of my distress, sir! I am to be pitied—not to be sold."

And she went out.

The notary remained dumbfounded, his eyes fixed on his fine embroidered slippers. They were a love gift, and their sight finally consoled him. Besides, he reflected that such an adventure might have carried him too far.

"The wretch! the scoundrel! . . . what an infamy!" she said to herself, as she fled with nervous steps under the aspens that lined the road. The disappointment of her failure increased the indignation of her outraged modesty; it seemed to her that Providence pursued her implacably, and, strengthening herself in her pride, she had never felt so much esteem for herself nor so much contempt for others. A spirit of warfare transformed her. She would have liked to strike all men, to spit in their faces, to crush them; she kept walking straight on, as quickly as she could, pale, shaking and furious, searching the empty horizon with tear-dimmed eyes, almost rejoicing in the hatred that was choking her.

When she saw her house a numbness came over her. She could not go on; yet she had to. Besides, what escape was there for her?

Félicité was waiting for her at the door.

"Well?"

"No!" said Emma.

And for a quarter of an hour the two of them went over the various persons in Yonville who might perhaps be inclined to help her. But each time that Félicité named some one Emma replied:

"Out of the question! they won't!"

"And the master'll soon be in."

"I know that well enough . . . Now leave me alone."

She had tried everything; there was nothing more to be done now; and when Charles came in she would have to tell him:

"Step aside! This rug on which you are walking is no longer ours. In your own house you don't own a chair, a pin, a straw, and it is I, poor man, who have ruined you."

Then there would be a great sob; next he would weep abundantly, and at last, the surprise past, he would forgive her.

"Yes," she murmured, grinding her teeth, "*he* will forgive me, the man I could never forgive for having known me, even if he had a million to spare! . . . Never! never!"

The thought of Bovary's magnanimity exasperated her. He was bound to find out the catastrophe, whether she confessed or not, now, soon, or to-morrow; so there was no escape from the horrible scene and she would have to bear the weight of his generosity. She wanted to return to Lheureux, but what good would it do? To write to her father—it was too late; and perhaps she began to repent now that she had not yielded to the notary, when she heard the trot of a horse in the alley. It was he; he was opening the gate; he was whiter than the plaster wall. Rushing to the stairs, she fled to the Square; and the wife of the mayor, who was talking to Lestiboudois in front of the church, saw her enter the house of the tax-collector.

She hurried off to tell Madame Caron, and the two ladies went up to the attic; hidden behind a sheet strung up on two poles, they stationed themselves comfortably in full command of Binet's room.

He was alone in his garret, busily copying in wood one of those indescribable bits of ivory, composed of crescents, of spheres hollowed out one within the other, the whole as straight as an obelisk, and of no use whatever; and he was beginning on the last piece—he was nearing his goal! In the twilight of the workshop the white dust was flying from his tools like a shower of sparks under the hoofs of a galloping horse; the two wheels were turning, droning; Binet smiled, his chin lowered, his nostrils distended. He seemed lost in the state of complete bliss that only the most menial tasks can offer: distracting the mind by easily overcome obstacles, they satisfy it completely, leading to a fulfilled achievement that leaves no room for dreams beyond.

"Ah! there she is!" exclaimed Madame Tuvache.

But the noise of the lathe made it impossible to hear what she was saying.

At last the two ladies thought they made out the word "francs," and Madame Tuvache whispered in a low voice:

"She's asking for extra time to pay her taxes."

"Apparently!" replied the other.

They saw her walking up and down, examining the napkin-rings, the candlesticks, the banister rails against the walls, while Binet stroked his beard with satisfaction.

"Do you think she wants to order something from him?" said Madame Tuvache.

"Why, he never sells anything," objected her neighbor.

The tax-collector seemed to be listening with wide-open eyes, as if he did not understand. She went on in a tender, suppliant manner. She came nearer to him, her breast heaving; they no longer spoke.

"Is she making advances to him?" said Madame Tuvache.

Binet was scarlet to his very ears. She took hold of his hands.

"Oh, it's too much!"

And no doubt she was suggesting something abominable to him; for the tax-collector—yet he was brave, had fought at Bautzen[65] and at Lützen,[66] had been through the French campaign,[67] and had even been proposed for the Croix de Guerre—suddenly, as at the sight of a serpent, recoiled as far as he could from her, exclaiming:

"Madame! How dare you? . . ."

"Women like that ought to be whipped," said Madame Tuvache.

"But where did she go?" Madame Caron asked. For while they talked, she had vanished out of sight, till they discovered her running up the Grande Rue and turning right as if making for the graveyard, leaving them lost in wonder.

"Mère Rollet," she cried on reaching the nurse's home, "I am choking; unlace me!" She fell sobbing on the bed. Nurse Rollet

65. Bautzen (in Saxony, now in Poland, called Budyszin) was the scene of a battle in 1813 where Napoleon defeated the Prussians and Russians.

66. Lützen, in Saxony, was the scene of another battle of Napoleon.

67. The French campaign refers to the battles in France before the Allies captured Paris and forced the abdication of Napoleon and his banishment to Elba in 1814.

covered her with a petticoat and remained standing by her side. Then, as she did not answer, the woman withdrew, took her wheel and began spinning flax.

"Please, stop that!" she murmured, fancying she heard Binet's lathe.

"What's bothering her?" said the nurse to herself. "Why has she come here?"

She had come, impelled by a kind of horror that drove her from her home.

Lying on her back, motionless, and with staring eyes, she saw things but vaguely, although she tried with idiotic persistence to focus her attention on them. She looked at the scaling walls, two logs smoking end to end in the fireplace, and a long spider crawling over her head in a cracked beam. At last she began to collect her thoughts. She remembered—one day, with Léon . . . Oh! how long ago that was—the sun was shining on the river, and the air full of the scent from the clematis . . . . Then, carried by her memories as by a rushing torrent, she soon remembered what had happened the day before.

"What time is it?" she asked.

Mère Rollet went out, raised the fingers of her right hand to that side of the sky that was brightest, and came back slowly, saying:

"Nearly three."

"Ah! thank you, thank you!"

For he would come, he was bound to. He would have found the money. But he would, perhaps, go down to her house, not guessing where she was, and she told the nurse to run and fetch him.

"Be quick!"

"I'm going, my dear lady, I'm going!"

She wondered now why she had not thought of him from the first. Yesterday he had given his word; he would not break it. And she already saw herself at Lheureux's spreading out her three banknotes on his desk. Then she would have to invent some story to explain matters to Bovary. What would she tell him?

The nurse, however, was a long time returning. But, as there was no clock in the cot, Emma feared she was perhaps exaggerating the length of time. She began walking round the garden, step by step; she went into the path by the hedge, and returned quickly, hoping that the woman would have come back by another road. At last, weary of waiting, assailed by fears that she thrust from her, no longer conscious whether she had been here a century or a moment, she sat down in a corner, closed her eyes, and stopped her ears. The gate grated; she sprang up. Before she could speak, Mère Rollet told her:

"There is no one at your house!"

"What?"

"He isn't there. And Monsieur is crying. He is calling for you. Everybody is looking for you."

Emma did not answer. She gasped with wild, rolling eyes, while the peasant woman, frightened at her face drew back instinctively, thinking her mad. Suddenly she struck her brow and uttered a cry; for the thought of Rodolphe, like a flash of lightning in a dark night, had struck into her soul. He was so good, so tender, so generous! And besides, should he hesitate to come to her assistance, she would know well enough how one single glance would reawaken their lost love. So she set out towards La Huchette, unaware that she was hastening to offer what had so angered her a while ago, not in the least conscious of her prostitution.

VIII

She asked herself as she walked along, "What am I going to say? How shall I begin?" And as she went on she recognised the thickets, the trees, the sea-rushes on the hill, the château beyond. All the sensations of her first love came back to her, and her poor oppressed heart expanded in the warmth of this tenderness. A warm wind blew in her face; melting snow fell drop by drop from the leave-buds onto the grass.

She entered, as in the past, through the small park-gate, reached the main courtyard, planted with a double row of lindens, their long whispering branches swaying in the wind. The dogs in their kennels barked, but their resounding voices brought no one out.

She went up the large straight staircase with wooden banisters that led to the hallway paved with dusty flagstones, into which a row of doors opened, as in a monastery or an inn. He was at the top, right at the end, on the left. When she placed her fingers on the lock her strength suddenly deserted her. She was afraid, almost wished he would not be there, though this was her only hope, her last chance of salvation. She collected her thoughts for one moment, and, strengthening herself by the feeling of present necessity, went in.

He was sitting in front of the fire, both his feet propped against the mantelpiece, smoking a pipe.

"Oh, it's you!" he said, getting up hurriedly.

"Yes, it is I . . . I have come, Rodolphe, to ask your advice."

And, despite all her efforts, it was impossible for her to open her lips.

"You have not changed; you're as charming as ever!"

"Oh," she replied bitterly, "they are poor charms since you disdained them."

Then he began a long justification of his conduct, excusing himself in vague terms, since he was unable to invent better.

She yielded to his words, still more to his voice and the sight of him, so that she pretended to believe, or perhaps believed, in the pretext he gave for their break; it was a secret on which depended the honor, the very life of a third person.

"Never mind," she said, looking at him sadly. "I have suffered much."

He replied philosophically:

"Life is that way!"

"Has life," Emma went on, "been kind to you at least since our separation?"

"Oh, neither good . . . nor bad."

"Perhaps it would have been better never to have parted."

"Yes, perhaps."

"You think so?" she said, drawing nearer.

Then, with a sigh:

"Oh, Rodolphe! if only you knew! . . . I loved you so!"

It was then that she took his hand, and they remained some time, their fingers intertwined, like that first day at the Agricultural Fair. With a gesture of pride he struggled against this emotion. But sinking upon his breast she told him:

"How did you think I could live without you? One cannot lose the habit of happiness. I was desperate, I thought I was going to die! I'll tell you about it . . . But you, you fled from me!"

With the natural cowardice that characterizes the stronger sex, he had carefully avoided her for the last three years; now Emma persisted, with coaxing little motions of the head, playful and feline:

"I know you love others, you may as well admit it. Oh! I don't blame them, I understand! You seduced them just as you seduced me. You're a man, a real man! you have all it takes to make yourself loved. But we'll start all over, won't we? We'll love each other as before! Look, I am laughing, I am happy! . . . Say something!"

She was irresistible, with a tear trembling in her eye, like a raindrop in a blue flower-cup, after the storm.

He had drawn her upon his knees, and with the back of his hand was caressing her smooth hair; a last ray of the sun was mirrored there, like a golden arrow. She lowered her head; at last he kissed her on the eyelids quite gently with the tips of his lips.

"Why, you have been crying! Why?"

She burst into tears. Rodolphe thought this was an outburst of her love. As she did not speak, he took this silence to be a last remnant of resistance, so he exclaimed:

"Oh, forgive me! You are the only one who really pleases me. I was a fool, a wicked fool! I love you, I'll always love you! What is the matter? Tell me . . ."

He knelt before her.

"Well, Rodolphe . . . I am ruined! You must lend me three thousand francs."

"But . . ." he said, as he slowly rose to his feet, "but . . ." His face assumed a grave expression.

"You know," she went on quickly, "that my husband had entrusted his money to a notary to invest, and he absconded. So we borrowed; the patients don't pay us. Moreover, the estate isn't settled yet; we shall have the money later on. But to-day, for want of three thousand francs, we are to be sold out, right now, this very minute. Counting on your friendship, I have come to you for help."

"Ah!" thought Rodolphe, turning very pale, "so that's what she came for."

At last he said, very calmly:

"My dear lady, I haven't got them."

He did not lie. If he had had it, he would probably have given the money, although it is generally unpleasant to do such fine things: a demand for money being, of all the winds that blow upon love, the coldest and most destructive.

She stared at him in silence for minutes.

"You haven't got them!"

She repeated several times:

"You haven't got them! . . . I ought to have spared myself this last shame. You never loved me. You are no better than the others."

She was losing her head, giving herself away.

Rodolphe interrupted her, declaring he was himself "hard up."

"Oh! I feel sorry for you!" said Emma, "exceedingly sorry!"

And fixing her eyes upon an embossed rifle that shone against its panoply:

"But when one is so poor one doesn't have silver on the butt of one's gun. One doesn't buy a clock inlaid with tortoiseshell," she went on, pointing to the Boulle clock, "nor silver-gilt whistles for one's whips," and she touched them, "nor charms for one's watch. Oh, he has all he needs! even a liqueur-stand in his bedroom; for you pamper yourself, you live well. You have a château, farms, woods; you go hunting; you travel to Paris. Why, if it were but that," she cried, taking up two cuff-links from the mantlepiece, "even for the least of these trifles, one could get money . . . Oh, I don't want anything from you; you can keep them!"

And she flung the links away with such force that their gold chain broke as it struck against the wall.

"But I! I would have given you everything. I would have sold all, worked for you with my hands, I would have begged on the highroads for a smile, for a look, to hear you say 'Thank you!' And you sit there quietly in your arm-chair, as if you had not made me suffer enough already! But for you, and you know it, I might have lived happily. What made you do it? Was it a bet? Yet you loved me . . . you said so. And but a moment ago . . . Ah! it would have been better to have driven me away. My hands are hot with your kisses, and there is the spot on the carpet where at my knees you swore an eternity of love! You made me believe you; for two years you held me in the most magnificent, the sweetest dream! . . . Our plans for the journey, do you remember? Oh, your letter! your letter! it tore my heart! And then when I come back to him—to him, rich, happy, free—to implore the help the first stranger would give, a suppliant, and bringing back to him all my tenderness, he repulses me because it could cost him three thousand francs!"

"I haven't got them," replied Rodolphe, with that perfect calm with which resigned rage covers itself as with a shield.

She went out. The walls trembled, the ceiling was crushing her, and she passed back through the long alley, stumbling against the heaps of dead leaves scattered by the wind. At last she reached the low hedge in front of the gate; she broke her nails against the lock in her haste to open it. Then a hundred paces beyond, breathless, almost falling, she stopped. And now turning round, she once more saw the impassive château, with the park, the gardens, the three courts, and all the windows of the façade.

She remained lost in stupor, and only conscious of herself through the beating of her arteries, that seemed to burst forth like a deafening music filling all the fields. The earth beneath her feet was more yielding than the sea, and the furrows seemed to her immense brown waves breaking into foam. All the memories and ideas that crowded her head seemed to explode at once like a thousand pieces of fireworks. She saw her father, Lheureux's closet, their room at home, another landscape. Madness was coming upon her; she grew afraid, and managed to recover herself, in a confused way, it is true, for she did not remember the cause of her dreadful confusion, namely the money. She suffered only in her love, and felt her soul escaping from her in this memory, as wounded men, dying, feel their life ebb from their bleeding wounds.

Night was falling, crows were flying about.

Suddenly it seemed to her that fiery spheres were exploding in the air like bullets when they strike, and were whirling, whirling, to melt at last upon the snow between the branches of the trees. In the midst of each of them appeared the face of Rodolphe. They multiplied and drew near, they penetrated her. It all disappeared; she recognised the lights of the houses that shone through the fog.

Now her plight, like an abyss, loomed before her. She was panting as if her heart would burst. Then in an ecstasy of heroism, that made her almost joyous, she ran down the hill, crossed the cow-plank, the footpath, the alley, the market, and reached the pharmacy. She was about to enter, but at the sound of the bell some one might come, and slipping in by the gate, holding her breath, feeling her way along the walls, she went as far as the door of the kitchen, where a candle was burning on the stove. Justin in his shirt-sleeves was carrying out a dish.

"Ah! they're eating; let's wait."

He returned; she tapped at the window. He came out.

"The key! the one for upstairs where he keeps the . . ."

"What?"

And he looked at her, astonished at the pallor of her face, that stood out white against the black background of the night. She seemed to him extraordinarily beautiful and majestic as a phantom. Without understanding what she wanted, he had the presentiment of something terrible.

But she went on quickly in a low voice that was sweet and melting:

"I want it; give it to me."

As the partition wall was thin, they could hear the clatter of the forks on the plates in the dining-room.

She pretended that she wanted to kill the rats that kept her from sleeping.

"I must go ask Monsieur."

"No, stay!"

Then with a casual air:

"Oh, it's not worth bothering him about, I'll tell him myself later. Come, hold the light for me."

She entered the corridor into which the laboratory door opened. Against the wall was a key labelled *Capharnaüm.*

"Justin!" called the pharmacist, growing impatient.

"Let's go up."

And he followed her. The key turned in the lock, and she went straight to the third shelf, so well did her memory guide her, seized the blue jar, tore out the cork, plunged in her hand, and withdrawing it full of white powder, she ate it greedily.

"Stop!" he cried, throwing himself upon her.

"Quiet! They might hear us . . ."

He was in despair, ready to call out.

"Say nothing, or all the blame will fall on your master."

Then she went home, suddenly calmed, with something of the serenity of one that has done his duty.

When Charles, thunderstruck at the news of the execution, rushed home, Emma had just gone out. He cried aloud, wept, fainted, but she did not return. Where could she be? He sent Félicité to Homais, to Monsieur Tuvache, to Lheureux, to the "Lion d'Or," everywhere, and in between the waves of his anxiety he saw his reputation destroyed, their fortune lost, Berthe's future ruined. By what?—Not a word! He waited till six in the evening. At last, unable to bear it any longer, and fancying she had gone to Rouen, he set out along the highroad, walked a mile, met no one, again waited, and returned home.

She had come back.

"What happened? . . . Why did you? . . . Tell me . . ."

She sat down at her writing-table and wrote a letter, which she sealed slowly, adding the date and the hour.

Then she said in a solemn tone:

"You are to read it to-morrow; till then, I beg you, don't ask me a single question. No, not one!"

"But . . ."

"Oh, leave me!"

She lay down full length on her bed.

A bitter taste in her mouth awakened her. She saw Charles, and again closed her eyes.

She was studying herself curiously, to detect the first signs of suffering. But no! nothing as yet. She heard the ticking of the clock, the crackling of the fire, and Charles breathing as he stood upright by her bed.

"Ah! it is but a little thing, death!" she thought. "I shall fall asleep and all will be over."

She drank a mouthful of water and turned her face to the wall. The frightful taste of ink persisted.

"I am thirsty; oh! so thirsty," she sighed.

"What is the matter?" said Charles, who was handing her a glass.

"It's nothing . . . Open the window, I'm choking."

She was seized with a sickness so sudden that she had hardly time to draw out her handkerchief from under the pillow.

"Take it away," she said quickly; "throw it away."

He spoke to her; she did not answer. She lay motionless, afraid that the slightest movement might make her vomit. But she felt an icy cold creeping from her feet to her heart.

"Ah! It's beginning," she murmured.

"What did you say?"

She gently rocked her head to and fro in anguish, opening her jaws as if something very heavy were weighing upon her tongue. At eight o'clock the vomiting began again.

Charles noticed that at the bottom of the basin there was a trace of white sediment sticking to the sides of the porcelain.

"This is extraordinary, very strange!" he repeated.

"No!" she loudly replied, "you are mistaken."

Then gently, almost caressingly, he passed his hand over her stomach. She uttered a sharp cry. He recoiled in terror.

Then she began to moan, faintly at first. Her shoulders were shaken by a strong shudder, and she was growing paler than the sheets in which she buried her clenched fists. Her unequal pulse was now almost imperceptible.

Drops of sweat oozed from her face, that had turned blue and rigid as under the effect of a metallic vapor. Her teeth chattered, her dilated eyes looked vaguely about her, and to all questions she replied only with a shake of the head; she even smiled once or twice. Gradually, her moaning grew louder; she couldn't repress a muffled scream; she pretended she felt better and that she'd soon get up. But she was seized with convulsions and cried out:

"God! It's horrible!"

He threw himself on his knees by her bed.

"Tell me! what have you eaten? Answer, for heaven's sake!"

And he looked at her with a tenderness in his eyes such as she had never seen.

"Well, there . . . there . . ." she said in a faltering voice.

He flew to the writing-table, tore open the seal, and read aloud: "Let no one be blamed . . ." He stopped, passed his hands over his eyes, and read it over again.

"What! . . . Help! Help!"

He could only keep repeating the word: "Poisoned! poisoned!" Félicité ran to Homais, who proclaimed it in the market-place; Madame Lefrançois heard it at the "Lion d'Or;" some got up to go and tell their neighbors, and all night the village was on the alert.

Distracted, stammering, reeling, Charles wandered about the room. He knocked against the furniture, tore his hair, and the pharmacist had never believed that there could be so terrible a sight.

He went home to write to Monsieur Canivet and to Doctor Larivière. His mind kept wandering, he had to start over fifteen times. Hippolyte went to Neufchâtel, and Justin so spurred Bovary's horse that he left it foundered and three parts dead by the hill at Bois-Guillaume.

Charles tried to look up his medical dictionary, but could not read it; the lines were jumping before his eyes.

"Be calm," said the pharmacist; "we must administer a powerful antidote. What is the poison?"

Charles showed him the letter. It was arsenic.

"Very well," said Homais, "we must make an analysis."

For he knew that in cases of poisoning an analysis must be made; and the other, who did not understand, answered:

"Oh, do it! Do anything! Save her . . ."

Then going back to her, he sank upon the carpet, and lay there with his head leaning against the edge of her bed, sobbing.

"Don't cry," she said to him. "Soon I won't trouble you any longer."

"Why did you do it? Who made you?"

She replied:

"There was no other way!"

"Weren't you happy? Is it my fault? But I did the best I could!"

"Yes, that's true . . . you're good, not like the others."

And she slowly passed her hand over his hair. The sweetness of this sensation deepened his sadness; he felt his whole being dissolving in despair at the thought that he must lose her, just when she was confessing more love for him than she ever did. He didn't know what to do, felt paralyzed by fear; the need for an immediate decision took away his last bit of self-control.

Emma thought that, at last, she was through with lying, cheating and with the numberless desires that had tortured her. She hated no one now; a twilight dimness was settling upon her thoughts, and, of all earthly noises, Emma heard none but the intermittent lamentations of this poor heart, sweet and remote like the echo of a symphony dying away.

"Bring me the child," she said, raising herself on her elbow.

"You're not feeling worse, are you?" asked Charles.

"No, no!"

The child, serious, and still half-asleep, was carried in on the maid's arm in her long white nightgown, from which her bare feet peeped out. She looked wonderingly at the disordered room, and half-closed her eyes, dazzled by the burning candles on the table. They reminded her, no doubt, of the morning of New Year's day and Mid-Lent, when thus awakened early by candlelight she came to her mother's bed to fetch her presents.

"But where is it, mamma?" she asked.

And as everybody was silent, "But I can't see my little stocking."

Félicité held her over the bed while she still kept looking towards the mantelpiece.

"Did nurse take it away?" she asked.

At the mention of this name, that carried her back to the memory of her adulteries and her calamities, Madame Bovary turned away her head, as at the loathing of another bitterer poison that rose to her mouth. But Berthe remained perched on the bed.

"Oh, how big your eyes are, mamma! How pale you are! how you sweat!"

Her mother looked at her.

"I'm frightened!" cried the child, recoiling.

Emma took her hand to kiss it; the child struggled.

"Enough! Take her away!" cried Charles, who was sobbing at the foot of the bed.

Then the symptoms ceased for a moment; she seemed less agitated; and at every insignificant word she spoke, every time she drew breath a little easier, his hopes revived. At last, when Canivet came in, he threw himself into his arms.

"Ah; it's you. Thank you! How good of you to come. But she's better. See! look at her."

His colleague was by no means of this opinion, and "never beating about the bush"—as he put it—he prescribed an emetic in order to empty the stomach completely.

She soon began vomiting blood. Her lips became drawn. Her limbs were convulsed, her whole body covered with brown spots, and her pulse slipped beneath the fingers like a stretched thread, like a harp-string about to break.

After this she began to scream horribly. She cursed the poison, railed at it, and implored it to be quick, and thrust away with her stiffened arms everything that Charles, in more agony than herself, tried to make her drink. He stood up, his handkerchief to his lips, moaning, weeping, and choked by sobs that shook his whole body. Félicité was running up and down the room. Homais, motionless, uttered great sighs; and Monsieur Canivet, always retaining his self-command, nevertheless began to feel uneasy.

"The devil! yet she has been purged, and since the cause has been removed . . ."

"The effect must cease," said Homais, "that's obvious."

"Oh, save her!" cried Bovary.

And, without listening to the pharmacist, who was still venturing the hypothesis. "It is perhaps a salutary paroxysm," Canivet was about to administer theriaca, when they heard the cracking of a whip; all the windows rattled, and a postchaise drawn by three horses abreast, up to their ears in mud, drove at a gallop round the corner of market. It was Doctor Larivière.

The apparition of a god would not have caused more commotion. Bovary raised his hands; Canivet stopped short; and Homais pulled off his cap long before the doctor had come in.

He belonged to that great school of surgeons created by Bichat,[68] to that generation, now extinct, of philosophical practitioners, who, cherishing their art with a fanatical love, exercised it with enthusiasm and wisdom. Every one in his hospital trembled when he was angry: and his students so revered him that they tried, as soon

68. Marie-Françoise-Xavier Bichat (1771–1802) was the author of an *Anatomie générale.*

as they were themselves in practice, to imitate him as much as possible. They could be found in all the neighboring towns wearing exactly the same merino overcoat and black frock. The doctor's buttoned cuffs slightly covered his fleshy hands—very beautiful hands, never covered by gloves, as though to be more ready to plunge into suffering. Disdainful of honors, of titles, and of academies, hospitable, generous, fatherly to the poor, and practising virtue without believing in it, he would almost have passed for a saint if the keenness of his intellect had not caused him to be feared as a demon. His glance, more penetrating than his scalpels, looked straight into your soul, and would detect any lie, regardless how well hidden. He went through life with the benign dignity that goes with the assurance of talent and wealth, with forty years of a hard-working, blameless life.

He frowned as soon as he had passed the door when he saw the cadaverous face of Emma stretched out on her back with her mouth open. Then, while apparently listening to Canivet, he rubbed his fingers up and down beneath his nostrils, repeating:

"I see, yes, yes . . ."

But he slowly shrugged his shoulders. Bovary watched him; they looked at one another; and this man, accustomed as he was to the sight of pain, could not keep back a tear that fell on his shirt front.

He tried to take Canivet into the next room. Charles followed him.

"She is sinking, isn't she? If we put on poultices? Anything! Oh, think of something, you who have saved so many!"

Charles put both arms around him, and looked at him in anxious supplication, half-fainting against his breast.

"Come, my poor boy, courage! There is nothing more to be done."

And Doctor Larivière turned away.

"You are leaving?"

"I'll be back."

He went out as if to give an order to the coachman, followed by Canivet, who was equally glad to escape from the spectacle of Emma dying.

The pharmacist caught up with them on the Square. He could not by temperament keep away from celebrities, so he begged Monsieur Larivière to do him the signal honor of staying for lunch.

He sent quickly to the "Lion d'Or" for some pigeons; to the butcher's for all the cutlets that could be found; to Tuvache for cream; and to Lestiboudois for eggs; and Homais himself aided in the preparations, while Madame Homais was saying as she tightened her apron-strings:

"I hope you'll forgive us, sir, for in this village, if one is caught unawares . . ."

"Stemmed glasses!" whispered Homais.

"If only we were in the city, I'd be able to find stuffed pig's feet . . ."

"Be quiet . . . Please doctor, à table!"

He thought fit, after the first few mouthfuls, to supply some details about the catastrophe.

"We first had a feeling of siccity in the pharynx, then intolerable pains at the epigastrium, super-purgation, coma."

"But how did she poison herself?"

"I don't know, doctor, and I don't even know where she can have procured the arsenious acid."

Justin, who was just bringing in a pile of plates, began to tremble.

"What's the matter?" said the pharmacist.

At this question the young man dropped the whole lot on the floor with a dreadful crash.

"Imbecile!" cried Homais, "clumsy lout! blockhead! confounded ass!"

But suddenly controlling himself:

"I wished, doctor, to make an analysis, and *primo* I delicately introduced a tube . . ."

"You would have done better," said the physician, "to introduce your fingers into her throat."

His colleague was silent, having just before privately received a severe lecture about his emetic, so that this good Canivet, so arrogant and so verbose at the time of the club-foot, was to-day very modest. He smiled an incessantly approving smile.

Homais dilated in Amphitryonic pride,[69] and the affecting thought of Bovary vaguely contributed to his pleasure by a kind ot selfish comparison with his own lot. Moreover, the presence of the surgeon exalted him. He displayed his erudition, spoke effusively about cantharides, upas, the manchineel, adder bites.

"I have even read that various persons have found themselves under toxicological symptoms, and, as it were, paralyzed by blood sausage that had been too strongly smoked. At least, this was stated in a very fine paper prepared by one of our pharmaceutical authorities, one of our masters, the illustrious Cadet de Gassicourt!"[70]

Madame Homais reappeared, carrying one of those shaky machines that are heated with spirits of wine; for Homais liked to make his coffee at the table, having, moreover, torrefied it, pulverised it, and mixed it himself.

69. Amphitryonic pride, a host's pride. *Amphitryon* is a comedy by Molière (1668). The verse:

Le véritable Amphitryon
Est l'Amphitryon où l'on dîne

has become a proverb. It means a man who brings companions to his table, a rich and powerful man whom we flatter.

70. Cadet de Gassicourt (1769–1821) was the pharmacist of Emperor Napoleon I who had considerable trouble under the Restoration because of his liberal ideas.

"*Saccharum*, doctor?" he said, offering sugar.

Then he had all his children brought down, anxious to have the physician's opinion on their constitutions.

At last Monsieur Larivière was about to leave, when Madame Homais asked for a consultation about her husband. He was making his blood too thick by falling asleep every evening after dinner.

"Oh, it isn't his blood I'd call too thick," said the physician.

And, smiling a little at his unnoticed joke, the doctor opened the door. But the shop was full of people; he had the greatest difficulty in getting rid of Monsieur Tuvache, who feared his wife would get pneumonia because she was in the habit of spitting on the ashes; then of Monseiur Binet, who sometimes experienced sudden attacks of great hunger; and of Madame Caron, who suffered from prickling sensations; of Lheureux, who had dizzy spells; of Lestiboudois, who had rheumatism; and of Madame Lefrançois, who had heartburn. At last the three horses started; and it was the general opinion that he had not shown himself at all obliging.

Public attention was distracted by the appearance of Monsieur Bournisien, who was going across the square carrying the holy oil.

Homais, as was due to his principles, compared priests to ravens attracted by the smell of death. The sight of an ecclesiastic was personally disagreeable to him, for the cassock made him think of the shroud, and his dislike of the one matched his fear of the other.

Nevertheless, not shrinking from what he called his "Mission," he returned to Bovary's house with Canivet, who had been strongly urged by Dr. Larivière to make this call; and he would, but for his wife's objections, have taken his two sons with him, in order to accustom them to great occasions; that this might be a lesson, an example, a solemn picture, that should remain in their heads later on.

The room when they went in was full of mournful solemnity. On the work-table, covered over with a white cloth, there were five or six small balls of cotton in a silver dish, near a large crucifix between two lighted candles.

Emma, her chin sunken upon her breast, had her eyes inordinately wide open, and her poor hands wandered over the sheets with that hideous and gentle movement of the dying, that seems as if they already wanted to cover themselves with the shroud. Pale as a statue and with eyes red as fire, Charles, beyond weeping, stood opposite her at the foot of the bed, while the priest, bending one knee, was muttering in a low voice.

She turned her face slowly, and seemed filled with joy on suddenly seeing the violet stole. She was doubtlessly reminded, in this moment of sudden serenity, of the lost bliss of her first mystical flights, mingling with the visions of eternal beatitude that were beginning.

The priest rose to take the crucifix; then she stretched forward her neck like one suffering from thirst, and glueing her lips to the body of the Man-God, she pressed upon it with all her expiring strength the fullest kiss of love that she had ever given. Then he recited the *Misereatur* and the *Indulgentiam*, dipped his right thumb in the oil, and began to give extreme unction. First, upon the eyes, that had so coveted all wordly goods; then upon the nostrils, that had been so greedy of the warm breeze and the scents of love; then upon the mouth, that had spoken lies, moaned in pride and cried out in lust; then upon the hands that had taken delight in the texture of sensuality; and finally upon the soles of the feet, so swift when she had hastened to satisfy her desires, and that would now walk no more.

The curé wiped his fingers, threw the bit of oil-stained cotton into the fire, and came and sat down by the dying woman, to tell her that she must now blend her sufferings with those of Jesus Christ and abandon herself to the divine mercy.

Finishing his exhortations, he tried to place in her hand a blessed candle, symbol of the celestial glory with which she was soon to be surrounded. Emma, too weak, could not close her fingers, and if it hadn't been for Monsieur Bournisien, the taper would have fallen to the ground.

Yet she was no longer quite so pale, and her face had an expression of serenity as if the sacrament had cured her.

The priest did not fail to point this out; he even explained to Bovary that the Lord sometimes prolonged the life of persons when he thought it useful for their salvation; and Charles remembered the day when, so near death, she had received communion. Perhaps there was no need to despair, he thought.

In fact, she looked around her slowly, as one awakening from a dream; then in a distinct voice she asked for her mirror, and remained bent over it for some time, until big tears fell from her eyes. Then she turned away her head with a sigh and fell back upon the pillows.

Her chest soon began heaving rapidly; the whole of her tongue protruded from her mouth; her eyes, as they rolled, grew paler, like the two globes of a lamp that is going out, so that one might have thought her already dead but for the fearful labouring of her ribs, shaken by violent breathing, as if the soul were struggling to free itself. Félicité knelt down before the crucifix, and the pharmacist himself slightly bent his knees, while Monsieur Canivet looked out vaguely at the Square. Bournisien had resumed his praying, his face bowed against the edge of the bed, his long black cassock trailing behind him in the room. Charles was on the other side, on his knees, his arms outstretched towards Emma. He had taken her hands and pressed them, shuddering at every heartbeat, as at the tremors of a falling ruin. As the death-rattle became stronger the priest prayed faster; his prayers mingled with Bovary's stifled sobs, and sometimes all seemed lost in the muffled murmur of the Latin syllables that sounded like a tolling bell.

Suddenly from the pavement outside came the loud noise of wooden shoes and the clattering of a stick; and a voice rose—a raucous voice—that sang

> Often the heat of a summer's day
> Makes a young girl dream her heart away.

Emma raised herself like a galvanised corpse, her hair streaming, her eyes fixed, staring.

> To gather up all the new-cut stalks
> Of wheat left by the scythe's cold swing,
> Nanette bends over as she walks
> Toward the furrows from where they spring.

"The blind man!" she cried.

And Emma began to laugh, an atrocious, frantic, desperate laugh, thinking she saw the hideous face of the poor wretch loom out of the eternal darkness like a menace.

> The wind blew very hard that day
> It blew her petticoat away.

A final spasm threw her back upon the mattress. They all drew near. She had ceased to exist.

IX

Someone's death always causes a kind of stupefaction; so difficult it is to grasp this advent of nothingness and to resign ourselves to the fact that it has actually taken place. But still, when he saw that she did not move, Charles flung himself upon her, crying:

"Farewell! farewell!"

Homais and Canivet dragged him from the room.

"Control yourself!"

"Yes," he said, struggling, "I'll be quiet. I won't do anything. But let me stay. I want to see her. She is my wife!"

And he wept.

"Cry," said the pharmacist; "let nature take its course; that will relieve you."

Weaker than a child, Charles let himself be led downstairs into the sitting-room, and Monsieur Homais soon went home. On the Square he was accosted by the blind man, who, having dragged himself as far as Yonville in the hope of getting the antiphlogistic salve, was asking every passer-by where the pharmacist lived.

"Good heavens, man, as if I didn't have other fish to fry! I can't help it, but you'll have to come back later."

And he hurried into the shop.

He had to write two letters, to prepare a soothing potion for Bovary, to invent some lie that would conceal the poisoning, and work it up into an article for the "Fanal," without counting the people who were waiting to get the news from him; and when the Yonvillers had all heard his story of the arsenic that she had mistaken for sugar in making a vanilla cream, Homais once more returned to Bovary's.

He found him alone (Monsieur Canivet had left), sitting in an arm-chair near the window, staring with a vacant look at the stone floor.

"Well," Homais said, "you ought yourself to fix the hour for the ceremony."

"Why? What ceremony?"

Then, in a stammering, frightened voice:

"Oh, no! not that. No! I want to keep her here."

Homais, to save face, took up a pitcher from the whatnot to water the geraniums.

"Ah! thank you," said Charles; "how kind of you!"

But he did not finish, choked by the flow of memories that Homais' action had released in him.

Then to distract him, Homais thought fit to talk a little about horticulture: plants wanted moisture. Charles bowed his head in approval.

"Besides, we'll soon be having fine weather again."

"Ah!" said Bovary.

The pharmacist, at his wit's end, gently drew aside the small window-curtain.

"Look! there's Monsieur Tuvache passing by."

Charles repeated mechanically:

"Monsieur Tuvache passing by!"

Homais did not dare to bring up the funeral arrangements again; it was the priest who finally convinced him of the necessity to bury Emma.

He shut himself up in his consulting-room, took a pen, and after sobbing for some time, wrote:

"I wish her to be buried in her wedding dress, with white shoes, and a wreath. Her hair is to be spread out over her shoulders. Three coffins, one oak, one mahogany, one of lead. Let no one try to overrule me; I shall have the strength to resist him. She is to be covered with a large piece of green velvet. This is my wish; see that it is done."

The two men were much taken aback by Bovary's romantic ideas. The pharmacist was first to remonstrate with him:

"This velvet seems excessive to me. Besides, think of the expense . . ."

"What's that to you?" cried Charles. "Leave me alone! You didn't love her. Go away!"

The priest took him by the arm for a walk in the garden. He discoursed on the vanity of earthly things. God was very great, very good: one must submit to his decrees without a murmur, even learn to be grateful for one's suffering.

Charles burst into blasphemy:

"I hate your God!"

"The spirit of rebellion is still upon you," sighed the priest.

Bovary was far away. He was striding along by the wall, near the espalier, and he ground his teeth; he raised to heaven looks of malediction, but not so much as a leaf stirred.

A fine rain was falling: Charles, whose chest was bare, at last began to shiver; he went in and sat down in the kitchen.

At six o'clock a noise like a clatter of old iron was heard on the square; it was the "Hirondelle" coming in, and he remained with his forehead pressed against the window-pane, watching all the passengers get out, one after the other. Félicité put down a mattress for him in the drawing-room. He threw himself upon it and fell asleep.

Although a philosopher, Monsieur Homais respected the dead. So bearing poor Charles no grudge, he returned in the evening to sit up with the body, bringing with him three books and a writing-pad for taking notes.

Monsieur Bournisien was there, and two large candles were burning at the head of the bed, which had been taken out of the alcove.

The pharmacist, unable to keep silent, soon began to express some regrets about this "unfortunate young woman," and the priest replied that there was nothing to do now but pray for her.

"Still," Homais insisted, "it is one of two things; either she died in a state of grace (as the Church calls it), and then she doesn't need our prayers; or else she died unrepentant (that is, I believe, the correct technical term), and then . . ."

Bournisien interrupted him, replying testily that it was none the less necessary to pray.

"But," the pharmacist objected, "since God knows all our needs, what can be the good of prayer?"

"What!" the priest exclaimed, "of prayer? Why, aren't you a Christian?"

"I beg your pardon," said Homais; "I admire Christianity. It freed the slaves, brought morality into the world . . ."

"That isn't the point. Look at the texts . . ."

"Oh! oh! As to texts, look at history; everybody knows that the Jesuits have falsified all the texts!"

Charles came in, and advancing towards the bed, slowly drew the curtains.

Emma's head was turned towards her right shoulder, the corner of her mouth, which was open, seemed like a black hole at the lower part of her face; her two thumbs were bent into the palms of her hands; a kind of white dust besprinkled her lashes, and her eyes were beginning to disappear in a viscous pallor, as if covered by a spiderweb. The sheet sunk in from her breast to her knees, and then rose at the tips of her toes, and it seemed to Charles that infinite masses, an enormous load, were weighing upon her.

The church clock struck two. They could hear the loud murmur of the river flowing in the darkness at the foot of the terrace. Monsieur Bournisien noisily blew his nose from time to time, and Homais' pen was scratching over the paper.

"Come, my good friend," he said, "don't stay here; the sight is too much for you."

When Charles had left, the pharmacist and the priest resumed their argument.

"Read Voltaire," said the one, "read D'Holbach, read the *Encyclopédie!*"[71]

"Read the 'Letters of some Portuguese Jews,' "[72] said the other; "read 'The Meaning of Christianity,'[73] by the former magistrate Nicolas."

They grew warm, they grew red, they both talked at once without listening to each other. Bournisien was scandalised at such audacity; Homais marvelled at such stupidity; and they were about to come to blows when Charles suddenly reappeared. He couldn't resist coming upstairs as though he were spellbound.

He stood at the foot of the bed to see her better, and he lost himself in a contemplation so deep that it was no longer painful.

He recalled stories of catalepsy, the marvels of magnetism, and he said to himself that by willing it with all his force he might perhaps succeed in reviving her. Once he even bent towards her, and cried in a low voice, "Emma! Emma!" His strong breathing made the flames of the candles tremble against the wall.

At daybreak the elder Madame Bovary arrived. As he embraced her, Charles burst into another flood of tears. She tried, as the pharmacist had done, to remonstrate with him on the expenses for the funeral. He became so angry that she was silent, and he even

71. Paul-Henri Dietrich, baron d' Holbach (1723–1789), friend and disciple of Diderot, was one of the most outspoken opponents of religion in the French Enlightenment. The *Encyclopédie*, a dictionary of the sciences, arts and letters, edited by Diderot and d'Alembert (1751–1772) is the intellectual monument of the French Enlightenment, a fountainhead of later secular and agnostic thought.

72. *Letters of Some Portuguese Jews* (1769) refers to a book by the Abbé Antoine Guéné directed against Voltaire.

73. *The Meaning of Christianity* is one of the many books defending Roman Catholicism by Jean-Jacques-Auguste Nicolas (1807–1888).

commissioned her to go to town at once and buy what was necessary.

Charles remained alone the whole afternoon; they had taken Berthe to Madame Homais'; Félicité was in the room upstairs with Madame Lefrançois.

In the evening he had some visitors. He rose and shook hands with them, unable to speak. Then they sat down together, and formed a large semicircle in front of the fire. With lowered head, they crossed and uncrossed their legs, and uttered from time to time a deep sigh. They were bored to tears, yet none would be the first to go.

Homais, when he returned at nine o'clock (for the last two days Homais seemed to have made the public Square his residence), was laden with a supply of camphor, benzoin and aromatic herbs. He also carried a large jar full of chlorine water, to keep off the miasma. Just then the servant, Madame Lefrançois and the elder Madame Bovary were busy getting Emma dressed, and they were drawing down the long stiff veil that covered her to her satin shoes.

Félicité was sobbing:

"Oh, my poor mistress! my poor mistress!"

"Look at her," said the innkeeper, sighing; "how pretty she still is! Now, couldn't you swear she was going to get up in a minute?"

Then they bent over her to put on her wreath. They had to raise the head a little, and a rush of black liquid poured from her mouth, as if she were vomiting.

"Heavens! Watch out for her dress!" cried Madame Lefrançois. "Now, just come and help us," she said to the pharmacist, "or are you afraid?"

"Afraid?" he replied, "I? As if I hadn't seen a lot worse when I was a student at the Hotel-Dieu. We used to make punch in the dissecting room! Nothingness does not frighten a philosopher; I have often said that I intend to leave my body to the hospitals, to serve the cause of science."

On arriving, the curé inquired after Monsieur Bovary and, at Homais' reply, he said:

"Of course, the blow is still too recent."

Then Homais congratulated him on not being exposed, like other people, to the loss of a beloved companion; this lead to a discussion on the celibacy of priests.

"You must admit," said the pharmacist, "that it is against nature for a man to do without women. There have been crimes . . ."

"For Heaven's sake!" exclaimed the priest, "how do you expect an individual who is married to keep the secrets of the confessional, for example?"

Homais attacked confession. Bournisien defended it; he discoursed on the acts of restitution that it brought about. He cited various anecdotes about thieves who had suddenly become honest. Military men on approaching the tribunal of penitence had finally seen the light. At Fribourg there was a minister . . .

His companion had fallen asleep. Then he felt somewhat stifled by the over-heavy atmosphere of the room; he opened the window; this awoke the pharmacist.

"Come, take a pinch of snuff," he told him. "Take it, it'll do you good."

A continual barking was heard in the distance.

"Do you hear that dog howling?" said the pharmacist.

"They smell the dead," replied the priest. "It's like bees; they leave their hives when there is a death in the neighborhood."

Homais failed to object to these prejudices, for he had again dropped asleep. Monsieur Bournisien, stronger than he, went on moving his lips and muttering for some time, then insensibly his chin sank down, he dropped his big black book, and began to snore.

They sat opposite one another, with bulging stomachs, puffed-up faces, and frowning looks, after so much disagreement uniting at last in the same human weakness, and they moved no more than the corpse by their side, that also seemed to be sleeping.

Charles coming in did not wake them. It was the last time; he came to bid her farewell.

The aromatic herbs were still smoking, and spirals of bluish vapour blended at the window with the entering fog. There were few stars, and the night was warm.

The wax of the candles fell in great drops upon the sheets of the bed. Charles watched them burn, straining his eyes in the glare of their yellow flame.

The watered satin of her gown shimmered white as moonlight. Emma was lost beneath it; and it seemed to him that, spreading beyond her own self, she blended confusedly with everything around her—the silence, the night, the passing wind, the damp odors rising from the ground.

Then suddenly he saw her in the garden at Tostes, on a bench against the thorn hedge, or else at Rouen in the streets, on the threshold of their house, in the yard at Bertaux. He again heard the laughter of the happy boys dancing under the appletrees: the room was filled with the perfume of her hair; and her dress rustled in his arms with a crackling noise. It was the same dress she was wearing now!

For a long while he thus recalled all his lost joys, her attitudes, her movements, the sound of her voice. Wave upon wave of despair came over him, like the tides of an overflowing sea.

He was seized by a terrible curiosity. Slowly, with the tips of his fingers, his heart pounding, he lifted her veil. But he uttered a cry of horror that awoke the other two.

They dragged him down into the sitting-room. Then Félicité came up to say that he wanted some of her hair.

"Cut some off," replied the pharmacist.

And as she did not dare to, he himself stepped forward, scissors in hand. He trembled so that he nicked the skin of the temple in several places. At last, stiffening himself against emotion, Homais gave two or three great cuts at random that left white patches amongst that beautiful black hair.

The pharmacist and the curé resumed their original occupations, not without time and again falling asleep—something of which they accused each other whenever they awoke. Monsieur Bournisien sprinkled the room with holy water and Homais threw a little chlorine on the floor.

Félicité had been so considerate as to put on the chest of drawers, for each of them, a bottle of brandy, some cheese, and a large brioche, and about four o'clock in the morning, unable to restrain himself any longer, the pharmacist sighed:

"I must say that I wouldn't mind taking some sustenance."

The priest did not need any persuading; he left to say mass and, upon his return, they ate and drank, chuckling a little without knowing why, stimulated by that vague gaiety that comes upon us after times of sadness. At the last glass the priest said to the pharmacist, as he clapped him on the shoulder:

"We'll end up good friends, you and I."

In the passage downstairs they met the undertaker's men, who were coming in. Then for two hours Charles had to suffer the torture of hearing the hammer resound against the wood. Next day they lowered her into her oak coffin, that was fitted into the other two; but as the bier was too large, they had to fill up the gaps with the wool of a mattress. At last, when the three lids had been planed down, nailed, soldered, it was placed outside in front of the door; the house was thrown open, and the people of Yonville began to flock round.

Old Rouault arrived, and fainted on the square at the sight of the black cloth.

X

He had only received Homais' letter thirty-six hours after the event; and, to cushion the blow, he had worded it in such a manner that it was impossible to make out just what had happened.

First, the old man had been shaken as if struck by apoplexy. Next, he understood that she was not dead, but she might be . . . At last, he had put on his smock, taken his hat, fastened his spurs to his boots, and set out at full speed; and the whole of the way old Rouault, panting, had been devoured by anxiety. He felt so dizzy that he was forced to dismount. He fancied he heard voices around him and thought he was losing his mind.

Day broke. He saw three black hens asleep in a tree. He shuddered, horrified at this omen. Then he promised the Holy Virgin three chasubles for the church, and vowed that he would go barefooted from the cemetery at Bertaux to the chapel of Vassonville.

He entered Maromme calling out ahead at the people of the inn, burst open the door with a thrust of his shoulder, made for a sack of oats and emptied a bottle of sweet cider into the manger; then he remounted his nag, whose feet struck sparks as it galloped along.

He told himself that they would certainly save her; the doctors were bound to discover a remedy. He remembered all the miraculous cures he had been told about.

Then she appeared to him dead: She was there, before his eyes, lying on her back in the middle of the road. He reined in his horse, and the hallucination disappeared.

At Quincampoix, to give himself heart, he drank three cups of coffee one after the other.

He imagined that they had written the wrong name on the letter. He looked for the letter in his pocket, felt it there, but did not dare to open it.

At last he began to think it was all a bad joke, a spiteful farce, somebody's idea of a fine prank; besides, if she were dead, he would have known. It couldn't be! the countryside looked as usual: the sky was blue, the trees swayed; a flock of sheep passed by. He reached the village; they saw him coming, hunched over his horse, whipping it savagely till its saddle-girths dripped with blood.

When he recovered consciousness, he fell, weeping, into Bovary's arms:

"My daughter! Emma! my child! tell me . . ."

The other replied between sobs:

"I don't know! I don't know! It's a curse!"

The pharmacist pulled them apart.

"Spare him the horrible details. I'll tell monsieur all about it. People are coming, show some dignity, for heaven's sake! Let's behave like philosophers."

Poor Charles tried as hard as he could, and repeated several times:

"Yes, be brave . . ."

"Damn it, I'll be brave," cried the old man, "I'll stay with her till the end!"

The bell was tolling. All was ready; they had to start.

Seated together in a stall of the choir, they saw the three chanting choristers continually pass and repass in front of them. The serpent-player was blowing with all his might. Monsieur Bournisien, in full regalia, was singing in a shrill voice. He bowed before the tabernacle, raising his hands, stretched out his arms. Lestiboudois went about the church with his verger's staff. The bier stood near the lectern, between four rows of candles. Charles felt an urge to get up and put them out.

Yet he tried to stir into himself the proper devotional feelings, to throw himself into the hope of a future life in which he would see her again. He tried to convince himself that she had gone on a long journey, far away, for a long time. But when he thought of her lying there, and that it was all over and that they would put her in the earth, he was seized with a fierce, gloomy, desperate rage. It seemed at times that he felt nothing, and he welcomed this lull in his pain, while blaming himself bitterly for being such a scoundrel.

The sharp noise of an iron-tipped stick was heard on the stones, striking them at irregular intervals. It came from the end of the church, and stopped short at the lower aisles. A man in a coarse brown jacket knelt down painfully. It was Hippolyte, the stable-boy at the "Lion d'Or." He had put on his new leg.

One of the choir boys came round the nave taking collection, and the coppers chinked one after the other on the silver plate.

"Oh hurry up!" cried Bovary, angrily throwing him a five-franc piece. "I can't stand it any longer."

The singer thanked him with a deep bow.

They sang, they knelt, they stood up; it was endless! He remembered how once, in the early days of their marriage, they had been to mass together, and they had sat down on the other side, on the right, by the wall. The bell began again. There was a great shuffling of chairs; the pall bearers slipped their three poles under the coffin, and every one left the church.

Then Justin appeared in the doorway of the pharmacy, but retreated suddenly, pale and staggering.

People stood at the windows to see the procession pass by. Charles walked first, as straight as he could. He tried to look brave and nodded to those who joined the crowd, coming from the side streets or from the open doors. The six men, three on either side, walked slowly, panting a little. The priests, the choristers, and the two choir-boys recited the *De profundis*, and their voices echoed over the fields, rising and falling with the shape of the hills. Sometimes they disappeared in the windings of the path; but the great silver cross always remained visible among the trees.

The women followed, wearing black coats with turned-down hoods; each of them carried a large lighted candle, and Charles felt himself grow faint at this continual repetition of prayers and torchlights, oppressed by the sweetish smell of wax and of cassocks. A fresh breeze was blowing; the rye and colza were turning green and along the roadside, dewdrops hung from the hawthorn hedges. All sorts of joyous sounds filled the air; the jolting of a cart rolling way off in the ruts, the crowing of a cock, repeated again and again, or the gamboling of a foal under the apple-trees. The pure sky was dappled with rosy clouds; a blueish haze hung over the iris-covered cottages. Charles recognized each courtyard as he passed. He remembered mornings like this, when, after visiting a patient, he left one of those houses to return home, to his wife.

The black cloth decorated with silver tears, flapped from time to time in the wind, baring the coffin underneath. The tired bearers walked more slowly, and the bier advanced jerkily, like a boat that pitches with every wave.

They reached the cemetery.

The men went right down to a place in the grass where a grave had been dug. They grouped themselves all round; and while the priest spoke, the red soil thrown up at the sides kept noiselessly slipping down at the corners.

Then, when the four ropes were laid out, the coffin was pushed onto them. He watched it go down; it seemed to go down forever.

At last a thud was heard; the ropes creaked and were drawn up. Then Bournisien took the spade handed to him by Lestiboudois; while his right hand kept sprinkling holy water, he vigorously threw in a spadeful of earth with the left; and the wood of the coffin, struck by the pebbles, gave forth that dread sound that seems to us the reverberation of eternity.

The priest passed the holy water sprinkler to his neighbor, Monsieur Homais. The pharmacist swung it gravely, then handed it to Charles, who sank to his knees and threw in handfuls of earth, crying, "Adieu!" He sent her kisses; he dragged himself towards the grave, as if to engulf himself with her.

They led him away, and he soon grew calmer, feeling perhaps, like the others, a vague satisfaction that it was all over.

Old Rouault on his way back began quietly smoking a pipe, to Homais' silent disapproval. He also noticed that Monsieur Binet had not come, that Tuvache had disappeared after mass, and that Theodore, the notary's servant, wore a blue coat—"as if he couldn't respect customs, and wear a black coat, for Heaven's sake!" And to share his observations with others he went from group to group. They were deploring Emma's death, especially Lheureux, who had not failed to come to the funeral.

"Poor little lady! What a blow for her husband!"

"Can you imagine," the pharmacist replied, "that he would have done away with himself if I hadn't intervened?"

"Such a fine person! To think that I saw her only last Saturday in my store."

"I haven't had leisure," said Homais, "to prepare a few words that I would cast over her tomb."

On getting home, Charles undressed, and old Rouault put on his blue smock. It was new, and as he had repeatedly wiped his eyes on the sleeves during his journey, the dye had stained his face, and traces of tears lined the layer of dust that covered it.

Mother Bovary joined them. All three were silent. At last the old man sighed:

"Do you remember, my friend, I came to Tostes once when you had just lost your first deceased? I consoled you that time. I could think of something to say then, but now . . ."

Then, with a loud groan that shook his whole chest,

"Ah! this is the end for me! I saw my wife go . . . then my son . . . and now today my daughter!"

He wanted to go back at once to Bertaux, saying that he couldn't sleep in this house. He even refused to see his grand-daughter.

"No, no! It would grieve me too much. You'll kiss her many times for me. Good bye . . . You're a good man! And I'll never forget this," he said, slapping his thigh. "Never fear, you shall always have your turkey."

But when he reached the top of the hill he turned back, as he had turned once before on the road of Saint-Victor when he had parted from her. The windows of the village were all ablaze in the slanting rays of the sun that was setting behind the meadow. He put his hand over his eyes, and saw at the horizon a walled enclosure, with black clusters of trees among the white stones; then he went on his way at a gentle trot, for his nag was limping.

Despite their fatigue, Charles and his mother stayed up talking very long that evening. They spoke of the days of the past and of the future. She would come to live at Yonville; she would keep house for him; they would never part again. She was subtly affectionate, rejoicing in her heart at regaining some of the tenderness that had wandered from her for so many years. Midnight struck. The village was silent as usual, and Charles lay awake, never ceasing to think of her.

Rodolphe, who, to distract himself, had been roaming in the woods all day, was quietly asleep in his château; and Léon, away in the city, also slept.

There was another who at that hour was not asleep.

On the grave between the pine-trees a child was on his knees weeping, and his heart, rent by sobs, was panting in the dark under the weight of an immense sorrow, tender as the moon and unfathomable as the night.

The gate suddenly grated. It was Lestiboudois coming to fetch the spade he had forgotten. He recognised Justin climbing over the wall, and knew at last who had been stealing his potatoes.

XI

The next day Charles had the child brought back. She asked for her mamma. They told her she was away; that she would bring her back some toys. Berthe mentioned her again several times, then finally forgot her. The child's gaiety broke Bovary's heart, and he had to put up besides with the intolerable consolations of the pharmacist.

Before long, money troubles started again. Monsieur Lheureux was putting his friend Vinçart back on the warpath, and before long Charles was signing notes for exorbitant amounts. For he would never consent to let the smallest of the things that had belonged to *her* be sold. His mother was exasperated with him; he grew even more angry than she did. He was a changed man. She left the house.

Then every one began to collect what they could. Mademoiselle Lempereur presented a bill for six months' teaching, although Emma had never taken a lesson (despite the receipted bill she had shown Bovary); it was an arrangement between the two women. The lending library demanded three years' subscriptions; Mère Rollet claimed postage for some twenty letters, and when Charles asked for an explanation, she was tactful enough to reply:

"Oh, I know nothing about it. It was her business."

With every debt he paid Charles thought he had reached the end. But others followed ceaselessly.

He tried to collect accounts due him from patients. He was shown the letters his wife had written. Then he had to apologise.

Félicité now wore Madame Bovary's dresses; not all, for he had kept some, and he locked himself up in Emma's room to look at them. Félicité was about her former mistress's height and often, on seeing her from behind, Charles thought she had come back and cried out:

"Oh, stay, don't go away!"

But at Pentecost she ran away from Yonville, carried off by Theodore, stealing all that was left of the wardrobe.

It was about this time that the widow Dupuis had the honor to inform him of the "marriage of Monsieur Léon Dupuis her son, notary at Yvetot, to Mademoiselle Léocadié Lebœuf Bondeville." Charles, among the other congratulations he sent him, wrote this sentence:

"How happy this would have made my poor wife!"

One day when, wandering aimlessly about the house, he had gone up to the attic, he felt a crumpled piece of paper under his slipper. He opened it and read: "Courage, Emma, courage. I would not bring misery into your life." It was Rodolphe's letter, fallen to the ground between the boxes, where it had remained till now, when the wind from the open dormer had blown it toward the door. And Charles stood, motionless and staring, in the very same place where, long ago, Emma, in despair, and paler even than he had thought of dying. At last he discovered a small R at the bottom of the second page. What did this mean? He remembered Rodolphe's attentions, his sudden disappearance, his embarrassed air on two or three subsequent occasions. But the respectful tone of the letter deceived him.

"Perhaps they loved one another platonically," he told himself.

Besides, Charles was not of those who go to the root of things; he shrank from the proofs, and his vague jealousy was lost in the immensity of his sorrow.

Every one, he thought, must have adored her; all men inevitably must have coveted her. This made her seem even more beautiful, and it awoke in him a fierce and persistent desire, which inflamed his despair and grew boundless, since it could never be assuaged.

To please her, as if she were still living, he adopted her taste, her ideas; he bought patent leather boots and took to wearing white cravats. He waxed his moustache and, just like her, signed promissory notes. She corrupted him from beyond the grave.

He was obliged to sell his silver piece by piece; next he sold the drawing-room furniture. All the rooms were stripped; but the bedroom, her own room, remained as before. After his dinner Charles went up there. He pushed the round table in front of the fire, and drew up *her* arm-chair. He sat down facing it. A candle burnt in one of the gilt candlesticks. Berthe, at his side, colored pictures.

He suffered, poor man, at seeing her so badly dressed, with laceless boots, and the arm-holes of her pinafore torn down to the hips; for the cleaning woman took no care of her. But she was so sweet, so pretty, and her little head bent forward so gracefully, letting her fair hair fall over her rosy cheeks, that an infinite joy came upon him, a happiness mingled with bitterness, like those ill-made wines that taste of resin. He mended her toys, made her puppets from cardboard, or sewed up half-torn dolls. Then, if his eyes fell upon the sewing kit, a ribbon lying about, or even a pin left in a crack of the table, he began to dream, and looked so sad that she became as sad as he.

No one now came to see them, for Justin had run away to Rouen, where he worked in a grocery, and the pharmacist's children saw less and less of the child. In view of the difference in their social positions, Monsieur Homais had chosen to discontinue the former intimacy.

The blind man, whom his salve had not cured, had gone back to the hill of Bois-Guillaume, where he told the travellers of his failure, to such an extent, that Homais when he went to town hid himself behind the curtains of the "Hirondelle" to avoid meeting him. He detested him, and wishing, in the interests of his own reputation, to get rid of him at all costs, he directed against him a secret campaign, that betrayed the depth of his intellect and the baseness of his vanity. Thus, for six consecutive months, one could read in the "Fanal de Rouen" editorials such as these:

"Anyone who has ever wended his way towards the fertile plains of Picardy has, no doubt, remarked, by the Bois-Guillaume hill, an unfortunate wretch suffering from a horrible facial wound. He bothers the passers by, pursues them and levies a regular tax on all travellers. Are we still living in the monstrous times of the Middle Ages, when vagabonds were permitted to display in our public places leprosy and scrofulas they had brought back from the Crusades?"

Or:

"In spite of the laws against vagrancy, the approaches to our great towns continue to be infected by bands of beggars. Some are seen going about alone, and these are, by no means, the least dangerous. Why don't our City Authorities intervene?"

Then Homais invented incidents:

"Yesterday, by the Bois-Guillaume hill, a skittish horse . . ." And then followed the story of an accident caused by the presence of the blind man.

He managed so well that the fellow was locked up. But he was released. He began again, and so did Homais. It was a struggle. Homais won out, for his foe was condemned to lifelong confinement in an asylum.

This success emboldened him, and henceforth there was no longer a dog run over, a barn burnt down, a woman beaten in the parish, of which he did not immediately inform the public, guided always by the love of progress and the hatred of priests. He instituted comparisons between the public and parochial schools to the detriment of the latter; called to mind the massacre of St. Bartholomew *à propos* of a grant of one hundred francs to the church; denounced abuses and kept people on their toes. That was his phrase. Homais was digging and delving; he was becoming dangerous.

However, he was stifling in the narrow limits of journalism, and soon a book, a major work, became a necessity. Then he composed "General Statistics of the Canton of Yonville, followed by Climatological Remarks." The statistics drove him to philosophy. He busied himself with great questions: the social problem, the moral plight of the poorer classes, pisciculture, rubber, railways, &c. He even began to blush at being a bourgeois. He affected bohemian manners, he smoked. He bought two *chic* Pompadour statuettes to adorn his drawing-room.

He by no means gave up his store. On the contrary, he kept well abreast of new discoveries. He followed the great trend towards chocolates; he was the first to introduce *Cho-ca* and *Revalenta* into the Seine-Inférieure. He was enthusiastic about the hydro-electric Pulvermacher health-belts; he wore one himself, and when at night he took off his flannel undershirt, Madame Homais was dazzled by the golden spiral that almost hid him from view. Her ardor would redouble for that man, swaddled more than a Scythian and as resplendent as one of the Magi.

He had fine ideas about Emma's tomb. First he proposed a broken column surmounted by a drapery, next a pyramid, then a Temple of Vesta, a sort of rotunda . . . or else a large pile of ruins. And in all his plans Homais always stuck to the weeping willow, which he looked upon as the indispensable symbol of sorrow.

Charles and he made a journey to Rouen together to look at some tombs, accompanied by an artist, one Vaufrylard, a friend of Bridoux's, who never ceased to make puns. At last, after having examined some hundred drawings, having ordered an estimate and made another journey to Rouen, Charles decided in favor of a mausoleum, whose two principal sides were to be decorated with "a spirit bearing an extinguished torch."

As to the inscription, Homais could think of nothing finer than *Sta viator*,[74] and he got no further; he racked his brain in vain; all that he could come up with was *Sta viator*. At last he hit upon *Amabilem conjugem calcas*,[75] which was adopted.

A strange thing was happening to Bovary: while continually thinking of Emma, he was nevertheless forgetting her. He grew desperate as he felt this image fading from his memory in spite of all efforts to retain it. Yet every night he dreamt of her; it was always the same dream. He approached her, but when he was about to embrace her she fell into decay in his arms.

For a week he was seen going to church in the evening. Monsieur Bournisien even paid him two or three visits, then gave him up. Moreover, the old man was growing bigoted and fanatic, according to Homais. He thundered against the spirit of the age, and never failed, every other week, in his sermon, to recount the death agony of Voltaire, who died devouring his excrements, as every one knows.

In spite of Bovary's thrifty life, he was far from being able to pay off his old debts. Lheureux refused to renew any more notes. Execution became imminent. Then he appealed to his mother, who consented to let him take a mortgage on her property, but with a great

74. *Sta viator*, "Stop, traveler."

75. *Amabilem conjugem calcas*, "you are treading upon the beloved spouse."

many recriminations against Emma; and in return for her sacrifice she asked for a shawl that had escaped from Félicité's raids. Charles refused to give it to her; they quarrelled.

She made the first peace overtures by offering to let the little girl, who could help her in the house, live with her. Charles consented to this, but when the time for parting came, all his courage failed him. Then there was a final, complete break between them.

As his affections vanished, he clung more closely to the love of his child. She worried him, however, for she coughed sometimes, and had red patches on her cheeks.

Across the square, facing his house, the prospering family of the pharmacist was more flourishing and thriving than ever. Napoleon helped him in the laboratory, Athalie embroidered him a skullcap, Irma cut out rounds of paper to cover the preserves, and Franklin recited the tables of Pythagoras by rote, without the slightest hesitation. He was the happiest of fathers, the most fortunate of men.

Not quite, however! A secret ambition devoured him. Homais hankered after the cross of the Legion of Honour. He had plenty of claims to it.

"First, having at the time of the cholera distinguished myself by a boundless devotion; second, by having published, at my expense, various works of public usefulness, such as" (and he recalled his pamphlet entitled, *On Cider, its Manufacture and Effects,* besides observations on the wooly aphis that he had sent to the Academy; his volume of statistics, and down to his pharmaceutical thesis); "without counting that I am a member of several learned societies" (he was member of a single one).

"And if this won't do," he said, turning on his heels, "there always is the assistance I give at fires!"

Homais' next step was trying to win over the Government to his cause. He secretly did the prefect several favors during the elections. He sold, in a word, prostituted himself. He even addressed a petition to the sovereign in which he implored him to "do him justice;" he called him "our good king," and compared him to Henri IV.

And every morning the pharmacist rushed for the paper to see if his nomination appeared. It was never there. At last, unable to bear it any longer, he had a grass plot in his garden designed to represent the Star of the Cross of Honour, with two little strips of grass running from the top to imitate the ribbon. He walked round it with folded arms, meditating on the folly of the Government and the ingratitude of men.

Out of respect, or because he took an almost sensuous pleasure in dragging out his investigations, Charles had not yet opened the secret drawer of Emma's rosewood desk. One day, however, he sat down before it, turned the key, and pressed the spring. All Léon's letters were there. There could be no doubt this time. He devoured them to the very last, ransacked every corner, all the furniture, all the drawers, behind the walls, sobbing and shouting in mad distress. He discovered a box and kicked it open. Rodolphe's portrait flew out at him, from among the pile of love-letters.

People wondered at his despondency. He never went out, saw no one, refused even to visit his patients. Then they said "he shut himself up to drink."

At times, however, someone would climb on the garden hedge, moved by curiosity. They would stare in amazement at this long-bearded, shabbily clothed, wild figure of a man, who wept aloud as he walked up and down.

On summer evenings, he would take his little girl with him to visit the cemetery. They came back at nightfall, when the only light left in the village was that in Binet's window.

He was unable, however, to savor his grief to the full, for he had no one to share it with. He paid visits to Madame Lefrançois to be able to speak of *her*. But the innkeeper only listened with half an ear, having troubles of her own. For Monsieur Lheureux had finally set up his own business, *les Favorites du Commerce*, and Hivert, every one's favorite messenger, threatened to go to work for the competition unless he received higher wages.

One day when he had gone to the market at Argueil to sell his horse—his last resource—he met Rodolphe.

They both turned pale when they caught sight of one another. Rodolphe, who had only sent his card for the funeral, first stammered some apologies, then grew bolder, and even invited Charles (it was in the month of August and very hot) to share a bottle of beer with him at the terrace of a café.

Leaning his elbows on the table, he chewed his cigar as he talked, and Charles was lost in reverie at the sight of the face she had loved. He seemed to find back something of her there. It was quite a shock to him. He would have liked to have been this man.

The other went on talking of agriculture, cattle and fertilizers, filling with banalities all the gaps where an allusion might slip in. Charles was not listening to him; Rodolphe noticed it, and he could follow the sequence of memories that crossed his face. This face gradually reddened; Charles's nostrils fluttered, his lips quivered. For a moment, Charles stared at him in somber fury and Rodolphe, startled and terrified, stopped talking. But soon the same look of mournful weariness returned to his face.

"I can't blame you for it," he said.

Rodolphe remained silent. And Charles, his head in his hands, went on in a broken voice, with the resigned accent of infinite grief:

"No, I can't blame you any longer."

He even made a phrase, the only one he'd ever made:

"Fate willed it this way."

Rodolphe, who had been the agent of this fate, thought him very meek for a man in his situation, comic even and slightly despicable.

The next day Charles sat down on the garden seat under the arbor. Rays of light were straying through the trellis, the vine leaves threw their shadows on the sand, jasmines perfumed the blue air, Spanish flies buzzed round the lilies in bloom, and Charles was panting like an adolescent under the vague desires of love that filled his aching heart.

At seven o'clock little Berthe who had not seen him all afternoon, came to fetch him for dinner.

His head was leaning against the wall, with closed eyes and open mouth, and in his hand was a long tress of black hair.

"Papa, come!"

And thinking he wanted to play, she gave him a gentle push. He fell to the ground. He was dead.

Thirty-six hours later, at the pharmacist's request, Monsieur Canivet arrived. He performed an autopsy, but found nothing.

When everything had been sold, there remained twelve francs and seventy-five centimes, just enough to send Mademoiselle Bovary off to her grandmother. The woman died the same year; and since Rouault was paralyzed, it was an aunt who took charge of her. She is poor, and sends her to a cotton-mill to earn a living.

Since Bovary's death three doctors have succeeded one another in Yonville without any success, so effectively did Homais hasten to eradicate them. He has more customers than there are sinners in hell; the authorities treat him kindly and he has the public on his side.

He has just been given the cross of the Legion of Honor.

FYODOR DOSTOEVSKY

(1821–1881)

Notes from Underground* [1]

Part I

UNDERGROUND

I

I am a sick man. . . . I am a spiteful man. I am an unattractive man. I believe my liver is diseased. However, I know nothing at all about my disease, and do not know for certain what ails me. I don't consult a doctor for it, and never have, though I have a respect for medicine and doctors. Besides, I am extremely superstitious, sufficiently so to respect medicine, anyway (I am well-educated enough not to be superstitious, but I am superstitious). No, I refuse to consult a doctor from spite. That you probably will not understand. Well, I understand it, though. Of course I can't explain who it is precisely that I am mortifying in this case by my spite: I am perfectly well aware that I cannot "pay out" the doctors by not consulting them; I know better than any one that by all this I am only injuring myself and no one else. But still, if I don't consult a doctor it is from spite. My liver is bad, well—let it get worse!

I have been going on like that for a long time—twenty years. Now I am forty. I used to be in the government service, but am no longer. I was a spiteful official. I was rude and took pleasure in being so. I did not take bribes, you see, so I was bound to find a recompense in that, at least. (A poor jest, but I will not scratch it out. I wrote it thinking it would sound very witty; but now that I have seen myself that I only wanted to show off in a despicable way, I will not scratch it out on purpose!)

When petitioners used to come for information to the table at which I sat, I used to grind my teeth at them, and felt intense enjoyment when I succeeded in making anybody unhappy. I almost always did succeed. For the most part they were all timid people—

* 1864. Translated by Constance Garnett. Reprinted in full. The punctuation ". . ." does not indicate omissions from this text.

1. The author of the diary and the diary itself are, of course, imaginary. Nevertheless it is clear that such persons as the writer of these notes not only may, but positively must, exist in our society, when we consider the circumstances in the midst of which our society is formed. I have tried to expose to the view of the public more distinctly than is commonly done, one of the characters of the recent past. He is one of the representatives of a generation still living. In this fragment, entitled "Underground," this person introduces himself and his views, and, as it were, tries to explain the causes owing to which he has made his appearance and was bound to make his appearance in our midst. In the second fragment there are added the actual notes of this person concerning certain events in his life. [Author's note.]

of course, they were petitioners. But of the uppish ones there was one officer in particular I could not endure. He simply would not be humble, and clanked his sword in a disgusting way. I carried on a feud with him for eighteen months over that sword. At last I got the better of him. He left off clanking it. That happened in my youth, though.

But do you know, gentlemen, what was the chief point about my spite? Why, the whole point, the real sting of it lay in the fact that continually, even in the moment of the acutest spleen, I was inwardly conscious with shame that I was not only not a spiteful but not even an embittered man, that I was simply scaring sparrows at random and amusing myself by it. I might foam at the mouth, but bring me a doll to play with, give me a cup of tea with sugar in it, and maybe I should be appeased. I might even be genuinely touched, though probably I should grind my teeth at myself afterwards and lie awake at night with shame for months after. That was my way.

I was lying when I said just now that I was a spiteful official. I was lying from spite. I was simply amusing myself with the petitioners and with the officer, and in reality I never could become spiteful. I was conscious every moment in myself of many, very many elements absolutely opposite to that. I felt them positively swarming in me, these opposite elements. I knew that they had been swarming in me all my life and craving some outlet from me, but I would not let them, would not let them, purposely would not let them come out. They tormented me till I was ashamed: they drove me to convulsions and—sickened me, at last, how they sickened me! Now, are not you fancying, gentlemen, that I am expressing remorse for something now, that I am asking your forgiveness for something? I am sure you are fancying that . . . However, I assure you I do not care if you are. . . .

It was not only that I could not become spiteful, I did not know how to become anything: neither spiteful nor kind, neither a rascal nor an honest man, neither a hero nor an insect. Now, I am living out my life in my corner, taunting myself with the spiteful and useless consolation that an intelligent man cannot become anything seriously, and it is only the fool who becomes anything. Yes, a man in the nineteenth century must and morally ought to be pre-eminently a characterless creature; a man of character, an active man is pre-eminently a limited creature. That is my conviction of forty years. I am forty years old now, and you know forty years is a whole lifetime; you know it is extreme old age. To live longer than forty years is bad manners, is vulgar, immoral. Who lives beyond forty? Answer that, sincerely and honestly. I will tell you who do: fools and worthless fellows. I tell all old men that to their face, all these venerable old men, all these silver-haired and reverend seniors! I tell the whole world that to its face! I have a right to say so, for I shall go on living to sixty myself. To seventy! To eighty! . . . Stay, let me take breath. . . .

You imagine no doubt, gentlemen, that I want to amuse you. You are mistaken in that, too. I am by no means such a mirthful person as you imagine, or as you may imagine; however, irritated by all this babble (and I feel that you are irritated) you think fit to ask me who am I—then my answer is, I am a collegiate assessor. I was in the service that I might have something to eat (and solely for that reason), and when last year a distant relation left me six thousand roubles in his will I immediately retired from the service and settled down in my corner. I used to live in this corner before, but now I have settled down in it. My room is a wretched, horrid one in the outskirts of the town. My servant is an old country-woman, ill-natured from stupidity, and, moreover, there is always a nasty smell about her. I am told that the Petersburg climate is bad for me, and that with my small means it is very expensive to live in Petersburg. I know all that better than all these sage and experienced counsellors and monitors. . . . But I am remaining in Petersburg; . . . I am not going away from Petersburg! I am not going away because . . . ech! Why, it is absolutely no matter whether I am going away or not going away.

But what can a decent man speak of with most pleasure?

Answer: Of himself.

Well, so I will talk about myself.

II

I want now to tell you, gentlemen, whether you care to hear it or not, why I could not even become an insect. I tell you solemnly, that I have many times tried to become an insect. But I was not equal even to that. I swear, gentlemen, that to be too conscious is an illness—a real thoroughgoing illness. For man's everyday needs, it would have been quite enough to have the ordinary human consciousness, that is, half or a quarter of the amount which falls to the lot of a cultivated man of our unhappy nineteenth century, especially one who has the fatal ill-luck to inhabit Petersburg, the most theoretical and intentional town on the whole terrestrial globe. (There are intentional and unintentional towns.) It would have been quite enough, for instance, to have the consciousness by which all so-called direct persons and men of action live. I bet you think I am writing all this from affectation, to be witty at the expense of men of action; and what is more, that from ill-bred affectation, I am clanking a sword like my officer. But, gentlemen, whoever can pride himself on his diseases and even swagger over them?

Though, after all, every one does do that; people do pride themselves on their diseases, and I do, may be, more than any one else. We will not dispute it; my contention was absurd. But yet I am firmly persuaded that a great deal of consciousness, every sort of consciousness, in fact, is a disease. I stick to that. Let us leave that, too, for a minute. Tell me this: why does it happen that at the very, yes, at the very moments when I am most capable of feeling every refinement of all that is "good and beautiful," as they used to say at one time, it would, as though of design, happen to me not only to feel but to do such ugly things, such that . . . Well, in short, actions that all, perhaps, commit; but which, as though purposely, occurred to me at the very time when I was most conscious that they ought not to be committed. The more conscious I was of goodness and of all that was "good and beautiful," the more deeply I sank into my mire and the more ready I was to sink in it altogether. But the chief point was that all this was, as it were, not accidental in me, but as though it were bound to be so. It was as though it were my most normal condition, and not in the least disease or depravity, so that at last all desire in me to struggle against this depravity passed. It ended by my almost believing (perhaps actually believing) that this was perhaps my normal condition. But at first, in the beginning, what agonies I endured in that struggle! I did not believe it was the same with other people, and all my life I hid this fact about myself as a secret. I was ashamed (even now, perhaps, I am ashamed): I got to the point of feeling a sort of secret abnormal, despicable enjoyment in returning home to my corner on some disgusting Petersburg night, acutely conscious that that day I had committed a loathsome action again, that what was done could never be undone, and secretly, inwardly gnawing, gnawing at myself for it, tearing and consuming myself till at last the bitterness turned into a sort of shameful accursed sweetness, and at last—into positive real enjoyment! Yes into enjoyment, into enjoyment! I insist upon that. I have spoken of this because I keep wanting to know for a fact whether other people feel such enjoyment? I will explain; the enjoyment was just from the too intense consciousness of one's own degradation; it was from feeling oneself that one had reached the last barrier, that it was horrible, but that it could not be otherwise; that there was no escape for you; that you never could become a different man; that even if time and faith were still left you to change into something different you would most likely not wish to change; or if you did wish to, even then you would do nothing; because perhaps in reality there was nothing for you to change into.

And the worst of it was, and the root of it all, that it was all in accord with the normal fundamental laws of over-acute consciousness, and with the inertia that was the direct result of those laws, and that consequently one was not only unable to change but could do absolutely nothing. Thus it would follow, as the result of acute consciousness, that one is not to blame in being a scoundrel; as though that were any consolation to the scoundrel once he has come to realize that he actually is a scoundrel. But enough. . . . Ech, I have talked a lot of nonsense, but what have I explained? How is enjoyment in this to be explained? But I will explain it. I will get to the bottom of it! That is why I have taken up my pen. . . .

I, for instance, have a great deal of *amour propre.* I am as suspicious and prone to take offence as a hunchback or a dwarf. But upon my word I sometimes have had moments when if I had happened to be slapped in the face I should, perhaps, have been positively glad of it. I say, in earnest, that I should probably have been able to discover even in that a peculiar sort of enjoyment—the enjoyment, of course, of despair; but in despair there are the most intense enjoyments, especially when one is very acutely conscious of the hopelessness of one's position. And when one is slapped in the face—why then the consciousness of being rubbed into a pulp would positively overwhelm one. The worst of it is, look at it which way one will, it still turns out that I was always the most to blame in everything. And what is most humiliating of all, to blame for no fault of my own but, so to say, through the laws of nature. In the first place, to blame because I am cleverer than any of the people surrounding me. (I have always considered myself cleverer than any of the people surrounding me, and sometimes, would you believe it, have been positively ashamed of it. At any rate, I have all my life, as it were, turned my eyes away and never could look people straight in the face.) To blame, finally, because even if I had had magnanimity, I should only have had more suffering from the sense of its uselessness. I should certainly have never been able to do anything from being magnanimous—neither to forgive, for my assailant would perhaps have slapped me from the laws of nature, and one cannot forgive the laws of nature; nor to forget, for even if it were owing to the laws of nature, it is insulting all the same. Finally, even if I had wanted to be anything but magnanimous, had desired on the contrary to revenge myself on my assailant, I could not have revenged myself on any one for anything because I should certainly never have made up my mind to do anything, even if I had been able to. Why should I not have made up my mind? About that in particular I want to say a few words.

III

With people who know how to revenge themselves and to stand up for themselves in general, how is it done? Why, when they are possessed, let us suppose, by the feeling of revenge, then for the time there is nothing else but that feeling left in their whole being. Such a gentleman simply dashes straight for his object like an infuriated bull with its horns down, and nothing but a wall will stop him. (By the way: facing the wall, such gentlemen—that is, the "direct" persons and men of action—are genuinely nonplussed. For them a wall is not an evasion, as for us people who think and consequently do nothing; it is not an excuse for turning aside, an excuse for which we are always very glad, though we scarcely believe in it ourselves, as a rule. No, they are nonplussed in all sincerity. The wall has for them something tranquillizing, morally soothing, final—maybe even something mysterious . . . but of the wall later.)

Well, such a direct person I regard as the real normal man, as his tender mother nature wished to see him when she graciously brought him into being on the earth. I envy such a man till I am green in the face. He is stupid. I am not disputing that, but perhaps the normal man should be stupid, how do you know? Perhaps it is very beautiful, in fact. And I am the more persuaded of that suspicion, if one can call it so, by the fact that if you take, for instance, the antithesis of the normal man, that is, the man of acute consciousness, who has come, of course, not out of the lap of nature but out of a retort (this is almost mysticism, gentlemen, but I suspect this, too), this retort-made man is sometimes so nonplussed in the presence of his antithesis that with all his exaggerated consciousness he genuinely thinks of himself as a mouse and not a man. It may be an acutely conscious mouse, yet it is a mouse, while the other is a man, and therefore, et cætera, et cætera. And the worst of it is, he himself, his very own self, looks on himself as a mouse; no one asks him to do so; and that is an important point. Now let us look at this mouse in action. Let us suppose, for instance, that it feels insulted, too (and it almost always does feel insulted), and wants to revenge itself, too. There may even be a greater accumulation of spite in it than in *l'homme de la nature et de la vérité*.[2] The base and nasty desire to vent that spite on its assailant rankles perhaps even more nastily in it than in *l'homme de la nature et de la vérité*. For through his innate stupidity the latter looks upon his revenge as justice pure and simple; while in consequence of his acute consciousness the mouse does not be-

2. "the man of nature and truth"; Rousseau's description of himself in the *Confessions* (1781–1788), which created an enormous stir because they professed to tell the whole truth about the author and were sometimes self-accusing.

lieve in the justice of it. To come at last to the deed itself, to the very act of revenge. Apart from the one fundamental nastiness the luckless mouse succeeds in creating around it so many other nastinesses in the form of doubts and questions, adds to the one question so many unsettled questions that there inevitably works up around it a sort of fatal brew, a stinking mess, made up of its doubts, emotions, and of the contempt spat upon it by the direct men of action who stand solemnly about it as judges and arbitrators, laughing at it till their healthy sides ache. Of course the only thing left for it is to dismiss all that with a wave of its paw, and, with a smile of assumed contempt in which it does not even itself believe, creep ignominiously into its mouse-hole. There in its nasty, stinking, underground home our insulted, crushed and ridiculed mouse promptly becomes absorbed in cold, malignant and, above all, everlasting spite. For forty years together it will remember its injury down to the smallest, most ignominious details, and every time will add, of itself, details still more ignominious, spitefully teasing and tormenting itself with its own imagination. It will itself be ashamed of its imaginings, but yet it will recall it all, it will go over and over every detail, it will invent unheard of things against itself, pretending that those things might happen, and will forgive nothing. Maybe it will begin to revenge itself, too, but, as it were, piecemeal, in trivial ways, from behind the stove, incognito, without believing either in its own right to vengeance, or in the success of its revenge knowing that from all its efforts at revenge it will suffer a hundred times more than he on whom it revenges itself, while he, I daresay, will not even scratch himself. On its deathbed it will recall it all over again, with interest accumulated over all the years and. . . .

But it is just in that cold, abominable half despair, half belief, in that conscious burying oneself alive for grief in the underworld for forty years, in that acutely recognized and yet partly doubtful hopelessness of one's position, in that hell of unsatisfied desires turned inward, in that fever of oscillations, or resolutions determined for ever and repented of again a minute later—that the savour of that strange enjoyment of which I have spoken lies. It is so subtle, so difficult of analysis, that persons who are a little limited, or even simply persons of strong nerves, will not understand a single atom of it. "Possibly," you will add on your own account with a grin, "people will not understand it either who have never received a slap in the face," and in that way you will politely hint to me that I, too, perhaps, have had the experience of a slap in the face in my life, and so I speak as one who knows. I bet that you are thinking that. But set your minds at rest, gentlemen, I have not received a slap in the face, though it is absolutely a matter of indifference to me what you may think about it. Possibly, I even regret, myself, that I have given so few slaps in the face during my life. But enough . . . not another word on that subject of such extreme interest to you.

I will continue calmly concerning persons with strong nerves who do not understand a certain refinement of enjoyment. Though in certain circumstances these gentlemen bellow their loudest like bulls, though this, let us suppose, does them the greatest credit, yet, as I have said already, confronted with the impossible they subside at once. The impossible means the stone wall! What stone wall? Why, of course, the laws of nature, the deductions of natural science, mathematics. As soon as they prove to you, for instance, that you are descended from a monkey, then it is no use scowling, accept it for a fact. When they prove to you that in reality one drop of your own fat must be dearer to you than a hundred thousand of your fellow-creatures, and that this conclusion is the final solution of all so-called virtues and duties and all such prejudices and fancies, then you have just to accept it, there is no help for it, for twice two is a law of mathematics. Just try refuting it.

"Upon my word," they will shout at you, "it is no use protesting: it is a case of twice two makes four! Nature does not ask your permission, she has nothing to do with your wishes, and whether you like her laws or dislike them, you are bound to accept her as she is, and consequently all her conclusions. A wall, you see, is a wall . . ." and so on, and so on.

Merciful Heavens! but what do I care for the laws of nature and arithmetic, when, for some reason I dislike those laws and the fact that twice two makes four? Of course I cannot break through the wall by battering my head against it if I really have not the strength to knock it down, but I am not going to be reconciled to it simply because it is a stone wall and I have not the strength.

As though such a stone wall really were a consolation, and really did contain some word of conciliation, simply because it is as true as twice two makes four. Oh, absurdity of absurdities! How much better it is to understand it all, to recognize it all, all the impossibilities and the stone wall; not to be reconciled to one of those impossibilities and stone walls if it disgusts you to be reconciled to it; by the way of the most inevitable, logical combinations to reach the most revolting conclusions on the everlasting theme, that even for the stone wall you are yourself somehow to blame, though again it is as clear as day you are not to blame in the least, and therefore grinding your teeth in silent impotence to sink into luxurious inertia, brooding on the fact that there is no one even for you to feel vindictive against, that you have not, and perhaps never will have, an object for your spite, that it is a sleight of hand, a bit of juggling, a card-sharper's trick, that it is simply a mess, no knowing what and no knowing who, but in spite of all these uncertainties and jugglings, still there is an ache in you, and the more you do not know, the worse the ache.

IV

"Ha, ha, ha! You will be finding enjoyment in toothache next," you cry, with a laugh.

"Well? Even in toothache there is enjoyment," I answer. I had toothache for a whole month and I know there is. In that case, of course, people are not spiteful in silence, but moan; but they are not candid moans, they are malignant moans, and the malignancy is the whole point. The enjoyment of the sufferer finds expression in those moans; if he did not feel enjoyment in them he would not moan. It is a good example, gentlemen, and I will develop it. Those moans express in the first place all the aimlessness of your pain, which is so humiliating to your consciousness; the whole legal system of nature on which you spit disdainfully, of course, but from which you suffer all the same while she does not. They express the consciousness that you have no enemy to punish, but that you have pain; the consciousness that in spite of all possible Wagenheims[3] you are in complete slavery to your teeth; that if some one wishes it, your teeth will leave off aching, and if he does not, they will go on aching another three months; and that finally if you are still contumacious and still protest, all that is left you for your own gratification is to thrash yourself or beat your wall with your fist as hard as you can, and absolutely nothing more. Well, these mortal insults, these jeers on the part of some one unknown, end at last in an enjoyment which sometimes reaches the highest degree of voluptuousness. I ask you, gentlemen, listen sometimes to the moans of an educated man of the nineteenth century suffering from toothache, on the second or third day of the attack, when he is beginning to moan, not as he moaned on the first day, that is, not simply because he has toothache, not just as any coarse peasant, but as a man affected by progress and European civilization, a man who is "divorced from the soil and the national elements," as they express it now-a-days. His moans become nasty, disgustingly malignant, and go on for whole days and nights. And of course he knows himself that he is doing himself no sort of good with his moans; he knows better than any one that he is only lacerating and harassing himself and others for nothing; he knows that even the audience before whom he is making his efforts. and his whole family, listen to him with loathing, do not put the

3. Wagenheim was apparently a German who advertised painless dentistry; he may have used hypnosis or autosuggestion.

least faith in him, and inwardly understand that he might moan differently, more simply, without trills and flourishes, and that he is only amusing himself like that from ill-humour, from malignancy. Well, in all these recognitions and disgraces it is that there lies a voluptuous pleasure. As though he would say: "I am worrying you, I am lacerating your hearts, I am keeping every one in the house awake. Well, stay awake then, you, too, feel every minute that I have toothache. I am not a hero to you now, as I tried to seem before, but simply a nasty person, an impostor. Well, so be it, then! I am very glad that you see through me. It is nasty for you to hear my despicable moans: well, let it be nasty; here I will let you have a nastier flourish in a minute. . . ." You do not understand even now, gentlemen? No, it seems our development and our consciousness must go further to understand all the intricacies of this pleasure. You laugh? Delighted. My jests, gentlemen, are of course in bad taste, jerky, involved, lacking self-confidence. But of course that is because I do not respect myself. Can a man of perception respect himself at all?

v

Come, can a man who attempts to find enjoyment in the very feeling of his own degradation possibly have a spark of respect for himself? I am not saying this now from any mawkish kind of remorse. And, indeed, I could never endure saying, "Forgive me, Papa, I won't do it again," not because I am incapable of saying that—on the contrary, perhaps just because I have been too capable of it, and in what a way, too! As though of design I used to get into trouble in cases when I was not to blame in any way. That was the nastiest part of it. At the same time I was genuinely touched and penitent, I used to shed tears and, of course, deceived myself, though I was not acting in the least and there was a sick feeling in my heart at the time. . . . For that one could not blame even the laws of nature, though the laws of nature have continually all my life offended me more than anything. It is loathsome to remember it all, but it was loathsome even then. Of course, a minute or so later I would realize wrathfully that it was all a lie, a revolting lie, an affected lie, that is, all this penitence, this emotion, these vows of reform. You will ask why did I worry myself with such antics: answer, because it was very dull to sit with one's hands folded, and so one began cutting capers. That is really it. Observe yourselves more carefully, gentlemen, then you will understand that it is so. I invented adventures for myself and made up a life, so as at least to live in some way. How many times it has happened to me—well, for instance, to take offence simply on purpose, for nothing; and one knows oneself, of course, that one is offended at nothing, that one is putting it on, but yet one brings oneself, at last to the point of being really offended. All my life I have had an impulse to play such pranks, so that in the end I could not control it in myself. Another time, twice, in fact, I tried hard to be in love. I suffered, too, gentlemen, I assure you. In the depth of my heart there was no faith in my suffering, only a faint stir of mockery, but yet I did suffer, and in the real, orthodox way; I was jealous, beside myself . . . and it was all from *ennui*, gentlemen, all from *ennui;* inertia overcame me. You know the direct, legitimate fruit of consciousness is inertia, that is, conscious sitting-with-the-hands-folded. I have referred to this already. I repeat, I repeat with emphasis: all "direct" persons and men of action are active just because they are stupid and limited. How explain that? I will tell you: in consequence of their limitation they take immediate and secondary causes for primary ones, and in that way persuade themselves more quickly and easily than other people do that they have found an infallible foundation for their activity, and their minds are at ease and you know that is the chief thing. To begin to act, you know, you must first have your mind completely at ease and no trace of doubt left in it. Why, how am I, for example to set my mind at rest? Where are the primary causes on which I am to build? Where are my foundations? Where am I to get them from? I exercise myself in reflection, and consequently with me every primary cause at once draws after itself another still more primary, and so on to infinity. That is just the essence of every sort of consciousness and reflection. It must be a case of the laws of nature again. What is the result of it in the end? Why, just the same. Remember I spoke just now of vengeance. (I am sure you did not take it in.) I said that a man revenges himself because he sees justice in it. Therefore he has found a primary cause, that is, justice. And so he is at rest on all sides, and consequently he carries out his revenge calmly and successfully, being persuaded that he is doing a just and honest thing. But I see no justice in it, I find no sort of virtue in it either, and consequently if I attempt to revenge myself, it is only out of spite. Spite, of course, might overcome everything, all my doubts, and so might serve quite successfully in place of a primary cause, precisely because it is not a cause. But what is to be done if I have not even spite (I began with that just now, you know). In consequence again of those accursed laws of consciousness, anger in me is subject to chemical disintegration. You look into it, the object flies off into air, your reasons evaporate, the criminal is not to be found, the wrong becomes not a wrong but a phantom, something like the toothache, for which no one is to blame, and consequently there is only the same outlet left again—that is, to beat the wall as hard as you can. So you give it up with a wave of the hand because you have not found a fundamental cause. And try letting yourself be carried away by your feelings, blindly, without reflection, without a primary cause, repelling consciousness at least for a time; hate or love, if only not to sit with your hands folded. The day after to-morrow, at the latest, you will begin despising yourself for having knowingly deceived yourself. Result: a soap-bubble and inertia. Oh, gentlemen, do you know, perhaps I consider myself an intelligent man, only because all my life I have been able neither to begin nor to finish anything. Granted I am a babbler, a harmless vexatious babbler, like all of us. But what is to be done if the direct and sole vocation of every intelligent man is babble, that is, the intentional pouring of water through a sieve?

VI

Oh, if I had done nothing simply from laziness! Heavens, how I should have respected myself, then. I should have respected myself because I should at least have been capable of being lazy; there would at least have been one quality, as it were, positive in me, in which I could have believed myself. Question: What is he? Answer: A sluggard; how very pleasant it would have been to hear that of oneself! It would mean that I was positively defined, it would mean that there was something to say about me. "Sluggard"—why, it is a calling and vocation, it is a career. Do not jest, it is so. I should then be a member of the best club by right, and should find my occupation in continually respecting myself. I knew a gentlemen who prided himself all his life on being a connoisseur of Lafitte. He considered this as his positive virtue, and never doubted himself. He died, not simply with a tranquil, but with a triumphant, conscience, and he was quite right, too. Then I should have chosen a career for myself, I should have been a sluggard and a glutton, not a simple one, but, for instance, one with sympathies for everything good and beautiful. How do you like that? I have long had visions of it. That "good and beautiful" weighs heavily on my mind at forty. But that is at forty; then—oh, then it would have been different! I should have found for myself a form of activity in keeping with it, to be precise, drinking to the health of everything "good and beautiful." I should have snatched at every opportunity to drop a tear into my glass and then to drain it to all that is "good and beautiful." I should then have turned everything into the good and the beautiful; in the nastiest, unquestionable trash, I should have sought out the good and the beautiful. I should have exuded tears like a wet sponge. An artist, for instance, paints a picture worthy of Gay.[4] At once I drink to the health of the artist who painted the picture worthy of Gay,

4. Nikolay Nikolaevich Gay (1831–1894), Russian painter of historical pictures who then had a great reputation. His father was a French emigrant.

because I love all that is "good and beautiful." An author has written *What you will:*[5] at once I drink to the health of "what you will" because I love all that is "good and beautiful."

I should claim respect for doing so. I should persecute any one who would not show me respect. I should live at ease, I should die with dignity, why, it is charming, perfectly charming! And what a good round belly I should have grown, what a triple chin I should have established, what a ruby nose I should have coloured for myself, so that every one would have said, looking at me: "Here is an asset! Here is something real and solid!" And, say what you like, it is very agreeable to hear such remarks about oneself in this negative age.

VII

But these are all golden dreams. Oh, tell me, who was it first announced, who was it first proclaimed, that man only does nasty things because he does not know his own interests; and that if he were enlightened, if his eyes were opened to his real normal interests, man would at once cease to do nasty things, would at once become good and noble because, being enlightened and understanding his real advantage, he would see his own advantage in the good and nothing else, and we all know that not one man can, consciously, act against his own interests, consequently, so to say, through necessity, he would begin doing good? Oh, the babe! Oh, the pure, innocent child! Why, in the first place, when in all these thousands of years has there been a time when man has acted only from his own interest? What is to be done with the millions of facts that bear witness that men, *consciously,* that is fully understanding their real interests, have left them in the background and have rushed headlong on another path, to meet peril and danger, compelled to this course by nobody and by nothing, but, as it were, simply disliking the beaten track, and have obstinately, wilfully, struck out another difficult, absurd way, seeking it almost in the darkness. So, I suppose, this obstinacy and perversity were pleasanter to them than any advantage. . . . Advantage! What is advantage? And will you take it upon yourself to define with perfect accuracy in what the advantage of man consists? And what if it so happens that a man's advantage, *sometimes,* not only may, but even must, consist in his desiring in certain cases what is harmful to himself and not advantageous. And if so, if there can be such a case, the whole principle falls into dust. What do you think—are there such cases? You laugh; laugh away, gentlemen, but only answer me: have man's advantages been reckoned up with perfect certainty? Are there not some which not only have

5. subtitle of Shakespeare's comedy *Twelfth Night,* generally used on the Continent instead of the main title, which is difficult to translate.

not been included but cannot possibly be included under any classification? You see, you gentlemen have, to the best of my knowledge, taken your whole register of human advantages from the averages of statistical figures and politico-economical formulas. Your advantages are prosperity, wealth, freedom, peace—and so on, and so on. So that the man who should, for instance, go openly and knowingly in opposition to all that list would, to your thinking, and indeed mine, too, of course, be an obscurantist or an absolute madman: would not he? But, you know, this is what is surprising: why does it so happen that all these statisticians, sages and lovers of humanity, when they reckon up human advantages invariably leave out one? They don't even take it into their reckoning in the form in which it should be taken, and the whole reckoning depends upon that. It would be no great matter, they would simply have to take it, this advantage, and add it to the list. But the trouble is, that this strange advantage does not fall under any classification and is not in place in any list. I have a friend for instance . . . Ech! gentlemen, but of course he is your friend, too; and indeed there is no one, no one, to whom he is not a friend! When he prepares for any undertaking this gentleman immediately explains to you, elegantly and clearly, exactly how he must act in accordance with the laws of reason and truth. What is more, he will talk to you with excitement and passion of the true normal interests of man; with irony he will upbraid the shortsighted fools who do not understand their own interests, nor the true significance of virtue; and, within a quarter of an hour, without any sudden outside provocation, but simply through something inside him which is stronger than all his interests, he will go off on quite a different tack—that is, act in direct opposition to what he has just been saying about himself, in opposition to the laws of reason, in opposition to his own advantage, in fact in opposition to everything . . . I warn you that my friend is a compound personality, and therefore it is difficult to blame him as an individual. The fact is, gentlemen, it seems there must really exist something that is dearer to almost every man than his greatest advantages, or (not to be illogical) there is a most advantageous advantage (the very one omitted of which we spoke just now) which is more important and more advantageous than all other advantages, for the sake of which a man if necessary is ready to act in opposition to all laws; that is, in opposition to reason, honour, peace, prosperity—in fact, in opposition to all those excellent and useful things if only he can attain that fundamental, most advantageous advantage which is dearer to him than all. "Yes, but it's advantage all the same" you will retort. But excuse me, I'll make the point clear, and it is not a case of playing upon words. What matters is, that this advantage is remarkable from the very fact that it breaks down all our classifications, and continually shatters every system constructed by lovers of mankind for the benefit of mankind. In fact, it upsets everything. But before I mention this advantage to you, I want to compromise myself personally, and therefore I boldly declare that all these fine systems, all these theories for explaining to mankind their real normal interests, in order that inevitably striving to pursue these interests they may at once become good and noble—are, in my opinion, so far, mere logical exercises! Yes, logical exercises. Why, to maintain this theory of the regeneration of mankind by means of the pursuit of his own advantage is to my mind almost the same thing as . . . as to affirm, for instance, following Buckle,[6] that through civilization mankind becomes softer, and consequently less bloodthirsty and less fitted for warfare. Logically it does seem to follow from his arguments. But man has such a predilection for systems and abstract deductions that he is ready to distort the truth intentionally, he is ready to deny the evidence of his senses only to justify his logic. I take this example because it is the most glaring instance of it. Only look about you: blood is being spilt in streams, and in the merriest way, as though it were champagne. Take the whole of the nineteenth century in which Buckle lived. Take Napoleon—the Great and also the present one. Take North America—the eternal union. Take the farce of Schleswig-Holstein.[7] . . . And what is it that civilization softens in us? The only gain of civilization for mankind is the greater capacity for variety of sensations—and absolutely nothing more. And through the development of this many-sidedness man may come to finding enjoyment in bloodshed. In fact, this has already happened to him. Have you noticed that it is the most civilized gentlemen who have been the subtlest slaughterers, to whom the Attilas[8] and Stenka Razins[9] could not hold a candle, and if they are not so conspicuous as the Attilas and Stenka Razins it is simply because they are so often met with, are so ordinary and have become so familiar to us. In any case civilization has made mankind if not more bloodthirsty, at least more vilely, more loathsomely bloodthirsty. In old days he saw justice in bloodshed and with his conscience at peace exterminated those he thought proper. Now we do think bloodshed abominable and yet we engage in this

6. Henry Thomas Buckle (1821–1862), the author of the *History of Civilization in England* (two volumes, 1857, 1861), which held that all progress is due to the march of mind. There is no moral progress except indirectly, as a result of intellectual enlightenment.

7. Austria and Prussia invaded Denmark and annexed its southernmost part, Schleswig-Holstein, in 1864.

8. Attila (406?–453 A.D.) was king of the Huns (433?–453). In 451 his armies penetrated as far as Orléans, in what today is France. He was defeated in the battle of Châlons on the Catalaunian plains and retired to Hungary. In 452 he led an expedition against Rome.

9. Stenka Razin was a Don Cossack leader who in 1670 conquered many cities along the Volga. He was finally defeated, captured, and executed in 1671.

abomination, and with more energy than ever. Which is worse? Decide that for yourselves. They say that Cleopatra (excuse an instance from Roman history) was fond of sticking gold pins into her slave-girls' breasts and derived gratification from their screams and writhings. You will say that that was in the comparatively barbarous times; that these are barbarous times too, because also, comparatively speaking, pins are stuck in even now; that though man has now learned to see more clearly than in barbarous ages, he is still far from having learnt to act as reason and science would dictate. But yet you are fully convinced that he will be sure to learn when he gets rid of certain old bad habits, and when common sense and science have completely re-educated human nature and turned it in a normal direction. You are confident that then man will cease from *intentional* error and will, so to say, be compelled not to want to set his will against his normal interests. That is not all; then, you say, science itself will teach man (though to my mind it's a superfluous luxury) that he never has really had any caprice or will of his own, and that he himself is something of the nature of a piano-key or the stop of an organ, and that there are, besides, things called the laws of nature; so that everything he does is not done by his willing it, but is done of itself, by the laws of nature. Consequently we have only to discover these laws of nature, and man will no longer have to answer for his actions and life will become exceedingly easy for him. All human actions will then, of course, be tabulated according to these laws, mathematically, like tables of logarithms up to 108,000, and entered in an index; or, better still, there would be published certain edifying works of the nature of encyclopædic lexicons, in which everything will be so clearly calculated and explained that there will be no more incidents or adventures in the world.

Then—this is all what you say—new economic relations will be established, all ready-made and worked out with mathematical exactitude, so that every possible question will vanish in the twinkling of any eye, simply because every possible answer to it will be provided. Then the "Crystal Palace"[10] will be built. Then . . . . In fact, those will be halcyon days. Of course there is no guaranteeing (this is my comment) that it will not be, for instance, frightfully dull then (for what will one have to do when everything will be calculated and tabulated), but on the other hand everything will be extraordinarily rational. Of course boredom may lead you to anything. It is boredom sets one sticking golden pins into people, but all that would not matter. What is bad (this is my

10. Dostoevsky has in mind the London Crystal Palace, a structure of glass and iron built in 1851–1854, and at that time admired as the newest wonder of architecture. The nave was five hundred yards long. The building burned down in 1936.

comment again) is that I dare say people will be thankful for the gold pins then. Man is stupid, you know, phenomenally stupid; or rather he is not at all stupid, but he is so ungrateful that you could not find another like him in all creation. I, for instance, would not be in the least surprised if all of a sudden, *à propos* of nothing, in the midst of general prosperity a gentleman with an ignoble, or rather with a reactionary and ironical, countenance were to arise and, putting his arms akimbo, say to us all: "I say, gentlemen, hadn't we better kick over the whole show and scatter rationalism to the winds, simply to send these logarithms to the devil, and to enable us to live once more at our own sweet foolish will!" That again would not matter, but what is annoying is that he would be sure to find followers—such is the nature of man. And all that for the most foolish reason, which, one would think, was hardly worth mentioning: that is, that man everywhere and at all times, whoever he may be, has preferred to act as he chose and not in the least as his reason and advantage dictated. And one may choose what is contrary to one's own interests, and sometimes one *positively ought* (that is my idea). One's own free unfettered choice, one's own caprice, however wild it may be, one's own fancy worked up at times to frenzy—is that very "most advantageous advantage" which we have overlooked, which comes under no classification and against which all systems and theories are continually being shattered to atoms. And how do these wiseacres know that man wants a normal, a virtuous choice? What has made them conceive that man must want a rationally advantageous choice? What man wants is simply *independent* choice, whatever that independence may cost and wherever it may lead. And choice, of course, the devil only knows what choice.

VIII

"Ha! ha! ha! But you know there is no such thing as choice in reality, say what you like," you will interpose with a chuckle. "Science has succeeded in so far analysing man that we know already that choice and what is called freedom of will is nothing else than——"

Stay, gentlemen, I meant to begin with that myself. I confess, I was rather frightened. I was just going to say that the devil only knows what choice depends on, and that perhaps that was a very good thing, but I remembered the teaching of science . . . and pulled myself up. And here you have begun upon it. Indeed, if there really is some day discovered a formula for all our desires and caprices—that is, an explanation of what they depend upon, by what laws they arise, how they develop, what they are aiming at in one case and in another and so on, that is a real mathematical formula—then, most likely, man will at once cease to feel desire, indeed, he will be certain to. For who would want to choose by rule? Besides, he will at once be transformed from a human being into an organ-stop or something of the sort; for what is a man without desires, without freewill and without choice, if not a stop in an organ? What do you think? Let us reckon the chances—can such a thing happen or not?

"H'm!" you decide. "Our choice is usually mistaken from a false view of our advantage. We sometimes choose absolute nonsense because in our foolishness we see in that nonsense the easiest means for attaining a supposed advantage. But when all that is explained and worked out on paper (which is perfectly possible, for it is contemptible and senseless to suppose that some laws of nature man will never understand), then certainly so-called desires will no longer exist. For if a desire should come into conflict with reason we shall then reason and not desire, because it will be impossible retaining our reason to be *senseless* in our desires, and in that way knowingly act against reason and desire to injure ourselves. And as all choice and reasoning can be really calculated—because there will some day be discovered the laws of our so-called freewill—so, joking apart, there may one day be something like a table constructed of them, so that we really shall choose in accordance with it. If, for instance, some day they calculate and prove to me that I make a long nose at some one because I could not help making a long nose at him and that I had to do it in that particular way, what *freedom* is left me, especially if I am a learned man and have taken my degree somewhere? Then I should be able to calculate my whole life for thirty years beforehand. In short, if this could be arranged there would be nothing left for us to do; anyway, we should have to understand that. And, in fact, we ought unwearyingly to repeat to ourselves that at such and such a time and in such and such circumstances nature does not ask our leave; that we have got to take her as she is and not fashion her to suit our fancy, and if we really aspire to formulas and tables of rules, and well, even . . . to the chemical retort, there's no help for it, we must accept the retort too, or else it will be accepted without our consent. . . ."

Yes, but here I come to a stop! Gentlemen, you must excuse me for being over-philosophical; it's the result of forty years underground! Allow me to indulge my fancy. You see, gentlemen, reason is an excellent thing, there's no disputing that, but reason is nothing but reason and satisfies only the rational side of man's nature, while will is a manifestation of the whole life, that is, of the whole human life including reason and all the impulses. And although our life, in this manifestation of it, is often worthless, yet it is life and not simply extracting square roots. Here I, for instance, quite naturally want to live, in order to satisfy all my capacities for life, and not simply my capacity for reasoning, that is, not simply one twentieth of my capacity for life. What does reason know? Reason only knows what it has succeeded in learning (some things, perhaps, it will never learn; this is a poor comfort, but why not say so frankly?) and human nature acts as a whole, with everything that is in it, consciously or unconsciously, and, even if it goes wrong, it lives. I suspect, gentlemen, that you are looking at me with compassion; you tell me again that an enlightened and developed man, such, in short, as the future man will be, cannot consciously desire anything disadvantageous to himself, that that can be proved mathematically. I thoroughly agree, it can—by mathematics. But I repeat for the hundredth time, there is one case, one only, when man may consciously, purposely, desire what is injurious to himself, what is stupid, very stupid—simply in order to have the right to desire for himself even what is very stupid and not to be bound by an obligation to desire only what is sensible. Of course, this very stupid thing, this caprice of ours, may be in reality, gentlemen, more advantageous for us than anything else on earth, especially in certain cases. And in particular it may be more advantageous than any advantage even when it does us obvious harm, and contradicts the soundest conclusions of our reason concerning our advantage—for in any circumstances it preserves for us what is most precious and most important—that is, our personality, our individuality. Some, you see, maintain that this really is the most precious thing for mankind; choice can, of course, if it chooses, be in agreement with reason; and especially if this be not abused but kept within bounds. It is profitable and sometimes even praiseworthy. But very often, and even most often, choice is utterly and stubbornly opposed to reason . . . and . . . and . . . do you know that that, too, is profitable, sometimes even praiseworthy? Gentlemen, let us suppose that man is not stupid. (Indeed one cannot refuse to suppose that, if only from the one consideration, that, if man is stupid, then who is wise?) But if he is not stupid, he is monstrously ungrateful! Phenomenally ungrateful. In fact, I believe that the best definition of man is the ungrateful biped. But that is not all, that is not his worst defect; his worst defect is his perpetual moral obliquity, perpetual —from the days of the Flood to the Schleswig-Holstein period. Moral obliquity and consequently lack of good sense; for it has long been accepted that lack of good sense is due to no other cause than moral obliquity. Put it to the test and cast your eyes upon the history of mankind. What will you see? Is it a grand spectacle?

Grand, if you like. Take the Colossus of Rhodes,[11] for instance, that's worth something. With good reason Mr. Anaevsky testifies of it that some say that it is the work of man's hands, while others maintain that it has been created by nature herself. Is it many-coloured? May be it is many-coloured, too: if one takes the dress uniforms, military and civilian, of all peoples in all ages—that alone is worth something, and if you take the undress uniforms you will never get to the end of it; no historian would be equal to the job. Is it monotonous? May be it's monotonous too: it's fighting and fighting; they are fighting now, they fought first and they fought last—you will admit, that it is almost too monotonous. In short, one may say anything about the history of the world—anything that might enter the most disordered imagination. The only thing one can't say is that it's rational. The very word sticks in one's throat. And, indeed, this is the odd thing that is continually happening: there are continually turning up in life moral and rational persons, sages and lovers of humanity who make it their object to live all their lives as morally and rationally as possible, to be, so to speak, a light to their neighbours simply in order to show them that it is possible to live morally and rationally in this world. And yet we all know that those very people sooner or later have been false to themselves, playing some queer trick, often a most unseemly one. Now I ask you: what can be expected of man since he is a being endowed with such strange qualities? Shower upon him every earthly blessing, drown him in a sea of happiness, so that nothing but bubbles of bliss can be seen on the surface; give him economic prosperity, such that he should have nothing else to do but sleep, eat cakes and busy himself with the continuation of his species, and even then out of sheer ingratitude, sheer spite, man would play you some nasty trick. He would even risk his cakes and would deliberately desire the most fatal rubbish, the most uneconomical absurdity, simply to introduce into all this positive good sense his fatal fantastic element. It is just his fantastic dreams, his vulgar folly that he will desire to retain, simply in order to prove to himself—as though that were so necessary—that men still are men and not the keys of a piano, which the laws of nature threaten to control so completely that soon one will be able to desire nothing but by the calendar. And that is not all: even if man really were nothing but a piano-key, even if this were proved to him by natural science and mathematics, even then he would not become reasonable, but would purposely do something perverse out of simple ingratitude, simply to gain his point. And if he does not find means he will contrive

11. a statue of Helios (Apollo) at Rhodes (an island in the Aegean Sea), about a hundred feet high, which was considered one of the Seven Wonders of the World. It was erected about 290 B.C.

destruction and chaos, will contrive sufferings of all sorts, only to gain his point! He will launch a curse upon the world, and as only man can curse (it is his privilege, the primary distinction between him and other animals), may be by his curse alone he will attain his object—that is, convince himself that he is a man and not a piano-key! If you say that all this, too, can be calculated and tabulated—chaos and darkness and curses, so that the mere possibility of calculating it all beforehand would stop it all, and reason would reassert itself, then man would purposely go mad in order to be rid of reason and gain his point! I believe in it, I answer for it, for the whole work of man really seems to consist in nothing but proving to himself every minute that he is a man and not a piano-key! It may be at the cost of his skin, it may be by cannibalism! And this being so, can one help being tempted to rejoice that it has not yet come off, and that desire still depends on something we don't know?

You will scream at me (that is, if you condescend to do so) that no one is touching my free will, that all they are concerned with is that my will should of itself, of its own free will, coincide with my own normal interests, with the laws of nature and arithmetic.

Good Heavens, gentlemen, what sort of free will is left when we come to tabulation and arithmetic, when it will all be a case of twice two makes four? Twice two makes four without my will. As if free will meant that!

IX

Gentlemen, I am joking, and I know myself that my jokes are not brilliant, but you know one can't take everything as a joke. I am, perhaps, jesting against the grain. Gentlemen, I am tormented by questions; answer them for me. You, for instance, want to cure men of their old habits and reform their will in accordance with science and good sense. But how do you know, not only that it is possible, but also that it is *desirable,* to reform man in that way? And what leads you to the conclusion that man's inclinations *need* reforming? In short, how do you know that such a reformation will be a benefit to man? And to go to the root of the matter, why are you so positively convinced that not to act against his real normal interests guaranteed by the conclusions of reason and arithmetic is certainly always advantageous for man and must always be a law for mankind? So far, you know, this is only your supposition. It may be the law of logic, but not the law of humanity. You think, gentlemen, perhaps that I am mad? Allow me to defend myself. I agree that man is pre-eminently a creative animal, predestined to strive consciously for an object and to engage in engineering—that is, incessantly and eternally to make new roads, *wherever they may lead*. But the reason why he wants sometimes to go off at a tangent may just be that he is *predestined* to make the road, and perhaps, too, that however stupid the "direct" practical man may be, the thought sometimes will occur to him that the road almost always does lead *somewhere*, and that the destination it leads to is less important than the process of making it, and that the chief thing is to save the well-conducted child from despising engineering, and so giving way to the fatal idleness, which, as we all know, is the mother of all the vices. Man likes to make roads and to create, that is a fact beyond dispute. But why has he such a passionate love for destruction and chaos also? Tell me that! But on that point I want to say a couple of words myself. May it not be that he loves chaos and destruction (there can be no disputing that he does sometimes love it) because he is instinctively afraid of attaining his object and completing the edifice he is constructing? Who knows, perhaps he only loves that edifice from a distance, and is by no means in love with it at close quarters; perhaps he only loves building it and does not want to live in it, but will leave it, when completed, for the use of *les animaux domestiques*—such as the ants, the sheep, and so on. Now the ants have quite a different taste. They have a marvellous edifice of that pattern which endures for ever—the ant-heap.

With the ant-heap the respectable race of ants began and with the ant-heap they will probably end, which does the greatest credit to their perseverance and good sense. But man is a frivolous and incongruous creature, and perhaps, like a chess player, loves the process of the game, not the end of it. And who knows (there is no saying with certainty), perhaps the only goal on earth to which mankind is striving lies in this incessant process of attaining, in other words, in life itself, and not in the thing to be attained, which must always be expressed as a formula, as positive as twice two makes four, and such positiveness is not life, gentlemen, but is the beginning of death. Anyway, man has always been afraid of this mathematical certainty, and I am afraid of it now. Granted that man does nothing but seek that mathematical certainty, he traverses oceans, sacrifices his life in the quest, but to succeed, really to find it, he dreads, I assure you. He feels that when he has found it there will be nothing for him to look for. When workmen have finished their work they do at least receive their pay, they go to the tavern, then they are taken to the police-station—and there is occupation for a week. But where can man go? Anyway, one can observe a certain awkwardness about him when he has attained such objects. He loves the process of attaining, but does not quite like to have attained, and that, of course, is very absurd. In fact, man is a comical creature; there seems to be a kind of jest in it all. But yet mathematical certainty is, after all, something insufferable. Twice two makes four seems to me simply a piece of insolence. Twice two makes four is a pert coxcomb who stands with arms akimbo barring your path and spitting. I admit that twice two makes four is an excellent thing, but if we are to give everything its due, twice two makes five is sometimes a very charming thing too.

And why are you so firmly, so triumphantly, convinced that only the normal and the positive—in other words, only what is conducive to welfare—is for the advantage of man? Is not reason in error as regards advantage? Does not man, perhaps, love something besides well-being? Perhaps he is just as fond of suffering? Perhaps suffering is just as great a benefit to him as well-being? Man is sometimes extraordinarily, passionately, in love with suffering, and that is a fact. There is no need to appeal to universal history to prove that; only ask yourself, if you are a man and have lived at all. As far as my personal opinion is concerned, to care only for well-being seems to me positively ill-bred. Whether it's good or bad, it is sometimes very pleasant, too, to smash things. I hold no brief for suffering nor for well-being either. I am standing for . . . my caprice, and for its being guaranteed to me when necessary. Suffering would be out of place in vaudevilles, for instance; I know that. In the "Crystal Palace" it is unthinkable; suffering means doubt, negation, and what would be the good of a crystal palace if there could be any doubt about it? And yet I think man will never renounce real suffering, that is, destruction and chaos. Why, suffering is the sole origin of consciousness. Though I did lay it down at the beginning that consciousness is the greatest misfortune for man, yet I know man prizes it and would not give it up for any satisfaction. Consciousness, for instance, is infinitely superior to twice two makes four. Once you have mathematical certainty there is nothing left to do or to understand. There will be nothing left but to bottle up your five senses and plunge into contemplation. While if you stick to consciousness, even though the same result is attained, you can at least flog yourself at times, and that will, at any rate, liven you up. Reactionary as it is, corporal punishment is better than nothing.

X[12]

You believe in a crystal palace that can never be destroyed—a palace at which one will not be able to put out one's tongue or make a long nose on the sly. And perhaps that is just why I am afraid of this edifice, that it is of crystal and can never be destroyed and that one cannot put one's tongue out at it even on the sly.

12. Section X was badly mutilated by the censor, as Dostoevsky makes clear in the letter to his brother Mikhail, dated March 26, 1864, which is quoted in our introduction.

You see, if it were not a palace, but a hen-house, I might creep into it to avoid getting wet, and yet I would not call the hen-house a palace out of gratitude to it for keeping me dry. You laugh and say that in such circumstances a hen-house is as good as a mansion. Yes, I answer, if one had to live simply to keep out of the rain.

But what is to be done if I have taken it into my head that that is not the only object in life, and that if one must live one had better live in a mansion. That is my choice, my desire. You will only eradicate it when you have changed my preference. Well, do change it, allure me with something else, give me another ideal. But meanwhile I will not take a hen-house for a mansion. The crystal palace may be an idle dream, it may be that it is inconsistent with the laws of nature and that I have invented it only through my own stupidity, through the old-fashioned irrational habits of my generation. But what does it matter to me that it is inconsistent? That makes no difference since it exists in my desires, or rather exists as long as my desires exist. Perhaps you are laughing again? Laugh away; I will put up with any mockery rather than pretend that I am satisfied when I am hungry. I know, anyway, that I will not be put off with a compromise, with a recurring zero, simply because it is consistent with the laws of nature and actually exists. I will not accept as the crown of my desires a block of slum tenements on a lease of a thousand years, and perhaps with a sign-board of Wagenheim the dentist hanging out. Destroy my desires, eradicate my ideals, show me something better, and I will follow you. You will say, perhaps, that it is not worth your trouble; but in that case I can give you the same answer. We are discussing things seriously; but if you won't deign to give me your attention, I will drop your acquaintance. I can retreat into my underground hole.

But while I am alive and have desires I would rather my hand were withered off than bring one brick to such a building! Don't remind me that I have just rejected the crystal palace for the sole reason that one cannot put out one's tongue at it. I did not say because I am so fond of putting my tongue out. Perhaps the thing I resented was, that of all your edifices there has not been one at which one could not put out one's tongue. On the contrary, I would let my tongue be cut off out of gratitude if things could be so arranged that I should lose all desire to put it out. It is not my fault that things cannot be so arranged, and that one must be satisfied with model flats. Then why am I made with such desires? Can I have been constructed simply in order to come to the conclusion that all my construction is a cheat? Can this be my whole purpose? I do not believe it.

But do you know what: I am convinced that we underground folk ought to be kept on a curb. Though we may sit forty years underground without speaking, when we do come out into the light of day and break out we talk and talk and talk. . . .

XI

The long and the short of it is, gentlemen, that it is better to do nothing! Better conscious inertia! And so hurrah for underground! Though I have said that I envy the normal man to the last drop of my bile, yet I should not care to be in his place such as he is now (though I shall not cease envying him). No, no; anyway the underground life is more advantageous. There, at any rate, one can. . . . Oh, but even now I am lying! I am lying because I know myself that it is not underground that is better, but something different, quite different, for which I am thirsting, but which I cannot find! Damn underground!

I will tell you another thing that would be better, and that is, if I myself believed in anything of what I have just written. I swear to you, gentlemen, there is not one thing, not one word of what I have written that I really believe. That is, I believe it, perhaps, but at the same time I feel and suspect that I am lying like a cobbler.

"Then why have you written all this?" you will say to me. "I ought to put you underground for forty years without anything to do and then come to you in your cellar, to find out what stage you have reached! How can a man be left with nothing to do for forty years?"

"Isn't that shameful, isn't that humiliating?" you will say, perhaps, wagging your heads contemptuously. "You thirst for life and try to settle the problems of life by a logical tangle. And how persistent, how insolent are your sallies, and at the same time what a scare you are in! You talk nonsense and are pleased with it; you say impudent things and are in continual alarm and apologizing for them. You declare that you are afraid of nothing and at the same time try to ingratiate yourself in our good opinion. You declare that you are gnashing your teeth and at the same time you try to be witty so as to amuse us. You know that your witticisms are not witty, but you are evidently well satisfied with their literary value. You may, perhaps, have really suffered, but you have no respect for your own suffering. You may have sincerity, but you have no modesty; out of the pettiest vanity you expose your sincerity to publicity and ignominy. You doubtlessly mean to say something, but hide your last word through fear, because you have not the resolution to utter it, and only have a cowardly impudence. You boast of consciousness, but you are not sure of your ground, for though your mind works, yet your heart is darkened and corrupt, and you cannot have a full, genuine consciousness without a pure heart. And how intrusive you are, how you insist and grimace! Lies, lies, lies!"

Of course I have myself made up all the things you say. That, too, is from underground. I have been for forty years listening to you through a crack under the floor. I have invented them myself, there was nothing else I could invent. It is no wonder that I have learned it by heart and it has taken a literary form. . .

But can you really be so credulous as to think that I will print all this and give it to you to read too? And another problem: why do I call you "gentlemen," why do I address you as though you really were my readers? Such confessions as I intend to make are never printed nor given to other people to read. Anyway, I am not strong-minded enough for that, and I don't see why I should be. But you see a fancy has occurred to me and I want to realize it at all costs. Let me explain.

Every man has reminiscences which he would not tell to every one, but only to his friends. He has other matters in his mind which he would not reveal even to his friends, but only to himself, and that in secret. But there are other things which a man is afraid to tell even to himself, and every decent man has a number of such things stored away in his mind. The more decent he is, the greater the number of such things in his mind. Anyway, I have only lately determined to remember some of my early adventures. Till now I have always avoided them, even with a certain uneasiness. Now, when I am not only recalling them, but have actually decided to write an account of them, I want to try the experiment whether one can, even with oneself, be perfectly open and not take fright at the whole truth. I will observe, in parenthesis, that Heine[13] says that a true autobiography is almost an impossibility, and that man is bound to lie about himself. He considers that Rousseau certainly told lies about himself in his *Confessions*, and even intentionally lied, out of vanity. I am convinced that Heine is right; I quite understand how sometimes one may, out of sheer vanity, attribute regular crimes to oneself, and indeed I can very well conceive that kind of vanity. But Heine judged of people who made their confessions to the public. I write only for myself, and I wish to declare once and for all that if I write as though I were addressing readers, that is simply because it is easier for me to write in that form. It is a form, an empty form—I shall never have readers. I have made this plain already. . .

I don't wish to be hampered by any restrictions in the compilation of my notes. I shall not attempt any system or method. I will jot things down as I remember them.

But here, perhaps, some one will catch at the word and ask me: if you really don't reckon on readers, why do you make such compacts with yourself—and on paper too—that is, that you won't at-

13. Dostoevsky alludes to *Confessions* (*Geständnisse*, 1854), fragmentary memoirs written by the German poet Heinrich Heine (1797–1856), in which on the very first page Heine speaks of Rousseau as lying and inventing disgraceful incidents about himself for his *Confessions*. (See footnote 2.)

tempt any system or method, that you jot things down as you remember them, and so on, and so on? Why are you explaining? Why do you apologize?

Well, there it is, I answer.

There is a whole psychology in all this, though. Perhaps it is simply that I am a coward. And perhaps that I purposely imagine an audience before me in order that I may be more dignified while I write. There are perhaps thousands of reasons. Again, what is my object precisely in writing? If it is not for the benefit of the public why should I not simply recall these incidents in my own mind without putting them on paper?

Quite so; but yet it is more imposing on paper. There is something more impressive in it; I shall be better able to criticize myself and improve my style. Besides, I shall perhaps obtain actual relief from writing. To-day, for instance, I am particularly oppressed by one memory of a distant past. It came back vividly to my mind a few days ago, and has remained haunting me like an annoying tune that one cannot get rid of. And yet I must get rid of it somehow. I have hundreds of such reminiscences; but at times some one stands out from the hundred and oppresses me. For some reason I believe that if I write it down I should get rid of it. Why not try?

Besides, I am bored, and I never have anything to do. Writing will be a sort of work. They say work makes man kind-hearted and honest. Well, here is a chance for me, anyway.

Snow is falling to-day, yellow and dingy. It fell yesterday, too, and a few days ago. I fancy it is the wet snow that has reminded me of that incident which I cannot shake off now. And so let it be a story *à propos* of the falling snow.

Part II

À PROPOS OF THE WET SNOW

When from dark error's subjugation
My words of passionate exhortation
  Had wrenched thy fainting spirit free;
And writhing prone in thine affliction
Thou didst recall with malediction
  The vice that had encompassed thee:
And when thy slumbering conscience, fretting
  By recollection's torturing flame,
Thou didst reveal the hideous setting
  Of thy life's current ere I came:
When suddenly I saw thee sicken,
  And weeping, hide thine anguished face,
Revolted, maddened, horror-stricken,
  At memories of foul disgrace, etc., etc., etc. . . .

NEKRASOV[14] (*translated by Juliet Soskice*)

14. Nikolay A. Nekrasov (1821–1878) was a famous Russian poet and editor of radical sympathies. The poem quoted dates from 1845, and is without title. The poem ends with the lines, "Into my house come bold and free, / Its rightful mistress there to be."

I

At that time I was only twenty-four. My life was even then gloomy, ill-regulated, and as solitary as that of a savage. I made friends with no one and positively avoided talking, and buried myself more and more in my hole. At work in the office I never looked at any one, and I was perfectly well aware that my companions looked upon me, not only as a queer fellow, but even looked upon me—I always fancied this—with a sort of loathing. I sometimes wondered why it was that nobody except me fancied that he was looked upon with aversion? One of the clerks had a most repulsive, pock-marked face, which looked positively villainous. I believe I should not have dared to look at any one with such an unsightly countenance. Another had such a very dirty old uniform that there was an unpleasant odor in his proximity. Yet not one of these gentlemen showed the slightest self-consciousness—either about their clothes or their countenance or their character in any way. Neither of them ever imagined that they were looked at with repulsion; if they had imagined it they would not have minded—so long as their superiors did not look at them in that way. It is clear to me now that, owing to my unbounded vanity and to the high standard I set for myself, I often looked at myself with furious discontent, which verged on loathing, and so I inwardly attributed the same feeling to every one. I hated my face, for instance: I thought it disgusting, and even suspected that there was something base in my expression, and so every day when I turned up at the office I tried to behave as independently as possible, and to assume a lofty expression, so that I might not be suspected of being abject. "My face may be ugly," I thought, "but let it be lofty, expressive, and, above all, *extremely* intelligent." But I was positively and painfully certain that it was impossible for my countenance ever to express those qualities. And what was worst of all, I thought it actually stupid looking, and I would have been quite satisfied if I could have looked intelligent. In fact, I would even have put up with looking base if, at the same time, my face could have been thought strikingly intelligent.

Of course, I hated my fellow clerks one and all, and I despised them all, yet at the same time I was, as it were, afraid of them. In fact, it happened at times that I thought more highly of them than of myself. It somehow happened quite suddenly that I alternated between despising them and thinking them superior to myself. A cultivated and decent man cannot be vain without setting a fearfully high standard for himself, and without despising and almost hating himself at certain moments. But whether I despised them or thought them superior I dropped my eyes almost every time I met any one. I even made experiments whether I could face so and so's looking at me, and I was always the first to drop my eyes. This worried me to distraction. I had a sickly dread, too, of being ridiculous, and so had a slavish passion for the conventional in everything external. I loved to fall into the common rut, and had a whole-hearted terror of any kind of eccentricity in myself. But how could I live up to it? I was morbidly sensitive, as a man of our age should be. They were all stupid, and as like one another as so many sheep. Perhaps I was the only one in the office who fancied that I was a coward and a slave, and I fancied it just because I was more highly developed. But it was not only that I fancied it, it really was so. I was a coward and a slave. I say this without the slightest embarrassment. Every decent man of our age must be a coward and a slave. That is his normal condition. Of that I am firmly persuaded. He is made and constructed to that very end. And not only at the present time owing to some casual circumstances, but always, at all times, a decent man is bound to be a coward and a slave. It is the law of nature for all decent people all over the earth. If any one of them happens to be valiant about something, he need not be comforted nor carried away by that; he would show the white feather just the same before something else. That is how it invariably and inevitably ends. Only donkeys and mules are valiant, and they only till they are pushed up to the wall. It is not worth while to pay attention to them for they really are of no consequence.

Another circumstance, too, worried me in those days: that there was no one like me and I was unlike any one else. "I am unique and they are all alike," I thought—and pondered.

From that it is evident that I was still a youngster.

The very opposite sometimes happened. It was loathsome sometimes to go to the office; things reached such a point that I often came home ill. But all at once, *à propos* of nothing, there would come a phase of scepticism and indifference (everything happened in phases to me), and I would laugh myself at my intolerance and fastidiousness, I would reproach myself with being *romantic*. At one time I was unwilling to speak to any one, while at other times I would not only talk, but go to the length of contemplating making friends with them. All my fastidiousness would suddenly, for no rhyme or reason, vanish. Who knows, perhaps I never had really had it, and it had simply been affected, and got out of books. I have not decided that question even now. Once I quite made friends with them, visited their homes, played preference, drank vodka, talked of promotions. . . . But here let me make a digression.

We Russians, speaking generally, have never had those foolish transcendental "romantics"—German, and still more French—on whom nothing produces any effect; if there were an earthquake, if all France perished at the barricades, they would still be the same, they would not even have the decency to affect a change, but would still go on singing their transcendental songs to the hour of their death, because they are fools. We, in Russia, have no fools; that is well known. That is what distinguishes us from foreign lands. Consequently these transcendental natures are not found amongst us in their pure form. The idea that they are is due to our "realistic" journalists and critics of that day, always on the look out for Kostanzhoglos[15] and Uncle Pyotr Ivanichs[16] and foolishly accepting them as our ideal; they have slandered our romantics, taking them for the same transcendental sort as in Germany or France. On the contrary, the characteristics of our "romantics" are absolutely and directly opposed to the transcendental European type, and no European standard can be applied to them. (Allow me to make use of this word "romantic"—an old-fashioned and much respected word which has done good service and is familiar to all). The characteristics of our romantic are to understand everything, *to see everything and to see it often incomparably more clearly than our most realistic minds see it;* to refuse to accept anyone or anything, but at the same time not to despise anything; to give way, to yield, from policy; never to lose sight of a useful practical object (such as rent-free quarters at the government expense, pensions, decorations), to keep their eye on that object through all the enthusiasms and volumes of lyrical poems, and at the same time to preserve "the good and the beautiful" inviolate within them to the hour of their death, and to preserve themselves also, incidentally, like some precious jewel wrapped in cotton wool if only for the benefit of "the good and the beautiful." Our "romantic" is a man of great breadth and the greatest rogue of all our rogues, I assure you. . . . I can assure you from experience, indeed. Of course, that is, if he is intelligent. But what am I saying! The romantic is always intelligent, and I only meant to observe that although we have had foolish romantics they don't count, and they were only so because in the flower of their youth they degenerated into Germans, and to preserve their precious jewel more comfortably, settled somewhere out there—by preference in Weimar or the Black Forest.

I, for instance, genuinely despised my official work and did not openly abuse it simply because I was in it myself and got a salary for it. Anyway, take note, I did not openly abuse it. Our romantic would rather go out of his mind—a thing, however, which very rarely happens—than take to open abuse, unless he had some other

15. Konstanzhoglo is the ideal efficient landowner in the second part of Gogol's novel *Dead Souls* (published posthumously in 1852).

16. Uncle Pyotr Ivanich, a character in Ivan Goncharov's novel *A Common Story* (1847), is a high bureaucrat, a factory owner who teaches lessons of sobriety and good sense to the romantic hero, Alexander Aduyev.

career in view; and he is never kicked out. At most, they would take him to the lunatic asylum as "the King of Spain"[17] if he should go very mad. But it is only the thin, fair people who go out of their minds in Russia. Innumerable "romantics" attain later in life to considerable rank in the service. Their many-sidedness is remarkable! And what a faculty they have for the most contradictory sensations! I was comforted by this thought even in those days, and I am of the same opinion now. That is why there are so many "broad natures" among us who never lose their ideal even in the depths of degradation; and though they never stir a finger for their ideal, though they are arrant thieves and knaves, yet they tearfully cherish their first ideal and are extraordinarily honest at heart. Yes, it is only among us that the most incorrigible rogue can be absolutely and loftily honest at heart without in the least ceasing to be a rogue. I repeat, our romantics, frequently, become such accomplished rascals (I use the term "rascals" affectionately), suddenly display such a sense of reality and practical knowledge that their bewildered superiors and the public generally can only ejaculate in amazement.

Their many-sidedness is really amazing, and goodness knows what it may develop into later on, and what the future has in store for us. It is not a poor material! I do not say this from any foolish or boastful patriotism. But I feel sure that you are again imagining that I am joking. Or perhaps it's just the contrary and you are convinced that I really think so. Anyway, gentlemen, I shall welcome both views as an honour and a special favour. And do forgive my digression.

I did not, of course, maintain friendly relations with my comrades and soon was at loggerheads with them, and in my youth and inexperience I even gave up bowing to them, as though I had cut off all relations. That, however, only happened to me once. As a rule, I was always alone.

In the first place I spent most of my time at home, reading. I tried to stifle all that was continually seething within me by means of external impressions. And the only external means I had was reading. Reading, of course, was a great help—exciting me, giving me pleasure and pain. But at times it bored me fearfully. One longed for movement in spite of everything, and I plunged all at once into dark, underground, loathsome vice of the pettiest kind. My wretched passions were acute, smarting, from my continual, sickly irritability. I had hysterical impulses, with tears and convulsions. I had no resource except reading, that is, there was nothing in my surroundings which I could respect and which attracted me. I was overwhelmed with depression, too; I had a hysterical craving for incongruity and

17. an allusion to Gogol's story "Memoirs of a Madman" (1835). The narrator imagines himself "the King of Spain" and is finally carried off to a lunatic asylum.

for contrast, and so I took to vice. I have not said all this to justify myself. . . . But, no! I am lying. I did want to justify myself. I make that little observation for my own benefit, gentlemen. I don't want to lie. I vowed to myself I would not.

And so, furtively, timidly, in solitude, at night, I indulged in filthy vice, with a feeling of shame which never deserted me, even at the most loathsome moments, and which at such moments nearly made me curse. Already even then I had my underground world in my soul. I was fearfully afraid of being seen, of being met, of being recognized. I visited various obscure haunts.

One night as I was passing a tavern I saw through a lighted window some gentlemen fighting with billiard cues, and saw one of them thrown out of a window. At other times I should have felt very much disgusted, but I was in such a mood at the time, that I actually envied the gentleman thrown out of a window—and I envied him so much that I even went into the tavern and into the billiard-room. "Perhaps," I thought, "I'll have a fight, too, and they'll throw me out of the window."

I was not drunk—but what is one to do—depression will drive a man to such a pitch of hysteria? But nothing happened. It seemed that I was not even equal to being thrown out of the window and I went away without having my fight.

An officer put me in my place from the first moment.

I was standing by the billiard-table and in my ignorance blocking up the way, and he wanted to pass; he took me by the shoulders and without a word—without a warning or explanation—moved me from where I was standing to another spot and passed by as though he had not noticed me. I could have forgiven blows, but I could not forgive his having moved me without noticing me.

Devil knows what I would have given for a real regular quarrel—a more decent, a more *literary* one, so to speak. I had been treated like a fly. This officer was over six foot, while I was a spindly little fellow. But the quarrel was in my hands. I had only to protest and I certainly would have been thrown out of the window. But I changed my mind and preferred to beat a resentful retreat.

I went out of the tavern straight home, confused and troubled, and the next night I went out again with the same lewd intentions, still more furtively, abjectly and miserably than before, as it were, with tears in my eyes—but still I did go out again. Don't imagine, though, it was cowardice made me slink away from the officer: I never have been a coward at heart, though I have always been a coward in action. Don't be in a hurry to laugh—I assure you I can explain it all.

Oh, if only that officer had been one of the sort who would consent to fight a duel! But no, he was one of those gentlemen (alas, long extinct!) who preferred fighting with cues or, like Gogol's Lieutenant Pirogov,[18] appealing to the police. They did not fight duels and would have thought a duel with a civilian like me an utterly unseemly procedure in any case—and they looked upon the duel altogether as something impossible, something free-thinking and French. But they were quite ready to bully, especially when they were over six foot.

I did not slink away through cowardice, but through an unbounded vanity. I was afraid not of his six foot, not of getting a sound thrashing and being thrown out of the window; I should have had physical courage enough, I assure you; but I had not the moral courage. What I was afraid of was that every one present, from the insolent marker down to the lowest little stinking, pimply clerk in a greasy collar, would jeer at me and fail to understand when I began to protest and to address them in literary language. For of the point of honour—not of honour, but of the point of honour (*point d'honneur*)—one cannot speak among us except in literary language. You can't allude to the "point of honour" in ordinary language. I was fully convinced (the sense of reality, in spite of all my romanticism!) that they would all simply split their sides with laughter, and that the officer would not simply beat me, that is, without insulting me, but would certainly prod me in the back with his knee, kick me round the billiard-table, and only then perhaps have pity and drop me out of the window.

Of course, this trivial incident could not with me end in that. I often met that officer afterwards in the street and noticed him very carefully. I am not quite sure whether he recognized me, I imagine not; I judge from certain signs. But I—I stared at him with spite and hatred and so it went on . . . for several years! My resentment grew even deeper with years. At first I began making stealthy inquiries about this officer. It was difficult for me to do so, for I knew no one. But one day I heard some one shout his surname in the street as I was following him at a distance, as though I were tied to him—and so I learnt his surname. Another time I followed him to his flat, and for ten kopecks learned from the porter where he lived, on which storey, whether he lived alone or with others, and so on—in fact, everything one could learn from a porter. One morning, though I had never tried my hand with the pen, it suddenly occurred to me to write a satire on this officer in the form of a novel which would unmask his villainy. I wrote the novel with relish. I did unmask his villainy, I even exaggerated it; at first I so altered his surname that it could easily be recognized, but on second thoughts

18. a character in Gogol's story "The Nevsky Prospekt" (1835). He pays violent court to the wife of a German tradesman and is thrown out by him and his friends. He does not actually call the police.

I changed it, and sent the story to the *Otechestvenniye Zapiski*.[19] But at that time such attacks were not the fashion and my story was not printed. That was a great vexation to me.

Sometimes I was positively choked with resentment. At last I determined to challenge my enemy to a duel. I composed a splendid, charming letter to him, imploring him to apologize to me, and hinting rather plainly at a duel in case of refusal. The letter was so composed that if the officer had had the least understanding of the good and the beautiful he would certainly have flung himself on my neck and have offered me his friendship. And how fine that would have been! How we should have got on together! "He could have shielded me with his higher rank, while I could have improved his mind with my culture, and, well . . . my ideas, and all sorts of things might have happened." Only fancy, this was two years after his insult to me, and my challenge would have been a ridiculous anachronism, in spite of all the ingenuity of my letter in disguising and explaining away the anachronism. But, thank God (to this day I thank the Almighty with tears in my eyes) I did not send the letter to him. Cold shivers run down my back when I think of what might have happened if I had sent it.

And all at once I revenged myself in the simplest way, by a stroke of genius! A brilliant thought suddenly dawned upon me. Sometimes on holidays I used to stroll along the sunny side of the Nevsky[20] about four o'clock in the afternoon. Though it was hardly a stroll so much as a series of innumerable miseries, humiliations and resentments; but no doubt that was just what I wanted. I used to wriggle along in a most unseemly fashion, like an eel, continually moving aside to make way for generals, for officers of the guards and the hussars, or for ladies. At such minutes there used to be a convulsive twinge at my heart, and I used to feel hot all down my back at the mere thought of the wretchedness of my attire, of the wretchedness and abjectness of my little scurrying figure. This was a regular martyrdom, a continual, intolerable humiliation at the thought, which passed into an incessant and direct sensation, that I was a mere fly in the eyes of all this world, a nasty, disgusting fly—more intelligent, more highly developed, more refined in feeling than any of them, of course—but a fly that was continually making way for every one, insulted and injured by every one. Why I inflicted this torture upon myself, why I went to the Nevsky, I don't know. I felt simply drawn there at every possible opportunity.

Already then I began to experience a rush of the enjoyment of

19. *Notes of the Fatherland*, the most famous radical Russian journal, founded in 1839.

20. Nevsky Prospekt, the most elegant main street in St. Petersburg, about three miles long; now called "Prospekt of the 25th October."

which I spoke in the first chapter. After my affair with the officer I felt even more drawn there than before: it was on the Nevsky that I met him most frequently, there I could admire him. He, too, went there chiefly on holidays. He, too, turned out of his path for generals and persons of high rank, and he, too, wriggled between them like an eel; but people, like me, or even better dressed like me, he simply walked over; he made straight for them as though there was nothing but empty space before him, and never, under any circumstances, turned aside. I gloated over my resentment watching him and . . . always resentfully made way for him. It exasperated me that even in the street I could not be on an even footing with him.

"Why must you invariably be the first to move aside?" I kept asking myself in hysterical rage, waking up sometimes at three o'clock in the morning. "Why is it you and not he? There's no regulation about it; there's no written law. Let the making way be equal as it usually is when refined people meet: he moves half-way and you move half-way; you pass with mutual respect."

But that never happened, and I always moved aside, while he did not even notice my making way for him. And lo and behold a bright idea dawned upon me! "What," I thought, "if I meet him and don't move on one side? What if I don't move aside on purpose, even if I knock up against him? How would that be?" This audacious idea took such a hold on me that it gave me no peace. I was dreaming of it continually, horribly, and I purposely went more frequently to the Nevsky in order to picture more vividly how I should do it when I did do it. I was delighted. This intention seemed to me more and more practical and possible.

"Of course I shall not really push him," I thought, already more good-natured in my joy. "I will simply not turn aside, will run up against him, not very violently, but just shouldering each other—just as much as decency permits. I will push against him just as much as he pushes against me." At last I made up my mind completely. But my preparations took a great deal of time. To begin with, when I carried out my plan I should need to be looking rather more decent, and so I had to think of my get-up. "In case of emergency, if, for instance, there were any sort of public scandal (and the public there is of the most *recherché*: the Countess walks there; Prince D. walks there; all the literary world is there), I must be well dressed; that inspires respect and of itself puts us on an equal footing in the eyes of society."

With this object I asked for some of my salary in advance, and bought at Churkin's a pair of black gloves and a decent hat. Black gloves seemed to me both more dignified and *bon ton* than the lemon-coloured ones which I had contemplated at first. "The colour is too gaudy, it looks as though one were trying to be conspicuous," and I did not take the lemon-coloured ones. I had got ready long beforehand a good shirt, with white bone studs; my overcoat was the only thing that held me back. The coat in itself was a very good one, it kept me warm; but it was wadded and it had a raccoon collar which was the height of vulgarity. I had to change the collar at any sacrifice, and to have a beaver one like an officer's. For this purpose I began visiting the Gostiny Dvor[21] and after several attempts I pitched upon a piece of cheap German beaver. Though these German beavers soon grow shabby and look wretched, yet at first they look exceedingly well, and I only needed it for one occasion. I asked the price; even so, it was too expensive. After thinking it over thoroughly I decided to sell my raccoon collar. The rest of the money—a considerable sum for me, I decided to borrow from Anton Antonich Syetochkin, my immediate superior, an unassuming person, though grave and judicious. He never lent money to any one, but I had, on entering the service, been specially recommended to him by an important personage who had got me my berth. I was horribly worried. To borrow from Anton Antonich seemed to me monstrous and shameful. I did not sleep for two or three nights. Indeed, I did not sleep well at that time, I was in a fever; I had a vague sinking at my heart or else a sudden throbbing, throbbing, throbbing! Anton Antonich was surprised at first, then he frowned, then he reflected, and did after all lend me the money, receiving from me a written authorization to take from my salary a fortnight later the sum that he had lent me.

In this way everything was at last ready. The handsome beaver replaced the mean-looking raccoon, and I began by degrees to get to work. It would never have done to act off-hand, at random; the plan had to be carried out skilfully, by degrees. But I must confess that after many efforts I began to despair: we simply could not run into each other. I made every preparation, I was quite determined—it seemed as though we should run into one another directly—and before I knew what I was doing I had stepped aside for him again and he had passed without noticing me. I even prayed as I approached him that God would grant me determination. One time I had made up my mind thoroughly, but it ended in my stumbling and falling at his feet because at the very last instant when I was six inches from him my courage failed me. He very calmly stepped over me, while I flew on one side like a ball. That night I was ill again, feverish and delirious.

And suddenly it ended most happily. The night before I had made up my mind not to carry out my fatal plan and to abandon it all, and

21. originally a guesthouse for foreign merchants; later used for displaying their wares.

with that object I went to the Nevsky for the last time, just to see how I would abandon it all. Suddenly, three paces from my enemy, I unexpectedly made up my mind—I closed my eyes, and we ran full tilt, shoulder to shoulder, against one another! I did not budge an inch and passed him on a perfectly equal footing! He did not even look round and pretended not to notice it; but he was only pretending, I am convinced of that. I am convinced of that to this day! Of course, I got the worst of it—he was stronger, but that was not the point. The point was that I had attained my object, I had kept up my dignity, I had not yielded a step, and had put myself publicly on an equal social footing with him. I returned home feeling that I was fully avenged for everything. I was delighted. I was triumphant and sang Italian arias. Of course, I will not describe to you what happened to me three days later; if you have read my first chapter you can guess that for yourself. The officer was afterwards transferred; I have not seen him now for fourteen years. What is the dear fellow doing now? Whom is he walking over?

II

But the period of my dissipation would end and I always felt very sick afterwards. It was followed by remorse—I tried to drive it away: I felt too sick. By degrees, however, I grew used to that too. I grew used to everything, or rather I voluntarily resigned myself to enduring it. But I had a means of escape that reconciled everything—that was to find refuge in "the good and the beautiful," in dreams, of course. I was a terrible dreamer, I would dream for three months on end, tucked away in my corner, and you may believe me that at those moments I had no resemblance to the gentleman who, in the perturbation of his chicken heart, put a collar of German beaver on his great coat. I suddenly became a hero. I would not have admitted my six-foot lieutenant even if he had called on me. I could not even picture him before me then. What were my dreams and how I could satisfy myself with them—it is hard to say now, but at the time I was satisfied with them. Though, indeed, even now, I am to some extent satisfied with them. Dreams were particularly sweet and vivid after a spell of dissipation; they came with remorse and with tears, with curses and transports. There were moments of such positive intoxication, of such happiness, that there was not the faintest trace of irony within me, on my honour. I had faith, hope, love. I believed blindly at such times that by some miracle, by some external circumstance, all this would suddenly open out, expand; that suddenly a vista of suitable activity—beneficent, good, and, above all *ready made* (what sort of activity I had no idea, but the great thing was that it should be all ready for me)—would rise up before me—and I should come out into the light of day, almost riding a white horse and crowned with laurel. Anything but the foremost place could not conceive for myself, and for that very reason I quite contentedly occupied the lowest in reality. Either to be a hero or to grovel in the mud—there was nothing between. That was my ruin, for when I was in the mud I comforted myself with the thought that at other times I was a hero, and the hero was a cloak for the mud: for an ordinary man it was shameful to defile himself, but a hero was too lofty to be utterly defiled, and so he might defile himself. It is worth noting that these attacks of the "good and the beautiful" visited me even during the period of dissipation and just at the times when I was touching bottom. They came in separate spurts, as though reminding me of themselves, but did not banish the dissipation by their appearance. On the contrary, they seemed to add a zest to it by contrast, and were only sufficiently present to serve as an appetizing sauce. That sauce was made up of contradictions and sufferings, of agonizing inward analysis, and all these pangs and pinpricks gave a certain piquancy, even a significance to my dissipation—in fact, completely answered the purpose of an appetizing sauce. There was a certain depth of meaning in it. And I could hardly have resigned myself to the simple, vulgar, direct debauchery of a clerk and have endured all the filthiness of it. What could have allured me about it then and have drawn me at night into the street? No, I had a lofty way of getting out of it all.

And what loving-kindness, oh Lord, what loving-kindness I felt at times in those dreams of mine! in those "flights into the good and the beautiful;" though it was fantastic love, though it was never applied to anything human in reality, yet there was so much of this love that one did not feel afterwards even the impulse to apply it in reality; that would have been superfluous. Everything, however, passed satisfactorily by a lazy and fascinating transition into the sphere of art, that is, into the beautiful forms of life, lying ready, largely stolen from the poets and novelists and adapted to all sorts of needs and uses. I, for instance, was triumphant over every one; every one, of course, was in dust and ashes, and was forced spontaneously to recognize my superiority, and I forgave them all. I was a poet and a grand gentleman, I fell in love; I came in for countless millions and immediately devoted them to humanity, and at the same time I confessed before all the people my shameful deeds, which, of course, were not merely shameful, but had in them much that was "good and beautiful" something in the Manfred[22] style. Every one would kiss me and weep (what idiots they would be if they did not), while I should go barefoot and hungry preaching new ideas and fighting a victorious Austerlitz[23] against the obscurantists. Then the

22. the hero of Lord Byron's verse drama *Manfred* (1817), who was oppressed by a mysterious guilt.

23. a village near Brno, the capital of Moravia, now in Czechoslovakia, where Napoleon defeated the combined Austrian and Russian armies in 1805.

band would play a march, an amnesty would be declared, the Pope would agree to retire from Rome to Brazil; then there would be a ball for the whole of Italy at the Villa Borghese[24] on the shores of the Lake of Como,[25] the Lake of Como being for that purpose transferred to the neighbourhood of Rome; then would come a scene in the bushes, and so on, and so on—as though you did not know all about it? You will say that it is vulgar and contemptible to drag all this into public after all the tears and transports which I have myself confessed. But why is it contemptible? Can you imagine that I am ashamed of it all, and that it was stupider than anything in your life, gentlemen? And I can assure you that some of these fancies were by no means badly composed. . . . It did not all happen on the shores of Lake Como. And yet you are right—it really is vulgar and contemptible. And most contemptible of all it is that now I am attempting to justify myself to you. And even more contemptible than that is my making this remark now. But that's enough, or there will be no end to it: each step will be more contemptible than the last. . . .

I could never stand more than three months of dreaming at a time without feeling an irresistible desire to plunge into society. To plunge into society meant to visit my superior at the office, Anton Antonich Syetochkin. He was the only permanent acquaintance I have had in my life, and wonder at the fact myself now. But I only went to see him when that phase came over me, and when my dreams had reached such a point of bliss that it became essential at once to embrace my fellows and all mankind; and for that purpose I needed, at least, one human being, actually existing. I had to call on Anton Antonich, however, on Tuesday—his at-home day; so I had always to time my passionate desire to embrace humanity so that it might fall on a Tuesday.

This Anton Antonich lived on the fourth storey in a house in Five Corners, in four low-pitched rooms, one smaller than the other, of a particularly frugal and sallow appearance. He had two daughters and their aunt, who used to pour out the tea. Of the daughters one was thirteen and another fourteen, they both had snub noses, and I was awfully shy of them because they were always whispering and giggling together. The master of the house usually sat in his study on a leather couch in front of the table with some grey-headed gentleman, usually a colleague from our office or some other department. I never saw more than two or three visitors there, always the same. They talked about the excise duty; about business in the Senate,[26] about salaries, about promotions, about His Excellency, and the best means of pleasing him, and so on. I had the patience to sit like a fool beside these people for four hours at a stretch, lis-

24. in Rome.

25. on the border of Italy and Switzerland.

26. The Russian Senate was at that time not a parliamentary body, but a high court.

tening to them without knowing what to say to them or venturing to say a word. I became stupefied, several times I felt myself perspiring, I was overcome by a sort of paralysis; but this was pleasant and good for me. On returning home I deferred for a time my desire to embrace all mankind.

I had however one other acquaintance of a sort, Simonov, who was an old schoolfellow. I had a number of schoolfellows, indeed, in Petersburg, but I did not associate with them and had even given up nodding to them in the street. I believe I had transferred into the department I was in simply to avoid their company and to cut off all connection with my hateful childhood. Curses on that school and all those terrible years of penal servitude! In short, I parted from my schoolfellows as soon as I got out into the world. There were two or three left to whom I nodded in the street. One of them was Simonov, who had been in no way distinguished at school, was of a quiet and equable disposition; but I discovered in him a certain independence of character and even honesty. I don't even suppose that he was particularly stupid. I had at one time spent some rather soulful moments with him, but these had not lasted long and had somehow been suddenly clouded over. He was evidently uncomfortable at these reminiscences, and was, I fancy, always afraid that I might take up the same tone again. I suspected that he had an aversion for me, but still I went on going to see him, not being quite certain of it.

And so on one occasion, unable to endure my solitude and knowing that as it was Thursday Anton Antonich's door would be closed, I thought of Simonov. Climbing up to his fourth storey I was thinking that the man disliked me and that it was a mistake to go and see him. But as it always happened that such reflections impelled me, as though purposely, to put myself into a false position, I went in. It was almost a year since I had last seen Simonov.

III

I found two of my old schoolfellows with him. They seemed to be discussing an important matter. All of them took scarcely any notice of my entrance, which was strange, for I had not met them for years. Evidently they looked upon me as something on the level of a common fly. I had not been treated like that even at school, though they all hated me. I knew, of course, that they must despise me now for my lack of success in the service, and for my having let myself sink so low, going about badly dressed and so on—which seemed to them a sign of my incapacity and insignificance. But I had not expected such contempt. Simonov was positively surprised at my turning up. Even in old days he had always seemed surprised at my coming. All this disconcerted me: I sat down, feeling rather miserable, and began listening to what they were saying.

They were engaged in warm and earnest conversation about a farewell dinner which they wanted to arrange for the next day to a comrade of theirs called Zverkov, an officer in the army, who was going away to a distant province. This Zverkov had been all the time at school with me too. I had begun to hate him particularly in the upper grades. In the lower grades he had simply been a pretty, playful boy whom everybody liked. I had hated him, however, even in the lower grades, just because he was a pretty and playful boy. He was always bad at his lessons and got worse and worse as he went on; however, he left with a good certificate, as he had powerful interest. During his last year at school he came in for an estate of two hundred serfs, and as almost all of us were poor he took up a swaggering tone among us. He was vulgar in the extreme, but at the same time he was a good-natured fellow, even in his swaggering. In spite of superficial, fantastic and sham notions of honour and dignity, all but very few of us positively grovelled before Zverkov, and the more so the more he swaggered. And it was not from any interested motive that they grovelled, but simply because he had been favoured by the gifts of nature. Moreover, it was, as it were, an accepted idea among us that Zverkov was a specialist in regard to tact and the social graces. This last fact particularly infuriated me. I hated the abrupt self-confident tone of his voice, his admiration of his own witticisms, which were often frightfully stupid, though he was bold in his language; I hated his handsome, but stupid face (for which I would, however, have gladly exchanged my intelligent one), and the free-and-easy military manners in fashion in the 'forties. I hated the way in which he used to talk of his future conquests of women (he did not venture to begin his attack upon women until he had the epaulettes of an officer, and was looking forward to them with impatience), and boasted of the duels he would constantly be fighting. I remember how I, invariably so taciturn, suddenly fastened upon Zverkov, when one day talking at a leisure moment with his schoolfellows of his future relations with the fair sex, and growing as sportive as a puppy in the sun, he all at once declared that he would not leave a single village girl on his estate unnoticed, that that was his *droit de seigneur*,[27] and that if the peasants dared to protest he would have them all flogged and double the tax on them, the bearded rascals. Our servile rabble applauded, but I attacked him, not from compassion for the girls and their fathers, but simply because they were applauding such an insect. I got the better of him on that occasion, but though Zverkov was stupid he was lively and impudent, and so laughed it off, and in such a way that my victory was not really complete: the laugh was on his side. He got the better of me on several occasions afterwards, but without malice, jestingly,

27. "the right of the master," i.e., to all the women serfs.

casually. I remained angrily and contemptuously silent and would not answer him. When we left school he made advances to me; I did not rebuff them, for I was flattered, but we soon parted and quite naturally. Afterwards I heard of his barrack-room success as a lieutenant, and of the fast life he was leading. Then there came other rumours—of his successes in the service. By then he had taken to cutting me in the street, and I suspected that he was afraid of compromising himself by greeting a personage as insignificant as me. I saw him once in the theatre, in the third tier of boxes. By then he was wearing shoulder-straps. He was twisting and twirling about, ingratiating himself with the daughters of an ancient General. In three years he had gone off considerably, though he was still rather handsome and adroit. One could see that by the time he was thirty he would be corpulent. So it was to this Zverkov that my schoolfellows were going to give a dinner on his departure. They had kept up with him for those three years, though privately they did not consider themselves on an equal footing with him, I am convinced of that.

Of Simonov's two visitors, one was Ferfichkin, a Russianized German—a little fellow with the face of a monkey, a blockhead who was always deriding every one, a very bitter enemy of mine from our days in the lower grades—a vulgar, impudent, swaggering fellow, who affected a most sensitive feeling of personal honour, though, of course, he was a wretched little coward at heart. He was one of those worshippers of Zverkov who made up to the latter from interested motives, and often borrowed money from him. Simonov's other visitor, Trudolyubov, was a person in no way remarkable—a tall young fellow, in the army, with a cold face, fairly honest, though he worshipped success of every sort, and was only capable of thinking of promotion. He was some sort of distant relation of Zverkov's, and this, foolish as it seems, gave him a certain importance among us. He always thought me of no consequence whatever; his behaviour to me, though not quite courteous, was tolerable.

"Well, with seven roubles each," said Trudolyubov, "twenty-one roubles between the three of us, we ought to be able to get a good dinner. Zverkov, of course, won't pay."

"Of course not, since we are inviting him," Simonov decided.

"Can you imagine," Ferfichkin interrupted hotly and conceitedly, like some insolent flunkey boasting of his master the General's decorations, "can you imagine that Zverkov will let us pay alone? He will accept from delicacy, but he will order half a dozen bottles of champagne."

"Do we want half a dozen for the four of us?" observed Trudolyubov, taking notice only of the half dozen.

"So the three of us, with Zverkov for the fourth, twenty-one roubles, at the Hôtel de Paris at five o'clock to-morrow," Simonov, who had been asked to make the arrangements, concluded finally.

"How twenty-one roubles?" I asked in some agitation, with a show of being offended; "if you count me it will not be twenty-one, but twenty-eight roubles."

It seemed to me that to invite myself so suddenly and unexpectedly would be positively graceful, and that they would all be conquered at once and would look at me with respect.

"Do you want to join, too?" Simonov observed, with no appearance of pleasure, seeming to avoid looking at me. He knew me through and through.

It infuriated me that he knew me so thoroughly.

"Why not? I am an old schoolfellow of his, too, I believe, and I must own I feel hurt that you have left me out," I said, boiling over again.

"And where were we to find you?" Ferfichkin put in roughly.

"You never were on good terms with Zverkov," Trudolyubov added, frowning.

But I had already clutched at the idea and would not give it up.

"It seems to me that no one has a right to form an opinion upon that," I retorted in a shaking voice, as though something tremendous had happened. "Perhaps that is just my reason for wishing it now, that I have not always been on good terms with him."

"Oh, there's no making you out . . . with these refinements," Trudolyubov jeered.

"We'll put your name down," Simonov decided, addressing me. "To-morrow at five o'clock at the Hôtel de Paris."

"What about the money?" Ferfichkin began in an undertone, indicating me to Simonov, but he broke off, for even Simonov was embarrassed.

"That will do," said Trudolyubov, getting up. "If he wants to come so much, let him."

"But it's a private thing, between us friends," Ferfichkin said crossly, as he, too, picked up his hat. "It's not an official gathering."

"We do not want at all, perhaps . . ."

They went away. Ferfichkin did not greet me in any way as he went out, Trudolyubov barely nodded. Simonov, with whom I was left *tête-à-tête*, was in a state of vexation and perplexity, and looked at me queerly. He did not sit down and did not ask me to.

"H'm . . . yes . . . to-morrow, then. Will you pay your subscription now? I just ask so as to know," he muttered in embarrassment.

I flushed crimson, and as I did so I remembered that I had owed Simonov fifteen roubles for ages—which I had, indeed, never forgotten, though I had not paid it.

"You will understand, Simonov, that I could have no idea when I came here. . . . I am very much vexed that I have forgotten. . . ."

"All right, all right, that doesn't matter. You can pay to-morrow after the dinner. I simply wanted to know. . . . Please don't . . ."

He broke off and began pacing the room still more vexed. As he walked he began to stamp with his heels.

"Am I keeping you?" I asked, after two minutes of silence.

"Oh!" he said, starting, "that is—to be truthful—yes. I have to go and see some one . . . not far from here," he added in an apologetic voice, somewhat abashed.

"My goodness, why didn't you say so?" I cried, seizing my cap, with an astonishingly free-and-easy air, which was the last thing I should have expected of myself.

"It's close by . . . not two paces away," Simonov repeated, accompanying me to the front door with a fussy air which did not suit him at all. "So five o'clock, punctually, to-morrow," he called down the stairs after me. He was very glad to get rid of me. I was in a fury.

"What possessed me, what possessed me to force myself upon them?" I wondered, grinding my teeth as I strode along the street, "for a scoundrel, a pig like that Zverkov! Of course, I had better not go; of course, I must just snap my fingers at them. I am not bound in any way. I'll send Simonov a note by to-morrow's post. . . ."

But what made me furious was that I knew for certain that I should go, that I should make a point of going; and the more tactless, the more unseemly my going would be, the more certainly I would go.

And there was a positive obstacle to my going: I had no money. All I had was nine roubles, I had to give seven of that to my servant, Apollon, for his monthly wages. That was all I paid him—he had to keep himself.

Not to pay him was impossible, considering his character. But I will talk about that fellow, about that plague of mine, another time.

However, I knew I should go and should not pay him his wages.

That night I had the most hideous dreams. No wonder; all the evening I had been oppressed by memories of my miserable days at school, and I could not shake them off. I was sent to the school by distant relations, upon whom I was dependent and of whom I have heard nothing since—they sent me there a forlorn, silent boy, already crushed by their reproaches, already troubled by doubt, and looking with savage distrust at every one. My schoolfellows met me with spiteful and merciless jibes because I was not like any of them. But I could not endure their taunts; I could not give in to them with the ignoble readiness with which they gave in to one another. I hated them from the first, and shut myself away from every one in timid, wounded and disproportionate pride. Their coarseness revolted me. They laughed cynically at my face, at my clumsy figure; and yet what stupid faces they had themselves. In our school the boys' faces seemed in a special way to degenerate and grow stupider. How many fine-looking boys came to us! In a few years they became repulsive. Even at sixteen I wondered at them morosely; even then I was struck by the pettiness of their thoughts, the stupidity of their pursuits, their games, their conversations. They had no understanding of such essential things, they took no interest in such striking, impressive subjects, that I could not help considering them inferior to myself. It was not wounded vanity that drove me to it, and for God's sake do not thrust upon me your hackneyed remarks, repeated to nausea, that "I was only a dreamer," while they even then had an understanding of life. They understood nothing, they had no idea of real life, and I swear that that was what made me most indignant with them. On the contrary, the most obvious, striking reality they accepted with fantastic stupidity and even at that time were accustomed to respect success. Everything that was just, but oppressed and looked down upon, they laughed at heartlessly and shamefully. They took rank for intelligence; even at sixteen they were already talking about a snug berth. Of course, a great deal of it was due to their stupidity, to the bad examples with which they had always been surrounded in their childhood and boyhood. They were monstrously depraved. Of course a great deal of that, too, was superficial and an assumption of cynicism; of course there were glimpses of youth and freshness even in their depravity; but even that freshness was not attractive, and showed itself in a certain rakishness. I hated them horribly, though perhaps I was worse than any of them. They repaid me in the same way, and did not conceal their aversion for me. But by then I did not desire their affection: on the contrary I continually longed for their humiliation. To escape from their derision I purposely began to make all the progress I could with my studies and forced my way to the very top. This impressed them. Moreover, they all began by degrees to grasp that I had already read books none of them could read, and understood things (not forming part of our school curriculum) of which they had not even heard. They took a savage and sarcastic view of it, but were morally impressed, especially as the teachers began to notice me on those grounds. The mockery ceased, but the hostility remained, and cold and strained relations became permanent between us. In the end I could not put up with it: with years a craving for society, for friends, developed in me. I attempted to get on friendly terms with some of my schoolfellows; but somehow or other my intimacy with them was always strained and soon ended of itself. Once, indeed, I did have a friend. But I was already a tyrant at heart; I wanted to exercise unbounded sway over him; I tried to instil into him a contempt for his surroundings; I required of him a disdainful and complete break with those surroundings. I frightened him with my passionate affection; I reduced him to tears, to hysterics. He was a simple and devoted soul; but when he devoted himself to me entirely I began to hate him immediately and repulsed him—as though all I needed him for was to win a victory over him, to subjugate him and nothing else. But I could not subjugate all of them; my friend was not at all like them either, he was, in fact, a rare exception. The first thing I did on leaving school was to give up the special job for which I had been destined so as to break all ties, to curse my past and shake the dust from off my feet. . . . And goodness knows why, after all that, I should go trudging off to Simonov's!

Early next morning I roused myself and jumped out of bed with excitement, as though it were all about to happen at once. But I believed that some radical change in my life was coming, and would inevitably come that day. Owing to its rarity, perhaps, any external event, however trivial, always made me feel as though some radical change in my life were at hand. I went to the office, however, as usual, but sneaked away home two hours earlier to get ready. The great thing, I thought, is not to be the first to arrive, or they will think I am overjoyed at coming. But there were thousands of such great points to consider, and they all agitated and overwhelmed me. I polished my boots a second time with my own hands; nothing in the world would have induced Apollon to clean them twice a day, as he considered that it was more than his duties required of him. I stole the brushes to clean them from the passage, being careful he should not detect it, for fear of his contempt. Then I minutely examined my clothes and thought that everything looked old, worn and threadbare. I had let myself get too slovenly. My uniform, perhaps, was tidy, but I could not go out to dinner in my uniform. The worst of it was that on the knee of my trousers was a big yellow stain. I had a foreboding that that stain would deprive me of nine-tenths of my personal dignity. I knew, too, that it was very bad to think so. "But this is no time for thinking: now I am in for the real thing," I thought, and my heart sank. I knew, too, perfectly well even then, that I was monstrously exaggerating the facts. But how could I help it? I could not control myself and was already shaking with fever. With despair I pictured to myself how coldly and disdainfully that "scoundrel" Zverkov would meet me; with what dull-witted, invincible contempt the blockhead Trudolyubov would look at me; with what impudent rudeness the insect Ferfichkin would snigger at me in order to curry favour with Zverkov; how completely Simonov would take it all in, and how he would despise me for the abjectness of my vanity and lack of spirit—and, worst of all, how paltry, *unliterary*, commonplace it would all be. Of course, the best thing would be not to go at all. But that was most impossible of all: if I feel impelled to do anything, I seem to be pitchforked into it. I should have jeered at myself ever afterwards: "So you funked it, you funked it, you funked the *real thing!*" On the contrary, I passionately longed to show all that "rabble" that I was by no means such a spiritless creature as I seemed to myself. What is more, even in the acutest paroxysm of this cowardly fever, I dreamed of getting the upper hand, of dominating them, carrying them away, making them like me—if only for my "elevation of thought and unmistakable wit." They would abandon Zverkov, he would sit on one side, silent and ashamed, while I should crush him. Then, perhaps, we would be reconciled and drink to our everlasting friendship; but what was most bitter and most humiliating for me was that I knew even then, knew fully and for certain, that I needed nothing of all this really, that I did not really want to crush, to subdue, to attract them, and that I did not care a straw really for the result, even if I did achieve it. Oh, how I prayed for the day to pass quickly! In unutterable anguish I went to the window, opened the movable pane and looked out into the troubled darkness of the thickly falling wet snow. At last my wretched little clock hissed out five. I seized my hat and trying not to look at Apollon, who had been all day expecting his month's wages, but in his foolishness was unwilling to be the first to speak about it, I slipt between him and the door and jumping into a high-class sledge, on which I spent my last half rouble, I drove up in grand style to the Hôtel de Paris.

IV

I had been certain the day before that I should be the first to arrive. But it was not a question of being the first to arrive. Not only were they not there, but I had difficulty in finding our room. The table was not laid even. What did it mean? After a good many questions I elicited from the waiters that the dinner had been ordered not for five, but for six o'clock. This was confirmed at the buffet too. I felt really ashamed to go on questioning them. It was only twenty-five minutes past five. If they changed the dinner hour they ought at least to have let me know—that is what the post is for, and not to have put me in an absurd position in my own eyes and . . . and even before the waiters. I sat down; the servant began laying the table; I felt even more humiliated when he was present. Towards six o'clock they brought in candles, though there were lamps burning in the room. It had not occurred to the waiter, however, to bring them in at once when I arrived. In the next room two gloomy, angry-looking persons were eating their dinners in silence at two different tables. There was a great deal of noise, even shouting, in a room further away; one could hear the laughter of a crowd of people, and nasty little shrieks in French: there were ladies at the dinner. It was sickening, in fact. I rarely passed more unpleasant moments, so much so that when they did arrive all together punctually at six I was overjoyed to see them, as though they were my deliverers, and even forgot that it was incumbent upon me to show resentment.

Zverkov walked in at the head of them; evidently he was the leading spirit. He and all of them were laughing; but, seeing me, Zverkov drew himself up a little, walked up to me deliberately with a slight, rather jaunty bend from the waist. He shook hands with me in a friendly, but not over-friendly, fashion, with a sort of circumspect courtesy like that of a General, as though in giving me his hand he were warding off something. I had imagined, on the contrary, that on coming in he would at once break into his habitual thin, shrill laugh and fall to making his insipid jokes and witticisms. I had been preparing for them ever since the previous day, but I had not expected such condescension, such high-official courtesy. So, then, he felt himself ineffably superior to me in every respect! If he only meant to insult me by that high-official tone, it would not matter, I thought—I could pay him back for it one way or another. But what if, in reality, without the least desire to be offensive, that sheepshead had a notion in earnest that he was superior to me and could only look at me in a patronizing way? The very supposition made me gasp.

"I was surprised to hear of your desire to join us," he began, lisping and drawling, which was something new. "You and I seem to have seen nothing of one another. You fight shy of us. You shouldn't. We are not such terrible people as you think. Well, anyway, I am glad to renew our acquaintance."

And he turned carelessly to put down his hat on the window.

"Have you been waiting long?" Trudolyubov inquired.

"I arrived at five o'clock as you told me yesterday," I answered aloud, with an irritability that threatened an explosion.

"Didn't you let him know that we had changed the hour?" said Trudolyubov to Simonov.

"No, I didn't. I forgot," the latter replied, with no sign of regret, and without even apologizing to me he went off to order the *hors d'œuvres.*

"So you've been here a whole hour? Oh, poor fellow!" Zverkov cried ironically, for to his notions this was bound to be extremely funny. That rascal Ferfichkin followed with his nasty little snigger like a puppy yapping. My position struck him, too, as exquisitely ludicrous and embarrassing.

"It isn't funny at all!" I cried to Ferfichkin, more and more irritated. "It wasn't my fault, but other people's. They neglected to let me know. It was . . . it was . . . it was simply absurd."

"It's not only absurd, but something else as well," muttered Trudolyubov, naïvely taking my part. "You are not hard enough upon it. It was simply rudeness—unintentional, of course. And how could Simonov . . . h'm!"

"If a trick like that had been played on me," observed Ferfichkin, "I should . . ."

"But you should have ordered something for yourself," Zverkov interrupted, "or simply asked for dinner without waiting for us."

"You will allow that I might have done that without your permission," I rapped out. "If I waited, it was . . ."

"Let us sit down, gentlemen," cried Simonov, coming in. "Everything is ready; I can answer for the champagne; it is capitally frozen. . . . You see, I did not know your address, where was I to look for you?" he suddenly turned to me, but again he seemed to avoid looking at me. Evidently he had something against me. It must have been what happened yesterday.

All sat down; I did the same. It was a round table. Trudolyubov was on my left, Simonov on my right. Zverkov was sitting opposite, Ferfichkin next to him, between him and Trudolyubov.

"Tell me, are you . . . in a government office?" Zverkov went on attending to me. Seeing that I was embarrassed he seriously thought that he ought to be friendly to me, and, so to speak, cheer me up.

"Does he want me to throw a bottle at his head?" I thought, in a fury. In my novel surroundings I was unnaturally ready to be irritated.

"In the N—— office," I answered jerkily, with my eyes on my plate.

"And ha-ave you a go-od berth? I say, what ma-a-de you leave your original job?"

"What ma-a-de me was that I wanted to leave my original job," I drawled more than he, hardly able to control myself. Ferfichkin went off into a guffaw. Simonov looked at me ironically. Trudolyubov left off eating and began looking at me with curiosity.

Zverkov winced, but he tried not to notice it.

"And the remuneration?"

"What remuneration?"

"I mean, your sa-a-lary?"

"Why are you cross-examining me?" However, I told him at once what my salary was. I turned horribly red.

"It is not very handsome," Zverkov observed majestically.

"Yes, you can't afford to dine at cafés on that," Ferfichkin added insolently.

"To my thinking it's very poor," Trudolyubov observed gravely.

"And how thin you have grown! How you have changed!" added Zverkov, with a shade of venom in his voice, scanning me and my attire with a sort of insolent compassion.

"Oh, spare his blushes," cried Ferfichkin, sniggering.

"My dear sir, allow me to tell you I am not blushing," I broke out at last; "do you hear? I am dining here, at this café, at my own expense, not at other people's—note that, Mr. Ferfichkin."

"Wha-at? Isn't every one here dining at his own expense? You would seem to be . . ." Ferfichkin flew out at me, turning as red as a lobster, and looking me in the face with fury.

"Tha-at," I answered, feeling I had gone too far, "and I imagine it would be better to talk of something more intelligent."

"You intend to show off your intelligence, I suppose?"

"Don't disturb yourself, that would be quite out of place here."

"Why are you clacking away like that, my good sir, eh? Have you gone out of your wits in your office?"

"Enough, gentlemen, enough!" Zverkov cried, authoritatively.

"How stupid it is!" muttered Simonov.

"It really is stupid. We have met here, a company of friends, for a farewell dinner to a comrade and you carry on an altercation," said Trudolyubov, rudely addressing himself to me alone. "You invited yourself to join us, so don't disturb the general harmony."

"Enough, enough!" cried Zverkov. "Give over, gentlemen, it's out of place. Better let me tell you how I nearly got married the day before yesterday. . . ."

And then followed a burlesque narrative of how this gentleman had almost been married two days before. There was not a word about the marriage, however, but the story was adorned with generals, colonels and gentlemen-in-waiting, while Zverkov almost took the lead among them. It was greeted with approving laughter; Ferfichkin positively squealed.

No one paid any attention to me, and I sat crushed and humiliated.

"Good Heavens, these are not the people for me!" I thought. "And what a fool I have made of myself before them! I let Ferfichkin go too far, though. The brutes imagine they are doing me an honour in letting me sit down with them. They don't understand that it's an honour to them and not to me! I've grown thinner! My clothes! Oh, damn my trousers! Zverkov noticed the yellow stain on the knee as soon as he came in. . . . But what's the use! I must get up at once, this very minute, take my hat and simply go without a word . . . with contempt! And to-morrow I can send a challenge. The scoundrels! As though I cared about the seven roubles. They may think. . . . Damn it! I don't care about the seven roubles. I'll go this minute!"

Of course I remained. I drank sherry and Lafitte by the glassful in my discomfiture. Being unaccustomed to it, I was quickly affected. My annoyance increased as the wine went to my head. I longed all at once to insult them all in a most flagrant manner and then go away. To seize the moment and show what I could do, so that they would say, "He's clever, though he is absurd," and . . . and . . . in fact, damn them all!

I scanned them all insolently with my drowsy eyes. But they seemed to have forgotten me altogether. They were noisy, vociferous, cheerful. Zverkov was talking all the time. I began listening. Zverkov was talking of some exuberant lady whom he had at last led on to declaring her love (of course, he was lying like a horse), and how he had been helped in this affair by an intimate friend of his, a Prince Kolya, an officer in the hussars, who had three thousand serfs.

"And yet this Kolya, who has three thousand serfs, has not put in an appearance here to-night to see you off," I cut in suddenly.

For a minute every one was silent. "You are drunk already." Trudolyubov deigned to notice me at last, glancing contemptuously in my direction. Zverkov, without a word, examined me as though I were an insect. I dropped my eyes. Simonov made haste to fill up the glasses with champagne.

Trudolyubov raised his glass, as did every one else but me.

"Your health and good luck on the journey!" he cried to Zverkov. "To old times, to our future, hurrah!"

They all tossed off their glasses, and crowded round Zverkov to kiss him. I did not move; my full glass stood untouched before me.

"Why, aren't you going to drink it?" roared Trudolyubov, losing patience and turning menacingly to me.

"I want to make a speech separately, on my own account . . . and then I'll drink it, Mr. Trudolyubov."

"Spiteful brute!" muttered Simonov. I drew myself up in my chair and feverishly seized my glass, prepared for something extraordinary, though I did not know myself precisely what I was going to say.

"*Silence!*" cried Ferfichkin. "Now for a display of wit!"

Zverkov waited very gravely, knowing what was coming.

"Mr. Lieutenant Zverkov," I began, "let me tell you that I hate phrases, phrasemongers and men in corsets . . . that's the first point, and there is a second one to follow it."

There was a general stir.

"The second point is: I hate ribaldry and ribald talkers. Especially ribald talkers! The third point: I love justice, truth and honesty." I went on almost mechanically, for I was beginning to shiver with horror myself and had no idea how I came to be talking like this. "I love thought, Monsieur Zverkov; I love true comradeship, on an equal footing and not . . . H'm . . . I love. . . . But, however, why not? I will drink your health, too, Mr. Zverkov. Seduce the Circassian girls, shoot the enemies of the fatherland and . . . and . . . to your health, Monsieur Zverkov!"

Zverkov got up from his seat, bowed to me and said:

"I am very much obliged to you." He was frightfully offended and turned pale.

"Damn the fellow!" roared Trudolyubov, bringing his fist down on the table.

"Well, he wants a punch in the face for that," squealed Ferfichkin.

"We ought to turn him out," muttered Simonov.

"Not a word, gentlemen, not a movement!" cried Zverkov solemnly, checking the general indignation. "I thank you all, but I can show him for myself how much value I attach to his words."

"Mr. Ferfichkin, you will give me satisfaction to-morrow for your words just now!" I said aloud, turning with dignity to Ferfichkin.

"A duel, you mean? Certainly," he answered. But probably I was so ridiculous as I challenged him and it was so out of keeping with my appearance that everyone, including Ferfichkin, was prostrate with laughter.

"Yes, let him alone, of course! He is quite drunk," Trudolyubov said with disgust.

"I shall never forgive myself for letting him join us," Simonov muttered again.

"Now is the time to throw a bottle at their heads," I thought to myself. I picked up the bottle . . . and filled my glass. . . . "No, I'd better sit on to the end," I went on thinking; "you would be pleased, my friends if I went away. Nothing will induce me to go. I'll go on sitting here and drinking to the end, on purpose, as a sign that I don't think you of the slightest consequence. I will go on sitting and drinking, because this is a public-house and I paid my entrance money. I'll sit here and drink, for I look upon you as so many pawns, as inanimate pawns. I'll sit here and drink . . . and sing if I want to, yes, sing, for I have the right to . . . to sing . . . H'm!"

But I did not sing. I simply tried not to look at any of them. I assumed most unconcerned attitudes and waited with impatience for them to speak *first*. But alas, they did not address me! And oh, how I wished, how I wished at that moment to be reconciled to them! It struck eight, at last nine. They moved from the table to the sofa. Zverkov stretched himself on a lounge and put one foot on a round table. Wine was brought there. He did, as a fact, order three bottles on his own account. I, of course, was not invited to join them. They all sat round him on the sofa. They listened to him, almost with reverence. It was evident that they were fond of him. "What for? What for?" I wondered. From time to time they were moved to drunken enthusiasm and kissed each other. They talked of the Caucasus, of the nature of true passion, of snug berths in the service, of the income of an hussar called Podkharzhevsky, whom none of them knew personally, and rejoiced in the largeness of it, of the extraordinary grace and beauty of a Princess D., whom none of them had ever seen; then it came to Shakespeare's being immortal.

I smiled contemptuously and walked up and down the other side of the room, opposite the sofa, from the table to the stove and back again. I tried my very utmost to show them that I could do without them, and yet I purposely made a noise with my boots, thumping with my heels. But it was all in vain. They paid no attention. I had the patience to walk up and down in front of them from eight o'clock till eleven, in the same place, from the table to the stove and back again. "I walk up and down to please myself and no one can prevent me." The waiter who came into the room stopped, from time to time, to look at me. I was somewhat giddy from turning round so often; at moments it seemed to me that I was in delirium. During those three hours I was three times soaked with sweat and dry again. At times, with an intense, acute pang I was stabbed to the heart by the thought that ten years, twenty years, forty years would pass, and that even in forty years I would remember with loathing and humiliation those filthiest, most ludicrous, and most awful moments of my life. No one could have gone out of his way to degrade himself more shamelessly, and I fully realized it, fully, and yet I went on pacing up and down from the table to the stove. "Oh, if you only knew what thoughts and feelings I am capable of, how cultured I am!" I thought at moments, mentally addressing the sofa on which my enemies were sitting. But my enemies behaved as though I were not in the room. Once —only once—they turned towards me, just when Zverkov was talking about Shakespeare, and I suddenly gave a contemptuous laugh. I laughed in such an affected and disgusting way that they all at once broke off their conversation, and silently and gravely for two minutes watched me walking up and down from the table to the stove, *taking no notice of them*. But nothing came of it: they said nothing, and two minutes later they ceased to notice me again. It struck eleven.

"Friends," cried Zverkov getting up from the sofa, "let us all be off now, *there!*"

"Of course, of course," the others assented. I turned sharply to Zverkov. I was so harassed, so exhausted, that I would have cut my throat to put an end to it. I was in a fever; my hair, soaked with perspiration, stuck to my forehead and temples.

"Zverkov, I beg your pardon," I said abruptly and resolutely. "Ferfichkin, yours too, and every one's, every one's: I have insulted you all!"

"Aha! A duel is not in your line, old man," Ferfichkin hissed venomously.

It sent a sharp pang to my heart.

"No, it's not the duel I am afraid of, Ferfichkin! I am ready to fight you to-morrow, after we are reconciled. I insist upon it, in fact, and you cannot refuse. I want to show you that I am not afraid of a duel. You shall fire first and I shall fire into the air."

"He is comforting himself," said Simonov.

"He's simply raving," said Trudolyubov.

"But let us pass. Why are you barring our way? What do you want?" Zverkov answered disdainfully.

They were all flushed, their eyes were bright: they had been drinking heavily.

"I ask for your friendship, Zverkov; I insulted you, but . . ."

"Insulted? *You* insulted *me?* Understand, sir, that you never, under any circumstances, could possibly insult *me*."

"And that's enough for you. Out of the way!" concluded Trudolyubov.

"Olympia is mine, friends, that's agreed!" cried Zverkov.

"We won't dispute your right, we won't dispute your right," the others answered, laughing.

I stood as though spat upon. The party went noisily out of the room. Trudolyubov struck up some stupid song. Simonov remained behind for a moment to tip the waiters. I suddenly went up to him.

"Simonov! give me six roubles!" I said, with desperate resolution.

He looked at me in extreme amazement, with vacant eyes. He, too, was drunk.

"You don't mean you are coming with us?"

"Yes."

"I've no money," he snapped out, and with a scornful laugh he went out of the room.

I clutched at his overcoat. It was a nightmare.

"Simonov, I saw you had money. Why do you refuse me? Am I a scoundrel? Beware of refusing me: if you knew, if you knew why I am asking! My whole future, my whole plans depend upon it!"

Simonov pulled out the money and almost flung it at me.

"Take it, if you have no sense of shame!" he pronounced pitilessly, and ran to overtake them.

I was left for a moment alone. Disorder, the remains of dinner, a broken wine-glass on the floor, spilt wine, cigarette ends, fumes of drink and delirium in my brain, an agonizing misery in my heart and finally the waiter, who had seen and heard all and was looking inquisitively into my face.

"I am going there!" I cried. "Either they shall all go down on their knees to beg for my friendship, or I will give Zverkov a slap in the face!"

V

"So this is it, this is it at last—contact with real life," I muttered as I ran headlong downstairs. "This is very different from the Pope's leaving Rome and going to Brazil, very different from the ball on Lake Como!"

"You are a scoundrel," a thought flashed through my mind, "if you laugh at this now."

"No matter!" I cried, answering myself. "Now everything is lost!"

There was no trace to be seen of them, but that made no difference—I knew where they had gone.

At the steps was standing a solitary night sledge-driver in a rough peasant coat, powdered over with the still falling, wet, and as it were warm, snow. It was hot and steamy. The little shaggy piebald horse was also covered with snow and coughing, I remember that very well. I made a rush for the roughly made sledge; but as soon as I raised my foot to get into it, the recollection of how Simonov had just given me six roubles seemed to double me up and I tumbled into the sledge like a sack.

"No, I must do a great deal to make up for all that," I cried. "But I will make up for it or perish on the spot this very night. Start!"

We set off. There was a perfect whirl in my head.

"They won't go down on their knees to beg for my friendship. That is a mirage, cheap mirage, revolting, romantic and fantastical—that's another ball on Lake Como. And so I am bound to slap Zverkov's face! It is my duty to. And so it is settled; I am flying to give him a slap in the face. Hurry up!"

The driver tugged at the reins.

"As soon as I go in I'll give it him. Ought I before giving him the slap to say a few words by way of preface? No. I'll simply go in and give it him. They will all be sitting in the drawing-room, and he with Olympia on the sofa. That damned Olympia! She laughed at my looks on one occasion and refused me. I'll pull Olympia's hair, pull Zverkov's ears! No, better one ear, and pull him by it round the room. Maybe they will all begin beating me and will kick me out. That's most likely, indeed. No matter! Anyway, I shall first slap him; the initiative will be mine; and by the laws of honour that is everything: he will be branded and cannot wipe off the slap by any blows, by nothing but a duel. He will be forced to fight. And let them beat me now. Let them, the ungrateful wretches! Trudolyubov will beat me hardest, he is so strong; Ferfichkin will be sure to catch hold sideways and tug at my hair. But no matter, no matter! That's what I am going for. The blockheads will be forced at last to see the tragedy of it all! When they drag me to the door I shall call out to them that in reality they are not worth my little finger. Get on, driver, get on!" I cried to the driver. He started and flicked his whip, I shouted so savagely.

"We shall fight at daybreak, that's a settled thing. I've done with the office. Ferfichkin made a joke about it just now. But where can I get pistols? Nonsense! I'll get my salary in advance and buy them. And powder, and bullets? That's the second's business. And how can it all be done by daybreak? And where am I to get a second? I have no friends. Nonsense!" I cried, lashing myself up more and more. "It's of no consequence! the first person I meet in the street is bound to be my second, just as he would be bound to pull a drowning man out of water. The most eccentric things may happen. Even if I were to ask the director himself to be my second to-morrow, he would be bound to consent, if only from a feeling of chivalry, and to keep the secret! Anton Antonich. . . ."

The fact is, that at that very minute the disgusting absurdity of my plan and the other side of the question was clearer and more vivid to my imagination than it could be to any one on earth. But. . . .

"Get on, driver, get on, you rascal, get on!"

"Ugh, sir!" said the son of toil.

Cold shivers suddenly ran down me.

Wouldn't it be better . . . to go straight home? My God, my God! Why did I invite myself to this dinner yesterday? But no, it's impossible. And my walking up and down for three hours from the table to the stove? No, they, they and no one else must pay for my walking up and down! They must wipe out this dishonour! Drive on!

And what if they give me into custody? They won't dare! They'll be afraid of the scandal. And what if Zverkov is so contemptuous that he refuses to fight a duel? He is sure to; but in that case I'll show them . . . I will turn up at the posting station when he is setting off to-morrow, I'll catch him by the leg, I'll pull off his coat when he gets into the carriage. I'll get my teeth into his hand, I'll bite him. "See what lengths you can drive a desperate man to!"

He may hit me on the head and they may belabour me from behind. I will shout to the assembled multitude: "Look at this young puppy who is driving off to captivate the Circassian girls after letting me spit in his face!"

Of course, after that everything will be over! The office will have vanished off the face of the earth. I shall be arrested, I shall be tried, I shall be dismissed from the service, thrown in prison, sent to Siberia. Never mind! In fifteen years when they let me out of prison I will trudge off to him, a beggar, in rags. I shall find him in some provincial town. He will be married and happy. He will have a grown-up daughter. . . . I shall say to him: "Look, monster, at my hollow cheeks and my rags! I've lost everything—my career, my happiness, art, science, *the woman I loved*, and all through you. Here are pistols. I have come to discharge my pistol and . . . and I . . . forgive you. Then I shall fire into the air and he will hear nothing more of me. . . ."

I was actually on the point of tears, though I knew perfectly well at that moment that all this was out of Pushkin's *Silvio*[28] and Lermontov's *Masquerade*.[29] And all at once I felt horribly ashamed, so ashamed that I stopped the horse, got out of the sledge, and stood still in the snow in the middle of the street. The driver gazed at me, sighing and astonished.

What was I to do? I could not go on there—it was evidently stupid, and I could not leave things as they were, because that would seem as though . . . Heavens, how could I leave things! And after such insults! "No!" I cried, throwing myself into the sledge again. "It is ordained! It is fate! Drive on, drive on!"

And in my impatience I punched the sledge-driver on the back of the neck.

"What are you up to? What are you hitting me for?" the peasant shouted, but he whipped up his nag so that it began kicking.

The wet snow was falling in big flakes; I unbuttoned myself, regardless of it. I forgot everything else, for I had finally decided on the slap, and felt with horror that it was going to happen *now, at once*, and that *no force could stop it*. The deserted street lamps gleamed sullenly in the snowy darkness like torches at a funeral. The snow drifted under my great-coat, under my coat, under my cravat, and melted there. I did not wrap myself up—all was lost, anyway.

At last we arrived. I jumped out, almost unconscious, ran up the steps and began knocking and kicking at the door. I felt fearfully weak, particularly in my legs and my knees. The door was opened

28. actually "The Shot" (1830), by the Russian Poet Alexander Pushkin (1799–1837), a story in which the hero, Silvio, finally gives up the idea of revenging himself for a slap in the face.

29. a verse play (1835) by the poet Mikhail Y. Lermontov (1814–1841).

quickly as though they knew I was coming. As a fact, Simonov had warned them that perhaps another gentleman would arrive, and this was a place in which one had to give notice and to observe certain precautions. It was one of those "millinery establishments" which were abolished by the police a good time ago. By day it really was a shop; but at night, if one had an introduction, one might visit it for other purposes.

I walked rapidly through the dark shop into the familiar drawing-room, where there was only one candle burning, and stood still in amazement: there was no one there. "Where are they?" I asked somebody. But by now, of course, they had separated. Before me was standing a person with a stupid smile, the "madam" herself, who had seen me before. A minute later a door opened and another person came in.

Taking no notice of anything I strode about the room, and, I believe, I talked to myself. I felt as though I had been saved from death and was conscious of this, joyfully, all over: I should have given that slap, I should certainly, certainly have given it! But now they were not here and . . . everything had vanished and changed! I looked round. I could not realize my condition yet. I looked mechanically at the girl who had come in: and had a glimpse of a fresh, young, rather pale face, with straight, dark eyebrows, and with grave, as it were wondering, eyes that attracted me at once; I should have hated her if she had been smiling. I began looking at her more intently and, as it were, with effort. I had not fully collected my thoughts. There was something simple and good-natured in her face, but something strangely grave. I am sure that this stood in her way here, and no one of those fools had noticed her. She could not, however, have been called a beauty, though she was tall, strong-looking, and well built. She was very simply dressed. Something loathsome stirred within me. I went straight up to her.

I chanced to look into the glass. My harassed face struck me as revolting in the extreme, pale, angry, abject, with dishevelled hair. "No matter, I am glad of it," I thought; "I am glad that I shall seem repulsive to her; I like that."

VI

. . . Somewhere behind a screen a clock began wheezing, as though oppressed by something, as though some one were strangling it. After an unnaturally prolonged wheezing there followed a shrill, nasty, and as it were unexpectedly rapid, chime—as though some one were suddenly jumping forward. It struck two. I woke up, though I had indeed not been asleep but lying half conscious.

It was almost completely dark in the narrow, cramped, low-pitched room, cumbered up with an enormous wardrobe and piles of cardboard boxes and all sorts of frippery and litter. The candle end that had been burning on the table was going out and gave a faint flicker from time to time. In a few minutes there would be complete darkness.

I was not long in coming to myself; everything came back to my mind at once, without an effort, as though it had been in ambush to pounce upon me again. And, indeed, even while I was unconscious a point seemed continually to remain in my memory unforgotten, and round it my dreams moved drearily. But strange to say, everything that had happened to me in that day seemed to me now, on waking, to be in the far, far away past, as though I had long, long ago lived all that down.

My head was full of fumes. Something seemed to be hovering over me, rousing me, exciting me, and making me restless. Misery and spite seemed surging up in me again and seeking an outlet. Suddenly I saw beside me two wide open eyes scrutinizing me curiously and persistently. The look in those eyes was coldly detached, sullen, as it were utterly remote; it weighed upon me.

A grim idea came into my brain and passed all over my body, as a horrible sensation, such as one feels when one goes into a damp and mouldy cellar. There was something unnatural in those two eyes, beginning to look at me only now. I recalled, too, that during those two hours I had not said a single word to this creature, and had, in fact, considered it utterly superfluous; in fact, the silence had for some reason gratified me. Now I suddenly realized vividly the hideous idea—revolting as a spider—of vice, which, without love, grossly and shamelessly begins with that in which true love finds its consummation. For a long time we gazed at each other like that, but she did not drop her eyes before mine and her expression did not change, so that at last I felt uncomfortable.

"What is your name?" I asked abruptly, to put an end to it.

"Liza," she answered almost in a whisper, but somehow far from graciously, and she turned her eyes away.

I was silent.

"What weather! The snow . . . it's disgusting!" I said, almost to myself, putting my arm under my head despondently, and gazing at the ceiling.

She made no answer. This was horrible.

"Have you always lived in Petersburg?" I asked a minute later, almost angrily, turning my head slightly towards her.

"No."

"Where do you come from?"

"From Riga," she answered reluctantly.

"Are you a German?"

"No, Russian."

"Have you been here long?"

"Where?"

"In this house?"

"A fortnight."

She spoke more and more jerkily. The candle went out; I could no longer distinguish her face.

"Have you a father and mother?"

"Yes . . . no . . . I have."

"Where are they?"

"There . . . in Riga."

"What are they?"

"Oh, nothing."

"Nothing? Why, what class are they?"

"Tradespeople."

"Have you always lived with them?"

"Yes."

"How old are you?"

"Twenty."

"Why did you leave them?"

"Oh, for no reason."

That answer meant "Let me alone; I feel sick, sad."

We were silent.

God knows why I did not go away. I felt myself more and more sick and dreary. The images of the previous day began of themselves, apart from my will, flitting through my memory in confusion. I suddenly recalled something I had seen that morning when, full of anxious thoughts, I was hurrying to the office.

"I saw them carrying a coffin out yesterday and they nearly dropped it," I suddenly said aloud, not that I desired to open the conversation, but as it were by accident.

"A coffin?"

"Yes, in the Haymarket; they were bringing it up out of a cellar."

"From a cellar?"

"Not from a cellar, but from a basement. Oh, you know . . . down below . . . from a house of ill-fame. It was filthy all round . . . Egg-shells, litter . . . stench. It was loathsome."

Silence.

"A nasty day to be buried," I began, simply to avoid being silent.

"Nasty, in what way?"

"The snow, the wet." (I yawned.)

"It makes no difference," she said suddenly, after a brief silence.

"No, it's horrid." (I yawned again.) "The gravediggers must have sworn at getting drenched by the snow. And there must have been water in the grave."

"Why water in the grave?" she asked, with a sort of curiosity, but speaking even more harshly and abruptly than before.

I suddenly began to feel provoked.

"Why, there must have been water at the bottom a foot deep. You can't dig a dry grave in Volkovo Cemetery."

"Why?"

"Why? Why, the place is waterlogged. It's a regular marsh. So they bury them in water. I've seen it myself . . . many times."

(I had never seen it once, indeed I had never been in Volkovo, and had only heard stories of it.)

"Do you mean to say, you don't mind how you die?"

"But why should I die?" she answered, as though defending herself.

"Why, some day you will die, and you will die just the same as that dead woman. She was . . . a girl like you. She died of consumption."

"A wench would have died in a hospital . . ." (She knows all about it already: she said "wench," not "girl.")

"She was in debt to her madam," I retorted, more and more provoked by the discussion; "and went on earning money for her up to the end, though she was in consumption. Some sledge-drivers standing by were talking about her to some soldiers and telling them so. No doubt they knew her. They were laughing. They were going to meet in a pot-house to drink to her memory."

A great deal of this was my invention. Silence followed, profound silence. She did not stir.

"And is it better to die in a hospital?"

"Isn't it just the same? Besides, why should I die?" she added irritably.

"If not now, a little later."

"Why a little later?"

"Why, indeed? Now you are young, pretty, fresh, you fetch a high price. But after another year of this life you will be very different—you will go off."

"In a year?"

"Anyway, in a year you will be worth less," I continued malignantly. "You will go from here to something lower, another house; a year later—to a third, lower and lower, and in seven years you will come to a basement in the Haymarket. That will be if you were lucky. But it would be much worse if you got some disease, consumption, say . . . and caught a chill, or something or other. It's not easy to get over an illness in your way of life. If you catch anything you may not get rid of it. And so you would die."

"Oh, well, then I shall die," she answered, quite vindictively, and she made a quick movement.

"But one is sorry."

"Sorry for whom?"

"Sorry for life."

Silence.

"Have you been engaged to be married? Eh?"

"What's that to you?"

"Oh, I am not cross-examining you. It's nothing to me. Why are you so cross? Of course you may have had your own troubles. What is it to me? It's simply that I felt sorry."

"Sorry for whom?"

"Sorry for you."

"No need," she whispered hardly audibly, and again made a faint movement.

That incensed me at once. What! I was so gentle with her, and she. . . .

"Why, do you think that you are on the right path?"

"I don't think anything."

"That's what's wrong, that you don't think. Realize it while there is still time. There still is time. You are still young, good-looking; you might love, be married, be happy. . . ."

"Not all married women are happy," she snapped out in the rude abrupt tone she had used at first.

"Not all, of course, but anyway it is much better than the life here. Infinitely better. Besides, with love one can live even without happiness. Even in sorrow life is sweet; life is sweet, however one lives. But here what is there but . . . filth? Phew!"

I turned away with disgust; I was no longer reasoning coldly. I began to feel myself what I was saying and warmed to the subject. I was already longing to expound the cherished ideas I had brooded over in my corner. Something suddenly flared up in me. An object had appeared before me.

"Never mind my being here, I am not an example for you. I am, perhaps, worse than you are. I was drunk when I came here, though," I hastened, however, to say in self-defence. "Besides, a man is no example for a woman. It's a different thing. I may degrade and defile myself, but I am not any one's slave. I come and go, and that's an end of it. I shake it off, and I am a different man But you are a slave from the start. Yes, a slave! You give up everything, your whole freedom. If you want to break your chains afterwards, you won't be able to: you will be more and more fast in the snares. It is an accursed bondage. I know it. I won't speak of any thing else, maybe you won't understand, but tell me: no doubt you are in debt to your madam? There, you see," I added, though she made no answer, but only listened in silence, entirely absorbed, "that's a bondage for you! You will never buy your freedom. They will see to that. It's like selling your soul to the devil. . . . And besides . . . perhaps I, too, am just as unlucky—how do you know

—and wallow in the mud on purpose, out of misery? You know, men take to drink from grief; well, maybe I am here from grief. Come, tell me, what is there good here? Here you and I . . . came together . . . just now and did not say one word to one another all the time, and it was only afterwards you began staring at me like a wild creature, and I at you. Is that loving? Is that how one human being should meet another? It's hideous, that's what it is!"

"Yes!" she assented sharply and hurriedly.

I was positively astounded by the promptitude of this "Yes." So the same thought may have been straying through her mind when she was staring at me just before. So she, too, was capable of certain thoughts? "Damn it all, this was interesting, this was a point of likeness!" I thought, almost rubbing my hands. And indeed it's easy to turn a young soul like that!

It was the exercise of my power that attracted me most.

She turned her head nearer to me, and it seemed to me in the darkness that she propped herself on her arm. Perhaps she was scrutinizing me. How I regretted that I could not see her eyes. I heard her deep breathing.

"Why have you come here?" I asked her, with a note of authority already in my voice.

"Oh, I don't know."

"But how nice it would be to be living in your father's house! It's warm and free; and you have a home of your own."

"But what if it's worse than this?"

"I must take the right tone," flashed through my mind. "I may not get far with sentimentality." But it was only a momentary thought. I swear she really did interest me. Besides, I was exhausted and moody. And cunning so easily goes hand-in-hand with feeling.

"Who denies it!" I hastened to answer. "Anything may happen. I am convinced that some one has wronged you, and that you are more sinned against than sinning. Of course, I know nothing of your story, but it's not likely a girl like you has come here of her own inclination. . . ."

"A girl like me?" she whispered, hardly audibly; but I heard it.

Damn it all, I was flattering her. That was horrid. But perhaps it was a good thing. . . . She was silent.

"See, Liza, I will tell you about myself. If I had had a home from childhood, I shouldn't be what I am now. I often think that. However bad it may be at home, anyway they are your father and mother, and not enemies, strangers. Once a year at least, they'll show their love of you. Anyway, you know you are at home. I grew up without a home; and perhaps that's why I've turned so . . . unfeeling."

I waited again. "Perhaps she doesn't understand," I thought, "and, indeed, it is absurd—it's moralizing."

"If I were a father and had a daughter, I believe I should love my daughter more than my sons, really," I began indirectly, as though talking of something else, to distract her attention. I must confess I blushed.

"Why so?" she asked.

Ah! so she was listening!

"I don't know, Liza. I knew a father who was a stern, austere man, but used to go down on his knees to his daughter, used to kiss her hands, her feet, he couldn't make enough of her, really. When she danced at parties he used to stand for five hours at a stretch, gazing at her. He was mad over her: I understand that! She would fall asleep tired at night, and he would wake to kiss her in her sleep and make the sign of the cross over her. He would go about in a dirty old coat, he was stingy to every one else, but would spend his last penny for her, giving her expensive presents, and it was his greatest delight when she was pleased with what he gave her. Fathers always love their daughters more than the mothers do. Some girls live happily at home! And I believe I should never let my daughters marry."

"What next?" she said, with a faint smile.

"I should be jealous, I really should. To think that she should kiss any one else! That she should love a stranger more than her father! It's painful to imagine it. Of course, that's all nonsense, of course every father would be reasonable at last. But I believe before I should let her marry, I should worry myself to death; I should find fault with all her suitors. But I should end by letting her marry whom she herself loved. The one whom the daughter loves always seems the worst to the father, you know. That is always so. So many family troubles come from that."

"Some are glad to sell their daughters, rather than marrying them honourably."

Ah, so that was it!

"Such a thing, Liza, happens in those accursed families in which there is neither love nor God," I retorted warmly, "and where there is no love, there is no sense either. There are such families, it's true, but I am not speaking of them. You must have seen wickedness in your own family, if you talk like that. Truly, you must have been unlucky. H'm! . . . that sort of thing mostly comes about through poverty."

"And is it any better with the gentry? Even among the poor, honest people live happily."

"H'm . . . yes. Perhaps. Another thing, Liza, man is fond of reckoning up his troubles, but does not count his joys. If he counted them up as he ought, he would see that every lot has enough happiness provided for it. And what if all goes well with the family, if the blessing of God is upon it, if the husband is a good one, loves you, cherishes you, never leaves you! There is happiness in such a family! Even sometimes there is happiness in the midst of sorrow; and indeed sorrow is everywhere. If you marry *you will find out for yourself*. But think of the first years of married life with one you love: what happiness, what happiness there sometimes is in it! And indeed it's the ordinary thing. In those early days even quarrels with one's husband end happily. Some women get up quarrels with their husbands just because they love them. Indeed, I knew a woman like that: she seemed to say that because she loved him, she would torment him and make him feel it. You know that you may torment a man on purpose through love. Women are particularly given to that, thinking to themselves 'I will love him so, I will make so much of him afterwards, that it's no sin to torment him a little now.' And all in the house rejoice in the sight of you, and you are happy and gay and peaceful and honourable. . . . Then there are some women who are jealous. If he went off anywhere—I knew one such woman, she couldn't restrain herself, but would jump up at night and run off on the sly to find out where he was, whether he was with some other woman. That's a pity. And the woman knows herself it's wrong, and her heart fails her and she suffers, but she loves—it's all through love. And how sweet it is to make it up after quarrels, to own herself in the wrong or to forgive him! And they are both so happy all at once—as though they had met anew, been married over again; as though their love had begun afresh. And no one, no one should know what passes between husband and wife if they love one another. And whatever quarrels there may be between them they ought not to call in their own mother to judge between them and tell tales of one another. They are their own judges. Love is a holy mystery and ought to be hidden from all other eyes, whatever happens. That makes it holier and better. They respect one another more, and much is built on respect. And if once there has been love, if they have been married for love, why should love pass away? Surely one can keep it! It is rare that one cannot keep it. And if the husband is kind and straightforward, why should not love last? The first phase of married love will pass, it is true, but then there will come a love that is better still. Then there will be the union of souls, they will have everything in common, there will be no secrets between them. And once they have children, the most difficult times will seem to them happy, so long as there is love and courage. Even toil will be a joy, you may deny yourself bread for your children and even that will be a joy. They will love you for it afterwards; so you are laying by for your future. As the children grow up you feel that you are an example, a support for them; that even after you die your children will always keep your thoughts and feelings, because they have received them from you, they will take on your semblance and likeness. So you see this is a great duty. How can it fail to draw the father and mother nearer? People say it's a trial to have children. Who says that? It is heavenly happiness! Are you fond of little children, Liza? I am awfully fond of them. You know—a little rosy baby boy at your bosom, and what husband's heart is not touched, seeing his wife nursing his child! A plump little rosy baby, sprawling and snuggling, chubby little hands and feet, clean tiny little nails, so tiny that it makes one laugh to look at them; eyes that look as if they understand everything. And while it sucks it clutches at your bosom with its little hand, plays. When its father comes up, the child tears itself away from the bosom, flings itself back, looks at its father, laughs, as though it were fearfully funny and falls to sucking again. Or it will bite its mother's breast when its little teeth are coming, while it looks sideways at her with its little eyes as though to say, 'Look, I am biting!' Is not all that happiness when they are the three together, husband, wife and child? One can forgive a great deal for the sake of such moments. Yes, Liza, one must first learn to live oneself before one blames others!"

"It's by pictures, pictures like that one must get at you," I thought to myself, though I did speak with real feeling, and all at once I flushed crimson. "What if she were suddenly to burst out laughing, what should I do then?" That idea drove me to fury. Towards the end of my speech I really was excited, and now my vanity was somehow wounded. The silence continued. I almost nudged her.

"Why are you——" she began and stopped. But I understood: there was a quiver of something different in her voice, not abrupt, harsh and unyielding as before, but something soft and shamefaced, so shamefaced that I suddenly felt ashamed and guilty.

"What?" I asked, with tender curiosity.

"Why, you . . ."

"What?"

"Why, you . . . speak somehow like a book," she said, and again there was a note of irony in her voice.

That remark sent a pang to my heart. It was not what I was expecting.

I did not understand that she was hiding her feelings under irony, that this is usually the last refuge of modest and chaste-souled people when the privacy of their soul is coarsely and intrusively invaded, and that their pride makes them refuse to surrender till the last moment and shrink from giving expression to their feelings before you. I ought to have guessed the truth from the timidity with which she had repeatedly approached her sarcasm, only bringing herself to utter it at last with an effort. But I did not guess, and an evil feeling took possession of me.

"Wait a bit!" I thought.

VII

"Oh, hush, Liza! How can you talk about being like a book, when it makes even me, an outsider, feel sick? Though I don't look at it as an outsider, for, indeed, it touches me to the heart. . . . Is it possible, is it possible that you do not feel sick at being here yourself? Evidently habit does wonders! God knows what habit can do with any one. Can you seriously think that you will never grow old, that you will always be good-looking, and that they will keep you here for ever and ever? I say nothing of the loathsomeness of the life here. . . . Though let me tell you this about it—about your present life, I mean; here though you are young now, attractive, nice, with soul and feeling, yet you know as soon as I came to myself just now I felt at once sick at being here with you! One can only come here when one is drunk. But if you were anywhere else, living as good people live, I should perhaps be more than attracted by you, should fall in love with you, should be glad of a look from you, let alone a word; I should hang about your door, should go down on my knees to you, should look upon you as my betrothed and think it an honour to be allowed to. I should not dare to have an impure thought about you. But here, you see, I know that I have only to whistle and you have to come with me whether you like it or not. I don't consult your wishes, but you mine. The lowest labourer hires himself as a workman, but he doesn't make a slave of himself altogether; besides, he knows that he will be free again presently. But when are you free? Only think what you are giving up here? What is it you are making a slave of? It is your soul, together with your body; you are selling your soul which you have no right to dispose of! You give your love to be outraged by every drunkard! Love! But that's everything, you know, it's a priceless diamond, it's a maiden's treasure, love—why, a man would be ready to give his soul, to face death to gain that love. But how much is your love worth now? You are sold, all of you, body and soul, and there is no need to strive for love when you can have everything without love. And you know there is no greater insult to a girl than that, do you understand? To be sure, I have heard that they comfort you, poor fools, they let you have lovers of your own here. But you know that's simply a farce, that's simply a sham, it's just laughing at you, and you are taken in by it! Why, do you suppose he really loves you, that lover of yours? I don't believe it. How can he love you when he knows you may be called away from him any minute?

He would be a low fellow if he did! Will he have a grain of respect for you? What have you in common with him? He laughs at you and robs you—that is all his love amounts to! You are lucky if he does not beat you. Very likely he does beat you, too. Ask him, if you have got one, whether he will marry you. He will laugh in your face, if he doesn't spit in it or give you a blow—though maybe he is not worth a bad halfpenny himself. And for what have you ruined your life, if you come to think of it? For the coffee they give you to drink and the plentiful meals? But with what object are they feeding you up? An honest girl couldn't swallow the food, for she would know what she was being fed for. You are in debt here, and, of course, you will always be in debt, and you will go on in debt to the end, till the visitors here begin to scorn you. And that will soon happen, don't rely upon your youth—all that flies by express train here, you know. You will be kicked out. And not simply kicked out; long before that she'll begin nagging at you, scolding you, abusing you, as though you had not sacrificed your health for her, had not thrown away your youth and your soul for her benefit, but as though you had ruined her, beggared her, robbed her. And don't expect any one to take your part: the others, your companions, will attack you, too, to win her favour, for all are in slavery here, and have lost all conscience and pity here long ago. They have become utterly vile, and nothing on earth is viler, more loathsome, and more insulting than their abuse. And you are laying down everything here, unconditionally, youth and health and beauty and hope, and at twenty-two you will look like a woman of five-and-thirty, and you will be lucky if you are not diseased, pray to God for that! No doubt you are thinking now that you have a gay time and no work to do! Yet there is no work harder or more dreadful in the world or ever has been. One would think that the heart alone would be worn out with tears. And you won't dare to say a word, not half a word when they drive you away from here; you will go away as though you were to blame. You will change to another house, then to a third, then somewhere else, till you come down at last to the Haymarket. There you will be beaten at every turn; that is good manners there, the visitors don't know how to be friendly without beating you. You don't believe that it is so hateful there? Go and look for yourself some time, you can see with your own eyes. Once, one New Year's Day, I saw a woman at a door. They had turned her out as a joke, to give her a taste of the frost because she had been crying so much, and they shut the door behind her. At nine o'clock in the morning she was already quite drunk, dishevelled, half-naked, covered with bruises, her face was powdered, but she had a black-eye, blood was trickling from her nose and her teeth; some cabman had just given her a drubbing. She was sitting on the stone steps, a salt fish of some sort was in her hand; she was crying, wailing something about her luck and beating with the fish on the steps, and cabmen and drunken soldiers were crowding in the doorway taunting her. You don't believe that you will ever be like that? I should be sorry to believe it, too, but how do you know; maybe ten years, eight years ago that very woman with the salt fish came here fresh as a cherub, innocent, pure, knowing no evil, blushing at every word. Perhaps she was like you, proud, ready to take offence, not like the others; perhaps she looked like a queen, and knew what happiness was in store for the man who should love her and whom she should love. Do you see how it ended? And what if at that very minute when she was beating on the filthy steps with that fish, drunken and dishevelled—what if at that very minute she recalled the pure early days in her father's house, when she used to go to school and the neighbour's son watched for her on the way, declaring that he would love her as long as he lived, that he would devote his life to her, and when they vowed to love one another for ever and be married as soon as they were grown up! No, Liza, it would be happy for you if you were to die soon of consumption in some corner, in some cellar like that woman just now. In the hospital, do you say? You will be lucky if they take you, but what if you are still of use to the madam here? Consumption is a queer disease, it is not like fever. The patient goes on hoping till the last minute and says he is all right. He deludes himself. And that just suits your madam. Don't doubt it, that's how it is; you have sold your soul, and what is more you owe money, so you daren't say a word. But when you are dying, all will abandon you, all will turn away from you, for then there will be nothing to get from you. What's more, they will reproach you for cumbering the place, for being so long over dying. However you beg you won't get a drink of water without abuse: 'Whenever are you going off, you nasty hussy, you won't let us sleep with your moaning, you make the gentlemen sick.' That's true, I have heard such things said myself. They will thrust you dying into the filthiest corner in the cellar—in the damp and darkness; what will your thoughts be, lying there alone? When you die, strange hands will lay you out, with grumbling and impatience; no one will bless you, no one will sigh for you, they only want to get rid of you as soon as may be; they will buy a coffin, take you to the grave as they did that poor woman to-day, and celebrate your memory at the tavern. In the gravest sleet, filth, wet snow—no need to put themselves out for you—'Let her down, Vanyukha; it's just like her luck—even here, she is headforemost, the hussy. Shorten the cord, you rascal.' 'It's all right as it is.' 'All right, is it? Why, she's on her side! She was a fellow-creature, after all! But, never mind, throw the earth on her.' And they won't care to waste much time quarrelling over you. They will scatter the wet blue clay as quick as they can and go off to the tavern . . . and there your memory on earth will end; other women have children to go to their graves, fathers, husbands. While for you neither tear, nor sigh, nor remembrance; no one in the whole world will ever come to you, your name will vanish from the face of the earth —as though you had never existed, never been born at all! Nothing but filth and mud, however you knock at your coffin lid at night, when the dead arise, however you cry: 'Let me out, kind people, to live in the light of day! My life was no life at all; my life has been thrown away like a dish-clout; it was drunk away in the tavern at the Haymarket; let me out, kind people, to live in the world again.' "

And I worked myself up to such a pitch that I began to have a lump in my throat myself, and . . . and all at once I stopped, sat up in dismay, and bending over apprehensively, began to listen with a beating heart. I had reason to be troubled.

I had felt for some time that I was turning her soul upside down and rending her heart, and—and the more I was convinced of it, the more eagerly I desired to gain my object as quickly and as effectually as possible. It was the exercise of my skill that carried me away; yet it was not merely sport. . . .

I knew I was speaking stiffly, artificially, even bookishly, in fact, I could not speak except "like a book." But that did not trouble me: I knew, I felt that I should be understood and that this very bookishness might be an assistance. But now, having attained my effect, I was suddenly panic-stricken. Never before had I witnessed such despair! She was lying on her face, thrusting her face into the pillow and clutching it in both hands. Her heart was being torn. Her youthful body was shuddering all over as though in convulsions. Suppressed sobs rent her bosom and suddenly burst out in weeping and wailing, then she pressed closer into the pillow: she did not want any one here, not a living soul, to know of her anguish and her tears. She bit the pillow, bit her hand till it bled (I saw that afterwards), or, thrusting her fingers into her dishevelled hair seemed rigid with the effort of restraint, holding her breath and clenching her teeth. I began saying something, begging her to calm herself, but felt that I did not dare; and all at once, in a sort of cold shiver, almost in terror, began fumbling in the dark, trying hurriedly to get dressed to go. It was dark: though I tried my best I could not finish dressing quickly. Suddenly I felt a box of matches and a candlestick with a whole candle in it. As soon as the room was lighted up, Liza sprang up, sat up in bed, and with a contorted face, with a half insane smile, looked at me almost senselessly. I sat down beside her and took her hands; she came to herself, made an impulsive movement towards me, would have caught hold of me, but did not dare, and slowly bowed her head before me.

"Liza, my dear, I was wrong . . . forgive me, my dear," I began, but she squeezed my hand in her fingers so tightly that I felt I was saying the wrong thing and stopped.

"This is my address, Liza, come to me."

"I will come," she answered resolutely, her head still bowed.

"But now I am going, good-bye . . . till we meet again."

I got up; she, too, stood up and suddenly flushed all over, gave a shudder, snatched up a shawl that was lying on a chair and muffled herself in it to her chin. As she did this she gave another sickly smile, blushed and looked at me strangely. I felt wretched; I was in haste to get away—to disappear.

"Wait a minute," she said suddenly, in the passage just at the doorway, stopping me with her hand on my overcoat. She put down the candle in hot haste and ran off; evidently she had thought of something or wanted to show me something. As she ran away she flushed, her eyes shone, and there was a smile on her lips—what was the meaning of it? Against my will I waited: she came back a minute later with an expression that seemed to ask forgiveness for something. In fact, it was not the same face, not the same look as the evening before: sullen, mistrustful and obstinate. Her eyes now were imploring, soft, and at the same time trustful, caressing, timid. The expression with which children look at people they are very fond of, of whom they are asking a favour. Her eyes were a light hazel, they were lovely eyes, full of life, and capable of expressing love as well as sullen hatred.

Making no explanation, as though I, as a sort of higher being, must understand everything without explanations, she held out a piece of paper to me. Her whole face was positively beaming at that instant with naïve, almost childish, triumph. I unfolded it. It was a letter to her from a medical student or some one of that sort—a very high-flown and flowery, but extremely respectful, love-letter. I don't recall the words now, but I remember well that through the high-flown phrases there was apparent a genuine feeling, which cannot be feigned. When I had finished reading it I met her glowing, questioning, and childishly impatient eyes fixed upon me. She fastened her eyes upon my face and waited impatiently for what I should say. In a few words, hurriedly, but with a sort of joy and pride, she explained to me that she had been to a dance somewhere in a private house, a family of "very nice people *who knew nothing*, absolutely nothing, for she had only come here so lately and it had all happened . . . and she hadn't made up her mind to stay and was certainly going away as soon as she had paid her debt . . ."

and at that party there had been the student who had danced with her all the evening. He had talked to her, and it turned out that he had known her in old days at Riga when he was a child, they had played together, but a very long time ago—and he knew her parents, but *about this* he knew nothing, nothing whatever, and had no suspicion! And the day after the dance (three days ago) he had sent her that letter through the friend with whom she had gone to the party . . . and . . . well, that was all.

She dropped her shining eyes with a sort of bashfulness as she finished.

The poor girl was keeping that student's letter as a precious treasure, and had run to fetch it, her only treasure, because she did not want me to go away without knowing that she, too, was honestly and genuinely loved; that she, too, was addressed respectfully. No doubt that letter was destined to lie in her box and lead to nothing. But none the less, I am certain that she would keep it all her life as a precious treasure, as her pride and justification, and now at such a minute she had thought of that letter and brought it with naïve pride to raise herself in my eyes that I might see, that I, too, might think well of her. I said nothing, pressed her hand and went out. I so longed to get away. . . . I walked all the way home, in spite of the fact that the melting snow was still falling in heavy flakes. I was exhausted, shattered, in bewilderment. But behind the bewilderment the truth was already gleaming. The loathsome truth.

VIII

It was some time, however, before I consented to recognize that truth. Waking up in the morning after some hours of heavy, leaden sleep, and immediately realizing all that had happened on the previous day, I was positively amazed at my last night's *sentimentality* with Liza, at all those "outcries of horror and pity." "To think of having such an attack of womanish hysteria, pah!" I concluded. And what did I thrust my address upon her for? What if she comes? Let her come, though; it doesn't matter. . . . But *obviously*, that was not now the chief and the most important matter: I had to make haste and at all costs save my reputation in the eyes of Zverkov and Simonov as quickly as possible; that was the chief business. And I was so taken up that morning that I actually forgot all about Liza.

First of all I had at once to repay what I had borrowed the day before from Simonov. I resolved on a desperate measure: to borrow fifteen roubles straight off from Anton Antonich. As luck would have it he was in the best of humours that morning, and gave it to me at once, on the first asking. I was so delighted at this that, as I signed the I O U with a swaggering air, I told him casually that the night before "I had been keeping it up with some friends at the Hôtel de Paris; we were giving a farewell party to a comrade, in fact,

I might say a friend of my childhood, and you know—a desperate rake, fearfully spoilt—of course, he belongs to a good family, and has considerable means, a brilliant career; he is witty, charming, a regular Lovelace, you understand; we drank an extra 'half-dozen' and . . ."

And it went off all right; all this was uttered very easily, unconstrainedly and complacently.

On reaching home I promptly wrote to Simonov.

To this hour I am lost in admiration when I recall the truly gentlemanly, good-humoured, candid tone of my letter. With tact and good-breeding, and, above all, entirely without superfluous words, I blamed myself for all that had happened. I defended myself, "if I really may be allowed to defend myself," by alleging that being utterly unaccustomed to wine, I had been intoxicated with the first glass, which I said, I had drunk before they arrived, while I was waiting for them at the Hôtel de Paris between five and six o'clock. I begged Simonov's pardon especially; I asked him to convey my explanations to all the others, especially to Zverkov, whom "I seemed to remember as though in a dream" I had insulted. I added that I would have called upon all of them myself, but my head ached, and besides I had not the face to. I was particularly pleased with a certain lightness, almost carelessness (strictly within the bounds of politeness, however), which was apparent in my style, and better than any possible arguments, gave them at once to understand that I took rather an independent view of "all that unpleasantness last night;" that I was by no means so utterly crushed as you, my friends, probably imagine; but on the contrary, looked upon it as a gentleman serenely respecting himself should look upon it. "On a young hero's past no censure is cast!"

"There is actually an aristocratic playfulness about it!" I thought admiringly, as I read over the letter. And it's all because I am an intellectual and cultivated man! Another man in my place would not have known how to extricate himself, but here I have got out of it and am as jolly as ever again, and all because I am "a cultivated and educated man of our day." And, indeed, perhaps, everything was due to the wine yesterday. H'm! . . . no, it was not the wine. I did not drink anything at all between five and six when I was waiting for them. I had lied to Simonov; I had lied shamelessly; and indeed I wasn't ashamed now. . . . Hang it all though, the great thing was that I was rid of it.

I put six roubles in the letter, sealed it up, and asked Apollon to take it to Simonov. When he learned that there was money in the letter, Apollon became more respectful and agreed to take it. Towards evening I went out for a walk. My head was still aching and giddy after yesterday. But as evening came on and the twilight grew denser, my impressions and, following them, my thoughts, grew more and more different and confused. Something was not dead within me, in the depths of my heart and conscience it would not die, and it showed itself in acute depression. For the most part I jostled my way through the most crowded business streets, along Myeshchansky Street, along Sadovy Street and in Yusupov Garden. I always liked particularly sauntering along these streets in the dusk, just when there were crowds of working people of all sorts going home from their daily work, with faces looking cross with anxiety. What I liked was just that cheap bustle, that bare prose. On this occasion the jostling of the streets irritated me more than ever. I could not make out what was wrong with me, I could not find the clue, something seemed rising up continually in my soul, painfully, and refusing to be appeased. I returned home completely upset, it was just as though some crime were lying on my conscience.

The thought that Liza was coming worried me continually. It seemed queer to me that of all my recollections of yesterday this tormented me, as it were, especially, as it were, quite separately. Everything else I had quite succeeded in forgetting by the evening; I dismissed it all and was still perfectly satisfied with my letter to Simonov. But on this point I was not satisfied at all. It was as though I were worried only by Liza. "What if she comes," I thought incessantly, "well, it doesn't matter, let her come! H'm! it's horrid that she should see, for instance, how I live. Yesterday I seemed such a hero to her, while now, h'm! It's horrid, though, that I have let myself go so, the room looks like a beggar's. And I brought myself to go out to dinner in such a suit! And my American leather sofa with the stuffing sticking out. And my dressing-gown, which will not cover me, such tatters, and she will see all this and she will see Apollon. That beast is certain to insult her. He will fasten upon her in order to be rude to me. And I, of course, shall be panic-stricken as usual, I shall begin bowing and scraping before her and pulling my dressing-gown round me, I shall begin smiling, telling lies. Oh, the beastliness! And it isn't the beastliness of it that matters most! There is something more important, more loathsome, viler! Yes, viler! And to put on that dishonest lying mask again!" . . .

When I reached that thought I fired up all at once.

"Why dishonest? How dishonest? I was speaking sincerely last night. I remember there was real feeling in me, too. What I wanted was to excite an honourable feeling in her. . . . Her crying was a good thing, it will have a good effect."

Yet I could not feel at ease. All that evening, even when I had come back home, even after nine o'clock, when I calculated that Liza could not possibly come, she still haunted me, and what was worse, she came back to my mind always in the same position. One moment out of all that had happened last night stood vividly before my imagination; the moment when I struck a match and saw her pale, distorted face, with its look of torture. And what a pitiful, what an unnatural, what a distorted smile she had at that moment! But I did not know then, that fifteen years later I should still in my imagination see Liza, always with the pitiful, distorted, inappropriate smile which was on her face at that minute.

Next day I was ready again to look upon it all as nonsense, due to over-excited nerves, and, above all, as *exaggerated*. I was always conscious of that weak point of mine, and sometimes very much afraid of it. "I exaggerate everything, that is where I go wrong," I repeated to myself every hour. But, however, "Liza will very likely come all the same," was the refrain with which all my reflections ended. I was so uneasy that I sometimes flew into a fury: "She'll come, she is certain to come!" I cried, running about the room, "if not to-day, she will come to-morrow; she'll find me out! The damnable romanticism of these pure hearts! Oh, the vileness—oh, the silliness—oh, the stupidity of these 'wretched sentimental souls!' Why, how fail to understand? How could one fail to understand? . . ."

But at this point I stopped short, and in great confusion, indeed.

And how few, how few words, I thought, in passing, were needed; how little of the idyllic (and affectedly, bookishly, artificially idyllic too) had sufficed to turn a whole human life at once according to my will. That's virginity, to be sure! Freshness of soil!

At times a thought occurred to me, to go to her, "to tell her all," and beg her not to come to me. But this thought stirred such wrath in me that I believed I should have crushed that "damned" Liza if she had chanced to be near me at the time. I should have insulted her, have spat at her, have turned her out, have struck her!

One day passed, however, another and another; she did not come and I began to grow calmer. I felt particularly bold and cheerful after nine o'clock, I even sometimes began dreaming, and rather sweetly: I, for instance, became the salvation of Liza, simply through her coming to me and my talking to her. . . . I develop her, educate her. Finally, I notice that she loves me, loves me passionately. I pretend not to understand (I don't know, however, why I pretend, just for effect, perhaps). At last all confusion, transfigured, trembling and sobbing, she flings herself at my feet and says that I am her saviour, and that she loves me better than anything in the world. I am amazed, but. . . . "Liza," I say, "can you imagine that I have not noticed your love, I saw it all, I divined it, but I did not dare to approach you first, because I had an influence over you and was afraid that you would force yourself, from gratitude, to respond to my love, would try to rouse in your heart a feeling which was perhaps absent, and I did not wish that . . . because it would be tyranny . . . it would be indelicate (in short, I launch off at that point into European, inexplicably lofty subtleties à la George Sand[30]), but now, now you are mine, you are my creation, you are pure, you are good, you are my noble wife.

> 'Into my house come bold and free,
> Its rightful mistress there to be.' "[31]

Then we begin living together, go abroad and so on, and so on. In fact, in the end it seemed vulgar to me myself, and I began putting out my tongue at myself.

Besides, they won't let her out, "the hussy!" I thought. They don't let them go out very readily, especially in the evening (for some reason I fancied she would come in the evening, and at seven o'clock precisely). Though she did say she was not altogether a slave there yet, and had certain rights; so, h'm! Damn it all, she will come, she is sure to come!

It was a good thing, in fact, that Apollon distracted my attention at that time by his rudeness. He drove me beyond all patience! He was the bane of my life, the curse laid upon me by Providence. We had been squabbling continually for years, and I hated him. My God, how I hated him! I believe I had never hated any one in my life as I hated him, especially at some moments. He was an elderly, dignified man, who worked part of his time as a tailor. But for some unknown reason he despised me beyond all measure, and looked down upon me insufferably. Though, indeed, he looked down upon every one. Simply to glance at that flaxen, smoothly brushed head, at the tuft of hair he combed up on his forehead and oiled with sunflower oil, at that dignified mouth, compressed into the shape of the letter V, made one feel one was confronting a man who never doubted of himself. He was a pedant, to the most extreme point, the greatest pedant I had met on earth, and with that had a vanity only befitting Alexander of Macedon. He was in love with every button on his coat, every nail on his fingers—absolutely in love with them, and he looked it! In his behaviour to me he was a perfect tyrant, he spoke very little to me, and if he chanced to glance at me he gave me a firm, majestically self-confident and invariably ironical look that drove me sometimes to fury. He did his work with the air of doing me the greatest favour. Though he did scarcely anything for me, and did not, indeed, consider himself bound to do anything. There could be no doubt that he looked upon me as the greatest fool on earth, and that "he did not get rid of me" was simply that

30. pseudonym of the French woman novelist Mme. Aurore Dudevant (1804–1876), famous also as a promoter of feminism.

31. the last lines of the poem by Nekrasov used as the epigraph of Part II of this story.

he could get wages from me every month. He consented to do nothing for me for seven roubles a month. Many sins should be forgiven me for what I suffered from him. My hatred reached such a point that sometimes his very step almost threw me into convulsions. What I loathed particularly was his lisp. His tongue must have been a little too long or something of that sort, for he continually lisped, and seemed to be very proud of it, imagining that it greatly added to his dignity. He spoke in a slow, measured tone, with his hands behind his back and his eyes fixed on the ground. He maddened me particularly when he read aloud the psalms to himself behind his partition. Many a battle I waged over that reading! But he was awfully fond of reading aloud in the evenings, in a slow, even, singsong voice, as though over the dead. It is interesting that that is how he has ended: he hires himself out to read the psalms over the dead, and at the same time he kills rats and makes blacking. But at that time I could not get rid of him, it was as though he were chemically combined with my existence. Besides, nothing would have induced him to consent to leave me. I could not live in furnished lodgings: my lodging was my private solitude, my shell, my cave, in which I concealed myself from all mankind, and Apollon seemed to me, for some reason, an integral part of that flat, and for seven years I could not turn him away.

To be two or three days behind with his wages, for instance, was impossible. He would have made such a fuss, I should not have known where to hide my head. But I was so exasperated with every one during those days, that I made up my mind for some reason and with some object to *punish* Apollon and not to pay him for a fortnight the wages that were owing him. I had for a long time—for the last two years—been intending to do this, simply in order to teach him not to give himself airs with me, and to show him that if I liked I could withhold his wages. I purposed to say nothing to him about it, and was purposely silent indeed, in order to score off his pride and force him to be the first to speak of his wages. Then I would take the seven roubles out of a drawer, show him I have the money put aside on purpose, but that I won't, I won't, I simply won't pay him his wages, I won't just because that is "what I wish," because "I am master, and it is for me to decide," because he has been disrespectful, because he has been rude; but if he were to ask respectfully I might be softened and give it to him, otherwise he might wait another fortnight, another three weeks, a whole month. . . .

But angry as I was, yet he got the better of me. I could not hold out for four days. He began as he always did begin in such cases, for there had been such cases already, there had been attempts (and it may be observed I knew all this beforehand, I knew his nasty tactics by heart). He would begin by fixing upon me an exceedingly severe stare, keeping it up for several minutes at a time, particularly on meeting me or seeing me out of the house. If I held out and pretended not to notice these stares, he would, still in silence, proceed to further tortures. All at once, *à propos* of nothing, he would walk softly and smoothly into my room, when I was pacing up and down or reading, stand at the door, one hand behind his back and one foot behind the other, and fix upon me a stare more than severe, utterly contemptuous. If I suddenly asked him what he wanted, he would make me no answer, but continue staring at me persistently for some seconds, then, with a peculiar compression of his lips and a most significant air, deliberately turn round and deliberately go back to his room. Two hours later he would come out again and again present himself before me in the same way. It had happened that in my fury I did not even ask him what he wanted, but simply raised my head sharply and imperiously and began staring back at him. So we stared at one another for two minutes; at last he turned with deliberation and dignity and went back again for two hours.

If I were still not brought to reason by all this, but persisted in my revolt, he would suddenly begin sighing while he looked at me, long, deep sighs as though measuring by them the depths of my moral degradation, and, of course, it ended at last by his triumphing completely: I raged and shouted, but still was forced to do what he wanted.

This time the usual staring manœuvres had scarcely begun when I lost my temper and flew at him in a fury. I was irritated beyond endurance apart from him.

"Stay," I cried, in a frenzy, as he was slowly and silently turning, with one hand behind his back, to go to his room, "stay! Come back, come back, I tell you!" and I must have bawled so unnaturally, that he turned round and even looked at me with some wonder. However, he persisted in saying nothing, and that infuriated me.

"How dare you come and look at me like that without being sent for? Answer!"

After looking at me calmly for half a minute, he began turning round again.

"Stay!" I roared, running up to him, "don't stir! There. Answer, now: what did you come in to look at?"

"If you have any order to give me it's my duty to carry it out," he answered, after another silent pause, with a slow, measured lisp, raising his eyebrows and calmly twisting his head from one side to another, all this with exasperating composure.

"That's not what I am asking you about, you torturer!" I shouted, turning crimson with anger. "I'll tell you why you came here myself: you see, I don't give you your wages, you are so proud you don't want to bow down and ask for it, and so you come to punish me with your stupid stares, to worry me and you have no sus . . . pic . . . ion how stupid it is—stupid, stupid, stupid, stupid!" . . .

He would have turned round again without a word, but I seized him.

"Listen," I shouted to him. "Here's the money, do you see, here it is" (I took it out of the table drawer); "here's the seven roubles complete, but you are not going to have it, you . . . are . . . not . . . going . . . to . . . have it until you come respectfully with bowed head to beg my pardon. Do you hear?"

"That cannot be," he answered, with the most unnatural self-confidence.

"It shall be so," I said, "I give you my word of honour, it shall be!"

"And there's nothing for me to beg your pardon for," he went on, as though he had not noticed my exclamations at all. "Why, besides, you called me a 'torturer,' for which I can summon you at the police-station at any time for insulting behaviour."

"Go, summon me," I roared, "go at once, this very minute, this very second! You are a torturer all the same! a torturer!"

But he merely looked at me, then turned, and regardless of my loud calls to him, he walked to his room with an even step and without looking round.

"If it had not been for Liza nothing of this would have happened," I decided inwardly. Then, after waiting a minute, I went myself behind his screen with a dignified and solemn air, though my heart was beating slowly and violently.

"Apollon," I said quietly and emphatically, though I was breathless, "go at once without a minute's delay and fetch the police-officer."

He had meanwhile settled himself at his table, put on his spectacles and taken up some sewing. But, hearing my order, he burst into a guffaw.

"At once, go this minute! Go on, or else you can't imagine what will happen."

"You are certainly out of your mind," he observed, without even raising his head, lisping as deliberately as ever and threading his needle. "Whoever heard of a man sending for the police against himself? And as for being frightened—you are upsetting yourself about nothing, for nothing will come of it."

"Go!" I shrieked, clutching him by the shoulder. I felt I should strike him in a minute.

But I did not notice the door from the passage softly and slowly open at that instant and a figure come in, stop short, and begin staring at us in perplexity. I glanced, nearly swooned with shame, and rushed back to my room. There, clutching at my hair with both hands, I leaned my head against the wall and stood motionless in that position.

Two minutes later I heard Apollon's deliberate footsteps. "There is some woman asking for you," he said, looking at me with peculiar severity. Then he stood aside and let in Liza. He would not go away, but stared at us sarcastically.

"Go away, go away," I commanded in desperation. At that moment my clock began whirring and wheezing and struck seven.

IX

"Into my house come bold and free,
Its rightful mistress there to be."
(From the same poem)

I stood before her crushed, crestfallen, revoltingly confused, and I believe I smiled as I did my utmost to wrap myself in the skirts of my ragged wadded dressing-gown—exactly as I had imagined the scene not long before in a fit of depression. After standing over us for a couple of minutes Apollon went away, but that did not make me more at ease. What made it worse was that she, too, was overwhelmed with confusion, more so, in fact, than I should have expected. At the sight of me, of course.

"Sit down," I said mechanically, moving a chair up to the table, and I sat down on the sofa. She obediently sat down at once and gazed at me open-eyed, evidently expecting something from me at once. This naïveté of expectation drove me to fury, but I restrained myself.

She ought to have tried not to notice, as though everything had been as usual, while instead of that, she . . . and I dimly felt that I should make her pay dearly for *all this.*

"You have found me in a strange position, Liza," I began, stammering and knowing that this was the wrong way to begin. "No, no, don't imagine anything," I cried, seeing that she had suddenly flushed. "I am not ashamed of my poverty. . . . On the contrary I look with pride on my poverty. I am poor but honourable. . . . One can be poor and honourable," I muttered. "However . . . would you like tea?". . .

"No," she was beginning.

"Wait a minute."

I leapt up and ran to Apollon. I had to get out of the room somehow.

"Apollon," I whispered in feverish haste, flinging down before him the seven roubles which had remained all the time in my clenched fist, "here are your wages, you see I give them to you; but for that you must come to my rescue: bring me tea and a dozen rusks from the restaurant. If you won't go, you'll make me a miserable man! You don't know what this woman is. . . . This is—everything! You may be imagining something. . . . But you don't know what that woman is!" . . .

Apollon, who had already sat down to his work and put on his spectacles again, at first glanced askance at the money without speaking or putting down his needle; then, without paying the slightest attention to me or making any answer he went on busying himself with his needle, which he had not yet threaded. I waited before him for three minutes with my arms crossed *à la Napoléon*. My temples were moist with sweat. I was pale, I felt it. But, thank God, he must have been moved to pity, looking at me. Having threaded his needle he deliberately got up from his seat, deliberately moved back his chair, deliberately took off his spectacles, deliberately counted the money, and finally asking me over his shoulder: "Shall I get a whole portion?" deliberately walked out of the room. As I was going back to Liza, the thought occurred to me on the way: shouldn't I run away just as I was in my dressing-gown, no matter where, and then let happen what would.

I sat down again. She looked at me uneasily. For some minutes we were silent.

"I will kill him," I shouted suddenly, striking the table with my fist so that the ink spurted out of the inkstand.

"What are you saying!" she cried, starting.

"I will kill him! kill him!" I shrieked, suddenly striking the table in absolute frenzy, and at the same time fully understanding how stupid it was to be in such a frenzy. "You don't know, Liza, what that torturer is to me. He is my torturer. . . . He has gone now to fetch some rusks; he . . ."

And suddenly I burst into tears. It was an hysterical attack. How ashamed I felt in the midst of my sobs; but still I could not restrain them.

She was frightened.

"What is the matter? What is wrong?" she cried, fussing about me.

"Water, give me water, over there!" I muttered in a faint voice, though I was inwardly conscious that I could have got on very well without water and without muttering in a faint voice. But I was, what is called, *putting it on*, to save appearances, though the attack was a genuine one.

She gave me water, looking at me in bewilderment. At that moment Apollon brought in the tea. It suddenly seemed to me that this commonplace, prosaic tea was horribly undignified and paltry after all that had happened, and I blushed crimson. Liza looked at Apollon with positive alarm. He went out without a glance at either of us.

"Liza, do you despise me?" I asked, looking at her fixedly, trembling with impatience to know what she was thinking.

She was confused, and did not know what to answer.

"Drink your tea," I said to her angrily. I was angry with myself, but, of course, it was she who would have to pay for it. A horrible spite against her suddenly surged up in my heart; I believe I could have killed her. To revenge myself on her I swore inwardly not to say a word to her all the time. "She is the cause of it all," I thought.

Our silence lasted for five minutes. The tea stood on the table; we did not touch it. I had got to the point of purposely refraining from beginning in order to embarrass her further; it was awkward for her to begin alone. Several times she glanced at me with mournful perplexity. I was obstinately silent. I was, of course, myself the chief sufferer, because I was fully conscious of the disgusting meanness of my spiteful stupidity, and yet at the same time I could not restrain myself.

"I want to . . . get away . . . from there altogether," she began, to break the silence in some way, but, poor girl, that was just what she ought not to have spoken about at such a stupid moment to a man so stupid as I was. My heart positively ached with pity for her tactless and unnecessary straightforwardness. But something hideous at once stifled all compassion in me; it even provoked me to greater venom. I did not care what happened. Another five minutes passed.

"Perhaps I am in your way," she began timidly, hardly audibly, and was getting up.

But as soon as I saw this first impulse of wounded dignity I positively trembled with spite, and at once burst out.

"Why have you come to me, tell me that, please?" I began, gasping for breath and regardless of logical connection in my words. I longed to have it all out at once, at one burst; I did not even trouble how to begin. "Why have you come? Answer, answer," I cried, hardly knowing what I was doing. "I'll tell you, my good girl, why you have come. You've come because I talked sentimental stuff to you then. So now you are soft as butter and longing for fine sentiments again. So you may as well know that I was laughing at you then. And I am laughing at you now. Why are you shuddering? Yes, I was laughing at you! I had been insulted just before, at dinner, by the fellows who came that evening before me. I came to you, meaning to thrash one of them, an officer; but I didn't succeed, I didn't find him; I had to avenge the insult on some one to get back my own again; you turned up, I vented my spleen on you and laughed at you. I had been humiliated, so I wanted to humiliate; I had been treated like a rag, so I wanted to show my power. . . . That's what it was, and you imagined I had come there on purpose to save you. Yes? You imagined that? You imagined that?"

I knew that she would perhaps be muddled and not take it all in exactly, but I knew, too, that she would grasp the gist of it, very well indeed. And so, indeed, she did. She turned white as a handkerchief, tried to say something, and her lips worked painfully; but she sank on a chair as though she had been felled by an axe. And all the time afterwards she listened to me with her lips parted and her eyes wide open, shuddering with awful terror. The cynicism, the cynicism of my words overwhelmed her. . . .

"Save you!" I went on, jumping up from my chair and running up and down the room before her. "Save you from what? But perhaps I am worse than you myself. Why didn't you throw it in my teeth when I was giving you that sermon: 'But what did you come here yourself for? was it to read us a sermon?' Power, power was what I wanted then, sport was what I wanted, I wanted to ring out your tears, your humiliation, your hysteria—that was what I wanted then! Of course, I couldn't keep it up then, because I am a wretched creature, I was frightened, and, the devil knows why, gave you my address in my folly. Afterwards, before I got home, I was cursing and swearing at you because of that address, I hated you already because of the lies I had told you. Because I only like playing with words, only dreaming, but, do you know, what I really want is that you should all go to hell. That is what I want. I want peace; yes, I'd sell the whole world for a farthing, straight off, so long as I was left in peace. Is the world to go to pot, or am I to go without my tea? I say that the world may go to pot for me so long as I always get my tea. Did you know that, or not? Well, anyway, I know that I am a blackguard, a scoundrel, an egoist, a sluggard. Here I have been shuddering for the last three days at the thought of your coming. And do you know what has worried me particularly for these three days? That I posed as such a hero to you, and now you would see me in a wretched torn dressing-gown, beggarly, loathsome. I told you just now that I was not ashamed of my poverty; so you may as well know that I am ashamed of it; I am more ashamed of it than of anything, more afraid of it than of being found out if I were a thief, because I am as vain as though I had been skinned and the very air blowing on me hurts. Surely by now you must realize that I shall never forgive you for having found me in this wretched dressing-gown, just as I was flying at Apollon like a spiteful cur. The saviour, the former hero, was flying like a mangy, unkempt sheep-dog at his lackey, and the lackey was jeering at him! And I shall never forgive you for the tears I could not help shedding before you just now, like some silly woman put to shame! And for what I am confessing to you now, I shall never forgive *you* either! Yes—you must answer for it all because you turned up like this, because

I am a blackguard, because I am the nastiest, stupidest, absurdest and most envious of all the worms on earth, who are not a bit better than I am, but, the devil knows why, are never put to confusion; while I shall always be insulted by every louse, that is my doom! And what is it to me that you don't understand a word of this! And what do I care, what do I care about you, and whether you go to ruin there or not? Do you understand? How I shall hate you now after saying this, for having been here and listening. Why, it's not once in a lifetime a man speaks out like this, and then it is in hysterics! . . . What more do you want? Why do you still stand confronting me, after all this? Why are you worrying me? Why don't you go?"

But at this point a strange thing happened. I was so accustomed to think and imagine everything from books, and to picture everything in the world to myself just as I had made it up in my dreams beforehand, that I could not all at once take in this strange circumstance. What happened was this: Liza, insulted and crushed by me, understood a great deal more than I imagined. She understood from all this what a woman understands first of all, if she feels genuine love, that is, that I was myself unhappy.

The frightened and wounded expression on her face was followed first by a look of sorrowful perplexity. When I began calling myself a scoundrel and a blackguard and my tears flowed (the tirade was accompanied throughout by tears) her whole face worked convulsively. She was on the point of getting up and stopping me; when I finished she took no notice of my shouting: "Why are you here, why don't you go away?" but realized only that it must have been very bitter to me to say all this. Besides, she was so crushed, poor girl; she considered herself infinitely beneath me; how could she feel anger or resentment? She suddenly leapt up from her chair with an irresistible impulse and held out her hands, yearning towards me, though still timid and not daring to stir. . . . At this point there was a revulsion in my heart, too. Then she suddenly rushed to me, threw her arms round me and burst into tears. I, too, could not restrain myself, and sobbed as I never had before.

"They won't let me . . . I can't be good!" I managed to articulate; then I went to the sofa, fell on it face downwards, and sobbed on it for a quarter of an hour in genuine hysterics. She came close to me, put her arms round me and stayed motionless in that position. But the trouble was that the hysterics could not go on for ever, and (I am writing the loathsome truth) lying face downwards on the sofa with my face thrust into my nasty leather pillow, I began by degrees to be aware of a far-away, involuntary but irresistible feeling that it would be awkward now for me to raise my head and look Liza straight in the face. Why was I ashamed? I don't know, but I was ashamed. The thought, too, came into my overwrought brain that our parts now were completely changed, that she was now the heroine, while I was just such a crushed and humiliated creature as she had been before me that night—four days before. . . . And all this came into my mind during the minutes I was lying on my face on the sofa.

My God! surely I was not envious of her then.

I don't know, to this day I cannot decide, and at the time, of course, I was still less able to understand what I was feeling than now. I cannot get on without domineering and tyrannizing over some one, but . . . there is no explaining anything by reasoning and so it is useless to reason.

I conquered myself, however, and raised my head; I had to do so sooner or later . . . and I am convinced to this day that it was just because I was ashamed to look at her that another feeling was suddenly kindled and flamed up in my heart . . . a feeling of mastery and possession. My eyes gleamed with passion, and I gripped her hands tightly. How I hated her and how I was drawn to her at that minute! The one feeling intensified the other. It was almost like an act of vengeance. At first there was a look of amazement, even of terror on her face, but only for one instant. She warmly and rapturously embraced me.

x

A quarter of an hour later I was rushing up and down the room in frenzied impatience, from minute to minute I went up to the screen and peeped through the crack at Liza. She was sitting on the ground with her head leaning against the bed, and must have been crying. But she did not go away, and that irritated me. This time she understood it all. I had insulted her finally, but . . . there's no need to describe it. She realized that my outburst of passion had been simply revenge, a fresh humiliation, and that to my earlier, almost causeless hatred was added a *personal hatred,* born of envy. . . . Though I do not maintain positively that she understood all this distinctly; but she certainly did fully understand that I was a despicable man, and what was worse, incapable of loving her.

I know I shall be told that this is incredible—but it is incredible to be as spiteful and stupid as I was; it may be added that it was strange I should not love her, or at any rate, appreciate her love. Why is it strange? In the first place, by then I was incapable of love, for I repeat, with me loving meant tyrannizing and showing my moral superiority. I have never in my life been able to imagine any other sort of love, and have nowadays come to the point of sometimes thinking that love really consists in the right—freely given by the beloved object—to tyrannize over her.

Even in my underground dreams I did not imagine love except as a struggle. I began it always with hatred and ended it with moral subjugation, and afterwards I never knew what to do with the subjugated object. And what is there to wonder at in that, since I had succeeded in so corrupting myself, since I was so out of touch with "real life," as to have actually thought of reproaching her, and putting her to shame for having come to me to hear "fine sentiments"; and did not even guess that she had come not to hear fine sentiments, but to love me, because to a woman all reformation, all salvation from any sort of ruin, and all moral renewal is included in love and can only show itself in that form.

I did not hate her so much, however, when I was running about the room and peeping through the crack in the screen. I was only insufferably oppressed by her being here. I wanted her to disappear. I wanted "peace," to be left alone in my underground world. Real life oppressed me with its novelty so much that I could hardly breathe.

But several minutes passed and she still remained, without stirring, as though she were unconscious. I had the shamelessness to tap softly at the screen as though to remind her. . . . She started, sprang up, and flew to seek her kerchief, her hat, her coat, as though making her escape from me. . . . Two minutes later she came from behind the screen and looked with heavy eyes at me. I gave a spiteful grin, which was forced, however, to *keep up appearances*, and I turned away from her eyes.

"Good-bye," she said, going towards the door.

I ran up to her, seized her hand, opened it, thrust something in it and closed it again. Then I turned at once and dashed away in haste to the other corner of the room to avoid seeing her, anyway. . . .

I did not mean a moment since to tell a lie—to write that I did this accidentally, not knowing what I was doing through foolishness, through losing my head. But I don't want to lie, and so I will say straight out that I opened her hand and put the money in it . . . from spite. It came into my head to do this while I was running up and down the room and she was sitting behind the screen. But this I can say for certain: though I did that cruel thing purposely, it was not an impulse from the heart, but came from my evil brain. This cruelty was so affected, so purposely made up, so completely a product of the brain, of books, that I could not even keep it up a minute—first I dashed away to avoid seeing her, and then in shame and despair rushed after Liza. I opened the door in the passage and began listening.

"Liza! Liza!" I cried on the stairs, but in a low voice, not boldly.

There was no answer, but I fancied I heard her footsteps, lower down on the stairs.

"Liza!" I cried, more loudly.

No answer. But at that minute I heard the stiff outer glass door open heavily with a creak and slam violently, the sound echoed up the stairs.

She had gone. I went back to my room in hesitation. I felt horribly oppressed.

I stood still at the table, beside the chair on which she had sat and looked aimlessly before me. A minute passed, suddenly I started; straight before me on the table I saw. . . . In short, I saw a crumpled blue five-rouble note, the one I had thrust into her hand a minute before. It was the same note; it could be no other, there was no other in the flat. So she had managed to fling it from her hand on the table at the moment when I had dashed into the further corner.

Well! I might have expected that she would do that. Might I have expected it? No, I was such an egoist, I was so lacking in respect for my fellow-creatures that I could not even imagine she would do so. I could not endure it. A minute later I flew like a madman to dress, flinging on what I could at random and ran headlong after her. She could not have got two hundred paces away when I ran out into the street.

It was a still night and the snow was coming down in masses and falling almost perpendicularly, covering the pavement and the empty street as though with a pillow. There was no one in the street, no sound was to be heard. The street lamps gave a disconsolate and useless glimmer. I ran two hundred paces to the cross-roads and stopped short.

Where had she gone? And why was I running after her?

Why? To fall down before her, to sob with remorse, to kiss her feet, to entreat her forgiveness! I longed for that, my whole breast was being rent to pieces, and never, never shall I recall that minute with indifference. But—what for? I thought. Should I not begin to hate her, perhaps, even to-morrow, just because I had kissed her feet to-day? Should I give her happiness? Had I not recognized that day, for the hundredth time, what I was worth? Should I not torture her?

I stood in the snow, gazing into the troubled darkness and pondered this.

"And will it not be better?" I mused fantastically, afterwards at home, stifling the living pang of my heart with fantastic dreams. "Will it not be better that she should keep the resentment of the insult for ever? Resentment—why, it is purification; it is a most stinging and painful consciousness! To-morrow I should have defiled her soul and have exhausted her heart, while now the feeling of insult will never die in her heart, and however loathsome the filth awaiting her—the feeling of insult will elevate and purify her . . .

by hatred . . . h'm! . . . perhaps, too, by forgiveness. . . . Will all that make things easier for her though? . . ."

And, indeed, I will ask on my own account here, an idle question: which is better—cheap happiness or exalted sufferings? Well, which is better?

So I dreamed as I sat at home that evening, almost dead with the pain in my soul. Never had I endured such suffering and remorse, yet could there have been the faintest doubt when I ran out from my lodging that I should turn back half-way? I never met Liza again and I have heard nothing of her. I will add, too, that I remained for a long time afterwards pleased with the phrase about the benefit from resentment and hatred in spite of the fact that I almost fell ill from misery.

Even now, so many years later, all this is somehow a very evil memory. I have many evil memories now, but . . . hadn't I better end my "Notes" here? I believe I made a mistake in beginning to write them, anyway I have felt ashamed all the time I've been writing this story; so it's hardly literature so much as a corrective punishment. Why, to tell long stories, showing how I have spoiled my life through morally rotting in my corner, through lack of fitting environment, through divorce from real life, and rankling spite in my underground world, would certainly not be interesting; a novel needs a hero, and all the traits for an anti-hero are *expressly* gathered together here, and what matters most, it all produces an unpleasant impression, for we are all divorced from life, we are all cripples, every one of us, more or less. We are so divorced from it that we feel at once a sort of loathing for real life, and so cannot bear to be reminded of it. Why, we have come almost to looking upon real life as an effort, almost as hard labour, and we are all privately agreed that it is better in books. And why do we fuss and fume sometimes? Why are we perverse and ask for something else? We don't know what ourselves. It would be the worse for us if our petulant prayers were answered. Come, try, give any one of us, for instance, a little more independence, untie our hands, widen the spheres of our activity, relax the control and we . . . yes, I assure you . . . we should be begging to be under control again at once. I know that you will very likely be angry with me for that, and will begin shouting and stamping. Speak for yourself, you will say, and for your miseries in your underground holes, and don't dare to say "all of us"—excuse me, gentlemen, I am not justifying myself with that "all of us." As for what concerns me in particular I have only in my life carried to an extreme what you have not dared to carry half-way, and what's more, you have taken your cowardice for good sense, and have found comfort in deceiving yourselves. So that perhaps, after all, there is more life in me than in you. Look into it more carefully! Why, we don't even know what living means now, what it is, and what it is called? Leave us alone without books and we shall be lost and in confusion at once. We shall not know what to join on to, what to cling to, what to love and what to hate, what to respect and what to despise. We are oppressed at being men—men with a real individual flesh and blood, we are ashamed of it, we think it a disgrace and try to contrive to be some sort of impossible generalized man. We are stillborn, and for generations past have been begotten, not by living fathers, and that suits us better and better. We are developing a taste for it. Soon we shall contrive to be born somehow from an idea. But enough; I don't want to write more from "Underground."

(*The notes of this paradoxalist do not end here, however. He could not refrain from going on with them, but it seems to us that we may stop here.*)

LEO TOLSTOY

(1828–1910)

The Death of Iván Ilyich*

I

During an interval in the Melvínski trial in the large building of the Law Courts the members and public prosecutor met in Iván Egórovich Shébek's private room, where the conversation turned on the celebrated Krasóvski case. Fëdor Vasílievich warmly maintained that it was not subject to their jurisdiction, Iván Egórovich maintained the contrary, while Peter Ivánovich, not having entered into the discussion at the start, took no part in it but looked through the *Gazette* which had just been handed in.

"Gentlemen," he said, "Iván Ilyich has died!"

"You don't say!"

"Here, read it yourself," replied Peter Ivánovich, handing Fëdor Vasílievich the paper still damp from the press. Surrounded by a black border were the words: "Praskóvya Fëdorovna Goloviná, with profound sorrow, informs relatives and friends of the demise of her beloved husband Iván Ilyich Golovín, Member of the Court of Justice, which occurred on February the 4th of this year 1882. The funeral will take place on Friday at one o'clock in the afternoon."

* 1886. Translated by Louise and Aylmer Maude.

Iván Ilyich had been a colleague of the gentlemen present and was liked by them all. He had been ill for some weeks with an illness said to be incurable. His post had been kept open for him, but there had been conjectures that in case of his death Alexéev might receive his appointment, and that either Vínnikov or Shtábel would succeed Alexéev. So on receiving the news of Iván Ilyich's death the first thought of each of the gentlemen in that private room was of the changes and promotions it might occasion among themselves or their acquaintances.

"I shall be sure to get Shtábel's place or Vínnikov's," thought Fëdor Vasílievich. "I was promised that long ago, and the promotion means an extra eight hundred rubles a year for me besides the allowance."

"Now I must apply for my brother-in-law's transfer from Kalúga," thought Peter Ivánovich. "My wife will be very glad, and then she won't be able to say that I never do anything for her relations."

"I thought he would never leave his bed again," said Peter Ivánovich aloud. "It's very sad."

"But what really was the matter with him?"

"The doctors couldn't say—at least they could, but each of them said something different. When last I saw him I thought he was getting better."

"And I haven't been to see him since the holidays. I always meant to go."

"Had he any property?"

"I think his wife had a little—but something quite trifling."

"We shall have to go to see her, but they live so terribly far away."

"Far away from you, you mean. Everything's far away from your place."

"You see, he never can forgive my living on the other side of the river," said Peter Ivánovich, smiling at Shébek. Then, still talking of the distances between different parts of the city, they returned to the Court.

Besides considerations as to the possible transfers and promotions likely to result from Iván Ilyich's death, the mere fact of the death of a near acquaintance aroused, as usual, in all who heard of it the complacent feeling that, "it is he who is dead and not I."

Each one thought or felt, "Well, he's dead but I'm alive!" But the more intimate of Iván Ilyich's acquaintances, his so-called friends, could not help thinking also that they would now have to fulfil the very tiresome demands of propriety by attending the funeral service and paying a visit of condolence to the widow.

Fëdor Vasílievich and Peter Ivánovich had been his nearest acquaintances. Peter Ivánovich had studied law with Iván Ilyich and had considered himself to be under obligations to him.

Having told his wife at dinner-time of Iván Ilyich's death, and of his conjecture that it might be possible to get her brother transferred to their circuit, Peter Ivánovich sacrificed his usual nap, put on his evening clothes, and drove to Iván Ilyich's house.

At the entrance stood a carriage and two cabs. Leaning against the wall in the hall downstairs near the cloak-stand was a coffin-lid covered with cloth of gold, ornamented with gold cord and tassels, that had been polished up with metal powder. Two ladies in black were taking off their fur cloaks. Peter Ivánovich recognized one of them as Iván Ilyich's sister, but the other was a stranger to him. His colleague Schwartz was just coming downstairs, but on seeing Peter Ivánovich enter he stopped and winked at him, as if to say: "Iván Ilyich has made a mess of things—not like you and me."

Schwartz's face with his Piccadilly whiskers, and his slim figure in evening dress, had as usual an air of elegant solemnity which contrasted with the playfulness of his character and had a special piquancy here, or so it seemed to Peter Ivánovich.

Peter Ivánovich allowed the ladies to precede him and slowly followed them upstairs. Schwartz did not come down but remained where he was, and Peter Ivánovich understood that he wanted to arrange where they should play bridge that evening. The ladies went upstairs to the widow's room, and Schwartz with seriously compressed lips but a playful look in his eyes, indicated by a twist of his eyebrows the room to the right where the body lay.

Peter Ivánovich, like everyone else on such occasions, entered feeling uncertain what he would have to do. All he knew was that at such times it is always safe to cross oneself. But he was not quite sure whether one should make obeisances while doing so. He therefore adopted a middle course. On entering the room he began crossing himself and made a slight movement resembling a bow. At the same time, as far as the motion of his head and arm allowed, he surveyed the room. Two young men—apparently nephews, one of whom was a high-school pupil—were leaving the room, crossing themselves as they did so. An old woman was standing motionless, and a lady with strangely arched eyebrows was saying something to her in a whisper. A vigorous, resolute Church Reader, in a frock-coat, was reading something in a loud voice with an expression that precluded any contradiction. The butler's assistant, Gerásim, stepping lightly in front of Peter Ivánovich, was strewing something on the floor. Noticing this, Peter Ivánovich was immediately aware of a faint odour of a decomposing body.

The last time he had called on Iván Ilyich, Peter Ivánovich had seen Gerásim in the study. Iván Ilyich had been particularly fond of him and he was performing the duty of a sick nurse.

Peter Ivánovich continued to make the sign of the cross slightly inclining his head in an intermediate direction between the coffin, the Reader, and the icons on the table in a corner of the room. Afterwards, when it seemed to him that this movement of his arm in crossing himself had gone on too long, he stopped and began to look at the corpse.

The dead man lay, as dead men always lie, in a specially heavy way, his rigid limbs sunk in the soft cushions of the coffin, with the head forever bowed on the pillow. His yellow waxen brow with bald patches over his sunken temples was thrust up in the way peculiar to the dead, the protruding nose seeming to press on the upper lip. He was much changed and had grown even thinner since Peter Ivánovich had last seen him, but, as is always the case with the dead, his face was handsomer and above all more dignified than when he was alive. The expression on the face said that what was necessary had been accomplished, and accomplished rightly. Besides this there was in that expression a reproach and a warning to the living. This warning seemed to Peter Ivánovich out of place, or at least not applicable to him. He felt a certain discomfort and so he hurriedly crossed himself once more and turned and went out of the door—too hurriedly and too regardless of propriety, as he himself was aware.

Schwartz was waiting for him in the adjoining room with legs spread wide apart and both hands toying with his top-hat behind his back. The mere sight of that playful, well-groomed, and elegant figure refreshed Peter Ivánovich. He felt that Schwartz was above all these happenings and would not surrender to any depressing influences. His very look said that this incident of a church service for Iván Ilyich could not be a sufficient reason for infringing the order of the session—in other words, that it would certainly not prevent his unwrapping a new pack of cards and shuffling them that evening while a footman placed four fresh candles on the table: in fact, that there was no reason for supposing that this incident would hinder their spending the evening agreeably. Indeed he said this in a whisper as Peter Ivánovich passed him, proposing that they should meet for a game at Fëdor Vasílievich's. But apparently Peter Ivánovich was not destined to play bridge that evening. Praskóvya Fëdorovna (a short, fat woman who despite all efforts to the contrary had continued to broaden steadily from her shoulders downwards and who had the same extraordinary arched eyebrows as the lady who had been standing by the coffin), dressed all in black, her head covered with lace, came out of her own room with some other ladies, conducted them to the room where the dead body lay, and said: "The service will begin immediately. Please go in."

Schwartz, making an indefinite bow, stood still, evidently neither accepting nor declining this invitation. Praskóvya Fëdorovna recognizing Peter Ivánovich, sighed, went close up to him, took his hand, and said: "I know you were a true friend to Iván Ilyich . . ." and looked at him awaiting some suitable response. And Peter Ivánovich knew that, just as it had been the right thing to cross himself in that room, so what he had to do here was to press her hand, sigh, and say, "Believe me . . ." So he did all this and as he did it felt that the desired result had been achieved: that both he and she were touched.

"Come with me. I want to speak to you before it begins," said the widow. "Give me your arm."

Peter Ivánovich gave her his arm and they went to the inner rooms, passing Schwartz who winked at Peter Ivánovich compassionately.

"That does for our bridge! Don't object if we find another player. Perhaps you can cut in when you do escape," said his playful look.

Peter Ivánovich sighed still more deeply and despondently, and Praskóvya Fëdorovna pressed his arm gratefully. When they reached the drawing-room, upholstered in pink cretonne and lighted by a dim lamp, they sat down at the table—she on a sofa and Peter Ivánovich on a low hassock, the springs of which yielded spasmodically under his weight. Praskóvya Fëdorovna had been on the point of warning him to take another seat, but felt that such a warning was out of keeping with her present condition and so changed her mind. As he sat down on the hassock Peter Ivánovich recalled how Iván Ilyich had arranged this room and had consulted him regarding this pink cretonne with green leaves. The whole room was full of furniture and knick-knacks, and on her way to the sofa the lace of the widow's black shawl caught on the carved edge of the table. Peter Ivánovich rose to detach it, and the springs of the hassock, relieved of his weight, rose also and gave him a push. The widow began detaching her shawl herself, and Peter Ivánovich again sat down, suppressing the rebellious springs of the hassock under him. But the widow had not quite freed herself and Peter Ivánovich got up again, and again the hassock rebelled and even creaked. When this was all over she took out a clean cambric handkerchief and began to weep. The episode with the shawl and the struggle with the hassock had cooled Peter Ivánovich's emotions and he sat there with a sullen look on his face. This awkward situation was interrupted by Sokolóv, Iván Ilyich's butler, who came to report that the plot in the cemetery that Praskóvya Fëdorovna had chosen would cost two hundred rubles. She stopped weeping and, looking at Peter Ivánovich with the air of a victim, remarked in French that it was very hard for her. Peter Ivánovich made a silent gesture signifying his full conviction that it must indeed be so.

"Please smoke," she said in a magnanimous yet crushed voice, and turned to discuss with Sokolóv the price of the plot for the grave.

Peter Ivánovich while lighting his cigarette heard her inquiring very circumstantially into the prices of different plots in the cemetery and finally decide which she would take. When that was done she gave instructions about engaging the choir. Sokolóv then left the room.

"I look after everything myself," she told Peter Ivánovich, shifting the albums that lay on the table; and noticing that the table was endangered by his cigarette-ash, she immediately passed him an ash-tray, saying as she did so: "I consider it an affectation to say that my grief prevents my attending to practical affairs. On the contrary, if anything can—I won't say console me, but—distract me, it is seeing to everything concerning him." She again took out her handkerchief as if preparing to cry, but suddenly, as if mastering her feeling, she shook herself and began to speak calmly. "But there is something I want to talk to you about."

Peter Ivánovich bowed, keeping control of the springs of the hassock, which immediately began quivering under him.

"He suffered terribly the last few days."

"Did he?" said Peter Ivánovich.

"Oh, terribly! He screamed unceasingly, not for minutes but for hours. For the last three days he screamed incessantly. It was unendurable. I cannot understand how I bore it; you could hear him three rooms off. Oh, what I have suffered!"

"Is it possible that he was conscious all that time?" asked Peter Ivánovich.

"Yes," she whispered. "To the last moment. He took leave of us a quarter of an hour before he died, and asked us to take Volódya away."

The thought of the sufferings of this man he had known so intimately, first as a merry little boy, then as a school-mate, and later as a grown-up colleague, suddenly struck Peter Ivánovich with horror, despite an unpleasant consciousness of his own and this woman's dissimulation. He again saw that brow, and that nose pressing down on the lip, and felt afraid for himself.

"Three days of frightful suffering and then death! Why, that might suddenly, at any time, happen to me," he thought, and for a moment felt terrified. But—he did not himself know how—the customary reflection at once occurred to him that this had happened to Iván Ilyich and not to him, and that it should not and could not happen to him, and that to think that it could would be yielding to depression which he ought not to do, as Schwartz's expression plainly showed. After which reflection Peter Ivánovich felt reassured, and began to ask with interest about the details of Iván Ilyich's death, as though death was an accident natural to Iván Ilyich but certainly not to himself.

After many details of the really dreadful physical sufferings Iván Ilyich had endured (which details he learnt only from the effect those sufferings had produced on Praskóvya Fëdorovna's nerves) the widow apparently found it necessary to get to business.

"Oh, Peter Ivánovich, how hard it is! How terribly, terribly hard!" and she again began to weep.

Peter Ivánovich sighed and waited for her to finish blowing her nose. When she had done so he said, "Believe me . . ." and she again began talking and brought out what was evidently her chief concern with him—namely, to question him as to how she could obtain a grant of money from the government on the occasion of her husband's death. She made it appear that she was asking Peter Ivánovich's advice about her pension, but he soon saw that she already knew about that to the minutest detail, more even than he did himself. She knew how much could be got out of the government in consequence of her husband's death, but wanted to find out whether she could not possibly extract something more. Peter Ivánovich tried to think of some means of doing so, but after reflecting for a while and, out of propriety, condemning the government for its niggardliness, he said he thought that nothing more could be got. Then she sighed and evidently began to devise means of getting rid of her visitor. Noticing this, he put out his cigarette, rose, pressed her hand, and went out into the anteroom.

In the dining-room where the clock stood that Iván Ilyich had liked so much and had bought at an antique shop, Peter Ivánovich met a priest and a few acquaintances who had come to attend the service, and he recognized Iván Ilyich's daughter, a handsome young woman. She was in black and her slim figure appeared slimmer than ever. She had a gloomy, determined, almost angry expression, and bowed to Peter Ivánovich as though he were in some way to blame. Behind her, with the same offended look, stood a wealthy young man, an examining magistrate, whom Peter Ivánovich also knew and who was her fiancé, as he had heard. He bowed mournfully to them and was about to pass into the death-chamber, when from under the stairs appeared the figure of Iván Ilyich's schoolboy son, who was extremely like his father. He seemed a little Iván Ilyich, such as Peter Ivánovich remembered when they studied law together. His tear-stained eyes had in them the look that is seen in the eyes of boys of thirteen or fourteen who are not pure-minded.

When he saw Peter Ivánovich he scowled morosely and shamefacedly. Peter Ivánovich nodded to him and entered the death-chamber. The service began: candles, groans, incense, tears, and sobs. Peter Ivánovich stood looking gloomily down at his feet. He did not look once at the dead man, did not yield to any depressing influence, and was one of the first to leave the room. There was no one in the anteroom, but Gerásim darted out of the dead man's room, rummaged with his strong hands among the fur coats to find Peter Ivánovich's and helped him on with it.

"Well, friend Gerásim," said Peter Ivánovich, so as to say something. "It's a sad affair, isn't it?"

"It's God's will. We shall all come to it some day," said Gerásim, displaying his teeth—the even, white teeth of a healthy peasant—and, like a man in the thick of urgent work, he briskly opened the front door, called the coachman, helped Peter Ivánovich into the sledge, and sprang back to the porch as if in readiness for what he had to do next.

Peter Ivánovich found the fresh air particularly pleasant after the smell of incense, the dead body, and carbolic acid.

"Where to, sir?" asked the coachman.

"It's not too late even now. . . . I'll call round on Fëdor Vasílievich."

He accordingly drove there and found them just finishing the first rubber, so that it was quite convenient for him to cut in.

II

Iván Ilyich's life had been most simple and most ordinary and therefore most terrible.

He had been a member of the Court of Justice, and died at the age of forty-five. His father had been an official who after serving in various ministries and departments in Petersburg had made the sort of career which brings men to positions from which by reason of their long service they cannot be dismissed, though they are obviously unfit to hold any responsible position, and for whom therefore posts are specially created, which though fictitious, carry salaries of from six to ten thousand rubles that are not fictitious, and in receipt of which they live on to a great age.

Such was the Privy Councillor and superfluous member of various superfluous institutions, Ilya Epímovich Golovín.

He had three sons, of whom Iván Ilyich was the second. The eldest son was following in his father's footsteps only in another department, and was already approaching that stage in the service at which a similar sinecure would be reached. The third son was a failure. He had ruined his prospects in a number of positions and was now serving in the railway department. His father and brothers, and still more their wives, not merely disliked meeting him, but avoided remembering his existence unless compelled to do so. His sister had married Baron Greff, a Petersburg official of her father's type. Iván Ilyich was *le phénix de la famille*[1] as people said. He was neither as cold and formal as his elder brother nor as wild as the younger, but was a happy mean between them—an intelligent, polished, lively and agreeable man. He had studied with his younger brother at the School of Law, but the latter had failed to complete the course and was expelled when he was in the fifth class. Iván Ilyich finished the course well. Even when he was at the School of Law he was just what he remained for the rest of his life: a capable, cheerful, good-natured, and sociable man, though strict in the fulfilment of what he considered to be his duty: and he considered his duty to be what was so considered by those in authority. Neither as a boy nor as a man was he a toady, but from early youth was by nature attracted to people of high station as a fly is drawn to the light, assimilating their ways and views of life and establishing friendly relations with them. All the enthusiasms of childhood and youth passed without leaving much trace on him; he succumbed to sensuality, to vanity, and latterly among the highest classes to liberalism, but always within limits which his instinct unfailingly indicated to him as correct.

At school he had done things which had formerly seemed to him very horrid and made him feel disgusted with himself when he did them; but when later on he saw that such actions were done by people of good position and that they did not regard them as wrong, he was able not exactly to regard them as right, but to forget about them entirely or not be at all troubled at remembering them.

Having graduated from the School of Law and qualified for the tenth rank of the civil service, and having received money from his father for his equipment, Iván Ilyich ordered himself clothes at Scharmer's, the fashionable tailor, hung a medallion inscribed *respice finem*[2] on his watch-chain, took leave of his professor and the prince who was patron of the school, had a farewell dinner with his comrades at Donon's first-class restaurant, and with his new and fashionable portmanteau, linen, clothes, shaving and other toilet appliances, and a travelling rug, all purchased at the best shops, he set off for one of the provinces where, through his father's influence, he had been attached to the governor as an official for special service.

In the province Iván Ilyich soon arranged as easy and agreeable a position for himself as he had had at the School of Law. He performed his official tasks, made his career, and at the same time amused himself pleasantly and decorously. Occasionally he paid

1. "the phoenix of the family." The word "phoenix" is used here to mean "rare bird," "prodigy."

2. "Regard the end" (a Latin motto).

official visits to country districts, where he behaved with dignity both to his superiors and inferiors, and performed the duties entrusted to him, which related chiefly to the sectarians,[3] with an exactness and incorruptible honesty of which he could not but feel proud.

In official matters, despite his youth and taste for frivolous gaiety, he was exceedingly reserved, punctilious, and even severe; but in society he was often amusing and witty, and always good-natured, correct in his manner, and *bon enfant*, as the governor and his wife —with whom he was like one of the family—used to say of him.

In the province he had an affair with a lady who made advances to the elegant young lawyer, and there was also a milliner; and there were carousals with aides-de-camp who visited the district, and after-supper visits to a certain outlying street of doubtful reputation; and there was too some obsequiousness to his chief and even to his chief's wife, but all this was done with such a tone of good breeding that no hard names could be applied to it. It all came under the heading of the French saying: "*Il faut que jeunesse se passe.*"[4] It was all done with clean hands, in clean linen, with French phrases, and above all among people of the best society and consequently with the approval of people of rank.

So Iván Ilyich served for five years and then came a change in his official life. The new and reformed judicial institutions were introduced, and new men were needed. Iván Ilyich became such a new man. He was offered the post of Examining Magistrate, and he accepted it though the post was in another province and obliged him to give up the connexions he had formed and to make new ones. His friends met to give him a send-off; they had a group-photograph taken and presented him with a silver cigarette-case, and he set off to his new post.

As examining magistrate Iván Ilyich was just as *comme il faut* and decorous a man, inspiring general respect and capable of separating his official duties from his private life, as he had been when acting as an official on special service. His duties now as examining magistrate were far more interesting and attractive than before. In his former position it had been pleasant to wear an undress uniform made by Scharmer, and to pass through the crowd of petitioners and officials who were timorously awaiting an audience with the governor, and who envied him as with free and easy gait he went straight into his chief's private room to have a cup of tea and a cigarette with him. But not many people had then been directly dependent on him—only police officials and the sectarians

3. the Old Believers, a large group of Russians (about twenty-five million in 1900), members of a sect which originated in a break with the Orthodox Church in the seventeenth century; they were subject to many legal restrictions.

4. Youth must have its fling. [Translator's note.]

when he went on special missions—and he liked to treat them politely, almost as comrades, as if he were letting them feel that he who had the power to crush them was treating them in this simple, friendly way. There were then but few such people. But now, as an examining magistrate, Iván Ilyich felt that everyone without exception, even the most important and self-satisfied, was in his power, and that he need only write a few words on a sheet of paper with a certain heading, and this or that important, self-satisfied person would be brought before him in the role of an accused person or a witness, and if he did not choose to allow him to sit down, would have to stand before him and answer his questions. Iván Ilyich never abused his power; he tried on the contrary to soften its expression, but the consciousness of it and of the possibility of softening its effect, supplied the chief interest and attraction of his office. In his work itself, especially in his examinations, he very soon acquired a method of eliminating all considerations irrelevant to the legal aspect of the case, and reducing even the most complicated case to a form in which it would be presented on paper only in its externals, completely excluding his personal opinion of the matter, while above all observing every prescribed formality. The work was new and Iván Ilyich was one of the first men to apply the new Code of 1864.[5]

On taking up the post of examining magistrate in a new town, he made new acquaintances and connexions, placed himself on a new footing, and assumed a somewhat different tone. He took up an attitude of rather dignified aloofness towards the provincial authorities, but picked out the best circle of legal gentlemen and wealthy gentry living in the town and assumed a tone of slight dissatisfaction with the government, of moderate liberalism, and of enlightened citizenship. At the same time, without at all altering the elegance of his toilet, he ceased shaving his chin and allowed his beard to grow as it pleased.

Iván Ilyich settled down very pleasantly in this new town. The society there, which inclined towards opposition to the governor, was friendly, his salary was larger, and he began to play *vint* [a form of bridge], which he found added not a little to the pleasure of life, for he had a capacity for cards, played good-humouredly, and calculated rapidly and astutely, so that he usually won.

After living there for two years he met his future wife, Praskóvya Fëdorovna Míkhel, who was the most attractive, clever, and brilliant girl of the set in which he moved, and among other amusements and relaxations from his labours as examining magistrate, Iván Ilyich established light and playful relations with her.

While he had been an official on special service he had been ac-

5. The emancipation of the serfs in 1861 was followed by a thorough all-round reform of judicial proceedings. [Translator's note.]

customed to dance, but now as an examining magistrate it was exceptional for him to do so. If he danced now, he did it as if to show that though he served under the reformed order of things, and had reached the fifth official rank, yet when it came to dancing he could do it better than most people. So at the end of an evening he sometimes danced with Praskóvya Fëdorovna, and it was chiefly during these dances that he captivated her. She fell in love with him. Iván Ilyich had at first no definite intention of marrying, but when the girl fell in love with him he said to himself: "Really, why shouldn't I marry?"

Praskóvya Fëdorovna came of a good family, was not bad looking, and had some little property. Iván Ilyich might have aspired to a more brilliant match, but even this was good. He had his salary, and she, he hoped, would have an equal income. She was well connected, and was a sweet, pretty, and thoroughly correct young woman. To say that Iván Ilyich married because he fell in love with Praskóvya Fëdorovna and found that she sympathized with his views of life would be as incorrect as to say that he married because his social circle approved of the match. He was swayed by both these considerations: the marriage gave him personal satisfaction, and at the same time it was considered the right thing by the most highly placed of his associates.

So Iván Ilyich got married.

The preparations for marriage and the beginning of married life, with its conjugal caresses, the new furniture, new crockery, and new linen, were very pleasant until his wife became pregnant—so that Iván Ilyich had begun to think that marriage would not impair the easy, agreeable, gay, and always decorous character of his life, approved of by society and regarded by himself as natural, but would even improve it. But from the first months of his wife's pregnancy, something new, unpleasant, depressing, and unseemly, and from which there was no way of escape, unexpectedly showed itself.

His wife, without any reason—*de gaieté de coeur* as Iván Ilyich expressed it to himself—began to disturb the pleasure and propriety of their life. She began to be jealous without any cause, expected him to devote his whole attention to her, found fault with everything, and made coarse and ill-mannered scenes.

At first Iván Ilyich hoped to escape from the unpleasantness of this state of affairs by the same easy and decorous relation to life that had served him heretofore: he tried to ignore his wife's disagreeable moods, continued to live in his usual easy and pleasant way, invited friends to his house for a game of cards, and also tried going out to his club or spending his evenings with friends. But one day his wife began upbraiding him so vigorously, using such coarse words, and continued to abuse him every time he did not fulfil her demands, so resolutely and with such evident determination not to give way till he submitted—that is, till he stayed at home and was bored just as she was—that he became alarmed. He now realized that matrimony—at any rate with Praskóvya Fëdorovna—was not always conducive to the pleasures and amenities of life, but on the contrary often infringed both comfort and propriety, and that he must therefore entrench himself against such infringement. And Iván Ilyich began to seek for means of doing so. His official duties were the one thing that imposed upon Praskóvya Fëdorovna, and by means of his official work and the duties attached to it he began struggling with his wife to secure his own independence.

With the birth of their child, the attempts to feed it and the various failures in doing so, and with the real and imaginary illnesses of mother and child, in which Iván Ilyich's sympathy was demanded but about which he understood nothing, the need of securing for himself an existence outside his family life became still more imperative.

As his wife grew more irritable and exacting and Iván Ilyich transferred the centre of gravity of his life more and more to his official work, so did he grow to like his work better and became more ambitious than before.

Very soon, within a year of his wedding, Iván Ilyich had realized that marriage, though it may add some comforts to life, is in fact a very intricate and difficult affair towards which in order to perform one's duty, that is, to lead a decorous life approved of by society, one must adopt a definite attitude just as towards one's official duties.

And Iván Ilyich evolved such an attitude towards married life. He only required of it those conveniences—dinner at home, housewife, and bed—which it could give him, and above all that propriety of external forms required by public opinion. For the rest he looked for light-hearted pleasure and propriety, and was very thankful when he found them, but if he met with antagonism and querulousness he at once retired into his separate fenced-off world of official duties, where he found satisfaction.

Iván Ilyich was esteemed a good official, and after three years was made Assistant Public Prosecutor. His new duties, their importance, the possibility of indicting and imprisoning anyone he chose, the publicity his speeches received, and the success he had in all these things, made his work still more attractive.

More children came. His wife became more and more querulous and ill-tempered, but the attitude Iván Ilyich had adopted towards his home life rendered him almost impervious to her grumbling.

After seven years' service in that town he was transferred to another province as Public Prosecutor. They moved, but were short of money and his wife did not like the place they moved to. Though the salary was higher the cost of living was greater, besides which two of their children died and family life became still more unpleasant for him.

Praskóvya Fëdorovna blamed her husband for every inconvenience they encountered in their new home. Most of the conversations between husband and wife, especially as to the children's education, led to topics which recalled former disputes, and those disputes were apt to flare up again at any moment. There remained only those rare periods of amorousness which still came to them at times but did not last long. These were islets at which they anchored for a while and then again set out upon that ocean of veiled hostility which showed itself in their aloofness from one another. This aloofness might have grieved Iván Ilyich had he considered that it ought not to exist, but he now regarded the position as normal, and even made it the goal at which he aimed in family life. His aim was to free himself more and more from those unpleasantnesses and to give them a semblance of harmlessness and propriety. He attained this by spending less and less time with his family, and when obliged to be at home he tried to safeguard his position by the presence of outsiders. The chief thing however was that he had his official duties. The whole interest of his life now centered in the official world and that interest absorbed him. The consciousness of his power, being able to ruin anybody he wished to ruin, the importance, even the external dignity of his entry into court, or meetings with his subordinates, his success with superiors and inferiors, and above all his masterly handling of cases, of which he was conscious—all this gave him pleasure and filled his life, together with chats with his colleagues, dinners, and bridge. So that on the whole Iván Ilyich's life continued to flow as he considered it should do—pleasantly and properly.

So things continued for another seven years. His eldest daughter was already sixteen, another child had died, and only one son was left, a schoolboy and a subject of dissensions. Iván Ilyich wanted to put him in the School of Law, but to spite him Praskóvya Fëdorovna entered him at the High School. The daughter had been educated at home and had turned out well: the boy did not learn badly either.

III

So Iván Ilyich lived for seventeen years after his marriage. He was already a Public Prosecutor of long standing, and had declined several proposed transfers while awaiting a more desirable post, when an unanticipated and unpleasant occurrence quite upset the peaceful course of his life. He was expecting to be offered the post of presiding judge in a University town, but Hoppe somehow came to the front and obtained the appointment instead. Iván Ilyich became irritable, reproached Hoppe, and quarrelled both with him and with his immediate superiors—who became colder to him and again passed him over when other appointments were made.

This was in 1880, the hardest year of Iván Ilyich's life. It was then that it became evident on the one hand that his salary was insufficient for them to live on, and on the other that he had been forgotten, and not only this, but that what was for him the greatest and most cruel injustice appeared to others a quite ordinary occurrence. Even his father did not consider it his duty to help him. Iván Ilyich felt himself abandoned by everyone, and that they regarded his position with a salary of 3,500 rubles as quite normal and even fortunate. He alone knew that with the consciousness of the injustices done him, with his wife's incessant nagging, and with the debts he had contracted by living beyond his means, his position was far from normal.

In order to save money that summer he obtained leave of absence and went with his wife to live in the country at her brother's place.

In the country, without his work, he experienced *ennui* for the first time in his life, and not only *ennui* but intolerable depression, and he decided that it was impossible to go on living like that, and that it was necessary to take energetic measures.

Having passed a sleepless night pacing up and down the veranda, he decided to go to Petersburg and bestir himself, in order to punish those who had failed to appreciate him and to get transferred to another ministry.

Next day, despite many protests from his wife and her brother, he started for Petersburg with the sole object of obtaining a post with a salary of five thousand rubles a year. He was no longer bent on any particular department, or tendency, or kind of activity. All he now wanted was an appointment to another post with a salary of five thousand rubles, either in the administration, in the banks, with the railways, in one of the Empress Márya's Institutions,[6] or even in the customs—but it had to carry with it a salary of five thousand rubles and be in a ministry other than that in which they had failed to appreciate him.

And this quest of Iván Ilyich's was crowned with remarkable and unexpected success. At Kursk an acquaintance of his, F. I. Ilyín, got into the first-class carriage, sat down beside Iván Ilyich, and told him of a telegram just received by the governor of Kursk announcing that a change was about to take place in the ministry: Peter Ivánovich was to be superseded by Iván Semënovich.

The proposed change, apart from its significance for Russia, had

6. reference to the charitable organization founded by the Empress Márya, wife of Paul I, late in the eighteenth century.

a special significance for Iván Ilyich, because by bringing forward a new man, Peter Petróvich, and consequently his friend Zachár Ivánovich, it was highly favourable for Iván Ilyich, since Zachár Ivánovich was a friend and colleague of his.

In Moscow this news was confirmed, and on reaching Petersburg Iván Ilyich found Zachár Ivánovich and received a definite promise of an appointment in his former department of Justice.

A week later he telegraphed to his wife: "Zachár in Miller's place. I shall receive appointment on presentation of report."

Thanks to this change of personnel, Iván Ilyich had unexpectedly obtained an appointment in his former ministry which placed him two stages above his former colleagues besides giving him five thousand rubles salary and three thousand five hundred rubles for expenses connected with his removal. All his ill humour towards his former enemies and the whole department vanished, and Iván Ilyich was completely happy.

He returned to the country more cheerful and contented than he had been for a long time. Praskóvya Fëdorovna also cheered up and a truce was arranged between them. Iván Ilyich told of how he had been fêted by everybody in Petersburg, how all those who had been his enemies were put to shame and now fawned on him, how envious they were of his appointment, and how much everybody in Petersburg had liked him.

Praskóvya Fëdorovna listened to all this and appeared to believe it. She did not contradict anything, but only made plans for their life in the town to which they were going. Iván Ilyich saw with delight that these plans were his plans, that he and his wife agreed, and that, after a stumble, his life was regaining its due and natural character of pleasant lightheartedness and decorum.

Iván Ilyich had come back for a short time only, for he had to take up his new duties on the 10th of September. Moreover, he needed time to settle into the new place, to move all his belongings from the province, and to buy and order many additional things: in a word, to make such arrangements as he had resolved on, which were almost exactly what Praskóvya Fëdorovna too had decided on.

Now that everything had happened so fortunately, and that he and his wife were at one in their aims and moreover saw so little of one another they got on together better than they had done since the first years of marriage. Iván Ilyich had thought of taking his family away with him at once, but the insistence of his wife's brother and her sister-in-law, who had suddenly become particularly amiable and friendly to him and his family, induced him to depart alone.

So he departed, and the cheerful state of mind induced by his success and by the harmony between his wife and himself, the one intensifying the other, did not leave him. He found a delightful house, just the thing both he and his wife had dreamt of. Spacious, lofty reception rooms in the old style, a convenient and dignified study, rooms for his wife and daughter, a study for his son—it might have been specially built for them. Iván Ilyich himself superintended the arrangements, chose the wallpapers, supplemented the furniture (preferably with antiques which he considered particularly *comme il faut*), and supervised the upholstering. Everything progressed and progressed and approached the ideal he had set himself: even when things were only half completed they exceeded his expectations. He saw what a refined and elegant character, free from vulgarity, it would all have when it was ready. On falling asleep he pictured to himself how the reception-room would look. Looking at the yet unfinished drawing-room he could see the fireplace, the screen, the what-not, the little chairs dotted here and there, the dishes and plates on the walls, and the bronzes, as they would be when everything was in place. He was pleased by the thought of how his wife and daughter, who shared his taste in this matter, would be impressed by it. They were certainly not expecting as much. He had been particularly successful in finding, and buying cheaply, antiques which gave a particularly aristocratic character to the whole place. But in his letters he intentionally understated everything in order to be able to surprise them. All this so absorbed him that his new duties—though he liked his official work—interested him less than he had expected. Sometimes he even had moments of absent-mindedness during the Court Sessions, and would consider whether he should have straight or curved cornices for his curtains. He was so interested in it all that he often did things himself, rearranging the furniture, or rehanging the curtains. Once when mounting a step-ladder to show the upholsterer, who did not understand, how he wanted the hangings draped, he made a false step and slipped, but being a strong and agile man he clung on and only knocked his side against the knob of the window frame. The bruised place was painful but the pain soon passed, and he felt particularly bright and well just then. He wrote: "I feel fifteen years younger." He thought he would have everything ready by September, but it dragged on till mid-October. But the result was charming not only in his eyes but to everyone who saw it.

In reality it was just what is usually seen in the houses of people of moderate means who want to appear rich, and therefore succeed only in resembling others like themselves: there were damasks, dark wood, plants, rugs, and dull and polished bronzes—all the things people of a certain class have in order to resemble other people of that class. His house was so like the others that it would never have been noticed, but to him it all seemed to be quite exceptional. He was very happy when he met his family at the station and brought them to the newly furnished house all lit up, where a footman in a white tie opened the door into the hall decorated with plants, and when they went on into the drawing room and the study uttering exclamations of delight. He conducted them everywhere, drank in their praises eagerly, and beamed with pleasure. At tea that evening, when Praskóvya Fëdorovna among other things asked him about his fall, he laughed, and showed them how he had gone flying and had frightened the upholsterer.

"It's a good thing I'm a bit of an athlete. Another man might have been killed, but I merely knocked myself, just here; it hurts when it's touched, but it's passing off already—it's only a bruise."

So they began living in their new home—in which, as always happens, when they got thoroughly settled in they found they were just one room short—and with the increased income, which as always was just a little (some five hundred rubles) too little, but it was all very nice.

Things went particularly well at first, before everything was finally arranged and while something had still to be done: this thing bought, that thing ordered, another thing moved, and something else adjusted. Though there were some disputes between husband and wife, they were both so well satisfied and had so much to do that it all passed off without any serious quarrels. When nothing was left to arrange it became rather dull and something seemed to be lacking, but they were then making acquaintances, forming habits, and life was growing fuller.

Iván Ilyich spent his mornings at the law court and came home to dinner, and at first he was generally in a good humour, though he occasionally became irritable just on account of his house. (Every spot on the tablecloth or the upholstery, and every broken window-blind string, irritated him. He had devoted so much trouble to arranging it all that every disturbance of it distressed him.) But on the whole his life ran its course as he believed life should do: easily, pleasantly, and decorously.

He got up at nine, drank his coffee, read the paper, and then put on his undress uniform and went to the law courts. There the harness in which he worked had already been stretched to fit him and he donned it without a hitch: petitioners, inquiries at the chancery, the chancery itself, and the sittings public and administrative. In all this the thing was to exclude everything fresh and vital, which always disturbs the regular course of official business, and to admit only official relations with people, and then only on official grounds. A man would come, for instance, wanting some information. Iván Ilyich, as one in whose sphere the matter did not lie, would have nothing to do with him: but if the man had some business with him in his official capacity, something that could be expressed on officially stamped paper, he would do everything, positively everything he could within the limits of such relations, and in doing so would maintain the semblance of friendly human relations, that is, would observe the courtesies of life. As soon as the official relations ended, so did everything else. Iván Ilyich possessed this capacity to separate his real life from the official side of affairs and not mix the two, in the highest degree, and by long practice and natural aptitude had brought it to such a pitch that sometimes, in the manner of a virtuoso, he would even allow himself to let the human and official relations mingle. He let himself do this just because he felt that he could at any time he chose resume the strictly official attitude again and drop the human relation. And he did it all easily, pleasantly, correctly, and even artistically. In the intervals between the sessions he smoked, drank tea, chatted a little about politics, a little about general topics, a little about cards, but most of all about official appointments. Tired, but with the feelings of a virtuoso—one of the first violins who has played his part in an orchestra with precision—he would return home to find that his wife and daughter had been out paying calls, or had a visitor, and that his son had been to school, had done his homework with his tutor, and was duly learning what is taught at High Schools. Everything was as it should be. After dinner, if they had no visitors, Iván Ilyich sometimes read a book that was being much discussed at the time, and in the evening settled down to work, that is, read official papers, compared the depositions of witnesses, and noted paragraphs of the Code applying to them. This was neither dull nor amusing. It was dull when he might have been playing bridge, but if no bridge was available it was at any rate better than doing nothing or sitting with his wife. Iván Ilyich's chief pleasure was giving little dinners to which he invited men and women of good social position, and just as his drawing-room resembled all other drawing-rooms so did his enjoyable little parties resemble all other such parties.

Once they even gave a dance. Iván Ilyich enjoyed it and everything went off well, except that it led to a violent quarrel with his wife about the cakes and sweets. Praskóvya Fëdorovna had made her own plans, but Iván Ilyich insisted on getting everything from an expensive confectioner and ordered too many cakes, and the quarrel occurred because some of those cakes were left over and the confectioner's bill came to forty-five rubles. It was a great and disagreeable quarrel. Praskóvya Fëdorovna called him "a fool and an imbecile," and he clutched at his head and made angry allusions to divorce.

But the dance itself had been enjoyable. The best people were there, and Iván Ilyich had danced with Princess Trúfonova, a sister of the distinguished founder of the Society "Bear my Burden."

The pleasures connected with his work were pleasures of ambition; his social pleasures were those of vanity; but Iván Ilyich's greatest pleasure was playing bridge. He acknowledged that whatever disagreeable incident happened in his life, the pleasure that beamed like a ray of light above everything else was to sit down to bridge with good players, not noisy partners, and of course to four-handed bridge (with five players it was annoying to have to stand out, though one pretended not to mind), to play a clever and serious game (when the cards allowed it) and then to have supper and drink a glass of wine. After a game of bridge, especially if he had won a little (to win a large sum was unpleasant), Iván Ilyich went to bed in specially good humour.

So they lived. They formed a circle of acquaintances among the best people and were visited by people of importance and by young folk. In their views as to their acquaintances, husband, wife, and daughter were entirely agreed, and tacitly and unanimously kept at arm's length and shook off the various shabby friends and relations who, with much show of affection, gushed into the drawing-room with its Japanese plates on the walls. Soon these shabby friends ceased to obtrude themselves and only the best people remained in the Golovíns' set.

Young men made up to Lisa, and Petríshchev, an examining magistrate and Dmítri Ivánovich Petríshchev's son and sole heir, began to be so attentive to her that Iván Ilyich had already spoken to Praskóvya Fëdorovna about it, and considered whether they should not arrange a party for them, or get up some private theatricals.

So they lived, and all went well, without change, and life flowed pleasantly.

IV

They were all in good health. It could not be called ill health if Iván Ilyich sometimes said that he had a queer taste in his mouth and felt some discomfort in his left side.

But this discomfort increased and, though not exactly painful, grew into a sense of pressure in his side accompanied by ill humour. And his irritability became worse and worse and began to mar the agreeable, easy, and correct life that had established itself in the Golovín family. Quarrels between husband and wife became more and more frequent, and soon the ease and amenity disappeared and even the decorum was barely maintained. Scenes again became frequent, and very few of those islets remained on which husband and wife could meet without an explosion. Praskóvya Fëdorovna now had good reason to say that her husband's temper was trying. With characteristic exaggeration she said he had always had a dreadful temper, and that it had needed all her good nature to put up with it for twenty years. It was true that now the quarrels were started by him. His bursts of temper always came just before dinner, often just as he began to eat his soup. Sometimes he noticed that a plate or dish was chipped, or the food was not right, or his son put his elbow on the table, or his daughter's hair was not done as he liked it, and for all this he blamed Praskóvya Fëdorovna. At first she retorted and said disagreeable things to him, but once or twice he fell into such a rage at the beginning of dinner that she realized it was due to some physical derangement brought on by taking food, and so she restrained herself and did not answer, but only hurried to get the dinner over. She regarded this self-restraint as highly praiseworthy. Having come to the conclusion that her husband had a dreadful temper and made her life miserable, she began to feel sorry for herself, and the more she pitied herself the more she hated her husband. She began to wish he would die; yet she did not want him to die because then his salary would cease. And this irritated her against him still more. She considered herself dreadfully unhappy just because not even his death could save her, and though she concealed her exasperation, that hidden exasperation of hers increased his irritation also.

After one scene in which Iván Ilyich had been particularly unfair and after which he had said in explanation that he certainly was irritable but that it was due to his not being well, she said that if he was ill it should be attended to, and insisted on his going to see a celebrated doctor.

He went. Everything took place as he had expected and as it always does. There was the usual waiting and the important air assumed by the doctor, with which he was so familiar (resembling that which he himself assumed in court), and the sounding and listening, and the questions which called for answers that were foregone conclusions and were evidently unnecessary, and the look of importance which implied that "if only you put yourself in our hands we will arrange everything—we know indubitably how it has to be done, always in the same way for everybody alike." It was all just as it was in the law courts. The doctor put on just the same air towards him as he himself put on towards an accused person.

The doctor said that so-and-so indicated that there was so-and-so inside the patient, but if the investigation of so-and-so did not confirm this, then he must assume that and that. If he assumed that and that, then . . . and so on. To Iván Ilyich only one question was important: was his case serious or not? But the doctor ignored that inappropriate question. From his point of view it was not the one under consideration, the real question was to decide between a floating kidney, chronic catarrh, or appendicitis. It was not a question of Iván Ilyich's life or death, but one between a floating kidney and appendicitis. And that question the doctor solved brilliantly, as it seemed to Iván Ilyich, in favour of the appendix, with the reservation that should an examination of the urine give fresh indications the matter would be reconsidered. All this was just what Iván Ilyich had himself brilliantly accomplished a thousand times in dealing with men on trial. The doctor summed up just as brilliantly, looking over his spectacles triumphantly and even gaily at the accused. From the doctor's summing up Iván Ilyich concluded that things were bad, but that for the doctor, and perhaps for everybody else, it was a matter of indifference, though for him it was bad. And this conclusion struck him painfully, arousing in him a great feeling of pity for himself and of bitterness towards the doctor's indifference to a matter of such importance.

He said nothing of this, but rose, placed the doctor's fee on the table, and remarked with a sigh: "We sick people probably often put inappropriate questions. But tell me, in general, is this complaint dangerous, or not? . . ."

The doctor looked at him sternly over his spectacles with one eye, as if to say: "Prisoner, if you will not keep to the questions put to you, I shall be obliged to have you removed from the court."

"I have already told you what I consider necessary and proper. The analysis may show something more." And the doctor bowed.

Iván Ilyich went out slowly, seated himself disconsolately in his sledge, and drove home. All the way home he was going over what the doctor had said, trying to translate those complicated, obscure, scientific phrases into plain language and find in them an answer to the question: "Is my condition bad? Is it very bad? Or is there as yet nothing much wrong?" And it seemed to him that the meaning of what the doctor had said was that it was very bad. Everything in the streets seemed depressing. The cabmen, the houses, the passers-by, and the shops, were dismal. His ache, this dull gnawing ache that never ceased for a moment, seemed to have acquired a new and more serious significance from the doctor's dubious remarks. Iván Ilyich now watched it with a new and oppressive feeling.

He reached home and began to tell his wife about it. She listened, but in the middle of his account his daughter came in with her hat on, ready to go out with her mother. She sat down reluctantly to listen to this tedious story, but could not stand it long, and her mother too did not hear him to the end.

"Well, I am very glad," she said. "Mind now to take your medicine regularly. Give me the prescription and I'll send Gerásim to the chemist's." And she went to get ready to go out.

While she was in the room Iván Ilyich had hardly taken time to breathe, but he sighed deeply when she left it.

"Well," he thought, "perhaps it isn't so bad after all."

He began taking his medicine and following the doctor's directions, which had been altered after the examination of the urine. But then it happened that there was a contradiction between the indications drawn from the examination of the urine and the symptoms that showed themselves. It turned out that what was happening differed from what the doctor had told him, and that he had either forgotten, or blundered, or hidden something from him. He could not, however, be blamed for that, and Iván Ilyich still obeyed his orders implicitly and at first derived some comfort from doing so.

From the time of his visit to the doctor, Iván Ilyich's chief occupation was the exact fulfilment of the doctor's instructions regarding hygiene and the taking of medicine, and the observation of his pain and his excretions. His chief interests came to be people's ailments and people's health. When sickness, deaths, or recoveries were mentioned in his presence, especially when the illness resembled his own, he listened with agitation which he tried to hide, asked questions, and applied what he heard to his own case.

The pain did not grow less, but Iván Ilyich made efforts to force himself to think that he was better. And he could do this so long as nothing agitated him. But as soon as he had any unpleasantness with his wife, any lack of success in his official work, or held bad cards at bridge, he was at once acutely sensible of his disease. He had formerly borne such mischances, hoping soon to adjust what was wrong, to master it and attain success, or make a grand slam. But now every mischance upset him and plunged him into despair. He would say to himself. "There now, just as I was beginning to get better and the medicine had begun to take effect, comes this accursed misfortune, or unpleasantness . . ." And he was furious with the mishap, or with the people who were causing the unpleasantness and killing him, for he felt that this fury was killing him but could not restrain it. One would have thought that it should have been clear to him that this exasperation with circumstances and people aggravated his illness, and that he ought therefore to ignore unpleasant occurrences. But he drew the very opposite conclusion: he said that he needed peace, and he watched for everything that might disturb it and became irritable at the slightest infringement of it. His condition was rendered worse by the fact that he read medical books and consulted doctors. The progress of his disease was so gradual that he could deceive himself when comparing one day with another—the difference was so slight. But when he consulted the doctors it seemed to him that he was getting worse, and even very rapidly. Yet despite this he was continually consulting them.

That month he went to see another celebrity, who told him almost the same as the first had done but put his questions rather differently, and the interview with this celebrity only increased Iván Ilyich's doubts and fears. A friend of a friend of his, a very good doctor, diagnosed his illness again quite differently from the others, and though he predicted recovery, his questions and suppositions bewildered Iván Ilyich still more and increased his doubts. A homeopathist diagnosed the disease in yet another way, and prescribed medicine which Iván Ilyich took secretly for a week. But after a week, not feeling any improvement and having lost confidence both in the former doctor's treatment and in this one's, he became still more despondent. One day a lady acquaintance mentioned a cure effected by a wonder-working icon. Iván Ilyich caught himself listening attentively and beginning to believe that it had occurred. This incident alarmed him. "Has my mind really weakened to such an extent?" he asked himself. "Nonsense! It's all rubbish. I mustn't give way to nervous fears but having chosen a doctor must keep strictly to his treatment. That is what I will do. Now it's all settled. I won't think about it, but will follow the treatment seriously till summer, and then we shall see. From now there must be no more of this wavering!" This was easy to say but impossible to carry out. The pain in his side oppressed him and seemed to grow worse and more incessant, while the taste in his mouth grew stranger and stranger. It seemed to him that his breath had a disgusting smell, and he was conscious of a loss of appetite and strength. There was no deceiving himself: something terrible, new, and more important than anything before in his life, was taking place within him of which he alone was aware. Those about him did not understand or would not understand it, but thought everything in the world was going on as usual. That tormented Iván Ilyich more than anything. He saw that his household, especially his wife and daughter who were in a perfect whirl of visiting, did not understand anything of it and were annoyed that he was so depressed and so exacting, as if he were to blame for it. Though they tried to disguise it he saw that he was an obstacle in their path, and that his wife had adopted a definite line in regard to his illness and kept to it regardless of anything he said or did. Her attitude was this: "You know," she would say to her friends, "Iván Ilyich can't do as other people do, and keep to the treatment prescribed for him. One day he'll take his drops and keep strictly to his diet and go to bed in good time, but the next day unless I watch him he'll suddenly forget his medicine, eat sturgeon—which is forbidden—and sit up playing cards till one o'clock in the morning."

"Oh, come, when was that?" Iván Ilyich would ask in vexation. "Only once at Peter Ivánovich's."

"And yesterday with Shébek."

"Well, even if I hadn't stayed up, this pain would have kept me awake."

"Be that as it may you'll never get well like that, but will always make us wretched."

Praskóvya Fëdorovna's attitude to Iván Ilyich's illness, as she expressed it both to others and to him, was that it was his own fault and was another of the annoyances he caused her. Iván Ilyich felt that this opinion escaped her involuntarily—but that did not make it easier for him.

At the law courts too, Iván Ilyich noticed, or thought he noticed, a strange attitude towards himself. It sometimes seemed to him that people were watching him inquisitively as a man whose place might soon be vacant. Then again, his friends would suddenly begin to chaff him in a friendly way about his low spirits, as if the awful, horrible, and unheard-of thing that was going on within him, incessantly gnawing at him and irresistibly drawing him away, was a very agreeable subject for jests. Schwartz in particular irritated him by his jocularity, vivacity, and *savoir-faire*, which reminded him of what he himself had been ten years ago.

Friends came to make up a set and they sat down to cards. They dealt, bending the new cards to soften them, and he sorted the diamonds in his hand and found he had seven. His partner said "No trumps" and supported him with two diamonds. What more could be wished for? It ought to be jolly and lively. They would make a grand slam. But suddenly Iván Ilyich was conscious of that gnawing pain, that taste in his mouth, and it seemed ridiculous that in such circumstances he should be pleased to make a grand slam.

He looked at his partner Mikháil Mikháylovich, who rapped the table with his strong hand and instead of snatching up the tricks pushed the cards courteously and indulgently towards Iván Ilyich that he might have the pleasure of gathering them up without the trouble of stretching out his hand for them. "Does he think I am too weak to stretch out my arm?" thought Iván Ilyich, and forgetting what he was doing he over-trumped his partner, missing the grand slam by three tricks. And what was most awful of all was that he saw how upset Mikháil Mikháylovich was about it but did not himself care. And it was dreadful to realize why he did not care.

They all saw that he was suffering, and said: "We can stop if you are tired. Take a rest." Lie down? No, he was not at all tired, and he finished the rubber. All were gloomy and silent. Iván Ilyich felt that he had diffused this gloom over them and could not dispel it. They had supper and went away, and Iván Ilyich was left alone with the consciousness that his life was poisoned and was poisoning the lives of others, and that this poison did not weaken but penetrated more and more deeply into his whole being.

With this consciousness, and with physical pain besides the terror, he must go to bed, often to lie awake the greater part of the night. Next morning he had to get up again, dress, go to the law courts, speak, and write; or if he did not go out, spend at home those twenty-four hours a day each of which was a torture. And he had to live thus all alone on the brink of an abyss, with no one who understood or pitied him.

V

So one month passed and then another. Just before the New Year his brother-in-law came to town and stayed at their house. Iván Ilyich was at the law courts and Praskóvya Fëdorovna had gone shopping. When Iván Ilyich came home and entered his study he found his brother-in-law there—a healthy, florid man—unpacking his portmanteau himself. He raised his head on hearing Iván Ilyich's footsteps and looked up at him for a moment without a word. That stare told Iván everything. His brother-in-law opened his mouth to utter an exclamation of surprise but checked himself, and that action confirmed it all.

"I have changed, eh?"

"Yes, there is a change."

And after that, try as he would to get his brother-in-law to return to the subject of his looks, the latter would say nothing about it. Praskóvya Fëdorovna came home and her brother went out to her. Iván Ilyich locked the door and began to examine himself in the glass, first full face, then in profile. He took up a portrait of himself taken with his wife, and compared it with what he saw in the glass. The change in him was immense. Then he bared his arms to the elbow, looked at them, drew the sleeves down again, sat down on an ottoman, and grew blacker than night.

"No, no, this won't do!" he said to himself, and jumped up, went to the table, took up some law papers and began to read them, but could not continue. He unlocked the door and went into the reception-room. The door leading to the drawing-room was shut. He approached it on tiptoe and listened.

"No, you are exaggerating!" Praskóvya Fëdorovna was saying.

"Exaggerating! Don't you see it? Why, he's a dead man! Look at his eyes—there's no light in them. But what is it that is wrong with him?"

"No one knows. Nikoláevich [that was another doctor] said something, but I don't know what. And Leshchetítsky [this was the celebrated specialist] said quite the contrary . . ."

Iván Ilyich walked away, went to his own room, lay down and began musing: "The kidney, a floating kidney." He recalled all the doctors had told him of how it detached itself and swayed about. And by an effort of imagination he tried to catch that kidney and arrest it and support it. So little was needed for this, it seemed to him. "No, I'll go to see Peter Ivánovich again." [That was the friend whose friend was a doctor.] He rang, ordered the carriage, and got ready to go.

"Where are you going, *Jean?*" asked his wife, with a specially sad and exceptionally kind look.

This exceptionally kind look irritated him. He looked morosely at her.

"I must go to see Peter Ivánovich."

He went to see Peter Ivánovich, and together they went to see his friend, the doctor. He was in, and Iván Ilyich had a long talk with him.

Reviewing the anatomical and physiological details of what in the doctor's opinion was going on inside him, he understood it all.

There was something, a small thing, in the vermiform appendix. It might all come right. Only stimulate the energy of one organ and check the activity of another, then absorption would take place and everything would come right. He got home rather late for dinner, ate his dinner, and conversed cheerfully, but could not for a long time bring himself to go back to work in his room. At last, however, he went to his study and did what was necessary, but the consciousness that he had put something aside—an important, intimate matter which he would revert to when his work was done—never left him. When he had finished his work he remembered that this intimate matter was the thought of his vermiform appendix. But he did not give himself up to it, and went to the drawing-room for tea. There were callers there, including the examining magistrate who was a desirable match for his daughter, and they were conversing, playing the piano, and singing. Iván Ilyich, as Praskóvya Fëdorovna remarked, spent that evening more cheerfully than usual, but he never for a moment forgot that he had postponed the important matter of the appendix. At eleven o'clock he said goodnight and went to his bedroom. Since his illness he had slept alone in a small room next to his study. He undressed and took up a novel by Zola,[7] but instead of reading it he fell into thought, and in his imagination that desired improvement in the vermiform appendix occurred. There was the absorption and evacuation and the re-

7. Émile Zola (1840–1902), French novelist, author of the *Rougon-Macquart* novels (*Nana, Germinal,* and so on). Tolstoy condemned Zola for his naturalistic theories and considered his novels crude and gross.

establishment of normal activity. "Yes, that's it!" he said to himself. "One need only assist nature, that's all." He remembered his medicine, rose, took it, and lay down on his back watching for the beneficent action of the medicine and for it to lessen the pain. "I need only take it regularly and avoid all injurious influences. I am already feeling better, much better." He began touching his side: it was not painful to the touch. "There, I really don't feel it. It's much better already." He put out the light and turned on his side . . . "The appendix is getting better, absorption is occurring." Suddenly he felt the old, familiar, dull, gnawing pain, stubborn and serious. There was the same familiar loathsome taste in his mouth. His heart sank and he felt dazed. "My God! My God!" he muttered. "Again, again! And it will never cease." And suddenly the matter presented itself in a quite different aspect. "Vermiform appendix! Kidney!" he said to himself. "It's not a question of appendix or kidney, but of life and . . . death. Yes, life was there and now it is going, going and I cannot stop it. Yes. Why deceive myself? Isn't it obvious to everyone but me that I'm dying, and that it's only a question of weeks, days . . . it may happen this moment. There was light and now there is darkness. I was here and now I'm going there! Where?" A chill came over him, his breathing ceased, and he felt only the throbbing of his heart.

"When I am not, what will there be? There will be nothing. Then where shall I be when I am no more? Can this be dying? No, I don't want to!" He jumped up and tried to light the candle, felt for it with trembling hands, dropped candle and candlestick on the floor, and fell back on his pillow.

"What's the use? It makes no difference," he said to himself, staring with wide-open eyes into the darkness. "Death. Yes, death. And none of them know or wish to know it, and they have no pity for me. Now they are playing." (He heard through the door the distant sound of a song and its accompaniment.) "It's all the same to them, but they will die too! Fools! I first, and they later, but it will be the same for them. And now they are merry . . . the beasts!"

Anger choked him and he was agonizingly, unbearably miserable. "It is impossible that all men have been doomed to suffer this awful horror!" He raised himself.

"Something must be wrong. I must calm myself—must think it all over from the beginning." And he again began thinking. "Yes, the beginning of my illness: I knocked my side, but I was still quite well that day and the next. It hurt a little, then rather more. I saw the doctors, then followed despondency and anguish, more doctors, and I drew nearer to the abyss. My strength grew less and I kept coming nearer and nearer, and now I have wasted away and there is no light in my eyes. I think of the appendix—but this is death! I think of mending the appendix, and all the while here is death! Can it really be death?" Again terror seized him and he gasped for breath. He leant down and began feeling for the matches, pressing with his elbow on the stand beside the bed. It was in his way and hurt him, he grew furious with it, pressed on it still harder, and upset it. Breathless and in despair he fell on his back, expecting death to come immediately.

Meanwhile the visitors were leaving. Praskóvya Fëdorovna was seeing them off. She heard something fall and came in.

"What has happened?"

"Nothing. I knocked it over accidentally."

She went out and returned with a candle. He lay there panting heavily, like a man who has run a thousand yards, and stared upwards at her with a fixed look.

"What is it, *Jean?*"

"No . . . o . . . thing. I upset it." ("Why speak of it? She won't understand," he thought.)

And in truth she did not understand. She picked up the stand, lit his candle, and hurried away to see another visitor off. When she came back he still lay on his back, looking upwards.

"What is it? Do you feel worse?"

"Yes."

She shook her head and sat down.

"Do you know, *Jean*, I think we must ask Leshchetísky to come and see you here."

This meant calling in the famous specialist, regardless of expense. He smiled malignantly and said "No." She remained a little longer and then went up to him and kissed his forehead.

While she was kissing him he hated her from the bottom of his soul and with difficulty refrained from pushing her away.

"Good-night. Please God you'll sleep."

"Yes."

VI

Iván Ilyich saw that he was dying, and he was in continual despair.

In the depth of his heart he knew he was dying, but not only was he not accustomed to the thought, he simply did not and could not grasp it.

The syllogism he had learned from Kiesewetter's *Logic*:[8] "Caius is a man, men are mortal, therefore Caius is mortal," had always seemed to him correct as applied to Caius, but certainly not as

8. Karl Kiesewetter (1766–1819) was a German popularizer of Kant's philosophy. His *Outline of Logic According to Kantian Principles* (1796) was widely used in Russian adaptations as a schoolbook.

applied to himself. That Caius—man in the abstract—was mortal, was perfectly correct, but he was not Caius, not an abstract man, but a creature quite, quite separate from all others. He had been little Ványa, with a mamma and a papa, with Mítya and Volódya, with the toys, a coachman and a nurse, afterwards with Kátenka and with all the joys, griefs, and delights of childhood, boyhood, and youth. What did Caius know of the smell of that striped leather ball Ványa had been so fond of? Had Caius kissed his mother's hand like that, and did the silk of her dress rustle so for Caius? Had he rioted like that at school when the pastry was bad? Had Caius been in love like that? Could Caius preside at a session as he did? Caius really was mortal, and it was right for him to die; but for me, little Ványa, Iván Ilyich, with all my thoughts and emotions, it's altogether a different matter. It cannot be that I ought to die. That would be too terrible."

Such was his feeling.

"If I had to die like Caius I should have known it was so. An inner voice would have told me so, but there was nothing of the sort in me and I and all my friends felt that our case was quite different from that of Caius. And now here it is!" he said to himself. "It can't be. It's impossible! But here it is. How is this? How is one to understand it?"

He could not understand it, and tried to drive this false, incorrect, morbid thought away and to replace it by other proper and healthy thoughts. But that thought, and not the thought only but the reality itself, seemed to come and confront him.

And to replace that thought he called up a succession of others, hoping to find in them some support. He tried to get back into the former current of thoughts that had once screened the thought of death from him. But strange to say, all that had formerly shut off, hidden, and destroyed, his consciousness of death, no longer had that effect. Iván Ilyich now spent most of his time in attempting to re-establish that old current. He would say to himself: "I will take up my duties again—after all I used to live by them." And banishing all doubts he would go to the law courts, enter into conversation with his colleagues, and sit carelessly as was his wont, scanning the crowd with a thoughtful look and leaning both his emaciated arms on the arms of his oak chair; bending over as usual to a colleague and drawing his papers nearer he would interchange whispers with him, and then suddenly raising his eyes and sitting erect would pronounce certain words and open the proceedings. But suddenly in the midst of those proceedings the pain in his side, regardless of the stage the proceedings had reached, would begin its own gnawing work. Iván Ilyich would turn his attention to it and try to drive the thought of it away, but without success. *It* would come and stand before him and look at him, and he would be petrified and the light would die out of his eyes, and he would again begin asking himself whether *It* alone was true. And his colleagues and subordinates would see with surprise and distress that he, the brilliant and subtle judge, was becoming confused and making mistakes. He would shake himself, try to pull himself together, manage somehow to bring the sitting to a close, and return home with the sorrowful consciousness that his judicial labours could not as formerly hide from him what he wanted them to hide, and could not deliver him from *It*. And what was worst of all was that *It* drew his attention to itself not in order to make him take some action but only that he should look at *It*, look it straight in the face: look at it without doing anything, suffer inexpressibly.

And to save himself from this condition Iván Ilyich looked for consolations—new screens—and new screens were found and for a while seemed to save him, but then they immediately fell to pieces or rather became transparent, as if *It* penetrated them and nothing could veil *It*.

In these latter days he would go into the drawing-room he had arranged—that drawing-room where he had fallen and for the sake of which (how bitterly ridiculous it seemed) he had sacrificed his life—for he knew that his illness originated with that knock. He would enter and see that something had scratched the polished table. He would look for the cause of this and find that it was the bronze ornamentation of an album, that had got bent. He would take up the expensive album which he had lovingly arranged, and feel vexed with his daughter and her friends for their untidiness—for the album was torn here and there and some of the photographs turned upside down. He would put it carefully in order and bend the ornamentation back into position. Then it would occur to him to place all those things in another corner of the room, near the plants. He would call the footman, but his daughter or wife would come to help him. They would not agree, and his wife would contradict him, and he would dispute and grow angry. But that was all right, for then he did not think about *It*. *It* was invisible.

But then, when he was moving something himself, his wife would say: "Let the servants do it. You will hurt yourself again." And suddenly *It* would flash through the screen and he would see it. It was just a flash, and he hoped it would disappear, but he would involuntarily pay attention to his side. "It sits there as before, gnawing just the same!" And he could no longer forget *It*, but could distinctly see it looking at him from behind the flowers. "What is it all for?"

"It really is so! I lost my life over that curtain as I might have done when storming a fort. Is that possible? How terrible and how stupid. It can't be true! It can't, but it is."

He would go to his study, lie down, and again be alone with *It:* face to face with *It.* And nothing could be done with *It* except to look at it and shudder.

VII

How it happened it is impossible to say because it came about step by step, unnoticed, but in the third month of Iván Ilyich's illness, his wife, his daughter, his son, his acquaintances, the doctors, the servants, and above all he himself, were aware that the whole interest he had for other people was whether he would soon vacate his place, and at last release the living from the discomfort caused by his presence and be himself released from his sufferings.

He slept less and less. He was given opium and hypodermic injections of morphine, but this did not relieve him. The dull depression he experienced in a somnolent condition at first gave him a little relief, but only as something new, afterwards it became as distressing as the pain itself or even more so.

Special foods were prepared for him by the doctors' orders, but all those foods became increasingly distasteful and disgusting to him.

For his excretions also special arrangements had to be made, and this was a torment to him every time—a torment from the uncleanliness, the unseemliness, and the smell, and from knowing that another person had to take part in it.

But just through this most unpleasant matter, Iván Ilyich obtained comfort. Gerásim, the butler's young assistant, always came in to carry the things out. Gerásim was a clean, fresh peasant lad, grown stout on town food and always cheerful and bright. At first the sight of him, in his clean Russian peasant costume, engaged on that disgusting task embarrassed Iván Ilyich.

Once when he got up from the commode too weak to draw up his trousers, he dropped into a soft armchair and looked with horror at his bare, enfeebled thighs with the muscles so sharply marked on them.

Gerásim with a firm light tread, his heavy boots emitting a pleasant smell of tar and fresh winter air, came in wearing a clean Hessian apron, the sleeves of his print shirt tucked up over his strong bare young arms; and refraining from looking at his sick master out of consideration for his feelings, and restraining the joy of life that beamed from his face, he went up to the commode.

"Gerásim!" said Iván Ilyich in a weak voice.

Gerásim started, evidently afraid he might have committed some blunder, and with a rapid movement turned his fresh, kind, simple young face which just showed the first downy signs of a beard.

"Yes, sir?"

"That must be very unpleasant for you. You must forgive me. I am helpless."

"Oh, why, sir," and Gerásim's eyes beamed and he showed his glistening white teeth, "what's a little trouble? It's a case of illness with you, sir."

And his deft strong hands did their accustomed task, and he went out of the room stepping lightly. Five minutes later he as lightly returned.

Iván Ilyich was still sitting in the same position in the armchair.

"Gerásim," he said when the latter had replaced the freshly-washed utensil. "Please come here and help me." Gerásim went up to him. "Lift me up. It is hard for me to get up, and I have sent Dmítri away."

Gerásim went up to him, grasped his master with his strong arms deftly but gently, in the same way that he stepped—lifted him, supported him with one hand, and with the other drew up his trousers and would have set him down again, but Iván Ilyich asked to be led to the sofa. Gerásim, without an effort and without apparent pressure, led him, almost lifting him, to the sofa and placed him on it.

"Thank you. How easily and well you do it all!"

Gerásim smiled again and turned to leave the room. But Iván Ilyich felt his presence such a comfort that he did not want to let him go.

"One thing more, please move up that chair. No, the other one—under my feet. It is easier for me when my feet are raised."

Gerásim brought the chair, set it down gently in place, and raised Iván Ilyich's legs on to it. It seemed to Iván Ilyich that he felt better while Gerásim was holding up his legs.

"It's better when my legs are higher," he said. "Place that cushion under them."

Gerásim did so. He again lifted the legs and placed them, and again Iván Ilyich felt better while Gerásim held his legs. When he set them down Iván Ilyich fancied he felt worse.

"Gerásim," he said. "Are you busy now?"

"Not at all, sir," said Gerásim, who had learnt from the townsfolk how to speak to gentlefolk.

"What have you still to do?"

"What have I to do? I've done everything except chopping the logs for to-morrow."

"Then hold my legs up a bit higher, can you?"

"Of course I can. Why not?" And Gerásim raised his master's legs higher and Iván Ilyich thought that in that position he did not feel any pain at all.

"And how about the logs?"

"Don't trouble about that, sir. There's plenty of time."

Iván Ilyich told Gerásim to sit down and hold his legs, and began to talk to him. And strange to say it seemed to him that he felt better while Gerásim held his legs up.

After that Iván Ilyich would sometimes call Gerásim and get him to hold his legs on his shoulders, and he liked talking to him. Gerásim did it all easily, willingly, simply, and with a good nature that touched Iván Ilyich. Health, strength, and vitality in other people were offensive to him, but Gerásim's strength and vitality did not mortify but soothed him.

What tormented Iván Ilyich most was the deception, the lie, which for some reason they all accepted, that he was not dying but was simply ill, and that he only need keep quiet and undergo a treatment and then something very good would result. He however knew that do what they would nothing would come of it, only still more agonizing suffering and death. This deception tortured him—their not wishing to admit what they all knew and what he knew, but wanting to lie to him concerning his terrible condition, and wishing and forcing him to participate in that lie. Those lies —lies enacted over him on the eve of his death and destined to degrade this awful, solemn act to the level of their visitings, their curtains, their sturgeon for dinner—were a terrible agony for Iván Ilyich. And strangely enough, many times when they were going through their antics over him he had been within a hairbreadth of calling out to them: "Stop lying! You know and I know that I am dying. Then at least stop lying about it!" But he had never had the spirit to do it. The awful, terrible act of his dying was, he could see, reduced by those about him to the level of a casual, unpleasant, and almost indecorous incident (as if someone entered a drawing-room diffusing an unpleasant odour) and this was done by that very decorum which he had served all his life long. He saw that no one felt for him, because no one even wished to grasp his position. Only Gerásim recognized and pitied him. And so Iván Ilyich felt at ease only with him. He felt comforted when Gerásim supported his legs (sometimes all night long) and refused to go to bed, saying: "Don't you worry, Iván Ilyich. I'll get sleep enough later on," or when he suddenly became familiar and exclaimed: "If you weren't sick it would be another matter, but as it is, why should I grudge a little trouble?" Gerásim alone did not lie; everything showed that he alone understood the facts of the case and did not consider it necessary to disguise them, but simply felt sorry for his emaciated and enfeebled master. Once when Iván Ilyich was sending him away he even said straight out: "We shall all of us die, so why should I grudge a little trouble?"—expressing the fact that he did not think his work burdensome, because he was doing it for a dying man and hoped someone would do the same for him when his time came.

Apart from this lying, or because of it, what most tormented Iván Ilyich was that no one pitied him as he wished to be pitied. At certain moments after prolonged suffering he wished most of all (though he would have been ashamed to confess it) for someone to pity him as a sick child is pitied. He longed to be petted and comforted. He knew he was an important functionary, that he had a beard turning grey, and that therefore what he longed for was impossible, but still he longed for it. And in Gerásim's attitude towards him there was something akin to what he wished for, and so that attitude comforted him. Iván Ilyich wanted to weep, wanted to be petted and cried over, and then his colleague Shébek would come, and instead of weeping and being petted, Iván Ilyich would assume a serious, severe, and profound air, and by force of habit would express his opinion on a decision of the Court of Appeal and would stubbornly insist on that view. This falsity around him and within him did more than anything else to poison his last days.

VIII

It was morning. He knew it was morning because Gerásim had gone, and Peter the footman had come and put out the candles, drawn back one of the curtains, and begun quietly to tidy up. Whether it was morning or evening, Friday or Sunday, made no difference, it was all just the same: the gnawing, unmitigated, agonizing pain, never ceasing for an instant, the consciousness of life inexorably waning but not yet extinguished, the approach of that ever dreaded and hateful Death which was the only reality, and always the same falsity. What were days, weeks, hours, in such a case?

"Will you have some tea, sir?"

"He wants things to be regular, and wishes the gentlefolk to drink tea in the morning," thought Iván Ilyich, and only said "No."

"Wouldn't you like to move onto the sofa, sir?"

"He wants to tidy up the room, and I'm in the way. I am uncleanliness and disorder," he thought, and said only:

"No, leave me alone."

The man went on bustling about. Iván Ilyich stretched out his hand. Peter came up, ready to help.

"What is it, sir?"

"My watch."

Peter took the watch which was close at hand and gave it to his master.

"Half-past eight. Are they up?"

"No sir, except Vladímir Ivánich" (the son) "who has gone to school. Praskóvya Fëdorovna ordered me to wake her if you asked for her. Shall I do so?"

"No, there's no need to." "Perhaps I'd better have some tea," he thought, and added aloud: "Yes, bring me some tea."

Peter went to the door, but Iván Ilyich dreaded being left alone. "How can I keep him here? Oh yes, my medicine." "Peter, give me my medicine." "Why not? Perhaps it may still do me some good." He took a spoonful and swallowed it. "No, it won't help. It's all tomfoolery, all deception," he decided as soon as he became aware of the familiar, sickly, hopeless taste. "No, I can't believe in it any longer. But the pain, why this pain? If it would only cease just for a moment!" And he moaned. Peter turned towards him. "It's all right. Go and fetch me some tea."

Peter went out. Left alone Iván Ilyich groaned not so much with pain, terrible though that was, as from mental anguish. Always and forever the same, always these endless days and nights. If only it would come quicker! If only *what* would come quicker? Death, darkness? . . . No, no! Anything rather than death!

When Peter returned with the tea on a tray, Iván Ilyich stared at him for a time in perplexity, not realizing who and what he was. Peter was disconcerted by that look and his embarrassment brought Iván Ilyich to himself.

"Oh, tea! All right, put it down. Only help me to wash and put on a clean shirt."

And Iván Ilyich began to wash. With pauses for rest, he washed his hands and then his face, cleaned his teeth, brushed his hair, and looked in the glass. He was terrified by what he saw, especially by the limp way in which his hair clung to his pallid forehead.

While his shirt was being changed he knew that he would be still more frightened at the sight of his body, so he avoided looking at it. Finally he was ready. He drew on a dressing-gown, wrapped himself in a plaid, and sat down in the armchair to take his tea. For a moment he felt refreshed, but as soon as he began to drink the tea he was again aware of the same taste, and the pain also returned. He finished it with an effort, and then lay down stretching out his legs, and dismissed Peter.

Always the same. Now a spark of hope flashes up, then a sea of despair rages, and always pain; always pain, always despair, and always the same. When alone he had a dreadful and distressing desire to call someone, but he knew beforehand that with others present it would be still worse. "Another dose of morphine—to lose consciousness. I will tell him, the doctor, that he must think of something else. It's impossible, impossible, to go on like this."

An hour and another pass like that. But now there is a ring at the door bell. Perhaps it's the doctor? It is. He comes in fresh, hearty, plump, and cheerful, with that look on his face that seems to say: "There now, you're in a panic about something, but we'll arrange it all for you directly!" The doctor knows this expression is out of place here, but he has put it on once for all and can't take it off—like a man who has put on a frock-coat in the morning to pay a round of calls.

The doctor rubs his hands vigorously and reassuringly.

"Brr! How cold it is! There's such a sharp frost; just let me warm myself!" he says, as if it were only a matter of waiting till he was warm, and then he would put everything right.

"Well now, how are you?"

Iván Ilyich feels that the doctor would like to say: "Well, how are our affairs?" but that even he feels that this would not do, and says instead: "What sort of a night have you had?"

Iván Ilyich looks at him as much as to say: "Are you really never ashamed of lying?" But the doctor does not wish to understand this question, and Iván Ilyich says: "Just as terrible as ever. The pain never leaves me and never subsides. If only something . . ."

"Yes, you sick people are always like that. . . . There, now I think I'm warm enough. Even Praskóvya Fëdorovna, who is so particular, could find no fault with my temperature. Well, now I can say good-morning," and the doctor presses his patient's hand.

Then, dropping his former playfulness, he begins with a most serious face to examine the patient, feeling his pulse and taking his temperature, and then begins the sounding and auscultation.

Iván Ilyich knows quite well and definitely that all this is nonsense and pure deception, but when the doctor, getting down on his knee, leans over him, putting his ear first higher then lower, and performs various gymnastic movements over him with a significant expression on his face, Iván Ilyich submits to it all as he used to submit to the speeches of the lawyers, though he knew very well that they were all lying and why they were lying.

The doctor, kneeling on the sofa, is still sounding him when Praskóvya Fëdorovna's silk dress rustles at the door and she is heard scolding Peter for not having let her know of the doctor's arrival.

She comes in, kisses her husband, and at once proceeds to prove that she has been up a long time already, and only owing to a misunderstanding failed to be there when the doctor arrived.

Iván Ilyich looks at her, scans her all over, sets against her the whiteness and plumpness and cleanness of her hands and neck, the gloss of her hair, and the sparkle of her vivacious eyes. He hates her with his whole soul. And the thrill of hatred he feels for her makes him suffer from her touch.

Her attitude towards him and his disease is still the same. Just as the doctor had adopted a certain relation to his patient which he could not abandon, so had she formed one towards him—that he was not doing something he ought to do and was himself to blame, and that she reproached him lovingly for this—and she could not now change that attitude.

"You see he doesn't listen to me and doesn't take his medicine at the proper time. And above all he lies in a position that is no doubt bad for him—with his legs up."

She described how he made Gerásim hold his legs up.

The doctor smiled with a contemptuous affability that said: "What's to be done? These sick people do have foolish fancies of that kind, but we must forgive them."

When the examination was over the doctor looked at his watch, and then Praskóvya Fëdorovna announced to Iván Ilyich that it was of course as he pleased, but she had sent to-day for a celebrated specialist who would examine him and have a consultation with Michael Danílovich (their regular doctor).

"Please don't raise any objections. I am doing this for my own sake," she said ironically, letting it be felt that she was doing it all for his sake and only said this to leave him no right to refuse. He remained silent, knitting his brows. He felt that he was so surrounded and involved in a mesh of falsity that it was hard to unravel anything.

Everything she did for him was entirely for her own sake, and she told him she was doing for herself what she actually was doing for herself, as if that was so incredible that he must understand the opposite.

At half-past eleven the celebrated specialist arrived. Again the sounding began and the significant conversations in his presence and in another room, about the kidneys and the appendix, and the questions and answers, with such an air of importance that again, instead of the real question of life and death which now alone confronted him, the question arose of the kidney and the appendix which were not behaving as they ought to and would now be attacked by Michael Danílovich and the specialist and forced to amend their ways.

The celebrated specialist took leave of him with a serious though not hopeless look, and in reply to the timid question Iván Ilyich, with eyes glistening with fear and hope, put to him as to whether there was a chance of recovery, said that he could not vouch for it but there was a possibility. The look of hope with which Iván Ilyich watched the doctor out was so pathetic that Praskóvya Fëdorovna, seeing it, even wept as she left the room to hand the doctor his fee.

The gleam of hope kindled by the doctor's encouragement did not last long. The same room, the same pictures, curtains, wallpaper, medicine bottles, were all there, and the same aching suffering body, and Iván Ilyich began to moan. They gave him a subcutaneous injection and he sank into oblivion.

It was twilight when he came to. They brought him his dinner and he swallowed some beef tea with difficulty, and then everything was the same again and night was coming on.

After dinner, at seven o'clock, Praskóvya Fëdorovna came into the room in evening dress, her full bosom pushed up by her corset, and with traces of powder on her face. She had reminded him in the morning that they were going to the theatre. Sarah Bernhardt was visiting the town and they had a box, which he had insisted on their taking. Now he had forgotten about it and her toilet offended him, but he concealed his vexation when he remembered that he had himself insisted on their securing a box and going because it would be an instructive and aesthetic pleasure for the children.

Praskóvya Fëdorovna came in, self-satisfied but yet with a rather guilty air. She sat down and asked how he was, but, as he saw, only for the sake of asking and not in order to learn about it, knowing that there was nothing to learn—and then went on to what she really wanted to say: that she would not on any account have gone but that the box had been taken and Helen and their daughter were going, as well as Petríshchev (the examining magistrate, their daughter's fiancé) and that it was out of the question to let them go alone; but that she would have much preferred to sit with him for a while; and he must be sure to follow the doctor's orders while she was away.

"Oh, and Fëdor Petróvich" (the fiancé) "would like to come in. May he? And Lisa?"

"All right."

Their daughter came in in full evening dress, her fresh young flesh exposed (making a show of that very flesh which in his own case caused so much suffering), strong, healthy, evidently in love, and impatient with illness, suffering, and death, because they interfered with her happiness.

Fëdor Petróvich came in too, in evening dress, his hair curled *à la Capoul*, a tight stiff collar round his long sinewy neck, an enormous white shirt-front and narrow black trousers tightly stretched over his strong thighs. He had one white glove tightly drawn on, and was holding his opera hat in his hand.

Following him the schoolboy crept in unnoticed, in a new uniform, poor little fellow, and wearing gloves. Terribly dark shadows showed under his eyes, the meaning of which Iván Ilyich knew well.

His son had always seemed pathetic to him, and now it was dreadful to see the boy's frightened look of pity. It seemed to Iván Ilyich that Vásya was the only one besides Gerásim who understood and pitied him.

They all sat down and again asked how he was. A silence followed

Lisa asked her mother about the opera-glasses, and there was an altercation between mother and daughter as to who had taken them and where they had been put. This occasioned some unpleasantness.

Fëdor Petróvich inquired of Iván Ilyich whether he had ever seen Sarah Bernhardt. Iván Ilyich did not at first catch the question, but then replied: "No, have you seen her before?"

"Yes, in *Adrienne Lecouvreur*."[9]

Praskóvya Fëdorovna mentioned some rôles in which Sarah Bernhardt was particularly good. Her daughter disagreed. Conversation sprang up as to the elegance and realism of her acting—the sort of conversation that is always repeated and is always the same.

In the midst of the conversation Fëdor Petróvich glanced at Iván Ilyich and became silent. The others also looked at him and grew silent. Iván Ilyich was staring with glittering eyes straight before him, evidently indignant with them. This had to be rectified, but it was impossible to do so. The silence had to be broken, but for a time no one dared to break it and they all became afraid that the conventional deception would suddenly become obvious and the truth become plain to all. Lisa was the first to pluck up courage and break that silence, but by trying to hide what everybody was feeling, she betrayed it.

"Well, if we are going it's time to start," she said, looking at her watch, a present from her father, and with a faint and significant smile at Fëdor Petróvich relating to something known only to them. She got up with a rustle of her dress.

They all rose, said good-night, and went away.

When they had gone it seemed to Iván Ilyich that he felt better; the falsity had gone with them. But the pain remained—that same pain and that same fear that made everything monotonously alike, nothing harder and nothing easier. Everything was worse.

Again minute followed minute and hour followed hour. Everything remained the same and there was no cessation. And the inevitable end of it all became more and more terrible.

"Yes, send Gerásim here," he replied to a question Peter asked.

IX

His wife returned late at night. She came in on tiptoe, but he heard her, opened his eyes, and made haste to close them again. She wished to send Gerásim away and to sit with him herself, but he opened his eyes and said: "No, go away."

"Are you in great pain?"

"Always the same."

"Take some opium."

9. a play (1849) by the French dramatist Eugène Scribe (1791–1861), in which the heroine was a famous actress of the eighteenth century. Tolstoy considered Scribe, who wrote over four hundred plays, a shoddy, commercial playwright.

He agreed and took some. She went away.

Till about three in the morning he was in a state of stupefied misery. It seemed to him that he and his pain were being thrust into a narrow, deep black sack, but though they were pushed further and further in they could not be pushed to the bottom. And this, terrible enough in itself, was accompanied by suffering. He was frightened yet wanted to fall through the sack, he struggled but yet co-operated. And suddenly he broke through, fell, and regained consciousness. Gerásim was sitting at the foot of the bed dozing quietly and patiently, while he himself lay with his emaciated stockinged legs resting on Gerásim's shoulders; the same shaded candle was there and the same unceasing pain.

"Go away, Gerásim," he whispered.

"It's all right, sir. I'll stay a while."

"No. Go away."

He removed his legs from Gerásim's shoulders, turned sideways onto his arm, and felt sorry for himself. He only waited till Gerásim had gone into the next room and then restrained himself no longer but wept like a child. He wept on account of his helplessness, his terrible loneliness, the cruelty of man, the cruelty of God, and the absence of God.

"Why hast Thou done all this? Why hast Thou brought me here? Why, dost Thou torment me so terribly?"

He did not expect an answer and yet wept because there was no answer and could be none. The pain again grew more acute, but he did not stir and did not call. He said to himself: "Go on! Strike me! But what is it for? What have I done to Thee? What is it for?"

Then he grew quiet and not only ceased weeping but even held his breath and became all attention. It was as though he were listening not to an audible voice but to a voice of his soul, to the current of thoughts arising within him.

"What is it you want?" was the first clear conception capable of expression in words, that he heard.

"What do you want? What do you want?" he repeated to himself.

"What do I want? To live and not to suffer," he answered.

And again he listened with such concentrated attention that even his pain did not distract him.

"To live? How?" asked his inner voice.

"Why, to live as I used to—well and pleasantly."

"As you lived before, well and pleasantly?" the voice repeated.

And in imagination he began to recall the best moments of his pleasant life. But strange to say none of those best moments of his pleasant life now seemed at all what they had then seemed—none of them except the first recollections of childhood. There, in childhood, there had been something really pleasant with which it would be possible to live if it could return. But the child who had experienced that happiness existed no longer, it was like a reminiscence of somebody else.

As soon as the period began which had produced the present Iván Ilyich, all that had then seemed joys now melted before his sight and turned into something trivial and often nasty.

And the further he departed from childhood and the nearer he came to the present the more worthless and doubtful were the joys. This began with the School of Law. A little that was really good was still found there—there was light-heartedness, friendship, and hope. But in the upper classes there had already been fewer of such good moments. Then during the first years of his official career, when he was in the service of the Governor, some pleasant moments again occurred: they were the memories of love for a woman. Then all became confused and there was still less of what was good; later on again there was still less that was good, and the further he went the less there was. His marriage, a mere accident, then the disenchantment that followed it, his wife's bad breath and the sensuality and hypocrisy: then that deadly official life and those preoccupations about money, a year of it, and two, and ten, and twenty, and always the same thing. And the longer it lasted the more deadly it became. "It is as if I had been going downhill while I imagined I was going up. And that is really what it was. I was going up in public opinion, but to the same extent life was ebbing away from me. And now it is all done and there is only death."

"Then what does it mean? Why? It can't be that life is so senseless and horrible. But if it really has been so horrible and senseless, why must I die and die in agony? There is something wrong!"

"Maybe I did not live as I ought to have done," it suddenly occurred to him. "But how could that be, when I did everything properly?" he replied, and immediately dismissed from his mind this, the sole solution of all the riddles of life and death, as something quite impossible.

"Then what do you want now? To live? Live how? Live as you lived in the law courts when the usher proclaimed 'The judge is coming!' The judge is coming, the judge!" he repeated to himself. "Here he is, the judge. But I am not guilty!" he exclaimed angrily. "What is it for?" And he ceased crying, but turning his face to the wall continued to ponder on the same question: Why, and for what purpose, is there all this horror? But however much he pondered he found no answer. And whenever the thought occurred to him, as it often did, that it all resulted from his not having lived as he ought to have done, he at once recalled the correctness of his whole life, and dismissed so strange an idea.

X

Another fortnight passed. Iván Ilyich now no longer left his sofa. He would not lie in bed but lay on the sofa, facing the wall nearly all the time. He suffered ever the same unceasing agonies and in his loneliness pondered always on the same insoluble question: "What is this? Can it be that it is Death?" And the inner voice answered: "Yes, it is Death."

"Why these sufferings?" And the voice answered, "For no reason—they just are so." Beyond and besides this there was nothing.

From the very beginning of his illness, ever since he had first been to see the doctor, Iván Ilyich's life had been divided between two contrary and alternating moods: now it was despair and the expectation of this uncomprehended and terrible death, and now hope and an intently interested observation of the functioning of his organs. Now before his eyes there was only a kidney or an intestine that temporarily evaded its duty, and now only that incomprehensible and dreadful death from which it was impossible to escape.

These two states of mind had alternated from the very beginning of his illness, but the further it progressed the more doubtful and fantastic became the conception of the kidney, and the more real the sense of impending death.

He had but to call to mind what he had been three months before and what he was now, to call to mind with what regularity he had been going downhill, for every possibility of hope to be shattered.

Latterly during that loneliness in which he found himself as he lay facing the back of the sofa, a loneliness in the midst of a populous town and surrounded by numerous acquaintances and relations but that yet could not have been more complete anywhere—either at the bottom of the sea or under the earth—during that terrible loneliness Iván Ilyich had lived only in memories of the past. Pictures of his past rose before him one after another. They always began with what was nearest in time and then went back to what was most remote—to his childhood—and rested there. If he thought of the stewed prunes that had been offered him that day, his mind went back to the raw shrivelled French plums of his childhood, their peculiar flavour and the flow of saliva when he sucked their stones, and along with the memory of that taste came a whole series of memories of those days: his nurse, his brother, and their toys. "No, I mustn't think of that. . . . It is too painful," Iván Ilyich said to himself, and brought himself back to the present—to the button on the back of the sofa and the creases in its morocco. "Morocco is expensive, but it does not wear well: there had been a quarrel about it. It was a different kind of quarrel and a different kind of morocco that time when we tore father's portfolio and were punished, and mamma brought us some tarts. . . ." And again his thoughts dwelt on his childhood, and again it was painful and he tried to banish them and fix his mind on something else.

Then again together with that chain of memories another series passed through his mind—of how his illness had progressed and grown worse. There also the further back he looked the more life there had been. There had been more of what was good in life and more of life itself. The two merged together. "Just as the pain went on getting worse and worse, so my life grew worse and worse," he thought. "There is one bright spot there at the back, at the beginning of life, and afterwards all becomes blacker and blacker and proceeds more and more rapidly—in inverse ratio to the square of the distance from death," thought Iván Ilyich. And the example of a stone falling downwards with increasing velocity entered his mind. Life, a series of increasing sufferings, flies further and further towards its end—the most terrible suffering. "I am flying. . . ." He shuddered, shifted himself, and tried to resist, but was already aware that resistance was impossible, and again with eyes weary of gazing but unable to cease seeing what was before them, he stared at the back of the sofa and waited—awaiting that dreadful fall and shock and destruction.

"Resistance is impossible!" he said to himself. "If I could only understand what it is all for! But that too is impossible. An explanation would be possible if it could be said that I have not lived as I ought to. But it is impossible to say that," and he remembered all the legality, correctitude, and propriety of his life. "That at any rate can certainly not be admitted," he thought, and his lips smiled ironically as if someone could see that smile and be taken in by it. "There is no explanation! Agony, death. . . . What for?"

XI

Another two weeks went by in this way and during that fortnight an event occurred that Iván Ilyich and his wife had desired. Petríshchev formally proposed. It happened in the evening. The next day Praskóvya Fëdorovna came into her husband's room considering how best to inform him of it, but that very night there had been a fresh change for the worse in his condition. She found him still lying on the sofa but in a different position. He lay on his back, groaning and staring fixedly straight in front of him.

She began to remind him of his medicines, but he turned his eyes towards her with such a look that she did not finish what she was saying; so great an animosity, to her in particular, did that look express.

"For Christ's sake let me die in peace!" he said.

She would have gone away, but just then their daughter came in and went up to say good morning. He looked at her as he had done at his wife, and in reply to her inquiry about his health said dryly that he would soon free them all of himself. They were both silent and after sitting with him for a while went away.

"Is it our fault?" Lisa said to her mother. "It's as if we were to blame! I am sorry for papa, but why should we be tortured?"

The doctor came at his usual time. Iván Ilyich answered "Yes" and "No," never taking his angry eyes from him, and at last said: "You know you can do nothing for me, so leave me alone."

"We can ease your sufferings."

"You can't even do that. Let me be."

The doctor went into the drawing-room and told Praskóvya Fëdorovna that the case was very serious and that the only resource left was opium to allay her husband's sufferings, which must be terrible.

It was true, as the doctor said, that Iván Ilyich's physical sufferings were terrible, but worse than the physical sufferings were his mental sufferings which were his chief torture.

His mental sufferings were due to the fact that that night, as he looked at Gerásim's sleepy, good-natured face with its prominent cheek-bones, the question suddenly occurred to him: "What if my whole life has really been wrong?"

It occurred to him that what had appeared perfectly impossible before, namely that he had not spent his life as he should have done, might after all be true. It occurred to him that his scarcely perceptible attempts to struggle against what was considered good by the most highly placed people, those scarcely noticeable impulses which he had immediately suppressed, might have been the real thing, and all the rest false. And his professional duties and the whole arrangement of his life and of his family, and all his social and official interests, might all have been false. He tried to defend all those things to himself and suddenly felt the weakness of what he was defending. There was nothing to defend.

"But if that is so," he said to himself, "and I am leaving this life with the consciousness that I have lost all that was given me and it is impossible to rectify it—what then?"

He lay on his back and began to pass his life in review in quite a new way. In the morning when he saw first his footman, then his wife, then his daughter, and then the doctor, their every word and movement confirmed to him the awful truth that had been revealed to him during the night. In them he saw himself—all that for which he had lived—and saw clearly that it was not real at all, but a terrible and huge deception which had hidden both life and death. This consciousness intensified his physical suffering tenfold. He groaned and tossed about, and pulled at his clothing which choked and stifled him. And he hated them on that account.

He was given a large dose of opium and became unconscious, but at noon his sufferings began again. He drove everybody away and tossed from side to side.

His wife came to him and said:

"*Jean*, my dear, do this for me. It can't do any harm and often helps. Healthy people often do it."

He opened his eyes wide.

"What? Take communion? Why? It's unnecessary! However . . ."

She began to cry.

"Yes, do, my dear. I'll send for our priest. He is such a nice man."

"All right. Very well," he muttered.

When the priest came and heard his confession, Iván Ilyich was softened and seemed to feel a relief from his doubts and consequently from his sufferings, and for a moment there came a ray of hope. He again began to think of the vermiform appendix and the possibility of correcting it. He received the sacrament with tears in his eyes.

When they laid him down again afterwards he felt a moment's ease, and the hope that he might live awoke in him again. He began to think of the operation that had been suggested to him. "To live! I want to live!" he said to himself.

His wife came in to congratulate him after his communion, and when uttering the usual conventional words she added:

"You feel better, don't you?"

Without looking at her he said "Yes."

Her dress, her figure, the expression of her face, the tone of her voice, all revealed the same thing. "This is wrong, it is not as it should be. All you have lived for and still live for is falsehood and deception, hiding life and death from you." And as soon as he admitted that thought, his hatred and his agonizing physical suffering again sprang up, and with that suffering a consciousness of the unavoidable, approaching end. And to this was added a new sensation of grinding shooting pain and a feeling of suffocation.

The expression of his face when he uttered that "yes" was dreadful. Having uttered it, he looked her straight in the eyes, turned on his face with a rapidity extraordinary in his weak state and shouted:

"Go away! Go away and leave me alone!"

XII

From that moment the screaming began that continued for three days, and was so terrible that one could not hear it through two closed doors without horror. At the moment he answered his wife he realized that he was lost, that there was no return, that the end had come, the very end, and his doubts were still unsolved and remained doubts.

"Oh! Oh! Oh!" he cried in various intonations. He had begun by screaming "I won't!" and continued screaming on the letter "o."

For three whole days, during which time did not exist for him, he struggled in that black sack into which he was being thrust by an invisible, resistless force. He struggled as a man condemned to death struggles in the hands of the executioner, knowing that he cannot save himself. And every moment he felt that despite all his efforts he was drawing nearer and nearer to what terrified him. He felt that his agony was due to his being thrust into that black hole and still more to his not being able to get right into it. He was hindered from getting into it by his conviction that his life had been a good one. That very justification of his life held him fast and prevented his moving forward, and it caused him most torment of all.

Suddenly some force struck him in the chest and side, making it still harder to breathe, and he fell through the hole and there at the bottom was a light. What had happened to him was like the sensation one sometimes experiences in a railway carriage when one thinks one is going backwards while one is really going forwards and suddenly becomes aware of the real direction.

"Yes, it was all not the right thing," he said to himself, "but that's no matter. It can be done. But what *is* the right thing?" he asked himself, and suddenly grew quiet.

This occurred at the end of the third day, two hours before his death. Just then his schoolboy son had crept softly in and gone up to the bedside. The dying man was still screaming desperately and waving his arms. His hand fell on the boy's head, and the boy caught it, pressed it to his lips, and began to cry.

At that very moment Iván Ilyich fell through and caught sight of the light, and it was revealed to him that though his life had not been what it should have been, this could still be rectified. He asked himself, "What *is* the right thing?" and grew still, listening. Then he felt that someone was kissing his hand. He opened his eyes, looked at his son, and felt sorry for him. His wife came up to him and he glanced at her. She was gazing at him open-mouthed, with undried tears on her nose and cheek and a despairing look on her face. He felt sorry for her too.

"Yes, I am making them wretched," he thought. "They are sorry, but it will be better for them when I die." He wished to say this but had not the strength to utter it. "Besides, why speak? I must act," he thought. With a look at his wife he indicated his son and said: "Take him away . . . sorry for him . . . sorry for you too. . . ." He tried to add, "forgive me," but said "forego" and waved his hand, knowing that He whose understanding mattered would understand.

And suddenly it grew clear to him that what had been oppressing him and would not leave him was all dropping away at once from two sides, from ten sides, and from all sides. He was sorry for them, he must act so as not to hurt them: release them and free himself from these sufferings. "How good and how simple!" he thought. "And the pain?" he asked himself. "What has become of it? Where are you, pain?"

He turned his attention to it.

"Yes, here it is. Well, what of it? Let the pain be."

"And death . . . where is it?"

He sought his former accustomed fear of death and did not find it. "Where is it? What death?" There was no fear because there was no death.

In place of death there was light.

"So that's what it is!" he suddenly exclaimed aloud. "What joy!"

To him all this happened in a single instant, and the meaning of that instant did not change. For those present his agony continued for another two hours. Something rattled in his throat, his emaciated body twitched, then the gasping and rattle became less and less frequent.

"It is finished!" said someone near him.

He heard these words and repeated them in his soul.

"Death is finished," he said to himself. "It is no more!"

He drew in a breath, stopped in the midst of a sigh, stretched out, and died.

HENRIK IBSEN

(1828–1906)

Hedda Gabler*

Characters

GEORGE TESMAN, *research graduate in cultural history*
HEDDA, *his wife*
MISS JULIANA TESMAN, *his aunt*
MRS. ELVSTED
JUDGE BRACK
EILERT LOEVBORG
BERTHA, *a maid*

The action takes place in TESMAN'S *villa in the fashionable quarter of town.*

Act I

SCENE—*A large drawing room, handsomely and tastefully furnished; decorated in dark colors. In the rear wall is a broad open doorway, with curtains drawn back to either side. It leads to a*

* Translated by Michael Meyer.

smaller room, decorated in the same style as the drawing room. In the right-hand wall of the drawing room, a folding door leads out to the hall. The opposite wall, on the left, contains french windows,[1] *also with curtains drawn back on either side. Through the glass we can see part of a verandah, and trees in autumn colors. Downstage stands an oval table, covered by a cloth and surrounded by chairs. Downstage right, against the wall, is a broad stove tiled with dark porcelain; in front of it stand a high-backed armchair, a cushioned footrest, and two footstools. Upstage right, in an alcove, is a corner sofa, with a small, round table. Downstage left, a little away from the wall, is another sofa. Upstage of the french windows, a piano. On either side of the open doorway in the rear wall stand what-nots holding ornaments of terra cotta and majolica. Against the rear wall of the smaller room can be seen a sofa, a table, and a couple of chairs. Above this sofa hangs the portrait of a handsome old man in general's uniform. Above the table a lamp hangs from the ceiling, with a shade of opalescent, milky glass. All round the drawing room bunches of flowers stand in vases and glasses. More bunches lie on the tables. The floors of both rooms are covered with thick carpets. Morning light. The sun shines in through the french windows.*

MISS JULIANA TESMAN, *wearing a hat and carrying a parasol, enters from the hall, followed by* BERTHA, *who is carrying a bunch of flowers wrapped in paper.* MISS TESMAN *is about sixty-five, of pleasant and kindly appearance. She is neatly but simply dressed in grey outdoor clothes.* BERTHA, *the maid, is rather simple and rustic-looking. She is getting on in years.*

MISS TESMAN. [*Stops just inside the door, listens, and says in a hushed voice*] No, bless my soul! They're not up yet.

BERTHA. [*Also in hushed tones*] What did I tell you, miss? The boat didn't get in till midnight. And when they did turn up—Jesus, miss, you should have seen all the things Madam made me unpack before she'd go to bed!

MISS TESMAN. Ah, well. Let them have a good lie in. But let's have some nice fresh air waiting for them when they do come down.

[*Goes to the french windows and throws them wide open*]

BERTHA. [*Bewildered at the table, the bunch of flowers in her hand*] I'm blessed if there's a square inch left to put anything. I'll have to let it lie here, miss.

[*Puts it on the piano*]

MISS TESMAN. Well, Bertha dear, so now you have a new mistress. Heaven knows it nearly broke my heart to have to part with you.

BERTHA. [*Snivels*] What about me, Miss Juju? How do you suppose I felt? After all the happy years I've spent with you and Miss Rena?

1. *French windows:* Door-sized windows through which people may pass, in this case opening to the outdoors.

MISS TESMAN. We must accept it bravely, Bertha. It was the only way. George needs you to take care of him. He could never manage without you. You've looked after him ever since he was a tiny boy.

BERTHA. Oh, but, Miss Juju, I can't help thinking about Miss Rena, lying there all helpless, poor dear. And that new girl! She'll never learn the proper way to handle an invalid.

MISS TESMAN. Oh, I'll manage to train her. I'll do most of the work myself, you know. You needn't worry about my poor sister, Bertha dear.

BERTHA. But Miss Juju, there's another thing. I'm frightened Madam may not find me suitable.

MISS TESMAN. Oh, nonsense, Bertha. There may be one or two little things to begin with——

BERTHA. She's a real lady. Wants everything just so.

MISS TESMAN. But of course she does! General Gabler's daughter! Think of what she was accustomed to when the General was alive. You remember how we used to see her out riding with her father? In that long black skirt? With the feather in her hat?

BERTHA. Oh, yes, miss. As if I could forget! But, Lord! I never dreamed I'd live to see a match between her and Master Georgie.

MISS TESMAN. Neither did I. By the way, Bertha, from now on you must stop calling him Master Georgie. You must say: Dr. Tesman.

BERTHA. Yes, Madam said something about that too. Last night —the moment they'd set foot inside the door. Is it true, then, miss?

MISS TESMAN. Indeed it is. Just imagine, Bertha, some foreigners have made him a doctor. It happened while they were away. I had no idea till he told me when they got off the boat.

BERTHA. Well, I suppose there's no limit to what he won't become. He's that clever. I never thought he'd go in for hospital work, though.

MISS TESMAN. No, he's not that kind of doctor. [*Nods impressively*] In any case, you may soon have to address him by an even grander title.

BERTHA. You don't say! What might that be, miss?

MISS TESMAN. [*Smiles*] Ah! If you only knew! [*Moved*] Dear God, if only poor dear Joachim could rise out of his grave and see what his little son has grown into! [*Looks round*] But Bertha, why have you done this? Taken the chintz covers off all the furniture!

BERTHA. Madam said I was to. Can't stand chintz covers on chairs, she said.

MISS TESMAN. But surely they're not going to use this room as a parlor?

BERTHA. So I gathered, miss. From what Madam said. He didn't say anything. The Doctor.

[GEORGE TESMAN *comes into the rear room, from the right,*

humming, with an open, empty travelling bag in his hand. He is about thirty-three, of medium height and youthful appearance, rather plump, with an open, round, contented face, and fair hair and beard. He wears spectacles, and is dressed in comfortable, indoor clothes.]

MISS TESMAN. Good morning! Good morning, George!

TESMAN. [*In open doorway*] Auntie Juju! Dear Auntie Juju! [*Comes forward and shakes her hand*] You've come all the way out here! And so early! What?

MISS TESMAN. Well, I had to make sure you'd settled in comfortably.

TESMAN. But you can't have had a proper night's sleep.

MISS TESMAN. Oh, never mind that.

TESMAN. We were so sorry we couldn't give you a lift. But you saw how it was—Hedda had so much luggage—and she insisted on having it all with her.

MISS TESMAN. Yes, I've never seen so much luggage.

BERTHA. [*To* TESMAN] Shall I go and ask Madam if there's anything I can lend her a hand with?

TESMAN. Er—thank you, Bertha; no, you needn't bother. She says if she wants you for anything she'll ring.

BERTHA. [*Over to right*] Oh. Very good.

TESMAN. Oh, Bertha—take this bag, will you?

BERTHA. [*Takes it.*] I'll put it in the attic.

[*Goes out into the hall*]

TESMAN. Just fancy, Auntie Juju, I filled that whole bag with notes for my book. You know, it's really incredible what I've managed to find rooting through those archives. By Jove! Wonderful old things no one even knew existed——

MISS TESMAN. I'm sure you didn't waste a single moment of your honeymoon, George dear.

TESMAN. No, I think I can truthfully claim that. But, Auntie Juju, do take your hat off. Here. Let me untie it for you. What?

MISS TESMAN. [*As he does so*] Oh dear, oh dear! It's just as if you were still living at home with us.

TESMAN. [*Turns the hat in his hand and looks at it*] I say! What a splendid new hat!

MISS TESMAN. I bought it for Hedda's sake.

TESMAN. For Hedda's sake? What?

MISS TESMAN. So that Hedda needn't be ashamed of me, in case we ever go for a walk together.

TESMAN. [*Pats her cheek*] You still think of everything, don't you, Auntie Juju? [*Puts the hat down on a chair by the table*] Come on, let's sit down here on the sofa. And have a little chat while we wait for Hedda.

[*They sit. She puts her parasol in the corner of the sofa.*]

MISS TESMAN. [*Clasps both his hands and looks at him*] Oh, George, it's so wonderful to have you back, and be able to see you with my own eyes again! Poor dear Joachim's own son!

TESMAN. What about me! It's wonderful for me to see you again, Auntie Juju. You've been a mother to me. And a father, too.

MISS TESMAN. You'll always keep a soft spot in your heart for your old aunties, won't you. George dear?

TESMAN. I suppose Auntie Rena's no better? What?

MISS TESMAN. Alas, no. I'm afraid she'll never get better, poor dear. She's lying there just as she has for all these years. Please God I may be allowed to keep her for a little longer. If I lost her I don't know what I'd do. Especially now I haven't you to look after.

TESMAN. [*Pats her on the back*] There, there, there!

MISS TESMAN. [*With a sudden change of mood*] Oh but George, fancy you being a married man! And to think it's you who've won Hedda Gabler! The beautiful Hedda Gabler! Fancy! She was always so surrounded by admirers.

TESMAN. [*Hums a little and smiles contentedly*] Yes, I suppose there are quite a few people in this town who wouldn't mind being in my shoes. What?

MISS TESMAN. And what a honeymoon! Five months! Nearly six.

TESMAN. Well, I've done a lot of work, you know. All those archives to go through. And I've had to read lots of books.

MISS TESMAN. Yes, dear, of course. [*Lowers her voice confidentially*] But tell me, George—haven't you any—any extra little piece of news to give me?

TESMAN. You mean, arising out of the honeymoon?

MISS TESMAN. Yes.

TESMAN. No, I don't think there's anything I didn't tell you in my letters. My doctorate, of course—but I told you about that last night, didn't I?

MISS TESMAN. Yes, yes, I didn't mean that kind of thing. I was just wondering—are you—are you expecting——?

TESMAN. Expecting what?

MISS TESMAN. Oh, come on George, I'm your old aunt!

TESMAN. Well actually—yes, I am expecting something.

MISS TESMAN. I knew it!

TESMAN. You'll be happy to hear that before very long I expect to become a professor.

MISS TESMAN. Professor?

TESMAN. I think I may say that the matter has been decided. But, Auntie Juju, you know about this.

MISS TESMAN. [*Gives a little laugh*] Yes, of course. I'd forgotten. [*Changes her tone*] But we were talking about your honeymoon. It must have cost a dreadful amount of money, George?

TESMAN. Oh well, you know, that big research grant I got helped a good deal.

MISS TESMAN. But how on earth did you manage to make it do for two?

TESMAN. Well, to tell the truth it was a bit tricky. What?

MISS TESMAN. Especially when one's traveling with a lady. A little bird tells me that makes things very much more expensive.

TESMAN. Well, yes, of course it does make things a little more expensive. But Hedda has to do things in style, Auntie Juju. I mean, she has to. Anything less grand wouldn't have suited her.

MISS TESMAN. No, no, I suppose not. A honeymoon abroad seems to be the vogue nowadays. But tell me, have you had time to look round the house?

TESMAN. You bet. I've been up since the crack of dawn.

MISS TESMAN. Well, what do you think of it?

TESMAN. Splendid. Absolutely splendid. I'm only wondering what we're going to do with those two empty rooms between that little one and Hedda's bedroom.

MISS TESMAN. [*Laughs slyly*] Ah, George dear, I'm sure you'll manage to find some use for them—in time.

TESMAN. Yes, of course, Auntie Juju, how stupid of me. You're thinking of my books. What?

MISS TESMAN. Yes, yes, dear boy. I was thinking of your books.

TESMAN. You know, I'm so happy for Hedda's sake that we've managed to get this house. Before we became engaged she often used to say this was the only house in town she felt she could really bear to live in. It used to belong to Mrs. Falk—you know, the Prime Minister's widow.

MISS TESMAN. Fancy that! And what a stroke of luck it happened to come into the market. Just as you'd left on your honeymoon.

TESMAN. Yes, Auntie Juju, we've certainly had all the luck with us. What?

MISS TESMAN. But, George dear, the expense! It's going to make a dreadful hole in your pocket, all this.

TESMAN. [*A little downcast*] Yes, I—I suppose it will, won't it?

MISS TESMAN. Oh, George, really!

TESMAN. How much do you think it'll cost? Roughly, I mean? What?

MISS TESMAN. I can't possibly say till I see the bills.

TESMAN. Well, luckily Judge Brack's managed to get it on very favorable terms. He wrote and told Hedda so.

MISS TESMAN. Don't you worry, George dear. Anyway I've stood security for all the furniture and carpets.

TESMAN. Security? But dear, sweet Auntie Juju, how could you possibly stand security?

MISS TESMAN. I've arranged a mortgage on our annuity.

TESMAN. [*Jumps up*] What? On your annuity? And—Auntie Rena's?

MISS TESMAN. Yes. Well, I couldn't think of any other way.

TESMAN. [*Stands in front of her*] Auntie Juju, have you gone completely out of your mind? That annuity's all you and Auntie Rena have.

MISS TESMAN. All right, there's no need to get so excited about it. It's a pure formality, you know. Judge Brack told me so. He was so kind as to arrange it all for me. A pure formality; those were his very words.

TESMAN. I dare say. All the same——

MISS TESMAN. Anyway, you'll have a salary of your own now. And, good heavens, even if we did have to fork out a little—tighten our belts for a week or two—why, we'd be happy to do so for your sake.

TESMAN. Oh, Auntie Juju! Will you never stop sacrificing yourself for me?

MISS TESMAN. [*Gets up and puts her hands on his shoulders*] What else have I to live for but to smooth your road a little, my dear boy? You've never had any mother or father to turn to. And now at last we've achieved our goal. I won't deny we've had our little difficulties now and then. But now, thank the good Lord, George dear, all your worries are past.

TESMAN. Yes, it's wonderful really how everything's gone just right for me.

MISS TESMAN. Yes! And the enemies who tried to bar your way have been struck down. They have been made to bite the dust. The man who was your most dangerous rival has had the mightiest fall. And now he's lying there in the pit he dug for himself, poor misguided creature.

TESMAN. Have you heard any news of Eilert? Since I went away?

MISS TESMAN. Only that he's said to have published a new book.

TESMAN. What! Eilert Loevborg? You mean—just recently? What?

MISS TESMAN. So they say. I don't imagine it can be of any value, do you? When your new book comes out, that'll be another story. What's it going to be about?

TESMAN. The domestic industries of Brabant[2] in the Middle Ages.

MISS TESMAN. Oh, George! The things you know about!

TESMAN. Mind you, it may be some time before I actually get down to writing it. I've made these very extensive notes, and I've got to file and index them first.

MISS TESMAN. Ah, yes! Making notes; filing and indexing; you've always been wonderful at that. Poor dear Joachim was just the same.

TESMAN. I'm looking forward so much to getting down to that. Especially now I've a home of my own to work in.

MISS TESMAN. And above all, now that you have the girl you set your heart on, George dear.

TESMAN. [*Embraces her*] Oh, yes, Auntie Juju, yes! Hedda's the loveliest thing of all! [*Looks towards the doorway*] I think I hear her coming. What?

[HEDDA *enters the rear room from the left, and comes into the drawing room. She is a woman of twenty-nine. Distinguished, aristocratic face and figure. Her complexion is pale and opalescent. Her eyes are steel-grey, with an expression of cold, calm serenity. Her hair is of a handsome auburn color, but is not especially abundant. She is dressed in an elegant, somewhat loose-fitting morning gown.*]

2. *Brabant:* In the Middle Ages, a duchy located in parts of what are now Belgium and the Netherlands.

MISS TESMAN. [*Goes to greet her*] Good morning, Hedda dear! Good morning!

HEDDA. [*Holds out her hand*] Good morning, dear Miss Tesman. What an early hour to call. So kind of you.

MISS TESMAN. [*Seems somewhat embarrassed*] And has the young bride slept well in her new home?

HEDDA. Oh—thank you, yes. Passably well.

TESMAN. [*Laughs*] Passably. I say, Hedda, that's good! When I jumped out of bed, you were sleeping like a top.

HEDDA. Yes. Fortunately. One has to accustom oneself to anything new, Miss Tesman. It takes time. [*Looks left*] Oh, that maid's left the french windows open. This room's flooded with sun.

MISS TESMAN. [*Goes towards the windows*] Oh—let me close them.

HEDDA. No, no, don't do that. Tesman dear, draw the curtains. This light's blinding me.

TESMAN. [*At the windows*] Yes, yes, dear. There, Hedda, now you've got shade and fresh air.

HEDDA. This room needs fresh air. All these flowers——But my dear Miss Tesman, won't you take a seat?

MISS TESMAN. No, really not, thank you. I just wanted to make sure you have everything you need. I must see about getting back home. My poor dear sister will be waiting for me.

TESMAN. Be sure to give her my love, won't you? Tell her I'll run over and see her later today.

MISS TESMAN. Oh yes, I'll tell her that. Oh, George——[*Fumbles in the pocket of her skirt*] I almost forgot. I've brought something for you.

TESMAN. What's that, Auntie Juju? What?

MISS TESMAN. [*Pulls out a flat package wrapped in newspaper and gives it to him*] Open and see, dear boy.

TESMAN. [*Opens the package*] Good heavens! Auntie Juju, you've kept them! Hedda, this is really very touching. What?

HEDDA. [*By the what-nots, on the right*] What is it, Tesman?

TESMAN. My old shoes! My slippers, Hedda!

HEDDA. Oh, them. I remember you kept talking about them on our honeymoon.

TESMAN. Yes, I missed them dreadfully. [*Goes over to her*] Here, Hedda, take a look.

HEDDA. [*Goes away towards the stove*] Thanks, I won't bother.

TESMAN. [*Follows her*] Fancy, Hedda, Auntie Rena's embroidered them for me. Despite her being so ill. Oh, you can't imagine what memories they have for me.

HEDDA. [*By the table*] Not for me.

MISS TESMAN. No, Hedda's right there, George.

TESMAN. Yes, but I thought since she's one of the family now——

HEDDA. [*Interrupts*] Tesman, we really can't go on keeping this maid.

MISS TESMAN. Not keep Bertha?

TESMAN. What makes you say that, dear? What?

HEDDA. [*Points*] Look at that! She's left her old hat lying on the chair.

TESMAN. [*Appalled, drops his slippers on the floor*] But, Hedda——!

HEDDA. Suppose someone came in and saw it?

TESMAN. But Hedda—that's Auntie Juju's hat.

HEDDA. Oh?

MISS TESMAN. [*Picks up the hat*] Indeed it's mine. And it doesn't happen to be old, Hedda dear.

HEDDA. I didn't look at it very closely, Miss Tesman.

MISS TESMAN. [*Tying on the hat*] As a matter of fact, it's the first time I've worn it. As the good Lord is my witness.

TESMAN. It's very pretty, too. Really smart.

MISS TESMAN. Oh, I'm afraid it's nothing much really. [*Looks round*] My parasol? Ah, here it is. [*Takes it*] This is mine, too. [*Murmurs*] Not Bertha's.

TESMAN. A new hat and a new parasol! I say, Hedda, fancy that!

HEDDA. Very pretty and charming.

TESMAN. Yes, isn't it? What? But Auntie Juju, take a good look at Hedda before you go. Isn't she pretty and charming?

MISS TESMAN. Dear boy, there's nothing new in that. Hedda's been a beauty ever since the day she was born.

[*Nods and goes right.*]

TESMAN. [*Follows her*] Yes, but have you noticed how strong and healthy she's looking? And how she's filled out since we went away?

MISS TESMAN. [*Stops and turns*] Filled out?

HEDDA. [*Walks across the room*] Oh, can't we forget it?

TESMAN. Yes, Auntie Juju—you can't see it so clearly with that dress on. But I've good reason to know——

HEDDA. [*By the french windows, impatiently*] You haven't good reason to know anything.

TESMAN. It must have been the mountain air up there in the Tyrol——

HEDDA. [*Curtly, interrupts him*] I'm exactly the same as when I went away.

TESMAN. You keep on saying so. But you're not. I'm right, aren't I, Auntie Juju?

MISS TESMAN. [*Has folded her hands and is gazing at her*] She's beautiful—beautiful. Hedda is beautiful. [*Goes over to* HEDDA, *takes her head between her hands, draws it down and kisses her hair*] God bless and keep you, Hedda Tesman. For George's sake.

HEDDA. [*Frees herself politely*] Oh—let me go, please.

MISS TESMAN. [*Quietly, emotionally*] I shall come see you both every day.

TESMAN. Yes, Auntie Juju, please do. What?

MISS TESMAN. Good-bye! Good-bye!

[*She goes out into the hall.* TESMAN *follows her. The door remains open.* TESMAN *is heard sending his love to* AUNT

RENA *and thanking* MISS TESMAN *for his slippers. Meanwhile* HEDDA *walks up and down the room raising her arms and clenching her fists as though in desperation. Then she throws aside the curtains from the french windows and stands there, looking out. A few moments later,* TESMAN *returns and closes the door behind him.*]

TESMAN. [*Picks up his slippers from the floor*] What are you looking at, Hedda?

HEDDA. [*Calm and controlled again*] Only the leaves. They're so golden. And withered.

TESMAN. [*Wraps up the slippers and lays them on the table*] Well, we're in September now.

HEDDA. [*Restless again*] Yes. We're already into September.

TESMAN. Auntie Juju was behaving rather oddly, I thought, didn't you? Almost as though she was in church or something. I wonder what came over her. Any idea?

HEDDA. I hardly know her. Does she often act like that?

TESMAN. Not to the extent she did today.

HEDDA. [*Goes away from the french windows*] Do you think she was hurt by what I said about the hat?

TESMAN. Oh, I don't think so. A little at first, perhaps——

HEDDA. But what a thing to do, throw her hat down in someone's drawing room. People don't do such things.

TESMAN. I'm sure Auntie Juju doesn't do it very often.

HEDDA. Oh well, I'll make it up with her.

TESMAN. Oh Hedda, would you?

HEDDA. When you see them this afternoon invite her to come out here this evening.

TESMAN. You bet I will! I say, there's another thing which would please her enormously.

HEDDA. Oh?

TESMAN. If you could bring yourself to call her Auntie Juju. For my sake, Hedda? What?

HEDDA. Oh no, really Tesman, you mustn't ask me to do that. I've told you so once before. I'll try to call her Aunt Juliana. That's as far as I'll go.

TESMAN. [*After a moment*] I say, Hedda, is anything wrong? What?

HEDDA. I'm just looking at my old piano. It doesn't really go with all this.

TESMAN. As soon as I start getting my salary we'll see about changing it.

HEDDA. No, no, don't let's change it. I don't want to part with it. We can move it into that little room and get another one to put in here.

TESMAN. [*A little downcast*] Yes, we—might do that.

HEDDA. [*Picks up the bunch of flowers from the piano*] These flowers weren't here when we arrived last night.

TESMAN. I expect Auntie Juju brought them.

HEDDA. Here's a card. [*Takes it out and reads*] "Will come back later today." Guess who it's from?

TESMAN. No idea. Who? What?

HEDDA. It says: "Mrs. Elvsted."

TESMAN. No, really? Mrs. Elvsted! She used to be Miss Rysing, didn't she?

HEDDA. Yes. She was the one with that irritating hair she was always showing off. I hear she used to be an old flame of yours.

TESMAN. [*Laughs*] That didn't last long. Anyway, that was before I got to know you, Hedda. By Jove, fancy her being in town!

HEDDA. Strange she should call. I only knew her at school.

TESMAN. Yes, I haven't seen her for—oh, heaven knows how long. I don't know how she manages to stick it out up there in the north. What?

HEDDA. [*Thinks for a moment, then says suddenly*] Tell me, Tesman, doesn't he live somewhere up in those parts? You know—Eilert Loevborg?

TESMAN. Yes, that's right. So he does.

[BERTHA *enters from the hall.*]

BERTHA. She's here again, madam. The lady who came and left the flowers. [*Points*] The ones you're holding.

HEDDA. Oh, is she? Well, show her in.

[BERTHA *opens the door for* MRS. ELVSTED *and goes out.* MRS. ELVSTED *is a delicately built woman with gentle, attractive features. Her eyes are light blue, large, and somewhat prominent, with a frightened, questioning expression. Her hair is extremely fair, almost flaxen, and is exceptionally wavy and abundant. She is two or three years younger than* HEDDA. *She is wearing a dark visiting dress, in good taste but not quite in the latest fashion.*]

HEDDA. [*Goes cordially to greet her*] Dear Mrs. Elvsted, good morning. How delightful to see you again after all this time.

MRS ELVSTED. [*Nervously, trying to control herself*] Yes, it's many years since we met.

TESMAN. And since *we* met. What?

HEDDA. Thank you for your lovely flowers.

MRS. ELVSTED. Oh, please—I wanted to come yesterday afternoon. But they told me you were away——

TESMAN. You've only just arrived in town, then? What?

MRS. ELVSTED. I got here yesterday, around midday. Oh, I became almost desperate when I heard you weren't here.

HEDDA. Desperate? Why?

TESMAN. My dear Mrs. Rysing—Elvsted——

HEDDA. There's nothing wrong, I hope?

MRS ELVSTED. Yes, there is. And I don't know anyone else here whom I can turn to.

HEDDA. [*Puts the flowers down on the table*] Come and sit with me on the sofa——

MRS. ELVSTED. Oh, I feel too restless to sit down.

HEDDA. You must. Come along, now.

[*She pulls* MRS. ELVSTED *down on to the sofa and sits beside her.*]

TESMAN. Well? Tell us, Mrs.—er——

HEDDA. Has something happened at home?

MRS. ELVSTED. Yes—that is, yes and no. Oh, I do hope you won't misunderstand me——

HEDDA. Then you'd better tell us the whole story, Mrs. Elvsted.

TESMAN. That's why you've come. What?

MRS. ELVSTED. Yes—yes, it is. Well, then—in case you don't already know—Eilert Loevborg is in town.

HEDDA. Loevborg here?

TESMAN. Eilert back in town? By Jove, Hedda, did you hear that?

HEDDA. Yes, of course I heard.

MRS. ELVSTED. He's been here a week. A whole week! In this city. Alone. With all those dreadful people——

HEDDA. But my dear Mrs. Elvsted, what concern is he of yours?

MRS. ELVSTED. [*Gives her a frightened look and says quickly*] He's been tutoring the children.

HEDDA. Your children?

MRS. ELVSTED. My husband's. I have none.

HEDDA. Oh, you mean your stepchildren.

MRS. ELVSTED. Yes.

TESMAN. [*Gropingly*] But was he sufficiently—I don't know how to put it—sufficiently regular in his habits to be suited to such a post? What?

MRS. ELVSTED. For the past two to three years he has been living irreproachably.

TESMAN. You don't say! By Jove, Hedda, hear that?

HEDDA. I hear.

MRS ELVSTED. Quite irreproachably, I assure you. In every respect. All the same—in this big city—with money in his pockets—I'm so dreadfully frightened something may happen to him.

TESMAN. But why didn't he stay up there with you and your husband?

MRS. ELVSTED. Once his book had come out, he became restless.

TESMAN. Oh, yes—Auntie Juju said he'd brought out a new book.

MRS. ELVSTED. Yes, a big new book about the history of civilization. A kind of general survey. It came out a fortnight ago. Everyone's been buying it and reading it—it's created a tremendous stir——

TESMAN. Has it really? It must be something he's dug up, then.

MRS. ELVSTED. You mean from the old days?

TESMAN. Yes.

MRS. ELVSTED. No, he's written it all since he came to live with us.

TESMAN. Well, that's splendid news, Hedda. Fancy that!

MRS. ELVSTED. Oh, yes! If only he can go on like this!

HEDDA. Have you met him since you came here?

MRS. ELVSTED. No, not yet. I had such dreadful difficulty finding his address. But this morning I managed to track him down at last.

HEDDA. [*Looks searchingly at her*] I must say I find it a little strange that your husband—hm——

MRS. ELVSTED. [*Starts nervously*] My husband! What do you mean?

HEDDA. That he should send you all the way here on an errand of this kind. I'm surprised he didn't come himself to keep an eye on his friend.

MRS. ELVSTED. Oh, no, no—my husband hasn't the time. Besides, I—er—wanted to do some shopping here.

HEDDA. [*With a slight smile*] Ah. Well, that's different.

MRS. ELVSTED. [*Gets up quickly, restlessly*] Please, Mr. Tesman, I beg you—be kind to Eilert Loevborg if he comes here. I'm sure he will. I mean, you used to be such good friends in the old days. And you're both studying the same subject, as far as I can understand. You're in the same field, aren't you?

TESMAN. Well, we used to be, anyway.

MRS. ELVSTED. Yes—so I beg you earnestly, do please, please, keep an eye on him. Oh, Mr. Tesman, do promise me you will.

TESMAN. I shall be only too happy to do so, Mrs. Rysing.

HEDDA. Elvsted.

TESMAN. I'll do everything for Eilert that lies in my power. You can rely on that.

MRS. ELVSTED. Oh, how good and kind you are! [*Presses his hands*] Thank you, thank you, thank you. [*Frightened*] My husband's so fond of him, you see.

HEDDA. [*Gets up*] You'd better send him a note, Tesman. He may not come to you of his own accord.

TESMAN. Yes, that'd probably be the best plan, Hedda. What?

HEDDA. The sooner the better. Why not do it now?

MRS. ELVSTED. [*Pleadingly*] Oh yes, if only you would!

TESMAN. I'll do it this very moment. Do you have his address, Mrs.—er—Elvsted?

MRS. ELVSTED. Yes.

[*Takes a small piece of paper from her pocket and gives it to him.*]

TESMAN. Good, good. Right, well I'll go inside and——[*Looks round*] Where are my slippers? Oh yes, here.

[*Picks up the package and is about to go*]

HEDDA. Try to sound friendly. Make it a nice long letter.

TESMAN. Right, I will.

MRS. ELVSTED. Please don't say anything about my having seen you.

TESMAN. Good heavens no, of course not. What?

[*Goes out through the rear room to the right*]

HEDDA. [*Goes over to* MRS. ELVSTED, *smiles, and says softly*] Well! Now we've killed two birds with one stone.

MRS. ELVSTED. What do you mean?

HEDDA. Didn't you realize I wanted to get him out of the room?

MRS. ELVSTED. So that he could write the letter?

HEDDA. And so that I could talk to you alone.

MRS. ELVSTED. [*Confused*] About this?

HEDDA. Yes, about this.

MRS. ELVSTED. [*In alarm*] But there's nothing more to tell, Mrs. Tesman. Really there isn't.

HEDDA. Oh, yes there is. There's a lot more. I can see that. Come along, let's sit down and have a little chat.

[*She pushes* MRS. ELVSTED *down into the armchair by the stove and seats herself on one of the footstools.*]

MRS. ELVSTED. [*Looks anxiously at her watch*] Really, Mrs. Tesman, I think I ought to be going now.

HEDDA. There's no hurry. Well? How are things at home?

MRS. ELVSTED. I'd rather not speak about that.

HEDDA. But my dear, you can tell me. Good heavens, we were at school together.

MRS. ELVSTED. Yes, but you were a year senior to me. Oh, I used to be terribly frightened of you in those days.

HEDDA. Frightened of me?

MRS. ELVSTED. Yes, terribly frightened. Whenever you met me on the staircase you used to pull my hair.

HEDDA. No, did I?

MRS. ELVSTED. Yes. And once you said you'd burn it all off.

HEDDA. Oh, that was only in fun.

MRS. ELVSTED. Yes, but I was so silly in those days. And then afterwards—I mean, we've drifted so far apart. Our backgrounds were so different.

HEDDA. Well, now we must try to drift together again. Now listen. When we were at school we used to call each other by our Christian names——

MRS. ELVSTED. No, I'm sure you're mistaken.

HEDDA. I'm sure I'm not. I remember it quite clearly. Let's tell each other our secrets, as we used to in the old days. [*Moves closer on her footstool*] There, now. [*Kisses her on the cheek*] You must call me Hedda.

MRS. ELVSTED. [*Squeezes her hands and pats them*] Oh, you're so kind. I'm not used to people being so nice to me.

HEDDA. Now, now, now. And I shall call you Tora, the way I used to.

MRS. ELVSTED. My name is Thea.

HEDDA. Yes, of course. Of course. I meant Thea. [*Looks at her sympathetically*] So you're not used to kindness, Thea? In your own home?

MRS. ELVSTED. Oh, if only I had a home! But I haven't. I've never had one.

HEDDA. [*Looks at her for a moment*] I thought that was it.

MRS. ELVSTED. [*Stares blankly and helplessly*] Yes—yes—yes.

HEDDA. I can't remember exactly now, but didn't you first go to Mr. Elvsted as a housekeeper?

MRS. ELVSTED. Governess, actually. But his wife—at the time, I mean—she was an invalid, and had to spend most of her time in bed. So I had to look after the house too.

HEDDA. But in the end, you became mistress of the house.

MRS. ELVSTED. [*Sadly*] Yes, I did.

HEDDA. Let me see. Roughly how long ago was that?

MRS. ELVSTED. When I got married, you mean?

HEDDA. Yes.

MRS. ELVSTED. About five years.

HEDDA. Yes; it must be about that.

MRS. ELVSTED. Oh, those five years! Especially the last two or three. Oh, Mrs. Tesman, if you only knew——

HEDDA. [*Slaps her hand gently*] Mrs. Tesman? Oh, Thea!

MRS. ELVSTED. I'm sorry, I'll try to remember. Yes—if you had any idea——

HEDDA. [*Casually*] Eilert Loevborg's been up there too, for about three years, hasn't he?

MRS. ELVSTED. [*Looks at her uncertainly*] Eilert Loevborg? Yes, he has.

HEDDA. Did you know him before? When you were here?

MRS. ELVSTED. No, not really. That is—I knew him by name, of course.

HEDDA. But up there, he used to visit you?

MRS. ELVSTED. Yes, he used to come and see us every day. To give the children lessons. I found I couldn't do that as well as manage the house.

HEDDA. I'm sure you couldn't. And your husband——? I suppose being a magistrate he has to be away from home a good deal?

MRS. ELVSTED. Yes. You see, Mrs.——you see, Hedda, he has to cover the whole district.

HEDDA. [*Leans against the arm of* MRS. ELVSTED'S *chair*] Poor, pretty little Thea! Now you must tell me the whole story. From beginning to end.

MRS. ELVSTED. Well—what do you want to know?

HEDDA. What kind of a man is your husband, Thea? I mean, as a person. Is he kind to you?

MRS. ELVSTED. [*Evasively*] I'm sure he does his best to be.

HEDDA. I only wonder if he isn't too old for you. There's more than twenty years between you, isn't there?

MRS. ELVSTED. [*Irritably*] Yes, there's that too. Oh, there are so many things. We're different in every way. We've nothing in common. Nothing whatever.

HEDDA. But he loves you, surely? In his own way?

MRS. ELVSTED. Oh, I don't know. I think he just finds me useful. And then I don't cost much to keep. I'm cheap.

HEDDA. Now you're being stupid.

MRS. ELVSTED. [*Shakes her head*] It can't be any different. With him. He doesn't love anyone except himself. And perhaps the children—a little.

HEDDA. He must be fond of Eilert Loevborg, Thea.

MRS. ELVSTED. [*Looks at her*] Eilert Loevborg? What makes you think that?

HEDDA. Well, if he sends you all the way down here to look for him——[*Smiles almost imperceptibly*] Besides, you said so yourself to Tesman.

MRS. ELVSTED. [*With a nervous twitch*] Did I? Oh yes, I suppose I did. [*Impulsively, but keeping her voice low*] Well, I might as well tell you the whole story. It's bound to come out sooner or later.

HEDDA. But my dear Thea——?

MRS. ELVSTED. My husband had no idea I was coming here.

HEDDA. What? Your husband didn't know?

MRS. ELVSTED. No, of course not. As a matter of fact, he wasn't even there. He was away at the assizes. Oh, I couldn't stand it any longer, Hedda! I just couldn't. I'd be so dreadfully lonely up there now.

HEDDA. Go on.

MRS. ELVSTED. So I packed a few things. Secretly. And went.

HEDDA. Without telling anyone?

MRS. ELVSTED. Yes. I caught the train and came straight here.

HEDDA. But my dear Thea! How brave of you!

MRS. ELVSTED. [*Gets up and walks across the room*] Well, what else could I do?

HEDDA. But what do you suppose your husband will say when you get back?

MRS. ELVSTED. [*By the table, looks at her*] Back there? To him?

HEDDA. Yes. Surely——?

MRS. ELVSTED. I shall never go back to him.

HEDDA. [*Gets up and goes closer*] You mean you've left your home for good?

MRS. ELVSTED. Yes. I didn't see what else I could do.

HEDDA. But to do it so openly!

MRS. ELVSTED. Oh, it's no use trying to keep a thing like that secret.

HEDDA. But what do you suppose people will say?

MRS. ELVSTED. They can say what they like. [*Sits sadly, wearily on the sofa*] I had to do it.

HEDDA. [*After a short silence*] What do you intend to do now? How are you going to live?

MRS. ELVSTED. I don't know. I only know that I must live wherever Eilert Loevborg is. If I am to go on living.

HEDDA. [*Moves a chair from the table, sits on it near* MRS. ELVSTED *and strokes her hands*] Tell me, Thea, how did this—friendship between you and Eilert Loevborg begin?

MRS. ELVSTED. Oh, it came about gradually. I developed a kind of—power over him.

HEDDA. Oh?

MRS. ELVSTED. He gave up his old habits. Not because I asked him to. I'd never have dared to do that. I suppose he just noticed I didn't like that kind of thing. So he gave it up.

HEDDA. [*Hides a smile*] So you've made a new man of him. Clever little Thea!

MRS. ELVSTED. Yes—anyway, he says I have. And he's made a—sort of—real person of me. Taught me to think—and to understand all kinds of things.

HEDDA. Did he give you lessons too?

MRS. ELVSTED. Not exactly lessons. But he talked to me. About—oh, you've no idea—so many things! And then he let me work with him. Oh, it was wonderful. I was so happy to be allowed to help him.

HEDDA. Did he allow you to help him!

MRS. ELVSTED. Yes. Whenever he wrote anything we always—did it together.

HEDDA. Like good pals?

MRS. ELVSTED. [*Eagerly*] Pals! Yes—why, Hedda, that's exactly the word he used! Oh, I ought to feel so happy. But I can't. I don't know if it will last.

HEDDA. You don't seem very sure of him.

MRS. ELVSTED. [*Sadly*] Something stands between Eilert Loevborg and me. The shadow of another woman.

HEDDA. Who can that be?

MRS. ELVSTED. I don't know. Someone he used to be friendly with in—in the old days. Someone he's never been able to forget.

HEDDA. What has he told you about her?

MRS. ELVSTED. Oh, he only mentioned her once, casually.

HEDDA. Well! What did he say?

MRS. ELVSTED. He said when he left her she tried to shoot him with a pistol.

HEDDA. [*Cold, controlled*] What nonsense. People don't do such things. The kind of people we know.

MRS. ELVSTED. No. I think it must have been that red-haired singer he used to——

HEDDA. Ah yes, very probably.

MRS. ELVSTED. I remember they used to say she always carried a loaded pistol.

HEDDA. Well then, it must be her.

MRS. ELVSTED. But Hedda, I hear she's come back, and is living here. Oh, I'm so desperate——!

HEDDA. [*Glances toward the rear room*] Ssh! Tesman's coming. [*Gets up and whispers*] Thea, we mustn't breathe a word about this to anyone.

MRS. ELVSTED. [*Jumps up*] Oh, no, no! Please don't!

[GEORGE TESMAN *appears from the right in the rear room with a letter in his hand, and comes into the drawing room.*]

TESMAN. Well, here's my little epistle all signed and sealed.

HEDDA. Good. I think Mrs. Elvsted wants to go now. Wait a moment—I'll see you as far as the garden gate.

TESMAN. Er—Hedda, do you think Bertha could deal with this?

HEDDA. [*Takes the letter*] I'll give her instructions.

[BERTHA *enters from the hall.*]

BERTHA. Judge Brack is here and asks if he may pay his respects to Madam and the Doctor.

HEDDA. Yes, ask him to be so good as to come in. And—wait a moment—drop this letter in the post box.

BERTHA. [*Takes the letter*] Very good, madam.

[*She opens the door for* JUDGE BRACK, *and goes out.* JUDGE BRACK *is forty-five; rather short, but well-built, and elastic in his movements. He has a roundish face with an aristocratic profile. His hair, cut short, is still almost black, and is carefully barbered. Eyes lively and humorous. Thick eyebrows. His moustache is also thick, and is trimmed square at the ends. He is wearing outdoor clothes which are elegant but a little too youthful for him. He has a monocle in one eye; now and then he lets it drop.*]

BRACK. [*Hat in hand, bows*] May one presume to call so early?

HEDDA. One may presume.

TESMAN. [*Shakes his hand*] You're welcome here any time. Judge Brack—Mrs. Rysing.

[HEDDA *sighs.*]

BRACK. [*Bows*] Ah—charmed——

HEDDA. [*Looks at him and laughs*] What fun to be able to see you by daylight for once, Judge.

BRACK. Do I look—different?

HEDDA. Yes. A little younger, I think.

BRACK. Obliged.

TESMAN. Well, what do you think of Hedda? What? Doesn't she look well? Hasn't she filled out——?

HEDDA. Oh, do stop it. You ought to be thanking Judge Brack for all the inconvenience he's put himself to——

BRACK. Nonsense, it was a pleasure——

HEDDA. You're a loyal friend. But my other friend is pining to get away. Au revoir, Judge. I won't be a minute.

[*Mutual salutations.* MRS. ELVSTED *and* HEDDA *go out through the hall.*]

BRACK. Well, is your wife satisfied with everything?

TESMAN. Yes, we can't thank you enough. That is—we may have to shift one or two things around, she tells me. And we're short of one or two little items we'll have to purchase.

BRACK. Oh? Really?

TESMAN. But you musn't worry your head about that. Hedda says she'll get what's needed. I say, why don't we sit down? What?

BRACK. Thanks, just for a moment. [*Sits at the table*] There's something I'd like to talk to you about, my dear Tesman.

TESMAN. Oh? Ah yes, of course. [*Sits*] After the feast comes the reckoning. What?

BRACK. Oh, never mind about the financial side—there's no hurry about that. Though I could wish we'd arranged things a little less palatially.

TESMAN. Good heavens, that'd never have done. Think of Hedda, my dear chap. You know her. I couldn't possibly ask her to live like a suburban housewife.

BRACK. No, no—that's just the problem.

TESMAN. Anyway, it can't be long now before my nomination[3]

3. *Nomination:* For the professorship. Professors at European universities were less numerous and more socially prominent than their contemporary American counterparts.

comes through.

BRACK. Well, you know, these things often take time.

TESMAN. Have you heard any more news? What?

BRACK. Nothing definite. [*Changing the subject*] Oh, by the way, I have one piece of news for you.

TESMAN. What?

BRACK. Your old friend Eilert Loevborg is back in town.

TESMAN. I know that already.

BRACK. Oh? How did you hear that?

TESMAN. She told me. That lady who went out with Hedda.

BRACK. I see. What was her name? I didn't catch it.

TESMAN. Mrs. Elvsted.

BRACK. Oh, the magistrate's wife. Yes, Loevborg's been living up near them, hasn't he?

TESMAN. I'm delighted to hear he's become a decent human being again.

BRACK. Yes, so they say.

TESMAN. I gather he's published a new book, too. What?

BRACK. Indeed he has.

TESMAN. I hear it's created rather a stir.

BRACK. Quite an unusual stir.

TESMAN. I say, isn't that splendid news! He's such a gifted chap—and I was afraid he'd gone to the dogs for good.

BRACK. Most people thought he had.

TESMAN. But I can't think what he'll do now. How on earth will he manage to make ends meet? What?

[*As he speaks his last words,* HEDDA *enters from the hall.*]

HEDDA. [*To* BRACK, *laughs slightly scornfully*] Tesman is always worrying about making ends meet.

TESMAN. We were talking about poor Eilert Loevborg, Hedda dear.

HEDDA. [*Gives him a quick look*] Oh, were you? [*Sits in the armchair by the stove and asks casually*] Is he in trouble?

TESMAN. Well, he must have run through his inheritance long ago by now. And he can't write a new book every year. What? So I'm wondering what's going to become of him.

BRACK. I may be able to enlighten you there.

TESMAN. Oh?

BRACK. You mustn't forget he has relatives who wield a good deal of influence.

TESMAN. Relatives? Oh, they've quite washed their hands of him, I'm afraid.

BRACK. They used to regard him as the hope of the family.

TESMAN. Used to, yes. But he's put an end to that.

HEDDA. Who knows? [*With a little smile*] I hear the Elvsteds have made a new man of him.

BRACK. And then this book he's just published——

TESMAN. Well, let's hope they find something for him. I've just written him a note. Oh, by the way, Hedda, I asked him to come over and see us this evening.

BRACK. But my dear chap, you're coming to me this evening. My bachelor party.[4] You promised me last night when I met you at the boat.

HEDDA. Had you forgotten, Tesman?

TESMAN. Good heavens, yes, I'd quite forgotten.

BRACK. Anyway, you can be quite sure he won't turn up here.

TESMAN. Why do you think that? What?

BRACK. [*A little unwillingly, gets up and rests his hands on the back of his chair*] My dear Tesman—and you, too, Mrs. Tesman—there's something I feel you ought to know.

TESMAN. Concerning Eilert?

BRACK. Concerning him and you.

TESMAN. Well, my dear Judge, tell us, please!

BRACK. You must be prepared for your nomination not to come through quite as quickly as you hope and expect.

TESMAN. [*Jumps up uneasily*] Is anything wrong? What?

BRACK. There's a possibility that the appointment may be decided by competition——

TESMAN. Competition! By Jove, Hedda, fancy that!

HEDDA. [*Leans further back in her chair*] Ah! How interesting!

TESMAN. But who else——? I say, you don't mean——?

BRACK. Exactly. By competition with Eilert Loevborg.

TESMAN. [*Clasps his hands in alarm*] No, no, but this is inconceivable! It's absolutely impossible! What?

BRACK. Hm. We may find it'll happen, all the same.

TESMAN. No, but—Judge Brack, they couldn't be so inconsiderate toward me! [*Waves his arms*] I mean, by Jove, I—I'm a married man! It was on the strength of this that Hedda and I *got* married! We ran up some pretty hefty debts. And borrowed money from Auntie Juju! I mean, good heavens, they practically promised me the appointment. What?

BRACK. Well, well, I'm sure you'll get it. But you'll have to go through a competition.

HEDDA. [*Motionless in her armchair*] How exciting, Tesman. It'll be a kind of duel, by Jove.

TESMAN. My dear Hedda, how can you take it so lightly?

HEDDA. [*as before*] I'm not. I can't wait to see who's going to win.

BRACK. In any case, Mrs. Tesman, it's best you should know how things stand. I mean before you commit yourself to these little items I hear you're threatening to purchase.

HEDDA. I can't allow this to alter my plans.

BRACK. Indeed? Well, that's your business. Good-bye. [*To* TESMAN] I'll come and collect you on the way home from my afternoon walk.

TESMAN. Oh, yes, yes. I'm sorry, I'm all upside down just now.

HEDDA. [*Lying in her chair, holds out her hand*] Good-bye, Judge. See you this afternoon.

BRACK. Thank you. Good-bye, good-bye.

4. *Bachelor party:* A party for men only, whether single or married.

TESMAN. [*Sees him to the door*] Good-bye, my dear Judge. You will excuse me, won't you?

[JUDGE BRACK *goes out through the hall.*]

TESMAN. [*Pacing up and down*] Oh, Hedda! One oughtn't to go plunging off on wild adventures. What?

HEDDA. [*Looks at him and smiles*] Like you're doing?

TESMAN. Yes. I mean, there's no denying it, it was a pretty big adventure to go off and get married and set up house merely on expectation.

HEDDA. Perhaps you're right.

TESMAN. Well, anyway, we have our home, Hedda. By Jove, yes. The home we dreamed of. And set our hearts on. What?

HEDDA. [*Gets up slowly, wearily*] You agreed that we should enter society. And keep open house. That was the bargain.

TESMAN. Yes. Good heavens, I was looking forward to it all so much. To seeing you play hostess to a select circle! By Jove! What? Ah, well, for the time being we shall have to make do with each other's company, Hedda. Perhaps have Auntie Juju in now and then. Oh dear, this wasn't at all what you had in mind——

HEDDA. I won't be able to have a liveried footman.[5] For a start.

TESMAN. Oh no, we couldn't possibly afford a footman.

HEDDA. And that thoroughbred horse you promised me——

TESMAN. [*Fearfully*] Thoroughbred horse!

HEDDA. I mustn't even think of that now.

TESMAN. Heaven forbid!

HEDDA. [*Walks across the room*] Ah, well. I still have one thing left to amuse myself with.

TESMAN. [*Joyfully*] Thank goodness for that. What's that, Hedda? What?

HEDDA. [*In the open doorway, looks at him with concealed scorn*] My pistols, George darling.

TESMAN. [*Alarmed*] Pistols!

HEDDA. [*Her eyes cold*] General Gabler's pistols.

[*She goes into the rear room and disappears.*]

TESMAN. [*Runs to the doorway and calls after her*] For heaven's sake, Hedda dear, don't touch those things. They're dangerous. Hedda—please—for my sake! What?

Act II

SCENE—*The same as in Act I except that the piano has been removed and an elegant little writing table, with a bookcase, stands in its place. By the sofa on the left a smaller table has been placed. Most of the flowers have been removed.* MRS. ELVSTED'S *bouquet stands on the larger table, downstage. It is afternoon.*

HEDDA, *dressed to receive callers, is alone in the room. She is*

5. *Liveried footman*: A uniformed manservant.

standing by the open french windows, loading a revolver. The pair to it is lying in an open pistol case on the writing table.

HEDDA. [*Looks down into the garden and calls*] Good afternoon, Judge.
BRACK. [*In the distance, below*] Afternoon, Mrs. Tesman.
HEDDA. [*Raises the pistol and takes aim*] I'm going to shoot you, Judge Brack.
BRACK. [*Shouts from below*] No no, no! Don't aim that thing at me!
HEDDA. This'll teach you to enter houses by the back door. [*Fires*]
BRACK. [*Below*] Have you gone completely out of your mind?
HEDDA. Oh dear! Did I hit you?
BRACK. [*Still outside*] Stop playing these silly tricks.
HEDDA. All right, Judge. Come along in.

[JUDGE BRACK, *dressed for a bachelor party, enters through the french windows. He has a light overcoat on his arm.*]

BRACK. For God's sake! Haven't you stopped fooling around with those things yet? What are you trying to hit?
HEDDA. Oh, I was just shooting at the sky.
BRACK. [*Takes the pistol gently from her hand*] By your leave, ma'am. [*Looks at it*] Ah, yes—I know this old friend well. [*Looks around*] Where's the case? Oh, yes. [*Puts the pistol in the case and closes it*] That's enough of that little game for today.
HEDDA. Well, what on earth *am* I to do?
BRACK. You haven't had any visitors?
HEDDA. [*Closes the french windows*] Not one. I suppose the best people are all still in the country.
BRACK. Your husband isn't home yet?
HEDDA. [*Locks the pistol case away in a drawer of the writing table*] No. The moment he'd finished eating he ran off to his aunties. He wasn't expecting you so early.
BRACK. Ah, why didn't I think of that? How stupid of me.
HEDDA. [*Turns her head and looks at him*] Why stupid?
BRACK. I'd have come a little sooner.
HEDDA. [*Walks across the room*] There'd have been no one to receive you. I've been in my room since lunch, dressing.
BRACK. You haven't a tiny crack in the door through which we might have negotiated?
HEDDA. You forgot to arrange one.
BRACK. Another stupidity.
HEDDA. Well, we'll have to sit down here. And wait. Tesman won't be back for some time.
BRACK. Sad. Well, I'll be patient.

[HEDDA *sits on the corner of the sofa.* BRACK *puts his coat over the back of the nearest chair and seats himself, keeping his hat in his hand. Short pause. They look at each other.*]

HEDDA. Well?
BRACK. [*In the same tone of voice*] Well?

HEDDA. I asked first.

BRACK. [*Leans forward slightly*] Yes, well, now we can enjoy a nice, cosy little chat—Mrs. Hedda.

HEDDA. [*Leans further back in her chair*] It seems such ages since we had a talk. I don't count last night or this morning.

BRACK. You mean: *à deux?*[6]

HEDDA. Mm—yes. That's roughly what I meant.

BRACK. I've been longing so much for you to come home.

HEDDA. So have I.

BRACK. You? Really, Mrs. Hedda? And I thought you were having such a wonderful honeymoon.

HEDDA. Oh, yes. Wonderful!

BRACK. But your husband wrote such ecstatic letters.

HEDDA. He! Oh, yes! He thinks life has nothing better to offer than rooting around in libraries and copying old pieces of parchment, or whatever it is he does.

BRACK. [*A little maliciously*] Well, that *is* his life. Most of it, anyway.

HEDDA. Yes, I know. Well, it's all right for him. But for me! Oh no, my dear Judge. I've been bored to death.

BRACK. [*Sympathetically*] Do you mean that? Seriously?

HEDDA. Yes. Can you imagine? Six whole months without ever meeting a single person who was one of us, and to whom I could talk about the kind of things we talk about.

BRACK. Yes, I can understand. I'd miss that, too.

HEDDA. That wasn't the worst, though.

BRACK. What was?

HEDDA. Having to spend every minute of one's life with—with the same person.

BRACK. [*Nods*] Yes. What a thought! Morning; noon; and——

HEDDA. [*Coldly*] As I said: every minute of one's life.

BRACK. I stand corrected. But dear Tesman is such a clever fellow, I should have thought one ought to be able——

HEDDA. Tesman is only interested in one thing, my dear Judge. His special subject.

BRACK. True.

HEDDA. And people who are only interested in one thing don't make the most amusing company. Not for long, anyway.

BRACK. Not even when they happen to be the person one loves?

HEDDA. Oh, don't use that sickly, stupid word.

BRACK. [*Starts*] But, Mrs. Hedda——!

HEDDA. [*Half laughing, half annoyed*] You just try it, Judge. Listening to the history of civilization morning, noon and——

BRACK. [*Corrects her*] Every minute of one's life.

HEDDA. All right. Oh, and those domestic industries of Brabant in the Middle Ages! That really is beyond the limit.

BRACK. [*Looks at her searchingly*] But, tell me—if you feel like this why on earth did you—? Ha——

6. *À deux:* Just the two of us.

HEDDA. Why on earth did I marry George Tesman?

BRACK. If you like to put it that way.

HEDDA. Do you think it so very strange?

BRACK. Yes—and no, Mrs. Hedda.

HEDDA. I'd danced myself tired, Judge. I felt my time was up—— [*Gives a slight shudder*] No, I mustn't say that. Or even think it.

BRACK. You've no rational cause to think it.

HEDDA. Oh—cause, cause——[*Looks searchingly at him*] After all, George Tesman—well, I mean, he's a very respectable man.

BRACK. Very respectable, sound as a rock. No denying that.

HEDDA. And there's nothing exactly ridiculous about him. Is there?

BRACK. Ridiculous? N-no, I wouldn't say that.

HEDDA. Mm. He's very clever at collecting material and all that, isn't he? I mean, he may go quite far in time.

BRACK. [*Looks at her a little uncertainly*] I thought you believed, like everyone else, that he would become a very prominent man.

HEDDA. [*Looks tired*] Yes, I did. And when he came and begged me on his bended knees to be allowed to love and to cherish me, I didn't see why I shouldn't let him.

BRACK. No, well—if one looks at it like that——

HEDDA. It was more than my other admirers were prepared to do, Judge dear.

BRACK. [*Laughs*] Well, I can't answer for the others. As far as I myself am concerned, you know I've always had a considerable respect for the institution of marriage. As an institution.

HEDDA. [*Lightly*] Oh, I've never entertained any hopes of you.

BRACK. All I want is to have a circle of friends whom I can trust, whom I can help with advice or—or by any other means, and into whose houses I may come and go as a—trusted friend.

HEDDA. Of the husband?

BRACK. [*Bows*] Preferably, to be frank, of the wife. And of the husband too, of course. Yes, you know, this kind of—triangle is a delightful arrangement for all parties concerned.

HEDDA. Yes, I often longed for a third person while I was away. Oh, those hours we spent alone in railway compartments——

BRACK. Fortunately your honeymoon is now over.

HEDDA. [*Shakes her head*] There's a long, long way still to go. I've only reached a stop on the line.

BRACK. Why not jump out and stretch your legs a little, Mrs. Hedda?

HEDDA. I'm not the jumping sort.

BRACK. Aren't you?

HEDDA. No. There's always someone around who——

BRACK. [*Laughs*] Who looks at one's legs?

HEDDA. Yes. Exactly.

BRACK. Well, but surely——

HEDDA. [*With a gesture of rejection*] I don't like it. I'd rather stay where I am. Sitting in the compartment. *À deux.*

BRACK. But suppose a third person were to step into the compartment?

HEDDA. That would be different.

BRACK. A trusted friend—someone who understood——

HEDDA. And was lively and amusing——

BRACK. And interested in—more subjects than one——

HEDDA. [*Sighs audibly*] Yes, that'd be a relief.

BRACK. [*Hears the front door open and shut*] The triangle is completed.

HEDDA. [*Half under breath*] And the train goes on.

[GEORGE TESMAN, *in grey walking dress with a soft felt hat, enters from the hall. He has a number of paper-covered books under his arm and in his pockets.*]

TESMAN. [*Goes over to the table by the corner sofa*] Phew! It's too hot to be lugging all this around. [*Puts the books down*] I'm positively sweating, Hedda. Why, hullo, hullo! You here already, Judge? What? Bertha didn't tell me.

BRACK. [*Gets up*] I came in through the garden.

HEDDA. What are all those books you've got there?

TESMAN. [*Stands glancing through them*] Oh, some new publications dealing with my special subject. I had to buy them.

HEDDA. Your special subject?

BRACK. His special subject, Mrs. Tesman.

[BRACK *and* HEDDA *exchange a smile.*]

HEDDA. Haven't you collected enough material on your special subject?

TESMAN. My dear Hedda, one can never have too much. One must keep abreast of what other people are writing.

HEDDA. Yes. Of course.

TESMAN. [*Rooting among the books*] Look—I bought a copy of Eilert Loevborg's new book, too. [*Holds it out to her*] Perhaps you'd like to have a look at it, Hedda? What?

HEDDA. No, thank you. Er—yes, perhaps I will, later.

TESMAN. I glanced through it on my way home.

BRACK. What's your opinion—as a specialist on the subject?

TESMAN. I'm amazed how sound and balanced it is. He never used to write like that. [*Gathers his books together*] Well, I must get down to these at once. I can hardly wait to cut the pages.[7] Oh, I've got to change, too. [*To* BRACK] We don't have to be off just yet, do we? What?

BRACK. Heavens, no. We've plenty of time yet.

TESMAN. Good, I needn't hurry, then. [*Goes with his books, but stops and turns in the doorway*] Oh, by the way, Hedda, Auntie Juju won't be coming to see you this evening.

HEDDA. Won't she? Oh—the hat, I suppose.

TESMAN. Good heavens, no. How could you think such a thing of

7. *Cut the pages:* Books used to be sold with the pages folded but uncut as they came fom the printing press; the owner had to cut the pages in order to read the book.

Auntie Juju? Fancy——! No, Auntie Rena's very ill.

HEDDA. She always is.

TESMAN. Yes, but today she's been taken really bad.

HEDDA. Oh, then it's quite understandable that the other one should want to stay with her. Well, I shall have to swallow my disappointment.

TESMAN. You can't imagine how happy Auntie Juju was in spite of everything. At your looking so well after the honeymoon!

HEDDA. [*Half beneath her breath, as she rises*] Oh, these everlasting aunts!

TESMAN. What?

HEDDA. [*Goes over to the french windows*] Nothing.

TESMAN. Oh. All right.

[*Goes into the rear room and out of sight*]

BRACK. What was that about the hat?

HEDDA. Oh, something that happened with Miss Tesman this morning. She'd put her hat down on a chair. [*Looks at him and smiles*] And I pretended to think it was the servant's.

BRACK. [*Shakes his head*] But my dear Mrs. Hedda, how could you do such a thing? To that poor old lady?

HEDDA. [*Nervously, walking across the room*] Sometimes a mood like that hits me. And I can't stop myself. [*Thows herself down in the armchair by the stove*] Oh, I don't know how to explain it.

BRACK. [*Behind her chair*] You're not really happy. That's the answer.

HEDDA. [*Stares ahead of her*] Why on earth should I be happy? Can you give me a reason?

BRACK. Yes. For one thing you've got the home you always wanted.

HEDDA. [*Looks at him*] You really believe that story?

BRACK. You mean it isn't true?

HEDDA. Oh, yes, it's partly true.

BRACK. Well?

HEDDA. It's true I got Tesman to see me home from parties last summer——

BRACK. It was a pity my home lay in another direction.

HEDDA. Yes. Your interests lay in another direction, too.

BRACK. [*Laughs*] That's naughty of you, Mrs. Hedda. But to return to you and Tesman——

HEDDA. Well, we walked past this house one evening. And poor Tesman was fidgeting in his boots trying to find something to talk about. I felt sorry for the great scholar——

BRACK. [*Smiles incredulously*] Did you? Hm.

HEDDA. Yes, honestly I did. Well, to help him out of his misery, I happened to say quite frivolously how much I'd love to live in this house.

BRACK. Was that all?

HEDDA. That evening, yes.

BRACK. But—afterwards?

HEDDA. Yes. My little frivolity had its consequences, my dear Judge.

BRACK. Our little frivolities do. Much too often, unfortunately.

HEDDA. Thank you. Well, it was our mutual admiration for the late Prime Minister's house that brought George Tesman and me together on common ground. So we got engaged, and we got married, and we went on our honeymoon, and—Ah well, Judge, I've —made my bed and I must lie in it, I was about to say.

BRACK. How utterly fantastic! And you didn't really care in the least about the house?

HEDDA. God knows I didn't.

BRACK. Yes, but now that we've furnished it so beautifully for you?

HEDDA. Ugh—all the rooms smell of lavender and dried roses. But perhaps Auntie Juju brought that in.

BRACK. [*Laughs*] More likely the Prime Minister's widow, rest her soul.

HEDDA. Yes, it's got the odor of death about it. It reminds me of the flowers one has worn at a ball—the morning after. [*Clasps her hands behind her neck, leans back in the chair and looks up at him*] Oh, my dear Judge, you've no idea how hideously bored I'm going to be out here.

BRACK. Couldn't you find some kind of occupation, Mrs. Hedda? Like your husband?

HEDDA. Occupation? That'd interest me?

BRACK. Well—preferably.

HEDDA. God knows what. I've often thought——[*Breaks off*] No, that wouldn't work either.

BRACK. Who knows? Tell me about it.

HEDDA. I was thinking—if I could persuade Tesman to go into politics, for example.

BRACK. [*Laughs*] Tesman! No, honestly, I don't think he's quite cut out to be a politician.

HEDDA. Perhaps not. But if I could persuade him to have a go at it?

BRACK. What satisfaction would that give you? If he turned out to be no good? Why do you want to make him do that?

HEDDA. Because I'm bored. [*After a moment*] You feel there's absolutely no possibility of Tesman becoming Prime Minister, then?

BRACK. Well, you know, Mrs. Hedda, for one thing he'd have to be pretty well off before he could become that.

HEDDA. [*Gets up impatiently*] There you are! [*Walks across the room*] It's this wretched poverty that makes life so hateful. And ludicrous. Well, it is!

BRACK. I don't think that's the real cause.

HEDDA. What is, then?

BRACK. Nothing really exciting has ever happened to you.

HEDDA. Nothing serious, you mean?

BRACK. Call it that if you like. But now perhaps it may.

HEDDA. [*Tosses her head*] Oh, you're thinking of this competition for that wretched professorship? That's Tesman's affair. I'm not going to waste my time worrying about that.

BRACK. Very well, let's forget about that then. But suppose you were to find yourself faced with what people call—to use the conventional phrase—the most solemn of human responsibilities? [*Smiles*] A new responsibility, little Mrs. Hedda.

HEDDA. [*Angrily*] Be quiet! Nothing like that's going to happen.

BRACK. [*Warily*] We'll talk about it again in a year's time. If not earlier.

HEDDA. [*Curtly*] I've no leanings in that direction, Judge. I don't want any—responsibilities.

BRACK. But surely you must feel some inclination to make use of that—natural talent which every woman—

HEDDA. [*Over by the french windows*] Oh, be quiet, I say! I often think there's only one thing for which I have any natural talent.

BRACK. [*Goes closer*] And what is that, if I may be so bold as to ask?

HEDDA. [*Stands looking out*] For boring myself to death. Now you know. [*Turns, looks toward the rear room and laughs*] Talking of boring, here comes the Professor.

BRACK. [*Quietly, warningly*] Now, now, now, Mrs. Hedda!

[GEORGE TESMAN, *in evening dress, with gloves and hat in his hand, enters through the rear room from the right.*]

TESMAN. Hedda, hasn't any message come from Eilert? What?

HEDDA. No.

TESMAN. Ah, then we'll have him here presently. You wait and see.

BRACK. You really think he'll come?

TESMAN. Yes, I'm almost sure he will. What you were saying about him this morning is just gossip.

BRACK. Oh?

TESMAN. Yes. Auntie Juju said she didn't believe he'd ever dare to stand in my way again. Fancy that!

BRACK. Then everything in the garden's lovely.

TESMAN. [*Puts his hat, with his gloves in it, on a chair, right*] Yes, but you really must let me wait for him as long as possible.

BRACK. We've plenty of time. No one'll be turning up at my place before seven or half past.

TESMAN. Ah, then we can keep Hedda company a little longer. And see if he turns up. What?

HEDDA. [*Picks up* BRACK'S *coat and hat and carries them over to the corner sofa*] And if the worst comes to the worst, Mr. Loevborg can sit here and talk to me.

BRACK. [*Offering to take his things from her*] No, please. What do you mean by "if the worst comes to the worst"?

HEDDA. If he doesn't want to go with you and Tesman.

TESMAN. [*Looks doubtfully at her*] I say, Hedda, do you think it'll be all right for him to stay here with you? What? Remember Auntie Juju isn't coming.

HEDDA. Yes, but Mrs. Elvsted is. The three of us can have a cup of tea together.

TESMAN. Ah, that'll be all right then.

BRACK. [*Smiles*] It's probably the safest solution as far as he's concerned.

HEDDA. Why?

BRACK. My dear Mrs. Tesman, you always say of my little bachelor parties that they should be attended only by men of the strongest principles.

HEDDA. But Mr. Loevborg is a man of principle now. You know what they say about a reformed sinner——

[BERTHA *enters from the hall.*]

BERTHA. Madam, there's a gentleman here who wants to see you——

HEDDA. Ask him to come in.

TESMAN. [*Quietly*] I'm sure it's him. By Jove. Fancy that!

[EILERT LOEVBORG *enters from the hall. He is slim and lean, of the same age as* TESMAN, *but looks older and somewhat haggard. His hair and beard are of a blackish-brown; his face is long and pale, but with a couple of reddish patches on his cheekbones. He is dressed in an elegant and fairly new black suit, and carries black gloves and a top hat in his hand. He stops just inside the door and bows abruptly. He seems somewhat embarrassed.*]

TESMAN. [*Goes over and shakes his hand*] My dear Eilert! How grand to see you again after all these years!

EILERT LOEVBORG. [*Speaks softly*] It was good of you to write, George. [*Goes nearer to* HEDDA] May I shake hands with you, too, Mrs. Tesman?

HEDDA. [*Accepts his hand*] Delighted to see you, Mr. Loevborg. [*With a gesture*] I don't know if you two gentlemen——

LOEVBORG. [*Bows slightly*] Judge Brack, I believe.

BRACK. [*Also with a slight bow*] Correct. We—met some years ago——

TESMAN. [*Puts his hands on* LOEVBORG'S *shoulders*] Now you're to treat this house just as though it were your own home, Eilert. Isn't that right, Hedda? I hear you've decided to settle here again? What?

LOEVBORG. Yes, I have.

TESMAN. Quite understandable. Oh, by the bye—I've just bought your new book. Though to tell the truth I haven't found time to read it yet.

LOEVBORG. You needn't bother.

TESMAN. Oh? Why?

LOEVBORG. There's nothing much in it.

TESMAN. By Jove, fancy hearing that from you!

BRACK. But everyone's praising it.

LOEVBORG. That was exactly what I wanted to happen. So I only wrote what I knew everyone would agree with.

BRACK. Very sensible.

TESMAN. Yes, but my dear Eilert——

LOEVBORG. I want to try to re-establish myself. To begin again—from the beginning.

TESMAN. [*A little embarrassed*] Yes, I—er—suppose you do. What?

LOEVBORG. [*Smiles, puts down his hat and takes a package wrapped in paper from his coat pocket*] But when this gets published—George Tesman—read it. This is my real book. The one in which I have spoken with my own voice.

TESMAN. Oh, really? What's it about?

LOEVBORG. It's the sequel.

TESMAN. Sequel? To what?

LOEVBORG. To the other book.

TESMAN. The one that's just come out?

LOEVBORG. Yes.

TESMAN. But my dear Eilert, that covers the subject right up to the present day.

LOEVBORG. It does. But this is about the future.

TESMAN. The future! But, I say, we don't know anything about that.

LOEVBORG. No. But there are one or two things that need to be said about it. [*Opens the package*] Here, have a look.

TESMAN. Surely that's not your handwriting?

LOEVBORG. I dictated it. [*Turns the pages*] It's in two parts. The first deals with the forces that will shape our civilization. [*Turns further on towards the end*] And the second indicates the direction in which that civilization may develop.

TESMAN. Amazing! I'd never think of writing about anything like that.

HEDDA. [*By the french windows, drumming on the pane*] No. You wouldn't.

LOEVBORG. [*Puts the pages back into their cover and lays the package on the table*] I brought it because I thought I might possibly read you a few pages this evening.

TESMAN. I say, what a kind idea! Oh, but this evening——? [*Glances at* BRACK] I'm not quite sure whether——

LOEVBORG. Well, some other time, then. There's no hurry.

BRACK. The truth is, Mr. Loevborg, I'm giving a little dinner this evening. In Tesman's honour, you know.

LOEVBORG. [*Looks round for his hat*] Oh—then I mustn't——

BRACK. No, wait a minute. Won't you do me the honor of joining us?

LOEVBORG. [*Curtly, with decision*] No I can't. Thank you so much.

BRACK. Oh, nonsense. Do—please. There'll only be a few of us. And I can promise you we shall have some good sport, as Mrs. Hed—as Mrs. Tesman puts it.

LOEVBORG. I've no doubt. Nevertheless——

BRACK. You could bring your manuscript along and read it to Tesman at my place. I could lend you a room.

TESMAN. By Jove, Eilert, that's an idea. What?

HEDDA. [*Interposes*] But Tesman, Mr. Loevborg doesn't want to go.

I'm sure Mr. Loevborg would much rather sit here and have supper with me.

LOEVBORG. [*Looks at her*] With you, Mrs. Tesman?

HEDDA. And Mrs. Elvsted.

LOEVBORG. Oh. [*Casually*] I ran into her this afternoon.

HEDDA. Did you? Well, she's coming here this evening. So you really must stay, Mr. Loevborg. Otherwise she'll have no one to see her home.

LOEVBORG. That's true. Well—thank you, Mrs. Tesman, I'll stay then.

HEDDA. I'll just tell the servant.

[*She goes to the door which leads into the hall, and rings.* BERTHA *enters.* HEDDA *talks softly to her and points towards the rear room.* BERTHA *nods and goes out.*]

TESMAN. [*To* LOEVBORG, *as* HEDDA *does this*] I say, Eilert. This new subject of yours—the—er—future—is that the one you're going to lecture about?

LOEVBORG. Yes.

TESMAN. They told me down at the bookshop that you're going to hold a series of lectures here during the autumn.

LOEVBORG. Yes, I am. I—hope you don't mind, Tesman.

TESMAN. Good heavens, no! But——?

LOEVBORG. I can quite understand it might queer your pitch a little.

TESMAN. [*Dejectedly*] Oh well, I can't expect you to put them off for my sake.

LOEVBORG. I'll wait till your appointment's been announced.

TESMAN. You'll wait! But—but—aren't you going to compete with me for the post? What?

LOEVBORG. No. I only want to defeat you in the eyes of the world.

TESMAN. Good heavens! Then Auntie Juju was right after all! Oh, I knew it, I knew it! Hear that, Hedda? Fancy! Eilert *doesn't* want to stand in our way.

HEDDA. [*Curtly*] Our? Leave me out of it, please.

[*She goes towards the rear room, where* BERTHA *is setting a tray with decanters and glasses on the table.* HEDDA *nods approval, and comes back into the drawing room.* BERTHA *goes out.*]

TESMAN. [*While this is happening*] Judge Brack, what do you think about all this? What?

BRACK. Oh, I think honor and victory can be very splendid things——

TESMAN. Of course they can. Still——

HEDDA. [*Looks at* TESMAN *with a cold smile*] You look as if you'd been hit by a thunderbolt.

TESMAN. Yes, I feel rather like it.

BRACK. There was a black cloud looming up, Mrs. Tesman. But it seems to have passed over.

HEDDA. [*Points towards the rear room*] Well, gentlemen, won't you go in and take a glass of cold punch?

BRACK. [*Glances at his watch*] A stirrup cup?[8] Yes, why not?

TESMAN. An admirable suggestion, Hedda. Admirable! Oh, I feel so relieved!

HEDDA. Won't you have one, too, Mr. Loevborg?

LOEVBORG. No, thank you. I'd rather not.

BRACK. Great heavens, man, cold punch isn't poison. Take my word for it.

LOEVBORG. Not for everyone, perhaps.

HEDDA. I'll keep Mr. Loevborg company while you drink.

TESMAN. Yes, Hedda dear, would you?

[*He and* BRACK *go into the rear room, sit down, drink punch, smoke cigarettes and talk cheerfully during the following scene.* EILERT LOEVBORG *remains standing by the stove.* HEDDA *goes to the writing table.*]

HEDDA. [*Raising her voice slightly*] I've some photographs I'd like to show you, if you'd care to see them. Tesman and I visited the Tyrol on our way home.

[*She comes back with an album, places it on the table by the sofa and sits in the upstage corner of the sofa.* EILERT LOEVBORG *comes toward her, stops and looks at her. Then he takes a chair and sits down on her left, with his back toward the rear room.*]

HEDDA. [*Opens the album*] You see these mountains, Mr. Loevborg? That's the Ortler group. Tesman has written the name underneath. You see: "The Ortler Group near Meran."[9]

LOEVBORG. [*Has not taken his eyes from her; says softly, slowly*] Hedda—Gabler!

HEDDA. [*Gives him a quick glance*] Ssh!

LOEVBORG. [*Repeats softly*] Hedda Gabler!

HEDDA. [*Looks at the album*] Yes, that used to be my name. When we first knew each other.

LOEVBORG. And from now on—for the rest of my life—I must teach myself never to say: Hedda Gabler.

HEDDA. [*Still turning the pages*] Yes, you must. You'd better start getting into practice. The sooner the better.

LOEVBORG. [*Bitterly*] Hedda Gabler married? And to George Tesman?

HEDDA. Yes. Well—that's life.

LOEVBORG. Oh, Hedda, Hedda! How could you throw yourself away like that?

HEDDA. [*Looks sharply at him*] Stop it.

LOEVBORG. What do you mean?

[TESMAN *comes in and goes toward the sofa.*]

8. *Stirrup cup:* A drink before parting. (Originally, it was taken by riders on horseback just before setting forth.)

9. *Meran:* Or Merano, a city in the Austrian Tyrol, since 1918 in Italy. The scenic features mentioned here and later are tourist attractions. The Ortler Group and the Dolomites are ranges of the Alps; the Ampezzo Valley lies beyond the Dolomites to the east; and the Brenner Pass is a major route through the Alps to Austria.

HEDDA. [*Hears him coming and says casually*] And this, Mr. Loevborg, is the view from the Ampezzo valley. Look at those mountains. [*Glances affectionately up at* TESMAN] What did you say those curious mountains were called, dear?

TESMAN. Let me have a look. Oh, those are the Dolomites.

HEDDA. Of course. Those are the Dolomites, Mr. Loevborg.

TESMAN. Hedda, I just wanted to ask you, can't we bring some punch in here? A glass for you, anyway. What?

HEDDA. Thank you, yes. And a biscuit[10] or two, perhaps.

TESMAN. You wouldn't like a cigarette?

HEDDA. No.

TESMAN. Right.

[*He goes into the rear room and over to the right.* BRACK *is sitting there, glancing occasionally at* HEDDA *and* LOEVBORG.]

LOEVBORG. [*Softly, as before*] Answer me, Hedda. How could you do it?

HEDDA. [*Apparently absorbed in the album*] If you go on calling me Hedda I won't talk to you any more.

LOEVBORG. Mayn't I even when we're alone?

HEDDA. No. You can think it. But you mustn't say it.

LOEVBORG. Oh, I see. Because you love George Tesman.

HEDDA. [*Glances at him and smiles*] Love? Don't be funny.

LOEVBORG. You don't love him?

HEDDA. I don't intend to be unfaithful to him. That's not what I want.

LOEVBORG. Hedda—just tell me one thing——

HEDDA. Ssh!

[TESMAN *enters from the rear room, carrying a tray.*]

TESMAN. Here we are! Here come the goodies!

[*Puts the tray down on the table*]

HEDDA. Why didn't you ask the servant to bring it in?

TESMAN. [*Fills the glasses*] I like waiting on you, Hedda.

HEDDA. But you've filled both glasses. Mr. Loevborg doesn't want to drink.

TESMAN. Yes, but Mrs. Elvsted'll be here soon.

HEDDA. Oh yes, that's true. Mrs. Elvsted——

TESMAN. Had you forgotten her? What?

HEDDA. We're so absorbed with these photographs. [*Shows him one*] You remember this little village?

TESMAN. Oh, that one down by the Brenner Pass. We spent a night there——

HEDDA. Yes, and met all those amusing people.

TESMAN. Oh yes, it was there, wasn't it? By Jove, if only we could have had you with us, Eilert! Ah, well.

[*Goes back into the other room and sits down with* BRACK]

LOEVBORG. Tell me one thing, Hedda.

10. *Biscuit:* Or tea biscuit; a cookie.

HEDDA. Yes?

LOEVBORG. Didn't you love me either? Not—just a little?

HEDDA. Well now, I wonder? No, I think we were just good pals—Really good pals who could tell each other anything. [*Smiles*] You certainly poured your heart out to me.

LOEVBORG. You begged me to.

HEDDA. Looking back on it, there was something beautiful and fascinating—and brave—about the way we told each other everything. That secret friendship no one else knew about.

LOEVBORG. Yes, Hedda, yes! Do you remember? How I used to come up to your father's house in the afternoon—and the General sat by the window and read his newspapers—with his back toward us——

HEDDA. And we sat on the sofa in the corner——

LOEVBORG. Always reading the same illustrated magazine——

HEDDA. We hadn't any photograph album.

LOEVBORG. Yes, Hedda. I regarded you as a kind of confessor. Told you things about myself which no one else knew about—then. Those days and nights of drinking and— Oh, Hedda, what power did you have to make me confess such things?

HEDDA. Power? You think I had some power over you?

LOEVBORG. Yes—I don't know how else to explain it. And all those —oblique questions you asked me——

HEDDA. You knew what they meant.

LOEVBORG. But that you could sit there and ask me such questions! So unashamedly——

HEDDA. I thought you said they were oblique.

LOEVBORG. Yes, but you asked them so unashamedly. That you could question me about—about that kind of thing!

HEDDA. You answered willingly enough.

LOEVBORG. Yes—that's what I can't understand—looking back on it. But tell me, Hedda—what you felt for me—wasn't that—love? When you asked me those questions and made me confess my sins to you, wasn't it because you wanted to wash me clean?

HEDDA. No, not exactly.

LOEVBORG. Why did you do it, then?

HEDDA. Do you find it so incredible that a young girl, given the chance to do so without anyone knowing, should want to be allowed a glimpse into a forbidden world of whose existence she is supposed to be ignorant?

LOEVBORG. So that was it?

HEDDA. One reason. One reason—I think.

LOEVBORG. You didn't love me, then. You just wanted—knowledge. But if that was so, why did you break it off?

HEDDA. That was your fault.

LOEVBORG. It was you who put an end to it.

HEDDA. Yes, when I realized that our friendship was threatening to develop into something—something else. Shame on you, Eilert Loevborg! How could you abuse the trust of your dearest friend?

LOEVBORG. [*Clenches his fists*] Oh, why didn't you do it? Why didn't you shoot me dead? As you threatened to?

HEDDA. I was afraid. Of the scandal.

LOEVBORG. Yes, Hedda. You're a coward at heart.

HEDDA. A dreadful coward. [*Changes her tone*] Luckily for you. Well, now you've found consolation with the Elvsteds.

LOEVBORG. I know what Thea's been telling you.

HEDDA. I dare say you told her about us.

LOEVBORG. Not a word. She's too silly to understand that kind of thing.

HEDDA. Silly?

LOEVBORG. She's silly about that kind of thing.

HEDDA. And I am a coward. [*Leans closer to him, without looking him in the eyes, and says quietly*] But let me tell you something. Something you don't know.

LOEVBORG. [*Tensely*] Yes?

HEDDA. My failure to shoot you wasn't my worst act of cowardice that evening.

LOEVBORG. [*Looks at her for a moment, realizes her meaning and whispers passionately*] Oh, Hedda! Hedda Gabler! Now I see what was behind those questions. Yes! It wasn't knowledge you wanted! It was life!

HEDDA. [*Flashes a look at him and says quietly*] Take care! Don't you delude yourself!

[*It has begun to grow dark.* BERTHA, *from outside, opens the door leading into the hall.*]

HEDDA. [*Closes the album with a snap and cries, smiling*] Ah, at last! Come in, Thea dear!

[MRS. ELVSTED *enters from the hall, in evening dress. The door is closed behind her.*]

HEDDA. [*On the sofa, stretches out her arms toward her*] Thea darling, I thought you were never coming!

[MRS. ELVSTED *makes a slight bow to the gentlemen in the rear room as she passes the open doorway, and they to her. Then she goes to the table and holds out her hand to* HEDDA. EILERT LOEVBORG *has risen from his chair. He and* MRS. ELVSTED *nod silently to each other.*]

MRS. ELVSTED. Perhaps I ought to go in and say a few words to your husband?

HEDDA. Oh, there's no need. They're happy by themselves. They'll be going soon.

MRS. ELVSTED. Going?

HEDDA. Yes, they're off on a spree this evening.

MRS. ELVSTED. [*Quickly, to* LOEVBORG] You're not going with them?

LOEVBORG. No.

HEDDA. Mr. Loevborg is staying here with us.

MRS. ELVSTED. [*Takes a chair and is about to sit down beside him*] Oh, how nice it is to be here!

HEDDA. No, Thea darling, not there. Come over here and sit beside me. I want to be in the middle.

MRS. ELVSTED. Yes, just as you wish.

[*She goes round the table and sits on the sofa, on* HEDDA'S *right.* LOEVBORG *sits down again in his chair.*]

LOEVBORG. [*After a short pause, to* HEDDA] Isn't she lovely to look at?

HEDDA. [*Strokes her hair gently*] Only to look at?

LOEVBORG. Yes. We're just good pals. We trust each other implicitly. We can talk to each other quite unashamedly.

HEDDA. No need to be oblique?

MRS. ELVSTED. [*Nestles close to* HEDDA *and says quietly*] Oh, Hedda I'm so happy. Imagine—he says I've inspired him!

HEDDA. [*Looks at her with a smile*] Dear Thea! Does he really?

LOEVBORG. She has the courage of her convictions, Mrs. Tesman.

MRS. ELVSTED. I? Courage?

LOEVBORG. Absolute courage. Where friendship is concerned.

HEDDA. Yes. Courage. Yes. If only one had that——

LOEVBORG. Yes?

HEDDA. One might be able to live. In spite of everything. [*Changes her tone suddenly*] Well, Thea darling, now you're going to drink a nice glass of cold punch.

MRS. ELVSTED. No, thank you. I never drink anything like that.

HEDDA. Oh. You, Mr. Loevborg?

LOEVBORG. Thank you, I don't either.

MRS. ELVSTED. No, he doesn't, either.

HEDDA. [*Looks into his eyes*] But if I want you to?

LOEVBORG. That doesn't make any difference.

HEDDA. [*Laughs*] Have I no power over you at all? Poor me!

LOEVBORG. Not where this is concerned.

HEDDA. Seriously, I think you should. For your own sake.

MRS. ELVSTED. Hedda!

LOEVBORG. Why?

HEDDA. Or perhaps I should say for other people's sake.

LOEVBORG. What do you mean?

HEDDA. People might think you didn't feel absolutely and unashamedly sure of yourself. In your heart of hearts.

MRS. ELVSTED. [*Quietly*] Oh, Hedda, no!

LOEVBORG. People can think what they like. For the present.

MRS. ELVSTED. [*Happily*] Yes, that's true.

HEDDA. I saw it so clearly in Judge Brack a few minutes ago.

LOEVBORG. Oh. What did you see?

HEDDA. He smiled so scornfully when he saw you were afraid to go in there and drink with them.

LOEVBORG. Afraid! I wanted to stay here and talk to you.

MRS. ELVSTED. That was only natural, Hedda.

HEDDA. But the Judge wasn't to know that. I saw him wink at Tesman when you showed you didn't dare to join their wretched little party.

LOEVBORG. Didn't dare! Are you saying I didn't dare?

HEDDA. I'm not saying so. But that was what Judge Brack thought.
LOEVBORG. Well, let him.
HEDDA. You're not going, then?
LOEVBORG. I'm staying here with you and Thea.
MRS. ELVSTED. Yes, Hedda, of course he is.
HEDDA. [*Smiles, and nods approvingly to* LOEVBORG] Firm as a rock! A man of principle! That's how a man should be! [*Turns to* MRS. ELVSTED *and strokes her cheek*] Didn't I tell you so this morning when you came here in such a panic——
LOEVBORG. [*Starts*] Panic?
MRS. ELVSTED. [*Frightened*] Hedda! But—Hedda!
HEDDA. Well, now you can see for yourself. There's no earthly need for you to get scared to death just because——[*Stops*] Well! Let's all three cheer up and enjoy ourselves.
LOEVBORG. Mrs. Tesman, would you mind explaining to me what this is all about?
MRS. ELVSTED. Oh, my God, my God, Hedda, what are you saying? What are you doing?
HEDDA. Keep calm. That horrid Judge has his eye on you.
LOEVBORG. Scared to death, were you? For my sake?
MRS. ELVSTED. [*Quietly, trembling*]Oh, Hedda! You've made me so unhappy!
LOEVBORG. [*Looks coldly at her for a moment. His face is distorted.*] So that was how much you trusted me.
MRS. ELVSTED. Eilert dear, please listen to me——
LOEVBORG. [*Takes one of the glasses of punch, raises it and says quietly, hoarsely*] Skoal, Thea!

[*Empties the glass, puts it down and picks up one of the others.*]

MRS. ELVSTED. [*Quietly*] Hedda, Hedda! Why did you want this to happen?
HEDDA. I—want it? Are you mad?
LOEVBORG. Skoal to you too, Mrs. Tesman. Thanks for telling me the truth. Here's to the truth!

[*Empties his glass and refills it*]

HEDDA. [*Puts her hand on his arm*] Steady. That's enough for now. Don't forget the party.
MRS. ELVSTED. No, no, no!
HEDDA. Ssh! They're looking at you.
LOEVBORG. [*Puts down his glass*] Thea, tell me the truth——
MRS. ELVSTED. Yes!
LOEVBORG. Did your husband know you were following me?
MRS. ELVSTED. Oh, Hedda!
LOEVBORG. Did you and he have an agreement that you should come here and keep an eye on me? Perhaps he gave you the idea? After all, he's a magistrate.[11] I suppose he needed me back in his office. Or did he miss my companionship at the card table?

11. ***Magistrate:*** Also translated ***sheriff.*** A civil official with duties associated with the courts.

MRS. ELVSTED. [*Quietly, sobbing*] Eilert, Eilert!

LOEVBORG. [*Seizes a glass and is about to fill it*] Let's drink to him, too.

HEDDA. No more now. Remember you're going to read your book to Tesman.

LOEVBORG. [*Calm again, puts down his glass*] That was silly of me, Thea. To take it like that, I mean. Don't be angry with me, my dear. You'll see—yes, and they'll see, too—that though I fell, I—I have raised myself up again. With your help, Thea.

MRS. ELVSTED. [*Happily*] Oh, thank God!

[BRACK *has meanwhile glanced at his watch. He and* TESMAN *get up and come into the drawing room.*]

BRACK. [*Takes his hat and overcoat*] Well, Mrs. Tesman. It's time for us to go.

HEDDA. Yes, I suppose it must be.

LOEVBORG. [*Gets up*] Time for me too, Judge.

MRS. ELVSTED. [*Quietly, pleadingly*] Eilert, please don't!

HEDDA. [*Pinches her arm*] They can hear you.

MRS. ELVSTED. [*Gives a little cry*] Oh!

LOEVBORG. [*To* BRACK] You were kind enough to ask me to join you.

BRACK. Are you coming?

LOEVBORG. If I may.

BRACK. Delighted.

LOEVBORG. [*Puts the paper package in his pocket and says to* TESMAN] I'd like to show you one or two things before I send it off to the printer.

TESMAN. I say, that'll be fun. Fancy——! Oh, but Hedda, how'll Mrs. Elvsted get home? What?

HEDDA. Oh, we'll manage somehow.

LOEVBORG. [*Glances over toward the ladies*] Mrs. Elvsted? I shall come back and collect her, naturally. [*Goes closer*] About ten o'clock, Mrs. Tesman? Will that suit you?

HEDDA. Yes. That'll suit me admirably.

TESMAN. Good, that's settled. But you mustn't expect me back so early, Hedda.

HEDDA. Stay as long as you c— as long as you like, dear.

MRS. ELVSTED. [*Trying to hide her anxiety*] Well then, Mr. Loevborg, I'll wait here till you come.

LOEVBORG. [*His hat in his hand*] Pray do, Mrs. Elvsted.

BRACK. Well, gentlemen, now the party begins. I trust that, in the words of a certain fair lady, we shall enjoy good sport.

HEDDA. What a pity the fair lady can't be there, invisible.

BRACK. Why invisible?

HEDDA. So as to be able to hear some of your uncensored witticisms, your honor.

BRACK. [*Laughs*] Oh, I shouldn't advise the fair lady to do that.

TESMAN. [*Laughs too*] I say, Hedda, that's good. By Jove! Fancy that!

BRACK. Well, good night, ladies, good night!

LOEVBORG. [*Bows farewell*] About ten o'clock, then.

[BRACK, LOEVBORG *and* TESMAN *go out through the hall. As they do so* BERTHA *enters from the rear room with a lighted lamp. She puts it on the drawing-room table, then goes out the way she came.*]

MRS. ELVSTED. [*Has got up and is walking uneasily to and fro*] Oh Hedda, Hedda! How is all this going to end?

HEDDA. At ten o'clock, then. He'll be here. I can see him. With a crown of vine-leaves in his hair.[12] Burning and unashamed!

MRS. ELVSTED. Oh, I do hope so!

HEDDA. Can't you see? Then he'll be himself again! He'll be a free man for the rest of his days!

MRS. ELVSTED. Please God you're right.

HEDDA. That's how he'll come! [*Gets up and goes closer*] You can doubt him as much as you like. I believe in him! Now we'll see which of us——

MRS. ELVSTED. You're after something, Hedda.

HEDDA. Yes, I am. For once in my life I want to have the power to shape a man's destiny.

MRS. ELVSTED. Haven't you that power already?

HEDDA. No, I haven't. I've never had it.

MRS. ELVSTED. What about your husband?

HEDDA. Him! Oh, if you could only understand how poor I am. And you're allowed to be so rich, so rich! [*Clasps her passionately*] I think I'll burn your hair off after all!

MRS. ELVSTED. Let me go! Let me go! You frighten me, Hedda!

BERTHA. [*In the open doorway*] I've laid tea in the dining room, madam.

HEDDA. Good, we're coming.

MRS. ELVSTED. No, no, no! I'd rather go home alone! Now—at once!

HEDDA. Rubbish! First you're going to have some tea, you little idiot. And then—at ten o'clock—Eilert Loevborg will come. With a crown of vine-leaves in his hair!

[*She drags* MRS. ELVSTED *almost forcibly toward the open doorway.*]

Act III

SCENE—*The same. The curtains are drawn across the open doorway, and also across the french windows. The lamp, half turned down, with a shade over it, is burning on the table. In the stove, the door of which is open, a fire has been burning, but it is now almost out.*

MRS. ELVSTED, *wrapped in a large shawl and with her feet resting on a footstool, is sitting near the stove, huddled in the armchair.*

12. *A crown . . . hair:* Like Bacchus, the god of wine, and his followers.

HEDDA *is lying asleep on the sofa, fully dressed, with a blanket over her.*

MRS. ELVSTED. [*After a pause, suddenly sits up in her chair and listens tensely. Then she sinks wearily back again and sighs.*] Not back yet! Oh, God! Oh, God! Not back yet!

[BERTHA *tiptoes cautiously in from the hall. She has a letter in her hand.*]

MRS. ELVSTED. [*Turns and whispers*] What is it? Has someone come?

BERTHA. [*Quietly*] Yes, a servant's just called with this letter.

MRS. ELVSTED. [*Quickly, holding out her hand*] A letter! Give it to me!

BERTHA. But it's for the Doctor, madam.

MRS. ELVSTED. Oh. I see.

BERTHA. Miss Tesman's maid brought it. I'll leave it here on the table.

MRS. ELVSTED. Yes, do.

BERTHA. [*Puts down the letter*] I'd better put the lamp out. It's starting to smoke.

MRS. ELVSTED. Yes, put it out. It'll soon be daylight.

BERTHA. [*Puts out the lamp*] It's daylight already, madam.

MRS. ELVSTED. Yes. Broad day. And not home yet.

BERTHA. Oh dear, I was afraid this would happen.

MRS. ELVSTED. Were you?

BERTHA. Yes. When I heard that a certain gentleman had returned to town, and saw him go off with them. I've heard all about him.

MRS. ELVSTED. Don't talk so loud. You'll wake your mistress.

BERTHA. [*Looks at the sofa and sighs*] Yes. Let her go on sleeping, poor dear. Shall I put some more wood on the fire?

MRS. ELVSTED. Thank you, don't bother on my account.

BERTHA. Very good.

[*Goes quietly out through the hall*]

HEDDA. [*Wakes as the door closes and looks up*] What's that?

MRS. ELVSTED. It was only the maid.

HEDDA. [*Looks round*] What am I doing here? Oh, now I remember. [*Sits up on the sofa, stretches herself and rubs her eyes*] What time is it, Thea?

MRS. ELVSTED. It's gone seven.

HEDDA. When did Tesman get back?

MRS. ELVSTED. He's not back yet.

HEDDA. Not home yet?

MRS. ELVSTED. [*Gets up*] No one's come.

HEDDA. And we sat up waiting for them till four o'clock.

MRS. ELVSTED. God! How I waited for him!

HEDDA. [*Yawns and says with her hand in front of her mouth*] Oh, dear. We might have saved ourselves the trouble.

MRS. ELVSTED. Did you manage to sleep?

HEDDA. Oh, yes. Quite well, I think. Didn't you get any?

MRS. ELVSTED. Not a wink. I couldn't, Hedda. I just couldn't.

HEDDA. [*Gets up and comes over to her*] Now, now, now. There's nothing to worry about. I know what's happened.

MRS. ELVSTED. What? Please tell me.

HEDDA. Well, obviously the party went on very late——

MRS. ELVSTED. Oh dear, I suppose it must have. But——

HEDDA. And Tesman didn't want to come home and wake us all up in the middle of the night. [*Laughs*] Probably wasn't too keen to show his face either, after a spree like that.

MRS. ELVSTED. But where could he have gone?

HEDDA. I should think he's probably slept at his aunts'. They keep his old room for him.

MRS. ELVSTED. No, he can't be with them. A letter came for him just now from Miss Tesman. It's over there.

HEDDA. Oh? [*Looks at the envelope*] Yes, it's Auntie Juju's handwriting. Well, he must still be at Judge Brack's, then. And Eilert Loevborg is sitting there, reading to him. With a crown of vine-leaves in his hair.

MRS. ELVSTED. Hedda, you're only saying that. You don't believe it.

HEDDA. Thea, you really are a little fool.

MRS. ELVSTED. Perhaps I am.

HEDDA. You look tired to death.

MRS. ELVSTED. Yes. I am tired to death.

HEDDA. Go to my room and lie down for a little. Do as I say, now; don't argue.

MRS. ELVSTED. No, no. I couldn't possibly sleep.

HEDDA. Of course you can.

MRS. ELVSTED. But your husband'll be home soon. And I must know at once——

HEDDA. I'll tell you when he comes.

MRS. ELVSTED. Promise me, Hedda?

HEDDA. Yes, don't worry. Go and get some sleep.

MRS. ELVSTED. Thank you. All right, I'll try.

[*She goes out through the rear room.* HEDDA *goes to the french windows and draws the curtains. Broad daylight floods into the room. She goes to the writing table, takes a small hand mirror from it and arranges her hair. Then she goes to the door leading into the hall and presses the bell. After a few moments,* BERTHA *enters.*]

BERTHA. Did you want anything, madam?

HEDDA. Yes, put some more wood on the fire. I'm freezing.

BERTHA. Bless you, I'll soon have this room warmed up. [*She rakes the embers together and puts a fresh piece of wood on them. Suddenly she stops and listens.*] There's someone at the front door, madam.

HEDDA. Well, go and open it. I'll see to the fire.

BERTHA. It'll burn up in a moment.

[*She goes out through the hall.* HEDDA *kneels on the foot-stool and puts more wood in the stove. After a few seconds,*

GEORGE TESMAN *enters from the hall. He looks tired, and rather worried. He tiptoes toward the open doorway and is about to slip through the curtains.*]

HEDDA. [*At the stove, without looking up*] Good morning.

TESMAN. [*Turns*] Hedda! [*Comes nearer*] Good heavens, are you up already? What?

HEDDA. Yes, I got up very early this morning.

TESMAN. I was sure you'd still be sleeping. Fancy that!

HEDDA. Don't talk so loud. Mrs. Elvsted's asleep in my room.

TESMAN. Mrs. Elvsted? Has she stayed the night here?

HEDDA. Yes. No one came to escort her home.

TESMAN. Oh. No, I suppose not.

HEDDA. [*Closes the door of the stove and gets up*] Well. Was it fun?

TESMAN. Have you been anxious about me? What?

HEDDA. Not in the least. I asked if you'd had fun.

TESMAN. Oh yes, rather! Well, I thought, for once in a while—The first part was the best; when Eilert read his book to me. We arrived over an hour too early—what about that, eh? By Jove! Brack had a lot of things to see to, so Eilert read to me.

HEDDA. [*Sits at the right-hand side of the table*] Well? Tell me about it.

TESMAN. [*Sits on a footstool by the stove*] Honestly, Hedda, you've no idea what a book that's going to be. It's really one of the most remarkable things that's ever been written. By Jove!

HEDDA. Oh, never mind about the book——

TESMAN. I'm going to make a confession to you, Hedda. When he'd finished reading a sort of beastly feeling came over me.

HEDDA. Beastly feeling?

TESMAN. I found myself envying Eilert for being able to write like that. Imagine that, Hedda!

HEDDA. Yes. I can imagine.

TESMAN. What a tragedy that with all those gifts he should be so incorrigible.

HEDDA. You mean he's less afraid of life than most men?

TESMAN. Good heavens, no. He just doesn't know the meaning of the word moderation.

HEDDA. What happened afterwards?

TESMAN. Well, looking back on it I suppose you might almost call it an orgy, Hedda.

HEDDA. Had he vine-leaves in his hair?

TESMAN. Vine-leaves? No, I didn't see any of them. He made a long, rambling oration in honor of the woman who'd inspired him to write this book. Yes, those were the words he used.

HEDDA. Did he name her?

TESMAN. No. But I suppose it must be Mrs. Elvsted. You wait and see!

HEDDA. Where did you leave him?

TESMAN. On the way home. We left in a bunch—the last of us, that is—and Brack came with us to get a little fresh air. Well, then, you see, we agreed we ought to see Eilert home. He'd had a drop too much.

HEDDA. You don't say?

TESMAN. But now comes the funny part, Hedda. Or I should really say the tragic part. Oh, I'm almost ashamed to tell you. For Eilert's sake, I mean——

HEDDA. Why, what happened?

TESMAN. Well, you see, as we were walking toward town I happened to drop behind for a minute. Only for a minute—er—you understand——

HEDDA. Yes, yes——?

TESMAN. Well then, when I ran on to catch them up, what do you think I found by the roadside. What?

HEDDA. How on earth should I know?

TESMAN. You mustn't tell anyone, Hedda. What? Promise me that—for Eilert's sake. [*Takes a package wrapped in paper from his coat pocket*] Just fancy! I found this.

HEDDA. Isn't this the one he brought here yesterday?

TESMAN. Yes! The whole of that precious, irreplaceable manuscript! And he went and lost it! Didn't even notice! What about that? By Jove! Tragic.

HEDDA. But why didn't you give it back to him?

TESMAN. I didn't dare to, in the state he was in.

HEDDA. Didn't you tell any of the others?

TESMAN. Good heavens, no. I didn't want to do that. For Eilert's sake, you understand.

HEDDA. Then no one else knows you have his manuscript?

TESMAN. No. And no one must be allowed to know.

HEDDA. Didn't it come up in the conversation later?

TESMAN. I didn't get a chance to talk to him any more. As soon as we got into the outskirts of town, he and one or two of the others gave us the slip. Disappeared, by Jove!

HEDDA. Oh? I suppose they took him home.

TESMAN. Yes, I imagine that was the idea. Brack left us, too.

HEDDA. And what have you been up to since then?

TESMAN. Well, I and one or two of the others—awfully jolly chaps, they were—went back to where one of them lived, and had a cup of morning coffee. Morning-after coffee—what? Ah, well. I'll just lie down for a bit and give Eilert time to sleep it off, poor chap, then I'll run over and give this back to him.

HEDDA. [*Holds out her hand for the package*] No, don't do that. Not just yet. Let me read it first.

TESMAN. Oh no, really, Hedda dear, honestly, I daren't do that.

HEDDA. Daren't?

TESMAN. No—imagine how desperate he'll be when he wakes up and finds his manuscript's missing. He hasn't any copy, you see. He told me so himself.

HEDDA. Can't a thing like that be rewritten?

TESMAN. Oh no, not possibly, I shouldn't think. I mean, the inspiration, you know——

HEDDA. Oh, yes. I'd forgotten that. [*Casually*] By the way, there's a letter for you.

TESMAN. Is there? Fancy that!

HEDDA. [*Holds it out to him*] It came early this morning.

TESMAN. I say, it's from Auntie Juju! What on earth can it be? [*Puts the package on the other footstool, opens the letter, reads it and jumps up*] Oh, Hedda! She says poor Auntie Rena's dying.

HEDDA. Well, we've been expecting that.

TESMAN. She says if I want to see her I must go quickly. I'll run over at once.

HEDDA. [*Hides a smile*] Run?

TESMAN. Hedda dear, I suppose you wouldn't like to come with me? What about that, eh?

HEDDA. [*Gets up and says wearily and with repulsion*] No, no, don't ask me to do anything like that. I can't bear illness or death. I loathe anything ugly.

TESMAN. Yes, yes. Of course. [*In a dither*] My hat? My overcoat? Oh yes, in the hall. I do hope I won't get there too late, Hedda? What?

HEDDA. You'll be all right if you run.

[BERTHA *enters from the hall.*]

BERTHA. Judge Brack's outside and wants to know if he can come in.

TESMAN. At this hour? No, I can't possibly receive him now.

HEDDA. I can. [*To* BERTHA] Ask his honor to come in.

[BERTHA *goes.*]

HEDDA. [*Whispers quickly*] The manuscript, Tesman.

[*She snatches it from the footstool.*]

TESMAN. Yes, give it to me.

HEDDA. No, I'll look after it for now.

[*She goes over to the writing table and puts it in the bookcase.* TESMAN *stands dithering, unable to get his gloves on.* JUDGE BRACK *enters from the hall.*]

HEDDA. [*Nods to him*] Well, you're an early bird.

BRACK. Yes, aren't I? [*To* TESMAN] Are you up and about, too?

TESMAN. Yes, I've got to go and see my aunts. Poor Auntie Rena's dying.

BRACK. Oh dear, is she? Then you mustn't let me detain you. At so tragic a——

TESMAN. Yes, I really must run. Good-bye! Good-bye!

[*Runs out through the hall*]

HEDDA. [*Goes nearer*] You seem to have had excellent sport last night—Judge.

BRACK. Indeed yes, Mrs. Hedda. I haven't even had time to take my clothes off.

HEDDA. *You* haven't either?

BRACK. As you see. What's Tesman told you about last night's escapades?

HEDDA. Oh, only some boring story about having gone and drunk coffee somewhere.

BRACK. Yes, I've heard about that coffee party. Eilert Loevborg wasn't with them, I gather?

HEDDA. No, they took him home first.

BRACK. Did Tesman go with him?

HEDDA. No, one or two of the others, he said.

BRACK. [*Smiles*] George Tesman is a credulous man, Mrs. Hedda.

HEDDA. God knows. But—has something happened?

BRACK. Well, yes, I'm afraid it has.

HEDDA. I see. Sit down and tell me.

[*She sits on the left of the table,* BRACK *at the long side of it, near her.*]

HEDDA. Well?

BRACK. I had a special reason for keeping track of my guests last night. Or perhaps I should say some of my guests.

HEDDA. Including Eilert Loevborg?

BRACK. I must confess—yes.

HEDDA. You're beginning to make me curious.

BRACK. Do you know where he and some of my other guests spent the latter half of last night, Mrs. Hedda?

HEDDA. Tell me. If it won't shock me.

BRACK. Oh, I don't think it'll shock you. They found themselves participating in an exceedingly animated *soirée*.[13]

HEDDA. Of a sporting character?

BRACK. Of a highly sporting character.

HEDDA. Tell me more.

BRACK. Loevborg had received an invitation in advance—as had the others. I knew all about that. But he had refused. As you know, he's become a new man.

HEDDA. Up at the Elvsteds', yes. But he went?

BRACK. Well, you see, Mrs. Hedda, last night at my house, unhappily, the spirit moved him.

HEDDA. Yes, I hear he became inspired.

BRACK. Somewhat violently inspired. And as a result, I suppose, his thoughts strayed. We men, alas, don't always stick to our principles as firmly as we should.

HEDDA. I'm sure you're an exception, Judge Brack. But go on about Loevborg.

BRACK. Well, to cut a long story short, he ended up in the establishment of a certain Mademoiselle Danielle.

HEDDA. Mademoiselle Danielle?

BRACK. She was holding the *soirée*. For a selected circle of friends and admirers.

HEDDA. Has she got red hair?

BRACK. She has.

HEDDA. A singer of some kind?

BRACK. Yes—among other accomplishments. She's also a celebrated

13. *Soirée:* Evening party.

huntress—of men, Mrs. Hedda. I'm sure you've heard about her. Eilert Loevborg used to be one of her most ardent patrons. In his salad days.[14]

HEDDA. And how did all this end?

BRACK. Not entirely amicably, from all accounts. Mademoiselle Danielle began by receiving him with the utmost tenderness and ended by resorting to her fists.

HEDDA. Against Loevborg?

BRACK. Yes. He accused her, or her friends, of having robbed him. He claimed his pocketbook had been stolen. Among other things. In short, he seems to have made a bloodthirsty scene.

HEDDA. And what did this lead to?

BRACK. It led to a general free-for-all, in which both sexes participated. Fortunately, in the end the police arrived.

HEDDA. The police too?

BRACK. Yes. I'm afraid it may turn out to be rather an expensive joke for Master Eilert. Crazy fool!

HEDDA. Oh?

BRACK. Apparently he put up a very violent resistance. Hit one of the constables on the ear and tore his uniform. He had to accompany them to the police station.

HEDDA. Where did you learn all this?

BRACK. From the police.

HEDDA. [*To herself*] So that's what happened. He didn't have a crown of vine-leaves in his hair.

BRACK. Vine-leaves, Mrs. Hedda?

HEDDA. [*In her normal voice again*] But, tell me, Judge, why do you take such a close interest in Eilert Loevborg?

BRACK. For one thing it'll hardly be a matter of complete indifference to me if it's revealed in court that he came there straight from my house.

HEDDA. Will it come to court?

BRACK. Of course. Well, I don't regard that as particularly serious. Still, I thought it my duty, as a friend of the family, to give you and your husband a full account of his nocturnal adventures.

HEDDA. Why?

BRACK. Because I've a shrewd suspicion that he's hoping to use you as a kind of screen.

HEDDA. What makes you think that?

BRACK. Oh, for heaven's sake, Mrs. Hedda, we're not blind. You wait and see. This Mrs. Elvsted won't be going back to her husband just yet.

HEDDA. Well, if there were anything between those two there are plenty of other places where they could meet.

BRACK. Not in anyone's home. From now on every respectable house will once again be closed to Eilert Loevborg.

HEDDA. And mine should be too, you mean?

14. *Salad days:* Indiscreet youth.

BRACK. Yes. I confess I should find it more than irksome if this gentleman were to be granted unrestricted access to this house. If he were superfluously to intrude into——

HEDDA. The triangle?

BRACK. Precisely. For me it would be like losing a home.

HEDDA. [*Looks at him and smiles*] I see. You want to be the cock of the walk.

BRACK. [*Nods slowly and lowers his voice*] Yes, that is my aim. And I shall fight for it with—every weapon at my disposal.

HEDDA. [*As her smile fades*] You're a dangerous man, aren't you? When you really want something.

BRACK. You think so?

HEDDA. Yes. I'm beginning to think so. I'm deeply thankful you haven't any kind of hold over me.

BRACK. [*Laughs equivocally*] Well, well, Mrs. Hedda—perhaps you're right. If I had, who knows what I might not think up?

HEDDA. Come, Judge Brack. That sounds almost like a threat.

BRACK. [*Gets up*] Heaven forbid! In the creation of a triangle—and its continuance—the question of compulsion should never arise.

HEDDA. Exactly what I was thinking.

BRACK. Well, I've said what I came to say. I must be getting back. Good-bye, Mrs. Hedda.

[*Goes toward the french windows*]

HEDDA. [*Gets up*] Are you going out through the garden?

BRACK. Yes, it's shorter.

HEDDA. Yes. And it's the back door, isn't it?

BRACK. I've nothing against back doors. They can be quite intriguing—sometimes.

HEDDA. When people fire pistols out of them, for example?

BRACK. [*In the doorway, laughs*] Oh, people don't shoot tame cocks.

HEDDA. [*Laughs too*] I suppose not. When they've only got one.

[*They nod good-bye, laughing. He goes. She closes the french windows behind him, and stands for a moment, looking out pensively. Then she walks across the room and glances through the curtains in the open doorway. Goes to the writing table, takes* LOEVBORG'S *package from the bookcase and is about to leaf through the pages when* BERTHA *is heard remonstrating loudly in the hall.* HEDDA *turns and listens. She hastily puts the package back in the drawer, locks it and puts the key on the inkstand.* EILBERT LOEVBORG, *with his overcoat on and his hat in his hand, throws the door open. He looks somewhat confused and excited.*]

LOEVBORG. [*Shouts as he enters*] I must come in, I tell you! Let me pass!

[*He closes the door, turns, see* HEDDA, *controls himself immediately and bows.*]

HEDDA. [*At the writing table*] Well, Mr. Loevborg, this is rather a late hour to be collecting Thea.

LOEVBORG. And an early hour to call on you. Please forgive me.

HEDDA. How do you know she's still here?

LOEVBORG. They told me at her lodgings that she has been out all night.

HEDDA. [*Goes to the table*] Did you notice anything about their behavior when they told you?

LOEVBORG. [*Looks at her, puzzled*] Notice anything?

HEDDA. Did they sound as if they thought it—strange?

LOEVBORG. [*Suddenly understands*] Oh, I see what you mean. I'm dragging her down with me. No, as a matter of fact I didn't notice anything. I suppose Tesman isn't up yet?

HEDDA. No, I don't think so.

LOEVBORG. When did he get home?

HEDDA. Very late.

LOEVBORG. Did he tell you anything?

HEDDA. Yes. I gather you had a merry party at Judge Brack's last night.

LOEVBORG. He didn't tell you anything else?

HEDDA. I don't think so. I was so terribly sleepy——

[MRS. ELVSTED *comes through the curtains in the open doorway.*]

MRS. ELVSTED. [*Runs toward him*] Oh, Eilert! At last!

LOEVBORG. Yes—at last. And too late.

MRS. ELVSTED. What is too late?

LOEVBORG. Everything—now. I'm finished, Thea.

MRS. ELVSTED. Oh, no, no! Don't say that!

LOEVBORG. You'll say it yourself, when you've heard what I——

MRS. ELVSTED. I don't want to hear anything!

HEDDA. Perhaps you'd rather speak to her alone? I'd better go.

LOEVBORG. No, stay.

MRS. ELVSTED. But I don't want to hear anything, I tell you!

LOEVBORG. It's not about last night.

MRS. ELVSTED. Then what——?

LOEVBORG. I want to tell you that from now on we must stop seeing each other.

MRS. ELVSTED. Stop seeing each other!

HEDDA. [*Involuntarily*] I knew it!

LOEVBORG. I have no further use for you, Thea.

MRS. ELVSTED. You can stand there and say that! No further use for me! Surely I can go on helping you? We'll go on working together, won't we?

LOEVBORG. I don't intend to do any more work from now on.

MRS. ELVSTED. [*Desperately*] Then what use have I for my life?

LOEVBORG. You must try to live as if you had never known me.

MRS. ELVSTED. But I can't!

LOEVBORG. Try to, Thea. Go back home——

MRS. ELVSTED. Never! I want to be wherever you are! I won't let myself be driven away like this! I want to stay here—and be with you when the book comes out.

HEDDA. [*Whispers*] Ah, yes! The book!

LOEVBORG. [*Looks at her*] Our book; Thea's and mine. It belongs to both of us.

MRS. ELVSTED. Oh, yes! I feel that, too! And I've a right to be with you when it comes into the world. I want to see people respect and honor you again. And the joy! The joy! I want to share it with you!

LOEVBORG. Thea—our book will never come into the world.

HEDDA. Ah!

MRS. ELVSTED. Not——?

LOEVBORG. It cannot. Ever.

MRS. ELVSTED. Eilert—what have you done with the manuscript? Where is it?

LOEVBORG. Oh Thea, please don't ask me that!

MRS. ELVSTED. Yes, yes—I must know. I've a right to know. Now!

LOEVBORG. The manuscript. I've torn it up.

MRS. ELVSTED. [*Screams*] No, no!

HEDDA. [*Involuntarily*] But that's not——!

LOEVBORG. [*Looks at her*] Not true, you think?

HEDDA. [*Controls herself*] Why—yes, of course it is, if you say so. It just sounded so incredible——

LOEVBORG. It's true, nevertheless.

MRS. ELVSTED. Oh, my God, my God, Hedda—he's destroyed his own book!

LOEVBORG. I have destroyed my life. Why not my life's work, too?

MRS. ELVSTED. And you—did this last night?

LOEVBORG. Yes, Thea. I tore it into a thousand pieces. And scattered them out across the fjord.[15] It's good, clean, salt water. Let it carry them away; let them drift in the current and the wind. And in a little while, they will sink. Deeper and deeper. As I shall, Thea.

MRS. ELVSTED. Do you know, Eilert—this book—all my life I shall feel as though you'd killed a little child?

LOEVBORG. You're right. It is like killing a child.

MRS. ELVSTED. But how could you? It was my child, too!

HEDDA. [*Almost inaudibly*] Oh—the child——!

MRS. ELVSTED. [*Breathes heavily*] It's all over, then. Well—I'll go now, Hedda.

HEDDA. You're not leaving town?

MRS. ELVSTED. I don't know what I'm going to do. I can't see anything except—darkness.

[*She goes out through the hall.*]

HEDDA. [*Waits a moment*] Aren't you going to escort her home, Mr. Loevborg?

LOEVBORG. I? Through the streets? Do you want me to let people see her with me?

HEDDA. Of course I don't know what else may have happened last night. But is it so utterly beyond redress?

15. *Fjord:* An inlet of the sea. [Pronounced *fyord.*]

LOEVBORG. It isn't just last night. It'll go on happening. I know it. But the curse of it is, I don't want to live that kind of life. I don't want to start all that again. She's broken my courage. I can't spit in the eyes of the world any longer.

HEDDA. [*As though to herself*] That pretty little fool's been trying to shape a man's destiny. [*Looks at him*] But how could you be so heartless toward her?

LOEVBORG. Don't call me heartless!

HEDDA. To go and destroy the one thing that's made her life worth living? You don't call that heartless?

LOEVBORG. Do you want to know the truth, Hedda?

HEDDA. The truth?

LOEVBORG. Promise me first—give me your word—that you'll never let Thea know about this.

HEDDA. I give you my word.

LOEVBORG. Good. Well; what I told her just now was a lie.

HEDDA. About the manuscript?

LOEVBORG. Yes. I didn't tear it up. Or throw it in the fjord.

HEDDA. You didn't? But where is it, then?

LOEVBORG. I destroyed it, all the same. I destroyed it, Hedda!

HEDDA. I don't understand.

LOEVBORG. Thea said that what I had done was like killing a child.

HEDDA. Yes. That's what she said.

LOEVBORG. But to kill a child isn't the worst thing a father can do to it.

HEDDA. What could be worse than that?

LOEVBORG. Hedda—suppose a man came home one morning, after a night of debauchery, and said to the mother of his child: "Look here. I've been wandering round all night. I've been to—such-and-such a place and such-and-such a place. And I had our child with me. I took him to—these places. And I've lost him. Just—lost him. God knows where he is or whose hands he's fallen into."

HEDDA. I see. But when all's said and done, this was only a book——

LOEVBORG. Thea's heart and soul were in that book. It was her whole life.

HEDDA. Yes. I understand.

LOEVBORG. Well, then you must also understand that she and I cannot possibly ever see each other again.

HEDDA. Where will you go?

LOEVBORG. Nowhere. I just want to put an end to it all. As soon as possible.

HEDDA. [*Takes a step toward him*] Eilert Loevborg, listen to me. Do it—beautifully!

LOEVBORG. Beautifully? [*Smiles*] With a crown of vine-leaves in my hair? The way you used to dream of me—in the old days?

HEDDA. No. I don't believe in that crown any longer. But—do it beautifully, all the same. Just this once. Good-bye. You must go now. And don't come back.

LOEVBORG. Adieu, madam. Give my love to George Tesman.
[*Turns to go*]

HEDDA. Wait. I want to give you a souvenir to take with you.
[*She goes over to the writing table, opens the drawer and the pistol-case, and comes back to* LOEVBORG *with one of the pistols.*]

LOEVBORG. [*Looks at her*] This? Is this the souvenir?

HEDDA. [*Nods slowly*] You recognize it? You looked down its barrel once.

LOEVBORG. You should have used it then.

HEDDA. Here! Use it now!

LOEVBORG. [*Puts the pistol in his breast pocket*] Thank you.

HEDDA. Do it beautifully, Eilert Loevborg. Only promise me that!

LOEVBORG. Good-bye, Hedda Gabler.
[*He goes out through the hall.* HEDDA *stands by the door for a moment, listening. Then she goes over to the writing table, takes out the package containing the manuscript, glances inside it, pulls some of the pages half out and looks at them. Then she takes it to the armchair by the stove and sits down with the package in her lap. After a moment, she opens the door of the stove; then she opens the packet.*]

HEDDA. [*Throws one of the pages into the stove and whispers to herself*] I'm burning your child, Thea! You with your beautiful wavy hair! [*She throws a few more pages into the stove.*] The child Eilert Loevborg gave you. [*Throws the rest of the manuscript in*] I'm burning it! I'm burning your child!

Act IV

SCENE—*The same. It is evening. The drawing room is in darkness. The small room is illuminated by the hanging lamp over the table. The curtains are drawn across the french windows.* HEDDA, *dressed in black, is walking up and down in the darkened room. Then she goes into the small room and crosses to the left. A few chords are heard from the piano. She comes back into the drawing room.*

BERTHA *comes through the small room from the right with a lighted lamp, which she places on the table in front of the corner sofa in the drawing room. Her eyes are red with crying, and she has black ribbons on her cap. She goes quietly out, right.* HEDDA *goes over to the french windows, draws the curtains slightly to one side and looks out into the darkness.*

A few moments later, MISS TESMAN *enters from the hall. She is dressed in mourning, with a black hat and veil.* HEDDA *goes to meet her and holds out her hand.*

MISS TESMAN. Well, Hedda, here I am in the weeds of sorrow. My poor sister has ended her struggles at last.

HEDDA. I've already heard. Tesman sent me a card.

MISS TESMAN. Yes, he promised me he would. But I thought, no, I must go and break the news of death to Hedda myself—here, in the house of life.

HEDDA. It's very kind of you.

MISS TESMAN. Ah, Rena shouldn't have chosen a time like this to pass away. This is no moment for Hedda's house to be a place of mourning.

HEDDA. [*Changing the subject*] She died peacefully, Miss Tesman?

MISS TESMAN. Oh, it was quite beautiful! The end came so calmly. And she was so happy at being able to see George once again. And say good-bye to him. Hasn't he come home yet?

HEDDA. No. He wrote that I mustn't expect him too soon. But please sit down.

MISS TESMAN. No, thank you, Hedda dear—bless you. I'd like to. But I've so little time. I must dress her and lay her out as well as I can. She shall go to her grave looking really beautiful.

HEDDA. Can't I help with anything?

MISS TESMAN. Why, you mustn't think of such a thing! Hedda Tesman mustn't let her hands be soiled by contact with death. Or her thoughts. Not at this time.

HEDDA. One can't always control one's thoughts.

MISS TESMAN. [*Continues*] Ah, well, that's life. Now we must start to sew poor Rena's shroud. There'll be sewing to be done in this house too before long, I shouldn't wonder. But not for a shroud, praise God.

[GEORGE TESMAN *enters from the hall.*]

HEDDA. You've come at last! Thank heavens!

TESMAN. Are you here, Auntie Juju? With Hedda? Fancy that!

MISS TESMAN. I was just on the point of leaving, dear boy. Well, have you done everything you promised me?

TESMAN. No, I'm afraid I forgot half of it. I'll have to run over again tomorrow. My head's in a complete whirl today. I can't collect my thoughts.

MISS TESMAN. But George dear, you mustn't take it like this.

TESMAN. Oh? Well—er—how should I?

MISS TESMAN. You must be happy in your grief. Happy for what's happened. As I am.

TESMAN. Oh, yes, yes. You're thinking of Aunt Rena.

HEDDA. It'll be lonely for you now, Miss Tesman.

MISS TESMAN. For the first few days, yes. But it won't last long, I hope. Poor dear Rena's little room isn't going to stay empty.

TESMAN. Oh? Whom are you going to move in there? What?

MISS TESMAN. Oh, there's always some poor invalid who needs care and attention.

HEDDA. Do you really want another cross like that to bear?

MISS TESMAN. Cross! God forgive you, child. It's been no cross for me.

HEDDA. But now—if a complete stranger comes to live with you——?

MISS TESMAN. Oh, one soon makes friends with invalids. And I need so much to have someone to live for. Like you, my dear. Well, I expect there'll soon be work in this house too for an old aunt, praise God!

HEDDA. Oh—please!

TESMAN. By Jove, yes! What a splendid time the three of us could have together if——

HEDDA. If?

TESMAN. [*Uneasily*] Oh, never mind. It'll all work out. Let's hope so—what?

MISS TESMAN. Yes, yes. Well, I'm sure you two would like to be alone. [*Smiles*] Perhaps Hedda may have something to tell you, George. Good-bye. I must go home to Rena. [*Turns to the door*] Dear God, how strange! Now Rena is with me and with poor dear Joachim.

TESMAN. Fancy that. Yes, Auntie Juju! What?

[MISS TESMAN *goes out through the hall.*]

HEDDA. [*Follows* TESMAN *coldly and searchingly with her eyes*] I really believe this death distresses you more than it does her.

TESMAN. Oh, it isn't just Auntie Rena. It's Eilert I'm so worried about.

HEDDA. [*Quickly*] Is there any news of him?

TESMAN. I ran over to see him this afternoon. I wanted to tell him his manuscript was in safe hands.

HEDDA. Oh? You didn't find him?

TESMAN. No. He wasn't at home. But later I met Mrs. Elvsted and she told me he'd been here early this morning.

HEDDA. Yes, just after you'd left.

TESMAN. It seems he said he'd torn the manuscript up. What?

HEDDA. Yes, he claimed to have done so.

TESMAN. You told him we had it, of course?

HEDDA. No. [*Quickly*] Did you tell Mrs. Elvsted?

TESMAN. No, I didn't like to. But you ought to have told him. Think if he should go home and do something desperate! Give me the manuscript, Hedda. I'll run over to him with it right away. Where did you put it?

HEDDA. [*Cold and motionless, leaning against the armchair*] I haven't got it any longer.

TESMAN. Haven't got it? What on earth do you mean?

HEDDA. I've burned it.

TESMAN. [*Starts, terrified*] Burned it! Burned Eilert's manuscript!

HEDDA. Don't shout. The servant will hear you.

TESMAN. Burned it! But in heaven's name——! Oh, no, no, no! This is impossible!

HEDDA. Well, it's true.

TESMAN. But Hedda, do you realize what you've done? That's appropriating lost property! It's against the law! By Jove! You ask Judge Brack and see if I'm not right.

HEDDA. You'd be well advised not to talk about it to Judge Brack or anyone else.

TESMAN. But how could you go and do such a dreadful thing? What on earth put the idea into your head? What came over you? Answer me! What?

HEDDA. [*Represses on almost imperceptible smile*] I did it for your sake, George.

TESMAN. For my sake?

HEDDA. When you came home this morning and described how he'd read his book to you——

TESMAN. Yes, yes?

HEDDA. You admitted you were jealous of him.

TESMAN. But, good heavens, I didn't mean it literally!

HEDDA. No matter. I couldn't bear the thought that anyone else should push you into the background.

TESMAN. [*Torn between doubt and joy*] Hedda—is this true? But—but—but I never realized you loved me like that! Fancy——

HEDDA. Well, I suppose you'd better know. I'm going to have—— [*Breaks off and says violently*] No, no—you'd better ask your Auntie Juju. She'll tell you.

TESMAN. Hedda! I think I understand what you mean. [*Clasps his hands*] Good heavens, can it really be true! What?

HEDDA. Don't shout. The servant will hear you.

TESMAN. [*Laughing with joy*] The servant! I say, that's good! The servant! Why, that's Bertha! I'll run out and tell her at once!

HEDDA. [*Clenches her hands in despair*] Oh, it's destroying me, all this—it's destroying me!

TESMAN. I say, Hedda, what's up? What?

HEDDA. [*Cold, controlled*] Oh, it's all so—absurd—George.

TESMAN. Absurd? That I'm so happy? But surely——? Ah, well—perhaps I won't say anything to Bertha.

HEDDA. No, do. She might as well know too.

TESMAN. No, no, I won't tell her yet. But Auntie Juju—I must let her know! And you—you called me George! For the first time! Fancy that! Oh, it'll make Auntie Juju so happy, all this! So very happy!

HEDDA. Will she be happy when she hears I've burned Eilert Loevborg's manuscript—for your sake?

TESMAN. No, I'd forgotten about that. Of course no one must be allowed to know about the manuscript. But that you're burning with love for me, Hedda, I must certainly let Auntie Juju know that. I say, I wonder if young wives often feel like that toward their husbands? What?

HEDDA. You might ask Auntie Juju about that too.

TESMAN. I will, as soon as I get the chance. [*Looks uneasy and thoughtful again*] But I say, you know, that manuscript. Dreadful business. Poor Eilert!

[MRS. ELVSTED, *dressed as on her first visit, with hat and overcoat, enters from the hall.*]

MRS. ELVSTED. [*Greets them hastily and tremulously*] Oh, Hedda dear, do please forgive me for coming here again.

HEDDA. Why, Thea, what's happened?

TESMAN. Is it anything to do with Eilert Loevborg? What?

MRS. ELVSTED. Yes—I'm so dreadfully afraid he may have met with an accident.

HEDDA. [*Grips her arm*] You think so?

TESMAN. But, good heavens, Mrs. Elvsted, what makes you think that?

MRS. ELVSTED. I heard them talking about him at the boarding-house, as I went in. Oh, there are the most terrible rumors being spread about him in town today.

TESMAN. Fancy. Yes, I heard about them too. But I can testify that he went straight home to bed. Fancy that!

HEDDA. Well—what did they say in the boarding-house?

MRS. ELVSTED. Oh, I couldn't find out anything. Either they didn't know, or else—— They stopped talking when they saw me. And I didn't dare to ask.

TESMAN. [*Fidgets uneasily*] We must hope—we must hope you misheard them, Mrs. Elvsted.

MRS. ELVSTED. No, no, I'm sure it was he they were talking about. I heard them say something about a hospital——

TESMAN. Hospital!

HEDDA. Oh no, surely that's impossible!

MRS. ELVSTED. Oh, I became so afraid. So I went up to his rooms and asked to see him.

HEDDA. Do you think that was wise, Thea?

MRS. ELVSTED. Well, what else could I do? I couldn't bear the uncertainty any longer.

TESMAN. But *you* didn't manage to find him either? What?

MRS. ELVSTED. No. And they had no idea where he was. They said he hadn't been home since yesterday afternoon.

TESMAN. Since yesterday? Fancy that!

MRS. ELVSTED. I'm sure he must have met with an accident.

TESMAN. Hedda, I wonder if I ought to go into town and make one or two enquiries?

HEDDA. No, no, don't you get mixed up in this.

[JUDGE BRACK *enters from the hall, hat in hand.* BERTHA, *who has opened the door for him, closes it. He looks serious and greets them silently.*]

TESMAN. Hullo, my dear Judge. Fancy seeing you!

BRACK. I had to come and talk to you.

TESMAN. I can see Auntie Juju's told you the news.

BRACK. Yes, I've heard about that too.

TESMAN. Tragic, isn't it?

BRACK. Well, my dear chap, that depends how you look at it.

TESMAN. [*Looks uncertainly at him*] Has something else happened?

BRACK. Yes.

HEDDA. Another tragedy?

BRACK. That also depends on how you look at it, Mrs. Tesman.

MRS. ELVSTED. Oh, it's something to do with Eilert Loevborg!

BRACK. [*Looks at her for a moment*] How did you guess? Perhaps you've heard already——?

MRS. ELVSTED. [*Confused*] No, no, not at all—I——

TESMAN. For heaven's sake, tell us!

BRACK. [*Shrugs his shoulders*] Well, I'm afraid they've taken him to the hospital. He's dying.

MRS. ELVSTED. [*Screams*] Oh God, God!

TESMAN. The hospital! Dying!

HEDDA. [*Involuntarily*] So quickly!

MRS. ELVSTED. [*Weeping*] Oh, Hedda! And we parted enemies!

HEDDA. [*Whispers*] Thea—Thea!

MRS. ELVSTED. [*Ignoring her*] I must see him! I must see him before he dies!

BRACK. It's no use, Mrs. Elvsted. No one's allowed to see him now.

MRS. ELVSTED. But what's happened to him? You must tell me!

TESMAN. He hasn't tried to do anything to himself? What?

HEDDA. Yes, he has. I'm sure of it.

TESMAN. Hedda, how can you——?

BRACK. [*Who has not taken his eyes from her*] I'm afraid you've guessed correctly, Mrs. Tesman.

MRS. ELVSTED. How dreadful!

TESMAN. Attempted suicide! Fancy that!

HEDDA. Shot himself!

BRACK. Right again, Mrs. Tesman.

MRS. ELVSTED. [*Tries to compose herself*] When did this happen, Judge Brack?

BRACK. This afternoon. Between three and four.

TESMAN. But, good heavens—where? What?

BRACK. [*A little hesitantly*] Where? Why, my dear chap, in his rooms of course.

MRS. ELVSTED. No, that's impossible. I was there soon after six.

BRACK. Well, it must have been somewhere else, then. I don't know exactly. I only know that they found him. He'd shot himself—through the breast.

MRS. ELVSTED. Oh, how horrible! That he should end like that!

HEDDA. [*To* BRACK] Through the breast, you said?

BRACK. That is what I said.

HEDDA. Not through the head?

BRACK. Through the breast, Mrs. Tesman.

HEDDA. The breast. Yes; yes. That's good, too.

BRACK. Why, Mrs. Tesman?

HEDDA. Oh—no, I didn't mean anything.

TESMAN. And the wound's dangerous, you say? What?

BRACK. Mortal. He's probably already dead.

MRS. ELVSTED. Yes, yes—I feel it! It's all over. All over. Oh Hedda——!

TESMAN. But, tell me, how did you manage to learn all this?

BRACK. [*Curtly*] From the police. I spoke to one of them.

HEDDA. [*Loudly, clearly*] At last! Oh, thank God!
TESMAN. [*Appalled*] For God's sake, Hedda, what are you saying?
HEDDA. I am saying there's beauty in what he has done.
BRACK. Mm—Mrs. Tesman——
TESMAN. Beauty! Oh, but I say!
MRS. ELVSTED. Hedda, how can you talk of beauty in connection with a thing like this?
HEDDA. Eilert Loevborg has settled his account with life. He's had the courage to do what—what he had to do.
MRS. ELVSTED. No, that's not why it happened. He did it because he was mad.
TESMAN. He did it because he was desperate.
HEDDA. You're wrong! I know!
MRS. ELVSTED. He must have been mad. The same as when he tore up the manuscript.
BRACK. [*Starts*] Manuscript? Did he tear it up?
MRS. ELVSTED. Yes. Last night.
TESMAN. [*Whispers*] Oh, Hedda, we shall never be able to escape from this.
BRACK. Hm. Strange.
TESMAN. [*Wanders round the room*] To think of Eilert dying like that. And not leaving behind him the thing that would have made his name endure.
MRS. ELVSTED. If only it could be pieced together again!
TESMAN. Yes, fancy! If only it could! I'd give anything——
MRS. ELVSTED. Perhaps it can, Mr. Tesman.
TESMAN. What do you mean?
MRS. ELVSTED. [*Searches in the pocket of her dress*] Look! I kept the notes he dictated it from.
HEDDA. [*Takes a step nearer*] Ah!
TESMAN. You kept them, Mrs. Elvsted! What?
MRS. ELVSTED. Yes, here they are. I brought them with me when I left home. They've been in my pocket ever since.
TESMAN. Let me have a look.
MRS. ELVSTED. [*Hands him a wad of small sheets of paper*] They're in a terrible muddle. All mixed up.
TESMAN. I say, just fancy if we can sort them out! Perhaps if we work on them together——?
MRS. ELVSTED. Oh, yes! Let's try, anyway!
TESMAN. We'll manage it. We must! I shall dedicate my life to this.
HEDDA. *You*, George? Your life?
TESMAN. Yes—well, all the time I can spare. My book'll have to wait. Hedda, you do understand? What? I owe it to Eilert's memory.
HEDDA. Perhaps.
TESMAN. Well, my dear Mrs. Elvsted, you and I'll have to pool our brains. No use crying over spilt milk, what? We must try to approach this matter calmly.

MRS. ELVSTED. Yes, yes, Mr. Tesman. I'll do my best.

TESMAN. Well, come over here and let's start looking at these notes right away. Where shall we sit? Here? No, the other room. You'll excuse us, won't you, Judge? Come along with me, Mrs. Elvsted.

MRS. ELVSTED. Oh, God! If only we can manage to do it!

[TESMAN *and* MRS. ELVSTED *go into the rear room. He takes off his hat and overcoat. They sit at the table beneath the hanging lamp and absorb themselves in the notes.* HEDDA *walks across to the stove and sits in the armchair. After a moment,* BRACK *goes over to her.*]

HEDDA. [*Half aloud*] Oh, Judge! This act of Eilert Loevborg's—doesn't it give one a sense of release!

BRACK. Release, Mrs. Hedda? Well, it's a release for him, of course——

HEDDA. Oh, I don't mean him—I mean me! The release of knowing that someone can do something really brave! Something beautiful!

BRACK. [*Smiles*] Hm—my dear Mrs. Hedda——

HEDDA. Oh, I know what you're going to say. You're a bourgeois at heart too, just like—ah, well!

BRACK. [*Looks at her*] Eilert Loevborg has meant more to you than you're willing to admit to yourself. Or am I wrong?

HEDDA. I'm not answering questions like that from you. I only know that Eilert Loevborg has had the courage to live according to his own principles. And now, at last, he's done something big! Something beautiful! To have the courage and the will to rise from the feast of life so early!

BRACK. It distresses me deeply, Mrs. Hedda, but I'm afraid I must rob you of that charming illusion.

HEDDA. Illusion?

BRACK. You wouldn't have been allowed to keep it for long, anyway.

HEDDA. What do you mean?

BRACK. He didn't shoot himself on purpose.

HEDDA. Not on purpose?

BRACK. No. It didn't happen quite the way I told you.

HEDDA. Have you been hiding something? What is it?

BRACK. In order to spare poor Mrs. Elvsted's feelings, I permitted myself one or two small—equivocations.

HEDDA. What?

BRACK. To begin with, he is already dead.

HEDDA. He died at the hospital?

BRACK. Yes. Without regaining consciousness.

HEDDA. What else haven't you told us?

BRACK. The incident didn't take place at his lodgings.

HEDDA. Well, that's utterly unimportant.

BRACK. Not utterly. The fact is, you see, that Eilert Loevborg was found shot in Mademoiselle Danielle's boudoir.

HEDDA. [*Almost jumps up, but instead sinks back in her chair*]

That's impossible. He can't have been there today.

BRACK. He was there this afternoon. He went to ask for something he claimed they'd taken from him. Talked some crazy nonsense about a child which had got lost——

HEDDA. Oh! So that was the reason!

BRACK. I thought at first he might have been referring to his manuscript. But I hear he destroyed that himself. So he must have meant his pocketbook—I suppose.

HEDDA. Yes, I suppose so. So they found him there?

BRACK. Yes; there. With a discharged pistol in his breast pocket. The shot had wounded him mortally.

HEDDA. Yes. In the breast.

BRACK. No. In the—hm—stomach. The—lower part——

HEDDA. [*Looks at him with an expression of repulsion*] That too! Oh, why does everything I touch become mean and ludicrous? It's like a curse!

BRACK. There's something else, Mrs. Hedda. It's rather disagreeable, too.

HEDDA. What?

BRACK. The pistol he had on him——

HEDDA. Yes? What about it?

BRACK. He must have stolen it.

HEDDA. [*Jumps up*] Stolen it! That isn't true! He didn't!

BRACK. It's the only explanation. He must have stolen it. Ssh!

[TESMAN *and* MRS. ELVSTED *have got up from the table in the rear room and come into the drawing room.*]

TESMAN. [*His hands full of papers*] Hedda, I can't see properly under that lamp. Think!

HEDDA. I am thinking.

TESMAN. Do you think we could possibly use your writing table for a little? What?

HEDDA. Yes, of course. [*Quickly*] No, wait! Let me tidy it up first.

TESMAN. Oh, don't you trouble about that. There's plenty of room.

HEDDA. No, no, let me tidy it up first, I say. I'll take this in and put them on the piano. Here.

[*She pulls an object, covered with sheets of music, out from under the bookcase, puts some more sheets on top and carries it all into the rear room and away to the left.* TESMAN *puts his papers on the writing table and moves the lamp over from the corner table. He and* MRS. ELVSTED *sit down and begin working again.* HEDDA *comes back.*]

HEDDA. [*Behind* MRS. ELVSTED'S *chair, ruffles her hair gently*] Well, my pretty Thea! And how is work progressing on Eilert Loevborg's memorial?

MRS. ELVSTED. [*Looks up at her, dejectedly*] Oh, it's going to be terribly difficult to get these into any order.

TESMAN. We've got to do it. We must! After all, putting other people's papers into order is rather my specialty, what?

[HEDDA *goes over to the stove and sits on one of the foot-*

stools. BRACK *stands over her, leaning against the armchair.*]

HEDDA. [*Whispers*] What was that you were saying about the pistol?

BRACK. [*Softly*] I said he must have stolen it.

HEDDA. Why do you think that?

BRACK. Because any other explanation is unthinkable, Mrs. Hedda, or ought to be.

HEDDA. I see.

BRACK. [*Looks at her for a moment*] Eilert Loevborg was here this morning. Wasn't he?

HEDDA. Yes.

BRACK. Were you alone with him?

HEDDA. For a few moments.

BRACK. You didn't leave the room while he was here?

HEDDA. No.

BRACK. Think again. Are you sure you didn't go out for a moment?

HEDDA. Oh—yes, I might have gone into the hall. Just for a few seconds.

BRACK. And where was your pistol-case during this time?

HEDDA. I'd locked it in that——

BRACK. Er—Mrs. Hedda?

HEDDA. It was lying over there on my writing table.

BRACK. Have you looked to see if both the pistols are still there?

HEDDA. No.

BRACK. You needn't bother. I saw the pistol Loevborg had when they found him. I recognized it at once. From yesterday. And other occasions.

HEDDA. Have you got it?

BRACK. No. The police have it.

HEDDA. What will the police do with this pistol?

BRACK. Try to trace the owner.

HEDDA. Do you think they'll succeed?

BRACK. [*Leans down and whispers*] No, Hedda Gabler. Not as long as I hold my tongue.

HEDDA. [*Looks nervously at him*] And if you don't?

BRACK. [*Shrugs his shoulders*] You could always say he'd stolen it.

HEDDA. I'd rather die!

BRACK. [*Smiles*] People say that. They never do it.

HEDDA. [*Not replying*] And suppose the pistol wasn't stolen? And they trace the owner? What then?

BRACK. There'll be a scandal, Hedda.

HEDDA. A scandal!

BRACK. Yes, a scandal. The thing you're so frightened of. You'll have to appear in court. Together with Mademoiselle Danielle. She'll have to explain how it all happened. Was it an accident, or was it—homicide? Was he about to take the pistol from his pocket to threaten her? And did it go off? Or did she snatch the pistol from his hand, shoot him and then put it back in his pocket? She might quite easily have done it. She's a resourceful lady, is Mademoiselle Danielle.

HEDDA. But I had nothing to do with this repulsive business.

BRACK. No. But you'll have to answer one question. Why did you give Eilert Loevborg this pistol? And what conclusions will people draw when it is proved you did give it to him?

HEDDA. [*Bows her head*] That's true. I hadn't thought of that.

BRACK. Well, luckily there's no danger as long as I hold my tongue.

HEDDA. [*Looks up at him*] In other words, I'm in your power, Judge. From now on, you've got your hold over me.

BRACK. [*Whispers, more slowly*] Hedda, my dearest—believe me—I will not abuse my position.

HEDDA. Nevertheless, I'm in your power. Dependent on your will, and your demands. Not free. Still not free! [*Rises passionately*] No. I couldn't bear that. No.

BRACK. [*Looks half-derisively at her*] Most people resign themselves to the inevitable, sooner or later.

HEDDA. [*Returns his gaze*] Possibly they do.

[*She goes across to the writing table.*]

HEDDA. [*Represses an involuntary smile and says in* TESMAN'S *voice*] Well, George. Think you'll be able to manage? What?

TESMAN. Heaven knows, dear. This is going to take months and months.

HEDDA. [*In the same tone as before*] Fancy that, by Jove! [*Runs her hands gently through* MRS. ELVSTED'S *hair*] Doesn't it feel strange, Thea? Here you are working away with Tesman just the way you used to work with Eilert Loevborg.

MRS. ELVSTED. Oh—if only I can inspire your husband too!

HEDDA. Oh, it'll come. In time.

TESMAN. Yes—do you know, Hedda, I really think I'm beginning to feel a bit—well—that way. But you go back and talk to Judge Brack.

HEDDA. Can't I be of use to you two in any way?

TESMAN. No, none at all. [*Turns his head*] You'll have to keep Hedda company from now on, Judge, and see she doesn't get bored. If you don't mind.

BRACK. [*Glances at* HEDDA] It'll be a pleasure.

HEDDA. Thank you. But I'm tired this evening. I think I'll lie down on the sofa in there for a little while.

TESMAN. Yes, dear—do. What?

[HEDDA *goes into the rear room and draws the curtains behind her. Short pause. Suddenly she begins to play a frenzied dance melody on the piano.*]

MRS. ELVSTED. [*Starts up from her chair*] Oh, what's that?

TESMAN. [*Runs to the doorway*] Hedda dear, please! Don't play dance music tonight! Think of Auntie Rena. And Eilert.

HEDDA. [*Puts her head out through the curtains*] And Auntie Juju. And all the rest of them. From now on I'll be quiet.

[*Closes the curtains behind her*]

TESMAN. [*At the writing table*] It distresses her to watch us doing this. I say, Mrs. Elvsted, I've an idea. Why don't you move in with Auntie Juju? I'll run over each evening, and we can sit and work there. What?

MRS. ELVSTED. Yes, that might be the best plan.

HEDDA. [*From the rear room*] I can hear what you're saying, Tesman. But how shall I spend the evenings out here?

TESMAN. [*Looking through his papers*] Oh, I'm sure Judge Brack'll be kind enough to come over and keep you company. You won't mind my not being here, Judge?

BRACK. [*In the armchair, calls gaily*] I'll be delighted, Mrs. Tesman. I'll be here every evening. We'll have great fun together, you and I.

HEDDA. [*Loud and clear*] Yes, that'll suit you, won't it, Judge? The only cock on the dunghill——!

[*A shot is heard from the rear room.* TESMAN, MRS. ELVSTED *and* JUDGE BRACK *start from their chairs.*]

TESMAN. Oh, she's playing with those pistols again.

[*He pulls the curtains aside and runs in.* MRS. ELVSTED *follows him.* HEDDA *is lying dead on the sofa. Confusion and shouting.* BERTHA *enters in alarm from the right.*]

TESMAN. [*Screams to* BRACK] She's shot herself! Shot herself in the head! By Jove! Fancy that!

BRACK. [*Half paralyzed in the armchair*] But, good God! People don't do such things!

ANTON CHEKHOV

(1860–1904)

The Cherry Orchard*

Characters

LUBOV ANDREYEVNA RANEVSKAYA, *a landowner*
ANYA, *her seventeen-year-old daughter*
VARYA, *her adopted daughter, twenty-two years old*
LEONID ANDREYEVICH GAYEV, *Mme. Ranevskaya's brother*
YERMOLAY ALEXEYEVICH LOPAHIN, *a merchant*
PYOTR SERGEYEVICH TROFIMOV, a student
SIMEONOV-PISHCHIK, *a landowner*
CHARLOTTA IVANOVNA, *a governess*
SEMYON YEPIHODOV, *a clerk*
DUNYASHA, *a maid*
FIRS (pronounced *fierce*), *a manservant, aged eighty-seven*

* Translated by Avraham Yarmolinsky.

YASHA, *a young valet*
A TRAMP
STATIONMASTER
POST OFFICE CLERK
GUESTS
SERVANTS

The action takes place on Mme. Ranevskaya's estate.

Act I

A room that is still called the nursery. One of the doors leads into ANYA*'s room. Dawn, the sun will soon rise. It is May, the cherry trees are in blossom, but it is cold in the orchard; there is a morning frost. The windows are shut. Enter* DUNYASHA *with a candle, and* LOPAHIN *with a book in his hand.*

LOPAHIN: The train is in, thank God. What time is it?

DUNYASHA: Nearly two. [*Puts out the candle.*] It's light already.

LOPAHIN: How late is the train, anyway? Two hours at least. [*Yawns and stretches.*] I'm a fine one! What a fool I've made of myself! I came here on purpose to meet them at the station, and then I went and overslept. I fell asleep in my chair. How annoying! You might have waked me . . .

DUNYASHA: I thought you'd left. [*Listens.*] I think they're coming!

LOPAHIN: [*Listens.*] No, they've got to get the luggage, and one thing and another . . . [*Pause.*] Lubov Andreyevna spent five years abroad, I don't know what she's like now. . . . She's a fine person—lighthearted, simple. I remember when I was a boy of fifteen, my poor father—he had a shop here in the village then—punched me in the face with his fist and made my nose bleed. We'd come into the yard, I don't know what for, and he'd had a drop too much. Lubov Andreyevna, I remember her as if it were yesterday—she was still young and so slim—led me to the washbasin, in this very room . . . in the nursery. "Don't cry, little peasant," she said, "it'll heal in time for your wedding . . ." [*Pause.*] Little peasant . . . my father was a peasant, it's true, and here I am in a white waistcoat and yellow shoes. A pig in a pastry shop, you might say. It's true I'm rich. I've got a lot of money. . . . But when you look at it closely, I'm a peasant through and through. [*Pages the book.*] Here I've been reading this book and I didn't understand a word of it. . . . I was reading it and fell asleep . . . [*Pause.*]

DUNYASHA: And the dogs were awake all night, they feel that their masters are coming.

LOPAHIN: Dunyasha, why are you so—

DUNYASHA: My hands are trembling. I'm going to faint.

LOPAHIN: You're too soft, Dunyasha. You dress like a lady, and look at the way you do your hair. That's not right. One should remember one's place.

[*Enter* YEPIHODOV *with a bouquet; he wears a jacket and highly polished boots that squeak badly. He drops the bouquet as he comes in.*]

YEPIHODOV: [*Picking up the bouquet.*] Here, the gardener sent these, said you're to put them in the dining room. [*Hands the bouquet to* DUNYASHA.]

LOPAHIN: And bring me some kvass.

DUNYASHA: Yes, sir. [*Exits.*]

YEPIHODOV: There's a frost this morning—three degrees below—and yet the cherries are all in blossom. I cannot approve of our climate. [*Sighs.*] I cannot. Our climate does not activate properly. And, Yermolay Alexeyevich, allow me to make a further remark. The other day I bought myself a pair of boots, and I make bold to assure you, they squeak so that it is really intolerable. What should I grease them with?

LOPAHIN: Oh, get out! I'm fed up with you.

YEPIHODOV: Every day I meet with misfortune. And I don't complain, I've got used to it, I even smile.

[DUNYASHA *enters, hands* LOPAHIN *the kvass.*]

YEPIHODOV: I am leaving [*Stumbles against a chair, which falls over.*] There! [*Triumphantly, as it were.*] There again, you see what sort of circumstance, pardon the expression. . . . It is absolutely phenomenal! [*Exits.*]

DUNYASHA: You know, Yermolay Alexeyevich, I must tell you, Yepihodov has proposed to me.

LOPAHIN: Ah!

DUNYASHA: I simply don't know . . . he's a quiet man, but sometimes when he starts talking, you can't make out what he means. He speaks nicely—and it's touching—but you can't understand it. I sort of like him though, and he is crazy about me. He's an unlucky man . . . every day something happens to him. They tease him about it here . . . they call him, Two-and-Twenty Troubles.

LOPAHIN: [*Listening.*] There! I think they're coming.

DUNYASHA: They *are* coming! What's the matter with me? I feel cold all over.

LOPAHIN: They really are coming. Let's go and meet them. Will she recognize me? We haven't seen each other for five years.

DUNYASHA: [*In a flutter.*] I'm going to faint this minute. . . . Oh, I'm going to faint!

[*Two carriages are heard driving up to the house.* LOPAHIN *and* DUNYASHA *go out quickly. The stage is left empty. There is a noise in the adjoining rooms.* FIRS, *who had driven to the station to meet* LUBOV ANDREYEVNA RANEVSKAYA, *crosses the stage hurriedly, leaning on a stick. He is wearing an old-fashioned livery and a tall hat. He mutters to himself indistinctly. The hubbub offstage increases.* A VOICE: "Come, let's go this way." *Enter* LUBOV ANDREYEVNA, ANYA, *and* CHARLOTTA IVANOVNA *with a pet dog on a leash, all in traveling dresses;* VARYA, *wearing a coat and kerchief;* GAYEV,

SIMEONOV-PISHCHIK, LOPAHIN, DUNYASHA *with a bag and an umbrella, servants with luggage. All walk across the room.*]

ANYA: Let's go this way. Do you remember what room this is, Mamma?

MME. RANEVSKAYA: [*Joyfully, through her tears.*] The nursery!

VARYA: How cold it is! My hands are numb. [*To* MME. RANEVSKAYA.] Your rooms are just the same as they were, Mamma, the white one and the violet.

MME. RANEVSKAYA: The nursery! My darling, lovely room! I slept here when I was a child . . . [*Cries.*] And here I am, like a child again! [*Kisses her brother and* VARYA, *and then her brother again.*] Varya's just the same as ever, like a nun. And I recognized Dunyasha. [*Kisses* DUNYASHA.]

GAYEV: The train was two hours late. What do you think of that? What a way to manage things!

CHARLOTTA: [*To* PISHCHIK.] My dog eats nuts, too.

PISHCHIK: [*In amazement.*] You don't say!

[*All go out, except* ANYA *and* DUNYASHA.]

DUNYASHA: We've been waiting for you for hours. [*Takes* ANYA'*s hat and coat.*]

ANYA: I didn't sleep on the train for four nights and now I'm frozen . . .

DUNYASHA: It was Lent when you left; there was snow and frost, and now . . . My darling! [*Laughs and kisses her.*] I have been waiting for you, my sweet, my darling! But I must tell you something . . . I can't put it off another minute . . .

ANYA: [*Listlessly.*] What now?

DUNYASHA: The clerk, Yepihodov, proposed to me, just after Easter.

ANYA: There you are, at it again . . . [*Straightening her hair.*] I've lost all my hairpins . . . [*She is staggering with exhaustion.*]

DUNYASHA: Really, I don't know what to think. He loves me—he loves me so!

ANYA: [*Looking toward the door of her room, tenderly.*] My own room, my windows, just as though I'd never been away. I'm home! Tomorrow morning I'll get up and run into the orchard. Oh, if I could only get some sleep. I didn't close my eyes during the whole journey—I was so anxious.

DUNYASHA: Pyotr Sergeyevich came the day before yesterday.

ANYA: [*Joyfully.*] Petya!

DUNYASHA: He's asleep in the bathhouse. He has settled there. He said he was afraid of being in the way. [*Looks at her watch.*] I should wake him, but Miss Varya told me not to. "Don't you wake him," she said.

[*Enter* VARYA *with a bunch of keys at her belt.*]

VARYA: Dunyasha, coffee, and be quick. . . . Mamma's asking for coffee.

DUNYASHA: In a minute. [*Exits.*]

VARYA: Well, thank God, you've come. You're home again. [*Fondling* ANYA.] My darling is here again. My pretty one is back.

ANYA: Oh, what I've been through!

VARYA: I can imagine.

ANYA: When we left, it was Holy Week, it was cold then, and all the way Charlotta chattered and did her tricks. Why did you have to saddle me with Charlotta?

VARYA: You couldn't have traveled all alone, darling—at seventeen!

ANYA: We got to Paris, it was cold there, snowing. My French is dreadful. Mamma lived on the fifth floor; I went up there, and found all kinds of Frenchmen, ladies, an old priest with a book. The place was full of tobacco smoke, and so bleak. Suddenly I felt sorry for Mamma, so sorry, I took her head in my arms and hugged her and couldn't let go of her. Afterward Mamma kept fondling me and crying . . .

VARYA: [*Through tears.*] Don't speak of it . . . don't.

ANYA: She had already sold her villa at Mentone, she had nothing left, nothing. I hadn't a kopeck left either, we had only just enough to get home. And Mamma wouldn't understand! When we had dinner at the stations, she always ordered the most expensive dishes, and tipped the waiters a whole ruble. Charlotta, too. And Yasha kept ordering, too—it was simply awful. You know Yasha's Mamma's footman now, we brought him here with us.

VARYA: Yes, I've seen the blackguard.

ANYA: Well, tell me—have you paid the interest?

VARYA: How could we?

ANYA: Good heavens, good heavens!

VARYA: In August the estate will be put up for sale.

ANYA: My God!

LOPAHIN: [*Peeps in at the door and bleats*]. Meh-h-h. [*Disappears.*]

VARYA: [*Through tears.*] What I couldn't do to him! [*Shakes her fist threateningly.*]

ANYA: [*Embracing* VARYA, *gently.*] Varya, has he proposed to you? [VARYA *shakes her head.*] But he loves you. Why don't you come to an understanding? What are you waiting for?

VARYA: Oh, I don't think anything will ever come of it. He's too busy, he has no time for me . . . pays no attention to me. I've washed my hands of him—I can't bear the sight of him. They all talk about our getting married, they all congratulate me—and all the time there's really nothing to it—it's all like a dream. [*In another tone.*] You have a new brooch—like a bee.

ANYA: [*Sadly.*] Mamma bought it. [*She goes into her own room and speaks gaily like a child.*] And you know, in Paris I went up in a balloon.

VARYA: My darling's home, my pretty one is back! [DUNYASHA *returns with the coffeepot and prepares coffee.* VARYA *stands at the door of* ANYA*'s room.*] All day long, darling, as I go about the house, I keep dreaming. If only we could marry you off to a rich man, I should feel at ease. Then I would go into a convent, and afterward to Kiev, to Moscow . . . I would spend my life going from one holy place to another . . . I'd go on and on. . . . What a blessing that would be!

ANYA: The birds are singing in the orchard. What time is it?

VARYA: It must be after two. Time you were asleep, darling. [*Goes into* ANYA's *room.*] What a blessing that would be!

[YASHA *enters with a plaid and a traveling bag, crosses the stage.*]

YASHA: [*Finically.*] May I pass this way, please?

DUNYASHA: A person could hardly recognize you, Yasha. Your stay aboard has certainly done wonders for you.

YASHA: Hm-m . . . and who are you?

DUNYASHA: When you went away I was that high—[*Indicating with her hand.*] I'm Dunyasha—Fyodor Kozoyedev's daughter. Don't you remember?

YASHA: Hm! What a peach! [*He looks round and embraces her. She cries out and drops a saucer.* YASHA *leaves quickly.*]

VARYA: [*In the doorway, in a tone of annoyance.*] What's going on here?

DUNYASHA: [*Through tears.*] I've broken a saucer.

VARYA: Well, that's good luck.

ANYA: [*Coming out of her room.*] We ought to warn Mamma that Petya's here.

VARYA: I left orders not to wake him.

ANYA: [*Musingly.*] Six years ago father died. A month later brother Grisha was drowned in the river. . . . Such a pretty little boy he was—only seven. It was more than Mamma could bear, so she went away, went away without looking back . . . [*Shudders.*] How well I understand her, if she only knew! [*Pauses.*] And Petya Trofimov was Grisha's tutor, he may remind her of it all . . .

[*Enter* FIRS, *wearing a jacket and a white waistcoat. He goes up to the coffeepot.*]

FIRS: [*Anxiously.*] The mistress will have her coffee here. [*Puts on white gloves.*] Is the coffee ready? [*Sternly, to* DUNYASHA.] Here, you! And where's the cream?

DUNYASHA: Oh, my God! [*Exits quickly.*]

FIRS: [*Fussing over the coffeepot.*] Hah! the addlehead! [*Mutters to himself.*] Home from Paris. And the old master used to go to Paris too . . . by carriage. [*Laughs.*]

VARYA: What is it, Firs?

FIRS: What is your pleasure, Miss? [*Joyfully.*] My mistress has come home, and I've seen her at last! Now I can die. [*Weeps with joy.*]

[*Enter* MME. RANEVSKAYA, GAYEV, *and* SIMEONOV-PISHCHIK. *The latter is wearing a tight-waisted, pleated coat of fine cloth, and full trousers.* GAYEV, *as he comes in, goes through the motions of a billiard player with his arms and body.*]

MME. RANEVSKAYA: Let's see, how does it go? Yellow ball in the corner! Bank shot in the side pocket!

GAYEV: I'll tip it in the corner! There was a time, Sister, when you and I used to sleep in this very room and now I'm fifty-one, strange as it may seem.

LOPAHIN: Yes, time flies.

GAYEV: Who?

LOPAHIN: I say, time flies.

GAYEV: It smells of patchouli here.

ANYA: I'm going to bed. Good night, Mamma. [*Kisses her mother.*]

MME. RANEVSKAYA: My darling child! [*Kisses her hands.*] Are you happy to be home? I can't come to my senses.

ANYA: Good night, Uncle.

GAYEV: [*Kissing her face and hands.*] God bless you, how like your mother you are! [*To his sister.*] At her age, Luba, you were just like her.

[ANYA *shakes hands with* LOPAHIN *and* PISHCHIK, *then goes out, shutting the door behind her.*]

MME. RANEVSKAYA: She's very tired.

PISHCHIK: Well, it was a long journey.

VARYA: [*To* LOPAHIN *and* PISHCHIK.] How about it, gentlemen? It's past two o'clock—isn't it time for you to go?

MME. RANEVSKAYA: [*Laughs.*] You're just the same as ever, Varya. [*Draws her close and kisses her.*] I'll have my coffee and then we'll all go. [FIRS *puts a small cushion under her feet.*] Thank you, my dear. I've got used to coffee. I drink it day and night. Thanks, my dear old man. [*Kisses him.*]

VARYA: I'd better see if all the luggage has been brought in. [*Exits.*]

MME. RANEVSKAYA: Can it really be I sitting here? [*Laughs.*] I feel like dancing, waving my arms about. [*Covers her face with her hands.*] But maybe I am dreaming! God knows I love my country, I love it tenderly; I couldn't look out of the window in the train, I kept crying so. [*Through tears.*] But I must have my coffee. Thank you, Firs, thank you, dear old man. I'm so happy that you're still alive.

FIRS: Day before yesterday.

GAYEV: He's hard of hearing.

LOPAHIN: I must go soon, I'm leaving for Kharkov about five o'clock. How annoying! I'd like to have a good look at you, talk to you. . . . You're just as splendid as ever.

PISHCHIK: [*Breathing heavily.*] She's even better-looking. . . . Dressed in the latest Paris fashion. . . . Perish my carriage and all its four wheels. . . .

LOPAHIN: Your brother, Leonid Andreyevich, says I'm a vulgarian and an exploiter. But it's all the same to me—let him talk. I only want you to trust me as you used to. I want you to look at me with your touching, wonderful eyes, as you used to. Dear God! My father was a serf of your father's and grandfather's, but you, you yourself, did so much for me once . . . so much . . . that I've forgotten all about that; I love you as though you were my sister —even more.

MME. RANEVSKAYA: I can't sit still, I simply can't. [*Jumps up and walks about in violent agitation.*] This joy is too much for me. . . . Laugh at me, I'm silly! My own darling bookcase! My darling table! [*Kisses it.*]

GAYEV: While you were away, nurse died.

MME. RANEVSKAYA: [*Sits down and takes her coffee.*] Yes, God rest her soul; they wrote me about it.

GAYEV: And Anastasy is dead. Petrushka Kossoy has left me and has gone into town to work for the police inspector. [*Takes a box of sweets out of his pocket and begins to suck one.*]

PISHCHIK: My daughter Dashenka sends her regards.

LOPAHIN: I'd like to tell you something very pleasant—cheering. [*Glancing at his watch.*] I am leaving directly. There isn't much time to talk. But I will put it in a few words. As you know, your cherry orchard is to be sold to pay your debts. The sale is to be on the twenty-second of August; but don't you worry, my dear, you may sleep in peace; there is a way out. Here is my plan. Give me your attention! Your estate is only fifteen miles from the town; the railway runs close by it; and if the cherry orchard and the land along the riverbank were cut up into lots and these leased for summer cottages, you would have an income of at least 25,000 rubles a year out of it.

GAYEV: Excuse me. . . . What nonsense.

MME. RANEVSKAYA: I don't quite understand you, Yermolay Alexeyevich.

LOPAHIN: You will get an annual rent of at least ten rubles per acre, and if you advertise at once, I'll give you any guarantee you like that you won't have a square foot of ground left by autumn, all the lots will be snapped up. In short, congratulations, you're saved. The location is splendid—by that deep river. . . . Only, of course, the ground must be cleared . . . all the old buildings, for instance, must be torn down, and this house, too, which is useless, and, of course, the old cherry orchard must be cut down.

MME. RANEVSKAYA: Cut down? My dear, forgive me, but you don't know what you're talking about. If there's one thing that's interesting—indeed, remarkable—in the whole province, it's precisely our cherry orchard.

LOPAHIN: The only remarkable thing about this orchard is that it's a very large one. There's a crop of cherries every other year, and you can't do anything with them; no one buys them.

GAYEV: This orchard is even mentioned in the encyclopedia.

LOPAHIN: [*Glancing at his watch.*] If we can't think of a way out, if we don't come to a decision, on the twenty-second of August the cherry orchard and the whole estate will be sold at auction. Make up your minds! There's no other way out—I swear. None, none.

FIRS: In the old days, forty or fifty years ago, the cherries were dried, soaked, pickled, and made into jam, and we used to—

GAYEV: Keep still, Firs.

FIRS: And the dried cherries would be shipped by the cartload. It meant a lot of money! And in those days the dried cherries were soft and juicy, sweet, fragrant. . . . They knew the way to do it, then.

MME. RANEVSKAYA: And why don't they do it that way now?

FIRS: They've forgotten. Nobody remembers it.

PISHCHIK: [*To* MME. RANEVSKAYA.] What's doing in Paris? Eh? Did you eat frogs there?

MME. RANEVSKAYA: I ate crocodiles.

PISHCHIK: Just imagine!

LOPAHIN: There used to be only landowners and peasants in the country, but now these summer people have appeared on the scene. . . . All the towns, even the small ones, are surrounded by these summer cottages; and in another twenty years, no doubt, the summer population will have grown enormously. Now the summer resident only drinks tea on his porch, but maybe he'll take to working his acre, too, and then your cherry orchard will be a rich, happy, luxuriant place.

GAYEV: [*Indignantly.*] Poppycock!

[*Enter* VARYA *and* YASHA.]

VARYA: There are two telegrams for you, Mamma dear. [*Picks a key from the bunch at her belt and noisily opens an old-fashioned bookcase.*] Here they are.

MME. RANEVSKAYA: They're from Paris. [*Tears them up without reading them.*] I'm through with Paris.

GAYEV: Do you know, Luba, how old this bookcase is? Last week I pulled out the bottom drawer and there I found the date burnt in it. It was made exactly a hundred years ago. Think of that! We could celebrate its centenary. True, it's an inanimate object, but nevertheless, a bookcase . . .

PISHCHIK: [*Amazed.*] A hundred years! Just imagine!

GAYEV: Yes. [*Tapping it.*] That's something. . . . Dear, honored bookcase, hail to you who for more than a century have served the glorious ideals of goodness and justice! Your silent summons to fruitful toil has never weakened in all those hundred years [*through tears*], sustaining, through successive generations of our family, courage and faith in a better future, and fostering in us ideals of goodness and social consciousness. . . . [*Pauses.*]

LOPAHIN: Yes . . .

MME. RANEVSKAYA: You haven't changed a bit, Leonid.

GAYEV: [*Somewhat embarrassed.*] I'll play it off the red in the corner! Tip it in the side pocket!

LOPAHIN: [*Looking at his watch.*] Well, it's time for me to go . . .

YASHA: [*Handing a pillbox to* MME. RANEVSKAYA.] Perhaps you'll take your pills now.

PISHCHIK: One shouldn't take medicines, dearest lady, they do neither harm nor good. . . . Give them here, my valued friend. [*Takes the pillbox, pours the pills into his palm, blows on them, puts them in his mouth, and washes them down with some kvass.*] There!

MME. RANEVSKAYA: [*Frightened.*] You must be mad!

PISHCHIK: I've taken all the pills.

LOPAHIN: What a glutton!

[*All laugh.*]

FIRS: The gentleman visited us in Easter week, ate half a bucket of pickles, he did . . . [*Mumbles.*]

MME. RANEVSKAYA: What's he saying?

VARYA: He's been mumbling like that for the last three years—we're used to it.

YASHA: His declining years!

[CHARLOTTA IVANOVNA, *very thin, tightly laced, dressed in*

white, a lorgnette at her waist, crosses the stage.]

LOPAHIN: Forgive me, Charlotta Ivanovna, I've not had time to greet you. [*Tries to kiss her hand.*]

CHARLOTTA: [*Pulling away her hand.*] If I let you kiss my hand, you'll be wanting to kiss my elbow next, and then my shoulder.

LOPAHIN: I've no luck today. [*All laugh.*] Charlotta Ivanovna, show us a trick.

MME. RANEVSKAYA: Yes, Charlotta, do a trick for us.

CHARLOTTA: I don't see the need. I want to sleep. [*Exits.*]

LOPAHIN: In three weeks we'll meet again. [*Kisses* MME. RANEVSKAYA'*s hand.*] Good-bye till then. Time's up. [*To* GAYEV.] Bye-bye. [*Kisses* PISHCHIK.] Bye-bye. [*Shakes hands with* VARYA, *then with* FIRS *and* YASHA.] I hate to leave. [*To* MME. RANEVSKAYA.] If you make up your mind about the cottages, let me know; I'll get you a loan of 50,000 rubles. Think it over seriously.

VARYA: [*Crossly.*] Will you never go!

LOPAHIN: I'm going, I'm going. [*Exits.*]

GAYEV: The vulgarian. But, excuse me . . . Varya's going to marry him, he's Varya's fiancé.

VARYA: You talk too much, Uncle.

MME. RANEVSKAYA: Well, Varya, it would make me happy. He's a good man.

PISHCHIK: Yes, one must admit, he's a most estimable man. And my Dashenka . . . she too says that . . . she says . . . lots of things. [*Snores; but wakes up at once.*] All the same, my valued friend, could you oblige me . . . with a loan of 240 rubles? I must pay the interest on the mortgage tomorrow.

VARYA: [*Alarmed.*] We can't, we can't!

MME. RANEVSKAYA: I really haven't any money.

PISHCHIK: It'll turn up. [*Laughs.*] I never lose hope, I thought everything was lost, that I was done for, when lo and behold, the railway ran through my land . . . and I was paid for it. . . . And something else will turn up again, if not today, then tomorrow . . . Dashenka will win two hundred thousand . . . she's got a lottery ticket.

MME. RANEVSKAYA: I've had my coffee, now let's go to bed.

FIRS: [*Brushes off* GAYEV; *admonishingly.*] You've got the wrong trousers on again. What am I to do with you?

VARYA: [*Softly.*] Anya's asleep. [*Gently opens the window.*] The sun's up now, it's not a bit cold. Look, Mamma dear, what wonderful trees. And heavens, what air! The starlings are singing!

GAYEV: [*Opens the other window.*] The orchard is all white. You've not forgotten it? Luba? That's the long alley that runs straight, straight as an arrow; how it shines on moonlight nights, do you remember? You've not forgotten?

MME. RANEVSKAYA: [*Looking out of the window into the orchard.*] Oh, my childhood, my innocent childhood. I used to sleep in this nursery—I used to look out into the orchard, happiness waked with me every morning, the orchard was just the same then . . . nothing has changed. [*Laughs with joy.*] All, all white! Oh, my orchard! After the dark, rainy autumn and the cold winter, you are young again, and full of happiness, the heavenly angels have not left you. . . . If I could free my chest and my shoulders from this rock that weighs on me, if I could only forget the past!

GAYEV: Yes, and the orchard will be sold to pay our debts, strange as it may seem.

MME. RANEVSKAYA: Look! There is our poor mother walking in the orchard . . . all in white . . . [*Laughs with joy.*] It is she!

GAYEV: Where?

VARYA: What are you saying, Mamma dear!

MME. RANEVSKAYA: There's no one there, I just imagined it. To the right, where the path turns toward the arbor, there's a little white tree, leaning over, that looks like a woman . . .

[TROFIMOV *enters, wearing a shabby student's uniform and spectacles.*]

MME. RANEVSKAYA: What an amazing orchard! White masses of blossom, the blue sky . . .

TROFIMOV: Lubov Andreyevna! [*She looks round at him.*] I just want to pay my respects to you, then I'll leave at once. [*Kisses her hand ardently.*] I was told to wait until morning, but I hadn't the patience . . . [MME. RANEVSKAYA *looks at him, perplexed.*]

VARYA: [*Through tears.*] This is Petya Trofimov.

TROFIMOV: Petya Trofimov, formerly your Grisha's tutor. . . . Can I have changed so much? [MME. RANEVSKAYA *embraces him and weeps quietly.*]

GAYEV: [*Embarrassed.*] Don't, don't, Luba.

VARYA: [*Crying.*] I told you, Petya, to wait until tomorrow.

MME. RANEVSKAYA: My Grisha . . . my little boy . . . Grisha . . . my son.

VARYA: What can one do, Mamma dear, it's God's will.

TROFIMOV: [*Softly, through tears.*] There . . . there.

MME. RANEVSKAYA: [*Weeping quietly.*] My little boy was lost . . . drowned. Why? Why, my friend? [*More quietly.*] Anya's asleep in there, and here I am talking so loudly . . . making all this noise. . . . But tell me, Petya, why do you look so badly? Why have you aged so?

TROFIMOV: A mangy master, a peasant woman in the train called me.

MME. RANEVSKAYA: You were just a boy then, a dear little student, and now your hair's thin—and you're wearing glasses! Is it possible you're still a student? [*Goes toward the door.*]

TROFIMOV: I suppose I'm a perpetual student.

MME. RANEVSKAYA: [*Kisses her brother, then* VARYA.] Now, go to bed. . . . You have aged, too, Leonid.

PISHCHIK: [*Follows her.*] So now we turn in. Oh, my gout! I'm staying the night here . . . Lubov Andreyevna, my angel, tomorrow morning . . . I do need 240 rubles.

GAYEV: He keeps at it.

PISHCHIK: I'll pay it back, dear . . . it's a trifling sum.

MME. RANEVSKAYA: All right, Leonid will give it to you. Give it to him, Leonid.

GAYEV: Me give it to him! That's a good one!

MME. RANEVSKAYA: It can't be helped. Give it to him! He needs it. He'll pay it back.

[MME. RANEVSKAYA, TROFIMOV, PISHCHIK, *and* FIRS *go out;* GAYEV, VARYA, *and* YASHA *remain.*]

GAYEV: Sister hasn't got out of the habit of throwing money around. [*To* YASHA.] Go away, my good fellow, you smell of the barnyard.

YASHA: [*With a grin.*] And you, Leonid Andreyevich, are just the same as ever.

GAYEV: Who? [*To* VARYA.] What did he say?

VARYA: [*To* YASHA.] Your mother's come from the village; she's been sitting in the servants' room since yesterday, waiting to see you.

YASHA: Botheration!

VARYA: You should be ashamed of yourself!

YASHA: She's all I needed! She could have come tomorrow. [*Exits.*]

VARYA: Mamma is just the same as ever; she hasn't changed a bit. If she had her own way, she'd keep nothing for herself.

GAYEV: Yes . . . [*Pauses.*] If a great many remedies are offered for some disease, it means it is incurable; I keep thinking and racking my brains; I have many remedies, ever so many, and that really means none. It would be fine if we came in for a legacy; it would be fine if we married off our Anya to a very rich man; or we might go to Yaroslavl and try our luck with our aunt, the Countess. She's very rich, you know . . .

VARYA: [*Weeping.*] If only God would help us!

GAYEV: Stop bawling. Aunt's very rich, but she doesn't like us. In the first place, Sister married a lawyer who was no nobleman . . . [ANYA *appears in the doorway.*] She married beneath her, and it can't be said that her behavior has been very exemplary. She's good, kind, sweet, and I love her, but no matter what extenuating circumstances you may adduce, there's no denying that she has no morals. You sense it in her least gesture.

VARYA: [*In a whisper.*] Anya's in the doorway.

GAYEV: Who? [*Pauses.*] It's queer, something got into my right eye—my eyes are going back on me. . . . And on Thursday, when I was in the circuit court—

[*Enter* ANYA.]

VARYA: Why aren't you asleep, Anya?

ANYA: I can't get to sleep, I just can't.

GAYEV: My little pet! [*Kisses* ANYA's *face and hands.*] My child! [*Weeps.*] You are not my niece, you're my angel! You're everything to me. Believe me, believe—

ANYA: I believe you, Uncle. Everyone loves you and respects you . . . but, Uncle dear, you must keep still. . . . You must. What were you saying just now about my mother? Your own sister? What made you say that?

GAYEV: Yes, yes . . . [*Covers his face with her hand.*] Really, that was awful! Good God! Heaven help me! Just now I made a speech to the bookcase . . . so stupid! And only after I was through, I saw how stupid it was.

VARYA: It's true, Uncle dear, you ought to keep still. Just don't talk, that's all.

ANYA: If you could only keep still, it would make things easier for you, too.

GAYEV: I'll keep still. [*Kisses* ANYA'*s and* VARYA'*s hands.*] I will. But now about business. On Thursday I was in court; well, there were a number of us there, and we began talking of one thing and another, and this and that, and do you know, I believe it will be possible to raise a loan on a promissory note to pay the interest at the bank.

VARYA: If only God would help us!

GAYEV: On Tuesday I'll go and see about it again. [*To* VARYA.] Stop bawling. [To ANYA.] Your mamma will talk to Lopahin, and he, of course, will not refuse her . . . and as soon as you're rested, you'll go to Yaroslavl to the Countess, your great-aunt. So we'll be working in three directions at once, and the thing is in the bag. We'll pay the interest—I'm sure of it. [*Puts a candy in his mouth.*] I swear on my honor, I swear by anything you like, the estate shan't be sold. [*Excitedly.*] I swear by my own happiness! Here's my hand on it, you can call me a swindler and a scoundrel if I let it come to an auction! I swear by my whole being.

ANYA: [*Relieved and quite happy again.*] How good you are, Uncle, and how clever! [*Embraces him.*] Now I'm at peace, quite at peace, I'm happy.

[*Enter* FIRS.]

FIRS: [*Reproachfully.*] Leonid Andreyevich, have you no fear of God? When are you going to bed?

GAYEV: Directly, directly. Go away, Firs, I'll . . . yes, I will undress myself. Now, children, 'nightie-'nightie. We'll consider details tomorrow, but now go to sleep. [Kisses ANYA *and* VARYA.] I am a man of the eighties; they have nothing good to say of that period nowadays. Nevertheless, in the course of my life, I have suffered not a little for my convictions. It's not for nothing that the peasant loves me; one should know the peasant; one should know from which—

ANYA: There you go again, Uncle.

VARYA: Uncle dear, be quiet.

FIRS: [*Angrily.*] Leonid Andreyevich!

GAYEV: I'm coming, I'm coming! Go to bed! Double bank shot in the side pocket! Here goes a clean shot . . .

[*Exits,* FIRS *hobbling after him.*]

ANYA: I am at peace now. I don't want to go to Yaroslavl—I don't like my great-aunt, but still, I am at peace, thanks to Uncle. [*Sits down.*]

VARYA: We must get some sleep. I'm going now. While you were away, something unpleasant happened. In the old servants' quarters, there are only the old people as you know; Yefim, Polya, Yevstigney, and Karp, too. They began letting all sorts of rascals in to spend the night. . . . I didn't say anything. Then I heard they'd been spreading a report that I gave them nothing but dried peas to eat—out of stinginess, you know . . . and it was all

Yevstigney's doing. . . . All right, I thought, if that's how it is, I thought, just wait. I sent for Yevstigney . . . [*Yawns.*] He comes. . . . "How's this, Yevstigney?" I say, "You fool . . ." [*Looking at* ANYA.] Anichka! [*Pauses.*] She's asleep. [*Puts her arm around* ANYA.] Come to your little bed. . . . Come . . . [*Leads her.*] My darling has fallen asleep. . . . Come.

[*They go out. Far away beyond the orchard, a shepherd is piping.* TROFIMOV *crosses the stage and, seeing* VARYA *and* ANYA, *stands still.*]

VARYA: Sh! She's asleep . . . asleep. . . . Come, darling.

ANYA: [*Softly, half-asleep.*] I'm so tired. Those bells . . . Uncle . . . dear. . . . Mamma and Uncle . . .

VARYA: Come, my precious, come along. [*They go into* ANYA'S *room.*]

TROFIMOV: [*With emotion.*] My sunshine, my spring!

Act II

A meadow. An old, long-abandoned, lopsided little chapel; near it a well, large slabs, which had apparently once served as tombstones, and an old bench. In the background the road to the Gayev estate. To one side poplars loom darkly, where the cherry orchard begins. In the distance a row of telegraph poles, and far off, on the horizon, the faint outline of a large city which is seen only in fine, clear weather. The sun will soon be setting. CHARLOTTA, YASHA, *and* DUNYASHA *are seated on the bench.* YEPIHODOV *stands near and plays a guitar. All are pensive.* CHARLOTTA *wears an old peaked cap. She has taken a gun from her shoulder and is straightening the buckle on the strap.*

CHARLOTTA: [*Musingly.*] I haven't a real passport, I don't know how old I am, and I always feel that I am very young. When I was a little girl, my father and mother used to go from fair to fair and give performances, very good ones. And I used to do the *salto mortale*, and all sorts of other tricks. And when papa and mamma died, a German lady adopted me and began to educate me. Very good. I grew up and became a governess. But where I come from and who am I, I don't know. . . . Who were my parents? Perhaps they weren't even married. . . . I don't know . . . [*Takes a cucumber out of her pocket and eats it.*] I don't know a thing. [*Pause.*] One wants so much to talk, and there isn't anyone to talk to. . . . I haven't anybody.

YEPIHODOV: [*Plays the guitar and sings.*] "What care I for the jarring world? What's friend or foe to me? . . ." How agreeable it is to play the mandolin.

DUNYASHA: That's a guitar, not a mandolin. [*Looks in a hand mirror and powders her face.*]

YEPIHODOV: To a madman in love it's a mandolin. [*Sings.*] "Would that the heart were warmed by the fire of mutual love!" [YASHA *joins in.*]

CHARLOTTA: How abominably these people sing. Pfui! Like jackals!

DUNYASHA: [*To* YASHA.] How wonderful it must be though to have stayed abroad!

YASHA: Ah, yes, of course, I cannot but agree with you there. [*Yawns and lights a cigar.*]

YEPIHODOV: Naturally. Abroad, everything has long since achieved full perplexion.

YASHA: That goes without saying.

YEPIHODOV: I'm a cultivated man, I read all kinds of remarkable books. And yet I can never make out what direction I should take, what is it that I want, properly speaking. Should I live, or should I shoot myself, properly speaking? Nevertheless, I always carry a revolver about me. . . . Here it is . . . [*Shows revolver.*]

CHARLOTTA: I've finished. I'm going. [*Puts the gun over her shoulder.*] You are a very clever man, Yepihodov, and a very terrible one; women must be crazy about you. Br-r-r! [*Starts to go.*] These clever men are all so stupid; there's no one for me to talk to . . . always alone, alone, I haven't a soul . . . and who I am, and why I am, nobody knows. [*Exits unhurriedly.*]

YEPIHODOV: Properly speaking and letting other subjects alone, I must say regarding myself, among other things, that fate treats me mercilessly, like a storm treats a small boat. If I am mistaken, let us say, why then do I wake up this morning, and there on my chest is a spider of enormous dimensions . . . like this . . . [*Indicates with both hands.*] Again, I take up a pitcher of kvass to have a drink, and in it there is something unseemly to the highest degree, something like a cockroach. [*Pause.*] Have you read Buckle?[1] [*Pause.*] I wish to have a word with you, Avdotya Fyodorovna, if I may trouble you.

DUNYASHA: Well, go ahead.

YEPIHODOV: I wish to speak with you alone. [*Sighs.*]

DUNYASHA: [*Embarrassed.*] Very well. Only first bring me my little cape. You'll find it near the wardrobe. It's rather damp here.

YEPIHODOV: Certainly, ma'am; I will fetch it, ma'am. Now I know what to do with my revolver. [*Takes the guitar and goes off playing it.*]

YASHA: Two-and-Twenty Troubles! An awful fool, between you and me. [*Yawns.*]

DUNYASHA: I hope to God he doesn't shoot himself! [*Pause.*] I've become so nervous, I'm always fretting. I was still a little girl when I was taken into the big house, I am quite unused to the simple life now, and my hands are white, as white as a lady's. I've become so soft, so delicate, so refined, I'm afraid of everything. It's so terrifying; and if you deceive me, Yasha, I don't know what will happen to my nerves. [YASHA *kisses her.*]

YASHA: You're a peach! Of course, a girl should never forget herself; and what I dislike more than anything is when a girl don't behave properly.

DUNYASHA: I've fallen passionately in love with you; you're educated—you have something to say about everything. [*Pause.*]

1. Henry Thomas Buckle (1821–1862) wrote a *History of Civilization in England* (1857–1861) which was considered daringly materialistic and free thinking.

YASHA: [*Yawns.*] Yes, ma'am. Now the way I look at it, if a girl loves someone, it means she is immoral. [*Pause.*] It's agreeable smoking a cigar in the fresh air. [*Listens.*] Someone's coming this way. . . . It's our madam and the others. [DUNYASHA *embraces him impulsively.*] You go home, as though you'd been to the river to bathe; go by the little path, or else they'll run into you and suspect me of having arranged to meet you here. I can't stand that sort of thing.

DUNYASHA: [*Coughing softly.*] Your cigar's made my head ache. [*Exits.* YASHA *remains standing near the chapel. Enter* MME. RANEVSKAYA, GAYEV, *and* LOPAHIN.]

LOPAHIN: You must make up your mind once and for all—there's no time to lose. It's quite a simple question, you know. Do you agree to lease your land for summer cottages or not? Answer in one word, yes or no; only one word!

MME. RANEVSKAYA: Who's been smoking such abominable cigars here? [*Sits down.*]

GAYEV: Now that the railway line is so near, it's made things very convenient. [*Sits down.*] Here we've been able to have lunch in town. Yellow ball in the side pocket! I feel like going into the house and playing just one game.

MME. RANEVSKAYA: You can do that later.

LOPAHIN: Only one word! [*Imploringly.*] Do give me an answer!

GAYEV: [*Yawning.*] Who?

MME. RANEVSKAYA: [*Looks into her purse.*] Yesterday I had a lot of money and now my purse is almost empty. My poor Varya tries to economize by feeding us just milk soup; in the kitchen the old people get nothing but dried peas to eat, while I squander money thoughtlessly. [*Drops the purse, scattering gold pieces.*] You see, there they go . . . [*Shows vexation.*]

YASHA: Allow me—I'll pick them up. [*Picks up the money.*]

MME. RANEVSKAYA: Be so kind. Yasha. And why did I go to lunch in town? That nasty restaurant, with its music and the tablecloth smelling of soap. . . . Why drink so much, Leonid? Why eat so much? Why talk so much? Today again you talked a lot, and all so inappropriately about the seventies, about the decadents.[2] And to whom? Talking to waiters about decadents!

LOPAHIN: Yes.

GAYEV: [*Waving his hand.*] I'm incorrigible; that's obvious. [*Irritably, to* YASHA.] Why do you keep dancing about in front of me?

YASHA: [*Laughs.*] I can't hear your voice without laughing—

GAYEV: Either he or I—

MME. RANEVSKAYA: Go away, Yasha; run along.

YASHA: [*Handing* MME. RANEVSKAYA *her purse.*] I'm going at once. [*Hardly able to suppress his laughter.*] This minute. [*Exits.*]

LOPAHIN: That rich man, Deriganov, wants to buy your estate. They say he's coming to the auction himself.

2. A group of French poets (Mallarmé is today the most famous) of the 1880's were labeled "decadents" by their enemies and sometimes adopted the name themselves, proud of their refinement and sensitivity.

MME. RANEVSKAYA: Where did you hear that?

LOPAHIN: That's what they are saying in town.

GAYEV: Our aunt in Yaroslavl has promised to help; but when she will send the money, and how much, no one knows.

LOPAHIN: How much will she send? A hundred thousand? Two hundred?

MME. RANEVSKAYA: Oh, well, ten or fifteen thousand; and we'll have to be grateful for that.

LOPAHIN: Forgive me, but such frivolous people as you are, so queer and unbusinesslike—I never met in my life. One tells you in plain language that your estate is up for sale, and you don't seem to take it in.

MME. RANEVSKAYA: What are we to do? Tell us what to do.

LOPAHIN: I do tell you, every day; every day I say the same thing! You must lease the cherry orchard and the land for summer cottages, you must do it and as soon as possible—right away. The auction is close at hand. Please understand! Once you've decided to have the cottages, you can raise as much money as you like, and you're saved.

MME. RANEVSKAYA: Cottages—summer people—forgive me, but it's all so vulgar.

GAYEV: I agree with you absolutely.

LOPAHIN: I shall either burst into tears or scream or faint! I can't stand it! You've worn me out! [*To* GAYEV.] You're an old woman!

GAYEV: Who?

LOPAHIN: An old woman! [*Gets up to go.*]

MME. RANEVSKAYA: [*Alarmed.*] No, don't go! Please stay, I beg you, my dear. Perhaps we shall think of something.

LOPAHIN: What is there to think of?

MME. RANEVSKAYA: Don't go, I beg you. With you here it's more cheerful anyway. [*Pause.*] I keep expecting something to happen, it's as though the house were going to crash about our ears.

GAYEV: [*In deep thought.*] Bank shot in the corner. . . . Three cushions in the side pocket. . . .

MME. RANEVSKAYA: We have been great sinners . . .

LOPAHIN: What sins could you have committed?

GAYEV: [*Putting a candy in his mouth.*] They say I've eaten up my fortune in candy! [*Laughs.*]

MME. RANEVSKAYA: Oh, my sins! I've squandered money away recklessly, like a lunatic, and I married a man who made nothing but debts. My husband drank himself to death on champagne, he was a terrific drinker. And then, to my sorrow, I fell in love with another man, and I lived with him. And just then—that was my first punishment—a blow on the head: my little boy was drowned here in the river. And I went abroad, went away forever . . . never to come back, never to see this river again . . . I closed my eyes and ran, out of my mind. . . . But he followed me, pitiless, brutal. I bought a villa near Mentone, because he fell ill there; and for three years, day and night, I knew no peace, no rest. The sick man wore me out, he sucked my soul dry. Then last year, when the villa was sold to pay my debts, I went to Paris, and there he robbed me, abandoned me, took up with another woman, I tried to poison myself—it was stupid, so shameful—and then suddenly I felt drawn back to Russia, back to my own country, to my little girl. [*Wipes her tears away.*] Lord, Lord! Be merciful, forgive me my sins—don't punish me anymore! [*Takes a telegram out of her pocket.*] This came today from Paris—he begs me to forgive him, implores me to go back . . . [*Tears up the telegram.*] Do I hear music? [*Listens.*]

GAYEV: That's our famous Jewish band, you remember? Four violins, a flute, and a double bass.

MME. RANEVSKAYA: Does it still exist? We ought to send for them some evening and have a party.

LOPAHIN: [*Listens.*] I don't hear anything. [*Hums softly.*] "The Germans for a fee will Frenchify a Russian." [*Laughs.*] I saw a play at the theater yesterday—awfully funny.

MME. RANEVSKAYA: There was probably nothing funny about it. You shouldn't go to see plays, you should look at yourselves more often. How drab your lives are—how full of unnecessary talk.

LOPAHIN: That's true; come to think of it, we do live like fools. [*Pause.*] My pop was a peasant, an idiot; he understood nothing, never taught me anything, all he did was beat me when he was drunk, and always with a stick. Fundamentally, I'm just the same kind of blockhead and idiot. I was never taught anything—I have a terrible handwriting. I write so that I feel ashamed before people, like a pig.

MME. RANEVSKAYA: You should get married, my friend.

LOPAHIN: Yes . . . that's true.

MME. RANEVSKAYA: To our Varya, she's a good girl.

LOPAHIN: Yes.

MME. RANEVSKAYA: She's a girl who comes of simple people, she works all day long; and above all, she loves you. Besides, you've liked her for a long time now.

LOPAHIN: Well, I've nothing against it. She's a good girl. [*Pause.*]

GAYEV: I've been offered a place in the bank—6,000 a year. Have you heard?

MME. RANEVSKAYA: You're not up to it. Stay where you are.

[FIRS *enters, carrying an overcoat.*]

FIRS: [*To* GAYEV.] Please put this on, sir, it's damp.

GAYEV: [*Putting it on.*] I'm fed up with you, brother.

FIRS: Never mind. This morning you drove off without saying a word. [*Looks him over.*]

MME. RANEVSKAYA: How you've aged, Firs.

FIRS: I beg your pardon?

LOPAHIN: The lady says you've aged.

FIRS: I've lived a long time; they were arranging my wedding and your papa wasn't born yet. [*Laughs.*] When freedom came I was already head footman. I wouldn't consent to be set free then; I stayed on with the master . . . [*Pause.*] I remember they were all very happy, but why they were happy, they didn't know themselves.

LOPAHIN: It was fine in the old days! At least there was flogging!

FIRS: [*Not hearing.*] Of course. The peasants kept to the masters, the masters kept to the peasants; but now they've all gone their own ways, and there's no making out anything.

GAYEV: Be quiet, Firs. I must go to town tomorrow. They've promised to introduce me to a general who might let us have a loan.

LOPAHIN: Nothing will come of that. You won't even be able to pay the interest, you can be certain of that.

MME. RANEVSKAYA: He's raving, there isn't any general. [*Enter* TROFIMOV, ANYA, *and* VARYA.]

GAYEV: Here come our young people.

ANYA: There's Mamma, on the bench.

MME. RANEVSKAYA: [*Tenderly.*] Come here, come along, my darlings. [Embraces ANYA and VARYA.] If you only knew how I love you both! Sit beside me—there, like that. [*All sit down.*]

LOPAHIN: Our perpetual student is always with the young ladies.

TROFIMOV: That's not any of your business.

LOPAHIN: He'll soon be fifty, and he's still a student!

TROFIMOV: Stop your silly jokes.

LOPAHIN: What are you so cross about, you queer bird?

TROFIMOV: Oh, leave me alone.

LOPAHIN: [*Laughs.*] Allow me to ask you, what do you think of me?

TROFIMOV: What I think of you, Yermolay Alexeyevich, is this: you are a rich man who will soon be a millionaire. Well, just as a beast of prey, which devours everything that comes in its way, is necessary for the process of metabolism to go on, so you, too, are necessary. [*All laugh.*]

VARYA: Better tell us something about the planets, Petya.

MME. RANEVSKAYA: No, let's go on with yesterday's conversation.

TROFIMOV: What was it about?

GAYEV: About man's pride.

TROFIMOV: Yesterday we talked a long time, but we came to no conclusion. There is something mystical about man's pride in your sense of the word. Perhaps you're right, from your own point of view. But if you reason simply, without going into subtleties, then what call is there for pride? Is there any sense in it, if man is so poor a thing physiologically, and if, in the great majority of cases, he is coarse, stupid, profoundly unhappy? We should stop admiring ourselves. We should work, and that's all.

GAYEV: You die, anyway.

TROFIMOV: Who knows? And what does it mean—to die? Perhaps man has a hundred senses, and at his death only the five we know perish, while the other ninety-five remain alive.

MME. RANEVSKAYA: How clever you are, Petya!

LOPAHIN: [*Ironically.*] Awfully clever!

TROFIMOV: Mankind goes forward, developing its powers. Everything that is now unattainable for it will one day come within man's reach and be clear to him; only we must work, helping with all our might those who seek the truth. Here among us in Russia only the very few work as yet. The great majority of the intelligentsia, as far as I can see, seek nothing, do nothing, are totally unfit for work of any kind. They call themselves the intelligentsia, yet they are uncivil to their servants, treat the peasants like animals, are poor students, never read anything serious, do absolutely nothing at all, only talk about science, and have little appreciation of the arts. They are all solemn, have grim faces, they all philosophize and talk of weighty matters. And meanwhile the vast majority of us, ninety-nine out of a hundred, live like savages. At the least provocation—a punch in the jaw, and curses. They eat disgustingly, sleep in filth and stuffiness, bedbugs everywhere, stench and damp and moral slovenliness. And obviously, the only purpose of all our fine talk is to hoodwink ourselves and others. Show me where the public nurseries are that we've heard so much about, and the libraries. We read about them in novels, but in reality they don't exist, there is nothing but dirt, vulgarity, and Asiatic backwardness. I don't like very solemn faces, I'm afraid of them, I'm afraid of serious conversations. We'd do better to keep quiet for a while.

LOPAHIN: Do you know, I get up at five o'clock in the morning, and I work from morning till night; and I'm always handling money, my own and other people's, and I see what people around me are really like. You've only to start doing anything to see how few honest, decent people there are. Sometimes when I lie awake at night, I think: "Oh, Lord, thou hast given us immense forests, boundless fields, the widest horizons, and living in their midst, we ourselves ought really to be giants."

MME. RANEVSKAYA: Now you want giants! They're only good in fairy tales; otherwise they're frightening.

[YEPIHODOV *crosses the stage at the rear, playing the guitar.*]

MME. RANEVSKAYA: [*Pensively.*] There goes Yepihodov.

GAYEV: Ladies and gentlemen, the sun has set.

TROFIMOV: Yes.

GAYEV: [*In a low voice, declaiming as it were.*] Oh, Nature, wondrous Nature, you shine with eternal radiance, beautiful and indifferent! You, whom we call our mother, unite within yourself life and death! You animate and destroy!

VARYA: [*Pleadingly.*] Uncle dear!

ANYA: Uncle, again!

TROFIMOV: You'd better bank the yellow ball in the side pocket.

GAYEV: I'm silent, I'm silent . . .

[*All sit plunged in thought. Stillness reigns. Only* FIRS'S *muttering is audible. Suddenly a distant sound is heard, coming from the sky as it were, the sound of a snapping string, mournfully dying away.*]

MME. RANEVSKAYA: What was that?

LOPAHIN: I don't know. Somewhere far away, in the pits, a bucket's broken loose; but somewhere very far away.

GAYEV: Or it might be some sort of bird, perhaps a heron.
TROFIMOV: Or an owl . . .
MME. RANEVSKAYA: [*Shudders.*] It's weird, somehow. [*Pause.*]
FIRS: Before the calamity the same thing happened—the owl screeched, and the samovar hummed all the time.
GAYEV: Before what calamity?
FIRS: Before the Freedom.[3] [*Pause.*]
MME. RANEVSKAYA: Come, my friends, let's be going. It's getting dark. [*To* ANYA.] You have tears in your eyes. What is it, my little one? [*Embraces her.*]
ANYA: I don't know, Mamma; it's nothing.
TROFIMOV: Somebody's coming.

[A TRAMP *appears, wearing a shabby white cap and an overcoat. He is slightly drunk.*]

TRAMP: Allow me to inquire, will this short cut take me to the station?
GAYEV: It will. Just follow that road.
TRAMP: My heartfelt thanks. [*Coughing.*] The weather is glorious. [*Recites.*] "My brother, my suffering brother.[4] . . . Go down to the Volga![5] Whose groans . . .?' [*To* VARYA.] Mademoiselle, won't you spare 30 kopecks for a hungry Russian?
VARYA: [*Frightened, cries out.*]
LOPAHIN: [*Angrily.*] Even panhandling has its proprieties.
MME. RANEVSKAYA: [*Scared.*] Here, take this. [*Fumbles in her purse.*] I haven't any silver . . . never mind, here's a gold piece.
TRAMP: My heartfelt thanks. [*Exits. Laughter.*]
VARYA: [*Frightened.*] I'm leaving. I'm leaving. . . . Oh, Mamma dear, at home the servants have nothing to eat, and you gave him a gold piece!
MME. RANEVSKAYA: What are you going to do with me? I'm such a fool. When we get home, I'll give you everything I have. Yermolay Alexeyevich, you'll lend me some more . . .
LOPAHIN: Yes, ma'am.
MME. RANEVSKAYA: Come, ladies and gentlemen, it's time to be going. Oh! Varya, we've settled all about your marriage. Congratulations!
VARYA: [*Through tears.*] Really, Mamma, that's not a joking matter.
LOPAHIN: "Aurelia, get thee to a nunnery, go . . ."[6]
GAYEV: And do you know, my hands are trembling: I haven't played billiards in a long time.
LOPAHIN: "Aurelia, nymph, in your orisons, remember me!"[6]
MME. RANEVSKAYA: Let's go, it's almost suppertime.
VARYA: He frightened me! My heart's pounding.
LOPAHIN: Let me remind you, ladies and gentlemen, on the twen-

3. refers to the emancipation of the serfs in 1861.
4. from a poem by Syomon Nadson (1862–1887).
5. comes from a poem by Nikolay Nekrasov (1821–1878).
6. Lopahin makes comic use of Hamlet's meeting with Ophelia (in the Russian distorted to "Okhmelia"). Hamlet, seeing her approaching, says: "Nymph, in thy orisons / Be all my sins remembered." (Act III, sc. 1, ll. 89–90), and later, suspecting her of spying for her father, sends her off with "Get thee to a nunnery" (l. 121).

ty-second of August the cherry orchard will be up for sale. Think about that! Think!

[*All except* TROFIMOV *and* ANYA *go out.*]

ANYA: [*Laughs.*] I'm grateful to that tramp, he frightened Varya and so we're alone.

TROFIMOV: Varya's afraid we'll fall in love with each other all of a sudden. She hasn't left us alone for days. Her narrow mind can't grasp that we're above love. To avoid the petty and illusory, everything that prevents us from being free and happy—that is the goal and meaning of our life. Forward! Do not fall behind, friends!

ANYA: [*Strikes her hands together.*] How well you speak! [*Pause.*] It's wonderful here today.

TROFIMOV: Yes, the weather's glorious.

ANYA: What have you done to me, Petya? Why don't I love the cherry orchard as I used to? I loved it so tenderly. It seemed to me there was no spot on earth lovelier than our orchard.

TROFIMOV: All Russia is our orchard. Our land is vast and beautiful, there are many wonderful places in it. [*Pause.*] Think of it, Anya, your grandfather, your great-grandfather and all your ancestors were serf owners, owners of living souls, and aren't human beings looking at you from every tree in the orchard, from every leaf, from every trunk? Don't you hear voices? Oh, it's terrifying! Your orchard is a fearful place, and when you pass through it in the evening or at night, the old bark on the trees gleams faintly, and the cherry trees seem to be dreaming of things that happened a hundred, two hundred years ago and to be tormented by painful visions. What is there to say? We're at least two hundred years behind, we've really achieved nothing yet, we have no definite attitude to the past, we only philosophize, complain of the blues, or drink vodka. It's all so clear: in order to live in the present, we should first redeem our past, finish with it, and we can expiate it only by suffering, only by extraordinary, unceasing labor. Realize that, Anya.

ANYA: The house in which we live has long ceased to be our own, and I will leave it, I give you my word.

TROFIMOV: If you have the keys, fling them into the well and go away. Be free as the wind.

ANYA: [*In ecstasy.*] How well you put that!

TROFIMOV: Believe me, Anya, believe me! I'm not yet thirty, I'm young, I'm still a student—but I've already suffered so much. In winter I'm hungry, sick, harassed, poor as a beggar, and where hasn't Fate driven me? Where haven't I been? And yet always, every moment of the day and night, my soul is filled with inexplicable premonitions. . . . I have a premonition of happiness, Anya. . . . I see it already!

ANYA: [*Pensively.*] The moon is rising.

[YEPIHODOV *is heard playing the same mournful tune on the guitar. The moon rises. Somewhere near the poplars* VARYA *is looking for* ANYA *and calling,* "Anya, where are you?"]

TROFIMOV: Yes, the moon is rising. [*Pause.*] There it is, happiness, it's approaching, it's coming nearer and nearer, I can already hear its footsteps. And if we don't see it, if we don't know it, what does it matter? Others will!

VARYA'S VOICE: Anya! Where are you?

TROFIMOV: That Varya again! [*Angrily.*] It's revolting!

ANYA: Never mind, let's go down to the river. It's lovely there.

TROFIMOV: Come on. [*They go.*]

VARYA'S VOICE: Anya! Anya!

Act III

A drawing room separated by an arch from a ballroom. Evening. Chandelier burning. The Jewish band is heard playing in the anteroom. In the ballroom they are dancing the Grand Rond. PISHCHIK *is heard calling,* "Promenade à une paire." PISHCHIK *and* CHARLOTTA, TROFIMOV *and* MME. RANEVSKAYA, ANYA *and the* POST OFFICE CLERK, VARYA *and the* STATIONMASTER, *and others enter the drawing room in couples.* DUNYASHA *is in the last couple.* VARYA *weeps quietly, wiping her tears as she dances. All parade through drawing room.* PISHCHIK *calling,* "Grand rond, balancez!" *and* "Les cavaliers à genoux et remerciez vos dames!" FIRS, *wearing a dress coat, brings in soda water on a tray.* PISHCHIK *and* TROFIMOV *enter the drawing room.*

PISHCHIK: I have high blood pressure; I've already had two strokes. Dancing's hard work for me; but as they say, "If you run with the pack, you can bark or not, but at least wag your tail." Still, I'm as strong as a horse. My late lamented father, who would have his joke, God rest his soul, used to say, talking about our origin, that the ancient line of the Simeonov-Pishchiks was descended from the very horse that Caligula had made a senator. [*Sits down.*] But the trouble is, I have no money. A hungry dog believes in nothing but meat. [*Snores, and wakes up at once.*] It's the same with me—I can think of nothing but money.

TROFIMOV: You know, there *is* something equine about your figure.

PISHCHIK: Well, a horse is a fine animal—one can sell a horse.

[*Sound of billiards being played in an adjoining room.* VARYA *appears in the archway.*]

TROFIMOV: [*Teasing her.*] Madam Lopahina! Madam Lopahina!

VARYA: [*Angrily.*] Mangy master!

TROFIMOV: Yes, I am a mangy master and I'm proud of it.

VARYA: [*Reflecting bitterly.*] Here we've hired musicians, and what shall we pay them with? [*Exits.*]

TROFIMOV: [*To* PISHCHIK.] If the energy you have spent during your lifetime looking for money to pay interest had gone into something else, in the end you could have turned the world upside down.

PISHCHIK: Nietzsche, the philosopher, the greatest, most famous of men, that colossal intellect, says in his works that it is permissible to forge banknotes.

TROFIMOV: Have you read Nietzsche?

PISHCHIK: Well . . . Dashenka told me. . . . And now I've got to the point where forging banknotes is the only way out for me. . . . The day after tomorrow I have to pay 310 rubles—I already have 130 . . . [*Feels in his pockets. In alarm.*] The money's gone! I've lost my money! [*Through tears.*] Where's my money? [*Joyfully.*] Here it is! Inside the lining . . . I'm all in a sweat . . .

[*Enter* MME. RANEVSKAYA *and* CHARLOTTA.]

MME. RANEVSKAYA: [*Hums the "Lezginka."*] Why isn't Leonid back yet? What is he doing in town? [*To* DUNYASHA.] Dunyasha, offer the musicians tea.

TROFIMOV: The auction hasn't taken place, most likely.

MME. RANEVSKAYA: It's the wrong time to have the band, and the wrong time to give a dance. Well, never mind. [*Sits down and hums softly.*]

CHARLOTTA: [*Hands* PISHCHIK *a pack of cards.*] Here is a pack of cards. Think of any card you like.

PISHCHIK: I've thought of one.

CHARLOTTA: Shuffle the pack now. That's right. Give it here, my dear Mr. Pishchik. *Eins, zwei, drei!*[7] Now look for it—it's in your side pocket.

PISHCHIK: [*Taking the card out of his pocket.*] The eight of spades! Perfectly right! Just imagine!

CHARLOTTA: [*holding the pack of cards in her hands. To* TROFIMOV.] Quickly, name the top card.

TROFIMOV: Well, let's see—the queen of spades.

CHARLOTTA: Right! [*To* PISHCHIK.] Now name the top card.

PISHCHIK: The ace of hearts.

CHARLOTTA: Right! [*Claps her hands and the pack of cards disappears.*] Ah, what lovely weather it is today! [*A mysterious feminine voice, which seems to come from under the floor, answers her:* "Oh, yes, it's magnificent weather, madam."] You are my best ideal. [*Voice:* "And I find you pleasing too, madam."]

STATIONMASTER: [*Applauding.*] The lady ventriloquist, bravo!

PISHCHIK: [*Amazed.*] Just imagine! Enchanting Charlotta Ivanovna, I'm simply in love with you.

CHARLOTTA: In love? [*Shrugs her shoulders.*] Are you capable of love? *Guter Mensch, aber schlechter Musikant!*[8]

TROFIMOV: [*Claps* PISHCHIK *on the shoulder.*] You old horse, you!

CHARLOTTA: Attention please! One more trick! [*Takes a plaid from a chair.*] Here is a very good plaid; I want to sell it. [*Shaking it out.*] Does anyone want to buy it?

PISHCHIK: [*In amazement.*] Just imagine!

CHARLOTTA: *Eins, zwei, drei!* [*Raises the plaid quickly, behind it stands* ANYA. *She curtsies, runs to her mother, embraces her, and runs back into the ballroom, amid general enthusiasm.*]

MME. RANEVSKAYA: [*Applauds.*] Bravo! Bravo!

7. German for "one, two, three."

8. ("A good man, but a bad musician") usually quoted in the plural: "*Gute Leute, schlechte Musikanten.*" It comes from *Das Buch le Grand* (1826) of German poet Heinrich Heine (1799–1856). Here it suggests that Pishchik may be a good man but a bad lover.

CHARLOTTA: Now again! *Eins, zwei, drei!* [*Lifts the plaid; behind it stands* VARYA, *bowing.*]

PISHCHIK: [*In amazement.*] Just imagine!

CHARLOTTA: The end! [*Throws the plaid at* PISHCHIK, *curtsies, and runs into the ballroom.*]

PISHCHIK: [*Running after her.*] The rascal! What a woman, what a woman! [*Exits.*]

MME. RANEVSKAYA: And Leonid still isn't here. What is he doing in town so long? I don't understand. It must be all over by now. Either the estate has been sold, or the auction hasn't taken place. Why keep us in suspense so long?

VARYA: [*Trying to console her.*] Uncle's bought it, I feel sure of that.

TROFIMOV: [*Mockingly.*] Oh, yes!

VARYA: Great-aunt sent him an authorization to buy it in her name, and to transfer the debt. She's doing it for Anya's sake. And I'm sure that God will help us, and Uncle will buy it.

MME. RANEVSKAYA: Great-aunt sent fifteen thousand to buy the estate in her name, she doesn't trust us, but that's not even enough to pay the interest. [*Covers her face with her hands.*] Today my fate will be decided, my fate—

TROFIMOV: [*Teasing* VARYA.] Madam Lopahina!

VARYA: [*Angrily.*] Perpetual student! Twice already you've been expelled from the university.

MME. RANEVSKAYA: Why are you so cross, Varya? He's teasing you about Lopahin. Well, what of it? If you want to marry Lopahin, go ahead. He's a good man, and interesting; if you don't want to, don't. Nobody's compelling you, my pet!

VARYA: Frankly, Mamma dear, I take this thing seriously; he's a good man and I like him.

MME. RANEVSKAYA: All right then, marry him. I don't know what you're waiting for.

VARYA: But, Mamma, I can't propose to him myself. For the last two years, everyone's been talking to me about him—talking. But he either keeps silent, or else cracks jokes. I understand; he's growing rich, he's absorbed in business—he has no time for me. If I had money, even a little, say, 100 rubles, I'd throw everything up and go far away—I'd go into a nunnery.

TROFIMOV: What a blessing . . .

VARYA: A student ought to be intelligent. [*Softly, with tears in her voice.*] How homely you've grown, Petya! How old you look! [*To* MME. RANEVSKAYA, *with dry eyes.*] But I can't live without work, Mamma dear; I must keep busy every minute.

[*Enter* YASHA.]

YASHA: [*Hardly restraining his laughter.*] Yepihodov has broken a billiard cue! [*Exits.*]

VARYA: Why is Yepihodov here? Who allowed him to play billiards? I don't understand these people! [*Exits.*]

MME. RANEVSKAYA: Don't tease her, Petya. She's unhappy enough without that.

TROFIMOV: She bustles so—and meddles in other people's business. All summer long she's given Anya and me no peace. She's afraid of a love affair between us. What business is it of hers? Besides, I've given no grounds for it, and I'm far from such vulgarity. We are above love.

MME. RANEVSKAYA: And I suppose I'm beneath love? [*Anxiously.*] What can be keeping Leonid? If I only knew whether the estate has been sold or not. Such a calamity seems so incredible to me that I don't know what to think—I feel lost. . . . I could scream. . . . I could do something stupid. . . . Save me, Petya, tell me something, talk to me!

TROFIMOV: Whether the estate is sold today or not, isn't it all one? That's all done with long ago—there's no turning back, the path is overgrown. Calm yourself, my dear. You mustn't deceive yourself. For once in your life you must face the truth.

MME. RANEVSKAYA: What truth? You can see the truth, you can tell it from falsehood, but I seem to have lost my eyesight, I see nothing. You settle every great problem so boldly, but tell me, my dear boy, isn't it because you're young, because you don't yet know what one of your problems means in terms of suffering? You look ahead fearlessly, but isn't it because you don't see and don't expect anything dreadful, because life is still hidden from your young eyes? You're bolder, more honest, more profound than we are, but think hard, show just a bit of magnanimity, spare me. After all, I was born here, my father and mother lived here, and my grandfather; I love this house. Without the cherry orchard, my life has no meaning for me, and if it really must be sold, then sell me with the orchard. [*Embraces* TROFIMOV, *kisses him on the forehead.*] My son was drowned here. [*Weeps.*] Pity me, you good, kind fellow!

TROFIMOV: You know, I feel for you with all my heart.

MME. RANEVSKAYA: But that should have been said differently, so differently! [*Takes out her handkerchief—a telegram falls on the floor.*] My heart is so heavy today—you can't imagine! The noise here upsets me—my inmost being trembles at every sound—I'm shaking all over. But I can't go into my own room; I'm afraid to be alone. Don't condemn me, Petya. . . . I love you as though you were one of us, I would gladly let you marry Anya—I swear I would—only, my dear boy, you must study—you must take your degree—you do nothing, you let yourself be tossed by Fate from place to place—it's so strange. It's true, isn't it? And you should do something about your beard, to make it grow somehow! [*Laughs.*] You're so funny!

TROFIMOV: [*Picks up the telegram.*] I've no wish to be a dandy.

MME. RANEVSKAYA: That's a telegram from Paris. I get one every day. One yesterday and one today. That savage is ill again—he's in trouble again. He begs forgiveness, implores me to go to him, and really I ought to go to Paris to be near him. Your face is stern, Petya; but what is there to do, my dear boy? What am I to do? He's ill, he's alone and unhappy, and who is to look after him, who is to keep him from doing the wrong thing, who is to give him his medicine on time? And why hide it or keep still about it—I love him! That's clear. I love him, love him! He's a millstone round my neck, he'll drag me to the bottom, but I love that stone, I can't live without it. [*Presses* TROFIMOV'S *hand*.] Don't think badly of me. Petya, and don't say anything, don't say . . .

TROFIMOV: [*Through tears*.] Forgive me my frankness in heaven's name; but, you know, he robbed you!

MME. RANEVSKAYA: No, no, no, you mustn't say such things! [*Covers her ears*.]

TROFIMOV: But he's a scoundrel! You're the only one who doesn't know it. He's a petty scoundrel—a nonentity!

MME. RANEVSKAYA: [*Controlling her anger*.] You are twenty-six or twenty-seven years old, but you're still a schoolboy.

TROFIMOV: That may be.

MME. RANEVSKAYA: You should be a man at your age. You should understand people who love—and ought to be in love yourself. You ought to fall in love! [*Angrily*.] Yes, yes! And it's not purity in you, it's prudishness, you're simple a queer fish, a comical freak!

TROFIMOV: [*Horrified*.] What is she saying?

MME. RANEVSKAYA: "I am above love!" You're not above love, but simply, as our Firs says, you're an addlehead. At your age not to have a mistress!

TROFIMOV: [*Horrified*.] This is frightful! What is she saying! [*Goes rapidly into the ballroom, clutching his head*.] It's frightful—I can't stand it, I won't stay! [*Exits, but returns at once*.] All is over between us! [*Exits into anteroom*.]

MME. RANEVSKAYA: [*Shouts after him*.] Petya! Wait! You absurd fellow, I was joking. Petya!

[*Sound of somebody running quickly downstairs and suddenly falling down with a crash.* ANYA *and* VARYA *scream. Sound of laughter a moment later*.]

MME. RANEVSKAYA: What's happened?

[ANYA *runs in*.]

ANYA: [*Laughing*.] Petya's fallen downstairs! [*Runs out*.]

MME. RANEVSKAYA: What a queer bird that Petya is!

[STATIONMASTER, *standing in the middle of the ballroom, recites Alexey Tolstoy's "Magdalene,"*[9] *to which all listen, but after a few lines, the sound of a waltz is heard from the anteroom and the reading breaks off. All dance.* TROFIMOV, ANYA, VARYA, *and* MME. RANEVSKAYA *enter from the anteroom*.]

MME. RANEVSKAYA: Petya, you pure soul, please forgive me. . . . Let's dance.

[*Dances with* PETYA. ANYA *and* VARYA *dance.* FIRS *enters, puts his stick down by the side door.* YASHA *enters from the drawing room and watches the dancers*.]

9. called "The Sinning Woman" in Russian, begins thus:

A bustling crowd with happy laughter,
with twangling lutes and clashing cymbals
with flowers and foliage all around
the colonnaded portico.

Alexey Tolstoy (1817–1875) was a distant relative of Leo Tolstoy, popular in his time as a dramatist and poet.

YASHA: Well, Grandfather?

FIRS: I'm not feeling well. In the old days it was generals, barons, and admirals that were dancing at our balls, and now we have to send for the Post Office Clerk and the Stationmaster, and even they aren't too glad to come. I feel kind of shaky. The old master that's gone, their grandfather, dosed everyone with sealing wax, whatever ailed 'em. I've been taking sealing wax every day for twenty years or more. Perhaps that's what's kept me alive.

YASHA: I'm fed up with you, Grandpop. [*Yawns.*] It's time you croaked.

FIRS: Oh, you addlehead! [*Mumbles.*]

[TROFIMOV *and* MME. RANEVSKAYA *dance from the ballroom into the drawing room.*]

MME. RANEVSKAYA: *Merci.* I'll sit down a while. [*Sits down.*] I'm tired.

[*Enter* ANYA.]

ANYA: [*Excitedly.*] There was a man in the kitchen just now who said the cherry orchard was sold today.

MME. RANEVSKAYA: Sold to whom?

ANYA: He didn't say. He's gone. [*Dances off with* TROFIMOV.]

YASHA: It was some old man gabbing, a stranger.

FIRS: And Leonid Andreyevich isn't back yet, he hasn't come. And he's wearing his lightweight between-season overcoat; like enough, he'll catch cold. Ah, when they're young they're green.

MME. RANEVSKAYA: This is killing me. Go, Yasha, find out to whom it has been sold.

YASHA: But the old man left long ago. [*Laughs.*]

MME. RANEVSKAYA: What are you laughing at? What are you pleased about?

YASHA: That Yepihodov is such a funny one. A funny fellow, Two-and-Twenty Troubles!

MME. RANEVSKAYA: Firs, if the estate is sold, where will you go?

FIRS: I'll go where you tell me.

MME. RANEVSKAYA: Why do you look like that? Are you ill? You ought to go to bed.

FIRS: Yes! [*With a snigger.*] Me go to bed, and who's to hand things round? Who's to see to things? I'm the only one in the whole house.

YASHA: [*To* MME. RANEVSKAYA.] Lubov Andreyevna, allow me to ask a favor of you, be so kind! If you go back to Paris, take me with you, I beg you. It's positively impossible for me to stay here. [*Looking around; sotto voce.*] What's the use of talking? You see for yourself, it's an uncivilized country, the people have no morals, and then the boredom! The food in the kitchen's revolting, and besides there's this Firs wanders about mumbling all sorts of inappropriate words. Take me with you, be so kind!

[*Enter* PISHCHIK.]

PISHCHIK: May I have the pleasure of a waltz with you, charming lady? [MME. RANEVSKAYA *accepts.*] All the same, enchanting lady, you must let me have 180 rubles. . . . You must let me have [*dancing*] just one hundred and eighty rubles. [*They pass into the ballroom.*]

YASHA: [*Hums softly.*] "Oh, wilt thou understand the tumult in my soul?"

[*In the ballroom a figure in a gray top hat and checked trousers is jumping about and waving its arms; shouts:* "Bravo, Charlotta Ivanovna!"]

DUNYASHA: [*Stopping to powder her face; to* FIRS.] The young miss has ordered me to dance. There are so many gentlemen and not enough ladies. But dancing makes me dizzy, my heart begins to beat fast, Firs Nikolayevich. The Post Office Clerk said something to me just now that quite took my breath away. [*Music stops.*]

FIRS: What did he say?

DUNYASHA: "You're like a flower," he said.

YASHA: [*Yawns.*] What ignorance. [*Exits.*]

DUNYASHA: "Like a flower!" I'm such a delicate girl. I simply adore pretty speeches.

FIRS: You'll come to a bad end.

[*Enter* YEPIHODOV.]

YEPIHODOV: [*To* DUNYASHA.] You have no wish to see me, Avdotya Fyodorovna . . . as though I was some sort of insect. [*Sighs.*] Ah, life!

DUNYASHA: What is it you want?

YEPIHODOV: Indubitably you may be right. [*Sighs.*] But of course, if one looks at it from the point of view, if I may be allowed to say so, and apologizing for my frankness, you have completely reduced me to a state of mind. I know my fate. Every day some calamity befalls me, and I grew used to it long ago, so that I look upon my fate with a smile. You gave me your word, and though I—

DUNYASHA: Let's talk about it later, please. But just now leave me alone, I am daydreaming. [*Plays with a fan.*]

YEPIHODOV: A misfortune befalls me every day; and if I may be allowed to say so, I merely smile, I even laugh.

[*Enter* VARYA.]

VARYA: [*To* YEPIHODOV.] Are you still here? What an impertinent fellow you are really! Run along, Dunyasha. [*To* YEPIHODOV.] Either you're playing billiards and breaking a cue, or you're wandering about the drawing room as though you were a guest.

YEPIHODOV: You cannot, permit me to remark, penalize me.

VARYA: I'm not penalizing you; I'm just telling you. You merely wander from place to place, and don't do your work. We keep you as a clerk, but heaven knows what for.

YEPIHODOV: [*Offended.*] Whether I work or whether I walk, whether I eat or whether I play billiards, is a matter to be discussed only by persons of understanding and of mature years.

VARYA: [*Enraged.*] You dare say that to me—you dare? You mean to say I've no understanding? Get out of here at once! This minute!

YEPIHODOV: [*Scared.*] I beg you to express yourself delicately.

VARYA: [*Beside herself.*] Clear out this minute! Out with you!

[YEPIHODOV *goes toward the door,* VARYA *following.*]

VARYA: Two-and-Twenty Troubles! Get out—don't let me set eyes on you again!

[*Exit* YEPIHODOV. *His voice is heard behind the door:* "I shall lodge a complaint against you!"]

VARYA: Oh, you're coming back? [*She seizes the stick left near door by* FIRS.] Well, come then . . . come . . . I'll show you. . . . Ah, you're coming? You're coming? . . . Come . . . [*Swings the stick just as* LOPAHIN *enters.*]

LOPAHIN: Thank you kindly.

VARYA: [*Angrily and mockingly.*] I'm sorry.

LOPAHIN: It's nothing. Thank you kindly for your charming reception.

VARYA: Don't mention it. [*Walks away, looks back and asks softly.*] I didn't hurt you, did I?

LOPAHIN: Oh, no, not at all. I shall have a large bump, though.

[*Voices from the ballroom:* "Lopahin is here! Lopahin!"]
[*Enter* PISHCHIK.]

PISHCHIK: My eyes do see, my ears do hear! [*Kisses* LOPAHIN.]

LOPAHIN: You smell of cognac, my dear friends. And we've been celebrating here, too.

[*Enter* MME. RANEVSKAYA.]

MME. RANEVSKAYA: Is that you, Yermolay Alexeyevich? What kept you so long? Where's Leonid?

LOPAHIN: Leonid Andreyevich arrived with me. He's coming.

MME. RANEVSKAYA: Well, what happened? Did the sale take place? Speak!

LOPAHIN: [*Embarrassed, fearful of revealing his joy.*] The sale was over at four o'clock. We missed the train—had to wait till half-past nine. [*Sighing heavily.*] Ugh. I'm a little dizzy.

[*Enter* GAYEV. *In his right hand he holds parcels, with his left he is wiping away his tears.*]

MME. RANEVSKAYA: Well, Leonid? What news? [*Impatiently, through tears.*] Be quick, for God's sake!

GAYEV: [*Not answering, simply waves his hand. Weeping, to* FIRS.] Here, take these; anchovies, Kerch herrings . . . I haven't eaten all day. What I've been through! [*The click of billiard balls comes through the open door of the billiard room and* YASHA*'s voice is heard:* "Seven and eighteen!" GAYEV*'s expression changes, he no longer weeps.*] I'm terribly tired. Firs, help me change. [*Exits, followed by* FIRS.]

PISHCHIK: How about the sale? Tell us what happened.

MME. RANEVSKAYA: Is the cherry orchard sold?

LOPAHIN: Sold.

MME. RANEVSKAYA: Who bought it?

LOPAHIN: I bought it.

[*Pause.* MME. RANEVSKAYA *is overcome. She would fall to the floor, were it not for the chair and table near which she stands.* VARYA *takes the keys from her belt, flings them on the floor in the middle of the drawing room and goes out.*]

LOPAHIN: I bought it. Wait a bit, ladies and gentlemen, please, my head is swimming, I can't talk. [*Laughs.*] We got to the auction and Deriganov was there already. Leonid Andreyevich had only 15,000 and straight off Deriganov bid 30,000 over and above the mortgage. I saw how the land lay, got into the fight, bid 40,000. He bid 45,000. I bid fifty-five. He kept adding five thousands, I ten. Well . . . it came to an end. I bid ninety above the mortgage and the estate was knocked down to me. Now the cherry orchard's mine! Mine! [*Laughs uproariously.*] Lord! God in Heaven! The cherry orchard's mine! Tell me that I'm drunk—out of my mind—that it's all a dream. [*Stamps his feet.*] Don't laugh at me! If my father and my grandfather could rise from their graves and see all that has happened—how their Yermolay, who used to be flogged, their half-literate Yermolay, who used to run about barefoot in winter, how that very Yermolay has bought the most magnificent estate in the world. I bought the estate where my father and grandfather were slaves, where they weren't even allowed to enter the kitchen. I'm asleep—it's only a dream—I only imagine it. . . . It's the fruit of your imagination, wrapped in the darkness of the unknown! [*Picks up the keys, smiling genially.*] She threw down the keys, wants to show she's no longer mistress here. [*Jingles keys.*] Well, no matter. [*The band is warming up.*] Hey, musicians! Strike up! I want to hear you! Come, everybody, and see how Yermolay Lopahin will lay the ax to the cherry orchard and how the trees will fall to the ground. We will build summer cottages there, and our grandsons and great-grandsons will see a new life here. Music! Strike up!

[*The band starts to play.* MME RANEVSKAYA *has sunk into a chair and is weeping bitterly.*]

LOPAHIN: [*Reproachfully.*] Why, why didn't you listen to me? My dear friend, my poor friend, you can't bring it back now. [*Tearfully.*] Oh, if only this were over quickly! Oh, if only our wretched, disordered life were changed!

PISHCHIK: [*Takes him by the arm; sotto voce.*] She's crying. Let's go into the ballroom. Let her be alone. Come. [*Takes his arm and leads him into the ballroom.*]

LOPAHIN: What's the matter? Musicians, play so I can hear you! Let me have things the way I want them. [*Ironically.*] Here comes the new master, the owner of the cherry orchard. [*Accidentally he trips over a little table, almost upsetting the candelabra.*] I can pay for everything. *Exits with* PISHCHIK.]

[MME. RANEVSKAYA, *alone, sits huddled up, weeping bitterly. Music plays softly. Enter* ANYA *and* TROFIMOV *quickly.* ANYA *goes to her mother and falls on her knees before her.* TROFIMOV *stands in the doorway.*]

ANYA: Mamma, Mamma, you're crying! Dear, kind, good Mamma, my precious, I love you, I bless you! The cherry orchard is sold, it's gone, that's true, quite true. But don't cry, Mamma, life is still before you, you still have your kind, pure heart. Let us go, let us go away from here, darling. We will plant a new orchard, even more luxuriant than this one. You will see it, you will understand, and like the sun at evening, joy—deep, tranquil joy—will sink into your soul, and you will smile, Mamma. Come, darling, let us go:

Act IV

Scene as in Act I. No window curtains or pictures, only a little furniture, piled up in a corner, as if for sale. A sense of emptiness. Near the outer door and at the back, suitcases, bundles, etc., are piled up. A door open on the left and the voices of VARYA *and* ANYA *are heard.* LOPAHIN *stands waiting.* YASHA *holds a tray with glasses full of champagne.* YEPIHODOV *in the anteroom is tying up a box. Behind the scene a hum of voices: peasants have come to say good-bye. Voice of* GAYEV: "Thanks, brothers, thank you."

YASHA: The country folk have come to say good-bye. In my opinion, Yermolay Alexeyevich, they are kindly souls, but there's nothing in their heads.

[*The hum dies away. Enter* MME. RANEVSKAYA *and* GAYEV. *She is not crying, but is pale, her face twitches and she cannot speak.*]

GAYEV: You gave them your purse, Luba. That won't do! That won't do!

MME. RANEVSKAYA: I couldn't help it! I couldn't! [*They go out.*]

LOPAHIN: [*Calls after them.*] Please, I beg you, have a glass at parting. I didn't think of bringing any champagne from town and at the station I could find only one bottle. Please, won't you? [*Pause.*] What's the matter, ladies and gentlemen, don't you want any? [*Moves away from the door.*] If I'd known, I wouldn't have bought it. Well, then I won't drink any, either. [YASHA *carefully sets the tray down on a chair.*] At least you have a glass, Yasha.

YASHA: Here's to the travelers! And good luck to those that stay! [*Drinks.*] This champagne isn't the real stuff, I can assure you.

LOPAHIN: Eight rubles a bottle. [*Pause.*] It's devilishly cold here.

YASHA: They didn't light the stoves today—it wasn't worth it, since we're leaving. [*Laughs.*]

LOPAHIN: Why are you laughing?

YASHA: It's just that I'm pleased.

LOPAHIN: It's October, yet it's as still and sunny as though it were summer. Good weather for building. [*Looks at his watch, and speaks off.*] Bear in mind, ladies and gentlemen, the train goes in forty-seven minutes, so you ought to start for the station in twenty minutes. Better hurry up!

[*Enter* TROFIMOV, *wearing an overcoat.*]

TROFIMOV: I think it's time to start. The carriages are at the door. The devil only knows what's become of my rubbers; they've disappeared. [*Calling off.*] Anya! My rubbers are gone. I can't find them.

LOPAHIN: I've got to go to Kharkov. I'll take the same train you do. I'll spend the winter in Kharkov. I've been hanging round here with you, till I'm worn out with loafing. I can't live without work—I don't know what to do with my hands, they dangle as if they didn't belong to me.

TROFIMOV: Well, we'll soon be gone, then you can go on with your useful labors again.

LOPAHIN: Have a glass.

TROFIMOV: No, I won't.

LOPAHIN: So you're going to Moscow now?

TROFIMOV: Yes, I'll see them into town, and tomorrow I'll go on to Moscow.

LOPAHIN: Well, I'll wager the professors aren't giving any lectures, they're waiting for you to come.

TROFIMOV: That's none of your business.

LOPAHIN: Just how many years have you been at the university?

TROFIMOV: Can't you think of something new? Your joke's stale and flat. [*Looking for his rubbers.*] We'll probably never see each other again, so allow me to give you a piece of advice at parting: don't wave your hands about! Get out of the habit. And another thing: building bungalows, figuring that summer residents will eventually become small farmers, figuring like that is just another form of waving your hands about. . . . Never mind, I love you anyway; you have fine, delicate fingers, like an artist; you have a fine, delicate soul.

LOPAHIN: [*Embracing him.*] Good-bye, my dear fellow. Thank you for everything. Let me give you some money for the journey, if you need it.

TROFIMOV: What for? I don't need it.

LOPAHIN: But you haven't any.

TROFIMOV: Yes, I have, thank you. I got some money for a translation—here it is in my pocket. [*Anxiously.*] But where are my rubbers?

VARYA: [*From the next room.*] Here! Take the nasty things. [*Flings a pair of rubbers onto the stage.*]

TROFIMOV: What are you so cross about, Varya? Hm . . . and these are not my rubbers.

LOPAHIN: I sowed three thousand acres of poppies in the spring, and now I've made 40,000 on them, clear profit; and when my poppies were in bloom, what a picture it was! So, as I say, I made 40,000; and I am offering you a loan because I can afford it. Why turn up your nose at it? I'm a peasant—I speak bluntly.

TROFIMOV: Your father was a peasant, mine was a druggist—that proves absolutely nothing whatever [LOPAHIN *takes out his wallet.*] Don't, put that away! If you were to offer me two hundred thousand, I wouldn't take it. I'm a free man. And everything that all of you, rich and poor alike, value so highly and hold so dear hasn't the slightest power over me. It's like so much fluff floating in the air. I can get on without you, I can pass you by, I'm strong and proud. Mankind is moving toward the highest truth, toward the highest happiness possible on earth, and I am in the front ranks.

LOPAHIN: Will you get there?

TROFIMOV: I will. [Pause.] I will get there, or I will show others the way to get there.

[*The sound of axes chopping down trees is heard in the distance.*]

LOPAHIN: Well, good-bye, my dear fellow. It's time to leave. We turn up our noses at one another, but life goes on just the same. When I'm working hard, without resting, my mind is easier, and it seems to me that I, too, know why I exist. But how many people are there in Russia, brother, who exist nobody knows why? Well, it doesn't matter. That's not what makes the wheels go round. They say Leonid Andreyevich has taken a position in the bank, 6,000 rubles a year. Only, of course, he won't stick to it, he's too lazy. . . .

ANYA: [*In the doorway.*] Mamma begs you not to start cutting down the cherry trees until she's gone.

TROFIMOV: Really, you should have more tact! [*Exits.*]

LOPAHIN: Right away—right away! Those men . . . [*Exits.*]

ANYA: Has Firs been taken to the hospital?

YASHA: I told them this morning. They must have taken him.

ANYA: [*To* YEPIHODOV, *who crosses the room.*] Yepihodov, please find out if Firs has been taken to the hospital.

YASHA: [*Offended.*] I told Yegor this morning. Why ask a dozen times?

YEPIHODOV: The aged Firs, in my definitive opinion, is beyond mending. It's time he was gathered to his fathers. And I can only envy him. [*Puts a suitcase down on a hat box and crushes it.*] There now, of course. I knew it! [*Exits.*]

YASHA: [*Mockingly.*] Two-and-Twenty Troubles!

VARYA: [*Through the door.*] Has Firs been taken to the hospital?

ANYA: Yes.

VARYA: Then why wasn't the note for the doctor taken too?

ANYA: Oh! Then someone must take it to him. [*Exits.*]

VARYA: [*From adjoining room.*] Where's Yasha? Tell him his mother's come and wants to say good-bye.

YASHA: [*Waves his hand.*] She tries my patience.

[DUNYASHA *has been occupied with the luggage. Seeing* YASHA *alone, she goes up to him.*]

DUNYASHA: You might just give me one little look, Yasha. You're going away. . . . You're leaving me . . . [*Weeps and throws herself on his neck.*]

YASHA: What's there to cry about? [*Drinks champagne.*] In six days I shall be in Paris again. Tomorrow we get into an express train and off we go, that's the last you'll see of us. . . . I can scarcely believe it. *Vive la France!* It don't suit me here, I just can't live here. That's all there is to it. I'm fed up with the ignorance here, I've had enough of it. [*Drinks champagne.*] What's there to cry about? Behave yourself properly, and you'll have no cause to cry.

DUNYASHA: [*Powders her face, looking in pocket mirror.*] Do send me a letter from Paris. You know I loved you, Yasha, how I loved you! I'm a delicate creature, Yasha.

YASHA: Somebody's coming! [*Busies himself with the luggage; hums softly.*]

[*Enter* MME. RANEVSKAYA, GAYEV, ANYA, *and* CHARLOTTA.]

GAYEV: We ought to be leaving. We haven't much time. [*Looks at* YASHA.] Who smells of herring?

MME. RANEVSKAYA: In about ten minutes we should be getting into the carriages. [*Looks around the room.*] Good-bye, dear old home, good-bye, grandfather. Winter will pass, spring will come, you will no longer be here, they will have torn you down. How much these walls have seen! [*Kisses* ANYA *warmly.*] My treasure, how radiant you look! Your eyes are sparkling like diamonds. Are you glad? Very?

ANYA: [*Gaily.*] Very glad. A new life is beginning, Mamma.

GAYEV: Well, really, everything is all right now. Before the cherry orchard was sold, we all fretted and suffered; but afterward, when the question was settled finally and irrevocably, we all calmed down, and even felt quite cheerful. I'm a bank employee now, a financier. The yellow ball in the side pocket! And anyhow, you are looking better, Luba, there's no doubt of that.

MME. RANEVSKAYA: Yes, my nerves are better, that's true. [*She is handed her hat and coat.*] I sleep well. Carry out my things, Yasha. It's time. [*To* ANYA.] We shall soon see each other again, my little girl. I'm going to Paris, I'll live there on the money your great-aunt sent us to buy the estate with—long live Auntie! But that money won't last long.

ANYA: You'll come back soon, soon, Mamma, won't you? Meanwhile I'll study. I'll pass my high school examination, and then I'll go to work and help you. We'll read all kinds of books together, Mamma, won't we? [*Kisses her mother's hands.*] We'll read in the autumn evenings, we'll read lots of books, and a new wonderful world will open up before us. [*Falls into a revery.*] Mamma, do come back.

MME. RANEVSKAYA: I will come back, my precious. [*Embraces her daughter. Enter* LOPAHIN *and* CHARLOTTA *who is humming softly.*]

GAYEV: Charlotta's happy: she's singing.

CHARLOTTA: [*Picks up a bundle and holds it like a baby in swaddling clothes.*] Bye, baby, bye. [*A baby is heard crying:* "Wah! Wah!"] Hush, hush, my pet, my little one. ["Wah! Wah!"] I'm so sorry for you! [*Throws the bundle down.*] You will find me a position, won't you? I can't go on like this.

LOPAHIN: We'll find one for you, Charlotta Ivanovna, don't worry.

GAYEV: Everyone's leaving us. Varya's going away. We've suddenly become of no use.

CHARLOTTA: There's no place for me to live in town, I must go away. [*Hums.*]

[*Enter* PISHCHIK.]

LOPAHIN: There's nature's masterpiece!

PISHCHIK: [*Gasping.*] Oh . . . let me get my breath . . . I'm in agony. . . . Esteemed friends . . . Give me a drink of water. . . .

GAYEV: Wants some money, I suppose. No, thank you . . . I'll keep out of harm's way. [*Exits.*]

PISHCHIK: It's a long while since I've been to see you, most charming lady. [*To* LOPAHIN.] So you are here . . . glad to see you, you intellectual giant . . . There . . . [*Gives* LOPAHIN *money.*] Here's 400 rubles, and I still owe you 840.

LOPAHIN: [*Shrugging his shoulders in bewilderment.*] I must be dreaming. . . . Where did you get it?

PISHCHIK: Wait a minute . . . it's hot. . . . A most extraordinary event! Some Englishmen came to my place and found some sort of white clay on my land . . . [*To* MME. RANEVSKAYA.] And 400 for you . . . most lovely . . . most wonderful . . . [*Hands her the money.*] The rest later. [*Drinks water.*] A young man in the train was telling me just now that a great philosopher recommends jumping off roofs. "Jump!" says he; "that's the long and the short of it!" [*In amazement.*] Just imagine! Some more water!

LOPAHIN: What Englishmen?

PISHCHIK: I leased them the tract with the clay on it for twenty-four years. . . . And now, forgive me, I can't stay. . . . I must be dashing on. . . . I'm going over to Znoikov . . . to Kardamanov . . . I owe them all money . . . [*Drinks water.*] Good-bye, everybody . . . I'll look in on Thursday . . .

MME. RANEVSKAYA: We're just moving into town; and tomorrow I go abroad.

PISHCHIK: [*Upset.*] What? Why into town? That's why the furniture is like that . . . and the suitcases. . . . Well, never mind! [*Through tears.*] Never mind . . . men of colossal intellect, these Englishmen. . . . Never mind . . . Be happy. God will come to your help. . . . Never mind . . . everything in this world comes to an end. [*Kisses* MME. RANEVSKAYA'*s hand.*] If the rumor reaches you that it's all up with me, remember this old . . . horse, and say: "Once there lived a certain . . . Simeonov-Pishchik . . . the kingdom of Heaven be his. . . ." Glorious weather! . . . Yes . . . [*Exits, in great confusion, but at once returns and says in the doorway.*] My daughter Dashenka sends her regards. [*Exits.*]

MME. RANEVSKAYA: Now we can go. I leave with two cares weighing on me. The first is poor old Firs. [*Glancing at her watch.*] We still have about five minutes.

ANYA: Mamma, Firs has already been taken to the hospital. Yasha sent him there this morning.

MME. RANEVSKAYA: My other worry is Varya. She's used to getting up early and working; and now, with no work to do, she is like a fish out of water. She has grown thin and pale, and keeps crying, poor soul. [*Pause.*] You know this very well, Yermolay Alexeyevich; I dreamed of seeing her married to you, and it looked as though that's how it would be. [*Whispers to* ANYA, *who nods to* CHARLOTTA *and both go out.*] She loves you. You find her attractive. I don't know, I don't know why it is you seem to avoid each other; I can't understand it.

LOPAHIN: To tell you the truth, I don't understand it myself. It's all a puzzle. If there's still time, I'm ready now, at once. Let's settle it straight off, and have done with it! Without you, I feel I'll never be able to propose.

MME. RANEVSKAYA: That's splendid. After all, it will only take a minute. I'll call her at once. . . .

LOPAHIN: And luckily, here's champagne, too. [*Looks at the glasses.*] Empty! Somebody's drunk it all. [*Yasha coughs.*] That's what you might call guzzling . . .

MME. RANEVSKAYA: [*Animatedly.*] Excellent! We'll go and leave you alone. Yasha, *allez!* I'll call her. [*At the door.*] Varya, leave everything and come here. Come! [*Exits with* YASHA.]

LOPAHIN: [*Looking at his watch.*] Yes . . . [*Pause behind the door, smothered laughter and whispering; at last, enter* VARYA.]

VARYA: [*Looking over the luggage in leisurely fashion.*] Strange, I can't find it . . .

LOPAHIN: What are you looking for?

VARYA: Packed it myself, and I don't remember . . . [*Pause.*]

LOPAHIN: Where are you going now, Varya?

VARYA: I? To the Ragulins'. I've arranged to take charge there—as housekeeper, if you like.

LOPAHIN: At Yashnevo? About fifty miles from here. [*Pause.*] Well, life in this house is ended!

VARYA: [*Examining luggage.*] Where is it? Perhaps I put it in the chest. Yes, life in this house is ended. . . . There will be no more of it.

LOPAHIN: And I'm just off to Kharkov—by this next train. I've a lot to do there. I'm leaving Yepihodov here . . . I've taken him on.

VARYA: Oh!

LOPAHIN: Last year at this time, it was snowing, if you remember, but now it's sunny and there's no wind. It's cold, though. . . . It must be three below.

VARYA: I didn't look. [*Pause.*] And besides, our thermometer's broken. [*Pause. Voice from the yard:* "Yermolay Alexeyevich!"]

LOPAHIN: [*As if he had been waiting for the call.*] This minute! [*Exits quickly.*]

[VARYA *sits on the floor and sobs quietly, her head on a bundle of clothes. Enter* MME. RANEVSKAYA *cautiously.*]

MME. RANEVSKAYA: Well? [*Pause.*] We must be going.

VARYA: [*Wiping her eyes.*] Yes, it's time, Mamma dear. I'll be able to get to the Ragulins' today, if only we don't miss the train.

MME. RANEVSKAYA: [*At the door.*] Anya, put your things on. [*Enter* ANYA, GAYEV, CHARLOTTA. GAYEV *wears a heavy overcoat with a hood. Enter servants and coachmen.* YEPIHODOV *bustles about the luggage.*]

MME. RANEVSKAYA: Now we can start on our journey.

ANYA: [*Joyfully.*] On our journey!

GAYEV: My friends, my dear, cherished friends, leaving this house forever, can I be silent? Can I, at leave-taking, refrain from giving utterance to those emotions that now fill my being?

ANYA: [*Imploringly.*] Uncle!

VARYA: Uncle, Uncle dear, don't.

GAYEV: [*Forlornly.*] I'll bank the yellow in the side pocket . . . I'll be silent . . .

[*Enter* TROFIMOV, *then* LOPAHIN.]

TROFIMOV: Well, ladies and gentlemen, it's time to leave.

LOPAHIN: Yepihodov, my coat.

MME. RANEVSKAYA: I'll sit down just a minute. It seems as though I'd never before seen what the walls of this house were like, the ceilings, and now I look at them hungrily, with such tender affection.

GAYEV: I remember when I was six years old sitting on that window sill on Whitsunday, watching my father going to church.

MME. RANEVSKAYA: Has everything been taken?

LOPAHIN: I think so. [*Putting on his overcoat.*] Yepihodov, see that everything's in order.

YEPIHODOV: [*In a husky voice.*] You needn't worry, Yermolay Alexeyevich.

LOPAHIN: What's the matter with your voice?

YEPIHODOV: I just had a drink of water. I must have swallowed something.

YASHA: [*Contemptuously.*] What ignorance!

MME. RANEVSKAYA: When we're gone, not a soul will be left here.

LOPAHIN: Until the spring.

[VARYA *pulls an umbrella out of a bundle, as though about to hit someone with it.* LOPAHIN *pretends to be frightened.*]

VARYA: Come, come, I had no such idea!

TROFIMOV: Ladies and gentlemen, let's get into the carriages—it's time. The train will be in directly.

VARYA: Petya, there they are, your rubbers, by that trunk. [*Tearfully.*] And what dirty old things they are!

TROFIMOV: [*Puts on rubbers.*] Let's go, ladies and gentlemen.

GAYEV: [*Greatly upset, afraid of breaking down.*] The train . . . the station. . . . Three cushions in the side pocket, I'll bank this one in the corner . . .

MME. RANEVSKAYA: Let's go.

LOPAHIN: Are we all here? No one in there? [*Locks the side door on the left.*] There are some things stored here, better lock up. Let us go!

ANYA: Good-bye, old house! Good-bye, old life!

TROFIMOV: Hail to you, new life!

[*Exits with* ANYA. VARYA *looks round the room and goes out slowly.* YASHA *and* CHARLOTTA *with her dog go out.*]

LOPAHIN: And so, until the spring. Go along, friends . . . Bye-bye! [*Exits.*]

[MME. RANEVSKAYA *and* GAYEV *remain alone. As though they had been waiting for this, they throw themselves on each other's necks, and break into subdued, restrained sobs, afraid of being overheard.*]

GAYEV: [*In despair.*] My sister! My sister!

MME. RANEVSKAYA: Oh, my orchard—my dear, sweet, beautiful orchard! My life, my youth, my happiness—good-bye! Good-bye! [*Voice of* ANYA, *gay and summoning:* "Mamma!" *Voice of* TROFIMOV, *gay and excited:* "Halloo!"]

MME. RANEVSKAYA: One last look at the walls, at the windows. . . . Our poor mother loved to walk about this room . . .

GAYEV: My sister, my sister! [*Voice of* ANYA: "Mamma!" *Voice of* TROFIMOV: "Halloo!"]

MME. RANEVSKAYA: We're coming.

[*They go out. The stage is empty. The sound of doors being locked, of carriages driving away. Then silence. In the stillness is heard the muffled sound of the ax striking a tree, a mournful, lonely sound.*

Footsteps are heard. FIRS *appears in the doorway on the right. He is dressed as usual in a jacket and white waistcoat and wears slippers. He is ill.*]

FIRS: [*Goes to the door, tries the handle.*] Locked! They've gone . . . [*Sits down on the sofa.*] They've forgotten me. . . . Never mind . . . I'll sit here a bit . . . I'll wager Leonid Andreyevich hasn't put his fur coat on, he's gone off in his light overcoat . . . [*Sighs anxiously.*] I didn't keep an eye on him. . . . Ah, when they're young, they're green . . . [*Mumbles something indistinguishable.*] Life has gone by as if I had never lived. [*Lies down.*] I'll lie down a while. . . . There's no strength left in you, old fellow; nothing is left, nothing. Ah, you addlehead! [*Lies motionless. A distant sound is heard coming from the sky, as it were, the sound of a snapping string mournfully dying away. All is still again, and nothing is heard but the strokes of the ax against a tree far away in the orchard.*]

Masterpieces of the Modern World

EDITED BY

KENNETH DOUGLAS
Late of Yale University

AND

SARAH N. LAWALL
Professor of Comparative Literature
University of Massachusetts, Amherst

Time has cast its definitive vote in favor of most of the earlier works in this anthology. Over the centuries, they have held the attention and aroused the enthusiasm of generations of readers; moreover, at the remove of a century or more, it is possible to see fairly clearly what qualities they have in common, so that such collective terms as "Neoclassicism," "Romanticism," and "Realism" have an agreed-upon meaning in literary history.

But what is "Modernism"? Is there such a thing? In our century, many authors have been widely appreciated, among them those included here, and their works hailed as modern masterpieces; and in some respects they are easier to assess, being close enough to our own time so that their vocabulary, and the historical and social contexts from which they spring, are reasonably familiar. Yet their very closeness in time puts them all in the foreground, so that it is hard to make out affinities and differences among them with any certainty. We can see them more sharply, in fact, if we look at them first in the light of some features of late nineteenth century writing that they simultaneously incorporate yet rebel against.

i.

The realist-naturalist movement, which dominated literature in the second half of the nineteenth century, claimed to focus on the actual world, viewing it without theological or moral presuppositions, in the manner of empirical science, and giving due weight to the social, political, and psychological forces influencing human behavior. At the same time, however, the introspective and visionary tradition of Romantic poetry was evolving into a new, subjective poetry taking reality only as a point of departure, as something not to be photographically described and scientifically analyzed but to be transformed into an imaginative vision of the "essence" of things. This new poetry was called "symbolist," after its use of symbolic language to evoke hidden meanings.

Of course the literary use of symbols is not new. Medieval literature, for example, alludes constantly to shared religious beliefs through a system of symbols where the rose symbolizes love, the dove the Holy Spirit, and the serpent Satan. Yet the nineteenth century symbolists developed their own approach, which focuses on a more personal, earthly vision and on an extreme self-consciousness in the use of language. A symbol, in their sense, is an image or cluster of images created in a particular poem to suggest another plane of reality, alluding to some idea that cannot be expressed in more direct and rational terms. Each poem offers its own vision or state of mind, and allows the reader to penetrate appearances through its unique transformation of perspective. Such intuitive penetration is held to be a fuller and more meaningful mode of thought and perception than mere objectivity. Its aim is to touch a primitive level of being where, for example, the five senses fuse: colors have taste, sights have physical texture, sounds have odor, and so on. (This fusion is called *synesthesia.*) Objective reality still exists, but appears transformed. An actual flower described in photographically realistic detail will not do; on the contrary, the poet must suggest the "idea of flower," an essence reflected in all real flowers, yet, as Mallarmé puts it, "absent from all bouquets." As can be seen, symbolist poetry can be very abstract in its implications, but it is also firmly based in concrete images and runs the gamut from the most material objects (a carcass, a deck of cards, a rainspout) to the most unreal: a "musician of silence," "hearses . . . parading in the brain," the "clash of icicles against stars." It is not, therefore, an escape from everyday reality so much as a transformation of it, the creation of a new world reassembled in the mind from pieces of the old.

The other great theme of symbolist poetry is language, especially the process of writing. The writer who must express underlying reality has an awesome responsibility to find the right words, a responsibility that Mallarmé found paralyzing as he faced "the empty paper whose blank whiteness defends it." The symbolist poet uses the same language as all of us, for there is no other, but this language must be purified into "poetic language" through a totally controlled arrangement of all possible levels of form. It is the relationship of words that counts, not just their dictionary definitions, as will be seen in the symbolist poems that follow. In Baudelaire's "Spleen," the combined use of so many words suggesting water (from the squeaky logs to the woman's dropsy) permeates the scene with unhealthy damp. Rimbaud's "Barbarian" introduces startling images, openly denies their reality ("they don't exist"), and then goes deeper into the world of the imagination by using more of the same kind of images. Many poems, like Baudelaire's "Windows," describe the process of writing itself; others, like Mallarmé's "Saint," evoke a focal point of ideal artistic creation which is that of poetry and music alike. The extraordinary self-consciousness of the symbolist poet became an element of the poem itself, focusing attention on its manipulations and distortions of language to assert, once and for all, that the only reality is that of the mind.

Symbolist writers frequently compared their poetry with music, whose characteristics they tried to reproduce. Both poetry and music they felt to be "pure" arts, where line and harmony mattered more than individual notes or words. They saw analogies, too, between their art and painting, whose distinctive new methods of depicting reality were being tried at the same period, as every visitor to a modern art gallery knows. Yet these moves away from the familiar seemed, in the poetic as in the art world, upsetting to the average citizen, whose common sense was outraged. Accused of being wilfully obscure, a number of these writers retired further into their own private worlds in the face of a hostile and unsympathetic society; the lesser among them lost touch with the very realities they claimed to transform. Yet, at its best, symbolist poetry remains a powerful example of the human imagination shaping its world—a challenge to the empirical observations of the scientist from what Rimbaud called, in his own writing, the "alchemy of the word."

ii.

Charles Baudelaire (1821–1867), the first of these symbolist writers, set out deliberately to startle the bourgeois, and he succeeded. His chief collection of poems bears the provocative title *Flowers of Evil* (*Les Fleurs du mal*) and includes invocations to Satan as well as half a dozen poems that in 1857, the year of the volume's publication (and the year of *Madame Bovary*), were banned as obscene. Yet Baudelaire's intentions reach far beyond sensationalism: the reader was to be started, but into serious involvement with the work. Baudelaire's verse preface involves both poet and reader in an overarching acknowledgment of human weakness and hypocrisy, made worse by an inertia of will causing and overshadowing all other sins. "Hypocritical reader,—my fellow,—my brother!" he ends, in a famous cry of common guilt that was later taken up by T. S. Eliot in *The Waste Land*.

Baudelaire is a master of precise and realistic description

used for effects that go beyond realism. The decaying, maggoty carcass of "A Carcass" ("Une Charogne") becomes the source of a strange and ironic beauty, a swarming, vibrating new life covering the outline of the old. A chill revelation of mortality emerges from the description of the city in "Spleen," where the mundane details, from the cat twisting and turning uncomfortably on cold tiles to the smelly deck of cards left behind by an old woman, exist not for themselves but to evoke an atmosphere of lethargy and decay climaxing in the tiny, altogether unrealistic final scene where two face cards talk sinisterly of their past loves.

Spleen

January, irritated with the whole city,
Pours from his urn great floods of gloomy cold
To the pale dwellers of the nearby graveyard
And death to the foggy outskirts of town.

My cat seeking a bed on the tiled floor
Moves ceaselessly his thin, mangy body;
The soul of an old poet wanders in the rainpipe
With the sad voice of a shivering ghost.

The great bell wails, and the smoking log
Accompanies in falsetto[1] the catarrhous clock,
While in a deck of cards full of dirty scents,

A mortal heritage from a dropsical old woman,
The handsome knave of hearts and the queen of spades
Converse covertly of their dead love affairs.

1. Pitched unnaturally high.

Baudelaire was also an experimenter with language, founder of the modern prose poem, and a visionary who wrote poetry about the act of writing. In "Windows," a prose poem of 1863, he ends an apparently realistic description of an old woman by saying that her story is not true—only a "legend"—or at least that he does not care whether it is true, so long as it provides a point of departure for his own imagination, letting him know "who he is, and what he is."

Windows

Looking from outside through an open window one never sees as many things as looking through a closed window. There is nothing more profound, more mysterious, more fruitful, more obscure, more dazzling than a candlelit window. What can be seen in the sunlight is always less interesting than what happens behind a windowpane. In that dark or luminous hole, life lives, life dreams, life suffers.

Beyond the waves of the roofs, I see a middle-aged woman, already wrinkled, poor, always bent over something, and who never goes out. With her face, with her clothes, with her gesture, with almost nothing, I have rewritten the story of that woman, or rather her legend, and sometimes I tell it to myself, crying.

Had it been a poor old man, I could have done the same to his story just as easily.

And I lie down, proud of having lived and suffered through others than myself.

Perhaps you will tell me: "Are you sure that this legend is the real one?" What does the nature of a reality which is not in me matter, if it helped me to live, to feel that I am and what I am?

One of Baudelaire's most influential poems is "Correspondences," a vision of the mystic unity of all nature revealed in the correspondence through synesthesia of our senses:

Correspondences

Nature is a temple where living pillars
Sometimes allow confused words to arise;
Man goes by through forests of symbols
Which observe him with familiar eyes.

Like long echoes which mingle far away
In a dark and unfathomable unity,
Vast as the night and as the light,
Perfumes, colors, and sounds answer one another.

Some perfumes are fresh as children's flesh,
Sweet as oboes, green as prairies,
And others, corrupt, rich and triumphant,

Possessing the expansion of infinite things,
Like amber, musk, benzoin and incense,
Which sing the raptures of the mind and the senses.[2]

The poem has, in fact, the shape of a logical argument; the thesis is set out in the first stanza, explained in the second, and illustrated with cumulative examples in the third and fourth. Nature, says Baudelaire, is a system of perpetual analogies. One thing corresponds to another: physical objects to each other (a pillar in a temple, for example, to a tree in the forest), spiritual reality to physical reality, and the senses (taste, smell, touch, sight, and hearing) among themselves to produce such combinations as *bitter green*, a *soft look*, a *harsh sound*. We are not usually aware of the "universal analogy"—the forest of the first stanza observes us without our knowing it—but the poet acts as seer and guide to urge us on toward a state of awareness where both "mind and senses" are transported into another dimension.

iii.

Arthur Rimbaud (1854–1891) and Stéphane Mallarmé (1842–1898) developed other aspects of the symbolist transformation of experience into vision. In a short and violent literary career —he wrote all his poetry between the ages of 15 and 20—Rimbaud moved from an aggressive, cynical realism to an attempt to transform both self and surroundings into a magically perfect whole. His autobiographical *A Season in Hell* (*Une Saison en enfer*, 1873) describes vividly his effort to reach the unknown by pure hallucination, a "derangement of all the senses." "I saw quite frankly a mosque in place of a factory, a school of drummers made up of angels—a parlor at the bottom of the lake. . . . I became a fabulous opera." At the end of *A Season in Hell*, he tells us that he has rejected these earlier illusions and embraced earth and rugged reality; but since he never wrote poetry to celebrate his newly rediscovered realism, he remains best

2. In the original French, both "Spleen" and "Correspondences" are sonnets.

known for the passion and beauty of his apocalyptic visions. "Barbarian" ("Barbare") is one of the later prose poems Rimbaud called *Illuminations.* Set outside normal time and space, "Long after the days and the seasons, and people and countries," it enacts a withdrawal that moves gradually from echoes of the real world to an elemental core of tenderness and beauty, completely inside the world of imagination.

Barbarian

Long after the days and the seasons, and people and countries,
The banner of raw meat against the silk of seas and arctic flowers; (they do not exist.)
Recovered from the old fanfares of heroism,—which still attack the heart and head,—far from the old assassins.
—Oh! the banner of raw meat against the silk of seas and arctic flowers; (they do not exist.)—
Bliss!
Live embers raining in gusts of frost.—Bliss!—fires in the rain of the wind of diamonds flung out by the earth's heart eternally carbonized for us.—O World!
(Far from the old retreats and the old flames, still heard, still felt.)
Fire and foam. Music, veerings of chasms and clash of icicles against the stars.
O bliss, O world, O music! And forms, sweat, eyes and long hair floating there. And white tears boiling,—O bliss!—and the feminine voice reaching to the bottom of volcanos and grottos of the arctic seas.
The banner . . .

Clearly the reader cannot approach this poem as if it were by Wordsworth—or even by Baudelaire. Rimbaud's vision has leaped beyond the picturing of actual scenes, whether a green pastoral landscape or a city room on a rainy day, and beyond the rational core that so often supports even a visionary poem—for example, the argument of Baudelaire's "Correspondence," describing the notion of transcendental vision and explaining how to reach it. Rimbaud, in fact, cuts short all explanations and simply presents the vision for itself. His poem is not, however, a merely impressionistic, unstructured collection of words. It is carefully organized according to an almost musical development of themes and pattern of oppositions. The poet first notifies his reader that this *is* a vision, taking place well apart from the world of real people, established nations, and the normal passage of time. He then proceeds to set out the particular materials with which he is going to build his world of the imagination. It is made of primitive, "barbarian" oppositions: red and white (raw meat and arctic flowers, embers and frost, fire and diamonds, flames and icicles), heat and cold, subterranean volcanos and starry sky. On a more fundamental level, it is a world that swings between the real and the ideal. Rimbaud moves from a quasi-autobiographical world of "old fanfares . . . old retreats" to an ideal world where there are ultimately no complete images, only "forms, sweat, eyes . . ." as component parts for a new creation. The types of images already symbolize this change. The "banner of raw meat" (a distortion of the expected silken banner) and the arctic flowers that do not exist are "hallucinated" from relatively familiar objects. In the second half of the poem, after the pivotal word "Bliss!", the chief images are cosmic and unimaginable as real scenes. Now it is the "old retreats" that are set aside, subordinated in parentheses, and the "veering of chasms" that becomes a new reality. The poem's second half also introduces the separate themes of bliss, world, and music, combining them musically in the final paragraph where everything poises on the end of new life, with the introduction of a feminine voice reaching into the very heart of this fiery, icy existence. "Barbarian" ends on a note of openness and ambiguity, as the cyclical opposition of reality and the imagination seem about to recommence with "The banner . . ." Rimbaud's poem typifies the symbolist doctrine of taking ordinary reality apart in order to assemble a new transcendent vision, employing to this end a subtly non-rational language as close to the patterns of music as possible.

Of all the symbolist writers, Mallarmé is the most thoroughly visionary. He chiefly uses ordinary words and images of ordinary things, but only as raw material for a wholly imaginary product. Avoiding the direct approach, he finds he can say more obliquely. So he suggests, rather than names; keeps several levels of meaning alive at the same time; complicates his syntax and even sometimes misleads us (to prolong the pleasure of discovery). An early poem titled "Saint" will illustrate many of his characteristics. The saint of the poem (according to an earlier title, Saint Cecilia, the patron saint of music) is seen as if in a stained-glass window before a cabinet where musical instruments are kept. The concealed cedarwood lute, which no longer gleams with gold as it did when formerly played with accompanying flute and mandola (an early mandolin), and the old book lying open at the Magnificat (a hymn of praise to God), establish the idea of an actual music that is now stilled. The last two stanzas evoke in contrast an ideal, soundless music symbolized by the saint who now plays an imaginary harp. She, the "musician of silence," has her finger poised on a golden harp shaped by the outstretched wing of a sculptured angel, a "feathered instrument" that receives from the evening sun all the gilding that was lost to the real instrument of the first stanza. The presence of the ideal music is felt more strongly by the end of the poem than was the discontinued actual music suggested by the poem's beginning.

Saint

At the window holding
The old cedarwood disgilt[3]
Of her lute shining
Once with flute or mandola,

Stands the pale saint spreading
The old book which unfolds
On the Magnificat glistening
Once for vespers and compline:[4]

At this monstrance window[5]
Brushed by the harp that an angel
Makes in his evening flight
For the delicate tip

3. Having lost its gilding, or gold decoration.

4. Evening church services.

5. An altar receptacle in which the Host is held: it has a small glass window in front.

Of the finger that without cedar
Or old book she balances
On the feathered instrument,
Musician of silence.

iv.

Again, what is "Modernism"? It has been called "the tradition of the new," consciously rejecting old habits of thought and familiar literary forms while striving to reflect our century's social and political changes, its dangers and anxieties, its rapid growth in technological and psychological knowledge. Modernism has also been called the "dehumanization of art," an overly self-conscious style that pushes into the background traditional humanistic notions of the individual and society. Yet modernism is not divorced from the past. It restates, in terms naturally influenced by the cultural crisis of our times, the same questions about existence and human nature that are implied in the nineteenth-century tension between realism and symbolism, rationality and intuition, representation and expression. Hardly a writer in this selection of modern masters—and they are an extraordinarily diverse group—has not learned from both realist and symbolist examples.

The term "Modernist" is usually reserved for more experimental and innovative modern works, those that view experience in new ways and adopt new forms. Not all writers included here are "modernist" in that special sense, for the modern tradition is pluralistic, marked by the many different ways, experimental and traditional, in which it embodies twentieth-century experience. But readers of the following selections must often be prepared to meet new styles and new world views, prepared also to examine these fictional worlds to see if they are really "dehumanized" or merely different.

Rather than a commonly accepted picture of reality, registered as if with a camera, one finds many perspectives, some seemingly objective and others shaped and distorted to suggest a special, personal view or to offer a non-literal level of understanding. One also finds great technical sophistication. Modern literature explodes the tightly organized plots, progressive character development, and chronological organization of nineteenth-century models, adopting instead freer, more associative patterns that represent the movement of consciousness. A novel may be organized so that themes and images are repeated and juxtaposed in musical rather than narrative ways; it may shift from "objective" third-person description to subjective stream-of-consciousness. Modern poetry often uses free verse and fragmentary discourse instead of traditional meters and narrative patterns; it can combine poetry with prose, inarticulate cries with extended philosophical meditation, startlingly new associations of images with complex allusions to sources both inside and outside the poem. Modernist literature is often highly self-conscious, unable to speak without being aware of speech, constantly questioning its own words and pointing at its own artistic techniques. While not all the works included here are innovative to the same degree, none is wholly untouched by visionary overtones or completely devoid of poetic manipulations of language.

The modern tradition is still evolving, and modernist works appear each year to challenge the insights of their predecessors and to exploit different aspects of form. The reader coming to these selections for the first time is invited to relate them to earlier works and to each other, to compare them with his or her own sense of modern culture, and finally to form a personal assessment of the way in which these texts are "modern"—a formal literature expressing our own era and pointing toward the future.

WILLIAM BUTLER YEATS

Yeats, who became the central figure of the Irish Literary Renaissance of the 1890's and subsequent decades, was born in Dublin in 1865 to moderately prosperous Protestant parents. After schooling in London and Dublin, holidays spent with relatives on his mother's side in County Sligo, in the northwest of Ireland, and a brief period in art school, he decided on a literary career. He developed an admirable prose style, writing fiction, literary essays, and autobiography.

Primarily, however, Yeats was a poet. Publishing his first volume of poems in 1889, he rapidly established his reputation in England. But he never looked on himself as anything but an Irishman and an Irish writer; he was convinced that the revivification of Irish materials (folk tales and Celtic mythology, with its gods and heroes) would both serve his country and provide the foundation for his own work. At the same time, he was aware of the literary currents of the day, notably the impact of French symbolism; he acquired, and maintained throughout his life, a keen interest in the occult and in Hindu thinking. It was here that he found a central core of meaning in history and in the individual life and was led to a conception of the richness of symbolic thinking and the essential role it could play in his poetry.

On the personal level, Yeats's prolonged, frustrated love for Maud Gonne, a fiery revolutionary beauty, left an indelible mark on his psyche and his art. Under her influence he became active, to some degree, in the politics of the Irish national revival. But he saw that the proper sphere for him was cultural. With Lady Gregory, a somewhat older woman, he founded what became the Dublin Abbey Theatre, remaining intensely involved in its fortunes for many years. For its stage, he wrote plays in both prose and verse using Irish themes, making dance an integral element in some after Ezra Pound had introduced him to the Japanese Noh plays. He served for a number of years in the Senate of the Irish Free State, where he conscientiously discharged his duties.

As a poet, Yeats first made himself known as an accomplished late romantic; his poems often evoked a misty, world-estranged atmosphere that is suggested by such titles as *The Shadowy Waters*. However, as early as the 1890's, he set out to acquire a leaner, harder style that would be less remote from the rhythms and, sometimes, the bluntness and coarseness of everyday speech. The unceasing struggle for self-renewal was rewarded by an exemption from that decline in talent that so frequently overtakes the aging creative writer. Indeed, in the 1920's, when Yeats was a sexagenarian, he produced a body of work unexcelled in its vigor and freshness. Most of the poems reproduced here date from that period.

The poems of his youth have an indefiniteness that he eliminated in his later work. The old poetic words were now employed less frequently, and the rhythms, which had always been subtly modulated, never falling into singsong, matched the new realism of thought and terminology by setting up at times an almost drastic clash between the stress pattern required by the sense of the phrase and the underlying metrical pattern, which nevertheless always makes its presence felt. The rhymes, sometimes imperfect, also vigorously impose a prosaic, nonpoetic countercurrent. The persona we seem to glimpse behind all this is passionate yet inexorably caught up in reflection, haughtily ambitious, and contemptuous of the beauty of any stray phrase, or even of any isolated poem, that could not be integrated into a vaster, meaningful pattern.

"The Stolen Child" was printed in Yeats's first collection of poems, *Crossways* (1889). Here, in a way eminently typical of him at this stage, reality and imagination contend; the intangibility of the faery speaker is balanced by the real place names of County Sligo, which the poet knew so well, and the faery's Puckish intimacy with nature is set off, in the fourth stanza, against a hauntingly nostalgic evocation of the cozy domestic joys that the child will know no more. Yeats himself realized, before the close of the 1880's, that evasion had been his favorite theme. He resolved to compel his poetry, in the future, to come to grips with the real.

Like the vast majority of his countrymen, he was taken totally by surprise when a rebellion against British rule broke out in Ireland in 1916. Though it was rapidly suppressed, the British, with the stupidity that seems to be de rigueur in such circumstances, executed a number of the ringleaders, among them a boy of sixteen, and opinion swung violently behind the rebels. Several months elapsed before Yeats could come sufficiently to terms with his emotions to make his own comments on the situation in "Easter 1916." He conveys his sense of shock by contrasting the then and the now of those who, "with vivid faces," had been planning the rebellion. Others, including Yeats, had found them ridiculous, looking on them as endless talkers, perhaps, or self-dramatizing fantasists. But with their deed, and their deaths, and the challenge they had hurled at the future, all was "changed utterly." They had run down the curtain on "the casual comedy" and arbitrarily forced "a terrible beauty" upon the world. Only those willing to make of their own minds a stonelike thing could have maintained such a resolve. In the third stanza he evokes, by way of contrast, that other beauty, the boundless anonymous relatedness and fluidity, outside history, of the natural world in which man, too, is immersed. This stanza does not again name the beauty that is "terrible." Instead, the last line names the "stone," the stumbling block. Was this hardening within a purpose, this exclusivism that led to death, worth the cost? For these men, Yeats decides, the dream and the passion were sufficient reward, apart from the possible outcome or the perhaps questionable value of their sacrifice. The poet thinks of them with a maternal tenderness, and fulfills his poet's role by "murmuring" their names into the future.

No lines by Yeats have been more often quoted in the 1970's than those of "The Second Coming." They were written under the impact of the exceptionally murderous World War I and its chaotic aftermath. Yeats was already working toward his cyclical theory of history (to be found in the prose work *A Vision,* second edition, 1937), a notion that readily jibed with his belief in reincarnation. His particular theory has convinced few, if any, however, and his actual sequences of historical epochs and turning points are even less compelling. But the poem is metaphor, not historical speculation, and as such is loaded with meaning for the poet's contemporaries. The sense of impending doom that he translates into visual terms still haunts us. It would be hard to find a more striking example of a poet thinking in images that are not strung together as mere conceits or developed into an overarching simile, but fuse into a single cry of passion, prophecy, and intellect.

"Sailing to Byzantium" bitterly ponders the contrast between the instinctive life of procreation, birth, and death, and the intellectual life that demands purpose, discipline, and achievement, if the aged man is not to be "paltry" as a scarecrow. To symbolize the willed perfection of the spirit, the poet chooses Byzantium, capital of the Eastern Empire of Christendom, whose austere religious art imposes on the fluctuation and fluency of the life of culture an ideal coherence of form, like a Bach fugue. It is a "holy city," and the poet calls on the divinely transfigured sages who people it to guide him toward eternity, which, like a poem, he conceives of as an "artifice." Once he has been removed from nature, he will himself become an artifact, a golden bird, whose task it is to keep a drowsy emperor awake with news of the time. "Eternity," William Blake declared, "is in love with the productions of time." Does Yeats's poem exemplify this, or does it depict time as in love with time?

"The Tower" is central in the work of the sexagenarian poet, who knows there is no escape from "Decrepit age." He brings to mind those who have lived before him, in his house or close at hand, for he would inquire whether they too had stormed against old age. Along with them he summons up his own creation Red Hanrahan, whose reckless, bawdy existence he has conceived as the antidote to Yeats's own circumspection. Cannot Hanrahan resolve the problem that can still eclipse the poet's sun and blot out the day:

"Does the imagination dwell the most/Upon a woman won or a woman lost?" In the poem's third section, Yeats bequeathes to these "upstanding men" he admires the pride and magnanimity he himself has inherited from his ancestors, and also his own faith in man's self-willed creativity. The final stanza names, because it would deprive them of their nameless horror, the indignities that waning years may yet inflict.

The remaining poems of our selection bear witness that the poetic gift did not abandon him. In "Coole Park and Ballylee, 1931," water and sky become transparent emblems for the human soul. The house they surround is Lady Gregory's (the older woman with whom Yeats was associated in the running of the Abbey Theatre, and but for whose firm guidance he felt he would have failed to accomplish anything of substance); here the house is celebrated as a kind of cloister that has sheltered and fostered cultural endeavor. Already it belongs to a vanished age, for the modern world has reverted to the instability of nomadism. "Lapis Lazuli" ironizes about hysterical anxiety in a menacing epoch and coolly finds all the world to be a stage upon which posturing and fretting are endlessly repeated. Yeats believed, as he wrote in a letter describing a piece of Chinese lapis lazuli that he owned, that "the east has its solutions always and therefore knows nothing of tragedy." The last stanza of the poem insinuates that the Chinese sages represented in the carving—or the carver himself, or his cultural milieu—have discovered the formula of great art, which enables gaiety and tranquility to survive in the midst of pain.

For himself, as a man, Yeats did not choose this path to a passionless summit. He asserted, rather, his kinship with the speaker in "The Wild Old Wicked Man," a poem with the tone of a ballad which reaches a somewhat oblique, balladlike intensity of feeling. The refrain, "Daybreak and a candle-end," has a terminal ring that extends beyond the obvious erotic connotation. With the conclusion ("But a coarse old man am I, I choose the second-best."), Yeats identifies himself fully with his personage. In "The Circus Animals' Desertion," this attitude is represented not as choice but as necessity, as the poet throws a wry backward glance at the now receding creatures of his imagination. Finally, in "Under Ben Bulben," which he arranged to have printed at the end of his last collection of poems, Yeats provided the epitaph that is now engraved upon his headstone. He proclaims the double truth of reincarnation, which hurls the individual soul on a perhaps ceaseless flight through eternity, but also sees to it that those who belong together stay together in their successive incarnations. And he imperiously states the purpose that drives on each great shaper or maker: "Profane perfection of mankind."

LUIGI PIRANDELLO

Pirandello at no time shared the extravagant hopes voiced by the youthful Rimbaud. He saw all things as garish, kaleidoscopic, hallucinatory, inextricably entangled, and irremediably ambiguous. An unbeliever, he gives the lie to the notion, dear to the believer, that a basic despair unfits a man for goal-oriented activity. Not only was he a prolific writer, but in his plays specifically he created his own genre, his own theater, and public, beyond Italian shores as well as at home, that was able to appreciate his work.

His success is bound up with a courageous refusal to accept the standard routines of middle-class theater and with the adoption of startling, even bewildering innovations which, to a considerable extent, were also the revival of age-old theatrical devices and situations. Plausibility flies out of the window, and there is no attempt to render the implausible more palatable by a shrewd measuring of the dosage. With the rapid, firecracker-like eruptions of unforeseeable occurrences, of reversals of fortune or behavior, that mark his plays, Pirandello calls into existence something akin to the Italian Renaissance's improvisatory Commedia dell'Arte (he calls one play *Tonight We Improvise*) and to the Roman comedies of Plautus, most familiar to today's audiences in the form of the musical *A Funny Thing Happened on the Way to the Forum*.

Yet this sophisticated, highly educated man did not simply purvey popular theatrical concoctions. He had his own attitude to life. Disabused without being cynical, he saw men as fraudulent not alone in their surface pretensions. What lay behind the surface was no less shoddy, uncertain, and vacillating. One mask, one facet of the personality, was replaced by another. There was no center that could impose a genuine order. Many of his personages are bitterly aware of their own incoherence, and their self-examination is both persistent and fruitless. Or it may occur that one especially lucid character acts as spokesman for the author. Even then, the feverish ratiocination and the eruptions of a multicolored unreality that thrill and amaze the theater public do not hide his sadness.

Pirandello's career proceeded from poetry through novels (seven of them) and short stories (they fill fifteen volumes) to plays. In every genre he began with his native Sicilian settings, and he translated several of his works into Sicilian dialect. But his most distinctive gifts required the greater complexity of thought and feeling associated with personages of less restricted horizons, and to such personages he turned, particularly in the three plays most frequently performed today: *Right You Are (If You Think So)*, *Henry IV*, and *Six Characters in Search of an Author*. The first of these exemplifies his skepticism concerning "truth." A family newly arrived in town shocks the natives and arouses their impertinent curiosity by its unorthodox living arrangements. It is discovered, through much prying, that the family's members cannot even agree on what their relationship to one another is though they are content to live with this ambiguity, or would be, were it not for their neighbors' shamelessness. Properly directed and performed, with brio, with rapierlike thrusts and a compelling drive, this play can transport audiences into a frenzy of intellectual excitement.

The "Six Characters" are, as the play's title declares, looking for an author. Restless, unhappy embryos of an act of literary conception that has never reached fulfillment in a completed work, they invade a stage where a play by Pirandello is being rehearsed and demand to be incarnated by the actors. The actors make the attempt, but their dissatisfaction with the unusually raw material that is offered them, and the characters' own disapproval of the actors' substitution of standardized banalities for the uniqueness of the events that make up the whole of the characters' shadow existence, constitute—in the form of a fiasco—a Pirandellian tour de force. He imprisons his audience in an avowed unreality that nevertheless seems to cast an intense (if fitful) light on the audience's own emotional and ideological world.

Henry IV may be regarded as the most massively successful embodiment of Pirandello's concern with the unanswerable question: What is Truth? Unlike Pilate, he could never wash his hands of it. The hero in this play has fallen from a horse and struck his head while participating in a pageant in the role of the medieval German emperor Henry IV. He emerges from unconsciousness but not from the role, and since he is wealthy he is able, with the connivance of friends and hirelings, to maintain it. This is the basic datum—but, since Pirandello is the author, the play bursts from these bonds. The ultimate sequence of reversals might be summarized as: role seen as role, role become reality, role again seen as role but not abandoned, role abandoned, role seen as role yet—for at this juncture something irremediable occurs—unwillingly reassumed. The hero remains locked forever, and consciously so, within a senseless farce. A similar forced wearing of a mask is performed by the French mime, Marcel Marceau: What had been tried on in jest becomes an inescapable destiny.

Pirandello did not comment on politics or social movements, but his writings make it plain that he looked on society as a burden inflicted upon the individual, with which he has to come to terms. He himself had been the obedient son of a father who derived his income from sulphur mines in Sicily. Never was he more disastrously obedient than in 1894, when he accepted as his wife a young woman he had not previously known, the daughter of his father's business partner. After some years of marriage, and with the collapse of the sulphur mining venture, Signora Pirandello's mind became affected. She raged against her husband with an insane jealousy nothing could assuage—though he handed over to her all his earnings, keeping only enough for streetcar fare. Even when her hostility turned also against their daughter, he decided not to have his wife institutionalized. The situation was terminated only with her death in 1918.

The close relationship between this tortured domesticity

and Pirandello's fascination by the polar opposites appearance and reality can hardly be denied. In view of accusations that he took a perverse delight in holding up to mockery the normal and respectable, it is important to point out that he was in fact an ethical and deeply responsible person who metamorphosed his own pain into an impressive body of work that has led to a renewed understanding of theater as theater.

ANDRÉ GIDE

The tremendous impact of André Gide on European letters early in the twentieth century was not due to the precision and clarity of his classically perfect style, although this was much admired; on the contrary, Gide's influence was that of a moral spokesman who rejected traditional wisdom, social customs, and an intellectualized or "literary" approach to life. Although accused by traditionalists of being immoral and perverse (possibly because he discerned some hypocrisy and self-serving righteousness in their own attitudes), Gide was constantly preoccupied by the need for honesty, rigorous self-analysis, and action based on moral commitment. His many novels, plays, and essays explore questions of human behavior and motivation, uncovering layer after layer of impulse and reaction and reaching for the very core of human personality.

Writers before Gide have of course pointed out the need for honesty and self-analysis: what was new in Gide's works was the strong emphasis on sensuality, and the rejection of a purely intellectualized view of life. From *Fruits of the Earth* (*Les Nourritures terrestres*) in 1897 to the *Journals* in 1950, Gide passionately upheld a sensuous and emotional appreciation of life as the basis for true honesty with oneself. He insisted on complete *disponibilité* or openness to all experience, on passion, spontaneity, and sincerity, on divesting oneself of all preestablished ideas, and on constant self-interrogation. Gide's own self-interrogation led him to recognize and reveal his homosexuality, and many of his most striking works (*The Immoralist, Strait is the Gate, The Counterfeiters*) consider the complex relationships of people in love.

Religion is another frequent theme in Gide's work, not only because of his personal quest (which he mentions in the beginning of "The Return of the Prodigal Son") but because it, like love, allows him to consider patterns of apparent selflessness and self-interest in human behavior. Sometimes the two themes are linked, as in *Strait Is the Gate* and *The Pastoral Symphony*; sometimes a religious theme is linked with a criticism of traditional institutions and established views, as in "The Return of the Prodigal Son."

Gide had an even more personal interest in writing "The Return." Toward the end of the nineteenth century, a number of prominent literary figures had either reaffirmed their Catholic faith after a period of disaffection, or had been converted to Catholicism. Militant Catholics such as the poets Paul Claudel and Francis Jammes felt it their duty to try to convert an important contemporary intellectual such as André Gide, especially when Gide himself was obviously preoccupied by moral questions and in fact entered into a correspondence with Claudel on the subject. Gide, however, came from a strong Protestant background and was most unwilling to give up his philosophical independence. When he heard rumors that people were boasting of his impending conversion, he wrote "The Return of the Prodigal Son" as an indirect assertion of independence, and as an explanation in parable form of his religious unwillingness to join an established church. Situating the story within a "frame," he imagines himself represented as kneeling, like the medieval donor of a religious painting, in a corner of the canvas. In this introductory section, and once again just before the Father's reprimand, Gide openly enters the tale to state its importance to himself, as narrator.

In retelling the New Testament parable, Gide further alters it by introducing a third, younger brother who will take up the unfinished quest of the defeated prodigal. To this younger brother, who idolizes him, the prodigal confesses that only a failure of nerve had induced him to return home. The hunger, the defeats, and the humiliations have been too much for him. Yet, in a sense, all is not lost. Confident that he is of tougher fiber, and can persist until he finds the longed-for Garden of Eden in the desert, the younger brother accepts the older brother's blessing and vanishes into the darkness to make his way alone.

To understand the "lesson" that this parable offered the readers of Gide's generation, the conversation with the older brother is particularly important. Gide erects a basic ideological barrier between the two brothers, going far beyond the fraternal rivalry and ill-feeling that the Bible story hints at. The prodigal had felt, and still believes, that only someone with the daring to shake off his inherited burden of advantages and responsibilities, and to plunge into the unknown, can win true riches. The elder brother, on the other hand, proudly accepts his place in the established order with its conventional wisdom—which, in his eyes, is unchallengeable truth. He is clearly portrayed as an establishment figure, in a very unsympathetic light. Gide cannot accept the elder son as the legitimate administrator of the interests on earth of a loving heavenly Father, for this elder son is a harsh authoritarian and disciplinarian who sees men as fundamentally evil, to be kept in bounds only by means of menaces and punishment.

There are political overtones to this 1907 story. In France at the time, a highly authoritarian trend, at bottom political rather than religious, was making itself heard. Its leaders would gladly have enlisted the Church in the service of their political goals. Their hatred of all undisciplined religiosity, of a "sentimental" personal attaching to Christ, for instance, knew no bounds. The perpetual threat of chaos required a ruthless repression of unchanneled impulse. Gide, on his side, was equally certain that both philosophical and political regimentation meant the death of the spirit.

MARCEL PROUST

Marcel Proust is known as the author of one book: an enormous, fifteen-volume exploration of time and consciousness called *Remembrance of Things Past* (*À la Recherche du temps perdu*). Written almost completely in the first person, and based on events in the author's life (though by no means purely autobiographical), the novel is famous as both an evocation of and a meditation on universal human emotions in the closed world of turn-of-the-century Parisian society.

The overall theme of the novel is suggested by a literal translation of its title: "In search of lost time." The narrator, partly the real Proust and partly an imagined "Marcel," is an old man weakened by a long illness who puzzles over the events of his past, trying to find in them a significant pattern. He begins with his childhood, ordered within the comfortable security of accepted manners and ideals in the family home at Combray. In succeeding volumes he goes out into the world, experiences love and disappointment, discovers the disparity between idealized images of places and people and their crude, sometimes banal reality, and is increasingly overcome by disillusionment with himself and society. Until the end of the novel Marcel remains a *grand nerveux*, an extremely sensitive person impelled by the large experiences of his life—love, art, separation, death—to discard early certainties and to seek out an intuited meaning for his life and for his dimly felt vocation as a writer.

In the short ending chapter, things suddenly come into focus as Marcel experiences tantalizing moments of spontaneous memory and recognizes the work of time in the aged and enfeebled figures of his old friends. Facing the approach of death with a joyful sense of existential continuity through memory, he realizes that his vocation as an artist lies in giving form to this concrete experience of time. The buried and apparently lost past is still alive within us, a part of our being, and memory can recapture it to give coherence to our present identity. "Marcel" has not yet begun to write by the end of the last volume, *Time Regained,* but paradoxically the book that fulfills his aims is already there: Proust's *Remembrance of Things Past.*

Love (both heterosexual and homosexual), art, death, pursuit of pleasure, isolation of the self in its own subjectivity, the fatal passage of time, the contradictions between imagination and reality: all these themes appear in passages of rich, minutely detailed sensuous description. For according to Proust, his novel of the human condition is not primarily philosophical, not an "analytical novel" but an "introspective" one; it avoids abstract arguments, expressing instead the texture of experience, a concrete perception of life as it grows and changes through time. (Proust's affirmation of life in its fully expressed wholeness is often compared with that of Henri Bergson, the twentieth-century French philosopher, remembered especially for his view of time as a reality to be lived rather than merely contemplated.) Marcel's awareness of his life in time comes about not through rational or "forced" memory but through spontaneous or "involuntary" memory—the chance recollection that occasionally wells up from his subconscious when he repeats a previous action such as drinking tea, stumbling, or opening a particular book. This memory is more powerful because it draws upon a buried level of experience where the five senses are still linked, where life still comes to us whole. Sounds are connected with color (the name *Brabant* with gold), and emotions with the settings in which they were experienced (sorrow with the smell of varnish on the stairway up to bed.) Involuntary memory recreates a whole past world in all its concrete reality—and so does art. When Proust attributes such an absolute value to art, and makes it the focus of his book, he joins the tradition of French moralist writers from Montaigne to Camus who speak directly of universal values.

When Proust's first volume (*Swann's Way*) appeared in 1913, it was immediately seen as a new kind of fiction. Unlike nineteenth century novels such as Flaubert's *Madame Bovary*, *Remembrance of Things Past* has no clear and continuous plot line building to a dénouement, nor (until the last volume, published in 1927) can the reader detect a consistent development of the central character, Marcel. Most of the novel sets forth a roughly chronological sequence of events, yet its opening pages swing through recollections of many times and places before settling on the narrator's childhood in Combray, and the second volume (*Swann in Love*) is a story told about another character and in the third person. Thus the novel proceeds by apparently discontinuous blocks of recollection, bound together by the central consciousness of the narrator. This was always Proust's plan—he repeatedly asserted that he had had in mind a fixed structure and goal for the novel when he wrote its first and last chapters in 1909, and that this plan was echoed in the "solidity of the smallest parts"—and his substantial revisions of the first draft enriched the already-existing structure without changing the sequence of scenes and events.

Proust's long sentences and mammoth paragraphs reflect the slow and careful progression of thought among the changing objects of its perception. Characters are remembered in different settings and perspectives: Charles Swann appears first as the visitor who often delays the child Marcel's bedtime kiss from his mother, next as an anxious and disappointed lover, and finally as a tragic, dying man rejected by his friends the Guermantes in their haste to get to a ball. Marcel's grandmother appears throughout the scenes in

Combray, later during a visit to the seaside resort of Balbec, still later in her death agonies when Marcel is unable truly to grieve, and finally as a sudden recollection when Marcel has trouble tying his shoelace in Balbec. The little musical phrase which Marcel first hears as part of a sonata by the composer Vinteuil, and which is associated with love in various settings, recurs toward the end of the novel as part of a septet and becomes a revelation of the subtle constructions of art. Places overlap in the memory: the imagined and the real Balbec or Venice confront one another, the church steeples of Vieuvicq and Martinville are juxtaposed. Proust's style is a flexible instrument sensitive to the vagaries of the mind, a quality also seen, although in very different forms, in such younger writers of the period as James Joyce and Virginia Woolf.

The opening chapter of the novel, "Overture," foreshadows the work's themes and methods rather like the overture of an opera. All but one of the main characters appear or are mentioned, and the patterns of future encounters are set. Marcel, waiting anxiously for his beloved mother's response to a note sent down to her during dinner, suffers the same agony of separation as does Swann in his love for the promiscuous Odette, or the older Marcel himself for Albertine. The strange world of half-sleep, half-waking with which the novel begins prefigures later awakenings of memory. Long passages of intricate introspection, and sudden shifts of time and space, introduce us to the style and point of view of the rest of the book. The narrator shares the painful anxiety of little Marcel's desperate wait for his mother's bedtime kiss; for though his observations and judgments are tempered with mature wisdom, he is only at the beginning of his progress to full consciousness. The remembrance of things past is a key to further discovery but not an end in itself.

"Overture" ends with Proust's most famous image, summing up for many readers the world, the style, and the process of discovery of the Proustian vision: nibbling at a madeleine (a small rich pastry) that he has dipped in lime-blossom tea, Marcel suddenly has an overwhelming feeling of happiness. He soon associates this tantalizing, puzzling phenomenon with the memory of earlier times when he sipped tea with his Aunt Leonie. He realizes that there is something valuable about such passive, spontaneous, and sensuous memory, quite different from the abstract operations of reason forcing itself to remember. Although the Marcel of "Combray" does not yet know it, he will pursue the elusive significance of this moment of happiness until, in *Time Regained*, he can as a complete artist bring it to the surface and link past and present time in a fuller and richer identity.

THOMAS MANN

When the German novelist Thomas Mann died in 1955, he had become an international figure to whom people looked for statements on art, modern society, and the human condition. His career spanned a time of great social and cultural change, and his work reflects both the upheavals of two world wars and the predicament of the artist, isolated from ordinary people by his or her special sensitivity. In stories about the role of the artist, or the decay of the great families of the prosperous middle class, Mann analyzes not only the culture of his time but also the universal human conflicts between art and life, sensuality and intellect, the individual and society. His most famous characters explore the limits of awareness, often ending in disease, madness, or death. Many of them symbolize human attitudes, but never abstractly: they are always described realistically, with pertinent attention to detail and with ironic perception and humor. Mann's novels are long and complex, highly organized with subtly interrelated themes and images that build up an increasingly rich association of ideas. In his own words, they constitute an "epic prose composition . . . understood by me as spiritual thematic pattern, as a musical complex of associations."

Mann drew heavily on personal experience for events and characters, and his letters and essays show that he felt deeply involved in the problems facing his fellow artists. But this was not merely a personal involvement, and Mann's protagonists symbolize much more than his own career. His first novel, *Buddenbrooks*, which describes the decline of a prosperous German family through four generations, is to some extent based on the history of the Mann family business; nonetheless, the elements of autobiography are quickly absorbed into the more universal themes of the inner decay of the German burgher tradition, its isolation from other segments of society, and in the portrait in Hanno Buddenbrooks of a developing artistic sensitivity and its relation to death. As artist and craftsman, Mann always insisted on distinguishing the work of art from its raw material, the emotions and experiences of life. He cultivated objectivity, distance, and irony in his own works, from the seemingly autobiographical *Tonio Kröger* to the humorous *Confessions of Felix Krull, Confidence Man*. No character, including the narrator, is immune from the author's critical eye.

Mann's fictional world is governed by a tension or dualism between sensuous experience and intellect or will. A diseased and alienated imaginative soul is set against a healthy, gregarious, somewhat obtuse normal citizen; the erratic and poor artist against the disciplined and prosperous burgher; the dark, brown-eyed Latin against the blond, blue-eyed Nordic; warm, unselfconscious feelings against icy, distant intellect; freedom against authority; immorality and decadence against moral respectability; a longing for the eternal and infinite against active participation in everyday life. There is no recommended resolution of these polarities, for if either overwhelms the other tragedy must follow. The artist, though representing one side of the dualism, is especially sensitive to the claims of both, and growing awareness of their combined importance is a sign of his or her maturation. The artist must live both extremes at once, in constant lucidity and pain, perpetually giving form to an underlying chaos of vital forces.

In a variety of circumstances throughout the novels, an artistic sensibility confronts different aspects of society and the human condition. The aspects are often linked, as in *Tonio Kröger*, where the budding artist Tonio is fascinated by the blond Teutonic normalcy of Hans and Ingeborg, and also in the overall history of the Buddenbrooks family, where the children of self-confident, agressive, and disciplined Consul Johann Buddenbrooks become increasingly introspective, hesitant, unhealthy, and artistic. The end of the family comes with young Hanno, a musical genius who is completely absorbed in his piano improvisations and fatal temptation to the infinite that music implies. Yet the artist-figure also confronts destiny on a larger scale than the fall of a prosperous merchant family. In *The Magic Mountain*, Hans Castorp has to decide how to live as he listens to the competing dogmas of the humanist Settembrini and the fanatic antirationalist Naphta, and undergoes a double temptation of oblivion through eroticism (Clavdia Chauchat) and death (symbolized by the mountain sanatorium). Mann's artist is not, however, merely a plaything of his environment: Hans Castorp turns to active participation in a world at war, and the Joseph of the biblical tetralogy *Joseph and His Brethren* controls not simply his destiny but that of others. The final, humorous metamorphosis of the artist-figure comes in the comic *Confessions of Felix Krull*, whose hero uses his skill and ironic insight to manipulate society to his advantage.

A much more somber vision of the artist, which offers something fairly close to a symbolic interpretation of contemporary history, is contained in the late novel *Doctor Faustus*, which Mann called "the novel of my epoch, dressed up in the story of a highly precarious and sinful artistic life." The composer Adrian Leverkühn sells his soul to the devil in order to become aware of the extremes of his own personality, thus enriching his experience and his composition. His music is determined by the patterns derived from the twelve-tone scale, and it opposes —in Leverkühn's composition, "Lamentation of Doctor Faustus"—the freer formal patterns of Beethoven's Ninth Symphony with its episodic choral finale, the "Ode to Joy." A compelling work, *Doctor Faustus* carries out one of the possibilities of the dialectic tension between art and life. It intensifies and pushes to an extreme the authoritarian arguments of Mann's own *Reflections of a Non-Political Man*, and reflects his horror at the negation of life inherent in Hitler's barbarism.

Many of Mann's themes derive, as he was aware, from the nineteenth-century German aesthetic tradition in which he grew up. The philosophers Schopenhauer and Nietzsche, and the composer Wagner had most influence on his development: Arthur Schopenhauer (1788–1860) for his vision of artistic suffering and development; Friedrich Nietzsche (1844–1900) for his portrait of the diseased artist overcoming chaos and decay to produce, through discipline and will, art works that justify existence; and Richard Wagner (1813–1883), for embodying in his own career Nietzsche's "diseased artist." Wagner planned to integrate completely all aspects of the art work, in his case opera, right down to the musical themes or *Leitmotifs* (pronounced "light-moteefs") each of which is associated with a particular person, thing, action, or state of being, and evokes those associations with increasing richness whenever the leitmotif is repeated. Mann's use of an analogous system of verbal leitmotifs is well known.

Tonio Kröger is an early work, written shortly after *Buddenbrooks,* and published in 1903. Since it describes the childhood and development of an artist in a burgher family, it is often taken as thinly veiled autobiography, or as at least a personal statement. Certainly it contains many elements from Mann's own life: the description of the home town, the Nordic father and Latin mother, recollections of particular childhood friends, boredom with school and enthusiasm for the poet Theodor Storm, a trip to Italy, and even the author's mistaken arrest for fraud when he returned home. The long central discussion of art and life also represents the central tension of Mann's major works. Yet *Tonio Kröger* is at the same time a highly structured novella (or short novel) that does not require any knowledge of its author's life to make clear the protagonist's growth toward self-knowledge.

The story falls roughly into three parts: Tonio Kröger's school years, with his infatuation with blond, blue-eyed Hans Hansen and his later adolescent love for blond, blue-eyed Ingeborg Holm; his early career as a writer, including a discussion on art with the Russian painter Lisabeta Ivanovna; and a visit to Denmark in which he comes to see Hans and Inge as idealized symbols of that "life" which is the counterpart of his own pull toward art. The point of view develops from an initial objectivity, in which Tonio's successive enthusiams, awkwardness, and disappointments are recorded with little overt interpretation, to a final assessment when the protagonist has earned the right to comment on his past life.

Tonio Kröger is in many ways a microcosm of themes and methods found in Mann's work as a whole. The familiar oppositions between bourgeois and artist, North and South, health and sickness, intellect and emotions, are all here, as well as the artist's final acceptance and transcendence of such oppositions. Leitmotifs, evocative phrases repeated almost word for word, link memories throughout the text and provide an overall emotional resonance: Tonio's "dark, fiery mother, who played the piano and mandolin," his father's "thoughtful blue eyes" and "wild flower in his buttonhole." The leitmotifs occur in Tonio's mind sometimes as clusters of associations: "the fountain, the old walnut tree, his fiddle, and away in the distance the North Sea" evoking his attachment to his childhood home, and the "gypsies living in a green wagon" symbolizing and representing an antithesis to Northern bourgeois respectability.

As the story progresses, the leitmotifs change and occasionally blend: on the boat to Denmark, Tonio recalls both the walnut tree and the "creaking of a garden gate" associated with Hans Hansen. The repetition and variation of leitmotifs unifies the tale, and it also reaffirms *Tonio Kröger* as the cumulative record of Tonio's life experience. The end of the story telescopes these fragments of memory in a half-real, half-imaginary encounter between Tonio and a Danish "Hans" and "Inge," an encounter that permits the mature Tonio to recognize the importance of this kind of recall for his role as an artist. Here both Tonio and the style of *Tonio Kröger* reach a level of awareness in which remembered experience becomes the material for art.

WALLACE STEVENS

The poetry of Wallace Stevens expresses the dualism between reality and imagination, between things as they really are and as we perceive and then shape them. For we can never really know reality directly; we see, touch, taste, smell, or hear what is outside us, constructing an image of the outside world, of everything we are not, but the outside world also exists in itself, beyond the grid of our image of it. Stevens' poetry lives in this paradox, swinging between the two poles, emphasizing now the shaping, creative imagination, now the material world of which we are only partly aware. The names of real Connecticut towns, an inventory of the trash on a dump, and descriptions of breakfast with coffee and oranges or of scars on an old piece of furniture, inhabit his poems side by side with the most abstract speculations, transformations of everyday scenes, visions of the edge of space, and a constant attitude of philosophical inquiry. Poetic artifice—the playful and imaginative use of language—clothes the most mundane observations, as if to assert a counterpoint between verbal style as an expression of imagination and the real subject about which it tries to speak. This balancing of dualities continues throughout Stevens' work, becoming more richly and subtly developed in his later poems.

"The Emperor of Ice Cream" is an early poem that already shows Stevens' absorption with this theme. The scene is a wake: a dead woman lies covered with the same sheet on which she once embroidered fantail pigeons. Stevens, however, begins his poem in the kitchen with the festivities in which the survivors are taking part. For the day is devoted not only to the dead but to the living, in whose imperial court the ice cream server is emperor, and the women dressed in their best clothes are handmaidens. Words with erotic overtones (*concupiscent*, *wenches*) reinforce the scene's essential hedonism, in which the only reality that counts is the pleasure of the moment.

Yet there is another reality, that of the dead woman, who has now become a mere object much like her own furniture, and Stevens painstakingly registers its details. The dresser is made of pine wood and lacks three glass knobs, the dead woman's calloused feet protrude from the too-short embroidered sheet. Such close-up observation puts the woman in a new imaginative context, in a world of lifeless inanimate things whose stillness comments with grim finality on the first stanza's boisterous celebration. The empire of ice cream contains both life and death; people, flowers, and yesterday's newspapers all ultimately come down to the same level of bare physicality. Wisdom lies in accepting the common outcome of all earthly appearances—"Let be be finale of seem"—and in celebrating life while it remains.

Stevens' juxtaposition of reality and our imaginative perception of it is echoed throughout his writing by a dialectic of other oppositions, one idea being raised seemingly only to be challenged and tested by another. Thus southern warmth and creativity in "The Idea of Order in Key West" oppose spare northern chill in "The Snow Man"; the color of red symbolizes reality and blue the imagination in "Large Red Man Reading"(and the colors combine to make purple); the glittering, reflecting surface of the river of rivers in Connecticut contrasts with its suggested depths and powerful flow. Frequently two points of view compete in the same poem: the argumentative birds in "Bantams in Pine Woods," pagan and orthodox Christian views in "Sunday Morning," nature and civilization in "Ancedote of the Jar." Stevens is not reaching for conclusive truths; he prefers questions to remain open so that explorations may continue.

Another recurring preoccupation of Stevens' work is with music. His poems are filled with the imagery of musical performance: the harpsichord of "Peter Quince at the Clavier," the singer in "The Idea of Order at Key West," the bird with its "foreign song" in "Of Mere Being." Other poems speak of a blue guitar, an old horn, a lute, citherns, saxophones, not to mention the "tink and tank and tunk-a-tunk-tunk" of an unnamed instrument (perhaps a banjo). Even the title of his first book is the name of a musical instrument, *Harmonium*, and he had wanted to name his collected poems *The Whole of Harmonium*. Music for Stevens was not however merely musical images in a poem, or the notion of "harmonizing" the sounds of words or holding contrasted ideas in "counterpoint." It implied for him a supreme, intuited language, the song of the golden bird on the edge of space in "Of Mere Being." The singer, bird or human, is the type of the poet, the "one of fictive music" who creates the world anew through the incantatory power of imagination.

The singer of "The Idea of Order at Key West" is such a poet, embodying imagination at its most ambitious: "She was the single artificer of the world /

In which she sang." Nature itself cannot create such a world, for it lacks the igniting spark; while the sea may imitate human gestures and sounds, it cannot truly speak, and makes only "meaningless plungings of water and wind." Imagination is supreme; the singer has "the maker's rage to order words" (*poet* comes from a Greek word meaning *maker*) and her song creates for herself and for her listeners a world of imagination in which lights from the fishing boats seem to map out the night against which they shine.

Stevens' poetry thus focuses on the ability of the individual imagination to conceive its own world. Whether expressed in realistic images or in abstract speculations, this theme could not please the politically-minded critics of the thirties, who accused him of being escapist and "a single artificer of his own world of mannerism." Stevens responded that he had "confidence in the spiritual role of the poet," and that this role was not to take sides on political issues, but to uncover for his society the possible relations between the subjective mind and the objective world in which it lives. Despite this, his early work was at first unappreciated; its gaudy exuberance made it seem less serious than the poetry of political commitment and visionary mysticism that Yeats was then writing, or Eliot's evocation in *The Waste Land* of a universal and profound despair. Only after the Second World War did Americans, and then Europeans, recognize that Stevens, too, was a master, worthy to stand beside his greatest contemporaries.

JAMES JOYCE

Et Tu, Healy! was the title of Joyce's first work. His father, a passionate adherent of Parnell in the controversy which split the Irish Parliamentary party and embittered Irish politics for many years to come, was so delighted by his nine-year-old son's essay attacking the virulent anti-Parnellite Timothy Healy that he arranged to have it printed. No copy is known to survive.

While Joyce certainly never renounced his Irish nationalism to become that contemner of things national, a "West Briton," his subsequent career diverged in almost every particular from the path he might have seemed destined to follow. In the language of the Church he announced his refusal to slide along the grooves of patriotic, cultural, and religious conformity: *Non serviam!* At the earliest possible moment he left Irish soil in favor of starvation in Paris, and he saw Ireland for the last time before the outbreak of World War I. The new Ireland, it is true, did nothing to indicate that Joyce would be persona grata within its bound-
of the Irish Free State, and until recently in the Republic of Ireland it was still impossible to purchase freely all of Joyce's works.

Yet this renunciation of residence in Ireland was accompanied by an unflagging interest in the Irish and, more particularly, in the Dublin scene. Friends sent him, at his request, all sorts of information and documentary material that kept him in touch with daily life. From *Dubliners* (1914) through A

Portrait of the Artist as a Young Man (1916), *Exiles* (1918), *Ulysses* (1922), and *Finnegans Wake* (1939), his works never cease to evoke his birthplace. And Joyce it is who has inscribed Dublin on the map of world literature.

Joyce attempted a supremely difficult task: to obtain the verdict of what has been called "contemporary posterity." He aimed, that is, at international acceptance, while yet loading his works with a wealth of topical and highly transitory allusions that might defeat—and frequently have defeated—the best-intentioned non-Irishmen. This approach has nothing in common with the method of the writer who seeks an entrée to the foreign market by exploiting the "picturesqueness" of his native land. Joyce made no concessions in order to attract an audience.

The homage paid to Ibsen by the young Joyce is often cited in order to establish his link with the naturalist school of writers, yet this admiration for the author of *Brand* (1866) and *Peer Gynt* (1867) is equally well fitted to show his kinship with the symbolists. By making that unwieldy and least naturally artistic art form, the novel, a miracle of controlled and infinitely rich and infinitely graduated echoes, Joyce proved himself the supreme symbolist. To attain his ends he did not scorn to use the humblest form of humor, of echo and suggestiveness—the pun; and he did so most liberally in his last work, *Finnegans Wake*. But the pun is not a mere conglomeration of sounds; it is an indissoluble unity of sound and significance. With Joyce it reached its apotheosis.

The symbolists in the main were poets, and to transfer their vision to the novel, that is to say, to pack every phrase of a lengthy tale with the wealth of meaning that each epithet of a brief lyric poem should convey, and more especially to relate coherently the larger blocks of this structure, was a formidable undertaking. To carry it out Joyce had recourse to the hierarchic sense found in medieval Catholicism, to its sense of pattern in human life and of kinship between macrocosm and microcosm. If the music of his work has a symbolist inspiration, its architecture is the gift of Mother Church.

Joyce certainly did not write to demonstrate the truth of revealed religion. Faithful, however, to his Catholic upbringing and his training in Thomistic Aristotelianism, he did aim at revealing the universal embodied in the particular. Thus in Joyce two traditions ran together: the symbolist "revival" of literature—a token of his attitude is his knowing Baudelaire's "Correspondences" by heart—and the Catholic conviction of an ordered and interpretable universe. Both, of course, are fundamentally at one in their affirmation of significance and their denial of all isolated "just-so-ness."

The opening of the *Portrait*, reproduced here, touches on Irish history and politics, the Church, and family relations, in the settings of school and home. All of Joyce's themes are here in a nutshell, in the seemingly artless and disconnected musings of the little Stephen. His father with the "hairy face" is, like God the Father, the first speaker. The story he tells serves to make the child aware of his separate identity: "He was baby tuckoo." Foreshadowing his vocation as a creative artist, Stephen makes the song he sings his own, prophetically enough, by taking liberties with everyday fact and ordinary language: "O, the green wothe botheth." Then comes the theme of the mother, the first incarnation for the artist-to-be of the Eternal Feminine and of the Muse. She plays on the piano so that he may dance. But this state of primal innocence and intimacy cannot endure. He hides under the table, and his mother asks for an apology. The threat which follows ("if not, the eagles will come and pull out his eyes") reminds us of Joyce's later near blindness. It becomes an insistent refrain:

> Pull out his eyes,
> Apologise,
> Apologise,
> Pull out his eyes.

Conscience is awakened. Here is the central theme of the *Portrait,* one critic (Hugh Kenner) insists, that of Sin: "the development of Stephen Dedalus from a bundle of sensations to a matured, self-conscious, dedicated, fallen being." The two later works, *Ulysses* and *Finnegans Wake,* will take up the phases, subsequent to the fall, of struggle and redemption.

Joyce placed comedy above tragedy. In other words, rather than hymn the nobility of heroic and inevitable defeat, he chose to affirm. And what Joyce affirmed, as in the repeated yes of Molly Bloom which marks the end of *Ulysses,* was the totality of things; a priori he excluded nothing. The artist's vocation is to understand, and hence—should he judge that men have erred—to forgive and ultimately to redeem.

To whatever degree they may remain caviar to the general, the impact of Joyce's works on numerous writers has been tremendous. For these writers they are not desiccating and defeatist, but lively stimuli to personal literary creativity. We may attribute this effect to Joyce's holding in a living tension those polar opposites—freedom bordering on chaos and a rigorous and fully conscious pattern. His handling of language revealed possibilities of which only traces can be found in earlier writers; he aroused the feeling that he had unhobbled and spurred on language so that for the first time its uttermost limits were explored. At the same time he showed that to construct the novel architectonically, with the minute care that had seemed appropriate only to the short lyric poem, was no vain endeavor.

VIRGINIA WOOLF

Virginia Woolf's fiction brings us to a world far removed from that of the realistic novel —the novel of plot, character, and social setting, with its "appalling narrative business of . . . getting from lunch to dinner," as she put it. Like Proust, whom she admired, Woolf writes of consciousness and mental perceptions, of exterior reality as filtered through a narrator's sensibility rather than presented directly as it is (or perhaps ought to be). But the traditional notions of character and point of view that still dominate Proust's writing are no part of hers. Woolf puts an extreme, almost poetic emphasis on form: on abrupt changes of point of view, on the interplay of inner monologues, on an intricate structure of interconnected and symbolic themes. She developed a fiction that can express an inner essential reality, self-contained: "Let us record the atoms as they fall upon the mind in the order in which they fall, let us trace the pattern, however disconnected and incoherent in appearance, which each sight or incident scores upon the consciousness."

Woolf's early critics attacked the apparent randomness of her style, accusing her of narrowness and aestheticism, of inability to structure a plot, of disregard or incomprehension of history. But her style is anything but random. Its qualities relate to what was happening in the visual arts at the time: if the traditional novel was like a realistic painting or a photograph, Woolf's was like post-Impressionistic art in its abstract arrangement of perspective, its concern with essences rather than surfaces. She called her novels "serious poetic experimental books," and they became more experimental as time passed. The first of them, *The Voyage Out* and *Night and Day*, were relatively traditional, but with *Jacob's Room* (1922) she eliminated the possibility of a settled, structured identification of the hero by having him described through a series of multiple and partial points of view. In *The Waves* (1931) there are not only soliloquies by six separate characters recalling their lives and relationships with the dead Percival, but also ten interludes by a different and omniscient narrator that describe the passage of a complete day from dawn to dusk. Woolf also experimented with the expansion and telescoping of time. In *Mrs. Dalloway* (1925), the preparations for Clarissa Dalloway's party and the party itself take place in one day, but concurrently her whole life story is recalled from childhood to her present age of fifty. Woolf's last novel, *Between the Acts* (1941), describes a country pageant in which all of English history is acted out, but the pageant itself is set within the framing story of Giles and Isa Oliver.

Such manipulations of time and point of view, however strange they may have seemed to Woolf's first readers, were in fact typical not only of her but of others whom we now see as modern masters: James Joyce, T. S. Eliot, Luigi Pirandello, and William Faulkner, to name but four. More individual was her view of the artist as androgynous, as possessing both masculine and feminine characteristics. In one of her essays she asserts that "the greatest writers lay no stress upon sex one way or another"—she argues that Lawrence, for example, weakens his work by a "display of self-conscious virility"—but the sexual identities of her own characters are not so much neutral as ambiguous. Some are homoerotic to a degree; others, the more individual and artistic personalities, blur in gender. *Orlando* (1928) tells of a protagonist who lives through centuries as both man and woman, maturing finally into acceptance of love and childbirth as a symbol of artistic vocation. Woolf's novels often portray such searches of incomplete personalities for full identity, in which the masculine and feminine are combined.

The climax of a Woolf story or novel is often an epiphany, a moment of heightened awareness in which a character suddenly gains an almost magical insight into the essence of a person or situation. The story "Moments of Being" turns on such an epiphany: Fanny Wilmot unexpectedly understands the significance of Julia Craye's courageous, independent, and slightly grotesque lifelong dedication to pure beauty. Julia is an artist who has chosen her own existence and given it shape by the power of her imagination; at the end of the story, the London night becomes "the effluence of her spirit" and a cloak she flings around her, while Julia herself blazes like a "dead white star."

"Moments of Being" uses the strategies of Woolf's novels: the telescoping of time, in which Miss Craye's life is recounted through several perspectives while Fanny drops her rose and picks it up again, the echoing of phrases and images (flowers, the pin), the central character's desperate search to possess essential being or beauty, and the author's subtle understanding of human feelings. The story has the narrow intimate focus for which Woolf has been criticized, but suggests an opening out into a larger context that includes both the shaping effect of Victorian society on the lives of early twentieth century people, and the struggles of human beings to fulfill their individual natures.

FRANZ KAFKA

It is not unusual to introduce Kafka in such a fashion that all but the boldest are frightened away from his writings. For tactical reasons, therefore, but also because it is true, let us begin by saying that Kafka's works are meticulously detailed accounts of happenings within the three dimensions and the time element of everyday reality. To see in the mind's eye what is represented as occurring presents no problem at all.

The dialogue, also, follows strictly all the normal rules of syntax; the sentences do not even approach those of Thomas Mann in complexity, the vocabulary is much more restricted than his. A great deal of this discourse, however, is of the "he said and she said" variety; that is, it records statements previously made by characters not present, perhaps reporting actions of yet other characters, or of personages who do not appear at all, or even passing on rumors and conflicting rumors. And nothing, and no one, is ever pinned down, a circumstance which is bound to give rise to bafflement and frustration.

The narrative sections, too, quite frequently expend their lucidity on the reporting of highly improbable or extremely curious incidents. Couples sink to the floor in loving embraces whose embarrassing interruption the circumstances make almost inevitable; mysterious agencies, inconclusively discussed by one or more characters, impinge on the hero decisively, yet in a way which leaves the purport of their intervention far from clear.

The result is that the reader tends to oscillate between the bafflement already alluded to and the search for, even the discovery of, a solution. But the very proponent of this solution may come to see that he has been unjustifiably dogmatic, while those who deny that any solution can be found slip all too easily, a little later, into some one-sided dogmatism of their own.

Most trenchantly characterizing this uneasy pendulum movement to which Kafka drives us is a phrase of Sartre's: "Kafka, or the impossibility of transcendence." For Kafka, unlike the positivists and the horizonless men of every age, saw this world of ours as a system incomplete in itself, traversed by fissures through which we glimpse something that for a moment seems to hold out the promise of a transcendent justification of all things and of ourselves. But then the vision disappears, and we fall back on the patchwork of immanence, of mundane reality. According to the religious interpretation of his work made by his biographer and friend Max Brod, Kafka depicts the world as it is—disconcerting, harsh, incurably ambiguous, the site of our logically undemonstrable conviction that God is good, but not of direct acquaintanceship with God—and does not share the view that a spiritual explanation of reality should try to win recruits by depicting the world as it is not. Yet according to another interpreter, Kafka mocks at the claims of the mystics and of religion in general.

Kafka's career as a whole was powerfully affected by the fact that he was a Jew. To be a Jew is to experience the impact of society in a way concerning which too few non-Jews trouble to inform themselves. Sooner or later the Jewish child is impressed, possibly as the result of some jeering remark or abusive epithet, with the sense of his *difference* from others, a difference about which nothing can be done. It does not stop there. The child learns that in the eyes of others the Jews are to blame, for anything or everything, and that he himself is guilty with the rest. But when such accusations from outside are repeated often enough, they arouse a sense of guilt within, also. Thus are born the conflicting impulses to admit guilt, yet to rebel against the unspecified and unproven accusation, proudly to refuse the assimilation which is denied and yet to long for it and strive toward it.

It should be mentioned, too, that Kafka's sense of guilt derived not only from these social pressures but also from his emotional involvement with his father, of whom he stood in awe and whose magnificent competence (so Franz Kafka saw it) contrasted with his own unreadiness to shoulder the burdens of marriage and a career. His first short story, "The Judgment" ("Das Urteil," 1913) most directly reveals the ambivalence of his attitude toward his father. Rebellion and repentance are intermingled. The story was written without a moment's hesitation in the course of one night, and the writing of the last sentence, very significantly, as Kafka told Brod, was accompanied by a sense of powerful sexual release.

Kafka's work is a great deal more, however, than an ingenious veiled portrayal of what it means to be a Jew in Western society. It does not affect us solely as the reflection of the situation of a minority to which we may not ourselves belong. For the suggestion may be advanced that the Jew, or the Wandering Jew, has come to be the archetype of Western man. The Jewish diaspora, the scattering of a people over the face of the earth, can be taken as the symbol of two things: of the increased uprootedness of individuals and populations all over the world, and of the state of consciousness induced by this separation from old values, old places, and old beloved objects.

"The Metamorphosis" ("Die Verwandlung," 1912) is the masterful and haunting expansion of a term of abuse. A human being is contemptuously called a louse, an insect. And usually that's all there is to it. Except that something remains—the wound, the sense of having been depreciated or degraded. Perhaps even an element of fear lurks in some crevice of the psyche, especially when the psyche is that of a child. Who knows, at what tender age, what dread transformations may sometimes occur!

Transformation is a common literary motif. Sometimes the fanciful and poetic predominated; sometimes the horrible. Here the horrible has the upper hand. It pounds at us all the more relentlessly because of the matter-of-fact tone used and the precise and circumstantial detailing of the embarrassments and physical difficulties that beset the transformed Gregor Samsa. Nor does he enjoy the privilege of suffering in isolation. The family is at once drawn in, and so is Gregor's employer, to whom the family is indebted. Gregor's uncomplaining readiness to support the entire family and the quiet sacrifice of his personal desires—all this goes unrecognized. The faults he attributes to himself and the sense of guilt they have instilled, built up to intolerable proportions by the massive disapproval of society and family—of his father, to be precise—set a gulf between him and human kind. Step by step, whatever is human recedes from him.

The peak of tension in this quietly told drama is reached when the father begins to pelt Gregor with apples. To this painful dilemma there can be only one solution. It happens, and at once. The family—sister, mother, and father—is bathed in light and joy; they experience a genuine renewal, for the monster is dead.

Few readers will fail to sense the persistent echo that this tale arouses in them. We were all once ten-year-olds; we still are a little. We do not have Kafka's gift for dredging up, in mythical form, the fears that afflicted us then, but we can recognize them when Kafka brings them to the light of day.

D. H. LAWRENCE

Of all the authors included in this section of the anthology, D. H. Lawrence is the only representative of those social classes whose members the spread of free popular education and the granting of scholarships enabled, in the nineteenth century, to rise intellectually "above their station." He was the son of a miner, and spent his childhood in a small mining town in the English Midlands. Despite his education and his travels, which took him through Europe, to Ceylon, Australia, Mexico, and the United States, and the contempt for his rough father which had been instilled in him by his bitter, "superior" mother, Lawrence remained in certain essentials very much his father's son.

When a writer of modest talent emerges from the people, his literary productions are likely to be rather palely derivative. He is conscious of the richer background of his social "betters," and treats too respectfully the established forms and conventions. But a young man driven on by the untamed forces that possessed Lawrence has an excellent opportunity to exceed in intensity and originality any similarly endowed but initially more cultivated writer. Did not Rimbaud bitterly condemn the education he felt had warped him, and express envy of the unspoiled illiterate?

Lawrence, however, could be classified as an unspoiled illiterate no more than any other writer. He read widely in English and other literatures, wrote a school text on European history, and explored a considerable range of topics—religion, psychology, myth, and so on. Not that he was ever in danger of becoming a scholar; he was interested more in finding confirmation of his own views and promptings that would aid their further development. But he is marked in spite of all by the narrowness of his early environment. The refinements, the smoothness, the avoidance of eccentricity, that come so easily to the young man from a cultivated home are rarely acquired later, and certainly not by a turbulent man of genius. In his life as in his writings, Lawrence was full of quirks, and it can surely be said that his books and articles contain more entirely preposterous assertions than those of any other writer represented in this section. But just as his most sensible friends, among them Aldous Huxley and Richard Aldington, and—above all—his wife, were able to discount in the man the elements of lesser value, since these were far outranked by his sterling qualities, so the perceptive reader, aided by the passage of time, will realize what genuine insight and passion inspire his works.

Lawrence's father was a quarrelsome, passionate man who found in the emotional ceremonies and hymn singing of the Nonconformist chapel a satisfaction that the politer religion of his wife could not provide. He worked in the bowels of the earth, and mounted again to the surface with an inner burden which required violent release. The son, though close to a mother ambitious on his behalf and possessive to a degree that for a while inhibited his relations with other women, not only came to feel, later, that he had wronged his father, but employed in his writings a symbolism that is reminiscent of the actual working conditions of his father's life. "Dark" is an adjective which he uses even to excess, and his concern is with the primitive, with the instinctual irrational urges without which the ingenious fabrics of our reasoning or rationalizations would never have been woven. This burrowing to the roots is often associated with the desire for a return to the womb of the mother, and it may be that in Lawrence the strong tug of repulsion-attraction, experienced with respect to both his parents, is to some extent responsible for the unique qualities, the richness and suggestiveness of his writing. There are other indications too that Lawrence could express the sexual state of innocent ambivalence (or polymorphism, as Freud calls it) which less gifted folk lose contact with after the years of earliest childhood. If Lawrence's creative imagination wafts us back to those days which have, for the isolated and responsible individual, the glamor of a lost paradise, it is indeed little wonder that he should hold and move us.

The story reprinted in these pages, "Odor of Chrysanthemums," recalls the harshly restrictive conditions that Lawrence knew during his own childhood. The little houses huddle close to the mouth of the coal mine, and coal dust covers everything. As in so much of Lawrence's fiction—even when English miners and rustics make way for middle-class people or aristocrats, or for exotic Mexicans and Indians—one protagonist in particular represents life's irrational forces. Lawrence's imagination runs the gamut from smoldering fires to a blazing intensity, but life, in this story, achieves only a "smoky burning." Another personage, closely linked with the first and usually of the opposite sex, fears or resists the forces of life or even, like the husband in *Lady Chatterly's Lover*, is cut off from life and hostile to it. In "Odor of Chrysanthemums," the woman is life's enemy since it is incarnated, for her, in her husband's underground delving in the mine, in his obscure rages and compulsive drunkenness. She has come to regard the fire in the grate as symbolic of his blind passion. On the pretext of "mending" the fire she actually "keeps wafflin' it about so's to make 'er slow," as her little boy remarks. The mother understands the meaning of her destructive attitude but refuses to acknowledge that it is indeed hers, and she reproaches the boy for his "evil imagination."

When the conditions of existence are felt with great intensity, symbols spring up unbidden on every side. One such provides the title of the story. Even around the dreary pit mouth, at the very entrance, as it were, to the infernal regions, hardy chrysanthemums bloom and spread their rather bitter smell. Almost as the story begins, the wife has the urge to associate herself with their unglamorous tenacity. As the story ends, she looks ahead to long, bleak years through which, somehow, this tenacity must carry her.

Lawrence likes to bring his short stories, as well as his novels, to a definite conclusion, if not to a total resolution of the preceding state of affairs. Here it is the husband's accidental death that writes finis to the flawed marriage relationship. The wife, alone in the presence of the corpse and absolved from her nagging plaints and resentments, no longer sees herself as a suffering individual with "rights" to which she would lay claim if she only knew how. From this moment on she has ceased to be an individual and has become nature's instrument. The regrets and the marital disputes already buried as her husband will be buried, she must live on in order that her children may live.

It is but an episode that Lawrence has related, yet he has involved us deeply in the essentials of existence. For a broader examination by Lawrence of the relationship between man and woman, than which no theme is more central to his concern, the reader may turn, for instance, to the novel *Sons and Lovers*.

T. S. ELIOT

Lucidly planned innovation carried out with superb generalship by a man who aimed at inserting his work in the long tradition of poetry in English—this is the tension of old and new that gives life and validity to Eliot's poetry. As a creative mind he had, of course, his own strongly felt, entirely legitimate likes and aversions. Less legitimate was his attempt to equate them with universal principles of right and wrong. He did this in a series of essays (among them *The Sacred Wood*, 1920, and *Homage to John Dryden*, 1924) which manifested depth, range, and considerable cogency and which, in combination with his poetic practice, established him over the years as the major and towering figure in the Anglo-American literary landscape.

What in particular he did not care for was the poetry of the romantics. Because of their self-indulgent laxness in word and thought, as he saw it, he was even ready to declare them outside the great "tradition." He found, too, little that was worthy of emulation in the production of his immediate predecessors, whose unimaginative handling of meter made it necessary for the fledgling poet to find or invent something else. (Yeats, with his insistence that poetry must always sing, was too incompatible to serve as a model for Eliot.) Especially attractive, on the other hand, were the Elizabethan and Jacobean poets, including the dramatists. Among the seventeenth-century poets he turned aside from Milton, finding his sublimity deficient in naturalness and his syntax too close to that of Latin. Instead, he praised John Donne's metaphysical poetry. Certain French poets also proved helpful to him in his search for stimulating models of tone and technique. The aseptic, sometimes parodistic, ironies and the offbeat imaginings of the late nineteenth-century Jules Laforgue caught his fancy, and at Ezra Pound's suggestion he studied some poems by Théophile Gautier as examples of chiseled, emotionally tightly controlled, precision. An advantage of reflecting on poetry written in a foreign language is that slavish adherence to the original is scarcely possible.

Eliot's poems, from the very outset, were entirely distinctive. This, in fact, was all that some early readers and critics could perceive. But a fellow craftsman, E. E. Cummings, already in 1920 had the eye to discern the "intensity" that arose from "a vocabulary almost brutally attuned to attain distinction; an extraordinarily tight orchestration of the shapes of sound; the delicate and careful murderings —almost invariably interpreted, internally as well as terminally, through near-rhyme and rhyme —of established tempos by oral rhythm." As for the emotional tone of this work, it had the pitch of disillusionment, a widespread reaction to the disasters and chaos of World War I and its aftermath. Eliot's firmly controlled lines conveyed the sense of a loss of control, of incoherence, of a void in danger of being occupied by demons if no beneficent force could assert its greater authority.

It came as a shock to some of his admirers when he announced his acceptance of the Christian revelation as this is interpreted by the Church of England. Yet there had been aspects of his poetry that foreshadowed this development. At the other extreme was the reaction of some Christians nonplussed by the modernity of Eliot's poetic stance. They were perhaps insufficiently aware that Eliot had not only steeped himself in centuries of literature reaching back beyond Christendom to antiquity but also, in his philosophical studies at Harvard and Oxford Universities, had explored the mystical tradition both Christian and pagan. Even Sanscrit, and the speculations of Hindu and Buddhist, had contributed to the patterning of his world. With *Murder in the Cathedral* (1935) he turned to drama—in this instance, drama liturgical rather than theatrical in nature, as befitted the theme, the assassination of Thomas à Becket. During the 1950's, in more conventionally theatrical pieces such as *The Cocktail Party*, he essayed a very loose free verse barely distinguishable from prose. These plays, though modern in setting, centered like his poems upon age-old moral dilemmas and spiritual turning points.

"The Love Song of J. Alfred Prufrock" was the first poem by Eliot to be published. Few other "first" poems could be cited that have so outstandingly triumphed over time and the fluctuations of literary taste. The maturity and mastery of the work cannot be called into question. It presents itself as the confession that one man makes to himself, not to any listener. The speaker, timid and no longer quite young, shrinks from the contempt and ridicule to which he believes he would be subjected were he to open his mind or his heart. He is walking, when the poem opens, through pallid evening light and along dismal streets that, like an incipient nightmare, threaten to confront him with what he fears to avow, possibly his own nullity or utter hopelessness.

The visit in prospect offers him respite.

The pervasive imprecision of the physical climate, a soft, damp October evening in London, also invades the London interior, seeming to sap any effort to act decisively. Prufock is convinced that others have seen into his internal disarray, and that he has been categorized and pinned down like an insect. Yet he is conscious of the cool elegance of the women in the room and even, from the far side of an untraversable barrier, of the animal warm-bloodedness that their elegance, by partially concealing it, reveals.

This rapid paraphrase of the poem's first sixty-nine lines is, it will be noted, explicit and abstract where the poem itself is concrete and allusive. From the "etherized" sky and "half-deserted streets" of the opening lines to Prufrock's necktie "asserted by a simple pin," it gives voice to Eliot's conviction that the poet must find an "objective correlative," something visible and concrete that will convey (by embodying) the mood that he desires to evoke. Prufrock—touchstone of the despair of each one of us, perhaps?—clinches his sense of human inadequacy by imagining a more appropriate milieu in which to behave as he does: he should have been a crab, "a pair of ragged claws" on the sea bottom, where communication with others is not yet invented.

Yet none of his rationalizing can quite silence the inner voice that bids him end his "policy of drift." For how uncouth, how embarrassing, the decisive deed or word would be! It is less painful for him to play a minor figure or accept a walk-on part. Does he even dare to eat a peach? Life, that is human and vaster than human, will withdraw and leave him to die.

With the *Ulysses* of James Joyce, Eliot's *Waste Land* is central to the literature of our time. This judgment, taken as expressing a historical fact, no historical revisionism will be able to annul—whatever the tastes or habits of future generations of readers may be. The two works, totally unimaginable before their appearance, immediately added to the complexity of the demands that could be made on a piece of writing.

The Waste Land illustrates throughout what Eliot means when he asserts that the whole body of poetry is one and indivisible—thus writing off in one sentence the emphasis of romanticism on the individual poet's personality, his "passion" and "sufferings," on the artist, and replacing it with a counteremphasis on the series of words committed to paper, on the art. In practical terms, it turns out that this conception of the "tradition" authorizes Eliot to incorporate in his poems echoes and direct quotations from previous poems, whether written in English, now translated, or cited in the original. Thus the newly written poem is not simply another bead to be added to the ever-growing, never completed string of English and European poetry; it is a web whose multiple threads (as in a carpet) or tessarae (as in a mosaic) repeat or allude to tones and patterns already utilized in the collective endeavor. For the reader, if he insists upon clarifying each reference, the burden of cogitation and research can be heavy. To lighten the task, Eliot himself wrote a number of explanatory notes, but few readers will find them sufficient. This reprinting provides additional notes, and, immediately below, a kind of scenario of the poem, to compensate for the poet's principled refusal to clutter the poem itself with explanatory transitional passages.

Eliot has acknowledged his general indebtedness both to Sir James Frazer's immense compendium of anthropological materials, *The Golden Bough* (twelve volumes, 1890–1915) and to Jessie L. Weston's *From Ritual to Romance* (1920), a study of the Grail legend. Behind this Christian legend Miss Weston found an older pagan tale, extant in many forms, of a fisher king whose land and people, because of some deficiency in him, lose their fertility and become "waste." In his poem, Eliot uses a great many motifs from mythological and religious sources to establish the character of the contemporary world as a new "waste land," a landscape of barren incoherence and papered-over terrors.

Section I is called "The Burial of the Dead." April, unconventionally, is named "the cruelest month," for it brings but a mockery of renewal, such a person as the countess, whose inane memoirs are next quoted, regarding a "season" as simply part of a fashionable round. The second block of verses echoes the denunciations of Old Testament prophets, and evokes both the end of Tristan's mythical love affair and the futilities of a more recent sexual encounter. Perhaps "the heart of light, the silence" of the next to last line is the poem's first hint that a moment of transcendence has been glimpsed, only to be left unexplored. The third sequence of this first section recounts the superstitious, mercenary exploitation of profound ancient symbols. To this sleazy level has the city (modern London or hell—as in Blake) sunk. The final lines babble hysterically and incoherently of the age-old myth of death and resurrection.

Section II, "A Game of Chess," depicts a lady of fashion amid the perfumes and the luxurious objects that feed, and imprison her in, her narcissism. The quotation marks in the passage that follows indicate either a dialogue or the lady's interior monologue, while the disenchanted observations not between quotation marks may convey her husband's unuttered reactions. A "knock" shifts the scene to a working-class pub just before closing time and to a discussion of abortion, of barrenness artificially induced. The barman's repeated "Hurry up please it's time" acquires an ominous resonance—which may also be a veiled call to repentance while there is still time.

"The Fire Sermon," Section III, contrasts the polluted Thames of today with the stream that poets of earlier centuries had celebrated. Now the water is associated only with decay. The next eight lines acquaint us with the basely commercial Mr. Eugenides, whose Syrian ancestors had spread fertility cults throughout Mediterranean lands. There follows a routine seduction scene. The remaining verses juxtapose literary echoes and fragmentary modern memories. The last five lines combine a quotation from the *Confessions* of St. Augustine of Hippo with a reference to the Buddha's "Fire Sermon."

Section IV, "Death by Water," in its brevity may or may not extend the promise of resurrection. At all events, there is a blunt final injunction to reflect on one's own transitoriness. "What the Thunder Said" is the fifth and last section of the poem. Without naming them—though Eliot does so in his notes—the poem utilizes three themes: Christ's journey to Emmaus, the approach to the Chapel Perilous in the Grail legend, and the condition of contemporary Eastern Europe. The images are of rock and of lack of water. But after a cock has crowed, the lightning flashes, and rain comes pouring down. The voice of the thunder, as in an ancient Hindu fable, is interpreted as calling for self-surrender, compassion, and domination of self. The final passage has a note of restrained hope that order can be restored. But again there are evocations of chaos, even of madness, and the Sanscrit benediction that ends the poem may be meant to suggest that what can be discovered in the remote past has not been awakened to life today.

The culmination of Eliot's work as a poet is represented by the *Four Quartets*, published in 1943. While considerable demands are again made on the reader, they are less of a literary than of a spiritual kind. In structure each poem is identical, being divided into five parts. As the overall title indicates, a musical analogy is intended and penetrates to the level of individual phrases which echo and are modulations of earlier phrases. The affirmed circularity of our deepest experience ("to arrive where we started," to cite but one phrase of many) also has its parallel in the structure of a piece of music.

"Little Gidding," reprinted here, is the last of the *Four Quartets*. The first of its five sections is itself divided into three parts which, successively, indicate the place and the time of year; the meaning, beyond mere conscious purpose, to which this place was dedicated; the identity of the quest in past and present. The second section reflects initially on metamorphosis and extinction, and then moves on to a much longer passage which, with its arrangement of masculine and feminine endings, suggests the chain-link distribution of the rhyming words in the terza rima of Dante's *Divine Comedy*. The setting utilizes Eliot's experiences as a fire warden in London during World War II, and imagines a conversation occurring between the living poet and an unnamed dead "master." They discuss the related topics of purification of speech and purgation of the soul.

The poem's third section considers the role of memory in achieving liberation and how all things are reconciled as they sink into the past, with the lesson that this contains for the living. The fourth section is short, and treats of fire as the symbol both of annihilation and of purgation. In the final, fifth section, the poet affirms the ultimate oneness of the transitory and the timeless.

A condition of complete simplicity
(Costing not less than everything)

allows the realization of this insight.

ANNA AKHMATOVA

The shape of Anna Akhmatova's poetic career cannot be understood apart from the influence of the Soviet government policies on the arts during the regime of Joseph Stalin. New works were closely examined for political correctness and social utility; writers who expressed subjective feelings and personal opinions instead of celebrating the heroes and heroic deeds of the masses were simply not published, and in many cases criticized officially in the most harsh and offensive terms. Akhmatova, for instance, though well known in Russian literary circles at the time of the Bolshevik Revolution of 1917, was allowed to publish no original work from Stalin's accession in 1923 until 1956, three years after his death. During the Second World War this ban was temporarily lifted, and she wrote the patriotic poems the times demanded, inspired rather by love of her country than by love of the regime. But in 1946 the Central Committee of the Communist Party again cracked down on "individualistic" writers, and her work was attacked by the Politburo's literary expert, A. A. Zhdanov, as the "poetry of an overwrought upper-class lady who frantically races back and forth between boudoir and chapel." (The allusion is to her aristocratic upbringing, her religious faith, and her poems' explorations of love.)

Akhmatova's early poetry is lyric and personal, experimental only in that it breaks away from the faded sentimentalities of late nineteenth-century Russian poetry to find a new clarity and directness. In a poem of 1910, she registers an intense aesthetic appreciation of a particular configuration of sight and sound: "The crow upon the wing with raucous caw, / And, down the dwindling path, the archway's curve." She also records the small details of behavior that reveal a state of mind, as in a poem where a distraught woman puts her glove on the wrong hand. Her work at this period often has for its theme unhappy love and separation, though expressed with honesty and indeed toughness: "Me, honor and obey? You've lost your mind! . . . Husband spells headsman to me, housed—confined." Though one or another poem may show her aware of the great movements of history around her, she is concerned mainly with personal meanings: "No one will listen now to songs. The tragic, / So long foreshadowed days have come around."

At no point in her long career was Akhmatova able to write the officially promoted socialist poetry that was required to gain acceptance and publication. She therefore suffered continuously from a feeling of internal exile; in "Not with a Loved One's Lyre," she refers to herself as a leper, and describes the painful isolation of one who is shunned not only by officialdom but also by the common people, who look on her as an outcast from their new society. To elude the ideological censor, she began to use historical or Biblical settings to hide contemporary references; thus in "Imitation from the Armenian," a bereaved mother sheep asks the Shah, "But what about my boy, did you enjoy his taste?" During the brief period of World War II when she was allowed to publish again, she seemed to be discovering a new role for herself as a national poet. Her poem "Courage," published in *Pravda* in 1942, rallies the Russian people to defend their homeland (and their language). Even the less "public" poems have a new tone, as she finds poetry in "An angry cry, the smell of fresh bitumen, / Along some wall a runic lichen sign, / And verses answer, tender, brash, and human, / For your delight and mine." The sharpness of perception is still there, but she now includes her readers with herself rather than setting herself apart. It was during these years that she wrote the cycle of poems called "Requiem," though it could not be published then and has not yet been published in its entirety in Russia.

"Requiem" shows vividly her reconciliation of personal and public voices. Its poems express not only her own grief and anxiety for an imprisoned son, but also the community of grief felt by all the women who had lost or were losing sons and husbands during the Stalinist purges of 1937–1938.

The title of the cycle, alluding to the Roman Catholic mass for the dead, is a protest against the official atheism of the state. The two prefaces establish the historical situation and Akhmatova's own role as speaker for the people. In the dedication and introduction, the scene is set in Leningrad and populated with grieving women who are defined not individually but as those—"The same everywhere"—who wait in fear. Epic in scope, the first poems recall a period when "only the dead smiled" and Russia seemed like an enormous prison camp. Subsequent poems shift to more personal feelings, as she speaks of her own as well as a more universal grief, of any mother's sense of loss and anxiety for a son. References to the arrest of Akhmatova's third husband Nikoali Punin (poem 1), the execution of her first husband Nikolai Gumilev (poem 2), and her son's imprisonment build rapidly into a picture of both individual and communal bereavement.

The speaker of these poems, the *I*, undergoes a certain dissociation of personality (poems 2 and 3), even the risk of madness (poem 9), and looks back unbelievingly at an earlier self (poem 4) in the struggle to free her son (poem 5). Ultimately, when the point of madness has been reached, the lyrical *I* gives way to a third-person description of the crucifixion (poem 10), and the theme of grieving mother and lost son moves to the transcendental level of Christian symbol. Though the tenth is the last numbered poem, two epilogues then reestablish the framework of memory and reassert the religious and historical motifs that have united the poems throughout. The immensity of the national grief is compared with the grandeur of the Russian landscape, especially its great rivers, yet is simultaneously seen as petrifying the soul and turning faces into tablets incised by suffering. At the very end, the poet herself reaches a stony immobility, metamorphosed by her suffering into the monument that is the traditional memorial to a national poet.

KATHERINE ANNE PORTER

The Modernist movement, with its special emphasis on form and on fluidity in time and perspective has by no means displaced more realistic and less experimental kinds of storytelling. Much of the fiction of Katherine Anne Porter is organized in ways a nineteenth-century writer would have understood: a single narrator tells the story from a consistent point of view, events follow upon each other in rational and usually chronological order. What makes her world distinctive is her precise thoughtful style that seeks the exact word to render each shade of intellectual and emotional perception, and her darkly pessimistic view of human life.

Porter is preoccupied by individuals caught within the broad movements of history. Ordinary people act out their destinies inside a culture and society —whether of the American South or West, Mexico, Europe, or an ocean liner—that shapes much of what they can be. Often the protagonist is an inquiring, independent, and uncompromising woman, like Miranda in *Pale Horse, Pale Rider,* who rejects the oversimplifications and stupidities of wartime propaganda and seeks refuge from its pressures in a love affair about which she is nonetheless fearfully hesitant, and who in the earlier "Old Mortality" learns to reject the different versions of her family history and seek out her own way. Porter's fiction is much concerned with relations between people, especially within the family, probing the ambiguous and often self-deluding attitudes inherent in the closest emotional ties. She observes, "My whole attempt has been to discover and understand human motives, human feelings, to make a distillation of what human relations and experiences my mind has been able to absorb."

But her mind and her work have never been exclusively concerned with individuals. Her apparently simple and straightforward stories open out upon larger historical and metaphysical planes. A pessimistic sense of history, which for her is the record of "the anguish that human beings inflict on each other—the never-ending wrong, forever incurable," informs much of her fiction: the First World War is not merely a setting for *Pale Horse, Pale Rider,* but the impetus behind what its characters do, say, and think. Anguish is the natural human condition, and no happy resolution is possible, only an increasing awareness of the conditions of existence which those who, like Miranda, resist the pressures of society and history, may earn through their sufferings. This view of human life as painful and incomplete is accompanied by a dedication to art, the "true testimony" that outlives its own society and civilization. "The arts," Porter has said, "represent the substance of faith and the only reality. They are what we find again when the ruins are cleared away." As with Mann, many of her protagonists are artists or have artistic sensibilities, and the clarity, balance, and fine discriminations of her own style become a way of ordering reality into art.

Reality is, however, a crucial raw material for Porter's fiction, which derives from the fusion of her experiences with what she invents. She describes the way that scattered memories of different people and scenes observed over the years can combine into a new tale with a structure all its own: "Now and again thousands of memories converge, harmonize, arrange themselves around a central idea in a coherent form, and I write a story." Her first collection, *Flowering Judas,* draws on her experiences in Mexico; some of the characters are based on actual persons—Uspensky in "Hacienda" suggests Sergei Eisenstein, the film director, who made a massive documentary about Mexico—and unknown people glimpsed for a moment are imagined as taking part in fictional anecdotes (as in the first published story, "Maria Concepcion"). But her stories aim always beyond experience, and at their best absorb historical events into the analytical framework of art.

This is certainly true of *Pale Horse, Pale Rider,* the longest of her stories and her announced favorite. It is based on her experiences during the wartime influenza epidemic of 1918, and the main character, Miranda, appears as a child in other stories reflecting Porter's early life. Yet the work is not autobiographical, but an impersonally presented description of Miranda's doomed love, illness, and numb return to life against the background of wartime America and in a larger, more universally human perspective suggested by biblical motifs.

The story has three parts covering Miranda's solitude and skepticism in the midst of hysterical wartime propaganda; her glimpse of a seemingly perfect love with Adam, shadowed by his preparations to go off to war and her own attack of influenza; and finally her struggle with death from which she emerges only to learn of the death of her hopes. The characters, realistically sketched, are driven by their inner needs and by the pressures of society, a society which Porter makes convincing and powerful through an abundance of pointed and authentic detail. The perspective extends beyond hsitory: Adam, golden, naturally and even stereotypically masculine, fated never to grow old, seems as perfect as his namesake in *Genesis,* created by the hand of God, and both the war and the epidemic seem as random and deadly as the pale horseman of the Apocalypse, franchised to kill with sword and with pestilence one-fourth of the inhabitants of the earth. Porter's craftsmanship is as evident in small details as in large—in the snatches of 1918 slang and popular songs, for example, and in the neutral gray of Miranda's dream-mount, Graylie, echoed in the clothes in which she chooses to reappear, like Lazarus, from the dead. The style is versatile, ranging from objective narrative to a stream-of-consciousness technique for the dreams. The full range of Porter's art is applied to her most characteristic theme, transforming *Pale Horse, Pale Rider* from a semi-autobiographical sketch into a fictional masterpiece.

WILLIAM FAULKNER

People often speak of Faulkner's style even before they speak of particular novels or stories. Like Joyce and Proust, he uses long, involved, and elaborate sentences to draw the reader into a special world of the imagination, sentences that follow the ebb and flow of his characters' thoughts, or meander like a narrative consciousness absorbed in the variety of the world it describes. The epic length of his sentences reflects one aspect of his sense of mythic grandeur, expressed also by historic and transcendental overtones found even in the most regional of tales. Faulkner's novels project such tales onto the large screen of contemporary historical change, presenting allegories of human endurance in an often-hostile universe, or alluding directly to earlier heroic expressions of the human condition in the Old Testament, Greek tragedy, and Shakespeare. Yet his world is by no means unrelievedly somber, and its realism and earthy humor have led to his being called a "comic" writer, in the broad sense that implies a panoramic vision encompassing the pettiness as well as the grandeur of human existence.

Novelist and storyteller of the American South, Faulkner created a whole fictional region called Yoknapatawpha County, modeled on parts of his native Mississippi. Here imaginary families such as the Compsons, Sutpens, and Snopeses rise to prosperity or fall into various kinds of degradation and death. Individual characters work out destinies that are already half-shaped by family tradition and invisible community pressures. They are caught in close and often incestuous blood relationships, and make their way in a world where the values, traditions, and privileges of an old plantation society are yielding to the values of a new mercantile class. A network of family dynasties illustrates this picture of a changing society: the decaying and impoverished Compson family (*The Sound and the Fury*), two generations of Sutpens rising to great wealth and dying in madness and isolation (*Absalom, Absalom!*), the McCaslin family with its history of incest, miscegenation, and guilt (*Go Down, Moses*), and the viciously grasping and ambitious "poor white" Snopes family (the Snopes trilogy). These are violent works, and the murders, lynchings and bestialities of all kinds that appear in them account for Faulkner's early American reputation as a lurid local writer. European critics, however, especially the French, who recognized his stature as early as 1931, were quick to recognize classical and Biblical prototypes in these tales of twisted family relationships. The titles themselves invite such observations, as do the names from Greek tragedy given some of the characters—Orestes Snopes, Clytemnestra Sutpen.

In Faulkner's world men and women are measured by the breadth of their compassion or the quality of their endurance. Few wholly negative characters appear, and these are seen as grotesque distortions of humanity: the cruel and frustrated Jason Compson, or the impotent rapist Popeye of *Sanctuary,* who "had that vicious depthless quality of stamped tin." The heroes tend to be larger than life, or even than death, as with Addie Bundren (*As I Lay Dying*), whose dying wish obliges her family to accompany her coffin across Mississippi in a miniature epic journey through flood and fire. They have the moral endurance of Bayard Sartoris II, who as a boy kills his grandmother's murderer and as a man has the courage not to avenge his father's death, or the physical endurance of the tall convict in *Old Man,* whose "whole purpose," according to Faulkner, was "to prove . . . just how much the human body could bear, stand, endure." Or they may be apparently ordinary people whose lives never draw attention, but whose perseverance and dedication to an idea, a person, or a way of life give them larger significance. They may also be thoughtful people driven to question their own identity and values, or idiots able only to feel a succession of emotions. Faulkner generally describes such figures from the outside. We see them act, and we may even follow their thoughts in an interior monologue, but these are only traces of a moment of basic moral choice that has already happened and from which we are excluded.

A variety of perspectives in Faulkner's novels elaborate varying versions of the truth. Three different narrators in *Absalom, Absalom!* tell the story of Thomas Sutpen. The four points of view of *The Sound and the Fury* move from the imagined inner monologue of an idiot to adult monologues and finally a third-person narrative focusing on Dilsey, the mammy who endures. Fifty-nine sections of interior monologue in *As I Lay Dying* express the inner relationships of the Bundren family. The convict in *Old Man* possesses a dogged, wilfully limited view of things modeled on simplistic cops-and-robbers stories and adventure tales; though he himself lives through a realistic version of the adventure tale, his sense of what is happening or may happen never moves onto the realistic plane. The narrative perspective itself may seem to shift in tone, as happens at the end of the epic coffin journey in *As I Lay Dying* when the widowed Anse Bundren returns happily from town with a new set of false teeth, a new wife, and a phonograph. Throughout, Faulkner's fluid style escapes rigid categories; it is a style of tension and contradictions, of tragedy and humor, realism and mythic outreach, now short and laconic, now long and rambling. In Faulkner's words, he was "trying to do the impossible . . . to say it all in one sentence, between one Cap and one period."

Although *Old Man* seems a relatively straightforward story of a convict's struggle for survival during the great Mississippi flood of 1927, it has its own complexity and is part of a larger whole. As first published in 1939, *Old Man* was half of the two-part novel *The Wild Palms*. Chapters from the two stories were printed in alternation, and the final chapter of each section located its protagonist in the Mississippi penitentiary at Parchman. Faulkner commented in an interview that he realized "something was missing" after the first section of *The Wild Palms* and wrote *Old Man* "to lift it like counterpoint in music." When *The Wild Palms* "began again to sag," he "raised it to pitch again with another section of its antithesis." Later editions printed the stories whole, one after the other in a single volume, and *Old Man* was published separately in 1946.

Though *Old Man* stands well by itself, the counterpoint with *The Wild Palms* does reveal something of what Faulkner intended by the nature of his characters and the relationships among them. In *The Wild Palms*, Charlotte Rittenmeyer runs away from her husband to experience "perfect," romantic love with intern Harry Wilbourne. The lovers seek to live at the highest pitch by rejecting any kind of security and respectability, and when Charlotte becomes pregnant she insists that Harry perform an abortion. The abortion is botched, Charlotte dies of toxemia, and Harry, arrested, refrains from suicide in order to keep alive the memory of Charlotte for the rest of his life in prison. In contrast, the nameless convict of *Old Man* is let loose on an apocalyptic flood to rescue a pregnant woman, helps her bear her baby on an island—an Indian mound—covered with poisonous snakes, supports them all for two weeks by killing alligators in an isolated swamp, and finally rejects the dangerous freedom of life "outside" by returning to the security of prison. Beyond the clear thematic contrasts between the two stories—for example, between birth and abortion—there are other less evident contrasts. *The Wild Palms* describes inner conflict and romantic agonies; *Old Man* focuses on action and unspoken choice. The wild palms that are the leading symbol of one story are opposed to the Old Man of the other, the Mississippi River; imagery of wind and yielding to water pervades the first tale, while the second is dominated by long struggle with and final conquest of the flood.

Reading *Old Man* without *The Wild Palms*, however, focuses attention more explicitly on elements of Faulkner's essential mythology: the human struggle for survival in a hostile universe, the archetypal experience of destruction and rebirth, the tension between the most basic human relationships and a distorting society. *Old Man* takes place on the edge of Yoknapatawpha County, and is one of the Southern regional stories that illustrate, with their realistic detail, heroic struggle, and grotesque humor, what Faulkner called in his Nobel Prize speech "the problem of the human heart in conflict with itself which alone can make good writing."

BERTOLT BRECHT

Bertolt Brecht is a dominant figure in modern drama not only as the author of half a dozen plays which rank as modern classics, but as the first master of a powerful new concept of theater. Dissatisfied with the traditional notion, derived from Aristotle's *Poetics*, that drama should draw its spectators into identification with and sympathy for the characters, and with the Realist aesthetic of naturalness and psychological credibility, he also believed that the modern stage should break open the closed world established as a dramatic convention by writers like Ibsen and Chekhov, whose audiences were to look at the action as if it were a slice of real life going on behind an invisible "fourth wall" between stage and audience. For Brecht, a radical Marxist, the modern audience must not be allowed to indulge in emotional identification at a safe distance; it must be educated and moved to political action. The movement called "epic theater," which was born in the twenties, suited his needs well, and through his plays, theoretical writings, and dramatic productions he developed its basic ideas into one of the most powerful theatrical styles of the century.

The name "epic theater" derives from a famous essay "On Epic and Dramatic Poetry" by Goethe and Schiller, who in 1797 described *dramatic* poetry as pulling the audience into emotional identification, in contrast to *epic* poetry, which by being distanced in the time, place, and nature of the action can be absorbed in calm contemplation. The idea of an epic theater is a paradox: how can a play engage an audience that is still held at a distance? Brecht's solution was to employ many "alienation effects" that were genuinely dramatic, but prevented total identification with the characters and forced spectators to think critically about what was taking place. These alienation effects have since become standard production techniques in the modern theater. In spite of Brecht's intentions and frequent revisions, however, the characters and situations of his plays remain emotionally engrossing, especially in his best-known works such as *Mother Courage and Her Children*.

Most of Brecht's plays are didactic, either openly or by implication. After he became a fervent Marxist in the mid-twenties, he wrote a number of plays intended to set forth Communist doctrine, instructing the workers of Germany in the meaning of social revolution. These plays were condemned as unattractive and "intellectualist" by the Communist press in Berlin and Moscow. In truth, Brecht's mind was too keen and questioning, too attracted by irony and paradox, for him to have a comfortable relation with authority, whether of the left or the right. His new ideas of theater, although he tactfully said that they were elements of a Marxist aesthetic, went directly against the prevailing Party view. After 1934 the Soviet bureaucracy of the arts supported as the official dramatic mode a style called "socialist realism," whose goal was to offer simple messages and foster identification with revolutionary heroes. Though the East German government subsidized Brecht's *Berliner Ensemble,* and refrained from interfering with the style of its productions, it also obliged him to defend some of his plays against charges of political unorthodoxy, and indeed to revise them. After Brecht settled in East Berlin in 1948, he wrote no major new plays but only minor propaganda pieces and adaptations of classical works such as Molière's *Don Juan* and Shakespeare's *Coriolanus.*

Brecht's concept of an epic theater touches on all aspects: dramatic structure, stage setting, music, and the actor's performance. The structure is to be open, episodic, and broken by dramatic or musical interludes. It is a "chronicle" that recounts events in an epic or distanced perspective. Episodes may be performed independently as self-contained dramatic parables, instead of being organically tied to a centrally-developing plot. Skits appear between scenes: in *A Man's a Man,* there is a fantastic interlude in which an elephant is accused of having murdered its mother. Sometimes a narrator comments on the action (*Three-Penny Opera, A Man's a Man*). The alienation effects are also heightened by setting most of the plays in far-away lands (China in *The Good Person of Setzuan,* India in *A Man's a Man,* England in *The Three-Penny Opera,* Russia in *The Caucasian Chalk Circle,* Chicago in *Saint Joan of the Stockyards* and *The Resistible Rise of Arturo Ui*), or times (the seventeenth century in *Mother Courage,* Renaissance Italy in *Galileo,* or an imagined ghostly afterlife in *The Trial of Lucullus*).

Stagecraft and performance further support Brecht's concept of a critical, intellectualized theater. Events on stage are announced beforehand by signs, or are accompanied by projected films and images during the action itself. Place names are printed on signs and suspended over the actors, and footlights and stage machinery are openly displayed. Songs that interrupt the dramatic action are addressed directly to the audience, and are often heralded by a sign Brecht called a "musical emblem: in *Mother Courage,* 'a trumpet, a drum, a flag, and electric globes that lit up.' " In addition, Brecht described a special kind of acting: actors should "demonstrate" their parts instead of being submerged in them. At rehearsals, Brecht often asked actors to speak their parts in the third person instead of the first. Masks were occasionally used for wicked people, or soldiers' faces chalked white to suggest a stylized fear. Such constant artificiality injected into all aspects of the performance makes it difficult for the audience to identify completely and unselfconsciously with the characters on stage.

Audiences may react emotionally to Brecht's plays and characters, but their reactions are unusually mixed and changing. Brecht's characters are complex and inhabit complex situations. Galileo is both a dedicated scientist who sacrifices his reputation for honesty so as to complete his work, and a weak sensualist who fails to recognize how his recantation will affect others' pursuit of scientific knowledge. In *The Good Person of Setzuan*, the overgenerous Shen Te can survive only by periodically adopting the mask of a harshly practical "cousin," Shui Ta. Mother Courage is both a tragic mother figure and a small-time profiteer who loses her children as she battens on war.

Brecht's work teems with such paradoxes, at all levels. He is a cynic who deflates religious zeal, militant patriotism, and heroic example as delusions that lead the masses on to futile sacrifice; yet an idealistic tone also pervades the plays, with prominent use of Biblical language and imagery and themes of individual sacrifice. Brecht's own zeal is directed toward enlightening the common man, giving him the force and clearsightedness to break out of a manipulative system. In *A Man's a Man*, the timid dock worker Galy Gay is transformed by fright and persuasion into another person, the ferociously successful soldier Jeriah Jip. When Jip turns up at the end of the play, he is given Gay's papers and forced to reassume Gay's identity. The play teaches that human personality can be broken down and reassembled like a machine; the only weapon against such mindless manipulation is awareness, an awareness that enables people to understand and control their destiny. Brecht's theater finds its dimension and purpose in achieving this complex and difficult goal.

Mother Courage was written shortly after Brecht turned forty, in a period of major plays including *Galileo, The Trial of Lucullus,* and *The Good Person of Setzuan*. It is set in Germany in the middle years of a war involving all of Europe, believed at the time Brecht was writing to have destroyed half the German population: the Thirty Years' War (1618–1648). But senseless violence, religious intolerance, artificial patriotism, and cynical opportunism were no more characteristic of seventeenth-century Germany than of the Nazi state, and the setting gave Brecht what he needed to write a strongly pacifist play in 1939, the year in which World War II was to begin.

Mother Courage evoked the sympathy of early audiences for her tragic inability to prevent her children's death. Such was not Brecht's intention, and he rewrote several sections of the play to bring out her avarice and blindness, her belief that she can use the war, by profiting from others' misery, without endangering her own family. For to Brecht, the tragedy of her life lay in her failure to relate the general fate of society to that of her own family.

In trying to manipulate the system for her personal advantage, she denies the human rights of others: she calls to others to enlist but not to her own children, and she would rather sell shirts to the officers than use them to bind a peasant's wounds. Yet the war that Mother Courage saw as a good provider ends by killing her three children, and even sooner because of their virtues (Eilif's martial zeal, Swisscheese's honesty, Kattrin's pity). Mother Courage is ruined, all the more so since she has learned nothing from the war and does not protest it. Instead, her bitter "Song of the Great Capitulation" presents compromise as inevitable, and at the end of the play she is chasing after a new regiment to continue her peddler's career.

Each of the twelve parable-like scenes of *Mother Courage* presents a particular aspect or lesson of the war. Setting and props encourage the audience to see the action as a "demonstration," by drawing attention to the way the play is put on. Signs or titles are projected onto a screen to announce what is about to happen; a revolving stage and projected backgrounds suggest the wagon's travels in a highly stylized way; a group of musicians sits in full view beside the stage to accompany the songs; realistic but sketchy three-dimensional structures represent buildings. The main piece of stage furniture is Mother Courage's canteen wagon, whose increasingly dilapidated appearance reveals her fall from prosperity into lonely poverty. In the first scene, the whole family appears with the wagon: at the end, Mother Courage pulls it alone.

Brecht hoped that *Mother Courage* would show its audiences "that in wartime the big profits are not made by little people. That war, which is a continuation of business by other means, makes the human virtues fatal even to their possessors. That no sacrifice is too great for the struggle against war." This last point is demonstrated by Kattrin's death, for she is the only one of Mother Courage's family whose virtue is not perverted by the war, and whose death is meant to provide a moral example. Drumming frantically to awaken the endangered city of Halle, she sacrifices her life to save the city's threatened children. Religious and secular themes join at this point, as they do so often in the course of the play, for Kattrin acts immediately after hearing the peasant family bemoan their helplessness and pray to God for miraculous aid. It is action, not passive prayer, that Brecht hopes to evoke with his epic theater. Both the play itself and its self-conscious, "alienated" staging try to move the audience toward a clearer understanding of forces in society, and to a responsible choice of their own roles.

JORGE LUIS BORGES

Jorge Luis Borges writes an intellectual and idealist literature. A Borges short story subordinates familiar notions of plot, character, setting, and narrative voice to a central idea, which is often a philosophical concept. But the philosophical concept is used not as a truth to be demonstrated but as a starting point for fantastic elaboration to entertain the reader. There is no doctrinal rock upon which Borges' world is constructed, but rather a "garden of forking paths" in which images of labyrinth and infinite mirroring, of cyclical repetition and recall, illustrate the quest of an elusive narrating voice to understand its own significance and that of the world.

"Time is the substance I am made of. Time is a river which sweeps me along, but I am the river; it is a tiger which destroys me, but I am the tiger; it is a fire which consumes me, but I am the fire. The world, unfortunately, is real; I, unfortunately, am Borges." Clearly the author of such ideas is not interested in literature that pretends to psychological realism. Borges dislikes what he calls "psychological fakery," and prefers writing that is openly artful, concerned with technique and invention, "a precise game of vigilances, echoes, and affinities" that has become, like his own work, a kind of verbal labyrinth—detective stories, for example, in which the search for an elusive explanation and carefully planted clues matter more than how believable the characters may be. In "Pierre Menard, Author of the Quixote," the narrator is a scholarly reviewer of a certain fictitious Menard, whose masterwork has been to rewrite *Don Quixote* from a twentieth-century point of view—not revise it, nor yet transcribe it, but actually reinvent it word for word. And he has succeeded: the texts are "verbally identical," we are told, yet Menard's is somehow "more ambiguous" than Cervantes' and thus "infinitely richer."

In "Tlön, Uqbar, Orbis Tertius" the narrator is engaged in tracking down mysterious encyclopedia references to a country called Tlön, whose language, science, and literature are exactly opposite (and perhaps related) to our own; for example, the Tlönians use verbs or adjectives instead of nouns, since they have no concept of objects in space, and their science consists of an association of ideas in which the most astounding theory is the best, whether or not it is true. In a postscript, the narrator states that the encyclopedia has turned out to be an immense scholarly hoax, yet also that strange and unearthly objects recognizably from Tlön have recently been found. The boundaries between fact and fiction are fluid in Borges' world, if indeed they exist at all in a universe composed of subjective perceptions and apprehensions. That universe is described as a library, or as a small iridescent sphere containing all of the points in space, or as a series of dreams within dreams, or as a lottery organizing universal chance into apparently meaningful order.

"The Lottery in Babylon" can be read as a parody of the growth of organized religion, with its priests, believers, and heretics and its various stages of doctrinal complication. Yet the narrator remains a puzzle. He was once a citizen of Babylon, but nothing is known of him now except that he is about to leave on a voyage. At the point in the story when the Company running the now compulsory "secret, free, and general" lottery introduces chance and ambiguity into its operations, one can no longer tell whether the Company itself any longer exists; the lottery has become indistinguishable from life, with its chances and coincidences. The assertion that there is nonetheless a lottery may show only that people need to impose an imagined order on what is really chaos, or that Borges the artist—whose infinitely forking paths imitate the game in which "no decision is final, all branch into others"—is actually giving another demonstration of the tantalizing, labyrinthine enigma of the universe.

VLADIMIR NABOKOV

"I have never been interested in what is called the literature of social comment," Vladimir Nabokov once remarked; "I am not 'sincere.' " Indeed, his fiction creates intricate, unrealistic mirror-worlds of verbal brilliance, sly and hidden allusions, and surprising shifts in narrative strategy. A devoted chess player, he has compared the plots and counterplots of his novels with those of chess. He is also a composer of chess problems, diagrams of positions to be solved by forcing checkmate within a specified number of moves. In a similar way, he challenges his readers to try to "solve" his novels. Since both the novels and the chess problems afford various solutions, simple as well as complex, the fun of the game is to recognize the several possibilities and seek out the least obvious but most elegant.

A Nabokov work offers puzzles of every kind. In his most famous novel, *Lolita*, the narrator Humbert Humbert first fears and then pursues his rival for Lolita's love, a mysterious figure whose appearance and other characterictics seem much like Humbert's own. For a moment it seems that the rival may be a figment of his imagination, a phantom double, yet Humbert murders the person after all—or perhaps he doesn't. Humbert's obsession with nymphets such as the twelve-year-old Lolita is on the one hand psychologically grounded in the frustration of his love as a boy for young Annabel Leigh, his subconscious forever scarred by the interruption of their lovemaking on the beach; but on the other hand the girl's name recalls ironically Edgar Allan Poe's sentimental poem of a lost seaside love, "Annabel Lee." (One critic has even observed that Lolita herself is described in terms that apply with remarkable precision to the butterfly *Lycaeides sublivens* Nabokov, a species which the author was first to identify—for he was also an expert lepidopterist.) A later novel, *Pale Fire*, begins as a critical edition of a 999-word poem by John Francis Shade carrying pedantic commentary by Charles Kinbote; but it then turns out to be the mad autobiography of the exiled King of Zembla, or of a man who thinks he is. An earlier "biography," *The Real Life of Sebastian Knight*, concludes by suggesting that the biography remains unwritten and that perhaps the man himself never existed.

Nabokov's fiction is thus always playful, always resisting

single interpretations. Yet it does return to certain images and themes. One recurring image is of an ideal setting or time that lies always just out of reach of the limits of sordid reality and offers a vision of aesthetic perfection. The beautiful and unattainable pastoral scene in "Cloud, Castle, Lake," made all the more poignant by the banality and cruelty of the world from which the unhappy Vasili Ivanovich hopes to find refuge there, is one such vision. Another is the precocious preadolescence that Humbert Humbert seeks in his nymphet lovers—a charmed age, as it seems to him, an "island of entranced time" lifted out of the stream of human mortality. To certain spirits these idealized realms offer a special kind of aesthetic ecstasy, an ecstasy such as Nabokov himself found in solving a particularly complicated chess problem or in finding a rare butterfly. His main characters generally show this kind of artistic sensitivity and the vulnerability that goes with it, while his secondary characters are often caricatures of uncaring, unimaginative people. The police state in *Bend Sinister*, for example, reduces its citizens to interchangeable personalities, complicated "anagrams" of one another. The tour members of "Cloud, Castle, Lake" cannot permit anyone to eat, read, sing, or think differently from themselves. The interaction of these two kinds of characters—not their development, for they do not change, instead carrying out to the end the roles he has assigned them—implies an important theme, a plea for the individuality of artistic consciousness as against a mechanical, conformist view of the imagination.

Although Nabokov disliked comparisons between his life and the situations in his work, it is often possible to discern echoes of one in the other. "Cloud, Castle, Lake," written in 1937 when the author had lived for several years in Hitler's Berlin, centers on another Russian refugee who is likewise living in Berlin in 1937, and the cruel conformity enforced by the tour guide and the noisy Philistine tourists sharply satirizes Nazi political and social attitudes: "Let us march and sweat together / With the steel-and-leather guys." Yet the story is more than social satire: Vasili at the end insists that he has "not the strength to belong to mankind any longer," and the narrator, suddenly assuming godlike authority, says, "Of course, I let him go." Such a role for the fictional narrator is not at all alien to Nabokov, who believes in total control of his literary universe and describes the narrator of another novel as "an anthropomorphic deity impersonated by me."

JEAN-PAUL SARTRE

Sartre is one of those rare authors who have been outstandingly successful in a great variety of genres. His publications embrace short stories, novels, plays, essays, psychology, philosophy, and public affairs. It would be misleading, however, not to indicate that, despite his prodigious literary activities and, probably, the many thousands of pages he has written but not published, he has not been equally active in every type of writing all the time. His five short stories all appeared in the 1930's. There was one prewar novel, *Nausea,* and in the 1950's he abandoned a novel, *Roads to Liberty,* after publishing the first three volumes. He has totally repudiated the 728 pages of *Being and Nothingness,* the philosophical work that aroused an extraordinary furor immediately after World War II and which, with the backing of several consistently successful plays, brought him world fame. The one thing that has remained constant, in this flood of words so diversely used, is the flood itself. It is in this sense that Sartre ironically gave the title *The Words* to a sketch of his early years.

No adequate account of this immense production can be given here. It is important to realize, however, that the reader whose interests are purely literary can gain only a fragmentary view of Sartre as writer, publicist, and ideologue. To complete the picture, he would have to plow through many pages that use several technical vocabularies and strange terms coined by Sartre himself. *Existentialism* was not his invention, actually, and it has also been applied, with excessive liberality, to the thinking of the German philosopher Martin Heidegger and of many others whose theories cannot possibly all be reconciled. Sartre's outlook, unlike Heidegger's, was rigidly dualistic. He maintained, in *Being and Nothingness,* that man had been regarded by philosophers and psychologists from the outside as though he were an object, and that previous attempts to deal with man's inwardness had actually smuggled the object inside him, in a disguised form. But the object is simply what it is, knowing no past and hoping for and fearing no future. Man, on the contrary, is divided against himself, looking backward and forward, and imagining how the present could be changed into what it is not (*néantiser,* "to nihilize," is Sartre's word for this procedure). Each man's project, no matter how varied the methods and envisaged goal may be, is fundamentally the endeavor to realize himself fully, like a solid object, but at the same time to realize, or be conscious, that he has become an unconscious object. He would thus have welded into unity the essence of the object and the existence of the subject. But this aim is self-contradictory, hence impossible, and man—to quote the last phrase of *Being and Nothingness*—"is a useless passion."

There are, on the path to this conclusion, many fascinating psychological analyses of great originality and depth. Some commentators have declared a number of the book's individual parts to be more impressive than the whole, and they find Sartre more successful as a psychologist than on the metaphysical level. For Sartre today, existentialism is but a trend, petit bourgeois in origin (since Sartre, its originator, is a petit bourgeois), within the one great ideology of the last hundred years and more: Marxism. Today, even when the psychology of one individual is at the center of his attention, he no longer finds it valid to consider this individual apart from the immediate social group and the wider society in which he has grown up and still lives.

One immense change that has taken place in Sartre's outlook can be simply stated. He had declared, in *Being and Nothingness,* that man was totally free—even though, as he paradoxically put it, man was "condemned to be free" and "free to commit himself." Now Sartre holds that man's freedom is but a nuance within societal patterns, whether these be firmly established, undergoing significant modification, or on the way out. However, freedom is no less precious and essential, because of that.

In this volume we present *No Exit,* one of Sartre's earliest and, almost certainly, the most frequently performed of his plays. The scene is laid in hell, and the play's three characters find themselves there not because one is a deserter and coward, another a Lesbian, and the third utterly frivolous—not even, really, because they have made a false use of their freedom, leading "inauthentic" lives. They are there because of their cruelty to other human beings on earth. They may be considered self-condemned to hell by their own self-centeredness, and by the need they have for other people, whom they nevertheless manipulate and abuse, to massage their egos. Now, in a hell that economizes on demons, instruments of torture, and so forth, they set about torturing each other.

Inès assumed that all was predestined because of her "nature." Garcin made all his actions—that is, those visible to the world at large—conform to his carefully cultivated image of himself as an idealist, intellectual, and courageous liberal. This imposed no restrictions on his private life, nor did it enable him to live up to his self-image and reputation in a moment of crisis. For Estelle, life was shaped exclusively by her inauthentic desire to be admired. To the mask of beauty and innocence, which she offered to the world, she sacrificed every other consideration. Like an actress, she assumed the roles assigned to her. It is because they have never made authentic decisions while alive that the three protagonists cannot decide to depart when the opportunity is offered them. Each becomes hell to the others, yet each needs the others, because none of the three can turn away from the past and confront an unknown future. Sartre has intensified this human drama of squandered human freedom by placing his characters in an Empire drawing room. It is this background of shabby gentility, a clinging to what is not, that symbolizes their outlook.

Many years ago, Sartre announced that he would undertake an "existential psychoanalysis" of Gustave Flaubert, while revealing on a number of occasions that he did not esteem the man behind the novels. In *L'Idiot de la famille* he has recently begun to carry out this promise. Two volumes, two thousand pages, perhaps one million words, lead us to the time when Flaubert published *Madame Bovary,* his first novel. In this connection, too, there has been a radical change in Sartre's outlook. First of all, the book could be written as currently conceived only because there is a huge amount of material available on Flaubert's childhood and the circumstances surrounding it. Reversing the old-fashioned deterministic practice of using an author's works simply as documents that throw light on the man, Sartre maintains that a man's life may enable us to understand better his writings, which realize in fantasy possibilities that the real world denies. But Sartre is not content merely to stand the old practice on its head. Utilizing the abundant materials and allowing himself, too, interpretative leaps that a cautious academic scholar would not even dream of, he works out and concretely exemplifies a method that flows in both directions: from milieu to individual, from individual to milieu. In this way, Sartre believes, it is possible to converge upon the complex truth of a man (a child, first of all) as society molds him, and also to illuminate more powerfully just what the individual has done with the measure of freedom that is his lot.

A study of these crushing dimensions is not going to be thoroughly read by very many people. It is conceivable, however, that the model Sartre has provided will significantly influence writers in the fields of literary history, social and political history, and sociology. In this way it may come to influence, at a considerable number of removes, and perhaps affecting public affairs as well as scholarly fields, the lives of people to whom the very name of Sartre is unknown. At all events, the serious investigator owes it to himself to examine whether he has anything to learn from this extraordinary work.

RICHARD WRIGHT

Richard Wright's fiction directly expresses the alienation and gradual coming to self-awareness of an individual trapped in a materialistic and repressive society. The first Afro-American writer to win prosperity and international fame, he is often seen as exclusively an exponent of black consciousness. This view is inadequate, though it is partly true: Wright did have a lifelong commitment to expressing Black and Third-World problems, writing not only literary but nonfictional works to that end, such as *Black Power*, a book about Ghana. But his sympathies and his writings range more widely. A Marxist who voluntarily exiled himself to France during the anti-Communist witchhunts of the late forties, he wrote of the economically as well as the racially oppressed, and he himself maintained that the characters in his novels transcend any purely racial identity, suffering from the more universal problem of maintaining their individuality in the face of social indifference or hostility.

Wright's first works drew upon his experience as a boy growing up in Mississippi during a time of savage racial persecution, an experience recounted in the autobiographical *Black Boy*. The violence and privation of those early years, Wright's rebellion against a fanatically severe religious upbringing, and his long puzzlement over racism —his grandmother was very light-skinned, and for a long time he simply did not perceive any difference—found direct expression in the stories of his first-published book, *Uncle Tom's Children* (1938), from which "Big Boy Leaves Home" is taken. In time, however, he widened his focus. The deprived and alienated Bigger Thomas of *Native Son* (1940) "was not black all the time, he was white, too"; an unpublished third novel, *Little Sister*, has as its central figure a woman whose fatal career results from her sex rather than her race; and Erskine Fowler of *Savage Holiday* (1954) is white. Noting this, some critics have argued that Wright's exile in Paris after 1946 cut him off from his roots and that the later works are comparatively weak. Yet all share Wright's great theme: the central figure of the novel must pass through a series of violent crises that force a coming to terms with his or her identity and role in society. Wright asserted that this theme is "the main burden of all serious fiction . . . character-destiny and the items, social, political, and personal, of that character-destiny."

Like other black writers of his generation, Wright found in the naturalist tradition of Europe and particularly America a style congenial to what he had to say. He was particularly struck by the direct, seemingly factual and objective manner of the American novelists Theodore Dreiser and Sinclair Lewis: "All my life had shaped me for the realism, the naturalism of the modern novel." His first-written, posthumously published novel, *Lawd Today*, contains pages of dialogue that read like transcriptions of overheard speech. Later works went beyond this documentary style, as Wright found affinities with the prose styles of Marcel Proust and the expatriate American poet Gertrude Stein, and as he came into contact with other American writers who could show him a variety of literary techniques adaptable to his own vision. He sought to define the matter and manner of a new "black novel," which would reject the exoticism of previous black writers and incorporate not only black folk material but also militant class consciousness and an awareness of the techniques of modern literature. Though Wright's own fiction remained essentially naturalistic in effect, it was far from photographic. The narrative is guided by his desire to reveal underlying truths, to teach, and as he once said of a fictional scene, "What I wanted [it] to say to the reader was *more important than its surface reality or plausibility*." He might have been speaking of the trial scene in *Native Son*, where Bigger Thomas' lawyer abandons any semblance of an effective defense of his client for a lengthy denunciation of the society which made him a criminal. Obsessive images also invite interpretations beyond surface realism. White is throughout Wright's work a vaguely threatening color, recurring often in nightmares. The famous opening scene of *Native Son*, in which Bigger Thomas kills a monstrous rat invading his home, sets an atmosphere of doom in a decaying society and prefigures Thomas' own destiny to be hunted and killed by society. Realistic narrative often gives way to an atmosphere of crisis and violence, of fantastic dreams and obsessed imaginings, which suggest the larger psychological or cultural forces that have done violence to the main character.

Wright's first book is *Uncle Tom's Children*, a collection of stories set in the South, all of them concerned with racism. The stories are violent, tense with terror, beatings, and murder, and in only one of them ("Fire and Cloud") is there any sense of momentary triumph for the oppressed blacks. "Big Boy Leaves Home" is the opening story, and was first published in 1936. At first its tone is carefree, but the idyllic vision of the truant boys' natural contentment is broken by the unnatural intrusion of white taboos and quickly changes to scenes of violence and terror, as a result of which Big Boy Morrison is expelled from his home into the same hostile world that confronts Wright's later protagonists (like Bigger Thomas). In spite of the force and immediacy of this and its companion stories, Wright felt that something was lacking: "I found that I had written a book which even bankers' daughters could read and weep over and feel good about. I swore that if I ever wrote another book, no one would weep over it. . . . they would have to face it without the consolation of tears." Perhaps he had in mind the philosophical and political dimension of his later novels, starting with *Native Son*; perhaps, like Bertolt Brecht, he felt he could not teach his audience unless he kept them from too close an identification with his characters. Most readers agree, however, that "Big Boy Leaves Home" is among Wright's finest achievements.

ALBERT CAMUS

Though Camus was a mature, established writer and recipient of the Nobel Prize for Literature at the time of his death in an automobile crash, it is nevertheless hard to shake off the feeling that his life's work had not been fully rounded out. Perhaps this is due to the shocking suddenness of his death, which was felt as a personal loss by many who had never known him. Perhaps he had arrived at a hiatus in his career, and stood on the verge of deciding, or discovering, in what direction he would next proceed. Or it may be that his writings themselves reveal him as a man dumbfounded, on the one hand, by the beauty of the world: a North African landscape shimmering in the heat, the swimmer's plunge and resurfacing in the sunlight, the unproblematical sensualities of growing up in the popular quarters of a French North African city. But the hideous, too, was a shock whose tremors refused to subside: shock at the callousness of men and at the yet grimmer reality of death and disease, to which even innocent children fall victim. Camus, though a professed unbeliever, nevertheless voiced his sense of outrage in terms that recall the questioning of Job and *The Brothers Karamazov* of Dostoevsky, along with countless others throughout history: How can unmerited suffering be reconciled with the existence of a God who is both all-powerful and good?

This questioning, or accusation, emerges most clearly at one stage of what is, in terms of length, Camus' most ambitious work, when a priest gives the orthodox Christian answer to this difficulty but fails to convince his hearer. *The Plague*—which, Camus insists, is a chronicle and not a novel—is related in the first person by a doctor who witnesses the outbreak and ravages of pestilence in a town which, because of this, is segregated from the rest of the country. The onset, worsening, and slow ebb of the malady form the setting against which men play their varied parts, which range from selfless dedication to a devil-may-care attitude that might have brought about the deaths of all. Some critics regard the work as that rare literary phenomenon in modern times, a piece of allegorical writing. The plague-bringing rats would then be the Nazis, and the isolated town would represent France or Nazi-occupied Europe. However, it is impossible to demonstrate that Camus' fiction and historical reality coincide in every essential feature. No one in the town, not even the most frivolous individual, was actually on the side of the rats. The situation in France under Nazi domination was distressingly different.

Dostoevskian questions had already been posed by Camus in his first novel, *The Stranger*, published in 1942. As in *The Brothers Karamazov*, a man is shot and an innocent man is absurdly convicted of the deed. Though innocent of his father's murder, Dimitrof was condemned because of a series of events that seemed to point to him as the culprit. Meursault, hero of *The Stranger*, did actually commit murder, but one might say that the deed was done "in all innocence." It was a reflex movement that, in the glaring heat of noon, made him reach for the revolver in his pocket when the Arab's knife flashed menacingly.

On legal grounds Meursault should have been acquitted, since he had acted in self-defense. But what rendered him suspect and intolerable was his general behavior, which threatened to expose the duplicity of accepted mores. The first slip had been his failure to weep during his mother's funeral. Society, acting as judge, could not understand this individual who did not pay homage to the forces of the universal cliché. Condemned to death for his strangeness, the stranger is turned in on himself and forced to reflect as he has never reflected before. He emerges from his anguished pondering still in rebellion against his fate but able to rejoice in the "tender indifference" of the natural world, with its stars, night odors, salty air.

The hero's previous attitude (nothing "made sense," it "didn't matter") is an essential component, and does much to explain the success of the book. The failure of this stranger to understand, to respect, to abide by the conventional petty hypocrisies that keep society moving smoothly in the old grooves, make of him an exemplar of "alienated" or "turned off" youth, just as, within the limits of possibility of time and place, he had become a dropout. The number of Meursaults in circulation was to multiply mightily, after the end of World War II.

The Myth of Sisyphus, also published in 1942, restates in a more theoretical way what *The Stranger* had expressed in novelistic terms. Sisyphus, condemned by the gods to a labor of utter futility, was for Camus the archetype of the "absurd hero." But his Sisyphus, in a sense, escapes his punishment. Knowing that his work is in vain, that the boulder, once he has pushed it to the mountain top, will inevitably roll to the bottom, Sisyphus joyously carries out his repetitive task. "One ought to be Sisyphus, and happy," that is the lesson to be drawn. Camus finds happiness in activity and in a full and sensuous union with the world. Yet one question continues to obtrude itself. In this godless universe, where "everything is permitted," that is, where man is not held back by fear of divine retribution, is everything, indeed, permitted? This Dostoevskian question pursues Camus through novels, essays, and plays until he reaches the conclusion that man, in relation to his fellow man, can sin.

The Fall (1957), which once more takes up this problem of man's guilt and the extent of his freedom, again reminds us of *The Brothers Karamazov,* especially of the chapter on the Grand Inquisitor. The narrator and protagonist identifies himself as a "judge-penitent" and confesses to a life filled with self-love and vanity: "I, I, I is the refrain of my whole life." Vanity has led to duplicity, for the self-created image of self established a role that must be maintained and that must be acknowledged by others. The more virtuous this image, in terms of what society expects, the greater the applause that will be won. Yet the individual, basking in the warmth of this applause, may be situated at a far remove from any reality corresponding to the image. But he continues to live his lie, to play the role assigned to him partly by himself and partly by others, until something occurs that shatters his complacency.

The "I" of this novel is not unique; it is really "we." And this is generally true of Camus' highly stylized characters. They remain lifelike, nevertheless; though we do not expect to meet any individual so generically simplified, like a clown or a personage from the commedia dell' arte, these characters nonetheless possess stark reality.

"The Renegade" is also a narrative in the first person. This is the most savage and the most impressive of the stories that make up *Exile and the Kingdom* (published in 1958). In it Camus has created a masklike living thing that is horrifyingly real. A slave speaks, and the story centers around the problem of man's freedom. In this "renegade," slavery seems to be innate. His changes of allegiance leave him ever both slave and prisoner. It matters little that one of his masters is the god of love and the other a god of hatred. His dedication to the god of love has led him to flee the confines of the seminary and to set himself up as a missionary among the most cruel savages. Eager to accept suffering and torture in the service of his lord, he believes that the faith radiating from him will conquer his oppressors. The actuality is very different.

In their harsh city of salt, these silent savages, dressed in black, are his undoubted masters, So he abandons the god of love (in actual fact, nothing of the sort but only the means by which he sought to establish his own domination) and pays homage to the Fetish, the god of hatred. Here, he believes, is "the principle of the world." Once more he is disappointed. The god of malice and hatred also turns out to be vulnerable. Soldiers arrive; they punish the worshippers of the Fetish. The missionary-turned-slave can achieve no second apostasy that would place him on the side of the big batallions. His tongueless mouth is stuffed with salt, and he dies a slave. Free men cannot be renegades because they have no masters. He who wanted to enslave others with the power of his word remains tongueless and can express his pain only in animallike grunts and cries.

The technique used by Camus in telling this story is rather extraordinary. It is an interior monologue. There is not even the nameless interlocutor of *The Fall*. Part of the story is a flashback. As he lies in wait for the new missionary, whom he has decided to kill, the renegade recapitulates his life. But though the flashback ends when, seemingly, he shoots the new missionary, the story goes on. Ramblingly, and between grunts of pain, the renegade finally acknowledges that the power of the sorcerer has been vanquished by the power of the soldiers, who are in the service of the god of love. Power replaces power, and the renegade's feeble gesture of aid has changed nothing. He dies, his mouth filled with salt. It is a bleak and despairing tale that Camus relates. We might do well to look back to his Sisyphus, happy in the recognition of the futility of his labor, in no man's service and rewarded by none.

LIVES, WRITINGS, AND CRITICISM

Biographical and critical works are listed only if they are available in English.

CHARLES BAUDELAIRE

LIFE. Born in Paris on April 9, 1821. In 1828 his widowed mother married Jacques Aupick, later to become a general and an ambassador. Throughout his life Baudelaire remained greatly attached to his mother and detested his stepfather. His independent behavior having caused alarm, in 1841 he was dispatched on a voyage to the tropics. The following year saw the beginning of his lifelong liaison with Jeanne Duval, a mulatto woman, and of his frequent changes of residence in Paris. Disturbed by his extravagance, the family in 1844 placed him under a financial tutelage which was never to be lifted. The revolutionary disturbances of 1848 awakened his enthusiasm, though later he expressed reactionary political views. The same year he published the first of his many translations from Edgar Allan Poe. His long-heralded collection of poems *Flowers of Evil (Les Fleurs du mal)*, which at last appeared in 1857, was judged to contain matter offensive to morals: author and publisher were fined, and obliged to omit six poems. Baudelaire, who had probably acquired a venereal infection many years before, noted in 1862 that he had felt on his forehead "the breeze from imbecility's wing." Two years later he left Paris, and his creditors, for Brussels. There, in 1866, he was stricken with aphasia and hemiplegia, and he was brought back to Paris. After prolonged suffering he died in his mother's arms, on August 31, 1867. He was interred beside the body of General Aupick.

CHIEF WRITINGS. *Flowers of Evil (Les Fleurs du mal,* 1857), translated by Lewis Piaget Shanks (1931), George Dillon and Edna St. Vincent Millay (1936), C. F. McIntyre (1947), Geoffrey Wagner (1949), Roy Campbell (1952), and William Aggeler (1954); *Artificial Paradises* (*Les Paradis artificiels,* 1860); *Aesthetic Curiosities* (*Curiosités esthétiques,* 1868); *Little Poems in Prose* (*Petits Poèmes en prose,* 1869) translated by A. Crowley (1928) and James Huneker (1929); *Romantic Art* (*L'Art romantique,* 1869); *Posthumous Works and Unedited Correspondence* (*Œuvres posthumes et correspondences inédites,* 1887), including material translated by Christopher Isherwood as *Intimate Journals* (1930); *Baudelaire as a Literary Critic* (1964), translated and edited by Lois B. and Francis E. Hyslop, Jr.; *Painter of Modern Life and Other Writings on Art* (1964), edited by Jonathan Mayne.

Biography and Criticism. François Porché, *Charles Baudelaire* (1928); Peter Quennell, *Baudelaire and the Symbolists* (1929); S. A. Rhodes, *The Cult of Beauty in Charles Baudelaire* (1929); Enid Starkie, *Baudelaire* (1933); Margaret Gilman, *Baudelaire the Critic* (1943); Joseph D. Bennett, *Baudelaire, a Criticism* (1944); Marcel Raymond, *From Baudelaire to Surrealism* (1949); Jean-Paul Sartre, *Baudelaire* (1950); P. M. Jones, *Baudelaire* (1952); Martin Turnell, *Baudelaire* (1954); D. J. Mossop, *Baudelaire's Tragic Hero* (1961); Henri Peyre (ed.), *Baudelaire* (1962); G. Poulet, *Who Was Baudelaire?* (1969); Pierre Emmanuel, *Baudelaire: The Paradox of Redemptive Satanism* (1970); Walter Benjamin, *Charles Baudelaire: A Lyric Poet in the Era of High Capitalism* (1973); Alex de Jonge, *Baudelaire, Prince of Clouds* (1976); Garnet Rees, *Baudelaire, Sartre and Camus: Lectures and Commentaries* (1976); and Alfred E. Carter, *Charles Baudelaire* (1977).

STÉPHANE MALLARMÉ

Life. Etienne (called Stéphane) Mallarmé was born in Paris on March 18, 1842, into a settled bourgeois family. His father was Deputy Clerk in the Registry, and ancestors on both sides of the family had been minor government bureaucrats as far back as the French Revolution. Mallarmé's mother died when he was five, and his sister in 1857; the pain of their loss recurs in images of his later poetry. After graduating from boarding school in 1860, he worked for two years in his grandfather's office before deciding to become a teacher of English. In 1863 he received a teaching position in the southeastern provincial town of Tournon and moved there with his new wife, a young German woman named Maria Gerhard. Their daughter, Geneviève, was born in 1864. A son, Anatole, was born in 1871 and died in 1879.

Mallarmé began publishing poems and articles in 1862, although his output was always meager and he did not produce a collection in book form until 1887. Much of his work was published separately in different journals. His first important group of poems was published in 1866 in the new literary magazine *Le Parnasse Contemporain,* and his translations of Edgar Allan Poe appeared in 1872. Mallarmé was eager to move to Paris, the capital of the arts, but as a young teacher in the state educational system he was dependent on governmental assignments. Sent in 1886 to Besançon, and in 1867 to Avignon, he was finally able to move to Paris in 1871 where he taught at the Lycée Fontanes. Mallarmé was not a particularly good language teacher, had little aptitude for drills and discipline, and was often a figure of fun for his students. On the other hand, he was an important and charismatic figure for the young writers, artists, and musicians who heard him talk about the nature of poetry at the "Tuesdays," gatherings held in Mallarmé's home every Tuesday evening from 1880 until shortly before his death. Mallarmé's influence was widespread. In 1876 Edouard Manet illustrated Mallarmé's "L'Après-midi d'un faune" ("Afternoon of a Faun"), and in 1894 Claude Debussy composed his musical "Prelude" to the same text. Verlaine included Mallarmé in his account of the new poets, *Les Poètes maudits* (*The Doomed Poets,* 1883), and after Verlaine's death Mallarmé was elected "Prince of Poets" by his colleagues in 1896. Upon his retirement from teaching in 1894, Mallarmé lectured on poetry and experimented with different kinds of poetic form, including the typographical arrangements of *Un Coup de dès* (*Dice Thrown,* 1897) that foreshadowed modern concrete poetry. For years, he had worked on the notion of a universal "Book," a complicated text that would be performed and not merely read. Yet he himself finally felt that his vision had outstripped technical possibilities, and when he died on September 9, 1898, the work remained incompleted.

Chief Writings. *Herodias,* translated by Clark Mills (1940); *Poems,* translated by Roger Fry (1951); *Selected Prose Poems, Essays, and Letters,* translated by Bradford Cook (1956); *Selected Poems,* translated by C. F. MacIntyre (1959); and *Mallarmé,* edited by Anthony Hartley (1965).

Biography and Criticism. Wallace Fowlie, *Mallarmé* (1953); Joseph Chiari, *Symbolisme from Poe to Mallarmé* (1956); A. R. Chisholm, *Mallarmé's "L'Après-midi d'un Faune," An Exegetical and Critical Study* (1958); Haskell Block, *Mallarmé and the Symbolist Drama* (1963); Charles Mauron, *Introduction to the Psychoanalysis of Mallarmé* (1963); Robert G. Cohn, *Toward the Poems of Mallarmé* (1965); Robert G. Cohn, *Mallarmé's Masterwork* (1966); Guy Michaud, *Mallarmé* (1966); Bernard Weinberg, *The Limits of Symbolism*

(1966); Norman Paxton, *The Development of Mallarmé's Prose Style* (1968); Frederic C. St. Aubyn, *Stéphane Mallarmé* (1969); Thomas A. Williams, *Mallarmé and the Language of Mysticism* (1970); Ursula Franklin, *An Anatomy of Poesis: the Prose Poems of Stéphane Mallarmé* (1976); Judy Kravis, *The Prose of Mallarmé: The Evolution of a Literary Language* (1976); and Paula G. Lewis, *The Aesthetics of Stéphane Mallarmé in Relation to His Public* (1976).

ARTHUR RIMBAUD

LIFE. Jean Nicholas Arthur Rimbaud was born on October 20, 1854, in Charleville, a town of northeastern France. He proved to be an unusually gifted student, and was encouraged in his literary tastes and endeavors, and also in his revolutionary ardor, by Georges Izambard, his teacher. In 1870 he made the first of his flights from home, and spent ten days in jail as a vagrant. The following year, the poet Paul Verlaine invited Rimbaud to Paris. It was the beginning of a stormy relationship. Together they visited London and Brussels, where, in 1873, Verlaine shot Rimbaud through the wrist and was sentenced to two years' imprisonment. In the same year, at the age of nineteen, Rimbaud gave up the writing of poetry. He found his way to many parts of Europe, to Cyprus, to Java, and to Aden, where he worked for an exporting firm, later moving to Harar, in Abyssinia. As an independent trader he went on expeditions in Abyssinia, and engaged in gunrunning, but it cannot be definitely established that he trafficked in slaves. Falling ill in 1891, he returned to France, and his leg, which was in horrible condition, was amputated at Marseilles. He died on November 10, 1891.

CHIEF WRITINGS. *A Season in Hell* (*Une Saison en enfer,* 1873), translated by Louise Varèse (1945), Norman Cameron (1950); *Illuminations* (*Les Illuminations,* 1887), partially translated by Louise Varèse in *Prose Poems from The Illuminations* (1946); *Complete Poems* (*Poésies complètes,* 1895); *Complete Works* (*Œuvres complètes,* 1946); *Works* (*Œuvres,* 1950). Other translations are to be found in Lionel Abel, *Some Poems of Rimbaud* (1939); Norman Cameron, *Selected Verse Poems* (1942); *Complete Works with Selected Letters,* translated by Wallace Fowlie (1966).

BIOGRAPHY AND CRITICISM. Peter Quennell, *Baudelaire and the Symbolists* (1929); Konrad Bercovici, *Savage Prodigal* (1948); Marcel Raymond, *From Baudelaire to Surrealism* (1949); W. M. Frohock, *Rimbaud's Poetic Practice* (1963); Gwendolyn Bays, *The Orphic Vision* (1964); Wallace Fowlie, *Rimbaud* (1966); Enid Starkie, *Arthur Rimbaud* (revised edition, 1968); Yves Bonnefoy, *Rimbaud* (1973); Robert G. Cohn, *The Poetry of Rimbaud* (1973); Nathaniel Wing, *Present Appearances: Aspects of Poetic Structure in Rimbaud's Illuminations* (1974); and F. C. St. Aubyn, *Arthur Rimbaud* (1975).

WILLIAM BUTLER YEATS

LIFE. Born on June 13, 1865, in Sandymount, a suburb of Dublin, Ireland, to a Protestant family which had settled in Ireland at the beginning of the eighteenth century. Yeats's father gave up the law for the study of painting, and moved to London, but the child spent much time also with relatives in Sligo, in the west of Ireland. The boy was not happy at school in England. The failure of rents compelled the family to return to Ireland in 1880; there Yeats attended first the High School, Dublin, and then the Dublin School of Art. In 1887, in London once more with his parents, he did ill-paid literary work. He founded the Rhymers' Club there, associated with William Morris, W. E. Henley, Arthur Symons, Lionel Johnson, and others, and became interested in both French symbolism and Celtic myth. In 1900, with Lady Gregory and Synge, he founded the theatrical venture which was to become, a little later, the Abbey Theatre. His meeting with Maud Gonne was a turning point in his life. He fell hopelessly in love with her, but throughout the years she steadfastly refused his suit, devoting herself to the aims of revolutionary Irish nationalism. Yeats eventually married Georgie Hyde-Lees, formerly his secretary, on October 21, 1917. He served for six years in the Irish Free State Senate, his most prominent speech being one in favor of divorce. In 1923 he was awarded the Nobel prize. His death occurred on January 28, 1939.

CHIEF WRITINGS. Poetry: *The Wind among the Reeds* (1899); *The Wild Swans at Coole* (1919); *The Tower* (1928); *The Collected Poems* (1933, new enlarged edition, 1950). Plays: *The Countess Cathleen* (1892); *The Land of Heart's Desire* (1894); *Collected Plays* (1934, new enlarged edition 1952); *Last Poems and Plays* (1940). Prose: *Dramatis Personae* (1936); *A Vision* (1937); *Letters to Katharine Tynan* (1953); and *Memoirs,* edited by Denis Donoghue (1972).

BIOGRAPHY AND CRITICISM. Edith Sitwell, *Aspects of Modern Poetry* (1934); Louis MacNeice, *The Poetry of W. B. Yeats* (1941); Joseph Hone, *W. B. Yeats* (1943); C. M. Bowra, *The Heritage of Symbolism* (1943); Richard Ellmann, *Yeats, The Man and the Mask* (1948); A. N. Jeffares, *W. B. Yeats, Man and Poet* (1949); Donald Stauffer, *The Golden Nightingale* (1940); Graham Hough, *The Last Romantics* (1950); J. Hall and M. Steinmann (eds.), *The Permanence of Yeats* (1950); T. R. Henn, *The Lonely Tower* (1950); Vivienne Koch, *W. B. Yeats: The Tragic Phase* (1951); T. Parkinson, *W. B. Yeats, Self-Critic* (1951); Richard Ellmann, *The Identity of Yeats* (1954); John Bayley, *Romantic Survival* (1957); John Unterecker, *Reader's Guide to William Butler Yeats* (1959); Francis Wilson, *Yeats' Iconography* (1960); V. K. N. Menon, *Development of William Butler Yeats* (1961); Benjamin L. Reid, *Yeats: The Lyric of Tragedy* (1961); Amy G. Stock, *Yeats: His Poetry and Thought* (1961); A. Norman Jeffares, *W. B. Yeats: The Poems* (1962); Morton I. Seiden, *Yeats: The Poet as Mythmaker* (1962); Edward Engelberg, *Vast Design: Patterns in W. B. Yeats' Aesthetic* (1963); Frank Kermode, *Romantic Image* (1963); Thomas Parkinson, *W. B. Yeats: The Later Poetry* (1963); Jon Stallworthy, *Between the Lines: Yeats's Poetry in the Making* (1963); John E. Unterecker (ed.), *Yeats: A Collection of Critical Essays* (1963); David R. Clark, *W. B. Yeats and the Theatre of Desolate Reality* (1964); Priscilla Shaw, *Rilke, Valéry and Yeats: The Domain of the Self* (1964); Richard Ellmann, *The Identity of Yeats* (second edition, 1964); Thomas R. Henn, *The Lonely Tower* (second edition, revised and enlarged, 1965); Richard Ellmann, *Eminent Domain: Yeats among Wilde, Joyce, Pound, Eliot, and Auden* (1970); Robert Beum, *The Poetic Art of William Butler Yeats* (1968); Harold Bloom, *Yeats* (1970); A. Norman Jeffares, *Commentary on the Collected Poems of W. B. Yeats* (1968, 1970); Marjorie Perloff, *Rhyme and Meaning in the Poetry of Yeats* (1970); K. Cross, *A Bibliography of Yeats Criticism*, 1887–1965 (1971); John R. Moore, *Masks of Love and Death: Yeats as Dramatist* (1971); John E. Stoll, *The Great Deluge: a Yeats Bibliography* (1971); Daniel Albright, *The Myth Against Myth* (1972); *William Butler Yeats, a Critical Anthology*, edited by Wm. Pritchard (1972); *William Butler Yeats; a Collection of Criticism*, edited by Patrick J. Keane (1973); Robert Snukal, *High Talk; The Philosophical Poetry of William Butler Yeats* (1973); Brenda S. Webster, *Yeats; a Psychoanalytic Study* (1973); Daniel Harris, *Yeats: Coole Park and Ballylee* (1974); Edward G. Malins, *A Preface to Yeats* (1974); Colin Meir, *The Ballads and Songs of William Butler Yeats* (1974); Frank H. Murphy, *Yeats' Early Poetry* (1975); Robert O'Driscoll, *Symbolism and Some Implications of the Symbolic Approach: William Butler Yeats during the Eighteen-nineties* (1975); Dudley Young, *Out of Ireland: A Reading of Yeats' Poetry* (1975); and Denis Donoghue, *Yeats* (1976).

LUIGI PIRANDELLO

LIFE. Pirandello was born in Girgenti, Sicily, in 1867. Having convinced his father that he had no head for business, he went off to study at the University of Rome, later transferring to the University of Bonn, in Germany. He wrote his Ph.D. dissertation on the dialect of his native town. He married in 1894 and settled in Rome. For ten years he was able to write without having to earn a livelihood, since his father gave him a generous allowance. The failure of the family business put an end to that, and for many years Pirandello taught in Rome at the equivalent of a normal school for women. His home life was made burdensome by his wife's increasingly serious mental derangement. She died in 1918. Pirandello achieved fame as a playwright about 1920, and thereupon gave up his teaching position. He traveled in Italy and elsewhere in Europe, and in America, with a theatrical troupe that performed his own plays. In 1934 he was awarded the Nobel Prize for Literature. He died in 1936.

CHIEF WRITINGS. *Naked Masks: Five Plays* (1922, 1952); *Each in His Own Way, and Two Other Plays* (1923); *The One-Act Plays* (1928); *The Old and the Young*, 2 volumes (1928); *As You Desire Me* (1931); *Horse in the Moon, Twelve Short Stories* (1932); *Tonight We Improvise* (1932); *One, None and a Hundred Thousand: A Novel* (1933); *The Naked Truth, and Eleven Other Stories* (1934); *Better Think Twice About It and Twelve Other Stories* (1935); *Six Characters in Search of an Author* (1935); *The Outcast: A Novel* (1935); *The Medals and Other Stories* (1939); *Right You Are* (1954); *When Someone Is Somebody* (1956); *The Mountain Giants* (1958); *Short Stories* (1959); *To Clothe the Naked, and Two Other Plays* (1962); *Pirandello's One-Act Plays* (1964); *The Late Mattia Pascal* (1923, 1964); *Short Stories* (1965).

BIOGRAPHY AND CRITICISM. John Palmer, *Studies in the Contemporary Theater* (1927); Stark Young, *Immortal Shadows* (1948); Francis Fergusson, *The Idea of a Theater* (1949); Lander MacClintock, *The Age of Pirandello* (1951); Thomas Bishop, *Pirandello and the French Theater* (1960); Walter Starkie, *Luigi Pirandello, 1867–1936*, third revised edition (1965); Oscar Büdel, *Pirandello* (1966); Glauco Cambon (ed.), *Pirandello: A Collection of Essays* (1967); Domenico Vittorini, *The Drama of Luigi Pirandello* (1957, 1969); Jörn Moestrup, *The Structural Patterns of Pirandello's Work* (1972); Anne Paolucci, *Pirandello's Theater* (1974); and Gaspare Giudice, *Pirandello: a Biography* (1975).

ANDRÉ GIDE

LIFE. Born on November 22, 1869, in Paris, to Protestant parents (his mother's family had recently been converted from Catholicism). His father died in 1880. He received an irregular education, attending the École Alsacienne for some time but also studying with private tutors. During the 1890's he frequented the gathering places of the symbolists, among them the salon of Stéphane Mallarmé, but felt ill at ease, owing to his piety, his awkwardness, and his slowness of speech. A trip to North Africa in the autumn of 1893 revolutionized his existence. He became seriously ill at Biskra, and during his convalescence fell in love with earthly delights—see his *Fruits of the Earth* (*Les Nourritures terrestres*), *The Immoralist* (*L'Immoraliste*), and the autobiographical *If It Die* (*Si le Grain ne meurt*). At this time he broke with symbolist literary ideals. On returning to Paris in 1895 he married his cousin Emmanuèle. Thereafter he divided his life between his two estates (in Normandy and in Paris) and extensive travels in Europe and North Africa. During World War I he spent some time working with Belgian refugees. A journey to the Congo led him to expose the abuses that occurred there, and in the early 1930's he announced his adherence to communism. But this new faith did not survive the test of a journey to Russia. A highly controversial career was crowned by the award of the Nobel prize in 1947. With his wide and penetrating reading, his sympathy for the young, his readiness to encourage budding talents, and his preaching of self-realization, Gide exercised a great influence in France and other European countries. Recently there has been increased interest in his writings in the United States. He died on February 19, 1951.

CHIEF WRITINGS. *Marshlands* (*Paludes,* 1895), translated by G. D. Painter in *Marshlands and Prometheus Misbound* (1953); *Fruits of the Earth* (*Les Nourritures terrestres,* 1897), translated by Dorothy Bussy (1949); *Prometheus Misbound* (*Le Prométhée mal enchainé,* 1899), translated by G. D. Painter in *Marshlands and Prometheus Misbound* (1953); *The Immoralist* (*L'Immoraliste,* 1902), translated by Dorothy Bussy (1930); *Saül* (1903), translated by Dorothy Bussy in *Return of the Prodigal . . . Saul* (1953); *Return of the Prodigal* (*Le Retour de l'enfant prodigue,* 1907), translated by Dorothy Bussy in *Return of the Prodigal . . . Saul* (1953); *Strait Is the Gate* (*La Porte étroite,* 1909), translated by Dorothy Bussy (1924); *Isabelle* (1911), translated by Dorothy Bussy in *Two Symphonies* (1931); *Corydon* (1911), translated by Hugh Gibb (1950); *The Vatican Swindle* (*Les Caves du Vatican,* 1914), translated by Dorothy Bussy as *Lafcadio's Adventures* (1927); *The Pastoral Symphony* (*La Symphonie pastorale,* 1919), translated by Dorothy Bussy in *Two Symphonies* (1931); *The Counterfeiters* (*Les Faux-monnayeurs,* 1925), translated by Dorothy Bussy (1928), and in 1951 published in one volume with *Journal of the Counterfeiters* (*Journal des faux-monnayeurs,* 1926), translated by Justin O'Brien; *If It Die* (*Si le Grain ne meurt,* 1926), translated by Dorothy Bussy (1935); *The Journals, 1889–1949* (1939–1950), translated by Justin O'Brien, 4 vols. (1947–1951); *Theseus* (*Thésée,* 1946), translated by John Russell in *Two Legends: Œdipus and Theseus* (1950); *Et nunc manet in te* (1947), translated by Justin O'Brien as *Madeleine* (1952); *Correspondence of André Gide and Edmund Gosse,* 1904–1928, edited and translated by Linette Brugmans (1959); André Gide and Paul Valéry, *Self-Portraits: The Gide-Valéry Letters,* translated by June Guicharnaud (1966); and *The Notebooks of André Walter* (*Les Cahiers d'André Walter,* 1891), translated by Wade Baskin (1968); see also, Arthur King Peters, *Jean Cocteau and André Gide: an Abrasive Friendship* (1973: contains complete Gide-Cocteau correspondence).

BIOGRAPHY AND CRITICISM. Montgomery Belgion, *Our Present Philosophy of Life* (1929); Léon Pierre-Quint, *André Gide: His Life and His Work* (1934); G. E. Lemaître, *Four French Novelists* (1938); Klaus Mann, *André Gide and the Crisis of Modern Thought* (1943)· Van Meter Ames, *André Gide* (1947); Harold March, *André Gide and the Hound of Heaven* (1951); G. D. Painter, *André Gide* (1952); L. Thomas, *André Gide* (1952); Justin O'Brien, *Portrait of André Gide* (1953); J. C. McLaren, *The Theatre of André Gide* (1953); R. Martin du Gard, *Recollections of André Gide* (1953); Germaine Brée, *André Gide* (1962); Jean Delay, *The Youth of André Gide* (1963); Ralph Freedman, *The Lyrical Novel* (1963); J. G. Brennan, *Three Philosophical Novelists* (1964); Wallace Fowlie, *André Gide: His Life and Art* (1965); Vinio Rossi, *André Gide: the Evolution of an Aesthetic* (1967); W. Wolfgang Holdheim, *Theory and Practice of the Novel. A Study of André Gide* (1968); George D. Painter, *André Gide: A Critical Biography* (1968); Thomas Cordle, *André Gide* (1969); Albert J. Guerard, *André Gide* (revised edition, 1969); Kenneth Perry, *Religious Symbolism of André Gide* (1969); G. W. Ireland, *André Gide: A Study of His Creative Writings* (1970); David Littlejohn (ed.), *Gide: A Collection of Critical Essays* (1970); Kurt Weinberg: *On Gide's Prométhée: Private Myth and*

Public Mystification (1972); Karin N. Ciholas, *Gide's Art of the Fugue* (1974); and C. D. E. Tolton, *André Gide and the Art of Autobiography* (1975).

MARCEL PROUST

LIFE. Proust was born on July 10, 1871, to a wealthy middle-class Parisian family. His father was a well-known doctor and professor of medicine, a Catholic of provincial background; his mother was a sensitive, intelligent woman of urban Jewish background who had much influence on her son. Proust fell ill with an asthma attack when he was nine, and thereafter spent his childhood holidays at a seaside resort, the model for Balbec, instead of in the country. In spite of his illness, Proust studied in Paris where he met many young writers and composers, and did a year of military service at Orleans. In 1890, he began to frequent the salons of the wealthy bourgeoisie and the aristocracy of the Faubourg Saint Germain, from which he drew much of the material for his portraits of society. He wrote for symbolist magazines like *Le Banquet* and *La Revue Blanche*, and published an elegant book, *Pleasures and Days* (1896), with drawings by Madeleine Lemaire and music by Reynaldo Hahn. In 1899 he also began to translate the English moralist and art critic, John Ruskin.

Proust's health started seriously to decline in 1902, and in addition he had lost both parents by 1905. The following year, his asthma worsening, he moved into a cork-lined, fumigated room at 102 Boulevard Haussmann, from which he emerged rarely and then only late at night for dinners with friends. There he wrote most of *Remembrance of Things Past*. Its first part (*Swann's Way*) was published at his own expense in 1913; World War I delayed publication of subsequent volumes, and Proust then began the painstaking revision and enlargement of the whole, from 1500 to 4000 pages, that was to occupy him until his death on November 18, 1922.

CHIEF WRITINGS. *Pleasures and Days* (*Les Plaisirs et les jours,* 1896); *Remembrance of Things Past* (*À la Recherche du temps perdu,* 1913–1927); *Sketches and Miscellanies* (*Pastiches et mélanges,* 1919); *Letters* (*Correspondance,* 6 vols. 1930–1936); *Jean Santeuil* (1952); *Contre Sainte-Beuve* (1954). Other volumes of translations: *Marcel Proust: A Selection from His Miscellaneous Writings*, edited by Gerard Hopkins (1948); *Marcel Proust on Art and Literature,* edited by Sylvia T. Warner (1958); *Letters of Marcel Proust*, edited by Mina Curtiss (1949); and *Letters to his Mother,* edited by George Painter (1957).

BIOGRAPHY AND CRITICISM. Samuel Beckett, *Proust* (1931); Harold March, *The Two Worlds of Marcel Proust* (1948); F. C. Green, *The Mind of Proust* (1949); André Maurois, *Proust, Portrait of a Genius* (1950); Charlotte Haldane, *Proust* (1951); Walter Strauss, *Proust and Literature: The Novelist as Critic* (1957); Richard Barker, *Marcel Proust, A Biography* (1958); George Painter, *Proust, The Early Years* (1959); *Proust: A Collection of Critical Essays,* edited by René Girard (1962); Milton Hindus, *A Reader's Guide to Marcel Proust* (1962); Howard Moss, *The Magic Lantern of Marcel Proust* (1962); William Bell, *Proust's Nocturnal Muse* (1963); Roger Shattuck, *Proust's Binoculars* (1963); Leo Bersani, *Marcel Proust: The Fictions of Life and Art* (1965); George Painter, *Proust: The Later Years* (1965); Germaine Brée, *Marcel Proust and Deliverance from Time* (revised edition 1969); George Stambolian, *Marcel Proust and The Creative Encounter* (1972); *In Search of Marcel Proust,* edited by Monique Chefdor (1973); P. A. Spalding and R. H. Cortie, *A Reader's Handbook to Proust* (1974); Wallace Fowlie, *A Reading of Proust* (revised 1975); and Céleste Albaret, *Monsieur Proust,* translated by B. Bray (1977).

THOMAS MANN

LIFE. Thomas Mann was born in the north German town of Lübeck on June 6, 1875. His father was a grain merchant and head of the family firm; his mother came from a German-Brazilian family and was known for her beauty and musical talent. Mann disliked the scientific emphasis of his secondary education and left school in 1894 after repeating two years. Rejoining his family in Munich, where they had moved after his father's death in 1891, he worked as an unpaid apprentice in a fire insurance business, but found more interest in university lectures in history, political economy, literature, and art. From 1896 to 1898 he lived and wrote in Italy, returning to Munich in 1898 for a two-year stint as manuscript reader for the satiric weekly *Simplicissimus.* He served less than three months in the Royal Bavarian Infantry, and after his discharge for poor health devoted himself to writing. In 1905 he married Katia Pringsheim; they had six children.

Through his writings up to and during World War I, Mann established himself as an important spokesman for modern Germany. His early conservatism and defense of authoritarian government later gave way to outspoken criticism of Nazi aims and methods. Mann went into voluntary exile on Hitler's becoming Chancellor in 1933. He had received the Nobel Prize in 1929, and was already an international figure. From 1933 to 1938 he lived in Switzerland, where he cofounded and edited the periodical *Measure and Worth.* In 1938 he came to America where he wrote, lectured, broadcast attacks on Hitlerism, and helped other exiles. Mann was Consultant in Germanic Literature to the Library of Congress in 1942 and became an American citizen in 1944. After the war, he visited Germany but refused to live there. He remained in America until 1952, when he moved to Switzerland. He died in Zurich on August 12, 1955.

CHIEF WRITINGS. *Buddenbrooks* (1900); "Tonio Kröger" (1903); *Royal Highness (Königliche Hoheit,* 1909); *Death in Venice (Der Tod in Venedig,* 1913); *Of the German Republic (Von deutscher Republik,* 1923); *The Magic Mountain (Der Zauerberg,* 1924); *Mario and the Magician (Mario und der Zauberer,* 1929); *Joseph and His Brethren (Joseph und seine Brüder,* 4 vols., 1933–1944); *Lotte in Weimar* (1939), translated as *The Beloved Returns* (1940); *Doctor Faustus (Doktor Faustus,* 19-47); *The Holy Sinner (Der Erwählte,* 1951); *Confessions of Felix Krull, Confidence Man (Bekenntnisse des Hochstaplers Felix Krull,* 1954). Other volumes of translations are *Stories of Three Decades* (1936); *Selected Essays* (1941); *Order of the Day* (1942); *Essays of Three Decades* (1946); *The Thomas Mann Reader,* edited by J. W. Angell (1950); and *Letters of Thomas Mann,* edited by Richard and Clara Winston (1970).

BIOGRAPHY AND CRITICISM. H. J. Weigand, *Thomas Mann's Novel Der Zauberberg* (1933); J. G. Brennan, *Thomas Mann's World* (1942); G. Lukacs, *Essays on Thomas Mann* (1949, revised and translated 1964); H. Hatfield, *Thomas Mann* (1951); K. W. Jonas, *Fifty Years of Thomas Mann Studies, A Bibliography of Criticism* (1955; new volumes forthcoming); R. H. Thomas, *Thomas Mann: The Meditation of Art* (1956); F. Kaufmann, *Thomas Mann: The World as Will and Representation* (1957); E. Heller, *The Ironic German* (1958); Thomas Mann, *A Sketch of My Life* (rev. ed. 1960); *Thomas Mann: A Collection of Critical Essays,* edited by H. Hatfield, (1964); H. Bürgin and H. O. Mayer, *Thomas Mann: A Chronicle of His Life* (1969); E. Kahler, *The Orbit of Thomas Mann* (1969); R. Hollingdale, *Thomas Mann: A Critical Study* (1971); W. A. Berendsohn, *Thomas Mann: Artist and Partisan in Troubled Times* (1973); and T. J. Reed, *Thomas Mann: The Uses of Tradition* (1974).

WALLACE STEVENS

LIFE. Wallace Stevens was born in Reading, Pennsylvania, on October 2, 1879, the second of five children. His father was a schoolteacher and then attorney with diverse business interests, and his mother also taught school. He enrolled at Harvard in 1897 as a special student (not in a degree program) and while at college contributed poems, stories, and sketches to the Harvard *Advocate* (of which he became president) and the Harvard *Monthly.* He also came to know the philosopher and writer George Santayana, by whose assertion of a common imaginative essence in religion and poetry he was much attracted.

Stevens left Harvard in 1900 to try journalism and then law school in New York; he received his degree and was admitted to the bar in 1904. After working as an attorney for several firms he finally entered the insurance business in 1908. In 1916 he joined a subsidiary of the Hartford Accident and Indemnity Company, becoming vice-president of the parent company in 1934 and remaining with them until his death in 1955; he dictated business correspondence and poems to the same secretary. In 1922 business affairs took him to Florida, and until 1940 he returned frequently to its landscape, which contributed many images to his poetry.

Stevens married Elsie V. Kachel in 1909. They had one daughter, Holly, in 1924, the year following publication of *Harmonium,* his first book of poems. He published little poetry after that until 1936, when *Ideas of Order* appeared. Later volumes included *The Man With the Blue Guitar* (1937), *Parts of a World* (1942), and a collection of prose essays called *The Necessary Angel* (1951). In the end, Stevens became a well-known and influential poet, winning the Bollingen Prize for Poetry in 1949, and the National Book Award in 1951 (for *The Auroras of Autumn*) and 1955 (for *The Collected Poems of Wallace Stevens*) shortly before his death from cancer on August 2, 1955.

CHIEF WRITINGS. Harmonium (1923); *Ideas of Order* (1936); *Parts of a World* (1942); *Transport to Summer* (1947); *The Auroras of Autumn* (1950); *The Necessary Angel* (1951); *The Collected Poems of Wallace Stevens* (1954); *Opus Posthumous* (1957); *The Palm at the End of the Mind* (1971); see also *Letters of Wallace Stevens,* edited by Holly Stevens (1966).

BIOGRAPHY AND CRITICISM. Robert Pack, *Wallace Stevens: An Approach to His Poetry* (1958); Frank Kermode, *Wallace Stevens* (1960); *The Achievement of Wallace Stevens,* edited by Ashley Brown and Robert Haller (1962); *Wallace Stevens: A Collection of Critical Essays,* edited by Marie Borroff (1963); Daniel Fuchs, *The Comic Spirit of Wallace Stevens* (1963); J. Hillis Miller, *Poets of Reality* (1965); *The Act of the Mind,* edited by Roy H. Pearce and J. Hillis Miller (1965); Joseph Riddel, *The Clairvoyant Eye* (1965); Frank Doggett, *Stevens' Poetry of Thought* (1966); Robert Buttel, *Wallace Stevens, The Making of Harmonium* (1967); James Baird, *The Dome and the Rock* (1968); Helen Vendler, *On Extended Wings* (1969); Samuel F. Morse, *Wallace Stevens; Poetry as Life* (1970); Edward Kessler,

Images of Wallace Stevens (1971); Michel Benamou, *Wallace Stevens and the Symbolist Imagination* (1972); A. W. Litz, *Introspective Voyager* (1972); Jerome Edelstein, *Wallace Stevens: a Descriptive Bibliography* (1973); *Sixteen Modern American Authors,* edited by Jackson Bryer (1973); Lucy Beckett, *Wallace Stevens* (1974); Adalaide Morris, *Wallace Stevens: Imagination and Faith* (1974); Harold Bloom, *Wallace Stevens: The Poems of Our Climate* (1977); and Susan Weston, *Wallace Stevens: An Introduction to the Poetry* (1977).

JAMES JOYCE

LIFE. James Augustine Aloysius Joyce, born on February 2, 1882, in Dublin, Ireland. His father, John Stanislaus Joyce, had political connections, and earned his living in a variety of makeshift occupations. Because of monetary difficulties, his family had to change residence frequently. Joyce was educated first at Clongowes Wood College, Clane, where he was a boarder for three years, and then, starting in 1891, at Belvedere College, Dublin, which he attended as a day pupil. Both these schools are under Jesuit direction. At the age of fifteen, he won a prize for an essay on "My Favorite Hero," in which his hero was Ulysses. He entertained but rejected the notion of becoming a Jesuit, and in 1898 entered the University College, Dublin, receiving a B.A. degree four years later. In October, 1902, he set off for Paris, where he nearly starved. The following year, receiving the news that his mother was dying, he made a hasty return journey to Ireland. In 1904 he left home to teach at the Clifton School in the Dublin seaside suburb of Dalkey, and lived for a while in the Martello Tower at Sandycove. At about this time he met Norah Barnacle of Galway, and he soon left with her for the Continent, in the belief that he had a position at the Berlitz School in Zurich. This proved to be a mistake, but he found a place instead at the Berlitz School in Trieste. There he became friendly with and encouraged the much older Italian novelist Italo Svevo. His last visit to Dublin occurred in 1912. After the outbreak of war in 1914, the Austrian authorities, because of his wretched eyesight, allowed him to leave the country on parole, and he settled in Zurich. In 1919 he returned to Trieste, but the following year he moved to Paris. At about this time, Harriet Weaver, the editor of the *Egoist,* freed him of financial worries by making over to him a sum of money sufficient to provide a lifelong income. With the collapse of armed resistance in France in World War II, the Joyces made their way to Vichy, and from there to Zurich, where Joyce was operated upon for malignant duodenal ulcer. He died on January 13, 1941.

CHIEF WRITINGS. *Chamber Music* (1907), edited by W. Y. Tindall (1954); *Dubliners* (1914); *A Portrait of the Artist as a Young Man* (1916); *Exiles* (1918); *Ulysses* (1922); *Finnegans Wake* (1939); *Stephen Hero* (1944); *Letters,* volume 1, edited by Stuart Gilbert (1957), volumes 2 and 3, edited by Richard Ellmann (1966); *First Draft of Finnegans Wake,* edited by David Hayman (1962); and *Selected Letters,* edited by Richard Ellmann (1971).

BIOGRAPHY AND CRITICISM. For biography see Frank Budgen, *James Joyce and the Making of Ulysses* (1934); Herbert Gorman, *James Joyce* (1939); Leon Edel, *James Joyce, the Last Journey* (1947); Stanislaus Joyce, *Recollections of James Joyce* (1950); J. F. Byrne, *The Silent Years* (1953); Richard Ellmann, *James Joyce* (1959); Stanislaus Joyce, *Dublin Diary* (1962). For criticism see Stuart Gilbert, *James Joyce's "Ulysses"* (1931, 2nd rev. ed., 1952); Edmund Wilson, *Axel's Castle* (1932); Samuel Beckett and others, *Examination . . . of Work in Progress* (1936); Harry Levin, *James Joyce,* (1941); D. S. Savage, *The Withered Branch* (1950); W. Y. Tindall, *James Joyce* (1950); William T. Noon, *Joyce and Aquinas* (1957); Richard M. Kain, *Fabulous Voyager* (1959); J. Mitchell Morse, *Sympathetic Alien* (1959); William Y. Tindall, *Reader's Guide to James Joyce* (1959); S. L. Goldberg, *The Classical Temper* (1961); A. Walton Litz, *The Art of James Joyce* (1961); Robert M. Adams, *Surface and Symbol* (1962); Thomas E. Connolly, *Joyce's Portrait: Criticisms and Critiques* (1962); Hugh Kenner, *Dublin's Joyce* (1962); Seon Givens (ed), *James Joyce: Two Decades of Criticism* (revised edition, 1962); Harry Blamires, *Bloomsday Book: A Guide through Joyce's Ulysses* (1966); Robert M. Adams, *Surface and Symbol: The Consistency of James Joyce's Ulysses* (1967); Cyril Pearl, *Dublin in Bloomtime: The City James Joyce Knew* (1969); John Gross, *James Joyce* (1970); Richard Ellmann, *Ulysses on the Liffey* (1972); Helene Cixous, *The Exile of James Joyce* (1972); Nathan Halper, *The Early James Joyce* (1973); Mark Shechner, *Joyce in Nighttown: A Psychoanalytic Inquiry into Ulysses* (1974); Stan G. Davies, *James Joyce: A Portrait of the Artist* (1975); Kenneth Grose, *James Joyce* (1975); and Charles Peake, *James Joyce, the Citizen and the Artist* (1977).

VIRGINIA WOOLF

LIFE. Adeline Virginia Stephen was born on January 25, 1882, in London, to a family of active intellectual and artistic interests. Her father was Leslie Stephen, an editor, historian, and literary critic, and her mother, Julia, who figures in several of Virginia's novels, was admired and sketched by some of the most famous Pre-Raphaelite artists. Virginia and her older sister Vanessa (later Vanessa Bell, the painter) were educated at home by their parents, while her brothers Adrian and Thoby were given a full formal and university education, an example of the characteristically different treatment accorded men and women which was always to absorb her. In 1892 her family took their summer holiday at a seaside home in St. Ives, Cornwall, whose landscape with waves and lighthouse was to reappear in her fiction. Her mother died in 1895 and Virginia, of fragile health since an attack of whooping cough at age six, suffered the first of several nervous breakdowns; the second, involving attempted suicide, followed in 1904, shortly after the death of her father.

In 1905 Virginia, Vanessa, and Adrian moved to a house in the Bloomsbury district of central London, where Virginia started writing reviews for the *Times Literary Supplement,* teaching literature and composition at Morley College (an institution with a volunteer, unpaid faculty that provided educational opportunities for workers), and working for the adult suffrage movement and a feminist group. Upon their sister's marriage to the art critic Clive Bell in 1907, Virginia and Adrian moved to another Bloomsbury home which became the center of a group of writers, artists, and intellectuals known today as the "Bloomsbury Group." United in protest against a staid Edwardian society, their number eventually included such major writers as E. M. Forster, Lytton Strachey, John Maynard Keynes, and the art critic Roger Fry, who introduced them to the works of post-Impressionist painters such as Manet and Cézanne.

In 1912 Virginia Stephen married Leonard Woolf, a University friend of her brothers'; he helped to achieve some stability in her life and encouraged her to write. Her first novel, *Voyage Out,* was published in 1915, and in 1917 the two of them established the Hogarth Press, publishing works by Katherine Mansfield, T. S. Eliot, Strachey, Forster, Maxim Gorki, and Middleton Murry in addition to Woolf's own novels. During the next two decades, she produced her best-known fiction, keeping up at the same time with a series of passionate and complicated friendships and family affairs, and coping with frequent bouts of physical and mental illness. She finished her last novel, *Between the Acts,* on February 26, 1941, and a month and two days later, sensing the approach of an even more serious attack of insanity, drowned herself in a river close by her Sussex home.

Chief Writings. *The Voyage Out* (1915); *Night and Day* (1919); *Monday or Tuesday* (1921); *Jacob's Room* (1922); *The Common Reader: First Series* (1925); *Mrs. Dalloway* (1925); *To the Lighthouse* (1927); *Orlando* (1928); *A Room of One's Own* (1929); *The Waves* (1931); *The Second Common Reader* (1932); *Three Guineas* (1938); *Roger Fry: A Biography* (1940); *Between the Acts* (1941); *A Haunted House and Other Short Stores* (1944); *A Writer's Diary,* edited by Leonard Woolf (1954); *Collected Essays* (4 vols.) (1967); *The Letters of Virginia Woolf, Vol. I: 1882–1912* (1975), *Vol. II: 1912–1922* (1976), *Vol. III: 1923–1928* (1977) edited by Nigel Nicolson and Joanne Trautmann; *Moments of Being, Unpublished Autobiographical Writings,* edited by J. Ferrone (1976); and *The Diary of Virginia Woolf, Vol. I: 1915–1919,* edited by Anne Olivier Bell (1977).

Biography and Criticism. Joan Bennett, *Virginia Woolf* (1945); Bernard Blackstone, *Virginia Woolf: A Commentary* (1949); James Hafley, *The Glass Roof* (1954); Jean Brownlee Kirkpatrick, *A Bibliography of Virginia Woolf* (1957, now being revised); A. D. Moody, *Virginia Woolf* (1963); Leonard Woolf, *Beginning Again* (1964); Jane Guiguet, *Virginia Woolf and Her Works* (1962, trans. 1965); Josephine Schaefer, *The Three-fold Nature of Reality in the Novels of Virginia Woolf* (1965); Leonard Woolf, *Downhill All the Way* (1967); Herbert Marder, *Feminism and Art: A Study of Virginia Woolf* (1968); Leonard Woolf, *The Journey Not the Arrival Matters* (1969); Jacqueline Latham, *Critics on Virginia Woolf* (1970); Jean Love, *Worlds in Consciousness* (1970); Harvena Richter, *Virginia Woolf: the Inward Voyage* (1970); *Virginia Woolf: a Collection of Critical Essays,* edited by Claire Sprague (1971); Quentin Bell, *Virginia Woolf: A Biography* (1972, 2 vols.); Joan Noble, *Recollections of Virginia Woolf* (1972); Nancy Bazin, *Virginia Woolf and the Androgynous Vision* (1973); Manly Johnson, *Virginia Woolf* (1973); Alice van Buren Kelley, *The Novels of Virginia Woolf* (1973); Allen McLaurin, *Virginia Woolf: the Echoes Enslaved* (1973); James Naremore, *The World Without a Self* (1973); Jean Alexander, *The Venture of Form in the Novels of Virginia Woolf* (1974); Avrom Fleishman, *Virginia Woolf* (1975); and John Lehmann, *Virginia Woolf and Her World* (1975).

FRANZ KAFKA

Life. Born on July 3, 1883, in Prague, then an important town of the Austro-Hungarian Empire. The son of a well-to-do middle-class Jewish merchant, he studied at the German University in Prague, obtaining his law degree in 1906. He then worked for many years in the workmen's insurance division of an insurance company that had official state backing. He was much impressed by his father and his father's satisfactory adjustment to life in the role of breadwinner and head of a family, and was troubled by a sense of his own contrasting inadequacy. For several years he entertained the idea of marriage, and he became engaged, but the projected marriage did not take place. In 1923 he met Dora Dymant, descendant of a prominent Eastern Jewish family, an excellent Hebrew scholar and a gifted actress. At the end of July he left Prague and established himself with her in Berlin. "I found an idyll," writes Max Brod of his visits to him there. "At last I saw my friend in a happy frame of mind; his physical condition however had grown worse." He had had several attacks of tuberculosis, and died, after considerable suffering, on June 3, 1924.

CHIEF WRITINGS. "The Judgment" ("Das Urteil," 1913), and "In the Penal Colony" ("In der Strafkolonie," 1919), translated in *The Penal Colony* (1948); *The Trial* (*Der Prozess,* 1925); *The Castle* (*Das Schloss,* 1926); *America* (*Amerika,* 1927); *Collected Works* (*Gesammelte Schriften,* 1935–1937); *The Diaries* (*Tagebücher,* 1951), translated (from the unpublished manuscript) by Joseph Kresh, 2 vols. (1948–1949); *Letters to Milena* (*Briefe an Milena,* 1952). Other translations are available in *Parables in German and English* (1947); *Selected Short Stories,* translated by Willa and Edwin Muir (1952); *Wedding Preparations in the Country, and Other Posthumous Writings,* translated by Ernest Kaiser and Eithne Wilkins (1954); and *I Am a Memory Come Alive; Autobiographical Writings,* edited by Nahum Glatzer (1974).

BIOGRAPHY AND CRITICISM. For biography see Max Brod, *Franz Kafka* (1947); G. Janouch, *Conversations with Kafka* (1953, 1971). For criticism see Paul Goodman, *Kafka's Prayer* (1947); Charles Neider, *Kafka: His Mind and Art* (1949); Antel Flores and Homer Swanda (eds.), *Franz Kafka Today* (1958); Ronald D. Gray (ed.), *Kafka* (1963); Mark Spilka, *Dickens and Kafka* (1963); Angel Flores (ed.), *The Kafka Problem* (1946, 1963); Margarete Buber-Neumann, *Mistress to Kafka: The Life and Death of Milena* (1966); Heinz Politzer, *Franz Kafka: Parable and Paradox* (1962, revised and enlarged edition, 1967); Martin Greenberg, *The Terror of Art: Kafka and Modern Literature* (1968); Herbert Tauber, *Franz Kafka: An Interpretation of His Works* (1968); Johann Bauer, *Kafka and Prague* (1971); Franz Baumer, *Franz Kafka* (1971); Anthony Thorlby, *Kafka: A Study* (1972); Deborah Crawford, *Franz Kafka: Man Out of Step* (1973); Patrick Bridgwater, *Kafka and Nietzsche* (1974); *Franz Kafka: A Collection of Criticism,* edited by Leo Hamalian (1974); Franz Kuna, *Kafka: Literature as Corrective Punishment* (1974); and John Hibberd, *Kafka in Context* (1975).

D. H. LAWRENCE

LIFE. David Herbert Lawrence, born on September 11, 1885, in Eastwood, a mining village with rural surroundings not far from Nottingham, England. His father was a coal miner, unschooled and of a violent temperament. His mother, better educated and ambitious for her sons, encouraged in her children a sense of superiority to their father. Lawrence was a good student, and a scholarship enabled him to go to secondary school. Poor health made it impossible for him to be a miner, and after a short spell of commercial employment, also brought to an end by ill health, he turned to teaching, which occupied him for the next three years. Then a scholarship took him to Nottingham University, and he spent two years there. In 1911, following the death of his mother and the publication of his first novel, he gave up teaching. The following year he met a German woman of good family, Frieda von Richthofen, then the wife of Professor Ernest Weekley of Nottingham University, and eloped with her. Their marriage, which at last became possible in 1914, was marked by reciprocal devotion and almost incessant quarreling. *The Rainbow,* published in 1915, was the first of Lawrence's books to be suppressed by the British authorities as obscene. The Lawrences went to live in Cornwall, but came under suspicion as spies and were ordered to leave the region. Lawrence was glad to get out of England in 1919, and made his way through Europe, Ceylon, and Australia to New Mexico and Mexico. He returned to Europe in 1923, and again, after bouts of dysentery and malaria in Mexico, in 1925. He was suffering from tuberculosis, and died at Vence, in the south of France, on March 2, 1930.

CHIEF WRITINGS. *The White Peacock* (1911); *Sons and Lovers* (1913); *The Rainbow* (1915); *Women in Love* (1920); *Kangaroo* (1923); *The Plumed Serpent* (1926); *Lady Chatterly's Lover* (1928); *Collected Poems* (1928); *Last Poems* (1932); *Letters* (1936); *Phoenix* (1936); *Tales* (1949); *The Later D. H. Lawrence* (1952); *Sex, Literature and Censorship* (1953); *Complete Poems* (1970); *D. H. Lawrence on Education,* edited by Joy and Raymond Williams (1973); and *The Escaped Cock,* edited and with commentary by Gerald M. Lacy (1973).

BIOGRAPHY AND CRITICISM. E. D.

McDonald, *A Bibliography of the Writings of D. H. Lawrence* (1925), and *A Bibliographical Supplement* (1931); Wyndham Lewis, *Paleface* (1929); F. R. Leavis, *D. H. Lawrence* (1930); Catherine Carswell, *Savage Pilgrimage* (1932); R. P. Blackmur, *The Double Agent* (1933); T. S. Eliot, *After Strange Gods* (1934); Earl and Achsah Brewster, *D. H. Lawrence, Reminiscences and Correspondence* (1934); Frieda Lawrence, *"Not I But the Wind . . ."* (1934); E. T. [Jessie Chambers], *D. H. Lawrence, A Personal Record* (1935); Diana Trilling (ed.), *The Portable Lawrence* (1947); J. M. Keynes, *Two Memoirs* (1949); Richard Aldington, *Portrait of a Genius but . . .* (1950); H. T. Moore, *The Life and Works of D. H. Lawrence* (1951); Anthony West, *D. H. Lawrence* (1951); Witter Bynner, *Journey with Genius* (1951); William Tiverton, *D. H. Lawrence and Human Existence* (1952); F. J. Hoffman and H. T. Moore (eds.), *The Achievement of D. H. Lawrence* (1953); Eliot Gilbert Fay, *Lorenzo in Search of the Sun* (1953); H. T. Moore, *The Intelligent Heart* (1954), republished in 1974 as *The Priest of Love*; H. T. Moore (ed.), *A D. H. Lawrence Miscellany* (1959); Eliseo Vivas, *D. H. Lawrence: The Triumph and Failure of Art* (1960); Eugene Goodheart, *The Utopian Vision of D. H. Lawrence* (1963); Julian Moynahan, *Deed of Life* (1963); Mark Spilka (ed.), *D. H. Lawrence: A Collection of Critical Essays* (1963); Daniel A. Weiss, *Oedipus in Nottingham* (1963); Kingsley Widmer, *The Art of Perversity* (1963); David Daiches, *D. H. Lawrence* (1963); George H. Ford, *Double Measure: A Study of the Novels and Stories of D. H. Lawrence* (1965, 1969); James C. Cowan (ed.), *D. H. Lawrence's American Journey* (1970); *D. H. Lawrence: The Critical Heritage*, edited by Ronald P. Draper (1970); Keith Alldritt, *Visual Imagination in D. H. Lawrence* (1971); Stephen J. Miko, *Toward Women in Love; The Emergence of a Lawrentian Aesthetic* (1971); Ronald E. Pritchard, *D. H. Lawrence: Body of Darkness* (1971); Emile Delavenay, *D. H. Lawrence, The Man and His Work; The Formative Years: 1885–1919* (1972); Sandra M. Gilbert: *Acts of Attention; The Poems of D. H. Lawrence* (1972); Frank Kermode, *Lawrence* (1973); Scott Sanders, *D. H. Lawrence: The World of the Major Novels* (1973); Stephen Spender, *D. H. Lawrence; Novelist, Poet, Prophet* (1973); Geoffrey Trease, *The Phoenix and the Flame: D. H. Lawrence; A Biography* (1973); F. R. Leavis, *Thought, Words, and Creativity: Art and Thought in Lawrence* (1976); and Marguerite Howe, *The Art of the Self in D. H. Lawrence* (1977).

T. S. ELIOT

LIFE. Thomas Stearns Eliot, born on September 26, 1888, in St. Louis, Missouri, to an old New England family. He was educated at Milton Academy and Harvard, where he took the B. A. degree in 1909 and the M. A. in 1910. He studied in Paris in 1911, at Harvard again in 1911–1914, and at Merton College, Oxford, in 1914–1915. In 1915 he married Vivienne Haigh, an Englishwoman. After teaching in a London school and working for Lloyd's Bank, he entered the publishing house of Faber & Faber, of which he was a director. In 1922 he founded the literary review *The Criterion*. He became a British subject in 1927, and a year later proclaimed himself an Anglo-Catholic and a royalist. The Nobel Prize for Literature was awarded him in 1948. Among the writers who influenced or attracted him he named Dante; the French poets Jules Laforgue, Tristan Corbière, and Baudelaire; the Elizabethan dramatists, particularly Webster, Shakespeare, Middleton, and Chapman; Dryden and the metaphysical poets; and, among his contemporaries, Ezra Pound. He died on January 4, 1965.

CHIEF WRITINGS. Poetry: *Prufrock and Other Observations* (1917); *Ara Vos Prec* (1920); *The Waste Land* (1922); *Collected Poems, 1909–1935* (1936); *Four Quartets* (1944); *Collected Poems, 1909–1962* (1963). Verse Plays: *The Rock* (1934); *Murder in the Cathedral* (1935); *The Family Reunion* (1939); *The Cocktail Party* (1950); *Collected Poems and Plays* (1952); *The Confidential Clerk* (1954). Criticism: *The Sacred Wood* (1920); *Selected Essays* (1932); *The Use of Poetry and the Use of Criticism* (1933); *Elizabethan Essays* (1934); *Essays Ancient and Modern* (1936); *Poetry and Drama* (1950). General: *The Idea of a Christian Society* (1939); *Notes toward the Definition of Culture* (1949); *The Waste Land: A Facsimile and Transcript of the Original Drafts, Including the Annotations of Ezra Pound,* edited by Valerie Eliot (1971).

BIOGRAPHY AND CRITICISM. F. O. Matthiessen, *The Achievement of T. S. Eliot* (revised edition, 1947); R. March and Tambimuttu (eds.), *T. S. Eliot, A Symposium* (1948). T. McGreevey, *Thomas Stearns Eliot, A Study* (1931); F. R. Leavis, *New Bearings in English Poetry* (1932); H. R. Williamson, *The Poetry of T. S. Eliot* (1932); R. Preston, *Four Quartets Rehearsed* (1946); F. O. Matthiessen, *The Achievement of T. S. Eliot,* rev. ed. (1947); B. Rajan (ed.), *T. S. Eliot, A Study of His Writings by Several Hands* (1947); L. Unger (ed.), *T. S. Eliot, A Selected Critique* (1948); F. C. A. Wilson, *Six Essays on the Development of T. S. Eliot* (1948); Victor H. Brombert, *The Criticism of T. S.*

Eliot (1949); E. A. Drew, *T. S. Eliot, The Design of His Poetry* (1949); H. L. Gardner, *The Art of T. S. Eliot* (1949); D. E. S. Maxwell, *The Poetry of T. S. Eliot* (1952); G. Williamson, *Reader's Guide to T. S. Eliot* (1953); Grover Smith, Jr., *T. S. Eliot's Poetry and Plays* (1956); Carl A. Bodelsen, *T. S. Eliot's Four Quartets* (1958); Neville Braybrooke (ed.), *T. S. Eliot, A Symposium* (1958); R. L. Brett, *Reason and Imagination* (1959); David E. Jones, *The Plays of T. S. Eliot* (1960); Ethel Cornwell, *Still Point* (1962); Hugh Kenner (ed.), *T. S. Eliot, A Collection of Critical Essays* (1962); Carol H. Smith, *T. S. Eliot's Dramatic Theory and Practice* (1963); Eric Thompson, *T. S. Eliot: The Metaphysical Perspective* (1963); Philip R. Headings, *T. S. Eliot* (1964); Fei-Pai Lu, *T. S. Eliot: The Dialectical Structure of His Theory of Poetry* (1966); J. Martin (ed.), *A Collection of Critical Essays on The Waste Land* (1967); B. Bergonzi, *T. S. Eliot* (1971); Russell Kirk, *Eliot and His Age* (1972); Roger Kojecky, *T. S. Eliot's Social Criticism* (1972); John D. Margolis, *T. S. Eliot's Intellectual Development* (1972); Joseph Chiari, *T. S. Eliot, Poet and Dramatist* (1972); *Eliot in His Time; Essays . . .* , edited by A. Walton Litz (1973); David Ward, *Thomas Stearns Eliot Between Two Worlds* (1973); Thomas S. Matthews, *Great Tom; Notes Towards the Definition of T. S. Eliot* (1974); Elisabeth W. Schneider, *Thomas Stearns Eliot: The Pattern in the Carpet* (1975); Stephen Spender, *Eliot* (1975); Derek A. Traversi, *Thomas Stearns Eliot: The Longer Poems* (1976); and Lyndall Gordon, *Eliot's Early Years* (1977).

ANNA AKHMATOVA

LIFE. Anna Andreevna Gorenko was born June 11, 1889, in a suburb of Odessa in Russia. Her father was a maritime engineer and mathematics professor; her mother was a strong-willed woman of populist sympathies who belonged to an early revolutionary group. (The *nom de plume* Akhmatova is the name of the poet's maternal great-grandmother.) The family was well off, and soon moved to Tsarskoe Selo, a small town outside St. Petersburg (now Leningrad) which had also been the summer residence of the tsars for more than a century.

Akhmatova turned to poetry after reading the work of Innokenti Annesky, a poet who had also been principal of the Tsarskoe Selo school. In 1910 she married a young poet Nikolai Gumilev; she visited Paris in 1910 and again in 1911, meeting many writers and artists, including Modigliani, who sketched her several times and read aloud with her the Symbolist poetry of Paul Verlaine. In 1912 she traveled with Gumilev in Northern Italy; in the same year, she published her first collection of poems, *Evening*, and gave birth to her only child, a son, Lev. Spending their winters in the literary society of St. Petersburg, Akhmatova, Gumilev, and Osip Mandelshtam were the leading figures of a small new literary movement, Acmeism, joining forces to reject the romantic quasi-religious aims of Russian Symbolism and to promote their own work.

Akhmatova's second volume of poetry, *The Rosary*, brought her wide fame and was quickly sold out; her third collection, *The White Flock*, published a month before the 1917 revolution, received little attention outside St. Petersburg. During the civil war that followed the execution of the Royal Family, Akhmatova refused to flee abroad, and her political difficulties began. Though she and Gumilev had been divorced in 1918, his arrest and execution for counter-revolutionary activities in 1921 put her own status into question, and after *Anno Domini MCMXXI* appeared in 1922 she was no longer able to publish, and was forced into the unwilling withdrawal from public activity that Russians of the time called "the internal emigration." Political harassment continued, however, aimed now at her son, who was arrested in 1934 and imprisoned again from 1937 to 1941, and yet again from 1949 to 1956. During the Second World War her patriotic activities and resistance poems earned her a brief rehabilitation; she was even allowed in 1940 to publish a new collection, *From Six Books*. But the edition was recalled by officials within six months, and in 1946 she was expelled from the Writer's Union. Unable to publish, Akhmatova supported herself between 1946 and 1958 by translating poetry from other languages; in 1950, hoping to obtain her son's release, Akhmatova wrote some peace poems in the approved Soviet style, but to no effect.

During the slow thaw that followed Stalin's death, Akhmatova was rehabilitated. In 1958 she was even elected to an honorary position on the executive council of the Writer's Union. She published a new collection called *Poems* in that same year, and in 1964 was allowed to travel to Italy to receive the Taormina poetry prize. She died on March 5, 1966.

CHIEF WRITINGS. *Evening* (1912); *Rosary* (1914); *White Flock* (1917); *Anno Domini MCMXXI* (1922); *From Six Books* (1940); *Poems* (1958); *A Poem Without a Hero* (1960); *Requiem* (1963); *The Course of Time* (1965). Translations: in *Modern Russian Poetry*, edited by Vladimir Markov and Merrill Sparks (1967), *Anna Akhmatova, Selected Poems*, translated by Richard McKane, essay by Andrei Sinyavaky (1969); *Poems of Akhmatova*, translated by Stanley Kunitz with Max Hayward (1973); and *Anna Akhmatova, Selected Poems,* translated by Walter Arndt, Robin Kemball, Carl Proffer (1976). The last three volumes also contain introductory material.

BIOGRAPHY AND CRITICISM. Sam Driver, *Anna Akhmatova* (1972); Jeanne van der Eng-Liedmeier and Kees Verheul, *Tale Without a Hero and Twenty-Two Poems by Anna Akhmatova* (1973); and Amanda Haight, *Anna Akhmatova: A Poetic Pilgrimage* (1977).

KATHERINE ANNE PORTER

LIFE. Katherine Anne Porter was born on May 15, 1890, in Indian Creek, Texas, the third of five children and the descendant of a "family of solid wealth and property in Kentucky, Louisiana, and Virginia" that had fallen on poorer days in Texas after the Civil War. Her mother died in 1892, and the family went to live with her paternal grandmother in Kyle, Texas; then, in 1903 or 1904, they moved to San Antonio. A rebellious student, she ran away from school at sixteen and married; at nineteen, she was divorced; at twenty-one she worked in Chicago on a newspaper and briefly as an extra in the movies; at twenty-four she returned to Texas, supporting herself as a ballad singer; and at twenty-eight she moved to a job as reporter for *The Rocky Mountain News* in Denver, where she nearly died during the great Influenza epidemic of 1918. Further travels took her to New York, then Mexico, and in 1921 to Fort Worth, where for the next ten years she wrote stories, reviews, and articles on Mexican culture and acted in amateur theater, traveling as often as she could. In 1927, in Boston, she took part in the demonstrations against the conviction and execution of Sacco and Vanzetti, and in 1930 published her first collection in New York: *Flowering Judas, and Other Stories.* A Guggenheim Fellowship in 1931 allowed her to live in Mexico again, and then to go to Europe on a cruise that became the basis of her 1961 novel, *Ship of Fools.* During the thirties and forties she was twice again married and twice divorced.

A perfectionist who has published only a small part of her writings, Porter worked for more then twenty years on *Ship of Fools.* Recognized as a consummate stylist, she has received a number of awards including the Pulitzer Prize and National Book Award for fiction in 1966. Her most recent book is an account of the Sacco-Vanzetti case called *The Never-Ending Wrong* (1977), and she is reportedly continuing work on a biography of Cotton Mather that has occupied her intermittently since the early 1920s.

CHIEF WRITINGS. *Flowering Judas and Other Stories* (1930); *Hacienda* (1934); *Flowering Judas and Other Stories* (expanded, 1935); *Noon Wine* (1937); *Pale Horse, Pale Rider: Three Short Novels* (1939); *The Leaning Tower and Other Stories* (1944); *The Days Before* (1952); *Ship of Fools* (1961); *The Collected Stories of Katherine Anne Porter* (1965); *A Christmas Story* (1967); *The Collected Essays and Occasional Writings of Katherine Anne Porter* (1970); and *The Never-Ending Wrong* (1977).

BIOGRAPHY AND CRITICISM. Harry J. Mooney, Jr., *The Fiction and Criticism of Katherine Anne Porter* (1957); Glenway Wescott, in *Images of Truth: Remembrances and Criticism* (1962); Ray B. West, Jr., *Katherine Anne Porter* (1963); William L. Nance, *Katherine Anne Porter and the Art of Rejection* (1964); George Hendrick, *Katherine Anne Porter* (1965); Winfred S. Emmons, *Katherine Anne Porter: The Regional Stories* (1967); *Paul Baumgartner, Katherine Anne Porter* (1969); *Katherine Anne Porter: A Critical Symposium,* edited by Lodwick Hartley and George Core (1960); Louise Waldrip and Shirley Ann Bauer, *A Bibliography of the Works of Katherine Anne Porter and a Bibliography of the Criticism of the Works of Katherine Anne Porter* (1969); Myron Liberman, *Katherine Anne Porter's Fiction* (1971); John E. Hardy, *Katherine Anne Porter* (1973); and *Katherine Anne Porter: A Collection of Critical Essays,* edited by Robert Penn Warren (1978).

WILLIAM FAULKNER

LIFE. William Cuthbert Falkner was born on September 25, 1897, in New Albany, Mississippi, to a prosperous family with many ties to Southern history. The eldest of four sons, Faulkner (he adopted this spelling in 1924) was named for a great-grandfather who commanded a Confederate regiment in the Civil War, built railroads, and wrote a novel. Faulkner's father worked for the family railroad until it was sold in 1902, afterwards moving the family to Oxford and eventually becoming business manager of the University of Mississippi. Young Faulkner left high school after two years to work as bookkeeper in his grandfather's bank. He read a great deal, borrowing books from a lawyer friend who encouraged his writing. From July 1918 to January 1919 he trained in Canada as a fighter pilot—then a common way of getting more quickly into combat in the First World War—and returned to Oxford after the Armistice to enroll at Ol' Miss. He published poetry, prose, and drawings in *The Mississippian* and worked on the yearbook, but left school in 1920 for a job in a New York Bookstore. He returned to Oxford in 1921 and became postmaster, but he was dismissed three years later for irresponsibility. In those years he wrote mainly poetry, and 1924 saw the publication of his first book, a collection of lyrics called *The Marble Faun.*

In 1925, in New Orleans, Faulkner

met Sherwood Anderson and a group of writers and artists associated with *The Double Dealer*, a literary magazine in which he himself soon published poems, essays, and prose sketches. His first novel, *Soldiers' Pay*, was written at this time, and after its completion he took a freighter to Europe, where he bicycled and hiked through Italy and France. In 1929 he married Estelle Oldham Franklin, with whom he had one child, Jill, in 1933. While writing his first novels, Faulkner worked on a shrimp trawler, in a lumber mill and a power plant, and as a carpenter, painter, and paper-hanger; gradually, however, he began to earn money from his short stories, of which he sold thirty between 1930 and 1932. When his 1931 bestseller, *Sanctuary*, was made into a movie, he was invited to work on movie scripts for a variety of Hollywood studios. Although Faulkner's reputation as a serious writer was slow to come in the United States, he was recognized in France as early as 1931 and by 1945, according to Jean-Paul Sartre, had become the idol of the young writers and intellectuals. He had already written most of his major works by 1946, when the *Portable Faulkner* anthology at last brought him to the attention of a wider American audience, and won the Nobel Prize for Literature in 1950 as a tribute to his entire career five years before being honored by the chief American literary awards, the Pulitzer Prize and the National Book Award, for *A Fable*. The Nobel Prize money was used to establish the William Faulkner Foundation, a fund charged with encouraging Latin American writers and with awarding educational scholarships to Mississippi blacks. Faulkner died of a heart attack in Oxford on July 6, 1962.

Chief Writings. *Soldiers' Pay* (1926); *Mosquitoes* (1927); *Sartoris* (1929); *The Sound and the Fury* (1929); *As I Lay Dying* (1930); *Sanctuary* (1931); *Idyll in the Desert* (1931); *Light in August* (1932); *Pylon* (1933); *Absalom, Absalom!* (1936); *The Unvanquished* (1938); *Wild Palms* (1939); *The Hamlet* (1940); *Go Down, Moses, and Other Stories* (1942); *Intruder in the Dust* (1948); *Knight's Gambit* (1949); *Collected Stories* (1950); *Requiem for a Nun* (1951); *A Fable* (1954); *The Marionettes*, edited by Noel Polk (1977). See also *Faulkner at Nagano*, edited by Robert Jelliffe (1956); *Selected Letters of William Faulkner*, edited by Joseph Blotner (1976); and *Faulkner at the University*, edited by Frederick Gwynn and Joseph Blotner (1977).

Biography and Criticism. Malcolm Cowley, *The Portable Faulkner* (1946); H. M. Campbell and R. E. Foster, *William Faulkner* (1951); Irving Howe, *William Faulkner* (1952); William Van O'Connor, *The Tangled Fire of William Faulkner* (1954); Robert Coughlan, *The Private World of William Faulkner* (1954); Hyatt Waggoner, *William Faulkner* (1959); *William Faulkner: Three Decades of Criticism*, edited by Frederick J. Hoffman and Olga W. Vickery (1960); Walter J. Slatoff, *Quest for Failure* (1960); Peter Swiggart, *The Art of Faulkner's Novels* (1962); John L. Longley, Jr., *The Tragic Mask: A Study of Faulkner's Heroes* (1963); Cleanth Brooks, *William Faulkner, The Yoknapatawpha Country* (1963); Edmond Volpe, *Reader's Guide to William Faulkner* (1964); Michael Millgate, *The Achievement of William Faulkner* (1965); Charles Nilon, *Faulkner and the Negro* (1965); Melvin Backman, *Faulkner: The Major Years* (1966); Malcolm Cowley, *The Faulkner-Cowley File* (1966); Robert Warren, *Faulkner: A Collection of Critical Essays* (1967); Richard P. Adams, *Faulkner: Myth and Motion* (1968); Maurice Coindreau, *The Time of William Faulkner: A French View of American Fiction*, edited and translated by George Reeves (1971); James Meriwether, *The Literary Career of William Faulkner* (1971); Charles Peavy: *Go Slow Now: Faulkner and the Race Question* (1971); Sally Page, *Faulkner's Women: Characterization and Meaning* (1972); Joseph Reed, *Faulkner's Narrative* (1973); Edwin Hunter, *William Faulkner: Narrative Practice and Prose Style* (1973); Joseph Blotner, *Faulkner: A Biography* (1974); Lewis M. Dabney, *The Indians of Yoknapatawpha* (1974); Panthea R. Broughton, *William Faulkner: The Abstract and the Actual* (1974); John Irwin, *Doubling and Incest/Repetition and Revenge* (1974); Warren Beck, *Faulkner: Essays* (1976); Calvin Brown, *A Glossary of Faulkner's South* (1976); Lynn G. Levins: *Faulkner's Heroic Design* (1976); Thomas McHaney, *William Faulkner: A Reference Guide* (1976); Cleanth Brooks, *William Faulkner: Toward Yoknapatawpha and Beyond* (1978); and Arthur Kinney, *Faulkner's Narrative Practice: Style as Vision* (1978).

BERTOLT BRECHT

Life. Eugen Berthold Brecht was born on February 10, 1898, in the medieval town of Augsburg, Bavaria. His father was a respected town citizen, director of a paper mill, and a Catholic. His mother, the daughter of a civil servant from the Black Forest, was a Protestant who raised young Berthold in her own faith (The spelling *Bertolt* was adopted later.) Brecht attended local schools until 1917, when he enrolled in Munich University to study natural sciences and medicine. He continued his studies while writing his first plays and acting as drama critic for an Augsburg newspaper, and in 1918 was mobilized as an orderly in a military hospital. In 1929 he married Helene Weigel, an actress who worked closely with him and for whom he wrote many leading roles. Together, they directed and made famous the theater group founded in 1949 for them in East Berlin: the *Berliner Ensemble.*

Brecht's unorthodoxy, his pacifism, his enthusiasm for Marx (whom he read in 1926), and his desire to create an activist popular theater that would embody a Marxist view of art, all put him at odds with the rising power of Hitler's National Socialism. He fled Germany for Denmark in 1933, before the Nazis could include him in their purge of left-wing intellectuals; in 1935, he was deprived of his German citizenship. Brecht was to flee several more times before the Nazi invasions: in 1939 to Sweden, in 1940 to Finland, and finally in 1941 to America, where he joined a colony of German exiles in Santa Monica, California, working for the film industry. Brecht continued to write and to arrange for translations of his work into English: *Galileo,* with Charles Laughton in the title role, was produced in 1947. In the same year, Brecht was questioned by the House Un-American Activities Committee. No charges were brought, but he left the United States the day after testifying before the Committee. A stateless man, Brecht lived in Switzerland until 1949, when the *Berliner Ensemble* was founded and he settled in East Berlin. He received Austrian citizenship (through his wife's nationality) in 1950. He died on August 14, 1956.

CHIEF WRITINGS. Plays: *Baal* (1918); *Drums in the Night* (*Trommeln in der Nacht,* 1918); *In the Jungle of the Cities* (*Im Dickicht der Städte,* 1921–23); *Life of Edward II of England* (*Leben Eduards des Zweiten von England,* with Lion Feuchtwanger, 1923–24); *A Man's a Man* (*Mann ist Mann,* 1924–25); *The Threepenny Opera* (*Die Dreigroschenoper,* 1928); *Rise and Fall of the City of Mahoganny* (*Aufstieg und Fall der Stadt Mahagonny,* 1928–29); *The Didactic Play of Baden: On Consent* (*Das Badener Lehrstück vom Einverständnis,* 1928–29); *St. Joan of the Stockyards* (*Die Heilige Johanna der Schlachthöfe,* 1929–30); *The Measures Taken* (*Die Massnahme,* 1930); *The Mother* (*Die Mutter,* 1930–32); *Fear and Misery of the Third Reich* (*Furcht und Elend des Dritten Reiches,* 1935–38); *Mother Courage and Her Children* (*Mutter Courage und ihre Kinder,* 1939); *The Trial of Lucullus* (*Las Verhör des Lukullus,* 1939); *Galileo* (*Leben des Galilei,* 1938–39); *The Good Person of Setzuan* (*Der gute Mensch von Sezuan,* 1938–40); *Mr. Puntila and His Hired Man, Matti* (*Herr Puntila und sein knecht Matti,* 1940–41); *The Resistible Rise of Arturo Ui* (*Der aufhaltsame Aufstieg des Arturo Ui,* 1941); *Schweik in the Second World War* (*Schweik im Zweiten Weltkrieg,* 1941–44); *The Caucasian Chalk Circle* (*Der Kaukasische Kreidedreis,* 1944–45). Poetry: *Manual of Piety* (*Die Hauspostille,* 1927); *Selected Poems* (1959). Prose: *Tales from The Calendar* (*Kalendergeschichten,* 1948); *Threepenny Novel* (*Dreigroschenroman,* 1934); *Brecht on Theatre* (collection, 1964); and *The Messingkauf Dialogues* (Der Messingkauf, 1937–51).

BIOGRAPHY AND CRITICISM. M. Esslin, *Brecht, The Man and His Work* (1959, revised 1974); J. Willett, *The Theatre of Bertolt Brecht* (1950, revised 1968); P. Demetz, *Brecht, A Collection of Critical Essays* (1962); W. Weideli, *The Art of Bertolt Brecht* (translation 1963); F. Ewen, *Bertolt Brecht, His Life, His Art, and His Times* (1967); C. Lyons, *Bertolt Brecht; the Despair and the Polemic* (1968); J. Fuegi, *The Essential Brecht* (1972); D. Suvin, "Brecht—An Essay at a Dramaturgic Bibliography" in *Brecht,* edited by E. Munk (1972); *Essays on Brecht: Theater and Politics,* edited by H. Knust and S. Mews (1974); *Brecht As They Knew Him,* edited by H. Witt and translated by J. Peet (1974); C. Hill, *Bertolt Brecht Chronicle* (translated in 1975); and R. Gray, *Brecht the Dramatist* (1976).

JORGE LUIS BORGES

LIFE. Jorge Luis Borges was born on August 24, 1899, in Buenos Aires, Argentina, to a prosperous family whose ancestors had been distinguished in Argentine history. His paternal grandmother was English, and the young Borges knew English as soon as Spanish. His father—a lawyer, teacher of psychology, and a writer and translator from English—was an atheist, his mother a practicing Roman Catholic. His parents moved early to a large house whose library and garden were to form an essential part of his literary imagination, and where he was to be educated by an English tutor until age nine. Caught in Geneva while traveling in Europe with his family at the outbreak of World War I, Borges attended secondary school in Switzerland throughout the war and there learned French and German. Later the family lived in Spain and Borges associated with a group of young experimental poets called Ultraists. When he returned to Buenos Aires in 1921, he founded his own group of Argentine Ultraists, whose mural-review, *Prisma,* was printed on sign paper and plastered on walls.

Following a second trip to Europe in 1923, Borges' life until 1961 was spent almost entirely in Argentina, in spite of the pressure of the military dictatorship of Juan Peron, which he opposed but left unmentioned in his fiction. He became close friends with the philosopher Macedonio Fernandez, whose dedication to pure thought and linguistic intricacies greatly influenced his own attitudes. He also wrote for the avant-garde review

Martin Fierro, which was at that time associated with an apolitical "art for art's sake" attitude and contrasted with the Boedo group of politically committed writers. Borges made his political views plain in speeches and non-literary writing, however, and in 1946 he was removed from his post as librarian by the Peron regime and offered the position of chicken inspector.

Borges explains that he began writing his mature stories as an experiment after a head injury and operation in 1938. In 1942, the noted magazine *Sur* devoted a special issue to him when, against all expectations, he was not awarded the National Prize for Literature. In 1955, after the fall of Peron, he was named Director of the National Library, a post traditionally given to an outstanding literary figure, and in 1956 he was appointed a professor of English literature at the University of Buenos Aires and awarded the National Prize which had been withheld from him before. Always nearsighted, he was by this time almost blind; his mother helped him by reading to him and taking dictation, but he was able to write only shorter pieces, and limited his verse to traditional forms and meters. In 1961 he shared the International Publishers' Prize with Samuel Beckett, after which he frequently traveled, lectured, and taught in Europe and the United States. In 1967 he married Else Astete Millan. He continues to live in Buenos Aires, the city of his youth.

Chief Works. *Fervor of Buenos Aires* (*Fervor de Buenos Aires,* 1923); *Inquisitions* (*Inquisiciones,* 1925); *Moon Across the Way* (*Luna de enfrente,* 1925); *Dimension of My Hope* (*El tamaño de mia esperanza,* 1926); *The Language of the Argentinians* (*El Idioma de los Argentinos,* 1928); *San Martin Notebook* (*Cuarderno San Martin,* 1929); *Discussion* (*Discusión,* 1932); *Universal History of Infamy* (*Historia universal de la infamia,* 1935); *History of Eternity* (*Historia de la eternidad,* 1936); *The Garden of Forking Paths* (*El Jardín de senderos que se bifurcan,* 1942); *Fictions* (*Ficciones,* 1944), translated as *Ficciones* (1962) and *Fictions* (1965) by Anthony Kerrigan and others; *New Refutation of Time* (*Nueva Refutación del Tiempo,* 1947); *The Aleph* (*El Aleph,* 1949); translated as *The Aleph and Other Stories* by Norman T. di Giovanni with the author (1970); *Labyrinths,* edited by Donald Yates and James Irby (a collection of stories and essays, 1962); *Other Inquisitions* (*Otras Inquisiciones* 1937–1952, translated by Ruth Simms (1964); *The Maker* (*El Hacedor,* 1960), translated as *Dreamtigers* by Mildred Boyer and Harold Moreland (1964); *A Personal Anthology* (*Antología Personal,* 1961), translated by Anthony Kerrigan (1967); *Selected Poems 1923–1967* (*Obra poética 1923–1967*), translated by Norman T. di Giovanni (1972); *Chronicles of Bustos Domecq* (*Crónicas de Bustos Domecq,* with Adolfo Bioy Casares, 1967), translated by Norman T. di Giovanni (1976); *The Book of Imaginary Beings* (*El Libro de los seres imaginarios,* with Margarita Guerrero, 1968), translated by Norman T. di Giovanni (1969); *In Praise of Darkness* (*Elogio de la sombra,* 1969), translated by Norman T. di Giovanni (1974); *The Other, the Same* (*El otro, el mismo,* 1960); *Brodie's Report* (*El Informe de Brodie,* 1970); translated as *Dr. Brodie's Report* by Norman T. di Giovanni (1972); and *Gold of the Tigers* (*El Oro de los Tigres,* 1972), translated by Alastair Reid (1977).

Biography and Criticism. Ana Maria Barrenechea, *Borges the Labyrinth Maker* (1957, translated in 1965); John Updike, "Books: The Author as Librarian" in Oct. 31, 1965 *New Yorker*; L. A. Murillo, *The Cyclical Night* (1968); Richard Burgin, *Conversations with Jorge Luis Borges* (1969); Ronald J. Christ, *The Narrow Act* (1969); Martin Stabb, *Jorge Luis Borges* (1970); Jaime Alazraki, *Jorge Luis Borges* (1971); *The Cardinal Points of Borges,* edited by Lowell Dunham and Ivar Ivask (1972); *Modern Fiction Studies, XIX* (issue devoted to Borges, 1973); Charles Newman and Marie Kinzie, *Prose for Borges* (1974); John O. Stark, *The Literature of Exhaustion: Borges, Nabokov, and Barth* (1974); and D. L. Shaw, *Borges Ficciones* (1976).

VLADIMIR NABOKOV

Life. Vladimir Vladimirovich Nabokov was born on April 23, 1899, in St. Petersburg (now Leningrad), Russia. He was the oldest of five children in a wealthy aristocratic family with strong liberal, artistic, and professional traditions. At first educated at home by tutors, he learned several languages, reading English before Russian, and traveled with his family often to Berlin, Paris, and resorts in the South of France and on the Adriatic. When he was seven Nabokov took up the study of butterflies, a field in which he was eventually to become a recognized authority. From 1911 to 1917 he attended the liberal Prince Tenishev School in St. Petersburg, but at the Bolshevik Revolution in 1917 the family fled to the Crimea and then again in 1919 to Germany; three years later Nabokov's father was shot and killed at a political rally in Berlin. Nabokov studied at Cambridge University from 1919 to 1922 before moving to Berlin. There he wrote his first published works (in Russian) and tutored students in English and French. He married Véra Evseevna Slonim in 1925; their one child, Dmitri was born in 1934.

Nabokov used the pen name Vladimir

Sirin for his Russian works: three volumes of poetry, many articles for the emigré press, and eight novels published between 1926 (*Mary*) and 1938 (*The Gift*). In 1937 he and his family fled Hitler's Germany for Paris, where he wrote his first novel in English, *The Real Life of Sebastian Knight* (published in 1941). The Nazi invasion of France in 1940 forced him to emigrate to America, where he became a citizen in 1945.

Once in America, Nabokov taught at several institutions before accepting a professorship at Cornell University from 1948 to 1959. He received Guggenheim Fellowships in 1943 and 1953, and a grant from the National Institute of Arts and Letters in 1951, continuing to publish novels, short stories, a critical biography of Gogol, and English translations of his earlier works in Russian. He first reached wide recognition, or perhaps notoriety, with the publication in Paris of *Lolita* (1955), the story of a middle-aged man and his twelve-year-old "nymphet" lover, Lolita. *Lolita's* success enabled Nabokov to retire from teaching in 1959 and devote all his time to writing. He then took up residence in Montreux, Switzerland, where he lived in the Palace Hotel overlooking Lake Geneva until his death. Among his new publications were a controversial four-volume translation of and commentary on Pushkin's *Eugene Onegin* (1964), a revision of his autobiography (*Speak, Memory*, 1966), several anthologies (including one that combines poetry and chess problems), and three new novels in English. Nabokov died in Switzerland on July 2, 1977.

Chief Writings. *Mary* (*Mashen'ka*, 1926), translated in 1970; *King, Queen, Knave* (*Korol', Dama, Valet*, 1928), translated in 1968; *The Luzhin Defense* (*Zashchita Luzhina*, 1930,) translated in 1964; *Glory* (*Podvig'*, 1932), translated in 1971; *Camera Obscura* (*Kamera Obskura*, 1933), translated in 1937, revised and translated as *Laughter in the Dark*, 1938; *Despair* (*Otchayanie*, 1936), translated in 1937, revised 1966; *Invitation to a Beheading* (*Priglashenie na Kazn'*, 1938), translated in 1959; *The Real Life of Sebastian Knight* (1941); *Nine Stories* (1947); *Bend Sinister* (1947); *The Gift* (*Dar*, 1952), translated in 1963; *Conclusive Evidence: A Memoir* (1951, revised in 1966 as *Speak, Memory: An Autobiography Revisited*); *Lolita* (1955), *Pnin* (1957); *Nabokov's Dozen* (1958); *Pale Fire* (1962); *Nabokov's Quartet* (1967); *Nabokov's Congeries* (1968); *Ada; or, Ardor* (1969); *Poems and Problems* (1971); *A Russian Beauty and Other Stories* (1973); *Transparent Things* (1973); *Strong Opinions* (1974); *Look at the Harlequins!* (1974); and *Tyrants Destroyed and Other Stories* (1975). See also translation of and commentary on Alexander Pushkin, *Eugene Onegin* (1964).

Biography and Criticism. Page Stegner, *The Art of Vladimir Nabokov: Escape into Aesthetics* (1966); Andrew Field, *Nabokov: His Life in Art* (1967); *Nabokov: The Man and His Work*, edited by L. S. Dembo (1967); Carl Proffer, *Keys to Lolita* (1968); *Nabokov: Criticisms, Reminiscences, Translations and Tributes*, edited by Alfred Appel, Jr. and Charles Newman (1970); Julian Moynahan, *Vladimir Nabokov* (1971); W. Woodlin Rowe, *Nabokov's Deceptive World* (1971); Julia Bader, *Crystal Land* (1972); Andrew Field, *Nabokov: A Bibliography* (1973); Donald Morton, *Vladimir Nabokov* (1974); Alfred Appel, Jr., *Nabokov's Dark Cinema* (1974); Douglas Fowler, *Reading Nabokov* (1974); *A Book of Things about Vladimir Nabokov*, edited by Carl R. Proffer (1974); and Andrew Field, *Nabokov: His Life in Part* (1977).

JEAN-PAUL SARTRE

Life. Sartre was born in Paris on June 21, 1905. His father, an officer in the French Navy, died while Sartre was still an infant, and his mother took him to live with her family. Sartre's mother remarried in 1916. After two years in a provincial secondary school, Sartre spent the rest of his schooldays in Paris, going on to study at the University of Paris. He became a secondary-school teacher. He was able to spend one year's leave of absence in Berlin. Made prisoner by the Germans after the French collapse of 1940, Sartre was released fairly soon and returned to teaching. He took part in the Resistance as a writer, though not as an activist, and became famous in 1943 with the performance of *The Flies* (*Les Mouches*) and the extraordinary success of his massive philosophical work *Being and Nothingness* (*L'Être et le Néant*). He gave up teaching the following year, and in 1945 founded the periodical *Les Temps Modernes*. Since then he has continued to write on philosophical, psychological, political, and topical matters, and has written many plays. His one postwar novel, *Roads to Freedom* (*Les Chemins de la Liberté*, 1945 and following years) remains unfinished. In 1962 he published the first volume of his autobiography, *The Words* (*Les Mots*), which deals with his childhood in grandfather Schweitzer's household. In 1964 he was awarded but refused to accept the Nobel Prize.

Chief Writings. *Nausea* (*La Nausée*, 1938), translated by Lloyd Alexander (1949); *The Wall* (*Le Mur*, 1939), translated also as *Intimacy and Other Stories* by Lloyd Alexander (1948); *Outline of a Theory of the Emotions* (*Esquisse d'une Théorie des Émotions*, 1940), translated by Bernard Frechtman (1948); *The Flies* (*Les Mouches*, 1942), translated by Stuart Gilbert (1947); *Being and Nothingness*

(*L'Être et le Néant,* 1943), translated by Hazel E. Barnes (1956); *No Exit* (*Huis-Clos,* 1944), translated by Stuart Gilbert (1947); *The Age of Reason, The Reprieve,* and *Troubled Sleep* (*L'Âge du Raison, Le Sursis,* and *La Mort dans l'Âme,* constituting three parts of *Les Chemins de la Liberté,* 1945–1949), translated by Eric Sutton (1947) and by Gerard Hopkins (1950); *Existentialism* (*L'Existentialisme est un Humanisme,* 1946), translated by Bernard Frechtman (1947); *Baudelaire* (1947), translated by Martin Turnell (1950); *Saint Genet, Actor and Martyr* (1952), translated by Bernard Frechtman (1962); *Literary Essays* (1957); *The Devil and the Good Lord, and Two Other Plays* (1960); *The Condemned of Altona* (1961); *Sartre on Cuba* (1961); *The Words* (*Les Mots,* 1962), translated by Bernard Frechtman (1964); *The Problem of Method* (1963); *Saint Genet, Actor and Martyr* (1968); *Situations* (1965); *Literary and Philosophical Essays* (1966); *The Communists and Peace* (1968); *The Ghost of Stalin* (1968); *On Genocide* (1968); *Sartre on Theater,* edited by Michel Contat and Michel Rybalka (*Un Théâtre de situations,* 1973), translated by Frank Jellinek (1976); and *Life/Situations (Situations, X),* translated by Paul Auster and Lydia Davis (1977).

BIOGRAPHY AND CRITICISM. Peter J. Dempsey, *The Psychology of Sartre* (1950); Hazel Barnes, *The Literature of Possibility* (1959); Robert Champigny, *Stages on Sartre's Way, 1938–1952* (1959); Wilfrid Desan, *The Tragic Finale: An Essay on the Philosophy of Jean-Paul Sartre* (revised edition, 1960); Norman H. Greene, *Jean-Paul Sartre: The Existentialist Ethic* (1960); Iris Murdoch, *Sartre: Romantic Rationalist* (1960); Philip Thody, *Jean-Paul Sartre: A Literary and Political Study* (1960); Fredric Jameson, *Sartre: The Origin of a Style* (1961); Edith Kern (ed.), *Sartre: A Collection of Critical Essays* (1962); René Marill-Albérès, *Jean-Paul Sartre, Philosopher without Faith* (1964); Mary Warnock, *The Philosophy of Sartre* (1965); Eugene H. Falk, *Types of Thematic Structure* (1967); George H. Bauer, *Sartre and the Artist* (1969); Dorothy McCall, *The Theatre of Jean-Paul Sartre* (1969); James F. Sheridan, *Sartre: The Radical Conversion* (1969); Edith Kern, *Existential Thought and Fictional Technique* (1970); Benjamin Suhl, *Jean-Paul Sartre: The Philosopher as Literary Critic* (1970); George Bauer, *Sartre and the Artist* (1969); Joseph H. McMahon, *Human Beings: The World of Jean-Paul Sartre* (1971); Philip M. W. Thody, *Sartre: A Biographical Introduction* (1971); *Sartre: A Collection of Critical Essays,* edited by Mary Warnock (1971); Germaine Brée, *Camus and Sartre: Crisis and Commitment* (1972); Hazel Barnes, *Sartre* (1973); Marjorie Grene, *Sartre* (1973); Michel Contat and M. Rybalka, *The Writings of Jean-Paul Sartre* (1974); Thomas M. King, *Sartre and the Sacred* (1974); Arthur C. Danto, *Jean-Paul Sartre* (1975); and Ian Craib, *Existentialism and Sociology: A Study of Jean-Paul Sartre* (1976).

RICHARD WRIGHT

LIFE. Richard Wright was born on a farm near Natchez, Mississippi, on September 4, 1908. His father was a poor and illiterate sharecropper; his mother taught in the black country schools. When Wright was five years old, his father deserted the family, and his mother had to work as a cook to support her two sons. The family remained extremely poor, and in 1916 Mrs. Wright was obliged to put her sons temporarily in an orphanage. Wright attended segregated black public schools and a Seventh Day Adventist school until ninth grade, but was frequently absent due to family illness or inability to buy books and clothes. The family moved often between Mississippi, Tennessee, and Arkansas, looking for jobs or visiting helpful relatives; living with an uncle in Arkansas brought a brief taste of prosperity in the summer of 1916, ended when the uncle was shot by envious whites and the entire family had to flee. In 1919 Wright's mother suffered a paralytic stroke and, unable to manage alone, moved the family to her parents' house in Jackson, Mississippi. Wright's grandmother and aunt, authoritarian Seventh Day Adventists, insisted on strong discipline and, believing fiction immoral, burned the novels he brought home to read. He graduated from junior high school in 1925, worked in Memphis, then moved to Chicago, one of the northern cities which then seemed to Southern blacks a haven of opportunity and acceptance.

Wright supported himself as a porter, dishwasher, and postal clerk, and brought his mother and brother to Chicago to live with him. He read Proust, Dostoevsky, Gertrude Stein, and studies in psychology and sociology. When he lost his job in the Depression, he went on relief sweeping streets. At about that time a friend introduced him to the John Reed Club, a Communist literary group, which led him to become a member of the Party in 1933. He worked energetically on its behalf in New York, where he had moved in 1937 and become Harlem correspondent for the Party's newspaper, the *Daily Worker*. However, there was constant conflict between Wright's commitment to literature, individualism, and civil rights, and the international Communist Party's demand for discipline and subordination to central authority. Though Wright remained actively committed to social reform, he withdrew from Party activity in 1942 and broke publicly in 1944 with a bitter essay entitled "I Tried to Be a Communist."

A brief marriage in 1939 to Dhima Rose Meadman was followed by a second marriage in 1941 to Ellen Poplar, with whom he had two daughters. After publishing his autobiography, *Black Boy,* in 1945, Wright moved with his family to France, where he associated with international writers and intellectuals such as Jean-Paul Sartre, André Gide, and Gunnar Myrdal, and became an active spokesman for Third World concerns, expressed in sociocultural commentaries based on travel in Africa, Asia, and Spain, and in a collection of European lectures called *White Man, Listen!* He died in Paris of a heart attack on November 28, 1960.

CHIEF WRITINGS. *Uncle Tom's Children* (1938, enlarged edition 1940); *Native Son* (1940); *Twelve Million Black Voices* (1941); *Black Boy* (1945); *The Outsider* (1953); *Black Power* (1954); *Savage Holiday* (1954); *The Color Curtain* (1956); *Pagan Spain* (1956); *White Man, Listen!* (1957); *The Long Dream* (1958); *Eight Men* (1961); *Lawd Today* (1963); *American Hunger* (1977); and *Richard Wright Reader* (edited by Ellen Wright and Michel Fabre, 1978).

BIOGRAPHY AND CRITICISM. Edwin Embree, *13 Against the Odds* (1944); Constance Webb, *Richard Wright* (1968); Robert Bone, *Richard Wright* (1969); Edward Margolies, *The Art of Richard Wright* (1969); Dan McCall, *The Example of Richard Wright* (1969); Richard Abcarian, *Richard Wright's Native Son* (1970); Carl Brignano, *Richard Wright: An Introduction to the Man and His Work* (1970); *Twentieth Century Interpretations of Native Son,* edited by Houston Baker, Jr. (1972); Keneth Kinnamon, *The Emergence of Richard Wright* (1972); Michel Fabre, *The Unfinished Quest of Richard Wright* (1973, translated by Isabel Barzun); *Richard Wright: Impressions and Perspectives* (1973, book form of Winter 1971 number of *New Letters*), edited by David Ray and Robert Farnsworth; and Fritz Gysin, *The Grotesque in American Negro Fiction* (1975).

ALBERT CAMUS

LIFE. Camus was born in Mondovi, Algeria, on November 7, 1913, to a working-class family. The father was killed early in World War I, and the mother, who was Spanish, moved to the city of Algiers. The boy grew up talking the mixed dialect—French, Spanish, Arabic—of the streets. A schoolteacher who took a special interest in Camus arranged for a scholarship to secondary school. After several years of university work, Camus turned to journalism, joined the Communist Party but stayed a member less than three years, and became very active in the theater. He moved to Paris in 1940. He first attracted wide attention as a writer in 1942 for the underground newspaper *Combat,* and after the war he continued to write editorials for it. His total work brought him the Nobel prize in 1957. He died on January 4, 1960, in a car accident.

CHIEF WRITINGS. *The Stranger* (*L'Étranger,* 1942); *The Myth of Sisyphus* (*Le mythe de Sisyphe,* 1942); *The Plague* (*La Peste,* 1948); *The Rebel* (*L'homme révolté,* 1954); *The Fall* (*La chute,* 1957); *Exile and the Kingdom* (*L'exil et la royaume,* 1958); *Caligula and Other Plays* (1958); *Possessed* (1960); *Resistance, Rebellion, and Death* (1960); *Notebook 1935–1942; Notebook, 1942–1951* (1965); *Lyrical and Critical Essays* (1968); *A Happy Death* (previously unpublished earlier version of *The Stranger*) (1972).

BIOGRAPHY AND CRITICISM. Albert Maquet, *Albert Camus: An Invincible Summer* (1958); John Cruickshank, *Albert Camus and the Literature of Revolt* (1959); Philip Thody, *Albert Camus* (1959); Thomas Hanna, *The Thought and Art of Albert Camus* (1959); and *Lyrical Existentialists* (1962); Germaine Brée, *Albert Camus* (1961) and *Camus: A Collection of Critical Essays* (1961); Adele King, *Albert Camus* (1964); Phillip H. Rhein, *Albert Camus* (1969); Maurice Friedman, *The Problematic Rebel* (revised edition, 1970); Conor C. O'Brien, *Albert Camus: Of Europe and Africa* (1970); Jean Onimus, *Albert Camus and Christianity* (1970); Morvan Lebesque, *Portrait of Camus: An Illustrated Biography* (1971); Paul Archambault, *Camus' Hellenic Sources* (1972); Germaine Brée, *Camus and Sartre* (1972); Donald Lazere, *The Unique Creation of Albert Camus* (1973); Lev Braun, *Witness of Decline: Albert Camus: Moralist of the Absurd* (1974); Irina Kirk, *Dostoevskij and Camus: The Themes of Unconsciousness, Isolation, Freedom and Love* (1974); Brian Masters, *Camus: A Study* (1974); and *Albert Camus' Literary Milieu: Arid Lands,* edited by W. T. Zyla (1976).

WILLIAM BUTLER YEATS

(1865–1939)

The Stolen Child*

WHERE dips the rocky highland
Of Sleuth Wood in the lake,
There lies a leafy island
Where flapping herons wake
The drowsy water-rats; 5
There we've hid our faery vats,
Full of berries
And of reddest stolen cherries.
Come away, O human child!
To the waters and the wild 10
With a faery, hand in hand,
For the world's more full of weeping than you
can understand.

Where the wave of moonlight glosses
The dim grey sands with light, 15
Far off by furthest Rosses
We foot it all the night,
Weaving olden dances,
Mingling hands and mingling glances
Till the moon has taken flight; 20
To and fro we leap
And chase the frothy bubbles,
While the world is full of troubles
And is anxious in its sleep.
Come away, O human child! 25
To the waters and the wild
With a faery, hand in hand,
For the world's more full of weeping than you
can understand.

Where the wandering water gushes 30
From the hills above Glen-Car,
In pools among the rushes
That scarce could bathe a star,
We seek for slumbering trout
And whispering in their ears 35
Give them unquiet dreams;

*** The selection from *Collected Poems* by William Butler Yeats. Copyright 1906 by The Macmillan Company; renewed 1934 by William Butler Yeats. Reprinted by permission of the publisher.**

2. *Sleuth Wood:* All the places mentioned in the poem are in a region of County Sligo, in northwestern Ireland, which Yeats knew well as a child—and where he is buried.

Leaning softly out
From ferns that drop their tears
Over the young streams.
Come away, O human child! 40
To the waters and the wild
With a faery, hand in hand,
For the world's more full of weeping than you
can understand.

Away with us he's going,
The solemn-eyed: 45
He'll hear no more the lowing
Of the calves on the warm hillside
Or the kettle on the hob
Sing peace into his breast,
Or see the brown mice bob 50
Round and round the oatmeal-chest.
For he comes, the human child,
To the waters and the wild
With a faery, hand in hand,
From a world more full of weeping than he
can understand. 55

Easter 1916*

I HAVE met them at close of day
Coming with vivid faces
From counter or desk among grey
Eighteenth-century houses.
I have passed with a nod of the head 5
Or polite meaningless words,
Or have lingered awhile and said
Polite meaningless words,
And thought before I had done
Of a mocking tale or a gibe 10
To please a companion
Around the fire at the club,
Being certain that they and I
But lived where motley is worn:
All changed, changed utterly: 15
A terrible beauty is born.

That woman's days were spent
In ignorant good-will,

* The selection from *Collected Poems* by William Butler Yeats. Copyright 1924 by The Macmillan Company; renewed 1952 by Bertha Georgie Yeats. Reprinted by permission of the publisher. A rebellion against British rule was launched by Irish nationalists on Easter Sunday, 1916, most of the action taking place in Dublin. After a week's fighting, which saw the main post office and much of Sackville Street go up in flames, the rebellion was suppressed. The British executed a number of the rebels.

17. *That woman's:* Constance, Countess Markiewicz (née Gore-Booth), of a prominent Sligo family, had turned against her family's traditions, becoming a fervent Irish nationalist and converting to Catholicism.

Her nights in argument
Until her voice grew shrill. 20
What voice more sweet than hers
When, young and beautiful,
She rode to harriers?
This man had kept a school
And rode our wingèd horse; 25
This other his helper and friend
Was coming into his force;
He might have won fame in the end,
So sensitive his nature seemed,
So daring and sweet his thought. 30
This other man I had dreamed
A drunken, vainglorious lout.
He had done most bitter wrong
To some who are near my heart,
Yet I number him in the song; 35
He, too, has resigned his part
In the casual comedy;
He, too, has been changed in his turn,
Transformed utterly:
A terrible beauty is born. 40

Hearts with one purpose alone
Through summer and winter seem
Enchanted to a stone
To trouble the living stream.
The horse that comes from the road, 45
The rider, the birds that range
From cloud to tumbling cloud,
Minute by minute they change;
A shadow of cloud on the stream
Changes minute by minute; 50
A horse-hoof slides on the brim,
And a horse plashes within it;
The long-legged moor-hens dive,
And hens to moor-cocks call;
Minute by minute they live: 55
The stone's in the midst of all.

Too long a sacrifice
Can make a stone of the heart.
O when may it suffice?
That is Heaven's part, our part 60
To murmur name upon name,
As a mother names her child
When sleep at last has come

24. *This man:* Patrick Pearse, schoolteacher, and a writer in English and Irish, was both a cultural and a political nationalist. The "helper and friend" was Thomas MacDonagh. Both were executed by the British.

32. *vainglorious lout:* Major John MacBride, whom Maud Gonne married in 1903. The marriage broke up two years later. MacBride was another of the leaders executed by the British.

On limbs that had run wild.
What is it but nightfall? 65
No, no, not night but death;
Was it needless death after all?
For England may keep faith
For all that is done and said.
We know their dream; enough 70
To know they dreamed and are dead;
And what if excess of love
Bewildered them till they died?
I write it out in a verse—
MacDonagh and MacBride 75
And Connolly and Pearse
Now and in time to be,
Wherever green is worn,
Are changed, changed utterly:
A terrible beauty is born. 80

September 25, 1916

76. *Connolly:* James Connolly, labor leader and nationalist. Executed by the British.

The Second Coming*

TURNING and turning in the widening gyre
The falcon cannot hear the falconer;
Things fall apart; the centre cannot hold;
Mere anarchy is loosed upon the world,
The blood-dimmed tide is loosed, and everywhere 5
The ceremony of innocence is drowned;
The best lack all conviction, while the worst
Are full of passionate intensity.

Surely some revelation is at hand;
Surely the Second Coming is at hand. 10
The Second Coming! Hardly are those words out
When a vast image out of *Spiritus Mundi*
Troubles my sight: somewhere in sands of the desert
A shape with lion body and the head of a man
A gaze blank and pitiless as the sun, 15
Is moving its slow thighs, while all about it

1. *gyre:* a circular or spiral turn. Yeats (who pronounced the g as in "guile") used the term to designate a cycle of history which reaches its end and is replaced by the opposing gyre. See the poet's prose work, *A Vision*.

10. *Second Coming:* The return of Christ on earth has been awaited all through the Christian era. But Yeats divorces the notion from Christian expectations and foresees the rise of a new age that will both regenerate and destroy. He had in mind the Russian Revolution of 1917 and, with the coming of Italian Fascism a few years later, he believed that the poem's clairvoyance had been demonstrated.

12. *Spiritus Mundi:* or "soul of the universe," akin in Yeats's thinking to the "collective unconscious" of the psychologist C. G. Jung.

Reel shadows of the indignant desert birds.
The darkness drops again; but now I know
That twenty centuries of stony sleep
Were vexed to nightmare by a rocking cradle, 20
And what rough beast, its hour come round at last,
Slouches towards Bethlehem to be born?

20. *rocking cradle:* that of the infant Christ.

Sailing to Byzantium*

I

That is no country for old men. The young
In one another's arms, birds in the trees
—Those dying generations—at their song,
The salmon-falls, the mackerel-crowded seas,
Fish, flesh, or fowl, commend all summer long 5
Whatever is begotten, born, and dies.
Caught in the sensual music all neglect
Monuments of unageing intellect.

II

An aged man is but a paltry thing,
A tattered coat upon a stick, unless 10
Soul clap its hands and sing, and louder sing
For every tatter in its mortal dress,
Nor is there singing school but studying
Monuments of its own magnificence;
And therefore I have sailed the seas and come 15
To the holy city of Byzantium.

III

O sages standing in God's holy fire
As in the gold mosaic of a wall,
Come from the holy fire, perne in a gyre,
And be the singing-masters of my soul. 20
Consume my heart away; sick with desire
And fastened to a dying animal

16. *Byzantium:* Yeats had been greatly impressed by the Byzantine mosaics he had seen in 1907 and 1924. The ancient city came to be for him a symbol of philosophical speculation allied with craftsmanship, a unique fusion of the spiritual and the aesthetic with practical skills.

17. *fire:* Fire symbolized for Yeats reconciliation in harmony and tranquility; the opposite pole was formed by terrestrial power, strain, and division.

19. *perne:* whirl. *gyre* (Yeats pronounced the *g* hard, as in "guile"): a whirling cone. The poet believed that historical epochs, in their characteristics and development, could be symbolized by two opposed, interpenetrating, revolving gyres.

It knows not what it is; and gather me
Into the artifice of eternity.

IV

Once out of nature I shall never take 25
My bodily form from any natural thing,
But such a form as Grecian goldsmiths make
Of hammered gold and gold enamelling
To keep a drowsy Emperor awake;
Or set upon a golden bough to sing 30
To lords and ladies of Byzantium
Of what is past, or passing, or to come.

29. *Emperor:* Yeats had read that a tree made of gold and silver stood in the palace at Byzantium, and that artificial birds sang on its branches.

The Tower*

I

What shall I do with this absurdity—
O heart, O troubled heart—this caricature,
Decrepit age that has been tied to me
As to a dog's tail?
Never had I more
Excited, passionate, fantastical 5
Imagination, nor an ear and eye
That more expected the impossible—
No, not in boyhood when with rod and fly,
Or the humbler worm, I climbed Ben Bulben's back
And had the livelong summer day to spend. 10
It seems that I must bid the Muse go pack,
Choose Plato and Plotinus for a friend
Until imagination, ear and eye,
Can be content with argument and deal
In abstract things; or be derided by 15
A sort of battered kettle at the heel.

II

I pace upon the battlements and stare
On the foundations of a house, or where
Tree, like a sooty finger, starts from the earth;
And send imagination forth 20

*** 1926. The selection from William Butler Yeats, *Collected Poems.* Copyright 1928 by The Macmillan Company and used with the publisher's permission. Yeats explains that the poem was written at Thoor Ballylee (Ballylee Castle), which he had bought. He refers to this castle in other poems also.**

9. *Ben Bulben:* a mountain in County Sligo. The churchyard where the poet's body now lies is in sight of it.

12. *Plotinus:* a Roman Neoplatonic philosopher (died 270 A.D.). He believed that ideal forms were the true reality. He is mentioned again in l. 146.

Under the day's declining beam, and call
Images and memories
From ruin or from ancient trees,
For I would ask a question of them all.

Beyond that ridge lived Mrs. French, and once 25
When every silver candlestick or sconce
Lit up the dark mahogany and the wine,
A serving man, that could divine
That most respected lady's every wish,
Ran and with the garden shears 30
Clipped an insolent farmer's ears
And brought them in a little covered dish.

Some few remembered still when I was young
A peasant girl commended by a song,
Who'd lived somewhere upon that rocky place, 35
And praised the colour of her face,
And had the greater joy in praising her,
Remembering that, if walked she there,
Farmers jostled at the fair
So great a glory did the song confer. 40

And certain men, being maddened by those rhymes,
Or else by toasting her a score of times,
Rose from the table and declared it right
To test their fancy by their sight;
But they mistook the brightness of the moon 45
For the prosaic light of day—
Music had driven their wits astray—
And one was drowned in the great bog of Cloone.

Strange, but the man who made the song was blind;
Yet, now I have considered it, I find 50
That nothing strange; the tragedy began
With Homer that was a blind man,
And Helen has all living hearts betrayed.
O may the moon and sunlight seem
One inextricable beam, 55
For if I triumph I must make men mad.

And I myself created Hanrahan
And drove him drunk or sober through the dawn

25. *Mrs. French:* an eighteenth-century resident of Peterswell, in the neighborhood of Thoor Ballylee.

34. *peasant girl:* Mary Hines. The poet who praised her was Blind Raftery (see l. 49).

48. *Cloone:* See *The Celtic Twilight* (1893), by Yeats, where the story summarized in this stanza is told.

54. *moon and sunlight:* In Yeats's own philosophy (see *A Vision*), moon and sun represent, respectively, the subjective and the objective components in man. In actual reality they are blended in "one inextricable beam."

57. *Hanrahan:* folk hero in Yeats's *Stories of Red Hanrahan* (1904).

From somewhere in the neighbouring cottages.
Caught by an old man's juggleries 60
He stumbled, tumbled, fumbled to and fro
And had but broken knees for hire
And horrible splendour of desire;
I thought it all out twenty years ago:

Good fellows shuffled cards in an old bawn; 65
And when that ancient ruffian's turn was on
He so bewitched the cards under his thumb
That all but the one card became
A pack of hounds and not a pack of cards,
And that he changed into a hare. 70
Hanrahan rose in a frenzy there
And followed up those baying creatures towards—

O towards I have forgotten what—enough!
I must recall a man that neither love
Nor music nor an enemy's clipped ear 75
Could, he was so harried, cheer;
A figure that has grown so fabulous
There's not a neighbour left to say
When he finished his dog's day:
An ancient bankrupt master of this house. 80

Before that ruin came, for centuries,
Rough men-at-arms, cross-gartered to the knees
Or shod in iron, climbed the narrow stair,
And certain men-at-arms there were
Whose images, in the Great Memory stored, 85
Come with loud cry and panting breast
To break upon a sleeper's rest
While their great wooden dice beat on the board.

As I would question all, come all who can;
Come old, necessitous, half-mounted man; 90
And bring beauty's blind rambling celebrant;
The red man the juggler sent
Through God-forsaken meadows; Mrs. French,
Gifted with so fine an ear;
The man drowned in a bog's mire, 95
When mocking Muses chose the country wench.

Did all old men and women, rich and poor,
Who trod upon these rocks or passed this door,
Whether in public or in secret rage
As I do now against old age? 100

65. *bawn:* cow barn.
80. *ancient bankrupt master:* He had lived about one hundred years before.
92. *red man:* Hanrahan.

But I have found an answer in those eyes
That are impatient to be gone;
Go therefore; but leave Hanrahan,
For I need all his mighty memories.

Old lecher with a love on every wind, 105
Bring up out of that deep considering mind
All that you have discovered in the grave,
For it is certain that you have
Reckoned up every unforeknown, unseeing
Plunge, lured by a softening eye, 110
Or by a touch or sigh,
Into the labyrinth of another's being;

Does the imagination dwell the most
Upon a woman won or a woman lost?
If on the lost, admit you turned aside 115
From a great labyrinth out of pride,
Cowardice, some silly over-subtle thought
Or anything called conscience once;
And that if memory recur, the sun's
Under eclipse and the day blotted out. 120

III

It is time that I wrote my will;
I choose upstanding men
That climb the streams until
The fountain leap, and at dawn
Drop their cast at the side 125
Of dripping stone; I declare
They shall inherit my pride,
The pride of people that were
Bound neither to Cause nor to State,
Neither to slaves that were spat on, 130
Nor to tyrants that spat,
The people of Burke and of Grattan
That gave, though free to refuse—
Pride, like that of the morn,
When the headlong light is loose, 135
Or that of the fabulous horn,
Or that of the sudden shower
When all the streams are dry,
Or that of the hour

105. *Old lecher:* Hanrahan in old age.

132. *of Burke and of Gratton:* Edmund Burke (1729–1797) and Henry Grattan (1746–1820); Yeats very much admired these Irish statesmen.

136. *horn:* which Roland, leader of Charlemagne's rear guard, refused to blow, as the Christian army left Spain. As a consequence, the Saracens who had ambushed Roland were able to kill him and his friend Oliver. See the *Song of Roland*, pp. 804–20.

When the swan must fix his eye 140
Upon a fading gleam,
Float out upon a long
Last reach of glittering stream
And there sing his last song.
And I declare my faith: 145
I mock Plotinus' thought
And cry in Plato's teeth,
Death and life were not
Till man made up the whole,
Made lock, stock and barrel 150
Out of his bitter soul,
Aye, sun and moon and star, all.
And further add to that
That, being dead, we rise,
Dream and so create 155
Translunar Paradise.
I have prepared my peace
With learned Italian things
And the proud stones of Greece,
Poet's imaginings 160
And memories of love,
Memories of the words of women,
All those things whereof
Man makes a superhuman
Mirror-resembling dream. 165

As at the loophole there
The daws chatter and scream,
And drop twigs layer upon layer.
When they have mounted up,
The mother bird will rest 170
On their hollow top,
And so warm her wild nest.

I leave both faith and pride
To young upstanding men
Climbing the mountain-side, 175
That under bursting dawn
They may drop a fly;
Being of that metal made
Till it was broken by
This sedentary trade. 180

Now shall I make my soul,
Compelling it to study
In a learned school
Till the wreck of body,

Slow decay of blood, 185
Testy delirium
Or dull decreptitude,
Or what worse evil come—
The death of friends, or death
Of every brilliant eye 190
That made a catch in the breath—
Seem but the clouds of the sky
When the horizon fades;
Or a bird's sleepy cry
Among the deepening shades. 195

Coole Park and Ballylee, 1931*

Under my window-ledge the waters race,
Otters below and moor-hens on the top,
Run for a mile undimmed in Heaven's face
Then darkening through 'dark' Raftery's 'cellar' drop,
Run underground, rise in a rocky place 5
In Coole demesne, and there to finish up
Spread to a lake and drop into a hole.
What's water but the generated soul?

Upon the border of that lake's a wood
Now all dry sticks under a wintry sun, 10
And in a copse of beeches there I stood,
For Nature's pulled her tragic buskin on
And all the rant's a mirror of my mood:
At sudden thunder of the mounting swan
I turned about and looked where branches break 15
The glittering reaches of the flooded lake.

Another emblem there! That stormy white
But seems a concentration of the sky;
And, like the soul, it sails into the sight
And in the morning's gone, no man knows why; 20
And is so lovely that it sets to right
What knowledge or its lack had set awry,

* The selection from *Collected Poems* by William Butler Yeats. Coole Park, on Galway Bay, was the property of Lady Gregory, who with Yeats had founded and labored over what became the Abbey Theatre. She played an essential part in his career, being a stabilizing and encouraging influence. Thoor Ballylee was the square tower, once part of the Coole estate, which Yeats purchased in 1917.

4. *Raftery's "cellar drop:* Raftery was an eighteenth-century Gaelic poet, almost blind, who in a poem on Mary Hines, a contemporary beauty, had referred to a "cellar in Ballylee." This is supposed to name a spot where the river flows underground.

8. *generated soul:* Since ancient times water, in its cyclical course from and to the heavens, has been looked on as a symbol for man's soul. Cr. the lyric poem by Goethe, "Die Seele des Menschen gleicht dem Wasser" (Man's soul resembles water).

12. *buskin:* the half-boot worn by the actors in Greek classical tragedy.

So arrogantly pure, a child might think
It can be murdered with a spot of ink.

Sound of a stick upon the floor, a sound 25
From somebody that toils from chair to chair;
Beloved books that famous hands have bound,
Old marble heads, old pictures everywhere;
Great rooms where travelled men and children found
Content or joy; a last inheritor 30
Where none has reigned that lacked a name and fame
Or out of folly into folly came.

A spot whereon the founders lived and died
Seemed once more dear than life; ancestral trees,
Or gardens rich in memory glorified 35
Marriages, alliances and families,
And every bride's ambition satisfied.
Where fashion or mere fantasy decrees
We shift about—all that great glory spent—
Like some poor Arab tribesman and his tent. 40
We were the last romantics—chose for theme
Traditional sanctity and loveliness;
Whatever's written in what poets name
The book of the people; whatever most can bless
The mind of man or elevate a rhyme; 45
But all is changed, that high horse riderless,
Though mounted in that saddle Homer rode
Where the swan drifts upon a darkening flood.

26. *chair to chair:* Lady Gregory, in her later years, had difficulty moving around.

Lapis Lazuli*

For Harry Clifton

I have heard that hysterical women say
They are sick of the palette and fiddle-bow,
Of poets that are always gay,
For everybody knows or else should know
That if nothing drastic is done 5
Aeroplane and Zeppelin will come out,
Pitch like King Billy bomb-balls in
Until the town lie beaten flat.

All perform their tragic play,
There struts Hamlet, there is Lear, 10

 Semiprecious stone, blue in color.

7. *King Billy:* William of Orange-Nassau, a Dutchman, who had become King William III of England in 1689. The following year he defeated James II at the Battle of the Boyne.

That's Ophelia, that Cordelia;
Yet they, should the last scene be there,
The great stage curtain about to drop,
If worthy their prominent part in the play,
Do not break up their lines to weep. 15
They know that Hamlet and Lear are gay;
Gaiety transfiguring all that dread.
All men have aimed at, found and lost;
Black out; Heaven blazing into the head:
Tragedy wrought to its uttermost. 20
Though Hamlet rambles and Lear rages,
And all the drop-scenes drop at once
Upon a hundred thousand stages,
It cannot grow by an inch or an ounce.

On their own feet they came, or on shipboard, 25
Camel-back, horse-back, ass-back, mule-back,
Old civilisations put to the sword.
Then they and their wisdom went to rack:
No handiwork of Callimachus,
Who handled marble as if it were bronze, 30
Made draperies that seemed to rise
When sea-wind swept the corner, stands;
His long lamp-chimney shaped like the stem
Of a slender palm, stood but a day;
All things fall and are built again, 35
And those that build them again are gay.

Two Chinamen, behind them a third,
Are carved in lapis lazuli,
Over them flies a long-legged bird,
A symbol of longevity; 40
The third, doubtless a serving-man,
Carries a musical instrument.

Every discoloration of the stone,
Every accidental crack or dent,
Seems a water-course or an avalanche, 45
Or lofty slope where it still snows
Though doubtless plum or cherry-branch
Sweetens the little half-way house
Those Chinamen climb towards, and I
Delight to imagine them seated there; 50
There, on the mountain and the sky,
On all the tragic scene they stare.
One asks for mournful melodies;
Accomplished fingers begin to play.
Their eyes mid many wrinkles, their eyes, 55
Their ancient, glittering eyes, are gay.

29. *Callimachus:* Greek sculptor of the fifth century B.C.

The Wild Old Wicked Man*

'Because I am mad about women
I am mad about the hills,'
Said that wild old wicked man
Who travels where God wills.
'Not to die on the straw at home, 5
Those hands to close these eyes,
That is all I ask, my dear,
From the old man in the skies.
Daybreak and a candle-end.

'Kind are all your words, my dear, 10
Do not the rest withhold.
Who can know the year, my dear,
When an old man's blood grows cold?
I have what no young man can have
Because he loves too much. 15
Words I have that can pierce the heart,
But what can he do but touch?'
Daybreak and a candle-end.

Then said she to that wild old man,
His stout stick under his hand, 20
'Love to give or to withhold
Is not at my command.
I gave it all to an older man:
That old man in the skies.
Hands that are busy with His beads 25
Can never close those eyes.'
Daybreak and a candle-end.

'Go your ways, O go your ways,
I choose another mark,
Girls down on the seashore 30
Who understand the dark;
Bawdy talk for the fishermen;
A dance for the fisher-lads;
When dark hangs upon the water
They turn down their beds. 35
Daybreak and a candle-end.

'A young man in the dark am I,
But a wild old man in the light,
That can make a cat laugh, or
Can touch by mother wit 40
Things hid in their marrow-bones

From time long passed away,
Hid from all those warty lads
That by their bodies lay.
Daybreak and a candle-end. 45

'All men live in suffering,
I know as few can know,
Whether they take the upper road
Or stay content on the low,
Rower bent in his row-boat 50
Or weaver bent at his loom,
Horseman erect upon horseback
Or child hid in the womb.
Daybreak and a candle-end.

'That some stream of lightning
From the old man in the skies
Can burn out that suffering
No right-taught man denies.
But a coarse old man am I,
I choose the second-best, 60
I forget it all awhile
Upon a woman's breast.'
Daybreak and a candle-end.

43. *warty:* in folk belief, an indicator of sexual prowess.

The Circus Animals' Desertion*

I

I sought a theme and sought for it in vain,
I sought it daily for six weeks or so.
Maybe at last, being but a broken man,
I must be satisfied with my heart, although
Winter and summer till old age began 5
My circus animals were all on show,
Those stilted boys, that burnished chariot,
Lion and woman and the Lord knows what.

II

What can I but enumerate old themes?
First that sea-rider Oisin led by the nose 10
Through three enchanted islands, allegorical dreams,

8. *Lion and woman:* a reference to the sphinx, which has the body of a lion with the head and torso of a woman.

10. *Oisin:* (pronounced Ushēn) hero of Irish mythology, who was led away to the "Isles of the Blest," returning over one hundred years later to find his friends all dead and pagan Ireland converted to Christianity. Subject of a long poem *The Wanderings of Oisin,* dated 1889.

Vain gaiety, vain battle, vain repose,
Themes of the embittered heart, or so it seems,
That might adorn old songs or courtly shows;
But what cared I that set him on to ride, 15
I, starved for the bosom of his faery bride?

And then a counter-truth filled out its play,
The Countess Cathleen was the name I gave it;
She, pity-crazed, had given her soul away,
But masterful Heaven had intervened to save it. 20
I thought my dear must her own soul destroy,
So did fanaticism and hate enslave it,
And this brought forth a dream and soon enough
This dream itself had all my thought and love.

And when the Fool and Blind Man stole the bread 25
Cuchulain fought the ungovernable sea;
Heart-mysteries there, and yet when all is said
It was the dream itself enchanted me:
Character isolated by a deed
To engross the present and dominate memory. 30
Players and painted stage took all my love,
And not those things that they were emblems of.

III

Those masterful images because complete
Grew in pure mind, but out of what began?
A mound of refuse or the sweepings of a street, 35
Old kettles, old bottles, and a broken can,
Old iron, old bones, old rags, that raving slut
Who keeps the till. Now that my ladder's gone,
I must lie down where all the ladders start,
In the foul rag-and-bone shop of the heart. 40

18. *The Countess Cathleen:* Play (1892) by Yeats. The heroine sells her soul to the devil to obtain food for starving people.

26. *Cuchulain:* (pronounced Cuhūlan) hero of Yeats's highly symbolic early play *On Baile's Strand* (1892).

Under Ben Bulben*

I

Swear by what the sages spoke
Round the Mareotic Lake
That the Witch of Atlas knew,
Spoke and set the cocks a-crow.

* The selection from *Collected Poems* by William Butler Yeats. Mountain in County Sligo, visible from the churchyard in Drumcliff, where Yeats's body is buried.

2. *Mareotic Lake:* near Alexandria. In the first century A.D. a school of Neo-Pythagorean philosophers was situated there and, two centuries later, a school of Christian Neo-Platonists.

3. *Witch of Atlas:* title of poem by Shelley. For Yeats, the witch symbolized absolute beauty.

Swear by those horsemen, by those women 5
Complexion and form prove superhuman,
That pale, long-visaged company
That air in immortality
Completeness of their passions won;
Now they ride the wintry dawn 10
Where Ben Bulben sets the scene.

Here's the gist of what they mean.

II

Many times man lives and dies
Between his two eternities,
That of race and that of soul, 15
And ancient Ireland knew it all.
Whether man die in his bed
Or the rifle knocks him dead,
A brief parting from those dear
Is the worst man has to fear. 20
Though grave-diggers' toil is long,
Sharp their spades, their muscles strong,
They but thrust their buried men
Back in the human mind again.

III

You that Mitchel's prayer have heard, 25
'Send war in our time, O Lord!'
Know that when all words are said
And a man is fighting mad,
Something drops from eyes long blind,
He completes his partial mind, 30
For an instant stands at ease,
Laughs aloud, his heart at peace.
Even the wisest man grows tense
With some sort of violence
Before he can accomplish fate, 35
Know his work or choose his mate.

IV

Poet and sculptor, do the work,
Nor let the modish painter shirk
What his great forefathers did,
Bring the soul of man to God. 40
Make him fill the cradles right.

Measurement began our might:
Forms a stark Egyptian thought,

25. *Mitchel's:* John Mitchel, Irish patriot who spent a great deal of time in prison and published his *Jail Journal.* Yeats knew him as a very old man.

44. *Phidias:* Greek sculptor of fifth century B.C.

6. *women . . superhuman:* fairies believed to ride past Ben Bulben.

Forms that gentler Phidias wrought.
Michael Angelo left a proof 45
On the Sistine Chapel roof,
Where but half-awakened Adam
Can disturb globe-trotting Madam
Till her bowels are in heat,
Proof that there's a purpose set 50
Before the secret working mind:
Profane perfection of mankind.

Quattrocento put in paint
On backgrounds for a God or Saint
Gardens where a soul's at ease; 55
Where everything that meets the eye,
Flowers and grass and cloudless sky,
Resemble forms that are or seem
When sleepers wake and yet still dream,
And when it's vanished still declare, 60
With only bed and bedstead there,
That heavens had opened.
Gyres run on;
When that greater dream had gone
Calvert and Wilson, Blake and Claude,
Prepared a rest for the people of God, 65
Palmer's phrase, but after that
Confusion fell upon our thought.

V

Irish poets, learn your trade,
Sing whatever is well made,
Scorn the sort now growing up 70
All out of shape from toe to top,
Their unremembering hearts and heads
Base-born products of base beds.
Sing the peasantry, and then
Hard-riding country gentlemen, 75
The holiness of monks, and after
Porter-drinkers' randy laughter;
Sing the lords and ladies gay
That were beaten into the clay
Through seven heroic centuries; 80
Cast your mind on other days
That we in coming days may be
Still the indomitable Irishry.

47. *Adam:* depicted by Michael Angelo on the roof of Sistine Chapel in Rome.
49. *in heat:* There is a similar reference in Yeats's poem "Long-legged Fly."
53. *Quattrocento:* the fifteenth century in Italy, fifteenth-century Italian art.
64. *Calvert . . . Claude:* Edward Calvert was a nineteenth-century wood-engraver, Richard Wilson an eighteenth-century landscape painter. William Blake, painter, poet, and visionary, was closely studied by Yeats. Claude Lorrain was a seventeenth-century French landscape painter, and Samuel Palmer, a nineteenth-century landscape painter and etcher. One of Palmer's works is called "The Lonely Tower."

VI

Under bare Ben Bulben's head
In Drumcliff churchyard Yeats is laid. 85
An ancestor was rector there
Long years ago, a church stands near,
By the road an ancient cross.
No marble, no conventional phrase;
On limestone quarried near the spot 90
By his command these words are cut:
Cast a cold eye
On life, on death.
Horseman, pass by!
September 4, 1938 95

LUIGI PIRANDELLO
(1867–1936)
Henry IV*

A Tragedy in Three Acts

Characters

HENRY IV[1]
THE MARCHIONESS MATILDA SPINA
FRIDA, *her daughter*
CHARLES DI NOLLI, *the young Marquis*
BARON TITO BELCREDI
DOCTOR DIONYSIUS GENONI
HAROLD (FRANK)
LANDOLPH (LOLO)
ORDULPH (MOMO)
BERTHOLD (FINO)
} *The four private counsellors (The names in brackets are nicknames)*
JOHN, *the old waiter*
THE TWO VALETS IN COSTUME

A Solitary Villa in Italy in Our Own Time

Act I

Salon in the villa, furnished and decorated so as to look exactly like the throne room of Henry IV in the royal residence at Goslar.[2] *Among the antique decorations there are two modern life-size portraits in oil*

* From *Naked Masks: Five Plays* by Luigi Pirandello. Translated by Edward Storer. Edited by Eric Bentley. Copyright 1922, 1952, by E. P. Dutton & Co., Inc. Renewal, 1950, by Stefano, Fausto, and Lietta Pirandello. Dutton Paperback Edition. Reprinted by permission of E. P. Dutton & Co., Inc.

1. German emperor, 1065–1106. During a reign filled with conflict, his greatest antagonist was Gregory VII, pope from 1073 to 1085. Twice excommunicated, Henry had on one occasion, at Canossa, to wait three days in the snow before Gregory received and pardoned him.

2. The permanent capital of Henry IV.

painting. They are placed against the back wall, and mounted in a wooden stand that runs the whole length of the wall. (It is wide and protrudes, so that it is like a large bench.) One of the paintings is on the right; the other on the left of the throne, which is in the middle of the wall and divides the stand.

The Imperial chair and Baldachin.[3]

The two portraits represent a lady and a gentleman, both young, dressed up in carnival costumes: one as "Henry IV," the other as the "Marchioness Matilda of Tuscany."[4] *Exits to right and left.*

When the curtain goes up, the two valets jump down, as if surprised, from the stand on which they have been lying, and go and take their positions, as rigid as statues, on either side below the throne with their halberds in their hands. Soon after, from the second exit, right, enter HAROLD, LANDOLPH, ORDULPH *and* BERTHOLD, *young men employed by the* MARQUIS CHARLES DI NOLLI *to play the part of "Secret Counsellors" at the court of "Henry IV." They are, therefore, dressed like German knights of the XIth century.* BERTHOLD, *nicknamed Fino, is just entering on his duties for the first time. His companions are telling him what he has to do and amusing themselves at his expense. The scene is to be played rapidly and vivaciously.*

LANDOLPH [*to* BERTHOLD *as if explaining*]. And this is the throne room.

HAROLD. At Goslar.

ORDULPH. Or at the castle in the Hartz, if you prefer.

HAROLD. Or at Wurms.

LANDOLPH. According as to what's doing, it jumps about with us, now here, now there.

ORDULPH. In Saxony.

HAROLD. In Lombardy.

LANDOLPH. On the Rhine.

ONE OF THE VALETS [*without moving, just opening his lips*]. I say . . .

HAROLD [*turning round*]. What is it?

FIRST VALET [*like a statue*]. Is he coming in or not? [*He alludes to* HENRY IV.]

ORDULPH. No, no, he's asleep. You needn't worry.

SECOND VALET [*releasing his pose, taking a long breath and going to lie down again on the stand*]. You might have told us at once.

FIRST VALET [*going over to* HAROLD]. Have you got a match, please?

LANDOLPH. What? You can't smoke a pipe here, you know.

FIRST VALET [*while* HAROLD *offers him a light*]. No; a cigarette. [*Lights his cigarette and lies down again on the stand.*]

BERTHOLD [*who has been looking on in amazement, walking round the room, regarding the costumes of the others*]. I say . . . this

3. A fixed canopy.

4. Henry's lifelong enemy, she owned the castle at Canossa.

room . . . these costumes . . . Which Henry IV is it? I don't quite get it. Is he Henry IV of France or not? [*At this* LANDOLPH, HAROLD, *and* ORDULPH, *burst out laughing.*]

LANDOLPH [*still laughing; and pointing to* BERTHOLD *as if inviting the others to make fun of him*]. Henry of France he says: ha! ha!

ORDULPH. He thought it was the king of France!

HAROLD. Henry IV of Germany, my boy: the Salian dynasty![5]

ORDULPH. The great and tragic Emperor!

LANDOLPH. He of Canossa. Every day we carry on here the terrible war between Church and State, by Jove.

ORDULPH. The Empire against the Papacy!

HAROLD. Anti-popes against the Pope!

LANDOLPH. Kings against anti-kings!

ORDULPH. War on the Saxons!

HAROLD. And all the rebels Princes!

LANDOLPH. Against the Emperor's own sons!

BERTHOLD [*covering his head with his hands to protect himself against this avalanche of information*]. I understand! I understand! Naturally, I didn't get the idea at first. I'm right then: these aren't costumes of the XVIth century?

HAROLD. XVIth century be hanged!

ORDULPH. We're somewhere between a thousand and eleven hundred.

LANDOLPH. Work it out for yourself: if we are before Canossa on the 25th of January, 1071 . . .[6]

BERTHOLD [*more confused than ever*]. Oh my God! What a mess I've made of it!

ORDULPH. Well, just slightly, if you supposed you were at the French court.

BERTHOLD. All that historical stuff I've swotted up!

LANDOLPH. My dear boy, it's four hundred years earlier.

BERTHOLD [*getting angry*]. Good Heavens! You ought to have told me it was Germany and not France. I can't tell you how many books I've read in the last fifteen days.

HAROLD. But I say, surely you knew that poor Tito was Adalbert of Bremen,[7] here?

BERTHOLD. Not a damned bit!

LANDOLPH. Well, don't you see how it is? When Tito died, the Marquis Di Nolli . . .

BERTHOLD. Oh, it was he, was it? He might have told me.

HAROLD. Perhaps he thought you knew.

LANDOLPH. He didn't want to engage anyone else in substitution. He thought the remaining three of us would do. But *he* began to cry out: "With Adalbert driven away . . .":[8] because, you see, he

5. Line of German emperors, in power from 1024 to 1125.

6. 1077 is the correct date.

7. Archbishop, appointed by Henry III, and regent until Henry IV came of age in 1066.

8. On acceding to the throne in 1066, Henry had been obliged to dismiss him.

didn't imagine poor Tito was dead; but that, as Bishop Adalbert, the rival bishops of Cologne and Mayence had driven him off . . .

BERTHOLD [*taking his head in his hand*]. But I don't know a word of what you're talking about.

ORDULPH. So much the worse for you, my boy!

HAROLD. But the trouble is that not even we know who you are.

BERTHOLD. What? Not even you? You don't know who I'm supposed to be?

ORDULPH. Hum! "Berthold."

BERTHOLD. But which Berthold? And why Berthold?

LANDOLPH [*solemnly imitating* HENRY IV]. "They've driven Adalbert away from me. Well then, I want Berthold! I want Berthold!" That's what he said.

HAROLD. We three looked one another in the eyes: who's got to be Berthold?

ORDULPH. And so here you are, "Berthold," my dear fellow!

LANDOLPH. I'm afraid you will make a bit of a mess of it.

BERTHOLD [*indignant, getting ready to go*]. Ah, no! Thanks very much, but I'm off! I'm out of this!

HAROLD [*restraining him with the other two, amid laughter*]. Steady now! Don't get excited!

LANDOLPH. Cheer up, my dear fellow! We don't any of us know who we are really. He's Harold; he's Ordulph! I'm Landolph! That's the way he calls us. We've got used to it. But who are we? Names of the period! Yours, too, is a name of the period: Berthold! Only one of us, poor Tito, had got a really decent part, as you can read in history: that of the Bishop of Bremen. He was just like a real bishop. Tito did it awfully well, poor chap!

HAROLD. Look at the study he put into it!

LANDOLPH. Why, he even ordered his Majesty about, opposed his views, guided and counselled him. We're "secret counsellors"—in a manner of speaking only; because it is written in history that Henry IV was hated by the upper aristocracy for surrounding himself at court with young men of the bourgeoisie.

ORDULPH. Us, that is.

LANDOLPH. Yes, small devoted vassals, a bit dissolute and very gay . . .

BERTHOLD. So I've got to be gay as well?

HAROLD. I should say so! Same as we are!

ORDULPH. And it isn't too easy, you know.

LANDOLPH. It's a pity; because the way we're got up, we could do a fine historical reconstruction. There's any amount of material in the story of Henry IV. But, as a matter of fact, we do nothing. We have the form without the content. We're worse than the real secret counsellors of Henry IV; because certainly no one had given them a part to play—at any rate, they didn't feel they had a part to play. It was their life. They looked after their own interests at the expense of others, sold investitures and—what not! We stop here in this magnificent court—for what?—Just doing nothing. We're like so many puppets hung on the wall, waiting for someone to come and move us or make us talk.

HAROLD. Ah, no, old sport, not quite that! We've got to give the proper answer, you know. There's trouble if he asks you something and you don't chip in with the cue.

LANDOLPH. Yes. that's true.

BERTHOLD. Don't rub it in too hard! How the devil am I to give him the proper answer, if I've swatted up Henry IV of France, and now he turns out to be Henry IV of Germany? [*The other three laugh.*]

HAROLD. You'd better start and prepare yourself at once.

ORDULPH. We'll help you out.

HAROLD. We've got any amount of books on the subject. A brief run through the main points will do to begin with.

ORDULPH. At any rate, you must have got some sort of general idea.

HAROLD. Look here! [*Turns him around and shows him the portrait of the Marchioness Matilda on the wall.*] Who's that?

BERTHOLD [*looking at it*]. That? Well, the thing seems to me somewhat out of place, anyway: two modern paintings in the midst of all this respectable antiquity!

HAROLD. You're right! They weren't there in the beginning. There are two niches there behind the pictures. They were going to put up two statues in the style of the period. Then the places were covered with those canvases there.

LANDOLPH [*interrupting and continuing*]. They would certainly be out of place if they really were paintings!

BERTHOLD. What are they, if they aren't paintings?

LANDOLPH. Go and touch them! Pictures all right . . . but for him! [*Makes a mysterious gesture to the right, alluding to* HENRY IV.] . . . who never touches them! . . .

BERTHOLD. No? What are they for him?

LANDOLPH. Well, I'm only supposing, you know; but I imagine I'm about right. They're images such as . . . well—such as a mirror might throw back. Do you understand? That one there represents himself, as he is in this throne room, which is all in the style of the period. What's there to marvel at? If we put you before a mirror, won't you see yourself, alive, but dressed up in ancient costume? Well, it's as if there were two mirrors there, which cast back living images in the midst of a world which, as you well see, when you have lived with us, comes to life too.

BERTHOLD. I say, look here . . . I've no particular desire to go mad here.

HAROLD. Go mad, be hanged! You'll have a fine time!

BERTHOLD. Tell me this: how have you all managed to become so learned?

LANDOLPH. My dear fellow, you can't go back over 800 years of history without picking up a bit of experience.

HAROLD. Come on! Come on! You'll see how quickly you get into it!

ORDULPH. You'll learn wisdom, too, at this school.

BERTHOLD. Well, for Heaven's sake, help me a bit! Give me the main lines, anyway.

HAROLD. Leave it to us. We'll do it all between us.

LANDOLPH. We'll put your wires on you and fix you up like a first-class marionette. Come along! [THEY *take him by the arm to lead him away.*]

BERTHOLD [*stopping and looking at the portrait on the wall*]. Wait a minute! You haven't told me who that is. The Emperor's wife?

HAROLD. No! The Emperor's wife is Bertha of Susa, the sister of Amadeus II of Savoy.

ORDULPH. And the Emperor, who wants to be young with us, can't stand her, and wants to put her away.

LANDOLPH. That is his most ferocious enemy: Matilda, Marchioness of Tuscany.

BERTHOLD. Ah, I've got it: the one who gave hospitality to the Pope!

LANDOLPH. Exactly: at Canossa!

ORDULPH. Pope Gregory VII!

HAROLD. Our *bête noir!* Come on! come on! [*All four move toward the right to go out, when, from the left, the old servant* JOHN *enters in evening dress.*]

JOHN [*quickly, anxiously*]. Hss! Hss! Frank! Lolo!

HAROLD [*turning round*]. What is it?

BERTHOLD [*marvelling at seeing a man in modern clothes enter the throne room*]. Oh! I say, this is a bit too much, this chap here!

LANDOLPH. A man of the XXth century, here! Oh, go away! [THEY *run over to him, pretending to menace him and throw him out.*]

ORDULPH [*heroically*]. Messenger of Gregory VII, away!

HAROLD. Away! Away!

JOHN [*annoyed, defending himself*]. Oh, stop it! Stop it, I tell you!

ORDULPH. No, you can't set foot here!

HAROLD. Out with him!

LANDOLPH [*to* BERTHOLD]. Magic, you know! He's a demon conjured up by the Wizard of Rome! Out with your swords! [*Makes as if to draw a sword.*]

JOHN [*shouting*]. Stop it, will you? Don't play the fool with me! The Marquis has arrived with some friends . . .

LANDOLPH. Good! Good! Are there ladies too?

ORDULPH. Old or young?

JOHN. There are two gentlemen.

HAROLD. But the ladies, the ladies, who are they?

JOHN. The Marchioness and her daughter.

LANDOLPH [*surprised*]. What do you say?

ORDULPH. The Marchioness?

JOHN. The Marchioness! The Marchioness!

HAROLD. Who are the gentlemen?

JOHN. I don't know.

HAROLD [*to* BERTHOLD]. They're coming to bring us a message from the Pope, do you see?

ORDULPH. All messengers of Gregory VII! What fun!

JOHN. Will you let me speak, or not?

ORDULPH. Come on then!

JOHN. One of the two gentlemen is a doctor, I fancy.

LANDOLPH. Oh, I see, one of the usual doctors.

HAROLD. Bravo Berthold, you'll bring us luck!
LANDOLPH. You wait and see how we'll manage this doctor!
BERTHOLD. It looks as if I were going to get into a nice mess right away.
JOHN. If the gentlemen would allow me to speak . . . they want to come here into the throne room.
LANDOLPH [*surprised*]. What? She? The Marchioness here?
HAROLD. Then this is something quite different! No play-acting this time!
LANDOLPH. We'll have a real tragedy: that's what!
BERTHOLD [*curious*]. Why? Why?
ORDULPH [*pointing to the portrait*]. She is that person there, don't you understand?
LANDOLPH. The daughter is the fiancée of the Marquis. But what have they come for, I should like to know?
ORDULPH. If he sees her, there'll be trouble.
LANDOLPH. Perhaps he won't recognize her any more.
JOHN. You must keep him there, if he should wake up . . .
ORDULPH. Easier said than done, by Jove!
HAROLD. You know what he's like!
JOHN. —even by force, if necessary! Those are my orders. Go on! Go on!
HAROLD. Yes, because who knows if he hasn't already wakened up?
ORDULPH. Come on then!
LANDOLPH [*going towards* JOHN *with the others*]. You'll tell us later what it all means.
JOHN [*shouting after them*]. Close the door there, and hide the key! That other door too. [*Pointing to the other door on right.*]
JOHN [*to the* TWO VALETS]. Be off, you two! There! [*Pointing to exit right.*] Close the door after you, and hide the key!

[*The* TWO VALETS *go out by the first door on right.* JOHN *moves over to the left to show in:* DONNA MATILDA SPINA, *the young* MARCHIONESS FRIDA, DR. DIONYSIUS GENONI, *the* BARON TITO BELCREDI *and the young* MARQUIS CHARLES DI NOLLI, *who, as master of the house, enters last.*

DONNA MATILDA SPINA *is about 45, still handsome, although there are too patent signs of her attempts to remedy the ravages of time with make-up. Her head is thus rather like a Walkyrie.*[9] *This facial make-up contrasts with her beautiful sad mouth. A widow for many years, she now has as her friend the* BARON TITO BELCREDI, *whom neither she nor anyone else takes seriously—at least so it would appear.*

What TITO BELCREDI *really is for her at bottom, he alone knows; and he is, therefore, entitled to laugh, if his friend feels the need of pretending not to know. He can always laugh at the jests which the beautiful Marchioness makes with the others at his expense. He is slim, prematurely gray, and younger than she is. His head is bird-like in shape. He would be a*

9. In Germanic mythology, female creature who rode over battlefields and gathered up spirits of dead warriors.

very vivacious person, if his ductile agility (which among other things makes him a redoubtable swordsman) were not enclosed in a sheath of Arab-like laziness, which is revealed in his strange, nasal drawn-out voice.

FRIDA, *the daughter of the Marchioness is 19. She is sad; because her imperious and too beautiful mother puts her in the shade, and provokes facile gossip against her daughter as well as against herself. Fortunately for her, she is engaged to the* MARQUIS CHARLES DI NOLLI.

CHARLES DI NOLLI *is a stiff young man, very indulgent towards others, but sure of himself for what he amounts to in the world. He is worried about all the responsibilities which he believes weigh on him. He is dressed in deep mourning for the recent death of his mother.*

DR. DIONYSIUS GENONI *has a bold rubicund Satyr-like face, prominent eyes, a pointed beard (which is silvery and shiny) and elegant manners. He is nearly bald. All enter in a state of perturbation, almost as if afraid, and all (except* DI NOLLI*) looking curiously about the room. At first, they speak sotto voce.*]

DI NOLLI [*to* JOHN]. Have you given the orders properly?

JOHN. Yes, my Lord; don't be anxious about that.

BELCREDI. Ah, magnificent! magnificent!

DOCTOR. How extremely interesting! Even in the surroundings his raving madness—is perfectly taken into account!

DONNA MATILDA [*glancing round for her portrait, discovers it, and goes up close to it*]. Ah! Here it is! [*Going back to admire it, while mixed emotions stir within her.*] Yes . . . yes . . . [*Calls her daughter* FRIDA.]

FRIDA. Ah, your portrait!

DONNA MATILDA. No, no . . . look again; it's you, not I, there!

DI NOLLI. Yes, it's quite true. I told you so. I . . .

DONNA MATILDA. But I would never have believed it! [*Shaking as if with a chill.*] What a strange feeling it gives one! [*Then looking at her daughter.*] Frida, what's the matter? [*She pulls her to her side, and slips an arm round her waist.*] Come: don't you see yourself in me there?

FRIDA. Well, I really . . .

DONNA MATILDA. Don't you think so? Don't you, really? [*Turning to* BELCREDI.] Look at it, Tito! Speak up, man!

BELCREDI [*without looking*]. Ah, no! I shan't look at it. For me, *a priori*, certainly not!

DONNA MATILDA. Stupid! You think you are paying me a compliment! [*Turning to* DOCTOR GENONI.] What do you say, Doctor? Do say something, please!

DOCTOR [*makes a movement to go near to the picture*].

BELCREDI [*with his back turned, pretending to attract his attention secretly*].—Hss! No, Doctor! For the love of Heaven, have nothing to do with it!

DOCTOR [*getting bewildered and smiling*]. And why shouldn't I?

DONNA MATILDA. Don't listen to him! Come here! He's insufferable!

FRIDA. He acts the fool by profession, didn't you know that?

BELCREDI [*to the* DOCTOR, *seeing him go over*]. Look at your feet, Doctor! Mind where you're going!

DOCTOR. Why?

BELCREDI. Be careful you don't put your foot in it!

DOCTOR [*laughing feebly*]. No, no. After all, it seems to me there's no reason to be astonished at the fact that a daughter should resemble her mother!

BELCREDI. Hullo! Hullo! He's done it now; he's said it.

DONNA MATILDA [*with exaggerated anger, advancing towards* BELCREDI]. What's the matter? What has he said? What has he done?

DOCTOR [*candidly*]. Well, isn't it so?

BELCREDI [*answering the* MARCHIONESS]. I said there was nothing to be astounded at—and you are astounded! And why so, then, if the thing is so simple and natural for you now?

DONNA MATILDA [*still more angry*]. Fool! fool! It's just because it is so natural! Just because it isn't my daughter who is there. [*Pointing to the canvas.*] That is my portrait; and to find my daughter there instead of me fills me with astonishment, an astonishment which, I beg you to believe, is sincere. I forbid you to cast doubts on it.

FRIDA [*slowly and wearily*]. My God! It's always like this . . . rows over nothing . . .

BELCREDI [*also slowly, looking dejected, in accents of apology*]. I cast no doubt on anything! I noticed from the beginning that you haven't shared your mother's astonishment; or, if something did astonish you, it was because the likeness between you and the portrait seemed so strong.

DONNA MATILDA. Naturally! She cannot recognize herself in me as I was at her age; while I, there, can very well recognize myself in her as she is now!

DOCTOR. Quite right! Because a portrait is always there fixed in the twinkling of an eye: for the young lady something far away and without memories, while, for the Marchioness, it can bring back everything: movements, gestures, looks, smiles, a whole heap of things . . .

DONNA MATILDA. Exactly!

DOCTOR [*continuing, turning towards her*]. Naturally enough, you can live all these old sensations again in your daughter.

DONNA MATILDA. He always spoils every innocent pleasure for me, every touch I have of spontaneous sentiment! He does it merely to annoy me.

DOCTOR [*frightened at the disturbance he has caused, adopts a professorial tone*]. Likeness, dear Baron, is often the result of imponderable things. So one explains that . . .

BELCREDI [*interrupting the discourse*]. Somebody will soon be finding a likeness between you and me, my dear Professor!

DI NOLLI. Oh! let's finish with this, please! [*Points to the two doors on the right, as a warning that there is someone there who may be listening.*] We've wasted too much time as it is!

FRIDA. As one might expect when *he's* present. [*Alludes to* BELCREDI.]

DI NOLLI. Enough! The Doctor is here; and we have come for a very serious purpose which you all know is important for me.

DOCTOR. Yes, that is so! But now, first of all, let's try to get some points down exactly. Excuse me, Marchioness, will you tell me why your portrait is here? Did you present it to him then?

DONNA MATILDA. No, not at all. How could I have given it to him? I was just like Frida then—and not even engaged. I gave it to him three or four years after the accident. I gave it to him because his mother wished it so much . . . [*Points to* DI NOLLI.]

DOCTOR. She was his sister? [*Alludes to* HENRY IV.]

DI NOLLI. Yes, Doctor; and our coming here is a debt we pay to my mother who has been dead for more than a month. Instead of being here, she and I [*Indicating Frida.*] ought to be traveling together . . .

DOCTOR. . . . taking a cure of quite a different kind!

DI NOLLI. —Hum! Mother died in the firm conviction that her adored brother was just about to be cured.

DOCTOR. And can't you tell me, if you please, how she inferred this?

DI NOLLI. The conviction would appear to have derived from certain strange remarks which he made, a little before mother died.

DOCTOR. Oh, remarks! . . . Ah! . . . It would be extremely useful for me to have those remarks, word for word, if possible.

DI NOLLI. I can't remember them. I know that mother returned awfully upset from her last visit with him. On her death-bed, she made me promise that I would never neglect him, that I would have doctors see him, and examine him.

DOCTOR. Um! Um! Let me see! let me see! Sometimes very small reasons determine . . . and this portrait here then? . . .

DONNA MATILDA. For Heaven's sake, Doctor, don't attach excessive importance to this. It made an impression on me because I had not seen it for so many years!

DOCTOR. If you please, quietly, quietly . . .

DI NOLLI. —Well, yes, it must be about fifteen years ago.

DONNA MATILDA. More, more: eighteen!

DOCTOR. Forgive me, but you don't quite know what I'm trying to get at. I attach a very great importance to these two portraits . . . They were painted, naturally, prior to the famous—and most regrettable pageant, weren't they?

DONNA MATILDA. Of course!

DOCTOR. That is . . . when he was quite in his right mind—that's what I've been trying to say. Was it his suggestion that they should be painted?

DONNA MATILDA. Lots of the people who took part in the pageant had theirs done as a souvenir . . .

BELCREDI. I had mine done—as "Charles of Anjou!"[10]

10. (1246–85). Founder of the line of Anjou.

DONNA MATILDA. . . . as soon as the costumes were ready.

BELCREDI. As a matter of fact, it was proposed that the whole lot of us should be hung together in a gallery of the villa where the pageant took place. But in the end, everybody wanted to keep his own portrait.

DONNA MATILDA. And I gave him this portrait of me without very much regret . . . since his mother . . . [*Indicates* DI NOLLI.]

DOCTOR. You don't remember if it was he who asked for it?

DONNA MATILDA. Ah, that I don't remember . . . Maybe it was his sister, wanting to help out . . .

DOCTOR. One other thing: was it his idea, this pageant?

BELCREDI [*at once*]. No, no, it was mine!

DOCTOR. If you please . . .

DONNA MATILDA. Don't listen to him! It was poor Belassi's idea.

BELCREDI. Belassi! What had he got to do with it?

DONNA MATILDA. Count Belassi, who died, poor fellow, two or three months after . . .

BELCREDI. But if Belasi wasn't there when . . .

DI NOLLI. Excuse me, Doctor; but is it really necessary to establish whose the original idea was?

DOCTOR. It would help me, certainly!

BELCREDI. I tell you the idea was mine? There's nothing to be proud of in it, seeing what the result's been. Look here, Doctor, it was like this. One evening, in the first days of November, I was looking at an illustrated German review in the club. I was merely glancing at the pictures, because I can't read German. There was a picture of the Kaiser, at some University town where he had been a student . . . I don't remember which.

DOCTOR. Bonn, Bonn!

BELCREDI. —You are right: Bonn! He was on horseback, dressed up in one of those ancient German student guild-costumes, followed by a procession of noble students, also in costume. The picture gave me the idea. Already someone at the club had spoken of a pageant for the forthcoming carnival. So I had the notion that each of us should choose for this Tower of Babel pageant to represent some character: a king, an emperor, a prince, with his queen, empress, or lady, alongside of him—and all on horseback. The suggestion was at once accepted.

DONNA MATILDA. I had my invitation from Belassi.

BELCREDI. Well, he wasn't speaking the truth! That's all I can say, if he told you the idea was his. He wasn't even at the club the evening I made the suggestion, just as he [*Meaning* HENRY IV.] wasn't there either.

DOCTOR. So he chose the character of Henry IV?

DONNA MATILDA. Because I . . . thinking of my name, and not giving the choice any importance, said I would be the Marchioness Matilda of Tuscany.

DOCTOR. I . . . don't understand the relation between the two.

DONNA MATILDA. —Neither did I, to begin with, when he said that in that case he would be at my feet like Henry IV at Canossa. I had heard of Canossa of course; but to tell the truth, I'd forgotten most of the story; and I remember I received a curious impression when I had to get up my part, and found that I was the faithful and zealous friend of Pope Gregory VII in deadly enmity with the Emperor of Germany. Then I understood why, since I had chosen to represent his implacable enemy, he wanted to be near me in the pageant as Henry IV.

DOCTOR. Ah, perhaps because . . .

BELCREDI. —Good Heavens, Doctor, because he was then paying furious court to her! [*Indicates the* MARCHIONESS.] And she, naturally . . .

DONNA MATILDA. Naturally? Not naturally at all . . .

BELCREDI [*pointing to her*]. She shouldn't stand him . . .

DONNA MATILDA. —No, that isn't true! I didn't dislike him. Not at all! But for me, when a man begins to want to be taken seriously, well . . .

BELCREDI [*continuing for her*]. He gives you the clearest proof of his stupidity.

DONNA MATILDA. No, dear; not in this case; because he was never a fool like you.

BELCREDI. Anyway, I've never asked you to take me seriously.

DONNA MATILDA. Yes, I know. But with him one couldn't joke. [*Changing her tone and speaking to the* DOCTOR.] One of the many misfortunes which happen to us women, Doctor, is to see before us every now and again a pair of eyes glaring at us with a contained intense promise of eternal devotion. [*Bursts out laughing.*] There is nothing quite so funny. If men could only see themselves with that eternal look of fidelity in their faces! I've always thought it comic; then more even than now. But I want to make a confession—I can do so after twenty years or more. When I laughed at him then, it was partly out of fear. One might have almost believed a promise from those eyes of his. But it would have been very dangerous.

DOCTOR [*with lively interest*]. Ah! ah! This is most interesting! Very dangerous, you say?

DONNA MATILDA. Yes, because he was very different from the others. And then, I am . . . well . . . what shall I say? . . . a little impatient of all that is pondered, or tedious. But I was too young then, and a woman. I had the bit between my teeth. It would have required more courage than I felt I possessed. So I laughed at him too—with remorse, to spite myself, indeed; since I saw that my own laugh mingled with those of all the others—the other fools—who made fun of him.

BELCREDI. My own case, more or less!

DONNA MATILDA. You make people laugh at you, my dear, with your trick of always humiliating yourself. It was quite a different affair with him. There's a vast difference. And you—you know—people laugh in your face!

BELCREDI. Well, that's better than behind one's back!
DOCTOR. Let's get to the facts. He was then already somewhat exalted, if I understand rightly.
BELCREDI. Yes, but in a curious fashion, Doctor.
DOCTOR. How?
BELCREDI. Well, cold-bloodedly so to speak.
DONNA MATILDA. Not at all! It was like this, Doctor! He was a bit strange, certainly; but only because he was fond of life: eccentric, there!
BELCREDI. I don't say he simulated exaltation. On the contrary, he was often genuinely exalted. But I could swear, Doctor, that he saw himself at once in his own exaltation. Moreover, I'm certain it made him suffer. Sometimes he had the most comical fits of rage against himself.
DOCTOR. Yes?
DONNA MATILDA. That is true.
BELCREDI [*to* DONNA MATILDA]. And why? [*To the* DOCTOR.] Evidently, because that immediate lucidity that comes from acting, assuming a part, at once put him out of key with his own feelings, which seemed to him not exactly false, but like something he was obliged to give the value there and then of—what shall I say—of an act of intelligence, to make up for that sincere cordial warmth he felt lacking. So he improvised, exaggerated, let himself go, so as to distract and forget himself. He appeared inconstant, fatuous, and —yes—even ridiculous, sometimes.
DOCTOR. And may we say unsociable?
BELCREDI. No, not at all. He was famous for getting up things: *tableaux vivants*,[11] dances, theatrical performances for charity: all for the fun of the thing, of course. He was a jolly good actor, you know!
DI NOLLI. Madness has made a superb actor of him.
BELCREDI. —Why, so he was even in the old days. When the accident happened, after the horse fell . . .
DOCTOR. Hit the back of his head, didn't he?
DONNA MATILDA. Oh, it was horrible! He was beside me! I saw him between the horse's hoofs! It was rearing!
BELCREDI. None of us thought it was anything serious at first. There was a stop in the pageant, a bit of disorder. People wanted to know what had happened. But they'd already taken him off to the villa.
DONNA MATILDA. There wasn't the least sign of a wound, not a drop of blood.
BELCREDI. We thought he had merely fainted.
DONNA MATILDA. But two hours afterwards . . .
BELCREDI. He reappeared in the drawing-room of the villa . . . that is what I wanted to say . . .
DONNA MATILDA. My God! What a face he had. I saw the whole thing at once!

11. People in costume, grouped to resemble a famous painting.

BELCREDI. No, no! that isn't true. Nobody saw it, Doctor, believe me!

DONNA MATILDA. Doubtless, because you were all like mad folk.

BELCREDI. Everybody was pretending to act his part for a joke. It was a regular Babel.

DONNA MATILDA. And you can imagine, Doctor, what terror struck into us when we understood that he, on the contrary, was playing his part in deadly earnest . . .

DOCTOR. Oh, he was there too, was he?

BELCREDI. Of course! He came straight into the midst of us. We thought he'd quite recovered, and was pretending, fooling, like all the rest of us . . . only doing it rather better; because, as I say, he knew how to act.

DONNA MATILDA. Some of them began to hit him with their whips and fans and sticks.

BELCREDI. And then—as a king, he was armed, of course—he drew out his sword and menaced two or three of us . . . It was a terrible moment, I can assure you!

DONNA MATILDA. I shall never forget that scene—all our masked faces hideous and terrified gazing at him, at that terrible mask of his face, which was no longer a mask, but madness, madness personified.

BELCREDI. He was Henry IV, Henry IV in person, in a moment of fury.

DONNA MATILDA. He'd got into it all the detail and minute preparation of a month's careful study. And it all burned and blazed there in the terrible obsession which lit his face.

DOCTOR. Yes, that is quite natural, of course. The momentary obsession of a dilettante became fixed, owing to the fall and the damage to the brain.

BELCREDI [*to* FRIDA *and* DI NOLLI]. You see the kind of jokes life can play on us. [*To* DI NOLLI.] You were four or five years old. [*To* FRIDA.] Your mother imagines you've taken her place there in that portrait; when, at the time, she had not the remotest idea that she would bring you into the world. My hair is already grey; and he—look at him—[*Points to portrait*]—ha! A smack on the head, and he never moves again: Henry IV for ever!

DOCTOR [*seeking to draw the attention of the others, looking learned and imposing*]. —Well, well, then it comes, we may say, to this . . .

[*Suddenly the first exit to right, the one nearest footlights, opens, and* BERTHOLD *enters all excited.*]

BERTHOLD [*rushing in*]. I say! I say! [*Stops for a moment, arrested by the astonishment which his appearance has caused in the others.*]

FRIDA [*running away terrified*]. Oh dear! oh dear! it's he, it's . . .

DONNA MATILDA [*covering her face with her hands so as not to see*]. Is it, is it he?

DI NOLLI. No, no, what are you talking about? Be calm!

DOCTOR. Who is it then?

BELCREDI. One of our masqueraders.

DI NOLLI. He is one of the four youths we keep here to help him out in his madness . . .

BERTHOLD. I beg your pardon, Marquis . . .

DI NOLLI. Pardon be damned! I gave orders that the doors were to be closed, and that nobody should be allowed to enter.

BERTHOLD. Yes, sir, but I can't stand it any longer, and I ask you to let me go away this very minute.

DI NOLLI. Oh, you're the new valet, are you? You were supposed to begin this morning, weren't you?

BERTHOLD. Yes, sir, and I can't stand it, I can't bear it.

DONNA MATILDA [*to* DI NOLLI *excitedly*]. What? Then he's not so calm as you said?

BERTHOLD [*quickly*]. —No, no, my lady, it isn't he; it's my companions. You say "help him out with his madness," Marquis; but they don't do anything of the kind. They're the real madmen. I come here for the first time, and instead of helping me . . .

[LANDOLPH *and* HAROLD *come in from the same door, but hesitate on the threshold.*]

LANDOLPH. Excuse me?

HAROLD. May I come in, my Lord?

DI NOLLI. Come in! What's the matter? What are you all doing?

FRIDA. Oh God! I'm frightened! I'm going to run away. [*Makes towards exit at left.*]

DI NOLLI [*restraining her at once*]. No, no, Frida!

LANDOLPH. My Lord, this fool here . . . [*Indicates* BERTHOLD.]

BERTHOLD [*protesting*]. Ah, no thanks, my friends, no thanks! I'm not stopping here! I'm off!

LANDOLPH. What do you mean—you're not stopping here?

HAROLD. He's ruined everything, my Lord, running away in here!

LANDOLPH. He's made him quite mad. We can't keep him in there any longer. He's given orders that he's to be arrested; and he wants to "judge" him at once from the throne: What is to be done?

DI NOLLI. Shut the door, man! Shut the door! Go and close that door! [LANDOLPH *goes over to close it.*]

HAROLD. Ordulph, alone, won't be able to keep him there.

LANDOLPH. —My Lord, perhaps if we could announce the visitors at once, it would turn his thoughts. Have the gentlemen thought under what pretext they will present themselves to him?

DI NOLLI. —It's all been arranged! [*To the* DOCTOR.] If you, Doctor, think it well to see him at once. . . .

FRIDA. I'm not coming! I'm not coming! I'll keep out of this. You too, mother, for Heaven's sake, come away with me!

DOCTOR. —I say . . . I suppose he's not armed, is he?

DI NOLLI. —Nonsense! Of course not. [*To* FRIDA.] Frida, you know this is childish of you. You wanted to come!

FRIDA. I didn't at all. It was mother's idea.

DONNA MATILDA. And I'm quite ready to see him. What are we going to do?

BELCREDI. Must we absolutely dress up in some fashion or other?

LANDOLPH. —Absolutely essential, indispensable, sir. Alas! as you see . . . [*Shows his costume*], there'd be awful trouble if he saw you gentlemen in modern dress.

HAROLD. He would think it was some diabolical masquerade.

DI NOLLI. As these men seem to be in costume to you, so we appear to be in costume to him, in these modern clothes of ours.

LANDOLPH. It wouldn't matter so much if he wouldn't suppose it to be the work of his mortal enemy.

BELCREDI. Pope Gregory VII?

LANDOLPH. Precisely. He calls him "a pagan."

BELCREDI. The Pope a pagan? Not bad that!

LANDOLPH. —Yes, sir,—and a man who calls up the dead! He accuses him of all the diabolical arts. He's terribly afraid of him.

DOCTOR. Persecution mania!

HAROLD. He'd be simply furious.

DI NOLLI [*to* BELCREDI]. But there's no need for you to be there, you know. It's sufficient for the Doctor to see him.

DOCTOR. —What do you mean? . . . I? Alone?

DI NOLLI. —But they are there. [*Indicates the three young men.*]

DOCTOR. I don't mean that . . . , I mean if the Marchioness . . .

DONNA MATILDA. Of course. I mean to see him too, naturally. I want to see him again.

FRIDA. Oh, why, mother, why? Do come away with me, I implore you!

DONNA MATILDA [*imperiously*]. Let me do as I wish! I came here for this purpose! [*To* LANDOLPH.] I shall be "Adelaide," the mother.

LANDOLPH. Excellent! The mother of the Empress Bertha. Good! It will be enough if her Ladyship wears the ducal crown and puts on a mantel that will hide her other clothes entirely. [*To* HAROLD.] Off you go, Harold!

HAROLD. Wait a moment! And this gentleman here? . . . [*Alludes to the* DOCTOR.]

DOCTOR. —Ah yes . . . we decided I was to be . . . the Bishop of Cluny, Hugh of Cluny!

HAROLD. The gentleman means the Abbot. Very good! Hugh of Cluny.[12]

LANDOLPH. —He's often been here before!

DOCTOR [*amazed*]. —What? Been here before?

LANDOLPH. —Don't be alarmed! I mean that it's an easily prepared disguise . . .

HAROLD. We've made use of it on other occasions, you see!

DOCTOR. But . . .

LANDOLPH. Oh, no there's no risk of his remembering. He pays more attention to the dress than to the person.

DONNA MATILDA. That's fortunate for me too then.

DI NOLLI. Frida, you and I'll get along. Come on, Tito!

BELCREDI. Ah no. If she [*Indicates the* MARCHIONESS.] stops here, so do I!

DONNA MATILDA. But I don't need you at all.

12. Godfather of Henry IV.

BELCREDI. You may not need me, but I should like to see him again myself. Mayn't I?

LANDOLPH. Well, perhaps it would be better if there were three.

HAROLD. How is the gentleman to be dressed then?

BELCREDI. Oh, try and find some easy costume for me.

LANDOLPH [*to* HAROLD]. Hum! Yes . . . he'd better be from Cluny too.

BELCREDI. What do you mean—from Cluny?

LANDOLPH. A Benedictine's habit of the Abbey of Cluny. He can be in attendance on Monsignor. [*To* HAROLD.] Off you go! [*To* BERTHOLD.] And you too get away and keep out of sight all today. No, wait a bit! [*To* BERTHOLD.] You bring here the costumes he will give you. [*To* HAROLD.] You go at once and announce the visit of the "Duchess Adelaide" and "Monsignor Hugh of Cluny." Do you understand? [HAROLD *and* BERTHOLD *go off by the first door on the right.*]

DI NOLLI. We'll retire now. [*Goes off with* FRIDA, *left.*]

DOCTOR. Shall I be a *persona grata*[13] to him, as Hugh of Cluny?

LANDOLPH. Oh, rather! Don't worry about that! Monsignor has always been received here with great respect. You too, my Lady, he will be glad to see. He never forgets that it was owing to the intercession of you two that he was admitted to the Castle of Canossa and the presence of Gregory VII, who didn't want to receive him.

BELCREDI. And what do I do?

LANDOLPH. You stand a little apart, respectfully: that's all.

DONNA MATILDA [*irritated, nervous*]. You would do well to go away, you know.

BELCREDI [*slowly, spitefully*]. How upset you seem! . . .

DONNA MATILDA [*proudly*]. I am as I am. Leave me alone!

[BERTHOLD *comes in with the costumes.*]

LANDOLPH [*seeing him enter*]. Ah, the costumes: here they are. This mantle is for the Marchioness . . .

DONNA MATILDA. Wait a minute! I'll take off my hat. [*Does so and gives it to* BERTHOLD.]

LANDOLPH. Put it down there! [*Then to the* MARCHIONESS, *while he offers to put the ducal crown on her head.*] Allow me!

DONNA MATILDA. Dear, dear! Isn't there a mirror here?

LANDOLPH. Yes, there's one there [*Points to the door on the left.*] If the Marchioness would rather put it on herself . . .

DONNA MATILDA. Yes, yes, that will be better. Give it to me! [*Takes up her hat and goes off with* BERTHOLD, *who carries the cloak and the crown.*]

BELCREDI. Well, I must say, I never thought I should be a Benedictine monk! By the way, this business must cost an awful lot of money.

THE DOCTOR. Like any other fantasy, naturally!

BELCREDI. Well, there's a fortune to go upon.

LANDOLPH. We have got there a whole wardrobe of costumes of the

13. Person declared to be officially acceptable.

period, copied to perfection from old models. This is my special job. I get them from the best theatrical costumers. They cost lots of money. [DONNA MATILDA *re-enters, wearing mantle and crown.*]

BELCREDI [*at once, in admiration*]. Oh magnificent! Oh, truly regal!

DONNA MATILDA [*looking at* BELCREDI *and bursting out into laughter*]. Oh no, no! Take it off! You're impossible. You look like an ostrich dressed up as a monk.

BELCREDI. Well, how about the Doctor?

THE DOCTOR. I don't think I looked so bad, do I?

DONNA MATILDA. No; the Doctor's all right . . . but you are too funny for words.

THE DOCTOR. Do you have many receptions here then?

LANDOLPH. It depends. He often gives orders that such and such a person appear before him. Then we have to find someone who will take the part. Women too . . .

DONNA MATILDA [*hurt, but trying to hide the fact*]. Ah, women too?

LANDOLPH. Oh, yes; many at first.

BELCREDI [*laughing*]. Oh, that's great! In costume, like the Marchioness?

LANDOLPH. Oh well, you know, women of the kind that lend themselves to . . .

BELCREDI. Ah, I see! [*Perfidiously to the* MARCHIONESS.] Look out, you know he's becoming dangerous for you.

[*The second door on the right opens, and* HAROLD *appears making first of all a discreet sign that all conversation should cease.*]

HAROLD. His Majesty, the Emperor!

[*The* TWO VALETS *enter first, and go and stand on either side of the throne. Then* HENRY IV *comes in between* ORDULPH *and* HAROLD, *who keep a little in the rear respectfully.*

HENRY IV *is about 50 and very pale. The hair on the back of his head is already grey; over the temples and forehead it appears blond, owing to its having been tinted in an evident and puerile fashion. On his cheek bones he has two small, doll-like dabs of color, that stand out prominently against the rest of his tragic pallor. He is wearing a penitent's sack over his regal habit, as at Canossa. His eyes have a fixed look which is dreadful to see, and this expression is in strained contrast with the sackcloth.* ORDULPH *carries the Imperial crown;* HAROLD, *the sceptre with eagle, and the globe with the cross.*]

HENRY IV [*bowing first to* DONNA MATILDA *and afterwards to the* DOCTOR]. My lady . . . Monsignor . . . [*Then he looks at* BELCREDI *and seems about to greet him too; when, suddenly, he turns to* LANDOLPH, *who has approached him, and asks him sotto voce and with diffidence.*] Is that Peter Damiani?[14]

LANDOLPH. No, Sire. He is a monk from Cluny who is accompanying

14. Cardinal-bishop of Ostia. He had tried to compel Henry IV to take back his first wife.

the Abbot.

HENRY IV [*looks again at* BELCREDI *with increasing mistrust, and then noticing that he appears embarrassed and keeps glancing at* DONNA MATILDA *and the* DOCTOR, *stands upright and cries out*]. No, it's Peter Damiani! It's no use, father, your looking at the Duchess. [*Then turning quickly to* DONNA MATILDA *and the* DOCTOR *as though to ward off a danger.*] I swear it! I swear that my heart is changed towards your daughter. I confess that if he [*Indicates* BELCREDI.] hadn't come to forbid it in the name of Pope Alexander, I'd have repudiated her. Yes, yes, there were people ready to favour the repudiation: the Bishop of Mayence would have done it for a matter of one hundred and twenty farms. [*Looks at* LANDOLPH *a little perplexed and adds.*] But I mustn't speak ill of the bishops at this moment! [*More humbly to* BELCREDI.] I am grateful to you, believe me, I am grateful to you for the hindrance you put in my way!—God knows, my life's been all made of humiliations: my mother,[15] Adalbert, Tribur,[16] Goslar! And now this sackcloth you see me wearing! [*Changes tone suddenly and speaks like one who goes over his part in a parenthesis of astuteness.*] It doesn't matter: clarity of ideas, perspicacity, firmness and patience under adversity that's the thing. [*Then turning to all and speaking solemnly.*] I know how to make amends for the mistakes I have made; and I can humiliate myself even before you, Peter Damiani. [*Bows profoundly to him and remains curved. Then a suspicion is born in him which he is obliged to utter in menacing tones, almost against his will.*] Was it not perhaps you who started that obscene rumor that my holy mother had illicit relations with the Bishop of Augusta?

BELCREDI [*since* HENRY IV *has his finger pointed at him*]. No, no, it wasn't I . . .

HENRY IV [*straightening up*]. Not true, not true? Infamy! [*Looks at him and then adds.*] I didn't think you capable of it! [*Goes to the* DOCTOR *and plucks his sleeve, while winking at him knowingly.*] Always the same, Monsignor, those bishops, always the same!

HAROLD [*softly, whispering as if to help out the doctor*]. Yes, yes, the rapacious bishops!

THE DOCTOR [*to* HAROLD, *trying to keep it up*]. Ah, yes, those fellows . . . ah yes . . .

HENRY IV. Nothing satisfies them! I was a little boy, Monsignor . . . One passes the time, playing even, when, without knowing it, one is a king.—I was six years old; and they tore me away from my mother, and made use of me against her without my knowing anything about it . . . always profaning, always stealing, stealing! . . . One greedier than the other . . . Hanno[17] worse than Stephen![18] Stephen worse than Hanno!

15. She had served as his first regent.

16. There Henry had been forced by the nobles and clergy of Saxony to seek Pope Gregory's pardon.

17. Archbishop of Cologne, Henry's second regent.

18. Probably Pope Stephen IX.

LANDOLPH [*sotto voce, persuasively, to call his attention*]. Majesty!

HENRY IV [*turning round quickly*]. Ah yes . . . this isn't the moment to speak ill of the bishops. But this infamy against my mother, Monsignor, is too much. [*Looks at the* MARCHIONESS *and grows tender.*] And I can't even weep for her, Lady . . . I appeal to you who have a mother's heart! She came here to see me from her convent a month ago . . . They had told me she was dead! [*Sustained pause full of feeling. Then smiling sadly.*] I can't weep for her; because if you are here now, and I am like this [*Shows the sackcloth he is wearing.*] it means I am twenty-six years old!

HAROLD. And that she is therefore alive, Majesty! . . .

ORDULPH. Still in her convent!

HENRY IV [*looking at them*]. Ah yes! And I can postpone my grief to another time. [*Shows the* MARCHIONESS *almost with coquetry the tint he has given to his hair.*] Look! I am still fair . . . [*Then slowly as if in confidence.*] For you . . . there's no need! But little exterior details do help! A matter of time, Monsignor, do you understand me? [*Turns to the* MARCHIONESS *and notices her hair.*] Ah, but I see that you too, Duchess . . . Italian, eh? [*As much as to say "false"; but without any indignation, indeed rather with malicious admiration.*] Heaven forbid that I should show disgust or surprise! Nobody cares to recognize that obscure and fatal power which sets limits to our will. But I say, if one is born and one dies . . . Did you want to be born, Monsignor? I didn't! And in both cases, independently of our wills, so many things happen we would wish didn't happen, and to which we resign ourselves as best we can! . . .

DOCTOR [*merely to make a remark, while studying* HENRY IV *carefully*]. Alas! Yes, alas!

HENRY IV. It's like this: When we are not resigned, out come our desires. A woman wants to be a man . . . an old man would be young again. Desires, ridiculous fixed ideas of course—But reflect! Monsignor, those other desires are not less ridiculous: I mean, those desires where the will is kept within the limits of the possible. Not one of us can lie or pretend. We're all fixed in good faith in a certain concept of ourselves. However, Monsignor, while you keep yourself in order, holding on with both your hands to your holy habit, there slips down from your sleeves, there peels off from you like . . . like a serpent . . . something you don't notice: life, Monsignor! [*Turns to the* MARCHIONESS.] Has it never happened to you, my Lady, to find a different self in yourself? Have you always been the same? My God! One day . . . how was it, how was it you were able to commit this or that action? [*Fixes her so intently in the eyes as almost to make her blanch.*] Yes, that particular action, that very one: we understand each other! But don't be afraid: I shall reveal it to none. And you, Peter Damiani, how could you be a friend of that man? . . .

LANDOLPH. Majesty!

HENRY IV [*at once*]. No, I won't name him! [*Turning to* BELCREDI.] What did you think of him? But we all of us cling tight to our conceptions of ourselves, just as he who is growing old dyes his hair. What does it matter that this dyed hair of mine isn't a reality for you, if it *is*, to some extent, for me?—you, you, my Lady, certainly don't dye your hair to deceive the others, nor even yourself; but only to cheat your own image a little before the looking-glass. I do it for a joke! You do it seriously! But I assure you that you too, Madam, are in masquerade, though it be in all seriousness; and I am not speaking of the venerable crown on your brows or the ducal mantle. I am speaking only of the memory you wish to fix in yourself of your fair complexion one day when it pleased you—or of your dark complexion, if you were dark: the fading image of your youth! For you, Peter Damiani, on the contrary, the memory of what you have been, of what you have done, seems to you a recognition of past realities that remain within you like a dream. I'm in the same case too: with so many inexplicable memories—like dreams! Ah! . . . There's nothing to marvel at in it, Peter Damiani! Tomorrow it will be the same thing with our life of today! [*Suddenly getting excited and taking hold of his sackcloth.*] This sackcloth here . . . [*Beginning to take it off with a gesture of almost ferocious joy while the* THREE VALETS *run over to him, frightened, as if to prevent his doing so.*] Ah, my God! [*Draws back and throws off sackcloth.*] Tomorrow, at Bressanone, twenty-seven German and Lombard bishops will sign with me the act of deposition of Gregory VII! No Pope at all! Just a false monk!

ORDULPH [*with the other three*]. Majesty! Majesty! In God's name! . . .

HAROLD [*inviting him to put on the sackcloth again*]. Listen to what he says, Majesty!

LANDOLPH. Monsignor is here with the Duchess to intercede in your favor. [*Makes secret signs to the* DOCTOR *to say something at once.*]

DOCTOR [*foolishly*]. Ah yes . . . yes . . . we are here to intercede . . .

HENRY IV [*repenting at once, almost terrified, allowing the three to put on the sackcloth again, and pulling it down over him with his own hands*]. Pardon . . . yes . . . yes . . . pardon, Monsignor: forgive me, my Lady . . . I swear to you I feel the whole weight of the anathema. [*Bends himself, takes his face between his hands, as though waiting for something to crush him. Then changing tone, but without moving, says softly to* LANDOLPH, HAROLD *and* ORDULPH.] But I don't know why I cannot be humble before that man there! [*Indicates* BELCREDI.]

LANDOLPH [*sotto voce*]. But why, Majesty, do you insist on believing he is Peter Damiani, when he isn't, at all?

HENRY IV [*looking at him timorously*]. He isn't Peter Damiani?

HAROLD. No, no, he is a poor monk, Majesty.

HENRY IV [*sadly with a touch of exasperation*]. Ah! None of us can estimate what we do when we do it from instinct . . . You perhaps, Madam, can understand me better than the others, since you are a woman and a Duchess. This is a solemn and decisive moment. I could, you know, accept the assistance of the Lombard bishops, arrest the Pope, lock him up here in the castle, run to Rome and elect an anti-Pope; offer alliance to Robert Guiscard[19]—and Gregory VII would be lost! I resist the temptation; and, believe me, I am wise in doing so. I feel the atmosphere of our times and the majesty of one who knows how to be what he ought to be! a Pope! Do you feel inclined to laugh at me, seeing me like this? You would be foolish to do so; for you don't understand the political wisdom which makes this penitent's sack advisable. The parts may be changed tomorrow. What would you do then? Would you laugh to see the Pope a prisoner? No! It would come to the same thing: I dressed as a penitent, today; he, as prisoner tomorrow! But woe to him who doesn't know how to wear his mask, be he king or Pope!—Perhaps he is a bit too cruel! No! Yes, yes, maybe!—You remember, my Lady, how your daughter Bertha, for whom, I repeat, my feelings have changed [*Turns to* BELCREDI *and shouts to his face as if he were being contradicted by him.*]—Yes, changed on account of the affection and devotion she showed me in that terrible moment . . . [*Then once again to the* MARCHIONESS.] . . . you remember how she came with me, my Lady, followed me like a beggar and passed two nights out in the open, in the snow?[20] You are her mother! Doesn't this touch your mother's heart? Doesn't this urge you to pity, so that you will beg His Holiness for pardon, beg him to receive us?

DONNA MATILDA [*trembling, with feeble voice*]. Yes, yes, at once . . .

DOCTOR. It shall be done!

HENRY IV. And one thing more! [*Draws them in to listen to him.*] It isn't enough that he should receive me! You know he can do *everything—everything*. I tell you! He can even call up the dead. [*Touches his chest.*] Behold me! Do you see me? There is no magic art unknown to him. Well, Monsignor, my Lady, my torment is really this: that whether here or there [*Pointing to his portrait almost in fear.*] I can't free myself from this magic. I am a penitent now, you see; and I swear to you I shall remain so until he receives me. But you two, when the excommunication is taken off, must ask the Pope to do this thing he can so easily do: to take me away from that; [*Indicating the portrait again.*] and let me live wholly and freely my miserable life. A man can't always be twenty-six, my Lady. I ask this of you for your daughter's sake too; that I may love her as she deserves to be loved, well disposed as I am now, all tender towards her for her pity. There: it's all there! I am in your hands! [*Bows.*] My Lady! Monsignor!

[*He goes off, bowing grandly, through the door by which he entered, leaving everyone stupefied, and the* MARCHIONESS *so profoundly touched, that no sooner has he gone than she breaks out into sobs and sits down almost fainting.*]

CURTAIN

19. A Norman prince, allied with Gregory VII.

20. Outside the castle of Canossa, in 1077.

Act II

Another room of the villa, adjoining the throne room. Its furniture is antique and severe. Principal exit at rear in the background. To the left, two windows looking on the garden. To the right, a door opening into the throne room.

Late afternoon of the same day.

DONNA MATILDA, *the* DOCTOR *and* BELCREDI *are on the stage engaged in conversation; but* DONNA MATILDA *stands to one side, evidently annoyed at what the other two are saying; although she cannot help listening, because, in her agitated state, everything interests her in spite of herself. The talk of the other two attracts her attention, because she instinctively feels the need for calm at the moment.*

BELCREDI. It may be as you say, Doctor, but that was my impression.

DOCTOR. I won't contradict you; but, believe me, it is only . . . an impression.

BELCREDI. Pardon me, but he even said so, and quite clearly [*Turning to the* MARCHIONESS.] Didn't he, Marchioness?

DONNA MATILDA [*turning round*]. What did he say? . . . [*Then not agreeing.*] Oh yes . . . but not for the reason you think!

DOCTOR. He was alluding to the costumes we had slipped on . . . Your cloak [*Indicating the* MARCHIONESS.] our Benedictine habits . . . But all this is childish!

DONNA MATILDA [*turning quickly, indignant*]. Childish? What do you mean, Doctor?

DOCTOR. From one point of view, it is—I beg you to let me say so, Marchioness! Yet, on the other hand, it is much more complicated than you can imagine.

DONNA MATILDA. To me, on the contrary, it is perfectly clear!

DOCTOR [*with a smile of pity of the competent person towards those who do not understand*]. We must take into account the peculiar psychology of madmen; which, you must know, enables us to be certain that they observe things and can, for instance, easily detect people who are disguised; can in fact recognize the disguise and yet believe in it; just as children do, for whom disguise is both play and reality. That is why I used the word childish. But the thing is extremely complicated, inasmuch as he must be perfectly aware of being an image to himself and for himself—that image there, in fact! [*Alluding to the portrait in the throne room, and pointing to the left.*]

BELCREDI. That's what he said!

DOCTOR. Very well then— An image before which other images, ours, have appeared: understand? Now he, in his acute and perfectly lucid delirium, was able to detect at once a difference between his image and ours: that is, he saw that ours were make-believes. So he suspected us; because all madmen are armed with a special diffidence. But that's all there is to it! Our make-believe, built up all round his, did not seem pitiful to him. While his seemed all the more tragic to us, in that he, as if in defiance—understand?—and induced by his suspicion, wanted to show us up merely as a joke. That was also partly the case with him, in coming before us with painted cheeks and hair, and saying he had done it on purpose for a jest.

DONNA MATILDA [*impatiently*]. No, it's not that, Doctor. It's not like that! It's not like that!

DOCTOR. Why isn't it, may I ask?

DONNA MATILDA [*with decision but trembling*]. I am perfectly certain he recognized me!

DOCTOR. It's not possible . . . it's not possible!

BELCREDI [*at the same time*]. Of course not!

DONNA MATILDA [*more than ever determined, almost convulsively*]. I tell you, he recognized me! When he came close up to speak to me—looking in my eyes, right into my eyes—he recognized me!

BELCREDI. But he was talking of your daughter!

DONNA MATILDA. That's not true! He was talking of me! Of me!

BELCREDI. Yes, perhaps, when he said . . .

DONNA MATILDA [*letting herself go*]. About my dyed hair! But didn't you notice that he added at once: "or the memory of your dark hair, if you were dark"? He remembered perfectly well that I was dark—then!

BELCREDI. Nonsense! nonsense!

DONNA MATILDA [*not listeng to him, turning to the* DOCTOR]. My hair, Doctor, is really dark—like my daughter's! That's why he spoke of her.

BELCREDI. But he doesn't even know your daughter! He's never seen her!

DONNA MATILDA. Exactly! Oh, you never understand anything! By my daughter, stupid, he meant me—as I was then!

BELCREDI. Oh, this is catching! This is catching, this madness!

DONNA MATILDA [*softly, with contempt*]. Fool!

BELCREDI. Excuse me, were you ever his wife? Your daughter is his wife—in his delirium: Bertha of Susa.

DONNA MATILDA. Exactly! Because I, no longer dark—as he remembered me—but *fair*, introduced myself as "Adelaide," the mother. My daughter doesn't exist for him: he's never seen her—you said so yourself! So how can he know whether she's fair or dark?

BELCREDI. But he said dark, speaking generally, just as anyone who wants to recall, whether fair or dark, a memory of youth in the color of the hair! And you, as usual, begin to imagine things! Doctor, you said I ought not to have come! It's she who ought not to have come!

DONNA MATILDA [*upset for a moment by* BELCREDI'S *remark, recovers herself. Then with a touch of anger, because doubtful*]. No, no . . . he spoke of me . . . He spoke all the time to me, with me, of me . . .

BELCREDI. That's not bad! He didn't leave me a moment's breathing space and you say he was talking all the time to you? Unless you think he was alluding to you too, when he was talking to Peter Damiani!

DONNA MATILDA [*defiantly, almost exceeding the limits of courteous discussion*]. Who knows? Can you tell me why, from the outset, he showed a strong dislike for you, for you alone? [*From the tone of the question, the expected answer must almost explicitly be: "because he understands you are my lover."* BELCREDI *feels this so well that he remains silent and can say nothing.*]

DOCTOR. The reason may also be found in the fact that only the visit of the Duchess Adelaide and the Abbot of Cluny was announced to him. Finding a third person present, who had not been announced, at once his suspicions . . .

BELCREDI. Yes, exactly! His suspicion made him see an enemy in me: Peter Damiani! But she's got it into her head, that he recognized her . . .

DONNA MATILDA. There's no doubt about it! I could see it from his eyes, doctor. You know, there's a way of looking that leaves no doubt whatever . . . Perhaps it was only for an instant, but I am sure!

DOCTOR. It is not impossible: a lucid moment . . .

DONNA MATILDA. Yes, perhaps . . . And then his speech seemed to me full of regret for his and my youth—for the horrible thing that happened to him, that has held him in that disguise from which he has never been able to free himself, and from which he longs to be free—he said so himself!

BELCREDI. Yes, so as to be able to make love to your daughter, or you, as you believe—having been touched by your pity.

DONNA MATILDA. Which is very great, I would ask you to believe.

BELCREDI. As one can see, Marchioness; so much so that a miracle-worker might expect a miracle from it!

DOCTOR. Will you let me speak? I don't work miracles, because I am a doctor and not a miracle-worker. I listened very intently to all he said; and I repeat that that certain analogical elasticity, common to all systematized delirium, is evidently with him much . . . what shall I say?—much relaxed! The elements, that is, of his delirium no longer hold together. It seems to me he has lost the equilibrium of his second personality and sudden recollections drag him—and this is very comforting—not from a state of incipient apathy, but rather from a morbid inclination to reflective melancholy, which shows a . . . a very considerable cerebral activity. Very comforting, I repeat! Now if, by this violent trick we've planned . . .

DONNA MATILDA [*turning to the window, in the tone of a sick person complaining*]. But how is it that the motor has not returned? It's three hours and a half since . . .

DOCTOR. What do you say?

DONNA MATILDA. The motor, Doctor! It's more than three hours and a half . . .

DOCTOR [*taking out his watch and looking at it*]. Yes, more than four hours, by this!

DONNA MATILDA. It could have reached here an hour ago at least! But, as usual . . .

BELCREDI. Perhaps they can't find the dress . . .

DONNA MATILDA. But I explained exactly where it was! [*Impatiently.*] And Frida . . . where is Frida?

BELCREDI [*looking out of the window*]. Perhaps she is in the garden with Charles . . .

DOCTOR. He'll talk her out of her fright.

BELCREDI. She's not afraid, Doctor; don't you believe it: the thing bores her rather . . .

DONNA MATILDA. Just don't ask anything of her! I know what she's like.

DOCTOR. Let's wait patiently. Anyhow, it will soon be over, and it has to be in the evening . . . It will only be the matter of a moment! If we can succeed in rousing him, as I was saying, and in breaking at one go the threads—already slack—which still bind him to this fiction of his, giving him back what he himself asks for—you remember, he said: "one cannot always be twenty-six years old, madam!" if we can give him freedom from this torment, which even *he* feels is a torment, then if he is able to recover at one bound the sensation of the distance of time . . .

BELCREDI [*quickly*]. He'll be cured! [*Then emphatically with irony.*] We'll pull him out of it all!

DOCTOR. Yes, we may hope to set him going again, like a watch which has stopped at a certain hour . . . just as if we had our watches in our hands and were waiting for that other watch to go again.—A shake—so—and let's hope it'll tell the time again after its long stop. [*At this point the* MARQUIS CHARLES DI NOLLI *enters from the principal entrance.*]

DONNA MATILDA. Oh, Charles! . . . And Frida? Where is she?

DI NOLLI. She'll be here in a moment.

DOCTOR. Has the motor arrived?

DI NOLLI. Yes.

DONNA MATILDA. Yes? Has the dress come?

DI NOLLI. It's been here some time.

DOCTOR. Good! Good!

DONNA MATILDA [*trembling*]. Where is she? Where's Frida?

DI NOLLI [*shrugging his shoulders and smiling sadly, like one lending himself unwillingly to an untimely joke*]. You'll see, you'll see! . . . [*Pointing towards the hall.*] Here she is! . . . [BERTHOLD *appears at the threshold of the hall, and announces with solemnity.*]

BERTHOLD. Her Highness the Countess Matilda of Canossa! [FRIDA *enters, magnificent and beautiful, arrayed in the robes of her mother as "Countless Matilda of Tuscany," so that she is a living copy of the portrait in the throne room.*]

FRIDA [*passing* BERTHOLD, *who is bowing, says to him with disdain*]. Of Tuscany, of Tuscany! Canossa is just one of my castles!

BELCREDI [*in admiration*]. Look! Look! She seems another person . . .

DONNA MATILDA. One would say it were I! Look!—Why, Frida, look! She's exactly my portrait, alive!

DOCTOR. Yes, yes . . . Perfect! Perfect! The portrait, to the life.

BELCREDI. Yes, there's no question about it. She *is* the portrait! Magnificent!

FRIDA. Don't make me laugh, or I shall burst! I say, mother, what a tiny waist you had? I had to squeeze so to get into this!

DONNA MATILDA [*arranging her dress a little*]. Wait! . . . Keep still! . . . These pleats . . . is it really so tight?

FRIDA. I'm suffocating! I implore you, to be quick! . . .

DOCTOR. But we must wait till it's evening!

FRIDA. No, no, I can't hold out till evening!

DONNA MATILDA. Why did you put it on so soon?

FRIDA. The moment I saw it, the temptation was irresistible . . .

DONNA MATILDA. At least you could have called me, or have had someone help you! It's still all crumpled.

FRIDA. So I saw, mother; but they are old creases; they won't come out.

DOCTOR. It doesn't matter, Marchioness! The illusion is perfect. [*Then coming nearer and asking her to come in front of her daughter, without hiding her.*] If you please, stay there, there . . . at a certain distance . . . now a little more forward . . .

BELCREDI. For the feeling of the distance of time . . .

DONNA MATILDA [*slightly turning to him*]. Twenty years after! A disaster! A tragedy!

BELCREDI. Now don't let's exaggerate!

DOCTOR [*embarrassed, trying to save the situation*]. No, no! I meant the dress . . . so as to see . . . You know . . .

BELCREDI [*laughing*]. Oh, as for the dress, Doctor, it isn't a matter of twenty years! It's eight hundred! An abyss! Do you really want to shove him across it [*Pointing first to* FRIDA *and then to* MARCHIONESS.] from there to here? But you'll have to pick him up in pieces with a basket! Just think now: for us it is a matter of twenty years, a couple of dresses, and a masquerade. But, if, as you say, Doctor, time has stopped for and around him: if he lives there [*Pointing to* FRIDA.] with her, eight hundred years ago . . . I repeat: the giddiness of the jump will be such, that finding himself suddenly among us . . . [*The* DOCTOR *shakes his head in dissent.*] You don't think so?

DOCTOR. No, because life, my dear baron, can take up its rhythms. This—our life—will at once become real also to him; and will pull him up directly, wresting from him suddenly the illusion, and showing him that the eight hundred years, as you say, are only twenty! It will be like one of those tricks, such as the leap into space, for instance, of the Masonic rite, which appears to be heaven knows how far, and is only a step down the stairs.

BELCREDI. Ah! An idea! Yes! Look at Frida and the Marchioness, doctor! Which is more advanced in time? We old people, Doctor! The young ones think they are more ahead; but it isn't true: we are more ahead, because time belongs to us more than to them.

DOCTOR. If the past didn't alienate us . . .

BELCREDI. It doesn't matter at all! How does it alienate us? They [*Pointing to* FRIDA *and* DI NOLLI.] have still to do what we have accomplished, Doctor: to grow old, doing the same foolish things, more or less, as we did . . . This is the illusion: that one comes forward through a door to life. It isn't so! As soon as one is born, one starts dying; therefore, he who started first is the most advanced of all. The youngest of us is father Adam! Look there: [*Pointing to* FRIDA.] eight hundred years younger than all of us—the Countess Matilda of Tuscany. [*He makes her a deep bow*.]

DI NOLLI. I say, Tito, don't start joking.

BELCREDI. Oh, you think I am joking? . . .

DI NOLLI. Of course, of course . . . all the time.

BELCREDI. Impossible! I've even dressed up as a Benedictine . . .

DI NOLLI. Yes, but for a serious purpose.

BELCREDI. Well, exactly. If it has been serious for the others . . . for Frida, now, for instance. [*Then turning to the* DOCTOR.] I swear, Doctor, I don't yet understand what you want to do.

DOCTOR [*annoyed*]. You'll see! Let me do as I wish . . . At present you see the Marchioness still dressed as . . .

BELCREDI. Oh, she also . . . has to masquerade?

DOCTOR. Of course! of course! In another dress that's in there ready to be used when it comes into his head he sees the Countess Matilda of Canossa before him.

FRIDA [*while talking quietly to* DI NOLLI *notices the doctor's mistake*]. Of Tuscany, of Tuscany!

DOCTOR. It's all the same!

BELCREDI. Oh, I see! He'll be faced by two of them . . .

DOCTOR. Two, precisely! And then . . .

FRIDA [*calling him aside*]. Come here, doctor! Listen!

DOCTOR. Here I am! [*Goes near the two young people and pretends to give some explanations to them*.]

BELCREDI [*softly to* DONNA MATILDA]. I say, this is getting rather strong, you know!

DONNA MATILDA [*looking him firmly in the face*]. What?

BELCREDI. Does it really interest you as much as all that—to make you willing to take part in . . . ? For a woman this is simply enormous! . . .

DONNA MATILDA. Yes, for an ordinary woman.

BELCREDI. Oh, no, my dear, for all women,—in a question like this! It's an abnegation.

DONNA MATILDA. I owe it to him.

BELCREDI. Don't lie! You know well enough it's not hurting you!

DONNA MATILDA. Well, then, where does the abnegation come in?

BELCREDI. Just enough to prevent you losing caste in other people's eyes—and just enough to offend me! . . .

DONNA MATILDA. But who is worrying about you now?

DI NOLLI [*coming forward*]. It's all right. It's all right. That's what we'll do! [*Turning toward* BERTHOLD.] Here you, go and call one of those fellows!

BERTHOLD. At once! [*Exit*.]

DONNA MATILDA. But first of all we've got to pretend that we are going away.

DI NOLLI. Exactly! I'll see to that . . . [*To* BELCREDI.] you don't mind staying here?

BELCREDI [*ironically*]. Oh, no, I don't mind, I don't mind! . . .

DI NOLLI. We must look out not to make him suspicious again, you know.

BELCREDI. Oh, Lord! *He* doesn't amount to anything!

DOCTOR. He must believe absolutely that we've gone away. [LANDOLPH *followed by* BERTHOLD *enters from the right.*]

LANDOLPH. May I come in?

DI NOLLI. Come in! Come in! I say—your name's Lolo, isn't it?

LANDOLPH. Lolo, or Landolph, just as you like!

DI NOLLI. Well, look here: the Doctor and the Marchioness are leaving, at once.

LANDOLPH. Very well. All we've got to say is that they have been able to obtain the permission for the reception from His Holiness. He's in there in his own apartments repenting of all he said—and in an awful state to have the pardon! Would you mind coming a minute? . . . If you would, just for a minute . . . put on the dress again . . .

DOCTOR. Why, of course, with pleasure . . .

LANDOLPH. Might I be allowed to make a suggestion? Why not add that the Marchioness of Tuscany has interceded with the Pope that he should be received?

DONNA MATILDA. You see, he has recognized me!

LANDOLPH. Forgive me . . . I don't know my history very well. I am sure you gentlemen know it much better! But I thought it was believed that Henry IV had a secret passion for the Marchioness of Tuscany.

DONNA MATILDA [*at once*]. Nothing of the kind! Nothing of the kind!

LANDOLPH. That's what I thought! But he says he's loved her . . . he's always saying it . . . And now he fears that her indignation for this secret love of his will work him harm with the Pope.

BELCREDI. We must let him understand that this aversion no longer exists.

LANDOLPH. Exactly! Of course!

DONNA MATILDA [*to* BELCREDI]. History says—I don't know whether you know it or not—that the Pope gave way to the supplications of the Marchioness Matilda and the Abbot of Cluny. And I may say, my dear Belcredi, that I intended to take advantage of this fact—at the time of the pageant—to show him my feelings were not so hostile to him as he supposed.

BELCREDI. You are most faithful to history, Marchioness . . .

LANDOLPH. Well then, the Marchioness could spare herself a double disguise and present herself with Monsignor [*Indicating the* DOCTOR.] as the Marchioness of Tuscany.

DOCTOR [*quickly, energetically*]. No, no! That won't do at all. It would ruin everything. The impression from the conformation must be a sudden one, give a shock! No, no, Marchioness, you will appear again as the Duchess Adelaide, the mother of the Empress. And then we'll go away. This is most necessary: that he should know we've gone away. Come on! Don't let's waste any more time! There's a lot to prepare.

[*Exeunt the* DOCTOR, DONNA MATILDA, *and* LANDOLPH, *right*.]

FRIDA. I am beginning to feel afraid again.

DI NOLLI. Again, Frida?

FRIDA. It would have been better if I had seen him before.

DI NOLLI. There's nothing to be frightened of, really.

FRIDA. He isn't furious, is he?

DI NOLLI. Of course not! he's quite calm.

BELCREDI [*with ironic sentimental affectation*]. Melancholy! Didn't you hear that he loves you?

FRIDA. Thanks! That's just why I am afraid.

BELCREDI. He won't do you any harm.

DI NOLLI. It'll only last a minute . . .

FRIDA. Yes, but there in the dark with him . . .

DI NOLLI. Only for a moment; and I will be near you, and all the others behind the door ready to run in. As soon as you see your mother, your part will be finished . . .

BELCREDI. I'm afraid of a different thing: that we're wasting our time . . .

DI NOLLI. Don't begin again! The remedy seems a sound one to me.

FRIDA. I think so too! I feel it! I'm all trembling!

BELCREDI. But, mad people, my dear friends—though they don't know it, alas—have this felicity which we don't take into account . . .

DI NOLLI [*interrupting, annoyed*]. What felicity? Nonsense!

BELCREDI [*forcefully*]. They don't reason!

DI NOLLI. What's reasoning got to do with it, anyway?

BELCREDI. Don't you call it reasoning that he will have to do—according to us—when he sees her [*Indicates* FRIDA.] and her mother? We've reasoned it all out, surely!

DI NOLLI. Nothing of the kind: no reasoning at all! We put before him a double image of his own fantasy, or fiction, as the doctor says.

BELCREDI [*suddenly*]. I say, I've never understood why they take degrees in medicine.

DI NOLLI [*amazed*]. Who?

BELCREDI. The alienists!

DI NOLLI. What ought they to take degrees in, then?

FRIDA. If they are alienists, in what else should they take degrees?

BELCREDI. In law, of course! All a matter of talk! The more they talk, the more highly they are considered. "Analogous elasticity," "the sensation of distance in time!" And the first thing they tell you is that they don't work miracles—when a miracle's just what is wanted! But they know that the more they say they are not miracle-workers, the more folk believe in their seriousness!

BERTHOLD [*who has been looking through the keyhole of the door on right*]. There they are! There they are! They're coming in here.

DI NOLLI. Are they?

BERTHOLD. He wants to come with them . . . Yes! . . . He's coming too!

DI NOLLI. Let's get away, then! Let's get away, at once! [*To* BERTHOLD.] You stop here!

BERTHOLD. Must I?

[*Without answering him,* DI NOLLI, FRIDA, *and* BELCREDI *go out by the main exit, leaving* BERTHOLD *surprised. The door on the right opens, and* LANDOLPH *enters first, bowing. Then* DONNA MATILDA *comes in, with mantle and ducal crown as in the first act; also the* DOCTOR *as the* ABBOT OF CLUNY. HENRY IV *is among them in royal dress.* ORDULPH *and* HAROLD *enter last of all.*]

HENRY IV [*following up what he has been saying in the other room*]. And now I will ask you a question: how can I be astute, if you think me obstinate?

DOCTOR. No, no, not obstinate!

HENRY IV [*smiling, pleased*]. Then you think me really astute?

DOCTOR. No, no, neither obstinate, nor astute.

HENRY IV [*with benevolent irony*]. Monsignor, if obstinacy is not a vice which can go with astuteness, I hoped that in denying me the former, you would at least allow me a little of the latter. I can assure you I have great need of it. But if you want to keep it all for yourself . . .

DOCTOR. I? I? Do I seem astute to you?

HENRY IV. No. Monsignor! What do you say? Not in the least! Perhaps in this case, I may seem a little obstinate to you [*Cutting short to speak to* DONNA MATILDA.] With your permission: a word in confidence to the Duchess. [*Leads her aside and asks her very earnestly.*] Is your daughter really dear to you?

DONNA MATILDA [*dismayed*]. Why, yes, certainly . . .

HENRY IV. Do you wish me to compensate her with all my love, with all my devotion, for the grave wrongs I have done her—though you must not believe all the stories my enemies tell about my dissoluteness!

DONNA MATILDA. No, no, I don't believe them. I never have believed such stories.

HENRY IV. Well, then are you willing?

DONNA MATILDA [*confused*]. What?

HENRY IV. That I return to love your daughter again? [*Looks at her and adds, in a mysterious tone of warning.*] You mustn't be a friend of the Marchioness of Tuscany!

DONNA MATILDA. I tell you again that she has begged and tried not less than ourselves to obtain your pardon . . .

HENRY IV [*softly, but excitedly*]. Don't tell me that! Don't say that to me! Don't you see the effect it has on me, my Lady?

DONNA MATILDA [*looks a him; then very softly as if in confidence*]. You love her still?

HENRY IV [*puzzled*]. Still? Still, you say? You know, then? But nobody knows! Nobody must know!

DONNA MATILDA. But perhaps she knows, if she has begged so hard for you!

HENRY IV [*looks at her and says*]. And you love your daughter? [*Brief pause. He turns to the* DOCTOR *with laughing accents.*] Ah, Monsignor, it's strange how little I think of my wife! It may be a sin, but I swear to you that I hardly feel her at all in my heart. What is stranger is that her own mother scarcely feels her in her heart. Confess, my Lady, that she amounts to very little for you. [*Turning to* DOCTOR.] She talks to me of that other woman, insistently, insistently, I don't know why! . . .

LANDOLPH [*humbly*]. Maybe, Majesty, it is to disabuse you of some ideas you have had about the Marchioness of Tuscany. [*Then, dismayed at having allowed himself this observation, adds.*] I mean just now, of course . . .

HENRY IV. You too maintain that she has been friendly to me?

LANDOLPH. Yes, at the moment, Majesty.

DONNA MATILDA. Exactly! Exactly! . . .

HENRY IV. I understand. That is to say, you don't believe I love her. I see! I see! Nobody's ever believed it, nobody's ever thought it. Better so, then! But enough, enough! [*Turns to the* DOCTOR *with changed expression.*] Monsignor, you see? The reasons the Pope has had for revoking the excommunication have got nothing at all to do with the reasons for which he excommunicated me originally. Tell Pope Gregory we shall meet again at Brixen. And you, Madame, should you chance to meet your daughter in the courtyard of the castle of your friend the Marchioness, ask her to visit me. We shall see if I succeed in keeping her close beside me as wife and Empress. Many women have presented themselves here already assuring me that they were she. And I thought to have her—yes, I tried sometimes—there's no shame in it, with one's wife!—But when they said they were Bertha, and they were from Susa, all of them—I can't think why—started laughing! [*Confidentially.*] Understand?—in bed—I undressed—so did she—yes, by God, undressed—a man and a woman—it's natural after all! Like that, we don't bother much about who we are. And one's dress is like a phantom that hovers always near one. Oh, Monsignor, phantoms in general are nothing more than trifling disorders of the spirit: images we cannot contain within the bounds of sleep. They reveal themselves even when we are awake, and they frighten us. I . . . ah . . . I am always afraid when, at night time, I see disordered images before me. Sometimes I am even afraid of my own blood pulsing loudly in my arteries in the silence of night, like the sound of a distant step in a lonely corridor! . . . But, forgive me! I have kept you standing too long already. I thank you, my Lady, I thank you, Monsignor. [DONNA MATILDA *and the* DOCTOR *go off bowing. As soon as they have gone,* HENRY IV *suddenly changes his tone.*] Buffoons, buffoons! One can play any tune on them! And that other fellow . . . Pietro Damiani! . . . Caught him out perfectly! He's afraid to appear before me again. [*Moves up and down excitedly while saying this; then sees* BER-

THOLD, *and points him out to the other three valets.*] Oh, look at this imbecile watching me with his mouth wide open! [*Shakes him.*] Don't you understand? Don't you see, idiot, how I treat them, how I play the fool with them, make them appear before me just as I wish? Miserable, frightened clowns that they are! And you [*Addressing the* VALETS.] are amazed that I tear off their ridiculous masks now, just as if it wasn't I who had made them mask themselves to satisfy this taste of mine for playing the madman!

LANDOLPH — HAROLD — ORDULPH [*bewildered, looking at one another*]. What? What does he say? What?

HENRY IV [*answers them imperiously*]. Enough! enough! Let's stop it. I'm tired of it. [*Then as if the thought left him no peace.*] By God! The impudence! To come here along with her lover! . . . And pretending to do it out of pity? So as not to infuriate a poor devil already out of the world, out of time, out of life! If it hadn't been supposed to be done out of pity, one can well imagine that fellow wouldn't have allowed it. Those people expect others to behave as they wish all the time. And, of course, there's nothing arrogant in that! Oh, no! Oh, no! It's merely their way of thinking, of feeling, of seeing. Everybody has his own way of thinking; you fellows, too. Yours is that of a flock of sheep—miserable, feeble, uncertain . . . But those others take advantage of this and make you accept their way of thinking; or, at least, they suppose they do; because, after all, what do they succeed in imposing on you? Words, words which anyone can interpret in his own manner! That's the way public opinion is formed! And it's a bad look out for a man who finds himself labelled one day with one of these words which everyone repeats; for example "madman," or "imbecile." Don't you think it is rather hard for a man to keep quiet, when he knows that there is a fellow going about trying to persuade everybody that he is as he sees him, trying to fix him in other people's opinion as a "madman"—according to him? Now I am talking seriously! Before I hurt my head, falling from my horse . . . [*Stops suddenly, noticing the dismay of the four young men.*] What's the matter with you? [*Imitates their amazed looks.*] What? Am I, or am I not, mad? Oh, yes! I'm mad all right! [*He becomes terrible.*] Well, then, by God, down on your knees, down on your knees! [*Makes them go down on their knees one by one.*] I order you to go down on your knees before me! And touch the ground three times with your foreheads! Down, down! That's the way you've got to be before madmen! [*Then annoyed with their facile humiliation.*] Get up, sheep! You obeyed me, didn't you? You might have put the strait jacket on me! . . . Crush a man with the weight of a word—it's nothing—a fly! all our life is crushed by the weight of words: the weight of the dead. Look at me here: can you really suppose that Henry IV is still alive? All the same, I speak, and order you live men about! Do you think it's a joke that the dead continue to live?—Yes, *here* it's a joke! But get out into the live world!—Ah, you say: what a beautiful sunrise—for us! All time is before us!—Dawn! We will do what we like with this day—.

Ah, yes! To Hell with tradition, the old conventions! Well, go on! You will do nothing but repeat the old, old words, while you imagine you are living! [*Goes up to* BERTHOLD *who has now become quite stupid*] You don't understand a word of this do you? What's your name?

BERTHOLD. I? . . . What? . . . Berthold . . .

HENRY IV. Poor Berthold! What's your name here?

BERTHOLD. I . . . I . . . my name is Fino.

HENRY IV [*feeling the warning and critical glances of the others, turns to them to reduce them to silence*]. Fino?

BERTHOLD. Fino Pagliuca, sire.

HENRY IV [*turning to* LANDOLPH]. I've heard you call each other by your nick-names often enough! Your name is Lolo isn't it?

LANDOLPH. Yes, sire . . . [*Then with a sense of immense joy.*] Oh Lord! Oh Lord! Then he is not mad . . .

HENRY IV [*brusquely*]. What?

LANDOLPH [*hesitating*]. No . . . I said . . .

HENRY IV. Not mad, any more. No. Don't you see? We're having a joke on those that think I am mad! [*To* HAROLD.] I say, boy, your name's Franco . . . [*To* ORDULPH] And yours . . .

ORDULPH. Momo.

HENRY IV. Momo, Momo . . . A nice name that!

LANDOLPH. So he isn't . . .

HENRY IV. What are you talking about? Of course not! Let's have a jolly, good laugh! . . . [*Laughs.*] Ah! . . . Ah! . . . Ah! . . .

LANDOLPH — HAROLD — ORDULPH [*looking at each other half happy and half dismayed*]. Then he's cured! . . . he's all right! . . .

HENRY IV. Silence! Silence! . . . [*To* BERTHOLD.] Why don't you laugh? Are you offended? I didn't mean it especially for you. It's convenient for everybody to insist that certain people are mad, so they can be shut up. Do you know why? Because it's impossible to hear them speak! What shall I say of these people who've just gone away? That one is a whore, another a libertine, another a swindler . . . don't you think so? You can't believe a word he says . . . don't you think so?—By the way, they all listen to me terrified. And why are they terrified, if what I say isn't true? Of course, you can't believe what madmen say—yet, at the same time, they stand there with their eyes wide open with terror!—Why? Tell me, tell me, why?—You see I'm quite calm now!

BERTHOLD. But perhaps, they think that . . .

HENRY IV. No, no, my dear fellow! Look me well in the eyes! . . . I don't say that it's true—nothing is true, Berthold! But . . . look me in the eyes!

BERTHOLD. Well . . .

HENRY IV. You see? You see? . . . You have terror in your own eyes now because I seem mad to you! There's the proof of it! [*Laughs.*]

LANDOLPH [*coming forward in the name of the others, exasperated*]. What proof?

HENRY IV. Your being so dismayed because now I seem again mad to you. You have thought me mad up to now, haven't you? You feel that this dismay of yours can become terror too—something to dash away the ground from under your feet and deprive you of the air you breathe! Do you know what it means to find yourselves face to face with a madman—with one who shakes the foundations of all you have built up in yourselves, your logic, the logic of all your constructions? Madmen, lucky folk! construct without logic, or rather with a logic that flies like a feather. Voluble! Voluble! Today like this and tomorrow—who knows? You say: "This cannot be"; but for them everything can be. You say: "This isn't true!" And why? Because it doesn't seem true to you, or you, or you . . . [*Indicates the three of them in succession.*] . . . and to a hundred thousand others! One must see what seems true to these hundred thousand others who are not supposed to be mad! What a magnificent spectacle they afford, when they reason! What flowers of logic they scatter! I know that when I was a child, I thought the moon in the pond was real. How many things I thought real! I believed everything I was told—and I was happy! Because it's a terrible thing if you don't hold on to that which seems true to you today—to that which will seem true to you tomorrow, even if it is the opposite of that which seemed true to you yesterday. I would never wish you to think, as I have done, on this horrible thing which really drives one mad: that if you were beside another and looking into his eyes—as I one day looked into somebody's eyes—you might as well be a beggar before a door never to be opened to you; for he who does enter there will never be you, but someone unknown to you with his own different and impenetrable world . . . [*Long pause. Darkness gathers in the room, increasing the sense of strangeness and consternation in which the four young men are involved.* HENRY IV *remains aloof, pondering on the misery which is not only his, but everybody's. Then he pulls himself up, and says in an ordinary tone.*] It's getting dark here . . .

ORDULPH. Shall I go for a lamp?

HENRY IV [*ironically*]. The lamp, yes the lamp! . . . Do you suppose I don't know that as soon as I turn my back with my oil lamp to go to bed, you turn on the electric light for yourselves, here, and even there, in the throne room? I pretend not to see it!

ORDULPH. Well, then, shall I turn it on now?

HENRY IV. No, it would blind me! I want my lamp!

ORDULPH. It's ready here behind the door. [*Goes to the main exit, opens the door, goes out for a moment, and returns with an ancient lamp which is held by a ring at the top.*]

HENRY IV. Ah, a little light! Sit there around the table, no, not like that; in an elegant, easy, manner! . . . [*To* HAROLD.] Yes, you, like that! [*Poses him.*] [*Then to* BERTHOLD.] You, so! . . . and I, here! [*Sits opposite them.*] We could do with a little decorative moonlight. It's very useful for us, the moonlight. I feel a real necessity for it, and pass a lot of time looking up at the moon from my window. Who would think, to look at her that she knows that eight hundred years have passed, and that I, seated at the window, cannot really be Henry IV gazing at the moon like any poor devil? But, look, look! See what a magnificent night scene we have here: the emperor surrounded by his faithful counsellors! . . . How do you like it?

LANDOLPH [*softly to* HAROLD, *so as not to break the enchantment*]. And to think it wasn't true!

HENRY IV. True? What wasn't true?

LANDOLPH [*timidly as if to excuse himself*]. No . . . I mean . . . I was saying this morning to him [*Indicates* BERTHOLD.]—he has just entered on service here—I was saying: what a pity that dressed like this and with so many beautiful costumes in the wardrobe . . . and with a room like that . . . [*Indicates the throne room.*]

HENRY IV. Well? what's the pity?

LANDOLPH. Well . . . that we didn't know . . .

HENRY IV. That it was all done in jest, this comedy?

LANDOLPH. Because we thought that . . .

HAROLD [*coming to his assistance*]. Yes . . . that it was done seriously!

HENRY IV. What do you say? Doesn't it seem serious to you?

LANDOLPH. But if you say that . . .

HENRY IV. I say that—you are fools! You ought to have known how to create a fantasy for yourselves, not to act it for me, or anyone coming to see me; but naturally, simply, day by day, before nobody, feeling yourselves alive in the history of the eleventh century, here at the court of your emperor, Henry IV! You, Ordulph [*Taking him by the arm.*], alive in the castle of Goslar, waking up in the morning, getting out of bed, and entering straightway into the dream, clothing yourself in the dream that would be no more a dream, because you would have lived it, felt it all alive in you. You would have drunk it in with the air you breathed; yet knowing all the time that it was a dream, so you could better enjoy the privilege afforded you of having to do nothing else but live this dream, this far off and yet actual dream! And to think that at a distance of eight centuries from this remote age of ours, so colored and so sepulchral, the men of the twentieth century are torturing themselves in ceaseless anxiety to know how their fates and fortunes will work out! Whereas you are already in history with me . . .

LANDOLPH. Yes, yes, very good!

HENRY IV. . . . Everything determined, everything settled!

ORDULPH. Yes, yes!

HENRY IV. And sad as is my lot, hideous as some of the events are, bitter the struggles and troublous the time—still all history! All history that cannot change, understand? All fixed for ever! And you could have admired at your ease how every effect followed obediently its cause with perfect logic, how every event took place precisely and coherently in each minute particular! The pleasure, the pleasure of history, in fact, which is so great, was yours.

LANDOLPH. Beautiful, beautiful!

HENRY IV. Beautiful, but it's finished! Now that you know, I could not do it any more! [*Takes his lamp to go to bed.*] Neither could you, if up to now you haven't understood the reason of it! I am sick of it now. [*Almost to himself with violent contained rage.*] By God, I'll make her sorry she came here! Dressed herself up as a mother-in-law for me . . . ! And he as an abbot . . . ! And they bring a doctor with them to study me . . . ! Who knows if they don't hope to cure me? . . . Clowns . . . ! I'd like to smack one of them at least in the face: yes, that one—a famous swordsman, they say! . . . He'll kill me . . . Well, we'll see, we'll see! . . . [*A knock at the door.*] Who is it?

THE VOICE OF JOHN. Deo Gratias!

HAROLD [*very pleased at the chance for another joke*]. Oh, it's John, it's old John, who comes every night to play the monk.

ORDULPH [*rubbing his hands*]. Yes, yes! Let's make him do it!

HENRY IV [*at once, severely*]. Fool, why? Just to play a joke on a poor old man who does it for love of me?

LANDOLPH [*to* ORDULPH]. It has to be as if it were true.

HENRY IV. Exactly, as if true! Because, only so, truth is not a jest [*Opens the door and admits* JOHN *dressed as a humble friar with a roll of parchment under his arm.*] Come in, come in, father! [*Then assuming a tone of tragic gravity and deep resentment.*] All the documents of my life and reign favorable to me were destroyed deliberately by my enemies. One only has escaped destruction, this, my life, written by a humble monk who is devoted to me. And you would laugh at him! [*Turns affectionately to* JOHN, *and invites him to sit down at the table.*] Sit down, father, sit down! Have the lamp near you! [*Puts the lamp near him.*] Write! Write!

JOHN [*opens the parchment and prepares to write from dictation*]. I am ready, your Majesty!

HENRY IV [*dictating*]. "The decree of peace proclaimed at Mayence helped the poor and the good, while it damaged the powerful and the bad. [*Curtain begins to fall.*] It brought wealth to the former, hunger and misery to the latter . . ."

CURTAIN

Act III

The throne room so dark that the wall at the bottom is hardly seen. The canvases of the two portraits have been taken away; and, within their frames, FRIDA, *dressed as the "Marchioness of Tuscany" and* CHARLES DI NOLLI, *as "Henry IV," have taken the exact positions of the portraits.*

For a moment, after the raising of curtain, the stage is empty. Then the door on the left opens; and HENRY IV, *holding the lamp by the ring on top of it, enters. He looks back to speak to the four young men, who, with* JOHN, *are presumedly in the adjoining hall, as at the end of the second act.*

HENRY IV. No, stay where you are, stay where you are. I shall manage all right by myself. Good night! [*Closes the door and walks, very sad and tired, across the hall towards the second door on the right, which leads into his apartments.*]

FRIDA [*as soon as she sees that he has just passed the throne, whispers from the niche like one who is on the point of fainting away with fright*]. Henry . . .

HENRY IV [*stopping at the voice, as if someone had stabbed him traitorously in the back, turns a terror-stricken face towards the wall at the bottom of the room; raising an arm instinctively, as if to defend himself and ward off a blow*]. Who is calling me? [*It is not a question, but an exclamation vibrating with terror, which does not expect a reply from the darkness and the terrible silence of the hall, which suddenly fills him with the suspicion that he is really mad.*]

FRIDA [*at his shudder of terror, is herself not less frightened at the part she is playing, and repeats a little more loudly*]. Henry! . . . [*But, although she wishes to act the part as they have given it to her, she stretches her head a little out of frame towards the other frame.*]

HENRY IV [*gives a dreadful cry; lets the lamp fall from his hands to cover his head with his arms, and makes a movement as if to run away*].

FRIDA [*jumping from the frame on to the stand and shouting like a mad woman*]. Henry! . . . Henry! . . . I'm afraid! . . . I'm terrified! . . .

[*And while* DI NOLLI *jumps in turn on to the stand and thence to the floor and runs to* FRIDA *who, on the verge of fainting, continues to cry out, the* DOCTOR, DONNA MATILDA, *also dressed as "Matilda of Tuscany,"* TITO BELCREDI. LANDOLPH, BERTHOLD *and* JOHN *enter the hall from the doors on the right and on the left. One of them turns on the light: a strange light coming from lamps hidden in the ceiling so that only the upper part of the stage is well lighted. The others without taking notice of* HENRY IV, *who looks on astonished by the unexpected inrush, after the moment of terror which still causes him to tremble, run anxiously to support and comfort the still shaking* FRIDA, *who is moaning in the arms of her fiancé. All are speaking at the same time.*]

DI NOLLI. No, no, Frida . . . Here I am . . . I am beside you!

DOCTOR [*coming with the others*]. Enough! Enough! There's nothing more to be done! . . .

DONNA MATILDA. He is cured, Frida. Look! He is cured! Don't you see?

DI NOLLI [*astonished*]. Cured?

BELCREDI. It was only for fun! Be calm!

FRIDA. No! I am afraid! I am afraid!

DONNA MATILDA. Afraid of what? Look at him! He was never mad at all! . . .

DI NOLLI. That isn't true! What are you saying? Cured?

DOCTOR. It appears so. I should say so . . .

BELCREDI. Yes, yes! They have told us so. [*Pointing to the four young men.*]

DONNA MATILDA. Yes, for a long time! He has confided in them, told them the truth!

DI NOLLI [*now more indignant than astonished*]. But what does it mean? If, up to a short time ago . . . ?

BELCREDI. Hum! He was acting, to take you in and also us, who in good faith . . .

DI NOLLI. Is it possible? To deceive his sister, also, right up to the time of her death?

HENRY IV [*remains apart, peering at one and now at the other under the accusation and the mockery of what all believe to be a cruel joke of his, which is now revealed. He has shown by the flashing of his eyes that he is meditating a revenge, which his violent contempt prevents him from defining clearly, as yet. Stung to the quick and with a clear idea of accepting the fiction they have insidiously worked up as true, he bursts forth at this point*]. Go on, I say! Go on!

DI NOLLI [*astonished at the cry*]. Go on! What do you mean?

HENRY IV. It isn't *your* sister only that is dead!

DI NOLLI. My sister? Yours, I say, whom you compelled up to the last moment, to present herself here as your mother Agnes!

HENRY IV. And was she not *your* mother?

DI NOLLI. My mother? Certainly my mother!

HENRY IV. But your mother is dead for me, *old and far away!* You have just got down now from there. [*Pointing to the frame from which he jumped down.*] And how do you know whether I have not wept her long in secret, dressed even as I am?

DONNA MATILDA [*dismayed, looking at the others*]. What does he say? [*Much impressed, observing him.*] Quietly! quietly, for Heaven's sake!

HENRY IV. What do I say? I ask all of you if Agnes was not the mother of Henry IV? [*Turns to* FRIDA *as if she were really the "Marchioness of Tuscany."*] You, Marchioness, it seems to me, ought to know.

FRIDA [*still frightened, draws closer to* DI NOLLI]. No, no, I don't know. Not I!

DOCTOR. It's the madness returning. . . . Quiet now, everybody!

BELCREDI [*indignant*]. Madness indeed, Doctor! He's acting again! . . .

HENRY IV [*suddenly*]. I? You have emptied those two frames over there, and he stands before my eyes as Henry IV . . .

BELCREDI. We've had enough of this joke now.

HENRY IV. Who said joke?

DOCTOR [*loudly to* BELCREDI]. Don't excite him, for the love of God!

BELCREDI [*without lending an ear to him, but speaking louder*]. But they have said so [*Pointing again to the four young men.*], they, they!

HENRY IV [*turning around and looking at them*]. You? Did you say it was all a joke?

LANDOLPH [*timid and embarrassed*]. No . . . really we said that you were cured.

BELCREDI. Look here! Enough of this! [*To* DONNA MATILDA.] Doesn't it seem to you that the sight of him, [*Pointing to* DI NOLLI.] Marchioness, and that of your daughter dressed so, is becoming an intolerable puerility?

DONNA MATILDA. Oh, be quiet! What does the dress matter, if he is cured?

HENRY IV. Cured, yes! I am cured! [*To* BELCREDI.] ah, but not to let it end this way all at once, as you suppose! [*Attacks him.*] Do you know that for twenty years nobody has ever dared to appear before me here like you and that gentleman? [*Pointing to the* DOCTOR.]

BELCREDI. Of course I know it. As a matter of fact, I too appeared before you this morning dressed . . .

HENRY IV. As a monk, yes!

BELCREDI. And you took me for Peter Damiani! And I didn't even laugh, believing, in fact, that . . .

HENRY IV. That I was mad! Does it make you laugh seeing her like that, now that I am cured? And yet you might have remembered that in my eyes her appearance now . . . [*Interrupts himself with a gesture of contempt.*] Ah! [*Suddenly turns to the* DOCTOR.] You are a doctor, aren't you?

DOCTOR. Yes.

HENRY IV. And you also took part in dressing her up as the Marchioness of Tuscany? To prepare a counterjoke for me here, eh?

DONNA MATILDA [*impetuously*]. No, no! What do you say? It was done for you! I did it for your sake.

DOCTOR [*quickly*]. To attempt, to try, not knowing . . .

HENRY IV [*cutting him short.* I understand. I say counter-joke, in his case [*Indicates* BELCREDI.] because he believes that I have been carrying on a jest . . .

BELCREDI. But excuse me, what do you mean? You say yourself you are cured.

HENRY IV. Let me speak! [*To the* DOCTOR.] Do you know, Doctor, that for a moment you ran the risk of making me mad again? By God, to make the portraits speak; to make them jump alive out of their frames . . .

DOCTOR. But you saw that all of us ran in at once, as soon as they told us . . .

HENRY IV. Certainly! [*Contemplates* FRIDA *and* DI NOLLI, *and then looks at the* MARCHIONESS, *and finally at his own costume.*] The combination is very beautiful . . . Two couples . . . Very good, very good, Doctor! For a madman, not bad! . . . [*With a slight wave of his hand to* BELCREDI.] It seems to him now to be a carnival out of season, eh? [*Turns to look at him.*] We'll get rid now of this masquerade costume of mine, so that I may come away with you. What do you say?

BELCREDI. With me? With us?

HENRY IV. Where shall we go? To the Club? In dress coats and with white ties? Or shall both of us go to the Marchioness' house?

BELCREDI. Wherever you like! Do you want to remain here still, to continue—alone—what was nothing but the unfortunate joke of a day of carnival? It is really incredible, incredible how you have been able to do all this, freed from the disaster that befell you!

HENRY IV. Yes, you see how it was! The fact is that falling from my horse and striking my head as I did, I was really mad for I know not how long . . .

DOCTOR. Ah! Did it last long?

HENRY IV [*very quickly to the* DOCTOR]. Yes, Doctor, a long time! I think it must have been about twelve years. [*Then suddenly turning to speak to* BELCREDI.] Thus I saw nothing, my dear fellow, of all that, after that day of carnival, happened for you but not for me: how things changed, how my friends deceived me, how my place was taken by another, and all the rest of it! And suppose my place had been taken in the heart of the woman I loved? . . . And how should I know who was dead or who had disappeared? . . . All this, you know, wasn't exactly a jest for me, as it seems to you . . .

BELCREDI. No, no! I don't mean that if you please. I mean after . . .

HENRY IV. Ah, yes? After? One day [*Stops and addresses the* DOCTOR.]—A most interesting case, Doctor! Study me well! Study me carefully! [*Trembles while speaking.*] All by itself, who knows how, one day the trouble here [*Touches his forehead.*] mended. Little by little, I open my eyes, and at first I don't know whether I am asleep or awake. Then I know I am awake. I touch this thing and that; I see clearly again . . . Ah!—then, as *he* says [*Alludes to* BELCREDI.] away, away with this masquerade, this incubus! Let's open the windows, breathe life once again! Away! Away! Let's run out! [*Suddenly pulling himself up.*] But where? And to do what? To show myself to all, secretly, as Henry IV, not like this, but arm in arm with you, among my dear friends?

BELCREDI. What are you saying?

DONNA MATILDA. Who could think it? It's not to be imagined. It was an accident.

HENRY IV. They all said I was mad before. [*To* BELCREDI.] And you know it! You were more ferocious than any one against those who tried to defend me.

BELCREDI. Oh, that was only a joke!

HENRY IV. Look at my hair! [*Shows him the hair on the nape of his neck.*]

BELCREDI. But mine is grey too!

HENRY IV. Yes, with this difference: that mine went grey here, as Henry IV, do you understand? And I never knew it! I perceived it all of a sudden, one day, when I opened my eyes; and I was terrified because I understood at once that not only had my hair gone grey, but that I was all grey, inside; that everything had fallen to pieces, that everything was finished; and I was going to arrive hungry as a wolf, at a banquet which had already been cleared away . . .

BELCREDI. Yes, but, what about the others? . . .

HENRY IV [*quickly*]. Ah, yes, I know! They couldn't wait until I was cured, not even those, who, behind my back, pricked my saddled horse till it bled. . . .

DI NOLLI [*agitated*]. What, what?

HENRY IV. Yes, treacherously, to make it rear and cause me to fall.

DONNA MATILDA [*quickly, in horror*]. This is the first time I knew that.

HENRY IV. That was also a joke, probably!

DONNA MATILDA. But who did it? Who was behind us, then?

HENRY IV. It doesn't matter who it was. All those that went on feasting and were ready to leave me their scrapings, Marchioness, of miserable pity, or some dirty remnant of remorse in the filthy plate! Thanks! [*Turning quickly to the* DOCTOR.] Now, Doctor, the case must be absolutely new in the history of madness; I preferred to remain mad—since I found everything ready and at my disposal for this new exquisite fantasy. I would live it—this madness of mine—with the most lucid consciousness; and thus revenge myself on the brutality of a stone which had dented my head. The solitude—this solitude—squalid and empty as it appeared to me when I opened my eyes again— I determined to deck it out with all the colors and splendors of that far off day of carnival, when you [*Looks at* DONNA MATILDA *and points* FRIDA *out to her.*]—when you, Marchioness, triumphed. So I would oblige all those who were around me to follow, by God, at my orders that famous pageant which had been—for you and not for me—the jest of a day. I would make it become—for ever—no more a joke but a reality, the reality of a real madness: here, all in masquerade, with throne room, and these my four secret counsellors: secret and, of course, traitors. [*He turns quickly towards them.*] I should like to know what you have gained by revealing the fact that I was cured! If I am cured, there's no longer any need of you, and you will be discharged! To give anyone one's confidence . . . that is really the act of a madman. But now I accuse you in my turn. [*Turning to othe others.*] Do you know? They thought [*Alludes to the* VALETS.] they could make fun of me too with you. [*Bursts out laughing. The others laugh, but shamefacedly, except* DONNA MATILDA.]

BELCREDI [*to* DI NOLLI]. Well, imagine that . . . That's not bad . . .

DI NOLLI [*to the* FOUR YOUNG MEN]. You?

HENRY IV. We must pardon them. This dress [*Plucking his dress*]. which is for me the evident, involuntary caricature of that other continuous, everlasting masquerade, of which we are the involuntary puppets [*Indicates* BELCREDI.], when, without knowing it, we mask ourselves with that which we appear to be . . . ah, that dress of theirs, this masquerade of theirs, of course, we must forgive it them, since they do not yet see it is identical with themselves . . . [*Turning again to* BELCREDI.] You know, it is quite easy to get accustomed to it. One walks about as a tragic character, just as if it were nothing . . . [*Imitates the tragic manner.*] in a room like this . . . Look here, doctor! I remember a priest, certainly Irish, a nice-looking priest, who was sleeping in the sun one November day, with his arm on the corner of the bench of a public garden.

He was lost in the golden delight of the mild sunny air which must have seemed for him almost summery. One may be sure that in that moment he did not know any more that he was a priest, or even where he was. He was dreaming . . . A little boy passed with a flower in his hand. He touched the priest with it here on the neck. I saw him open his laughing eyes, while all his mouth smiled with the beauty of his dream. He was forgetful of everything . . . But all at once, he pulled himself together, and stretched out his priest's cassock; and there came back to his eyes the same seriousness which you have seen in mine; because the Irish priests defend the seriousness of their Catholic faith with the same zeal with which I defend the sacred rights of hereditary monarchy! I am cured, gentlemen: because I can act the madman to perfection, here; and I do it very quietly, I'm only sorry for you that have to live your madness so agitatedly, without knowing it or seeing it.

BELCREDI. It comes to this, then, that it is we who are mad. That's what it is!

HENRY IV [*containing his irritation*]. But if you weren't mad, both you and she [*Indicating the* MARCHIONESS.] would you have come here to see me?

BELCREDI. To tell the truth, I came here believing that you were the madman.

HENRY IV [*suddenly indicating the* MARCHIONESS]. And she?

BELCREDI. Ah, as for her . . . I can't say. I see she is all fascinated by your words, by this *conscious* madness of yours. [*Turns to her.*] Dressed as you are [*Speaking to her.*], you could even remain here to live it out, Marchioness.

DONNA MATILDA. You are insolent!

HENRY IV [*conciliatingly*]. No, Marchioness, what he means to say is that the miracle would be complete, according to him, with you here, who—as the Marchioness of Tuscany, you well know,—could not be my friend, save, as at Canossa, to give me a little pity . . .

BELCREDI. Or even more than a little! She said so herself!

HENRY IV [*to the* MARCHIONESS, *continuing*]. And even, shall we say, a little remorse! . . .

BELCREDI. Yes, that too she has admitted.

DONNA MATILDA [*angry*]. Now look here . . .

HENRY IV [*quickly, to placate her*]. Don't bother about him! Don't mind him! Let him go on infuriating me—though the Doctor's told him not to. [*Turns to* BELCREDI.] But do you suppose I am going to trouble myself any more about what happened between us—the share you had in my misfortune with her [*Indicates the* MARCHIONESS *to him and pointing* BELCREDI *out to her.*] the part he has now in your life? This is my life! Quite a different thing from your life! Your life, the life in which you have grown old—I have not lived that life. [*To* DONNA MATILDA.] Was this what you wanted to show me with this sacrifice of yours, dressing yourself up like this, according to the Doctor's idea? Excellently done, Doctor! Oh, an excellent idea:—"As we were then, eh? and as we are now?" But I am not a madman according to your way of thinking, Doctor. I know very well that that man there [*Indicates* DI NOLLI.] cannot be me; because I am Henry IV, and have been, these twenty years, cast in this eternal masquerade. She has lived these years! [*Indicates the* MARCHIONESS.] She has enjoyed them and has become—look at her!—a woman I can no longer recognize. It is so that I knew her! [*Points to* FRIDA *and draws near her.*] This is the Marchioness I know, always this one! . . . You seem a lot of children to be so easily frightened by me . . . [*To* FRIDA.] And you're frightened too, little girl, aren't you, by the jest that they made you take part in—though they didn't understand it wouldn't be the jest they meant it to be, for me? Oh miracle of miracles! Prodigy of prodigies! The dream alive in you! More than alive in you! It was an image that wavered there and they've made you come to life! Oh, mine! You're mine, mine, mine, in my own right! [HE *holds her in his arms, laughing like a madman, while all stand still terrified. Then as they advance to tear* FRIDA *from his arms, he becomes furious, terrible and cries imperiously to his* VALETS.] Hold them! Hold them! I order you to hold them!

[*The* FOUR YOUNG MEN *amazed, yet fascinated, move to execute his orders, automatically, and seize* DI NOLLI, *the* DOCTOR, *and* BELCREDI.]

BELCREDI [*freeing himself*]. Leave her alone! Leave her alone! You're no madman!

HENRY IV [*in a flash draws the sword from the side of* LANDOLPH, *who is close to him*]. I'm not mad, eh! Take that, you! . . . [*Drives sword into him. A cry of horror goes up. All rush over to assist* BELCREDI, *crying out together.*]

DI NOLLI. Has he wounded you?

BERTHOLD. Yes, yes, seriously!

DOCTOR. I told you so!

FRIDA. Oh God, oh God!

DI NOLLI. Frida, come here!

DONNA MATILDA. He's mad, mad!

DI NOLLI. Hold him!

BELCREDI [*while* THEY *take him away by the left exit,* HE *protests as he is borne out*]. No, no, you're not mad! You're not mad. He's not mad!

[THEY *go out by the left amid cries and excitement. After a moment, one hears a still sharper, more piercing cry from* DONNA MATILDA, *and then, silence.*]

HENRY IV [*who has remained on the stage between* LANDOLPH, HAROLD *and* ORDULPH, *with his eyes almost starting out of his head, terrified by the life of his own masquerade which has driven him to crime.*] Now, yes . . . we'll have to [*Calls his* VALETS *around him as if to protect him.*] here we are . . . together . . . for ever!

CURTAIN

ANDRÉ GIDE

(1869–1951)

The Return of the Prodigal Son*

As was done in old triptychs,[1] I have painted here, for my secret pleasure, the parable[2] told to us by Our Lord Jesus Christ. Leaving scattered and indistinct the double inspiration which moves me, I have not tried to prove the victory of any god over me—or my victory. And yet, if the reader demands of me some expression of piety, he will not perhaps look for it in vain in my painting, where, like a donor in the corner of the picture, I am kneeling, a pendant to the prodigal son, smiling like him and also like him, my face soaked with tears.

The Prodigal Son

When, after a long absence, tired of his fancies and as if fallen out of love with himself, the prodigal son, from the depths of that destitution he sought, thinks of his father's face; of that not too

* Reprinted from *French Stories*, edited and translated by Wallace Fowlie. Reprinted with permission of the publishers.

1. sets of three painted or sculptured panels, often placed behind the altar.

2. A certain man had two sons: And the younger of them said to his father, Father, give me the portion of goods that falleth to me. And he divided unto them his living.

And not many days after the younger son gathered all together, and took his journey into a far country, and there wasted his substance with riotous living. And when he had spent all, there arose a mighty famine in that land; and he began to be in want. And he went and joined himself to a citizen of that country; and he sent him into the fields to feed swine. And he would fain have filled his belly with the husks that the swine did eat: and no man gave unto him.

And when he came to himself, he said, How many hired servants of my father's have bread enough and to spare, and I perish with hunger! I will arise and go to my father, and will say unto him, Father, I have sinned against heaven, and before thee, and am no more worthy to be called thy son: make me as one of thy hired servants.

And he arose, and came to his father. But when he was yet a great way off, his father saw him, and had compassion, and ran, and fell on his neck, and kissed him. And the son said unto him, Father, I have sinned against heaven, and in thy sight, and am no more worthy to be called thy son.

But the father said to his servants, Bring forth the best robe, and put it on him; and put a ring on his hand, and shoes on his feet: and bring hither the fatted calf, and kill it; and let us eat, and be merry: For this my son was dead, and is alive again; he was lost, and is found. And they began to be merry.

Now his elder son was in the field: and as he came and drew nigh to the house, he heard musick and dancing. And he called one of the servants, and asked what these things meant. And he said unto him, Thy brother is come; and thy father hath killed the fatted calf, because he hath received him safe and sound. And he was angry, and would not go in: therefore came his father out, and intreated him.

And he answering said to his father, Lo, these many years do I serve thee, neither transgressed I at any time thy commandment; and yet thou never gavest me a kid, that I might make merry with my friends: but as soon as this thy son was come, which hath devoured thy living with harlots, thou hast killed for him the fatted calf.

And he said unto him, Son, thou art ever with me, and all that I have is thine. It was meet that we should make merry, and be glad: for this thy brother was dead, and is alive again; and was lost, and is found (Luke 15:11–22).

small room where his mother used to bend over his bed; of that garden, watered with a running stream, but enclosed and from which he had always wanted to escape; of his thrifty older brother whom he never loved, but who still holds, in the expectation of his return, that part of his fortune which, as a prodigal, he was not able to squander—the boy confesses to himself that he did not find happiness, nor even succeed in prolonging very much that disorderly excitement which he sought in place of happiness. "Ah!" he thinks, "if my father, after first being angry with me, believed me dead, perhaps, in spite of my sins, he would rejoice at seeing me again. Ah, if I go back to him very humbly, my head bowed and covered with ashes, and if, bending down before him and saying to him: 'Father, I have sinned against heaven, and before you,' what shall I do if, raising me with his hand, he says, 'Come into the house, my son'?" And already the boy is piously on his way.

When from the top of the hill he sees at last the smoking roofs of the house, it is evening. But he waits for the shadows of night in order to veil somewhat his poverty. In the distance he hears his father's voice. His knees give way. He falls and covers his face with his hands because he is ashamed of his shame, and yet he knows that he is the lawful son. He is hungry. In a fold of his tattered cloak he has only one handful of those sweet acorns which were his food, as they were the food of the swine he herded. He sees the preparations for supper. He makes out his mother coming on to the doorstep. . . . He can hold back no longer. He runs down the hill and comes into the courtyard where his dog, failing to recognize him, barks. He tries to speak to the servants. But they are suspicious and move away in order to warn the master. Here he is!

Doubtless he was expecting his prodigal son, because he recognizes him immediately. He opens his arms. The boy then kneels before him, and hiding his forehead with one arm, he raises his right hand for pardon:

"Father! Father! I have gravely sinned against heaven and against you. I am not worthy to be called your son. But at least, like one of your servants, the humblest, let me live in a corner of our house."

The father raises him and embraces him.

"My son, blessed is this day when you come back to me!" And his joy weeps as it overflows his heart. He raises his head from his son's brow which he was kissing, and turns toward his servants:

"Bring forth the best robe. Put shoes on his feet, and a precious ring on his finger. Look in our stables for the fattest calf and kill it. Prepare a joyful feast, for my son whom I thought dead is alive."

And as the news spreads rapidly, he hastens. He does not want another to say:

"Mother, the son we wept for has returned to us."

Everyone's joy mounting up like a hymn troubles the older son. He sits down at the common table because his father invites him and urges him forcibly. Alone, among all the guests, for even the humblest servant is invited, he shows an angry expression. To the repentant sinner why is there more honor than to himself, who has never sinned? He esteems order more than love. If he consents to appear at the feast, it is because by giving credit to his brother, he can lend him joy for one evening. It is also because his father and mother have promised him to rebuke the prodigal tomorrow, and because he himself is preparing to admonish him seriously.

The torches send up their smoke toward heaven. The meal is over. The servants have cleared the tables. Now, in the night, when not a breath is stirring, soul after soul, in the weary house, goes to sleep. And yet, in the room next to the prodigal's, I know a boy, his younger brother, who throughout the night until dawn will try in vain to sleep.

The Father's Reprimand

Lord, like a child I kneel before You today, my face soaked with tears. If I remember and transcribe here your compelling parable, it is because I know who your prodigal child was. I see myself in him. At times I hear in myself and repeat in secret those words which, from the depth of his great distress, You have him cry:

"How many hirelings of my father have bread enough and to spare, and I perish with hunger!"

I imagine the father's embrace, and in the warmth of such love my heart melts. I imagine an earlier distress, and even—ah! I imagine all kinds of things. This I believe: I am the very one whose heart beats when, from the top of the hill, he sees again the blue roofs of the house he left. What keeps me then from running toward my home and going in?—I am expected. I can see the fatted calf they are preparing. . . . Stop! Do not set up the feast too quickly!—Prodigal son, I am thinking of you. Tell me first what your Father said to you the next day, after the feast of welcome. Ah! even if the elder son prompts you, Father, let me hear your voice sometimes through his words!

"My son, why did you leave me?"

"Did I really leave you? Father, are you not everywhere? Never did I cease loving you."

"Let us not split hairs. I had a house which kept you in. It was built for you. Generations worked so that in it your soul could find shelter, luxury worthy of it, comfort and occupation. Why did you, the heir, the son, escape from the House?"

"Because the House shut me in. The House is not You, Father."

"It is I who built it, and for you."

"Ah! you did not say that, my brother did. You built the whole world, the House and what is not the House. The House was built by others. In your name, I know, but by others."

"Man needs a roof under which he can lay his head. Proud boy! Do you think you can sleep in the open?"

"Do you need pride to do that? Some poorer than I have done so."

"They are the poor. You are not poor. No one can give up his wealth. I had made you rich above all men."

"Father, you know that when I left, I took with me all the riches I could. What do I care about goods that cannot be carried away?"

"All that fortune you took away, you have spent recklessly."

"I changed your gold into pleasures, your precepts into fantasy, my chastity into poetry, and my austerity into desires."

"Was it for that your thrifty parents strove to instill into you so much virtue?"

"So that I should burn with a brighter flame perhaps, being kindled by a new fervor."

"Think of that pure flame Moses saw on the sacred bush. It shone, but without consuming."

"I have known love which consumes."

"The love which I want to teach you, refreshes. After a short time, what did you have left, prodigal son?"

"The memory of those pleasures."

"And the destitution which comes after them."

"In that destitution, I felt close to you, Father."

"Was poverty needed to drive you back to me?"

"I do not know. I do not know. It was in the dryness of the desert that I loved my thirst more."

"Your poverty made you feel more deeply the value of riches."

"No, not that! Can't you understand me, Father? My heart, emptied of everything, became filled with love. At the cost of all my goods, I bought fervor."

"Were you happy, then, far from me?"

"I did not feel far from you."

"Then, what made you come back? Tell me."

"I don't know. Laziness perhaps."

"Laziness, my son? What! Wasn't it love?"

"Father, I have told you. I never loved you better than in the desert. But each morning I was tired of looking for my subsistence. In the House, at least there is food to eat."

"Yes, servants look after that. So, what brought you back was hunger."

"Cowardice also perhaps, and sickness. . . . In the end, that food I was never sure of finding weakened me. Because I fed on wild fruit and locusts and honey. I grew less and less able to stand the discomfort which at first quickened my fervor. At night, when I was cold, I thought of my tucked-in bed in my father's house. When I fasted, I thought of my father's home where the abundance of food served always exceeded my hunger. I weakened; I didn't feel enough courage, enough strength to struggle much longer and yet . . ."

"So yesterday's fatted calf seemed good to you?"

The prodigal son throws himself down sobbing, with his face against the ground.

"Father! Father! The wild taste of sweet acorns is still in my mouth, in spite of everything. Nothing could blot out their savor."

"Poor child!" says the father as he raises him up."I spoke to you perhaps too harshly. Your brother wanted me to. Here it is he who makes the law. It is he who charged me to say to you: 'Outside of the House, there is no salvation for you.' But listen. It was I who made you. I know what is in you. I know what sent you out on your wanderings. I was waiting for you at the end of the road. If you had called me . . . I was there."

"Father! might I then have found you without coming back?"

"If you felt weak, you did well to come back. Go now. Go back to the room I had prepared for you. Enough for today. Rest. Tomorrow you will speak with your brother."

The Elder Brother's Reprimand

The prodigal son first tries to bluster.

"Big brother," he begins, "we aren't very much alike. Brother, we aren't alike at all."

The elder brother says:

"It's your fault."

"Why mine?"

"Because I live by order. Whatever differs from it is the fruit or the seed of pride."

"Am I different only in my faults?"

"Only call quality what brings you back to order, and curtail all the rest."

"It is that mutilation I fear. What you plan to suppress comes also from the Father."

"Not suppress—curtail, I said."

"I understand. All the same, that is how I curtailed my virtues."

"And that is also why now I still see them in you. You must exaggerate them. Understand me. It is not a diminution of yourself, but an exaltation I propose, in which the most diverse, the most unruly elements of your flesh and your spirit must join together harmoniously, in which the worst in you must nourish the best, in which the best must submit to . . ."

"It was exaltation which I also sought and found in the desert—and perhaps not very different from the one you propose to me."

"To tell the truth, I wanted to impose it on you."

"Our Father did not speak so harshly."

"I know what the Father said to you. It was vague. He no longer expresses himself very clearly, so that he can be made to say what one wants. But I understand his thought very well. With the servants, I am the one interpreter, and who wants to understand the Father must listen to me."

"I understand him quite easily without you."

"You thought you did. But you understood incorrectly. There are not several ways of understanding the Father. There are not several ways of listening to him. There are not several ways of loving him, so that we may be united in his love."

"In his House."

"This love brings one back here. You see this, for you have come back. Tell me now, what impelled you to leave?"

"I felt too clearly that the House is not the entire universe. I myself am not completely in the boy you wanted me to be. I could not help imagining other cultures, other lands, and roads by which to reach them, roads not yet traced. I imagined in myself the new being which I felt rushing down those roads. I ran away."

"Think what could have happened if, like you, I had deserted our Father's House. Servants and thieves would have pillaged all our goods."

"That would not have mattered to me, since I was catching sight of other goods . . ."

"Which your pride exaggerated. My brother, indiscipline is over. You will learn, if you don't yet know it, out of what chaos man has emerged. He has just barely emerged. With all of his artless weight, he falls back into it as soon as the Spirit no longer supports him above it. Do not learn this at your own expense. The well-ordered elements which make up your being wait only for an acquiescence, a weakening on your part in order to return to anarchy . . . But what you will never know is the length of time that was needed for man to elaborate man. Now that we have the model, let us keep it. 'Hold that fast which thou hast,' says the Spirit to the Angel of the Church, and He adds, 'that no man taketh thy crown.'[3] The *which thou hast* is your crown, that royalty over others and over yourself. The usurper lies in wait for your crown. He is everywhere. He

3. Revelation 3:11.

prowls around you and in you. *Hold fast*, my brother! Hold fast."

"Too long ago I let go my hold. And now I cannot close my hand over my own wealth."

"Yes, you can. I will help you. I have watched over your wealth during your absence."

"And moreover, I know those words of the Spirit. You did not quote them all."

"You are right. It goes on: 'Him that overcometh will I make a pillar in the temple of my God, and he shall go no more out.' "[4]

" 'And he shall go no more out.' That is precisely what terrifies me."

"If it is for his happiness."

"Oh! I understand. But I had been in that temple . . ."

"You found you were wrong to have left, since you wanted to return."

"I know, I know. I am back now. I agree."

"What good can you look for elsewhere, which here you do not find in abundance? Or better—here alone your wealth is to be found."

"I know that you kept my riches for me."

"The part of your fortune which you did not squander, namely that part which is common to all of us: the property."

"Then do I personally own nothing else?"

"Yes. That special allotment of gifts which perhaps our Father will still consent to grant you."

"That is all I want. I agree to own only that."

"How proud you are! You will not be consulted. Between you and me, that portion is risky. I would advise your giving it up. It was that allotment of personal gifts which already brought on your downfall. That was the wealth you squandered immediately."

"The other kind I couldn't take with me."

"Therefore you will find it intact. Enough for today. Find rest now in the House."

"That suits me well, for I am tired."

"Then blessed be your fatigue! Now go and sleep. Tomorrow your mother will speak to you."

The Mother

Prodigal son, whose mind still rebels against the words of your brother, let your heart now speak. How sweet it is, as you lie at the feet of your mother, with your head hidden on her lap, to feel her caressing hand bow your stubborn neck!

4. Revelation 3:12.

"Why did you leave me for so long a time?"

And since you answer only with tears:

"Why weep now, my son? You have been given back to me. In waiting for you, I have shed all my tears."

"Were you still waiting for me?"

"Never did I give up hoping for you. Before going to sleep, every evening I would think: if he returns tonight, will he be able to open the door? And it took me a long time to fall asleep. Every morning, before I was totally awake, I would think: isn't it today he will come back? Then I prayed. I prayed so hard that it was not possible for you not to come back."

"Your prayers forced me to come back."

"Don't smile because of me, my child."

"Oh mother, I have come back to you very humble. See how I place my forehead lower than your heart! There is not one of my thoughts of yesterday which does not become empty today. When close to you, I can hardly understand why I left the house."

"You will not leave it again?"

"I cannot leave it again."

"What then attracted you outside?"

"I don't want to think of it any more. Nothing . . . Myself . . ."

"Did you think then that you would be happy away from us?"

"I was not looking for happiness."

"What were you looking for?"

"I was looking for . . . who I was."

"Oh! son of your parents, and brother among your brothers."

"I was not like my brothers. Let's not talk any more about it. I have come back now."

"Yes, let's talk of it further. Do not believe that your brothers are so unlike you."

"Henceforth my one care is to be like all of you."

"You say that as if with resignation."

"Nothing is more fatiguing than to realize one's difference. Finally my wandering tired me out."

"You have aged, that is true."

"I have suffered."

"My poor child! Doubtless your bed was not made every evening, nor the table set for all your meals?"

"I ate what I found and often it was green or spoiled fruit which my hunger made into food."

"At least did you suffer only from hunger?"

"The sun at mid-day, the cold wind in the heart of the night, the shifting sand of the desert, the thorns which made my feet bloody, nothing of all that stopped me, but—I didn't tell this to my brother—I had to serve . . ."

"Why did you conceal it?"

"Bad masters who harmed me bodily, exasperated my pride, and gave me barely enough to eat. That is when I thought: 'Serving for the sake of serving! . . .' In dreams I saw my house, and I came home."

The prodigal son again lowers his head and his mother caresses it tenderly.

"What are you going to do now?"

"I have told you. Try to become like my big brother, look after our property, like him choose a wife . . ."

"You have doubtless someone in mind, as you say that."

"Oh, anyone at all will be my first preference, as soon as you have chosen her. Do as you did for my brother."

"I should have preferred someone you love."

"What does it matter? My heart had made a choice. I renounce the pride which took me far away from you. Help me in my choice. I submit, I tell you. And I will have my children submit also. In that way, my adventure will not seem pointless to me."

"Listen to me. There is at this moment a child you could take on already as a charge."

"What do you mean and of whom are you speaking?"

"Of your younger brother who was not ten when you left, whom you hardly recognized, but who . . ."

"Go on, mother! What are you worried about now?"

"In whom you might well have recognized yourself because he is like what you were when you left."

"Like me?"

"Like what you were, I said, not yet, alas, what you have become."

"What he will become."

"What you must make him become immediately. Speak to him. He will listen to you, doubtless, you the prodigal. Tell him what disappointment you met on your way. Spare him . . ."

"But what causes you such alarm about my brother? Perhaps simply a resemblance of features . . ."

"No, no! the resemblance between you two is deeper. I worry now for him about what first did not worry me enough for you. He reads too much, and doesn't always prefer good books."

"Is that all it is?"

"He is often perched on the highest part of the garden, from where, as you know, you can see the countryside over the walls."

"I remember. Is that all?"

"He spends less time with us than in the farm."

"Ah! what does he do there?"

"Nothing wrong. But it is not the farmers he stays with, it is the farm hands who are as different from us as possible and those who are not from this country. There is one in particular, who comes from some distance, and who tells him stories.

"Ah! the swineherd."

"Yes. Did you know him? . . . Your brother each evening in order to listen to him, follows him into the pigsties. He comes back only for dinner, but with no appetite, and his clothes reeking. Remonstrances have no effect. He stiffens under constraint. On certain mornings, at dawn, before any of us are up, he runs off to accompany that swineherd to the gate when he is leading off his herd to graze."

"He knows he must not leave."

"You knew also! One day he will escape from me, I am sure. One day he will leave . . ."

"No, I will speak to him, mother. Don't be alarmed."

"I know he will listen to a great deal from you. Did you see how he watched you that first evening, with what prestige your rags were covered, and the purple robe your father put on you! I was afraid that in his mind he will confuse one with the other, and that he is attracted first by the rags. But now this idea seems ridiculous to me. For if you, my child, had been able to foresee such unhappiness, you would not have left us, would you?"

"I don't know now how I was able to leave you, you who are my mother."

"Well, tell him all that."

"I will tell him that tomorrow evening. Now kiss me on my forehead as you used to when I was small and you watched me fall asleep. I am sleepy."

"Go to bed. I am going to pray for all of you."

Dialogue with the Younger Brother

Beside the prodigal's, there is a room not too small, with bare walls. The prodigal, a lamp in his hand, comes close to the bed were his younger brother is lying, his face toward the wall. He begins in a low voice, so as not to disturb him if the boy is sleeping.

"I would like to talk to you, brother."

"What is stopping you?"

"I thought you were sleeping."

"I don't have to sleep in order to dream."

"You were dreaming? Of what?"

"What do you care? If I can't understand my dreams, I don't think you will be able to explain them to me."

"Are they that subtle, then? If you told them to me, I would try."

"Do you choose your dreams? Mine are what they want to be,

and are freer than I . . . What have you come here for? Why are you disturbing me in my sleep?"

"You aren't sleeping, and I'm here to speak gently to you."

"What have you to say to me?"

"Nothing, if that is the tone you take."

"Then goodbye."

The prodigal goes toward the door, but puts the lamp on the floor so that the room is barely lighted. Then, coming back, he sits on the edge of the bed and in the dark strokes for a long time the boy's forehead which is kept turned away.

"You answer me more gruffly than I ever did your brother. Yet I too rebelled against him."

The stubborn boy suddenly sat up.

"Tell me, is it my brother that sent you?"

"No, not he, but our mother."

"So, you wouldn't have come of your own accord."

"But I came as a friend."

Half sitting up on his bed, the boy looks straight at the prodigal.

"How could one of my family be my friend?"

"You are mistaken about our brother . . ."

"Don't speak to me about him! I hate him. My whole heart cries out against him. He's the reason for my answering you gruffly."

"Explain why."

"You wouldn't understand."

"Tell me just the same."

The prodigal rocks his brother in his arms and already the boy begins to yield.

"The evening you returned, I couldn't sleep. All night I kept thinking: I had another brother, and I didn't know it. . . . That is why my heart beat so hard when, in the courtyard of our house, I saw you come covered with glory."

"Alas, I was covered then with rags."

"Yes, I saw you. You were already glorious. And I saw what our father did. He put a ring on your finger, a ring the like of which our brother does not have. I did not want to question anyone about you. All that I knew was that you had come from very far away, and that your eyes, at table . . ."

"Were you at the feast?"

"Oh! I know you did not see me. During the whole meal you looked far off without seeing anything. And it was all right when on the second evening you spoke with our father, but on the third . . ."

"Go on."

"Ah! you could have said to me at least one word of love!"

"You were expecting me then?"

"Impatiently! Do you think I would hate our brother so much if you had not gone to talk with him that evening and for so long? What did you find to say to each other? You certainly know, if you are like me, that you can have nothing in common with him."

"I had behaved very wrongly toward him."

"Is that possible?"

"At any rate toward our father and mother. You know that I ran away from home."

"Yes, I know. A long time ago, wasn't it?"

"When I was about your age."

"Ah! And that's what you call behaving wrong?"

"Yes, it was wrong, it was my sin."

"When you left, did you feel you were doing wrong?"

"No, I felt duty-bound to leave."

"What has happened since then to change your first truth into an error?"

"I suffered."

"And is that what makes you say: I did wrong?"

"No, not exactly. That is what made me reflect."

"Then, before, you didn't reflect?"

"Yes, but my weak reason let itself be conquered by my desires."

"As later by your suffering. So that today you have come back . . . conquered."

"No, not exactly—resigned."

"At any rate, you have given up being what you wanted to be."

"What my pride persuaded me to be."

The boy remains silent a moment, then suddenly cries with a sob:

"Brother! I am the boy you were when you left. Tell me. Did you find nothing but disappointments on your wanderings? Is all that I imagine outside and different from here, only an illusion? All the newness I feel in me, is that madness? Tell me, what did you meet on your way that seemed so tragic? Oh! what made you come back?"

"The freedom I was looking for, I lost. When captive, I had to serve."

"I am captive here."

"Yes, but I mean serving bad masters. Here you are serving your parents."

"Ah! serving for the sake of serving! At least don't we have the freedom of choosing our bondage?"

"I had hoped for that. As far as my feet carried me, I walked, like Saul in search of his she-asses, in search of my desire. But there where a kingdom was waiting for him, I found wretchedness. And yet . . ."

"Didn't you mistake the road?"

"I walked straight ahead."

"Are you sure? And yet there are still other kingdoms, and lands without kings, to discover."

"Who told you?"

"I know it, I feel it. I have already the impression of being the lord over them."

"Proud boy!"

"Ah! ah! that's something our brother said to you. Why do you repeat it to me now? Why didn't you keep that pride? You would not have come back."

"Then I would never have known you."

"Yes, yes, out there where I would have joined you, you would have recognized me as your brother. It seems to me even that I am leaving in order to find you."

"That you are leaving?"

"Haven't you understood? Aren't you yourself encouraging me to leave?"

"I wanted to spare your returning, but by sparing your departure."

"No, no, don't tell me that. No, you don't mean that. You yourself left like a conqueror, didn't you?"

"And that is what made my bondage seem harder to me."

"Then, why did you give in to it? Were you already so tired?"

"No, not then. But I had doubts."

"What do you mean?"

"Doubts about everything, about myself. I wanted to stop and settle down somewhere. The comfort which this master promised me was a temptation . . . Yes, I feel it clearly now. I failed."

The prodigal bows his head and hides his face in his hands.

"But at first?"

"I had walked for a long time through large tracts of wild country."

"The desert?"

"It wasn't always the desert."

"What were you looking for there?"

"I myself do not understand now."

"Get up from my bed. Look, on the table beside it, there, near that torn book."

"I see a pomegranate split open."

"The swineherd brought it to me the other evening, after he had not been back for three days."

"Yes, it is a wild pomegranate."

"I know. It is almost unbearably bitter. And yet I feel, if I were sufficiently thirsty, I would bite into it."

"Ah! now I can tell you. That is the thirst I was looking for in the desert."

"A thirst which that sour fruit alone can quench . . ."

"No, but it makes you love that thirst."

"Do you know where it can be picked?"

"In a small deserted orchard you reach before evening. No longer does any wall separate it from the desert. A stream flowed through it. Some half-ripe fruit hung from the branches."

"What fruit?"

"The same which grows in our garden, but wild. It had been very hot all day."

"Listen. Do you know why I was expecting you this evening? I am leaving before the end of the night. Tonight, this night, as soon as it grows pale . . . I have girded my loins. Tonight I have kept on my sandals."

"So, what I was not able to do, you will do?"

"You opened the way for me, and it will help me to think of you."

"It is for me to admire you, and for you to forget me, on the contrary. What are you taking with you?"

"You know that as the youngest, I have no share in the inheritance. I am taking nothing."

"That is better."

"What are you looking at through the window?"

"The garden where our dead forefathers are sleeping."

"Brother . . ." (and the boy, who has gotten out of bed, puts, around the prodigal's neck, his arm which has become as tender as his voice)—"Come with me."

"Leave me! leave me! I am staying to console our mother. Without me you will be braver. It is time now. The sky turns pale. Go without making any noise. Come! kiss me, my young brother, you are taking with you all my hopes. Be strong. Forget us. Forget me. May you never come back . . . Go down quietly, I am holding the lamp . . ."

"Ah! give me your hand as far as the door."

"Be careful of the steps as you go down."

MARCEL PROUST

(1871–1922)

Remembrance of Things Past*[1]

(*À la Recherche du temps perdu*)

For a long time I used to go to bed early. Sometimes, when I had put out my candle, my eyes would close so quickly that I had not even time to say "I'm going to sleep." And half an hour later the thought that it was time to go to sleep would awaken me; I would try to put away the book which, I imagined, was still in my hands, and to blow out the light; I had been thinking all the time, while I was asleep, of what I had just been reading, but my thoughts had run into a channel of their own, until I myself seemed actually to have become the subject of my book: a church, a quartet, the rivalry between François I and Charles V.[2] This impression would persist for some moments after I was awake; it did not disturb my mind, but it lay like scales upon my eyes and prevented them from registering the fact that the candle was no longer burning. Then it would begin to seem unintelligible, as the thoughts of a former existence must be to a reincarnate spirit; the subject of my book would separate itself from me, leaving me free to choose whether I would form part of it or no; and at the same time my sight would return and I would be astonished to find myself in a state of darkness, pleasant and restful enough for the eyes, and even more, perhaps, for my mind, to which it appeared incomprehensible, without a cause, a matter dark indeed.

I would ask myself what o'clock it could be; I could hear the whistling of trains, which, now nearer and now farther off, punctuating the distance like the note of a bird in a forest, showed me in perspective the deserted countryside through which a traveler

* Published 1913–1927. Translated by C. K. Scott Moncrieff.

1. This selction, "Overture," is the opening section of Combray, the first volume of *Swann's Way* (*Du Côté de chez Swann*, 1913), itself the first full volume of Proust's novel. "Swann's way" is one of the two directions in which Marcel's family used to take walks from their home in Combray, toward Tansonville, home of Charles Swann, and is associated with various scenes and anecdotes of love and private life. The longer walk toward the estate of the Guermantes (*Guermantes Way*, 1921, the novel's third volume), a fictional family of the highest aristocracy appearing frequently in the novel, evokes an aura of high society and French history, a more public sphere. The narrator is Marcel as an old man. The verb tense of the French original through all but the final volume of the novel is typically the imperfect, a tense of uncompleted action. Fictional people and places mingle with the real; where a name is not annotated, it is Proust's invention.

2. Francis I (1496–1567), King of France, and Charles V (1500–1558), Holy Roman Emperor and King of Spain, fought four wars over the Empire's expansion in Europe.

would be hurrying toward the nearest station: the path that he followed being fixed for ever in his memory by the general excitement due to being in a strange place, to doing unusual things, to the last words of conversation, to farewells exchanged beneath an unfamiliar lamp which echoed still in his ears amid the silence of the night; and to the delightful prospect of being once again at home.

I would lay my cheeks gently against the comfortable cheeks of my pillow, as plump and blooming as the cheeks of babyhood. Or I would strike a match to look at my watch. Nearly midnight. The hour when an invalid, who has been obliged to start on a journey and to sleep in a strange hotel, awakens in a moment of illness and sees with glad relief a streak of daylight showing under his bedroom door.[3] Oh, joy of joys! it is morning. The servants will be about in a minute: he can ring, and some one will come to look after him. The thought of being made comfortable gives him strength to endure his pain. He is certain he heard footsteps: they come nearer, and then die away. The ray of light beneath his door is extinguished. It is midnight; some one has turned out the gas; the last servant has gone to bed, and he must lie all night in agony with no one to bring him any help.

I would fall asleep,[4] and often I would be awake again for short snatches only, just long enough to hear the regular creaking of the wainscot,[5] or to open my eyes to settle the shifting kaleidoscope of the darkness, to savor, in an instantaneous flash of perception, the sleep which lay heavy upon the furniture, the room, the whole surroundings of which I formed but an insignificant part and whose unconsciousness I should very soon return to share. Or, perhaps, while I was asleep I had returned without the least effort to an earlier stage in my life, now for ever outgrown; and had come under the thrall of one of my childish terrors, such as that old terror of my great-uncle's pulling my curls, which was effectually dispelled on the day—the dawn of a new era to me—on which they were finally cropped from my head. I had forgotten that event during my sleep; I remembered it again immediately I had succeeded in making myself wake up to escape my great uncle's fingers; still, as a measure of precaution, I would bury the whole of my head in the pillow before returning to the world of dreams.

Sometimes, too, just as Eve was created from a rib of Adam, so a woman would come into existence while I was sleeping, conceived from some strain in the position of my limbs. Formed by the

3. The point of view is no longer the child's, nor yet that of the old man, but reflects Marcel's adult experience as an invalid traveler.

4. The narrator returns to the child's perspective in a typical alternation of two narrative views, two layers of the same existence.

5. The wooden paneling of the walls.

appetite that I was on the point of gratifying, she it was, I imagined, who offered me that gratification. My body, conscious that its own warmth was permeating hers, would strive to become one with her, and I would awake. The rest of humanity seemed very remote in comparison with this woman whose company I had left but a moment ago: my cheek was still warm with her kiss, my body bent beneath the weight of hers. If, as would sometimes happen, she had the appearance of some woman whom I had known in waking hours, I would abandon myself altogether to the sole quest of her, like people who set out on a journey to see with their own eyes some city that they have always longed to visit, and imagine that they can taste in reality what has charmed their fancy. And then, gradually, the memory of her would dissolve and vanish, until I had forgotten the maiden of my dream.

When a man is asleep, he has in a circle round him the chain of the hours, the sequence of the years, the order of the heavenly host.[6] Instinctively, when he awakes, he looks to these, and in an instant reads off his own position on the earth's surface and the amount of time that has elapsed during his slumbers; but this ordered procession is apt to grow confused, and to break its ranks. Suppose that, toward morning, after a night of insomnia, sleep descends upon him while he is reading, in quite a different position from that in which he normally goes to sleep, he has only to lift his arm to arrest the sun and turn it back in its course,[7] and, at the moment of waking, he will have no idea of the time, but will conclude that he has just gone to bed. Or suppose that he gets drowsy in some even more abnormal position; sitting in an armchair, say, after dinner: then the world will fall topsy-turvy from its orbit, the magic chair will carry him at full speed through time and space, and when he opens his eyes again he will imagine that he went to sleep months earlier and in some far distant country. But for me it was enough if, in my own bed, my sleep was so heavy as completely to relax my consciousness; for then I lost all sense of the place in which I had gone to sleep, and when I awoke at midnight, not knowing where I was, I could not be sure at first who I was; I had only the most rudimentary sense of existence, such as may lurk and flicker in the depths of an animal's consciousness; I was more destitute of human qualities than the cave-dweller; but then the memory, not yet of the place in which I was, but of various other places where I had lived, and might now very possibly be, would come like a rope let down from heaven to draw me up out of the

6. Theologians divide the angels into nine ranks or choirs of precedence.

7. If his uplifted arm prevents him from seeing the sunlight, he will think it is still night.

abyss of not-being, from which I could never have escaped by myself: in a flash I would traverse and surmount centuries of civilization, and out of a half-visualized succession of oil-lamps, followed by shirts with turned-down collars,[8] would put together by degrees the component parts of my ego.

Perhaps the immobility of the things that surround us is forced upon them by our conviction that they are themselves, and not anything else, and by the immobility of our conceptions of them. For it always happened that when I awoke like this, and my mind struggled in an unsuccessful attempt to discover where I was, everything would be moving round me through the darkness: things, places, years. My body, still too heavy with sleep to move, would make an effort to construe the form which its tiredness took as an orientation of its various members, so as to induce from that where the wall lay and the furniture stood, to piece together and to give a name to the house in which it must be living. Its memory, the composite memory of its ribs, knees, and shoulder blades offered it a whole series of rooms in which it had at one time or another slept; while the unseen walls kept changing, adapting themselves to the shape of each successive room that it remembered, whirling madly through the darkness. And even before my brain, lingering in consideration of when things had happened and of what they had looked like, had collected sufficient impressions to enable it to identify the room, it, my body, would recall from each room in succession what the bed was like, where the doors were, how daylight came in at the windows, whether there was a passage outside, what I had had in my mind when I went to sleep, and had found there when I awoke. The stiffened side underneath my body would, for instance, in trying to fix its position, imagine itself to be lying, face to the wall, in a big bed with a canopy; and at once I would say to myself, "Why, I must have gone to sleep after all, and Mamma never came to say good night!" for I was in the country with my grandfather, who died years ago; and my body, the side upon which I was lying, loyally preserving from the past an impression which my mind should never have forgotten, brought back before my eyes the glimmering flame of the night light in its bowl of Bohemian glass,[9] shaped like an urn and hung by chains from the ceiling, and the chimney piece of Siena marble[10] in my bedroom at Combray, in my great-aunt's house, in those far distant days which, at the moment of waking, seemed present without being clearly defined,

8. The narrator's memory links successive segments of the past to recreate his personal identity, just as evolution links stages in the growth from caveman to the modern Parisian, with his reading lamps and fashionable shirts.

9. Likely to have been ornately engraved. (Bohemia, the western part of Czechoslovakia, was a major center of the glass industry).

10. The marble from Siena, in central Italy, mottled and reddish in color.

but would become plainer in a little while when I was properly awake.

Then would come up the memory of a fresh position; the wall slid away in another direction; I was in my room in Mme. de Saint-Loup's[11] house in the country; good heavens, it must be ten o'clock, they will have finished dinner! I must have overslept myself, in the little nap which I always take when I come in from my walk with Mme. de Saint-Loup, before dressing for the evening. For many years have now elapsed since the Combray days, when, coming in from the longest and latest walks, I would still be in time to see the reflection of the sunset glowing in the panes of my bedroom window. It is a very different kind of existence at Tansonville now with Mme. de Saint-Loup, and a different kind of pleasure that I now derive from taking walks only in the evenings, from visiting by moonlight the roads on which I used to play, as a child, in the sunshine; while the bedroom, in which I shall presently fall asleep instead of dressing for dinner, from afar off I can see it, as we return from our walk, with its lamp shining through the window, a solitary beacon in the night.

These shifting and confused gusts of memory never lasted for more than a few seconds; it often happened that, in my spell of uncertainty as to where I was, I did not distinguish the successive theories of which that uncertainty was composed any more than, when we watch a horse running, we isolate the successive positions of its body as they appear upon a bioscope.[12] But I had seen first one and then another of the rooms in which I had slept during my life, and in the end I would revisit them all in the long course of my waking dream: rooms in winter, where on going to bed I would at once bury my head in a nest, built up out of the most diverse materials, the corner of my pillow, the top of my blankets, a piece of a shawl, the edge of my bed, and a copy of an evening paper, all of which things I would contrive, with the infinite patience of birds building their nests, to cement into one whole; rooms where, in a keen frost, I would feel the satisfaction of being shut in from the outer world (like the sea-swallow which builds at the end of a dark tunnel and is kept warm by the surrounding earth), and where, the fire keeping in all night, I would sleep wrapped up, as it were, in a great cloak of snug and savory air, shot with the glow of the logs which would break out again in flame: in a sort of alcove without walls, a cave of warmth dug out of the heart of the room itself, a zone of heat whose boundaries were constantly shifting and altering in temperature as gusts of air ran across them to strike freshly upon

11. Charles Swann's daughter, Gilberte, who has married Robert de Saint-Loup, a nephew of the Guermantes.

12. An early moving-picture machine that showed photographs in rapid succession.

my face, from the corners of the room, or from parts near the window or far from the fireplace which had therefore remained cold —or rooms in summer, where I would delight to feel myself a part of the warm evening, where the moonlight striking upon the half-opened shutters would throw down to the foot of my bed its enchanted ladder; where I would fall asleep, as it might be in the open air, like a titmouse[13] which the breeze keeps poised in the focus of a sunbeam—or sometimes the Louis XVI room,[14] so cheerful that I could never feel really unhappy, even on my first night in it: that room where the slender columns which lightly supported its ceiling would part, ever so gracefully, to indicate where the bed was and to keep it separate; sometimes again that little room with the high ceiling, hollowed in the form of a pyramid out of two separate stories, and partly walled with mahogany, in which from the first moment my mind was drugged by the unfamiliar scent of flowering grasses,[15] convinced of the hostility of the violet curtains and of the insolent indifference of a clock that chattered on at the top of its voice as though I were not there; while a strange and pitiless mirror with square feet, which stood across one corner of the room, cleared for itself a site I had not looked to find tenanted in the quiet surroundings of my normal field of vision:[16] that room in which my mind, forcing itself for hours on end to leave its moorings, to elongate itself upward so as to take on the exact shape of the room, and to reach to the summit of that monstrous funnel, had passed so many anxious nights while my body lay stretched out in bed, my eyes staring upward, my ears straining, my nostrils sniffing uneasily, and my heart beating; until custom[17] had changed the color of the curtains, made the clock keep quiet, brought an expression of pity to the cruel, slanting face of the glass, disguised or even completely dispelled the scent of flowering grasses, and distinctly reduced the apparent loftiness of the ceiling. Custom! that skillful but unhurrying manager who begins by torturing the mind for weeks on end with her provisional arrangements; whom the mind, for all that, is fortunate in discovering, for without the help of custom it would never contrive, by its own efforts, to make any room seem habitable.

Certainly I was now well awake; my body had turned about for the last time and the good angel of certainty had made all the surrounding objects stand still, had set me down under my bedclothes,

13. Small, sparrow-like bird.

14. Furnished in late-18th-century style, named for the French monarch of the time, and marked by great elegance. The room is that in which Marcel visits Robert de Saint-Loup in *Guermantes Way.*

15. *Vetiver*, the aromatic root of a tropical grass packaged as a moth-preventive.

16. The narrator's room at the fictional seaside resort of Balbec, a setting in *Within a Budding Grove* (1918, the novel's second volume).

17. Literally, "habit."

in my bedroom, and had fixed, approximately in their right places in the uncertain light, my chest of drawers, my writing-table, my fireplace, the window overlooking the street, and both the doors. But it was no good my knowing that I was not in any of those houses of which, in the stupid moment of waking, if I had not caught sight exactly, I could still believe in their possible presence; for memory was now set in motion; as a rule I did not attempt to go to sleep again at once, but used to spend the greater part of the night recalling our life in the old days at Combray with my great-aunt, at Balbec, Paris, Doncières, Venice,[18] and the rest; remembering again all the places and people that I had known, what I had actually seen of them, and what others had told me.

At Combray, as every afternoon ended, long before the time when I should have to go up to bed, and to lie there, unsleeping, far from my mother and grandmother, my bedroom became the fixed point on which my melancholy and anxious thoughts were centered. Someone had had the happy idea of giving me, to distract me on evenings when I seemed abnormally wretched, a magic lantern,[19] which used to be set on top of my lamp while we waited for dinner time to come: in the manner of the master-builders and glass-painters of gothic days it substituted for the opaqueness of my walls an impalpable iridescence, supernatural phenomena of many colors, in which legends were depicted, as on a shifting and transitory window. But my sorrows were only increased, because this change of lighting destroyed, as nothing else could have done, the customary impression I had formed of my room, thanks to which the room itself, but for the torture of having to go to bed in it, had become quite endurable. For now I no longer recognized it, and I became uneasy, as though I were in a room in some hotel or furnished lodging, in a place where I had just arrived, by train, for the first time.

Riding at a jerky trot, Golo,[20] his mind filled with an infamous design, issued from the little three-cornered forest which dyed dark-green the slope of a convenient hill, and advanced by leaps and bounds toward the castle of poor Geneviève de Brabant. This castle was cut off short by a curved line which was in fact the circumference of one of the transparent ovals in the slides which were pushed into position through a slot in the lantern. It was only the wing of a castle, and in front of it stretched a moor on which Geneviève stood, lost in contemplation, wearing a blue girdle.[21] The castle and the moor were yellow, but I could tell their color without wait-

18. Main settings for the rest of the novel. Doncières, like Balbec, is a fictional locale.

19. A kind of slide projector.

20. Villain of a fifth-century legend. He falsely accuses Geneviève de Brabant of adultery. (Brabant was a principality in what is now Belgium)

21. Belt.

ing to see them, for before the slides made their appearance the old-gold sonorous name of Brabant had given me an unmistakable clue. Golo stopped for a moment and listened sadly to the little speech read aloud by my great-aunt,[22] which he seemed perfectly to understand, for he modified his attitude with a docility not devoid of a degree of majesty, so as to conform to the indications given in the text; then he rode away at the same jerky trot. And nothing could arrest his slow progress. If the lantern were moved I could still distinguish Golo's horse advancing across the window-curtains, swelling out with their curves and diving into their folds. The body of Golo himself, being of the same supernatural substance as his steed's, overcame all material obstacles—everything that seemed to bar his way—by taking each as it might be a skeleton and embodying it in himself: the door-handle, for instance, over which, adapting itself at once, would float invincibly his red cloak or his pale face, never losing its nobility or its melancholy, never showing any sign of trouble at such a transubstantiation.

And, indeed, I found plenty of charm in these bright projections, which seemed to have come straight out of a Merovingian[23] past, and to shed around me the reflections of such ancient history. But I cannot express the discomfort I felt at such an intrusion of mystery and beauty into a room which I had succeeded in filling with my own personality until I thought no more of the room than of myself. The anesthetic effect of custom being destroyed, I would begin to think and to feel very melancholy things. The door handle of my room, which was different to me from all the other door handles in the world, inasmuch as it seemed to open of its own accord and without my having to turn it, so unconscious had its manipulation become; lo and behold, it was now an astral body[24] for Golo. And as soon as the dinner bell rang I would run down to the dining room, where the big hanging lamp, ignorant of Golo and Bluebeard[25] but well acquainted with my family and the dish of stewed beef, shed the same light as on every other evening; and I would fall into the arms of my mother, whom the misfortunes of Geneviève de Brabant had made all the dearer to me, just as the crimes of Golo had driven me to a more than ordinarily scrupulous examination of my own conscience.

But after dinner, alas, I was soon obliged to leave Mamma, who stayed talking with the others, in the garden if it was fine, or in the

22. Marcel's great-aunt is reading the story to him as they wait for dinner.

23. The first dynasty of French kings, 500-751 A.D.

24. Spiritual counterpart of the physical body; according to the doctrine of Theosophy (a spiritualist movement originating in 1875), the astral body survives the death of the physical body.

25. The legendary wife-murderer, presumably depicted on another set of slides.

little parlor where everyone took shelter when it was wet. Everyone except my grandmother, who held that "It is a pity to shut oneself indoors in the country," and used to carry on endless discussions with my father on the very wettest days, because he would send me up to my room with a book instead of letting me stay out of doors. "That is not the way to make him strong and active," she would say sadly, "especially this little man, who needs all the strength and character that he can get." My father would shrug his shoulders and study the barometer, for he took an interest in meteorology, while my mother, keeping very quiet so as not to disturb him, looked at him with tender respect, but not too hard, not wishing to penetrate the mysteries of his superior mind. But my grandmother, in all weathers, even when the rain was coming down in torrents and Françoise had rushed indoors with the precious wicker armchairs, so that they should not get soaked—you would see my grandmother pacing the deserted garden, lashed by the storm, pushing back her grey hair in disorder so that her brows might be more free to imbibe the life-giving drafts of wind and rain. She would say, "At last one can breathe!" and would run up and down the soaking paths—too straight and symmetrical for her liking, owing to the want of any feeling for nature in the new gardener, whom my father had been asking all morning if the weather were going to improve—with her keen, jerky little step regulated by the various effects wrought upon her soul by the intoxication of the storm, the force of hygiene, the stupidity of my education and of symmetry in gardens, rather than by any anxiety (for that was quite unknown to her) to save her plum-colored skirt from the spots of mud under which it would gradually disappear to a depth which always provided her maid with a fresh problem and filled her with fresh despair.

When these walks of my grandmother's took place after dinner there was one thing which never failed to bring her back to the house: that was if (at one of those points when the revolutions of her course brought her, moth-like, in sight of the lamp in the little parlor where the liqueurs were set out on the card table) my great-aunt called out to her: "Bathilde! Come in and stop your husband from drinking brandy!" For, simply to tease her (she had brought so foreign a type of mind into my father's family that everyone made a joke of it), my great-aunt used to make my grandfather, who was forbidden liqueurs, take just a few drops. My poor grandmother would come in and beg and implore her husband not to taste the brandy; and he would become annoyed and swallow his few drops all the same, and she would go out again sad and discouraged, but still smiling, for she was so humble and so sweet that her gentleness toward others, and her continual subordination of herself and of her own troubles, appeared on her face blended in a smile which, unlike those seen on the majority of human faces, had no trace in it of irony, save for herself, while for all of us kisses seemed to spring from her eyes, which could not look upon those she loved without yearning to bestow upon them passionate caresses. The torments inflicted on her by my great-aunt, the sight of my grandmother's vain entreaties, of her in her weakness conquered before she began, but still making the futile endeavor to wean my grandfather from his liqueur glass—all these were things of the sort to which, in later years, one can grow so well accustomed as to smile at them, to take the tormentor's side with a happy determination which deludes one into the belief that it is not, really, tormenting; but in those days they filled me with such horror that I longed to strike my great-aunt. And yet, as soon as I heard her "Bathilde! Come in and stop your husband from drinking brandy!" in my cowardice I became at once a man, and did what all we grown men do when face to face with suffering and injustice; I preferred not to see them; I ran up to the top of the house to cry by myself in a little room beside the schoolroom and beneath the roof which smelt of orris root,[26] and was scented also by a wild currant bush which had climbed up between the stones of the outer wall and thrust a flowering branch in through the half-opened window. Intended for a more special and a baser use,[27] this room, from which, in the daytime, I could see as far as the keep of Roussainville-le-Pin,[28] was for a long time my place of refuge, doubtless because it was the only room whose door I was allowed to lock, whenever my occupation was such as required an inviolable solitude; reading or dreaming, secret tears or paroxysms of desire. Alas! I little knew that my own lack of will power, my delicate health, and the consequent uncertainty as to my future weighed far more heavily on my grandmother's mind than any little breach of the rules by her husband, during those endless perambulations, afternoon and evening, in which we used to see passing up and down, obliquely raised toward the heavens, her handsome face with its brown and wrinkled cheeks, which with age had acquired almost the purple hue of tilled fields in autumn, covered, if she were walking abroad, by a half-lifted veil, while upon them either the cold or some sad reflection invariably left the drying traces of an involuntary tear.

My sole consolation when I went upstairs for the night was that Mamma would come in and kiss me after I was in bed. But this

26. A powder then used as a deodorizer for rooms.

27. As a toilet.

28. The *keep* is the best-fortified tower of a medieval castle.

good night lasted for so short a time: she went down again so soon that the moment in which I heard her climb the stairs, and then caught the sound of her garden dress of blue muslin, from which hung little tassels of plaited straw, rustling along the double-doored corridor, was for me a moment of the keenest sorrow. So much did I love that good night that I reached the stage of hoping that it would come as late as possible, so as to prolong the time of respite during which Mamma would not yet have appeared. Sometimes when, after kissing me, she opened the door to go, I longed to call her back, to say to her "Kiss me just once again," but I knew that then she would at once look displeased, for the concession which she made to my wretchedness and agitation in coming up to me with this kiss of peace always annoyed my father, who thought such ceremonies absurd, and she would have liked to try to induce me to outgrow the need, the custom of having her there at all, which was a very different thing from letting the custom grow up of my asking her for an additional kiss when she was already crossing the threshold. And to see her look displeased destroyed all the sense of tranquillity she had brought me a moment before, when she bent her loving face down over my bed, and held it out to me like a Host,[29] for an act of Communion in which my lips might drink deeply the sense of her real presence, and with it the power to sleep. But those evenings on which Mamma stayed so short a time in my room were sweet indeed compared to those on which we had guests to dinner, and therefore she did not come at all. Our "guests" were practically limited to M. Swann, who, apart from a few passing strangers, was almost the only person who ever came to the house at Combray, sometimes to a neighborly dinner (but less frequently since his unfortunate marriage,[30] as my family did not care to receive his wife) and sometimes after dinner, uninvited. On those evenings when, as we sat in front of the house beneath the big chestnut tree and round the iron table, we heard, from the far end of the garden, not the large and noisy rattle which heralded and deafened as he approached with its ferruginous,[31] interminable, frozen sound any member of the household who had put it out of action by coming in "without ringing," but the double peal—timid, oval, gilded—of the visitors' bell, everyone would at once exclaim, "A visitor! Who in the world can it be?" but they knew quite well that it could only be M. Swann. My great-aunt, speaking in a loud voice, to set an example, in a tone which she endeavored to make sound natural, would tell the others not to whisper so; that nothing could be more unpleasant for a stranger coming in, who would be led to think that

29. Communion wafer.
30. To his mistress, Odette de Crécy, whose reputation for promiscuity would continue.
31. Iron-like

people were saying things about him which he was not meant to hear; and then my grandmother would be sent out as a scout, always happy to find an excuse for an additional turn in the garden, which she would utilize to remove surreptitiously, as she passed, the stakes of a rose-tree or two, so as to make the roses look a little more natural, as a mother might run her hand through her boy's hair, after the barber had smoothed it down, to make it stick out properly round his head.

And there we would all stay, hanging on the words which would fall from my grandmother's lips when she brought us back her report of the enemy, as though there had been some uncertainty among a vast number of possible invaders, and then, soon after, my grandfather would say: "I can hear Swann's voice." And, indeed, one could tell him only by his voice, for it was difficult to make out his face with its arched nose and green eyes, under a high forehead fringed with fair, almost red hair, dressed in the Bressant style,[32] because in the garden we used as little light as possible, so as not to attract mosquitoes: and I would slip away as though not going for anything in particular, to tell them to bring out the syrups;[33] for my grandmother made a great point, thinking it "nicer," of their not being allowed to seem anything out of the ordinary, which we kept for visitors only. Although a far younger man, M. Swann was very much attached to my grandfather, who had been an intimate friend, in his time, of Swann's father, an excellent but an eccentric man in whom the least little thing would, it seemed, often check the flow of his spirits and divert the current of his thoughts. Several times in the course of a year I would hear my grandfather tell at table the story, which never varied, of the behavior of M. Swann the elder upon the death of his wife, by whose bedside he had watched day and night. My grandfather, who had not seen him for a long time, hastened to join him at the Swanns' family property on the outskirts of Combray, and managed to entice him for a moment, weeping profusely, out of the death chamber, so that he should not be present when the body was laid in its coffin. They took a turn or two in the park, where there was a little sunshine. Suddenly M. Swann seized my grandfather by the arm and cried, "Oh, my dear old friend, how fortunate we are to be walking here together on such a charming day! Don't you see how pretty they are, all these trees—my hawthorns, and my new pond, on which you have never congratulated me? You look as glum as a nightcap. Don't you feel this little breeze? Ah! whatever you may say, it's good to be alive all the same, my dear Amédée!" And then,

32. Close-cropped, like a crew cut; named after a French actor.

33. Such as Grenadine, a sweet, nonalcoholic drink served as a cordial.

abruptly, the memory of his dead wife returned to him, and probably thinking it too complicated to inquire into how, at such a time, he could have allowed himself to be carried away by an impulse of happiness, he confined himself to a gesture which he habitually employed whenever any perplexing question came into his mind: that is, he passed his hand across his forehead, dried his eyes, and wiped his glasses. And he could never be consoled for the loss of his wife, but used to say to my grandfather, during the two years for which he survived her, "It's a funny thing, now; I very often think of my poor wife, but I cannot think of her very much at any one time." "Often, but a little at a time, like poor old Swann," became one of my grandfather's favorite phrases, which he would apply to all kinds of things. And I should have assumed that this father of Swann's had been a monster if my grandfather, whom I regarded as a better judge than myself, and whose word was my law and often led me in the long run to pardon offences which I should have been inclined to condemn, had not gone on to exclaim, "But after all, he had a heart of gold."

For many years, albeit—and especially before his marriage—M. Swann the younger came often to see them at Combray, my great-aunt and grandparents never suspected that he had entirely ceased to live in the kind of society which his family had frequented, or that, under the sort of incognito which the name of Swann gave him among us, they were harboring—with the complete innocence of a family of honest innkeepers who have in their midst some distinguished highwayman and never know it—one of the smartest[34] members of the Jockey Club, a particular friend of the Comte de Paris and of the Prince of Wales, and one of the men most sought after in the aristocratic world of the Faubourg Saint-Germain.[35]

Our utter ignorance of the brilliant part which Swann was playing in the world of fashion was, of course, due in part to his own reserve and discretion, but also to the fact that middle-class people in those days took what was almost a Hindu view of society,[36] which they held to consist of sharply defined castes, so that everyone at his birth found himself called to that station in life which his parents already occupied, and nothing, except the chance of a

34. Most stylish.

35. The Faubourg Saint-Germain is a fashionable area of Paris on the left bank of the Seine; many of the French aristocracy lived there. The Jockey Club was an exclusive men's club devoted not only to horseracing but to other diversions (such as the Opera). The Comte de Paris (1838–1894) was heir apparent to the French throne, in the unlikely chance that the monarchy were reinstated, and the Prince of Wales became in 1901 King Edward VII of England. The implication is that Swann's social connections were not merely of the highest but of an idle and somewhat hedonistic sort.

36. Which divides all of its members into four distinct hereditary castes, with relative restrictions on occupations and marriage.

brilliant career or of a "good" marriage, could extract you from that station or admit you to a superior caste. M. Swann, the father, had been a stockbroker; and so "young Swann" found himself immured for life in a caste where one's fortune, as in a list of taxpayers, varied between such and such limits of income. We knew the people with whom his father had associated, and so we knew his own associates, the people with whom he was "in a position to mix." If he knew other people besides, those were youthful acquaintances on whom the old friends of the family, like my relatives, shut their eyes all the more good-naturedly that Swann himself, after he was left an orphan, still came most faithfully to see us; but we would have been ready to wager that the people outside our acquaintance whom Swann knew were of the sort to whom he would not have dared to raise his hat, had he met them while he was walking with ourselves. Had there been such a thing as a determination to apply to Swann a social coefficient peculiar to himself, as distinct from all the other sons of other stockbrokers in his father's position, his coefficient would have been rather lower than theirs, because, leading a very simple life, and having always had a craze for "antiques" and pictures, he now lived and piled up his collections in an old house which my grandmother longed to visit, but which stood on the Quai d'Orléans,[37] a neighborhood in which my great-aunt thought it most degrading to be quartered. "Are you really a connoisseur, now?" she would say to him; "I ask for your own sake, as you are likely to have 'fakes' palmed off on you by the dealers," for she did not, in fact, endow him with any critical faculty, and had no great opinion of the intelligence of a man who, in conversation, would avoid serious topics and showed a very dull preciseness, not only when he gave us kitchen recipes, going into the most minute details, but even when my grandmother's sisters were talking to him about art. When challenged by them to give an opinion, or to express his admiration for some picture, he would remain almost impolitely silent, and would then make amends by furnishing (if he could) some fact or other about the gallery in which the picture was hung, or the date at which it had been painted. But as a rule he would content himself with trying to amuse us by telling us the story of his latest adventure—and he would have a fresh story for us on every occasion—with someone whom we ourselves knew, such as the Combray chemist,[38] or our cook, or our coachman. These stories certainly used to make my great-aunt laugh, but she could never tell whether that was on account of the absurd parts which Swann invariabley made himself play in the adventures, or of the wit that he showed in telling us of

37. A beautiful though less fashionable section in the heart of Paris, along the Seine.

38. Pharmacist.

them. "It is easy to see that you are a regular 'character,' M. Swann!"

As she was the only member of our family who could be described as a trifle "common," she would always take care to remark to strangers, when Swann was mentioned, that he could easily, if he had wished to, have lived in the Boulevard Haussmann or the Avenue de l'Opéra,[39] and that he was the son of old M. Swann who must have left four or five million francs, but that it was a fad of his. A fad which, moreover, she thought was bound to amuse other people so much that in Paris, when M. Swann called on New Year's Day bringing her a little pack of *marrons glacés*,[40] she never failed, if there were strangers in the room, to say to him: "Well, M. Swann, and do you still live next door to the Bonded Vaults,[41] so as to be sure of not missing your train when you go to Lyons?" and she would peep out of the corner of her eye, over her glasses, at the other visitors.

But if anyone had suggested to my aunt that this Swann, who, in his capacity as the son of old M. Swann, was "fully qualified" to be received by any of the "upper middle class," the most respected barristers and solicitors[42] of Paris (though he was perhaps a trifle inclined to let this hereditary privilege go into abeyance), had another almost secret existence of a wholly different kind: that when he left our house in Paris, saying that he must go home to bed, he would no sooner have turned the corner than he would stop, retrace his steps, and be off to some drawing room on whose like no stockbroker or associate of stockbrokers had ever set eyes—that would have seemed to my aunt as extraordinary as, to a woman of wider reading, the thought of being herself on terms of intimacy with Aristaeus,[43] of knowing that he would, when he had finished his conversation with her, plunge deep into the realms of Thetis, into an empire veiled from mortal eyes, in which Virgil depicts him as being received with open arms; or—to be content with an image more likely to have occurred to her, for she had seen it painted on the plates we used for biscuits at Combray—as the thought of having had to dinner Ali Baba,[44] who, as soon as he found himself alone and unobserved, would make his way into the cave, resplendent with its unsuspected treasures.

One day when he had come to see us after dinner in Paris, and

39. Two large modern avenues where the wealthy *bourgeoisie* (or middle class) liked to live.

40. Candied chestnuts, a traditional gift on New Year's Day, then a more common day for exchanging gifts than Christmas.

41. A wine warehouse in southeastern Paris, close to the *Gare de Lyon*, the terminal from which trains depart for the industrial city of Lyon and other destinations in southeastern France.

42. Trial lawyers and lawyers of other kinds.

43. Son of the Greek god Apollo. In Virgil's *Fourth Georgic*, Aristaeus seeks help from the sea nymph Thetis.

44. Hero of an *Arabian Nights* tale, a poor youth who discovers a robber's cave filled with treasure.

had begged pardon for being in evening clothes, Françoise, when he had gone, told us that she had got it from his coachman that he had been dining "with a princess." "A pretty sort of princess,"[45] drawled my aunt; "I know them," and she shrugged her shoulders without raising her eyes from her knitting, serenely ironical.

Altogether, my aunt used to treat him with scant ceremony. Since she was of the opinion that he ought to feel flattered by our invitations, she thought it only right and proper that he should never come to see us in summer without a basket of peaches or raspberries from his garden, and that from each of his visits to Italy he should bring back some photographs of old masters for me.

It seemed quite natural, therefore, to send to him whenever we wanted a recipe for some special sauce or for a pineapple salad for one of our big dinner parties, to which he himself would not be invited, not seeming of sufficient importance to be served up to new friends who might be in our house for the first time. If the conversation turned upon the Princes of the House of France,[46] "Gentlemen you and I will never know, will we, and don't want to, do we?" my great-aunt would say tartly to Swann, who had, perhaps, a letter from Twickenham[47] in his pocket; she would make him play accompaniments and turn over music on evenings when my grandmother's sister sang; manipulating this creature, so rare and refined at other times and in other places, with the rough simplicity of a child who will play with some curio from the cabinet no more carefully than if it were a penny toy. Certainly the Swann who was a familiar figure in all the clubs of those days differed hugely from the Swann created in my great-aunt's mind when, of an evening, in our little garden at Combray, after the two shy peals had sounded from the gate, she would vitalize, by injecting into it everything she had ever heard about the Swann family, the vague and unrecognizable shape which began to appear, with my grandmother in its wake, against a background of shadows, and could at last be identified by the sound of its voice. But then, even in the most insignificant details of our daily life, none of us can be said to constitute a material whole, which is identical for everyone, and need only be turned up like a page in an account-book or the record of a will; our social personality is created by the thoughts of other people. Even the simple act which we describe as "seeing someone we know" is, to some extent, an intellectual process. We pack the physical outline of the creature we see with all the ideas we have already formed about him, and in the complete picture of him which we compose in our minds those ideas have certainly the prin-

45. That is, a "princess" of some shady level of society.

46. The male members of the French royal family, such as the Comte de Paris. The spirit of the times was anti-Royalist, and in fact all claimants to the French throne and their heirs were banished from France by law in 1886.

47. Fashionable London suburb. The French royal family had a house there.

cipal place. In the end they come to fill out so completely the curve of his cheeks, to follow so exactly the line of his nose, they blend so harmoniously in the sound of his voice that these seem to be no more than a transparent envelope, so that each time we see the face or hear the voice it is our own ideas of him which we recognize and to which we listen. And so, no doubt, from the Swann they had built up for their own purposes my family had left out, in their ignorance, a whole crowd of the details of his daily life in the world of fashion, details by means of which other people, when they met him, saw all the Graces[48] enthroned in his face and stopping at the line of his arched nose as at a natural frontier; but they contrived also to put into a face from which its distinction had been evicted, a face vacant and roomy as an untenanted house, to plant in the depths of its unvalued eyes a lingering sense, uncertain but not unpleasing, half memory and half oblivion, of idle hours spent together after our weekly dinners, round the card table or in the garden, during our companionable country life. Our friend's bodily frame had been so well lined with this sense, and with various earlier memories of his family, that their own special Swann had become to my people a complete and living creature; so that even now I have the feeling of leaving someone I know for another quite different person when, going back in memory, I pass from the Swann whom I knew later and more intimately to this early Swann —this early Swann in whom I can distinguish the charming mistakes of my childhood, and who, incidentally, is less like his successor than he is like the other people I knew at that time, as though one's life were a series of galleries in which all the portraits of any one period had a marked family likeness, the same (so to speak) tonality—this early Swann abounding in leisure, fragrant with the scent of the great chestnut tree, of baskets of raspberries and of a sprig of tarragon.

And yet one day, when my grandmother had gone to ask some favor of a lady whom she had known at the Sacré Coeur[49] (and with whom, because of our caste theory, she had not cared to keep up any degree of intimacy in spite of several common interests), the Marquise de Villeparisis,[50] of the famous house of Bouillon, this lady had said to her:

"I think you know M. Swann very well; he is a great friend of my nephews, the des Laumes."

My grandmother had returned from the call full of praise for the house, which overlooked some gardens, and in which Mme. de Villeparisis had advised her to rent a flat; and also for a repairing tailor and his daughter, who kept a little shop in the courtyard, into

48. Greek divinities, young women who personified beauty and grace.
49. A convent school in Paris, attended by daughters of the aristocracy and the wealthy *bourgeoisie*.

which she had gone to ask them to put a stitch in her skirt, which she had torn on the staircase. My grandmother had found these people perfectly charming: the girl, she said, was a jewel, and the tailor a most distinguished man, the finest she had ever seen. For in her eyes distinction was a thing wholly independent of social position. She was in ecstasies over some answer the tailor had made, saying to Mamma:

"Sévigné[51] would not have said it better!" and, by the way of contrast, of a nephew of Mme. de Villeparisis whom she had met at the house:

"My dear, he is so common!"

Now, the effect of that remark about Swann had been, not to raise him in my great-aunt's estimation, but to lower Mme. de Villeparisis. It appeared that the deference which, on my grandmother's authority, we owed to Mme. de Villeparisis imposed on her the reciprocal obligation to do nothing that would render her less worthy of our regard, and that she had failed in her duty in becoming aware of Swann's existence and in allowing members of her family to associate with him. "How should she know Swann? A lady who, you always made out, was related to Marshal MacMahon!"[52] This view of Swann's social atmosphere which prevailed in my family seemed to be confirmed later on by his marriage with a woman of the worst class, you might almost say a "fast" woman, whom, to do him justice, he never attempted to introduce to us, for he continued to come to us alone, though he came more and more seldom; but from whom they thought they could establish, on the assumption that he had found her there, the circle, unknown to them, in which he ordinarily moved.

But on one occasion my grandfather read in a newspaper that M. Swann was one of the most faithful attendants at the Sunday luncheons given by the Duc de X———, whose father and uncle had been among our most prominent statesmen in the reign of Louis Philippe.[53] Now my grandfather was curious to learn all the little details which might help him to take a mental share in the private lives of men like Molé, the Duc Pasquier, or the Duc de Broglie.[54] He was delighted to find that Swann associated with people who had known them. My great-aunt, however, interpreted

50. Member of the Guermantes family. Proust enhances the apparent reality of the Guermantes by relating them to the historical house of Bouillon, a famous aristocratic family tracing its descent from the Middle Ages. The des Laumes, on the other hand, are fictional.

51. The Marquise de Sévigné (1626–1696), known for the lively style of her letters.

52. (1808–1893), Marshal of France, elected President of the French Republic in 1873.

53. King of France from 1830 to 1848, father of the Comte de Paris.

54. Comte Louis Mathieu Molé (1781–1855) held various cabinet positions before becoming premier of France in 1836; Duc Etienne Denis de Pasquier (1767–1862) also held important public positions up to 1837; and Duc Achille Charles Leonce Victor de Broglie (1785–1870) had a busy public career that ended in 1851. All were active during the reign of Louis Philippe.

this piece of news in a sense discreditable to Swann; for anyone who chose his associates outside the caste in which he had been born and bred, outside his "proper station," was condemned to utter degradation in her eyes. It seemed to her that such a one abdicated all claim to enjoy the fruits of those friendly relations with people of good position which prudent parents cultivate and store up for their children's benefit, for my great-aunt had actually ceased to "see" the son of a lawyer we had known because he had married a "Highness" and had thereby stepped down—in her eyes—from the respectable position of a lawyer's son to that of those adventurers, upstart footmen or stable-boys mostly, to whom we read that queens have sometimes shown their favors. She objected, therefore, to my grandfather's plan of questioning Swann, when next he came to dine with us, about these people whose friendship with him we had discovered. On the other hand, my grandmother's two sisters, elderly spinsters who shared her nobility of character but lacked her intelligence, declared that they could not conceive what pleasure their brother-in-law could find in talking about such trifles. They were ladies of lofty ambition, who for that reason were incapable of taking the least interest in what might be called the "pinchbeck"[55] things of life, even when they had an historic value, or, generally speaking, in anything that was not directly associated with some object esthetically precious. So complete was their negation of interest in anything which seemed directly or indirectly a part of our everyday life that their sense of hearing—which had gradually come to understand its own futility when the tone of the conversation, at the dinner table, became frivolous or merely mundane, without the two old ladies' being able to guide it back to the topic dear to themselves—would leave its receptive channels unemployed, so effectively that they were actually becoming atrophied. So that if my grandfather wished to attract the attention of the two sisters, he would have to make use of some such alarm signals as mad-doctors adopt in dealing with their distracted patients; as by beating several times on a glass with the blade of a knife, fixing them at the same time with a sharp word and a compelling glance, violent methods which the said doctors are apt to bring with them into their everyday life among the sane, either from force of professional habit or because they think the whole world a trifle mad.

Their interest grew, however, when, the day before Swann was to dine with us, and when he had made them a special present of a case of Asti,[56] my great-aunt, who had in her hand a copy of the *Figaro*[57] in which to the name of a picture then on view in a Corot[58] exhibition were added the words, "from the collection of

55. Petty or spurious; here, gossip or small talk.
56. An Italian white wine.
57. Leading Parisian newspaper.
58. (1796–1875), French landscape painter, very popular at the time.

M. Charles Swann," asked: "Did you see that Swann is 'mentioned' in the *Figaro*?"

"But I have always told you," said my grandmother, "that he had plenty of taste."

"You would, of course," retorted my great-aunt, "say anything just to seem different from *us*." For, knowing that my grandmother never agreed with her, and not being quite confident that it was her own opinion which the rest of us invariably endorsed, she wished to extort from us a wholesale condemnation of my grandmother's views, against which she hoped to force us into solidarity with her own.

But we sat silent. My grandmother's sisters having expressed a desire to mention to Swann this reference to him in the *Figaro*, my great-aunt dissuaded them. Whenever she saw in others an advantage, however trivial, which she herself lacked, she would persuade herself that it was no advantage at all, but a drawback, and would pity so as not to have to envy them.

"I don't think that would please him at all; I know very well, I should hate to see my name printed like that, as large as life, in the paper, and I shouldn't feel at all flattered if anyone spoke to me about it."

She did not, however, put any very great pressure upon my grandmother's sisters, for they, in their horror of vulgarity, had brought to such a fine art the concealment of a personal allusion in a wealth of ingenious circumlocution, that it would often pass unnoticed even by the person to whom it was addressed. As for my mother, her only thought was of managing to induce my father to consent to speak to Swann, not of his wife, but of his daughter, whom he worshipped, and for whose sake it was understood that he had ultimately made his unfortunate marriage.

"You need only say a word; just ask him how she is. It must be so very hard for him."

My father, however, was annoyed: "No, no; you have the most absurd ideas. It would be utterly ridiculous."

But the only one of us in whom the prospect of Swann's arrival gave rise to an unhappy foreboding was myself. And that was because on the evenings when there were visitors, or just M. Swann in the house, Mamma did not come up to my room. I did not, at that time, have dinner with the family: I came out to the garden after dinner, and at nine I said good night and went to bed. But on these evenings I used to dine earlier than the others, and to come in afterwards and sit at table until eight o'clock, when it was understood that I must go upstairs; that frail and precious kiss which Mamma used always to leave upon my lips when I was in bed and just going to sleep I had to take with me from the dining room to my own, and to keep inviolate all the time that it took me to undress, without letting its sweet charm be broken, without letting its volatile essence diffuse itself and evaporate; and just on those very evenings when I must needs take most pains to receive it with due formality, I had to snatch it, to seize it instantly and in public, without even having the time or being properly free to apply to what I was doing the punctiliousness which madmen use who compel themselves to exclude all other thoughts from their minds while they are shutting a door, so that when the sickness of uncertainty sweeps over them again they can triumphantly face and overcome it with the recollection of the precise moment in which the door was shut.

We were all in the garden when the double peal of the gatebell sounded shyly. Everyone knew that it must be Swann, and yet they looked at one another inquiringly and sent my grandmother scouting.

"See that you thank him intelligibly for the wine," my grandfather warned his two sisters-in-law; "you know how good it is, and it is a huge case."

"Now, don't start whispering!" said my great-aunt. "How would you like to come into a house and find everyone muttering to themselves?"

"Ah! there's M. Swann," cried my father. "Let's ask him if he thinks it will be fine tomorrow."

My mother fancied that a word from her would wipe out all the unpleasantness which my family had contrived to make Swann feel since his marriage. She found an opportunity to draw him aside for a moment. But I followed her: I could not bring myself to let her go out of reach of me while I felt that in a few minutes I should have to leave her in the dining room and go up to my bed without the consoling thought, as on ordinary evenings, that she would come up, later, to kiss me.

"Now, M. Swann," she said, "do tell me about your daughter; I am sure she shows a taste already for nice things, like her papa."

"Come along and sit down there with us all on the verandah," said my grandfather, coming up to him. My mother had to abandon the quest, but managed to extract from the restriction itself a further refinement of thought, as great poets do when the tyranny of rhyme forces them into the discovery of their finest lines.

"We can talk about her again when we are by ourselves," she said, or rather whispered to Swann. "It is only a mother who can understand. I am sure that hers would agree with me."

And so we all sat down round the iron table. I should have liked not to think of the hours of anguish which I should have to spend, that evening, alone in my room, without the possibility of going to sleep: I tried to convince myself that they were of no importance, really, since I should have forgotten them next morning, and to fix my mind on thoughts of the future which would carry me, as on a bridge, across the terrifying abyss that yawned at my feet. But my mind, strained by this foreboding, distended like the look which I shot at my mother, would now allow any other impression to enter. Thoughts did, indeed, enter it, but only on the condition that they left behind them every element of beauty, or even of quaintness, by which I might have been distracted or beguiled. As a surgical patient, by means of a local anesthetic, can look on with a clear consciousness while an operation is being performed upon him and yet feel nothing, I could repeat to myself some favorite lines, or watch my grandfather attempting to talk to Swann about the Duc d'Audriffet-Pasquier,[59] without being able to kindle any emotion from one or amusement from the other. Hardly had my grandfather begun to question Swann about that orator when one of my grandmother's sisters, in whose ears the question echoed like a solemn but untimely silence which her natural politeness bade her interrupt, addressed the other with:

"Just fancy, Flora, I met a young Swedish governess today who told me some most interesting things about the cooperative movement in Scandinavia. We really must have her to dine here one evening."

"To be sure!" said her sister Flora, "but I haven't wasted my time either. I met such a clever old gentleman at M. Vinteuil's[60] who knows Maubant[61] quite well, and Maubant has told him every little thing about how he gets up his parts. It is the most interesting thing I ever heard. He is a neighbor of M. Vinteuil's, and I never knew; and he is so nice besides."

"M. Vinteuil is not the only one who has nice neighbors," cried my aunt Céline in a voice which seemed loud because she was so timid, and seemed forced because she had been planning the little speech for so long; darting, as she spoke, what she called a "significant glance" at Swann. And my aunt Flora, who realized that this veiled utterance was Céline's way of thanking Swann intelligibly for the Asti, looked at him with a blend of congratulation and irony, either just because she wished to underline her sister's little epigram, or because she envied Swann his having inspired it, or merely because she imagined that he was embarrassed, and could not help having a little fun at his expense.

"I think it would be worth while," Flora went on, "to have this old gentleman to dinner. When you get him upon Maubant or Mme. Materna[62] he will talk for hours on end."

59. A fictitious nobleman.

60. A fictitious composer and neighbor of the family.

61. Actor at the Comédie Francaise, the French national theater.

62. Austrian soprano, who took part in the premiere of Wagner's *Ring* cycle at Bayreuth in 1876.

"That must be delightful," sighed my grandfather, in whose mind nature had unfortunately forgotten to include any capacity whatsoever for becoming passionately interested in the cooperative movement among the ladies of Sweden or in the methods employed by Maubant to get up his parts, just as it had forgotten to endow my grandmother's two sisters with a grain of that precious salt which one has oneself to "add to taste" in order to extract any savor from a narrative of the private life of Molé or of the Comte de Paris.

"I say!" exclaimed Swann to my grandfather, "what I was going to tell you has more to do than you might think with what you were asking me just now, for in some respects there has been very little change. I came across a passage in Saint-Simon[63] this morning which would have amused you. It is in the volume which covers his mission to Spain; not one of the best, little more in fact than a journal, but at least it is a journal wonderfully well written, which fairly distinguishes it from the devastating journalism that we feel bound to read in these days, morning, noon and night."

"I do not agree with you: there are some days when I find reading the papers very pleasant indeed!" my aunt Flora broke in, to show Swann that she had read the note about his Corot in the *Figaro*.

"Yes," aunt Céline went one better. "When they write about things or people in whom we are interested."

"I don't deny it," answered Swann in some bewilderment. "The fault I find with our journalism is that it forces us to take an interest in some fresh triviality or other every day, whereas only three or four books in a lifetime give us anything that is of real importance. Suppose that, every morning, when we tore the wrapper off our paper with fevered hands, a transmutation were to take place, and we were to find inside it—oh! I don't know; shall we say Pascal's *Pensées*?"[64] He articulated the title with an ironic emphasis so as not to appear pedantic. "And then, in the gilt and tooled volumes which we open once in ten years," he went on, showing that contempt for the things of this world which some men of the world like to affect, "we should read that the Queen of the Hellenes had arrived at Cannes, or that the Princesse de Léon had given a fancy dress ball. In that way we should arrive at the right proportion between 'information' and 'publicity.'" But at once regretting that he had allowed himself to speak, even in jest, of serious matters, he added ironically: "We are having a most entertaining conversation; I cannot think why we climb to these lofty summits," and then, turning to my grandfather: "Well, Saint-Simon tells how Maule-

63. The memoirs of the Duc de Saint-Simon (1675–1755) describe court life and intrigue during the reigns of Louis XIV and Louis XV. He was sent to Spain in 1721 to arrange the marriage of Louis XV and the daughter of the King of Spain.

64. The *Thoughts* of the French mathematician and religious philosopher Blaise Pascal (1623–1662) are comments on the human condition, and one of the triumphant works of French classicism.

vrier had had the audacity to offer his hand to his sons. You remember how he says of Maulevrier, 'Never did I find in that coarse bottle anything but ill-humor, boorishness, and folly.' "[65]

"Coarse or not, I know bottles in which there is something very different!" said Flora briskly, feeling bound to thank Swann as well as her sister, since the present of Asti had been addressed to them both. Céline began to laugh.

Swann was puzzled, but went on: " 'I cannot say whether it was his ignorance or a trap,' writes Saint-Simon; 'he wished to give his hand to my children. I noticed it in time to prevent him.' "

My grandfather was already in ecstasies over "ignorance or a trap," but Miss Céline—the name of Saint-Simon, a "man of letters," having arrested the complete paralysis of her sense of hearing—had grown angry.

"What! You admire that, do you? Well, it is clever enough! But what is the point of it? Does he mean that one man isn't as good as another? What difference can it make whether he is a duke or a groom so long as he is intelligent and good? He had a fine way of bringing up his children, your Saint-Simon, if he didn't teach them to shake hands with all honest men. Really and truly, it's abominable. And you dare to quote it!"

And my grandfather, utterly depressed, realizing how futile it would be for him, against this opposition, to attempt to get Swann to tell him the stories which would have amused him, murmured to my mother: "Just tell me again that line of yours which always comforts me so much on these occasions. Oh, yes:

What virtues, Lord, Thou makest us abhor![66]

Good, that is, very good."

I never took my eyes off my mother. I knew that when they were at table I should not be permitted to stay there for the whole of dinner time, and that Mamma, for fear of annoying my father, would not allow me to give her in public the series of kisses that she would have had in my room. And so I promised myself that in the dining room, as they began to eat and drink and as I felt the hour approach, I would put beforehand into this kiss, which was bound to be so brief and stealthy in execution, everything that my own efforts could put into it; would look out very carefully first the exact spot on her cheek where I would imprint it, and would so prepare my thoughts that If might be able, thanks to these mental preliminaries, to consecrate the whole of the minute Mamma would allow me to the sensation of her cheek against my lips, as a painter who

65. Maulevrier was the French ambassador to Spain. Saint-Simon considered him of inferior birth, and refused to let his own children shake Maulevrier's hand. (*Memoirs*, vol. XXXIX.)

66. From *Pompey's Death* (line 1072), a tragedy by the French dramatist Pierre Corneille (1606–1684).

can have his subject for short sittings only prepares his palette, and from what he remembers and from rough notes does in advance everything which he possibly can do in the sitter's absence. But tonight, before the dinner bell had sounded, my grandfather said with unconscious cruelty: "The little man looks tired; he'd better go up to bed. Besides, we are dining late tonight."

And my father, who was less scrupulous than my grandmother or mother in observing the letter of a treaty, went on: "Yes, run along; to bed with you."

I would have kissed Mamma then and there, but at that moment the dinner bell rang.

"No, no, leave your mother alone. You've said good night quite enough. These exhibitions are absurd. Go on upstairs."

And so I must set forth without viaticum;[67] must climb each step of the staircase "against my heart," as the saying is, climbing in opposition to my heart's desire, which was to return to my mother, since she had not, by her kiss, given my heart leave to accompany me forth. That hateful staircase, up which I always passed with such dismay, gave out a smell of varnish which had to some extent absorbed, made definite and fixed the special quality of sorrow that I felt each evening, and made it perhaps even more cruel to my sensibility because, when it assumed this olfactory guise, my intellect was powerless to resist it. When we have gone to sleep with a maddening toothache and are conscious of it only as a little girl whom we attempt, time after time, to pull out of the water, or as a line of Molière[68] which we repeat incessantly to ourselves, it is a great relief to wake up, so that our intelligence can disentangle the idea of toothache from any artificial semblance of heroism or rhythmic cadence. It was the precise converse of this relief which I felt when my anguish at having to go up to my room invaded my consciousness in a manner infinitely more rapid, instantaneous almost, a manner at once insidious and brutal as I breathed in—a far more poisonous thing than any moral penetration—the peculiar smell of the varnish upon that staircase.

Once in my room I had to stop every loophole, to close the shutters, to dig my own grave as I turned down the bedclothes, to wrap myself in the shroud of my nightshirt. But before burying myself in the iron bed which had been placed there because, on summer nights, I was too hot among the rep curtains of the four-poster,[69] I was stirred to revolt, and attempted the desperate stratagem of a condemned prisoner. I wrote to my mother begging her to come upstairs for an important reason which I could not put in writing.

67. The communion wafer and wine given to the dying in Catholic rites.

68. (1622–1673), French dramatist.

69. Bed with corner pillars to support a canopy and curtains. *rep*: a heavy, ribbed fabric.

My fear was the Françoise, my aunt's cook who used to be put in charge of me when I was at Combray, might refuse to take my note. I had a suspicion that, in her eyes, to carry a message to my mother when there was a stranger in the room would appear flatly inconceivable, just as it would be for the door keeper of a theatre to hand a letter to an actor upon the stage. For things which might or might not be done she possessed a code at once imperious, abundant, subtle, and uncompromising on points themselves imperceptible or irrelevant, which gave it a resemblance to those ancient laws which combine such cruel ordinances as the massacre of infants at the breast with prohibitions, of exaggerated refinement, against "seething the kid in his mother's milk," or "eating of the sinew which is upon the hollow of the thigh."[70] This code, if one could judge it by the sudden obstinacy which she would put into her refusal to carry out certain of our instructions, seemed to have foreseen such social complications and refinements of fashion as nothing in Françoise's surroundings or in her career as a servant in a village household could have put into her head; and we were obliged to assume that there was latent in her some past existence in the ancient history of France, noble and little understood, just as there is in those manufacturing towns where old mansions still testify to their former courtly days, and chemical workers toil among delicately sculptured scenes of the Miracle of Theophilus or the Quatre Fils Aymon.[71]

In this particular instance, the article of her code which made it highly improbable that—barring an outbreak of fire—Françoise would go down and disturb Mamma when M. Swann was there for so unimportant a person as myself was one embodying the respect she showed not only for the family (as for the dead, for the clergy, or for royalty), but also for the stranger within our gates; a respect which I should perhaps have found touching in a book, but which never failed to irritate me on her lips, because of the solemn and gentle tones in which she would utter it, and which irritated me more than usual this evening when the sacred character in which she invested the dinner party might have the effect of making her decline to disturb its ceremonial. But to give myself one chance of success I lied without hesitation, telling her that it was not in the least myself who had wanted to write to Mamma, but Mamma who, on saying good night to me, had begged me not to forget to send her an answer about something she had asked me to find, and that she would certainly be very angry if this note were not taken to

70. Refers to the strict dietary laws of *Deuteronomy* 14:21 (the kid) and *Genesis* 32:32 the thigh).

71. Theophile was saved from damnation by the Virgin Mary after having signed a pact with the devil, and the four sons of Aymon were heroic knights who together rode the magic horse Bayard.

her. I think that Françoise disbelieved me, for, like those primitive men whose senses weres so much keener than our own, she could immediately detect, by signs imperceptible to the rest of us, the truth or falsehood of anything that we might wish to conceal from her. She studied the envelope for five minutes as though an examination of the paper itself and the look of my handwriting could enlighten her as to the nature of the contents, or tell her to which article of her code she ought to refer the matter. Then she went out with a air of resignation which seemed to imply: "What a dreadful thing for parents to have a child like this!"

A moment later she returned to say that they were still at the ice stage and that it was impossible for the butler to deliver the note at once, in front of everybody; but that when the finger bowls were put round he would find a way of slipping it into Mamma's hand. At once my anxiety subsided; it was now no longer (as it had been a moment ago) until tomorrow that I had lost my mother, for my little line was going—to annoy her, no doubt, and doubly so because this contrivance would make me ridiculous in Swann's eyes —but was going all the same to admit me, invisibly and by stealth, into the same room as herself, was going to whisper from me into her ear; for that forbidden and unfriendly dining room, where but a moment ago the ice itself—with burned nuts in it—and the finger bowls seemed to me to be concealing pleasures that were mischievous and of a mortal sadness because Mamma was tasting of them and I was far away, had opened its doors to me and, like a ripe fruit which bursts through its skin, was going to pour out into my intoxicated heart the gushing sweetness of Mamma's attention while she was reading what I had written. Now I was no longer separated from her; the barriers were down; an exquisite thread was binding us. Besides, that was not all, for surely Mamma would come.

As for the agony through which I had just passed, I imagined that Swann would have laughed heartily at it if he had read my letter and had guessed its purpose; whereas, on the contrary, as I was to learn in due course, a similar anguish[72] had been the bane of his life for many years, and no one perhaps could have understood my feelings at that moment so well as himself; to him, that anguish which lies in knowing that the creature one adores is in some place of enjoyment where oneself is not and cannot follow— to him that anguish came through Love, to which it is in a sense predestined, by which it must be equipped and adapted; but when, as had befallen me, such an anguish possesses one's soul before Love has yet entered into one's life, then it must drift, awaiting Love's coming, vague and free, without precise attachment, at the

72. That is, his unhappy love for Odette de Crécy, described in *Swann in Love*.

disposal of one sentiment today, of another tomorrow, of filial piety or affection for a comrade. And the joy with which I first bound myself apprentice, when Françoise returned to tell me that my letter would be delivered; Swann, too, had known well that false joy which a friend can give us, or some relative of the woman we love, when on his arrival at the house or theatre where she is to be found, for some ball or party or "first night" at which he is to meet her, he sees us wandering outside, desperately awaiting some opportunity of communicating with her. He recognizes us, greets us familiarly, and asks what we are doing there. And when we invent a story of having some urgent message to give to his relative or friend, he assures us that nothing could be more simple, takes us in at the door, and promises to send her down to us in five minutes. How much we love him—as at that moment I loved Françoise—the good-natured intermediary who by a single word has made supportable, human, almost propitious the inconceivable, infernal scene of gaiety in the thick of which we have been imagining swarms of enemies, perverse and seductive, beguiling away from us, even making laugh at us, the woman whom we love. If we are to judge of them by him, this relative who has accosted us and who is himself an initiate in those cruel mysteries, then the other guests cannot be so very demoniacal. Those inaccessible and torturing hours into which she had gone to taste of unknown pleasures—behold, a breach in the wall, and we are through it. Behold, one of the moments whose series will go to make up their sum, a moment as genuine as the rest, if not actually more important to ourself because our mistress is more intensely a part of it; we picture it to ourselves, we possess it, we intervene upon it, almost we have created it: namely, the moment in which he goes to tell her that we are waiting there below. And very probably the other moments of the party will not be essentially different, will contain nothing else so exquisite or so well able to make us suffer, since this kind friend has assured us that "Of course, she will be delighted to come down! It will be far more amusing for her to talk to you than to be bored up there." Alas! Swann had learned by experience that the good intentions of a third party are powerless to control a woman who is annoyed to find herself pursued even into a ballroom by a man whom she does not love. Too often, the kind friend comes down again alone.

My mother did not appear, but with no attempt to safeguard my self-respect (which depended upon her keeping up the fiction that she had asked me to let her know the result of my search for something or other) made Françoise tell me, in so many words "There is no answer"—words I have so often, since then, heard the hall-porters in "minions" and the flunkeys in gambling clubs and the like, repeat to some poor girl, who replies in bewilderment: "What! he's said nothing? It's not possible. You did give him my letter, didn't you? Very well, I shall wait a little longer." And just as she invariably protests that she does not need the extra gas which the porter offers to light for her, and sits on there, hearing nothing further, except an occasional remark on the weather which the porter exchanges with a messenger whom he will send off suddenly, when he notices the time, to put some customer's wine on the ice; so, having declined Françoise's offer to make me some tea or to stay beside me, I let her go off again to the servants' hall, and lay down and shut my eyes, and tried not to hear the voices of my family who were drinking their coffee in the garden.

But after a few seconds I realized that, by writing that line to Mamma, by approaching—at the risk of making her angry—so near to her that I felt I could reach out and grasp the moment in which I should see her again, I had cut myself off from the possibility of going to sleep until I actually had seen her, and my heart began to beat more and more painfully as I increased my agitation by ordering myself to keep calm and to acquiesce in my ill-fortune. Then, suddenly, my anxiety subsided, a feeling of intense happiness coursed through me, as when a strong medicine begins to take effect and one's pain vanishes: I had formed a resolution to abandon all attempts to go to sleep without seeing Mamma, and had decided to kiss her at all costs, even with the certainty of being in disgrace with her for long afterward, when she herself came up to bed. The tranquillity which followed my anguish made me extremely alert, no less than my sense of expectation, my thirst for and my fear of danger.

Noiselessly I opened the window and sat down on the foot of my bed; hardly daring to move in case they should hear me from below. Things outside seemed also fixed in mute expectation, so as not to disturb the moonlight which, duplicating each of them and throwing it back by the extension, forward, of a shadow denser and more concrete than its substance, had made the whole landscape seem at once thinner and longer, like a map which, after being folded up, is spread out upon the ground. What had to move—a leaf of the chestnut tree, for instance—moved. But its minute shuddering, complete, finished to the least detail and with utmost delicacy of gesture, made no discord with the rest of the scene, and yet was not merged on it, remaining clearly outlined. Exposed upon this surface of silence, which absorbed nothing from them, the most distant sounds, those which must have come from gardens at the far end of the town, could be distinguished with such exact "finish" that the impression they gave of coming from a distance seemed due only to their "pianissimo" execution, like those movements on muted strings so well performed by the orchestra of the Conservatoire[73]

73. The national music conservatory in Paris.

that, although one does not lose a single note, one thinks all the same that they are being played somewhere outside, a long way from the concert hall, so that all the old subscribers, and my grandmother's sisters too, when Swann had given them his seats, used to strain their ears as if they had caught the distant approach of an army on the march, which had not yet rounded the corner of the Rue de Trévise.[74]

I was well aware that I had placed myself in a position than which none could be counted upon to involve me in graver consequences at my parents' hands; consequences far graver, indeed, than a stranger would have imagined, and such as (he would have thought) could follow only some really shameful fault. But in the system of education which they had given me faults were not classified in the same order as in that of other children, and I had been taught to place at the head of the list (doubtless because there was no other class of faults from which I needed to be more carefully protected) those in which I can now distinguish the common feature that one succumbs to them by yielding to a nervous impulse. But such words as these last had never been uttered in my hearing; no one had yet accounted for my temptations in a way which might have led me to believe that there was some excuse for my giving in to them, or that I was actually incapable of holding out against them. Yet I could easily recognize this class of transgressions by the anguish of mind which preceded, as well as by the rigor of the punishment which followed them; and I knew that what I had just done was in the same category as certain other sins for which I had been severely chastised, though infinitely more serious than they. When I went out to meet my mother as she herself came up to bed, and when she saw that I had remained up so as to say good night to her again in the passage, I should not be allowed to stay in the house a day longer, I should be packed off to school[75] next morning; so much was certain. Very good: had I been obliged, the next moment, to hurl myself out of the window, I should still have preferred such a fate. For what I wanted now was Mamma, and to say good night to her; I had gone too far along the road which led to the realization of this desire to be able to retrace my steps.

I could hear my parents' footsteps as they went with Swann; and, when the rattle of the gate assured me that he had really gone, I crept to the window. Mamma was asking my father if he had thought the lobster good, and whether M. Swann had had some of the coffee-and-pistachio ice. "I thought it rather so-so," she was saying; "next time we shall have to try another flavor."

"I can't tell you," said my great-aunt, "what a change I find in Swann. He is quite antiquated!" She had grown so accustomed to

74. A street in Combray.

75. Boarding school.

seeing Swann always in the same stage of adolescence that it was a shock to her to find him suddenly less young than the age she still attributed to him. And the others too were beginning to remark in Swann that abnormal, excessive, scandalous senescence, meet only in a celibate, is one of that class for whom it seems that the great day which knows no morrow must be longer than for other men, since for such a one it is void of promise, and from its dawn the moments steadily accumulate without any subsequent partition[76] among his offspring.

"I fancy he has a lot of trouble with that wretched wife of his, who 'lives' with a certain Monsieur de Charlus,[77] as all Combray knows. It's the talk of the town."

My mother observed that, in spite of this, he had looked much less unhappy of late. "And he doesn't nearly so often do that trick of his, so like his father, of wiping his eyes and passing his hand across his forehead. I think myself that in his heart of hearts he doesn't love his wife any more."

"Why, of course he doesn't," answered my grandfather. "He wrote me a letter about it, ages ago, to which I took care to pay no attention, but it left no doubt as to his feelings, let alone his love for his wife. Hullo! you two; you never thanked him for the Asti!" he went on, turning to his sisters-in-law.

"What! we never thanked him? I think, between you and me, that I put it to him quite neatly," replied my aunt Flora.

"Yes, you managed it very well; I admired you for it," said my aunt Céline.

"But you did it very prettily, too."

"Yes; I liked my expression about 'nice neighbors.' "

"What! Do you call that thanking him?" shouted my grandfather. "I heard that all right, but devil take me if I guessed it was meant for Swann. You may be quite sure he never noticed it."

"Come, come; Swann is not a fool. I am positive he appreciated the compliment. You didn't expect me to tell him the number of bottles, or to guess what he paid for them."

My father and mother were left alone and sat down for a moment; then my father said: "Well, shall we go up to bed?"

"As you wish, dear, though I don't feel in the least like sleeping. I don't know why; it can't be the coffee ice—it wasn't strong enough to keep me awake like this. But I see a light in the servants' hall: poor Françoise has been sitting up for me, so I will get her to unhook me while you go and undress."

My mother opened the latticed door which led from the hall to the staircase. Presently I heard her coming upstairs to close her

76. Sharing, as under a will.

77. Brother of the Duc de Guermantes.

window. I went quietly into the passage; my heart was beating so violently that I could hardly move, but at least it was throbbing no longer with anxiety, but with terror and with joy. I saw in the well of the stair a light coming upward, from Mamma's candle. Then I saw Mamma herself: I threw myself upon her. For an instant she looked at me in astonishment, not realizing what could have happened. Then her face assumed an expression of anger. She said not a single word to me; and, for that matter, I used to go for days on end without being spoken to, for far less offences than this. A single word from Mamma would have been an admission that further intercourse with me was within the bounds of possibility, and that might perhaps have appeared to me more terrible still, as indicating that, with such a punishment as was in store for me, mere silence, and even anger, were relatively puerile.

A word from her then would have implied the false calm in which one converses with a servant to whom one has just decided to give notice: the kiss one bestows on a son who is being packed off to enlist, which would have been denied him if it had merely been a matter of being angry with him for a few days. But she heard my father coming from the dressing room, where he had gone to take off his clothes, and, to avoid the "scene" which he would make if he saw me, she said, in a voice half stifled by her anger; "Run away at once. Don't let your father see you standing there like a crazy jane!"[78]

But I begged her again to "Come and say good night to me!" terrified as I saw the light from my father's candle already creeping up the wall, but also making use of his approach as a means of blackmail, in the hope that my mother, not wishing him to find me there, as find me he must if she continued to hold out, would give in to me, and say: "Go back to your room. I will come."

Too late: my father was upon us. Instinctively I murmured, though no one heard me, "I am done for!"

I was not, however. My father used constantly to refuse to let me do things which were quite clearly allowed by the more liberal charters granted me by my mother and grandmother, because he paid no heed to "Principles," and because in his sight there were no such things as "Rights of Man."[79] For some quite irrelevant reason, or for no reason at all, he would at the last moment prevent me from taking some particular walk, one so regular and so consecrated to my use that to deprive me of it was a clear breach of faith; or again, as he had done this evening, long before the

78. Lunatic.

79. Reference to the "Declaration of the Rights of Man" in the preamble to the French Constitution of 1791, and to Thomas Paine's *Rights of Man* (1791–1792), a passionate defense of republicanism. Marcel sees the relationship between himself and his mother and grandmother as somehow democratic; his father plays the role of tyrant in their small society.

appointed hour he would snap out: "Run along up to bed now; no excuses!" But then again, simply because he was devoid of principles (in my grandmother's sense), so he could not, properly speaking, be called inexorable. He looked at me for a moment with an air of annoyance and surprise, and then when Mamma had told him, not without some embarrassment, what had happened, said to her: "Go along with him, then; you said just now that you didn't feel like sleep, so stay in his room for a little. I don't need anything."

"But dear," my mother answered timidly, "whether or not I feel like sleep is not the point; we must not make the child accustomed . . ."

"There's no question of making him accustomed," said my father, with a shrug of the shoulders; "you can see quite well that the child is unhappy. After all, we aren't jailers. You'll end by making him ill, and a lot of good that will do. There are two beds in his room; tell Françoise to make up the big one for you, and stay beside him for the rest of the night. I'm off to bed, anyhow; I'm not nervous like you. Good night."

It was impossible for me to thank my father; what he called my sentimentality would have exasperated him. I stood there, not daring to move; he was still confronting us, an immense figure in his white nightshirt, crowned with the pink and violet scarf of Indian cashmere in which, since he had begun to suffer from neuralgia,[80] he used to tie up his head, standing like Abraham in the engraving after Benozzo Gozzoli[81] which M. Swann had given me, telling Sarah that she must tear herself away from Isaac. Many years have passed since that night. The wall of the staircase, up which I had watched the light of his candle gradually climb, was long ago demolished. And in myself, too, many things have perished which, I imagined, would last for ever, and new structures have arisen, giving birth to new sorrows and new joys which in those days I could not have foreseen, just as now the old are difficult of comprehension. It is a long time, too, since my father has been able to tell Mamma to "Go with the child." Never again will such hours be possible for me. But of late I have been increasingly able to catch, if I listen attentively, the sound of the sobs which I had the strength to control in my father's presence, and which broke out only when I found myself alone with Mamma. Actually, their echo has never ceased: it is only because life is now growing more and more quiet round about me that I hear them afresh, like those convent bells which are so effectively drowned during the day by the noises of the streets that one would suppose them to have been stopped forever, until they sound out again through the silent evening air.

80. neuralgia: Headache.

81. (1420–1497). Florentine painter whose frescoes at Pisa contain scenes from the life of the Hebrew patriarch Abraham.

Mamma spent that night in my room: when I had just committed a sin so deadly that I was waiting to be banished from the household, my parents gave me a far greater concession than I should ever have won as the reward of a good action. Even at the moment when it manifested itself in this crowning mercy, my father's conduct toward me was still somewhat arbitrary, and regardless of my deserts, as was characteristic of him and due to the fact that his actions were generally dictated by chance expediencies rather than based on any formal plan. And perhaps even what I called his strictness, when he sent me off to bed, deserved that title less, really, than my mother's or grandmother's attitude, for his nature, which in some respects differed more than theirs from my own, had probably prevented him from guessing, until then, how wretched I was every evening, a thing which my mother and grandmother knew well; but they loved me enough to be unwilling to spare me that suffering, which they hoped to teach me to overcome, so as to reduce my nervous sensibility and to strengthen my will. As for my father, whose affection for me was of another kind, I doubt if he would have shown so much courage, for as soon as he had grasped the fact that I was unhappy he had said to my mother: "Go and comfort him."

Mamma stayed all night in my room, and it seemed that she did not wish to mar by recrimination those hours, so different from anything that I had had a right to expect; for when Françoise (who guessed that something extraordinary must have happened when she saw Mamma sitting by my side, holding my hand and letting me cry unchecked) said to her: "But, Madame, what is little Master crying for?" she replied: "Why, Françoise, he doesn't know himself: it is his nerves. Make up the big bed for me quickly and then go off to your own." And thus for the first time my unhappiness was regarded no longer as a fault for which I must be punished, but as an involuntary evil which had been officially recognized a nervous condition for which I was in no way responsible: I had the consolation that I need no longer mingle apprehensive scruples with the bitterness of my tears; I could weep henceforward without sin. I felt no small degree of pride, either, in Françoise's presence at this return to humane conditions which, not an hour after Mamma had refused to come up to my room and had sent the snubbing message that I was to go to sleep, raised me to the dignity of a grown-up person, brought me of a sudden to a sort of puberty of sorrow, to emancipation from tears. I ought then to have been happy; I was not. It struck me that my mother had just made a first concession which must have been painful to her, that it was a first step down from the ideal she had formed for me, and that for the first time she, with all her courage, had to confess herself beaten. It struck me that if I had just scored a victory it was over her; that I had succeeded, as sickness or sorrow or age might have succeeded, in relaxing her will, in altering her judgment; that this evening opened a new era, must remain a black date in the calendar. And if I had dared now, I should have said to Mamma; "No, I don't want you; you mustn't sleep here." But I was conscious of the practical wisdom, of what would be called nowadays the realism with which she tempered the ardent idealism of my grandmother's nature, and I knew that now the mischief was done she would prefer to let me enjoy the soothing pleasure of her company, and not to disturb my father again. Certainly my mother's beautiful features seemed to shine again with youth that evening, as she sat gently holding my hands and trying to check my tears; but, just for that reason, it seemed to me that this should not have happened; her anger would have been less difficult to endure than this new kindness which my childhood had not known; I felt that I had with an impious and secret finger traced a first wrinkle upon her soul and made the first white hair show upon her head. This thought redoubled my sobs, and then I saw that Mamma, who had never allowed herself to go to any length of tenderness with me, was suddenly overcome by my tears and had to struggle to keep back her own. Then, as she saw that I had noticed this, she said to me, with a smile: "Why, my little buttercup, my little canary boy, he's going to make Mamma as silly as himself if this goes on. Look, since you can't sleep, and Mamma can't either, we mustn't go on in this stupid way; we must do something; I'll get one of your books." But I had none there. "Would you like me to get out the books now that your grandmother is going to give you for your birthday? Just think it over first, and don't be disappointed if there is nothing new for you then."

I was only too delighted, and Mamma went to find a parcel of books in which I could not distinguish, through the paper in which it was wrapped, any more than its squareness and size, but which, even at this first glimpse, brief and obscure as it was, bade fair to eclipse already the paint box of last New Year's Day and the silkworms of the year before. It contained *La Mare au Diable, Françoise le Champi, La Petite Fadette,* and *Les Maîtres Sonneurs.*[82] My grandmother, as I learned afterward, had at first chosen Musset's poems, a volume of Rousseau, and *Indiana*; for while she considered light reading as unwholesome as sweets and cakes, she did not reflect that the strong breath of genius must have upon the very soul of a child an influence at once more dangerous

82. *The Devil's Pool, François the Foundling Discovered in the Fields, Little Fadette,* and *The Master Bellringers,* novels of idealized country life by the French woman writer George Sand (1806–1876).

and less quickening than those of fresh air and country breezes upon his body. But when my father had seemed almost to regard her as insane on learning the names of the books she proposed to give me,[83] she had journeyed back by herself to Jouy-le-Viccomte to the bookseller's, so that there should be no fear of my not having my present in time (it was a burning hot day, and she had come home so unwell that the doctor had warned my mother not to allow her again to tire herself in that way), and had there fallen back upon the four pastoral novels of George Sand.

"My dear," she had said to Mamma, "I could not allow myself to give the child anything that was not well written."

The truth was that she could never make up her mind to purchase anything from which no intellectual profit was to be derived, and, above all, that profit which good things bestowed on us by teaching us to seek our pleasures elsewhere than in the barren satisfaction of worldly wealth. Even when she had to make someone a present of the kind called "useful," when she had to give an armchair or some table silver or a walking-stick, she would choose "antiques," as though their long desuetude had effaced from them any semblance of utility and fitted them rather to instruct us in the lives of the men of other days than to serve the common requirements of our own. She would have liked me to have in my room photographs of ancient buildings or of beautiful places. But at the moment of buying them, and for all that the subject of the picture had an esthetic value of its own, she would find that vulgarity and utility had too prominent a part in them, through the mechanical nature of their reproduction by photography. She attempted by a subterfuge, if not to eliminate altogether their commercial banality, at least to minimize it, to substitute for the bulk of it what was art still, to introduce, as it might be, several "thicknesses" of art; instead of photographs of Chartres Cathedral, of the Fountains of Saint-Cloud, or of Vesuvius she would inquire of Swann whether some great painter had not made pictures of them, and preferred to give me photographs of "Chartres Cathedral" after Corot, of the "Fountains of Saint-Cloud" after Hubert Robert, and of 'Vesuvius" after Turner,[84] which were a stage higher in the scale of art. But although the photographer had been prevented from reproducing directly the masterpieces or the beauties of nature, and had there been replaced by a great artist, he resumed his odious position when it came to reproducing the artist's interpretation. Accordingly,

83. The works of Alfred de Musset (1810–1857) and Jean-Jacques Rousseau (1712–1778), often romantic and sometimes confessional, and some by Sand (*Indiana* was a novel of free love), would be thought unsuitable reading for a young child.

84. The Cathedral of Chartres, painted in 1830 by Corot; the fountains in the old park at Saint-Cloud, outside Paris, painted by Hubert Robert (1733–1809), and Vesuvius, the famous volcano near Naples, painted by W. M. J. Turner (1775–1851).

having to reckon again with vulgarity, my grandmother would endeavor to postpone the moment of contact still further. She would ask Swann if the picture had not been engraved, preferring, when possible, old engravings with some interest of association apart from themselves, such, for example, as show us a masterpiece in a state in which we can no longer see it today, as Morghen's print of the "Cenacolo" of Leonardo before it was spoiled by restoration.[85] It must be admitted that the results of this method of interpreting the art of making presents were not always happy. The idea which I formed of Venice, from a drawing by Titian[86] which is supposed to have the lagoon in the background, was certainly far less accurate than what I have since derived from ordinary photographs. We could no longer keep count in the family (when my great-aunt tried to frame an indictment of my grandmother) of all the armchairs she had presented to married couples, young and old, which on a first attempt to sit down upon them had at once collapsed beneath the weight of their recipient. But my grandmother would have thought it sordid to concern herself too closely with the solidity of any piece of furniture in which could still be discerned a flourish, a smile, a brave conceit of the past. And even what in such pieces supplied a material need, since it did so in a manner to which we are no longer accustomed, was as charming to her as one of those old forms of speech in which we can still see traces of a metaphor whose fine point has been worn away by the rough usage of our modern tongue. In precisely the same way the pastoral novels of George Sand, which she was giving me for my birthday, were regular lumber rooms of antique furniture, full of expressions that have fallen out of use and returned as imagery, such as one finds now only in country dialects. And my grandmother had bought them in preference to other books, just as she would have preferred to take a house that had a gothic dovecot, or some other such piece of antiquity as would have a pleasant effect on the mind, filling it with a nostalgic longing for impossible journeys through the realms of time.

Mamma sat down by my bed; she had chosen *François le Champi,* whose reddish cover and incomprehensible title[87] gave it a distinct personality in my eyes and a mysterious attraction. I had not then read any real novels. I had heard it said that George Sand was a typical novelist. That prepared me in advance to imagine that *François le Champi* contained something inexpressibly delicious. The course of the narrative, where it tended to arouse curiosity or

85. Leonardo da Vinci's *Last Supper* was the subject of a famous engraving by Morghen, a late eighteenth-century engraver. The paints in the original fresco had deteriorated rapidly, and a major restoration took place in the nineteenth century.

86. Venetian painter (1477–1576).

87. *Champi* (see note 82) is an old French word the child Marcel would not have known.

melt to pity, certain modes of expression which disturb or sadden the reader, and which, with a little experience, he may recognize as "common form" in novels, seemed to me then distinctive—for to me a new book was not one of a number of similar objects, but was like an individual man, unmatched, and with no cause of existence beyond himself—an intoxicating whiff of the peculiar essence of *François le Champi.* Beneath the everyday incidents, the commonplace thoughts and hackneyed words, I could hear, or overhear, an intonation, a rhythmic utterance fine and strange. The "action" began: to me it seemed all the more obscure because in those days, when I read to myself, I used often, while I turned the pages, to dream of something quite different. And to the gaps which this habit made in my knowledge of the story more were added by the fact that when it was Mamma who was reading to me aloud she left all the love scenes out. And so all the odd changes which take place in the relations between the miller's wife and the boy, changes which only the birth and growth of love can explain, seemed to me plunged and steeped in a mystery, the key to which (as I could readily believe) lay in that strange and pleasant-sounding name of *Champi,* which draped the boy who bore it, I knew not why, in its own bright color, purpurate and charming. If my mother was not a faithful reader, she was, none the less, admirable when reading a work in which she found the note of true feeling by the respectful simplicity of her interpretation and by the sound of her sweet and gentle voice. It was the same in her daily life, when it was not works of art but men and women whom she was moved to pity or admire: it was touching to observe with what deference she would banish from her voice, her gestures, from her whole conversation, now the note of joy which might have distressed some mother who had long ago lost a child, now the recollection of an event or anniversary which might have reminded some old gentleman of the burden of his years, now the household topic which might have bored some young man of letters. And so, when she read aloud the prose of George Sand, prose which is everywhere redolent of that generosity and moral distinction which Mamma had learned from my grandmother to place above all other qualities in life, and which I was not to teach her until much later to refrain from placing, in the same way, above all other qualities in literature; taking pains to banish from her voice any weakness or affectation which might have blocked its channel for that powerful stream of language, she supplied all the natural tenderness, all the lavish sweetness which they demanded to phrases which seemed to have been composed for her voice, and which were all, so to speak, within her compass. She came to them with the tone that they required, with the cordial accent which existed before they were, which dictated them, but which is not to be found in the words themselves, and by these means she smoothed away, as she read on, any harshness there might be or disordance in the tenses of verbs, endowing the imperfect and preterite[88] with all the sweetness which there is in generosity, all the melancholy which there is in love; guided the sentence that was drawing to an end toward that which was waiting to begin, now hastening, now slackening the pace of the syllables so as to bring them, despite their difference of quantity, into a uniform rhythm, and breathed into this quite ordinary prose a kind of life, continuous and full of feeling.

My agony was soothed; I let myself be borne upon the current of this gentle night on which I had my mother by my side. I knew that such a night could not be repeated; that the strongest desire I had in the world, namely, to keep my mother in my room through the sad hours of darkness, ran too much counter to general requirements and to the wishes of others for such a concession as had been granted me this evening to be anything but a rare and casual exception. Tomorrow night I should again be the victim of anguish and Mamma would not stay by my side. But when these storms of anguish grew calm I could no longer realize their existence; besides, tomorrow evening was still a long way off; I reminded myself that I should still have time to think about things, albeit that remission of time could bring me no access of power, albeit the coming event was in no way dependent upon the exercise of my will, and seemed not quite inevitable only because it was still separated from me by this short interval.

And so it was that, for a long time afterwards, when I lay awake at night and revived old memories of Combray, I saw no more of it than this sort of luminous panel, sharply defined against a vague and shadowy background, like the panels which a Bengal fire[89] or some electric sign will illuminate and dissect from the front of a building the other parts of which remain plunged in darkness: broad enough at its base, the little parlor, the dining room, the alluring shadows of the path along which would come M. Swann, the unconscious author of my sufferings, the hall through which I would journey to the first step of that staircase, so hard to climb, which constituted, all by itself, the tapering "elevation" of an irregular pyramid; and, at the summit, my bedroom, with the little passage through whose glazed[90] door Mamma would enter; in a word,

88. The imperfect is the tense of continued and incomplete action in the past, while the preterite describes a single completed action. The mother's gentle voice renders harmonious Sand's occasional awkwardness in the use of these tenses.

89. Fireworks.

90. I.e., with glass panes.

seen always at the same evening hour, isolated from all its possible surroundings, detached and solitary against its shadowy background, the bare minimum of scenery necessary (like the setting one sees printed at the head of an old play, for its performance in the provinces) to the drama of my undressing, as though all Combray had consisted of but two floors joined by a slender staircase, and as though there had been no time there but seven o'clock at night. I must own[91] that I could have assured any questioner that Combray did include other scenes and did exist at other hours than these. But since the facts which I should then have recalled would have been prompted only by an exercise of the will, by my intellectual memory, and since the pictures which that kind of memory shows us of the past preserve nothing of the past itself, I should never have had any wish to ponder over this residue of Combray. To me it was in reality all dead.

Permanently dead? Very possibly.

There is a large element of hazard in these matters, and a second hazard, that of our own death, often prevents us from awaiting for any length of time the favors of the first.

I feel that there is much to be said for the Celtic belief that the souls of those whom we have lost are held captive in some inferior being, in an animal, in a plant, in some inanimate object, and so effectively lost to us until the day (which to many never comes) when we happen to pass by the tree or to obtain possession of the object which forms their prison.[92] Then they start and tremble, they call us by our name, and as soon as we have recognized their voice the spell is broken. We have delivered them: they have overcome death and return to share our life.

And so it is with our own past. It is a labor in vain to attempt to recapture it: all the efforts of our intellect must prove futile. The past is hidden somewhere outside the realm, beyond the reach of intellect, in some material object (in the sensation which that material object will give us) which we do not suspect. And as for that object, it depends on chance whether we come upon it or not before we ourselves must die.

Many years had elapsed during which nothing of Combray, save what was comprised in the theatre and the drama of my going to bed there, had any existence for me, when one day in winter, as I came home, my mother, seeing that I was cold, offered me some tea, a thing I did not ordinarily take. I declined at first, and then, for no particular reason, changed my mind. She sent out for one of those short, plump little cakes called "petites madeleines," which look as though they had been molded in the fluted scallop of a pil-

91. Admit.
92. A belief attributed to Druids, the priests of the Celtic peoples.

grim's shell.[93] And soon, mechanically, weary after a dull day with the prospect of a depressing morrow, I raised to my lips a spoonful of the tea in which I had soaked a morsel of the cake. No sooner had the warm liquid, and the crumbs with it, touched my palate than a shudder ran through my whole body, and I stopped, intent upon the extraordinary changes that were taking place. An exquisite pleasure had invaded my senses, but individual, detached, with no suggestion of its origin. And at once the vicissitudes of life had become indifferent to me, its disasters innocuous, its brevity illusory—this new sensation having had on me the effect which love has of filling me with a precious essence; or rather this essence was not in me, it was myself. I had ceased now to feel mediocre, accidental, mortal. Whence could it have come to me, this all-powerful joy? I was conscious that it was connected with the taste of tea and cake, but that it infinitely transcended those savors, could not, indeed, be of the same nature as theirs. Whence did it come? What did it signify? How could I seize upon and define it?

I drink a second mouthful, in which I find nothing more than in the first, a third, which gives me rather less than the second. It is time to stop; the potion is losing its magic. It is plain that the object of my quest, the truth, lies not in the cup but in myself. The tea has called up in me, but does not itself understand, and can only repeat indefinitely with a gradual loss of strength, the same testimony; which I, too, cannot interpret, though I hope at least to be able to call upon the tea for it again and to find it there presently, intact and at my disposal, for my final enlightenment. I put down my cup and examine my own mind. It is for it to discover the truth. But how? What an abyss of uncertainty whenever the mind feels that some part of it has strayed beyond its own borders; when it, the seeker, is at once the dark region through which it must go seeking, where all its equipment will avail it nothing. Seek? More than that: create. It is face to face with somthing which does not so far exist, to which it alone can give reality and substance, which it alone can bring into the light of day.

And I begin again to ask myself what it could have been, this unremembered state which brought with it no logical proof of its existence, but only the sense that it was a happy, that it was a real state in whose presence other states of consciousness melted and vanished. I decide to attempt to make it reappear. I retrace my thoughts to the moment at which I drank the first spoonful of tea. I find again the same state, illumined by no fresh light. I compel my mind to make one further effort, to follow and recapture once again the fleeting sensation. And that nothing may interrupt it in

93. The scallop shell was a badge worn by Christian pilgrims to holy places.

its course I shut out every obstacle, every extraneous idea, I stop my ears and inhibit all attention to the sounds which come from the next room. And then, feeling that my mind is growing fatigued without having any success to report, I compel it for a change to enjoy that distraction which I have just denied it, to think of other things, to rest and refresh itself before the supreme attempt. And then for the second time I clear an empty space in front of it. I place in position before my mind's eye the still recent taste of that first mouthful, and I feel something start within me, something that leaves its resting place and attempts to rise, something that has been embedded like an anchor at a great depth; I do not know yet what it is, but I can feel it mounting slowly; I can measure the resistance, I can hear the echo of great spaces traversed.

Undoubtedly what is thus palpitating in the depths of my being must be the image, the visual memory which, being linked to that taste, has tried to follow it into my conscious mind. But its struggles are too far off, too much confused; scarcely can I perceive the colorless reflection in which are blended the uncapturable whirling medley of radiant hues, and I cannot distinguish its form, cannot invite it, as the one possible interpreter, to translate to me the evidence of its contemporary, its inseparable paramour, the taste of cake soaked in tea; cannot ask it to inform me what special circumstance is in question, of what period in my past life.

Will it ultimately reach the clear surface of my consciousness, this memory, this old, dead moment which the magnetism of an identical moment has traveled so far to importune, to disturb, to raise up out of the very depths of my being? I cannot tell. Now that I feel nothing, it has stopped, has perhaps gone down again into its darkness, from which who can say whether it will ever rise? Ten times over I must essay the task, must lean down over the abyss. And each time the natural laziness which deters us from every difficult enterprise, every work of importance, has urged me to leave the thing alone, to drink my tea and to think merely of the worries of today and of my hopes for tomorrow, which let themselves be pondered over without effort or distress of mind.

And suddenly the memory returns. The taste was that of the little crumb of madeleine which on Sunday mornings at Combray (because on those mornings I did not go out before church time), when I went to say good day to her in her bedroom, my aunt Léonie used to give me, dipping it first in her own cup of real or of lime-flower tea. The sight of the little madeleine had recalled nothing to my mind before I tasted it; perhaps because I had so often seen such things in the interval, without tasting them, on the trays in pastry-cooks' windows, that their image had dissociated itself from those Combray days to take its place among others more recent; perhaps because of those memories, so long abandoned and put out of mind, nothing now survived, everything was scattered; the forms of things, including that of the little scallop shell of pastry, so richly sensual under its severe, religious folds, were either obliterated or had been so long dormant as to have lost the power of expansion which would have allowed them to resume their place in my consciousness. But when from a long-distant past nothing subsists, after the people are dead, after the things are broken and scattered, still, alone, more fragile, but with more vitality, more unsubstantial, more persistent, more faithful, the smell and taste of things remain poised a long time, like souls, ready to remind us, waiting and hoping for their moment, amid the ruins of all the rest; and bear unfaltering, in the tiny and almost impalpable drop of their essence, the vast structure of recollection.

And once I had recognized the taste of the crumb of madeleine soaked in her decoction of lime flowers which my aunt used to give me (although I did not yet know and must long postpone the discovery of why this memory made me so happy) immediately the old grey house upon the street, where her room was, rose up like the scenery of a theatre to attach itself to the little pavilion, opening on to the garden, which had been built out behind it for my parents (the isolated panel which until that moment had been all that I could see); and with the house the town, from morning to night and in all weathers, the Square where I was sent before luncheon, the streets along which I used to run errands, the country roads we took when it was fine. And just as the Japanese amuse themselves by filling a porcelain bowl with water and steeping in it little crumbs of paper which until then are without character or form, but, the moment they become wet, stretch themselves and bend, take on color and distinctive shape, become flowers or houses or people, permanent and recognizable, so in that moment all the flowers in our garden and in M. Swann's park, and the water lilies on the Vivonne[94] and the good folk of the village and their little dwellings and the parish church and the whole of Combray and of its surroundings, taking their proper shapes and growing solid, sprang into being, town and gardens alike, from my cup of tea.

94. The local river.

THOMAS MANN*

1875–1955

Tonio Kröger

The winter sun, poor ghost of itself, hung milky and wan behind layers of cloud above the huddled roofs of the town. In the gabled streets it was wet and windy and there came in gusts a sort of soft hail, not ice, not snow.

School was out. The hosts of the released streamed over the paved court and out at the wrought-iron gate, where they broke up and hastened off right and left. Elder pupils held their books in a strap high on the left shoulder and rowed, right arm against the wind, toward dinner. Small people trotted gaily off, splashing the slush with their feet, the tools of learning rattling amain in their walrus-skin satchels. But one and all pulled off their caps and cast down their eyes in awe before the Olympian hat and ambrosial beard[1] of a master moving homeward with measured stride. . . .

"Ah, there you are at last, Hans," said Tonio Kröger. He had been waiting a long time in the street and went up with a smile to the friend he saw coming out of the gate in talk with other boys and about to go off with them. . . . "What?" said Hans, and looked at Tonio. "Right-oh! We'll take a little walk, then."

Tonio said nothing and his eyes were clouded. Did Hans forget, had he only just remembered that they were to take a walk together today? And he himself had looked forward to it with almost incessant joy.

"Well, good-bye, fellows," said Hans Hansen to his comrades. "I'm taking a walk with Kröger." And the two turned to their left, while the others sauntered off in the opposite direction.

Hans and Tonio had time to take a walk after school because in neither of their families was dinner served before four o'clock. Their fathers were prominent business men, who held public office and were of consequence in the town. Hans' people had owned for some generations the big wood yards down by the river, where powerful machine saws hissed and spat and cut up timber; while Tonio was the son of Consul Kröger,[2] whose grain sacks with the firm name in great black letters you might see any day driven through the streets; his large, old ancestral home was the finest house in all the town. The two friends had to keep taking off their hats to their many acquaintances; some folk did not even wait for the fourteen-year-old lads to speak first, as by rights they should.

* Published in 1903. Translated by H. T. Lowe-Porter.

1. That is, divine-seeming attributes.

2. Title given to a member of the City Council, the main governing body of independent city-states such as Lübeck, on the north coast of Germany.

Both of them carried their satchels across their shoulders and both were well and warmly dressed: Hans in a short sailor jacket, with the wide blue collar of his sailor suit turned out over shoulders and back, and Tonio in a belted grey overcoat. Hans wore a Danish sailor cap with black ribbons, beneath which streamed a shock of straw-colored hair. He was uncommonly handsome and well built, broad in the shoulders and narrow in the hips, with keen, far-apart, steel-blue eyes; while beneath Tonio's round fur cap was a brunette face with the finely chiseled features of the south; the dark eyes, with delicate shadows and too heavy lids, looked dreamily and a little timorously on the world. Tonio's walk was idle and uneven, whereas the other's slim legs in their black stockings moved with an elastic, rhythmic tread.

Tonio did not speak. He suffered. His rather oblique brows were drawn together in a frown, his lips were rounded to whistle, he gazed into space with his head on one side. Posture and manner were habitual.

Suddenly Hans shoved his arm into Tonio's, with a sideways look —he knew very well what the trouble was. And Tonio, though he was silent for the next few steps, felt his heart soften.

"I hadn't forgotten, you see, Tonio," Hans said, gazing at the pavement, "I only thought it wouldn't come off today because it was so wet and windy. But I don't mind that at all, and it's jolly of you to have waited. I thought you had gone home, and I was cross. . . ."

Everything in Tonio leaped and jumped for joy at the words.

"All right; let's go over the wall," he said with a quaver in his voice. "Over the Millwall and the Holstenwall,[3] and I'll go as far as your house with you, Hans. Then I'll have to walk back alone, but that doesn't matter; next time you can go round my way."

At bottom he was not really convinced by what Hans said; he quite knew the other attached less importance to this walk than he did himself. Yet he saw Hans was sorry for his remissness and willing to be put in a position to ask pardon, a pardon that Tonio was far indeed from withholding.

The truth was, Tonio loved Hans Hansen, and had already suffered much on his account. He who loves the more is the inferior and must suffer; in this hard and simple fact his fourteen-year-old soul had already been instructed by life; and he was so organized that he received such experiences consciously, wrote them down as it were inwardly, and even, in a certain way, took pleasure in them, though without ever letting them mold his conduct, indeed, or drawing any practical advantage from them. Being what he was, he found this knowledge far more important and far more interesting

3. Park-like walks built on the top of the old city walls.

than the sort they made him learn in schools; yes, during his lesson hours in the vaulted Gothic classrooms he was mainly occupied in feeling his way about among these intuitions of his and penetrating them. The process gave him the same kind of satisfaction as that he felt when he moved about in his room with his violin—for he played the violin—and made the tones, brought out as softly as ever he knew how, mingle with the plashing of the fountain that leaped and danced down there in the garden beneath the branches of the old walnut tree.

The fountain, the old walnut tree, his fiddle, and away in the distance the North Sea, within sound of whose summer murmurings he spent his holidays—these were the things he loved, within these he enfolded his spirit, among these things his inner life took its course. And they were all things whose names were effective in verse and occurred pretty frequently in the lines Tonio Kröger sometimes wrote.

The fact that he had a notebook full of such things, written by himself, leaked out through his own carelessness and injured him no little with the masters as well as among his fellows. On the one hand, Consul Kröger's son found their attitude both cheap and silly, and despised his schoolmates and his masters as well, and in his turn (with extraordinary penetration) saw through and disliked their personal weaknesses and bad breeding. But then, on the other hand, he himself felt his verse-making extravagant and out of place and to a certain extent agreed with those who considered it an unpleasing occupation. But that did not enable him to leave off.

As he wasted his time at home, was slow and absent-minded at school, and always had bad marks from the masters, he was in the habit of bringing home pitifully poor reports, which troubled and angered his father, a tall, fastidiously dressed man, with thoughtful blue eyes, and always a wild flower in his buttonhole. But for his mother, she cared nothing about the reports—Tonio's beautiful black-haired mother, whose name was Consuelo, and who was so absolutely different from the other ladies in the town, because father had brought her long ago from some place far down on the map.

Tonio loved his dark, fiery mother, who played the piano and mandolin so wonderfully, and he was glad his doubtful standing among men did not distress her. Though at the same time he found his father's annoyance a more dignified and respectable attitude and despite his scoldings understood him very well, whereas his mother's blithe indifference always seemed just a little wanton. His thoughts at times would run something like this: "It is true enough that I am what I am and will not and cannot alter: heedless, self-willed, with my mind on things nobody else thinks of. And so it is right they should scold and punish me and not smother things all up with kisses and music. After all, we are not gypsies living in a green wagon; we're respectable people, the family of Consul Kröger." And not seldom he would think: "Why is it I am different, why do I fight everything, why am I at odds with the masters and like a stranger among the other boys? The good scholars, and the solid majority—they don't find the masters funny, they don't write verses, their thoughts are all about things that people do think about and can talk about out loud. How regular and comfortable they must feel, knowing that everybody knows just where they stand! It must be nice! But what is the matter with me, and what will be the end of it all?"

These thoughts about himself and his relation to life played an important part in Tonio's love for Hans Hansen. He loved him in the first place because he was handsome; but in the next because he was in every respect his own opposite and foil. Hans Hansen was a capital scholar, and a jolly chap to boot, who was head at drill,[4] rode and swam to perfection, and lived in the sunshine of popularity. The masters were almost tender with him, they called him Hans and were partial to him in every way; the other pupils curried favor with him; even grown people stopped him on the street, twitched the shock of hair beneath his Danish sailor cap, and said; "Ah, here you are, Hans Hansen, with your pretty blond hair! Still head of the school? Remember me to your father and mother, that's a fine lad!"

Such was Hans Hansen; and ever since Tonio Kröger had known him, from the very minute he set eyes on him, he had burned inwardly with a heavy, envious longing. "Who else has blue eyes like yours, or lives in such friendliness and harmony with all the world? You are always spending your time with some right and proper occupation. When you have done your prep[5] you take your riding lesson, or make things with a fret-saw; even in the holidays, at the seashore, you row and sail and swim all the time, while I wander off somewhere and lie down in the sand and stare at the strange and mysterious changes that whisk over the face of the sea. And all that is why your eyes are so clear. To be like you . . ."

He made no attempt to be like Hans Hansen, and perhaps hardly even seriously wanted to. What he did ardently, painfully want was that just as he was, Hans Hansen should love him; and he wooed Hans Hansen in his own way, deeply, lingeringly, devotedly, with a melancholy that gnawed and burned more terribly than all the sudden passion one might have expected from his exotic looks.

And he wooed not in vain. Hans respected Tonio's superior

4. Gymnastics.
5. Homework. *Fret-saw*: A coping-saw or jigsaw.

power of putting certain difficult matters into words; moreover, he felt the lively presence of an uncommonly strong and tender feeling for himself; he was grateful for it, and his response gave Tonio much happiness—though also many pangs of jealousy and disillusion over his futile efforts to establish a communion of spirit between them. For the queer thing was that Tonio, who after all envied Hans Hansen for being what he was, still kept on trying to draw him over to his own side; though of course he could succeed in this at most only at moments and superficially. . . .

I have just been reading something so wonderful and splendid . . ." he said. They were walking and eating together out of a bag of fruit toffees they had bought at Iverson's sweet shop in Mill Street for ten pfennigs.[6] "You must read it, Hans, it is Schiller's *Don Carlos*[7] . . . I'll lend it to you if you like; . . ."

"Oh, no," said Hans Hansen, "you needn't, Tonio, that's not anything for me. I'll stick to my horse books. There are wonderful cuts in them, let me tell you. I'll show them to you when you come to see me. They are instantaneous photography—the horse in motion; you can see him trot and canter and jump, in all positions, that you never can get to see in life, because they happen so fast. . . ."

"In all positions?" asked Tonio politely. "Yes, that must be great. But about *Don Carlos*—it is beyond anything you could possibly dream of. There are places in it that are so lovely they make you jump . . . as though it were an explosion—"

"An explosion?" asked Hans Hansen. "What sort of an explosion?"

"For instance, the place where the king has been crying because the marquis betrayed him . . . . but the marquis did it only out of love for the prince, you see, he sacrifices himself for his sake. And the word comes out of the cabinet[8] into the antechamber that the king has been weeping. 'Weeping? The king been weeping?' All the courtiers are fearfully upset, it goes through and through you, for the king has always been so frightfully stiff and stern. But it is so easy to understand why he cried, and I feel sorrier for him than for the prince and the marquis put together. He is always so alone, nobody loves him, and then he thinks he has found one man, and then *he* betrays him. . . ."

Hans Hansen looked sideways into Tonio's face, and something in it must have won him to the subject, for suddenly he shoved his arm once more into Tonio's and said;

"How had he betrayed him, Tonio?"

6. Pennies. 100 pfennigs equal 1 mark.

7. An historical drama by the German Romantic author Friedrich von Schiller (1759–1805). In the passage mentioned later, the king has just learned, by reading captured letters destined for rebels in Brabant and Flanders, that the Marquis of Posa has betrayed him.

8. Private chamber, study.

Tonio went on.

"Well," he said, "you see all the letters for Brabant and Flanders—"

"There comes Irwin Immerthal," said Hans.

Tonio stopped talking. If only the earth would open and swallow Immerthal up! "Why does he have to come disturbing us? If he only doesn't go with us all the way and talk about the riding lessons!" For Irwin Immerthal had riding lessons too. He was the son of the bank president and lived close by, outside the city wall. He had already been home and left his bag, and now he walked toward them through the avenue. His legs were crooked and his eyes like slits.

" 'lo, Immerthal," said Hans. "I'm taking a little walk with Kröger. . . ."

"I have to go into town on an errand," said Immerthal. "But I'll walk a little way with you. Are those fruit toffees you've got? Thanks, I'll have a couple. Tomorrow we have our next lesson, Hans." He meant the riding lesson.

"What larks!" said Hans. "I'm going to get the leather gaiters for a present, because I was top lately in our papers."

"You don't take riding lessons, I suppose, Kröger?" asked Immerthal, and his eyes were only two gleaming cracks.

"No . . ." answered Tonio, uncertainly.

"You ought to ask your father," Hans Hansen remarked, "so you could have lessons too, Kröger."

"Yes . . ." said Tonio. He spoke hastily and without interest; his throat had suddenly contracted, because Hans had called him by his last name. Hans seemed conscious of it too, for he said by way of explanation: "I call you Kröger because your first name is so crazy. Don't mind my saying so, I can't do with it all. Tonio—why, what sort of name is that? Though of course I know it's not your fault in the least."

"No, they probably called you that because it sounds so foreign and sort of something special," said Immerthal, obviously with intent to say just the right thing.

Tonio's mouth twitched. He pulled himself together and said:

"Yes, it's a silly name—Lord knows I'd rather be called Heinrich or Wilhelm. It's all because I'm named after my mother's brother Antonio. She comes from down there,[9] you know. . . ."

There he stopped and let the others have their say about horses and saddles. Hans had taken Immerthal's arm; he talked with a fluency that *Don Carlos* could never have roused in him. . . . Tonio felt a mounting desire to weep pricking his nose from time to time; he had hard work to control the trembling of his lips.

9. Italy.

Hans could not stand his name—what was to be done? He himself was called Hans, and Immerthal was called Irwin; two good, sound, familiar names, offensive to nobody. And Tonio was foreign and queer. Yes, there was always something queer about him, whether he would or no, and he was alone, the regular and usual would none of him; although after all he was no gypsy in a green wagon, but the son of Consul Kröger, a member of the Kröger family. But why did Hans call him Tonio as long as they were alone and then feel ashamed as soon as anybody else was by? Just now he had won him over, they had been close together, he was sure. "How had he betrayed him, Tonio?" Hans asked, and took his arm. But he had breathed easier directly Immerthal came up, he had dropped him like a shot, even gratuitously taunted him with his outlandish name. How it hurt to have to see through all this! . . . Hans Hansen did like him a little, when they were alone, that he knew. But let a third person come, he was ashamed, and offered up his friend. And again he was alone. He thought of King Philip. The king had wept. . . .

"Goodness, I have to go," said Irwin Immerthal. "Good-bye, and thanks for the toffee." He jumped upon a bench that stood by the way, ran along it with his crooked legs, jumped down, and trotted off.

"I like Immerthal," said Hans, with emphasis. He had a spoilt and arbitrary way of announcing his likes and dislikes, as though graciously pleased to confer them like an order on this person and that. . . . He went on talking about the riding lessons where he had left off. Anyhow, it was not very much farther to his house; the walk over the walls was not a long one. They held their caps and bent their heads before the strong, damp wind that rattled and groaned in the leafless trees. And Hans Hansen went on talking, Tonio throwing in a forced yes or no from time to time. Hans talked eagerly, had taken his arm again; but the contact gave Tonio no pleasure. The nearness was only apparent, not real; it meant nothing. . . .

They struck away from the walls close to the station, where they saw a train puff busily past, idly counted the coaches, and waved to the man who was perched on top of the last one bundled in a leather coat. They stopped in front of the Hansen villa on the Lindenplatz, and Hans went into detail about what fun it was to stand on the bottom rail of the garden gate and let it swing on its creaking hinges. After that they said good-bye.

"I must go in now," said Hans. "Good-bye, Tonio. Next time I'll take you home, see if I don't."

"Good-bye, Hans," said Tonio. "It was a nice walk."

They put out their hands, all wet and rusty from the garden gate.

But as Hans looked into Tonio's eyes, he bethought himself, a look of remorse came over his charming face.

"And I'll read *Don Carlos* pretty soon, too," he said quickly. "That bit about the king in his cabinet must be nuts." Then he took his bag under his arm and ran off through the front garden. Before he disappeared he turned and nodded once more.

And Tonio went off as though on wings. The wind was at his back; but it was not the wind alone that bore him along so lightly.

Hans would read *Don Carlos*, and then they would have something to talk about, and neither Irwin Immerthal nor another could join in. How well they understood each other! Perhaps—who knew? —some day he might even get Hans to write poetry! . . . No, no, that he did not ask. Hans must not become like Tonio, he must stop just as he was, so strong and bright, everybody loved him as he was, and Tonio most of all. But it would do him no harm to read *Don Carlos*. . . . Tonio passed under the squat old city gate, along by the harbor, and up the steep, wet, windy, gabled street to his parents' house. His heart beat richly: longing was awake in it, and a gentle envy; a faint contempt, and no little innocent bliss.

Ingeborg Holm, blonde little Inge, the daugher of Dr. Holm, who lived on Market Square opposite the tall old Gothic fountain with its manifold spires—she it was Tonio Kröger loved when he was sixteen years old.

Strange how things come about! He had seen her a thousand times; then one evening he saw her again; saw her in a certain light, talking with a friend in a certain saucy way, laughing and tossing her head; saw her lift her arm and smooth her back hair with her schoolgirl hand, that was by no means particularly fine or slender, in such a way that the thin white sleeve slipped down from her elbow; heard her speak a word or two, a quite indifferent phrase, but with a certain intonation, with a warm ring in her voice; and his heart throbbed with ecstasy, far stronger than that he had once felt when he looked at Hans Hansen long ago, when he was still a little, stupid boy.

That evening he carried away her picture in his eye: the thick blond plait, the longish, laughing blue eyes, the saddle of pale freckles across the nose. He could not go to sleep for hearing that ring in her voice; he tried in a whisper to imitate the tone in which she had uttered the commonplace phrase, and felt a shiver run through and through him. He knew by experience that this was love. And he was accurately aware that love would surely bring him much pain, affliction, and sadness, that it would certainly destroy his peace, filling his heart to overflowing with melodies which would be no good to him because he would never have the time or tranquillity to give them permanent form. Yet he received this love with joy, surrendered himself to it, and cherished it with all the strength of his being; for he knew that love made one vital and rich, and he longed to be vital and rich, far more than he did to work tranquilly on anything to give it permanent form.

Tonio Kröger fell in love with merry Ingeborg Holm in Frau Consul[10] Hustede's drawing room on the evening when it was emptied of furniture for the weekly dancing class. It was a private class, attended only by members of the first families; it met by turns in the various parental houses to receive instruction from Knaak, the dancing-master, who came from Hamburg expressly for the purpose.

François Knaak was his name, and what a man he was! "*J'ai l'honneur de me vous représenter*," he would say, "*mon nom est Knaak*. . . .[11] This is not said during the bowing, but after you have finished and are standing up straight again. In a low voice, but distinctly. Of course one does not need to introduce oneself in French every day in the week, but if you can do it correctly and faultlessly in French you are not likely to make a mistake when you do it in German." How marvelously the silky black frock coat fitted his chubby hips! His trouser legs fell down in soft folds upon his patent leather pumps with their wide satin bows, and his brown eyes glanced about him with languid pleasure in their own beauty.

All this excess of self-confidence and good form was positively overpowering. He went trippingly—and nobody tripped like him, so elastically, so weavingly, rockingly, royally—up to the mistress of the house, made a bow, waited for a hand to be put forth. This vouchsafed, he gave murmurous voice to his gratitude, stepped buoyantly back, turned on his left foot, swiftly drawing the right one backwards on its toe-tip, and moved away, with his hips shaking.

When you took leave of a company you must go backward out at the door; when you fetched a chair, you were not to shove it along the floor or clutch it by one leg; but gently, by the back, and set it down without a sound. When you stood, you were not to fold your hands on your tummy or seek with your tongue the corners of your mouth. If you did, Herr Knaak had a way of showing you how it looked that filled you with disgust for the particular gesture all the rest of your life.

This was deportment. As for dancing, Herr Knaak was, if possible, even more of a master at that. The salon was emptied of furniture and lighted by a gas chandelier in the middle of the ceiling and candles on the mantel shelf. The floor was strewn with talc, and the

10. "Mrs. Consul"; the wife of a dignitary would be formally addressed using her husband's title.

11. "I am honored to represent myself to you . . . my name is Knaak." French was the accepted language for elegant society at that time, particularly in the ballroom. *Represent* rather than *present* is bad French, and undermines Knaak's claim to faultless elegance.

pupils stood about in a dumb semicircle. But in the next room, behind the portières,[12] mothers and aunts sat on plush-upholstered chairs and watched Herr Knaak through their lorgnettes,[13] as in little springs and hops, curtsying slightly, the hem of his frock coat held up on each side by two fingers, he demonstrated the single steps of the mazurka.[14] When he wanted to dazzle his audience completely he would suddenly and unexpectedly spring from the ground, whirling his two legs about each other with bewildering swiftness in the air, as it were trilling with them, and then, with a subdued bump, which nevertheless shook everything within him to its depths, return to earth.

"What an unmentionable monkey!" thought Tonio Kröger to himself. But he saw the absorbed smile on jolly little Inge's face as she followed Herr Knaak's movements; and that, though not that alone, roused in him something like admiration of all this wonderfully controlled corporeality How tranquil, how imperturbable was Herr Knaak's gaze! His eyes did not plumb the depth of things to the place where life becomes complex and melancholy; they knew nothing save that they were beautiful brown eyes. But that was just why his bearing was so proud. To be able to walk like that, one must be stupid; then one was loved, then one was lovable. He could so well understand how it was that Inge, blonde, sweet little Inge, looked at Herr Knaak as she did. But would never a girl look at him like that?

Oh, yes, there would, and did. For instance, Magdalena Vermehren, Attorney Vermehren's daughter, with the gentle mouth and the great, dark, brilliant eyes, so serious and adoring. She often fell down in the dance; but when it was "ladies' choice" she came up to him; she knew he wrote verses and twice she had asked him to show them to her. She often sat at a distance, with drooping head, and gazed at him. He did not care. It was Inge he loved, blonde, jolly Inge, who most assuredly despised him for his poetic effusions . . . he looked at her, looked at her narrow blue eyes full of fun and mockery, and felt an envious longing; to be shut away from her like this, to be forever strange—he felt it in his breast, like a heavy, burning weight.

"First couple *en avant*,"[15] said Herr Knaak; and no words can tell how marvelously he pronounced the nasal. They were to practice the quadrille, and to Tonio Kröger's profound alarm he found himself in the same set with Inge Holm. He avoided her where he could, yet somehow was forever near her; kept his eyes away from her person and yet found his gaze ever on her. There she came, trip-

12. Curtains hung as a screen across the doorway.

13. Eyeglasses with a short handle.

14. The mazurka, the quadrille, and the polonaise—all used by Mann in this story—are ballroom dances involving patterns performed by a series of couples.

15. Forward.

ping up hand-in-hand with red-headed Ferdinand Matthiessen; she flung back her braid, drew a deep breath, and took her place opposite Tonio. Herr Heinzelmann, at the piano, laid bony hands upon the keys, Herr Knaak waved his arm, the quadrille began.

She moved to and fro before his eyes, forward and back, pacing and swinging; he seemed to catch a fragrance from her hair or the folds of her thin white frock, and his eyes grew sadder and sadder. "I love you, dear, sweet Inge," he said to himself, and put into his worlds all the pain he felt to see her so intent upon the dance with not a thought of him. Some lines of an exquisite poem by Storm came into his mind: "I would sleep, but thou must dance."[16] It seemed against all sense, and most depressing, that he must be dancing when he was in love. . . .

"First couple *en avant*," said Herr Knaak; it was the next figure. "*Compliment! Moulinet des dames! Tour de main!*"[17] and he swallowed the silent *e* in the "*de*," with quite indescribable ease and grace.

"Second couple *en avant*!" This was Tonio Kröger and his partner. "*Compliment!*" And Tonio Kröger bowed. "*Moulinet des dames!*" And Tonio Kröger, with bent head and gloomy brows, laid his hand on those of the four ladies, on Ingeborg Holm's hand, and danced the *moulinet*.

Roundabout rose a tittering and laughing. Herr Knaak took a ballet pose conventionally expressive of horror. "Oh, dear! Oh, dear!" he cried. "Stop! Stop! Kröger among the ladies! *En arrière*, Fräulein Kröger, step back, *fi donc*![18] Everybody else understood it but you. Shoo! Get out! Get away!" He drew out his yellow silk handkerchief and flapped Tonio Kröger back to his place.

Everyone laughed, the girls and the boys and the ladies beyond the portières; Herr Knaak had made something too utterly funny out of the little episode, it was as amusing as a play. But Herr Heinzelmann at the piano sat and waited, with a dry, business-like air, for a sign to go on; he was hardened against Herr Knaak's effects.

Then the quadrille went on. And the intermission followed. The parlormaid came clinking in with a tray of wine-jelly[19] glasses, the cook followed in her wake with a load of plum cake. But Tonio Kröger stole away. He stole out into the corridor and stood there, his hands behind his back, in front of a window with the blind

16. From the poem "Hyacinth" by Theodor Storm (1817–1888), German poet and novella writer noted for his poetic realism. His lyrics and early stories (such as *Immensee,* whose theme is the lost happiness of childhood) express a tone of melancholy resignation, and were much read by the young Thomas Mann.

17. "Bow and curtsey! Windmill for the ladies! Change hands;" Instructions for ballroom dancing would normally be given in French. The dance figure described here is a "windmill" in which the women join right hands and walk around the center.

18. "Back, Miss Kröger . . . shame on you!" (Tonio is mockingly called Fraülein, i.e., "Miss.")

19. A gelatin dessert made with wine.

down. He never thought that one could not see through the blind and that it was absurd to stand there as though one were looking out.

For he was looking within, into himself, the theatre of so much pain and longing. Why, why was he here? Why was he not sitting by the window in his own room, reading Storm's *Immensee* and lifting his eyes to the twilight garden outside, where the old walnut tree moaned? That was the place for him! Others might dance, others bend their fresh and lively minds upon the pleasure in hand! . . . But no, no, after all, his place was here, where he could feel near Inge even though he stood lonely and aloof, seeking to distinguish the warm notes of her voice amid the buzzing, clattering, and laughter within. Oh, lovely Inge, blonde Inge of the narrow, laughing blue eyes! So lovely and laughing as you are one can only be if one does not read *Immensee* and never tries to write things like it. And that was just the tragedy!

Ah, she *must* come! She *must* notice where he had gone, must feel how he suffered! She must slip out to him, even pity must bring her, to lay her hand on his shoulder and say: "Do come back to us, ah, don't be sad—I love you, Tonio." He listened behind him and waited in frantic suspense. But not in the least. Such things did not happen on this earth.

Had she laughed at him too like all the others? Yes, she had, however gladly he would have denied it for both their sakes. And yet it was only because he had been so taken up with her that he had danced the *moulinet des dames*. Suppose he had—what did that matter? Had not a magazine accepted a poem of his a little while ago—even though the magazine had failed before his poem could be printed? The day was coming when he would be famous, when they would print everything he wrote; and *then* he would see if that made any impression on Inge Holm! No, it would make no impression at all; that was just it. Magdalena Vermehren, who was always falling down in the dances, yes, she would be impressed. But never Ingeborg Holm, never blue-eyed, laughing Inge. So what was the good of it?

Tonio Kröger's heart contracted painfully at the thought. To feel stirring within you the wonderful and melancholy play of strange forces and to be aware that those others you yearn for are blithely inaccessible to all that moves you—what a pain is this! And yet! He stood there aloof and alone, staring hopelessly at a drawn blind and making, in his distraction, as though he could look out. But yet he was happy. For he lived. His heart was full; hotly and sadly it beat for thee, Ingeborg Holm, and his soul embraced thy blonde, simple, pert, commonplace little personality in blissful self-abnegation.

Often after that he stood thus, with burning cheeks, in lonely corners, whither the sound of music, the tinkling of glasses and fragrance of flowers came but faintly, and tried to distinguish the ringing tones of thy voice amid the distant happy din; stood suffering for thee—and still was happy! Often it angered him to think that he might talk with Magdalena Vermehren, who always fell down in the dance. She understood him, she laughed or was serious in the right places; while Inge the fair, let him sit never so near her, seemed remote and estranged, his speech not being her speech. And still—he was happy. For happiness, he told himself, is not in being loved—which is a satisfaction of the vanity and mingled with disgust. Happiness is in loving, and perhaps in snatching fugitive little approaches to the beloved object. And he took inward note of this thought, wrote it down in his mind; followed out all its implications and felt it to the depths of his soul.

"Faithfulness," thought Tonio Kröger. "Yes, I will be faithful, I will love thee, Ingeborg, as long as I live!" He said this in the honesty of his intentions. And yet a still small voice whispered misgivings in his ear: after all, he had forgotten Hans Hansen utterly, even though he saw him every day! And the hateful, the pitiable fact was that this still, small, rather spiteful voice was right: time passed and the day came when Tonio Kröger was no longer so unconditionally ready as once he had been to die for the lively Inge, because he felt in himself desires and powers to accomplish in his own way a host of wonderful things in this world.

And he circled with watchful eye the sacrificial altar, where flickered the pure, chaste flame of his love; knelt before it and tended and cherished it in every way, because he so wanted to be faithful. And in a little while, unobservably, without sensation or stir, it went out after all.

But Tonio Kröger still stood before the cold altar, full of regret and dismay at the fact that faithfulness was impossible upon this earth. Then he shrugged his shoulders and went away.

He went the way that go he must, a little idly, a little irregularly, whistling to himself, gazing into space with his head on one side; and if he went wrong it was because for some people there is no such thing as a right way. Asked what in the world he meant to become, he gave various answers, for he was used to say (and had even already written it) that he bore within himself the possibility of a thousand ways of life, together with the private conviction that they were all sheer impossibilities.

Even before he left the narrow streets of his native city, the threads that bound him to it had gently loosened. The old Kröger family gradually declined, and some people quite rightly considered

Tonio Kröger's own existence and way of life as one of the signs of decay. His father's mother, the head of the family, had died, and not long after his own father followed, the tall, thoughtful, carefully dressed gentleman with the field flower in his buttonhole. The great Kröger house, with all its stately tradition, came up for sale, and the firm was dissolved. Tonio's mother, his beautiful, fiery mother, who played the piano and mandolin so wonderfully and to whom nothing mattered at all, she married again after a year's time; married a musician, moreover, a virtuoso with an Italian name, and went away with him into remote blue distances. Tonio Kröger found this a little irregular, but who was he to call her to order, who wrote poetry himself and could not even give an answer when asked what he meant to do in life?

And so he left his native town and its tortuous, gabled streets with the damp wind whistling through them; left the fountain in the garden and the ancient walnut tree, familiar friends of his youth; left the sea too, that he loved so much, and felt no pain to go. For he was grown up and sensible and had come to realize how things stood with him; he looked down on the lowly and vulgar life he had led so long in these surroundings.

He surrendered utterly to the power that to him seemed the highest on earth, to whose service he felt called, which promised him elevation and honors: the power of intellect, the power of the Word, that lords it with a smile over the unconscious and inarticulate. To this power he surrendered with all the passion of youth, and it rewarded him with all it had to give, taking from him inexorably, in return, all that it is wont to take.

It sharpened his eyes and made him see through the large words which puff out of the bosoms of mankind; it opened for him men's souls and his own, made him clairvoyant, showed him the inwardness of the world and the ultimate behind men's words and deeds. And all that he saw could be put in two words: the comedy and the tragedy of life.

And then, with knowledge, its torment and its arrogance, came solitude; because he could not endure the blithe and innocent with their darkened understanding, while they in turn were troubled by the sign on his brow.[20] But his love of the world kept growing sweeter and sweeter, and his love of form; for he used to say (and had already said it in writing) that knowledge of the soul would unfailingly make us melancholy if the pleasures of expression did not keep us alert and of good cheer.

He lived in large cities and in the south, promising himself a lux-

20. In the Old Testament, Cain, who had killed his brother Abel, is set apart from the rest of mankind by a mark which God puts on his forehead. [*Genesis* 4:15.]

uriant ripening of his art by southern suns; perhaps it was the blood of his mother's race that drew him thither. But his heart being dead and loveless, he fell into adventures of the flesh, descended into the depths of lust and searing sin, and suffering unspeakably thereby. It might have been his father in him, that tall, thoughtful, fastidiously dressed man with the wild flower in his buttonhole, that made him suffer so down there in the south; now and again he would feel a faint, yearning memory of a certain joy that was of the soul; once it had been his own, but now, in all his joys, he could not find it again.

Then he would be seized with disgust and hatred of the senses; pant after purity and seemly peace, while still he breathed the air of art, the tepid, sweet air of permanent spring, heavy with fragrance where it breeds and brews and burgeons in the mysterious bliss of creation. So for all result he was flung to and fro forever between two crass extremes: between icy intellect and scorching sense, and what with his pangs of conscience led an exhausting life, rare, extraordinary, excessive, which at bottom he, Tonio Kröger, despised. "What a labyrinth!" he sometimes thought. "How could I possibly have got into all these fantastic adventures? As though I had a wagonful of traveling gypsies for my ancestors!"

But as his health suffered from these excesses, so his artistry was sharpened; it grew fastidious, precious, *raffiné*,[21] morbidly sensitive in questions of tact and taste, rasped by the banal. His first appearance in print elicited much applause; there was joy among the elect, for it was a good and workmanlike performance, full of humor and acquaintance with pain. In no long time his name—the same by which his masters had reproached him, the same he had signed to his earlierst verses on the walnut tree and the fountain and the sea, those syllables compact of the north and the south, that good middle-class name with the exotic twist to it—became a synonym for excellence; for the painful thoroughness of the experiences he had gone through, combined with a tenacious ambition and a persistent industry, joined battle with the irritable fastidiousness of his taste and under grinding torments issued in work of a quality quite uncommon.

He worked, not like a man who works that he may live; but as one who is bent on doing nothing but work; having no regard for himself as a human being but only as a creator; moving about grey and unobtrusive among his fellows like an actor without his make-up, who counts for nothing as soon as he stops representing something else. He worked withdrawn out of sight and sound of the small fry, for whom he felt nothing but contempt, because to them a talent was a social asset like another; who, whether they were poor

21. Refined, exquisite.

or not, went about ostentatiously shabby or else flaunted startling cravats,[22] all the time taking jolly good care to amuse themselves, to be artistic and charming without the smallest notion of the fact that good work only comes out under pressure of a bad life; that he who lives does not work; that one must die to life in order to be utterly a creator.

"Shall I disturb you?" asked Tonio Kröger on the threshold of the atelier.[23] He held his hat in his hand and bowed with some ceremony, although Lisabeta Ivanovna was a good friend of his, to whom he told all his troubles.

"Mercy on you, Tonio Kröger! Don't be so formal," answered she, with her lilting intonation. "Everybody knows you were taught good manners in your nursery." She transferred her brush to her left hand, that held the palette, reached him her right, and looked him in the face, smiling and shaking her head.

"Yes, but you are working," he said. "Let's see. Oh, you've been getting on," and he looked at the color sketches leaning against chairs at both sides of the easel and from them to the large canvas covered with a square linen mesh, where the first patches of color were beginning to appear among the confused and schematic lines of the charcoal sketch.

This was in Munich, in a back building in Schellingstrasse, several stories up. Beyond the wide window facing the north were blue sky, sunshine, birds twittering; the young sweet breath of spring streaming through an open pane mingled with the smells of paint and fixative.[24] The afternoon light, bright golden, flooded the spacious emptiness of the atelier; it made no secret of the bad flooring or the rough table under the window, covered with little bottles, tubes, and brushes; it illumined the unframed studies on the unpapered walls, the torn silk screen that shut off a charmingly furnished little living-corner near the door; it shone upon the inchoate work on the easel, upon the artist and the poet there before it.

She was about the same age as himself—slightly past thirty. She sat there on a low stool, in her dark blue apron, and leant her chin in her hand. Her brown hair, compactly dressed, already a little grey at the sides, was parted in the middle and waved over the temples, framing a sensitive, sympathetic, dark-skinned face, which was Slavic in its facial structure, with flat nose, strongly accentuated cheek bones, and little bright black eyes. She sat there measuring her work with her head on one side and her eyes screwed up; her features were drawn with a look of misgiving, almost of vexation.

22. Neckties.
23. Artist's studio.
24. Liquid preservative applied to water color paintings or charcoal drawings.

He stood beside her, his right hand on his hip, with the other furiously twirling his brown moustache. His dress, reserved in cut and a soothing shade of grey, was punctilious and dignified to the last degree. He was whistling softly to himself, in the way he had, and his slanting brows were gathered in a frown. The dark brown hair was parted with severe correctness, but the labored forehead beneath showed a nervous twitching, and the chiseled southern features were sharpened as though they had been gone over again with a graver's tool. And yet the mouth—how gently curved it was, the chin how softly formed! . . . After a little he drew his hand across his brow and eyes and turned away.

"I ought not to have come," he said.

"And why not, Tonio Kröger?"

"I've just got up from my desk, Lisabeta, and inside my head it looks just the way it does on this canvas. A scaffolding, a faint first draft smeared with corrections and a few splotches of color; yes, and I come up here and see the same thing. And the same conflict and contradiction in the air," he went on, sniffing, "that has been torturing me at home. It's extraordinary. If you are possessed by an idea, you find it expressed everywhere, you even *smell* it. Fixative and the breath of spring; art and—what? Don't say nature, Lisabeta, 'nature' isn't exhausting. Ah, no, I ought to have gone for a walk, though it's doubtful if it would have made me feel better. Five minutes ago, not far from here, I met a man I know, Adalbert, the novelist. 'God damn the spring!' says he in the aggressive way he has. 'It is and always has been the most ghastly time of the year. Can you get hold of a single sensible idea, Kröger? Can you sit still and work out even the smallest effect, when your blood tickles till it's positively indecent and you are teased by a whole host of irrelevant sensations that when you look at them turn out to be unworkable trash? For my part, I am going to a café. A café is neutral territory, the change of the seasons doesn't affect it; it represents, so to speak, the detached and elevated sphere of the literary man, in which one is only capable of refined ideas.' And he went into the café . . . and perhaps I ought to have gone with him."

Lisabeta was highly entertained.

"I like that, Tonio Kröger. That part about the indecent tickling is good. And he is right too, in a way, for spring is really not very conducive to work. But now listen. Spring or no spring, I will just finish this little place—work out this little effect, as your friend Adalbert would say. Then we'll go into the 'salon' and have tea, and you can talk yourself out, for I can perfectly well see you are too full for utterance. Will you just compose yourself somewhere—on that chest, for instance, if you are not afraid for your aristocratic garments—"

"Oh, leave my clothes alone, Lisabeta Ivanovna! Do you want me to go about in a ragged velveteen jacket or a red waistcoat? Every artist is as bohemian as the deuce, inside! Let him at least wear proper clothes and behave outwardly like a respectable being. No, I am not too full for utterance," he said as he watched her mixing her paints. "I've told you, it is only that I have a problem and a conflict, that sticks in my mind and disturbs me at my work. . . . Yes, what was it we were just saying? We were talking about Adalbert, the novelist, that stout and forthright man. 'Spring is the most ghastly time of the year,' says he, and goes into a café. A man has to know what he needs, eh? Well, you see he's not the only one; the spring makes me nervous, too; I get dazed with the triflingness and sacredness of the memories and feelings it evokes; only that I don't succeed in looking down on it; for the truth is it makes me ashamed; I quail before its sheer naturalness and triumphant youth. And I don't know whether I should envy Adalbert or despise him for his ignorance. . . .

"Yes, it is true; spring is a bad time for work; and why? Because we are feeling too much. Nobody but a beginner imagines that he who creates must feel. Every real and genuine artist smiles at such naïve blunders as that. A melancholy enough smile, perhaps, but still a smile. For what an artist talks about is never the main point; it is the raw material, in and for itself indifferent, out of which, with bland and serene mastery, he creates the work of art. If you care too much about what you have to say, if your heart is too much in it, you can be pretty sure of making a mess. You get pathetic, you wax sentimental; something dull and doddering, without roots or outlines, with no sense of humor—something tiresome and banal grows under your hand, and you get nothing out of it but apathy in your audience and disappointment and misery in yourself. For so it is, Lisabeta; feeling, warm, heartfelt feeling, is always banal and futile; only the irritations and icy ecstasies of the artist's corrupted nervous system are artistic. The artist must be unhuman, extra-human; he must stand in a queer aloof relationship to our humanity; only so is he in a position, I ought to say only so would he be tempted, to represent it, to present it, to portray it to good effect. The very gift of style, of form and expression, is nothing else than this cool and fastidious attitude toward humanity; you might say there has to be this impoverishment and devastation as a preliminary condition. For sound natural feeling, say what you like, has no taste. It is all up with the artist as soon as he becomes a man and begins to feel. Adalbert knows that; that's why he betook himself to the café, the neutral territory—God help him!"

"Yes, God help him, Batushka,"[25] said Lisabeta, as she washed

25. Literally, "Little Father," an affectionate Russian diminutive.

her hands in a tin basin. "You don't need to follow his example."

"No, Lisabeta, I am not going to; and the only reason is that I am now and again in a position to feel a little ashamed of the springtime of my art. You see sometimes I get letters from strangers, full of praise and thanks and admiration from people whose feelings I have touched. I read them and feel touched myself at these warm if ungainly emotions I have called up; a sort of pity steals over me at this naïve enthusiasm; and I positively blush at the thought of how these good people would freeze up if they were to get a look behind the scenes. What they, in their innocence, cannot comprehend is that a properly constituted, healthy, decent man never writes, acts, or composes—all of which does not hinder me from using his admiration for my genius to goad myself on; nor from taking it in deadly earnest and aping the airs of a great man. Oh, don't talk to me, Lisabeta. I tell you I am sick to death of depicting humanity without having any part or lot in it. . . . Is an artist a male, anyhow? Ask the females! It seems to me we artists are all of us something like those unsexed papal singers[26] . . . we sing like angels; but—"

"Shame on you, Tonio Kröger. But come to tea. The water is just on the boil, and here are some *papyros*.[27] You were talking about singing soprano, do go on. But really you ought to be ashamed of yourself. If I did not know your passionate devotion to your calling and how proud you are of it—"

"Don't talk about 'calling,' Lisabeta Ivanovna. Literature is not a calling, it is a curse, believe me! When does one begin to feel the curse? Early, horribly early. At a time when one ought by rights still to be living in peace and harmony with God and the world. It begins by your feeling yourself set apart, in a curious sort of opposition to the nice, regular people; there is a gulf of ironic sensibility, of knowledge, scepticism, disagreement between you and the others; it grows deeper and deeper, you realize that you are alone; and from then on any *rapprochement*[28] is simply hopeless! What a fate! That is, if you still have enough heart, enough warmth of affections, to feel how frightful it is! . . . Your self-consciousness is kindled, because you among thousands feel the sign on your brow and know that everyone else sees it. I once knew an actor, a man of genius, who had to struggle with a morbid self-consciousness and instability. When he had no role to play, nothing to represent, this man, consummate artist but impoverished human being, was overcome by an exaggerated consciousness of his ego. A genuine artist

26. *Castrati* were singers castrated as young boys to preserve their soprano voices. The practice stopped in 1878, but the pope's chapel employed them as late as 1903 because women were not permitted to become part of the papal establishment.

27. Cigarettes.

28. Reconciliation.

—not one who has taken up art as a profession like another, but artist foreordained and damned—you can pick out, without boasting very sharp perceptions, out of a group of men. The sense of being set apart and not belonging, of being known and observed, something both regal and incongruous shows in his face. You might see something of the same sort on the features of a prince walking through a crowd in ordinary clothes. But no civilian clothes are any good here, Lisabeta. You can disguise yourself, you can dress up like an attaché or a lieutenant of the guard on leave; you hardly need to give a glance or speak a word before everyone knows you are not a human being, but something else: something queer, different, inimical.

"But what is it, to be an artist? Nothing shows up the general human dislike of thinking, and man's innate craving to be comfortable, better than his attitude to this question. When these worthy people are affected by a work of art, they say humbly that that sort of thing is a 'gift.' And because in their innocence they assume that beautiful and uplifting results must have beautiful and uplifting causes, they never dream that the 'gift' in question is a very dubious affair and rests upon extremely sinister foundations. Everybody knows that artists are 'sensitive' and easily wounded; just as everybody knows that ordinary people, with a normal bump of self-confidence, are not. Now you see, Lisabeta, I cherish at the bottom of my soul all the scorn and suspicion of the artist gentry—translated into terms of the intellectual—that my upright old forebears there on the Baltic would have felt for any juggler or mountebank that entered their houses. Listen to this. I know a banker, grey-haired business man, who has a gift for writing stories. He employs this gift in his idle hours, and some of his stories are of the first rank. But despite—I say despite—this excellent gift his withers are by no means unwrung:[29] on the contrary, he has had to serve a prison sentence, on anything but trifling grounds. Yes, it was actually first *in prison* that he became conscious of his gift, and his experiences as a convict are the main theme in all his works. One might be rash enough to conclude that a man has to be at home in some kind of jail in order to become a poet. But can you escape the suspicion that the source and essence of his being an artist had less to do with his life in prison than they had with the reasons that *brought him there?* A banker who writes—that is a rarity, isn't it? But a banker who isn't a criminal, who is irreproachably respectable, and yet writes—he doesn't exist. Yes, you are laughing, and yet I am more than half serious. No problem, none in the world, is more tormenting than this of the artist and his human aspect. Take the most

29. I.e., he is by no means untroubled.

miraculous case of all, take the most typical and therefore the most powerful of artists, take such a morbid and profoundly equivocal work as *Tristan and Isolde*,[30] and look at the effect it has on a healthy young man of thoroughly normal feelings. Exaltation, encouragement, warm, downright enthusiasm, perhaps incitement to 'artistic' creation of his own. Poor young dilettante![31] In us artists it looks fundamentally different from what he wots[32] of, with his 'warm heart' and 'honest enthusiasm.' I've seen women and youths go mad over artists . . . and I *knew* about them . . . ! The origin, the accompanying phenomena, and the conditions of the artist life—good Lord, what I haven't observed about them, over and over!"

"Observed, Tonio Kröger? If I may ask, only 'observed'?"

He was silent, knitting his oblique brown brows and whistling softly to himself.

"Let me have your cup, Tonio. The tea is weak. And take another cigarette. Now, you perfectly know that you are looking at things as they do not necessarily have to be looked at. . . ."

"That is Horatio's answer, dear Lisabeta. ' 'Twere to consider too curiously,[33] to consider so.' "

"I mean, Tonio Kröger, that one can consider them just exactly as well from another side. I am only a silly painting female, and if I can contradict you at all, if I can defend your own profession a little against you, it is not by saying anything new, but simply by reminding you of some things you very well know yourself: of the purifying and healing influence of letters, the subduing of the passions by knowledge and eloquence; literature as the guide to understanding, forgiveness, and love, the redeeming power of the Word, literary art as the noblest manifestation of the human mind, the poet as the most highly developed of human beings, the poet as saint. Is it to consider things not curiously enough, to consider them so?"

"You may talk like that, Lisabeta Ivanovna, you have a perfect right. And with reference to Russian literature, and the words of your poets, one can really worship them; they really come close to being that elevated literature you are talking about. But I am not ignoring your objections, they are part of the things I have in my mind today. . . . Look at me, Lisabeta. I don't look any too cheerful, do I? A little old and tired and pinched, eh? Well, now to

30. Opera by Richard Wagner on the legendary doomed love of the knight Tristan and his uncle's wife, Queen Isolde. The sensuous appeal of the lovers' longing for night, death, and erotic transcendence, and the revolutionary example of Wagner's new musical forms, overwhelmed young artists and amateurs in the late 19th and early 20th centuries.

31. A dabbler or amateur of the arts.

32. Knows (consciously archaic language).

33. I.e., "too closely"—the words with which Horatio reproaches Hamlet(V,i, 106) for adopting a morbid perspective.

come back to the 'knowledge.' Can't you imagine a man, born orthodox, mild-mannered, well-meaning, a bit sentimental, just simply over-stimulated by his psychological clairvoyance, and going to the dogs? Not to let the sadness of the world unman you; to read, mark, learn, and put to account even the most torturing things and to be of perpetual good cheer, in the sublime consciousness of moral superiority over the horrible invention of existence—yes, thank you! But despite all the joys of expression once in a while the thing gets on your nerves. '*Tout comprendre c'est tout pardonner*.'[34] I don't know about that. There is something I call being sick of knowledge, Lisabeta; when it is enough for you to see through a thing in order to be sick to death of it, and not in the least in a forgiving mood. Such was the case of Hamlet the Dane, that typical literary man. He knew what it meant to be called to knowledge without being born to it. To see things clear, if even through your tears, to recognize, notice, observe—and have to put it all down with a smile, at the very moment when hands are clinging, and lips meeting, and the human gaze is blinded with feeling—it is infamous, Lisabeta, it is indecent, outrageous—but what good does it do to be outraged?

"Then another and no less charming side of the thing, of course, is your ennui,[35] your indifferent and ironic attitude toward truth. It is a fact that there is no society in the world so dumb and hopeless as a circle of literary people who are hounded to death as it is. All knowledge is old and tedious to them. Utter some truth that it gave you considerable youthful joy to conquer and possess—and they will all chortle at you for your naïveté. Oh, yes, Lisabeta, literature is a wearing job. In human society, I do assure you, a reserved and skeptical man can be taken for stupid, whereas he is really only arrogant and perhaps lacks courage. So much for 'knowledge.' Now for the 'Word.' It isn't so much a matter of the 'redeeming power' as it is of putting your emotions on ice and serving them up chilled! Honestly, don't you think there's a good deal of cool cheek in the prompt and superficial way a writer can get rid of his feelings by turning them into literature? If your heart is too full, if you are overpowered with the emotions of some sweet or exalted moment—nothing simpler! Go to the literary man, he will put it all straight for you instanter.[36] He will analyze and formulate your affair, label it and express it and discuss it and polish it off and make you indifferent to it for time and eternity—and not charge you a farthing.[37] You will go home quite relieved, cooled off, enlightened; and wonder what it was all about and why you were so might-

34. "To understand everything is to forgive everything." [Voltaire.]
35. Boredom.
36. Right away.
37. A quarter of a penny.

ily moved. And will you seriously enter the lists in behalf of this vain and frigid charlatan? What is uttered, so runs this *credo*,[38] is finished and done with. If the whole world could be expressed, it would be saved, finished and done. . . . Well and good. But I am not a nihilist—"

"You are not a—" said Lisabeta. . . . She was lifting a teaspoonful of tea to her mouth and paused in the act to stare at him.

"Come, come, Lisabeta, what's the matter? I say I am not a nihilist,[39] with respect, that is, to lively feeling. You see, the literary man does not understand that life may go on living, unashamed, even after it has been expressed and therewith finished. No matter how much it has been redeemed by becoming literature, it keeps right on sinning—for all action is sin in the mind's eye—

"I'm nearly done, Lisabeta. Please listen. I love life—this is an admission. I present it to you, you may have it. I have never made it to anyone else. People say—people have even written and printed—that I hate life, or fear or despise or abominate it. I liked to hear this, it has always flattered me; but that does not make it true. I love life. You smile; and I know why, Lisabeta. But I implore you not to take what I am saying for literature. Don't think of Caesar Borgia[40] or any drunken philosophy that has him for a standard-bearer. He is nothing to me, your Caesar Borgia. I have no opinion of him, and I shall never comprehend how one can honor the extraordinary and demonic[41] as an ideal. No, life as the eternal antinomy of mind and art does not represent itself to us as a vision of savage greatness and ruthless beauty; we who are set apart and different do not conceive it as, like us, unusual; it is the normal, respectable, and admirable that is the kingdom of our longing: life, in all its seducitve banality! That man is very far from being an artist, my dear, whose last and deepest enthusiasm is the *raffiné*, the eccentric and satanic; who does not know a longing for the innocent, the simple, and the living, for a little friendship, devotion, familiar human happiness—the gnawing, surreptitious hankering, Lisabeta, for the bliss of the commonplace. . . .

"A genuine human friend. Believe me, I should be proud and happy to possess a friend among men. But up to now all the friends I have had have been demons, kobolds,[42] impious monsters, and specters dumb with excess of knowledge—that is to say, literary men.

"I may be standing upon some platform, in some hall in front of people who have come to listen to me. And I find myself looking

38. Statement of faith (Latin, *I believe*).

39. One who denies all social order and collective values.

40. Caesar (Cesare) Borgia (1467–1507), ruthless ruler and patron of the arts in Renaissance Italy, taken by Machiavelli as the model for his essay on government, *The Prince*.

41. Possessed of supernatural genius.

42. Mischievous elves in German folklore.

round among my hearers, I catch myself secretly peering about the auditorium, and all the while I am thinking who it is that has come here to listen to me, whose grateful applause is in my ears, with whom my art is making me one. . . . I do not find what I seek, Lisabeta, I find the herd. The same old community, the same old gathering of early Christians, so to speak: people with fine souls in uncouth bodies, people who are always falling down in the dance, if you know what I mean; the kind to whom poetry serves as a sort of mild revenge on life. Always and only the poor and suffering, never any of the others, the blue-eyed ones, Lisabeta—they do not need mind. . . .

"And, after all, would it not be a lamentable lack of logic to want it otherwise? It is against all sense to love life and yet bend all the powers you have to draw it over to your own side, to the side of finesse and melancholy and the whole sickly aristocracy of letters. The kingdom of art increases and that of health and innocence declines on this earth. What there is left of it ought to be carefully preserved; one ought not to tempt people to read poetry who would much rather read books about the instantaneous photography of horses.

"For, after all, what more pitiable sight is there than life led astray by art? We artists have a consummate contempt for the dilettante, the man who is leading a living life and yet thinks he can be an artist too if he gets the chance. I am speaking from personal experience, I do assure you. Suppose I am in a company in a good house, with eating and drinking going on, and plenty of conversation and good feeling: I am glad and grateful to be able to lose myself among good regular people for a while. Then all of a sudden —I am thinking of something that actually happened—an officer gets up, a lieutenant, a stout, good-looking chap, whom I could never have believed guilty of any conduct unbecoming his uniform, and actually in good set terms asks the company's permission to read some verses of his own composition. Everybody looks disconcerted, they laugh and tell him to go on, and he takes them at their word and reads from a sheet of paper he has up to now been hiding in his coat-tail pocket—something about love and music, as deeply felt as it is inept. But I ask you: a lieutenant! A man of the world! He surely did not need to. . . . Well, the inevitable result is long faces, silence, a little artificial applause, everybody thoroughly uncomfortable. The first sensation I am conscious of is guilt—I feel partly responsible for the disturbance this rash youth has brought upon the company; and no wonder, for I, as a member of the same guild, am a target for some of the unfriendly glances. But next minute I realize something else: this man for whom just now I felt the greatest respect has suddenly sunk in my eyes. I feel a benevolent pity. Along with some other brave and good-natured gentlemen

I go up and speak to him. 'Congratulations, Herr Lieutenant,' I say, 'that is a very pretty talent you have. It was charming.' And I am within an ace of clapping him on the shoulder. But is that the way one is supposed to feel toward a lieutenant—benevolent? . . . It was his own fault. There he stood, suffering embarrassment for the mistake of thinking that one may pluck a single leaf from the laurel tree of art[43] without paying for it with his life. No, there I go with my colleague, the convict banker—but don't you find, Lisabeta, that I have quite a Hamlet-like flow of oratory today?"

"Are you done, Tonio Kröger?"

"No. But there won't be any more."

"And quite enough too. Are you expecting a reply?"

"Have you one ready?"

"I should say. I have listened to you faithfully, Tonio, from beginning to end, and I will give you the answer to everything you have said this afternoon and the solution of the problem that has been upsetting you. Now: the solution is that you, as you sit there, are, quite simply, a bourgeois."

"Am I?" he asked a little crestfallen.

"Yes, that hits you hard, it must. So I will soften the judgment just a little. You are a bourgeois on the wrong path, a bourgeois *manqué*."[44]

Silence. Then he got up resolutely and took his hat and stick.

"Thank you, Lisabeta Ivanovna; now I can go home in peace. I am expressed."[45]

Toward autumn Tonio Kröger said to Lisabeta Ivanovna:

"Well, Lisabeta, I think I'll be off. I need a change of air. I must get away, out into the open."

"Well, well, well, little Father! Does it please your Highness to go down to Italy again?"

"Oh, get along with your Italy, Lisabeta. I'm fed up with Italy, I spew it out of my mouth. It's a long time since I imagined I could belong down there. Art, eh? Blue-velvet sky, ardent wine, the sweets of sensuality. In short, I don't want it—I decline with thanks. The whole *bellezza*[46] business makes me nervous. All those frightfully animated people down there with their black animal-like eyes; I don't like them either. These Romance peoples have no soul in their eyes. No, I'm going to take a trip to Denmark."

"To Denmark?"

43. The laurel tree was sacred to Apollo, the Greek god of poetry and prophecy.

44. The German says literally, a *bourgeois gone astray*. Tonio is caught between two worlds; he can neither reject nor live up to his bourgeois heritage.

45. In recognizing and accepting Lisabeta's description of himself, Tonio uses the same word (*erledigt*) that was earlier translated as "get rid of," "polished off," and "finished" in the discussion of the fixative role of art.

46. "Beauty" (Italian).

"Yes. I'm quite sanguine of the results. I happen never to have been there, though I lived all my youth so close to it. Still I have always known and loved the country. I suppose I must have this northern tendency from my father, for my mother was really more for the *bellezza,* in so far, that is, as she cared very much one way or the other. But just take the books that are written up there, that clean, meaty, whimsical Scandinavian literature. Lisabeta, there's nothing like it, I love it. Or take the Scandinavian meals, those incomparable meals, which can only be digested in strong sea air (I don't know whether I can digest them in any sort of air); I know them from my home too, because we ate that way up there. Take even the names, the given names that people rejoice in up north; we have a good many of them in my part of the country too: Ingeborg, for instance, isn't it the purest poetry—like a harp-tone? And then the sea—up there it's the Baltic! . . . In a word, I am going, Lisabeta, I want to see the Baltic again and read the books and hear the names on their native heath; I want to stand on the terrace at Kronberg,[47] where the ghost appeared to Hamlet, bringing despair and death to that poor, noble-souled youth. . . ."

"How are you going, Tonio, if I may ask? What route are you taking?"

"The usual one," he said, shrugging his shoulders, and blushed perceptibly. "Yes, I shall touch my—my point of departure, Lisabeta, after thirteen years, and that may turn out rather funny."

She smiled.

"That is what I wanted to hear, Tonio Kröger. Well, be off, then, in God's name. Be sure to write to me, do you hear? I shall expect a letter full of your experiences in—Denmark."

And Tonio Kröger traveled north. He traveled in comfort (for he was wont to say that anyone who suffered inwardly more than other people had a right to a little outward ease); and he did not stay until the towers of the little town he had left rose up in the grey air. Among them he made a short and singular stay.

The dreary afternoon was merging into evening when the train pulled into the narrow, reeking shed, so marvelously familiar. The volumes of thick smoke rolled up to the dirty glass roof and wreathed to and fro there in long tatters, just as they had, long ago, on the day when Tonio Kröger, with nothing but derision in his heart, had left his native town.—He arranged to have his luggage sent to his hotel and walked out of the station.

There were the cabs, those enormously high, enormously wide black cabs drawn by two horses, standing in a rank. He did not take one, he only looked at them, as he looked at everything: the narrow

47. Castle in Helsingör (Elsinore), the supposed setting of Shakespeare's *Hamlet.*

gables, and the pointed towers peering above the roofs close at hand; the plump, fair, easy-going populace, with their broad yet rapid speech. And a nervous laugh mounted in him, mysteriously akin to a sob.—He walked on, slowly, with the damp wind constantly in his face, across the bridge, with the mythological statues on the railings, and some distance along the harbor.

Good Lord, how tiny and close it all seemed! The comical little gabled streets were climbing up just as of yore from the port to the town! And on the ruffled waters the smokestacks and masts of the ships dipped gently in the wind and twilight. Should he go up that next street, leading, he knew, to a certain house? No, tomorrow. He was too sleepy. His head was heavy from the journey, and slow, vague trains of thought passed through his mind.

Sometimes in the past thirteen years, when he was suffering from indigestion, he had dreamed of being back home in the echoing old house in the steep, narrow street. His father had been there too, and reproached him bitterly for his dissolute manner of life, and this, each time, he had found quite as it should be. And now the present refused to distinguish itself in any way from one of those tantalizing dream fabrications in which the dreamer asks himself if this be delusion or reality and is driven to decide for the latter, only to wake up after all in the end. . . . . He paced through the half-empty streets with his head inclined against the wind, moving as though in his sleep in the direction of the hotel, the first hotel in the town, where he meant to sleep. A bow-legged man, with a pole at the end of which burned a tiny fire, walked before him with a rolling, seafaring gait and lighted the gas lamps.

What was at the bottom of this? What was it burning darkly beneath the ashes of his fatigue, refusing to burst out into a clear blaze? Hush, hush, only no talk. Only don't make words! He would have liked to go on so, for a long time, in the wind, through the dusky, dreamily familiar streets—but everything was so little and close together here. You reached your goal at once.

In the upper town there were arc-lamps,[48] just lighted. There was the hotel with the two black lions in front of it; he had been afraid of them as a child. And there they were, still looking at each other as though they were about to sneeze; only they seemed to have grown much smaller. Tonio Kröger passed between them into the hotel.

As he came on foot, he was received with no great ceremony. There was a porter, and a lordly gentleman dressed in black, to do the honors; the latter, shoving back his cuffs with his little fingers, measured him from the crown of his head to the soles of his boots, obviously with intent to place him, to assign him to his proper cate-

48. Electrical street lights.

gory socially and hierarchically speaking and then mete out the suitable degree of courtesy. He seemed not to come to any clear decision and compromised on a moderate display of politeness. A mild-mannered waiter with yellow-white side whiskers, in a dress suit shiny with age, and rosettes on his soundless shoes, led him up two flights into a clean old room furnished in patriarchal style. Its windows gave on a twilight view of courts and gables, very medieval and picturesque, with the fantastic bulk of the old church close by. Tonio Kröger stood awhile before this window; then he sat down on the wide sofa, crossed his arms, drew down his brows, and whistled to himself.

Lights were brought and his luggage came up. The mild-mannered waiter laid the hotel register on the table, and Tonio Kröger, his head on one side, scrawled something on it that might be taken for a name, a station, and a place of origin. Then he ordered supper and went on gazing into space from his sofa-corner. When it stood before him he let it wait long untouched, then took a few bites and walked up and down an hour in his room, stopping from time to time and closing his eyes. Then he very slowly undressed and went to bed. He slept long and had curiously confused and ardent dreams.

It was broad day when he woke. Hastily he recalled where he was and got up to draw the curtains; the pale-blue sky, already with a hint of autumn, was streaked with frayed and tattered cloud; still, above his native city the sun was shining.

He spent more care than usual upon his toilette,[49] washed and shaved and made himself fresh and immaculate as though about to call upon some smart family where a well-dressed and flawless appearance was *de rigueur*;[50] and while occupied in this wise he listened to the anxious beating of his heart.

How bright it was outside! He would have liked better a twilight air like yesterday's, instead of passing through the streets in the broad sunlight, under everybody's eye. Would he meet people he knew, be stopped and questioned and have to submit to be asked how he had spent the last thirteen years? No, thank goodness, he was known to nobody here; even if anybody remembered him, it was unlikely he would be recognized—for certainly he had changed in the meantime! He surveyed himself in the glass and felt a sudden sense of security behind his mask, behind his work-worn face, that was older than his years. . . . He sent for breakfast, and after that he went out; he passed under the disdainful eye of the porter and the gentleman in black, through the vestibule and between the two lions, and so into the street.

Where was he going? He scarcely knew. It was the same as yes-

49. Grooming.

50. Expected by etiquette.

terday. Hardly was he in the midst of this long-familiar scene, this stately conglomeration of gables, turrets, arcades, and fountains, hardly did he feel once more the wind in his face, that strong current wafting a faint and pungent aroma from far-off dreams, when the same mistiness laid itself like a veil about his senses. . . . The muscles of his face relaxed, and he looked at men and things with a look grown suddenly calm. Perhaps right there, on that street corner, he might wake up after all. . . .

Where was he going? It seemed to him the direction he took had a connection with his sad and strangely rueful dreams of the night. . . . He went to Market Square, under the vaulted arches of the Rathaus,[51] where the butchers were weighing out their wares red-handed, where the tall old Gothic fountain stood with its manifold spires. He paused in front of a house, a plain narrow building, like many another, with a fretted[52] baroque gable; stood there lost in contemplation. He read the plate on the door, his eyes rested a little while on each of the windows. Then slowly he turned away.

Where did he go? Toward home. But he took a round-about way outside the walls—for he had plenty of time. He went over the Millwall and over the Holstenwall, clutching his hat, for the wind was rushing and moaning through the trees. He left the wall near the station, where he saw a train puffing busily past, idly counted the coaches, and looked after the man who sat perched upon the last. In the Lindenplatz he stopped at one of the pretty villas, peered long into the garden and up at the windows, lastly conceived the idea of swinging the gate to and fro upon its hinges till it creaked. Then he looked awhile at his moist, rust-stained hand and went on, went through the squat old gate, along the harbor, and up the steep, windy street to his parents' house.

It stood aloof from its neighbors, its gable towering above them; grey and somber, as it had stood these three hundred years; and Tonio Kröger read the pious, half-illegible motto above the entrance. Then he drew a long breath and went in.

His heart gave a throb of fear, lest his father might come out of one of the doors on the ground floor, in his office coat, with the pen behind his ear, and take him to task for his excesses. He would have found the reproach quite in order; but he got past unchidden. The inner door was ajar, which appeared to him reprehensible though at the same time he felt as one does in certain broken dreams, where obstacles melt away of themselves, and one presses onward in marvelous favor with fortune. The wide entry, paved with great square flags, echoed to his tread. Opposite the silent kitchen was the curious projecting structure, of rough boards, but cleanly varnished, that had been the servants' quarters. It was quite high up and could

51. Town hall.
52. Decorated with elaborately carved ornaments.

only be reached by a sort of ladder from the entry. But the great cupboards and carven presses were gone. The son of the house climbed the majestic staircase, with his hand on the white-enameled, fret-work balustrade. At each step he lifted his hand, and put it down again with the next as though testing whether he could call back his ancient familiarity with the stout old railing. . . . But at the landing of the entresol[53] he stopped. For on the entrance door was a white plate; and on it in black letters he read; "Public Library."

"Public Library?" thought Tonio Kröger. What were either literature or the public doing here? He knocked . . . heard a "come in," and obeying it with gloomy suspense gazed upon a scene of most unhappy alteration.

The story was three rooms deep, and all the doors stood open. The walls were covered nearly all the way up with long rows of books in uniform bindings, standing in dark-colored bookcases. In each room a poor creature of a man sat writing behind a sort of counter. The farthest two just turned their heads, but the nearest got up in haste and, leaning with both hands on the table, stuck out his head, pursed his lips, lifted his brows, and looked at the visitor with eagerly blinking eyes.

"I beg pardon," said Tonio Kröger without turning his eyes from the bookshelves. "I am a stranger here, seeing the sights. So this is your Public Library? May I examine your collection a little?"

"Certainly, with pleasure," said the official, blinking still more violently. "It is open to everybody. . . . Pray look about you. Should you care for a catalogue?"

"No, thanks," answered Tonio Kröger, "I shall soon find my way about." And he began to move slowly along the walls, with the appearance of studying the rows of books. After a while he took down a volume, opened it, and posted himself at the window.

This was the breakfast room. They had eaten here in the morning instead of in the big dining room upstairs, with its white statues of gods and goddesses standing out against the blue walls. . . . Beyond there had been a bedroom, where his father's mother had died—only after a long struggle, old as she was, for she had been of a pleasure-loving nature and clung to life. And his father too had drawn his last breath in the same room; tht tall, correct, slightly melancholy and pensive gentleman with the wild flower in his buttonhole. . . . Tonio had sat at the foot of his death bed, quite given over to unutterable feelings of love and grief. His mother had knelt at the bedside, his lovely, fiery mother, dissolved in hot tears, and after that she had withdrawn with her artist into the far blue south. . . . And beyond still, the small third room, likewise full of books

53. Mezzanine.

and presided over by a shabby man—that had been for years on end his own. Thither he had come after school and a walk—like today's; against that wall his table had stood with the drawer where he had kept his first clumsy, heartfelt attempts at verse. . . . The walnut tree . . . a pang went through him. He gave a sidewise glance out at the window. The garden lay desolate, but there stood the old walnut tree where it used to stand, groaning and creaking heavily in the wind. And Tonio Kröger let his gaze fall upon the book he had in his hands, an excellent piece of work, and very familiar. He followed the black lines of print, the paragraphs, the flow of words that flowed with so much art, mounting in the ardor of creation to a certain climax and effect and then as artfully breaking off.

"Yes, that was well done," he said; put back the book and turned away. Then he saw that the fuctionary still stood bolt-upright, blinking with a mingled expression of zeal and misgiving. "A capital collection, I see," said Tonio Kröger. "I have already quite a good idea of it. Much obliged to you. Good-bye." He went out; but it was a poor exit, and he felt sure the official would stand there perturbed and blinking for several minutes.

He felt no desire for further researches. He had been home. Strangers were living upstairs in the large rooms behind the pillared hall; the top of the stairs was shut off by a glass door which used not to be there, and on the door was a plate. He went away, down the steps, across the echoing corridor, and left his parental home. He sought a restaurant, sat down in a corner, and brooded over a heavy, greasy meal. Then he returned to his hotel.

"I am leaving," he said to the fine gentleman in black. "This afternoon." And he asked for his bill, and for a carriage to take him down to the harbor where he should take the boat for Copenhagen. Then he went up to his room and sat there stiff and still, with his cheek on his hand, looking down on the table before him with absent eyes. Later he paid his bill and packed his things. At the appointed hour the carriage was announced and Tonio Kröger went down in travel array.

At the foot of the stairs the gentleman in black was waiting.

"Beg pardon," he said, shoving back his cuffs with his little fingers. . . . "Beg pardon, but we must detain you just a moment. Herr Seehaase, the proprietor, would like to exchange two words with you. A matter of form. . . . He is back there. . . . If you will have the goodness to step this way. . . . It is *only* Herr Seehaase, the proprietor."

And he ushered Tonio Kröger into the background of the vestibule. . . . There, in fact, stood Herr Seehaase. Tonio Kröger recognized him from old time. He was small, fat, and bow-legged. His shaven sidewhisker was white, but he wore the same old low-cut dress coat and little velvet cap embroidered in green. He was not alone. Beside him, at a little high desk fastened into the wall, stood a policeman in a helmet, his gloved right hand resting on a document in colored inks; he turned towards Tonio Kröger with his honest, soldierly face as though he expected Tonio to sink into the earth at his glance.

Tonio Kröger looked at the two and confined himself to waiting.

"You came from Munich?" the policeman asked at length in a heavy, good-natured voice.

Tonio Kröger said he had.

"You are going to Copenhagen?"

"Yes, I am on the way to a Danish seashore resort."

"Seashore resort? Well, you must produce your papers," said the policeman. He uttered the last word with great satisfaction.

"Papers . . . ?" He had no papers. He drew out his pocketbook and looked into it; but aside from notes there was nothing there but some proof-sheets of a story which he had taken along to finish reading. He hated relations with officials and had never got himself a passport. . . .

"I am sorry," he said, "but I don't travel with papers."

"Ah!" said the policeman. "And what might be your name?"

Tonio replied.

"Is that a fact?" asked the policeman, suddenly erect, and expanding his nostrils as wide as he could. . . .

"Yes, that is a fact," answered Tonio Kröger.

"And what are you, anyhow?"

Tonio Kröger gulped and gave the name of his trade in a firm voice. Herr Seehaase lifted his head and looked him curiously in the face.

"H'm," said the policeman. "And you give out that you are not identical with an individdle named"—he said "individdle" and then, referring to his document in colored inks, spelled out an involved, fantastic name which mingled all the sounds of all the races—Tonio Kröger forgot it next minute—"of unknown parentage and unspecified means," he went on, "wanted by the Munich police for various shady transactions, and probably in flight toward Denmark?"

"Yes, I give out all that, and more," said Tonio Kröger, wriggling his shoulders. The gesture made a certain impression.

"What? Oh, yes, of course," said the policeman. "You say you can't show any papers—"

Herr Seehaase threw himself into the breach.

"It is only a formality," he said pacifically, "nothing else. You must bear in mind the official is only doing his duty. If you could only identify yourself somehow—some document . . ."

They were all silent. Should he make an end of the business, by revealing to Herr Seehaase that he was no swindler without specified means, no gypsy in a green wagon, but the son of the late Consul Kröger, a member of the Kröger family? No, he felt no desire to do that. After all, were not these guardians of civic order within their right? He even agreed with them—up to a point. He shrugged his shoulders and kept quiet.

"What have you got, then?" asked the policeman. "In your portfoly, I mean?"

"Here? Nothing. Just a proof-sheet," answered Tonio Kröger.

"Proof-sheet? What's that? Let's see it."

And Tonio Kröger handed over his work. The policeman spread it out on the shelf and began reading. Herr Seehaase drew up and shared it with him. Tonio Kröger looked over their shoulders to see what they read. It was a good moment, a little effect he had worked out to a perfection. He had a sense of self-satisfaction.

"You see," he said, "there is my name. I wrote it, and it is going to be published, you understand."

"All right, that will answer," said Herr Seehaase with decision, gathered up the sheets and gave them back. "That will have to answer, Petersen," he repeated crisply, shutting his eyes and shaking his head as though to see and hear no more. "We must not keep the gentleman any longer. The carriage is waiting. I implore you to pardon the little inconvenience, sir. The officer has only done his duty, but I told him at once he was on the wrong track. . . ."

"Indeed!" thought Tonio Kröger.

The officer seemed still to have his doubts; he muttered something else about individdle and document. But Herr Seehaase, overflowing with regrets, led his guest through the vestibule, accompanied him past the two lions to the carriage, and himself, with many respectful bows, closed the door upon him. And then the funny, high, wide old cab rolled and rattled and bumped down the steep, narrow street to the quay.

And such was the manner of Tonio Kröger's visit to his ancestral home.

Night fell and the moon swam up with silver gleam as Tonio Kröger's boat reached the open sea. He stood at the prow wrapped in his cloak against a mounting wind, and looked beneath into the dark going and coming of the waves as they hovered and swayed and came on, to meet with a clap and shoot erratically away in a bright gush of foam.

He was lulled in a mood of still enchantment. The episode at the hotel, their wanting to arrest him for a swindler in his own home, had cast him down a little, even though he found it quite in order

—in a certain way. But after he came on board he had watched, as he used to do as a boy with his father, the lading of goods into the deep bowels of the boat, amid shouts of mingled Danish and Plattdeutsch;[54] not only boxes and bales, but also a Bengal tiger and a polar bear were lowered in cages with stout iron bars. They had probably come from Hamburg and were destined for a Danish menagerie. He had enjoyed these distractions. And as the boat glided along between flat riverbanks he quite forgot Officer Petersen's inquisition; while all the rest—his sweet, sad, rueful dreams of the night before, the walk he had taken, the walnut tree—had welled up again in his soul. The sea opened out and he saw in the distance the beach where he as a lad had been let to listen to the ocean's summer dreams; saw the flashing of the lighthouse tower and the lights of the Kurhaus[55] where he and his parents had lived. . . . The Baltic! He bent his head to the strong salt wind; it came sweeping on, it enfolded him, made him faintly giddy and a little deaf; and in that mild confusion of the senses all memory of evil, of anguish and error, effort and exertion of the will, sank away into joyous oblivion and were gone. The roaring, foaming, flapping, and slapping all about him came to his ears like the groan and rustle of an old walnut tree, the creaking of a garden gate. . . . More and more the darkness came on.

"The stars! Oh, by Lord, look at the stars!" a voice suddenly said, with a heavy singsong accent that seemed to come out of the inside of a tun.[56] He recognized it. It belonged to a young man with red-blond hair who had been Tonio Kröger's neighbor at dinner in the salon. His dress was very simple, his eyes were red, and he had the moist and chilly look of a person who has just bathed. With nervous and self-conscious movements he had taken unto himself an astonishing quantity of lobster omelet. Now he leaned on the rail beside Tonio Kröger and looked up at the skies, holding his chin between thumb and forefinger. Beyond a doubt he was in one of those rare and festal and edifying moods that cause the barriers between man and man to fall; when the heart opens even to the stranger, and the mouth utters that which otherwise it would blush to speak. . . .

"Look, by dear sir, just look at the stars. There they stahd and glitter; by goodness, the whole sky is full of theb! And I ask you, when you stahd ahd look up at theb, ahd realize that bany of theb are a huddred tibes larger thad the earth, how does it bake you feel? Yes, we have idvehted the telegraph and the telephode and all the triuphs of our bodern tibes. But whed we look up there, after all we have to recogdize and uhderstad that we are worbs, biserable worbs,

54. A northern German dialect.

55. Boarding house (at a health resort or spa).

56. Large barrel or vat.

ahd dothing else. Ab I right, sir, or ab I wrog? Yes, we are worbs," he answered himself, and nodded meekly and abjectly in the direction of the firmament.

"Ah, no, he has no literature in his belly," thought Tonio Kröger. And he recalled something he had lately read, an essay by a famous French writer on cosmological and psychological philosophies, a very delightful *causerie*.[57]

He made some sort of reply to the young man's feeling remarks, and they went on talking, leaning over the rail, and looking into the night with its movement and fitful lights. The young man, it seemed, was a Hamburg merchant on his holiday.

"Y'ought to travel to Copedhagen on the boat, thigks I, and so here I ab, and so far it's been fide. But they shouldn't have given us the lobster obelet, sir, for it's going to be storby—the captain said so hibself—and that's do joke with indigestible food like that in your stobach. . . ."

Tonio Kröger listened to all this engaging artlessness and was privately drawn to it.

"Yes," he said, "all the food up here is too heavy. It makes one lazy and melancholy."

"Belancholy?" repeated the young man, and looked at him, taken aback. Then he asked, suddenly: "You are a stradger up here, sir?"

"Yes, I come from a long way off," answered Tonio Kröger vaguely, waving his arm.

"But you're right," said the youth; "Lord knows you are right about the belancholy. I am dearly always belancholy, but specially on evedings like this when there are stars in the sky." And he supported his chin again with thumb and forefinger.

"Surely this man writes verses," thought Tonio Kröger; "business man's verses, full of deep feeling and single-mindedness."

Evening drew on. The wind had grown so violent as to prevent them from talking. So they thought they would sleep a bit, and wished each other good-night.

Tonio Kröger stretched himself out on the narrow cabin bed, but he found no repose. The strong wind with its sharp tang had power to rouse him; he was strangely restless with sweet anticipations. Also he was violently sick with the motion of the ship as she glided down a steep mountain of wave and her screw[58] vibrated as in agony, free of the water. He put on all his clothes again and went up to the deck.

Clouds raced across the moon. The sea danced. It did not come on in full-bodied, regular waves; but far out in the pale and flickering light the water was lashed, torn, and tumbled; leaped upward

57. Chat. According to a letter of July 21, 1954, the reference is to an essay on the "cosmological and psychological perspective" by the French novelist and essayist, Paul Bourget (1852–1935).

58. Propeller.

like great licking flames; hung in jagged and fantastic shapes above dizzy abysses, where the foam seemed to be tossed by the playful strength of colossal arms and flung upward in all directions. The ship had a heavy passage; she lurched and stamped and groaned through the welter; and far down in her bowels the tiger and the polar bear voiced their acute discomfort. A man in an oilskin, with the hood drawn over his head and a lantern strapped to his chest, went straddling painfully up and down the deck. And at the stern, leaning far out, stood the young man from Hamburg suffering the worst. "Lord!" he said, in a hollow, quavering voice, when he saw Tonio Kröger. "Look at the uproar of the elebents, sir!" But he could say no more—he was obliged to turn hastily away.

Tonio Kröger clutched at a taut rope and looked abroad into the arrogance of the elements. His exultation outvied storm and wave; within himself he chanted a song to the sea, instinct with love of her: "O thou wild friend of my youth, Once more I behold thee—" But it got no further, he did not finish it. It was not fated to receive a final form nor in tranquillity to be welded to a perfect whole. For his heart was too full. . . .

Long he stood; then stretched himself out on a bench by the pilot-house and looked up at the sky, where stars were flickering. He even slept a little. And when the cold foam splashed his face it seemed in his half-dreams like a caress.

Perpendicular chalk-cliffs, ghostly in the moonlight, came in sight. They were nearing the island of Möen.[59] Then sleep came again, broken by salty showers of spray that bit into his face and made it stiff. . . . When he really roused, it was broad day, fresh and palest grey, and the sea had gone down. At breakfast he saw the young man from Hamburg again, who blushed rosy-red for shame of the poetic indiscretions he had been betrayed into by the dark, ruffled up his little red-blond moustache with all five fingers, and called out a brisk and soldierly good-morning—after that he studiously avoided him.

And Tonio Kröger landed in Denmark. He arrived in Copenhagen, gave tips to everybody who laid claim to them, took a room at a hotel, and roamed the city for three days with a open guidebook and the air of an intelligent foreigner bent on improving his mind. He looked at the King's New Market and the "Horse" in the middle of it, gazed respectfully up the columns of the Frauenkirch, stood long before Thorwaldsen's noble and beautiful statuary, climbed the round tower, visited castles, and spent two lively evenings in the Tivoli.[60] But all this was not exactly what he saw.

59. Danish island in the Baltic Sea.

60. Scenic spots and monuments in Copenhagen, the capital of Denmark. The King's New Market is a large square with a statue of King Christian V on a horse; the Frauenkirch (or Vor Frue Kirke, in Danish) is the Cathedral of Our Lady; Bertel Thorwaldsen (1770–1844) was a famous Danish sculptor; Tivoli is a large recreation park with lake, restaurants, theatre and concert halls, and an amusement midway.

The doors of the houses—so like those in his native town, with open-work gables of baroque shape—bore names known to him of old; names that had a tender and precious quality, and withal in their syllables an accent of plaintive reproach, of repining after the lost and gone. He walked, he gazed, drawing deep, lingering drafts of moist sea air; and everywhere he saw eyes as blue, hair as blond, faces as familiar, as those that had visited his rueful dreams the night he had spent in his native town. There in the open street it befell him that a glance, a ringing word, a sudden laugh would pierce him to his marrow.

He could not stand the bustling city for long. A restlessness, half memory and half hope, half foolish and half sweet, possessed him; he was moved to drop this role of ardently inquiring tourist and lie somewhere, quite quietly, on a beach. So he took ship once more and traveled under a cloudy sky, over a black water, northward along the coast of Seeland[61] toward Helsingör. Thence he drove, at once, by carriage, for three-quarters of an hour, along and above the sea, reaching at length his ultimate goal, the little white "bath-hotel" with green blinds. It stood surrounded by a settlement of cottages, and its shingled turret tower looked out on the beach and the Swedish coast. Here he left the carriage, took possession of the light room they had ready for him, filled shelves and presses with his kit, and prepared to stop awhile.

It was well on in September; not many guests were left in Aalsgaard.[62] Meals were served on the ground floor, in the great beamed dining room, whose lofty windows led out upon the veranda and the sea. The landlady presided, an elderly spinster with white hair and faded eyes, a faint color in her cheek and a feeble twittering voice. She was forever arranging her red hands to look well upon the tablecloth. There was a short-necked old gentleman, quite blue in the face, with a grey sailor beard; a fish-dealer he was, from the capital, and strong at the German. He seemed entirely congested and inclined to apoplexy; breathed in short gasps, kept putting his beringed first finger to one nostril, and snorting violently to get a passage of air through the other. Notwithstanding, he addressed himself constantly to the whisky bottle, which stood at his place at luncheon and dinner, and breakfast as well. Besides him the company consisted only of three tall American youths with their governor or tutor, who kept adjusting his glasses in unbroken silence. All day long he played football with his charges, who had narrow, taciturn faces and reddish-yellow hair parted in the middle. "Please pass the *wurst*," said one. "That's not *wurst*, it's

61. Seeland or Zealand is the largest of the Danish islands; Copenhagen is located on Seeland.

62. A fishing village close to Elsinore; the seaside here is directly opposite the Swedish coast.

schinken,"[63] said the other, and this was the extent of their conversation, as the rest of the time they sat there dumb, drinking hot water.

Tonio Kröger could have wished himself no better table companions. He reveled in the peace and quiet, listened to the Danish palatals,[64] the clear and the clouded vowels in which the fish-dealer and the landlady desultorily conversed; modestly exchanged views with the fish-dealer on the state of the barometer, and then left the table to go through the veranda and onto the beach once more, where he had already spent long, long morning hours.

Sometimes it was still and summery there. The sea lay idle and smooth, in stripes of blue and russet and bottle-green, played all across with glittering silvery lights. The seaweed shriveled in the sun and the jellyfish lay steaming. There was a faintly stagnant smell and a whiff of tar from the fishing boat against which Tonio Kröger leaned, so standing that he had before his eyes not the Swedish coast but the open horizon, and in his face the pure, fresh breath of the softly breathing sea.

Then grey, stormy days would come. The waves lowered their heads like bulls and charged against the beach; they ran and ramped high up the sands and left them strewn with shining wet sea grass, driftwood, and mussels. All abroad beneath an overcast sky extended ranges of billows, and between them foaming valleys palely green; but above the spot where the sun hung behind the cloud a patch like white velvet lay on the sea.

Tonio Kröger stood wrapped in wind and tumult, sunk in the continual dull, drowsy uproar that he loved. When he turned away it seemed suddenly warm and silent all about him. But he was never unconscious of the sea at his back; it called, it lured, it beckoned him. And he smiled.

He went landward, by lonely meadow paths, and was swallowed up in the beech groves that clothed the rolling landscape near and far. Here he sat down on the moss, against a tree, and gazed at the strip of water he could see between the trunks. Sometimes the sound of surf came on the wind—a noise like boards collapsing at a distance. And from the treetops over his head a cawing—hoarse, desolate, forlorn. He held a book on his knee, but did not read a line. He enjoyed profound forgetfulness, hovered disembodied above space and time; only now and again his heart would contract with a fugitive pain, a stab of longing and regret, into whose origin he was too lazy to inquire.

Thus passed some days. He could not have said how many and had no desire to know. But then came one on which something

63. *Wurst*: sausage; *schinken*: ham.

64. For example, in the Danish pronunciation of Copenhagen: *Tyubbenhaven.*

happened; happened while the sun stood in the sky and people were about; and Tonio Kröger, even, felt no vast surprise.

The very opening of the day had been rare and festal. Tonio Kröger woke early and suddenly from his sleep, with a vague and exquisite alarm; he seemed to be looking at a miracle, a magic illumination. His room had a glass door and balcony facing the sound; a thin white gauze curtain divided it into living- and sleeping-quarters, both hung with delicately tinted paper and furnished with an airy good taste that gave them a sunny and friendly look. But now to his sleep-drunken eyes it lay bathed in a serene and roseate light, an unearthly brightness that gilded walls and furniture and turned the gauze curtain to radiant pink cloud. Tonio Kröger did not at once understand. Not until he stood at the glass door and looked out did he realize that this was the sunrise.

For several days there had been clouds and rain; but now the sky was like a piece of pale-blue silk, spanned shimmering above sea and land, and shot with light from red and golden clouds. The sun's disk rose in splendor from a crisply glittering sea that seemed to quiver and burn beneath it. So began the day. In a joyous daze Tonio Kröger flung on his clothes, and breakfasting in the veranda before everybody else, swam from the little wooden bathhouse some distance out into the sound, then walked for an hour along the beach. When he came back, several omnibuses[65] were before the door, and from the dining room he could see people in the parlor next door where the piano was, in the veranda, and on the terrace in front; quantities of people sitting at little tables enjoying beer and sandwiches amid lively discourse. There were whole families, there were old and young, there were even a few children.

At second breakfast—the table was heavily laden with cold viands,[66] roast, pickled, and smoked—Tonio Kröger inquired what was going on.

"Guests," said the fish-dealer. "Tourists and ball-guests from Helsingör. Lord help us, we shall get no sleep this night! There will be dancing and music, and I fear me it will keep up till late. It is a family reunion, a sort of celebration and excursion combined; they all subscribe to it and take advantage of the good weather. They came by boat and bus and they are having breakfast. After that they go on with their drive, but at night they will all come back for a dance here in the hall. Yes, damn it, you'll see we shan't get a wink of sleep."

"Oh, it will be a pleasant change," said Tonio Kröger.

After that there was nothing more said for some time. The landlady arranged her red fingers on the cloth, the fish-dealer blew through his nostril, the Americans drank hot water and made long faces.

65. Buses.

66. Meats.

Then all at once a thing came to pass: *Hans Hansen and Ingeborg Holm walked through the room.*

Tonio Kröger, pleasantly fatigued after his swim and rapid walk, was leaning back in his chair and eating smoked salmon on toast; he sat facing the veranda and the ocean. All at once the door opened and the two entered hand-in-hand—calmly and unhurried. Ingeborg, blonde Inge, was dressed just as she used to be at Herr Knaak's dancing class. The light flowered frock reached down to her ankles and it had a tulle fichu[67] draped with a pointed opening that left her soft throat free. Her hat hung by its ribbons over her arm. She, perhaps, was a little more grown up than she used to be, and her wonderful plait of hair was wound round her head; but Hans Hansen was the same as ever. He wore his sailor overcoat with gilt buttons, and his wide blue sailor collar lay across his shoulders and back; the sailor cap with its short ribbons he was dangling carelessly in his hand. Ingeborg's narrow eyes were turned away; perhaps she felt shy before the company at table. But Hans Hansen turned his head straight toward them, and measured one after another defiantly with his steel-blue eyes; challengingly, with a sort of contempt. He even dropped Ingeborg's hand and swung his cap harder than ever, to show what manner of man he was. Thus the two, against the silent, blue-dyed sea, measured the length of the room and passed through the opposite door into the parlor.

This was at half past eleven in the moning. While the guests of the house were still at table the company in the veranda broke up and went away by the side door. No one else came into the dining room. The guests could hear them laughing and joking as they got into the omnibuses, which rumbled away one by one. . . . "So they are coming back?" asked Tonio Kröger.

"That they are," said the fish-dealer. "More's the pity. They have ordered music, let me tell you—and my room is right above the dining room."

"Oh, well, it's a pleasant change," repeated Tonio Kröger. Then he got up and went away.

The day he spent as he had the others, on the beach and in the wood, holding a book on his knee and blinking in the sun. He had but one thought; they were coming back to have a dance in the hall, the fish-dealer had promised they would; and he did nothing but be glad of this, with a sweet and timorous gladness such as he had not felt through all these long dead years. Once he happened, by some chance association, to think of his friend Adalbert, the novelist, the man who had known what he wanted and betaken himself to the café to get away from the spring. Tonio Kröger shrugged his shoulders at the thought of him.

Luncheon was served earlier than usual, also supper, which they

67. A cloak or shawl made of lacy, netlike fabric.

ate in the parlor because the dining room was being got ready for the ball, and the whole house flung in disorder for the occasion. It grew dark; Tonio Kröger sitting in his room heard on the road and in the house the sounds of approaching festivity. The picknickers were coming back; from Helsingör, by bicycle and carriage, new guests were arriving; a fiddle and a nasal clarinet might be heard practicing down in the dining room. Everything promised a brilliant ball. . . .

Now the little orchestra struck up a march; he could hear the notes, faint but lively. The dancing opened with a polonaise. Tonio Kröger sat for a while and listened. But when he heard the march time go over into a waltz he got up and slipped noiselessly out of his room.

From his corridor it was possible to go by the side stairs to the side entrance of the hotel and thence to the veranda without passing through a room. He took this route, softly and stealthily as though on forbidden paths, feeling along through the dark, relentlessly drawn by this stupid jigging music that now came up to him loud and clear.

The veranda was empty and dim, but the glass door stood open into the hall, where shone two large oil lamps, furnished with bright reflectors. Thither he stole on soft feet; and his skin prickled with the thievish pleasure of standing unseen in the dark and spying on the dancers there in the brightly lighted room. Quickly and eagerly he glanced about for the two whom he sought. . . .

Even though the ball was only half an hour old, the merriment seemed in full swing; however, the guests had come hither already warm and merry, after a whole day of carefree, happy companionship. By bending forward a little, Tonio Kröger could see into the parlor from where he was. Several old gentlemen sat there smoking, drinking, and playing cards; others were with their wives on the plush-upholstered chairs in the foreground watching the dance. They sat with their knees apart and their hands resting on them, puffing out their cheeks with a prosperous air; the mothers, with bonnets perched on their parted hair, with their hands folded over their stomachs and their heads on one side, gazed into the whirl of dancers. A platform had been erected on the long side of the hall, and on it the musicians were doing their utmost. There was even a trumpet, that blew with a certain caution, as though afraid of its own voice, and yet after all kept breaking and cracking. Couples were dipping and circling about, others walked arm-in-arm up and down the room. No one wore ballroom clothes; they were dressed as for an outing in the summertime: the men in countrified suits which were obviously their Sunday wear; the girls in light-colored frocks with bunches of field flowers in their bodices. Even a few children were there, dancing with each other in their own way, even after the music stopped. There was a long-legged man in a coat with a little swallow-tail, a provincial lion with an eyeglass and frizzed hair, a post office clerk or some such thing; he was like a comic figure stepped bodily out of a Danish novel; and he seemed to be the leader and manager of the ball. He was everywhere at once, bustling, perspiring, officious, utterly absorbed; setting down his feet, in shiny, pointed, military half-boots, in a very artificial and involved manner, toes first; waving his arms to issue an order, clapping his hands for the music to begin; here, there, and everywhere, and glancing over his shoulder in pride at his great bow of office, the streamers of which fluttered grandly in his rear.

Yes, there they were, those two, who had gone by Tonio Kröger in the broad light of day; he saw them again—with a joyful start he recognized them almost at the same moment. Here was Hans Hansen by the door, quite close; his legs apart, a little bent over, he was eating with circumspection a large piece of sponge cake, holding his hand cupwise under his chin to catch the crumbs. And there by the wall sat Ingeborg Holm, Inge the fair; the post office clerk was just mincing up to her with an exaggerated bow and asking her to dance. He laid one hand on his back and gracefully shoved the other into his bosom. But she was shaking her head in token that she was a little out of breath and must rest awhile, whereat the post office clerk sat down by her side.

Tonio Kröger looked at them both, these two for whom he had in time past suffered love—at Hans and Ingeborg. They were Hans and Ingeborg not so much by virtue of individual traits and similarity of costume as by similarity of race and type. This was the blonde, fair-haired breed of the steel-blue eyes, which stood to him for the pure, the blithe, the untroubled in life; for a virginal aloofness that was at once both simple and full of pride. . . . He looked at them. Hans Hansen was standing there in his sailor suit, lively and well built as ever, broad in the shoulders and narrow in the hips; Ingeborg was laughing and tossing her head in a certain high-spirited way she had; she carried her hand, a schoolgirl hand, not at all slender, not at all particularly aristocratic, to the back of her head in a certain manner so that the thin sleeve fell away from her elbow—and suddenly such a pang of homesickness shook his breast that involuntarily he drew farther back into the darkness lest someone might see his features twitch.

"Had I forgotten you?" he asked. "No, never. Not thee, Hans, not thee, Inge the fair! It was always you I worked for; when I heard applause I always stole a look to see if you were there. . . . Did you read *Don Carlos*, Hans Hansen, as you promised me at the garden gate? No, don't read it! I do not ask it any more. What have you to do with a king who weeps for loneliness? You must not cloud your clear eyes or make them dreamy and dim by peering into melancholy poetry. . . . To be like you! To begin again, to grow up like you, regular like you, simple and normal and cheerful, in conformity and understanding with God and man, beloved of the innocent and happy. To take you, Ingeborg Holm, to wife, and have a son like you, Hans Hansen—to live free from the curse of knowledge and the torment of creation, live and praise God in blessed mediocrity! Begin again? But it would do no good. It would turn out the same—everything would turn out the same as it did before. For some go of necessity astray, because for them there is no such thing as a right path."

The music ceased; there was a pause in which refreshments were handed round. The post office assistant tripped about in person with a trayful of herring salad and served the ladies; but before Ingeborg Holm he even went down on one knee as he passed her the dish, and she blushed for pleasure.

But now those within began to be aware of a spectator behind the glass door; some of the flushed and pretty faces turned to measure him with hostile glances; but he stood his ground. Ingeborg and Hans looked at him too, at almost the same time, both with that utter indifference in their eyes that looks so like contempt. And he was conscious too of a gaze resting on him from a different quarter; turned his head and met with his own the eyes that had sought him out. A girl stood not far off, with a fine, pale little face—he had already noticed her. She had not danced much, she had few partners, and he had seen her sitting there against the wall, her lips closed in a bitter line. She was standing alone now too; her dress was a thin light stuff, like the others, but beneath the transparent frock her shoulders showed angular and poor, and the thin neck was thrust down so deep between those meager shoulders that as she stood there motionless she might almost be thought a little deformed. She was holding her hands in their thin mitts across her flat breast, with the finger tips touching; her head was drooped, yet she was looking up at Tonio Kröger with black swimming eyes. He turned away. . . .

Here, quite close to him, were Ingeborg and Hans. He had sat down beside her—she was perhaps his sister—and they ate and drank together surrounded by other rosy-cheeked folk; they chattered and made merry, called to each other in ringing voices, and laughed aloud. Why could he not go up and speak to them? Make some trivial remark to him or her, to which they might at least answer with a smile? It would make him happy—he longed to do it; he would go back more satisfied to his room if he might feel he had established a little contact with them. He thought out what he might say; but he had not the courage to say it. Yes, this too was just as it had been: they would not understand him, they would listen like strangers to anything he was able to say. For their speech was not his speech.

It seemed the dance was about to begin again. The leader developed a comprehensive activity. He dashed hither and thither, adjuring everybody to get partners; helped the waiters to push chairs and glasses out of the way, gave orders to the musicians, even took some awkward people by the shoulders and shoved them aside. . . . What was coming? They formed squares of four couples each. . . . A frightful memory brought the color to Tonio Kröger's cheeks. They were forming for a quadrille.

The music struck up, the couples bowed and crossed over. The leader called off; he called off—Heaven save us—in French! And pronounced the nasals with great distinction. Ingeborg Holm danced close by, in the set nearest the glass door. She moved to and fro before him, forward and back, pacing and turning; he caught a waft from her hair or the thin stuff of her frock, and it made him close his eyes with the old, familiar feeling, the fragrance and bittersweet enchantment he had faintly felt in all these days, that now filled him utterly with irresistible sweetness. And what was the feeling? Longing, tenderness? Envy? Self-contempt? . . . *Moulinet des dames!* "Did you laugh, Ingeborg the blonde, did you laugh at me when I disgraced myself by dancing the *moulinet*? And would you still laugh today even after I have become something like a famous man? Yes, that you would, and you would be right to laugh. Even if I in my own person had written the nine symphonies and *The World as Will and Idea* and painted the Last Judgment,[68] you would still be eternally right to laugh. . . ." As he looked at her he thought of a line of verse once so familiar to him, now long forgotten: "I would sleep, but thou must dance." How well he knew it, that melancholy northern mood it evoked—its heavy inarticulateness. To sleep. . . . To long to be allowed to live the life of simple feeling, to rest sweetly and passively in feeling alone, without compulsion to act and achieve—and yet to be forced to dance, dance the cruel and perilous sword dance of art; without even being allowed to forget the melancholy conflict within oneself; to be forced to dance, the while one loved. . . .

A sudden wild extravagance had come over the scene. The sets had broken up, the quadrille was being succeeded by a galop, and all the couples were leaping and gliding about. They flew past Tonio Kröger to a maddeningly quick tempo, crossing, advancing, retreating, with quick, breathless laughter. A couple came rushing

68. The nine symphonies of Beethoven, Schopenhauer's philosophical work *The World as Will and Idea*, and Michelangelo's Last Judgment, painted in the Sistine Chapel, were regarded as the greatest achievements of mind and art.

and circling toward Tonio Kröger; the girl had a pale, refined face and lean, high shoulders. Suddenly, directly in front of him, they tripped and slipped and stumbled. . . . The pale girl fell, so hard and violently it almost looked dangerous; and her partner with her. He must have hurt himself badly, for he quite forgot her, and, half rising, began to rub his knee and grimace; while she, quite dazed, it seemed, still lay on the floor. Then Tonio Kröger came forward, took her gently by the arms, and lifted her up. She looked dazed, bewildered, wretched; then suddenly her delicate face flushed pink.

"*Tak, O, mange tak!*"[69] she said, and gazed up at him with dark, swimming eyes.

"You should not dance any more, Fräulein,"[70] he said gently. Once more he looked round at *them*, at Ingeborg and Hans, and then he went out, left the ball and the veranda and returned to his own room.

He was exhausted with jealousy, worn out with the gaiety in which he had had no part. Just the same, just the same as it had always been. Always with burning cheeks he had stood in his dark corner and suffered for you, you blond, you living, you happy ones! And then quite simply gone away. Somebody *must* come now! Ingeborg *must* notice he had gone, must slip after him, lay a hand on his shoulder and say: "Come back and be happy. I love you!" But she came not at all. No, such things did not happen. Yes, all was as it had been, and he too was happy, just as he had been. For his heart was alive. But between that past and this present what had happened to make him become that which he now was? Icy desolation, solitude: mind, and art, forsooth!

He undressed, lay down, put out the light. Two names he whispered into his pillow, the few chaste northern syllables that meant for him his true and native way of love, of longing and happiness; that meant to him life and home, meant simple and heartfelt feeling. He looked back on the years that had passed. He thought of the dreamy adventures of the senses, nerves, and mind in which he had been involved; saw himself eaten up with intellect and introspection, ravaged and paralyzed by insight, half worn out by the fevers and frosts of creation, helpless and in anguish of conscience between two extremes, flung to and fro between austerity and lust; *raffiné*, impoverished, exhausted by frigid and artificially heightened ecstasies; erring, forsaken, martyred, and ill—and sobbed with nostalgia and remorse.

Here in his room it was still and dark. But from below life's lulling, trivial waltz-rhythm came faintly to his ears.

69. "Thanks, oh many thanks" (Danish).

70. Miss.

Tonio Kröger sat up in the north, composing his promised letter to his friend Lisabeta Ivanovna.

"Dear Lisabeta down there in Arcady,[71] whither I shall shortly return," he wrote: "Here is something like a letter, but it will probably disappoint you, for I mean to keep it rather general. Not that I have nothing to tell; for indeed, in my way, I have had experiences; for instance, in my native town they were even going to arrest me. . . . but of that by word of mouth. Sometimes now I have days when I would rather state things in general terms than go on telling stories.

"You probably still remember, Lisabeta, that you called me a *bourgeois, a bourgeois manqué?* You called me that in an hour when, led on by other confessions I had previously let slip, I confessed to you my love of life, or what I call life. I ask myself if you were aware how very close you came to the truth, how much my love of 'life' is one and the same thing as my being a *bourgeois*. This journey of mine has given me much occasion to ponder the subject.

"My father, you know, had the temperament of the north: solid, reflective, puritanically correct, with a tendency to melancholia. My mother, of indeterminate foreign blood, was beautiful, sensuous, naïve, passionate, and careless at once, and, I think, irregular by instinct. The mixture was no doubt extraordinary and bore with it extraordinary dangers. The issue of it, a *bourgeois* who strayed off into art, a bohemian who feels nostalgic yearnings for respectability, an artist with a bad conscience. For surely it is my *bourgeois* conscience makes me see in the artist life, in all irregularity and all genius, something profoundly suspect, profoundly disreputable; that fills me with this lovelorn *faiblesse*[72] for the simple and good, the comfortably normal, the average unendowed respectable human being.

"I stand between two worlds. I am at home in neither, and I suffer in consequence. You artists call me a *bourgeois,* and the *bourgeois* try to arrest me. . . . I don't know which makes me feel worse. The *bourgeois* are stupid; but you adorers of the beautiful, who call me phlegmatic and without aspirations, you ought to realize that there is a way of being an artist that goes so deep and is so much a matter of origins and destinies that no longing seems to it sweeter and more worth knowing than longing after the bliss of the commonplace.

"I admire those proud, cold beings who adventure upon the paths of great and demonic beauty and despise 'mankind'; but I do

71. A magical land of happy pastoral innocence.

72. Weakness (French).

not envy them. For if anything is capable of making a poet of a literary man, it is my *bourgeois* love of the human, the living and usual. It is the source of all warmth, goodness, and humor; I even almost think it is itself that love of which it stands written that one may speak with the tongues of men and of angels and yet having it not is as sounding brass and tinkling cymbals.[73]

"The work I have so far done is nothing or not much—as good as nothing. I will do better, Lisabeta—this is a promise. As I write, the sea whispers to me and I close my eyes. I am looking into a world unborn and formless, that needs to be ordered and shaped; I see into a whirl of shadows of human figures who beckon to me to weave spells to redeem them: tragic and laughable figures and some that are both together—and to these I am drawn. But my deepest and secretest love belongs to the blond and blue-eyed, the fair and living, the happy, lovely, and commonplace.

"Do not chide this love, Lisabeta; it is good and fruitful. There is longing in it, and a gentle envy; a touch of contempt and no little innocent bliss."

1903

73. Luther's translation from the Bible, *I Corinthians* 13:1. The Bible goes on to define this kind of love as "patient and kind . . . not jealous or boastful . . . not arrogant or rude; [it] does not insist on its own way, . . . is not irritable or resentful . . . does not rejoice at wrong, but rejoices in the right. Love bears all things, believes all things, hopes all things, endures all things [and] never ends."

WALLACE STEVENS

(1879–1955)

Sunday Morning

I

Complacencies of the peignoir, and late
Coffee and oranges in a sunny chair,
And the green freedom of a cockatoo
Upon a rug mingle to dissipate
The holy hush of ancient sacrifice. 5
She dreams a little, and she feels the dark
Encroachment of that old catastrophe,
As a calm darkens among water-lights.

Title: Although the central figure of the poem is clearly a woman sitting over late breakfast on Sunday morning instead of going to church, Stevens comments that "this is not essentially a woman's meditation on religion and the meaning of life. It is anybody's meditation." [Stevens, *Letters*, p. 250.]

2. *peignoir*: Negligée.

5. *Sacrifice*: Throughout the stanza, there are hints of Christ's Crucifixion and the celebration of the Mass.

The pungent oranges and bright, green wings
Seem things in some procession of the dead, 10
Winding across wide water, without sound.
The day is like wide water, without sound,
Stilled for the passing of her dreaming feet
Over the seas, to silent Palestine,
Dominion of the blood and sepulchre. 15

II

Why should she give her bounty to the dead?
What is divinity if it can come
Only in silent shadows and in dreams?
Shall she not find in comforts of the sun,
In pungent fruit and bright, green wings, or else 20
In any balm or beauty of the earth,
Things to be cherished like the thought of heaven?
Divinity must live within herself:
Passions of rain, or moods in falling snow;
Grievings in loneliness, or unsubdued 25
Elations when the forest blooms; gusty
Emotions on wet roads on autumn nights;
All pleasures and all pains, remembering
The bough of summer and the winter branch.
These are the measures destined for her soul. 30

III

Jove in the clouds had his inhuman birth.
No mother suckled him, no sweet land gave
Large-mannered motions to his mythy mind
He moved among us, as a muttering king,
Magnificent, would move among his hinds, 35
Until our blood, commingling, virginal,
With heaven, brought such requital to desire
The very hinds discerned it, in a star.
Shall our blood fail? Or shall it come to be
The blood of paradise? And shall the earth 40
Seem all of paradise that we shall know?
The sky will be much friendlier then than now,
A part of labor and a part of pain,
And next in glory to enduring love,
Not this dividing and indifferent blue. 45

IV

She says, "I am content when wakened birds,
Before they fly, test the reality

16–22: *Why should . . . heaven?*: "The poem is simply an expression of paganism." [Stevens, *Letters*, p. 250.]

31. *Jove*: Ruler of the gods in Roman myth.

35. *hinds*: Shepherds.

38. Alludes to the star that led the shepherds to the manger where Christ was born.

Of misty fields, by their sweet questionings;
But when the birds are gone, and their warm fields
Return no more, where, then, is paradise?" 50
There is not any haunt of prophecy,
Nor any old chimera of the grave,
Neither the golden underground, nor isle
Melodious, where spirits gat them home,
Nor visionary south, nor cloudy palm 55
Remote on heaven's hill, that has endured
As April's green endures; or will endure
Like her remembrance of awakened birds,
Or her desire for June and evening, tipped
By the consummation of the swallow's wings. 60

V

She says, "But in contentment I still feel
The need of some imperishable bliss."
Death is the mother of beauty; hence from her,
Alone, shall come fulfilment to our dreams
And our desires. Although she strews the leaves 65
Of sure obliteration on our paths,
The path sick sorrow took, the many paths
Where triumph rang its brassy phrase, or love
Whispered a little out of tenderness,
She makes the willow shiver in the sun 70
For maidens who were wont to sit and gaze
Upon the grass, relinquished to their feet.
She causes boys to pile new plums and pears
On disregarded plate. The maidens taste
And stray impassioned in the littering leaves. 75

VI

Is there no change of death in paradise?
Does ripe fruit never fall? Or do the boughs
Hang always heavy in that perfect sky,
Unchanging, yet so like our perishing earth,
With rivers like our own that seek for seas 80
They never find, the same receding shores
That never touch with inarticulate pang?
Why set the pear upon those river-banks
Or spice the shores with odors of the plum?

51. *haunt of prophecy*: Like, for example, the oracle at Delphi.

52. *chimera*: Fantastic image; literally, a mythological monster.

53–54. *golden underground nor isle melodious*: The Elysian Fields, or Isles of the Blessed, where the heroes of Greek myth went after death.

71. *were wont to*: used to.

74. *disregarded plate*: "Plate is used in the sense of so-called family plate. Disregarded refers to the disuse into which things fall that have been possessed for a long time. I mean, therefore, that death releases and renews. What the old have come to disregard, the young inherit and make use of." [Stevens, *Letters*, p. 183.]

Alas, that they should wear our colors there, 85
The silken weavings of our afternoons,
And pick the strings of our insipid lutes!
Death is the mother of beauty, mystical,
Within whose burning bosom we devise
Our earthly mothers waiting, sleeplessly. 90

VII

Supple and turbulent, a ring of men
Shall chant in orgy on a summer morn
Their boisterous devotion to the sun,
Not as a god, but as a god might be,
Naked among them, like a savage source. 95
Their chant shall be a chant of paradise,
Out of their blood, returning to the sky;
And in their chant shall enter, voice by voice,
The windy lake wherein their lord delights,
The trees, like serafin, and echoing hills, 100
That choir among themselves long afterward.
They shall know well the heavenly fellowship
Of men that perish and of summer morn.
And whence they came and whither they shall go
The dew upon their feet shall manifest. 105

VIII

She hears, upon that water without sound,
A voice that cries, "The tomb in Palestine
Is not the porch of spirits lingering.
It is the grave of Jesus, where he lay."
We live in an old chaos of the sun, 110
Or old dependency of day and night,
Or island solitude, unsponsored, free,
Of that wide water, inescapable.
Deer walk upon our mountains, and the quail
Whistle about us their spontaneous cries; 115
Sweet berries ripen in the wilderness;
And, in the isolation of the sky,
At evening, casual flocks of pigeons make
Ambiguous undulations as they sink.
Downward to darkness, on extended wings. 120

1923

100. *serafin*: Angels of the highest rank.

104–105. *And whence . . . manifest*: "Life is as fugitive as dew upon the feet of men dancing in dew. Men do not either come from any direction or disappear in any direction. Life is as meaningless as dew." [Stevens, *Letters*, p. 250.]

108. *spirits lingering*: That is, remaining on earth after the body is dead.

Peter Quince at the Clavier

I

Just as my fingers on these keys
Make music, so the selfsame sounds
On my spirit make a music, too.

Music is feeling, then, not sound;
And thus it is that what I feel, 5
Here in this room, desiring you,

Thinking of your blue-shadowed silk,
Is music. It is like the strain
Waked in the elders by Susanna.

Of a green evening, clear and warm, 10
She bathed in her still garden, while
The red-eyed elders watching, felt

The basses of their beings throb
In witching chords, and their thin blood
Pulse pizzicati of Hosanna. 15

II

In the green water, clear and warm,
Susanna lay.
She searched
The touch of springs,
And found 20
Concealed imaginings.
She sighed,
For so much melody.

Upon the bank, she stood
In the cool 25
Of spent emotions.
She felt, among the leaves,
The dew
Of old devotions.

She walked upon the grass, 30
Still quavering.
The winds were like her maids,

Title: In Shakespeare's *Midsummer Night's Dream,* Peter Quince is the carpenter-playwright who directs his own play about the tragic lovers Pyramus and Thisbe. Both the play and the production amuse the noble audience. *clavier:* General term in Shakespeare's day for a keyboard instrument, such as a harpsichord.

9. *Susanna*: In the Apocrypha, a Babylonian woman falsely accused of adultery by lecherous elders who spied on her bathing.

15. *Hosanna*: A cry of praise to God. *pizzicati*: Notes sounded by plucking a string (as on a violin).

On timid feet,
Fetching her woven scarves,
Yet wavering. 35

A breath upon her hand
Muted the night.
She turned—
A cymbal crashed,
And roaring horns. 40

III

Soon, with a noise like tambourines,
Came her attendant Byzantines.

They wondered why Susanna cried
Against the elders by her side;

And as they whispered, the refrain 45
Was like a willow swept by rain.

Anon, their lamps' uplifted flame
Revealed Susanna and her shame.

And then, the simpering Byzantines
Fled, with a noise like tambourines. 50

IV

Beauty is momentary in the mind—
The fitful tracing of a portal;
But in the flesh it is immortal.
The body dies; the body's beauty lives.
So evenings die, in their green going, 55
A wave, interminably flowing.
So gardens die, their meek breath scenting
The cowl of winter, done repenting.
So maidens die, to the auroral
Celebration of a maiden's choral. 60
Susanna's music touched the bawdy strings
Of those white elders; but, escaping,
Left only Death's ironic scraping.
Now, in its immortality, it plays
On the clear viol of her memory, 65
And makes a constant sacrament of praise.

1923

42. *Byzantines*: Inhabitants of ancient Byzantium, a Christian empire of the Near East. "Somebody once called my attention to the fact that there were no Byzantines in Susanna's time. I hope that that bit of precious pedantry will seem as unimportant to you as it does to me." [Stevens, *Letters*, p. 250.]
47. *anon*: Soon.
58. *cowl*: Monk's hood.
59. *So maidens die*: As maidens; i.e., on becoming women. *auroral*: At dawn.
60. *Choral*: I.e., choral song.
63. *Death's . . . scraping*: Rasping fiddle-music.
65. *viol*: A stringed instrument of the 16th and 17th centuries, played with a bow.

Anecdote of the Jar

I placed a jar in Tennessee.
And round it was, upon a hill.
It made the slovenly wilderness
Surround that hill.

The wilderness rose up to it, 5
And sprawled around, no longer wild.
The jar was round upon the ground
And tall and of a port in air.

It took dominion everywhere.
The jar was gray and bare. 10
It did not give of bird or bush,
Like nothing else in Tennessee.

1923

8. *port*: Dignified bearing, manner.

The Snow Man

One must have a mind of winter
To regard the frost and the boughs
Of the pine-trees crusted with snow;

And have been cold a long time
To behold the junipers shagged with ice, 5
The spruces rough in the distant glitter

Of the January sun; and not to think
Of any misery in the sound of the wind,
In the sound of a few leaves,

Which is the sound of the land 10
Full of the same wind
That is blowing in the same bare place

For the listener, who listens in the snow.
And, nothing himself, beholds
Nothing that is not there and the nothing that is. 15

1923

The Emperor of Ice-Cream

Call the roller of big cigars,
The muscular one, and bid him whip

Title: "I think I should select from my poems as my favorite 'The Emperor of Ice-Cream.' This wears a deliberately commonplace costume, and yet seems to me to contain something of the essential gaudiness of poetry; that is the reason why I like it." (1933) [Stevens, *Letters*, p. 263.]

In kitchen cups concupiscent curds.
Let the wenches dawdle in such dress
As they are used to wear, and let the boys 5
Bring flowers in last month's newspapers.
Let be be finale of seem.
The only emperor is the emperor of ice-cream.

Take from the dresser of deal,
Lacking the three glass knobs, that sheet 10
On which she embroidered fantails once
And spread it so as to cover her face.
If her horny feet protrude, they come
To show how cold she is, and dumb.
Let the lamp affix its beam. 15
The only emperor is the emperor of ice-cream.

1923

3. *concupiscent*: Lusty, sensual. "The words 'concupiscent curds' . . . express the concupiscence of life, but, by contrast with the things in relation to them in the poem, they express or accentuate life's destitution." [Stevens, *Letters*, p. 500.]
7. *Let be . . . seem*: ". . . the true sense of 'Let be be the finale of seem' is let being become the conclusion or denouement of appearing to be: in short, icecream is an absolute good. The poem is obviously not about icecream, but about being as distinguished from seeming to be." [Stevens, *Letters*, p. 341.]
9. *deal*: Fir or pine wood.
11. *fantails*: Fantail pigeons.

Bantams in Pine-Woods

Chieftain Iffucan of Azcan in caftan
Of tan with henna hackles, halt!

Damned universal cock, as if the sun
Was blackamoor to bear your blazing tail.

Fat! Fat! Fat! Fat! I am the personal. 5
Your world is you. I am my world.

You ten-foot poet among inchlings. Fat!
Begone! An inchling bristles in these pines,

Bristles, and points their Appalachian tangs,
And fears not portly Azcan nor his hoos. 10

1923

1. *Chief Iffucan of Azcan*: Stevens parodies the long genealogical names given to prize bantams, like race horses or pedigreed dogs and cats.
1–2. *In caftan . . . hackles*: The cock's crest.
4. *blackamoor*: African black; here, a servant carrying the tail as if it were the hem of a long cloak.
5. *Fat!*: The bantam's cry.
8. *inchling*: The smaller bantam.
9. *tangs*: Scents.
10. *Portly*: Pompous, corpulent. *hoos*: The cock's cry.

The Idea of Order at Key West

She sang beyond the genius of the sea.
The water never formed to mind or voice,
Like a body wholly body, fluttering
Its empty sleeves; and yet its mimic motion
Made constant cry, caused constantly a cry, 5
That was not ours although we understood,
Inhuman, of the veritable ocean.

The sea was not a mask. No more was she.
The song and water were not medleyed sound
Even if what she sang was what she heard. 10
Since what she sang was uttered word by word.
It may be that in all her phrases stirred
The grinding water and the gasping wind;
But it was she and not the sea we heard.

For she was the maker of the song she sang. 15
The ever-hooded, tragic-gestured sea
Was merely a place by which she walked to sing.
Whose spirit is this? we said, because we knew
It was the spirit that we sought and knew
That we should ask this often as she sang. 20

If it was only the dark voice of the sea
That rose, or even colored by many waves;
If it was only the outer voice of sky
And cloud, of the sunken coral water-walled,
However clear, it would have been deep air, 25
The heaving speech of air, a summer sound
Repeated in a summer without end
And sound alone. But it was more than that,
More even than her voice, and ours, among
The meaningless plungings of water and the wind, 30
Theatrical distances, bronze shadows heaped
On high horizons, mountainous atmospheres
Of sky and sea.
It was her voice that made
The sky acutest at its vanishing. 35
She measured to the hour its solitude.
She was the single artificer of the world
In which she sang. And when she sang, the sea,

Title: Published in *Ideas of Order* (1936). "In 'The Idea of Order at Key West' life has ceased to be a matter of chance. It may be that every man introduces his own order into the life about him . . . But still there is order . . . These are tentative ideas for the purposes of poetry." [Stevens, *Letters*, p. 293.] Key West is the southernmost of the Florida keys, and Stevens spent midwinter vacations there for almost twenty years.

1. *Beyond the genius of the sea*: I.e., beyond the power of the sea to respond.

2–8. *The water . . . not a mask*: The movement of the waves, imitating fluttering sleeves, also emits an inhuman cry. The sea mimics the human body, but without a mind; it is not even as close as the mask worn by actors in ancient Greek drama.

37. *artificer*: creator and shaper.

Whatever self it had, became the self
That was her song, for she was the maker. Then we, 40
As we beheld her striding there alone,
Knew that there never was a world for her
Except the one she sang and, singing, made.

Ramon Fernandez, tell me, if you know,
Why, when the singing ended and we turned 45
Toward the town, tell why the glassy lights,
The lights in the fishing boats at anchor there,
As the night descended, tilting in the air,
Mastered the night and portioned out the sea,
Fixing emblazoned zones and fiery poles, 50
Arranging, deepening, enchanting night.

Oh! Blessed rage for order, pale Ramon,
The maker's rage to order words of the sea,
Words of the fragrant portals, dimly-starred,
And of ourselves and of our origins, 55
In ghostlier demarcations, keener sounds.

1935

44. *Ramon Fernandez*: (1894–1944), French critic who described the way impressionistic techniques in literature impose a subjective order on reality. Stevens had read some of Fernandez' criticism, but denied that he intended any specific reference here.
50. *emblazoned*: Ornamented, usually with heraldic symbols. *zones . . . poles*: As with the geographic zones and poles of the earth.

The Man on the Dump

Day creeps down. The moon is creeping up.
The sun is a corbeil of flowers the moon Blanche
Places there, a bouquet. Ho-ho . . . The dump is full
Of images. Days pass like papers from a press.
The bouquets come here in the papers. So the sun, 5
And so the moon, both come, and the janitor's poems
Of every day, the wrapper on the can of pears,
The cat in the paper-bag, the corset, the box
From Esthonia: the tiger chest, for tea.

The freshness of night has been fresh a long time. 10
The freshness of morning, the blowing of day, one says
That it puffs as Cornelius Nepos reads, it puffs
More than, less than or it puffs like this or that.
The green smacks in the eye, the dew in the green
Smacks like fresh water in a can, like the sea 15

2. *corbeil*: Basket. *Blanche*: A name signifying whiteness.
4. *images*: Introduces the poem's implied comparison between a dump and poetry, whose history is seen as an accumulation of outworn images in the search for perfect expression. *papers:* Newspapers.
9. *Esthonia:* A Baltic republic, since 1940 part of the U.S.S.R.
12. *Cornelius Nepos*: Roman historian (first century B.C.), now little read, the author of brief anecdotal and highly moralized *Lives of Famous Men.*

On a cocoanut—how many men have copied dew
For buttons, how many women have covered themselves
With dew, dew dresses, stones and chains of dew, heads
Of the floweriest flowers dewed with the dewiest dew.
One grows to hate these things except on the dump. 20

Now, in the time of spring (azaleas, trilliams,
Myrtle, viburnums, daffodils, blue phlox),
Between that disgust and this, between the things
That are on the dump (azaleas and so on)
And those that will be (azaleas and so on). 25
One feels the purifying change. One rejects
The trash.

That's the moment when the moon creeps up
To the bubbling of bassoons. That's the time
One looks at the elephant-colorings of tires: 30
Everything is shed; and the moon comes up as the moon
(All its images are in the dump) and you see
As a man (not like an image of a man),
You see the moon rise in the empty sky.

One sits and beats an old tin can, lard pail. 35
One beats and beats for that which one believes.
That's what one wants to get near. Could it after all
Be merely oneself, as superior as the ear
To a crow's voice? Did the nightingale torture the ear,
Pack the heart and scratch the mind? And does the ear 40
Solace itself in peevish birds? Is it peace,
Is it a philosopher's honeymoon, one finds
On the dump? Is it to sit among mattresses of the dead,
Bottles, pots, shoes and grass and murmur *aptest eve*:
Is it to hear the blatter of grackles and say 45
Invisible priest; is it to eject, to pull
The day to pieces and cry *stanza my stone*?
Where was it one first heard of the Truth? The the.

1942

22–23. *azaleas . . . blue phlox*: Spring flowers.
40. *nightingale*: Traditional image for lyric poetry, for example in Keats's *Ode to a Nightingale* (p. 563).
43. *a philosopher's honeymoon*: I.e., a respite from philosophizing.
45–48. *Aptest eve / stanza my stone*: Suggests a romantic, mystical "nightingale" poetry that turns its back on material reality.
46. *grackles*: Noisy birds.
48. *the truth? The the*: "The truth" is an intangible absolute (like "*the* good"); what it specifies cannot be defined. The *the* itself however represents an urge to seek absolute meaning: to say *the*, not merely *a*.

Large Red Man Reading

There were ghosts that returned to earth to hear his phrases,
As he sat there reading, aloud, the great blue tabulae.

2. *tabulae*: Tablets used for early writing. For Stevens, blue is the color symbolic of the imagination, red of reality.

They were those from the wilderness of stars that had expected
more.

There were those that returned to hear him read from the poem of
life,
Of the pans above the stove, the pots on the table, the tulips
among them. 5
They were those that would have wept to step barefoot into reality,

That would have wept and been happy, have shivered in the frost
And cried out to feel it again, have run fingers over leaves
And against the most coiled thorn, have seized on what was ugly

And laughed, as he sat there reading, from out of the purple tabu-
lae, 10
The outlines of being and its expressings, the syllables of its law:
Poesis, poesis, the literal characters, the vatic lines,

Which in those ears and in those thin, those spended hearts,
Took on color, took on shape and the size of things as they are
And spoke the feeling for them, which was what they had lacked. 15

1950

12. *Poesis*: Poetry. *vatic*: Prophetic, oracular.

13. *spended*: Spent, exhausted.

Lebensweisheitspielerei

Weaker and weaker, the sunlight falls
In the afternoon. The proud and the strong
Have departed.

Those that are left are the unaccomplished,
The finally human, 5
Natives of a dwindled sphere.

Their indigence is an indigence
That is an indigence of the light,
A stellar pallor that hangs on the threads.

Little by little, the poverty 10
Of autumnal space becomes
A look, a few words spoken.

Each person completely touches us
With what he is and as he is,
In the stale grandeur of annihilation. 15

1953

Title: Playing around with life-wisdom (German); pronounced "*lay*bens-*vize*-height-shpeeler*eye*."

The River of Rivers in Connecticut

There is a great river this side of Stygia,
Before one comes to the first black cataracts
And trees that lack the intelligence of trees.

In that river, far this side of Stygia,
The mere flowing of the water is a gayety, 5
Flashing and flashing in the sun. On its banks,

No shadow walks. The river is fateful,
Like the last one. But there is no ferryman.
He could not bend against its propelling force.

It is not to be seen beneath the appearances 10
That tell of it. The steeple at Farmington
Stands glistening and Haddam shines and sways.

It is the third commonness with light and air,
A curriculum, a vigor, a local abstraction . . .
Call it, once more, a river, an unnamed flowing, 15

Space-filled, reflecting the seasons, the folk-lore
Of each of the senses; call it, again and again,
The river that flows nowhere, like a sea.

1957

Title: The Connecticut River, the largest in New England.
1. *Stygia*: Hades, the Greek underworld, bounded by the wide black river Styx.
9. *ferryman*: In Greek mythology, Charon ferried the souls of the dead across the Styx.
11. *Farmington*: Town in Connecticut.
12. *Haddam*: Town in Connecticut. "I just like the name. It is an old whaling town, I believe. In any case, it has a completely Yankee sound." [Stevens, *Letters*, p. 786.]
14. *curriculum*: Flowing or course (Latin).

Of Mere Being

The palm at the end of the mind,
Beyond the last thought, rises
In the bronze decor,

A gold-feathered bird
Sings in the palm, without human meaning, 5
Without human feeling, a foreign song.

You know then that it is not the reason
That makes us happy or unhappy.
The bird sings. Its feathers shine.

The palm stands on the edge of space. 10
The wind moves slowly in the branches.
The bird's fire-fangled feathers dangle down.

1957

JAMES JOYCE
(1882–1941)
A Portrait of the Artist as a Young Man*

Once upon a time and a very good time it was there was a moocow coming down along the road and this moocow that was down along the road met a nicens little boy named baby tuckoo. . . .

His father told him that story: his father looked at him through a glass: he had a hairy face.

He was baby tuckoo. The moocow came down the road where Betty Byrne lived: she sold lemon platt.

O, the wild rose blossoms
On the little green place.

He sang that song. That was his song.

O, the green wothe botheth.

When you wet the bed, first it is warm then it gets cold. His mother put on the oilsheet. That had the queer smell.

His mother had a nicer smell than his father. She played on the piano the sailor's hornpipe for him to dance. He danced:

Tralala, lala,
Tralala tralaladdy,
Tralala, lala,
Tralala lala.

Uncle Charles and Dante clapped. They were older than his father and mother but Uncle Charles was older than Dante.

Dante had two brushes in her press. The brush with the maroon velvet back was for Michael Davitt[1] and the brush with the green velvet back was for Parnell.[2] Dante gave him a cachou every time he brought her a piece of tissue paper.

The Vances lived in number seven. They had a different father and mother. They were Eileen's father and mother. When they were grown up he was going to marry Eileen. He hid under the table. His mother said:

—O, Stephen will apologise.

* From *A Portrait of the Artist as a Young Man* by James Joyce, included in *The Portable James Joyce.* According to Joyce the book was begun in 1904, in Dublin, and finished in 1914, in Trieste. It was published in 1916. The first two parts of the first chapter are reprinted here. The punctuation ". . ." does not indicate omissions from this text.

1. Irish patriot (1846–1906) who, like the majority of the Irish nationalist politicians, broke with Parnell when the latter's adultery with Mrs. O'Shea became known.

2. Charles Parnell (1846–1891), the leader of the Irish Parliamentary Party in the British House of Commons. Party and country were split on the question of his suitability as leader after Captain O'Shea named him as corespondent in a divorce suit (1889) against Mrs. O'Shea.

Dante said:

—O, if not, the eagles will come and pull out his eyes—

Pull out his eyes,
Apologise,
Apologise,
Pull out his eyes.

Apologise,
Pull out his eyes,
Pull out his eyes,
Apologise.

* * *

The wide playgrounds were swarming with boys. All were shouting and the prefects urged them on with strong cries. The evening air was pale and chilly and after every charge and thud of the footballers the greasy leather orb flew like a heavy bird through the grey light. He kept on the fringe of his line, out of sight of his prefect, out of the reach of the rude feet, feigning to run now and then. He felt his body small and weak amid the throng of players and his eyes were weak and watery. Rody Kickham was not like that: he would be captain of the third line all the fellows said.

Rody Kickham was a decent fellow but Nasty Roche was a stink. Rody Kickham had greaves in his number[3] and a hamper in the refectory. Nasty Roche had big hands. He called the Friday pudding dog-in-the-blanket. And one day he had asked:

—What is your name?

Stephen had answered: Stephen Dedalus.

Then Nasty Roche had said:

—What kind of a name is that?

And when Stephen had not been able to answer Nasty Roche had asked:

—What is your father?

Stephen had answered:

—A gentleman.

Then Nasty Roche had asked:

—Is he a magistrate?

He crept about from point to point on the fringe of his line, making little runs now and then. But his hands were bluish with cold. He kept his hands in the side pockets of his belted grey suit. That was a belt round his pocket. And belt was also to give a fellow a belt. One day a fellow had said to Cantwell:

—I'd give you such a belt in a second.

Cantwell had answered:

—Go and fight your match. Give Cecil Thunder a belt. I'd like to see you. He'd give you a toe in the rump for yourself.

3. sediment of melted animal fat in his locker.

That was not a nice expression. His mother had told him not to speak with the rough boys in the college. Nice mother! The first day in the hall of the castle[4] when she had said goodbye she had put up her veil double to her nose to kiss him: and her nose and eyes were red. But he had pretended not to see that she was going to cry. She was a nice mother but she was not so nice when she cried. And his father had given him two five-shilling pieces for pocket money. And his father had told him if he wanted anything to write home to him and, whatever he did, never to peach[5] on a fellow. Then at the door of the castle the rector had shaken hands with his father and mother, his soutane[6] fluttering in the breeze, and the car had driven off with his father and mother on it. They had cried to him from the car, waving their hands:

—Good-bye, Stephen, goodbye!

—Good-bye, Stephen, goodbye!

He was caught in the whirl of a scrimmage and, fearful of the flashing eyes and muddy boots, bent down to look through the legs. The fellows were struggling and groaning and their legs were rubbing and kicking and stamping. Then Jack Lawton's yellow boots dodged out the ball and all the other boots and legs ran after. He ran after them a little way and then stopped. It was useless to run on. Soon they would be going home for the holidays. After supper in the study hall he would change the number pasted up inside his desk from seventyseven to seventysix.

It would be better to be in the study hall than out there in the cold. The sky was pale and cold but there were lights in the castle He wondered from which window Hamilton Rowan had thrown his hat on the haha and had there been flowerbeds at that time under the windows. One day when he had been called to the castle the butler had shown him the marks of the soldiers' slugs in the wood of the door and had given him a piece of shortbread that the community ate. It was nice and warm to see the lights in the castle. It was like something in a book. Perhaps Leicester Abbey was like that. And there were nice sentences in Doctor Cornwell's Spelling Book. They were like poetry but they were only sentences to learn the spelling from.

> Wolsey died in Leicester Abbey
> Where the abbots buried him.
> Canker is a disease of plants,
> Cancer one of animals.

It would be nice to lie on the hearthrug before the fire, leaning his head upon his hands, and think on those sentences. He shivered as if he had cold slimy water next his skin. That was mean of Wells to shoulder him into the square ditch because he would not

4. The Jesuit school of Clongowes is housed in an old castle.

5. tell, inform.

6. cassock.

swop his little snuffbox for Wells's seasoned hacking chestnut, the conqueror of forty. How cold and slimy the water had been! A fellow had once seen a big rat jump into the scum. Mother was sitting at the fire with Dante waiting for Brigid to bring in the tea. She had her feet on the fender and her jewelly slippers were so hot and they had such a lovely warm smell. Dante knew a lot of things. She had taught him where the Mozambique Channel was and what was the longest river in America and what was the name of the highest mountain in the moon. Father Arnall knew more than Dante because he was a priest but both his father and Uncle Charles said that Dante was a clever woman and a wellread woman. And when Dante made that noise after dinner and then put up her hand to her mouth: that was heartburn.

A voice cried far out on the playground:

—All in!

Then other voices cried from the lower and third lines:

—All in! All in!

The players closed around, flushed and muddy, and he went among them, glad to go in. Rody Kickham held the ball by its greasy lace. A fellow asked him to give it one last: but he walked on without even answering the fellow. Simon Moonan told him not to because the prefect was looking. The fellow turned to Simon Moonan and said:

—We all know why you speak. You are McGlade's suck.

Suck was a queer word. The fellow called Simon Moonan that name because Simon Moonan used to tie the prefect's false sleeves behind his back and the prefect used to let on to be angry. But the sound was ugly. Once he had washed his hands in the lavatory of the Wicklow Hotel and his father pulled the stopper up by the chain after and the dirty water went down through the hole in the basin. And when it had all gone down slowly the hole in the basin had made a sound like that: suck. Only louder.

To remember that and the white look of the lavatory made him feel cold and then hot. There were two cocks that you turned and water came out: cold and hot. He felt cold and then a little hot: and he could see the names printed on the cocks. That was a very queer thing.

And the air in the corridor chilled him too. It was queer and wettish. But soon the gas would be lit and in burning it made a light noise like a little song. Always the same: and when the fellows stopped talking in the playroom you could hear it.

It was the hour for sums. Father Arnall wrote a hard sum on the board and then said:

—Now then, who will win? Go ahead, York! Go ahead, Lancaster![7]

7. The two sections of the class were named after York and Lancaster, the opposing factions in the Wars of the Roses, the English civil wars of the fifteenth century.

Stephen tried his best but the sum was too hard and he felt confused. The little silk badge with the white rose on it that was pinned on the breast of his jacket began to flutter. He was no good at sums but he tried his best so that York might not lose. Father Arnall's face looked very black but he was not in a wax:[8] he was laughing. Then Jack Lawton cracked his fingers and Father Arnall looked at his copybook and said:

—Right. Bravo Lancaster! The red rose wins. Come on now, York! Forge ahead!

Jack Lawton looked over from his side. The little silk badge with the red rose on it looked very rich because he had a blue sailor top on. Stephen felt his own face red too, thinking of all the bets about who would get first place in Elements, Jack Lawton or he. Some weeks Jack Lawton got the card for first and some weeks he got the card for first. His white silk badge fluttered and fluttered as he worked at the next sum and heard Father Arnall's voice. Then all his eagerness passed away and he felt his face quite cool. He thought his face must be white because it felt so cool. He could not get out the answer for the sum but it did not matter. White roses and red roses: those were beautiful colours to think of. And the cards for first place and third place were beautiful colours too: pink and cream and lavender. Lavender and cream and pink roses were beautiful to think of. Perhaps a wild rose might be like those colours and he remembered the song about the wild rose blossoms on the little green place. But you could not have a green rose. But perhaps somewhere in the world you could.

The bell rang and then the classes began to file out of the rooms and along the corridors towards the refectory. He sat looking at the two prints of butter on his plate but could not eat the damp bread. The tablecloth was damp and limp. But he drank off the hot weak tea which the clumsy scullion,[9] girt with a white apron, poured into his cup. He wondered whether the scullion's apron was damp too or whether all white things were cold and damp. Nasty Roche and Saurin drank cocoa that their people sent them in tins. They said they could not drink the tea; that it was hogwash. Their fathers were magistrates, the fellows said.

All the boys seemed to him very strange. They had all fathers and mothers and different clothes and voices. He longed to be at home and lay his head on his mother's lap. But he could not: and so he longed for the play and study and prayers to be over and to be in bed.

He drank another cup of hot tea and Fleming said:

—What's up? Have you a pain or what's up with you?

—I don't know, Stephen said.

—Sick in your bread basket, Fleming said, because your face looks white. It will go away.

—O yes, Stephen said.

8. bad temper.

9. kitchen boy.

But he was not sick there. He thought that he was sick in his heart if you could be sick in that place. Fleming was very decent to ask him. He wanted to cry. He leaned his elbows on the table and shut and opened the flaps of his ears. Then he heard the noise of the refectory every time he opened the flaps of his ears. It made a roar like a train at night. And when he closed the flaps the roar was shut off like a train going into a tunnel. That night at Dalkey[10] the train had roared like that and then, when it went into the tunnel, the roar stopped. He closed his eyes and the train went on, roaring and then stopping; roaring again, stopping. It was nice to hear it roar and stop and then roar out of the tunnel again and then stop.

Then the higher line fellows began to come down along the matting in the middle of the refectory, Paddy Rath and Jimmy Magee and the Spaniard who was allowed to smoke cigars and the little Portuguese who wore the woolly cap. And then the lower line tables and the tables of the third line. And every single fellow had a different way of walking.

He sat in a corner of the playroom pretending to watch a game of dominos and once or twice he was able to hear for an instant the little song of the gas. The prefect was at the door with some boys and Simon Moonan was knotting his false sleeves. He was telling them something about Tullabeg.

Then he went away from the door and Wells came over to Stephen and said:

—Tell us, Dedalus, do you kiss your mother before you go to bed?

Stephen answered:

—I do.

Wells turned to the other fellows and said:

—O, I say, here's a fellow says he kisses his mother every night before he goes to bed.

The other fellows stopped their game and turned round, laughing. Stephen blushed under their eyes and said:

—I do not.

Wells said:

—O, I say, here's a fellow says he doesn't kiss his mother before he goes to bed.

They all laughed again. Stephen tried to laugh with them. He felt his whole body hot and confused in a moment. What was the right answer to the question? He had given two and still Wells laughed. But Wells must know the right answer for he was in third of grammar. He tried to think of Wells's mother but he did not dare to raise his eyes to Wells's face. He did not like Wells's face. It was Wells who had shouldered him into the square ditch the day before because he would not swop his little snuffbox for Wells's seasoned hacking chestnut, the conqueror of forty. It was a mean thing to do; all the fellows said it was. And how cold and slimy the

10. on the coast. It could be reached from Dublin by train or streetcar.

water had been! And a fellow had once seen a big rat jump plop into the scum.

The cold slime of the ditch covered his whole body; and, when the bell rang for study and the lines filed out of the playrooms, he felt the cold air of the corridor and staircase inside his clothes. He still tried to think what was the right answer. Was it right to kiss his mother or wrong to kiss his mother? What did that mean, to kiss? You put your face up like that to say goodnight and then his mother put her face down. That was to kiss. His mother put her lips on his cheek; her lips were soft and they wetted his cheek; and they made a tiny little noise: kiss. Why did people do that with their two faces?

Sitting in the study hall he opened the lid of his desk and changed the number pasted up inside from seventyseven to seventysix. But the Christmas vacation was very far away: but one time it would come because the earth moved round always.

There was a picture of the earth on the first page of his geography: a big ball in the middle of clouds. Fleming had a box of crayons and one night during free study he had coloured the earth green and the clouds maroon. That was like the two brushes in Dante's press, the brush with the green velvet back for Parnell and the brush with the maroon velvet back for Michael Davitt. But he had not told Fleming to colour them those colours. Fleming had done it himself.

He opened the geography to study the lesson; but he could not learn the names of places in America. Still they were all different places that had different names. They were all in different countries and the countries were in continents and the continents were in the world and the world was in the universe.

He turned to the flyleaf of the geography and read what he had written there: himself, his name and where he was.

Stephen Dedalus
Class of Elements
Clongowes Wood College
Sallins
County Kildare
Ireland
Europe
The World
The Universe

That was in his writing: and Fleming one night for a cod[11] had written on the opposite page:

Stephen Dedalus is my name,
Ireland is my nation.
Clongowes is my dwellingplace
And heaven my expectation.

11. joke.

He read the verses backwards but then they were not poetry. Then he read the flyleaf from the bottom to the top till he came to his own name. That was he: and he read down the page again. What was after the universe? Nothing. But was there anything round the universe to show where it stopped before the nothing place began? It could not be a wall but there could be a thin thin line there all round everything. It was very big to think about everything and everywhere. Only God could do that. He tried to think what a big thought that must be but he could think only of God. God was God's name just as his name was Stephen. *Dieu* was the French for God and that was God's name too; and when anyone prayed to God and said *Dieu* then God knew at once that it was a French person that was praying. But though there were different names for God in all the different languages in the world and God understood what all the people who prayed said in their different languages still God remained always the same God and God's real name was God.

It made him very tired to think that way. It made him feel his head very big. He turned over the flyleaf and looked wearily at the green round earth in the middle of the maroon clouds. He wondered which was right, to be for the green or for the maroon, because Dante had ripped the green velvet back off the brush that was for Parnell one day with her scissors and had told him that Parnell was a bad man. He wondered if they were arguing at home about that. That was called politics. There were two sides in it: Dante was on one side and his father and Mr. Casey were on the other side but his mother and Uncle Charles were on no side. Every day there was something in the paper about it.

It pained him that he did not know well what politics meant and that he did not know where the universe ended. He felt small and weak. When would he be like the fellows in Poetry and Rhetoric? They had big voices and big boots and they studied trigonometry. That was very far away. First came the vacation and then the next term and then vacation again and then again another term and then again the vacation. It was like a train going in and out of tunnels and that was like the noise of the boys eating in the refectory when you opened and closed the flaps of the ears. Term, vacation; tunnel, out; noise, stop. How far away it was! It was better to go to bed to sleep. Only prayers in the chapel and then bed. He shivered and yawned. It would be lovely in bed after the sheets got a bit hot. First they were so cold to get into. He shivered to think how cold they were first. But then they got hot and then he could sleep. It was lovely to be tired. He yawned again. Night prayers and then bed: he shivered and wanted to yawn. It would be lovely in a few minutes. He felt a warm glow creeping up from the cold shivering sheets, warmer and warmer till he felt warm all over, ever so warm and yet he shivered a little and still wanted to yawn.

The bell rang for night prayers and he filed out of the study hall after the others and down the staircase and along the corridors to the chapel. The corridors were darkly lit and the chapel was darkly lit. Soon all would be dark and sleeping. There was cold night air in the chapel and the marbles were the colour the sea was at night. The sea was cold day and night: but it was colder at night. It was cold and dark under the seawall beside his father's house. But the kettle would be on the hob to make punch.

The prefect of the chapel prayed above his head and his memory knew the responses:

> O Lord, open our lips
> And our mouths shall announce Thy praise.
> Incline unto our aid, O God!
> O Lord, make haste to help us!

There was a cold night smell in the chapel. But it was a holy smell. It was not like the smell of the old peasants who knelt at the back of the chapel at Sunday mass. That was a smell of air and rain and turf and corduroy. But they were very holy peasants. They breathed behind him on his neck and sighed as they prayed. They lived in Clane, a fellow said: there were little cottages there and he had seen a woman standing at the halfdoor of a cottage with a child in her arms, as the cars had come past from Sallins. It would be lovely to sleep for one night in that cottage before the fire of smoking turf, in the dark lit by the fire, in the warm dark, breathing the smell of the peasants, air and rain and turf and corduroy. But, O, the road there between the trees was dark! You would be lost in the dark. It made him afraid to think of how it was.

He heard the voice of the prefect of the chapel saying the last prayer. He prayed it too against the dark outside under the trees.

> Visit, we beseech Thee, O Lord, this habitation and drive away from it all the snares of the enemy. May Thy holy angels dwell herein to preserve us in peace and may Thy blessing be always upon us through Christ our Lord. Amen.

His fingers trembled as he undressed himself in the dormitory. He told his fingers to hurry up. He had to undress and then kneel and say his own prayers and be in bed before the gas was lowered so that he might not go to hell when he died. He rolled his stockings off and put on his nightshirt quickly and knelt trembling at his bedside and repeated his prayers quickly, fearing that the gas would go down. He felt his shoulders shaking as he murmured:

> God bless my father and my mother and spare them to me!
> God bless my little brothers and sisters and spare them to me!
> God bless Dante and Uncle Charles and spare them to me!

He blessed himself and climbed quickly into bed and, tucking the end of the nightshirt under his feet, curled himself together under the cold white sheets, shaking and trembling. But he would not go to hell when he died; and the shaking would stop. A voice bade the boys in the dormitory goodnight. He peered out for an instant over the coverlet and saw the yellow curtains round and before his bed that shut him off on all sides. The light was lowered quietly.

The prefect's shoes went away. Where? Down the staircase and along the corridors or to his room at the end? He saw the dark. Was it true about the black dog that walked there at night with eyes as big as carriagelamps? They said it was the ghost of a murderer. A long shiver of fear flowed over his body. He saw the dark entrance hall of the castle. Old servants in old dress were in the ironingroom above the staircase. It was long ago. The old servants were quiet. There was a fire there but the hall was still dark. A figure came up the staircase from the hall. He wore the white cloak of a marshal; his face was pale and strange; he held his hand pressed to his side. He looked out of strange eyes at the old servants. They looked at him and saw their master's face and cloak and knew that he had received his death wound. But only the dark was where they looked: only dark silent air. Their master had received his death wound on the battlefield of Prague far away over the sea. He was standing on the field; his hand was pressed to his side; his face was pale and strange and he wore the white cloak of a marshal.

O how cold and strange it was to think of that! All the dark was cold and strange. There were pale strange faces there, great eyes like carriagelamps. They were the ghosts of murderers, the figures of marshals who had received their deathwound on battlefields far away over the sea. What did they wish to say that their faces were so strange?

> Visit, we beseech Thee, O Lord, this habitation and drive away from it all . . .

Going home for the holidays! That would be lovely: the fellows had told him. Getting up on the cars in the early wintry morning outside the door of the castle. The cars were rolling on the gravel. Cheers for the rector!

Hurray! Hurray! Hurray!

The cars drove past the chapel and all caps were raised. They drove merrily along the country roads. The drivers pointed with their whips to Bodenstown. The fellows cheered. They passed the farmhouse of the Jolly Farmer. Cheer after cheer after cheer. Through Clane they drove, cheering and cheered. The peasant women stood at the halfdoors, the men stood here and there. The lovely smell there was in the wintry air: the smell of Clane: rain and wintry air and turf smouldering and corduroy.

The train was full of fellows: a long long chocolate train with cream facings. The guards went to and fro opening, closing, locking, unlocking the doors. They were men in dark blue and silver; they had silvery whistles and their keys made a quick music: click, click: click, click.

And the train raced on over the flat lands and past the Hill of Allen. The telegraphpoles were passing, passing. The train went on and on. It knew. There were lanterns in the hall of his father's house and ropes of green branches. There were holly and ivy round the pierglass[12] and holly and ivy, green and red, twined round the chandeliers. There were red holly and green ivy round the old portraits on the walls. Holly and ivy for him and for Christmas.

Lovely . . .

All the people. Welcome home, Stephen! Noises of welcome. His mother kissed him. Was that right? His father was a marshal now: higher than a magistrate. Welcome home, Stephen!

Noises . . .

There was a noise of curtainrings running back along the rods, of water being splashed in the basins. There was a noise of rising and dressing and washing in the dormitory: a noise of clapping of hands as the prefect went up and down telling the fellows to look sharp. A pale sunlight showed the yellow curtains drawn back, the tossed beds. His bed was very hot and his face and body were very hot.

He got up and sat on the side of his bed. He was weak. He tried to pull on his stocking. It had a horrid rough feel. The sunlight was queer and cold.

Fleming said:

—Are you not well?

He did not know; and Fleming said:

—Get back into bed. I'll tell McGlade you're not well.

—He's sick.

—Who is?

—Tell McGlade.

—Get back into bed.

—Is he sick?

A fellow held his arms while he loosened the stocking clinging to his foot and climbed back into the hot bed.

He crouched down between the sheets, glad of their tepid glow. He heard the fellows talk among themselves about him as they dressed for mass. It was a mean thing to do, to shoulder him into the square ditch, they were saying.

12. a tall mirror.

Then their voices ceased; they had gone. A voice at his bed said:

—Dedalus, don't spy on us, sure you won't?

Wells's face was there. He looked at it and saw that Wells was afraid.

—I didn't mean to. Sure you won't?

His father had told him, whatever he did, never to peach on a fellow. He shook his head and answered no and felt glad.

Wells said:

—I didn't mean to, honour bright. It was only for cod. I'm sorry.

The face and the voice went away. Sorry because he was afraid. Afraid that it was some disease. Canker was a disease of plants and cancer one of animals: or another different. That was a long time ago then out on the playgrounds in the evening light, creeping from point to point on the fringe of his line, a heavy bird flying low through the grey light. Leicester Abbey lit up. Wolsey died there. The abbots buried him themselves.

It was not Wells's face, it was the prefect's. He was not foxing.[13] No, no: he was sick really. He was not foxing. And he felt the prefect's hand on his forehead; and he felt his forehead warm and damp against the prefect's cold damp hand. That was the way a rat felt, slimy and damp and cold. Every rat had two eyes to look out of. Sleek slimy coats, little little feet tucked up to jump, black slimy eyes to look out of. They could understand how to jump. But the minds of rats could not understand trigonometry. When they were dead they lay on their sides. Their coats dried then. They were only dead things.

The prefect was there again and it was his voice that was saying that he was to get up, that Father Minister had said he was to get up and dress and go to the infirmary. And while he was dressing himself as quickly as he could the prefect said:

—We must pack off to Brother Michael because we have the collywobbles!

He was very decent to say that. That was all to make him laugh. But he could not laugh because his cheeks and lips were all shivery. and then the prefect had to laugh by himself.

The prefect cried:

—Quick march! Hayfoot! Strawfoot!

They went together down the staircase and along the corridor and past the bath. As he passed the door he remembered with a vague fear the warm turf-coloured bogwater, the warm moist air, the noise of plunges, the smell of the towels, like medicine.

Brother Michael was standing at the door of the infirmary and from the door of the dark cabinet on his right came a smell like medicine. That came from the bottles on the shelves. The prefect

13. pretending.

spoke to Brother Michael and Brother Michael answered and called the prefect sir. He had reddish hair mixed with grey and a queer look. It was queer that he would always be a brother. It was queer too that you could not call him sir because he was a brother and had a different kind of look. Was he not holy enough or why could he not catch up on the others?

There were two beds in the room and in one bed there was a fellow: and when they went in he called out:

—Hello! It's young Dedalus! What's up?

—The sky is up, Brother Michael said.

He was a fellow out of the third of grammar and, while Stephen was undressing, he asked Brother Michael to bring him a round of buttered toast.

—Ah, do! he said.

—Butter you up! said Brother Michael. You'll get your walking papers in the morning when the doctor comes.

—Will I? the fellow said. I'm not well yet.

Brother Michael repeated:

—You'll get your walking papers. I tell you.

He bent down to rake the fire. He had a long back like the long back of a tramhorse. He shook the poker gravely and nodded his head at the fellow out of third of grammar.

Then Brother Michael went away and after a while the fellow out of third of grammar turned in towards the wall and fell asleep.

That was the infirmary. He was sick then. Had they written home to tell his mother and father? But it would be quicker for one of the priests to go himself to tell them. Or he would write a letter for the priest to bring.

Dear Mother,

I am sick. I want to go home. Please come and take me home. I am in the infirmary.

Your fond son,

Stephen.

How far away they were! There was cold sunlight outside the window. He wondered if he would die. You could die just the same on a sunny day. He might die before his mother came. Then he would have a dead mass in the chapel like the way the fellows had told him it was when Little had died. All the fellows would be at the mass, dressed in black, all with sad faces. Wells too would be there but no fellow would look at him. The rector would be there in a cope[14] of black and gold and there would be tall yellow candles on the altar and round the catafalque. And they would carry the coffin out of the chapel slowly and he would be buried in the little

14. a long mantle worn over the surplice in processions and the like.

graveyard of the community off the main avenue of limes.[15] And Wells would be sorry then for what he had done. And the bell would toll slowly.

He could hear the tolling. He said over to himself the song that Brigid had taught him.

> Dingdong! The castle bell!
> Farewell, my mother!
> Bury me in the old churchyard
> Beside my eldest brother.
> My coffin shall be black,
> Six angels at my back,
> Two to sing and two to pray
> And two to carry my soul away.

How beautiful and sad that was! How beautiful the words were where they said *Bury me in the old churchyard!* A tremor passed over his body. How sad and how beautiful! He wanted to cry quietly but not for himself: for the words, so beautiful and sad, like music. The bell! The bell! Farewell! O farewell!

The cold sunlight was weaker and Brother Michael was standing at his bedside with a bowl of beeftea. He was glad for his mouth was hot and dry. He could hear them playing in the playgrounds. And the day was going on in the college just as if he were there.

Then Brother Michael was going away and the fellow out of third of grammar told him to be sure and come back and tell him all the news in the paper. He told Stephen that his name was Athy and that his father kept a lot of racehorses that were spiffing[16] jumpers and that his father would give a good tip to Brother Michael any time he wanted it because Brother Michael was very decent and always told him the news out of the paper they got every day up in the castle. There was every kind of news in the paper: accidents, shipwrecks, sports and politics.

—Now it is all about politics in the papers, he said. Do your people talk about that too?

—Yes, Stephen said.

—Mine too, he said.

Then he thought for a moment and said:

—You have a queer name, Dedalus, and I have a queer name too, Athy. My name is the name of a town. Your name is like Latin.

Then he asked:

—Are you good at riddles?

Stephen answered:

—Not very good.

Then he said:

15. linden trees.

16. top-notch, excellent.

—Can you answer me this one? Why is the county of Kildare like the leg of a fellow's breeches?

Stephen thought what could be the answer and then said:

—I give it up.

—Because there is a thigh in it, he said. Do you see the joke? Athy[17] is the town in the county Kildare, and a thigh is the other thigh.

—O, I see, Stephen said.

—That's an old riddle, he said.

After a moment he said:

—I say!

—What? asked Stephen.

—You know, he said, you can ask that riddle another way.

—Can you? said Stephen.

—The same riddle, he said. Do you know the other way to ask it?

—No, said Stephen.

—Can you not think of the other way? he said.

He looked at Stephen over the bedclothes as he spoke. Then he lay back on the pillow and said:

—There is another way but I won't tell you what it is.

Why did he not tell it? His father, who kept the racehorses, must be a magistrate too like Saurin's father and Nasty Roche's father. He thought of his own father, of how he sang songs while his mother played and of how he always gave him a shilling when he asked for sixpence and he felt sorry for him that he was not a magistrate like the other boys' fathers. Then why was he sent to that place with them? But his father had told him that he would be no stranger there because his granduncle had presented an address to the Liberator[18] there fifty years before. You could know the people of that time by their old dress. It seemed to him a solemn time: and he wondered if that was the time when the fellows in Clongowes wore blue coats with brass buttons and yellow waistcoats and caps of rabbitskin and drank beer like grownup people and kept greyhounds of their own to course the hares with.

He looked at the window and saw that the daylight had grown weaker. There would be cloudy grey light over the playgrounds. There was no noise on the playgrounds. The class must be doing the themes or perhaps Father Arnall was reading out of the book.

It was queer that they had not given him any medicine. Perhaps Brother Michael would bring it back when he came. They said you got stinking stuff to drink when you were in the infirmary. But he felt better now than before. It would be nice getting better slowly. You could get a book then. There was a book in the library about

17. pronounced "a thigh."

18. Daniel O'Connell (1775–1847), Irish political leader.

Holland. There were lovely foreign names in it and pictures of strangelooking cities and ships. It made you feel so happy.

How pale the light was at the window! But that was nice. The fire rose and fell on the wall. It was like waves. Someone had put coal on and he heard voices. They were talking. It was the noise of the waves. Or the waves were talking among themselves as they rose and fell.

He saw the sea of waves, long dark waves rising and falling, dark under the moonless night. A tiny light twinkled at the pierhead where the ship[19] was entering: and he saw a multitude of people gathered by the waters' edge to see the ship that was entering their harbour. A tall man stood on the deck, looking out towards the flat dark land: and by the light at the pierhead he saw his face, the sorrowful face of Brother Michael.

He saw him lift his hand towards the people and heard him say in a loud voice of sorrow over the waters:

—He is dead. We saw him lying upon the catafalque.

A wail of sorrow went up from the people.

—Parnell! Parnell! He is dead!

They fell upon their knees, moaning in sorrow.

And he saw Dante in a maroon velvet dress and with a green velvet mantle hanging from her shoulders walking proudly and silently past the people who knelt by the waters' edge.

A great fire, banked high and red, flamed in the grate and under the ivytwined branches of the chandelier the Christmas table was spread. They had come home a little late and still dinner was not ready: but it would be ready in a jiffy, his mother had said. They were waiting for the door to open and for the servants to come in, holding the big dishes covered with their heavy metal covers.

All were waiting: Uncle Charles, who sat far away in the shadow of the window, Dante and Mr Casey, who sat in the easychairs at either side of the hearth, Stephen, seated on a chair between them, his feet resting on the toasted boss.[20] Mr Dedalus looked at himself in the pierglass above the mantelpiece, waxed out his moustache ends and then, parting his coat tails, stood with his back to the glowing fire: and still from time to time he withdrew a hand from his coat tail to wax out one of his moustache ends. Mr Casey leaned his head to one side and, smiling, tapped the gland of his neck with his fingers. And Stephen smiled too for he knew now that it was not true that Mr Casey had a purse of silver in his throat. He smiled to think how the silvery noise which Mr Casey used to make had deceived him. And when he had tried to open Mr Casey's hand

19. Stephen in his semidelirium evokes what he has heard of the return of Parnell's body to Ireland on Sunday, October 11, 1891. There were great popular demonstrations.

20. hassock.

to see if the purse of silver was hidden there he had seen that the fingers could not be straightened out: and Mr Casey had told him that he had got those three cramped fingers[21] making a birthday present for Queen Victoria.

Mr Casey tapped the gland of his neck and smiled at Stephen with sleepy eyes: and Mr Dedalus said to him:

—Yes. Well now, that's all right. O, we had a good walk, hadn't we, John? Yes . . . I wonder if there's any likelihood of dinner this evening. Yes. . . . O, well now, we got a good breath of ozone round the Head[22] today. Ay, bedad.

He turned to Dante and said:

—You didn't stir out at all, Mrs Riordan?

Dante frowned and said shortly:

—No.

Mr Dedalus dropped his coat tails and went over to the sideboard. He brought forth a great stone jar of whisky from the locker and filled the decanter slowly, bending now and then to see how much he had poured in. Then replacing the jar in the locker he poured a little of the whisky into two glasses, added a little water and came back with them to the fireplace.

—A thimbleful, John, he said, just to whet your appetite.

Mr Casey took the glass, drank, and placed it near him on the mantelpiece. Then he said:

—Well, I can't help thinking of our friend Christopher manufacturing . . .

He broke into a fit of laughter and coughing and added:

—. . . manufacturing that champagne for those fellows.

Mr Dedalus laughed loudly.

—Is it Christy? he said. There's more cunning in one of those warts on his bald head than in a pack of jack foxes.

He inclined his head, closed his eyes, and, licking his lips profusely, began to speak with the voice of the hotel keeper.

—And he has such a soft mouth when he's speaking to you, don't you know. He's very moist and watery about the dewlaps, God bless him.

Mr Casey was still struggling through his fit of coughing and laughter. Stephen, seeing and hearing the hotel keeper through his father's face and voice, laughed.

Mr Dedalus put up his eyeglass and, staring down at him, said quietly and kindly:

—What are you laughing at, you little puppy, you?

The servants entered and placed the dishes on the table. Mrs Dedalus followed and the places were arranged.

21. perhaps due to some patriotic misadventure with explosives. Mr. Casey is an ardent nationalist.

22. Howth Head, the promontory forming the northern side of Dublin Bay.

—Sit over, she said.

Mr Dedalus went to the end of the table and said:

—Now, Mrs Riordan, sit over. John, sit you down, my hearty.

He looked round to where Uncle Charles sat and said:

—Now then, sir, there's a bird here waiting for you.

When all had taken their seats he laid his hand on the cover and then said quickly, withdrawing it:

—Now, Stephen.

Stephen stood up in his place to say the grace before meals:

> Bless us, O Lord, and these Thy gifts which through Thy bounty we are about to receive through Christ our Lord. Amen.

All blessed themselves and Mr Dedalus with a sigh of pleasure lifted from the dish the heavy cover pearled around the edge with glistening drops.

Stephen looked at the plump turkey which had lain, trussed and skewered, on the kitchen table. He knew that his father had paid a guinea for it in Dunn's of D'Olier Street and that the man had prodded it often at the breastbone to show how good it was: and he remembered the man's voice when he had said:

—Take that one, sir. That's the real Ally Daly.

Why did Mr Barrett in Clongowes call his pandybat[23] a turkey? But Clongowes was far away: and the warm heavy smell of turkey and ham and celery rose from the plates and dishes and the great fire was banked high and red in the grate and the green ivy and red holly made you feel so happy and when dinner was ended the big plum pudding would be carried in, studded with peeled almonds and sprigs of holly, with bluish fire running around it and a little green flag flying from the top.

It was his first Christmas dinner and he thought of his little brothers and sisters who were waiting in the nursery, as he had often waited, till the pudding came. The deep low collar and the Eton jacket made him feel queer and oldish: and that morning when his mother had brought him down to the parlour, dressed for mass, his father had cried. That was because he was thinking of his own father. And Uncle Charles had said so too.

Mr Dedalus covered the dish and began to eat hungrily. Then he said:

—Poor old Christy, he's nearly lopsided now with roguery.

—Simon, said Mrs Dedalus, you haven't given Mrs Riordan any sauce.

Mr Dedalus seized the sauceboat.

23. for inflicting corporal punishment.

—Haven't I? he cried. Mrs Riordan, pity the poor blind.

Dante covered her plate with her hands and said:

—No, thanks.

Mr Dedalus turned to Uncle Charles.

—How are you off, sir?

—Right as the mail, Simon.

—You, John?

—I'm all right. Go on yourself.

—Mary? Here, Stephen, here's something to make your hair curl.

He poured sauce freely over Stephen's plate and set the boat again on the table. Then he asked Uncle Charles was it tender. Uncle Charles could not speak because his mouth was full but he nodded that it was.

—That was a good answer our friend made to the canon. What? said Mr Dedalus.

—I didn't think he had that much in him, said Mr Casey.

—*I'll pay your dues, father, when you cease turning the house of God into a pollingbooth.*[24]

—A nice answer, said Dante, for any man calling himself a catholic to give to his priest.

—They have only themselves to blame, said Mr Dedalus suavely. If they took a fool's advice they would confine their attention to religion.

—It is religion, Dante said. They are doing their duty in warning the people.

—We go to the house of God, Mr Casey said, in all humility to pray to our Maker and not to hear election addresses.

—It is religion, Dante said again. They are right. They must direct their flocks.

—And preach politics from the altar, is it? asked Mr Dedalus.

—Certainly, said Dante. It is a question of public morality. A priest would not be a priest if he did not tell his flock what is right and what is wrong.

Mrs Dedalus laid down her knife and fork, saying:

—For pity sake and for pity sake let us have no political discussion on this day of all days in the year.

—Quite right, ma'am, said Uncle Charles. Now Simon, that's quite enough now. Not another word now.

—Yes, yes, said Mr Dedalus quickly.

He uncovered the dish boldly and said:

—Now then, who's for more turkey?

Nobody answered. Dante said:

24. There had been clerical opposition to the continued leadership of Parnell.

—Nice language for any catholic to use!

—Mrs Riordan, I appeal to you, said Mrs Dedalus, to let the matter drop now.

Dante turned on her and said:

—And am I to sit here and listen to the pastors of my church being flouted?

—Nobody is saying a word against them, said Mr Dedalus, so long as they don't meddle in politics.

—The bishops and priests of Ireland have spoken, said Dante, and they must be obeyed.

—Let them leave politics alone, said Mr Casey, or the people may leave their church alone.

—You hear? said Dante turning to Mrs Dedalus.

—Mr Casey! Simon! said Mrs Dedalus, let it end now.

—Too bad! Too bad! said Uncle Charles.

What? cried Mr Dedalus. Were we to desert him at the bidding of the English people?[25]

—He was no longer worthy to lead, said Dante. He was a public sinner.

—We are all sinners and black sinners, said Mr Casey coldly.

—*Woe be to the man by whom the scandal cometh!* said Mrs. Riordan. *It would be better for him that a millstone were tied about his neck and that he were cast into the depths of the sea rather than that he should scandalise one of these, my least little ones.*[26] That is the language of the Holy Ghost.

—And very bad language if you ask me, said Mr Dedalus coolly.

—Simon! Simon! said Uncle Charles. The boy.

—Yes, yes, said Mr Dedalus. I meant about the . . . I was thinking about the bad language of that railway porter. Well now, that's all right. Here, Stephen, show me your plate, old chap. Eat away now. Here.

He heaped up the food on Stephen's plate and served Uncle Charles and Mr Casey to large pieces of turkey and splashes of sauce. Mrs Dedalus was eating little and Dante sat with her hands in her lap. She was red in the face. Mr Dedalus rooted with the carvers at the end of the dish and said:

—There's a tasty bit here we call the pope's nose. If any lady or gentleman . . .

He held a piece of fowl up on the prong of the carvingfork. Nobody spoke. He put it on his own plate, saying:

—Well, you can't say but you were asked. I think I had better eat it myself because I'm not well in my health lately.

25. English Nonconformist disapproval of the adulterer Parnell had forced Prime Minister Gladstone to refuse all dealings with him.

26. See Luke 17:1–2.

He winked at Stephen and, replacing the dishcover, began to eat again.

There was a silence while he ate. Then he said:

—Well now, the day kept up fine after all. There were plenty of strangers down too.

Nobody spoke. He said again:

—I think there were more strangers down than last Christmas.

He looked round at the others whose faces were bent towards their plates and, receiving no reply, waited for a moment and said bitterly:

—Well, my Christmas dinner has been spoiled anyhow.

—There could be neither luck nor grace, Dante said, in a house where there is no respect for the pastors of the church.

Mr Dedalus threw his knife and fork noisily on his plate.

—Respect! he said. Is it for Billy with the lip[27] or for the tub of guts up in Armagh?[28] Respect!

—Princes of the church, said Mr Casey with slow scorn.

—Lord Leitrim's[29] coachman, yes, said Mr Dedalus.

—They are the Lord's anointed, Dante said. They are an honour to their country.

—Tub of guts, said Mr Dedalus coarsely. He has a handsome face, mind you, in repose. You should see that fellow lapping up his bacon and cabbage of a cold winter's day. O Johnny!

He twisted his features into a grimace of heavy bestiality and made a lapping noise with his lips.

—Really, Simon, you should not speak that way before Stephen. It's not right.

—O, he'll remember all this when he grows up, said Dante hotly —the language he heard against God and religion and priests in his own home.

—Let him remember too, cried Mr Casey to her from across the table, the language with which the priests and the priests' pawns broke Parnell's heart and hounded him into his grave. Let him remember that too when he grows up.

—Sons of bitches! cried Mr Dedalus. When he was down they turned on him to betray him and rend him like rats in a sewer. Lowlived dogs! And they look it! By Christ, they look it!

—They behaved rightly, cried Dante. They obeyed their bishops and their priests. Honour to them!

—Well, it is perfectly dreadful to say that not even for one day

27. presumably a reference to William J. Walsh (1841–1921), archbishop of Dublin from 1885.

28. Archbishop of Armagh at this time was Michael Logue (1840–1924), later cardinal.

29. Lord Leitrim was an Irish landlord.

in the year, said Mrs Dedalus, can we be free from these dreadful disputes!

Uncle Charles raised his hands mildly and said:

—Come now, come now, come now! Can we not have our opinions whatever they are without this bad temper and this bad language? It is too bad surely.

Mrs Dedalus spoke to Dante in a low voice but Dante said loudly:

—I will not say nothing. I will defend my church and my religion when it is insulted and spit on by renegade catholics.

Mr Casey pushed his plate rudely into the middle of the table and, resting his elbows before him, said in a hoarse voice to his host:

—Tell me, did I tell you that story about a very famous spit?

—You did not, John, said Mr Dedalus.

Why then, said Mr Casey, it is a most instructive story. It happened not long ago in the county Wicklow where we are now.

He broke off and, turning towards Dante, said with quiet indignation:

—And I may tell you, ma'am, that I, if you mean me, am no renegade catholic. I am a catholic as my father was and his father before him and his father before him again when we gave up our lives rather than sell our faith.

—The more shame to you now, Dante said, to speak as you do.

—The story, John, said Mr Dedalus smiling. Let us have the story anyhow.

—Catholic indeed! repeated Dante ironically. The blackest protestant in the land would not speak the language I have heard this evening.

Mr Dedalus began to sway his head to and fro, crooning like a country singer.

—I am no protestant, I tell you again, said Mr Casey flushing.

Mr Dedalus, still crooning and swaying his head, began to sing in a grunting nasal tone:

O, come all you Roman catholics
That never went to mass.

He took up his knife and fork again in good humour and set to eating, saying to Mr Casey:

—Let us have the story, John. It will help us to digest.

Stephen looked with affection at Mr Casey's face which stared across the table over his joined hands. He liked to sit near him at the fire, looking up at his dark fierce face. But his dark eyes were never fierce and his slow voice was good to listen to. But why was he then against the priests? Because Dante must be right then. But he had heard his father say that she was a spoiled nun and that she had come out of the convent in the Alleghanies when her brother had got the money from the savages for the trinkets and the chainies. Perhaps that made her severe against Parnell. And she did not like him to play with Eileen because Eileen was a protestant and when she was young she knew children that used to play with protestants and the protestants used to make fun of the litany of the Blessed Virgin. *Tower of Ivory,* they used to say, *House of Gold!* How could a woman be a tower of ivory or a house of gold? Who was right then? And he remembered the evening in the infirmary in Clongowes, the dark waters, the light at the pierhead and the moan of sorrow from the people when they had heard.

Eileen had long white hands. One evening when playing tig[30] she had put her hands over his eyes: long and white and thin and cold and soft. That was ivory: a cold white thing. That was the meaning of *Tower of Ivory.*

—The story is very short and sweet, Mr Casey said. It was one day down in Arklow, a cold bitter day, not long before the chief died. May God have mercy on him!

He closed his eyes wearily and paused. Mr Dedalus took a bone from his plate and tore some meat from it with his teeth, saying:

—Before he was killed, you mean.

Mr Casey opened his eyes, sighed and went on:

—He was down in Arklow one day. We were down there at a meeting and after the meeting was over we had to make our way to the railway station through the crowd. Such booing and baaing, man, you never heard. They called us all the names in the world. Well there was one old lady, and a drunken old harridan she was surely, that paid all her attention to me. She kept dancing along beside me in the mud bawling and screaming into my face: *Priest-hunter! The Paris Funds!*[31] *Mr Fox!*[32] *Kitty O'Shea!*

—And what did you do, John? asked Mr Dedalus.

—I let her bawl away, said Mr Casey. It was a cold day and to keep up my heart I had (saving your presence, ma'am) a quid of Tullamore[33] in my mouth and sure I couldn't say a word in any case because my mouth was full of tobacco juice.

—Well, John?

—Well. I let her bawl away, to her heart's content, *Kitty O'Shea* and the rest of it till at last she called that lady a name that I won't sully this Christmas board nor your ears, ma'am, nor my own lips by repeating.

He paused. Mr Dedalus, lifting his head from the bone, asked:

30. the game of tag.

31. This money, contributed by Irish-Americans, had been held in Paris at Parnell's disposal. After his death, the use he had made of it became a bone of contention between Parnellite and anti-Parnellite factions.

32. Parnell had used this name when registering at boardinghouses with Mrs. O'Shea.

33. a chewing tobacco.

—And what did you do, John?

—Do! said Mr Casey. She stuck her ugly old face up at me when she said it and I had my mouth full of tobacco juice. I bent down to her and *Phth!* says I to her like that.

He turned aside and made the act of spitting.

—Phth! says I to her like that, right into her eye.

He clapped a hand to his eye and gave a hoarse scream of pain.

—*O Jesus, Mary and Joseph!* says she. *I'm blinded! I'm blinded and drownded!*

He stopped in a fit of coughing and laughter, repeating:

—*I'm blinded entirely.*

Mr Dedalus laughed loudly and lay back in his chair while Uncle Charles swayed his head to and fro.

Dante looked terribly angry and repeated while they laughed:

—Very nice! Ha! Very nice!

It was not nice about the spit in the woman's eye.

But what was the name the woman had called Kitty O'Shea that Mr Casey would not repeat? He thought of Mr Casey walking through the crowds of people and making speeches from a wagonette. That was what he had been in prison for and he remembered that one night Sergeant O'Neill had come to the house and had stood in the hall, talking in a low voice with his father and chewing nervously at the chinstrap of his cap. And that night Mr Casey had not gone to Dublin by train but a car had come to the door and he had heard his father say something about the Cabinteely road.

He was for Ireland and Parnell and so was his father: and so was Dante too for one night at the band on the esplanade she had hit a gentleman on the head with her umbrella because he had taken off his hat when the band played *God save the Queen* at the end.

Mr Dedalus gave a snort of contempt.

—Ah, John, he said. It is true for them. We are an unfortunate priestridden race and always were and always will be till the end of the chapter.

Uncle Charles shook his head, saying:

—A bad business! A bad business!

Mr Dedalus repeated:

—A priestridden Godforsaken race!

He pointed to the portrait of his gandfather on the wall to his right.

—Do you see that old chap up there, John? he said. He was a good Irishman when there was no money in the job. He was condemned to death as a whiteboy.[34] But he had a saying about our clerical friends, that he would never let one of them put his two feet under his mahogany.[35]

34. one of a group of peasants who, from 1761 onward, resisted paying tithes to the Anglican Church. On their nocturnal excursions they hid their faces under white shirts.

35. dining-room table.

Dante broke in angrily:

—If we are a priestridden race we ought to be proud of it! They are the apple of God's eye. *Touch them not*, says Christ, *for they are the apple of My eye.*

—And can we not love our country then? asked Mr Casey. Are we not to follow the man that was born to lead us?

—A traitor to his country! replied Dante. A traitor, an adulterer! The priests were right to abandon him. The priests were always the true friends of Ireland.

—Were they, faith? said Mr Casey.

He threw his fist on the table and, frowning angrily, protruded one finger after another.

—Didn't the bishops of Ireland betray us in the time of the union[36] when Bishop Lanigan presented an address of loyalty to the Marquess Cornwallis? Didn't the bishops and priests sell the aspirations of their country in 1829 in return for catholic emancipation?[37] Didn't they denounce the fenian movement[38] from the pulpit and in the confession box? And didn't they dishonour the ashes of Terence Bellew MacManus?[39]

His face was glowing with anger and Stephen felt the glow rise to his own cheek as the spoken words thrilled him. Mr Dedalus uttered a guffaw of coarse scorn.

—O, by God, he cried, I forgot little old Paul Cullen![40] Another apple of God's eye!

Dante bent across the table and cried to Mr Casey:

—Right! Right! They were always right! God and morality and religion come first.

Mrs Dedalus, seeing her excitement, said to her:

—Mrs Riordan, don't excite yourself answering them.

God and religion before everything! Dante cried. God and religion before the world!

Mr Casey raised his clenched fist and brought it down on the table with a crash.

—Very well, then, he shouted hoarsely, if it comes to that, no God for Ireland!

—John! John! cried Mr Dedalus, seizing his guest by the coat sleeve.

36. The Irish parliament, representing the Anglo-Irish gentry, was abolished in 1802, and thereafter members for Ireland sat in the British House of Commons.

37. the legislation which freed Catholics from civil disabilities.

38. a secret society whose aim was Irish independence. It was formed in New York about 1854.

39. Irish rebel (1823–1860). He escaped from penal servitude, to which the British had condemned him, and died in the United States. His body was returned to Ireland.

40. Irish prelate (1803–1878). His expression of disapproval of Irish nationalism, when he was papal legate, disappointed the nationalists. He was later archbishop of Dublin, and cardinal.

Dante started across the table, her cheeks shaking. Mr Casey struggled up from his chair and bent across the table towards her, scraping the air from before his eyes with one hand as though he were tearing aside a cobweb.

—No God for Ireland! he cried. We have had too much God in Ireland. Away with God!

—Blasphemer! Devil! screamed Dante, starting to her feet and almost spitting in his face.

Uncle Charles and Mr Dedalus pulled Mr Casey back into his chair again, talking to him from both sides reasonably. He stared before him out of his dark flaming eyes, repeating:

—Away with God, I say!

Dante shoved her chair violently aside and left the table, upsetting her napkinring which rolled slowly along the carpet and came to rest against the foot of an easychair. Mrs Dedalus rose quickly and followed her towards the door. At the door Dante turned round violently and shouted down the room, her cheeks flushed and quivering with rage:

—Devil out of hell! We won! We crushed him to death! Fiend!

The door slammed behind her.

Mr Casey, freeing his arms from his holders, suddenly bowed his head on his hands with a sob of pain.

—Poor Parnell! he cried loudly. My dead king!

He sobbed loudly and bitterly.

Stephen, raising his terrorstricken face, saw that his father's eyes were full of tears.

VIRGINIA WOOLF
(1882–1941)

Moments of Being

"Slater's Pins Have No Points"[1]

"Slater's pins have no points—don't you always find that?" said Miss Craye, turning round as the rose fell out of Fanny Wilmot's dress, and Fanny stopped, with her ears full of the music, to look for the pin on the floor.

The words gave her an extraordinary shock, as Miss Craye struck the last chord of the Bach fugue.[2] Did Miss Craye actually go to Slater's and buy pins then, Fanny Wilmot asked herself, transfixed for a moment. Did she stand at the counter waiting like anybody

1. The title under which "Moments of Being" was first published in 1928.
2. Intricate musical form favored by Johann Sebastian Bach (1683–1750), eighteenth-century German composer.

else, and was she given a bill with coppers[3] wrapped in it, and did she slip them into her purse and then, an hour later, stand by her dressing table and take out the pins? What need had she of pins? For she was not so much dressed as cased, like a beetle compactly in its sheath, blue in winter, green in summer. What need had she of pins—Julia Craye—who lived, it seemed, in the cool glassy world of Bach fugues, playing to herself what she liked, and only consenting to take one or two pupils at the Archer Street College of Music (so the Principal, Miss Kingston, said) as a special favor to herself, who had "the greatest admiration for her in every way." Miss Craye was left badly off, Miss Kingston was afraid, at her brother's death. Oh, they used to have such lovely things, when they lived at Salisbury,[4] and her brother Julius was, of course, a very well-known man: a famous archeologist. It was a great privilege to stay with them, Miss Kingston said ("My family had always known them—they were regular Canterbury[5] people," Miss Kingston said), but a little frightening for a child; one had to be careful not to slam the door or bounce into the room unexpectedly. Miss Kingston, who gave little character sketches like this on the first day of term while she received checks and wrote out receipts for them, smiled here. Yes, she had been rather a tomboy; she had bounced in and set all those Roman glasses[6] and things jumping in their case. The Crayes were not used to children. The Crayes were none of them married. They kept cats; the cats, one used to feel, knew as much about the Roman urns and things as anybody.

"Far more than I did!" said Miss Kingston brightly, writing her name across the stamp[7] in her dashing, cheerful, full-bodied hand, for she had always been practical. That was how she made her living, after all.

Perhaps then, Fanny Wilmot thought, looking for the pin, Miss Craye said that about "Slater's pins having no points," at a venture.[8] None of the Crayes had ever married. She knew nothing about pins—nothing whatever. But she wanted to break the spell that had fallen on the house; to break the pane of glass which separated them from other people. When Polly Kingston, that merry little girl, had slammed the door and made the Roman vases jump, Julius, seeing that no harm was done (that would be his first instinct) looked, for the case was stood in the window, at Polly skipping home across the fields; looked with the look his sister often had, that lingering, driving look.

3. Pennies.

4. Cathedral city in the country about eighty miles southwest of London.

5. Cathedral city fifty-five miles east of London.

6. Archeological finds.

7. In England, postage stamps used to be affixed to receipts as a way of paying a tax on certain business transactions. One signed across the stamp to prevent it from being soaked off and reused.

8. I.e., to see what would happen.

"Stars, sun, moon," it seemed to say, "the daisy in the grass, fires, frost on the window-pane, my heart goes out to you. But," it always seemed to add, "you break, you pass, you go." And simultaneously it covered the intensity of both these states of mind with "I can't reach you—I can't get at you," spoken wistfully, frustratedly. And the stars faded, and the child went. That was the kind of spell that was the glassy surface, that Miss Craye wanted to break by showing, when she had played Bach beautifully as a reward to a favorite pupil (Fanny Wilmot knew that she was Miss Craye's favorite pupil), that she, too, knew, like other people, about pins. Slater's pins had no points.

Yes, the "famous archeologist" had looked like that too. "The famous archeologist"—as she said that, endorsing checks, ascertaining the day of the month, speaking so brightly and frankly, there was in Miss Kingston's voice an indescribable tone which hinted at something odd; something queer in Julius Craye; it was the very same thing that was odd perhaps in Julia too. One could have sworn, thought Fanny Wilmot, as she looked for the pin, that at parties, meetings (Miss Kingston's father was a clergyman), she had picked up some piece of gossip, or it might only have been a smile, or a tone when his name was mentioned, which had given her "a feeling" about Julius Craye. Needless to say, she had never spoken about it to anybody. Probably she scarcely knew what she meant by it. But whenever she spoke of Julius, or heard him mentioned, that was the first thing that came to mind; and it was a seductive thought; there was something odd about Julius Craye.

It was so that Julia looked too, as she sat half turned on the music stool, smiling. It's on the field, it's on the pane, it's in the sky—beauty; and I can't get at it; I can't have it—I, she seemed to add, with that little clutch of the hand which was so characteristic, who adore it so passionately, would give the whole world to possess it! And she picked up the carnation which had fallen on the floor, while Fanny searched for the pin. She crushed it, Fanny felt, voluptuously in her smooth veined hands stuck about with water-colored rings set in pearls. The pressure of her fingers seemed to increase all that was most brilliant in the flower; to set it off; to make it more frilled, fresh, immaculate. What was odd in her, and perhaps in her brother, too, was that this crush and grasp of the finger was combined with a perpetual frustration. So it was even now with the carnation. She had her hands on it; she pressed it; but she did not possess it, enjoy it, not entirely and altogether.

None of the Crayes had married, Fanny Wilmot remembered. She had in mind how one evening when the lesson had lasted longer than usual and it was dark, Julia Craye had said "it's the use of men, surely, to protect us," smiling at her that same odd smile, as she stood fastening her cloak, which made her, like the flower, conscious to her finger tips of youth and brilliance, but, like the flower, too, Fanny suspected, made her feel awkward.

"Oh, but I don't want protection," Fanny had laughed, and when Julia Craye, fixing on her that extraordinary look, had said she was not so sure of that, Fanny positively blushed under the admiration in her eyes.

It was the only use of men, she had said. Was it for that reason then, Fanny wondered, with her eyes on the floor, that she had never married? After all, she had not lived all her life in Salisbury. "Much the nicest part of London," she had said once, "(but I'm speaking of fifteen or twenty years ago) is Kensington.[9] One was in the Gardens in ten minutes—it was like the heart of the country. One could dine out in one's slippers without catching cold. Kensington—it was like a village then, you know," she had said.

Here she broke off, to denounce acridly the drafts in the Tubes.[10]

"It was the use of men," she had said, with a queer wry acerbity. Did that throw any light on the problem why she had not married? One could imagine every sort of scene in her youth, when with her good blue eyes, her straight firm nose, her air of cool distinction, her piano playing, her rose flowering with chaste passion in the bosom of her muslin dress, she had attracted first the young men to whom such things, the china tea cups and the silver candlesticks and the inlaid table, for the Crayes had such nice things, were wonderful; young men not sufficiently distinguished; young men of the cathedral town with ambitions. She had attracted them first, and then her brother's friends from Oxford or Cambridge. They would come down in the summer; row her on the river; continue the argument about Browning[11] by letter; and arrange perhaps, on the rare occasions when she stayed in London, to show her—Kensington Gardens?

"Much the nicest part of London—Kensington (I'm speaking of fifteen or twenty years ago)," she had said once. One was in the Gardens in ten minutes—in the heart of the country. One could make that yield what one liked, Fanny Wilmot thought, single out, for instance, Mr. Sherman, the painter, an old friend of hers; make him call for her by appointment, one sunny day in June; take her to have tea under the trees. (They had met, too, at those parties to which one tripped in slippers without fear of catching cold.) The aunt or other elderly relative was to wait there while they looked at

9. A fashionable district of London, between Hyde Park and the Thames River. Kensington Gardens is a large public park adjoining Hyde Park to the west.

10. Subway.

11. Robert Browning (1812–1883), English poet.

the Serpentine.[12] They looked at the Serpentine. He may have rowed her across. They compared it with the Avon.[13] She would have considered the comparison very furiously. Views of rivers were important to her. She sat hunched a little, a little angular, though she was graceful then, steering. At the critical moment, for he had determined that he must speak now—it was his only chance of getting her alone—he was speaking with his head turned at an absurd angle, in his great nervousness, over his shoulder—at that very moment she interrupted fiercely. He would have them into the Bridge,[14] she cried. It was a moment of horror, of disillusionment, of revelation, for both of them. I can't have it, I can't possess it, she thought. He could not see why she had come then. With a great splash of his oar he pulled the boat round. Merely to snub him? He rowed her back and said goodbye to her.

The setting of that scene could be varied as one chose, Fanny Wilmot reflected. (Where had that pin fallen?) It might be Ravenna;[15] or Edinburgh,[16] where she had kept house for her brother. The scene could be changed; and the young man and the exact manner of it all, but one thing was constant—her refusal, and her frown, and her anger with herself afterward, and her argument, and her relief—yes, certainly her immense relief. The very next day, perhaps, she would get up at six, put on her cloak, and walk all the way from Kensington to the river. She was so thankful that she had not sacrificed her right to go and look at things when they are at their best—before people are up, that is to say she could have her breakfast in bed if she liked. She had not sacrificed her independence.

Yes, Fanny Wilmot smiled, Julia had not endangered her habits. They remained safe; and her habits would have suffered if she had married. "They're ogres," she had said one evening, half laughing, when another pupil, a girl lately married, suddenly bethinking her that she would miss her husband, had rushed off in haste.

"They're ogres," she had said, laughing grimly. An ogre would have interfered perhaps with breakfast in bed; with walks at dawn down to the river. What would have happened (but one could hardly conceive this) had she had children? She took astonishing precautions against chills, fatigue, rich food, the wrong food, drafts, heated rooms, journeys in the Tube, for she could never determine which of these it was exactly that brought on those terrible headaches that gave her life the semblance of a battlefield. She was always engaged in outwitting the enemy, until it seemed as if the

12. Small lake in Hyde Park, with swimming and boating facilities.
13. English river, also much used for boating.
14. The bridge across the Serpentine.
15. Ancient city in northern Italy, known for its art treasures.
16. Capital of Scotland.

pursuit had its interest; could she have beaten the enemy finally she would have found life a little dull. As it was, the tug-of-war was perpetual—on the one side the nightingale or the view which she loved with passion—yes, for views and birds she felt nothing less than passion; on the other the damp path or the horrid long drag up a steep hill which would certainly make her good for nothing next day and bring on one of her headaches. When, therefore, from time to time, she managed her forces adroitly and brought off a visit to Hampton Court[17] the week the crocuses—those glossy bright flowers were her favorite—were at their best, it was a victory. It was something that lasted; something that mattered for ever. She strung the afternoon on the necklace of memorable days, which was not too long for her to be able to recall this one or that one; this view, that city; to finger it, to feel it, to savor, sighing, the quality that made it unique.

"It was so beautiful last Friday," she said, "that I determined I must go there." So she had gone off to Waterloo[18] on her great undertaking—to visit Hampton Court—alone. Naturally, but perhaps foolishly, one pitied her for the thing she never asked pity for (indeed she was reticent habitually, speaking of her health only as a warrior might speak of his foe)—one pitied her for always doing everything alone. Her brother was dead. Her sister was asthmatic. She found the climate of Edinburgh good for her. It was too bleak for Julia. Perhaps, too, she found the associations painful, for her brother, the famous archeologist, had died there; and she had loved her brother. She lived in a little house off the Brompton Road[19] entirely alone.

Fanny Wilmot saw the pin; she picked it up. She looked at Miss Craye. Was Miss Craye so lonely? No, Miss Craye was steadily, blissfully, if only for that moment, a happy woman. Fanny had surprised her in a moment of ecstasy. She sat there, half turned away from the piano, with her hands clasped in her lap holding the carnation upright, while behind her was the sharp square of the window, uncurtained, purple in the evening, intensely purple after the brilliant electric lights which burnt unshaded in the bare music room. Julia Craye, sitting hunched and compact holding her flower, seemed to emerge out of the London night, seemed to fling it like a cloak behind her, it seemed, in its bareness and intensity, the effluence of her spirit, something she had made which surrounded her. Fanny stared.

All seemed transparent, for a moment, to the gaze of Fanny Wilmot, as if looking through Miss Craye, she saw the very foun-

17. Palace outside London famous for its gardens.

18. Waterloo Bridge, from which boats depart for Hampton Court.

19. Major street in the Kensington area.

tain of her being spurting its pure silver drops. She saw back and back into the past behind her. She saw the green Roman vases stood in their case; heard the choristers playing cricket;[20] saw Julia quietly descend the curving steps on to the lawn; then saw her pour out tea beneath the cedar tree; softly enclosed the old man's hand in hers; saw her going round and about the corridors of the ancient Cathedral dwelling place with towels in her hand to mark them; lamenting, as she went, the pettiness of daily life; and slowly aging, and putting away clothes when summer came, because at her age they were too bright to wear; and tending her father's sickness; and cleaving her way ever more definitely as her will stiffened toward her solitary goal; traveling frugally; counting the cost and measuring out of her tight shut purse the sum needed for this journey or for that old mirror; obstinately adhering, whatever people might say, in choosing her pleasures for herself. She saw Julia—

Julia blazed. Julia kindled. Out of the night she burnt like a dead white star. Julia opened her arms. Julia kissed her on the lips. Julia possessed it.

"Slater's pins have no points," Miss Craye said, laughing queerly and relaxing her arms, as Fanny Wilmot pinned the flower to her breast with trembling fingers.

20. Probably the boys in the cathedral choir. Cricket is an English game somewhat like baseball.

FRANZ KAFKA

(1883–1924)

The Metamorphosis (Die Verwandlung) *

As Gregor Samsa awoke one morning from uneasy dreams he found himself transformed in his bed into a gigantic insect. He was lying on his hard, as it were armor-plated, back and when he lifted his head a little he could see his dome-like brown belly divided into stiff arched segments on top of which the bed quilt could hardly keep in position and was about to slide off completely. His numerous legs, which were pitifully thin compared to the rest of his bulk, waved helplessly before his eyes.

What has happened to me? he thought. It was no dream. His

room, a regular human bedroom, only rather too small, lay quiet between the four familiar walls. Above the table on which a collection of cloth samples was unpacked and spread out—Samsa was a commercial traveler—hung the picture which he had recently cut out of an illustrated magazine and put into a pretty gilt frame. It showed a lady, with a fur cap on and a fur stole, sitting upright and holding out to the spectator a huge fur muff into which the whole of her forearm had vanished!

Gregor's eyes turned next to the window, and the overcast sky—one could hear rain drops beating on the window gutter—made him quite melancholy. What about sleeping a little longer and forgetting all this nonsense, he thought, but it could not be done, for he was accustomed to sleep on his right side and in his present condition he could not turn himself over. However violently he forced himself towards his right side he always rolled on to his back again. He tried it at least a hundred times, shutting his eyes to keep from seeing his struggling legs, and only desisted when he began to feel in his side a faint dull ache he had never experienced before.

Oh God, he thought, what an exhausting job I've picked on! Traveling about day in, day out. It's much more irritating work than doing the actual business in the office, and on top of that there's the trouble of constant traveling, of worrying about train connections, the bed and irregular meals, casual acquaintances that are always new and never become intimate friends. The devil take it all! He felt a slight itching up on his belly; slowly pushed himself on his back nearer to the top of the bed so that he could lift his head more easily; identified the itching place which was surrounded by many small white spots the nature of which he could not understand and made to touch it with a leg, but drew the leg back immediately, for the contact made a cold shiver run through him.

He slid down again into his former position. This getting up early, he thought, makes one quite stupid. A man needs his sleep. Other commercials live like harem women. For instance, when I come back to the hotel of a morning to write up the orders I've got, these others are only sitting down to breakfast. Let me just try that with my chief; I'd be sacked on the spot. Anyhow, that might be quite a good thing for me, who can tell? If I didn't have to hold my hand because of my parents I'd have given notice long ago, I'd have gone to the chief and told him exactly what I think of him. That would knock him endways from his desk! It's a queer way of doing, too, this sitting on high at a desk and talking down to employees, especially when they have to come quite near because the chief is hard of hearing. Well, there's still hope; once I've saved enough money to pay back my parents' debts to him—that should take another five or six years—I'll do it without fail. I'll cut myself completely loose then. For the moment, though, I'd better get up, since my train goes at five.

He looked at the alarm clock ticking on the chest. Heavenly Father! he thought. It was half-past six o'clock and the hands were quietly moving on, it was even past the half-hour, it was getting on toward a quarter to seven. Had the alarm clock not gone off? From the bed one could see that it had been properly set for four o'clock; of course it must have gone off. Yes, but was it possible to sleep quietly through that ear-splitting noise? Well, he had not slept quietly, yet apparently all the more soundly for that. But what was he to do now? The next train went at seven o'clock; to catch that he would need to hurry like mad and his samples weren't even packed up, and he himself wasn't feeling particularly fresh and active. And even if he did catch the train he wouldn't avoid a row with the chief, since the firm's porter would have been waiting for the five o'clock train and would have long since reported his failure to turn up. The porter was a creature of the chief's, spineless and stupid. Well, supposing he were to say he was sick? But that would be most unpleasant and would look suspicious, since during his five years' employment he had not been ill once. The chief himself would be sure to come with the sick-insurance doctor, would reproach his parents with their son's laziness and would cut all excuses short by referring to the insurance doctor, who of course regarded all mankind as perfectly healthy malingerers. And would he be so far wrong on this occasion? Gregor really felt quite well, apart from a drowsiness that was utterly superfluous after such a long sleep, and he was even unusually hungry.

As all this was running through his mind at top speed without his being able to decide to leave his bed—the alarm clock had just struck a quarter to seven—there came a cautious tap at the door behind the head of his bed. "Gregor," said a voice—it was his mother's—"it's a quarter to seven. Hadn't you a train to catch?" That gentle voice! Gregor had a shock as he heard his own voice answering hers, unmistakably his own voice, it was true, but with a persistent horrible twittering squeak behind it like an undertone, that left the words in their clear shape only for the first moment and then rose up reverberating round them to destroy their sense, so that one could not be sure one had heard them rightly. Gregor wanted to answer at length and explain everything, but in the circumstances he confined himself to saying: "Yes, yes, thank you, Mother, I'm getting up now." The wooden door between them must have kept the change in his voice from being noticeable outside, for his mother contented herself with this statement and shuffled away. Yet this brief exchange of words had made the other members of the family aware that Gregor was still in the house, as they had not expected, and at one of the side doors his father was already knocking, gently, yet with his fist. "Gregor, Gregor," he called, "what's the matter with you?" And after a little while he called again in a deeper voice: "Gregor! Gregor!" At the other side door his sister was saying in a low, plaintive tone: "Gregor? Aren't you well? Are you needing anything?" He answered them both at once: "I'm just ready," and did his best to make his voice sound as normal as possible by enunciating the words very clearly and leaving long pauses between them. So his father went back to his breakfast, but his sister whispered: "Gregor, open the door, do." However, he was not thinking of opening the door, and felt thankful for the prudent habit he had acquired in traveling of locking all doors during the night, even at home.

His immediate intention was to get up quietly without being disturbed, to put on his clothes and above all eat his breakfast, and only then to consider what else was to be done, since in bed, he was well aware, his meditations would come to no sensible conclusion. He remembered that often enough in bed he had felt small aches and pains, probably caused by awkward postures, which had proved purely imaginary once he got up, and he looked forward eagerly to seeing this morning's delusions gradually fall away. That the change in his voice was nothing but the precursor of a severe chill, a standing ailment of commercial travelers, he had not the least possible doubt.

To get rid of the quilt was quite easy; he had only to inflate himself a little and it fell off by itself. But the next move was difficult, especially because he was so uncommonly broad. He would have needed arms and hands to hoist himself up; instead he had only the numerous little legs which never stopped waving in all directions and which he could not control in the least. When he tried to bend one of them it was the first to stretch itself straight; and did he succeed at last in making it do what he wanted, all the other legs meanwhile waved the more wildly in a high degree of unpleasant agitation. "But what's the use of lying idle in bed," said Gregor to himself.

He thought that he might get out of bed with the lower part of his body first, but this lower part, which he had not yet seen and of which he could form no clear conception, proved too difficult to move; it shifted so slowly; and when finally, almost wild with annoyance, he gathered his forces together and thrust out recklessly, he had miscalculated the direction and bumped heavily against the lower end of the bed, and the stinging pain he felt informed him that precisely this lower part of his body was at the moment probably the most sensitive.

So he tried to get the top part of himself out first, and cautiously moved his head towards the edge of the bed. That proved easy enough, and despite its breadth and mass the bulk of his body at last slowly followed the movement of his head. Still, when he finally got his head free over the edge of the bed he felt too scared to go on advancing, for after all if he let himself fall in this way it would take a miracle to keep his head from being injured. And at all costs he must not lose consciousness now, precisely now; he would rather stay in bed.

But when after a repetition of the same efforts he lay in his former position again, sighing, and watched his little legs struggling against each other more wildly than ever, if that were possible, and saw no way of bringing any order into this arbitrary confusion, he told himself again that it was impossible to stay in bed and that the most sensible course was to risk everything for the smallest hope of getting away from it. At the same time he did not forget meanwhile to remind himself that cool reflection, the coolest possible, was much better than desperate resolves. In such moments he focused his eyes as sharply as possible on the window, but, unfortunately, the prospect of the morning fog, which muffled even the other side of the narrow street, brought him little encouragement and comfort. "Seven o'clock already," he said to himself when the alarm clock chimed again, "seven o'clock already and still such a thick fog." And for a little while he lay quiet, breathing lightly, as if perhaps expecting such complete repose to restore all things to their real and normal condition.

But then he said to himself: "Before it strikes a quarter past seven I must be quite out of this bed, without fail. Anyhow, by that time someone will have come from the office to ask for me, since it opens before seven." And he set himself to rocking his whole body at once in a regular rhythm, with the idea of swinging it out of the bed. If he tipped himself out in that way he could keep his head from injury by lifting it at an acute angle when he fell. His back seemed to be hard and was not likely to suffer from a fall on the carpet. His biggest worry was the loud crash he would not be able to help making, which would probably cause anxiety, if not terror, behind all the doors. Still, he must take the risk.

When he was already half out of the bed—the new method was more a game than an effort, for he needed only to hitch himself across by rocking to and fro—it struck him how simple it would be if he could get help. Two strong people—he thought of his father and the servant girl—would be amply sufficient; they would only have to thrust their arms under his convex back, lever him out of the bed, bend down with their burden and then be patient enough to let him turn himself right over on the the floor, where it was to be hoped his legs would then find their proper function. Well, ignoring the fact that the doors were all locked, ought he really to call for help? In spite of his misery he could not suppress a smile at the very idea of it.

He had got so far that he could barely keep his equilibrium when he rocked himself strongly, and he would have to nerve himself very soon for the final decision since in five minutes' time it would be a quarter past seven—when the front door bell rang. "That's someone from the office," he said to himself, and grew almost rigid, while his little legs only jigged about all the faster. For a moment everything stayed quiet. "They're not going to open the door," said Gregor to himself, catching at some kind of irrational hope. But then of course the servant girl went as usual to the door with her heavy tread and opened it. Gregor needed only to hear the first good morning of the visitor to know immediately who it was—the chief clerk himself. What a fate, to be condemned to work for a firm where the smallest omission at once gave rise to the gravest suspicion! Were all employees in a body nothing but scoundrels, was there not among them one single loyal devoted man who, had he wasted only an hour or so of the firm's time in a morning, was so tormented by conscience as to be driven out of his mind and actually incapable of leaving his bed? Wouldn't it really have been sufficient to send an apprentice to inquire—if any inquiry were necessary at all—did the chief clerk himself have to come and thus indicate to the entire family, an innocent family, that this suspicious circumstance could be investigated by no one less versed in affairs than himself? And more through the agitation caused by these reflections than through any act of will Gregor swung himself out of bed with all his strength. There was a loud thump, but it was not really a crash. His fall was broken to some extent by the carpet, his back, too, was less stiff than he thought, and so there was merely a dull thud, not so very startling. Only he had not lifted his head carefully enough and had hit it; he turned it and rubbed it on the carpet in pain and irritation.

"That was something falling down in there," said the chief clerk in the next room to the left. Gregor tried to suppose to himself that something like what had happened to him today might some day happen to the chief clerk; one really could not deny that it was possible. But as if in brusque reply to this supposition the chief clerk took a couple of firm steps in the next-door room and his patent leather boots creaked. From the right-hand room his sister was whispering to inform him of the situation: "Gregor, the chief clerk's here." "I know," muttered Gregor to himself; but he didn't dare to make his voice loud enough for his sister to hear it.

"Gregor," said his father now from the left-hand room, "the chief clerk has come and wants to know why you didn't catch the early train. We don't know what to say to him. Besides, he wants to talk to you in person. So open the door, please. He will be good enough to excuse the untidiness of your room." "Good morning, Mr. Samsa," the chief clerk was calling amiably meanwhile. "He's not well," said his mother to the visitor, while his father was still speaking through the door, "he's not well, sir, believe me. What else would make him miss a train! The boy thinks about nothing but his work. It makes me almost cross the way he never goes out in the evenings; he's been here the last eight days and has stayed at home every single evening. He just sits there quietly at the table reading a newspaper or looking through railway timetables. The only amusement he gets is doing fretwork. For instance, he spent two or three evenings cutting out a little picture frame; you would be surprised to see how pretty it is; it's hanging in his room; you'll see it in a minute when Gregor opens the door. I must say I'm glad you've come, sir; we should never have got him to unlock the door by ourselves; he's so obstinate; and I'm sure he's unwell, though he wouldn't have it to be so this morning." "I'm just coming," said Gregor slowly and carefully, not moving an inch for fear of losing one word of the conversation. "I can't think of any other explanation, madam," said the chief clerk, "I hope it's nothing serious. Although on the other hand I must say that we men of business—fortunately or unfortunately—very often simply have to ignore any slight indisposition, since business must be attended to." "Well, can the chief clerk come in now?" asked Gregor's father impatiently, again knocking on the door. "No," said Gregor. In the left-hand room a painful silence followed this refusal, in the right-hand room his sister began to sob.

Why didn't his sister join the others? She was probably newly out of bed and hadn't even begun to put on her clothes yet. Well, why was she crying? Because he wouldn't get up and let the chief clerk in, because he was in danger of losing his job, and because the chief would begin dunning his parents again for the old debts? Surely these were things one didn't need to worry about for the present. Gregor was still at home and not in the least thinking of deserting the family. At the moment, true, he was lying on the carpet and no one who knew the condition he was in could seriously expect him to admit the chief clerk. But for such a small discourtesy, which could plausibly be explained away somehow later on, Gregor could hardly be dismissed on the spot. And it seemed to Gregor that it would be much more sensible to leave him in peace for the present than to trouble him with tears and entreaties. Still, of course, their uncertainty bewildered them all and excused their behavior.

"Mr. Samsa," the chief clerk called now in a louder voice, "what's the matter with you? Here you are, barricading yourself in your room, giving only 'yes' and 'no' for answers, causing your parents a lot of unnecessary trouble and neglecting—I mention this only in passing—neglecting your business duties in an incredible fashion. I am speaking here in the name of your parents and of your chief, and I beg you quite seriously to give me an immediate and precise explanation. You amaze me, you amaze me. I thought you were a quiet, dependable person, and now all at once you seem bent on making a disgraceful exhibition of yourself. The chief did hint to me early this morning a possible explanation for your disappearance—with reference to the cash payments that were entrusted to you recently—but I almost pledged my solemn word of honor that this could not be so. But now that I see how incredibly obstinate you are, I no longer have the slightest desire to take your part at all. And your position in the firm is not so unassailable. I came with the intention of telling you all this in private, but since you are wasting my time so needlessly I don't see why your parents shouldn't hear it too. For some time past your work has been most unsatisfactory; this is not the season of the year for a business boom, of course, we admit that, but a season of the year for doing no business at all, that does not exist, Mr. Samsa, must not exist."

"But, sir," cried Gregor, beside himself and in his agitation forgetting everything else, "I'm just going to open the door this very minute. A slight illness, an attack of giddiness, has kept me from getting up. I'm still lying in bed. But I feel all right again. I'm getting out of bed now. Just give me a moment or two longer! I'm not quite so well as I thought. But I'm all right, really. How a thing like that can suddenly strike one down! Only last night I was quite well, my parents can tell you, or rather I did have a slight presentiment. I must have showed some sign of it. Why didn't I report it at the office! But one always thinks that an indisposition can be got over without staying in the house. Oh sir, do spare my parents! All that you're reproaching me with now has no foundation; no one has ever said a word to me about it. Perhaps you haven't looked at the last orders I sent in. Anyhow, I can still catch the eight o'clock train, I'm much the better for my few hours' rest. Don't let me detain you here, sir; I'll be attending to business very soon, and do be good enough to tell the chief so and to make my excuses to him!"

And while all this was tumbling out pell-mell and Gregor hardly knew what he was saying, he had reached the chest quite easily, perhaps because of the practice he had had in bed, and was now trying to lever himself upright by means of it. He meant actually to open the door, actually to show himself and speak to the chief clerk; he was eager to find out what the others, after all their insistence, would say at the sight of him. If they were horrified then the responsibility was no longer his and he could stay quiet. But if they took it calmly, then he had no reason either to be upset, and could really get to the station for the eight o'clock train if he hurried. At first he slipped down a few times from the polished surface of the chest, but at length with a last heave he stood upright; he paid no more attention to the pains in the lower part of his body, however they smarted. Then he let himself fall against the back of a near-by chair, and clung with his little legs to the edges of it. That brought him into control of himself again and he stopped speaking, for now he could listen to what the chief clerk was saying.

"Did you understand a word of it?" the chief clerk was asking; "surely he can't be trying to make fools of us?" "Oh dear," cried his mother, in tears, "perhaps he's terribly ill and we're tormenting him. Grete! Grete!" she called out then. "Yes Mother?" called his sister from the other side. They were calling to each other across Gregor's room. "You must go this minute for the doctor. Gregor is ill. Go for the doctor, quick. Did you hear how he was speaking?" "That was no human voice," said the chief clerk in a voice noticeably low beside the shrillness of the mother's. "Anna! Anna!" his father was calling through the hall to the kitchen, clapping his hands, "get a locksmith at once!" And the two girls were already running through the hall with a swish of skirts—how could his sister have got dressed so quickly?—and were tearing the front door open. There was no sound of its closing again; they had evidently left it open, as one does in houses where some great misfortune has happened.

But Gregor was now much calmer. The words he uttered were no longer understandable, apparently, although they seemed clear enough to him, even clearer than before, perhaps because his ear had grown accustomed to the sound of them. Yet at any rate people now believed that something was wrong with him, and were ready to help him. The positive certainty with which these first measures had been taken comforted him. He felt himself drawn once more into the human circle and hoped for great and remarkable results from both the doctor and the locksmith, without really distinguishing precisely between them. To make his voice as clear as possible for the decisive conversation that was now imminent he coughed a little, as quietly as he could, of course, since this noise too might not sound like a human cough for all he was able to judge. In the next room meanwhile there was complete silence. Perhaps his parents were sitting at the table with the chief clerk, whispering, perhaps they were all leaning against the door and listening.

Slowly Gregor pushed the chair towards the door, then let go of it, caught hold of the door for support—the soles at the end of his little legs were somewhat sticky—and rested against it for a moment after his efforts. Then he set himself to turning the key in the lock with his mouth. It seemed, unhappily, that he hadn't really any teeth—what could he grip the key with?—but on the other hand his jaws were certainly very strong; with their help he did manage to set the key in motion, heedless of the fact that he was undoubtedly damaging them somewhere, since a brown fluid issued from his mouth, flowed over the key and dripped on the floor. "Just listen to that," said the chief clerk next door; "he's turning the key." That was a great encouragement to Gregor; but they should all have shouted encouragement to him, his father and mother too: "Go on, Gregor," they should have called out, "keep going, hold on to that key!" And in the belief that they were all following his efforts intently, he clenched his jaws recklessly on the key with all the force at his command. As the turning of the key progressed he circled round the lock, holding on now only with his mouth, pushing on the key, as required, or pulling it down again with all the weight of his body. The louder click of the finally yielding lock literally quickened Gregor. With a deep breath of relief he said to himself: "So I didn't need the locksmith," and laid his head on the handle to open the door wide.

Since he had to pull the door towards him, he was still invisible when it was really wide open. He had to edge himself slowly round the near half of the double door, and to do it very carefully if he was not to fall plump upon his back just on the threshold. He was still carrying out this difficult manoeuvre, with no time to observe anything else, when he heard the chief clerk utter a loud "Oh!"—it sounded like a gust of wind—and now he could see the man, standing as he was nearest to the door, clapping one hand before his open mouth and slowly backing away as if driven by some invisible steady pressure. His mother—in spite of the chief clerk's being there her hair was still undone and sticking up in all directions—first clasped her hands and looked at his father, then took two steps towards Gregor and fell on the floor among her outspread skirts, her face quite hidden on her breast. His father knotted his fist with a fierce expression on his face as if he meant to knock Gregor back into his room, then looked uncertainly round the living room, covered his eyes with his hands and wept till his great chest heaved.

Gregor did not go now into the living room, but leaned against the inside of the firmly shut wing of the door, so that only half his body was visible and his head above it bending sideways to look at the others. The light had meanwhile strengthened; on the other side of the street one could see clearly a section of the endlessly long, dark gray building opposite—it was a hospital—abruptly punctuated by its row of regular windows; the rain was still falling, but only in large singly discernible and literally singly splashing drops. The breakfast dishes were set out on the table lavishly, for breakfast was the most important meal of the day to Gregor's father, who lingered it out for hours over various newspapers. Right opposite Gregor on the wall hung a photograph of himself on military service, as a lieutenant, hand on sword, a carefree smile on his face, inviting one to respect his uniform and military bearing. The door leading to the hall was open, and one could see that the front door stood open too, showing the landing beyond and the beginning of the stairs going down.

"Well," said Gregor, knowing perfectly that he was the only one who had retained any composure, "I'll put my clothes on at once, pack up my samples and start off. Will you only let me go? You see, sir, I'm not obstinate, and I'm willing to work; traveling is a hard life, but I couldn't live without it. Where are you going, sir? To the office? Yes? Will you give a true account of all this? One can be temporarily incapacitated, but that's just the moment for remembering former services and bearing in mind that later on, when the incapacity has been got over, one will certainly work with all the more industry and concentration. I'm loyally bound to serve the chief, you know that very well. Besides, I have to provide for my parents and my sister. I'm in great difficulties, but I'll get out of them again. Don't make things any worse for me than they are. Stand up for me in the firm. Travelers are not popular there, I know. People think they earn sacks of money and just have a good time. A prejudice there's no particular reason for revising. But you, sir, have a more comprehensive view of affairs than the rest of the staff, yes, let me tell you in confidence, a more comprehensive view than the chief himself, who, being the owner, lets his judgment easily be swayed against one of his employees. And you know very well that the traveler, who is never seen in the office almost the whole year round, can so easily fall a victim to gossip and ill luck and unfounded complaints, which he mostly knows nothing about, except when he comes back exhausted from his rounds, and only then suffers in person from their evil consequences, which he can no longer trace back to the original causes. Sir, sir, don't go away without a word to me to show that you think me in the right at least to some extent!"

But at Gregor's very first words the chief clerk had already backed away and only stared at him with parted lips over one twitching shoulder. And while Gregor was speaking he did not stand still one moment but stole away towards the door, without taking his eyes off Gregor, yet only an inch at a time, as if obeying some secret injunction to leave the room. He was already at the hall, and the suddenness with which he took his last step out of the living room would have made one believe he had burned the sole of his foot. Once in the hall he stretched his right arm before him towards the staircase, as if some supernatural power were waiting there to deliver him.

Gregor perceived that the chief clerk must on no account be allowed to go away in this frame of mind if his position in the firm were not to be endangered to the utmost. His parents did not understand this so well; they had convinced themselves in the course of years that Gregor was settled for life in this firm, and besides they were so preoccupied with their immediate troubles that all foresight had forsaken them. Yet Gregor had this foresight. The chief clerk must be detained, soothed, persuaded and finally won over; the whole future of Gregor and his family depended on it! If only his sister had been there! She was intelligent; she had begun to cry while Gregor was still lying quietly on his back. And no doubt the chief clerk, so partial to ladies, would have been guided by her; she would have shut the door of the flat and in the hall talked him out of his horror. But she was not there, and Gregor would have to handle the situation himself. And without remembering that he was still unaware what powers of movement he possessed, without even remembering that his words in all possibility, indeed in all likelihood, would again be unintelligible, he let go the wing of the door, pushed himself through the opening, started to walk towards the chief clerk, who was already ridiculously clinging with both hands to the railing on the landing; but immediately, as he was feeling for a support, he fell down with a little cry upon all his numerous legs. Hardly was he down when he experienced for the first time this morning a sense of physical comfort; his legs had firm ground under them; they were completely obedient, as he noted with joy; they even strove to carry him forward in whatever direction he chose; and he was inclined to believe that a final relief from all his sufferings was at hand. But in the same moment as he found himself on the floor, rocking with suppressed eagerness to move, not far from his mother, indeed just in front of her, she, who had seemed so completely crushed, sprang all at once to her feet, her arms and fingers outspread, cried: "Help, for God's sake, help!" bent her head down as if to see Gregor better, yet on the contrary kept backing senselessly away; had quite forgotten that the laden table stood behind her; sat upon it hastily, as if in absence of mind, when she bumped into it; and seemed altogether unaware that the big coffee pot beside her was upset and pouring coffee in a flood over the carpet.

"Mother, Mother," said Gregor in a low voice, and looked up at her. The chief clerk, for the moment, had quite slipped from his mind; instead, he could not resist snapping his jaws together at the sight of the streaming coffee. That made his mother scream again, she fled from the table and fell into the arms of his father, who hastened to catch her. But Gregor had now no time to spare for his parents; the chief clerk was already on the stairs; with his chin on the banisters he was taking one last backward look. Gregor made a spring, to be as sure as possible of overtaking him; the chief clerk must have divined his intention, for he leaped down several steps and vanished; he was still yelling "Ugh!" and it echoed through the whole staircase.

Unfortunately, the flight of the chief clerk seemed completely to upset Gregor's father, who had remained relatively calm until now, for instead of running after the man himself, or at least not hindering Gregor in his pursuit, he seized in his right hand the walking stick which the chief clerk had left behind on a chair, together with a hat and greatcoat, snatched in his left hand a large newspaper from the table and began stamping his feet and flourishing the stick and the newspaper to drive Gregor back into his room. No entreaty of Gregor's availed, indeed no entreaty was even understood, however humbly he bent his head his father only stamped on the floor the more loudly. Behind his father his mother had torn open a window, despite the cold weather, and was leaning far out of it with her face in her hands. A strong draught set in from the street to the staircase, the window curtains blew in, the newspapers on the table fluttered, stray pages whisked over the floor. Pitilessly Gregor's father drove him back, hissing and crying "Shoo!" like a savage. But Gregor was quite unpracticed in walking backwards, it really was a slow business. If he only had a chance to turn round he could get back to his room at once, but he was afraid of exasperating his father by the slowness of such a rotation and at any moment the stick in his father's hand might hit him a fatal blow on the back or on the head. In the end, however, nothing else was left for him to do since to his horror he observed that in moving backwards he could not even control the direction he took; and so, keeping an anxious eye on his father all the time over his shoulder, he began to turn round as quickly as he could, which was in reality very slowly. Perhaps his father noted his good intentions, for he did not interfere except every now and then to help him in the manoeuvre from a distance with the point of the stick. If only he would have stopped making that unbearable hissing noise! It made Gregor quite lose his head. He had turned almost completely round when the hissing noise so distracted him that he even turned a little the wrong way again. But when at last his head was fortunately right in front of the doorway, it appeared that his body was too broad simply to get through the opening. His father, of course, in his present mood was far from thinking of such a thing as opening the other half of the door, to let Gregor have enough space. He had merely the fixed idea of driving Gregor back into his room as quickly as possible. He would never have suffered Gregor to make the circumstantial preparations for standing up on end and perhaps slipping his way through the door. Maybe he was now making more noise than ever to urge Gregor forward, as if no obstacle impeded him; to Gregor, anyhow, the noise in his rear sounded no longer like the voice of one single father; this was really no joke, and Gregor thrust himself —come what might—into the doorway. One side of his body rose up, he was tilted at an angle in the doorway, his flank was quite bruised, horrid blotches stained the white door, soon he was stuck fast and, left to himself, could not have moved at all, his legs on one side fluttered trembling in the air, those on the other were crushed painfully to the floor—when from behind his father gave him a strong push which was literally a deliverance and he flew far into the room, bleeding freely. The door was slammed behind him with the stick, and then at last there was silence.

II

Not until it was twilight did Gregor awake out of a deep sleep, more like a swoon than a sleep. He would certainly have waked up of his own accord not much later, for he felt himself sufficiently rested and well-slept, but it seemed to him as if a fleeting step and a cautious shutting of the door leading into the hall had aroused him. The electric lights in the street cast a pale sheen here and there on the ceiling and the upper surfaces of the furniture, but down below, where he lay, it was dark. Slowly, awkwardly trying out his feelers, which he now first learned to appreciate, he pushed his way to the door to see what had been happening there. His left side felt like one single long, unpleasantly tense scar, and he had actually to limp on his two rows of legs. One little leg, moreover, had been severely damaged in the course of that morning's events—it was almost a miracle that only one had been damaged—and trailed uselessly behind him.

He had reached the door before he discovered what had really drawn him to it: the smell of food. For there stood a basin filled with fresh milk in which floated little sops of white bread. He could almost have laughed with joy, since he was now still hungrier than in the morning, and he dipped his head almost over the eyes straight into the milk. But soon in disappointment he withdrew it again; not only did he find it difficult to feed because of his tender left side—and he could only feed with the palpitating collaboration of his whole body—he did not like the milk either, although milk had been his favorite drink and that was certainly why his sister had set it there for him, indeed it was almost with repulsion that he turned away from the basin and crawled back to the middle of the room.

He could see through the crack of the door that the gas was turned on in the living room, but while usually at this time his father made a habit of reading the afternoon newspaper in a loud voice to his mother and occasionally to his sister as well, not a sound was now to be heard. Well, perhaps his father had recently given up this habit of reading aloud, which his sister had mentioned so often in conversation and in her letters. But there was the same silence all around, although the flat was certainly not empty of occupants. "What a quiet life our family has been leading," said Gregor to himself, and as he sat there motionless staring into the darkness he felt great pride in the fact that he had been able to provide such a life for his parents and sister in such a fine flat. But what if all the quiet, the comfort, the contentment were now to end in horror? To keep himself from being lost in such thoughts Gregor took refuge in movement and crawled up and down the room.

Once during the long evening one of the side doors was opened a little and quickly shut again, later the other side door too; someone had apparently wanted to come in and then thought better of it. Gregor now stationed himself immediately before the living room door, determined to persuade any hesitating visitor to come in or at least to discover who it might be; but the door was not opened again and he waited in vain. In the early morning, when the doors were locked, they had all wanted to come in, now that he had opened one door and the other had apparently been opened during the day, no one came in and even the keys were on the other side of the doors.

It was late at night before the gas went out in the living room, and Gregor could easily tell that his parents and his sister had all stayed awake until then, for he could clearly hear the three of them stealing away on tiptoe. No one was likely to visit him, not until the morning, that was certain; so he had plenty of time to meditate at his leisure on how he was to arrange his life afresh. But the lofty, empty room in which he had to lie flat on the floor filled him with an apprehension he could not account for, since it had been his very own room for the past five years—and with a half-unconscious action, not without a slight feeling of shame, he scuttled under the sofa, where he felt comfortable at once, although his back was a little cramped and he could not lift his head up, and his only regret was that his body was too broad to get the whole of it under the sofa.

He stayed there all night, spending the time partly in a light slumber, from which his hunger kept waking him up with a start, and partly in worrying and sketching vague hopes, which all led to the same conclusion, that he must lie low for the present and, by exercising patience and the utmost consideration, help the family to bear the inconvenience he was bound to cause them in his present condition.

Very early in the morning, it was still almost night, Gregor had the chance to test the strength of his new resolutions, for his sister, nearly fully dressed, opened the door from the hall and peered in. She did not see him at once, yet when she caught sight of him under the sofa—well, he had to be somewhere, he couldn't have flown away, could he?—she was so startled that without being able to help it she slammed the door shut again. But as if regretting her behavior she opened the door again immediately and came in on tiptoe, as if she were visiting an invalid or even a stranger. Gregor had pushed his head forward to the very edge of the sofa and watched her. Would she notice that he had left the milk standing, and not for lack of hunger, and would she bring in some other kind of food more to his taste? If she did not do it of her own accord, he would rather starve than draw her attention to the fact, although he felt a wild impulse to dart out from under the sofa, throw himself at her feet and beg her for something to eat. But his sister at once noticed, with surprise, that the basin was still full, except for a little milk that had been spilt all around it, she lifted it immediately, not with her bare hands, true, but with a cloth and carried it away. Gregor was wildly curious to know what she would bring instead, and made various speculations about it. Yet what she actually did next, in the goodness of her heart, he could never have guessed at. To find out what he liked she brought him a whole selection of food, all set out on an old newspaper. There were old, half-decayed vegetables, bones from last night's supper covered with a white sauce that had thickened; some raisins and almonds; a piece of cheese that Gregor would have called uneatable two days ago; a dry roll of bread, a buttered roll, and a roll both buttered and salted. Besides all that, she set down again the same basin, into which she had poured some water, and which was apparently to be reserved for his exclusive use. And with fine tact, knowing that Gregor would not eat in her presence, she withdrew quickly and even turned the key, to let him understand that he could take his ease as much as he liked. Gregor's legs all whizzed towards the food. His wounds must have healed completely, moreover, for he felt no disability, which amazed him and made him reflect how more than a month ago he had cut one finger a little with a knife and had still suffered pain from the wound only the day before yesterday. Am I less sensitive now? he thought, and sucked greedily at the cheese, which above all the other edibles attracted him at once and strongly. One after another and with tears of satisfaction in his eyes he quickly devoured the cheese, the vegetables and the sauce; the fresh food, on the other hand, had no charms for him, he could not even stand the smell of it and actually dragged away to some little distance the things he could eat. He had long finished his meal and was only lying lazily on the same spot when his sister turned the key slowly as a sign for him to retreat. That roused him at once, although he was nearly asleep, and he hurried under the sofa again. But it took considerable self-control for him to stay under the sofa, even for the short time his sister was in the room, since the large meal had swollen his body somewhat and he was so cramped he could hardly breathe. Slight attacks of breathlessness afflicted him and his eyes were starting a little out of his head as he watched his unsuspecting sister sweeping together with a broom not only the remains of what he had eaten but even the things he had not touched, as if these were now of no use to anyone, and hastily shoveling it all into a bucket, which she covered with a wooden lid and carried away. Hardly had she turned her back when Gregor came from under the sofa and stretched and puffed himself out.

In this manner Gregor was fed, once in the early morning while his parents and the servant girl were still asleep, and a second time after they had all had their midday dinner, for then his parents took a short nap and the servant girl could be sent out on some errand or other by his sister. Not that they would have wanted him to starve, of course, but perhaps they could not have borne to know more about his feeding than from hearsay, perhaps too his sister wanted to spare them such little anxieties wherever possible, since they had quite enough to bear as it was.

Under what pretext the doctor and the locksmith had been got rid of on that first morning Gregor could not discover, for since what he said was not understood by the others it never struck any of them, not even his sister, that he could understand what they said, and so whenever his sister came into his room he had to content himself with hearing her utter only a sigh now and then and an occasional appeal to the saints. Later on, when she had got a little used to the situation—of course she could never get completely used to it—she sometimes threw out a remark which was kindly meant or could be so interpreted. "Well, he liked his dinner today," she would say when Gregor had made a good clearance of his food; and when he had not eaten, which gradually happened more and more often, she would say almost sadly: "Everything's been left standing again."

But although Gregor could get no news directly, he overheard a lot from the neighboring rooms, and as soon as voices were audible, he would run to the door of the room concerned and press his whole body against it. In the first few days especially there was no conversation that did not refer to him somehow, even if only indirectly. For two whole days there were family consultations at every mealtime about what should be done; but also between meals the same subject was discussed, for there were always at least two members of the family at home, since no one wanted to be alone in the flat and to leave it quite empty was unthinkable. And on the very first of these days the household cook—it was not quite clear what and how much she knew of the situation—went down on her knees to his mother and begged leave to go, and when she departed, a quarter of an hour later, gave thanks for her dismissal with tears in her eyes as if for the greatest benefit that could have been conferred on her, and without any prompting swore a solemn oath that she would never say a single word to anyone about what had happened.

Now Gregor's sister had to cook too, helping her mother; true, the cooking did not amount to much, for they ate scarcely anything. Gregor was always hearing one of the family vainly urging another to eat and getting no answer but: "Thanks, I've had all I want," or something similar. Perhaps they drank nothing either. Time and again his sister kept asking his father if he wouldn't like some beer and offered kindly to go and fetch it herself, and when he made no answer suggested that she could ask the concierge to fetch it, so that he need feel no sense of obligation, but then a round "No" came from his father and no more was said about it.

In the course of that very first day Gregor's father explained the family's financial position and prospects to both his mother and his sister. Now and then he rose from the table to get some voucher or memorandum out of the small safe he had rescued from the collapse of his business five years earlier. One could hear him opening the complicated lock and rustling papers out and shutting it again. This statement made by his father was the first cheerful information Gregor had heard since his imprisonment. He had been of the opinion that nothing at all was left over from his father's business, at least his father had never said anything to the contrary, and of course he had not asked him directly. At that time Gregor's sole desire was to do his utmost to help the family to forget as soon as possible the catastrophe which had overwhelmed the business and thrown them all into a state of complete despair. And so he had set to work with unusual ardor and almost overnight had become a commercial traveler instead of a little clerk, with of course much greater chances of earning money, and his success was immediately translated into good round coin which he could lay on the table for his amazed and happy family. These had been fine times, and they had never recurred, at least not with the same sense of glory, although later on Gregor had earned so much money that he was able to meet the expenses of the whole household and did so. They had simply got used to it, both the family and Gregor; the money was gratefully accepted and gladly given, but there was no special uprush of warm feeling. With his sister alone had he remained intimate, and it was a secret plan of his that she, who loved music, unlike himself, and could play movingly on the violin, should be sent next year to study at the Conservatorium, despite the great expense that would entail, which must be made up in some other way. During his brief visits home the Conservatorium was often mentioned in the talks he had with his sister, but always merely as a beautiful dream which could never come true, and his parents discouraged even these innocent references to it; yet Gregor had made up his mind firmly about it and meant to announce the fact with due solemnity on Christmas Day.

Such were the thoughts, completely futile in his present condition, that went through his head as he stood clinging upright to the door and listening. Sometimes out of sheer weariness he had to give up listening and let his head fall negligently against the door, but he always had to pull himself together again at once, for even the slight sound his head made was audible next door and brought all conversation to a stop. "What can he be doing now?" his father would say after a while, obviously turning towards the door, and only then would the interrupted conversation gradually be set going again.

Gregor was now informed as amply as he could wish—for his father tended to repeat himself in his explanations, partly because it was a long time since he had handled such matters and partly because his mother could not always grasp things at once—that a certain amount of investments, a very small amount it was true, had survived the wreck of their fortunes and had even increased a little because the dividends had not been touched meanwhile. And besides that, the money Gregor brought home every month—he had kept only a few dollars for himself—had never been quite used up and now amounted to a small capital sum. Behind the door Gregor nodded his head eagerly, rejoiced at this evidence of unexpected thrift and foresight. True, he could really have paid off some more of his father's debts to the chief with this extra money, and so brought much nearer the day on which he could quit his job, but doubtless it was better the way his father had arranged it.

Yet this capital was by no means sufficient to let the family live on the interest of it; for one year, perhaps, or at the most two, they could live on the principal, that was all. It was simply a sum that ought not to be touched and should be kept for a rainy day; money for living expenses would have to be earned. Now his father was still hale enough but an old man, and he had done no work for the past five years and could not be expected to do much; during these five years, the first years of leisure in his laborious though unsuccessful life, he had grown rather fat and become sluggish. And Gregor's old mother, how was she to earn a living with her asthma, which troubled her even when she walked through the flat and kept her lying on a sofa every other day panting for breath beside an open window? And was his sister to earn her bread, she who was still a child of seventeen and whose life hitherto had been so pleasant, consisting as it did in dressing herself nicely, sleeping long, helping in the housekeeping, going out to a few modest entertainments and above all playing the violin? At first whenever the need for earning money was mentioned Gregor let go his hold on the door and threw himself down on the cool leather sofa beside it, he felt so hot with shame and grief.

Often he just lay there the long nights through without sleeping at all, scrabbling for hours on the leather. Or he nerved himself to the great effort of pushing an armchair to the window, then crawled up over the window sill and, braced against the chair, leaned against the window panes, obviously in some recollection of the sense of freedom that looking out of a window always used to give him. For in reality day by day things that were even a little way off were growing dimmer to his sight; the hospital across the street, which he used to execrate for being all too often before his eyes, was now quite beyond his range of vision, and if he had not known that he lived in Charlotte Street, a quiet street but still a city street, he might have believed that his window gave on a desert waste where gray sky and gray land blended indistinguishably into each other. His quick-witted sister only needed to observe twice that the armchair stood by the window; after that whenever she had tidied the room she always pushed the chair back to the same place at the window and even left the inner casements open.

If he could have spoken to her and thanked her for all she had to do for him, he could have borne her ministrations better; as it was, they oppressed him. She certainly tried to make as light as possible of whatever was disagreeable in her task, and as time went on she succeeded, of course, more and more, but time brought more enlightenment to Gregor too. The very way she came in distressed him. Hardly was she in the room when she rushed to the window, without even taking time to shut the door, careful as she was usually to shield the sight of Gregor's room from the others, and as if she were almost suffocating tore the casements open with hasty fingers, standing then in the open draught for a while even in the bitterest cold and drawing deep breaths. This noisy scurry of hers upset Gregor twice a day; he would crouch trembling under the sofa all the time, knowing quite well that she would certainly have spared him such a disturbance had she found it at all possible to stay in his presence without opening the window.

On one occasion, about a month after Gregor's metamorphosis, when there was surely no reason for her to be still startled at his appearance, she came a little earlier than usual and found him gazing out of the window, quite motionless, and thus well placed to look like a bogey. Gregor would not have been surprised had she not come in at all, for she could not immediately open the window while he was there, but not only did she retreat, she jumped back as if in alarm and banged the door shut; a stranger might well have thought that he had been lying in wait for her there meaning to bite her. Of course he hid himself under the sofa at once, but he had to wait until midday before she came again, and she seemed more ill at ease than usual. This made him realize how repulsive the sight of him still was to her, and that it was bound to go on being repulsive, and what an effort it must cost her not to run away even from the sight of the small portion of his body that stuck out from under the sofa. In order to spare her that, therefore, one day he carried a sheet on his back to the sofa—it cost him four hours' labor—and arranged it there in such a way as to hide him completely, so that even if she were to bend down she could not see him. Had she considered the sheet unnecessary, she would certainly have stripped it off the sofa again, for it was clear enough that this curtaining and confining of himself was not likely to conduce to Gregor's comfort, but she left it where it was, and Gregor even fancied that he caught a thankful glance from her eye when he lifted the sheet carefully a very little with his head to see how she was taking the new arrangement.

For the first fortnight his parents could not bring themselves to the point of entering his room, and he often heard them expressing their appreciation of his sister's activities, whereas formerly they had frequently scolded her for being as they thought a somewhat useless daughter. But now, both of them often waited outside the door, his father and his mother, while his sister tidied his room, and as soon as she came out she had to tell them exactly how things were in the room, what Gregor had eaten, how he had conducted himself this time and whether there was not perhaps some slight improvement in his condition. His mother, moreover, began relatively soon to want to visit him, but his father and sister dissuaded her at first with arguments which Gregor listened to very attentively and altogether approved. Later, however, she had to be held back by main force, and when she cried out: "Do let me in to Gregor, he is my unfortunate son! Can't you understand that I must go to him?" Gregor thought that it might be well to have her come in, not every day, of course, but perhaps once a week; she understood things, after all, much better than his sister, who was only a child despite the efforts she was making and had perhaps taken on so difficult a task merely out of childish thoughtlessness.

Gregor's desire to see his mother was soon fulfilled. During the daytime he did not want to show himself at the window, out of consideration for his parents, but he could not crawl very far around the few square yards of floor space he had, nor could be bear lying quietly at rest all during the night, while he was fast losing any interest he had ever taken in food, so that for mere recreation he had formed the habit of crawling crisscross over the walls and ceiling. He especially enjoyed hanging suspended from the ceiling; it was much better than lying on the floor; one could breathe more freely; one's body swung and rocked lightly; and in the almost blissful absorption induced by this suspension it could happen to his own surprise that he let go and fell plump on the floor. Yet he now had his body much better under control than formerly, and even such a big fall did him no harm. His sister at once remarked the new distraction Gregor had found for himself—he left traces behind him of the sticky stuff on his soles wherever he crawled—and she got the idea in her head of giving him as wide a field as possible to crawl in and of removing the pieces of furniture that hindered him, above all the chest of drawers and the writing desk. But that was more than she could manage all by herself; she did not dare ask her father to help her; and as for the servant girl, a young creature of sixteen who had had the courage to stay on after the cook's departure, she could not be asked to help, for she had begged as an especial favor that she might keep the kitchen door locked and open it only on a definite summons; so there was nothing left but to apply to her mother at an hour when her father was out. And the old lady did come, with exclamations of joyful eagerness, which, however, died away at the door of Gregor's room. Gregor's sister, of course, went in first, to see that everything was in order before letting his mother enter. In great haste Gregor pulled the sheet lower and rucked it more in folds so that it really looked as if it had been thrown accidentally over the sofa. And this time he did not peer out from under it; he renounced the pleasure of seeing his mother on this occasion and was only glad that she had come at all. "Come in, he's out of sight," said his sister, obviously leading her mother in by the hand. Gregor could now hear the two women struggling to shift the heavy old chest from its place, and his sister claiming the greater part of the labor for herself, without listening to the admonitions of her mother who feared she might overstrain herself. It took a long time. After at least a quarter of an hour's tugging his mother objected that the chest had better be left where it was, for in the first place it was too heavy and could never be got out before his father came home, and standing in the middle of the room like that it would only hamper Gregor's movements, while in the second place it was not at all certain that removing the furniture would be doing a service to Gregor. She was inclined to think to the contrary; the sight of the naked walls made her own heart heavy, and why shouldn't Gregor have the same feeling, considering that he had been used to his furniture for so long and might feel forlorn without it. "And doesn't it look," she concluded in a low voice—in fact she had been almost whispering all the time as if to avoid letting Gregor, whose exact whereabouts she did not know, hear even the tones of her voice, for she was convinced that he could not understand her words—"doesn't it look as if we were showing him, by taking away his furniture, that we have given up hope of his ever getting better and are just leaving him coldly to himself? I think it would be best to keep his room exactly as it has always been, so that when he comes back to us he will find everything unchanged and be able all the more easily to forget what has happened in between."

On hearing these words from his mother Gregor realized that the lack of all direct human speech for the past two months together with the monotony of family life must have confused his mind, otherwise he could not account for the fact that he had quite earnestly looked forward to having his room emptied of furnishing. Did he really want his warm room, so comfortably fitted with old family furniture, to be turned into a naked den in which he would certainly be able to crawl unhampered in all directions but at the price of shedding simultaneously all recollection of his human background? He had indeed been so near the brink of forgetfulness that only the voice of his mother, which he had not heard for so long, had drawn him back from it. Nothing should be taken out of his room; everything must stay as it was; he could not dispense with the good influence of the furniture on his state of mind; and even if the furniture did hamper him in his senseless crawling round and round, that was no drawback but a great advantage.

Unfortunately his sister was of the contrary opinion; she had grown accustomed, and not without reason, to consider herself an expert in Gregor's affairs as against her parents, and so her mother's advice was now enough to make her determined on the removal not only of the chest and the writing desk, which had been her first intention, but of all the furniture except the indispensable sofa. This determination was not, of course, merely the outcome of childish recalcitrance and of the self-confidence she had recently developed so unexpectedly and at such cost; she had in fact perceived that Gregor needed a lot of space to crawl about in, while on the other hand he never used the furniture at all, so far as could be seen. Another factor might have been also the enthusiastic temperament of an adolescent girl, which seeks to indulge itself on every opportunity and which now tempted Grete to exaggerate the horror of her brother's circumstances in order that she might do all the more for him. In a room where Gregor lorded it all alone over empty walls no one save herself was likely ever to set foot.

And so she was not to be moved from her resolve by her mother, who seemed moreover to be ill at ease in Gregor's room and therefore unsure of herself, was soon reduced to silence and helped her daughter as best she could to push the chest outside. Now, Gregor could do without the chest, if need be, but the writing desk he must retain. As soon as the two women had got the chest out of his room, groaning as they pushed it, Gregor stuck his head out from under the sofa to see how he might intervene as kindly and cautiously as possible. But as bad luck would have it, his mother was the first to return, leaving Grete clasping the chest in the room next door where she was trying to shift it all by herself, without of course moving it from the spot. His mother however was not accustomed to the sight of him, it might sicken her and so in alarm Gregor backed quickly to the other end of the sofa, yet could not prevent the sheet from swaying a little in front. That was enough to put her on the alert. She paused, stood still for a moment and then went back to Grete.

Although Gregor kept reassuring himself that nothing out of the way was happening, but only a few bits of furniture were being changed round, he soon had to admit that all this trotting to and fro of the two women, their little ejaculations and the scraping of furniture along the floor affected him like a vast disturbance coming from all sides at once, and however much he tucked in his head and legs and cowered to the very floor he was bound to confess that he would not be able to stand it for long. They were clearing his room out; taking away everything he loved; the chest in which he kept his fret saw and other tools was already dragged off; they were now loosening the writing desk which had almost sunk into the floor, the desk at which he had done all his homework when he was at the commercial academy, at the grammar school before that, and, yes, even at the primary school—he had no more time to waste in weighing the good intentions of the two women, whose existence he had by now almost forgotten, for they were so exhausted that they were laboring in silence and nothing could be heard but the heavy scuffling of their feet.

And so he rushed out—the women were just leaning against the writing desk in the next room to give themselves a breather—and four times changed his direction, since he really did not know what to rescue first, then on the wall opposite, which was already otherwise cleared, he was struck by the picture of the lady muffled in so much fur and quickly crawled up to it and pressed himself to the glass, which was a good surface to hold on to and comforted his hot belly

This picture at least, which was entirely hidden beneath him, was going to be removed by nobody. He turned his head towards the door of the living room so as to observe the women when they came back.

They had not allowed themselves much of a rest and were already coming; Grete had twined her arm round her mother and was almost supporting her. "Well, what shall we take now?" said Grete, looking round. Her eyes met Gregor's from the wall. She kept her composure, presumably because of her mother, bent her head down to her mother, to keep her from looking up, and said, although in a fluttering, unpremeditated voice: "Come, hadn't we better go back to the living room for a moment?" Her intentions were clear enough to Gregor, she wanted to bestow her mother in safety and then chase him down from the wall. Well, just let her try it! He clung to his picture and would not give it up. He would rather fly in Grete's face.

But Grete's words had succeeded in disquieting her mother, who took a step to one side, caught sight of the huge brown mass on the flowered wallpaper, and before she was really conscious that what she saw was Gregor screamed in a loud, hoarse voice: "Oh God, oh God!" fell with outspread arms over the sofa as if giving up and did not move. "Gregor!" cried his sister, shaking her fist and glaring at him. This was the first time she had directly addressed him since his metamorphosis. She ran into the next room for some aromatic essence with which to rouse her mother from her fainting fit. Gregor wanted to help too—there was still time to rescue the picture—but he was stuck fast to the glass and had to tear himself loose; he then ran after his sister into the next room as if he could advise her, as he used to do; but then had to stand helplessly behind her; she meanwhile searched among various small bottles and when she turned round started in alarm at the sight of him; one bottle fell on the floor and broke; a splinter of glass cut Gregor's face and some kind of corrosive medicine splashed him; without pausing a moment longer Grete gathered up all the bottles she could carry and ran to her mother with them; she banged the door shut with her foot. Gregor was now cut off from his mother, who was perhaps nearly dying because of him; he dared not open the door for fear of frightening away his sister, who had to stay with her mother; there was nothing he could do but wait; and harassed by self-reproach and worry he began now to crawl to and fro, over everything, walls, furniture and ceiling, and finally in his despair, when the whole room seemed to be reeling round him, fell down on to the middle of the big table.

A little while elapsed, Gregor was still lying there feebly and all around was quiet, perhaps that was a good omen. Then the doorbell rang. The servant girl was of course locked in her kitchen, and Grete would have to open the door. It was his father. "What's been happening?" were his first words; Grete's face must have told him everything. Grete answered in a muffled voice, apparently hiding her head on his breast: "Mother has been fainting, but she's better now. Gregor's broken loose." "Just what I expected," said his father, "just what I've been telling you, but you women would never listen." It was clear to Gregor that his father had taken the worst interpretation of Grete's all too brief statement and was assuming that Gregor had been guilty of some violent act. Therefore Gregor must now try to propitiate his father, since he had neither time nor means for an explanation. And so he fled to the door of his own room and crouched against it, to let his father see as soon as he came in from the hall that his son had the good intention of getting back into his room immediately and that it was not necessary to drive him there, but that if only the door were opened he would disappear at once.

Yet his father was not in the mood to perceive such fine distinctions. "Ah!" he cried as soon as he appeared, in a tone which sounded at once angry and exultant. Gregor drew his head back from the door and lifted it to look at his father. Truly, this was not the father he had imagined to himself; admittedly he had been too absorbed of late in his new recreation of crawling over the ceiling to take the same interest as before in what was happening elsewhere in the flat, and he ought really to be prepared for some changes. And yet, and yet, could that be his father? The man who used to lie wearily sunk in bed whenever Gregor set out on a business journey; who welcomed him back of an evening lying in a long chair in a dressing gown; who could not really rise to his feet but only lifted his arms in greeting, and on the rare occasions when he did go out with his family, on one or two Sundays a year and on high holidays, walked between Gregor and his mother, who were slow walkers anyhow, even more slowly than they did, muffled in his old greatcoat, shuffling laboriously forward with the help of his crook-handled stick which he set down most cautiously at every step and, whenever he wanted to say anything, nearly always came to a full stop and gathered his escort around him? Now he was standing there in fine shape; dressed in a smart blue uniform with gold buttons, such as bank messengers wear; his strong double chin bulged over the stiff high collar of his jacket; from under his bushy eyebrows his black eyes darted fresh and penetrating glances; his onetime tangled white hair had been combed flat on either side of a shining and carefully exact parting. He pitched his cap, which bore a gold monogram, probably the badge of some bank, in a wide sweep across the whole room on to a sofa and with the tail-ends of his jacket thrown back, his hands in his trouser pockets, advanced with a grim visage towards Gregor. Likely enough he did not himself know what he meant to do, at any rate he lifted his feet uncommonly high, and Gregor was dumbfounded at the enormous size of his shoe soles. But Gregor could not risk standing up to him, aware as he had been from the very first day of his new life that his father believed only the severest measures suitable for dealing with him. And so he ran before his father, stopping when he stopped and scuttling forward again when his father made any kind of move. In this way they circled the room several times without anything decisive happening, indeed the whole operation did not even look like a pursuit because it was carried out so slowly. And so Gregor did not leave the floor, for he feared that his father might take as a piece of peculiar wickedness any excursion of his over the walls or the ceiling. All the same, he could not stay this course much longer, for while his father took one step he had to carry out a whole series of movements. He was already beginning to feel breathless, just as in his former life his lungs had not been very dependable. As he was staggering along, trying to concentrate his energy on running, hardly keeping his eyes open; in his dazed state never even thinking of any other escape than simply going forward; and having almost forgotten that the walls were free to him, which in this room were well provided with finely carved pieces of furniture full of knobs and crevices—suddenly something lightly flung landed close behind him and rolled before him. It was an apple; a second apple followed immediately; Gregor came to a stop in alarm; there was no point in running on, for his father was determined to bombard him. He had filled his pockets with fruit from the dish on the sideboard and was now shying apple after apple, without taking particularly good aim for the moment. The small red apples rolled about the floor as if magnetized and cannoned into each other. An apple thrown without much force grazed Gregor's back and glanced off harmlessly. But another following immediately landed right on his back and sank in; Gregor wanted to drag himself forward, as if this startling, incredible pain could be left behind him; but he felt as if nailed to the spot and flattened himself out in a complete derangement of all his senses. With his last conscious look he saw the door of his room being torn open and his mother rushing out ahead of his screaming sister, in her underbodice, for her daughter had loosened her clothing to let her breathe more freely and recover from her swoon, he saw his mother rushing towards his father, leaving one after another behind her on the floor her loosened petticoats, stumbling over her petticoats straight to his father and embracing him, in complete union with him—but here Gregor's sight began to fail—with her hands clasped round his father's neck as she begged for her son's life.

III

The serious injury done to Gregor, which disabled him for more than a month—the apple went on sticking in his body as a visible reminder, since no one ventured to remove it—seemed to have made even his father recollect that Gregor was a member of the family, despite his present unfortunate and repulsive shape, and ought not to be treated as an enemy, that, on the contrary, family duty required the suppression of disgust and the exercise of patience, nothing but patience.

And although his injury had impaired, probably for ever, his powers of movement, and for the time being it took him long, long minutes to creep across his room like an old invalid—there was no question now of crawling up the wall—yet in his own opinion he was sufficiently compensated for this worsening of his condition by the fact that towards evening the living-room door, which he used to watch intently for an hour or two beforeheand, was always thrown open, so that lying in the darkness of his room, invisible to the family, he could see them all at the lamp-lit table and listen to their talk, by general consent as it were, very different from his earlier eavesdropping.

True, their intercourse lacked the lively character of former times, which he had always called to mind with a certain wistfulness in the small hotel bedrooms where he had been wont to throw himself down, tired out, on damp bedding. They were now mostly very silent. Soon after supper his father would fall asleep in his armchair; his mother and sister would admonish each other to be silent; his mother, bending low over the lamp, stitched at fine sewing for an underwear firm; his sister, who had taken a job as a salesgirl, was learning shorthand and French in the evenings on the chance of bettering herself. Sometimes his father woke up, and as if quite unaware that he had been sleeping said to his mother: "What a lot of sewing you're doing today!" and at once fell asleep again, while the two women exchanged a tired smile.

With a kind of mulishness his father persisted in keeping his uniform on even in the house; his dressing gown hung uselessly on its peg and he slept fully dressed where he sat, as if he were ready for service at any moment and even here only at the beck and call of his superior. As a result, his uniform, which was not brand-new to start with, began to look dirty, despite all the loving care of the mother and sister to keep it clean, and Gregor often spent whole evenings gazing at the many greasy spots on the garment, gleaming with gold buttons always in a high state of polish, in which the old man sat sleeping in extreme discomfort and yet quite peacefully.

As soon as the clock struck ten his mother tried to rouse his father with gentle words and to persuade him after that to get into bed, for sitting there he could not have a proper sleep and that was what he needed most, since he had to go on duty at six. But with the mulishness that had obsessed him since he became a bank messenger he always insisted on staying longer at the table, although he regularly fell asleep again and in the end only with the greatest trouble could be got out of his armchair and into his bed. However insistently Gregor's mother and sister kept urging him with gentle reminders, he would go on slowly shaking his head for a quarter of an hour, keeping his eyes shut, and refuse to get to his feet. The mother plucked at his sleeve, whispering endearments in his ear, the sister left her lessons to come to her mother's help, but Gregor's father was not to be caught. He would only sink down deeper in his chair. Not until the two women hoisted him up by the armpits did he open his eyes and look at them both, one after the other, usually with the remark: "This is a life. This is the peace and quiet of my old age." And leaning on the two of them he would heave himself up, with difficulty, as if he were a great burden to himself, suffer them to lead him as far as the door and then wave them off and go on alone, while the mother abandoned her needlework and the sister her pen in order to run after him and help him farther.

Who could find time, in this overworked and tired-out family, to bother about Gregor more than was absolutely needful? The household was reduced more and more; the servant girl was turned off; a gigantic bony charwoman with white hair flying round her head came in morning and evening to do the rough work; everything else was done by Gregor's mother, as well as great piles of sewing. Even various family ornaments, which his mother and sister used to wear with pride at parties and celebrations, had to be sold, as Gregor discovered of an evening from hearing them all discuss the prices obtained. But what they lamented most was the fact that they could not leave the flat which was much too big for their present circumstances, because they could not think of any way to shift Gregor. Yet Gregor saw well enough that consideration for him was not the main difficulty preventing the removal, for they could have easily shifted him in some suitable box with a few air holes in it; what really kept them from moving into another flat was rather their own complete hopelessness and the belief that they had been singled out for a misfortune such as had never happened to any of their relations or acquaintances. They fulfilled to the uttermost all that the world demands of poor people, the father fetched breakfast for the small clerks in the bank, the mother devoted her energy to making underwear for strangers, the sister trotted to and fro behind the counter at the behest of customers, but more than this they had not the strength to do. And the wound in Gregor's back began to nag at him afresh when his mother and sister, after getting his father into bed, came back again, left their work lying, drew close to each other and sat cheek to cheek; when his mother, pointing towards his room, said: "Shut that door now, Grete," and he was left again in darkness, while next door the women mingled their tears or perhaps sat dry-eyed staring at the table.

Gregor hardly slept at all by night or by day. He was often haunted by the idea that next time the door opened he would take the family's affairs in hand again just as he used to do; once more, after this long interval, there appeared in his thoughts the figures of the chief and the chief clerk, the commercial travelers and the apprentices, the porter who was so dull-witted, two or three friends in other firms, a chambermaid in one of the rural hotels, a sweet and fleeting memory, a cashier in a milliner's shop, whom he had wooed earnestly but too slowly—they all appeared, together with strangers or people he had quite forgotten, but instead of helping him and his family they were one and all unapproachable and he was glad when they vanished. At other times he would not be in the mood to bother about his family, he was only filled with rage at the way they were neglecting him, and although he had no clear idea of what he might care to eat he would make plans for getting into the larder to take the food that was after all his due, even if he were not hungry. His sister no longer took thought to bring him what might especially please him, but in the morning and at noon before she went to business hurriedly pushed into his room with her foot any food that was available, and in the evening cleared it out again with one sweep of the broom, heedless of whether it had been merely tasted, or—as most frequently happened—left untouched. The cleaning of his room, which she now did always in the evenings, could not have been more hastily done. Streaks of dirt stretched along the walls, here and there lay balls of dust and filth. At first Gregor used to station himself in some particularly filthy corner when his sister arrived, in order to reproach her with it, so to speak. But he could have sat there for weeks without getting her to make any improvement; she could see the dirt as well as he did, but she had simply made up her mind to leave it alone. And yet, with a touchiness that was new to her, which seemed anyhow to have infected the whole family, she jealously guarded her claim to be the sole caretaker of Gregor's room. His mother once subjected his room to a thorough cleaning, which was achieved only by means of several buckets of water—all this dampness of course upset Gregor too and he lay widespread, sulky and motionless on the sofa—but she was well punished for it. Hardly had his sister noticed the changed aspect of his room that evening than she rushed in high dudgeon into the living room and, despite the imploringly raised hands of her mother, burst into a storm of weeping, while her parents—her father had of course been startled out of his chair—looked on at first in helpless amazement; then they too began to go into action; the father reproached the mother on his right for not having left the cleaning of Gregor's room to his sister; shrieked at the sister on his left that never again was she to be allowed to clean Gregor's room; while the mother tried to pull the father into his bedroom, since he was beyond himself with agitation; the sister, shaken with sobs, then beat upon the table with her small fists; and Gregor hissed loudly with rage because not one of them thought of shutting the door to spare him such a spectacle and so much noise.

Still, even if the sister, exhausted by her daily work, had grown tired of looking after Gregor as she did formerly, there was no need for his mother's intervention or for Gregor's being neglected at all. The charwoman was there. This old widow, whose strong bony frame had enabled her to survive the worst a long life could offer, by no means recoiled from Gregor. Without being in the least curious she had once by chance opened the door of his room and at the sight of Gregor, who, taken by surprise, began to rush to and fro although no one was chasing him, merely stood there with her arms folded. From that time she never failed to open his door a little for a moment, morning and evening, to have a look at him. At first she even used to call him to her, with words which apparently she took to be friendly, such as: "Come along, then, you old dung beetle!" or "Look at the old dung beetle, then!" To such allocutions Gregor made no answer, but stayed motionless where he was, as if the door had never been opened. Instead of being allowed to disturb him so senselessly whenever the whim took her, she should rather have been ordered to clean out his room daily, that charwoman! Once, early in the morning—heavy rain was lashing on the windowpanes, perhaps a sign that spring was on the way—Gregor was so exasperated when she began addressing him again that he ran at her, as if to attack her, although slowly and feebly enough. But the charwoman instead of showing fright merely lifted high a chair that happened to be beside the door, and as she stood there with her mouth wide open it was clear that she meant to shut it only when she brought the chair down on Gregor's back. "So you're not coming any nearer?" she asked, as Gregor turned away again, and quietly put the chair back into the corner.

Gregor was now eating hardly anything. Only when he happened to pass the food laid out for him did he take a bit of something in his mouth as a pastime, kept it there for an hour at a time and usually spat it out again. At first he thought it was chagrin over the state of his room that prevented him from eating, yet he soon got used to the various changes in his room. It had become a habit in the family to push into his room things there was no room for elsewhere, and there were plenty of these now, since one of the rooms had been let to three lodgers. These serious gentlemen—all three of them with full beards, as Gregor once observed through a crack in the door—had a passion for order, not only in their own room but, since they were now members of the household, in all its arrangements, especially in the kitchen. Superfluous, not to say dirty, objects they could not bear. Besides, they had brought with them most of the furnishings they needed. For this reason many things could be dispensed with that it was no use trying to sell but that should not be thrown away either. All of them found their way into Gregor's room. The ash can likewise and the kitchen garbage can. Anything that was not needed for the moment was simply flung into Gregor's room by the charwoman, who did everything in a hurry; fortunately Gregor usually saw only the object, whatever it was, and the hand that held it. Perhaps she intended to take the things away again as time and opportunity offered, or to collect them until she could throw them all out in a heap, but in fact they just lay wherever she happened to throw them, except when Gregor pushed his way through the junk heap and shifted it somewhat, at first out of necessity, because he had not room enough to crawl, but later with increasing enjoyment, although after such excursions, being sad and weary to death, he would lie motionless for hours. And since the lodgers often ate their supper at home in the common living room, the living-room door stayed shut many an evening, yet Gregor reconciled himself quite easily to the shutting of the door, for often enough on evenings when it was opened he had disregarded it entirely and lain in the darkest corner of his room, quite unnoticed by the family. But on one occasion the charwoman left the door open a little and it stayed ajar even when the lodgers came in for supper and the lamp was lit. They set themselves at the top end of the table where formerly Gregor and his father and mother had eaten their meals, unfolded their napkins and took knife and fork in hand. At once his mother appeared in the other doorway with a dish of meat and close behind her his sister with a dish of potatoes piled high. The food steamed with a thick vapor. The lodgers bent over the food set before them as if to scrutinize it before eating, in fact the man in the middle, who seemed to pass for an authority with the other two, cut a piece of meat as it lay on the dish, obviously to discover if it were tender or should be sent back to the kitchen. He showed satisfaction, and Gregor's mother and sister, who had been watching anxiously, breathed freely and began to smile.

The family itself took its meals in the kitchen. None the less, Gregor's father came into the living room before going into the kitchen and with one prolonged bow, cap in hand, made a round of the table. The lodgers all stood up and murmured something in their beards. When they were alone again they ate their food in almost complete silence. It seemed remarkable to Gregor that among the various noises coming from the table he could always distinguish the sound of their masticating teeth, as if this were a sign to Gregor that one needed teeth in order to eat, and that with toothless jaws even of the finest make one could do nothing. "I'm hungry enough," said Gregor sadly to himself, "but not for that kind of food. How these lodgers are stuffing themselves, and here am I dying of starvation!"

On that very evening—during the whole of his time there Gregor could not remember ever having heard the violin—the sound of violin-playing came from the kitchen. The lodgers had already finished their supper, the one in the middle had brought out a newspaper and given the other two a page apiece, and now they were leaning back at ease reading and smoking. When the violin began to play they pricked up their ears, got to their feet, and went on tiptoe to the hall door where they stood huddled together. Their movements must have been heard in the kitchen, for Gregor's father called out: "Is the violin-playing disturbing you, gentlemen? It can be stopped at once." "On the contrary," said the middle lodger, "could not Fräulein Samsa come and play in this room, beside us, where it is much more convenient and comfortable?" "Oh certainly," cried Gregor's father, as if he were the violin-player. The lodgers came back into the living room and waited. Presently Gregor's father arrived with the music stand, his mother carrying the music and his sister with the violin. His sister quietly made everything ready to start playing; his parents, who had never let rooms before and so had an exaggerated idea of the courtesy due to lodgers, did not venture to sit down on their own chairs; his father leaned against the door, the right hand thrust between two buttons of his livery coat, which was formally buttoned up; but his mother was offered a chair by one of the lodgers and, since she left the chair just where he had happened to put it, sat down in a corner to one side.

Gregor's sister began to play; the father and mother, from either side, intently watched the movements of her hands. Gregor, attracted by the playing, ventured to move forward a little until his head was actually inside the living room. He felt hardly any surprise at his growing lack of consideration for the others; there had been a time when he prided himself on being considerate. And yet just on this occasion he had more reason than ever to hide himself, since owing to the amount of dust which lay thick in his room and rose into the air at the slightest movement, he too was covered with dust; fluff and hair and remnants of food trailed with him, caught on his back and along his sides; his indifference to everything was much too great for him to turn on his back and scrape himself clean on the carpet, as once he had done several times a day. And in spite of his condition, no shame deterred him from advancing a little over the spotless floor of the living room.

To be sure, no one was aware of him. The family was entirely absorbed in the violin-playing; the lodgers, however, who first of all had stationed themselves, hands in pockets, much too close behind the music stand so that they could all have read the music, which must have bothered his sister, had soon retreated to the window, half-whispering with downbent heads, and stayed there while his father turned an anxious eye on them. Indeed, they were making it more than obvious that they had been disappointed in their expectation of hearing good or enjoyable violin-playing, that they had had more than enough of the performance and only out of courtesy suffered a continued disturbance of their peace. From the way they all kept blowing the smoke of their cigars high in the air through nose and mouth one could divine their irritation. And yet Gregor's sister was playing so beautifully. Her face leaned sideways, intently and sadly her eyes followed the notes of music. Gregor crawled a little farther forward and lowered his head to the ground so that it might be possible for his eyes to meet hers. Was he an animal, that music had such an effect upon him? He felt as if the way were opening before him to the unknown nourishment he craved. He was determined to push forward till he reached his sister, to pull at her skirt and so let her know that she was to come into his room with her violin, for no one here appreciated her playing as he would appreciate it. He would never let her out of his room, at least, not so long as he lived; his frightful appearance would become, for the first time, useful to him; he would watch all the doors of his room at once and spit at intruders; but his sister should need no constraint, she should stay with him of her own free will; she should sit beside him on the sofa, bend down her ear to him and hear him confide that he had had the firm intention of sending her to the Conservatorium, and that, but for his mishap, last Christmas—surely Christmas was long past?—he would have announced it to everybody without allowing a single objection. After this confession his sister would be so touched that she would burst into tears, and Gregor would then raise himself to her shoulder and kiss her on the neck, which, now that she went to business, she kept free of any ribbon or collar.

"Mr. Samsa!" cried the middle lodger, to Gregor's father, and pointed, without wasting any more words, at Gregor, now working himself slowly forwards. The violin fell silent, the middle lodger first smiled to his friends with a shake of the head and then looked at Gregor again. Instead of driving Gregor out, his father seemed to think it more needful to begin by soothing down the lodgers, although they were not at all agitated and apparently found Gregor more entertaining than the violin-playing. He hurried towards them and spreading out his arms, tried to urge them back into their own room and at the same time to block their view of Gregor. They now began to be really a little angry, one could not tell whether because of the old man's behavior or because it had just dawned on them that all unwittingly they had such a neighbor as Gregor next door. They demanded explanations of his father, they waved their arms like him, tugged uneasily at their beards, and only with reluctance backed towards their room. Meanwhile Gregor's sister, who stood there as if lost when her playing was so abruptly broken off, came to life again, pulled herself together all at once after standing for a while holding violin and bow in nervelessly hanging hands and staring at her music, pushed her violin into the lap of her mother, who was still sitting in her chair fighting asthmatically for breath, and ran into the lodgers' room to which they were now being shepherded by her father rather more quickly than before. One could see the pillows and blankets on the beds flying under her accustomed fingers and being laid in order. Before the lodgers had actually reached their room she had finished making the beds and slipped out.

The old man seemed once more to be so possessed by his mulish self-assertiveness that he was forgetting all the respect he should show to his lodgers. He kept driving them on and driving them on until in the very door of the bedroom the middle lodger stamped his foot loudly on the floor and so brought him to a halt. "I beg to announce," said the lodger, lifting one hand and looking also at Gregor's mother and sister, "that because of the disgusting conditions prevailing in this household and family"—here he spat on the floor with emphatic brevity—"I give you notice on the spot. Naturally I won't pay you a penny for the days I have lived here, on the contrary I shall consider bringing an action for damages against you, based on claims—believe me—that will be easily susceptible of proof." He ceased and stared straight in front of him, as if he expected something. In fact his two friends at once rushed into the breach with these words: "And we too give notice on the spot." On that he seized the door-handle and shut the door with a slam.

Gregor's father, groping with his hands, staggered forward and fell into his chair; it looked as if he were stretching himself there for his ordinary evening nap, but the marked jerkings of his head, which was as if uncontrollable, showed that he was far from asleep. Gregor had simply stayed quietly all the time on the spot where the lodgers had espied him. Disappointment at the failure of his plan, perhaps also the weakness arising from extreme hunger, made it impossible for him to move. He feared, with a fair degree of certainty, that at any moment the general tension would discharge itself in a combined attack upon him, and he lay waiting. He did not react even to the noise made by the violin as it fell off his mother's lap from under her trembling fingers and gave out a resonant note.

"My dear parents," said his sister, slapping her hand on the table by way of introduction, "things can't go on like this. Perhaps you don't realize that, but I do. I won't utter my brother's name in the presence of this creature, and so all I say is: we must try to get rid of it. We've tried to look after it and to put up with it as far as is humanly possible, and I don't think anyone could reproach us in the slightest."

"She is more than right," said Gregor's father to himself. His mother, who was still choking for lack of breath, began to cough hollowly into her hand with a wild look in her eyes.

His sister rushed over to her and held her forehead. His father's thoughts seemed to have lost their vagueness at Grete's words, he sat more upright, fingering his service cap that lay among the plates still lying on the table from the lodgers' supper, and from time to time looked at the still form of Gregor.

"We must try to get rid of it," his sister now said explicitly to her father, since her mother was coughing too much to hear a word, "it will be the death of both of you, I can see that coming. When one has to work as hard as we do, all of us, one can't stand this continual torment at home on top of it. At least I can't stand it any longer." And she burst into such a passion of sobbing that her tears dropped on her mother's face, where she wiped them off mechanically.

"My dear," said the old man sympathetically, and with evident understanding, "but what can we do?"

Gregor's sister merely shrugged her shoulders to indicate the feeling of helplessness that had now overmastered her during her weeping fit, in contrast to her former confidence.

"If he could understand us," said her father, half questioningly; Grete, still sobbing, vehemently waved a hand to show how unthinkable that was.

"If he could understand us," repeated the old man, shutting his eyes to consider his daughter's conviction that understanding was impossible, "then perhaps we might come to some agreement with him. But as it is—"

"He must go," cried Gregor's sister, "that's the only solution, Father. You must just try to get rid of the idea that this is Gregor. The fact that we've believed it for so long is the root of all our trouble. But how can it be Gregor? If this were Gregor, he would have realized long ago that human beings can't live with such a creature, and he'd have gone away on his own accord. Then we wouldn't have any brother, but we'd be able to go on living and keep his memory in honor. As it is, this creature persecutes us, drives away our lodgers, obviously wants the whole apartment to himself and would have us all sleep in the gutter. Just look, Father," she shrieked all at once, "he's at it again!" And in an access of panic that was quite incomprehensible to Gregor she even quitted her mother, literally thrusting the chair from her as if she would rather sacrifice her mother than stay so near to Gregor, and rushed behind her father, who also rose up, being simply upset by her agitation, and half-spread his arms out as if to protect her.

Yet Gregor had not the slightest intention of frightening anyone, far less his sister. He had only begun to turn round in order to crawl back to his room, but it was certainly a startling operation to watch, since because of his disabled condition he could not execute the difficult turning movements except by lifting his head and then bracing it against the floor over and over again. He paused and looked round. His good intentions seemed to have been recognized; the alarm had only been momentary. Now they were all watching him in melancholy silence. His mother lay in her chair, her legs stiffly outstretched and pressed together, her eyes almost closing for sheer weariness; his father and his sister were sitting beside each other, his sister's arm around the old man's neck.

Perhaps I can go on turning round now, thought Gregor, and began his labors again. He could not stop himself from panting with the effort, and had to pause now and then to take breath. Nor did anyone harass him, he was left entirely to himself. When he had completed the turn-round he began at once to crawl straight back. He was amazed at the distance separating him from his room and could not understand how in his weak state he had managed to accomplish the same journey so recently, almost without remarking it. Intent on crawling as fast as possible, he barely noticed that not a single word, not an ejaculation from his family, interfered with his progress. Only when he was already in the doorway did he turn his head round, not completely, for his neck muscles were getting stiff, but enough to see that nothing had changed behind him except that his sister had risen to her feet. His last glance fell on his mother, who was not quite overcome by sleep.

Hardly was he well inside his room when the door was hastily pushed shut, bolted and locked. The sudden noise in his rear startled him so much that his little legs gave beneath him. It was his sister who had shown such haste. She had been standing ready waiting and had made a light spring forward, Gregor had not even heard her coming, and she cried "At last!" to her parents as she turned the key in the lock.

"And what now?" said Gregor to himself, looking round in the darkness. Soon he made the discovery that he was now unable to stir a limb. This did not surprise him, rather it seemed unnatural that he should ever actually have been able to move on these feeble little legs. Otherwise he felt relatively comfortable. True, his whole body was aching, but it seemed that the pain was gradually growing less and would finally pass away. The rotting apple in his back and the inflamed area around it, all covered with soft dust, already hardly troubled him. He thought of his family with tenderness and love. The decision that he must disappear was one that he held to even more strongly than his sister, if that were possible. In this state of vacant and peaceful meditation he remained until the tower clock struck three in the morning. The first broadening of light in the world outside the window entered his consciousness once more. Then his head sank to the floor of its own accord and from his nostrils came the last faint flicker of his breath.

When the charwoman arrived early in the morning—what between her strength and her impatience she slammed all the doors so loudly, never mind how often she had been begged not to do so, that no one in the whole apartment could enjoy any quiet sleep after her arrival—she noticed nothing unusual as she took her customary peep into Gregor's room. She thought he was lying motionless on purpose, pretending to be in the sulks; she credited him with every kind of intelligence. Since she happened to have the long-handled broom in her hand she tried to tickle him up with it from the doorway. When that too produced no reaction she felt provoked and poked at him a little harder, and only when she had pushed him along the floor without meeting any resistance was her attention aroused. It did not take her long to establish the truth of the matter, and her eyes widened, she let out a whistle, yet did not waste much time over it but tore open the door of the Samsas' bedroom and yelled into the darkness at the top of her voice: "Just look at this, it's dead; it's lying here dead and done for!"

Mr. and Mrs. Samsa started up in their double bed and before they realized the nature of the charwoman's announcement had some difficulty in overcoming the shock of it. But then they got out of bed quickly, one on either side, Mr. Samsa throwing a blanket over his shoulders, Mrs. Samsa in nothing but her nightgown; in this array they entered Gregor's room. Meanwhile the door of the living room opened, too, where Grete had been sleeping since the advent of the lodgers; she was completely dressed as if she had not been to bed, which seemed to be confirmed also by the paleness of her face. "Dead?" said Mrs. Samsa, looking questioningly at the charwoman, although she could have investigated for herself, and the fact was obvious enough without investigation. "I should say so," said the charwoman, proving her words by pushing Gregor's corpse a long way to one side with her broomstick. Mrs. Samsa made a movement as if to stop her, but checked it. "Well," said Mr. Samsa, "now thanks be to God." He crossed himself, and the three women followed his example. Grete, whose eyes never left the corpse, said: "Just see how thin he was. It's such a long time since he's eaten anything. The food came out again just as it went in." Indeed, Gregor's body was completely flat and dry, as could only now be seen when it was no longer supported by the legs and nothing prevented one from looking closely at it.

"Come in beside us, Grete, for a little while," said Mrs. Samsa with a tremulous smile, and Grete, not without looking back at the corpse, followed her parents into their bedroom. The charwoman shut the door and opened the window wide. Although it was so early in the morning a certain softness was perceptible in the fresh air. After all, it was already the end of March.

The three lodgers emerged from their room and were surprised to see no breakfast; they had been forgotten. "Where's our breakfast?" said the middle lodger peevishly to the charwoman. But she put her finger to her lips and hastily, without a word, indicated by gestures that they should go into Gregor's room. They did so and stood, their hands in the pockets of their somewhat shabby coats, around Gregor's corpse in the room where it was now fully light.

At that the door of the Samsas' bedroom opened and Mr. Samsa appeared in his uniform, his wife on one arm, his daughter on the other. They all looked a little as if they had been crying; from time to time Grete hid her face on her father's arm.

"Leave my house at once!" said Mr. Samsa, and pointed to the door without disengaging himself from the women. "What do you mean by that?" said the middle lodger, taken somewhat aback, with a feeble smile. The two others put their hands behind them and kept rubbing them together, as if in gleeful expectation of a fine set-to in which they were bound to come off the winners. "I mean just what I say," answered Mr. Samsa, and advanced in a straight line with his two companions towards the lodger. He stood his ground at first quietly, looking at the floor as if his thoughts were taking a new pattern in his head. "Then let us go, by all means," he said, and looked up at Mr. Samsa as if in a sudden access of humility he were expecting some renewed sanction for this decision. Mr. Samsa merely nodded briefly once or twice with meaning eyes. Upon that the lodger really did go with long strides into the hall, his two friends had been listening and had quite stopped rubbing their hands for some moments and now went scuttling after him as if afraid that Mr. Samsa might get into the hall before them and cut them off from their leader. In the hall they all three took their hats from the rack, their sticks from the umbrella stand, bowed in silence and quitted the apartment. With a suspiciousness which proved quite unfounded Mr. Samsa and the two women followed them out to the landing; leaning over the banister they watched the three figures slowly but surely going down the long stairs, vanishing from sight at a certain turn of the staircase on every floor and coming into view again after a moment or so; the more they dwindled, the more the Samsa family's interest in them dwindled, and when a butcher's boy met them and passed them on the stairs coming up proudly with a tray on his head, Mr. Samsa and the two women soon left the landing and as if a burden had been lifted from them went back into their apartment.

They decided to spend this day in resting and going for a stroll; they had not only deserved such a respite from work, but absolutely needed it. And so they sat down at the table and wrote three notes of excuse, Mr. Samsa to his board of management, Mrs. Samsa to her employer and Grete to the head of her firm. While they were writing, the charwoman came in to say that she was going now, since her morning's work was finished. At first they only nodded without looking up, but as she kept hovering there they eyed her irritably. "Well?" said Mr. Samsa. The charwoman stood grinning in the doorway as if she had good news to impart to the family but meant not to say a word unless properly questioned. The small ostrich feather standing upright on her hat, which had annoyed Mr. Samsa ever since she was engaged, was waving gaily in all directions. "Well, what is it then?" asked Mrs. Samsa, who obtained more respect from the charwoman than the others. "Oh," said the charwoman, giggling so amiably that she could not at once continue, "just this, you don't need to bother about how to get rid of the thing next door. It's been seen to already." Mrs. Samsa and Grete bent over their letters again, as if preoccupied; Mr. Samsa, who perceived that she was eager to begin describing it all in detail, stopped her with a decisive hand. But since she was not allowed to tell her story, she remembered the great hurry she was in, being obviously deeply huffed: "Bye, everybody," she said, whirling off violently, and departed with a frightful slamming of doors.

"She'll be given notice tonight," said Mr. Samsa, but neither from his wife nor his daughter did he get any answer, for the charwoman seemed to have shattered again the composure they had barely achieved. They rose, went to the window and stayed there, clasping each other tight. Mr. Samsa turned in his chair to look at them and quietly observed them for a little. Then he called out: "Come along, now, do. Let bygones by bygones. And you might have some consideration for me." The two of them complied at once, hastened to him, caressed him and quickly finished their letters.

Then they all three left the apartment together, which was more than they had done for months, and went by tram into the open country outside the town. The tram, in which they were the only passengers, was filled with warm sunshine. Leaning comfortably back in their seats they canvassed their prospects for the future, and it appeared on closer inspection that these were not at all bad, for the jobs they had got, which so far they had never really discussed with each other, were all three admirable and likely to lead to better things later on. The greatest immediate improvement in their condition would of course arise from moving to another house; they wanted to take a smaller and cheaper but also better situated and more easily run apartment than the one they had, which Gregor had selected. While they were thus conversing, it struck both Mr. and Mrs. Samsa, almost at the same moment, as they became aware of their daughter's increasing vivacity, that in spite of all the sorrow of recent times, which had made her cheeks pale, she had bloomed into a pretty girl with a good figure. They grew quieter and half unconsciously exchanged glances of complete agreement, having come to the conclusion that it would soon be time to find a good husband for her. And it was like a confirmation of their new dreams and excellent intentions that at the end of their journey their daughter sprang to her feet first and stretched her young body.

D. H. LAWRENCE

(1885–1930)

Odor of Chrysanthemums*

I

The small locomotive engine, Number 4, came clanking, stumbling down from Selston with seven full wagons. It appeared round the corner with loud threats of speed, but the colt that it startled from among the gorse,[1] which still flickered indistinctly in the raw afternoon, out-distanced it at a canter. A woman, walking up the railway line to Underwood, drew back into the hedge, held her basket aside, and watched the footplate of the engine advancing. The trucks thumped heavily past, one by one, with slow inevitable movement, as she stood insignificantly trapped between the jolting black wagons and the hedge; then they curved away towards the coppice where the withered oak leaves dropped noiselessly, while the birds, pulling at the scarlet hips beside the track, made off into the dusk that had already crept into the spinney. In the open, the smoke from the engine sank and cleaved to the rough grass. The fields were dreary and forsaken, and in the marshy strip that led to the whimsey, a reedy pit pond, the fowls had already abandoned their run among the alders, to roost in the tarred fowl house. The pit bank[2] loomed up beyond the pond, flames like red sores licking its ashy sides, in the afternoon's stagnant light. Just beyond rose the tapering chimneys and the clumsy black headstocks[3] of Brinsley Colliery. The two wheels were spinning fast up against the sky, and the winding engine rapped out its little spasms. The miners were being turned up.

* The selection from *The Complete Short Stories of D. H. Lawrence*.

1. furze, a prickly shrub with yellow blossoms.

2. bank formed by waste materials extracted from the mine.

3. above-ground structures over mine shafts.

The engine whistled as it came into the wide bay of railway lines beside the colliery, where rows of trucks stood in harbor.

Miners, single, trailing, and in groups, passed like shadows diverging home. At the edge of the ribbed level of sidings squat[4] a low cottage, three steps down from the cinder track. A large bony vine clutched at the house, as if to claw down the tiled roof. Round the bricked yard grew a few wintry primroses. Beyond, the long garden sloped down to a bush-covered b ook course. There were some twiggy apple trees, winter-crack trees, and ragged cabbages. Beside the path hung disheveled pink chrysanthemums, like pink cloths hung on bushes. A woman came stooping out of the felt-covered fowl house, halfway down the garden. She closed and padlocked the door, then drew herself erect, having brushed some bits from her white apron.

She was a tall woman of imperious mien, handsome, with definite black eyebrows. Her smooth black hair was parted exactly. For a few moments she stood steadily watching the miners as they passed along the railway: then she turned towards the brook course. Her face was calm and set, her mouth was closed with disillusionment. After a moment she called:

"John!" There was no answer. She waited, and then said distinctly:

"Where are you?"

"Here!" replied a child's sulky voice from among the bushes. The woman looked piercingly through the dusk.

"Are you at that brook?" she asked sternly.

For answer the child showed himself before the raspberry canes that rose like whips. He was a small, sturdy boy of five. He stood quite still, defiantly.

"Oh!" said the mother, conciliated. "I thought you were down at that wet brook—and you remember what I told you——"

The boy did not move or answer.

"Come, come on in," she said more gently, "it's getting dark. There's your grandfather's engine coming down the line!"

The lad advanced slowly, with resentful, taciturn movement. He was dressed in trousers and waistcoat of cloth that was too thick and hard for the size of the garments. They were evidently cut down from a man's clothes.

As they went slowly towards the house he tore at the ragged wisps of chrysanthemums and dropped the petals in handfuls among the path.

"Don't do that—it does look nasty," said his mother. He refrained, and she, suddenly pitiful, broke off a twig with three or four wan flowers and held them against her face. When mother and son reached the yard her hand hesitated, and instead of laying the flower aside, she pushed it in her apron-band. The mother and son

4. squatted.

stood at the foot of the three steps looking across the bay of lines at the passing home of the miners. The trundle of the small train was imminent. Suddenly the engine loomed past the house and came to a stop opposite the gate.

The engine-driver, a short man with round gray beard, leaned out of the cab high above the woman.

"Have you got a cup of tea?" he said in a cheery, hearty fashion.

It was her father. She went in, saying she would mash. Directly, she returned.

"I didn't come to see you on Sunday," began the little gray-bearded man.

"I didn't expect you," said his daughter.

The engine driver winced; then, reassuming his cheery, airy manner, he said:

"Oh, have you heard then? Well, and what do you think——?"

"I think it is soon enough," she replied.

At her brief censure the little man made an impatient gesture, and said coaxingly, yet with dangerous coldness:

"Well, what's a man to do? It's no sort of life for a man of my years, to sit at my own hearth like a stranger. And if I'm going to marry again it may as well be soon as late—what does it matter to anybody?"

The woman did not reply, but turned and went into the house. The man in the engine-cab stood assertive, till she returned with a cup of tea and a piece of bread and butter on a plate. She went up the steps and stood near the footplate of the hissing engine.

"You needn't 'a' brought me bread an' butter," said her father. "But a cup of tea"—he sipped appreciatively—"it's very nice." He sipped for a moment or two, then: "I hear as Walter's got another bout on," he said.

"When hasn't he?" said the woman bitterly.

"I heerd tell of him in the Lord Nelson braggin' as he was going to spend that b—— afore he went: half a sovereign that was."

"When?" asked the woman.

"A' Sat'day night—I know that's true."

"Very likely," she laughed bitterly. "He gives me twenty-three shillings."

"Aye, it's a nice thing, when a man can do nothing with his money but make a beast of himself!" said the gray whiskered man. The woman turned her head away. Her father swallowed the last of his tea and handed her the cup.

"Aye," he sighed, wiping his mouth. "It's a settler,[5] it is——"

He put his hand on the lever. The little engine strained and groaned, and the train rumbled towards the crossing. The woman again looked across the metals. Darkness was settling over the spaces of the railway and trucks: the miners, in gray somber groups, were

5. grave problem, something hard to bear.

still passing home. The winding engine pulsed hurriedly, with brief pauses. Elizabeth Bates looked at the dreary flow of men, then she went indoors. Her husband did not come.

The kitchen was small and full of firelight; red coals piled glowing up the chimney mouth. All the life of the room seemed in the white, warm hearth and the steel fender reflecting the red fire. The cloth was laid for tea; cups glinted in the shadows. At the back, where the lowest stairs protruded into the room, the boy sat struggling with a knife and a piece of white wood. He was almost hidden in the shadow. It was half-past four. They had but to await the father's coming to begin tea. As the mother watched her son's sullen little struggle with the wood, she saw herself in his silence and pertinacity; she saw the father in her child's indifference to all but himself. She seemed to be occupied by her husband. He had probably gone past his home, slunk past his own door, to drink before he came in, while his dinner spoiled and wasted in waiting. She glanced at the clock, then took the potatoes to strain them in the yard. The garden and fields beyond the brook were closed in uncertain darkness. When she rose with the saucepan, leaving the drain steaming into the night behind her, she saw the yellow lamps were lit along the high road that went up the hill away beyond the space of the railway lines and the field.

Then again she watched the men trooping home, fewer now and fewer.

Indoors the fire was sinking and the room was dark red. The woman put her saucepan on the hob, and set a batter pudding near the mouth of the oven. Then she stood unmoving. Directly, gratefully, came quick young steps to the door. Someone hung on the latch a moment, then a little girl entered and began pulling off her outdoor things, dragging a mass of curls, just ripening from gold to brown, over her eyes with her hat.

Her mother chid[6] her for coming late from school, and said she would have to keep her at home the dark winter days.

"Why, mother, it's hardly a bit dark yet. The lamp's not lighted, and my father's not home."

"No, he isn't. But it's a quarter to five! Did you see anything of him?"

The child became serious. She looked at her mother with large, wistful blue eyes.

"No, mother, I've never seen him. Why? Has he come up an' gone past, to Old Brinsley? He hasn't, mother, 'cos I never saw him."

"He'd watch that," said the mother bitterly, "he'd take care as you didn't see him. But you may depend upon it, he's seated in the Prince o' Wales. He wouldn't be this late."

The girl looked at her mother piteously.

6. chided, scolded.

"Let's have our teas, mother, should we?" said she.

The mother called John to table. She opened the door once more and looked out across the darkness of the lines. All was deserted: she could not hear the winding engines.[7]

"Perhaps," she said to herself, "he's stopped to get some ripping done."

They sat down to tea. John, at the end of the table near the door, was almost lost in the darkness. Their faces were hidden from each other. The girl crouched against the fender slowly moving a thick piece of bread before the fire. The lad, his face a dusky mark on the shadow, sat watching her who was transfigured in the red glow.

"I do think it's beautiful to look in the fire," said the child.

"Do you?" said her mother. "Why?"

"It's so red, and full of little caves—and it feels so nice, and you can fair smell it."

"It'll want mending directly," replied her mother, "and then if your father comes he'll carry on and say there never is a fire when a man comes home sweating from the pit. A public house is always warm enough."

There was silence till the boy said complainingly: "Make haste, our Annie."

"Well, I am doing! I can't make the fire do it no faster, can I?"

"She keeps wafflin'[8] it about so's to make 'er slow," grumbled the boy.

"Don't have such an evil imagination, child," replied the mother.

Soon the room was busy in the darkness with the crisp sound of crunching. The mother ate very little. She drank her tea determinedly, and sat thinking. When she rose her anger was evident in the stern unbending of her head. She looked at the pudding in the fender, and broke out:

"It is a scandalous thing as a man can't even come home to his dinner! If it's crozzled[9] up to a cinder I don't see why I should care. Past his very door he goes to get to a public house, and here I sit with his dinner waiting for him——"

She went out. As she dropped piece after piece of coal on the red fire, the shadows fell on the walls, till the room was almost in total darkness.

"I canna see," grumbled the invisible John. In spite of herself, the mother laughed.

"You know the way to your mouth," she said. She set the dustpan outside the door. When she came again like a shadow on the hearth, the lad repeated, complaining sulkily:

"I canna see."

7. for raising and lowering men and materials.

8. separating, breaking up embers.

9. burnt up.

"Good gracious!" cried the mother irritably, "you're as bad as your father if it's a bit dusk!"

Nevertheless, she took a paper spill[10] from a sheaf on the mantelpiece and proceeded to light the lamp that hung from the ceiling in the middle of the room. As she reached up, her figure displayed itself just rounding with maternity.

"Oh, mother——!" exclaimed the girl.

"What?" said the woman, suspended in the act of putting the lamp glass over the flame. The copper reflector shone handsomely on her, as she stood with uplifted arm, turning to face her daughter.

"You've got a flower in your apron!" said the child, in a little rapture at this unusual event.

"Goodness me!" exclaimed the woman, relieved. "One would think the house was afire." She replaced the glass and waited a moment before turning up the wick. A pale shadow was seen floating vaguely on the floor.

"Let me smell!" said the child, still rapturously, coming forward and putting her face to her mother's waist.

"Go along, silly!" said the mother, turning up the lamp. The light revealed their suspense so that the woman felt it almost unbearable. Annie was still bending at her waist. Irritably, the mother took the flowers out from her apron band.

"Oh, mother—don't take them out!" Annie cried, catching her hand and trying to replace the sprig.

"Such nonsense!" said the mother, turning away. The child put the pale chrysanthemums to her lips, murmuring:

"Don't they smell beautiful!"

Her mother gave a short laugh.

"No," she said, "not to me. It was chrysanthemums when I married him, and chrysanthemums when you were born, and the first time they ever brought him home drunk, he'd got brown chrysanthemums in his buttonhole."

She looked at the children. Their eyes and their parted lips were wondering. The mother sat rocking in silence for some time. Then she looked at the clock.

"Twenty minutes to six!" In a tone of fine bitter carelessness she continued: "Eh, he'll not come now till they bring him. There he'll stick! But he needn't come rolling in here in his pit dirt, for *I* won't wash him. He can lie on the floor——Eh, what a fool I've been, what a fool! And this is what I came here for, to this dirty hole, rats and all, for him to slink past his very door. Twice last week—he's begun now——"

She silenced herself, and rose to clear the table.

While for an hour or more the children played, subduedly intent, fertile of imagination, united in fear of the mother's wrath,

10. long twist of paper.

and in dread of their father's home-coming, Mrs. Bates sat in her rocking chair making a "singlet" of thick cream-colored flannel, which gave a dull wounded sound as she tore off the gray edge. She worked at her sewing with energy, listening to the children, and her anger wearied itself, lay down to rest, opening its eyes from time to time and steadily watching, its ears raised to listen. Sometimes even her anger quailed and shrank, and the mother suspended her sewing, tracing the footsteps that thudded along the sleepers outside; she would lift her head sharply to bid the children "hush," but she recovered herself in time, and the footsteps went past the gate, and the children were not flung out of their play-world.

But at last Annie sighed, and gave in. She glanced at her wagon of slippers, and loathed the game. She turned plaintively to her mother.

"Mother!"—but she was inarticulate.

John crept out like a frog from under the sofa. His mother glanced up.

"Yes," she said, "just look at those shirt-sleeves!"

The boy held them out to survey them, saying nothing. Then somebody called in a hoarse voice away down the line, and suspense bristled in the room, till two people had gone by outside, talking.

"It is time for bed," said the mother.

"My father hasn't come," wailed Annie plaintively. But her mother was primed with courage.

"Never mind. They'll bring him when he does come—like a log." She meant there would be no scene. "And he may sleep on the floor till he wakes himself. I know he'll not go to work tomorrow after this!"

The children had their hands and faces wiped with a flannel. They were very quiet. When they had put on their nightdresses, they said their prayers, the boy mumbling. The mother looked down at them, at the brown silken bush of intertwining curls in the nape of the girl's neck, at the little black head of the lad, and her heart burst with anger at their father, who caused all three such distress. The children hid their faces in her skirts for comfort.

When Mrs. Bates came down, the room was strangely empty, with a tension of expectancy. She took up her sewing and stitched for some time without raising her head. Meantime her anger was tinged with fear.

II

The clock struck eight and she rose suddenly, dropping her sewing on her chair. She went to the stair-foot door, opened it, listening. Then she went out, locking the door behind her.

Something scuffled in the yard, and she started, though she knew it was only the rats with which the place was over-run. The night was very dark. In the great bay of railway lines, bulked with trucks, there was no trace of light, only away back she could see a few yellow lamps at the pit top, and the red smear of the burning pit bank on the night. She hurried along the edge of the track, then, crossing the converging lines, came to the stile by the white gates, whence she emerged on the road. Then the fear which had led her shrank. People were walking up to New Brinsley; she saw the lights in the houses; twenty yards farther on were the broad windows of the Prince of Wales, very warm and bright, and the loud voices of men could be heard distinctly. What a fool she had been to imagine that anything had happened to him! He was merely drinking over there at the Prince of Wales. She faltered. She had never yet been to fetch him, and she never would go. So she continued her walk towards the long straggling line of houses, standing back on the highway. She entered a passage between the dwellings.

"Mr. Rigley?—Yes! Did you want him? No, he's not in at this minute."

The raw-boned woman leaned forward from her dark scullery and peered at the other, upon whom fell a dim light through the blind of the kitchen window.

"Is it Mrs. Bates?" she asked in a tone tinged with respect.

"Yes. I wondered if your Master was at home. Mine hasn't come yet."

" 'Asn't 'e! Oh, Jack's been 'ome an' 'ad 'is dinner an' gone out. 'E's just gone for 'alf an hour afore bedtime. Did you call at the Prince of Wales?"

"No——"

"No, you didn't like——! It's not very nice." The other woman was indulgent. There was an awkward pause. "Jack never said nothink about—about your Master,"[11] she said.

"No!—I expect he's stuck in there!"

Elizabeth Bates said this bitterly, and with recklessness. She knew that the woman across the yard was standing at her door listening, but she did not care. As she turned:

"Stop a minute! I'll just go an' ask Jack if 'e knows anythink," said Mrs. Rigley.

"Oh no—I wouldn't like to put——!"

"Yes, I will, if you'll just step inside an' see as th' childer doesn't come downstairs and set theirselves afire."

Elizabeth Bates, murmuring a remonstrance, stepped inside. The other woman apologized for the state of the room.

The kitchen needed apology. There were little frocks and trousers and childish undergarments on the squab[12] and on the

11. husband. 12. couch.

floor, and a litter of playthings everywhere. On the black American cloth[13] of the table were pieces of bread and cake, crusts, slops,[14] and a teapot with cold tea.

"Eh, ours is just as bad," said Elizabeth Bates, looking at the woman, not at the house. Mrs. Rigley put a shawl over her head and hurried out, saying:

"I shanna be a minute."

The other sat, noting with faint disapproval the general untidiness of the room. Then she fell to counting the shoes of various sizes scattered over the floor. There were twelve. She sighed and said to herself: "No wonder!"—glancing at the litter. There came the scratching of two pairs of feet on the yard, and the Rigleys entered. Elizabeth Bates rose. Rigley was a big man, with very large bones. His head looked particularly bony. Across his temple was a blue scar, caused by a wound got in the pit, a wound in which the coal dust remained blue like tattooing.

" 'Asna 'e come whoam yit?"[15] asked the man, without any form of greeting, but with deference and sympathy. "I couldna say wheer he is—'e's non ower theer!"[16]—he jerked his head to signify the Prince of Wales.

" 'E's 'appen[17] gone up to th' Yew," said Mrs. Rigley.

There was another pause. Rigley had evidently something to get off his mind:

"Ah[18] left 'im finishin' a stint," he began. "Loose-all[19] 'ad bin gone about ten minutes when we com'n away, an' I shouted: 'Are ter[20] comin', Walt?' an' 'e said: 'Go on, Ah shanna be but a'ef a minnit,' so we com'n ter th' bottom, me an' Bowers, thinkin' as 'e wor just behint, an' 'ud come up i' th' next bantle[21]——"

He stood perplexed, as if answering a charge of deserting his mate. Elizabeth Bates, now again certain of disaster, hastened to reassure him:

"I expect 'e's gone up to th' Yew Tree, as you say. It's not the first time. I've fretted myself into a fever before now. He'll come home when they carry him."

"Ay, isn't it too bad!" deplored the other woman.

"I'll just step up to Dick's an' see if 'e *is* theer," offered the man, afraid of appearing alarmed, afraid of taking liberties.

"Oh, I wouldn't think of bothering you that far," said Elizabeth Bates, with emphasis, but he knew she was glad of his offer.

As they stumbled up the entry, Elizabeth Bates heard Rigley's wife run across the yard and open her neighbor's door. At this,

13. oilcloth.
14. undrunk remains of tea, emptied out of the cups into a "slop bowl."
15. "Hasn't he come home yet?"
16. not over there.
17. "He may have."
18. I.
19. end of day's shift.
20. art thou, are you.
21. platform of elevator in mine shaft.

suddenly all the blood in her body seemed to switch away from her heart.

"Mind!" warned Rigley. "Ah've said many a time as Ah'd fill up them ruts in this entry, sumb'dy 'll be breakin' their legs yit."

She recovered herself and walked quickly along with the miner.

"I don't like leaving the children in bed, and nobody in the house," she said.

"No, you dunna!" he replied courteously. They were soon at the gate of the cottage.

"Well, I shanna be many minnits. Dunna you be frettin' now, 'e'll be all right," said the butty.[22]

"Thank you very much, Mr. Rigley," she replied.

"You're welcome!" he stammered, moving away. "I shanna be many minnits."

The house was quiet. Elizabeth Bates took off her hat and shawl, and rolled back the rug. When she had finished, she sat down. It was a few minutes past nine. She was startled by the rapid chuff of the winding engine at the pit, and the sharp whirr of the brakes on the rope as it descended. Again she felt the painful sweep of her blood, and she put her hand to her side, saying aloud: "Good gracious!—it's only the nine o'clock deputy going down," rebuking herself.

She sat still, listening. Half an hour of this, and she was wearied out.

"What am I working myself up like this for?" she said pitiably to herself, "I s'll only be doing myself some damage."

She took out her sewing again.

At a quarter to ten there were footsteps. One person! She watched for the door to open. It was an elderly woman, in a black bonnet and a black woolen shawl—his mother. She was about sixty years old, pale, with blue eyes, and her face all wrinkled and lamentable. She shut the door and turned to her daughter-in-law peevishly.

"Eh, Lizzie, whatever shall we do, whatever shall we do!" she cried.

Elizabeth drew back a little, sharply.

"What is it, mother?" she said.

The elder woman seated herself on the sofa.

"I don't know, child, I can't tell you!"—she shook her head slowly. Elizabeth sat watching her, anxious and vexed.

"I don't know," replied the grandmother, sighing very deeply. "There's no end to my troubles, there isn't. The things I've gone through, I'm sure it's enough——!" She wept without wiping her

22. work companion, buddy.

eyes, the tears running.

"But, mother," interrupted Elizabeth, "what do you mean? What is it?"

The grandmother slowly wiped her eyes. The fountains of her tears were stopped by Elizabeth's directness. She wiped her eyes slowly.

"Poor child! Eh, you poor thing!" she moaned. "I don't know what we're going to do, I don't—and you as you are—it's a thing, it is indeed!"

Elizabeth waited.

"Is he dead?" she asked, and at the words her heart swung violently, though she felt a slight flush of shame at the ultimate extravagance of the question. Her words sufficiently frightened the old lady, almost brought her to herself.

"Don't say so, Elizabeth! We'll hope it's not as bad as that; no, may the Lord spare us that, Elizabeth. Jack Rigley came just as I was sittin' down to a glass afore going to bed, an' 'e said: ' 'Appen[23] you'll go down th' line, Mrs. Bates. Walt's had an accident. 'Appen you'll go an' sit wi' 'er till we can get him home.' I hadn't time to ask him a word afore he was gone. An' I put my bonnet on an' come straight down, Lizzie. I thought to myself: 'Eh, that poor blessed child, if anybody should come an' tell her of a sudden, there's no knowin' what'll 'appen to 'er.' You mustn't let it upset you, Lizzie—or you know what to expect. How long is it, six months—or is it five, Lizzie? Ay!"—the old woman shook her head—"time slips on, it slips on! Ay!"

Elizabeth's thoughts were busy elsewhere. If he was killed—would she be able to manage on the little pension and what she could earn?—she counted up rapidly. If he was hurt—they wouldn't take him to the hospital—how tiresome he would be to nurse!—but perhaps she'd be able to get him away from the drink and his hateful ways. She would—while he was ill. The tears offered to come to her eyes at the picture. But what sentimental luxury was this she was beginning? She turned to consider the children. At any rate she was absolutely necessary for them. They were her business.

"Ay!" repeated the old woman, "it seems but a week or two since he brought me his first wages. Ay—he was a good lad, Elizabeth, he was, in his way. I don't know why he got to be such a trouble, I don't. He was a happy lad at home, only full of spirits. But there's no mistake he's been a handful of trouble, he has! I hope the Lord'll spare him to mend his ways. I hope so, I hope so. You've had a sight o' trouble with him, Elizabeth, you have indeed. But he was a jolly enough lad wi' me, he was, I can assure you. I

23. maybe.

don't know how it is. . . ."

The old woman continued to muse aloud, a monotonous irritating sound, while Elizabeth thought concentratedly, startled once, when she heard the winding engine chuff quickly, and the brakes skirr with a shriek. Then she heard the engine more slowly, and the brakes made no sound. The old woman did not notice. Elizabeth waited in suspense. The mother-in-law talked, with lapses into silence.

"But he wasn't your son, Lizzie, an' it makes a difference. Whatever he was, I remember him when he was little, an' I learned to understand him and to make allowances. You've got to make allowances for them——"

It was half-past ten, and the old woman was saying: "But it's trouble from beginning to end; you're never too old for trouble, never too old for that——" when the gate banged back, and there were heavy feet on the steps.

"I'll go, Lizzie, let me go," cried the old woman, rising. But Elizabeth was at the door. It was a man in pit clothes.

"They're bringin' 'im, Missis," he said. Elizabeth's heart halted a moment. Then it surged on again, almost suffocating her.

"Is he—is it bad?" she asked.

The man turned away, looking at the darkness:

"The doctor says 'e'd been dead hours. 'E saw 'im i' th' lamp-cabin."

The old woman, who stood just behind Elizabeth, dropped into a chair, and folded her hands, crying: "Oh, my boy, my boy!"

"Hush!" said Elizabeth, with a sharp twitch of a frown. "Be still, mother, don't waken th' children: I wouldn't have them down for anything!"

The old woman moaned softly, rocking herself. The man was drawing away. Elizabeth took a step forward.

"How was it?" she asked.

"Well, I couldn't say for sure," the man replied, very ill at ease. " 'E wor finishin' a stint an' th' butties 'ad gone, an' a lot o' stuff come down atop 'n 'im."

"And crushed him?" cried the widow, with a shudder.

"No," said the man, "it fell at th' back of 'im. 'E wor under th' face[24] an' it niver touched 'im. It shut 'im in. It seems 'e wor smothered."

Elizabeth shrank back. She heard the old woman behind her cry:

"What?—what did 'e say it was?"

The man replied, more loudly: " 'E wor smothered!"

Then the old woman wailed aloud, and this relieved Elizabeth.

24. coal face.

"Oh, mother," she said, putting her hand on the old woman, "don't waken th' children, don't waken th' children."

She wept a little, unknowing, while the old mother rocked herself and moaned. Elizabeth remembered that they were bringing him home, and she must be ready. "They'll lay him in the parlor," she said to herself, standing a moment pale and perplexed.

Then she lighted a candle and went into the tiny room. The air was cold and damp, but she could not make a fire, there was no fireplace. She set down the candle and looked round. The candlelight glittered on the luster-glasses, on the two vases that held some of the pink chrysanthemums, and on the dark mahogany. There was a cold, deathly smell of chrysanthemums in the room. Elizabeth stood looking at the flowers. She turned away, and calculated whether there would be room to lay him on the floor, between the couch and the chiffonier.[25] She pushed the chairs aside. There would be room to lay him down and to step round him. Then she fetched the old red tablecloth, and another old cloth, spreading them down to save her bit of carpet. She shivered on leaving the parlor; so, from the dresser drawer she took a clean shirt and put it at the fire to air. All the time her mother-in-law was rocking herself in the chair and moaning.

"You'll have to move from there, mother," said Elizabeth. "They'll be bringing him in. Come in the rocker."

The old mother rose mechanically, and seated herself by the fire, continuing to lament. Elizabeth went into the pantry for another candle, and there, in the little penthouse under the naked tiles, she heard them coming. She stood still in the pantry doorway, listening. She heard them pass the end of the house, and come awkwardly down the three steps, a jumble of shuffling footsteps and muttering voices. The old woman was silent. The men were in the yard.

Then Elizabeth heard Matthews, the manager of the pit, say: "You go in first, Jim. Mind!"

The door came open, and the two women saw a collier backing into the room, holding one end of a stretcher, on which they could see the nailed pit boots of the dead man. The two carriers halted, the man at the head stooping to the lintel of the door.

"Wheer will you have him?" asked the manager, a short, white-bearded man.

Elizabeth roused herself and came from the pantry carrying the unlighted candle.

"In the parlor," she said.

"In there, Jim!" pointed the manager, and the carriers backed

25. high chest of drawers, buffet.

round into the tiny room. The coat with which they had covered the body fell off as they awkwardly turned through the two doorways, and the women saw their man, naked to the waist, lying stripped for work. The old woman began to moan in a low voice of horror.

"Lay th' stretcher at th' side," snapped the manager, "an' put 'im on th' cloths. Mind now, mind! Look you now——!"

One of the men had knocked off a vase of chrysanthemums. He stared awkwardly, then they set down the stretcher. Elizabeth did not look at her husband. As soon as she could get in the room, she went and picked up the broken vase and the flowers.

"Wait a minute!" she said.

The three men waited in silence while she mopped up the water with a duster.

"Eh, what a job, what a job, to be sure!" the manager was saying, rubbing his brow with trouble and perplexity. "Never knew such a thing in my life, never! He'd no business to ha' been left. I never knew such a thing in my life! Fell over him clean as a whistle, an' shut him in. Not four foot of space, there wasn't—yet it scarce bruised him."

He looked down at the dead man, lying prone, half naked, all grimed with coal dust.

"''Sphyxiated', the doctor said. It *is* the most terrible job I've ever known. Seems as if it was done o' purpose. Clean over him, an' shut 'im in, like a mouse-trap"—he made a sharp, descending gesture with his hand.

The colliers standing by jerked aside their heads in hopeless comment.

The horror of the thing bristled upon them all.

Then they heard the girl's voice upstairs calling shrilly: "Mother, mother—who is it? Mother, who is it?"

Elizabeth hurried to the foot of the stairs and opened the door: "Go to sleep!" she commanded sharply. "What are you shouting about? Go to sleep at once—there's nothing——"

Then she began to mount the stairs. They could hear her on the boards, and on the plaster floor of the little bedroom. They could hear her distinctly:

"What's the matter now?—what's the matter with you, silly thing?"—her voice was much agitated, with an unreal gentleness.

"I thought it was some men come," said the plaintive voice of the child. "Has he come?"

"Yes, they've brought him. There's nothing to make a fuss about. Go to sleep now, like a good child."

They could hear her voice in the bedroom, they waited whilst she covered the children under the bedclothes.

"Is he drunk?" asked the girl, timidly, faintly.

"No! No—he's not! He—he's asleep."

"Is he asleep downstairs?"

"Yes—and don't make a noise."

There was silence for a moment, then the men heard the frightened child again:

"What's that noise?"

"It's nothing, I tell you, what are you bothering for?"

The noise was the grandmother moaning. She was oblivious of everything, sitting on her chair rocking and moaning. The manager put his hand on her arm and bade her "Sh—sh! !"

The old woman opened her eyes and looked at him. She was shocked by this interruption, and seemed to wonder.

"What time is it?" the plaintive thin voice of the child, sinking back unhappily into sleep, asked this last question.

"Ten o'clock," answered the mother more softly. Then she must have bent down and kissed the children.

Matthews beckoned to the men to come away. They put on their caps and took up the stretcher. Stepping over the body, they tiptoed out of the house. None of them spoke till they were far from the wakeful children.

When Elizabeth came down she found her mother alone on the parlor floor, leaning over the dead man, the tears dropping on him.

"We must lay him out," the wife said. She put on the kettle, then returning knelt at the feet, and began to unfasten the knotted leather laces. The room was clammy and dim with only one candle, so that she had to bend her face almost to the floor. At last she got off the heavy boots and put them away.

"You must help me now," she whispered to the old woman. Together they stripped the man.

When they arose, saw him lying in the naïve dignity of death, the woman stood arrested in fear and respect. For a few moments they remained still, looking down, the old mother whimpering. Elizabeth felt countermanded.[26] She saw him, how utterly inviolable he lay in himself. She had nothing to do with him. She could not accept it. Stooping, she laid her hand on him, in claim. He was still warm, for the mine was hot where he had died. His mother had his face between her hands, and was murmuring incoherently. The old tears fell in succession as drops from wet leaves; the mother was not weeping, merely her tears flowed. Elizabeth embraced the body of her husband, with cheek and lips. She seemed to be listening, inquiring, trying to get some connection. But she could not. She was driven away. He was impregnable.

She rose, went into the kitchen, where she poured warm

26. dismissed, rendered useless.

water into a bowl, brought soap and flannel and a soft towel. "I must wash him," she said.

Then the old mother rose stiffly, and watched Elizabeth as she carefully washed his face, carefully brushing his big blond moustache from his mouth with the flannel. She was afraid with a bottomless fear, so she ministered to him. The old woman, jealous, said:

"Let me wipe him!"—and she kneeled on the other side drying slowly as Elizabeth washed, her big black bonnet sometimes brushing the dark head of her daughter-in-law. They worked thus in silence for a long time. They never forgot it was death, and the touch of the man's dead body gave them strange emotions, different in each of the women; a great dread possessed them both, the mother felt the lie was given to her womb, she was denied; the wife felt the utter isolation of the human soul, the child within her was a weight apart from her.

At last it was finished. He was a man of handsome body, and his face showed no traces of drink. He was blond, full fleshed, with fine limbs. But he was dead.

"Bless him," whispered his mother, looking always at his face, and speaking out of sheer terror. "Dear lad—bless him!" She spoke in a faint, sibilant ecstasy of fear and mother love.

Elizabeth sank down again to the floor, and put her face against his neck, and trembled and shuddered. But she had to draw away again. He was dead, and her living flesh had no place against his. A great dread and weariness held her: she was so unavailing. Her life was gone like this.

"White as milk he is, clear as a twelve-month baby, bless him, the darling!" the old mother murmured to herself. "Not a mark on him, clear and clean and white, beautiful as ever a child was made," she murmured with pride. Elizabeth kept her face hidden.

"He went peaceful, Lizzie—peaceful as sleep. Isn't he beautiful, the lamb? Ay—he must ha' made his peace, Lizzie. 'Appen he made it all right, Lizzie, shut in there. He'd have time. He wouldn't look like this if he hadn't made his peace. The lamb, the dear lamb. Eh, but he had a hearty laugh. I loved to hear it. He had the heartiest laugh, Lizzie, as a lad——"

Elizabeth looked up. The man's mouth was fallen back, slightly open under the cover of the moustache. The eyes, half shut, did not show glazed in the obscurity. Life with its smoky burning gone from him, had left him apart and utterly alien to her. And she knew what a stranger he was to her. In her womb was ice of fear, because of this separate stranger with whom she had been living as one flesh. Was this what it all meant—utter, intact separateness, obscured by heat of living? In dread she turned her face away. The fact was too deadly. There had been nothing between them, and yet they had come together, exchanging their nakedness repeatedly. Each time he had taken her, they had been two isolated beings, far apart as now. He was no more responsible than she. The child was like ice in her womb. For as she looked at the dead man, her mind, cold and detached, said clearly: "Who am I? What have I been doing? I have been fighting a husband who did not exist. *He* existed all the time. What wrong have I done? What was that I have been living with? There lies the reality, this man." And her soul died in her for fear: she knew she had never seen him, he had never seen her, they had met in the dark and had fought in the dark, not knowing whom they met or whom they fought. And now she saw, and turned silent in seeing. For she had been wrong. She had said he was something he was not; she had felt familiar with him. Whereas he was apart all the while, living as she never lived, feeling as she never felt.

In fear and shame she looked at his naked body, that she had known falsely. And he was the father of her children. Her soul was torn from her body and stood apart. She looked at his naked body and was ashamed, as if she had denied it. After all, it was itself. It seemed awful to her. She looked at his face, and she turned her own face to the wall. For his look was other than hers, his way was not her way. She had denied him what he was—she saw it now. She had refused him as himself. And this had been her life, and his life. She was grateful to death, which restored the truth. And she knew she was not dead.

And all the while her heart was bursting with grief and pity for him. What had he suffered? What stretch of horror for this helpless man! She was rigid with agony. She had not been able to help him. He had been cruelly injured, this naked man, this other being, and she could make no reparation. There were the children—but the children belonged to life. This dead man had nothing to do with them. He and she were only channels through which life had flowed to issue in the children. She was a mother—but how awful she knew it now to have been a wife. And he, dead now, how awful he must have felt it to be a husband. She felt that in the next world he would be a stranger to her. If they met there, in the beyond, they would only be ashamed of what had been before. The children had come, for some mysterious reason, out of both of them. But the children did not unite them. Now he was dead, she knew how eternally he was apart from her, how eternally he had nothing more to do with her. She saw this episode of her life closed. They had denied each other in life. Now he had withdrawn. An anguish came over her. It was finished then: it had become hopeless between them long before he died. Yet he had been her husband. But how little!

"Have you got his shirt, 'Lizabeth?"

Elizabeth turned without answering, though she strove to weep and behave as her mother-in-law expected. But she could not, she was silenced. She went into the kitchen and returned with the garment.

"It is aired," she said, grasping the cotton shirt here and there to try. She was almost ashamed to handle him; what right had she or anyone to lay hands on him; but her touch was humble on his body. It was hard work to clothe him. He was so heavy and inert. A terrible dread gripped her all the while: that he could be so heavy and utterly inert, unresponsive, apart. The horror of the distance between them was almost too much for her—it was so infinite a gap she must look across.

At last it was finished. They covered him with a sheet and left him lying, with his face bound. And she fastened the door of the little parlor, lest the children should see what was lying there. Then, with peace sunk heavy on her heart, she went about making tidy the kitchen. She knew she submitted to life, which was her immediate master. But from death, her ultimate master, she winced with fear and shame.

T. S. ELIOT

(1888–1965)

The Love Song of J. Alfred Prufrock*

S'io credesse che mia risposta fosse
A persona che mai tornasse al mondo,
Questa fiamma staria senza piu scosse.
Ma perciocche giammai di questo fondo
Non torno vivo alcun, s'i'odo il vero,
Senza tema d'infamia ti rispondo.†

Let us go then, you and I,
When the evening is spread out against the sky
Like a patient etherized upon a table;
Let us go, through certain half-deserted streets,
The muttering retreats 5
Of restless nights in one-night cheap hotels
And sawdust restaurants with oyster shells:

* Selection from *Collected Poems 1909–1962* by T. S. Eliot, copyright, 1936, by Harcourt Brace Jovanovich, Inc.; copyright © 1963, 1964 by T. S. Eliot. Reprinted by permission of the publishers.

† *ti rispondo:* Dante, *Inferno,* 27. 61–66. Speaking from within a flickering flame is the spirit of Guido da Montefeltro: "If I thought my answer were given to anyone who would ever return to the world, this flame would stand still without moving any further. But since never from this abyss has anyone ever returned alive, if what I hear is true without fear of infamy I answer thee."

Streets that follow like a tedious argument
Of insidious intent
To lead you to an overwhelming question . . . 10
Oh, do not ask, "What is it?"
Let us go and make our visit.

In the room the women come and go
Talking of Michelangelo.

The yellow fog that rubs its back upon the windowpanes, 15
The yellow smoke that rubs its muzzle on the windowpanes
Licked its tongue into the corners of the evening,
Lingered upon the pools that stand in drains,
Let fall upon its back the soot that falls from chimneys,
Slipped by the terrace, made a sudden leap, 20
And seeing that it was a soft October night,
Curled once about the house, and fell asleep.

And indeed there will be time
For the yellow smoke that slides along the street,
Rubbing its back upon the windowpanes; 25
There will be time, there will be time
To prepare a face to meet the faces that you meet;
There will be time to murder and create,
And time for all the works and days of hands
That lift and drop a question on your plate; 30
Time for you and time for me,
And time yet for a hundred indecisions,
And for a hundred visions and revisions,
Before the taking of a toast and tea.

In the room the women come and go 35
Talking of Michelangelo.

And indeed there will be time
To wonder, "Do I dare?" and, "Do I dare?"
Time to turn back and descend the stair,
With a bald spot in the middle of my hair— 40
(They will say: "How his hair is growing thin!")
My morning coat, my collar mounting firmly to the chin,
My necktie rich and modest, but asserted by a simple pin—
(They will say: "But how his arms and legs are thin!")
Do I dare 45
Disturb the universe?
In a minute there is time
For decisions and revisions which a minute will reverse.

For I have known them all already, known them all—
Have known the evenings, mornings, afternoons, 50

29. *works and days:* This may allude, by way of contrast, to the genuine labors described in the *Works and Days* of Hesiod, the Greek writer who in the eighth century B.C. wrote this didactic poem on country life.

I have measured out my life with coffee spoons;
I know the voices dying with a dying fall
Beneath the music from a farther room.
  So how should I presume?

And I have known the eyes already, known them all— 55
The eyes that fix you in a formulated phrase,
And when I am formulated, sprawling on a pin,
When I am pinned and wriggling on the wall,
Then how should I begin
To spit out all the butt-ends of my days and ways? 60
  And how should I presume?

And I have known the arms already, known them all—
Arms that are braceleted and white and bare
(But in the lamplight, downed with light brown hair!)
Is it perfume from a dress 65
That makes me so digress?
Arms that lie along a table, or wrap about a shawl.
  And should I then presume?
  And how should I begin?

. . . . .

Shall I say, I have gone at dusk through narrow streets 70
And watched the smoke that rises from the pipes
Of lonely men in shirt-sleeves, leaning out of windows? . . .

I should have been a pair of ragged claws
Scuttling across the floors of silent seas.

. . . . .

And the afternoon, the evening, sleeps so peacefully! 75
Smoothed by long fingers,
Asleep . . . tired . . . or it malingers,
Stretched on the floor, here beside you and me.
Should I, after tea and cakes and ices,
Have the strength to force the moment to its crisis? 80
But though I have wept and fasted, wept and prayed,
Though I have seen my head (grown slightly bald) brought in upon
  a platter,
I am no prophet—and here's no great matter;
I have seen the moment of my greatness flicker,
And I have seen the eternal Footman hold my coat, and snicker, 85
And in short, I was afraid.

And would it have been worth it, after all,
After the cups, the marmalade, the tea,

52. *dying fall:* reminiscent of Orsino's speech in Shakespeare's *Twelfth Night* (I.i.4).
82. *upon a platter:* See Matthew 14: 1–12, which relates how Salome asked for and obtained the head of John the Baptist on a platter.

Among the porcelain, among some talk of you and me,
Would it have been worth while, 90
To have bitten off the matter with a smile,
To have squeezed the universe into a ball
To roll it toward some overwhelming question,
To say: "I am Lazarus, come from the dead,
Come back to tell you all, I shall tell you all"— 95
If one, settling a pillow by her head,
Should say: "That is not what I meant at all.
That is not it, at all."

And would it have been worth it, after all,
Would it have been worth while, 100
After the sunsets and the dooryards and the sprinkled streets,
After the novels, after the teacups, after the skirts that trail along the floor—
And this, and so much more?—
It is impossible to say just what I mean!
But as if a magic lantern threw the nerves in patterns on a screen: 105
Would it have been worth while
If one, settling a pillow or throwing off a shawl,
And turning toward the window, should say:
"That is not it at all,
That is not what I meant, at all." 110

. . . . .

No! I am not Prince Hamlet, nor was meant to be;
Am an attendant lord, one that will do
To swell a progress, start a scene or two,
Advise the prince; no doubt, an easy tool,
Deferential, glad to be of use, 115
Politic, cautious, and meticulous;
Full of high sentence, but a bit obtuse;
At times, indeed, almost ridiculous—
Almost, at times, the Fool.

I grow old . . . I grow old . . . 120
I shall wear the bottoms of my trousers rolled.

Shall I part my hair behind? Do I dare to eat a peach?
I shall wear white flannel trousers, and walk upon the beach.
I have heard the mermaids singing, each to each.

I do not think that they will sing to me. 125

94. *Lazarus:* The account of the resurrection of Lazarus is given in John 11:1–44.
113. *a progress:* term used in the Elizabethan period to denote the official journey of a monarch or great personage.
117. *high sentence:* sententiously expressed opinions.

I have seen them riding seaward on the waves
Combing the white hair of the waves blown back
When the wind blows the water white and black.

We have lingered in the chambers of the sea
By sea-girls wreathed with seaweed red and brown 130
Till human voices wake us, and we drown.

The Waste Land*

"Nam Sibyllam quidem Cumis ego ipse oculis meis vidi in ampulla pendere, et cum illi pueri dicerent: Σίβυλλα τί θέλεις; respondebat illa: ἀποθανεῖν θέλω."†

FOR EZRA POUND‡

il miglior fabbro

I. The Burial of the Dead§

April is the cruelest month, breeding
Lilacs out of the dead land, mixing
Memory and desire, stirring
Dull roots with spring rain.
Winter kept us warm, covering 5
Earth in forgetful snow, feeding
A little life with dried tubers.
Summer surprised us, coming over the Starnbergersee
With a shower of rain; we stopped in the colonnade,
And went on in sunlight, into the Hofgarten, 10
And drank coffee, and talked for an hour.
Bin gar keine Russin, stamm' aus Litauen, echt deutsch.
And when we were children, staying at the archduke's,
My cousin's, he took me out on a sled,
And I was frightened. He said, Marie, 15
Marie, hold on tight. And down we went.
In the mountains, there you feel free.
I read, much of the night, and go south in the winter.

* Selection from *Collected Poems 1909–1962* by T. S. Eliot, copyright, 1936, by Harcourt Brace Jovanovich, Inc.; copyright © 1963, 1964 by T. S. Eliot. Reprinted by permission of the publishers.

† From Petronius's *Satyricon*, written in the first century A.D. "For once with my own eyes I saw the Cumaean Sybil hanging in a cage, and when the boys said to her, 'What do you want?' she answered, 'I want to die.' " Virgil, in the *Aeneid*, gave Aeneas this prophetess as a guide through Hades. Other prophets mentioned in the poem are Madame Sosostris and Tiresias.

‡ The manuscript of *The Waste Land*, with remarks made and excisions suggested by Pound, has now been published. See Eliot, Chief Writings, p. 1403. *fabbro:* Dante, *Purgatory,* 26. 117, described as "the best craftsman" the Provençal poet Arnaut Daniel.

§ The title comes from the Anglican burial service.

1. *cruelest month:* Because, instead of a genuine renewal of life, there is only the onset of another dreary round of chatter and meaningless get-togethers for society people, like the countess cited in lines 8 ff.

8. *Starnbergersee:* lake near Munich. This passage is suggested by *My Past,* the memoirs of Countess Marie Larisch.

10. *Hofgarten:* public garden in Munich.

12. *echt deutsch:*. "There's nothing Russian about me, I'm from Lithuania, and German through and through." Many Germans had settled in Lithuania and deemed themselves the superiors of Slavs.

What are the roots that clutch, what branches grow
Out of this stony rubbish? Son of man,
You cannot say, or guess, for you know only 20
A heap of broken images, where the sun beats,
And the dead tree gives no shelter, the cricket no relief,
And the dry stone no sound of water. Only
There is shadow under this red rock,
(Come in under the shadow of this red rock), 25
And I will show you something different from either
Your shadow at morning striding behind you
Or your shadow at evening rising to meet you;
I will show you fear in a handful of dust.
Frisch weht der Wind 30
Der Heimat zu
Mein Irisch Kind,
Wo weilest du?
"You gave me hyacinths first a year ago;
They called me the hyacinth girl." 35
—Yet when we came back, late, from the Hyacinth garden,
Your arms full, and your hair wet, I could not
Speak, and my eyes failed, I was neither
Living nor dead, and I knew nothing,
Looking into the heart of light, the silence. 40
Oed' und leer das Meer.

Madame Sosostris, famous clairvoyante,
Had a bad cold, nevertheless
Is known to be the wisest woman in Europe,
With a wicked pack of cards. Here, said she, 45
Is your card, the drowned Phoenician Sailor,

20. *Son of man:* "Cf. Ezekiel II, i" [Eliot's note]. There God addresses Ezekiel: "Son of man, stand upon thy feet, and I will speak unto thee." The whole passage paints a desolate picture of old age.

23. *no relief:* "Cf. Ecclesiastes XII, v" [Eliot's note]. There "the Preacher" paints a scene of desolation and decay.

34. *weilest du:* "V. *Tristan und Isolde,* I, verses 5–8" [Eliot's note]. In Wagner's opera the sailor sings, "Cool blows the wind toward the homeland, Where are you lingering, my Irish sweetheart?"

42. *das Meer:* "Id. III, verse 24" [Eliot's note]. In the third act of the opera Tristan lies dying, and awaits the arrival of Isolde from Cornwall. The watcher can only report, "Waste and empty is the sea."

43. *Sosostris:* This invented name is vaguely Egyptian in sound, and harmonizes with the rest of this scene of dreary charlatanism.

46. *pack of cards:* the Tarot deck of cards. Eliot writes, in his note,

> I am not familiar with the exact constitution of the Tarot pack of cards, from which I have obviously departed to suit my own convenience. The Hanged Man, a member of the traditional pack, fits my purpose in two ways: because he is associated in my mind with the Hanged God of Frazer, and because I associate him with the hooded figure in the passage of the disciples to Emmaus in Part V. The Phoenician Sailor and the Merchant appear later; also the 'crowds of people,' and Death by Water is executed in Part IV. The Man with Three Staves (an authentic member of the Tarot pack) I associate, quite arbitrarily, with the Fisher King himself.

The Tarot deck, still used for purposes of divination, has as its four suits cup, lance, sword and dish, which in the Grail legend are symbols of life.

47. *Phoenician Sailor:* He is related to or identical with Mr. Eugenides (Part III) and Phlebas the Phoenician (Part IV).

(Those are pearls that were his eyes. Look!)
Here is Belladonna, the Lady of the Rocks,
The lady of situations.
Here is the man with three staves, and here the Wheel, 50
And here is the one-eyed merchant, and this card,
Which is blank, is something he carries on his back,
Which I am forbidden to see. I do not find
The Hanged Man. Fear death by water.
I see crowds of people, walking round in a ring. 55
Thank you. If you see dear Mrs. Equitone,
Tell her I bring the horoscope myself:
One must be so careful these days.

Unreal City, 60
Under the brown fog of a winter dawn,
A crowd flowed over London Bridge, so many,
I had not thought death had undone so many.
Sighs, short and infrequent, were exhaled,
And each man fixed his eyes before his feet. 65
Flowed up the hill and down King William Street,
To where Saint Mary Woolnoth kept the hours
With a dead sound on the final stroke of nine.
There I saw one I knew, and stopped him, crying: "Stetson!
You who were with me in the ships at Mylae! 70
That corpse you planted last year in your garden,
Has it begun to sprout? Will it bloom this year?
Or has the sudden frost disturbed its bed?
Oh keep the Dog far hence, that's friend to men,

48. *that were his eyes:* from Ariel's song in Shakespeare's *The Tempest,* act I, sc. ii, ll. 398. Since the passage is concerned with a drowning, it ties in with the other references to death by drowning. Water as a purifier, and immersion symbolizing, as in baptism, a return to the living depths, are also hinted at here—though everything is garbled and reduced to incoherence by the fortune teller.

49. *Belladonna:* Italian for "beautiful lady," also the deadly nightshade, used for eyeshadow. The "Lady of the Rocks" is a painting of the Virgin Mary by Leonardo da Vinci. Here again Eliot evokes the ambiguity, the conflicting meanings, that haunt the same symbol: the rock as barrenness, or that rock on which Christ founded his Church—the Virgin Mary, mediatrix between God and man, or the meretriciousness of a painted seductress.

51. *three staves:* See note to line 46. The "Wheel" is Fortune's Wheel.

55. *Hanged man:* in the Tarot deck, a symbol of death and resurrection.

60. *Unreal City:* "Cf. Baudelaire: 'Fourmillante cité, cité pleine de rêves,/ Où le spectre en plein jour raccroche le passant" [Eliot's note]. "Swarming city, city filled with dreams, where in broad daylight the specter accosts the passerby."

63. *so many:* "Cf. *Inferno* III, 55–57 . . ." [Eliot's note]. On arriving in Hell, Dante sees "So long a train of people; I never should have believed Death had undone so many." Eliot associates the nonentities that make up the crowd with those Dante saw outside the portals of hell: "the wretched souls of those who lived without disgrace and without praise."

64. *exhaled:* "Cf. *Inferno* IV, 25–27" [Eliot's note]. Dante is referring to the virtuous pagans, who occupy the first circle of Hell: "Here, so far as I could tell by listening, there was no lamentation except sighs, which caused the eternal air to tremble."

68. *stroke of nine:* "A phenomenon which I have often noticed" [Eliot's note]. Saint Mary Woolnoth is a church in the City (the financial district of London) where King William Street is also located.

70. *Mylae:* naval battle in the Punic War (260 B.C.). The sameness of the killing in the remote and in the recent past is underlined by the association of a modern name with this remote event.

Or with his nails he'll dig it up again! 75
You! hypocrite lecteur!—mon semblable—mon frère!"

II. A Game of Chess*

The Chair she sat in, like a burnished throne,
Glowed on the marble, where the glass
Held up by standards wrought with fruited vines
From which a golden Cupidon peeped out 80
(Another hid his eyes behind his wing)
Doubled the flames of sevenbranched candelabra
Reflecting light upon the table as
The glitter of her jewels rose to meet it,
From satin cases poured in rich profusion; 85
In vials of ivory and colored glass
Unstoppered, lurked her strange synthetic perfumes,
Unguent, powdered, or liquid—troubled, confused
And drowned the sense in odors; stirred by the air
That freshened from the window, these ascended 90
In fattening the prolonged candle flames,
Flung their smoke into the laquearia,
Stirring the pattern on the coffered ceiling.
Huge sea-wood fed with copper
Burned green and orange, framed by the colored stone, 95
In which sad light a carvéd dolphin swam.
Above the antique mantel was displayed
As though a window gave upon the sylvan scene
The change of Philomel, by the barbarous king
So rudely forced; yet there the nightingale 100
Filled all the desert with inviolable voice
And still she cried, and still the world pursues,

75. *up again:* "Cf. the Dirge in Webster's *The White Devil*" [Eliot's note], act V, sc. iv. The lines are: "But keep the wolf far thence, that's foe to men,/ For with his nails he'll dig them up again." The substitution of dog for wolf may have the aim of stressing the suburban banality to which everything, terror and the promise of resurrection alike (the sprouting corpse) have been reduced.

76. "V. Baudelaire, Preface to *Fleurs du Mal*" [Eliot's note]. The line means, "Hypocritical reader, my fellow and my brother!" The poem asserts that reader and poet alike are sunk in contemptible vices, of which the worst is ennui or boredom. Eliot adopts the same shock tactics, since a "conviction of sin" is the first step on the path of repentance.

* *A Game of Chess:* The title recalls two plays by Thomas Middleton (1570–1627), *A Game at Chesse* and *Women Beware Women.* In the latter a seduction scene is paralleled move by move by a chess game.

77. *burnished throne:* "Cf. *Antony and Cleopatra,* II, ii, l. 190" [Eliot's note]. Enobarbus's description of Cleopatra begins, "The barge she sat in, like a burnish'd throne,/Burn'd on the water." Once again there is a diminution of the glories of the past in the tawdry present.

92. *laquearia:* "Laquearia. V. *Aeneid,* I, 726 . . ." [Eliot's note]. The word denotes a "paneled ceiling," and occurs in a passage that means, "Blazing torches hang from the gold-paneled ceiling, and torches conquer the night with flames." Dido, Queen of Carthage (which is mentioned later in the poem as a site for unhallowed loves), is entertaining Aeneas at a banquet.

98. *sylvan scene:* "Sylvan scene. V. Milton, *Paradise Lost,* IV, 140" [Eliot's note]. This phrase occurs in the description of Eden, as first it is seen by Satan.

99. *Philomel:* "V. Ovid, Metamorphoses, VI, Philomela" [Eliot's note]. The gods turned Philomela into a nightingale. She had been raped, and her tongue cut out, by her brother-in-law King Tereus.

100. *nightingale:* "Cf. Part III, l. 204" [Eliot's note].

"Jug Jug" to dirty ears.
And other withered stumps of time
Were told upon the walls; staring forms 105
Leaned out, leaning, hushing the room enclosed.
Footsteps shuffled on the stair.
Under the firelight, under the brush, her hair
Spread out in fiery points
Glowed into words, then would be savagely still. 110

"My nerves are bad tonight. Yes, bad. Stay with me.
Speak to me. Why do you never speak. Speak.
What are you thinking of? What thinking? What?
I never know what you are thinking. Think."

I think we are in rats' alley 115
Where the dead men lost their bones.

"What is that noise?"
The wind under the door.
"What is that noise now? What is the wind doing?"
Nothing again nothing. 120
"Do
You know nothing? Do you see nothing? Do you remember
Nothing?"

I remember
Those are pearls that were his eyes. 125
"Are you alive, or not? Is there nothing in your head?"
But
O O O O that Shakespeherian Rag—
It's so elegant
So intelligent 130
"What shall I do now? What shall I do?"
"I shall rush out as I am, and walk the street
With my hair down, so. What shall we do tomorrow?
What shall we ever do?"

The hot water at ten. 135
And if it rains, a closed car at four.
And we shall play a game of chess,
Pressing lidless eyes and waiting for a knock upon the door.

When Lil's husband got demobbed, I said—
I didn't mince my words, I said to her myself, 140
HURRY UP PLEASE ITS TIME
Now Albert's coming back, make yourself a bit smart.

103. *"Jug Jug":* conventional representation of nightingale's song in Elizabethan verse.

115. *rats' alley:* "Cf. Part III, l. 195" [Eliot's note].

118. *under the door:* "Cf. Webster: 'Is the wind in that door still?' " [Eliot's note]. This occurs in John Webster's play *The Devil's Law Case* (1623), act III, sc. ii.

125. *his eyes:* "Cf. Part I, ll. 37, 48" [Eliot's note].

137. *chess:* "Cf. the game of chess in Middleton's *Women Beware Women*" [Eliot's note].

139. *demobbed*: demobilized (British slang of the period).

141. *TIME:* British bartender's announcement that the legal closing time has arrived.

He'll want to know what you done with that money he gave you
To get yourself some teeth. He did, I was there.
You have them all out, Lil, and get a nice set, 145
He said, I swear, I can't bear to look at you.
And no more can't I, I said, and think of poor Albert,
He's been in the army four years, he wants a good time,
And if you don't give it him, there's others will, I said.
Oh is there, she said. Something o' that, I said. 150
Then I'll know who to thank, she said, and give me a straight look.
HURRY UP PLEASE ITS TIME
If you don't like it you can get on with it, I said.
Others can pick and choose if you can't.
But if Albert makes off, it won't be for lack of telling. 155
You ought to be ashamed, I said, to look so antique.
(And her only thirty-one.)
I can't help it, she said, pulling a long face,
It's them pills I took, to bring it off, she said.
(She's had five already, and nearly died of young George.) 160
The chemist said it would be all right, but I've never been the same.
You *are* a proper fool, I said.
Well, if Albert won't leave you alone, there it is, I said,
What you get married for if you don't want children?
HURRY UP PLEASE ITS TIME 165
Well, that Sunday Albert was home, they had a hot gammon,
And they asked me in to dinner, to get the beauty of it hot—
HURRY UP PLEASE ITS TIME
HURRY UP PLEASE ITS TIME
Goonight Bill. Goonight Lou. Goonight May. Goonight. 170
Ta ta. Goonight. Goonight.
Good night, ladies, good night, sweet ladies, good night, good night.

*III. The Fire Sermon**

The river's tent is broken: the last fingers of leaf
Clutch and sink into the wet bank. The wind
Crosses the brown land, unheard. The nymphs are departed. 175
Sweet Thames, run softly, till I end my song.
The river bears no empty bottles, sandwich papers,
Silk handkerchiefs, cardboard boxes, cigarette ends
Or other testimony of summer nights. The nymphs are departed.
And their friends, the loitering heirs of city directors; 180
Departed, have left no addresses.
By the waters of Leman I sat down and wept . . .

161. *chemist:* druggist.

166. *gammon:* bacon or ham.

172. *good night:* Cf. *Hamlet*, act IV, sc. v. Spoken by Ophelia at the end of the madness scene.

* *Fire Sermon:* Buddha's sermon dealing with the fires of the passions. See note by Eliot to line 308 below.

176. *song:* "V. Spenser, *Prothalamion*" [Eliot's note]. Spenser's marriage song also has a Thames setting.

182. *Leman:* another name for Lake Geneva. Also, the Old English word *leman* meant a mistress. *and wept:* See first verse of 137th Psalm: "By the rivers of Babylon, there we sat down, yea, we wept, when we remembered Zion." Thus the nobility of the Psalm is reduced to evoking the tawdry conclusion of trivial erotic relationships.

Sweet Thames, run softly till I end my song,
Sweet Thames, run softly, for I speak not loud or long.
But at my back in a cold blast I hear 185
The rattle of the bones, and chuckle spread from ear to ear.
A rat crept softly through the vegetation
Dragging its slimy belly on the bank
While I was fishing in the dull canal
On a winter evening round behind the gashouse 190
Musing upon the king my brother's wreck
And on the king my father's death before him.
White bodies naked on the low damp ground
And bones cast in a little low dry garret,
Rattled by the rat's foot only, year to year. 195
But at my back from time to time I hear
The sound of horns and motors, which shall bring
Sweeney to Mrs. Porter in the spring.
O the moon shone bright on Mrs. Porter
And on her daughter 200
They wash their feet in soda water
Et O ces voix d'enfants, chantant dans la coupole!

Twit twit twit
Jug jug jug jug jug jug
So rudely forc'd. 205
Tereu

Unreal City
Under the brown fog of a winter noon
Mr. Eugenides, the Smyrna merchant
Unshaven, with a pocket full of currants 210
C.i.f. London: documents at sight,
Asked me in demotic French
To luncheon at the Cannon Street Hotel
Followed by a weekend at the Metropole.

185. *I hear:* Andrew Marvell, in *To His Coy Mistress*, wrote: "But ever at my back I hear/Time's wingéd chariot, hurrying near." The ominous, too, has been trivialized.

191. *brother's wreck:* "Cf. *The Tempest,* I, ii" [Eliot's note].

196. *I hear:* "Cf. Marvell, *To His Coy Mistress*" [Eliot's note].

197. *sound of horns:* "Cf. Day, *Parliament of Bees:* When of the sudden,. listening, you shall hear,/A noise of horns and hunting, which shall bring/Actaeon to Diana in the spring,/Where all shall see her naked skin . . ." [Eliot's note.] For having looked on the goddess Diana naked, Actaeon was transformed into a stag, hunted, and killed. Sweeney need fear no such fate.

199. *Mrs. Porter:* "I do not know the origin of the ballad from which these lines are taken: it was reported to me from Sydney, Australia" [Eliot's note]. There are other, less printable version of the ballad.

202. *coupole:* "V. Verlaine, *Parsifal*" [Eliot's note]. The line means: "And oh, those children's voices, singing from the cupola." Verlaine's Parsifal resists all temptation, while the Parsifal of Wagner's opera has his feet washed before he dare set eyes on the Holy Grail.

206. *Tereu:* regularly used by Elizabethan poets to represent nightingale's song; also a form of the name Tereus (see note to line 99).

211. *documents at sight:* "The currants were quoted at a price 'carriage and insurance free to London'; and the Bill of Lading etc. were to be handed to the buyer upon payment of the sight draft" [Eliot's note].

212. *demotic:* vulgar, popular.

213. *Cannon Street Hotel:* commercial hotel popular with foreign businessmen at the time this poem was written.

214. *Metropole:* probably the hotel at Brighton, on the south coast of England.

At the violet hour, when the eyes and back 215
Turn upward from the desk, when the human engine waits
Like a taxi throbbing waiting,
I Tiresias, though blind, throbbing between two lives,
Old man with wrinkled female breasts, can see
At the violet hour, the evening hour that strives 220
Homeward, and brings the sailor home from sea,
The typist home at teatime, clears her breakfast, lights
Her stove, and lays out food in tins.
Out of the window perilously spread
Her drying combinations touched by the sun's last rays. 225
On the divan are piled (at night her bed)
Stockings, slippers, camisoles, and stays.
I Tiresias, old man with wrinkled dugs
Perceived the scene, and foretold the rest—
I too awaited the expected guest. 230
He, the young man carbuncular, arrives,
A small house agent's clerk, with one bold stare,
One of the low on whom assurance sits
As a silk hat on a Bradford millionaire.
The time is now propitious, as he guesses, 235
The meal is ended, she is bored and tired,
Endeavors to engage her in caresses
Which still are unreproved, if undesired.
Flushed and decided, he assaults at once;
Exploring hands encounter no defense; 240
His vanity requires no response,
And makes a welcome of indifference.
(And I Tiresias have foresuffered all
Enacted on this same divan or bed;
I who have sat by Thebes below the wall 245
And walked among the lowest of the dead.)
Bestows one final patronizing kiss,
And gropes his way, finding the stairs unlit . . .

She turns and looks a moment in the glass,
Hardly aware of her departed lover; 250
Her brain allows one half-formed thought to pass;
"Well now that's done: and I'm glad it's over."

218. *Tiresias:* "Tiresias, although a mere spectator and not indeed a 'character,' is yet the most important personage in the poem, uniting all the rest. Just as the one-eyed merchant, seller of currants, melts into the Phoenician Sailor, and the latter is not wholly distinct from Ferdinand Prince of Naples [The Tempest], so all the women are one woman, and the two sexes meet in Tiresias. The whole passage from Ovid is of great anthropological interest" [Eliot's note]. Eliot then quotes Ovid's *Metamorphoses* 3: 320–38, which relates how Tiresias spent seven years of his life transformed into a woman.

221. *from sea:* "This may not appear as exact as Sappho's lines, but I had in mind the 'longshore' or 'dory' fisherman, who returns at nightfall" [Eliot's note]. One fragment of a poem by Sappho is addressed to the Evening Star, "which summons back all that the light Dawn scattered." The line also echoes Robert Louis Stevenson's "Requiem": "Home is the sailor, home from the sea."

234. *Bradford:* woolen manufacturing town in Yorkshire; profited greatly during World War I.

246. *the dead:* Tiresias prophesied in Thebes for many years, dying only when the city was destroyed. He continued to prophesy in Hades.

When lovely woman stoops to folly and
Paces about her room again, alone,
She smoothes her hair with automatic hand, 255
And puts a record on the gramophone.

"This music crept by me upon the waters"
And along the Strand, up Queen Victoria Street.
O City city, I can sometimes hear
Beside a public bar in Lower Thames Street, 260
The pleasant whining of a mandolin
And a clatter and a chatter from within
Where fishmen lounge at noon: where the walls
Of Magnus Martyr hold
Inexplicable splendor of Ionian white and gold 265

The river sweats
Oil and tar
The barges drift
With the turning tide
Red sails 270
Wide
To leeward, swing on the heavy spar.
The barges wash
Drifting logs
Down Greenwich reach 275
Past the Isle of Dogs.
Weialala leia
Wallala leialala

Elizabeth and Leicester
Beating oars 280
The stern was formed
A gilded shell
Red and gold

256. *gramophone:* "V. Goldsmith, the song in *The Vicar of Wakefield*" [Eliot's note], chap. 24. The text is,

When lovely woman stoops to folly
And finds too late that men betray
What charm can soothe her melancholy,
What art can wash her guilt away?
The only art her guilt to cover,
To hide her shame from every eye,
To give repentance to her lover
And wring his bosom—is to die.

257. *waters:* "V. *The Tempest,* as above" [Eliot's note].

264. *Magnus Martyr:* "The interior of St. Magnus Martyr is to my mind one of the finest among Wren's interiors. See *The Proposed Demolition of Nineteen City Churches:* (P. S. King & Son, Ltd.)" [Eliot's note]. The church was designed by Christopher Wren and is situated in Lower Thames Street, just below London Bridge.

266. *river sweats:* "The Song of the (three) Thames-daughters begins here. From line 292 to 306 inclusive they speak in turn. V. *Götterdämmerung,* III, i: the Rhine-daughters" [Eliot's note], who bewail the river's lost beauty. Eliot imitates here the rhythm of Wagner's lines.

275–76. *Greenwich . . . Dogs:* dock area of the Thames.

278. *leialala;* This refrain is borrowed from Wagner's *Götterdämmerung.*

279. *Leicester:* "V. Froude [*Reign of*] *Elizabeth,* Vol. I, ch. iv, letter of De Quadra to Philip of Spain: 'In the afternoon we were in a barge, watching the games on the river. (The queen) was alone with the Lord Robert, and myself on the poop, when they began to talk nonsense, and went so far that Lord Robert at last said, as I was on the spot there was no reason why they should not be married if the queen pleased'" [Eliot's note]. Sir Robert Dudley was the Earl of Leicester, and a favorite of the queen's.

The brisk swell
Rippled both shores 285
Southwest wind
Carried down stream
The peal of bells
White towers
Weialala leia 290
Wallala leialala

"Trams and dusty trees.
Highbury bore me. Richmond and Kew
Undid me. By Richmond I raised my knees
Supine on the floor of a narrow canoe." 295

"My feet are at Moorgate, and my heart
Under my feet. After the event
He wept. He promised 'a new start.'
I made no comment. What should I resent?"

"On Margate Sands. 300
I can connect
Nothing with nothing.
The broken fingernails of dirty hands.
My people humble people who expect
Nothing." 305
la la

To Carthage then I came

Burning burning burning burning
O Lord Thou pluckest me out
O Lord Thou pluckest 310

burning

IV. *Death by Water*

Phlebas the Phoenician, a fortnight dead,
Forgot the cry of gulls, and the deep sea swell

294. *undid me:* "Cf. *Purgatorio,* V, 133 . . ." [Eliot's note]. These lines, parodied by Eliot, mean, "Remember me, who am La Pia./Siena made me, Maremma unmade me." La Pia was killed by her husband in a castle in Maremma. *Highbury . . Richmond and Kew:* Highbury is a lower middle-class suburb of London; Richmond and Kew, where this "Thames daughter" was undone, are riverside haunts of the fashionable.

296. *Moorgate:* Area in the heart of the financial district, where *this* Thames daughter may have been a secretary.

300. *Margate:* seaside resort in Kent.

306. *I came:* "V. St. Augustine's *Confessions:* 'to Carthage then I came, where a caldron of unholy loves sang all about mine ears'" [Eliot's note]. The saint is speaking of his youthful libertinism. Cf. line 92.

308. *pluckest me out:* "From St. Augustine's *Confessions* again. The collocation of these two representatives of eastern and western asceticism, as the culmination of this part, is not an accident" [Eliot's note]. *Burning:* "The complete text of the Buddha's Fire Sermon (which corresponds in importance to the Sermon on the Mount) from which these words are taken, will be found translated in the late Henry Clarke Warren's *Buddhism in Translation* (Harvard Oriental Series). Mr. Warren was one of the great pioneers of Buddhist studies in the Occident" [Eliot's note].

And the profit and loss.
A current under sea
Picked his bones in whispers. As he rose and fell 315
He passed the stages of his age and youth
Entering the whirlpool.
Gentile or Jew
O you who turn the wheel and look to windward,
Consider Phlebas, who was once handsome and tall as you. 320

V. *What the Thunder Said**

After the torchlight red on sweaty faces
After the frosty silence in the gardens
After the agony in stony places
The shouting and the crying
Prison and palace and reverberation 325
Of thunder of spring over distant mountains
He who was living is now dead
We who were living are now dying
With a little patience

Here is no water but only rock 330
Rock and no water and the sandy road
The road winding above among the mountains
Which are mountains of rock without water
If there were water we should stop and drink
Amongst the rock one cannot stop or think 335
Sweat is dry and feet are in the sand
If there were only water amongst the rock
Dead mountain mouth of carious teeth that cannot spit
Here one can neither stand nor lie nor sit
There is not even silence in the mountains 340
But dry sterile thunder without rain
There is not even solitude in the mountains
But red sullen faces sneer and snarl
From doors of mudcracked houses
If there were water 345
And no rock
If there were rock
And also water
And water
A spring 350
A pool among the rock
If there were the sound of water only

* "In the first part of Part V three themes are employed: the journey to Emmaus, the approach to the Chapel Perilous (see Miss Weston's book), and the present decay of eastern Europe" [Eliot's note]. The journey to Emmaus is an important episode in the life of Christ. Entrance to the chapel at first seems to establish the quest as barren, until a fertilizing rain begins to fall.

323. *gardens:* One of these was Gethsemane (Matthew 26: 36–45), where Christ prayed; the other was Golgotha, the hill of the Crucifixion, where the disciples buried Christ's body in a garden. This passage recalls the successive steps of the Passion, leading to death on the cross, and burial.

Not the cicada
And dry grass singing 355
But sound of water over a rock
Where the hermit thrush sings in the pine trees
Drip drop drip drop drop drop drop
But there is no water

Who is the third who walks always beside you? 360
When I count, there are only you and I together
But when I look ahead up the white road
There is always another one walking beside you
Gliding wrapped in a brown mantle, hooded
I do not know whether a man or a woman 365
—But who is that on the other side of you?

What is that sound high in the air
Murmur of maternal lamentation
Who are those hooded hordes swarming
Over endless plains, stumbling in cracked earth 370
Ringed by the flat horizon only
What is the city over the mountains
Cracks and reforms and bursts in the violet air
Falling towers
Jerusalem Athens Alexandria 375
Vienna London
Unreal

A woman drew her long black hair out tight
And fiddled whisper music on those strings
And bats with baby faces in the violet light 380
Whistled, and beat their wings
And crawled head downward down a blackened wall
And upside down in air were towers
Tolling reminiscent bells, that kept the hours
And voices singing out of empty cisterns and exhausted wells. 385

In this decayed hole among the mountains
In the faint moonlight, the grass is singing
Over the tumbled graves, about the chapel
There is the empty chapel, only the wind's home.
It has no windows, and the door swings, 390

357. *pine trees:* "This is . . . the hermit-thrush which I have heard in Quebec Province . . . Its 'water-dripping song' is justly celebrated" [Eliot's note].

361. *you and I together:* "The following lines were stimulated by the account of one of the Antarctic expeditions (I forget which, but I think one of Shackleton's): it was related that the party of explorers, at the extremity of their strength, had the constant delusion that there was *one more member* than could actually be counted" [Eliot's note].

367. *high in the air:* In his note to this passage, Eliot quotes from Hermann Hesse's *Blick ins Chaos* (*Looking into Chaos*). An English rendering is, "Already half Europe, already at least half of Eastern Europe is on the road to Chaos, drives drunken in holy madness along the abyss and sings the while, sings drunk and hymn-like as Dimitri Karamazov sang. The bourgeois laughs, offended, at these songs, the saint and the prophet hear them with tears."

Dry bones can harm no one.
Only a cock stood on the rooftree
Co co rico co co rico
In a flash of lightning. Then a damp gust
Bringing rain 395

Ganga was sunken, and the limp leaves
Waited for rain, while the black clouds
Gathered far distant, over Himavant.
The jungle crouched, humped in silence.
Then spoke the thunder 400
DA
Datta: what have we given?
My friend, blood shaking my heart
The awful daring of a moment's surrender
Which an age of prudence can never retract 405
By this, and this only, we have existed
Which is not to be found in our obituaries
Or in memories draped by the beneficent spider
Or under seals broken by the lean solicitor
In our empty rooms 410
DA
Dayadhvam: I have heard the key
Turn in the door once and turn once only
We think of the key, each in his prison
Thinking of the key, each confirms a prison 415
Only at nightfall, ethereal rumours
Revive for a moment a broken Coriolanus
DA
Damyata: The boat responded
Gaily, to the hand expert with sail and oar 420
The sea was calm, your heart would have responded
Gaily, when invited, beating obedient
To controlling hands

393. *co co rico:* cockadoodledoo. As Jesus had predicted, after Peter had three times denied his Lord, "immediately the cock crew" (Matthew 26: 34, 74).

396. *Ganga:* the River Ganges.

398. *Himavant:* a peak in the Himalayas.

401. *have we given:* " 'Datta, dayadhvam, damyata' (Give, sympathize, control). The fable of the meaning of the Thunder is found in the *Brihadaranyaka-Upanishad*, 5. I. A translation is found in Deussen's *Sechzig Upanishads des Veda*, p. 489" [Eliot's note].

In this Hindu fable, gods, men, and demons in turn ask their father Prajapati for a word. To each he replies "DA." The gods interpret this as Datta, a command to give alms. Men hear it as Dayadhvam, a call for compassion, and the demons as Damyata, urging self-control. The divine voice of the thunder, the fable tells us in conclusion, saying DA DA DA, bids us practice alms-giving, self-control, and compassion.

408. *spider:* "Cf. Webster, *The White Devil*, V, vi: '. . . they'll remarry/Ere the worm pierce your winding-sheet, ere the spider/Make a thin curtain for your epitaphs' " [Eliot's note].

412. *key:* In his note, Eliot refers to the passage in the *Inferno* where Ugolino relates how he and his young sons were left to starve to death. The line echoed (*Inferno*, 33. 46) means, "and I heard below the door of the horrible tower nailed up."

417. *Coriolanus:* In his play, which is based on Plutarch's *Lives*, Shakespeare presents Coriolanus as a great warrior whose scorn of the populace leads to his downfall: he is a man very much locked up in the prison of himself.

I sat upon the shore
Fishing, with the arid plain behind me 425
Shall I at least set my lands in order?
London Bridge is falling down falling down falling down
Poi s'ascose nel foco che gli affina
Quando fiam uti chelidon—O swallow swallow
Le Prince d'Aquitaine à la tour abolie 430
These fragments I have shored against my ruins
Why then Ile fit you. Hieronymo's mad againe.
Datta. Dayadhvam. Damyata.
Shantih shantih shantih

425. *Fishing:* "V. Weston: *From Ritual to Romance*; chapter on the Fisher King" [Eliot's note].

427. *falling down:* This nursery rhyme contains the line, "Take the key and lock her up, my fair lady."

428. *che gli affina:* "V. *Purgatorio*, XXVI, 148 . . ." [Eliot's note]. The lines quoted are uttered by the Provençal poet Arnaut Daniel, who is purging the lusts in which he indulged on earth. They mean, " 'And so I pray you, by that Virtue which guides you to the top of the stair, be reminded in time of my pain.' Then he hid himself in the fire that purifies them."

429. *chelidon:* "V. *Pervigilium Veneris.* Cf. Philomela in Parts I and II" [Eliot's note]. The line means, "When shall I become as the swallow?" The poem, *The Vigil of Venus*, is a late Latin work that celebrates the spring festival. In it, Philomela is identified with the swallow.

430. *abolie:* "V. Gérard de Nerval, Sonnet *El Desdichado*" [Eliot's note]. The Spanish title means "the disinherited," the line means, "The Prince of Aquitaine with the deserted tower." There may be an association with the Tarot card representing a ruined tower, and which symbolizes the decline of old traditions.

432. *mad againe:* "V. Kyd's *Spanish Tragedy*" [Eliot's note]. The play, written in 1594, has as its subtitle: *Hieronymo's Mad Againe.* Hieronymo, driven mad by his son's death, "fits" the parts in a court masque so that he has the opportunity to kill his son's murderers.

434. *Shantih:* "Shantih. Repeated as here, a formal ending to an Upanishad. 'The Peace which passeth understanding' is our nearest equivalent to this word" [Eliot's note]. The Upanishads comment in verse, in dialogue form, on Hindu metaphysics, and sometimes directly on the Hindu scriptures, the Vedas. While this conclusion suggests that a healing process may occur, the remoteness of the language used might be taken to imply that the requisite contemporary applications of this age-old wisdom remain to be made.

From *Four Quartets*

*Little Gidding**

I

Midwinter spring is its own season
Sempiternal though sodden towards sundown,
Suspended in time, between pole and tropic.
When the short day is brightest, with frost and fire,
The brief sun flames the ice, on pond and ditches, 5
In windless cold that is the heart's heat,
Reflecting in a watery mirror
A glare that is blindness in the early afternoon.

* Selection from *Collected Poems 1909–1962* by T. S. Eliot, copyright, 1936, by Harcourt Brace Jovanovich, Inc.; copyright © 1963, 1964 by T. S. Eliot. Reprinted by permission of the publishers. In Huntingdonshire, site of an Anglican community established in 1625 by Nicholas Ferrar. The chapel, which was rebuilt in the nineteenth century, still exists. Eliot saw it one midwinter day.

2. *Sempiternal:* everlasting.

And glow more intense than blaze of branch, or brazier,
Stirs the dumb spirit: no wind, but pentecostal fire
In the dark time of the year. Between melting and freezing 10
The soul's sap quivers. There is no earth smell
Or smell of living thing. This is the springtime
But not in time's covenant. Now the hedgerow
Is blanched for an hour with transitory blossom
Of snow, a bloom more sudden 15
Than that of summer, neither budding nor fading,
Not in the scheme of generation.
Where is the summer, the unimaginable
Zero summer?

20

If you came this way,
Taking the route you would be likely to take
From the place you would be likely to come from,
If you came this way in may time, you would find the hedges
White again, in May, with voluptuary sweetness.
It would be the same at the end of the journey, 25
If you came at night like a broken king,
If you came by day not knowing what you came for,
It would be the same, when you leave the rough road
And turn behind the pigsty to the dull façade
And the tombstone. And what you thought you came for 30
Is only a shell, a husk of meaning
From which the purpose breaks only when it is fulfilled
If at all. Either you had no purpose
Or the purpose is beyond the end you figured
And is altered in fulfillment. There are other places 35
Which also are the world's end, some at the sea jaws,
Or over a dark lake, in a desert or a city—
But this is the nearest, in place and time,
Now and in England.

40

If you came this way,
Taking any route, starting from anywhere,
At any time or at any season,
It would always be the same: you would have to put off
Sense and notion. You are not here to verify,
Instruct yourself, or inform curiosity 45
Or carry report. You are here to kneel
Where prayer has been valid. And prayer is more
Than an order of words, the conscious occupation
Of the praying mind, or the sound of the voice praying.
And what the dead had no speech for, when living, 50
They can tell you, being dead: the communication
Of the dead is tongued with fire beyond the language of the living.

10. *pentecostal fire:* As recorded in Acts 2, on the Pentecost day following Christ's death and resurrection, the apostles saw "cloven tongues like as of fire," and were "filled with the Holy Ghost."

27. *broken king:* Charles I, who visited the Little Gidding community on several occasions, is said to have returned in secret after the total collapse of his cause in the Civil War.

Here, the intersection of the timeless moment
Is England and nowhere. Never and always. 55

II

Ash on an old man's sleeve
Is all the ash the burnt roses leave.
Dust in the air suspended
Marks the place where a story ended.
Dust inbreathed was a house— 60
The wall, the wainscot, and the mouse.
The death of hope and despair,
    This is the death of air.

There are flood and drouth
Over the eyes and in the mouth, 65
Dead water and dead sand
Contending for the upper hand.
The parched eviscerate soil
Gapes at the vanity of toil,
Laughs without mirth. 70
    This is the death of earth.

Water and fire succeed
The town, the pasture, and the weed.
Water and fire deride
The sacrifice that we denied. 75
Water and fire shall rot
The marred foundations we forgot,
Of sanctuary and choir.
    This is the death of water and fire.

In the uncertain hour before the morning 80
  Near the ending of interminable night
  At the recurrent end of the unending
After the dark dove with the flickering tongue
  Had passed below the horizon of his homing
  While the dead leaves still rattled on like tin 85
Over the asphalt where no other sound was
  Between three districts whence the smoke arose
  I met one walking, loitering and hurried
As if blown towards me like the metal leaves
  Before the urban dawn wind unresisting. 90
  And as I fixed upon the down-turned face
That pointed scrutiny with which we challenge
  The first-met stranger in the waning dusk
  I caught the sudden look of some dead master
Whom I had known, forgotten, half recalled 95
  Both one and many; in the brown baked features

63. *death of air:* reminiscence of a theory concerning the conflict of the four elements, voiced by the pre-Socratic Greek philosopher Heraclitus (fifth to fourth century B.C.): "Fire is the death of air; air lives in the death of fire." The latter declaration is not reflected in the poem.

The eyes of a familiar compound ghost
Both intimate and unidentifiable.
So I assumed a double part, and cried
And heard another's voice cry: "What! are *you* here?" 100
Although we were not. I was still the same,
Knowing myself yet being someone other—
And he a face still forming; yet the words sufficed
To compel the recognition they preceded.
And so, compliant to the common wind, 105
Too strange to each other for misunderstanding,
In concord at this intersection time
Of meeting nowhere, no before and after,
We trod the pavement in a dead patrol.
I said: "The wonder that I feel is easy, 110
Yet ease is cause of wonder. Therefore speak:
I may not comprehend, may not remember."
And he: "I am not eager to rehearse
My thought and theory which you have forgotten.
These things have served their purpose: let them be. 115
So with your own, and pray they be forgiven
By others, as I pray you to forgive
Both bad and good. Last season's fruit is eaten
And the fullfed beast shall kick the empty pail.
For last year's words belong to last year's language 120
And next year's words await another voice.
But, as the passage now presents no hindrance
To the spirit unappeased and peregrine
Between two worlds become much like each other,
So I find words I never thought to speak 125
In streets I never thought I should revisit
When I left my body on a distant shore.
Since our concern was speech, and speech impelled us
To purify the dialect of the tribe
And urge the mind to aftersight and foresight, 130
Let me disclose the gifts reserved for age
To set a crown upon your lifetime's effort.
First, the cold friction of expiring sense
Without enchantment, offering no promise
But bitter tastelessness of shadow fruit 135
As body and soul begin to fall asunder.
Second, the conscious impotence of rage
At human folly, and the laceration
Of laughter at what ceases to amuse.

97. *familiar compound ghost:* echo of Shakespeare's Sonnet LXXXVI: "that affable familiar ghost." W. B. Yeats is part of this "compound ghost."

99. *double part:* Eliot may be referring to his "other self," or perhaps he is recalling Dante's questioning of souls in Hell and Purgatory.

123. *peregrine:* foreign, wandering (cognate with *pilgrim*).

129. *dialect of the tribe:* a free rendering of Mallarmé's line "Donner un sens plus pur aux mots de la tribu" (To give the words of the multitude a purer sense), in the sonnet "Le Tombeau d'Edgar Poe."

And last, the rending pain of re-enactment 140
Of all that you have done, and been; the shame
Of motives late revealed, and the awareness
Of things ill done and done to others' harm
Which once you took for exercise of virtue.
Then fools' approval strings, and honor stains. 145
From wrong to wrong the exasperated spirit
Proceeds, unless restored by that refining fire
Where you must move in measure, like a dancer."
The day was breaking. In the disfigured street
He left me, with a kind of valediction, 150
And faded on the blowing of the horn.

III

There are three conditions which often look alike
Yet differ completely, flourish in the same hedgerow:
Attachment to self and to things and to persons, detachment
From self and from things and from persons; and, growing between
them, indifference 155
Which resembles the others as death resembles life,
Being between two lives—unflowering, between
The live and the dead nettle. This is the use of memory:
For liberation—not less of love but expanding
Of love beyond desire, and so liberation 160
From the future as well as the past. Thus, love of a country
Begins as attachment to our own field of action
And comes to find that action of little importance
Though never indifferent. History may be servitude,
History may be freedom. See, now they vanish, 165
The faces and places, with the self which, as it could, loved them,
To become renewed, transfigured, in another pattern.

Sin is Behovely, but
All shall be well, and
All manner of things shall be well. 170
If I think, again, of this place,
And of people, not wholly commendable,
Of no immediate kin or kindness,
But some of peculiar genius,
All touched by a common genius, 175
United in the strife which divided them;
If I think of a king at nightfall,
Of three men, and more, on the scaffold
And a few who died forgotten

147. *refining fire:* Line 428 of *The Waste Land* cites in the original Italian the text of Dante, *Purgatorio* 26.148.

151. *blowing of the horn:* reminiscence of *Hamlet* act I, sc. ii, l. 157: "It faded on the crowing of the cock."

168. *Behovely:* inevitable. The sentence is taken from the writings of Dame Juliana of Norwich, a fourteenth-century mystic: "Sin is behovabil, but all shall be well and all manner of thing shall be well." As elsewhere in the poem, here too is voiced the theme of the ultimate reconciliation of hostile forces.

In other places, here and abroad, 180
And of one who died blind and quiet
Why should we celebrate
These dead men more than the dying?
It is not to ring the bell backward
Nor is it an incantation 185
To summon the specter of a Rose.
We cannot revive old factions
We cannot restore old policies
Or follow an antique drum.
These men, and those who opposed them 190
And those whom they opposed
Accept the constitution of silence
And are folded in a single party.
Whatever we inherit from the fortunate
We have taken from the defeated 195
What they had to leave us—a symbol:
A symbol perfected in death.
And all shall be well and
All manner of thing shall be well
By the purification of the motive 200
In the ground of our beseeching.

IV

The dove descending breaks the air
With flame of incandescent terror
Of which the tongues declare
The one discharge from sin and error. 205
The only hope, or else despair
  Lies in the choice of pyre or pyre—
  To be redeemed from fire by fire.

Who then devised the torment? Love.
Love is the unfamiliar Name 210
Behind the hands that wove
The intolerable shirt of flame
Which human power cannot remove.
  We only live, only suspire
  Consumed by either fire or fire. 215

V

What we call the beginning is often the end
And to make an end is to make a beginning.
The end is where we start from. And every phrase
And sentence that is right (where every word is at home,

181. *blind and quiet:* The reference is to Milton.

212. *shirt of flame:* the poisoned "shirt of Nessus," which Deianeira gave to Hercules, believing it would increase his love for her. Instead, it ate into his flesh and could not be removed. To put an end to his agony Hercules mounted his funeral pyre, from where he was transported to the heavens.

Taking its place to support the others, 220
The word neither diffident nor ostentatious,
An easy commerce of the old and the new,
The common word exact without vulgarity,
The formal word precise but not pedantic,
The complete consort dancing together) 225
Every phrase and every sentence is an end and a beginning,
Every poem an epitaph. And any action
Is a step to the block, to the fire, down the sea's throat
Or to an illegible stone: and that is where we start.
We die with the dying: 230
See, they depart, and we go with them.
We are born with the dead:
See, they return, and bring us with them.
The moment of the rose and the moment of the yew tree
Are of equal duration. A people without history 235
Is not redeemed from time, for history is a pattern
Of timeless moments. So, while the light fails
On a winter's afternoon, in a secluded chapel
History is now and England.
With the drawing of this Love and the voice of this Calling 240

We shall not cease from exploration
And the end of all our exploring
Will be to arrive where we started
And know the place for the first time.
Through the unknown, remembered gate 245
When the last of earth left to discover
Is that which was the beginning;
At the source of the longest river
The voice of the hidden waterfall
And the children in the apple tree 250
Not known, because not looked for
But heard, half-heard, in the stillness
Between two waves of the sea.
Quick now, here, now, always—
A condition of complete simplicity 255
(Costing not less than everything)
And all shall be well and
All manner of thing shall be well
When the tongues of flame are in-folded
Into the crowned knot of fire 260
And the fire and the rose are one.

225. *consort:* The word has a dual meaning: "company" and also "harmony of sounds."

240. *voice of this Calling:* from the *Cloud of Unknowing*, a fourteenth-century work that contains suggestions for those who would practice religious meditation.

250. *apple tree: Burnt Norton*, the first of the *Four Quartets*, similarly refers to
the hidden laughter
Of children in the foliage
Quick now, here, now, always.
Symbolized by both passages is the moment of insight that may occur when the busy external mind has for a moment been lulled into passivity.

ANNA AKHMATOVA

(1889–1966)

Requiem

No, not far beneath some foreign sky then,
Not with foreign wings to shelter me,—
I was with my people then, close by them
Where my luckless people chanced to be.

1916

By Way of a Preface

In the terrible years of the Yezhovshchina, I spent seventeen months in the prison queues in Leningrad. Somehow, one day, someone "identified" me. Then a woman standing behind me, whose lips were blue with cold, and who, naturally enough, had never even heard of my name, emerged from that state of torpor common to us all and, putting her lips close to my ear (there, everyone spoke in whispers), asked me:

—And could you describe *this?*

And I answered her:

—I can.

Then something vaguely like a smile flashed across what once had been her face.

1 April 1957
Leningrad

Dedication

Mountains bow beneath that boundless sorrow,
And the mighty river stops its flow.
But those prison bolts are tried and thorough,
And beyond them, every "convict's burrow"
Tells a tale of mortal woe. 5
Someone, somewhere, feels the cool wind, bracing,
Sees the sun go nestling down to rest—
We know nothing, we, together facing
Still the sickening clank of keys, the pacing
Of the sentries with their heavy steps. 10

Title: A lament for the poet's son, arrested in 1937 and then imprisoned in Leningrad. A *Requiem* is a mass sung for the dead. Typically, Akhmatova's experience is blended with that of others—here, the women mourning relatives taken during the Stalinist purges of 1937–1938. The sections of "Requiem" were composed at different times, and the verse and prose prefaces were written later than the body of the poem. The complete work was first published in Munich in 1963. Only excerpts have appeared in the Soviet Union. The translation is by Robin Kemble.

By Way of a Preface: In 1937–1938, mass arrests were carried out by the secret police. *Yezhovshchina* means "Yezhov's tricks," referring to the head of the secret police, Nicolai Yezhov.

8. *We*: Women waiting before prison gates.

We'd rise, as for early Mass, each morning,
Cross the callous city, wend our way,
Meet, more lifeless than the dead, half mourning,
Watch the sun sink, the Neva mist forming,
But with hope still singing far away. 15
Sentenced . . . And at once the tears come rolling,
Cut off from the world, quite on her own,
Heart reduced to shreds, and almost falling,
Just as if some lout had sent her sprawling,
Still . . . She staggers on her way . . . Alone . . . 20
Where are now the friends of my misfortune,
Those that shared my own two years of hell?
What do the Siberian snow-winds caution,
What bodes the moon circle for their fortunes?
Theirs be this, my greeting and farewell. 25

March, 1940

Prelude

It was when no one smiled any longer
Save the dead, who were glad of release.
And when Leningrad dangled, incongruous,
By its prisons—a needless caprice.
And when, out of their minds with sheer suffering, 30
The long lines of the newly condemned
Heard the engines' shrill whistles go sputtering
A brief song of farewell to their friends.
Stars of death stood above us, and Russia,
In her innocence, twisted in pain 35
Under blood-spattered boots, and the shudder
Of the Black Marias in their train.

1

It was dawn when they took you. I followed,
As a widow walks after the bier.
By the icons—a candle, burnt hollow; 40
In the bed-room—the children, in tears.
Your lips—cool from the kiss of the icon,
Still to think—the cold sweat on your brow . . .
Like the wives of the Streltsy, now I come
To wait under the Kremlin's gaunt towers. 45

1935

14. *Neva*: The large river that flows through Leningrad.

21. *friends of my misfortune*: The women the poet met while waiting before the prison.

23. *Siberian*: Victims of the purges who were not executed were condemned to prison camps in Siberia.

24. *moon circle*: A ring around the moon, seen refracted through the snow.

34. *stars of death*: Stars in the sky, and perhaps also the stars on soldiers' caps and uniforms.

37. *Black Marias*: Police cars for conveying those arrested.

38. Akhmatova's third husband, the art historian Nikolai Punin, was arrested at dawn.

42. *Icon*: Small religious painting. He has kissed it before being taken away.

44. *Streltsy*: Household troops of the Tsar, who revolted in the time of Peter I. A thousand were executed in 1698 before the Kremlin, in the sight of their wives and mothers.

2

Silent flows the silent Don,
Yellow moon looks quietly on,

Cap askew, looks in the room,
Sees a shadow in the gloom.

Sees this woman, sick, at home, 50
Sees this woman, all alone,

Husband buried, then to see
Son arrested . . . Pray for me.

3

No, this is not me, this is somebody else that suffers.
I could never face that, and all that has happened: 55
Let sackcloth and ashes enshroud it,
And see all the lamps are removed . . .
Night.

4

You, my mocking one, pet of society,
And gay sinner of Tsarskoe Selo: 60
Had you dreamt, in your sweet notoriety,
Of the future that lay in store—
How you'd stand at the Crosses, three-hundredth
In the queue, each bleak New Year,
Hug your precious parcel of comforts, 65
Melt the ice with your hot bright tears.
There the poplar, used to imprisonment,
Sways aloft. Not a sound. But think
Of the numbers rotting there, innocent . . .

5

For seventeen long months my pleas, 70
My cries have called you home.
I've begged the hangman on my knees,
My son, my dread, my own.
My mind's mixed up for good, and I'm
No longer even clear 75
Who's man, who's beast, nor how much time

46. *Don*: The great Russian river. The first four lines of this section resemble a Russian lullabye.
52. *Husband buried*: Akhmatova's first husband, the poet Nikolai Gumilev, was shot in 1921.
60. *Tsarskoe Selo*: Or "The Tsar's Village," a town near Leningrad where Akhmatova spent her childhood, built around the Tsar's Summer Palace.
63. A prison in Leningrad whose buildings form a cross.
72. *the hangman*: Stalin. Akhmatova wrote a letter to him pleading unsuccessfully for the release of her son.

Before the end draws near.
And only flowers decked with dust,
And censers ringing, footprints thrust
Somewhere-nowhere, afar. 80
And, staring me straight in the eye
And warning me that death is nigh—
One monumental star.

1939

6

Weeks fly past in light profusion,
How to fathom what's been done; 85
How those long white nights, dear son,
Watched you in your cell's seclusion.

How once more they watch you there,
Eyes like hawks' that burn right through you,
Speak to you of death, speak to you 90
Of the lofty cross you bear.

1939

7

Sentence

And the word in stone has fallen heavy
On my breast, which was alive till now.
Never mind—for, mark you, I was ready,
I shall get along somehow. 95

So much to be done before tomorrow:
Crush the memory till no thoughts remain,
Carve a heart in stone, immune to sorrow,
Teach myself to face life once again,—

And if not . . . The rustling heat of summer 100
Fills my window with its festive tone.
I long since foresensed that there would come a
Sunny day like this—and empty home.

1939, Summer

8

To Death

You'll come in any case—then why not right away?
I'm waiting—life has dragged me under. 105
I've put the lamp out, left the door to show the way

79. *censers*: Incense holders used during religious rites.

When you come in your simple wonder.
For that, choose any guise you like: Burst in on me,
A shell with poison-gas container,
Or bandit with a heavy weight, creep up on me, 110
Or poison me with typhus vapor,
Or be a fable, known *ad nauseam*
To everyone denounced in error,
So I may see the top of that blue cap, and scan
The face of the house-porter, white with terror. 115
But nothing matters now. The Yenisey swirls by,
The Pole star shines above the torrent.
And the glint of those beloved eyes
Conceals the last, the final horror.

19 August 1939
Fontanny Dom

9

So madness now has wrapped its wings 120
Round half my soul and plies me, heartless,
With drafts of fiery wine, begins
To lure me toward the vale of darkness.

And I can see that I must now
Concede the victory—as I listen, 125
The dream that dogged my fevered brow
Already seems an outside vision.

And though I go on bended knee
To plead, implore its intercession,
There's nothing I may take with me, 130
It countenances no concession:

Nor yet my son's distracted eyes—
The rock-like suffering rooted in them,
The day the storm broke from clear skies,
The hour spent visiting the prison, 135

Nor yet the kind, cool clasp of hands,
The lime-tree shadows' fitful darting,
The far light call across the land—
The soothing words exchanged on parting.

4 May 1940
Fontanny Dom

112. *ad nauseam*: To the point of nausea. Denunciations for "counterrevolutionary" activity were common.
114. *blue cap*: Worn by the secret police.
116. *Yenisey*: River in Siberia along which there were many prison camps.

10

Crucifixion

Weep not for Me, Mother,
that I am in the grave.

I

The angels hailed that solemn hour and stately, 140
the heavens dissolved in tongues of fire. And He
Said to the Father; "Why didst Thou forsake Me!"
And to His Mother: "Weep thou not for Me . . ."

II

Magdalena sobbed, and the disciple,
He whom Jesus loved, stood petrified. 145
But there, where His Mother stood in silence,
No one durst so much as lift their eyes.

1940–43

Epilogue

I

I've learned how faces droop and then grow hollow,
How fear looks out from underneath the lids,
How cheeks, carved out of suffering and of sorrow, 150
Take on the lines of rough cuneiform scripts.
How heads of curls, but lately black or ashen,
Turn suddenly to silver overnight,
Smiles fade on lips reduced to dread submission,
A hoarse dry laugh stands in for trembling fright. 155
I pray, not for myself alone, my cry
Goes up for all those with me there—for all,
In heart of winter, heat-wave of July,
Who stood beneath that blind, deep-crimson wall.

II

The hour of remembrance is with us again. 160
I see you, I hear you, I feel you as then:

There's one they scarce dragged to the window, and one
Whose days in the land of her forebears are done,

And one tossed her beautiful head back when shown
Her corner, and said; "It's like being back home!" 165

142. *"Why . . . Me!"*: Christ's last words from the Cross. [*Matthew* 27:46.]
143. *"Weep . . Me"*: These words and the epigraph refer to a line from the Russian Orthodox prayer sung at services on Easter Saturday: "Weep not for Me, Mother, when thou lookest in the grave." Christ is comforting Mary with the promise of his resurrection.
151. *cuneiform*: Ancient Babylonian writing, carved on tablets.

I'd like to remember each one by her name,
But they took the list, and there's no more remain.

I've worked them a funeral shroud from each word
Of pain that escaped them, and I overheard.

I'll think of them everywhere, always, each one. 170
I shall not forget them in dark days to come.

And should they once silence my mortified lips,
Let one hundred millions for whom my voice speaks—

Let *them* take my place, and remember each year
Whenever my day of remembrance draws near. 175

And should they one day, in this country, agree
To raise a memorial somewhere to me,

I'd willingly give my consent to their plan,
But on one condition, which is—that it stand,

Not down by the sea, where I entered this world 180
(I've cut the last links that once bound us of old),

Nor yet by the tree-stump in old Tsarsky Sad,
Whose shade seeks me still with disconsolate love,

But here, where they let me stand three hundred hours,
And never so much as unbolted the doors. 185

For even in death I still fear to forget
The grim Black Marias, their thundering tread,

The sickening slam of that loathsome cell-door,
The old woman's howl, like a wounded beast's roar.

And may the snow, melting, well forth clear and strong, 190
Like tears from my eyelids, unmoving, like bronze,

And may the lone prison-dove coo from afar,
And boats travel silently down the Neva.

1940, March

168. *funeral shroud*: Distant reference to a tenth-century appearance of the Virgin in a church, where she extended her veil over the people in protection—the occasion of a religious festival celebrated on October 1.

182. *Tsarsky Sad*: The park and garden surrounding the Tsar's Summer Palace. The "shade" in the garden is a ghost, either the restless spirit of Akhmatova's executed husband Gumilev or the Russian poet Pushkin (1799–1837), who once lived in Tsarskoe Selo. In other poems, Akhmatova writes of a favorite willow, later only a stump, and of Pushkin whom she describes as walking in the park.

191. Akhmatova imagines herself memorialized as a national poet, and demands that her statue be placed here where she has experienced both public and private tragedy.

KATHERINE ANNE PORTER

(1890–   )

Pale Horse, Pale Rider*[1]

In sleep she knew she was in her bed, but not the bed she had lain down in a few hours since, and the room was not the same but it was a room she had known somewhere. Her heart was a stone lying upon her breast outside of her; her pulses lagged and paused, and she knew that something strange was going to happen, even as the early morning winds were cool through the lattice, the streaks of light were dark blue and the whole house was snoring in its sleep.

Now I must get up and go while they are all quiet. Where are my things? Things have a will of their own in this place and hide where they like. Daylight will strike a sudden blow on the roof startling them all up to their feet; faces will beam asking, Where are you going, What are you doing, What are you thinking, How do you feel, Why do you say such things, What do you mean? No more sleep. Where are my boots and what horse shall I ride? Fiddler or Graylie or Miss Lucy with the long nose and the wicked eye? How I have loved this house in the morning before we are all awake and tangled together like badly cast fishing lines. Too many people have been born here, and have wept too much here, and have laughed too much, and have been too angry and outrageous with each other here. Too many have died in this bed already, there are far too many ancestral bones propped up on the mantelpieces, there have been too damned many antimacassars[2] in this house, she said loudly, and oh, what accumulation of storied dust never allowed to settle in peace for one moment.

And the stranger? Where is that lank greenish stranger I remember hanging about the place, welcomed by my grandfather, my great-aunt, my five times removed cousin, my decrepit hound and my silver kitten? Why did they take to him, I wonder? And where are they now? Yet I saw him pass the window in the evening. What else besides them did I have in the world? Nothing. Nothing is mine, I have only nothing but it is enough, it is beautiful and it is all mine. Do I even walk about in my own skin or is it something I have borrowed to spare my modesty? Now what horse shall I borrow for this journey I do not mean to take, Graylie or Miss Lucy

* Published in 1939.

1. *Revelation* 6:8—"And I looked, and behold a pale horse: and his name that sat on him was Death, and Hell followed with him, and they were given power over a fourth of the earth, to kill with sword and with famine and with pestilence. . . ."

2. Protective coverings for the backs of chairs and sofas.

or Fiddler who can jump ditches in the dark and knows how to get the bit between his teeth? Early morning is best for me because trees are trees in one stroke, stones are stones set in shades known to be grass, there are no false shapes or surmises, the road is still asleep with the crust of dew unbroken. I'll take Graylie because he is not afraid of bridges.[3]

Come now, Graylie, she said, taking his bridle, we must outrun Death and the Devil. You are no good for it, she told the other horses standing saddled before the stable gate, among them the horse of the stranger, gray also, with tarnished nose and ears. The stranger swung into his saddle beside her, leaned far towards her and regarded her without meaning, the blank still stare of mindless malice that makes no threats and can bide its time. She drew Graylie around sharply, urged him to run. He leaped the low rose hedge and the narrow ditch beyond, and the dust of the lane flew heavily under his beating hoofs. The stranger rode beside her, easily, lightly, his reins loose in his half-closed hand, straight and elegant in dark shabby garments that flapped upon his bones; his pale face smiled in an evil trance, he did not glance at her. Ah, I have seen this fellow before, I know this man if I could place him. He is no stranger to me.

She pulled Graylie up, rose in her stirrups and shouted, I'm not going with you this time—ride on! Without pausing or turning his head the stranger rode on. Graylie's ribs heaved under her, her own ribs rose and fell, Oh, why am I so tired, I must wake up. "But let me get a fine yawn first," she said, opening her eyes and stretching, "a slap of cold water in my face, for I've been talking in my sleep again, I heard myself but what was I saying?"

Slowly, unwillingly, Miranda drew herself up inch by inch out of the pit of sleep, waited in a daze for life to begin again. A single word struck in her mind, a gong of warning, reminding her for the daylong what she forgot happily in sleep, and only in sleep. The war,[4] said the gong, and she shook her head. Dangling her feet idly with their slippers hanging, she was reminded of the way all sorts of persons sat upon her desk at the newspaper office. Every day she found someone there, sitting upon her desk instead of the chair provided, dangling his legs, eyes roving, full of his important affairs, waiting to pounce about something or other. "*Why* don't they sit in the chair? Should I put a sign on it, saying, 'For God's sake, sit here'?"

Far from putting up a sign, she did not even frown at her visitors. Usually she did not notice them at all until their determination to be seen was greater than her determination not to see them.

3. According to superstition, evil spirits cannot cross running water.

4. The story is set during the First World War.

Saturday, she thought, lying comfortably in her tub of hot water, will be payday, as always. Or I hope always. Her thoughts roved hazily in a continual effort to bring together and unite firmly the disturbing oppositions in her day-to-day existence, where survival, she could see clearly, had become a series of feats of sleight of hand. I owe—let me see, I wish I had pencil and paper—well, suppose I *did* pay five dollars now on a Liberty Bond,[5] I couldn't possibly keep it up. Or maybe. Eighteen dollars a week. So much for rent, so much for food, and I mean to have a few things besides. About five dollars' worth. Will leave me twenty-seven cents. I suppose I can make it. I suppose I should be worried. I am worried. Very well, now I am worried and what next? Twenty-seven cents. That's not so bad. Pure profit, really. Imagine if they should suddenly raise me to twenty I should then have two dollars and twenty-seven cents left over. But they aren't going to raise me to twenty. They are in fact going to throw me out if I don't buy a Liberty Bond. I hardly believe that. I'll ask Bill. (Bill was the city editor.) I wonder if a threat like that isn't a kind of blackmail. I don't believe even a Lusk Committeeman[6] can get away with that.

Yesterday there had been two pairs of legs dangling, on either side of her typewriter, both pairs stuffed thickly into funnels of dark expensive-looking material. She noticed at a distance that one of them was oldish and one was youngish, and they both of them had a stale air of borrowed importance which apparently they had got from the same source. They were both much too well nourished and the younger one wore a square little mustache. Being what they were, no matter what their business was it would be something unpleasant. Miranda had nodded at them, pulled out her chair and without removing her cap or gloves had reached into a pile of letters and sheets from the copydesk as if she had not a moment to spare. They did not move, or take off their hats. At last she had said "Good morning" to them, and asked if they were, perhaps, waiting for her?

The two men slid off the desk, leaving some of her papers rumpled, and the oldish man had inquired why she had not bought a Liberty Bond. Miranda had looked at him then, and got a poor impression. He was a pursy-faced man, gross-mouthed, with little lightless eyes, and Miranda wondered why nearly all of those selected to do the war work at home were of his sort. He might be anything at all, she thought; advance agent for a road show, promoter of a wildcat oil company, a former saloon keeper announcing

5. Savings bonds were sold by the government to help finance the War.

6. State Senator Clayton R. Lusk was chairman of the New York State legislative "Joint Committee Investigating Seditious Activities," a committee active between March 27, 1919, and April 24, 1920, in seeking out those suspected of having been pro-German during the War. For the purposes of the story, Porter has changed the time and scope of the Committee's operations.

the opening of a new cabaret, an automobile salesman—any follower of any one of the crafty, haphazard callings. But he was now all Patriot, working for the government. "Look here," he asked her, "do you know there's a war, or don't you?"

Did he expect an answer to that? Be quiet, Miranda told herself, this was bound to happen. Sooner or later it happens. Keep your head. The man wagged his finger at her. "Do you?" he persisted, as if he were prompting an obstinate child.

"Oh, the war," Miranda had echoed on a rising note and she almost smiled at him. It was habitual, automatic, to give that solemn, mystically uplifted grin when you spoke the words or heard them spoken. "*C'est la guerre,*"[7] whether you could pronounce it or not, was even better, and always, always, you shrugged.

"Yeah," said the younger man in a nasty way, "the war." Miranda, startled by the tone, met his eye; his stare was really stony, really viciously cold, the kind of thing you might expect to meet behind a pistol on a deserted corner. This expression gave temporary meaning to a set of features otherwise nondescript, the face of those men who have no business of their own. "We're having a war, and some people are buying Liberty Bonds and others just don't seem to get around to it," he said. "That's what we mean."

Miranda frowned with nervousness, the sharp beginnings of fear. "Are you selling them?" she asked, taking the cover off her typewriter and putting it back again.

"No, we're not selling them," said the older man. "We're just asking you why you haven't bought one." The voice was persuasive and ominous.

Miranda began to explain that she had no money, and did not know where to find any, when the older man interrupted: "That's no excuse, no excuse at all, and you know it, with the Huns overrunning martyred Belgium."[8]

"With our American boys fighting and dying in Belleau Wood,"[9] said the younger man, "anybody can raise fifty dollars to help beat the Boche."

Miranda said hastily, "I have eighteen dollars a week and not another cent in the world. I simply cannot buy anything."

"You can pay for it five dollars a week," said the older man (they had stood there cawing back and forth over her head), "like a lot of other people in this office, and a lot of other offices besides are doing."

7. "That's war."

8. *Hun* was a slang word for *German*; another was *Boche*. The German Army invaded neutral Belgium in August 1914, bringing Great Britain into the war—but not the United States, which held back until April 1917.

9. A forest in Northern France where in June 1918 United States Marines blocked the German drive on Paris, losing nearly eight thousand men.

Miranda, desperately silent, had thought, "Suppose I were not a coward, but said what I really thought? Suppose I said to hell with this filthy war? Suppose I asked that little thug, What's the matter with you, why aren't you rotting in Belleau Wood? I wish you were. . . ."

She began to arrange her letters and notes, her fingers refusing to pick up things properly. The older man went on making his little set speech. It was hard, of course. Everybody was suffering, naturally. Everybody had to do his share. But as to that, a Liberty Bond was the safest investment you could make. It was just like having the money in the bank. Of course. The government was back of it and where better could you invest?

"I agree with you about that," said Miranda, "but I haven't any money to invest."

And of course, the man had gone on, it wasn't so much her fifty dollars that was going to make any difference. It was just a pledge of good faith on her part. A pledge of good faith that she was a loyal American doing her duty. And the thing was safe as a church. Why, if he had a million dollars he'd be glad to put every last cent of it in these Bonds. . . . "You can't lose by it," he said, almost benevolently, "and you can lose a lot if you don't. Think it over. You're the only one in this whole newspaper office that hasn't come in. And every firm in this city has come in one hundred per cent. Over at the *Daily Clarion* nobody had to be asked twice."

"They pay better over there," said Miranda. "But next week, if I can. Not now, next week."

"See that you do," said the younger man. "This ain't any laughing matter."

They lolled away, past the Society Editor's desk, past Bill the City Editor's desk, past the long copydesk where old man Gibbons sat all night shouting at intervals, "Jarge! Jarge!" and the copyboy would come flying. "Never say *people* when you mean *persons*," old man Gibbons had instructed Miranda, "and never say *practically*, say *virtually*, and don't for God's sake ever so long as I am at this desk use the barbarism *inasmuch* under any circumstances whatsoever. Now you're educated, you may go." At the head of the stairs her inquisitors had stopped in their fussy pride and vainglory, lighting cigars and wedging their hats more firmly over their eyes.

Miranda turned over in the soothing water, and wished she might fall asleep there, to wake up only when it was time to sleep again. She had a burning slow headache, and noticed it now, remembering she had waked up with it and it had in fact begun the evening before. While she dressed she tried to trace the insidious career of her headache, and it seemed reasonable to suppose it had started with the war. "It's been a headache, all right, but not quite like this." After the Committeemen had left, yesterday, she had gone to the cloakroom and had found Mary Townsend, the Society Editor, quietly hysterical about something. She was perched on the edge of the shabby wicker couch with ridges down the center, knitting on something rose-colored. Now and then she would put down her knitting, seize her head with both hands and rock, saying, "My *God*," in a surprised, inquiring voice. Her column was called Ye Towne Gossyp, so of course everybody called her Towney. Miranda and Towney had a great deal in common, and liked each other. They had both been real reporters once, and had been sent together to "cover" a scandalous elopement in which no marriage had taken place, after all, and the recaptured girl, her face swollen, had sat with her mother who was moaning steadily under a mound of blankets. They had both wept painfully and implored the young reporters to suppress the worst of the story. They had suppressed it, and the rival newspaper printed it all the next day. Miranda and Towney had then taken their punishment together, and had been degraded publicly to routine female jobs, one to the theaters, the other to society. They had this in common, that neither of them could see what else they could possibly have done, and they knew they were considered fools by the rest of the staff—nice girls, but fools. At sight of Miranda, Towney had broken out in a rage, "I can't do it, I'll never be able to raise the money, I told them, I can't, I can't, but they wouldn't listen."

Miranda said, "I knew I wasn't the only person in this office who couldn't raise five dollars. I told them I couldn't, too, and I can't."

"My *God*," said Towney, in the same voice, "they told me I'd lose my job—"

"I'm going to ask Bill," Miranda said; "I don't believe Bill would do that."

"It's not up to Bill," said Towney. "He'd have to if they got after him. Do you suppose they could put us in jail?"

"I don't know," said Miranda. "If they do, we won't be lonesome." She sat down beside Towney and held her own head. "What kind of soldier are you knitting that for? It's a sprightly color, it ought to cheer him up."

"Like hell," said Towney, her needles going again. "I'm making this for myself. That's that."

"Well," said Miranda, "we won't be lonesome and we'll catch up on our sleep." She washed her face and put on fresh makeup. Taking clean gray gloves out of her pocket she went out to join a group of young women fresh from the country club dances, the morning bridge, the charity bazaar, the Red Cross workrooms, who were wallowing in good works. They gave tea dances and raised money, and with the money they bought quantities of sweets, fruit, cigarettes, and magazines for the men in the cantonment[10] hospitals. With this loot they were now setting out, a gay procession of high-powered cars and brightly tinted faces to cheer the brave boys who already, you might very well say, had fallen in defense of their country. It must be frightfully hard on them, the dears, to be floored like this when they're all crazy to get overseas and into the trenches as quickly as possible. Yes, and some of them are the cutest things you ever saw, I didn't know there were so many good-looking men in this country, good heavens, I said, where do they come from? Well, my dear, you may ask yourself that question, who knows where they did come from? You're quite right, the way I feel about it is this, we must do everything we can to make them contented, but I draw the line at talking to them. I told the chaperons at those dances for enlisted men, I'll dance with them, every dumbbell who asks me, but I will NOT talk to them, I said, even if there is a war. So I danced hundreds of miles without opening my mouth except to say, Please keep your knees to yourself. I'm glad we gave those dances up. Yes, and the men stopped coming, anyway. But listen, I've heard that a great many of the enlisted men come from very good families; I'm not good at catching names, and those I did catch I'd never heard before, so I don't know . . . but it seems to me if they were from good families, you'd know it, wouldn't you? I mean, if a man is well bred he doesn't step on your feet, does he? At least not that. I used to have a pair of sandals ruined at every one of those dances. Well, I think any kind of social life is in very poor taste just now, I think we should all put on our Red Cross headdresses and wear them for the duration of the war—

Miranda, carrying her basket and her flowers, moved in among the young women, who scattered out and rushed upon the ward uttering girlish laughter meant to be refreshingly gay, but there was a grim determined clang in it calculated to freeze the blood. Miserably embarrassed at the idiocy of her errand, she walked rapidly between the long rows of high beds, set foot to foot with a narrow aisle between. The men, a selected presentable lot, sheets drawn up to their chins, not seriously ill, were bored and restless, most of them willing to be amused at anything. They were for the most part picturesquely bandaged as to arm or head, and those who were not visibly wounded invariably replied "Rheumatism" if some tactless girl, who had been solemnly warned never to ask this question, still forgot and asked a man what his illness was. The good-natured, eager ones, laughing and calling out from their hard narrow beds, were soon surrounded. Miranda, with her wilting bouquet and her basket of sweets and cigarettes, looking about, caught the unfriendly bitter eye of a young fellow lying on his back, his right leg in a cast

10. Temporary hospitals for military personnel.

and pulley. She stopped at the foot of his bed and continued to look at him, and he looked back with an unchanged, hostile face. Not having any, thank you and be damned to the whole business, his eyes said plainly to her, and will you be so good as to take your trash off my bed? For Miranda had set it down, leaning over to place it where he might be able to reach it if he would. Having set it down, she was incapable of taking it up again, but hurried away, her face burning, down the long aisle and out into the cool October sunshine, where the dreary raw barracks swarmed and worked with an aimless life of scurrying, dun-colored insects; and going around to a window near where he lay, she looked in, spying upon her soldier. He was lying with his eyes closed, his eyebrows in a sad bitter frown. She could not place him at all, she could not imagine where he came from nor what sort of being he might have been "in life," she said to herself. His face was young and the features sharp and plain, the hands were not laborer's hands but not well-cared-for hands either. They were good useful properly shaped hands, lying there on the coverlet. It occurred to her that it would be her luck to find him, instead of a jolly hungry puppy glad of a bite to eat and a little chatter. It is like turning a corner absorbed in your painful thoughts and meeting your state of mind embodied, face to face, she said. "My own feelings about this whole thing, made flesh. Never again will I come here, this is no sort of thing to be doing. This is disgusting," she told herself plainly. "Of course I would pick him out," she thought, getting into the back seat of the car she came in, "serves me right, I know better."

Another girl came out looking very tired and climbed in beside her. After a short silence, the girl said in a puzzled way, "I don't know what good it does, really. Some of them wouldn't take anything at all. I don't like this, do you?"

"I hate it," said Miranda.

"I suppose it's all right, though," said the girl, cautiously.

"Perhaps," said Miranda, turning cautious also.

That was for yesterday. At this point Miranda decided there was no good in thinking of yesterday, except for the hour after midnight she had spent dancing with Adam. He was in her mind so much, she hardly knew when she was thinking about him directly. His image was simply always present in more or less degree, he was sometimes nearer the surface of her thoughts, the pleasantest, the only really pleasant thought she had. She examined her face in the mirror between the windows and decided that her uneasiness was not all imagination. For three days at least she had felt odd and her expression was unfamiliar. She would have to raise that fifty dollars somehow, she supposed, or who knows what can happen? She was hardened to stories of personal disaster, of outrageous accusations and extraordinarily bitter penalties that had grown monstrously out of incidents very little more important than her failure—her refusal—to buy a Bond. No, she did not find herself a pleasing sight, flushed and shiny, and even her hair felt as if it had decided to grow in the other direction. I must do something about this, I can't let Adam see me like this, she told herself, knowing that even now at that moment he was listening for the turn of her doorknob, and he would be in the hallway, or on the porch when she came out, as if by sheerest coincidence. The noon sunlight cast cold slanting shadows in the room where, she said, I suppose I live, and this day is beginning badly, but they all do now, for one reason or another. In a drowse, she sprayed perfume on her hair, put on her moleskin cap and jacket, now in their second winter, but still good, still nice to wear, again being glad she had paid a frightening price for them. She had enjoyed them all this time, and in no case would she have had the money now. Maybe Maybe she could manage for that Bond. She could not find the lock without leaning to search for it, then stood undecided a moment possessed by the notion that she had forgotten something she would miss seriously later on.

Adam was in the hallway, a step outside his own door; he swung about as if quite startled to see her, and said, "Hello. I don't have to go back to camp today after all—isn't that luck?"

Miranda smiled at him gaily because she was always delighted at the sight of him. He was wearing his new uniform, and he was all olive and tan and tawny, hay colored and sand colored from hair to boots. She half noticed again that he always began by smiling at her; that his smile faded gradually; that his eyes became fixed and thoughtful as if he were reading in a poor light.

They walked out together into the fine fall day, scuffling bright ragged leaves under their feet, turning their faces up to a generous sky really blue and spotless. At the first corner they waited for a funeral to pass, the mourners seated straight and firm as if proud in their sorrow.

"I imagine I'm late," said Miranda, "as usual. What time is it?"

"Nearly half past one," he said, slipping back his sleeve with an exaggerated thrust of his arm upward. The young soldiers were still self-conscious about their wristwatches. Such of them as Miranda knew were boys from southern and southwestern towns, far off the Atlantic seaboard, and they had always believed that only sissies wore wristwatches. "I'll slap you on the wristwatch," one vaudeville comedian would simper to another, and it was always a good joke, never stale.

"I think it's a most sensible way to carry a watch," said Miranda. "You needn't blush."

"I'm nearly used to it," said Adam, who was from Texas. "We've been told time and again how all the hemanly regular army men wear them. It's the horrors of war," he said; "are we downhearted?[11] I'll say we are."

It was the kind of patter going the rounds. "You look it," said Miranda.

He was tall and heavily muscled in the shoulders, narrow in the waist and flanks, and he was infinitely buttoned, strapped, harnessed into a uniform as tough and unyielding in cut as a straitjacket, though the cloth was fine and supple. He had his uniforms made by the best tailor he could find, he confided to Miranda one day when she told him how squish he was looking in his new soldier suit. "Hard enough to make anything of the outfit, anyhow," he told her. "It's the least I can do for my beloved country, not to go around looking like a tramp." He was twenty-four years old and a Second Lieutenant in an Engineers Corps, on leave because his outfit expected to be sent over shortly. "Came in to make my will," he told Miranda, "and get a supply of toothbrushes and razor blades. By what gorgeous luck do you suppose," he asked her, "I happened to pick on your rooming house? How did I know you were there?"

Strolling, keeping step, his stout polished well-made boots setting themselves down firmly beside her thinsoled black suede, they put off as long as they could the end of their moment together, and kept up as well as they could their small talk that flew back and forth over little grooves worn in the thin upper surface of the brain, things you could say and hear clink reassuringly at once without disturbing the radiance which played and darted about the simple and lovely miracle of being two persons named Adam and Miranda, twenty-four years old each, alive and on the earth at the same moment: "Are you in the mood for dancing, Miranda?" and "I'm always in the mood for dancing, Adam!" but there were things in the way, the day that ended with dancing was a long way to go.

He really did look, Miranda thought, like a fine healthy apple this morning. One time or another in their talking, he had boasted that he had never had a pain in his life that he could remember. Instead of being horrified at this monster, she approved his monstrous uniqueness. As for herself, she had had too many pains to mention, so she did not mention them. After working for three years on a morning newspaper she had an illusion of maturity and experience; but it was fatigue merely, she decided, from keeping what she had been brought up to believe were unnatural hours, eating casually at dirty little restaurants, drinking bad coffee all night, and smoking too much. When she said something of her way

11. A rallying cry used to whip up audience enthusiasm. It was supposed to be answered by a resounding "No!"

of living to Adam, he studied her face a few seconds as if he had never seen it before, and said in a forthright way, "Why, it hasn't hurt you a bit, I think you're beautiful," and left her dangling there, wondering if he had thought she wished to be praised. She did wish to be praised, but not at that moment. Adam kept unwholesome hours too, or had in the ten days they had known each other, staying awake until one o'clock to take her out for supper; he smoked also continually, though if she did not stop him he was apt to explain to her exactly what smoking did to the lungs. "But," he said, "does it matter so much if you're going to war, anyway?"

"No," said Miranda, "and it matters even less if you're staying at home knitting socks. Give me a cigarette, will you?" They paused at another corner, under a half-foliaged maple, and hardly glanced at a funeral procession approaching. His eyes were pale tan with orange flecks in them, and his hair was the color of a haystack when you turn the weathered top back to the clear straw beneath. He fished out his cigarette case and snapped his silver lighter at her, snapped it several times in his own face, and they moved on, smoking.

"I can see you knitting socks," he said. "That would be just your speed. You know perfectly well you can't knit."

"I do worse," she said, soberly; "I write pieces advising other young women to knit and roll bandages and do without sugar and help win the war."

"Oh, well," said Adam, with the easy masculine morals in such questions, "that's merely your job, that doesn't count."

"I wonder," said Miranda. "How did you manage to get an extension of leave?"

"They just gave it," said Adam, "for no reason. The men are dying like flies out there, anyway. This funny new disease. Simply knocks you into a cocked hat."

"It seems to be a plague," said Miranda, "something out of the Middle Ages. Did you ever see so many funerals, ever?"

"Never did. Well, let's be strong-minded and not have any of it. I've got four days more straight from the blue and not a blade of grass must grow under our feet. What about tonight?"

"Same thing," she told him, "but make it about half past one. I've got a special job beside my usual run of the mill."

"What a job you've got," said Adam, "nothing to do but run from one dizzy amusement to another and then write a piece about it."

"Yes, it's too dizzy for words," said Miranda. They stood while a funeral passed, and this time they watched it in silence. Miranda pulled her cap to an angle and winked in the sunlight, her head swimming slowly "like goldfish," she told Adam, "my head swims.

I'm only half awake, I must have some coffee."

They lounged on their elbows over the counter of a drugstore. "No more cream for the stay-at-homes," she said, "and only one lump of sugar. I'll have two or none; that's the kind of martyr I'm being. I mean to live on boiled cabbage and wear shoddy from now on and get in good shape for the next round. No war is going to sneak up on me again."

"Oh, there won't be any more wars, don't you read the newspapers?"[12] asked Adam. "We're going to mop 'em up this time, and they're going to stay mopped, and this is going to be all."

"So they told me," said Miranda, tasting her bitter lukewarm brew and making a rueful face. Their smiles approved of each other, they felt they had got the right tone, they were taking the war properly. Above all, thought Miranda, no tooth-gnashing, no hair-tearing, it's noisy and unbecoming and it doesn't get you anywhere.

"Swill," said Adam rudely, pushing back his cup. "Is that all you're having for breakfast?"

"It's more than I want," said Miranda,

"I had buckwheat cakes, with sausage and maple syrup, and two bananas, and two cups of coffee, at eight o'clock, and right now, again, I feel like a famished orphan left in the ashcan. I'm all set, said Adam, "for broiled steak and fried potatoes and—"

"Don't go on with it," said Miranda, "it sounds delirious to me. Do all that after I'm gone." She slipped from the high seat, leaned against it slightly, glanced at her face in her round mirror, rubbed rouge on her lips and decided that she was past praying for.

"There's something terribly wrong," she told Adam. "I feel too rotten. It can't just be the weather, and the war."

"The weather is perfect," said Adam, "and the war is simply too good to be true. But since when? You were all right yesterday."

"I don't know," she said slowly, her voice sounding small and thin. They stopped as always at the open door before the flight of littered steps leading up to the newspaper loft. Miranda listened for a moment to the rattle of typewriters above, the steady rumble of presses below. "I wish we were going to spend the whole afternoon on a park bench," she said, "or drive to the mountains."

"I do too," he said: "let's do that tomorrow."

"Yes, tomorrow, unless something else happens. I'd like to run away," she told him; "let's both."

"Me?" said Adam. "Where I'm going there's no running to speak of. You mostly crawl about on your stomach here and there among the debris. You know, barbed wire and such stuff. It's going to be the kind of thing that happens once in a lifetime." He reflected a moment, and went on, "I don't know a darned thing

12. Politicians called the First World War a "war to end all wars."

about it, really, but they make it sound awfully messy. I've heard so much about it I feel as if I had been there and back. It's going to be an anticlimax," he said, "like seeing the pictures of a place so often you can't see it at all when you actually get there. Seems to me I've been in the army all my life."

Six months, he meant. Eternity. He looked so clear and fresh, and he had never had a pain in his life. She had seen them when they had been there and back and they never looked like this again. "Already the returned hero," she said, "and don't I wish you were."

"When I learned the use of the bayonet in my first training camp," said Adam, "I gouged the vitals out of more sandbags and sacks of hay than I could keep track of. They kept bawling at us, 'Get him, get that Boche, stick him before he sticks you'—and we'd go for those sandbags like wildfire, and honestly, sometimes I felt a perfect fool for getting so worked up when I saw the sand trickling out. I used to wake up in the night sometimes feeling silly about it."

"I can imagine," said Miranda. "It's perfect nonsense." They lingered, unwilling to say good-by. After a little pause, Adam, as if keeping up the conversation, asked, "Do you know what the average life expectation of a sapping party[13] is after it hits the job?"

"Something speedy, I suppose."

"Just nine minutes," said Adam; "I read that in your own newspaper not a week ago."

"Make it ten and I'll come along," said Miranda.

"Not another second," said Adam, "exactly nine minutes, take it or leave it."

"Stop bragging," said Miranda. "Who figured that out?"

"A noncombatant," said Adam, "a fellow with rickets."

This seemed very comic, they laughed and leaned toward each other and Miranda heard herself being a little shrill. She wiped the tears from her eyes. "My, it's a funny war," she said; "isn't it? I laugh every time I think about it."

Adam took her hand in both of his and pulled a little at the tips of her gloves and sniffed them. "What nice perfume you have," he said, "and such a lot of it, too. I like a lot of perfume on gloves and hair," he said, sniffing again.

"I've got probably too much," she said. "I can't smell or see or hear today. I must have a fearful cold."

"Don't catch cold," said Adam; "my leave is nearly up and it will be the last, the very last." She moved her fingers in her gloves as he pulled at the fingers and turned her hands as if they were something new and curious and of great value, and she turned shy and

13. A unit of military engineers sent to mine and blow up enemy fortifications.

quiet. She liked him, she liked him, and there was more than this but it was no good even imagining, because he was not for her nor for any woman, being beyond experience already, committed without any knowledge or act of his own to death. She took back her hands. "Good-by," she said finally, "until tonight."

She ran upstairs and looked back from the top. He was still watching her, and raised his hand without smiling. Miranda hardly ever saw anyone look back after he had said good-by. She could not help turning sometimes for one glimpse more of the person she had been talking with, as if that would save too rude and too sudden a snapping of even the lightest bond. But people hurried away, their faces already changed, fixed, in their straining towards their next stopping place, already absorbed in planning their next act or encounter. Adam was waiting as if he expected her to turn, and under his brows fixed in a strained frown, his eyes were very black.

At her desk she sat without taking off jacket or cap, slitting envelopes and pretending to read the letters. Only Chuck Rouncivale, the sports reporter, and Ye Towne Gossyp were sitting on her desk today, and them she liked having there. She sat on theirs when she pleased. Towney and Chuck were talking and they went on with it.

"They say," said Towney, "that it is really caused by germs brought by a German ship to Boston, a camouflaged ship, naturally, it didn't come in under its own colors. Isn't that ridiculous?"

"Maybe it was a submarine," said Chuck, "sneaking in from the bottom of the sea in the dead of night. Now that sounds better."

"Yes, it does," said Towney; "they always slip up somewhere in these details . . . and they think the germs were sprayed over the city—it started in Boston, you know—and somebody reported seeing a strange, thick, greasy-looking cloud float up out of Boston Harbor and spread slowly all over that end of town. I think it was an old woman who saw it."

"Should have been," said Chuck.

"I read it in a New York newspaper," said Towney; "so it's bound to be true."

Chuck and Miranda laughed so loudly at this that Bill stood up and glared at them. "Towney still reads the newspapers," explained Chuck.

"Well, what's funny about that?" asked Bill, sitting down again and frowning into the clutter before him.

"It was a noncombatant saw that cloud," said Miranda.

"Naturally," said Towney.

"Member of the Lusk Committee, maybe," said Miranda.

"The Angel of Mons,"[14] said Chuck, "or a dollar-a-year man."[15]

14. An angelic figure said to have appeared on the side of the Allies over the battlefield of Mons in Belgium, 1918.

15. A business executive working for the government at a nominal salary of a dollar a year.

Miranda wished to stop hearing and talking, she wished to think for just five minutes of her own about Adam, really to think about him, but there was no time. She had seen him first ten days ago, and since then they had been crossing streets together, darting between trucks and limousines and pushcarts and farm wagons; he had waited for her in doorways and in little restaurants that smelled of stale frying fat; they had eaten and danced to the urgent whine and bray of jazz orchestras, they had sat in dull theaters because Miranda was there to write a piece about the play. Once they had gone to the mountains and, leaving the car, had climbed a stony trail, and had come out on a ledge upon a flat stone, where they sat and watched the lights change on a valley landscape that was, no doubt, Miranda said, quite apocryphal—"We need not believe it, but it is fine poetry," she told him; they had leaned their shoulders together there, and had sat quite still, watching. On two Sundays they had gone to the geological museum, and had pored in shared fascination over bits of meteors, rock formations, fossilized tusks and trees, Indian arrows, grottoes from the silver and gold lodes. "Think of those old miners washing out their fortunes in little pans beside the streams," said Adam, "and inside the earth there was this——" and he had told her he liked better those things that took long to make; he loved airplanes too, all sorts of machinery, things carved out of wood or stone. He knew nothing much about them, but he recognized them when he saw them. He had confessed that he simply could not get through a book, any kind of book except textbooks on engineering; reading bored him to crumbs; he regretted now he hadn't brought his roadster, but he hadn't thought he would need a car; he loved driving, he wouldn't expect her to believe how many hundreds of miles he could get over in a day . . . he had showed her snapshots of himself at the wheel of his roadster; of himself sailing a boat, looking very free and windblown, all angles, hauling on the ropes; he would have joined the air force but his mother had hysterics every time he mentioned it. She didn't seem to realize that dogfighting in the air was a good deal safer than sapping parties on the ground at night. But he hadn't argued, because of course she did not realize about sapping parties. And here he was, stuck, on a plateau a mile high with no water for a boat and his car at home, otherwise they could really have had a good time. Miranda knew he was trying to tell her what kind of person he was when he had his machinery with him. She felt she knew pretty well what kind of person he was, and would have liked to tell him that if he thought he had left himself at home in a boat or an automobile, he was much mistaken. The telephones were ringing, Bill was shouting at somebody who kept saying, "Well, but listen, well, but listen—" but nobody was going to listen, of course, nobody. Old man Gibbons bellowed in despair, "Jarge, Jarge—"

"Just the same," Towney was saying in her most complacent patriotic voice, "Hut Service[16] is a fine idea, and we should all volunteer even if they don't want us." Towney does well at this, thought Miranda, look at her; remembering the rose-colored sweater and the tight rebellious face in the cloakroom. Towney was now all open-faced glory and goodness, willing to sacrifice herself for her country. "After all," said Towney, "I *can* sing and dance well enough for the Little Theater, and I could write their letters for them, and at a pinch I might drive an ambulance. I have driven a Ford for years."

Miranda joined in: "Well, I can sing and dance too, but who's going to do the bed-making and the scrubbing up? Those huts are hard to keep, and it would be a dirty job and we'd be perfectly miserable; and as I've got a hard dirty job and am perfectly miserable, I'm going to stay at home."

"I think the women should keep out of it," said Chuck Rouncivale. "They just add skirts to the horrors of war." Chuck had bad lungs and fretted a good deal about missing the show. "I could have been there and back with a leg off by now; it would have served the old man right. Then he'd either have to buy his own hooch or sober up."

Miranda had seen Chuck on payday giving the old man money for hooch. He was a good-humored ingratiating old scoundrel, too, that was the worst of him. He slapped his son on the back and beamed upon him with the bleared eye of paternal affection while he took his last nickel.

"It was Florence Nightingale[17] ruined wars," Chuck went on. "What's the idea of petting soldiers and binding up their wounds and soothing their fevered brows? That's not war. Let 'em perish where they fall. That's what they're there for."

"You can talk," said Towney, with a slantwise glint at him.

"What's the idea?" asked Chuck, flushing and hunching his shoulders. "You know I've got this lung, or maybe half of it anyway by now."

"You're much too sensitive," said Towney. "I didn't mean a thing."

Bill had been raging about, chewing his half-smoked cigar, his hair standing up in a brush, his eyes soft and lambent but wild, like a stag's. He would never, thought Miranda, be more than fourteen years old if he lived for a century, which he would not at the rate he was going. He behaved exactly like city editors in the moving

16. Red Cross canteens in Europe, staffed by women volunteers.

17. Nursing pioneer (1820–1910), who in 1854 organized a unit of female nurses to staff a field hospital near the front lines of the Crimean War and care for wounded soldiers there.

pictures, even to the chewed cigar. Had he formed his style on the films, or had scenario writers seized once for all on the type Bill in its inarguable purity? Bill was shouting to Chuck: "*And* if he comes back here take him up the alley and saw his head off *by hand!*"

Chuck said, "He'll be back, don't worry." Bill said mildly, already off on another track, "Well, saw him off." Towney went to her own desk, but Chuck sat waiting amiably to be taken to the new vaudeville show. Miranda, with two tickets, always invited one of the reporters to go with her on Monday. Chuck was lavishly hardboiled and professional in his sports writing, but he had told Miranda that he didn't give a damn about sports, really; the job kept him out in the open, and paid him enough to buy the old man's hooch. He preferred shows and didn't see why women always had the job.

"Who does Bill want sawed today?" asked Miranda.

"That hoofer[18] you panned in this morning's," said Chuck. "He was up here bright and early asking for the guy that writes up the show business. He said he was going to take the goof who wrote that piece up the alley and bop him in the nose. He said . . ."

"I hope he's gone," said Miranda; "I do hope he had to catch a train."

Chuck stood up and arranged his maroon-colored turtle-necked sweater, glanced down at the peasoup tweed plus fours[19] and the hobnailed tan boots which he hoped would help to disguise the fact that he had a bad lung and didn't care for sports, and said, "He's long gone by now, don't worry. Let's get going; you're late as usual."

Miranda, facing about, almost stepped on the toes of a little drab man in a derby hat. He might have been a pretty fellow once, but now his mouth dropped where he had lost his side teeth, and his sad red-rimmed eyes had given up coquetry. A thin brown wave of hair was combed out with brilliantine and curled against the rim of the derby. He didn't move his feet, but stood planted with a kind of inert resistance, and asked Miranda: "Are you the so-called dramatic critic on this hick newspaper?"

"I'm afraid I am," said Miranda.

"Well," said the little man, "I'm just asking for one minute of your valuable time." His underlip shot out, he began with shaking hands to fish about in his waistcoat pocket. "I just hate to let you get away with it, that's all." He riffled through a collection of shabby newspaper clippings. "Just give these the once-over, will you? And then let me ask you if you think I'm gonna stand for

18. Dancer.
19. Loose sporting trousers, cut and gartered four inches below the knee.

being knocked by a tanktown critic," he said, in a toneless voice: "look here, here's Buffalo, Chicago, Saint Looey, Philadelphia, Frisco, besides New York. Here's the best publications in the business, *Variety*, the *Billboard*, they all broke down and admitted that Danny Dickerson knows his stuff. So you don't think so, hey? That's all I wanta ask you."

"No, I don't," said Miranda, as bluntly as she could, "and I can't stop to talk about it."

The little man leaned nearer, his voice shook as if he had been nervous for a long time. "Look here, what was there you didn't like about me? Tell me that."

Miranda said, "You shouldn't pay any attention at all. What does it matter what I think?"

"I don't care what you think, it ain't that," said the little man, "but these things get round and booking agencies back East don't know how it is out here. We get panned in the sticks and they think it's the same as getting panned in Chicago, see? They don't know the difference. They don't know that the more high class an act is the more the hick critics pan it. But I've been called the best in the business by the best in the business and I wanta know what you think is wrong with me."

Chuck said, "Come on, Miranda, curtain's going up." Miranda handed the little man his clippings, they were mostly ten years old, and tried to edge past him. He stepped before her again and said without much conviction. "If you was a man I'd knock your block off." Chuck got up at that and lounged over, taking his hands out of his pockets, and said, "Now you've done your song and dance you'd better get out. Get the hell out now before I throw you downstairs."

The little man pulled at the top of his tie, a small blue tie with red polka dots, slightly frayed at the knot. He pulled it straight and repeated as if he had rehearsed it, "Come out in the alley." The tears filled his thickened red lids. Chuck said, "Ah, shut up," and followed Miranda, who was running towards the stairs. He overtook her on the sidewalk. "I left him sniveling and shuffling his publicity trying to find the joker," said Chuck, "the poor old heel."

Miranda said, "There's too much of everything in this world just now. I'd like to sit down here on the curb, Chuck, and die, and never again see—I wish I could lose my memory and forget my own name. . . . I wish—"

Chuck said, "Toughen up, Miranda. This is no time to cave in. Forget that fellow. For every hundred people in show business, there are ninety-nine like him. But you don't manage right, anyway. You bring it on yourself. All you have to do is play up the headliners, and you needn't even mention the also-rans. Try to keep in mind that Rypinsky has got show business cornered in this town; please Rypinsky and you'll please the advertising department, please them and you'll get a raise. Hand-in-glove, my poor dumb child, will you never learn?"

"I seem to keep learning all the wrong things," said Miranda hopelessly.

"You do for a fact," Chuck told her cheerfully. "You are as good at it as I ever saw. Now do you feel better?"

"This is a rotten show you've invited me to," said Chuck. "Now what are you going to do about it? If I were writing it up. I'd—"

"Do write it up," said Miranda. "You write it up this time. I'm getting ready to leave, anyway, but don't tell anybody yet."

"You mean it? All my life," said Chuck, "I've yearned to be a so-called dramatic critic on a hick newspaper, and this is positively my first chance."

"Better take it," Miranda told him. "It may be your last." She thought, This is the beginning of the end of something. Something terrible is going to happen to me. I shan't need bread and butter where I'm going. I'll will it to Chuck, he has a venerable father to buy hooch for. I hope they let him have it. Oh, Adam, I hope I see you once more before I go under with whatever is the matter with me. "I wish the war were over," she said to Chuck, as if they had been talking about that. "I wish it were over and I wish it had never begun."

Chuck had got out his pad and pencil and was already writing his review. What she had said seemed safe enough but how would he take it? "I don't care how it started or when it ends," said Chuck, scribbling away. "I'm not going to be there."

All the rejected men talked like that, thought Miranda. War was the only thing they wanted, now they couldn't have it. Maybe they had wanted badly to go, some of them. All of them had a sidelong eye for the women they talked with about it, a guarded resentment which said, "Don't pin a white feather[20] on me, you bloodthirsty female. I've offered my meat to the crows and they won't have it." The worst thing about war for the stay-at-homes is there isn't anyone to talk to any more. The Lusk Committee will get you if you don't watch out. Bread will win the war. Work will win, sugar will win, peach pits will win the war. Nonsense. *Not* nonsense, I tell you, there's some kind of valuable high explosive to be got out of peach pits. So all the happy housewives hurry during the canning season to lay their baskets of peach pits on the altar of their country. It keeps them busy and makes them feel useful, and all these women running wild with the men away are dangerous, if they

20. Badge of cowardice.

aren't given something to keep their little minds out of mischief. So rows of young girls, the intact cradles of the future, with their pure serious faces framed becomingly in Red Cross wimples,[21] roll cock-eyed bandages that will never reach a base hospital, and knit sweaters that will never warm a manly chest, their minds dwelling lovingly on all the blood and mud and the next dance at the Acanthus Club for the officers of the flying corps. Keeping still and quiet will win the war.

"I'm simply not going to be there," said Chuck, absorbed in his review. No, Adam will be there, thought Miranda. She slipped down in the chair and leaned her head against the dusty plush, closed her eyes and faced for one instant that was a lifetime the certain, the overwhelming and awful knowledge that there was nothing at all ahead for Adam and for her. Nothing. She opened her eyes and held her hands together palms up, gazing at them and trying to understand oblivion.

"Now look at this," said Chuck, for the lights had come on and the audience was rustling and talking again. "I've got it all done, even before the headliner comes on. It's old Stella Mayhew, and she's always good, she's been good for forty years, and she's going to sing 'O the blues ain't nothin' but the easy-going heart disease.' That's all you need to know about her. Now just glance over this. Would you be willing to sign it?"

Miranda took the pages and stared at them conscientiously, turning them over, she hoped, at the right moment, and gave them back. "Yes, Chuck, yes, I'd sign that. But I won't. We must tell Bill you wrote because it's your start, maybe."

"You don't half appreciate it," said Chuck. "You read it too fast. Here, listen to this—" and he began to mutter excitedly. While he was reading she watched his face. It was a pleasant face with some kind of spark of life in it, and a good severity in the modeling of the brow above the nose. For the first time since she had known him she wondered what Chuck was thinking about. He looked preoccupied and unhappy, he wasn't so frivolous as he sounded. The people were crowding into the aisle, bringing out their cigarette cases ready to strike a match the instant they reached the lobby; women with waved hair clutched at their wraps, men stretched their chins to ease them of their stiff collars, and Chuck said, "We might as well go now." Miranda, buttoning her jacket, stepped into the moving crowd, thinking, What did I ever know about them? There must be a great many of them here who think as I do, and we dare not say a word to each other of our desperation, we are speechless animals letting ourselves be destroyed, and why? Does anybody here believe the things we say to each other?

21. Headdresses, like those worn by nuns.

Stretched in unease on the ridge of the wicker couch in the cloakroom, Miranda waited for time to pass and leave Adam with her. Time seemed to proceed with more than usual eccentricity, leaving twilight gaps in her mind for thirty minutes which seemed like a second, and then hard flashes of light that shone clearly on her watch proving that three minutes is an intolerable stretch of waiting, as if she were hanging by her thumbs. At last it was reasonable to imagine Adam stepping out of the house in the early darkness into the blue mist that might soon be rain, he would be on the way, and there was nothing to think about him, after all. There was only the wish to see him and the fear, the present threat, of not seeing him again; for every step they took towards each other seemed perilous, drawing them apart instead of together, as a swimmer in spite of his most determined strokes is yet drawn slowly backward by the tide. "I don't want to love," she would think in spite of herself, "not Adam, there is no time and we are not ready for it and yet this is all we have—"

And there he was on the sidewalk, with his foot on the first step, and Miranda almost ran down to meet him. Adam, holding her hands, asked, "Do you feel well now? Are you hungry? Are you tired? Will you feel like dancing after the show?"

"Yes to everything," said Miranda, "yes, yes. . . ." Her head was like a feather, and she steadied herself on his arm. The mist was still mist that might be rain later, and though the air was sharp and clean in her mouth, it did not, she decided, make breathing any easier. "I hope the show is good, or at least funny," she told him, "but I promise nothing."

It was a long, dreary play, but Adam and Miranda sat very quietly together waiting patiently for it to be over. Adam carefully and seriously pulled off her glove and held her hand as if he were accustomed to holding her hand in theaters. Once they turned and their eyes met, but only once, and the two pairs of eyes were equally steady and noncommittal. A deep tremor set up in Miranda, and she set about resisting herself methodically as if she were closing windows and doors and fastening down curtains against a rising storm. Adam sat watching the monotonous play with a strange shining excitement, his face quite fixed and still.

When the curtain rose for the third act, the third act did not take place at once. There was instead disclosed a backdrop almost covered with an American flag improperly and disrespectfully exposed, nailed at each upper corner, gathered in the middle and nailed again, sagging dustily. Before it posed a local dollar-a-year man, now doing his bit as a Liberty Bond salesman. He was an ordinary man past middle life, with a neat little melon buttoned into his trousers and waistcoat, an opinionated tight mouth, a face and figure in which nothing could be read save the inept sensual record of fifty years. But for once in his life he was an important fellow in an impressive situation, and he reveled, rolling his words in an actorish tone.

"Looks like a penguin," said Adam. They moved, smiled at each other, Miranda reclaimed her hand, Adam folded his together and they prepared to wear their way again through the same old moldy speech with the same old dusty backdrop. Miranda tried not to listen, but she heard. These vile Huns—glorious Belleau Wood—our keyword is Sacrifice—Martyred Belgium—give till it hurts—our noble boys Over There—Big Berthas[22]—the death of civilization—the Boche—

"My head aches," whispered Miranda. "Oh, why won't he hush?"

"He won't," whispered Adam. "I'll get you some aspirin."

"In Flanders Field the poppies grow. Between the crosses row on row"[23]—"He's getting into the home stretch," whispered Adam—atrocities, innocent babes hoisted on Boche bayonets—your child and my child—if our children are spared these things, then let us say with all reverence that these dead have not died in vain—the war, the *war*, the WAR to end WAR, war for Democracy, for humanity, a safe world forever and ever—and to prove our faith in Democracy to each other, and to the world, let everybody get together and buy Liberty Bonds and do without sugar and wool socks—was that it? Miranda asked herself, Say that over, I didn't catch the last line. Did you mention Adam? If you didn't I'm not interested. What about Adam, you little pig? And what are we going to sing this time, "Tipperary" or "There's a Long, Long Trail"?[24] Oh, please do let the show go on and get over with. I must write a piece about it before I can go dancing with Adam and we have no time. Coal, oil, iron, gold, international finance, why don't you tell us about them, you little liar?

The audience rose and sang "There's a Long, Long Trail A-winding," their opened mouths black and faces pallid in the reflected footlights; some of the faces grimaced and wept and had shining streaks like snail's tracks on them. Adam and Miranda joined in at the tops of their voices, grinning shamefacedly at each other once or twice.

In the street, they lit their cigarettes and walked slowly as always. "Just another nasty old man who would like to see the young ones

22. Huge German guns used to bombard cities from many miles away.

23. Lines from a famous wartime poem, "In Flanders Fields," written by John McCrae in 1915. Tens of thousands of Allied soldiers were slaughtered in the trench warfare in Flanders (part of Belgium) and northern France during the first year of the war. The speech is a jumble of patriotic references and slogans.

24. Sentimental songs of separation popular during the War—but not actually about the war itself.

killed," said Miranda in a low voice; "the tomcats try to eat the little tomkittens, you know. They don't fool you really, do they, Adam?"

The young people were talking like that about the business by then. They felt they were seeing pretty clearly through that game. She went on, "I hate these potbellied baldheads, too fat, too old, too cowardly, to go to war themselves, they know they're safe; it's you they are sending instead—"

Adam turned eyes of genuine surprise upon her. "Oh, *that* one," he said. "Now what could the poor sap do if they did take him? It's not his fault," he explained, "he can't do anything but talk." His pride in his youth, his forbearance and tolerance and contempt for that unlucky being breathed out of his very pores as he strolled, straight and relaxed in his strength. "What *could* you expect of him, Miranda?"

She spoke his name often, and he spoke hers rarely. The little shock of pleasure the sound of her name in his mouth gave her stopped her answer. For a moment she hesitated, and began at another point of attack. "Adam," she said, "the worst of war is the fear and suspicion and the awful expression in all the eyes you meet . . . as if they had pulled down the shutters over their minds and their hearts and were peering out at you, ready to leap if you make one gesture or say one word they do not understand instantly. It frightens me; I live in fear too, and no one should have to live in fear. It's the skulking about, and the lying. It's what war does to the mind and the heart, Adam, and you can't separate these two—what it does to them is worse than what it can do to the body."

Adam said soberly, after a moment, "Oh, yes, but suppose one comes back whole? The mind and the heart sometimes get another chance, but if anything happens to the poor old human frame, why, it's just out of luck, that's all."

"Oh, yes," mimicked Miranda. "It's just out of luck, that's all."

"If I didn't go," said Adam, in a matter-of-fact voice, "I couldn't look myself in the face."

So that's all settled. With her fingers flattened on his arm, Miranda was silent, thinking about Adam. No, there was no resentment or revolt in him. Pure, she thought, all the way through, flawless, complete, as the sacrificial lamb must be. The sacrificial lamb strode along casually, accommodating his long pace to hers, keeping her on the inside of the walk in the good American style, helping her across street corners as if she were a cripple—"I hope we don't come to a mud puddle, he'll carry me over it"—giving off whiffs of tobacco smoke, a manly smell of scentless soap, freshly cleaned leather and freshly washed skin, breathing through his nose and carrying his chest easily. He threw back his head and smiled into the sky which still misted, promising rain. "Oh, boy," he said, "what a night. Can't you hurry that review of yours so we can get started?"

He waited for her before a cup of coffee in the restaurant next to the pressroom, nicknamed The Greasy Spoon. When she came down at last, freshly washed and combed and powdered, she saw Adam first, sitting near the dingy big window, face turned to the street, but looking down. It was an extraordinary face, smooth and fine and golden in the shabby light, but now set in a blind melancholy, a look of pained suspense and disillusion. For just one split second she got a glimpse of Adam when he would have been older, the face of the man he would not live to be. He saw her then, rose, and the bright glow was there.

Adam pulled their chairs together at their table; they drank hot tea and listened to the orchestra jazzing "Pack Up Your Troubles."

"In an old kit bag, and smoil, smoil, smoil," shouted half a dozen boys under the draft age, gathered around a table near the orchestra. They yelled incoherently, laughed in great hysterical bursts of something that appeared to be merriment, and passed around under the tablecloth flat bottles containing a clear liquid—for in this western city founded and built by roaring drunken miners, no one was allowed to take his alcohol openly—splashed it into their tumblers of ginger ale, and went on singing, "It's a Long Way to Tipperary." When the tune changed to "Madelon,"[25] Adam said, "Let's dance." It was a tawdry little place, crowded and hot and full of smoke, but there was nothing better. The music was gay; and life is completely crazy anyway, thought Miranda, so what does it matter? This is what we have, Adam and I, this is all we're going to get, this is the way it is with us. She wanted to say, "Adam, come out of your dream and listen to me. I have pains in my chest and my head and my heart and they're real. I am in pain all over, and you are in such danger as I can't bear to think about, and why can we not save each other?" When her hand tightened on his shoulder his arm tightened about her waist instantly, and stayed there, holding firmly. They said nothing but smiled continually at each other, odd changing smiles as though they had found a new language. Miranda, her face near Adam's shoulder, noticed a dark young pair sitting at a corner table, each with an arm around the waist of the other, their heads together, their eyes staring at the same thing, whatever it was, that hovered in space before them. Her right hand lay on the table, his hand over it, and her face was a blur with weeping. Now and then he raised her hand and kissed it, and set it down and held it, and her eyes would fill again. They were not

25. A brisk French song popular at the time.

shameless, they had merely forgotten where they were, or they had no other place to go, perhaps. They said not a word, and the small pantomime repeated itself, like a melancholy short film running monotonously over and over again. Miranda envied them. She envied that girl. At least she can weep if that helps, and he does not even have to ask, What is the matter? Tell me. They had cups of coffee before them, and after a long while—Miranda and Adam had danced and sat down again twice—when the coffee was quite cold, they drank it suddenly, then embraced as before, without a word and scarcely a glance at each other. Something was done and settled between them, at least; it was enviable, enviable, that they could sit quietly together and have the same expression on their faces while they looked into the hell they shared, no matter what kind of hell, it was theirs, they were together.

At the table nearest Adam and Miranda a young woman was leaning on her elbow, telling her young man a story. "And I don't like him because he's too fresh. He kept on asking me to take a drink and I kept telling him, I don't drink and he said, Now look here, I want a drink the worst way and I think it's mean of you not to drink with me, I can't sit up here and drink by myself, he said. I told him, You're not by yourself in the first place; I like that, I said, and if you want a drink go ahead and have it, I told him, why drag *me* in? So he called the waiter and ordered ginger ale and two glasses and I drank straight ginger ale like I always do but he poured a shot of hooch in his. He was awfully proud of that hooch, said he made it himself out of potatoes. Nice homemade likker, warm from the pipe, he told me, three drops of this and your ginger ale will taste like Mumm's Extry.[26] But I said, No, and I mean no, can't you get that through your bean? He took another drink and said, Ah, come on, honey, don't be so stubborn, this'll make your shimmy shake. So I just got tired of the argument, and I said, I don't need to drink, to shake my shimmy, I can strut my stuff on tea, I said. Well, why don't you then, he wanted to know, and I just told him—"

She knew she had been asleep for a long time when all at once without even a warning footstep or creak of the door hinge, Adam was in the room turning on the light, and she knew it was he, though at first she was blinded and turned her head away. He came over at once and sat on the side of the bed and began to talk as if he were going on with something they had been talking about before. He crumpled a square of paper and tossed it in the fireplace.

"You didn't get my note," he said. "I left it under the door. I was called back suddenly to camp for a lot of inoculations. They

26. Mumm's Extra Dry, a well-known French champagne.

kept me longer than I expected, I was late. I called the office and they told me you were not coming in today. I called Miss Hobbe here and she said you were in bed and couldn't come to the telephone. Did she give you my message?"

"No," said Miranda drowsily, "but I think I have been asleep all day. Oh, I do remember. There was a doctor here. Bill sent him. I was at the telephone once, for Bill told me he would send an ambulance and have me taken to the hospital. The doctor tapped my chest and left a prescription and said he would be back, but he hasn't come."

"Where is it, the prescription?" asked Adam.

"I don't know. He left it, though, I saw him."

Adam moved about searching the tables and the mantelpiece. "Here it is," he said. "I'll be back in a few minutes. I must look for an all-night drugstore. It's after one o'clock. Good-by."

Good-by, good-by. Miranda watched the door where he had disappeared for quite a while, then closed her eyes, and thought, When I am not here I cannot remember anything about this room where I have lived for nearly a year, except that the curtains are too thin and there was never any way of shutting out the morning light. Miss Hobbe had promised heavier curtains, but they had never appeared. When Miranda in her dressing gown had been at the telephone that morning, Miss Hobbe had passed through, carrying a tray. She was a little red-haired nervously friendly creature, and her manner said all too plainly that the place was not paying and she was on the ragged edge.

"My dear *child,*" she said sharply, with a glance at Miranda's attire, "what is the matter?"

Miranda, with the receiver to her ear, said, "Influenza, I think."

"*Horrors,*" said Miss Hobbe, in a whisper, and the tray wavered in her hands. "Go back to bed at once . . . go at *once*!"

"I must talk to Bill first," Miranda had told her, and Miss Hobbe had hurried on and had not returned. Bill had shouted directions at her, promising everything, doctor, nurse, ambulance, hospital, her check every week as usual, everything, but she was to get back to bed and stay there. She dropped into bed, thinking that Bill was the only person she had ever seen who actually tore his own hair when he was excited enough . . . I suppose I should ask to be sent home, she thought, it's a respectable old custom to inflict your death on the family if you can manage it. No, I'll stay here, this is my business, but not in this room, I hope. . . . I wish I were in the cold mountains in the snow, that's what I should like best; and all about her rose the measured ranges of the Rockies wearing their perpetual snow, their majestic blue laurels of cloud, chilling her to the bone with their sharp breath. Oh, no, I must have warmth—

and her memory turned and roved after another place she had known first and loved best, that now she could see only in drifting fragments of palm and cedar, dark shadows and a sky that warmed without dazzling, as this strange sky had dazzled without warming her; there was the long slow wavering of gray moss in the drowsy oak shade, the spacious hovering of buzzards overhead, the smell of crushed water herbs along a bank, and without warning a broad tranquil river into which flowed all the rivers she had known. The walls shelved away in one deliberate silent movement on either side, and a tall sailing ship was moored near by, with a gangplank weathered to blackness touching the foot of her bed. Back of the ship was jungle, and even as it appeared before her, she knew it was all she had ever read or had been told or felt or thought about jungles; a writhing terribly alive and secret place of death, creeping with tangles of spotted serpents, rainbow-colored birds with malign eyes, leopards with humanly wise faces and extravagantly crested lions; screaming long-armed monkeys tumbling among broad fleshy leaves that glowed with sulphur-colored light and exuded the ichor of death, and rotting trunks of unfamiliar trees sprawled in crawling slime. Without surprise, watching from her pillow, she saw herself run swiftly down this gangplank to the slanting deck, and standing there, she leaned on the rail and waved gaily to herself in bed, and the slender ship spread its wings and sailed away into the jungle. The air trembled with the shattering scream and the hoarse bellow of voices all crying together, rolling and colliding above her like ragged stormclouds, and the words became two words only rising and falling and clamoring about her head. Danger, danger, danger, the voices said, and War, war, war. There was her door half open, Adam standing with his hand on the knob, and Miss Hobbe with her face all out of shape with terror was crying shrilly, "I tell you, they must come for her *now*, or I'll put her on the sidewalk. . . . I tell you, this is a plague, a plague, my God, and I've got a houseful of people to think about!"

Adam said, "I know that. They'll come for her tomorrow morning."

"Tomorrow morning, my God, they'd better come now!"

"They can't get an ambulance," said Adam, "and there aren't any beds. And we can't find a doctor or a nurse. They're all busy. That's all there is to it. You stay out of the room, and I'll look after her."

"Yes, you'll look after her, I can see that," said Miss Hobbe, in a particularly unpleasant tone.

"Yes, that's what I said," answered Adam, drily, "and you keep out."

He closed the door carefully. He was carrying an assortment of misshapen packages, and his face was astonishingly impassive.

"Did you hear that?" he asked, leaning over and speaking very quietly.

"Most of it," said Miranda, "it's a nice prospect, isn't it?"

"I've got your medicine," said Adam, "and you're to begin with it this minute. She can't put you out."

"So it's really as bad as that," said Miranda.

"It's as bad as anything can be," said Adam, "all the theaters and nearly all the shops and restaurants are closed, and the streets have been full of funerals all day and ambulances all night—"

"But not one for me," said Miranda, feeling hilarious and light-headed. She sat up and beat her pillow into shape and reached for her robe. "I'm glad you're here, I've been having a nightmare. Give me a cigarette, will you, and light one for yourself and open all the windows and sit near one of them. You're running a risk," she told him, "don't you know that? Why do you do it?"

"Never mind," said Adam, "take your medicine," and offered her two large cherry-colored pills. She swallowed them promptly and instantly vomited them up. "*Do* excuse me," she said, beginning to laugh. "I'm so sorry." Adam without a word and with a very concerned expression washed her face with a wet towel, gave her some cracked ice from one of the packages, and firmly offered her two more pills. "That's what they always did at home," she explained to him, "and it worked." Crushed with humiliation, she put her hands over her face and laughed again, painfully.

"There are two more kinds yet," said Adam, pulling her hands from her face and lifting her chin. "You've hardly begun. And I've got other things, like orange juice and ice cream—they told me to feed you ice cream—and coffee in a thermos bottle, and a thermometer. You have to work through the whole lot so you'd better take it easy."

"This time last night we were dancing," said Miranda, and drank something from a spoon. Her eyes followed him about the room, as he did things for her with an absentminded face, like a man alone; now and again he would come back, and slipping his hand under her head, would hold a cup or a tumbler to her mouth, and she drank, and followed him with her eyes again, without a clear notion of what was happening.

"Adam," she said, "I've just thought of something. Maybe they forgot St. Luke's Hospital. Call the sisters there and ask them not to be so selfish with their silly old rooms. Tell them I only want a very small dark ugly one for three days, or less. Do try them, Adam."

He believed, apparently, that she was still more or less in her right mind, for she heard him at the telephone explaining in his deliberate voice. He was back again almost at once, saying, "This seems to be my day for getting mixed up with peevish old maids.

The sister said that even if they had a room you couldn't have it without doctor's orders. But they didn't have one, anyway. She was pretty sour about it."

"Well," said Miranda in a thick voice, "I think that's abominably rude and mean, don't you?" She sat up with a wide gesture of both arms, and began to retch again, violently.

"Hold it, as you were," called Adam, fetching the basin. He held her head, washed her face and hands with ice water, put her head straight on the pillow, and went over and looked out the window. "Well," he said at last, sitting beside her again, "they haven't got a room. They haven't got a bed. They haven't even got a baby crib, the way she talked. So I think that's straight enough, and we may as well dig in."

"Isn't the ambulance coming?"

"Tomorrow, maybe."

He took off his tunic and hung it on the back of a chair. Kneeling before the fireplace, he began carefully to set kindling sticks in the shape of an Indian tepee, with a little paper in the center for them to lean upon. He lighted this and placed other sticks upon them, and larger bits of wood. When they were going nicely he added still heavier wood, and coal a few lumps at a time, until there was a good blaze, and a fire that would not need rekindling. He rose and dusted his hands together, the fire illuminated him from the back and his hair shone.

"Adam," said Miranda, "I think you're very beautiful." He laughed out at this, and shook his head at her. "What a hell of a word," he said, "for me." "It was the first that occurred to me," she said, drawing up on her elbow to catch the warmth of the blaze. "That's a good job, that fire."

He sat on the bed again, dragging up a chair and putting his feet on the rungs. They smiled at each other for the first time since he had come in that night. "How do you feel now?" he asked.

"Better, much better," she told him. "Let's talk. Let's tell each other what we meant to do."

"You tell me first," said Adam. "I want to know about you."

"You'd get the notion I had a very sad life," she said, "and perhaps it was, but I'd be glad enough to have it now. If I could have it back, it would be easy to be happy about almost anything at all. That's not true, but that's the way I feel now." After a pause, she said, "There's nothing to tell, after all, if it ends now, for all this time I was getting ready for something that was going to happen later, when the time came. So now it's nothing much."

"But it must have been worth having until now, wasn't it?" he asked seriously as if it were something important to know.

"Not if this is all," she repeated obstinately.

"Weren't you ever—happy?" asked Adam, and he was plainly afraid of the word; he was shy of it as he was of the word *love*, he seemed never to have spoken it before, and was uncertain of its sound or meaning.

"I don't know," she said, "I just lived and never thought about it. I remember things I liked, though, and things I hoped for."

"I was going to be an electrical engineer," said Adam. He stopped short. "And I shall finish up when I get back," he added, after a moment.

"Don't you love being alive?" asked Miranda. "Don't you love weather and the colors at different times of the day, and all the sounds and noises like children screaming in the next lot, and automobile horns and little bands playing in the street and the smell of food cooking?"

"I love to swim, too," said Adam.

"So do I," said Miranda; "we never did swim together."

"Do you remember any prayers?" she asked him suddenly. "Did you ever learn anything at Sunday School?"

"Not much," confessed Adam without contrition. "Well, the Lord's Prayer."

"Yes, and there's Hail Mary," she said, "and the really useful one beginning, I confess to Almighty God and to blessed Mary ever virgin and to the holy Apostles Peter and Paul—"

"Catholic," he commented.

"Prayers just the same, you big Methodist. I'll bet you *are* a Methodist."

"No, Presbyterian."

"Well, what others do you remember?"

"Now I lay me down to sleep—" said Adam.

"Yes, that one, and Blessed Jesus meek and mild—you see that my religious education wasn't neglected either. I even know a prayer beginning O Apollo.[27] Want to hear it?"

"No," said Adam, "you're making fun."

"I'm not," said Miranda, "I'm trying to keep from going to sleep. I'm afraid to go to sleep, I may not wake up. Don't let me go to sleep, Adam. Do you know Matthew, Mark, Luke and John? Bless the bed I lie upon?"

"If I should die before I wake, I pray the Lord my soul to take. Is that it?" asked Adam. "It doesn't sound right, somehow."

"Light me a cigarette, please, and move over and sit near the window. We keep forgetting about fresh air. You must have it." He lighted the cigarette and held it to her lips. She took it between her fingers and dropped it under the edge of her pillow. He found it and crushed it out in the saucer under the water tumbler. Her head

27. Greek god of many attributes, including healing.

swam in darkness for an instant, cleared, and she sat up in panic, throwing off the covers and breaking into a sweat. Adam leaped up with an alarmed face, and almost at once was holding a cup of hot coffee to her mouth.

"You must have some too," she told him, quiet again, and they sat huddled together on the edge of the bed, drinking coffee in silence.

Adam said, "You must lie down again. You're awake now."

"Let's sing," said Miranda. "I know an old spiritual, I can remember some of the words." She spoke in a natural voice. "I'm fine now." She began in a hoarse whisper, " 'Pale horse, pale rider, done taken my lover away. . . .' Do you know that song?"

"Yes," said Adam, "I heard Negroes in Texas sing it, in an oil field."

"I heard them sing it in a cotton field," she said; "it's a good song."

They sang that line together. "But I can't remember what comes next," said Adam.

" 'Pale horse, pale rider,' " said Miranda. "(We really need a good banjo) 'done taken my lover away—' " Her voice cleared and she said, "But we ought to get on with it. What's the next line?"

"There's a lot more to it than that," said Adam, "about forty verses, the rider done taken away mammy, pappy, brother, sister, the whole family besides the lover—"

"But not the singer, not yet," said Miranda. "Death always leaves one singer to mourn. 'Death,' " she sang, " 'oh, leave one singer to mourn—' "

" 'Pale horse, pale rider,' " chanted Adam, coming in on the beat, " 'done taken my lover away!' (I think we're good, I think we ought to get up an act—)"

"Go in Hut Service," said Miranda, "entertain the poor defenseless heroes Over There."

"We'll play banjos," said Adam; "I always wanted to play the banjo."

Miranda sighed, and lay back on the pillow and thought, I must give up, I can't hold out any longer. There was only that pain, only that room, and only Adam. There were no longer any multiple planes of living, no tough filaments of memory and hope pulling taut backwards and forwards holding her upright between them. There was only this one moment and it was a dream of time, and Adam's face, very near hers, eyes still and intent, was a shadow, and there was to be nothing more. . . .

"Adam," she said out of the heavy soft darkness that drew her down, down, "I love you, and I was hoping you would say that to me, too."

He lay down beside her with his arm under her shoulder, and pressed his smooth face against hers, his mouth moved towards her mouth and stopped. "Can you hear what I am saying? . . . What do you think I have been trying to tell you all this time?"

She turned towards him, the cloud cleared and she saw his face for an instant. He pulled the covers about her and held her, and said, "Go to sleep, darling, darling, if you will go to sleep now for one hour I will wake you up and bring you hot coffee and tomorrow we will find somebody to help. I love you, go to sleep—"

Almost with no warning at all, she floated into the darkness, holding his hand, in sleep that was not sleep but clear evening light in a small green wood, an angry dangerous wood full of inhuman concealed voices singing sharply like the whine of arrows and she saw Adam transfixed by a flight of these singing arrows that struck him in the heart and passed shrilly cutting their path through the leaves. Adam fell straight back before her eyes, and rose again unwounded and alive; another flight of arrows loosed from the invisible bow struck him again and he fell, and yet he was there before her untouched in a perpetual death and resurrection. She threw herself before him, angrily and selfishly she interposed, between him and the track of the arrow, crying, No, no, like a child cheated in a game, It's my turn now, why must you always be the one to die? and the arrows struck her cleanly through the heart and through his body and he lay dead, and she still lived, and the wood whistled and sang and shouted, every branch and leaf and blade of grass had its own terrible accusing voice. She ran then, and Adam caught her in the middle of the room, running, and said, "Darling, I must have been asleep too. What happened, you screamed terribly?"

After he had helped her to settle again, she sat with her knees drawn up under her chin, resting her head on her folded arms and began carefully searching for her words because it was important to explain clearly. "It was a very odd sort of dream, I don't know why it could have frightened me. There was something about an old-fashioned valentine. There were two hearts carved on a tree, pierced by the same arrow—you know, Adam—"

"Yes, I know, honey," he said in the gentlest sort of way, and sat kissing her on the cheek and forehead with a kind of accustomedness, as if he had been kissing her for years, "one of those lace paper things."

"Yes, and yet they were alive, and were us, you understand—this doesn't seem to be quite the way it was, but it was something like that. It was in a wood—"

"Yes," said Adam. He got up and put on his tunic and gathered up the thermos bottle. "I'm going back to that little stand and get us some ice cream and hot coffee," he told her, "and I'll be back in five minutes, and you keep quiet. Good-by for five minutes," he said, holding her chin in the palm of his hand and trying to catch her eye, "and you be very quiet."

"Good-by," she said. "I'm awake again." But she was not, and the two alert young internes from the County hospital who had arrived, after frantic urgings from the noisy city editor of the Blue Mountain *News*, to carry her away in a police ambulance, decided that they had better go down and get the stretcher. Their voices roused her, she sat up, got out of bed at once and stood glancing about brightly. "Why, you're all right," said the darker and stouter of the two young men, both extremely fit and competent-looking in their white clothes, each with a flower in his buttonhole. "I'll just carry you." He unfolded a white blanket and wrapped it around her. She gathered up the folds and asked, "But where is Adam?" taking hold of the doctor's arm. He laid a hand on her drenched forehead, shook his head, and gave her a shrewd look. "Adam?"

"Yes," Miranda told him, lowering her voice confidentially, "he was here and now he is gone."

"Oh, he'll be back," the interne told her easily, "he's just gone round the block to get cigarettes. Don't worry about Adam. He's the least of your troubles."

"Will he know where to find me?" she asked, still holding back.

"We'll leave him a note," said the interne. "Come now, it's time we got out of here."

He lifted and swung her up to his shoulder. "I feel very badly," she told him; "I don't know why."

"I'll bet you do," said he, stepping out carefully, the other doctor going before them, and feeling for the first step of the stairs. "Put your arms around my neck," he instructed her. "It won't do you any harm and it's a great help to me."

"What's your name?" Miranda asked as the other doctor opened the front door and they stepped out into the frosty sweet air.

"Hildesheim," he said, in the tone of one humoring a child.

"Well, Dr. Hildesheim, aren't we in a pretty mess?"

"We certainly are," said Dr. Hildesheim.

The second young interne, still quite fresh and dapper in his white coat, though his carnation was withering at the edges, was leaning over listening to her breathing through a stethoscope, whistling thinly, "There's a Long, Long Trail—" From time to time he tapped her ribs smartly with two fingers, whistling. Miranda observed him for a few moments until she fixed his bright busy hazel eye not four inches from hers. "I'm not unconscious," she explained, "I know what I want to say." Then to her horror she heard herself babbling nonsense, knowing it was nonsense though she could not hear what she was saying. The flicker of attention in the eye near her vanished, the second interne went on tapping and listening, hissing softly under his breath.

"I wish you'd stop whistling," she said clearly. The sound stopped. "It's a beastly tune," she added. Anything, anything at all to keep her small hold on the life of human beings, a clear line of communication, no matter what, between her and the receding world. "Please let me see Dr. Hildesheim," she said, "I have something important to say to him. I must say it now." The second interne vanished. He did not walk away, he fled into the air without a sound, and Dr. Hildesheim's face appeared in his stead.

"Dr. Hildesheim, I want to ask you about Adam."

"That young man? He's been here, and left you a note, and has gone again," said Dr. Hildesheim, "and he'll be back tomorrow and the day after." His tone was altogether too merry and flippant.

"I don't believe you," said Miranda bitterly, closing her lips and eyes and hoping she might not weep.

"Miss Tanner," called the doctor, "have you got that note?"

Miss Tanner appeared beside her, handed her an unsealed envelope, took it back, unfolded the note and gave it to her.

"I can't see it," said Miranda, after a pained search of the page full of hasty scratches in black ink.

"Here, I'll read it," said Miss Tanner. "It says, 'They came and took you while I was away and now they will not let me see you. Maybe tomorrow they will, with my love, Adam,' " read Miss Tanner in a firm dry voice, pronouncing the words distinctly. "Now, do you see?" she asked soothingly.

Miranda, hearing the words one by one, forgot them one by one. "Oh, read it again, what does it say?" she called out over the silence that pressed upon her, reaching towards the dancing words that just escaped as she almost touched them. "That will do," said Dr. Hildesheim, calmly authoritarian. "Where is that bed?"

"There is no bed yet," said Miss Tanner, as if she said, We are short of oranges. Dr. Hildesheim said, "Well, we'll manage something," and Miss Tanner drew the narrow trestle with bright crossed metal supports and small rubbery wheels into a deep jut of the corridor, out of the way of the swift white figures darting about, whirling and skimming like water flies all in silence. The white walls rose sheer as cliffs, a dozen frosted moons followed each other in perfect self-possession down a white lane and dropped mutely one by one into a snowy abyss.

What is this whiteness and silence but the absence of pain? Miranda lay lifting the nap of her white blanket softly between eased fingers, watching a dance of tall deliberate shadows moving behind a wide screen of sheets spread upon a frame. It was there, near her, on her side of the wall where she could see it clearly and enjoy it, and it was so beautiful she had no curiosity as to its meaning. Two dark figures nodded, bent, curtsied to each other, retreated and bowed again, lifted long arms and spread great hands against the white shadow of the screen; then with a single round movement, the sheets were folded back, disclosing two speechless men in white, standing, and another speechless man in white, lying on the bare springs of a white iron bed. The man on the springs was swathed smoothly from head to foot in white, with folded bands across the face, and a large stiff bow like merry rabbit ears dangled at the crown of his head.

The two living men lifted a mattress standing hunched against the wall, spread it tenderly and exactly over the dead man. Wordless and white they vanished down the corridor, pushing the wheeled bed before them. It had been an entrancing and leisurely spectacle, but now it was over. A pallid white fog rose in their wake insinuatingly and floated before Miranda's eyes, a fog in which was concealed all terror and all weariness, all the wrung faces and twisted backs and broken feet of abused, outraged living things, all the shapes of their confused pain and their estranged hearts; the fog might part at any moment and loose the horde of human torments. She put up her hands and said, Not yet, not yet, but it was too late. The fog parted and two executioners, white clad, moved towards her pushing between them with marvelously deft and practiced hands the misshapen figure of an old man in filthy rags whose scanty beard waggled under his opened mouth as he bowed his back and braced his feet to resist and delay the fate they had prepared for him. In a high weeping voice he was trying to explain to them that the crime of which he was accused did not merit the punishment he was about to receive; and except for this whining cry there was silence as they advanced. The soiled cracked bowls of the old man's hands were held before him beseechingly as a beggar's as he said, "Before God I am not guilty," but they held his arms and drew him onward, passed, and were gone.

The road to death is a long march beset with all evils, and the heart fails little by little at each new terror, the bones rebel at each step, the mind sets up its own bitter resistance and to what end? The barriers sink one by one, and no covering of the eyes shuts out the landscape of disaster, nor the sight of crimes committed there. Across the field came Dr. Hildesheim, his face a skull beneath his German helmet, carrying a naked infant writhing on the point of his bayonet, and a huge stone pot marked Poison in Gothic letters. He stopped before the well that Miranda remembered in a pasture on her father's farm, a well once dry but now bubbling with living water, and into its pure depths he threw the child and the poison, and the violated water sank back soundlessly into the earth. Miranda, screaming, ran with her arms above her head; her voice echoed and came back to her like a wolf's howl, Hildesheim is a Boche, a spy, a Hun, kill him, kill him before he kills you. . . . She woke howling, she heard the foul words accusing Dr. Hildesheim tumbling from her mouth; opened her eyes and knew she was in a bed in a small white room, with Dr. Hildesheim sitting beside her, two firm fingers on her pulse. His hair was brushed sleekly and his buttonhole flower was fresh. Stars gleamed through the window, and Dr. Hildesheim seemed to be gazing at them with no particular expression, his stethoscope dangling around his neck. Miss Tanner stood at the foot of the bed writing something on a chart.

"Hello," said Dr. Hildesheim, "at least you take it out in shouting. You don't try to get out of bed and go running around." Miranda held her eyes open with a terrible effort, saw his rather heavy, patient face clearly even as her mind tottered and slithered again, broke from its foundation and spun like a cast wheel in a ditch. "I didn't mean it, I never believed it, Dr. Hildesheim, you mustn't remember it—" and was gone again, not being able to wait for an answer.

The wrong she had done followed her and haunted her dream: this wrong took vague shapes of horror she could not recognize or name, though her heart cringed at sight of them. Her mind, split in two, acknowledged and denied what she saw in the one instant, for across an abyss of complaining darkness her reasoning coherent self watched the strange frenzy of the other coldly, reluctant to admit the truth of its visions, its tenacious remorses and despairs.

"I know those are your hands," she told Miss Tanner, "I know it but to me they are white tarantulas, don't touch me."

"Shut your eyes," said Miss Tanner.

"Oh, no," said Miranda, "for then I see worse things," but her eyes closed in spite of her will, and the midnight of her internal torment closed about her.

Oblivion, thought Miranda, her mind feeling among her memories of words she had been taught to describe the unseen, the unknowable, is a whirlpool of gray water turning upon itself for all eternity . . . eternity is perhaps more than the distance to the farthest star. She lay on a narrow ledge over a pit that she knew to be bottomless, though she could not comprehend it; the ledge was her childhood dream of danger, and she strained back against a reassuring wall of granite at her shoulders, staring into the pit, thinking, There it is, there it is at last, it is very simple; and soft carefully shaped words like oblivion and eternity are curtains hung before nothing at all. I shall not know when it happens, I shall not feel or remember, why can't I consent now, I am lost, there is no hope for me. Look, she told herself, there it is, that is death and there is nothing to fear. But she could not consent, still shrinking stiffly against the granite wall that was her childhood dream of safety, breathing slowly for fear of squandering breath, saying desperately, Look, don't be afraid, it is nothing, it is only eternity.

Granite walls, whirlpools, stars, are things. None of them is death, nor the image of it. Death is death, said Miranda, and for the dead it has no attributes. Silenced, she sank easily through deeps under deeps of darkness until she lay like a stone at the farthest bottom of life, knowing herself to be blind, deaf, speechless, no longer aware of the members of her own body, entirely withdrawn from all human concerns, yet alive with a peculiar lucidity and coherence; all notions of the mind, the reasonable inquiries of doubt, all ties of blood and the desires of the heart, dissolved and fell away from her, and there remained of her only a minute fiercely burning particle of being that knew itself alone, that relied upon nothing beyond itself for its strength; not susceptible to any appeal or inducement, being itself composed entirely of one single motive, the stubborn will to live. This fiery motionless particle set itself unaided to resist destruction, to survive and to be in its own madness of being, motiveless and planless beyond that one essential end. Trust me, the hard unwinking angry point of light said. Trust me. I stay.

At once it grew, flattened, thinned to a fine radiance, spread like a great fan and curved out into a rainbow through which Miranda, enchanted, altogether believing, looked upon a deep clear landscape of sea and sand, of soft meadow and sky, freshly washed and glistening with transparencies of blue. Why, of course, of course, said Miranda, without surprise but with serene rapture as if some promise made to her had been kept long after she had ceased to hope for it. She rose from her narrow ledge and ran lightly through the tall portals of the great bow that arched in its splendor over the burning blue of the sea and the cool green of the meadow on either hand.

The small waves rolled in and over unhurriedly, lapped upon the sand in silence and retreated; the grasses flurried before a breeze that made no sound. Moving towards her leisurely as clouds through the shimmering air came a great company of human beings, and Miranda saw in an amazement of joy that they were all the living she had known. Their faces were transfigured, each in its own beauty, beyond what she remembered of them, their eyes were clear and untroubled as good weather, and they cast no shadows. They were pure identities and she knew them every one without calling their names or remembering what relation she bore to them. They surrounded her smoothly on silent feet, then turned their entranced faces again towards the sea, and she moved among them easily as a wave among waves. The drifting circle widened, separated, and each figure was alone but not solitary; Miranda, alone too, questioning nothing, desiring nothing, in the quietude of her ecstasy, stayed where she was, eyes fixed on the overwhelming deep sky where it was always morning.

Lying at ease, arms under her head, in the prodigal warmth which flowed evenly from sea and sky and meadow, within touch but not touching the serenely smiling familiar beings about her, Miranda felt without warning a vague tremor of apprehension, some small flick of distrust in her joy; a thin frost touched the edges of this confident tranquillity; something, somebody, was missing, she had lost something, she had left something valuable in another country, oh, what could it be? There are no trees, no trees here, she said in fright, I have left something unfinished. A thought struggled at the back of her mind, came clearly as a voice in her ear. Where are the dead? We have forgotten the dead, oh, the dead, where are they? At once as if a curtain had fallen, the bright landscape faded, she was alone in a strange stony place of bitter cold, picking her way along a steep path of slippery snow, calling out, Oh, I must go back! But in what direction? Pain returned, a terrible compelling pain running through her veins like heavy fire, the stench of corruption filled her nostrils, the sweetish sickening smell of rotting flesh and pus; she opened her eyes and saw pale light through a coarse white cloth over her face, knew that the smell of death was in her own body, and struggled to lift her hand. The cloth was drawn away; she saw Miss Tanner filling a hypodermic needle in her methodical expert way, and heard Dr. Hildesheim saying, "I think that will do the trick. Try another." Miss Tanner plucked firmly at Miranda's arm near the shoulder, and the unbelievable current of agony ran burning through her veins again. She struggled to cry out, saying, Let me go, let me go; but heard only incoherent sounds of animal suffering. She saw doctor and nurse glance at each other with the glance of initiates at a mystery, nodding in silence, their eyes alive with knowledgeable pride. They looked briefly at their handiwork and hurried away.

Bells screamed all off key, wrangling together as they collided in midair, horns and whistles mingled shrilly with cries of human distress; sulphur-colored light exploded through the black windowpane and flashed away in darkness. Miranda waking from a dreamless sleep asked without expecting an answer, "What is happening?" for there was a bustle of voices and footsteps in the corridor, and a sharpness in the air; the far clamor went on, a furious exasperated shrieking like a mob in revolt.

The light came on, and Miss Tanner said in a furry voice, "Hear that? They're celebrating. It's the Armistice.[28] The war is over, my dear." Her hands trembled. She rattled a spoon in a cup, stopped to

28. November 11, 1918.

listen, held the cup out to Miranda. From the ward for old bedridden women down the hall floated a ragged chorus of cracked voices singing, "My country, 'tis of thee . . ."

Sweet land . . . oh, terrible land of this bitter world where the sound of rejoicing was a clamor of pain, where ragged tuneless old women, sitting up waiting for their evening bowl of cocoa, were singing, "Sweet land of Liberty—"

"Oh, say, can you see?" their hopeless voices were asking next, the hammer strokes of metal tongues drowning them out. "The war is over," said Miss Tanner, her underlip held firmly, her eyes blurred. Miranda said, "Please open the window, please, I smell death in here."

Now if real daylight such as I remember having seen in this world would only come again, but it is always twilight or just before morning, a promise of day that is never kept. What has become of the sun? That was the longest and loneliest night and yet it will not end and let the day come. Shall I ever see light again?

Sitting in a long chair, near a window, it was in itself a melancholy wonder to see the colorless sunlight slanting on the snow, under a sky drained of its blue. "Can this be my face?" Miranda asked her mirror. "Are these my own hands?" she asked Miss Tanner, holding them up to show the yellow tint like melted wax glimmering between the closed fingers. The body is a curious monster, no place to live in, how could anyone feel at home there? Is it possible I can ever accustom myself to this place? she asked herself. The human faces around her seemed dulled and tired, with no radiance of skin and eyes as Miranda remembered radiance; the once white walls of her room were now a soiled gray. Breathing slowly, falling asleep and waking again, feeling the splash of water on her flesh, taking food, talking in bare phrases with Dr. Hildesheim and Miss Tanner, Miranda looked about her with the covertly hostile eyes of an alien who does not like the country in which he finds himself, does not understand the language nor wish to learn it, does not mean to live there and yet is helpless, unable to leave it at his will.

"It is morning," Miss Tanner would say, with a sigh, for she had grown old and weary once for all in the past month, "morning again, my dear," showing Miranda the same monotonous landscape of dulled evergreens and leaden snow. She would rustle about in her starched skirts, her face bravely powdered, her spirit unbreakable as good steel, saying, "Look, my dear, what a heavenly morning, like a crystal," for she had an affection for the salvaged creature before her, the silent ungrateful human being whom she, Cornelia Tanner, a nurse who knew her business, had snatched back from death with her own hands. "Nursing is nine-tenths, just the same," Miss Tanner would tell the other nurses; "keep that in mind." Even the sunshine was Miss Tanner's own prescription for the further recovery of Miranda, this patient the doctors had given up for lost, and who yet sat here, visible proof of Miss Tanner's theory. She said, "Look at the sunshine, now," as she might be saying, "I ordered this for you, my dear, do sit up and take it."

"It's beautiful," Miranda would answer, even turning her head to look, thanking Miss Tanner for her goodness, most of all her goodness about the weather, "beautiful, I always loved it." And I might love it again if I saw it, she thought, but truth was, she could not see it. There was no light, there might never be light again, compared as it must always be with the light she had seen beside the blue sea that lay so tranquilly along the shore of her paradise. That was a child's dream of the heavenly meadow, the vision of repose that comes to a tired body in sleep, she thought, but I have seen it when I did not know it was a dream. Closing her eyes she would rest for a moment remembering that bliss which had repaid all the pain of the journey to reach it; opening them again she saw with a new anguish the dull world to which she was condemned, where the light seemed filmed over with cobwebs, all the bright surfaces corroded, the sharp planes melted and formless, all objects and beings meaningless, ah, dead and withered things that believed themselves alive!

At night, after the long effort of lying in her chair, in her extremity of grief for what she had so briefly won, she folded her painful body together and wept silently, shamelessly, in pity for herself and her lost rapture. There was no escape. Dr. Hildesheim, Miss Tanner, the nurses in the diet kitchen, the chemist, the surgeon, the precise machine of the hospital, the whole humane conviction and custom of society, conspired to pull her inseparable rack of bones and wasted flesh to its feet, to put in order her disordered mind, and to set her once more safely in the road that would lead her again to death.

Chuck Rouncivale and Mary Townsend came to see her, bringing her a bundle of letters they had guarded for her. They brought a basket of delicate small hothouse flowers, lilies of the valley with sweet peas and feathery fern, and above these blooms their faces were merry and haggard.

Mary said, "You *have* had a tussle, haven't you?" and Chuck said, "Well, you made it back, didn't you?" Then after an uneasy pause, they told her that everybody was waiting to see her again at her desk. "They've put me back on sports already, Miranda," said Chuck. For ten minutes Miranda smiled and told them how gay and what a pleasant surprise it was to find herself alive. For it will not do to betray the conspiracy and tamper with the courage of the living; there is nothing better than to be alive, everyone has agreed on that; it is past argument, and who attempts to deny it is justly outlawed. "I'll be back in no time at all," she said; "this is almost over."

Her letters lay in a heap in her lap and beside her chair. Now and then she turned one over to read the inscription, recognizing this handwriting or that, examined the blotted stamps and the postmarks, and let them drop again. For two or three days they lay upon the table beside her, and she continued to shrink from them. "They will all be telling me again how good it is to be alive, they will say again they love me, they are glad I am living too, and what can I answer to that?" and her hardened, indifferent heart shuddered in despair of itself, because before it had been tender and capable of love.

Dr. Hildesheim said, "What, all these letters not opened yet?" and Miss Tanner said, "Read your letters, my dear, I'll open them for you." Standing beside the bed, she slit them cleanly with a paper knife. Miranda, cornered, picked and chose until she found a thin one in an unfamiliar handwriting. "Oh, no, now," said Miss Tanner, "take them as they come. Here, I'll hand them to you." She sat down, prepared to be helpful to the end.

What a victory, what triumph, what happiness to be alive, sang the letters in a chorus. The names were signed with flourishes like the circles in air of bugle notes, and they were the names of those she had loved best; some of those she had known well and pleasantly; and a few who meant nothing to her, then or now. The thin letter in the unfamiliar handwriting was from a strange man at the camp where Adam had been, telling her that Adam had died of influenza in the camp hospital. Adam had asked him, in case anything happened, to be sure to let her know.

If anything happened. To be sure to let her know. If anything happened. "Your friend, Adam Barclay," wrote the strange man. It had happened—she looked at the date—more than a month ago.

"I've been here a long time, haven't I?" she asked Miss Tanner, who was folding letters and putting them back in their proper envelopes.

"Oh, quite a while," said Miss Tanner, "but you'll be ready to go soon now. But you must be careful of yourself and not overdo, and you should come back now and then and let us look at you, because sometimes the after effects are very—"

Miranda, sitting up before the mirror, wrote carefully: "One lipstick, medium, one ounce flask Bois d'Hiver perfume, one pair of gray suede gauntlets[29] without straps, two pair gray sheer stockings without clocks—"[30]

Towney, reading after her, said, "Everything without something so that it will be almost impossible to get?"

"Try it, though," said Miranda, "they're nicer without. One

29. Gloves.

30. Ornamental figures down the sides.

walking stick of silvery wood with a silver knob."

"That's going to be expensive," warned Towney. "Walking is hardly worth it."

"You're right," said Miranda, and wrote in the margin, "a nice one to match my other things. Ask Chuck to look for this, Mary. Good-looking and not too heavy." Lazarus,[31] come forth. Not unless you bring me my top hat and stick. Stay where you are then, you snob. Not at all, I'm coming forth. "A jar of cold cream," wrote Miranda, "a box of apricot powder—and, Mary, I don't need eye shadow, do I?" She glanced at her face in the mirror and away again. "Still, no one need pity this corpse if we look properly to the art of the thing."

Mary Townsend said, "You won't recognize yourself in a week."

"Do you suppose, Mary," asked Miranda, "I could have my old room back again?"

"That should be easy," said Mary. "We stored away all your things there with Miss Hobbe." Miranda wondered again at the time and trouble the living took to be helpful to the dead. But not quite dead now, she reassured herself, one foot in either world now; soon I shall cross back and be at home again. The light will seem real and I shall be glad when I hear that someone I know has escaped from death. I shall visit the escaped ones and help them dress and tell them how lucky they are, and how lucky I am still to have them. Mary will be back soon with my gloves and my walking stick, I must go now, I must begin saying good-by to Miss Tanner and Dr. Hildesheim. Adam, she said, now you need not die again, but still I wish you were here; I wish you had come back, what do you think I came back for, Adam, to be deceived like this?

At once he was there beside her, invisible but urgently present, a ghost but more alive then she was, the last intolerable cheat of her heart; for knowing it was false she still clung to the lie, the unpardonable lie of her bitter desire. She said, "I love you," and stood up trembling, trying by the mere act of her will to bring him to sight before her. If I could call you up from the grave I would, she said, if I could see your ghost I would say, I believe. . . . "I believe," she said aloud. "Oh, let me see you once more." The room was silent, empty, the shade was gone from it, struck away by the sudden violence of her rising and speaking aloud. She came to herself as if out of sleep. Oh, no, that is not the way, I must never do that, she warned herself. Miss Tanner said, "Your taxicab is waiting, my dear," and there was Mary. Ready to go.

No more war, no more plague, only the dazed silence that follows the ceasing of the heavy guns; noiseless houses with the shades drawn, empty streets, the dead cold light of tomorrow. Now there would be time for everything.

31. Man raised by Jesus from the dead [*John* 11:1–44, 12:1–5.]

WILLIAM FAULKNER

(1897–1962)

Old Man*

I

Once (it was in Mississippi, in May, in the flood year 1927[1]) there were two convicts. One of them was about twenty-five, tall, lean, flat-stomached, with a sunburned face and Indian-black hair and pale, china-colored outraged eyes—an outrage directed not at the men who had foiled his crime, not even at the lawyers and judges who had sent him here, but all the writers, the uncorporeal names attached to the stories, the paper novels—the Diamond Dicks and Jesse Jameses[2] and such—whom he believed had led him into his present predicament through their own ignorance and gullibility regarding the medium in which they dealt and took money for, in accepting information on which they placed the stamp of verisimilitude and authenticity (this so much the more criminal since there was no sworn notarized statement attached and hence so much the quicker would the information be accepted by one who expected the same unspoken good faith, demanding, asking, expecting no certification, which he extended along with the dime or fifteen cents to pay for it) and retailed for money and which on actual application proved to be impractical and (to the convict) criminally false; there would be times when he would halt his mule and plow in midfurrow (there is no walled penitentiary in Mississippi; it is a cotton plantation[3] which the convicts work under the rifles and shotguns of guards and trustees) and muse with a kind of enraged impotence, fumbling among the rubbish left him by his one and only experience with courts and law, fumbling until the meaningless and verbose shibboleth[4] took form at last (himself seeking justice at the same blind fount where he had met justice and been hurled back and down): Using the mails to defraud: who felt that he had been defrauded by the third-class mail system not of crass and stupid money which he did not particularly want anyway, but of liberty and honor and pride.

He was in for fifteen years (he had arrived shortly after his nineteenth birthday) for attempted train robbery. He had laid his plans

* Published in 1939 as chapters alternating with another story, *The Wild Palms*.

1. The disastrous Mississippi River floods of 1927 lasted more than six weeks, caused over three hundred deaths, and destroyed some $250 million worth of property.

2. Robber heroes of popular adventure stories.

3. The State Penal Farm at Parchman, Mississippi.

4. Password.

in advance, he had followed his printed (and false) authority to the letter; he had saved the paper-backs for two years, reading and rereading them, memorizing them, comparing and weighing story and method against story and method, taking the good from each and discarding the dross as his workable plan emerged, keeping his mind open to make the subtle last-minute changes, without haste and without impatience, as the newer pamphlets appeared on their appointed days as a conscientious dressmaker makes the subtle alterations in a court presentation costume as the newer bulletins[5] appear. And then when the day came, he did not even have a chance to go through the coaches and collect the watches and the rings, the brooches and the hidden money-belts, because he had been captured as soon as he entered the express car where the safe and the gold would be. He had shot no one because the pistol which they took away from him was not that kind of a pistol although it was loaded; later he admitted to the District Attorney that he had got it, as well as the dark lantern in which a candle burned and the black handkerchief to wear over the face, by peddling among his pinehill neighbors subscriptions to the *Detectives' Gazette*. So now from time to time (he had ample leisure for it) he mused with that raging impotence, because there was something else he could not tell them at the trial, did not know how to tell them. It was not the money he had wanted. It was not riches, not the crass loot; that would have been merely a bangle to wear upon the breast of his pride like the Olympic runner's amateur medal—a symbol, a badge to show that he too was the best at his chosen gambit[6] in the living and fluid world of his time. So that at times as he trod the richly shearing black earth behind his plow or with a hoe thinned the sprouting cotton and corn or lay on his sullen back in his bunk after supper, he cursed in a harsh steady unrepetitive stream, not at the living men who had put him where he was but at what he did not even know were pennames, did not even know were not actual men but merely the designations of shades who had written about shades.

The second convict was short and plump. Almost hairless, he was quite white. He looked like something exposed to light by turning over rotting logs or planks and he too carried (though not in his eyes like the first convict) a sense of burning and impotent outrage. So it did not show on him and hence none knew it was there. But then nobody knew very much about him, including the people who had sent him here. His outrage was directed at no printed word but at the paradoxical fact that he had been forced to come here of his

5. Issued by a royal court, for example, as to the style of dress to be worn when being presented to a member of the royal family.

6. Opening move, as in chess.

own free choice and will. He had been forced to choose between the Mississippi State penal farm and the Federal Penitentiary at Atlanta, and the fact that he, who resembled a hairless and pallid slug, had chosen the out-of-doors and the sunlight was merely another manifestation of the close-guarded and solitary enigma of his character, as something recognizable roils momentarily into view from beneath stagnant and opaque water, then sinks again. None of his fellow prisoners knew what his crime had been, save that he was in for a hundred and ninety-nine years—this incredible and impossible period of punishment or restraint itself carrying a vicious and fabulous quality which indicated that his reason for being here was such that the very men, the paladins[7] and pillars of justice and equity who had sent him here had during that moment become blind apostles not of mere justice but of all human decency, blind instruments not of equity but of all human outrage and vengeance, acting in a savage personal concert, judge, lawyer and jury, which certainly abrogated justice and possibly even law. Possibly only the Federal and State's Attorneys knew what the crime actually was There had been a woman in it and a stolen automobile transported across a State line, a filling station robbed and the attendant shot to death. There had been a second man in the car at the time and anyone could have looked once at the convict (as the two attorneys did) and known he would not even have had the synthetic courage of alcohol to pull trigger on anyone. But he and the woman and the stolen car had been captured while the second man, doubtless the actual murderer, had escaped, so that, brought to bay at last in the State's Attorney's office, harried, dishevelled and snarling, the two grimly implacable and viciously gleeful attorneys in his front and the now raging woman held by two policemen in the anteroom in his rear, he was given his choice. He could be tried in Federal Court under the Mann Act and for the automobile,[8] that is, by electing to pass through the anteroom where the woman raged he could take his chances on the lesser crime in Federal Court, or by accepting a sentence for manslaughter in the State Court he would be permitted to quit the room by a back entrance, without having to pass the woman. He had chosen; he stood at the bar and heard a judge (who looked down at him as if the District Attorney actually had turned over a rotten plank with his toe and exposed him) sentence him to a hundred and ninety-nine years at the State Farm. Thus (he had ample leisure too; they had tried to teach him to plow and had failed, they had put him in the blacksmith shop and the fore-

7. Knights of medieval romance, who acted as champions of accuser and accused in trials by battle.

8. Federal laws punish crimes involving the crossing of state lines. The convict may be tried for transporting the automobile across state lines or, under the Mann Act, for transporting the woman allegedly for purposes of prostitution.

man trusty himself had asked to have him removed: so that now, in a long apron like a woman, he cooked and swept and dusted in the deputy wardens' barracks) he too mused at times with that sense of impotence and outrage though it did not show on him as on the first convict since he leaned on no halted broom to do it and so none knew it was there.

It was this second convict who, toward the end of April, began to read aloud to the others from the daily newspapers when, chained ankle to ankle and herded by armed guards, they had come up from the fields and had eaten supper and were gathered in the bunkhouse. It was the Memphis newspaper which the deputy wardens had read at breakfast; the convict read aloud from it to his companions who could have had but little active interest in the outside world, some of whom could not have read it for themselves at all and did not even know where the Ohio and Missouri river basins were, some of whom had never even seen the Mississippi River although for past periods ranging from a few days to ten and twenty and thirty years (and for future periods ranging from a few months to life) they had plowed and planted and eaten and slept beneath the shadow of the levee[9] itself, knowing only that there was water beyond it from hearsay and because now and then they heard the whistles of steamboats from beyond it and, during the last week or so had seen the stacks and pilot houses moving along the sky sixty feet above their heads.

But they listened, and soon even those who like the taller convict had probably never before seen more water than a horse pond would hold knew what thirty feet on a river gauge at Cairo or Memphis[10] meant and could (and did) talk glibly of sandboils.[11] Perhaps what actually moved them were the accounts of the conscripted levee gangs, mixed blacks and whites working in double shifts against the steadily rising water; stories of men, even though they were negroes,[12] being forced like themselves to do work for which they received no other pay than coarse food and a place in a mudfloored tent to sleep on—stories, pictures, which emerged from the shorter convict's reading voice: the mudsplashed white men with the inevitable shot-guns, the antlike lines of negroes carrying sandbags, slipping and crawling up the steep face of the revetment[13] to hurl their futile ammunition into the face of a flood and return for more. Or perhaps it was more than this. Per-

9. Wall built along a river bank to contain floods.

10. Key points along the Mississippi for measuring the river's height on a "river gauge." Cairo, Illinois is at the entry of the Ohio River into the Mississippi; a water height there of 50 feet assures a major flood, and the height in 1927 was 56.4 feet.

11. Water forced by flood pressure through a levee and bursting out at its back.

12. I.e., the convicts acknowledged that the Negroes were men like themselves.

13. Barricade.

haps they watched the approach of the disaster with that same amazed and incredulous hope of the slaves—the lions and bears and elephants, the grooms and bathmen and pastrycooks—who watched the mounting flames of Rome from Ahenobarbus' gardens.[14] But listen they did and presently it was May and the wardens' newspaper began to talk in headlines two inches tall—those black staccato slashes of ink which, it would almost seem, even the illiterate should be able to read: *Crest Passes Memphis at Midnight 4000 Homeless in White River Basin Governor Calls out National Guard Martial Law Declared in Following Counties Red Cross Train with Secretary Hoover*[15] *Leaves Washington Tonight*; then, three evenings later (It had been raining all day—not the vivid brief thunderous downpours of April and May, but the slow steady gray rain of November and December before a cold north wind. The men had not gone to the fields at all during the day, and the very second-hand optimism of the almost twenty-four-hour-old news seemed to contain its own refutation.): *Crest Now Below Memphis 22,000 Refugees Safe at Vicksburg*[16] *Army Engineers Say Levees Will Hold.*

"I reckon that means it will bust tonight," one convict said.

"Well, maybe this rain will hold on until the water gets here," a second said. They all agreed to this because what they meant, the living unspoken thought among them, was that if the weather cleared, even though the levees broke and the flood moved in upon the Farm itself, they would have to return to the fields and work, which they would have had to do. There was nothing paradoxical in this, although they could not have expressed the reason for it which they instinctively perceived: that the land they farmed and the substance they produced from it belonged neither to them who worked it nor to those who forced them at guns' point to do so, that as far as either—convicts or guards—were concerned, it could have been pebbles they put into the ground and papier-mâché cotton- and corn-sprouts which they thinned. So it was that, what between the sudden wild hoping and the idle day and the evening's headlines, they were sleeping restlessly beneath the sound of the rain on the tin roof when at midnight the sudden glare of the electric bulbs and the guards' voices waked them and they heard the throbbing of the waiting trucks.

"Turn out of there!" the deputy shouted. He was fully dressed—rubber boots, slicker and shotgun. "The levee went out at Mound's Landing[17] an hour ago. Get up out of it!"

14. Nero (37–68 A.D.), Roman emperor of the Ahenobarbus family, was supposed to have burned Rome in 64 A.D.

15. Herbert Hoover, then Secretary of Commerce, was an all-purpose domestic trouble-shooter for the Coolidge Aministration.

16. City on the Yazoo River just above its junction with the Mississippi, and at the south end of that region of Mississippi called "the Delta."

17. On the Mississippi River, forty miles southwest of Parchman. The great flood of 1927 began when the levee broke here on April 21.

II

When the belated and streaming dawn broke the two convicts, along with twenty others, were in a truck. A trusty drove, two armed guards sat in the cab with him. Inside the high, stall-like topless body the convicts stood, packed like matches in an upright box or like the pencil-shaped ranks of cordite in a shell,[1] shackled by the ankles to a single chain which wove among the motionless feet and swaying legs and a clutter of picks and shovels among which they stood, and was riveted by both ends to the steel body of the truck.

Then and without warning they saw the flood about which the plump convict had been reading and they listening for two weeks or more. The road ran south. It was built on a raised levee, known locally as a dump, about eight feet above the flat surrounding land, bordered on both sides by the barrow pits from which the earth of the levee had been excavated. These barrow pits had held water all winter from the fall rains, not to speak of the rain of yesterday, but now they saw that the pit on either side of the road had vanished and instead there lay a flat still sheet of brown water which extended into the fields beyond the pits, raveled out into long motionless shreds in the bottom of the plow furrows and gleaming faintly in the gray light like the bars of a prone and enormous grating. And then (the truck was moving at good speed) as they watched quietly (they had not been talking much anyway but now they were all silent and quite grave, shifting and craning as one to look soberly off to the west side of the road) the crests of the furrows vanished too and they now looked at a single perfectly flat and motionless steel-colored sheet in which the telephone poles and the straight hedgerows which marked section lines seemed to be fixed and rigid as though set in concrete.

It was perfectly motionless, perfectly flat. It looked, not innocent, but bland. It looked almost demure. It looked as if you could walk on it. It looked so still that they did not realize it possessed motion until they came to the first bridge. There was a ditch under the bridge, a small stream, but ditch and stream were both invisible now, indicated only by the rows of cypress and bramble which marked its course. Here they both saw and heard movement—the slow profound eastward and upstream ("It's running backward," one convict said quietly.) set of the still rigid surface, from beneath which came a deep faint subaquean[2] rumble which (though none in the truck could have made the comparison) sounded like a subway train passing far beneath the street and which inferred a terrific and secret speed. It was as if the water itself were in three strata, separate and distinct, the bland and unhurried surface bear-

1. Artillery shells were packed with this explosive, which resembled brown twine.

2. Underwater.

ing a frothy scum and a miniature flotsam of twigs and screening as though by vicious calculation the rush and fury of the flood itself, and beneath this in turn the original stream, trickle, murmuring along in the opposite direction, following undisturbed and unaware its appointed course and serving its Lilliputian end, like a thread of ants between the rails on which an express train passes, they (the ants) as unaware of the power and fury as if it were a cyclone crossing Saturn.

Now there was water on both sides of the road and now, as if once they had become aware of movement in the water the water seemed to have given over deception and concealment, they seemed to be able to watch it rising up the flanks of the dump; trees which a few miles back had stood on tall trunks above the water now seemed to burst from the surface at the level of the lower branches like decorative shrubs on barbered lawns. The truck passed a negro cabin. The water was up to the window ledges. A woman clutching two children squatted on the ridgepole, a man and a halfgrown youth, standing waist-deep, were hoisting a squealing pig onto the slanting roof of a barn, on the ridgepole of which sat a row of chickens and a turkey. Near the barn was a haystack on which a cow stood tied by a rope to the center pole and bawling steadily; a yelling negro boy on a saddleless mule which he flogged steadily, his legs clutching the mule's barrel and his body leaned to the drag of a rope attached to a second mule, approached the haystack, splashing and floundering. The woman on the housetop began to shriek at the passing truck, her voice carrying faint and melodious across the brown water, becoming fainter and fainter as the truck passed and went on, ceasing at last, whether because of distance or because she had stopped screaming those in the truck did not know.

Then the road vanished. There was no perceptible slant to it yet it had slipped abruptly beneath the brown surface with no ripple, no ridgy demarcation, like a flat thin blade slipped obliquely into flesh by a delicate hand, annealed into the water without disturbance, as if it had existed so for years, had been built that way. The truck stopped. The trusty descended from the cab and came back and dragged two shovels from among their feet, the blades clashing against the serpentining of the chain about their ankles. "What is it?" one said. "What are you fixing to do?" The trusty didn't answer. He returned to the cab, from which one of the guards had descended, without his shotgun. He and the trusty, both in hip boots and each carrying a shovel, advanced into the water, gingerly, probing and feeling ahead with the shovel handles. The same convict spoke again. He was a middle-aged man with a wild thatch of iron-gray hair and a slightly mad face. "What the hell are they doing?" he said. Again nobody answered him. The truck moved, on into the water, behind the guard and the trusty, beginning to push ahead of itself a thick slow viscid ridge of chocolate water. Then the gray-haired convict began to scream. "God damn it, unlock the chain!" He began to struggle, thrashing violently about him, striking at the men nearest him until he reached the cab, the roof of which he now hammered on with his fists, screaming. "God damn it, unlock us! Unlock us! Son of a bitch!" he screamed, addressing no one. "They're going to drown us! Unlock the chain!" But for all the answer he got the men within radius of his voice might have been dead. The truck crawled on, the guard and the trusty feeling out the road ahead with the reversed shovels, the second guard at the wheel, the twenty-two convicts packed like sardines into the truck bed and padlocked by the ankles to the body of the truck itself. They crossed another bridge—two delicate and paradoxical iron railings slanting out of the water, traveling parallel to it for a distance, then slanting down into it again with an outrageous quality almost significant yet apparently meaningless like something in a dream not quite nightmare. The truck crawled on.

Along toward noon they came to a town, their destination. The streets were paved; now the wheels of the truck made a sound like tearing silk. Moving faster now, the guard and the trusty in the cab again, the truck even had a slight bone in its teeth,[3] its bow-wave spreading beyond the submerged sidewalks and across the adjacent lawns, lapping against the stoops and porches of houses where people stood among piles of furniture. They passed through the business district; a man in hip boots emerged knee-deep in water from a store, dragging a flat-bottomed skiff containing a steel safe.

At last they reached the railroad. It crossed the street at right angles, cutting the town in two. It was on a dump, a levee, also, eight or ten feet above the town itself; the street ran blankly into it and turned at right angles beside a cotton compress[4] and a loading platform on stilts at the level of a freight car door. On this platform was a khaki army tent and a uniformed National Guard sentry with a rifle and bandolier.[5]

The truck turned and crawled out of the water and up the ramp which cotton wagons used and where trucks and private cars filled with household goods came and unloaded into the platform. They were unlocked from the chain in the truck and shackled ankle to ankle in pairs they mounted the platform and into an apparently inextricable jumble of beds and trunks, gas and electric stoves, radios and tables and chairs and framed pictures which a chain of

3. A white bow wave, such as a moving ship makes.
4. Machine for compressing cotton into bales.
5. Ammunition belt.

negroes under the eye of an unshaven white man in muddy corduroy and hip boots carried piece by piece into the compress, at the door of which another guardsman stood with his rifle, they (the convicts) not stopping here but herded on by the two guards with their shotguns, into the dim and cavernous building where among the piled heterogeneous furniture the ends of cotton bales and the mirrors on dressers and sideboards gleamed with an identical mute and unreflecting concentration of pallid light.

They passed on through, onto the loading platform where the army tent and the first sentry were. They waited here. Nobody told them for what nor why. While the two guards talked with the sentry before the tent the convicts sat in a line along the edge of the platform like buzzards on a fence, their shackled feet dangling above the brown motionless flood out of which the railroad embankment rose, pristine and intact, in a kind of paradoxical denial and repudiation of change and portent, not talking, just looking quietly across the track to where the other half of the amputated town seemed to float, house shrub and tree, ordered and pageant-like and without motion, upon the limitless liquid plain beneath the thick gray sky.

After a while the other four trucks from the Farm arrived. They came up, bunched closely, radiator to tail light, with their four separate sounds of tearing silk and vanished beyond the compress. Presently the ones on the platform heard the feet, the mute clashing of the shackles, the first truckload emerged from the compress, the second, the third; there were more than a hundred of them now in their bed-ticking[6] overalls and jumpers and fifteen or twenty guards with rifles and shotguns. The first lot rose and they mingled, paired, twinned by their clanking and clashing umbilicals; then it began to rain, a slow steady gray drizzle like November instead of May. Yet not one of them made any move toward the open door of the compress. They did not even look toward it, with longing or hope or without it. If they thought at all, they doubtless knew that the available space in it would be needed for furniture, even if it were not already filled. Or perhaps they knew that, even if there were room in it, it would not be for them, not that the guards would wish them to get wet but that the guards would not think about getting them out of the rain. So they just stopped talking and with their jumper collars turned up and shackled in braces like dogs at a field trial they stood, immobile, patient, almost ruminant, their backs turned to the rain as sheep and cattle do.

After another while they became aware that the number of soldiers had increased to a dozen or more, warm and dry beneath rubberized ponchos, there was an officer with a pistol at his belt, then and without making any move toward it, they began to smell food

6. Strong fabric for covering mattresses.

and, turning to look, saw an army field kitchen set up just inside the compress door. But they made no move, they waited until they were herded into line, they inched forward, their heads lowered and patient in the rain, and received each a bowl of stew, a mug of coffee, two slices of bread. They ate this in the rain. They did not sit down because the platform was wet, they squatted on their heels as country men do, hunching forward, trying to shield the bowls and mugs into which nevertheless the rain splashed steadily as into miniature ponds and soaked, invisible and soundless, into the bread.

After they had stood on the platform for three hours, a train came for them. Those nearest the edge saw it, watched it—a passenger coach apparently running under its own power and trailing a cloud of smoke from no visible stack, a cloud which did not rise but instead shifted slowly and heavily aside and lay upon the surface of the aqueous earth with a quality at once weightless and completely spent. It came up and stopped, a single old fashioned open-ended wooden car coupled to the nose of a pushing switch engine[7] considerably smaller. They were herded into it, crowding forward to the other end where there was a small cast iron stove. There was no fire in it, nevertheless they crowded about it—the cold and voiceless lump of iron stained with fading tobacco and hovered about by the ghosts of a thousand Sunday excursions to Memphis or Moorhead[8] and return—the peanuts, the bananas, the soiled garments of infants—huddling, shoving for places near it. "Come on, come on," one of the guards shouted. "Sit down, now." At last three of the guards, laying aside their guns, came among them and broke up the huddle, driving them back and into seats.

There were not enough seats for all. The other stood in the aisle, they stood braced, they heard the air hiss out of the released brakes, the engine whistled four blasts, the car came into motion with a snapping jerk; the platform, the compress fled violently as the train seemed to transpose from immobility to full speed with that same quality of unreality with which it had appeared, running backward now though with the engine in front where before it had moved forward but with the engine behind.

When the railroad in its turn ran beneath the surface of the water, the convicts did not even know it. They felt the train stop, they heard the engine blow a long blast which wailed away unechoed across the waste, wild and forlorn, and they were not even curious; they sat or stood behind the rain-streaming windows as the train crawled on again, feeling its way as the truck had while the brown water swirled between the trucks[9] and among the spokes of the driving wheels and lapped in cloudy steam against the dragging

7. A small railway engine, normally used for making trains up rather than hauling them.
8. Memphis, Tennessee, is just across the Mississippi state line; Moorhead is a town about 130 miles south of Memphis.
9. Wheels.

fire-filled belly of the engine; again it blew four short harsh blasts filled with the wild triumph and defiance yet also with repudiation and even farewell, as if the articulated steel itself knew it did not dare stop and would not be able to return. Two hours later in the twilight they saw through the streaming windows a burning plantation house. Juxtaposed to nowhere and neighbored by nothing it stood, a clear steady pyre-like flame rigidly fleeing its own reflection, burning in the dusk above the watery desolation with a quality paradoxical, outrageous and bizarre.

Sometime after dark the train stopped. The convicts did not know where they were. They did not ask. They would no more have thought of asking where they were than they would have asked why and what for. They couldn't even see, since the car was unlighted and the windows fogged on the outside by rain and on the inside by the engendered heat of the packed bodies. All they could see was a milky and sourceless flick and glare of flashlights. They could hear shouts and commands, then the guards inside the car began to shout; they were herded to their feet and toward the exit, the ankle chains clashing and clanking. They descended into a fierce hissing of steam, through ragged wisps of it blowing past the car. Laid-to alongside the train and resembling a train itself was a thick blunt motor launch to which was attached a string of skiffs and flat boats. There were more soldiers; the flashlights played on the rifle barrels and bandolier buckles and flicked and glinted on the ankle chains of the convicts as they stepped gingerly down into knee-deep water and entered the boats; now car and engine both vanished completely in steam as the crew began dumping the fire from the firebox.

After another hour they began to see lights ahead—a faint wavering row of red pin-pricks extending along the horizon and apparently hanging low in the sky. But it took almost another hour to reach them while the convicts squatted in the skiffs, huddled into the soaked garments (they no longer felt the rain any more at all as separate drops) and watched the lights draw nearer and nearer until at last the crest of the levee defined itself; now they could discern a row of army tents stretching along it and people squatting about the fires, the wavering reflections from which, stretching across the water, revealed an involved mass of other skiffs tied against the flank of the levee which now stood high and dark overhead. Flashlights glared and winked along the base, among the tethered skiffs; the launch, silent now, drifted in.

When they reached the top of the levee they could see the long line of khaki tents, interspersed with fires about which people—men, women and children, negro and white—crouched or stood among shapeless bales of clothing, their heads turning, their eyeballs glinting in the firelight as they looked quietly at the striped garments and the chains; further down the levee, huddled together too though untethered, was a drove of mules and two or three cows. Then the taller convict became conscious of another sound. He did not begin to hear it all at once, he suddenly became aware that he had been hearing it all the time, a sound so much beyond all his experience and his powers of assimilation that up to this point he had been as oblivious of it as an ant or a flea might be of the sound of the avalanche on which it rides; he had been traveling upon water since early afternoon and for seven years now he had run his plow and harrow and planter within the very shadow of the levee on which he now stood, but this profound deep whisper which came from the further side of it he did not at once recognize. He stopped. The line of convicts behind jolted into him like a line of freight cars stopping, with an iron clashing like cars. "Get on!" a guard shouted.

"What's that?" the convict said. A negro man squatting before the nearest fire answered him:

"Dat's him. Dat's de Ole Man."

"The old man?" the convict said.

"Get on! Get on up there!" the guard shouted. They went on; they passed another huddle of mules, the eyeballs rolling too, the long morose faces turning into and out of the firelight; they passed them and reached a section of empty tents, the light pup tents of a military campaign, made to hold two men. The guards herded the convicts into them, three brace[10] of shackled men to each tent.

They crawled in on all fours, like dogs into cramped kennels, and settled down. Presently the tent became warm from their bodies. Then they became quiet and then all of them could hear it, they lay listening to the bass whisper deep, strong and powerful. "The old man?" the train-robber convict said.

"Yah," another said. "He dont have to brag."

At dawn the guards waked them by kicking the soles of the projecting feet. Opposite the muddy landing and the huddle of skiffs an army field kitchen was set up, already they could smell the coffee. But the taller convict at least, even though he had had but one meal yesterday and that at noon in the rain, did not move at once toward the food. Instead and for the first time he looked at the River within whose shadow he had spent the last seven years of his life but had never seen before; he stood in quiet and amazed surmise and looked at the rigid steel-colored surface not broken into waves but merely slightly undulant. It stretched from the level on which he stood, further than he could see—a slowly and heavily rolling chocolate-frothy expanse broken only by a thin line a mile

10. Pairs; normally used in describing wild game, not men.

away as fragile in appearance as a single hair, which after a moment he recognized. *It's another levee,* he thought quietly. *That's what we look like from there. That's what I am standing on looks like from there.* He was prodded from the rear; a guard's voice carried forward: "Go on! Go on! You'll have plenty of time to look at that!"

They received the same stew and coffee and bread as the day before; they squatted again with their bowls and mugs as yesterday, though it was not raining yet. During the night an intact wooden barn had floated up. It now lay jammed by the current against the levee while a crowd of negroes swarmed over it, ripping off the shingles and planks and carrying them up the bank; eating steadily and without haste, the taller convict watched the barn dissolve rapidly down to the very water-line exactly as a dead fly vanished beneath the moiling industry of a swarm of ants.

They finished eating. Then it began to rain again, as upon a signal, while they stood or squatted in their harsh garments which had not dried out during the night but had merely become slightly warmer than the air. Presently they were haled to their feet and told off into two groups, one of which was armed from a stack of mud-clogged picks and shovels nearby, and marched away up the levee. A little later the motor launch with its train of skiffs came up across what was, fifteen feet beneath its keel, probably a cotton field, the skiffs loaded to the gunwales with negroes and a scattering of white people nursing bundles on their laps. When the engine shut off the faint plinking of a guitar came across the water; The skiffs warped in[11] and unloaded; the convicts watched the men and women and children struggle up the muddy slope, carrying heavy towsacks and bundles wrapped in quilts. The sound of the guitar had not ceased and now the convicts saw him—a young, black, lean-hipped man, the guitar slung by a piece of cotton plow line about his neck. He mounted the levee, still picking it. He carried nothing else, no food, no change of clothes, not even a coat.

The taller convict was so busy watching this that he did not hear the guard until the guard stood directly beside him shouting his name. "Wake up!" the guard shouted. "Can you fellows paddle a boat?"

"Paddle a boat where?" the taller convict said.

"In the water," the guard said. "Where in hell do you think?"

"I aint going to paddle no boat nowhere out yonder," the tall convict said, jerking his head toward the invisible river beyond the levee behind him.

"No, it's on this side," the guard said. He stooped swiftly and unlocked the chain which joined the tall convict and the plump hairless one. "It's just down the road a piece." He rose. The two

11. Were tied up at the bank.

convicts followed him down to the boats. "Follow them telephone poles until you come to a filling station. You can tell it, the roof is still above water. It's on a bayou[12] and you can tell the bayou because the tops of the trees are sticking up. Follow the bayou until you come to a cypress snag with a woman in it. Pick her up and then cut straight back west until you come to a cotton house with a fellow sitting on the ridgepole—" He turned, looking at the two convicts, who stood perfectly still, looking first at the skiff and then at the water with intense sobriety. "Well? What are you waiting for?"

"I cant row a boat," the plump convict said.

"Then it's high time you learned," the guard said. "Get in."

The tall convict shoved the other forward. "Get in," he said. "That water aint going to hurt you. Aint nobody going to make you take a bath."

As, the plump one in the bow and the other in the stern, they shoved away from the levee, they saw other pairs being unshackled and manning the other skiffs. "I wonder how many more of them fellows are seeing this much water for the first time in their lives too," the tall convict said. The other did not answer. He knelt in the bottom of the skiff, pecking gingerly at the water now and then with his paddle. The very shape of his thick soft back seemed to wear that expression of wary and tense concern.

Some time after midnight a rescue boat filled to the guard rail with homeless men and women and children docked at Vicksburg. It was a steamer, shallow of draft; all day long it had poked up and down cypress- and gum-choked[13] bayous and across cotton fields (where at times instead of swimming it waded) gathering its sorry cargo from the tops of houses and barns and even out of trees, and now it warped into that mushroom city of the forlorn and despairing where kerosene flares smoked in the drizzle and hurriedly strung electrics glared upon the bayonets of martial policemen and the red cross brassards[14] of doctors and nurses and canteen-workers. The bluff overhead was almost solid with tents, yet still there were more people than shelter for them; they sat or lay, single and by whole families, under what shelter they could find or sometimes under the rain itself, in the little death of profound exhaustion while the doctors and the nurses and the soldiers stepped over and around and among them.

Among the first to disembark was one of the penitentiary deputy wardens, followed closely by the plump convict and another white man—a small man with a gaunt unshaven wan face still wearing an expression of incredulous outrage. The deputy warden seemed to

12. A slow-moving, marshy stream or river.
13. That is, choked with wood from gum-trees.
14. Identifying armbands.

know exactly where he wished to go. Followed closely by his two companions he threaded his way swiftly among the piled furniture and the sleeping bodies and stood presently in a fiercely lighted and hastily established temporary office, almost a military post of command in fact, where the Warden of the Penitentiary sat with two army officers wearing majors' leaves. The deputy warden spoke without preamble. "We lost a man," he said. He called the tall convict's name.

"Lost him?" the Warden said.

"Yah. Drowned." Without turning his head he spoke to the plump convict. "Tell him," he said.

"He was the one that said he could row a boat," the plump convict said. "I never. I told him myself—" he indicated the deputy warden with a jerk of his head "—I couldn't. So when we got to the bayou—"

"What's this?" the Warden said.

"The launch brought word in," the deputy warden said. "Woman in a cypress snag on the bayou, then this fellow—" he indicated the third man; the Warden and the two officers looked at the third man "—on a cotton house.[15] Never had room in the launch to pick them up. Go on."

"So we come to where the bayou was," the plump convict continued in a voice perfectly flat, without any inflection whatever. "Then the boat got away from him. I dont know what happened. I was just sitting there because he was so positive he could row a boat. I never saw any current. Just all of a sudden the boat whirled clean around and begun to run fast backward like it was hitched to a train and it whirled around again and I happened to look up and there was a limb right over my head and I grabbed it just in time and that boat was snatched out from under me like you'd snatch off a sock and I saw it one time more upside down and that fellow that said he knew all about rowing holding to it with one hand and still holding the paddle in the other—" He ceased. There was no dying fall to his voice, it just ceased and the convict stood looking quietly at a half-full quart of whiskey sitting on the table.

"How do you know he's drowned?" the Warden said to the deputy. "How do you know he didn't just see his chance to escape, and took it?"

"Escape where?" the other said. "The whole Delta's flooded. There's fifteen foot of water for fifty miles, clean back to the hills.[16] And that boat was upside down."

"That fellow's drowned," the plump convict said. "You dont need to worry about him. He's got his pardon; it wont cramp nobody's hand signing it, neither."

15. A small house with a sheet-iron roof, used for storing cotton.

16. I.e., covering the entire plain for fifty miles east of the river.

"And nobody else saw him?" the Warden said. "What about the woman in the tree?"

"I dont know," the deputy said. "I aint found her yet. I reckon some other boat picked her up. But this is the fellow on the cotton house."

Again the Warden and the two officers looked at the third man, at the gaunt, unshaven wild face in which an old terror, an old blending of fear and impotence and rage still lingered. "He never came for you?" the Warden said. "You never saw him?"

"Never nobody came for me," the refugee said. He began to tremble though at first he spoke quietly enough. "I set there on that sonabitching cotton house, expecting hit to go any minute. I saw that launch and them boats come up and they never had no room for me. Full of bastard niggers and one of them setting there playing a guitar but there wasn't no room for me. A guitar!" he cried; now he began to scream, trembling, slavering, his face twitching and jerking. "Room for a bastard nigger guitar but not for me—"

"Steady now," the Warden said. "Steady now."

"Give him a drink," one of the officers said. The Warden poured the drink. The deputy handed it to the refugee, who took the glass in both jerking hands and tried to raise it to his mouth. They watched him for perhaps twenty seconds, then the deputy took the glass from him and held it to his lips while he gulped, though even then a thin trickle ran from each corner of his mouth, into the stubble on his chin.

"So we picked him and—" the deputy called the plump convict's name now "—both up just before dark and come on in. But that other fellow is gone."

"Yes," the Warden said. "Well. Here I haven't lost a prisoner in ten years, and now, like this—I'm sending you back to the Farm tomorrow. Have his family notified, and his discharge papers filled out at once."

"All right," the deputy said. "And listen, chief. He wasn't a bad fellow and maybe he never had no business in that boat. Only he did say he could paddle one. Listen. Suppose I write on his discharge, Drowned while trying to save lives in the great flood of ninety twenty-seven, and send it down for the Governor to sign it. It will be something nice for his folks to have, to hang on the wall when neighbors come in or something. Maybe they will even give his folks a cash bonus because after all they sent him to the Farm to raise cotton, not to fool around in a boat in a flood."

"All right," the Warden said. "I'll see about it. The main thing is to get his name off the books as dead before some politician tries to collect his food allowance."[17]

17. I.e., as if the dead man were alive and on welfare.

"All right," the deputy said. He turned and herded his companions out. In the drizzling darkness again he said to the plump convict; "Well, your partner beat you. He's free. He's done served his time out but you've got a right far piece to go yet."

"Yah," the plump convict said. "Free. He can have it."

As the short convict had testified, the tall one, when he returned to the surface, still retained what the short one called the paddle. He clung to it, not instinctively against the time when he would be back inside the boat and would need it, because for a time he did not believe he would ever regain the skiff or anything else that would support him, but because he did not have time to think about turning it loose. Things had moved too fast for him. He had not been warned, he had felt the first snatching tug of the current, he had seen the skiff begin to spin and his companion vanish violently upward like in a translation out of Isaiah,[1] then he himself was in the water, struggling against the drag of the paddle which he did not know he still held each time he fought back to the surface and grasped at the spinning skiff which at one instant was ten feet away and the next poised above his head as though about to brain him, until at last he grasped the stern, the drag of his body becoming a rudder to the skiff, the two of them, man and boat and with the paddle perpendicular above them like a jackstaff,[2] vanishing from the view of the short convict (who had vanished from that of the tall one with the same celerity though in a vertical direction) like a tableau[3] snatched offstage intact with violent and incredible speed.

He was now in the channel of a slough,[4] a bayou, in which until today no current had run probably since the old subterranean outrage[5] which had created the country. There was plenty of current in it now though; from his trough behind the stern he seemed to see the trees and sky rushing past with vertiginous speed, looking down at him between the gouts of cold yellow in lugubrious and mournful amazement. But they were fixed and secure in something; he thought of that, he remembered in an instant of despairing rage the firm earth fixed and founded strong and cemented fast and stable forever by the generations of laborious sweat, somewhere beneath him, beyond the reach of his feet, when, and again without warning, the stern of the skiff struck him a stunning blow across the bridge of his nose. The instinct which had caused him to cling to it now caused him to fling the paddle into the boat in order to grasp the gunwale[6] with both hands just as the skiff pivoted and spun

1. Biblical book named for the Old Testament prophet, who was "translated" or carried up into the heavens to receive a vision of the future.

2. A staff on which a small flag or "jack" is hoisted.

3. Posed group.

4. Marsh.

5. Underground upheaval.

6. Top of the boat's side.

away again. With both hands free he now dragged himself over the stern and lay prone on his face, streaming with blood and water and panting, not with exhaustion but with that furious rage which is terror's aftermath.

But he had to get up at once because he believed he had come much faster (and so farther) then he had. So he rose, out of the watery scarlet puddle in which he had lain, streaming, the soaked denim heavy as iron on his limbs, the black hair plastered to his skull, the blood-infused water streaking his jumper, and dragged his forearm gingerly and hurriedly across his lower face and glanced at it then grasped the paddle and began to try to swing the skiff back upstream. It did not even occur to him that he did not know where his companion was, in which tree among all which he had passed or might pass. He did not even speculate on that for the reason that he knew so incontestably that the other was upstream from him, and after his recent experience the mere connotation of the term upstream carried a sense of such violence and force and speed that the conception of it as other than a straight line was something which the intelligence, reason, simply refused to harbor, like the notion of a rifle bullet the width of a cotton field.

The bow began to swing back upstream. It turned readily, it outpaced the aghast and outraged instant in which he realized it was swinging far too easily, it had swung on over the arc and lay broadside to the current and began again that vicious spinning while he sat, his teeth bared in his bloody streaming face while his spent arms flailed the impotent paddle at the water, that innocent-appearing medium which at one time had held him in iron-like and shifting convolutions like an anaconda yet which now seemed to offer no more resistance to the thrust of his urge and need than so much air, like air; the boat which had threatened him and at last actually struck him in the face with the shocking violence of a mule's hoof now seemed to poise weightless upon it like a thistle bloom, spinning like a wind vane while he flailed at the water and thought of, envisioned, his companion safe, inactive and at ease in the tree with nothing to do but wait, musing with impotent and terrified fury upon that arbitrariness of human affairs which had abrogated to the one the secure tree and to the other the hysterical and unmanageable boat for the very reason that it knew that he alone of the two of them would make any attempt to return and rescue his companion.

The skiff had paid off[7] and now ran with the current again. It seemed again to spring from immobility into incredible speed, and he thought he must already be miles away from where his companion had quitted him, though actually he had merely described a big circle since getting back into the skiff, and the object (a clump of

7. I.e., the bow swung away from the wind.

cypress trees choked by floating logs and debris) which the skiff was now about to strike was the same one it had careened into before when the stern had struck him. He didn't know this because he had not yet ever looked higher than the bow of the boat. He didn't look higher now, he just saw that he was going to strike; he seemed to feel run through the very insentient fabric of the skiff a current of eager gleeful vicious incorrigible wilfulness; and he who had never ceased to flail at the bland treacherous water with what he had believed to be the limit of his strength now from somewhere, some ultimate absolute reserve, produced a final measure of endurance, will to endure which adumbrated mere muscle and nerves, continuing to flail the paddle right up to the instant of striking, completing one last reach thrust and recover out of pure desperate reflex, as a man slipping on ice reaches for his hat and money-pocket, as the skiff struck and hurled him once more flat on his face in the bottom of it.

This time he did not get up at once. He lay flat on his face, slightly spread-eagled and in an attitude almost peaceful, a kind of abject meditation. He would have to get up sometime, he knew that, just as all life consists of having to get up sooner or later and then having to lie down again sooner or later after a while. And he was not exactly exhausted and he was not particularly without hope and he did not especially dread getting up. It merely seemed to him that he had accidentally been caught in a situation in which time and environment, not himself, was mesmerized; he was being toyed with by a current of water going nowhere, beneath a day which would wane toward no evening; when it was done with him it would spew him back into the comparatively safe world he had been snatched violently out of and in the meantime it did not much matter just what he did or did not do. So he lay on his face, now not only feeling but hearing the strong quiet rustling of the current on the underside of the planks, for a while longer. Then he raised his head and this time touched his palm gingerly to his face and looked at the blood again, then he sat up onto his heels and leaning over the gunwale he pinched his nostrils between thumb and finger and expelled a gout of blood and was in the act of wiping his fingers on his thigh when a voice slightly above his line of sight said quietly, "It's taken you a while," and he who up to this moment had had neither reason nor time to raise his eyes higher than the bows looked up and saw, sitting in a tree and looking at him, a woman. She was not ten feet away. She sat on the lowest limb of one of the trees holding the jam he had grounded on, in a calico wrapper and an army private's tunic and a sunbonnet, a woman whom he did not even bother to examine since that first startled glance had been ample to reveal to him all the generations of her life and background, who could have been his sister if he had a sister, his wife if he had not entered the penitentiary at an age scarcely out of adolescence and some years younger than that at which even his prolific and monogamous kind married—a woman who sat clutching the trunk of the tree, her stockingless feet in a pair of man's unlaced brogans less than a yard from the water, who was very probably somebody's sister and quite certainly (or certainly should have been) somebody's wife, though this too he had entered the penitentiary too young to have had more than mere theoretical female experience to discover yet. "I thought for a minute you wasn't aiming to come back."

"Come back?"

"After the first time. After you run into this brush pile the first time and got into the boat and went on." He looked about, touching his face tenderly again; it could very well be the same place where the boat had hit him in the face.

"Yah," he said. "I'm here now though."

"Could you maybe get the boat a little closer? I taken a right sharp strain getting up here; maybe I better . . ." He was not listening; he had just discovered that the paddle was gone; this time when the skiff hurled him forward he had flung the paddle not into it but beyond it. "It's right there in them brush tops," the woman said. "You can get it. Here. Catch a holt of this." It was a grapevine. It had grown up into the tree and the flood had torn the roots loose. She had taken a turn with it about her upper body; she now loosed it and swung it out until he could grasp it. Holding to the end of the vine he warped[8] the skiff around the end of the jam, picking up the paddle, and warped the skiff on beneath the limb and held it and now he watched her move, gather herself heavily and carefully to descend—that heaviness which was not painful but just excruciatingly careful, that profound and almost lethargic awkwardness which added nothing to the sum of that first aghast amazement which had served already for the catafalque[9] of invincible dream since even in durance he had continued (and even with the old avidity, even though they had caused his downfall) to consume the impossible pulp-printed fables carefully censored and as carefully smuggled into the penitentiary; and who to say what Helen, what living Garbo,[10] he had not dreamed of rescuing from what craggy pinnacle or dragoned keep[11] when he and his companion embarked in the skiff. He watched her, he made no further effort to help her beyond holding the skiff savagely steady while she

8. I.e., pulled.
9. Coffin.
10. Greta Garbo (b. 1905) had already appeared in several romantic American films by 1927. Helen, the fabled beauty of ancient Greece, was carried off to Troy by Paris and was the cause of the Trojan War.
11. The most impenetrable part of a castle.

lowered herself from the limb—the entire body, the deformed swell of belly bulging the calico, suspended by its arms, thinking, *And this is what I get. This, out of all the female meat that walks, is what I have to be caught in a runaway boat with.*

"Where's that cottonhouse?" he said.

"Cottonhouse?"

"With that fellow on it. The other one."

"I dont know. It's a right smart of[12] cottonhouses around here. With folks on them too, I reckon." She was examining him. "You're bloody as a hog," she said. "You look like a convict."

"Yah," he said, snarled. "I feel like I done already been hung. Well, I got to pick up my pardner and then find that cottonhouse." He cast off. That is, he released his hold on the vine. That was all he had to do, for even while the bow of the skiff hung high on the log jam and even while he held it by the vine in the comparatively dead water behind the jam, he felt steadily and constantly the whisper, the strong purring power of the water just one inch beyond the frail planks on which he squatted and which, as soon as he released the vine, took charge of the skiff not with one powerful clutch but in a series of touches light, tentative, and catlike; he realized now that he had entertained a sort of foundationless hope that the added weight might make the skiff more controllable. During the first moment or two he had a wild (and still foundationless) belie that it had; he had got the head upstream and managed to hold i so by terrific exertion continued even after he discovered that the were traveling straight enough but stern-first and continued some how even after the bow began to wear away and swing: the old irre sistible movement which he knew well by now, too well to figh against it, so that he let the bow swing on downstream with th hope of utilizing the skiff's own momentum to bring it through th full circle and so upstream again, the skiff traveling broadside the bow-first then broadside again, diagonally across the channel toward the other wall of submerged trees; it began to flee beneat him with terrific speed, they were in an eddy but did not know i he had no time to draw conclusions or even wonder; he crouche his teeth bared in his blood-caked and swollen face, his lungs burst ing, flailing at the water while the trees stooped hugely down a him. The skiff struck, spun, struck again; the woman half lay in th bow, clutching the gunwales, as if she were trying to crouch behin her own pregnancy; he banged now not at the water but at th living sapblooded wood with the paddle, his desire now not to g anywhere, reach any destination, but just to keep the skiff fro beating itself to fragments against the tree trunks. Then somethin exploded, this time against the back of his head, and stooping tre

12. **I.e., there are a lot of.**

and dizzy water, the woman's face and all, fled together and vanished in bright soundless flash and glare.

An hour later the skiff came slowly up an old logging road and so out of the bottom, the forest, and into (or onto) a cottonfield—a gray and limitless desolation now free of turmoil, broken only by a thin line of telephone poles like a wading millipede. The woman was now paddling, steadily and deliberately, with that curious lethargic care, while the convict squatted, his head between his knees, trying to stanch the fresh and apparently inexhaustible flow of blood from his nose with handfuls of water. The woman ceased paddling, the skiff drifted on, slowing, while she looked about. "We're done out," she said.

The convict raised his head and also looked about. "Out where?"

"I thought maybe you might know."

"I dont even know where I used to be. Even if I knowed which way was north, I wouldn't know if that was where I wanted to go." He cupped another handful of water to his face and lowered his hand and regarded the resulting crimson marbling on his palm, not with dejection, not with concern, but with a kind of sardonic and vicious bemusement. The woman watched the back of his head.

"We got to get somewhere."

"Dont I know it? A fellow on a cottonhouse. Another in a tree. And now that thing in your lap."

"It wasn't due yet. Maybe it was having to climb that tree quick yesterday, and having to set in it all night. I'm doing the best I can. But we better get somewhere soon."

"Yah," the convict said. "I thought I wanted to get somewhere too and I aint had no luck at it. You pick out a place to get to now and we'll try yours. Gimme that oar." The woman passed him the paddle. The boat was a double-ender; he had only to turn around.

"Which way you fixing to go?" the woman said.

"Never you mind that. You just keep on holding on." He began to paddle, on across the cottonfield. It began to rain again, though not hard at first. "Yah," he said. "Ask the boat. I been in it since breakfast and I aint never knowed, where I aimed to go or where I was going either."

That was about one o'clock. Toward the end of the afternoon the skiff (they were in a channel of some sort again, they had been in it for some time; they had got into it before they knew it and too late to get out again, granted there had been any reason to get out, as, to the convict anyway, there was certainly none and the fact that their speed had increased again was reason enough to stay in it) shot out upon a broad expanse of debris-filled water which the convict recognized as a river and, from its size, the Yazoo River though it was little enough he had seen of this country which he had not quitted for so much as one single day in the last seven years of his life. What he did not know was that it was now running backward. So as soon as the drift of the skiff indicated the set of the current, he began to paddle in that direction which he believed to be downstream, where he knew there were towns—Yazoo City,[13] and as a last resort, Vicksburg, if his luck was that bad, if not, smaller towns whose names he did not know but where there would be people, houses, something, anything he might reach and surrender his charge to and turn his back on her forever, on all pregnant and female life forever and return to that monastic existence of shotguns and shackles where he would be secure from it. Now, with the imminence of habitations, release from her, he did not even hate her. When he looked upon the swelling and unmanageable body before him it seemed to him that it was not the woman at all but rather a separate demanding threatening inert yet living mass of which both he and she were equally victims; thinking, as he had been for the last three or four hours, of that minute's—nay, second's—aberration of eye or hand which would suffice to precipitate her into the water to be dragged down to death by that senseless millstone which in its turn would not even have to feel agony, he no longer felt any glow of revenge toward her as its custodian, he felt sorry for her as he would for the living timber in a barn which had to be burned to rid itself of vermin.

He paddled on, helping the current, steadily and strongly, with a calculated husbandry of effort, toward what he believed was downstream, towns, people, something to stand upon, while from time to time the woman raised herself to bail the accumulated rain from the skiff. It was raining steadily now though still not hard, still without passion, the sky, the day itself dissolving without grief; the skiff moved in a nimbus, an aura of gray gauze which merged almost without demarcation with the roiling spittle-frothed debris-choked water. Now the day, the light, definitely began to end and the convict permitted himself an extra notch or two of effort because it suddenly seemed to him that the speed of the skiff had lessened. This was actually the case though the convict did not know it. He merely took it as a phenomenon of the increasing obfuscation, or at most as a result of the long day's continuous effort with no food, complicated by the ebbing and fluxing phases of anxiety and impotent rage at his absolutely gratuitous predicament. So he stepped up his stroke a beat or so, not from alarm but on the contrary, since he too had received that lift from the mere presence of a known stream, a river known by its ineradicable name to generations of men who had been drawn to live beside it as man always has been drawn to dwell beside water, even before he had a name

13. Yazoo City is about fifty miles up the Yazoo River from Vicksburg.

for water and fire, drawn to the living water, the course of his destiny and his actual physical appearance rigidly coerced and postulated by it. So he was not alarmed. He paddled on, upstream without knowing it, unaware that all the water which for forty hours now had been pouring through the levee break to the north was somewhere ahead of him, on its way back to the River.

It was full dark now. That is, night had completely come, the gray dissolving sky had vanished, yet as though in perverse ratio surface visibility had sharpened, as though the light which the rain of the afternoon had washed out of the air had gathered upon the water as the rain itself had done, so that the yellow flood spread on before him now with a quality almost phosphorescent, right up to the instant where vision ceased. The darkness in fact had its advantages; he could now stop seeing the rain. He and his garments had been wet for more than twenty-four hours now so he had long since stopped feeling it, and now that he could no longer see it either it had in a certain sense ceased for him. Also, he now had to make no effort even not to see the swell of his passenger's belly. So he was paddling on, strongly and steadily, not alarmed and not concerned but just exasperated because he had not yet begun to see any reflection on the clouds which would indicate the city or cities which he believed he was approaching but which were actually now miles behind him, when he heard a sound. He did not know what it was because he had never heard it before and he would never be expected to hear such again since it is not given to every man to hear such at all and to none to hear it more than once in his life. And he was not alarmed now either because there was not time, for although the visibility ahead, for all its clarity, did not extend very far, yet in the next instant to the hearing he was also seeing something such as he had never seen before. This was that the sharp line where the phosphorescent water met the darkness was now about ten feet higher than it had been an instant before and that it was curled forward upon itself like a sheet of dough being rolled out for a pudding. It reared, stooping; the crest of it swirled like the mane of a galloping horse and, phosphorescent too, fretted and flickered like fire. And while the woman huddled in the bows, aware or not aware the convict did not know which, he (the convict), his swollen and blood-streaked face gaped in an expression of aghast and incredulous amazement, continued to paddle directly into it. Again he simply had not had time to order his rhythm-hypnotized muscles to cease. He continued to paddle though the skiff had ceased to move forward at all but seemed to be hanging in space while the paddle still reached thrust recovered and reached again; now instead of space the skiff became abruptly surrounded by a welter of fleeing debris—planks, small buildings, the bodies of drowned yet antic animals, entire trees leaping and diving like porpoises above which the skiff seemed to hover in weightless and airy indecision like a bird above a fleeing countryside, undecided where to light or whether to light at all, while the convict squatted in it still going through the motions of paddling, waiting for an opportunity to scream. He never found it. For an instant the skiff seemed to stand erect on its stern and then shoot scrabbling and scrambling up the curling wall of water like a cat, and soared on above the licking crest itself and hung cradled into the high actual air in the limbs of a tree, from which bower of new-leafed boughs and branches the convict, like a bird in its nest and still waiting his chance to scream and still going through the motions of paddling though he no longer even had the paddle now, looked down upon a world turned to furious motion and in incredible retrograde.[14]

Some time about midnight, accompanied by a rolling cannonade of thunder and lightning like a battery going into action, as though some forty hours' constipation of the elements, the firmament itself, were discharging in clapping and glaring salute to the ultimate acquiescence to desperate and furious motion, and still leading its charging welter of dead cows and mules and outhouses and cabins and hencoops, the skiff passed Vicksburg. The convict didn't know it. He wasn't looking high enough above the water; he still squatted, clutching the gunwales and glaring at the yellow turmoil about him out of which entire trees, the sharp gables of houses, the long mournful heads of mules which he fended off with a splintered length of plank snatched from he knew not where in passing (and which seemed to glare reproachfully back at him with sightless eyes, in limber-lipped and incredulous amazement) rolled up and then down again, the skiff now traveling forward now sideways now sternward, sometimes in the water, sometimes riding for yards upon the roofs of houses and trees and even upon the backs of the mules as though even in death they were not to escape that burden-bearing doom with which their eunuch race was cursed. But he didn't see Vicksburg; the skiff, traveling at express speed, was in a seething gut[15] between soaring and dizzy banks with a glare of light above them but he did not see it; he saw the flotsam ahead of him divide violently and begin to climb upon itself, mounting, and he was sucked through the resulting gap too fast to recognize it was the trestling of a railroad bridge; for a horrible moment the skiff seemed to hang in static indecision before the looming flank of a steamboat as though undecided whether to climb over it or dive under it, then a hard icy wind filled with the smell and taste and sense of wet and boundless desolation blew upon him; the skiff made one long bounding lunge as the convict's native state, in a

14. The boat is now moving backward, to the south.

15. Narrows.

funal paroxysm, regurgitated him onto the wild bosom of the Father of Waters.

This is how he told about it seven weeks later, sitting in new bed-ticking garments, shaved and with his hair cut again, on his bunk in the barracks:

During the next three or four hours after the thunder and lightning had spent itself the skiff ran in pitch streaming darkness upon a roiling expanse which, even if he could have seen, apparently had no boundaries. Wild and invisible, it tossed and heaved about and beneath the boat, ridged with dirty phosphorescent foam and filled with a debris of destruction—objects nameless and enormous and invisible which struck and slashed at the skiff and whirled on. He did not know he was now upon the River. At that time he would have refused to believe it, even if he had known. Yesterday he had known he was in a channel by the regularity of the spacing between the bordering trees. Now, since even by daylight he could have seen no boundaries, the last place under the sun (or the streaming sky rather) he would have suspected himself to be would have been a river; if he had pondered at all about his present whereabouts, about the geography beneath him, he would merely have taken himself traveling at dizzy and inexplicable speed above the largest cottonfield in the world; if he who yesterday had known he was in a river, had accepted that fact in good faith and earnest, then had seen that river turn without warning and rush back upon him with furious and deadly intent like a frenzied stallion in a lane—if he had suspected for one second that the wild and limitless expanse on which he now found himself was a river, consciousness would simply have refused; he would have fainted.

When daylight—a gray and ragged dawn filled with driving scud between icy rain-squalls—came and he could see again, he knew he was in no cottonfield. He knew that the wild water on which the skiff tossed and fled flowed above no soil tamely trod by man, behind the straining and surging buttocks of a mule. That was when it occurred to him that its present condition was no phenomenon of a decade, but that the intervening years during which it consented to bear upon its placid and sleepy bosom the frail mechanicals of man's clumsy contriving was the phenomenon and this the norm and the river was now doing what it liked to do, had waited patiently the ten years in order to do, as a mule will work for you ten years for the privilege of kicking you once. And he also learned something else about fear too, something he had even failed to discover on that other occasion when he was really afraid—that three or four seconds of that night in his youth while he looked down the twice-flashing pistol barrel of the terrified mail clerk before the clerk could be persuaded that his (the convict's) pistol would not shoot: that if you just held on long enough a time would come in fear after which it would no longer be agony at all but merely a kind of horrible outrageous itching, as after you have been burned bad.

He did not have to paddle now, he just steered (who had been without food for twenty-four hours now and without any sleep to speak of for fifty) while the skiff sped on across that boiling desolation where he had long since begun to not dare believe he could possibly be where he could not doubt he was, trying with his fragment of splintered plank merely to keep the skiff intact and afloat among the houses and trees and dead animals (the entire towns, stores, residences, parks and farmyards, which leaped and played about him like fish), not trying to reach any destination, just trying to keep the skiff afloat until he did. He wanted so little. He wanted nothing for himself. He just wanted to get rid of the woman, the belly, and he was trying to do that in the right way, not for himself, but for her. He could have put her back into another tree at any time—

"Or you could have jumped out of the boat and let her and it drown," the plump convict said. "Then they could have given you the ten years for escaping and then hung you for the murder and charged the boat to your folks."

"Yah," the tall convict said.—But he had not done that. He wanted to do it the right way, find somebody, anybody he could surrender her to, something solid he could set her down on and then jump back into the river, if that would please anyone. That was all he wanted—just to come to something, anything. That didn't seem like a great deal to ask. And he couldn't do it. He told how the skiff fled on—

"Didn't you pass nobody?" the plump convict said. "No steamboat, nothing?"

"I don't know," the tall one said.—while he tried merely to keep it afloat, until the darkness thinned and lifted and revealed—

"Darkness?" the plump convict said. "I thought you said it was already daylight."

"Yah," the tall one said. He was rolling a cigarette, pouring the tobacco carefully from a new sack, into the creased paper. "This was another one. They had several while I was gone."—the skiff to be moving still rapidly up a winding corridor bordered by drowned trees which the convict recognized again to be a river running again in the direction that, until two days ago, had been upstream. He was not exactly warned through instinct that this one, like that of two days ago, was in reverse. He would not say that he now believed himself to be in the same river, though he would not have been surprised to find that he did believe this, existing now, as he did and had and apparently was to continue for an unnamed period, in a state in which he was toy and pawn on a vicious and inflammable geography. He merely realized that he was in a river again, with all the subsequent inferences of a comprehensible, even if not familiar, portion of the earth's surface. Now he believed that all he had to do would be to paddle far enough and he would come to something horizontal and above water even if not dry and perhaps even populated; and, if fast enough, in time, and that his only other crying urgency was to refrain from looking at the woman who, as vision, the incontrovertible and apparently inescapable presence of his passenger, returned with dawn, had ceased to be a human being and (you could add twenty-four more hours to the first twenty-four and the first fifty now, even counting the hen. It was dead, drowned, caught by one wing under a shingle on a roof which had rolled momentarily up beside the skiff yesterday and he had eaten some of it raw though the woman would not) had become instead one single inert monstrous sentient womb from which, he now believed, if he could only turn his gaze away and keep it away, would disappear, and if he could only keep his gaze from pausing again at the spot it had occupied, would not return. That's what he was doing this time when he discovered the wave was coming.

He didn't know how he discovered it was coming back. He heard no sound, it was nothing felt nor seen. He did not even believe that finding the skiff to be now in slack water—that is, that the motion of the current which, whether right or wrong, had at least been horizontal, had now stopped that and assumed a vertical direction—was sufficient to warn him. Perhaps it was just an invincible and almost fanatic faith in the inventiveness and innate viciousness of that medium on which his destiny was now cast, apparently forever; a sudden conviction far beyond either horror or surprise that now was none too soon for it to prepare to do whatever it was it intended doing. So he whirled the skiff, spun it on its heel like a running horse, whereupon, reversed, he could not even distinguish the very channel he had come up. He did not know whether he simply could not see it or if it had vanished some time ago and he not aware at the time; whether the river had become lost in a drowned world or if the world had become drowned in one limitless river. So now he could not tell if he were running directly before the wave or quartering[16] across its line of charge; all he could do was keep that sense of swiftly accumulating ferocity behind him and paddle as fast as his spent and now numb muscles could be driven, and try not to look at the woman, to wrench his gaze from her and keep it away until he reached something flat and above water. So, gaunt, hollow-eyed, striving and wrenching almost physically at his eyes as if they were two of those suction-tipped rubber arrows shot from the toy gun of a child, his spent muscles obeying

16. Running diagonally.

not will now but that attenuation beyond mere exhaustion which, mesmeric, can continue easier than cease, he once more drove the skiff full tilt into something it could not pass and, once more hurled violently forward onto his hands and knees, crouching, he glared with his wild swollen face up at the man with the shotgun and said in a harsh, croaking voice: "Vicksburg? Where's Vicksburg?"

Even when he tried to tell it, even after the seven weeks and he safe, secure, riveted warranted and doubly guaranteed by the ten years they had added to his sentence for attempted escape, something of the old hysteric incredulous outrage came back into his face, his voice, his speech. He never did even get on the other boat. He told how he clung to a strake[17] (it was a dirty unpainted shanty boat with a drunken rake of tin stove pipe, it had been moving when he struck it and apparently it had not even changed course even though the three people on it must have been watching him all the while—a second man, barefoot and with matted hair and beard also at the steering sweep,[18] and then—he did not know how long—a woman leaning in the door, in a filthy assortment of men's garments, watching him too with the same cold speculation) being dragged violently along, trying to state and explain his simple (and to him at least) reasonable desire and need; telling it, trying to tell it, he could feel again the old unforgettable affronting like an ague fit[19] as he watched the abortive tobacco rain steadily and faintly from between his shaking hands and then the paper itself part with a thin dry snapping report:

"Burn my clothes?" the convict cried. "Burn them?"

"How in hell do you expect to escape in them billboards?" the man with the shotgun said. He (the convict) tried to tell it, tried to explain as he had tried to explain not to the three people on the boat alone but to the entire circumambience—desolate water and forlorn trees and sky—not for justification because he needed none and knew that his hearers, the other convicts, required none from him, but rather as, on the point of exhaustion, he might have picked dreamily and incredulously at a suffocation. He told the man with the gun how he and his partner had been given the boat and told to pick up a man and a woman, how he had lost his partner and failed to find the man, and now all in the world he wanted was something flat to leave the woman on until he could find an officer, a sheriff. He thought of home, the place where he had lived almost since childhood, his friends of years whose ways he knew and who knew his ways, the familiar fields where he did work he had learned to do well and to like, the mules with characters he knew and respected as he knew and respected the characters of cer-

17. A line of planking in the boat's hull.

18. Oar used for steering.

19. A fit of shivering.

tain men; he thought of the barracks at night, with screens against the bugs in summer and good stoves in winter and someone to supply the fuel and the food too; the Sunday ball games and the picture shows—things which, with the exception of the ball games, he had never known before. But most of all, his own character (Two years ago they had offered to make a trusty of him. He would no longer need to plow or feed stock, he would only follow those who did with a loaded gun, but he declined. "I reckon I'll stick to plowing," he said, absolutely without humor. "I done already tried to use a gun one time too many.") his good name, his responsibility not only toward those who were responsible toward him but to himself, his own horror in the doing of what was asked of him, his pride in being able to do it, no matter what it was He thought of this and listened to the man with the gun talking about escape and it seemed to him that, hanging there, being dragged violently along (It was here he said that he first noticed the goats' beards of moss in the trees, though it could have been there for several days so far as he knew. It just happeneds that he first noticed it here.) that he would simply burst.

"Cant you get it into your head that the last thing I want to do is run away?" he cried. "You can set there with that gun and watch me; I give you fair lief.[20] All I want is to put this woman—"

"And I told you she could come aboard," the man with the gun said in his level voice. "But there ain't no room on no boat of mine for nobody hunting a sheriff in no kind of clothes, let alone a penitentiary suit."

"When he steps aboard, knock him in the head with the gun barrel," the man at the sweep said. "He's drunk."

"He aint coming aboard," the man with the gun said. "He's crazy."

Then the woman spoke. She didn't move, leaning in the door, in a pair of faded and patched and filthy overalls like the two men: "Give them some grub and tell them to get out of here." She moved, she crossed the deck and looked down at the convict's companion with her cold sullen face. "How much more time have you got?"

"It wasn't due till next month," the woman in the boat said. "But I—" The woman in overalls turned to the man with the gun. "Give them some grub," she said. But the man with the gun was still looking down at the woman in the boat.

"Come on," he said to the convict. "Put her aboard, and beat it."

"And what'll happen to you," the woman in overalls said, "when you try to turn her over to an officer. When you lay alongside a

20. Permission.

sheriff and the sheriff asks you who you are?" Still the man with the gun didn't even look at her. He hardly even shifted the gun across his arm as he struck the woman across the face with the back of his other hand, hard. "You son of a bitch," she said. Still the man with the gun did not even look at her.

"Well?" he said to the convict.

"Dont you see I cant?" the convict cried. "Cant you see that?"

Now, he said, he gave up. He was doomed. That is, he knew now that he had been doomed from the very start never to get rid of her, just as the ones who sent him out with the skiff knew that he never would actually give up; when he recognized one of the objects which the woman in overalls was hurling into the skiff to be a can of condensed milk, he believed it to be a presage, gratuitous and irrevocable as a death-notice over the telegraph, that he was not even to find a flat stationary surface in time for the child to be born on it. So he told how he held the skiff alongside the shanty-boat while the first tentative toying of the second wave made up beneath him, while the woman in overalls passed back and forth between house and rail, flinging the food—the hunk of salt meat, the ragged and filthy quilt, the scorched lumps of cold bread which she poured into the skiff from a heaped dishpan like so much garbage—while he clung to the strake against the mounting pull of the current, the new wave which for the moment he had forgotten because he was still trying to state the incredible simplicity of his desire and need until the man with the gun (the only one of the three who wore shoes) began to stamp at his hands, he snatching his hands away one at a time to avoid the heavy shoes, then grasping the rail again until the man with the gun kicked at his face, he flinging himself sideways to avoid the shoe and so breaking his hold on the rail, his weight canting the skiff off at a tangent on the increasing current so that it began to leave the shanty boat behind and he paddling again now, violently, as a man hurries toward the precipice for which he knows at last he is doomed, looking back at the other boat, the three faces sullen derisive and grim and rapidly diminishing across the widening water and at last, apoplectic, suffocating with the intolerable fact not that he had been refused but that he had been refused so little, had wanted so little, asked for so little, yet there had been demanded of him in return the one price out of all breath which (they must have known) if he could have paid it, he would not have been where he was, asking what he asked, raising the paddle and shaking it and screaming curses back at them even after the shotgun flashed and the charge went scuttering past along the water to one side.

So he hung there, he said, shaking the paddle and howling, when suddenly he remembered that other wave, the second wall of water full of houses and dead mules building up behind him back in the swamp. So he quit yelling then and went back to paddling. He was not trying to outrun it. He just knew from experience that when it overtook him, he would have to travel in the same direction it was moving in anway, whether he wanted to or not, and when it did overtake him, he would begin to move too fast to stop, no matter what places he might come to where he could leave the woman, land her in time. Time: that was his itch now, so his only chance was to stay ahead of it as long as he could and hope to reach something before it struck. So he went on, driving the skiff with muscles which had been too tired so long they had quit feeling it, as when a man has had bad luck for so long that he ceases to believe it is even bad, let alone luck. Even when he ate—the scorched lumps the size of baseballs and the weight and durability of cannel coal[21] even after having lain in the skiff's bilge where the shanty boat woman had thrown them—the iron-like lead-heavy objects which no man would have called bread outside of the crusted and scorched pan in which they had cooked—it was with one hand, begruding even that from the paddle.

He tried to tell that too—that day while the skiff fled on among the bearded trees while every now and then small quiet tentative exploratory feelers would come up from the wave behind and toy for a moment at the skiff, light and curious, then go on with a faint hissing sighing, almost a chuckling, sound, the skiff going on, driving on with nothing to see but trees and water and solitude: until after a while it no longer seemed to him that he was trying to put space and distance behind him or shorten space and distance ahead but that both he and the wave were now hanging suspended simultaneous and unprogressing in pure time, upon a dreamy desolation in which he paddled on not from any hope even to reach anything at all but merely to keep intact what little of distance the length of the skiff provided between himself and the inert and inescapable mass of female meat before him; then night and the skiff rushing on, fast since any speed over anything unknown and invisible is too fast, with nothing before him and behind him the outrageous idea of a volume of moving water toppling forward, its crest frothed and shredded like fangs, and then dawn again (another of those dreamlike alterations day to dark then back to day again with that quality truncated, anachronic and unreal as the waxing and waning of lights in a theatre scene) and the skiff emerging now with the woman no longer supine beneath the shrunken soaked private's coat but sitting bolt upright, gripping the gunwales with both hands, her eyes closed and her lower lip caught between her teeth and he driving the splintered board furiously now, glaring at her out of his wild

21. A hard gray bituminous coal.

swollen sleepless face and crying, croaking, "Hold on! For God's sake hold on!"

"I'm trying to," she said. "But hurry! Hurry!" He told it, the unbelievable: hurry, hasten: the man falling from a cliff being told to catch onto something and save himself; the very telling of it emerging shadowy and burlesque, ludicrous, comic and mad, from the ague of unbearable forgetting with a quality more dreamily furious than any fable behind proscenium[22] lights:

He was in a basin now—"A basin?" the plump convict said. "That's what you wash in."

"All right," the tall one said, harshly, above his hands. "I did." With a supreme effort he stilled them long enough to release the two bits of cigarette paper and watched them waft in light fluttering indecision to the floor between his feet, holding his hands motionless even for a moment longer—a basin, a broad peaceful yellow sea which had an abruptly and curiously ordered air, giving him, even at that moment, the impression that it was accustomed to water even if not total submersion; he even remembered the name of it, told to him two or three weeks later by someone: Atchafalaya[23]—

"Louisiana?" the plump convict said. "You mean you were clean out of Mississippi? Hell fire." He stared at the tall one. "Shucks," he said. "That aint but just across from Vicksburg."

"They never named any Vicksburg across from where I was," the tall one said. "It was Baton Rouge[24] they named." And now he began to talk about a town, a little neat white portrait town nestling among enormous very green trees, appearing suddenly in the telling as it probably appeared in actuality, abrupt and airy and miragelike and incredibly serene before him behind a scattering of boats moored to a line of freight cars standing flush to the doors in water. And now he tried to tell that too: how he stood waist-deep in water for a moment looking back and down at the skiff in which the woman half lay, her eyes still closed, her knuckles white on the gunwales and a tiny thread of blood creeping down her chin from her chewed lip, and he looking down at her in a kind of furious desperation.

"How far will I have to walk?" she said.

"I dont know, I tell you!" he cried. "But it's land somewhere yonder! It's land, houses."

"If I try to move, it wont even be born inside a boat," she said. You'll have to get closer."

"Yes," he cried, wild, desperate, incredulous. "Wait. I'll go and surrender, then they will have—" He didn't finish, wait to finish; he

22. Theater (literally, the arched opening between stage and audience).

23. A river of southern Louisiana, parallel to the Mississippi.

24. The capital of Louisiana, about 175 miles downriver from Vicksburg.

told that too; himself splashing, stumbling, trying to run, sobbing and gasping; now he saw it—another loading platform standing above the yellow flood, the khaki figures on it as before, identical, the same; he said how the intervening days since that first innocent morning telescoped, vanished as if they had never been, the two contiguous succeeding instants (succeeding? simultaneous) and he transported across no intervening space but merely turned in his own footsteps, plunging, splashing, his arms raised, croaking harshly. He heard the startled shout, "There's one of them!" the command, the clash of equipment, the alarmed cry: "There he goes! There he goes!"

"Yes!" he cried, running, plunging, "here I am! Here! Here!" running on, into the first scattered volley, stopping among the bullets, waving his arms, shrieking, "I want to surrender! I want to surrender!" watching not in terror but in amazed and absolutely unbearable outrage as a squatting clump of the khaki figures parted and he saw the machine gun, the blunt thick muzzle slant and drop and probe toward him and he still screaming in his hoarse crow's voice, "I want to surrender! Cant you hear me?" continuing to scream even as he whirled and plunged splashing, ducking, went completely under and heard the bullets going thuck-thuck-thuck on the water above him and he scrabbling still on the bottom, still trying to scream even before he regained his feet and still all submerged save his plunging unmistakable buttocks, the outraged screaming bubbling from his mouth and about his face since he merely wanted to surrender. Then he was comparatively screened, out of range, though not for long. That is (he didn't tell how nor where) there was a moment in which he paused, breathed for a second before running again, the course back to the skiff open for the time being though he could still hear the shouts behind him and now and then a shot, and he panting, sobbing, a long savage tear in the flesh of one hand, got when and how he did not know, and he wasting precious breath, speaking to no one now any more than the scream of the dying rabbit is addressed to any mortal ear but rather an indictment of all breath and its folly and suffering, its infinite capacity for folly and pain, which seems to be its only immortality: "All in the world I want is just to surrender."

He returned to the skiff and got in and took up his splintered plank. And now when he told this, despite the fury of element which climaxed it, it (the telling) became quite simple; he now even creased another cigarette paper between fingers which did not tremble at all and filled the paper from the tobacco sack without spilling a flake, as though he had passed from the machine-gun's barrage into a bourne[25] beyond any more amazement: so that the

25. Destination.

subsequent part of his narrative seemed to reach his listeners as though from beyond a sheet of slightly milky though still transparent glass, as something not heard but seen—a series of shadows, edgeless yet distinct, and smoothly flowing, logical and unfrantic and making no sound: They were in the skiff, in the center of the broad placid trough which had no boundaries and down which the tiny forlorn skiff flew to the irresistible coercion of a current going once more he knew not where, the neat small liveoak-bowered towns unattainable and miragelike and apparently attached to nothing upon the airy and unchanging horizon. He did not believe them, they did not matter, he was doomed; they were less than the figments of smoke or of delirium, and he driving his unceasing paddle without destination or even hope now, looking now and then at the woman sitting with her knees drawn up and locked and her entire body one terrific clench while the threads of bloody saliva crept from her teeth-clenched lower lip. He was going nowhere and fleeing from nothing, he merely continued to paddle because he had paddled so long now that hed believed if he stopped his muscles would scream in agony. So when it happened he was not surprised. He heard the sound which he knew well (he had heard it but once before, true enough, but no man needed hear it but once) and he had been expecting it; he looked back, still driving the paddle, and saw it, curled, crested with its strawlike flotsam of trees and debris and dead beasts and he glared over his shoulder at it for a full minute out of that attenuation far beyond the point of outragement where even suffering, the capability of being further affronted, had ceased, from which he now contemplated with savage and invulnerable curiosity the further extent to which his now anesthetized nerves could bear, what next could be invented for them to bear, until the wave actually began to rear above his head into its thunderous climax. Then only did he turn his head. His stroke did not falter, it neither slowed nor increased; still paddling with that spent hypnotic steadiness, he saw the swimming deer. He did not know what it was nor that he had altered the skiff's course to follow it, he just watched the swimming head before him as the wave boiled down and the skiff rose bodily in the old familiar fashion on a welter of tossing trees and houses and bridges and fences, he still paddling even while the paddle found no purchase save air and still paddled even as he and the deer shot forward side by side at arm's length, he watching the deer now, watching the deer begin to rise out of the water bodily until it was actually running along upon the surface, rising still, soaring clear of the water altogether, vanishing upward in a dying crescendo of splashings and snapping branches, its damp scut flashing upward, the entire animal vanishing upward as smoke vanishes. And now the skiff struck and canted and he was out of it too, standing knee-deep, springing out and falling to his knees, scrambling up, glaring after the vanished deer. "Land!" he croaked. "Land! Hold on! Just hold on!" He caught the woman beneath the arms, dragging her out of the boat, plunging and panting after the vanished deer. Now earth actually appeared—an acclivity smooth and swift and steep, bizarre, solid and unbelievable; an Indian mound,[26] and he plunging at the muddy slope, slipping back, the woman struggling in his muddy hands.

"Let me down!" she cried. "Let me down!" But he held her, panting, sobbing, and rushed again at the muddy slope; he had almost reached the flat crest with his now violently unmanageable burden when a stick under his foot gathered itself with thick convulsive speed. *It was a snake,* he thought as his feet fled beneath him and with the indubitable last of his strength he half pushed and half flung the woman up the bank as he shot feet first and face down back into that medium upon which he had lived for more days and nights than he could remember and from which he himself had never completely emerged, as if his own failed and spent flesh were attempting to carry out his furious unflagging will for severance at any price, even that of drowning, from the burden with which, unwitting and without choice, he had been doomed. Later it seemed to him that he had carried back beneath the surface with him the sound of the infant's first mewling cry.

IV

When the woman asked him if he had a knife, standing there in the streaming bedticking garments which had got him shot at, the second time by a machine gun, on the two occasions when he had seen any human life after leaving the levee four days ago, the convict felt exactly as he had in the fleeing skiff when the woman suggested that they had better hurry. He felt the same outrageous affronting of a condition purely moral, the same raging impotence to find any answer to it; so that, standing above her, spent suffocating and inarticulate, it was a full minute before he comprehended that she was now crying. "The can! The can in the boat!" He did not anticipate what she could want with it; he did not even wonder nor stop to ask. He turned running; this time he thought, *It's another moccasin*[1] as the thick body truncated in that awkward reflex which had nothing of alarm in it but only alertness, he not even shifting his stride though he knew his running foot would fall within a yard of the flat head. The bow of the skiff was well up the slope now where the wave had set it and there was another snake

26. Large earthworks shaped like truncated pyramids. Their purpose is unknown.

1. Water moccasin, a poisonous snake that lives in the swamps and bayous of the Southeast.

just crawling over the stern into it and as he stooped for the bailing can he saw something else swimming toward the mound, he didn't know what—a head, a face at the apex of a vee of ripples. He snatched up the can; by pure juxtaposition of it and water he scooped it full, already turning. He saw the deer again, or another one. That is, he saw a deer—a side glance, the light smoke-colored phantom in a cypress vista then gone, vanished, he not pausing to look after it, galloping back to the woman and kneeling with the can to her lips until she told him better.

It had contained a pint of beans or tomatoes, something, hermetically sealed and opened by four blows of an axe heel, the metal flap turned back, the jagged edges razor-sharp. She told him how, and he used this in lieu of a knife, he removed one of his shoelaces and cut it in two with the sharp tin.[2] Then she wanted warm water—"If I just had a little hot water," she said in a weak serene voice without particular hope; only when he thought of matches it was again a good deal like when she had asked him if he had a knife, until she fumbled in the pocket of the shrunken tunic (it had a darker double vee on one cuff and a darker blotch on the shoulder where service stripes and a divisional emblem[3] has been ripped off but this meant nothing to him) and produced a match-box contrived by telescoping two shotgun shells. So he drew her back a little from the water and went to hunt wood dry enough to burn, thinking this time, *It's just another snake*, only, he said, he should have thought *ten thousand other snakes*: and now he knew it was not the same deer because he saw three at one time, does or bucks he did not know which since they were all antlerless in May and besides he had never seen one of any kind anywhere before except on a Christmas card; and then the rabbit, drowned, dead anyway, already torn open, the bird, the hawk, standing upon it—the erected crest, the hard vicious patrician nose, the intolerant omnivorous yellow eye—and he kicking at it, kicking it lurching and broadwinged into the actual air.

When he returned with the wood and the dead rabbit, the baby, wrapped in the tunic, lay wedged between two cypress-knees and the woman was not in sight, though while the convict knelt in the mud, blowing and nursing his meagre flame, she came slowly and weakly from the direction of the water. Then, the water heated at last and there produced from some where he was never to know, she herself perhaps never to know until the need comes, no woman perhaps ever to know, only no woman will even wonder, that square of something somewhere between sackcloth and silk—squatting,

2. The baby's umbilical cord is cut and tied.

3. Service stripes tell how many years a soldier has been in the Army; the divisional emblem, the Army unit in which he had last served.

his own wet garments steaming in the fire's heat, he watched her bathe the child with a savage curiosity and interest that became amazed unbelief, so that at last he stood above them both, looking down at the tiny terra-cotta colored creature resembling nothing, and thought, *And this is all. This is what severed me violently from all I ever knew and did not wish to leave and cast me upon a medium I was born to fear, to fetch up at last in a place I never saw before and where I do not even know where I am.*

Then he returned to the water and refilled the bailing can. It was drawing toward sunset now (or what would have been sunset save for the high prevailing overcast) of this day whose beginning he could not even remember; when he returned to where the fire burned in the interlaced gloom of the cypresses, even after this short absence, evening had definitely come, as though darkness too had taken refuge upon that quarter-acre mound, that earthen Ark out of Genesis, that dim wet cypress-choked life-teeming constricted desolation in what direction and how far from what and where he had no more idea than of the day of the month, and had now with the setting of the sun crept forth again to spread upon the waters. He stewed the rabbit in sections while the fire burned redder and redder in the darkness where the shy wild eyes of small animals—once the tall mild almost plate-sized stare of one of the deer—glowed and vanished and glowed again, the broth hot and rank after the four days; he seemed to hear the roar of his own saliva as he watched the woman sip the first canful. Then he drank too; they ate the other fragments which had been charring and scorching on willow twigs; it was full night now. "You and him better sleep in the boat," the convict said. "We want to get an early start tomorrow." He shoved the bow of the skiff off the land so it would lie level, he lengthened the painter[4] with a piece of grapevine and returned to the fire and tied the grapevine about his wrist and lay down. It was mud he lay upon, but it was solid underneath, it was earth, it did not move; if you fell upon it you broke your bones against its incontrovertible passivity sometimes but it did not accept you substanceless and enveloping and suffocating, down and down and down; it was hard at times to drive a plow through, it sent you spent, weary, and cursing its light-long insatiable demands back to your bunk at sunset at times but it did not snatch you violently out of all familiar knowing and sweep you thrall and impotent for days against any returning. *I dont know where I am and I dont reckon I know the way back to where I want to go,* he thought. *But at least the boat has stopped long enough to give me a chance to turn it around.*

He waked at dawn, the light faint, the sky jonquil-colored;[5] the

4. Towrope fastened at the bow.

5. Yellow.

day would be fine. The fire had burned out; on the opposite side of the cold ashes lay three snakes motionless and parallel as underscoring, and in the swiftly making light others seemed to materialize: earth which an instant before had been mere earth broke up into motionless coils and loops, branches which a moment before had been mere branches now become immobile ophidian festoons even as the convict stood thinking about food, about something hot before they started. But he decided against this, against wasting this much time, since there still remained in the skiff quite a few of the rocklike objects which the shanty woman had flung into it, besides (thinking this) no matter how fast nor successfully he hunted, he would never be able to lay up enough food to get them back to where they wanted to go. So he returned to the skiff, paying himself back to it by his vine-spliced painter, back to the water on which a low mist thick as cotton batting (though apparently not very tall, deep) lay, into which the stern of the skiff was already beginning to disappear although it lay with its prow almost touching the mound. The woman waked, stirred. "We fixing to start now?" she said.

"Yah," the convict said. "You aint aiming to have another one this morning, are you?" He got in and shoved the skiff clear of the land, which immediately began to dissolve into the mist. "Hand me the oar," he said over his shoulder, not turning yet.

"The oar?"

He turned his head. "The oar. You're laying on it." But she was not, and for an instant during which the mound, the island continued to fade slowly into the mist which seemed to enclose the skiff in weightless and impalpable wool like a precious or fragile bauble or jewel, the convict squatted not in dismay but in that frantic and astonished outrage of a man who, having just escaped a falling safe, is struck by the following two-ounce paper weight which was sitting on it: this the more unbearable because he knew that never in his life had he less time to give way to it. He did not hesitate. Grasping the grapevine end he sprang into the water, vanishing in the violent action of climbing and reappeared still climbing and (who had never learned to swim) plunged and threshed on toward the almost-vanished mound, moving through the water then upon it as the deer had done yesterday and scrabbled up the muddy slope and lay gasping and panting, still clutching the grapevine end.

Now the first thing he did was to choose what he believed to be the most suitable tree (for an instant in which he knew he was insane he thought of trying to saw it down with the flange of the bailing can) and build a fire against the butt of it. Then he went to seek food. He spent the next six days seeking it while the tree burned through and fell and burned through again at the proper length and he nursing little constant cunning flames along the flanks of the log to make it paddle-shaped, nursing them at night too while the woman and baby (it was eating, nursing now, he turning his back or even returning into the woods each time she prepared to open the faded tunic) slept in the skiff. He learned to watch for stooping hawks and so found more rabbits and twice possums; they ate some drowned fish which gave them both a rash and then a violent flux[6] and one snake which the woman thought was turtle and which did them no harm, and one night it rained and he got up and dragged brush, shaking the snakes (he no longer thought, *It aint nothing but another moccasin,* he just stepped aside for them as they, when there was time, telescoped sullenly aside for him) out of it with the old former feeling of personal invulnerability and built a shelter and the rain stopped at once and did not recommence and the woman went back to the skiff.

Then one night—the slow tedious charring log was almost a paddle now—one night and he was in bed, in his bed in the bunkhouse and it was cold, he was trying to pull the covers up only his mule wouldn't let him, prodding and bumping heavily at him, trying to get into the narrow bed with him and now the bed was cold too and wet and he was trying to get out of it only the mule would not let him, holding him by his belt in its teeth, jerking and bumping him back into the cold wet bed and, leaning, gave him a long swipe across the face with its cold limber masculated tongue and he waked to no fire, no coal even beneath where the almost-finished paddle had been charring and something else prolonged and coldly limber passed swifly across his body where he lay in four inches of water while the nose of the skiff alternately tugged at the grapevine tied about his waist and bumped and shoved him back into the water again. Then something else came up and began to nudge at his ankle (the log, the oar, it was) even as he groped frantically for the skiff, hearing the swift rustling going to and fro inside the hull as the woman began to thrash about and scream. "Rats!" she cried. "It's full of rats!"

"Lay still!" he cried. "It's just snakes. Cant you hold still long enough for me to find the boat?" Then he found it, he got into it with the unfinished paddle; again the thick muscular body convulsed under his foot; it did not strike; he would not have cared, glaring astern where he could see a little—the faint outer luminosity of the open water. He poled toward it, thrusting aside the snake-looped branches, the bottom of the skiff resounding faintly to thick solid plops, the woman shrieking steadily. Then the skiff was clear of the trees, the mound, and now he could feel the bodies whipping about his ankles and hear the rasp of them as they went over the gunwale. He drew the log in and scooped it forward along

6. Diarrhea.

the bottom of the boat and up and out; against the pallid water he could see three more of them in lashing convolutions before they vanished. "Shut up!" he cried. "Hush! I wish I was a snake so I could get out too!"

When once more the pale and heatless wafer disc of the early sun stared down at the skiff (whether they were moving or not the convict did not know) in its nimbus of fine cotton batting, the convict was hearing again that sound which he had heard twice before and would never forget—that sound of deliberate and irresistible and monstrously disturbed water. But this time he could not tell from what direction it came. It seemed to be everywhere, waxing and fading; it was like a phantom behind the mist, at one instant miles away, the next on the point of overwhelming the skiff within the next second; suddenly, in the instant he would believe (his whole weary body would spring and scream) that he was about to drive the skiff point-blank into it and with the unfinished paddle of the color and texture of sooty bricks, like something gnawed out of an old chimney by beavers and weighing twenty-five pounds, he would whirl the skiff frantically and find the sound dead ahead of him again. Then something bellowed tremendously above his head, he heard human voices, a bell jangled and the sound ceased and the mist vanished as when you draw your hand across a frosted pane, and the skiff now lay upon a sunny glitter of brown water flank to flank with, and about thirty yards away from, a steamboat. The decks were crowded and packed with men, women and children sitting or standing beside and among a homely conglomeration of hurried furniture, who looked mournfully and silently down into the skiff while the convict and the man with a megaphone in the pilot house talked to each other in alternate puny shouts and roars above the chuffing of the reversed engines:

"What in hell are you trying to do? Commit suicide?"

"Which is the way to Vicksburg?"

"Vicksburg? Vicksburg? Lay alongside and come aboard."

"Will you take the boat too?"

"Boat? Boat?" Now the megaphone cursed, the roaring waves of blasphemy and biological supposition empty cavernous and bodiless in turn, as if the water, the air, the mist had spoken it, roaring the words then taking them back to itself and no harm done, no scar, no insult left anywhere. "If I took aboard every floating sardine can you sonabitchin mushrats want me to I wouldn't even have room forrard for a leadsman.[7] Come aboard! Do you expect me to hang here on stern engines till hell freezes?"

"I aint coming without the boat," the convict said. Now another voice spoke, so calm and mild and sensible that for a moment it

7. Crewman who tells the depth of water with a weighted line. *Forrard*: on the forward deck. *On stern engines*: I.e., with engines reversed.

sounded more foreign and out of place than even the megaphone's bellowing and bodiless profanity:

"Where is it you are trying to go?"

"I aint trying," the convict said. "I'm going. Parchman."[8] The man who had spoken last turned and appeared to converse with a third man in the pilot house. Then he looked down at the skiff again.

"Carnarvon?"[9]

"What?" the convict said. "Parchman?"

"All right. We're going that way. We'll put you off where you can get home. Come aboard."

"The boat too?"

"Yes, yes. Come along. We're burning coal just to talk to you." So the convict came alongside then and watched them help the woman and baby over the rail and he came aboard himself, though he still held to the end of the vine-spliced painter until the skiff was hoisted onto the boiler deck. "My God," the man, the gentle one, said, "is that what you have been using for a paddle?"

"Yah," the convict said. "I lost the plank."

"The plank," the mild man (the convict told how he seemed to whisper it), "the plank. Well. Come along and get something to eat. Your boat is all right now."

"I reckon I'll wait here," the convict said. Because now, he told them, he began to notice for the first time that the other people, the other refugees who crowded the deck, who had gathered in a quiet circle about the upturned skiff on which he and the woman sat, the grapevine painter wrapped several times about his wrist and clutched in his hand, staring at him and the woman with queer hot mournful intensity, were not white people—

"You mean niggers?" the plump convict said.

"No. Not Americans."

"Not Americans? You was clean out of *America* even?"

"I dont know," the tall one said. "They called it Atchafalaya."— Because after a while he said, "What?" to the man and the man did it again, gobble-gobble—

"Gobble-gobble?" the plump convict said.

"That's the way they talked," the tall one said. "Gobble-gobble, whang, caw-caw-to-to"[10]—And he sat there and watched them gobbling at one another and then looking at him again, then they fell

8. Parchman (and the Penal Farm) is about one hundred miles north of Vicksburg, and over three hundred miles north of where the convict is now. A Louisiana steamboat captain would never have heard of it.

9. A Louisiana town fourteen miles downriver from New Orleans. The levee there was dynamited on April 29 to relieve the pressure of flood waters on the New Orleans levee.

10. The convict's impression of the dialect spoken by Cajuns, Louisianans of French-Canadian descent. The Cajuns were originally expelled by the British from the east Canadian province of Acadia in the 18th century.

back and the mild man (he wore a Red Cross brassard) entered, followed by a waiter with a tray of food. The mild man carried two glasses of whiskey.

"Drink this," the mild man said. "This will warm you." The woman took hers and drank it but the convict told how he looked at his and thought, *I ain't tasted whiskey in seven years.* He had not tasted it but once before that; it was at the still itself back in a pine hollow; he was seventeen, he had gone there with four companions, two of whom were grown men, one of twenty-two or -three, the other about forty; he remembered it. That is, he remembered perhaps a third of that evening—a fierce turmoil in the hell-colored firelight, the shock and shock of blows about his head (and likewise of his own fists on other hard bone), then the waking to a splitting and blinding sun in a place, a cowshed, he had never seen before and which later turned out to be twenty miles from his home. He said he thought of this and he looked about at the faces watching him and he said,

"I reckon not."

"Come, come," the mild man said. "Drink it."

"I dont want it."

"Nonsense," the mild man said. "I'm a doctor. Here. Then you can eat." So he took the glass and even then he hesitated but again the mild man said, "Come along, down with it; you're still holding us up," in that voice still calm and sensible but a little sharp too—the voice of a man who could keep calm and affable because he wasn't used to being crossed—and he drank the whiskey and even in the second between the sweet full fire in his belly and when it began to happen he was trying to say, "I tried to tell you! I tried to!" But it was too late now in the pallid sun-glare of the tenth day of terror and hopelessness and despair and impotence and rage and outrage and it was himself and the mule, his mule (they had let him name it—John Henry) which no man save he had plowed for five years now and whose ways and habits he knew and respected and who knew his ways and habits so well that each of them could anticipate the other's very movements and intentions; it was himself and the mule, the little gobbling faces flying before them, the familiar hard skull-bones shocking against his fists, his voice shouting, "Come on, John Henry! Plow them down! Gobble them down, boy!" even as the bright hot red wave turned back, meeting it joyously, happily, lifted, poised, then hurling through space triumphant and yelling, then again the old shocking blow at the back of his head: he lay on the deck, flat on his back and pinned arm and leg and cold sober again, his nostrils gushing again, the mild man stopping over him with behind the thin rimless glasses the coldest eyes the convict had ever seen—eyes which the convict said were not looking at him but at the gushing blood with nothing in the world in them but complete impersonal interest.

"Good man," the mild man said. "Plenty of life in the old carcass yet, eh? Plenty of good red blood too. Anyone ever suggest to you that you were hemophilic? ("What? the plump convict said. "Hemophilic? You know what that means?" The tall convict had his cigarette going now, his body jackknifed backward into the coffinlike space between the upper and lower bunks, lean, clean, motionless, the blue smoke wreathing across his lean dark aquiline shaven face. "That's a calf that's a bull and a cow at the same time."

"No, it aint," a third convict said. "It's a calf or a colt that aint neither one."[11]

"Hell fire," the plump one said. "He's got to be one or the other to keep from drounding." He had never ceased to look at the tall one in the bunk; now he spoke to him again: "You let him call you that?") The tall one had done so. He did not answer the doctor (this was where he stopped thinking of him as the mild man) at all. He could not move either, though he felt fine, he felt better than he had in ten days. So they helped him to his feet and steadied him over and lowered him onto the upturned skiff beside the woman, where he sat bent forward, elbows on knees in the immemorial attitude, watching his own bright crimson staining the mud-trodden deck, until the doctor's clean clipped hand appeared under his nose with a phial.

"Smell," the doctor said. "Deep." The convict inhaled, the sharp ammoniac sensation burned up his nostrils and into his throat. "Again," the doctor said. The convict inhaled obediently. This time he choked and spat a gout of blood, his nose now had no more feeling than a toenail, other than it felt about the size of a ten-inch shovel, and as cold.

"I ask you to excuse me," he said. "I never meant—"

"Why?" the doctor said. "You put up as pretty a scrap against forty or fifty men as I ever saw. You lasted a good two seconds. Now you can eat something. Or do you think that will send you haywire again?"

They both ate, sitting on the skiff, the gobbling faces no longer watching them now, the convict gnawing slowly and painfully at the thick sandwich, hunched, his face laid sideways to the food and parallel to the earth as a dog chews; the steamboat went on. At noon there were bowls of hot soup and bread and more coffee; they ate this too, sitting side by side on the skiff, the grapevine still wrapped about the convict's wrist. The baby waked and nursed and slept again and they talked quietly:

11. The convicts have confused *hemophilic,* subject to excessive bleeding, with *hermaphroditic,* of both sexes.

"Was it Parchman he said he was going to take us?"

"That's where I told him I wanted to go."

"It never sounded exactly like Parchman to me. It sounded like he said something else." The convict had thought that too. He had been thinking about that fairly soberly ever since they boarded the steamboat and soberly indeed ever since he had remarked the nature of the other passengers, those men and women definitely a little shorter than he and with skin a little different in pigmentation from any sunburn, even though the eyes were sometimes blue or gray, who talked to one another in a tongue he had never heard before and who apparently did not understand his own, people the like of whom he had never seen about Parchman nor anywhere else and whom he did not believe were going there or beyond there either. But after his hill-billy country fashion and kind he would not ask, because to his raising asking information was asking a favor and you did not ask favors of strangers; if they offered them perhaps you accepted and you expressed gratitude almost tediously recapitulant, but you did not ask. So he would watch and wait, as he had done before, and do or try to do to the best of his ability what the best of his judgment dictated.

So he waited, and in midafternoon the steamboat chuffed and thrust through a willow-choked gorge and emerged from it, and now the convict knew it was the River. He could believe it now—the tremendous reach, yellow and sleepy in the afternoon—("Because it's too big," he told them soberly. "Ain't no flood in the world big enough to make it do more than stand a little higher so it can look back and see just where the flea is, just exactly where to scratch. It's the little ones, the little piddling creeks that run backward one day and forward the next and come busting down on a man full of dead mules and hen houses.")—and the steamboat moving up this now (*like a ant crossing a plate*, the convict thought, sitting beside the woman on the upturned skiff, the baby nursing again, apparently looking too out across the water where, a mile away on either hand, the twin lines of levee resembled parallel unbroken floating thread) and then it was nearing sunset and he began to hear, to notice, the voices of the doctor and of the man who had first bawled at him through the megaphone now bawling again from the pilot house overhead:

"Stop? Stop? Am I running a street car?"

"Stop for the novelty then," the doctor's pleasant voice said. "I dont know how many trips back and forth you have made in yonder nor how many of what you call mushrats you have fetched out. But this is the first time you ever had two people—no, three—who not only knew the name of some place they wished to go to but were actually trying to go there." So the convict waited while the sun slanted more and more and the steamboat-ant crawled steadily on across its vacant and gigantic plate turning more and more to copper. But he did not ask, he just waited. *Maybe it was Carrollton*[12] *he said,* he thought. *It begun with a* C. But he did not believe that either. He did not know where he was, but he did know that this was not anywhere near the Carrollton he remembered from that day seven years ago when, shackled wrist to wrist with the deputy sheriff, he had passed through it on the train—the slow spaced repeated shattering banging of trucks where two railroads crossed, a random scattering of white houses tranquil among trees on green hills lush with summer, a pointing spire, the finger of the hand of God. But there was no river there. *And you aint never close to this river without knowing it,* he thought. *I don't care who you are nor where you have been all your life.* Then the head of the steamboat began to swing across the stream, its shadow swinging too, traveling long before it across the water, toward the vacant ridge of willow-massed earth empty of all life. There was nothing there at all, the convict could not even see either earth or water beyond it; it was as though the steamboat were about to crash slowly through the thin low frail willow barrier and embark into space, or lacking this, slow and back and fill and disembark him into space, granted it was about to disembark him, granted this was that place which was not near Parchman and was not Carrollton either, even though it did begin with C. Then he turned his head and saw the doctor stooping over the woman, pushing the baby's eyelid up with his forefinger, peering at it.

"Who else was there when he came?" the doctor said.

"Nobody," the convict said.

"Did it all yourselves, eh?"

"Yes," the convict said. Now the doctor stood up and looked at the convict.

"This is Carnarvon," he said.

"Carnarvon?" the convict said. "That aint—" Then he stopped, ceased. And now he told about that—the intent eyes as dispassionate as ice behind the rimless glasses, the clipped quick-tempered face that was not accustomed to being crossed or lied to either. ("Yes," the plump convict said. "That's what I was aiming to ask. Them clothes. Anybody would know them. How if this doctor was as smart as you claim he was—"

"I had slept in them for ten nights, mostly in the mud," the tall one said. "I had been rowing since midnight with that sapling oar I had tried to burn out that I never had time to scrape the soot off. But it's being scared and worried and then scared and then worried

12. Another Mississippi town, between Jackson, the state capital in which the convict was presumably tried, and Parchman.

again in clothes for days and days and days that changes the way they look. I dont mean just your pants." He did not laugh. "Your face too. That doctor knowed."

"All right," the plump one said. "Go on.")

"I know it," the doctor said. "I discovered that while you were lying on the deck yonder sobering up again. Now dont lie to me. I dont like lying. This boat is going to New Orleans."

"No," the convict said immediately, quietly, with absolute finality. He could hear them again—the thuck-thuck-thuck on the water where an instant before he had been. But he was not thinking the bullets. He had forgotten them, forgiven them. He was thinking of himself crouching, sobbing, panting before running again—the voice, the indictment, the cry of final and irrevocable repudiation of the old primal faithless Manipulator of all the lust and folly and injustice: *All in the world I wanted was just to surrender;* thinking of it, remembering it but without heat now, without passion now and briefer than an epitaph: *No. I tried that once. They shot at me.*

"So you dont want to go to New Orleans. And you didn't exactly plan to go to Carnarvon. But you will take Carnarvon in preference to New Orleans." The convict said nothing. The doctor looked at him, the magnified pupils like the heads of two bridge nails. "What were you in for? Hit him harder than you thought, eh?"

No. I tried to rob a train."

"Say that again." The convict said it again. "Well? Go on. You dont say that in the year 1927 and just stop, man." So the convict told it, dispassionately too—about the magazines, the pistol which would not shoot, the mask and the dark lantern in which no draft had been arranged to keep the candle burning so that it died almost with the match but even then left the metal too hot to carry, won with subscriptions. *Only it aint my eyes or my mouth either he's watching,* he thought. *It's like he is watching the way my hair grows on my head.* "I see," the doctor said. "But something went wrong. But you've had plenty of time to think about it since. To decide what was wrong, what you failed to do."

"Yes, the convict said. "I've thought about it a right smart since."

"So next time you are not going to make that mistake."

"I don't know," the convict said. "There aint going to be a next time."

"Why? If you know what you did wrong, they wont catch you next time."

The convict looked at the doctor steadily. They looked at each other steadily; the two sets of eyes were not so different after all. "I reckon I see what you mean," the convict said presently. "I was eighteen then. I'm twenty-five now."

"Oh," the doctor said. Now (the convict tried to tell it) the doctor did not move, he just simply quit looking at the convict. He produced a pack of cheap cigarettes from his coat. "Smoke?" he said.

"I wouldn't care for none," the convict said.

"Quite," the doctor said in that affable clipped voice. He put the cigarettes away. "There has been conferred upon my race (the Medical race) also the power to bind and to loose,[13] if not by Jehovah perhaps, certainly by the American Medical Association—on which incidentally, in this day of Our Lord, I would put my money, at any odds, at any amount, at any time. I dont know just how far out of bounds I am on this specific occasion but I think we'll put it to the touch." He cupped his hands to his mouth, toward the pilot house overhead. "Captain!" he shouted. "We'll put these three passengers ashore here." He turned to the convict again. "Yes," he said, "I think I shall let your native State lick its own vomit. Here." Again his hand emerged from his pocket, this time with a bill in it.

"No," the convict said.

"Come, come; I dont like to be disputed either."

"No," the convict said. "I aint got any way to pay it back."

"Did I ask you to pay it back?"

"No," the convict said. "I never asked to borrow it either."

So once more he stood on dry land, who had already been toyed with twice by that risible and concentrated power of water, once more than should have fallen to the lot of any one man, any one lifetime, yet for whom there was reserved still another unbelievable recapitulation, he and the woman standing on the empty levee, the sleeping child wrapped in the faded tunic and the grapevine painter still wrapped about the convict's wrist, watching the steamboat back away and turn and once more crawl onward up the platter-like reach of vacant water burnished more and more to copper, its trailing smoke roiling in slow copper-edged gouts, thinning out along the water, fading, stinking away across the vast serene desolation, the boat growing smaller and smaller until it did not seem to crawl at all but to hang stationary in the airy substanceless sunset, dissolving into nothing like a pellet of floating mud.

Then he turned and for the first time looked about him, behind him, recoiling, not through fear but through pure reflex and not physically but the soul, the spirit, that profound sober alert attentiveness of the hillman who will not ask anything of strangers, not even information, thinking quietly. *No. This aint Carrollton neither.* Because he now looked down the almost perpendicular

13. The power conferred by Jesus on Peter, and on the Popes: "Whatsoever thou shalt bind on earth shall be bound in heaven; and whatsoever thou shalt loose on earth shall be loosed in heaven." [*Matthew* 16:19.]

landward slope of the levee through sixty feet of absolute space, upon a surface, a terrain flat as a waffle and of the color of a waffle or perhaps of the summer coat of a claybank horse and possessing that same piled density of a rug or peltry,[14] spreading away without undulation yet with that curious appearance of imponderable solidity like fluid, broken here and there by thick humps of arsenical green which nevertheless still seemed to possess no height and by writhen veins of the color of ink which he began to suspect to be actual water but with judgment reserved, with judgment still reserved even when presently he was walking in it. That's what he said, told: So they went on. He didn't tell how he got the skiff singlehanded up the revetment and across the crown and down the opposite sixty-foot drop, he just said he went on, in a swirling cloud of mosquitoes like hot cinders, thrusting and plunging through the saw-edged grass which grew taller than his head and which whipped back at his arms and face like limber knives, dragging by the vine-spliced painter the skiff in which the woman sat, slogging and stumbling knee-deep in something less of earth than water, along one of those black winding channels less of water than earth: and then (he was in the skiff too now, paddling with the charred log, what footing there had been having given away beneath him without warning thirty minutes ago, leaving only the air-filled bubble of his jumper-back ballooning lightly on the twilit water until he rose to the surface and scrambled into the skiff) the house, the cabin a little larger than a horse-box, of cypress boards and an iron roof, rising on ten-foot stilts slender as spiders' legs, like a shabby and death-stricken (and probably poisonous) wading creature which had got that far into the flat waste and died with nothing nowhere in reach or sight to lie down upon, a pirogue[15] tied to the foot of a crude ladder, a man standing in the open door holding a lantern (it was that dark now) above his head, gobbling down at them.

He told it—of the next eight or nine or ten days, he did not remember which, while the four of them—himself and the woman and baby and the little wiry man with rotting teeth and soft wild bright eyes like a rat or a chipmunk, whose language neither of them could understand—lived in the room and a half. He did not tell it that way, just as he apparently did not consider it worth the breath to tell how he had got the hundred-and-sixty-pound skiff singlehanded up and across and down the sixty-foot levee. He just said, "After a while we come to a house and we stayed there eight or nine days when they blew up the levee with dynamite so we had to leave." That was all. But he remembered it, but quietly now, with the cigar now, the good one the Warden had given him (though not lighted yet) in his peaceful and steadfast hand,

14. Animal skins. **15. Dugout canoe.**

remembering that first morning when he waked on the thin pallet beside his host (the woman and baby had the one bed) with the fierce sun already latticed through the warped rough planking of the wall, and stood on the rickety porch looking out upon that flat fecund waste neither earth nor water, where even the senses doubted which was which, which rich and massy air and which mazy and impalpable vegetation, and thought quietly, *He must do something here to eat and live. But I dont know what. And until I can go on again, until I can find where I am and how to pass that town without them seeing me I will have to help him do it so we can eat and live too, and I dont know what.* And he had a change of clothing too, almost at once on that first morning, not telling any more than he had about the skiff and the levee how he had begged borrowed or bought from the man whom he had not laid eyes on twelve hours ago and with whom on the day he saw him for the last time he still could exchange no word, the pair of dungaree pants which even the Cajun had discarded as no longer wearable, filthy, buttonless, the legs slashed and frayed into fringe like that on an 1890 hammock, in which he stood naked from the waist up and holding out to her the mud-caked and soot-stained jumper and overall when the woman waked on that first morning in the crude bunk nailed into one corner and filled with dried grass, saying, "Wash them. Good. I want all them stains out. All of them."

"But the jumper," she said. "Aint he got ere old shirt too? That sun and them mosquitoes—" But he did not even answer, and she said no more either, though when he and the Cajun returned at dark the garments were clean, stained a little still with the old mud and soot, but clean, resembling again what they were supposed to resemble as (his arms and back already a fiery red which would be blisters by tomorrow) he spread the garments out and examined them and then rolled them up carefully in a six-months-old New Orleans paper and thrust the bundle behind a rafter, where it remained while day followed day and the blisters on his back broke and suppurated and he would sit with his face expressionless as a wooden mask beneath the sweat while the Cajun doped his back with something on a filthy rag from a filthy saucer, she still saying nothing since she too doubtless knew what his reason was, not from that rapport of the wedded conferred upon her by the two weeks during which they had jointly suffered all the crises emotional social economic and even moral which do not always occur even in the ordinary fifty married years (the old married: you have seen them, the electroplate reproductions, the thousand identical coupled faces with only a collarless stud or a fichu out of Louisa Alcott[16] to

16. (1832–1888), author of *Little Women*. *Fichu*: A three-cornered cape or shawl worn by women on the head or shoulders.

denote the sex, looking in pairs like the winning braces of dogs after a field trial, out from among the packed columns of disaster and alarm and baseless assurance and hope and incredible insensitivity and insulation from tomorrow propped by a thousand morning sugar bowls or coffee urns; or singly, rocking on porches or sitting in the sun beneath the tobacco-stained porticoes of a thousand county courthouses, as though with the death of the other having inherited a sort of rejuvenescence, immortality; relict, they take a new lease on breath and seem to live forever, as though that flesh which the old ceremony or ritual had morally purified and made legally one had actually become so with long tedious habit and he or she who entered the ground first took all of it with him or her, leaving only the old permanent enduring bone, free and trammelless)—not because of this but because she too had stemmed at some point from the same dim hill-bred Abraham.[17]

So the bundle remained behind the rafter and day followed day while he and his partner (he was in partnership now with his host, hunting alligators on shares, on the halvers he called it—"Halvers?" the plump convict said. "How could you make a business agreement with a man you claim you couldn't even talk to?"

"I never had to talk to him," the tall one said. "Money aint got but one language.") departed at dawn each day, at first together in the pirogue but later singly, the one in the pirogue and the other in the skiff, the one with the battered and pitted rifle, the other with the knife and a piece of knotted rope and a lightwood club the size and weight and shape of a Thuringian mace, stalking their pleistocene[18] nightmares up and down the secret inky channels which writhed the flat brass-colored land. He remembered that too: the first morning when turning in the sunrise from the rickety platform he saw the hide nailed drying to the wall and stopped dead, looking at it quietly, thinking quietly and soberly, *So that's it. That's what he does in order to eat and live,* knowing it was a hide, a skin, but from what animal, by association, ratiocination or even memory of any picture out of his dead youth, he did not know but knowing that it was the reason, the explanation, for the little lost spider-legged house (which had already begun to die, to rot from the legs upward almost before the roof was nailed on) set in that teeming and myriad desolation, enclosed and lost within the furious embrace of flowing mare earth and stallion sun, divining through pure rapport of kind for kind, hill-billy and bayou-rat, the two one and identical because of the same grudged dispensation and niggard[19] fate of hard and unceasing travail not to gain future security, a

17. All Hebrews are said to be descended from the Old Testament patriarch Abraham.

18. Stone Age. The Thuringians were a pre-Christian Germanic tribe.

19. Misery, grudging.

balance in the bank or even in a buried soda can for slothful and easy old age, but just permission to endure and endure to buy air to feel and sun to drink for each's little while, thinking (the convict), *Well, anyway I am going to find out what it is sooner than I expected to,* and did so, re-entered the house where the woman was just waking in the one sorry built-in straw-filled bunk which the Cajun had surrendered to her, and ate the breakfast (the rice, a semi-liquid mess violent with pepper and mostly fish considerably high,[20] the chicory-thickened coffee) and, shirtless, followed the little scuttling bobbing bright-eyed rotten-toothed man down the crude ladder and into the pirogue. He had never seen a pirogue either and he believed that it would not remain upright—not that it was light and precariously balanced with its open side upward but that there was inherent in the wood, the very log, some dynamic and unsleeping natural law, almost will, which its present position outraged and violated—yet accepting this too as he had the fact that that hide had belonged to something larger than any calf or hog and that anything which looked like that on the outside would be more than likely to have teeth and claws too, accepting this, squatting in the pirogue, clutching both gunwales, rigidly immobile as though he had an egg filled with nitroglycerin in his mouth and scarcely breathing, thinking. *If that's it, then I can do it too and even if he cant tell me how I reckon I can watch him and find out.* And he did this too, he remembered it, quietly even yet, thinking, *I thought that was how to do it and I reckon I would still think that even if I had it to do again now for the first time*—the brazen day already fierce upon his naked back, the crooked channel like a voluted thread of ink, the pirogue moving steadily to the paddle which both entered and left the water without a sound; then the sudden cessation of the paddle behind him and the fierce hissing, gobble of the Cajun at his back and he squatting bate-breathed and with that intense immobility of complete sobriety of a blind man listening while the frail wooden shell stole on at the dying apex of its own parted water. Afterward he remembered the rifle too—the rust-pitted single-shot weapon with a clumsily wired stock and a muzzle you could have driven a whiskey cork into, which the Cajun had brought into the boat—but not now; now he just squatted, crouched, immobile, breathing with infinitesimal care, his sober unceasing gaze going here and there constantly as he thought, *What? What? I not only dont know what I am looking for, I dont even know where to look for it.* Then he felt the motion of the pirogue as the Cajun moved and then the tense gobbling hissing actually, hot rapid and repressed, against his neck and ear, and

20. Smelly, rotten.

glancing downward saw projecting between his own arm and body from behind the Cajun's hand holding the knife, and glaring up again saw the flat thick spit of mud which as he looked at it divided and became a thick mud-colored log which in turn seemed, still immobile, to leap suddenly against his retinae in three—no, four—dimensions: volume, solidity, shape, and another: not fear but pure and intense speculation and he looking at the scaled motionless shape, thinking not, *It looks dangerous* but *It looks big,* thinking, *Well, maybe a mule standing in a lot looks big to a man that never walked up to one with a halter before,* thinking, *Only if he could just tell me what to do it would save time,* the pirogue drawing nearer now, creeping now, with no ripple now even and it seemed to him that he could even hear his companion's held breath and he taking the knife from the other's hand now and not even thinking this since it was too fast, a flash; it was not a surrender, not a resignation, it was too calm, it was a part of him, he had drunk it with his mother's milk and lived with it all his life: *After all a man cant only do what he has to do, with what he has to do it with, with what he has learned, to the best of his judgment. And I reckon a hog is still a hog, no matter what it looks like. So here goes,* sitting still for an instant longer until the bow of the pirogue grounded lighter than the falling of a leaf and stepped out of it and paused just for one instant while the words *It does look big* stood for just a second, unemphatic and trivial, somewhere where some fragment of his attention could see them and vanished, and stopped straddling, the knife driving even as he grasped the near foreleg, this all in the same instant when the lashing tail struck him a terrific blow upon the back. But the knife was home, he knew that even on his back in the mud, the weight of the thrashing beast longwise upon him, its ridged back clutched to his stomach, his arm about its throat, the hissing head clamped against his jaw, the furious tail lashing and flailing, the knife in his other hand probing for the life and finding it, the hot fierce gush: and now sitting beside the profound up-bellied carcass, his head again between his knees in the old attitude while his own blood freshened the other which drenched him, thinking, *It's my durn nose again.*

So he sat there, his head, his streaming face, bowed between his knees in an attitude not of dejection but profoundly bemused, contemplative, while the shrill voice of the Cajun seemed to buzz at him from an enormous distance; after a time he even looked up at the antic wiry figure bouncing hysterically about him, the face wild and grimacing, the voice gobbling and high; while the convict, holding his face carefully slanted so the blood would run free, looked at him with the cold intentness of a curator or custodian paused before one of his own glass cases, the Cajun threw up the rifle, cried "Boom-boom-boom!" flung it down and in pantomime re-enacted the recent scene then whirled his hands again, crying "Magnifique! Magnifique! Cent d'argent! mille d'argent! Tout l'argent sous le ciel de Dieu!"[21] But the convict was already looking down again, cupping the coffee-colored water to his face, watching the constant bright carmine marble it, thinking, *It's a little late to be telling me that now,* and not even thinking this long because presently they were in the pirogue again, the convict squatting again with that unbreathing rigidity as though he were trying by holding his breath to decrease his very weight, the bloody skin in the bows before him and he looking at it, thinking, *And I cant even ask him how much my half will be.*

But this not for long either, because, as he was to tell the plump convict later, money has but one language. He remembered that too (they were at home now, the skin spread on the platform, where for the woman's benefit now the Cajun once more went through the pantomime—the gun which was not used, the hand-to-hand battle; for the second time the invisible alligator was slain amid cries, the victor rose and found this time that not even the woman was watching him. She was looking at the once more swollen and inflamed face of the convict. "You mean it kicked you right in the face?" she said.

"Nah," the convict said harshly, savagely. "It never had to. I done seem to got to where if that boy was to shoot me in the tail with a bean blower my nose would bleed.")—remembered that too but he did not try to tell it. Perhaps he could not have—how two people who could not even talk to one another made an agreement which both not only understood but which each knew the other would hold true and protect (perhaps for this reason) better than any written and witnessed contract. They even discussed and agreed somehow that they should hunt separately, each in his own vessel, to double the chances of finding prey. But this was easy; the convict could almost understand the words in which the Cajun said, "You do not need me and the rifle; we will only hinder you, be in your way." And more than this, they even agreed about the second rifle: that there was someone, it did not matter who—friend, neighbor, perhaps one in business in that line—from whom they could rent a second rifle; in their two patois,[22] the one bastard English, the other bastard French—the one volatile, with his wild bright eyes and his voluble mouth full of stumps of teeth, the other sober, almost grim, swollen-faced and with his naked back blistered and scoriated like so much beef—they discussed this, squatting on either

21. "Wonderful! Wonderful! A hundred dollars! A thousand dollars! All the money under God's heaven!" (French)

22. Dialects.

side of the pegged-out hide like two members of a corporation facing each other across a mahogany board table, and decided against it, the convict deciding: "I reckon not," he said. "I reckon if I had knowed enough to wait to start out with a gun, I still would. But since I done already started out without one, I dont reckon I'll change." Because it was a question of the money in terms of time, days. (Strange to say, that was the one thing which the Cajun could not tell him: how much the half would be. But the convict knew it was half.) He had so little of them. He would have to move on soon, thinking (the convict), *All this durn foolishness will stop soon and I can get on back,* and then suddenly he found that he was thinking, *Will have to get on back,* and he became quite still and looked about at the rich strange desert which surrounded him, in which he was temporarily lost in peace and hope and into which the last seven years had sunk like so many trivial pebbles into a pool, leaving no ripple, and he thought quietly, with a kind of bemused amazement, *Yes. I reckon I had done forgot how good making money was. Being let to make it.*

So he used no gun, his the knotted rope and the Thuringian mace, and each morning he and the Cajun took their separate ways in the two boats to comb and creep the secret channels about the lost land from (or out of) which now and then still other pint-sized dark men appeared gobbling, abruptly and as though by magic from nowhere, in other hollowed logs, to follow quietly and watch him at his single combats—men named Tine and Toto and Theule, who were not much larger than and looked a good deal like the muskrats which the Cajun (the host did this too, supplied the kitchen too, he expressed this too like the rifle business, in his own tongue, the convict comprehending this too as though it had been English: "Do not concern yourself about food, O Hercules.[23] Catch alligators; I will supply the pot.") took now and then from traps as you take a shoat pig at need from a pen, and varied the eternal rice and fish (the convict did tell this: how at night, in the cabin, the door and one sashless window battened against mosquitoes—a form, a ritual, as empty as crossing the fingers or knocking on wood—sitting beside the bug-swirled lantern on the plank table in a temperature close to blood heat he would look down at the swimming segment of meat on his sweating plate and think, *It must be Theule. He was the fat one.*)—day following day, unemphatic and identical, each like the one before and the one which would follow while his theoretical half of a sum to be reckoned in pennies, dollars, or tens of dollars he did not know, mounted—the mornings when he set forth to find waiting for him like the *matador* his *aficionados*[24] the small

23. Strong hero of Greek and Roman myth, who as a baby in the cradle strangled two serpents barehanded.

24. Like the bullfighter his fans.

clump of constant and deferential pirogues, the hard noons when ringed half about by little motionless shells he fought his solitary combats, the evenings, the return, the pirogues departing one by one into inlets and passages which during the first few days he could not even distinguish, then the platform in the twilight where before the static woman and the usually nursing infant and the one or two bloody hides of the day's take the Cajun would perform his ritualistic victorious pantomime before the two growing rows of knife marks in one of the boards of the wall; then the nights when, the woman and child in the single bunk and the Cajun already snoring on the pallet and the reeking lantern set close, he (the convict) would sit on his naked heels, sweating steadily, his face worn and calm, immersed and indomitable, his bowed back raw and savage as beef beneath the suppurant old blisters and the fierce welts of tails, and scrape and chip at the charred sapling which was almost a paddle now, pausing now and then to raise his head while the cloud of mosquitoes about it whined and whirled, to stare at the wall before him until after a while the crude boards themselves must have dissolved away and let his blank unseeing gaze go on and on unhampered, through the rich oblivious darkness, beyond it even perhaps, even perhaps beyond the seven wasted years during which, so he had just realized, he had been permitted to toil but not to work. Then he would retire himself, he would take a last look at the rolled bundle behind the rafter and blow out the lantern and lie down as he was beside his snoring partner, to lie sweating (on his stomach, he could not bear the touch of anything on his back) in the whining ovenlike darkness filled with the forlorn bellowing of alligators, thinking not, *They never gave me time to learn* but *I had forgot how good it is to work.*

Then on the tenth day it happened. It happened for the third time. At first he refused to believe it, not that he felt that now he had served out and discharged his apprenticeship to mischance, had with the birth of the child reached and crossed the crest of his Golgotha[25] and would now be, possibly not permitted so much as ignored, to descend the opposite slope free-wheeling. That was not his feeling at all. What he declined to accept was the fact that a power, a force such as that which had been consistent enough to concentrate upon him with deadly undeviation for weeks, should with all the wealth of cosmic violence and disaster to draw from, have been so barren of invention and imagination, so lacking in pride of artistry and craftmanship, as to repeat itself twice. Once he had accepted, twice he even forgave, but three times he simply declined to believe, particularly when he was at last persuaded to realize that his third time was to be instigated not by the blind

25. The hill on which Christ was crucified.

potency of volume and motion but by human direction and hands: that now the cosmic joker, foiled twice, had stooped in its vindictive concentration to the employing of dynamite.

He did not tell that. Doubtless he did not know himself how it happened, what was happening. But he doubtless remembered it (but quietly above the thick rich-colored pristine cigar in his clean steady hand), what he knew, divined of it. It would be evening, the ninth evening, he and the woman on either side of their host's empty place at the evening meal, he hearing the voices from without but not ceasing to eat, still chewing steadily, because it would be the same as though he were seeing them anyway—the two or three or four pirogues floating on the dark water beneath the platform on which the host stood, the voices gobbling and jabbering, incomprehensible and filled not with alarm and not exactly with rage or even perhaps absolute surprise but rather just cacophony like those of disturbed marsh fowl, he (the convict) not ceasing to chew but just looking up quietly and maybe without a great deal of interrogation or surprise too as the Cajun burst in and stood before them, wild-faced, glaring, his blackened teeth gaped against the inky orifice of his distended mouth, watching (the convict) while the Cajun went through his violent pantomime of violent evacuation, ejection, scooping something invisible into his arms and hurling it out and downward and in the instant of completing the gesture changing from instigator to victim of that which he had set into pantomimic motion, clasping his head and, bowed over and not otherwise moving, seeming to be swept on and away before it, crying "Boom! Boom! Boom!", the convict watching him, his jaw not chewing now, though for just that moment, thinking, *What? What is it he is trying to tell me?* thinking (this a flash too, since he could not have expressed this, and hence did not even know that he had ever thought it) that though his life had been cast here, circumscribed by this environment, accepted by this environment and accepting it in turn (and he had done well here—this quietly, soberly indeed, if he had been able to phrase it, think it instead of merely knowing it—better than he had ever done, who had not even known until now how good work, making money, could be) yet it was not his life, he still and would ever be no more than the water bug upon the surface of the pond, the plumbless and lurking depths of which he would never know, his only actual contact with it being the instants when on lonely and glaring mudspits under the pitiless sun and amphitheatred by his motionless and riveted semicircle of watching pirogues, he accepted the gambit which he had not elected, entered the lashing radius of the armed tail and beat at the thrashing and hissing head with his lightwood club, or this failing, embraced without hesitation the armored body itself with the frail web of flesh and bone in which he walked and lived and sought the raging life with an eight-inch knife-blade.

So he and the woman merely watched the Cajun as he acted out the whole charade of eviction—the little wiry man gesticulant and wild, his hysterical shadow leaping and falling upon the rough wall as he went through the pantomime of abandoning the cabin, gathering in pantomime his meagre belongings from the walls and corners—objects which no other man would want and only some power or force like blind water or earthquake or fire would ever dispossess him of, the woman watching too, her mouth slightly open upon a mass of chewed food, on her face an expression of placid astonishment, saying, "What? What's he saying?"

"I dont know," the convict said. "But I reckon if it's something we ought to know we will find it out when it's ready for us to." Because he was not alarmed, though by now he had read the other's meaning plainly enough. *He's fixing to leave*, he thought. *He's telling me to leave too*—this later, after they had quitted the table and the Cajun and the woman had gone to bed and the Cajun had risen from the pallet and approached the convict and once more went through the pantomime of abandoning the cabin, this time as one repeats a speech which may have been misunderstood, tediously, carefully repetitional as to a child, seeming to hold the convict with one hand while he gestured, talked, with the other, gesturing as though in single syllables, the convict (squatting, the knife open and the almost-finished paddle across his lap) watching, nodding his head, even speaking in English: "Yah; sure. You bet. I got you." —trimming again at the paddle but no faster, with no more haste than on any other night, serene in his belief that when the time came for him to know whatever it was, that would take care of itself, having already and without even knowing it, even before the possibility, the question, ever arose, declined, refused to accept even the thought of moving also, thinking about the hides, thinking, *If there was just some way he could tell me where to carry my share to get the money* but thinking this only for an instant between two delicate strokes of the blade because almost at once he thought, *I reckon as long as I can catch them I wont have no big trouble finding whoever it is that will buy them.*

So the next morning he helped the Cajun load his few belongings —the pitted rifle, a small bundle of clothing (again they traded, who could not even converse with one another, this time the few cooking vessels, a few traps by definite allocation, and something embracing and abstractional which included the stove, the crude bunk, the house or its occupancy—something—in exchange for one alligator hide)—into the pirogue, then, squatting and as two children divide sticks they divided the hides, separating them into two piles, one-for-me-and-one-for-you, two-for-me-and-two-for-you, and the Cajun loaded his share and shoved away from the platform and paused again, though this time he only put the paddle down, gathered something invisibly into his two hands and flung it violently upward, crying "Boom? Boom?" on a rising inflection, nodding violently to the half-naked and savagely scoriated man on the platform who stared with a sort of grim equability back at him and said, "Sure. Boom. Boom." Then the Cajun went on. He did not look back. They watched him, already paddling rapidly, or the woman did; the convict had already turned.

"Maybe he was trying to tell us to leave too," she said.

"Yah," the convict said. "I thought of that last night. Hand me the paddle." She fetched it to him—the sappling, the one he had been trimming at nightly, not quite finished yet though one more evening would do it (he had been using a spare one of the Cajun's. The other had offered to let him keep it, to include it perhaps with the stove and the bunk and the cabin's freehold but the convict had declined. Perhaps he had computed it by volume against so much alligator hide, this weighed against one more evening with the tedious and careful blade.) and he departed too with his knotted rope and mace, in the opposite direction, as though not only not content with refusing to quit the place he had been warned against, he must establish and affirm the irrevocable finality of his refusal by penetrating even further and deeper into it. And then and without warning the high fierce drowsing of his solitude gathered itself and struck at him.

He could not have told this if he had tried—this not yet midmorning and he going on, alone for the first time, no pirogue emerging anywhere to fall in behind him, but he had not expected this anyway, he knew that the others would have departed too; it was not this, it was his very solitude, his desolation which was now his alone and in full since he had elected to remain; the sudden cessation of the paddle, the skiff shooting on for a moment yet while he thought, *What? What?* Then, *No. No. No,* as the silence and solitude and emptiness roared down upon him in a jeering bellow: and now reversed, the skiff spun violently on its heel, he the betrayed driving furiously back toward the platform where he knew it was already too late, that citadel where the crux and dear breath of his life—the being allowed to work and earn money, that right and privilege which he believed he had earned to himself unaided, asking no favor of anyone or anything save the right to be let alone to pit his will and strength against the sauric protagonist of a land, a region, which he had not asked to be projected into—was being threatened, driving the home-made paddle in grim fury, coming in sight of the platform at last and seeing the motor launch lying alongside it with no surprise at all but actually with a kind of pleasure as though at a visible justification of his outrage and fear, the privilege of saying *I told you so* to his own affronting, driving on toward it in a dreamlike state in which there seemed to be no progress at all, in which, unimpeded and suffocating, he strove dreamily with a weightless oar, with muscles without strength or resiliency, at a medium without resistance, seeming to watch the skiff creep infinitesimally across the sunny water and up to the platform while a man in the launch (there were five of them in all) gobbled at him in that same tongue he had been hearing constantly now for ten days and still knew no word of, just as a second man, followed by the woman carrying the baby and dressed again for departure in the faded tunic and the sunbonnet, emerged from the house, carrying (the man carried several other things but the convict saw nothing else) the paper-wrapped bundle which the convict had put behind the rafter ten days ago and no other hand had touched since, he (the convict) on the platform too now, holding the skiff's painter in one hand and the bludgeon-like paddle in the other, contriving to speak to the woman at last in a voice dreamy and suffocating and incredibly calm: "Take it away from him and carry it back into the house."

"So you can talk English, can you?" the man in the launch said. "Why didn't you come out like they told you to last night?"

"Out?" the convict said. Again he even looked, glared, at the man in the launch, contriving even again to control his voice: "I aint got time to take trips. I'm busy," already turning to the woman again, his mouth already open to repeat as the dreamy buzzing voice of the man came to him and he turning once more, in a terrific and absolutely unbearable exasperation, crying, "Flood? What flood? Hell a mile, it's done passed me twice months ago! It's gone! What flood?" and then (he did not think this in actual words either but he knew it, suffered that flashing insight into his own character or destiny: how there was a peculiar quality of repetitiveness about his present fate, how not only the almost seminal crises recurred with a certain monotony, but the very physical circumstances followed a stupidly unimaginative pattern) the man in the launch said, "Take him" and he was on his feet for a few minutes yet, lashing and striking in panting fury, then once more on his back on hard unyielding planks while the four men swarmed over him in a fierce wave of hard bones and panting curses and at last the thin dry vicious snapping of handcuffs.

"Damn it, are you mad?" the man in the launch said. "Cant you understand they are going to dynamite that levee at noon today?— Come on," he said to the others. "Get him aboard. Let's get out of here."

"I want my hides and boat," the convict said.

"Damn your hides," the man in the launch said. "If they dont get that levee blowed pretty soon you can hunt plenty more of them on the capitol steps at Baton Rouge. And this is all the boat you will need and you can say your prayers about it.",

"I aint going without my boat," the convict said. He said it calmly and with complete finality, so calm, so final that for almost a minute nobody answered him, they just stood looking quietly down at him as he lay, half-naked, blistered and scarred, helpless and manacled hand and foot, on his back, delivering his ultimatum in a voice peaceful and quiet as that in which you talk to your bedfellow before going to sleep. Then the man in the launch moved; he spat quietly over the side and said in a voice as calm and quiet as the convict's:

"All right. Bring his boat." They helped the woman, carrying the baby and the paper-wrapped parcel, into the launch. Then they helped the convict to his feet and into the launch too, the shackles on his wrists and ankles clashing. "I'd unlock you if you'd promise to behave yourself," the man said. The convict did not answer this at all.

"I want to hold the rope," he said.

"The rope?"

"Yes," the convict said. "The rope." So they lowered him into the stern and gave him the end of the painter after it had passed the towing cleat,[26] and they went on. The convict did not look back. But then, he did not look forward either, he lay half sprawled, his shackled legs before him, the end of the skiff's painter in one shackled hand. The launch made two other stops; when the hazy wafer of the intolerable sun began to stand once more directly overhead there were fifteen people in the launch; and then the convict, sprawled and motionless, saw the flat brazen land begin to rise and become a greenish-black mass of swamp, bearded and convoluted, this in turn slopping short off and there spread before him an expanse of water embraced by a blue dissolution of shore line and glittering thinly under the noon, larger than he had ever seen before, the sound of the launch's engine ceasing, the hull sliding on behind its fading bow-wave. "What are you doing?" the leader said.

"It's noon," the helmsman said. "I thought we might hear the dynamite." So they all listened, the launch lost of all forward motion, rocking slightly, the glitter-broken small waves slapping and whispering at the hull, but no sound, no tremble even, came anywhere under the fierce hazy sky; the long moment gathered itself and turned on and noon was past. "All right," the leader said.

26. Fitting to which ropes may be fastened.

"Let's go." The engine started again, the hull began to gather speed. The leader came aft and stooped over the convict, key in hand. "I guess you'll have to behave now, whether you want to or not," he said, unlocking the manacles. "Wont you?"

"Yes," the convict said. They went on; after a time the shore vanished completely and a little sea got up. The convict was free now but he lay as before, the end of the skiff's painter in his hand, bent[27] now with three or four turns about his wrist; he turned his head now and then to look back at the towing skiff as it slewed and bounced in the launch's wake; now and then he even looked out over the lake,[28] the eyes alone moving, the face grave and expressionless, thinking, *This is a greater immensity of water, of waste and desolation, than I have ever seen before*; perhaps not; thinking three or four hours later, the shoreline raised again and broken into a clutter of sailing sloops[29] and power cruisers, *These are more boats than I believed existed, a maritime race of which I also had no cognizance* or perhaps not thinking it but just watching as the launch opened the shored gut of the ship canal, the low smoke of the city beyond it, then a wharf, the launch slowing in; a quiet crowd of people watching with that same forlorn passivity he had seen before and whose race he did recognize even though he had not seen Vicksburg[30] when he passed it—the brand, the unmistakable hallmark of the violently homeless, he more so than any, who would have permitted no man to call him one of them.

"All right," the leader said to him. "Here you are."

"The boat," the convict said.

"You've got it. What do you want me to do—give you a receipt for it?"

"No," the convict said. "I just want the boat."

"Take it. Only you ought to have a bookstrap or something to carry it in." ("Carry it in?" the plump convict said. "Carry it where? Where would you have to carry it?"),

He (the tall one) told that: how he and the woman disembarked and how one of the men helped him haul the skiff up out of the water and how he stood there with the end of the painter wrapped around his wrist and the man bustled up, saying, "All right. Next load! Next load!" and how he told this man too about the boat and the man cried, "Boat? Boat?" and how he (the convict) went with them when they carried the skiff over and racked, berthed, it with the others and how he lined himself up by a Coca-Cola sign and the arch of a draw bridge so he could find the skiff again quick when he returned, and how he and the woman (he carrying the paper-wrapped parcel) were herded into a truck and after a while the

27. Fastened.

28. Lake Pontchartrain, the great lake of New Orleans, 625 square miles in size.

29. Single-masted cruising boats.

30. Which had been refuge for twenty thousand people dispossessed by the flood.

truck began to run in traffic, between close houses, then there was a big building, an armory—

"Armory?" the plump one said. "You mean a jail."

"No. It was a kind of warehouse, with people with bundles laying on the floor." And how he thought maybe his partner might be there and how he even looked about for the Cajun while waiting for a chance to get back to the door again, where the solider was and how he got back to the door at last, the woman behind him and his chest actually against the dropped rifle.

"Gwan, gwan," the soldier said. "Get back. They'll give you some clothes in a minute. You cant walk around the streets that way. And something to eat too. Maybe your kinfolks will come for you by that time." And he told that too: how the woman said,

"Maybe if you told him you had some kinfolks here he would let us out." And how he did not; he could not have expressed this either, it too deep, too ingrained; he had never yet had to think it into words through all the long generations of himself—his hillman's sober and jealous respect not for truth but for the power, the strength of lying—not to be niggard with lying but rather to use it with respect and even care, delicate quick and strong, like a fine and fatal blade. And how they fetched him clothes—a blue jumper and overalls, and then food too (a brisk starched young woman saying, "But the baby must be bathed, cleaned. It will die if you dont" and the woman saying, "Yessum. He might holler some, he aint never been bathed before. But he's a good baby.") and now it was night, the unshaded bulbs harsh and savage and forlorn above the snorers and he rising, gripping the woman awake, and then the window. He told that: how there were doors in plenty, leading he did not know where, but he had a hard time finding a window they could use but he found one at last, he carrying the parcel and the baby too while he climbed through first—"You ought to tore up a sheet and slid down it," the plump convict said. But he needed no sheet, there were cobbles under his feet now, in the rich darkness. The city was there too but he had not seen it yet and would not—the low constant glare; Bienville had stood there too, it had been the figment of an emasculate also calling himself Napoleon but no more, Andrew Jackson had found it one step from Pennsylvania Avenue.[31] But the convict found it considerably further than one step back to the ship canal and the skiff, the Coca-Cola sign dim now, the draw bridge arching spiderly against the jonquil sky at dawn: nor did he tell, any more than about the sixty-foot levee, how he got the skiff

31. Allusions to the history of New Orleans, founded in 1718 by the colonizer and first governor of Louisiana, Jean Baptiste le Moyne, Sieur de Bienville (1680–1768). Napoleon Bonaparte, ruler of France from 1799 to 1814, sold the Louisiana Territory to the United States in 1803; Andrew Jackson (1767–1845), the popular hero of the Battle of New Orleans (1815), became president in 1829. The White House is on Pennsylvania Avenue.

back into the water. The lake was behind him now; there was but one direction he could go. When he saw the River again he knew it at once. He should have; it was now ineradicably a part of his past, his life; it would be a part of what he would bequeath, if that were in store for him. But four weeks later it would look different from what it did now, and did; he (the old man) had recovered from his debauch, back in banks again, the Old Man, rippling placidly toward the sea, brown and rich as chocolate between levees whose inner faces were wrinkled as though in a frozen and aghast amazement, crowned with the rich green of summer in the willows; beyond them, sixty feet below, slick mules squatted against the broad pull of middle-busters[32] in the richened soil which would not need to be planted, which would need only to be shown a cotton seed to sprout and make; there would be the symmetric miles of strong stalks by July, purple bloom in August, in September the black fields snowed over, spilled, the middles dragged smooth by the long sacks, the long black limber hands plucking, the hot air filled with the whine of gins,[33] the September air then but now June air heavy with locust and (the towns) the smell of new paint and the sour smell of the paste which holds wall paper—the towns, the villages, the little lost wood landings on stilts on the inner face of the levee, the lower storeys bright and rank under the new paint and paper and even the marks on spile[34] and post and tree of May's raging waterheight fading beneath each bright silver gust of summer's loud and inconstant rain; there was a store at the levee's lip, a few saddled and rope-bridled mules in the sleepy dust, a few dogs, a handful of negroes sitting on the steps beneath the chewing tobacco and malaria medicine signs, and three white men, one of them a deputy sheriff canvassing for votes to beat his superior (who had given him his job) in the august primary, all pausing to watch the skiff emerge from the glitter-glare of the afternoon water and approach and land, a woman carrying a child stepping out, then a man, a tall man who, approaching, proved to be dressed in a faded but recently washed and quite clean suit of penitentiary clothing, stopping in the dust where the mules dozed and watching with pale cold humorless eyes while the deputy sheriff was still making toward his armpit that gesture which everyone present realized was to have produced a pistol in one flashing motion for a considerable time while still nothing came of it. It was apparently enough for the newcomer, however.

"You a officer?" he said.

"You damn right I am," the deputy said. "Just let me get this damn gun—"

"All right," the other said. "Yonder's your boat, and here's the woman. But I never did find that bastard on the cottonhouse."

32. Plows. They "busted" the sod.
33. Machines to separate cotton seeds from the fiber.
34. A foundation post or piling.

V

One of the Governor's young men arrived at the Penitentiary the next morning. That is, he was fairly young (he would not see thirty again though without doubt he did not want to, there being that about him which indicated a character which never had and never would want anything it did not, or was not about to, possess), a Phi Beta Kappa out of an Eastern university, a colonel on the Governor's staff who did not buy it with a campaign contribution, who had stood in his negligent Eastern-cut clothes and his arched nose and lazy contemptuous eyes on the galleries of any number of little lost backwoods stores and told his stories and received the guffaws of his overalled and spitting hearers and with the same look in his eyes fondled infants named in memory of the last administration and in honor (or hope) of the next, and (it was said of him and doubtless not true) by lazy accident the behinds of some who were not infants any longer though still not old enough to vote. He was in the Warden's office with a briefcase, and presently the deputy warden of the levee was there too. He would have been sent for presently though not yet, but he came anyhow, without knocking, with his hat on, calling the Governor's young man loudly by a nickname and striking him with a flat hand on the back and lifted one thigh to the Warden's desk, almost between the Warden and the caller, the emissary. Or the vizier with the command, the knotted cord,[1] as began to appear immediately.

"Well," the Governor's young man said, "you've played the devil, haven't you?" The Warden had a cigar. He had offered the caller one. It had been refused, though presently, while the Warden looked at the back of his neck with hard immobility even a little grim, the deputy leaned and reached back and opened the desk drawer and took one.

"Seems straight enough to me," the Warden said. "He got swept away against his will. He came back as soon as he could and surrendered."

"He even brought that damn boat back," the deputy said. "If he'd a throwed the boat away he could a walked back in three days. But no sir. He's got to bring the boat back. 'Here's your boat and here's the woman but I never found no bastard on no cottonhouse.' " He slapped his knee, guffawing. "Them convicts. A mule's got twice as much sense."

"A mule's got twice as much sense as anything except a rat," the emissary said in his pleasant voice. "But that's not the trouble."

"What is the trouble?" the Warden said.

1. Used by oriental torturers to strangle their victims; the "vizier" (a high officer in the old Turkish Empire) is bringing the "command" for someone's dispatch.

"This man is dead."

"Hell fire, he ain't dead," the deputy said. "He's up yonder in that bunkhouse right now, lying his head off probly. I'll take you up there and you can see him." The Warden was looking at the deputy.

"Look," he said. "Bledsoe was trying to tell me something about that Kate mule's leg. You better go up to the stable and—"

"I done tended to it," the deputy said. He didn't even look at the Warden. He was watching, talking to, the emissary. "No sir. He aint—"

"But he has received an official discharge as being dead. Not a pardon nor a parole either: a discharge. He's either dead, or free. In either case he doesn't belong here." Now both the Warden and the deputy looked at the emissary, the deputy's mouth open a little, the cigar poised in his hand to have its tip bitten off. The emissary spoke pleasantly, extremely distinctly: "On a report of death forwarded to the Governor by the Warden of the Penitentiary." The deputy closed his mouth, though otherwise he didn't move. "On the official evidence of the officer delegated at the time to the charge and returning to the body of the prisoner to the Penitentiary." Now the deputy put the cigar into his mouth and got slowly off the desk, the cigar rolling across his lip as he spoke:

"So that's it. I'm to be it, am I?" He laughed shortly, a stage laugh, two notes. "When I done been right three times running through three separate administrations? That's on a book somewhere too. Somebody in Jackson can find that too.[2] And if they cant, I can show—"

"Three administrations?" the emissary said. "Well, well. That's pretty good."

"You damn right it's good," the deputy said. "The woods are full of folks that didn't." The Warden was again watching the back of the deputy's neck.

"Look," he said. "Why dont you step up to my house and get that bottle of whiskey out of the sideboard and bring it down here?"

"All right," the deputy said. "But I think we better settle this first. I'll tell you what we'll do—"

"We can settle it quicker with a drink or two," the Warden said. "You better step on up to your place and get a coat so the bottle—"

"That'll take too long," the deputy said. "I won't need no coat." He moved to the door, where he stopped and turned. "I'll tell you what to do. Just call twelve men in here and tell him it's a jury—he

2. A suggestion that the Governor's young man check the deputy Warden's political record with the Governor's political aides.

never seen but one before and he wont know no better—and try him over for robbing that train. Hamp can be the judge."

"You cant try a man twice for the same crime," the emissary said. "He might know that even if he doesn't know a jury when he sees one."

"Look," the Warden said.,

"All right. Just call it a new train robbery. Tell him it happened yesterday, tell him he robbed another train while he was gone and just forgot it. He couldn't help himself. Besides, he wont care. He'd just as lief[3] be here as out. He wouldn't have nowhere to go if he was out. None of them do. Turn one loose and be damned if he aint right back here by Christmas like it was a reunion or something, for doing the very same thing they caught him at before." He guffawed again. "Them convicts."

"Look," the Warden said. "While you're there, why dont you open the bottle and see if the liquor's any good. Take a drink or two. Give yourself time to feel it. If it's not good, no use in bringing it."

"O.K.," the deputy said. He went out this time.

"Couldn't you lock the door?" the emissary said. The Warden squirmed faintly. That is, he shifted his position in his chair.

"After all, he's right," he said. "He's guessed right three times now. And he's kin to all the folks in Pittman County[4] except the niggers."

"Maybe we can work fast then." The emissary opened the briefcase and took out a sheaf of papers. "So there you are," he said.

"There what are?"

"He escaped."

"But he came back voluntarily and surrendered."

"But he escaped."

"All right," the Warden said. "He escaped. Then what?" Now the emissary said look. That is, he said,

"Listen. I'm on per diem.[5] That's tax-payers, votes. And if there's any possible chance for it to occur to anyone to hold an investigation about this, there'll be ten senators and twenty-five representatives here on a special train maybe. On per diem. And it will be mighty hard to keep some of them from going back to Jackson by way of Memphis or New Orleans—on per diem."[6]

"All right," the Warden said. "What does he say to do?"

"This. The man left here in charge of one specific officer. But he was delivered back here by a different one."

3. Just as soon.

4. The only fictional geography in *Old Man*.

5. That is, with a daily allowance for expenses, usually a generous one.

6. In other words, take a detour of two or three hundred miles to one of the pleasure spots of the South, at government expense.

"But he surren—" This time the Warden stopped of his own accord. He looked, stared almost, at the emissary. "All right. Go on."

"In specific charge of an appointed and delegated officer, who returned here and reported that the body of the prisoner was no longer in his possession; that, in fact, he did not know where the prisoner was. That's correct, isn't it?" The Warden said nothing. "Isn't that correct?" the emissary said, pleasantly, insistently.

"But you cant do that to him. I tell you he's kin to half the—"

"That's taken care of. The Chief has made a place for him on the highway patrol."

"Hell," the Warden said. "He cant ride a motorcycle. I dont even let him try to drive a truck."

"He wont have to. Surely an amazed and grateful State can supply the man who guessed right three times in succession in Mississippi general elections with a car to ride in and somebody to run it if necessary. He wont even have to stay in it all the time. Just so he's near enough so when an inspector sees the car and stops and blows the horn of it he can hear it and come out."

"I still dont like it," the Warden said.

"Neither do I. Your man could have saved all of this if he had just gone on and drowned himself, as he seems to have led everybody to believe he had. But he didn't. And the Chief says do. Can you think of anything better?" The Warden sighed.

"No," he said.

"All right." The emissary opened the papers and uncapped a pen and began to write. "Attempted escape from the Penitentiary, ten years' additional sentence," he said. "Deputy Warden Buckworth transferred to Highway Patrol. Call it for meritorious service even if you want to. It wont matter now. Done?"

"Done," the Warden said.

"Then suppose you send for him. Get it over with." So the Warden sent for the tall convict and he arrived presently, saturnine and grave, in his new bedticking, his jowls blue and close under the sunburn, his hair recently cut and neatly parted and smelling faintly of the prison barber's (the barber was in for life, for murdering his wife, still a barber) pomade. The Warden called him by name.

"You had bad luck, didn't you?" The convict said nothing. "They are going to have to add ten years to your time."

"All right," the convict said.

"It's hard luck. I'm sorry."

"All right," the convict said. "If that's the rule." So they gave him the ten years more and the Warden gave him the cigar and now he sat, jackknifed backward into the space between the upper and lower bunks, the unlighted cigar in his hand while the plump convict and four others listened to him. Or questioned him, that is, since it was all done, finished, now and he was safe again, so maybe it wasn't even worth talking about any more.

"All right," the plump one said. "So you come back into the River. Then what?"

"Nothing. I rowed."

"Wasn't it pretty hard rowing coming back?"

"The water was still high. It was running pretty hard still. I never made much speed for the first week or two. After that it got better." Then, suddenly and quietly, something—the inarticulateness, the innate and inherited reluctance for speech, dissolved and he found himself, listened to himself, telling it quietly, the words coming fast but easily to the tongue as he required them: How he paddled on (he found out by trying it that he could make better speed, if you could call it speed, next the bank—this after he had been carried suddenly and violently out to midstream before he could prevent it and found himself, the skiff, traveling back toward the region from which he had just escaped and he spent the better part of the morning getting back inshore and up to the canal again from which he had emerged at dawn) until night came and they tied up to the bank and ate some of the food he had secreted in his jumper before leaving the armory in New Orleans and the woman and the infant slept in the boat as usual and when daylight came they went on and tied up again that night too and the next day the food gave out and he came to a landing, a town, he didn't notice the name of it, and he got a job. It was a cane farm—

"Cane?" one of the other convicts said. "What does anybody want to raise cane for? You cut cane. You have to fight it where I come from. You burn it just to get shut of it."

"It was sorghum,"[7] the tall convict said.

"Sorghum?" another said. "A whole farm just raising sorghum? *Sorghum?* What did they do with it?" The tall one didn't know. He didn't ask, he just came up the levee and there was a truck waiting full of niggers and a white man said, "You there. Can you run a shovel plow?" and the convict said, "Yes," and the man said, "Jump in then," and the convict said, "Only I've got a—"

"Yes," the plump one said. "That's what I been aiming to ask. What did—" The tall convict's face was grave, his voice was calm, just a little short:

"They had tents for the folks to live in. They were behind." The plump one blinked at him.

"Did they think she was your wife?"

"I dont know. I reckon so." The plump one blinked at him.

7. Plant grown for sugar and fodder.

"Wasn't she your wife? Just from time to time kind of, you might say?" The tall one didn't answer this at all. After a moment he raised the cigar and appeared to examine a loosening of the wrapper because after another moment he licked the cigar carefully near the end. "All right," the plump one said. "Then what?" So he worked there four days. He didn't like it. Maybe that was why: that he too could not quite put credence in that much of what he believed to be sorghum. So when they told him it was Saturday and paid him and the white man told him about somebody who was going to Baton Rouge the next day in a motor boat, he went to see the man and took the six dollars he had earned and bought food with it and tied the skiff behind the motor boat and went to Baton Rouge. It didn't take long and even after they left the motor boat at Baton Rouge and he was paddling again it seemed to the convict that the River was lower and the current not so fast, so hard, so they made fair speed, tying up to the bank at night among the willows, the woman and baby sleeping in the skiff as of old. Then the food gave out again. This time it was a wood landing, the wood stacked and waiting, a wagon and team being unladen of another load. The men with the wagon told him about the sawmill and helped him drag the skiff up the levee; they wanted to leave it there but he would not so they loaded it onto the wagon too and he and the woman got on the wagon too and they went to the sawmill. They gave them one room in a house to live in there. They paid two dollars a day and furnish. The work was hard. He liked it. He stayed there eight days.

"If you liked it so well, why did you quit?" the plump one said. The tall convict examined the cigar again, holding it up where the light fell upon the rich chocolate-colored flank.

"I got in trouble," he said.

"What trouble?"

"Woman. It was a fellow's wife."

"You mean you had been toting one piece up and down the country day and night for over a month, and now the first time you have a chance to stop and catch your breath almost you got to get in trouble over another one?" The tall convict had thought of that. He remembered it: how there were times, seconds, at first when if it had not been for the baby he might have, might have tried. But they were just seconds because in the next instant his whole being would seem to flee the very idea in a kind of savage and horrified revulsion; he would find himself looking from a distance at this millstone which the force and power of blind and risible Motion had fastened upon him, thinking, saying aloud actually, with harsh and savage outrage even though it had been two years since he had had a woman and that a nameless and not young negress, a casual, a straggler whom he had caught more or less by chance on one of the fifth-Sunday visiting days, the man—husband or sweetheart—whom she had come to see having been shot by a trusty a week or so previous and she had not heard about it: "She aint even no good to me for that."

"But you got this one, didn't you?" the plump convict said.

"Yah," the tall one said. The plump one blinked at him.

"Was it good?"

"It's all good," one of the others said. "Well? Go on. How many more did you have on the way back? Sometimes when a fellow starts getting it it looks like he just cant miss even if—" That was all, the convict told them. They left the sawmill fast, he had no time to buy food until they reached the next landing. There he spent the whole sixteen dollars he had earned and they went on. The River was lower now, there was no doubt of it, and sixteen dollars' worth looked like a lot of food and he thought maybe it would do, would be enough. But maybe there was more current in the River still than it looked like. But this time it was Mississippi, it was cotton; the plow handles felt right to his palms again, the strain and squat of the slick buttocks against the middle buster's blade was what he knew, even though they paid but a dollar a day here. But that did it. He told it: they told him it was Saturday again and paid him and he told about it—night, a smoked lantern in a disc of worn and barren earth as smooth as silver, a circle of crouching figures, the importunate murmurs and ejaculations, the meagre piles of worn bills beneath the crouching knees, the dotted cubes clicking and scuttering in the dust; that did it. "How much did you win?" the second convict said.

"Enough," the tall one said. It was enough exactly; he gave it all to the man who owned the second motor boat (he would not need food now), he and the woman in the launch now and the skiff towing behind, the woman with the baby and the paper-wrapped parcel beneath his peaceful hand, on his lap; almost at once he recognized, not Vicksburg because he had never seen Vicksburg, but the trestle beneath which on his roaring wave of trees and houses and dead animals he had shot, accompanied by thunder and lightning, a month and three weeks ago; he looked at it once without heat, even without interest as the launch went on. But now he began to watch the bank, the levee. He didn't know how he would know but he knew he would, and then it was early afternoon and sure enough the moment came and he said to the launch owner: "I reckon this will do."

"Here?" the launch owner said. "This dont look like anywhere to me."

"I reckon this is it," the convict said. So the launch put inshore, the engine ceased, it drifted up and lay against the levee and the owner cast the skiff loose.

"You better let me take you on until we come to something," he said. "That was what I promised."

"I reckon this will do," the convict said. So they got out and he stood with the grapevine painter in his hand while the launch purred again and drew away, already curving; he did not watch it. He laid bundle down and made the painter fast to a willow root and picked up the bundle and turned. He said no word, he mounted the levee, passing the mark, the tide-line of the old raging, dry now and lined, traversed by shallow and empty cracks like foolish and deprecatory senile grins, and entered a willow clump and removed the overalls and shirt they had given him in New Orleans and dropped them without even looking to see where they fell and opened the parcel and took out the other, the known, the desired, faded a little, stained and worn, but clean, recognizable, and put them on and returned to the skiff and took up the paddle. The woman was already in it.

The plump convict stood blinking at him. "So you come back," he said. "Well well." Now they all watched the tall convict as he bit the end from the cigar neatly and with complete deliberation and spat it out and licked the bite smooth and damp and took a match from his pocket and examined the match for a moment as though to be sure it was a good one, worthy of the cigar perhaps, and raked it up his thigh with the same deliberation—a motion almost too slow to set fire to it, it would seem—and held it until the flame burned clear and free of sulfur, then put it to the cigar. The plump one watched him, blinking rapidly and steadily. "And they give you ten years more for running. That's bad. A fellow can get used to what they give him at first, to start off with, I dont care how much it is, even a hundred and ninety-nine years. But ten more years. Ten years more, on top of that. When you never expected it. Ten more years to have to do without no society, no female companionship—" He blinked steadily at the tall convict. But he (the tall convict) had thought of that too. He had had a sweetheart. That is, he had gone to church singings and picnics with her—a girl a year or so younger than he, short-legged, with ripe breasts and a heavy mouth and dull eyes like ripe muscadines,[8] who owned a baking-powder can almost full of ear-rings and brooches and rings bought (or presented at suggestion) from ten-cent stores. Presently he had divulged his plan to her, and there were times later when, musing, the thought occurred to him that

8. Grapes.

possibly if it had not been for her he would not actually have attempted it—this a mere feeling, unworded, since he could not have phrased this either: that who to know what Capone's uncandled bridehood[9] she might not have dreamed to be her destiny and fate, what fast car filled with authentic colored glass and machine guns, running traffic lights. But that was all past and done when the notion first occurred to him, and in the third month of his incarceration she came to see him. She wore ear-rings and a bracelet or so which he had never seen before and it never became quite clear how she had got that far from home, and she cried violently for the first three minutes though presently (and without his ever knowing either exactly how they had got separated or how she had made the acquaintance) he saw her in animated conversation with one of the guards. But she kissed him before she left that evening and said she would return the first chance she got, clinging to him, sweating a little, smelling of scent and soft female flesh, slightly pneumatic. But she didn't come back though he continued to write to her, and seven months later he got an answer. It was a postcard, a colored lithograph of a Birmingham hotel, a childish X inked heavily across one window, the heavy writing on the reverse slanted and primer-like too: *This is where were honnymonning at. Your friend (Mrs) Vernon Waldrip*

The plump convict stood blinking at the tall one, rapidly and steadily. "Yes, sir," he said. "It's them ten more years that hurt. Ten more years to do without a woman, no woman a tall a fellow wants—" He blinked steadily and rapidly, watching the tall one. The other did not move, jacknifed backward between the two bunks, grave and clean, the cigar burning smoothly and richly in his clean steady hand, the smoke wreathing upward across his face saturnine, humorless, and calm "Ten more years—"

"Women . . .t!" the tall convict said.

9. I.e., unsanctified union, as between mistress.
the Chicago gangster Al Capone and his

BERTOLT BRECHT
(1898–1956)

Mother Courage and Her Children*

A Chronicle of the Thirty Years' War[1]

Characters

MOTHER COURAGE
KATTRIN, *her mute daughter*
EILIF, *her elder son*
SWISS CHEESE, *her younger son*
THE RECRUITER
THE SERGEANT
THE COOK
THE GENERAL
THE CHAPLAIN
THE ORDNANCE OFFICER
YVETTE POTTIER
THE MAN WITH THE PATCH OVER HIS EYE
THE OTHER SERGEANT
THE OLD COLONEL
A CLERK
A YOUNG SOLDIER
AN OLDER SOLDIER
A PEASANT
THE PEASANT'S WIFE
THE YOUNG MAN
THE OLD WOMAN
ANOTHER PEASANT
THE PEASANT WOMAN
A YOUNG PEASANT
THE LIEUTENANT
SOLDIERS
A VOICE

* Written in 1939; first performed in Zurich in 1941. Translated by Ralph Manheim.

1. The Thirty Years' War, actually a series of wars fought in central Europe from 1618 to 1648, began with a Protestant revolt in Bohemia (now western Czechoslovakia) that deposed King Ferdinand, then head of the Catholic Habsburg dynasty that ruled Austria from 1282 to 1919. He immediately was elected Holy Roman Emperor and, as chief of a loose confederation of Catholic European princes, organized a confederation that put down the Bohemian revolt, but the war spread quickly into Germany. The Protestant side drew first Denmark and then, after the Danes' quick defeat, Sweden into the conflict.

At the time *Mother Courage* opens, in 1624, a Swedish army has been fighting in Poland for three years. After winning the coastal province of Livonia (now part of the U.S.S.R.), it invades Germany in 1630 under the command of King Gustavus Adolphus. The king however fails to relieve the siege of Magdeburg by the imperial general Johan Tserclaes, Count of Tilly, and the Protestant bishopric is burned to the ground. Gustavus Adolphus later defeats Tilly in two major battles, but in 1632 both are killed, and two years later the Swedish force is destroyed by the Imperial army. The ensuing peace is brief, for in 1635 a new Swedish army, joined by troops from Catholic France, renews the fighting. (Religious justifications for the war early lost their strength, and were overshadowed by territorial and dynastic ambitions.) This last phase of the war has just begun at the end of *Mother Courage*, and lasting peace will come only twelve years later.

Brecht is true to history as he knew it; only recently have historians disputed the traditional belief that the war devastated Germany and halved its population. He does not mention the most famous Imperial general, Wallenstein, a swashbuckling and romantic figure who was the subject of plays and stories Brecht's German audience knew; such an adventurer has no place in an allegory against war, as Brecht is concerned not with the exploits of heroes but with the plight of common people trampled by forces they can neither control nor understand.

1

Spring, 1624. General Oxenstjerna recruits troops in Dalarna for the Polish campaign. The canteen woman, Anna Fierling, known as Mother Courage, loses a son.[2]

Highway near a city.

A sergeant and a recruiter stand shivering.

THE RECRUITER. How can anybody get a company together in a place like this? Sergeant, sometimes I feel like committing suicide. The general wants me to recruit four platoons by the twelfth, and the people around here are so depraved I can't sleep at night. I finally get hold of a man, I close my eyes and pretend not to see that he's chicken-breasted and he's got varicose veins, I get him good and drunk and he signs up. While I'm paying for the drinks, he steps out, I follow him to the door because I smell a rat: Sure enough, he's gone, like a fart out of a goose. A man's word doesn't mean a thing, there's no honor, no loyalty. This place has undermined my faith in humanity, sergeant.

THE SERGEANT. It's easy to see these people have gone too long without a war. How can you have morality without a war, I ask you? Peace is a mess, it takes a war to put things in order. In peacetime the human race goes to the dogs. Man and beast are treated like so much dirt. Everybody eats what they like, a big piece of cheese on white bread, with a slice of meat on top of the cheese. Nobody knows how many young men or good horses there are in that town up ahead, they've never been counted. I've been in places where they hadn't had a war in as much as seventy years, the people had no names, they didn't even know who they were. It takes a war before you get decent lists and records; then your boots are done up in bales and your grain in sacks, man and beast are properly counted and marched away, because people realize that without order they can't have a war.

THE RECRUITER. How right you are!

THE SERGEANT. Like all good things, a war is hard to get started. But once it takes root, it's vigorous; then people are as scared of peace as dice players are of laying off, because they'll have to reckon up their losses. But at first they're scared of war. It's the novelty.

THE RECRUITER. Say, there comes a wagon. Two women and two young fellows. Keep the old woman busy, sergeant. If this is another flop, you won't catch me standing out in this April wind any more.

2. The heading for this and each new scene is projected on a screen on stage; it situates the action and tells what will happen. *General Oxenstjerna*: One of the Swedish generals. *Dalarna*: a rural province in central Sweden. A canteen woman sells provisions to soldiers; Mother Courage's wagon is "a cross between a military vehicle and a general store." [Brecht's note.]

[*A Jew's harp*[3] *is heard. Drawn by two young men, a covered wagon approaches. In the wagon sit Mother Courage and her mute daughter Kattrin*]

MOTHER COURAGE. Good morning, sergeant.

SERGEANT. [*Barring the way*] Good morning, friends. Who are you?

MOTHER COURAGE. Business people. [*Sings*]

Hey, Captains, make the drum stop drumming
And let your soldiers take a seat.
Here's Mother Courage, with boots she's coming
To help along their aching feet.
How can they march off to the slaughter
With baggage, cannon, lice and fleas
Across the rocks and through the water
Unless their boots are in one piece?
  The spring is come. Christian, revive![4]
  The snowdrifts melt. The dead lie dead.
  And if by chance you're still alive
  It's time to rise and shake a leg.

O Captains, don't expect to send them
To death with nothing in their crops.
First you must let Mother Courage mend them
In mind and body with her schnapps.[5]
On empty bellies it's distressing
To stand up under shot and shell.
But once they're full, you have my blessing
To lead them to the jaws of hell.
  The spring is come. Christian, revive!
  The snowdrifts melt, the dead lie dead.
  And if by chance you're still alive
  It's time to rise and shake a leg.

THE SERGEANT. Halt, you scum. Where do you belong?

THE ELDER SON. Second Finnish Regiment.

THE SERGEANT. Where are your papers?

MOTHER COURAGE. Papers?

THE YOUNGER SON. But she's Mother Courage!

THE SERGEANT. Never heard of her. Why Courage?

MOTHER COURAGE. They call me Courage, sergeant, because when I saw ruin staring me in the face I drove out of Riga through cannon fire with fifty loaves of bread in my wagon. They were getting moldy, it was high time, I had no choice.

THE SERGEANT. No wisecracks. Where are your papers?

3. A small, twangy instrument held against the teeth, associated with country music.

4. The phrase in German parodies religious announcements of Easter and Christ's resurrection.

5. Liquor, especially gin. (The original says *wein*, or wine.)

MOTHER COURAGE. [*Fishing a pile of papers out of a tin box and climbing down*] Here are my papers sergeant. There's a whole missal, picked it up in Alt-Ötting[6] to wrap cucumbers in, and a map of Moravia, God knows if I'll ever get there, if I don't it's total loss. And this here certifies that my horse hasn't got hoof-and-mouth disease, too bad, he croaked on us, he cost fifteen guilders,[7] but not out of my pocket, glory be. Is that enough paper?

THE SERGEANT. Are you trying to pull my leg? I'll teach you to get smart. You know you need a license.

MOTHER COURAGE. You mind your manners and don't go telling my innocent children that I'd go anywhere near your leg, it's indecent. I want no truck with you. My license in the Second Regiment is my honest face, and if you can't read it, that's not my fault. I'm not letting anybody put his seal on it.

THE RECRUITER. Sergeant, I detect a spirit of insubordination in this woman. In our camp we need respect for authority.

MOTHER COURAGE . Wouldn't sausage be better?

THE SERGEANT. Name.

MOTHER COURAGE. Anna Fierling.

THE SERGEANT. Then you're all Fierlings?

MOTHER COURAGE. What do you mean? Fierling is my name. Not theirs.

THE SERGEANT. Aren't they all your children?

MOTHER COURAGE. That they are, but why should they all have the same name? [*Pointing at the elder son*] This one, for instance. His name is Eilif Nojocki. How come? Because his father always claimed to be called Kojocki or Mojocki. The boy remembers him well, except the one he remembers was somebody else, a Frenchman with a goatee. But aside from that, he inherited his father's intelligence; that man could strip the pants off a peasant's ass without his knowing it. So, you see, we've each got our own name.

THE SERGEANT. Each different, you mean?

MOTHER COURAGE. Don't act so innocent.

THE SERGEANT. I suppose that one's a Chinaman? [*Indicating the younger son*]

MOTHER COURAGE. Wrong. He's Swiss.

THE SERGEANT. After the Frenchman?

MOTHER COURAGE. What Frenchman? I never heard of any Frenchman. Don't get everything balled up or we'll be here all day. He's Swiss, but his name is Fejos, the name has nothing to do with his father. He had an entirely different name, he was an engineer, built fortifications, but he drank.

[*Swiss Cheese nods, beaming; the mute Kattrin is also tickled*]

6. A place of pilgrimage fifty miles east of Munich in the south German kingdom of Bavaria. *Missal*: Prayer book.

7. The basic unit of Dutch money, also called a *florin*. When Brecht was writing; one guilder was worth about twenty-five cents.

THE SERGEANT. Then how can his name be Fejos?

MOTHER COURAGE. I wouldn't want to offend you, but you haven't got much imagination. Naturally his name is Fejos because when he came I was with a Hungarian, it was all the same to him, he was dying of kidney trouble though he never touched a drop, a very decent man. The boy takes after him

THE SERGEANT. But you said he wasn't his father?

MOTHER COURAGE. He takes after him all the same. I call him Swiss Cheese, how come, because he's good at pulling the wagon. [*Pointing at her daughter*] Her name is Kattrin Haupt, she's half German.

THE SERGEANT. A fine family, I must say.

MOTHER COURAGE. Yes, I've been all over the world with my wagon.

THE SERGEANT. It's all being taken down. [*He takes it down*] You're from Bamberg,[8] Bavaria. What brings you here?

MOTHER COURAGE. I couldn't wait for the war to kindly come to Bamberg.

THE REECRUITER. You wagon pullers ought to be called Jacob Ox and Esau Ox.[9] Do you ever get out of harness?

EILIF. Mother, can I clout him one on the kisser? I'd like to.

MOTHER COURAGE. And I forbid you. You stay put. And now, gentlemen, wouldn't you need a nice pistol, or a belt buckle, yours is all worn out, sergeant.

THE SERGEANT. I need something else. I'm not blind. Those young fellows are built like tree trunks, big broad chests, sturdy legs. Why aren't they in the army? That's what I'd like to know.

MOTHER COURAGE. [*Quickly*] Nothing doing, sergeant. My children aren't cut out for soldiers.

THE RECRUITER. Why not? There's profit in it, and glory. Peddling shoes is woman's work. [*To Eilif*] Step up; let's feel if you've got muscles or if you're a sissy.

MOTHER COURAGE. He's a sissy. Give him a mean look and he'll fall flat on his face.

THE RECRUITER. And kill a calf if it happens to be standing in the way. [*Tries to lead him away*]

MOTHER COURAGE. Leave him alone, He's not for you.

THE RECRUITER. He insulted me. He referred to my face as a kisser. Him and me will now step out in the field and discuss this thing as man to man.

EILIF. Don't worry, mother. I'll take care of him.

MOTHER COURAGE. You stay put. You no-good! I know you, always fighting. He's got a knife in his boot, he's a knifer.

THE RECRUITER. I'll pull it out of him like a milk tooth. Come on, boy.

MOTHER COURAGE. Sergeant, I'll report you to the colonel. He'll throw you in the lock-up. The lieutenant is courting my daughter.

8. German city of northern Bavaria.
9. Biblical twin brothers. [*Genesis* 25–7.]

THE SERGEANT. No rough stuff, brother. [*To Mother Courage*] What have you got against the army? Wasn't his father a soldier? Didn't he die fair and square? You said so yourself.

MOTHER COURAGE. He's only a child. You want to lead him off to slaughter, I know you. You'll get five guilders for him.

THE RECRUITER. He'll get a beautiful cap and top boots.

EILIF. Not from you.

MOTHER COURAGE. Oh, won't you come fishing with me? said the fisherman to the worm. [*To Swiss Cheese*] Run and yell that the they're trying to steal your brother. [*She pulls a knife*] Just try to steal him. I'll cut you down, you dogs. I'll teach you to put him in your war! We do an honest business in ham and shirts, we're peaceful folk.

THE SERGEANT. I can see by the knife how peaceful you are. You ought to be ashamed of yourself, put that knife away, you bitch. A minute ago you admitted you lived off war, how else would you live, on what? How can you have a war without soldiers?

MOTHER COURAGE. It doesn't have to be my children.

THE SERGEANT. I see. You'd like the war to eat the core and spit out the apple. You want your brood to batten on war, tax-free. The war can look out for itself, is that it? You call yourself Courage, eh? And you're afraid of the war that feeds you. Your sons aren't afraid of it, I can see that.

EILIF. I'm not afraid of any war.

THE SERGEANT. Why should you be? Look at me: Has the soldier's life disagreed with me? I was seventeen when I joined up.

MOTHER COURAGE. You're not seventy yet.

THE SERGEANT. I can wait.

MOTHER COURAGE. Sure. Under ground.

THE SERGEANT. Are you trying to insult me? Telling me I'm going to die?

MOTHER COURAGE. But suppose it's the truth? I can see the mark on you. You look like a corpse on leave.

SWISS CHEESE. She's got second sight. Everybody says so. She can tell the future.

THE RECRUITER. Then tell the sergeant his future. It might amuse him.

THE SERGEANT. I don't believe in that stuff.

MOTHER COURAGE. Give me your helmet. [*He gives it to her*]

THE SERGEANT. It doesn't mean any more than taking a shit in the grass. But go ahead for the laugh.

MOTHER COURAGE. [*Takes a sheet of parchment and tears it in two*] Eilif, Swiss Cheese, Kattrin: That's how we'd all be torn apart if we got mixed up too deep in the war. [*To the sergeant*] Seeing it's you, I'll do it for nothing. I make a black cross on this piece. Black is death.

SWISS CHEESE. She leaves the other one blank. Get it?

MOTHER COURAGE. Now I fold them, and now I shake them up together. Same as we're all mixed up together from the cradle to the grave. And now you draw, and you'll know the answer.

[*The sergeant hesitates*]

THE RECRUITER. [*To Eilif*] I don't take everybody, I'm known to be picky and choosey, but you've got spirit, I like that.

THE SERGEANT. [*Fishing in the helmet*] Damn foolishness! Hocus-pocus!

SWISS CHEESE. He's pulled a black cross. He's through.

THE RECRUITER. Don't let them scare you, there's not enough bullets for everybody.

THE SERGEANT. [*Hoarsely*] You've fouled me up.

MOTHER COURAGE. You fouled yourself up the day you joined the army. And now we'll be going, there isn't a war every day, I've got to take advantage.

THE SERGEANT. Hell and damnation! Don't try to hornswoggle me. We're taking your bastard to be a soldier.

EILIF. I'd like to be a soldier, mother.

MOTHER COURAGE. You shut your trap, you Finnish devil.

EILIF. Swiss Cheese wants to be a soldier too.

MOTHER COURAGE. That's news to me. I'd better let you draw too, all three of you. [*She goes to the rear to mark crosses on slips of parchment*]

THE RECRUITER. [*To Eilif*] It's been said to our discredit that a lot of religion goes on in the Swedish camp, but that's slander to blacken our reputation. Hymn singing only on Sunday, one verse! And only if you've got a voice.

MOTHER COURAGE. [*Comes back with the slips in the sergeant's helmet*] Want to sneak away from their mother, the devils, and run off to war like calves to a salt lick. But we'll draw lots on it, then they'll see that the world is no vale of smiles[10] with a "Come along, son, we're short on generals." Sergeant, I'm very much afraid they won't come through the war. They've got terrible characters, all three of them. [*She holds out the helmet to Eilif*] There. Pick a slip. [*He picks one and unfolds it. She snatches it away from him*] There you have it. A cross! Oh, unhappy mother that I am, Oh, mother of sorrows. Has he got to die? Doomed to perish in the springtime of his life? If he joins the army, he'll bite the dust, that's sure. He's too brave, just like his father. If he's not smart, he'll go the way of all flesh, the slip proves it. [*She roars at him*] Are you going to be smart?

EILIF. Why not?

MOTHER COURAGE. The smart thing to do is to stay with your mother, and if they make fun of you and call you a sissy, just laugh.

THE RECRUITER. If you're shitting in your pants, we'll take your brother.

MOTHER COURAGE. I told you to laugh. Laugh! And now you pick, Swiss Cheese. I'm not so worried about you, you're honest. [*He picks a slip*] Oh! Why, have you got that strange look? It's got to be blank. There can't be a cross on it. No, I can't lose you.

10. Parodying the traditional description of this world as a "vale of tears."

[*She takes the slip*] A cross? Him too? Maybe it's because he's so stupid. Oh, Swiss Cheese, you'll die too, unless you're very honest the whole time, the way I've taught you since you were a baby, always bringing back the change when I sent you to buy bread. That's the only way you can save yourself. Look sergeant, isn't that a black cross?

THE SERGEANT. It's a cross all right. I don't see how I could have pulled one. I always stay in the rear. [*To the recruiter*] It's on the up and up. Her own get it too.

SWISS CHEESE. I get it too. But I can take a hint.

MOTHER COURAGE. [*To Kattrin*] Now you're the only one I'm sure of, you're a cross yourself[11] because you've got a good heart. [*She holds up the helmet to Kattrin in the wagon, but she herself takes out the slip*] It's driving me to despair. It can't be right, maybe I mixed them wrong. Don't be too good-natured, Kattrin, don't, there's a cross on your path too. Always keep very quiet, that ought to be easy seeing you're dumb. Well, now you know. Be careful, all of you, you'll need to be. And now we'll climb up and drive on. [*She returns the sergeant's helmet and climbs up into the wagon*]

THE RECRUITER. [*To the sergeant*] Do something!

THE SERGEANT. I'm not feeling so good.

THE RECRUITER. Maybe you caught cold when you took your helmet off in the wind. Tell her you want to buy something. Keep her busy. [*Aloud*] You could at least take a look at that buckle, sergeant. After all, selling things is these good people's living. Hey, you, the sergeant wants to buy that belt buckle.

MOTHER COURAGE. Half a guilder. A buckle like that is worth two guilders. [*She climbs down*]

THE SERGEANT. It's not new. This wind! I can't examine it here. Let's go where it's quiet. [*He goes behind the wagon with the buckle*]

MOTHER COURAGE. I haven't noticed any wind.,

THE SERGEANT. Maybe it is worth half a guilder. It's silver.

MOTHER COURAGE. [*Joins him behind the wagon*] Six solid ounces.

THE RECRUITER. [*To Eilif*] And then we'll have a drink, just you and me. I've got your enlistment bonus right here. Come on.

[*Eilif stands undecided*]

MOTHER COURAGE. All right. Half a guilder.

THE SERGEANT. I don't get it. I always stay in the rear. There's no safer place for a sergeant. You can send the men up forward to win glory. You've spoiled my dinner. It won't go down, I know it, not a bite.

MOTHER COURAGE. Don't take it to heart. Don't let it spoil your appetite. Just keep behind the lines. Here, take a drink of schnapps, man. [*She hands him the bottle*]

THE RECRUITER. [*Has taken Eilif's arm and is pulling him away toward the rear*] A bonus of ten guilders, and you'll be a brave

11. I.e., a heavy burden.

man and you'll fight for the king, and the women will tear each other's hair out over you. And you can clout me one on the kisser for insulting you. [*Both go out*]

[*Mute Kattrin jumps down from the wagon and emits raucous sounds*]

MOTHER COURAGE. Just a minute, Kattrin, Just a minute. The sergeant's paying up. [*Bites the half guilder*] I'm always suspicious of money. I'm a burnt child, sergeant. But your coin is good. And now we'll be going. Where's Eilif?

SWISS CHEESE. He's gone with the recruiter.

MOTHER COURAGE. [*Stands motionless, then*] You simple soul. [*To Kattrin*] I know. You can't talk, you couldn't help it.

THE SERGEANT. You could do with a drink yourself, mother. That's the way it goes. Soldiering isn't the worst thing in the world. You want to live off the war, but you want to keep you and yours out of it. Is that it?

MOTHER COURAGE. Now you'll have to pull with your brother, Kattrin.

[*Brother and sister harness themselves to the wagon and start pulling. Mother Courage walks beside them. The wagon rolls off*]

THE SERGEANT. [*Looking after them*]
If you want the war to work for you
You've got to give the war its due.

2

In 1625 and 1626 Mother Courage crosses Poland in the train of the Swedish armies. Outside the fortress of Wallhof[1] she meets her son again.—A capon is successfully sold, the brave son's fortunes are at their zenith.

The general's tent.

Beside it the kitchen. The thunder of cannon. The cook is arguing with Mother Courage, who is trying to sell him a capon.

THE COOK. Sixty hellers[2] for that pathetic bird?

MOTHER COURAGE. Pathetic bird? You mean this plump beauty? Are you trying to tell me that a general who's the biggest eater for miles around—God help you if you haven't got anything for his dinner—can't afford a measly sixty hellers?

THE COOK. I can get a dozen like it for ten hellers right around the corner.

MOTHER COURAGE. What, you'll find a capon like this right around the corner? With a siege on and everybody so starved you can see right through them. Maybe you'll scare up a rat, maybe, I say, 'cause they've all been eaten, I've seen five men chasing a

1. *in the train*: I.e., with the supplies and baggage at the end of the line of march. Wallhof: Fictional city.

2. A small coin formerly used in Austria and Germany.

starved rat for hours. Fifty hellers for a giant capon in the middle of a siege.

THE COOK. We're not besieged; they are. We're the besiegers, can't you get that through your head?

MOTHER COURAGE. But we haven't got anything to eat either, in fact we've got less than the people in the city. They've hauled it all inside. I hear their life is one big orgy. And look at us. I've been around to the peasants, they haven't got a thing.

THE COOK. They've got plenty. They hide it.

MOTHER COURAGE. [*Triumphantly*] Oh, no! They're ruined, that's what they are. They're starving. I've seen them. They're so hungry they're digging up roots. They lick their fingers when they've eaten a boiled strap. That's the situation. And here I've got a capon and I'm supposed to let it go for forty hellers.

THE COOK. Thirty, not forty. Thirty, I said.

MOTHER COURAGE. It's no common capon. They tell me this bird was so talented that he wouldn't eat unless they played music, he had his own favorite march. He could add and subtract, that's how intelligent he was. And you're trying to tell me forty hellers is too much. The general will bite your head off if there's nothing to eat.

THE COOK. You know what I'm going to do? [*He takes a piece of beef and sets his knife to it*] Here I've got a piece of beef. I'll roast it. Think it over. This is your last chance.

MOTHER COURAGE. Roast and be damned. It's a year old.

THE COOK. A day old. That ox was running around only yesterday afternoon, I saw him with my own eyes.

MOTHER COURAGE. Then he must have stunk on the hoof.

THE COOK. I'll cook it five hours if I have to. We'll see if it's still tough. [*He cuts it*]

MOTHER COURAGE. Use plenty of pepper, maybe the general won't notice the stink.

[*The general, a chaplain and Eilif enter the tent*]

THE GENERAL. [*Slapping Eilif on the back*] All right, son, into your general's tent you go, you'll sit at my right hand. You've done a heroic deed and you're a pious trooper, because this is a war of religion and what you did was done for God, that's what counts with me. I'll reward you with a gold bracelet when I take the city. We come here to save their souls and what do those filthy, shameless peasants do? They drive their cattle away. And they stuff their priests with meat, front and back. But you taught them a lesson. Here's a tankard of red wine for you. [*He pours*] We'll down it in one gulp. [*They do so*] None for the chaplain, he's got his religion. What would you like for dinner, sweetheart?

EILIF. A scrap of meat. Why not?

THE GENERAL. Cook! Meat!

THE COOK. And now he brings company when there's nothing to eat.

[*Wanting to listen, Mother Courage makes him stop talking*]

EILIF. Cutting down peasants whets the appetite.

MOTHER COURAGE. God, it's my Eilif.

THE COOK. Who?

MOTHER COURAGE. My eldest. I haven't seen hide nor hair of him in two years, he was stolen from me on the highway. He must be in good if the general invites him to dinner, and what have you got to offer? Nothing. Did you hear what the general's guest wants for dinner? Meat! Take my advice, snap up this capon. The price is one guilder.

THE GENERAL. [*Has sat down with Eilif. Bellows*] Food, Lamb, you lousy, no-good cook, or I'll kill you.

THE COOK. All right, hand it over. This is extortion.

MOTHER COURAGE. I thought it was a pathetic bird.

THE COOK. Pathetic is the word. Hand it over. Fifty hellers! It's highway robbery

MOTHER COURAGE. One guilder, I say. For my eldest son, the general's honored guest, I spare no expense.

THE COOK. [*Gives her the money*] Then pluck it at least while I make the fire.

MOTHER COURAGE. [*Sits down to pluck the capon*] Won't he be glad to see me! He's my brave, intelligent son. I've got a stupid one too, but he's honest. The girl's a total loss. But at least she doesn't talk, that's something.

THE GENERAL. Take another drink, son, it's my best Falerno,[3] I've only got another barrel or two at the most, but it's worth it to see that there's still some true faith in my army. The good shepherd here just looks on, all he knows how to do is preach. Can he do anything? No. And now, Eilif my son, tell us all about it, how cleverly you hoodwinked those peasants and captured those twenty head of cattle. I hope they'll be here soon.

EILIF. Tomorrow. Maybe the day after.

MOTHER COURAGE. Isn't my Eilif considerate, not bringing those oxen in until tomorrow, or you wouldn't have even said hello to my capon.

EILIF. Well, it was like this: I heard the peasants were secretly—mostly at night—rounding up the oxen they'd hidden in a certain forest. The city people had arranged to come and get them. I let them round the oxen up, I figured they'd find them easier than I would. I made my men ravenous for meat, put them on short rations for two days until their mouths watered if they even heard a word beginning with *me* . . . like measles.

THE GENERAL. That was clever of you.

EILIF. Maybe. The rest was a pushover. Except the peasants had clubs and there were three times more of them and they fell on us like bloody murder. Four of them drove me into a clump of bushes, they knocked my sword out of my hand and yelled: Surrender! Now what'll I do, I says to myself, they'll make hash out of me.

3. A famous wine made from grapes grown in Falerno in Italy.

THE GENERAL. What did you do?

EILIF. I laughed.

THE GENERAL. You laughed?

EILIF. I laughed. Which led to a conversation. The first thing you know, I'm bargaining. Twenty guilders is too much for that ox, I say, how about fifteen? Like I'm meaning to pay. They're flummoxed, they scratch their heads. Quick, I reach for my sword and mow them down. Necessity knows no law. See what I mean?

THE GENERAL. What do you say to that, shepherd?

CHAPLAIN. Strictly speaking, that maxim is not in the Bible. But our Lord was able to turn five loaves into five hundred.[4] So there was no question of poverty; he could tell people to love their neighbors because their bellies were full. Nowadays it's different.

THE GENERAL. [*Laughs*] Very different. All right, you Pharisee,[5] take a swig. [*To Eilif*] You mowed them down, splendid, so my fine troops could have a decent bite to eat. Doesn't the Good Book say: "Whatsoever thou doest for the least of my brethren, thou doest for me"?[6] And what have you done for them? You've got them a good chunk of beef for their dinner. They're not used to moldy crusts; in the old days they had a helmetful of white bread and wine before they went out to fight for God.

EILIF. Yes, I reached for my sword and I mowed them down.

THE GENERAL. You're a young Caesar. You deserve to see the king.

EILIF. I have, in the distance. He shines like a light. He's my ideal.

THE GENERAL. You're something like him already, Eilif. I know the worth of a brave soldier like you. When I find one, I treat him like my own son. [*He leads him to the map*] Take a look at the situation, Eilif; we,ve still got a long way to go.

MOTHER COURAGE. [*Who has been listening starts plucking her capon furiously*] He must be a rotten general.

THE COOK. Eats like a pig, but why rotten?

MOTHER COURAGE. Because he needs brave soldiers, that's why. If he planned his campaigns right, what would he need brave soldiers for? The run-of-the-mill would do. Take it from me, whenever you find a lot of virtues, it shows that something's wrong.

THE COOK. I'd say it proves that something is all right.

MOTHER COURAGE. No, that something's wrong. See, when a general or a king is real stupid and leads his men up shit creek, his troops need courage, that's a virtue. If he's stingy and doesn't hire enough soldiers, they've all got to be Herculeses. And if he's a slob and lets everything go to pot, they've got to be as sly as serpents or they're done for. And if he's always expecting too much of them, they need an extra dose of loyalty. A country that's run right, or a good king or a good general, doesn't need any of these virtues. You don't need virtues in a decent country, the people

4. Reference to the episode in the Gospels when Jesus fed five thousand people with five loaves and two fishes. [See *Matthew* 15:33 ff.]

5. Biblical: Religious hyprocrite, quibbler on religious doctrine.

6. Spoken by Jesus in the Gospels. [See *Matthew* 25:40 ff.]

can all be perfectly ordinary, medium-bright, and cowards too for my money.

THE GENERAL. I bet your father was a soldier.

EILIF. A great soldier, I'm told. My mother warned me about it. Makes me think of a song.

THE GENERAL. Sing it! [*Bellowing*] Where's that food!

EILIF. It is called: The Song of the Old Wife and the Soldier.

[*He sings, doing a war dance with his saber*]

A gun or a pike[7] they can kill who they like
And the torrent will swallow a wader
You had better think twice before battling with ice
Said the old wife to the soldier.
Cocking his rifle he leapt to his feet
Laughing for joy as he heard the drum beat
The wars cannot hurt me, he told her.
He shouldered his gun and he picked up his knife
To see the wide world. That's the soldier's life.
Those were the words of the soldier.

Ah, deep will they lie who wise counsel defy
Learn wisdom from those that are older
Oh, don't venture too high or you'll fall from the sky
Said the old wife to the soldier.
But the young soldier with knife and with gun
Only laughed a cold laugh and stepped into the run.
The water can't hurt me, he told her.
And when the moon on the rooftop shines white
We'll be coming back. You can pray for that night.
Those were the words of the soldier.

MOTHER COURAGE. [*In the kitchen, continues the song, beating a pot with a spoon*]

Like the smoke you'll be gone and no warmth linger on
And your deeds only leave me the colder!
Oh, see the smoke race. Oh, dear God keep him safe!
That's what she said of the soldier.

EILIF. What's that?

MOTHER COURAGE. [*Goes on singing*]

And the young soldier with knife and with gun
Was swept from his feet till he sank in the run
And the torrent swallowed the waders.
Cold shone the moon on the rooftop white
But the soldier was carried away with the ice
And what was it she heard from the soldiers?

7. Long spear used by the infantry.

Like the smoke he was gone and no warmth lingered on
And his deeds only left her the colder.
Ah, deep will they lie who wise counsel defy!
That's what she said to the soldiers.

THE GENERAL. What do they think they're doing in my kitchen?

EILIF. [*Has gone into the kitchen. He embraces his mother*] Mother! It's you! Where are the others?

MOTHER COURAGE. [*In his arms*] Snug as a bug in a rug. Swiss Cheese is paymaster of the Second Regiment; at least he won't be fighting, I couldn't keep him out altogether.

EILIF. And how about your feet?

MOTHER COURAGE. Well, it's hard getting my shoes on in the morning.

THE GENERAL. [*Has joined them*] Ah, so you're his mother. I hope you've got more sons for me like this fellow here.

EILIF. Am I lucky! There you're sitting in the kitchen hearing your son being praised.

MOTHER COURAGE. I heard it all right! [*She gives him a slap in the face*]

EILIF. [*Holding his cheek*] For capturing the oxen?

MOTHER COURAGE. No. For not surrendering when the four of them were threatening to make hash out of you! Didn't I teach you to take care of yourself? You Finnish devil!

[*The general and the chaplain laugh*]

3

Three years later Mother Courage and parts of a Finnish[1] regiment are taken prisoner. She is able to save her daughter and her wagon, but her honest son dies.

Army camp.

Afternoon. On a pole the regimental flag. Mother Courage has stretched a clothesline between her wagon, on which all sorts of merchandise is hung in display, and a large cannon. She and Kattrin are folding washing and piling it on the cannon. At the same time she is negotiating with an ordnance officer[2] *over a sack of bullets. Swiss Cheese, now in the uniform of a paymaster, is looking on. A pretty woman, Yvette Pottier, is sitting with a glass of brandy in front of her, sewing a gaudy-colored hat. She is in her stocking feet, her red high-heeled shoes are on the ground beside her.*

THE ORDNANCE OFFICER. I'll let you have these bullets for two guilders. It's cheap, I need the money, because the colonel's been drinking with the officers for two days and we're out of liquor.

MOTHER COURAGE. That's ammunition for the troops. If it's found

1. Finland was under Swedish rule at this time.

2. Officer in charge of weapons, particularly explosives.

here, I'll be court-martialed. You punks sell their bullets and the men have nothing to shoot at the enemy.

THE ORDNANCE OFFICER. Don't be hard-hearted, you scratch my back, I'll scratch yours.

MOTHER COURAGE. I'm not taking any army property. Not at that price.

THE ORDNANCE OFFICER. You can sell it for five guilders, maybe eight, to the ordnance officer of the Fourth before the day is out, if you're quiet about it and give him a receipt for twelve. He hasn't an ounce of ammunition left.

MOTHER COURAGE. Why don't you do it yourself?

THE ORDNANCE OFFICER. Because I don't trust him, he's a friend of mine.

MOTHER COURAGE. [*Takes the sack*] Hand it over. [*To Kattrin*] Take it back there and pay him one and a half guilders. [*In response to the ordnance officer's protest*] One and a half guilders, I say. [*Kattrin drags the sack behind the wagon, the ordnance officer follows her. Mother Courage to Swiss Cheese*] Here's your underdrawers, take good care of them, this is October, might be coming on fall, I don't say it will be, because I've learned that nothing is sure to happen the way we think, not even the seasons. But whatever happens, your regimental funds have to be in order. Are your funds in order?

SWISS CHEESE. Yes, mother.

MOTHER COURAGE. Never forget that they made you paymaster because you're honest and not brave like your brother, and especially because you're too simple-minded to get the idea of making off with the money. That's a comfort to me. And don't go mislaying your drawers.

SWISS CHEESE. No, mother. I'll put them under my mattress.

[*Starts to go*]

ORDNANCE OFFICER. I'll go with you, paymaster.

MOTHER COURAGE. Just don't teach him any of your tricks.

[*Without saying good-bye the ordnance officer goes out with Swiss Cheese*]

YVETTE. [*Waves her hand after the ordnance officer*] You might say good-bye officer.

MOTHER COURAGE. [*To Yvette*] I don't like to see those two together. He's not the right kind of company for my Swiss Cheese. But the war's getting along pretty well. More countries are joining in all the time, it can go on for another four, five years, easy. With a little planning ahead, I can do good business if I'm careful. Don't you know you shouldn't drink in the morning with your sickness?.

YVETTE. Who says I'm sick, it's slander.

MOTHER COURAGE. Everybody says so.

YVETTE. Because they're all liars. Mother Courage, I'm desperate. They all keep out of my way like I'm a rotten fish on account of those lies. What's the good of fixing my hat? [*She throws it down*] That's why I drink in the morning, I never used to, I'm getting crow's-feet, but it doesn't matter now. In the Second Finnish Regiment they all know me. I should have stayed home when my first love walked out on me. Pride isn't for the likes of us. If we can't put up with shit, we're through.

MOTHER COURAGE. Just don't start in on your Pieter and how it all happened in front of my innocent daughter.

YVETTE. She's just the one to hear it, it'll harden her against love.

MOTHER COURAGE. Nothing can harden them.

YVETTE. Then I'll talk about it because it makes me feel better. It begins with my growing up in fair Flanders, because if I hadn't I'd never have laid eyes on him and I wouldn't be here in Poland now, because he was an army cook, blond, a Dutchman, but skinny. Kattrin, watch out for the skinny ones, but I didn't know that then, and another thing I didn't know is that he had another girl even then, and they all called him Pete the Pipe, because he didn't even take his pipe out of his mouth when he was doing it, that's all it meant to him. [*She sings the Song of Fraternization*]

When I was only sixteen
The foe came into our land.
He laid aside his saber
And with a smile he took my hand.
  After the May parade
  The May light starts to fade.
  The regiment dressed by the right[3]
  Then drums were beaten, that's the drill.[4]
  The foe took us behind the hill
  And fraternized all night.

There were so many foes came
And mine worked in the mess.[5]
I loathed him in the daytime.
At night I loved him none the less.
  After the May parade
  The May light starts to fade.
  The regiment dressed by the right
  Then drums were beaten, that's the drill.
  The foe took us behind the hill
  And fraternized all night.

The love which came upon me
Was wished on me by fate.
My friends could never grasp why
I found it hard to share their hate.

3. I.e., each man aligned himself with the man on his right to form straight ranks for the parade.

4. I.e., that's the usual thing.

5. The kitchen.

The fields were wet with dew
When sorrow first I knew.
The regiment dressed by the right
Then drums were beaten, that's the drill.
And then the foe, my lover still
Went marching from our sight.

Well, I followed him, but I never found him. That was five years ago. [*She goes behind the wagon with an unsteady gait*]

MOTHER COURAGE. You've left your hat.

YVETTE. Anybody that wants it can have it.

MOTHER COURAGE. Let that be a lesson to you, Kattrin. Have no truck with soldiers. It's love that makes the world go round, so you'd better watch out. Even with a civilian it's no picnic. He says he'd kiss the ground you put your little feet on, talking of feet, did you wash yours yesterday, and then you're his slave. Be glad you're dumb, that way you'll never contradict yourself or want to bite your tongue off because you've told the truth, it's a gift of God to be dumb. Here comes the general's cook, I wonder what he wants.

[*The cook and the chaplain enter*]

THE CHAPLAIN. I've got a message for you from your son Eilif. The cook here thought he'd come along, he's taken a shine to you.

THE COOK. I only came to get a breath of air.

MOTHER COURAGE. You can always do that here if you behave, and if you don't, I can handle you. Well, what does he want? I've got no money to spare.

THE CHAPLAIN. Actually he wanted me to see his brother, the paymaster.

MOTHER COURAGE. He's not here any more, or anywhere else either. He's not his brother's paymaster. I don't want him leading him into temptation and being smart at his expense [*Gives him money from the bag slung around her waist*] Give him this, it's a sin, he's speculating on mother love and he ought to be ashamed.

THE COOK. He won't do it much longer, then he'll be marching off with his regiment, maybe to his death, you never can tell. Better make it a little more, you'll be sorry later. You women are hard-hearted, but afterwards you're sorry. A drop of brandy wouldn't have cost much when it was wanted, but it wasn't given, and later, for all you know, he'll be lying in the cold ground and you can't dig him up again.

THE CHAPLAIN. Don't be sentimental, cook. There's nothing wrong with dying in battle, it's a blessing, and I'll tell you why. This is a war of religion. Not a common war, but a war for the faith, and therefore pleasing to God.

THE COOK. That's a fact. In a way you could call it a war, because of the extortion and killing and looting, not to mention a bit of rape, but it's a war of religion, which makes it different from all other wars, that's obvious. But it makes a man thirsty all the same, you've got to admit that.

THE CHAPLAIN. [*To Mother Courage, pointing at the cook*] I tried to discourage him, but he says you've turned his head, he sees you in his dreams.

THE COOK. [*Lights a short-stemmed pipe*] All I want is a glass of brandy from your fair hand, nothing more sinful. I'm already so shocked by the jokes the chaplain's been telling me, I bet I'm still red in the face.

MOTHER COURAGE. And him a clergyman! I'd better give you fellows something to drink or you'll be making me immoral propositions just to pass the time.

THE CHAPLAIN. This is temptation, said the deacon, and succumbed to it. [*Turning toward Kattrin as he leaves*] And who is this delightful young lady?

MOTHER COURAGE. She's not delightful, she's a respectable young lady.

[*The chaplain and the cook go behind the wagon with Mother Courage. Kattrin looks after them, then she walks away from the washing and approaches the hat. She picks it up, sits down and puts on the red shoes. From the rear Mother Courage is heard talking politics with the chaplain and the cook*]

MOTHER COURAGE. The Poles here in Poland shouldn't have butted in. All right, our king marched his army into their country. But instead of keeping the peace, the Poles start butting into their own affairs and attack the king while he's marching quietly through the landscape. That was a breach of the peace and the blood is on their head.

THE CHAPLAIN. Our king had only one thing in mind; freedom. The emperor had everybody under his yoke, the Poles as much as the Germans; the king had to set them free.

THE COOK. I see it this way, your brandy's first-rate, I can see why I liked your face, but we were talking about the king. This freedom he was trying to introduce into Germany cost him a fortune, he had to levy a salt tax in Sweden, which, as I said, cost the poor people a fortune. Then he had to put the Germans in jail and break them on the rack because they liked being the emperor's slaves. Oh yes, the king made short shrift of anybody that didn't want to be free. In the beginning he only wanted to protect Poland against wicked people, especially the emperor, but the more he ate the more he wanted, and pretty soon he was protecting all of Germany.[6] But the Germans didn't take it lying down and the king got nothing but trouble for all his kindness and expense, which he naturally had to defray from taxes, which made for bad blood, but that didn't discourage him. He had one

6. Allusion to Hitler's expansion of German territory allegedly to protect German-speaking peoples, first in Bohemia and then, in 1938, through the annexation of Austria.

thing in his favor, the word of God, which was lucky, because otherwise people would have said he was doing it all for himself and what he hoped to get out of it. As it was, he always had a clear conscience and that was all he really cared about.

MOTHER COURAGE. It's easy to see you're not a Swede, or you wouldn't talk like that about the Hero-King.

THE CHAPLAIN. You're eating his bread, aren't you?

THE COOK. I don't eat his bread, I bake it.

MOTHER COURAGE. He can't be defeated because his men believe in him. [*Earnestly*] When you listen to the big wheels talk, they're making war for reasons of piety, in the name of everything that's fine and noble. But when you take another look, you see that they're not so dumb; they're making war for profit. If they weren't, the small fry like me wouldn't have anything to do with it.[7]

THE COOK. That's a fact.

THE CHAPLAIN. And it wouldn't hurt you as a Dutchman to take a look at that flag up there before you express opinions in Poland.

MOTHER COURAGE. We're all good Protestants here! Prosit![8] [*Kattrin has started strutting about with Yvette's hat on, imitating Yvette's gait.*]

[*Suddenly cannon fire and shots are heard. Drums. Mother Courage, the cook and the chaplain run out from behind the wagon, the two men still with glasses in hand. The ordnance officer and a soldier rush up to the cannon and try to push it away*]

MOTHER COURAGE. What's going on? Let me get my washing first, you lugs. [*She tries to rescue her washing*]

THE ORDNANCE OFFICER. The Catholics. They're attacking. I don't know as we'll get away. [*To the soldier*] Get rid of the gun! [*Runs off*]

THE COOK. Christ, I've got to find the general. Courage, I'll be back for a little chat in a day or two. [*Rushes out*]

MOTHER COURAGE. Stop, you've forgotten your pipe.

THE COOK. [*From the distance*] Keep it for me! I'll need it.

MOTHER COURAGE. Just when we were making a little money!

THE CHAPLAIN. Well, I guess I'll be going too. It might be dangerous though, with the enemy so close. Blessed are the peaceful[9] is the best motto in wartime. If only I had a cloak to cover up with.

MOTHER COURAGE. I'm not lending any cloaks, not on your life. I've had bitter experience in that line.

THE CHAPLAIN. But my religion puts me in special danger.

MOTHER COURAGE. [*Bringing him a cloak*] It's against my better conscience. And now run along.

7. The German expression can also be translated, "Wouldn't be doing the same thing."

8. Cheers!

9. A parody of Jesus' Sermon on the Mount: "Blessed are the peacemakers, for they shall be called sons of God." [*Matthew* 5:9.]

THE CHAPLAIN. Thank you kindly, you've got a good heart. But maybe I'd better sit here a while. The enemy might get suspicious if they see me running.

MOTHER COURAGE. [*To the soldier*] Leave it lay, you fool, you won't get paid extra. I'll take care of it for you, you'd only get killed.

THE SOLDIER. [*Running away*] I tried. You're my witness.

MOTHER COURAGE. I'll swear it on the Bible. [*Sees her daughter with the hat*] What are you doing with that floozy hat? Take it off, have you gone out of your mind? Now of all times, with the enemy on top of us? [*She tears the hat off Kattrin's head*] You want them to find you and make a whore out of you? And those shoes! Take them off, you woman of Babylon![10] [*She tries to pull them off*] Jesus Christ, chaplain, make her take those shoes off! I'll be right back. [*She runs to the wagon*]

YVETTE. [*Enters, powdering her face*] What's this I hear? The Catholics are coming? Where is my hat? Who's been stamping on it? I can't be seen like this if the Catholics are coming. What'll they think of me? I haven't even got a mirror. [*To the chaplain*] How do I look? Too much powder?

THE CHAPLAIN. Just right.

YVETTE. And where are my red shoes? [*She doesn't see them because Kattrin hides her feet under her skirt*] I left them here. I've got to get back to my tent. In my bare feet. It's disgraceful! [*Goes out*]

[*Swiss Cheese runs in carrying a small box*]

MOTHER COURAGE. [*Comes out with her hands full of ashes. To Kattrin*] Ashes. [*To Swiss Cheese*] What you got there?

SWISS CHEESE. The regimental funds.

MOTHER COURAGE. Throw it away! No more paymastering for you.

SWISS CHEESE. I'm responsible for it. [*He goes rear*]

MOTHER COURAGE. [*To the chaplain*] Take your clergyman's coat off, chaplain, or they'll recognize you, cloak or no cloak. [*She rubs Kattrin's face with ashes*] Hold still! There. With a little dirt you'll be safe. What a mess! The sentries were drunk. Hide your light under a bushel,[11] as the Good Book says. When a soldier, especially a Catholic, sees a clean face, she's a whore before she knows it. Nobody feeds them for weeks. When they finally loot some provisions, the next thing they want is women. That'll do it. Let me look at you. Not bad. Like you'd been wallowing in a pigsty. Stop shaking. You're safe now. [*To Swiss Cheese*] What did you do with the cashbox?

SWISS CHEESE. I thought I'd put it in the wagon.

MOTHER COURAGE. [*Horrified*] What! In my wagon? Of all the sinful stupidity! If my back is turned for half a second! They'll hang us all!

10. Sinful woman. The ancient Asian city of Babylon is a Biblical locus for sin and decadence: "Babylon the great, mother of harlots and of earth's abominations. [*Revelations* 17:5.]

11. Also parodies the Sermon on the Mount: "Nor do men light a lamp and put it under a bushel [basket] but on a stand, and it gives light to all in the house." [*Matthew* 5:15.]

SWISS CHEESE. Then I'll put it somewhere else, or I'll run away with it.

MOTHER COURAGE. You'll stay right here. It's too late.

THE CHAPLAIN. [*Still changing, comes forward*] Heavens, the flag!

MOTHER COURAGE. [*Takes down the regimental flag*] Bozhe moi![12] I'm so used to it I don't see it. Twenty-five years I've had it.

[*The cannon fire grows louder*]

[*Morning, three days later. The cannon is gone. Mother Courage, Kattrin, the chaplain and Swiss Cheese are sitting dejectedly over a meal*]

SWISS CHEESE. This is the third day I've been sitting here doing nothing; the sergeant has always been easy on me, but now he must be starting to wonder: where can Swiss Cheese be with the cashbox?

MOTHER COURAGE. Be glad they haven't tracked you down.

THE CHAPLAIN. What about me? I can't hold a service here either. The Good Book says: "Whosoever hath a full heart, his tongue runneth over."[13] Heaven help me if mine runneth over.

MOTHER COURAGE. That's the way it is. Look what I've got on my hands: one with a religion and one with a cashbox. I don't know which is worse.

THE CHAPLAIN. Tell yourself that we're in the hands of God.

MOTHER COURAGE. I don't think we're that bad off, but all the same I can't sleep at night. If it weren't for you, Swiss Cheese, it'd be easier. I think I've put myself in the clear. I told them I was against the antichrist;[14] he's a Swede with horns, I told them, and I'd noticed the left horn was kind of worn down. I interrupted the questioning to ask where I could buy holy candles cheap. I knew what to say because Swiss Cheese's father was a Catholic and he used to make jokes about it. They didn't really believe me, but their regiment had no provisioner, so they looked the other way. Maybe we stand to gain. We're prisoners, but so are lice on a dog.

THE CHAPLAIN. This milk is good. Though there's not very much of it or of anything else. Maybe we'll have to cut down on our Swedish appetites. But such is the lot of the vanquished.

MOTHER COURAGE. Who's vanquished? Victory and defeat don't always mean the same thing to the big wheels up top and the small fry underneath. Not by a long shot. In some cases defeat is a blessing to the small fry. Honor's lost, but nothing else. One time in Livonia[15] our general got such a shellacking from the

12. My God! [Polish and Russian expression.]

13. "Out of the abundance of the heart the mouth speaketh," Biblical proverb meaning that one's words reflect the good or evil in one's heart. [Jesus to the Pharisees, *Matthew* 12:34.]

14. Figure of evil, whose appearance on earth is supposed to prefigure the end of the world and the coming of the Last Judgment.

15. Region of the east Baltic, now part of the U.S.S.R.

enemy that in the confusion I laid hands on a beautiful white horse from the baggage train. That horse pulled my wagon for seven months, until we had a victory and they checked up. On the whole, you can say that victory and defeat cost us plain people plenty. The best thing for us is when politics gets bogged down. [*To Swiss Cheese*] Eat!

SWISS CHEESE. I've lost my appetite. How's the sergeant going to pay the men?

MOTHER COURAGE. Troops never get paid when they're running away.

SWISS CHEESE. But they've got it coming to them. If they're not paid, they don't need to run. Not a step.

MOTHER COURAGE. Swiss Cheese, you're too conscientious, it almost frightens me. I brought you up to be honest, because you're not bright, but somewhere it's got to stop. And now me and the chaplain are going to buy a Catholic flag and some meat. Nobody can buy meat like the chaplain, he goes into a trance and heads straight for the best piece, I guess it makes his mouth water and that shows him the way. At least they let me carry on my business. Nobody cares about a shopkeeper's religion, all they want to know is the price. Protestant pants are as warm as any other kind.

THE CHAPLAIN. Like the friar[16] said when somebody told him the Lutherans were going to stand the whole country on its head. They'll always need beggars, he says. [*Mother Courage disappears into the wagon*] But she's worried about that cashbox. They've taken no notice of us so far, they think we're all part of the wagon, but how long can that go on?

SWISS CHEESE. I can take it away.

THE CHAPLAIN. That would be almost more dangerous. What if somebody sees you? They've got spies. Yesterday morning, just as I'm relieving myself, one of them jumps out of the ditch. I was so scared I almost let out a prayer. That would have given me away. I suppose they think they can tell a Protestant by the smell of his shit. He was a little runt with a patch over one eye.

MOTHER COURAGE. [*Climbing down from the wagon with a basket*] Look what I've found. You shameless slut! [*She hold up the red shoes triumphantly*] Yvette's red shoes! She's swiped them in cold blood. It's your fault. Who told her she was a delightful young lady? [*She puts them into the basket*] I'm giving them back. Stealing Yvette's shoes! She ruins herself for money, that I can understand. But you'd like to do it free of charge, for pleasure. I've told you, you'll have to wait for peace. No soldiers! Just wait for peace with your worldly ways.

THE CHAPLAIN. She doesn't seem very worldly to me.

MOTHER COURAGE. Too worldly for me. In Dalarna she was like a stone, which is all they've got around there. The people used to say: We don't see the cripple. That's the way I like it. That way

16. A mendicant or beggar monk.

she's safe. [*To Swiss Cheese*] You leave that box where it is, hear? And keep an eye on your sister, she needs it. The two of you will be the death of me. I'd sooner take care of a bag of fleas. [*She goes off with the chaplain. Kattrin starts clearing away the dishes*]

SWISS CHEESE. Won't be many more days when I can sit in the sun in my shirtsleeves. [*Kattrin points to a tree*] Yes, the leaves are all yellow. [*Kattrin asks him, by means of gestures, whether he wants a drink*] Not now. I'm thinking. [*Pause*] She says she can't sleep. I'd better get the cashbox out of here, I've found a hiding place. All right, get me a drink. [*Kattrin goes behind the wagon*] I'll hide it in the rabbit hole down by the river until I can take it away. Maybe late tonight. I'll go get it and take it to the regiment. I wonder how far they've run in three days? Won't the sergeant be surprised! Well, Swiss Cheese, this is a pleasant disappointment, that's what he'll say. I trust you with the regimental cashbox and you bring it back.

[*As Kattrin comes out from behind the wagon with a glass of brandy, she comes face to face with two men. One is a sergeant. The other removes his hat and swings it through the air in a ceremonious greeting. He has a patch over one eye*]

THE MAN WITH THE PATCH. Good morning, my dear. Have you by any chance seen a man from the headquarters of the Second Finnish Regiment?

[*Scared out of her wits, Kattrin runs front, spilling the brandy. The two exchange looks and withdraw after seeing Swiss Cheese sitting there*]

SWISS CHEESE. [*Starting up from his thoughts*] You've spilled half of it. What's the fuss about? Poke yourself in the eye? I don't understand you. I'm getting out of here, I've made up my mind, it's best. [*He stands up. She does everything she can think of to call his attention to the danger. He only evades her*] I wish I could understand you. Poor thing, I know you're trying to tell me something, you just can't say it. Don't worry about spilling the brandy, I'll be drinking plenty more. What's one glass? [*He takes the cashbox out of the wagon and hides it under his jacket*] I'll be right back. Let me go, you're making me angry. I know you mean well. If only you could talk.

[*When she tries to hold him back, he kisses her and tears himself away. He goes out. She is desperate, she races back and forth, uttering short inarticulate sounds. The chaplain and Mother Courage come back. Kattrin gesticulates wildly at her mother*]

MOTHER COURAGE. What's the matter? You're all upset. Has somebody hurt you? Where's Swiss Cheese? Tell it to me in order, Kattrin. Your mother understands you. What, the no-good's taken the cashbox? I'll hit him over the head with it, the sneak. Take your time, don't talk nonsense, use your hands, I don't like it when you howl like a dog, what will the chaplain think? It gives him the creeps. A one-eyed man?

THE CHAPLAIN. The one-eyed man is a spy. Did they arrest Swiss Cheese? [*Kattrin shakes her head and shrugs her shoulders*] We're done for.

MOTHER COURAGE. [*Takes a Catholic flag out of her basket. The chaplain fastens it to the flagpole*] Hoist the new flag!

THE CHAPLAIN. [*Bitterly*] All good Catholics here.

[*Voices are heard from the rear. The two men bring in Swiss Cheese*]

SWISS CHEESE. Let me go, I haven't got anything. Stop twisting my shoulder, I'm innocent.

THE SERGEANT. He belongs here. You know each other.

MOTHER COURAGE. What makes you think that?

SWISS CHEESE. I don't know them. I don't even know who they are. I had a meal here, it cost me ten hellers. Maybe you saw me sitting here, it was too salty.

THE SERGEANT. Who are you anyway?

MOTHER COURAGE. We're respectable people. And it's true. He had a meal here. He said it was too salty.

THE SERGEANT. Are you trying to tell me you don't know each other?

MOTHER COURAGE. Why should I know him? I don't know everybody. I don't ask people what their name is or if they're heathens; if they pay, they're not heathens. Are you a heathen?

SWISS CHEESE. Of course not.

THE CHAPLAIN. He ate his meal and he behaved himself. He didn't open his mouth except when he was eating. Then you have to.

THE SERGEANT. And who are you?

MOTHER COURAGE. He's only my bartender. You gentlemen must be thirsty, I'll get you a drink of brandy, you must be hot and tired.

THE SERGEANT. We don't drink on duty. [*To Swiss Cheese*] You were carrying something. You must have hidden it by the river. You had something under your jacket when you left here.

MOTHER COURAGE. Was it really him?

SWISS CHEESE. I think you must have seen somebody else. I saw a man running with something under his jacket. You've got the wrong man.

MOTHER COURAGE. That's what I think too, it's a misunderstanding. These things happen. I'm a good judge of people. I'm Mother Courage, you've heard of me, everybody knows me. Take it from me, this man has an honest face.

THE SERGEANT. We're looking for the cashbox of the Second Finnish Regiment. We know what the man in charge of it looks like. We've been after him for two days. You're him.

SWISS CHEESE. I'm not.

THE SERGEANT. Hand it over. If you don't you're a goner, you know that. Where is it?

MOTHER COURAGE. [*With urgency*] He'd hand it over, wouldn't he, knowing he was a goner if he didn't? I've got it, he'd say, take it, you're stronger. He's not that stupid. Speak up, you stupid idiot, the sergeant's giving you a chance.

SWISS CHEESE. But I haven't got it.

THE SERGEANT. In that case come along. We'll get it out of you.

[*They lead him away*]

MOTHER COURAGE. [*Shouts after them*] He'd tell you. He's not that stupid. And don't twist his shoulder off! [*Runs after them*]

[*The same evening. The chaplain and mute Kattrin are washing dishes and scouring knives*]

THE CHAPLAIN. That boy's in trouble. There are cases like that in the Bible. Take the Passion of our Lord and Savior. There's an old song about it. [*He sings the Song of the Hours*]

In the first hour Jesus mild
Who had prayed since even[17]
Was betrayed and led before
Pontius[18] the heathen.

Pilate found him innocent
Free from fault and error.
Therefore, having washed his hands
Sent him to King Herod.

In the third hour he was scourged
Stripped and clad in scarlet
And a plaited crown of thorns
Set upon his forehead.

On the Son of Man they spat
Mocked him and made merry.
Then the cross of death was brought
Given him to carry.

At the sixth hour with two thieves
To the cross they nailed him
And the people and the thieves
Mocked him and reviled him.

This is Jesus King of Jews
Cried they in derision
Till the sun withdrew its light
From that awful vision.

At the ninth hour Jesus wailed
Why hast thou me forsaken?

17. Evening.
18. Pontius Pilate: Roman judge before whom Jesus was arraigned by the Scribes. [*Matthew* 27:1–24.]

Soldiers brought him vinegar
Which he left untaken.

Then he yielded up the ghost
And the earth was shaken.
Rended was the temple's veil[19]
And the saints were wakened.

Soldiers broke the two thieves' legs
As the night descended
Thrust a spear in Jesus' side
When his life had ended.

Still they mocked, as from his wound
Flowed the blood and water
Thus blasphemed the Son of Man
With their cruel laughter.

MOTHER COURAGE. [*Enters in a state of agitation*] His life's at stake. But they say the sergeant will listen to reason. Only it mustn't come out that he's our Swiss Cheese, or they'll say we've been giving him aid and comfort. All they want is money. But where will we get the money? Hasn't Yvette been here? I met her just now, she's latched onto a colonel, he's thinking of buying her a provisioner's business.

THE CHAPLAIN. Are you really thinking of selling?

MOTHER COURAGE. How else can I get the money for the sergeant?

THE CHAPLAIN. But what will you live on?

MOTHER COURAGE. That's the hitch.

[*Yvette Pottier comes in with a doddering colonel*]

YVETTE. [*Embracing Mother Courage*] My dear Mother Courage. Here we are again! [*Whispering*] He's willing. [*Aloud*] This is my dear friend who advises me on business matters. I just chanced to hear that you wish to sell your wagon, due to circumstances. I might be interested.

MOTHER COURAGE. Mortgage it, not sell it, let's not be hasty. It's not so easy to buy a wagon like this in wartime.

YVETTE. [*Disappointed*] Only mortgage it? I thought you wanted to sell it. In that case, I don't know if I'm interested. [*To the colonel*] What do you think?

THE COLONEL. Just as you say, my dear.

MOTHER COURAGE. It's only being mortgaged.

YVETTE. I thought you needed money.

MOTHER COURAGE. [*Firmly*] I need the money, but I'd rather run myself ragged looking for an offer than sell now. The wagon is our livelihood. It's an opportunity for you, Yvette, God knows

19. Matthew reports that at the moment of Jesus' death, the veil or curtain in the temple which set off the sanctuary was torn from top to bottom; the earth shook, and dead men rose from their graves. [*Matthew* 27:51–3.]

when you'll find another like it and have such a good friend to advise you. See what I mean?

YVETTE. My friend thinks I should snap it up, but I don't know. If it's only being mortgaged . . . Don't you agree that we ought to buy?

THE COLONEL. Yes, my dear.

MOTHER COURAGE. Then you'll have to look for something that's for sale, maybe you'll find something if you take your time and your friend goes around with you. Maybe in a week or two you'll find the right thing.

YVETTE. Then we'll go looking, I love to go looking for things, and I love to go around with you, Poldi,[20] it's a real pleasure. Even if it takes two weeks. When would you pay the money back if you get it?

MOTHER COURAGE. I can pay it back in two weeks, maybe one.

YVETTE. I can't make up my mind, Poldi, chéri,[21] tell me what to do. [*She takes the colonel aside*] I know she's got to sell, that's definite. The lieutenant, you know who I mean, the blond one, he'd be glad to lend me the money. He's mad about me, he says I remind him of somebody. What do you think?

THE COLONEL. Keep away from that lieutenant. He's no good. He'll take advantage. Haven't I told you I'd buy you something, pussykins?

YVETTE. I can't accept it from you. But then if you think the lieutenant might take advantage . . . Poldi, I'll accept it from you.

THE COLONEL. I hope so.

YVETTE. Your advice is to take it?

THE COLONEL. That's my advice.

YVETTE. [*Goes back to Mother Courage*] My friend advises me to do it. Write me out a receipt, say the wagon belongs to me complete with stock and furnishings when the two weeks are up. We'll take inventory right now, then I'll bring you the two hundred guilders. [*To the colonel*] You go back to camp, I'll join you in a little while, I've got to take inventory, I don't want anything missing from my wagon. [*She kisses him. He leaves. She climbs up in the wagon*] I don't see very many boots.

MOTHER COURAGE. Yvette. This is no time to inspect your wagon if it is yours. You promised to see the sergeant about my Swiss Cheese, you've got to hurry. They say he's to be court-martialed in an hour.

YVETTE. Just let me count the shirts.

MOTHER COURAGE. [*Pulls her down by the skirt*] You hyena, it's Swiss Cheese, his life's at stake. And don't tell anybody where the offer comes from, in heaven's name say it's your gentleman friend, or we'll all get it, they'll say we helped him.

YVETTE. I've arranged to meet One-Eye in the woods, he must be there already.

20. Pet name for Leopold.

21. Darling.

THE CHAPLAIN. And there's no need to start out with the whole two hundred, offer a hundred and fifty, that's plenty.

MOTHER COURAGE. Is it your money? You just keep out of this. Don't worry, you'll get your bread and soup. Go on now and don't haggle. It's his life. [*She gives Yvette a push to start her on her way*]

THE CHAPLAIN. I didn't mean to butt in, but what are we going to live on? You've got an unemployable daughter on your hands.

MOTHER COURAGE. You muddlehead, I'm counting on the regimental cashbox. They'll allow for his expenses, won't they?

THE CHAPLAIN. But will she handle it right?

MOTHER COURAGE. It's in her own interest. If I spend her two hundred, she gets the wagon. She's mighty keen on it, how long can she expect to hold on to her colonel? Kattrin, you scour the knives, use pumice. And you, don't stand around like Jesus on the Mount of Olives,[22] bestir yourself, wash those glasses, we're expecting at least fifty for dinner, and then it'll be the same old story: "Oh my feet, I'm not used to running around, I don't run around in the pulpit." I think they'll set him free. Thank God they're open to bribery. They're not wolves, they're human and out for money. Bribe-taking in humans is the same as mercy in God. It's our only hope. As long as people take bribes, you'll have mild sentences and even the innocent will get off once in a while.

YVETTE. [*Comes in panting*] They want two hundred. And we've got to be quick. Or it'll be out of their hands. I'd better take One-Eye to see my colonel right away. He confessed that he'd had the cashbox, they put the thumb screws on him. But he threw it in the river when he saw they were after him. The box is gone. Should I run and get the money from my colonel?

MOTHER COURAGE. The box is gone? How will I get my two hundred back?

YVETTE. Ah, so you thought you could take it out of the cashbox? You thought you'd put one over on me. Forget it. If you want to save Swiss Cheese, you'll just have to pay, or maybe you'd like me to drop the whole thing and let you keep your wagon?

MOTHER COURAGE. This is something I hadn't reckoned with. But don't rush me, you'll get the wagon, I know it's down the drain, I've had it for seventeen years. Just let me think a second, it's all so sudden. What'll I do, I can't give them two hundred, I guess you should have bargained. If I haven't got a few guilders to fall back on, I'll be at the mercy of the first Tom, Dick, or Harry. Say I'll give them a hundred and twenty, I'll lose my wagon anyway.

YVETTE. They won't go along. One-Eye's in a hurry, he's so keyed-up he keeps looking behind him. Hadn't I better give them the whole two hundred?

MOTHER COURAGE. [*In despair*] I can't do it. Thirty years I've worked. She's twenty-five and no husband. I've got her to keep too. Don't needle me, I know what I'm doing. Say a hundred

22. The ridge of hills outside Jerusalem where Jesus waited after the Last Supper to be captured and taken before the high priest.

and twenty or nothing doing.

YVETTE. It's up to you. [*Goes out quickly*]

[*Mother Courage looks neither at the chaplain nor at her daughter. She sits down to help Kattrin scour the knives*]

MOTHER COURAGE. Don't break the glasses. They're not ours any more. Watch what you're doing, you'll cut yourself. Swiss Cheese will be back, I'll pay two hundred if I have to. You'll have your brother. With eighty guilders we can buy a peddler's pack and start all over. Worse things have happened.

THE CHAPLAIN. The Lord will provide.

MOTHER COURAGE. Rub them dry. [*They scour the knives in silence. Suddenly Kattrin runs sobbing behind the wagon*]

YVETTE. [*Comes running*] They won't go along. I warned you. One-Eye wanted to run out on me, he said it was no use. He said we'd hear the drums any minute, meaning he'd been sentenced. I offered a hundred and fifty. He didn't even bother to shrug his shoulders. When I begged and pleaded, he promised to wait till I'd spoken to you again.

MOTHER COURAGE. Say I'll give him the two hundred. Run. [*Yvette runs off. They sit in silence. The chaplain has stopped washing the glasses*]

Maybe I bargained too long. [*Drums are heard in the distance. The chaplain stands up and goes to the rear. Mother Courage remains seated. It grows dark. The drums stop. It grows light again. Mother Courage has not moved*]

YVETTE. [*Enters, very pale*] Now you've done it with your haggling and wanting to keep your wagon. Eleven bullets he got, that's all. I don't know why I bother with you any more, you don't deserve it. But I've picked up a little information. They don't believe the cashbox is really in the river. They suspect it's here and they think you were connected with him. They're going to bring him here, they think maybe you'll give yourself away when you see him. I'm warning you: You don't know him, or you're all dead ducks. I may as well tell you, they're right behind me. Should I keep Kattrin out of the way? [*Mother Courage shakes her head*] Does she know? Maybe she didn't hear the drums or maybe she didn't understand.

MOTHER COURAGE. She knows. Get her.

[*Yvette brings Kattrin, who goes to her mother and stands beside her. Mother Courage takes her by the hand. Two soldiers come in with a stretcher on which something is lying under a sheet. The sergeant walks beside them. They set the stretcher down*]

THE SERGEANT. We've got a man here and we don't know his name. We need it for the records. He had a meal with you. Take a look, see if you know him. [*He removes the sheet*] Do you know him? [*Mother Courage shakes her head*] What? You'd never seen him before he came here for a meal? [*Mother Courage shakes her head*] Pick him up. Throw him on the dump. Nobody knows him. [*They carry him away*]

4

Mother Courage sings the Song of the Great Capitulation.

Outside an officer's tent.

Mother Courage is waiting. A clerk looks out of the tent.

THE CLERK. I know you. You had a Protestant paymaster at your place, he was hiding. I wouldn't put in any complaints if I were you.

MOTHER COURAGE. I'm putting in a complaint. I'm innocent. If I take this lying down, it'll look as if I had a guilty conscience. First they ripped up my whole wagon with their sabers, then they wanted me to pay a fine of five talers[1] for no reason at all.

THE CLERK. I'm advising you for your own good: Keep your trap shut. We haven't got many provisioners and we'll let you keep on with your business, especially if you've got a guilty conscience and pay a fine now and then.

MOTHER COURAGE. I'm putting in a complaint.

THE CLERK. Have it your way. But you'll have to wait till the captain can see you. [*Disappears into the tent*]

A YOUNG SOLDIER. [*Enters in a rage*] Bouque la Madonne![2] Where's that stinking captain? He embezzled my reward and now he's drinking it up with his whores. I'm going to get him!

AN OLDER SOLDIER. [*Comes running after him*] Shut up. They'll put you in the stocks!

THE YOUNG SOLDIER. Come on out, you crook! I'll make chops out of you. Embezzling my reward! Who jumps in the river? Not another man in the whole squad, only me. And I can't even buy myself a beer. I won't stand for it. Come on out and let me cut you to pieces!

THE OLDER SOLDIER. Holy Mary! He'll ruin himself.

MOTHER COURAGE. They didn't give him a reward?

THE YOUNG SOLDIER. Let me go. I'll run you through too, the more the merrier.

THE OLDER SOLDIER. He saved the colonel's horse and they didn't give him a reward. He's young, he hasn't been around long.

MOTHER COURAGE. Let him go, he's not a dog, you don't have to tie him up. Wanting a reward is perfectly reasonable. Why else would he distinguish himself?

THE YOUNG SOLDIER. And him drinking in there! You're all a lot of yellowbellies. I distinguished myself and I want my reward.

MOTHER COURAGE. Young man, don't shout at me. I've got my own worries and besides, go easy on your voice, you may need it. You'll be hoarse when the captain comes out, you won't be able to say boo and he won't be able to put you in the stocks till you're blue in the face. People that yell like that don't last long, maybe half an hour, then they're so exhausted you have to sing

1. German silver coins.

2. Screw the Virgin!

them to sleep.

THE YOUNG SOLDIER. I'm not exhausted and who wants to sleep? I'm hungry. They make our bread out of acorns and hemp seed, and they skimp on that. He's whoring away my reward and I'm hungry. I'll murder him.

MOTHER COURAGE. I see. You're hungry. Last year your general made you cut across the fields to trample down the grain. I could have sold a pair of boots for ten guilders if anybody'd had ten guilders and if I'd had any boots. He thought he'd be someplace else this year, but now he's still here and everybody's starving. I can see that you might be good and mad.

THE YOUNG SOLDIER. He can't do this to me, save your breath, I won't put up with injustice.

MOTHER COURAGE. You're right, but for how long? How long won't you put up with injustice? An hour? Two hours? You see, you never thought of that, though it's very important, because it's miserable in the stocks when it suddenly dawns on you that you *can* put up with injustice.

THE YOUNG SOLDIER. I don't know why I listen to you. Bouque la Madonne! Where's the captain?

MOTHER COURAGE. You listen to me because I'm not telling you anything new. You know your temper has gone up in smoke, it was a short temper and you need a long one, but that's a hard thing to come by.

THE YOUNG SOLDIER. Are you trying to say I've no right to claim my reward?

MOTHER COURAGE. Not at all. I'm only saying your temper isn't long enough, it won't get you anywhere. Too bad. If you had a long temper, I'd even egg you on. Chop the bastard up, that's what I'd say, but suppose you don't chop him up, because your tail's drooping and you know it. I'm left standing there like a fool and the captain takes it out on me.

THE OLDER SOLDIER. You're right. He's only blowing off steam.

THE YOUNG SOLDIER. We'll see about that. I'll cut him to pieces. [*He draws his sword*] When he comes, I'll cut him to pieces.

THE CLERK. [*Looks out*] The captain will be here in a moment. Sit down

[*The young soldier sits down*]

MOTHER COURAGE. There he sits. What did I tell you? Sitting, aren't you? Oh, they know us like a book, they know how to handle us. Sit down! And down we sit. You can't start a riot sitting down. Better not stand up again, you won't be able to stand the way you were standing before. Don't be embarrassed on my account, I'm no better, not a bit of it. We were full of piss and vinegar, but they've bought it off. Look at me. No back talk, it's bad for business. Let me tell you about the great capitulation. [*She sings the Song of the Great Capitulation*][3]

3. Mother Courage punctuates the story of her own gradual disillusionment with proverbs and common sayings that represent a folk wisdom of successful adjustment.

When I was young, no more than a spring chicken
I too thought that I was really quite the cheese
(No common peddler's daughter, not I with my looks and my
talent and striving for higher things!)
One little hair in the soup would make me sicken
And at me no man would dare to sneeze.
(It's all or nothing, no second best for me. I've got what it
takes, the rules are for somebody else!)
But a chickadee
Sang wait and see!
And you go marching with the show
In step, however fast or slow
And rattle off your little song:
It won't be long.
And then the whole thing slides.
You think God provides—
But you've got it wrong.

And before one single year had wasted
I had learned to swallow down the bitter brew
(Two kinds on my hands and the price of bread and who do they
take me for anyway!)
Man, the double-edged shellacking that I tasted
On my ass and knees I was when they were through.
(You've got to get along with people, one good turn deserves
another, no use trying to ram your head through the wall!)
And the chickadee
Sang wait and see!
And she goes marching with the show
In step, however fast or slow
And rattles off her little song:
It won't be long.
And then the whole thing slides
You think God provides—
But you've got it wrong.

I've seen many fired by high ambition
No star's big or high enough to reach out for.
(It's ability that counts, where there's a will there's a way, one
way or another, we'll swing it!)
Then while moving mountains they get a suspicion
That to wear a straw hat is too big a chore.
(No use being too big for your britches!)
And the chickadee
Sings wait and see!
And they go marching with the show
In step, however fast or slow
And rattle off their little song:
It won't be long.

And then the whole thing slides!
You think God provides—
But you've got it wrong!

MOTHER COURAGE. [*To the young soldier*] So here's what I think: Stay here with your sword if your anger's big enough, I know you have good reason, but if it's a short quick anger, better make tracks!

THE YOUNG SOLDIER. Kiss my ass! [*He staggers off, the older soldier after him*]

THE CLERK. [*Sticking his head out*] The captain is here. You can put in your complaint now.

MOTHER COURAGE. I've changed my mind. No complaint. [*She goes out*]

5

Two years have passed. The war has spread far and wide. With scarcely a pause Mother Courage's little wagon rolls through Poland, Moravia, Bavaria, Italy, and back again to Bavaria in 1631. Tilly's victory at Magdeburg[1] costs Mother Courage four officers' shirts.

Mother Courage's wagon has stopped in a devastated village.

Thin military music is heard from the distance. Two soldiers at the bar are being waited on by Kattrin and Mother Courage. One of them is wearing a lady's fur coat over his shoulders.

MOTHER COURAGE. What's that? You can't pay? No money, no schnapps. Plenty of victory marches for the Lord but no pay for the men.

THE SOLDIER. I want my schnapps. I came too late for the looting. The general skunked us: permission to loot the city for exactly one hour. Says he's not a monster; the mayor must have paid him.

THE CHAPLAIN. [*Staggers in*] There's still some wounded in the house. The peasant and his family. Help me, somebody, I need linen.

[*The second soldier goes out with him. Kattrin gets very excited and tries to persuade her mother to hand out linen*

MOTHER COURAGE. I haven't got any. The regiment's bought up all my bandages. You think I'm going to rip up my officers' shirts for the likes of them?

THE CHAPLAIN. [*Calling back*] I need linen, I tell you.

MOTHER COURAGE. [*Sitting down on the wagon steps to keep Kat-*

1. City eighty miles west of Berlin, besieged by the Imperial Army in 1630.

trin out] Nothing doing. They don't pay, they got nothing to pay with.

THE CHAPLAIN. [*Bending over a woman whom he has carried out*] Why did you stay here in all that gunfire?

THE PEASANT WOMAN. [*Feebly*] Farm.

MOTHER COURAGE. You won't catch them leaving their property. And I'm expected to foot the bill. I won't do it.

THE FIRST SOLDIER. They're Protestants. Why do they have to be Protestants?

MOTHER COURAGE. Religion is the least of their worries. They've lost their farm.

THE SECOND SOLDIER. They're no Protestants. They're Catholics like us.

THE FIRST SOLDIER. How do we know who we're shooting at?

A PEASANT. [*Whom the Chaplain brings in*] They got my arm.

THE CHAPLAIN. Where's the linen?

[*All look at Mother Courage, who does not move*]

MOTHER COURAGE. I can't give you a thing. What with all my taxes, duties, fees and bribes! [*Making guttural sounds, Kattrin picks up a board and threatens her mother with it*] Are you crazy? Put that board down, you slut, or I'll smack you. I'm not giving anything, you can't make me, I've got to think of myself. [*The chaplain picks her up from the step and puts her down on the ground. Then he fishes out some shirts and tears them into strips*]

My shirts! Half a guilder apiece! I'm ruined!

[*The anguished cry of a baby is heard from the house*]

THE PEASANT. The baby's still in there!

[*Kattrin runs in*]

THE CHAPLAIN. [*To the woman*] Don't move. They're bringing him out.

MOTHER COURAGE. Get her out of there. The roof'll cave in.

THE CHAPLAIN. I'm not going in there again.

MOTHER COURAGE. [*Torn*] Don't run hog-wild with my expensive linen.

[*Kattrin emerges from the ruins carrying an infant*]

MOTHER COURAGE. Oh, so you've found another baby to carry around with you? Give that baby back to its mother this minute, or it'll take me all day to get it away from you. Do you hear me? [*To the second soldier*] Don't stand there gaping, go back and tell them to stop that music, I can see right here that they've won a victory. Your victory's costing me a pretty penny.

[*Kattrin rocks the baby in her arms, humming a lullaby*]

MOTHER COURAGE. There she sits, happy in all this misery; give it back this minute, the mother's coming to. [*She pounces on the first soldier who has been helping himself to the drinks and is now making off with the bottle*] Pshagreff![2] Beast! Haven't you had enough victories for today? Pay up.

2. Son of a bitch! (Polish)

FIRST SOLDIER. I'm broke.
MOTHER COURAGE. [*Tears the fur coat off him*] Then leave the coat here, it's stolen anyway.
THE CHAPLAIN. There's still somebody in there.

6

Outside Ingolstadt[1] in Bavaria Mother Courage attends the funeral of Tilly, the imperial field marshal. Conversations about heroes and the longevity of the war. The chaplain deplores the waste of his talents. Mute Kattrin gets the red shoes. 1632.

Inside Mother Courage's tent.

A bar open to the rear. Rain. In the distance drum rolls and funeral music. The chaplain and the regimental clerk are playing a board game. Mother Courage and her daughter are taking inventory.

THE CHAPLAIN. The procession's starting.
MOTHER COURAGE. It's a shame about the general—socks: twenty-two pairs—I hear he was killed by accident. On account of the fog in the fields. He's up front encouraging the troops. "Fight to the death, boys," he sings out. Then he rides back, but he gets lost in the fog and rides back forward. Before you know it he's in the middle of the battle and stops a bullet—lanterns: we're down to four. [*A whistle from the rear. She goes to the bar*] You men ought to be ashamed, running out on your late general's funeral! [*She pours drinks*]
THE CLERK. They shouldn't have been paid before the funeral. Now they're getting drunk instead.
THE CHAPLAIN. [*To the clerk*] Shouldn't you be at the funeral?
THE CLERK. In this rain?
MOTHER COURAGE. With you it's different, the rain might spoil your uniform. It seems they wanted to ring the bells, naturally, but it turned out the churches had all been shot to pieces by his orders, so the poor general won't hear any bells when they lower him into his grave. They're going to fire a three-gun salute instead, so it won't be too dull—seventeen sword belts.
CRIES. [*From the bar*] Hey! Brandy!
MOTHER COURAGE. Money first! No, you can't come into my tent with your muddy boots! You can drink outside, rain or no rain. [*To the clerk*] I'm only letting officers in. It seems the general had been having his troubles. Mutiny in the Second Regiment because he hadn't paid them. It's a war of religion, he says, should they profit by their faith?

[*Funeral march. All look to the rear*]

1. City forty miles north of Munich.

THE CHAPLAIN. Now they're marching past the body.

MOTHER COURAGE. I feel sorry when a general or an emperor passes away like this, maybe he thought he'd do something big, that posterity would still be talking about and maybe put up a statue in his honor, conquer the world, for instance, that's a nice ambition for a general, he doesn't know any better. So he knocks himself out, and then the common people come and spoil it all, because what do they care about greatness, all they care about is a mug of beer and maybe a little company. The most beautiful plans have been wrecked by the smallness of the people that are supposed to carry them out. Even an emperor can't do anything by himself, he needs the support of his soldiers and his people. Am I right?

THE CHAPLAIN. [*Laughing*] Courage, you're right, except about the soldiers. They do their best. With those fellows out there, for instance, drinking their brandy in the rain. I'll undertake to carry on one war after another for a hundred years, two at once if I have to, and I'm not a general by trade.

MOTHER COURAGE. Then you don't think the war might stop?

THE CHAPLAIN. Because the general's dead? Don't be childish. They grow by the dozen, there'll always be plenty of heroes.

MOTHER COURAGE. Look here, I'm not asking you for the hell of it. I've been wondering whether to lay in supplies while they're cheap, but if the war stops, I can throw them out the window.

THE CHAPLAIN. I understand. You want a serious answer. There have always been people who say: "The war will be over some day." I say there's no guarantee the war will ever be over. Naturally a brief intermission is conceivable. Maybe the war needs a breather, a war can even break its neck, so to speak. There's always a chance of that, nothing is perfect here below. Maybe there never will be a perfect war, one that lives up to all our expectations. Suddenly, for some unforeseen reason, a war can bog down, you can't think of everything. Some little oversight and your war's in trouble. And then you've got to pull it out of the mud. But the kings and emperors, not to mention the pope, will always come to its help in adversity. On the whole, I'd say this war has very little to worry about, it'll live to a ripe old age.

A SOLDIER. [*Sings at the bar*]

A drink, and don't be slow!
A soldier's got to go
And fight for his religion.

Make it double, this is a holiday.

MOTHER COURAGE. If I could only be sure . . .

THE CHAPLAIN. Figure it out for yourself. What's to stop the war?

THE SOLDIER. [*Sings*]

Your breasts, girl, don't be slow!
A soldier's got to go
And ride away to Pilsen.[2]

THE CLERK. [*Suddenly*] But why can't we have peace? I'm from Bohemia, I'd like to go home when the time comes.

THE CHAPLAIN. Oh, you'd like to go home? Ah, peace! What becomes of the hole when the cheese has been eaten?

THE SOLDIER. [*Sings*]

Play cards, friends, don't be slow!
A soldier's got to go
No matter if it's Sunday.

A prayer, priest, don't be slow!
A soldier's got to go
And die for king and country.

THE CLERK. In the long run nobody can live without peace.

THE CHAPLAIN. The way I see it, war gives you plenty of peace. It has its peaceful moments. War meets every need, including the peaceful ones, everything's taken care of, or your war couldn't hold its own. In a war you can shit the same as in the dead of peace, you can stop for a beer between battles, and even on the march you can always lie down on your elbows and take a little nap by the roadside. You can't play cards when you're fighting; but then you can't when you're plowing in the dead of peace either, but after a victory the sky's the limit. Maybe you've had a leg shot off, at first you raise a howl; you make a big thing of it. But then you calm down or they give you schnapps, and in the end you're hopping around again and the war's no worse off than before. And what's to prevent you from multiplying in the thick of the slaughter, behind a barn or someplace, in the long run how can they stop you, and then the war has your progeny to help it along. Take it from me, the war will always find an answer. Why would it have to stop?

[*Kattrin has stopped working and is staring at the chaplain*]

MOTHER COURAGE. Then I'll buy the merchandise. You've convinced me. [*Kattrin suddenly throws down a basket full of bottles and runs out*] Kattrin! [*Laughs*] My goodness, the poor thing's been hoping for peace. I promised her she'd get a husband when peace comes. [*She runs after her*]

THE CLERK. [*Getting up*] I win, you've been too busy talking. Pay up.

MOTHER COURAGE. [*Comes back with Kattrin*] Be reasonable, the war'll go on a little longer and we'll make a little more money,

2. A city in Bohemia, near the German border.

then peace will be even better. Run along to town now, it won't take you ten minutes, and get the stuff from the Golden Lion, only the expensive things, we'll pick up the rest in the wagon later, it's all arranged, the regimental clerk here will go with you. They've almost all gone to the general's funeral, nothing can happen to you. Look sharp, don't let them take anything away from you, think of your dowry.

[*Kattrin puts a kerchief over her head and goes with the clerk*]

THE CHAPLAIN. Is it all right letting her go with the clerk?

MOTHER COURAGE. Who'd want to ruin her? She's not pretty enough.

THE CHAPLAIN. I've come to admire the way you handle your business and pull through every time. I can see why they call you Mother Courage.

MOTHER COURAGE. Poor people need courage. Why? Because they're sunk. In their situation it takes gumption just to get up in the morning. Or to plow a field in the middle of a war. They even show courage by bringing children into the world, because look at the prospects. The way they butcher and execute each other, think of the courage they need to look each other in the face. And putting up with an emperor and a pope takes a whale of a lot of courage, because those two are the death of the poor. [*She sits down, takes a small pipe from her pocket and smokes*] You could be making some kindling.

THE CHAPLAIN. [*Reluctantly takes his jacket off and prepares to chop*] Chopping wood isn't really my trade, you know, I'm a shepherd of souls.

MOTHER COURAGE. Sure. But I have no soul and I need firewood.

THE CHAPLAIN. What's that pipe?

MOTHER COURAGE. Just a pipe.

THE CHAPLAIN. No, it's not "just a pipe," it's a very particular pipe.

MOTHER COURAGE. Really?

THE CHAPLAIN. It's the cook's pipe from the Oxenstjerna regiment.

MOTHER COURAGE. If you know it all, why the mealy-mouthed questions?

THE CHAPLAIN. I didn't know if *you* knew. You could have been rummaging through your belongings and laid hands on some pipe and picked it up without thinking.

MOTHER COURAGE. Yes. Maybe that's how it was.

THE CHAPLAIN. Except it wasn't. You knew who that pipe belongs to.

MOTHER COURAGE. What of it?

THE CHAPLAIN. Courage, I'm warning you. It's my duty. I doubt if you ever lay eyes on the man again, but that's no calamity, in fact you're lucky. If you ask me, he wasn't steady. Not at all.

MOTHER COURAGE. What makes you say that? He was a nice man.

THE CHAPLAIN. Oh, you think he was nice? I differ. Far be it from me to wish him any harm, but I can't say he was nice. I'd say he was a scheming Don Juan.[3] If you don't believe me, take a look at his pipe. You'll have to admit that it shows up his character.

MOTHER COURAGE. I don't see anything. It's beat up.

THE CHAPLAIN. It's half bitten through. A violent man. That is the pipe of a ruthless, violent man, you must see that if you've still got an ounce of good sense.

MOTHER COURAGE. Don't wreck my chopping block.

THE CHAPLAIN. I've told you I wasn't trained to chop wood. I studied theology. My gifts and abilities are being wasted on muscular effort. The talents that God gave me are lying fallow. That's a sin. You've never heard me preach. With one sermon I can whip a regiment into such a state that they take the enemy for a flock of sheep. Then men care no more about their lives than they would about a smelly old sock that they're ready to throw away in hopes of final victory. God has made me eloquent. You'll swoon when you hear me preach.

MOTHER COURAGE. I don't want to swoon. What good would that do me?

THE CHAPLAIN. Courage, I've often wondered if maybe you didn't conceal a warm heart under that hard-bitten talk of yours. You too are human, you need warmth.

MOTHER COURAGE. The best way to keep this tent warm is with plenty of firewood.

THE CHAPLAIN. Don't try to put me off. Seriously, Courage, I sometimes wonder if we couldn't make our relationship a little closer. I mean, seeing that the whirlwind of war has whirled us so strangely together.

MOTHER COURAGE. Seems to me it's close enough. I cook your meals and you do chores, such as chopping wood, for instance.

THE CHAPLAIN. [*Goes toward her*] You know what I mean by "closer"; it has nothing to do with meals and chopping wood and such mundane needs. Don't harden your heart, let it speak.

MOTHER COURAGE. Don't come at me with that ax. That's too close a relationship.

THE CHAPLAIN. Don't turn it to ridicule. I'm serious. I've given it careful thought.

MOTHER COURAGE. Chaplain, don't be silly. I like you, I don't want to have to scold you. My aim in life is to get through, me and my children and my wagon. I don't think of it as mine and besides I'm not in the mood for private affairs. Right now I'm taking a big risk, buying up merchandise with the general dead and everybody talking peace. What'll you do if I'm ruined? See? You don't know. Chop that wood, then we'll be warm in the evening, which is a good thing in times like these. Now what? [*She stands up*]

[*Enter Kattrin out of breath, with a wound across her forehead and over one eye. She is carrying all sort of things, packages, leather goods, a drum, etc.*]

3. Philanderer.

MOTHER COURAGE. What's this? Assaulted? On the way back? She was assulted on the way back. Must have been that soldier that got drunk here! I shouldn't have let you go! Throw the stuff down! It's not bad, only a flesh wound. I'll bandage it, it'll heal in a week. They're worse than wild beasts. [*She bandages the wound*]

THE CHAPLAIN. I can't find fault with them. At home they never raped anybody. I blame the people that start wars, they're the ones that dredge up man's lowest instincts.

MOTHER COURAGE. Didn't the clerk bring you back? That's because you're respectable, they don't give a damn. It's not a deep wound, it won't leave a mark. There, all bandaged. Don't fret, I've got something for you. I've been keeping it for you on the sly, it'll be a surprise. [*She fishes Yvette's red shoes out of a sack*] See? You've always wanted them. Now you've got them. Put them on quick before I regret it. It won't leave a mark, though I wouldn't mind if it did. The girls that attract them get the worst of it. They drag them around till there's nothing left of them. If you don't appeal to them, they won't harm you. I've seen girls with pretty faces, a few years later they'd have given a wolf the creeps. They can't step behind a bush without fearing the worst. It's like trees. The straight tall ones get chopped down for ridgepoles, the crooked ones enjoy life. In other words, it's a lucky break. The shoes are still in good condition, I've kept them nicely polished.

[*Kattrin leaves the shoes where they are and crawls into the wagon*]

THE CHAPLAIN. I hope she won't be disfigured.

MOTHER COURAGE. There'll be a scar. She can stop waiting for peace.

THE CHAPLAIN. She didn't let them take anything.

MOTHER COURAGE. Maybe I shouldn't have drummed it into her. If I only knew what went on in her head. One night she stayed out, the only time in all these years. Afterwards she traipsed around as usual, except she worked harder. I never could find out what happened. I racked my brains for quite some time. [*She picks up the articles brought by Kattrin and sorts them angrily*] That's war for you! A fine way to make a living!

[*Cannon salutes are heard*]

THE CHAPLAIN. Now they're burying the general. This is a historic moment.

MOTHER COURAGE. To me it's a historic moment when they hit my daughter over the eye. She's a wreck, she'll never get a husband now, and she's so crazy about children. It's the war that made her dumb too, a soldier stuffed something in her mouth when she was little. I'll never see Swiss Cheese again and where Eilif is, God knows. God damn the war.

7

Mother Courage at the height of her business career.

Highway.

The chaplain, Mother Courage and her daughter Kattrin are pulling the wagon. New wares are hanging on it. Mother Courage is wearing a necklace of silver talers.

MOTHER COURAGE. Stop running down the war. I won't have it. I know it destroys the weak, but the weak haven't a chance in peacetime either. And war is a better provider. [*Sings*]

If you're not strong enough to take it
The victory will find you dead.
A war is only what you make it.
It's business, not with cheese but lead.

And what good is it staying in one place? The stay-at-homes are the first to get it. [*Sings*]

Some people think they'd like to ride out
The war, leave danger to the brave
And dig themselves a cozy hideout—
They'll dig themselves an early grave.
I've seen them running from the thunder
To find a refuge from the war
But once they're resting six feet under
They wonder what they hurried for.

[*They plod on*]

8

In the same year Gustavus Adolphus, King of Sweden, is killed at the battle of Lützen.[1] Peace threatens to ruin Mother Courage's business. Her brave son performs one heroic deed too many and dies an ignominious death.

A camp.

A summer morning. An old woman and her son are standing by the wagon. The son is carrying a large sack of bedding.

MOTHER COURAGE'S VOICE. [*From the wagon*] Does it have to be at this unearthly hour?

THE YOUNG MAN. We've walked all night, twenty miles, and we've got to go back today.

MOTHER COURAGE'S VOICE. What can I do with bedding? The people haven't any houses.

1. Town a few miles from the great Protestant city of Leipzig.

THE YOUNG MAN. Wait till you've seen it.

THE OLD WOMAN. She won't take it either. Come on.

THE YOUNG MAN. They'll sell the roof from over our heads for taxes. Maybe she'll give us three guilders if you throw in the cross. [*Bells start ringing*] Listen, mother!

VOICES. [*From the rear*] Peace! The king of Sweden is dead!

MOTHER COURAGE. [*Sticks her head out of the wagon. She has not yet done her hair*] Why are the bells ringing in the middle of the week?

THE CHAPLAIN. [*Crawls out from under the wagon*] What are they shouting?

MOTHER COURAGE. Don't tell me peace has broken out when I've just taken in more supplies.

THE CHAPLAIN. [*Shouting toward the rear*] Is it true? Peace?

VOICE. Three weeks ago, they say. But we just found out.

THE CHAPLAIN. [*To Mother Courage*] What else would they ring the bells for?

VOICE. There's a whole crowd of Lutherans, they've driven their carts into town. They brought the news.

THE YOUNG MAN. Mother, it's peace. What's the matter?

[*The old woman has collapsed*]

MOTHER COURAGE. [*Going back into the wagon*] Heavenly saints! Kattrin, peace! Put your black dress on! We're going to church. We owe it to Swiss Cheese. Can it be true?

THE YOUNG MAN. The people here say the same thing. They've made peace. Can you get up? [*The old woman stands up, still stunned*] I'll get the saddle shop started again. I promise. Everything will be all right. Father will get his bed back. Can you walk? [*To the chaplain*] She fainted. It was the news. She thought peace would never come again. Father said it would. We'll go straight home. [*Both go out*]

MOTHER COURAGE'S VOICE. Give her some brandy.

THE CHAPLAIN. They're gone.

MOTHER COURAGE'S VOICE. What's going on in camp?

THE CHAPLAIN. A big crowd. I'll go see. Shouldn't I put on my clericals?

MOTHER COURAGE'S VOICE. Better make sure before you step out in your antichrist costume. I'm glad to see peace, even if I'm ruined. At least I've brought two of my children through the war. Now I'll see my Eilif again.

THE CHAPLAIN. Look who's coming down the road. If it isn't the general's cook!

THE COOK. [*Rather bedraggled, carrying a bundle*] Can I believe my eyes? The chaplain!

THE CHAPLAIN. Courage! A visitor!

[*Mother Courage climbs down*]

THE COOK. Didn't I promise to come over for a little chat as soon as I had time? I've never forgotten your brandy, Mrs. Fierling.

MOTHER COURAGE. Mercy, the general's cook! After all these years! Where's Eilif, my eldest?

THE COOK. Isn't he here yet? He left ahead of me, he was coming to see you too.

THE CHAPLAIN. I'll put on my clericals, wait for me. [*Goes out behind the wagon*]

MOTHER COURAGE. Then he'll be here any minute. [*Calls into the wagon*] Kattrin, Eilif's coming! Bring the cook a glass of brandy! [*Kattrin does not appear*] Put a lock of hair over it, and forget it! Mr. Lamb is no stranger. [*Gets the brandy herself*] She won't come out. Peace doesn't mean a thing to her, it's come too late. They hit her over the eye, there's hardly any mark, but she thinks people are staring at her.

THE COOK. Ech, war! [*He and Mother Courage sit down*]

MOTHER COURAGE. Cook, you find me in trouble. I'm ruined.

THE COOK. What? Say, that's a shame.

MOTHER COURAGE. Peace has done me in. Only the other day I stocked up. The chaplain's advice. And now they'll all demobilize and leave me sitting on my merchandise.

THE COOK. How could you listen to the chaplain? If I'd had time, I'd have warned you against him, but the Catholics came too soon. He's a fly-by-night. So now he's the boss here?

MOTHER COURAGE. He washed my dishes and helped me pull the wagon.

THE COOK. Him? Pulling? I guess he's told you a few of his jokes too, I wouldn't put it past him, he has an unsavory attitude toward women, I tried to reform him, it was hopeless. He's not steady.

MOTHER COURAGE. Are you steady?

THE COOK. If nothing else, I'm steady. Prosit!

MOTHER COURAGE. Steady is no good. I've only lived with one steady man, thank the Lord. I never had to work so hard, he sold the children's blankets when spring came, and he thought my harmonica was unchristian. In my opinion you're not doing yourself any good by admitting you're steady.

THE COOK. You've still got your old bite, but I respect you for it.

MOTHER COURAGE. Don't tell me you've been dreaming about my old bite.

THE COOK. Well, here we sit, with the bells of peace and your world-famous brandy, that hasn't its equal.

MOTHER COURAGE. The bells of peace don't strike my fancy right now. I don't see them paying the men, they're behindhand already. Where does that leave me with my famous brandy? Have you been paid?

THE COOK. [*Hesitantly*] Not really. That's why we demobilized ourselves. Under the circumstances, I says to myself, why should I stay on? I'll go see my friends in the meantime. So here we are.

MOTHER COURAGE. You mean you're out of funds?

THE COOK. If only they'd stop those damn bells! I'd be glad to go into some kind of business. I'm sick of being a cook. They give me roots and shoe leather to work with, and then they throw the hot soup in my face. A cook's got a dog's life these days. I'd rather be in combat, but now we've got peace. [*The chaplain appears in his original dress*] We'll discuss it later.

THE CHAPLAIN. It's still in good condition. There were only a few moths in it.

THE COOK. I don't see why you bother. They won't take you back. Who are you going to inspire now to be an honest soldier and earn his pay at the risk of his life? Besides, I've got a bone to pick with you. Advising this lady to buy useless merchandise on the ground that the war would last forever.

THE CHAPLIN. [*Heatedly*] And why, I'd like to know, is it any of your business?

THE COOK. Because it's unscrupulous. How can you meddle in other people's business and give unsolicited advice?

THE CHAPLAIN. Who's meddling? [*To Mother Courage*] I didn't know you were accountable to this gentleman, I didn't know you were so intimate with him.

MOTHER COURAGE. Don't get excited, the cook is only giving his private opinion. And you can't deny that your war was a dud.

THE CHAPLAIN. Courage, don't blaspheme against peace. You're a battlefield hyena.

MOTHER COURAGE. What am I?

THE COOK. If you insult this lady, you'll hear from me.

THE CHAPLAIN. I'm not talking to you. Your intentions are too obvious. [*To Mother Courage*] But when I see you picking up peace with thumb and forefinger like a snotty handkerchief, it revolts my humanity; you don't want peace, you want war, because you profit by it, but don't forget the old saying: "He hath need of a long spoon that eateth with the devil."

MOTHER COURAGE. I've no use for war and war hasn't much use for me. Anyway, I'm not letting anybody call me a hyena, you and me are through.

THE CHAPLAIN. How can you complain about peace when it's such a relief to everybody else? On account of the old rags in your wagon?

MOTHER COURAGE. My merchandise isn't old rags, it's what I live off, and so did you.

THE CHAPLAIN. Off war, you mean. Aha!

THE COOK. [*To the chaplain*] You're a grown man, you ought to know there's no sense in giving advice. [*To Mother Courage*] The best thing you can do now is to sell off certain articles quick, before the prices hit the floor. Dress yourself and get started, there's no time to lose.

MOTHER COURAGE. That's very sensible advice. I think I'll do it.

THE CHAPLAIN. Because the cook says so!

MOTHER COURAGE. Why didn't *you* say so? He's right, I'd better run over to the market. [*She goes into the wagon*]

THE COOK. My round, chaplain. No presence of mind. Here's what you should have said: me give you advice? All I ever did was talk politics! Don't try to take me on. Cockfighting is undignified in a clergyman.

THE CHAPLAIN. If you don't shut up, I'll murder you, undignified or not.

THE COOK. [*Taking off his shoe and unwinding the wrappings from his feet*] If the war hadn't made a godless bum out of you, you could easily come by a parsonage now that peace is here. They won't need cooks, there's nothing to cook, but people still do a lot of believing, that hasn't changed.

THE CHAPLAIN. See here, Mr. Lamb. Don't try squeeze me out. Being a bum has made me a better man. I couldn't preach to them any more.

[*Yvette Pottier enters, elaborately dressed in black, with a cane. She is much older and fatter and heavily powdered. Behind her a servant*]

YVETTE. Hello there! Is this the residence of Mother Courage?

THE CHAPLAIN. Right you are. With whom have we the pleasure?

YVETTE. The Countess Starhemberg, my good people. Where is Mother Courage.

THE CHAPLAIN. [*Calls into the wagon*] Countess Starhemberg wishes to speak to you!

MOTHER COURAGE. I'm coming.

YVETTE. It's Yvette!

MOTHER COURAGE'S VOICE. My goodness! It's Yvette!

YVETTE. Just dropped in to see how you're doing. [*The cook has turned around in horror*] Pieter!

THE COOK. Yvette!

YVETTE. Blow me down! How did you get here?

THE COOK. In a cart.

THE CHAPLAIN. Oh, you know each other? Intimately?

YVETTE. I should think so. [*She looks the cook over*] Fat!

THE COOK. You're not exactly willowy yourself.

YVETTE. All the same I'm glad I ran into you, you bum. Now I can tell you what I think of you.

THE CHAPLAIN. Go right ahead, spare no details, but wait until Courage comes out.

MOTHER COURAGE. [*Comes out with all sorts of merchandise*] Yvette! [*They embrace*] But what are you in mourning for?

YVETTE. Isn't it becoming? My husband the colonel died a few years ago.

MOTHER COURAGE. The old geezer that almost bought my wagon?

YVETTE. His elder brother.

MOTHER COURAGE. You must be pretty well fixed. It's nice to find somebody that's made a good thing out of the war.

YVETTE. Oh well, it's been up and down and back up again.

MOTHER COURAGE. Let's not say anything bad about colonels. They make money by the bushel.

THE CHAPLAIN. If I were you, I'd put my shoes back on again. [*To Yvette*] Countess Starhemberg, you promised to tell us what you think of this gentleman.

THE COOK. Don't make a scene here.

MOTHER COURAGE. He's a friend of mine, Yvette.

YVETTE. He's Pete the Pipe, that's who he is.

THE COOK. Forget the nicknames, my name is Lamb.

MOTHER COURAGE. [*Laughs*] Pete the Pipe! That drove the women crazy! Say, I've saved your pipe.

THE CHAPLAIN. And smoked it.

YVETTE. It's lucky I'm here to warn you. He's the worst rotter that ever infested the coast of Flanders. He ruined more girls than he's got fingers.

THE COOK. That was a long time ago. I've changed.

YVETTE. Stand up when a lady draws you into a conversation! How I loved this man! And all the while he was seeing a little bandy-legged brunette, ruined her too, naturally.

THE COOK. Seems to me I started you off on a prosperous career.

YVETTE. Shut up, you depressing wreck! Watch your step with him, his kind are dangerous even when they've gone to seed.

MOTHER COURAGE. [*To Yvette*] Come along, I've got to sell my stuff before the prices drop. Maybe you can help me, with your army connections. [*Calls into the wagon*] Kattrin, forget about church, I'm running over to the market. When Eilif comes, give him a drink. [*Goes out with Yvette*]

YVETTE. [*In leaving*] To think that such a man could lead me astray! I can thank my lucky stars that I was able to rise in the world after that. I've put a spoke in your wheel, Pete the Pipe, and they'll give me credit for it in heaven when my time comes.

THE CHAPLAIN. Our conversation seems to illustrate the old adage: The mills of God grind slowly.[2] What do you think of my jokes now?

THE COOK. I'm just unlucky. I'll come clean: I was hoping for a hot meal. I'm starving. And now they're talking about me, and she'll get the wrong idea. I think I'll beat it before she comes back.

THE CHAPLAIN. I think so too.

THE COOK. Chaplain, I'm fed up on peace already. Men are sinners from the cradle, fire and sword are their natural lot. I wish I were cooking for the general again. God knows where he is, I'd roast a fine fat capon, with mustard sauce and a few carrots.

THE CHAPLAIN. Red cabbage. Red cabbage with capon.

THE COOK. That's right, but he wanted carrots.

THE CHAPLAIN. He was ignorant.

THE COOK. That didn't prevent you from gorging yourself.

THE CHAPLAIN. With repugnance.

THE COOK. Anyway you'll have to admit those were good times.

THE CHAPLAIN. I might admit that.

THE COOK. Now you've called her a hyena, your good times here are over. What are you staring at?

THE CHAPLAIN. Eilif? [*Eilif enters, followed by soldiers with pikes. His hands are fettered. He is deathly pale*] What's wrong?

2. From a saying by Friedrich von Logan (1605–1655), as translated by Longfellow: "Though the mills of God grind slowly, / Yet they grind exceeding small."

EILIF. Where's mother?

THE CHAPLAIN. Gone to town.

EILIF. I heard she was here. They let me come and see her.

THE COOK. [*To the soldiers*] Where are you taking him?

A SOLDIER. No good place.

THGE CHAPLAIN. What has he done?

THE SOILDIER. Broke into a farm. The peasant's wife is dead.

THE CHAPLAIN. How could you do such a thing?

EILIF. It's what I've been doing all along.

THE COOK. But in peacetime!

EILIF. Shut your trap. Can I sit down till she comes?

THE SOLDIER. We haven't time.

THE CHAPLAIN. During the war they honored him for it, he sat at the general's right hand. Then it was bravery. Couldn't we speak to the officer?

THE SOLDIER. No use. What's brave about taking a peasant's cattle?

THE COOK. It was stupid.

EILIF. If I'd been stupid. I'd have starved, wise guy.

THE COOK. And for being smart your head comes off.

THE CHAPLAIN. Let's get Kattrin at least.

EILIF. Leave her be. Get me a drink of schnapps.

THE SOLDIER. No time. Let's go!

THE CHAPLAIN. And what should we tell your mother?

EILIF. Tell her it wasn't any different, tell her it was the same. Or don't tell her anything.

[*The soldiers drive him away*]

THE CHAPLAIN. I'll go with you on your hard journey.

EILIF. I don't need any sky pilot.

THE CHAPLAIN. You don't know yet. [*He follows him*]

THE COOK. [*Calls after them*] I'll have to tell her, she'll want to see him.

THE CHAPLAIN. Better not tell her anything. Or say he was here and he'll come again, maybe tomorrow. I'll break it to her when I get back.[*Hurries out*]

[*The cook looks after them, shaking his head, then he walks anxiously about. Finally he approaches the wagon*]

THE COOK. Hey! Come on out! I can see why you'd hide from peace. I wish I could do it myself. I'm the general's cook, remember? Wouldn't you have a bite to eat, to do me till your mother gets back? A slice of ham or just a piece of bread while I'm waiting. [*He looks in*] She's buried her head in a blanket.

[*The sound of gunfire in the rear*]

MOTHER COURAGE. [*Runs in. She is out of breath and still has her merchandise*] Cook, the peace is over, the war started up again three days ago. I hadn't sold my stuff yet when I found out. Heaven be praised! They're shooting each other up in town, the Catholics and Lutherans. We've got to get out of here. Kattrin, start packing. What have *you* got such a long face about? What's wrong?

THE COOK. Nothing.

MOTHER COURAGE. Something's wrong, I can tell by your expression.

THE COOK. Maybe it's the war starting up again. Now I probably won't get anything hot to eat before tomorrow night.

MOTHER COURAGE. That's a lie, cook.

THE COOK. Eilif was here. He couldn't stay.

MOTHER COURAGE. He was here? Then we'll see him on the march. I'm going with our troops this time. How does he look?

THE COOK. The same.

MOTHER COURAGE. He'll never change. The war couldn't take him away from me. He's smart. Could you help me pack? [*She starts packing*] Did he tell you anything? Is he in good with the general? Did he say anything about his heroic deeds?

THE COOK. [*Gloomily*] They say he's been at one of them again.

MOTHER COURAGE. Tell me later, we've got to be going. [*Kattrin emerges*] Kattrin, peace is over. We're moving. [*To the cook*] What's the matter with you?

THE COOK. I'm going to enlist.

MOTHER COURAGE. I've got a suggestion. Why don't . . .? Where's the chaplain?

THE COOK. Gone to town with Eilif.

MOTHER COURAGE. Then come a little way with me, Lamb. I need help.

THE COOK. That incident with Yvette . . .

MOTHER COURAGE. It hasn't lowered you in my estimation. Far from it. Where there's smoke there's fire. Coming?

THE COOK. I won't say no.

MOTHER COURAGE. The Twelfth Regiment has shoved off. Take the shaft. Here's a chunk of bread. We'll have to circle around to meet the Lutherans. Maybe I'll see Eilif tonight. He's my favorite. It's been a short peace. And we're on the move again. [*She sings, while the cook and Kattrin harness themselves to the wagon*]

From Ulm to Metz, from Metz to Pilsen[3]
Courage is right there in the van.
The war both in and out of season
With shot and shell will feed its man.
But lead alone is not sufficient
The war needs soldiers to subsist!
Its diet elseways is deficient.
The war is hungry! So enlist!

3. Ulm is about eighty miles west of Munich. Metz, in the province of Lorraine (ceded to France at the end of the Thirty Years' War), is about two hundred miles west of Ulm; to travel from Metz to Pilsen one must cross the whole of Germany.

9

The great war of religion has been going on for sixteen years. Germany has lost more than half its population. Those whom the slaughter has spared have been laid low by epidemics. Once-flourishing countrysides are ravaged by famine. Wolves prowl through the charred ruins of the cities. In the fall of 1634 we find Mother Courage in Germany, in the Fichtelgebirge[1] at some distance from the road followed by the Swedish armies. Winter comes early and is exceptionally severe. Business is bad, begging is the only resort. The cook receives a letter from Utrecht[2] and is dismissed.

Outside a half-demolished presbytery.

Gray morning in early winter. Gusts of wind. Mother Courage and the cook in shabby sheepskins by the wagon.

THE COOK. No light. Nobody's up yet.

MOTHER COURAGE. But it's a priest. He'll have to crawl out of bed to ring the bells. Then he'll get himself a nice bowl of hot soup.

THE COOK. Go on, you saw the village, everything's been burned to a crisp.

MOTHER COURAGE. But somebody's here, I heard a dog bark.

THE COOK. If the priest's got anything, he won't give it away.

MOTHER COURAGE. Maybe if we sing . . .

THE COOK. I've had it up to here. [*Suddenly*] I got a letter from Utrecht. My mother's died of cholera and the tavern belongs to me. Here's the letter if you don't believe me. It's no business of yours what my aunt says about my evil ways, but never mind, read it.

MOTHER COURAGE[3] [*Reads the letter*] Lamb, I'm sick of roaming around, myself. I feel like a butcher's dog that pulls the meat cart but doesn't get any for himself. I've nothing left to sell and the people have no money to pay for it. In Saxony a man in rags tried to foist a cord[4] of books on me for two eggs, and in Württemberg they'd have let their plow go for a little bag of salt. What's the good of plowing? Nothing grows but brambles. In Pomerania[5] they say the villagers have eaten up all the babies, and that nuns have been caught at highway robbery.

THE COOK. It's the end of the world.

MOTHER COURAGE. Sometimes I have visions of myself driving

1. A range of mountains in Germany near the Bohemian border.
2. City in the south of Holland.
3. In this scene, Mother Courage and the Cook for the first time use *du*, the familiar form of *you* in German. (The familiar form is used between lovers, close friends and family, and young people; the formal *sie* is used otherwise.)
4. A large quantity; the same volume as a cord of wood.
5. Saxony, Württemberg, and Pomerania are German principalities.

through hell, selling sulfur and brimstone, or through heaven peddling refreshments to the roaming souls. If me and the children I've got left could find a place where there's no shooting, I wouldn't mind a few years of peace and quiet.

THE COOK. We could open up the tavern again. Think it over. Anna. I made up my mind last night; with or without you, I'm going back to Utrecht. In fact I'm leaving today.

MOTHER COURAGE. I'll have to talk to Kattrin. It's kind of sudden, and I don't like to make decisions in the cold with nothing in my stomach. Kattrin! [*Kattrin climbs out of the wagon*] Kattrin, I've got something to tell you. The cook and me are thinking of going to Utrecht. They've left him a tavern there. You'd be living in one place, you'd meet people. A lot of men would be glad to get a nice, well-behaved girl, looks aren't everything. I'm all for it. I get along fine with the cook. I've got to hand it to him: He's got a head for business. We'd eat regular meals, wouldn't that be nice? And you'd have your own bed, wouldn't you like that? It's no life on the road, year in year out. You'll go to rack and ruin. You're crawling with lice already. We've got to decide, you see, we could go north with the Swedes, they must be over there. [*She points to the left*] I think we'll do it, Kattrin.

THE COOK. Anna, could I have a word with you alone?

MOTHER COURAGE. Get back in the wagon, Kattrin.

[*Kattrin climbs back in*]

THE COOK. I interrupted you because I see there's been a misunderstanding, I thought it was too obvious to need saying. But if it isn't, I'll just have to say it. You can't take her, it's out of the question. Is that plain enough for you?

[*Kattrin sticks her head out of the wagon and listens*]

MOTHER COURAGE. You want me to leave Kattrin?

THE COOK. Look at it this way. There's no room in the tavern. It's not one of those places with three taprooms. If the two of us put our shoulder to the wheel, we can make a living, but not three, it can't be done. Kattrin can keep the wagon.

MOTHER COURAGE. I'd been thinking she could find a husband in Utrecht.

THE COOK. Don't make me laugh! How's she going to find a husband? At her age? And dumb! And with that scar!

MOTHER COURAGE. Not so loud.

THE COOK. Shout or whisper, the truth's the truth. And that's another reason why I can't have her in the tavern. The customers won't want a sight like that staring them in the face. Can you blame them?

MOTHER COURAGE. Shut up. Not so loud, I say.

THE COOK. There's a light in the presbytery.[6] Let's sing.

MOTHER COURAGE. How could she pull the wagon by herself? She's afraid of the war. She couldn't stand it. The dreams she must have! I hear her groaning at night. Especially after battles. What

6. That part of a church in which the bishop and clergy sit.

she sees in her dreams, God knows. It's pity that makes her suffer so. The other day the wagon hit a hedgehog, I found it hidden in her blanket.

THE COOK. The tavern's too small. [*He calls*] Worthy gentleman and members of the household! We shall now sing the Song of Solomon, Julius Caesar, and other great men, whose greatness didn't help them any. Just to show you that we're God-fearing people ourselves, which makes it hard for us, especially in the winter. [*They sing*]

You saw the wise King Solomon[7]
You know what came of him.
To him all hidden things were plain.
He cursed the hour gave birth to him
And saw that everything was vain.
How great and wise was Solomon!
Now think about his case. Alas
A useful lesson can be won.
It's wisdom that had brought him to that pass!
How happy is the man with none!

Our beautiful song proves that virtues are dangerous things, better steer clear of them, enjoy life, eat a good breakfast, a bowl of hot soup, for instance. Take me, I haven't got any soup and wish I had, I'm a soldier, but what has my bravery in all those battles got me, nothing, I'm starving, I'd be better off if I'd stayed home like a yellowbelly. And I'll tell you why.

You saw the daring Caesar[8] next
You know what he became.
They deified him in his life
But then they killed him just the same.
And as they raised the fatal knife
How loud he cried: "You too, my son!"
Now think about his case. Alas
A useful lesson can be won.
It's daring that had brought him to that pass!
How happy is the man with none!

[*In an undertone*] They're not even looking out. Worthy gentleman and members of the household! Maybe you'll say, all right, if bravery won't keep body and soul together, try honesty. That may fill your belly or at least get you a drop to drink. Let's look into it.

You've heard of honest Socrates[9]
Who never told a lie.
They weren't so grateful as you'd think

7. Old Testament ruler celebrated for his wisdom. In line 4 of the stanza, the cook confuses Solomon with the Biblical Job, who does curse the day he was born. [*Job* 3:1.]

8. [100–44 B.C.], Roman general and dictator, assassinated by a republican clique including his young friend Brutus when suspected of imperial ambitions.

9. Greek philosopher, condemned to death in 399 B.C. for teaching the young to question accepted beliefs.

Instead they sentenced him to die
And handed him the poisoned drink.
How honest was the people's noble son!
Now think about his case. Alas
A useful lesson can be won.
His honesty had brought him to that pass.
How happy is the man with none!

Yes, they tell us to be charitable and to share what we have, but what if we haven't got anything? Maybe philanthropists have a rough time of it too, it stands to reason, they need a little something for themselves. Yes, charity is a rare virtue, because it doesn't pay.

St. Martin[10] couldn't bear to see
His fellows in distress.
He saw a poor man in the snow.
"Take half my cloak!" He did, and lo!
They both of them froze none the less.
He thought his heavenly reward was won.
Now think about his case. Alas
A useful lesson can be won.
Unselfishness had brought him to that pass.
How happy is the man with none!

That's our situation. We're God-fearing folk, we stick together, we don't steal, we don't murder, we don't set fire to anything! You could say that we set an example which bears out the song, we sink lower and lower, we seldom see any soup, but if we were different, if we were thieves and murderers, maybe our bellies would be full. Because virtue isn't rewarded, only wickedness, the world needn't be like this, but it is.

And here you see God-fearing folk
Observing God's ten laws.
So far He hasn't taken heed.
You people sitting warm indoors
Help to relieve our bitter need!
Our virtue can be counted on.
Now think about our case. Alas
A useful lesson can be won.
The fear of God has brought us to this pass.
How happy is the man with none!

VOICE. [*From above*] Hey, down there! Come on up! We've got some good thick soup.

MOTHER COURAGE. Lamb, I couldn't get anything down. I know what you say makes sense, but is it your last word? We've always been good friends.

THE COOK. My last word. Think it over.

10. (330–397 A.D.) As a young soldier in the Roman army, Martin divided his military cloak with a beggar. He dreamed of Christ that night and was baptized thereafter, later becoming Bishop of Tours.

MOTHER COURAGE. I don't need to think it over. I won't leave her.

THE COOK. It wouldn't be wise, but there's nothing I can do. I'm not inhuman, but it's a small tavern. We'd better go in now, or there won't be anything left, we'll have been singing in the cold for nothing.

MOTHER COURAGE. I'll get Kattrin.

THE COOK. Better bring it down for her. They'll get a fright if the three of us barge in. [*They go out*]

[*Kattrin climbs out of the wagon. She is carrying a bundle. She looks around to make sure the others are gone. Then she spreads out an old pair of the cook's trousers and a skirt belonging to her mother side by side on a wheel of the wagon so they can easily be seen. She is about to leave with her bundle when Mother Courage comes out of the house*]

MOTHER COURAGE. [*With a dish of soup*] Kattrin! Stop! Kattrin! Where do you think you're going with that bundle? Have you taken leave of your wits? [*She examines the bundle*] She's packed her things. Were you listening? I've told him it's no go with Utrecht and his lousy tavern, what would we do there? A tavern's no place for you and me. The war still has a thing or two up its sleeve for us. [*She sees the trousers and skirt*] You're stupid. Suppose I'd seen that and you'd been gone? [*Kattrin tries to leave, Mother Courage holds her back*] And don't go thinking I've given him the gate on your account. It's the wagon. I won't part with the wagon, I'm used to it, it's not you, it's the wagon. We'll go in the other direction, we'll put the cook's stuff out here where he'll find it, the fool. [*She climbs up and throws down a few odds and ends to join the trousers*] There. Now we're shut of him, you won't see me taking anyone else into the business. From now on it's you and me. This winter will go by like all the rest. Harness up, it looks like snow.

[*They harness themselves to the wagon, turn it around and pull it away. When the cook comes out he sees his things and stands dumbfounded*]

10

Throughout 1635 Mother Courage and her daughter Kattrin pull the wagon over the roads of central Germany in the wake of the increasingly bedraggled armies.

Highway.

Mother Courage and Kattrin are pulling the wagon. They come to a peasant's house. A voice is heard singing from within.

THE VOICE.

The rose bush in our garden
Rejoiced our hearts in spring
It bore such lovely flowers.

We planted it last season
Before the April showers.
A garden is a blessèd thing
It bore such lovely flowers.

When winter comes a-stalking
And gales great snow storms bring
They trouble us but little.
We've lately finished caulking
The roof with moss and wattle.[1]
A sheltering roof's a blessèd thing
When winter comes a-stalking.

[*Mother Courage and Kattrin have stopped to listen. Then they move on*]

1. Sticks and branches.

11

January 1636. The imperial troops threaten the Protestant city of Halle.[1] The stone speaks. Mother Courage loses her daughter and goes on alone. The end of the war is not in sight.

The wagon, much the worse for wear, is standing beside a peasant house with an enormous thatch roof. The house is built against the side of a stony hill. Night.

A lieutenant and three soldiers in heavy armor step out of the woods.

THE LIEUTENANT. I don't want any noise. If anybody yells, run him through with your pikes.

FIRST SOLDIER. But we need a guide. We'll have to knock if we want them to come out.

THE LIEUTENANT. Knocking sounds natural. It could be a cow bumping against the barn wall.

[*The soldiers knock on the door. A peasant woman opens. They hold their hands over her mouth. Two soldiers go in*]

A MAN'S VOICE. [*Inside*] Who's there?

[*The soldiers bring out a peasant and his son*]

THE LIEUTENANT. [*Points to the wagon, in which Kattrin has appeared*] There's another one. [*A soldier pulls her out*] Anybody else live here?

THE PEASANT COUPLE. This is our son.—That's a dumb girl.—Her mother's gone into the town on business—Buying up people's belongings, they're selling cheap because they're getting out.—They're provisioners.

THE LIEUTENANT. I'm warning you to keep quiet, one squawk and

1. Protestant city twenty miles northwest of Leipzig.

you'll get a pike over the head. All right. I need somebody who can show us the path to the city. [*Points to the young peasant*] You. Come here!

THE YOUNG PEASANT. I don't know no path.

THE SECOND SOLDIER. [*Grinning*] He don't know no path.

THE YOUNG PEASANT. I'm not helping the Catholics.

THE LIEUTENANT. [*To the second soldier*] Give him a feel of your pike!

THE YOUNG PEASANT. [*Forced down on his knees and threatened with the pike*] You can kill me. I won't do it.

THE FIRST SOLDIER. I know what'll make him think twice. [*He goes over to the barn*] Two cows and an ox. Get this: If you don't help us, I'll cut them down.

THE YOUNG PEASANT. Not the animals!

THE PEASANT WOMAN. [*In tears*] Captain, spare our animals or we'll starve.

THE LIEUTENANT. If he insists on being stubborn, they're done for.

THE FIRST SOLDIER. I'll start with the ox.

THE YOUNG PEASANT. [*To the old man*] Do I have to? [*The old woman nods*] I'll do it.

THE PEASANT WOMAN. And thank you kindly for your forbearance, Captain, for ever and ever, amen.

[*The peasant stops her from giving further thanks*]

THE FIRST SOLDIER. Didn't I tell you? With them it's the animals that come first.

[*Led by the young peasant, the lieutenant and the soldiers continue on their way*]

THE PEASANT. I wish I knew what they're up to. Nothing good.

THE PEASANT WOMAN. Maybe they're only scouts.—What are you doing?

THE PEASANT. [*Putting a ladder against the roof and climbing up*] See if they're alone. [*On the roof*] Men moving in the woods. All the way to the quarry. Armor in the clearing. And a cannon. It's more than a regiment. God have mercy on the city and everybody in it.

THE PEASANT WOMAN. See any light in the city?

THE PEASANT. No. They're all asleep. [*He climbs down*] If they get in, they'll kill everybody.

THE PEASANT WOMAN. The sentry will see them in time.

THE PEASANT. They must have killed the sentry in the tower on the hill, or he'd have blown his horn.

THE PEASANT WOMAN. If there were more of us . . .

THE PEASANT. All by ourselves up here with a cripple . . .

THE PEASANT WOMAN. We can't do a thing. Do you think . . .

THE PEASANT. Not a thing.

THE PEASANT WOMAN. We couldn't get down there in the dark.

THE PEASANT. The whole hillside is full of them. We can't even give a signal.

THE PEASANT WOMAN. They'd kill us.

THE PEASANT. No, we can't do a thing.

THE PEASANT WOMAN. [*To Kattrin*] Pray, poor thing, pray! We can't stop the bloodshed. If you can't talk, at least you can pray. He'll hear you if nobody else does. I'll help you. [*All kneel, Kattrin behind the peasants*] Our Father which art in heaven, hear our prayer. Don't let the town perish with everybody in it, all asleep and unsuspecting. Wake them, make them get up and climb the walls and see the enemy coming through the night with cannon and pikes, through the fields and down the hillside. [*Back to Kattrin*] Protect our mother and don't let the watchman sleep, wake him before it's too late. And succor our brother-in-law, he's in there with his four children, let them not perish, they're innocent and don't know a thing. [*To Kattrin, who groans*] The littlest is less than two, the oldest is seven. [*Horrified, Kattrin stands up*] Our Father, hear us, for Thou alone canst help, we'll all be killed, we're weak, we haven't any pikes or anything, we are powerless and in Thine hands, we and our animals and the whole farm, and the city too, it's in Thine hands, and the enemy is under the walls with great might.

[*Kattrin has crept unnoticed to the wagon, taken something out of it, put it under her apron and climbed up the ladder to the roof of the barn*]

THE PEASANT WOMAN. Think upon the children in peril, especially the babes in arms and the old people that can't help themselves and all God's creatures.

THE PEASANT. And forgive us our trespasses as we forgive them that trespass against us. Amen.

[*Kattrin, sitting on the roof, starts beating the drum that she has taken out from under her apron*]

THE PEASANT WOMAN. Jesus! What's she doing?

THE PEASANT. She's gone crazy.

THE PEASANT WOMAN. Get her down, quick!

[*The peasant runs toward the ladder, but Kattrin pulls it up on the roof*]

THE PEASANT WOMAN. She'll be the death of us all.

THE PEASANT. Stop that, you cripple!

THE PEASANT WOMAN. She'll have the Catholics down on us.

THE PEASANT. [*Looking around for stones*] I'll throw rocks at you.

THE PEASANT WOMAN. Have you no pity? Have you no heart? We're dead if they find out it's us! They'll run us through!

[*Kattrin stares in the direction of the city, and goes on drumming*]

THE PEASANT WOMAN. [*To the peasant*] I told you not to let those tramps stop here. What do they care if the soldiers drive our last animals away?

THE LIEUTENANT. [*Rushes in with his soldiers and the young peasant*] I'll cut you to pieces!

THE PEASANT WOMAN. We're innocent, captain. We couldn't help it. She sneaked up there. We don't know her.

THE LIEUTENANT. Where's the ladder?

THE PEASANT. Up top.

THE LIEUTENANT. [*To Kattrin*] Throw down that drum. It's an order!

[*Kattrin goes on drumming*]

THE LIEUTENANT. You're all in this together! This'll be the end of you!

THE PEASANT. They've felled some pine trees in the woods over there. We could get one and knock her down . . .

THE FIRST SOLDIER. [*To the Lieutenant*] Request permission to make a suggestion. [*He whispers something in the lieutenant's ear. He nods*] Listen. We've got a friendly proposition. Come down, we'll take you into town with us. Show us your mother and we won't touch a hair of her head.

[*Kattrin goes on drumming*]

THE LIEUTENANT. [*Pushes him roughly aside*] She doesn't trust you. No wonder with your mug. [*He calls up*] If I give you my word? I'm an officer, you can trust my word of honor.

[*She drums still louder*]

THE LIEUTENANT. Nothing is sacred to her.

THE YOUNG PEASANT. It's not just her mother, lieutenant!

THE FIRST SOLDIER. We can't let this go on. They'll hear it in the city.

THE LIEUTENANT. We'll have to make some kind of noise that's louder than the drums. What could we make noise with?

THE FIRST SOLDIER. But we're not supposed to make noise.

THE LIEUTENANT. An innocent noise, stupid. A peaceable noise.

THE PEASANT. I could chop wood.

THE LIEUTENANT. That's it, chop! [*The peasant gets an ax and chops at a log*] Harder! Harder! You're chopping for your life.

[*Listening, Kattrin has been drumming more softly. Now she looks anxiously around and goes on drumming as before*]

THE LIEUTENANT. [*To the peasant*] Not loud enough. [*To the first soldier*] You chop too.

THE PEASANT. There's only one ax. [*Stops chopping*]

THE LIEUTENANT. We'll have to set the house on fire. Smoke her out.

THE PEASANT. That won't do any good, Captain. If the city people see fire up here, they'll know what's afoot.

[*Still drumming, Kattrin has been listening again. Now she laughs*]

THE LIEUTENANT. Look, she's laughing at us. I'll shoot her down, regardless. Get the musket!

[*Two soldiers run out. Kattrin goes on drumming*]

THE PEASANT WOMAN. I've got it, captain. That's their wagon over there. If we start smashing it up, she'll stop. The wagon's all they've got.

THE LIEUTENANT. [*To the young peasant*] Smash away. [*To Kattrin*] *We'll* smash your wagon if you don't stop.

[*The young peasant strikes a few feeble blows at the wagon*]

THE PEASANT WOMAN. Stop it, you beast!

[*Kattrin strares despairingly at the wagon and emits pitiful sounds. But she goes on drumming*]

THE LIEUTENANT. Where are those stinkers with the musket?

THE FIRST SOLDIER. They haven't heard anything in the city yet, or we'd hear their guns.

THE LIEUTENANT. [*To Kattrin*] They don't hear you. And now we're going to shoot you down. For the last time: Drop that drum!

THE YOUNG PEASANT. [*Suddenly throws the plank away*] Keep on drumming! Or they'll all be killed! Keep on drumming, keep on drumming . . .

[*The soldier throws him down and hits him with his pike. Kattrin starts crying, but goes on drumming*]

THE PEASANT WOMAN. Don't hit him in the back! My God, you're killing him.

[*The soldiers run in with the musket*]

THE SECOND SOLDIER. The colonel's foaming at the mouth. We'll be court-martialed.

THE LIEUTENANT. Set it up! Set it up! [*To Kattrin, while the musket is being set up on its stand*] For the last time: Stop that drumming! [*Kattrin in tears drums as loud as she can*] Fire!

[*The soldiers fire, Kattrin is hit. She beats the drum for a few times more and then slowly collapses*]

THE LIEUTENANT. Now we'll have some quiet.

[*But Kattrin's last drumbeats are answered by the city's cannon. A confused hubbub of alarm bells and cannon is heard in the distance*]

THE FIRST SOLDIER. She's done it.

12

Night, toward morning. The fifes and drums of troops marching away.

Outside the wagon Mother Courage sits huddled over her daughter. The peasant couple are standing beside them.

THE PEASANT. [*Hostile*] You'll have to be going, woman. There's only one more regiment to come. You can't go alone.[1]

MOTHER COURAGE. Maybe I can get her to sleep. [*She sings*]

Lullaby baby
What stirs in the hay?
The neighbor brats whimper
Mine are happy and gay.
They go in tatters
And you in silk down
Cut from an angel's
Best party gown.

1. I.e., for protection and for customers Mother Courage must travel with the army.

They've nothing to munch on
And you will have pie
Just tell your mother
In case it's too dry.
Lullaby baby
What stirs in the hay?
That one lies in Poland
The other—who can say?

Now she's asleep. You shouldn't have told her about your brother-in-law's children.

THE PEASANT. Maybe it wouldn't have happened if you hadn't gone to town to swindle people.

MOTHER COURAGE. I'm glad she's sleeping now.

THE PEASANT WOMAN. She's not sleeping, you'll have to face it, she's dead.

THE PEASANT. And it's time you got started. There are wolves around here, and what's worse, marauders.

MOTHER COURAGE. Yes. [*She goes to the wagon and takes out a sheet of canvas to cover the body with*]

THE PEASANT WOMAN. Haven't you anybody else? Somebody you can go to?

MOTHER COURAGE. Yes, there's one of them left. Eilif.

THE PEASANT. [*While Mother Courage covers the body*] Go find him. We'll attend to this one, give her a decent burial. Set your mind at rest.

MOTHER COURAGE. Here's money for your expenses. [*She gives the peasant money*]

[*The peasant and his son shake hands with her and carry Kattrin away*]

THE PEASANT WOMAN. [*On the way out*] Hurry up!

MOTHER COURAGE. [*Harnesses herself to the wagon*] I hope I can pull the wagon alone. I'll manage, there isn't much in it. I've got to get back in business.

[*Another regiment marches by with fifes and drums in the rear*]

MOTHER COURAGE. Hey, take me with you! [*She starts to pull*]

[*Singing is heard in the rear:*]

With all the killing and recruiting
The war will worry on a while.
In ninety years they'll still be shooting.
It's hardest on the rank-and-file.
Our food is swill, our pants all patches
The higher-ups steal half our pay
And still we dream of God-sent riches.
Tomorrow is another day!
The spring is come! Christian, revive!
The snowdrifts melt, the dead lie dead!
And if by chance you're still alive
It's time to rise and shake a leg.

JORGE LUIS BORGES
(1899–)

The Lottery in Babylon[1]

Like all men in Babylon, I have been proconsul;[2] like all, a slave. I have also known omnipotence, opprobrium, imprisonment. Look: the index finger on my right hand is missing. Look: through the rip in my cape you can see a vermilion tattoo on my stomach. It is the second symbol, Beth. This letter, on nights when the moon is full, gives me power over men whose mark is Gimmel, but it subordinates me to the men of Aleph,[3] who on moonless nights owe obedience to those marked with Gimmel. In the half light of dawn, in a cellar, I have cut the jugular vein of sacred bulls before a black stone. During a lunar year[4] I have been declared invisible. I shouted and they did not answer me; I stole bread and they did not behead me. I have known what the Greeks do not know, incertitude. In a bronze chamber, before the silent handkerchief of the strangler, hope has been faithful to me, as has panic in the river of pleasure. Heraclides Ponticus[5] tells with amazement that Pythagoras remembered having been Pyrrhus and before that Euphorbus[6] and before that some other mortal. In order to remember similar vicissitudes I do not need to have recourse to death or even to deception.

I owe this almost atrocious variety to an institution which other republics do not know or which operates in them in an imperfect and secret manner: the lottery. I have not looked into its history; I know that the wise men cannot agree. I know of its powerful purposes what a man who is not versed in astrology can know about the moon. I come from a dizzy land where the lottery is the basis of reality. Until today I have thought as little about it as I have about the conduct of indecipherable divinities or about my heart. Now, far from Babylon and its beloved customs, I think with a certain amount of amazement about the lottery and about the blasphemous conjectures which veiled men murmur in the twilight.

My father used to say that formerly—a matter of centuries, of years?—the lottery in Babylon was a game of plebian character. He

1. Capital of ancient Babylonia, the Biblical "Babylon the great . . . dwelling place of demons, a haunt of every foul spirit." [*Revelation* 18:2.] The story was first published in 1942; the translation is by John M. Fein.

2. A high administrative official.

3. Aleph, Beth, and Gimmel are the first three letters of the Hebrew alphabet.

4. A cycle of twelve full moons.

5. Greek philosopher (fourth century B.C.) who, like his teacher Plato, wrote dialogues.

6. Pythagoras (sixth century B.C.), the Greek philosopher and mathematician, taught the doctrine of the transmigration of souls. In Horace's *Ode* I:28–29 he recalls being Euphorbus, the Trojan hero killed by Menelaus [*Iliad* 17:45]; according to Borges he also remembered having been Pyrrhus, the son of Achilles and Deidameia. [*Odyssey* 4.5–9.]

recounted (I don't know whether rightly) that barbers sold, in exchange for copper coins, squares of bone or of parchment adorned with symbols.[7] In broad daylight a drawing took place. Those who won received silver coins without any other test of luck. The system was elementary, as you can see.,

Naturally these "lotteries" failed. Their moral virtue was nil. They were not directed at all of man's faculties, but only at hope. In the face of public indifference, the merchants who founded these venal lotteries began to lose money. Someone tried a reform: The interpolation of a few unfavorable tickets in the list of favorable numbers. By means of this reform, the buyers of numbered squares ran the double risk of winning a sum and of paying a fine that could be considerable. This slight danger (for every thirty favorable numbers there was one unlucky one) awoke, as is natural, the interest of the public. The Babylonians threw themselves into the game. Those who did not acquire chances were considered pusillanimous, cowardly. In time, that justified disdain was doubled. Those who did not play were scorned, but also the losers who paid the fine were scorned. The Company (as it came to be known then) had to take care of the winners, who could not cash in their prizes if almost the total amount of the fines was unpaid. It started a lawsuit against the losers. The judge condemned them to pay the original fine and costs or spend several days in jail. All chose jail in order to defraud the Company. The bravado of a few is the source of the omnipotence of the Company and of its metaphysical and ecclesiastical power.

A little while afterward the lottery lists omitted the amounts of fines and limited themselves to publishing the days of imprisonment that each unfavorable number indicated. That laconic spirit, almost unnoticed at the time, was of capital importance. *It was the first appearance in the lottery of nonmonetary elements*. The success was tremendous. Urged by the clientele, the Company was obliged to increase the unfavorable numbers.

Everyone knows that the people of Babylon are fond of logic and even of symmetry. It was illogical for the lucky numbers to be computed in round coins and the unlucky ones in days and nights of imprisonment. Some moralists reasoned that the possession of money does not always determine happiness and that other forms of happiness are perhaps more direct.

Another concern swept the quarters of the poorer classes. The members of the college of priests multiplied their stakes and enjoyed all the vicissitudes of terror and hope; the poor (with reasonable or unavoidable envy) knew that they were excluded from that notoriously delicious rhythm. The just desire that all, rich and

7. **Barbers sell lottery tickets in modern Argentina.**

poor, should participate equally in the lottery, inspired an indignant agitation, the memory of which the years have not erased. Some obstinate people did not understand (or pretended not to understand) that it was a question of a new order, of a necessary historical stage. A slave stole a crimson ticket, which in the drawing credited him with the burning of his tongue. The legal code fixed that same penalty for the one who stole a ticket. Some Babylonians argued that he deserved the burning irons in his status of a thief; others, generously, that the executioner should apply it to him because chance had determined it that way. There were disturbances, there were lamentable drawings of blood, but the masses of Babylon finally imposed their will against the opposition of the rich. The people achieved amply its generous purposes. In the first place, it caused the Company to accept total power. (That unification was necessary, given the vastness and complexity of the new operations.) In the second place, it made the lottery secret, free and general. The mercenary sale of chances was abolished. Once initiated in the mysteries of Baal, every free man automatically participated in the sacred drawings, which took place in the labyrinths of the god every sixty nights and which determined his destiny until the next drawing. The consequences were incalculable. A fortunate play could bring about his promotion to the council of wise men or the imprisonment of an enemy (public or private) or finding, in the peaceful darkness of his room, the woman who begins to excite him and whom he never expected to see again. A bad play: mutilation, different kinds of infamy, death. At times one single fact—the vulgar murder of C, the mysterious apotheosis of B—was the happy solution of thirty or forty drawings. To combine the plays was difficult, but one must remember that the individuals of the Company were (and are) omnipotent and astute. In many cases the knowledge that certain happinesses were the simple product of chance would have diminished their virtue. To avoid that obstacle, the agents of the Company made use of the power of suggestion and magic. Their steps, their maneuverings, were secret. To find out about the intimate hopes and terrors of each individual, they had astrologists and spies. There were certain stone lions, there was a sacred latrine called Qaphqas,[8] there were fissures in a dusty aqueduct which, according to general opinion, *led to the Company*; malignant or benevolent persons deposited information in these places. An alphabetical file collected these items of varying truthfulness.

Incredibly, there were complaints. The Company, with its usual discretion, did not answer directly. It preferred to scrawl in the rubbish of a mask factory a brief statement which now figures in the

8. Pronounced *Kafka*.

sacred scriptures. This doctrinal item observed that the lottery is an interpolation of chance in the order of the world and that to accept errors is not to contradict chance: it is to corroborate it. It likewise observed that those lions and that sacred receptacle, although not disavowed by the Company (which did not abandon the right to consult them), functioned without official guarantee.

This declaration pacified the public's restlessness. It also produced other effects, perhaps unforeseen by its writer. It deeply modified the spirit and the operations of the Company. I don't have much time left; they tell us that the ship is about to weigh anchor. But I shall try to explain it.

However unlikely it might seem, no one had tried out before then a general theory of chance. Babylonians are not very speculative. They revere the judgments of fate, they deliver to them their lives, their hopes, their panic, but it does not occur to them to investigate fate's labyrinthine laws nor the gyratory spheres[9] which reveal it. Nevertheless, the *unofficial* declaration that I have mentioned inspired many discussions of judicial-mathematical character. From some one of them the following conjecture was born: If the lottery is an intensification of chance, a periodical infusion of chaos in the cosmos, would it not be right for chance to intervene in all stages of the drawing and not in one alone? Is it not ridiculous for chance to dictate someone's death and have the circumstances of that death—secrecy, publicity, the fixed time of an hour or a century—not subject to chance? These just scruples finally caused a considerable reform, whose complexities (aggravated by centuries' practice) only a few specialists understand, but which I shall try to summarize, at least in a symbolic way.

Let us imagine a first drawing, which decrees the death of a man. For its fulfillment one proceeds to another drawing, which proposes (let us say) nine possible executors. Of these executors, four can initiate a third drawing which will tell the name of the executioner, two can replace the adverse order with a fortunate one (finding a treasure, let us say), another will intensify the death penalty (that is, will make it infamous or enrich it with tortures), others can refuse to fulfill it. This is the symbolic scheme. In reality *the number of drawings is infinite*. No decision is final, all branch into others. Ignorant people suppose that infinite drawings require an infinite time; actually it is sufficient for time to be infinitely subdivisible, as the famous parable of the contest with the tortoise[10] teaches. This infinity harmonizes admirably with the sinuous num-

9. The circling movements of heavenly bodies which, according to astrology, reveal human destinies.

10. One of the paradoxes of the Greek philosopher Zeno (fifth century B.C.); swift Achilles can never overtake the tortoise because, each time he reaches the place where the tortoise was, the tortoise has moved on.

bers of Chance and with the Celestial Archetype of the Lottery, which the Platonists[11] adore. Some warped echo of our rites seems to have resounded on the Tiber: Ellus Lampridius, in the *Life of Antoninus Heliogabalus;*[12] tells that this emperor wrote on shells the lots that were destined for his guests, so that one received ten pounds of gold and another ten flies, ten dormice, ten bears. It is permissible to recall that Heliogabalus was brought up in Asia Minor, among the priests of the eponymous god.

There are also impersonal drawings with an indefinite purpose. One decrees that a sapphire of Taprobana be thrown into the waters of the Euphrates;[13] another, that a bird be released from the roof of a tower; another, that each century there be withdrawn (or added) a grain of sand from the innumerable ones on the beach. The consequences are, at times, terrible.

Under the beneficent influence of the Company, our customs are saturated with chance. The buyer of a dozen amphoras of Damascene[14] wine will not be surprised if one of them contains a talisman or a snake. The scribe who writes a contract almost never fails to introduce some erroneous information. I myself, in this hasty declaration, have falsified some splendor, some atrocity. Perhaps, also, some mysterious monotony . . . Our historians, who are the most penetrating on the globe, have invented a method to correct chance. It is well known that the operations of this method are (in general) reliable, although, naturally, they are not divulged without some portion of deceit. Furthermore, there is nothing so contaminated with fiction as the history of the Company. A paleographic document, exhumed in a temple, can be the result of yesterday's lottery or of an age-old lottery. No book is published without some discrepancy in each one of the copies. Scribes take a secret oath to omit, to interpolate, to change. The indirect lie is also cultivated.

The Company, with divine modesty, avoids all publicity. Its agents, as is natural, are secret. The orders which it issues continually (perhaps incessantly) do not differ from those lavished by impostors. Moreover, who can brag about being a mere impostor? The drunkard who improvises an absurd order, the dreamer who awakens suddenly and strangles the woman who sleeps at his side, do they not execute, perhaps, a secret decision of the Company? That silent

11. Followers of the Greek philosopher Plato (fourth century B.C.), who held that earthly objects are imperfect copies or reflections of an absolute Idea; thus, all beds are separate versions of the abstract notion of Bed. [*Republic* X.]

12. Roman emperor (204–222 A.D.) known for his extravagance, the subject of a biography by the Roman historian Ellus Lampridius (fourth century A.D.). Originally named Varius Bassanius, the emperor adopted the name of Elagabalus, a Syrian sun god. (The river Tiber flows through Rome.)

13. The river on which ancient Babylon was situated. *Taprobana*: Legendary islands of the Far East.

14. From Damascus, the ancient capital of Syria.

functioning, comparable to God's, gives rise to all sorts of conjectures. One abominably insinuates that the Company has not existed for centuries and that the sacred disorder of our lives is purely hereditary, traditional. Another judges it eternal and teaches that it will last until the last night, when the last god annihilates the world. Another declares that the Company is omnipotent, but that it only has influence in tiny things: in a bird's call, in the shadings of rust and of dust, in the half dreams of dawn. Another, in the words of masked heresiarchs,[15] *that it has never existed and will not exist.* Another, no less vile, reasons that it is indifferent to affirm or deny the reality of the shadowy corporation, because Babylon is nothing else than an infinite game of chance.

15. Heretical thinkers.

VLADIMIR NABOKOV

(1899–1977)

Cloud, Castle, Lake*

One of my representatives—a modest, mild bachelor, very efficient—happened to win a pleasure trip at a charity ball given by Russian refugees.[1] That was in 1936 or 1937. The Berlin summer was in full flood (it was the second week of damp and cold, so that it was a pity to look at everything which had turned green in vain, and only the sparrows kept cheerful); he did not care to go anywhere, but when he tried to sell his ticket at the office of the Bureau of Pleasantrips he was told that to do so he would have to have special permission from the Ministry of Transportation; when he tried them, it turned out that first he would have to draw up a complicated petition at a notary's on stamped paper; and besides, a so-called "certificate of non-absence from the city for the summertime" had to be obtained from the police.[2]

So he sighed a little, and decided to go. He borrowed an aluminum flask from friends, repaired his soles, bought a belt and a fancy-style flannel shirt—one of those cowardly things which shrink in the first wash. Incidentally, it was too large for that likable little

* Written in Russian and published in 1937; translated into English by the author and Peter Pertzov in 1941.

1. Those who fled Russia after the 1917 Revolution. Berlin and Paris were the main centers for the refugee "White Russian" communities.

2. "Our utter physical dependence on this or that nation, which had coldly granted us political refuge, became painfully evident when some trashy 'visa,' some diabolical 'identity card' had to be obtained or prolonged, for then an avid bureaucratic hell would attempt to close upon the petitioner and he might wilt while his dossier waxed fatter and fatter." (*Speak, Memory*)

man, his hair always neatly trimmed, his eyes so intelligent and kind. I cannot remember his name at the moment. I think it was Vasili Ivanovich.

He slept badly the night before the departure. And why? Because he had to get up unusually early, and hence took along into his dreams the delicate face of the watch ticking on his night table; but mainly because that very night, for no reason at all, he began to imagine that this trip, thrust upon him by a feminine Fate in a low-cut gown,[3] this trip which he had accepted so reluctantly, would bring him some wonderful, tremulous happiness. This happiness would have something in common with his childhood, and with the excitement aroused in him by Russian lyrical poetry, and with some evening sky line once seen in a dream, and with that lady, another man's wife, whom he had hopelessly loved for seven years—but it would be even fuller and more significant than all that. And besides, he felt that the really good life must be oriented toward something or someone.

The morning was dull, but steam-warm and close, with an inner sun, and it was quite pleasant to rattle in a streetcar to the distant railway station where the gathering place was: several people, alas, were taking part in the excursion. Who would they be, these drowsy beings, drowsy as seem all creatures still unknown to us? By Window No. 6, at 7 A.M., as was indicated in the directions appended to the ticket, he saw them (they were already waiting; he had managed to be late by about three minutes).

A lanky blond young man in Tyrolese garb[4] stood out at once. He was burned the color of a cockscomb, had huge brick-red knees with golden hairs, and his nose looked lacquered. He was the leader furnished by the Bureau, and as soon as the newcomer had joined the group (which consisted of four women and as many men) he led it off toward a train lurking behind other trains, carrying his monstrous knapsack with terrifying ease, and firmly clanking with his hob-nailed boots.

Everyone found a place in an empty car, unmistakably third-class,[5] and Vasili Ivanovich, having sat down by himself and put a peppermint into his mouth, opened a little volume of Tyutchev,[6] whom he had long intended to re-read; but he was requested to put the book aside and join the group. An elderly bespectacled post-office clerk, with skull, chin, and upper lip a bristly blue as if he had

3. The woman who presented him with his prize at the ball, as Fate personified.

4. From the Austrian or Italian Tyrol, Alpine country popular with hikers and mountain-climbers. Tyrolese garb includes leather shorts, hiking boots, a mountaineer's stick (or Alpenstock), and a cap with a feather in it.

5. The cheapest and most spartan accommodations on the train.

6. Fedor Ivanovich Tyutchev, Russian poet and diplomat (1803–1873). Tyutchev lived twenty-two years in Western Europe, and was known for poetry that sang the praises of his native land.

shaved off some extraordinarily luxuriant and tough growth especially for this trip, immediately announced that he had been to Russia and knew some Russian—for instance, *patzlui*[7]—and, recalling philanderings in Tsaritsyn, winked in such a manner that his fat wife sketched out in the air the outline of a backhand box on the ear. The company was getting noisy. Four employees of the same building firm were tossing each other heavyweight jokes: a middle-aged man, Schultz; a younger man, Schultz also, and two fidgety young women with big mouths and big rumps. The red-headed, rather burlesque widow in a sport skirt knew something too about Russia (the Riga[8] beaches). There was also a dark young man by the name of Schramm, with lusterless eyes and a vague velvety vileness about his person and manners, who constantly switched the conversation to this or that attractive aspect of the excursion, and who gave the first signal for rapturous appreciation; he was, as it turned out later, a special stimulator from the Bureau of Pleasantrips.

The locomotive, working rapidly with its elbows, hurried through a pine forest, then—with relief—among fields. Only dimly realizing as yet all the absurdity and horror of the situation, and perhaps attempting to persuade himself that everything was very nice, Vasili Ivanovich contrived to enjoy the fleeting gifts of the road. And indeed, how enticing it all is, what charm the world acquires when it is wound up and moving like a merry-go-round! The sun crept toward a corner of the window and suddenly spilled over the yellow bench. The badly pressed shadow of the car sped madly along the grassy bank, where flowers blended into colored streaks. A crossing: a cyclist was waiting, one foot resting on the ground. Trees appeared in groups and singly, revolving coolly and blandly, displaying the latest fashions. The blue dampness of a ravine. A memory of love, disguised as a meadow. Wispy clouds—greyhounds of heaven.

We both, Vasili Ivanovich and I, have always been impressed by the anonymity of all the parts of a landscape, so dangerous for the soul, the impossibility of ever finding out where that path you see leads—and look, what a tempting thicket! It happened that on a distant slope or in a gap in the trees there would appear and, as it were, stop for an instant, like air retained in the lungs, a spot so enchanting—a lawn, a terrace—such perfect expression of tender well-meaning beauty—that it seemed that if one could stop the train and go thither, forever, to you, my love . . . But a thousand beech trunks were already madly leaping by, whirling in a sizzling

7. A garbled version of the Russian word for *kiss*. *Tsaritsyn*: Former name for Stalingrad, now Volgograd, a city on the Volga in southwestern Russia.

8. Major seaport on the Baltic.

sun pool, and again the chance for happiness was gone.

At the stations, Vasili Ivanovich would look at the configuration of some entirely insignificant objects—a smear on the platform, a cherry stone, a cigarette butt—and would say to himself that never, never would he remember these three little things here in that particular interrelation, this pattern, which he now could see with such deathless precision; or again, looking at a group of children waiting for a train, he would try with all his might to single out at least one remarkable destiny—in the form of a violin or a crown, a propeller or a lyre[9]—and would gaze until the whole party of village schoolboys appeared as on an old photograph, now reproduced with a little white cross above the face of the last boy on the right: the hero's childhood.

But one could look out of the window only by snatches. All had been given sheet music with verses from the Bureau:

> Stop that worrying and moping,
> Take a knotted stick and rise,
> Come a-tramping in the open
> With the good, the hearty guys!
>
> Tramp your country's grass and stubble,
> With the good, the hearty guys,
> Kill the hermit and his trouble
> And to hell with doubts and sighs!
>
> In a paradise of heather
> Where the field mouse screams and dies,
> Let us march and sweat together
> With the steel-and-leather guys!

This was to be sung in chorus: Vasili Ivanovich, who not only could not sing but could not even pronounce German words clearly, took advantage of the drowning roar of mingling voices and merely opened his mouth while swaying slightly, as if he were really singing—but the leader, at a sign from the subtle Schramm, suddenly stopped the general singing and, squinting askance at Vasili Ivanovich, demanded that he sing solo. Vasili Ivanovich cleared his throat, timidly began, and after a minute of solitary torment all joined in; but he did not dare thereafter to drop out.

He had with him his favorite cucumber from the Russian store, a loaf of bread, and three eggs. When evening came, and the low crimson sun entered wholly the soiled seasick car, stunned by its own din, all were invited to hand over their provisions, in order to divide them evenly—this was particularly easy, as all except Vasili

9. Stringed instrument resembling a harp, emblematic of musical and poetic inspiration.

Ivanovich had the same things. The cucumber amused everybody, was pronounced inedible, and was thrown out of the window. In view of the insufficiency of his contribution, Vasili Ivanovich got a smaller portion of sausage.

He was made to play cards. They pulled him about, questioned him, verified whether he could show the route of the trip on a map —in a word, all busied themselves with him, at first good-naturedly, then with malevolence, which grew with the approach of night. Both girls were called Greta; the red-headed widow somehow resembled the rooster-leader; Schramm, Schultz, and the other Schultz, the post-office clerk and his wife, all gradually melted together, merged together, forming one collective, wobbly, many-handed being, from which one could not escape. It pressed upon him from all sides. But suddenly at some station all climbed out, and it was already dark, although in the west there still hung a very long, very pink cloud, and farther along the track, with a soul-piercing light, the star of a lamp trembled through the slow smoke of the engine, and crickets chirped in the dark, and from somewhere there came the odor of jasmine and hay, my love.

They spent the night in a tumble-down inn. A mature bedbug is awful, but there is a certain grace in the motions of silky silverfish.[10] The post-office clerk was separated from his wife, who was put with the widow; he was given to Vasili Ivanovich for the night. The two beds took up the whole room. Quilt on top, chamber pot below. The clerk said that somehow he did not feel sleepy, and began to talk of his Russian adventures, rather more circumstantially than in the train. He was a great bully of a man, thorough and obstinate, clad in long cotton drawers, with mother-of-pearl claws on his dirty toes, and bear's fur between fat breasts. A moth dashed about the ceiling, hobnobbing with its shadow. "In Tsaritsyn," the clerk was saying, "there are now three schools, a German, a Czech, and a Chinese one. At any rate, that is what my brother-in-law says; he went there to build tractors."

Next day, from early morning to five o'clock in the afternoon, they raised dust along a highway, which undulated from hill to hill; then they took a green road through a dense fir wood. Vasili Ivanovich, as the least burdened, was given an enormous round loaf of bread to carry under his arm. How I hate you, our daily! But still his precious, experienced eyes noted what was necessary. Against the background of fir-tree gloom a dry needle was hanging vertically on an invisible thread.

Again they piled into a train, and again the small partitionless car was empty. The other Schultz began to teach Vasili Ivanovich how to play the mandolin. There was much laughter. When they got

10. A wingless household pest.

tired of that, they thought up a capital game, which was supervised by Schramm. It consisted of the following: the women would lie down on the benches they chose, under which the men were already hidden, and when from under one of the benches there would emerge a ruddy face with ears, or a big outspread hand, with a skirt-lifting curve of the fingers (which would provoke much squealing), then it would be revealed who was paired off with whom. Three times Vasili Ivanovich lay down in filthy darkness, and three times it turned out that there was no one on the bench when he crawled out from under. He was acknowledged the loser and was forced to eat a cigarette butt.

They spent the night on straw mattresses in a barn, and early in the morning set out again on foot. Firs, ravines, foamy streams. From the heat, from the songs which one had constantly to bawl, Vasili Ivanovich became so exhausted that during the midday halt he fell asleep at once, and awoke only when they began to slap at imaginary horseflies on him. But after another hour of marching, that very happiness of which he had once half dreamt was suddenly discovered.

It was a pure, blue lake, with an unusual expression of its water. In the middle, a large cloud was reflected in its entirety. On the other side, on a hill thickly covered with verdure (and the darker the verdure, the more poetic it is), towered, arising from dactyl to dactyl,[11] an ancient black castle. Of course, there are plenty of such views in Central Europe, but just this one—in the inexpressible and unique harmoniousness of its three principal parts, in its smile, in some mysterious innocence it had, my love! my obedient one!—was something so unique, and so familiar, and so long-promised, and it so *understood* the beholder that Vasili Ivanovich even pressed his hand to his heart, as if to see whether his heart was there in order to give it away.

At some distance, Schramm, poking into the air with the leader's alpenstock, was calling the attention of the excursionists to something or other; they had settled themselves around on the grass in poses seen in amateur snapshots, while the leader sat on a stump, his behind to the lake, and was having a snack. Quietly, concealing himself in his own shadow, Vasili Ivanovich followed the shore, and came to a kind of inn. A dog still quite young greeted him; it crept on its belly; its jaws laughing, its tail fervently beating the ground. Vasili Ivanovich accompanied the dog into the house, a piebald two-storied dwelling with a winking window beneath a convex tiled eyelid; and he found the owner, a tall old man vaguely resembling a Russian war veteran, who spoke German so poorly and with such a

11. Digit or joint: segments of the castle walls. Also echoes "poetic," since a dactyl is a rhythmic unit of a poetic meter.

soft drawl that Vasili Ivanovich changed to his own tongue, but the man understood as in a dream and continued in the language of his environment, his family.

Upstairs was a room for travelers. "You know, I shall take it for the rest of my life," Vasili Ivanovich is reported to have said as soon as he had entered it. The room itself had nothing remarkable about it. On the contrary, it was a most ordinary room, with a red floor, daisies daubed on the white walls, and a small mirror half filled with the yellow infusion of the reflected flowers—but from the window one could clearly see the lake with its cloud and its castle, in a motionless and perfect correlation of happiness. Without reasoning, without considering, only entirely surrendering to an attraction the truth of which consisted in its own strength, a strength which he had never experienced before, Vasili Ivanovich in one radiant second realized that here in this little room with that view, beautiful to the verge of tears, life would at last be what he had always wished it to be. What exactly it would be like, what would take place here, that of course he did not know, but all around him were help, promise, and consolation—so that there could not be any doubt that he must live here. In a moment he figured out how he would manage it so as not to have to return to Berlin again, how to get the few possessions that he had—books, the blue suit, her photograph. How simple it was turning out! As my representative, he was earning enough for the modest life of a refugee Russian.

"My friends," he cried, having run down again to the meadow by the shore, "my friends, good-by. I shall remain for good in that house over there. We can't travel together any longer. I shall go no farther. I am not going anywhere. Good-by!"

"How is that?" said the leader in a queer voice, after a short pause, during which the smile on the lips of Vasili Ivanovich slowly faded, while the people who had been sitting on the grass half rose and stared at him with stony eyes.

"But why?" he faltered. "It is here that . . ."

"Silence!" the post-office clerk suddenly bellowed with extraordinary force. "Come to your senses, you drunken swine!"

"Wait a moment, gentlemen," said the leader, and, having passed his tongue over his lips, he turned to Vasili Ivanovich.

"You probably have been drinking," he said quietly. "Or have gone out of your mind. You are taking a pleasure trip with us. Tomorrow, according to the appointed itinerary—look at your ticket—we are all returning to Berlin. There can be no question of anyone—in this case you—refusing to continue this communal journey. We were singing today a certain song—try and remember what it said. That's enough now! Come, children, we are going on."

"There will be beer at Ewald," said Schramm in a caressing voice. "Five hours by train. Hikes. A hunting lodge. Coal mines. Lots of interesting things."

"I shall complain," wailed Vasili Ivanovich. "Give me back my bag. I have the right to remain where I want. Oh, but this is nothing less than an invitation to a beheading"[12]—he told me he cried when they seized him by the arms.

"If necessary we shall carry you," said the leader grimly, "but that is not likely to be pleasant. I am responsible for each of you, and shall bring back each of you, alive or dead."

Swept along a forest road as in a hideous fairy tale, squeezed, twisted, Vasili Ivanovich could not even turn around, and only felt how the radiance behind his back receded, fractured by trees, and then it was no longer there, and all around the dark firs fretted but could not interfere. As soon as everyone had got into the car and the train had pulled off, they began to beat him—they beat him a long time, and with a good deal of inventiveness. It occurred to them, among other things, to use a corkscrew on his palms; then on his feet. The post-office clerk, who had been to Russia, fashioned a knout[13] out of a stick and a belt, and began to use it with devilish dexterity. Atta boy! The other men relied more on their iron heels, whereas the women were satisfied to pinch and slap. All had a wonderful time.

After returning to Berlin, he called on me, was much changed, sat down quietly, putting his hands on his knees, told his story; kept on repeating that he must resign his position, begged me to let him go, insisted that he could not continue, that he had not the strength to belong to mankind any longer. Of course, I let him go.[14]

Marienbad, 1937

12. *Invitation to a Beheading*, title of a book by Nabokov first published in 1938.

13. A leather whip used to flog criminals in Russia.

14. In an interview, Nabokov later added this comment about Vasili: "He will never find it again. If I let him go, it is in the hope that he might find a less dangerous job than that of my agent."

JEAN-PAUL SARTRE
(born 1905)

No Exit (Huis Clos) *

A Play in One Act

Characters in the Play

VALET ESTELLE
GARCIN INEZ

Huis Clos (No Exit) was presented for the first time at the Théâtre du Vieux-Colombier, Paris, in May 1944.

SCENE—*A drawing-room in Second Empire style. A massive bronze ornament stands on the mantelpiece.*

GARCIN. [*Enters accompanied by the* ROOM-VALET, *and glances around him*] Hm! So here we are?

VALET. Yes, Mr. Garcin.

GARCIN. And this is what it looks like?

VALET. Yes.

GARCIN. Second Empire furniture, I observe. . . . Well, well, I dare say one gets used to it in time.

VALET. Some do. Some don't.

GARCIN. Are all the other rooms like this one?

VALET. How could they be? We cater for all sorts: Chinamen and Indians, for instance. What use would they have for a Second Empire chair?

GARCIN. And what use do you suppose *I* have for one? Do you know who I was? . . . Oh, well, it's no great matter. And, to tell the truth, I had quite a habit of living among furniture that I didn't relish, and in false positions. I'd even come to like it. A false position in a Louis-Philippe dining-room—you know the style?—well, that had its points, you know. Bogus in bogus, so to speak.

VALET. And you'll find that living in a Second Empire drawing-room has its points.

GARCIN. Really? . . . Yes, yes, I dare say. . . . [*He takes another look around.*] Still, I certainly didn't expect—this! You know what they tell us down there?

VALET. What about?

GARCIN. About [*Makes a sweeping gesture*] this—er—residence.

VALET. Really, sir, how could you belive such cock-and-bull stories? Told by people who'd never set foot here. For, of course, if they had—

* 1945. Reprinted from *No Exit and The Flies* by Jean-Paul Sartre, translated by Stuart Gilbert, by permission of Alfred A. Knopf. The punctuation ". . ." does not indicate omissions from this text.

GARCIN. Quite so. [*Both laugh. Abruptly the laugh dies from* GARCIN'S *face.*] But, I say, where are the instruments of torture?

VALET. The what?

GARCIN. The racks and red-hot pincers and all the other paraphernalia?

VALET. Ah, you must have your little joke, sir!

GARCIN. My little joke? Oh, I see. No, I wasn't joking. [*A short silence. He strolls around the room.*] No mirrors, I notice. No windows. Only to be expected. And nothing breakable. [*Bursts out angrily.*] But, damn it all, they might have left me my toothbrush!

VALET. That's good! So you haven't yet got over your—what-do-you-call-it?—sense of human dignity? Excuse me smiling.

GARCIN. [*Thumping ragefully the arm of an armchair*] I'll ask you to be more polite. I quite realize the position I'm in, but I won't tolerate . . .

VALET. Sorry, sir. No offense meant. But all our guests ask me the same questions. Silly questions, if you'll pardon me saying so. Where's the torture-chamber? That's the first thing they ask, all of them. They don't bother their heads about the bathroom requisites, that I can assure you. But after a bit, when they've got their nerve back, they start in about their toothbrushes and whatnot. Good heavens, Mr. Garcin, can't you use your brains? What, I ask you, would be the point of brushing your teeth?

GARCIN. [*More calmly*] Yes, of course you're right. [*He looks around again.*] And why should one want to see oneself in a looking-glass? But that bronze contraption on the mantelpiece, that's another story. I suppose there will be times when I stare my eyes out at it. Stare my eyes out—see what I mean? . . . All right, let's put our cards on the table. I assure you I'm quite conscious of my position. Shall I tell you what it feels like? A man's drowning, choking, sinking by inches, till only his eyes are just above water. And what does he see? A bronze atrocity by—what's the fellow's name?—Barbedienne. A collector's piece. As in a nightmare. That's their idea, isn't it? . . . No, I suppose you're under orders not to answer questions; and I won't insist. But don't forget, my man, I've a good notion of what's coming to me, so don't you boast you've caught me off my guard. I'm facing the situation, facing it. [*He starts pacing the room again.*] So that's that; no toothbrush. And no bed, either. One never sleeps, I take it?

VALET. That's so.

GARCIN. Just as I expected. *Why* should one sleep? A sort of drowsiness steals on you, tickles you behind the ears, and you feel your eyes closing—but why sleep? You lie down on the sofa and—in a flash, sleep flies away. Miles and miles away. So you rub your eyes, get up, and it starts all over again.

VALET. Romantic, that's what you are.

GARCIN. Will you keep quiet, please! . . . I won't make a scene, I shan't be sorry for myself, I'll face the situation, as I said just now. Face it fairly and squarely. I won't have it springing at me from behind, before I've time to size it up. And you call that being "romantic"! . . . So it comes to this; one doesn't need rest. Why bother about sleep if one isn't sleepy? That stands to reason, doesn't it? Wait a minute, there's a snag somewhere; something disagreeable. Why, now, should it be disagreeable? . . . Ah, I see; it's life without a break.

VALET. What do you mean by that?

GARCIN. What do I mean? [*Eyes the* VALET *suspiciously.*] I thought as much. That's why there's something so beastly, so damn bad-mannered, in the way you stare at me. They're paralyzed.

VALET. What are you talking about?

GARCIN. Your eyelids. We move ours up and down. Blinking, we call it. It's like a small black shutter that clicks down and makes a break. Everything goes black; one's eyes are moistened. You can't imagine how restful, refreshing, it is. Four thousand little rests per hour. Four thousand little respites—just think! . . . So that's the idea. I'm to live without eyelids. Don't act the fool, you know what I mean. No eyelids, no sleep; it follows, doesn't it? I shall never sleep again. But then—how shall I endure my own company? Try to understand. You see, I'm fond of teasing, it's a second nature with me—and I'm used to teasing myself. Plaguing myself, if you prefer; I don't tease nicely. But I can't go on doing that without a break. Down there I had my nights. I slept. I always had good nights. By way of compensation, I suppose. And happy little dreams. There was a green field. Just an ordinary field. I used to stroll in it. . . . Is it daytime now?

VALET. Can't you see? The lights are on.

GARCIN. Ah yes, I've got it. It's *your* daytime. And outside?

VALET. Outside?

GARCIN. Damn it, you know what I mean. Beyond that wall.

VALET. There's a passage.

GARCIN. And at the end of the passage?

VALET. There's more rooms, more passages, and stairs.

GARCIN. And what lies beyond them?

VALET. That's all.

GARCIN. But surely you have a day off sometimes. Where do you go?

VALET. To my uncle's place. He's the head valet here. He has a room on the third floor.

GARCIN. I should have guessed as much. Where's the light-switch?

VALET. There isn't any.

GARCIN. What? Can't one turn off the light?

VALET. Oh, the management can cut off the current if they want to. But I can't remember their having done so on this floor. We have all the electricity we want.

GARCIN. So one has to live with one's eyes open all the time?

VALET. To *live*, did you say?

GARCIN. Don't let's quibble over words. With one's eyes open. Forever. Always broad daylight in my eyes—and in my head. [*Short silence.*] And suppose I took that contraption on the mantelpiece and dropped it on the lamp—wouldn't it go out?

VALET. You can't move it. It's too heavy.

GARCIN. [*Seizing the bronze ornament and trying to lift it*] You're right. It's too heavy.

[*A short silence follows.*]

VALET. Very well, sir, if you don't need me any more, I'll be off.

GARCIN. What? You're going? [*The* VALET *goes up to the door.*] Wait. [VALET *looks round.*] That's a bell, isn't it? [VALET *nods.*] And if I ring, you're bound to come?

VALET. Well, yes, that's so—in a way. But you can never be sure about that bell. There's something wrong with the wiring, and it doesn't always work. [GARCIN *goes to the bell-push and presses the button. A bell purrs outside.*]

GARCIN. It's working all right.

VALET. [*Looking surprised*] So it is. [*He, too, presses the button.*] But I shouldn't count on it too much if I were you. It's—capricious. Well, I really must go now. [GARCIN *makes a gesture to detain him.*] Yes, sir?

GARCIN. No, never mind. [*He goes to the mantelpiece and picks up a paper-knife.*] What's this?

VALET. Can't you see? An ordinary paper-knife.

GARCIN. Are there books here?

VALET. No.

GARCIN. Then what's the use of this? [VALET *shrugs his shoulders.*] Very well. You can go. [VALET *goes out.*]

[GARCIN *is by himself. He goes to the bronze ornament and strokes it reflectively. He sits down; then gets up, goes to the bell-push, and presses the button. The bell remains silent. He tries two or three times, without success. Then he tries to open the door, also without success. He calls the* VALET *several times, but gets no result. He beats the door with his fists, still calling. Suddenly he grows calm and sits down again. At the moment the door opens and* INEZ *enters, followed by the* VALET.]

VALET. Did you call sir?

GARCIN. [*On the point of answering "Yes"—but then his eyes fall on* INEZ.] No.

VALET. [*Turning to* INEZ] This is your room, madam, [INEZ *says nothing.*] If there's any information you require—? [INEZ *still keeps silent, and the* VALET *looks slightly huffed.*] Most of our guests have quite a lot to ask me. But I won't insist. Anyhow, as regards the toothbrush, and the electric bell, and that thing on the mantelshelf, this gentleman can tell you anything you want to know as well as I could. We've had a little chat, him and me. [VALET *goes out.*]

[GARCIN *refrains from looking at* INEZ, *who is inspecting the room. Abruptly she turns to* GARCIN.]

INEZ. Where's Florence? [*Garcin does not reply.*] Didn't you hear? I asked you about Florence. Where is she?

GARCIN. I haven't an idea.

INEZ. Ah, that's the way it works, is it? Torture by separation. Well, as far as I'm concerned, you won't get anywhere. Florence was a tiresome little fool, and I shan't miss her in the least.

GARCIN. I beg your pardon. Who do you suppose I am?

INEZ. You? Why, the torturer, of course.

GARCIN. [*Looks startled, then bursts out laughing*] Well, that's a good one! Too comic for words. I the torturer! So you came in, had a look at me, and thought I was—er—one of the staff. Of course, it's that silly fellow's fault; he should have introduced us. A torturer indeed! I'm Joseph Garcin, journalist and man of letters by profession. And as we're both in the same boat, so to speak, might I ask you, Mrs.—?

INEZ. [*Testily*] Not "Mrs." I'm unmarried.

GARCIN. Right. That's a start, anyway. Well, now that we've broken the ice, do you *really* think I look like a torturer? And, by the way, how does one recognize torturers when one sees them? Evidently you've ideas on the subject.

INEZ. They look frightened.

GARCIN. Frightened! But how ridiculous! Of whom should they be frightened? Of their victims?

INEZ. Laugh away, but I know what I'm talking about. I've often watched my face in the glass.

GARCIN. In the glass? [*He looks around him.*] How beastly of them! They've removed everything in the least resembling a glass. [*Short silence*] Anyhow, I can assure you I'm not frightened. Not that I take my position lightly; I realize its gravity only too well. But I'm not afraid.

INEZ. [*Shrugging her shoulders*] That's your affair. [*Silence*] Must you be here all the time, or do you take a stroll outside, now and then?

GARCIN. The door's locked.

INEZ. Oh! . . . That's too bad.

GARCIN. I can quite understand that it bores you having me here. And I, too—well, quite frankly, I'd rather be alone. I want to think things out, you know; to set my life in order, and one does that better by oneself. But I'm sure we'll manage to pull along together somehow. I'm no talker, I don't move much; in fact I'm a peaceful sort of fellow. Only, if I may venture on a suggestion, we should make a point of being extremely courteous to each other. That will ease the situation for us both.

INEZ. I'm not polite.

GARCIN. Then I must be polite for two.

[*A longish silence.* GARCIN *is sitting on a sofa, while* INEZ *paces up and down the room.*]

INEZ. [*Fixing her eyes on him*] Your mouth!

GARCIN. [*As if waking from a dream*] I beg your pardon.

INEZ. Can't you keep your mouth still? You keep twisting it about all the time. It's grotesque.

GARCIN. So sorry. I wasn't aware of it.

INEZ. That's just what I reproach you with. [GARCIN'S *mouth twitches.*] There you are! You talk about politeness, and you don't even try to control your face. Remember you're not alone; you've no right to inflict the sight of your fear on me.

GARCIN. [*Getting up and going towards her*] How about you? Aren't you afraid?

INEZ. What would be the use? There was some point in being afraid *before*; while one still had hope.

GARCIN. [*In a low voice*] There's no more hope—but it's still "before." We haven't yet begun to suffer.

INEZ. That's so. [*A short silence*] Well? What's going to happen?

GARCIN. I don't know. I'm waiting.

[*Silence again.* GARCIN *sits down and* INEZ *resumes her pacing up and down the room.* GARCIN'S *mouth twitches; after a glance at* INEZ *he buries his face in his hands. Enter* ESTELLE *with the* VALET. ESTELLE *looks at* GARCIN, *whose face is still hidden by his hands.*]

ESTELLE. [*To* GARCIN] No! Don't look up. I know what you're hiding with your hands. I know you've no face left. [GARCIN *removes his hands.*] What! [*A short pause. Then, in a tone of surprise*] But I don't know you!

GARCIN. I'm not the torturer, madam.

ESTELLE. I never thought you were. I—I thought someone was trying to play a rather nasty trick on me. [*To the* VALET] Is anyone else coming?

VALET. No, madam. No one else is coming.

ESTELLE. Oh! Then we're to stay by ourselves, the three of us, this gentleman, this lady, and myself. [*She starts laughing.*]

GARCIN. [*Angrily*] There's nothing to laugh about.

ESTELLE. [*Still laughing*] It's those sofas. They're so hideous. And just look how they've been arranged. It makes me think of New Year's Day—when I used to visit that boring old aunt of mine, Aunt Mary. Her house is full of horrors like that. . . . I suppose each of us has a sofa of his own. Is that one mine? [*To the* VALET] But you can't expect me to sit on that one. It would be too horrible for words. I'm in pale blue and it's vivid green.

INEZ. Would you prefer mine?

ESTELLE. That claret-colored one, you mean? That's very sweet of you, but really—no, I don't think it'd be so much better. What's the good of worrying, anyhow? We've got to take what comes to us, and I'll stick to the green one. [*Pauses*] The only one which might do, at a pinch, is that gentleman's. [*Another pause*]

INEZ. Did you hear, Mr. Garcin?

GARCIN. [*With a slight start*] Oh—the sofa, you mean. So sorry. [*He rises.*] Please take it, madam.

ESTELLE. Thanks. [*She takes off her coat and drops it on the sofa. A short silence.*] Well, as we're to live together, I suppose we'd better introduce ourselves. My name's Rigault. Estelle Rigault. [GARCIN *bows and is going to announce his name, but* INEZ *steps in front of him.*]

INEZ. And I'm Inez Serrano. Very pleased to meet you.

GARCIN. [*Bowing again*] Joseph Garcin.

VALET. Do you require me any longer?

ESTELLE. No, you can go. I'll ring when I want you.

[*Exit* VALET, *with polite bows to everyone.*]

INEZ. You're very pretty. I wish we'd had some flowers to welcome you with.

ESTELLE. Flowers? Yes, I loved flowers. Only they'd fade so quickly here, wouldn't they? It's so stuffy. Oh, well, the great thing is to keep as cheerful as we can, don't you agree? Of course, you, too, are—[1]

INEZ. Yes. Last week. What about you?

ESTELLE. I'm—quite recent. Yesterday. As a matter of fact, the ceremony's not quite over. [*Her tone is natural enough, but she seems to be seeing what she describes.*] The wind's blowing my sister's veil all over the place. She's trying her best to cry. Come, dear! Make another effort. That's better. Two tears, two little tears are twinkling under the black veil. Oh dear! What a sight Olga looks this morning! She's holding my sister's arm, helping her along. She's not crying, and I don't blame her; tears always mess one's face up, don't they? Olga was my bosom friend, you know.

INEZ. Did you suffer much?

ESTELLE. No. I was only half conscious, mostly.

INEZ. What was it?

ESTELLE. Pneumonia. [*In the same tone as before*] It's over now, they're leaving the cemetery. Good-by. Good-by. Quite a crowd they are. My husband's stayed at home. Prostrated with grief, poor man. [*To* INEZ] How about you?

1. The word left unuttered is "dead."

INEZ. The gas stove.

ESTELLE. And you, Mr. Garcin?

GARCIN. Twelve bullets through my chest. [ESTELLE *makes a horrified gesture.*] Sorry! I fear I'm not good company among the dead.

ESTELLE. Please, please don't use that word. It's so—so crude. In terribly bad taste, really. It doesn't mean much anyhow. Somehow I feel we've never been so much alive as now. If we've absolutely got to mention this—this state of things, I suggest we call ourselves—wait!—absentees. Have you been—been absent for long?

GARCIN. About a month.

ESTELLE. Where do you come from?

GARCIN. From Rio.

ESTELLE. I'm from Paris. Have you anyone left down there?

GARCIN. Yes, my wife. [*In the same tone as* ESTELLE *has been using*] She's waiting at the entrance of the barracks. She comes there every day. But they won't let her in. Now she's trying to peep between the bars. She doesn't yet know I'm—absent, but she suspects it. Now she's going away. She's wearing her black dress. So much the better, she won't need to change. She isn't crying, but she never did cry, anyhow. It's a bright sunny day and she's like a black shadow creeping down the empty street. Those big tragic eyes of hers—with that martyred look they always had. Oh, how she got on my nerves!

[*A short silence.* GARCIN *sits on the central sofa and buries his head in his hands.*]

INEZ. Estelle!

ESTELLE. Please, Mr. Garcin!

GARCIN. What is it?

ESTELLE. You're sitting on my sofa.

GARCIN. I beg your pardon. [*He gets up.*]

ESTELLE. You looked so—so far away. Sorry I disturbed you.

GARCIN. I was setting my life in order. [INEZ *starts laughing.*] You may laugh, but you'd do better to follow my example.

INEZ. No need. My life's in perfect order. It tidied itself up nicely of its own accord. So I needn't bother about it now.

GARCIN. Really? You imagine it's so simple as that. [*He runs his hand over his forehead.*] Whew! How hot it is here! Do you mind if—? [*He begins taking off his coat.*]

ESTELLE. How dare you! [*More gently*] No, please don't. I loathe men in their shirt sleeves.

GARCIN. [*Putting on his coat again*] All right. [*A short pause*] Of course, I used to spend my nights in the newspaper office, and it was a regular Black Hole, so we never kept our coats on. Stiflingly hot it could be. [*Short pause. In the same tone as previously*] Stiffling, that it *is*. It's night now.

ESTELLE. That's so. Olga's undressing; it must be after midnight.

How quickly the time passes, on earth!

INEZ. Yes, after midnight. They've sealed up my room. It's dark, pitch-dark, and empty.

GARCIN. They've slung their coats on the backs of the chairs and rolled up their shirt-sleeves above the elbow. The air stinks of men and cigar-smoke. [*A short silence*] I used to like living among men in their shirt-sleeves.

ESTELLE. [*Aggressively*] Well, in that case our tastes differ. That's all it proves. [*Turning to* INEZ] What about you? Do you like men in their shirt-sleeves?

INEZ. Oh, I don't care much for men any way.

ESTELLE. [*Looking at the other two with a puzzled air*] Really I can't imagine why they put us three together. It doesn't make sense.

INEZ. [*Stifling a laugh*] What's that you said?

ESTELLE. I'm looking at you two and thinking that we're going to live together. . . . It's so absurd. I expected to meet old friends, or relatives.

INEZ. Yes, a charming old friend—with a hole in the middle of his face.

ESTELLE. Yes, him too. He danced the tango so divinely. Like a professional. . . . But why, why should we of all people be put together?

GARCIN. A pure fluke, I should say. They lodge folks as they can, in the order of their coming. [*To* INEZ] Why are you laughing?

INEZ. Because you amuse me, with your "flukes." As if they left anything to chance! But I suppose you've got to reassure yourself somehow.

ESTELLE. [*Hesitantly*] I wonder, now. Don't you think we may have met each other at some time in our lives?

INEZ. Never. I shouldn't have forgotten you.

ESTELLE. Or perhaps we have friends in common. I wonder if you know the Dubois-Seymours?

INEZ. Not likely.

ESTELLE. But *everyone* went to their parties.

INEZ. What's their job?

ESTELLE. Oh, they don't do anything. But they have a lovely house in the country, and hosts of people visit them.

INEZ. I didn't. I was a post-office clerk.

ESTELLE. [*Recoiling a little*] Ah. yes. . . . Of course, in that case—[*A pause*] And you, Mr. Garcin?

GARCIN. We've never met. I always lived in Rio.

ESTELLE. Then you must be right. It's mere chance that has brought us together.

INEZ. Mere chance? Then it's by chance this room is furnished as we see it. It's an accident that the sofa on the right is a livid green, and that one on the left's wine-red. Mere chance? Well, just try to shift the sofas and you'll see the difference quick enough. And that statue on the mantelpiece, do you think it's there by accident? And what about the heat here? How about that? [*A short silence*] I tell you they've thought it all out. Down to the last detail. Nothing was left to chance. This room was all set for us.

ESTELLE. But really! Everything here's so hideous; all in angles, so uncomfortable. I always loathed angles.

INEZ. [*Shrugging her shoulders*] And do you think I lived in a Second Empire drawing-room?

ESTELLE. So it was all fixed up beforehand?

INEZ. Yes. And they've put us together deliberately.

ESTELLE. Then it's not mere chance that *you* precisely are sitting opposite *me?* But what can be the idea behind it?

INEZ. Ask me another! I only know they're waiting.

ESTELLE. I never could bear the idea of anyone's expecting something from me. It always made me want to do just the opposite.

INEZ. Well, do it. Do it if you can. You don't even know what they expect.

ESTELLE. [*Stamping her foot*] It's outrageous! So something's coming to me from you two? [*She eyes each in turn.*] Something nasty, I suppose. There are some faces that tell me everything at once. Yours don't convey anything.

GARCIN. [*Turning abruptly towards* INEZ] Look here! Why are we together? You've given us quite enough hints, you may as well come out with it.

INEZ. [*In a surprised tone*] But I know nothing, absolutely nothing about it. I'm as much in the dark as you are.

GARCIN. We've got to know. [*Ponders for a while*]

INEZ. If only each of us had the guts to tell—

GARCIN. Tell what?

INEZ. Estelle!

ESTELLE. Yes?

INEZ. What have you done? I mean, why have they sent you here?

ESTELLE. [*Quickly*] That's just it. I haven't a notion, not the foggiest. In fact, I'm wondering if there hasn't been some ghastly mistake. [*To* INEZ] Don't smile. Just think of the number of people who—who become absentees every day. There must be thousands and thousands, and probably they're sorted out by—by understrappers, you know what I mean. Stupid employees who don't know their job. So they're bound to make mistakes sometimes. . . . Do stop smiling. [*To* GARCIN] Why don't you speak? If they made a mistake in my case, they may have done the same about you. [*To* INEZ] And you, too. Anyhow, isn't it better to think we've got here by mistake?

INEZ. Is that all you have to tell us?

ESTELLE. What else should I tell? I've nothing to hide. I lost my parents when I was a kid, and I had my young brother to bring up. We were terribly poor and when an old friend of my people asked me to marry him I said yes. He was very well off, and quite nice. My brother was a very delicate child and needed all sorts of attention, so really that was the right thing for me to do, don't you agree? My husband was old enough to be my father, but for six years we had a happy married life. Then two years ago I met the man I was fated to love. We knew it the moment we set eyes on each other. He asked me to run away with him, and I refused. Then I got pneumonia and it finished me. That's the whole story. No doubt, by certain standards, I did wrong to sacrifice my youth to a man nearly three times my age. [*To* GARCIN] Do *you* think that could be called a sin?

GARCIN. Certainly not. [*A short silence*] And now, tell me, do you think it's a crime to stand by one's principles?

ESTELLE. Of course not. Surely no one could blame a man for that!

GARCIN. Wait a bit! I ran a pacifist newspaper. Then war broke out. What was I to do? Everyone was watching me, wondering: "Will he dare?" Well, I dared. I folded my arms and they shot me. Had I done anything wrong?

ESTELLE. [*Laying her hand on his arm*] Wrong? On the contrary. You were—

INEZ. [*Breaks in ironically*]—a hero! And how about your wife, Mr. Garcin?

GARCIN. That's simple. I'd rescued her from—from the gutter.

ESTELLE. [*To* INEZ] You see! You see!

INEZ. Yes, I see. [*A pause*] Look here! What's the point of play-acting, trying to throw dust in each other's eyes? We're all tarred with the same brush.

ESTELLE. [*Indignantly*] How dare you!

INEZ. Yes, we are criminals—murderers—all three of us. We're in hell, my pets; they never make mistakes, and people aren't damned for nothing.

ESTELLE. Stop! For heaven's sake—

INEZ. In hell! Damned souls—that's us, all three!

ESTELLE. Keep quiet! I forbid you to use such disgusting words.

INEZ. A damned soul—that's you, my little plaster saint. And ditto our friend there, the noble pacifist. We've had our hour of pleasure, haven't we? There have been people who burned their lives out for our sakes—and we chuckled over it. So now we have to pay the reckoning.

GARCIN. [*Raising his fist*] Will you keep your mouth shut, damn it!

INEZ. [*Confronting him fearlessly, but with a look of vast surprise*] Well, well! [A *pause*] Ah, I understand now. I know why they've put us three together.

GARCIN. I advise you to—to think twice before you say any more.

INEZ. Wait! You'll see how simple it is. Childishly simple. Obviously there aren't any physical torments—you agree, don't you? And yet we're in hell. And no one else will come here. We'll stay in this room together, the three of us, for ever and ever. . . . In short, there's someone absent here, the official torturer.

GARCIN. [*Sotto voce*] I'd noticed that.

INEZ. It's obvious what they're after—an economy of man-power—or devil-power, if you prefer. The same idea as in the cafeteria, where customers serve themselves.

ESTELLE. What ever do you mean?

INEZ. I mean that each of us will act as torturer of the two others.

[*There is a short silence while they digest this information.*]

GARCIN. [*Gently*] No, I shall never be your torturer. I wish neither of you any harm, and I've no concern with you. None at all. So the solution's easy enough, each of us stays put in his or her corner and takes no notice of the others. You here, you here, and I there. Like soldiers at our posts. Also, we mustn't speak. Not one word. That won't be difficult; each of us has plenty of material for self-communings. I think I could stay ten thousand years with only my thoughts for company.

ESTELLE. Have *I* got to keep silent, too?

GARCIN. Yes. And that way we—we'll work out our salvation. Looking into ourselves, never raising our heads. Agreed?

INEZ. Agreed.

ESTELLE. [*After some hesitation*] I agree.

GARCIN. Then—good-by.

[*He goes to his sofa and buries his head in his hands. There is a long silence; then* INEZ *begins singing to herself.*]

INEZ. [*Singing*]

What a crowd in Whitefriars Lane!
They've set trestles in a row,
With a scaffold and the knife,
And a pail of bran below.
Come, good folks, to Whitefriars Lane.
Come to see the merry show!

The headsman rose at crack of dawn,
He'd a long day's work in hand,
Chopping heads off generals,
Priests and peers and admirals,
All the highest in the land.
What a crowd in Whitefriars Lane!

See them standing in a line,
Ladies all dressed up so fine.
But their heads have got to go,
Heads and hats roll down below.
Come, good folks, to Whitefriars Lane,
Come to see the merry show!

[*Meanwhile* ESTELLE *has been plying her powder-puff and lipstick. She looks round for a mirror, fumbles in her bag, then turns towards* GARCIN.]

ESTELLE. Excuse me, have you a glass? [GARCIN *does not answer.*] Any sort of glass, a pocket-mirror will do. [GARCIN *remains silent.*] Even if you won't speak to me, you might lend me a glass.

[*His head still buried in his hands,* GARCIN *ignores her.*]

INEZ. [*Eagerly*] Don't worry. I've a glass in my bag. [*She opens her bag. Angrily*] It's gone! They must have taken it from me at the entrance.

ESTELLE. How tiresome!

[*A short silence.* ESTELLE *shuts her eyes and sways, as if about to faint.* INEZ *turns forward and holds her up.*]

INEZ. What's the matter?

ESTELLE. [*Opens her eyes and smiles*] I feel so queer. [*She pats herself.*] Don't you ever get taken that way? When I can't see myself I begin to wonder if I really and truly exist. I pat myself just to make sure, but it doesn't help much.

INEZ. You're lucky. I'm always conscious of myself—in my mind. Painfully conscious.

ESTELLE. Ah yes, in your mind. But everything that goes on in one's head is so vague, isn't it? It makes one want to sleep. [*She is silent for a while.*] I've six big mirrors in my bedroom. There they are. I can see them. But they don't see me. They're reflecting the carpet, the settee, the window—but how empty it is, a glass in which I'm absent! When I talked to people I always made sure there was one near by in which I could see myself. I watched myself talking. And somehow it kept me alert, seeing myself as the others saw me. . . . Oh dear! My lipstick! I'm sure I've put it on all crooked. No, I can't do without a looking-glass for ever and ever, I simply can't.

INEZ. Suppose I try to be your glass? Come and pay me a visit, dear. Here's a place for you on my sofa.

ESTELLE. But—[*Points to* GARCIN]

INEZ. Oh, he doesn't count.

ESTELLE. But we're going to—to hurt each other. You said it youself.

INEZ. Do I look as if I wanted to hurt you?

ESTELLE. One never can tell.

INEZ. Much more likely *you'll* hurt *me*. Still, what does it matter?

If I've got to suffer, it may as well be at your hands, your pretty hands. Sit down. Come closer. Closer. Look into my eyes. What do you see?

ESTELLE. Oh, I'm there! But so tiny I can't see myself properly.

INEZ. But *I* can. Every inch of you. Now ask me questions. I'll be as candid as any looking-glass.

[ESTELLE *seems rather embarrassed and turns to* GARCIN, *as if appealing to him for help.*]

ESTELLE. Please, Mr. Garcin. Sure our chatter isn't boring you?

[GARCIN *makes no reply.*]

INEZ. Don't worry about him. As I said, he doesn't count. We're by ourselves. . . . Ask away.

ESTELLE. Are my lips all right?

INEZ. Show! No, they're a bit smudgy.

ESTELLE. I thought as much. Luckily [*Throws a quick glance at* GARCIN] no one's seen me. I'll try again.

INEZ. That's better. No. Follow the line of your lips. Wait! I'll guide your hand. There. That's quite good.

ESTELLE. As good as when I came in?

INEZ. Far better. Crueler. Your mouth looks quite diabolical that way.

ESTELLE. Good gracious! And you say you like it! How maddening, not being able to see for myself! You're quite sure, Miss Serrano, that it's all right now?

INEZ. Won't you call me Inez?

ESTELLE. Are you sure it looks all right?

INEZ. You're lovely, Estelle.

ESTELLE. But how can I rely upon your taste? Is it the same as *my* taste? Oh, how sickening it all is, enough to drive one crazy!

INEZ. I *have* your taste, my dear, because I like you so much. Look at me. No, straight. Now smile. I'm not so ugly, either. Am I not nicer than your glass?

ESTELLE. Oh, I don't know. You scare me rather. My reflection in the glass never did that; of course, I knew it so well. Like something I had tamed. . . . I'm going to smile, and my smile will sink down into your pupils, and heaven knows what it will become.

INEZ. And why shouldn't you "tame" *me*? [*The women gaze at each other,* ESTELLE *with a sort of fearful fascination.*] Listen! I want you to call me Inez. We must be great friends.

ESTELLE. I don't make friends with women very easily.

INEZ. Not with postal clerks, you mean? Hullo, what's that—that nasty red spot at the bottom of your cheek? A pimple?

ESTELLE. A pimple? Oh, how simply foul! Where?

INEZ. There. . . . You know the way they catch larks—with a mirror? I'm your lark-mirror, my dear, and you can't escape me. . . . There isn't any pimple, not a trace of one. So what about it?

Suppose the mirror started telling lies? Or suppose I covered my eyes—as he is doing—and refused to look at you, all that loveliness of yours would be wasted on the desert air. No, don't be afraid, I can't help looking at you, I shan't turn my eyes away. And I'll be nice to you, ever so nice. Only you must be nice to me, too.

[*A short silence*]

ESTELLE. Are you really—attracted by me?

INEZ. Very much indeed.

[*Another short silence*]

ESTELLE. [*Indicating* GARCIN *by a slight movement of her head*] But I wish he'd notice me, too.

INEZ. Of course! Because he's a Man! [*To* GARCIN] You've won. [GARCIN *says nothing.*] But look at her, damn it! [*Still no reply from* GARCIN] Don't pretend. You haven't missed a word of what we've said.

GARCIN. Quite so; not a word. I stuck my fingers in my ears, but your voices thudded in my brain. Silly chatter. Now will you leave me in peace, you two? I'm not interested in you.

INEZ. Not in me, perhaps—but how about this child? Aren't you interested in her? Oh, I saw through your game; you got on your high horse just to impress her.

GARCIN. I asked you to leave me in peace. There's someone talking about me in the newspaper office and I want to listen. And, if it'll make you any happier, let me tell you that I've no use for the "child," as you call her.

ESTELLE. Thanks.

GARCIN. Oh, I didn't mean it rudely.

ESTELLE. You cad!

[*They confront each other in silence for some moments.*]

GARCIN. So's that's that. [*Pause*] You know I begged you not to speak.

ESTELLE. It's *her* fault; she started. I didn't ask anything of her and she came and offered me her—her glass.

INEZ. So you say. But all the time you were making up to him, trying every trick to catch his attention.

ESTELLE. Well, why shoudn't I?

GARCIN. You're crazy, both of you. Don't you see where this is leading us? For pity's sake, keep your mouths shut. [*Pause*] Now let's all sit down again quite quietly; we'll look at the floor and each must try to forget the others are there.

[*A longish silence.* GARCIN *sits down. The women return hesitantly to their places. Suddenly* INEZ *swings round on him.*]

INEZ. To forget about the others? How utterly absurd! I *feel* you there, in every pore. Your silence clamors in my ears. You can nail up your mouth, cut your tongue out—but you can't prevent your *being there*. Can you stop your thoughts? I hear them ticking away like a clock, tick-tock, tick-tock, and I'm certain you hear mine. It's all very well skulking on your sofa, but you're everywhere, and every sound comes to me soiled, because you've intercepted it on its way. Why, you've even stolen my face; you know it and I don't! And what about her, about Estelle? You've stolen her from me, too; if she and I were alone do you suppose she'd treat me as she does? No, take your hands from your face, I won't leave you in peace—that would suit your book too well. You'd go on sitting there, in a sort of trance, like a yogi, and even if I didn't see her I'd feel it in my bones—that she was making every sound, even the rustle of her dress, for your benefit, throwing you smiles you didn't see. . . . Well, I won't stand for that, I prefer to choose my hell; I prefer to look you in the eyes and fight it out face to face.

GARCIN. Have it your own way. I suppose we were bound to come to this; they knew what they were about, and we're easy game. If they'd put me in a room with men—men can keep their mouths shut. But it's no use wanting the impossible. [*He goes to* ESTELLE *and lightly fondles her neck.*] So I attract you, little girl? It seems you were making eyes at me?

ESTELLE. Don't touch me.

GARCIN. Why not? We might, anyhow, be natural. . . . Do you know, I used to be mad about women? And some were fond of me. So we may as well stop posing, we've nothing to lose. Why trouble about politeness, and decorum, and the rest of it? We're between ourselves. And presently we shall be naked as—as new-born babes.

ESTELLE. Oh, let me be!

GARCIN. As new-born babes. Well, I'd warned you, anyhow. I asked so little of you, nothing but peace and a little silence. I'd put my fingers in my ears. Gomez was spouting away as usual, standing in the center of the room, with all the pressmen listening. In their shirtsleeves. I tried to hear, but it wasn't too easy. Things on earth move so quickly, you know. Couldn't you have held your tongues? Now it's over, he's stopped talking, and what he thinks of me has gone back into his head. Well, we've got to see it through somehow. . . . Naked as we were born. So much the better; I want to know whom I have to deal with.

INEZ. You know already. There's nothing more to learn.

GARCIN. You're wrong. So long as each of us hasn't made a clean breast of it—why they've damned him or her—we know nothing. Nothing that counts. You, young lady, you shall begin. Why? Tell us why. If you are frank, if we bring our specters into the open, it may save us from disaster. So—out with it! Why?

ESTELLE. I tell you I haven't a notion. They wouldn't tell me why.

GARCIN. That's so. They wouldn't tell me, either. But I've a pretty good idea. . . . Perhaps you're shy of speaking first? Right. I'll lead off. [*A short silence*] I'm not a very estimable person.

INEZ. No need to tell us that. We know you were a deserter.

GARCIN. Let that be. It's only a side-issue. I'm here because I treated my wife abominably. That's all. For five years. Naturally, she's suffering still. There she is: the moment I mention her, I see her. It's Gomez who interests me, and it's she I see. Where's Gomez got to? For five years. There! They've given her back my things; she's sitting by the window, with my coat on her knees. The coat with the twelve bullet-holes. The blood's like rust; a brown ring round each hole. It's quite a museum-piece, that coat; scarred with history. And I used to wear it, fancy! . . . Now, can't you shed a tear, my love? Surely you'll squeeze one out—at last? No? You can't manage it? . . . Night after night I came home blind drunk, stinking of wine and women. She'd sat up for me, of course. But she never cried, never uttered a word of reproach. Only her eyes spoke. Big, tragic eyes. I don't regret anything. I must pay the price, but I shan't whine. . . . It's snowing in the street. Won't you cry, confound you? That woman was a born martyr, you know; a victim by vocation.

INEZ. [*Almost tenderly*] Why did you hurt her like that?

GARCIN. It was so easy. A word was enough to make her flinch. Like a sensitive-plant. But never, never a reproach. I'm fond of teasing. I watched and waited. But no, not a tear, not a protest. I'd picked her up out of the gutter, you understand. . . . Now she's stroking the coat. Her eyes are shut and she's feeling with her fingers for the bullet-holes. What are you after? What do you expect? I tell you I regret nothing. The truth is, she admired me too much. Does that mean anything to you?

INEZ. No. Nobody admired *me*.

GARCIN. So much the better. So much the better for you. I suppose all this strikes you as very vague. Well, here's something you can get your teeth into. I brought a half-caste girl to stay in our house. My wife slept upstairs; she must have heard—everything. She was an early riser and, as I and the girl stayed in bed late, she served us our morning coffee.

INEZ. You brute!

GARCIN. Yes, a brute, if you like. But a well-beloved brute. [*A far-away look comes to his eyes*] No, it's nothing. Only Gomez, and he's not talking about *me*. . . . What were you saying? Yes, a brute. Certainly. Else why should I be here? [*To* INEZ] Your turn.

INEZ. Well, I was what some people down there called "a damned bitch." Damned already. So it's no surprise, being here.

GARCIN. Is that all you have to say?

INEZ. No. There was that affair with Florence. A dead men's tale.

With three corpses to it. He to start with; then she and I. So there's no one left, I've nothing to worry about; it was a clean sweep. Only that room. I see it now and then. Empty, with the doors locked. . . . No, they've just unlocked them. "To Let." It's to let; there's a notice on the door. That's—too ridiculous.

GARCIN. Three. Three deaths, you said?

INEZ. Three.

GARCIN. One man and two women?

INEZ. Yes.

GARCIN. Well, well. [*A pause*] Did he kill himself?

INEZ. He? No, he hadn't the guts for that. Still, he'd every reason; we led him a dog's life. As a matter of fact, he was run over by a tram. A silly sort of end. . . . I was living with them; he was my cousin.

GARCIN. Was Florence fair?

INEZ. Fair? [*Glances at* ESTELLE] You know, I don't regret a thing; still, I'm not so very keen on telling you the story.

GARCIN. That's all right. . . . So you got sick of him?

INEZ. Quite gradually. All sorts of little things got on my nerves. For instance, he made a noise when he was drinking—a sort of gurgle. Trifles like that. He was rather pathetic really. Vulnerable. Why are you smiling?

GARCIN. Because I, anyhow, am *not* vulnerable.

INEZ. Don't be too sure. . . . I crept inside her skin, she saw the world through my eyes. When she left him, I had her on my hands. We shared a bed-sitting-room at the other end of the town.

GARCIN. And then?

INEZ. Then that tram did its job. I used to remind her every day: "Yes, my pet, we killed him between us." [*A pause*] I'm rather cruel, really.

GARCIN. So am I.

INEZ. No, you're not cruel. It's something else.

GARCIN. What?

INEZ. I'll tell you later. When I say I'm cruel, I mean I can't get on without making people suffer. Like a live coal. A live coal in others' hearts. When I'm alone I flicker out. For six months I flamed away in her heart, till there was nothing but a cinder. One night she got up and turned on the gas while I was asleep. Then she crept back into bed. So now you know.

GARCIN. Well! Well!

INEZ. Yes? What's in your mind?

GARCIN. Nothing. Only that it's not a pretty story.

INEZ. Obviously. But what matter?

GARCIN. As you say, what matter? [*To* ESTELLE] Your turn. What have you done?

ESTELLE. As I told you, I haven't a notion. I rack my brain, but it's no use.

GARCIN. Right. Then we'll give you a hand. That fellow with the smashed face, who was he?

ESTELLE. Who—who do you mean?

INEZ. You know quite well. The man you were so scared of seeing when you came in.

ESTELLE. Oh, him! A friend of mine.

GARCIN. Why were you afraid of him?

ESTELLE. That's my business, Mr. Garcin.

INEZ. Did he shoot himself on your account?

ESTELLE. Of course not. How absurd you are!

GARCIN. Then why should you have been so scared? He blew his brains out, didn't he? That's how his face got smashed.

ESTELLE. Don't! Please don't go on.

GARCIN. Because of you. Because of you.

INEZ. He shot himself because of you.

ESTELLE. Leave me alone! It's—it's not fair, bullying me like that. I want to go! I want to go!

[*She runs to the door and shakes it.*]

GARCIN. Go if you can. Personally, I ask for nothing better. Unfortunately, the door's locked.

[ESTELLE *presses the bell-push, but the bell does not ring.* INEZ *and* GARCIN *laugh.* ESTELLE *swings round on them, her back to the door.*]

ESTELLE. [*In a muffled voice*] You're hateful, both of you.

INEZ. Hateful? Yes, that's the word. Now get on with it. That fellow who killed himself on your account—you were his mistress, eh?

GARCIN. Of course she was. And he wanted her to have her to himself alone. That's so, isn't it?

INEZ. He danced the tango like a professional, but he was poor as a church mouse—that's right, isn't it?

[*A short silence*]

GARCIN. Was he poor or not? Give a straight answer.

ESTELLE. Yes, he was poor.

GARCIN. And then you had your reputation to keep up. One day he came and implored you to run away with him, and you laughed in his face.

INEZ. That's it. You laughed at him. And so he killed himself.

ESTELLE. Did you use to look at Florence in that way?

INEZ. Yes.

[*A short pause, then* ESTELLE *bursts out laughing.*]

ESTELLE. You've got it all wrong, you two. [*She stiffens her shoulders, still leaning against the door, and faces them. Her voice grows shrill, truculent.*] He wanted me to have a baby. So there!

GARCIN. And you didn't want one?

ESTELLE. I certainly didn't. But the baby came, worse luck. I went to Switzerland for five months. No one knew anything. It was a girl. Roger was with me when she was born. It pleased him no end, having a daughter. It didn't please *me!*

GARCIN. And then?

ESTELLE. There was a balcony overlooking the lake. I brought a big stone. He could see what I was up to and he kept on shouting: "Estelle, for God's sake, don't!" I hated him then. He saw it all. He was leaning over the balcony and he saw the rings spreading on the water—

GARCIN. Yes? And then?

ESTELLE. That's all. I came back to Paris—and he did as he wished.

GARCIN. You mean he blew his brains out?

ESTELLE. It was absurd of him, really, my husband never suspected anything. [*A pause*] Oh, how I loathe you! [*She sobs tearlessly.*]

GARCIN. Nothing doing. Tears don't flow in this place.

ESTELLE. I'm a coward. A coward! [*Pause*] If you knew how I hate you!

INEZ. [*Taking her in her arms*] Poor child! [*To* GARCIN] So the hearing's over. But there's no need to look like a hanging judge.

GARCIN. A hanging judge? [*He glances around him.*] I'd give a lot to be able to see myself in a glass. [*Pause*] How hot it is! [*Unthinkingly he takes off his coat.*] Oh, sorry! [*He starts putting it on again.*]

ESTELLE. Don't bother. You can stay in your shirt-sleeves. As things are—

GARCIN. Just so. [*He drops his coat on the sofa.*] You mustn't be angry with me, Estelle.

ESTELLE. I'm not angry with you.

INEZ. And what about me? Are you angry with me?

ESTELLE. Yes.

[*A short silence*]

INEZ. Well, Mr. Garcin, now you have us in the nude all right. Do you understand things any better for that?

GARCIN. I wonder. Yes, perhaps a trifle better. [*Timidly*] And now suppose we start trying to help each other.

INEZ. I don't need help.

GARCIN. Inez, they've laid their snare damned cunningly—like a cobweb. If you make any movement, if you raise your hand to fan yourself, Estelle and I feel a little tug. Alone, none of us can save himself or herself; we're linked together inextricably. So you can take your choice. [*A pause*] Hullo? What's happening?

INEZ. They've let it. The windows are wide open, a man is sitting on my bed. *My* bed, if you please! They've let it, let it! Step in, step in, make yourself at home, you brute! Ah, there's a woman, too. She's going up to him, putting her hands on his shoulders. . . . Damn it, why don't they turn the lights on? It's getting dark. Now he's going to kiss her. But that's my room, *my* room. Pitch-dark now. I can't see anything, but I hear them whispering, whispering. Is he going to make love to her on *my* bed? What's that she said? That it's noon and the sun is shining? I must be going blind. [*A pause*] Blacked out. I can't see or hear a thing. So I'm done with the earth, it seems. No more alibis for me! [*She shudders*] I feel so empty, desiccated—really dead at last. All of me's here in this room. [*A pause*] What were you saying? Something about helping me, wasn't it?

GARCIN. Yes.

INEZ. Helping me to do what?

GARCIN. To defeat their devilish tricks.

INEZ. And what do you expect me to do, in return?

GARCIN. To help *me*. It only needs a little effort, Inez; just a spark of human feeling.

INEZ. Human feeling. That's beyond my range. I'm rotten to the core.

GARCIN. And how about me? [*A pause*] All the same, suppose we try?

INEZ. It's no use. I'm all dried up. I can't give and I can't receive. How could *I* help you? A dead twig, ready for the burning. [*She falls silent, gazing at* ESTELLE, *who has buried her head in her hands.*] Florence was fair, a natural blonde.

GARCIN. Do you realize that this young woman's fated to be your torturer?

INEZ. Perhaps I've guessed it.

GARCIN. It's through her they'll get you. I, of course, I'm different—aloof. I take no notice of her. Suppose you had a try—

INEZ. Yes?

GARCIN. It's a trap. They're watching you, to see if you'll fall into it.

INEZ. I know. And you're another trap. Do you think they haven't foreknown every word you say? And of course there's a whole nest of pitfalls that we can't see. Everything here's a booby-trap. But what do I care? I'm a pitfall, too. For her, obviously. And perhaps I'll catch her.

GARCIN. You won't catch anything. We're chasing after each other, round and round in a vicious circle, like the horses on a roundabout. That's part of their plan, of course. . . . Drop it, Inez. Open your hands and let go of everything. Or else you'll bring disaster on all three of us.

INEZ. Do I look the sort of person who lets go? I know what's coming to me. I'm going to burn, and it's to last forever. Yes, I *know* everything. But do you think I'll let go? I'll catch her, she'll see you through my eyes, as Florence saw that other man. What's the good of trying to enlist my sympathy? I assure you I know everything, and I can't feel sorry even for myself. A trap! Don't I know it, and that I'm in a trap myself, up to the neck, and there's nothing to be done about it? And if it suits their book, so much the better!

GARCIN. [*Gripping her shoulders*] Well, *I*, anyhow, can feel sorry for you, too. Look at me, we're naked, naked right through, and I can see into your heart. That's one link between us. Do you think I'd want to hurt you? I don't regret anything, I'm dried up, too. But for you I can still feel pity.

INEZ. [*Who has let him keep his hands on her shoulders until now, shakes herself loose*] Don't. I hate being pawed about. And keep your pity for yourself. Don't forget, Garcin, that there are traps for you, too, in this room. All nicely set for you. You'd do better to watch your own interests. [*A pause.*] But, if you will leave us in peace, this child and me, I'll see I don't do you any harm.

GARCIN. [*Gazes at her for a moment, then shrugs his shoulders*] Very well.

ESTELLE. [*Raising her head*] Please, Garcin.

GARCIN. What do you want of me?

ESTELLE. [*Rises and goes up to him*] You can help *me*, anyhow.

GARCIN. If you want help, apply to her.

[INEZ *has come up and is standing behind* ESTELLE, *but without touching her. During the dialogue that follows she speaks almost in her ear. But* ESTELLE *keeps her eyes on* GARCIN, *who observes her without speaking, and she addresses her answers to him, as if it were he who is questioning her.*]

ESTELLE. I implore you, Garcin—you gave me your promise, didn't you? Help me quick. I don't want to be left alone. Olga's taken him to a cabaret.

INEZ. Taken whom?

ESTELLE. Peter. . . . Oh, now they're dancing together.

INEZ. Who's Peter?

ESTELLE. Such a silly boy. He called me his glancing stream—just fancy! He was terribly in love with me. . . . She's persuaded him to come out with her tonight.

INEZ. Do you love him?

ESTELLE. They're sitting down now. She's puffing like a grampus. What a fool the girl is to insist on dancing! But I dare say she does it to reduce. . . . No, of course I don't love him; he's only eighteen, and I'm not a baby-snatcher.

INEZ. Then why bother about them? What difference can it make?

ESTELLE. He belonged to me.

INEZ. Nothing on earth belongs to you any more.

ESTELLE. I tell you he was mine. All mine.

INEZ. Yes, he was yours—once. But now— Try to make him hear, try to touch him. Olga can touch him, talk to him as much as she likes. That's so, isn't it? She can squeeze his hands, rub herself against him—

ESTELLE. Yes, look! She's pressing her great fat chest against him, puffing and blowing in his face. But, my poor little lamb, can't you see how ridiculous she is? Why don't you laugh at her? Oh, once I'd have only had to glance at them and she'd have slunk away. Is there really nothing, nothing left of me?

INEZ. Nothing whatever. Nothing of you's left on earth—not even a shadow. All you own is here. Would you like that paper-knife? Or that ornament on the mantelpiece? That blue sofa's yours. And I, my dear, am yours forever.

ESTELLE. You mine! That's good! Well, which of you two would dare to call me his glancing stream, his crystal girl? You know too much about me, you know I'm rotten through and through. . . . Peter dear, think of me, fix your thoughts on me, and save me. All the time you're thinking "my glancing stream, my crystal girl," I'm only half here, I'm only half wicked, and half of me is down there with you, clean and bright and crystal-clear as running water. . . . Oh, just look at her face, all scarlet, like a tomato. No, it's absurd, we've laughed at her together, you and I, often and often. . . . What's that tune?—I always loved it. Yes, the *St. Louis Blues*. . . . All right, dance away, dance away. Garcin, I wish you could see her, you'd die of laughing. Only—she'll never know I see her. Yes, I see you Olga, with your hair all anyhow, and you do look a dope, my dear. Oh, now you're treading on his toes. It's a scream! Hurry up! Quicker! Quicker! He's dragging her along, bundling her round and round—it's too ghastly! He always said I was so light, he loved to dance with me. [*She is dancing as she speaks.*] I tell you, Olga, I can see you. No, she doesn't care, she's dancing through my gaze. What's that? What's that you said? "Our poor dear Estelle"? Oh, don't be such a humbug! You didn't even shed a tear at the funeral. . . . And she has the nerve to talk to him about her poor dear friend Estelle! How dare she discuss me with Peter? Now then, keep time. She never could dance and talk at once. Oh, what's that? No, no. Don't tell him. Please, please don't tell him. You can keep him, do what you like with him, but please don't tell him about—that! [*She has stopped dancing.*] All right. You can have him now. Isn't it *foul*, Garcin? She's told him everything, about Roger, my trip to Switzerland, the baby. "Poor Estelle wasn't exactly—" No, I wasn't exactly— True enough. He's looking grave, shaking his head, but he doesn't seem so very much surprised, not what one would expect. Keep him, then—I won't haggle with you over his long eyelashes, his pretty girlish face. They're yours for the asking. His glancing stream, his crystal. Well, the crystal's shattered into bits. "Poor Estelle!" Dance, dance, dance. On with it. But do keep time. One, two. One, two. How I'd love to go down to earth for just a moment, and dance with him again. [*She dances again for some moments.*] The music's growing fainter. They've turned down the lights, as they do for a tango. Why are they playing so softly? Louder, please. I can't hear. It's so far away, so far away. I—I can't hear a sound. [*She stops dancing.*] All over. It's the end. The earth has left me. [*To* GARCIN] Don't turn from me—please. Take me in your arms. [*Behind* ESTELLE'S *back,* INEZ *signs to* GARCIN *to move away.*]

INEZ. [*Commandingly*] Now then, Garcin!

[GARCIN *moves back a step, and, glancing at* ESTELLE, *points to* INEZ.]

GARCIN. It's to her you should say that.

ESTELLE. [*Clinging to him*] Don't turn away. You're a man, aren't you, and surely I'm not such a fright as all that! Everyone says I've lovely hair and, after all, a man killed himself on my account. You have to look at something, and there's nothing here to see except the sofas and that awful ornament and the table. Surely I'm better to look at than a lot of stupid furniture. Listen! I've dropped out of their hearts like a little sparrow fallen from its nest. So gather me up, dear, fold me to your heart—and you'll see how nice I can be.

GARCIN. [*Freeing himself from her, after a short struggle*] I tell you it's to that lady you should speak.

ESTELLE. To her? But she doesn't count, she's a woman.

INEZ. Oh, I don't count? Is that what you think? But, my poor little fallen nestling, you've been sheltering in my heart for ages, though you didn't realize it. Don't be afraid; I'll keep looking at you for ever and ever, without a flutter of my eyelids, and you'll live in my gaze like a mote in a sunbeam.

ESTELLE. A sunbeam indeed! Don't talk such rubbish! You've tried that trick already, and you should know it doesn't work.

INEZ. Estelle! My glancing stream! My crystal!

ESTELLE. *Your* crystal? It's grotesque. Do you think you can fool me with that sort of talk? Everyone knows by now what I did to my baby. The crystal's shattered, but I don't care. I'm just a hollow dummy, all that's left of me is the outside—but it's not for you.

INEZ. Come to me, Estelle. You shall be whatever you like: a glancing stream, a muddy stream. And deep down in my eyes you'll see yourself just as you want to be.

ESTELLE. Oh, leave me in peace. You haven't any eyes. Oh, damn it, isn't there anything I can do to get rid of you? I've an idea. [*She spits in* INEZ's *face.*] There!

INEZ. Garcin, you shall pay for this.

[*A pause,* GARCIN *shrugs his shoulders and goes to* ESTELLE.]

GARCIN. So it's a man you need?

ESTELLE. Not *any* man. You.

GARCIN. No humbug now. Any man would do your business. As I happen to be here, you want me. Right!—[*He grips her shoulders.*] Mind, I'm not your sort at all, really; I'm not a young nincompoop and I don't dance the tango.

ESTELLE. I'll take you as you are. And perhaps I shall change you.

GARCIN. I doubt it. I shan't pay much attention; I've other things to think about.

ESTELLE. What things?

GARCIN. They wouldn't interest you.

ESTELLE. I'll sit on your sofa and wait for you to take some notice of me. I promise not to bother you at all.

INEZ. [*With a shrill laugh*] That's right, fawn on him, like the silly bitch you are. Grovel and cringe! And he hasn't even good looks to commend him!

ESTELLE. [*To* GARCIN] Don't listen to her. She has no eyes, no ears. She's—nothing.

GARCIN. I'll give you what I can. It doesn't amount to much. I shan't love you; I know you too well.

ESTELLE. Do you want me, anyhow?

GARCIN. Yes.

ESTELLE. I ask no more.

GARCIN. In that case—[*He bends over her.*]

INEZ. Estelle! Garcin! You must be going crazy. You're not alone. I'm here too.

GARCIN. Of course—but what does it matter?

INEZ. Under my eyes? You couldn't—couldn't dc it.

ESTELLE. Why not? I often undressed with my maid looking on.

INEZ. [*Gripping* GARCIN's *arm*] Let her alone. Don't paw her with your dirty man's hands.

GARCIN. [*Thrusting her away roughly*] Take care. I'm no gentleman, and I'd have no compunction about striking a woman.

INEZ. But you promised me; you promised. I'm only asking you to keep your word.

GARCIN. Why should I, considering you were the first to break our agreement?

[INEZ *turns her back on him and retreats to the far end of the room.*]

INEZ. Very well, have it your own way. I'm the weaker party, one against two. But don't forget I'm here, and watching. I shan't take my eyes off you, Garcin; when you're kissing her, you'll feel them boring into you. Yes, have it your own way, make love and get it over. We're in hell; my turn will come.

[*During the following scene she watches them without speaking.*]

GARCIN. [*Coming back to* ESTELLE *and grasping her shoulders*] Now then. Your lips. Give me your lips.

[*A pause. He bends to kiss her, then abruptly straightens up.*]

ESTELLE. [*Indignantly*] Really! [*A pause*] Didn't I tell you not to pay any attention to her?

GARCIN. You've got it wrong. [*Short silence*] It's Gomez; he's back in the press-room. They've shut the windows; it must be winter down there. Six months since I—Well, I warned you I'd be absent-minded sometimes, didn't I? They're shivering, they've kept their coats on. Funny they should feel the cold like that, when I'm feeling so hot. Ah, this time he's talking about me.

ESTELLE. Is it going to last long? [*Short silence*] You might at least tell me what he's saying.

GARCIN. Nothing. Nothing worth repeating. He's a swine, that's all. [*He listens attentively.*] A god-damned bloody swine. [*He turns to* ESTELLE.] Let's come back to—to ourselves. Are you going to love me?

ESTELLE. [*Smiling*] I wonder now !

GARCIN. Will you trust me?

ESTELLE. What a quaint thing to ask! Considering you'll be under my eyes all the time, and I don't think I've much to fear from Inez, so far as you're concerned.

GARCIN. Obviously. [*A pause. He takes his hands off* ESTELLE*'s shoulders.*] I was thinking of another kind of trust. [*Listens*] Talk away, talk away, you swine. I'm not there to defend myself. [*To* ESTELLE] Estelle, you must give me your trust.

ESTELLE. Oh, what a nuisance you are! I'm giving you my mouth, my arms, my whole body—and everything could be so simple. . . . My trust! I haven't any to give, I'm afraid, and you're making me terribly embarrassed. You must have something pretty ghastly on your conscience to make such a fuss about my trusting you.

GARCIN. They shot me.

ESTELLE. I know. Because you refused to fight. Well, why shouldn't you?

GARCIN. I—I didn't exactly refuse. [*In a far-away voice*] I must say he talks well, he makes out a good case against me, but he never says what I should have done instead. Should I have gone to the general and said: "General, I decline to fight"? A mug's game; they'd have promptly locked me up. But I wanted to show my colors, my true colors, do you understand? I wasn't going to be silenced. [*To* ESTELLE] So I—I took the train. . . . They caught me at the frontier.

ESTELLE. Where were you trying to go?

GARCIN. To Mexico. I meant to launch a pacifist newspaper down there. [*A short silence*] Well, why don't you speak?

ESTELLE. What could I say? You acted quite rightly, as you didn't want to fight. [GARCIN *makes a fretful gesture.*] But, darling, how on earth can I guess what you want me to answer?

INEZ. Can't you guess? Well, *I* can. He wants you to tell him that he bolted like a lion. For "bolt" he did, and that's what's biting him.

GARCIN. "Bolted," "went away"—we won't quarrel over words.

ESTELLE. But you *had* to run away. If you'd stayed they'd have sent you to jail, wouldn't they?

GARCIN. Of course. [*A pause*] Well, Estelle, am I a coward?

ESTELLE. How can I say? Don't be so unreasonable, darling. I can't put myself in your skin. You must decide that for yourself.

GARCIN. [*Wearily*] I can't decide.

ESTELLE. Anyhow, you must remember. You must have had reasons for acting as you did.

GARCIN. I had.

ESTELLE. Well?

GARCIN. But were they the real reasons?

ESTELLE. You've a twisted mind, that's your trouble. Plaguing yourself over such trifles!

GARCIN. I'd thought it all out, and I wanted to make a stand. But was that my real motive?

INEZ. Exactly. That's the question. Was that your real motive? No doubt you argued it out with yourself, you weighed the pros and cons, you found good reasons for what you did. But fear and hatred and all the dirty little instincts one keeps dark—they're motives too. So carry on, Mr. Garcin, and try to be honest with yourself—for once.

GARCIN. Do I need you to tell me that? Day and night I paced my cell, from the window to the door, from the door to the window. I pried into my heart, I sleuthed myself like a detective. By the end of it I felt as if I'd given my whole life to introspection. But always I harked back to the one thing certain—that I had acted as I did, I'd taken that train to the frontier. But why? Why? Finally I thought: My death will settle it. If I face death courageously, I'll prove I am no coward.

INEZ. And how did you face death?

GARCIN. Miserably. Rottenly. [INEZ *laughs.*] Oh, it was only a physical lapse—that might happen to anyone; I'm not ashamed of it.

Only everything's been left in suspense, forever. [*To* ESTELLE] Come here, Estelle. Look at me. I want to feel someone looking at me while they're talking about me on earth. . . . I like green eyes.

INEZ. Green eyes! Just hark to him! And you, Estelle, do you like cowards?

ESTELLE. If you knew how little I care! Coward or hero, it's all one—provided he kisses well.

GARCIN. There they are, slumped in their chairs, sucking at their cigars. Bored they look. Half-asleep. They're thinking: "Garcin's a coward." But only vaguely, dreamily. One's got to think of something. "That chap Garcin was a coward." That's what they've decided, those dear friends of mine. In six months' time they'll be saying: "Cowardly as that skunk Garcin." You're lucky, you two; no one on earth is giving you another thought. But I—I'm long in dying.

INEZ. What about your wife, Garcin?

GARCIN. Oh, didn't I tell you? She's dead.

INEZ. Dead?

GARCIN. Yes, she died just now. About two months ago.

INEZ. Of grief?

GARCIN. What else should she die of? So all is for the best, you see; the war's over, my wife's dead, and I've carved out my place in history.

[*He gives a choking sob and passes his hand over his face.* ESTELLE *catches his arm.*]

ESTELLE. My poor darling! Look at me. Please look. Touch me. Touch me. [*She takes his hand and puts it on her neck.*] There! Keep your hand there. [GARCIN *makes a fretful movement.*] No, don't move. Why trouble what those men are thinking? They'll die off one by one. Forget them. There's only me, now.

GARCIN. But *they* won't forget *me*, not they! They'll die, but others will come after them to carry on the legend. I've left my fate in their hands.

ESTELLE. You think too much, that's your trouble.

GARCIN. What else is there to do now? I was a man of action once. . . . Oh, if only I could be with them again, for just one day—I'd fling their lie in their teeth. But I'm locked out; they're passing judgment on my life without troubling about me, and they're right, because I'm dead. Dead and done with. [*Laughs*] A back number.

[*A short pause*]

ESTELLE. [*Gently*] GARCIN.

GARCIN. Still there? Now listen! I want you to do me a service. No, don't shrink away. I know it must seem strange to you, having someone asking you for help; you're not used to that. But if you'll make the effort, if you'll only *will* it hard enough, I dare say we can really love each other. Look at it this way. A thousand of them are proclaiming I'm a coward; but what do numbers matter? If there's someone, just one person, to say quite positively I did not run away, that I'm not the sort who runs away, that I'm brave and decent and the rest of it—well, that one person's faith would save me. Will you have that faith in me? Then I shall love you and cherish you for ever. Estelle—will you?

ESTELLE. [*Laughing*] Oh, you dear silly man, do you think I could love a coward?

GARCIN. But just now you said—

ESTELLE. I was only teasing you. I like men, my dear, who're real men, with tough skin and strong hands. You haven't a coward's chin, or a coward's mouth, or a coward's voice, or a coward's hair. And it's for your mouth, your hair, your voice, I love you.

GARCIN. Do you mean this? *Really* mean it?

ESTELLE. Shall I swear it?

GARCIN. Then I snap my fingers at them all, those below and those in here. Estelle, we shall climb out of hell. [INEZ *gives a shrill laugh. He breaks off and stares at her.*] What's that?

INEZ. [*Still laughing*] But she doesn't mean a word of what she says. How can you be such a simpleton? "Estelle, am I a coward?" As if she cared a damn either way.

ESTELLE. Inez, how dare you? [*To* GARCIN] Don't listen to her. If you want me to have faith in you, you must begin by trusting me.

INEZ. That's right! That's right! Trust away! She wants a man—that far you can trust her—she wants a man's arm round her waist, a man's smell, a man's eyes glowing with desire. And that's all she wants. She'd assure you you were God Almighty if she thought it would give you pleasure.

GARCIN. Estelle, is this true? Answer me. Is it true?

ESTELLE. What do you expect me to say? Don't you realize how maddening it is to have to answer questions one can't make head or tail of? [*She stamps her foot.*] You do make things difficult. . . . Anyhow, I'd love you just the same, even if you were a coward. Isn't that enough?

[*A short pause*]

GARCIN. [*To the two women*] You disgust me, both of you. [*He goes towards the door.*]

ESTELLE. What are you up to?

GARCIN. I'm going.

INEZ. [*Quickly*] You won't get far. The door is locked.

GARCIN. I'll make them open it. [*He presses the bell-push. The bell does not ring.*]

ESTELLE. Please! Please!

INEZ. [*To* ESTELLE] Don't worry, my pet. The bell doesn't work.

GARCIN. I tell you they shall open. [*Drums on the door*] I can't endure it any longer, I'm through with you both. [ESTELLE *runs to him; he pushes her away.*] Go away. You're even fouler than she. I won't let myself get bogged in your eyes. You're soft and slimy. Ugh! [*Bangs on the door again*] Like an octopus. Like a quagmire.

ESTELLE. I beg you, oh, I beg you not to leave me. I'll promise not to speak again, I won't trouble you in any way—but don't go. I daren't be left alone with Inez, now she's shown her claws.

GARCIN. Look after yourself. I never asked you to come here.

ESTELLE. Oh, how mean you are! Yes, it's quite true you're a coward.

INEZ. [*Going up to* ESTELLE] Well, my little sparrow fallen from the nest, I hope you're satisfied now. You spat in my face—playing up to him, of course—and we had a tiff on his account. But he's going, and a good riddance it will be. We two women will have the place to ourselves.

ESTELLE. You won't gain anything. If that door opens, I'm going, too.

INEZ. Where?

ESTELLE. I don't care where. As far from you as I can.

[GARCIN *has been drumming on the door while they talk.*]

GARCIN. Open the door! Open, blast you! I'll endure anything, your red-hot tongs and molten lead, your racks and prongs and garrotes—all your fiendish gadgets, everything that burns and flays and tears—I'll put up with any torture you impose. Anything, anything would be better than this agony of mind, this creeping pain that gnaws and fumbles and caresses one and never hurts quite enough. [*He grips the door-knob and rattles it.*] Now will you open? [*The door flies open with a jerk, and he just avoids falling.*] Ah! [*A long silence*]

INEZ. Well, Garcin? You're free to go.

GARCIN. [*Meditatively*] Now I wonder why that door opened.

INEZ. What are you waiting for? Hurry up and go.

GARCIN. I shall not go.

INEZ. And you, Estelle? [ESTELLE *does not move.* INEZ *bursts out laughing.*] So what? Which shall it be? Which of the three of us will leave? The barrier's down, why are we waiting? . . . But what a situation! It's a scream! We're—inseparables!

[ESTELLE *springs at her from behind.*]

ESTELLE. Inseparables? Garcin, come and lend a hand. Quickly. We'll push her out and slam the door on her. That'll teach her a lesson.

INEZ. [*Struggling with* ESTELLE] Estelle! I beg you, let me stay. I won't go, I won't go! Not into the passage.

GARCIN. Let go of her.

ESTELLE. You're crazy. She hates you.

GARCIN. It's because of her I'm staying here.

[ESTELLE *releases* INEZ *and stares dumbfoundedly at* GARCIN.]

INEZ. Because of me? [*Pause*] All right, shut the door. It's ten times hotter here since it opened. [GARCIN *goes to the door and shuts it.*] Because of me, you said?

GARCIN. Yes. *You*, anyhow, know what it means to be a coward.

INEZ. Yes, I know.

GARCIN. And you know what wickedness is, and shame, and fear. There were days when you peered into yourself, into the secret places of your heart, and what you saw there made you faint with horror. And then, next day, you didn't know what to make of it, you couldn't interpret the horror you had glimpsed the day before. Yes, you know what evil *costs*. And when you say I'm a coward, you know from experience what that means. Is that so?

INEZ. Yes.

GARCIN. So it's you whom I have to convince; you are of my kind. Did you suppose I meant to go? No, I couldn't leave you here, gloating over my defeat, with all those thoughts about me running in your head.

INEZ. Do you really wish to convince me?

GARCIN. That's the one and only thing I wish for now. I can't hear them any longer, you know. Probably that means they're through with me. For good and all. The curtain's down, nothing of me is left on earth—not even the name of coward. So, Inez, we're alone. Only you two remain to give a thought to me. She—she doesn't count. It's you who matter; you who hate me. If you'll have faith in me I'm saved.

INEZ. It won't be easy. Have a look at me. I'm a hard-headed woman.

GARCIN. I'll give you all the time that's needed.

INEZ. Yes, we've lots of time in hand. *All* time.

GARCIN. [*Putting his hands on her shoulders*] Listen! Each man has an aim in life, a leading motive; that's so, isn't it? Well, I didn't give a damn for wealth, or for love. I aimed at being a real man. A tough, as they say. I staked everything on the same horse. . . . Can one possibly be a coward when one's deliberately courted danger at every turn? And can one judge a life by a single action?

INEZ. Why not? For thirty years you dreamt you were a hero, and condoned a thousand petty lapses—because a hero, of course, can do no wrong. An easy method, obviously. Then a day came when you were up against it, the red light of real danger—and you took the train to Mexico.

GARCIN. I "dreamt," you say. It was no dream. When I chose the hardest path, I made my choice deliberately. A man is what he wills himself to be.

INEZ. Prove it. Prove it was no dream. It's what one does, and nothing else, that shows the stuff one's made of.

GARCIN. I died too soon. I wasn't allowed time to—to do my deeds.

INEZ. One always dies too soon—or too late. And yet one's whole life is complete at that moment, with a line drawn neatly under it, ready for the summing up. You are—your life, and nothing else.

GARCIN. What a poisonous woman you are! With an answer for everything.

INEZ. Now then! Don't lose heart. It shouldn't be so hard, convincing me. Pull yourself together, man, rake up some arguments. [GARCIN *shrugs his shoulders.*] Ah, wasn't I right when I said you were vulnerable? Now you're going to pay the price, and what a price! You're a coward, Garcin, because I wish it. I wish it—do you hear? —I wish it. And yet, just look at me, see how weak I am, a mere breath on the air, a gaze observing you, a formless thought that thinks you. [*He walks towards her, opening his hands.*] Ah, they're open now, those big hands, those coarse, man's hands! But what do you hope to do? You can't throttle thoughts with hands. So you've no choice, you must convince me, and you're at my mercy.

ESTELLE. Garcin!

GARCIN. What?

ESTELLE. Revenge yourself.

GARCIN. How?

ESTELLE. Kiss me, darling—then you'll hear her squeal.

GARCIN. That's true, Inez. I'm at your mercy, but you're at mine as well. [*He bends over* ESTELLE. INEZ *gives a little cry.*]

INEZ. Oh, you coward, you weakling, running to women to console you!

ESTELLE. That's right, Inez. Squeal away.

INEZ. What a lovely pair you make! If you could see his big paw splayed out on your back, rucking up your skin and creasing the silk. Be careful, though! He's perspiring, his hand will leave a blue stain on your dress.

ESTELLE. Squeal away, Inez, squeal away! . . . Hug me tight, darling; tighter still—that'll finish her off, and a good thing too!

INEZ. Yes, Garcin, she's right. Carry on with it, press her to you till you feel your bodies melting into each other; a lump of warm, throbbing flesh. . . . Love's a grand solace, isn't it, my friend? Deep and dark as sleep. But I'll see you don't sleep.

[GARCIN *makes a slight movement.*]

ESTELLE. Don't listen to her. Press your lips to my mouth. Oh, I'm yours, yours, yours.

INEZ. Well, what are you waiting for? Do as you're told. What a lovely scene: coward Garcin holding baby-killer Estelle in his manly arms! Make your stakes, everyone. Will coward Garcin kiss the lady, or won't he dare? What's the betting? I'm watching you, everybody's watching, I'm a crowd all by myself. Do you hear the crowd? Do you hear them muttering, Garcin? Mumbling and muttering. "Coward! Coward! Coward! Coward!"—that's what they're saying. . . . It's no use trying to escape, I'll never let you go. What do you hope to get from her silly lips? Forgetfulness? But I shan't forget you, not I! "It's I you must convince." So come to me. I'm waiting. Come along, now. . . . Look how obedient he is, like a well-trained dog who comes when his mistress calls. You can't hold him, and you never will.

GARCIN. Will night never come?

INEZ. Never.

GARCIN. You will always see me?

INEZ. Always.

[GARCIN *moves away from* ESTELLE *and takes some steps across the room. He goes to the bronze ornament.*]

GARCIN. This bronze. [*Strokes it thoughtfully*] Yes, now's the moment; I'm looking at this thing on the mantelpiece, and I understand that I'm in hell. I tell you, everything's been thought out beforehand. They knew I'd stand at the fireplace stroking this thing of bronze, with all those eyes intent on me. Devouring me. [*He swings round abruptly.*] What? Only two of you? I thought there were more; many more. [*Laughs*] So this is hell. I'd never have believed it. You remember all we were told about the torture-chambers, the fire and brimstone, the "burning marl."[2] Old wives' tales! There's no need for red-hot pokers. Hell is—other people!

ESTELLE. My darling! Please—

GARCIN. [*Thrusting her away*] No, let me be. She is between us. I cannot love you when she's watching.

ESTELLE. Right! In that case, I'll stop her watching. [*She picks up the paper-knife from the table, rushes at* INEZ, *and stabs her several times.*]

INEZ. [*Struggling and laughing*] But, you crazy creature, what do you think you're doing? You know quite well I'm dead.

ESTELLE. Dead?

[*She drops the knife. A pause.* INEZ *picks up the knife and jabs herself with it regretfully.*]

INEZ. Dead! Dead! Dead! Knives, poison, ropes—all useless. It has happened already, do you understand? Once and for all. So here we are, forever. [*Laughs*]

ESTELLE. [*With a peal of laughter*] Forever. My God, how funny! Forever.

2. earth.

GARCIN. [*Looks at the two women, and joins in the laughter*] For ever, and ever, and ever.

[*They slump onto their respective sofas. A long silence. Their laughter dies away and they gaze at each other.*]

GARCIN. Well, well, let's get on with it. . . .

CURTAIN

RICHARD WRIGHT
(1908–1960)

Big Boy Leaves Home*

I

Yo mama don wear no drawers . . .

Clearly, the voice rose out of the woods, and died away. Like an echo another voice caught it up:

Ah seena when she pulled em off . . .

Another, shrill, cracking, adolescent:

N she washed 'em in alcohol . . .

Then a quartet of voices, blending in harmony, floated high above the tree tops:

N she hung 'em out in the hall . . .

Laughing easily, four black boys came out of the woods into cleared pasture. They walked lollingly in bare feet, beating tangled vines and bushes with long sticks.

"Ah wished Ah knowed some mo lines t tha song."

"Me too."

"Yeah, when yuh gits t where she hangs em out in the hall yuh has t stop."

"Shucks, whut goes wid *hall*?"

"*Call.*"

"*Fall.*"

"*Wall.*"

"*Quall.*"

They threw themselves on the grass, laughing.

"Big Boy?"

"Huh?"

"Yuh know one thing?"

"Whut?"

"Yuh sho is crazy!"

"Crazy?"

"Yeah, yuh crazys a bed-bug!"

* Published in 1936.

"Crazy bout whut?"

"Man, whoever hearda *quall?*"

"Yuh said yuh wanted something to go wid *hall*, didn't yuh?"

"Yeah, but whuts a *quall?*"

"Nigger, a *qualls* a *quall*."

They laughed easily, catching and pulling long green blades of grass with their toes.

"Waal, ef a *qualls* a *quall*, whut IS a *quall?*"

"Oh, Ah know."

"Whut?"

"Tha ol song goes something like this:

Yo mama don wear no drawers,
Ah seena when she pulled em off,
N she washed em in alcohol,
N she hung em out in the hall,
N then she put em back on her QUALL!"

They laughed again. Their shoulders were flat to the earth, their knees propped up, and their faces square to the sun.

"Big Boy, yuhs CRAZY!"

"Don ax me nothin else."

"Nigger, yuhs CRAZY!"

They fell silent, smiling, dropping the lids of their eyes softly against the sunlight.

"Man, don the groun feel warm?"

"Jus lika bed."

"Jeeesus, Ah could stay here ferever."

"Me too."

"Ah kin feel tha ol sun goin all thu me."

"Feels like mah bones is warm."

In the distance a train whistled mournfully.

"There goes number fo!"

"Hittin on all six!"

"Highballin it down the line!"

"Boun fer up Noth, Lawd, bound fer up Noth!"

They began to chant, pounding bare heels in the grass.

Dis train bound fo Glory
Dis train, Oh Hallelujah
Dis train bound fo Glory
Dis train, Oh Hallelujah
Dis train bound fo Glory
Ef yuh ride no need for fret er worry
Dis train, Oh Hallelujah
Dis train . . .
Dis train don carry no gambler

Dis train, Oh Hallelujah
Dis train don carry no gambler
Dis train, Oh Hallelujah
Dis train don carry no gambler
No fo day creeper er midnight rambler
Dis train, Oh Hallelujah
Dis train . . .

When the song ended they burst out laughing, thinking of a train bound for Glory.

"Gee, thas a good ol song!"

"Huuuuummmmmmmman . . ."

"Whut?"

"Geeee whiiiiiiz . . ."

"Whut?"

"Somebody done let win! Das whut!"

Buck, Bobo and Lester jumped up. Big Boy stayed on the ground, feigning sleep.

"Jeeesus, tha sho stinks!"

"Big Boy!"

Big Boy feigned to snore.

"Big Boy!"

Big Boy stirred as though in sleep.

"Big Boy!"

"Hunh?"

"Yuh rotten inside!"

"Rotten?"

"Lawd, cant yuh smell it?"

"Smell whut?"

"Nigger, yuh mus gotta bad col!"

"*Smell whut?*"

"NIGGER, YUH BROKE WIN!"

Big Boy laughed and fell back on the grass, closing his eyes.

"The hen whut cackles is the hen whut laid the egg."

"We ain no hens."

"Yuh cackled, didnt yuh?"

The three moved off with noses turned up.

"C mon!"

"Where yuh-all goin?"

"T the creek fer a swim."

"Yeah, les swim."

"Naw buddy naw!" said Big Boy, slapping the air with a scornful palm.

"Aa, c mon! Don be a heel!"

"N git *lynched*? Hell naw!"

"He ain gonna see us."

"How yuh know?"

"Cause he ain."

"Yuh-all go on. Ahma stay right here," said Big Boy.

"Hell, let im stay! C mon, les go," said Buck.

The three walked off, swishing at grass and bushes with sticks. Big Boy looked lazily at their backs.

"Hey!"

Walking on, they glanced over their shoulders.

"Hey, niggers!"

"C mon!"

Big Boy grunted, picked up his stick, pulled to his feet, and stumbled off.

"Wait!"

"C mon!"

He ran, caught up with them, leaped upon their backs, bearing them to the ground.

"Quit, Big Boy!"

"Gawddam, nigger!"

"Git t hell offa me!"

Big Boy sprawled in the grass beside them, laughing and pounding his heels in the ground.

"Nigger, whut yuh think we is, hosses?"

"How come yuh awways hoppin on us?"

"Lissen, wes gonna doubt-team[1] on yuh one of these days n beat yo ol ass good."

Big Boy smiled.

"Sho nough?"

"Yeah, don yuh like it?"

"We gonna beat yuh sos yuh cant walk!"

"N dare yuh t do nothin erbout it!"

Big Boy bared his teeth.

"C mon! Try it now!"

The three circled around him.

"Say, Buck, yuh grab his feets!"

"N yuh git his head, Lester!"

"N Bobo, yuh get berhin n grab his arms!"

Keeping more than arm's length, they circled round and round Big Boy.

"C mon!" said Big Boy, feinting at one and then the other.

Round and round they circled, but could not seem to get any closer. Big Boy stopped and braced his hands on his hips.

"Is all three of yuh-all scareda me?"

"Les git im some other time," said Bobo, grinning.

"Yeah, we kin ketch yuh when yuh ain thinkin," said Lester.

1. I.e., double-team, "gang up."

"We kin trick yuh," said Buck.

They laughed and walked together.

Big Boy belched.

"Ahm hongry," he said.

"Me too."

"Ah wished Ah hada big hot pota belly-busters!"

"Cooked wid some good ol saltry ribs . . ."

"N some good ol egg cornbread . . ."

"N some buttermilk . . ."

"N some hot peach cobbler[2] swimmin in juice . . ."

"Nigger, hush!"

They began to chant, emphasizing the rhythm by cutting at grass with sticks.

Bye n bye
Ah wanna piece of pie
Pies too sweet
Ah wanna piece of meat
Meats too red
Ah wanna piece of bread
Breads too brown
Ah wanna go t town
Towns too far
Ah wanna ketch a car
Cars too fas
Ah fall n break mah ass
Ahll understan it better by n bye . . .

They climbed over a barbed-wire fence and entered a stretch of thick woods. Big Boy was whistling softly, his eyes half-closed.

"LES GIT IM!"

Buck, Lester, and Bobo whirled, grabbed Big Boy about the neck, arms, and legs, bearing him to the ground. He grunted and kicked wildly as he went back into weeds.

"Hol im tight!"

"Git his arms! Git his arms!"

"Set on his legs so he cant kick!"

Big Boy puffed heavily, trying to get loose.

"WE GOT YUH NOW, GAWDDAMMIT, WE GOT YUH NOW!"

"Thas a Gawddam lie!" said Big Boy. He kicked, twisted, and clutched for a hold on one and then the other.

"Say, yuh-all hep me hol his arms!" said Bobo.

"Aw, we got this bastard now!" said Lester.

"Thas a Gawddam lie!" said Big Boy again.

"Say, yuh-all hep me hol his arms!" called Bobo.

2. A deep-dish pie.

Big Boy managed to encircle the neck of Bobo with his left arm. He tightened his elbow scissors-like and hissed through his teeth:

"Yuh got me, ain yuh?"

"Hol im!"

"Les beat this bastard's ass!"

"Say, hep me hol his *arms*! Hes got aholda mah *neck*!" said Bobo.

Big Boy squeezed Bobo's neck and twisted his head to the ground.

"Yuh got me, ain yuh?"

"Quit, Big Boy, yuh chokin me! Yuh hurtin mah neck!" cried Bobo.

"Turn me loose!" said Big Boy.

"Ah ain't got yuh! Its the others whut got yuh!" pleaded Bobo.

"Tell them others t git t hell offa me or Ahma break yo neck," said Big Boy.

"Ssssay, yyyuh-al gggit ooooffa Bbig Boy. Hhhes got me," gurgled Bobo.

"Cant yuh hol im?"

"Nnaw, hhes ggot mmah nneck . . ."

Big Boy squeezed tighter.

"N Ahma break it too les yuh tell em t git t hell offa me!"

"Ttturn mmmeee llloose," panted Bobo, tears gushing.

"Cant yuh hol im, Bobo?" asked Buck.

"Nnaw, yuh-all tturn im lloose; hhhes got mah nnneck . . ."

"Grab his neck, Bobo . . ."

"Ah cant; yugurgur . . ."

To save Bobo, Lester and Buck got up and ran to a safe distance. Big Boy released Bobo, who staggered to his feet, slobbering and trying to stretch a crick out of his neck.

"Shucks, nigger, yuh almos broke mah neck," whimpered Bobo.

"Ahm gonna break yo ass next time," said Big Boy.

"Ef Bobo coulda hel yuh we woulda had yuh," yelled Lester.

"Ah waznt gonna let im do that," said Big Boy.

They walked together again, swishing sticks.

"Yuh see," began Big Boy, "when a ganga guys jump on yuh, all yuh gotta do is put the heat on one of them n make im tell the others t let up, see?"

"Gee, thas a good idee!"

"Yeah, thas a good idee!"

"But yuh almos broke mah neck, man," said Bobo.

"Ahma smart nigger," said Big Boy, thrusting out his chest.

II

They came to the swimming hole.

"Ah ain goin in," said Bobo.

"Done got scared?" asked Big Boy.

"Naw, Ah ain scared . . ."

"How come yuh ain goin in?"

"Yuh know ol man Harvey don erllow no niggers t swim in this hole."

"N just las year he took a shot at Bob fer swimming in here," said Lester.

"Shucks, ol man Harvey ain studyin' bout[3] us niggers," said Big Boy.

"Hes at home thinking about his jelly-roll,"[4] said Buck.

They laughed.

"Buck, yo mins lowern a snakes belly," said Lester.

"Ol man Harveys too doggone ol t think erbout jelly-roll," said Big Boy.

"Hes dried up; all the saps done lef im," said Bobo.

"C mon, les go!" said Big Boy.

Bobo pointed.

"See tha sign over yonder?"

"Yeah."

"Whut it say?"

"NO TRESPASSIN," read Lester.

"Know whut that mean?"

"Mean ain no dogs n niggers erllowed," said Buck.

"Waal, wes here now," said Big Boy. "Ef he ketched us even like this thered be trouble, so we just as waal go on in . . ."

"Ahm wid the nex one!"

"Ahll go ef anybody else goes!"

Big Boy looked carefully in all directions. Seeing nobody, he began jerking off his overalls.

"LAS ONE INS A OL DEAD DOG!"

"THAS YO MA!"

"THAS YO PA!"

"THAS BOTH YO MA N YO PA!"

They jerked off their clothes and threw them in a pile under a tree. Thirty seconds later they stood, black and naked, on the edge of the hole under a sloping embankment. Gingerly Big Boy touched the water with his foot.

"Man, this waters col," he said.

"Ahm gonna put mah cloes back on," said Bobo, withdrawing his foot.

Big Boy grabbed him about the waist.

"Like hell yuh is!"

"Git outta the way, nigger!" Bobo yelled.

"Thow im in!" said Lester.

"Duck im!"

Bobo crouched, spread his legs, and braced himself against Big

3. Paying any attention to.

4. Slang for female genitals; here, sex.

Boy's body. Locked in each other's arms, they tussled on the edge of the hole, neither able to throw the other.

"C mon, les me n yuh push em in."

"O.K."

Laughing, Lester and Buck gave the two locked bodies a running push. Big Boy and Bobo splashed, sending up silver spray in the sunlight. When Big Boy's head came up he yelled:

"Yuh bastard!"

"Tha wuz yo ma yuh pushed!" said Bobo, shaking his head to clear the water from his eyes.

They did a surface dive, came up and struck out across the creek. The muddy water foamed. They swam back, waded into shallow water, breathing heavily and blinking eyes.

"C mon in!"

"Man, the water's fine!"

Lester and Buck hesitated.

"Les wet em," Big Boy whispered to Bobo.

Before Lester and Buck could back away, they were dripping wet from handfuls of scooped water.

"Hey, quit!"

"Gawddam, nigger; tha waters col!"

"C mon in!" called Big Boy.

"We just as wall go on in now," said Buck.

"Look n see ef anybody's comin."

Kneeling, they squinted among the trees.

"Ain nobody."

"C mon, les go."

They waded in slowly, pausing each few steps to catch their breath. A desperate water battle began. Closing eyes and backing away, they shunted water into one another's faces with the flat palms of hands.

"Hey, cut it out!"

"Yeah, Ahm bout drownin!"

They came together in water up to their navels, blowing and blinking. Big Boy ducked, upsetting Bobo.

"Look out, nigger!"

"Don holler so loud!"

"Yeah, they kin hear yo ol big mouth a mile erway."

"This waters too col fer me."

"Thas cause it rained yistiddy."

They swam across and back again.

"Ah wish we hada bigger place t swim in."

"The white folks got plenty swimming pools n we ain got none."

"Ah useta swim in the ol Missippi when we lived in Vicksburg."[5]

Big Boy put his head under the water and blew his breath. A

5. City in Mississippi, near the junction of the Yazoo and Mississippi Rivers.

sound came like that of a hippopotamus.

"C mon, les be hippos."

Each went to a corner of the creek and put his mouth just below the surface and blew like a hippopotamus. Tiring, they came and sat under the embankment.

"Look like Ah gotta chill."

"Me too."

"Les stay here n dry off."

"Jeeesus, Ahm col!"

They kept still in the sun, suppressing shivers. After some of the water had dried off their bodies they began to talk through chattering teeth.

"Whut would yuh do ef ol man Harveyd come erlong right now?"

"Run like hell!"

"Man, Ahd run so fas hed thinka black streaka lightnin shot pass im."

"But spose he hada gun?"

"Aw, nigger, shut up!"

They were silent. They ran their hands over wet, trembling legs, brushing water away. Then their eyes watched the sun sparkling on the restless creek.

Far away a train whistled.

"There goes number seven!"

"Headin fer up Noth!"

"Blazin it down the line!"

"Lawd, Ahm going Noth some day."

"Me too, man."

"They say colored folks up Noth is got ekual rights."

They grew pensive. A black winged butterfly hovered at the water's edge. A bee droned. From somewhere came the sweet scent of honeysuckles. Dimly they could hear sparrows twittering in the woods. They rolled from side to side, letting sunshine dry their skins and warm their blood. They plucked blades of grass and chewed them.

"Oh!"

They looked up, their lips parting.

"Oh!"

A white woman, poised on the edge of the opposite embankment, stood directly in front of them, her hat in her hand and her hair lit by the sun.

"Its a woman!" whispered Big Boy in an underbreath. "A *white* woman!"

They stared, their hands instinctively covering their groins. Then they scrambled to their feet. The white woman backed slowly out of sight. They stood for a moment, looking at one another.

"Les git outta here!" Big Boy whispered.

"Wait till she goes erway."

"Les run, they'll ketch us here naked like this!"

"Mabbe theres a man wid her."

"C mon, les git our cloes," said Big Boy.

They waited a moment longer, listening.

"What t hell! Ahma git mah cloes," said Big Boy.

Grabbing at short tufts of grass, he climbed the embankment.

"Don run out there now!"

"C mon back, fool!"

Bobo hesitated. He looked at Big Boy, and then at Buck and Lester.

"Ahm goin wid Big Boy n git mah cloes," he said.

"Don run out there naked like tha, fool!" said Buck. "Yuh don know whos out there!"

Big Boy was climing over the edge of the embankment.

"C mon," he whispered.

Bobo climed after. Twenty-five feet away the woman stood. She had one hand over her mouth. Hanging by fingers, Buck and Lester peeped over the edge.

"C mon back; that womans scared," said Lester.

Big Boy stopped, puzzled. He looked at the woman. He looked at the bundle of clothes. Then he looked at Buck and Lester.

"C mon, les git our cloes!"

He made a step.

"Jim!" the woman screamed.

Big Boy stopped and looked around. His hands hung loosely at his side. The woman, her eyes wide, her hand over her mouth, backed away to the tree where their clothes lay in a heap.

"Big Boy, come back here n wait till shes gone!"

Bobo ran to Big Boy's side.

"Les go home! They'll ketch us here," he urged.

Big Boy's throat felt tight.

"Lady, we wanna git our cloes," he said.

Buck and Lester climbed the embankment and stood indecisively. Big Boy ran toward the tree.

"Jim!" the woman screamed. "Jim! Jim!"

Black and naked, Big Boy stopped three feet from her.

"We wanna git our cloes," he said again, his words coming mechanically.

He made a motion.

"You go away! You go away! I tell you, you go away!"

Big Boy stopped again, afraid. Bobo ran and snatched the clothes. Buck and Lester tried to grab theirs out of his hands.

"You go away! You go away! You go away!" the woman screamed.

"Les go!" said Bobo, running toward the woods.

CRACK!

Lester grunted, stiffened, and pitched forward. His forehead struck a toe of the woman's shoes.

Bobo stopped, clutching the clothes. Buck whirled. Big Boy stared at Lester, his lips moving.

"Hes gotta gun; hes gotta gun!" yelled Buck, running wildly.

CRACK!

Buck stopped at the edge of the embankment, his head jerked backward, his body arched stiffly to one side; he toppled headlong, sending up a shower of bright spray to the sunlight. The creek bubbled.

Big Boy and Bobo backed away, their eyes fastened fearfully on a white man who was running toward them. He had a rifle and wore an army officer's uniform. He ran to the woman's side and grabbed her hand.

"You hurt, Bertha, you hurt?"

She stared at him and did not answer.

The man turned quickly. His face was red. He raised the rifle and pointed it at Bobo. Bobo ran back, holding the clothes in front of his chest.

"Don shoot me, Mistah, don shoot me . . ."

Big Boy lunged for the rifle, grabbing the barrel.

"You black sonofabitch!"

Big Boy clung desperately.

"Let go, you black bastard!"

The barrel pointed skyward.

CRACK!

The white man, taller and heavier, flung Big Boy to the ground. Bobo dropped the clothes, ran up, and jumped onto the white man's back.

"You black sonsofbitches!"

The white man released the rifle, jerked Bobo to the ground, and began to batter the naked boy with his fists. Then Big Boy swung, striking the man in the mouth with the barrel. His teeth caved in, and he fell, dazed. Bobo was on his feet.

"C mon, Big Boy, les go!"

Breathing hard, the white man got up and faced Big Boy. His lips were trembling, his neck and chin wet with blood. He spoke quietly.

"Give me that gun, boy!"

Big Boy leveled the rifle and backed away.

The white man advanced.

"Boy, I say give me that gun!"

Bobo had the clothes in his arms.

"Run, Big Boy, run!"

The man came at Big Boy.

"Ahll kill yuh; Ahll kill yuh!" said Big Boy.

His finger fumbled for the trigger.

The man stopped, blinked, spat blood. His eyes were bewildered. His face whitened. Suddenly, he lunged for the rifle, his hands outstretched.

CRACK!

He fell forward on his face.

"Jim!"

Big Boy and Bobo turned in surprise to look at the woman.

"Jim!" she screamed again, and fell weakly at the foot of the tree.

Big Boy dropped the rifle, his eyes wide. He looked around. Bobo was crying and clutching the clothes.

"Big Boy, Big Boy . . ."

Big Boy looked at the rifle, started to pick it up, but didn't. He seemed at a loss. He looked at Lester, then at the white man; his eyes followed a thin stream of blood that seeped to the ground.

"Yuh done killed im," mumbled Bobo.

"Les go home!"

Naked, they turned and ran toward the wood. When they reached the barbed-wire fence they stopped.

"Les git our cloes on," said Big Boy.

They slipped quickly into overalls. Bobo held Lester's and Buck's clothes.

"Whut we gonna do wid these?"

Big Boy stared. His hands twitched.

"Leave em."

They climbed the fence and ran through the woods. Vines and leaves switched their faces. Once Bobo tripped and fell.

"C mon!" said Big Boy.

Bobo started crying, blood streaming from his scratches.

"Ahm scared!"

"C mon! Don cry! We wanna git home fo they ketches us!"

"Ahm scared!" said Bobo again, his eyes full of tears.

Big Boy grabbed his hand and dragged him along.

"C mon!"

III

They stopped when they got to the end of the woods. They could see the open road leading home, to ma and pa. But they hung back, afraid. The thick shadows cast from the trees were friendly and sheltering. But the wide glare of sun stretching out over the fields was pitiless. They crouched behind an old log.

"We gotta git home," said Big Boy.

"Theys gonna lynch us," said Bobo, half-questioningly.

Big Boy did not answer.

"Theys gonna lynch us," said Bobo again.

Big Boy shuddered.

"Hush!" he said. He did not want to think of it. He could not think of it; there was but one thought, and he clung to that one blindly. He had to get home, home to ma and pa.

Their heads jerked up. Their ears had caught the rhythmic jingle of a wagon. They fell to the ground and clung flat to the side of a log. Over the crest of the hill came the top of a hat. A white face. Then shoulders in a blue shirt. A wagon drawn by two horses pulled into full view.

Big Boy and Bobo held their breath, waiting. Their eyes followed the wagon till it was lost in dust around a bend of the road.

"We gotta git home," said Big Boy.

"Ahm scared," said Bobo.

"C mon! Les keep t the fields."

They ran till they came to the cornfields. Then they went slower, for last year's corn stubbles bruised their feet.

They came in sight of a brickyard.

"Wait a minute," gasped Big Boy.

They stopped.

"Ahm goin on t mah home n yuh better go on t yos."

Bobo's eyes grew round.

"Ahm scared!"

"Yuh better go on!"

"Lemme go wid yuh; theyll ketch me . . ."

"Ef yuh kin git home mabbe yo folks kin hep yuh t git erway."

Big Boy started off. Bobo grabbed him.

"Lemme go wid yuh!"

Big Boy shook free.

"Ef yuh stay here theys gonna lynch yuh!" he yelled, running.

After he had gone about twenty-five yards he turned and looked; Bobo was flying through the woods like the wind.

Big Boy slowed when he came to the railroad. He wondered if he ought to go through the streets or down the track. He decided on the tracks. He could dodge a train better than a mob.

He trotted along the ties, looking ahead and back. His cheek itched, and he felt it. His hand came away smeared with blood. He wiped it nervously on his overalls.

When he came to his back fence he heaved himself over. He landed among a flock of startled chickens. A bantam rooster tried to spur him. He slipped and fell in front of the kitchen steps, grunting heavily. The ground was slick with greasy dishwater.

Panting, he stumbled through the doorway.

"Lawd, Big Boy, whuts wrong wid yuh?"

His mother stood gaping in the middle of the floor. Big Boy flopped wordlessly onto a stool, almost toppling over. Pots simmered on the stove. The kitchen smelled of food cooking.

"Whuts the matter, Big Boy?"

Mutely, he looked at her. Then he burst into tears. She came and felt the scratches on his face.

"Whut happened t yuh, Big Boy? Somebody been botherin yuh?"

"They after me, Ma! They after me . . ."

"Who?"

"Ah . . . Ah . . . We . . ."

"Big Boy, whuts wrong wid yuh?"

"He killed Lester n Buck," he muttered simply.

"Killed!"

"Yessum."

"Lester n Buck!"

"Yessum, Ma!"

"How killed?"

"He shot em, Ma!"

"Lawd Gawd in Heaven, have mercy on us all! This is mo trouble, mo trouble," she moaned, wringing her hands.

"N Ah killed im, Ma . . ."

She stared, trying to understand.

"Whut happened, Big Boy?"

"We tried t git our cloes from the tree . . ."

"Whut tree?"

"We wuz swimmin, Ma. N the white woman . . ."

"*White* woman? . . ."

"Yessum. She wuz at the swimmin hole . . ."

"Lawd have mercy! Ah knowed yuh boys wuz gonna keep on till yuh got into somethin like this!"

She ran into the hall.

"Lucy!"

"Mam?"

"C mere!"

"Mam?"

"C mere, Ah say!"

"Whutcha wan, Ma? Ahm sewin."

"Chile, will yuh c mere like Ah ast yuh?"

Lucy came to the door holding an unfinished apron in her hands. When she saw Big Boy's face she looked wildly at her mother.

"Whuts the matter?"

"Wheres Pa?"

"Hes out front, Ah reckon."

"Git im, quick!"

"Whuts the matter, Ma?"

"Go git yo Pa, Ah say!"

Lucy ran out. The mother sank into a chair, holding a dish rag. Suddenly, she sat up.

"Big Boy, Ah thought yuh wuz at school?"

Big Boy looked at the floor.

"How come yuh didn't go t school?"

"We went t the woods."

She sighed.

"Ah done done al Ah kin fer yuh, Big Boy. Only Gawd kin help yuh now."

"Ma, don let em git me; don let em git me . . ."

His father came into the doorway. He stared at Big Boy, then at his wife.

"Whuts Big Boy inter now?" he asked sternly.

"Saul, Big Boys done gone n got inter trouble wid the white folks."

The old man's mouth dropped, and he looked from one to the other.

"Saul, we gotta git im erway from here."

"Open yo mouth n talk! What yuh been doin?" The old man gripped Big Boy's shoulders and peered at the scratches on his face.

"Me n Lester n Buck n Bobo wuz out on ol man Harveys place swimmin . . ."

"Saul, its a *white* woman!"

Big Boy winced. The old man compressed his lips and stared at his wife. Lucy gaped at her brother as though she had never seen him before.

"Whut happened? Cant yuh all talk?" the old man thundered, with a certain helplessness in his voice.

"We wuz swimmin," Big Boy began, "n then a white woman comes up t the hole. We got up right erway to git our cloes sos we could git erway, n she started screamin. Our cloes wuz right by the tree where she wuz standin, n when we started t git em she jus screamed. We told her we wanted our cloes . . . Yuh see, Pa, she was standin' right *by* our cloes; n when we went t git em she just screamed . . . Bobo got the cloes, n then he shot Lester . . ."

"*Who* shot Lester?"

"The white man."

"Whut white man?"

"Ah dunno, Pa. He wuz a soljer, n he had a rifle."

"A soljer?"

"Yessuh."

"A *soljer*?"

"Yessuh, Pa. A soljer."

The old man frowned.

"N then what yuh-all do?"

"Waal, Buck said, 'Hes gotta gun! N we started runnin. N then he shot Buck, ne he fell in the swimmin hole. We didn't see im no mo . . . He wuze close on us then. He looked at the white woman n then he started t shoot Bobo. Ah grabbed the gun, n we started fightin. Bobo jumped on his back. He started beatin Bobo. Then Ah hit im wid the gun. Then he started at me n Ah shot im. Then we run . . ."

"Who seen?"

"Nobody."

"Wheres Bobo?"

"He went home."

"Anybody run after yuh-all?"

"Nawsuh."

"Yuh see anybody?"

"Nawsuh. Nobody but a white man. But he didnt see us."

"How long fo yuh-all lef the swimmin hole?"

"Little while ergo."

The old man nervously brushed his hand across his eyes and walked to the door. His lips moved, but no words came.

"Saul, whut we gonna do?"

"Lucy," began the old man, "go t Brother Sanders n tell im Ah said c mere; n go t Brother Jenkins n tell im Ah said c mere; n go t Elder Peters[6] n tell im Ah said c mere. N don say nothin t nobody but whut Ah tol yuh. N when yuh git thu come straight back. Now go!"

Lucy dropped her apron across the back of a chair and ran down the steps. The mother bent over, crying and praying. The old man walked slowly over to Big Boy.

"Big Boy?"

Big Boy swallowed.

"Ahm talkin t yuh!"

"Yessuh."

"How come yuh didnt go t school this mawnin?"

"We went t the woods."

"Didnt yo ma send yuh t school?"

"Yessuh."

"How come yuh didnt go?"

"We went t the woods."

6. An Elder (deacon or trustee) in the local Baptist church, and thus an important figure in his community. Members of the congregation address each other as Brother and Sister.

"Don yuh know thas wrong?"

"Yessuh."

"How come yuh go?"

Big Boy looked at his finger, knotted them, and squirmed in his seat.

"AHM TALKIN T YUH!"

His wife straightened up and said reprovingly:

"Saul!"

The old man desisted, yanking nervously at the shoulder straps of his overalls.

"How long wuz the woman there?"

"Not long."

"Wuz she young?"

"Yessuh. Lika gal."

"Did yuh-all say anythin t her?"

"Nawsuh. We jes said we wanted our cloes."

"N what she say?"

"Nothin, Pa. She jus backed erway t the tree n screamed."

The old man stared, his lips trying to form a question.

"Big Boy, did yuh-all bother her?"

"Nawsuh, Pa. We didnt *touch* her."

"How long fo the white man come up?"

"Right erway."

"Whut he say?"

"Nothin. He jus cussed us."

Abruptly the old man left the kitchen.

"Ma, cant Ah go fo they ketches me?"

"Sauls doin whut he kin."

"Ma, Ma, Ah don want em t ketch me . . ."

"Sauls doin what he kin. Nobody but the good Lawd kin hep us now."

The old man came back with a shotgun and leaned it in a corner. Fascinatedly, Big Boy looked at it.

There was a knock at the front door.

"Liza, see whos there."

She went. They were silent, listening. They could hear her talking.

"Whos there?"

"Me."

"Who?"

"Me, Brother Sanders."

"C mon in. Sauls waitin fer yuh."

Sanders paused in the doorway, smiling.

"Yuh sent fer me, Brother Morrison?"

"Brother Sanders, wes in deep trouble here."

Sanders came all the way into the kitchen.

"Yeah?"

"Big Boy done gone n killed a white man."

Sanders stopped short, then came forward, his face thrust out, his mouth open. His lips moved several times before he could speak.

"A *white* man?"

"They gonna kill me; they gonna kill me!" Big Boy cried, running to the old man.

"Saul, cant we git im erway somewhere?"

"Here now, take it easy; take it easy," said Sanders, holding Big Boy's wrists.

"They gonna kill me; they gonna lynch me!"

Big Boy slipped to the floor. They lifted him to a stool. His mother held him closely, pressing his head to her bosom.

"Whut we gonna do?" asked Sanders.

"Ah done sent fer Brother Jenkins n Elder Peters."

Sanders leaned his shoulders against the wall. Then, as the full meaning of it came to him, he exclaimed:

"Theys gonna git a mob! . . ." His voice broke off and his eyes fell on the shotgun.

Feet came pounding on the steps. They turned toward the door. Lucy ran in crying, Jenkins followed. The old man met him in the middle of the room, taking his hand.

"Wes in bad trouble here, Brother Jenkins. Big Boy's done gone n killed a white man. Yuh-alls gotta hep me . . ."

Jenkins looked hard at Big Boy.

"Elder Peters says hes comin," said Lucy.

"When all this happen?" asked Jenkins.

"Near bout a hour ergo, now," said the old man.

"Whut we gonna do?" asked Jenkins.

"Ah wanna wait till Elder Peters come," said the old man helplessly.

"But we gotta work fas ef we gonna do anythin," said Sanders. "We'll git in trouble jus standin here like this."

Big Boy pulled away from his mother.

"Pa, lemma go now! Lemma go now!"

"Be still, Big Boy!"

"Where kin yuh go?"

"Ah could ketch a freight!"

"Thas *sho* death!" said Jenkins. "They'll be watchin em all!"

"Kin yuh-all hep me wid some money?" the old man asked.

They shook their heads.

"Saul, whut kin we do? Big Boy cant stay here."

There was another knock at the door.

The old man backed stealthily to the shotgun.

"Lucy, go!"

Lucy looked at him, hesitating.

"Ah better go," said Jenkins.

It was Elder Peters. He came in hurriedly.

"Good evenin, everybody!"

"How yuh, Elder?"

"Good evenin."

"How yuh today?"

Peters looked around the crowded kitchen.

"Whuts the matter?"

"Elder, wes in deep trouble," began the old man. "Big Boy n some mo boys . . ."

". . . Lester n Buck n Bobo . . ."

". . . wuz over on ol man Harveys place swimmin . . ."

"N he don like us niggers *none*," said Peters emphatically. He widened his legs and put his thumbs in the armholes of his vest.

". . . n some white woman . . ."

"Yeah?" said Peters, coming closer.

". . . comes erlong n the boys tries t git their cloes where they done lef em under a tree. Waal, she started screamin n all, see? Reckon she thought the boys wuz after her. Then a white man in a soljers suit shoots two of em . . ."

". . . Lester n Buck . . ."

"Huummm," said Peters. "Tha wuz old man Harveys son."

"Harveys son?"

"Yuh mean the one that wuz in the Army?"

"Yuh mean Jim?"

"Yeah," said Peters. "The papers said he wuz here fer a vacation from his regiment. N tha woman the boys saw wuz jus erbout his wife . . ."

They stared at Peters. Now that they knew what white person had been killed, their fears became definite.

"N whut else happened?"

"Big Boy shot the man . . ."

"Harveys *son*?"

"He had t, Elder. He wuz gonna shoot im ef he didnt . . ."

"Lawd!" said Peters. He looked around and put his hat back on.

"How long ergo wuz this?"

"Mighty near an hour, now. Ah reckon."

"Do the white folks know yit?"

"Don know, Elder."

"Yuh-all better git this boy outta here right now," said Peters. "Cause ef yuh don theres gonna be a lynchin . . ."

"Where kin Ah go, Elder?" Big Boy ran up to him.

They crowded around Peters. He stood with his legs wide apart, looking up at the ceiling.

"Mabbee we kin hide im in the church till he kin git erway," said Jenkins.

Peters' lips flexed.

"Naw, Brother, thall never do! Theyll git im there sho. N anyhow, ef they ketch im there itll ruin us all. We gotta git the boy outta town . . ."

Sanders went up to the old man.

"Lissen," he said in a whisper. "Mah son, Will, the one whut drives fer the Magnolia Express Comny, is takin a truck o goods t Chicawgo in the mawnin. If we kin hide Big Boy somewhere till then, we kin put him on the truck . . ."

"Pa, please, lemme go wid Will when he goes in the mawnin," Big Boy begged.

The old man stared at Sanders.

"Yuh reckon thas safe?"

"Its the only thing yuh *kin* do," said Peters.

"But where we gonna hide im till then?"

"Whut time yo boy leavin out in the mawnin?"

"At six."

They were quiet, thinking. The water kettle on the stove sang.

"Pa, Ah knows where Will passes erlong wid the truck out on Bullards Road. Ah kin hide in one of them ol kilns . . ."

"Where?"

"In one of them kilns we built . . ."

"But they'll git yuh there," wailed the mother.

"But there ain no place else fer im t go."

"Theres some holes big enough fer me t git in n stay till Will comes erlong," said Big Boy. "Please, Pa, lemme go fo they ketches me . . ."

"Let im go!"

"Please, Pa . . ."

The old man breathed heavily.

"Lucy, git his things!"

"Saul, theyll git im out there!" wailed the mother, grabbing Big Boy.

Peters pulled her away.

"Sister Morrison, ef yuh don let im go n git erway from here hes gonna be caught shos theres a Gawd in Heaven!"

Lucy came running with Big Boy's shoes and pulled them on his feet. The old man thrust a battered hat on his head. The mother went to the stove and dumped the skillet of corn pone[7] into her apron. She wrapped it, and unbuttoning Big Boy's overalls, pushed it into his bosom.

7. A kind of corn bread made without eggs, shaped into ovals and cooked on a griddle.

"Heres something fer yuh t eat; n pray, Big Boy, cause thas all anybody kin do now . . ."

Big Boy pulled to the door, his mother clinging to him.

"Let im go, Sister Morrison!"

"Run fas, Big Boy!"

Big Boy raced across the yard, scattering the chickens. He paused at the fence and hollered back:

"Tell Bobo where Ahm hidin n tell im t c mon!"

IV

He made for the railroad, running straight toward the sunset. He held his left hand tightly over his heart, holding the hot pone of corn bread there. At times he stumbled over the ties, for his shoes were tight and hurt his feet. His throat burned from thirst; he had had no water since noon.

He veered off the track and trotted over the crest of a hill, following Bullard's Road. His feet slipped and slid in the dust. He kept his eyes straight ahead, fearing every clump of shrubbery, every tree. He wished it were night. If he could only get to the kilns without meeting anyone. Suddenly a thought came to him like a blow. He recalled hearing the old folks tell tales of blood-hounds, and fear made him run slower. None of them had thought of that. Spose blood-houns wuz put on his trail? Lawd! Spose a whole pack of em, foamin n howlin, tore im t pieces? He went limp and his feet dragged. Yeah, thas whut they wuz gonna send after im, blood-houns! N then thered be no way fer im t dodge! Why hadnt Pa let im take tha shotgun? He stopped. He oughta go back n git tha shotgun. And then when the mob came he would take some with him.

In the distance he heard the approach of a train. It jarred him back to a sharp sense of danger. He ran again, his big shoes sopping up and down in the dust. He was tired and his lungs were bursting from running. He wet his lips, wanting water. As he turned from the road across a plowed field he heard the train roaring at his heels. He ran faster, gripped in terror.

He was nearly there now. He could see the black clay on the sloping hillside. Once inside a kiln he would be safe. For a little while, at least. He thought of the shotgun again. If he only had something! Someone to talk to . . . Thas right! Bobo! Bobod be wid im. Hed almost fergot Bobo. Bobod bringa gun; he knowed he would. N tergether they could kill the whole mob. Then in the mawning theyd git inter Will's truck n go far erway, t Chicawgo . . .

He slowed to a walk, looking back and ahead. A light wind skipped over the grass. A beetle lit on his cheek and he brushed it off. Behind the dark pines hung a red sun. Two bats flapped against that sun. He shivered, for he was growing cold; the sweat on his body was drying.

He stopped at the foot of the hill, trying to choose between two patches of black kilns high above him. He went to the left, for there lay the ones he, Bobo, Lester, and Buck had dug only last week. He looked around again; the landscape was bare. He climbed the embankment and stood before a row of black pits sinking four and five feet deep into the earth. He went to the largest and peered in. He stiffened when his ears caught the sound of a whir. He ran back a few steps and poised on his toes. Six foot of snake slid out of the pit and went into coil. Big Boy looked around wildly for a stick. He ran down the slope, peering into the grass. He stumbled over a tree limb. He picked it up and tested it by striking it against the ground.

Warily, he crept back up the slope, his stick poised. When about seven feet from the snake he stopped and waved the stick. The coil grew tighter, the whir sounded louder, and a flat head reared to strike. He went to the right, and the flat head followed him, the blue-black tongue darting forth; he went to the left, and the flat head followed him there too.

He stopped, teeth clenched. He had to kill this snake. Jus had t kill im! This wuz the safest pit on the hillside. He waved the stick again, looking at the snake before, thinking of a mob behind. The flat head reared higher. With stick over shoulder, he jumped in, swinging. The stick sang through the air, catching the snake on the side of the head, sweeping him out of coil. There was a brown writhing mass. Then Big Boy was upon him, pounding blows home, one on top of the other. He fought viciously, his eyes red, his teeth bared in a snarl. He beat till the snake lay still; then he stomped it with his heel, grinding its head into the dirt.

He stopped, limp, wet. The corners of his lips were white with spittle. He spat and shuddered.

Cautiously, he went to the hole and peered. He longed for a match. He imagined whole nests of them in there waiting. He put the stick into the hole and waved it around. Stooping, he peered again. It mus be awright. He looked over the hillside, his eyes coming back to the dead snake. Then he got to his knees and backed slowly into the hole.

When inside he felt there must be snakes about him, ready to strike. It seemed he could see and feel them there, waiting tensely in coil. In the dark he imagined long, white fangs ready to sink into his neck, his side, his legs. He wanted to come out, but kept still. Shucks, he told himself, ef there wuz any snakes in here they sho woulda done bit me by now. Some of his fear left, and he relaxed.

With elbows on ground and chin on palms, he settled. The clay was cold to his knees and thighs, but his bosom was kept warm by the hot pone of corn bread. His thirst returned and he longed for a drink. He was hungry, too. But he did not want to eat the corn pone. Naw, not now. Mabbe after erwhile, after Bobo came. Then theyd both eat the corn pone.

The view from his hole was fringed by the long tufts of grass. He could see all the way to Bullard's Road, and even beyond. The wind was blowing, and in the east the first touch of dusk was rising. Every now and then a bird floated past, a spot of wheeling black printed against the sky. Big Boy sighed, shifted his weight, and chewed at a blade of grass. A wasp droned. He heard number nine, far away and mournful.

The train made him remember how they had dug these kilns on long hot summer days, how they had made boilers out of big tin cans, filled them with water, fixed stoppers for steam, cemented them in holes with wet clay, and built fires under them. He recalled how they had danced and yelled when a stopper blew out of a boiler, letting out a big spout of steam and a shrill whistle. There were times when they had the whole hillside blazing and smoking. Yeah, yuh see, Big Boy wuz Casey Jones n wuz speedin it down the gleamin rails of the Southern Pacific. Bobo had number two on the Santa Fe. Buck wuz on the Illinoy Central. Lester the Nickel Plate. Lawd, how they sheveled the wood in! The boiling water would almost jar the cans loose from the clay. More and more pine-knots and dry leaves would be piled under the cans. Flames would grow so tall they would have to shield their eyes. Sweat would pour off their faces. Then, suddenly, a peg would shoot high into the air, and

Psssseeeezzzzzzzzzzzzzzzz . . .

Big Boy sighed and stretched out his arm, quenching the flames and scattering the smoke. Why didnt Bobo c mon? He looked over the fields; there was nothing but dying sunlight. His mind drifted back to the kilns. He remembered the day when Buck, jealous of his winning, had tried to smash his kiln. Yeah, that ol sonofabitch! Naw, Lawd! He didnt go t say tha! Whut wu he thinkin erbout? Cussin the dead! Yeah, po ol Buck wuz dead now. N Lester too. Yeah, it wuz awright fer Buck t smash his kiln. Sho. N he wished he hadnt socked ol Buck so hard tha day. He wuz sorry fer Buck now. N he sho wished he hadnt cussed po ol Bucks ma, neither. Tha wuz sinful! Mabbe Gawd would git im fer that? But he didnt go t do it! Po Buck! Po Lester! Hed never treat anybody like tha ergin, never . . .

Dusk was slowly deepening. Somewhere, he could not tell exactly where, a cricket took up a fitful song. The air was growing soft and heavy. He looked over the fields, longing for Bobo . . .

He shifted his body to ease the cold damp of the ground, and thought back over the day. Yeah, hed been dam right erbout not wantin t go swimmin. N ef hed followed his right mind hed neverve gone n got inter all this trouble. At first hed said naw. But shucks, somehow hed just went on wid the res. Yeah he shoulda went on t school tha mawnin, like Ma told im t do. But, hell, who wouldnt git tireda awways drivin a guy t school! Tha wuz the big trouble awways drivin a guy t school. He wouldnt be in all this trouble now if it wuznt fer that Gawddam school! Impatiently, he took the grass out of his mouth and threw it away, demolishing the little red school house . . .

Yeah, if they had all kept still n quiet when tha ol white woman showed-up, mabbe shedve went on off. But yuh never kin tell erbout these white folks. Mabbe she wouldntve went. Mabbe tha white man woulda killed all of em! All *fo* of em! Yeah, yuh never kin tell erbout white folks. Then, ergin, mabbe tha white woman woulda went on off n laffed. Yeah, mabbe tha white man woulda said: *Yuh nigger bastards git t hell outta here! Yuh know Gawdam well yuh don berlong here*! N then they woulda grabbed their cloes n run like all hell . . . He blinked the white man away. Where wuz Bobo? Why didnt he hurry up n c mon?

He jerked another blade and chewed. Yeah, ef Pa had only let im have tha shotgun! He could stan off a whole mob wid a shotgun. He looked at the ground as he turned a shotgun over in his hands. Then he leveled it at an advancing white man. *Boooom*! The man curled up. Another came. He reloaded quickly, and let him have what the other had got. He too curled up. Then another came. He got the same medicine. Then the whole mob swirled around him, and he blazed away, getting as many as he could. They closed in; but, by Gawd, he had done his part, hadnt he? N the newspapersd say; NIGGER KILLS DOZEN OF MOB BEFO LYNCHED! Er mabbe theyd say: TRAPPED NIGGER SLAYS TWENTY BEFO KILLED! He smiled a little. Tha wouldnt be so bad, would it? Blinking the newspaper away, he looked over the fields. Where wuz Bobo? Why didnt he hurry up n c mon?

He shifted, trying to get a crick out of his legs. Shucks, he wuz gettin tireda this. N it wuz almos dark now. Yeah, there wuz a little bittie star way over yonder in the eas. Mabbe tha white man wuznt dead? Mabbe they wuznt even lookin fer im? Mabbe he could go back home now? Naw, better wait erwhile. Thad be bes. But, Lawd, ef he only had some water! He could hardly swallow, his throat was so dry. Gawddam them white folks! Thas all they wuz good fer, t run a nigger down lika rabbit! Yeah, they git yuh in a corner n then they let yuh have it. A thousan of em! He shivered, for the cold of the clay was chilling his bones. Lawd, spose they found im here in this hole? N wid nobody t help im? . . . But ain no use in thinkin erbout tha; wait till trouble come fo yuh start fightin it. But if tha mob came one by one hed wipe em all out. Clean up the whole bunch. He caught one by the neck and choked him long and hard, choked him till his tongue and eyes popped out. Then he jumped upon his chest and stomped him like he had stomped that snake. When he had finished with one, another came. He choked him too. Choked till he sank slowly to the ground, gasping . . .

"Hoalo!"

Big Boy snatched his fingers from the white man's neck and looked over the fields. He saw nobody. Had someone spied him? He was sure that somebody had hollered. His heart pounded. But, shucks, nobody couldnt see im here in this hole . . . But mabbe theyd seen im when he wuz comin n had laid low n wuz now closin in on im! Praps they wuz signalin fer the others? Yeah, they wuz creepin up on im! Mabbe he oughta git up n run . . . Oh! Mabbe tha wuz Bobo! Yeah, Bobo! He oughta clim out n see if Bobo wuz lookin fer im . . . He stiffened.

"Hoalo!"

"Hoalo!"

"Wheres yuh?"

"Over here on Bullards Road!"

"C mon over!"

"Awright!"

He heard footsteps. Then voices came again, low and far away this time.

"Seen anybody?"

"Naw. Yuh?"

"Naw."

"Yuh reckon they got erway?"

"Ah dunno. Its hard t tell."

"Gawddam them sonofabitchin niggers!"

"We oughta kill ever black bastard in this country!"

"Waal, Jim got two of em, anyhow."

"But Bertha said there wuz *fo!*"

"Where in hell they hidin?"

"She said one of em wuz named Big Boy, or somethin like tha."

"We went t his shack lookin fer im."

"Yeah?"

"But we didnt fin im."

"These niggers stick together; they don never tell on each other."

"We looked all thu the shack n couldnt fin hide ner hair of im. Then we drove the ol woman n man out n set the shack on fire . . ."

"Jeesus! Ah wished Ah coulda been there!"

"Yuh shoulda heard the ol nigger woman howl . . ."

"Hoalo!"

"C mon over!"

Big Boy eased to the edge and peeped. He saw a white man with a gun slung over his shoulder running down the slope. Wuz they gonna search the hill? Lawd, there wuz no way fer im t git erway now; he wuz caught! He should knowed theyd git im here. N he didnt hava thing, notta thing t fight wid. Yeah, soon as the bloodhouns came theyd fin im. Lawd, have mercy! Theyd lynch im right here on the hill . . . Theyd git im n tie im t a stake n burn im erlive! Lawd! Nobody but the good Lawd could hep im now, nobody . . .

He heard more feet running. He nestled deeper. His chest ached. Nobody but the good Lawd could hep now. They wuz crowdn all round im n when they hada big crowd theyd close in on im. Then itd be over . . . The good Lawd would have t hep him, cause nobody could hep im now, nobody . . .

And then he went numb when he remembered Bobo. Spose Bobod come now? Hed be caught sho! Both of em would be caught! Theyd make Bobo tell where he wuz! Bobo oughta not try to come now. Somebody oughta tell im . . . But there wuz nobody; there wuz no way . . .

He eased slowly back to the opening. There was a large group of men. More were coming. Many had guns. Some had coils of rope slung over shoulders.

"Ah tell yuh they still here, somewhere . . ."

"But we looked all over!"

"What t hell! Wouldnt do t let em git erway!"

"Naw. Ef they git erway notta woman in this town would be safe."

"Say, whuts tha yuh got?"

"Er pillar."

"Fer whut?"

"Feathers, fool!"

"Chris! Thisll be hot if we kin ketch them niggers!"

"Ol Anderson said he wuz gonna bringa barrela tar!"

"Ah got some gasolin in mah car if yuh need it."

Big Boy had no feelings now. He was waiting. He did not wonder if they were coming after him. He just waited. He did not wonder about Bobo. He rested his cheek against the cold clay, waiting.

A dog barked. He stiffened. It barked again. He balled himself into a knot at the bottom of the hole, waiting. Then he heard the patter of dog feet.

"Look!"

"Whuts he got?"

"Its a snake!"

"Yeah, the dogs foun a snake!"

"Gee, its a big one!"

"Shucks, Ah wish he could fin one of them sonofabitchin niggers!"

The voices sank to low murmurs. Then he heard number twelve, its bell tolling and whistle crying as it slid along the rails. He flattened himself against the clay. Someone was singing:

We'll hang ever nigger t a sour apple tree . . .[8]

When the song ended there was hard laughter. From the other side of the hill he heard the dog barking furiously. He listened. There was more than one dog now. There were many and they were barking their throats out.

"Hush. Ah hear them dogs!"

"When theys barkin like tha theys foun somethin!"

"Here they come over the hill!"

"WE GOT IM! WE GOT IM!"

There came a roar. Tha must be Bobo; tha mus be Bobo . . . In spite of his fear, Big Boy looked. The road, and half of the hillside across the road, were covered with men. A few were at the top of the hill, stenciled against the sky. He could see dark forms moving up the slopes. They were yelling.

"By Gawd, we got im!"

"C mon!"

"Where is he?"

"Theyre bringin im over the hill!"

"Ah got a rope fer im!"

"Say, somebody go n git the others!"

"Where is he? Cant we see im, Mister?"

"They say Berthas comin, too."

"Jack! Jack! Don leave me! Ah wanna see im!"

"Theyre bringin im over the hill, sweetheart!"

"AH WANNA BE THE FIRS T PUT A ROPE ON THA BLACK BASTARDS NECK!"

"Les start the fire!"

"Heat the tar!"

"Ah got some chains t chain im."

"Bring im over this way!"

"Chris, Ah wished Ah hada drink . . ."

Big Boy saw men moving over the hill. Among them was a long dark spot. Tha mus be Bobo; tha mus be Bobo theys carryin . . .

8. A parody of "We'll hang Jeff Davis to a sour apple tree," sung by Union soldiers to the tune of "The Battle Hymn of the Republic."

Theyll git im here. He oughta git up n run. He clamped his teeth and ran his hand across his forehead, bringing it away wet. He tried to swallow, but could not; his throat was dry.

They had started the song again:

We'll hang ever nigger t a sour apple tree . . .

There were women singing now. Their voices made the song round and full. Song waves rolled over the top of pine trees. The sky sagged low, heavy with clouds. Wind was rising. Sometimes cricket cries cut surprisingly across the mob song. A dog had gone to the utmost top of the hill. At each lull of the song his howl floated full into the night.

Big Boy shrank when he saw the first flame light the hillside. Would they see im here? Then he remembered you could not see into the dark if you were standing in the light. As flames leaped higher he saw two men rolling a barrel up the slope.

"Say, gimme a han here, will yuh?"

"Awright, heave!"

"C mon! Straight up! Git t the other end!"

"Ah got the feathers here in this pillar!"

"BRING SOME MO WOOD!"

Big Boy could see the barrel surrounded by flames. The mob fell back, forming a dark circle. Theyd fin im here! He had a wild impulse to climb out and fly across the hills. But his legs would not move. He stared hard, trying to find Bobo. His eyes played over a long, dark spot near the fire. Fanned by wind, flames leaped higher. He jumped. That dark spot had moved. Lawd, thas Bobo; thas Bobo . . .

He smelt the scent of tar, faint at first, then stronger. The wind brought it full into his face, then blew it away. His eyes burned and he rubbed them with his knuckles. He sneezed.

"LES GIT SOURVINEERS!"

He saw the mob close in around the fire. Their faces were hard and sharp in the light of the flames. More men and women were coming over the hill. The long, dark spot was smudged out.

"Everybody git back!"

"Look! Hes gotta finger!"

"C MON! GIT THE GALS BACK FROM THE FIRE!"

"He's got one of his ears, see?"

"Whuts the matter!"

"A woman fell out! Fainted, Ah reckon . . ."

The stench of tar permeated the hillside. The sky was black and the wind was blowing hard.

"HURRY UP N BURN THE NIGGER FO IT RAINS!"

Big Boy saw the mob fall back, leaving a small knot of men about the fire. Then, for the first time, he had a full glimpse of Bobo. A black body flashed in the light. Bobo was struggling, twisting; they were binding his arms and legs.

When he saw them tilt the barrel he stiffened. A scream quivered. He knew the tar was on Bobo. The mob fell back. He saw a tar-drenched body glistening and turnbing.

"THE BASTARDS GOT IT!"

There was a sudden quiet. Then he shrank violently as the wind carried, like a flurry of snow, a widening spiral of white feathers into the night. The flames leaped tall as the trees. The scream came again. Big Boy trembled and looked. The mob was running down the slopes, leaving the fire clear. Then he saw a writhing white mass cradled in yellow flame, and heard screams, one on top of the other, each shriller and shorter than the last. The mob was quiet now, standing still, looking up the slopes at the writhing white mass gradually growing black, growing black in a cradle of yellow flame.

"PO ON MO GAS!"

"Gimme a lif, will yuh!"

Two men were struggling, carrying between them a heavy can. They set it down, tilted it, leaving it so that the gas would trickle down to the hollowed earth around the fire.

Big Boy slid back into the hole, his face buried in clay. He had no feelings now, no fears. He was numb, empty, as though all blood had been drawn from him. Then his muscles flexed taut when he heard a faint patter. A tiny stream of cold water seeped to his knees, making him push back to a drier spot. He looked up; rain was beating in the grass.

"It's rainin!"

"C mon, les git t town!"

". . . don worry, when the fire git thu wid im hell be gone . . ."

"Wait, Charles! Don leave me; its slippery here . . ."

"Ahll take some of yuh ladies back in mah car . . ."

Big Boy heard the dogs barking again, this time closer. Running feet pounded past. Cold water chilled his ankles. He could hear raindrops steadily hissing.

Now a dog was barking at the mouth of the hole, barking furiously, sensing a presence there. He balled himself into a knot and clung to the bottom, his knees and shins buried in water. The bark came louder. He heard paws scraping and felt the hot scent of dog breath on his face. Green eyes glowed and drew nearer as the barking, muffled by the closeness of the hole, beat upon his eardrums. Backing till his shoulders pressed against the clay, he held his breath. He pushed out his hands, his fingers stiff. The dog yawped louder, advancing, his bark rising sharp and thin. Big Boy rose to his knees, his hands before him. Then he flattened out still more against the bottom, breathing lungsful of hot dog scent, breathing it slowly, hard, but evenly. The dog came closer, bringing hotter dog scent. Big Boy could go back no more. His knees were slipping and slopping in the water. He braced himself, ready. Then, he never exactly knew how—he never knew whether he had lunged or the dog had lunged—they were together, rolling in the water. The green eyes were beneath him, between his legs. Dognails bit into his arms. His knees slipped backward and he landed full on the dog; the dog's breath left in a heavy gasp. Instinctively, he fumbled for the throat as he felt the dog twisting between his knees. The dog snarled, long and low, as though gathering strength. Big Boy's hands traveled swiftly over the dog's back, groping for the throat. He felt dognails again and saw green eyes, but his fingers had found the throat. He choked, feeling his fingers sink; he choked, throwing back his head and stiffening his arms. He felt the dog's body heave, felt dognails digging into his loins. With strength flowing from fear, he closed his fingers, pushing his full weight on the dog's throat. The dog heaved again, and lay still . . . Big Boy heard the sound of his own breathing filling the hole, and heard shouts and footsteps above him going past.

For a long time he held the dog, held it long after the last footstep had died out, long after the rain had stopped.

v

Morning found him still on his knees in a puddle of rainwater, staring at the stiff body of a dog. As the air brightened he came to himself slowly. He held still for a long time, as though waking from a dream, as though trying to remember.

The chug of a truck came over the hill. He tried to crawl to the opening. His knees were stiff and a thousand needlelike pains shot from the bottom of his feet to the calves of his legs. Giddiness made his eyes blur. He pulled up and looked. Through brackish light he saw Will's truck standing some twenty-five yards away, the engine running. Will stood on the running board, looking over the slopes of the hill.

Big Boy scuffled out, falling weakly in the wet grass. He tried to call to Will, but his dry throat would make no sound. He tried again.

"Will!"

Will heard, answering:

"Big Boy, c mon!"

He tried to run, and fell. Will came, meeting him in the tall grass.

"C mon," Will said, catching his arm.

They struggled to the truck.

"Hurry up!" said Will, pushing him onto the running-board.

Will pushed back a square trapdoor which swung above the back of the driver's seat. Big Boy pulled through, landing with a thud on the bottom. On hands and knees he looked around in the semi-darkness.

"Wheres Bobo?"

Big Boy stared.

"Wheres Bobo?"

"They got im."

"When?"

"Las night."

"The mob?"

Big Boy pointed in the direction of a charred sapling on the slope of the opposite hill. Will looked. The trapdoor fell. The engine purred, the gears whined, and the truck lurched forward over the muddy road, sending Big Boy on his side.

For a while he lay as he had fallen, on his side, too weak to move. As he felt the truck swing around a curve he straightened up and rested his back against a stack of wooden boxes. Slowly, he began to make out objects in the darkness. Through two long cracks fell thin blades of daylight. The floor was of smooth steel, and cold to his thighs. Splinters and bits of sawdust danced with the rumble of the truck. Each time they swung around a curve he was pulled over the floor; he grabbed at corners of boxes to steady himself. Once he heard the crow of a rooster. It made him think of home, of ma and pa. He thought he remembered hearing somewhere that the house had burned, but could not remember where . . . It all seemed unreal now.

He was tired. He dozed, swaying with the lurch. Then he jumped awake. The truck was running smoothly, on gravel. Far away he heard two short blasts from the Buckeye Lumber Mill. Unconsciously, the thought sang through his mind: Its six erclock . . .

The trapdoor swung in. Will spoke through a corner of his mouth.

"How yuh comin?"

"Awright."

"How they git Bobo?"

"He wuz comin over the hill."

"Whut they do?"

"They burnt im . . . Will, Ah wan some water; mah throats like fire . . ."

"Well git some when we pas a fillin station."

Big Boy leaned back and dozed. He jerked awake when the truck stopped. He heard Will get out. He wanted to peep through the trapdoor, but was afraid. For a moment, the wild fear he had known in the hole came back. Spose theyd search n fin im? He quieted when he heard Will's footsteps on the running-board. The trapdoor pushed in. Will's hat came through, dripping.

"Take it, quick!"

Big Boy grabbed, spilling water into his face. The truck lurched. He drank. Hard cold lumps of brick rolled into his hot stomach. A dull pain made him bend over. His intestines seemed to be drawing into a tight knot. After a bit it eased, and he sat up, breathing softly.

The truck swerved. He blinked his eyes. The blades of daylight had turned brightly golden. The sun had risen.

The truck sped over the asphalt miles, sped northward, jolting him, shaking out of his bosom the crumbs of corn bread, making them dance with the splinters and sawdust in the golden blades of sunshine.

He turned on his side and slept.

ALBERT CAMUS

(1913–1960)

The Renegade (Le Renégat)*

"What a jumble! What a jumble! I must tidy up my mind. Since they cut out my tongue, another tongue, it seems, has been constantly wagging somewhere in my skull, something has been talking, or someone, that suddenly falls silent and then it all begins again—oh, I hear too many things I never utter, what a jumble, and if I open my mouth it's like pebbles rattling together. Order and method, the tongue says, and then goes on talking of other matters simultaneously—yes, I always longed for order. At least one thing is certain, I am waiting for the missionary who is to come and take my place. Here I am on the trail, an hour away from Taghâsa, hidden in a pile of rocks, sitting on my old rifle. Day is breaking over the desert, it's still very cold, soon it will be too hot, this country drives men mad and I've been here I don't know how many years. . . . No, just a little longer. The missionary is to come this morning, or this evening. I've heard he'll come with a guide, perhaps they'll have but one camel between them. I'll wait, I am waiting, it's only the cold making me shiver. Just be patient a little longer, lousy slave!

But I have been patient for so long. When I was home on that

* 1957. Copyright 1958 by Alfred A Knopf, Inc. Reprinted from *Exile and the Kingdom* by Albert Camus, translated by Justin O'Brien, by permission of Alfred A. Knopf, Inc.

high plateau of the Massif Central,[1] my coarse father, my boorish mother, the wine, the pork soup every day, the wine above all, sour and cold, and the long winter, the frigid wind, the snowdrifts, the revolting bracken—oh, I wanted to get away, leave them all at once and begin to live at last, in the sunlight, with fresh water. I believed the priest, he spoke to me of the seminary, he tutored me daily, he had plenty of time in that Protestant region, where he used to hug the walls as he crossed the village. He told me of the future and of the sun, Catholicism is the sun, he used to say, and he would get me to read, he beat Latin into my hard head ('The kid's bright but he's pig-headed'), my head was so hard that, despite all my falls, it has never once bled in my life: 'Bull-headed,' my pig of a father used to say. At the seminary they were proud as punch, a recruit from the Protestant region was a victory, they greeted me like the sun at Austerlitz.[2] The sun was pale and feeble, to be sure, because of the alcohol, they have drunk sour wine and the children's teeth are set on edge, *gra gra,*[3] one really ought to kill one's father, but after all there's no danger that *he*'ll hurl himself into missionary work since he's now long dead, the tart wine eventually cut through his stomach, so there's nothing left but to kill the missionary.

I have something to settle with him and with his teachers, with my teachers who deceived me, with the whole of lousy Europe, everybody deceived me. Missionary work, that's all they could say, go out to the savages and tell them: 'Here is my Lord, just look at him, he never strikes or kills, he issues his orders in a low voice, he turns the other cheek, he's the greatest of masters, choose him, just see how much better he's made me, offend me and you will see.' Yes, I believed, *gra gra,* and I felt better, I had put on weight, I was almost handsome, I wanted to be offended. When we would walk out in tight black rows, in summer, under Grenoble's hot sun and would meet girls in cotton dresses, I didn't look away, I despised them, I waited for them to offend me, and sometimes they would laugh. At such times I would think: 'Let them strike me and spit in my face,' but their laughter, to tell the truth, came to the same thing, bristling with teeth and quips that tore me to shreds, the offense and the suffering were sweet to me! My confessor couldn't understand when I used to heap accusations on myself: 'No, no, there's good in you!' Good! There was nothing but sour wine in me, and that was all for the best, how can a man become better if he's not bad, I had grasped that in everything they taught me. That's the only thing I did grasp, a single idea, and, pig-headed bright boy, I carried it to its logical conclusion, I went out of my way for punishments, I groused at the normal, in short I too wanted to be an example in order to be noticed and so that

1. the mountainous region that covers one fifth of the area of France.
2. Here, in 1805, Napoleon defeated the Austrians and Russians.
3. an inarticulate sound.

after noticing me people would give credit to what had made me better, through me praise my Lord.

Fierce sun! It's rising, the desert is changing, it has lost its mountain-cyclamen color, O my mountain, and the snow, the soft enveloping snow, no, it's a rather grayish yellow, the ugly moment before the great resplendence. Nothing, still nothing from here to the horizon over yonder where the plateau disappears in a circle of still soft colors. Behind me, the trail climbs to the dune hiding Taghâsa, whose iron name has been beating in my head for so many years. The first to mention it to me was the half-blind old priest who had retired to our monastery, but why do I say the first, he was the only one, and it wasn't the city of salt, the white walls under the blinding sun, that struck me in his account but the cruelty of the savage inhabitants and the town closed to all outsiders, only one of those who had tried to get in, one alone, to his knowledge, had lived to relate what he had seen. They had whipped him and driven him out into the desert after having put salt on his wounds and in his mouth, he had met nomads who for once were compassionate, a stroke of luck, and since then I had been dreaming about his tale, about the fire of the salt and the sky, about the House of the Fetish and his slaves, could anything more barbarous, more exciting be imagined, yes, that was my mission and I had to go and reveal to them my Lord.

They all expatiated on the subject at the seminary to discourage me, pointing out the necessity of waiting, that it was not missionary country, that I wasn't ready yet, I had to prepare myself specially, know who I was, and even then I had to go through tests, then they would see! But go on waiting, ah, no!—yes, if they insisted, for the special preparation and the tryouts because they took place at Algiers and brought me closer, but for all the rest I shook my pig-head and repeated the same thing, to get among the most barbarous and live as they did, to show them at home, and even in the House of the Fetish, through example, that my Lord's truth would prevail. They would offend me, of course, but I was not afraid of offenses, they were essential to the demonstration, and as a result of the way I endured them I'd get the upper hand of those savages like a strong sun. Strong, yes, that was the word I constantly had on the tip of my tongue, I dreamed of absolute power, the kind that makes people kneel down, that forces the adversary to capitulate, converts him in short, and the blinder, the crueler he is, the more he's sure of himself, mired in his own conviction, the more his consent establishes the royalty of whoever brought about his collapse. Converting good folk who had strayed somewhat was the shabby ideal of our priests, I despised them for daring so little when they could do so much, they lacked faith and I had it, I wanted to be acknowledged by the torturers themselves, to fling them on their knees and make them say: 'O Lord, here is thy victory,' to rule in short by the sheer force of words over an army of the wicked. Oh, I was sure of reasoning logically on that subject, never quite sure of myself otherwise, but once I get an idea I don't let go of it, that's my strong point, yes the strong point of the fellow they all pitied!

The sun has risen higher, my forehead is beginning to burn. Around me the stones are beginning to crack open with a dull sound, the only cool thing is the rifle's barrel, cool as the fields, as the evening rain long ago when the soup was simmering, they would wait for me, my father and mother who would occasionally smile at me, perhaps I loved them. But that's all in the past, a film of heat is beginning to rise from the trail, come on, missionary, I'm waiting for you, now I know how to answer the message, my new masters taught me, and I know they are right, you have to settle accounts with that question of love. When I fled the seminary in Algiers I had a different idea of the savages and only one detail of my imaginings was true, they are cruel. I had robbed the treasurer's office, cast off my habit, crossed the Atlas,[4] the upper plateaus and the desert, the bus-driver of the Trans-Sahara line made fun of me: 'Don't go there,' he too, what had got into them all, and the gusts of sand for hundreds of wind-blown kilometers, progressing and backing in the face of the wind, then the mountains again made up of black peaks and ridges sharp as steel, and after them it took a guide to go out on the endless sea of brown pebbles, screaming with heat, burning with the fires of a thousand mirrors, to the spot on the confines of the white country and the land of the blacks where stands the city of salt. And the money the guide stole from me, ever naïve I had shown it to him, but he left me on the trail—just about here, it so happens—after having struck me: 'Dog, there's the way, the honor's all mine, go ahead, go on, they'll show you,' and they did show me, oh yes, they're like the sun that never stops, except at night, beating sharply and proudly, that is beating me hard at this moment, too hard, with a multitude of lances burst from the ground, oh shelter, yes shelter, under the big rock, before everything gets muddled.

The shade here is good. How can anyone live in the city of salt, in the hollow of that basin full of dazzling heat? On each of the sharp right-angle walls cut out with a pickax and coarsely planed, the gashes left by the pickax bristle with blinding scales, pale scattered sand yellows them somewhat except when the wind dusts the upright walls and terraces, then everything shines with dazzling whiteness under a sky likewise dusted even to its blue rind. I was going blind during those days when the stationary fire would crackle for hours on the surface of the white terraces that all seemed to meet as if, in the remote past, they had all together tackled a mountain of salt, flattened it first, and then had hollowed out streets, the insides of houses and windows directly in the mass, or as

4. a range of mountains in Morocco, Algeria, and Tunisia.

if—yes, this is more like it, they had cut out their white, burning hell with a powerful jet of boiling water just to show that they could live where no one ever could, thirty days' travel from any living thing, in this hollow in the middle of the desert where the heat of day prevents any contact among creatures, separates them by a portcullis of invisible flames and of searing crystals, where without transition the cold of night congeals them individually in their rock-salt shells, nocturnal dwellers in a dried-up icefloe, black Eskimoes suddenly shivering in their cubical igloos. Black because they wear long black garments, and the salt that collects even under their nails, that they continue tasting bitterly and swallowing during the sleep of those polar nights, the salt they drink in the water from the only spring in the hollow of a dazzling groove, often spots their dark garments with something like the trail of snails after a rain.

Rain, O Lord, just one real rain, long and hard, rain from your heaven! Then at last the hideous city, gradually eaten away, would slowly and irresistibly cave in and, utterly melted in a slimy torrent, would carry off its savage inhabitants toward the sands. Just one rain, Lord! But what do I mean, what Lord, they are the lords and masters! They rule over their sterile homes, over their black slaves that they work to death in the mines and each slab of salt that is cut out is worth a man in the region to the south, they pass by, silent, wearing their mourning veils in the mineral whiteness of the streets, and at night, when the whole town looks like a milky phantom, they stoop down and enter the shade of their homes, where the salt walls shine dimly. They sleep with a weightless sleep and, as soon as they wake, they give orders, they strike, they say they are a united people, that their god is the true god, and that one must obey. They are my masters, they are ignorant of pity and, like masters, they want to be alone, to progress alone, to rule alone, because they alone had the daring to build in the salt and the sands a cold torrid city. And I . . .

What a jumble when the heat rises, I'm sweating, they never do, now the shade itself is heating up, I feel the sun on the stone above me, it's striking, striking like a hammer on all the stones and it's the music, the vast music of noon, air and stones vibrating over hundreds of kilometers, *gra*, I hear the silence as I did once before. Yes, it was the same silence, years ago, that greeted me when the guards led me to them, in the sunlight, in the center of the square, whence the concentric terraces rose gradually toward the lid of hard blue sky sitting on the edge of the basin. There I was, thrown on my knees in the hollow of that white shield, my eyes corroded by the swords of salt and fire issuing from all the walls, pale with fatigue, my ear bleeding from the blow given by my guide, and they, tall and black, looked at me without saying a word. The day was at its midcourse. Under the blows of the iron sun the sky resounded at length, a sheet of white-hot tin, it was the same silence, and they stared at me, time passed, they kept on staring at me, and I couldn't face their stares, I panted more and more violently, eventually I wept, and suddenly they turned their backs on me in silence and all together went off in the same direction. On my knees, all I could see, in the red-and-black sandals, was their feet sparkling with salt as they raised the long black gowns, the tip rising somewhat, the heel striking the ground lightly, and when the square was empty I was dragged to the House of the Fetish.

Squatting, as I am today in the shelter of the rock and the fire above my head pierces the rock's thickness, I spent several days within the dark of the House of the Fetish, somewhat higher than the others, surrounded by a wall of salt, but without windows, full of a sparkling night. Several days, and I was given a basin of brackish water and some grain that was thrown before me the way chickens are fed, I picked it up. By day the door remained closed and yet the darkness became less oppressive, as if the irresistible sun managed to flow through the masses of salt. No lamp, but by feeling my way along the walls I touched garlands of dried palms decorating the walls and, at the end, a small door, coarsely fitted, of which I could make out the bolt with my fingertips. Several days, long after—I couldn't count the days or the hours, but my handful of grain had been thrown me some ten times and I had dug out a hole for my excrements that I covered up in vain, the stench of an animal den hung on anyway—long after, yes, the door opened wide and they came in.

One of them came toward me where I was squatting in a corner. I felt the burning salt against my cheek, I smelled the dusty scent of the palms, I watched him approach. He stopped a yard away from me, he stared at me in silence, a signal, and I stood up, he stared at me with his metallic eyes that shone without expression in his brown horse-face, then he raised his hand. Still impassive, he seized me by the lower lip, which he twisted slowly until he tore my flesh and, without letting go, made me turn around and back up to the center of the room, he pulled on my lip to make me fall on my knees there, mad with pain and my mouth bleeding, then he turned away to join the others standing against the walls. They watched me moaning in the unbearable heat of the unbroken daylight that came in the wide-open door, and in that light suddenly appeared the Sorcerer with his raffia hair, his chest covered with a breastplate of pearls, his legs bare under a straw skirt, wearing a mask of reeds and wire with two square openings for the eyes. He was followed by musicians and women wearing heavy motley gowns that revealed nothing of their bodies. They danced in front of the door at the end, but a coarse, scarcely rhythmical dance, they just barely moved, and finally the Sorcerer opened the little door behind me, the masters did not stir, they were watching me, I turned around and saw the Fetish, his double ax-head, his iron nose twisted like a snake.

I was carried before him, to the foot of the pedestal, I was made to drink a black, bitter, bitter water, and at once my head began to burn, I was laughing, that's the offense, I have been offended. They undressed me, shaved my head and body, washed me in oil, beat my face with cords dipped in water and salt, and I laughed and turned my head away, but each time two women would take me by the ears and offer my face to the Sorcerer's blows while I could see only his square eyes, I was still laughing, covered with blood. They stopped, no one spoke but me, the jumble was beginning in my head, then they lifted me up and forced me to raise my eyes toward the Fetish, I had ceased laughing. I knew that I was now consecrated to him to serve him, adore him, no, I was not laughing any more, fear and pain stifled me. And there, in that white house, between those walls that the sun was assiduously burning on the outside, my face taut, my memory exhausted, yes, I tried to pray to the Fetish, he was all there was and even his horrible face was less horrible than the rest of the world. Then it was that my ankles were tied with a cord that permitted just one step, they danced again, but this time in front of the Fetish, the masters went out one by one.

The door once closed behind them, the music again, and the Sorcerer lighted a bark fire around which he pranced, his long silhouette broke on the angles of the white walls, fluttered on the flat surfaces, filled the room with dancing shadows. He traced a rectangle in a corner to which the women dragged me, I felt their dry and gentle hands, they set before me a bowl of water and a little pile of grain and pointed to the Fetish, I grasped that I was to keep my eyes fixed on him. Then the Sorcerer called them one after the other over to the fire, he beat some of them who moaned and who then went and prostrated themselves before the Fetish my god, while the Sorcerer kept on dancing and he made them all leave the room until only one was left, quite young, squatting near the musicians and not yet beaten. He held her by a shock of hair which he kept twisting around his wrist, she dropped backward with eyes popping until she finally fell on her back. Dropping her, the Sorcerer screamed, the musicians turned to the wall, while behind the square-eyed mask the scream rose to an impossible pitch, and the woman rolled on the ground in a sort of fit and, at last on all fours, her head hidden in her locked arms, she too screamed, but with a hollow, muffled sound, and in this position, without ceasing to scream and to look at the Fetish, the Sorcerer took her nimbly and nastily, without the woman's face being visible, for it was covered with the heavy folds of her garment. And, wild as a result of the solitude, *I* screamed too, yes, howled with fright toward the Fetish until a kick hurled me against the wall, biting the salt as I am biting this rock today with my tongueless mouth, while waiting for the man I must kill.

Now the sun has gone a little beyond the middle of the sky. Through the breaks in the rock I can see the hole it makes in the white-hot metal of the sky, a mouth voluble as mine, constantly vomiting rivers of flame over the colorless desert. On the trail in front of me, nothing, no cloud of dust on the horizon, behind me they must be looking for me, no, not yet, it's only in the late afternoon that they opened the door and I could go out a little, after having spent the day cleaning the House of the Fetish, set out fresh offerings, and in the evening the ceremony would begin, in which I was sometimes beaten, at others not, but always I served the Fetish, the Fetish whose image is engraved in iron in my memory and now in my hope also. Never had a god so possessed or enslaved me, my whole life day and night was devoted to him, and pain and the absence of pain, wasn't that joy, were due him and even, yes, desire, as a result of being present, almost every day, at that impersonal and nasty act which I heard without seeing it inasmuch as I now had to face the wall or else be beaten. But, my face up against the salt, obsessed by the bestial shadows moving on the wall, I listened to the long scream, my throat was dry, a burning sexless desire squeezed my temples and my belly as in a vise. Thus the days followed one another, I barely distinguished them as if they had liquefied in the torrid heat and the treacherous reverberation from the walls of salt, time had become merely a vague lapping of waves in which there would burst out, at regular intervals, screams of pain or possession, a long ageless day in which the Fetish ruled as this fierce sun does over my house of rocks, and now, as I did then, I weep with unhappiness and longing, a wicked hope consumes me, I want to betray, I lick the barrel of my gun and its soul inside, its soul, only guns have souls—oh, yes! the day they cut out my tongue, I learned to adore the immortal soul of hatred!

What a jumble, what a rage, *gra gra*, drunk with heat and wrath, lying prostrate on my gun. Who's panting here? I can't endure this endless heat, this waiting, I must kill him. Not a bird, not a blade of grass, stone, an arid desire, their screams, this tongue within me talking, and since they mutilated me, the long, flat, deserted suffering deprived even of the water of night, the night of which I would dream, when locked in with the god, in my den of salt. Night alone with its cool stars and dark fountains could save me, carry me off at last from the wicked gods of mankind, but ever locked up I could not contemplate it. If the newcomer tarries more, I shall see it at least rise from the desert and sweep over the sky, a cold golden vine that will hang from the dark zenith and from which I can drink at length, moisten this black dried hole that no muscle of live flexible flesh revives now, forget at last that day when madness took away my tongue.

How hot it was, really hot, the salt was melting or so it seemed to me, the air was corroding my eyes, and the Sorcerer came in without his mask. Almost naked under grayish tatters, a new woman followed him and her face, covered with a tattoo reproducing the mask of the Fetish, expressed only an idol's ugly stupor. The only thing alive about her was her thin flat body that flopped at the foot of the god when the Sorcerer opened the door of the niche. Then he went out without looking at me, the heat rose, I didn't stir, the Fetish looked at me over that motionless body whose muscles stirred gently and the woman's idol-face didn't change when I approached. Only her eyes enlarged as she stared at me, my feet touched hers, the heat then began to shriek, and the idol, without a word, still staring at me with her dilated eyes, gradually slipped onto her back, slowly drew her legs up and raised them as she gently spread her knees. But, immediately afterward, *gra,* the Sorcerer was lying in wait for me, they all entered and tore me from the woman, beat me dreadfully on the sinful place, what sin, I'm laughing, where is it and where is virtue, they clapped me against a wall, a hand of steel gripped my jaws, another opened my mouth, pulled on my tongue until it bled, was it I screaming with that bestial scream, a cool cutting caress, yes cool at last, went over my tongue. When I came to, I was alone in the night, glued to the wall, covered with hardened blood, a gag of strange-smelling dry grasses filled my mouth, it had stopped bleeding, but it was vacant and in that absence the only living thing was a tormenting pain. I wanted to rise, I fell back, happy, desperately happy to die at last, death too is cool and its shadow hides no god.

I did not die, a new feeling of hatred stood up one day, at the same time I did, walked toward the door of the niche, opened it, closed it behind me, I hated my people, the Fetish was there and from the depth of the hole in which I was I did more than pray to him, I believed in him and denied all I had believed up to then. Hail! he was strength and power, he could be destroyed but not converted, he stared over my head with his empty, rusty eyes. Hail! he was the master, the only lord, whose indisputable attribute was malice, there are no good masters. For the first time, as a result of offenses, my whole body crying out a single pain, I surrendered to him and approved his maleficent order, I adored in him the evil principle of the world. A prisoner of his kingdom—the sterile city carved out of a mountain of salt, divorced from nature, deprived of those rare and fleeting flowerings of the desert, preserved from those strokes of chance or marks of affection such as an unexpected cloud or a brief violent downpour that are familiar even to the sun or the sands, the city of order in short, right angles, square rooms, rigid men—I freely became its tortured, hate-filled citizen, I repudiated the long history that had been taught me. I had been misled, solely the reign of malice was devoid of defects, I had been misled, truth is square, heavy, thick, it does not admit distinctions, gold is an idle dream, an intention constantly postponed and pursued with exhausting effort, a limit never reached, its reign is impossible. Only evil can reach its limits and reign absolutely, it must be served to establish its visible kingdom, then we shall see, but what does 'then' mean, only evil is present, down with Europe, reason, honor, and the cross. Yes, I was to be converted to the religion of my masters, yes indeed, I was a slave, but if I too become vicious I cease to be a slave, despite my shackled feet and my mute mouth. Oh, this heat is driving me crazy, the desert cries out everywhere under the unbearable light, and he, the Lord of kindness, whose very name revolts me, I disown him, for I know him now. He dreamed and wanted to lie, his tongue was cut out so that his word would no longer be able to deceive the world, he was pierced with nails even in his head, his poor head, like mine now, what a jumble, how weak I am, and the earth didn't tremble, I am sure, it was not a righteous man they had killed, I refuse to believe it, there are no righteous men but only evil masters who bring about the reign of relentless truth. Yes, the Fetish alone has power, he is the sole god of this world, hatred is his commandment, the source of all life, the cool water, cool like mint that chills the mouth and burns the stomach.

Then it was that I changed, they realized it, I would kiss their hands when I met them, I was on their side, never wearying of admiring them, I trusted them, I hoped they would mutilate my people as they had mutilated me. And when I learned that the missionary was to come, I knew what I was to do. That day like all the others, the same blinding daylight that had been going on so long! Late in the afternoon a guard was suddenly seen running along the edge of the basin, and, a few minutes later, I was dragged to the House of the Fetish and the door closed. One of them held me on the ground in the dark, under threat of his cross-shaped sword, and the silence lasted for a long time until a strange sound filled the ordinarily peaceful town, voices that it took me some time to recognize because they were speaking my language, but as soon as they rang out the point of the sword was lowered toward my eyes, my guard stared at me in silence. Then two voices came closer and I can still hear them, one asking why that house was guarded and whether they should break in the door, Lieutenant, the other said: 'No' sharply, then added, after a moment, that an agreement had been reached, that the town accepted a garrison of twenty men on condition that they would camp outside the walls and respect the customs. The private laughed, 'They're knuckling under,' but the officer didn't know, for the first time in any case they were willing to receive someone to take care of the children and that would be the chaplain, later on they would see about the territory. The other said they would cut off the chaplain's you know what if the soldiers were not there. 'Oh, no!' the officer answered. 'In fact, Father Beffort will come before the garrison; he'll be here in two days.' That was all I heard, motionless, lying under the sword, I was in pain, a wheel of needles and knives was whirling in me. They were crazy, they were crazy, they were allowing a hand to be laid on the city, on their invincible power, on the true god, and the fellow who was to come would not have his tongue cut out, he would show off his insolent goodness without paying for it, without enduring any offense. The reign of evil would be postponed, there would be doubt again, again time would be wasted dreaming of the impossible good, wearing oneself out in fruitless efforts instead of hastening the realization of the only possible kingdom and I looked at the sword threatening me, O sole power to rule over the world! O power, and the city gradually emptied of its sounds, the door finally opened, I remained alone, burned and bitter, with the Fetish, and I swore to him to save my new faith, my true masters, my despotic God, to betray well, whatever it might cost me.

Gra, the heat is abating a little, the stone has ceased to vibrate, I can go out of my hole, watch the desert gradually take on yellow and ocher tints that will soon be mauve. Last night I waited until they were asleep, I had blocked the lock on the door, I went out with the same step as usual, measured by the cord, I knew the streets, I knew where to get the old rifle, what gate wasn't guarded, and I reached here just as the night was beginning to fade around a handful of stars while the desert was getting a little darker. And now it seems days and days that I have been crouching in these rocks. Soon, soon, I hope he comes soon! In a moment they'll begin to look for me, they'll speed over the trails in all directions, they won't know that I left for them and to serve them better, my legs are weak, drunk with hunger and hate. Oh! over there, *gra*, at the end of the trail, two camels are growing bigger, ambling along, already multiplied by short shadows, they are running with that lively and dreamy gait they always have. Here they are, here at last!

Quick, the rifle, and I load it quickly. O Fetish, my god over yonder, may your power be preserved, may the offense be multipled, may hate rule pitilessly over a world of the damned, may the wicked forever be masters, may the kingdom come, where in a single city of salt and iron black tyrants will enslave and possess without pity! And now, *gra gra,* fire on pity, fire on impotence and its charity, fire on all that postpones the coming of evil, fire twice, and there they are toppling over, falling, and the camels flee toward the horizon, where a geyser of black birds has just risen in the unchanged sky. I laugh, I laugh, the fellow is writhing in his detested habit, he is raising his head a little, he sees me—me his all-powerful shackled master, why does he smile at me, I'll crush that smile! How pleasant is the sound of a rifle butt on the face of goodness, today, today at last, all is consummated and everywhere in the desert, even hours away from here, jackals sniff the nonexistent wind, then set out in a patient trot toward the feast of carrion awaiting them. Victory! I raise my arms to a heaven moved to pity, a lavender shadow is just barely suggested on the opposite side, O nights of Europe, home, childhood, why must I weep in the moment of triumph?

He stirred, no the sound comes from somewhere else, and from the other direction here they come rushing like a flight of of dark birds, my masters, who fall upon me, seize me, ah yes! strike, they fear their city sacked and howling, they fear the avenging soldiers I called forth, and this is only right, upon the sacred city. Defend yourselves now, strike! strike me first, you possess the truth! O my masters, they will then conquer the soldiers, they'll conquer the word and love, they'll spread over the deserts, cross the seas, fill the light of Europe with their black veils—strike the belly, yes, strike the eyes—sow their salt on the continent, all vegetation, all youth will die out, and dumb crowds with shackled feet will plod beside me in the world-wide desert under the cruel sun of the true faith, I'll not be alone. Ah! the pain, the pain they cause me, their rage is good and on this cross-shaped war-saddle where they are now quartering me, pity! I'm laughing, I love the blow that nails me down crucified.

* * *

How silent the desert is! Already night and I am alone, I'm thirsty. Still waiting, where is the city, those sounds in the distance, and the soldiers perhaps the victors, no, it can't be, even if the soldiers are victorious, they're not wicked enough, they won't be able to rule, they'll still say one must become better, and still millions of men between evil and good, torn, bewildered, O Fetish, why hast thou forsaken me? All is over, I'm thirsty, my body is burning, a darker night fills my eyes.

This long, this long dream, I'm awaking, no, I'm going to die, dawn is breaking, the first light, daylight for the living, and for me the inexorable sun, the flies. Who is speaking, no one, the sky is not opening up, no, no, God doesn't speak in the desert, yet whence comes that voice saying: 'If you consent to die for hate and power, who will forgive us?' Is it another tongue in me or still that other fellow refusing to die, at my feet, and repeating: 'Courage! courage! courage!'? Ah! supposing I were wrong again! Once fraternal men, sole recourse, O solitude, forsake me not! Here, here who are you, torn, with bleeding mouth, is it you, Sorcerer, the soldiers defeated you, the salt is burning over there, it's you my beloved master! Cast off that hate-ridden face, be good now, we were mistaken, we'll begin all over again, we'll rebuild the city of mercy, I want to go back home. Yes, help me, that's right, give me your hand. . . .'

A handful of salt fills the mouth of the garrulous slave.

This long, this [illegible] going to [illegible] day is [illegible] the [illegible], [illegible] to the [illegible] and for the [illegible], the [illegible] is [illegible] the [illegible] God doesn't [illegible] the [illegible] and power, who will forgive us? If it [illegible] tongue [illegible] to the [illegible] and [illegible] if we [illegible] wrong again [illegible] with [illegible] you [illegible] as your [illegible] beloved [illegible] now, we [illegible] again, [illegible] only on [illegible] [illegible]

A [illegible] of salt like the mouth of the [illegible] eye.

A Note on Translation

Reading literature in translation is a pleasure on which it is fruitless to frown. The purist may insist that we ought always read in the original languages, and we know ideally that he is right. But his counsel is a counsel of perfection, quite impractical even for him, since no man in one lifetime can master all the languages whose literatures he might wish to explore. Master languages as fast as we may, we shall always have to read to some extent in translation, and this means we must be alert to what we are about: if in reading a work of literature in translation we are not reading the "original," what precisely are we reading? This is a question of great complexity, to which justice cannot be done in a brief note. Nevertheless, the following sketch of some of the considerations that a mature answer would involve may be helpful to those who are coming into a self-conscious relation with literature in translation for the first time.

One of the memorable scenes of ancient literature is the meeting of Hector and Andromache in Book VI of Homer's *Iliad*. Hector, leader and mainstay of the armies defending Troy, is implored by his wife Andromache to withdraw within the city walls and carry on the defense from there, where his life will not be constantly at hazard. In Homer's text her opening words to him are these: δαιμόνιε, φθίσει σε τὸ σὸν μένος (daimonie, phthisei se to son menos). How should they be translated into English?

Here is how they have actually been translated into English by capable translators, at various periods, in verse and prose.

1. George Chapman, 1598

O noblest in desire,
Thy mind, inflamed with others' good, will set thy self on fire.

2. John Dryden, 1693

Thy dauntless heart (which I foresee too late),
Too daring man, will urge thee to thy fate.

3. Alexander Pope, 1715

Too daring Prince! ...
For sure such courage length of life denies,
And thou must fall, thy virtue's sacrifice.

4. William Cowper, 1791

> Thy own great courage will cut short thy days,
> My noble Hector. . . .

5. Lang, Leaf, and Myers, 1883 (prose)

> Dear my lord, this thy hardihood will undo thee. . . .

6. A. T. Murray, 1924 (prose, Loeb Library)

> Ah, my husband, this prowess of thine will be thy doom. . . .

7. E. V. Rieu, 1950 (prose)

> "Hector," she said, "you are possessed. This bravery of yours will be your end."

8. I.A. Richards, 1950 (prose)

> "Strange man," she said, "your courage will be your destruction."

9. Robert Fitzgerald, 1976

> Oh, my wild one, your bravery will be
> your own undoing!

From these strikingly different renderings of the same six words, certain facts about the nature of translation begin to emerge. We notice, for one thing, that Homer's word *μένος* (menos) is diversified by the translators into "mind," "dauntless heart," "such courage," "great courage," "hardihood," "prowess," "bravery," "courage," and again "bravery." The word has in fact all these possibilities. Used of things, it normally means "force"; of animals, "fierceness" or "brute strength" or (in the case of horses) "mettle"; of men, "passion" or "spirit" or even "purpose." Homer's application of it in the present case points our attention equally—whatever particular sense we may imagine Andromache to have uppermost—to Hector's force, strength, fierceness in battle, spirited heart and mind. But since English has no matching term of like inclusiveness, the passage as the translators give it to us reflects this lack and we find one attribute singled out to the exclusion of the rest.

Here then is the first and most crucial fact about any work of literature read in translation. It cannot escape the linguistic characteristics of the language into which it is turned: the grammatical, syntactical, lexical, and phonetic boundaries which constitute collectively the individuality or "genius" of that language. A Greek play or a Russian novel in English will be governed first of all by the resources of the English language, resources which are certain to be in every instance very different, as the efforts with *μένος* show, from those of the original.

Turning from *μένος* to *δαιμόνιε* (daimonie) in Homer's clause, we encounter a second crucial fact about translations. Nobody knows exactly what shade of meaning δαιμόνιε had for Homer. In later writers the word normally suggests divinity, something miraculous, wondrous; but in Homer it appears as a vocative of address for both chieftain and commoner, man and wife. The coloring one gives it must therefore be determined either by the way one thinks a Greek wife of Homer's era might actually address her husband (a subject on which we have no information whatever), or in the way one thinks it suitable for a hero's wife to address her husband in an epic poem, that is to say, a highly stylized and formal work. In general, the translators of our century will be seen to have eschewed formality in order to stress the intimacy, the wifeliness, and, especially in Fitzgerald's case, a certain motherliness, in Andromache's appeal: (6) "Ah, my husband," (7) "Hector" (with perhaps a hint, in "you are possessed," of the alarmed distaste with which wives have so often viewed their husbands' bellicose moods), (8) "Strange man," (9) "Oh, my wild one." On the other hand, the older translators have obviously removed Andromache to an epic or heroic distance from her beloved, whence she sees and kindles to his selfless courage, acknowledging, even in the moment of pleading with him to be otherwise, his moral grandeur and the tragic destiny this too certainly implies: (1) "On noblest in desire, . . . inflamed by others' good"; (2) "Thy dauntless heart (which I foresee too late), / Too daring man"; (3) "Too daring Prince! . . . / And thou must fall, thy virtue's sacrifice"; (4) "My noble Hector." Even the less specific "Dear my lord" of Lang, Leaf, and Myers looks in the same direction because of its echo of the speech of countless Shakespearean men and women who have shared this powerful moral sense: "Dear my lord, make me acquainted with your cause of grief"; "Perseverance, dear my lord, keeps honor bright"; etc.

The fact about translation which emerges from all this is that just as the translated work reflects the individuality of the language it is turned into, so it reflects the individuality of the age in which it is done, and the age will permeate it everywhere like yeast in dough. We think of one kind of permeation when we think of the governing verse forms and attitudes toward verse at a given epoch. In Chapman's time, experiments seeking an "heroic" verse form for English were widespread, and accordingly he tries a "fourteener" couplet (two rhymed lines of seven stresses each) in his *Iliad* and a pentameter couplet in his *Odyssey*. When Dryden and Pope wrote, a closed pentameter couplet had become established as the heroic form *par excellence*. By Cowper's day, thanks largely to the prestige of *Paradise Lost*, the couplet had gone out of fashion for narrative poetry in favor of blank verse. Our age, inclining to prose and in verse to proselike informalities and relaxations, has, predictably, produced half a dozen excellent prose translations of the *Iliad*, but only two in verse (Fitzgerald's and that of Richmond Lattimore), both relying on rhythms that are much of the time closer to the verse of William Carlos Williams and some of the prose of novelists like Faulkner than to the swift firm tread of Homer's Greek. For if it is true that what we translate from a given work is what, wearing the spectacles of our time, we see in it, it is also true that we see in it what we have the power to translate.

Of course there are other effects of the translator's epoch on his translation besides those exercised by contemporary taste in verse and verse forms. Chapman writes in a great age of poetic metaphor and therefore almost instinctively translates his understanding of Homer's verb *φθίσει* (phthisei, "to cause to wane, consume, waste, pine") into metaphorical terms of flame, presenting his Hector to us as a man of burning generosity who will be consumed by his very ardor. This is a conception rooted in large part in the psychology of the Elizabethans, who had the habit of speaking of the soul as "fire," of one of the four temperaments as "fiery," of even the more material bodily processes, like digestion, as if they were carried on by the heat of fire ("concoction," "decoction"). It is rooted too in that characteristic Renaissance élan so unforgettably expressed in characters like Tamburlaine and Dr. Faustus, the former of whom exclaims to the stars above:

> . . . I, the chiefest lamp of all the earth,
> First rising in the East with mild aspect,
> But fixèd now in the meridian line,
> Will send up fire to your turning spheres,
> And cause the sun to borrow light of you. . . .

Pope and Dryden, by contrast, write to audiences for whom strong metaphor has become suspect. They therefore reject the fire image (which we must recall is not present in the Greek) in favor of a form of speech more congenial to their age, the *sententia* or aphorism, and give it extra vitality by making it the scene of a miniature drama: in Dryden's case, the hero's dauntless heart "urges" him (in the double sense of physical as well as moral pressure) to his fate; in Pope's, the hero's courage, like a judge, "denies" continuance of life, with the consequence that he "falls"—and here Pope's second line suggests analogy to the sacrificial animal—the victim of his own essential nature, of what he is.

To pose even more graphically the pressures that a translator's period brings, consider the following lines from Hector's reply to Andromache's appeal that he withdraw, first in Chapman's Elizabethan version, then in Fitzgerald's twentieth-century one:

Chapman, 1598:

The spirit I did first breathe
Did never teach me that—much less since the contempt of death
Was settled in me, and my mind knew what a Worthy was,
Whose office is to lead in fight and give no danger pass
Without improvement. In this fire must Hector's trial shine.
Here must his country, father, friends be in him made divine.

Fitzgerald, 1976:

. . . Long ago I learned
how to be brave, how to go forward always
and to contend for honor, Father's and mine.

If one may exaggerate to make a necessary point, the world of Henry V and Othello suddenly gives way here to our own, a world so embarrassed by heroic language that "to lead in fight" reshapes itself to the much more neutral "to go forward always," while terms of really large implication like "brave" and "honor" are left to jostle uncomfortably against a phrase banal enough to refer easily to a piece of real estate or the family car: "Father's and mine."

Besides the two factors so far mentioned, language and period, as affecting the character of a translation, there is inevitably a third—the translator himself, with his particular degree of talent, his personal way of regarding the work to be translated, his own special hierarchy of values, moral, esthetic, metaphysical (which may or may not be summed up in a "world view"), his unique style or lack of it. But this influence all readers are likely to bear in mind, and it needs no laboring here. That, for example, two translators of Hamlet, one a Freudian, the other an Existentialist, will produce impressively different translations is obvious from the fact that when Freudian and Existentialist argue about the play in English they often seem to have different plays in mind.

We can now return to the question from which we started. After all allowances have been made for language, age, and individual translator, is anything of the original left? What, in short, does the reader of translations read? Let it be said at once that in utility prose—prose whose function is mainly referential—he reads everything that matters. "*Nicht Rauchen,*" "*Défense de Fumer,*" and "*No Smoking,*" posted in a railway car, make their point, and the differences between them in sound and form have no significance for us in that context. Since the prose of a treatise and of most fiction is preponderantly referential, we rightly feel, when we have paid close attention to Cervantes or Montaigne or Machiavelli or Tolstoy in a good English translation, that we have had roughly the same experience as a native Spaniard, Frenchman, Italian, or Russian. But "roughly" is the correct word; for good prose points iconically *to* itself as well as referentially beyond itself, and everything that it points to in itself in the original (rhythms, sounds, idioms, word play, etc.) must alter radically in being translated. The best analogy is to imagine a Van Gogh painting reproduced in the medium of tempera, etching, or engraving: the "picture" remains, but the intricate interanimation of volumes with colorings with brushstrokes has disappeared.

When we move on to poetry, even in its longer narrative and dramatic forms—plays like *Oedipus*, poems like the *Iliad* or the *Divine Comedy*—our situation as English readers worsens appreciably, as the many unlike versions of Andromache's appeal to Hector make very clear. But, again, only appreciably. True, this is the point at which the fact that a translation is *always* an interpretation explodes irresistibly on our attention; but if it is a good translation, the result will be a sensitive interpretation and also a work with intrinsic interest in its own right—at very best, a true work of art, a new poem. It is only when the shorter, primarily lyrical forms of poetry are presented that the reader of translations faces insuperable disadvantage. In these forms, the referential aspect of language has a tendency to disappear into, or, more often, draw its real meaning and accreditation from, the iconic aspect. Let us look for just a moment at a brief poem by Federico García Lorca and its English translation (by Stephen Spender and J. L. Gili):

¡Alto pinar!
Cuatro palomas por el aire van.

Cuatro palomas
vuelan y tornan.
Llevan heridas
sus cuatro sombras.

¡Bajo pinar!
Cuatro palomas en la tierra están.

Above the pine trees:
Four pigeons go through the air.

Four pigeons
fly and turn round.
They carry wounded
their four shadows.

Below the pine trees:
Four pigeons lie on the earth.

In this translation the referential sense of the English words follows with remarkable exactness the referential sense of the Spanish words they replace. But the life of Lorca's poem does not lie in that sense. It lies in such matters as the abruptness, like an intake of breath at a sudden revelation, of the two exclamatory lines (1 and 7), which then exhale musically in images of flight and death; or as the echoings of *palomas* in *heridas* and *sombras,* bringing together (as in fact the hunter's gun has done) these unrelated nouns and the unrelated experiences they stand for in a sequence that seems, momentarily, to have all the logic of a tragic action, in which *doves* become *wounds* become *shadows;* or as the external and internal rhyming among the five verbs, as though all motion must (as in fact it must) end with *están.*

Since none of this can be brought over into another tongue (least of all Lorca's rhythms), the translator must decide between leaving his reader to wonder why Lorca is a poet to be bothered about at all, and making a new but true poem of his own, whose merit will almost certainly be in inverse ratio to its likeness to the original. Samuel Johnson made such a poem in translating Horace's famous *Diffugere nives,* and so did A. E. Housman. If we juxtapose the last two stanzas of each translation, and the corresponding Latin, we can see at a glance that each has the consistency and inner life of a genuine poem, and that neither of them (even if we consider only what is obvious to the eye, the line-lengths) is very close to Horace.

Cum semel occideris, et de te splendida Minos
fecerit arbitria,
non, Torquate, genus, non te facundia, non te
restituet pietas.

Infernis neque enim tenebris Diana pudicum
liberat Hippolytum
nec Lethaea valet Theseus abrumpere caro
vincula Pirithoo.

Johnson:

Not you, Torquatus, boast of Rome,
When Minos once has fixed your doom,
Or eloquence, or splendid birth,
Or virtue, shall restore to earth.
Hippolytus, unjustly slain,
Diana calls to life in vain;
Nor can the might of Theseus rend
The chains of hell that hold his friend.

Housman:

When thou descendest once the shades among,
The stern assize and equal judgment o'er,
Not thy long lineage nor thy golden tongue,
No, nor thy righteousness, shall friend thee more.

Night holds Hippolytus the pure of stain,
Diana steads him nothing, he must stay;
And Theseus leaves Pirithous in the chain
The love of comrades cannot take away.

The truth of the matter is that when the translator of short poems chooses to be literal, he loses most or all of the poetry; and when he chooses to make his own poetry, he loses most or all of the author. There is no way out of this dilemma, and in our own selection of short poems for this edition we have acknowledged the problem by excluding translations in favor of short poems written originally in English.

We may assure ourselves, then, that the reading of literature in translation is not the disaster it has sometimes been represented. It is true that, however good the translation, we remain at a remove from the original, the remove becoming closest to impassable in the genre of the lyric poem. But with this exception, it is obvious that translation brings us closer by far to the work than we could be if we did not read it at all, or read it with a defective knowledge of the language. "To a thousand cavils," said Samuel Johnson, "one answer is sufficient; the purpose of a writer is to be read, and the criticism which would destroy the power of pleasing must be blown aside." Johnson was defending Pope's Homer for those marks of its own time and place that make it the great interpretation it is; but Johnson's exhilarating common sense applies equally to the problem we are considering here. Literature is to be read, and the criticism that would destroy the reader's power to make some form of contact with much of the world's great writing must indeed be blown aside.

MAYNARD MACK

Index